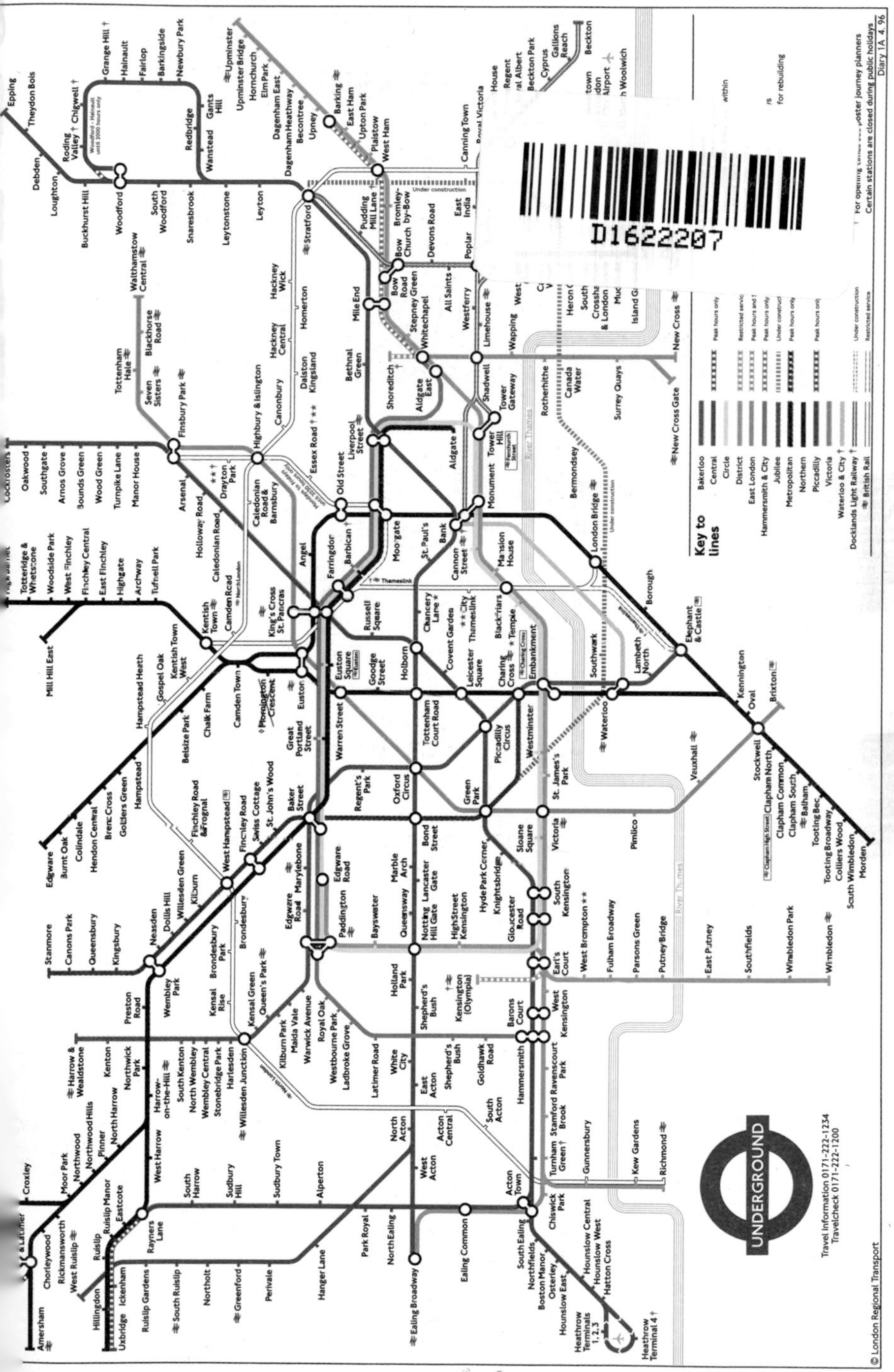

KL22NQ

LRT Registered User No. 97/2726

London
Regent's Park
Inner Circle
Chester Rd.
Outer Circle
Park Rd.
Albany St.
Euston Rd.
Hampstead Rd.
Eversholt St.
Maida Vale
Abercorn Pl.
Abbey Rd.
Grove End Rd.
Hall Rd.
Circus Rd.
Wellington Rd.
Prince Albert Rd.
St. John's Wood Rd.
Lisson Grove
Clifton Rd.
Bloomfield Rd.
Edgware Rd.
Harrow Rd.
Marylebone Flyover
Marylebone Rd.
Devonshire St.
Marylebone High St.
Harley St.
Portland Pl.
Gt. Portland St.
Cleveland St.
Tottenham
Berners St.
Crawford St.
Upper Montague St.
Gloucester Pl.
Baker St.
Seymour Pl.
Manchester Square
Wigmore St.
Bishop's Bridge Rd.
Paddington Station
Praed St.
Sussex Gdns.
Oxford Circus
Oxford
Marble Arch
Oxford St.
Duke St.
Brook St.
Bond St.
Regent St.
Queensway
Craven Hill
Bayswater Rd.
N. Carriage Dr.
Speaker's Corner
Grosvenor Square
Grosvenor St.
U.S. Embassy
Berkeley Square
Park Lane
Sth. Audley St.
Curzon St.
Jermyn St.
Kensington Gardens
Hyde Park
W. Carriage Dr.
The Serpentine
Kensington Palace
Piccadilly
St. James's Palace
Green Park
Hyde Park Corner
Constitution Hill
St. James Park
S. Carriage Rd.
Kensington Rd.
Kensington Gore
Knightsbridge
Royal Albert Hall
Prince Consort Rd.
Exhibition Rd.
Victoria & Albert Museum
Palace Gate
Gloucester Rd.
Queen's Gate
Brompton Rd.
Basil St.
Sloane St.
Pavilion Rd.
Cadogan Pl.
Grosvenor Pl.
Belgrave Square
Eaton Square
Buckingham Palace Rd.
Victoria Station
Wilton Rd.
Cromwell Rd.
Natural History Museum
Walton St.
Pont St.
Draycott Ave.
Sloane Ave.
Sloane Sq.
Coach Station
Warwick Way
Old Brompton Rd.
Ixworth Pl.
Cale St.
Pimlico Rd.
Sutherland St.
Lupus St
King's Rd.
Sydney St.
Old Church St.
Flood St.
Royal Hospital Rd.
Chelsea Br. Rd.
Ebury Br. Rd.
Royal Hospital
Grosvenor Rd.
Redcliffe Gdns.
Finborough Rd.
Fulham Rd.
Oakley St.
Carlyle's House
Cheyne Walk
Chelsea Embankment
Chelsea Br.
River Thames
Beaufort St.
Albert Br.
Battersea Park

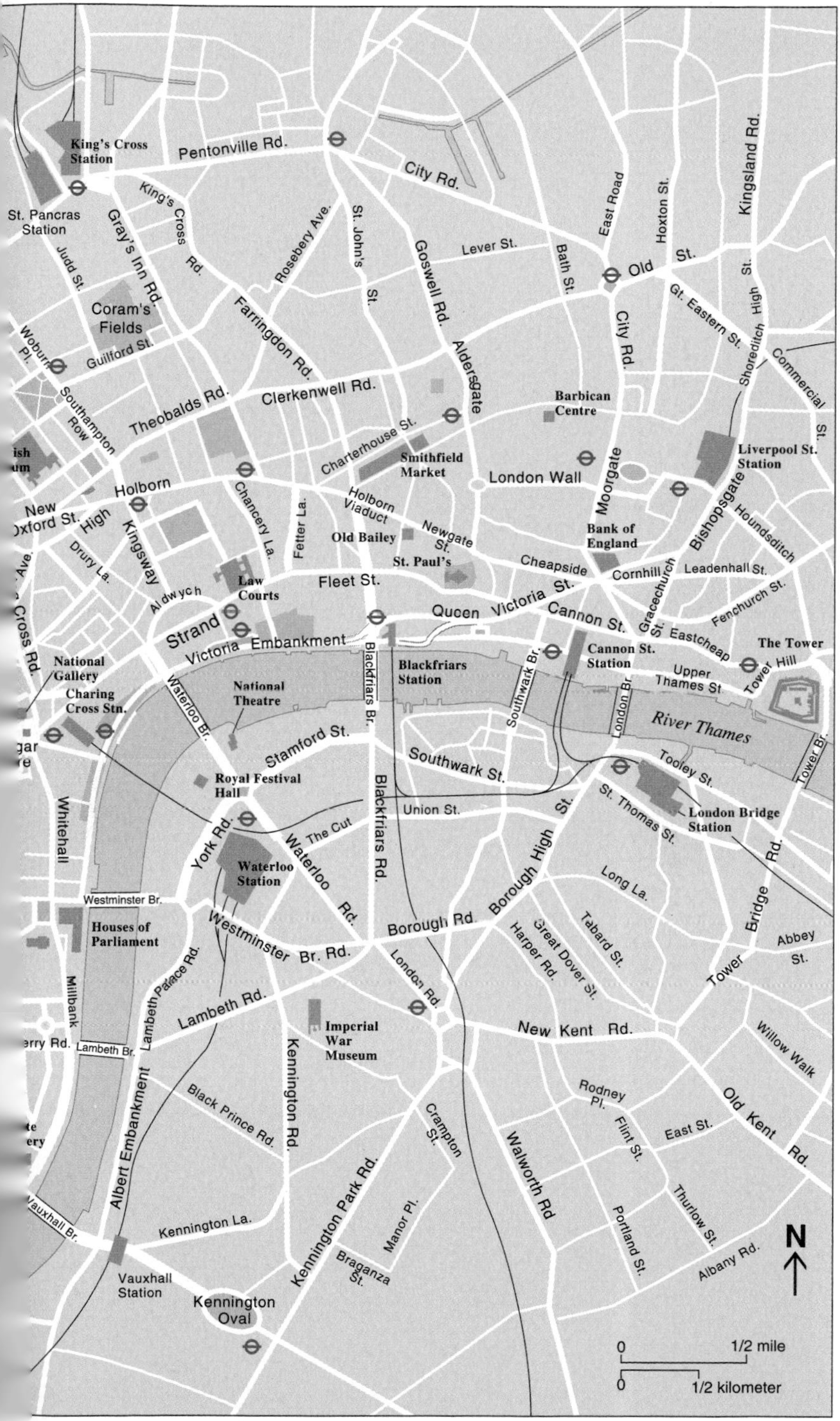
King's Cross Station
St. Pancras Station
Pentonville Rd.
City Rd.
King's Cross Rd.
Gray's Inn Rd.
Judd St.
Rosebery Ave.
St. John's St.
Goswell Rd.
Lever St.
Bath St.
East Road
Hoxton St.
Kingsland Rd.
Old St.
Shoreditch High St.
Gt. Eastern St.
Commercial St.
Coram's Fields
Guilford St.
Woburn Pl.
Southampton Row
Farringdon Rd.
Theobalds Rd.
Clerkenwell Rd.
Aldersgate
City Rd.
Barbican Centre
Charterhouse St.
Smithfield Market
London Wall
Moorgate
Liverpool St. Station
Holborn
New Oxford St.
High
Kingsway
Chancery La.
Fetter La.
Holborn Viaduct
Newgate St.
Old Bailey
St. Paul's
Bank of England
Bishopsgate
Houndsditch
Drury La.
Law Courts
Fleet St.
Cheapside
Cornhill
Gracechurch St.
Leadenhall St.
Fenchurch St.
Aldwych
Strand
Queen Victoria St.
Cannon St.
Eastcheap
Victoria Embankment
Blackfriars Br.
Blackfriars Station
Southwark Br.
Cannon St. Station
Upper Thames St.
The Tower
Tower Hill
National Gallery
Charing Cross Stn.
Waterloo Br.
National Theatre
London Br.
River Thames
Tower Br.
Stamford St.
Southwark St.
Tooley St.
Royal Festival Hall
Union St.
St. Thomas St.
London Bridge Station
Whitehall
York Rd.
The Cut
Waterloo Rd.
Blackfriars Rd.
Borough High St.
Waterloo Station
Long La.
Westminster Br.
Houses of Parliament
Westminster Br. Rd.
Borough Rd.
Great Dover St.
Harper Rd.
Tabard St.
Tower Bridge Rd.
Abbey St.
Lambeth Palace Rd.
London Rd.
Millbank
Lambeth Rd.
Imperial War Museum
New Kent Rd.
Willow Walk
Lambeth Br.
Kennington Rd.
Rodney Pl.
Albert Embankment
Black Prince Rd.
Crampton St.
Flint St.
East St.
Old Kent Rd.
Walworth Rd
Kennington Park Rd.
Manor Pl.
Portland St.
Thurlow St.
Vauxhall Br.
Kennington La.
Braganza St.
Albany Rd.
Vauxhall Station
Kennington Oval
N
0
1/2 mile
0
1/2 kilometer

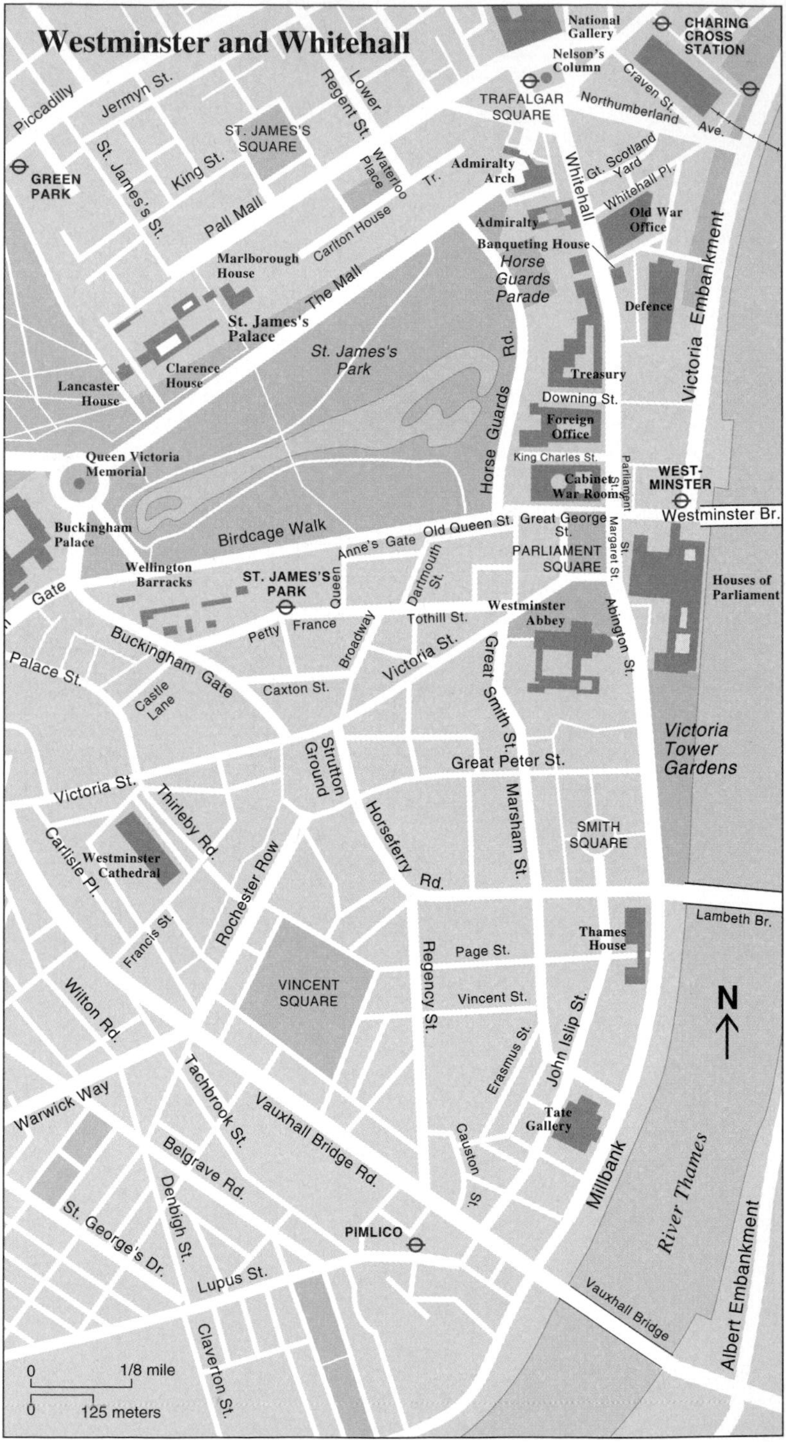
Westminster and Whitehall
National Gallery
CHARING CROSS STATION
Nelson's Column
TRAFALGAR SQUARE
Craven St.
Northumberland Ave.
Piccadilly
Jermyn St.
Regent St.
Lower
ST. JAMES'S SQUARE
St. James's St.
King St.
GREEN PARK
Waterloo Place
Tr.
Admiralty Arch
Whitehall
Gt. Scotland Yard
Whitehall Pl.
Pall Mall
Carlton House
Admiralty
Old War Office
Banqueting House
Horse Guards Parade
Marlborough House
The Mall
Defence
Victoria Embankment
St. James's Palace
St. James's Park
Horse Guards Rd.
Clarence House
Lancaster House
Treasury
Downing St.
Foreign Office
King Charles St.
Queen Victoria Memorial
Cabinet War Rooms
Parliament St.
WEST-MINSTER
Westminster Br.
Buckingham Palace
Birdcage Walk
Old Queen St.
Great George St.
Anne's Gate
Queen
Dartmouth St.
PARLIAMENT SQUARE
St. Margaret St.
Houses of Parliament
Wellington Barracks
ST. JAMES'S PARK
Gate
Westminster Abbey
Abington St.
Tothill St.
Petty France
Broadway
Buckingham Gate
Palace St.
Victoria St.
Great Smith St.
Castle Lane
Caxton St.
Victoria Tower Gardens
Strutton Ground
Great Peter St.
Victoria St.
Thirleby Rd.
Marsham St.
Horseferry Rd.
SMITH SQUARE
Carlisle Pl.
Westminster Cathedral
Rochester Row
Lambeth Br.
Francis St.
Thames House
Page St.
Regency St.
VINCENT SQUARE
Vincent St.
Wilton Rd.
John Islip St.
N
Erasmus St.
Warwick Way
Tachbrook St.
Vauxhall Bridge Rd.
Tate Gallery
Causton St.
Belgrave Rd.
Millbank
River Thames
St. George's Dr.
Denbigh St.
PIMLICO
Albert Embankment
Lupus St.
Vauxhall Bridge
Claverton St.
0
1/8 mile
0
125 meters

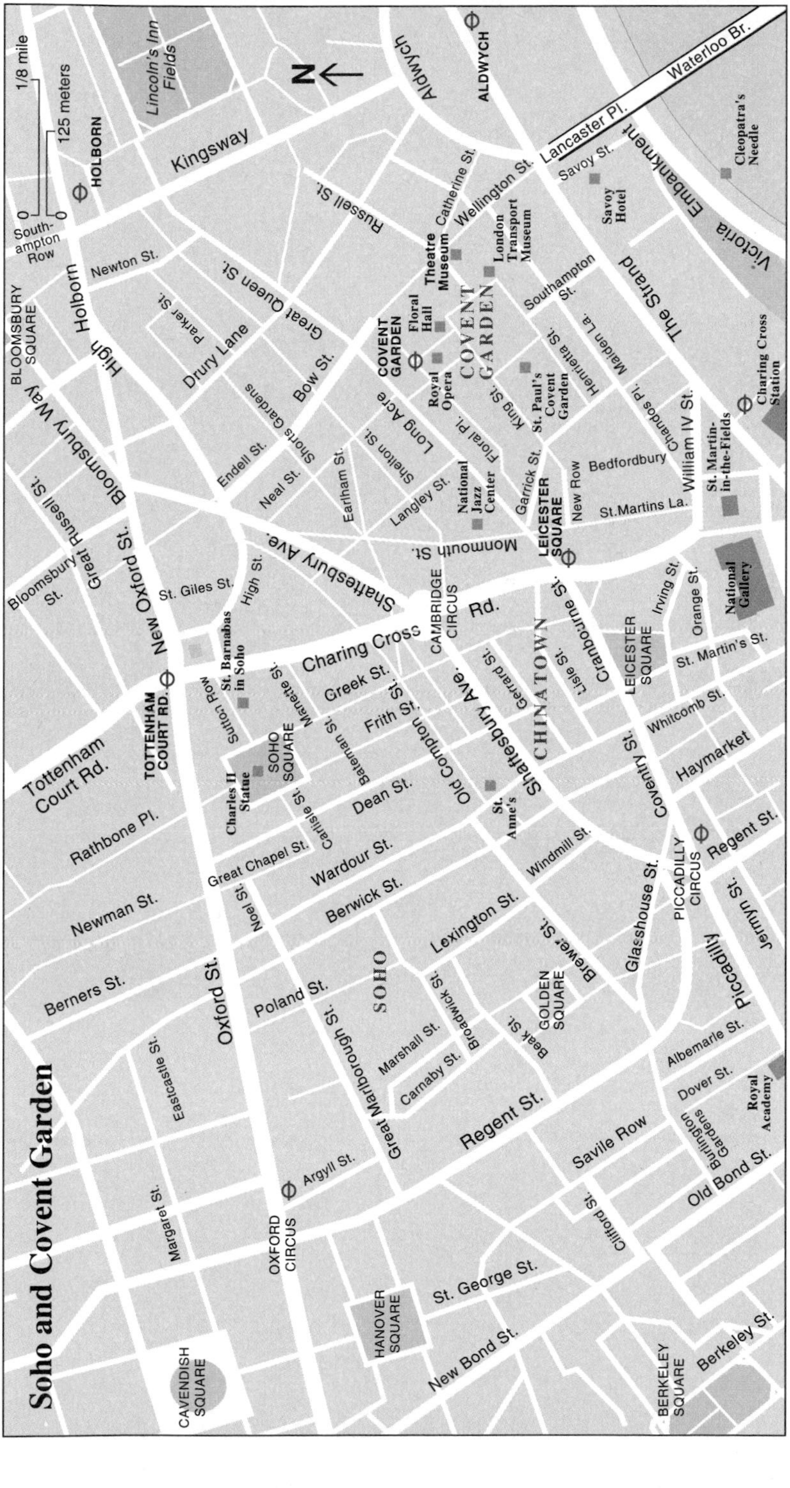

Soho and Covent Garden
1/8 mile
125 meters
0
0
N
HOLBORN
Lincoln's Inn Fields
Kingsway
Aldwych
ALDWYCH
Waterloo Br.
Lancaster Pl.
Savoy St.
Savoy Hotel
Cleopatra's Needle
Victoria Embankment
Wellington St.
Catherine St.
Russell St.
Theatre Museum
London Transport Museum
Southampton Row
Newton St.
Great Queen St.
Parker St.
Drury Lane
BLOOMSBURY SQUARE
High Holborn
Bow St.
Floral Hall
COVENT GARDEN
Royal Opera
COVENT GARDEN
Southampton St.
The Strand
Maiden La.
Henrietta St.
St. Paul's Covent Garden
King St.
Floral Pl.
Long Acre
Shorts Gardens
Endell St.
Neal St.
Earlham St.
Shelton St.
Langley St.
National Jazz Center
Garrick St.
Chandos Pl.
Bedfordbury
New Row
William IV St.
St. Martin-in-the-Fields
Charing Cross Station
LEICESTER SQUARE
St.Martins La.
Monmouth St.
Shaftesbury Ave.
Bloomsbury Way
Great Russell St.
Bloomsbury St.
New Oxford St.
St. Giles St.
High St.
CAMBRIDGE CIRCUS
Charing Cross Rd.
National Gallery
Irving St.
Orange St.
LEICESTER SQUARE
St. Martin's St.
Cranbourne St.
Lisle St.
Gerrard St.
CHINATOWN
Shaftesbury Ave.
St. Barnabas in Soho
Sutton Row
Manette St.
Greek St.
Frith St.
Old Compton St.
TOTTENHAM COURT RD.
SOHO SQUARE
Charles II Statue
Bateman St.
Carlisle St.
Dean St.
St. Anne's
Coventry St.
Whitcomb St.
Haymarket
Tottenham Court Rd.
Rathbone Pl.
Great Chapel St.
Wardour St.
Windmill St.
PICCADILLY CIRCUS
Regent St.
Newman St.
Noel St.
Berwick St.
Lexington St.
Brewer St.
Glasshouse St.
Jermyn St.
Piccadilly
Berners St.
Oxford St.
Poland St.
SOHO
Broadwick St.
GOLDEN SQUARE
Beak St.
Eastcastle St.
Great Marlborough St.
Marshall St.
Carnaby St.
Albemarle St.
Dover St.
Royal Academy
Regent St.
Burlington Gardens
Savile Row
Old Bond St.
Argyll St.
OXFORD CIRCUS
Margaret St.
Clifford St.
St. George St.
HANOVER SQUARE
New Bond St.
Berkeley St.
BERKELEY SQUARE
CAVENDISH SQUARE

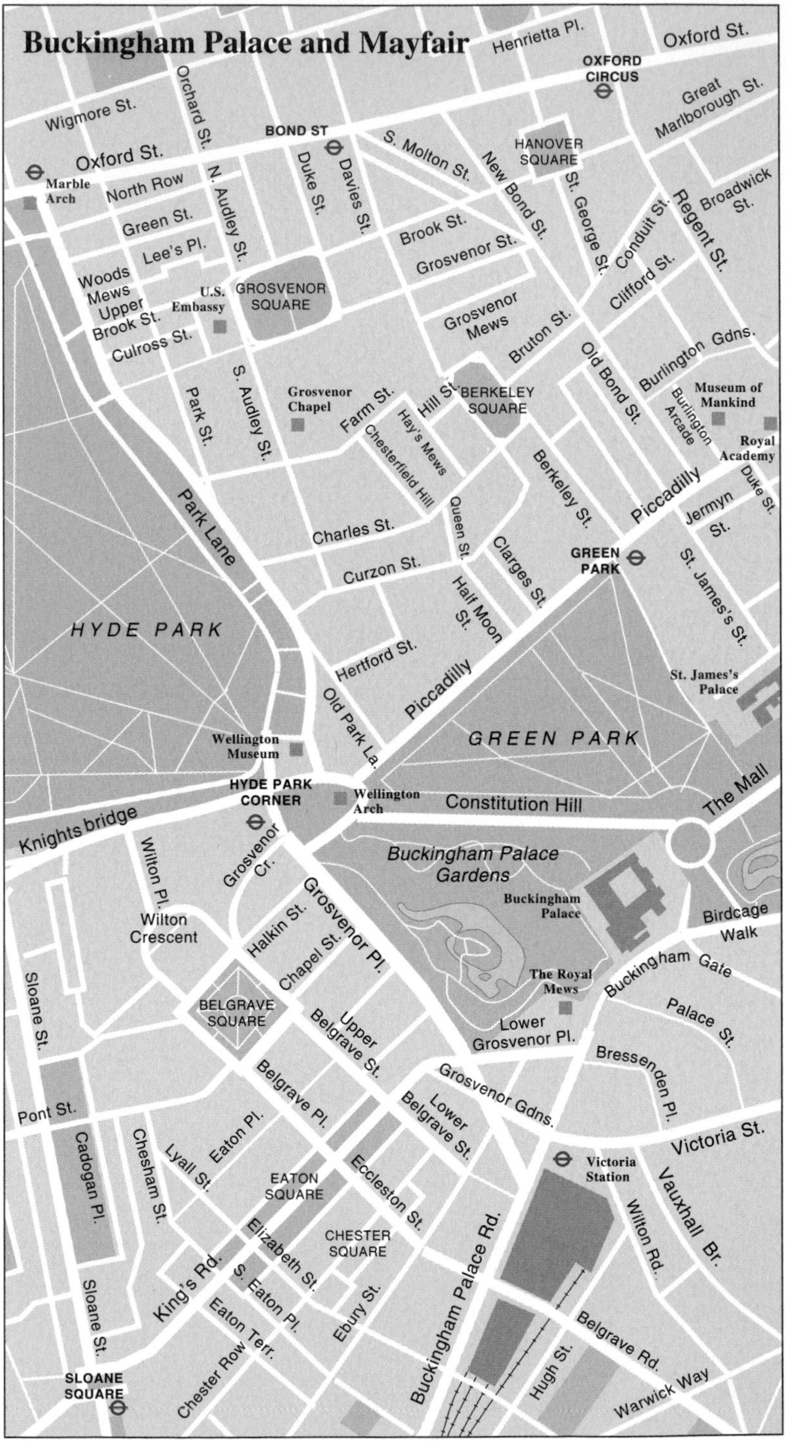
Buckingham Palace and Mayfair
Henrietta Pl.
Oxford St.
OXFORD CIRCUS
Great Marlborough St.
Wigmore St.
Orchard St.
BOND ST
Oxford St.
S. Molton St.
HANOVER SQUARE
Marble Arch
North Row
N. Audley St.
Duke St.
Davies St.
New Bond St.
St. George St.
Regent St.
Broadwick St.
Green St.
Lee's Pl.
Brook St.
Grosvenor St.
Conduit St.
Clifford St.
Woods Mews
Upper Brook St.
U.S. Embassy
GROSVENOR SQUARE
Grosvenor Mews
Bruton St.
Culross St.
Old Bond St.
Burlington Gdns.
Park St.
S. Audley St.
Grosvenor Chapel
Farm St.
Hill St.
BERKELEY SQUARE
Burlington Arcade
Museum of Mankind
Hay's Mews
Chesterfield Hill
Royal Academy
Berkeley St.
Piccadilly
Duke St.
Jermyn St.
Park Lane
Charles St.
Queen St.
Clarges St.
GREEN PARK
St. James's St.
Curzon St.
Half Moon St.
HYDE PARK
Hertford St.
Piccadilly
St. James's Palace
Old Park La.
GREEN PARK
Wellington Museum
HYDE PARK CORNER
Wellington Arch
Constitution Hill
The Mall
Knights bridge
Wilton Pl.
Grosvenor Cr.
Buckingham Palace Gardens
Grosvenor Pl.
Buckingham Palace
Birdcage Walk
Wilton Crescent
Halkin St.
Chapel St.
The Royal Mews
Buckingham Gate
Sloane St.
BELGRAVE SQUARE
Upper Belgrave St.
Lower Grosvenor Pl.
Palace St.
Belgrave Pl.
Bressenden Pl.
Grosvenor Gdns.
Lower Belgrave St.
Pont St.
Eaton Pl.
Victoria St.
Cadogan Pl.
Chesham St.
Lyall St.
EATON SQUARE
Eccleston St.
Victoria Station
Vauxhall Br.
Wilton Rd.
Elizabeth St.
CHESTER SQUARE
King's Rd.
S. Eaton Pl.
Ebury St.
Buckingham Palace Rd.
Sloane St.
Eaton Terr.
Belgrave Rd.
Hugh St.
Chester Row
Warwick Way
SLOANE SQUARE

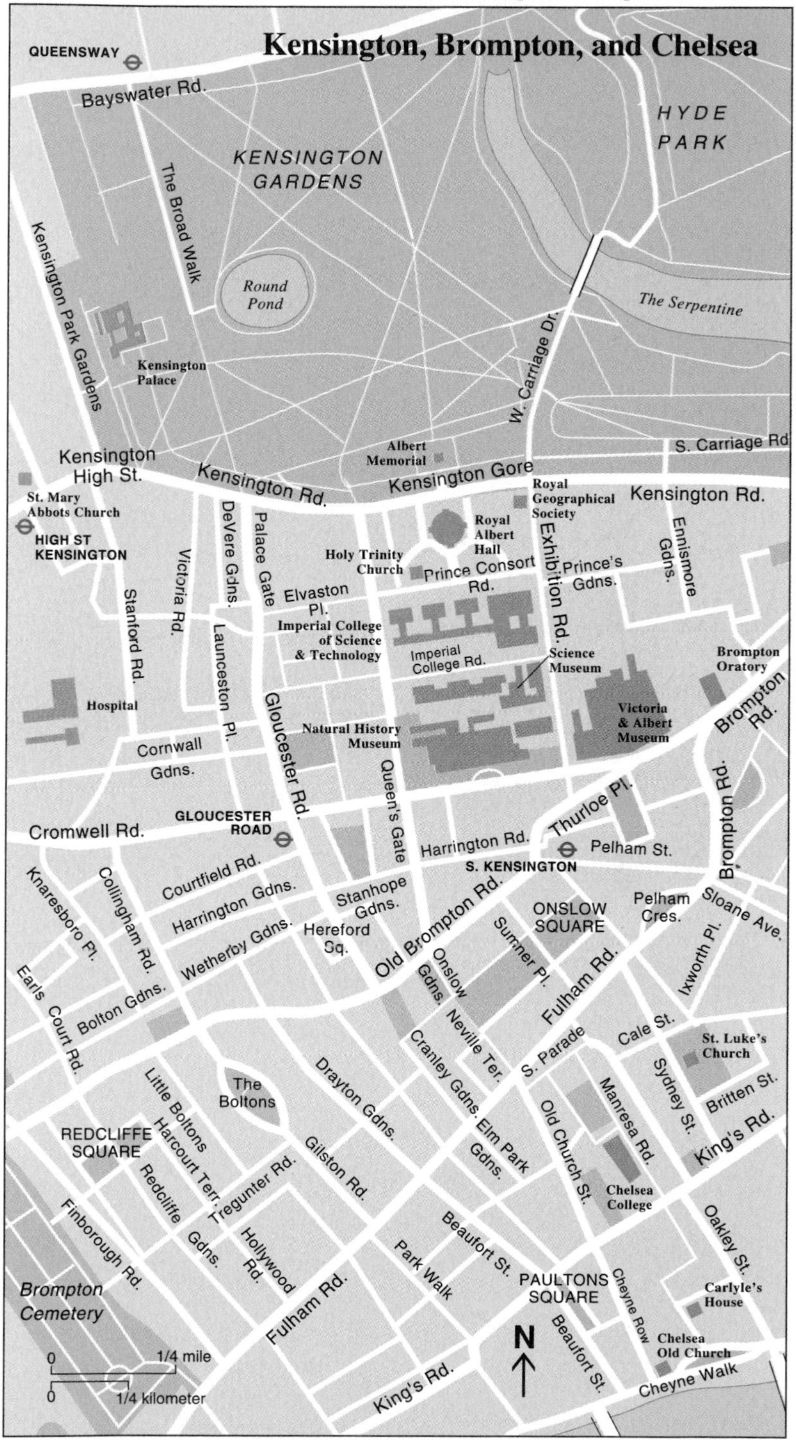

Kensington, Brompton, and Chelsea
QUEENSWAY
Bayswater Rd.
KENSINGTON GARDENS
HYDE PARK
The Broad Walk
Kensington Park Gardens
Round Pond
The Serpentine
Kensington Palace
W. Carriage Dr.
Albert Memorial
S. Carriage Rd
Kensington High St.
Kensington Rd.
Kensington Gore
Royal Geographical Society
Kensington Rd.
St. Mary Abbots Church
HIGH ST KENSINGTON
Royal Albert Hall
Ennismore Gdns.
Victoria Rd.
DeVere Gdns.
Palace Gate
Holy Trinity Church
Exhibition Rd.
Prince Consort Rd.
Prince's Gdns.
Stanford Rd.
Elvaston Pl.
Imperial College of Science & Technology
Launceston Pl.
Imperial College Rd.
Science Museum
Brompton Oratory
Hospital
Gloucester Rd.
Victoria & Albert Museum
Brompton Rd.
Natural History Museum
Cornwall Gdns.
Queen's Gate
Thurloe Pl.
Brompton Rd.
Cromwell Rd.
GLOUCESTER ROAD
Harrington Rd.
Pelham St.
S. KENSINGTON
Knaresboro Pl.
Collingham Rd.
Courtfield Rd.
Harrington Gdns.
Stanhope Gdns.
Old Brompton Rd.
ONSLOW SQUARE
Pelham Cres.
Sloane Ave.
Wetherby Gdns.
Hereford Sq.
Sumner Pl.
Earls Court Rd.
Bolton Gdns.
Onslow Gdns.
Fulham Rd.
Ixworth Pl.
Neville Ter.
Cale St.
St. Luke's Church
S. Parade
Cranley Gdns.
The Boltons
Drayton Gdns.
Sydney St.
Britten St.
Little Boltons
Manresa Rd.
Old Church St.
Elm Park Gdns.
REDCLIFFE SQUARE
Harcourt Terr.
King's Rd.
Gilston Rd.
Redcliffe Gdns.
Tregunter Rd.
Chelsea College
Oakley St.
Finborough Rd.
Hollywood Rd.
Beaufort St.
Park Walk
Fulham Rd.
PAULTONS SQUARE
Cheyne Row
Carlyle's House
Brompton Cemetery
Beaufort St.
Chelsea Old Church
N
0
1/4 mile
0
1/4 kilometer
King's Rd.
Cheyne Walk

London: City of London

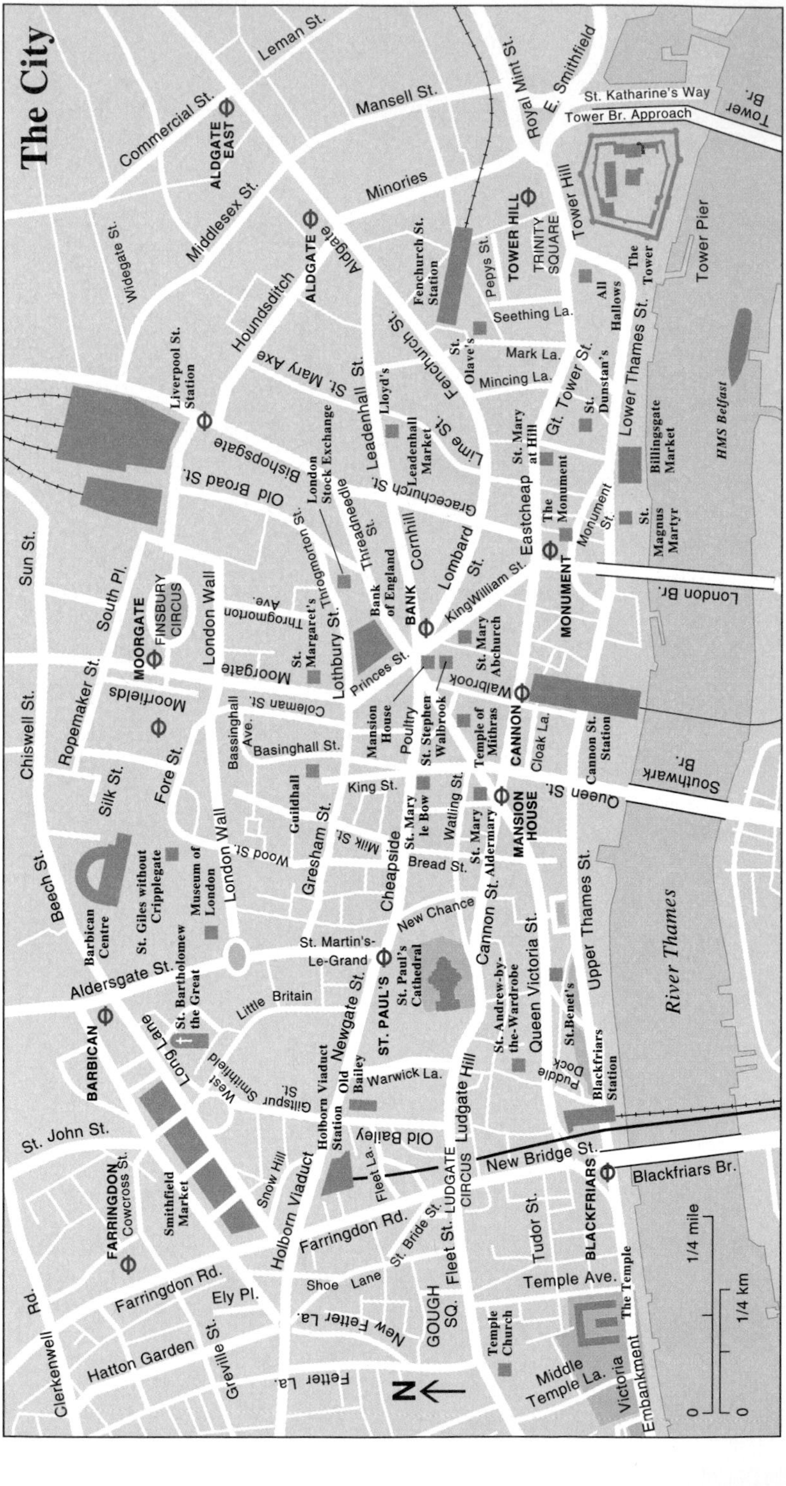

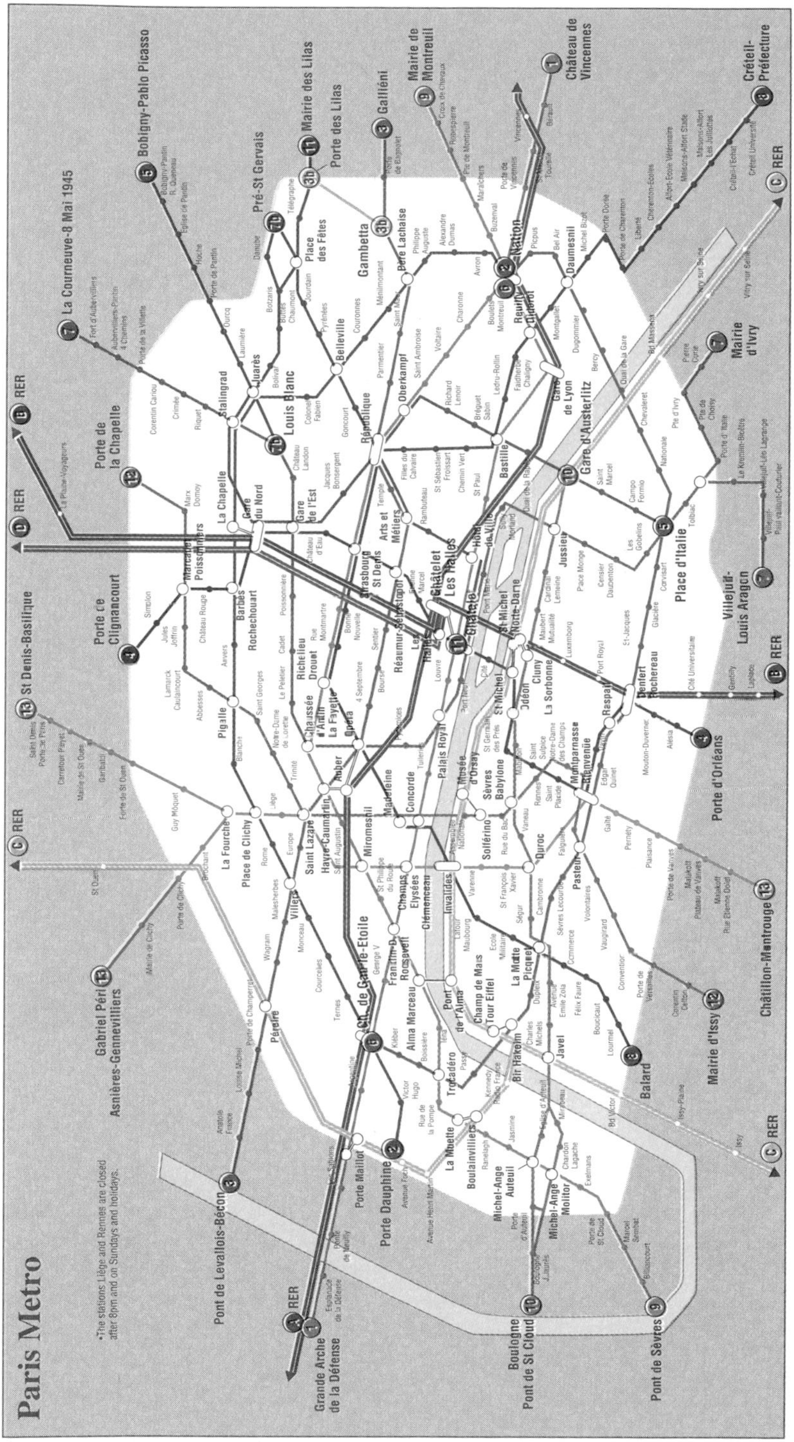
Paris Metro
•The stations Liège and Rennes are closed after 8pm and on Sundays and holidays.
Grande Arche de la Défense
Pont de Levallois-Bécon
Gabriel Péri Asnières-Gennevilliers
St Denis-Basilique
Porte de Clignancourt
Porte de la Chapelle
La Courneuve-8 Mai 1945
Bobigny-Pablo Picasso
Pré-St Gervais
Mairie des Lilas
Porte des Lilas
Gallieni
Mairie de Montreuil
Château de Vincennes
Créteil-Préfecture
Mairie d'Ivry
Villejuif-Louis Aragon
Porte d'Orléans
Châtillon-Montrouge
Mairie d'Issy
Balard
Pont de Sèvres
Boulogne Pont de St Cloud
Porte Dauphine
RER

Paris: Overview and Arrondissements
1 Cimetière de Montmartre
2 Sacré Coeur Basilica
3 Parc La Villette
4 Parc des Buttes Chaumont
5 Jardins du Trocadero
6 Palais Chaillot
7 Cimetière de Passy
8 American Embassy
9 British Embassy
10 Petit Palais
11 Grand Palais
12 Arc de Triomphe
13 Madeleine
14 Gare St-Lazare
15 Parc Monceau
16 Palais de la Découverte
17 Opéra Garnier
18 Galeries Lafayette
19 Printemps
20 Gare du Nord
21 Gare de l'Est
22 Opéra Bastille
23 Palais Omnisports de Bercy
24 Ministère des Finances
25 Gare de Lyon
26 Parc de Montsouris
27 Cité Universitaire
28 Cimetière Montparnasse
29 Gare Montparnasse
30 Bureau des Objets Trouvés (Lost and Found)
31 Louvre
32 Palais Royale
33 Forum des Halles
34 Musée de l'Orangerie
35 Central Post Office
36 Bourse
37 Bibliothèque Nationale
38 Ecole des Arts et Métiers
39 Archives Nationales
40 Musée Carnavalet
41 Musée Picasso
42 Centre George Pompidou
43 place des Vosges
44 Musée Victor Hugo
45 Notre Dame
46 Mémorial de la Déportation
47 Université de Paris (Sorbonne)
48 Ecole Normal Supérieure
49 Musée de Cluny
50 Museum Nationale d'Histoire Naturelle
51 Panthéon
52 Eglise St-Etienne du Mont
53 La Mosquée
54 Jardin des Plantes
55 Jardins du Luxembourg
56 Eglise St-Sulpice
57 Théâtre Nationale de l'Odéon
58 Eiffel Tower
59 Champs de Mars
60 Ecole Militaire
61 UNESCO
62 Hôtel des Invalides
63 Assemblée Nationale
64 Musée d'O₁ say
65 Cimetière de l'Est du Pere Lachaise
17e
8e
16e
7e
15e
14e
Bois de Boulogne
Seine
PORTE DE CLICHY
PÉREIRE LEVALLOIS
PL. DU MAL JUIN
NEUILLY/ PORT MAILLOT
TO LA DÉFENSE
PL. DES TERNES
PL. CHARLES DE GAULLE/ ETOILE
PL. ST-AUGUSTIN
PL. DE L'EUROPE
AUBER
PL. DE LA CONCORDE
AV FOCH
PL. DU TROCADERO
AV HENRI MARTIN
BOULAINVILLIERS LA MUETTE
PT DE ALMA
INVALIDES
MUSÉE D'ORSAY
PL. DES INVALIDES
CHAMP DE MARS/TOUR EIFFEL
KENNEDY/ MAISON RADIO
PL. VAUBAN
PL. JEAN-LORRAIN
JAVEL
BD VICTOR
Pont du Garigliano
Pont de Bir Hakeim
Pont d'Iéna
GARE PARIS-VAUGIRARD
bd. Bessières
rue Victor Hugo
rue du Président Wilson
bd. Victor Hugo
bd. Bineau
bd. Berthier
bd. Reims
bd. Péreire
rue de Tocqueville
av. de Villiers
bd. des Batignolles
bd. de Courcelles
bd. Malesherbes
rue du Rocher
av. de la Grande Armée
av. Foch
av. Victor Hugo
av. Kléber
av. Marceau
av. d'Iéna
av. Friedland
av. Hoche
bd. Haussmann
rue du Faubourg St-Honoré
av. des Champs Elysées
av. Montaigne
cours de la Reine
quai d'Orsay
rue de l'Université
rue St- Dominique
av. de la Bourdonnais
rue de Varenne
rue de Babylone
rue de Sèvres
bd. du Montparnasse
bd. Raspail
bd. de Grenelle
rue du Théâtre
av. Emile Zola
rue de la Convention
rue de Vaugirard
rue Lacourbe
bd. Lefebvre
bd. Brune
rue d'Alésia
av. du Maine
bd. Murat
bd. Exelmans
rue Molitor
bd. Suchet
av. Mozart
rue du Ranelagh
av. Henri Martin
av. Paul Doumer
av. de New York
bd. Garibaldi
av. de Suffren
bd. Pasteur
bd. Victor
quai André Citroën

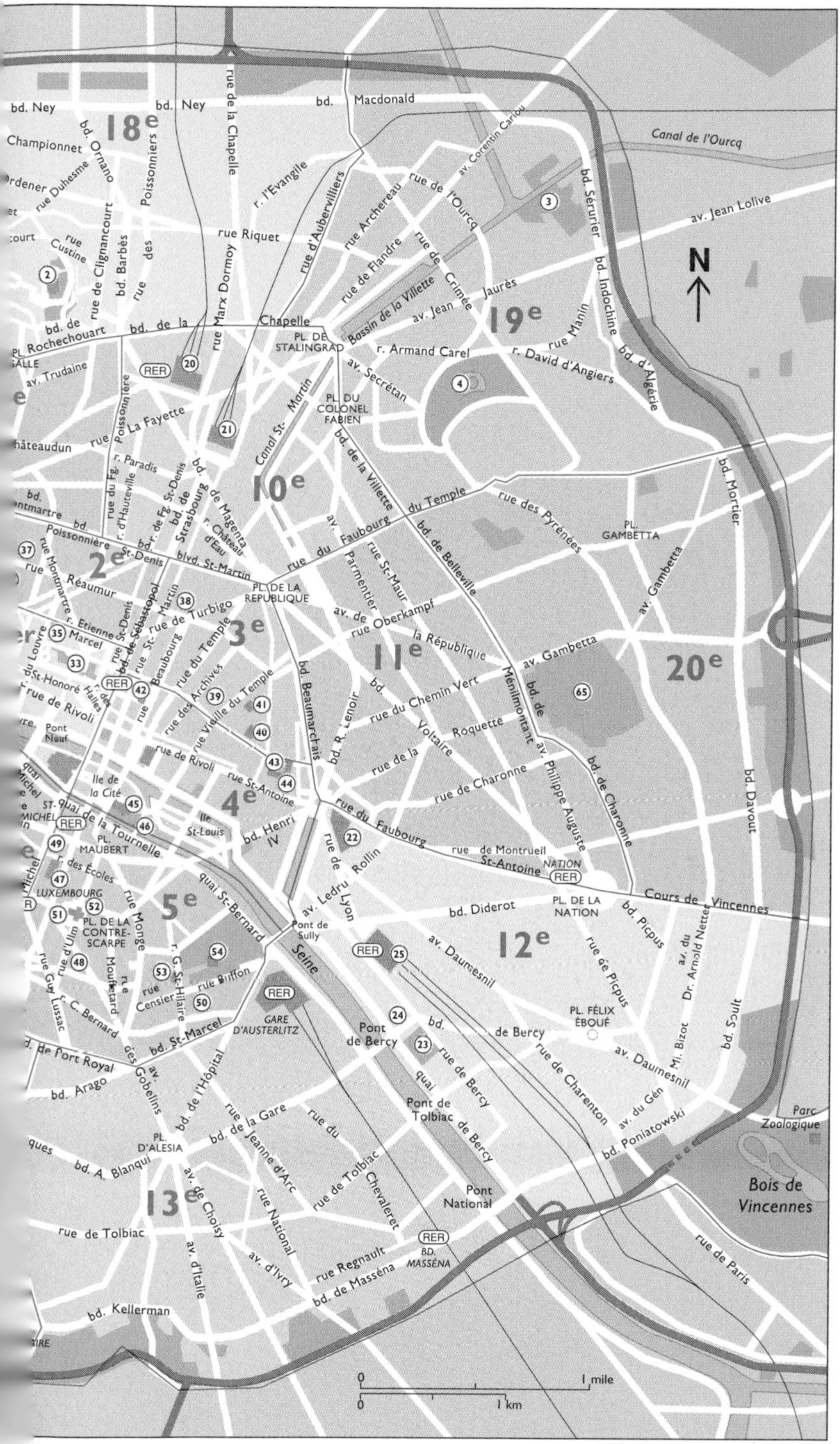
18e
19e
10e
2e
3e
11e
20e
4e
5e
12e
13e
N
bd. Ney
bd. Macdonald
Canal de l'Ourcq
Championnet
bd. Ornano
rue Duhesme
rue de la Chapelle
Poissonniers
r. l'Evangile
rue d'Aubervilliers
av. Corentin Cariou
bd. Sérurier
rue de l'Ourcq
rue Archereau
av. Jean Lolive
rue Riquet
rue Custine
rue de Clignancourt
bd. Barbès
rue des
rue Marx Dormoy
rue de Flandre
rue de Crimée
Bassin de la Villette
av. Jean Jaurès
bd. Indochine
rue Manin
bd. d'Algérie
bd. de Rochechouart
bd. de la Chapelle
PL. DE STALINGRAD
r. Armand Carel
r. David d'Angiers
av. Trudaine
RER
av. Secrétan
PL. DU COLONEL FABIEN
Canal St-Martin
rue La Fayette
rue Poissonnière
r. Paradis
bd. de la Villette
bd. Mortier
rue du Fg. Poissonnière
r. d'Hauteville
r. de Fg. St-Denis
bd. de Strasbourg
bd. de Magenta
r. Château d'Eau
rue du Faubourg du Temple
rue des Pyrénées
PL. GAMBETTA
bd. Poissonnière
St-Denis
blvd. St-Martin
av. Parmentier
rue St-Maur
bd. de Belleville
av. Gambetta
rue Montmartre
rue Réaumur
PL. DE LA REPUBLIQUE
rue Oberkampf
av. de la République
r. Etienne Marcel
bd. de Sébastopol
rue St-Martin
rue de Turbigo
rue Beaubourg
rue du Temple
bd. Beaumarchais
rue du Chemin Vert
Ménilmontant
bd. de Ménilmontant
rue St-Honoré
r. des Halles
rue de Rivoli
rue des Archives
rue Vieille du Temple
bd. R. Lenoir
bd. Voltaire
rue de la Roquette
Pont Neuf
rue de Rivoli
rue St-Antoine
rue de Charonne
av. Philippe Auguste
bd. de Charonne
bd. Davout
Ile de la Cité
Ile St-Louis
bd. Henri IV
quai de la Tournelle
rue du Faubourg St-Antoine
rue de Lyon
rue de Montreuil
NATION
PL. MAUBERT
r. des Écoles
quai St-Bernard
av. Ledru Rollin
Cours de Vincennes
LUXEMBOURG
PL. DE LA CONTRE-SCARPE
rue Monge
Pont de Sully
bd. Diderot
PL. DE LA NATION
bd. Picpus
Seine
av. Daumesnil
rue de Picpus
av. du Dr. Arnold Netter
rue d'Ulm
rue Mouffetard
r. G. St-Hilaire
rue Buffon
rue Censier
GARE D'AUSTERLITZ
rue Gay Lussac
r. C. Bernard
bd. de Port Royal
bd. St-Marcel
Pont de Bercy
bd. de Bercy
PL. FÉLIX ÉBOUÉ
av. Daumesnil
Mi. Bizot
bd. Soult
bd. Arago
av. des Gobelins
bd. de l'Hôpital
rue de Bercy
quai de Bercy
rue de Charenton
av. du Gén
bd. Poniatowski
Parc Zoologique
Pont de Tolbiac
rue de la Gare
rue du Chevaleret
PL. D'ALESIA
bd. A. Blanqui
rue Jeanne d'Arc
rue de Tolbiac
Bois de Vincennes
av. de Choisy
rue National
Pont National
rue de Paris
rue de Tolbiac
rue Regnault
BD. MASSÉNA
bd. de Masséna
av. d'Italie
av. d'Ivry
bd. Kellerman
0
1 mile
1 km

Paris: 1er and 2e

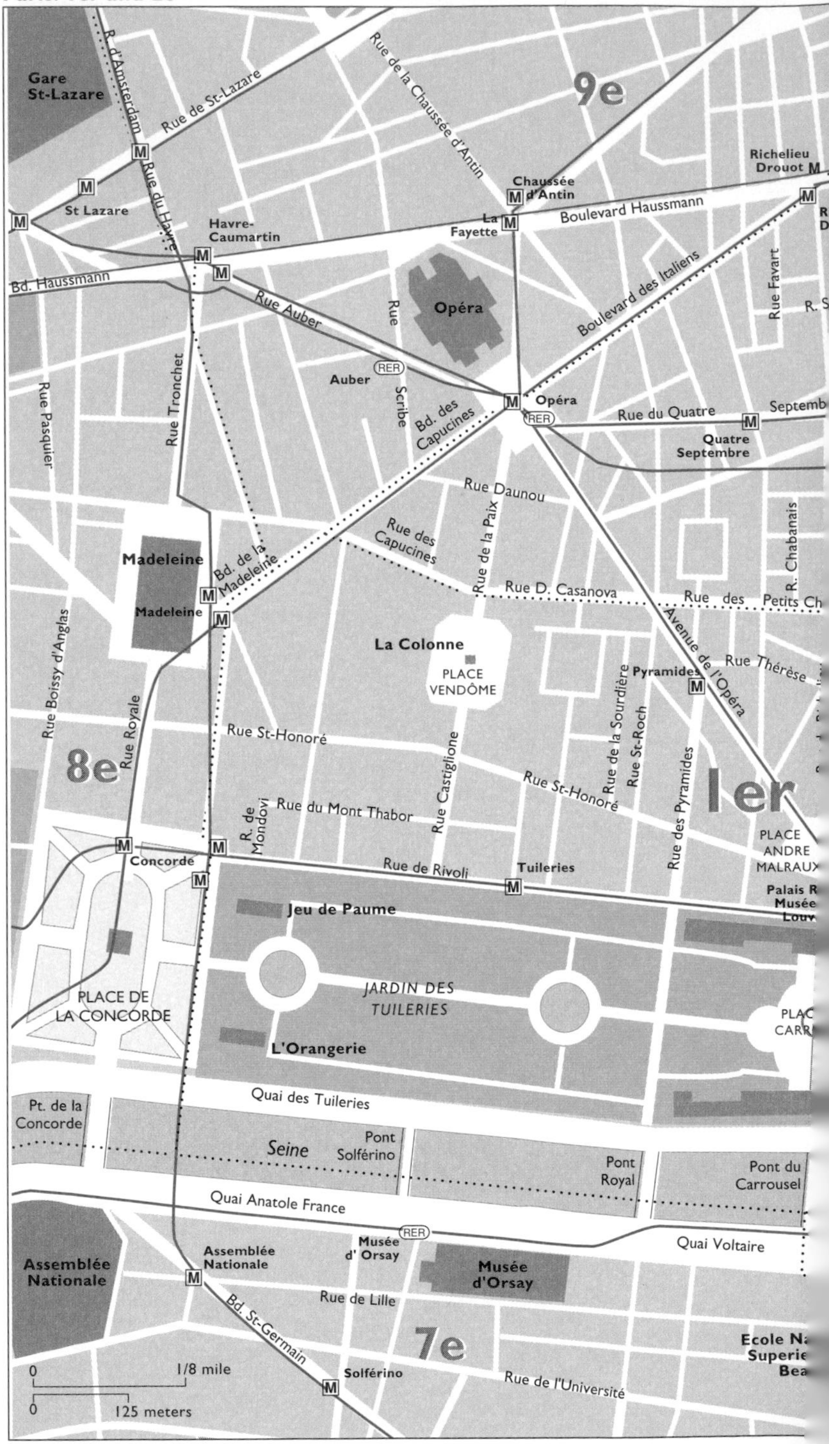
Gare St-Lazare
R. d'Amsterdam
Rue de St-Lazare
Rue de la Chaussée d'Antin
9e
Richelieu Drouot
Rue du Havre
St Lazare
Chaussée d'Antin
La Fayette
Boulevard Haussmann
Havre-Caumartin
Bd. Haussmann
Rue Auber
Rue Scribe
Opéra
Boulevard des Italiens
Rue Favart
Auber
RER
Rue Pasquier
Rue Tronchet
Bd. des Capucines
Opéra
Rue du Quatre Septembre
Quatre Septembre
Rue Daunou
Rue des Capucines
R. Chabanais
Madeleine
Bd. de la Madeleine
Rue de la Paix
Rue D. Casanova
Rue des Petits Ch
Avenue de l'Opéra
La Colonne
PLACE VENDÔME
Pyramides
Rue Thérèse
Rue Boissy d'Anglas
Rue Royale
Rue St-Honoré
Rue Castiglione
Rue de la Sourdière
Rue St-Roch
Rue des Pyramides
8e
1er
R. de Mondovi
Rue du Mont Thabor
PLACE ANDRE MALRAUX
Concorde
Rue de Rivoli
Tuileries
Jeu de Paume
JARDIN DES TUILERIES
PLACE DE LA CONCORDE
L'Orangerie
Quai des Tuileries
Pt. de la Concorde
Seine
Pont Solférino
Pont Royal
Pont du Carrousel
Quai Anatole France
Quai Voltaire
Assemblée Nationale
Musée d'Orsay
Rue de Lille
Bd. St-Germain
7e
Solférino
Rue de l'Université
0
1/8 mile
125 meters

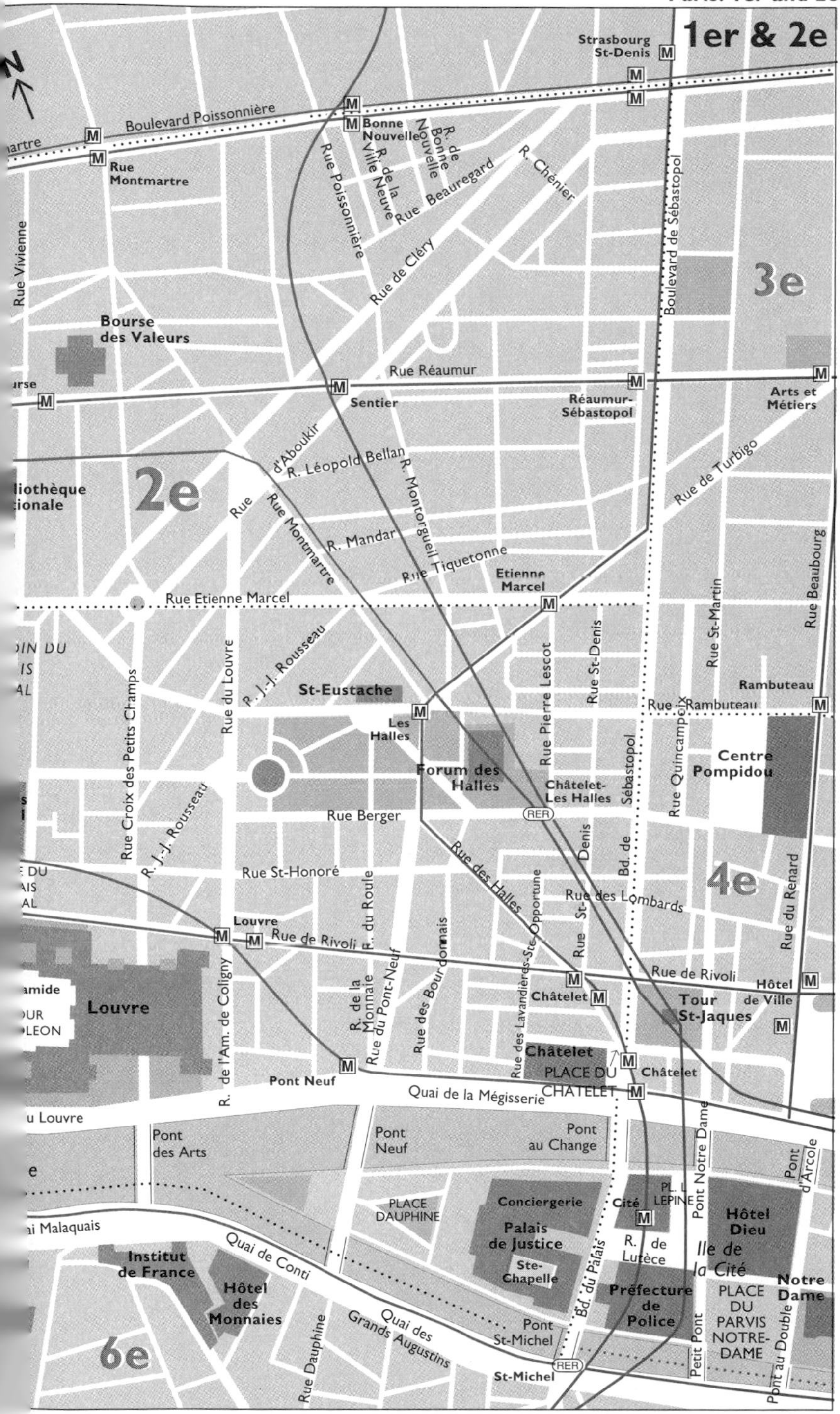
1er & 2e
Strasbourg St-Denis
Boulevard Poissonnière
Bonne Nouvelle
Rue Montmartre
R. de Bonne Nouvelle
R. de la Ville Neuve
Rue Poissonnière
Rue Beauregard
R. Chénier
Rue de Cléry
Boulevard de Sébastopol
3e
Rue Vivienne
Bourse des Valeurs
Rue Réaumur
Sentier
Réaumur-Sébastopol
Arts et Métiers
Rue d'Aboukir
R. Léopold Bellan
R. Montorgueil
Rue de Turbigo
2e
Rue Montmartre
R. Mandar
Rue Tiquetonne
Etienne Marcel
Rue Etienne Marcel
Rue Beaubourg
R. J.-J. Rousseau
Rue du Louvre
Rue Croix des Petits Champs
St-Eustache
Les Halles
Forum des Halles
Rue Pierre Lescot
Rue St-Denis
Rue St-Martin
Rambuteau
Rue Rambuteau
Rue Quincampoix
Centre Pompidou
Châtelet-Les Halles
Bd. de Sébastopol
Rue Berger
RER
Rue des Halles
Rue St-Honoré
4e
Rue des Lombards
Rue du Renard
Louvre
Rue de Rivoli
R. du Roule
Rue du Pont-Neuf
R. de la Monnaie
Rue des Bourdonnais
Rue des Lavandières-Ste-Opportune
Rue St-Denis
Châtelet
Hôtel de Ville
Tour St-Jaques
Louvre
R. de l'Am. de Coligny
Pont Neuf
PLACE DU CHATELET
Quai de la Mégisserie
Pont des Arts
Pont au Change
Pont Notre Dame
Pont d'Arcole
PLACE DAUPHINE
Conciergerie
Cité
PL. L LEPINE
Hôtel Dieu
Palais de Justice
Ste-Chapelle
R. de Lutèce
Ile de la Cité
Quai Malaquais
Quai de Conti
Institut de France
Hôtel des Monnaies
Bd. du Palais
Préfecture de Police
PLACE DU PARVIS NOTRE-DAME
Notre Dame
Quai des Grands Augustins
Pont St-Michel
Petit Pont
Pont au Double
6e
Rue Dauphine
St-Michel

Paris: 5e and 6e

Palais du Louvre
Pont Neuf
Châtelet
1er
Quai du Louvre
Pont du Carrousel
Pont des Arts
Pont au Change
Conciergerie
Cité
Hôtel Dieu
Quai Malaquais
Quai de Conti
Ste-Chapelle
Ile de la Cité
Bd. du Palais
Rue de la Cité
Ecole Nationale Superieure des Beaux Arts
Institut de France
Hôtel des Monnaies
Quai des Grands Augustins
Pont St-Michel
Pont St-Michel
RER
St-Michel
R. Bonaparte
Rue des Sts-Pères
Rue Jacob
Rue de Seine
Rue Mazarine
Rue Dauphine
Rue St-André des Arts
Rue Danton
Pl. St-Michel
Rue St-Jacques
R. de l'Abbaye
PLACE ST-GERMAIN-DES-PRÉS
St-Germain Des Prés
Bd. St-Germain
Bd. St-Germain
St-Germain des Prés
Mabillon
Odéon
Musée du Cluny
7e
R. du Four
Rue de l'Odeon
Rue de Tournon
Rue Racine
Boulevard St-Michel
Sorbonne
R. de Sevres
R. du Vieux Colombier
R. du Saint Sulpice
PLACE ST-SULPICE
St-Sulpice
PLACE DE L'ODÉON
PLACE DE LA SORBONNE
St-Sulpice
R. du Cherche Midi
R. de Rennes
R. d'Assas
Palais du Luxembourg
Rue Soufflot
Luxembourg
Bd. Raspail
R. de Vaugirard
6e
Rennes
Rue Gay-Lussac
JARDIN DU LUXEMBOURG
St Placide
Notre-Dame des Champs
Rue d'Assas
Rue du Montparnasse
Rue Vavin
Rue Notre-Dame des Champs
Boulevard St-Michel
Rue St-Jacques
Montparnasse Bienvenüe
Vavin
Avenue de la Observatoire
Boulevard du Montparnasse
Port Royal
Boulevard Raspail
R. du Depart
14e
Edgar Quinet
Boulevard Edgar Quinet

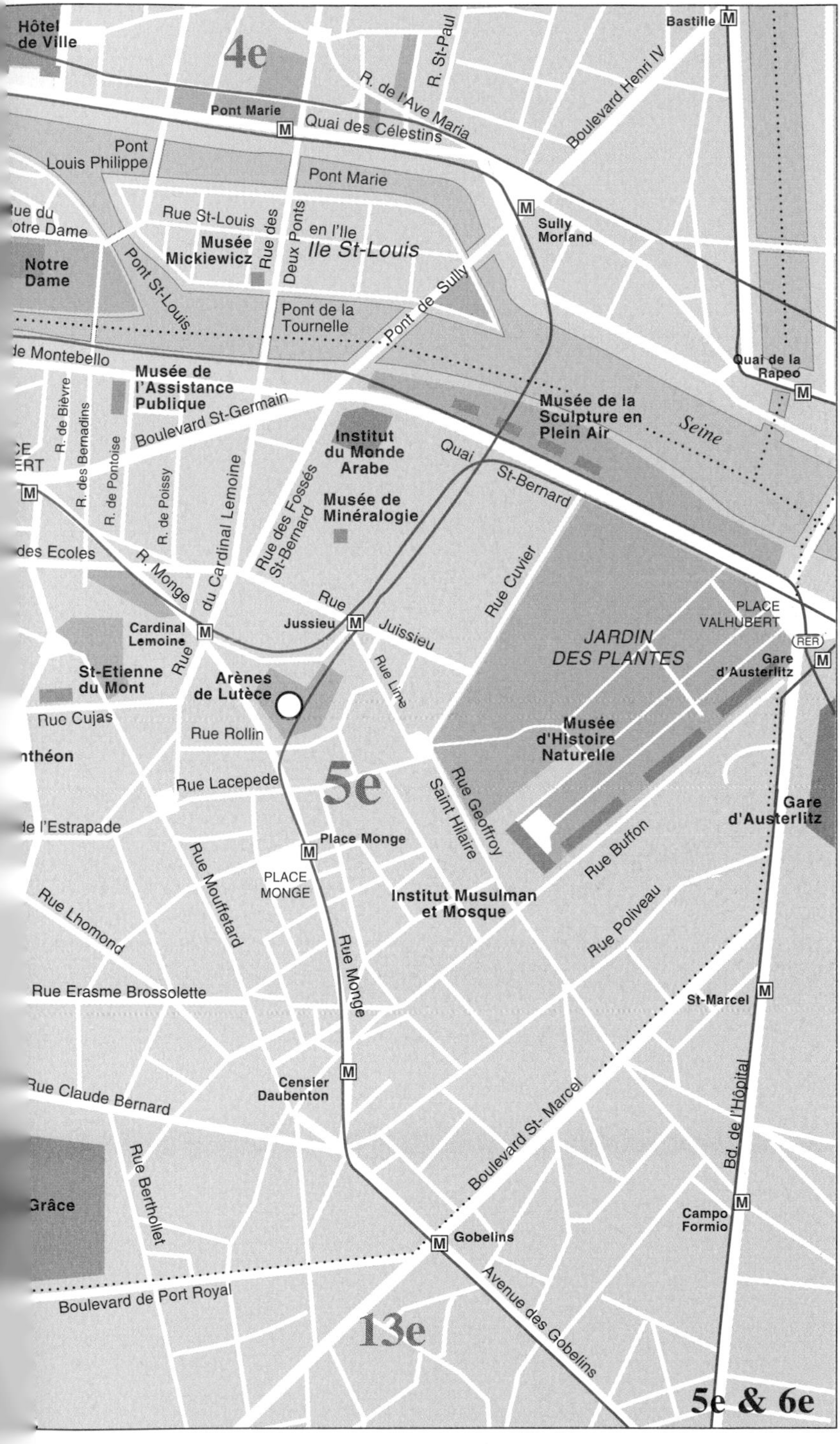
Hôtel de Ville
4e
Pont Marie
Quai des Célestins
R. St-Paul
R. de l'Ave Maria
Bastille
Boulevard Henri IV
Pont Louis Philippe
Pont Marie
Rue du Notre Dame
Rue St-Louis
Rue des Deux Ponts
en l'Ile
Ile St-Louis
Musée Mickiewicz
Sully Morland
Notre Dame
Pont St-Louis
Pont de Sully
Pont de la Tournelle
de Montebello
Quai de la Rapeo
Musée de l'Assistance Publique
Boulevard St-Germain
Musée de la Sculpture en Plein Air
Seine
R. de Bièvre
R. des Bernadins
R. de Pontoise
R. de Poissy
Rue du Cardinal Lemoine
Rue des Fossés St-Bernard
Institut du Monde Arabe
Quai St-Bernard
Musée de Minéralogie
des Ecoles
R. Monge
Rue Cuvier
Rue Jussieu
PLACE VALHUBERT
Cardinal Lemoine
Jussieu
JARDIN DES PLANTES
RER
Gare d'Austerlitz
St-Etienne du Mont
Rue
Rue Linné
Arènes de Lutèce
Rue Cujas
Rue Rollin
Musée d'Histoire Naturelle
nthéon
Rue Lacepede
5e
Rue Geoffroy Saint Hilaire
Gare d'Austerlitz
de l'Estrapade
Place Monge
PLACE MONGE
Rue Mouffetard
Rue Buffon
Institut Musulman et Mosque
Rue Lhomond
Rue Poliveau
Rue Monge
Rue Erasme Brossolette
St-Marcel
Censier Daubenton
Rue Claude Bernard
Boulevard St- Marcel
Bd. de l'Hôpital
Rue Berthollet
Grâce
Campo Formio
Gobelins
Boulevard de Port Royal
Avenue des Gobelins
13e
5e & 6e

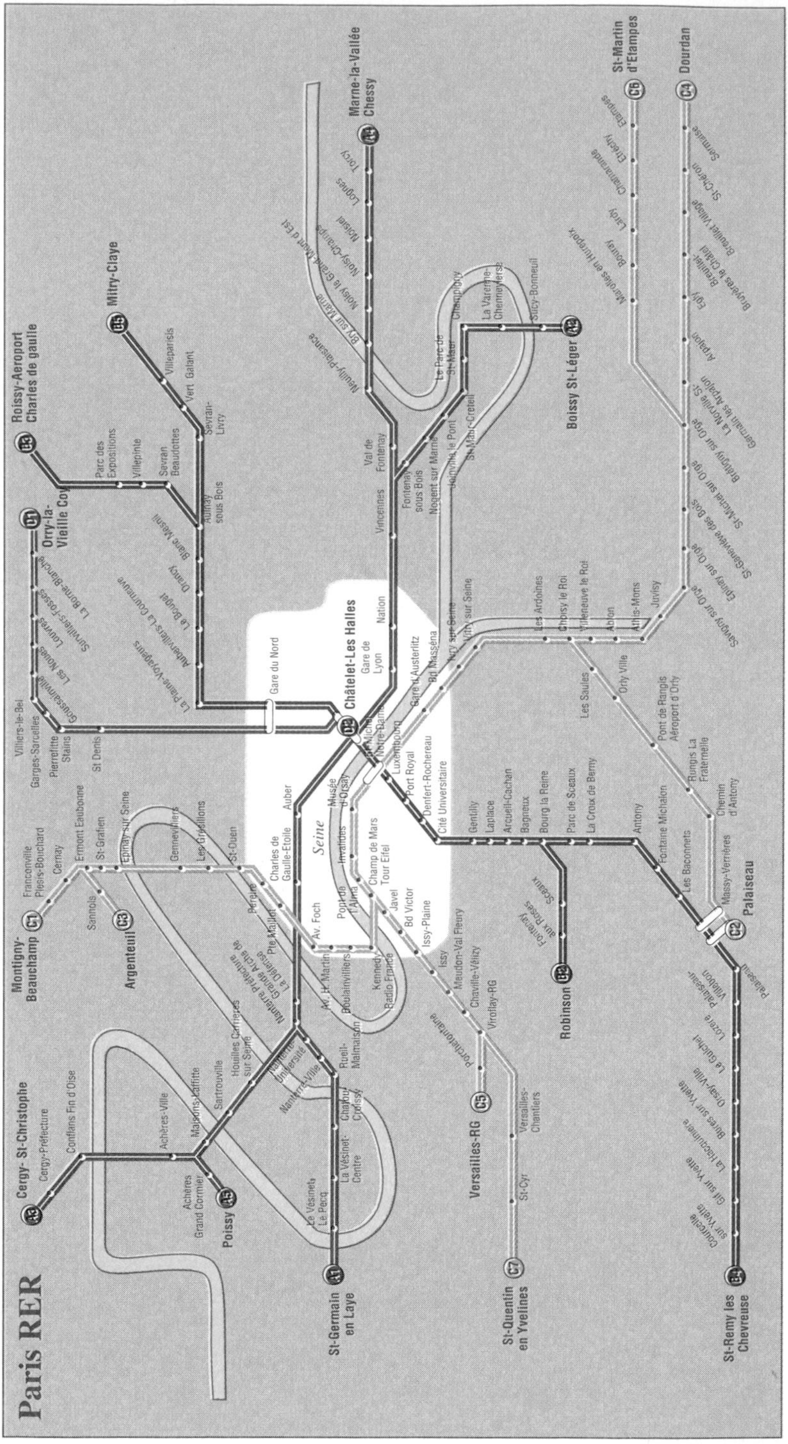

Paris RER
Cergy- St-Christophe
Poissy
St-Germain en Laye
Montigny-Beauchamp
Argenteuil
Versailles-RG
St-Quentin en Yvelines
Robinson
St-Remy les Chevreuse
Palaiseau
Boissy-Aeroport Charles de gaulle
Mitry-Claye
Orry-la-Vieille Coy
Marne-la-Vallée Chessy
Boissy St-Léger
St-Martin d'Etampes
Dourdan
Châtelet-Les Halles
Gare du Nord
Gare de Lyon
Nation
Auber
Charles de Gaulle-Etoile
Seine

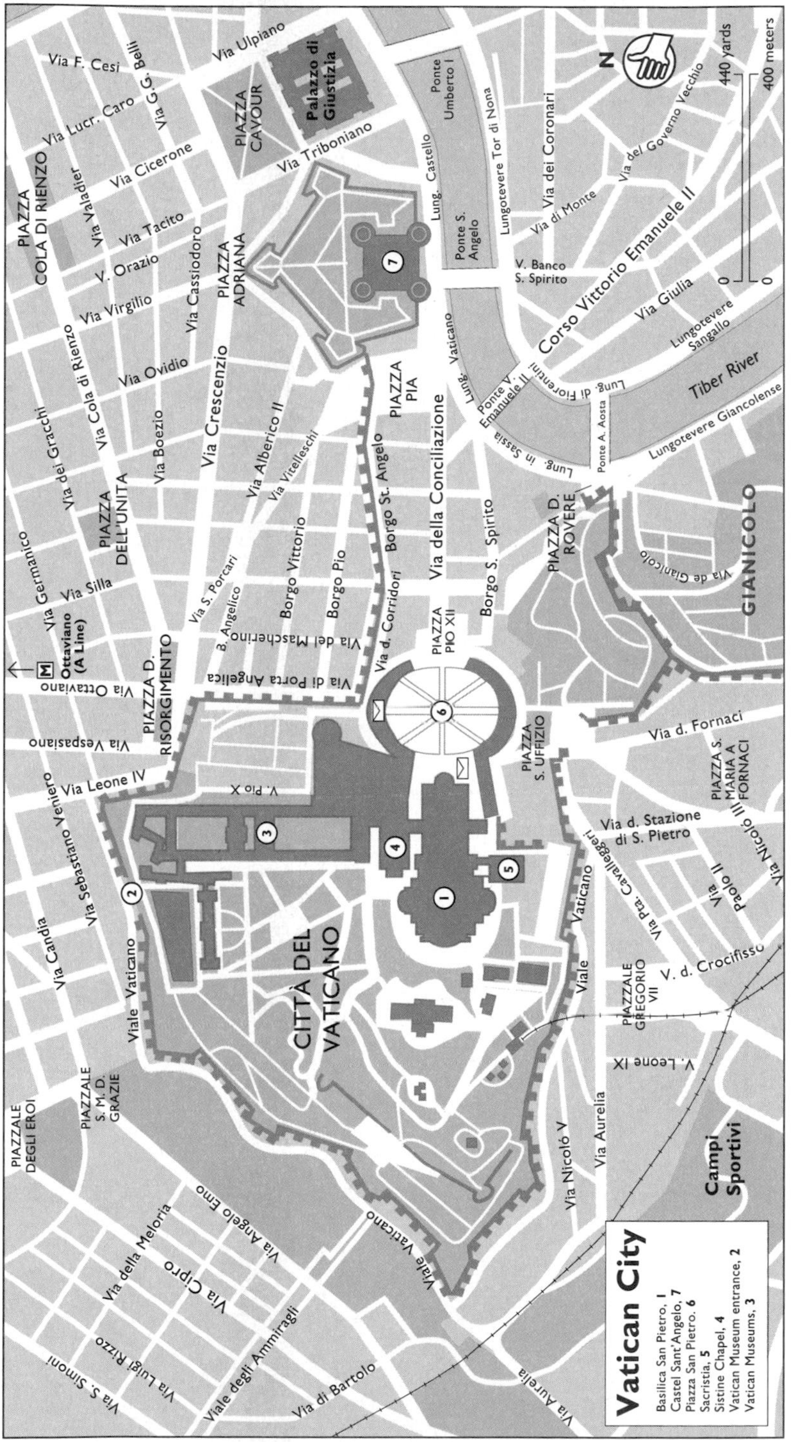
Vatican City
Basilica San Pietro, 1
Castel Sant'Angelo, 7
Piazza San Pietro, 6
Sacristia, 5
Sistine Chapel, 4
Vatican Museum entrance, 2
Vatican Museums, 3
N
0
440 yards
400 meters
CITTÀ DEL VATICANO
PIAZZA COLA DI RIENZO
PIAZZA CAVOUR
Palazzo di Giustizia
PIAZZA ADRIANA
PIAZZA PIA
PIAZZA DELL'UNITÀ
PIAZZA D. RISORGIMENTO
PIAZZA PIO XII
PIAZZA D. ROVERE
PIAZZA S. UFFIZIO
PIAZZA S. MARIA A FORNACI
PIAZZALE GREGORIO VII
PIAZZALE S. M. D. GRAZIE
PIAZZALE DEGLI EROI
GIANICOLO
Campi Sportivi
Tiber River
Ottaviano (A Line)
Via F. Cesi
Via Ulpiano
Via Lucr. Caro
Via G.G. Belli
Via Cicerone
Via Tribonian o
Via Valadier
Via Tacito
V. Orazio
Via Cassiodoro
Via Virgilio
Via Cola di Rienzo
Via Ovidio
Via Crescenzio
Via dei Gracchi
Via Boezio
Via Alberico II
Via Vitelleschi
Borgo St. Angelo
Via della Conciliazione
Borgo S. Spirito
Via Germanico
Via Silla
Via S. Porcari
B. Angelico
Borgo Vittorio
Borgo Pio
Via d. Corridori
Via del Mascherino
Via di Porta Angelica
Via Ottaviano
Via Vespasiano
Via Leone IV
V. Pio X
Via Sebastiano Veniero
Via Candia
Viale Vaticano
Ponte Umberto I
Lung. Castello
Ponte S. Angelo
Lungotevere Tor di Nona
Via dei Coronari
Via del Governo Vecchio
Via di Monte
V. Banco S. Spirito
Corso Vittorio Emanuele II
Via Giulia
Lungotevere Sangallo
Lung. Vaticano
Ponte V. Emanuele II
Lung. di Fiorentini
Lung. in Sassia
Ponte A. Aosta
Lungotevere Gianicolense
Via de Gianicolo
Via d. Fornaci
Via d. Stazione di S. Pietro
Via Pta. Cavalleggeri
Via Paolo II
Via Nicolò III
V. d. Crocifisso
Viale Vaticano
V. Leone IX
Via Aurelia
Via Nicolò V
Via Angelo Emo
Via della Meloria
Via Cipro
Via Luigi Rizzo
Via S. Simoni
Viale degli Ammiragli
Via di Bartolo
Via Aurelia

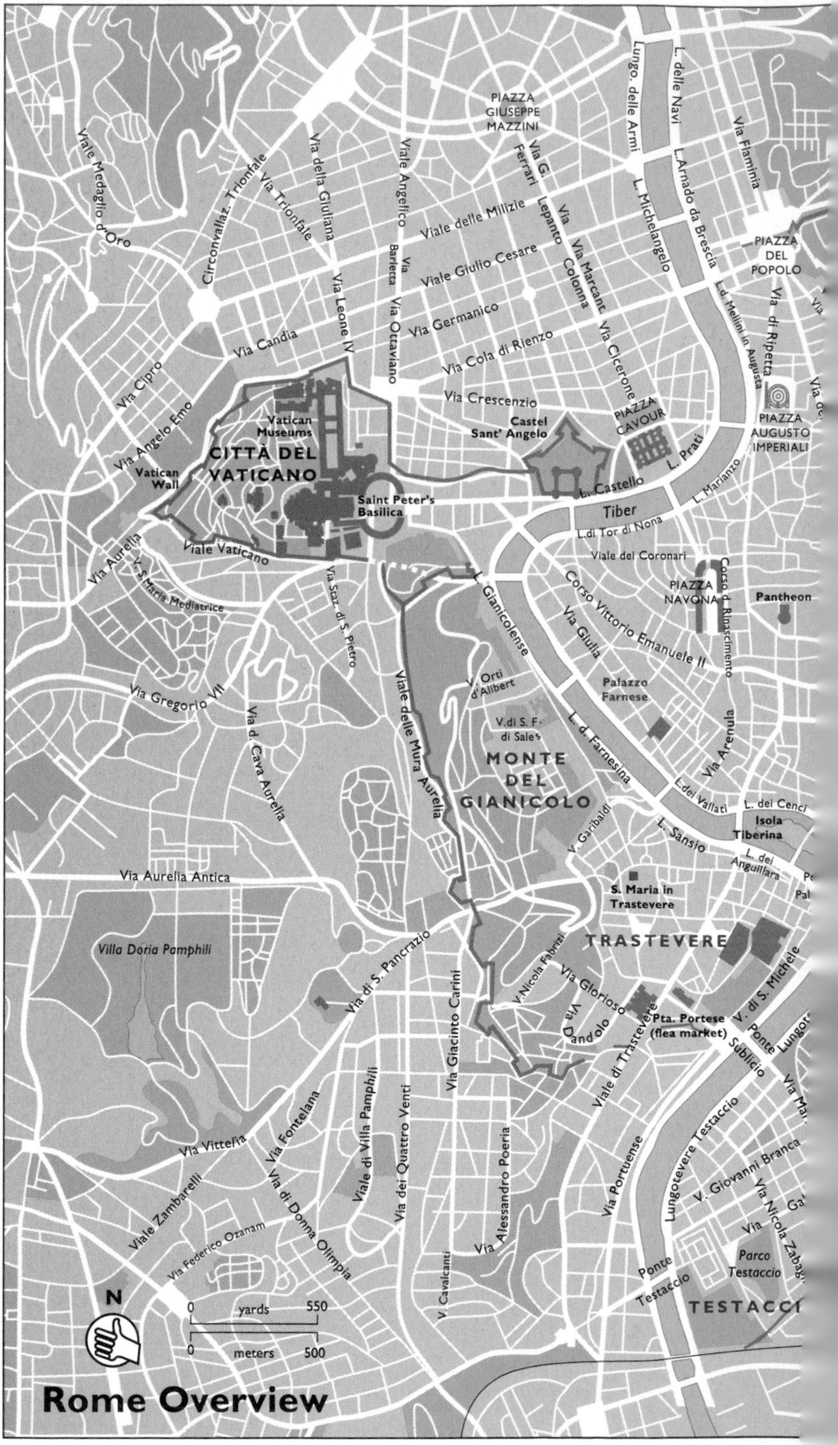
PIAZZA GIUSEPPE MAZZINI
PIAZZA DEL POPOLO
PIAZZA CAVOUR
PIAZZA AUGUSTO IMPERIALE
PIAZZA NAVONA
CITTÀ DEL VATICANO
Vatican Museums
Vatican Wall
Saint Peter's Basilica
Castel Sant' Angelo
Pantheon
Tiber
MONTE DEL GIANICOLO
Palazzo Farnese
Isola Tiberina
S. Maria in Trastevere
TRASTEVERE
Pta. Portese (flea market)
Villa Doria Pamphili
Parco Testaccio
TESTACCI
Viale Medaglie d'Oro
Circonvallaz. Trionfale
Via Trionfale
Via della Giuliana
Via Leone IV
Viale Angelico
Via Barletta
Via Ottaviano
Via G. Ferrari
Via Lepanto
Via Marcant. Colonna
Via Cicerone
Lungo. delle Armi
L. delle Navi
L. Michelangelo
L. Arnado da Brescia
Via Flaminia
Viale delle Milizie
Viale Giulio Cesare
Via Germanico
Via Cola di Rienzo
Via Crescenzio
Via Candia
Via Cipro
Via Angelo Emo
L.d. Mellini in Augusta
Via di Ripetta
L. Prati
L. Castello
L. Marianzo
L.di Tor di Nona
Viale dei Coronari
Corso Vittorio Emanuele II
Corso d. Rinascimento
Via Giulia
Via Aurelia
V. S. Maria Mediatrice
Viale Vaticano
Via Staz. di S. Pietro
L. Gianicolense
V. Orti d'Alibert
V.di S. F. di Sales
Via Gregorio VII
Via d. Cava Aurelia
Viale delle Mura Aurelia
L. d. Farnesina
Via Arenula
L.dei Vallati
L. dei Cenci
L. Sansio
L. dei Anguillara
V. Garibaldi
Via Aurelia Antica
Via di S. Pancrazio
Via Giacinto Carini
V. Nicola Fabrizi
Via Glorioso
Via Dandolo
Viale di Trastevere
V. di S. Michele
Ponte Sublicio
Via Vittelia
Via Fontelana
Viale di Villa Pamphili
Via dei Quattro Venti
Via Alessandro Poeria
Via Portuense
Lungotevere Testaccio
V. Giovanni Branca
Via Nicola Zabaglia
Viale Zambarelli
Via di Donna Olimpia
Via Federico Ozanam
V. Cavalcanti
Ponte Testaccio
N
0 yards 550
0 meters 500
Rome Overview

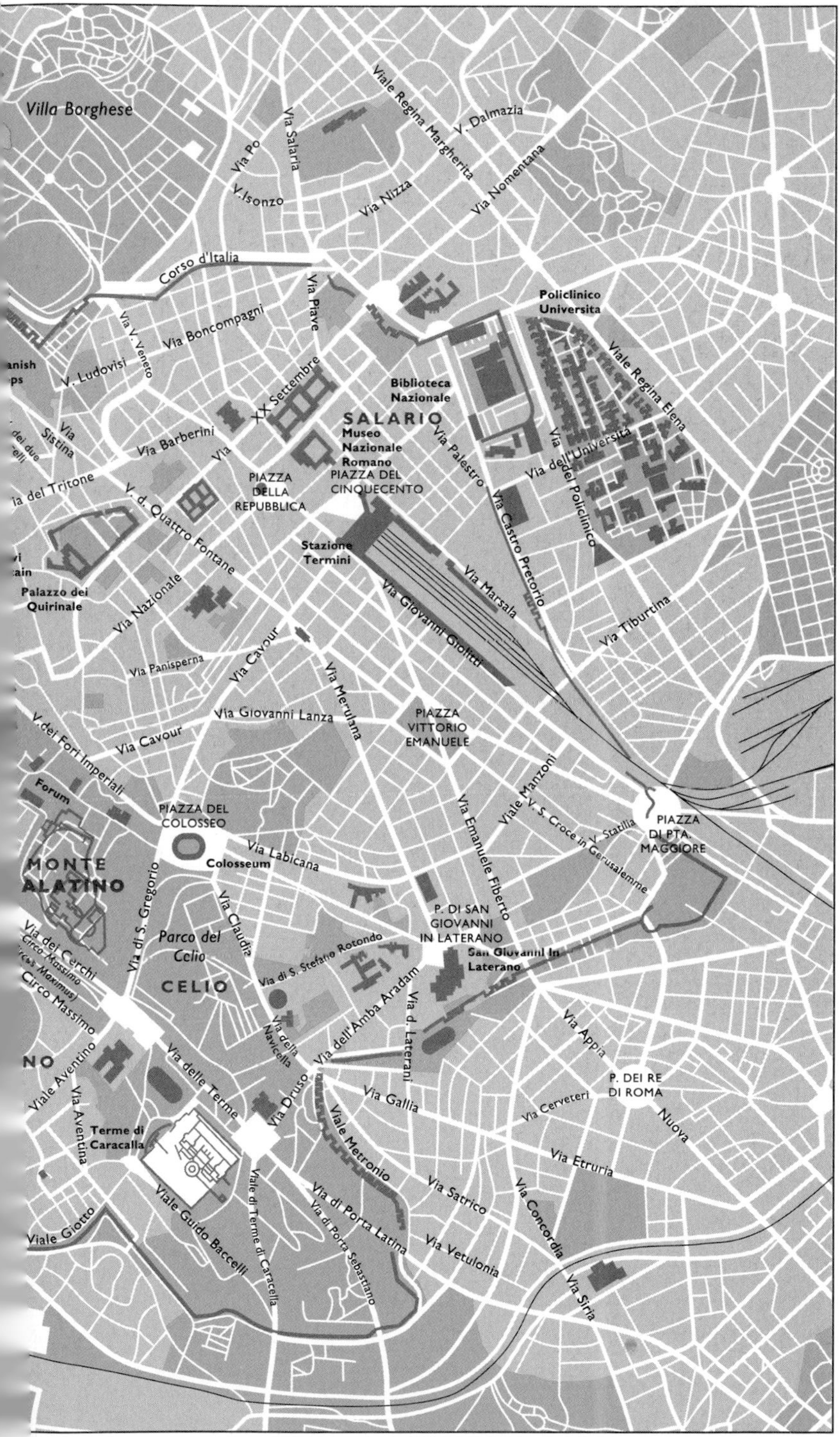
Villa Borghese
Via Po
V. Isonzo
Via Salaria
Viale Regina Margherita
V. Dalmazia
Via Nizza
Via Nomentana
Corso d'Italia
Via Piave
Via V. Veneto
Via Boncompagni
V. Ludovisi
Policlinico Universita
Viale Regina Elena
Biblioteca Nazionale
SALARIO
Museo Nazionale Romano
XX Settembre
Via Barberini
Via Sistina
Via del Tritone
V. d. Quattro Fontane
PIAZZA DELLA REPUBBLICA
PIAZZA DEL CINQUECENTO
Via Palestro
Via dell'Università
Via del Policlinico
Via Castro Pretorio
Stazione Termini
Via Marsala
Via Giovanni Giolitti
Palazzo dei Quirinale
Via Nazionale
Via Tiburtina
Via Panisperna
Via Cavour
Via Merulana
Via Giovanni Lanza
PIAZZA VITTORIO EMANUELE
V. dei Fori Imperiali
Via Cavour
Forum
PIAZZA DEL COLOSSEO
Colosseum
Via Labicana
Viale Manzoni
V. S. Croce in Gerusalemme
V. Statilia
PIAZZA DI PTA. MAGGIORE
Via Emanuele Filiberto
MONTE
ALATINO
Via di S. Gregorio
Via Claudia
Parco del Celio
CELIO
P. DI SAN GIOVANNI IN LATERANO
San Giovanni In Laterano
Via di S. Stefano Rotondo
Via dei Cerchi
Circo Massimo
Via della Navicella
Via dell'Amba Aradam
Via d. Laterani
Via Appia
Viale Aventino
Via delle Terme
Via Druso
Via Gallia
P. DEI RE DI ROMA
Via Cerveteri
Nuova
Via Aventina
Terme di Caracalla
Viale Metronio
Via Etruria
Via Satrico
Via Concordia
Viale di Terme di Caracalla
Via di Porta Latina
Via di Porta Sebastiano
Via Vetulonia
Viale Giotto
Viale Guido Baccelli
Via Siria

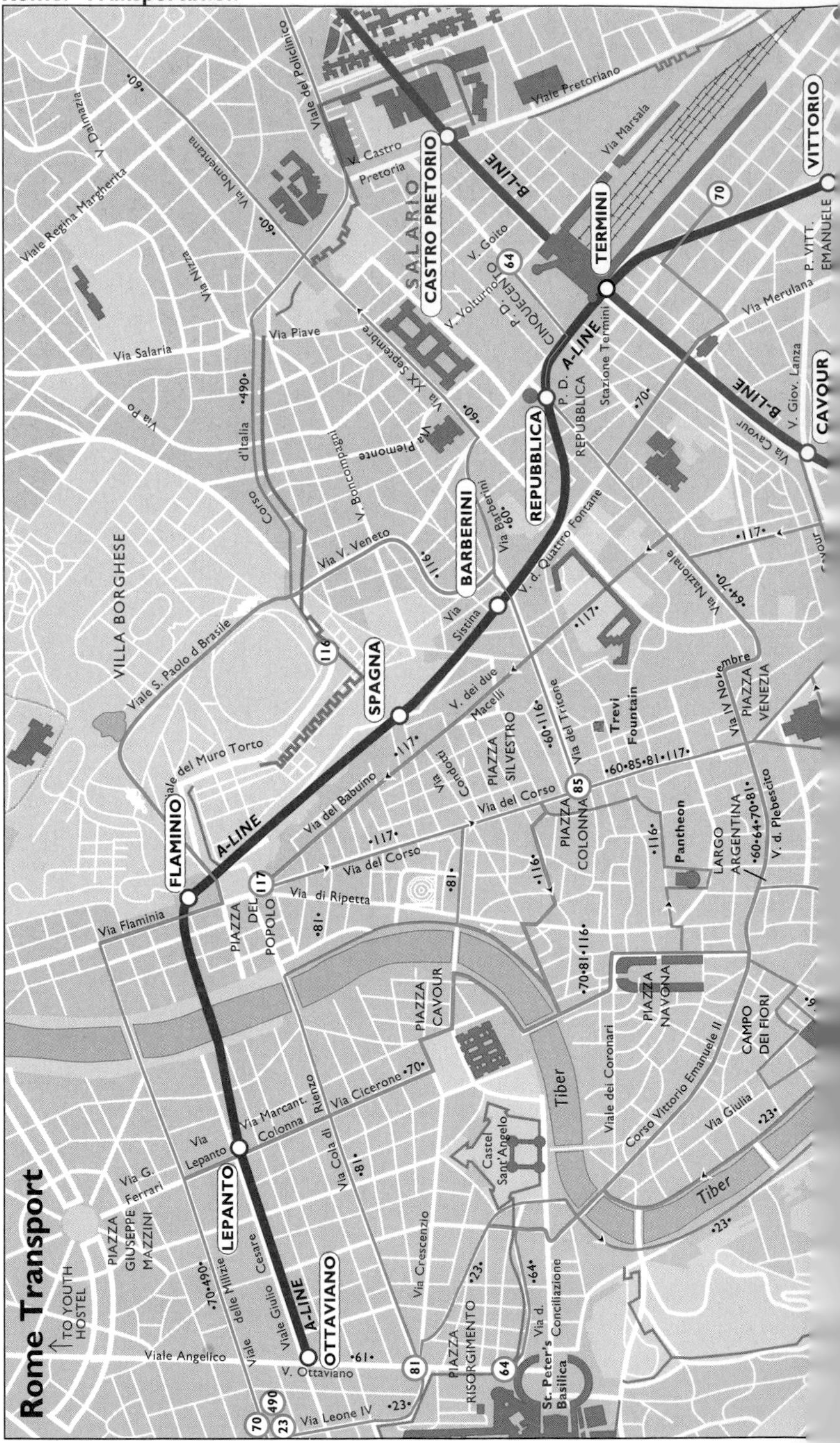
Rome Transport
TO YOUTH HOSTEL
A-LINE
B-LINE
OTTAVIANO
LEPANTO
FLAMINIO
SPAGNA
BARBERINI
REPUBBLICA
TERMINI
CASTRO PRETORIO
VITTORIO
CAVOUR
VILLA BORGHESE
SALARIO
PIAZZA GIUSEPPE MAZZINI
PIAZZA DEL POPOLO
PIAZZA CAVOUR
PIAZZA RISORGIMENTO
PIAZZA SILVESTRO
PIAZZA COLONNA
PIAZZA NAVONA
PIAZZA VENEZIA
LARGO ARGENTINA
CAMPO DEI FIORI
P. D. REPUBBLICA
P. D. CINQUECENTO
P. VITT. EMANUELE
Castel Sant'Angelo
St. Peter's Basilica
Pantheon
Trevi Fountain
Tiber
Viale Angelico
V. Ottaviano
Via Leone IV
Viale Giulio Cesare
Viale delle Milizie
Via G. Ferrari
Via Lepanto
Via Marcant. Colonna
Via Cola di Rienzo
Via Cicerone
Via Crescenzio
Via d. Conciliazione
Via Flaminia
Viale del Muro Torto
Viale S. Paolo d Brasile
Via di Ripetta
Via del Corso
Via del Babuino
Via Condotti
V. dei due Macelli
Via Sistina
Via del Tritone
Via Barberini
V. d. Quattro Fontane
Via Nazionale
Via IV Novembre
V. d. Plebescito
Corso Vittorio Emanuele II
Viale dei Coronari
Via Giulia
Via V. Veneto
V. Boncompagni
Corso d'Italia
Via Piemonte
Via XX Settembre
Via Piave
Via Salaria
Via Po
Via Nizza
Viale Regina Margherita
V. Dalmazia
Via Nomentana
Viale del Policlinico
V. Castro Pretoria
V. Volturno
V. Goito
Viale Pretoriano
Via Marsala
Stazione Termini
Via Merulana
V. Giov. Lanza
Via Cavour
70
490
23
81
64
117
116
85
•70•490•
•61•
•23•
•81•
•64•
•60•
•490•
•117•
•116•
•70•81•116•
•60•85•81•117•
•60•64•70•81•
•64•70•
•70•

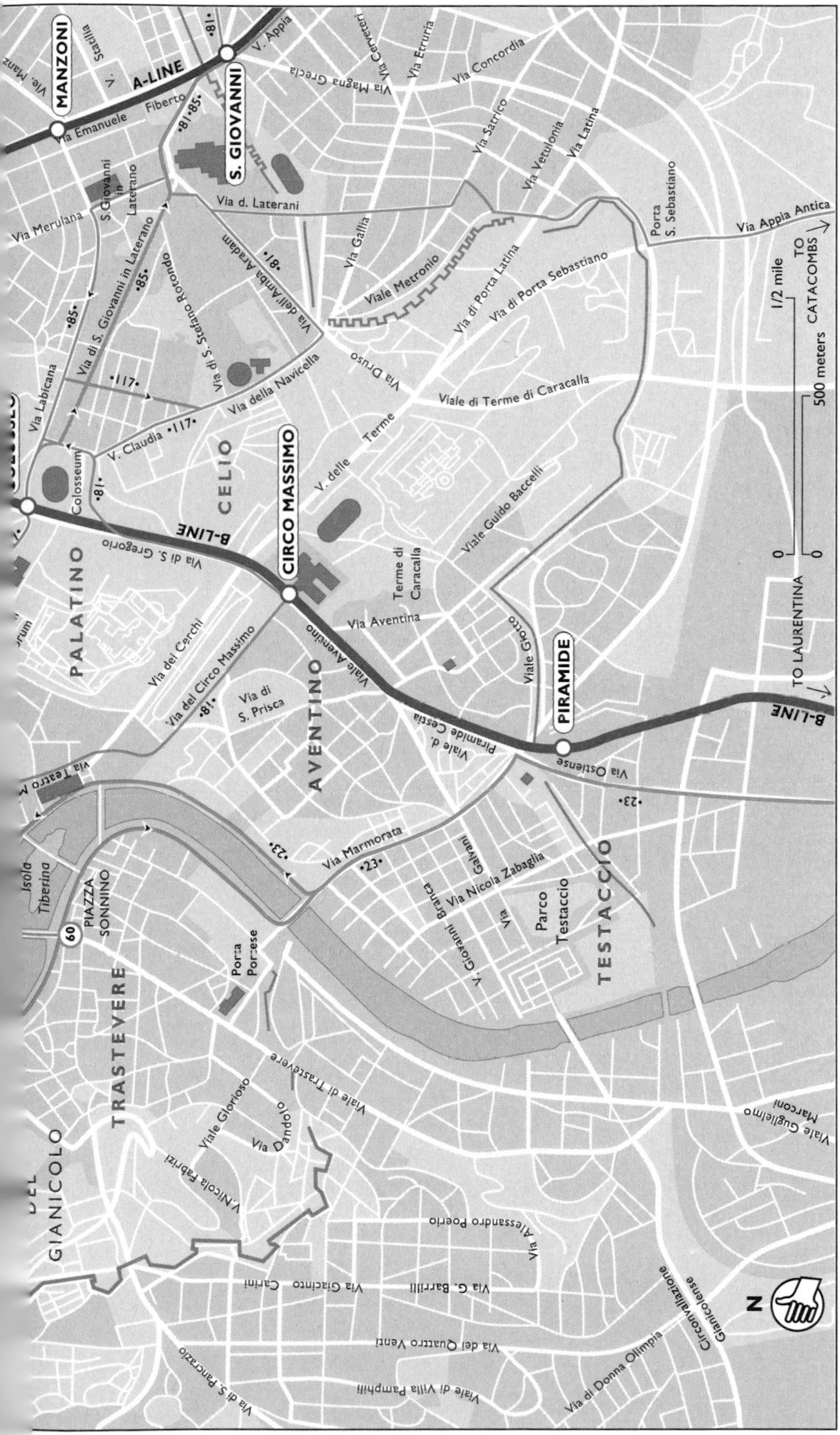
MANZONI
S. GIOVANNI
A-LINE
B-LINE
CIRCO MASSIMO
PIRAMIDE
Colosseum
PALATINO
CELIO
AVENTINO
TESTACCIO
TRASTEVERE
GIANICOLO
Isola Tiberina
PIAZZA SONNINO
Porta Portese
Parco Testaccio
Terme di Caracalla
Porta S. Sebastiano
Via Appia Antica
TO CATACOMBS
TO LAURENTINA
1/2 mile
500 meters
Via Emanuele Filiberto
Via Merulana
Via Labicana
Via d. Laterani
Via di S. Giovanni in Laterano
Via di S. Stefano Rotondo
Via dell'Amba Aradam
Via della Navicella
V. Claudia
Via di S. Gregorio
Via dei Cerchi
Via del Circo Massimo
Via di S. Prisca
Viale Aventino
Via Aventina
Viale Guido Baccelli
Viale di Terme di Caracalla
V. delle Terme
Via Druso
Viale Metronio
Via di Porta Latina
Via di Porta Sebastiano
Via Gallia
Via Latina
Via Vetulonia
Via Satrico
Via Concordia
Via Etruria
Via Cerveteri
Via Magna Grecia
V. Appia
Viale Giotto
Viale d. Piramide Cestia
Via Ostiense
Via Marmorata
Via Nicola Zabaglia
V. Giovanni Branca
Via Galvani
Viale di Trastevere
Viale Glorioso
Via Dandolo
V. Nicola Fabrizi
Via Alessandro Poerio
Via Giacinto Carini
Via G. Barrili
Via dei Quattro Venti
Viale di Villa Pamphili
Via di S. Pancrazio
Via di Donna Olimpia
Circonvallazione Gianicolense
Viale Guglielmo Marconi
Via Teatro Marcello
•81•
•85•
•117•
•23•
60
N

Central Rome
Ara Pacis, 3
Campo dei Fiori, 27
Captioline Hill and Museums, 22
Castel Sant'Angelo, 9
Chiesa Nuova, 10
Il Gesù, 23
Galleria Corsini, 31
Galleria Doria Pamphilij, 19
Galleria Spada, 28
Mausoleum of Augustus, 4
Museo Barrocco, 26
Museo Mario Praz, 7
Museo Napoleonico, 7
Museo di Palazzo Venezia, 18
Palazzo di Giustizia, 8
Pantheon, 13
P. Farnese, 29
P. Navona, 11
P. del Popolo, 2
P. della Rotonda, 13
P. di Spagna, 5
P. Venezia, 20
Sant'Agnese in Agone, 11
Sant'Andrea delle valle, 25
Sant'Antonio dei Portoghesi, 6
Santi Apostoli, 17
Sant'Ignazio, 15
San Luigi dei Francesci, 12
San Marcello, 16
Santa Maria sopra Minerva, 14
Santa Maria del Popolo, 1
Spanish Steps, 5
Theater of Marcellus, 24
Trevi Fountain, 16
Villa Farnesina, 30
Vittorio Emanuele II Monument, 21
VILLA BORGHESE
VILLA MEDICI
PIAZZA DEL POPOLO
PIAZZA D. LIBERTA
PIAZZA CAVOUR
PIAZZA ADRIANA
PIAZZA DEI TRIBUNALI
PIAZZA PIA
PIAZZA D. PORTO DI RIPETTA
PIAZZA AUGUSTO IMPERATORE
PIAZZA DI SPAGNA
PIAZZA TRINITÀ D. MONTE
PIAZZA DEL PARLIAMENTO
PIAZZA S. SILVESTRO
LARGO CHIGI
Tiber River
Ponte Margherita
Ponte Cavour
Ponte Umberto I
Ponte S. Ange
Spagna
TO ST. PETER'S
Via del Corso
Via di Ripetta
Via del Babuino
Via Margutta
Via Cola di Rienzo
Via Crescenzio
Lungotevere Castello
Lungotevere Vaticano
Lungotevere Marzio
Lung. in Augusta
Lung. dei Mellini
Lung. Prati
Passeggiata di Ripetta
V. d. Conciliazione
Via Porta Castello
Via Tomacelli
Via dell' Arancio
Via Condotti
Via Borgognona
Via Frattina
Via delle Vite
Via della Mercede
Via del Tritone
Via Sistina
Via Trinità dei Monti
Via Belvedere
V. del Muro Torto
Viale G. d'Annunzio

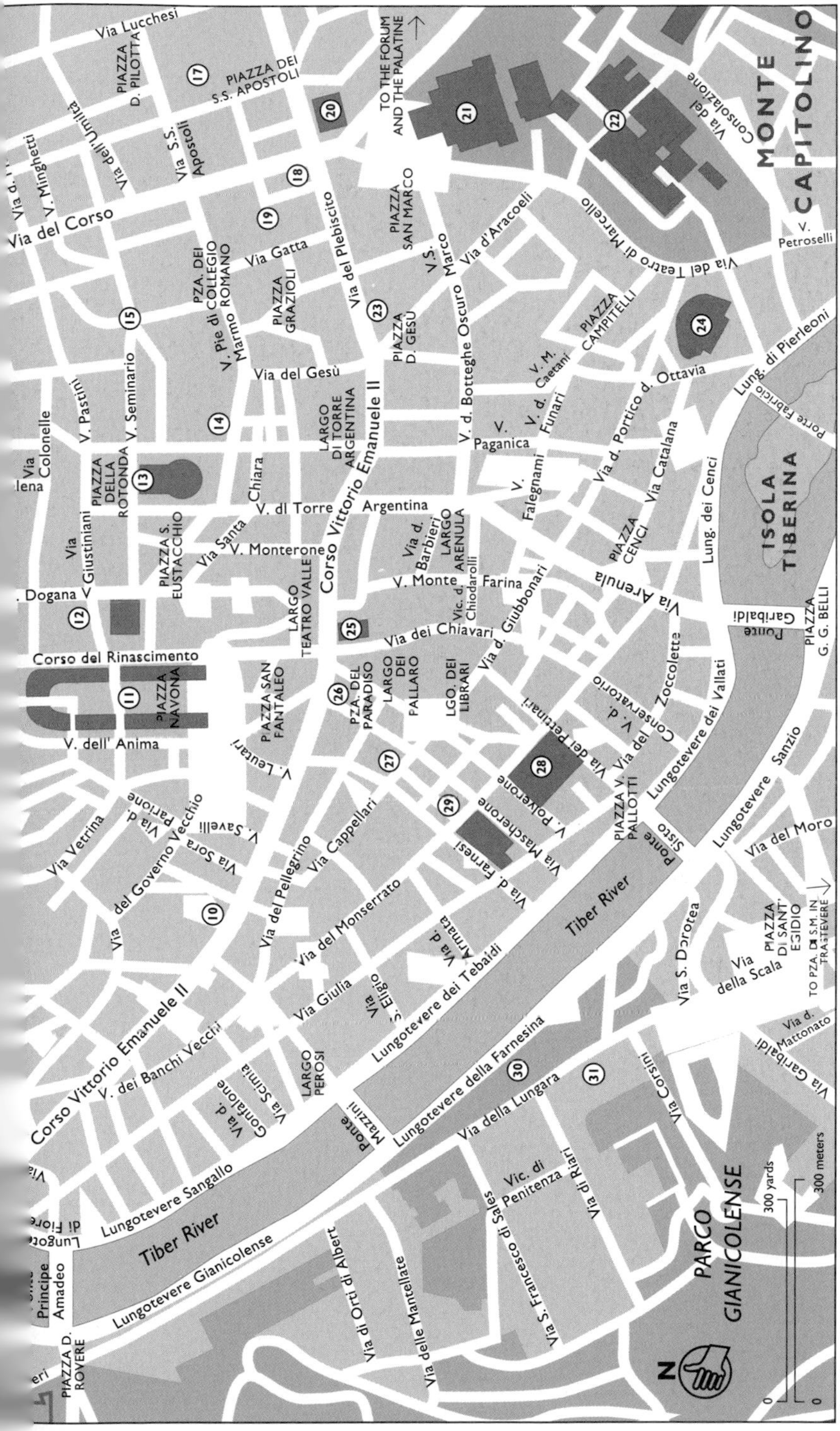
MONTE CAPITOLINO
ISOLA TIBERINA
PARCO GIANICOLENSE
TO THE FORUM AND THE PALATINE
TO PZA. DI S.M. IN TRASTEVERE
Via Lucchesi
PIAZZA D. PILOTTA
PIAZZA DEI S.S. APOSTOLI
Via dell'Umiltà
V. Minghetti
Via S.S. Apostoli
Via del Corso
PIAZZA SAN MARCO
V.S. Marco
Via d'Aracoeli
Via del Plebiscito
PZA. DEI COLLEGIO ROMANO
Via Gatta
PIAZZA GRAZIOLI
V. Pie di Marmo
Via del Gesù
PIAZZA D. GESÙ
V. d. Botteghe Oscure
Via della Consolazione
Via del Teatro di Marcello
V. Petroselli
PIAZZA CAMPITELLI
V. M. Caetani
V. d. Funari
V. Paganica
V. Falegnami
Via d. Portico d. Ottavia
Lung. di Pierleoni
Ponte Fabricio
Via Catalana
Lung. dei Cenci
PIAZZA CENCI
Via Arenula
Ponte Garibaldi
PIAZZA G. G. BELLI
LARGO DI TORRE ARGENTINA
Corso Vittorio Emanuele II
V. dl Torre Argentina
Via d. Barbieri
LARGO ARENULA
Vic. d. Chiodaroli
V. Monte Farina
Via d. Giubbonari
Via dei Chiavari
LARGO TEATRO VALLE
V. Monterone
Via Santa Chiara
PIAZZA S. EUSTACCHIO
PIAZZA DELLA ROTONDA
V. Seminario
V. Pastini
Via Colonelle
Via Giustiniani
Dogana V.
Corso del Rinascimento
PIAZZA NAVONA
V. dell' Anima
PIAZZA SAN PANTALEO
PZA. DEL PARADISO
LARGO DEI FALLARO
LGO. DEI LIBRARI
Via dei Pettinari
V. d. Conservatorio
Via del Zoccoletta
Lungotevere dei Vallati
PIAZZA V. PALLOTTI
Ponte Sisto
Lungotevere Sanzio
Via del Moro
V. Leutari
Via d. Parione
V. Savelli
Via Sora
Via del Governo Vecchio
Via Vetrina
Via del Pellegrino
Via Cappellari
V. Polverone
Via Mascherone
Via d. Farnesi
Via del Monserrato
Via d. Armata
Tiber River
Via S. Dorotea
Via della Scala
PIAZZA DI SANT' EGIDIO
Via Giulia
Via S. Eligio
Lungotevere dei Tebaldi
Lungotevere della Farnesina
Via d. Mattonato
Via Garibaldi
Via Corsini
Via della Lungara
Corso Vittorio Emanuele II
V. dei Banchi Vecchi
Via d. Gonfalone
Via Scimia
LARGO PEROSI
Ponte Mazzini
Lungotevere Sangallo
Lungotevere di Fiore
Ponte Principe Amadeo
Lungotevere Gianicolense
PIAZZA D. ROVERE
Via di Orti di Albert
Via delle Mantellate
Via S. Francesco di Sales
Vic. di Penitenza
Via di Riari
300 yards
300 meters
N
10
11
12
13
14
15
17
18
19
20
21
22
23
24
25
26
27
28
29
30
31

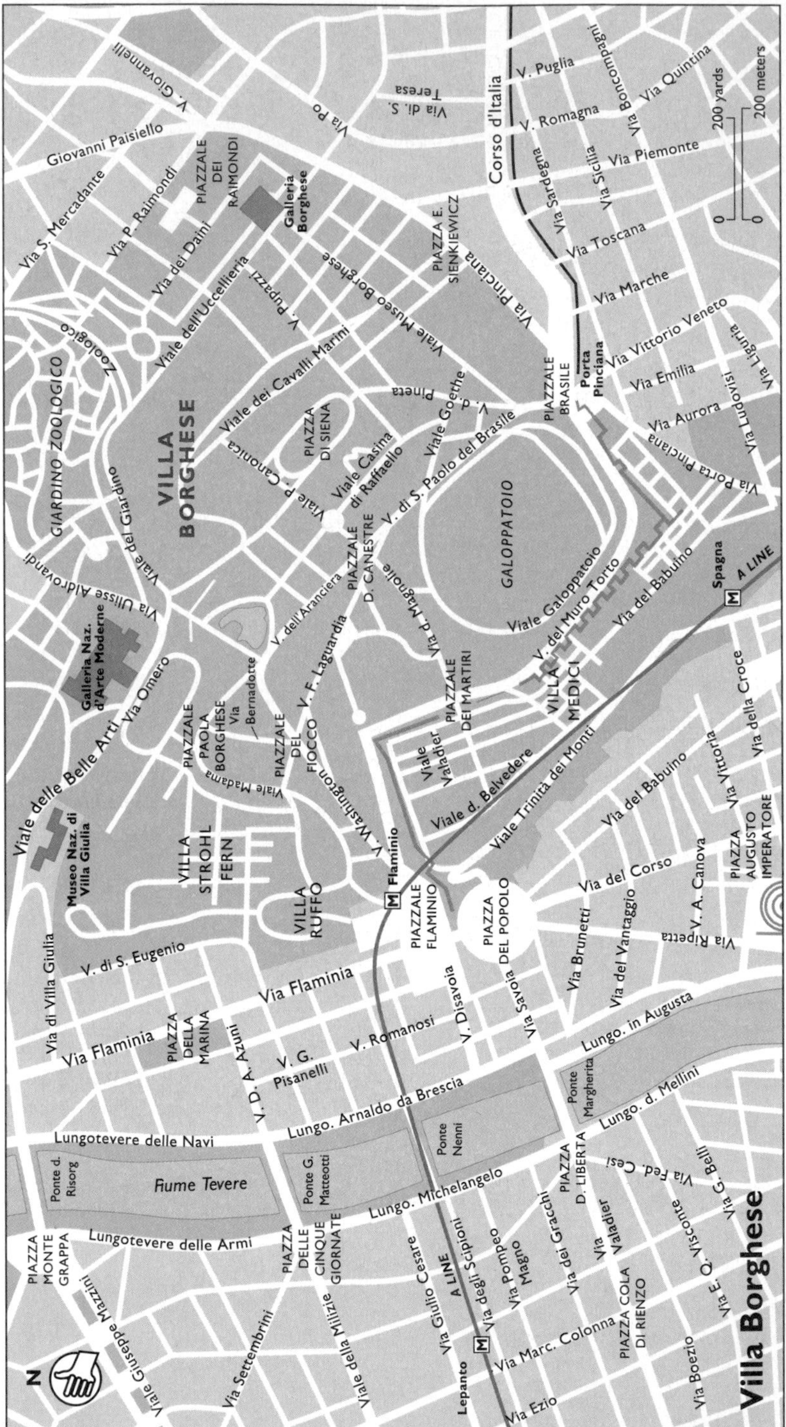
Villa Borghese
VILLA BORGHESE
GIARDINO ZOOLOGICO
GALOPPATOIO
Galleria Borghese
Galleria Naz. d'Arte Moderne
Museo Naz. di Villa Giulia
VILLA STROHL FERN
VILLA RUFFO
VILLA MEDICI
PIAZZA DEL POPOLO
PIAZZALE FLAMINIO
Flaminio
Spagna
Lepanto
A LINE
Porta Pinciana
PIAZZALE BRASILE
PIAZZA DI SIENA
PIAZZALE DEI RAIMONDI
PIAZZA E. SIENKIEWICZ
PIAZZALE D. CANESTRE
PIAZZALE DEL FIOCCO
PIAZZALE PAOLA BORGHESE
PIAZZALE DEI MARTIRI
PIAZZA AUGUSTO IMPERATORE
PIAZZA DELLA MARINA
PIAZZA MONTE GRAPPA
PIAZZA DELLE CINQUE GIORNATE
PIAZZA D. LIBERTÀ
PIAZZA COLA DI RIENZO
Fiume Tevere
Ponte d. Risorg
Ponte G. Matteotti
Ponte Nenni
Ponte Margherita
Corso d'Italia
Via Pinciana
Via Po
Via di. S. Teresa
V. Giovannelli
Giovanni Paisiello
Via S. Mercadante
Via P. Raimondi
Via dei Daini
Viale dell'Uccelliera
Viale Museo Borghese
Viale dei Cavalli Marini
V. Pupazzi
Zoologico
Viale del Giardino
Via Ulisse Aldrovandi
Viale P. Canonica
Viale Casina di Raffaello
V. di S. Paolo del Brasile
Viale Goethe
V. d. Pineta
V. dell'Aranciera
Via d. Magnolie
V. F. Laguardia
Via Bernadotte
Viale Madama
V. Washington
Via Omero
Viale delle Belle Arti
Viale Galoppatoio
V. del Muro Torto
Viale Valadier
Viale d. Belvedere
Viale Trinità dei Monti
Via del Babuino
Via della Croce
Via Vittoria
Via del Corso
V. A. Canova
Via Ripetta
Via Brunetti
Via del Vantaggio
Via Savoia
V. Disavoia
V. di S. Eugenio
Via Flaminia
Via di Villa Giulia
V. D. A. Azuni
V. G. Pisanelli
V. Romanosi
Lungo. Arnaldo da Brescia
Lungo. in Augusta
Lungo. d. Mellini
Lungotevere delle Navi
Lungo. Michelangelo
Lungotevere delle Armi
Viale Giuseppe Mazzini
Via Settembrini
Viale della Milizie
Via Giulio Cesare
Via degli Scipioni
Via Pompeo Magno
Via dei Gracchi
Via Valadier
Via Marc. Colonna
Via Fed. Cesi
Via G. Belli
Via E. Q. Visconte
Via Boezio
Via Ezio
V. Puglia
V. Romagna
Via Boncompagni
Via Quintina
Via Piemonte
Via Sardegna
Via Sicilia
Via Toscana
Via Marche
Via Vittorio Veneto
Via Emilia
Via Liguria
Via Aurora
Via Ludovisi
Via Porta Pinciana
200 yards
200 meters
N

LET'S GO:
Europe

"Lighthearted and sophisticated, informative and fun to read. *[Let's Go]* helps the novice traveler navigate like a knowledgeable old hand."

—Atlanta Journal-Constitution

"The guides are aimed not only at young budget travelers but at the independent traveler, a sort of streetwise cookbook for traveling alone."

—The New York Times

Let's Go writers travel on your budget.

"Retains the spirit of the student-written publication it is: candid, opinionated, resourceful, amusing info for the traveler of limited means but broad curiosity." ***—Mademoiselle***

"The writers seem to have experienced every rooster-packed bus and lunar-surfaced mattress about which they write." ***—The New York Times***

"All the dirt, dirt cheap." ***—People***

Great for independent travelers.

"A world-wise traveling companion—always ready with friendly advice and helpful hints, all sprinkled with a bit of wit." ***—The Philadelphia Inquirer***

"Lots of valuable information for any independent traveler."

—The Chicago Tribune

Let's Go is completely revised each year.

"Unbeatable: good sight-seeing advice; up-to-date info on restaurants, hotels, and inns; a commitment to money-saving travel; and a wry style that brightens nearly every page." ***—The Washington Post***

"Its yearly revision by a new crop of Harvard students makes it as valuable as ever." ***—The New York Times***

All the important information you need.

"Enough information to satisfy even the most demanding of budget travelers...*Let's Go* follows the creed that you don't have to toss your life's savings to the wind to travel—unless you want to."

—The Salt Lake Tribune

"Value-packed, unbeatable, accurate, and comprehensive."

—The Los Angeles Times

Let's Go Publications

Let's Go: Alaska & the Pacific Northwest 1998
Let's Go: Australia 1998 **New title!**
Let's Go: Austria & Switzerland 1998
Let's Go: Britain & Ireland 1998
Let's Go: California 1998
Let's Go: Central America 1998
Let's Go: Eastern Europe 1998
Let's Go: Ecuador & the Galápagos Islands 1998
Let's Go: Europe 1998
Let's Go: France 1998
Let's Go: Germany 1998
Let's Go: Greece & Turkey 1998
Let's Go: India & Nepal 1998
Let's Go: Ireland 1998
Let's Go: Israel & Egypt 1998
Let's Go: Italy 1998
Let's Go: London 1998
Let's Go: Mexico 1998
Let's Go: New York City 1998
Let's Go: New Zealand 1998 **New title!**
Let's Go: Paris 1998
Let's Go: Rome 1998
Let's Go: Southeast Asia 1998
Let's Go: Spain & Portugal 1998
Let's Go: USA 1998
Let's Go: Washington, D.C. 1998

Let's Go Map Guides

Berlin	*New Orleans*
Boston	*New York City*
Chicago	*Paris*
London	*Rome*
Los Angeles	*San Francisco*
Madrid	*Washington, D.C.*

Coming Soon: *Amsterdam, Florence*

Let's Go Publications

Let's Go Europe 1998

Caroline R. Sherman
Editor

Rachel A. Farbiarz
Associate Editor

Catharine M. Hornby
Associate Editor

St. Martin's Press New York

HELPING LET'S GO

If you want to share your discoveries, suggestions, or corrections, please drop us a line. We read every piece of correspondence, whether a postcard, a 10-page email, or a coconut. Please note that mail received after May 1998 may be too late for the 1999 book, but will be kept for future editions. **Address mail to:**

Let's Go: Europe
67 Mount Auburn Street
Cambridge, MA 02138
USA

Visit Let's Go at **http://www.letsgo.com,** or send email to:

fanmail@letsgo.com
Subject: "Let's Go: Europe"

In addition to the invaluable travel advice our readers share with us, many are kind enough to offer their services as researchers or editors. Unfortunately, our charter enables us to employ only currently enrolled Harvard-Radcliffe students.

Distributed outside the USA and Canada by Macmillan.

ISBN: 0-312-16888-8

First edition
10 9 8 7 6 5 4 3 2 1

Let's Go: Europe is written by Let's Go Publications, 67 Mount Auburn Street, Cambridge, MA 02138, USA.

Printed in the USA on recycled paper with biodegradable soy ink.

ADVERTISING DISCLAIMER

All advertisements appearing in Let's Go publications are sold by an independent agency not affiliated with the production of the guides. Advertisers are never given preferential treatment, and the guides are researched, written, and published independent of advertising. Advertisements do not imply endorsement of products or services by Let's Go. If you are interested in purchasing advertising space in a Let's Go publication, contact: Let's Go Advertising Sales, 67 Mount Auburn Street, Cambridge, MA 02138, USA.

About Let's Go

THIRTY-EIGHT YEARS OF WISDOM

Back in 1960, a few students at Harvard University banded together to produce a 20-page pamphlet offering a collection of tips on budget travel in Europe. This modest, mimeographed packet, offered as an extra to passengers on student charter flights to Europe, met with instant popularity. The following year, students traveling to Europe researched the first, full-fledged edition of *Let's Go: Europe,* a pocket-sized book featuring honest, irreverent writing and a decidedly youthful outlook on the world. Throughout the 60s, our guides reflected the times; the 1969 guide to America led off by inviting travelers to "dig the scene" at San Francisco's Haight-Ashbury. During the 70s and 80s, we gradually added regional guides and expanded coverage into the Middle East and Central America. With the addition of our in-depth city guides, handy map guides, and extensive coverage of Asia and Australia, the 90s are also proving to be a time of explosive growth for Let's Go, and there's certainly no end in sight. The first editions of *Let's Go: Australia* and *Let's Go: New Zealand* hit the shelves this year, expanding our coverage to six continents, and research for next year's series has already begun.

We've seen a lot in 38 years. *Let's Go: Europe* is now the world's bestselling international guide, translated into seven languages. And our new guides bring Let's Go's total number of titles, with their spirit of adventure and their reputation for honesty, accuracy, and editorial integrity, to 40. But some things never change: our guides are still researched, written, and produced entirely by students who know first-hand how to see the world on the cheap.

HOW WE DO IT

Each guide is completely revised and thoroughly updated every year by a well-traveled set of over 200 students. Every winter, we recruit over 140 researchers and 60 editors to write the books anew. After several months of training, Researcher-Writers hit the road for seven weeks of exploration, from Anchorage to Adelaide, Estonia to El Salvador, Iceland to Indonesia. Hired for their rare combination of budget travel sense, writing ability, stamina, and courage, these adventurous travelers know that train strikes, stolen luggage, food poisoning, and marriage proposals are all part of a day's work. Back at our offices, editors work from spring to fall, massaging copy written on Himalayan bus rides into witty yet informative prose. A student staff of typesetters, cartographers, publicists, and managers keeps our lively team together. In September, the collected efforts of the summer are delivered to our printer, who turns them into books in record time, so that you have the most up-to-date information available for your vacation. And even as you read this, work on next year's editions is well underway.

WHY WE DO IT

We don't think of budget travel as the last recourse of the destitute; we believe that it's the only way to travel. Living cheaply and simply brings you closer to the people and places you've been saving up to visit. Our books will ease your anxieties and answer your questions about the basics—so you can get off the beaten track and explore. Once you learn the ropes, we encourage you to put *Let's Go* down now and then to strike out on your own. As any seasoned traveler will tell you, the best discoveries are often those you make yourself. When you find something worth sharing, drop us a line. We're Let's Go Publications, 67 Mount Auburn Street, Cambridge, MA 02138, USA (email fanmail@letsgo.com).

HAPPY TRAVELS!

Contents

Let's Go Picks

This book itself is a kind of "Greatest Hits" compilation—the best of Europe in under a thousand pages. But below we've chosen the true *crème de la crème:* the places and events that we'd most recommend. The list is subjective, of course; drop us a line and tell us what gets your thumb of approval.

Europe's Biggest Party: Los San Fermines (July 6-14) brings over a week of craziness in Pamplona, Spain (see p. 808). **The Love Parade** (usually the second weekend of July), in Berlin, celebrates Germany's infatuation with techno (see p. 373), while the festivities continue to a different beat at the annually inebriating **Oktoberfest** (Sept. 19-Oct. 4) in Munich (see p. 422). The flowers and festivities of **Carnaval** (Feb. 14-March 1) turn Nice into something a little naughty (see p. 339). The beaches and bars in Portugal's **Algarve** region should become even more packed in 1998 as visitors to Lisbon's **Expo '98** (May 22-Sept. 30), the largest World Fair of the century, head south for more sun (see p. 714 and 709). **EuroPride '98,** the largest Gay and Lesbian PrideFest in the world (July 18-26), will coincide with **Stockholm's** reign as the 1998 **Cultural Capital of Europe** (see p. 855).

Best Hiking: Sweden's **Lappland** offers untouched wilderness, reindeer herds, and the Midnight Sun (see p. 866). Rough terrain and harsh climate have isolated **Dartmoor National Park,** England, leaving the area and its prehistoric remains with a solitary beauty (see p. 150). Italy's **Dolomites** present stunning limestone spires and pine forests (see p. 559). **Snowdonia,** Wales, has hikes for all experience levels among its misty crags and mountains (see p. 174). The **Tirol** region in western Austria offers some of the world's most spectacular hiking (see p. 76).

Best Architecture: Spain's **Barcelona** (see p. 811) shocks with the bizarre splendor of Gaudí's creations, while to the north **Bilbao's** (see p. 805) miraculous new Guggenheim museum beckons from beyond winding streets. The skyline of **Istanbul,** Turkey (see p. 900), still dazzles with graceful minarets as it did five centuries ago. All your modernist yearnings will be fulfilled at the abstract cube houses in **Rotterdam,** Netherlands (see p. 642). Amidst silver canals and rows of stone houses in **Bruges,** Belgium (see p. 117), reside some of the best examples of northern Renaissance architecture. The modest 16th-century monasteries with their painted frescoes await discovery in the green hills of **Bukovina,** Romania (see p. 735).

Best Food and Drink: Against the culinary dreamscape of Italy, **Naples** (see p. 587) earns its reputation for the world's best pizza. **Lyon** allows even budget travelers to partake in *haute cuisine* (see p. 349). Paprika embraces eats in amazing ways in **Budapest** (see p. 464). Inside its coffeehouses, **Vienna** lovingly offers sumptuous pastries (see p. 77). Bountiful berries make for some delicious pie in **Kuhmo,** Finland (see p. 283). To wash it all down, Europe is a continent of superlative spirits, with the exceptional ports flowing from **Porto,** Portugal (see p. 721), and the most authentic servings of the revered Guinness in **Killarney,** Ireland (see p. 517).

Tomorrow's Hot Destinations: Having escaped mass Sovietization and retained its majestic, Baroque beauty, **Vilnius,** Lithuania, is experiencing a cultural and financial Renaissance (see p. 607). A fascinating and troubled past lends darkness and intrigue to trendy **Kraków,** Poland (see p. 692). Those flying affordable Icelandair to other destinations can exploit the layover option to explore utopian **Reykjavík,** Iceland (see p. 487). Long protected from tourism, **Chios,** Greece, has gorgeous (and undiscovered) volcanic beaches and medieval villages (see p. 458). Discover **Berlin** all over again as restorations work their magic on this uniquely energetic and cutting-edge city (see p. 362).

Maps

Color Maps

Acknowledgments

Perhaps more than any other guide in the series, the Europe book is dependent on the expertise and work of others. Our R-Ws, Brian, Brittany, Carolyn, and Josh, entertained and amazed us with their adventures and rescarch. Ķŕźyśźțof, our Managing Editor, was as clever with his editing as he was wise about Ēăśțēŗń Ēūŗōþē. Sara and her cohorts Luke and Jed inspired us to revise those maps. The book would have been lost without the infinite patience and helpfulness of Melanie and Dave. Jake and Anne kept us happy and on cue. The regional teams were an unbelievable source of knowledge: those fabulous Eastern Europeans (Ruth, Rachel, Bede), the sharp-witted Germans (Måns, Alex, Jenny), the warm—yet efficient, of course—Austrians and Swiss (Lisa, Nic), the simply splendid British (Eric, Olivia), the pull-no-punches Irish (Sam, Dan), the jolly Londoners (Nick, Dave), the alarmingly organized French (Rob, Hillary, Matt), the wacky and wonderful Italians (Katie, Clint, Matt), the inimitable Romans (Ian, Mei-Mei), the cool and collected Parisian (Andrés), the boisterous Greeks and Turks (Patrick, Ziad, James), and *los valorosos*—the Spaniards and Portugese (Derek, Amir, James). Also invaluable were BSI, the Finnish Tourist Board, RailEurope, Norway Rail, the Belgian Tourist Office, the Icelandic Tourist Board and tourist offices, Norwegian tourist offices, Rick Steves, and the Danish Tourist Board. A thousand blessings to Adam, Andrés, Andrew, Bede, DanO, Jenny, Lisa, Mai, Matt, Melissa, Nic, Pooja, Rachel E., and Sam for last-minute help. Thanks to Adam H. for keeping us legal, Måns for proofing half the book, and, of course, Belle and Sebastian.

Caroline thanks: Rachel and Catharine—trusted partners, untiring sources of ideas and energy, and valued friends. Special thanks to Catharine for her encyclopedic knowledge and eye for detail, and to Rachel for her creativity and for using her green pen so well. Rachel E., with best wishes for her NYC career. Tom, David, and Dave for being a set of first-class fellows. My various roommates for inspiration. LRA for its many investments in my education. Professor Blair for her instruction and compassion. Phil for always having a story to tell. Todd and Josh in the hopes of another Oberlin summer. Evan for still being epic. Private Rachel Dahl, who doesn't even begin to know how wonderful she is. Adam for being the older brother I never had. Simon for putting me up and putting up with me. The many members of my family, for whom distance has only meant an increased awareness of how much I love them.

Rachel thanks: Caroline for unflagging clarity and commitment and Mather hall confidences. Catharine for amazing precision, X-files, and Ana's Taqueria. And to both the madams de la Europa for being true track & field stars. Katie, Clint, Ian, Mai, los citos queridos, Derek, Krzysztof, Pooja, and all of the dancing fools at studio 67 for a superlative summer. My partner in crime JS4, golden HRS, MOU (who transcends modifiers), homies ASL & DPB, big-eyed LMM, summer roomies LZF & DPB, and of course, SFH and SAM for being my life's disco balls. My grandparents for love and strudel, my parents for always being a shuttle ride away, and my brothers Michael and Adam for being my best friends and co-armchair-analysts. Acharon, acharon chaviv, my work on this book is dedicated to the loving memory of Shlomo and Yakkov Levy.

Catharine thanks: Caroline, for bringing about this book while allowing us the flexibility to have a part in what it turned out to be, and Rachel, for your boundless spirit and devotion; both of you were a joy to work with. Caroline, I have complete confidence you will do an excellent job as Publishing Director, and I wish both of you the best of luck. Mike, thanks for making a Klein bottle with me and for making Boston our city. Niffer, Christine, Cricket, and Isabel, thanks for being such wonderful roommates and friends. Max, thank you for a treasured friendship and best of luck at Stanford. Love to my family, especially my parents, Lucy, Rob, Grandma, Grosla, Liz, and Voncile, my family in Cambridge. Finally, I dedicate my work on this book to the memory of Lars and to the hope of a bright future for Helga, Tom, and Lara Day.

Staff

Editor	Caroline R. Sherman
Associate Editor	Rachel A. Farbiarz
Associate Editor	Catharine M. Hornby
Managing Editor	Krzysztof Owerkowicz
Regional Guide Staffs	
Austria & Switzerland	Lisa M. Nosal, Nicolas R. Rapold
Britain and Ireland	Eric Giroux, Olivia Choe
Eastern Europe	Ruth M. Halikman, Rachel Eelkema, Bede M. Sheppard
France	Robert C. Lagueux, Hillary B. Read, Matthew J. Bester
Germany	Måns O. Larsson, Alexander Z. Speier, Jennifer R. Weiss
Greece & Turkey	Patrick K. Lyons, Ziad W. Munson, James J. Castanino
Ireland	Sam Bull, Dan Visel
Italy	Katherine T. Model, Clint D. Thacker, Matthew J. Bester
London	Nicholas A. Stoller, David J. Eilenberg
Paris	Andrés Colapinto
Rome	Hsiao-Yun Chu, Ian Z. Pervil
Spain & Portugal	Derek M. Glanz, Amir D. Perlson, James J. Castanino
Publishing Director	John R. Brooks
Production Manager	Melanie Quintana Kansil
Associate Production Manager	David Collins
Cartography Manager	Sara K. Smith
Editorial Manager	Melissa M. Reyen
Editorial Manager	Emily J. Stebbins
Financial Manager	Krzysztof Owerkowicz
Personnel Manager	Andrew E. Nieland
Publicity Manager	Nicholas Corman
Publicity Manager	Kate Galbraith
New Media Manager	Daniel O. Williams
Assistant Cartographer	Joseph E. Reagan
Assistant Cartographer	Luke Z. Fenchel
Director of Advertising Sales	Todd L. Glaskin
Senior Sales Executives	Matthew R. Hillery, Joseph W. Lind Peter J. Zakowich, Jr.
President	Amit Tiwari
General Manager	Richard Olken
Assistant General Manager	Anne E. Chisholm

Researcher-Writers

Brittany Applestein *Northern Sweden and Finland*
Our favorite rower, Brittany powered her way through Sweden and Finland. Her energy amazed us, especially when peddling 60km to the ever-elusive Umeå. Never wasting a moment, Brittany turned months into days and still managed to ensure that beloved Helsinki and the depths of northern Sweden were thoroughly and accurately covered. Although she sometimes doubled the populations of the towns she visited, Brittany left her heart in Gävle...or was it Switzerland?

Joshua Derman *Iceland and Norway*
We sent a bespectacled New York poet to the top of the world and got back a Viking. Fighting through the media hordes, forging shifting alliances with the Germanic peoples, and ravenously devouring rotten shark, Josh turned his pen towards the oft-neglected regions of the world. Sensitive to the needs of tourists, the improvements he made to our coverage were much appreciated. Josh does not recommend swimming in rësërvöirs, gläcïër-riddën fjörds, ör völcänïc crätërs—it's too Ð*Þ#ðþ!!! cold!

Carolyn Magill *Belgium, Luxembourg, and the Netherlands*
Whether wandering through the streets of Amsterdam, getting to know the locals at Amersfort, or introducing the Macarena to the wilds of Benelux, Carolyn had an action-packed summer. With a practiced Let's Go eye and a commitment to making the guide everything it could be, Carolyn dazzled us with her diligence, attentive reporting, and historical sense. Her expanded Amsterdam coverage was especially awe-inspiring. Sweet as the Belgian chocolate she sent, Carolyn never melted under pressure.

Brian Martin *Denmark, Oslo, and Southern Sweden*
Wonderful, wonderful Brian. A veteran Let's Go researcher and Scandinavian enthusiast, Brian lovingly crafted copy that was a collage of extensive, insightful, and scented research. He proved that the Scandinavia of hurdy-gurdys and oom-pah-loom-pah is *soooo* last year and let us know that the future begins in Stockholm and high-heeled tennis shoes are forever. Determined to make 1998 the year of *Let's Go: Scandinavia (including Europe),* only he could have endured being underdressed in Copenhagen. Hardly a B&T kind of guy, Brian is the real thing.

Regional Researcher-Writers
Sixty researchers documented the other European countries in this book for the 12 regional guides. Adventurers, wits, hikers, sophisticates, they made us alternately giggle, commiserate, and curse some awful handwriting.

Adriana Abdenur *Portugal*
Alexander Atanasov *Yugoslavia, Bosnia, Dubrovnik*
Heidi Barrett *Zurich, Central Switzerland, Interlaken, Italian Switzerland*
Elif Batuman *Central Anatolia, Turkish Mediterranean Coast*
Megan Brenn-White *Eastern Germany*
Chris Brooke *Czech Republic, Slovakia*
Hsiao-Yun Chu *Rome*
Pablo Colapinto *Madrid, Extremadura, Castilla La Mancha*
Mark Coumounduros *Aegean Coast, Northwestern Turkey*
Alexandra DeLaite *Mainland Greece, Sporades, Corfu, Istanbul*
Katia Dianina *Central and Northwest Russia*
Elgin Eckert *Trentino-Alto Adige, Friuli-Venezia Giulia, the Veneto*
David Eilenberg *London*
Aykan Erdemir *Istanbul, Northwestern Turkey*

Dan Epstein	*Bulgaria, Moldova, Odessa*
Greg Feifer	*Estonia, Latvia, Lithuania*
S. Monica Ferrell	*Paris*
Shalimar Abigail Fojas	*Geneva, Lausanne, Western Switzerland, Basel*
Anton Ford	*Paris*
J. Michael Friedman	*Malta*
Jean Galbraith	*Heart of England, North England, Scotland*
Elizabeth Hanify	*Dublin, Southeast Ireland*
Christopher Hilton	*Western Ireland*
Daniel Horwitz	*Abruzzo, Apulia, Basilicata, Campania*
Estibaliz Iturralde	*Andalucía*
Katherine R. Ives	*The Alps, Lyon, Burgundy, Franche-Comte*
Albert Khine	*North England, Scotland, Highlands and Islands*
Sara Kimberlin	*Western Austria, Innsbruck, Salzburg, Liechtenstein*
Elizabeth Kivowitz	*Castilla y León, Navarra, Aragón, La Rioja*
Demetra Koutsoukos	*Athens, Cyclades, Dodecanese*
Eric Kurlander	*Northwestern Germany*
Jesse Lichtenstein	*Castilla y León, Galicia, Asturias and Cantabria*
Christian Lorentzen	*Cyprus, Crete, Lefkoşa, Black Sea Coast*
Kate McCarthy	*Bavaria*
Ryan McKittrick	*Catalunya, Islas Baleares, Valencia and Murcia*
Michaella E. Maloney	*Bordeaux, Pays Basque, Languedoc, Marseille*
James Markham	*Southern Russia, Eastern Ukraine, Moscow*
Gene Mazo	*Belarus, Moscow, Vilnius*
Thomas F. Moore	*Normandy, Brittany*
Douglas S. Muller	*Southwestern Germany*
Benjamin Paloff	*Poland*
Megan Peimer	*Northern Ireland, Donegal*
Ian Pervil	*Rome*
Sasha Radin	*Kraków, Eastern Slovakia, Eastern Hungary, Western Ukraine*
Brian Saccente	*Paris*
Stu Shapley	*Berlin and Northeast Germany*
Isabel Smith	*Liguria, Piedmont, Lombardy, Emilia-Romagna*
Mark Staloff	*Burgundy, Alsace-Lorraine, Champagne, The North*
John Stephenson	*Corsica, The Côte d'Azur, The Rhône Valley*
Nicholas Stoller	*London*
Christina Svendsen	*Sardinia, Tuscany, Umbria*
Catherine Toal	*Wales, Central & North England*
Anne Merrill Toole	*Romania*
Jasmine Vasavada	*Eastern Austria, Vienna, Southern Austria*
David Weld	*Southwest Ireland*
Tobie Whitman	*South England, Heart of England, East Anglia*
Chad Wolfe	*Calabria, Sicily*
Emily Wong	*Peloponnese, Ionian Islands, Saronic Gulf Islands*
Bojan Žagrović	*Slovenia, Croatia, Western Hungary*
William D. A. Zerhouni	*Loire Valley, Poitou-Charentes, Aquitaine*

How to Use This Book

Once upon a time, in not-so-distant history, the Grand Tour of Europe was the privilege of the aristocratic class. Often the finishing touch to an education, a trip around Europe was taken very seriously, with earnest intentions to broaden one's mind by meeting polite company in foreign lands, observing the countryside through the window of a coach, and recording curiosities in a journal to be passed around to friends at home. *Let's Go* believes that this kind traveling only distances the traveler from the land—budget travel is not only a method for stretching your funds farther, but brings you closer to the actual people and culture of the country. Today you need not have a noble lineage (or even a Eurail pass) to experience the best of Europe—all that's required is an adventurous spirit and a trusty guide.

Let's Go: Europe opens with a chapter of **Essentials** to guide you through the quagmire of preparations, with tips on passport and visa acquisition, packing, getting to Europe, and the budget travel opportunities once you're there. It also addresses specific concerns, such as those of women, bisexuals, gays, lesbians, travelers with disabilities, senior citizens, and travelers with children.

The rest of the book lists individual countries in alphabetical order. The 1998 covers roughly forty countries, including Bosnia, Malta, and Yugoslavia for the first time. England, Wales, Scotland, and the Isle of Man are grouped under Britain, while Northern Ireland is in the Ireland chapter (no political statement is intended by this arrangement). Each chapter begins with an overview of that country's history and culture as well as country-specific Essentials, where you'll find such tidbits as visa requirements and the scoop on transportation, accommodations, regional cuisine, and a few helpful phrases in the national language.

For each major city, the **Orientation and Practical Information** section outlines the city's layout, shows you how to get there and to connecting cities, and explains how to communicate with folks back home. These sections also tell you where to go and whom to call in medical emergencies and crisis situations. Then we shower you with information on **Accommodations, Camping, Food, Sights,** and **Entertainment.** Smaller towns are usually divided in half: first we describe the sights, then we dig into the nitty-gritty: practical information, accommodations, and food. This year, we have expanded coverage of entertainment and nightlife throughout the guide, as well as information on how to **access the Internet** while abroad. Gray boxes provide more detailed information on particular sights, history and art, and local customs and festivals. At the end of the book, the **Rail Planner** is intended to help you make your way.

Although our intrepid researcher-writers beat a trail across the continent annually, there are countless undiscovered travel gems in Europe. Keep an eye out for any amazing places we've missed, follow your own spirit and imagination, and feel free to write us about what you find.

A NOTE TO OUR READERS

The information for this book is gathered by *Let's Go*'s researchers from late May through August. Each listing is derived from the assigned researcher's opinion based upon his or her visit at a particular time. The opinions are expressed in a candid and forthright manner. Other travelers might disagree. Those traveling at a different time may have different experiences since prices, dates, hours, and conditions are always subject to change. You are urged to check beforehand to avoid inconvenience and surprises. Travel always involves a certain degree of risk, especially in low-cost areas. When traveling, especially on a budget, always take particular care to ensure your safety.

N
Reykjavík
ICELAND
0
400 miles
0
400 kilometers
Norwegian Sea
Faroe Islands
Trondheim
Shetland Islands
ATLANTIC OCEAN
NORWAY
Bergen
Oslo
Orkney Islands
NORTHERN IRELAND
SCOTLAND
North Sea
SWEDEN
Glasgow
Edinburgh
Gothenburg
Belfast
IRELAND
DENMARK
GREAT BRITAIN
Dublin
Copenhagen
Hamburg
WALES
ENGLAND
Cardiff
NETHERLANDS
London
Amsterdam
Berlin
Brussels
GERMANY
Bonn
BELGIUM
Frankfurt
Prague
LUXEMBOURG
Paris
CZECH REPUBLIC
Nantes
LIECHTENSTEIN
Munich
Zurich
Vienna
Bay of Biscay
SWITZERLAND
Bern
AUSTRIA
Geneva
Ljubljana
Bordeaux
Lyon
Milan
Venice
SLOVENIA
Santiago de Campostela
FRANCE
CROATIA
Adriatic
Marseille
Nice
Florence
BOSNIA AND HERZEGOVINA
PORTUGAL
ANDORRA
MONACO
SAN MARINO
Dubrovnik
Lisbon
Madrid
Barcelona
Corsica (Fr.)
Sea
SPAIN
Rome
ITALY
València
Naples
Seville
Balearic Islands (Sp.)
Sardinia (It.)
Tyrrhenian Sea
Granada
Tangier
GIBRALTAR
Mediterranean
Sicily
Rabat
Tunis
MOROCCO
ALGERIA
TUNISIA
MALTA
Sea

Map of Europe
Honnigsvåg
Rovaniemi
Umeå
Gulf of Bothnia
FINLAND
L. Onega
L. Ladoga
Helsinki
Tallinn
St. Petersburg
Stockholm
ESTONIA
Volga R.
Nizhny
Novgorod
Rīga
Moscow
LATVIA
Baltic
Sea
LITHUANIA
Vilnius
RUSSIA
RUSSIA
Gdańsk
Minsk
Warsaw
BELARUS
KAZAKHSTAN
Volgograd
POLAND
Kiev
Kharkiv
Kraków
Dnieper River
Lviv
UKRAINE
SLOVAKIA
Bratislava
Caspian
Sea
MOLDOVA
Budapest
Sea of
Azov
HUNGARY
Odessa
Rostov-na-Donu
ROMANIA
Yalta
GEORGIA
Belgrade
Bucharest
YUGOSLAVIA
Black Sea
ARMENIA
Sarajevo
BULGARIA
MONTENEGRO
Sofia
AZERBAIJAN
Istanbul
Tiranë
FYR
MACEDONIA
Ankara
IRAN
Thessaloniki
ALBANIA
TURKEY
Aegean
Sea
Izmir
Ionian
Sea
Athens
SYRIA
IRAQ
GREECE
Sea of Crete
Crete
LEBANON
CYPRUS

ESSENTIALS

Touring through the entirety of Europe, or even just a chunk of it, can be a daunting, albeit exciting, prospect. Where to begin? Fortunately, there are countless resources devoted to helping travelers plan a journey through Europe. The organizations, publications, and tourist offices listed below can provide you with more than enough literature on your destination countries. All you need to do is dive in and plan a trip tailored to your specific interests and needs without losing sight of the fact that this is a vacation. Don't overplan your itinerary so that the trip becomes one big blur; just relax and wander through Europe at your own pace.

PLANNING YOUR TRIP

Give careful consideration to when and with whom you travel. Summer is the high season for traveling in Europe. The masses come around July and August; June or September may be a better time to go. Traveling companions may insulate you from local culture, but they do share in food and lodging costs, as well as providing energy, comfort, and extra safety. If you choose to travel with others, discuss your trip in detail before you leave to make sure your interests are compatible. Going solo gives you freedom of movement but also the danger of loneliness and the need for extra safety precautions, particularly for women. A budget travel subculture fills Europe's hostels, ensuring that you will only be as lonely as you want to be.

Useful Information

GOVERNMENT INFORMATION OFFICES

The following are **embassies** or **consulates** unless otherwise indicated.

Austria: Australia and New Zealand (National Tourist Office), 36 Carrington St. 1st fl., Sydney NSW 2000 (tel. (02) 9299 3621; fax 9299 3808). **Canada (National Tourist Office),** 1010 Ouest rue Sherbourne #1410, Montréal, QUE. H3A 2R7 (tel. (514) 849-3709; fax 849-9577) and Granville Sq. #1380, 200 Granville St., Vancouver, BC V6C 1S4 (tel. (604) 683-8695; fax 662-8528). **South Africa,** P.O. Box 95572 Waterkloof, Pretoria 0145 (tel. (012) 46 24 83; fax 46 11 51); **National Tourist Office,** Private Bag X18, Parklands, 2121 Johannesburg (tel. (011) 442 72 35; fax 442 83 04). **U.K. (Tourist Office),** 30 St. George St., London W1R 0AL (tel. (0171) 629 04 61; fax 499 60 38). **U.S. (Tourist Office),** P.O. Box 1142, New York, NY 10108-1142 (tel. (212) 944-6880; fax 730-4568).

Belarus: U.K., 6 Kensington Court, London, W8 5DL (tel. (0171) 937 32 88; fax 361 00 05). **U.S.,** 1619 New Hampshire Ave. NW, Washington, D.C. 20009 (tel. (202) 986-1604; fax 986-1805).

Belgium: Belgium (Tourist Board), Grasmarkt 63, B-1000 Brussels (tel. (02) 504 03 90; fax 504 02 80). **Canada (Tourist Board),** P.O. Box 760, Succursdale N.D.G., Montréal, QUE H4A 3S2 (tel. (514) 484-3594; fax 489-8965). **South Africa,** 625 Leyds St., Muckleneuk, Pretoria, 0002 (tel. (012) 44 32 01; fax 44 32 16). **U.K. (Tourist Board),** 29 Prince St., London W1R 7RG. **U.S. (Tourist Board),** 780 Third Ave., #1501, New York, NY 10017 (tel. (212) 758-8130; fax 355-7675).

Bosnia-Herzegovina: Australia, (tel. (02) 6257 5798); fax 6257 7855) in Canberra. **U.K.,** 320 Regent St., London W1R 5AB (tel. (0171) 255 3758; fax 255 3760). **U.S.,** 1707 L. St. NW, Washington 20036 (tel. (202) 833-3612; fax 833-2061) or 866 U.N. Plaza, # 580, New York, NY 10017 (tel. (212) 593-1042; fax 751-9019.

Britain: Australia (Tourist Authority), Level 16, Gateway Bldg., 1 Macquarie Pl., Sydney NSW 2000 (tel. (02) 9377 4400). **Canada (Tourist Authority),** 111 Avenue Rd., Ste. 450, Toronto, ONT M5R 3J8 (tel. (888) 847-4885 or (416) 925-6326). **New Zealand (Tourist Authority),** Dilworth Bldg., Ste. 305, Corner Queen & Customs St., Auckland 1 (tel. (09) 303 14 46. **South Africa,** Southern Life Bldg., 8 Riebeeck St., Cape Town, 8001 (tel. (21) 25 36 70); **Tourist Authority,** Lancaster Gate, Hyden Ln., Hyde Park, Sandton 2196 (tel. (011) 325 03 43. **U.S.,** 551 Fifth Ave., Ste. 701, New York, NY 10176 (tel. (800) 462-2748).

Bulgaria: Australia, 1/4 Carlotta Rd., Double Bay, Sydney, NSW 2028 (tel. (02) 9327 7581; fax 9327 8067). **Canada,** 325 Stewart St., Ottawa, ONT K1N 6K5 (tel. (613) 789-3215; fax 789-3523). **U.K.,** 186-188 Queensgate, London SW7 5HL (tel. (0171) 584 9400; fax 584 4948). **U.S.,** 1621 22nd St. NW, Washington, D.C. 20008 (tel. (202) 387-7969; fax 234-7973).

Croatia: Australia, 14 Jindalee Crescent, O'Malley, Canberra ACT 2606 (tel. (02) 6286 6988; fax 6286 3544). **Canada,**130 Albert St., #1700, Ottawa, ONT K1 P5 G4 (tel. (613) 230-7351; fax 230-7388). **New Zealand,** 131 Lincoln Rd., Henderson, P.O. Box 83200, Edmonton, Auckland (tel. (09) 836 55 81; fax 836 54 81). **South Africa,** 1160 Church Street, P.O. Box 11335, 0028 Hatfield, 083 Colbyn Pretoria (tel. (012) 342 12 06; fax 342 18 19). **U.K.,** 21 Conway St., London W1P 5HL (tel. (0171) 387 20 22; fax 387 05 74). **U.S.,** 2343 Massachusetts Ave. NW, Washington, D.C. 20008 (tel. (202) 588-5899; fax 588-8936).

Cyprus: South Africa, 1 Lakeside Pl., Ernest Oppenheimer Ave., Bruma 2198 (tel. (011) 622 45 17; fax 622 13 13). **U.K. (Tourist Office),** 213 Regent St., London W1R 8DA (tel. (0171) 734 98 22; fax 287 65 34; email cto@cyta.xom.cy). **U.S. (Tourist Office),** 13 E. 40th St., New York, NY 10016 (tel. (212) 683-5280; fax 683-5282; email gocyprus@aol.com; http://www.cyprustourism.org).

Czech Republic: Australia, 38 Culgoa Circuit, O'Malley, Canberra, ACT 2606 (tel. (02) 6290 1386; fax 6290 0006). **Canada,** 541 Sussex Dr., Ottawa, ONT K1N 6Z6 (tel. (613) 562-3875; fax 562-3878); **Tourist Board,** P.O. Box 198, Exchange Tower, 2 First Canadian Place, Toronto, ONT M5X 1A6 (tel. (416) 367-3432; fax 367-3492). **Ireland,** 57 Northumberland Rd., Ballsbridge, Dublin 4 (tel. (031) 668 1135; fax 668 1660). **New Zealand,** 48 Hair St., Wainuiomata, Wellington (tel. (04) 564 6001; fax 564 9022). **South Africa,** 936 Pretorius St., Arcadia, Pretoria 0083, or P.O. Box 3326, Pretoria 0001 (tel. (012) 342 34 77; fax 43 20 33). **U.K.,** 26 Kensington Palace Gardens, London W8 4QY (tel. (0171) 243 1115; fax 727 9654); **Tourist Board,** 95 Great Portland St., London W1N 5RA (tel. (0171) 291 9920; fax 436 8300). **U.S.,** 3900 Spring of Freedom St. NW, Washington, D.C. 20008 (tel. (202) 274-9100; fax 966-8540) or 10990 Wilshire Blvd., #1100, Los Angeles, CA 90024 (tel. (310) 473-0889; fax 473-9813); **Tourist Board,** 1109-1111 Madison Ave., New York, NY 10028 (tel. (212) 288-0830; fax 288-0971).

Denmark: U.S. (Tourist Board), P.O. Box 4649, Grand Central Station, New York, NY 10163 (tel. (212) 885-9700; fax 885-9710; http://www.visitdenmark.com). **South Africa,** PO Box 2942, Pretoria, 001 (tel. (012) 322 05 95; fax 322 05 96).

Estonia: Australia, 86 Louisa Rd., Birchgrove 2041, NSW (tel. (02) 9810 7468; fax 9818 1779). **Canada,** 958 Broadview Ave., Toronto, ONT M4K 2R6 (tel. (416) 461-0764; fax 461-0448). **South Africa,** 16 Hofmeyr St., Welgemoed 7530 (tel. (021) 913 2579; fax 933 5048). **U.K.,** 16 Hyde Park Gate, London SW7 5DG (tel. (0171) 589 3428; fax 589 3430). **U.S.,** 2131 Massachusetts Ave. NW, Washington, D.C. 20008 (tel. (202) 588-0101; fax 588-0108).

Finland: Australia (Tourist Board), Level 4, 81 York St., Sydney NSW 2000 (tel. (02) 9290 1850; fax (02) 9290 1981). **New Zealand (Tourist Board),** 3rd fl., 20 Fort St., Auckland (tel. 909) 379 97 16; fax 379 88 740. **South Africa,** PO Box 443, Pretoria, 0001 (tel. (012) 343 02 75; fax 343 30 95). **U.K. (Tourist Board),** 30-35 Pall Mall, London SW1Y 5LP (tel. (0171) 839 40 48; fax 321 06 96).**U.S. (Tourist Board),** P.O. Box 4649, Grand Central Station, New York, NY 10163-4649 (tel. (212) 885-9700; fax 885-9710; http://www.travelfile.com/get/finninfo).

France: Australia, 31 Market St., 26th Fl., Sydney, NSW 2000 (tel. (02) 9262 5779); **Government Tourist Office,** 25 Bligh St. Sydney NSW 2000 (tel. (61) 92 31 52 44). **Canada (Tourist Office),** 1981 Ave. McGill College, Ste. 490, Montréal, PQ H3A 2W9 (tel. (514) 288-4264). **Ireland (Tourist Office),** 35 Lower Abbey St., Dublin 1 (tel. (01) 703 40 46). **New Zealanders** should contact this branch or the Consular Section within the French Embassy at 1 Willeston St., Wellington (tel. (64) 44 72 02 00). **South Africa (Embassy),** 807 George Ave., Arcadia, 0083 (tel. (012) 43 55 64 or 43 55 65; fax 43 34 81). **U.K. (Tourist Office),** 178 Piccadilly, London W1V OAL (tel. (0171) 629 12 72). **U.S. (Tourist Office),** 444 Madison Ave., 16th fl., New York, NY 10022 (tel. (900) 990-0040, costs US$0.50 per min.)

Germany: Australia (National Tourist Office), German-Australia Chamber of Industry of Commerce, PO Box A 980, Sydney South, NSW 1235 (tel. (02) 9267 8148; fax 9267 9035). **Canada (National Tourist Office),** 175 Bloor St. E., North Tower, Ste. 604, Toronto, ONT M4W 3R8 (tel. (416) 968-1570; fax 968-1986; email germanto@idirect.com). **South Africa,** P.O. Box 2023, Pretoria, 0001 (tel. (012) 344 38 54; fax 343 94 01); **National Tourist Office,** 22 Girton Rd., Parktown, PO Box 10883, Johannesburg 2000 (tel. (27 11) 643 16 15; fax 484 27 50). **U.K. (National Tourist Office),** 34 Belgrave Sq.,London SW1X 8QB (tel. (0171) 824 13 00; fax 824 15 66; http://www.german-embassy.org.uk). **U.S. (National Tourist Office),** 122 E. 42nd St., 52nd fl., New York, NY 10168 (tel. (212) 661-7200; fax 661-7174; email gntony@aol.com).

Greece: Australia (National Tourist Organization), 3rd Fl. 51 Pitt St., Sydney, NSW 2000 (tel. (02) 9241 1663; fax 9235 2174).**Canada (National Tourist Organization),** 1300 Bay St., Toronto, ONT M5R 3K8 (tel. (416) 968-2220; fax 968-6533). **South Africa,** 995 Pretorius St., Arcadia, 0083 (tel. (012) 43 73 51; fax 43 43 13). **U.K. (National Tourist Organization),** 4 Conduit St., London W1R 0DJ (tel. (0171) 734 59 97). **U.S. (National Tourist Organization),** Olympic Tower, 645 5th Ave., 5th fl., New York, NY 10022 (tel. (212) 421-5777; fax 826-6940).

Hungary: Australia, Edgecliff Centre 203-233, #405, Head Rd., Edgecliff, Sydney, NSW 2027 (tel. (02) 9328 7859; fax 9327 1829). **Canada,** 299 Waverley St., Ottawa, ONT K2P 0Z9 (tel. (613) 230-2717; fax 230-7560). **Ireland,** 2 Fitzwilliam Pl., Dublin 2 (tel. (01) 661 2903; fax 661 2880). **South Africa,** P.O. Box 27077, Sunnyside 0132, 959 Arcadia St., Arcadia, Pretoria (tel. (012) 43 30 30; fax 43 30 29). **U.K.,** 35/B Eaton Pl., London SW1X 8BY (tel. (0171) 235 7191; fax 823 1348); **Tourist Board,** 46 Eaton Pl., London SW1 X8AL (tel. (0171) 823 1032; fax 823 1459). **U.S.,** 3910 Shoemaker St. NW, Washington, D.C. 20008 (tel. (202) 362-6730; fax 686-6412) or 11766 Wilshire Blvd., #410, Los Angeles, CA 90025 (tel. (310) 473-9344; fax 479-0456); **Tourist Board,** 150 E. 58th St., 33rd Fl., New York, NY 10155 (tel. (212) 355-0240; fax 207-4103; email huntour@gramercy.los.com).

Iceland: U.S. (Tourist Board), P.O. Box 4649, Grand Central Station, New York, NY 10163-4649 (tel. (212) 885-9700; fax 885-9710; http://www/arctic.is/ITB/)

Ireland: Australia (Tourist Board), Level 5, 36 Carrington St., Sydney NSW 2000 (tel. (02) 9299 6177; fax 9299 6323).**Canada (Tourist Board),** 160 Bloor St. E., Ste. 1150, Toronto, ONT M4W 1B9 (tel. (800) 223-6470 or (416) 929-2777; fax 929-6783). **South Africa,** P.O. Box 4174, Pretoria, 001 (tel. (012) 342 50 62; fax 342 18 78). **U.K. (Tourist Board),** 150 New Bond St., London W1Y 0AQ (tel. (0171) 518 08 00; fax 493 90 65). **U.S. (Tourist Board),** 345 Park Ave., New York, NY 10154 (tel. (800) 223-6470 or (212) 418-0800; fax 371-9052).

Italy: Canada (Tourist Board), 1 Pl. Ville Marie, #1914, Montréal, QUE H3B 3M9 (tel. (514) 866-7667; fax 392-1429). **South Africa,** 796 George Ave., Arcadia, Pretoria (tel. (012) 43 55 41; fax 43 55 47). **U.K. (Tourist Board),** 1 Princes St., London W1R 8AY (tel. (0171) 408 12 54; fax 493 66 95). **U.S. (Tourist Board),** 630 5th Ave., #1565, New York, NY 10111 (tel. (212) 245-4822; fax 586-9249) or 12400 Wilshire Blvd., #550, Los Angeles, CA 90025 (tel. (310) 820-0098; fax 820-6357).

Latvia: Australia, P.O. Box 457, Strathfield NSW 2135 (tel. (02) 9744 5981; fax 9747 6055). **Canada,** 112 Kent St., Place de Ville, Tower B, #208, Ottawa, ONT K1P 5P2 (tel. (613) 238-6014; fax 238-7044). **Ireland,** 88-95 Grafton St., Dublin 2, Ireland (tel. (01) 679 56 66; fax 679 52 60). **South Africa,** P.O. Box 34, Cyrildene, Johannesburg 2198 (tel. (011) 782 58 12; fax. 888 55 00). **U.K.,** 45 Nottingham Pl., London W1M 3FE (tel. (0171) 312 00 40; fax 312 00 42). **U.S.,** 4325 17th St. NW, Washington, D.C. 20011 (tel. (202) 726-8213; fax 726-6785).

Lithuania: Australia, 40B Fiddens Wharf Rd., Killara NSW 2071 (tel. (02) 9498 2571; fax 9498 2571). **Canada,** 130 Albert St., #204, Ottawa, ONT K1P 5G4 (tel. (613) 567-5458; fax 567-5315). **South Africa,** P.O. Box 1737, Houghton 20141 (tel. (011)

486 36 60; fax 486 36 50). **U.K.,** 84 Gloucester Pl., London W1H 3HN (tel. (0171) 486 64 01; fax 486 64 03). **U.S.,** 2622 16th St. NW, Washington, D.C. 20009 (tel. (202) 234-5860; fax 328-0466).

Luxembourg: Luxembourg, P.O. Box 1001, L-1010 Luxembourg (tel. (352) 40 08 08; fax 40 47 48). **South Africa,** P.O. Box 3431, Parklands 2121 (tel. (011) 447 64 34; fax 477 54 96). **U.K. (Tourist Office),** 122 Regent St., London W1R 5FE (tel. (0171) 434 28 00; fax 734 12 05; http://www.luxcentral.com). **U.S. (Tourist Office),** 17 Beekman Pl., New York, NY 10022 (tel. (212) 935-8888; fax 935-5896; email Luxnto@aol.com).

Malta: Australia, 261 La Perouse St., Red Hill, Canberra A.C.T. 2603 (tel. (02) 6295 5196; fax 6239 6084). **South Africa,** P.O. Box 2441, Parklands, 2121 (tel. (011) 706 05 12; fax 706 03 01). **U.K.,** 16 Kensington Square, London W8 5HH (tel. (071) 938 17 12; fax 937 86 64); **Malta House,** 36-39 Piccadilly, London WIV OPP (tel. (0171) 292 49 00; fax 734 18 80). **U.S.,** 2017 Connecticut Ave. NW, Washington DC 20008 (tel. (202) 462-3611); **Malta National Tourist Office,** Empire State Bldg., 350 Fifth Avenue, Ste. 4412, New York, NY 10118 (tel. (212) 695-9520).

Netherlands: Australia and New Zealand, contact local KLM (airline) offices. **Canada and U.S. (Board of Tourism),** 225 N. Michigan Ave., Ste. 1854, Chicago, IL 60601 (tel. (888) 464-6552, for a representative (312) 819-1500; fax 819-1740; http://www.nbt.nl/holland). **Ireland and U.K. (Board of Tourism),** P.O. Box 523, London SW 1E 6NT (tel. (0171) 891 717 777; fax 828 7941). **South Africa,** P.O. Box 117, Pretoria, 0001 (tel. (012) 344 39 10; fax 343 99 50). **Board of Tourism,** P.O. Box 781738, Sandton 2146 (tel. (11) 884 8184; fax 883 5573).

Northern Ireland Tourist Board: Head Office, 59 North St., Belfast, BT1 1NB, Northern Ireland (tel. (01232) 24 66 09; fax 24 09 60). **Canada,** 111 Avenue Rd., Ste. 450, Toronto, ONT M5R 3J8 (tel. (416) 925-6368; fax 961-2175). **Ireland,** 16 Nassau St., Dublin 2 (tel. (01) 679 19 77; CallSave (01850) 23 02 30; fax (01) 677 15 87. **U.K.,** British Travel Centre, 12 Lower Regent St., London SW1Y 4PQ (tel. (0171) 839 84 17; fax 839 61 79. **U.S.,** 551 Fifth Ave., Ste. 701, New York, NY 10176 (tel. (800) 326-0036 or (212) 922-0101; fax 922-0099).

Norway: South Africa, PO Box 9843, Pretoria, 0001 (tel. (012) 323 47 90; fax 323 47 89). **U.K. (Tourist Board),** Charles House, 5 Regent St., London SW1Y 4LR (tel. (0171) 839 62 55 or 839 26 50; fax 839 60 14). **U.S. (Tourist Board),** P.O. Box 4649, Grand Central Station, New York, NY 10163-4649 (tel. (212) 885-9700; fax 885-9710; email gonorway@interport.net; http://www.norway.org).

Poland: Australia, 7 Turrana St., Yarralumla ACT 2600 Canberra (tel. (02) 6273 1208 or 6273 1211; fax 6273 3181). **Canada,** 443 Daly St., Ottawa, ONT, K1N 6H3 (tel. (613) 789-0468; fax 789-1218). **Ireland,** 5 Ailesbury Rd., Dublin 4 (tel. (01) 283 08 55; fax 283 75 62). **New Zealand,** 17 Upland Rd., Kelburn, Wellington (tel. (04) 71 24 56; fax 71 24 55). **South Africa,** 14 Amos St., Colbyn, Pretoria 0083 (tel. (012) 43 26 21; fax 43 26 08). **U.K.,** 47 Portland Place, London W1N 4JH (tel. (0171) 580 43 24; fax 323 40 18); **Tourist Board,** 1st fl., Remo House, 310-312 Regent St., London W2R 5AJ (tel. (0171) 580 8811; fax 580 8866). **U.S.,** 2640 16th St. NW, Washington, D.C. 20009 (tel. (202) 234-3800; fax 328-6271); **Tourist Board,** 275 Madison Ave., Ste. 1711, New York, NY 10016 (tel. (212) 338-9412; fax 338-9283; http://www.polandtour.org).

Portugal: Canada (Trade and Tourist Office), 60 Bloor St. W., Ste. 1005, Toronto, ON M4W 3B8 (tel. (416) 921-7376; fax 921-1353) and 500 Sherbrooke St. W, Ste. 940, Montréal, QUE H3A 3C6 (tel. (514) 282-1264; fax 499-1450). **Ireland (Trade and Tourist Office),** 54 Dawson St., Dublin 2 (tel. (01) 670 91 33 or 670 91 34; fax 670 91 41). **South Africa,** P.O. Box 27102, Sunnyside, 0132 (tel. (27 11) 484 34 87; fax 484 54 16). **U.K. (Trade and Tourist Office),** 22-25A Sackville St., London W1X 1DE (tel. (0171) 494 14 41; fax 494 18 68). **U.S. (Trade and Tourist Office),** 590 5th Ave., 4th fl., New York, NY 10036-4704 (tel.(212) 354-4403, 354-4404 or (800) 767-8842; http://www.portugal.org).

Romania: Australia, 333 Old South Head Rd., Bondi, Sydney (tel. (02) 9130 5718; fax 9365 3238). **Canada,** 655 Rideau St., Ottawa, ONT K1N 6A3 (tel. (613) 789-5345; fax 789-4365). **South Africa,** 117 Charles St., Brooklyn 0011, POB 11295, Pretoria (tel. (012) 466 941; fax 466 947). **U.K.,** 4 Palace Green, Kensington, London W8 4QD (tel. (0171) 937 9666; fax 937 8069); **Tourist Office,** 823a Marylebone High St., London

W1M 3RD (tel./fax (0171) 224 3692). **U.S.,** 1607 23rd St. NW, Washington, D.C. 20008 (tel. (202) 332-4846; fax 232-4748); **Tourist Office,** 342 Madison Ave., #210, New York, NY 10173 (tel. (212) 697-6971; fax 697-6972).

Russia: Australia, 78 Canberra Ave., Griffith ACT 2603 Canberra (tel. (02) 6295 9033; fax 6295 1847). **Canada,** 285 Charlotte St., Ottawa, ONT K1N 8L5 (tel. (613) 235-4341; fax 236-6342) or 52 Range Rd., Ottawa, ONT K1N 8J5 (tel. (613) 236-6215; fax 238-6158); **Travel Information Office,** 1801 McGill College Ave., #930, Montréal, QUE H3A 2N4 (tel. (514) 849-6394; fax 849-6743). **Ireland,** 186 Orwell Rd., Dublin 14 (tel. (01) 492 3525). **New Zealand,** 57 Messines Rd., Karori, Wellington (tel. (04) 476 61 13; fax 476 38 43). **U.K.** 13 Kensington Palace Gardens, London W84 QX (tel. (0171) 229 36 28; fax 727 86 25); **Travel Information Office,** 219 Marsh Wall, London E14 9PD (tel. (0171) 538 86 00; fax 538 59 67; email info@intourus.demm.co.uk). **U.S.,** 1706 18th St. NW, Washington, D.C. 20009 (info tel. (202) 232-6020; Consular tel. 939-8907; fax 328-0137), 9 East 91st St., New York, NY 10128 (tel. (212) 348-0926; fax 831-9162), or 2790 Green St., San Francisco, CA 94123 (tel. (415) 202-9800); **Travel Information Office,** Intourist, 610 5th Ave., #603, New York, NY, 10020 (tel. (212) 757-3884; fax 459-0031).

Slovakia: Australia, 47 Culgoa Circuit, O'Malley, Canberra ACT 2606 (tel. (02) 6290 1516; fax 6290 1755). **Canada,** 50 Rideau Terrace, Ottawa, ONT K1M 2A1 (tel. (613) 749-4442; fax 749-4989). **South Africa,** P.O. Box 12736, Hatfield 0028, Pretoria (tel. (012) 342 20 51; fax 342 36 88). **U.K.,** 25 Kensington Palace Gardens, London W8T 4QY (tel. (0171) 243 0803; fax 727 5824). **U.S.,** 2201 Wisconsin Ave. NW, #250, Washington, D.C. 20007 (tel. (202) 965-5161; fax 965-5166); **Tourist Board,** 10 E. 40th St., Ste. 3604, New York, NY 10016 (tel. (212) 213-3865).

Slovenia: Australia, P.O. Box 1301, Level 6, 60 Marcus Clarke St., Canberra ACT 2601 (tel. (02) 6243 4830). **Canada,** 150 Metcalfe St., #2101, Ottawa, ONT K2P 1P1 (tel. (613) 565-5781; fax 565-5783). **U.K.,** Cavendish Court 11 15, #1, Wigmore St., London W1H 9LA (tel. (0171) 495 7775; fax 495 7776); **Tourist Board,** 2 Canfield Pl., London NW6 3BT (tel. (0171) 372 3767; fax 372 3763). **U.S.,** 1525 New Hampshire Ave. NW, Washington, D.C. 20036 (tel. (202) 667-5363; fax 667-4563); **Tourist Board,** 345 E. 12th St., New York, NY 10003 (tel. (212) 358-9686; fax 358-9025; http://sloveniatravel.com).

Spain: Canada (Tourist Board), 2 Bloor St. W., 34th fl., Toronto, ON M4W 3E2 (tel. (416) 961-3131; fax 961-1992). **South Africa,** 37 Shortmarket St., Cape Town 8001 (tel. (012) 222 326; fax 222 328). 169 Pine St., Arcadia, Pretoria 0083 (tel. (012) 344 3875/76; fax 343 4891). **U.K. (Tourist Board),** 57-58 Saint James's St., London SW1A 1LD (tel. (171) 499 09 01; fax 629 42 57). 24hr. brochure request line (tel. 8910 66 99 20). **U.S. (Tourist Board),** 666 5th Ave., 35th fl., New York, NY 10022 (tel. (212) 265-8822; fax 265-8864; email oet.ny@here-i.com; http://www.OKSPAIN.org) or San Vincente Plaza Building, 8383 Wilshire Blvd., Suite 960, Beverly Hills, CA 90211 (tel. (213) 658 7188; fax 658-1061).

Sweden: South Africa, PO Box 2289, Pretoria, 0001 (tel. (012) 43 67 07; fax 43 67 71). **U.K. (Tourist Board),** 11 Montagu Place, London W1H 2AL (tel. (0171) 724 5868; fax 724 5872). **U.S. (Tourist Board),** 655 Third Ave., New York, NY 10017-5617 (tel. (212) 885-9700; fax 885-9710).

Switzerland (including Liechtenstein): U.S. (National Tourist Board), 608 5th Ave., New York, NY 10020 (tel. (212) 757-5944; fax 262-6116) and 150 N. Michigan Ave., Ste. 2930, Chicago, IL 60601 (tel. (312) 630-5840; fax 630-5848). **Canada (National Tourist Board),** 926 East Mall, Etobicoke, ONT M9B 6K1 (tel. (416) 695-2090; fax 695-2774). **South Africa,** PO Box 2289, 0001 Pretoria (tel. (012) 43 67 07; fax 43 67 71). **U.K. (National Tourist Board),** Swiss Centre, Swiss Court, London W1V 8EE (tel. (0171) 734 19 21; fax 437 45 77).

Turkey: Australia (Information Office), Ste. 101, 280 George St., Sydney, NSW 2000 (tel. (02) 9223 3055; fax 9223 3204). **Canada (Information Office),** Constitution Sq., 360 Albert St., Ste. 801, Ottawa, ONT K1R 7X7 (tel. 613) 230-8654; fax 230-3683). **South Africa,** PO Box 56014, Arcadia, 0007 (tel. (012) 342 60 53; fax 342 60 52). **U.K. (Information Office),** 1st fl., 170-173 Piccadilly, London W1V 9DD (tel. (0171) 629 77 11; fax 491 07 73; email eb25@cityscape.co.uk). **U.S. (Information Office),** Turkish Centre, 821 United Nations Plaza, New York, NY 10017 (tel. (212) 687-2194; fax 599-7568; email tourny@soho.ios.com).

Ukraine: Australia, #3, Ground Floor, 902-912 Mt. Alexander Road, Essendon, Victoria 3040. **Canada,** 310 Somerset St. West, Ottawa, ONT K2P 0J9 (tel. (613) 230-2961; fax 230-2400). **South Africa,** 398 Marais Street, Pretoria (tel. (12) 46 19 43; fax 46 19 44). **U.K.,** 78 Kensington Park Rd., London W1 12PL (tel. (0171) 727 6312; fax 792 1708). **U.S.,** 3350 M St. NW, Washington, D.C. 20007 (tel. (202) 333-0606; fax 333-0817).

Yugoslavia: Australia, 11 Nuyts St., Red Hill, Canberra (tel. (02) 6295 1458; fax 6239 6178). **Canada,** 17 Blackburn Ave., Ottawa, ONT KIN 8A2 (tel. (613) 233-6289; fax 233-7850). **U.K.,** 5-7 Lexham Gardens, London W8 5JU (tel. (0171) 370 6105; fax 370 3838). **U.S.,** 2410 California St. NW, Washington, D.C. 20008 (tel. (202) 462-6566; fax 462-2508).

USEFUL TRAVEL ORGANIZATIONS

Council on International Educational Exchange (CIEE), 205 E. 42nd St., New York, NY 10017-5706 (tel. (888) COUNCIL (268-6245); fax (212) 822-2699; http://www.ciee.org). A private, not-for-profit organization, Council has world-wide work, volunteer, academic, and professional programs. They also offer identity cards (ISIC, ITIC, and GO25) and publications like *Student Travels* (free).

Federation of International Youth Travel Organizations (FIYTO), Bredgade 25H, DK-1260 Copenhagen K, Denmark (tel. (45) 33 33 96 00; fax 33 93 96 76; email mailbox@fiyto.org; http://www.fiyto.org), is an international organization promoting travel for young people. Member organizations include language schools, educational travel companies, national tourist boards, and accommodation centers. FIYTO sponsors the GO25 Card (http://www.go25.org).

International Student Travel Confederation, Herengracht 479, 1017 BS Amsterdam, The Netherlands (tel. (31) 20 421 28 00; fax 20 421 28 10; email istcinfo@istc.org; http://www.istc.org), a confederation of student travel organizations which promotes and facilitates travel among young people. Member organizations include International Student Surface Travel Association (ISSA), Student Air Travel Association (SATA), IASIS Travel Insurance, and International Association for Educational and Work Exchange Programs (IAEWEP).

USEFUL PUBLICATIONS

Although *Let's Go* tries to cover all aspects of budget travel, we can't put *everything* in our guides. You might supplement your *Let's Go* library with more specific publications. Language tapes and **Handy Dictionaries** (US$9-13) can be obtained through Hippocrene Books, Inc., 171 Madison Ave., New York, NY 10016 (tel. (212) 685-4371, orders (718) 454-2366; fax (718) 454-1391; email hippocre@ix.netcom.com; http://www.netcom.com/~hippocre). Books, cassettes, atlases, dictionaries, and maps are available from Travel Books & Language Center, Inc., 4931 Cordell Ave., Bethesda, MD 20814 (tel. (800) 220-2665; fax (301) 951-8546; email travelbks@aol.com). Hard-to-find **maps** are stocked by Wide World Books and Maps, 1911 N. 45th St., Seattle, WA 98103 (tel. (206) 634-3453; fax 634-0558; email travel@speakeasy.org; http://www.travelbooksandmaps.com). **Michelin** publishes detailed road maps and atlases, as well as the **Green Guides** (US$18-20), with in-depth maps, suggested tours, and area background. Visit a bookstore or contact Michelin Tyre, the Edward Hyde Bldg., 38 Clarendon Rd., Watford WD1 1SX, U.K. (tel. (01923) 41 50 00; fax 41 50 52); in the U.S., Michelin Tire Corporation, P.O. Box 19008, Greenville, SC 29602-9001 (tel. (800) 423-0485; fax (803) 458-5665). Travel gear, guidebooks, railpasses, and hostel memberships can be purchased from the **Forsyth Travel Library,** 1750 East 131st Street, P.O. Box 480800 Kansas City, MO 64148 (tel. (800) 367-7984; fax (816) 942-6969; email forsyth@avi.net; http://www.forsyth.com). Books on packing, global weather patterns, and safety concerns (US$9-10 each) are available from **Ten Speed Press,** P.O. Box 7123, Berkeley, CA 94707 (tel. (800) 841-2665; fax (510) 559-1629; email order@tenspeed.com). For *Background Notes* (US$1 each) on all countries, and *Health Information for International Travel* (US$14) contact the **Superintendent of Documents,** P.O. Box 371954, Pitts-

EAST COAST <> EUROPE $169
WESTCOAST <> EUROPE $249
MIDWEST <> EUROPE $199
OTHER DESTINATIONS CHEAP
DISCOUNTED BUS/RAIL PASSES + CAR RENTALS
EUROPE SUCKS
WHY SPEND MORE THAN $169 GETTING THERE
AIR-TECH UNLTD.
(800) 575-TECH
HTTP://CAMPUS.NET/AEROTECH
INFO@AEROTECH.COM

burgh, PA 15250 (tel. (202) 512-1800; fax 512-2250; email gpoaccess@gpo.gov; http://www.access.gpo.gov/su_docs).

Festivals, a free booklet from the European Festivals Association, 120B, rue de Lausanne, CH-1202 Geneva, Switzerland (tel. (22) 732 28 03; fax 738 40 12; email aef@vtx.ch), lists the dates and programs of major European festivals. In the U.S., enclose 5 International Reply Coupons to order it from Dailey-Thorp Travel, Inc., 330 West 58th Street, New York, NY 10018-1817. Peruse **Mona Winks: Self-Guided Tours of Europe's Top Museums** (US$19) with "Professor" Rick Steves, a veteran traveler who offers great advice in **Europe Through the Back Door** (US$20). Both are available from John Muir Publications, P.O. Box 613, Santa Fe, NM 87504 (tel. (800) 888-7504; fax (505) 988-1680). For the inside story on **Charming Small Hotels** in England, France, Germany, Italy, Tuscany, or Switzerland (US$15 each), contact Hunter Publishing, P.O. Box 7816, Edison, NJ 08818 (tel. (908) 225-1900; fax 417-0482; email hunterpub@emi.net; http://www.hunterpublishing.com). The **Specialty Travel Index,** 305 San Anselmo Ave., #313, San Anselmo, CA 94960 (tel. (415) 459-4900; fax 459-4974; email spectrav@ix.netcom.com; http://www.spectrav.com), is a listing of tour operators (US$6; 2 copies $10).

INTERNET RESOURCES

Budget travel is moving rapidly into the information age. On today's **Internet,** people can become their own budget travel agents by making airline, hostel, or car rental reservations. There are a number of ways to access the 'net. Most popular are commercial Internet services, such as **America Online** (tel. (800) 827-6364) and **CompuServe** (tel. (800) 433-0389). Many employers and schools offer gateways to the Internet at no cost, unlike commercial gateways. The Internet can be used in many ways, but the World Wide Web and Usenet newsgroups are the most helpful.

The World Wide Web

Increasingly the Internet forum of choice, the **World Wide Web** provides graphics, sound, and text. This and the proliferation of web pages (individual sites) have made the Web the most active and exciting use of the Internet. It has also become the newest path from corporate advertisers to the minds of the masses; be sure to distinguish between information and marketing. Another difficulty with the Web is its lack of hierarchy—it is a web, after all. **Search engines,** which look for web pages under specific subjects, help the process. **Lycos** (http://a2z.lycos.com) and **Infoseek** (http://guide.infoseek.com) are popular. **Yahoo!** is slightly more organized; check out its travel links at http://www.yahoo.com/Recreation/Travel.

If you know one good site, you can start "surfing" from there, through links from one web page to another. *Let's Go* recommends the following sites for budget travel info: **Big World Magazine** (http://boss.cpcnet.com/personal/bigworld/bigworld.htm), **The CIA World Factbook** (http://www.odci.gov/cia/publications), **City.Net** (http://www.city.net), **Cybercafe Guide** (http://www.cyberiacafe.net/cyberia/guide/ccafe.htm), **Foreign Language for Travelers** (http://www.travelang.com), **Rent-A-Wreck's Travel Links** (http://www.rent-a-wreck.com/raw/travlist.htm), **The Student and Budget Travel Guide** (http://asa.ugl.lib.umich.edu/chdocs/travel/travel-guide.html), and **TravelHUB** (http://www.travelhub.com). We list other relevant web sites throughout the book, but as the turnover of good web sites is high, it is important that you head out on your own.

Usenet Newsgroups

Newsgroups are forums for discussion of specific topics. One user "posts" a written question, which other users read and respond to. Information is available on almost any imaginable topic. But proliferation can become over-extension; the quality of discussion can be poor, and you often have to wade through piles of nonsense to find useful information. **Usenet,** the family of newsgroups, can be accessed easily from most Internet gateways. In UNIX systems, a good newsreader is "tin" (just type "tin" at the prompt). Most commercial providers offer access to Usenet and often also have

ESSENTIALS

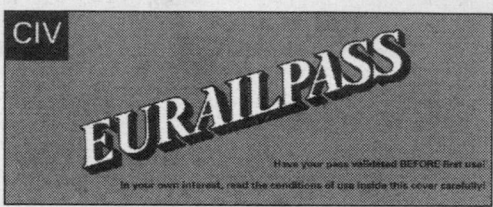

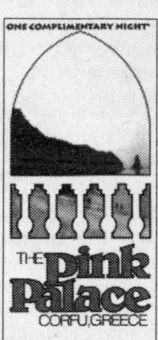

Get the MCI Card.
The Smart and Easy Card.

The MCI Card with WorldPhone Service is designed specifically to keep you in touch with people that matter the most to you. We make international calling as easy as possible.

The MCI Card with WorldPhone Service....

- Provides access to the US from over 125 countries and places worldwide.
- Country to country calling from over 70 countries
- Gives you customer service 24 hours a day
- Connects you to operators who speak your language
- Provides you with MCI's low rates with no sign-up or monthly fees
- Even if you don't have an MCI Card, you can still reach a WorldPhone Operator and place collect calls to the U.S. Simply dial the access code of the country you are calling from and hold for a WorldPhone operator.

For more information or to apply for a Card call:

1-800-444-1616

Outside the U.S., call MCI collect (reverse charge) at:

1-916-567-5151

MCI

The MCI Card with WorldPhone Service... The easy way to call when traveling worldwide.

For more information or to apply for a Card call: 1-800-444-1616

Outside the U.S., call MCI collect (reverse charge) at: 1-916-567-5151

Please cut out and save this reference guide for convenient U.S. and worldwide calling with the MCI Card with WorldPhone Service.

COUNTRY		WORLDPHONE TOLL-FREE ACCESS #
#American Samoa		633-2MCI (633-2624)
#Antigua	(Available from public card phones only)	#2
#Argentina (CC)		0800-5-1002
#Aruba ✣		800-888-8
#Australia (CC) ◆	To call using OPTUS ■	1-800-551-111
	To call using TELSTRA ■	1-800-881-100
#Austria (CC) ◆		022-903-012
#Bahamas		1-800-888-8000
#Bahrain		800-002
#Barbados		1-800-888-8000
#Belarus (CC)	From Brest, Vitebsk, Grodno, Minsk	8-800-103
	From Gomel and Mogilev regions	8-10-800-103
#Belgium (CC) ◆		0800-10012
#Belize	From Hotels	557
	From Payphones	815
# Bermuda ✣		1-800-888-8000
#Bolivia ◆		0-800-2222
#Brazil (CC)		000-8012
#British Virgin Islands ✣		1-800-888-8000
#Brunei		800-011
#Bulgaria		00800-0001
#Canada (CC)		1-800-888-8000
#Cayman Islands		1-800-888-8000
#Chile (CC)	To call using CTC ■	800-207-300
	To call using ENTEL ■	800-360-180
#China ❖	(Available from most major cities)	108-12
	For a Mandarin-speaking Operator	108-17
#Colombia (CC) ◆		980-16-0001
	Colombia IIIC Access in Spanish	980-16-1000
#Costa Rica ◆		0800-012-2222
#Cote D'Ivoire		1001
#Croatia (CC) ★		0800-22-0112
#Cyprus ◆		080-90000
#Czech Republic (CC) ◆		00-42-000112
#Denmark (CC) ◆		8001-0022
#Dominica		1-800-888-8000
#Dominican Republic (CC) ✣		1-800-888-8000
	Dominican Republic IIIC Access in Spanish	1121
#Ecuador (CC) ✣		999-170
#Egypt ◆	(Outside of Cairo, dial 02 first)	355-5770
El Salvador ◆		800-1767
#Federated States of Micronesia		624

FOLD

COUNTRY		WORLDPHONE TOLL-FREE ACCESS #
#Fiji		004-890-1002
#Finland (CC) ◆		08001-102-80
#France (CC) ◆		0800-99-0019
#French Antilles (CC)	(includes Martinique, Guadeloupe)	0800-99-0019
French Guiana (CC)		0-800-99-0019
#Gabon		00-005
#Gambia ◆		00-1-99
#Germany (CC)		0130-0012
#Greece (CC) ◆		00-800-1211
#Grenada ✣		1-800-888-8000
#Guam (CC)		950-1022
Guatemala (CC) ◆		99-99-189
#Guyana		177
#Haiti ✣		193
	Haiti IIIC Access in French/Creole	190
Honduras ✣		122
#Hong Kong (CC)		800-96-1121
#Hungary (CC) ◆		00▼800-01411
#Iceland (CC) ◆		800-9002
#India (CC) ❖	(Available from most major cities)	000-127
#Indonesia (CC) ◆		001-801-11
Iran ✣		(SPECIAL PHONES ONLY)
#Ireland (CC)		1-800-55-1001
#Israel (CC)		177-150-2727
#Italy (CC) ◆		172-1022
#Jamaica ✣		1-800-888-8000
	(From Special Hotels only)	873
	Jamaica IIIC Access	#2-from public phones
#Japan (CC) ◆	To call using KDD ■	0039-121▶
	To call using IDC ■	0066-55-121
	To call using ITJ ■	0044-11-121
#Jordan		18-800-001
#Kazakhstan (CC)		8-800-131-4321
#Kenya ❖	(Available from most major cities)	080011
#Korea (CC)	To call using KT ■	009-14
	To call using DACOM ■	00309-12
	Phone Booths✣	Press red button, 03, then ✱
	Military Bases	550-2255
#Kuwait		800-MCI (800-624)
Lebanon ✣		600-MCI (600-624)
#Liechtenstein (CC) ◆		0800-89-0222
#Luxembourg		0800-0112

FOLD

COUNTRY		WORLDPHONE TOLL-FREE ACCESS #
#Macao		0800-131
#Macedonia (CC) ◆		99800-4266
#Malaysia (CC) ◆		800-0012
#Malta		0800-89-0120
#Marshall Islands		1-800-888-8000
#Mexico	Avantel (CC)	91-800-021-8000
	Telmex ▲	95-800-674-7000
	Mexico IIIC Access	91-800-021-1000
#Micronesia		624
#Monaco (CC) ◆		800-99-019
#Montserrat		1-800-888-8000
#Morocco		00-211-0012
#Netherlands (CC) ◆		0800-022-9122
#Netherlands Antilles (CC) ✣		001-800-888-8000
#New Zealand (CC)		000-912
Nicaragua (CC)	(Outside of Managua, dial 02 first)	166
Nicaragua IIIC Access in Spanish		*2 from any public payphone
#Norway (CC) ◆		800-19912
#Pakistan		00-800-12-001
#Panama		108
	Military Bases	2810-108
#Papua New Guinea (CC)		05-07-19140
#Paraguay ✣		008-112-800
#Peru		0-800-500-10
#Philippines (CC) ◆	To call using PLDT ■	105-14
	To call using PHILCOM ■	1026-14
	Philippines IIIC via PLDT in Tagalog	105-15
	Philippines IIIC via PhilCom in Tagalog	1026-12
#Poland (CC) ✣		00-800-111-21-22
#Portugal (CC) ✣		05-017-1234
#Puerto Rico (CC)		1-800-888-8000
#Qatar ★		0800-012-77
Romania (CC) ✣		01-800-1800
#Russia (CC) ◆✣	To call using ROSTELCOM ■	747-3322
	(For Russian speaking operator)	747-3320
	To call using SOVINTEL ■	960-2222
#Saipan (CC) ✣		950-1022
#San Marino (CC) ◆		172-1022
#Saudi Arabia (CC)		1-800-11
#Singapore		8000-112-112
#Slovak Republic (CC)		00421-00112
#Slovenia		080-8808

MCI

their own version limited to the members of the provider. There are a number of different hierarchies, including "soc" (society and culture), "rec" (recreation), and "alt" (alternative; varied topics). "Clari-net" posts AP news wires. Since the quality of discussion changes so rapidly and new groups are always appearing, it's best to scan through to find appropriate topics.

Documents and Formalities

Be sure to file all applications several weeks or months in advance of your planned departure date. Remember that you are relying on government agencies and that a backlog in processing can spoil your plans.

When you travel, always carry on your person two or more forms of identification, including at least one photo ID. A passport combined with a driver's license or birth certificate is usually enough, but many establishments require several IDs before cashing traveler's checks. Don't carry all of your IDs together—that risks disaster in the case of theft or loss. Also, be sure to bring half a dozen extra passport-size photos for the other IDs and railpasses you will acquire.

ENTRANCE REQUIREMENTS

Citizens of Australia, Canada, Ireland, New Zealand, South Africa, the U.K., and the U.S. all need valid **passports** to enter any European country and to re-enter their own country. Some countries do not allow entrance if the holder's passport expires in under six months, and returning to the U.S. with an expired passport may result in a fine. Some countries in Europe also require a **visa;** an **invitation** from a sponsoring individual or organization is required by a few Eastern European countries.

Upon entering a country, you must declare certain items from abroad and must pay a duty on the value of those articles that exceed the allowance established by that country's **customs** service. Holding onto receipts for purchases made abroad will help establish values when you return. It is wise to make a list, including serial numbers, of valuables that you bring from home; if you register this with customs before your departure, you will avoid import duty charges and ensure an easy return. Be especially careful to document items manufactured abroad.

When you enter a country, dress neatly and carry proof of your financial independence, such as a visa to the next country on your itinerary, an airplane ticket to depart, enough money to cover the cost of your living expenses, etc. Admission as a visitor does not include the right to work, which is authorized only by a work permit (see **Work and Volunteer,** p. 31). Entering certain countries to study requires a special visa, and immigration officers may also want to see proof of acceptance from a school, proof that the course of study will take up most of your time in the country, and as always, proof that you can support yourself.

PASSPORTS

Before you leave, photocopy the page of your passport that contains your photograph and identifying information, especially your passport number. Carry this photocopy in a safe place apart from your passport and leave another copy at home. These measures will help prove your citizenship and facilitate the issuing of a new passport if you lose the original document. Consulates also recommend you carry an expired passport or an official copy of your birth certificate in a part of your baggage separate from other documents. You can request a duplicate birth certificate from the Bureau of Vital Records and Statistics in your state or province of birth.

If you lose your passport, notify the local police and the nearest embassy or consulate of your home government. It may take weeks to process a replacement, and your new one may be valid for only a limited time. Also, any visas stamped in your old passport will be irretrievable. To expedite its replacement, you will need to know all information previously recorded and show identification and proof of citizenship. In an emergency, ask for immediate temporary traveling papers that will permit you to

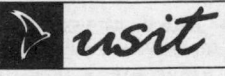

reenter your home country. Your passport is a public document belonging to your nation's government. You may have to surrender it to a foreign government official; but, if you don't get it back, inform the nearest mission of your home country. For extended stays, register your passport with the nearest embassy or consulate.

Australia Citizens must apply for a passport at a post office, a passport office, or an Australian diplomatic mission overseas. An appointment may be necessary. Passport offices are located in Adelaide, Brisbane, Canberra City, Darwin, Hobart, Melbourne, Newcastle, Perth, and Sydney. A parent may file an application for a child who is under 18 and unmarried. Adult passports cost AUS$126 (32 pages, valid for 5 years) or AUS$188 (64 pages, valid for 10), and a child's is AUS$63 (32 pages, valid for 5 years) or AUS$94 (64 pages, valid for 5 years). For more info, call toll-free (in Australia) 13 12 32.

Canada Application forms in English and French are available at all passport offices, Canadian missions, many travel agencies, and Northern stores in northern communities. Travel agents can direct citizens to the nearest location of the 28 regional Passport Offices. Canadian citizens residing abroad should contact the nearest Canadian embassy or consulate. Children under 16 may be included on a parent's passport. Passports cost CDN$60, are valid for five years, and are not renewable. Processing takes approximately five business days for in-person applications; 10 days by mail. For additional info, contact the Canadian Passport Office, Department of Foreign Affairs and International Trade, Ottawa, ON, K1A 0G3 (tel. (613) 994-3500; http://www.dfait-maeci.gc.ca/passport) or call (800) 567-6868 (24hr.); in Toronto (416) 973-3251; in Vancouver (604) 775-6250; in Montréal (514) 283-2152. For further help and a list of Canadian embassies and consulates abroad, refer to the booklet *Bon Voyage, But...,* free at any passport office or by calling InfoCentre at (800) 267-8376. You can also find entry and background information for various countries by contacting the Consular Affairs Bureau in Ottawa (tel. (800) 267-6788 (24hr.) or (613) 944-6788).

Ireland Citizens can apply for a passport by mail to either the Department of Foreign Affairs, Passport Office, Setanta Centre, Molesworth St., Dublin 2 (tel. (01) 671 1633), or the Passport Office, Irish Life Building, 1A South Mall, Cork (tel. (021) 272 525). Get an application at a local Garda station or request one from a passport office. The new Passport Express Service, available through post offices, allows citizens to get a passport in two weeks for an extra IR£3. Passports cost IR£45 and are valid for 10 years. Citizens under 18 or over 65 can request a three-year passport that costs IR£10.

New Zealand Application forms are available in New Zealand from travel agents and Department of Internal Affairs Link Centres in main cities and towns. Overseas, forms and services are provided by New Zealand embassies, high commissions, and consulates. Applications may also be sent to the Passport Office, P.O. Box 10526, Wellington, New Zealand. Standard processing time in New Zealand is 10 working days. Passports are valid for 10 years (NZ$80). Children must apply for their own passports (NZ$40). Urgent passport service is an extra NZ$80. Different fees apply at overseas posts: nine posts including London, Sydney, and Los Angeles offer both standard and urgent services (adult NZ$130, child NZ$65, plus NZ$130 if urgent). At other overseas posts the passports will process within three working days (NZ$260, child NZ$195).

South Africa Citizens can apply for a passport at any **Home Affairs Office** or **South African Mission.** Tourist passports are valid for 10 years (SAR80). Children under 16 must be issued their own passports, valid for 5 years (SAR60). If a passport is needed in a hurry, an **emergency passport** may be issued for SAR50. An application for a permanent passport must accompany the emergency passport application. Time for the application's completion is normally 3 months or more from the time of

submission. Current passports less than 10 years old may be **renewed** until December 31, 1999; every citizen whose passport's validity does not extend far beyond this date is urged to renew it as soon as possible, to avoid the expected glut of applications as 2000 approaches. Renewal is free, and turnaround time is usually 2 weeks. For further information, contact the nearest Department of Home Affairs Office.

United Kingdom British citizens, British Dependent Territories citizens, British Nationals (overseas), and British Overseas citizens may apply for a 10-year passport (5-year if under 16). The British Visitor's Passport has been abolished; every traveler over 16 now needs a 10-year, standard passport. Applications are available at passport offices, main post offices, many travel agents, and branches of Lloyds Bank and Artac World Choice. Apply in person or by mail to one of the passport offices in London, Liverpool, Newport, Peterborough, Glasgow, or Belfast (UK£18). Children under 16 may be included on a parent's passport. Processing by mail usually takes 4-6 weeks. The London office offers same-day, walk-in rush service; arrive early. Call the U.K. Passport Agency at (0990) 21 04 10, or get info at http://www.open.gov.uk/ukpass.

United States Citizens may apply for a passport at any federal or state courthouse or post office authorized to accept passport applications, or at a U.S. Passport Agency, located in Boston, Chicago, Honolulu, Houston, Los Angeles, Miami, New Orleans, New York, Philadelphia, San Francisco, Seattle, Stamford, and Washington, D.C. Refer to the "U.S. Government, State Department" section of the telephone directory or the local post office for addresses. Parents must apply in person for children under age 13. You must apply in person if this is your first passport, if you're under age 18, or if your current passport is more than 12 years old or was issued before your 18th birthday. Passports are valid for 10 years (5 years if under 18) and cost US$65 (under 18 US$40). Passports may be renewed by mail or in person for US$55. Processing takes 3-4 weeks. Rush service is available for a surcharge of US$30 with proof of departure within 10 working days, or for travelers leaving in 2-3 weeks who require visas. Given proof of citizenship, a U.S. embassy or consulate abroad can usually issue a new passport. Report in writing a passport lost or stolen in the U.S. to Passport Services, 1425 K St., N.W., U.S. Department of State, Washington D.C., 20524 or to the nearest passport agency. For more info, contact the U.S. Passport Information's 24-hour recorded message (tel. (202) 647-0518). Citizens may receive consular info sheets, travel warnings, and public announcements at any passport agency, U.S. embassy, or consulate, or by sending a self-addressed stamped envelope to: Overseas Citizens Services, Room 4811, Department of State, Washington, D.C. 20520-4818 (tel. (202) 647-5225; fax 647-3000). Additional info (including publications) about documents, formalities, and travel abroad is available through the Bureau of Consular Affairs homepage at http://travel.state.gov, or through the State Department site at http://www.state.gov.

VISAS

A visa is an endorsement that a foreign government stamps into a passport, allowing the bearer to stay in that country for a specified period of time. Most visas (US$10-70) give you a month within six months to a year from the date of issue.

Most Western European nations do not require visas of American, Canadian, British, Irish, Australian, or New Zealand citizens staying for less than three months; France requires a visa from Australians. South Africans generally need visas for any European country. Eastern European countries' visa requirements vary greatly for citizens of different countries. Check your destination country's specific visa requirements in the country's **Getting There** section of this book as early as possible.

If you want to stay longer, apply for a visa at the country's embassy or consulate in your home country before your departure. Unless you are a student, extending your stay once abroad is difficult, if not impossible. Contact the country's immigration officials or police long before your time is up, and show proof of financial resources.

For more information, send for *Foreign Entry Requirements* (US$0.50) from the **Consumer Information Center,** Department 363D, 18th and F St. NW, Room G-142, Washington, D.C. 20405 (tel. (719) 948-4000; http://www.pueblo.gsa.gov), or contact the **Center for International Business and Travel (CIBT),** 25 West 43rd St. #1420, New York, NY 10036 (tel. (800) 925-2428 or (212) 575-2811 from NYC), which secures visas for travel to and from all countries for a variable service charge.

CUSTOMS: GOING HOME

Upon returning home, you must declare all articles you acquired abroad and pay a duty on the value of articles that exceeds the allowance established by your country's customs service; see **Entrance Requirements,** p. 13, for hints on ensuring an easy return passage. Goods and gifts purchased at duty-free shops abroad are not exempt from duty or sales tax at your point of return; you must declare these items, as well.

Australia Citizens may import AUS$400 (under 18 AUS$200) of goods duty-free, in addition to 1.125L alcohol and 250 cigarettes or 250g tobacco. You must be over 18 to import alcohol or tobacco. There is no limit to the amount of Australian and/or foreign cash that may be brought into or taken out of the country, but amounts of AUS$10,000 or more, or the equivalent, must be reported. All foodstuffs and animal products must be declared. For info, contact the Regional Director, Australian Customs Service, GPO Box 8, Sydney NSW 2001 (tel. (02) 9213 2000; fax 9213 4000).

Canada Citizens abroad for at least one week may bring back up to CDN$500 worth of goods duty-free. Citizens or residents traveling for a period between 48 hours and six days can bring back up to CDN$200. Both of these exemptions may include tobacco and alcohol. You may ship goods except tobacco and alcohol home under the CDN$500 exemption as long as you declare them upon arrival. Goods under the CDN$200 exemption, as well as all alcohol and tobacco, must be in your hand or checked luggage. Citizens of legal age (varies by province) may import in-person up to 200 cigarettes, 50 cigars or cigarillos, 400g loose tobacco, 400 tobacco sticks, 1.14L wine or alcohol, and 24 355mL cans/bottles of beer; the value of these products is included in the CDN$200 or CDN$500. For more info, write Canadian Customs, 2265 St. Laurent Blvd., Ottawa, ONT K1G 4K3 (tel. (613) 993-0534), phone the 24-hour Info Service at (800) 461-9999, or visit Revenue Canada at http://www.revcan.ca.

Ireland Citizens must declare everything in excess of IR£142 (under 15 IR£73) obtained outside the EU or duty- and tax-free in the EU above the allowances of 200 cigarettes, 100 cigarillos, 50 cigars, or 250g tobacco; 1L liquor or 2L wine; 2L still wine; 50g perfume; and 250mL toilet water. Duty and tax-paid goods from another EU country up to IR£460 (under 15 IR£115) are not subject to customs duties. Citizens under 17 may not import tobacco or alcohol. Contact The Revenue Commissioners, Dublin Castle (tel. (01) 679 27 77; fax 671 20 21; email taxes@iol.ie; http://www.revenue.ie) or The Collector of Customs and Excise, The Custom House, Dublin 1 for info.

New Zealand Citizens may import up to NZ$700 worth of goods duty-free if they are intended for personal use or are unsolicited gifts. The concession is 200 cigarettes (1 carton) or 250g tobacco or 50 cigars or a combination of all three not to exceed 250g. You may also bring in 4.5L of beer or wine and 1.125L of liquor. Only travelers over 17 may import tobacco or alcohol. For more information, contact New Zealand Customs, 50 Anzac Ave., Box 29, Auckland (tel. (09) 377 35 20; fax 309 29 78).

South Africa Citizens may import duty-free: 400 cigarettes, 50 cigars, 250g tobacco, 2L wine, 1L of spirits, 250mL toilet water, and 50mL perfume, and other consumable items up to a value of SAR500. Goods up to a value of SAR10,000

over and above this duty-free allowance are dutiable at 20%; such goods are also exempted from the VAT. Items acquired abroad and sent to the Republic as unaccompanied baggage do not qualify for any allowances. You may not export or import South African bank notes in excess of SAR2000. For more information, consult the free pamphlet *South African Customs Information,* available in airports or from the Commissioner for Customs and Excise, Private Bag X47, Pretoria 0001 (tel. (012) 314 99 11; fax 328 64 78).

United Kingdom Citizens or visitors arriving in the U.K. from outside the EU must declare goods in excess of the following allowances: 200 cigarettes, 100 cigarillos, 50 cigars, or 250g tobacco; still table wine (2L); strong liquours over 22% volume (1L), or fortified or sparkling wine and other liqueurs (2L); perfume (60 cc/mL); toilet water (250 cc/mL); and UK£136 worth of all other goods including gifts and souvenirs. You must be over 17 to import liquor or tobacco. These allowances also apply to duty-free purchases within the EU, except for the "other goods" category, which has an allowance of UK£71. Goods obtained duty and tax paid for personal use (regulated by set guide levels) within the EU do not require any further customs duty. For more info contact Her Majesty's Customs and Excise, Custom House, Nettleton Road, Heathrow Airport, Hounslow, Middlesex TW6 2LA (tel. (0181) 910 37 44; fax 910 37 65).

United States Citizens may import US$400 worth of accompanying goods duty-free and must pay a 10% tax on the next US$1000. You must declare all purchases, so have sales slips ready. The US$400 personal exemption covers goods purchased for personal or household use (this includes gifts) and cannot include more than 100 cigars, 200 cigarettes (1 carton), and 1L of wine or liquor. You must be over 21 to bring liquor into the U.S. If you mail home personal goods of U.S. origin, you can avoid duty charges by marking the package "American goods returned." For more information, consult the free brochure *Know Before You Go,* available from the U.S. Customs Service, Box 7407, Washington D.C. 20044 (tel. (202) 927-6724).

YOUTH, STUDENT, & TEACHER IDENTIFICATION

The **International Student Identity Card (ISIC)** is the most widely accepted form of student identification and will procure discounts throughout Europe for sights, theaters, museums, accommodations, train, ferry, and airplane travel, and other services. Present the card wherever you go, and always ask about discounts. It also provides insurance benefits, including US$100 per day of in-hospital sickness for a maximum of 60 days, and US$300 accident-related medical reimbursement for each accident (see **Insurance,** p. 30). Cardholders also have access to a 24-hour ISIC helpline whose multilingual staff can provide help in overseas emergencies.

Many student travel offices issue ISICs: STA Travel in Australia and New Zealand; Travel CUTS in Canada; USIT in Ireland and Northern Ireland; SASTS in South Africa; Campus Travel and STA Travel in the U.K.; Council Travel, Let's Go Travel, and STA Travel in the U.S.; and any of the other organizations under the auspices of the International Student Travel Confederation (ISTC). When you apply for the card, request a copy of the *International Student Identity Card Handbook,* which lists some available discounts. You can also write to Council for a copy (see **Useful Travel Organizations,** p. 9). The card is valid from September to December of the following year. The fee is US$19. Applicants must be at least 12 years old and degree-seeking students of a secondary or post-secondary school. Because of the proliferation of phony ISICs, many airlines and other services require other proof of student identity: a signed letter from the registrar attesting to your student status and stamped with the school seal and/or your school ID card. The US$20 **International Teacher Identity Card (ITIC)** offers similar but limited discounts as well as medical insurance coverage. For more info, email isicinfo@istc.org or consult http://www.istc.org.

Federation of International Youth Travel Organizations (FIYTO) issues the **GO25 Card,** a discount card for non-students who are under 26. This one-year card offers benefits similar to the ISIC and can be obtained at most organizations that sell the ISIC. A free brochure listing discounts comes with purchase of the card. To apply, you need a passport, valid driver's license, or copy of a birth certificate; and a passport-sized photo with your name printed on the back. The fee is US$19, CDN$15, or UK£5. Info is available at http://www.fiyto.org and http://www.go25.org, or by contacting Travel CUTS in Canada, STA Travel in the U.K., Council Travel in the U.S., or FIYTO headquarters in Denmark (see **Useful Travel Organizations,** p. 9).

DRIVING PERMITS AND INSURANCE

Unless you have a valid driver's license from an EU country, you must have an **International Driving Permit (IDP)** to drive in Europe, though certain countries allow travelers to drive with a valid American or Canadian license for a limited number of months. Most car rental agencies don't require the permit. A valid driver's license from your home country must always accompany the IDP. Call an automobile association to find out if your destination country requires the IDP. It may be a good idea to get one anyway, in case you're in a position (such as an accident or stranded in a smaller town) where the police may not read or speak English.

Your IDP, valid for one year, must be issued before departure. An application usually includes one or two photos, a current local license, an additional ID, and a fee. **Australians** can obtain an IDP (AUS$12) by contacting their local Royal Automobile Club (RAC) or the National Royal Motorist Association (NRMA) if in NSW or the ACT. **Canadian** license holders can obtain an IDP (CDN$10) through Canadian Automobile Association (CAA) branch offices, or by writing to CAA Central Ontario, 60 Commerce Valley Drive East, Thornhill, ONT L3T 7P9 (tel. (416) 221-4300). **Irish** citizens can pick up an IDP (IR£4) at the nearest Automobile Association (AA) or phone (1) 283 3555 for a postal application form. In **New Zealand,** contact the local Automobile Association (AA) or their main office at 99 Albert Street, PO Box 5, Auckland (tel. (09) 377 4660; fax 309 4564). IDPs cost NZ$8 (postage NZ$2). In **South Africa** get an IDP (SAR25) from your local Automobile Association of South Africa office. For more info phone (011) 466 6641 or write to P.O. Box 596, 2000 Johannesburg. In the **U.K.** IDPs (UK£4) can be picked up at your local AA Shop, or call (01256) 49 39 32 for a postal application form (allow 2-3 weeks). **U.S.** license holders can get an IDP (US$10) at any American Automobile Association (AAA) office or by writing to AAA Florida, Travel Agency Services Department, 1000 AAA Drive (mail stop 28), Heathrow, FL 32746-5080 (tel. (800) 222-4357 or (407) 444-4245; fax 444-4247; http://www.aaa.com).

Most credit cards cover standard insurance. If you rent, lease, or borrow a car, you will need a **green card,** or **International Insurance Certificate,** to prove that you have liability insurance. Obtain it through the car rental agency; most include coverage in their prices. If you lease a car, you can obtain a green card from the dealer. Some travel agents offer the card, and it may be available at the border. Verify whether your auto insurance applies abroad; even if it does, you will still need a green card to certify this to foreign officials. If you have a collision while in Europe, the accident will show up on your domestic records if you report it to your company. Rental agencies may require you to purchase theft insurance in some countries, such as Italy or sometimes Switzerland, that they consider to have a high risk of auto theft.

Money Matters

If you stay in hostels and prepare your own food, expect to spend US$10-60 per day plus transportation, depending on the local cost of living and your needs. Don't sacrifice safety and health for a cheaper tab.

CURRENCY AND EXCHANGE

Banks in Europe often use a three-letter code based on the name of the country and the name of the currency (for example, Norwegian kroner are NOK). We list this code at the beginning of each country's section with the abbreviation we use and the

September 1997 exchange rates between local currency and U.S. dollars (US$), Canadian dollars (CDN$), British pounds (UK£), Irish pounds (IR£), Australian dollars (AUS$), New Zealand dollars (NZ$) and South African Rand (SAR). Check a large newspaper's financial pages for the latest exchange rates.

It is more expensive to buy foreign currency than domestic. In other words, Dutch guilders are cheaper in the Netherlands than in the U.S. However, converting some money before you arrive will allow you to zip through the airport rather than languishing in exchange lines, and prevents being stuck with no money after banking hours or on a holiday. You should bring enough foreign currency to last the first 24-72 hours, depending on the day of the week you arrive. Observe commission rates closely: banks generally have the best rates, but sometimes tourist offices or exchange kiosks are better. Airports and railroad stations generally have poor rates. A good rule of thumb is to go only to banks or bureaux de change which have no more than a 5% margin between buy and sell prices. Be sure that both prices are listed.

Since you lose money with every transaction, convert large sums (unless the currency is depreciating rapidly), but don't convert more of any currency than you'll need, since it may be difficult to change it back to your home currency, or to a new one. Some countries, such as the Czech Republic, Slovakia, and Russia, may require transaction receipts to reconvert local currency. A few (generally in Eastern Europe) will not allow you to convert local currency back at all.

If you are using traveler's checks or bills, be sure to carry some in small denominations (US$50 or less), especially for times when you are forced to exchange money at disadvantageous rates. However, you should generally carry a range of denominations since, in some countries, charges are levied per check cashed.

It may be difficult to exchange your home currency abroad—tellers may not recognize Australian and New Zealand dollars—so it's a good idea to have a few U.S. dollars or German marks on hand. In some places (e.g. Eastern European hotels), Western currency is preferred to local. Find out which establishments require hard currency, and don't use Western money when you don't have to. Throwing dollars around is offensive, attracts theft, and invites many locals to jack prices up.

TRAVELER'S CHECKS

Traveler's checks are one of the safest means of carrying money. Agencies and banks sell them for face value plus a 1% commission. (Members of the American Automobile Association can get American Express checks commission-free through AAA). **American Express** and **Visa** are the most widely recognized. Order checks well in advance. If your checks get lost or stolen, you will be reimbursed by the check issuer; you may need a police report verifying the loss or theft. Inquire about toll-free refund hotlines and the location of refund centers when you purchase your checks. Keep check receipts and a record of which checks you've cashed in a separate place from the checks themselves. Leave a list of check numbers with someone at home in case of loss. Never countersign checks until you're ready to cash them. Be sure to keep cash for less touristy regions and emergencies. You may find it hard to change traveler's checks outside major cities in Eastern Europe. Finally, always bring your passport with you when you plan to use the checks.

American Express (AmEx): Call (800) 221-7282 in the U.S. and Canada; in the U.K. (0800) 52 13 13; in New Zealand (0800) 44 10 68; in Australia (008) 25 19 02). Elsewhere, call U.S. collect (801) 964-6665. AmEx Traveler's Cheques are widely recognized and easy to replace. Buy them for a small fee at AmEx Travel Service Offices, banks, and AAA offices (commission-free for AAA members). Members can also buy checks at AmEx Dispensers at Travel Service Offices, at airports, or by phone (tel. (800) 673-3782). AmEx offices cash their checks commission-free, with slightly worse rates than banks. Cheques for Two available; request AmEx's *Traveler's Companion.* Checks available over America Online (tel. (800) 297-1234).

Citicorp: Call (800) 645-6556 in the U.S. and Canada; in Europe (44) 171 508 7007. Elsewhere, call U.S. collect (813) 623-1709. Citicorp and Citicorp Visa traveler's checks (1-2% commission). Checkholders are enrolled for 45 days in the Travel

Assist Program (hotline (800) 250-4377 or collect (202) 296-8728) providing English-speaking doctors and lawyers, interpreter referrals, and check refund assistance. Worldwide delivery of traveler's checks.

Thomas Cook MasterCard: Call in U.S. and Canada (800) 223-9920; in U.K. (0800) 622 101 or collect (1733) 502 995. Elsewhere, call U.S. collect (609) 987-7300. Checks (1-2% commission). Thomas Cook offices cash checks commission-free.

Visa: Call in U.S. (800) 227-6811; in U.K. (0800) 89 54 92. Elsewhere, call the U.K. collect at (1733) 31 89 49. Sells checks by mail; call (800) 235-7366. Any Visa traveler's check can be reported lost at the Visa number.

CREDIT CARDS

Credit cards can be invaluable or frustrating, as levels of acceptance vary. Major credit cards—**MasterCard** and **Visa** are the most welcomed—instantly extract cash advances from associated banks and teller machines throughout Western Europe (and sometimes elsewhere) in local currency. This can be a bargain because credit card companies get the wholesale exchange rate, which is generally better than the banks' retail rate, but you will be charged ruinous interest rates if you don't pay the bill quickly. **American Express** cards also work in some ATMs, as well as at AmEx offices and major airports. AmEx Cardmembers can enroll in **Express Cash.** For a 2% transaction fee for each withdrawal with a US$2.50 minimum, card holders may withdraw up to US$1000 in a seven-day period from their bank account or line of credit (tel. (800) 227-4669; outside the U.S., call collect (904) 565-7875).

All ATMs require a **Personal Identification Number (PIN).** Ask AmEx, MasterCard, or Visa to assign you one if they haven't upon issuing the card. MasterCard and Visa have different names elsewhere ("EuroCard" or "Access" for MasterCard and "Carte Bleue" or "Barclaycard" for Visa). Credit cards are invaluable in a financial emergency and may offer other services, like insurance and emergency help.

American Express (tel. (800) 528-4800) has a hefty annual fee (US$55), but cardholders can cash personal checks at AmEx offices and use a 24-hour medical and legal assistance hotline (tel. (800) 554-2639 in U.S. and Canada; elsewhere call U.S. collect (301) 214-8228). Another benefit is the **AmEx Travel Service,** which sends mailgrams and cables, holds mail at AmEx offices, and helps change airline, hotel, and car rental reservations. **MasterCard** (tel. (800) 999-0454) and **Visa** (tel. (800) 336-8472) are issued by individual banks and organizations, each with different services.

CASH CARDS

Cash cards—popularly called **ATM cards**—are widespread in Europe, especially the **Cirrus** (U.S. tel. (800) 424-7787) and **PLUS** (U.S. tel. (800) 843-7587) money networks. Cirrus has cash machines in 80 countries and territories and charges US$3-5 to withdraw abroad. PLUS covers over 100 countries. Depending on your bank at home, you will probably be able to access your personal account. Happily, the ATM machines get the same wholesale exchange rate as credit cards. Unhappily, there is often a daily limit on withdrawal amounts, and computer network failures are common. Memorize your PIN code in numeral form, as machines abroad may not have letters on the keys, and talk to your bank if your PIN is longer than four digits. Many ATMs are outdoors; use discretion and don't get distracted while at the machine.

One innovation worth investigating is Visa's **TravelMoney,** an ATM card that doesn't require a bank or credit card account. Travelers buy it from one of over 20 banks worldwide by paying whatever they want to have on the card plus a commission of a few percent. The PIN and quick replacement policy (1-2 days) make TravelMoney a convenient and secure way to avoid changing money or have money sent from home. For more info, call from the U.S. and Canada (800) 847-2399; from the U.K. (0800) 96 38 33; elsewhere U.S. collect (410) 581-9091.

GETTING MONEY FROM HOME

One of the easiest ways to get money from home is to bring an **American Express** card. AmEx allows card holders to draw cash from their checking accounts at any of its major offices and many of its representatives' offices, up to US$1000 every 21 days (no service charge, no interest). Unless using the AmEx service, avoid cashing checks in foreign currencies; they usually take weeks and a US$30 fee to clear.

Money can be wired abroad through **Western Union** (tel. (800) 325-6000; (800) 225-5227 to cable money in the U.S.). Credit card transfers do not work overseas; you must send cash. Some people also choose to send money abroad in cash via **Federal Express** to avoid transmission fees and taxes. FedEx is reasonably reliable; however, this method may be illegal, it involves an element of risk, and it requires that you remain at a legitimate address for a day or two to wait for the money's arrival.

In emergencies, U.S. citizens can have money sent via the State Department's **Overseas Citizens Service,** American Citizens Services, Consular Affairs, Room 4811, 2201 C St. NW, U.S. Department of State, Washington, D.C. 20520 (tel. (202) 647-5225, after hours (202) 647-4000; fax 647-3000; http://travel.state.gov). For US$15, the State Department forwards money within hours to the nearest consular office.

Safety and Security

SAFETY

Blend in as much as possible. Walking inside to check your map is better than brandishing it on the street. Muggings are often impromptu; acting nervous implies that you have something valuable. Act confident and as if you know where you're going.

When exploring new **cities,** you need extra vigilance, but no city should turn precautions into panic. Find out about unsafe areas from *Let's Go,* tourist offices, lodging managers, or a local, but, above all, trust what your eyes tell you. If you feel uncomfortable, leave quickly, but don't let fear close off new worlds. Leave your itinerary with someone, especially if you are traveling alone, which you should never admit. A **whistle** can scare off attackers and attract attention. Know the police phone number. At night, stay near crowded, well-lit areas, and don't cross deserted neighborhoods.

If you take a **car,** park your vehicle only in a garage or well-traveled areas and learn local driving signals. The leading cause of travel deaths in many parts of the world is motor vehicle crashes. Wearing a seatbelt is law in many areas. Children under 40 lbs. should ride in specially designed carseats, obtainable from most car rental agencies. For long journeys, you may want to bring some spare parts. Learn your route before you depart; some roads have poor (or nonexistent) shoulders, few gas stations, or loose animals. In many regions, you will need to drive more slowly and cautiously than you would at home. Details and statistics on road safety are available from the **Association for Safe International Road Travel (ASIRT).** See **By Car,** p. 53.

Sleeping in a car is foolish, but if you must, do so close to a police station or 24-hour service station. Sleeping outside can be even more dangerous—camp only in campsites or wilderness backcountry. Exercise extreme caution when using **pools** or **beaches;** hidden rocks and shallow depths can cause injury or depth. Heed warnings about undertows. If you rent scubadiving equipment, make sure that it works.

A good self-defense course might cost you more than the trip. **Impact, Prepare,** and **Model Mugging** (tel. (800) 345-KICK; US$50-400) can refer you to courses in the U.S. Community colleges frequently offer inexpensive self-defense classes. Get more complete safety info from the **United States Department of State** (tel. (202) 647-5225 (24hr.); http://travel.state.gov). To order the free *A Safe Trip Abroad,* contact the Superintendent of Documents (see **Useful Publications,** p. 9). Find official warnings from the **United Kingdom Foreign and Commonwealth Office** at http://www.fco.gov.uk, or call (0171) 238-4503, and from the **Canadian Department of Foreign Affairs and International Trade** (DFAIT) at http://www.dfait-maeci.gc.ca (tel. (613) 944-6788 in Ottawa, (800) 267-6788 elsewhere in Canada).

SECURITY

Among the most colorful aspects of large cities are **con artists,** who often work in groups. Children are among the most effective. Don't respond or make eye contact, walk away quickly, and keep a grip on your belongings. Contact the police if a hustler is insistent or aggressive. *Don't put money in a wallet in your back pocket.* Carry as little money as possible and never count it in public. A **money belt,** sold at camping supply stores, is the best way to carry cash, especially the nylon, zippered pouch with belt that sits inside a waistband. A **neck pouch,** although less accessible, is equally safe. Avoid fanny-packs: even on your stomach, your valuables will be visible and easy to steal. Be alert in public telephone booths and discrete about revealing your calling-card number.

Be particularly watchful of your belongings on **buses** (carry your backpack in front of you), don't check baggage on trains, and don't trust anyone to watch your bag. **Trains** are notoriously easy for thieves, who strike when tourists fall asleep. When traveling in pairs, alternate sleeping; when alone, never stay in an empty compartment. Keep documents and valuables on you, and sleep on top bunks with your luggage stored above or with you. Try not to leave possessions in your **car** while away. If the tape deck or radio is not removable, conceal it under a lot of junk. Put baggage in the trunk if you must, but savvy thieves can tell a heavily loaded car by its tires.

Label every piece of luggage both inside and out. For packs, buy small combination **padlocks** to slip through the two zippers, securing the pack shut. Padlocks can also secure hostel lockers, which are useful but unwise for storing valuables. Never leave your belongings unattended anywhere, especially hostels. If you feel unsafe, look for a place with a curfew or night attendant. Be extra-vigilant in low-budget hotels, where others may have keys, and in dorm-style lodgings. Making **photocopies** of important documents will let you recover them if they are lost or filched. Carry one copy separately and leave another copy at home. Keep some money separate as well.

Travel Assistance International by Worldwide Assistance Services, Inc., 1133 15th St. NW, #400, Washington, D.C. 20005-2710 (tel. (800) 821-2828 or (202) 828-5894; fax 828-5896; email wassist@aol.com) provides its members with a 24-hour hotline for emergencies and referrals. Their Per-Trip (starting at US$65) and Frequent Traveler (starting at US$235) plans include medical, travel, and communication assistance services. The **American Society of Travel Agents,** 1101 King St., Alexandria, VA 22313 (http://www.astanet.com), publishes the free brochure, *Travel Safety.*

DRUGS AND ALCOHOL

Check alcohol, drunk driving, and drug laws for your destinations. The drinking age in Europe is lower than in the U.S. Avoid public drunkenness; it is often against the law and can jeopardize your safety. If you carry **prescription drugs,** keep a copy of the prescriptions—some drugs allowed in your home country may be illegal abroad. **Illegal drug laws** all over the world are different; such drugs are best avoided altogether. Remember that you are subject to the laws of the country you're traveling in and that it is your responsibility to familiarize yourself with those laws. Embassies will not help you if you are arrested on drug charges, which are punishable by anything from a prison sentence to the death penalty—a definite vacation-ruiner.

Health

BEFORE YOU GO

Take measures before leaving to prepare for emergencies. Write **emergency contact names,** allergies, and medical conditions in your passport. Always go prepared with any **medication** you take or may need, plus a copy of the prescription and/or a statement from your doctor, particularly for insulin, syringes, or any narcotics. Consult a doctor before leaving, especially for longer stays and rural or unindustrialized regions. If you wear **glasses** or **contact lenses,** carry an extra prescription and arrange to have someone send a replacement pair in an emergency. If you wear contacts, take a pair of glasses in case of loss or simply to rest your eyes. Bring extra solutions, enzyme tablets, and eyedrops, because prices can be sky-high. A **first-aid kit** should include bandages, pain killers, antiseptic soap or antibiotic cream, a thermometer, tweezers, motion sickness remedy, moleskin, sunscreen, insect repellent, burn ointment, and medicine for diarrhea, constipation, or stomach problems.

Look at your **immunization** records before you go; some countries require vaccination certificates. Travelers over two years old should be sure that the following vaccines are up to date: Measles, Mumps, and Rubella (MMR); Diphtheria, Tetanus, and Pertussis (DTP or DTap)—particularly advisable for those traveling to the former Soviet Union, where diphtheria is epidemic; Polio (OPV); Haemophilus Influenza B (HbCV); and Hepatitis B (HBV) if you plan to be sexually active. A booster of Tetanus-diphtheria (Td) is recommended every 10 years, and adults traveling to the former Soviet Union should consider an additional dose of Polio vaccine if they have not had one during adulthood. Hepatitis A vaccine and/or Immune Globulin (IG) is recommended for those going to Eastern or Southern Europe.

For information about region-specific vaccinations and health data, contact the **United States Centers for Disease Control and Prevention (CDC).** The CDC maintains an international travelers' hotline (tel. (404) 332-4559; fax 332-4565; http://www.cdc.gov), and publishes the booklet *Health Information for International Travelers* (US$20), a global rundown of disease, immunization, and health advice for particular countries. (Send a check or money order to the Superintendent of Documents. See **Useful Publications,** p. 9) Call (202) 512-1800 for credit card orders.

The **United States Department of State** compiles Consular Information Sheets on health and entry requirements for all countries. To receive these by fax, dial (202) 647-3000 directly from a fax machine and follow the instructions. For travel warnings call the Overseas Citizens' Services (tel. (202) 647-5225). You can also get all of this information by contacting the State Department's regional passport agencies in the U.S., field offices of the U.S. Chamber of Commerce, and U.S. embassies and consulates abroad, or by sending a stamped, self-addressed envelope to the **Overseas Citizens' Services,** see **Getting Money From Home,** p. 26. For general health info, contact the **American Red Cross,** 285 Columbus Ave., Boston, MA 02116-5114 (tel. (800) 564-1234), which publishes a *First-Aid and Safety Handbook* (US$15).

Travelers with specific medical conditions (diabetes, epilepsy, heart conditions, allergies, etc.) may want the **Medic Alert Identification Tag** (US$35 the first year, US$15 annually thereafter) from the Medic Alert Foundation, 2323 Colorado Ave., Turlock, CA 95382 (tel. (800) 825-3785). Membership to the foundation provides the disease-identifying tag and gives a 24-hour collect-call hotline. The **American Diabetes Association,** 1660 Duke St., Alexandria, VA 22314 (tel. (800) 232-3472), provides *Travel and Diabetes* and multilingual diabetic ID cards.

If you are concerned about medical support while traveling, contact **Global Emergency Medical Services (GEMS),** 2001 Westside Dr., #120, Alpharetta, GA 30201 (tel. (800) 860-1111; fax (770) 475-0058), which provides 24-hour medical assistance through registered nurses with on-line access to your medical info, primary physician, and a worldwide network of screened English-speaking doctors. Subscribers get a pocket-sized, personal medical record with vital info. The **International Association for Medical Assistance to Travelers (IAMAT)** offers a free membership ID card, a world-wide directory of English-speaking doctors, and charts on immunization, diseases, climate, and sanitation. In the U.S., contact 417 Center St., Lewiston, NY 14092 (tel. (716) 754-4883; fax (519) 836-3412; email iamat@sentex.net; http://www.sentex.net/~iamat); in **Canada,** 40 Regal Rd., Guelph, ONT N1K 1B5 (tel. (519) 836-0102) or 1287 St. Clair Ave. W., Toronto, ONT M6E 1B8 (tel. (416) 652-0137; fax (519) 836-3412); in **New Zealand,** P.O. Box 5049, Christchurch 5.

ON-THE-ROAD AILMENTS

Common sense is the simplest prescription for good health: eat well, drink lots of fluids, get enough sleep, and don't overexert yourself. Keep strong with high-protein, low-sugar snacks. You may experience fatigue, discomfort, or mild diarrhea as your body adapts to a new environment. Many people take over-the-counter remedies for **diarrhea,** although these can complicate infections. Avoid anti-diarrheals if you suspect exposure to contaminated food or water. The most dangerous side effect of diarrhea is **dehydration;** one anti-dehydration formula is 8oz. of water with ½ tsp. of sugar or honey and a pinch of salt—down several doses a day, rest, and wait for the malady to run its course. If you develop a fever or your symptoms last longer than five days, you may have a **food- or water-borne disease,** which can be quite serious—consult a doctor. **Cholera,** an intestinal bacterial disease carried in contaminated food, is a danger in Eastern Europe. First symptoms are watery diarrhea, dehydration, vomiting, and muscle cramps. Untreated cholera quickly becomes fatal. Antibiotics are available, but it is vital to rehydrate. **Hepatitis A** is an intermediate risk in Eastern Europe and the former Soviet Union. It is a viral infection of the liver acquired primarily through sexual contact and contaminated water, ice, shellfish, unpeeled fruits, and vegetables. Symptoms include fatigue, fever, loss of appetite, nausea, dark urine, jaundice, vomiting, aches and pains, and light stools. Ask your doctor about the vaccine "Havrix" or for an injection of immune globulin (IG). To avoid food- and water-borne diseases, watch what you eat and drink. Peel your own fruit and never eat raw foods, especially seafood. Be sure that the cooked food is hot (breads are safe cold). Boil, treat with iodine, or pass through a water purifier all water, drink only bottled beverages, and don't trust ice. Be cautious with food from street vendors.

Watch out for **heatstroke** in which sweating stops, body temperature rises, and an intense headache develops. Left untreated, it is followed by confusion and ultimately death. Cool victims off with fruit juice or salted water, wet towels, and shade, then rush them to a hospital. For protection, wear a hat and light long-sleeved shirt. Extreme cold is also dangerous. Signs of **hypothermia** include rapidly dropping body temperature, shivering, poor coordination, irritability, and exhaustion, followed by slurred speech, sleepiness, hallucinations, and amnesia. *Do not let hypothermia victims fall asleep*—unconsciousness can lead to death. To avoid hypothermia, keep dry, wear wool, dress in layers, and wear a hat. **Frostbite** turns the skin white, cold, and waxy. Never rub or apply hot water to frostbite; frozen skin is easily damaged. Instead, slowly warm the frostbitten area in dry fabric or with steady body contact. Take serious cases to a doctor immediately. Take a few days to adjust to lower oxygen levels at **high altitudes** before exerting yourself on long hikes. At oxygen-thin altitudes any alcohol will do you in quickly. Foreign alcoholic drinks are often strong.

Wet or forested areas have **insects**—mosquitoes, fleas, ticks, and lice—which carry many diseases. **Ticks**—responsible for Lyme disease, among others—can be particularly dangerous. Brush ticks off when walking and inspect your scalp carefully. Wear repellent and clothing covering as much skin as possible. To remove a tick, grasp it close to your skin and apply slow, steady traction. Topical cortisones may help itching. **Parasites** hide in unsafe water and food; some are also transmitted by insects. Symptoms of parasitic infections include swollen glands or lymph nodes, fever, rashes or itchiness, digestive problems, eye problems, and anemia. Wear shoes and follow the precautions for avoiding food- and water-borne diseases. Animal bites can mean **rabies;** clean wounds thoroughly and seek medical help right away.

Women traveling in unsanitary conditions are vulnerable to **urinary tract and bladder infections,** common bacterial diseases which cause a burning sensation and painful and/or frequent urination. Drink lots of water and cranberry juice. See a doctor if symptoms persist. For more info, see **Women Travelers,** p. 33.

HIV, AIDS, AND STDS

HIV causes **AIDS,** crippling the immune system and making victims susceptible to even minor illnesses. While not everyone who is HIV-positive has AIDS, *any person who is HIV-positive can transmit this currently fatal virus*. The easiest mode of HIV transmission is through direct blood-to-blood contact: *never* share intravenous drug, tattooing, or other needles. The most common mode of transmission is sexual intercourse (contact of infected semen or vaginal secretions with blood or mucous membranes). Over 90% of newly infected adults acquired their infection through heterosexual sex; women now represent 50% of all new infections. Always assume your partner to be HIV-positive. Bring latex condoms with Nonoxynol-9 spermicide with you, and *use them.* Saliva, urine, and casual contact are not believed to be risky.

If you are HIV-positive, write to the Bureau of Consular Affairs for country-specific entry requirements at Room 6831, Department of State, Washington, DC 20520 (http://travel.state.gov.). Many countries require an **HIV Antibody Test** for extended stays or work permits. For more info on HIV/AIDS, call the **U.S. Center for Disease Control's 24-hour Hotline** (tel. (800) 342-2437) or the **World Health Organization (WHO)** (tel. (202) 861-3200; http://www.paho.org/english/techinfo.htm). Statistics are available at the WHO, Attn.: Global Program on AIDS, 20 Avenue Appia, 1211 Geneva 27, Switzerland (tel. (022) 791 21 11). Council's brochure, *Travel Safe: AIDS and International Travel,* available at all Council Travel offices (see **Budget Travel Agencies,** p. 41), describes different countries' regulations.

Always be aware of the risks of sexually transmitted diseases **(STDs)** such as gonorrhea, chlamydia, genital warts, syphilis, and herpes. Safer sex involves following the guidelines recommended for avoiding HIV and using common sense, but remember that condoms can break or slip off. An STD can be a permanent souvenir from your vacation. Try *looking* at your partner's genitals before sex, and if anything is amiss, just don't do it. The U.S. Center for Disease Control has an **STDs hotline** (tel. (800) 227-8922). If you may be sexually active, if you will be a health worker abroad, or if you are working or living in rural areas (particularly in Eastern Europe), you are advised to get the **Hepatitis B** vaccination, which begins six months before travel.

Insurance

Beware of buying unnecessary travel coverage—your regular policies may extend to travel-related accidents. **Medical insurance** (especially university policies) often covers costs incurred abroad. **Medicare's** "foreign travel" coverage is valid only in Canada and Mexico. **Canadians** are protected by their home province's health insurance plan for up to 90 days after leaving Canada; check with the provincial Ministry of Health or Health Plan Headquarters. **Australia** has Reciprocal Health Care Agreements (RHCAs) with several countries; when traveling in those nations, Australians are entitled to many services they receive at home. Contact the Commonwealth Department of Human Services and Health. An E111 form (available from local national health authorities) covers **EU citizens** for emergency treatment throughout the EU. **Homeowners' insurance** (or your family's coverage) often covers theft during travel and loss of travel documents (passport, plane ticket, etc.) up to US$500.

ISIC and **ITIC** provide US$3000 of accident-related medical reimbursement and US$100 per day up to 60 days of hospitalization. The cards give access to a toll-free Traveler's Assistance hotline (tel. (800) 626-2427 in the U.S. and Canada; elsewhere U.S. collect (713) 267-2525) whose multilingual staff can help in emergencies. **Council** and **STA** offer a range of plans that can supplement your basic insurance coverage, including medical treatment and hospitalization, accidents, baggage loss, or even charter flights missed due to illness. **American Express** cardholders receive automatic car rental insurance and travel accident coverage on flight purchases made with the card. See **Budget Travel Agencies,** p. 41, or see **Money Matters,** p. 22.

Insurance companies usually require a copy of police reports for thefts, or evidence of having paid medical expenses before they will honor a claim. There may be time limits on filing for reimbursement. Check with each insurance carrier for specific policies. Always carry policy numbers and proof of insurance. Most carriers have 24-hour hotlines. Insurance companies include: **Access America,** 6600 West Broad St., P.O. Box 11188, Richmond, VA 23230 (tel. (800) 284-8300; fax (804) 673-1491), **The Berkely Group/Carefree Travel Insurance,** 100 Garden City Plaza, P.O. Box 9366, Garden City, NY 11530-9366 (tel. (800) 323-3149 or (516) 294-0220; fax 294-1096), **Globalcare Travel Insurance,** 220 Broadway, Lynnfield MA, 01940 (tel. (800) 821-2488; fax (617) 592-7720; email global@nebc.mv.com; http://

www.nebc.mv.com/globalcare), **Travel Guard International,** 1145 Clark St., Stevens Point, WI 54481 (tel. (800) 826-1300; fax (715) 345-0525; http://www.travelguard.com), **Travel Assistance International (TAI),** by Worldwide Assistance Services, Inc., 1133 15th St. NW, #400, Washington, D.C. 20005-2710 (tel. (800) 821-2828 or (202) 828-5894; fax 828-5896; email wassist@aol.com), and **Wallach and Company, Inc.,** 107 West Federal St., P.O. Box 480, Middleburg, VA 20118-0480 (tel. (800) 237-6615, fax (540) 687-3172; email wallach.r@mediasoft.net).

Alternatives to Tourism

STUDY

Foreign study programs vary tremendously in expense, academic quality, living conditions, degree of contact with local students, and exposure to culture and language. There is a plethora of high school exchange programs. Most American undergraduates enroll in university-sponsored programs, and many colleges staff offices with study abroad information. Ask for the names of recent participants and get in touch.

American Field Service (AFS), 198 Madison Ave., 8th Fl., New York, NY 10016 (tel. students (800) 237-4636, administration (800) 876-2376; fax (503) 241-1653; email afsinfo@afs.org; http://www.afs.org/usa). Offers homestay exchange programs for high school students and recent graduates. Financial aid available.

American Institute for Foreign Study, College Division, 102 Greenwich Ave., Greenwich, CT 06830 (tel. (800) 727-2437). Organizes programs for high school and college study in universities throughout Europe. Scholarships available.

College Semester Abroad, School for International Training, Kipling Rd., P.O. Box 676, Brattleboro, VT 05302 (tel. (800) 336-1616; fax (802) 258-3500). Offers semester-long programs, including tuition, room and board, and airfare (US$9300-11,500). Scholarships are available; federal financial aid is usually transferable.

Council on International Education Exchange, 205 E. 42nd St., New York, NY 10017 (tel. (888) COUNCIL (268-6245); fax (212) 822-2699; email info@ciee.org; http://www.ciee.org). Sponsors over 40 study abroad programs throughout the world. Contact them for more information (see **Work and Volunteer,** p. 31).

Institute of International Education (IIE), 809 United Nations Plaza, New York, NY 10017-3580 (tel. (212) 984-5413; fax 984-5358). Book orders: IIE Books, Institute of International Education, P.O. Box 371, Annapolis Junction, MD 20701 (tel. (800) 445-0443; fax (301) 206-9789; email iiebooks@pmds.com). IIE's library of study abroad resources is open to the public Tues.-Thurs. 11am-3:45pm. Publishes *Academic Year Abroad* (US$43, US$5 postage) and *Vacation Study Abroad* (US$37, US$5 postage). Write for a complete list of publications.

Transitions Abroad, P.O. Box 1300, 18 Hulst Rd., Amherst, MA 01004-1300 (tel. (800) 293-0373; fax 256-0373; email trabroad@aol.com; http://transabroad.com). Magazine lists publications and resources for overseas study, work, and volunteering (US$25 for 6 issues, single copy $6.25). Publishes *The Alternative Travel Directory,* a guide to living, learning, and working overseas (US$20; postage $4).

WORK AND VOLUNTEER

There's no better way to submerge yourself in a foreign culture than to become part of its economy. It's easy to find a temporary job, but it will rarely be glamorous or lucrative. Officially, you can hold a job in Europe only with a **work permit,** obtained by your employer, usually demonstrating that you have skills that locals lack. European friends can expedite permits or arrange work-for-accommodations swaps. Be an au pair; advertise to teach English. Many permit-less agricultural workers go untroubled. European Union citizens can work in any EU country, and if your parents were born in an EU country, you may be able to claim dual citizenship or the right to a permit, but beware of countries where citizenship entails military service. Check with universities' foreign language departments for job opening connections, and contact the Consulate or Embassy of your destination country for more information.

If you are a full-time student at a U.S. university, the simplest way to get a job abroad is through **Council on International Educational Exchange (Council)** and its member organizations (see **Useful Travel Organizations,** p. 9). Council can procure three- to six-month work permits (and a work and housing handbook) for France, Germany, Spain, and the U.K. (US$25 application fee). French and German positions require language skills; British and Irish programs are best for neophytes, since Council helps with finding accommodations, openings, and connections. **U.S. permanent residents** can get work permits for France and Ireland.

Vacation Work Publications, 9 Park End St., Oxford OX1 1HJ, England (tel. (01865) 24 19 78; fax 79 08 85), publishes *Work Your Way Around the World* (UK£11, UK£1.50-2.50 postage). **Surrey Books,** 230 E. Ohio St., #120, Chicago, IL 60611 (tel. (800) 326-4430; fax (312) 751-7330) publishes *How to Get a Job in Europe: The Insider's Guide* (US$18). **InterExchange,** 161 Sixth Ave., New York, NY 10013 (tel. (212) 924-0446; fax 924-0575), has info on teaching and au pair programs. **Now Hiring! Jobs in Eastern Europe** (US$15), Independent Publishers Group, 814 N. Franklin St., Chicago, IL 60610 (tel. 312) 337-0747) covers finding work and accommodation in Eastern Europe. **Transitions Abroad Publishing, Inc.,** 18 Hulst Rd., P.O. Box 1300, Amherst, MA 01004-1300 (tel. (800) 293-0373; fax (413) 256-0373; email trabroad@aol.com), publishes a bimonthly magazine on opportunities abroad.

Volunteer jobs are readily available almost everywhere. You may receive room and board in exchange for your labor; the work can be fascinating (or stultifying). You can sometimes avoid the high application fees charged by the placement organizations by contacting the individual workcamps directly; check with the organizations. Listings in Vacation Work Publications's *International Directory of Voluntary Work* (UK£10; postage UK£2.50) can be helpful. (See above.) Also try:

Council has a Voluntary Services Department offering 2- to 4-week environmental or community services projects in over 30 countries. Must be at least 18 years old. Minimum US$295 placement fee. See **Useful Travel Organizations,** p. 9.

Peace Corps, 1990 K St. NW, Room 8508, Washington, D.C. 20526 (tel. (800) 424-8580; fax (202) 606-4469; http://www.peacecorps.gov). Write for their "blue" brochure, detailing applicant requirements. Opportunities in developing nations in Central and Eastern Europe and the former Soviet Union. Must be U.S. citizen, age 18 or over, and willing to make a 2yr. commitment. Bachelor's degree preferred.

Volunteers for Peace, 43 Tiffany Rd., Belmont, VT 05730 (tel. (802) 259-2759; fax 259-2922; email vfp@vfp.com; http://www.vfp.com). Arranges speedy placement in 2- to 3-week workcamps of 10-15 people (US$200). Listings in annual *International Workcamp Directory* (US$15). Free newsletter.

Willing Workers on Organic Farms (WWOOF) distributes a list of organic farmers offering room and board for workers. Contact: WWOOF, Postfact 59, CH-8124 Maur, Switzerland; or 50 Hans Crescent, London SWIX ONA, England (tel. (0171) 823-9937; email wwoof@dataway.c); include an international postal reply coupon.

Specific Concerns

WOMEN TRAVELERS

Women exploring on their own inevitably face additional safety concerns. Trust your instincts: if you'd feel safer elsewhere, move on. Always carry money for a phone call, bus, or taxi. Consider staying in hostels with single rooms that lock from the inside or in religious organizations that provide rooms for women only; avoid "communal" showers. Stick to centrally located lodgings, and avoid late-night treks or metro rides. Hitching is never safe for lone women, even in pairs. Choose train compartments occupied by other women or couples; ask the conductor to put together a women-only compartment. In some parts of Europe, women are frequently beset by unwelcome followers. Exercise caution without avoiding all local men.

The less you resemble a tourist, the better off you'll be. Always look as if you know where you're going, and ask women or couples for directions if you're lost. Try to dress conservatively, especially in rural areas. Shorts and t-shirts may identify you as a foreigner and should be avoided. Observe the way local women dress and invest in clothing to blend in. Wearing a conspicuous wedding band may help prevent unpleasantness, but in cities you may be harassed no matter how you're dressed. In crowds, you may be pinched or squeezed by over/under-sexed slimeballs. Your best answer to verbal harassment is no answer at all (a reaction is what the harasser wants). Feigning deafness or sitting motionless may do a world of good. The extremely persistent may be dissuaded by a firm, loud, and very public "Go away!" in the appropriate language. If need be, turn to an older woman for help; her rebukes will usually embarrass the most persistent jerks.

Women traveling alone should not attempt to challenge local custom or assert strong feminist beliefs. You won't change anything but may endanger yourself. You might even want to refer to your (fictional) "over-protective husband" who is waiting back at your hotel. Don't hesitate to seek out a police officer or a passerby. *Let's Go* lists emergency numbers (including rape crisis lines) in the **Practical Information** listings of most large cities; memorize the local numbers. Carry a whistle or an airhorn on your keychain for emergencies. A **model mugging** course will prepare you for a potential mugging and will raise your level of awareness and confidence (see **Safety and Security,** p. 26). Women face additional health concerns when traveling (see **Health,** p. 27). These warnings and suggestions should not discourage women from traveling. Don't take unnecessary risks, but don't lose your spirit of adventure either.

For information in the U.S., contact the **National Organization for Women (NOW),** which has branches across the country. Main offices are 22 W. 21st St., 7th fl., **New York,** NY 10010 (tel. (212) 260-4422); 1000 16th St. NW, 7th fl., **Washington,** D.C. 20004 (tel. (202) 331-0066); and 3543 18th St., **San Francisco,** CA 94110 (tel. (415) 861-8960; fax 861-8969; email sfnow@sirius.com; http://www.sirius.com/~sfnow/now.html). The following publications offer tips for women travelers:

Handbook For Women Travelers, by Maggie and Gemma Moss (UK£9). From Piatkus Books, 5 Windmill St., London W1P 1HF (tel. (0171) 631 07 10).

A Foxy Old Woman's Guide to Traveling Alone, by Jay Ben-Lesser (Crossing Press, US $11). Info, informal advice, and a resource list on solo budget travel.

A Journey of One's Own, by Thalia Zepatos (US$17). Good advice and a bibliography of resources. Order from The Eighth Mountain Press, 624 Southeast 29th Ave., Portland, OR 97214 (tel. (503) 233-3936; fax 233-0774; email eightmt@aol.com).

Women Going Places, a travel guide emphasizing women-owned enterprises. Geared towards lesbians but offers advice for all women. US$15 from Inland Book Company, 1436 W. Randolph St., Chicago, IL 60607 (tel. (800) 243-0138; fax (800) 334-3892), or a local bookstore.

Women Travel: Adventures, Advice & Experience, by Miranda Davies and Natania Jansz (Penguin, US$13). Information on specific foreign countries plus a decent bibliography and resource index. The sequel, *More Women Travel,* is US$15. Both from Rough Guides, 375 Hudson St. 3rd fl., New York, NY 10014.

OLDER TRAVELERS

Senior Citizens are eligible for a wide array of discounts. If you don't see a senior citizen price listed, ask. Proof of senior citizen status is often required. Agencies for senior group travel such as **Eldertreks,** 597 Markham St., Toronto, ONT Canada, M6G 2L7 (tel. (416) 588-5000; fax 588-9839; email passages@inforamp.net) and **Walking the World,** P.O. Box 1186, Fort Collins, CO 80522 (tel. (970) 225-0500; fax 225-9100; email walktworld@aol.com), are growing in popularity and enrollment.

AARP (American Association of Retired Persons), 601 E St. NW, Washington, D.C. 20049 (tel. (202) 434-2277). Members 50 and over receive discounts, benefits and services, including the AARP Motoring Plan from AMOCO (tel. (800) 334-3300). Annual fee US$8 per couple;$20 for three years; lifetime membership US$75.

Elderhostel, 75 Federal St., 3rd fl., Boston, MA 02110-1941 (tel. (617) 426-7788; fax 426-8351; email Cadyg@elderhostel.org; http://www.elderhostel.org). For those 55 or over (spouse of any age). Programs (1-4 weeks) in over 70 countries.

Gateway Books, 2023 Clemens Rd., Oakland, CA 94602 (tel. (510) 530-0299, credit card orders (800) 669-0773; fax (510) 530-0497; email donmerwin@aol.com; http://www.discoverypress.com/gateway.html). Publishes *Europe the European Way: A Traveler's Guide to Living Affordably in the World's Great Cities* (US$14) offering hints for the budget-conscious senior considering a long stay or retiring abroad.

National Council of Senior Citizens, 8403 Colesville Rd., Silver Springs, MD 20910-31200 (tel. (301) 578-8800; fax 578-8999). Memberships US$13 a year, US$33 for 3 years; or US$175 for a lifetime. Individuals or couples receive hotel and auto rental discounts, a senior newspaper, and use of a discount travel agency.

Pilot Books, 127 Sterling Ave., P.O. Box 2102, Greenport, NY 11944 (tel. (516) 477-1094 or (800) 79PILOT; fax (516) 477-0978; email feedback@pilotbooks.com; http://www.pilotbooks.com). Helpful guides including **Doctor's Guide to Protecting Your Health Before, During, and After International Travel** (US$10, postage US$2) and **The Senior Citizens' Guide to Budget Travel in Europe** (US$6, postage US$2, new edition next year). Call or write for a list of titles.

No Problem! Worldwise Tips for Mature Adventurers, by Janice Kenyon. Advice and info on insurance, finances, security, health, packing. Useful appendices. US$16 from Orca Book Publishers, P.O. Box 468, Custer, WA 98240-0468.

Unbelievably Good Deals and Great Adventures That You Absolutely Can't Get Unless You're Over 50, by Joan Rattner Heilman. Great tips on senior discounts. US$10 from Contemporary Books.

BISEXUAL, GAY, AND LESBIAN TRAVELERS

Attitudes toward bisexual, gay, and lesbian travelers are, naturally, particular to each place. Listed below are organizations and publishers which address those concerns.

Are You Two...Together? A Gay and Lesbian Travel Guide to Europe. Includes overviews of regional laws and lists of gay/lesbian organizations and establishments catering to or indifferent to gays and lesbians. Random House (US$18).

Damron Travel Guides, P.O. Box 422458, San Francisco, CA 94142 (tel. (415) 255-0404 or (800) 462-6654; email damronco@ud.com; http://www.damron.co). *The Damron Road Atlas* (US$16) contains maps of major European cities and gay and lesbian resorts, and lists bars and accommodations. *Damron's Accommodations* lists world-wide gay/lesbian hotels (US$19). Mail order available; US$5 shipping.

Ferrari Publications, Inc., P.O. Box 37887, Phoenix, AZ 85069 (tel. (602) 863-2408; fax 439-3952; email ferrari@q-net.com; http://www.q-net.com). *Ferrari's Guides' Gay Travel A to Z* (US$16), *Ferrari's Guides' Men's Travel in Your Pocket* (US$16), *Ferrari's Guides' Women's Travel in Your Pocket* (US$14), *Ferrari Guides' Inn Places* (US$16), and *Ferrari Guides' Gay Paris*. Available in bookstores or by mail order. (Postage/handling US$4.50 for the first item, US$1 for each additional item within the U.S. Overseas, call or write for shipping cost.)

Gay Europe (Perigee Books, US$14), by David Andrusia. A look at gay life throughout Europe, including restaurants, clubs, and beaches. Introductions cover laws and gay-friendliness. Available in bookstores.

Gay's the Word, 66 Marchmont St., London WC1N 1AB (tel. (0171) 278 76 54). Largest gay/lesbian bookshop in the U.K. Mail order service. Provides a list of titles on a given subject. Open Mon.-Sat. 10am-6pm, Thurs. 10am-7pm, Sun. 2-6pm.

Giovanni's Room, 345 S. 12th St., Philadelphia, PA 19107 (tel. (215) 923-2960; fax 923-0813; email giolphilp@netaxs.com). International feminist, lesbian, and gay bookstore with mail-order service. Carries many of the publications listed here.

International Gay and Lesbian Travel Association, P.O. Box 4974, Key West, FL 33041 (tel. (800) 448-8550; fax (305) 296-6633; email IGTA@aol.com; http:www.rainbow-mall.com/igta). Over 1300 companies. Lists of travel agents, accommodations, and events.

International Lesbian and Gay Association (ILGA), 81, rue Marché-au-Charbon, B-1000 Bruxelles, Belgium (tel./fax 32 2 502 24 71; email ilga@ilga.org). Not a travel service. Provides political information, such as homosexuality laws.

Spartacus International Gay Guides (US$33), published by Bruno Gmunder, Postfach 61 01 04, D-10921 Berlin, Germany (tel. (30) 615 00 3 42; fax 615 91 34). Lists bars, restaurants, hotels, and bookstores catering to gays. Includes homosexuality laws and hotlines. Available in bookstores and in the U.S. from Lambda Rising, 1625 Connecticut Ave. NW, Washington, D.C., 20009-1013 (tel. (202) 462-6969).

Women Going Places (Inland Book Company, US$14). Emphasizes women-owned enterprises, geared toward lesbians. See **Women Travelers,** p. 33.

DISABLED TRAVELERS

Countries vary in accessibility to travelers with disabilities. Some national and regional tourist boards provide directories on the accessibility of various accommodations and transportation services. If these services are not available, contact institutions of interest directly. You should inform airlines and hotels of disabilities when making arrangements, so they can prepare special accommodations. Hotels and hostels are becoming more accessible to disabled persons, and many attractions are trying to make exploring the outdoors more feasible. Call ahead to restaurants, parks, and other facilities to find out about ramps, door widths, elevator dimensions, etc.

Arrange transportation well in advance. If you give sufficient notice, some major car rental agencies (**Hertz, Avis,** and **National**) may offer hand-controlled vehicles. **Rail** is probably most convenient: large stations in Britain are equipped with wheelchair facilities, and the French national railroad offers wheelchair compartments on all TGV (high speed) and Conrail trains. Guide dog owners will need to provide a certificate of immunization against rabies and should inquire as to the specific quarantine policies of destination countries. The following organizations provide info:

Access Project (PHSP), 39 Bradley Gardens, West Ealing, London W13 8HE, U.K. Distributes access guides to London and Paris (UK£5). Researched by persons with disabilities. They cover traveling, accommodations, and access to sights and entertainment. Includes a "Loo Guide" with a list of wheelchair-accessible toilets.

American Foundation for the Blind, 11 Penn Plaza, New York, NY 10011 (tel. (212) 502-7600). Provides information and services Mon.-Fri. 8:30am-4:30pm. For their *Consumer's Catalogue,* contact Lighthouse Enterprises, 36-20 Northern Boulevard, Long Island City, NY 11101 (tel. (800) 829-0500).

Directions Unlimited, 720 N. Bedford Rd., Bedford Hills, NY 10507 (tel. (800) 533-5343; in NY (914) 241-1700; fax 241-0243). Specializes in arranging individual and group vacations, tours, and cruises for the physically disabled.

Flying Wheels Travel Service, 143 W. Bridge St., Owatonne, MN 55060 (tel. (800) 535-6790; fax 451-1685). Arranges trips for groups and individuals in wheelchairs or with other sorts of limited mobility.

Graphic Language Press, P.O. Box 270, Cardiff by the Sea, CA 92007 (tel. (760) 944-9594; email niteowl@cts.com; http://www.geocities.com/Paris/1502). Publishers of **Wheelchair Through Europe** (US$13). Comprehensive advice for the wheelchair-bound travelers. Their web site Global Access features worldwide trip reports from disabled travelers, tips, resources, and networking.

The Guided Tour Inc., Elkins Park House, 114B, 7900 Old York Rd., Elkins Park, PA 19027-2339 (tel. (800) 783-5841 or (215) 782-1370; fax 635-2637). Organizes travel programs for persons with developmental and physical challenges and those requiring renal dialysis. Call, fax, or write for a free brochure.

Mobility International, USA (MIUSA), P.O. Box 10767, Eugene, OR 97440 (tel. (514) 343-1284 voice and TDD; fax 343-6812; email info@miusa.org; http//miusa.org). Headquarters in Brussels, 25, rue de Manchester, Brussels, Belgium B-1070 (tel. (322) 410 62 97; fax 410 68 74). Info on travel programs, work/volunteer camps, accommodations, access guides, and organized tours. Membership US$30. Sells *A World of Options* (US$30, nonmembers US$35; organizations $40).

Moss Rehab Hospital Travel Information Service, (tel. (215) 456-9600, TDD (215) 456-9602). Resource center on accessibility and other travel concerns.

Society for the Advancement of Travel for the Handicapped (SATH), 347 Fifth Ave., #610, New York, NY 10016 (tel. (212) 447-1928; fax 725-8253; email sath-travel@aol.com; http://www.sath.org). Publishes a quarterly magazine *OPEN WORLD* (subscription US$13; free for members) and sheets on disability travel and accessible destinations. Annual membership US$45, students and seniors US$30.

Twin Peaks Press, P.O. Box 129, Vancouver, WA 98666-0129 (tel. (360) 694-2462, orders only MC and Visa (800) 637-2256; fax (360) 696-3210; email 73743.2634@compuserve.com; http://netm.com/mall/infoprod/twinpeak/helen.htm). Publishes *Travel for the Disabled* (US$20), *Directory for Travel Agencies of the Disabled* (US$20), *Wheelchair Vagabond* (US$15), and *Directory of Accessible Van Rentals* (US$10). Postage US$3.50 for first book, US$1.50 each additional.

DIETARY CONCERNS

Vegetarians should have no problem finding suitable cuisine. In city listings, *Let's Go* notes many restaurants which cater to vegetarians or which offer good vegetarian selections. The **Vegetarian Society of the UK** (VSUK), Parkdale, Dunham Rd., Altringham, Cheshire WA14 4QG, U.K. (tel. (0161) 928 0793), publishes *The European Vegetarian Guide to Hotels and Restaurants* as well as back copies of *The International Vegetarian Travel Guide* (UK£2, last published in 1991) and other titles. Call or send a self-addressed, stamped envelope for a listing.

Travelers who keep **kosher** should contact synagogues in larger cities about kosher restaurants; your own synagogue or college Hillel should have lists of Jewish institutions. **The Jewish Travel Guide** lists synagogues, kosher restaurants, and Jewish institutions in over 80 countries. It is available from Ballantine-Mitchell Publishers, Newbury House, 890-900 Eastern Ave., Newbury Park, Ilford, Essex IG2 7HH, U.K. (tel. (0181) 599 88 66; fax 599 09 84), and from Sepher-Hermon Press, 1265 46th St., Brooklyn, NY 11219 (tel. (718) 972-9010; US$15, US$2.50 shipping).

TRAVELING WITH CHILDREN

Family vacations can be rewarding or frustrating. Plan ahead, slow the pace, and adapt plans to the interests and patience of all the travelers. Make sure your accommodations are child-friendly, or ask if a hostel has rooms for families. If you rent a car, ask if the rental company provides a car seat for younger children. Traveling by car is an easy way to keep an eye on young children, but teenagers may prefer train. A papoose-style device for babies may be easier to manoeuver than a stroller.

Restaurants often have children's menus and discounts, and virtually all museums and tourist attractions have a children's rate. Make your child carry some sort of ID in case of an emergency, and arrange a reunion spot in case of separation when sightseeing. Children under two generally fly for 10% of the adult airfare on international flights (not necessarily including a seat). International fares are usually discounted 25% for children ages two to 11. Breast-feeding is often a problem while traveling.

Backpacking with Babies and Small Children (US$10) is published by Wilderness Press, 2440 Bancroft Way, Berkeley, CA 94704 (tel. (800) 443-7227 or (510) 843-8080; fax 548-1355; email wpress@ix.netcom.com). The **Kidding Around** series (US$8, postage under US$5), with illustrated children's books about Spain, Paris, and London, is available from John Muir Publications, P.O. Box 613, Santa Fe, NM 87504 (tel. (800) 285-4078; fax (505) 988-1680; contact Kathleen Chambers). **Take Your Kids to Europe** by Cynthia W. Harriman (US$17), published by Globe-Pequot Press, 6 Business Park Rd., Old Saybrook, CT 06475 (tel. (800) 285-4078; fax (860) 395-1418; email charriman@masongrant.com), has lots of tips for trips with older children. **Travel with Children** by Maureen Wheeler (US$12, postage US$1.50) is published by Lonely Planet Publications, Embarcadero West, 155 Filbert St., #251, Oakland, CA 94607 (tel. (800) 275-8555 or (510) 893-8555; fax 893-8563; email info@lonelyplanet.com), and P.O. Box 617, Hawthorn, Victoria 3122, Australia.

Packing

PACK LIGHT! Plan your packing according to the climate and the type of travel you'll be doing. Before you leave, strap your packed bag on and imagine yourself walking uphill on hot asphalt for three hours. A good rule is to pack what you need, then take half the clothes and twice the money. Leave room for souvenirs and gifts.

LUGGAGE

If you plan to cover most of your itinerary on foot, a sturdy **backpack** with padded hip belt and external compartments is unbeatable. In general, internal-frame packs are easier to carry and more efficient. For extensive camping or hiking, look into an **external-frame** pack, which offers added support, distributes weight better, and allows for a sleeping bag to be strapped on. Tie down loose straps to escape conveyor belt mangling. Whichever you choose, make sure your pack has a strong, padded hip belt, which transfers the weight from the shoulders to the legs. Sturdy backpacks cost anywhere from US$150-470. This is one area where it doesn't pay to economize—cheaper packs may be less comfortable, and the straps are more likely to fray or rip. A **suitcase** suffices for the less mobile, but weight and maneuverability should be considered. An empty, light-weight **shoulder bag** packed inside your luggage will be useful for purchases or laundry. A small **daypack** with secure closures allows you to dive into the city with just the essentials—lunch, camera, water bottle, and *Let's Go.* Guard money, passport, railpass, and other important articles in a **moneybelt or neck pouch,** and keep it with you always (see **Safety and Security,** p. 26).

CLOTHING AND FOOTWEAR

The **clothing** you bring will depend on when and where you plan to travel. If visiting places of worship, wear clothes that cover the shoulders and knees. Light natural fibers are the best in heat. For colder weather, you need a few heavier layers; have at least one layer that will insulate while wet. Make sure your clothing can survive wrinkles and adverse cleansings. Always bring a jacket or wool sweater. **Walking shoes** (well-cushioned sneakers and well-ventilated hiking boots) are not a place to skimp, and be sure to waterproof them. A double pair of socks—light silk or polypropylene inside and thick wool outside—will cushion feet, keep them dry, and help prevent blisters. Bring flip-flops for protection from fungi in showers. Talcum powder can prevent foot sores, and moleskin is bliss for blisters. *Break in your shoes before you leave home.* **Rain gear** is essential. A waterproof jacket and backpack cover will shield you and your stuff. A **poncho** is bulkier and may tear, but is lighter and can serve as ground cloths or camper lean-tos. Gore-Tex® is waterproof and breathable.

MISCELLANEOUS

The following list is not exhaustive: pocketknife, alarm clock, sewing kit, water bottle, flashlight, towel, compass, bungee cord, toilet paper—the European kind is rough—plastic baggies, waterproof matches, moleskin, whistle, rubber bands, insect repellant, electrical tape (for patching tears), clothespins, maps and phrasebooks, tweezers, sunscreen, vitamins, cold medicine, tissues, an antiseptic, safety pins, and padlock. Condoms, tampons, and your favorite brand of deodorant and razor may be hard to find on the road. A **first-aid kit** is good but bulky. **Laundry** facilities are sometimes hard to find. Washing clothes in hotel sinks is often a better option. Bring a bar of detergent soap, a sink-stopper (a squash ball works), and a travel clothesline or string. If staying in youth hostels, make the requisite **sleepsack** by folding a full-size sheet in half the long way, then sewing two sides closed. **Contact lens** supplies are rare and expensive, so bring saline and cleaner or wear glasses. **Film** is pricey, so buy it at home. Consider bringing a **disposable camera** or two rather than an expensive permanent one. Despite disclaimers, airport security X-rays *can* fog film.

Call USTn
for the
Best Deals in
Student Travel
• Student Discount Airfares
• Eurail & BritRail Passes
• ISIC & Hostel Cards
• Student Tours
University and Student Travel Nationwide (USTN) Call now!
Arizona State U Tempe (ASU) (800) 815-6455
California State Polytechnic San Luis Obispo (SLO) (800) 321-8728
California State U San Diego (CSUSD) (800) 662-6282
U of California Berkeley (UCB) (510) 843-1000
U of California Irvine (UCI) (800) 278-1132
U of California Santa Barbara (UCSB) (800) 595-0019
U of Colorado Boulder (800) LETS - GO-1
U of Florida Gainesville (800) 723-9005
Oregon State U Corvallis (OSU) (800) 858-3399
U of Oregon Eugene (UO) (800) 835-4745
U of Washington Seattle (800) 753-6636
American University Washington, D.C. (888) 364-2100
Gallaudet University Washington, D.C. Services for hearing impaired (888) 651-5227
We recommend only the best, including ...
Contiki
The World's Biggest Travel Company For 18-35 Year Olds

European **electricity** is usually 220 volts AC, which fries 110V North American appliances. Hardware stores have **adapters** (for the plug shape) and **converters** (which change the voltage). Use both, or you'll melt your appliance.

GETTING THERE

Budget Travel Agencies

Students and those under 26 qualify for reduced airfares from student travel agencies such as **Council Travel, STA, Let's Go Travel,** and **Travel CUTS.** These agencies resell bulk ticket purchases; in 1997, peak season student round-trips from the East Coast of North America to even the offbeat corners of Europe rarely topped US$800, with off-season fares considerably lower. Round-trip (regular) fares from Australia or New Zealand through STA were about US$1900. Student travel agencies also serve people over 26, although many discounts are specifically for the young.

Council Travel (http://www.ciee.org/cts/ctshome.htm), offers railpasses, discount airfares, hosteling cards, guidebooks, budget tours, travel gear, and student (ISIC), youth (GO25), and teacher (ITIC) identity cards. U.S. offices include: Emory Village, 1561 N. Decatur Rd., **Atlanta,** GA 30307 (tel. (404) 377-9997); 729 Boylston St., **Boston,** MA 02116 (tel. (617) 266-1926); 1153 N. Dearborn, **Chicago,** IL 60610 (tel. (312) 951-0585); 10904 Lindbrook Dr., **Los Angeles,** CA 90024 (tel. (310) 208-3551); 1501 University Ave. SE, **Minneapolis,** MN 55414 (tel. (612) 379-2323); 205 E. 42nd St., **New York,** NY 10017 (tel. (212) 822-2700); 953 Garnet St., **San Diego,** CA 92109 (tel. (619) 270-6401); 530 Bush St., **San Francisco,** CA 94108 (tel. (415) 421-3473); 1314 N.E. 43rd St., **Seattle,** WA 98105 (tel. (206) 632-2448); 3300 M St. NW, **Washington, D.C.** 20007 (tel. (202) 337-6464). **For U.S. cities not listed,** call 800-2-COUNCIL (226-8624). Also 28A Poland St. (Oxford Circus), **London,** W1V 3DB (tel. (0171) 287 3337).

Rail Europe Inc., 226 Westchester Ave., White Plains, NY 10604 (tel. (800) 438-7245; fax 432-1329; http://www.raileurope.com). Sells all Eurail products and passes, national railpasses including Brit Rail and German Rail, and point-to-point tickets. Up-to-date info on rail travel including Eurostar, the English Channel train.

STA Travel, 6560 North Scottsdale Rd., #F100, Scottsdale, AZ 85253 (tel. (800) 777-0112; fax (602) 922-0793; http://sta.-travel.com). A student and youth travel organization with over 150 offices worldwide offering discount airfares, railpasses, accommodations, tours, insurance, and ISICs. Offices in the U.S. include: 297 Newbury St., **Boston,** MA 02115 (tel. (617) 266-6014); 429 S. Dearborn St., **Chicago,** IL 60605 (tel. (312) 786-9050); 7202 Melrose Ave., **Los Angeles,** CA 90046 (tel. (213) 934-8722); **Miami,** FL 33133 (tel. (305) 284-1044); 10 Downing St., #G, **New York,** NY 10003 (tel. (212) 627-3111); 51 Grant Ave., **San Francisco,** CA 94108 (tel. (415) 391-8407); 4341 University Way NE, **Seattle,** WA 98105 (tel. (206) 633-5000); and 2401 Pennsylvania Ave., **Washington, D.C.** 20037 (tel. (202) 887-0912). Overseas offices include: Priory House, 6 Wrights Ln., **London** W8 6TA, U.K. (tel. (0171) 938 47 11); 10 High St., **Auckland,** New Zealand (tel. (09) 309 97 23); and 222 Faraday St., **Melbourne** VIC 3050, Australia (tel. (03) 9349 6911).

Let's Go Travel, Harvard Student Agencies, 17 Holyoke St., Cambridge, MA 02138 (tel. (617) 495-9649; fax 496-8015; email travel@hsa.net; http://hsa.net/travel). Railpasses, HI-AYH memberships, ISICs, ITICs, FIYTO cards, guidebooks, maps, bargain flights, and travel gear. Call or write for a catalogue (or see insert).

Campus Travel, 52 Grosvenor Gardens, London SW1W OAG (http://www.campus-travel.co.uk). Branches across U.K. Student and youth fares on transportation. Flexible airline tickets. Discount and ID cards for youths, travel insurance, maps, guides, and booklets. Telesales and bookings for **Europe** tel. (0171) 730 34 02; **North America** (0171) 730 21 01; **worldwide** (0171) 730 81 11; in Manchester (0161) 273 17 21; in Scotland (0131) 668 33 03.

Travel CUTS (Canadian University Travel Services, Ltd.), 187 College St., Toronto, ONT M5T 1P7, Canada (tel. (416) 979-2406; fax 979-8167; email mail@travelcuts). Also 295-A Regent St., **London** W1R 7YA, U.K. (tel. (0171) 637 31 61). Discounted airfares; student fares with ISIC. Issues ISIC, FIYTO, GO25, HI cards, and railpasses. Free *Student Traveller* and info on the Student Work Abroad Program (SWAP).

Travel Management International (TMI), 1129 East Wayzata, Wayzata, MN 55391 (tel. (612) 404-7164 or (800) 245-3672). Student fares and discounts.

Unitravel, 117 North Warson Rd., St. Louis, MO 63132 (tel. (800) 325 2222; fax (314) 569 2503). Offers discounted airfares on major scheduled airlines.

USIT Youth and Student Travel, 19-21 Aston Quay, O'Connell Bridge, Dublin 2, Ireland (tel. (01) 677 81 17; fax 679 88 33). Also New York Student Center, 895 Amsterdam Ave., New York, NY 10025 (tel. (212) 663-5435; email usitny@aol.com). Additional offices throughout Ireland and Greece. Low-cost tickets and flexible travel arrangements. ISIC and FIYTO-GO 25 cards in Ireland only.

Wasteels, 7041 Grand National Drive, #207, Orlando, FL 32819 (tel. (407) 351-2537; in **London** (0171) 834 70 66). A huge chain in Europe, with 200,000 locations. Information in English can be requested from the London office (tel. (4471) 834 70 66; fax 630 76 28). Sells Wasteels BIJ tickets, which are discounted (30-45% off regular fare) 2nd class international point-to-point train tickets with unlimited stopovers, available only to those under 26 and sold *only* in Europe.

By Plane

The first budget challenge is getting there: airlines attempt to squeeze every dollar; finding a cheap flight in their deliberately confusing jungle will be easier if you understand the system. Call every toll-free number, and ask about discounts. Use several **travel agents;** better yet, have an agent who is a regional specialist. Travel agents on commission may not want to spend time finding you the cheapest fares. **TravelHUB** (http://www.travelhub.com) can help you find Web travel agencies.

Students and "youth" (people under 26) should never pay full price for a ticket. Seniors can also get great deals. Sunday newspapers may have travel sections with local bargains. Australians should consult the Saturday *Sydney Morning Herald* and the ethnic press. Outsmart airline reps with the *Official Airline Guide* (US$359/yr; with fares, US$479; check your local library), a monthly guide listing nearly every scheduled flight in the world and toll-free phone numbers to call for reservations. *Guide*'s flight schedules and information on hotels, cruises, and rail and ferry schedules is on the web at http://www.oag.com (one-time hook-up fee US$25 and a user's fee of 17-47¢/min). Michael McColl's *The Worldwide Guide to Cheap Airfare* (US$15) is also useful, or try the **Air Traveler's Handbook** (http://www.cis.ohio-state.edu/hypertext/faq/usenet/travel/air/handbook/top.html).

Most airfares peak between mid-June and early September. Midweek (Mon.-Thurs. morning) round-trip flights run about US$40-50 cheaper than on weekends; weekend flights are generally less crowded. Traveling from hub to hub (for example, Los Angeles to Sydney) will win a more competitive fare than from smaller cities. Return-date flexibility is usually not an option for budget travelers; traveling with an "open return" ticket can be pricier than fixing a date and paying to change it. Whenever flying internationally, pick up your ticket well in advance of the departure date, have the flight confirmed, and arrive at the airport at least two hours before your flight.

COMMERCIAL AIRLINES

The commercial airlines' lowest regular offer is **APEX** (Advance Purchase Excursion Fare); advertised specials may be cheaper but have more restrictions and lower availability. APEXs provide confirmed reservations and allow "open-jaw" tickets (landing in and returning from different cities). Generally, reservations must be made seven to 21 days in advance, with seven- to 14-day minimum and up to 90-day maximum stay limits, and hefty cancellation and change penalties. Book APEX fares early for peak season; by May it may be difficult getting the summer departure date you want.

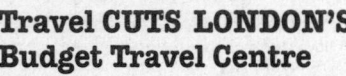

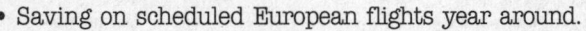

If you pay an airline's lowest published fare, you may waste hundreds of dollars; find out the average commercial price in order to assess your "bargain." Look into flights to less-popular destinations or on smaller carriers. **Icelandair** (tel. (800) 223-5500) has last-minute offers and a standby fare from New York to Luxembourg (April-June 1 and Sept.-Oct. US$410; June 1-Aug. US$610). Reserve within three days of departure. **Finnair** (tel. (800) 950-5000) offers US$111 round-trip fares to Helsinki. Icelandair (http://www.centrum.is/icelandair) and Finnair (http://www.us.finnair.com) also hold ticket auctions on their websites. **Martinair** (tel. (800) 627-8462 or (800) MARTINAIR) offers one-way only standby fares (US$210) from New York to Amsterdam (you're responsible for the ticket home). **TowerAir** offers round-trip flights to Paris (US$534), Athens, and Rome.

TICKET CONSOLIDATORS

Ticket consolidators sell unsold tickets on commercial and charter airlines at unpublished fares and are the best deal for traveling on short notice, on a high-priced trip, to an off-beat destination, or in peak season. Consolidators fares are generally much cheaper—a 30-40% price reduction is not uncommon. There are rarely age or stay constraints, but there is little flexibility in changing flights, and you must go back to the consolidator to get a refund for a missed flight. These tickets are often for connecting (not direct) flights on foreign airlines and do not credit frequent-flyer miles.

Consolidators come in three varieties: wholesale only; specialty agencies (both wholesale and retail); and "bucket shops," or discount retail agencies. As a private consumer, you can deal only with retail, but you can also have access to wholesale through a travel agent. Look for bucket shops' tiny ads in weekend papers (in the U.S., try the *Sunday New York Times*). In London, the real bucket shop center is the **Air Travel Advisory Bureau** (tel. (0171) 636 50 00).

Be a smart and careful shopper. Phone around, and pay with a credit card (in spite of the 2-5% fee) so you can stop payment if you never receive your tickets. Research the agency and get a copy of their refund policy. Ask about accommodations and car rental discounts. Insist on a receipt that gives full details about the tickets, refunds, and restrictions, and record the agent with whom you spoke and when. If they refuse to give you a receipt, or seem clueless or shady, use a different company. Beware the "bait and switch" gag: some firms will advertise a super-low fare and then tell a caller that it has been sold. Although this is a viable excuse, if they can't offer you a price near the advertised fare, it's a scam—report them to the Better Business Bureau.

Try **Airfare Busters** (tel. (800) 232-8783); **Pennsylvania Travel** (tel. (800) 331-0947); **Cheap Tickets** (tel. (800) 377-1000); or **Rebel** (tel. (800) 227-3235 or (800) 732-3588); fax (805) 294-0981; email travel@rebeltours.com; http://www.rebeltours.com). **Moment's Notice** (tel. (718) 234-6295; fax 234-6450; http://www.moments-notice.com) offers air tickets, tours, and hotels (US$25 annual fee). **NOW Voyager,** 74 Varick St. #307, New York, NY 10013 (tel. (212) 431-1616; fax (212) 334-5243; email info@nowvoyagertravel.com; http://www.nowvoyagertravel.com), acts as a consolidator and books discounted flights, mostly from New York, as well as courier flights, for a registration fee of US$50. For a processing fee, depending on the itinerary and number of travelers, **Travel Avenue** (tel. (800) 333-3335; fax (312) 876-1254; http://www.travelavenue.com) will search for the lowest airfare available and give you a rebate on fares over US$300.

Kelly Monaghan's *Consolidators: Air Travel's Bargain Basement* (US$7 plus US$2 shipping), from the Intrepid Traveler, P.O. Box 438, New York, NY 10034 (email intreptrav@aol.com), lists consolidators by location and destination. Find the **World Wide Wanderer Cyberian Bucket Shop Guide** at http://www.tmn.com/wwwanderer/WWWanderer_home_page.html.

STANDBY FLIGHTS

Very flexible budget travelers might try standby flights, for which you buy a promise that you will get to a destination near where you're going within a window of time (usually 5 days) from a location in a specified region. You call in before your date-

range to hear all of your flight options for the next week or so, and your probability of boarding. You then decide which flights you want to try to make and present a voucher at the airport which grants you the right to board a flight on a space-available basis. This procedure repeats for the return trip. When flying standby, be sure to read all the fine print in agreements. It may be difficult to receive refunds, and vouchers will not be honored if the airline fails to receive payment in time. **Air-Tech, Ltd.,** 588 Broadway, #204, New York, NY 10012 (tel. (212) 219-7000; fax 219-0066), sells standby tickets for around US$169-239 one way, and also arranges courier flights and regular confirmed-reserved flights at discount rates. With **Airhitch,** 2641 Broadway, 3rd fl., New York, NY 10025 (tel. (800) 326-2009 or (212) 864-2000; fax 864-5489), and Los Angeles, CA (tel. (310) 726-5000), one way runs US$175-269. Several European offices handle return registration; the main one is in Paris (tel. (01) 47 00 16 30).

CHARTER FLIGHTS

Charters are flights a tour operator contracts with an airline to fly extra loads of passengers to peak-season destinations. Charter flights fly less often and have more restrictions, notably on refunds. They are almost always fully booked, and schedules may change or be canceled last minute without a full refund. Pay with a credit card and consider insurance against trip interruption. Try **Interworld** (tel. (305) 443-4929; fax 443-0351); **Travac** (tel. (800) 872-8800; fax (212) 714-9063; email mail@travac.com; http://www.travac.com); or **Rebel,** (see **Ticket Consolidators,** p. 45).

Eleventh-hour **discount clubs** and **fare brokers** offer members savings on European travel, including charters and tour packages. Study contracts closely and avoid overnight layovers. Some options are **Last Minute Travel Club,** 100 Sylvan Rd., Woburn, MA 01801, one of the few without a membership fee (tel. (800) 527-8646 or (617) 267-9800), and **Travelers Advantage,** Stamford, CT (tel. (800) 548-1116; http://www.travelersadvantage.com; US$49 annual fee). Other clubs double as ticket consolidators, including **Moment's Notice** (US$25 annual fee), and **Travel Avenue.**

COURIER COMPANIES

Those who travel light should consider being a **courier.** The company hiring you uses your checked luggage space for freight; you only bring carry-ons. You must be over 21 (sometimes 18), have a passport, and procure any necessary visas. Most flights are round-trip with fixed-length stays (usually a week) and depart from New York. Round-trip fares to Western Europe from the U.S. range from US$250-550. **NOW Voyager** (see ticket consolidators above), acts as an agent, with last-minute deals from US$200 round-trip plus US$50 registration fee. Another agent to try is **Halbart Express,** 147-05 176th St., Jamaica, NY 11434 (tel. (718) 656-5000; fax 917-0708; offices in Chicago, Los Angeles, and London). Check a bookstore or library for *Air Courier Bargains* (US$15, plus US$2.50 shipping from the Intrepid Traveler, P.O. Box 438, New York, NY 10034; email intreptrav@aol.com). *The Courier Air Travel Handbook* (US$10, plus US$3.50 shipping) contains names and phone numbers. Order it from Bookmasters, Inc., P.O. Box 2039, Mansfield, OH 44905 (tel. (800) 507-2665). Always read the fine print. There are cheap fares out there, but you won't get something for nothing.

ONCE THERE

Getting Around

BY TRAIN

European trains retain the charm and romance of an era when travelers experienced the distances between the destinations. But charm and romance never did satisfy

ESSENTIALS

earthly needs, so bring food and water to avoid pricey on-board cafes and undrinkable water. Lock your compartment door and keep your valuables on your person.

Many train stations have separate counters for domestic and international tickets, seat reservations, and info—check before lining up. Even with a railpass, reservations are often required on major lines, and are advisable during holiday seasons. Make them at least a few hours in advance at the station (US$3-10). While many high speed trains (such as EuroCity, InterCity, Sweden's X2000, or France's TGV) are included in a railpass, other trains (such as Spain's AVE and Talgo, Finland's Pendolino S220, Germany's ICE, or Italy's ETR500 and Pendolino) require a supplement (around US$10).

For overnight travel, a tight, open bunk called a **couchette** is an affordable luxury (about US$20; reserve at the station at least several days in advance). Some countries give students or young people direct discounts on regular domestic rail tickets, while some others sell a student or youth card valid for 20-50% off a series of tickets.

Railpasses Buying a railpass is a popular and sensible option under many circumstances. Ideally conceived, a railpass allows you to jump on any train in Europe and go wherever you want whenever you want. The handbook that comes with your railpass tells you everything you need to know and includes a timetable for major routes, a map, and details possible ferry, steamer, bus, car rental, hotel, and **Eurostar** (the high speed train linking London and Paris or Brussels) discounts. In practice, you still must stand in line to pay for seat reservations, supplements, and couchette reservations, and to have your pass validated when you first use it.

More importantly, railpasses don't always pay off. For ballpark estimates, consult **Rick Steves' Europe Through the Back Door** newsletter or the **DERTravel** or **RailEurope** railpass brochure for prices of point-to-point tickets. Add them up and compare with railpass prices. You may find it tough to make your railpass pay for itself in Belgium, Greece, Ireland, Italy, Luxembourg, the Netherlands, Portugal, Spain, and all of Eastern Europe, where train fares are reasonable or distances short. If, however, the total cost of your trips nears the price of the pass, the convenience of avoiding ticket lines may be worth the difference.

Eurail remains the best option for many non-EU travelers. Eurail passes are valid in most of Western Europe (although not Britain). Eurail passes and Europasses are designed by the EU, and are purchasable only by non-Europeans from non-European distributors. The EU sets the prices, so no one travel agent is preferable.

The first-class Eurail pass rarely pays off; it is offered for 15 days (US$522), 21 days (US$678), one month (US$838), two months (US$1188), or three months (US$1468). You might prefer the **Eurail Saverpass**, which allows unlimited first-class travel for 15 days (US$444), 21 days (US$576), one month (US$712), two months (US$1010), or three months (US$1248) per person in groups of two or more. Travelers under age 26 can buy a **Eurail Youthpass**, good for 15 days (US$365), 21 days (US $475), one month (US$587), two months (US$832), or three months (US $1028) of second class travel. **Eurail Flexipasses** allow limited first-class travel within a two-month period: 10 days (US$616), 15 days (US$812). **Youth Flexipasses**, for those under 26 who wish to travel second-class, are available for US$431 or US$568, respectively.

The **Europass** combines France, Germany, Italy, Spain, and Switzerland in one plan. With a Europass you can travel in any of these five countries for five to fifteen days within a window of two months. First-class adult prices begin at US$316 for five days and increase by US$42 for each extra day. With a first-class ticket you can buy an identical second ticket for 40% off. Second-class youth tickets begin at US$210 for the first five days plus $29 for each additional day. Children aged 4 to 11 travel for half the price of a first-class ticket. Associate countries (Austria/Hungary, Belgium/Luxembourg/Netherlands, Greece, and Portugal) cost a nominal fee. The Europass introduces complications since you may only travel in countries you've "purchased." If you cut through a country you haven't purchased you will be fined.

You should plan your itinerary before buying a Europass. It will save you money if your travels are confined to between three and five adjacent Western European countries, or if you know that you want to go only to large cities. Europasses are not appro-

ESSENTIALS

priate if you like to take lots of side trips—you'll waste rail days. If you're tempted to add lots of rail days and associate countries, consider the Eurailpass.

It's best to buy a Eurailpass before you leave; all Eurailpasses and point-to-point tickets can be purchased from **Rail Europe, Inc.,** 226-230 Westchester Ave., White Plains, NY 10604 (tel. (800) 438-7245; fax (800) 432-1329 in the U.S.; and tel. (800) 361-7245; fax (905) 602-4198 in Canada; http://www.raileurope.com), which offers special group rates for six or more, or from **DERTravel Services,** 9501 W. Devon Ave., #400, Rosemont, IL 60018 (tel. (800) 421-2929, fax (800) 282-7474; http://www.dertravel.com). You can also contact Council Travel, Travel CUTS, Let's Go Travel (see **Budget Travel Agencies,** p. 41), or any other travel agent. If you're already in Europe, call an American agent, who should express mail a pass. Eurailpasses are not refundable once validated. You can get a replacement for a lost pass only if you have purchased insurance on it under the Pass Protection Plan (US$10).

InterRail Passes may be purchased by European residents of at least six months. The Under 26 InterRail Card (from UK£189) allows either 15 days or one month of unlimited travel within one, two, three or all of the seven zones into which InterRail divides Europe; the cost is determined by the number of zones the pass covers. The Over 26 InterRail Card offers unlimited second-class travel in 19 countries in Europe for 15 days or one month for UK£215 and UK£275, respectively. Contact **Student Travel Center,** 24 Rupert St., 1st fl., London W1V7FN, U.K. (tel. (0171) 437 01 21, 437 63 70, or 434 13 06; fax 734 38 36; http://www.hols.com/studentt/). Passes are also available from travel agents or main train stations throughout Europe.

If your travels will be limited to one country, consider a national railpass or regional passes such as the **Scanrail Passes** for Scandinavia; **Benelux Tourrail Passes** for Belgium, the Netherlands, and Luxembourg; the **Balkan Flexipasses,** which allow you travel throughout Turkey and the Balkan countries; and the **European East Passes,** which cover Austria, the Czech Republic, Hungary, Poland, and Slovakia. In addition, many countries (and Europass and Eurail) offer rail and drive passes, which combine car rental with rail travel—a good option for travelers who wish both to visit cities accessible by rail and make side trips into the surrounding areas. Several national and regional passes offer companion fares, allowing two adults traveling together 50% off the price of one pass. Some passes can be bought only in Europe and some others only outside of Europe; check with a railpass agent or with national tourist offices.

Rail Tickets For travelers under 26, **BIJ** tickets (Billets Internationals de Jeunesse, sold under the names **Wasteels, Eurotrain,** and **Route 26**) are a great alternative. Available for international trips within Europe and for travel within France as well as most ferry services, they knock 25-40% off second-class fares. Tickets are good for two months and allow a number of stopovers along the direct route. Issued for a specific international route between two points, they must be bought in Europe and used in the direction and order of the designated route. They are available from European travel agents, at Wasteels or Eurotrain offices (in or near train stations), and sometimes at ticket counters. Contact Wasteels in Victoria Station, adjacent to Platform 2, London SW1V 1JT, U.K. (tel. (0171) 834 70 66; fax 630 76 28).

Useful Resources The ultimate reference for rail trips is the **Thomas Cook European Timetable** (US$28; US$39 with a train and ferry map of Europe; postage US$4.50). This timetable covers all major and most minor train routes. In the U.S. and Canada, order from **Forsyth Travel Library** (see **Useful Publications,** p. 9). In Europe find it at any **Thomas Cook Money Exchange Center.** Also from Forsyth is Jay Burnoose's **Traveling Europe's Trains** (US$15), with maps and sightseeing suggestions. The annual **Eurail Guide to Train Travel in the New Europe** (US$15) from **Houghton Mifflin Co.,** 222 Berkeley St., Boston, MA 02116 (tel. (800) 225-3362; fax (800) 634-7568), gives timetables, instructions, and prices. The free annual railpass edition of **Rick Steves' Europe Through the Back Door,** 120 Fourth Ave. N., P.O. Box 2009, Edmonds, WA 98020 (tel. (425) 771-8303; fax 771-0833; email ricksteves@aol.com; http://www.ricksteves.com), compares passes and point-to-point tickets. **Hunter**

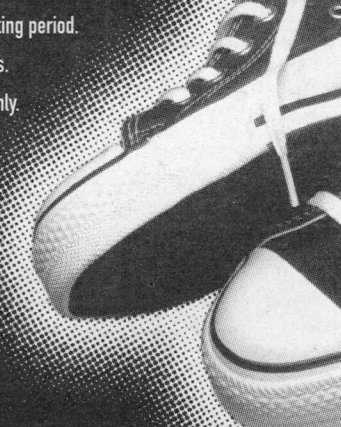

Publishing, P.O. Box 7816, Edison, NJ 08818 (tel. (908) 225-1900; fax 417-0482; email hunterpub@emi.net; http://www.hunterpublishing.com), offers rail atlases and guides including **Britain on the Backroads** and **The Trans-Siberian Rail Guide.**

BY BUS

The bus networks of Britain, Ireland, Portugal, Greece, Turkey, the Czech Republic, and the former Yugoslavia are more extensive and convenient, and in Iceland buses are the only ground transportation available. Elsewhere, destination determines the choice between bus and train. They may be cramped, but short-haul buses can reach rural areas inaccessible by train. Amsterdam, Athens, Istanbul, London, Munich, and Oslo are centers for long-distance lines.

Eurolines, 4 Cardiff Rd., Luton LU1 1PP, U.K. (tel. (01582) 40 45 11; fax (01582) 40 06 94; in London, 52 Grosvenor Gardens, Victoria; (tel.(0171) 730 82 35), is Europe's largest operator of Europe-wide coach services, including Eastern Europe and Russia. A Eurolines Pass offers unlimited 30-day (under 26 and over 60 UK£159; 26-60 UK £199) or 60-day (under 26 and over 60, UK£199, 26-60 UK£249) travel between 20 major tourist destinations. Eurolines also offers **Euro Explorers,** eight complete travel loops throughout Europe with set fares and itineraries. **Eurobus,** P.O. Box 3016, Workingham, Berkshire RG40 2YP, U.K. (tel.(0118) 936 23 21; fax (0118) 936 23 22; http://www.eurobus.uk.com), offers cheap bus trips in 25 major cities in 10 major European countries for those between ages 16 and 38. The buses, with English speaking guides and drivers, stop door-to-door at one hostel or budget hotel per city, and let you hop on and off. Tickets are sold by zone (one zone US$225, two zones US$400, all three zones US$525). Included with purchase of all three zones or added for a nominal fee with other tickets is **London Link,** a London/Paris return ticket. Travelers under 26 are eligible for discounts on all tickets. For purchase in the United States contact Council Travel or STA; in Canada contact Travel CUTS (see **Budget Travel Agencies,** p. 41). For discounted bus tickets between Athens and Rome check out **Magic Travel Services** in Athens (see **By Plane,** p. 55).

BY CAR

Yes, there really is no speed limit on the Autobahn. Cars offer speed, freedom, access to the countryside, and an escape from the town-to-town mentality of trains. Unfortunately, they also insulate you from the *esprit de corps* of rail traveling. Although a single traveler won't save by renting a car, four usually will. If you can't decide between train and car travel, you may benefit from a combination of the two; Rail Europe and other railpass vendors and travel agents offer rail-and-drive packages.

You can **rent** a car from a U.S.-based firm (Alamo, Avis, Budget, or Hertz) with European offices, from a European-based company (Europcar), or from a tour operator (Auto Europe, Bon Voyage By Car, Europe By Car, and Kemwel Holiday Autos), which will arrange a rental for you from a European company. Multinationals offer greater flexibility, but tour operators often strike better deals. Rentals vary by company, season, and pick-up point; picking up your car in Belgium, Germany or Holland is usually cheaper than renting from Paris. Expect to pay US$80-400 per week, plus tax (5-25%), for a teensy car. Reserve well before leaving for Europe and pay in advance if you can. It is always significantly less expensive to reserve a car from the U.S. than from Europe. Always check if prices quoted include tax and collision insurance; some credit card companies will cover this automatically. Ask about discounts and check the terms of insurance, particularly the size of the deductible. Rates are lowest in Belgium, Germany, Holland, and the U.K.; they are highest in Scandinavia and Eastern Europe. Ask your airline about special packages; you may get up to a week of free rental. Minimum age varies by country, but is usually 21-25. At most agencies, all that's needed to rent a car is a driver's license and proof that you've had it for a year. In Hungary and Spain you will need an international driver's license.

Try **Alamo,** not available for France, (tel. (800) 522-9696; http://www.goalamo.com); **Auto Europe,** 39 Commercial St., P.O. Box 7006, Portland, ME (tel. (800) 223-5555; fax (800) 235-6321; http://www.auto-europe.com); **Avis Rent a Car** (tel.

(800) 331-1084; http://www.avis.com); **Bon Voyage By Car** (tel. (800) 272-3299; in Canada (800) 253-3876); **Budget Rent a Car** (tel. (800) 472-3325); **Europe by Car,** One Rockefeller Plaza, New York, NY 10020 (tel. (800) 223-1516, (212) 581-3040; in California (800) 252-9401; fax (212) 246-1458; http://www.europebycar.com); **Europcar,** 145 Avenue Malekoff, 75016 Paris, France (tel. (800) 227-3876, in Canada (800) 227-7368, in France 01 45 00 08 06); **France Auto Vacances** (tel. (800) 234-1426); **Hertz Rent a Car** (tel. (800) 654-3001; http://www.hertz.com); **Kemwel Holiday Autos** (tel. (800) 678-0678; http://www.kemwel.com); **Maiellano Travel Auto** (for Italy) 445 Forest Ave., Staten Island, NY 10301 (tel. (800) 223-1616; fax (718) 727-0399); or **Payless Car Rental** (tel. (800) 729-5377).

For longer than 17 days, **leasing** can be cheaper than renting and is sometimes the only option for those ages 18-21. The cheapest leases are agreements to buy the car and sell it back at a prearranged price. In practice they don't entail enormous financial transactions. Leases include insurance and are not taxed. The most affordable originate in France, Belgium, Germany, or Italy (about US$1200 for 60 days). Contact Bon Voyage By Car, Europe by Car, France Auto-Vacance, or Auto Europe in advance.

If you know what you're doing, **buying** a used car or van in Europe and selling it before you leave can provide the cheapest wheels for longer trips. Check with consulates for import-export laws on used vehicles, registration, and safety and emission standards. Camper-vans and motor homes save you the hassle and expense of finding lodgings. Most of these vehicles are diesel-powered and deliver roughly 24 to 30 miles per gallon of diesel fuel, which is cheaper than gas. David Shore and Patty Campbell's **Europe by Van and Motorhome** (US$14; postage US$2, overseas US$6) guides you through the entire process of renting, leasing, buying, and selling vehicles in Britain and on the Continent, including buy-back options, registration, insurance, and dealer listings. To order, write or call Shore/Campbell Publications, 1842 Santa Margarita Dr., Fallbrook, CA 92028 (tel./fax (800) 659-5222 or (760) 723-6184).

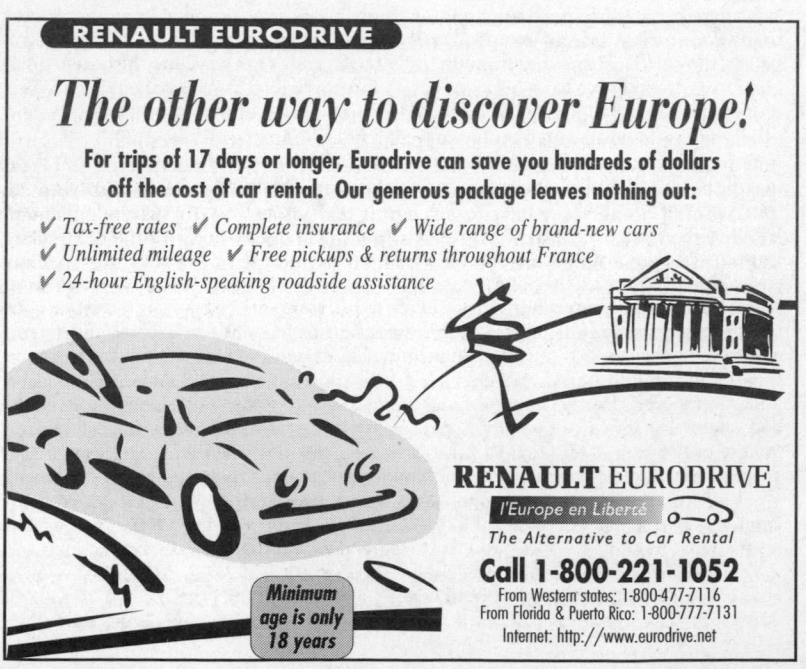

Eric Bredesen's **Moto-Europa** (US$16; shipping US$3, overseas US$7), available from Seren Publishing, 2935 Saint Anne Dr., Dubuque, IA 52001 (tel. (800) 387-6728; fax (319) 583-7853), is a thorough guide to all these options and includes itinerary suggestions, a motorist's phrasebook, and chapters on leasing and buying vehicles. More general info is available from the **American Automobile Association (AAA)** (see **Driving Permits and Insurance,** p. 22). For regional numbers of the **Canadian Automobile Association (CAA),** call (800) 222-4357.

Before setting off, know the laws of the countries in which you'll be driving (e.g., both seat belts and headlights must be on at all times in Scandinavia, and keep left in Ireland and the U.K.). European road conditions are rarely as good as they are in the States. The **Association for Safe International Road Travel (ASIRT),** 5413 West Cedar Ln., #103C, Bethesda, MD 20814 (tel. (301) 983-5252; fax 983-3663; http://www.horizon-web.com/asirt), can provide specific information. ASIRT considers road travel (by car or bus) to be relatively safe in Denmark, Ireland, The Netherlands, Norway, Sweden, Switzerland, and the U.K., and relatively unsafe in Portugal, Latvia, Turkey, Bulgaria, Greece, and Poland. Scandinavians and Western Europeans use unleaded gas almost exclusively, but it's not available in much of Eastern Europe.

BY PLANE

Flying across Europe on regularly scheduled flights can devour your budget. **Alitalia** (tel. (800) 223-5730) sells "Europlus": in conjunction with a transatlantic flight, for US$299 you can purchase a package of three flight coupons good within Europe; unlimited additional tickets cost $100. To U.S. residents, **Lufthansa** (tel. (800) 645-3880) offers "Discover Europe," a package of three flight coupons (US$125-200 each); up to six additional tickets are US$105-175 each. Student travel agencies sell cheap tickets, and budget fares are frequently available in the spring and summer on high-volume routes between northern Europe and resort areas in Italy, Greece, and Spain. Consult budget travel agents and local newspapers. The **Air Travel Advisory Bureau** in London (tel. (0171) 636 50 00) can find discount flights. **Magic Travel Services** in Athens (tel. (01) 323 74 71) is inexpensive. Many European airlines offer ticket packages which give intercontinental passengers discounts on flights within Europe, accommodations, and car rentals—check with a travel agent.

BY BOAT

Travel by boat is a bewitching alternative favored by Europeans but overlooked by foreigners. Most European ferries are comfortable and well-equipped. Even the cheapest fare class sometimes includes a reclining chair or couchette. Be aware, however, that school groups frequently travel on ferries. For a prime spot, check in at least two hours early and allow plenty of time for getting to the port. Avoid the astronomically priced cafeteria cuisine by bringing your own food. Fares jump sharply in July and August. Ask for discounts; ISIC holders can often get student fares, and Eurail passholders get many reductions and free trips (check the brochure with your railpass). You'll occasionally have to pay a port tax (under US$10). Advance planning and reserved tickets can spare you days of waiting in dreary ports for the next sailing.

Mediterranean ferries are the most glamorous and the most rocky. Reservations are recommended, especially in July and August. Bring toilet paper. Ferries run on erratic schedules, with similar routes and varying prices. Shop around, and beware of dinky, unreliable companies which don't take reservations. Ferries across the **English Channel** are frequent and dependable; see the Britain **Getting There** section (p. 126). Ferries in the **North Sea** and **Baltic Sea** are reliable and go everywhere. Those content with deck passage rarely need to book ahead. **Riverboats** acquaint you with towns that trains only wink at. The Moselle, Rhine, and Danube steamers are overrun by tourists; less commercial lines can be more attractive.

For complete schedules and fares for European ferries, steamers, and cruises find a copy of the quarterly **Official Steamship Guide International** at your travel agent. **Thomas Cook** also lists complete ferry schedules. (See **By Train,** p. 47). Links to some major European ferry companies can be found at http://www.youra.com/intnl-ferries.html. For info on European long river and sea cruises and visa-free cruises to Russia contact **EuroCruises,** 303 W. 13th St., New York, NY 10014 (tel. (800) 688-3876, (212) 691-2099, or (212) 366-4747; email eurocruises@compuserve.com).

BY BICYCLE

Today, biking is one of the key elements of the classic budget Eurovoyage. With the proliferation of mountain bikes, you can do some serious natural sight-seeing. Remember that touring involves pedaling both yourself and whatever you store in the **panniers** (bags which strap to your bike). Take some reasonably challenging day-long rides at home to prepare yourself before you leave, and have your bike tuned up. Wear visible clothing, drink plenty of water (even if you're not thirsty), and ride on the same side as the traffic. Learn and use the international signals for turns. Practice fixing a modern derailleur-equipped mount and changing a tire. A few simple tools and a good bike manual will be invaluable. For info about touring routes, consult national tourist offices or any of these publications. **The Mountaineers Books,** 1001 S.W. Klickitat Way, #201, Seattle, WA 98134 (tel. (800) 553-4453 or (206) 223-6303; fax 223-6306; mbooks@mountaineers.org), offers nation-specific tour books (especially France, Germany, Ireland, and the U.K.), as well as **Europe By Bike,** by Karen and Terry Whitehill (US$15; shipping $3), a great source of specific area tours in 11 countries. Send for a catalogue. **Cycling Europe: Budget Bike Touring in the Old World** (US$13), by N. Slavinski, from National Book Network, 15200 NBN Way, PO Box 190, Blue Ridge Summit, PA 17214-0190 (tel. (800) 462-6420), may also be helpful. **Michelin road maps** are clear and detailed (see **Useful Publications,** p. 9).

If you are nervous about striking out on your own, **Blue Marble Travel** offers bike tours for adults aged 20 to 50. (in U.S. tel. (800) 258-8689 or (201) 326-9533; fax 326-8939; in Paris (01) 42 36 02 34; fax 42 21 14 77; http://www.blumarbl.com). Pedal with or without 10 to 15 companions through the Alps, France, Italy, Portugal, Scandinavia, and Spain. Grad students get a 15% discount, and "stand-by" fares may be obtained in Europe. **CBT Bicycle Tours** offers one- to seven-week tours (around US$95 a day), including lodging and breakfasts, one-third of dinners, complete van and staff support, airport transfers, and extensive route notes and maps. Tours run May through August in Belgium, England, France, Germany, Holland, Italy, Ireland, Luxembourg, and Switzerland. Contact CBT Bicycle Tours, 415 W. Fullerton, #1003, Chicago, IL 60614 (tel. (800) 736-BIKE (2453) or (773) 404-1710; fax 404-1833).

Many airlines will count your bike as your second free piece of luggage; a few charge. The additional or automatic fee runs about US$60-110 each way. Bikes must be packed in a cardboard box with the pedals and front wheel detached. Airlines sell bike boxes at airports (US$10). Most ferries let you take your bike for free or a small fee. You can ship your bike on trains, though the cost varies from small to substantial.

Riding a bike with a frame pack strapped on it or your back is about as safe as pedaling blindfolded over a sheet of ice. Panniers are essential. The first thing to buy is a suitable **bike helmet.** At about US$25-50, they're a much better buy than head injury or death. U-shaped **Citadel** or **Kryptonite locks** are expensive (starting at US$30), but the companies insure their locks against theft of your bike for one to two years. **Bike Nashbar,** 4111 Simon Rd., Youngstown, OH 44512 (tel. (800) 627-4227; fax (800) 456-1223; http://www.nashbar.com), has excellent prices, ships anywhere in the U.S. or Canada, and cheerfully beats advertised competitors' offers by US$0.05.

Renting a bike beats bringing your own if your touring will be confined to one or two regions. *Let's Go* lists rental shops for most larger cities and towns. Some hostels rent bicycles cheaply. In Switzerland, train stations rent bikes and often allow you to drop them off elsewhere; check stations throughout Europe for similar deals.

BY MOPED AND MOTORCYCLE

Motorized bikes have long spiced up southern European roads with their flashy colors and perpetual buzz. They offer an enjoyable, relatively inexpensive way to tour coastal areas and countryside, particularly where there are few cars. They don't use much gas, can be put on trains and ferries, and are a good compromise between the high cost of car travel and the limited range of bicycles. However, they're uncomfortable for long distances, dangerous in the rain, and unpredictable on rough roads and gravel. Always wear a helmet, and never ride with a backpack. If you've never been

SCOTLAND
HAGGIS
HAGGIS TOURS
Backpackers
6 DAY TOUR
A 6 day adventure of a lifetime exploring the West coast, the Isle of Skye, the North West Highlands and Loch Ness. Perfect for those with a week to really discover Scotland.
JUMP ON-JUMP -OFF-
The ultimate in Backpackers Travel! A totally flexible tour pass, ideal for those independent travellers wishing to explore Scotland at their own pace.
3 DAY TOUR
A Truly Fabulous 3 day, 2 night adventure to the magnificent Highlands and Isle of Skye. Excellent for those short of time.
HAGGIS
The Ultimate Backpackers tours of Scotland for independent travellers*.
Regular departures, tours run all year round!
To make a reservation call our office or call into any branch of Campus Travel, STA Travel and other independent travel agencies throughout the UK.
(*fully guided tours - whilst we do go for short treks/hikes, we are not a specialised walking/hiking tour company.)
Tel: (+44) 0131 557 9393
WEBSITE: http\\:www.haggis-backpackers.com
11 Blackfriars Street, Edinburgh EH1 1NB
Fax: (+44) 0131 558 1177

on a moped before, a twisting Alpine road is not the place to start. Expect to pay about US$20-35 per day; try auto repair shops, and remember to bargain. Motorcycles normally require a license. Before renting, ask if the quoted price includes tax and insurance, or you may be hit with an unexpected additional fee. Avoid handing your passport over as a deposit; if you have an accident or mechanical failure you may not get it back until you cover all repairs. Pay ahead of time instead.

BY THUMB

Let's Go strongly urges you to consider seriously the risks before you choose to hitch. We do not recommend hitching as a safe means of transportation, and none of the information presented here is intended to do so.

Not everyone can be an airplane pilot, but any bozo can drive a car. Hitching means entrusting your life to a random person and risking theft, assault, sexual harassment, and unsafe driving. Depending on the circumstances and the norms of the country, men and women in groups and men traveling alone might consider hitching (called "autostop" in much of Europe) beyond the range of bus or train routes. If you're a woman traveling alone or with another woman, don't hitch. It's too dangerous. A man and a woman are a safer combination, two men will have a harder time, and three will go nowhere. Safety-minded hitchers avoid getting in the back of a two-door car and never let go of their backpacks. They will not get into a car that they can't get out of in a hurry. If they ever feel threatened, they insist on being let off, regardless of location. Acting as if they are going to open the car door or vomit on the upholstery will usually get a driver to stop. Hitchhiking at night can be particularly treacherous.

Experienced hitchers pick a spot outside of built-up areas, where drivers can pull off and return to the road safely, and have time to look over potential passengers. Hitching (or even standing) on super-highways is usually illegal: one may only thumb at rest stops or at entrance ramps. Most Europeans signal with an open hand, and write their destination on a sign in large letters with a smiley-face under it. Drivers prefer hitchers who are wholesome. No one stops for anyone wearing sunglasses.

Britain and Ireland are the easiest places in Western Europe to get a lift. Hitching in Scandinavia is slow but steady. Long-distance hitching in northwestern Europe demands close attention to expressway junctions and rest stop locations. Hitching in southern Europe is generally mediocre; France is the worst. Hitching remains common in Eastern Europe, though Westerners can be a target for theft and the line between hitching and taking a taxi is quite thin.

Most Western European countries offer a ride service (listed in the **Practical Information** for major cities) which pairs drivers with riders. The fee varies according to destination. **Eurostop International** (**Verband der Deutschen Mitfahrzentralen** in Germany and **Allostop** in France) is one of the largest in Europe. Not all of these organizations screen drivers and riders; ask in advance.

BY FOOT

Europe's grandest scenery can often be seen only by foot. *Let's Go* describes many daytrips for those who want to hoof it, but native inhabitants (Europeans are fervent, almost obsessive hikers), hostel proprietors, and fellow travelers are the best source of tips. Many European countries have hiking and mountaineering organizations; alpine clubs in Germany, Austria, Switzerland, and Italy, as well as tourist organizations in Scandinavia, provide inexpensive, simple accommodations in splendid settings. **Walking Europe from Top to Bottom,** by S. Margolis and G. Harmon, details one of Europe's most popular trails (US$11); check your local bookstore for others.

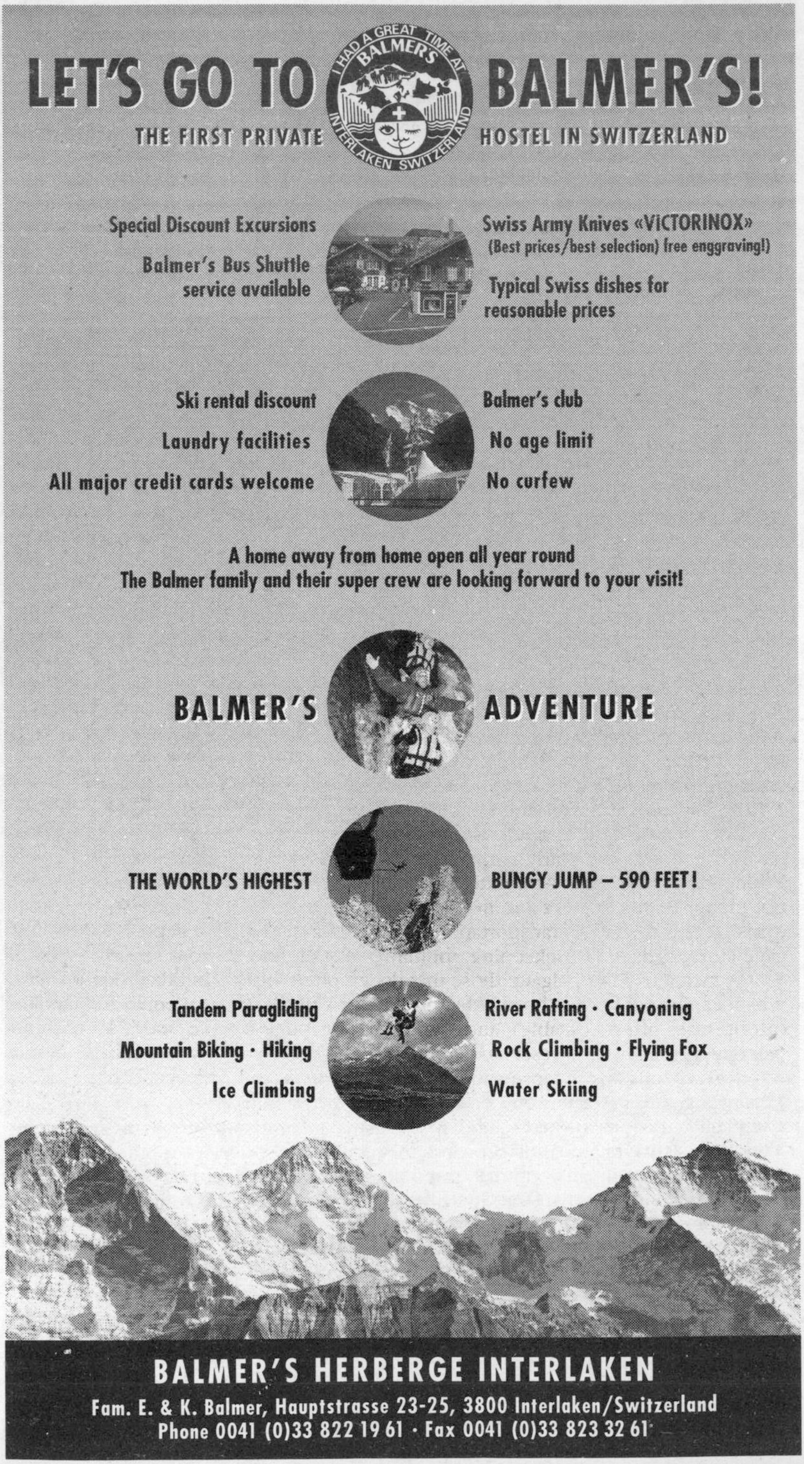
LET'S GO TO BALMER'S!
I HAD A GREAT TIME AT BALMER'S
INTERLAKEN SWITZERLAND
THE FIRST PRIVATE HOSTEL IN SWITZERLAND
Special Discount Excursions
Balmer's Bus Shuttle service available
Swiss Army Knives «VICTORINOX»
(Best prices/best selection) free enggraving!)
Typical Swiss dishes for reasonable prices
Ski rental discount
Laundry facilities
All major credit cards welcome
Balmer's club
No age limit
No curfew
A home away from home open all year round
The Balmer family and their super crew are looking forward to your visit!
BALMER'S ADVENTURE
THE WORLD'S HIGHEST BUNGY JUMP – 590 FEET!
Tandem Paragliding
Mountain Biking · Hiking
Ice Climbing
River Rafting · Canyoning
Rock Climbing · Flying Fox
Water Skiing
BALMER'S HERBERGE INTERLAKEN
Fam. E. & K. Balmer, Hauptstrasse 23-25, 3800 Interlaken/Switzerland
Phone 0041 (0)33 822 19 61 · Fax 0041 (0)33 823 32 61

Accommodations

When arriving in a town without a reservation, stop first at the tourist office, which should distribute accommodations listings and reserve rooms for a small fee. Prices often rise each January. Hostel proprietors or locals with rooms may approach you in ports or train stations, an accepted custom with no guarantee of trustworthiness or quality. Carry your own baggage, ask for ID, and have them write down the price.

HOSTELS

Europe in the summer is overrun by young budget travelers. Hostels are the hub of this subculture, providing opportunities to meet youth from all over the world, find traveling partners, trade stories, and learn about places to visit. At US$5-25 per night, prices are low; only camping is cheaper. Guests tend to be in their teens and twenties, but most hostels welcome travelers of all ages. In northern Europe, where hotel prices are high, hostels have special family rooms. In the average hostel, though, you and 1-50 roommates will sleep in a gender-segregated room of bunk beds, with common bathrooms and a lounge down the hall. The hostel warden may be a laid-back student, a hippie dropout, or a crotchety disciplinarian. Most hostels have well-equipped kitchens; some serve hot meals. The **Internet Guide to Hostelling** (http://hostels.com) has more information, as does **Eurotrip** (http://www.eurotrip.com).

The basic disadvantage of hostels is their regimentation. Most have an early curfew—a distinct cramp in your style if you plan to rage in town. There is also usually a lockout from morning to mid-afternoon. Conditions are generally spartan and crowded, and you may run into screaming pre-teen tour groups. Hostel quality varies dramatically. Some are set in gorgeous castles, others in run-down barracks far from the town center. Rural hostels are often the most appealing. Hostels usually prohibit sleeping bags and provide blankets and sheets instead. Some require sleepsacks; you can make your own from a sheet or order one (about US$14) from Let's Go Travel (see **Budget Travel Agencies,** p. 41) or a youth hostel federation. Large hostels are reluctant to take telephone reservations; citing an exact train arrival time or promising to call to confirm may help. In hostels in large Western European cities, take advantage of hostel-to-hostel fax booking services (US$2-5).

Privately owned hostels are found in major tourist centers and throughout some countries (particularly Ireland). No membership is required, and you won't always have to contend with early curfews or daytime lockouts, but their quality varies. **Young Men's Christian Association (YMCA)** rates are usually lower than a hotel's but higher than a hostel's and may include the use of TV, air conditioning, pools, gyms, access to public transportation, tourist information, safe deposit boxes, luggage storage, daily housekeeping, multilingual staff, and 24-hour security. Not all YMCA locations offer lodging; those that do are often located in urban downtowns, which can be convenient but a little gritty. Many YMCAs accept women and families (group rates often available), and some will not lodge people under 18 without parental permission. All reservations must be made and paid for in advance, with a traveler's check (signed top and bottom), U.S. money order, certified check, Visa, or MasterCard in US dollars. For information or reservations (reservation fee US$3 U.S. and Canada, US$5 elsewhere), write to **Y's Way International,** 224 E. 47th St., New York, NY 10017 (212-308-2899; fax 308-3161; and http://www.ymca.org for links to branches worldwide, but not to Y's Way). Y's Way "Travel Partners" are in Holland, Belgium, Austria, Dusseldorf, Switzerland, Paris, London, and Malta.

Most **Young Women's Christian Associations (YWCA)** accommodate women and, sometimes, couples. Nonmembers are often required to join when lodging. Write to **YWCA-USA,** 726 Broadway, New York, NY 1000, or call (212) 614-2700. A world-wide directory (US$10) features names, addresses, restrictions, and other info.

Hostel Membership

Hostelling International (HI) is a federation of national hosteling associations. All of the HI national affiliates listed below comply with HI standards and regulations. Offi-

cial youth hostels will normally display a blue triangle with the symbol of the national hostel association. The International Youth Hostel Federation, 9 Guessens Road, Welwyn Garden City, Hertfordshire AL8 6QW, U.K., publishes **Hostelling International: Europe** (UK£7/US$14, including postage), which lists HI affiliated hostels throughout Europe and details the **International Booking Network (IBN)** which makes confirmed reservations at any of more than 300 hostels throughout the world (US$5 fee; US$2 in person; 1-week advance notice required, 1½ weeks when reserving from overseas). To make prepaid reservations, call or visit any hostel on the IBN or an HI branch. For US$5, reservations can be made for up to six nights and up to nine people, and changes can be made from three to eight days before the date of the reservation. Credit card (MC, Discover, or Visa) guarantee required.

A one-year HI membership permits you to stay at youth hostels all over Europe at unbeatable prices, and with few exceptions (such as Bavaria), you need not be a youth to take advantage of HI. Prospective hostel-goers should become members of the youth hostel association in their own country in order to become HI members. If you didn't get a membership at home, you can ask an HI hostel for a blank membership card with space for six validation stamps. Each night you'll pay a nonmember supplement (one-sixth the membership fee) and earn one Guest Stamp; get six stamps, and you're a member. This system works well in most of Western Europe, though in some countries you may need to remind the hostel reception. In Eastern Europe, many hostels are not HI members. (There is one HI hostel in Russia but more in Poland, the Czech Republic, and Hungary.) Most student travel agencies (see **Budget Travel Agencies,** p. 41) sell HI cards; or contact one of the national hostel organizations listed below. The **Internet Guide to Hosteling** is at http://hostels.com.

Hostelling International-American Youth Hostels (HI-AYH), 733 15th St. NW, Suite 840, Washington, D.C. 20005 (202-783-6161; fax 783-6171; email hiayhserv@hiayh.org; http://www.hiayh.org). Memberships also available at travel agencies: one year US$25; under 18 US$10; over 54 US$15; family US$35.

Hostelling International-Canada (HI-C), 400-205 Catherine St., Ottawa, ONT K2P 1C3, Canada (613-237-7884; fax 237-7868). IBN booking centers in Edmonton, Montreal, Ottawa, and Vancouver. Membership packages: 1yr, under 18 CDN$12; 1yr., over 18 CDN$25; 2yr., over 18 CDN$35; lifetime CDN$175.

Youth Hostels Association of England and Wales (YHA), Trevelyan House, 8 St. Stephen's Hill, St. Albans, Hertfordshire AL1 2DY, U.K. (tel. (01727) 855215; fax 844126). Enrollment fees are: UK£9.50; under 18 UK£3.50; UK£9.50 per parent with children under 18 enrolled free; UK£130 for lifetime membership. Overnight prices for under 18 UK£4.25-17.20; for adults UK£6.25-20.50.

An Óige (Irish Youth Hostel Association), 61 Mountjoy St., Dublin 7, Ireland (tel. (01) 830 4555; fax 830 5808; anoige@iol.ie; http://www.irelandyha.org). 1yr. membership is IR£7.50; under 18 IR£4; family membership IR£7.50 for each adult with children under 16 free. IR£4.50-9.50 a night. 37 locations.

Youth Hostels Association of Northern Ireland (YHANI), 22 Donegall Rd., Belfast BT12 5JN, U.K. (tel. (01232) 324733 or 315435; fax 439699). Annual memberships UK£7; under 18 UK£3; family UK£14 for up to 6 children.

Scottish Youth Hostels Association (SYHA), 7 Glebe Crescent, Stirling FK8 2JA (tel. (01786) 891400; fax 891333; email syha@syha.org.uk; http://www.syha.org.uk). Membership UK£6; under 18 UK£2.50.

Australian Youth Hostels Association (AYHA), Level 3, 10 Mallett St., Camperdown NSW 2050, Australia (tel. (02) 9565 1699; fax 9565 1325; email YHA@zeta.org.au). Memberships AUS$44, renewal AUS$27; under 18 AUS$13.

Youth Hostels Association of New Zealand (YHANZ), P.O. Box 436, 173 Gloucester St., Christchurch 1, New Zealand (tel. (643) 379 9970; fax 365 4476; email info@yha.org.nz; http://www.yha.org.nz). Annual membership fee NZ$24.

Hostel Association of South Africa, P.O. Box 4402, Cape Town 8000, South Africa (tel. (021) 24 2511; fax 24 4119; email hisa@gem.co.za; http://www.gen.com/hisa). Membership SAR45; group SAR120; family SAR90; lifetime SAR250.

HOTELS, GUEST HOUSES, AND PRIVATE HOMES

Hotels are quite expensive in Britain, Switzerland, Austria, and northern Europe. Rock bottom for one or two people is US$25 each. Elsewhere, couples can usually get by fairly well (rooms with a double bed are generally cheaper than those with two twin beds), as can larger groups, but inexpensive European hotels may come as a shock to pampered North Americans. You'll share a hall bathroom; one of your own will cost extra. Hot showers may also cost extra. In Britain and Ireland, a large breakfast is often included; elsewhere a continental breakfast of a roll, jam, coffee or tea, and maybe an egg is served. Some hotels offer "full pension" (all meals) and "half pension" (no lunch). Unmarried couples will generally have no trouble getting a room together, although couples under 21 may encounter resistance.

Smaller **guest houses** and **pensions** are often cheaper than hotels. Even less expensive are rooms in **private homes**—the local tourist office usually has a list. If you're traveling alone, this is an economical way to get a single and meet real Europeans. The British and Irish **bed and breakfast** is a breed of private room that's extra heavy on the bacon and eggs. Private rooms are an excellent option in Eastern Europe, where youth hostels are non-existent outside of cities; tourist offices and travel agencies book most private rooms, and proprietors flag down tourists at the train station.

If you reserve in writing, indicate your night of arrival and the number of nights you plan to stay. The hotel will send you a confirmation and may request payment for the first night. Not all hotels take reservations, and few accept checks in foreign currency. Enclosing two International Reply Coupons will ensure a prompt reply (each US$1.05, good for ½ ounce; available at any post office).

CAMPING

Camping in Europe can rock or suck. **Organized campgrounds** exist in most European cities, accessible by foot, car, or public transportation. Showers, bathrooms, and a small restaurant or store are common; some sites have more elaborate facilities. Prices are US$5-15 per person with an additional charge for a tent. Money and time spent in getting to the campsite may eat away at your budget and patience.

Europa Camping and Caravan Guide, an annually updated catalogue of European campsites, is available for $20 through Recreational Equipment, Inc. (REI), P.O. Box 1700, Sumner, WA 98352-0001 (tel. (800) 426-4840). The Automobile Association, AA Publishing, P.O. Box 194, Rochester, Kent, ME2 4QG, U.K. (tel. (01634) 29 71 23; fax 29 80 00 or 29 80 02), publishes a wide range of maps, atlases, and travel guides, including **Camping and Caravanning: Europe** and **Camping and Caravanning: Britain & Ireland** (each UK£8). An **International Camping Carnet** (membership card) is required by some campgrounds but can usually be bought on the spot. The card entitles you to some discounts. It's available for US$35 through Family Campers and RVers, 4804 Transit Rd., Bldg. #2, Depew, NY 14043 (tel. (716) 668-6242; price includes their publication *Camping Today* and a membership fee).

Prospective campers will need to invest money in equipment and energy in carrying it. Use reputable mail-order firms to gauge prices; order from them if you can't do as well locally, and buy before you leave. In the fall, the previous year's merchandise may be discounted. **Campmor,** P.O. Box 700, Saddle River, NJ 07458-0700 (tel. (800) 526-4784, outside the U.S. call (201) 825-8300; email customer-service@campmor.com; http://www.campmor.com), has brandname equipment at low prices. **REI** (see above) stocks a wide range of gear and has seasonal sales. And 24 hours a day, 365 days a year, **L.L. Bean,** Freeport, ME 04033 (tel. (800) 341-4341), supplies its own equipment and national-brand merchandise with a 100% satisfaction guarantee.

Good **sleeping bags**—made of down (lightweight and warm) or synthetic (faster drying, heavier, more durable, and warmer when wet)—have ratings for minimum temperatures. The lower the mercury, the higher the price. Estimate the most severe conditions you may encounter, subtract a few degrees, and then choose your bag. Do not buy a down bag if you will be in a rainy climate. Expect to pay US$65-100 for a summer synthetic bag and US$250-550 for a good down bag for sub-freezing temper-

atures. **Sleeping bag pads** cost US$15 and up, while **air mattresses** are about US$25-50. The best **tents** are free-standing, have their own frames and suspension systems, and require no staking. Low profile dome tents are good all-around, with little unnecessary bulk. Remember to seal the seams against water. Backpackers and cyclists will require small, lightweight models, costing US$125 and up. Try L.L. Bean or **Sierra Designs,** 1255 Powell St., Emeryville, CA 94608 (tel. (510) 450-9555; fax 654-0705), which carries all seasons and types of lightweight tent models.

For info on picking a pack, see **Packing,** p. 39. Weight should be centered on the hips for women and a little higher on the back for men, and tighten the hip strap on your pelvic bones. Be sure to wear **hiking boots** with good ankle support—see **Clothing and Footware,** p. 39. Other camping basics include **rain gear,** which should be a jacket and pants, rather than a poncho which can catch and tear. **Synthetics,** like polypropylene tops, socks, and long underwear, along with a synthetic or wool jacket, will keep you warm even when wet, unlike cotton. When camping in autumn, winter, or spring, bring along a **"space blanket,"** which helps you to retain your body heat and doubles as a groundcloth (US$5-15). Plastic **water bottles** are virtually shatter- and leak-proof. Bring **water-purification tablets** for when you can't boil water. For those places that forbid fires or the gathering of firewood (this includes virtually every organized campground in Europe), you'll need a **camp stove**. The classic Coleman starts at about US$30. Consider the "GAZ" butane/propane stove; its little blue cylinders can be purchased anywhere on the continent—just don't take them on a plane. A **first aid kit, Swiss army knife, insect repellent,** and **waterproof matches** or a **lighter** are essential camping items. Other items include: a collapsible **water sack**, a battery-operated **flash-light,** a **plastic groundcloth,** a **nylon tarp,** a **waterproof backpack cover** (although you can also store your belongings in plastic bags inside your backpack), and a **"stuff sack"** and plastic bag to keep your sleeping bag dry. **Wilderness Press,** 2440 Bancroft Way, Berkeley, CA 94704-1676 (tel. (800) 443-7227 or (510) 843-8080; fax 548-1355; email wpress@ix.netcom.com) publishes useful books like *Backpacking Basics* (US$10, postage US$1). **The Caravan Club,** East Grinstead House, East Grinstead, West Sussex, RH19 1UA, U.K. (tel. (0342) 32 69 44; fax 41 02 58), produces one of the most detailed English-language guides to campsites in Europe and the U.K.

The Great Outdoors

The first thing to preserve in the wilderness is yourself—health, safety, and food should be your primary concerns. See **Health** (p. 27) for info about basic concerns and first-aid. Many water bodies have bacteria like giardia, which causes gas, cramps, loss of appetite, and diarrhea and may last for months. To avoid this, always boil your water for at least five minutes or use an iodine solution. Filters do not remove all bacteria. *Never go camping or hiking by yourself for any significant time or distance.* If you're going into an area that is not well-traveled or marked, let someone know where you're hiking and for how long. Stay warm and drink water constantly.

The second thing to protect is the wilderness. Make small fires using only dead branches or brush; using a campstove is more cautious. Some parks and sites prohibit campfires. Pitch your tent on high, dry ground, don't cut vegetation, and don't clear sites. If there are no toilet facilities, bury human waste at least 4 in. deep and 100 ft. from any water supplies or campsites. Use only biosafe soap or detergents. Always carry your trash to the next trash can; burning and burying pollute the environment.

ALTERNATIVE ACCOMMODATIONS

In university towns, **student dormitories** may be open to travelers when school is not in session. Many **monasteries** and **convents** will open their doors, particularly in Italy. Though sleeping in train stations may be tolerated by authorities, it's neither comfortable nor safe, and don't spend the night in an urban park unless you place a similarly low value on your life. Several host networks can help you find lodging with families; see **Work and Volunteer,** p. 31.

Keeping in Touch

MAIL

Mail can be sent internationally through **Poste Restante** (the international phrase for General Delivery) to any city or town. Mark the envelope "HOLD" and address it, for example, "Michael DYBBS, Poste Restante, City, Country (with country code)." The last name should be capitalized and underlined. The mail will go to a special desk in the central post office, unless you specify a post office by street address or postal code. For towns in the Czech Republic and Slovakia, write a "1" after the city name to ensure that mail goes to the central post office. As a rule, it's best to use the largest post office in the area; sometimes, mail will be sent there regardless of what you write. When possible, it is safer and quicker to send mail express or registered.

It helps to use the appropriate translation of **Poste Restante** (*Lista de Correos* in Spanish, *Fermo Posta* in Italian, and *Postlagernde Briefe* in German). Bring your passport and other ID to pick up your mail. If the clerk insists that there is nothing for you, check under your first name. Some places may charge a minimal fee. *Let's Go* lists post offices in the **Practical Information** section for cities and most towns.

Aerogrammes, printed sheets that fold into envelopes (no enclosures) and travel via airmail, are available at post offices. It helps to mark "airmail" in the appropriate language (*par avion* in French, *por avión* in Spanish, *mit luftpost* in German, *per via aerea* in Italian, *poczta lotnicza* in Polish, *leteky* in Czech), though *par avion* is universally understood. Airmail between Europe and the U.S. averages one to two weeks. Allow at least two weeks for Australia, New Zealand, and most of Africa.

If regular airmail is too slow, there are a few faster, more expensive, options. Federal Express (tel. (800) 463-3339) can get a letter from New York to Paris in two days for US$29.07. By U.S. Express Mail, the same letter would arrive in two to three days and would cost US$21. Fed-Ex rates from non-U.S. locations are prohibitively expensive (Paris to New York, for example, costs upwards of US$60). **Surface mail** is by far the cheapest and slowest way to send mail. It takes one to three months to cross the Atlantic, appropriate for sending large quantities of items you won't need for a while. Do not send items of great value (either monetary or sentimental) by surface mail. It is vital to distinguish airmail from surface mail by explicitly labeling "airmail" in the appropriate language. When ordering materials from abroad, always include one or two **International Reply Coupons**—a way of providing the postage to cover delivery. IRCs should be available from your local post office (US$1.05 for ½ oz.).

American Express offices throughout Europe will act as a mail service for cardholders if you contact them in advance. Under this free **Client Letter Service,** they will hold mail for 30 days, forward upon request, and accept telegrams. The last name of the person to whom the mail is addressed should be capitalized and underlined. Some offices will offer these services to non-cardholders (especially those who have purchased AmEx Traveler's Cheques). Check the **Practical Information** section in *Let's Go* for the cities you plan to visit. A complete list is available free from AmEx (tel. (800) 528-4800) in the booklet *Traveler's Companion* or online at http://www.americanexpress.com/shared/cgibin/tsoserve.cgi?travel/index.

TELEPHONES

The **country code** is listed with exchange rates at the beginning of each chapter. **City codes** are listed at the end of the Practical Information section for large cities and in parentheses with the phone numbers for smaller cities and regions.

You can place **international calls** from most phones. To call from the U.S., dial the international access code (011), then the country code, the city code, and the local number. Country codes and city codes may sometimes be listed with a zero in front (e.g., 033), but when using 011 (or whatever your international access code happens

to be), drop successive zeros (e.g., 011 33). You may have to go through the operator or wait for a tone after the international access code. Note: Wherever possible, save money by using a calling card (see below) for international phone calls.

You can usually make direct international calls from **pay phones,** but you may need to drop coins as quickly as words. Pay phones may be card-operated or accept major credit cards. Be wary of more expensive, private pay phones; look for pay phones in public areas, like train stations. In-room hotel phone calls often include a sky-high surcharge (up to US$10). It's a better idea to find a phone in the lobby.

English-speaking operators are often available for both local and international assistance. Operators in most European countries will place **collect calls** for you. It's cheaper to find a pay phone and deposit just enough money to be able to say "Call me," but some pay phones in Europe can't receive calls). Some companies, seizing on this "call-me-back" concept, have created callback phone services. Under these plans, you call a specified number, ring once, and hang up. The company's computer calls back and gives you a dial tone. You can then make as many calls as you want, at rates reduced 20-60% (monthly US$10-25 minimum billing). For info, call **America Tele-Fone** (tel. (800) 321-5817), **Globaltel** (tel. (770) 449-1295), **International Telephone** (tel. (800) 638-5558), or **Telegroup** (tel. (800) 338-0225).

A **calling card** is a cheaper alternative; your local long-distance phone company will have a number for you to dial while in Europe (either toll-free or a local call) to connect to an operator at home. The calls (plus a small surcharge) are then billed collect or to a calling card. Call **AT&T** about its **US Direct** and **World Connect** service (tel. (888) 288-4685, from abroad (810) 262-6644 collect), **Sprint** (tel. (800) 877-4646, from abroad call (913) 624-5335 collect), or **MCI WorldPhone** and **World Reach** (tel. (800) 444-4141; from abroad dial the country's MCI access number). MCI's WorldPhone provides access to MCI's **Traveler's Assist** for legal and medical advice, exchange rate information, and translation services. For similar services for countries outside the U.S., contact your local phone company. In Canada, contact **Canada Direct** (tel. (800) 565-4708); in the U.K., British Telecom **BT Direct** (tel. (800) 34 51 44); in Ireland, Telecom Éireann **Ireland Direct** (tel. (800) 25 02 50); in Australia, Telsta **Australia Direct** (tel. 13 22 00); in New Zealand, **Telecom New Zealand** (tel. 123); and in South Africa, **Telkom South Africa** (tel. 09 03).

In many countries, you can also buy **pre-paid phone cards**, which carry a certain amount of phone time depending on the card's denomination. The time is measured in minutes or talk units (e.g. one unit/one minute), and the card usually has a toll-free access telephone number and a personal identification number (PIN). To make a phone call, dial the access number, enter your PIN, and at the voice prompt, enter the phone number of the party you're trying to reach.

Phone rates are highest in the morning, lower in the evening, and lowest on Sundays and at night. Remember **time differences** when you call. Britain, Ireland, Portugal, and Iceland are on Greenwich Mean Time (GMT)—five hours ahead of Eastern Standard Time. Finland, Estonia, Latvia, Lithuania, western Russia, Romania, Bulgaria, Greece, and Turkey are two hours ahead of GMT. Moscow is three hours ahead. Everywhere else in this book is 1 hour ahead of GMT. Some countries (like Iceland) ignore daylight savings time, and fall and spring switchover times vary.

OTHER COMMUNICATION

Domestic and international **telegrams** offer an option slower than phone but faster than post. Fill out a form at any post or telephone office; cables arrive in one or two days. Telegrams can be quite expensive; **Western Union** (tel. (800) 325-6000), for example, adds a surcharge to the per-word rate depending on the country. You may wish to consider **faxes** for more immediate, personal, and cheaper communication. Major cities have bureaus where you can pay to send and receive faxes.

If you're spending a year abroad and want to keep in touch with friends or colleagues, **electronic mail (email)** is an attractive option. You can set up a free **web-**

based account at http://www.hotmail.com, which will allow you to exchange email. You can also get a free account at http://www.juno.com. Check the Index of this book under "Internet Access" for places to get onto the electronic highway while you're on the road, or search through http://www.cyberiacafe.net/cyberia/guide/ccafe.htm to find a list of **cybercafés,** where you can drink a cup of joe and email him too.

Parting Words

One of the quickest ways to learn about a different culture is to dissolve discreetly in it. As a foreigner, you will probably stand out, but a sincere effort to fit in will receive a warm reception. Hanging out exclusively with compatriots will insulate you from the local culture. You might as well stay home, an even cheaper alternative to budget travel. Get out and explore—culture shock may set in, but go for the *kringle* and goulash anyway and save McDonald's for home.

Language differences can be a bridge rather than a barrier between you and the people you meet, if you don't assume that other people speak English. Humbly asking "Do you speak English?"—or stumbling through the appropriate translation—expresses a genuine desire to communicate. Do your homework; play language tapes while you pack, and flip through a phrase book. You can learn the numbers from one to ten, how to order ice cream, and "please" and "thank you" in minutes.

But there is no substitute for practicing with native speakers and making friends in the process. While the history, architecture, and natural wonders of your destination country are fascinating, what makes your trip special is the people you'll meet. A photo of the Eiffel Tower, however elegantly silhouetted against the setting sun, won't evoke as many memories as a snapshot of Irma Moosbrugger who put you up for the night in Amsterdam. Part of meeting people is respecting their culture. Americans have acquired a reputation as arrogant boors, which may explain the little maple leaves that Canadian (and some American) tourists sew on their backpacks. However, the stereotype of the Ugly American need not haunt beer-swillling Yanks if they show that they're making an effort to understand your hosts. Europeans have a strong sense of their cultural history; if you belittle it, you'll only seem ignorant.

A word of warning: Many travelers succumb to a budget obsession on the road. Perhaps *Let's Go*'s greatest sin is that it perpetuates this mentality—to eat at the cheapest restaurant and stay at the cheapest hostel no matter how grimy or tacky. If you find yourself stuck in the doldrums, spend the extra 50 francs for a hearty meal or a night at a soothing pension. After all, your trip is supposed to be fun.

Andorra

Embracing fewer than 500 sq. km between France and Spain in the hermetic confines of the Pyrenees, pint-sized Andorra (pop. 65,000) might sell its soul, duty-free, if it could get a good price. Souvenir-seeking tourists flock to the neon-lit streets for tax-free shopping, but outside the crowded boutiques await serene hamlets, mountain lakes, and some of the best ski slopes in Europe. Catalan is the official language, though French and Spanish are spoken widely. Every establishment is legally bound to accept both pesetas and francs, although pesetas are more prevalent. **Phones** require an STA *teletarjeta* (telecard; from 500ptas), available at post offices and kiosks. For **directory assistance,** dial 111. Andorra's **telephone code** is 376.

French and Spanish border police require presentation of a valid passport or an EU identity card to enter the country. All traffic from France must enter Andorra at the town **Pas de la Casa;** on the Spanish side, **La Seu d'Urgell** is the gateway town. **Andor-Inter/Samar** buses (in Madrid tel. (91) 230 31 31; in Toulouse 05 61 58 14 53; in Andorra 82 62 89) run to Madrid (9hr., 4700ptas). Andorra la Vella's main **bus station** is at Pl. Guillemó, off Av. Princep Benlloch at the end of C. Doctor Negüi. An efficient system of **inter-city buses** connects villages lying along Andorra's three major highways (110-590ptas). For a map of Andorra, see the Spain country map.

Andorra la Vella

Andorra la Vella is little more than a narrow, cluttered road flanked by shop after duty-free shop. To get to the **tourist office,** Av. Doctor Villanova (tel. 82 02 14), from the bus stop on Av. Princep Benlloch, continue east just past the *plaça* on your left, then take C. Dr. Villanova. (Open July-Sept. Mon.-Sat. 9am-1pm and 3-7pm; Oct.-June Mon.-Sat. 10am-1pm and 3-7pm, Sun. 10am-1pm.) **Pensió La Rosa,** Antic Carrer Major, 18 (tel. 82 18 10), just south of Av. Princep Benlloch, provides immaculate rooms (singles 1700ptas, doubles 3000ptas; breakfast 350ptas). Better to save your travel budget for a different country, but if you can't wait, hunt for restaurants along the busy **Avinguda Meritxell** and on the quieter streets near **Plaça Princep Benlloch.** The tourist office sells tickets to the August music and dance **festival.**

The Countryside

The *parròquia* (parish) of **La Massana,** easily accessible by bus from Andorra la Vella (10min., 110ptas), provides an excellent base for exploring Andorra's spectacular mountains. The **tourist office** (tel. 83 56 93) is in a steep-roofed cabin just ahead of the bus stop (open Mon.-Sat. 9am-1pm and 3-7pm, Sun. 9am-1pm and 3-6pm). To reach the **Alberg Borda Jovell,** Av. Jovell, Sispony (tel. 83 65 20; fax 83 57 76), from La Massana's bus stop, walk 75m back toward Andorra la Vella and turn right at the main intersection, then follow the signs south for 1.3km (midnight curfew; 2200ptas). The least populated of the parish towns, **Ordino,** 5km northeast of La Massana, gives you a glimpse of Andorra before the Reebok and Sony invasion. Slink toward **Escaldes-Engordany,** just outside Andorra la Vella, for the pleasures of **Caldea Spa,** Parc de la Mola, 10 (tel. 82 86 00), with massages and Roman baths (2200ptas for 3hr., plus fees for each service; open daily 10am-11pm).

With its many trails, Andorra lends itself well to **hiking** and **mountain biking;** check at the tourist office for info on cycling routes and the *Grandes-Randonnées* hiking trails. Several superb **ski** resorts lie within Andorra's boundaries, and all rent equipment. **Pal** (tel. 83 62 36), 10km from La Massana, is one of the largest; take the daily bus from La Massana at 10am (returns 5pm; 250ptas each way). Cross-country and downhill aficionados flock to **Soldeu-El Tarter** (tel. 82 11 97), 15km from the French border between Andorra la Vella and Pas de la Casa. Get the tourist office's *Mountains of Snow,* or call **SKI Andorra** (tel. 86 43 89) for more info on the resorts.

Austria (Österreich)

US$1= 13.14AS (Austrian Schillings) | **10AS = US$0.76**
CDN$1= 9.58AS | **10AS = CDN$1.04**
UK£1= 21.38AS | **10AS = UK£0.47**
IR£1= 19.13AS | **10AS = IR£0.52**
AUS$1= 9.79AS | **10AS = AUS$1.02**
NZ$1= 8.53AS | **10AS = NZ$1.17**
SAR1= 2.86AS | **10AS = SAR3.50**
Country Code: 43 | **International Dialing Prefix: 00**
from Vienna: 900

Surrounded by seven countries, the Federal Republic of Austria binds Eastern and Western Europe. Austria is what remains of the once mighty Austro-Hungarian Empire which under the Hapsburg dynasty dominated eastern Europe. The mid-eighteenth through the nineteenth century was the heyday of Viennese culture, when Hadyn, Mozart, Beethoven, Schubert, the Strauss Family, and Mahler changed music forever. Things fell apart, however, in the twentieth century. A weakened Austro-Hungary pulled the rest of Europe into the First World War, and at the war's end, the Empire ended also. The glory of the nineteenth century gave way to Freud's critiques of middle class unhappiness, and a troubled Austria did not resist the 1938 Nazi invasion. Yet the post-war years have brought about an Austria that is less concerned with world power and more concerned with mountains, music, and tourism.

Despite Austria's political and economic importance and the rise of urban giants like Vienna and Salzburg, the country retains an overpowering physical beauty. With onion-domed churches set against snow-capped Alpine peaks, lush meadows blanketed with edelweiss, pristine mountain lakes, dark forests, and mighty castles towering above the Danube, Austria generates tourism year-round. Alpine sports dominate the winter scene, while lakeside frolicking and hiking takes over during the summer.

For extensive and entertaining information on the country, pick up a copy of *Let's Go: Austria and Switzerland 1998.*

GETTING THERE AND GETTING AROUND

The **Österreichische Bundesbahn (ÖBB),** Austria's federal railroad, operates an amazingly efficient 5760km network of track accommodating frequent, fast, and comfortable trains. The ÖBB publishes the yearly *Fahrpläne Kursbuch Bahn-Inland,* a massive compilation of all rail, ferry, and cable-car transportation schedules in Austria (100AS). Over 130 stations accept major credit cards as well as AmEx Traveler's Cheques and Eurocheques. **Eurail** passes are valid on the Austrian rail network. The **Austrian Railpass** allows four days of travel within any 10-day period on all rail lines, including Wolfgangsee ferries and private rail lines; it also entitles holders to a 50% discount on bicycle rental at train stations as well as the steamers of Erste Donau Dampfschiffahrts Gesellschaft operating between Passau, Linz, and Vienna (US$111 for second-class travel or US$165 for first class).

The efficient Austrian bus system consists mainly of orange **BundesBuses,** which cover mountain areas inaccessible by train. They usually cost about as much as trains—railpasses are not valid. Buy tickets on-board or at a ticket office at the station. **Bikes** are also a great way to get around; countless private companies and over 160 train stations rent them (90AS per day, 50AS with a railpass or valid train ticket from that day). If you get a bike at a train station, you can return it to any participating station. Look for the *Gepäckbeforderung* symbol (a little bicycle) on departure schedules to see if bikes are permitted in the baggage car. If your bike breaks down on the road, some auto clubs may rescue you; try the **Austrian Automobile, Motorcycle, and Touring Club (ÖAMTC)** (tel. 120) or **ARBÖ** (tel. 123).

Austria is often a **hitchhiker's** nightmare—Austrians rarely pick them up, and many mountain roads are all but deserted. Generally, hitchhikers stand on highway *Knoten*

(on-ramps) and wait. The thumb signal is recognized, but signs with a destination and the word *bitte* (please) are just as common. **Mitfahrzentrale** offices in most larger cities match travelers with drivers heading in the same direction.

ESSENTIALS

Virtually every town in Austria has a **tourist office,** most marked by a standard green "i" sign, and nearly all have a wealth of info on tourist attractions, activities, and accommodations. You may run into language difficulties in the small-town offices.

The unit of **currency** is the Schilling, abbreviated AS here and often simply S in Austria. **Exchange rates** are standardized among banks and exchange counters, while stores, hotels, and restaurants that accept U.S. dollars apply a slightly lower rate of exchange. Every establishment that exchanges currency charges at least 14AS. Many banks offer cash advances to Visa and MasterCard holders.

Most stores in Austria close Saturday afternoons and Sundays, and some museums take Mondays off. Stores in many small towns close for lunch breaks from noon to 3pm. **Holidays** include Epiphany (Jan. 6), Easter (April 12 in 1998), Labor Day (May 1), Ascension Day (May 21), Whit Sunday and Monday (May 31-June 1), Corpus Christi Day (June 11), Feast of the Assumption (Aug. 15), Flag Day (Oct. 26), All Saints' Day (Nov. 1), and the Feast of the Immaculate Conception (Dec. 8).

Communication Austria maintains an efficient **postal system.** Airmail letters take five to seven days to reach North America, although they make take up to two and a half weeks to reach Australia and New Zealand.

The Austrian **phone system** is equally reliable. You can usually make direct international calls from a pay phone, but remember to bring a handful of coins. A better option might be to buy **telephone cards** *(Wertkarten),* available in post offices, train stations, and *Tabak/Trafik* in 50AS and 100AS denominations (for 48AS and 95AS respectively). The quickest and cheapest way to call abroad collect is to go to a post office and ask for a *Zurückrufen,* or return call. You will receive a card with a number on it. Call your party and tell them to call you back at that number, and at the end of the conversation pay for the original call. For **AT&T Direct,** dial 022 90 30 11; for **MCI WorldPhone,** 022 90 30 12; for **Sprint Access,** 022 90 30 14; for **Canada Direct,** 022 90 30 13; for **BT Direct,** 022 90 30 44; for **Australia Direct,** 022 90 30 61; for **NZ Direct,** 022 90 30 64; and for **South Africa Direct,** 155 85 35. Note that the use of these services is considered a local call, so you must have coins or a phone card. The number for the **police** is 133; for an **ambulance** 144; for **fire** 122.

English is the most common second language in Austria, but any effort to use the mother tongue will win fans. *Grüss Gott* (Greet God) is the typical Austrian greeting. For a language chart, see the Germany **Essentials,** p. 361.

Accommodations and Camping Rooms in Austria are usually spotless; even the most odious of Austria's **youth hostels** *(Jugendherbergen)* are quite tolerable. Most hostels charge US$8-25 a night for shared rooms, although rooms in larger cities may cost slightly more. Nonmembers are normally charged an extra fee and sometimes turned away completely. Many hostels are somewhat cramped and offer little privacy; prepubescent hordes may also try your patience.

Hotels are usually quite expensive. If you're on a tight budget, look instead for *Zimmer Frei* or *Privatzimmer* signs; they advertise rooms in private houses for a more reasonable 150-300AS. Otherwise, smaller pensions and *Gastehäuser* are often within the budget traveler's range. With over 400 sites throughout the country, **camping** is another popular option. Pitching a tent, however, is often not significantly cheaper than staying in a hostel; prices range from 50-70AS per person and 25-60AS per tent, and a tax of 8-10AS is added for campers over 15 years old. Lists of all types of accommodations, including campgrounds, are available at tourist offices; many offices will also reserve rooms for a small fee.

Skiing and Hiking Western Austria is one of the world's best skiing and hiking regions, and the areas around Innsbruck and Kitzbühel in the Tirol are saturated with lifts and runs. High season runs from mid-December to mid-January and from February to March. Local tourist offices provide information on regional skiing and can point you to budget travel agencies that offer ski packages. Unless you're on top of a mountain, Austria doesn't usually get brutally cold. Nevertheless, warm sweaters are the rule from September to May, with a parka, hat, and gloves added in the winter months. Summertime brings frequent rains and high humidity—almost every other day in Salzburg, and nearly as often to the east—so suitable gear is a must.

Thanks to the extensive network of hiking trails and Alpine refuges, Austria's Alps are as accessible as they are gorgeous. A membership in the **Österreichischer Alpenverein** provides half-off the cost of staying at a series of **huts** across the Tirol and throughout Austria, all located a day's hike apart from each other. A place in any of the huts is always assured, along with use of the kitchen facilities and provisions. Third-party insurance, accident provision, travel discounts, and a wealth of maps and mountain information are also included with membership. For membership information call or write to: Österreichischer Alpenverein, Willhelm-Greil-Str. 15, A-6010 Innsbruck (tel. 58 78 28; fax 58 88 42). Membership (US$55, students under 25 US$40, one-time fee US$10) also includes use of some of the **Deutscher Alpenverein** (German Alpine Club) huts, all of which have beds.

Even if you're going for only a day hike, check terrain and weather conditions; weather in the Alps changes instantaneously. *Always* carry waterproof clothing and some high-energy food, wear durable footwear, and tell someone where you're going. Staying at Alpine refuges adds another safety precaution: you're expected to list your next destination in the refuge book, thus alerting search-and-rescue teams if you become lost or stranded.

Food and Drink One of life's great enigmas is how a country with such unremarkable cuisine can produce such heavenly desserts. In mid-afternoon, Austrians flock to *Café-Konditoreien* to nurse the national sweet tooth with *Kaffee und Kuchen* (coffee and cake). Try *Sacher Torte,* a rich chocolate pastry layered with marmalade, *Linzer Torte,* a nutty pastry with raspberry filling, *Apfel Strudel,* and a multitude of other delights. Staple foods include *Schweinfleisch* (pork), *Kalbsfleisch* (veal), *Wurst* (sausage), *Eier* (eggs), *Käse* (cheese), *Brot* (bread), and *Kartoffeln* (potatoes). Austria's best-known dish is *Schnitzel,* a meat cutlet (usually veal or pork) fried in butter with bread crumbs. The best discount supermarkets in Austria are **Billa, Hofer,** and **Konsum.** Most restaurants expect you to seat yourself, and a small

tip (usually rounding up the bill) is customary. The server won't bring your check without first being asked; say *zahlen, bitte* (TSAH-len BIT-uh) to settle up.

Of course, you'll need something to wash all those pastries down. The most famous Austrian wine is probably *Gumpoldskirchen* from Lower Austria, the largest wine-producing province. *Klosterneuburger,* produced near Vienna, is both reasonably priced and dry. Austrian beers are outstanding—try *Stiegl Bier,* a Salzburg brew, *Zipfer Bier* from upper Austria, and *Gösser Bier* from Graz. Austria imports lots of Budweiser beer (the famous Czech *Budvar,* not the American brew).

Vienna (Wien)

Smoke lingering in brooding coffehouses, bronze palace roofs faded gentle green, the hush that awaits the conductor's baton—the serene and softly aged Vienna is grand in a way that cradles rather than confronts. The center of the Hapsburg empire and a prime mover in the world of the European history book, Vienna treats cobblestone dreamers to a collection bin of imperial tastes and proportions. Yet as buildings rose and coffeehouse klatschers scribbled, Vienna's *fin de siècle* veneer provided a fine gloss for the slow boil of Zionism, Nazism, and the Viennese schizophrenia that kept Freud's waiting room full. The memory of condoned atrocities still lurks in the collective conscience of Vienna, a black pall that spurs the city on to entertaining the international scepter. But political energy quiets every evening as the city makes a turn towards dusk, only to enter the next morning bejeweled and elegant.

AUSTRIA

ORIENTATION AND PRACTICAL INFORMATION

Vienna is in eastern Austria, 40km from the Hungarian, Czech, and Slovak borders. The city is divided into 23 **districts** *(Bezirke),* with the old *Innere Stadt* (inner city) occupying the first district. From this center, the city spreads out in a series of concentric rings. The first ring, which surrounds the *Innere Stadt,* is the **Ringstraße,** known simply as the Ring. Many of Vienna's attractions are located in this area, including several museums and the *Rathaus.* Along the southern section of the ring, the intersection of **Opernring, Kärntner Ring,** and **Kärntner Straße** forms the epicenter of the city; the Opera House, tourist office, and the **Karlsplatz** U-Bahn stop are nearby. Roman numerals have been added to most of the addresses listed below to indicate the district in which particular establishments are located.

Vienna is a metropolis with crime like any other; be extra careful in the beautiful Karlsplatz, home to many pushers and junkies, and avoid areas in the 5th, 10th, and 14th districts, as well as Landstr.-Hauptstr. Beware of pickpockets in the parks and on **Kärntner Straße,** where tourists make tempting targets. Vienna's skin trade operates in some sections of the Gürtel; **Prater Park** is also questionable at night.

> The Austrian telephone network is becoming digitized, and phone numbers may change without notice after this book goes to press.

Tourist Offices: I, Kärntnerstr. 38 (tel. 58 86 60), behind the Opera House. The small bureau dispenses a city map for free. *Youth Scene* provides vital info for travelers of all ages. The office also books rooms (300-400AS) for a 40AS fee and the first night's deposit. Open daily 8am-5pm. **Branch offices** at Westbahnhof (open daily 6:15am-11pm), Südbahnhof (open May-Oct. daily 6:30am-9pm), and the airport (open June-Sept. 8:30am-9pm). **Jugend-Info Wien** (Vienna Youth Information Service), Bellaria-Passage (tel. 17 99; email jugendinfo.vie@blackbox.ping.at), in the underground passage at the Bellaria intersection. Enter at the "Dr.-Karl-Renner-Ring/Bellaria" tram stop (lines 1, 2, 46, 49, D, and J) or the "Volkstheater" U-Bahn station. The hip and knowledgeable staff has an accommodations list, cheap tickets, and *Jugend in Wien.* Open Mon.-Fri. noon-7pm, Sat. 10am-7pm.

Budget Travel: Österreichisches Verkehrsbüro (Austrian National Travel Office), I, Operngasse 3-5 (tel. 588 62 38), opposite the Opera House. Sells BIJ tickets and the *Thomas Cook Timetable* (270AS). Open Mon.-Fri. 9am-6pm, Sat. 9am-noon. For special deals on **airplane tickets** call the state's information hotline (tel. 15 54).

Embassies and Consulates: Australia, IV, Mattiellistr. 2-4 (tel. 512 85 80), behind the Karlskirche. Open Mon.-Thurs. 8:30am-1pm and 2-5:30pm, Fri. 8:30am-1:15pm. **Canada,** I, Laurenzerburg 2, 3rd fl. (tel. 531 38, ext. 3000). Open Mon.-Fri. 8:30am-12:30pm and 1:30-3:30pm. **Ireland,** III, Hilton Center, 16th fl., Landstraßer Hauptstr. 2 (tel. 715 42 47; fax 713 60 04). **New Zealand,** XIX, Springsiedlegasse 28 (tel. 318 85 05; fax 37 76 60). **South Africa,** XIX, Sandgasse 33 (tel. 32 46 93). **U.K.,** III, Jauresgasse 10 (tel. 716 13 53 38). Open Mon.-Fri. 9:15am-noon and 2-4pm. **U.S.,** IX, Boltzmangasse 16, off Währingerstr.

Currency Exchange: Most **banks** are open Mon.-Wed. and Fri. 8am-3pm, Thurs. 8am-5:30pm, with a break from 12:30-1:30pm. Bank and airport exchanges have the same official exchange rates; expect a minimum 50AS commission for traveler's checks, 10AS for cash. Longer hours and smaller commissions are available at the **train stations.** The 24hr. exchange at the **main post office** has excellent rates.

American Express: I, Kärntnerstr. 21-23, P.O. Box 28, A-1015 (tel. 515 40), down from Stephansplatz. Cashes AmEx (commission free) and Thomas Cook (3% commission) checks. Holds members' mail for 4 weeks. Open Mon.-Fri. 9am-5:30pm, Sat. 9am-noon.

Flights: For flight info, call 711 10, ext. 22 33. **Wien Schwechat** airport is 18km from Vienna, accessible by public transportation from the city center. One option is to take U-3 or U-4 to "Wien Mitte/Landstraße," and then the S-7 to "Flughafen/Wolfsthal" (34AS, Eurail not valid). The train from Wien Nord to the airport accepts Eurail (30min.). **Austrian Airlines** (tel. 17 89) flies to London (round-trip 3540AS), Rome (round-trip 2990AS), and Berlin (round-trip 4190AS). Travelers under 26 qualify for youth tickets.

Trains: For train info tel. 17 17, staffed 24hr. (http://www.bahn.at). 3 main stations in the city. The **Westbahnhof,** XV, Mariahilferstr. 132, serves Salzburg (3hr., 396AS), Innsbruck (6hr., 690AS), Budapest (3-4hr., 348AS) and major western cities including Amsterdam, Paris, and Munich. To reach the city center, take U-3 "Erdberg" to "Volkstheater" or "Stephansplatz." The **Südbahnhof,** X, Wiedner Gürtel 1a, travels to Prague (5½hr., 468AS), Rome (14hr., 987AS), and Venice (7½hr., 660AS). If you arrive at this station, take tram D "Nußdorf" from the right side of the station or the S-Bahn (1, 2, 3, or 15) to "Südtirolerplatz," and then enter the U-Bahn system. The **Franz-Josefs Bahnhof,** IX, Althamstr. 10, handles commuter trains but also serves Berlin (12hr., 1002AS). There are two smaller stations: **Bahnhof Wien Mitte,** in the center of town, serves commuter trains and the shuttle to the airport; **Bahnhof Wien-Nord,** by the Prater on the north side of the Danube Canal, is one of the main S-Bahn and U-Bahn links for trains heading north.

Buses: For bus information, call 711 01, staffed daily 7am-7pm. Catch buses at the **City Bus Terminals** at Wien-Mitte/Landstraße, Hüttelsdorf, Heiligenstadt, Floridsdorf, Kagran, Erdberg, or Reumannplatz. Domestic BundesBuses run from these stations to local and international destinations. Ticket counters open Mon.-Fri. 6am-5:50pm, Sat.-Sun. 6am-3:50pm. Bus travel is often as expensive as train travel.

Public Transportation: Excellent **U-Bahn** (subway), **bus,** and **S-bahn** (tram) systems cover the city. Single fare is 20AS (17AS if purchased in advance at a ticket office or tobacco shop); a 24hr. pass costs 50AS, a 72hr. pass 130AS, a week pass (Mon.-Mon.) 142AS. All passes allow unlimited travel on the system, except on special night buses. To validate a ticket, punch it immediately upon entering the bus, tram, etc. in the orange machine. Unstamped ticket holders risk a 500AS fine. Tickets can be purchased from *Tabak* kiosks or *Automaten* in major U-Bahn stations. Trams and subways close from 12:30-5:30am, but **night buses** run on reduced routes (25AS, passes not valid). Night bus stops are designated by "N" signs. Streetcar lines and U-Bahn stops are listed on a free city map, available at the tourist office; ticket counters sell comprehensive maps for 15AS. The public transportation **information** number (tel. 587 31 86; German-speaking) will give you directions to any point in the city. Staffed Mon.-Fri. 6:30am-6:30pm, Sat.-Sun. 8:30am-4pm. Information stands around the city will also help you out, or check http://www.weinnet.at/efa for the shortest route between two points.

Ferries: Cruise with **DDSG Donaureisen** (tel. 523 80) to Budapest for 750AS, round-trip 1100AS (daily April 8-Oct. 29). Buy tickets at tourist offices. Boats dock at the *Reichsbrücke* on the New Danube; take U-1 to "Vorgartenstr."

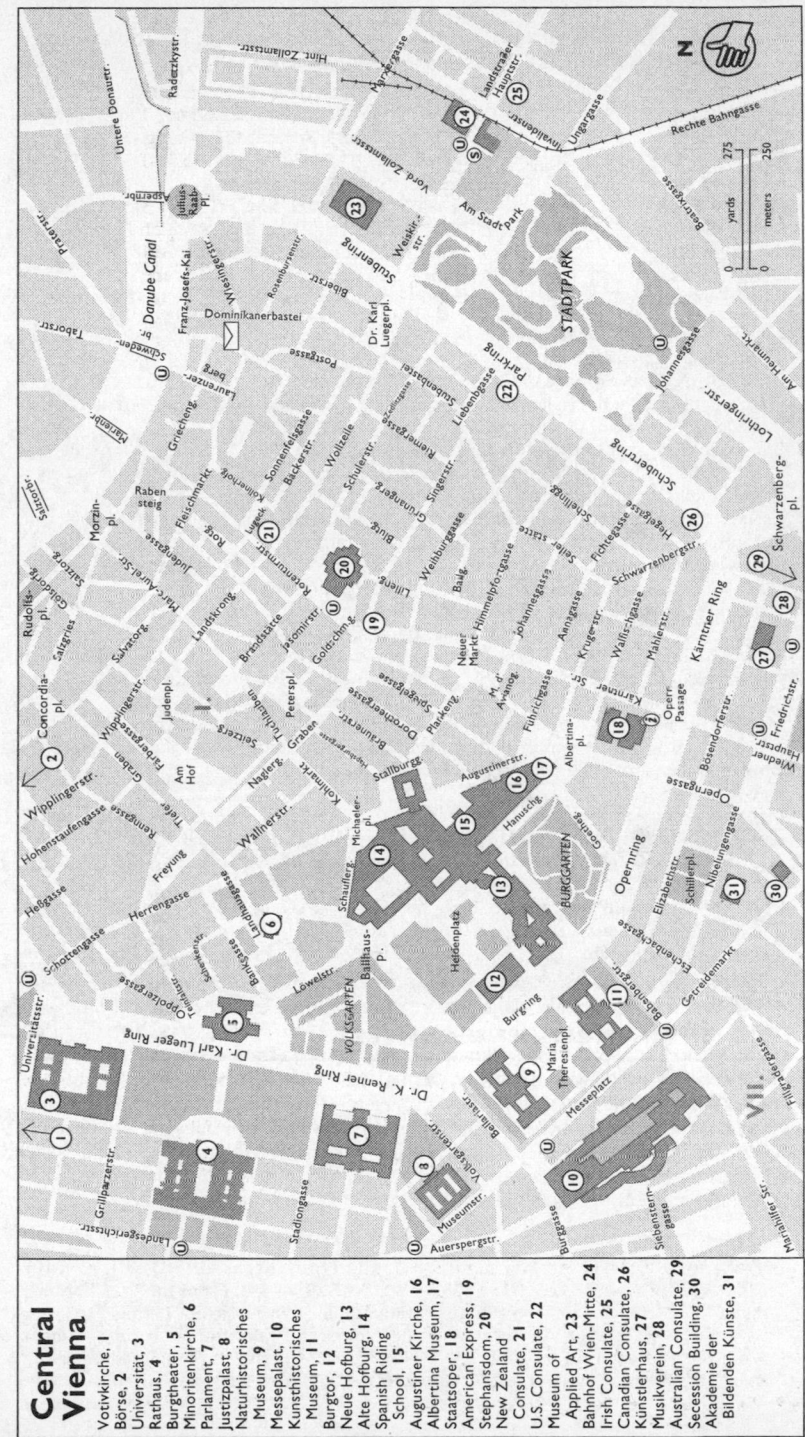

Central Vienna

Votivkirche, 1
Börse, 2
Universität, 3
Rathaus, 4
Burgtheater, 5
Minoritenkirche, 6
Parlament, 7
Justizpalast, 8
Naturhistorisches Museum, 9
Messepalast, 10
Kunsthistorisches Museum, 11
Burgtor, 12
Neue Hofburg, 13
Alte Hofburg, 14
Spanish Riding School, 15
Augustiner Kirche, 16
Albertina Museum, 17
Staatsoper, 18
American Express, 19
Stephansdom, 20
New Zealand Consulate, 21
U.S. Consulate, 22
Museum of Applied Art, 23
Bahnhof Wien-Mitte, 24
Irish Consulate, 25
Canadian Consulate, 26
Künstlerhaus, 27
Musikverein, 28
Australian Consulate, 29
Secession Building, 30
Akademie der Bildenden Künste, 31

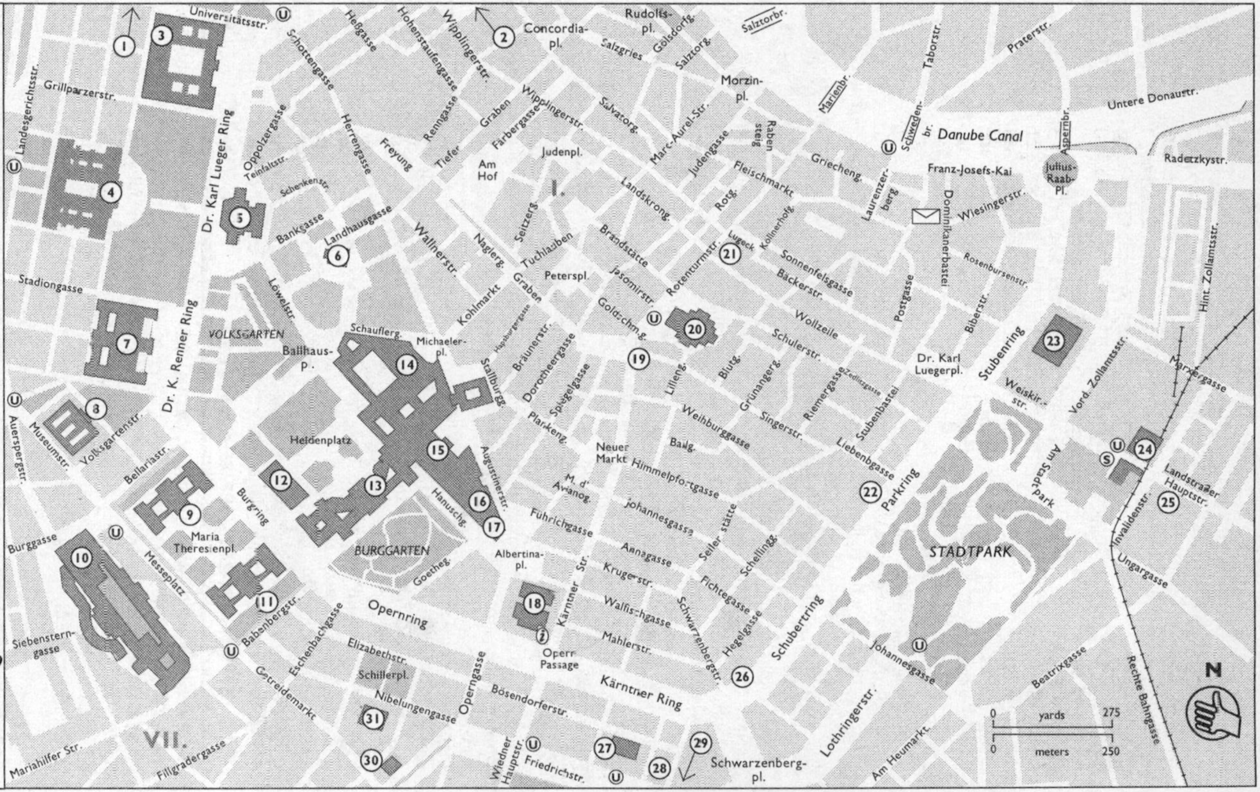

AUSTRIA

Taxis: (tel. 313 00, 401 00, 601 60, 814 00, or 910 11). Stands at Westbahnhof, Südbahnhof, and Karlspl. in the city center. Accredited taxis have yellow and black signs on the roof. Basic rate generally 27AS, plus a per km charge. 16AS surcharge for taxis called by radiophone; 10AS surcharge on Sun., holidays, and nights (11pm-6am); 12AS surcharge for luggage over 20kg, 24AS for over 50kg.

Bike Rental: At Wien Nord and the Westbahnhof. 150AS per day, 90AS with a train ticket from the day of arrival. Elsewhere in the city, including Donauinsel, rentals average 30AS per hr. Pick up *Vienna By Bike* at the tourist office for details.

Hitchhiking: Those who hitch to Salzburg take U-4 to "Hütteldorf"; the highway leading to the Autobahn is about 10km farther out. Those hitching south try the traffic circle near Laaerberg (streetcar 67 to the last stop). **Mitfahrzentrale Wien,** VIII, Daungasse 1a (tel. 408 22 10), off Laudongasse, pairs drivers and riders. Open Mon.-Wed. 10am-5pm, Thurs.-Fri. 10am-6pm, Sat.-Sun. 10am-2pm.

Luggage Storage: Lockers (40AS per 24hr.) at all train stations. Adequate for sizable backpacks. **Luggage watch** 30AS. Open daily 4am-1:15am.

Bookstores: Shakespeare & Company, I, Sterngasse 2 (tel. 535 50 53; fax 535 50 53 16; email bookseller@shakespeare.co.at). Eclectic and intelligent. Great English magazine selection. Open Mon.-Fri. 9am-7pm, Sat. 9am-5pm.

Bisexual, Gay, and Lesbian Organizations: Rosa Lila Villa, VI, Linke Wienzeile 102 (tel. 586 81 50), is a favored resource. Friendly staff provides counseling, information, a lending library, and nightclub listings. Open Mon.-Fri. 5-8pm.

Laundromat: Schnell und Sauber, VII, Westbahnhofstr. 60; U-6 to "Burggasse Stadthalle." Wash 60AS for 6kg. Detergent included. Spin-dry 10AS. Open 24hr.

Snow reports: Vienna, Lower Austria, and Styria (tel. 15 83); Salzburg, Upper Austria, and Carinthia (tel. 15 84); Tirol and the Voralberg (tel. 15 85).

Crisis Hotlines: House for Threatened and Battered Women: (tel. 545 48 00 or 202 55 00). 24hr. emergency hotline. **Rape Crisis Hotline:** (tel. 523 22 22). Open Mon. 10am-6pm, Tues. 2-6pm, Wed. 10am-2pm, Thurs. 5-11pm. 24hr. immediate help: tel. 717 19. **English-language "Befrienders" Suicide Hotline:** (tel. 713 33 74). Open Mon.-Fri. 9:30am-1pm and 6:30-10pm, Sat.-Sun. 6:30-10pm.

Medical Assistance: Allgemeines Krankenhaus, IX, Währinger Gürtel 18-20 (tel. 404 00). A consulate can provide a list of English-speaking physicians.

Emergencies: Ambulance: tel. 144. **Fire:** tel. 122.

Police: tel. 133.

Internet Access: Libro, Donauzentrum (tel. 202 52 55). Free access at its 6 terminals. **Public Netbase, VII,** Museumsquartier, Museumpl. I (tel. 522 18 34). Free surfing 2-7pm. **Jugend-Info des Bundesministeriums,** Franz-Josefs-Kai 51 (tel. 533 70 30). Free access at 1 PC. Mon.-Fri 11am-6pm.

Post Offices: Hauptpostamt, I, Fleischmarkt 19. Exchange windows, telephones, faxes, and mail services. Open 24hr. Address *Poste Restante* to "Postlagernde Briefe, Hauptpostamt, Fleischmarkt 19, A-1010 Wien." **Postal Codes:** In the 1st district A-1010, in the 2nd A-1020, in the 3rd A-1030, and so on, to the 23rd A-1230.

Telephone Code: 0222 from within Austria, 1 from outside the country.

ACCOMMODATIONS AND CAMPING

One of the few unpleasant aspects of Vienna is the hunt for cheap rooms during the summer season. Write or call for reservations at least five days ahead, and pick up lists of hostels and hotels from the tourist office. University dorms alleviate the problem slightly in July when they metamorphose into hostels. Those unable to find a hostel bed or dorm room should consider a one-star *Pension,* common in the seventh, eighth, and ninth districts (singles around 350AS, doubles around 500AS).

Hostels

Myrthengasse (HI), VII, Myrthengasse 7, and **Neustiftgasse (HI),** VII, Neustiftgasse 85 (both tel. 523 63 16 or 523 94 29; fax 523 58 49). From the Westbahnhof take U-6 ("Heiligenstadt") to "Burggasse-Stadthalle," then bus 48A ("Ring") to "Neubaugasse." Walk back on Burggasse one block, and take the 1st right (15min.). From the Südbahnhof, take bus 13A ("Skodagasse/Alerstr.") to "Kellermanngasse," then walk 2 blocks to your left on Neustiftgasse and turn left on Myrthengasse. The hostels, under the same management, are around the corner from each other. Comfortable, modern rooms with pine furniture, and lockers. Curfew 1am. Lockout 9am-3:45pm. 160-190AS. Laundry 50AS. Reserve ahead.

Believe-It-Or-Not, VIII, Myrthengasse 10, #14 (ring bell; tel. 526 46 58), across the street from the Myrthengasse (see above). Funky and social. Kitchen, living room, and 2 bedrooms with high ceilings. Zany caretaker's personal crash-course on Vienna is a must. Reception open 8am until early afternoon. 160AS. Reserve ahead.

Jugendgästehaus Wien Brigittenau (HI), XX, Friedrich-Engels-Pl. 24 (tel. 332 82 940 or 330 05 98; fax 330 83 79). Ride U-1 or U-4 to "Schwedenplatz," then tram N to "Floridsdorferbrücke/Friedrich-Engels-Pl.," and follow the signs. Spacious hostel with exceptional facilities for the disabled. Reception open 24hr. Dorms 160-190AS. Lockers and breakfast included.

Kolpingfamilie Wien-Meidling (HI), XIII, Bendlgasse 10-12 (tel. 813 54 87; fax 812 21 30). Take U-4 or U-6 to "Niederhofstr.," head right on Niederhofstr., and take the fourth right. Well-lit and modern. Reception open daily 6am-midnight. Dorms 100-155AS. Doubles 430AS. Nonmembers add 20AS. Breakfast 45AS. Linen 65AS.

Schloßherberge am Wilhelminenberg (HI), XVI, Savoyenstr. 2 (tel. 485 85 03, ext. 700; fax 485 85 037, ext. 02). Take U-6 to "Thaliastr.," then tram 46 ("Joachimsthalerplatz") to "Maroltingergasse," then bus 146B (46 in Vienna) to "Schloß Wilhelminenberg." The trip is undoubtedly worth it. The building is to the left of a palatial castle and offers fantastic views of Vienna. 220AS. Reserve ahead.

Hostel Zöhrer, VIII, Skodagasse 26 (tel. 406 07 30; fax 408 04 09). From Westbahnhof, take U-6 ("Heiligenstadt") to "Alserstr.," then streetcar 43 ("Schottentor") to "Skodagasse." From Südbahnhof, take bus 13A to "Alserstr./Skodag." Crowded but comfortable. Kitchen. Reception 7:30am-10pm. Check-out 9am. No curfew. Dorms with showers 170AS. 2-bed dorms 230AS. Breakfast and sheets included. Laundry 60AS. Front door/locker key deposit 100AS, with ID 50AS.

Jugendgästehaus Hütteldorf-Hacking (HI), XIII, Schloßberggasse 8 (tel. 877 15 01 or 877 02 63; fax 877 02 632). From Karlspl., take U-4 to "Hütteldorf," take the Hadikg. exit, cross the footbridge, and follow the signs (10min.). From Westbahnhof, take S-50 to "Hütteldorf." Sits in one of Vienna's most affluent districts. Reception 6:30am-11:45pm. Lockout 9am-4pm. Curfew 11:45pm; keycard 25AS. 153AS, with shower 183AS. Breakfast included. Laundry 70AS.

AUSTRIA

University Dormitories

Many dorms become summer hostels from July to September. Although lacking character, their cleanliness and relatively low cost should satisfy budget travelers.

Porzellaneum der Wiener Universität, IX, Porzellangasse 30 (tel. 31 77 28 20). From Südbahnhof, tram D ("Nußdorf") to "Fürstengasse." From Westbahnhof, tram 5 to "Franz-Josefs Bahnhof," then tram D ("Südbahnhof"). Reception open 24hr. Singles 175AS. Doubles 350AS. Sheets and showers included. Reserve ahead.

Ruddfinum, IV, Mayerhofgasse 3 (tel. 505 53 84). U-1 to "Taubstummengasse." Why should your vacation differ from college life? Reception open 24hr. Singles 270AS. Doubles 480AS. Triples 600AS. Sheets, showers, and breakfast included.

Gästehaus Pfeilgasse, VIII, Pfeilgasse 6 (tel. 401 74; fax 401 76 20). U-2 to "Lerchenfelderstr." Right on Lerchenfelderstr., right on Lange Gasse, then left on Pfeilgasse. Reception open 24hr. Singles 260AS. Doubles 440AS. Breakfast included.

Katholisches Studentenhaus, XIX, Peter-Jordanstr. 29 (tel. 34 92 64). From Westbahnhof, U-6 ("Heiligenstadt") to "Nußdorferstr.," then tram 38 to "Hardtgasse" and turn left. From Südbahnhof, take tram D to "Schottentor," then tram 38. Singles 230AS. Doubles 340AS. Showers and sheets included. Call ahead.

Hotels and Pensions

F. Kaled and Tina, VII, Lindengasse 42 (tel. 523 90 13). U-3 to "Ziedergasse." Follow Ziedergasse 2 blocks to Lindengasse; the hotel is on the right. Lovely private rooms. Singles 400AS, with bath 450AS. Doubles 550-650AS. Triples 800AS.

Hotel Quisisana, VI, Windmühlgasse 6 (tel. 587 71 55; fax 587 71 56). U-2 to "Babenbergerstr.," turn right on Mariahilferstr., go 3 blocks, and bear left on Windmühlgasse. An old-fashioned hotel run by a charming older couple. Singles 320AS, with shower 370AS. Doubles 500-600AS. Triples 750AS. Quads 1000AS.

Pension Hargita, VII, Andreasgasse (tel. 526 19 28). U-3 to "Zieglergasse" then head down Mariahilferstr. Singles 400AS, with shower 450AS. Doubles 550-800AS.

Pension Wild, VIII, Lange Gasse 10 (tel. 435 174; fax 526 04 92). U-3 to "Volkstheater," then U-2 to "Lerchenfelderstr." and take the first right. From Südbahnhof, bus 13A ("Alserstr./Skodagasse") to "Piaristengasse." Turn left onto Lerchenfelderstr. and left again onto Lange Gasse. Kitchen. Reception open 7am-10pm. No curfew, but grab a late night key. Singles 460-550AS. Doubles 590-690AS. Triples 860-960AS. Breakfast and shower included. Reserve ahead.

Camping

Wien-West, Hüttelbergstr. 80 (tel. 914 35 94 or 914 23 14). Take U-4 to Hütteldorf, then bus 14B or 152 ("Campingpl.") to "Wien West." Laundry machines, grocery stores, and cooking facilities. 63AS per person, 40AS per tent. Closed Feb.

FOOD

In a capricious and uncertain world, the Viennese take it as a given that the least you can do is face it all with a full stomach. Culinary offerings in the city reflect the patchwork empire of the Hapsburgs. *Serbische Bohnensuppe* (Serbian bean soup) and *Ungärische Gulaschsuppe* (Hungarian goulash) exemplify the Eastern European influence. *Knödel,* bread dumplings found in most side dishes, originated in the former Czechoslovakia. Even the famed *Wiener Schnitzel* (fried and breaded veal cutlets) was first cooked in Milan. Vienna is perhaps most renowned for its sublime desserts and chocolates; they're unbelievably rich, but most are priced for patrons who are likewise blessed. *Sacher Torte, Imperial Torte,* and even *Apfel Strudel* cost up to 40AS, though most residents maintain that they are worth every *Groschen.*

Restaurants in the touristy **Kärntnerstraße** area are generally overpriced. A better bet is the neighborhood just north of the university where **Universitätsstraße** and **Währingerstraße** meet; reasonably priced *Gaststätten, Kneipen* (bars), and restaurants are easy to find. The **Rathausplatz** hosts inexpensive food stands most of the year. The aromatic delicacies at the open-air **Naschmarkt** are an especially filling option for vegetarians who travel to this carnivorous city; to reach the market, take U-Bahn 4 to "Kettenbrückengasse" (open Mon.-Fri. 7am-6pm, Sat. 7am-1pm). For discount supermarket fare, try the ubiquitous **Billa, Konsum,** or **Hoffer,** and **Sparmarkt.** To conquer the summer heat, try the ice cream at **Gelateria Hoher Markt,** I, Hoher Markt, just off Rotenturmstr. (open March-Oct. daily 9am-11pm). Be aware that grocery stores and most restaurants close from Saturday afternoon to Monday morning.

Restaurants

Trześniewski, I, Dorotheergasse 1, 3 blocks down the Graben from the Stephansdom. A famous stand-up restaurant that has been serving petite open-faced sandwiches for over 80 years. The preferred locale of Franz Kafka. Lots of veggie options. Open Mon.-Fri. 8:30am-7:30pm, Sat. 9am-1pm; first Sat. of the month 9am-6pm. **Branch** at VII, Mariahilferstr. 26-30 in the Hermansky store. Same hours.

Levante, I, Wallnerstr. 2. Greek-Turkish restaurant features heaps of affordable dishes, including vegetarian delights. Entrees 78-130AS. **Branches** at I, Wollzeile 19; Mariahilferstr. 88a; and VIII, Josefstädterstr. 14. All open daily 11am-11:30pm.

Brezelgwölb, I, Lederhof 9 (tel./fax 533 88 11). Excellent hearty cuisine even the Viennese call *"Altwiener"* (old Viennese). Rare standing pieces of the medieval city wall reside in the courtyard—the rest was torn down to build the Ringstraße. Reserve in the evening. Open daily 11:30am-1am.

Tunnel, VIII, Florianigasse 39. U-2 to "Rathaus." Dark and smoky, prized for its dilapidated hipness, live music, and really affordable food. Open daily 9am-2am.

Blue Box, VII, Richtergasse 8. U-3 to "Neubaugasse." You absolutely can't come to Vienna and miss this place. Dishes are fresh, flamboyant, and above all, original. Choose from Viennese, French, English, vegetarian, you name it. Open Tues.-Thurs. 10am-2am, Fri.-Sat. 10am-4am, Sun. 10am-2am, Mon. 6pm-2am.

Cafés and Konditoreien

The café is a centerpiece of Vienna's unhurried charm. The waiter will serve you as soon as you sit down, but will leave you alone with your coffee, newspaper, and book for the rest of the stay. The *Konditoreien* are no less traditional, but here the focus shifts from coffee to delectable pastries.

Café Hawelka, I, Dorotheergasse 6, 3 blocks down Graben from the Stephansdom. The award-winning Hawelka is shabby and glorious. *Buchteln* (sweet dumplings filled with preserves, served only at 10pm) 35AS. Coffee 30-50AS. Open Mon. and Wed.-Sat. 8am-2am, Sun. 4pm-2am.

Café Museum, I, Friedrichstr. 6. Near the Opera; head away from the *Innere Stadt* to the corner of Operngasse and Friedrichstr. Built in 1899 by Adolf Loos with striking, curved red leather and lots of space. Open daily 7am-11pm.

Café Central, I, at the corner of Herrengasse and Strauchgasse, inside Palais Ferstel. Former patrons include Lenin and Trotsky, who played chess here, fingering imperialist miniatures with cool anticipation, and Sigmund Freud. Oh, the café serves coffee, too. Open Mon.-Sat. 9am-8pm. Live piano music 4-7pm.

Demel, I, Kohlmarkt 14. Walk 5min. from the Stephansdom down Graben. The premier Viennese *Konditorei.* The atmosphere is divine in this legendary *fin-de-siècle* cathedral of sweets. Waitresses in convent-black serve the tasty confections (35-50AS). Don't miss the *crème-du-jour.* Open daily 10am-6pm.

Hotel Sacher, I, Philharmonikerstr. 4, around the corner from the main tourist information office. This historic sight has been serving the world-famous *Sacher Torte* (50AS) in red velvet opulence for years. Open daily 7am-11:30pm.

Café Sperl, VI, Gumpendorferstr. 11, 15min. from the Westbahnhof. One of Vienna's oldest and most beautiful cafés. Coffee 30-50AS. Open Mon.-Sat. 7am-11pm, Sun. 5-11pm; July-Aug. closed Sun.

AUSTRIA

SIGHTS

Vienna from A to Z (60AS from the tourist office, more in bookstores) gives all you need for a self-created tour. The free *Museums* brochure from the tourist office lists all opening hours and admission prices. Museum tickets usually cost 20-80AS.

The Innere Stadt If you begin your tour from the main tourist office, the first prominent building in view will be the **State Opera House,** or *Staatsoper.* Apart from St. Stephan's Cathedral, no other building is as close to the hearts of the Viennese as the opera house. The cheapest way to see the glittering gold, crystal, and red-velvet interior may be to see an opera; standing-room tickets with excellent views are only 20AS. If can't find tickets, tours of the house cost 40AS, students 25AS (July-Aug. daily 11am-3pm on the hour; Sept.-June upon request). Alfred Hrdlicka's poignant 1988 sculpture **Monument Gregen Krieg und Faschismus** (Memorial Against War and Fascism), behind the opera on Albertinaplatz, memorializes the suffering of Austria's people—especially its Jews—during World War II. From Albertinaplatz, Tegetthoffstr. leads to the spectacular **Neuer Markt,** where a graceful fountain and 17th-century church greet visitors. Continue north from here to reach Vienna's most revered landmark, the Gothic **Stephansdom;** the cathedral's smoothly tapering South Tower has become Vienna's emblem. Take a lap around the building before checking out the view from the **Nordturm** (North Tower). In the catacombs, the **vault** stores Hapsburgs' innards. (Tours of the cathedral in English Mon.-Sat. 10:30am and 3pm, Sun. 3pm. 30AS. Spectacular July-Sept. evening tour Sat. 7pm. 100AS. North Tower open April-Sept. daily 9am-6pm; Oct.-March 8am-5pm. Elevator ride 50AS. Tours of the vault Mon.-Sat. 10am-noon and 2-4:30pm, Sun. 2-5pm. 50AS.)

The **Hofburg** (Imperial Palace), rising from the southeast of the Michaelerplatz, was inhabited by the Hapsburg emperors until 1918, and now houses the President's office. The enormous complex also includes the **Burggarten** (Gardens of the Imperial Palace), the **Burgkapelle** (where the Vienna Boys' Choir sings Mass on Sun. and religious holidays), and the **Schauräume** (State rooms), the former private rooms of

Emperor Franz Josef and Empress Elisabeth. Perhaps the grandest part of the complex is the **Neue Hofburg** (New Palace); the double-headed golden eagle crowning the roof symbolizes the double empire of Austria-Hungary. Also check out the **Nationalbibliothek** (National Library), which has outstanding papyrus scriptures and musical manuscripts. Keep walking around the Hofburg, away from the Michaelerkirche, to wander through the Baroque **Josefsplatz,** which features an equestrian monument to Emperor Josef II and the stunning 14th-century **Augustinerkirche.** Between Josefsplatz and Michaelerplatz, the Palace Stables *(Stallburg)* are home to the famous Royal Lipizzaner stallions of the **Spanische Reitschule** (Spanish Riding School). Performances (April-June and Sept. Sun. at 10:45am and Wed. at 7pm; March and Nov. to mid-Dec. Sun. at 10:45am) are always sold out; write for reservations six months in advance (do not send money) to Spanische Reitschule, Hofburg, A-1010 Wien (tickets 250-900AS, standing-room 200AS). Watching the horses train is much cheaper. (March-June and Nov. to mid-Dec. Tues.-Sat. 10am-noon; Feb. Mon.-Sat. 10am-noon, except when the horses tour. Tickets sold at door at Josefsplatz, Gate 2, from about 8:30am. 100AS.)

The Hofburg's Heldenplatz gate presides over the Burgring segment of the **Ringstraße.** In 1857, Emperor Franz Josef commissioned this 187ft. wide and 2½mi. long boulevard to replace the Medieval city walls that separated Vienna's center from the suburban districts. Follow Burgring west through the **Volksgarten's** hundreds of varieties of roses to reach the Neoclassical, sculpture-adorned **Parliament** building. Just up Dr.-Karl-Renner-Ring is the **Rathaus,** an intriguing remnant of late 19th-century neo-Gothic with Victorian mansard roofs and red geraniums in the windows. There are numerous art exhibits inside, and the city holds outdoor festivals in the square outside. Opposite the Rathaus, the **Burgtheater** contains frescoes by Klimt. Immediately to the north on Dr.-Karl-Lueger-Ring is the **Universität,** and the surrounding sidestreets overflow with cafés, bookstores, and bars.

Outside the Ring Music lovers trek out to the **Zentralfriedhof** (Central Cemetery), XI, Simmeringer Hauptstr. 234; the second gate leads to the graves of Beethoven, Strauss, and Schönberg, and an honorary monument to Mozart. (Open May-Aug. daily 7am-7pm; March-April and Sept.-Oct. 7am-6pm; Nov.-Feb. 8am-5pm.) To reach the Zentralfriedhof, take streetcar 71 from Schwarzenbergplatz (35min.). If you need some cheering up after this experience, visit the **Hundertwasser Haus,** at the corner of Löwenstraße and Kegelgasse in the third district. A wild fantasia of pastel colors, ceramic mosaics, and oblique tile columns contribute to the eccentricity of this blunt rejection of architectural orthodoxy.

Another must-see is the **Schloß Schönbrunn** and its surrounding gardens, which comprise one of the greatest palace complexes in Europe. Tours of some of the palaces' 1500 rooms reveal the elaborate taste of Maria Theresa's era. The six-year-old Mozart played in the **Hall of Mirrors** at the whim of the Empress, and to the profit of the boy's father. The **Great Gallery's** frescoes are a highlight, but the **Million Gulden Room** wins the prize for excessiveness; Indian miniatures cover the chamber's walls. In summer, many concerts and festivals take place in the palace. (Palace apartments open April-Oct. daily 8:30am-5pm; Nov.-March 8:30am-4:30pm. 100AS, tours in English 40AS.) To reach the palace, take U-4 to "Schönbrunn."

The **Prater,** extending southeast from the Wien-Nord Bahnhof, is a notoriously touristed amusement park that functioned as a private game reserve for the Imperial family until 1766. The park is dotted with various arcades, restaurants, and casinos. Rides range from garish thrill machines to merry-go-rounds to the stately 65m **Riesenrad** (Giant Ferris Wheel), which offers one of the best views of Vienna. (Open Feb.-Oct. daily 10am-10pm, sometimes until midnight; Nov. 10am-8pm. Entrance to the complex is free, but each attraction charges admission.) Beloved by children during the day, the Prater becomes less wholesome and more dangerous after sunset.

Museums On the Burgring in what used to be the *Neue Hofburg* is the famous **Kunsthistorisches Museum.** The building is home to one of the world's best art collections, including Brueghels, Vermeer's *Allegory of Painting,* and numerous works by Rembrandt, Rubens, Titian, Dürer, and Velázquez. Cellini's famous golden salt cellar is here, along with a superb collection of ancient art and a transplanted Egyptian burial chamber. Gustav Klimt decorated the lobby. (Picture gallery open Tues.-Wed. and Fri.-Sun. 10am-6pm, Thurs. 10am-9pm. 100AS, students 50AS.) Across the way sits the **Naturhistorisches Museum,** identical in appearance but less interesting in content. Fans of Klimt and fellow radicals Schiele and Kokoschka should visit the **Austrian Gallery,** in the **Belvedere Palace,** entrance at Prinz-Eugenstr. 27. The Lower Belvedere houses the Baroque Museum and the Museum of Medieval Austrian Art (both museums open Tues.-Sun. 10am-5pm; 60AS, students 30AS).

The greatest monument of *fin-de-siècle* Vienna is the **Secession Building,** I, Friedrichstr. 12, built by Wagner's pupil Josef Maria Olbrich to accommodate the artists, led by Gustav Klimt, who scorned the historical style and broke with the uptight Viennese art establishment. Olbrich designed this extraordinary ivory-and-gold edifice as a reaction against the overblown Neoclassicism of the Ring museums. Exhibits by contemporary artists adorn the walls, as does Klimt's 30m *Beethoven Frieze* (open Tues.-Fri. 10am-6pm, Sat.-Sun. 10am-4pm; 30AS, students 15AS). The **Künstlerhaus,** from which the Secession seceded, is to the east at Karlsplatz 5 (open Mon.-Wed. and Fri.-Sun. 10am-6pm, Thurs. 10am-9pm; 90AS, students 40AS).

For more of the Art Nouveau movement, visit the **Österreichisches Museum für Angewandte Kunst** (Museum of Applied Art), I, Stubenring 5, the oldest museum of applied arts in Europe. Otto Wagner furniture and Klimt sketches pose amid crystal, china, furniture, and rugs from the Middle Ages to the present (open Tues.-Wed. and Fri.-Sun. 10am-6pm, Thurs. 10am-9pm. 90AS, students 45AS). Other marvelous creations by Otto Wagner are scattered around town; his **Pavilion** is at Karlsplatz, the major U-Bahn station, his **Postsparkassenamt** is on the Postgasse, and his **Kirche am Steinhof** resides at XIV, Baumgartner Höhe 1 (bus 48). The acoustics of the church have the longest reverberations in the world, fully 27 seconds in some cases. The exterior is even more stunning, combining Wagner's functionalism with a decidedly Byzantine influence (open only Sat. 3-4pm, free).

Kunst Haus Wien, III, Untere Weißgerberstr. 13, built for the works of Hundertwasser, is one of his greatest works in and of itself. This crazily pastiched building also hosts international contemporary exhibits (open daily 10am-7pm; 90AS, students 50AS). The **Historisches Museum der Stadt Vienna** (Historical Museum of the City of Vienna), IV, Karlspl. 5, to the left of the Karlskirche, houses collections of historical artifacts and paintings that document the city's evolution from the Roman Vindobona encampment through 640 years of Hapsburg rule to the present (open Tues.-Sun. 9am-4:30pm; 50AS, students 20AS).

ENTERTAINMENT

Music and Theater

You can enjoy Viennese opera in the imperial splendor of the **State Opera House** for a mere 20-50AS. Get in line on the west side about three hours before curtain for standing room *(Stehplätze)* tickets, sold only on the day of performance. Get tickets for the center to enjoy the best views, and bring a scarf to tie on the rail to save your place during the show. Costlier advance tickets (100-850AS) are on sale at the **Bundestheaterkasse,** I, Hanuschgasse 3 (tel. 514 44 22 60), next to the opera along the Burggarten (university ID—not ISIC—required; open Mon.-Fri. 8am-6pm, Sun. 9am-noon). Get there at 6-7am opening day for a good seat. They also sell tickets for Vienna's other public theaters: the **Volksoper, Burgtheater,** and **Akademietheater.**

Vienna, the most musical of cities, quiets somewhat in summer; the Staatsoper, the Philharmonic Orchestra, and the **Wiener Sängerknaben** (Vienna Boys' Choir) vacation during July and August. During the rest of the year, the pre-pubescent prodigies sing 9:15am mass each Sunday at the **Burgkapelle** (Royal Chapel) of the Hofburg. Reserve tickets (60-280AS) at least two months in advance from Hofmusikkapelle, Hofburg, Schweizerhof, A-1010 Wien. Do not enclose money. Unreserved seats are

AUSTRIA

sold starting at 5pm on the preceding Friday; standing room is free. The **Wiener Philharmoniker** (Vienna Philharmonic Orchestra) is also world-renowned, performing in the **Musikverein,** I, Dumbastr. 3 (tel. 505 81 90), on the northeast side of Karlsplatz. Another great option is to listen to **Sunday masses** in Augustinerkirche, Michaelerkirche, and Stephansdom; the accompanying choral and organ music is divine. The **Theater an der Wien,** VI, Linke Wienzeile 6 (tel. 588 30), premiered Beethoven's *Fidelio* and Mozart's *Magic Flute,* and now features modern musicals and other performances. The **Wiener Kammeroper** (Chamber Opera) performs during the summer in Schönbrunner Schloßpark.

English-language drama is performed at **Vienna's English Theater,** VIII, Josefsgasse 12 (tel. 402 12 60); tickets run 150-420AS, but students snatch up seats for 100AS on the night of performance (box office open Mon.-Fri. 10am-6pm, Sat.-Sun. 10am-4pm). If you yearn to hear still more English, head to the **International Theater,** IX, Porzellangasse 8 (tel. 319 62 72; tickets 220AS, under 26 120AS).

Heurigen and Nightlife

Vienna is almost as famous for its *Heurigen* (wine gardens with outside seating at picnic tables) as for its art and music. Unique to Vienna, *Heurigen* began when Emperor Josef II, in a fit of largesse, allowed the local wine-growers to sell and serve their wine in their homes at certain times of the year. The worn picnic benches and old shade trees provide an ideal spot to contemplate, converse, or listen to *Schrammelmusik* (sentimental folk songs played by aged musicians inhabiting the *Heurigen*). Most *Heurigen* also serve simple buffets (grilled chicken, salads, pretzels, etc.) that make for an enjoyable and inexpensive meal. In the middle of the summer, *Stürm* (sweet, cloudy, unpasteurized wine) is available. **Grinzing** is the largest *Heurigen* area, but atmosphere and prices are better in **Sievering, Neustift am Wald, Stammersdorf,** and **Neuwaldegg.** Hidden from tourists and therefore beloved by locals, **Buschenschank Heinrich Niersche,** XIX, Strehlgasse 21, overlooks the field of Grinzing. Take U-Bahn 1 to "Währingerstraße/Volksoper," then bus 41A to "Pötzleindorfer Höhe," walk uphill one block, and make a right on Strehlgasse. (*Weiße G'spritzer,* white wine with tonic water, 18AS. Open Wed.-Mon. 3pm-midnight.)

The city parties until dawn, though public transportation stops around midnight. Pick up a copy of *Falter* (28AS) for the best entertainment listings. Revelers tend to lose themselves in the infamous **Bermuda Dreieck** (Triangle), a collection of a dozen or so bars down Rotenturmstr., away from the Stephansdom. The revelry begins along the cobblestone streets and outdoor seating in this area, and then moves indoors from 11pm until 2am or even 4am. You can also take U-Bahn 3 to **"Stubentor"** to reach a solid stomping ground of the hip. Other locals congregate in the cool, ancient grottos of the **Bäckerstraße** area behind the Stephansdom, or in the eighth district behind the university. Once you're in the swing of things, use the Viennese terms for bars, *Biesel* or *Lokal,* when asking a sloshed native where you should go.

Benjamin, I, Salzgries 11-13, just outside of the Triangle. Go down the steps from Ruprecht's church, left onto Josefs Kai, and left on Salzgries. Persian rugs, velvet lounge, soul grooves, and airplane seats. *Budvar* and *Kapsreiter* 37AS and 43AS, respectively. Open Sun.-Thurs. 7pm-2am, Fri.-Sat. 7pm-4am.

Krah Krah, I, Rabensteig 8. From Stephanspl., head down Rotenturmstr., and continue slightly to your left on Rabensteig. 50 kinds of beer on tap. Outdoor seating until 10pm. Open Sun.-Wed. 11am-2am, Thurs.-Sat. 11am-3am.

Zwölf Apostellenkeller, I, Sonnenfelsgasse 3, behind the Stephansdom. To reach this underground tavern, walk into the archway, take a right, go down the long staircase, and discover grottoes that date back to 1561. Beer 37AS. *Viertel* of wine from 25AS. Open Aug.-June daily 4:30pm-midnight.

Esterházykeller, I, Haarhof 1, off Naglergasse. Vienna's least expensive *Weinkeller.* Try the Burgenlander *Grüner Veltliner* wine (26AS). Open in summer Mon.-Fri. 11am-11pm; off-season Mon.-Fri. 11am-11pm and Sat.-Sun. 4-11pm.

Kaktus, I, Seitenstettengasse 5, in the heart of the triangle. Packed with the bombed and the beautiful. Open Sun.-Thurs. 6pm-2am, Fri.-Sat. 6pm-4am.

Alsergrunder Kulturpark, IX, Alserstr. 4 (tel. 407 82 14). Not one bar but many. All sorts of people and all sorts of nightlife—just about anything you might want for a happening night out. Frequent concerts. Open daily April.-Oct. 4pm-2am.

U-4, XII, Schönbrunnerstr. 222 (tel. 85 83 18). U-4 to "Meidling Hauptstr." Once *the* disco in Vienna and still packed. Five floors and theme nights please a varied clientele. Thurs. is "Gay Heavens Night." Cover 50-100AS. Open daily 11pm-5am.

Why Not, I, Tiefer Graben 22 (tel. 535 11 58). A gay bar/disco for women and men. Open Fri.-Sat. 11pm-6am, Sun. 9pm-2am. Women-only one Thurs. per month.

Near Vienna: Baden bei Wien

Since the age of Roman rule, bathers have cherished the Baden bei Wien for the therapeutic effects of its hot sulfur springs. Emperor Franz I moved the summer court here in 1803, attracting notables such as Mozart, Schubert, Strauss, and Beethoven. The largest bath, the **Strandbad,** is at Helenenstr. 19-21. (Mon.-Fri. 79AS, Sat.-Sun. 92AS; after 1pm, 66AS and 79AS. Swimming pool only 25AS.) The **Kurdirektion,** Brusattipl. 4 (tel. (02252) 445 31), is the center of all curative spa treatments, housing an indoor thermal pool mainly for patients but also open to visitors (72AS). The spa has sulfur mud baths (305AS). Centered around Hauptpl., Baden's lovely *Fußgängerzone* features the **Dreifaltigkeitsäule** (Trinity Column), erected in 1718 to thank God for keeping the plague from Baden; the **Rathaus;** and Franz Josef I's summer residence at #17. At Rathausgasse 10 is the **Beethovenhaus,** where the composer wrote much of his *Ninth Symphony* (open Tues.-Fri. 4-6pm, Sat.-Sun. 9-11am and 4-6pm). From Vienna, take the Süd Autobahn and exit at "Baden," or the **Badner Bahn,** a tram that runs every 15 minutes between Josefpl. and the Opera House in Vienna. Baden's **tourist office** is at Brusattipl. 3 (tel. (02252) 868 00; fax 441 47); from the Josefpl. tram stop, walk toward the fountain and follow Erzherzog-Rainer-Ring to the second left (open May-Oct. Mon.-Sat. 9am-12:30pm and 2-6pm, Sun. 9am-12:30pm).

Salzburg

For the city of Salzburg, the three most important factors are Mozart, Mozart, and Mozart. Though wedged between three foliage-covered peaks and dotted with church spires, medieval turrets, and resplendent palaces, Salzburg considers its forte to be not its spectacular sights but the music of favorite son Wolfgang Amadeus Mozart. The city's adulation reaches a deafening roar every summer during the Salzburger Festspiele, a five-week festival featuring hundreds of operas, concerts, plays, and open-air performances. And no tour guide will let you forget that Salzburg is also the place to pay homage to *The Sound of Music*'s trilling von Trapp family.

ORIENTATION AND PRACTICAL INFORMATION

Salzburg hugs both sides of the **Salzach River** a few kilometers from the German border. On the west bank is the *Altstadt* and the heavily touristed pedestrian district; on the east side is the *Neustadt,* with the **Mirabellplatz** at its heart. To reach the downtown area from the *Hauptbahnhof,* take bus 1 ("Maxglan"), bus 5 ("Birkensiedlung"), bus 6 ("Parsch"), bus 51 ("Salzburg Süd"), or bus 55 ("Rif"). On foot, exit the station, turn left, and follow Rainerstr. until it becomes Mirabellpl. (15min.).

Tourist Office: Mozartpl. 5 (tel. 84 75 68 or 88 98 73 30; fax 88 98 73 42), in the *Altstadt.* From the station, take bus 5, 6, 51, or 55 to "Mozartsteg," and curve around the building into Mozartpl. On foot, turn left on Rainerstr., follow it to the end, cross the river over the Salzach, and follow it upstream. Staff will help you find rooms. The free hotel map is the same as the 10AS city map. Open July-Aug. daily 9am-8pm; Sept.-June 9am-6pm. **Branch offices** at the train station, platform 2a (open Mon.-Sat. 8:45am-8pm), and the airport (open daily 9am-9pm).

Budget Travel: ÖKISTA, Wolf-Dietrich-Str. 31 (tel. 88 32 52; fax 88 18 19), near the International Youth Hotel. Open Mon.-Fri. 9am-5:30pm. **Young Austria,** Alpenstr.

108a (tel. 625 75 80; fax 62 57 58 21). Open Mon.-Fri. 9am-5pm, Sat. 9am-noon. Both have discounts, especially for travelers under 26.

Consulates: South Africa, Erzabt-Klotz-Str. 4 (tel. 84 33 28; fax 84 37 78 80). Open Mon.-Fri. 8am-1pm and 2-5pm. **U.K.,** Alter Markt 4 (tel. 843 133). Open Mon.-Fri. 9am-noon. **U.S.,** Herbert-von-Karajan-Pl. 1 (tel. 848 776; fax 849 777), in the *Altstadt.* Open Mon., Wed., and Fri. 9am-noon.

Currency Exchange: Banking hours are Mon.-Fri. 8am-12:30pm and 2-4:30pm. Currency exchange at the train station is open daily 7am-9pm. Banks offer better rates for cash than AmEx, but commissions are often higher.

American Express: Mozartpl. 5 (tel. 80 80; fax 808 01 78). No commission on own checks. Holds mail for check- or card-holders, books tours, and reserves music festival tickets. Open Mon.-Fri. 9am-5:30pm, Sat. 9am-noon.

Airport: The cheapest way to fly to Salzburg is to land in Munich and then take the train. Salzburg's own **Flughafen Salzburg** (tel. 858 02 51) is 4km west of the city center. For flight info, call **Austrian Airlines/SwissAir** (tel. 85 45 11). Bus 77 ("Bahnhof") runs to the train station every 15-30min. (5:55am-11:26pm).

Trains: Hauptbahnhof, Südtiroler Pl. (tel. 17 17), in the *Neustadt* north of town. To: Vienna (3½hr., 396AS), Munich (2hr., 294AS), Budapest (7½hr., 736AS), Innsbruck (2hr., 336AS), Venice (7½hr., 470AS), and Prague via Linz (544AS).

Buses: The bus depot (tel. (0660) 51 88) is right outside the main train station. The **BundesBus** makes outstanding connections to the Salzkammergut region.

Local Public Transportation: Extensive bus network. Info at the Lokalbahnhof, next to the station (tel. 87 21 45). 21AS per ride if you pay the driver, 15AS from a *Tabak* stand (in packs of five) or a vending machine. Day pass 32AS from a *Tabak.*

Bike Rental: At the train station, platform 3 (tel. 88 87 31 63). 150AS per day, 90AS with a train ticket from that day. 670AS per week.

Hitchhiking: Hitchers headed to Innsbruck, Munich, or Italy (except Venice) first take bus 77 to the German border. Thumbers bound for Vienna or Venice take bus 29 ("Forellenwegsiedlung") to the *Autobahn* entrance at "Schmiedlingerstr." They also take bus 15 ("Bergheim") to the *Autobahn* entrance at "Grüner Wald."

Luggage Storage: At the train station. Large lockers 30AS for two calendar days, small lockers 20AS. Luggage check 30AS per piece per calendar day. Open 24hr.

Lesbian Organizations: Frauenkulturzentrum (Women's Center), Elisabethstr. 17 (tel./fax 87 16 39). Open Mon. noon-4pm, Tues.-Thurs. 10am-4pm.

Laundromat: Norge Exquisit Textil Reinigung, Paris-Lodronstr. 16, on the corner of Wolf-Dietrich-Str. Wash and dry 82AS. Open Mon.-Fri. 7:30am-4pm, Sat. 8-10am.

Crisis Lines: Rape: tel. 88 11 00. **AIDS:** tel. 88 14 88.

Pharmacies: Elisabeth-Apotheke, Elisabethstr. 1 (tel. 87 14 84), a few blocks left of the train station. Most pharmacies are open Mon.-Fri. 8am-12:30pm and 2:30-6pm, Sat. 8am-noon. Closed pharmacies post lists of those open for emergencies.

Medical Assistance: When the dog bites, when the bee stings, when you're feeling sad... **Hospital,** Müllner-Hauptstr. 48 (tel. 44 82).

Emergencies: Ambulance: tel. 144. **Fire:** tel. 122.

Police: tel. 133. Headquarters at Alpenstr. 90 (tel. 63 83).

Post Office: Mail your brown paper packages tied up with strings by the train station. Address *Poste Restante* to "Postlagernde Briefe, Bahnhofspostamt, A-5020 Salzburg." Open daily 6am-11pm. **Branch office** at Residenzpl. 9. Open Mon.-Fri. 7am-7pm, Sat. 8-10am. **Postal Code:** A-5020.

Telephones: At the train station, main post office, Residenzpl. post office, and throughout the city center. **Telephone Code:** 0662.

ACCOMMODATIONS AND CAMPING

Most of Salzburg's affordable accommodations are located on the outskirts of town, easily accessible by local transportation. For *Pensionen* and private homes, start by asking for the tourist office's list of private rooms. The office also books rooms, but charges a fee of 7.2% of the room price. You must have a reservation or plan of action if you are arriving during the summer music festival.

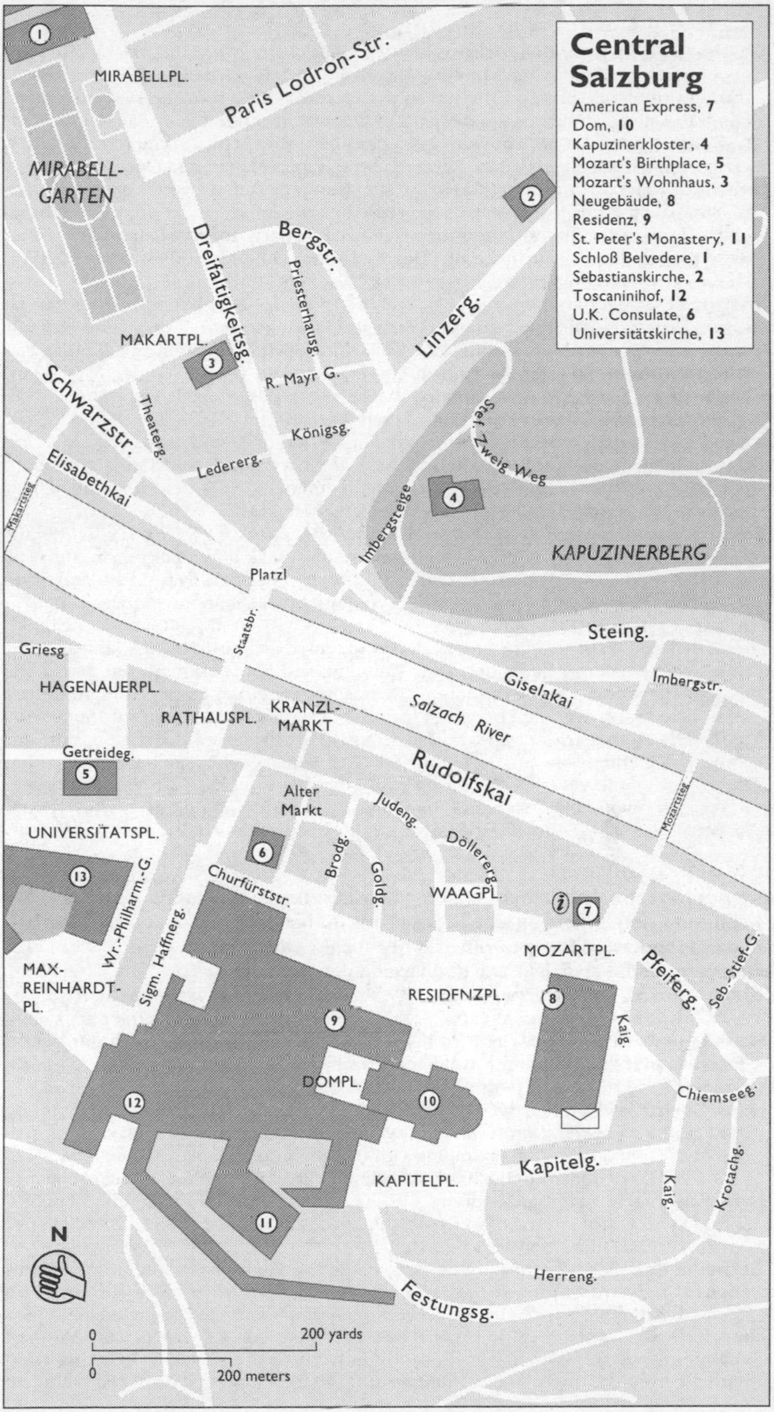
Central Salzburg
American Express, 7
Dom, 10
Kapuzinerkloster, 4
Mozart's Birthplace, 5
Mozart's Wohnhaus, 3
Neugebäude, 8
Residenz, 9
St. Peter's Monastery, 11
Schloß Belvedere, 1
Sebastianskirche, 2
Toscaninihof, 12
U.K. Consulate, 6
Universitätskirche, 13
MIRABELLPL.
Paris Lodron-Str.
MIRABELL-GARTEN
Dreifaltigkeitsg.
Bergstr.
Priesterhausg.
Linzerg.
MAKARTPL.
R. Mayr G.
Schwarzstr.
Theaterg.
Königsg.
Stef. Zweig Weg
Lederer g.
Elisabethkai
Makartsteg
Imbergsteige
KAPUZINERBERG
Platzl
Staatsbr.
Steing.
Griesg.
HAGENAUERPL.
RATHAUSPL.
KRANZL-MARKT
Giselakai
Imbergstr.
Salzach River
Getreideg.
Rudolfskai
Alter Markt
Judeng.
UNIVERSITATSPL.
Döllererg.
Mozartsteg
Brodg.
Goldg.
Wr.-Philharm.-G.
Churfürststr.
WAAGPL.
MOZARTPL.
Sigm. Haffnerg.
MAX-REINHARDT-PL.
Pfeiferg.
Seb.-Stief-G.
RESIDFNZPL.
Kaig.
DOMPL.
Chiemseeg.
Kapitelg.
KAPITELPL.
Krotachg.
N
Herreng.
Festungsg.
0
200 yards
0
200 meters

AUSTRIA

Hostels and Dormitories

Gasthaus Naturfreundehaus/Bürgerwehr, Mönchsberg 19c (tel. 84 17 29), towers over the old town. Take bus 1 ("Maxglan") to "Mönchsbergaufzug" then walk through the stone arch on the left to the elevator. Ride it to the top, turn right, climb the steps, and go down the path to the left. Reception daily 8am-10pm. Curfew 1am. Dorms 120AS. Showers 10AS per 4min. Breakfast (on the terrace with a great view) 30AS. Sheets 10AS. Reserve ahead. Open May to mid-Oct.

International Youth Hotel (YoHo), Paracelsusstr. 9 (tel. 87 96 49 or 834 60; fax 87 88 10), off Franz-Josef-Str. Exit the station to the left, turn left onto Gabelsbergerstr. through the tunnel, then turn right. A frat party for foreigners. Reception daily 8am-midnight. Curfew 1am. Dorms 140AS. Doubles 360AS. Quads 640AS. Showers 10AS per 6min. Breakfast 30-55AS. Lockers 10AS.

Institut St. Sebastian, Linzergasse 41 (tel. 87 13 86; fax 87 13 86 85). From the station, turn left on Rainerstr., go past Mirabellpl., turn left onto Bergstr., and turn left at the end. The hostel is through the arch on the left. Reception open 24hr.; call ahead. Dorms 170AS. Singles 300-360AS. Doubles 600-630AS. Triples 690-780AS. Dorm sheets 30AS. Kitchen. Laundry 40AS. Only dorms available Oct.-June.

Jugendgästehaus Salzburg (HI), Josef-Preis-Allee 18 (tel. 84 26 70 or 84 68 57; fax 84 11 01), southeast of the *Altstadt.* Take bus 5, 51, or 55 to "Justizgebäude." Curfew midnight. Dorms 160-164AS. Doubles 520-528AS. Quads 840-856AS. Nonmembers add 40AS first night. Breakfast and sheets included. Kitchen, laundry, and lockers. Reserve ahead. Outstanding wheelchair facilities.

Eduard-Heinrich-Haus (HI), Eduard-Heinrich-Str. 2 (tel. 62 59 76; fax 62 79 80). Take bus 51 ("Salzburg Süd") to "Polizeidirektion." Walk down Billrothstr., turn left on the Robert-Stolz-Promenade, then right. Reception open daily 7-9am and 5pm-midnight. Lockout 9am-5pm. Dorms 160AS with breakfast, nonmembers 200AS.

Haunspergstraße (HI), Haunspergstr. 27 (tel. 87 50 30; fax 88 34 77), near the train station. Walk straight out Kaiserschützenstr. which becomes Jahnstr., and turn left. No groups! Reception daily 7am-2pm and 5pm-midnight, but hostel fills by late afternoon. Curfew midnight. Dorms 160AS. Nonmembers add 40AS first night. Sheets, shower, and breakfast included. Laundry 80AS. Open July-Aug.

Aigen (HI), Aignerstr. 34 (tel. 62 32 48; fax 232 48 13). From the station, bus 5 to "Mozartsteg" then bus 49 ("Josef-Käut-Str.") to "Finanzamt," and walk 5min. along the road. It's the yellow building on your right. Bare rooms with wooden floors. Reception open daily 7-9am and 5pm-midnight. Curfew midnight. Dorms 180AS, nonmembers 220AS. Breakfast, showers, and sheets included.

Hotels and Pensions

Distrust proprietors at the train station who offer rooms. *Pensionen* within the city are scarce and expensive; look on the outskirts for better prices and quality. The bargain rooms on **Kasern Berg** are officially outside the city; the tourist office doesn't list them. To reach this area, take any northbound regional train to "Salzburg-Maria Plain" (every 30min. 6:17am-11:17pm, 4min., 17AS, Eurail valid), and walk up the road.

Haus Lindner, Panoramaweg 5 (tel. 45 66 81). Spacious rooms with hardwood floors. Families with children welcome (playground in rear). No singles. Doubles, triples, quads 160-200AS per person. Breakfast and shower included. Call ahead.

Haus Christine, Panoramaweg 3 (tel. 45 67 73), next to Haus Lindner and run by Frau Lindner's sister. Comfortable, newly renovated rooms. Breakfast room features huge windows with a stunning view of Salzburg. Doubles 320AS-400AS. Triples 480–600AS. Quads 640-800AS. Shower and breakfast included. Call ahead.

Haus Rosemarie Seigmann, Kasern Berg 66 (tel. 45 00 01). Welcoming, English-speaking host. Stone terrace overlooks the Alps. Doubles and triples 170-200AS per person. Breakfast and showers included.

Germana Kapeller, Kasern Berg 64 (tel. 45 66 71). English-speaking host oversees enchantingly traditional rooms and screens *The Sound of Music* daily upon demand. 170-200AS per person. Showers and complete breakfast included.

Haus Ballwein, Moostr. 69 (tel./fax 82 40 29). Take bus 1 from the station, then change to bus 60, which stops directly in front of the pension. Relaxing rural reprieve from the bustle of city tourism. 200-240AS per person. Breakfast included.

AUSTRIA

Haus Kernstock, Karolingerstr. 29 (tel. 82 74 69). Take bus 77 ("Flughafen") to "Karolingerstr." Friendly host, commodious rooms, and private baths. Laundry 80AS. Doubles, triples, and quads 220-250AS per person. Breakfast included.

Pension Sandwirt, Lastenstr. 6a (tel./fax 87 43 51), near the train station. From the station, exit from the platform 13 staircase, making a right on the footbridge. At the bottom, turn right; the pension is behind the building with the large post sign (3min). Singles 280-300AS. Doubles 440-550AS. Triples 570AS. Breakfast included.

Camping

Camping Stadtblick, Rauchenbichlerstr. 21 (tel. 45 06 52), next to Haus Elisabeth. The site offers a sweeping view of the city. 65AS per person. 15AS per tent, 80AS for a bed in a tent, 25AS per car. Ask about *Let's Go* discounts.

Camping Nord-Sam, Samstr. 22-A (tel. 66 04 94). Take bus 33 "Obergnigl" to "Langmoosweg." Shady, flower-bedecked campsites, and a small swimming pool. Late June-Aug. 53AS per person, 99AS per site; April to mid-June and Sept.-Oct. 40AS per person, 76AS per site. Laundry 75AS. Open April-Oct.

FOOD

AUSTRIA

Blessed with fantastic **beer gardens** and **Konditoreien** (pastry shops), Salzburg begs its guests to eat outdoors. The Salzburger *Nockerl* is the local specialty—a large soufflé of eggs, sugar, and raspberry filling, baked into three mounds representing the three hills of Salzburg. **Mozartkugeln** (Mozart's balls—er, chocolate) are one of Salzburg's favorite confections. Supermarkets include the ubiquitous **SPAR,** e.g. at Mirabellapl. **EuroSPAR** is next to the train station bus terminal (supermarkets generally open Mon.-Fri. 8am-6pm, Sat. 8am-noon). Open-air **markets** fill the Universitätsplatz in the *Altstadt* (open Mon.-Fri. 6am-7pm, Sat. 6am-1pm).

Restaurant Zur Bürgerwehr-Einkehr, Mönchsberg 19c. The owners of the Gasthaus Naturfreundehaus (see above) run this appealing restaurant at the top of the Mönchsberg. Take in some of the best views in town as you enjoy huge meals for 68-108AS. Kitchen open May-Oct. Sat.-Thurs. 10am-9pm.

Humboldt-Stuben, Gstättengasse 6, across the street from the Mönchsberg elevator. Specialty bacon and egg hamburger 59AS. *Pinzgauer Kasnock'n* 98AS. *Salzburger Nockerl* for two 92AS. Veggie-friendly salad bar. Open daily 10am-1:30am.

Zum Fidelen Affen, Priesterhausgasse 8, off Linzergasse. Phenomenal food in a darkwood, pleasantly crowded pub. Drinks 30AS. Spinach *Spätzle* (potato-based noodles) 88AS. Full meal of salad and main course 87-110AS. Open daily 5:30-11pm.

Der Wilde Mann, Getreidegasse 20, in the passage. Huge portions of *Wiener Schnitzel,* potatoes, and *Stiegl Bier* for the wild man (or woman) in us all. Less-touristed than nearby bistros. Entrees 70-120AS. Open Mon.-Sat. 9am-9pm.

Vegy, Schwarzstr. 21. Vegetarian restaurant with a domestic, relaxing atmosphere. Have a seat at a table or buy a quick meal to go. Very filling food. Daily *menu* with entree and soup 78AS. Open Mon.-Fri. 10:30am-6pm.

Fischmarkt, at Hanuschpl. on the *Altstadt* side of the river. Two huge trees reach through the roof of this casual, crowded restaurant. Savor Danish seafood. Fish sandwiches 22-35AS. Beer 21AS. Open Mon.-Fri. 8:30am-6:30pm, Sat. 8:30am-1pm.

Trześniewski, Getreidegasse 9. Kafka's Vienna hangout now has a franchise on the ground floor of Mozart's birthplace. Wonderful sandwiches 9AS; about four make a good lunch. Open Mon.-Fri. 8:30am-6pm, Sat. 8:30am-1pm.

Café im Kunstlerhaus, Hellbrunnerstr. 3. Low-key café popular with students, artists, and their fans. Wide variety of drinks—treat yourself. Local bands play Tues. and Thurs. nights. Sat. is lesbian night. Open Mon.-Fri. 11am-11pm.

SIGHTS

Salzburg sprang up under the protective watch of the hilltop fortress **Hohensalzburg,** built atop the Mönchsberg between 1077 and 1681 by the ruling archbishops. Tours wind through staterooms, torture chambers, and the watchtower. The **Rainer Museum** displays medieval weapons and instruments of torture. (Fortress open July-Sept. daily 8am-7pm; Oct.-March 9am-5pm; April-June 9am-6pm. 35AS. Castle tours in

English and German July-Aug. daily 9:30am-5:30pm, April-June and Sept.-Oct. 9:30am-5pm, Nov.-March 10am-4:30pm. Tour, museum, and fortress 65AS.) The cable car from Festungsgasse to the fortress runs every 10 minutes (round-trip 69AS).

At the bottom of the Festungsbahn is **Kapitelplatz,** housing a giant chess grid and horse-bath fountain. Standing at the chess grid, the entrance to **St. Peter's Monastery,** through the cemetery, is at the back right corner. The cemetery, **Petersfriedhof,** is one of the most peaceful places in Salzburg and is best known as the spot where Liesl's Nazi boyfriend Rolf blew the whistle on the von Trapp family in *The Sound of Music* (open April-Sept. daily 6:30am-7pm; Oct.-March 6:30am-6pm). On the left side of the cemetery is the entrance to the **Katakomben** (catacombs), where Christians allegedly worshipped as early as 250. (Tours in English and German every hr. May-Sept. daily 10am-5pm; Oct.-April 11am-noon and 1:30-3:30pm. 12AS, students 8AS.) Exit the cemetery down the little path in the opposite corner from the entrance off Kapitelplatz, and head to the courtyard in front of the church. **St. Peter's Church,** once a Romanesque basilica, received a Rococo facelift in the 18th century (open daily 9am-12:15pm and 2:30-6:30pm).

AUSTRIA

The distinctive dome of the **Universitätskirche** (University Church) stands watch over the Universitätsplatz, near the daily farmer's market. Generally considered Fischer von Erlach's masterpiece, the massive chapel is one of the largest on the continent and quite celebrated in European Baroque circles. From the Universitätsplatz, several passages lead through tiny courtyards filled with geraniums and ivy. They eventually give way to the stampede of **Getreidegasse,** a labyrinth of winding pathways and well preserved facades dating to the 17th and 18th centuries.

Wolfgang Amadeus Mozart was unleashed upon the world from what is now called **Mozarts Geburtshaus** (birthplace), at Getreidegasse 9. The house exhibits the boy wonder's first viola, some pictures, letters, and incredible stage sets for his operas. (Open July-Aug. daily 9am-6:25pm; Sept.-June 9am-5:25pm; in the summer arrive before 11am to beat the crowds. 65AS, students 50AS.) Turn right at the *Alter Markt* and venture down to Residenzpl. to find the 35-bell **Glockenspiel** which rings to a Mozart tune at 7am, 11am, and 6pm, and Archbishop Wolf Dietrich's palace, the **Residenz,** featuring Baroque staterooms and a gallery with works by Rubens, Breughel, and Titian. (Tours in German July-Aug. daily every 30min. 10am-4:30pm; Sept.-June Mon.-Fri. 10am-3pm. 50AS, students 40AS.) Mozart was christened in the adjacent Baroque **Dom** in 1756 and later worked there as *Konzertmeister* and court organist. The connecting **Dom Museum** holds the **Kunst- und Wunderkammer** (art and miracles chamber), which includes conch shells, mineral formations, and a two-foot whale's tooth (open mid-May to mid-Oct. daily 10am-5pm; 50AS, students 25AS).

Cross the river on the Staatsbrücke into the *Neustadt;* it's the only bridge from the *Altstadt* over the Salzach open to motorized traffic. In the New City, the bridge opens into **Linzergasse,** an enchanting medieval street. Ascend the stairs from under the stone arch on the right side of Linzergasse 14 to the **Kapuzinerkloster** (Capuchin Monastery). Legend has it that the resident monks clad in coffee-colored robes with white hoods inspired the world's first cup of *cappuccino.* Turning onto Dreifaltigkeitgasse will bring you to Makartpl. and Mozart's **Wohnhaus** (residence). It suffered major damage in World War II air raids but was renovated and reopened on Mozart's 240th birthday, January 27, 1996. Continue down this street to Mirabellplatz to discover the marvelous 17th-century **Schloß Mirabell.** Next to the palace, the manicured **Mirabellgarten** includes extravagant rose beds, labyrinths of shrubs, and 15 grotesque marble likenesses of Wolf Dietrich's court jesters. Students from nearby Mozarteum often perform here. Maria also made this one of her stops in *The Sound of Music* as the children danced around and sang "do-re-mi." **Salzburg Sightseeing Tours** (tel. 88 16 16; fax 87 87 76) traces the movie through the city. Tours leave from Mirabellpl. daily at 9:30am and 2pm (350AS, students 315AS; *Let's Go* discount).

ENTERTAINMENT

The Music Festivals

The renowned **Salzburger Festspiele** run from late July to the beginning of September. During the festivities, almost every public space is overrun with operas, dramas, films, and concerts. The complete program of events, which lists all important concert locations and dates, is printed a year in advance (10AS) and is available from any tourist office. For the best seats, requests must be made in person or by mail months in advance. Write with orders to **Kartenbüro der Salzburger Festspiele,** Postfach 140, A-5010 Salzburg (fax 84 66 82), by early January. Cheap tickets (100-300AS) are gobbled up quickly; don't be surprised if you're offered tickets for up to 1000AS. Those under 26 can try writing eight months in advance to Direktion der Salzburger Festspiele, attn: Carl-Philip von Maldeghem, Hofstallg. 1, A-5020 Salzburg. American Express sells marked-up cheap tickets. If you have no luck, or can't afford what's offered, try to take advantage of the **Fest zur Eröffungsfest** (Opening Day Festival), when concerts, shows, and films are either very cheap or free. Tickets for these events are available on a first-come, first-serve basis the week of the opening.

Even when the *Festpiele* are not in full force, there are a lot of other concerts and shows staged throughout the city. The **Mozarteum** (Music School; tel. 87 31 54; fax 87 29 96) performs a number of concerts on a rotating schedule, available at the tourist office. For a bit more money, check out the **Mozart Serendaden** (Mozart's Serenades) at Hellbrunn. These are evening concerts where Mozart favorites are performed with the musicians dressed in traditional Mozart garb; an intermission buffet is also included. For information and tickets, call or write Konzertdirektion Nerat, A-5020 Salzburg, Lieferinger Hauptstr. 136 (tel. 43 68 70; fax 43 69 70). For a particularly enchanting atmosphere, attend one of the **Festungskonzerte** (Fortress Concerts). There is a concert nightly, and tickets cost 270AS. For more information, contact Festungkonzerte Anton-Adlgasserweg 22, A-5020 Salzburg (tel. 82 58 58; fax 82 58 59). Throughout the summer there are various outdoor performances in the Mirabellgarten, including concerts, folk-singing, and dancing. The tourist office has information, but strolling through in the evening might prove just as effective.

Beer Gardens and Bars

Salzburg prides itself on the charm of its beer gardens, many of which serve generous portions of food. They do, however, tend to close early. For those who want to tipple later, simply head to one of the more conventional bars.

Augustiner Bräu, Augustinergasse 4. From the *Altstadt,* pick up the footpath at Hanuschplatz and follow the river (walking with the current). Go left up the flight of stairs past the Riverside Café, cross Müllner Hauptstr., continue up the hill, and take the first left. A Salzburg legend. Great beer is poured into massive steins from even more massive wooden kegs. Concession stands inside calm grumbling stomachs. Liters 56AS. Half-liters 28AS. Open Mon.-Fri. 3-11pm, Sat.-Sun. 2:30-11pm.

Sternbräu, Getreidegasse 34. Located in the *Altstadt,* this place has two beer gardens, a restaurant, and a self-service snack bar. Get there by ducking into any number of passages at the end of Getreidegasse. Open daily 9am-11pm.

K&K Stieglkeller, Festungsgasse 10, off Kapitelplatz near the Festungsbahn. Halfway up the mountain on the way to the *Festung,* this garden has a fantastic view of the *Altstadt.* Good Stiegl beer on tap and reasonably priced food. Open May-Sept. daily 10am-10pm. Sound of Music Live dinner show around 7:30pm.

Pub Passage, Rudolfskai 22-26, under the Radisson Hotel by Mozartsteg. A shopping promenade for youthful clubbing. All these bars are located in corridors of the "mall" and are open daily until 2-4am. Each has its own gimmick: **Tom's Bierklinik** brags beers from all over; **The Black Lemon** hosts Latino night on Wed.; **Bräu zum Frommen Hell** burns with 80s music; and **Hell** is a TV sports bar.

2 Stein, Giselakai 9. Possibly the coolest bar in town. Previously a gay bar, 2 Stein now caters to a mixed clientele of both genders. Open daily 5pm-4am.

Frauen Café, Sittikusstr. 17. Mellow lesbian hangout. Open Wed.-Sat. 8pm-midnight.

AUSTRIA

Near Salzburg: Lustschloß Hellbrunn

Just south of Salzburg lies the unforgettable **Lustschloß Hellbrunn** (tel. 82 03 72; fax 82 03 72 31), a one-time pleasure palace for Wolf Dietrich's nephew, the Archbishop Markus Sittikus. The sprawling estate includes fish ponds, gardens, a gazebo, and tree-lined footpaths. The neighboring **Wasserspielen** (Water Gardens) are perennial favorites; Markus amused himself with elaborate water-powered figurines and a booby-trapped table which spouted water on drunken guests. (Open July-Aug. daily 9am-10pm; May-June and Sept. 9am-5pm; April and Oct. 9am-4:30pm. Castle tour 30AS, students 20AS. Wasserspiele tour 70AS, 35AS. Tours of both 90AS, 45AS.) The **Steintheater,** on the palace grounds, is the oldest natural theater north of the Alps. To reach the palatial grounds, take bus 55 ("Anif") from the train station, Mirabellpl., or Mozartsteg to Hellbrunn, or bike 40 minutes down beautiful Hellbrunner Allee.

AUSTRIA

Salzkammergut

East of Salzburg, the landscape swells into towering mountains interspersed with unfathomably deep lakes. The region is remarkably accessible, with 2000km of footpaths, 12 cablecars and chairlifts, and dozens of hostels.

Transportation and Accommodations The Vienna-Salzburg **rail** line skirts the northern edge of the Salzkammergut. Within the region, a network of **buses** operate. Most routes run four to 12 times per day, and since the mountainous area is barren of rail tracks, buses are the most efficient method travel through the lake region. Check at the Bad Ischl Kiosk (tel. (06132) 231 13) or any other Salzkammergut town bus station for detailed info. Look especially for the *Postbus: Salzkammergut* brochure, a map of the area which also details local bus routes. **Hitchers** from Salzburg reportedly take bus 29 to Gnigl and come into the Salzkammergut at Bad Ischl. The lake district itself is known as one of the rare Austrian regions in which hitchhikers make good time. Nevertheless, it's safer and more enjoyable to **bike** around the lake and through the mountain passes; most train stations in the region rent bikes. On the lakes themselves, reasonably priced **ferries** connect major towns. The **Wolfgangsee** line is operated by the Austrian railroad, so railpass holders enjoy free passage; other lines offer discounts to those with railpasses.

Hostels abound, though you can often find far superior rooms in private homes and *Pensionen* at just slightly higher prices. *"Zimmer Frei"* signs peek out from virtually every house. **Campgrounds** dot the region, but many are trailer-oriented; away from large towns, some travelers camp discreetly almost anywhere without trouble. Hikers can capitalize on dozens of **cable cars** in the area to gain altitude before setting out on their own, and almost every community has a local trail map posted in a public area or available at the tourist office. At higher elevations, **alpine huts** supply mountain info of all sorts. These huts are leased through the **Österreichischer Alpenverein** (Austrian Alpine Club); their main office is in Innsbruck (tel. (0512) 594 47), with a branch office in Linz (tel. (0732) 773 22 95).

Hallstatt In a valley surrounded on all sides by the sheer rocky cliffs of the Dachstein mountains, **Hallstatt** is quite simply, in the words of Alex V. Humboldt, "the most beautiful lakeside village in the world." In the 19th century, Hallstatt was the site of one of the largest Iron Age archeological finds in history, and the **Prähistorisches Museum** (Prehistoric Museum), across from the tourist office, displays artifacts unearthed in the region (open May-Sept. daily 10am-6pm; Oct.-April Thurs.-Tues. 10am-4pm, Wed. 2-4pm). The **Heimatmuseum** around the corner has exhibits on daily life in historic Hallstatt. (Open May-Sept. daily 10am-6pm; Oct.-April 10am-4pm. Both museums 40AS, students 20AS.) Depending on your point of view, a visit to St. Michael's Chapel at the **Pfarrkirche** can be macabre, poignant, or intrusive; next to the chapel you can enter the parish "charnel house," a bizarre repository for skeletons. (Open May-Sept. daily 10am-6pm; off-season call (06134) 82 79 for an appointment. 10AS.) The 2500-year-old **Salzbergwerke** is the oldest saltworks in the world. (Open June to mid-Sept. 9:30am-4:30pm; April-May and mid-Sept. to Oct. 9:30am-3pm. 135AS, with guest card 120AS, students 60AS.) To reach the mines, wander up the path near the Pfarrkirche to the top (1hr.), or follow the black signs with the yellow eyes to the train station and take the **Salzbergbahn.** (In service June to mid-Sept. 9am-6pm; April-May and mid-Sept. to Oct. 9am-4:30pm. One way 55AS, with guest card 45AS. Round-trip 97AS and 85AS, respectively.) Hallstatt is also the starting point for some of the most spectacular **hiking** trails in the region. The tourist office sells a 70AS guide which details over 35 additional trails, including the **Echental** hike and the **Glacier Gardens** hike, through valleys carved out by glaciers.

To reach Hallstatt from Salzburg, **buses** are the best option; you'll have to transfer in Bad Ischl, and perhaps also at Gosamühle (144AS). The **train station** lies on the opposite bank of the lake from downtown; when you arrive, take the ferry into town (ferry 20AS; train from Salzburg via Attnang-Puchheim 262AS). The **tourist office,** Seestr. 169 (tel. (06134) 82 08; fax 83 52), in the Kultur und Kongresshaus, finds cheap rooms for no fee. (Open July-Aug. Mon.-Fri. 8:30am-6pm, Sat. 10am-6pm, Sun. 10am-2pm; Sept.-June Mon.-Fri. 9am-noon and 1-5pm.) Wherever you stay, ask the proprietor for the free **guest card,** which offers discounts on various attractions throughout town. The **youth hostel,** Salzbergstr. 50, is limited to groups, but **Gasthaus zur Mühle,** Kirchenweg 36 (tel. (06134) 8318), is a quasi-hostel with lots of backpackers. (Reception open daily 8am-2pm and 4-10pm. 100AS. Showers and lockers included. Sheets 35AS.) **Frühstuckspension Sarstein,** Gosaumühlstr. 83 (tel. (06134) 82 17), offers the prettiest accommodations in town. From the tourist office, head toward the ferry dock, and continue along the road nearest the lake past the Pfarrkircher steps (190-300AS, breakfast included).

AUSTRIA

Dachstein Ice Caves At the other end of the lake in Obertraun, the **Dachstein Ice Caves** give eloquent testimony to the geological hyperactivity that forged the region's natural beauty (open May to mid-Oct. daily 9am-5pm; each of 2 caves 85AS, combined 125AS). From Hallstatt, take the bus to Obertraun (35AS) and ride the Dachstein cable car up 1350m to Schönbergalm (round-trip 165AS). For more information on the caves, call (06131) 362.

Hohe Tauern National Park

The enormous **Hohe Tauern range** in the Austrian Central Alps spans about 10 towns across the south of Austria and boasts 246 glaciers and 304 mountains over 3000m. The national park, the largest in all of Europe, encloses 29 towns with a total of 60,000 residents. The **Glocknergruppe,** in the heart of the park, boasts the highest of the Hohe Tauern peaks and dazzling glaciers. The **Krimmler Wasserfälle** is in the far west. For general information about the park, contact **Nationalparkverwaltung Hohe Tauern,** 5741 Neukirchen Nr. 306, Austria (tel. (06565) 655 80; fax 65 58 18). Heavy snowfall forces many roads to close from November to April.

More than a million visitors annually brave the hairpin-fraught trek to gaze and gawk at the superlative-stumping **Großglockner Straße,** one of Austria's most popular attractions, which runs through the park from north to south. Skirting the country's loftiest mountains, Bundesstraße 107 winds for 50km amid silent Alpine valleys, meadows of (small and white, clean and bright) edelweiss, tumbling waterfalls, and a staggering glacier. The trip up to Kaiser-Franz-Josefs-Höhe (the midway point of the Großglockner Straße) and Edelweißspitze (the highest point) takes you from the flora and fauna of Austria into Arctic-like environments. Although tours generally run from **Zell am See** or **Lienz** to the park, the highway is officially only the 6.4km stretch from **Bruck an der Großglockner** to **Heiligenblut.** Coming from Zell am See, you'll pass the **Alpine Nature Exhibit** on the way up to Kaiser-Franz-Josefs-Höhe (open daily 9am-5pm; free). From Kaiser-Franz-Josefs-Höhe, you can gaze on Austria's highest peak, the **Großglockner** (3797m), and ride the **Gletscherbahn** funicular to Austria's longest glacier, the **Pasterze** (mid-May to Oct. every hr.; round-trip 95AS).

Wise budget travelers choose **BundesBus,** which offers daily return trips from Zell am See or Lienz to Kaiser-Franz-Josefs-Höhe. From the **north,** bus 3064 leaves from Zell am See's main bus station behind the post office, swinging by the stop directly across from the train station (round-trip 226AS). Zell am See's **Haus der Jugend (HI),** Seespitzstr. 13 (tel. 551 71 or 571 85; fax 57 18 54), offers immaculate rooms. Exit the back of the train station, turn right, and walk along the well-lit footpath beside the lake; at the end, take a left. (Reception open daily 7-9am and 4-10pm. Curfew 10pm. Dorms 145-170AS. Tax for guests over 25 9.50-10.50AS. Breakfast and sheets included. Open Dec.-Oct.) From the **south,** the odyssey begins in Lienz (185AS). For more details, check *Der BundesBus ist WanderFreundlich,* available at the bus stations in Lienz and Zell am See and the tourist offices in Lienz and Heiligenblut.

AUSTRIA

Kitzbühel

Kitzbühel welcomes tourists with glitzy casinos and countless pubs, yet few visitors remain at ground level long enough to enjoy them. The mountains surrounding the city attract skiers and hikers of all stripes. One of the best in the world, the Kitzbühel **ski area** challenges with its ethereal network of lifts, runs, and trails. In January, the city hosts the true *crème de la crème* during the **Hahnenkamm Ski Competition,** part of the annual World Cup (entry tickets available at the gate). For amateurs, a one-day ski pass (385-410AS) grants passage on 64 lifts and connecting shuttle buses. Passes may be purchased at any of the lifts or the Kurhaus Aquarena. The **Kitzbüheler Alpen Ski Pass** gives access to 260 lifts for six—not necessarily consecutive—days (1990AS). **Ski rental** is available from virtually any sports shop in the area; try **Kitzsport Schlechter,** Jochbergerstr. 7. Downhill equipment runs 180-350AS per day, and snowboards cost 270-380AS per day.

An extensive network of 70 **hiking trails** snakes up the mountains surrounding the city. The tourist office stocks English maps and organizes excellent hiking excursions for guest-card holders. Most of the trails are accessible by bus from the Hahnenkamm parking lot (hourly from 8am-5:10pm; 26AS, with guest card 20AS); after ski season, ride the **Hahnenkammbahn** to reach some of the loftier paths (daily 8am-5:30pm; 160AS, with guest card 140AS) or climb up to the trails yourself (about 2hr.). For budding botanists, the **Kitzbüheler Hornbahn** lift ascends to the **Alpenblumengarten,** where 120 different types of Alpine flowers blossom each spring (cable car 80AS per section; garden open late May to mid-Oct.). Before setting out for **mountian biking,** buy a booklet detailing the bike paths at the tourist office (54AS). If you need a bike, rent one at **Stanger Radsport,** Josef-Pirchlstr. 42 (tel. (05356) 25 49; 250AS per day).

Practical Information, Accommodations, and Food Most **phone numbers** in Kitzbühel are adding a "6" to the beginning of the local number. Kitzbühel has two **train stations** (info tel. (05356) 405 53 85), one at each side of the "U" formed by the rail tracks. Direct connections are available to Innsbruck (1hr., 125AS), Salzburg (3hr., 228AS), Vienna (6hr., 560AS), and other cities. The **tourist office,** Hinterstadt 18 (tel. (05356) 21 55 or 22 72; fax 23 07), offers tours and information; use the free telephone at the electronic accommodations board outside to secure a room. (Open July-Sept. and mid-Dec. to late April Mon.-Fri. 8:30am-6:30pm, Sat. 8:30am-noon and 4-6pm, Sun. 10am-noon and 4-6pm; Oct. to mid-Dec. and late April-June Mon.-Fri. 8:30am-12:30pm and 2:30-6pm.) Kitzbühel has more guest beds than inhabitants, but you'll pay for the convenience. Wherever you stay, be sure to ask for your **guest card** upon registration—it entitles you to discounts on many attractions. The **Hotel Kaiser,** Bahnhofstr. 2 (tel. (05356) 47 09), down the street from the main train station, offers a friendly staff, sun terrace, and an inexpensive bar (singles 250AS, doubles 200AS; breakfast included). To get to **Camping Schwarzsee,** Reitherstr. 24 (tel. (05356) 28 06; fax 44 79 30), take the train to "Schwarzsee" and walk toward the lake (76-85AS per person, 92AS per tent, 90-100AS per caravan; guest tax 6AS). Grocery shoppers can load up at the **SPAR Markt,** Bichlstr. 22, on the corner of Ehrengasse and Bichlstr. (open Mon.-Fri. 8am-6:30pm, Sat. 7:30am-1pm).

Innsbruck

With Baroque facades, rose bushes, and a ring of snow-capped mountains, Innsbruck is the quiet, provincial counterpart to Vienna's sprawling dominance and Salzburg's musical noteriety. Thrust into the international limelight by the Winter Olympics of 1964 and 1976, Innsbruck continues to draw athletes of all ilks to its more than 150 cable cars and chairlifts and extensive network of mountains paths which radiate from the city to the mountians.

ORIENTATION AND PRACTICAL INFORMATION

Lying along the eastern bank of the **River Inn,** Innsbruck is very walkable. **Maria-Theresien-Straße,** the main thoroughfare, offers excellent mountain views. To reach the **Altstadt** from the main train station, turn right and walk until you reach Museumstr., then turn left and walk for about 10 minutes. You can also take tram 3 or 6, or city bus A, F, or K from the station to "Maria-Theresien-Str." Continue down Museumstr. and toward the river (curving to the left onto Burggraben, across Maria-Theresien-Str., and onto Marktgraben) to reach the **University district.**

Tourist Office: Innsbruck-Information, Burggraben 3 (tel. 53 56; fax 53 56 14), on the edge of the *Altstadt* just off the end of Museumstr. Sells the **Innsbruck Card,** which gives unlimited access to sights and public transportation (200-350AS). Open Mon.-Sat. 8am-7pm, Sun. 9am-6pm. **Branch** offices are located at train station and major motor exits. **Tirol Information Office,** Maria-Theresien-Str. 55 (tel. 512 72 72; fax 51 27 27 27), gives Tirol info. Open Mon.-Fri. 8am-6pm.

Currency Exchange: Main post office and its branch in the train station. Open daily 7:30am-9pm. Better rates at **banks.** Open Mon. Fri. 8am-noon and 2:30-4pm.

American Express: Brixnerstr. 3 (tel. 58 24 91). Go right from train station, then first left. Mail held; all bank services. Open Mon.-Fri. 9am-5:30pm, Sat. 9am-noon.

Trains: Hauptbahnhof, on Südtirolerpl. (tel. 17 17; open 7:30am-9pm). Daily trains to Bergenz (2¾hr.), Salzburg (3hr.), Vienna (5½hr.), Basel (5hr.), Zurich (4hr.), Munich (2hr.), Hamburg (11hr.), Brussels (12hr.), Paris (11hr.), and Rome (9hr).

Buses: To get to the rest of Tirol, take a **Bundesbus** from the station on Sterzingerstr., next to the *Hauptbahnhof* and to the left of the main station.

Bike Rental: At the main train station (tel. 503 53 95). 150-200AS per day, 96-160AS with Eurailpass or train ticket from that day. Open April-early Nov.

Ski Rental: Skischule Innsbruck, Leopoldstr. 4 (tel. 58 23 10). 250AS including insurance. **Stubaier Gletscherbahn** (tel. 681 41). 270AS, with insurance.

Medical Assistance: University Hospital, Anichstr. 35 (tel. 50 40).

Emergencies: Ambulance: tel. 144. **Fire:** tel. 122. **Mountain Rescue:** 140. **Police:** tel. 133. Headquarters at Kaiserjägerstr. 8 (tel. 590 00).

Post Office: Maximilianstr. 2 (tel. 500), down from the Triumph Arch. Open 24hr. Branch next to the train station. Open Mon.-Fri. 7am-8pm, Sat. 8am-6pm. **Postal Code:** A-6020.

Telephones: In post office or train station near info office. **Telephone Code:** 0512.

ACCOMMODATIONS, CAMPING, AND FOOD

Beds are scarce in June, when only two hostels are open. In July, university housing opens up to travelers, easing the crunch; try **Technikerhaus,** Fischnalerstr. 26 (tel. 28 21 10) or **Internationales Studentenhaus,** Rechengasse 7 (tel. 50 15 92).

Hostel Torsten Arneus-Schwedenhaus (HI), Rennweg 17b (tel. 58 58 14), along the river. Take bus C from the station to "Handelsakademie." Front-yard view of the river. Reception open daily 7-10am and 5-10:30pm. Lockout 9am-5pm. Curfew 10:30pm. 120AS, shower included. Breakfast 45AS. Reserve ahead. Open July-Aug.

Jugendherberge Innsbruck (HI), Reichenauerstr. 147 (tel. 34 61 79 or 34 61 80). From the train station take bus R to "König-Laurin Str.," and then bus O to "Jugendherberge." Good facilities and staff. Reception open daily 7-10am and 5-10pm. Curfew 11pm. 145-175AS, nonmembers 185-215AS. Price drops after one night. Breakfast and sheets included. Phone reservations honored until 5pm.

Jugenherberge St. Nikolaus (HI), Innstr. 95 (tel. 28 65 15; fax 28 65 15 14). From the train station take bus K to "Schmelzergasse" and walk across the street. Come for the happening scene, not the facilities. Reception open daily 5-8pm. Lockout 10am-5pm. Get a key if you're out past 1AM. 145AS, nonmembers 160AS.

Haus Wolf, Dorfstr. 48 (tel. 54 86 73), in the suburb of Mutters. Take the Stubaitalbahn tram to "Birchfeld" and walk down Dorfstr. in the direction the tram continues. Let proprietor Titti Wolf spoil you with comfy beds and great views. Singles, doubles, and triples 190AS per person. Breakfast and shower included.

Haus Kaltenberger, Schulgasse 15 (tel. 54 85 76), just down the road from Haus Wolf in Mutters. Take the Stubaitalbahn to "Mutters," then walk towards the church, turn right on Dorfstr., and take the first left. Gorgeous mountain view. 200AS. Breakfast and shower included.

Camping Innsbruck Kranebitten, Kranebitter Allee 214 (tel. 28 41 80). From train station, take bus LK at Bozner Pl. to "Klammstr." After hours, find a site and check in the next morning. 60AS per person, 40AS per tent, 45AS per car. Guest tax 6AS.

Rather than gawk at the overpriced delis and *Konditoreien* on Maria-Theresien-Str., cross the river to **Innstr.** to find a myriad of ethnic restaurants, cheap *Schnitzel Stuben,* and Turkish grocers. There's a farmer's **market** in the *Markthalle* next to the river on the corner of Innrain and Marktgraben (open Mon.-Fri. 7am-6:30pm, Sat. 7am-1pm). Delight in pasta and veggie options at the candlelit, wooded **Al Dente,** Meranestr. 7 (entrees 82-142AS; open Mon.-Sat. 7am-11pm, Sun. and holidays 11am-11pm) or indulge in more veggie fare at **Philippine Vegetarische Küche,** Müllerstr. 9, at Lieberstr. one block from the post office (entrees 82-168AS; specials 45-98AS; open Mon.-Sat. 10am-11pm). **Gasthof Weißes Lamm,** Mariahilfstr. 12, serves up Tirolian fare and is popular with the locals. (Soup, entree, and salad 80-115AS. Open Mon.-Wed. and Fri.-Sun. 11:30am-2pm and 6-10pm.) **University Mensa,** Herzog-Siegmund-Ufer 15, on the 2nd floor of the new university at Blasius-Hueber-Str., near the bridge, is a student cafeteria open to public (meals 35-65AS). Both **Churrasco la Mamma,** Innrain 2, and **Crocodiles,** Maria-Theresien-Str. 49, offer brick-oven pizza.

SIGHTS AND ENTERTAINMENT

Beneath 2657 gilded shingles, the **Goldenes Dachl** (Golden Roof) on Herzog-Friedrich-Str. is the center of the *Altstadt.* Inside the building, the new **Maximilianeum** museum commemorates Innsbruck's favorite ruler. (Open May-Sept. daily 10am-6pm; Oct.-April Tues.-Sun. 10am-12:30pm and 2-5pm. 60AS, students 30AS.) Climb the stairs of the 15th-century **Stadtturm** (city tower) to soak in a panoramic view (open in summer daily 10am-5pm; off-season 10am-4pm; 22AS, students 11AS). At Rennweg and Hofgasse stand the **Hofburg** (Imperial Palace), **Hofkirche** (Imperial Church), and **Hofgarten** (take a guess). Built between the 16th and 18th centuries, the Hofburg brims with dynastic trappings (open daily 9am-5pm; last entrance 4:30pm; 55AS, students 35AS). The Hofkirche holds an intricate sarcophagus decorated with scenes from Maximilian I's life, as well as 28 mammoth bronze statues guarding the tomb. The punchline: the monument was never completed to Maxi's wishes, and he was buried near Vienna instead (open July-Aug. daily 9am-5:30pm; Sept.-June closes 5pm; 20AS, students 14AS). A special ticket (50AS) will also admit you to the collection of the **Tiroler Volkskunstmuseum,** which provides a thorough introduction to Tirolean culture (museum alone 40AS, students 25AS).

Backtrack a bit, cross the covered bridge over the Inn, and follow signs up to the **Alpenzoo,** with vertebrate species indigenous to the Alps. Descend on the network of trails that weave across the hillside. If you'd rather ride to the zoo, catch tram 1 or 4 or bus C, D, or E to "Hungerburg" and take the cable car up the mountain (zoo open in summer daily 9am-6pm; off-season 9am-5pm; 70AS, students 30AS).

Outside the city proper, Archduke Ferdinand of Tirol left behind piles of 16th-century armor and artwork (including pieces by Velazquez and Titian) at **Schloß Ambras,** one of the most beautiful Renaissance castles in Austria. A portrait gallery depicts European dynasties from the 14th to the 19th centuries. To reach the palace, take streetcar 6 ("Igls") to "Schloß Ambras," and follow the signs (open daily 10am-5pm; 60AS, students 30AS). On the hill overlooking the city perches the **Olympische Schischanze** (Olympic Ski Jump). Farther down the motorway, spanning the Sil River, is the tallest bridge on the continent, the **Europabrücke.**

A **Club Innsbruck** membership, available if you register at any central-Innsbruck accommodation, provides you with discounts on museums, free bike tours, **ski bus service,** and the option to join the club's fine **hiking** program (June-Sept.). Hikers meet in front of the Congress Center at 8:30am and return from the mountain range by 5pm. In winter, Club members hop on the complimentary ski shuttle (schedules at the tourist office) to any suburban cable car. From there, a comprehensive **lift ticket** to all 52 lifts in the region costs 1180AS for three days or 2140AS for six days (with Club membership 980AS or 1780AS). Innsbruck-Information and its train station branch offer the most reliable daily **glacier ski packages:** 660AS in summer (including bus, lift, and ski rental) and 540AS in winter. The tourist offices also carry mountain guide booklets for hikers and plenty of info on skiing. During August, Innsbruck hosts the **Festival of Early Music,** with concerts by some of the world's leading soloists on period instruments at the Schloß Ambras, and organ recitals on the Hofkirche's 16th-century Ebert organ (for tickets call 53 56 21; fax 53 56 43).

Though most visitors collapse into bed after a full day of Alpine adventure, there is still enough action to keep a few party-goers from their pillows. Much of the lively nightlife revolves around the **university quarter. Hofgarten Café,** hidden inside the Hofgarten park, draws students and professionals alike. A series of tents shelter different bars and dance floors. Use the park's back entrance after 10pm to get to the café. (Snacks 50-100AS. Beer 28AS. Open in summer daily 10am-1am; off-season Mon.-Sat. 5pm-1am, Sun. 10am-6pm.) **Treibhaus,** Angerzellgasse 8, is Innsbruck's favorite student hangout and has a musical bent (food 50-95AS; open Mon.-Fri. 9am-1am, Sat.-Sun. 10am-1am). **Jimmy's,** Wilhelm-Greil-Str. 17, on the Landhauspl., is packed with students who revere rock music (50-105AS; open Mon.-Fri. 11am-1am, Sat.-Sun. 7pm-1am). Amber walls and sleek black railings line **Krah Vogel,** Anichstr. 12, a hip, modern bar (beer 29-37AS; open Mon.-Sat. 9:30am-1am, Sun. 4pm-1am).

Bregenz

When the Romans conquered Brigantium two millennia ago, they set up a thriving bath and spa center. Ever since those first sun-worshippers, Bregenz has been a shrine to the principles of pleasure. Today the city is a kind of tourist nirvana, and thousands come—Speedo-clad—to bake on the banks of the lake and hike in the nearby mountains. The **Martinturm,** Bregenz's landmark, rules the Oberstadt and boasts Europe's largest onion dome. The second and third floors of the tower house the **Voralberg Military Museum,** whose view of the Boden expanse is worth the 10AS entrance fee (open May-Sept. Tues.-Sun. 9am-6pm). But the main attraction of the town is the **Bodensee,** where all along the waterfront carefully groomed paths surround fantastic playgrounds and paddleboat rental shops. Hop aboard a ferry to the **Blumeninsel Mainau** (Mainau Flower Isle) and take a tour of the island's Baroque castle, tropical palm house, and butterfly house. (Ferries depart Bregenz May-Sept. daily at 11am and return at 4pm. Round-trip 280AS. Tours 116AS.)

The **train station** (tel. (05574) 675 50) serves as the departure point for **BundesBus** connections to the rest of Austria. For maps and hotel reservations (30AS), head to the **tourist office** at Anton-Schneider-Str. (tel. (05574) 43 39 10; fax 433 91 10; email tourismus@bregenz.vol.at). From the train station, go left along Bahnhofstr., turn right onto Rathausstr., and then take the first left. In May/June 1998 the office will move to the Tourismushaus, Bahnhofstr. 14, a block to the left of the train station. In terms of location and price, the **Jugendherberge (HI),** Belrupstr. 16a (tel. (05574) 228 67), can't be beat (reception open 5-8pm; 126AS; open April-Sept.). More expensive and nicer is the **Pension Sonne,** Kaiserstr. 8 (tel. (05574) 425 72), off Bahnhofstr. (singles 330-490AS, doubles 600-940AS). **Seecamping** (tel. (05574) 718 96 or 718 95) is a long but pleasant walk from the train station, bearing left along Strandweg on the lake. (60AS per person and per tent, showers included. Guest tax 17AS. Open May 15-Sept. 15.) **SPAR Café Restaurant,** on the first floor of the GWL building at the corner of Kaiserstr. and Römerstr., has a self-serve salad bar and cafeteria-style entrees (56-98AS; open Mon.-Fri. 8:30am-6pm, Sat. 8:30am-4pm).

Linz an der Donau

The third largest city in Austria and home of Kepler, Beethoven, Bruckner, and *Linzer torte,* Linz rules over the industrial and modern sector of Austria. Its annual festivals—the **Brucknerfest** celebrating 19th-century symphonic composer Anton Bruckner (contact Brucknerhauskasse, Untere Donaulände 7, A-4010 Linz; http://www.brucknerhaus.linz.at) and the **Pflasterspektakel** (a street performer's fair during the third weekend in July)—draw artists and crowds from all over the world.

Hugging the Danube's bank, the enormous **Hauptplatz** was built in the 14th and 15th centuries from the wealth the town gathered taxing the salt and iron that passed through it. The 18th-century marble **trinity column** symbolizes the city's escape from the horrors of war, famine, and the plague. An astronomical clock crowns the Baroque **Altes Rathaus.** Only two people have ever addressed the public from its balcony: Adolf Hitler and Pope John Paul II. Johannes Kepler, who hypothesized the elliptical geometry of planetary orbit, wrote his major work, *Harmonices Mundi,* while living around the corner at Rathausgasse 5. On nearby Domgasse stands Linz's twin-towered **Alter Dom** (old cathedral), where Bruckner was once church organist (open daily 8am-noon and 3-6:30pm). To the south, the enormous neo-Gothic **Neuer Dom** (new cathedral) is the largest in Austria.

Across Nibelungenbrücke, the left bank of the Danube boasts a captivating view of Linz from the apex of the **Pöstlingberg** (537m). Tram 3 ("Bergbahnhof Urfahr") runs to the base of the summit. From there, hike 0.5km up Hagenstr. or hop aboard the steep trolley car **Pöstlingbergbahn** (25AS, round-trip 40AS). The twin-towered **Pöstlingbergkirche** (parish church), the city's symbol, stands guard from the hill's crest. The **Grottenbahn** chugs through the **fairy-tale caves** of Pöstlingberg. (Open April-Nov. Mon.-Fri. 9am-6pm, Sat.-Sun. 10am-5pm; Dec. daily 10am-5pm. 45AS.) The **Neue Galerie,** Blütenstr. 15, also on the left bank, boasts one of Austria's best modern and contemporary art collections. (Open June-Sept. Mon.-Fri. 10am-6pm, Thurs. until 10pm, Sat. 10am-1pm; Oct.-May closed Sat. 60AS, students 30AS.) The new **Ars Electronica,** Hauptstr. 2 (email info@aec.at; http://www.aec.at), just over the bridge from Hauptpl., sends you soaring over Upper Austria with a full-body flight simulator (open Wed.-Sun. 11am-7pm; 80AS, students and seniors 40AS).

Practical Information, Accommodations, and Food Linz is a transportation hub for both Austria and Eastern Europe. Frequent **trains** (tel. (0732) 17 17) from Bahnhofpl. grind to Vienna (2hr., 264AS), Salzburg (1½hr., 192AS), Innsbruck (3½hr., 516AS), Munich (3hr., 400AS), and Prague (4hr., 265AS). The **tourist office,** Hauptpl. 1 (tel. (0732) 70 70 17 77; fax 77 28 73), in the Altes Rathaus, helps find rooms at no charge. (Open May-Sept. Mon.-Fri. 7am-7pm, Sat. 9am-7pm, Sun. 10am-7pm; Oct.-April Mon.-Fri. 8am-6pm, Sat. 9am-6pm, Sun. 10am-6pm.)

Linz suffers from a lack of cheap rooms; reserve ahead. **Jugendherberge Linz (HI),** Kapuzinerstr. 14 (tel. (0732) 78 27 20 or 77 87 77), near Hauptpl., offers the cheapest beds in town at an excellent location. From the train station, take tram 3 to "Taubenmarkt" then cross Landstr., walk down Promenade, continue on Klammstr., and turn left on Kapuzinerstr. (reception open 8-10am and 5-8pm; 150AS, nonmembers 190AS). Another hostel, the **Jugendgästehaus (HI),** awaits at Stanglhofweg 3 (tel. (0732) 66 44 34). From Blumauerpl., near the train station, take bus 27 ("Schiffswerft") to "Froschberg." Walk straight on Ziegeleistr. and turn right on Roseggerstr. (Reception open daily 8am-4pm and 6-11pm. Singles 303AS; doubles 406AS. Guest tax 8AS. Breakfast included.) **Goldenes Dachl,** Hafnerstr. 27 (tel. (0732) 67 54 80), has comfortable, large rooms. From the train station, take bus 21 to "Auerspergpl." Continue in the same direction along Herrenstr., then turn left onto Wurmstr., then right (singles 260AS, doubles 460-90AS). **Camping Pleschinger See** (tel. (0732) 24 78 70) is on the Linz-Vienna biking path on Pleschinger Lake (45AS per person, 45AS per tent; open May-late Sept). **Mangolds,** Hauptpl. 3., is a Vegetarian Valhalla (entrees 43-68AS; open Mon.-Fri. 11am-8pm, Sat. 11am-5pm). Sail bravely into the **Bermuda Dreieck** (Bermuda Triangle), behind the west side of Hauptpl, for Linzer nightlife.

Graz

Since Charlemagne claimed this strategic crossroads, Graz has witnessed over a thousand years of hostility. The ruins of the fortress perched on the **Schloßberg** withstood battering by the Ottoman Turks, Napoleon's armies (three times), and the Soviet Union. Today Austria's second-largest city provides respite from the throngs of more touristy locales. The central *Altstadt* packs dozens of classical arches and domes into a twisting maze of cobblestone streets, while the stark modern buildings of Technical University a few blocks away demonstrate the influence of Graz's famous School of Architecture. A sight in itself, the tourist office is situated in the **Landhaus,** remodeled in 1557 in masterful Lombard style. Nearby, you'll find the **Landeszeughaus** (Provincial Arsenal), Herrengasse 16, the world's largest armory with 30,000 harnesses and weapons dating from the late Middle Ages to the early 19th century (open April-Oct. Mon.-Fri. 9am-5pm, Sat.-Sun. 9am-1pm; 25AS, students free). Dominating the inner city of Graz is the towering **Schloßberg** (castle hill), the one-time site of a medieval fortress razed by Napoleon. Only the 16th-century **bell tower** and the 13th-century **clock tower** remain. Graz's remarkable **Opernhaus** (opera house), at Opernring and Burggasse (tel. (0316) 80 08), sells standing-room tickets at the door an hour before curtain call (tickets 490-1750AS; standing-room from 100AS, student rush from 150AS). Regular tickets are available at the **Theaterkasse,** Kaiser-Josef-Pl. 10 (tel. (0316) 80 00; open Mon.-Fri. 8am-6:30pm, Sat. 8am-1pm).

The **Hauptbahnhof,** Europapl. (info tel. (0316) 17 17), lies on the other side of the river, a short ride from Hauptpl. on tram 1, 3, or 6. **Trains** chug to Salzburg (4¼hr., 396AS), Innsbruck (6hr., 540AS), Vienna (2½hr., 296AS), and Munich (6hr., 690AS). The **Graz-Köflach Bus** (GKB; tel. (0316) 59 87) departs from Griespl. for West Styria. For the remainder of Austria, the **BundesBus** departs from Europapl. 6 (next to the train station) or, more often, from Andreas-Hofer-Pl. The **tourist office,** Herrengasse 16 (tel. (0316) 807 50; fax 807 55 55), books rooms (30AS) and gives away a map. (Open in summer Mon.-Fri. 9am-7pm, Sat. 9am-6pm, Sun. 10am-3pm; off-season Mon.-Sat. 9am-6pm, Sun. 10am-3pm.) There is a branch office (tel. (0316) 91 68 37) at the main train station (open Mon.-Sat. 9am-6pm, Sun. 10am-3pm).

Sniffing out a cheap bed in Graz may require detective work. Ask the tourist office about *Privatzimmer* (most 150-300AS). **Jugendgästehaus Graz (HI),** Idlhofgasse 74 (tel. (0316) 914 876; fax 914 87 688), is 15 minutes from the train station. (Dorms 135AS; doubles 400AS; quads 540AS. First night 20AS extra. Nonmembers add 40AS. Breakfast included. **Internet access** 15AS for 15min.) **Hotel Strasser,** Eggenberger Gürtel 11 (tel. (0316) 91 39 77; fax 91 68 56), five minutes from the train station, has large rooms. Exit the station, cross the street, and head right on Bahnhofgürtel. (Singles 340-440AS; doubles 560-660AS; triples 840AS; quads 1000AS. Breakfast included.) For **Hotel Zur Stadt Feldbach,** Conrad-von-Hötzendorf-Str. 58 (tel. (0316) 82 94 68; fax 84 73 71), take tram 4 ("Liebnau") or 5 ("Puntigam") to "Jakominigürtel." (Reception open 24hr. on the 2nd floor. Singles 350AS; doubles 500-650AS; triples 750AS.) **Internet Café,** Andreas-Hoger-Pl. 9, has 'net access (40AS for 30min.). **University Mensa,** Sonnenfelspl. 1, just east of the Stadtpark at the intersection of Zinzendorfgasse and Leechgasse, provides the best deal (*menus* 47-51AS; open Mon.-Fri. 11am-2:30pm). **Gastwirtschaft Wartburgasse,** Halbärthgasse 4, serves up tasty food (lunch specials 50-60AS; open Mon.-Thurs. 9am-1am, Fri. 9am-4am, Sat. 6pm-1am). After-hours activity is found in the **Bermuda Triangle,** an area of the old city behind Hauptpl. and bordered by Mehlpl., Färbergasse, and Prokopiagasse.

Belarus (Беларусь)

US$1	**= 27,500BR (Belarusian rubles)**	**10,000BR =**	**US$0.36**
CDN$1	**= 20,430BR**	**10,000BR =**	**CDN$0.49**
UK£1	**= 43,170BR**	**10,000BR =**	**UK£0.23**
IR£1	**= 44,800BR**	**10,000BR =**	**IR£0.23**
AUS$1	**= 20,480BR**	**10,000BR =**	**AUS$0.49**
NZ$1	**= 18,220BR**	**10,000BR =**	**NZ$0.55**
SAR1	**= 7600BR**	**10,000BR =**	**SAR1.32**

Country Code: 375 **International Dialing Prefix: 810**

Inflation is rampant in Belarus, so prices are likely to be significantly higher than those listed here. Prices listed in U.S. dollars are more likely to be stable.

The fall of the USSR left Belarus directionless and lacking a national identity. While other republics were toppling their statues of Lenin, Belarusians polished theirs. Soviet bureaucracy persists needlessly: businesses lack effective management and services; border and travel regulations discourage tourism and restrict natives; and taxes and prohibitive legislation make living devastatingly difficult. Belarus's president, Aleksandr Lukashenka, has become Europe's most ruthless totalitarian ruler, and the Chernobyl accident affected Belarus even more than the Ukraine (although it poses no risk to tourists). But there are reasons besides the train routes to Russia to put Belarus on your itinerary: Minsk is developing a reputation as a trendy city, the Belarusian countryside is lovely, and visiting the country is as close to getting a peek behind the Iron Curtain as you can find in post-1989 Europe.

Lift the Belarusian curtain of your mind with *Let's Go: Eastern Europe 1998.*

BELARUS

ESSENTIALS

Belarus is very useful as a transportation link to Russia (see the Russia country map for a map of Belarus). If you're just passing through, **transit visas** (US$20-30; valid for 48hr.) are issued at consulates and at the border. For longer visits, you must secure an invitation and a visa—an expensive and head-spinning process. If an acquaintance in Belarus can procure you an invitation, you can get a single-entry (5-day service US$50, next-day US$100) or a multiple-entry (US$300) visa at an embassy or consulate (see **Government Information Offices,** p. 1). If you use **Host Families Association, HOFA,** 5-25 Tavricheskaya, 193015 St. Petersburg, Russia (tel./fax 812 275 1992; email hofa@usa.net), to find housing, they will provide invitations (homestays US$30-50). You may also obtain an invitation from a **Belintourist** office, which will give you documentation after you pre-pay all your hotel nights.

Be sure to carry a supply of hard **cash;** U.S. dollars, Deutschmarks, and Russian rubles are the preferred mediums of exchange; you will have a great deal of trouble with any other currency, even British pounds. There are one or two ATM machines in Minsk and some hotels do take **credit cards,** but traveler's checks are rarely accepted. Local **phone calls** must be paid for with tokens, Belarusian rubles, or cards available at the post office. Long-distance phone calls usually must be made at a telephone office or from a hotel. To reach the **BT Direct** operator, dial 8 800 44. For **AT&T Direct,** dial 8 800 101. For **MCI WorldPhone,** dial 8 800 103 from Minsk, Hrodna, Brest, and Vitebsk, or 8 10 80 01 03 from Gomel and Mogilev. Belarusians speak primarily Russian, but Polish is also fairly common in Hrodna and Brest. There are no hostels in Belarus, and many **hotels** charge a much higher rate for foreigners. If you do stay at a hotel, keep all the slips of paper you receive to avoid paying fines on your way out of the country. **Private rooms,** often US$10 or less, are worth a shot. The after-effects of **Chernobyl** are unlikely to harm short-term visitors, but it is wise to avoid all but imported dairy products and to drink bottled water.

Minsk Мінск

If you're looking for the supreme Soviet city, skip Moscow and head to Minsk, where the fall of Communism has meant only a reluctant shuffle toward the West. Lenin's statue stands in pl. Nezalezhnastsi (Незалежнасці), and monuments to Felix Dzerzhinski, the Belarusian founder of the KGB, line avenues bearing his name. Flattened in World War I, the city was redesigned as a showpiece of Soviet style, with wide avenues and stereotypical Stalinist architecture.

On **pl. Nezalezhnastsi,** one block north of the train station, the grandiose giant at the far west end of the square was the headquarters of the KGB. On pl. Svobody (Свободы), east of the "Nyamiha" Metro stop, stands the dazzling and recently restored **Svetadukha Kafedralny Sobor** (Светадуха Кафедралный Собор; Cathedral of the Holy Spirit), vul. Mefodiya 3. Built in 1642 as a Bernardine monastery, the building later burned down, and was rebuilt by the Russian Orthodox Church. Just west, about 200m down vul. Nyamiha, stands the yellow **Petropavilsky Sobor** (Петропавилский Собор; Cathedral of St. Peter and St. Paul), vul. Rakovskaya 4 (Раковская; tel. 26 74 75), the oldest church in Minsk, built in 1612.

Minsk's reconstructed **Old Town,** east of vul. Nyamiha on the north bank of the Svisloch, is a nice area for a mid-afternoon stroll through souvenir shops and beer gardens. A **Jewish memorial stone** stands on vul. Zaslavskaya (Заславская), behind Gastinitsa Yubileynaya, to commemorate the more than 5000 Jews who were shot and buried on this spot by the Nazis in 1941. The **Muzey Velikoy Otechestvennoy Voyny** (Музей Великой Отечественной Войны; Museum of the Great Patriotic War; tel. (0172) 26 15 44), pr. F. Skaryny 25a, explores World War II in Belarus, which lost 20% of its population (open Tues.-Sun. 10am-6pm; 9000BR; call for a tour in English, 60,000BR). The **National History and Culture Museum,** vul. K. Marxa 12 (К. Маркса), explores the history of everything Belarusian (open Thurs.-Tues. 11am-7pm; 7000BR). Soviet Minsk is completed by the city's parks; wander up pr. F. Skaryny to **Park Gorkoho** (Парк Горкого) and **Yanka Kupala Park** (Янка Купала Парк).

BELARUS

Practical Information, Accommodations, and Food Buy **train** tickets to destinations outside Belarus at the **Advance-Booking Office,** vul. Chkalova 9 (tel. (0172) 296 30 67; open Mon.-Sat. 9am-1pm and 2-6pm). Trains run to Moscow (10-14hr., 650,000BR), Vilnius (4½hr., 200,000BR), and Warsaw (12hr., US$30). There are two Minsk bus stations. **Avtovakzal Tsentralny** (Автовакзал Центральный; tel. (0172) 227 78 20, to Western Europe 227 04 73), east of the train station at vul. Babruskaya 12 (Бабруйская), serves Vilnius (4hr., 77,000BR), Warsaw (11hr., 245,000BR), and western cities. Take trolleybus 20 from vul. Kirava (Кирава), near Avtovakzal Tsentralny, to "Автовакзал Восточний" (**Avtovakzal Vostochny;** tel. (0172) 248 08 81), at vul. Vaneyeva 34 (Ванэева), for buses within Belarus. The **Belintourist** (Белінтурист) office is at pr. Masherava 19 (tel. (0172) 226 98 40), next to Gastsinitsa Yubileyni (metro: Nyamiha; open Mon.-Fri. 9am-6pm). The **Belarusian Society for Friendship and Cultural Relations with Foreign Countries,** vul. Zakharava 28 (Захарава; tel. (0172) 233 15 02), is effusively helpful (open Mon.-Fri. 9am-6pm).

Hotels are universally expensive: pick up *Minsk in Your Pocket* (US$1) for a fighting chance at a decent room. **Gastsinitsa Svisloch** (Гасцініца Свислочь),vul. Kirava 13 (Кірава; tel. (0172) 20 97 83), has singles for 370,000BR and doubles for 680,000-860,000BR, but may not have hot water. **Gastsinitsa Minsk** (Гасцініца Мінск), pr. F. Skaryny 11 (tel. (0172) 20 01 32), in the center of town, offers renovated singles for US$41 and doubles for US$60 (breakfast included). Private rooms run about US$10. **Restaran Uzbekistan** (Рэстаран Узбекистан), vul. Y. Kupaly 17, serves up Uzbek dishes in a tiny co-op restaurant. *Plov po uzbeski* (плов по узбески) is a rice dish with lamb (78,200BR; open daily 8am-11am, noon-4:30pm, and 6pm-midnight). Minsk's world-renowned **Opera and Ballet Theater,** vul. E. Pashkevich 23 (Пашкевич; tel. (0172) 233 17 90), showcases one of the best ballets in the former USSR. Tickets (10,000-150,000BR) can be purchased from the **Central Ticket Office,** pr. F. Skaryny 13 (tel. (0172) 20 25 70; open Mon.-Sat. 9am-8pm, Sun. 11am-5pm).

Hrodna and Brest Гродна и Брэст

Hrodna A city where the towers to God overpower the towers to Stalin, Hrodna (pronounced *grodna* in Russian) is a rarity in Belarus. World War II was brief here. Among the many churches is the pale-white 16th-century **Barnardinski Kostyol** (Барнардінскі костёл; Bernadine church) on vul. Krupskay (Крупскай), whose bright interior holds frescoes of Jesus and angels. But Hrodna's greatest sights are its two castles, reached by heading up vul. Zamkava (Замкава). The **Stary Zamak** (Стары замак, old castle), on the right, was built in the 1570s on the ruins of a 15th-century castle used by Lithuanian Grand Duke Vytautus. Inside, a museum recalls its history (open Mon.-Sat. 9am-6pm; *kassa* closes 5pm; 15,000BR; tours 60,000BR). On the opposite side of the hill, **Novy Zamak** (Новы замак, New Castle), destroyed in World War II and rebuilt in 1951, houses a worthwhile **History and Archeology Museum,** where exhibits are devoted to the Hrodna's history from its first written mention in 1128 (open Mon.-Sat. 10am-6pm; *kassa* closes 5pm; 10,000BR; tours 60,000BR).

The **train station,** vul. Budonova (Будонова; tel. (0152) 44 85 56), lies 2km northeast of the city center at the end of vul. Azheshka (Ажэшка). Trains run to Minsk (6-9hr., 75,000-100,000BR), Vilnius (175,000BR), and Warsaw (1 per day, 5½hr., US$10). The **bus station** (автовокзал; *avtovokzal*), vul. Krasnoarmeyskaya 7a (Красноармейская; tel. (0152) 72 37 24), sits 1.5km south of the train station. Bus 15 connects the stations (2000BR). **Buses** run to Minsk (5½hr., 135,000BR), Brest (7½hr., 135,000BR), and Warsaw (6hr., 185,000BR). The **tourist office,** vul. Azheshka 49, 2nd floor (tel. (0152) 72 17 79), offers assistance in Russian, finds rooms, and arranges city tours with prior notice (open Mon.-Fri. 8:30am-5pm, Sat. 8-11am). Take bus 3 or 14 from the train station to **Gastinitsa Neman** (Гасцініца Неман), vul. Stefana Batorya 8 (Стэфана Баторыя; tel. (0152) 72 19 36), for simple rooms with TVs (singles 255,000BR, doubles 400,000BR; bring your own toilet paper). **Gastinitsa Belarus** (Беларусь), vul. Kalinovskovo 1 (Каліновского; tel. (0152) 44 16 74), has cozy singles (310,000BR) and doubles (525,000BR) with toilet and shower (MC, V). Take bus 15 from the train station and get off at "Kinoteatr Kosmos" (Кінотеатр Космос), the fifth stop. Next door to the hotel, the **Restaurant Belarus** sells *cheburiki* (чебурики, beef fried in a flaky shell, 8000BR) and other cuisine (open noon-5pm and 6pm-1am).

Brest Traded to the Germans in the 1918 Treaty of Brest-Litovsk, Polish between the wars, and Russian again after 1939, Brest today is a hectic border town that sees legions of traders crossing back and forth across the Polish-Belarusian border. The massive brick walls, moats, and encasements of **Krepasts Brest-Litoisk** (Крэпасць Брэст-Літоўск; Brest Fortress) withstood a six-week German siege during World War II. Patriotic Red Army songs and the sounds of gunfire emanate eerily from openings above your head at the **Galoiny Ivakhod** (Галоўны ўваход; Principal Entrance), at the end of vul. Maskaiskaya. To the right lies **Uskhodni Fort** (Усходні Форт; Eastern Fort), a football-field-sized complex where isolated Russians held their ground for three weeks. To the north, **Painochnaya Brama** (Паўночная Брама; Northern Gate) is the only gate still fully intact. To gain a sense of the fortress's former magnitude, remember that the whole place used to look like this. Around the base of the soldier-in-the-boulder monolith to the right of the main gate are **memorials** to the defenders and an eternal flame dedicated to all 13 of the Soviet Union's "Hero Cities."

The English-speaking **Belintourist** office, vul. Maskaiskaya 15 (Маскаўская; tel. (0162) 25 10 71), in Gastsinitsa Intourist, has maps and brochures (open Mon.-Fri. 8am-6pm). The **train station,** north of vul. Ardzhanikidze (Арджанікідзе; tel. (0162) 005), connects to Prague (18hr., US$45), Warsaw (US$15), and Minsk (7hr., 80,0000BR). The **bus station** (tel. (0162) 225 51 36), at the corner of vul. Kuybysheva (Куйбышева) and vul. Mitskevicha (Міцкевіча), serves Hrodna (7½hr., 134,500BR) and Warsaw (6hr., 185,000BR). **Gastsinitsa Instituta** (Гасцініца Института), vul. Pushkinskaya 16/1 (tel. (0162) 23 93 72), is a budget oasis (singles 120,000-170,000BR, doubles 240,000-340,000BR). **Restaurant India** (Рестаран Індіа), vul. Gogolya 29 (Гоголя), is said to be the best Indian restaurant west of Delhi (open daily noon-11pm).

BELARUS

Belgium (Belgique, België)

US$1 = 37.21BF (Belgian francs)
CDN$1 = 26.94BF
UK£1 = 59.15BF
IR£1 = 55.26BF
AUS$1 = 27.16BF
NZ$1 = 23.65BF
SAR1 = 7.94BF
Country Code: 32

10BF = US$0.27
10BF = CDN$0.37
10BF = UK£0.17
10BF = IR£0.18
10BF = AUS$0.37
10BF = NZ$0.42
10BF = SAR 1.26
International Dialing Prefix: 00

As you enter Belgium by train from the south or east, you may wonder if urban development will ever interrupt the countless miles of rolling countryside, rows of trees, and occasional small farmhouses. Suddenly, however, the swift blur of gold and green is replaced by grey, red, and brown brick. Major centers such as Antwerp bustle and thrive, and the cultural treasure troves of Bruges and Ghent await discovery. The capital city Brussels, home to NATO and the European Union, buzzes with leaders who quietly make the decisions you'll read about in tomorrow's paper. If you don't get off the train, though, the urban hustle will just as quickly vanish into the wide expanse of colorful Belgian countryside.

The first stop on the military tours of many would-be European conquerors, Belgium bears the scars of a troubled European history. Today division persists between Flemish-speaking nationalists of the northern province of Flanders and French-speaking Walloons. But some things transcend political tensions; from the Ardennes forests and the white sands of the North Sea coast to the cobblestoned medieval passageways, Belgium's beauty is even richer than its chocolate.

GETTING THERE AND GETTING AROUND

Belgium's **train network** is one of the most reliable in Europe. Prices are low, and the country is at most four hours across by rail. **Eurail** is valid on intercity buses as well as trains. The **Benelux Tourrail Pass** is a decent option, covering five days of travel in Belgium, the Netherlands, and Luxembourg during a one-month period (3100BF, over 26 4220BF). A five-day pass for travel in Belgium costs 2060BF. The best deal may be the **Go Pass,** which allows 10 trips within Belgium for 1390BF. A **Half-Fare Card** (590BF for one month) is also available, and tourist offices sell a **24-hour pass** covering all municipal transport in the country (230BF).

Biking is very popular, and many roads are equipped with bike lanes (which you must use even if they're studded with potholes). When you see two paths next to the street, the one by the street is for bicycles and mopeds, the one by the storefront is for pedestrians. You can rent bikes at 31 of Belgium's train stations. Inquire at stations about train and bike **passes,** and pick up the brochure *Train et Vélo/Trein en Fiets.* **Hitchhiking** is losing popularity in Belgium and is not recommended as a safe means of transport, but hitchers still report a fair amount of success in some areas. Bilingual signs ("please" is *s.v.p.* in French, *a.u.b.* in Flemish) are abundant. **Taxi Stop** (tel. (02) 223 23 10) has offices in major cities and matches travelers with Belgian drivers for destinations all over Europe (1.3BF per km, 200-800BF per trip). **Ferries** from Zeebrugge and Oostende, near Bruges, cross to Dover and other British ports.

ESSENTIALS

Belgium's network of tourist offices is supplemented by **Infor-Jeunes/Info-Jeugd,** a service which helps young people secure accommodations. The English-language *Bulletin* (85BF at newsstands) lists everything from movies to job opportunities.

Most pay **phones** require a 200BF phone card, available at **PTT** (post, telephone, and telegraph) offices and magazine stands; the rarer coin-operated phones are more expensive. Calls are cheapest from 8pm to 8am and on weekends. For operator assistance within Belgium-Netherlands-Luxembourg, dial 13 07; for international assistance, 13 04 (10BF). To reach an **AT&T Direct** operator, dial 0800 100 10; **MCI WorldPhone,** 0800 100 12; **Sprint Access,** 0800 100 14; **Canada Direct,** 0800 100 19; **BT Direct,** 0800 100 44; **Ireland Direct,** 0800 103 53; **Australia Direct,** 078 11 00 61; **New Zealand Direct,** 0800 100 64; **South Africa Direct,** 0800 100 27.

Public holidays in Belgium are Jan. 1 (New Year's Day), April 12-13 (Easter), May 5 (Labour Day), May 21 (Feast of the Ascension), June 1 (Whit Monday), July 11 (Flemish Community Day), July 21 (National Day), August 15 (Feast of the Assumption), September 27 (French Community Day), Nov. 1 (All Saints Day), Nov. 11 (Armistice Day), and Dec. 25 (Christmas).

Accommodations, Camping, Food, and Drink **Hotels** in Belgium are fairly expensive, with "trench-bottom" prices for singles starting at 800BF and doubles at 1000-1100BF. Avoid bankruptcy by staying in one of the 31 **HI hostels,** which charge about 335BF per night. They are generally modern and often boast extremely cheap bars. Pick up *Budget Holidays* or the free *Camping* at any tourist office for complete listings of hostels and campsites. **Campgrounds** charge about 130BF per night. Many visitors make the mistake of staying in Brussels and day-tripping to neighboring cities; try using the nearby Bruges, Ghent, or Antwerp as a base instead. Private hostels in Bruges are fun and lively, and the city is a welcoming refuge at night.

Belgian cuisine can be wonderful, but a native dish may cost as much as a night in a decent hotel. Steamed mussels (*moules*) are usually tasty and reasonably affordable (a whole pot for around 430BF). Other specialities include *lapin* (rabbit) and *canard* (duck). Belgian beer is both a national pride and a national pastime; more varieties (over 500, ranging from the ordinary Jupiler to the religiously brewed Chimay) are produced here than in any other country. Regular or quirky blonde goes for as little as 30BF, and dark beers cost about 60-90BF. Leave room in the wallet and belly for Belgian *gaufres* (waffles) and famous Godiva chocolates.

Brussels (Bruxelles, Brussel)

Instantly associated with NATO and the European Union, Brussels is more than just a political and economic capital. In the Grand-Place, center of the old city, you'll find the essence of Belgium, from waffles and beer to the *Mannekin Pis*. Where Antwerp claims Rubens, Brussels's cultural icon is no less than Hergé's androgynous comic strip creations Tintin and his dog Snowy, who peer at you from city shop windows. Architect Victor Horta was the innovator of and inspiration for many of Brussels's most fascinating interiors and exteriors, but Brussels' more recent architects have mingled garish glass and concrete behind gothic spires. Still Brussels has carefully preserved its Old Town, to the delight of travelers who flock to its narrow streets.

ORIENTATION AND PRACTICAL INFORMATION

Brussels's trinity of train stations consists of **Brussels Midi** (serving the south part of the city), **Brussels Central** (gateway to the Grand-Place), and **Brussels Nord** (near the Botanical Gardens). Most of Brussels's major attractions are clustered around these stations, near the **Bourse** (Stock Market) to the west and the **Parc de Bruxelles** to the east. Travel within the center of the city is easy, but trekking from the north end to the south is quite a hike. A 200BF **tourist passport** secures one day's public transportation, a map, a slew of reductions on museum admissions, and other bonuses (available at the TIB and almost every bookshop). If you're on an extended visit, you may want to attack the city by area. Be aware that public transportation stops completely at midnight. Walking from a disco in the south back to Gare du Nord is not a good idea. Although Brussels is a bilingual city, some maps may only be in Flemish. *Let's Go* uses French as it is usually more familiar to travelers.

Tourist Offices: National, 63, rue du Marché aux Herbes (tel. 504 03 90; fax 504 02 70). From Grand-Place walk 1 block from Town Hall. Books rooms all over Belgium and has the free *What's On* brochures. Open June-Sept. daily 9am-7pm; April, May, and Oct. 9am-6pm; Nov.-March Mon.-Sat. 9am 6pm, Sun. 1-5pm. **TIB (Tourist Information Brussels),** in the Town Hall (tel. 513 89 40), charges at least 35BF for reservations. Sells tourist passport and has *Brussels Guide and Map* (100BF). Info on the 350BF guided walks. Theater, opera, and ballet tickets sold Mon.-Sat. 11am-5pm. Open April-Sept. daily 9am-6pm; Oct.-March 10am-2pm.

Budget Travel: Acotra World, 51, rue de la Madeleine (tel. 512 55 40). Free room-finding service. Also finds flights for those under 26. Open Mon.-Sat. 10am-5:30pm. **Infor-Jeunes,** 27, rue du Marché-aux-Herbes. Budget bonanza. Open Mon.-Fri. noon-5:30pm. Also at Gare du Midi (tel. 522 58 56; March-Oct.).

Embassies: Australia, 6, rue Guimard (tel. 231 05 16). **Canada,** 2, av. Tervueren (tel. 741 06 11). **New Zealand,** 47, bd. du Régent (tel. 512 10 40). **South Africa,** 26 rue de la Loi (tel. 230 68 45). Generally open weekdays between 9am and 5pm. **U.K.,** 85, rue Arlon (tel. 287 62 11). **U.S.,** 27, bd. du Régent (tel. 513 38 30); **consulate,** 25 bd. du Régent (tel. 513 38 30) for lost passport help (open 9am-noon).

Currency Exchange: At **Gare du Nord** (150BF commission; open daily 8am-8pm), **Gare Centrale** (no commission but mediocre rates; open daily 7am-9pm), and **Gare du Midi** (30BF commission; open daily 6:45am-10:30pm). Most banks and change booths charge 100-150BF to cash checks, but banks have better rates.

BELGIUM

American Express: 2, pl. Louise (tel. 676 27 27). M: Louise. Decent exchange rates. Mail held for 30 days. 50BF mail retrieval if you don't have an AmEx card or checks. Wires money for a significant charge. Open Mon.-Fri. 9am-5pm, Sat. 9:30am-noon.

Flights: (tel. 722 31 11, info 723 60 10). Trains to **Brussels International Airport** (25min., 90BF) leave Gare Centrale 5:39am-11:14pm; all stop at Gare du Nord.

Trains: For info, call 555 25 55. Most stop at **Gare Centrale** and many also stop at either **Gare du Nord** or **Gare du Midi.** Traffic to **Gare du Quartier Leopold** generally passes through one of the main stations. To: Amsterdam (3hr., 920BF), Bruges (45-60min., 370BF), Antwerp (30min., 190BF), and Paris (2hr., 900BF). **Eurostar** goes directly from London to Brussels (3¼hr., from US$75 one way).

Buses: STIB (Société des Transports Intercommunaux Bruxellois). Offices in Gare du Midi (open Mon.-Fri. 7:30am-5pm, Sat. 8:30am-4:30pm), and at 20, Galeries de la Toison d'Or, 6th fl. (tel. 515 30 64). **L'Épervier,** 50, pl. de Brouckère (tel. 217 00 25). M: Brouckère. Eurobus representative. Open Mon.-Fri. 9am-6pm, Sat. 9am-noon and 1:30-4pm.

Public Transportation: 50BF buys 1hr. of travel on buses, the **Métro (M),** and trams. Day pass 130BF. 10-trip pass 320BF. Buy tickets at any Métro or train station, or on the bus. Public transportation runs daily 6am-midnight.

Hitchhiking: Hitchhiking is illegal on motorways and sliproads. To Antwerp or Amsterdam, hitchers reportedly take tram 52 or 92 from Gare du Midi or Gare du Nord to Heysel. To Ghent, Bruges, and Oostende, they take bus 85 from the Bourse to one stop before the terminus and follow E40 signs. To Paris, hitchers take tram 52, 55, or 91 to rue de Stalle and walk toward the E19.

Luggage Storage: Lockers and offices at the three major train stations. Bag check 60BF, lockers 80BF, oversize lockers 100BF.

Gay Services: tel. 733 10 24. Lists local events. Staffed daily 9am-9pm. *The Gay Guide to Belgium,* available at the tourist office (350BF) lists gay establishments.

Laundromat: Salon Lavoir, 5, rue Haute, around the corner from Bruegel's youth hostel. M: Gare Centrale. Wash and dry 240BF. Open Mon.-Fri. 8am-6pm.

Crisis Hotline: SOS-Jeunes, 27, rue Mercellis (tel. 512 90 20). For concerns about rape, drug use, and emotional trauma. Staffed 24hr. by English speaking operators.

Pharmacies: Pharma-Congrès, 56, rue du Congrès, at rue du Nord, near the Jacques Brel hostel. M: Gare Centrale. Open Mon.-Fri. 8:30am-1pm and 1:30-5:30pm. **Neos-Bourse Pharmacie** (tel. 218 06 40), bd. Anspach at rue du Marché-aux-Polets. M: Bourse. Open Mon.-Fri. 8:30am-6:30pm, Sat. 9am-6:30pm.

Medical Assistance: Free Clinic, 154a, chaussée de Wavre (tel. 512 13 14). Don't be misled by the name; you do have to pay for medical attention. Open Mon.-Fri. 9am-6pm. **24hr. medical services:** tel. 479 18 18 or 648 80 00.

Emergencies: Ambulance or **First Aid:** tel. 112.

Police: tel. 101.

Internet Access: Cyber Bar de l'Amour Fou, 185 ch. d'Ixelles, and **1101 Cybercafé,** 1101 ch. de Wavre, offer Internet and email access (150BF per 30min.).

Post Office: M: de Brouckère. **Main office** on the 2nd floor of the Centre Monnaie, the tall building on pl. de la Monnaie. Open Mon.-Fri. 9am-5pm, Sat. 9am-noon. **Postal Code:** 1000 Bruxelles.

Telephones: 17, bd. de l'Impératrice, near Gare Centrale. Rates superior to those of privately owned competitors. Open daily 8am-10pm. Privately owned **Public Phone,** 30a, rue de Lombard, has higher rates but a more pleasant atmosphere. Open daily 10am-10pm. For operator assistance, dial 1280. **Telephone Code:** 02.

ACCOMMODATIONS AND CAMPING

Accommodations in Brussels are fairly easy to come by. In general hotels and hostels are very well kept; any that you choose will provide a good springboard to the city.

Centre Vioncent Van Gogh-CHAB, 8, rue Traversière (tel. 217 01 58; fax 219 79 95). M: Botanique; walk toward the Jardin Botanique on rue Royale and turn right. 10min. walk from Gare du Nord; from Gare Centrale, take bus 65 or 66 to rue du Méridien. Colorful, artsy rooms. Internet access. Reception open daily 7am-2am. Dorms 300-440BF. Singles 650BF. Doubles 1040BF. Sheets 100BF. Laundry 200BF.

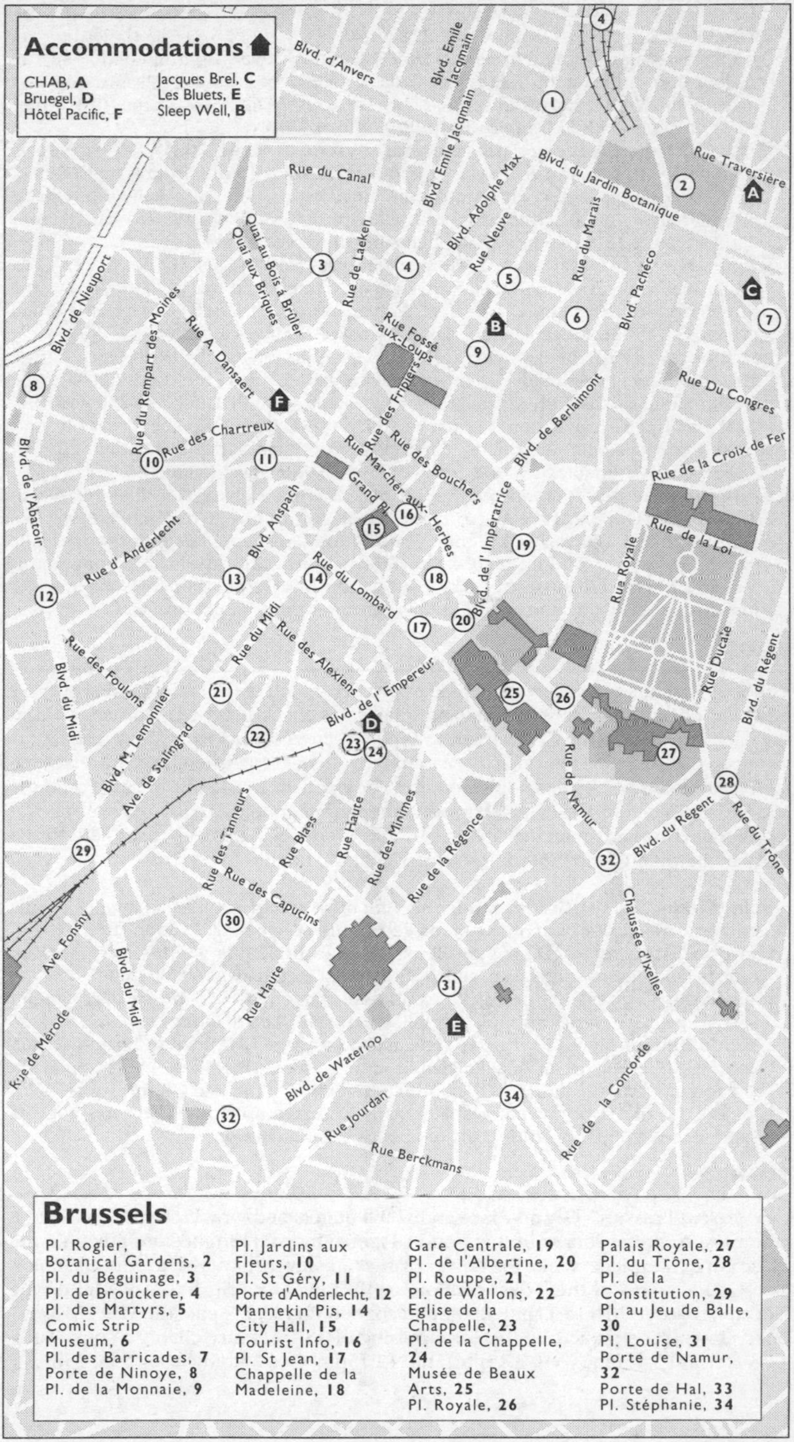
Accommodations
CHAB, A
Bruegel, D
Hôtel Pacific, F
Jacques Brel, C
Les Bluets, E
Sleep Well, B
Blvd. d'Anvers
Blvd. Emile Jacqmain
Rue du Canal
Blvd. Emile Jacqmain
Blvd. Adolphe Max
Blvd. du Jardin Botanique
Rue Traversière
Quai au Bois à Brûler
Quai aux Briques
Rue de Laeken
Rue Neuve
Rue du Marais
Blvd. Pachéco
Blvd. de Nieuport
Rue du Rempart des Moines
Rue A. Dansaert
Rue Fossé -aux-Loups
Rue Du Congres
Blvd. de Berlaimont
Rue des Chartreux
Rue des Fripiers
Rue des Bouchers
Rue Marché aux Herbes
Grand Pl.
Rue de la Croix de Fer
Rue de la Loi
Blvd. de l'Abatoir
Blvd. Anspach
Rue d' Anderlecht
Blvd. de l' Impératrice
Rue Royale
Rue du Lombard
Rue du Midi
Rue des Alexiens
Rue des Foulons
Blvd. du Midi
Blvd. M. Lemonnier
Ave. de Stalingrad
Blvd. de l' Empereur
Rue Ducale
Blvd. du Régent
Rue de Namur
Blvd. du Régent
Rue du Trône
Rue des Tanneurs
Rue Blaes
Rue Haute
Rue des Minimes
Rue de la Régence
Rue des Capucins
Chaussée d'Ixelles
Ave. Fonsny
Blvd. du Midi
Rue Haute
Rue de Mérode
Blvd. de Waterloo
Rue de la Concorde
Rue Jourdan
Rue Berckmans
Brussels
Pl. Rogier, 1
Botanical Gardens, 2
Pl. du Béguinage, 3
Pl. de Brouckere, 4
Pl. des Martyrs, 5
Comic Strip Museum, 6
Pl. des Barricades, 7
Porte de Ninoye, 8
Pl. de la Monnaie, 9
Pl. Jardins aux Fleurs, 10
Pl. St Géry, 11
Porte d'Anderlecht, 12
Mannekin Pis, 14
City Hall, 15
Tourist Info, 16
Pl. St Jean, 17
Chappelle de la Madeleine, 18
Gare Centrale, 19
Pl. de l'Albertine, 20
Pl. Rouppe, 21
Pl. de Wallons, 22
Eglise de la Chappelle, 23
Pl. de la Chappelle, 24
Musée de Beaux Arts, 25
Pl. Royale, 26
Palais Royale, 27
Pl. du Trône, 28
Pl. de la Constitution, 29
Pl. au Jeu de Balle, 30
Pl. Louise, 31
Porte de Namur, 32
Porte de Hal, 33
Pl. Stéphanie, 34

Sleep Well, 23, rue du Daumier (tel. 218 50 50; fax 218 13 13). From Gare Centrale, walk right down bd. de l'Imperatrice, left on Stormstraat, right on Montagne aux Herbes, left onto Rue du Fosse Aux Loupes, then the first right. Clean rooms and private showers. Reception open 24hr. Lockout 10am-2pm. Dorms (July-Aug.) 340BF. Singles 650BF. Doubles 1040BF. Triples 1320BF.

Gîtes d'Etape: Auberge de Jeunesse "Jacques Brel" (HI), 30, rue de la Sablonnière (tel. 218 01 87), on the pl. des Barricades. 15min. from Gare Centrale. M: Botanique. Spacious, colorful rooms. Reception open daily 8am-7pm. Dorms 395BF. Singles 660BF. Doubles 1080BF. Triples 1350BF. Quads 1800BF. Dinner 270BF. Sheets 120BF. Wheelchair accessible. Reserve ahead.

Jeugdherberg Bruegel (HI), 2, Heilige Geeststr. (tel. 511 04 36; fax 512 07 11). From the back exit of Central Station, right on Cantersteen/bd. de l'Empereur, then the second left after Pl. de la Justice. Well-maintained, friendly, and quiet. 3-8 bed dorms 395-450BF. Singles 660BF. Doubles 1080BF. Sheets 125BF.

Les Bluets, 124 rue Beckermans (tel./fax 534 39 38). Near the posh Place Louise area, this hotel is a paradise—complete with gardens and chirping birds—for the weary. Large rooms with sitting areas. Singles 900-1350BF. Doubles 1250-2450BF.

Hôtel Pacific, 57, rue Antoine Dansaert (tel. 511 84 59). M: Bourse; cross bd. Anspach. Excellent location, friendly, English-speaking staff. Flexible midnight curfew. Singles 950BF. Doubles 1500BF. Showers 100BF. Breakfast included.

Camping: The best site is **Paul Rosmant,** 52 Warandeberg (tel. 782 10 09), in Wezembeck-Oppem. Take metro 1B to "Kraainem" or bus 30 to "Sint-Petersplein." Sun. take metro 1B to Stockel then tram 39 to Marcelisstr. Reception open daily 9am-12:30pm and 2-10pm. 250BF per person. North of Brussels in Grimbergen is **Veldkant,** 64 Veldkantstr. (tel. 269 25 97). Take bus G from Gare du Nord then follow signs. 125BF per person, 125BF per tent. Both sites open April-Oct.

BELGIUM

FOOD

Although restaurants in Brussels can be expensive, much of the street food costs very little. For cheap cafeteria style food and small cafés check out the arcade across from the back entrance to the Central Station (open Mon.-Sat. 6am-5pm). Many restaurants are near the Grand-Place. Visit the **rue des Bouchers,** just north of the Place, to admire the piles of exotic shellfish on ice. The open air **market** at pl. Ste-Catherine (open daily 7am-5pm) offers fresh produce and other goodies. Load up on supplies at a **GB supermarket;** branches are at 248, rue Vierge Noire (M: Bourse), and in the "City 2" shopping center, 50m from Sleep Well (M: Rogier).

Sole d'Italia, 67, rue Grétry. A huge serving of spaghetti with bread is only 195BF, and other specialties are only a bit more expensive. Open daily noon-late.

Dandon Biscuiterie, 31, rue au Beurre, serves delicious waffles, scrumptious crepes, and yummy pancakes, all for 75-210BF. Open daily 8:30am-7pm.

Maison des Crepes, 42, rue des Pierres. Popular among locals, this small restaurant serves specialty crepes starting at 80BF. Open daily 9am-6:30pm.

L'Ecole Buissonnière, 13, rue de Traversière, opposite CHAB youth hostel. M: Botanique. Affordable traditional Belgian food (most meals 165-345BF). Ask to dine on the terrace or in the garden. Open Mon.-Fri. noon-2:30pm and 6-8pm.

L'orfeo, 12, rue Haute. Comfortable restaurant serves up fresh salads and hot pita sandwiches from 160-240BF. Lots of good vegetarian options.

SIGHTS

One look at Brussels's **Grand-Place** and you'll understand why Victor Hugo called it "the most beautiful square in the world." Framed by gold-trimmed architecture, the Place is a masterpiece, while the flower market and feverish tourist activity add color. The Gothic spires of the **Town Hall** pierce the sky. From April to Aug and during December around 10 to 11pm, 800 multi-colored floodlights give the Hall a psychedelic glow accompanied by the eerie pulsing of 15th-century chants. (Tours Tues. 11:30am and 3:15pm, Wed. 3:15pm, Sun. 12:15pm; Oct.-March closed Sun. 75BF.)

Three blocks behind the Town Hall on rue de l'Etuve at rue du Chêne is Brussels' most giggled-at sight, the **Mannekin-Pis,** a statue of an impudent boy (with an apparently gargantuan bladder) steadily urinating. One story goes that a 17th-century mayor promised to build a statue in the position that his lost son was found; another says it commemorates a boy who (à la Gulliver) ingeniously defused a bomb. Locals have created hundreds of outfits for him, each with a little hole for you-know-what.

For more intellectual stimulation, visit the two **Royal Museums of Fine Arts.** The **Musée d'Art Ancien,** 3, rue de la Régence (M: Gare Centrale or Parc), houses a huge collection of the Flemish masters, including Brueghel the Elder's *Fall of Icarus* and *Census in Bethlehem* and Rubens's *Martyrdom of St. Levinius* and *Calvary.* Next door at the **Musée d'Art Moderne,** you'll find everything form the brilliant to the banal—an extensive Magritte collection (in 1998), works by Miró, Picasso, and Dalí, and Andy Warhol's portrait of hockey star Wayne Gretzky (both open Tues.-Sun. 10am-5pm; 150BF, students 100BF). The **Musées Royaux d'Art et d'Histoire,** 10, parc du Cinquantenaire (M: Mérode), cover a wide variety of periods and parts—Roman torsos without heads, Syrian heads without torsos, and Egyptian caskets with feet (open Tues.-Sat. 9:30am-4:45pm, Sun.9:30am-6pm; 120BF, students 90BF).

The symbol of the 1958 World's Fair and Brussels' answer to the Eiffel tower, the shining aluminum and steel **Atomium** (M: Heysel, in the Bruparck entertainment complex) represents a cubic iron crystal structure 102m high, or magnified 165 billion times. It's now a **science museum** featuring fauna and minerals from around the world (open April-Aug. daily 9am-8pm; Sept.-March 10am-6pm; 200BF).

The **Musée Horta,** 25, rue Américaine, is early 20th century Art Nouveau master Baron Victor Horta's home (open Tues.-Sun. 2-5:30pm; 150BF during the week, 200BF on the weekend). For more Art Nouveau architecture, plus all the French and Belgian comic strips *(bande desinée)* you crave, visit the **Belgian Comic Strip Centre,** 20, rue des Sables, in a renovated Art Deco warehouse a few blocks from Sleep Well. Brussels, the "Comic Strip Capital of the World," even has a comic strip **library** complete with a reproduction of Tintin's rocket ship and works of over 700 artists (open Tues.-Sun. noon–6pm; 150BF). For Tintin souvenirs, check out the museum store or the **Tintin Boutique** near the Grand-Place. When you tire of ol' Tintin, escape to the **Botanical Gardens,** rue Royale (M: Botanique; open daily 10am-10pm; free).

Victor Hugo described the **Saints Michel et Gudule Cathedral,** just north of Central Station at pl. St-Gudule, as the "purest flowering of the Gothic style." Built over the course of six centuries, this magnificent cathedral represents Romanesque and modern architecture as well (open daily 8am-7pm; free).

ENTERTAINMENT

Theater and Cinema

The flagship of Brussels's theater network is the beautiful **Théâtre Royal de la Monnaie,** pl. de la Monnaie (M: de Brouckère; tel. 218 12 11). Renowned throughout the world for its opera and ballet, the theater actually has affordable performances (tourist office has schedules; tickets 250-3000BF; open Tues.-Sat. 11am-6pm). In the shadow of the Atomium, **Kinepolis** (M: Heysel), with 26 screens and a spectacular 600 sq. m Imax theater, is the largest movie theater in Europe (tickets from 300BF). In summer, concerts pop up on the **Grand-Place** and in the **Parc de Bruxelles.** The **Théâtre Royal des Galleries** offers popular theater in French (tel. 513 23 28; tickets 150-800BF). For info on events, snag *What's On* or call **BBB Agenda** (tel. 512 82 77).

Bars and Nightclubs

The Scene in Brussels is intensely European—patrons dress stylishly but retain a casual air. At night the Grand-Place and the streets surrounding it come to life with street performers and live concerts in the square. Leave your valuables at home if you join the nocturnal frenzy around **av. Louise.**

La Mort Subite, 7, rue Montagne-aux-Herbes-Potagères. One of Brussels's oldest and best-known cafés, across from the entrance to Galeries St. Hubert, opposite the Grand-Place. Beer 50-90BF. Coffee 60BF. Open daily 10:30am-midnight.

Le Cercueil ("the coffin"), 10, rue des Harengs, off the Grand-Place. Younger crowd illuminated by blacklights. Drinks are expensive as Hell. Beer from 100BF, cocktails from 250BF. Open weekdays 11am-3am, weekends until 5am.

Blues Corner, 12, rue des Chapeliers, off the Grand-Place. Hear Credence Clearwater Revival with a Flemish accent or classic blues live every night. Open 10pm-late.

L'Incognito, 36, rue des Pierres. Gay men of all ages socialize in a mellow, friendly atmosphere that picks up as the morning draws near. Open nightly 4pm-dawn.

La Lunette, 3, pl. de la Monnaie. Student bar featuring cheap drinks and snacks (beer 40BF, *croque-monsieur*, ham and cheese, 95BF). Open daily noon-late.

The Garage, 16, rue Dequesnoy. A swarm of sweaty bodies, and that's just to go through the cover charge line. Popular, fashionable crowd. Live bands often. Cover from 200BF includes a free drink. Open Wed.-Sun. 11pm-late. Sun. is gay night.

Le Feminin, 9, rue Borgval. Women only. Open Tues. and Fri.-Sun. 10pm-dawn.

FLANDERS (VLAANDEREN)

Nearly all the major Belgian cities are in Flanders whose inhabitants speak Flemish, a language close to Dutch. Historically, the delta of the river Schelde at Antwerp provided the region with a major seaport, and the production and trade of linen, wool, and diamonds underwrote the cultural transformation of the Northern Renaissance. Flemish cities were among the largest in 16th-century Europe; today they are marvelously close together, rich in art, and vibrant with multilingual, friendly people.

Mechelen

Mechelen, situated between Antwerp and Brussels, has enough sights to keep a visitor occupied for days. Lack of affordable accommodations and a mild nightlife, however, reduce it to an enjoyable daytrip. As the ecclesiatical capital of Belgium, Mechelen's main claim to fame is its *carillon* (set of 49 bells) performances (June-Sept. Mon. 8:30pm). **St. Rumbold's Tower,** rising 97m over **Grote Markt,** down Consciencestr. from the station, contains two *carillons*. Climb to the top for a view of the town. The early Renaissance buildings in the Grote Markt include the 14th-century **Stadhuis** (city hall). The **De Wit Tapestry factory** on Schoutetstraat (off Wollemarkt) offers tours (Aug.-June Sat. at 10:30am; 50BF). Passing the factory and heading right on De Deckerstr., then left on Stassartstr., brings you to the **Museum of Nazi Deportation and Resistance;** during the Holocaust, Mechelen served as a temporary camp for Jews who were being sent to Auschwitz-Birkenau (open Sun.-Thurs. 10am-5pm, Fri. 10am-1pm). The **Gouden Carolus Brewery** tours explain the brewing process that has been used since 1471. The highlight, of course, is the tasting of one of its three beers (tours April-Aug. daily at 3pm; 100BF).

The **tourist office** (tel. (015) 29 76 55; fax 29 76 53) in the Stadhuis is brochure-laden; ask for the free booklet with museum info and a map. (Open Easter-Sept. Mon.-Fri. 8am-6pm, Sat.-Sun. 9:30am-12:30pm and 1:30-5pm; Oct.-Easter Mon.-Fri. 8am-5pm, Sat.-Sun. 10am-noon and 2-4:30pm.) Ask also about the frequent **music festivals;** the most raucous is **Op Signoorke** on the second Sunday of September. Trains frequently shuttle to and from Brussels and Antwerp (each 15min. and 110BF). **Carlton,** Grote Markt 3, serves simple dishes (75-200BF; daily 11am-8pm). Alternatively, you can grab some grub at the **grocery store GB,** de Stassartstr. 30 (open Mon. 8:30am-2pm, Tues.-Sat. 8am-6pm, and Fri.until 7pm).

Antwerp (Antwerpen)

Antwerp rose to prominence early as a commercial center and by the 16th century claimed a place among the most powerful cities in Europe. It was the city of Rubens and Van Dyck, of wool and diamonds. Now Belgium's second largest city, Antwerp offers over 20 museums featuring the finest examples of art, architecture, and literature. Bells chiming from the cathedral announce each hour, but they cannot interrupt the constant bustle of activity on the cobblestoned streets below. Bars stay open "until late," which usually means after sunrise.

ORIENTATION AND PRACTICAL INFORMATION

Antwerp rests 40km north of Brussels on the Amsterdam-Brussels-Paris rail line. **Centraal Station** is located smack in the middle of town, with the **zoo** next to it. The **Meir,** an avenue lined with museums, shops and eateries, connects the station to the **Grote Markt** and **Groenplaats,** Antwerp's two major squares (15min. walk).

Tourist Office: Municipal Tourist Office, Grote Markt 15 (tel. 232 01 03; fax 231 19 37). From Centraal Station, turn left onto De Keyserlei, which becomes Meir. Follow Meir to Groenplaats (15min.; bear right at Meirbrug), then bear left down Bromstr. and past the cathedral to Maalderijstr. Free hotel reservations and map. City map with street index 20BF; info packet with map 20BF. Free guide to gay establishments. Open Mon.-Sat. 9am-7:45pm, Sun. 9am-4:45pm.

Budget Travel: VTB, St. Jacobsmarkt 45-47 (tel. 234 34 34). Travel info and youth tickets. Open Mon.-Fri. 9am-5:30pm, Sat. 9am-12:30pm. **Jeugd-Info-Antwerpen,** Apostelstr. 20-22 (tel. 232 27 18). Open Mon.-Fri. 10am-7:30pm, Sat. 2-5pm.

Currency Exchange: Bureaus at Centraal Station have poor rates (10-50BF commission), but one has longer hours (open daily 8am-11pm). If the banks are closed, the best rates are at **American Express** and the **Thomas Cook** bureau on Koningen Astridplein, in front of the train station.

American Express: Frankrijklei 21 (tel. 232 59 20). Exchange and mail desks close Mon.-Fri. at 5pm. Those without AmEx card or checks pay 50BF to retrieve mail.

Trains: Centraal Station, 15min. from the Grote Markt and most of the sights. Trains run frequently to Rotterdam (1hr., 600BF), Amsterdam (2hr., 740BF), and Brussels (45min., 190BF).

Public Transportation: In Flanders, mostly run by de Lijn; a pass from one city (Antwerp, Bruges, Ghent, Mechelen) will work in another. Trams and buses 40BF. 10-ride ticket (280BF) or day pass (110BF) available at Centraal Station, tram and subway stops, or at the tourist office. Subway runs daily 6am-midnight.

Bike Rental: Cyclorent, Sint Katelynevest 12 (tel. 226 95 59; fax 226 42 29), with a touch of India. 300BF per day, 1440BF per week. Open Mon.-Sat. 10am-6pm.

Hitchhiking: Those heading to Germany, the Netherlands, and Ghent reportedly take bus 20 from the train station to the big interchange (Plantin en Moretuslei) outside town. Those going to Brussels and points south take tram 2 to the intersection of Jan Devoslei and Jan van Rijswijklaan.

Luggage Storage: At the train station. Baggage check 60BF. Lockers 60-100BF.

Gay Organization: Amok, Vrijdagmarkt 11, has an info and help line: tel. 232 16 19. Open Mon., Tues., Thurs., and Fri., 11am-3pm, Wed. noon-5pm.

Laundromat: Was-A-Tom, Lange Koepoort 34, near the Grote Markt. Wash 120-150BF, dry 20-40BF. **Wassalon Sickle,** Volkstr. 23, near Boomerang. Wash 80-100BF, dry 20-40BF. Both open daily 7am-10pm.

Pharmacy: Onze Apotheek, Nationalestr. 5, near downtown Antwerp. Open Mon.-Fri. 9am-12:30pm and 2-6:30pm. Pharmacies post the current *pharmacie de garde.* Pharmacies are everywhere—look for big, green, neon crosses.

Medical Assistance: Saint Elisabeth Hospital, Lange Gasthuisstr. 45 (tel. 223 56 11 or 223 56 20).

Emergencies: Ambulance: tel. 100.

Police: tel. 101. Police headquarters are located at Oudlaan 5 (tel. 202 55 11).

Post Office: Main office and *Poste Restante* on Groenplaats. **Postal Code:** 2000.

Telephones: RTT, Jezusstr. 1. Open daily 8am-8pm. Also at Centraal Station. Open Mon.-Fri. 9am-noon and 12:30-5:15pm. **Telephone Code:** 03.

ACCOMMODATIONS AND CAMPING

Budget accommodations are somewhat scarce and less than spectacular. Some cafés around the train station advertising "rooms for tourists" rent lodgings by the hour.

Boomerang Youth Hostel, Volkstr. 49 (tel. 238 47 82). From Centraal Station, take bus 23 (across the street in front of the hotel) to "Museum," or walk 25min. Best hostel location. Eclectic decor. Clean rooms, hot shower, free breakfast, movie every night, and terrace with grill. Reception open daily 9am-10pm. Dorms 385BF. Free lockers, 200BF deposit on locks. Sheets 100BF.

Scoutel, Stoomstr. 3 (tel. 226 46 06; fax 232 63 92). Follow Pelikaanstr., go under 2nd underpass, and take the first right. New and sporting: all rooms have a bathroom and shower. Kitchen and TV room. Reception open daily 9am-6pm. Check in before 8pm (Fri.-Sat. before 10pm). Singles 950BF. Doubles 1470BF. Triples 1810BF. Free luggage storage at reception. Sheets included, towels 25BF.

New International Youth Hotel, Provinciestr. 256 (tel. 230 05 22). Take tram 11 from Centraal Station, or walk left down Pelikaanstr., and turn left under the 5th underpass. Comfortable, if not exciting. Good rates for currency exchange. Reception open daily 8am-11pm. Dorms 430BF. Singles 920BF. Doubles 1320-1780BF. Triples 1950BF. Quads 2300BF. Breakfast included. Sheets 120BF.

Jeugdherberg Op-Sinjoorke (HI), Eric Sasselaan 2 (tel. 238 02 73). Take tram 2 ("Hoboken") to "Bouwcentrum," walk right, take first left, and follow HI signs over the river and through the woods, or take bus 27 to "Camille Huysmanslaan." 45min. walk from any nightlife. Clean, modern, and somewhat strict. Kitchen, laundry. 375BF, nonmembers 475BF. Breakfast included. Sheets 125BF.

Camping: Jan van Rijswijklaan, on Vogelzanglaan (tel. 238 57 17). Reception open daily 7am-9pm. 85BF per person, 35BF per tent. Shower included. **De Molen,** on St. Annastrand (tel. 219 60 90). Reception open daily 7am-10pm. 45BF per person, 45BF per tent. Shower 20BF. Both open April-Sept.

BELGIUM

FOOD

Finding inexpensive food in Antwerp can be a crusade, but it's hard to get tired of that old standby—Italian. Avoid touristed areas and wander south of Groenplaats along the river to the area around the **Waalse Kaai** and the **Museum of Fine Arts,** or head north to **Suiker Rui.** A meal for 200BF is a good deal. **GB** (Grand Bazar), Groenplaats's subterranean supermarket, is great; go down into the Groenplaats tram station and follow the signs for Winkelcentrum (open Mon.-Thurs. and Sat. 9am-8pm, Fri. 9am-9pm). Pelikaanstraat leads south to the kosher world of the **Jewish District.**

Beleejde Broodjes, Melmarket 5, 2min. from Groenpl. Best prices around for decent meals. Spaghetti 195BF. Open Mon.-Sat. 6:30am-8pm, Sun 11am-7pm.

Atlantis, Korte Nieuwstr. 6. Tasty vegetarian meals including omelettes, pasta, and cheese toast at bargain prices (about 180-250BF). Open Wed.-Mon. 5-9:30pm.

Gringo's Mexican Restaurant, Ernest van Dijckaai 24. Funny masks, colorful parrots, and great deals. Meals from around 200BF. Open daily 6-11:30pm.

't Oerwoud, a hip little place on the corner of Suiker Rui and Ernest van Dijckaai. Serves pub fare, spaghetti, and pasta from 225BF. Kitchen open daily 5pm-late.

Dof Jus, Woolstr. 11. A cozy place with a variety of vegetarian standards. Most meals under 280BF. Open Mon.-Fri. noon-3pm and 5:30-9pm, Sat. noon-3pm.

Tavern Jan Zonder Brees, Krabbenstr. 2. Relaxed atmosphere and great food; less touristy than most. Meals from 200BF. Open daily 9am-2am, later on Fri.-Sat.

Den Beiaard, Handschoenmarket 21. Large gay clientele (both men and women) and long hours. Meals from 200BF. Open daily 9am-late.

SIGHTS AND ENTERTAINMENT

Many of the best sights in Antwerp are free. A walk along the **Cogels Osylei** will take you past fanciful Art Nouveau mansions built with the wealth of the city's Golden Age. **Centraal Station** itself is beautiful, and the shops and buildings lining the **Meir** are excellent examples of Antwerp old and new. Not free but still impressive is the world-famous **Antwerp Zoo**, right next to the train station, a serene and exotic natural environment with fascinating wildlife (open daily 9am-6pm; 340BF, students 270BF). Combine your trip to the zoo with a 50-minute tour of the **River Schelde** on the *Flandria* (ask for info at the zoo or the tourist office).

The **Stadhuis** (city hall), in Grote Markt in the **oude stad** (old city), is a dignified example of Renaissance architecture (open for tours Mon.-Wed. and Fri. 9am-3pm, Sat. noon-3:30pm; 30BF). The nearby **Kathedraal van Onze-Lieve-Vrouw,** Groenplaats 21, has a showy Gothic tower and an interior decorated with stained glass and Flemish masterpieces, notably Rubens's *Descent from the Cross* and *Exaltation of the Cross* (open Mon.-Fri. 10am-5pm, Sat. 10am-3pm, Sun. 1-4pm; 60BF). The little-known **Mayer van den Bergh Museum** at Lange Gasthuisstr. 19 harbors Brueghel's *Mad Meg* (open Tues.-Sun. 10am-5pm; 75BF, students 30BF). Antwerp's famed son built **Rubens Huis,** Wapper 9, off Meir, and filled it with art (open Tues.-Sun. 10am-4:45pm; 75BF). The **Royal Museum of Fine Art,** Leopold De Waelplaats 1-9, showcases one of the best collections of Old Flemish Masters in the world (from the 14th-17th centuries). Natural lighting and the originality of its exhibit designs have made this gallery a model for many others (open Tues.-Sun. 10am-5pm; 150BF, students 120BF, Fri. free). From June to mid-July, the **Whitsun Fair,** across from the museum, offers a tangle of bright neon and gut-wrenching rides. The **Film Museum,** Meir 50 (tel. 233 86 71), shows outdoor movies (100-150BF) in the summer. For an events guide, pick up *Antwerpen* at the tourist office.

Antwerp is famously well-endowed with 300 bars and nightclubs. International DJs spin house music in near-rave conditions at **Café d'Anvers,** Verversrui 16 (cover 200BF; open Sat.-Sun. from midnight). Live jazz bands on Sunday and Monday nights feature at the **Swing Café,** on Suiker Rui (no cover; open daily noon-late). The streets behind the cathedral are always crowded. **Bierland,** Korte Nieuwstr. 28, is the most popular student hang-out, with special drink promotions. **Zottekot,** Vlaamse Kaai 23, indulges in theme nights, such as Monday's "DJ plays cupid" (cover 200BF; open Thurs.-Mon. 7pm-late). Alternatively, for a quiet evening of conversation, try the **Pelgrom,** Pelgrimstr. 15, a 16th-century cellar with vaulted ceilings (open daily noon-midnight). Most gay bars and discos cluster along Van Schoonhovenstr., just north of Centraal Station. Closer to Grote Markt is **Rotskam,** Vridagmarkt 12, where both men and women enjoy Belgian beer (open Sat.-Thurs. 3pm-late, Fri. 9am-late).

Ghent (Gent)

Ghent is quite possibly the most underrated town in Belgium. Back in the 14th century, when it reigned as the center of Europe's garment industry, Ghent was second only to Paris in size and prestige. Although no longer a European powerhouse, Ghent still contends for the title of *la ville lumière* with buildings bathed nocturnally in multicolored splendor. During the day, the impressive remnants of the Middle Ages provide hours of exploration.

PRACTICAL INFORMATION

Tourist Office: Municipal Tourist Office, in the belfry (tel. 224 15 55). Take tram 1 or 12 from the train station to the main post office (looks more like a castle than a post office), then head down Klein Turkije. Free map, guide to restaurants and sights, and guide to gay-friendly restaurants and bars. Open April-Oct. daily 9:30am-6:30pm; Nov.-March 9:30am-12:30pm and 1:15-4:30pm.

Budget Travel: JOKER/Acotra, Overpoorstr. 58 (tel. 221 97 94). The office sells BIJ tickets and offers helpful advice. Open Mon.-Fri. 10am-1pm and 2-6pm, Sat. 10am-1pm. **Taxi-Stop,** Onderbergen 51 (tel. 223 23 10). Matches drivers with riders (1.3BF per km), books cheap last-minute flights (tel. 224 00 23), and sells **Eurolines** bus tickets. Open Mon.-Fri. 9am-6pm.

Trains: Trams 1, 10, 11, and 12 run between **Sint-Pietersstation** (tel. 222 44 44), on the city's south edge and Korenmarkt in the old city center. Frequent trains to Bruges (15min., 170BF), Brussels (35min., 235BF), and Antwerp (1½hr., 245BF).

BELGIUM

Hitchhiking: Ghent lies at the intersection of the E40, connecting Brussels and Germany with Oostende, and the E17, linking Paris and Amsterdam. Hitchers reportedly turn right out of the station onto Clementinalaan, which becomes Burggravenlaan, and continue until they reach the E17.

Gay and Lesbian Organizations: Men call 222 83 01; **'T'Aksent Op Roze** (tel. 224 35 82) for women. Info on activities and establishments in Flanders.

Laundromat: St. Jacobsnieuwstr. 85. Wash and dry 140BF. Bring plenty of 20BF coins. Open daily 8am-10pm.

Emergencies: tel. 100.

Police: tel. 101. For police headquarters, dial 266 88 16.

Post Office: Korenmarkt 16 (tel. 225 20 34). *Poste Restante.* One of the lovelier buildings in town. Open Mon.-Fri. 8am-6pm, Sat. 9am-noon. **Postal Code:** 9000.

Telephones: Keizer Karelstr. 1. Buy phone cards here or at any newsstand. Open Mon.-Thurs. 8am-4pm, Fri. 8am-6pm. Coin phones rare. **Telephone Code:** 09.

ACCOMMODATIONS, CAMPING, AND FOOD

The youth hostel **De Draeke (HI),** St-Widostraat 11 (tel. 233 70 50; fax 233 80 01), elegant, modern, clean, and in the shadow of a castle, is the best place to stay in Ghent. From the station, take tram 1, 10, or 11 to "Gravensteen" (15min.). Walk left, then take the first right on Gewad, and then right on St-Widostr. The hotel offers **currency exchange** at good rates, and its dorms (375BF) and doubles (450BF) have bathrooms and showers. (Reception open daily 7:30am-11pm. Nonmembers 100BF extra. Breakfast included. Sheets 125BF.) Rooms are also available at the **university** (singles 500BF, breakfast and shower included; open July 15-Sept. 15). Call the office at Stalhof 6 (tel. 264 71 00; fax 264 72 96) for info. **Den Ijzer,** Vlaanderenstr. 177 (tel. 225 98 73), is a back-up plan; take tram 12 from the station to Kouter (1150BF; breakfast included). To get to **Camping Blaarmeersen,** Zuiderlaan 12 (tel. 221 53 99), walk 15 blocks or ride bus 38 northwest of Sint-Pietersstation (120BF per person, 130BF per tent; open March to mid-Oct.).

BELGIUM

With luck, you'll be able to find a good meal for about 200BF. The best areas are around **Korenmarkt,** just in front of the post office, **Vrijtagmarkt,** a few blocks from the town hall, and **St.-Pietersnieuwstraat,** down by the university. The gay-friendly **Backstage,** on the corner of St.-Pietersnieuwstr. and J. Plateaustr., serves salads from 200BF and omelettes from 130BF, and doubles as a theater (open daily 11:30am-1am). Next door at **La Rustica,** the cooks dole out tasty pizza (180-200BF; open daily 6-11pm, also Mon.-Fri. 12:30-2:30pm). Tucked away at Plotersgracht 11 is **Amadeus,** where Belgians come from out of town for the superb all-you-can-eat spare ribs (425BF; open Mon.-Tues. 7-11pm, Fri.-Sun. 6pm-midnight). **Fritz Pannakoen,** Donkersteeg 28, serves *croque monsieurs* (115-165BF), spaghetti (185BF), and veggie lasagne (220BF; open Mon.-Sat. 8am-6:30pm). At Koornmarket 19, **Damberd** serves sandwiches (100BF) and coffee to a mostly gay and lesbian clientele.

SIGHTS AND ENTERTAINMENT

Connoisseurs of fine architecture relish a trip to Ghent, which has the most protected monuments of any Belgian city. The tourist office offers guided city tours. **Gravensteen,** the Castle of the Counts, is a sprawling medieval fortress complete with ramparts, chambers, and a torture room. (Open April-Sept. daily 9am-6pm; Oct.-March 9am-5pm. Last admission 45min. before closing. 200BF, students 100BF.) Wind your way up the towering **Belfort** (belfry) and experience some classic Hitchcock vertigo. The dragon weather vane that sits on top is the *de facto* symbol of Ghent. In the Middle Ages, a man hiding inside the great bronze dragon shot fire from its mouth with a torch and fireworks (open daily 10am-12:30pm and 2-5:30pm; 100BF with guide, 80BF without). The **Stadhuis** (town hall) is an arresting juxtaposition of Gothic and Renaissance architecture. A block away on Limburgstr. stands **Sint-Baafskathedraal,** built between the 14th and 16th centuries. Its claim to fame is Jan van Eyck's *Adoration of the Mystic Lamb,* an imposing polyptych on wood panels. (Open Easter-Oct. Mon.-Sat. 9:30-11:45am and 2-5:45pm, Sun. 1-5:45pm; Nov.-Easter Mon.-Sat. 10:30-

11:50am and 2:30-4pm, Sun. 2-4:45pm. Cathedral free. *Adoration* 60BF, students 40BF.) Also worth a visit is the **Museum voor Schone Kunsten** (Museum of Fine Arts) in the Citadel Park, home to a strong Flemish collection and an exhibit of modern art (open Tues.-Sun. 9:30am-5pm; 80BF).

Ghent is home to a large university, the **Rijksuniversiteit Ghent,** and the city's nightlife thrives with its student population. From October to July 15, young scholars cavort in the cafés and discos near the university restaurant on **Overpoortstr. Vooruit,** a huge art-deco bar on St-Pietersnieuwstr., once the meeting place of the socialist party, was occupied by Nazis during World War II and is now popular with students (open Aug. 13-July 16 daily 10pm-3am). The bar's concert hall (tel. (09) 223 82 01) features everything from rock to jazz to avant-garde. **De Tap en de Tepal,** on Gewad by the youth hostel, serves wine and cheese from 100-200BF. On the Vrijtagmarkt at the wood-paneled **Dulle Grief,** beer lovers lament that they can't sample every one of the over 250 Belgian beers (open Mon. 4:30pm-1am, Tues.-Sat. noon-1am, Sun. 3-7pm). Ghent is a popular destination for gay men and women; the disco **Cherry Lane,** Meersenierstr. 3, attracts lesbians (no cover; Mon.-Wed. 8pm-late), while men dance the night away at **De Pintelier,** Pintestr. 76.

Bruges (Brugge)

Visitors to Bruges seem to believe that they are the first to discover its charms. Less well-known than other Flemish towns, the capital of Flanders is one of the most beautiful cities in Europe. As you walk from the train station to the city center, silver canals carve their way through rows of stone houses; the entire city remains one of the best-preserved examples of northern Renaissance architecture. The beauty belies the destruction this region sustained in World War I; eight decades after the war, farmers uncover 200 tons of artillery every year as they plough their fields.

ORIENTATION AND PRACTICAL INFORMATION

Although it may seem logical to make Bruges a daytrip from Brussels, there is good reason to reverse your itinerary and visit the capital city from Bruges, where natives are warm and welcoming to visitors. The dizzying **Belfort** (belfry) towers high at the center of town, presiding over the **Markt,** a handsome square. Outside the ring of canals, south of the center of the city, stands the train station.

Tourist Office: Burg 11 (tel. 44 86 86), just east of the Markt. Turn left out of the station and walk to 't Zand Sq., then turn right on Zuid-Zuidzandstr., then right through the Markt on Breidelstr. to Burg, another square (15min.). The office books rooms (400BF deposit) and sells a good map (25BF). Open April-Sept. Mon.-Fri. 9:30am-6:30pm, Sat.-Sun. 10am-noon and 2-6:30pm; Oct.-March Mon.-Fri. 9:30am-1pm, 2-5:30pm, Sat. 9:30am-12:45pm and 2-5pm. There is a smaller office at the **train station.** Open March-Oct. Mon.-Sat. 2:45-9pm; Nov.-Feb. Mon.-Sat. 1:45-8pm. **Youth Information Center: JAC,** Kleine Hertsbergestr. 1 (tel. 33 83 06), near the Burg, the 2nd right off Hoogstraat. The center lists cheap rooms and restaurants and has a youth crisis center. Open Mon. and Wed. 9am-noon and 1:30-8pm, Tues. 1:30-8pm, Fri. 9am-noon and 1:30-6pm, Sat. 10am-12:30pm.

Currency Exchange: Burg 11, inside the tourist office.

Trains: The station is on Stationsplein (tel. 38 23 82), 15min. south of the city center. To: Antwerp (1hr., 385BF), Brussels (1hr., 365BF), Ghent (15min., 170BF).

Bike Rental: At train station; 345BF per day. **Koffieboontje,** Hallestr. 4 (tel. 33 80 27), off the Markt by the belfry. 250BF a day, students 150BF; 850-1000BF a week.

Hitchhiking: Those hitching to Brussels take bus 7 to St. Michiels or pick up the highway behind the station.

Luggage Storage: At the train station; 60BF. **Lockers** (15BF) at the tourist office.

Laundromat: Belfort, Ezelstr. 51, next to Snuffel's Sleep-In. Wash 'n' dry 130-250BF. Open daily 7am-10pm. **Mister Wash** is next door (160-280BF).

Emergencies: tel. 100.

Police: tel. 101.

BELGIUM

Internet Access: Huysderkunsten, Kordevuldersstr. 30 (tel. 34 70 09). 150BF per 30min. Open Mon.-Fri. noon-8pm, Sat. noon-5pm.

Post Office: Markt 5. *Poste Restante.* Open Mon.-Fri. 9am-6pm, Sat. 9am-noon. **Postal Code:** 8000.

Telephones: Find a coin phone at the tourist office, post office, or your hostel; card phones dot the streets. **Telephone Code:** 050.

ACCOMMODATIONS AND CAMPING

Hostels fill up quickly in June, July, and August. Call ahead or to show up early in the morning. The first three hostels listed here have standardized their prices: dorms 380BF, singles 550BF, doubles 950BF, triples 1290BF, and quads 1720BF.

The Passage, Dweersstr. 26 (tel. 34 02 32; fax 34 01 40). At 't Zand turn right on Zuidzandstr., then take your first left. Airy rooms, ideal location, and good restaurant (entrees 195BF-395BF; 1 free beer for guests; open daily 6pm-midnight). Reception open daily 8:30am-midnight. Free city map. Dorms and doubles available. 5% discount on some rooms with *Let's Go* or a youth hostel card. Credit cards accepted. Free if it's your birthday. Or try **The Hotel Passage** next door. Reception open 8am-10pm. Singles 1200BF. Doubles 1800BF.

Bauhaus International Youth Hotel, Langestr. 135-137 (tel. 34 10 93 or 33 41 80); take bus 6 from the station to Kruispoort; ask bus driver to tell you when to get off (40BF). A piece of America transplanted into a few square feet, and a frenzy of activity at night. Reception (and bar) open daily 8am-2am. Free beer with hearty dinners (200-400BF). Lockers 30BF.

Snuffel's Sleep-In, Ezelstr. 49 (tel. 33 31 33; fax 33 32 50), 10min. from the Markt; follow Sint-Jakobstr., which turns into Ezelstr. Or, take bus 3, 8, 9, or 13 from the station. All proceeds go to charity. Kitchen access; laundromat and groceries next door. The only drawback is the trot through the lively bar to the shower. Reception open daily 8am-midnight. Ask about doing chores for a free night's stay.

Europa International Youth Hostel (HI), Baron 143 (tel. 35 26 79; fax 35 37 72), 15min. walk from station, away from the Markt. Turn right from the station and follow Buiten Katelijnevest to Baron Ruzettelaan; or take bus 2 to the third stop. Stay here if the other hostels are full or for a quiet night's sleep. Dorms 372BF. Doubles 1090BF. Quads 1880BF. Breakfast included.

't Keizershof, Oostmeers 126 (tel. 33 87 28). 5min. walk from the station; walk left and take first right. Unexciting but clean and comfortable. Singles 925BF. Doubles 1300BF. Triples 1900BF. Quads 2300BF. No credit cards.

Hotel Salvators, St-Salvatorsherhof 17 (tel. 33 19 21; fax 33 94 64). From 't Zand walk down Zuidzandstraat and take a right. Great for groups. Kitchen, TV, and common area. Bar open daily 5-10pm. Doubles 1500BF, with bath 2300BF. Triples 2700BF and quads 3000BF, both with bath. Breakfast included.

Hotel Lybeer, Korte Vulderstr. 31 (tel. 33 43 55), just off 't Zand Sq.; take the first right off Zuidzandstr., then a quick left. Pleasant rooms and comfortable lounge area. Reception open daily 8am-midnight. Singles 900BF, with bath 1990BF. Doubles 1550BF, with bath 2350BF. Triples 2100BF, with bath 3500BF. Continental breakfast included, English breakfast 100BF.

Camping: St. Michiel, Tillegemstr. (tel. 38 08 19; fax 80 68 24). Take bus 7 from the station. 25min. walk from the Markt. Camping with a restaurant, café, and style. 130BF per tent. Showers 30BF.

FOOD

There are inexpensive eats around Bruges if you *search*. To avoid high prices, stay away from the Markt and 't Zand. Instead, look a block or two away from the town center. From the Burg, cross the river and turn left to find the **Vismarkt,** which sells fresh seafood. An even cheaper option is the **Nopri Supermarket,** Noordzandstr. 4, just off 't Zand or **Battard,** 55 Langestr., close to Bauhaus (both closed Sun.). **Markets** open on 't Zand every Saturday morning and the Burg every Wednesday morning.

Cafe Craenenburg, Markt 16. The exception to the rule that good location means high prices. Munch on a simple meals and people-watch from the terrace. Sandwiches 130-180BF. Omelettes 180BF. Spaghetti 210BF. Open daily 7:30am-11pm.

The Lotus, Wappenmakerstr. 5, 3rd left off Philipstockstr. from the Markt. Serves vegetarian lunches in an attractive building. Meals from 210-260BF. Open mid-Aug. to July daily 11:45am-1:45pm.

Ganzespel, Ganzestr. 37. From Burg, turn up Hoogstr.; 3rd right after the river. Hearty portions for a local clientele. Square meal 245BF. Open Wed.-Sat. noon-2pm and 6-10pm, Sun. noon-10pm.

Bistro de Kluiver, Hoogstr. 12. Tasty, diverse menu and cozy mood. Veggie pasta 220BF. Spare ribs and salad 350BF. Escargots 130BF. Open Wed.-Sun. 7pm-1am.

Cactus Cafe, Sint-Jakobsstr. 33. Lively restaurant a 5min. walk from the Markt. Italian is cheap: calzones, veggie pasta or lasagne 180BF. Open Mon.-Sat. 11:30am-2pm, Wed.-Sat. also 6:30pm-3am, Sun. 6:30pm-midnight.

SIGHTS AND ENTERTAINMENT

Bruges is best seen on foot; the tourist office suggests excellent walking tours. Rising precipitously from the Markt, the **Belfort** towers above the center of the city. Climb its dizzying 366 steps during the day for a view of surrounding areas, then come back at night when it serves as the city's torch. (Open April-Oct. daily 9:30am-5pm; Nov.-March 9:30am-12:30pm and 1:30-5pm; tickets sold until 4:15pm. 100BF, students 80BF.) Up the street at the Burg, the 14th-century **Stadhuis** (town hall) has beautiful paintings and furniture behind its flamboyant Gothic front (open April-Sept. daily 9:30am-5pm; Oct.-March 9:30am-noon and 2-5pm; 100BF, students 80BF). More macabre personalities should check out the **Groeninge Museum** on Dijverstr., with works depicting decapitations, flaying, boiling in oil, and drawing and quartering by the Flemish Primitivists (Jan van Eyck, Hans Memling) and the master of medieval macabre, Hieronymous Bosch. (Open April-Sept. daily 9:30am-5pm; Oct.-March Wed.-Mon. 9:30am-noon and 2-5pm. 200BF, students 150BF.) Next door is the **Gruuthuse Museum,** the 15th-century home of beer magnates, which shelters an amazing collection of weapons, tapestries, musical instruments, and coins dating back to the 6th century. (Open April-Sept. daily 9:30am-5pm; Oct.-March Wed.-Mon. 9:30am-noon and 2-5pm. 130BF, students 100BF.) Nearby, the **Memling Museum,** Mariastr. 38, showcases one of the oldest surviving medieval hospitals (Open April-Sept. daily 9:30am-5pm; Oct.-March Thurs.-Tues. 9:30am-12:30pm and 2-5pm.)

Hidden away in the **Church of Our Lady** is the oft-photographed Michelangelo sculpture *Madonna and Child,* his only work to leave Italy during his lifetime. (Open April-Sept. Mon.-Sat. 10-11:30am and 2:30-5pm, Sun. 2:30-5pm; Oct.-March closes 30min. earlier in the evenings. Free.) A relic supposedly containing the blood of Christ is held in the **Basilica of the Holy Blood,** on the corner of the Burg. (Open April-Sept daily 9:30-noon and 2-6pm; Oct.-March 10am-noon and 2-4pm; closed Wednesday afternoon. Free.) **Minnewater** (the Lake of Love) lies on the south side of the city. Don't get too excited—this romantic spot, once the home of an ammunition dump, is more for the contemplation, not the consummation, of love. Just when you thought the 17th century was over, the **Museum voor Volkskunde,** Rolweg 40, reconstructs life in that era. Take Hoogstr. from the Burg to Molenmeers. (Open April-Sept. daily 9:30am-5pm; Oct.-March 9:30am-12:30pm and 2-5pm, closed Tues.) For a view of an 18th-century windmill, head right on Rolweg to Kruisvest to the **Sint-Janshuismolen** (open May-Sept. daily 9:30am-12:30pm and 1:15-5pm).

If you're ready for cycling, the **Back Road Bike Co.** explores windmills, castles, and World War II bunkers. Tour groups leave from the main tourist office. (Tours March-Oct. daily at 1pm, 3hr., 450BF; June-Sept. and holidays, Sat.-Sun. also 10am, 2hr., 400BF. Call 34 30 45 for info; fax reservations to 34 57 18.) **Boat tours** along Bruges's canals leave every 30 minutes (daily 10am-6pm; 150BF); call the tourist office for info.

The best nightlife in Bruges is just wandering through the romantic streets and over cobblestone bridges after sunset, but if that isn't intoxicating enough for you, try sampling some of the 300 varieties of beer at **Brugs Beertje,** Kemelstr. 5 (open Mon.-

Tues. and Thurs. 4pm-1am, Fri.-Sat. 4pm-2am; from 50BF). Next door, the *jenever*, Dutch gin, is tantalizingly fruity at **Dreiple Huis** (open daily 5pm-1am, Fri.-Sat. until 2am). The flavors slyly mask the very high alcohol content. **Rikka Rock,** on 't Zand, is where the twenty-something locals hang out (beers from 50BF; open daily noon-1am). After hours head next door to **L'ObCéDé** for pulsating music and low purple lights (no cover; open daily 8pm-3am).

Near Bruges

Informative **Quasimodo** tours (tel. (050) 37 04 70) provide a terrific way to explore Flanders while keeping Bruges as a base. The "Flanders Fields" tour somberly patrols the battlefields of World War I where thousands of soldiers died (open Sun., Tues., and Thurs.; 1400BF, under 26 1000BF), while the "Triple Treat" tour offers a little of everything, stopping for waffles, chocolate, and beer along the way (Mon., Wed., and Fri.; same prices). Conducted in English, these tours leave various hostels and hotels as well as the central train station between 8:45 and 9:20am, return around 5pm.

The towns along the North Sea coast of Belgium win fans largely for their beaches. **Zeebrugge** is little more than a port, but **Oostende** and **Knokke** boast beautiful beaches and stylish stores, just an hour's easy bike ride from Bruges. Ferries, ships, and jetfoils chug daily to the U.K. from Zeebrugge and Oostende, easily accessible by train from Bruges (1 per hr., 30min., 150BF). Get tickets from travel agents, at ports, or in the Oostende train station. **P&O European Ferries** (Brussels tel. (02) 231 19 37; Oostende tel. (059) 70 76 01; Zeebrugge tel. (050) 54 22 22) sail to Dover and Felixstowe. Another option is **Oostende Lines** and its mighty freighter, the *Prins Filip* (tel. (059) 55 99 55; fax 80 94 17), which goes to Ramsgate, England, which is 2 hours from London's Victoria Station (8 per day, 599BF in July-Aug., 499BF off-season). In Oostende, the **De Ploate Youth Hostel (HI),** Langestr. 82 (tel. (059) 80 52 97), is close to the station (strict midnight curfew; 465BF). Campgrounds freckle the coast, including **De Vuurtoren,** Heistlaan 168 (tel. (050) 51 17 82), in Knokke (2 people 470BF; open mid-March to mid-Oct.), and **Jamboree,** Polderlaan 55 (tel. (050) 41 45 45), in Blankenberge (1-person tent 310BF; 2-person tent 460BF).

WALLONIE

The dense forests of Belgium's middle marked the edge of Roman influence in the third century, and seventeen centuries later the division remains. While Germanic tribes settled the cities of modern day Flanders, Romanized Celts retained their French culture and language. Wallonie lacks the world class cities of the north, but offers instead the peaceful beauty of the Ardennes.

Tournai

The first city liberated by the Allied forces, Tournai escaped major damage in World War II. Yet the city is not without a turbulent history—it has belonged to Germany, France, Belgium, and England. The city's most spectacular structure is the Romanesque and Gothic **cathedral,** whose **treasure room** houses a collection of medieval goldware and some of St. Thomas Becket's threads. The **Museum of Fine Arts,** Enclos Saint-Martin, is as remarkable for its Art Nouveau design as it is for its works by Breughel, Rubens, and Van Gogh. The **Museum of Folklore,** housed in 17th-century buildings on Rédiut de Sions, recreates historic Tournai (both open Wed.-Mon. 10am-noon and 2-5:30pm; 80BF, students 50BF).

To get to Tournai's **tourist office,** 14, Vieux Marché Aux Poteries (tel. (069) 22 20 45; fax 21 62 22), exit the station, walk straight for 15 minutes to the city center, and go around the left side of the cathedral. They have brochures and maps (open Mon.-Fri. 9am-7pm, Sat. 10am-1pm and 3-6pm, Sun. 10am-noon and 2-6pm). The **Auberge de Tournai,** rue St-Martin (tel. (069) 21 61 36), housed in an 18th-century abbey, has tapestries worthy of museums and offers clean rooms (reception open 8am-1pm and 5-10pm; 345BF, nonmembers 445BF; sheets 125BF). The **Pita Pyramid,** 7, rue de la Tête d'Or, stuffs its fare into pockets. (140-210BF. Open Mon.-Thurs. 11:30am-2:30pm and 5:30pm-1am, Fri.-Sun. until 3am.) Nightlife centers around the Grand-Place and along the canals. **La Fabrique,** 13 Quai du Marché Aux Poissons, is a popular nightspot (open daily 11am-11pm, Sun. closes at 5pm).

Waterloo

Napoleon was caught with both hands in his shirt at Waterloo, just south of Brussels. Modern residents are more likely to have their hands in your pockets, as history buffs and fans of the diminutive dictator pay for a glimpse at the town's little slice of history. For 385BF (students 315BF), you can buy a pass that grants admission to the six main sights: Wellington's Museum, Napoleon's Museum, the Waxwork Museum, the Lion's Mound, the Visitors Center, and the battlefield panorama. To get to Waterloo, take bus W (every 30min, 76BF one way) from pl. Rouppe in Brussels (accessible via tram 90), or take the train from Brussels (135-185BF round-trip), and then walk 1km to the center of town. You can purchase the discount pass at the **tourist office,** 149, chausée de Bruxelles (tel. (02) 354 99 10; fax 354 22 23; open daily 9:30am-6:30pm).

Namur and the Ardennes

The small city of **Namur,** in the heart of Wallonie an hour's train ride from Brussels, is the last remaining outpost before the vast wilderness of the Ardennes. As such, the city serves as an excellent base for hiking, biking, caving, and climbing excursions. The first noticeable sight is the foreboding **citadel,** rooted on the top of a rocky hill to the south. You can do the adventurous thing and climb to the top, or take a mini-train (Tues.-Sun. 10am-4pm; 160BF, round-trip 190BF). For another 195BF, you can check out the fortress. For a little adrenaline, rent a mountain bike from the high station of the *télésiège* (150BF per hr., 600BF per day). For spiritual uplift, in both senses, check out the monastery and brewery of the **Abbaye de Floreffe.** To get there, take bus 10 ("Chatelineau") to Floreffe (open March-Oct. daily 10:30am-6pm; 80BF; beer 60BF).

The **tourist office,** just a few blocks to the left of the train station of Place Léopold (tel. (081) 22 28 59), has discount packages for Namur's main attractions (open daily 9am-12:30pm and 1-6pm). Get a free map here or at the train station. The **provincial tourist office,** 3 rue de Notre Dame (tel. (081) 22 29 98), helps plan trips into deep green the Ardennes forest (open Mon.-Fri. 8am-noon and 1-5pm). Namur's youth hostel, the **Auberge Félicien Rops (HI),** 8, av. Félicien Rops (tel. (081) 22 36 88), named for one of Namur's best known artists, is among the friendliest and best equipped lodges around, with laundry facilities (240BF), a kitchen, bike rental (400BF), and tasty meals (250BF for dinner). To reach the hostel, take bus 3 directly to the door, or take bus 4 or 5 to "Les Marroniers" (members only; reception open 24hr.; 375BF, breakfast included) **Les Trieux,** 99, rue des Tris (tel. (081) 44 55 83), in Malonne, is the best camping option; to get there, ride bus 6 for 6km (75BF per person, 75BF per tent; cold showers free; open April-Oct.). For a great view of the area, take bus 433 ("Lustin"; 50BF) to the **Belevdere** restaurant on a 300 ft. cliff on the banks of the Meuse (meals from 300BF). Try the regional Ardennes ham at one of the sandwich stands throughout the city or stop at **Maison St-Aubain supermarket,** on rue de Fer.

Bosnia-Herzegovina

US$1	**= 182BHD (Bosnian dinars)**	**100BHD =**	**US$0.55**
CDN$1	**= 132BHD**	**100BHD =**	**CDN$0.76**
UK£1	**= 290BHD**	**100BHD =**	**UK£0.35**
IR£1	**= 267BHD**	**100BHD =**	**IR£0.38**
AUS$1	**= 133BHD**	**100BHD =**	**AUS$0.75**
NZ$1	**= 116BHD**	**100BHD =**	**NZ$0.87**
SAR1	**= 39BHD**	**100BHD =**	**SAR2.58**

Country Code: 387 **International Dialing Prefix: 00**

Defying the odds, the nation of Bosnia-Herzegovina persists, the mountainous centerpiece of the former Yugoslavia. Bosnia's distinction, and its troubles, spring from its self-regard as a mixing ground for Muslims, Croats, and Serbs. In Sarajevo that ideal is at least verbally maintained, but in the smaller towns, ethnic problems continue. Bosnia was once a beautiful country of rolling green hills and valleys; today the road to Sarajevo passes through endless fields guarded by roofless, abandoned houses. A large part of the population are refugees, displaced and scattered. The future is uncertain, particularly with the scheduled withdrawal of NATO troops in summer 1999. But the people of Bosnia are resilient, and the process of rebuilding is underway.

Learn more about Bosnia's past and present in *Let's Go: Eastern Europe 1998.*

> The U.S. Department of State issued a **Travel Warning** in June 1996 advising against unnecessary travel to Bosnia. Check http://travel.state.gov/travel_warnings.html for updates. If the 30,000-strong peace implementation force (SFOR) pulls out as planned in June 1998, Bosnia may be quite unstable.

ESSENTIALS

Citizens of U.S. and Ireland do not need **visas** to enter Bosnia, but citizens of Australia, New Zealand, the U.K., and South Africa do. Visa applications require you to submit your passport, a visa application, and a small fee (US$15). Register with your embassy upon arrival, and keep your papers with you at all times. **Croatia Airlines** (tel. in Zagreb (41) 42 77 52, in Split (21) 36 22 02) has service to Zagreb, Zurich, Ljubljana, and Istanbul. To buy a ticket in Sarajevo, you must pay in cash. **Trains** are barely functional, but **buses** run between Sarajevo and Split, Dubrovnik, and Zagreb.

Outside Sarajevo, **do not set foot off the pavement** under any circumstances. Even in Sarajevo, use caution. Millions of **landmines** and **unexploded ordinances (UXOs)** lace the country. Many landmine injuries occur on **road shoulders.**

Tourist services are limited, although in Sarajevo and (to some extent) Mostar, travelers are welcomed. In Sarajevo, a fledgling **tourist office** provides guidance. The **U.S. Embassy,** equipped with full-time consul, is also useful. Bosnia's currency, the **dinar,** is firmly attached to the **Deutschmark** at an exchange rate of 100 dinars per DM1. Transactions take place in either or both currencies. The Croatian **kuna** was also named an official currency in late summer 1997. **ATMs** are non-existent. **Traveler's checks** can be exchanged in Sarajevo and Mostar. **Cash** is almost exclusively the method of payment. *Poste Restante* is unavailable. Post offices are marked by small yellow signs with diagonal lines through them. Dialing into and out of Bosnia is no longer problematic. To call **AT&T Direct,** dial 008 00 00 10. For the **police,** dial 66 42 11; in case of **fire,** dial 93; in case of **emergency,** dial 94.

Sarajevo

Tall, Communist-era buildings tower silently, abandoned, their windows jagged black holes. The city streets, which thronged with Olympic fervor 14 years ago, bear the

marks of grenades and shrapnel. Sarajevans speak of their city's prewar beauty; now it possesses a sad and scarred nobility, and a determination to restore what was lost.

Many of Sarajevo's traditional tourist sites were damaged during the war; inquire at the U.S. Embassy or at the tourist agency for an update. **Maršala Titova** (a.k.a. Maršala Tita) is the main street (*ulica*), running east to west through town. The **eternal flame** is a 1945 marker to all Sarajevans who died in World War II. Evidence of the recent four-year siege is not hard to find; the souvenir cartoon-style map (DM10) sold at **Šahinpašić,** Mustafe Bašeskije 1, highlights points of interest. At least half of Sarajevo's buildings sustained damage as a result of the war. The **National Library,** at the east end of town on Obala Kulina Bana, was once regarded as the most beautiful building in Sarajevo. It is now an open-air structure housing piles of rubble. Up in the hills, a **treeline** is sharply evident, demarcating the front lines.

The four different religious structures in town are representative of Sarajevo's diversity: a Catholic church, an Orthodox church, a mosque, and a synagogue, all in the downtown area. The cobbled **Baščaršija** (known as the Turkish quarter) lies on the east end of town, farther east on Ferhadija. The **Gazi Husref-Gebova Mosque** has towered over Ferhadija since its 1530 construction by the Ottoman Turks. Renovations should be completed by 1998; meanwhile, the mosque is open to visitors daily from 5am to 11pm. On the corner of Obala Kulina Bana and Zelenih Beretki, a plaque on a building wall commemorates the birthplace of **World War I.** It was here that Gavrilo Princip shot Austrian Archduke Franz Ferdinand on June 28, 1914.

Practical Information, Accommodations, and Food Some kiosks and bookstores stock city **maps** (DM10). Incoming citizens should register immediately with their embassy: **Canada,** Logavina 7 (tel. (071) 447 900; fax 447 901); **U.K.,** Tina Ujevića 8 (tel. (071) 66 61 29; fax 66 11 31); and **U.S.,** Alipašina 43 (tel. (071) 65 99 69 or 65 97 43; fax 65 97 22). **Australians** should contact their embassy in Vienna (see p. 78), and **New Zealanders** should contact their embassy in Rome (see p. 536). A **tourist bureau,** Zelenih Beretki 22a (tel. (071) 53 22 81; fax 53 26 06), provides hotel info (open Mon.-Fri. 8am-3pm, Sat. 8am-2pm). **Central Banka,** Zelenih Beretki 54 (tel. (071) 530 66 88; fax 53 24 06 or 66 38 55), exchanges money. The **train station** (tel. (071) 61 75 84) has limited service. The **bus station,** Kranjčevića 9 (tel. (071) 67 01 80 or 44 54 42, info 21 31 00), is behind the Holiday Inn. **Centrotrans** (tel. (071) 53 28 74; fax 67 06 99) runs to Dubrovnik (8hr., DM40), Frankfurt (3 per week, 15hr., DM180), Split (8hr., DM35), and Zagreb (10hr., DM60).

Housing is absurdly expensive. Private rooms are the only realistic options. **Euro-Club,** Valtera Perica 20 (tel. (071) 66 62 40; fax 20 79 60), in Skenderija, can sometimes help (contact them a week in advance; open Mon.-Sat. 10am-7pm). **Bosnia Tours,** Maršala Titova 54 (tel. (071) 20 22 06; tel./fax 20 22 07), is a private accommodations service (call ahead; DM60, 2 beds DM100; open Mon.-Sat. 8am-8pm). Scour the Turkish quarter for **Čevabdžinića** shops. A convenient **market** lies on Mula Mustafe Bašekija (open Mon.-Sat. 8am-5pm, Sun. 8am-noon). **Klub Preporod,** Branilaca Sarajeva 30, has classic Bosnian fare (DM7-12; open Mon.-Sat. 8am-10pm). The international crowd plugs in at the **Internet Cafe,** Maršala Titova 5, which boasts Czech *Budvar* (open Sun.-Thurs. 10am-1am, Fri.-Sat. until 3am). **Senator,** Štosmajerova bb, harbors the best **disco** in town on Friday and Saturday nights (open 8pm until people leave). In mid-September, the **Sarajevo Film Festival** gets rolling, organized by the Obala Art Center, Obala Kulina Bana 10 (tel. (071) 52 41 27; fax 66 45 47).

Mostar

For 400 years, Mostar beguiled visitors with its 16th-century Turkish bridge, which rose in a slender cobalt arc. Tragically, in November 1993, the bridge was destroyed by shelling; a swinging metal bridge stands as a replacement. As the main city in Herzeg-Bosna (the mostly Croat-controlled part of Bosnia), Mostar suffered severely from the recent war. Most of the sights that survived the war or have been reconstructed are in the **old Turkish quarter,** including 14th-century **mosques** and the **Turkish house,** Biscevica 13, which is always open. In his **workshop** at Kujundziluk 4 (tel. 55 00 22), master Ramiz Pandur fashions his world-famous etchings and reliefs. The **Neretva River** serves as a rough borderline between the Muslim eastern side, and the Croatian western side. Locals rarely cross over and no one can know what will happen if the international military force pulls out as scheduled on June 30, 1998. Violence in Mostar surrounding the Bosnian elections in September of 1997 illustrate the not-so-hidden tension between the two sides. As always, exercise caution.

The **bus station** (tel. (88) 56 04 95) in the Muslim part of town, services Sarajevo (4 per day, 2½hr., DM10), Zagreb (8:45am, 18hr., DM40), Dubrovnik (10am, 3hr., DM27), and Split (10:30am, 4hr., DM16). **Tourist agencies Atlas,** Kardinala Stepinca bb (tel./fax (88) 31 87 71), and **Reise Service** (tel./fax (88) 31 56 66) sit next to each other in **Hotel Ero;** walk across the bridge opposite the bus station into the Croat part of town and continue about 100m. Both agencies specialize in organizing vacations for locals but can also answer general questions and provide photocopied **maps** (both open Mon.-Fri. 8am-4pm and Sat. 8am-12pm). Exchange **traveler's checks** at **Hrvatska banka** (tel./fax (88) 31 21 20), in the same building. Hotels lie on the Croat side. **Hotel Ero,** Ante Starcevica bb (tel. (88) 31 71 66; fax 31 43 94), has singles (DM70) and doubles (DM120) with TV. Several kilometers from the bus station is the cheaper private hotel **Nikola Coric,** Fra Didaka Buntica 125a (tel. (88) 31 95 60; fax 31 95 59; DM50). The food on the Croatian side is unexceptional. You can get pizza (25kn) and *kava* (3kn) at **Cafe-Pizzeria Milano,** K. Tomislava (open Mon.-Fri. 8am-11pm, Sat.-Sun. 8am-midnight). On the Muslim side, **Babylon,** Tapmana bb, offers roasted trout (DM10) and brains in bread crumbs (DM10; open daily 9am-11pm).

Britain

US$1 = £0.61 (British pounds) — **£1 = US$1.64**
CDN$1 = £0.45 — **£1 = CDN$2.25**
IR£1 = £1.13 — **£1 = IR£0.89**
AUS$1 = £0.45 — **£1 = AUS$2.20**
NZ$1 = £0.40 — **£1 = NZ$2.53**
SAR = £0.13 — **£1 = SAR7.56**
Country Code: 44 — **International Dialing Prefix: 00**

English, a language of many fragmented dialects created by invaded and colonized peoples, is today the true *lingua franca*. One need only review the history of Britain to appreciate this paradox. Once considered too common for scholarship or rule, the tongue later became a tool in England's subjection of Wales, Scotland, and Ireland, and was integral to the creation of the modern British state—from mercantilism to Empire and beyond. "England" originally referred to a group of Anglo-Saxon principalities united in the 9th century, though it eventually came to mean the areas of most centralized power. In 1603, the union of England, Wales, and Scotland effectively occurred when Elizabeth I died and James VI of Scotland ascended to the throne as James I of England. After the French Revolution inspired the 1798 revolt in Ireland, Britain abolished Irish "self-government," and in 1801, the "United Kingdom of Great Britain and Ireland" was proclaimed. But in the 20th century, this union began to disintegrate, foreshadowing the collapse of the overseas Empire. Most of Ireland won independence in 1921; Scotland and Wales were promised regional autonomy in 1975. As the ongoing Troubles in Northern Ireland reflect, questions of union and nationalism will be contested for years to come. It's been a while since the Union Jack flew over two-fifths of the earth's surface, but the Empire's heirs retain a proud, sometimes arrogant, detachment toward the rest of the world.

Names, like language, hold a certain political force. Deciding just what to call this part of the world can incite local tempers and fuel debates. "Great Britain" refers to England, Scotland, and Wales (and don't call a Scot or Welshman "English"—it's neither accurate nor polite); the political terms "United Kingdom" and "Britain" refer to these regions, Northern Ireland, and the Isle of Man. Because of distinctions in laws and currency, *Let's Go* uses the term "Britain" to refer to England, Scotland, Wales, and the Isle of Man. Coverage of Northern Ireland is in the Ireland chapter for geographical convenience; no political statement is intended. Britain may be small but is clearly not homogeneous. For the traveler, such topographical, cultural, and economic difference so close together makes for an extremely rich journey. Look beyond London, allowing time for both the cities and the isolated, wild hills and sea.

For more detailed, exhilarating coverage of Britain and London, pore over *Let's Go: Britain & Ireland 1998* or *Let's Go: London 1998.*

GETTING THERE

In May 1994, the **Channel Tunnel** (Chunnel) was completed, physically connecting England and France (the horror!/*l'horreur!*). **Eurostar** operates rather like an airline, with similar discounts, reservations, and restrictions. Return tickets start at US$150, and 12 trains per day run from London and Paris. While France, Brit, BritFrance, Eurailpass, and Europasses are not tickets to ride, they are tickets to a discount, as is being a youth. From the U.S. call (800) EUROSTAR (387-6782) to purchase your ticket. In the U.K., call (01233) 61 75 75 for more information.

Stena Sealink (tel. (01233) 64 70 47 or 24 02 80) and **P&O** (tel. (0990) 98 09 80) offer extensive **ferry** service across the channel between France (Calais and Le Havre) and England (Dover or Portsmouth). Always ask about reduced fares—an HI card or ISIC with Travelsave stamps might win a 25-50% discount on your fare. Book ahead June through August. Other routes between the Continent and England include Bergen, Norway to Lerwick or Newcastle; Esbjerg, Denmark to Harwich; Gothenburg, Sweden to Harwich or Newcastle; Hamburg to Harwich or Newcastle; Oostende, Belgium to Ramsgate, near Dover; and Hook of Holland to Harwich.

Bus/ferry combinations are the best way to get from **Ireland** to Britain. **Supabus** (contact **Bus Éireann** in Cork, tel. (021) 50 60 66) runs a bus/ferry deal from Dublin to London twice a day. Depart Dublin at 10am (single IR£17, youth IR£15; IR£5 tax) and at 8:45pm (single IR£26, youth IR£24; IR£5 tax). Return prices range from IR£30-£43. Prices from London are the same, without the IR£5 tax. Supabus connects in London to the Eurolines network. **Bus Éireann** also offers daily service from Cork to London (IR£39-45, return IR£49-59; IR£5 tax).

GETTING AROUND

Fares on all modes of public transportation in Britain are generally labeled either single (one way) or return (round-trip). Period returns require you to return within a specific number of days; day returns are same-day round-trips.

Long-distance **coach** (bus) travel in Britain is more extensive than in most European countries and is the cheapest option. **National Express** (tel. (0990) 80 80 80) is the principal operator of long-distance coach services. For information contact **Eurolines (U.K.) Limited,** 23 Crawley Road, Luton LU1 1PP, England. Those 60 or over or 16-25 are eligible for Seniors' and Young Persons' **Discount Coach Cards** (£8), which reduce standard coach fares on National Express by about 30%.

Britain's **British Rail** service is extensive but expensive. If you plan to travel a great deal within Britain, the **BritRail Pass** can be a good buy. *You must buy BritRail Passes before arriving in Britain.* They allow unlimited travel in England, Wales, and Scotland; British Rail does not operate in Northern Ireland or the Republic of Ireland. In 1997, BritRail Passes cost US$249 for eight days (ages 16-25 US$199) and US$485 for 22 days (ages 16-25 US$389). BritRail Travel also offers **Flexipasses,** allowing travel on a limited number of days within a specific time period. The **Young Person's Railcard** (£16, valid for one year) offers 33% off most fares and discounts on Stena Sealink Line to Continental and Irish ports. You can buy this pass at major British Rail Travel Centres in the U.K. You must prove you're either between 16 and 25 (with a birth certificate or passport) or a full-time student over 23 at a British school, and submit two passport-sized photos. Families, seniors, and travelers in wheelchairs have their own Railcards. The **Eurail pass** is *not* accepted in Britain.

Much of Britain's countryside is well suited for **biking.** Many cities and villages have bike rental shops and maps of local cycle routes; ask at the tourist office. Large-scale Ordnance Survey maps detail the extensive system of long-distance **hiking** paths. Tourist offices and National Park Information Centres can provide extra information about routes. *Let's Go* does not recommend **hitchhiking,** but for those who decide to try, Vacation Work Publications publishes the *Hitch-Hikers' Manual: Britain,* which contains practical info on hitching laws, techniques, and the best places to hitch from 200 British towns (£4 plus £2.50 shipping).

ESSENTIALS

There are local **tourist offices** everywhere in Great Britain; most will book a place to stay for around £2. Most offices also offer a "book-a-bed-ahead" service; for about £2.50 (less in Wales), they will reserve a room in the next town you visit. Proprietors who have not paid a fee to be listed with a tourist office may be less visible.

The pound sterling (£) is the main unit of **currency** in the United Kingdom. One pound equals 100 pence (p). Northern Ireland, Scotland, and the Channel Islands have their own bank notes, which are identical in value to other British notes and can be used interchangeably with standard currency. Isle of Man notes can only be used within the Isle of Man, and you may have difficulty using Scottish £1 notes outside Scotland. Northern Ireland currency is not accepted in the rest of Britain. Most banks are open Monday through Friday 9:30am to 5pm, although the hours in small villages may be reduced. Britain closes for **bank holidays** on Jan. 1, Easter (April 10-13, 1998), May 4, May 25, Aug. 23, and Christmas (Dec. 25-26). Discount rates for students, seniors, children, and the unemployed are often grouped under the catch-all term "concessions." The U.K. charges a **value-added tax (VAT),** a national sales tax on most goods and some services; the rate is 17.5% on many services and all goods except books, medicine, and food. This tax is generally included in the listed price. Should you wish to receive a VAT refund, you must ask the shopkeeper from whom you buy your goods for the appropriate form, which customs officials will sign and stamp when you take your purchases through customs. Once home, send the form and a self-addressed, British-stamped envelope to the shopkeeper, who will mail your refund. You will, at some point, begin to wonder if that 17.5% is really worth it.

Communication British **pay phones** charge 10p for local calls. A series of harsh beeps will warn you to insert more money when your time is up. For the rest of the call, a display ticks off your credit in suspenseful 1p increments. Unused coins (not change) are returned (maybe). You may use remaining credit on a second call by pressing the "follow on call" button (often marked "FC"). Phones don't accept 1p, 2p, or 5p coins. If you plan to make several calls, pick up a **Phonecard,** available in denominations of £2, £5, £10, and £20. Get them at post offices, newsagents, or John Menzies stationery shops. Phone booths that take cards are labeled in green and are common except in rural areas; coin booths are labeled in red.

To make **international calls,** call direct or access an operator in the country you're dialing—rates for operator-assisted calls are often cheaper and the service a bit speedier. For **AT&T Direct,** dial 0800 89 00 11; **MCI WorldPhone,** 0800 89 02 22; **Canada Direct,** 0800 89 00 16; **Australia Direct,** 0800 89 00 61; **New Zealand Direct,** 0800 89 00 64. For the operator, dial 100; directory inquires, 192; international directory inquiries, 153; the international operator, 155. The general **emergency** number for Britain and Ireland is 999; no coins needed.

Accommodations Britain has hundreds of **youth hostels,** both HI and independent. **YHA** (England and Wales) and **SYHA** (Scotland) are the national HI affiliates in Britain. Hostels here are sometimes closed from 10am to 5pm, and some impose an 11pm curfew. Some require sleep sacks; most prohibit sleeping bags. If these regulations cramp your style, stick to looser independent establishments. Remember, quality can vary dramatically. Always book ahead in high season.

Native to Britain, the term **bed and breakfast** generally means a small place that offers basic accommodations and breakfast at a reasonable price, often in private homes. B&Bs (usually £10-24, in London £16-60) are extremely widespread; when one is full, ask the owner for a referral. Some proprietors grant considerable rate reductions to guests who pay in advance or by the week and offer discounts between September and May. **Bed and Breakfast (GB),** PO Box 66, 94 Bell St., Henley-on-Thames, Oxon, England RG9 1XS (tel. (01491) 57 88 03; fax 41 08 06), covers London, England, Scotland, Wales, and Ireland for £30 and up. Cheap hotels, often called guest houses, can sometimes offer even better bargains than B&Bs.

Food and Drink British cuisine's deservedly modest reputation redeems itself in a few areas. Britain is largely a nation of carnivores; the best native dishes are roasts—beef, lamb, and Wiltshire hams. And meat isn't just for dinner; the British like their famed breakfasts meaty and cholesterol-filled. Typical breakfast fare includes orange juice, cereal, eggs, bacon, sausage, toast, butter, grilled tomatoes, mushrooms, and, in winter, porridge. Veggies are the weakest, mushiest part of any meal. Salads often mean a mixture of mayo and something else. Before you leave the country, you must try any of the sweet, glorious British puddings.

Pub grub (food served in bars) is fast, filling, and generally cheap. The "ploughman's lunch" (a product of a 60s advertising campaign) consists of cheese, bread, pickle, chutney, and a tomato. Fish and chips are traditionally drowned in vinegar and salt. Caffs (full meals £5-6) are the British equivalent of U.S. diners. To escape English food, try Chinese, Greek, and especially Indian cuisines. Most restaurants figure a service charge into the bill, but if not, leave a 10-15% tip.

British "tea" refers both to a drink and a social ritual. Tea the drink is served strong and milky; if you want it any other way, say so in advance. Tea the social can be a meal unto itself. Afternoon high tea as it is still served in rural Britain includes cooked meats, salad, sandwiches, and pastries. Cream tea, a specialty of Cornwall and Devon, includes toast, shortbread, crumpets, scones, jam, and clotted cream.

The British pub is a social institution where individuals and communities come together for conversation and relaxation. This attitude is reflected in the careful furnishing of pubs, which resemble the private living rooms they have come to replace. Drinks are generally served from 11am to 11pm, Sundays noon to 10:30pm. Beer is the standard drink. Bear in mind that British beer may have a higher alcohol content than what you're accustomed to, and that British beer is usually served room temperature. Lager (the European equivalent of American beer) is served at a colder temperature. Traditional cider, a fermented apple juice served sweet or dry, is a potent and tasty alternative to beer. Remember never to tip at a pub!

ENGLAND

A land where there is the promise of a cup of tea just beyond even the darkest moor, England, for better or worse, has determined the meaning of "civilized" for many peoples and cultures. The driving force behind the brilliant expansion of the British empire, it is only since the end of World War II that England has been forced to play a more modest role and pay cultural atonement for its imperialist past. With its economy in trouble and Irish, Welsh, and Scottish nationalism on the rise, an uneasy sense of emptiness has settled over the land. Now that the sun has almost set on the British empire, the English, who have always termed themselves as British, are searching for an identity of their own. Out of the decay has come a new culture—everyone from punk rockers to tabloid writers are defining "English" as the antithesis of everything "British" used to mean. Tourists today can choose to linger in the glorious past, or to do as the English do and saucily throw off the burdens of civilization.

London

At first glance, London is kind to the expectations of visitors stuffing their mental baggage with bobbies and Beefeaters, nursery rhymes and "Masterpiece Theatre," Sherlock Holmes and history books. The relatively small area embraced by the Underground's Circle Line seems to burst with "big sights," and all the city's double-decker red buses appear to spin around the mad whirl of Piccadilly Circus. But central London is just a speck on the Greater London map. Beyond Tower Bridge looms the pyramid-tipped Canary Wharf skyscraper, centerpiece of the world's largest and most controversial redevelopment. The Victorian doorway crafted with Anglican piety may belong to a Sikh or a Muslim in a city internalizing its imperial past. Part of what makes London fascinating is this tension between the close quarters of central London and the expansive boroughs; between the cluttered, "familiar," sometimes fictional past of the heritage industry and a riotously modern present.

For an absolutely smashing little book packed with first-rate information on this city, grab a copy of *Let's Go: London 1998.*

ORIENTATION AND PRACTICAL INFORMATION

London is divided into boroughs and postal code areas, and into informal districts. Both the borough name and postal code prefix appear at the bottom of most street signs. The city has grown by absorbing nearby towns, an expansion reflected in borough names such as "City of Westminster" and "City of London" (or "The City").

Central London, on the north side of the Thames and bounded roughly by the Underground's Circle Line, contains most of the major sights. Within central London, the vaguely defined **West End** incorporates the understated elegance of Mayfair, the shopping streets around Oxford Circus, the theaters and tourist traps of Piccadilly Circus and Leicester Square, the exotic labyrinth of Soho, chic Covent Garden, and London's unofficial center, **Trafalgar Square.** East of the West End lies **Holborn,** center of legal activity, and **Fleet Street,** the journalists' traditional haunt.

Around the southeastern corner of the Circle Line is **The City:** London's financial district, with the Tower of London at its eastern edge and St. Paul's Cathedral nearby. Farther east is the ethnically diverse and working-class **East End** and the epic construction site of **Docklands.** Moving back west, along the river and the southern part of the Circle Line is the district of **Westminster,** the royal, political, and ecclesiastical center of England, where you'll find Buckingham Palace, the Houses of Parliament,

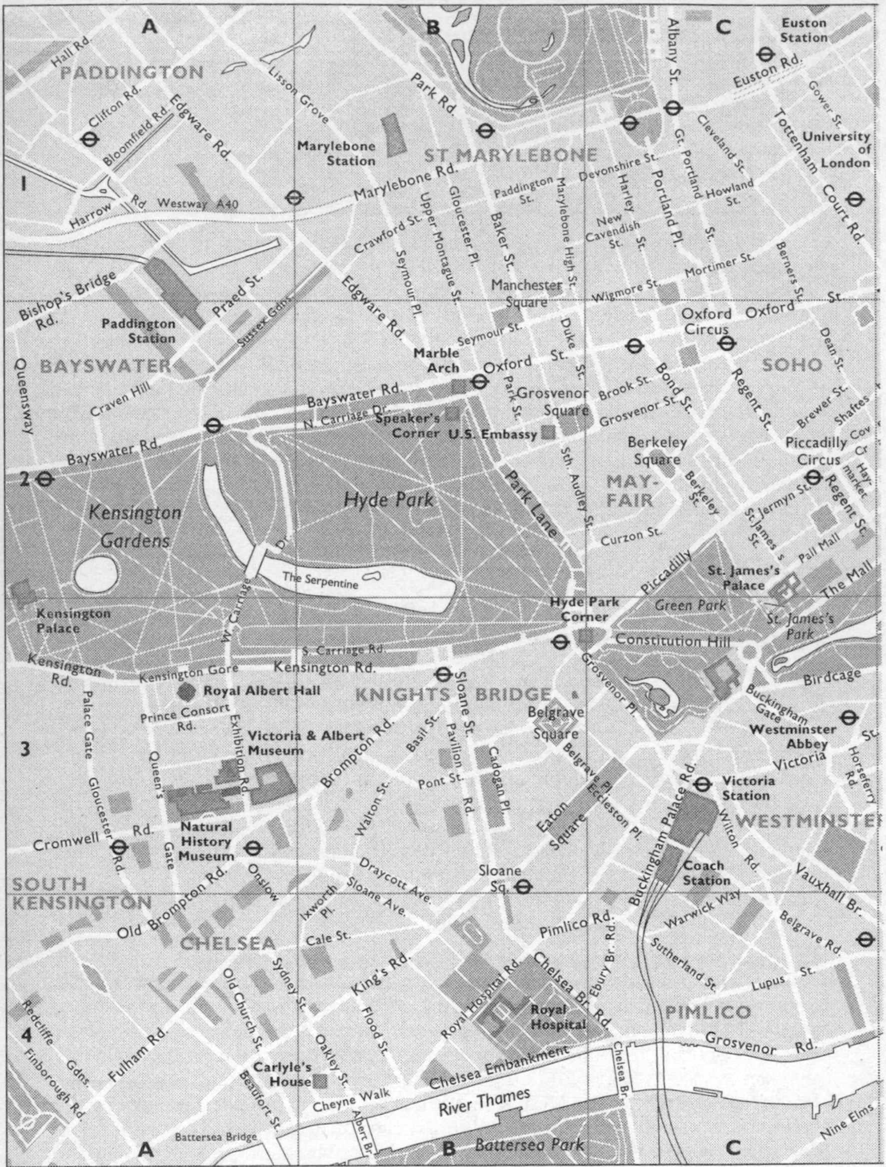

Central London: Major Street Finder

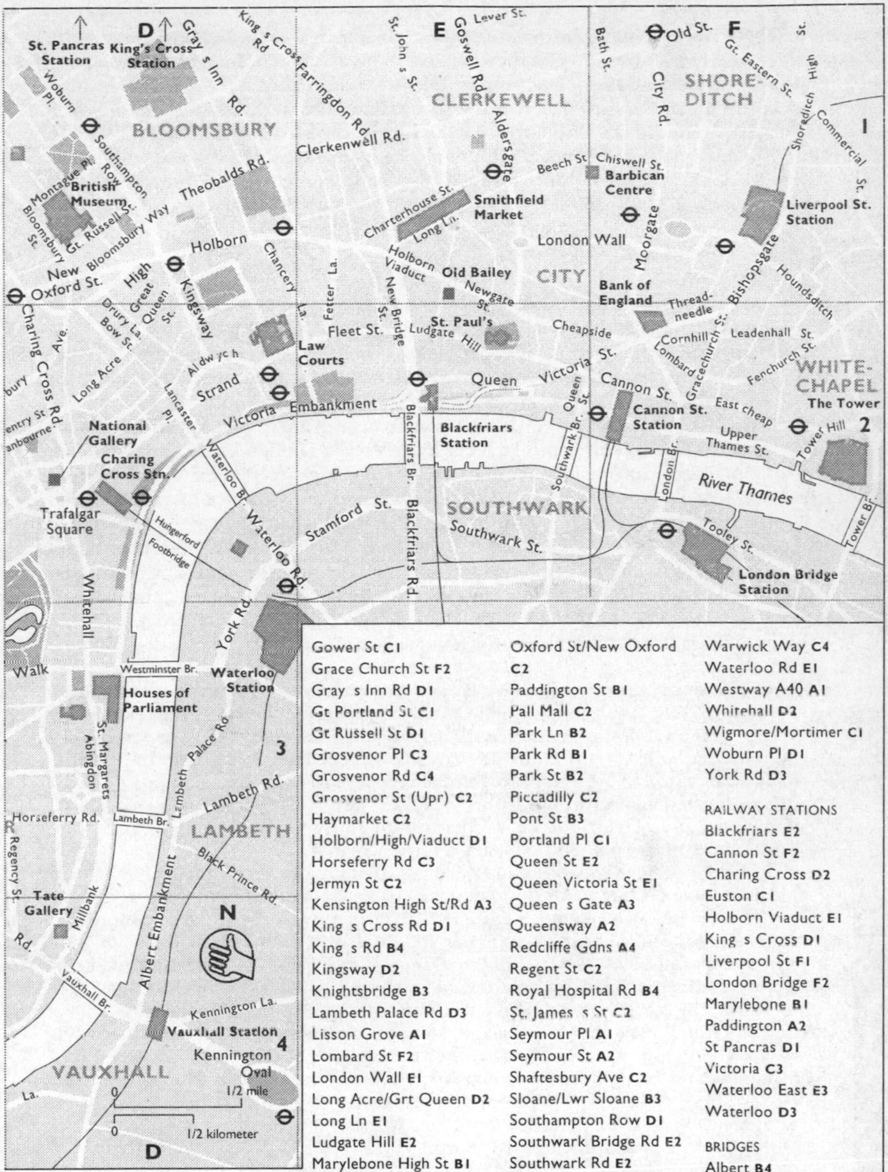

Edgware Rd **A1**
Euston Rd **C1**
Exhibition Rd **A3**
Farringdon Rd **E1**
Fenchurch/Aldgate **F2**
Fleet St **E2**
Fulham Rd **A4**
Gloucester Pl **B1**
Gloucester Rd **A3**
Goswell Rd **E1**
Gower St **C1**
Grace Church St **F2**
Gray s Inn Rd **D1**
Gt Portland St **C1**
Gt Russell St **D1**
Grosvenor Pl **C3**
Grosvenor Rd **C4**
Grosvenor St (Upr) **C2**
Haymarket **C2**
Holborn/High/Viaduct **D1**
Horseferry Rd **C3**
Jermyn St **C2**
Kensington High St/Rd **A3**
King s Cross Rd **D1**
King s Rd **B4**
Kingsway **D2**
Knightsbridge **B3**
Lambeth Palace Rd **D3**
Lisson Grove **A1**
Lombard St **F2**
London Wall **E1**
Long Acre/Grt Queen **D2**
Long Ln **E1**
Ludgate Hill **E2**
Marylebone High St **B1**
Marylebone Rd **B1**
Millbank **D4**
Montague Pl **D1**
Moorgate **F1**
New Bridge St **E2**
New Cavendish **C1**
Newgate St **E1**
Nine Elms Ln **C4**
Oakley St **B4**
Old St **F1**
Old Brompton Rd **A4**
Onslow Sq/St **A3**
Oxford St/New Oxford **C2**
Paddington St **B1**
Pall Mall **C2**
Park Ln **B2**
Park Rd **B1**
Park St **B2**
Piccadilly **C2**
Pont St **B3**
Portland Pl **C1**
Queen St **E2**
Queen Victoria St **E1**
Queen s Gate **A3**
Queensway **A2**
Redcliffe Gdns **A4**
Regent St **C2**
Royal Hospital Rd **B4**
St. James s St **C2**
Seymour Pl **A1**
Seymour St **A2**
Shaftesbury Ave **C2**
Sloane/Lwr Sloane **B3**
Southampton Row **D1**
Southwark Bridge Rd **E2**
Southwark Rd **E2**
St. Margarets/Abingdon **D3**
Stamford St **E2**
Strand **D2**
Sydney St **A4**
Thames St(Upr&Lwr) **F2**
The Mall **C2**
Theobald s Rd **D1**
Threadneedle St **F2**
Tottenham Ct Rd **C1**
Vauxhall Br. Rd **C4**
Victoria Embankment **D2**
Victoria St **C3**
Warwick Way **C4**
Waterloo Rd **E1**
Westway A40 **A1**
Whitehall **D2**
Wigmore/Mortimer **C1**
Woburn Pl **D1**
York Rd **D3**

RAILWAY STATIONS

Blackfriars **E2**
Cannon St **F2**
Charing Cross **D2**
Euston **C1**
Holborn Viaduct **E1**
King s Cross **D1**
Liverpool St **F1**
London Bridge **F2**
Marylebone **B1**
Paddington **A2**
St Pancras **D1**
Victoria **C3**
Waterloo East **E3**
Waterloo **D3**

BRIDGES

Albert **B4**
Battersea **A4**
Blackfriars **E2**
Chelsea **C4**
Hungerford Footbridge **D2**
Lambeth **D3**
London Bridge **F2**
Southwark **E2**
Tower Bridge **F2**
Waterloo **D2**
Westminster **D3**

and Westminster Abbey. In the southwest corner of the Circle Line, below the expanse of **Hyde Park,** are gracious **Chelsea,** embassy-laden **Belgravia,** and **Kensington,** adorned with London's posher shops and restaurants.

Around the northwest corner of the Circle Line, tidy terraces border **Regent's Park;** nearby are the faded squares of **Paddington** and **Notting Hill Gate,** home to large Indian and West Indian communities. Moving east toward the Circle Line's northeast corner leads to **Bloomsbury,** which harbors the British Museum, London University colleges, art galleries, and specialty bookshops. Trendy residential districts stretch to the north, including **Hampstead** and **Highgate,** with the enormous Hampstead Heath and fabulous views of the city.

Trying to reach a **specific destination** in London can be frustrating. Numbers often go up one side of a street and down the other. One road may change names four times in fewer miles, and a single name may designate a street, lane, square, and row. **Postal code prefixes,** which often appear on London street signs and in street addresses, may help you find your way. The letters stand for compass directions, with reference to the central district (itself divided into WC and EC, for West Central and East Central). All districts that border this central district are numbered "1." There are no S or NE codes. A **good map** is key. For a day's walk, London Transport's free map will do, but visitors staying longer ought to buy a London street index. *London A to Z* (that's "ay to *zed,*" by the way) and *Nicholson's Streetfinder* (from £2) are excellent.

For the most part, London is a tourist-friendly city. It's hard to wander unwittingly into unnerving neighborhoods; these areas, in parts of Hackney, Tottenham, and South London, lie well away from central London. The areas around King's Cross/St. Pancras and Notting Hill Gate tube stations are a bit seedy at night. In general, unattended packages will be taken either by thieves or by the police, who are remarkably anxious (and rightly so) about terrorist bombs. Leave nothing unattended.

Tourist Offices: London Tourist Board Information Centre: Victoria Station Forecourt, SW1 (tel. (0839) 123 432; recorded message only; 39-49p per min.). Tube: Victoria. Info on London and England and an accommodations service (£5 booking fee, plus 15% refundable deposit). Expect long waits. Open April-Nov. daily 8am-7pm; Dec.-March Mon.-Sat. 8am-7pm, Sun. 8am-5pm. Additional tourist offices located at Heathrow Airport (open April-Nov. daily 9am-6pm; Dec.-March 9am-5pm) and "Liverpool St." Underground Station (open Mon. 8:15am-7pm, Tues.-Sat. 8:15am-6pm, Sun. 8:30am-4:45pm). **British Travel Centre:** 12 Regent St. Tube: Piccadilly Circus. Down Regent St. from the "Lower Regent St." tube exit. Ideal for travelers bound for destinations outside of London. Combines the services of the BTA, British Rail, and a Traveller's Exchange with an accommodations service (£5 plus 15% deposit). Open May-Oct. Mon.-Fri. 9am-6:30pm, Sat. 9am-5pm, Sun. 10am-4pm; Nov.-April Mon.-Fri. 9am-6:30pm, Sat.-Sun. 10am-4pm. **City of London Information Centre:** St. Paul's Churchyard, EC4 (tel. 606 30 30). Tube: St. Paul's. Info on the City of London. Open daily 9am-5pm.

Budget Travel: London is *the* place to shop for cheap bus, plane, and train tickets to anywhere. Browse ads in *Time Out* or the *Evening Standard.*

Embassies and High Commissions: Australia, Australia House, The Strand, WC2 (tel. 379 43 34). Tube: Aldwych or Temple. Open Mon.-Fri. 9:30am-3:30pm. **Canada,** MacDonald House, 1 Grosvenor Sq., W1 (tel. 258 66 00). Tube: Bond St. or Oxford Circus. **Ireland,** 17 Grosvenor Pl., SW1 (tel. 235 21 71). Tube: Hyde Park Corner. Open Mon.-Fri. 9:30am-1pm and 2:15-5pm. **New Zealand,** New Zealand House, 80 Haymarket, SW1 (tel. 930 84 22). Tube: Charing Cross. Open Mon.-Fri. 10am-noon and 2-4pm. **South Africa,** South Africa House, Trafalgar Sq., WC2 (tel. 451 72 99). Tube: Charing Cross. Open 10am-noon and 2-4pm. **U.S.,** 24 Grosvenor Sq., W1 (tel. 499 90 00). Tube: Bond St. Phones answered 24hr.

Flights: Heathrow Airport (tel. (0181) 759 43 21) is the world's busiest airport. From Heathrow, take the **Underground** to central London (45min.). London Transport's **Airbus** (tel. 222 12 34) zips from Heathrow to central points, including hotels (6:15am-8:30pm, 1hr., £6). From **Gatwick Airport** (tel. (01293) 53 53 53), take the BR Gatwick Express train to Victoria Station (daily 5:30am-11pm every 15min., 11pm-1am and 4-5:30am every 30min., 1-4am every hr. on the hr.; 35min.; day return £8.50-10). **National Express** (tel. (0990) 80 80 80) buses run from Victoria Station to Gatwick (every hr., 5:30am-10pm; 1hr.; £7.50, return £11). Taxis take twice as long and cost 5 times as much. British Rail's **Stansted Express** runs to **Stansted Airport** (tel. (01279) 68 05 00) from Liverpool St. station (£10).

Trains: 8 major stations: Charing Cross, Euston, King's Cross, Liverpool St., Paddington, St. Pancras, Victoria, and Waterloo. All stations linked by Underground. For train info stop by ticket offices at the stations or any LTB or BTA tourist office, or call **British Rail** at (0345) 48 49 50 (24hr.). For info on traveling to Europe, try (0990) 84 88 48. For **Eurostar** info (through the Chunnel), call (0345) 88 18 81.

Buses: Victoria Coach Station (tube: Victoria), located on Buckingham Palace Rd., is the hub of Britain's denationalized coaches. **National Express** (tel. (0990) 80 80 80) services an expansive network. Greater London area served by **Green Line** (tel. (0181) 668 72 61), which leaves frequently from Eccleston Bridge behind Victoria Station. Purchase tickets from the driver. Deals include the one-day **Rover** ticket (£7, valid on almost every Green Line coach and London Country bus Mon.-Fri. after 9am, Sat.-Sun. all day).

Public Transportation: London is divided into 6 concentric transport zones; fares depend on the distance of the journey and the number of zones crossed. Call the 24hr. help line (222 12 34) for a live operator, who will help you plan subway and bus travel. The **Underground** (or **tube**) is fast, efficient, and crowded. It opens about 6am; the last train runs around midnight. Buy your ticket before you board and pass it through automatic gates at both ends of your journey. On-the-spot £10 fine if you're caught without a valid ticket. The **Travelcard** is a must for budget travelers. One-day Travelcards cannot be used before 9:30am Mon.-Fri. and are not valid on night buses (adult one-day Travelcard, zones 1 & 2, £3.20). Travelcards can be used on the Underground, regular buses, British Rail (Network SouthEast), and the Docklands Light Railway. The one-week and one-month Travelcards can be used at any time and are valid for Night Bus travel. (1-week Travelcard, zones 1&2, £15.70; 1-month Travelcard, zones 1&2, £60.30. Bring a passport-sized photo.) **Night buses** (the "N" routes) run frequently throughout London 11:30pm-6am. All pass through Trafalgar Sq. Pick up a free brochure about night buses, which includes times of the last British Rail and Underground trains. The **bus** network is divided into 4 zones. In and around central London, one-way fares range from 50p to £1.20, depending on the number of zones you cross. Bus 11 (originating at Liverpool St. station) and Bus 14 (beginning in Riverside-Putney) offer excellent sightseeing opportunities. Pick up free maps and guides at **London Transport's Information Centres** (look for the lower-case "i" logo on signs) at the following tube stations: Euston, Victoria, King's Cross, Liverpool St., Oxford Circus, Piccadilly, St. James's Park, and at Heathrow Terminals 1, 2, and 4.

Taxis: A light signifies that they're empty. Fares are steep, and 10% tip is standard.

Hitchhiking: Anyone who values safety will take a train or bus out of London. Hitchers check the University of London Union's **ride board,** on the ground floor of 1 Malet St., WC1 (tube: Russell Sq.), or ask at youth hostels. **Freewheelers** is a rideshare agency. £10 annual membership required. Each match-up costs £3. Single-sex matching available. Email freewheelers@freewheelers.co.uk, check out http://www.freewheelers.co.uk/freewheelers, or write Freewheelers, Ltd., 25 Low Friar St., Newcastle upon Tyne, NE1 5UE.

Bisexual, Gay, and Lesbian Information: London Lesbian and Gay Switchboard: tel. 837 73 24. 24hr. advice and support service. **Bisexual Helpline:** tel. (0181) 569 75 00. Tues.-Wed. 7:30-9:30pm. **Lesbian Line:** tel. 251 69 11. Mon. 6-10pm, Tues.-Thurs. 7-10pm, Fri. 3-6pm.

Crisis Lines: Samaritans: 46 Marshall St., W1 (tel. 734 28 00). Tube: Oxford Circus. Highly respected 24hr. crisis hotline listens (rather than advises) to callers with suicidal depression and other problems. **The London Rape Crisis Centre's Rape Crisis Hotline,** P.O. Box 69, WC1 (tel. 837 16 00). Phones answered Mon.-Fri. 6-10pm, Sat.-Sun. 10am-10pm. **National AIDS Helpline:** tel. (0800) 567 123. 24hr.

Information for Travelers with Disabilities: RADAR, 12 City Forum, 250 City Rd., EC1V 8AF (tel. 250 32 22). Open Mon.-Fri. 10am-4pm.

Pharmacies: Police stations keep lists of emergency doctors and pharmacists. Listings under "Chemists" in the Yellow Pages. **Bliss Chemists** at Marble Arch (5 Marble Arch, W1; tel. 723 61 16) is open daily 9am-midnight.

Medical Assistance: In an emergency, you can be treated at no charge in the A&E ward of a hospital. Socialized medicine has lowered fees here, so don't ignore any health problem merely because you are low on cash. The following have 24hr. walk-in A&E (also known as casualty) departments: **Royal London Hospital,** Whitechapel (tel. 377 70 00; tube: Whitechapel); **Royal Free Hospital,** Pond St., NW3 (tel. 794 05 00; tube: Belsize Park or British Rail: Hampstead Heath); **Charing Cross Hospital,** Fulham Palace Rd. (entrance St. Dunstan's Rd.), W6 (tel. (0181) 846 12 34; tube: Baron's Ct. or Hammersmith); **St. Thomas' Hospital,** Lambeth Palace Rd., SE1 (tel. 928 92 92; tube: Westminster); **University College Hospital,** Gower St. (entrance on Grafton Way), WC1 (tel. 387 93 00; tube: Euston or Warren St.). Or, look under "Hospitals" in the gray Businesses and Services phone book.

Emergency: Dial 999; no coins required.

Internet Access: Webshack, 15 Dean St., W1 (tel. 439 80 00). Tube: Leicester Sq. or Tottenham Ct. £3 for 30min. £5 for 1hr. Open Mon.-Sat. 11am-midnight. **Cyberia,** 39 Whitfeld St., W1. Tube: Goodge St. £3 for 30min., concessions £2.40. Open Mon.-Fri. 9:30am-10pm, Sat.-Sun. 10am-9pm.

Post Office: Save hassle and have mail sent to **Trafalgar Sq.,** 24-28 William IV St., London WC2N 4DL (tel. 930 95 80). Tube: Charing Cross. Open Mon.-Thurs. and Sat. 8am-8pm, Fri. 8:30am-8pm.

Telephones: Most phones accept change and phonecards, but some accept only phonecards. London has 2 **city codes:** 0171 (central London) and 0181 (outer London). Use the code only if you are calling from one area to the other. **All London numbers listed in Let's Go are 0171 unless otherwise indicated.**

ACCOMMODATIONS

Write well in advance to reserve rooms for summer—landing in London without reservations is like landing on a bicycle that has no seat. B&Bs are a bargain for groups of two or more, but hostels are the cheapest (and most social) option for small groups. Check for reduced weekly rates in hotels. Colleges and universities rent out rooms during the summer, offering the best deals to students with ID.

YHA/HI Hostels

Cheap and cheery, London's YHA hostels can be a welcome relief from dreary urban B&Bs. Reserve ahead for July and August; if not, it's still worth calling (central tel. 248 65 47; Mon.-Sat. 9:30am-5:30pm). Bring a padlock to secure your personal locker.

Oxford Street, 14-18 Noel St., W1 (tel. 734 16 18; fax 734 16 57). Tube: Oxford Circus. Walk east on Oxford St. and turn right on Poland St. Close to the Soho action. TV lounge, kitchen, and currency exchange. 24hr. security; no curfew. Superb location makes up for the expense: £18-19.50. Book at least 3-4 wks. in advance; full payment required to reserve. No children. Reception open 7am-11pm. MC, V.

Hampstead Heath, 4 Wellgarth Rd., NW11 (tel. (0181) 458 90 54, -70 96; fax 209 05 46). Tube: Golders Green, then bus 210 or 268 toward Hampstead, or on foot by turning left from the station onto North End Rd. and then left again onto Wellgarth Rd. (10min.). A beautiful, sprawling hostel. Kitchen and laundry facilities. Lovely backyard and outdoor walkway. 24hr. security and check-in. No curfew. Book in advance. £15; under 18 £12.80. Special family rates. MC, V.

City of London, 36 Carter Ln., EC4 (tel. 236 49 65; fax 236 76 81). Tube: St. Paul's. From the City Information Centre on the opposite side of St. Paul's Cathedral, go left down Godliman St., then take the first right onto Carter Lane. Antiseptic cleanliness, secure luggage storage, currency exchange, laundry facilities, theater box office, and 24hr. security. Reception open 7am-11pm. Single-sex rooms only. £18.50-23.50, under 18 £16-20. Call at least a week in advance. MC, V.

Earl's Court, 38 Bolton Gdns., SW5 (tel. 373 70 83; fax 835 20 34). Tube: Earl's Ct. Exit from the tube station onto Earl's Court Rd. and turn right; Bolton Gdns. is the 5th street on your left. A converted townhouse in a leafy residential neighborhood. Kitchen and laundry access. Reception open 7am-11pm. 24hr. security. No curfew. All rooms single-sex. £18, under 18 £15.80. Nonmembers £1.50 extra. £1 student discount. Breakfast included. MC, V.

Holland House, Holland Walk, W8 (tel. 937 07 48; fax 376 06 67). Tube: High St. Ken. Handsome Jacobean mansion and nondescript modern addition. HI membership required. Laundry and kitchen facilities. Reception open 7:30am-11:30pm. 24hr. access. Quiet room with **Internet** capability. £18. MC, V.

King's Cross/St. Pancras, 79-81 Euston Rd., N1 (tel. 248 65 47; fax 236 65 47). Tube: King's Cross/St. Pancras or Euston. Set to open in October 1997. Centrally located. Prices are expected to hover around £20. MC, V.

Private Hostels

Private hostels, which do not require an HI card, generally have a youthful clientele and often sport a vaguely bohemian atmosphere. Some have kitchen facilities and curfews are rare.

Central University of Iowa Hostel, 7 Bedford Pl., WC1 (tel. 580 11 21; fax 580 56 38). Tube: Holborn or Russell Sq. From "Russell Sq." tube stop, head left and turn left onto Southampton Row, then turn right onto Russell Sq.; Bedford Pl. is the first left. Bright, spartan rooms with bunk beds, new wood furniture, and bookshelves. Laundry facilities, towels and linen, TV lounge. Reception open 9am-1pm and 3-8:30pm. No curfew. Singles £20. Doubles £18. Triples or quads £16. £10 key deposit. Breakfast included. Open mid-May to mid-Aug. AmEx, MC, V.

Astor's Museum Inn, 27 Montague St., WC1 (tel. 580 53 60; fax 636 79 48). Tube: Holborn, Tottenham Ct. Rd., or Russell Sq. Off Bloomsbury Sq. The prime location compensates for standard dorms. If they're full, they'll direct you to 1 of 3 other Astor's hostels and pay for your tube or cab fare. Adequate linens provided. Reception open 24hr. No curfew. Coed dorms almost inevitable. £13-17. Discounts available Oct.-March. Breakfast included. Book about a month ahead. MC, V.

Tonbridge School Clubs, Ltd. (tel. 837 44 06), Judd and Cromer St., WC1. Tube: King's Cross/St. Pancras. Follow Euston Rd. to the site of the new British Library and turn left onto Judd St.; the hostel is 3 blocks down. Students with non-British passports only. No frills and no privacy, but dirt cheap. Blankets and foam pads provided. Lockout 9am-9pm. Lights off 11:30pm. Use caution when walking in the area at night. Floor space £5. Men are advised to call ahead.

Quest Hotel, 45 Queensborough Terr., W2 (tel. 229 77 82). Tube: Queensway. From the tube, take a left onto Bayswater, walk 2 blocks and turn left onto Queensborough Terr. Communal, clean, and sociable. Kitchen. 10am checkout. No curfew or lock-out. £12.50-17. Breakfast and sheets included. Key deposit £3. MC, V.

Palace Hotel, 31 Palace Ct., W2 (tel. 221 56 28; fax 243 81 57). Tube: Notting Hill Gate or Queensway. From Notting Hill Gate, walk east until Notting Hill Gate turns into Bayswater, then turn left onto Palace Ct. From Queensway, walk west on Bayswater and take a right onto Palace Ct. Young community atmosphere and bright dorm rooms. Shower facilities are immaculate. Reception open 24hr. No curfew. Laundry. £12. Weekly: £60. Breakfast included. Cash only.

Albert Hotel, 191 Queens Gate, SW7 (tel. 584 30 19; fax 823 85 20). Tube: Gloucester Rd., or Bus 2 from South Kensington. A substantial walk from the tube; take a right on Cromwell and a left on Queen's Gate. Beautiful, Gothic entrance leads into elegant, wood-paneled hostel with sweeping staircases. Laundry. Reception open 24hr. Dorms £11-15. Singles or twins £40. Weekly: dorm only, £66. Breakfast and linen included. Reserve with 1 night's deposit. MC, V (over £50).

O'Callaghan's Hotel, 205 Earl's Ct. Rd., SW5 (tel. 370 30 00; fax 370 26 23). Tube: Earl's Court. A bare bones place to hit the hay; guests like the relaxed atmosphere as well as the prices. Friendly management will pick you up from Victoria and drive you to two other branches if first hostel is full. Reception open 24hr. Dorms £10. Doubles £24. Weekly: dorms £60; doubles £140. Winter discounts.

Victoria Hotel, 71 Belgrave Rd. SW1 (tel. 834 30 77; fax 932 06 93). Tube: Pimlico. From the station, take the Bessborough St. (south side) exit and go left along Lupus St., then take a right at St. George's Sq. Belgrave Rd. starts on the other side. A clean, friendly, bohemian hostel. Kitchen. Reception open 24hr. £12.50-15. Luggage storage and breakfast included. MC, V.

University Halls of Residence

London's university residences often accommodate visitors during the summer break (early June to mid-Sept.) and Easter vacations. Many of these halls have box-like rooms and institutional furniture. Most charge £18-25 and contain all singles. Call well in advance (by April for July reservations), as conference groups snatch up rooms early. The **King's Campus Vacation Bureau** (write to 127 Stanford Street, SE1 9NQ; tel. 928 37 77) controls bookings for a number of residential halls.

High Holborn Residence, 178 High Holborn, WC1 (tel. 379 55 89; fax 379 56 40). Tube: Holborn. An amazing combination of comfort and affordability. Singles are spacious and immaculately furnished. You could eat off the bathroom floors, if so inclined. Usually booked far in advance. Continental breakfast. Lounge and bar. Laundry facilities. Reception open daily 7am-11pm. Singles £27. Twins £45, with bath £52. Discounts for longer stays. Open July to mid-Sept.

Wellington Hall, 71 Vincent Sq., Westminster, SW1 (tel. 834 47 40; fax 233 77 09). Tube: Victoria. Walk 1 long block along Vauxhall Bridge Rd.; turn left on Rochester Row. Charming Edwardian hall on pleasant, quiet square. Memorable oak panels and stained-glass windows in dining room. Spacious rooms. English breakfast. Reserve through King's Campus Vacation Bureau (see above). Singles £23. Doubles £35. Discounts for longer stays. Rooms generally available June-Sept. and Easter.

Carr Saunders Hall, 18-24 Fitzroy St., W1 (tel. 323 97 12; fax 580 47 18). Tube: Warren St. Reception open Sun.-Thurs. 8:30am-midnight, Fri.-Sat. 8:30am-2am. Singles £23. Doubles £42. MC, V.

John Adams Hall, 15-23 Endsleigh St., WC1 (tel. 387 40 86; fax 383 01 64). Tube: Euston. Heading right on Euston Rd., take 1st right onto Gordon St. and 1st left onto Endsleigh Gdns.; Endsleigh St. is the 2nd right. Elegant Georgian building. English breakfast. Laundry facilities, TV lounge, and 5 pianos. Reception open Mon.-Fri. 8am-1pm and 2-10pm, Sat. 8am-1pm and 5:30-10pm, Sun. 9am-1pm and 5:30-10pm. Singles £21.40. Doubles £37. 5 or more days: singles £19; doubles £33. Open July-Aug. and Easter, but a few rooms free all year. MC, V.

Bed & Breakfasts

The number of B&Bs boggles the mind. While some are about as indistinct as blades of grass, many feature unique furnishings and a warm, welcoming atmosphere.

Near Victoria Station

B&Bs around Victoria Station are close to London's attractions as well as transportation connections. In the summer, prudent visitors make reservations well in advance.

Melbourne House, 79 Belgrave Rd., SW1 (tel. 828 35 16; fax 828 71 20). Past Warwick Sq. Closer to "Pimlico" than "Victoria"; from "Pimlico," take the Bessborough St. (south side) exit and go left along Lupus St. Turn right at St. George's Sq.; Belgrave Rd. starts on the other side of the square. Recent refurbishments have improved an already top choice. English breakfast. Singles £28. Doubles or twins £68. Triples £85. Family quads £100. Winter discount. Book ahead. MC, V.

Oxford House, 92-94 Cambridge St., SW1 (tel. 834 64 67; fax 834 02 25), close to the church. From St. George's Sq. (see directions above to St. George's), turn right onto Clarendon St., then take the 1st left onto Cambridge St. A true B&B, guests are welcomed into the family. Fabulous English breakfast. Singles £34. Doubles £44-46. Triples £56-59. Quads £76-80. By reservation only. MC, V (5% surcharge).

Georgian House Hotel, 35 St. George's Dr., SW1 (tel. 834 14 38; fax 976 60 85). Terrific discounts on rooms on the 3rd and 4th floors. Huge English breakfast. Ask about rooms in the annex. Reception open 8am-11pm. Singles £19-29, with bath £36-39. Doubles with bath £32-55. Triples with bath £45-68. Quads £54-75. MC, V.

Eaton House Hotel, 125 Ebury St., SW1 (tel./fax 730 87 81). Kind hosts (former tour guides) serve up Belgravian comfort at more than reasonable prices. English breakfast. Singles £35. Doubles £50. Triples £70. 10% discount in winter. AmEx, MC, V.

Earl's Court

The area feeds on the tourist trade: travel agencies, currency exchanges, and souvenir shops dominate. The area also has a vibrant gay and lesbian population. Rooms tend to be dirt cheap, but ask to see a room to make sure the "dirt" isn't literal. Beware overeager guides willing to lead you from the station to a hostel.

York House Hotel, 27-29 Philbeach Gdns., SW5 (tel. 373 75 19; fax 370 46 41). Special features include a mod, 60s-style TV lounge and a lovely garden. Extraordinarily clean. English breakfast. Singles £28. Doubles £45, with bath £62. Triples £55, with bath £75. Quads £63. AmEx, DC, MC, V.

Mowbray Court Hotel, 28-32 Penywern Rd., SW5 (tel. 373 82 85 or 370 36 90; fax 370 56 93). Staff incredibly helpful. Superb breakfast. Singles £40, with bath £48. Doubles £50, with bath £60. Triples £63, with bath £72. Family rooms for 4 people £76, with bath £85. Quints £90, with bath £100. Sextets £106, with bath £110. Negotiable discounts. Reserve ahead; no deposit required. AmEx, DC, MC, V.

Oxford Hotel, 24 Penywern Rd., SW5 (tel. 370 11 61; fax 373 82 56). Musty orange bedspreads are mitigated by soaring ceilings and flamboyant moldings. Singles £30, with bath and TV £42. Doubles £45, with bath and TV £55. Triples £55, with bath and TV £63. Quads £64, with bath and TV £72. Quints with bath and TV £85. Winter and weekly rates may be 10-15% lower. Reserve ahead. No credit cards.

Half Moon Hotel, 10 Earl's Ct. Sq., SW5 (tel. 373 99 56; fax 373 84 56). Inexpensive, adequate rooms. TV in every room. Continental breakfast. Singles £25-40. Doubles £35-60. Triples £55-75. Quads £90. MC, V (4% surcharge).

Kensington & Chelsea

These hotels prove convenient for those who wish to visit the stunning array of museums that line the southwest side of Hyde Park. Prices are a bit higher, but hotels here tend to be significantly more sober and comfortable than many at Earl's Court.

Abbey House Hotel, 11 Vicarage Gate, W8 (tel. 727 25 94). Tube: High St. Kensington. After a series of renovations, the hotel has achieved a level of comfort that can't be rivaled at these prices. Palatial rooms. English breakfast. Singles £38. Doubles £60. Triples £74. Quads £86. Quints £96. Book ahead. No credit cards.

Vicarage Hotel, 10 Vicarage Gate, W8 (tel. 229 40 30; fax 792 59 89). Tube: High St. Kensington. Comfortable and immaculate. English breakfast. Singles £38. Doubles £60. Triples £75. Quads £84. No credit cards.

Oakley Hotel, 73 Oakley St., SW3 (tel. 352 55 99, -66 10; fax 727 11 90). Tube: Sloane Sq. or Victoria, then Bus 11, 19, or 22; or Kensington, then Bus 49. Turn left onto Oakley St. from King's Rd. at the Chelsea Fire Station. One of the best bargains in London. Lovely bedrooms. Kitchen. Singles £29. Twins £44, with bath £52. Triples £57, with bath £66. Quads £64. Quints £74. 4-bed dorms (women only) £14, £75 per week. Winter and long-term discounts. Reserve ahead. AmEx, MC, V.

Bloomsbury

Despite its proximity to the West End, Bloomsbury maintains a fairly residential demeanor, with gracious, tree-filled squares and a prime location.

Arosfa Hotel, 83 Gower St., WC1 (tel./fax 636 21 15). Spacious rooms and immaculate facilities. Singles £29. Doubles £42, with bath £55. Triples £56, with bath £67. Quads £57, with bath £77.

Arran House, 77-79 Gower St., WC1 (tel. 636 21 86 or 637 11 40; fax 436 53 28; email arran@dircon.co.uk). Laundry facilities. English breakfast. Singles £35-46. Doubles £47-65. Triples £63-79. Quads £68-82. Quints £78. MC, V.

Celtic Hotel, 62 Guilford St., WC1 (tel. 837 92 58 or 837 67 37). Go left when exiting the station. Take a left onto Herbrand St., and another left onto Guilford. Basic, sparsely furnished rooms and clean facilities. English breakfast. Singles £32.50. Doubles £44.50. Triples £66. Quads £76. Quints £95.

Euro Hotel, 51-53 and 58-60 Cartwright Gdns., WC1 (tel. 387 43 21; fax 383 50 44). Large rooms and spotless bathrooms. Full English breakfast. Singles £43.50. Doubles £59. Triples £72. Quads £80. AmEx, MC, V.

George Hotel, 60 Cartwright Gdns., WC1 (tel. 387 87 77; fax 387 86 66). Newly renovated hotel. English breakfast. Singles £39.50. Doubles £49.50-64.50. Triples £68-82. Quads £80. Children stay free on weekends. MC, V.

Alhambra Hotel, 17-19 Argyle St., WC1 (tel. 837 95 75; fax 916 24 76). Singles £27-55. Doubles £38-55. Triples £50-70. Quads £90. AmEx, MC, V.

Jesmond Dene Hotel, 27 Argyle St., WC1 (tel. 837 46 54; fax 833 16 33). Newly renovated hotel offers spotless, tasteful rooms. English breakfast. Singles £28-40. Doubles £36-50. Triples £50-65. Quads £70-85. MC, V.

Paddington & Bayswater

B&Bs, some slightly decrepit, cluster around Norfolk Square and Sussex Gardens.

Hyde Park Rooms Hotel, 137 Sussex Gdns., W2 (tel. 723 02 25 or 723 09 65). Tube: Paddington. Bright, airy rooms. An outstanding value. English breakfast. Singles £26-38. Doubles £38-48. Triples £57-72. AmEx, MC, V (5% surcharge).

Dean Court Hotel, 57 Inverness Terr., W2 (tel. 229 29 61; fax 727 11 90). Tube: Bayswater or Queensway. From Queensway, make a left onto Bayswater Rd.—Inverness is your first left. Clean rooms with firm mattresses, English breakfast, and a friendly atmosphere. **New Kent** next door has the same prices and management. No private facilities. Doubles £38. Twins £49. Triples £54. AmEx, MC, V.

Garden Court Hotel, 30-31 Kensington Gdns. Sq., W2 (tel. 229 25 53; fax 727 27 49). Tube: Bayswater. From the Tube, make a left onto Queensway, a left onto Porchester Gdns., and then a right onto Kensington Gdns. Sq. Firm yet bouncy mattresses add to the "real" hotel ambience. English breakfast. Singles £32-46. Doubles £48-72. Triples £63-78. Family £70-86. £25 deposit required. MC, V.

FOOD

London presents a tantalizing range of foreign and English specialties. Indian, Lebanese, Greek, Chinese, Thai, Italian, West Indian, and African food is inexpensive and readily available. If you eat but one meal in London, let it be Indian—London's Indian food is rivaled only by India's. Meals are less expensive on Westbourne Grove (Tube: Bayswater) or near Euston Station than in the West End.

The West End

Mandeer, 21 Hanway Place W1. Tube: Tottenham Ct. Road. North Indian food is exceedingly fresh, primarily organic, and all vegetarian. The best deal in the house is the lunch buffet (from £2.90). Open Mon.-Sat. noon-3pm and 5:30-10pm.

The Stockpot, 18 Old Compton St., W1. Tube: Leicester Sq. or Piccadilly. The cheapest place in Soho to soak up style. Open Mon.-Tues. 11:30am-11:30pm, Wed.-Sat. 11:30am-11:45pm, Sun. noon-11pm. Also at 40 Panton St.

The Wren Café at St. James's, 35 Jermyn St., SW1. Tube: Piccadilly Circus or Green Park. Wholefood/vegetarian delights served in the shadow of a Christopher Wren church. Open Mon.-Fri. 7:30am-7pm, Sat. 8am-7pm, Sun. 10am-5pm.

Sofra, 36 Tavistock St., WC2. Tube: Covent Garden. Turkish restaurant with fresh food. Dinner £6. Open Mon.-Fri. 7am-midnight, Sat.-Sun. 7am-10pm.

Golden Dragon, 28-29 Gerrard St., W1. Tube: Leicester Sq. One of the best Chinese restaurants. Regular meals are expensive, but the *dim sum* is affordable. Open Mon.-Fri. noon-11:30pm, Sat. noon-midnight, Sun. 11am-11pm. *Dim Sum* served Mon.-Sat. noon-4:45pm, Sun. 11am-4:45pm.

Neal's Yard Salad Bar, 2 Neal's Yard, WC2. Carry out or sit outside at this simple vegetarian's nirvana. Tempting salads from £2. Open daily 10am-8pm.

Belgo Centraal, 50 Earlham St., WC2. Waiters in monk's cowls and bizarre 21st-century beerhall interior make this one of Covent Garden's most popular restaurants. Weekday lunchtime wild boar sausage, Belgian mash, and a beer for £5. Come early at dinner to get the best deal. Open Mon.-Sat. noon-11:30pm, Sun. noon-10:30pm.

City of London & East End

The Place Below, in St. Mary-le-Bow Church crypt, Cheapside, EC2. Tube: St. Paul's. Attractive and generous vegetarian dishes served in the unexpectedly light stone church basement. Second dining room moonlights as an ecclesiastical court, where the Archbishop of Canterbury still settles cases and swears in new bishops. Quiche and salad £5.75. Open Mon.-Fri. 7:30am-2:30pm.

Bengal Cuisine, 12 Brick Ln., E1. Tube: Aldgate East. Quick service. Tasty chicken curry £3.95-4.95. 10% student discount on weekends. Open daily noon-midnight.

Lahore Kebab House, 2 Umberston St., E1. Tube: Whitechapel or Shadwell DLR. Off Commercial Rd. Some of the best, cheapest Indian and Pakistani cuisine in the city. No dish over £4. Feel free to bring your own beer. Open daily noon-midnight.

Kensington, Knightsbridge, Chelsea, & Victoria

Ciaccio, 5 Warwick Way, SW1. Tube: Victoria. An intimate Italian eatery. Pick a container of pasta and a sauce (pesto, veggie, tomato, and meat), and they'll heat it up for £1.69-2.85. Open Mon.-Fri. 10am-7pm, Sat. 9:30am-6pm.

Apadna, 351 Kensington High St., W8. Savory *kabas* in fresh-baked *naan* £2.70. Open daily 11am-11pm.

Chelsea Kitchen, 98 King's Rd., SW3. Tube: Sloane Sq. Eclectic menu of cheap, filling, tasty food. Open Mon.-Sat. 8am-11:30pm, Sun. 9am-11:30pm.

Bloomsbury and North London

Wagamama, 4a Streatham St., WC1. Tube: Tottenham Ct. Rd. Fast food: waitstaff takes your orders on hand-held electronic radios that transmit directly to the kitchen. Noodles £3.80-5.70. Open Mon.-Sat. noon-11pm, Sat. 12:30-10pm.

The Coffee Gallery, 23 Museum St. Tube: Tottenham Ct. Rd. or Holborn. Delicious, fresh Italian garden food. Open Mon.-Fri. 8am-5:30pm, Sat. 10am-5:30pm.

Diwana Bhel Poori House, 121 Drummond St., NW1. Tube: Warren St. Tasty Indian vegetarian food in a clean and airy restaurant. Lunch buffet £4 (noon-2:30pm). Open daily noon-11:30pm.

Café Olé, 119 Upper St., N1. Tube: Angel. A hip Mediterranean bar/café. Lunch menu items £1-4.80. Entrees around £5. Open Mon.-Sat. 8am-11pm.

LeMercury, 140a Upper St., N1. Tube: Angel or Highbury and Islington. French restaurant with the quintessential candle-lit effect. All main courses £5.45. Open Mon.-Sat. 11am-1am, Sun. noon-11.30pm.

Notting Hill & Ladbroke Grove

Manzara, 24 Pembridge Rd., W11. Tube: Notting Hill Gate. Afternoon, pizzas are £3, and sandwiches are £1. Evenings, they offer a £6 all-you-can-eat Greek and Turkish array. Take-away discount. Open daily 8am-midnight.

The Grain Shop, 269a Portobello Rd., W11. Tube: Ladbroke Grove. Direct the staff to fill various-sized take-away containers with any combination of the 6 hot vegetarian dishes—large £4.10, medium £3, small £2. Open Mon.-Sat. 10am-6pm.

PUBS

The clientele of London's 700 pubs varies widely from one neighborhood to the next. Avoid touristy pubs near train stations. For the best prices head to the East End. Stylish, lively pubs cluster around the fringes of the West End. Many historic ale-houses lend an ancient air to areas swallowed up by the urban sprawl, such as Highgate and Hampstead. Don't be afraid to leave a good pub—making a circuit, or **pub crawl,** lets you experience the diversity of a neighborhood's nightlife.

The Dog and Duck, 8 Bateman St., W1. Tube: Tottenham Ct. Rd. Frequent winner of the Best Pub in Soho award, its size keeps the crowd down. Inexpensive pints (£1.95-2.20). Evenings bring locals, theater-goers, and, yes, some tourists. Open Mon.-Fri. noon-11pm, Sat. 6-11pm, Sun. 7-10:30pm.

The Three Greyhounds, 25 Greek St., W1. Tube: Leicester Sq. This medieval-styled pub provides welcome respite from the posturing of Soho. 1996 winner of the Best Pub in Soho award. Open Mon.-Sat. 11:30am-11pm, Sun. 4-10:30pm.

Riki Tik, 23-24 Bateman St., W1. Tube: Leicester Square, Tottenham Ct. Rd., or Piccadilly Circus. A hyped, hip, and tremendously swinging bar specializing in orgasmic flavored vodka shots (£2.60). Come during happy hour (5:30-7:30pm) for near-bargains. Open Mon.-Sat. noon-1am. £3 cover after 11pm.

Lamb and Flag, 33 Rose St., WC2, off Garrick St. Tube: Covent Garden or Leicester Sq. A traditional pub, with no music and 2 sections—the public bar for the working class and the saloon bar for the businessmen, though today the classes mix. Open Mon.-Thurs. 11am-11pm, Fri.-Sat. 11am-10:45pm, Sun. noon-10:30pm.

World's End Distillery, 459 King's Rd. near World's End Pass before Edith Grove. Tube: Sloane Sq. Cavernous, imposing 1-room pub in Chelsea. Open Mon.-Sat. 11am-11pm, Sun. noon-3pm and 7-10:30pm.

Filthy MacNasty's Whiskey Café, 68 Amwell St. Tube: Angel. Celtic drawings line the fire-colored walls; former Pogues singer Shane MacGowan frequently appears for last call. Renowned for traditional Irish music. Live shows Thurs.-Sun. all day. Open daily 11am-11pm. Wheelchair accessible.

SIGHTS

London is best explored on foot. But if you have only one day here, a tour may be a good way to intensify your sight-seeing experience. The **Original London Sightseeing Tour** (tel. (0181) 877 17 22) provides a convenient, albeit cursory, overview of London's attractions from a double-decker bus. Tours lasting two hours depart from Baker St., Haymarket (near Piccadilly Circus), Marble Arch, Embankment, and near Victoria Station. The route includes views of Buckingham Palace, the Houses of Parliament, Westminster Abbey, the Tower of London, St. Paul's, and Piccadilly Circus. A ticket allows you to ride the buses for a 24-hour period—permitting visitors to hop off at major sights and hop on a later bus to finish the tour (tours daily 9am-5:30pm, buses come every 5-10min.; £12). Walking tours can fill in the specifics of London that bus tours run right over. Among the best is **The Original London Walks** (tel. 624 39 78), two-hour tours led by well-regarded guides (£4.50, students £3.50).

Mayfair to Parliament An auspicious beginning to a day's wander is **Piccadilly Circus** and its towering neon bluffs (Tube: Piccadilly Circus). At the center of the Nash's swirling hub stands a fountain topped by a statue everyone calls Eros but is actually supposed to be the Angel of Christian Charity. North are the tiny shops of Regent St. and the renovated seediness of **Soho,** a region which sports a vibrant sidewalk café culture, where pornography once reigned supreme. Outdoor cafés, upscale shops, and slick crowds huddle in **Covent Garden,** to the northeast. Paths across **Green Park** lead to **Buckingham Palace** (Tube: Victoria or Green Park), now partially open to tourists (£9, seniors £6.50, children £5; call 930 48 32 for more info). The **Changing of the Guard** occurs daily (April to late Aug.) or every other day (Sept.-March) at 11:30am, unless it's raining. Arrive early or you won't see a thing.

The Mall, a wide processional, leads from the palace to **Admiralty Arch** and **Trafalgar Square.** South of the Mall, **St. James's Park** shelters a duck preserve and a flock of lawn chairs (70p/4hr.). The center of a vicious traffic roundabout, Trafalgar Square (Tube: Charing Cross) centers on Nelson's Column, a 40-ft. high statue astride a 132-ft. column. Political Britain branches off **Whitehall,** just south of Trafalgar. Draped in black velvet, Charles I was led out of the **Banqueting House** (corner of Horse Guards Ave. and Whitehall) and beheaded. The building now hosts less lethal state dinners. (Open Mon.-Sat. 10am-5pm but closed for government functions. Last admission 4:30pm. £3, concessions £2.25.) The Prime Minister resides off Whitehall at **10 Downing Street,** now closed to tourists. In the middle of Whitehall is the **Cenotaph,** a monument to Britain's war dead. Whitehall ends by the sprawling **Houses of Parliament** (Tube: Westminster). Access to the House of Commons and the House of Lords is extremely restricted since a member was killed in a bomb blast in 1979. Queue up outside when either are in session in order to sit in the upper galleries of the Lords or Commons. You can hear **Big Ben** but not see him; Big Ben is neither the tower nor the clock, but the 14-ton bell, cast when a similarly proportioned Sir Benjamin Hall served as Commissioner of Works. Church and state tie the knot in **Westminster Abbey,** coronation chamber to English monarchs for the past 684 years and the site of **Poet's Corner,** the **Grave of the Unknown Warrior,** the **Stone of Scone,** and the elegantly perpendicular **Chapel of Henry VII.** Britain bestows no greater honor than burial within these walls. The abbey plumber is buried here along with Elizabeth I, Darwin, Dickens, and Newton. Ask about the story surrounding the Stone of Scone. (Abbey open Mon.-Sat. 7:30am-6pm, Wed. also 6-7:45pm, Sun. in-between services. Free. Chapels and transepts open Mon.-Fri. 9am-4:45pm, Wed. also 6-7:45pm, Sat. 9am-2:45pm and 3:45-5:45pm. £5, concessions £3; all parts of the abbey £2 Wed. evenings. Photography permitted Wed. evenings only.)

Hyde Park & Kensington to Chelsea **Hyde Park** shows its best face on Sundays from 11am to dusk, when soapbox orators take freedom of speech to the limit at **Speaker's Corner** (Tube: Marble Arch, *not* Hyde Park Corner). To the west, **Kensington Gardens,** an elegant relic of Edwardian England, celebrates the glories of model yacht racing in the squarish Round Pound. From the gardens, you can catch a glimpse of Kensington Palace. The **Royal Albert Hall,** on the south edge of Hyde Park, hosts the **Proms,** a gloriously British festival of music. Up Brompton Rd. near Knightsbridge, **Harrods** (Tube: Knightsbridge) vends under their humble motto, *Omnia Omnibus Ubique.* ("All things for all people, everywhere." Open Mon.-Tues. and Sat. 10am-6pm, Wed.-Fri. 10am-7pm.) Still-fashionable **King's Road** (Tube: Sloane Sq.), south in **Chelsea,** attempts to do justice to its bohemian past—past residents include Oscar Wilde and the Sex Pistols.

Regent's Park to Fleet Street Take a picnic from Harrods to the expanse of **Regent's Park,** northeast of Hyde Park across Marylebone (Tube: Regent's Park). The **London Zoo,** in the north end, harbors such exotic animals as mambos, Asian lions, and piranhas. (Open April-Sept. daily 10am-5:30pm; Oct.-March 10am-4pm. Last admission 1hr. before closing. £8, concessions £7.) **Camden Town** (Tube: Camden Town), bordering the park to the northeast, sports rollicking street markets. **Bloomsbury**—eccentric, erudite, and disorganized—is known for its literary and scholarly connections, including the **British Museum.** Although nearly all the papers have moved to cheaper real estate, **Fleet Street** is the traditional den of the British press. Close by are the **Inns of Court,** which have controlled access to the English Bar since the 13th century.

City of London & the East End Once upon a time, "London" meant the square-mile enclave of the **City of London;** the rest of today's metropolis were far-flung towns and villages. The **Tower of London,** the grandest fortress in medieval Europe, was the palace and prison of English monarchs for over 500 years. Its best-known edifice, the **White Tower,** was begun by William the Conqueror. In 1483, the "Princes in the Tower" (Edward V and his brother) were murdered in the **Bloody Tower** in one of the great unsolved mysteries of history. Two of the wives of jolly King Henry VIII were beheaded in the courtyard, and in 1941 Rudolf Hess was sent to the Tower after his parachute dumped him in Scotland. The **Crown Jewels** include the Stars of Africa, cut from the enormous Cullinan Diamond, which was mailed third-class from the Transvaal in an unmarked brown paper package. (Tube: Tower Hill. Open March-Oct. Mon.-Sat. 9am-6pm, Sun. 10am-6pm; Nov.-Feb. Mon.-Sat. 9am-5pm, Sun. 10am-5pm. £8.50, concessions £6.40.) Next to the tower is **Tower Bridge,** one of London's best-known landmarks. Other fragments of history are scattered throughout the City, among them 24 Christopher Wren churches interspersed among the soaring steel of modern skyscrapers. Peruse smaller churches, such as the Strand's **St. Clement Danes** of "Oranges and Lemons" fame or the superb **St. Stephen Walbrook** near the Bank of England (Tube: Bank). True-blue cockney Londoners are born within earshot of the famous bells of **St. Mary-le-Bow,** Cheapside. In the German Blitz in 1940, **St. Paul's Cathedral** stood firm in a sea of fire. Climb above the graves of Wren, Nelson, and Wellington in the crypt to the dizzying top of the dome; the view is unparalleled. (Tube: St. Paul's. Open Mon.-Sat. 8:30am-4pm. Ambulatory and galleries open Mon.-Sat. 8:45am-4:15pm. Cathedral, ambulatory, crypt, and galleries £6, students £5.) The **Barbican Centre** (tube: Barbican or Moorgate) is one of the most impressive and controversial post-Blitz rebuilding projects.

The **East End** is a relatively poor section of London with a history of racial conflict. A large working-class population moved into the district during the Industrial Revolution, soon followed by a wave of Jewish immigrants fleeing persecution in Eastern Europe who settled around **Whitechapel.** Notable remnants of the former East End community include the city's oldest standing synagogue, **Bevis Marks Synagogue** (Bevis Marks and Heneage Ln., EC3. Tel. 626 12 74. Tube: Aldgate; from Aldgate High St. turn right onto Houndsditch. Creechurch Lane on the left leads to Bevis Marks.) In 1978, the latest immigration wave brought a large Muslim Bangladeshi community to the East End. At the heart of this community is **Brick Lane** (Tube: Aldgate East), a street lined with Indian and Bangladeshi restaurants, colorful textile shops, and ethnic groceries. (To reach Brick Lane, head left up Whitechapel as you exit the tube station; turn left onto Osbourne St., which turns into Brick Lane.) On Sundays, market stalls selling books, bric-a-brac, leather jackets, and sandwiches flank this street and Middlesex St., better known as **Petticoat Lane.**

The South & Outskirts Lesser-known but equally rewarding treasures lie south of the river, the area currently experiencing a cultural and economic renewal. **Southwark Cathedral,** a smallish, quiet church, boasts London's second-best Gothic structure and a chapel dedicated to John Harvard (Tube: London Bridge). West along the riverbank, a reconstruction of **Shakespeare's Globe Theatre** is used for performances. (Tel. 620 02 02. Open for tours May-Sept. daily 9am-12:15pm and 2-4pm; Oct.-April 10am-5pm. £5, concessions £4.) South London's entertainment history lives on in the festive **South Bank Arts Centre** (Tube: Waterloo).

The genteel Victorian shopping and residential district of Brixton (Tube: Brixton) became the locus of a Caribbean and African community who followed large-scale Commonwealth immigration in the 1950s and 1960s. Most of the activity in Brixton centers around the **Brixton Market** at Electric Ave., Popes Rd., and Brixton Station Rd. Choose from among the stalls of fresh fish, vegetables, and West Indian cuisine, or browse through the stalls of African crafts and discount clothing. Nearby, on the corner of Coldharbor and Atlantic, the **Black Cultural Archives,** 378 Coldharbor Lane, SW9 (tel. 738 45 91), mounts small but informative exhibits on black history.

The transport system that encouraged London's urban sprawl blurs the distinction between city and surroundings. If Hyde Park seemed small, **Highgate** and **Hampstead Heath** will prove that there is an English countryside. To the east, Karl Marx and George Eliot repose in the Gothic tangle of **Highgate Cemetery,** Swains Lane. (Tube: Archway. **Eastern Cemetery** open Mon.-Fri. 11am-4:30pm, Sat.-Sun. 10am-4:30pm. £1. **Western Cemetery** access by guided tour only Mon.-Fri. at noon, 2, and 4pm, Sat.-Sun. every hr. 11am to 4pm. £3. Camera permit £1.)

London **Docklands,** the largest commercial development in Europe, has utterly changed the face of East London within the space of 10 years. As part of Thatcher's privatization program, redevelopment of the area was handed over to the private sector—in the form of the **London Docklands Development Corporation (LDDC)**—along with a generous helping of public funds. The best way to see the region is via the **Docklands Light Railway (DLR)** (tel. 918 40 00), a futuristic, totally automatic, driverless elevated rail system. All tickets, Travelcards, and passes issued by London Transport, London Underground, and British Rail are valid on the DLR provided they cover the correct zones. The first stop for any Docklands tour should be the **Docklands Visitors Centre.** (Tel. 512 11 11. DLR: Crossharbor, then left up the road. Open Mon.-Fri. 8:30am-6pm, Sat.-Sun. 9:30am-5pm.)

Head by train or boat to red-brick **Hampton Court Palace** (tel. (0181) 781 95 00) for a quirky change of pace. Its grounds contain the famous **hedgerow maze** (British Rail: Hampton Court). From the Monday before Easter until the end of September, a boat runs from Westminster Pier to Hampton Court, leaving in the morning at 10:30, 11:15am, and noon, and returning from Hampton Court at 3, 4, and 5pm. The trip takes three to four hours one way. (£7, return £10. Hampton Court open March-late Oct. Mon. 10:15am-6pm, Tues.-Sun. 9:30am-6pm; late Oct.-March Mon. 10:15am-4:30pm, Tues.-Sun. 9:30am-4:30pm. Last admission 45min. before closing.

Gardens open at the same time but close at 9pm or dusk, whichever comes first. Free. All-encompassing admission £8.50, concessions £6.40. Admission to maze or Privy Garden £2.)

Windsor Castle (tel. (01753) 86 82 86 or 83 11 18 for 24hr. information line) is the Queen's spectacular country retreat. British Rail serves Windsor and Eton Central station and Windsor and Eton Riverside station, both of which are near Windsor Castle. (Open daily 10am-5:30pm; last admission 4pm; Nov.-March 10am-4pm; last admission at 3pm. £8.80, seniors £6.20.)

Just west of central London on the Thames lie the serene and exotic **Kew Gardens.** Lose yourself in the controlled wilderness of the grounds, or explore the Victorian and modern glasshouses containing thousands of plant species. (Tube or British Rail: Kew Gardens. Gardens open Mon.-Fri. 9:30am-6:30pm, last admission 6pm, Sat.-Sun. 9:30am-7:30pm, last admission 7pm. Conservatories close at 5:30pm. Closing times may vary by season. £5, students and seniors £3, after 4:45pm £3. Tours leave Victoria Gate daily at 11am and 2pm, £1.)

Museums

British Museum, Great Russell St. (tel. 580 17 88 for recorded info). Tube: Tottenham Ct. Rd. or Holborn. The closest thing to a complete record of the rise and ruin of world cultures. Among the plunder on display are the **Rosetta Stone** (whose inscriptions allowed French scholar Champollion to decipher hieroglyphics) and the Elgin Marbles. See an early *Beowulf* and 2 of 4 surviving copies of the *Magna Carta.* Open Mon.-Sat. 10am-5pm, Sun. 2:30-6pm. Free, suggested donation £2.

National Gallery, Trafalgar Sq. (tel. 747 28 85 for recorded info). Tube: Charing Cross. One of the world's best collections of European paintings. The Micro Gallery can print out a free personalized tour. Open Mon.-Sat. 10am-6pm, Wed. also 6-8pm, Sun. noon-6pm. Free.

National Portrait Gallery, St. Martin's Pl., opposite St. Martin's in the Fields. Tube: Charing Cross. Mugs from Queen Elizabeth II to John Lennon. Doubles as *Who's Who in Britain.* Open Mon.-Sat. 10am-6pm, Sun. noon-6pm. Free.

Tate Gallery, Millbank, up the Thames from Parliament Sq. (tel. 887 80 00 for recorded info). Tube: Pimlico. The best of British artists, along with Monet, Dalí, Picasso, and Matisse. The best place for contemporary art fans in London. The vast J.M.W. Turner collection rests in the Clore Gallery. Open daily 10am-5:50pm. Free.

Victoria and Albert Museum, Cromwell Rd. (tel. 938 84 41 for recorded info). Tube: South Kensington. An array of fine and applied arts. Open Mon. noon-5:50pm, Tues.-Sun. 10am-5:50pm. £5, concessions £3, students free.

Madame Tussaud's, Marylebone Rd., NW1. Tube: Baker St. The classic waxwork museum. Might not be worth the wait and the cost. Open Mon.-Fri. 10am-5:30pm, Sat.-Sun. 9:30am-5:30pm. £9, seniors £6.75.

Museum of London, 150 London Wall, EC2 (tel. 600 08 07 for 24hr. info). Tube: St. Paul's or Barbican. From Londinium to the 1996 European Soccer Championships. Free lectures Wed.-Fri. 1:10pm. Open Tues.-Sat. 10am-5:50pm, Sun. noon-5:50pm, last entry 5:30pm. £3.50, students £1.75. Free after 4:30pm. Wheelchair accessible.

Museum of the Moving Image (MOMI), South Bank Centre, SE1 (tel. 401 26 36 for 24hr. info). Tube: Waterloo. The entertaining museum charts the development of image-making with light, from shadow puppets to film and telly. Open daily 10am-6pm. Last admission 5pm. £6, students £4.85, seniors £4.

Science Museum, Exhibition Rd., SW7. Tube: South Kensington. Closet science geeks will be outed by their orgasmic cries as they enter this wonderland of motors, springs, and spaceships. This 5-story collection rivals the best science museums around. Open daily 10am-6pm. £5, concessions £2.90. Free 4:30-6pm.

London Transport Museum, Covent Garden, WC2 (tel. 836 85 57 for recorded info). Tube: Covent Garden. Although ground floor traffic flows through a maze of historic trains, trams, and buses, the museum offers much more than a history of public transport vehicles. Open Sat.-Thurs. 10am-6pm, Fri. 11am-6pm. Last admission 5:15pm. £4.50, concessions £2.50. Wheelchair accessible.

Royal Air Force Museum, Grahame Park Way, NW9 (tel. 0181 205 22 66 for 24hr. info). Tube: Colindale. Exit left and head straight for about 15min., or take bus 303 from the tube station. Even those uninterested in aerial combat will have a tough time being bored. Open daily 10am-6pm. Last admission 5:30pm. Adults £5.85, students £2.95. Wheelchair accessible.

Imperial War Museum, Lambeth Rd., SE1 (tel. 416 50 00). Tube: Lambeth North or Elephant & Castle. The atrium is filled with tanks and planes; gripping exhibits illuminate every aspect of two world wars in every possible medium. Open daily 10am-6pm. £4.70, students £3.70. Free daily 4:30-6pm. Wheelchair accessible.

The Wallace Collection, Hertford House, Manchester Sq., W1 (tel. 935 06 87). Tube: Bond St. Outstanding works include Hals's *The Laughing Cavalier,* Delacroix's *Execution of Marino Faliero,* Fragonard's *The Swing,* and Rubens's *Christ on the Cross.* Home to the largest armor and weaponry collection outside of the Tower of London. Open Mon.-Sat. 10am-5pm, Sun. 11am-5pm. Guided tours Mon.-Tues. 1pm, Wed. 11:30am and 1pm, Thurs.-Fri. 1pm, Sat. 11:30am, Sun. 3pm. Free.

ENTERTAINMENT

On any given day or night, Londoners and visitors can choose from the widest range of entertainment. For guidance consult *Time Out* (£1.70) or *What's On* (£1.30).

Theater, Music, & Film

London **theater** is unrivalled. Seats cost £8-30 and up, and student/senior standby (with an "S" or "concessions" in listings) puts even the best seats within reach—£7-10 just before curtain (come two hours early). **Day seats** are sold cheaply (9-10am, the day of performance) to all; queue up earlier. The **Leicester Square Ticket Booth** sells half-price tickets on the day of major plays (open Mon.-Sat. noon-6:30pm; long wait. £2 fee; cash only). Standby tickets for the **Royal National Theatre,** on the South Bank Centre (tel. 928 22 52; tube: Waterloo), sell two hours beforehand (£8-12; students £7, 45min. before). The **Barbican Theatre** (24hr. info tel. 382 72 72, reservations 638 88 91; tube: Barbican or Moorgate), London home of the Royal Shakespeare Co., has student standbys for £6 from 9am on the performance day. Exciting cheaper performances are found on the **Fringe,** in less commercial theaters.

Most major **classical music** is staged at the acoustically superb **Royal Festival Hall** (tel. 960 42 42; Tube: Waterloo) and the **Barbican Hall. Marble Hill House** has low-priced outdoor concerts on summer weekends (tel. 413 14 43). Londoners have been lining up for standing room in the **Royal Albert Hall's "Proms"** (BBC Henry Wood Promenade Concerts; tel. 589 82 12) for nearly a century. **Pop music** performers from the world over cannot keep away from London. **Brixton Academy** (tel. 924 99 99; Tube: Brixton) is a larger, rowdy venue for a variety of music including rock and reggae (advance tickets £8-25). **Ronnie Scott's,** 47 Frith St., W1 (tel. 439 07 47; tube: Leicester Sq. or Piccadilly Circus), has London's greatest jazz (cover from £12).

The Prince Charles, Leicester Pl., WC2 (tel. 437 81 81; tube: Leicester Sq.), is a Soho institution. The four shows a day (cheerily deconstructed on the recorded phone message) are generally second runs but also include a sprinkling of classics for only £1.75-2.25. **Everyman Cinema,** Hollybush Vale, Hampstead, NW3 (tel. 435 15 25; tube: Hampstead), has double and triple bills based on either a theme or a classic celluloid figure (membership 60p per year; Mon.-Fri. £4.50, Sat.-Sun. £5, students Mon.-Fri. £3.50). **Gate Cinema,** Notting Hill Gate Rd. (tel. 727 40 43; tube: Notting Hill Gate), shows art house films (£3-6).

Dance Clubs

London pounds to 100% groovy Liverpool tunes, ecstatic Manchester rave, hometown soul and house, U.S. hip-hop, and Jamaican reggae. Many clubs host a variety of provocative one-night stands (like "Get Up and Use Me") throughout the week. Check listings in *Time Out* for the latest.

Iceni, 11 White Horse St., W1 (tel. 495 53 33). Tube: Green Park. Off Curzon Street. 3 floors of deep funk in this Mayfair hotspot. £5-8. Open Wed.-Sat. 10pm-3am.

Ministry of Sound, 103 Gaunt St., SE1. Tube: Elephant & Castle. Night Bus N12, N62, N65, N72, N77, or N78. Another south of the Thames mega-club, with the long queues, beefy covers, beautiful people, and pumping house tunes. Fri. £10, Sat. £15. Open Fri. 11pm-8am, Sat. 11pm-9am.

The Hanover Grand, 6 Hanover St., W1. Tube: Oxford Circus. Loud, funkified atmosphere. £5-15. Open Wed.-Sat. 10:30pm-5am.

The Fridge, Town Hall Parade, Brixton Hill, SW2 (tel. 326 51 00). Tube: Brixton. Night bus N2. A serious dance dive with a stylish multi-ethnic crowd. Saturday's "Love Muscle," the ultimate London one-nighter, packs in lesbians. £10, with flyer £8. Open Fri.-Sat. 10pm-6am.

BISEXUAL, GAY, & LESBIAN LONDON

London has a very visible gay scene, covering everything from the flamboyant to the mainstream. *Time Out* has a section devoted to gay listings, and gay newspapers include *Capital Gay* (free, caters to men), *Pink Paper,* and *Shebang* (for women). *Gay Times* (£3) is the British counterpart to the *Advocate; Diva* (£2) is a monthly lesbian mag. Islington, Earl's Court, and Soho (especially **Old Compton Street**) are all gay-friendly areas. For further info contact the **gay, lesbian, bisexual helplines,** p. 133.

Comptons of Soho, 53 Old Compton St., W1. Tube: Leicester Sq. or Piccadilly Circus. Soho's "official" gay pub, always busy with a crowd of all ages. Open Mon.-Sat. noon-11pm, Sun. noon-10:30pm.

Drill Hall Women-Only Bar, 16 Chenies St., WC1. Tube: Goodge St. A much anticipated one-nighter located in the lobby of one of London's biggest alternative theaters. Crowded and laid-back. Open Mon. 6-11pm.

Old Compton Café, 35 Old Compton St., W1. Tube: Leicester Sq. Open 24hr. in the geographic epicenter of Soho, this is *the* gay café. Tables and people (mostly twenty- and thirty-something males) overflow onto the street.

Substation Soho, Falconberg Ct., W1. Tube: Tottenham Ct. Rd. For men who find the Old Compton St. scene too tame. A cruisy, late-night testosterone fest. Open Mon.-Thurs. 10pm-3am, Fri. 10pm-4am, Sat. 10:30pm-6am.

Heaven, Villiers St., WC2, underneath The Arches. Tube: Embankment or Charing Cross (Villiers is off the Strand). The oldest and biggest European gay disco. Bumping garage music Fri. and Sat. at 10pm. Cover £6-8.

"G.A.Y.," at London Astoria 1 (Sat.), and 2 (Thurs. and Mon.), 157 Charing Cross Rd., WC2. Tube: Tottenham Ct. Rd. Pop extravaganza amidst chrome and disco balls. Unpretentious mixed clientele. Open Mon., Thurs., and Sat. from 10:30pm (Sat. until 5am). Cover £3, Sat. £6. Discounts with flyers.

SOUTH ENGLAND

Kent

Canterbury Chaucer didn't intend the tourists when he wrote "And specially from every shires ende, Of engelond to canterbury they wende." His sometimes lewd, sometimes reverent tale, instead speaks of the pilgrims of Middle Ages, en route from London to **Canterbury Cathedral** on England's busiest road. Here, Archbishop Thomas à Becket met his demise after an irate Henry II asked, "Will no one rid me of this troublesome priest?" and a few of his henchmen took the hint. (Open Easter-Oct. Mon.-Sat. 8:45am-7pm, Sun. 11am-2:30pm and 4:30-5:30pm; Nov.-Easter 8:45am-5pm. Choral evensong Mon.-Fri. 5:30pm, Sat.-Sun. 3:15pm. Donation £2. Check nave pulpit for times of guided tours. £3, students £2. Headphone tour £2.50.) The **Canterbury Tales** visitor attraction, St. Margaret's St., recreates the tales with a gap-toothed Wife of Bath, her waxen companions, and authentic olfactory stimulation. (Open July-Aug. daily 9am-6pm; March-June and Sept.-Oct. 9:30am-5:30pm; Nov.-Feb. Sun.-Fri. 10am-4:30pm, Sat. 9:30am-5:30pm. £4.85, students £3.95.) The rest of the city brims with more religious monuments. On Stour St., **Greyfriars,** the first Franciscan friary in England, maintains charming riverside gardens. Also on Stour St., the **Canterbury Heritage Museum** features medieval pilgrim badges and reconstructions of the historical Canterbury. (Open Nov.-May Mon.-Sat. 10:30am-5pm; June-Oct. also Sun. 1:30-5pm. £1.90, students £1.25.) The **Roman Museum,** Butchery Ln., houses artifacts from Cantebury's Roman inhabitants (open Mon.-Sat. 10am-5pm, last admission 4pm; £1.90, students £1.25). Little remains of **St. Augustine's Abbey,** but older Roman ruins and the site of St. Augustine's first tomb can be viewed near the cathedral (open in summer daily 10am-6pm; off-season Mon.-Sat. 10am-4pm; £2, students £1.50). Around the corner, **St. Martin's** is the oldest parish church in England.

Canterbury's **tourist office,** 34 St. Margaret's St. (tel. (01227) 76 65 67; fax 45 98 40), books accommodations (£2.50 and 10% deposit) and carries maps and guides for Kent. (Open aprill with his shoures soote-Oct. daily 9:30am-6pm; Nov.-the droghte of march 9:30am-5pm.) **Trains** from London's Victoria Station arrive at Canterbury's East Station; from Charing Cross and Waterloo Station, trains arrive at West Station (1½hr., £13.10). **Buses** (tel. (01227) 47 20 82) to Canterbury leave London's Victoria Coach Station (1¾hr., £8). **B&Bs** bunch near both train stations and on London and Whitstable Rd. The **YHA Youth Hostel** at 54 New Dover Rd. (tel. (01227) 46 29 11) may be packed and chaotic (reception open daily 7-10am and 1-11pm; £9.40; open Feb.-Dec daily). **The Tudor House,** 6 Best Ln. (tel. (01227) 76 56 50), and **Let's Stay,** Mrs. Connolly, 26 New Dover Rd. (tel. (01227) 46 36 28), offer clean rooms in attractive old houses (£9-16). The streets around the cathedral teem with bakeries and sweet shops. **Café Venezia,** 60-61 Palace St., serves cheap pizza (open July-Aug. daily 9am-11pm; Sept.-June 9am-6pm), while the **The Famous Sandwich Shop,** 16 St. Dunstans St, creates fresh sandwiches (open Mon,-Sat. 8:15am-4pm). **Simple Simon's,** 3-9 Church Ln., draws students to sample its publy wares (open daily 11am-11pm; live music usually Tues. and Thurs.).

Dover The roar of the English Channel at Dover has been drowned out by the puttering of ferries, the hum of hovercraft, and the chatter of French families *en vacances.* Yet the city has retained its dignified maritime identity despite the clamor of tourist traffic. The view from Castle Hill Rd. reveals why **Dover Castle** is famed both for its setting and for its impregnability. Dover's **tourist office,** Townwall St. (tel. (01304) 20 51 08), has accommodations info and ferry and hoverport tickets (open July-Aug. daily 8:30am-7:30pm; Sept.-June 9am-6pm). The **YHA Charlton House Youth Hostel,** 306 London Rd. (tel. (01304) 20 13 14), is a half-mile walk from the train station (lockout 10am-1pm; curfew 11pm; £9.40). **Amanda Guest House,** 4 Harold St. (tel. (01304) 20 17 11), and **Victoria Guest House,** 1 Laureston Pl. (tel. (01304) 20 51 40), offer gracious Victorian accommodations (£24-40). Cheap **food** fries from dawn to dusk in the fish-and-chip shops on London Rd. and Biggin St. Enjoy a decent pub lunch almost anywhere in the city center.

Trains for Dover's Priory Station leave from London's Victoria, Waterloo East, London Bridge, and Charing Cross stations approximately every 45 minutes (2hr., £17). Beware when you board as many trains branch off *en route;* check schedules and displays to see which trains split. National Express **buses** run regularly from London's Victoria Coach Station to the Eastern Docks after stopping at the bus station (tel. (01304) 24 00 24, info (01813) 58 13 33) on Pencester Rd. (2¾hr., £13). Buses also make trips to Canterbury (£4). **Stena Sealink** (tel. (01233) 64 70 47 or 24 02 80) and **P&O** (tel. (01304) 21 21 21) both send **ferries** daily to Calais, France. Stena Sealink fares at peak season (July-Sept.) are £24 single, students £20. P&O offers a £24 single with five-day return, children £12. **Hovercraft** leave from Dover's Hoverport (tel. (01304) 24 02 41), at the Prince of Wales Pier for Calais (£25 return) or Boulogne (same rates). Book a few days in advance.

Sussex

Brighton According to legend, the soon-to-be King George slinked into Brighton for some hanky-panky around 1784. Still the unrivaled home of the "dirty weekend," Brighton sparkles with a risque, tawdry luster all its own. Before indulging, check out

England's long-time fascination with the Far East incarnate at the **Royal Pavilion** on Pavilion Parade, next to Old Steine (open June-Sept. daily 10am-6pm; Oct.-May 10am-5pm; £4.10, students £3). Around the corner stands the **Brighton Museum and Art Gallery** on Church St., with paintings, English pottery, and a wild deco and Art Nouveau collection. Leer at Salvador Dalí's sexy red sofa, *Mae West's Lips* (open Mon.-Tues. and Thurs.-Sat. 10am-5pm, Sun. 2-5:30pm; free).

Brighton brims with nightlife options. It is *the* gay nightlife spot in Britain outside London. Check out *The Punter, What's On,* and *Gay Times* (£2.20) for info on the rapidly changing club and bar scenes. Earlier in the evening folks gather to drink at **Fortune of War** and **Cuba,** both on the beach between West and Palace Pier. The most technically armed and massively populated clubs are **Paradox** and **Event II,** both on West. St. Paradox gets a bit dressy toward the end of the week. The monthly "Wild Fruit" gay night is popular with a mixed crowd. The **Combler Club,** on the King's Rd. has a mixed crowd grinding by the water's edge. Revelers flock form as far as Amsterdam for dark rendezvous and hard-core dirty dancing under the converted arches of World War II tunnels at **Zap Club,** King's Rd.

The **tourist office,** 10 Bartholomew Sq. (tel. (01273) 32 37 55), offers a free map and books rooms for £2.50 plus a 10% deposit (open Mon.-Fri. 9am-5pm, Sat. 10am-5pm, Sun. 10am-4pm). **Trains** roll regularly from London to Brighton (1¼hr., £12.60) on their way to Arundel via Ford (50min., £6) and Portsmouth (1½hr., £11.10). National Express **buses** also head to Brighton from London (2hr., £8). Brighton's best bets for budget lodging are its hostels. Cheaper and shabbier **B&Bs** collect west of the West Pier and east of Palace Pier. The **Brighton Backpackers Hostel,** 75-76 Middle St. (tel. (01273) 77 77 17), is an independent hostel just 50m from the waterfront (£9; weekly rate £50). **Baggies Back-packers,** 33 Oriental Pl. (tel. (01273) 73 37 40), has mellow vibes and exquisite murals (£8-9, doubles £23). The **YHA Youth Hostel,** Patcham Pl. (tel. (01273) 55 61 96), has rooms that look new even though they're 400 years old (curfew 11pm; £9.40). Take Patcham Bus 5 or 5A from Old Steine in front of the Royal Pavilion to the Black Lion Hotel. Prowl The Lanes between North and Prince Albert St. in search of sustenance. **Food for Friends,** 17a Prince Albert St., has well-seasoned vegetarian meals (£3-6; open daily 8am-10:30pm).

Arundel and Chichester The tea rooms and antique shops of **Arundel** surround its castle like stone minions, always in the shadow of towers, ramparts, and cathedral spires. **Arundel Castle** is the third oldest in Britain and the seat of the Duke of Norfolk, Earl Marshal of England (open April-Oct. Sun.-Fri. noon-5pm; last admission 4pm; £5.50). In late August, the castle hosts the **Arundel Festival,** 10 days of concerts, jousting, and outdoor theater; a fringe schedule offers less expensive events (info tel. (01903) 88 36 90). The **tourist office,** 61 High St. (tel. (01903) 88 22 68), offers the free *Town Guide.* (Open in summer Mon.-Fri. 9am-5pm, Sat.-Sun. 10am-5pm; off-season Mon.-Fri. 9am-3pm, Sat.-Sun. 10am-3pm.) **Trains** leave London's Victoria Station for Arundel (1¼hr., day return £13.50). Most other train and bus routes require connections at Littlehampton to the south or Barnham to the east. If you're up for the 1½ mi. walk from town, the **YHA Warningcamp Youth Hostel** (tel. (01903) 88 22 04) cheerfully offers a place to prop up your feet. (Curfew 11pm. £7.70, camping £3.85. Open July-Aug. daily; April-June Mon.-Sat.; Sept.-Oct. Tues.-Sat.; Nov.-Dec. Sun.-Thurs. Closed Jan.-March.) Otherwise, prepare to pay at least £15-20 for **B&Bs** along the River Arun. Locals frequent **Belinda's,** 13 Tarrant St., a 16th-century tea room with a bird-filled garden and large wine selection (open Tues.-Sat. 9:30am-5:30pm, Sun. 11am-5:30pm). Bus 11 travels to the nearby **Littlehampton,** where **The Body Shop Tour** (tel. (01903) 84 40 44) takes visitors behind the scenes at the retail chain's factory (open Mon.-Fri.; £4, students £3).

The remains of Roman walls and an imposing Norman cathedral provide the backdrop for **Chichester's** superb theater, arts festival, and gallery exhibits. The **Cathedral,** begun in 1091, features a glorious stained-glass window by Chagall (open daily 7:30am-6pm; off-season until 5pm; £2 donation encouraged). During the first half of July, the cathedral hosts the **Chichester Festivities,** one of the finest spells of concentrated musical and artistic creativity in all of England (info tel. (01243) 78 57 18). The **Roman Palace** in nearby Fishbourne is the largest Roman residence excavated in Britain. Go west along Westgate, which becomes Fishbourne Rd. (the A259) for 1½ mi., or take bus 700 or 701 from Chichester center. (Open March-July and Sept.-Oct. daily 10am-5pm; Aug. 10am-6pm; Nov.-Dec. and Feb. 10am-4pm; Jan. Sun. only 10am-4pm. £3.80, students £3.20.)

The **tourist office,** South St. (tel. (01243) 77 58 88; fax 53 94 49), has a 24-hour computer information guide listing vacancies. (Open July-Aug. Mon.-Fri. 9:15am-6pm, Sat. 9am-5:15pm, Sun. 10am-4pm; Sept.-May Mon.-Sat. 9:15am-5:15pm.) **Trains** run to and from London's Victoria Station (1½hr., £15.40), Brighton (1hr., £6.90), and Portsmouth (1hr., £4.20). National Express **buses** run less frequently to London (period return £10); Coastline buses 700 and 701 serve Brighton (2hr., £4.40) and Portsmouth (1hr., £3.90). The bus station (tel. (01903) 23 76 61) lies diagonally across from the train station on Southgate. Rooms for under £15 are virtually nonexistent here. **Hedgehogs,** 45 Whyke Ln. (tel. (01243) 78 00 22), offers cozy rooms near the town center (£16-22). Camp at **Southern Leisure Centre,** Vinnetrow Rd. (tel. (01243) 78 77 15), a 15-minute walk southeast of town (£8 per tent, £2 per person; £2 more in July and Aug.; open April-Oct.). **Blanc Boulangerie and Patisserie,** 56 South St., will make any Francophone's mouth water.

Hampshire

Portsmouth Over 900 years old and site of the D-Day launching in 1944, Portsmouth boasts an incomparable naval heritage and magnificent seafaring relics. Henry VIII's beloved **Mary Rose** set sail in 1545 only to keel over and sink before the monarch's eyes. The vessel, raised from its watery grave in 1982, is now on display along with Tudor artifacts salvaged from the wreck. Nearby, Admiral Nelson's flagship **HMS Victory** won the Battle of Trafalgar against the French and Spanish in 1805, but a careful look reveals the dismal, cramped conditions endured by recruits. Entrance to just the **Historic Dockyard** is free. (Open July-Aug. daily 10am-7pm; March-June and Sept.-Oct. 10am-6pm; Nov.-Feb. 10am-5:30pm.) Each ship within charges admission (£5.50, students £4).

Portsmouth has **tourist offices** on The Hard (tel. (01705) 82 67 22), by the entrance to the ships (open daily 9:30am-5:45pm), and at 102 Commercial Rd. (tel. (01705) 83 83 82), next to the train station (open Mon.-Sat. 9:30am-5:30pm). **Trains** (tel. (01705) 22 93 93) arrive from London Waterloo (1½hr., return £16.80); National Express **buses** run from London (2½hr., return £12.50) and Salisbury (2hr., £7). **B&Bs** clutter Southsea, a resort town 1½ mi. east; cheaper lodgings lie two or three blocks inland. The **YHA Youth Hostel** is in Wymering Manor, Old Wymering Lane, Medina Rd. (tel. (01705) 37 56 61), in Cosham (£8.50; open Feb.-Aug. daily; Oct.-Nov. Fri.-Sat.; closed Dec.-Jan.). Take any bus to Cosham and follow the signs. The **Southsea Backpackers Lodge,** 4 Florence Rd. (tel. (01705) 83 24 95), offers ample facilities (dorms £8, singles £12, doubles £22). Mrs. Parkes watches over her spotless **Testudo House,** 19 Whitwell Rd., Southsea (tel. (01705) 82 43 24; £17.50-34). **Restaurants** line Osborne, Palmerston, and Clarendon Rd. in the Southsea shopping district. Near The Hard, **pubs** greet weary sailors and tourists.

Winchester Winchester's glory days echo from the shadowy Middle Ages. William the Conqueror and Alfred the Great (whose statued image still looms) based their kingdoms here, and Charles II moved to Winchester during the Great Plague of 1665 to keep track of his properties and occasionally inquire about his subjects' deaths. The city still makes a great daytrip from Salisbury or Portsmouth. At 556 ft., the **Winchester Cathedral** is the longest medieval building in Europe. The interior is scattered with scaffoldings but the magnificent medieval tiles and Jane Austen's grave are still visible (open daily 7:15am-6:30pm; East End closes 5pm; £2.50, students £2). Founded in 1382, most of **Winchester College's** 14th-century buildings remain intact (tour booking tel. (01962) 87 74 74).

The **tourist office,** The Guildhall, Broadway (tel. (01962) 84 05 00 or 84 81 80; fax 84 13 65), books rooms (£2.50 fee plus 10% deposit), gives out maps, and arranges walking tours. (Open June-Sept. Mon.-Sat. 10am-6pm, Sun. 11am-2pm; Oct.-May Mon.-Sat. 10am-5pm.) **Trains** (tel. (0345) 48 49 50) run from London (1hr., £15.40-18.10) and depart for Chichester (1hr., £8.70), Portsmouth (1hr., £6.20), Oxford (2½hr., £6.50), and Gatwick (£10.50). National Express **buses** run to London via Heathrow (1½hr., £9-12), and to Oxford and Gatwick; Hampshire buses head to Salisbury (1½hr., £4) and Portsmouth (1½hr., return £4). For bus schedules call (01256) 46 45 01. There is no luggage storage at any public facility.

The **YHA youth hostel,** 1 Water Ln. (tel. (01962) 85 37 23), is well-located (lockout 10am-5pm; curfew 11pm; expect a chore or two; £8.50; call ahead). **B&Bs** cluster on Christchurch and St. Cross Rd. near Ranelagh Rd. **Mrs. Tisdall's,** 32 Hyde St. (tel. (01962) 85 16 21), is comfortable and convenient (£19-32; 10% *Let's Go* discount; breakfast included). Camp at **Mornhill,** two miles outside the city center, at the top of Alresford Rd. (£5 pitch fee; £2.60-4 per person; laundry £1.40; open March-Oct.). Restaurants line Jewry St., and most pubs serve good fare. **Royal Oak,** off High St., claims fame as the country's oldest pub, while the more recent **Mash Tun,** Eastgate St., has a psychedelic flare (open daily noon-11pm).

Salisbury and Stonehenge

Salisbury revolves around the axis of the **Salisbury Cathedral,** whose spire—the tallest in England—rises 404 ft. from its grassy close. (Open July-Aug. daily 8am-8pm; Sept.-June 8am-6:30pm. £2.50, students £1.50. Tours Mon.-Sat. 11:15am and 2:15pm. Tower tours Mon.-Sat. 11am, 2, 3, and 6:30pm, Sun. 4:30pm. £2.) One of four surviving copies of the *Magna Carta* rests in the **Chapter House,** which is surrounded by detailed medieval friezes. (Open March-Oct. Mon.-Sat. 9:30am-4:45pm, Sun. 1-4:45pm; Nov.-Feb. Mon.-Sat. 11am-3pm, Sun. 1-3:15pm. 30p.)

The helpful **tourist office,** Fish Row (tel. (01722) 33 49 56; fax 42 20 59), Guildhall in Market Sq., books rooms (with a deposit) and offers tours (1½hr, £2). (Open July-Aug. Mon.-Sat. 9:30am-7pm, Sun. 10:30am-5pm; June and Sept. Mon.-Sat. 9:30am-6pm, Sun. 10:30am-4:30pm; Oct.-May Mon.-Sat. 9:30am-5pm; May also Sun. 10:30am-4:30pm.) **Trains** depart Salisbury Station, South Western Rd. (tel. in Southampton (0345) 48 49 50), for Winchester (change at Southampton, 1½hr., £8.80), Portsmouth (1½hr., £10.40), and London (1½hr., £19.50). National Express **buses** run from London's Victoria Station (2¾hr., £10.50). Wilts and Dorset buses serve Bath and Stonehenge (1-day bus pass £4.40). The **YHA youth hostel,** Milford Hill House, Milford Hill (tel. (01722) 32 75 72), is surrounded by two acres of gardens (curfew 11:30pm; £9.40; camping £4.70 per person). **Matt and Tiggy's,** 51 Salt Ln. (tel. (01722) 32 74 43), is just up from the bus station (£9.50; breakfast £2; sheets 80p). **The Old Bakery,** 35 Bedwin St. (tel. (01722) 32 01 00), is a comfy resting spot (singles £15, doubles £14-18, mention *Let's Go;* breakfast £3). Sip your brew at the **Old Mill** or the not-so-**New Inn**, two of the 60-odd watering holes.

The 22-feet high boulders of **Stonehenge** (tel. (01980) 62 53 68) were carried and placed from 2800 to 1500 BC, some from as far away as Ireland. Capture a good view from Amesbury Hill, 1½ mi. up the A303, or pay admission for a closer look. (Open June-Aug. daily 9am-7pm; Sept. to mid-Oct. and mid-March to May 9:30am-6pm; mid-Oct. to mid-March 9:30am-4pm. £3.70, students £2.80.)

SOUTHWEST ENGLAND

Myths and legends shroud the counties of Dorset, Somerset, Devon, and Cornwall in England's West Country, home to Bronze Age barrows and King Arthur. Although you will undoubtedly encounter industrial cities and annoying "Mayflour" bake shops, the region's timeless terrain is unfailingly beautiful.

British Rail **trains** from London frequently pass through Plymouth and Exeter on their way to Penzance. From Glasgow and Edinburgh, a line passes though Bristol and Exeter before ending at Plymouth. National Express **buses** run to major points along the north coast via Bristol and to points along the south coast via Exeter and Plymouth. Local bus service is less expensive and more extensive than the local trains. For hikers and bikers, the longest coastal path in England, the **South West Peninsula Coast Path,** originates in Dorset and runs through South Devon, Cornwall, and North Devon, ending in Somerset. The path is divided into four, more manageable parts based on the national parks and counties through which it passes.

Exeter

Exeter withstood an 18-day siege by William the Conqueror in 1068 but was flattened during a few perilous days of German bombing in 1942. Frantic rebuilding has resulted in an odd mixture of the venerable and the banal: Roman and Norman ruins poke up from delicatessen parking lots, and department store cash registers ring atop medieval catacombs. This jigsaw cityscape and a large university community may have fostered Exeter's diverse population, noteworthy in homogenous Devon.

Exeter Cathedral, low-slung and lovely, overlooks the commercial clutter of High St. Although the cathedral was heavily damaged in World War II, intricate details abound: a gilded ceiling boss depicts the murder of St. Thomas of Becket, the west front holds hundreds of stone figures, and misericordia (small seats against a wall) retain carvings of elephants and basilisks. On display in the cathedral library, the **Exeter Book** is the richest treasury of early Anglo-Saxon poetry in the world. (Cathedral open daily 7am-6:30pm. Library open Mon.-Fri. 2-5pm. £2 donation. Free guided tours April-Oct. Mon.-Fri. 11:30am and 2:30pm, Sat. 11am.)

National Express **buses** (tel. (0990) 80 80 80) provide the cheapest transportation to Exeter; a student coach card grants passage from London Victoria Coach Station (4hr.) for £22.50. Buses also drive from Bristol (£10) and Bath (£14.50). The bus station (tel. (01392) 562 31) is on Paris St., off High St. just outside the city walls. **Trains** arrive at Exeter St. David's Station, St. David's Hill, from London's Paddington and Waterloo Stations (3hr., £36 and £39 respectively); a few trains from Waterloo Station arrive at Exeter Central Station, Queen St. The **tourist office,** Civic Centre, Paris St. (tel. (01392) 26 57 00), books rooms (10% deposit; open Mon.-Fri. 9am-5pm, Sat. 9am-1pm and 2-5pm). The **YHA youth hostel,** 47 Countess Wear Rd. (tel. (01392) 87 33 29; fax 87 69 39), is spacious and cheery (£9.40; breakfast £2.70). Cheap eateries cluster along Queen St., near the Central Station. If you're heading north or west to one of the national parks, pick up a supplies at **Marks and Spencer** on High St. The newest, best watering hole is the airy **Imperial,** New North Rd., just up from St. David's Station (two dinners for £5). Two doors down from Central Station, **Internet Express** has The Access you've been looking for (£2.50 per 30min.).

Dartmoor National Park

> The Ministry of Defense uses much of the northern moor for target practice; consult the *Dartmoor Visitor* or an Ordnance Survey map for the boundaries of the danger area, or call (01392) 27 01 64 for recorded info, cowboy.

The lush, green forests and windy moors of Dartmoor National Park challenge visitors with treacherous terrain and capricious weather, but reward hearty explorers with an unparalleled sense of beauty and serenity. Prehistoric remains lurk about the moor near **Princetown,** at the southern edge of the park's north-central plateau. The moor was the setting for the famous Sherlock Holmes tale *The Hound of the Baskervilles.* The rugged eastern part of the park centers on **Hay Tor.** Two miles north of this village lies **Hound Tor,** where excavations have unearthed the remains of 13th-century huts and longhouses. Don't be surprised if a weary traveler approaches you and asks for a rubber stamp (or "traveler"). Yes, a rubber stamp. Throughout the park are hidden **Dartmoor Letterboxes,** containing stamps to prove you were here; finding them is hardly elementary (stamp and clue books are available in area stores), and the quest captivates some avid Dartmoorians.

Contact the Exeter **bus station** (tel. (01392) 42 77 11), the Plymouth bus station (tel. (01752) 22 26 66), or the Devon County Council's **Public Transportation Helpline** (tel. (01392) 38 28 00; Mon.-Fri. 8:30am-5pm) for info on transportation to Dartmoor. **Hiking** and **cycling** are the way to go once inside the park. Whatever method you choose, make sure you have an Ordnance Survey Map (about £5), waterproof gear, and a compass. Ask questions and pick up the essential *Dartmoor Visitor* from one of the National Park Information Centres: **Tavistock** (tel. (01822) 61 29 38), **Ivybridge** (tel. (01752) 89 70 35), **Newbridge** (tel. (01364) 63 13 03), **Okehampton** (tel. (01837) 530 20), **Postbridge** (tel. (01822) 88 02 72), and **Princetown** (High Moorland Visitor Centre; tel. (01822) 89 04 14).

B&B signs are frequently displayed in pubs and farmhouses along the roads, and the information centers hand out free accommodation lists. **YHA Steps Bridge** (tel. (01647) 25 24 35) is in Dunsford, near the eastern edge of the park (£6.75; open July-Aug. daily; April-June and Sept. Fri.-Tues.). The popular **YHA Bellever** (tel. (01822) 88 02 27), in Yelverton, is 1 mi. southeast of Postbridge village; take bus 359 or 82 from Exeter or bus 82 from Plymouth and ask to be let off as close to the hostel as possible (£8.80; open July-Aug. daily; April-June and Sept.-Oct. Mon.-Sat.). Although official campsites exist, many travelers camp on the open moor. Ask permission before crossing or camping on private land.

Plymouth

Plymouth has long been a city of departures: Sir Francis Drake, Captain Cook, the Pilgrims, Lord Nelson, and millions of emigrants to the United States and New Zealand have immortalized Plymouth in their haste to get away from it. The city offers only a few attractions for stranded travelers. At the foot of the Hoe, the **Plymouth Dome** mixes life-size dioramas and more traditional displays to recreate Plymouth life since the Tudors. (Open April-Sept. daily 9am-7:30pm, last entry 6pm; Oct.-March 9am-6pm, last entry 5pm. £4.) The blackened shell of **Charles Church,** largely destroyed by a bomb in 1941, stands in the middle of the Charles Cross traffic circle as a memorial to the Plymouth citizens killed during World War II.

The **tourist office,** Island House, 9 The Barbican (tel. (01752) 26 48 49; fax 25 79 55), answers questions and dispenses a free city map (open Mon.-Sat. 9am-5pm, Sun. 10am-4pm). **Trains** run hourly to London (3½hr., £41), Penzance (1¾hr., £10), and Bristol (3½hr., £28). National Express **buses** (tel. (0990) 80 80 80) also serve London (4½hr., £27) and Bristol (2½hr., £20). Stagecoach Devon buses connect to Exeter (1¼hr., £4). **Ferries** leave Millbay Docks (tel. (0990) 36 03 60) for Roscoff, France (6hr., £20-58), and Santander, Spain (24hr., £80-145). Check in an hour before departure; disabled travelers should arrive two hours early.

Low-priced **B&Bs** grace Citadel Rd. and Athenaeum St. between the west end of Royal Parade and the Hoe; prices run £12-15. Check on availability at the tourist office. Call ahead for the excellent **YHA Youth Hostel,** Belmont House, Belmont Place, Stoke (tel. (01752) 56 21 89), which has spacious rooms and an elegant dining hall. Take bus 15 or 81 to "Stoke," and the hostel will appear on your left (lock-out 10am-5pm; curfew 11pm; £9.40; breakfast £2.85). The closer **Plymouth Backpackers Hotel,** 172 Citadel Rd., The Hoe (tel. (01752) 22 51 58), has basic hostel dorm rooms from £7.50. Reel in the catch of the day at **Cap'n Jaspers,** a stand by the Barbican side of the Harbor (open Mon.-Sat. 6:30am-11:45pm, Sun. 10am-11:45pm).

The Cornish Coast

Penzance and St. Ives On Cornwall's Penwith Peninsula, sunny **Penzance** is the very model of an ancient English pirate town. A stone sailor greets visitors to the life of 18th-century seamen at the **Maritime Museum,** halfway down Chapel St.

(open May-Oct. Mon.-Sat. 10:30am-4:30pm; £2). Across the bay from Penzance at Marazion, **St. Michael's Mount** monastery was built on the site of a supposed sighting of Archangel Michael by 5th-century fishermen. (Open April-Oct. Mon.-Fri. 10:30am-5:45pm; in summer also most weekends; off-season as weather permits. Island £4.) Penzance's **train station** (tel. (0345) 48 49 50) and **bus station** (tel. (01209) 71 99 88) stand conveniently together in the same square on Wharf Rd., at the head of Albert Pier. The **tourist office** (tel. (01736) 36 22 07), also in the square, books rooms. (£2.75. Open Mon.-Fri. 9am-5pm, Sat. 10am-1pm; in summer also Sat. 9am-4pm and Sun. 10am-1pm.) The super-friendly **YHA Youth Hostel,** Castle Horneck (tel. (01736) 36 26 66), provides newly refurbished rooms in a restored 18th-century mansion (reception open daily 5-11pm; £9.40; **campsites** £4.70). **The Turk's Head,** 46 Chapel St., serves yummy food in a 13th-century pub. (Meals from £4-5. Open Mon.-Sat. 11am-2:30pm and 6-10pm, Sun. noon-2:30pm and 6-10pm.)

Ten miles north of Penzance, **St. Ives** perches on a rounded spit of land lined by pastel beaches and azure waters. A white **lighthouse,** thought to be an inspiration for Virginia Woolf's masterpiece *To The Lighthouse,* watches over the town. The **tourist office** (tel. (01736) 79 62 97) is in the Guildhall on Street-an-Pol (open Mon.-Sat. 9:30am-5:30pm, Sun. 10am-1pm; off-season closed Sat.-Sun.). **Trains** on the Plymouth-Penzance line stop at St. Erth, a 10-minute shuttle from St. Ives. **Buses** run to St. Ives from Penzance (£1.80). Although the closest youth hostel beckons from Penzance, **B&Bs** line every alley and cluster on Park Ave. and Tregenna Terr. (from £15). Prices dip farther from the water and higher up the gusty hillside. Campsites are abundant in nearby Hayle; try **Trevalgan Camping Park** (tel. (01736) 79 64 33), with cooking facilities and access to the coastal path. Storefront blackboards will tempt you with **Cornish cream tea** (a pot of tea with scones, jam, and Cornish clotted cream). Try it at **Bumble's Tea Room** at Digey Square near the Tate (£2.50; open Mon.-Sat. 10am-4:30pm, Sun. 11am-4:30pm; off-season closed Sun.).

Falmouth Two spectacular castles eye each other across the world's third largest natural harbor in Falmouth, situated along the Penryn River. **Pendennis Castle,** built by Henry VIII to keep out French frigates, now features a walk-through diorama and superb views (open April-Oct. daily 10am-6pm; Nov.-March 10am-4pm; £2.70, students £2). **St. Mawes Castle,** a 20-minute ferry ride from Falmouth to St. Mawes village (for ferry info, call (01326) 31 32 01 or 31 38 13; return £3.50), was expected to gun down any Frenchmen Pendennis spared. (Open April-Oct. daily 10am-6pm; Nov.-March Wed.-Sun. 10am-4pm. £2.20, students £1.70.)

Falmouth is accessible by **rail** from any stop on the London-Penzance line, including Exeter and Plymouth; change at Truro and go three stops (30min., £2.40). Western National **buses** (tel. (0990) 80 80 80) serve Falmouth from Truro (£2.20) and Penzance (£3.50). The **tourist office,** 28 Killigrew St. (tel. (01326) 31 23 00), will help you find a room. (Open July-Aug. Mon.-Thurs. 9am-5pm, Fri. 9am-4:45pm, Sun. 10am-4pm; Sept.-June closed Sun.) The **YHA Youth Hostel,** Pendennis Castle (tel. (01326) 31 14 35; fax 31 54 73), is 30 minutes from town ending with an uphill seaside hike. Book far ahead. (Reception open daily 8:30am-10am and 5-10:30pm. Curfew 11pm. £8.50. Open Feb.-Sept. daily; Oct.-Nov. Tues.-Sat. Closed Dec.-Jan.)

Newquay An outpost of surfer subculture, **Newquay** (NEW-key) is an enclave of neon youth—come for the beaches. The town's **tourist office** (tel. (01637) 87 13 45) sits atop Marcus Hill (open Mon.-Sat. 9am-6pm, Sun. 10am-5pm; in winter shortened hours). All **trains** to Newquay run through the small town of Par on the main London-Penzance line. National Express **buses** (tel. (0990) 80 80 80) run directly to Newquay from London; Western National buses connect Newquay and St. Ives. Get a crash course in surfer life at **Fistral Backpackers,** 18 Headland Rd. (tel. (01637) 87 31 46; £6.50; July-Aug. £7.50) or **Towan Beach Backpackers,** 16 Beachfield Ave. (tel. (01637) 87 46 68; £5-7). The restaurants in Newquay are expensive; keep an eye out for three-course "early bird" specials. **Food for Thought,** 33A Bank St., at the corner of Beachfield Ave., offers takeout "Californian" salads and sandwiches (under £2;

open daily 8:30am-10pm). Newquay's nightlife rises at 9pm and reigns until dawn; clubs are open until 1am. Those on the trail of surfer bars begin at **The Red Lion,** wash over to pubs on Fore St., and crash at **The Newquay Arms.**

HEART OF ENGLAND

Oxford

Named for the place where oxen could ford the Thames, Oxford, the city of dreaming spires, is a furiously rushing commercial town which shelters England's oldest university. Despite an appalling number of buses, the hoards of commercial and professional people, bikes, and vehicles are largely concentrated in a small district in the city center. To escape, leave the busy streets and alleys and enter into the quiet world of the medieval college quadrangle, enhanced by meticulously cared-for lawns and vibrantly colorful gardens, or walk along Christ Church meadow down to the Thames, obscurely called the Isis for these few miles only.

ORIENTATION AND PRACTICAL INFORMATION

Queen, High, St. Aldates, and Cornmarket St. meet at right angles in **Carfax,** the town center. The colleges surround Carfax to the east along High St. and Broad St.; the train and bus stations lie to the west.

Tourist Office: The Old School, Gloucester Green (tel. 72 68 71; fax 24 02 61). From Carfax, follow signposts up Cornmarket St., left onto Georger St., and right into Gloucester Green. A pamphleteer's paradise. Accommodations list 50p. Street map 70p. Books rooms for £2.50 and a 10% deposit. Open Mon -Sat. 9:30am-5pm, Sun. 10am-3:30pm.

Currency Exchange: Several banks line Carfax. **Barclays,** 54 Cornmarket St. Open Mon.-Fri. 9:30am-4:30pm, Wed. only until 5pm, Sat. 10am-noon.

American Express: 4 Queen St. (tel. 79 20 66). Open Mon.-Tues. and Thurs.- Fri. 9am-5:30pm, Wed. 9:30am-5:30pm, Sat. 9am-5pm; in summer also Sun. 11am-3pm.

Trains: Park End St., west of Carfax (tel. 79 44 22 for recorded schedules). Local trains (1hr.) run every 15-30min. from London's Paddington Station. Ticket office open Mon.-Fri. 5:50am-8pm, Sat. 6:45am-8pm, Sun. 7:45am-8pm.

Buses: Station on Gloucester Green (follow arrows from Carfax). **Oxford Tube** (tel. 77 22 50) and **Oxford CityLink** (tel. 71 13 12 or 77 22 50 for timetable) send buses to and from London. **Carfax Travel,** 138 High St. (tel. 72 61 72), books for National Express, British Rail, and ferries (open Mon.-Fri. 9am-5pm, Sat. 9am-1pm). Most local buses board on the streets adjacent to Carfax.

Luggage Storage: Pensioners Club (tel. 24 22 37), Gloucester Green. Stores luggage from 9am-4:45pm for £1 per bag. Ask for permission to leave bags longer.

Crisis Lines: Samaritans: 123 Iffley Rd. (24hr. tel. 72 21 22). Drop-in daily 8am-10pm. **Rape Crisis:** tel. 72 62 95. Open Mon.-Tues. and Thurs. 7-9pm, Wed. 4-6pm, Sun. 6-8pm; answering machine other times.

Pharmacy: Boots, 6-8 Cornmarket St. (tel. 24 74 61). Open Mon.-Wed. 9am-6pm, Thurs. 8:45am-7pm, Fri.-Sat. 8:45am-6pm, Sun. 11am-5pm.

Hospital: John Radcliffe, Headley Way (tel. 74 11 66). Take bus 13B or 14A.

Emergency: Dial 999; no coins required.

Police: St. Aldates and Speedwell St. (tel. 26 60 00).

Internet Access: Westgate Library, on the corner of Castle and New. £1.25 for 15min. **Daily Information,** 31 Warnborough Rd. (tel. 31 00 11). £6 per hr.

Post Office: 124 St. Aldates St. (tel. 20 28 63). Open Mon.-Fri. 9am-5:30pm, Sat. 9am-6pm. **Postal Code:** OX1 1ZZ.

Telephones: Card and coin phones available at Carfax, on Cornmarket St., and on St. Aldates St. **Telephone Code:** 01865.

ACCOMMODATIONS AND CAMPING

B&Bs line the main roads out of town, all of them a vigorous walk (15-20min.) from Carfax. You'll find cheaper B&Bs on Iffley Rd. and Cowley Road, both served by frequent buses from Carfax (4 and 51). Expect to pay £16-22 per person.

YHA Youth Hostel, 32 Jack Straw's Ln., Headington (tel. 76 29 97; fax 76 94 02). Catch Citylink Bus 13 or 14 (60p) away from Carfax on High St. and ask the driver to stop. The hostel is an 8min. walk up a hill. One of England's larger hostels (114 beds), with a kitchen, laundry, lockers, and a food shop. Campers can use facilities for half-price. Reserve ahead.

Tara, 10 Holywell St. (the proprietors are deaf, so use phone *Typetalk* (free) at (51) 494 20 22; within the UK (0800) 51 51 52; give the operator Tara's phone number 20 29 53; fax 20 02 97). A great find on the oldest medieval street in Oxford. Singles £28. Doubles £44. Triples £55. Book 2 weeks ahead.

Heather House, 192 Iffley Rd. (tel./fax 24 97 57). Take a bus marked "Rose Hill" from the bus station, train station, or Carfax Tower. Clean and modern, with an friendly Austrian proprietor. Singles £20. Larger rooms £18-23 per person.

Bravalla, 242 Iffley Rd. (tel. 24 13 26; fax 25 05 11). Sunny rooms with soothing floral patterns and pastels. Singles £25. Doubles with bath £40-44.

Old Mitre Rooms, 4B Turl St. (tel. 27 98 21). Recently refurbished dorm rooms. Singles £19. Doubles £37, with bath £40. Triples £45. Open July-early Sept.

Oxford Backpacker's Hotel, 9a Hythe Bridge St. (tel. 72 17 61). Right between the bus and train stations. Laundry facilities and kitchen. £9-10 a night.

Camping: Oxford Camping International, 426 Abingdon Rd. (tel. 24 65 51, after 5:30pm 72 56 46). Take any bus in the 30s from Carfax. 129 nondescript sites. Laundry. Up to 2 adults £7.85, each additional adult £1.55. Showers (20p).

FOOD

Oxford offers a mix of typical college-town eateries and more upscale ethnic restaurants. **Harvey's of Oxford,** 58 High St., is one of the better take-aways. (Mighty sandwiches £1-2.75. Open Mon.-Fri. 8:30am-5:30pm, Sat. 8:30am-6:30pm, Sun. 9:30am-6:30pm.) **Fasta Pasta** in the covered market hawks cheap, gourmet sandwiches and bagels and an impressive selection of olives. When students tire of burgers and pizza, they stock up at the **Co-op** supermarket on Cornmarket St. (open Mon.-Fri. 8am-7pm, Sat. 8am-6pm) or at the **market** at Gloucester Green (open Wed. all day).

The Nosebag, 6-8 St. Michael's, overcomes a silly name with excellent food: gourmet meals served cafeteria-style. (£5-7. Open Mon. 9:30am-5:30pm, Tues.-Thurs. and Sun. 9:30am-9pm, Fri.-Sat. 9:30am-10:30pm.) Across Magdalen Bridge, **Hi-Lo Jamaican Eating House, Kashmir Halal,** and **The Pak Fook,** all on Cowley Rd., are good bets. **Chiang Mai,** in an alley at 130A High St., has spicy Thai food and vegetarian offerings (£5-8; open Mon.-Sat. noon-2:30pm and 6-11pm). **Heroes,** 8 Ship St., serves up sandwiches on a variety of fresh breads with a super selection of stuffings (£1.70-3.30; open Mon.-Fri. 8am-7pm, Sat. 8:30am-6pm, Sun. 10am-5pm).

SIGHTS AND ENTERTAINMENT

Start your walking tour at Carfax ("four-forked"), the center of activity, with a hike up the 99 spiral stairs of **Carfax Tower** for an overview of the city (open April to Oct. daily 10am-5:30pm, Nov.-March daily 10am-3:30pm; £1.20).

King Henry II founded Britain's first university in 1167, and today Oxford's alumni register reads like a who's who of British history, literature, and philosophy. Down St. Aldates St., **Christ Church** names 13 prime ministers among its former students (open Mon.-Sat. 9am-6pm, Sun. 11:30am-6pm; £3, students £2). The 13th-century **University College,** on High St., welcomed Bill Clinton during his Rhodes Scholar days but once expelled Percy Bysshe Shelley for writing about atheism; a monument recalls his watery death. Nearby, the idyllic **Botanic Garden** is perfect for a late-afternoon stroll (open daily 9am-5pm; glasshouses open daily 2-4pm; £1). Flamboyant

Oscar Wilde attended **Magdalen College,** considered by many Oxford's most handsome college (open daily 11am-6pm; £2, students £1).

Follow Catte St. to the **Bodleian Library,** Oxford's principal reading and research library with over five million books. No one has ever been permitted to check one out, not even Cromwell. Well, especially not Cromwell (open Mon.-Fri. 9am-6pm, Sat. 9am-12:30pm). Across Broad St. you could browse for days at **Blackwell's,** the world-famous bookstore (open Mon.-Sat. 9am-6pm, Sun. 11am-5pm). The **Sheldonian Theatre**, set beside the Bodleian, is a Roman-style jewel of an auditorium. Graduation ceremonies, conducted in Latin, take place here. The cupola of the theater affords an inspiring view of the spires of Oxford (open Mon.-Sat. 10am-12:30pm, and 2-3:30pm, subject to change; £1.50). The **Cast Gallery,** behind the **Ashmolean Museum** on Beaumont St., stores over 250 casts of Greek sculptures. While the museum undergoes renovation, the entire display is exhibited—the finest classical collection outside London (open Tues.-Sat. 10am-4pm, Sun. 2-4pm; free). The five blocks of **Cowley Road** nearest the Magdalen Bridge feature a fascinating clutter of ethnic restaurants, small bookstores, and alternative shops.

Music and drama at Oxford are cherished arts. Try to attend a concert at one of the colleges or a performance at the **Holywell Music Rooms,** the oldest in the country. **City of Oxford Orchestra,** the city's professional symphony orchestra (tel. 25 23 65, tickets 26 13 84), plays in the Sheldonian Theatre and various college chapels (shows at 8pm; tickets £12-15, 25% student discount). The **Apollo Theatre,** George St. (tel. 24 45 44), presents performances ranging from lounge-lizard jazz to the Welsh National Opera (tickets from £6, discounts for seniors and students). During summer, college **theater groups** stage productions in local gardens and cloisters.

Pubs far outnumber colleges in Oxford; *Good Pubs of Oxford* (£3 at the tourist office) is an indispensable guide to the town's offerings. **The Bear,** on Aldred St., opened in 1242, is decorated with some 5000 ties while **The King's Arms,** Holywell St, is Oxford's unofficial student union. **The Eagle and Child,** 49 Giles St., known to all as the Bird and Baby, served C.S. Lewis and J.R.R. Tolkien for a quarter-century. For more sober entertainment, head to the River Thames, where **punting** is a favorite pastime among Oxford students and visitors.

■ Near Oxford: Woodstock

The largest private home in England and one of the loveliest, **Blenheim Palace** (tel. (01993) 81 13 25) features rambling grounds, a nearby lake, and a fantastic garden. While attending a party here, Churchill's mother gave birth to the future Prime Minister in a closet. (Open mid-March to Oct. daily 10:30am-5:30pm; grounds open daily 9am-5:30pm. £7.80, seniors and students £5.80, includes a boat trip on the lake.) Blenheim sprawls in **Woodstock,** 8 mi. north of Oxford on the A44; **Thames Transit** runs several buses (20, 20a, 20b, and 20c) from the Gloucester Green bus station in Oxford (2 per hr., 30min., return £2.70). **Spires and Shires** (tel. (01865) 25 17 85) offers daily bus tours to Blenheim from Broad St. and the Oxford train station (2 each morning; £13.50, seniors and students £12.50; includes admission to the palace). Churchill is buried in the nearby village churchyard of **Bladon.**

Cotswolds

Stretching across western England, the whimsical hills of the **Cotswolds** enfold old Roman settlements and tiny Saxon villages hewn from the famed Cotswold stone. Although not readily accessible by public transportation, the glorious Cotswolds demand entry into any itinerary. The hills lie mostly in **Gloucestershire,** bounded by **Banbury** in the northeast, **Bradford-upon-Avon** in the southwest, **Cheltenham** in the north, and **Malmesbury** in the south. **Trains** and **buses** frequent the area's major gateways—Cheltenham, Bath, and Gloucester—but buses between the villages are rare. Snag the comprehensive *Connection* timetable free from all area bus stations and tourist offices. *Getting There from Cheltenham* is also invaluable. Local roads are perfect for **cycling,** and the closely spaced villages make ideal watering holes. **Cotswold Way,** spanning 100 mi. from Bath to Chipping Camden, should appeal to those interested in **hiking** the hills. When you're ready to call it a day, the *Cotswold Way Handbook* (£1.50) lists **B&Bs** along the Cotswold Way. Most **campsites** are close to Cheltenham, but Bourton-on-the-Water, Stow-on-the-Wold, and Moreton-on-the-Marsh also have places to put your Tent-on-the-Ground. The annually updated *Gloucestershire Caravan and Camping Guide* is free from local tourist centers.

Stow-on-the-Wold, Winchcombe, and Cirencester Experience the Cotswolds as the English have for centuries by treading well-worn footpaths from village to village. **Stow-on-the-Wold** is a sleepy town with fine views, cold winds, and authentic stocks. The **YHA youth hostel** (tel. (01451) 83 04 97) stands just a few yards from the stocks. (Open April-Aug. daily; Sept.-Oct. Mon.-Sat; Nov.-Dec weekends. £7.70, students £6.70. Closed Jan.-March. Call ahead.) West of Stow-on-the-Wold and 6 mi. north of Cheltenham on the A46, **Sudeley Castle,** once the manor of King Ethelred the Unready, enserfs the town of **Winchcombe** and holds regular falconry shows (open April-Oct. daily 10:30am-5pm; £4). Archaeologists have discovered prehistoric paths and habitation sites across the Cotswolds. **Belas Knap,** a 4000-year-old burial mound, lies less than 2 mi. southwest of Sudeley Castle.

The Cotswolds boast some of the best examples of Roman settlements in Britain, most notably in **Cirencester.** Its **Corinium Museum,** Park St., houses a formidable collection of Roman artifacts. (Open April-Oct. Mon.-Sat. 10am-5pm, Sun. 2-5pm; Nov.-March Tues.-Sat. 10am-5pm, Sun. 2-5pm. £1.75, students £1.) The **tourist office** is in Corn Hall, Market Pl. (tel. (01285) 65 41 80). Stay in Cheltenham (see below) and make the ruins a daytrip. On Fridays, the town becomes a bedlamic **antique marketplace.** Quaff a pint at the **Golden Cross,** on Black Jack St., or the **Crown,** at West Market Pl. near the abbey.

Cheltenham A spa town second only to Bath, Cheltenham epitomizes elegance and proudly possesses the only naturally alkaline water in Great Britain. Enjoy the diuretic and laxative effects of the waters at the **Town Hall** (open Mon.-Fri. 9am-1pm and 2:15pm-5pm; free) or at the **Pittville Pump Room** in Pittville Park (tel. (01242) 52 38 52). Manicured gardens adorn shops and houses around town, but for a real floral fix, sunbathe at the exquisite **Imperial Gardens,** just past The Promenade away from the center of town. The **tourist office,** Municipal Offices, 77 The Promenade (tel. (01242) 52 28 78), one block east of the bus station, posts vacancies after hours. (Open July-Aug. Mon.-Sat. 9:30am-6pm, Sun. 9:30am-1:30pm; Sept.-June Mon.-Sat. 9:30am-5:15pm.) **Trains** run regularly to London (2hr., £26), Bath (1½hr., £11.40), and Exeter (2hr., £25.70). National Express **buses** run to London (3hr., £9.50) and Exeter (3½hr., £17) as well. The well-located **YMCA,** Vittoria Walk (tel. (01242) 52 40 24), is clean and accepts both men and women. From Town Hall, turn left off Promenade and go three blocks (reception open 24hr.; singles £13.50). **Bentons Guest House,** 71 Bath Rd. (tel. (01242) 51 74 17), and **Cross Ways,** 57 Bath Rd. (tel. (01242) 52 76 83), boast well-kept rooms (£18-20). Fruit stands and **bakeries** dot High St. For a relaxing pint, try **Dobell's,** 24 The Promenade (open Mon.-Sat. 11am-11pm, Sun. noon-2:30pm and 7-10:30pm).

Stratford-upon-Avon

Shakespeare lived here, and the area's industry is now the Bard. Knick-knack huts hawk "Will Power" T-shirts, and all the perfumes of Arabia will not sweeten the tour-bus-exhausted air in Stratford's center. Diehard fans should purchase the **combination ticket** (£8.50, students £7.50), which offers admission to five Shakespeare sights, but the least crowded way to pay homage is to visit Shakespeare's grave in **Holy Trinity Church,** Trinity St. (60p, students 40p). Bring your *Complete Works* to the riverbank outside. In town, begin your walking tour at **Shakespeare's Birthplace** (tel. 26 98 90) on Henley St. The Birthplace is half period recreation and half Shakespeare life-and-work exhibition. **New Place,** Chapel St., was Stratford's hippest home when Shakespeare bought it in 1597 after writing some hits in London. Only the foundation remains—it can be viewed from the street above. Down Chapel Lane, the **Great Garden** and the more attractive exterior of New Place can be viewed for free from the bowers around back.

Recent sons of the world-famous **Royal Shakespeare Company** include Kenneth Branagh and Ralph Fiennes; get thee to a performance. To reserve seats (£5-48) call the box office (tel. (01789) 29 56 23, 24hr. recording 26 91 91; fax 26 19 74). The box office opens at 9:30am; a group gathers outside about 20 minutes before opening for same-day sales. Phones open at 9am. Student and senior standbys for £11 exist in principle. The **Stratford Festival** (for 2 weeks in July) manages to celebrate artistic achievement other than Shakespeare's. The festival typically features world-class art from all arenas of performance (ticket info (01789) 41 45 13).

Practical Information, Accommodations, and Food Stratford lies about two hours from London by **Thames trains** (tel. 57 94 53). National Express **buses** run to and from London's Victoria Station (3 per day, 3hr., day return £14).The **tourist office,** Bridgefoot, across Warwick Rd. at Bridge St. toward the waterside park (tel. (01789) 29 31 27), books rooms for £3 and a 10% deposit. (Open April-Sept. Mon.-Sat. 9am-6pm, Sun. 11am-5pm; Oct.-March Mon.-Sat. 9am-5pm.)

To B&B or not to B&B? If you can find one with a vacancy it's probably a good investment; the nearest youth hostel is more than 2 mi. out of town and, with a return bus fare, costs as much as an inexpensive B&B. Guest houses (£15-22) line **Grove Road, Evesham Place,** and **Evesham Road. Greensleeves,** 46 Alcester Rd. (tel. (01789) 29 21 31), on the way to the train station, is a cheerful home with delicious food and a grandmotherly proprietor (£15, students £14). **Field View Guest House,** 35 Banbury Rd. (tel. (01789) 29 26 94), offers clean singles (£16) and doubles (£32). The **HI youth hostel,** Hemmingford House, Wellesbourne Rd., Alveston (tel (01789) 29 70 93), has large, attractive grounds; take bus 18 (£1.50) from Wood St., across from the McDonald's (members only; reception open daily 7am-midnight; £13, student discounts). Closer to town, **Nando's,** 18 Evesham Pl. (tel./fax (01789) 20 49 07), has delightful owners and comfortable rooms (£22-42). **Elms,** Tiddington Rd. (tel. (01789) 29 23 12), over 1 mi. northeast of Stratford on the B4086, offers **camping** grounds (£3.50, each additional person £2; open April-Oct.).

Hussain's Indian Cuisine, 6a Chapel St., is Stratford's best Indian cuisine, with a slew of tandoori (lunch £6; entrees £5.75 and up; open daily noon-2pm and 5pm-midnight). **Dirty Duck Pub,** Southern Ln. River, serves a traditional pub lunch for £2-4.50; double that for dinners (open Mon.-Sat. 11am-11pm, Sun noon-10pm). A Safeway **supermarket** awaits on Alcester Rd.

Bath

Supposedly founded by an exiled leprous prince after the hot springs cured his disease, Bath ironically went on to become one of the great hubs of social networking. Queen Anne's visit in 1701 established Bath as a meeting place for 18th-century artists and intellectuals, and authors like Fielding, Austen, and Dickens immortalized the city in their works. Today, more hair salons than literary salons grace the streets, but the elegant Georgian city retains a beauty worthy of its distinguished history.

The excellent **Roman Baths Museum** (tel. (01225) 47 77 84) explores the architectural remains, engineering achievements, and bits and pieces from the daily life of the Roman spa city Aquae Sulis. The ruins of the city were discovered by sewer-diggers in 1880. (Open April-July and Sept. daily 9am-6pm; Aug. 9am-6pm and 8-10pm; Oct.-March Mon.-Sat. 9:30am-5pm, Sun. 10:30am-5pm. £6. Partial wheelchair access.) Next door, the towering and tombstoned 15th-century **Bath Abbey** has a whimsical west facade showing several angels climbing ladders up to heaven and, curiously enough, two climbing down (open April-Sept. daily 9am-6pm; Oct.-March 9am-4pm; £1.50). The dazzling **Museum of Costume** on Bennett St. will satisfy any fashion fetish. (Open Mon.-Sat. 10am-5pm, Sun. 11am-5pm. £3.60, joint ticket to Museum and Roman Baths £8.) Walk up Gay St. to **The Circus,** which has attracted illustrious residents for two centuries; blue plaques mark the houses of Thomas Gainsborough, William Pitt, and David Livingstone. Up Brock St. resides the **Royal Crescent,** a half-moon of Gregorian townhouses. **Royal Victoria Park,** nearby, contains one of the finest collections of trees in the country, and its **botanical gardens** nurture 5000 species of plants (open Mon.-Sat. 9am-dusk, Sun. 10am-dusk; free).

Practical Information, Accommodations, and Food From Bath, **trains** travel to London Paddington (1½hr., £27), Exeter (1¾hr., £19), and Bristol (15min., £4.40); National Express **buses** (tel. (0990) 80 80 80) run to and from London Victoria (3hr., £9.70 return) and Oxford (2hr., £12). The train and bus stations are near the south end of Manvers St. From either terminal, walk up Manvers St. to the Orange Grove roundabout, and turn left to reach the efficient **tourist office** (tel. (01225) 47 71 01) in the Abbey Churchyard. (Open June-Sept. Mon.-Sat. 9:30am-7pm, Sun. 10am-6pm; Oct.-May Mon.-Sat. 9:30am-5pm, Sun. 10am-4pm.)

B&Bs (£16-18) cluster on Pulteney Road and Pulteney and Crescent Gardens. For a more relaxed setting, take the footpath behind the rail station to **Widcombe Hill,** where rooms start at £17. The **YHA youth hostel,** Bathwick Hill (tel. (01225) 46 56 74), is in a secluded and clean mansion overlooking the city (£9.40). Badgerline "University" Bus 18 runs to the hostel from the bus station and the Orange Grove roundabout (until 11pm, return 75p). Savor **Mrs. Guy's** exquisite Georgian house and homemade jams at 14 Raby Pl. (tel. (01225) 46 51 20; fax 46 52 83). From N. Parade, turn left onto Pulteney Rd., then right up Bathwick Hill, and Raby Pl. will appear on the left (singles £20, doubles £36-40). Look for the *Let's Go* sign in the window of **Lynn Shearn,** Prior House, 3 Marlborough Lane (tel. (01225) 31 35 87); the warm reception continues inside (doubles £26, breakfast included). The **International Backpackers Hostel,** 13 Pierrepont St. (tel. (01225) 44 67 87), has a great location (£9.50; £11 with breakfast).

Fruits and vegetables are ripe for the picking at the **Guildhall Market,** between High St. and Grand Parade (open Mon.-Sat. 8am-5:30pm). Indulge in a cream tea (£5.25) at the palatial Victorian **Pump Room,** Abbey Churchyard (open Mon.-Sat. 9:30am-5pm), or an excellent vegetarian dish at **Demuths Restaurant,** 2 North Parade Passage, off Abbey Green (open Mon.-Fri. 9am-10pm, Sat. 9am-11pm, Sun. 10am-10pm). A night on the town could begin and end at **P. J. Peppers** on George St. The **Pig and Fiddle** on the corner of Saracen and Broad packs in a young crowd.

EAST ANGLIA

The plush green farmlands and watery fens of East Anglia stretch northeast from London, cloaking the counties of Cambridgeshire, Norfolk, and Suffolk. Although industry is modernizing the economies of Cambridge and Peterborough, the college town and cathedral city are still linked by flat fields sliced into irregular tiles by windbreaks, hedges, and stone walls. East Anglia's flat terrain and relatively low annual rainfall are a boon to bikers and hikers. The area's two longest walking trails, **Peddar's Way** and **Weaver's Way,** together cover over 200 miles.

Cambridge

Cambridge's university began a mere 785 years ago when rebels "defected" from nearby Oxford to this settlement on the River Cam. Today these rebels can be seen maneuvering around the prohibited lush campus lawns and scurrying nightly to meet the closing college gates. Since third-year finals shape many students' futures, most colleges close to visitors during official quiet periods in May and early June. But when exams end, cobblestoned Cambridge explodes with gin-soaked glee. May Week (in mid-June, naturally) launches a dizzying schedule of cocktail parties and festivities, including The Bumps (rowing races where the winners celebrate by burning a boat) and the aptly named Suicide Sunday.

ORIENTATION AND PRACTICAL INFORMATION

Cambridge (pop. 105,000), 60 mi. north of London, has two main avenues. The main shopping street starts at **Magdalene Bridge** and becomes **Bridge St., Sidney St., St. Andrew's St., Regent St.,** and finally **Hills Rd.** The other main street also suffers from an identity crisis, changing names four times from **St. John's St.** to **Trumpington Rd.** This is the academic thoroughfare, with several colleges lying between the road and the River Cam. From the bus station, a quick walk down **Emmanuel St.** leads to a shopping district near the tourist office. To reach the center of town from the train station, go west along Station Rd. and turn right onto Hills Rd.

Tourist Office: Wheeler St. (tel. 32 26 40; fax 45 75 88), a block south of the marketplace. Books rooms (£3 fee, 10% deposit). *Cambridge: The Complete Guide* has a street-indexed map (£1.30). Open April-Oct. Mon.-Tues. and Thurs.-Fri. 9am-6pm, Wed. 9:30am-6pm, Sat. 9am-5pm, Sun. 10:30am-3:30pm; Nov.-March closes at 5:30pm during the week. Info on city events is available at **Corn Exchange box office,** Corn Exchange St. (tel. 35 78 51), adjacent to the tourist office.

Currency Exchange: Lloyds Bank and the American Express office cluster on Sidney St. **Thomas Cook** is at 18 Market St.

American Express: 25 Sidney St. (tel. 35 16 36). Open Mon.-Wed. and Fri. 9am-5:30pm, Thurs. 9:30am-5:30pm, Sat. 9am-5pm.

Train Station: Station Rd. (BritRail tel. (0345) 48 49 50). Open daily 5am-11pm for ticket purchases. Trains to Cambridge run from both London's King's Cross and Liverpool Street stations (1hr., £14.50).

Bus Station: Drummer St. **National Express** (info tel. (0900) 80 80 80) arrives from London's Victoria Station (2hr., from £8). National Express buses and **Cambridge Coaches** travel to Oxford every 2hr. from 8:40am to 5:40pm (3hr., return £8, students £6). **Cambus** (tel. 42 35 54) handles local service (60p-£1).

Bike Rental: Geoff's Bike Rental, 65 Devonshire Rd. (tel. 36 56 29). £6 per day. June-Aug. £15 per week; Sept.-May £12 per week. Open daily 9am-6pm.

Crisis Lines: Crime Victims: tel. 36 30 24. **Rape Crisis:** tel. 35 83 14.

Medical Assistance: Addenbrookes Hospital, Hill Rd. (tel. 24 51 51). Catch Cambus 95 from Emmanuel St. (95p).

Emergency: Dial 999; no coins required.

Police: Parkside (tel. 35 89 66).

Internet Access: Cambridge Arms, 3-4 King St. (tel. 50 50 15). £3.25 for 30min.

Post Office: 9-11 St. Andrew's St. (tel. 32 33 25). Open Mon.-Tues. and Thurs.-Fri. 9am-5:30pm, Wed. 9:30am-5pm, Sat. 9am-12:30pm. *Poste Restante* and currency exchange. **Postal Code:** CB2 3AA.

Telephone Code: 01223.

ACCOMMODATIONS, CAMPING, AND FOOD

The lesson this university town teaches is to book ahead. Many of the **B&Bs** around Portugal St. and Tenison Rd. are open only in July and August. Check the comprehensive list at the tourist office, or pick up the guide to accommodations there (50p).

YHA Youth Hostel, 97 Tenison Rd. (tel. 35 46 01; fax 31 27 80). Relaxed, welcoming atmosphere. Well-equipped kitchen, laundry room, and TV lounge. Spiffy cafeteria. 3- to 4-bed rooms £10.30, students £9.30, under 18 £7. Crowded March-Oct.; in summer call ahead with a credit card.

Mrs. McCann, 40 Warkworth St. (tel. 31 40 98). A jolly hostess with comfortable twin rooms in a quiet neighborhood near the bus station. Rates go down after three nights. £15 per person. Breakfast included.

Warkworth Guest House, Warkworth Terr. (tel. 36 36 82). Sunny rooms with TV near the bus station. Singles £20. Doubles £35. Breakfast included.

Tenison Towers Guest House, 148 Tenison Rd. (tel. 56 65 11). Fresh flowers grace impeccable rooms near the train station. Singles in summer £14-18; off-season £18-20. Doubles £28-32. Triples £42. Quads £48-56.

Home from Home B&B, Liz Fasano, 39 Milton Rd. (tel. 32 35 55). Sparkling rooms and an accommodating hostess. Singles £30. Doubles £40. Breakfast included.

Highfield Farm Camping Park, Long Rd., Comberton (tel. 26 23 08); take Cambus 118 from the Drummer St. station. Flush toilets, showers, and laundry facilities. £5 per tent. Open April-Oct.

Tatties, 26-28 Regent St., boasts delectable baked potatoes to please any palate (platters with vegetable skewers £4-5; open daily 10am-10:30pm). **Rainbow's Vegetarian Bistro,** 9A King's Parade, is a tiny burrow serving vegetarian fare (open daily 9am-9pm). **Nadia's,** 11 St. John's St., is an uncommonly good bakery at commoner's prices (take-out only; open Mon.-Sat. 7:30am-5:30pm, Sun. 7:30am-5pm). Foreigners and beautiful people meet for cappuccino and quiche at **Clowns Coffee Bar,** 54 King St. (open daily 9am-midnight). **Hobbs' Pavillion,** Parker's Piece, off Park Terr., is renowned for delicious pancakes (open Tues.-Sat. noon-2:15pm and 7-9:45pm).

Market Square has bright pyramids of fruit and vegetables (open Mon.-Sat. 8am-5pm). Students buy their gin and corn flakes at **Sainsbury's,** 44 Sidney St., the only grocery store in the middle of town (open Mon.-Fri. 8am-8pm, Sat. 8am-7pm, Sun. 10am-4pm). The alcohol-serving **curry houses** on Castle Hill are also popular.

SIGHTS AND ENTERTAINMENT

Cambridge is an architect's dream, packing some of the most breathtaking examples of English architecture into less than 1 sq. mile. If you are pressed for time, visit at least one chapel (preferably King's), one garden (try Christ's), one library (Trinity's is the most interesting), and one dining hall. Cambridge is most exciting during the university's three terms: Michaelmas (Oct.-Dec.), Lent (Jan.-March), and Easter (April-June). Most of the colleges are open daily from 9am to 5:30pm, although a few are closed to sightseers during the Easter term and virtually all are closed during exam period (mid-May to mid-June). The colleges' hours may vary and are often mysteriously obscure; call to find out.

Cambridge's colleges stretch along the River Cam. **King's College** (tel. 33 11 00), on King's Parade, possesses a spectacular Gothic chapel. Rubens's magnificent *Adoration of the Magi* hangs behind the altar. (College open Mon.-Fri. 9:30am-4:30pm, Sun. 10am-5pm. £2.50, students £1.50. Chapel open term-time Mon.-Sat. 9:30am-3:30pm, Sun. 1:15-2:15pm and 5-5:30pm; chapel and exhibitions open during college vacations 9:30am-4:30pm. Free.) **Trinity College** (tel. 33 84 00), on Trinity St., of *Chariots of Fire* fame, is the University's purse and houses the stunning **Wren Library,** which keeps such notable treasures as A.A. Milne's handwritten manuscript of *Winnie-the-Pooh* and less momentous achievements by Milton, Byron, Tennyson, and Thackeray (library open Mon.-Fri. noon-2pm; £1.50). **Queens' College** (tel. 33 55 11), possesses the only unaltered Tudor courtyard in Cambridge (college open daily 1:45-4:30pm; summer also 10:30am-12:45pm; £1), while **Christ's College** (tel. 33 49 00), founded as "God's house" in 1448, boasts gorgeous gardens. (Open in summer Mon.-Fri. 10:30am-noon; in session Mon.-Fri. 10:30am-12:30pm and 2-4pm.) The **Fitzwilliam Museum,** Trumpington Rd., houses paintings by da Vinci, Michelangelo, Picasso, Monet, and Seurat and an eclectic collection of antiques only the Brits could have assembled (open Tues.-Sat. 10am-5pm, Sun. 2:15-5pm; free).

Just 15 mi. north of Cambridge, the massive **Ely cathedral** and its **stained glass museum** merit a morning or afternoon excursion. (Cathedral open Easter-Sept. daily 7am-7pm; Oct.-Easter Mon.-Fri. 7:30am-6pm, Sun. 7:30am-5pm. £3, students £2.20. Museum open daily 10:30am-4:30pm. £2.50, students £1.50.) Trains run from Cambridge to Ely daily (20min., day return £3.80).

The best source of information on student activities is the *Varsity;* the tourist office's free *Cambridge Nightlife Guide* is helpful as well. Cambridge hangouts offer good pub-crawling year-round, though they lose some of their character and their best customers in the summer. Students drink at the **Anchor,** Silver St., and **The Mill,** Mill Ln., pouring out with their pints onto Silver St. Bridge and a riverside park when weather permits. A quieter riverside alternative is the **Rat and Parrot,** Thompsons Ln. **Pickerel,** on Bridge St., is Cambridge's oldest pub. **The Eagle,** Benet St., is where Nobel laureates Watson and Crick rushed in breathless to announce their discovery of the DNA double helix—unimpressed, the barmaid insisted they settle their four-shilling back-tab before she'd serve them a toast. **Burleigh Arms,** 9-11 Newmarket Rd., serves up beer and lager to its primarily gay clientele. Dancing rears its rocking rump at **The Junction,** Clifton Rd., off Cherry Rd. (Fri.-Sat.), and at **5th Avenue,** upstairs at Lion Yard, every night except Sunday (cover £3-5; open 9pm-2am).

Norwich

One of England's largest and most populous cities before the Norman invasion, Norwich (NOR-ridge, like porridge) wears medieval garbs under modern attire. The 11th-century **Norwich Cathedral** and the 12th-century **Norwich Castle,** where King John signed the Magna Carta in 1215, reign over puzzling, winding streets unaffected by modern gridding. (Cathedral open mid-May to mid-Sept. daily 7:30-am-7pm; mid-Sept. to mid-May 7:30am-6pm. Free.) **Regional railways** (tel. (0345) 48 49 50) run trains to the station at the corner of Riverside and Thorpe Rd. from Cambridge (1½hr., £8.75) and London (4hr., £27.40). National express **buses** (tel. (0990) 80 80 80) travel from the station on Surrey St. to and from Cambridge (2½hr., return £8.75) and London (3hr., £14.50) as well. The **tourist office** is at Guildhall, Gaol Hill (tel. (01603) 66 60 71), in front of city hall. (Open June-Sept. Mon.-Sat. 10am-5pm; Oct.-May Mon.-Fri. 10am-4pm, Sat. 10am-2pm.) The **YMCA,** 46-52 Giles St. (tel. (01603) 62 02 69), has gender-segregated wings (dorms £8.50, singles £12.50). In the heart of the city is one of England's largest and oldest open-air **markets** (open Mon.-Sat. 8am-4:30pm).

CENTRAL ENGLAND

The 19th century swept into central England in an industrial sandstorm, revolutionizing quiet village life. By the beginning of the 20th century, the "dark satanic mills" foreseen by William Blake had indeed overrun the Midlands. Yet several cities preserved their architectural and artistic treasures, and others embraced artists and musicians to counterbalance the harms of industrialization. Today, Manchester and Liverpool are home to innovative music and arts scenes as well as some of the U.K.'s most vibrant nightlife, while Lincoln and Chester tell many of their tales in Latin.

Lincoln

Medieval streets, half-timbered Tudor houses, and a 12th-century cathedral are all relative newcomers to **Lincoln,** built for retired Roman legionnaires. The king of the hill is undoubtedly the magnificent **Lincoln Cathedral.** (Open Mon.-Sat. 7:15am-8pm, Sun. 7:15am-5pm. £3. Free tours March-Dec. Mon.-Fri. 11am and 2pm; Jan.-Feb. Sat. only.) **Lincoln Castle** still retains its Norman walls and houses one of the four surviving copies of the *Magna Carta.* (Open April-Oct. Mon.-Sat. 9:30am-5:30pm, Sun. 11am-5:30pm; Nov.-March Mon.-Sat. 9:30am-4pm. £2.)

The main **tourist office,** 9 Castle Hill (tel. (01522) 52 98 28), atop the hill near the cathedral, distributes *Where to Stay* and *What's On In Lincoln* (open Mon.-Thurs. 9am-5:30pm, Fri. 9am-5pm, Sat.-Sun. 10am-5pm). The station on St. Mary's St. (tel. (01522) 34 02 22) welcomes **trains** from London's King Cross Station (2hr., £34). National Express **buses** (tel. (0990) 80 80 80) roll from the Melville St. station, across from the train station (to London 5hr., £20). Carline and Yarborough Rd., west of the cathedral, are lined with **B&Bs** (£14-18). **Bradford Guest House,** 67 Monks Rd. (tel. (01522) 52 39 47), across from North Lincolnshire College, is only five minutes from the town center (singles £16, doubles £30; includes breakfast). A **YHA youth hostel,** 77 S. Park (tel. (01522) 52 20 76), is opposite South Common at the end of Canwick Rd. (Reception closed daily 10am-5pm. £8.50, students £7.50. Open April-June Mon.-Sat.; July-Aug. daily; Sept.-Oct. and mid-Feb. to March Tues.-Sat.; Nov. to mid-Dec. Fri.-Sat.) **The Spinning Wheel,** 39 Steep Hill Rd., just south of the tourist office, serves vegetarian dishes (£3.75-5, open daily 11am-10pm).

Peak National Park

Covering 555 sq. mi., Peak National Park lies at the southern end of the Pennines, with Manchester, Sheffield, Nottingham, and Stoke-on-Trent at its corners. In the northern Dark Peak area, deep gullies gouge the hard peat moorland against a backdrop of gloomy cliffs. Well-marked public footpaths (sometimes turning into small steams) lead over mildly rocky hillsides to village clusters in the Northern Peak area. Abandoned milestones, derelict lead mines, and country homes are scattered throughout the southern White Peak.

Practical Information Public transport and bus tours bring mobs of visitors on sunny summer weekends; for a more tranquil visit, try to catch the infrequent buses to the more remote northern moors. Two **rail lines** originate in Manchester and enter the park from the northwest: one line stops at Buxton near the park's western edge, while the Hope Valley line continues across the park to Sheffield, Hope, and Hathersage. **Bus TP** winds through the park for 3½ hours from Manchester to Nottingham every two hours, stopping at Buxton, Bakewell, Matlock, Derby, and other towns. Those who plan to ride frequently should buy a **Derbyshire Wayfarer** (£7), which covers virtually all transport services. The invaluable *Peak District Timetable* (60p, available in Peak tourist offices) has bus and train routes and a map.

Write to Peak District National Park, National Park Office, Aldern House, Barlow Rd., Bakewell DE4 5AE for info and publications. The **National Park Information Centres** at **Bakewell** (tel. (01629) 81 32 27), **Castleton** (tel. (01433) 62 06 79), and **Edale** (tel. (01433) 67 02 07) have walking guides and some have accommodations services. You can also ask questions at **tourist offices** in **Ashbourne** (tel. (01335) 34 36 66), **Buxton** (tel. (01298) 731 53), and **Matlock Bath** (tel. (01629) 550 82). Many farmers allow camping on their land; **YHA youth hostels** in the park cost around £8. **Bakewell** (tel. (01629) 81 23 13), **Buxton** (tel. (01298) 222 87), **Edale** (tel. (01433) 67 03 02), **Matlock** (tel. (01629) 58 29 83), and **Castleton** (tel (01433) 62 02 35), are all good options. The park authority operates six **Cycle Hire Centres,** where you can rent bikes (about £7.70). Call **Ashbourne** (tel. (01335) 34 31 56) or **Heyfield** (tel. (01663) 74 62 22) for info.

Bakewell, Edale, and Castleton The Southern Peak is better served than the Northern Peak by buses and trains, and is consequently more trampled than its counterpart. Thirty miles southeast of Manchester, **Bakewell** is the best base for exploring the southern portion of the park. Located near several scenic walks through the White Peaks, the town is known for its delicious Bakewell pudding, created when a flustered cook, trying to make a tart, poured an egg mixture over strawberry jam instead of mixing it into the dough. **The Old Original Bakewell Pudding Shop,** on Rutland Sq., sells lunches and delicious desserts in addition to the pudding (open July-Aug. daily 8:30am-9pm; Sept.-June Mon.-Thurs. 9am-6pm). Bakewell's **National Park Information Center** is at the intersection of Bridge and Market St. The intimate and cozy **YHA Youth Hostel,** Fly Hill, is a three-minute walk from the info center (open mid-April to Oct. Mon.-Sat.; Nov. to mid-April Fri.-Sat.).

The northern Dark Peak area contains some of the wildest and most rugged hill country in England. Cradled in the deep dale of the River Noe, with gentle, gray-green hills sweeping up on two sides, **Edale** has little in the way of civilization other than a church, café, pub, school, and nearby youth hostel. Its environs, however, are arguably the most spectacular in Northern England. If there's no room at the youth hostel, try camping at **Fieldhead** (tel. (01433) 67 03 86), behind the tourist office (£3 per person) or the **Cooper's Camp and Caravan Site** (tel. (01433) 67 03 72), near the school (£2.25 per person). From Edale, the 7½ mi. path to **Castleton** affords a breathtaking view of both the dark gritstone Edale Valley (Dark Peak) and the lighter limestone Hope Valley (White Peak) to the south. If picturesque Castleton persuades you to stay for awhile, check out the amazing caverns in the area. The **Blue John Cavern** (tel. (01433) 62 06 42) and **Treak Cliff Cavern** (tel. (01433) 62 05 71) are about 1½ mi. west of town on the A625. (Blue John open daily 9:30am-6pm; 45min. tours every 10min. £4.50. Treak Cliff open Dec.-Oct. daily 9:30am-5pm; Nov. 10am-4pm. £4.50.) Gigantic **Peak Cavern** (tel. (01433) 62 02 85) was known in the 18th century as the "Devil's Arse" and features the second-largest aperture in the world (open Easter-Aug. daily 10am-5pm; Dec.-Easter. 10am-4:30pm; £4). In town, stay at the excellent **YHA Youth Hostel** (open mid-Feb. to late Dec; £8.50) or **Cryer House** (tel. (01433) 62 02 44), across from the tourist office (£18).

Manchester

The Industrial Revolution quickly transformed this once unremarkable village into a bustling northern hub. Derided by Ruskin as a "devil's darkness," the partially gentrified city is still considered slightly dangerous but draws thousands with its pulsing nightlife and its vibrant arts scene. The towering neo-Gothic **Manchester Town Hall** at Lloyd and Cooper St. in St. Peter's Sq., is a gem in a city not known for its architecture, but is surpassed by the **Central Library** behind it. One of the largest municipal libraries in Europe, the domed building houses a music and theater library, an exceptional language and literature library, and an extensive Judaica collection (open Mon.-Thurs. 10am-8pm, Fri.-Sat. 10am-5pm). In the **Museum of Science and Industry,** Castlefield, on Liverpool Rd., working steam engines and looms provide a dramatic vision of Britain's industrialization (open daily 10am-5pm; £5, students £3).

Manchester has notably energetic and exciting theater and music. For a list of everything that's going on, get *City Life* (£1.40) at newsstands. The **Royal Exchange Theatre** (tel. (0161) 833 98 33), temporarily at Upper Camfield Market at the intersection of Liverpool and Deansgate, performs a diverse program in a space-age theater-in-the-round at its temporary location until November 1998. Box office temporarily at Albert Sq., across from City Hall. (Open Mon.-Sat. 10am-7:30pm. From £5; concessions £4 when booked 3 days in advance with ID.) Manchester's dance club and live music scene remains a national trendsetter. Most clubs lie within a few blocks of Whitworth St. The **Hacienda (HAC),** 11-13 Whitworth St. West, packs in students. Saturday remains Freak Night, and legendary gay "HAC Flesh" night is on the last Wednesday of the month. Nearby, the **Venue,** 17 Whitworth St. West, plays indie and alternative. Down Little Peter St., the large **Boardwalk** features Friday disco, Saturday indie, and alternative Tuesdays. East of Princess St., the **Gay Village** rings merrily all night. Evening crowds drink at the bars lining **Canal St.;** the purple **Manto's** fills up with all ages, genders, and orientations, with its weekend "Breakfast Club" lasting until 6am (£2).

Practical Information, Accommodations, and Food The **tourist office,** Town Hall Extension on Lloyd St. (tel. (0161) 234 31 57), provides guides to accommodations, food, and sights (open Mon.-Sat. 10am-5:30pm, Sun. 11am-4pm). **Trains** leave Piccadilly Station on London Rd. and Victoria Station on Victoria St. for London (2[hr., £54.50), Liverpool (1hr., £6), and Chester (1hr., £7). **Buses** serve about 50 stops around Piccadilly Gardens; pick up an immense, free, fold-out route map at the station (open Mon.-Sat. 7am-6:30pm, Sun. 10am-6pm). National Express buses use the Chorlton St. station (to London 4hr., £18).

The highest concentration of budget accommodations is located 2-3 mi. south of the city center in the suburbs of **Fallowfield, Withington,** and **Didsbury** (take bus 42 or 45). Closer to the heart of the city, the **YHA Manchester Youth Hostel** (tel. (0161) 839 99 60), near the Museum of Science, offers modern, efficient facilities including a huge kitchen, laundry, and cafeteria (reception open 24hr.; from £11). Manage a meal at the pricey Chinatown restaurants by eating their multi-course "Businessman's Lunch." **Café Loco,** on Whitworth St. West, offers fast food, a 10% student discount, and long hours for late-night revelers. (Pizza and burgers £1.60-3.70. Open Mon.-Tues. 5pm-2:30am, Wed. noon-3am, Thurs. 5pm-3am, Fri.-Sat. 5pm-4:30am, Sun. 5pm-11pm.) **Cornerhouse Café,** 70 Oxford St., near the city center, sports a bar (open until 11pm), art galleries, cinemas, and trendy crowds (entrees from £3.50; hot meals served noon-2:30pm and 5-7pm).

Chester

Strategically located near Wales and a deep harbor, Chester was first inhabited by Romans keeping a nervous eye on the frontier of their empire. After the empire crumbled the Anglo-Saxons moved in, then with the Norman Conquest land-hungry Frenchmen overran the city. The city has recently changed hands again: today, shops rule, and it at times resembles an American theme-park pastiche of Ye Olde English Village. The famous **city walls** completely encircle the town, and you can walk on them for free. The original **Northgate,** with a fine-grained view of the Welsh hills, was rebuilt in 1808 to house the city's jail. Just outside Newgate lies the half-unearthed base of the largest **Roman amphitheater** in Britain (open April-Sept. daily 10am-6pm; Oct.-March 10am-1pm and 2-4pm; free). Fight your way through the throngs for a visit to the awe-inspiring **cathedral.** Every aspect of the cathedral is outstanding, from the intersecting stone arches to the brilliant stained-glass windows. The cloisters, with their garden, should not be missed (cathedral open daily 7am-6:30pm). During the last week in June and first week of July, a river carnival and raft race highlight the **Sports and Leisure Fortnight;** contact the tourist office for more details. The **Chester Summer Music Festival** draws musical groups from across Britain during the third and fourth weeks of July. Contact the Chester Summer Music Festival Office, 8 Abbey Sq., Chester CH1 2HH (tel. (01244) 32 07 00 or 34 12 00).

British Rail **trains** run from the station on City Rd. to London Euston (3hr., £47), Holyhead (1 per hr., £13.30), and Manchester (1hr., £7). National Express **buses** leave from Delamere St. for London (5½hr., £19.50), and Manchester (1hr., £5.75). The **tourist office,** Town Hall, Northgate St. (tel. (01244) 31 83 56 or 31 31 26), offers a useful city map for £1. (Open May-Oct. Mon.-Sat. 9am-7:30pm, Sun. 10am-4pm; Nov.-April Mon.-Sat. 9am-5:30pm, Sun. 10am-4pm.) A smaller branch is located at the train station (open daily 10am-8pm). Decent **B&Bs** (from £14) line Hoole Rd., a five-minute walk from the train station (or take bus 21, C30, or 53 from the city center). The **YHA youth hostel,** Hough Green House, 40 Hough Green (tel. (01244) 68 00 56), 1½ mi. from the city center, is a beautiful Victorian house; take bus 7, 8, 16, 19, or any bus headed for "Mold" (£9.40; closed late Dec.). **Bridge Guest House,** 18-20 Crewe St. (tel. (01244) 34 04 38), will shelter the weary for £16-28. **Tesco supermarket** is hidden at the end of an alley off Frodsham St. (open Mon.-Sat. 8am-10pm, Sun. 11am-5pm). For cheeses and fresh produce, stop at the indoor **market** beside the Town Hall. **Hattie's Tea Shop,** 5 Rufus Ct., off Northgate, offers homemade cakes and snacks (open Mon.-Fri. 9am-5pm, Sat. 9am-7pm, Sun. 11am-4pm).

Liverpool

Although Liverpool still clings to its status as the birthplace of the Beatles, the city also nurtures an enormous cathedral, docklands transformed to attract tourists instead of ships, and a modern, thriving cultural and artistic life. The Anglican **Liverpool Cathedral,** Upper Duke St., begun in 1904, boasts the highest Gothic arches ever built, the largest vault and organ, and the highest and heaviest bells in the world. Climb to the top of the tower for a view to North Wales. (Cathedral open daily 9am-6pm; tower open 11am-4pm, weather permitting. Tower £1.50. Free organ recitals in summer Sat. 3:30pm.) In contrast, the **Metropolitan Cathedral of Christ the King,** Mt. Pleasant, looks more like a rocket launcher than a house of worship (open daily

8am-6pm; in winter Sun. closes 5pm). **Albert Dock,** at the western end of Hanover St., is a series of 19th-century warehouses transformed into a complex of shops, restaurants, and museums. A cornerstone of this development is the **Tate Gallery** (a branch of the London dive), with scads of modern art (open Tues.-Sun. 10am-6pm; free). Also at Albert Dock, **The Beatles Story** pays tribute to the group's work with John Lennon's white piano, a recreation of the Cavern Club, and, of course, a yellow submarine (open April-Sept. daily 10am-6pm; Oct.-March 10am-5pm; £6). Pick up the **Beatles Map** (£1.50) at the tourist office, which leads you to Strawberry Fields and Penny Lane. Nearby, the **Beatles Shop,** 31 Matthew St., is loaded with souvenirs and memorabilia (open Mon.-Sat. 9:30am-5:30pm, Sun. 11am-4pm).

The **tourist office** (tel. (0151) 709 36 32), in the Clayton Sq. Shopping Centre, stocks a guide to the city (£1) and books rooms for a 10% deposit, and they do appreciate you coming 'round (open Mon.-Sat. 9:30am-5:30pm). A smaller branch is located at **Atlantic Pavilion,** Albert Dock (tel. (0151) 708 88 54; open daily 10am-5:30pm). **Trains** run to Manchester (2hr., £5.80), Birmingham (2hr., £17.40), and London (2hr., £52.50). National Express **buses** (tel. (0990) 80 80 80) head to London (4-5hr., £21), Manchester (1hr., £6), and Birmingham (2½hr., £9.75). Head to Lord Nelson St., adjacent to the train station, or Mount Pleasant, for modest hotels. After a hard day's night head to the beautiful old house at the **Embassie Youth Hostel,** 1 Faulkner Sq. (tel. (0151) 707 10 89), in the southeast part of town (£9.50). Single women will find sparkling clean rooms at the **YWCA,** 1 Rodney St. (tel. (0151) 709 77 91; singles £12, doubles £22). Hardman St. has many budget and ethnic restaurants. The gay-friendly **Everyman Bistro,** 9-11 Hope St., off Mt. Pleasant by the university, has vegetarian selections (£3-5; open Mon.-Sat. noon-midnight).

Liverpool has a thriving arts scene and an energetic nightlife. *In Touch* (£1), available at the tourist office and newsstands, and *Liverpool Echo* (28p), sold on street corners, detail the city's offerings. The bookstore **News From Nowhere,** 96 Bold St., has info on special events at gay and lesbian clubs. Fight your way inside **Flanagan's Apple,** Matthew St., which offers the best Irish music in town nightly. The **Cavern Club,** Matthew St., where the Fab Four first gained prominence, features live music Saturday afternoons and a disco Thursday-Monday (free before 9pm). The **Baa Bar,** 43-45 Fleet St., off Bold St., attracts a lesbian, gay, trendy, and far from sheepish crowd for cappuccino and cheap beers (open Mon.-Sat. 9am-2am, Sun. noon-6pm).

NORTH ENGLAND

Between Central England's industrial belt and Scotland's rugged wilderness is a quiet area of natural beauty. Sliced by the Pennine Mountains, North England's main attractions lie enshrined in four national parks and several calm coastal areas. Walkers and ramblers flock here, and no trail tests their stamina more than the Pennine Way, the country's first official long-distance path and still its longest. Isolated villages along the trails continue a pastoral tradition that contrasts with the polluted enormity and din of many English cities to the south.

Pennine Way

The Pennine Peaks form the spine of England, arching south to north up the center of Britain from the Peak National Park to the Scottish border. The 250 mi. **Pennine Way** crowns the central ridge. Hard-core hikers have completed the hike in 10 days, but most walkers spend three weeks on the long, green trail. The classic Wainwright's *Pennine Way Companion* (£10), available from bookstores, is a good supplement to the Ordnance Survey maps, which run about £6 at Peak Information Centers. **YHA youth hostels** are spaced within a day's hike (7-29 mi.) of one another. Send a self-addressed envelope to YHA Northern Region, P.O. Box 11, Matlock, Derbyshire DE4 2XA (tel. (01629) 82 58 50), for info on the **Pennine Way Package** which allows you to book a route of 18 or more hostels along the walk (50p booking fee per hostel). Any National Park Information Centre can also supply details on trails and alternative accommodations, or you can consult the invaluable *Pennine Way Accommodations and Catering Guide* (90p). In the High Penines, YHA operates three **camping barns.** To book call and send a check to YHA (see above).

South Pennines In the midst of the gorse-strewn moorland of the **South Pennines,** the tiny villages of **Haworth** and **Hebden Bridge** provide hospitable civilization breaks for an overnight or daytrip from Manchester. From Hebden Bridge, you can make day-hikes to the nearby villages of Blackshaw Head, Cragg Vale, or **Hepstonstall,** where you'll find the ruins of a 13th-century church and a 1764 octagonal church, the oldest Methodist house of worship in the world. Two **rail** lines go through the region—get the free *West Yorkshire Train Times.* Hebden Bridge's **tourist office,** 1 Bridge Gate (tel. (01422) 84 38 31), is equipped with indexed maps (25p) and many free walking guides and leaflets on local attractions. (Open mid-March to Oct. Mon.-Sat. 10am-5pm, Sun. 11am-5pm; Oct. to mid-March daily 10am-4pm.) Brontë fans must see the **parsonage** near the tourist office in Haworth, where Emily, Charlotte, and Anne lived with their father and their brother Branwell. (Open April-Sept. daily 10am-5pm; Oct.-March 11am-4:30pm. £3.80, students £2.80.) Haworth's **tourist office,** 2-4 West Ln. (tel. (01535) 64 23 29), at the summit of Main St., stocks maps and guides (open Easter-Nov. daily 9:30am-5:30pm; Nov.-Easter closes 5pm). The town's **YHA Youth Hostel,** Longlands Dr. (tel. (01535) 64 22 34), tops a hill a mile from the tourist office. (Curfew 11pm. £8.50. Open April-Sept. daily; Feb.-March and Oct. to late Dec. Mon.-Sat.) **B&Bs** are at 4, 6, and 8 Main St., and up the hill to the tourist office (about £16-17).

High Pennines This largely untouristed area stretches from below Barnard Castle in the south to Hadrian's Wall in the north, about 20 mi. west of Durham City. The Pennines are best suited to **hiking** or **biking;** cars can successfully navigate the roads, but buses tackle the region with distressing hesitancy. Twenty miles southwest of Durham by the River Tees, the peaceful market town of **Barnard Castle** makes an excellent base for exploring the castles of Teesdale and the North Pennine peaks and waterfalls. Along the river sprawl the ruins of the 13th-century Norman **castle.** (Open April-Sept. daily 10am-6pm; Oct.-March Wed.-Sun. 10am-4pm. £2, students £1.50.) A mechanized silver swan merits a visit to the **Bowes Museum,** a 17th-century-style French château with landscaped gardens. (Open May-Sept. Mon.-Sat. 10am-5:30pm, Sun. 2-5pm; March-April and Oct. Mon.-Sat. 10am-5pm, Sun. 2-5pm; Nov.-Feb. Mon.-Sat. 10am-4pm, Sun. 2-4pm. £3.50 Free tours June-Sept. Tues.-Fri. 11:15am and 2pm, Sat. 2pm, Sun. 2:15pm.) Barnard Castle has no youth hostel but boasts many excellent **B&Bs,** including **Mrs. Fry,** 66 Newgate (tel. (01833) 63 72 40; £14). Guided walks leave from the **tourist office,** 43 Galgate (tel. (01833) 69 09 09; open Easter-Sept. daily 10am-6pm; Oct.-Easter 11am-4pm).

Durham City

Twisting medieval streets, footbridges, and restricted vehicle access make cliff-top Durham a foot-friendly area, although its only claim to being a "city" is the presence of **Durham Cathedral,** England's greatest Norman cathedral. At one end lies the **tomb of the Venerable Bede,** author of *The Ecclesiastical History of the English People.* The view from the **tower** compensates for the 325-step climb. (Cathedral open May-Sept. Mon.-Sat. 7:15am-8pm, Sun. 8am-8pm; Oct.-April closes 6pm. Free. Tower open daily 10am-4pm. £2.) **Durham Castle,** once a key defensive fortress, has become a residence for university students (tours July-Sept. daily 10am-noon and 2-4pm; Oct.-June 2-4:30pm; £2.75). If your legs are Wear-y, rent a rowboat from **Brown's Boathouse Centers,** Elvet Bridge, and explore the winding River Wear while dodging scullers and ducks (£2.50).

The **tourist office** (tel. (0191) 384 37 20) is at Market Place; if you're arriving at the train station, you might want to call ahead for directions. (Open July-Aug. Mon.-Sat. 9:30am-6pm, Sun. 2-5pm; June and Sept. Mon.-Sat. 10am-5:30pm; Oct.-May Mon.-Fri. 10am-5pm, Sat. 9:30am-1pm.) **Trains** leave from the station (tel. (0191) 232 62 62) north of town to London (3hr., £61), York (1hr., £21.50), and Newcastle (20min., £3.20). **Buses** also regularly serve London and Newcastle from the station on North Rd. A large supply of cheap dormitory rooms, available from July to September and during school vacations, rings the cathedral. **University College,** Durham Castle (tel. (0191) 374 38 63), and **St. John's College,** 3 South Bailey (tel. (0191) 374 35 66), provide rooms (£16-19.50). **Mrs. Koltai** runs an attractive B&B at 10 Gilesgate (tel. (0191) 386 20 26; singles £15, doubles £30). Chain stores and bakeries with £1 pastries crowd the center of town, while vegetables and fruits fill the stands of **Market Hall** (open daily 9am-5pm). Grab a sandwich from **Marks and Spencer,** on Silver St. across from the post office (open Mon.-Thurs. 9am-5:30pm, Fri.-Sat. 8:30am-5:30pm). Students gather at **Brewer and Firkin,** 58 Saddler St., to dance and drink the local specialty, Lindisfarne mead.

Newcastle upon Tyne

Hardworking Newcastle is not known for dreamy spires or evening hush, but for the legendary local pub and club scene. While you can still see straight, explore the masterful **Tyne Bridge** and the elegant tower of the **Cathedral Church of St. Nicholas** (church open Mon.-Fri. 7am-6pm, Sat. 8am-4pm, Sun. 9am-noon and 4-7pm; free). At night, head to **Bigg Market,** a rowdy haven that frowns on underdressed student types. Some of the milder pubs in this area are **Blackie Boy** and **Macy's.** The **Quayside** is a slightly more relaxed, student-friendly area of town; **The Red House,** 32 Sandhill, and **The Cooperage,** past the swing bridge, offer good drinks. Revelers begin swaying even before they've imbibed at **The Tuxedo Royale,** a boat/dance club under the Tyne Bridge. Gays and lesbians flock to the corner of Waterloo and Sunderland St. to drink at **The Village** and dance at **Powerhouse.**

The **tourist office** (tel. (0191) 261 06 10), at the Central Library off New Bridge St., offers an essential street map. (Open Mon. and Thurs. 9:30am-8pm, Tues.-Wed. and Fri. 9:30am-5pm, Sat. 9am-5pm.) There is also a branch office at Central Station, from which **trains** (tel. (0191) 232 62 62) leave for London (3hr., £61) and Edinburgh (1½hr., £26-7). **Buses** depart Gallowgate Coach Station for London (6hr., £15) and Edinburgh (3hr., £16.50) as well. Lodgings typically begin at £15, but the **YHA youth hostel,** 107 Jesmond Rd. (tel. (0191) 281 25 70), offers cheap and crowded rooms. (Curfew 11pm; ask for the late entry code. Lockout 10am-5pm. £7.70, under 26 £6.70. Closed Dec.-Jan.) **Café Procope,** 35 The Side, specializes in international cuisine. Expect cheap food and paranormal activity at the **Supernatural Vegetarian Restaurant,** 2 Princess Sq. (open Mon.-Sat. 10:30am-7:30pm).

York

York looks and feels as different from nearby Manchester and Liverpool as it does from its American namesake. Yet the well-preserved city walls that once foiled marauding invaders cannot protect York from hordes of equally determined tourists. The visitors' quarry is a city strewn with medieval cottages and Georgian townhouses, all in the shadow of Britain's largest Gothic cathedral.

The best introduction to the city is a 2½mi. walk along its medieval walls; you can sign up for one of countless **walking tours** at a tourist center. The **Association of Voluntary Guides** runs a particularly good architectural tour. (2hr.; April-Oct. daily 10:15am and 2:15pm; July-Aug. also 7pm. Meet in front of the York City Art Gallery directly across from the tourist office.) The tourist stampede abates in the early morning and toward dusk, but everyone and everything converges at the enormous **York Minster,** built between 1220 and 1470. Half of all the medieval stained glass in England glitters here. The **Great East Window,** depicting the beginning and ending of the world, holds over a hundred scenes and is the largest medieval glass window on Earth. It's a mere 275 steps to the top of the **Central Tower,** from which you can stare down on York's red roofs. (Cathedral open in summer daily 7am-8:30pm; off-season 7am-5pm. Donation £2. Tower open daily 9:30am-6:30pm or until dark in winter. £2.) The **Yorkshire Museum,** in the gardens off Museum St., presents an elaborate display of Roman, Anglo-Saxon, and Viking art galleries, as well as the gorgeous £2.5 million **Middleham Jewel.** (Open April-Oct. daily 10am-5pm; Nov.-March Mon.-Sat. 10am-5pm, Sun. 1-5pm. Last admission 4:30pm. £3, concessions £2.) In the museum gardens, peacocks strut among the haunting ruins of **St. Mary's Abbey,** once the most influential Benedictine monastery in northern England.

Near York presides **Castle Howard** (tel. (01653) 64 83 33), featured as Sebastian's family home in the TV version of Evelyn Waugh's *Brideshead Revisited* and still inhabited by the Howard family. The English Baroque hall and the 999 acres of grounds, including gardens, fountains, and lakes, are stunning. **York Pullman** (tel. (01904) 62 29 92) in Bootham Tower, Exhibition Square, offers half-day excursions to the castle for £3.75. (Castle open March-Oct. daily 11am-4:45pm. Grounds open from 10am. Call for off-season hours. £6.50, students £5.50.)

Practical Information, Accommodations, and Food The main **tourist office** (tel. (01904) 62 17 56) in De Grey Rooms, Exhibition Sq., finds rooms for a £2 fee. Ask for free leaflets. (Open July-Aug. Mon.-Sat. 9am-7pm, Sun. 9:30am-6pm; Sept.-June Mon.-Sat. 9am-6pm, Sun. 9:30am-6pm.) **Trains** arrive at Station Rd. from London's King's Cross Station (2hr., £52.50), Manchester's Piccadilly Station (1½hr., £12.80), and Edinburgh (2-3hr., £43.50). National Express **buses** (tel. (0990) 80 80 80) run less frequently to London (4hr., £15), Manchester (3hr., £8), and Edinburgh (5hr., £25.50) from the station on Rougier St.

Competition for inexpensive **B&Bs** (from £13) can be fierce in the summer. Try side streets along Bootham/Clifton or The Mount area (past the train station and down Blossom St.), Haxby Road. (Take bus 2a or walk from the tourist office to the end of Gillygate and take the right fork.) **Avenue Guest House,** 6 The Avenue (tel. (01904) 62 05 75), and **Clifton View Guest House,** 118/120 Clifton (tel. (01904) 62 50 47), ¾ mi. from town, both provide comfortable rooms (£13-18 per person). **YHA Youth Hostel,** Water End, Clifton (tel. (01904) 65 31 47), 1 mi. from the town center, is a super-grade hostel with excellent facilities. From the tourist office, walk about ¾ mi. out Bootham/Clifton and take a left at Water End, or take a bus to Clifton Green and walk ¼ mi. (Reception open daily 7am-11:30pm. £13.85; singles £17; doubles £35; family rooms £69. Breakfast included. Closed early Jan.)

Expensive tea rooms, medium-priced bistros, fudge shops, and cheap eateries bump elbows even in the remote alleyways of York. Fruit and vegetable grocers peddle their wares at the **market** behind the Shambles (open Mon.-Sat. 8am-5pm). Enjoy sandwiches (£1.50-1.80) and salads in the attractive, windowed **Theatre Royal Café Bar,** St. Leonard's Pl. (open Mon.-Sat. 10am-7pm), or eat upstairs overlooking the market at **Little Shambles Café,** Little Shambles off Shambles, open for English breakfast (£1.90), lunch, and tea, daily 7am to 4pm. **La Romantica** is open later and serves delicious pastas and pizzas (£5-7) in a candlelit setting (open Mon.-Sat. noon-2:30pm and 5-11pm, Sun. 5-11pm). **Ye Old Starre,** the city's oldest pub, and the **Punch Bowl,** both on Stonegate, stand out among countless bars throughout the city. For other entertainment options, pick up the weekly *What's On* guide and the seasonal *Evening Entertainment* brochure from the tourist office.

Lake District National Park

Although rugged hills make up much of England's landscape, only in the Lake District of the northwest corner do sparkling waterholes fill the spaces in between. Windermere, Ambleside, Grasmere, and Keswick make good bases for exploring. In summer, tourists in exhaust-spewing tour buses can be as numerous as sheep and cattle, so ascend into the hills and wander through the smaller towns, especially those in the more remote northern and western areas. The farther west you go from the busy bus route serving the towns along the A591, the more countryside you'll have to yourself.

Getting There and Getting Around The best way to reach the Lake District is to take public transportation to Windermere or Oxenholme, and then hike or take a local bus to more remote regions. British Rail **trains** service Oxenholme; **National Express buses** run to Windermere from Manchester, Birmingham, and London (call the Windermere tourist office for info, tel. (015394) 464 99). Two rail lines flank the park: the **Preston-Lancaster-Carlisle line** runs south to north along the east edge, while the **Barrow-Carlisle line** serves the west coast. **Stagecoach Cumberland buses** (tel. (01946) 632 22) serve over 25 towns and villages; tourist offices provide the essential and free *Explore Lakeland by Bus,* which has timetables.

Psych yourself up for a hilly challenge if you decide to **bike.** Two-wheelers can be rented in most towns. **Hikers** will find an abundance of trails and often an overabundance of fellow walkers. If you plan to take a long or difficult hike, check first with the Park Service, get a good map (e.g. Ordnance Survey), call for **weather** information (tel. (017687) 757 57), and leave your route with your B&B or hostel proprietor.

Practical Information and Accommodations For an introduction to the Lake District, visit the beautiful grounds and house of the **National Park Visitor Centre** (tel. (015394) 466 01) in **Brockhole,** halfway between Windermere and Ambleside (open March-Nov. daily 10am-5pm). The following **National Park Information Centres** provide expert info, sell a camping guide (£1), and book accommodations: **Ambleside** (tel. (015394) 327 29), **Bowness Bay** (tel. (015394) 428 95), **Coniston** (tel. (015394) 415 33), **Grasmere** (tel. (015394) 352 45), **Hawkshead** (tel. (015394) 365 25), **Keswick** (tel. (017687) 728 03), **Pooley Bridge** (tel. (017684) 865 30), **Seatoller Barn** (tel. (017687) 772 94), and **Ullswater** (tel. (017684) 824 14). **B&Bs** line nearly every street in every town (£13-16), and the Lakes have the highest concentration of **YHA youth hostels** in the world, but lodgings fill in July and August. Campers should pick up the National Park's *Caravan and Tent Guide* (£1) and the free *Camping Barn Network* which list campground locations.

Windermere and Bowness A first stop for many travelers, **Windermere** and **Bowness** fill to the gills in summer as myriads of boaters and water-skiers swarm over Lake Windermere. **Windermere Lake Cruises** (tel. (015394) 885 10) runs a Lake Information Centre at the north end of the pier, rents boats, and books passage on popular cruises to Ambleside (return £5.20) and south to Lakeside (return £5.50). Stop in the Windermere **tourist office** next to the rail station (tel. (015394) 464 99) to book National Express buses, exchange foreign currency (£2.50 commission), or get a guide to lake walks and local restaurants (open Easter-Oct. daily 9am-6pm; Nov.-Easter 9am-5pm). The **YHA youth hostel** (tel. (015394) 435 43), 1 mi. north of Windermere off the A591, is a spacious house with lovely grounds, panoramic views, and lots of kids (£7.70; open Jan.-Oct. daily). Bowness and Windermere are chock-full of convenient **B&Bs,** but you'll still have to book ahead. In Bowness, try **Brendan Chase,** 1-3 College Road (tel. (015394) 456 38; £10-15), **The Haven,** 10 Birch St. (tel. (015394) 440 17; £15), or **Dalecott,** 13 Upper Oak St. (tel. (015394) 451 21; £13.50-16.50). The nearest campground, **Limefitt Park** (tel. (015394) 323 00), 4½ mi. north of Bowness on the A592, offers every amenity except public transport (2-person tent £15). In Windermere, stop in the **Coffee Pot,** 15 Main Rd., for sandwiches (open Mon.-Wed. and Fri.-Sat. 10am-5:30pm, Sun. 1-5pm). In Bowness, try the **Hedgerow Teashop** on Lake Rd. for a ploughman's lunch (£4; open Wed.-Mon. 10:30am-5pm).

Ambleside and Grasmere The villages of **Ambleside** and **Grasmere** offer Lake District beauty at a less frenetic pace than Windermere. *Ambleside Walks in the Countryside* (20p) lists three gentle walks from the town's center. The Ambleside **tourist office** (tel. (015394) 325 82) sits on Church St. (Open Easter-Oct. daily 9am-5pm; Nov.-Easter Tues.-Thurs. 10am-1pm and 2-5pm, Fri.-Sat. 9am-1pm and 2-5pm.)

B&Bs cluster on Church St. and Compston Rd. but fill up quickly (£14.50-16). Ambleside's **YHA youth hostel** (tel. (015394) 323 04), 1 mi. south on Windermere Rd. (the A591), has a bit of a country-club atmosphere; you can even swim off the pier (£9.10; open year-round daily). On Compton Rd., **Scoffs** serves up a huge selection of sandwiches on baguettes (from £1.25; open Mon.-Fri. 10am-4pm, Sat.-Sun. 8:30am-4pm).

During quiet mornings in **Grasmere,** you can savor the peace that Wordsworth so enjoyed here. Visit **Dove Cottage** where the poet lived with his wife, his sister, Samuel Taylor Coleridge, De Quincey, and assorted children and literati. (Open mid-Feb. to mid-Jan. daily 9:30am-5:30pm. £4.25. Admission covers museum next door.) The 6 mi. **Wordsworth Walk** circumnavigates the two lakes of the Rothay River, passing by the poet's grave, Dove cottage, and Rydal Mount along the way. Star-seeking fell-climbers can tackle the path from Rydal to Legburthwaite (near Keswick) in an athletic day, passing the towering Great Rigg and Melvellyn on the way. Bus 555 will bring you back to Ambleside. There are two **YHA youth hostels** within 1 mi. north of Grasmere. **Butterlip How** (tel. (015394) 353 16) is a Victorian house with flowering gardens (£8.25; open April-Sept. daily; Oct. and Jan.-March Tues.-Sun.). **Thorney How** (tel. (015394) 355 91) is a converted farmhouse; follow the road to Easedale, turn right at the fork, then turn left (£8.25; open daily April-Aug.; Feb.-March and Sept.-Dec. Thurs.-Mon.). For a tasty snack, try Sarah Nelson's famous Grasmere Gingerbread at **Church Cottage,** just by St. Oswald's.

Keswick Sandwiched between towering Skiddaw peak and the northern edge of Lake Derwentwater, **Keswick** (KEZ-ick) rivals Windermere as the region's tourist capital. The **tourist office,** Moot Hall, Market Sq. (tel. (017687) 726 45), finds B&Bs for a 10% deposit and sells both a £1 lodgings booklet and a 20p map. (Open mid-July to Aug. daily 9:30am-7pm; April to mid-July and Sept.-Oct. 9:30am-5:30pm; Nov.-March 10am-4pm.) **B&Bs** nestle between Station St., St. John St., and Penrith Rd. (£10-16).

Nine miles south of Keswick lies the harrowing **Honister Pass,** gateway to the wildest parts of the Lake District, including craggy Great Gable and Green Gable (take bus 77 in summer, or bus 79 to "Seatoller," 1½ mi. away). **Honister Hause youth hostel** (tel. (017687) 772 67) sits at the Pass' summit (£6.75; open July-Aug. Fri.-Wed.; April-June and Sept.-early Nov. Fri.-Tues.). No serious mountain climber's Lakeland experience would be complete without a hike up nearby **Scafell Pike** in the magnificent Langdale Fells. At 3221 ft., it's the highest peak in England.

WALES

As churning coal and steel mines fall victim to Britain's faltering economy, Wales has turned its economic base from heavy industry to tourism. Travelers from near and far crowd Welch towns on their way to miles of sandy beaches, grassy cliffs, and dramatic mountains. Nevertheless, Wales clings steadfastly to its Celtic heritage, continuing a struggle for independence that has been surging for over a millennium. Especially in the North, which is even more fiercely nationalistic and linguistically independent of England than South Wales, the Welsh language endures in conversation, commerce, and literature. Enjoy the landscapes and cultures that make this area unique, and avoid calling the Welsh "English" at all costs.

Cardiff (Caerdydd)

One of the few urban centers in a land of small villages, Cardiff mined its wealth out of the coal industry and today mixes youthful flair and traditional culture. Begin with tradition by visiting the opulent interior, beautiful gardens, and Norman keep of **Cardiff Castle.** (Open April-Sept. daily 9:30am-6pm; March and Oct. 9:30am-5pm; Nov.-Feb. 9:30am-4:00pm. £4.) The domed **National Museum of Wales** includes a hoard of Impressionist art and startling audio-visual exhibits outlining "The Evolution of Wales" (open Tues.-Sun. 10am-5pm; £3.25, students £2).

National Express **Rapide coaches** (tel. (0990) 80 80 80) careen to Cardiff from London's Victoria Station (5 per day, 3hr., £22), Heathrow Airport (7 per day, 3hr., £28), and Gatwick Airport (8 per day, 4hr., £31); buses also arrive from Glasgow (3 per day, 8½hr., £42-50). British Rail **trains** chug into the station in Central Square (tel. (0345) 48 49 50) from London's Paddington Station (1-2 per hour, 2hr., £34). The **tourist office** (tel. (01222) 22 72 81) at the train station provides a free accommodations list and booking service. (Open April-Sept. Mon.-Sat. 9am-6:30pm, Sun. 10am-4pm; Oct.-March Mon.-Sat. 9am-5:30pm, Sun. 10am-4pm.)

Budget accommodations are scarce in the center of Cardiff, but the tourist office lists reasonably priced **B&Bs** (£16-18) on the outskirts. The best deals are found in the smaller neighborhoods around Cathedral Rd. (take bus 32 or walk 15min. from the castle). To room at the comfortable Cardiff **youth hostel (YHA),** 2 Wedal Rd., Roath Park (tel. (01222) 46 23 03), 2 mi. from the city center, take bus 80 or 82 from Central Station. (Check-in after 3pm. Lockout 10am-3pm. Curfew 11pm. £9.40. Open March-Oct. daily; Jan.-Feb. and Nov. Mon.-Sat.)

Cardiff's specialty is **Brains S.A.** (Special Ale), known by locals as "Brains Skull Attack." Tours of **Brains Brewery** on Caroline St. can be arranged by calling Donna Locke (tel. (01222) 39 40 22) on weekdays between 3 and 5pm. **Celtic Cauldron Wholefoods,** 47-49 Castle Arcade, is vegetarian-friendly and offers a beginning Welsh class on weekdays at 5:30pm (open Mon.-Fri. 9am-9pm, Sat. 9am-6pm, Sun. 11am-4pm). Byte into a bagel at the **Cardiff Cybercafé,** 9 Duke St. (£4.50 per hour; open daily 10am-10pm), or buy anything from peaches to octupi from the **Central Market** between St. Mary and Trinity St. (open Mon.-Sat. 8am-5:30pm). Head to the Welsh-speaking **Clwb Ifor Bach,** 11 Womanby St., for the local music scene (cover £2-3; open Mon.-Fri until 2am, Sat. until 4am, and Sun. until 10:30pm). **Club X,** 37-39 Charles St., is a happening gay venue (cover £2-4; open Wed.-Sat. 10pm-2am).

Wye Valley

The "fever of the world" with which Wordsworth juxtaposed the tranquility of the Wye River now enters its valley in the form of the tourist trade. Even so, much of this region, where the Wye River (Afon Gwy) winds down the hills of central Wales, remains unsullied. Below Monmouth, the Wye forms the border between England and Wales and flows between Wordsworth's "steep cliffs," tufted orchards," and "pastoral farms," green to the very door.

Stagecoach Red and White **buses** (tel. (01633) 26 63 36) are the primary means of transport in the area (there is virtually no Sunday service), but hikers enjoy walks of all difficulties and lengths. The **Wye Valley Walk** starts from Chepstow and goes to Tintern Abbey and other sites. Across the river, **Offa's Dyke Path** encompasses 177 mi. of trails and runs along the entire English/Welsh border.

Chepstow Chepstow's strategic position at the mouth of the river and the base of the English border made it an important fortification and commercial center in Norman times. **Chepstow Castle** is Britain's oldest stone castle and one of its longest. (Open April-Sept. daily 10am-6pm; Oct.-March 10am-4pm, Sun. 11am-4pm. £3, students £2.) Nearby, the **tourist office** (tel. (01291) 62 37 72) provides info on the castle and the valley's treasures (open May-Sept. daily 10am-6pm; Oct.-April 10am-4pm). **Trains** arrive at Station Rd.; **National Express** buses stop above the town gate in front of the Somerfield supermarket. Ask about bus tickets at **Fowler's Travel,** 9 Moor St. The **YHA Youth Hostel** (tel. (01594) 53 02 72), 4 mi. northeast of Tintern, occupies a 12th-century castle with a dungeon. To get there from the A466 (bus 69 from Chepstow) or Offa's Dyke, follow signs for 2 mi. from Bigsweir Bridge to St. Briavel's (curfew 11:30pm; £9.40, under 18 £6.30; closed Jan.). In Chepstow, stay at **Lower Hardwick House,** Mt. Pleasant (tel. (01291) 62 21 62), 300 yards up the hill from the bus station (£15-18, doubles £32; camping £5 per tent).

Tintern, Monmouth, and Hay-on-Wye Five miles north of Chepstow on the A466, the delicate arches of **Tintern Abbey** (tel. (01291) 68 92 51) shade crowds of tourists in the summer. Wordsworth's praise is fitting; the windswept abbey is beautiful against the open sky and surrounding hills. (Open mid-March to mid-Oct. daily 9:30am-6:30pm; mid-Oct. to mid-March Mon.-Sat. 9:30am-4pm, Sun. 11am-4pm. £2.20, students £1.70.) Near the footbridge, a path leads to the **Devil's Pulpit** (1hr.), a huge stone from which Satan is said to have tempted the monks working in the fields. The market town of **Monmouth,** birthplace of Geoffrey of Monmouth (whose *History of the Kings of Britain* gives some credibility to King Arthur), lies 8 mi. north of Tintern. The **tourist office** (tel. (01600) 71 38 99) hides in Shire Hall on Agincourt Sq. where leaders of the Chartist movement were tried (open April-Oct. daily 10am-6pm). Geoffrey is thought to have studied at the school that now houses the **YHA youth hostel** (tel. (01600) 71 51 16), near the town center (£7, under 18 £4.75; open daily March-Oct.). **Wye Avon,** Dixton Rd. (tel. (01600) 71 33 22), gives board in a beautiful Monmouth house (singles £16, doubles £32).

Hay-on-Wye boasts 35 second-hand and antiquarian book shops, and hosts a 10-day literary festival in late May at which luminaries like Elie Weisel give readings while Salman Rushdie darts nervously about. The **tourist office,** Oxford Rd. (tel. (01497) 82 01 44), books beds (£2; open April-Oct. daily 10am-1pm and 2-5pm; Nov.-March 11am-1pm and 2-4pm). If you're willing to walk, stay at the beautifully restored **Old Post Office** (tel. (01497) 82 00 08), 2 mi. away in the sleepy village of Llanigon. Take the Brecon Rd. (B4350) out of Hay, turn left at the Llanigon sign, and follow the road for ½ mi. (doubles £15 per person).

Brecon Beacons National Park (Bannau Brycheiniog)

Brecon Beacons National Park (Bannau Brycheiniog) encompasses 519 sq. mi. of barren peaks, thick forests, and spectacular waterfalls. The park is crisscrossed by four mountain ranges. At the center is the impressive **Brecon Beacons;** the most pleasant hiking route starts in nearby **Llanfaes** and follows leafy roads up to trails past streams and waterfalls. The **Black Mountains,** in the easternmost section of the park, offer long and lofty ridges and 80 sq. mi. of solitude; **Crickhowell,** on the A40, is the easiest starting point for forays into this area. About 7 mi. southwest of the Beacons, the **waterfall district** features forest rivers tumbling through rapids, gorges, and amazing falls. Near **Abercrave,** off the A4067, the stunning **Dan-yr-Ogof Showcaves** (tel. (01639) 73 02 84) showcase enormous stalagmites.

The market towns on the fringe of the park, especially **Brecon** and **Abergavenny,** make pleasant touring bases. The Paddington Station (London)-South Wales **train** line runs via Cardiff to Abergavenny at the park's southeast corner; call National Rail Inquiries at (0345) 48 49 50. **Red and White** buses (tel. (01633) 48 51 18) regularly cross the park en route from Brecon, on the northern side of the park to Abergavenny, Brecon, and Hay-on-Wye. Once in town, stop at a **National Park Information Centre.** Ordnance Survey maps 12 and 13 (£6 each) are indispensable, both for exploring and reaching safety in bad weather. The centers also provide weather reports and brochures on hiking. In **Abergavenny,** the info center is on Monmouth Rd., in the tourist office opposite the bus station (tel. (01873) 85 32 54; open Easter-Oct. daily 9:30am-5:30pm). In **Brecon,** go to Cattle Market Car Park, next to the tourist info office off Lion St. (tel. (01874) 62 31 56; open April-Oct. daily 9:30am-5:30pm). The main park office is around the corner on Glamorgan St.

Several HI youth hostels are scattered throughout the park. **Llwyn-y-Celyn HI Youth Hostel** (tel. (01874) 62 42 61), 8 mi. south of Brecon (take bus 43), is convenient to the Beacons range. (Lockout 10am-5pm. £6.95. Open July-Aug. daily; mid-Feb. to June and Sept.-Nov. Mon.-Sat.) **Ystradfellte HI Youth Hostel** (tel. (01639) 72 03 01) is near the waterfall district. (£6.10, under 18 £4. Open April to mid-July Fri.-Wed; mid-July to Aug. daily; Sept.-Oct. Fri.-Wed.; Nov. to mid-Dec. and mid-Jan. to

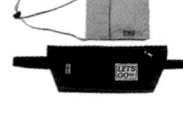

LET'S GO ORDER FORM

Last Name	First Name	Date of Birth
Street	*We cannot ship to Post Office Boxes*	
City	State	Zip Code
Phone (very important)	Citizenship (Country)	
School/College		Date of Travel

Description, Size	Color	Quantity	Unit Price	Total Price

Total Purchase Price	
Shipping and Handling	
MA Residents add 5% sales tax on gear and books	
TOTAL	

From which Let's Go Guide are you ordering? ❑ Europe ❑ USA ❑ Other________

❑ Mastercard ❑ Visa

Cardholder name:

Card number:

Expiration date:

Shipping and Handling

Eurail Passes do not factor into merchandise value.

Domestic 2-3 Weeks
Merchandise value under $30 .... $4
Merchandise value $30-$100 .... $6
Merchandise value over $100 .... $8

Domestic 2-3 Days
Merchandise value under $30 .... $14
Merchandise value $30-$100 .... $16
Merchandise value over $100 .... $18

Domestic Overnight
Merchandise value under $30 .... $24
Merchandise value $30-$100 .... $26
Merchandise value over $100 .... $28

All international shipping $30

Make check or money order payable to:
Let's Go Travel
17 Holyoke Street
Cambridge MA, 02138
(617) 495-9649

1-800-5-LETSGO

http://www.hsa.net/travel/letsgo.html

March Fri.-Sat.) **Capel-y-ffin HI Youth Hostel** (tel. (01873) 89 06 50; **camping** allowed; £6.95), at the eastern edge of the Black Mountains near Hay-on-Wye, is an excellent base for ridge-walking. The Brecon tourist office's free *Where to Stay in Brecon's National Park* maps 14 camp sites in the park (about £2-5.50 per tent).

Pembrokeshire Coast National Park

The Pembrokeshire Coast National Park features harbors, hills, and quaint villages amid 225 sq. mi. of beautiful coastal scenery. The best way to enter the region is from **Haverfordwest,** on the main **rail** line from London (£52) to Cardiff (£13.20). **Buses** have more frequent and comprehensive service; schedules are compiled in the helpful *Guide to Local Bus Services,* available at regional tourist offices. In town, the **Tourist Information Centre,** The Old Bridge (tel. (01437) 76 31 10), has info about the entire park (open June-Sept. daily 10am-5:30pm; April-May 10am-5pm). Another point of entry into the park is the town of **Pembroke.** The **Pembroke Castle** is among the most impressive fortresses in South Wales and the birthplace of Henry VII. (Open April-Sept. daily 9:30am-6pm; March and Oct. 10am-5pm; Nov.-Feb. Mon.-Sat. 10am-4pm. £2.95.) The **tourist office,** Commons Rd. (tel. (01646) 62 23 88), offers info on bus routes and tons of brochures. (Open Easter-Oct. daily 10am-5:30pm; Nov.-Easter Tues., Thurs., and Sat. 10am-4pm; Dec.-Jan. often closed.) Stay at the **Merton Place House,** 3 East Block (tel. (01646) 68 47 96; £15).

Once in the park, check out one of the **Outdoor Activity Centres,** which rent canoes, kayaks, and bicycles (£10-20 a day). For short hikes, stick to the more accessible St. David's Peninsula in the northwest; otherwise, set out on the coastal path, which is marked with acorn symbols. Near the western extremity of the coastal path is **St. David's,** medieval Wales's largest and richest diocese. A chest in the **cathedral** holds the bones of St. David, patron saint of Wales (donation £2). The **Bishop's Palace** resembles a castle. (Open April-Oct. daily 9:30am-6:30pm; Nov.-March Mon.-Sat. 9:30am-4pm, Sun. noon-4pm. £1.70, students £1.20.) **YHA youth hostels** are spaced along the coastal path. **Marloes Sands** (tel. (01646) 63 66 67) is near the Dale Peninsula (£6.25; open July-Aug. daily; mid-April to June and Sept. Mon.-Sat.). **Broad Haven** (tel. (01437) 78 16 88), on St. Bride's Bay, has 75 beds (£8.50; open mid-March to Sept. daily; Oct. Mon.-Sat.). **St. David's** (tel. (01437) 72 03 45), lies near St. David's Head (£6.25; open April-June and Sept.-Oct. Fri.-Wed.; July-August daily).

Aberystwyth

Along the sweeping Cardigan Bay coastline, the university town of Aberystwyth offers easy access to all of Wales and plenty of pubs to entertain you as you wait for your connection. If it's a long wait, check out the **National Library of Wales,** off Penglais Rd., which houses the earliest surviving manuscript of the *Canterbury Tales* and almost every book written in Welsh or pertaining to Wales (open Mon.-Fri. 9:30am-6pm, Sat. 9:30am-5pm; free). The gray-stoned ruins of the 13th-century **Aberystwyth Castle** afford a magnificent view of the coastline and surrounding hills.

The city rests at the western end of the mid-Wales rail line; **British Rail,** Alexandra Rd. (tel. (01654) 70 23 11), provides service to major cities. For destinations on the northern coast, change at Machynlleth (30min., £3.70). **TrawsCambria** runs a daily bus to Aberystwyth from Cardiff (£9.70). The **tourist office,** Lisburne House, Terrace Rd. (tel. (01970) 61 21 25), has B&B info (open July-Aug. daily 10am-6pm; Sept.-June 10am-5pm). The nearest **HI youth hostel** is 9 mi. north in Borth (tel. (01970) 87 14 98; £8.50). Take the train to Borth Station (10min.) or Crosville Bus 511 or 512. The city boasts over 50 pubs; relax at **Rummer's,** on Trefecher Bridge of Bridge St., or the oldest pub in town, **The Angel,** 57-59 Upper Great Darkgate St.

Snowdonia Forest and National Park

The 840 sheep-dotted sq. mi. of Snowdonia National Park, stretching from Machynlleth in the south to Bangor and Conwy in the north, embrace narrow-cut valleys, elevated moorland, and the sun-pierced coves of the Llŷn Peninsula, but are dominated by the rough countenance of the ancient mountains. At 3560 ft., **Mount Snowdon** is one of the highest peaks in Britain and the most popular mountain for hiking.

Practical Information and Accommodations Tourist offices and National Park Information Centres stock leaflets on walks (40p), drives, and accommodations, as well as Ordnance Survey maps (£5-6). Contact the **Snowdonia National Park Headquarters,** Penrhyndeudraeth, Gwynedd, Wales LL48 6LF (tel. (01766) 77 02 74), for full details. Among the other information centers, **Betws-y-coed,** Royal Oak Stables (tel. (01690) 71 06 65 or 71 04 26), is the busiest and best-stocked (open April-Oct. daily 10am-6pm; Nov.-March 9:30am-4:30pm). Call **Mountaincall Snowdonia** (tel. (01839) 50 53 30) for the local forecast, ground conditions, and a three- to five-day forecast. If hiking isn't your thing, the **Snowdon Mountain Railway** (tel. (01286) 87 02 23), opened in 1896 and operated by coal-fired steam locomotives, travels from Llanberis to Snowdonia's summit. (2hr. round-trip; 30min. stop at the peak. Return £14. Weary hikers can try for a £6 standby back down.) The **Ffestiniog Railway** (tel. (01766) 51 23 40) romps through the mountains from Porthmadog (return £8.20-12.40). A **Red Rover ticket** (£4.20) buys unlimited travel on the **Snowdon Sherpa buses** which run between the park's towns and trailheads.

The eight **YHA youth hostels** in the mountain area are some of the best in Wales. Plenty of sheep, cows, and bulls keep hostelers company at **Llanberis** (tel. (01286) 87 02 80) as they take in the splendid views of Lake Peris and Llŷn Padarn below and Mt. Snowdon above (£7.70; open April-Aug. daily; Sept.-Oct. Tues.-Sat. Jan.-March Fri.-Sun.; closed Nov.-Dec.). **Snowdon Ranger,** Llyn Cwellyn (tel. (01286) 65 03 91), is at the base of great hiking trails; take bus 95. (£8.50. Open April-Aug. daily; mid-Feb. to end of March and Nov.-Dec. Fri.-Sun.; Sept.-Oct. Wed.-Sun.) In the mountains, **camping** is permitted as long as you leave no mess, but the Park Service discourages it because of recent erosion. In the valleys, owner's consent is needed.

Llanberis and Harlech Distinguished mainly by the mountain looming over it, **Llanberis** is the largest town in the park and has flocks of B&Bs. To reach **Ceunant Mawr,** one of Wales's most impressive waterfalls, walk along the footpath on Victoria Terr. by Victoria Hotel, take the first right, then the first left (about 1mi.). The **tourist office,** 41A High St. (tel. (01286) 87 07 65), books rooms and doles out maps and hiking tips (open daily 10am-6pm). Llanberis is a short ride from Caernarfon (**KMP** bus 88; tel. (01286) 87 08 80) or Bangor (Crosville bus 77; tel. (01970) 61 79 51).

Just shy of the Llŷn Peninsula, the tiny town of **Harlech** affords a haunting view of the misty, craggy mountains of Snowdownia to the north. Edward I chose the strategic spot for his third in-your-face fortress—**Harlech Castle.** (Open April-Oct. daily 9:30am-6:30pm; Nov.-March Mon.-Sat. 9:30am-4pm, Sun. 11am-4pm. £3, students £2.) The **tourist office** at Gwyddfor House, Stryd Fawr (tel. (01341) 78 06 58), will book you a room, or try the **YHA Llanbedr Hostel** (tel. (01341) 24 12 87), 4 mi. south; take the train to Llanbedr or bus 38. (Open May-Aug. daily; Sept.-Oct. and mid-Feb. to April Thurs.-Mon.; Jan. to mid-Feb. Fri.-Sun.)

Llŷn Peninsula and Northern Coast

The Llŷn has been a hotspot for tourism since the Middle Ages, when crowds of religious pilgrims tramped through on their way to Bardsey Island off the peninsula's western tip. Now sun worshippers make the trek to the endless, sandy beaches along the coast. **Porthmadog** is the southeast gateway to the peninsula. The town's principal attraction is the steam **Ffestiniog Railway** (tel. (01766) 51 23 40), which runs through the hills of Snowdonia (1hr., £12.40). The **tourist office** is at the end of Stryd Fawr (tel. (01766) 51 29 81). An eccentric landmark of Italy-fixation, the private village of **Portmeirion** stands 2 mi. east of Porthmadog. The various buildings, all of which were transported from faraway places, are washed with cool Mediterranean colors. Statues in classical, Indian, and mythical styles await discovery.

The Menai Strait Perched on the edge of the bay of the same name, **Caernarfon** (can-AR-von) lures visitors with Wales's grandest medieval castle. Built by Edward I in 1283, the overwhelming **Caernarfon Castle** features rapid-arrow slits (the only surviving in the world) and decorative bands of colored stone. (Open April-Oct. daily 9:30am-6:30pm; Nov.-March Mon.-Sat. 9:30am-4pm, Sun. 11am-4pm. £3.80, students £2.80.) The **tourist office,** Castle St., Oriel Pendeitsh (tel. (01286) 67 22 32), offers a helpful street map and accommodations listings. (Open April-Oct. daily 10am-6pm; Nov.-March Mon.-Tues. and Thurs.-Fri. 9:30am-5pm, Sat. and Sun. 9am-4:30pm.) Stay at the hostel **Totters,** 2 High St. (tel. (01286) 67 29 63), in its polished wood bunks (£9). The delightful B&B **Bryn Hyfyrd,** St. David's Rd. (tel (01286) 67 38 40), offers spacious rooms (£14-20). Bakeries and cafés crowd Pool St. Watch the sunset with pint in hand at the **Anglesey Arms,** the Promenade.

Buses 5 and 5B run every 15 minutes between Caernarfon and **Bangor,** where you can visit the **Bangor Cathedral** and walk along the coast to the Victorian pier. **Beaumaris,** across the Menai Strait, features the magnificent **Beaumaris Castle,** the largest of Edward I's chain of Welsh fortresses. (Open April-Oct. daily 9:30am-6:30pm; Nov.-March Mon.-Sat. 9:30am-4pm, Sun. 11am-4pm. £2.20, students £1.40.) The **Sun-y-Don,** 7 Bulkeley Terrace (tel. (01248) 81 07 94), has £38 doubles.

Holyhead and Conwy On the Isle of Anglesey, **Holyhead** has one sure lure for the traveler: **ferries** to Ireland. **Irish Ferries** leave Holyhead daily for Dublin (4hr., £25 one way), and accepts bookings at its Holyhead offices. In the U.K., call (0990) 17 17 17, after hours (01) 661 0715; in Dublin call (01) 661 05 11. **Stena Sealink** (tel. (01233) 64 70 47) sails to **Dun Laoghaire** which has bus/rail connections to Dublin (4hr., one way £26-35). **National Express** hits Holyhead from most major cities. The town is also the terminus of the North Wales Coast **rail** line with hourly trains to Bangor (30min., £5.20), Chester (1½hr., £13.30), and London (6hr., £44). **British Rail** runs from Holyhead to Cardiff (£48.30). If you miss your boat, check room vacancies at the **tourist office** (tel. (01407) 76 26 22), in a booth in the rail station (open in summer daily 10am-6pm; off-season 9:30am-5pm).

Edward I's 13th-century **castle** solemnly guards over the walled town of **Conwy,** which has an agelessness that even the countless tourist buses cannot kill. In the 14th-century **Aberconwy House** on High St. and Castle St., tilted floors and windows frame displays of armor and period furnishings (open April-Oct. Wed.-Mon. 11am-5:30pm; last admission 5pm; £2). Conwy's **tourist office** (tel. (01492) 59 22 48) is at the entrance to the castle (open Easter-Oct. daily 9:30am-6:30pm; Nov.-Easter Mon.-Sat. 10am-4pm). **B&Bs** cluster in the Cadnant Park area, a 10-minute walk from the castle. To get to the fabulous **YHA Conwy** from Lancaster Sq. (tel. (01492) 59 35 71), head down Bangor Rd., turn left up Mt. Pleasant, and go right at the top of the hill (£9.40). Crosville (tel. (01970) 61 79 51) **buses** 5 and 5B follow a coastal route from Caernarfon to Llandudno, stopping in Bangor and Conwy along the way.

SCOTLAND

At its best, Scotland is a world apart, a defiantly distinct nation within the United Kingdom with a culture and worldview all its own. Exuberant Glasgow has a mind-bending nightlife, Aberdeen's grand architecture sprawls regally, and Edinburgh is the epicenter of Scottish culture during its famed International Festival in August. A little over half the size of England but with one tenth its population, Scotland revels in stark and open spaces. The heather-covered mountains and glassy lochs of the west coast and luminescent mists of the Hebrides demand worship, while the farmlands to the south and the rolling river valleys of the east coast display a gentler beauty.

Edinburgh

In the early 18th century, the dark alleys of Edinburgh (ED-in-bur-ra) hosted an outpouring of talent that turned the Calvinist Kingdom of God into a capital of the Enlightenment. The philosopher David Hume presided over a republic of letters that included Adam Smith, Robert Louis Stevenson, and Sir Walter Scott, and the New Town city planning project rejected the Old Town's tenements, closes, and wynds in favor of the graceful Gregorian symmetry and orderly gridwork. Today Edinburgh is a meeting place of opposing forces—natural rock and hewn stone, wild landscapes and terraced gardens, distant bagpipes and roaring traffic.

ORIENTATION AND PRACTICAL INFORMATION

Edinburgh lies 45 mi. east of Glasgow and 405 mi. northwest of London on Scotland's east coast. **Princes Street** is the main road in the New Town, in the northern section of the city; the **Royal Mile** (Lawnmarket, High St., and Canongate) is the main street in the Old Town. **North Bridge, Waverly Bridge,** and **The Mound** connect the Old and New Towns. The train station lies between North Bridge and Waverley Bridge near the center of town; the bus station is three blocks from the east end of Princes St. Edinburgh is easily explored on foot, but **Lothian Regional Transport** (tel. 554 44 94) and **SMT** (tel. 557 50 61) sell bus passes for extensive travel.

Tourist Office: Edinburgh and Scotland Information Centre, Waverley Market, 3 Princes St. (tel. 557 17 00), next to Waverley train station. Busy but efficient accommodations service (£3); outside, a 24hr. computer gives availability updates. Pick up *Day by Day* and an accommodations booklet (both free), as well as *The Essential Guide to Edinburgh* (50p). Bus and theater tickets. *Bureau de change.* Open July-Aug. Mon.-Sat. 9am-8pm, Sun. 10am-8pm; May-June and Sept. Mon.-Sat. 9am-7pm, Sun. 10am-7pm; Oct.-April Mon.-Sat. 9am-5pm, Sun. 10am-5pm.

Budget Travel Services: Edinburgh Travel Centre, Potterow Union, Bristo Sq. (tel. 668 22 21). Open Mon.-Fri. 9am-5:30pm. Offices at 196 Rose St. (tel. 226 20 19) and 92 S. Clark St. (tel. 667 94 88) also open Sat. 10am-1pm. **Campus Travel,** 53 Forrest Rd. (tel. 225 61 00). Open Mon.-Tues. and Thurs.-Fri. 9am-5:30pm.

Currency Exchange: Try **Barclays,** 18 South Saint Andrews St., and the **Royal Bank of Scotland,** on North Bridge. Both have **ATM** machines.

American Express: 139 Princes St. EH2 4BR (tel. 225 78 81), 5 blocks from Waverley Station. Mail held. Open Mon.-Wed. 9am-5:30pm, Thurs. 9:30am-5:30pm, Sat. 9am-4pm.

Trains: Waverley Station (tel. (0345) 484 49 50), in the center of town. To: Glasgow (£7), Aberdeen (£31), Oban (£23), Inverness (£28), and other cities. For schedules, call **Scotrail** at (0345) 48 49 50).

Buses: St. Andrew Square Bus Station, St. Andrew Square (info tel. 558 16 16). **Scottish Citylink** (tel. (0990) 50 50 50) serves Glasgow (£4.50), Inverness (£12), and Aberdeen (£12.50). **National Express** (tel. 452 87 77) sends buses to London (£20.50). To avoid long lines, simply buy your ticket on the bus.

Taxis: City Cabs, tel. 228 12 11; **Central Radio Taxis,** tel. 229 24 68. Taxi stands are located at both stations and on almost every corner on Princes St.

Bike Rental: Edinburgh Cycle Hire, 29 Blackfriars St. (tel. 556 55 60), off High St. Bikes £7-15 per day.

Bisexual, Gay, and Lesbian Services: West and Wilde Bookshop, 25A Dundas St. (tel. 556 00 79). Open Tues.-Sat. 10am-7pm, Sun. noon-5pm. **Gay Switchboard:** tel. 556 40 49; staffed Mon. and Thurs. 7:30-10pm. **Lesbian Line:** tel. 557 07 51; staffed Mon. and Thurs. 7:30-10pm. **Bisexual Line:** tel. 557 36 20; staffed Thurs. 7:30-9:30pm. Pick up *Gay Scotland* or drop by the **Stonewall Café-Bar,** 60 Broughton St. (tel. 478 70 69). Open daily 11am-11pm.

Crisis Lines: Nightline: tel. 557 44 44; staffed daily 6pm-8am. **Rape Crisis Center:** tel. 556 94 37; staffed Mon. 7-9pm, Tues. 10-11:30am, Thurs. 1-3pm, Sat. 9-11am. **Women's Aid:** tel. 229 14 19; staffed Mon.-Fri. 10am-3:30pm.

Hospital: Royal Infirmary of Edinburgh, 1 Lauriston Pl. (tel. 536 10 00). From The Mound, take bus 23 or 27.

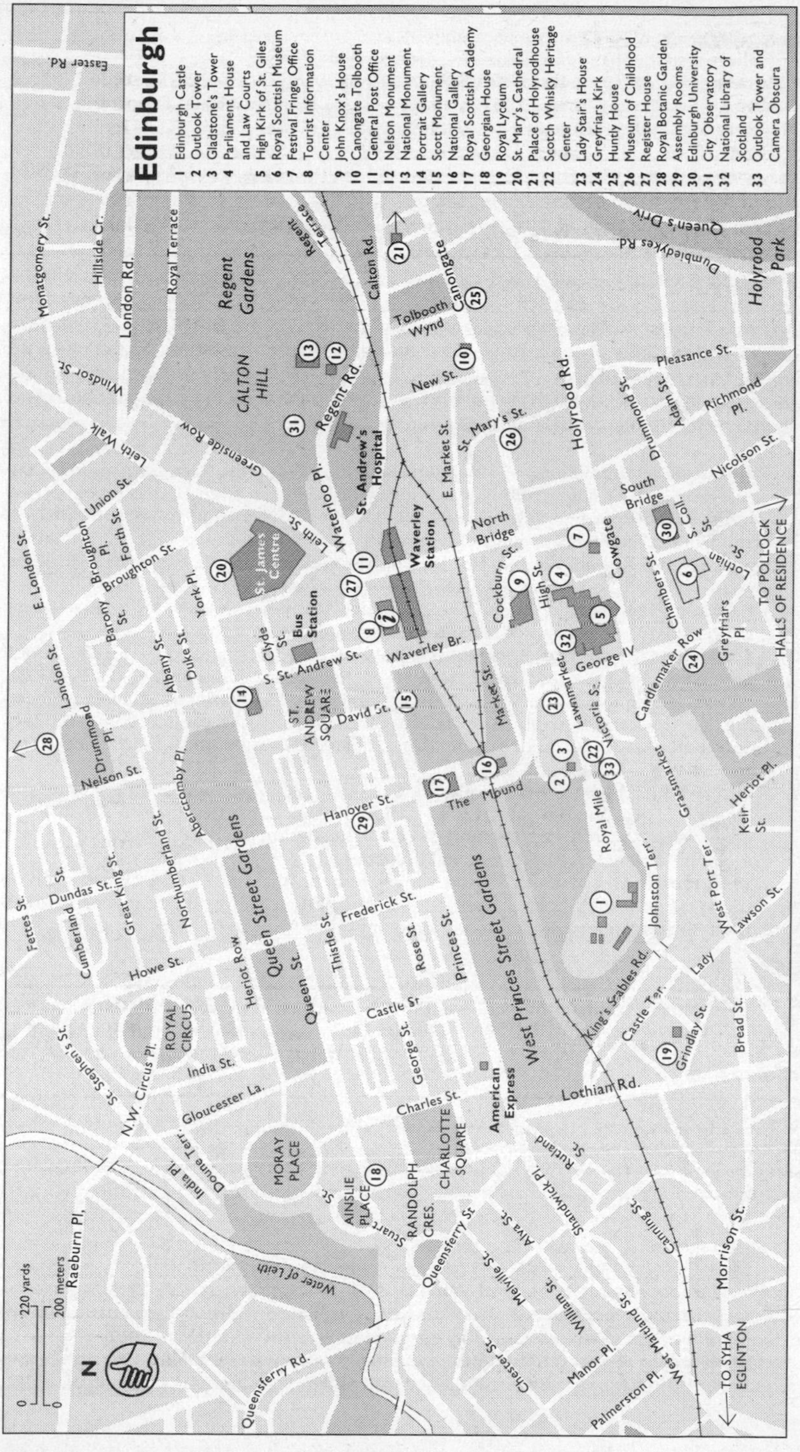
Edinburgh
1 Edinburgh Castle
2 Outlook Tower
3 Gladstone's Tower
4 Parliament House and Law Courts
5 High Kirk of St. Giles
6 Royal Scottish Museum
7 Festival Fringe Office
8 Tourist Information Center
9 John Knox's House
10 Canongate Tolbooth
11 General Post Office
12 Nelson Monument
13 National Monument
14 Portrait Gallery
15 Scott Monument
16 National Gallery
17 Royal Scottish Academy
18 Georgian House
19 Royal Lyceum
20 St. Mary's Cathedral
21 Palace of Holyrodhouse
22 Scotch Whisky Heritage Center
23 Lady Stair's House
24 Greyfriars Kirk
25 Huntly House
26 Museum of Childhood
27 Register House
28 Royal Botanic Garden
29 Assembly Rooms
30 Edinburgh University
31 City Observatory
32 National Library of Scotland
33 Outlook Tower and Camera Obscura
N
0 220 yards
0 200 meters
CALTON HILL
Regent Gardens
Holyrood Park
Waverley Station
St. Andrew's Hospital
Bus Station
St. James Centre
ST. ANDREW SQUARE
CHARLOTTE SQUARE
MORAY PLACE
ROYAL CIRCUS
AINSLIE PLACE
RANDOLPH CRES.
American Express
Queen Street Gardens
Princes Street Gardens
West Princes Street Gardens
Royal Mile
Water of Leith
TO SYHA EGLINTON
TO POLLOCK HALLS OF RESIDENCE

BRITAIN

Emergency: tel. 999; no coins required.
Police: Headquarters at 5 Fettes Ave. (tel. 311 31 31).
Internet Access: electricFROG, 42-44 Cockburn St. (tel. 226 15 05). £2.50 for 30min, students £2; email 15min. £1.20. Open Mon.-Sat. 10am-10pm, Sun. noon-8pm; during Festival Mon.-Sat. 10am-midnight.
Post Office: 8-10 St. James Centre (tel. 556 95 46), near the bus station. Open Mon. 9am-5:30pm, Tues.-Fri. 8:30am-5:30pm, Sat. 8:30am-6pm. **Postal Code:** EH1 3SR.
Telephone Code: 0131.

ACCOMMODATIONS

The tourist office will find you a room for £3, but the private service in the train station will do the same for free (open Mon.-Sat. 8am-8pm, Sun. 9:30am-7:30pm). During festival season (Aug. 16-Sept. 5) there are few available rooms. The *Where to Stay 1998* register (free at the tourist office) lists Edinburgh's countless **B&Bs;** most are open between May and September and cost £11-16. Slightly more elegant **guest houses** run £15-25 and remain open year-round. Edinburgh's hostels are cheap and convenient but fill up fast. Call ahead when possible.

Edinburgh Backpackers, 65 Cockburn St. (tel. 225 62 09). This new hostel occupies prime real estate; from North Bridge, turn right on High St. and take the first right. Reception open 24hr. £10-12.50. Also has doubles and twins with kitchen and laundry facilities at 34a Cockburn (£35).
Backpackers' Royal Mile Hostel, 105 High St. (tel. 557 61 20), boasts new facilities and fewer beds to a room. £9.90-10.20, seventh night free.
14 Argyle Pl. (Iolaire) (tel. 667 99 91), south of the Meadows and the Royal Mile. Expect a welcoming cup of tea and excellent advice on sights. TVs. £10-11.
SYHA Hostel Eglinton, 18 Eglinton Crescent EH12 5DD (tel. 337 11 20), about 1mi. west of town center, near Haymarket train station. Take bus 3, 4, 12, 13, 22, 26, 28, 31, 33, or 44 from Princes St. to Palmerston Pl. Laundry machines, kitchen, luggage, lockers. Reception open 7am-midnight. Curfew 2am. £10.95, students and seniors £9.45. Continental breakfast included. Evening meal £4.20. Paid reservations urged Easter-Sept. Open Jan.-Nov.
Belford Youth Hostel, 6-8 Douglas Gardens (tel. 225 62 09), about 1mi. west of the city center near the Haymarket train station. Elegant converted church. Light sleepers beware. Kitchen, laundry, and cable TV. Reception open 8am-3am. £9.50, linen included. Doubles £30. Continental breakfast £1.75.
SYHA Hostel Bruntsfield, 7 Bruntsfield Crescent (tel. 447 29 94), 1½mi. south of the west end of Princes St. A trek, but sparkling facilities make it worthwhile. Kitchen and laundry. Reception open daily 7am-11pm. £6.75-9.15.

FOOD

As the capital of Scottish tourism, Edinburgh is compelled to offer traditional Scottish fare—whisky, haggis, turnips, and so on—with much ceremony and great cost. If your budget is too meager for restaurant prices, **Littlewoods Department Store,** 92 Princes St., has a salad bar (£1.59-4) and groceries. (Open Mon. 9:30am-5:30pm, Tues.-Wed. 9am-5pm, Thurs. 9am-7pm, Fri.-Sat. 9am-6pm, Sun. 12:30-5pm). You can also shop at **Presto's foodmarket** at the St. James Shopping Centre (open Mon.-Wed. and Fri.-Sat. 8:30am-6pm, Thurs. 8:30am-8pm).

Kalpna, 2 St. Patrick Sq. (tel. 667 98 90). Superb Indian vegetarian fare in a smoke-free setting. All-you-can-eat buffet lunch £4.50. Dinner buffet once a week £9. Curry, *korma,* and wild vegetable dishes £4-7. Reserve for dinner. Open in summer Mon.-Fri. noon-2pm and 5:30-11pm, Sat. noon-2pm, Sun. 6-10:30pm.
Henderson's Salad Table and Wine Bar, 94 Hanover St. (tel. 225 21 31), between George and Queen St. Great salads and hot dishes from £2. Live music nightly 7:30pm. Open Mon.-Sat. 10am-10:45pm, during Festival Sun. 9am-9pm.
Parrots, 3-5 Viewforth (tel. 229 32 52). Good veggie selection. Moussaka £3.75. Baltistan dishes £5.75. Open Sun. and Tues.-Thurs. 6-10:30pm, Fri.-Sat. 5-10:30pm;

under 18 admitted Fri-Sat. 5-8pm only. Closing hours flexible; call if arriving after 10:30pm. Reservations recommended.

Susie's Diner, 53 W. Nicolson St. Hardcore vegetarian fare. Specials under £3. Open Mon.-Sat. 9am-10pm, Sun. 1-9pm; later during the Festival.

Kebab Mahal, 7 Nicolson Sq. Among the best of Edinburgh's many kebaberies. Kebabs £2-4. Hummus £1.55. Lamb curry £3. Open Sun.-Thurs. noon-midnight, Fri.-Sat. noon-2am. All dishes are Halal.

SIGHTS

The **Royal Mile** (Lawnmarket, High St., and Canongate) defines the length of Old Town, the medieval center of Edinburgh. At the top of the Royal Mile, **Edinburgh Castle** glowers over the city from the peak of an extinct volcano. The Scottish Crown Jewels and Regalia lie within, as well as **St. Margaret's Chapel,** a 12th-century Norman church. (Open daily April-Sept. 9:30am-6pm; Oct.-March 9:30am-5pm. Last admission 45min. before closing. £5.50.) The walk along Royal Mile from the castle passes some of Edinburgh's oldest attractions. The 1617 tenement **Gladstone's Land** is well worth a visit; everything inside remains as it was almost 400 years ago. (Open April-Oct. Mon.-Sat. 10am-5pm, Sun. 2-5pm. Last admission 4:30pm. £2.60, students £1.70.) Through the passage at 477 Lawnmarket awaits **Lady Stair's House,** a 17th-century townhouse home to **The Writer's Museum,** with memorabilia of Robert Burns, Sir Walter Scott, and Robert Louis Stevenson (open Mon.-Sat. 10am-5pm; during Festival also Sun. 2-5pm; free).

Where Lawnmarket becomes High St., the Mile is dominated by **St. Giles Cathedral.** From the pulpit of St. Giles, John Knox delivered fiery Presbyterian sermons to rally the populace against Mary, Queen of Scots. (Open Easter-Aug. Mon.-Sat. 9am-7pm; Sept.-Easter 9am-5pm; year-round Sun. 1-5pm. £1 donation requested.) **Canongate,** the steep hill at the of the Mile, has three free museums; if you've had your fill of museum etiquette, check out the toys and games at the **Museum of Childhood,** 42 High St. The spectacular **Palace of Holyroodhouse** at the eastern end of the Mile, once the home of Mary, Queen of Scots, is now Queen Elizabeth II's official residence in Scotland. (Open April-Oct. Mon.-Sat. 9:30am-5:15pm, Sun. 9:30am-4:30pm; Nov.-March Mon.-Sat. 9:30am-3:45pm; closed in late May and late June-early July. £5.30.) While in town, royalty attend services at **Canongate Kirk,** a 17th-century chapel and the resting place of Adam Smith.

On the way to the New Town, on The Mound, the **National Gallery of Scotland** has a small but superb collection of Renaissance, Romantic, and Impressionist works. (Open Mon.-Sat. 10am-5pm, Sun. 2-5pm; during Festival Mon.-Sat. 10am-6pm, Sun. 11am-6pm. Free.) Edinburgh's New Town is a masterpiece of Georgian planning. James Craig won the city-planning contest in 1767 with his rectangular gridiron of three main parallel streets (Queen, George, and Princes) linking two large squares (Charlotte and St. Andrew). The **New Town Conservation Centre,** 13a Dundas St., can answer questions about the area (open Mon.-Fri. 9am-1pm and 2-5pm). A must-see is the elegant **Georgian House,** 7 Charlotte Sq. (open April-Oct. Mon.-Sat. 10am-5pm, Sun. 2-5pm; £4, students £2.70). The chandeliered **Assembly Rooms,** east of Charlotte Sq. on George St., shine as one of the glories of classical Edinburgh and host varied performances during the summer. On Princes St., between The Mound and Waverley Bridge, sits the **Walter Scott Monument**—a grotesque Gothic "steeple without a church" with statues of Scott and his dog inside. Climb the winding 287-step staircase for £2 and get an eagle's-eye view of Princes St. Gardens, the castle, and Old Town's Market St. (open April-Sept. Mon.-Sat. 9am-6pm; Oct.-March Mon.-Sat. 9am-3pm). The **Scottish National Portrait Gallery,** 1 Queen St., north of St. Andrew Sq., mounts the mugs of famous Scots (open Mon.-Sat. 10am-5pm, Sun. 2-5pm; free).

ENTERTAINMENT AND FESTIVALS

The summer season overflows with music in the gardens and many theater and film events around town. In winter, shorter days and the crush of students promote a flourishing nightlife. For details, find a copy of *The List* (£1.90).

Theater, Music, and Nightlife

In Bruntsfield, **King's Theatre,** 2 Leven St. (tel. 220 43 49), sponsors touring productions of musicals and plays while the **Royal Lyceum Theatre,** 30 Grindlay St. (tel. 229 96 97), presents well-known comedies. Both may be closed this summer, though they will remain open though during the Festival. The **Playhouse Theatre,** Greenside Pl. (tel. 557 25 90), often hosts musicals. **Usher Hall** (tel. 228 11 55), on Lothian Rd., hosts orchestral events (box office open Mon.-Sat. 10am-5pm); it may, however, also be closed this summer. Jazz enthusiasts crowd **L'attache,** below **Platform I,** Rutland St., **Navaar House Hotel** on Mayfield Gardens, and **The Cellar Bar,** Chambers St. For rock and progressive shows, try **The Venue** (tel. 557 30 73) and **Calton Studios** (tel. 556 70 66), both on Calton Rd. **Whistle Binkies,** 4 Niddry St. (tel. 557 51 14), has nightly live music from country to punk rock (open daily 5pm-3am). You'll find Scottish bands and country dancing at the **Ross Open-Air Theatre** (tel. 529 79 05), under the tent in Princes St. Gardens (from about 7pm), and at a number of smaller pubs.

There's a pub in sight from everywhere in Edinburgh. Royal Mile pubs draw an older crowd, but **Scruffy Murphy's,** 50 George IV Bridge near St. Giles, and **The Tron Ceilidh Bar,** off High St. at South Bridge, attract many students. Some of the best pubs in the Old Town are clustered around the university. Students booze it up at the **Pear Tree,** 38 W. Nicolson St., with a large outdoor courtyard, and **Greyfriars Bobby's Bar,** 34 Candlemaker Row. Nearby, at 9B Victoria St., are **Finnigan's Wake** and its neighbor **Buddy Mulligan's.** The New Town has several gay pubs, concentrated in the Broughton St. area. **The Basement,** on Broughton St., is a local favorite.

Festivals

In August, the spectacular **Edinburgh International Festival** (Aug. 16-Sept. 5 in 1998) features a kaleidoscopic program of music, drama, dance, and art. For tickets and a schedule of events, contact the **Festival Box Office,** 21 Market St. EH1 1BW (inquiries tel. 473 20 01, bookings 473 20 00; fax 473 20 03). Tickets (£5-30) are sold by phone and over the counter starting the third week in April, and by post or fax from the second week in April. You can also get tickets at the door for most events. Look for half-price tickets after 1pm on the day of the performance.

Around the festival has grown a more spontaneous **Festival Fringe** (Aug. 9-31 in 1998), which now includes over 500 amateur and professional companies presenting theater, comedy, children's shows, folk and classical music, poetry, dance, opera, and various exhibits (tickets £6-10, students £3-6). The *Fringe Programme* (available from the end of June) and the *Daily Diary* list info on performances; get brochures and tickets by mail from the **Fringe Festival Office,** 180 High St., Edinburgh, Scotland EH1 1QS. (Include 75p postage from Britain, £1.50 from EU countries, £3 from everywhere else. Cash, stamps, and foreign currency accepted.) Bookings can be made by post starting mid-June, by phone beginning late June (inquiries 226 52 57, bookings 226 51 38), and in person from July 28. (Box office open Mon.-Fri. 10am-6pm; Aug. and during the Festival daily 10am-7pm.) The **Military Tattoo** (provisional 1998 dates Aug. 7-29), is performed every Monday to Saturday night in the Esplanade—a spectacle of military bands, bagpipes, and drums. For tickets (£7.50-16), contact the **Tattoo Ticket Sale Office,** 33-34 Market St. (tel. 225 11 88; fax 225 86 27), which accepts bookings from early January (open Mon.-Fri. 10am-4:30pm or until the show).

St. Andrews

In St. Andrews, golf is the game. At the northwest edge of town, St. Andrews' **Old Course,** the golf pilgrim's Canterbury and frequent venue for the British Open, stretches out regally to a gorgeous beach. (Call (01334) 47 57 57 or fax 47 70 36 to enter the lottery for starting times or make a reservation for a nearby course. £50-70 per round on the Old Course, £15-30 on other courses.) The **British Golf Museum,** next to the Old Course, details the origins of the game. (Open Easter-Oct. daily 9:30am-5:30pm; Oct.-Easter Thurs.-Mon. 11am-3pm. £3.75, students £2.75.)

Despite the onslaught of pastel and polyester, one need not worship the wedge to love St. Andrews. With its restored medieval streets, ruins of an enormous cathedral, ancient university, and magnificent beaches, St. Andrews possesses a rare and compelling beauty. In the Middle Ages, pilgrims journeyed to **St. Andrews Cathedral** to pray at the Saint's Shrine; today, only a facade and the outline of the walls remain. Nearby, **St. Andrews Castle** maintains secret tunnels, bottle-shaped dungeons, and high stone walls to keep out rebellious heretics. (Cathedral and castle open April-Sept. Mon.-Sat. 9:30am-6:30pm, Sun. noon-6:30pm; Oct.-March Mon.-Sat. 9:30am-4:30pm, Sun. 2-4:30pm. Joint ticket £3.30.) **St. Andrews University,** founded in the 15th century, lies just west of the castle between North St. and The Scores.

Five Scottish **buses** follow the scenic coastal route every day from Edinburgh to St. Andrews (2hr., £4). For more info, call the St. Andrew Sq. station in Edinburgh (tel. (0131) 558 16 16). Scotrail **trains** stop 5 mi. away at **Leuchars** (from Edinburgh 1hr., £6.10); from there, buses travel to St. Andrews. The marvelous **tourist office** is at 70 Market St. (tel. (01334) 47 20 21; fax 47 84 22); from the bus station, turn right on City Rd. and take the first left. (Open June and Sept.-Oct. Mon.-Sat. 9:30am-7pm, Sun. 11am-6pm; July-Aug. Mon.-Sat. 9:30am-8pm, Sun. 11am-6pm; Nov.-March Mon.-Sat. 9:30am-5:30pm.) The office gives out lists of local **B&Bs.** The thrifty traveler should make St. Andrews a daytrip from Edinburgh or Glasgow. **Mr. Pennington's Bunkhouse** (tel. (01334) 31 07 68), in West Pitkierie, 8 mi. south of St. Andrews, is a rustic 700-year-old fortified farmhouse (£6-8.50, sheets 50p). **Gannochy House** (tel. (01334) 46 48 70), next to Younger Hall on North Street, is centrally located, albeit an eye-sore (reception open 2-6pm; £10; open June- Aug.).

Glasgow

Due west of Edinburgh in central Scotland, Glasgow is really a tale of two cities. A mile northwest of the downtown area, the West End matches Edinburgh's class with boundless energy and a continental elegance all its own. Farther east, however, pastoral beauty gives way to a concrete grid of streets and buildings where the economy includes a booming trade in stolen wallets. The one constant throughout the city is an innovative arts community: three universities and 13,000 students provide the energy and creativity, and numerous theaters and concert halls provide the setting for everything from opera to bagpiping to fabulous drag shows.

ORIENTATION AND PRACTICAL INFORMATION

George Square is the physical center of Glasgow; the tourist office and cathedral are within a few blocks of the square. To get there from Central Station, exit left onto Union St., walk two blocks, and turn right onto St. Vincent St. From Buchanan Station, exit right onto North Hanover at the end of the station opposite the info booth.

Tourist Office: 11 George St. (tel. 204 44 00), off George Sq. U: Buchanan St. Free local accommodations and bus bookings. Pick up the *Essential Guide to Glasgow* and *Where To Stay* (£1.50). Open July-Aug. Mon.-Sat. 9am-8pm, Sun. 10am-6pm; Sept.-May Mon.-Sat. 9am-6pm; June Mon.-Sat. 9am-7pm, Sun. 10am-6pm.

Currency Exchange: At tourist office. **Barclays,** 90 Vincent St., about a block from the tourist office, has an **ATM** networked to the Cirrus and Plus systems. Most banks are open Mon.-Fri. 9:30am-5pm. A few have Sat. hours.

American Express: 115 Hope St. (tel. 221 43 66; fax 204 26 85). Client mail held. Open Mon.-Fri. 8:30am-5:30pm, Sat. 9am-noon.

Flights: Glasgow Airport (tel. 887 11 11), 10 mi. west in Abbotsinch. Citylink runs to Glasgow's Buchanan station (20min., £2) and to Edinburgh (1¾hr., £6.50).

Trains: With credit card purchases, call (0800) 45 04 50. **Central Station,** Gordon St., serves southern Scotland, England, and Wales. U: St. Enoch. To: Stranraer (2½hr., £22), Dumfries (1¾hr., £15.40), and London via York and Newcastle (5-6hr., about £63). **Queen St. Station,** beside Coppthorne Hotel, George Sq., covers routes to the north and east. U: Buchanan St. To: Edinburgh (50min., £6.90), Aberdeen (2½hr., £34), Inverness (3¼hr., £28), and Fort William (3¾hr., £22).

Buses: Buchanan Station, N. Hanover St. (tel. 332 71 33), 2 blocks north of George Sq. Bus transportation is much cheaper than train service. National Express (tel. (0990) 80 80 80) and/or Scottish Citylink (tel. (0990) 50 50 50) serve Edinburgh (50min., £4.50), Oban (3hr., £9.80), Inverness (4hr., £11), and London (8hr., £13).

Public Transportation: Glasgow's transportation system includes suburban rail, a dazzling variety of private bus services, and the **Underground (U),** a circular subway line, a.k.a. the Clockwork Orange (runs Mon.-Sat. 6:30am-11pm, Sun. 11am-6pm; 65p). Wave wildly to stop buses and carry exact change (usually 55-80p).

Laundry: Coin-Op Laundromat, 39-41 Bank St. U: Kelvinbridge. Soap and change available. Open Mon.-Fri. 9am-8pm, Sat.-Sun. 9am-5pm.

Gay and Lesbian Switchboard: tel. 332 83 72. Staffed Wed. 7-10pm.

Pharmacy: Boots, 200 Sauchiehall St. (tel. 332 07 74 or 332 19 25). Open Mon.-Wed. 8:30am-6pm, Thurs. 8:30am-7pm, Fri.-Sat. 8:30am-6pm, Sun. 10am-5pm.

Emergencies: Dial 999; no coins required.

Police: Stewart St. (tel. 532 30 00).

Internet Access: The Internet Café, 569 Sauchiehall St. (tel. 564 1052). £2.50 for 30min.; students £2. Open Mon.-Fri. 9am-11pm, Sat. 10am-11pm, Sun. 11am-11pm.

Post Office: Post offices are sprinkled about. Near George Sq., try 47 St. Vincent St., open Mon.-Fri. 8:30am-5:45pm, Sat. 9am-12:30pm. **Postal Code:** G2 5QX.

Telephone Code: 0141.

ACCOMMODATIONS

In the summer, try to reserve rooms a month in advance, or call the **SYHA hostel** in Loch Lomond, less than an hour north (see p. 185). In addition to the places listed below, the universities in town provide dorm accommodations during the summer. The **University of Glasgow,** 52 Hillhead St. (tel. 330 53 85; open Mon.-Fri. 9am-5pm), offers housing in six dorms, including **Queen Margaret Hall,** 55 Bellshaugh Rd. (tel. 334 21 92), near Byres Rd. (£20.50, students £14.75). The **University of Strathclyde** has rooms at **Baird Hall,** 460 Sauchiehall St. (tel. 332 64 15; £15-19.50); and at the **Campus Village** dorms (tel. 552 06 26; £9-22.50) off Cathedral St. Glasgow's **B&Bs** cluster on both sides of Great Western Rd. in the University area, or east of the necropolis near Westercriags Rd.

SYHA Youth Hostel, 7-8 Park Terr. (tel. 332 30 04), in a beautiful residential area. U: St. George's Cross. From Central Station, take bus 44 or 59 to the first stop on Woodlands Rd. (at Lynedoch St.); from Queen St. Station or Buchanan bus station, take bus 11. Once the home of an English nobleman, the hostel retains an air of luxury. Bike shed and laundry facilities. £11.50-12.50. Breakfast included.

Glasgow Backpackers Hostel, Kelvin Lodge, 8 Park Circus (tel. 332 54 12). U: St. George's Cross. Sunny, spacious, and laid-back. Roomy kitchen. Night keys available. Dorms £9.50. Doubles £21. Open July to mid-Sept.

Alamo Guest House, 46 Gray St. (tel. 339 23 95). Quiet, spacious rooms and plenty of bathrooms. Singles £18, with bath £20. Doubles £34.

McLay's Guest House, 268 Renfrew St. (tel. 332 47 96). Near the intense scene at the Glasgow School of Art and Sauchiehall St. Its size makes it feel more like a hotel than a B&B. Singles £18.50-21. Doubles £35-39. Family rooms for 4 £48-55.

FOOD

Like many university towns, Glasgow has many cheap restaurants with great food. Cafés cluster behind Byres Rd. on **Ashton Lane,** a cobblestone alley lined with 19th-century brick facades. For groceries, try **Safeway,** 373 Byers Rd. (open Mon.-Sat. 8am-8pm, Sun. 9am-6pm), or **Grassroots,** 48 Woodlands Rd. (Open Mon.-Wed. and Fri. 8:45am-6pm, Thurs. 8:45am-7pm, Sat. 9am-6pm, Sun. 11am-3pm.)

The Bay Tree Vegetarian Café, 403 Great Western Rd. Vegans and vegetarians rejoice! Superb hot meals £4. Large salad £3.50. Hot breakfast all day Sun. £3.25. 10% student discount. Open Mon.-Fri. 8:30am-9pm, Sat. 9am-9pm, Sun. 11am-8pm.

Pierre Victoire, at three locations: 16 Byers Rd., 91 Miller St., and 415 Sauciehall St. French, reasonably priced, and delicious. 2- and 3-course menus £4.90-6.95. Open Mon.-Sat. noon-3pm and 6-11pm, Sun. noon-3pm and 6:30-10pm.

The Willow Tea Room, 217 Sauchiehall St., upstairs from Henderson the Jewellers. Over 28 kinds of tea (£1.30 a pot) and marvelous sweets. Meringues with strawberries and cream £2. Open Mon.-Sat. 9:30am-4:30pm, Sun. 11:30am-4:15pm.

Insomnia Café, 38-40 Woodlands Rd., near the hostels. Open 24hr. Sleepless students. Samosas with riata and onion £2.45. Breakfast quesadilla £2.75.

Grosvenor Café, 31-35 Ashton Lane, behind U: Hillhead. Stuff yourself silly from the endless menu—most dishes under £1. More elaborate dinner menu Tues. 7-11pm. Open Mon. 9am-7pm, Tues.-Sat. 9am-11pm, Sun. 11am-5:30pm and 7-11pm.

SIGHTS

The Gothic **Glasgow Cathedral,** at the eastern end of Cathedral St., which runs behind Queen St. Station, was the only full-scale cathedral spared the fury of the 16th-century Scottish Reformation. (Open April-Sept. Mon.-Sat. 9:30am-6pm, Sun. 2-5pm; Oct.-March Mon.-Sat. 9:30am-4pm, Sun. 2-4pm.) Next door is the entrance to the giant **necropolis,** a terrifying hilltop cemetery. Nearby, the **St. Mungo Museum of Religious Life and Art** surveys world religions from Hindu to Yoruba and boasts an impressive array of sacred objects (open Mon. and Wed.-Sat. 10am-5pm, Sun. 11am-5pm; free). Charles Rennie Mackintosh, Scotland's most famous architect, designed the **Glasgow School of Art,** 167 Renfrew St. (tours Mon.-Fri. 11am-2pm, Sat. 10:30am; £3.50, students £2). **Queen's Cross,** 870 Garscube Rd., designed by the batty genius, houses a society dedicated to him (open Mon.-Fri. 10:30am-5pm; free).

The West End's residential **Park Circus** area features elegant parks and intact examples of early Victorian terracing. A block west, students come to tan on the grassy slopes of **Kelvingrove Park,** a large wooded expanse on the banks of the River Kelvin. In the southwest corner of the park, just off the intersection of Argyle and Sauchichall St., the spired **Art Gallery and Museum** displays works by Rembrandt and Van Gogh as well as exhibits on armor, bee keeping, and natural history (open Mon.-Sat. 10am-5pm, Sun. 11am-5pm; free). The **Museum of Transport,** on Dumbarton Rd., displays a collection of full-scale original trains, trams, and automobiles in a huge warehouse (open Mon.-Sat. 10am-5pm, Sun. 11am-5pm; free). To the west, on the bridge over the river, you can see the soaring tower of the **University of Glasgow**'s central building. Founded in 1451, the university is Britain's fourth oldest. The central university building is off Byres Rd. on University Ave. These newly refurbished arches support the **Hunterian Museum,** the oldest museum in town, which includes an interesting ancient coin collection (open Mon.-Sat. 9:30am-5pm; free).

ENTERTAINMENT

Glaswegians play more and party harder than Edinburgh's inhabitants. The **Ticket Centre,** City Hall, Candleriggs (tel. 227 55 11; phones staffed Mon.-Sat. 9am-9pm, Sun. noon-5pm), will tell you what's playing at the city's dozen-odd theaters. Pick up a free copy of the *City Live!* events calendar here as well (open Mon.-Sat. 9:30am-6:30pm, Sun. noon-5pm). The arts scene intensifies during several spring and summer festivals. The **Mayfest** arts festival offers a good program of Scottish and international theater and music; for information, write to 18 Albion St., Glasgow, G1 1LH (tel. 552 84 44). The annual **Glasgow International Jazz Festival** (June 26-July 5 in 1998) brings such greats as B. B. King and Betty Carter to town (same address as Mayfest; tel. 552 35 52), while in early August, the city hosts the largest **International Early Music Festival** in the U.K. (call 333 11 78 for more info). During the **World Pipe Band Championships** in mid-August, the skirling of bagpipes is heard for miles.

No matter where you end your day of sight-seeing, you won't be more than a block or so from a welcoming pub. The infamous Byres Road pub crawl usually starts with a trip to **Tennant's Bar** and then proceeds toward the River Clyde. At **The Ubiquitous Chip Bar,** 12 Ashton Lane, near U: Hillhead off Byres Rd., local academics and writers converse amid old wood, stained glass, and quiet tables (open Mon.-Thurs.

11am-11pm, Fri.-Sat. 11am-midnight, Sun. 12:30-11pm). **Halt Bar,** 160 Woodlands Rd., 2 blocks from the youth hostel, attracts all sorts. One side is dark and deafening, the other hot and humid (open Mon.-Thurs. 11am-11pm, Fri.-Sat. 11am-midnight). **The Horseshoe Bar,** 17-21 Drury St., in the city center, is a magnificent Victorian bar with etched mirrors and carved wooden walls. As many as 25 bartenders are needed to preside over the longest continuous bar in the U.K. (open daily 8:30pm-midnight).

The city's sizable student population guarantees a lively club scene as well. *The List* (£1.90 from newsstands) is the best source of info on the Glasgow-Edinburgh club scene. Unless specified otherwise, club hours are generally 11pm to 3am; cover charges run £2-8 with occasional student discounts. Head to **Nice n' Sleazy,** 421 Sauchiehall St., where patrons enjoy music and choose from 15 flavors of Absolut vodka (open daily 11:30am-midnight). Look for two skeletons just outside the second floor windows of **Archaos,** 25 Queen St. With frequent student discounts, musical variety, and several floors, it's no wonder that it's packed. Across the street, **Garage,** 490 Sauchiehall St., swallows hordes of students into its vortex of Mad Hatter decor. Grunge and indie resound in the **Cathouse,** 15 Union St., with mostly student patrons. **Bennet's,** 80 Glassford St., attracts a gay crowd with upbeat dance music.

■ Near Glasglow: Arran

Billed as "Scotland in Miniature," the **Isle of Arran,** is easily accessible from Glasgow's Central Station. Take the **train** west to Ardrossan on the Firth of Clyde (45min., £4), and from there take the **Calmac ferry** (tel. (01770) 30 21 66) which makes the crossing to **Brodick,** Arran's largest town. Brodick's **tourist office** (tel. (01770) 30 23 95), in the round building at the base of the pier, distributes free maps and info on the island's numerous **hiking options** (open May-Sept. Mon.-Sat. 9am-7:30pm, Sun. 10am-5pm). **Brodick Cycles,** down Shore Rd. (tel./fax (01770) 30 22 72), rents bikes. (£2-5 per hr.; £4.50-9 per day. Open mid-March to mid-Oct. daily 9am-1pm and 2-6pm.) The popular ascent of **Goatfell** (2866 ft.; 4-5hr.) lies between the **Brodick castle** and the heritage museum; the views from the top are stellar. As the Ancient seat of the Dukes of Hamilton, the castle has a fine porcelain collection and scores of dead beasties. (Open April-Oct. daily 11:30am-5pm. Last admission 4:30pm. Castle and gardens £4.50, students £1.50.) To rest your weary bones try **Mrs. Wilkie** (tel. (01770) 30 28 28) at Cala Sona at the top of Alma Pk. (£13), and stock up on necessities at the **Co-op,** across from the ferry terminal (open Mon.-Sat. 8am-8pm, Sun. 10am-6pm). The small town of **Lochranza,** 14 mi. from Broddick, offers opportunities to explore the northern areas of the island, while **Blackwaterfoot,** is a good base for jaunts to the prehistoric sites in the west. **Bus** transport throughout the island is convenient and cheap; just flag down a driver and hop on.

Loch Lomond and the Trossachs

Loch Lomond The hills of the Scottish uplands begin to swell 30 mi. from Glasgow and grow into majestic peaks as they undulate northward. Just 45 minutes northwest of Glasgow, **Loch Lomond** is the closest that most foreigners get to the Highlands. Visitors who undertake hikes in such roadless areas as the northeastern edge of Loch Lomond are rewarded with quiet splendor. Small, rough beaches make fine spots for lazy picnics and paddles. **West Highland Way** snakes along the entire eastern side of the Loch, 95 mi. from Milngavie north to Fort William.

Balloch, at the Loch's south tip, is the "major" town in the area. Across the River Leven, the **Balloch Castle Country Park** provides 200 acres of beach, woods, gardens, ancient ruins, and a **Visitor's Centre/Ranger Station** (open Easter-Oct. daily 10am-6pm). The town's **tourist office,** Old Station Building, Balloch Rd. (tel. (01389) 75 35 33), books rooms and sells walking guides and maps. (Open July-Aug. daily 9:30am-7:30pm; June 9:30am-6pm; Sept. 9:30am-7pm; April-May and Oct. 10am-5pm.) **Trains** run from the station across the street from the tourist office on Balloch Rd. to Glasgow's Queen Station (45min.; £2.85). The **bus station** is a few paces down

Balloch Rd., but buses bypassing the town pick up passengers on the A82 near the roundabout. **Sweeney's Cruises** run boat tours of Loch Lomond starting on the tourist office's side of the River Leven (1hr.; £4). **Buses** 305 and 307 also make the trek (£2.80) and continue to **Luss** on the Loch's western side (from Glasgow £3.70). To reach the eastern side, take bus 309 from Balloch to **Balmaha** (40min.).

The **SYHA Loch Lomond Youth Hostel** (tel. (01389) 85 02 26) is a stunning 19th-century castle-like building 2 mi. north of Balloch. Call ahead to book a room (£8.15-9.15). The **SYHA Rowardennan Youth Hostel** (tel. (01360) 87 02 59) is the first hostel along the West Highland Way (£7.75; open March-Oct.). To get there, take the Inverbeg ferry (tel. (01301) 70 23 56) across the Loch to Rowardennan (April-Sept. 3 per day; £3). In bad weather, summon the small launch from Rowardennan by jumping up and down and raising an orange ball on a flagpole. In Balloch, **B&Bs** congregate on Balloch Rd. The **Tullichewan Caravan and Camping Site** (tel. (01389) 75 94 75) is located on Old Luss Rd. up Balloch Rd. from the tourist office (tent and 2 people £9; closed Nov.). They also rent mountain bikes (£10 per 8hr.).

Trossachs The gentle mountains and lochs of the **Trossachs** form the southern boundary of the Highlands, northeast of Loch Lomond. A few buses link Glasgow to **Aberfoyle** and **Callander,** the area's two main towns. The A821 winds through the heart of the Trossachs between Aberfoyle and Callander, passing near beautiful **Loch Katrine,** the Trossachs' original lure and the setting of Scott's *The Lady of the Lake.* A road for walkers and cyclists traces the Loch's shoreline. Cyclists can rent bikes on the pier (tel. (01877) 38 26 14; £10 per day; open April-Sept. daily 10am-5:30pm). Nearby, 1207 ft. **Ben A'an'** hulks over the Trossachs; the rocky one-hour hike up begins a mile from the pier, along the A821. The **S.S. Sir Walter Scott** (tel. (0141) 955 01 28) steams between Loch Katrine's Trossachs Pier and Stronachlachar (April-Oct.; £3.70). Getting to this area is tough: your best bet is to ask in Aberfoyle or Callander about **post buses.** Or try **The Trossachs Trundler,** which creaks to Callander, Aberfoyle, and Trossachs Pier in time for the sailing of the *Sir Walter Scott* (buses run July-Sept.; Day Rover £4.50). Service Bus 59 leaving from Stirling bus station connects with the Trundler in Callander (Stirling Trossachs Trundler Rover £7.40). Call the **Stirling Council Public Transport Helpline** at (01786) 44 27 07 for info.

Stranraer

Located on the westernmost peninsula of Dumfries and Galloway, Stranraer is the place to get a ferry to Northern Ireland—don't ask for more. **Stena Sealink** (tel. (01233) 64 70 47) leave for Belfast (2-3½hr.; return £44-52, students £32-38, bikes free). Arrive an hour before departures; ferries sometimes leave early depending on weather conditions. The **Seacat Hoverspeed** (tel. (0345) 52 35 23) shudders through the Irish Sea to Belfast (1hr.; £25-32, students £16-22, bikes £5). **Trains** connect Glasgow to Stranraer (2½hr., £18.50); **buses** run to Glasgow (3-4hr.) and to London (9hr.) via Manchester (6½hr.). The **tourist office,** 1 Bridge St. (tel. (01776) 70 25 95), posts a list of **B&Bs** and books rooms for a deposit. (Open June-Sept. Mon.-Sat. 9:30am-6pm, Sun. 10am-6pm; April-May and Oct. Mon.-Sat.9:30am-5pm, Sun. 10am-4pm; Nov.-March Mon.-Sat. 10am-4pm.) Should you fancy some munchies for the ride, visit the **Tesco supermarket** near the ferry terminal.

Aberdeen

The center of Britain's North Sea oil industry, Aberdeen offsets its dirt and smog with attractive parks, a vibrant university, and proximity to some of the finest castles and least crowded Scottish countrysides. **Old Aberdeen** and **Aberdeen University** are a short bus ride (1, 2, 7, or 15) from the city center. Squirm to see the intricately carved "misery seats" in the 16th-century **King's College Chapel** (open daily 9am-4:30pm). The twin-spired, 14th-century **St. Machar's Cathedral** has less torturous features, including a heraldic ceiling and stained glass (open daily 9am-5pm). The impressive

Aberdeen Art Gallery, Schoolhill (tel. (01224) 64 63 33), houses many English, French, and Scottish paintings, and hosts summertime drama and music performances (open Mon.-Sat. 10am-5pm, Sun. 2-5pm; free). Aberdeen's largest park, **Hazlehead,** off Queen's Rd., has an aviary and extensive woodlands. Take bus 14 or 15 to Queen's Rd. and walk 1 mi. on Hazlehead Ave. A sandy **beach** stretches north for about 2 mi. from Aberdeen's old fishing community at Footdee.

The **tourist office,** St. Nicholas House, Broad St. (tel. (01224) 63 27 27, 24hr. info 63 63 63), books rooms. Ask for *It's Free in Aberdeen.* (Open July-Aug. Mon.-Sat. 9am-7pm, Sun. 10am-5pm; Sept. and June Mon.-Sat. 9am-5pm, Sun. 10am-2pm; Oct.-May Mon.-Fri. 9am-5pm, Sat. 10am-noon.) **Trains** zip from the station on Guild St. to Edinburgh (£31), Glasgow (£34), London (£78), and Inverness (£18). National Express and Scottish Citylink **buses** travel from the station on Guild St. (tel. (01224) 21 22 66) to the same cities for half the price. The **Aberdeen Ferry Terminal,** Jamieson's Quay (tel. (01224) 57 26 15), is the only place on mainland Britain where ferries go to Lerwick on the Shetland Islands and Stromness on the Orkney Islands. **Mrs. Hoffman,** 201 Great Western Rd. (tel. (01224) 58 78 23), and other B&Bs on the same street provide rooms (£15-23). Take bus 17, 18, or 19 or walk 20 minutes from the train and bus stations. The enormous **SYHA George VI Memorial Hostel,** 8 Queen's Rd. (tel. (01224) 64 69 88), has spacious dorms (£7.10-9.60; lights out 11:30pm; curfew 2am). For camping, try **Hazlehead Park** (tel. (01224) 32 12 68) on Groats Rd. Take bus 14 or 15 (£3.50-7 per tent). The **Safeway supermarket** is at 215 King St. (open Mon.-Thurs. and Sat. 8am-8pm, Fri. 8am-10pm, Sun. 9am-6pm).

Inverness

The charms of Inverness, like the Loch Ness monster herself, are somewhat elusive, but persistent visitors won't be disappointed. In town, don't expect many reminders of Shakespeare's *Macbeth;* nothing of the "auld Castlehill" remains, and Banquo's ghost has no ruins to haunt. Instead, visit the **Balnain House,** 40 Huntley St., try your hand at the bagpipe or *clarsach* (harp), and hear live Highland music daily. (July-Aug. Mon.-Fri. 10am-8pm, Sat.-Sun. 10am-6pm; June Tues.-Sun.10am-5pm; Sept.-May Tues.-Sat. 10am-5pm.) Just 5 mi. south of Inverness, unfathomably deep and unbelievably famous, **Loch Ness** guards its secrets. An easy way to see the loch is on the tour run by **Inverness Traction,** leaving from the tourist office at 10:30am, 11:15am, and 2:30pm (£7.50, students £6). A mile south of Culloden, to the east of Inverness, the chambered cairns (mounds of rough stones) of the **Cairns of Clava** recall Bronze Age civilizations. Nearby, the restored **Castle Stuart** was the residence of the Earls of Moray and the Stuart family in the 17th century. (Open Easter to mid Oct. 10am-5pm; mid-Oct. to Easter 11am-4pm. £3.50, students £2.50.) The **Cawdor Castle** and its stunning garden maze, have entertained the Thane's descendants since the 15th century (open May to mid-Oct. daily 10am-5pm; £5, students £4).

The **tourist office,** Bridge St. (tel. (01463) 23 43 53), can put you on the trail of Nessie. (Open July to mid-Sept. Mon.-Sat. 9am-8:30pm, Sun. 9:30am-6pm; mid-May to June Mon.-Sat. 9am-6pm, Sun. 9:30am-5:30pm; call for off-season hours.) Buy a **Tourist Trail Day Rover** (£6, students £4) to travel by bus from Inverness to Cawdor Castle, Castle Stuart, other sites near Culloden, and back to Inverness. **Trains** run from Station Sq. (tel. (01463) 23 89 24) to Aberdeen (£18), Edinburgh and Glasgow (£28), and London (£78). Scottish Citylink provides frequent **bus** service to most destinations, including London (£41), Edinburgh (£12), and Glasgow (£11). Stay at the **Inverness Student Hotel,** 8 Culduthel Rd. (tel. (01463) 23 65 56); the extroverted staff also runs a resource center (reception open daily 6:30am-2:30am; £8.50-8.90). From the stations, walk left along Academy St., turn right onto Union and left on the pedestrian Drummond St., then look for signs for the **Ho-Ho Hostel,** 23a High St., (tel./fax (01463) 22 12 25; dorms £8.50, twins or doubles £9.50).

HIGHLANDS AND ISLANDS

The Highlands Boundary Fault stretches northeast from Arran Island to Aberdeen, marking the southern boundary of the Highlands and Islands. Scotland's frayed northwest coast, cut by sea lochs and girded by islands, remains the most beautiful region in Scotland and one of the last stretches of true wilderness in Europe. Even in tourist season, you can easily hike for a full day without seeing another human being. The mainland towns of Oban, Fort William, Glencoe, Ullapool, and Thurso allow access to the islands. Although bus routes criss-cross the region and boat services connect more than 40 islands to the mainland, you often can't make more than one or two journeys a day on any form of transportation, even in high season.

Caledonian MacBrayne Ferries (tel. (01475) 65 01 00; fax 65 02 62)), known locally as "Cal-Mac" or "MacBrayne," sail from Oban to most southern Hebrides islands. Ferries go to Craignure on Mull (40min., £3.15); Coll and Tiree, two islands west of Mull, stopping at Tobermory on Mull (Mon., Wed., and Sat.; Tues. and Fri. without the Tobermory stop; to Tobermory 1¾hr., £7.50; to Coll 3hr. or Tiree 4¼hr., £10.15); and Barra (Mon. and Wed.-Sat.; 5hr., £16).

Oban and the Lower Hebrides

Three hours by bus or train from Glasgow, **Oban** (OH-ben), the busiest ferry port on the west coast, endears itself with sporadic outbursts of small-town warmth. If you tire of the busy pier, gaze at the bay from **McCaig's Tower,** built between 1902 and 1906 to employ local masons, or walk 15 minutes north of town to the crumbling tower of **Dunollie Castle.** The **tourist office,** Argyll Sq. (tel. (01631) 56 31 22), is friendly but very busy. (Open July-Aug. Mon.-Sat. 9am-9pm, Sun. 9am-5pm; off-season reduced hours.) Sleep in peach bunkbeds at **Oban Backpackers Lodge,** 21 Breadalbande St. (tel. (01631) 56 21 07; £8.90). The **SYHA Youth Hostel,** Corran Esplanade (tel. (01631) 56 20 25), hugs the waterfront (£8.60-9.60; open March-Dec.).

The **tourist office,** St. Nicholas House, Broad St. (tel. (01224) 63 27 27; 24hr. info 63 63 63), books rooms. Ask for *It's Free in Aberdeen.* (Open July-Aug. Mon.-Sat. 9am-7pm, Sun. 10am-5pm; Sept. and June Mon.-Sat. 9am-5pm, Sun. 10am-2pm; Oct.-May Mon.-Fri. 9am-5pm, Sat. 10am-noon.) **Trains** zip from the station on Guild St. to Edinburgh (£31), Glasgow (£34), London (£78), and Inverness (£18). National Express and Scottish Citylink **buses** travel from the station on Guild St. (tel. (01224) 21 22 66) to the same cities for half the price. The **Aberdeen Ferry Terminal,** Jamieson's Quay (tel. (01224) 57 26 15), is the only place on mainland Britain where ferries go to Lerwick on the Shetland Islands and Stromness on the Orkney Islands. **Mrs. Hoffman's,** 201 Great Western Rd. (tel. (01224) 58 78 23), and other B&Bs on the same street provide rooms (£15-23). Take bus 17, 18, or 19 or walk 20 minutes from the train and bus stations. The enormous **SYHA George VI Memorial Hostel,** 8 Queen's Rd. (tel. (01224) 64 69 88), has spacious dorms (£7.10-9.60; lights out 11:30pm; curfew 2am). For camping, try **Hazlehead Park** (tel. (01224) 32 12 68) on Groats Rd. Take bus 14 or 15 (£3.50-7 per tent). The **Safeway supermarket** is at 215 King St. (open Mon.-Thurs., Sat. 8am-8pm, Fri. 8am-10pm, Sun. 9am-6pm).

Fort William and the Road to the Isles

Fort William no longer has a fort, but it could use one to fend off summer tourists. Mountaineers come for the challenge of 4406 ft. **Ben Nevis,** one of the highest peaks in Britain. The main trail starts just past the town park; allow eight to nine hours for the hike to the top and back. Visitors to the **Nevis Range** ski area (tel. (01397) 70 58 25) enjoy Scotland's longest ski run and a state-of-the-art **gondola** (return £6). The **tourist office** (tel. (01397) 70 37 81) provides information on the area's attractions. (Open May-Sept. Mon.-Sat. 9am-8pm, Sun. 9am-6pm; Oct.-April Mon.-Thurs. 10am-

4pm, Fri. 10am-5pm; Jan.-April Sat.-Sun. 10am-1pm.) Just five minutes from town, the **Ft. William Backpackers Guesthouse** (tel. (01397) 70 07 11), Alma Rd., welcomes visitors with a hot cup of tea and a cozy bed (£8.90; breakfast £1.40). The **SYHA Glen Nevis Youth Hostel** (tel. (01397) 70 23 36) stands 3 mi. east of town on the Glen Nevis Rd. (curfew 2am; £8.90). On the opposite side of the River Nevis, the **Ben Nevis Bunkhouse** (tel. (01397) 70 22 40) lies 2 mi. from town along Achintee Rd. (£8). The **Glen Nevis Caravan & Camping Park** (tel. (01397) 70 21 91) is on Glen Nevis Rd., half a mile before the SYHA hostel (£1.30, tents £4.60-5.78, reduced prices off season; open mid-March to Nov.).

Trains wind coastward through the mountains from Fort William to **Mallaig** along the famous "Road to the Isles." On the way, disembark at Arisaig or Morar to reach the **Silver Sands** (white beaches). Walk 3 mi. along the A830 from the station at Arisaig or Morar to reach a **campsite** near secluded beaches. The **tourist office** (tel. (01687) 46 21 70) in Mallaig is around the block from the rail station. (Open July-Aug. Mon-Sat. 9am-8pm, Sun. 10am-5pm; Easter-June and early-late Sept. Mon.-Sat. 9am-6:30pm, Sun. 10am-5pm; mid-March to April and late Sept. to mid-Oct. Mon.-Sat. 10am-6:30pm.) In town, catch up on sleep in a roomy bed at **Sheena's Backpackers Lodge** (tel. (01687) 46 27 64; £8.50-12).

Skye

Often described as the shining jewel in the Hebridean crown, Skye radiates unparalleled natural splendor. The **Cuillin Hills,** volcanic peaks surging boldly into a halo of clouds, offer perhaps the most dramatic mountain vistas in Britain. Lush peninsulas and bays mark the extremes of the island near Staffin and Armadale. The new **Skye Bridge** includes a footpath for pedestrians and sends shuttle buses (55p) to Skye. Four Scottish Citylink and Skye-Ways **coaches** run daily from Glasgow to **Kyle of Lochalsh** (5½hr.), on the western edge of mainland Scotland; a similar service also runs from Inverness (2hr.). **Trains** arrive at the Kyle of Lochalsh from Inverness (2½hr.). Transportation on the island is difficult; bus service is infrequent and expensive. Biking or hiking may be better options; many hitch. **Badger Tours** (tel. (01599) 53 41 69) offers a thoroughly enjoyable, full-day tour of Skye's scattered sights for £10 per person. The **tourist office** in Kyle of Lochalsh (tel. (01599) 53 42 76) books B&Bs for £1 on either side of the channel.

Once you've seen the harbor in Kyleakin, move on to the ruins of the **Castle Moil;** legend relates that the original castle on this site was built by "Saucy Mary," a Norwegian princess who stretched a stout chain across the Kyle and charged ships a fee to come through the narrows. Eight miles east along the A87, on an islet in Loch Duich, perches **Eilean Donan Castle,** the restored 13th-century seat of the MacKenzies. Or visit the ruins of **Duntulm Castle,** which guard the tip of the peninsula. The castle was the MacDonald's formidable stronghold until a nurse dropped the chief's baby from the window, cursing the house.

Skye's attractive **SYHA hostels** are distressingly oversubscribed in the summer; call in advance. **Glenbrittle** (tel. (01478) 64 02 78) is in the heart of the Cuillins, accessible only to hikers and those with their own transportation (£6.10; open mid-March to Oct.). **Uig** (tel. (01470) 54 22 11), overlooking the bay on the northern peninsula, is a tough 45-minute walk from the ferry on the A586 (£6.10; open mid-March to Oct.). **Broadford** (tel. (01471) 82 24 42) is the most central, close to both mountains and beaches (£7.75; open April-Dec.). **Armadale** (tel. (01471) 84 42 60; £6.10; open mid-March to Sept.), on the southern tip of Skye, is near the Mallaig ferry and serves as a base for touring the verdant **Sleat Peninsula.** The top-notch **Kyleakin** (tel. (01599) 53 45 85) fills very quickly (£8.15). Several independent hostels await. The **Skye Backpackers** (tel. (01599) 53 45 10) in Kyleakin offers relaxed comfort for £8.90-9.50. Near Broadford, **Fossil Bothy** (tel. (01471) 82 26 44 or 82 22 97) sleeps eight cozily (£7). In Portree, Skye's capital, stay at the **Portree Backpackers Hostel,** 6 Woodpark, Dunvegan Rd. (tel. (01478) 61 36 41; £8.50).

Outer Hebrides

The landscape of the Outer Hebrides is astoundingly ancient; much of the exposed rock here is about three billion years old. The culture and customs of the Hebridean people have also resisted change. Most old and some young islanders still speak Gaelic among themselves. The vehemently Calvinist islands of Lewis and Harris observe the Sabbath strictly: all shops and restaurants close, and public transportation stops on Sundays. Television and tourism are diluting some local customs, but the islands are large and remote enough to retain much of their beauty and charm.

Caledonian MacBrayne ships travelers out. Ferries and infrequent buses connect the islands, and hitchers and cyclists enjoy success except during frequent rain storms. Since ferries arrive at odd hours, try to arrange a bed ahead. The Outer Hebrides are home to the **Gatliff Hebridean Trust Hostels** (Urras Osdailean Nan Innse Gall Gatliff), four 19th-century thatched croft houses converted into simple hostels, open year-round, with enough authenticity and atmosphere to more than compensate for crude facilities (each £4.65). **Camping** is allowed on public land, but freezing winds and sodden ground often make it miserable. For more information, snag a copy of *The Outer Hebrides Handbook and Guide* (£8 at tourist offices).

Lewis and Harris The island of **Lewis** is famous for its atmosphere: pure light and drifting mists off the Atlantic Ocean shroud the untouched miles of moorland and small lochs in quiet luminescence. The unearthly setting is ideal for exploring the **Callanish Stones,** an extraordinary (and isolated) Bronze Age circle. Caledonian MacBrayne **ferries** from Ullapool on the mainland serve **Stornoway,** the biggest town in the Outer Hebrides (Mon.-Sat., £11.40). The **tourist office** (tel. (01851) 70 30 88) is at 26 Cromwell St.; turn right from the ferry terminal, then left on Cromwell St. (open variable hours). The **Stornoway Backpackers Hostel,** 47 Keith St. (tel. (01851) 70 36 28), has free tea, coffee, and cereal and is always open (£8).

Although **Harris** is part of the same island as Lewis, it preserves its separate identity behind the curiously treeless **Forest of Harris** (actually a mountain range). Open hills, softened by a carpet of *machair* and wildflowers, make for wonderful off-trail rambling. **Ferries** (tel. (01859) 50 24 44) serve unlovely **Tarbert** from Uig on Skye (£7.60). The chipper **tourist office** awaits on Pier Rd. (tel. (01859) 50 20 11; open late March to mid-Oct. Mon.-Sat. 9am-5pm and for late ferry arrivals). Rent a bike from **Mr. Mackenzie,** across from the tourist office (£6 per day). The nearest **SYHA Youth Hostel** is 7 mi. away in **Stockinish** (tel. (01859) 53 03 73; £4.65; open mid-March to Sept.), but there are many **B&Bs** near the tourist office.

Barra Little Barra, the southern outpost of the outer isles, is indescribably beautiful—but we'll try. On a sunny day, the island's colors are unforgettable: grassy sand dunes and flawless beaches complement dazzling blue waters wreathed below by dimly visible red, brown, and green kelp. **Kisimul Castle,** bastion of the old Clan MacNeil, inhabits an islet in Castlebay Harbor (boat trips out Mon., Wed., and Sat. 2-5pm; £2.20). West of Castlebay, near Borve, is one squat **standing stone** which allegedly was erected in memory of a Viking galley captain who lost a bet with a Barra man; Archaeologists who excavated the site did indeed find a skeleton and Nordic armor. To see the whole island rent a bike from **Castlebay Cycle Hire** (tel. (01871) 81 02 84; £8) and follow A888, which makes a 14 mi. circle around the rather steep slopes of **Ben Havel.** A Caledonian MacBrayne **ferry** makes the trip between Castlebay on Barra and Oban or Mallaig on the mainland (Mon.-Tues., Thurs.-Fri., and Sun.; 7hr., £16.45). The Castlebay **tourist office** (tel. (01871) 81 03 36) is around the bend to the right from the pier. (Open roughly April to mid-Oct. Mon.-Fri. 9am-5pm, Sat. 9am-4pm, Sun. 11:30am-12:30pm, and for late ferry arrivals.)

Orkney Islands

Orkney rarely fails to enchant visitors with its natural wonders, ancient and medieval artifacts and monuments, and hospitality. Several ferries connect mainland Scotland to the islands. The **Orkney Bus,** which departs daily (May-early Sept.) from the Inverness bus station's platform 10am at 2:20pm, rides to **John O'Groats,** where ferries sail for **Burwick** on the southern tip of Orkney (£36). Two **P&O Scottish Ferries** originating in Aberdeen stop in Stromness most weeks on their way to Lerwick, Shetland. (June-Aug. Sun. and Tues. noon; May and Sept. Sat. noon; Oct.-Dec. Sat. 6pm; Jan.-April times vary. Tel. (01224) 57 26 15 for exact schedule.) On the main island, the largest and busiest city, Kirkwall, lies north of Burwick and east of Stromness; frequent buses connect the three. From the Kirkwall pier, the **Orkney Islands Shipping Co.** (tel. (01856) 87 20 44) ferries passengers to **Sanday** and the smaller islands.

Kirkwall and Stromness **Kirkwall** is the administrative and social center of the Orkney Islands. The sandstone **St. Magnus Cathedral,** begun in 1137, and a few age-old structures at the town center attest to the city's long history. The **tourist office,** 6 Broad St. (tel. (01856) 87 28 56), down the main road from the cathedral, books B&Bs and dispenses advice (open mid-April to Sept. daily 8:30am-8pm; Oct. to mid-April Mon.-Sat. 9:30am-5pm). The friendly **Kirkwall Youth Hostel (SYHA),** Skapa Rd. (tel. (01856) 87 22 43), has affordable prices (open mid-March to Oct.; £7.75). For quiet rooms, try **Vanglee** (tel. (01856) 87 30 13), on Weyland Park off Cromwell Rd. (£12.50). Camping is available off the A965 at the **Pickaquoy Caravan & Camping Site** (tel. (01856) 87 35 35; £3.50-4.15). Stock up on supplies at the **Safeway Supermarket** on Broad St.

Stromness was founded in the 16th century as a fishing and whaling port. The helpful **tourist office** (tel. (01856) 85 07 16) resides in an old warehouse on the pier (usually open for ferry arrivals and departures; call for hours). Nearby, **Brown's Hostel,** 45-7 Victoria St. (tel. (01856) 85 06 61), offers warm, comfortable rooms for £7.50-8. The **SYHA hostel** (tel. (01856) 85 05 89) on Hellihole Rd. doesn't deserve its infernal address (£6.10; open mid-March to Oct.). **The Café** at 22 Victoria St. serves cheap meals (£3-6; open Mon.-Sat. 9am-9pm, Sun. 10am-9pm). The bars at **The Ferry Inn** and **The Stromness Hotel** are popular nightspots for both locals and tourists.

Many important archaeological sites are around Stromness and Kirkwall. **Skara Brae** was once a busy Stone Age village. Nearby on A965, **Standing Stones of Stenness** may be the site of a priests' settlement. On the southern tip of Ronaldsay, 35 mi. from Stromness, perches the **Tomb of Eagles** where you can handle Stone Age tools and skulls and saunter through a Bronze Age house (call ahead (01856) 83 13 39; £2).

Shetland Islands

The Shetland Islands, as well the Orkneys, became part of Scotland in the 15th century when King Christian I of Norway and Denmark mortgaged them to pay for his daughters dowry. Nowhere on the islands can you be farther than 3 mi. from the sea, and they are therefore very vulnerable to nature' whims.

The fastest transit to Shetland is the **British Airways/BABA special** from Kirkwall; ask at the tourist offices in Stromness, Kirkwall, or Lerwick for discounts and booking. **British Airways** (tel. (0345) 22 21 11) also flies from Aberdeen, Edinburgh, and Glasgow. All flights are met by buses to Lerwick (45min., £1.80). **P&O Scottish Ferries** leave weekdays at 6pm (June-Aug. Tues. at noon) from Aberdeen for Lerwick (14hr., £47.50-51). A ferry runs from Stromness on Orkney to Lerwick (Tues. 10pm, Sun. noon; Sept.-May Sun. noon only; 8hr., £36). P&O sends ferries from Shetland to Bergen, Norway (June-Aug. Sat. 10am, £57, berth from £62); Bookings and info are available from P&O Scottish Ferries, P.O. Box 5, Jamieson's Quay, Aberdeen AB11 5NP (tel. (01224) 57 26 15). On the island, tourist offices offer ferry and plane schedules (70p). Shetland's main bus lines are **John Leask & Son** (tel. (01595) 69 31 62) and **Shalder Coaches** (tel. (01595) 88 02 17).

Lerwick and Environs The main city on Shetland, Lerwick lies on the eastern coast of the main island and is served by the A970. The best views of the city and its harbor are from the giant **Fort Charlotte,** a relic of the Cromwellian era. Only 1 mi. west of the town center on Clickimin Rd., the ruins of **Clickimin Broch,** a stronghold from the 4th century BC, still look strong enough to repel invaders (both free).

Ferries arrive at Holmsgarth Terminal, a 20-minute walk northwest of the city center, and smaller Victoria Pier, across from the tourist office downtown. **Shetland Islands Tourism** (tel. (01595) 34 34), at Market Cross, books rooms anywhere on the islands for £1. (Open May-Sept. Mon.-Fri. 8am-6pm, Sat. 8am-4pm, Sun. 10am-1pm; July-Aug. also Sun. 2-5pm; Oct.-April Mon.-Fri. 9am-5pm.) The newly refurbished **SYHA Youth Hostel,** Islesburgh House (tel. (01595) 69 21 14), at King Harald and Union St., is extraordinarily well-equipped (£7.35). Farther from the city, enjoy the panoramic harbor views at **Mrs. Nicholson's,** 133 North Rd. (tel. (01595) 69 33 62; £15-16). You can camp almost anywhere on the island with the landowner's permission. Inexpensive eats cluster in the center of town. The **Hostel Café** offers healthy options at wallet-friendly prices. The **Co-op supermarket** on Commercial Rd. should satisfy all. **The Lounge,** 4 Mounthooly St., is the town's liveliest pub.

Near Lerwick at the southern tip of Mainland is **Jarlshof,** one of the most remarkable archaeological sites in Europe. Here are stacked the remains of human settlement layers from the Neolithic to the Renaissance (open April-Sept. Mon.-Sat. 9:30am-6:30pm, Sun. 2-6:30pm; £2). The north Mainland, largely accessible by car, has wild and deserted coastal scenery; in the northwest, explore the jagged volcanic forms on **Esha Ness.** Hourly ferries (£1) sail to the isle of **Bressay,** an ideal spot ideal for a gentle amble. Hike to the summit of **Ward of Bressay** for a sweeping view of the sea.

Isle of Man

Between Ireland and Britain, the Isle of Man is a pint-sized anomaly in the middle of the Irish Sea. The inhabitants are British and swear allegiance to Queen Elizabeth, but the island proudly touts its own legislature, flag, currency, and language. Politics aside, the island is beautiful—ringed by cliffs, sliced by deep valleys, and criss-crossed by lovable antique trains. Manx's kippers (smoked herring), its most famous delicacy, are boasted to be tastier and oilier (that's a good thing) than the English variety.

The Isle of Man shares the British international **phone code** (44) and accepts British currency, but Manx notes are *not* accepted in the rest of the U.K. The **Isle of Man Steam Packet Company** monopolizes **ferry** service on the island. For reservations, call the Douglas office (tel. (01624) 66 16 61; fax 66 10 65) or the Belfast office (tel. (0345) 52 35 23); bookings can also be made through travel agents or by emailing res@steam-packet.com. Combination **Sail/Rail tickets** to Douglas are available from any British Rail, National Express, or SeaCat station (from London, return £49-65).

Douglas The capital of the island, **Douglas** was once a popular Victorian resort, and the city still maintains railway and horse-tram networks, promenades, and the **Gaiety Theater,** whose gilded and cherubic interior is amazing (tours every Sat. 10:30am; July-Aug. also Thurs. 2:30pm; free). South of the theater, the **Manx Museum** chronicles the island's natural and human history from the Ice Age to the present (open Mon.-Sat. 10am-5pm; free). **Cyberia Internet Café,** 1st. floor, Crescent Leisure Centre, Central Promenade, will get you connected, and the **Cul-de-Sac Bar and Pizzeria,** 3 Market Hill, provides music, drinks, and crowds. **Bushy's Bar,** will hopefully have moved to Loch Promenade by summer 1998. The "madness and capers" associated with this island institution should continue unadulterated (Bushy's beer UK£1.30-1.50). The **tourist office,** Sea Terminal Building (tel. (01624) 68 67 66), has the helpful *What's on the Isle of Man* and a free map of Douglas. (Open Easter-Sept. daily 9am-7:30pm; Oct.-Easter Mon.-Thurs. 9am-5:30pm, Fri. 9am-5pm, Sat. 9am-1pm. Always open for early evening ferry.) Find sunny rooms and a private bar at the **Glen Villa,** 5 Broadway (tel. (01624) 67 33 94; UK£13), or seek out the homey **Seaside Hotel,** 9 Empress Dr. (tel. (01624) 67 47 65; fax 61 50 41; UK£14).

Bulgaria (България)

US$1	**= 1810 lv (Bulgarian leva)**	**100 lv=**	**US$0.06**
CDN$1	**= 1309 lv**	**100 lv=**	**CDN$0.08**
UK£1	**= 2879 lv**	**100 lv=**	**UK£0.04**
IR£1	**= 2654 lv**	**100 lv=**	**IR£0.04**
AUS$1	**= 1317 lv**	**100 lv=**	**AUS$0.08**
NZ$1	**= 1149 lv**	**100 lv=**	**NZ$0.09**
SAR1	**= 385 lv**	**100 lv=**	**SAR0.26**
Country Code: 359		**International Dialing Prefix: 00**	

From the pine-clad slopes of the Rila, Pirin, and Rodopi mountains to the beaches of the beautiful Black Sea, Bulgaria pleases the eye. Evidence of its long history appears in tiny National Revival villages, Greco-Thracian ruins, and 9th-century citadels. But today the desperate pursuit of the West in a country too poor to hide its flaws illustrates that while Bulgaria may love its history and culture, it hates its immediate past.

In the height of Bulgaria's autonomy in the 13th century its borders stretched from the Black Sea to the Aegean and the Adriatic Seas. Many monasteries, palaces, and churches were erected during these years before Ottoman Turks invaded in the 14th century. The Ottoman Empire ruled the land for the next 500 years, until the weakening of the Empire allowed the development of Bulgarian pride. During the National Revival of the late 19th century, Bulgarians reestablished an independent church and championed the use of the Bulgarian language, but the country did not profit from the wars of the 19th and 20th centuries. Post World War II elections made Bulgaria a Communist republic, and the nation failed to realize the post-war boom of the West. In 1989, the Bulgarian Communist Party lost control of the country, but chaotic privatization attempts shifted favor back toward ex-Communists. Elections in the 1990s have produced a rapid parade of non-Communist and ex-Communist governments, while a financial crisis in 1996 raised inflation over 700% and led to massive unemployment. Bulgaria today is among the poorest countries in Europe, and greater political freedom has been balanced by economic hardship.

For more detailed coverage of Bulgaria, peruse *Let's Go: Eastern Europe 1998.*

GETTING THERE

U.S. and EU citizens can visit Bulgaria **visa-free** for up to 30 days. Citizens of other countries, or anyone planning to stay longer than 30 days, must obtain a visa (single-entry US$53, multiple-entry US$123, transit US$43) from their local consulate (see **Government Information Offices,** p. 1). Visas take about 10 days to process, unless you opt for rush service (US$68-88). The application requires a passport, a photograph, and payment by cash or money order. Visas can be extended at a Bureau for Foreigners, located in every major Bulgarian city. The visa price includes a US$20 border tax which the visa-less are required to pay upon entering the country.

For info on traveling to Bulgaria, contact **Balkan Holidays,** 317 Madison Ave., #508, New York, NY 10017 (tel. (212) 573-5530; fax 573-5538). **Train** links from Bulgaria through the former Yugoslavia to Western Europe are now being reestablished. The office for international train tickets is usually in the town center (look for **Rila Travel;** Рила), or you can go to the international ticket counter at Sofia Central Railway Station. Balkan Air, Lufthansa, and British Airways **fly** to Sofia for relatively little. You can also take a **bus** from neighboring countries, or a **ferry** from Istanbul.

GETTING AROUND

The **train** system is comprehensive but slow, crowded, and aged. Direct trains run from Sofia to major towns throughout the country. There are three train types: express (експрес), fast (бърз; *burz*), and slow (пътнически; *putnicheski*). Avoid the

slow trains, which stop at any sign of civilization. Arrive early for a seat. Stations are poorly marked, often only in Cyrillic. Some useful words are: влак (*vlak*—train); автобус (*avtobus*—bus); гара (*gara*—station); перон (*peron*—platform); коловоз (*kolovoz*—track); билет (*bilet*—ticket); заминаващи (*zaminavashti*—departure); пристигащи (*pristigashti*—arrival); спален вагон (*spalen vagon*—sleeping car); първа класа (*purva klasa*—first class); and втора класа (*vtora klasa*—second class).

Slow trains and rising ticket prices make **bus** travel an attractive option. For long distances, the private companies **Group Travel** and **Etap** offer modern buses with A/C, bathrooms, and even VCRs at around 1.5 times the price of train tickets. Buy a seat in advance from the agency office or pay when boarding. Some buses have set departure times; others leave when full. Private companies have great package deals on international travel. **Balkan Air** fares have swollen enormously (Sofia to Varna or Burgas US$159), and there are no youth discounts on domestic flights.

Taxis are everywhere in cities and larger towns. Avoid private taxis, refuse to pay in dollars, and insist on a metered ride *(sus apparata)*. Ask the distance and price per km to do your own calculations. At the Sofia airport, don't pay more than US$10 to reach the center. **Hitchhiking** is risky, but the patient may succeed.

ESSENTIALS

Balkantourist, the former national tourist bureau, maintains offices throughout the country. The offices often change money and book hotel rooms and private accommodations. In a few cities, it may be difficult to get information unless you're booking an expensive excursion or room, but at least they speak English. If you have no luck at the tourist offices, keep in mind that many hotels also provide valuable tourist info.

The **lev** (lv, plural *leva*) is the standard monetary unit, but *Let's Go* lists some prices in U.S. dollars due to recent chaos in the lev's value. As of July 1, 1997, the lev is pegged to the Deutschmark; 1000lv=DM1. Private **exchange bureaus** may be open 24 hours, but often buy only U.S. dollars and major European currencies. Exchange bureaus have a lower rate for AmEx Traveler's Cheques than for cash. You can also change currency or cash AmEx Traveler's Cheques in *leva* (sometimes dollars) at major **banks** such as **BulBank** or **Biohim Bank,** and **Obedinena Bulgarska Banka.** Most banks also accept major credit cards for cash advances (especially MC); otherwise you can use credit cards in larger hotels and more expensive resorts. **ATMs** are becoming an alternative to carrying Deutschmarks or dollars; most are linked to Cirrus, EC, and MC. Bills from before 1974 are worthless.

Public **bathrooms** are often nothing more than a hole in the ground; pack a small bar of soap and toilet paper, and expect to pay 20-50lv for the toilet paper. **Safety concerns** are of special importance in a country where hard currency is desirable; avoid walking alone after dark, even if you know where you're going. *Pedestrians do not have the right of way* in Bulgaria, and some drivers choose to park on sidewalks. There is a growing but very limited acceptance of **homosexuality.**

Communication Making international **telephone** calls from Bulgaria requires tremendous patience. To call collect, dial 0123 for an international operator or have the telephone office or hotel receptionist order the call for you. The operator invariably won't speak English. You can also make international calls at most post offices, but connections are poor outside large cities. Calls to the U.S. average US$2 per minute, but expect to pay up to US$4 per minute at major hotels and resorts. **AT&T Direct** (tel. 008 00 00 10), **Australia Direct** (tel. 1 800 03 23 29), **British Telecom** (tel. 00 800 99 44), **Sprint Access** (tel. 008 00 10 10), and **MCI** (tel. 008 00 00 01) provide direct calling card connections via English-speaking operators. In an **emergency,** dial 150 for fire, 166 for police, and 150 if you need an ambulance.

Some English is often spoken by young people and in tourist areas, but in the countryside you're on your own. The Bulgarian transliteration is much the same as the Russian except that х is *h,* щ is *sht,* and ъ is sometimes transliterated as *â* (pronounced as in English b*u*g). For Cyrillic characters, see p. 740. Keep in mind that Bulgarians shake their heads to indicate "yes" and nod to indicate "no." Also, be aware that many street names will be changed as the country moves further from its communist past; try to find the most recent map.

Yes/no	Да/Не	dah/neh
Hello	Добър ден	DOH-bur den
Please	Моля	MOE-lya
Thank you	Благодаря	blahg-oh-dahr-YA
Where is...?	Къде е...?	kuh-DEH EH
How much does this cost?	Колко струва?	KOHL-ko STROO-va
Do you speak English?	Говорите ли английски?	goh-VOH-rih-tih lih ahn-GLIH-skih
I don't understand	Не разбирам	neh rahz-BIH-rahm
Help!	Помощ	POH-mosht

Accommodations and Camping When you cross the border you will probably be given a yellow **statistical card** to document where you stay each night. If you get one and lose it, you may have difficulty getting a hotel room. Those who do not need a visa to enter the country sometimes do not receive a card.

Private rooms are arranged through Balkantourist or other tourist offices for US$3-11 a night. Be sure to ask for a central location and try to find out if any family members speak English. Or, look for signs reading частни квартири (private rooms). Bulgarian **hotels** are classed by stars; rooms in one-star hotels are almost identical to those in two- and three-star hotels but have no private bathrooms; they average about US$8 for singles and US$30 for doubles. Foreigners are always charged much higher prices than Bulgarians. The majority of Bulgarian **youth Hostels** are located in the countryside and are popular with student groups; try to make reservations through **ORBITA,** Hristo Botev 48 (Христо Ботев; tel. (02) 80 01 02; fax 88 58 14), which can also find rooms in university dorms. Outside major towns, **campgrounds** give you a chance to meet backpackers. Free-lance camping is popular, but you risk a fine and your safety.

Food and Drink Food from kiosks is cheap (1000-2000lv), and restaurants average 4000lv per meal. Kiosks sell *kebabcheta* (кебабчета; small sausage-shaped hamburgers), salami sandwiches, pizzas, *banitsa sus sirene* (баница със сирене; cheese-filled pastries), and filled rolls. Fruits and vegetables are sold in a *plod-zelenchuk* (плод-зеленчук), *pazar* (пазар), and on the street. In summer, Bulgaria is blessed with delicious fruits and vegetables, especially tomatoes and peaches. Try *shopska salata* (шопска салата), an addictive salad of tomatoes, peppers, cucumbers, onions, and feta cheese. *Gyuvech* (гювеч) is mixed stew with meat, onion, peppers, potatoes, and other veggies. Also try *tarator* (таратор)—a cold soup made with yogurt, cucumber, and garlic. Not withstanding these vegetarian delights, Bulgarians put a heavy emphasis on meat. Try *kavarma* (каварма)—a meat dish with lots of onions and sometimes an egg on top. There are also many organ-based dishes such as *mozik* (мозик; brain) or *ezik* (език; tongue). Bulgarians are known for their cheeses and yogurts.

Well-stirred *airan* (айран; yogurt with water and ice cubes) and *boza* (боза; same ingredients as beer, but sweet and thicker) are popular national drinks, excellent with breakfast. Bulgaria exports mineral water; locals swear by its healing qualities (good brands are Gorna Banya and Hissaria). Melnik is famous for its red wine. A 10% **tip** is appreciated but not obligatory.

Sofia София

Sofia's skyline illustrates the many phases of its 1500-year history: both modern Socialist- and capitalist-style high-rises share space with spires, monuments, and minarets. Below, amid the fumes of buses, BMWs, and Moskviches, dwell more than a million Bulgarians, some wearing business suits and talking on cellular phones, some parading around in rags with dancing bears. Sofia is no Prague or Budapest, but that's why you can get coffee and pastries for dimes, and culture and nightlife for quarters.

ORIENTATION AND PRACTICAL INFORMATION

Current **maps** are sold in hotels, tourist agencies, kiosks, and change bureaus. **Bul. Patriarh Evtimii** (бул. Патриарх Евтимий), **bul. Hristo Botev** (Христо Ботев), **bul. Aleksandr Stamboliiski** (Александър Стамболийски), **bul. Knyaz Aleksandr Dondukov** (Княз Александър Дондуков), and **bul. Vasil Levski** (Васил Левски) surround the most administrative and tourist sights. **Pl. Sveta Nedelya** (пл. Света Неделя), the center of Sofia, is recognizable by St. Nedelya Church, the Sheraton Hotel, and Tsentralen Universalen Magazin (TSUM). South from pl. Sveta Nedelya runs the pedestrian bul. Vitosha (Витоша). To the north **bul. Knyaginya Maria Luiza** (Княгиня Мария Луиза) connects to the central **train station,** *tsentralna gara* (централна гара). Young people meet at **Popa,** the irreverent nickname of **Patriarch Evtimii's monument,** where Patriarh Evtimii meets Vasil Levski and **Graf Ignatiev** (Граф Игнатиев). Pick up the *Sofia City Guide* (free at the airport, hotels, and travel agencies) and the *Sofia Guide* (1000lv at Balkan Tour) for sight guides and phone numbers.

Tourist Office: BalkanTour Ltd., Stamboliiski 27/37 (tel. 987 72 33 or 988 52 56; fax 88 07 95 or 83 20 88), 3 blocks from pl. Sveta Nedelya. Books rooms (US$15-44), exchanges currency and traveler's checks, and sells current maps. Arranges bus travel to Istanbul, Prague, Budapest, and other cities. Open daily 8am-7pm.

Budget Travel: ORBITA Travel, Hristo Botev 48 (tel. 80 15 06 or 80 01 02; fax 988 58 14). From pl. Sveta Nedelya, walk up Stamboliiski, and take a left. Finds rooms. Issues and renews ISICs. Open Mon.-Fri. 9am-5:30pm.

Embassies: Citizens of **Canada, Australia,** and **New Zealand** should contact the British embassy. **South Africa,** Vasil Aprilov ul. 3 (Васил Априлов; tel. 44 29 16). **U.K.,** Vasil Levski 38 (tel. 980 12 20 or 980 12 21), 3 blocks northwest of the Palace of Culture (NDK). Open Mon.-Thurs. 8:30am-12:30pm and 1:30-5pm, Fri. 8:30am-1pm. **U.S.,** ul. Suborna 1a (Суборна; tel. 88 48 01 through 05), 3 blocks from pl. Sveta Nedelya behind the Sheraton. Americans are advised to register with the **Consular section,** Kapitan Andreev 1 (Капитан Андреев; tel. 65 94 59), behind Economic Tehnikum. Open Mon.-Fri. 9am-4:30pm.

Currency Exchange: The largest concentrations of exchange bureaus are along bul. Vitosha, Stamboliiski, and Graf Ignatiev. **Bulbank** (Булбанк), pl. Sv. Nedelya 7 (tel. 84 91), across from the Sheraton, cashes traveler's checks (US$1 per transaction). Open Mon.-Fri. 8:30am-12:30pm and 1-4:30pm. **7M** has many branches and gives Visa cash advances for a 6% commission. Open Mon.-Fri. 9am-5pm, Sat. 10am-1pm. **ATMs** accepting Cirrus, Eurocard, and MC, are located at Bulbank and at **Purva Investitsionna Banka** (Първа Инвестиционна Банка), Stefan Karadzha 51 (Стефан Караджа), next to the telephone office.

American Express: Megatours, ul. (*not* bul.) Levski 1 (tel. 981 42 01 or 981 21 67). Take Tsar Osvoboditel (Цар Освободител) to the left of the Mausoleum. Cashes traveler's checks (4.5% commission), replaces cards, and sells plane and bus tickets. The office in Hotel Rila, ul. Kaloyan 6 (Калоян; tel. 980 88 89), Sofia 1000, holds mail. Open Mon.-Fri. 9am-6:30pm, Sat. 9am-noon.

Flights: Airport Sofia (tel. 79 32 11, info tel. 72 24 14, international flights tel. 79 32 11 22). To get to city center, take bus 84 (100lv). The bus stop is on the left from international arrivals; ask for *tsentur* (център). Some airlines offer youth fares. **Balkan Airlines,** pl. Narodno Subranie 12 (Народно Събрание; tel. 88 06 63, reservations 68 41 48; fax 68 94 18), flies to Moscow, Warsaw, Prague, London, Athens, and Istanbul. Open Mon.-Fri. 8am-7pm, Sat. 8am-2pm. **Lufthansa,** Suborna 9 (tel. 980 41 41; fax 981 29 11). Open Mon.-Fri. 9am-5:30pm.

Trains: Sofia's central **train station** is north of the center on Knyaginya Maria Luiza. Trams 1 and 7 travel to pl. Sv. Nedelya; trams 9 and 12 head down Hristo Botev. Buses 85, 213, 305, and 313 get you there from different points in town. Tickets for Northern Bulgaria are sold on the ground floor, while tickets for Southern Bulgaria and international destinations are in the basement. Or pick up domestic and international tickets at the all-purpose **ticket office** (Bulgarian tickets tel. 65 84 02, international tickets 65 71 86), down the stairs in front of the main entry of NDK. Trains run to Athens (50,000lv), Budapest (70,000lv), Istanbul (30,000lv), and Thessaloniki (36,000lv). Open Mon.-Fri. 7am-3pm, Sat. 7am-2pm.

Buses: The bus station at **Ovcha Kupel** (Овча Купел), along Tsar Boris III bul. (Цар Борис III), serves domestic and international travelers. The station can be reached by tram 5 from the Natsionalen Prirodonauchen Muzey near Sv. Nedelya or tram 4 from the train station. For info and tickets, try the office under the NDK (tel. 65 71 87). Private **international and domestic** buses leave from the parking lot across from the central train station. Get tickets at the Billetni Tsentur (Биллетни Център) kiosks, or check on the buses themselves. Pay in leva, US$, or DM. The private bus company **Group Travel,** Ivan Vazov 13 (tel. 981 07 04), goes everywhere in and around Bulgaria. From the Sheraton, walk up Knyaz Dondukov bul. and take a left on Rakovski. To Budapest (US$40) and Prague (DM65). **Matpu** (Матпу), ul. Damyan Gruev 23 (Дамян Груев; tel. 52 50 04 or 51 92 01), services Balkan connections and Athens (US$37, students $30), Belgrade (US$21), Istanbul (US$20), Skopje (US$10), and Tirana (US$26). Pay in leva.

Public Transportation: The system of trams and buses is gleefully cheap (100lv per ride, day-pass 400lv). Buy tickets at kiosks or from the driver. Operating hours are officially 4am-1am, but most lines don't run later than 11pm or earlier than 6am.

Hitchhiking: Hitching in the Sofia area is said to be becoming increasingly dangerous, and drivers rarely stop. Those hitching to Rila Monastery reportedly take tram 5 to highway E79; those headed to Koprivshtitsa take tram 3 from Sofia.

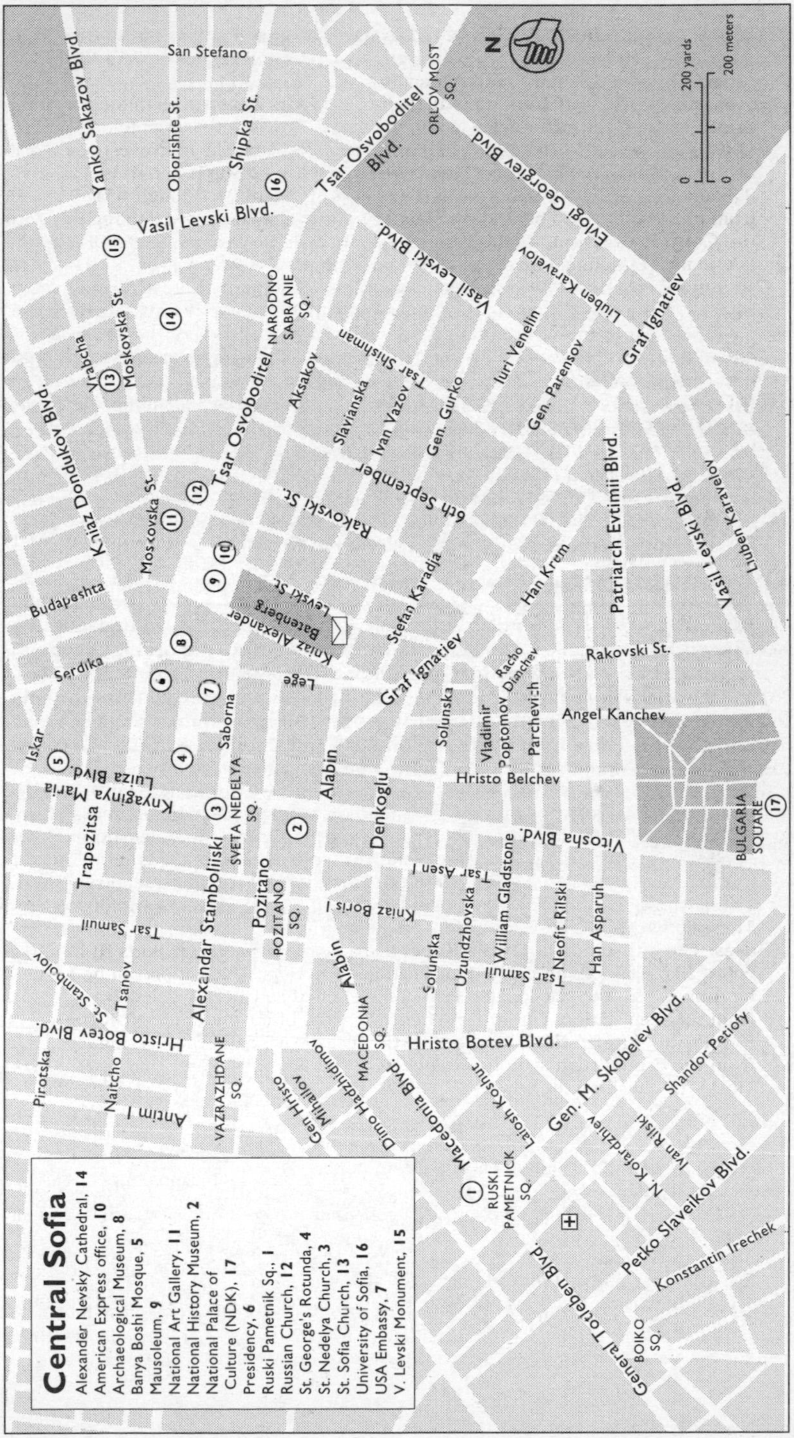
Central Sofia
Alexander Nevsky Cathedral, 14
American Express office, 10
Archaeological Museum, 8
Banya Boshi Mosque, 5
Mausoleum, 9
National Art Gallery, 11
National History Museum, 2
National Palace of Culture (NDK), 17
Presidency, 6
Ruski Pametnik Sq., 1
Russian Church, 12
St. George's Rotunda, 4
St. Nedelya Church, 3
St. Sofia Church, 13
University of Sofia, 16
USA Embassy, 7
V. Levski Monument, 15
N
0
200 yards
200 meters
San Stefano
Yanko Sakazov Blvd.
Oborishte St.
Shipka St.
Tsar Osvoboditel Blvd.
ORLOV MOST SQ.
Evlogi Georgiev Blvd.
Vasil Levski Blvd.
NARODNO SABRANIE SQ.
Moskovska St.
Vrabcha
Kniaz Dondukov Blvd.
Aksakov
Tsar Shishman
Slavianska
Ivan Vazov
Gen. Gurko
Iuri Venelin
Luiben Karavelov
Gen. Parensov
Graf Ignatiev
6th Septemver
Rakovski St.
Patriarch Evtimii Blvd.
Budapeshta
Serdika
Iskar
Kniaz Alexander Batenberg
Levski St.
Stefan Karadja
Han Krem
Lege
Saborna
Knyaginya Maria Luiza Blvd.
SVETA NEDELYA SQ.
Alabin
Solunska
Vladimir Poptomov
Racho Dianchev
Parchevich
Angel Kanchev
Hristo Belchev
Denkoglu
Trapezitsa
Alexandar Stamboliiski
Pozitano
POZITANO SQ.
Vitosha Blvd.
BULGARIA SQUARE
Tsar Asen I
Kniaz Boris I
Tsar Samuil
Uzundzhovska
William Gladstone
Neofit Rilski
Han Asparuh
St. Stambolov
Tsanov
Hristo Botev Blvd.
MACEDONIA SQ.
Pirotska
Naitcho
Antim I
VAZRAZHDANE SQ.
Gen Hristo Mihailov
Dimo Hadzhidimov
Macedonia Blvd.
Laiosh Koshut
Gen. M. Skobelev Blvd.
Shandor Petiofy
RUSKI PAMETNICK SQ.
N. Kofardzhiev
Ivan Rilski
Petko Slaveikov Blvd.
Konstantin Irechek
General Totleben Blvd.
BOIKO SQ.

BULGARIA

Luggage Storage: Downstairs at the central train station. Look for "гардероб" *(garderob)* signs. 300lv per piece. Open 5:30am-midnight.

Laundromats: None really. Hosts of private rooms may do it for a minimal charge. A good dry cleaner is **Svezhest** (Свежест), Vasil Kolarov 19 (Васил Коларов). Open Mon.-Fri. 7am-8pm, Sat. 8am-2pm.

Pharmacies: Purva Chastna Apteka (Първа Частна Аптека), Tsar Asen 43 (Цар Асен). Open *dyenonoshte* (денонощe; 24hr.). **Megapharma,** Vitosha 69 (tel. 980 53 99), across from the NDK. Open daily 8am-11pm.

Medical Assistance: State-owned hospitals offer foreigners emergency aid free of charge. **Pirogov emergency hospital,** Gen. Totleben bul. 21 (Ген. Тотлебен; tel. 515 32 43), across from Hotel Rodina. Open 24hr. Dr. Anton Filchev is an English-speaking **dentist** (tel. 66 29 84). Embassies have more info about medical care.

Emergencies: Ambulance: tel. 150. **Fire:** tel. 160.

Police: tel. 166.

Internet Access: ICN (tel. 916 62 213), on the lower floor of NDK. 5000lv per hr. Also in the **Business Center** in the basement of the Sheraton. US$6 per hr.

Post Office: General Gurko 2 (Ген. Гърко). Walk down Suborna behind pl. Sv. Nedelya, turn right on Knyaz Batenberg (Княз Батенберг), and head left on Gurko. Open for *Poste Restante* (60lv charge) Mon.-Fri. 8am-8pm. Many hotels also provide postal services. **Postal Code:** 1000.

Telephones: On ul. Stefan Karadzhna, near the post office. Use 10lv coins. For collect or card calls, dial 00 800 0010 for **AT&T,** 00 800 0001 for **MCI,** and 00 800 1010 for **Sprint Access.** Open 24hr. **Telephone Code:** 02.

ACCOMMODATIONS AND CAMPING

Hotels are rarely worth their price, but private rooms are better. Apart from ORBITA (see above), which arranges student hotel discounts (US$6-10 per person) and dorm rooms (US$3-4 per person), try **Markella** (Маркела), Knyaginya Maria Luiza 17 (tel. 981 64 21), across from TSUM. They will stamp your statistical card and give you keys and directions (US$4-5 per person; open Mon.-Sat. 8:30am-8:30pm). **Camping Vrana** (tel. 78 12 13) is 10km from the center on E-80, and **Cherniya Kos** (tel. 57 11 29) 11km from the center on E-79; ask at Balkan Tour for details.

Instead of staying in the expensive, sometimes unpleasant hotels in central Sofia, many choose the suburb **Dragalevtsi** (Драгалевци), which offers many private, clean, and cheap hotels. Take tram 9 or 12 to the last stop, then bus 64; get off after 5 stops in the main square. **Hotel Orhideya** (Орхидея), Angel Bukoreshtliev 9 (Ангел Букорешлиев; tel. 67 27 39), and **Hotel Darling** (Дарлинг), Yabulkova Gradina 14 (tel. 67 19 86), the unvarnished house next to Hotel Orhideya, are good bets.

Orbita Hotel, James Baucher bul. 76 (Джеймс Баучер; tel. 639 39), next to Hotel Vitosha. Take tram 9 south past NDK to Anton Ivanov. A 2-star behemoth. Clean, plain rooms have private baths and fridges. Singles US$35. Doubles US$46. Students US$16 and US$20, respectively. Breakfast included with non-discount rates.

Hotel Baldjieva (Балдиева), Tsar Asen 23 (Цар Асен; tel. 87 29 14 or 87 37 84). Walking from pl. Sv. Nedelya to the NDK, Tsar Asen is on the right, parallel to Vitosha. Small rooms with fridges and laundry. Shared bathrooms. Doubles US$35.

Hotel Niky, Neofit Rilski 16 (Неофит Рилски; tel. 51 19 15 or 951 51 04), off Vitosha (Витоша). Wood-paneled rooms have private showers and satellite TV. Shared toilets. Singles US$20. Doubles US$40. Pay in dollars, DM, or leva.

Hotel Tsar Asen (Цар Асен), Tsar Asen 68 (tel. 54 78 01 or 70 59 20). Walking toward the NDK on Tsar Asen, cross Patr. Evtimii and continue 40m. Ring doorbell at the gate. Cable TV and private shower. Singles US$28. Doubles US$34.

Slavyanska Beseda (Славянска Беседа), Slavyanska 3 (tel. 88 04 41; fax 981 25 23), near the post office. From pl. Slaveikov (Славейков) take Rakovski towards Tsar Osvoboditel. Dingy halls lead to clean rooms with bath, TV, phone, and fridge. Ask about hot water. Singles US$30. Doubles US$40. Pay in dollars or leva.

FOOD

From fast food to Bulgarian specialties, inexpensive meals are easy to find. Supermarket **Zornitsa** (Зорница), Denkogli 34 (Денкогли), off Vitosha, is well-stocked (open Mon.-Sat. 8am-8pm). All-night markets lie along Vitosha. An **open market,** known as the women's market (женски пазар; *zhenski pazar*), extends for several blocks. Take Knyaginya Maria Luiza from pl. Sveta Nedelya and make a left on Ekzarh Yosif (Екзарх Йосиф); bring a bag for fresh fruit and vegetables (open daily).

Kushtata (Къщата, "house"), Verila 4 (Верила) off Vitosha near the NDK. A beautiful old house. Entrees 4000-8000lv. Salads 800-3000lv. Soups 860-2400lv. English menu. Open daily noon-midnight.

Borsalino (Борсалино), Chervena Stena 10 (Червена Стена), behind Hotel Orbita. Tasty Bulgarian specialties like *sarmi lozov list* (meat-stuffed vine leaves with sour cream, 1980lv), or *svinsko sus zele* (stewed pork with cabbage, 2400lv). English menu. Open 24hr. At night, take a taxi (about 2000lv).

Eddy's Tex-Mex Diner, Vitosha 4. Break through the saloon doors into one of Sofia's hippest eateries. Buffalo wings (2500lv) and fajitas (4000lv). Open 12:30pm until the customer leaves. Live music nightly from 9:30pm.

Korona (Корона; the Crown), Rakovski 163A. Go up Rakovski from pl. Slaveikov. Vegetarians may like *grutski sumichki* (stuffed vine leaves, 860lv) or "cheeses on grill Bella" (2500lv). Carnivorous main dishes 3000-5000lv. A/C. English menu and English spoken. Open daily 11am-10:30pm.

Café Luciano (Лучано), Rakovski 137. A chain of cafés worth visiting each time you pass one. Low prices and excellent, jet-black caffeine. Open daily 9am-midnight.

SIGHTS AND ENTERTAINMENT

Sofia's two most venerable churches, the late Roman **Sv. Georgi** (Св. Георги; St. George's Rotunda) and the early Byzantine **Sv. Sofia,** date from the 4th and 6th centuries, respectively. St. George's hides in the courtyard of the Sheraton Hotel, accompanied by a complex of ruins that used to be an ancient canal system. St. Sofia, the city's namesake since the 14th century, has 5th-century floor mosaics that have been preserved intact to this day. Across the square from St. Sofia looms the gold-domed **Sv. Aleksandr Nevsky** (Свэ Александър Невски), erected between 1904-1912 in memory of the 200,000 Russians who died in the 1877-78 Russo-Turkish War. The **crypt** houses a spectacular array of painted icons and religious artifacts. (Cathedral open daily 9:30am-7pm; 1500lv, English tour 4500lv. Crypt open Wed.-Mon. 10:30am-12:30pm and 2-6:30pm.) In an underpass between pl. Sveta Nedelya and TSUM, the tiny 14th-century **Tsurkva Hram Sv. Petya Samardzhiiska** (Църква Храм Св. Петя Самарджийска; Church of St. Petya Samardzhiiska) has intriguing frescoes (open Mon.-Sat. 8am-6pm, Sun. 8am-3pm).

Along the way to the central train station from pl. Sveta Nedelya sits the 16th-century **Banya Bashi Mosque** (Баня Баши; open daily 9am-10pm; no shorts, remove shoes at door). Across the street, the **Tsentralen Sinagog** (Централен Синагог), Ekzarh Yosif 16, is one of Europe's largest synagogues. Down Tsar Osvoboditel from pl. Sv. Nedelya, the beautiful 1913 **Sv. Nikolai** (Св. Николай) has five onion domes and was built in accordance with Moscow architectural and decorative styles (open Thurs.-Sun. 9am-10pm). A few interesting museums complement the city's architectural monuments. The labels in the **Natsionalen Istoricheski Muzey** (Национален Исторически Музей; National Museum of History), Vitosha 2, are in Bulgarian only, but a guided tour in English can be arranged. (Open May-Sept. Mon.-Fri. 9:30am-6:30pm; Oct.-April Mon.-Fri. 9:30am-4:30pm. Box office closes at 3:45pm. 5000lv, students 2500lv.) Traditional Bulgaria is preserved at the **Natsionalen Etnograficheski Muzey** (Национален Етнографически) in the Royal Palace building (open Wed.-Sun. 10:30am-5pm; 3000lv, students 1500lv). The **Natsionalna Hudozhestvena Galeriya** (Национална Художествена Галерия; Museum of Fine Arts), with a permanent exhibit of Bulgarian masterpieces, is also located in the Royal Palace (open Tues.-Sun. 10:30am-6pm; 1500lv, students 750lv).

Rakovski is Bulgaria's Broadway, with half a dozen theaters along a half-mile stretch. The **National Opera House,** Rakovski 59 (main entrance at Vrabcha 1; Врабча; tel. 87 13 66), has tickets at the box office to the right of the main entrance (300-10,000lv; open Mon. 9am-5:30pm, Tues.-Fri. 8:30am-7:30pm, Sat. 9am-7pm). The **Natsionalen Dvorets Kultura** (Национален Дворец Култура; National Palace of Culture, NDK), at the end of Vitosha, contains restaurants, theaters, and the country's best cinema; subtitled American movies run 1000lv. The nightlife in Sofia gets wilder every year. Outdoor cafés and bars share **bul. Vitosha** with musicians and dancing bears. **Frankie's Jazz Club/Piano Bar,** Kurnigradska 15 (Кърниградска), off Vitosha across from the American Center, hosts some of Bulgaria's best jazz musicians (cover 500lv; no music in summer; open 10am-2am). Smartly dressed Sofians go to the cafés around the park near the NDK to scam and be scammed, while regulars head to **Yalta** (Ялта), one of Sofia's most venerable discos (cover 1000lv). Euro-techno pop brings down the house at the **Orbilux** disco at Hotel Orbita, Anton Ivanov 76 (Антон Иванов). Music starts around 10pm (cover 200lv; women free). The exceedingly exclusive **Spartakus** (Спартакус), under the Grand Hotel Sofia by pl. Narodno Subranie (Народно Събрание), serves gay and straight clientele.

■ Near Sofia: Rila Monastery

Rilski Manastir (Рилски Манастир), 120km south of Sofia, is the largest and most famous monastery in Bulgaria. Built by Holy Ivan of Rila in the 10th century, the monastery maintained the arts of icon painting and manuscript copying through Byzantine and Ottoman occupations. The 1200 frescoes on the central **chapel** and surrounding walls form an outdoor gallery. The monastery also houses **museums** with religious objects, coins, weapons, and jewelry. (Monastery open daily 6am-dusk; services 6:30am and 4:30pm. Museums 1500lv; English tours 4000lv.) Maps and suggested routes for excellent **hiking** in the nearby hills are posted outside the monastery. Trails are marked by colored lines on a white background.

To reach the monastery, take a **bus** to Rila from Sofia's Ovcha Kupel station (4 per week, 2½hr., 1500lv), or from Sofia's Novotel Europa via Blagoevgrad (Sofia-Blagoevgrad 8-10 per day, 2hr., 1200lv; Blagoevgrad-Rila 6 per day, 1½hr., 600lv); and then take a bus from Rila (2 per day, 1hr., 500lv, last bus at 3:15pm). To stay the night, inquire in room 170 (tel. (099 7054) 22 08) or ask any monk for a heated **monastery cell** (reception open daily 9am-noon and 2-4pm, after 6pm try Room 74; US$15). The **Turisticheska Spalnya** (Туристическа Спалня) next door has packed rooms and showerless bathrooms with holes for toilets (15,000lv), or you can stay at the three-star **Hotel Rilets** (Рилец; tel. (099 7054) 21 06), 15 minutes from the monastery (singles US$24, doubles US$36). **Restaurant Rila,** by the monastery, serves delicious trout (балканска пастърва, 4000lv; open daily 7:30am-11:30pm). The **monastery bakery** sells loaves of bread for 600lv (open daily 7am-6:30pm).

Melnik Мелник

This is what you came to Bulgaria for. Deep in a sandstone gorge, tiny Melnik quietly produces delicious wine in well-preserved National Revival houses. **Kordopulova Kushta** (Кордопулова Къща; Kordopulova's House), the biggest National Revival house in Bulgaria, with a comparably sized wine cellar, was built in 1754 by the Greek Manolous Kordopolous family, who settled here to make and trade wine. Formerly a national museum, it has recently been returned to the heirs of its last owners. To get there, take the right fork of the town's road and look for the biggest house on the hillside to your left (open daily dawn-dusk; free). Mitko Manolev's **Izba za Degustatsiya na Vino** (Изба за Дегустация на Вино; wine tasting cellar; tel. (0997437) 234) is a 200-year-old establishment offering the freshness of its naturally air-conditioned caverns and some of the best Melnik wine (glass 300-400lv, bottle 1200-2000lv; open daily 8am-9pm). To visit, turn left at the fork and climb the hillside on the right through the ruins of the 10th-century **Bolyarska Kushta** (Болярска Къща; Bolyar's House). More ruins dot the hills overlooking the town.

Buses arrive here via Sandanski (Sofia-Sandanski 1 per day, 2½hr., 2400lv; Sandanski-Melnik 4 per day, 40 min., 6000lv) or Blagoevgrad (1 per day, 1hr., 7000lv; Sofia-Blagoevgrad 8-10 per day, 2hr., 1200lv). Although there is no tourist office, maps are sold at hotels and restaurants (1000lv). Private rooms are widely available (2000-4000lv). **Hotel-Vinarna MNO** (Хотел. Ресторант. Винарна; tel. (0997437) 249), on the left 50m past the post office, has 30 beds split between large doubles and triples with private showers (15,000lv or US$10). The **Mencheva Kushta** (Менчева Къща), on the right fork of the town street, serves up a hearty dish of beef, potatoes, cheese, mushrooms, and egg (повече по чорбаджийск; 2400lv) as well as a host of vegetarian and meat dishes (450-3800lv). The owners rent three doubles (10,000lv).

Plovdiv Пловдив

Bulgaria's second city, Plovdiv is a microcosmic kaleidoscope of Bulgarian history and culture. Pass quickly by Soviet-style apartment blocks and stroll into the convoluted **Stari Grad** (Град Пловдив; Old Town), where National Revival houses protrude over the cobblestones below, windows stare into alleys at impossible angles, and churches and mosques hide in secluded corners.

With over 150 houses designated cultural monuments, Plovdiv's *Stari Grad* is a giant historical museum. The area's most ancient treasure is the 2nd-century Roman Marble **Antichen Teatr** (Античен Театр; amphitheater), which now hosts a **Festival of the Arts** in summer and early fall and an **Opera Festival** in June (contact Puldin Tours, below, for details). Take a right off Knyaz Aleksander (Княз Александър) to Stanislav Dospevski (Станислав Доспевски) and walk ahead to reach the theater. In the middle of pl. Dzhumaya (Джумая) lies the **Philipoplis Stadium;** see if you can spot the ancient stones beneath the more recent trash. The mosque that gave its name to pl. Dzhumaya is the **Dzhumaya Dzhamiya** (Джамия), whose colorful minaret peeks between other buildings. At the end of Suborna (Съборна), the **Etnografski Muzei** (Етнографски Музей; Museum of Ethnography) displays ancient Bulgarian crafts including an interesting exhibit on the production of precious rose oil (open Tues.-Sun. 9am-noon and 1-5pm). On a cool evening, head to the fountainside café in the **Tsentralni Park** (Централни Парк), near pl. Tsentralen (пл. Централен), illuminated by multicolored strobes. One of the many **movie theaters** on Knyaz Aleksander is bound to be showing a film in English.

Practical Information, Accommodations, and Food English-speaking **Puldin Tours** (Пълдин), bul. Bulgaria 106 (България; tel. (032) 55 38 48), offers maps in English (but usually with Communist-era street names), finds rooms (US$13-20), and changes money. From the train station in the southwestern corner of the rectangular downtown, ride trolley 102 or 2 (150lv) nine stops to bul. Bulgaria and backtrack a block; look for the office in the northeastern corner of the rectangle (open Mon.-Fri. 9am-5:30pm; until 9pm during fairs). If you can figure out Cyrillic, street vendors sell good maps for 3000lv. **Trains** arrive from Sofia (every hr., 2½hr., 1820lv) on their way to Istanbul and Burgas; **buses** arrive from and leave for Sofia at Yug (Юг) station on the north side of Hristo Botev (Христо Ботев) (every hour, 1hr., 2000lv). **Prima Vista Agency** (Прима Виста), Ivan Vazov 74 (Иван Вазов; tel. (032) 27 27 78; fax 27 20 54) finds private lodgings for visitors (open daily 10am-6pm). **Hostel Touristicheski Dom** (Туристически Дом; tel. (032) 23 32 11), P.R. Slaveykov 5 (П.Р. Славейков) in the Old Town, has clean one- and two-bed dorms with sinks in a National Revival building listed among Plovdiv's monuments. From Knyaz Aleksander (Княз Александър), take Patriarch Evtimii (Патриарх Евтимий), passing under Tsar Boris, into town and hang a left on Slaveykov (lockout midnight; 18,000lv per room). From pl. Tsentralen, walk across Tsar Boris to reach **Hotel Feniks** (Феникс), Kapitan Raicho 79, 3rd fl. (Капитан Райчо; tel. (032) 22 47 29), which has unintentionally antique furniture, laundry, and shared bathrooms (singles US$15, doubles US$30).

Kambanata (Камбаната), Suborna 2B (tel.(032) 26 06 65), has a large number of traditional vegetarian dishes for under US$0.50, but the chef's specialty is "Kambanata," a concoction of filet of pork or veal, cream, mushrooms, smoked cheese and spaghetti (US$2; open daily 10:30am-midnight). **Union Club** (Юнитын Клуб), Hayne 5 (Хайне; new name Metropolit Paisii; Метрополит Пайсий), is run by a master chef and has a 230-item English menu. To get there, walk up Suborna and turn right up an alley before the church, going through the wooden gate (open daily 9am-late).

■ Near Plovdiv: Bachkovo Monastery

About 28km south of Plovdiv lies the 11th-century Bachkovski Manastir (Бачковски Манастир), the second largest in the country. The monastery's treasure is the miracle-working icon of the Virgin Mary and Child, kept in the **Holy Trinity Church** (open daily 7am-dark). To get to Bachkovo, take a **train** from Plovdiv to Asenovgrad (every 30min., 25min., 600lv), then catch a **bus** to the monastery (10min., 250lv). Inquire about the spartan **accommodations** at the administrative office on the monastery's second floor; ask for Brother German (tel. (03327) 277; 10- to 20-bed dorms 2000lv). The monks allow visitors to pitch tents on the lawn for free.

Valley of Roses

Stretching across central Bulgaria along the rail line east from Sofia, the famed Valley of Roses preserves much of the architecture and heritage of the 19th-century National Revival. Unsurprisingly, the smell of roses wafts through the area.

Koprivshtitsa The seemingly sleepy little wood and stone houses of **Koprivshtitsa** (Копривщица) conceal its revolutionary roots. Todor Kableshkov's 1876 "letter of blood" announcing uprising against Ottoman rule was drafted here; the Turks' brutal oppression led to the Russo-Turkish War of 1877-78 and, eventually, Bulgarian independence. Many homes of the uprising leaders are now museums (Къщата-музей): the 1845 house of **Todor Kableshkov** (Тодор Каблешков) has ingeniously carved ceilings (open Tues.-Sun. 8am-noon and 1:30-5:30pm). The house of **Georgi Benkovski** (Георги Бенковски) pays tribute to the leader of the "Flying Troop" of horsemen (closed Tues.). The birthplace of **Dimcho Debelyanov** (Димчо Дебелянов) showcases one of Bulgaria's best lyric poets (closed Mon.). A 1500lv ticket grants entry to all museum houses. The 1817 **Uspenie Bogorodichno** (Успение Богородично; Assumption Church) is said to have been built in 11 days.

Trains from Sofia (1½-2hr., 500lv) stop 10km from Koprivshtitsa. Get off at the stop after Anton, or, on a *burz* (бърз; fast) train, the one after Pirdop. A bus awaits to take you into town (10min., 300lv), but it drives off quickly, so hurry. Get off at the Koprivshtitsa **bus station** (a dark wooden building), which posts the bus and train schedules. To reach the main square, where you'll find a **bank, pharmacy,** and **post office,** backtrack along the river. **Hotel Byalo Konche** (Бяло Конче; tel. (997184) 22 50), up the steep street from the main square, has five doubles, with shared shower and toilet, in a classic Koprivshtitsa house (US$8 per person, breakfast included). **Hotel Dalmatinets** (Далматинец), Georgi Benkovski 62 (Георги Бенковски; tel. (997184) 29 04), is near the end of town, upstream from the Biohim (Биохим) Bank. Five doubles with private showers and 24-hour hot water go for US$10 (US$12 with breakfast). Arrange **private rooms** through the English-speaking owner of the souvenir shop advertising *chastni kvartiri* (частни квартири; tel. (997184) 21 64) in the main square (US$5 per person; open daily 10am-6pm). **Byaloto Konche** has a separate tavern offering splendid full meals for around 2500lv (open daily 8am-late). The **food market** by the stream, past the buses and post office, stocks essentials.

Kazanluk The town of **Kazanluk** (Казанлък) has long been the center of Bulgaria's rose-growing world. During the Rose Festival in the first week of June, the town drowns in a sweet scent which lovingly envelops the song-and-dance troupes, comedians, and soccer stars. Half an hour away from pl. Sevtopolis (Севтополис) awaits the

More Precious than Gold

More expensive by weight than gold and used in luxurious perfumes, over 70% of the world's rose oil is produced in Bulgaria. Workers in the famed Valley of Roses fields pick rose petals, one by one, in late May and early June. A single gram of "attar of roses" (rose oil) requires 2000 petals picked before sunrise. The first roses were grown here by Thracians, and modern rose cultivation began in the 17th century under the Ottomans. Apart from perfume and rose water, Bulgarian rose petals have been used in medicine, jam, tea, vodka, sweet liquor, and syrup. Rose-picking season ends with the annual **rose festival** (Прозник на Розата), held during the first June weekend in Karlovo and Kazanluk.

Muzey na Rozata (Музей на Розата; Rose Museum), which illustrates the history of rose oil production. Next door are **gardens** with over 250 rose varieties (open March 15-Oct. 15 daily 8:30am-5pm; US$1, students US$0.50). To reach the museum from the square, take Gen. Skobelev (Скобелев), go right at the fork, and continue on bul. Osvobozhdenie (Освобождение) towards Gabrovo; buses 5 and 6 run irregularly across from Hotel Kazanluk (100lv). Kazanluk's **Trakiiska Grobnitsa** (Тракийска Гробница; Thracian Tomb) is a 10-minute walk from pl. Sevtopolis. Climb the stairs to the top of the park's hill, the resting place of the original tomb that dates from the turn of the 3rd century BC. The inside has been recreated 20m away (open March-Oct. daily 8:30am-noon and 1:30-6pm; US$1, students US$0.50). Ten kilometers to the south, the man-made **Lake Koprinka** (Копринка) floods the remains of the Thracian city of Sevtopolis. Take bus 3 from the train station (120lv).

Trains arrive often from Sofia (3hr., 1960lv), Burgas (3hr., 1960lv), and Karlovo (1½hr., 800lv); **buses** make the trip from Plovdiv's Sever station (2 per day). From the train station, bul. Rozova Dolina leads to pl. Sevtopolis (пл. Севтополис). Off the square at 23 Pehoten Shipchenski Polk 16 (23 Пехотен Шипченски Полк), the **Bookstore Tezi** (Тези) sells English maps of town. Limited accommodations include **Hotel Voenen Klub** (Военен Клуб), bul. Rozova Dolina 8 (tel. (0431) 221 64), with lived-in rooms, private showers and hot water (6000lv per person) and the **Hotel Vesta** (Веста; tel. (0431) 477 40), Chavdar Voivoda 3 (Чавдар Войвода), behind the monolithic cultural center, with newer rooms and 24-hour hot water (singles US$43, doubles US$48). Part of a new tourist complex, **Campground Krunsko Hanche** (Крънско Ханче; tel. (0431) 242 39 or 270 91), 3km from the city (take a bus to Gabrovo or city bus 6; ask the driver to stop), has two bungalows (for 2 people) at US$5 per person. Pitch a tent for US$4 per person. For budget dining, search out **Starata Kushta** (Старата Къща), Dr. Baev 2. From pl. Sevtapolis, take a left on Gen. M. Skobelev, then right on Gen. Gurko (Ген. Гурко); Dr. Baev (Др. Баев) is the first right (open 24hr.).

Etura Etura (Етъра) is a worthwhile two-hour stopover en route from Kazanluk (7 buses each way per day, 40min.) to Veliko Turnovo. Buses stop in **Gabrovo.** Once there, take trolley 32 or bus 1 to the end-stop at "Bolshevik" (15min., 150lv), then ride bus 7 or 8 and ask to be dropped off at Etura (5min., 150lv). The town's attraction is a little **outdoor museum** (open May-Aug. daily 8am-6pm; Sept.-April 8am-4pm; 3900lv, students 2300lv) with National Revival style buildings, workshops, and mills. Climb through tiny doors and narrow staircases into artisan shops that look as they did a hundred years ago. Visit the candy store for sticky sesame and honey bars (300lv), or the bakery for sweet breads and pastries (400lv).

Veliko Turnovo Велико Турново

Perched high above the Yantra River, Veliko Turnovo has been watching over Bulgaria for 5000 years. The city's residents led the national uprising against Byzantine rule in 1185, and the fortress walls and battle towers have stood since Veliko Turnovo was the capital of Bulgaria's Second Kingdom. Bulgaria's biggest treasure trove of ruins also has a relaxed atmosphere, beyond the narrow streets of the Old Town.

The remains of the **Tsarevets** (Царевец), a fortress which once housed a cathedral and the royal palace, stretch across an overgrown hilltop overlooking the city (open in summer daily 8am-7pm; off-season 8am-5pm; 2500lv, students 1500lv). At the top of the hill stands **Tsurkva Vuzneseniegospodne** (Възнесениегосподне; Church of the Ascension), restored in 1981 on the 1300th anniversary of the Bulgarian state. Near the fortress off ul. Ivan Vazov (Иван Вазов), the **Muzey Vtoroto Bulgarsko Tsarstvo** (Музей Второто Българско Царство; Museum of the Second Bulgarian Kingdom) traces the region's history with Thracian pottery, a collection of medieval crafts, and copies of religious frescoes (open Tues.-Fri. 8am-noon and 1-6pm; 2500lv, students 1500lv). Next door, the **Muzey na Vuzrazhdaneto** (Възраждането; National Revival) documents Bulgaria's 19th-century cultural and religious resurgence (open Wed.-Mon. 8am-noon and 1-6pm; 2500lv, students 1500lv).

Veliko Turnovo sends frequent **trains** to Burgas (2480lv), Sofia (2480lv), Varna (3½hr., 2480lv), Ruse (1280lv), and Pleven (1½hr., 1440lv). Almost any city bus from the station goes to the town center, but ask *"za tsentur?"* to be sure (150lv). There is no official tourist office, but a bookstore (Книжарница) near the gates to the Tsarevets fortress has good maps (500lv). Fortunately, you shouldn't need a lot of help finding a room. Backpacker-oriented triples and quads await at **Hotel Orbita** (Хотел Орбита), Hristo Botev 15 (Христо Ботев; tel. (062) 220 41; 10,000lv per person). **Hotel Trapezitsa (HI)** (Хотел Трапезица), Stefan Stambolov 79 (tel. (062) 220 61), is an excellent youth hostel with clean rooms, some with views of the river. From the post office, walk straight, and turn right with the street (doubles 12,000lv, nonmembers 18,000lv). **Hotel Komfort,** Panayot Tipografov 5 (Панайот Типографов; tel. (062) 287 28), has tidy rooms and beautiful bathrooms. From Stambolov, walk left of Rakovski (Раковски), turn left on the small square, and search for the street sign (US$15 per person). A large outdoor **market** sells fresh produce daily from dawn to dusk at the corner of Bulgaria (България) and Nikola Gabrovski (Никола Габровски). Several taverns occupy the balconies of old houses overlooking the river.

■ Ruse Русе

For centuries, foreigners drifted down the Danube to Ruse, and the city eagerly adopted the Baroque, Renaissance, and Art Deco styles of its guests. Recently, the war in the former Yugoslavia has weakened Ruse's links to the west, and today most of the city's museums are closed, but the city center remains one of the liveliest and most beautiful in all of Bulgaria. **Pl. Svoboda** (пл. Свобода), in the city center, features many fountains and trees, an Italian-style monument, and a magnificent theater. On the right side of the square is the **Opera House** and **Sveta Troitsa** (Света Троица; Holy Trinity Church), erected in 1632 during the Ottoman occupation (open Sat.-Sun. 6am-8:30pm). **Sveti Pavel** (Свети Павел; St. Paul's), one of the few Catholic churches in Bulgaria, is on a small street off Knyazheska (Княжеска). In the evening, come for a stroll in the popular **Mladezhki Park** (Младежки Парк) on the east side of the city, complete with a swimming pool. At night, try one of the **movie theaters** on Aleksandrovska (Александровска) or the **discos** in the Riga and Dunav Hotels.

Dunav Tours (Дунав Турс), pl. Han Kubrat (Хан Кубрат; tel. (082) 22 30 88 or 22 52 50), arranges private rooms (singles US$9, doubles US$13) and provides maps and brochures; from pl. Svoboda, take Aleksandrovska in the direction indicated by the statue's left hand. **Trains** run to Sofia (7hr., 3740lv), Varna (4hr., 2120lv), and Bucharest (6hr., 4250lv). Ruse is accessible by **bus** from Pleven (2hr., 2400lv) and Varna (3½hr., 2400lv); **Group Travel,** pl. Svoboda (tel. (082) 23 20 08), at Dunav Hotel, sends buses to Sofia (5hr., 4700lv). Securing a private room through Dunav Tours is the best bet for accommodations. **Hotel Helios** (Хелиос), ul. Nikolaevska 1 (Николаевска; tel. (082) 22 56 61), has bland but clean rooms with small private bathrooms. The hotel is at the end of Aleksandrovska, across the small park and to the left (singles US$20, doubles US$30). Food in Ruse centers around Aleksandrovska, with the **Hali** (Хали) supermarket at the intersection with Tsar Osvoboditel (Цар Освободител; open Mon.-Sat. 8am-8pm, Sun. 8am-2pm). **Leventa** (Левента; tel. (082) 282

90), underneath the tallest TV tower in the Balkans (take bus 17), serves main courses (2500-4600lv) and vegetarian dishes (800-2000lv; open daily 11:30am-midnight).

BLACK SEA COAST

The Black Sea is a sentimental journey for many Bulgarians: bare-bottomed childhood vacations, summer jobs flipping *kebabche,* and first loves. The campgrounds and international youth centers have long been popular with young party-bound backpackers. Ancient ruins, modern resorts, fishing villages, sandy beaches, and sports from parasailing to horseback riding are within the budget traveler's reach. Go north for rocky cliffs and small villages; go south for popular resorts and beautiful beaches.

Varna Варна

Varna has been crawling with sunburned visitors since 600 BC, when Greek sailors frequented the young port city then known as Odessos. By the time Romans arrived in the 2nd century AD, Varna was a busy trading port and cosmopolitan cultural center. These days, Bulgaria's third-largest city harbors an alluring Old Town, Roman ruins, seaside gardens, and a beach ideal for rollerblading.

The **beach** is accessible through the **Seaside Gardens.** As you stroll along the gardens, peep inside the **Voennomorski Muzey** (Военноморски Музей; Marine Museum), which presents regional navigation history (open daily 10am-6pm; last entrance 5:30pm; 2000lv, students 1000lv). Also see the **Akvarium** (Аквариум), which has a stuffed monarch seal and lively fish (open Mon. noon-7pm, Tues.-Sun. 9am-7pm; 1000lv). The well-preserved **Rimski Termi** (Римски Терми; Roman Baths) stand on San Stefano (open Tues.-Sun. 10am-5pm; 1000lv) in the city's old quarter—**Grutska Mahala** (Гръцка Махала). Bulgaria's second-largest cathedral, **Sv. Bogoroditsa,** is in the city center across from the post office between Maria Luiza and Suborni. It was built in 1882-86 in honor of the Russian soldiers who fought for Bulgaria's liberation.

The **Opera House** (tel. 22 33 88, reservations 22 30 89) on the main square, has a reduced summer schedule (tickets 1000lv). Nightlife centers on bul. Slivnitsa and Knyaz Boris I. The **Festivalen Complex,** with a cinema and disco, attracts younger crowds. In summer, many discos and bars open by the beach. Dance all night under glowing arachnids at **Spider,** near the port (500lv). **Spartakus** (Спартакус), a "private mixed club welcoming all sexual orientations," is in the Opera House.

Practical Information, Accommodations, and Food The Varnenski Bryag (Варненски Бряг) **tourist office,** Musala 3 (Мусала, tel. (052) 22 55 24; fax 25 30 83), between Preslav and Knyaz Boris I off pl. Nezavisimost, has transportation info and arranges private rooms for US$10-14 (open June daily 8am-7pm; July-Aug. 7am-8pm; Sept.-May 8am-5pm). A **branch office** (tel. (052) 22 22 06), at pl. Slaveykov 6, across from the train station, is marked only "Частни Квартири." **Trains** roll to Sofia (7hr., 3900lv, *couchette* 2200lv extra), Plovdiv (5½-7hr., 3000lv), and elsewhere from the commercial port by the shore. The helpful **Rila** international trains bureau, Preslav 13 (tel. (052) 22 62 73 or 22 62 88), sells tickets to Budapest, Athens, and Istanbul (open Mon.-Fri. 8am-6:30pm, Sat. 8am-3pm). **Buses** are the best means of getting to and from Burgas (3hr., 3500lv). **Group Travel,** Knyaz Boris I 6 (tel. (052) 25 67 34), hidden under a SONY sign, sends buses to Sofia (6½hr., 4700lv).

Along with Varnenski Bryag's two offices (see above), **Isak** (Исак; tel. (052) 60 23 18), at the train station, also finds rooms for US$5-7 per person (open daily 5am-10pm). **Hotel Musala** (Мусала), Musala 3 (tel. 22 39 25), next to Varnenski Bryag, is mediocre but affordable (singles with sink US$14, doubles US$20, triples US$24). **Voenno-Morski Klub Hotel** (Военно-Морски), Vladislav Vorhenski 2 (Владислав Ворхенски), is right across from the cathedral. (singles 10,200-20,400lv, doubles 20,400-34,000lv). **Knyaz Boris I** and **Slivnitsa** swarm with cafés, kiosks, and vendors selling everything from foot-long hot dogs to cotton candy. A block up Preslav from pl. Garov, **"Happy" English Pub** bursts with youth and serves all your favorite Bulgarian dishes at moderate prices. The specialty is pork filet stuffed with ham and mushrooms (4150lv; English menu; open daily 8am-midnight). The **Restaurant Musala** (Мусала), pl. Nezavisimost, stirs up goulash (5700lv) and southeast Asian specials like sweet and sour chicken (8000lv; open daily 8:30am-11:30pm, music from 8pm).

■ Near Varna: Balchik

An overlooked jewel among the northern seaside resorts, **Balchik** (Балчик) captivates with a simple and unspoiled beauty, dotted with white houses and orange roofs carved into rocky cliffs. The **public beach** is small but clean, with showers, changing rooms, bar, volleyball, umbrellas, and paddleboat rental (3000lv per hr.). A smaller, less-crowded beach lies 0.5km in the other direction along the public beach. Above the slightly rocky shoreline lies Romanian Queen Marie's **summer palace,** where you can sit in her marble throne and tour the **rose garden** and the largest **cactus collection** in the Balkans (open daily 8am-8pm; entry to both 4000lv, students 500lv). To reach Balchik, take a **bus** or a quicker **minivan** from Varna (1hr., 1350lv), then walk down Cherno More (Черно Море) to the main square; Primorska (Приморска) runs to the shore. **Hotel Esperanza** (Хотел Есперанса), Cherno More 16 (tel. (0579) 51 48), is a small establishment with spacious rooms (US$7 per person). About 15 summer restaurants serve 3000lv meals along the beach. At night, relax at a beachside café or dance at **Cariba disco,** right on the beach (open 10pm-sunrise; free).

Burgas Бургас

Used mainly as a transport link to the south coast, Burgas is underrated by tourists. The consummate Bulgarian beach town, Burgas is filled with people strolling just about, especially through the lively, colorful center—Aleksandrovska and Bogoridi—and its seaside gardens. The two main sights are the **Armenian Church,** Bogoridi, behind Hotel Bulgaria (open Tues.-Fri. 9am-1pm and 3-6pm, Sat.-Sun. 9am-1pm), and the **Archeological Museum,** Bogorodi 21. (Open in summer Mon.-Sat. 9am-5pm; off-season Mon.-Fri. 9am-5pm. US$1, students US$0.50. Free English guidebook.)

Ten daily **trains** travel to Sofia (6-7hr., 4100lv) via Plovdiv or Karlovo and Ruse (6hr., 244lv), and two to Varna (4½hr., 1960lv). **Primorets Tourist,** pl. Garov (пл. Гаров; tel. (056) 427 27), a block east of Aleksandrovska under the sign "Частни Квартири," offers private rooms (US$4; open 8am-8pm). **Hotel Park** (tel. (056) 319 51), in the northern part of the seaside gardens, offers clean rooms with balcony and shower; take bus 4 from the center (singles 45,000lv, doubles 60,000lv). **Kraimorie Campground** (Къмпинг Крайморие; tel. (056) 240 25), 10km from Burgas by hourly bus 17, rents out motel rooms by wide, clean beaches (doubles US$20, bungalows US$12). **Bogoridi** and the area near the beach are full of restaurants and cafés. **Taverna Neptune** serves delicious fish. Next door is the open-air **Dance Club Strena.**

■ Near Burgas: Nesebur, Sozopol, and Ahtopol

Nesebur (Несебър), a museum town atop the peninsula at the south end of Sunny Beach, is a nice alternative to generic coastal resorts, although it too gets crowded during the summer. A walk through the **Stari Grad** is a walk through time. Stone fortress walls from the 3rd century AD stand on the north shore, and a Byzantine gate and port date from the 5th century. The 6th-century church **Starata Mitropoliya** (Старата Митрополия; Old Metropolitan) survives roofless in the center of town, and the 11th-century **Tsurkvata Sveti Stefan** (Църквата Свети Стефан; Church of St. Stephen) is plastered in 16th-century frescoes. The **Archaeological Museum,** to the right of the town gate, exhibits a collection of ceramics, coins, and naval implements (open May-Oct. daily 9am-6pm; Nov.-April closed weekends; 1500lv, students 250lv).

Buses from Burgas (every 40min., 40min., 1250lv) stop at the Old Nesebur port and gate leading to town. From the bus stop, bear right (staying on the main road) and stop by **Tourist Bureau Mesembria** (Месембрия; tel. (0554) 60 91) for a free map. The bureau arranges rooms at US$8 per person (open daily 9am-8:30pm). In high season, it may be difficult to find accommodations for fewer than three nights, but families can be approached on the street to ask about rooms (US$3-5). **Mesembria Hotel,** Mesembria 14a (tel. (0554) 32 55), near the post office, has rooms for 50,000lv per person. **Kapitanska Sreshta** (Капитанска Среща; Captain's Meeting), on Chayka (Чайка), serves up treasures of the sea (open daily 10am-midnight; live music 6-11pm). Other edibles are sold at kiosks along the harbor.

Sozopol (Созопол) was once the resort of choice for Bulgaria's artistic community and still caters to a more creative set than its Black Sea neighbors, quieter and less expensive than Nesebur. To reach Sozopol from Burgas, take the hourly **bus** (6am-8pm, 45min., 960lv). From the bus station, walk to the end of the park, turn left on Republikanska (Републиканска), and walk toward the New Town. The tourist bureau **Lotos** operates offices at the bus station (tel./fax (5514) 282) and at Ropotomo 1 (tel. (5514) 429), in the New Town main square. The clerks organize trips and arrange private rooms for US$7 per person (open daily 8am-5pm). The cheapest hotel is the **Voenski Club** (Военски Клуб; tel. (5514) 283), at the intersection of Republikanska and Ropotomo (doubles US$10-12). The **Lotos** offices have info on campsites in the area as well. **Apolonia** is the site of a crafts fair and home to many **kiosks** offering fresh fish and calamari. For a delicious meal, walk to restaurant **Vyaturna Melnitsa** (Вятърна Мелница), Morski Skali (Морски Скали), the street running along the peninsula tip (entrees 2300-12,400lv; open daily 8am-midnight).

Ahtopol (Ахтопол), 25km from the Turkish border, is a humble town of 1400 inhabitants. Its man-made attractions are few. Yet hidden rocky bays with crystal-clear water and the highest seawater temperature of all Bulgarian resorts more than make up the difference. The public **beach** competes with several small bays (try the one at the lighthouse). Get there by **bus** from Burgas (2 per day, 2½hr., 2500lv). The bus station is on the main **Trakia** (Тракия) street. All points of interest are within a 15-minute walking radius. To get to the beach from the bus station, take Levski (Левски) to the end, then follow the paved path past the sign which reads "ЖП РАЙОН ПЛОВДИВ." **Tourist bureau CREDO-OK** is at the bus station (tel. (995563) 340). Helpful staff provides free maps and **private rooms** (US$4 per person) and sells **bus tickets** to Sofia (1 per day, 7½hr., US$5) and arranges bus excursions to Istanbul (US$60). An **exchange bureau** is on the way to the post office (open daily 9am-1pm and 4-7pm).

Private rooms are the accommodations of choice (US$3-4), but a few private hotels also exist. Try **Valdi** (Валди; tel. (995563) 320), Cherno More 22a (Черно Море). Take a left on Veleka (Велека) from Trakia, then a right on Cherno More (clean doubles with shower 25,000lv). The small town leads a surprisingly active culinary life. It is busiest along **Kraymorska** (Крайморска)—left and right off Trakia at the quay. On the other side of Trakia, **Restaurant Sirius** (Сириус), Kraymorska, offers cheap grills (700-1000lv) and fish (750-3000lv) amid live music and mythic Greek scenes painted on the fence (open daily 11am-midnight). Left and up the street is **Chetirimata Kapitana** (Четиримата Капитана), Kraymorska 29. Draped in fishing nets, it offers imaginatively named and prepared dishes (2200-4800lv; open daily 11am-3pm and 6pm-midnight). A couple of **discos** operate until sunrise by the beach.

Croatia (Hrvatska)

US$1	= 6.40kn (Croatian kuna)	1kn =	US$0.16
CDN$1	= 4.63kn	1kn =	CDN$0.22
UK£1	= 10.19kn	1kn =	UK£0.10
IR£1	= 9.39kn	1kn =	IR£0.11
AUS$1	= 4.66kn	1kn =	AUS$0.22
NZ$1	=4.06kn	1kn =	NZ$0.25
SAR1	= 1.36kn	1kn =	SAR0.73

Country Code: 385 **International Dialing Prefix: 00**

Sprawled along the spectacular Dalmatian coast, Croatia came away from the 1991 breakup of Yugoslavia with some of the finest resort towns in Europe. The war dampened tourism, but peacetime is luring European visitors back in droves to sail the blue Adriatic sea, sip coffee in Zagreb's cafés, and explore the historic walled cities of Dubrovnik and Split. A stiff police presence remains visible throughout the country, and ethnic tension continues, but Croatia savors its long-sought independence.

For more detailed coverage of Croatia, refer to *Let's Go: Eastern Europe 1998.*

GETTING THERE AND GETTING AROUND

Citizens of Australia, Ireland, New Zealand, the U.K, and the U.S. don't need **visas** to enter Croatia. South African citizens require visas; send an application, two passport-sized photos, and a 29SAR check or money order to the nearest embassy and consulate (see **Government Information Offices,** p. 1). Citizens of any country staying more than 90 days should fill out an extension of stay form at a local police station.

By land or air, Zagreb is the main entry point. **Croatia Airlines** (tel. (041) 45 12 44; fax 45 14 15) flies here from many cities, including Chicago, Frankfurt, London, New York, Paris, and Toronto. **Trains** travel to Zagreb from Budapest, Ljubljana, and Vienna, and continue to cities throughout Croatia. **Buses** are sometimes more convenient than trains, but are usually slow and crowded. **Ferry** service is run by **Jadrolinija.** Boats sail the Rijeka-Split-Dubrovnik route, stopping at some islands along the way. Ferries also chug from Split to Ancona, Italy, and from Dubrovnik to Bari, Italy.

ESSENTIALS

Most major cities have a tourist office *(turist biro),* which generally does not arrange accommodations. New private agencies include the two conglomerates **Kompas** and **Atlas** (associated with American Express). Most tourist offices, banks, hotels, and transportation stations offer **currency exchange,** but traveler's checks are accepted by only a smattering of banks. The country's few **ATMs** are in major cities. Croatia's monetary unit, the **kuna,** is theoretically convertible, but impossible to exchange abroad (except in Hungary and Slovenia). Most banks give Visa or MasterCard **cash advances,** but only pricey stores, restaurants, and hotels accept plastic.

Post offices usually have **telephones** available to the public. Phones requiring a **telekarta** (phone card), available at most newspaper stands and the post office, are gradually phasing out token phones. For **AT&T Direct,** dial 993 85 42 88; **BT Direct,** 99 38 00 44; **MCI World Phone,** 993 85 01 12. The Croats speak a southern Slavic language very similar to Serbian, but write in Latin rather than Cyrillic characters. In Zagreb and tourist offices, many know English, but the most popular coastal languages are Italian and German.

Although Croatia is currently at peace, travel to Slavonia and Krajina is extremely dangerous due to unexploded mines. Travel to the coast and islands is considered relatively safe, but check on the situation in nearby Bosnia. The police require foreigners to register with them within 24 hours of arriving in a new city; hotels, campsites, and accommodation agencies should do this for you. Women travelers usually feel safe. Tolerance for homosexuality, while growing, is low; discretion is advisable.

Most **hotels** are expensive, and a 20-50% tourist surcharge will be added to your bill, but you can often avoid the surcharge by asking to pay in kuna. *Sobe* (rooms to let) can be great, but prices are increasing. Organized **campgrounds** speckle the country but are usually packed. Keep in mind that all rooms are subject to a tourist tax of 5-10kn, and that arriving during the weekend may cause lodging problems.

Zagreb

After bearing much of the weight of the war, Zagreb is passionately embracing the role of a modern central European capital. This mid-sized city has a magic to it, from the towering arches of St. Stephen's cathedral to the Austro-Hungarian architecture of many of the downtown buildings. Organized tours of Zagreb leave from the TIC office at Zrinjevac 14, every Wednesday at 10am (minibus 75kn, on foot 45kn). Solo strolls through old Zagreb generally begin around the huge statue and beautiful facades of **Trg bana Josipa Jelačića.** The **Zagrebačka katedrala,** visible from many parts of the city, lies just around the corner (tours Mon.-Sat. 10am-5pm, Sun. and holy days 1-5pm). The **Mimara Museum,** Rooseveltiv trg 4, has a strong collection, which combines history with globe-spinning art (open Mon. 2-8pm, Tues.-Sun. 10am-6pm; 20kn, students 10kn, Mon. free). The former clerical city of Kapitol and craftsmen's province of Gradec comprise the area called **Gornji Grad** (Upper Town). The medieval core remains intact, including the **Kamenita Vrata** (Stone Gate) on Radićeva ulica and **Crkva sv. Mark** (Church of St. Mark) with its charming painted roof. Visitors tend to head straight for the **Lotrščak tower,** Strossmayerovo šetalište 9, with its splendid city panorama (open Tues.-Fri. 10am-6pm, Sat.-Sun. 10am-1pm; 7kn).

CROATIA

The Glavni Kolodvor **train station,** Trg kralja Tomislava 12 (tel. (01) 27 23 42), provides efficient service to coastal Croatia as well as Budapest (7hr., 165kn), Ljubljana (2½hr., 41kn), Venice (8hr., 152kn), and Vienna (6½hr., 262kn). Croatia's **bus** system is better developed than its rail system; the station (tel. (01) 615 71 11), south of the railway tracks on Držićeva Cesta, serves Frankfurt (5 per week, DM142), Ljubljana (3hr., 55kn), Sarajevo (9hr., DM60), and Vienna (8hr., 173kn). The main **tourist office,** Trg J. Jelačića 11 (tel. (01) 481 40 54; fax 481 40 56), in the square's southeast corner, has free maps (open Mon.-Fri. 8am-8pm, Sat.-Sun. 9am-6pm). Rooms in Zagreb are expensive, but **Student Hotel Cvjetno,** Odranska 8 (tel. (01) 611 84 44), has converted dorm rooms available from July 15 through October (singles 200kn, doubles 270kn). **Omladinski Turistički Centar (HI),** Petrinjska 77 (tel. (01) 42 64 61; fax 42 76 27), has clean but worn out rooms with tiny bathrooms (dorms 70kn, singles 132-190kn, doubles 355-310kn). Across from the train station, an escalator leads to a huge underground mall with a food court.

Poreč

Although Poreč has been a municipality since before Caesar's time, it has never been so lively as today. Along the polished stone pavement, buildings glisten, ice-cream vendors tout their wares, and live bands stake out every street corner. The Old Town's main street is the historic **Dekumana,** lined with shops and restaurants. From Trg Slobode, walk past the **Pentagon Tower,** a relic of Poreč's Venetian days; the emblematic lion remains visible today on the 15th-century Gothic tower. The **Euphrasius Basilica,** one block north of Dekumana, is the city's most important monument. The basilica has late Gothic choir stalls, a Renaissance belltower, and stunning Byzantine mosaics inside. The best beaches are south of the Marina, around the **Plava Laguna** (Blue Lagoon) and **Zelena Laguna** (Green Lagoon). Shed your fig leaf for **Solan's** nudist camp (tel. (52) 44 34 00), next to Laterna.

The **bus station,** five minutes south of the town center at Rade Končara 1 (tel. (52) 321 53), serves Ljubljana (4½hr., 83kn) and Zagreb (5hr., 74-105kn). The **information center,** Zagrebačka 11 (tel. (52) 45 14 58; fax 45 16 65), provides free maps and pamphlets (open in summer daily 8am-10pm; off-season 9am-4pm). Ask at the info center about Poreč's several hotels, most with a DM2 daily tourist tax. For **private rooms,** try **Passage,** Zagrebačka 17 (tel. (52) 43 17 81; fax 43 17 38), near the tourist office. (Singles DM12-27; doubles DM40-67; apartments DM40. Open daily 8:30am-9:30pm.) If these rooms are full, there are agencies on every corner. **Laternacamp** (tel. (52) 44 34 88; fax 44 30 93), far to the east, has good facilities (DM13 per night plus DM6 per person; open April-Oct.). Ten daily buses go to Laterna.

Split

With an Old Town wedged between a high mountain range and a palm-lined waterfront, Split lures visitors with Roman ruins, multiple museums, and, above all, stirring natural beauty. The eastern half of the **Old Town** was once the summer residence of the Roman Emperor Diocletian. A **portal,** just past the line of taxis on the south side of the city, leads into the cellars of the city; at the entrance, turn either direction to wander around the labyrinth and explore the archaeological finds (portal open daily 9am-10pm). Straight through the cellars and up the stairs, you will find yourself in the open-air **peristyle,** a colonnaded square. The phenomenal **cathedral** on the west end of the peristyle is one of architecture's great ironies—it was originally the mausoleum of Diocletian, an emperor known largely for his violent persecution of Christians (open daily 7am-noon and 4-7pm). Split has **beaches** on both its north and south ends. The best ones require a ride on bus 60 outside the city.

Trains (tel. (021) 35 53 88) don't serve many cities, but do run to Zagreb (9hr., 106kn); **buses** run to Dubrovnik (4½hr., 70kn), and Zagreb (6½-9hr., 60-99kn). From the stations, follow Obala kneza Domagoja to Obala hrvatskog narodnog preporoda, where the **tourist office** (tel. (021) 34 21 42), at #12, answers questions (in English) and provides maps and brochures (open Mon.-Fri. 7:30am-8pm, Sat. 8am-1pm). The tourist office also finds private singles for 50-95kn, doubles for 70-145kn. **Prenoćište Slavija,** Buvinova 2 (tel. (021) 470 53), in the Old Town, is sparkling clean (singles 160kn, with bath 200kn; doubles 200-240kn; tourist tax 7kn). Inquire at the tourist office about **camping** in and around Split. Heavenly **Dionis,** Marmontaova 3, on the west side of the Old Town, pleases with a large, hearty *menü* for 25kn (open daily 7am-11pm). **Delta,** Trumbićeva Obala 12, offers sandwiches (10kn), pizza, and alluring pastries (open daily 7am-1am). Split's nightlife far surpasses that of its posher island rivals. On weekends the guests in the **Discoteque Night Café,** Osječka 66, at the Koteks center, are counted in the thousands (open nightly 9pm-3am).

■ Near Split: Hvar

The island of **Hvar** may well be one of the most beautiful islands in the world. More of a phantasmagorical palette than an island, Hvar's fields of lavender challenge the blue of the sea; the yellow facades dance with the ivory white cobblestone. The only easy way to get here is on the **Jadrolinija Ferry,** which connects to Split (2hr., 23kn). Another ferry stops by Hvar on its way from Split to Dubrovnik (Tues., Wed., Fri., and Sun., 2hr., 50kn) or back (Mon., Tues., and Sat., 6-8hr., 60kn). North from the ferry landing, the **tourist office** (tel. (021) 74 22 50) rents singles for 70kn and doubles for 120kn (open Mon.-Sat. 9am-noon and 6-9pm, Sun. 6-8pm). The nearby **Mengola** (tel. (021) 74 20 99) also has private rooms (singles 88kn, doubles 132kn). The well-stocked **Razvitka market** is on the north side of the main square (open Mon.-Sat. 6am-9:30pm, Sun. 7am-noon).

Dubrovnik

Picturesquely sandwiched between the Dinaric Alps and the calm Adriatic, Dubrovnik's image appears in every piece of Croatian tourist literature. Those expecting to see still-smoking ruins from the war will find that the damage is hardly noticeable: Dubrovnik's vibrant café culture brims with energy and pride. The most impressive legacy of this former naval city-state are the awesome **city walls.** Stretching up to 25m high, they were mostly completed in the 14th century. Climbing to the top affords a glorious view of the old city and the sparkling blue Adriatic; budget an hour if you want to walk the full 2km circumference (open daily 9am-9pm). Entering the Old Town on its main street, the **Franjevački samostan** (Franciscan monastery) is on the left and the **Dominikanski samostan** (Dominican monastery) awaits at the other end. The latter has a rich collection of Renaissance paintings, art, and books (open daily 9am-6pm; 5kn). Nearby, the street opens into a large square, with **Crkva sv. Vlaha** (St. Blaise's Church) sitting on the same side as the **katedrala.** Between the two is the town's best museum, the 1441 **Knežev dvor** (Rector's Palace), which holds furniture, paintings, coins, and weaponry, all dating from the 16th and 17th centuries (open Mon.-Sat. 9am-1pm and 4-7pm, Sun. 9am-1pm; 10kn).

The **bus station** (tel. (020) 230 88), about 2km north of the Old Town, serves Split (5hr., 46-71kn) and Zagreb (11hr., 135kn). A few hundred meters north of the station, the **ferry** landing (tel. (020) 41 10 00) sends boats to Split (8hr., 70kn). From this area, you can take a bus to the Old Town gates (any except bus 7; 5kn on board or 4kn from kiosks). The **tourist office** (tel. (020) 263 54) is just through the main gates, on the right (open Mon.-Sat. 8am-9pm, Sun. 9am–1pm). The **HI youth hostel,** Bana J. Jelačića 15/17 (tel. (020) 232 41; fax 41 25 92), is ultra-clean and friendly. From the bus station, walk up Starčevića about 10 minutes, turn right at the traffic light, and then right again after 30m. Pass a short chain of small bars and watch for a sign on the left (reception open daily 7am-2pm; 60kn; breakfast 7kn). Women at the bus station offer private rooms (singles 80kn, doubles 130kn). **Raguse 2,** Zamanjina 2, cooks up spaghetti (30kn), octopus salad (30kn), and *mussels bouzzara* (30kn; open daily 8am-11pm). For disco deca*dance,* follow the noise in Stari Grad to the **Arsenal** (open nightly 11pm-5am; cover 10kn).

The Republic of Cyprus (ΚΥΠΡΟΣ)

US$1 = C£0.54 (Cypriot Pounds)	**C£1 = US$1.83**
CDN$1 = C£0.39	**C£1 = CDN$2.56**
UK£1 = C£0.87	**C£1 = UK£1.15**
IR£1 = C£0.79	**C£1 = IR£0.90**
AUS$1 = C£0.41	**C£1 = AUS$1.94**
NZ$1 = C£0.35	**C£1 = NZ$2.25**
SAR1 = C£0.11	**C£1 = SAR6.81**
Country Code: 357	**International Dialing Prefix: 080**

Journeys to northern Cyprus require careful planning and must usually begin in Turkey. For info on northern Cyprus, see *Let's Go: Greece and Turkey 1998.*

Aphrodite blessed the island of Cyprus with an abundance of natural beauty, from the sandy beaches of Agia Napa to the serene Troodos Mountains. Unfortunately, the beautiful is also desirable, and the ancient temples, Roman mosaics, crusader castles, magnificent mosques, and English street signs all attest to the succession of settlements by those who would have control over the spectacular isle. The struggle for ownership continues today as the Greek forces in the Republic of Cyprus cast an angry and suspicious eye on their Turkish neighbors in northern Cyprus.

ESSENTIALS

The third largest island in the Mediterranean after Sicily and Sardinia, Cyprus lies 64km from Turkey and 480km from the nearest Greek island. Stretching across the island, the infamous **Green Line** divides the Greek southern portion of Cyprus from the Turkish Republic of Northern Cyprus, or northern Cyprus. The Republic of Cyprus occupies 63% of the island, but restrictions prohibit travel from north to south except for tourists to return from short daytrips. No Greek Cypriot has entered northern Cyprus for over 20 years. If planning to cross over, head to the **Ledra Palace Checkpoint** in Nicosia and prepare for lots of restrictions and requirements. You can enter northern Cyprus only between 8am and 1pm, and you must return by 5pm. Do not let Turkish officials stamp your passport; if they do, you can never return to Greek Cyprus. They should stamp a separate form instead.

Olympic Airlines (tel. (800) 223-1226), **Egypt Air** (tel. (800) 334-6787), and **Cyprus Airways** (tel. (212) 714-2310) offer **flights** to the Republic of Cyprus; student fare from Athens is about US$190 round-trip. Many **boat** agencies connect Cyprus to Greece, including **Afroessa Lines S.A.,** 1 Charilaou Trikoupi St. (tel. 418 37 77), and **Stability Line,** 11 Sachtouri St. (tel. 413 2392), in Peirais. Inquire at ferry docks and tourist offices for more information. Once in the Republic of Cyprus, cars drive on the *left* side of the road and driving conditions can be intimidating. **Buses** and **taxis** connect towns, and tourist offices stock an island-wide bus schedule. Transportation is largely nonexistent after 7pm—not even taxis run.

Cyprus' extremely helpful **tourist offices** provide free maps and plenty of info on buses, museums, and cultural activities. Southern Cyprus has a fairly good **telephone** system; direct overseas calls can be made from nearly all public phones if you have enough change, and telecards (sold at banks and kiosks) are convenient for making international calls. To call **AT&T Direct,** dial 080 900 10; **MCI WorldPhone,** 080 900 00; **Sprint Access,** 080 900 01. Cheap, clean hotels are rare, but Nicosia, Paphos, and Larnaka all have **HI youth hostels.** Cyprus has only a few **campgrounds,** but you may sleep on beaches and in forests; exercise caution.

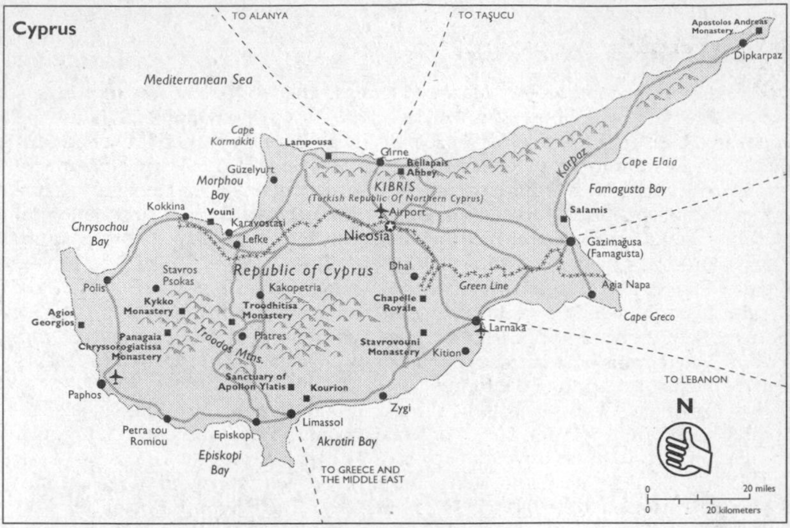

Nicosia (Lefkosia) ΛΕΥΚΩΣΙΑ

Landlocked Nicosia, the capital of the Republic of Cyprus, is a city of walls. The ramparts and barbed wire of the **Green Line** run east-west at the north end of the city to separate it from the Turkish-occupied area, and the enormous circular walls left by the Venetians distinguish the New City from the Old. Geared more towards bureaucrats than backpackers, Nicosia is best seen as a daytrip. The **Makarios Cultural Center** occupies the Old City buildings of Archbishopric Kyprianos Sq., where several interesting museums are clustered, including the **Byzantine Art Gallery,** with the island's largest collection of icons (open Mon.-Fri. 9am-4:30pm; £1), the **Folk Art Museum** (open Mon.-Fri. 9am-5pm, Sat. 10am-1pm; £1), and the Greek **Independence War Gallery,** with relics from the struggle for *enosis,* the union of Cyprus with Greece (open Mon.-Fri. 9am-4:30pm, Sat. 9am-1pm; £0.50). Nearby is the **Ömeriye Mosque,** easily recognizable by its large minaret, and the **Turkish Baths,** 8 Tillirias St. (Open for women Wed. and Fri. 8am-3pm. Open for men Wed. and Fri. 3-7pm, Tues., Thurs., and Sat-Sun. 8am-7pm. £4.) In the *Laiki Yitonia,* the pedestrian shopping district, the **Leventis Municipal Museum** on Hippocratis St., chronicles the history of Nicosia (open Tues.-Sun. 10am-4:30pm; free). In the New City, the **Cyprus Museum** has the most extensive collection of ancient artifacts on the island (open Mon.-Sat. 9am-5pm, Sun. 10am-1pm; £1.50).

There are two bus stations in town: **Kemek,** 34 Leonides St. (tel. (02) 463989), south of Solonos Sq., and **Kolo Kassi** (tel. (02) 347774), on Salaminos St. by the entrance to the Old City. Buses run to Limassol (3-4 per day, £1.50), Larnaka (4-7 per day, £1.50), and Platres (5 per week, £2). The **tourist office,** 35 Aristokypros St. (tel. (02) 444264), in the *Laiki Yitonia,* has maps, bus info, and free copies of *Nicosia: This Month* (open Mon.-Fri. 8:30am-4pm, Sat. 8:30am-2pm). The southern part of the Old City contains most budget lodgings, but the New City is the center of the nightlife. The popular and international **youth hostel (HI),** I Hadjidaki St. (tel. (02) 444808), a bit of a walk into the New City, has a communal kitchen (£4; sheets £1). **Royal Hotel,** 17 Euripides St. (tel. (02) 463245), on a sidestreet off Ledra in the middle of the Old City, has clean rooms with fans (singles £8.25, doubles £13.50). The **municipal market** on the corner of Digenis Akritas and Kallipolis Ave. has a variety of food stands.

Larnaka ΛΑΡΝΑΚΑ

One of the oldest continuously inhabited cities in the world, **Larnaka** surprisingly draws tourists not with history but with **beaches**. The city does, however, house the uncovered treasures of several archaeological digs. Larnaka was built over ancient Kition, whose ruins reveal part of an ancient Cyclopean wall, the **Temple of Astarte** (the Phoenician goddess of fertility), and four small temples (open Mon.-Fri. 7:30am-2:30pm, also Sept.-June Thurs. 3-6pm; £0.75). The **Larnaka District Archaeological Museum** and **Kition Archaeological Site** have objects from Neolithic to Roman times (open Mon.-Fri. 7:30am-2:30pm, Sept.-June also Thurs. 3-6pm; £0.75). The private **Pierides Foundation Museum** on Zinonos St. showcases artifacts from 3000 years of Cypriot history, including prehistoric idols and antique maps. (Open in summer Mon.-Fri. 9am-1pm and 3-6pm, Sat. 9am-1pm, Sun. 10am-1pm; reduced hours in winter. £1.) The remains of Lazarus lie (permanently, this time) in the **Church of St. Lazarus,** at the first left north of the fortress.

Most **flights** into Cyprus land at the Larnaka airport; take bus 19 (Mon.-Sat. 6:20am-7pm, in winter until 5:45pm; £0.50) or a taxi (about £3) from the airport into town. From Athinon Ave., **buses** leave for Nicosia (4-7 per day, £1.30) and Limassol (3-4 per day, £1.50). A **tourist office** is located at the airport (open 24hr.), and another resides at Vasileos Pavlou Sq. (tel. (04) 654322; hours vary). The **HI youth hostel** (tel. (04) 621188), Nikolaou Rossou St. in St. Lazarus Sq., has three large 10-bed dorms (reception open 24hr.; £3.50, sheets £1). Seek out the **Web Internet Café,** 54 Lordou Vyronou St. (tel. (04) 654954), for the tastiest burger in town (£2.80) and access to the web, email, and chat rooms (£2 per hr.). The **1900 Art Cafe,** 6 Stasinou St., fosters the exchange of intellectual and artistic ideas over carafes of local wine (£2.50; vegetarian-friendly menu).

From Larnaka, many visitors bus north to **Agia Napa** (£1), a tourist center with white sandy beaches and a raucous nightlife dominated by foreigners. **Xenis Rooms** (tel. (03) 721086), run out of a private home, shelters tourists. To get there, go up the road to Paralimni until you have to turn. A left and then a right at Mary's Supermarket will take you to the top of the hill (2-night min. stay; doubles £10).

Limassol (Lemesos) ΛΕΜΕΣΟΣ

The island's second largest city and port of entry for most passenger ferries, industrial **Limassol** is a cordial introduction to a striking island. The **Limassol Castle** has changed hands many times since its construction in the 12th century, but its latest incarnation is as the **Cyprus Medieval Museum.** (Open in summer Mon.-Fri. 7:30am-5pm, Sat. 9am-5pm, Sun. 10am-1pm; off-season Mon.-Sat. 7:30am-5pm. £1.) For sunbathing, the gorgeous **Dassoudi Beach,** 3km east of town (bus 3 from the market on Kanaris St.), and the ebullient **Ladies Mile Beach** at the new port (bus 1), are both popular. The extensive Roman and Hellenistic ruins of **Kourion,** 10km out of town, boast a **sanctuary to Apollo** from the 8th century BC and a **stadium** built in the 2nd century AD. Buses to Kourion leave from Limassol Castle (every hr. on the hr. 9am-2pm, return at 11:50am, 2:50 and 4:50pm; £0.60).

Limassol's **tourist office,** 15 Spiro Araouzos St. (tel. (05) 362756), on the waterfront one block east of the castle, provides maps and schedules. (Open July-Aug. Mon. and Thurs. 8:15am-2:15pm and 4-6:30pm, Tues.-Wed. and Fri. 8:15am-2:15pm, Sat. 8:15am-1:15pm; call for off-season hours.) The **bus terminal,** at the corner of Irenis and Enosis St., serves Nicosia (3-4 per day, £1.50), Paphos (1 per day, £1.50), and Larnaka (2-4 per day, £1.70). In town, **Guest House Ikaros,** 61 Eleftherias St. (tel. (05) 354348), has large, pleasant rooms (singles £5, doubles £10), and its neighbor **Stalis Guest House** (tel. 05) 368197) has budget accommodations (singles £3, doubles £5.80). The **central market** is the best option for the health- and wealth-conscious traveler (open Mon.-Tues. and Thurs.-Fri. 6am-1pm and 4-6pm, Wed. 6am-1pm). Limassol residents are especially spirited during the **wine festival** from late August to early September (Dionyssian revelries 6-11pm; £1.50).

Paphos ΠΑΦΟΣ

Paphos' glory days as the capital under the Egyptian Ptolemies were ended in the 4th century by an earthquake, and the city remained a small village until Turkish occupation rendered northern Cyprus' tourist areas inaccessible to Southern Cypriots. Since then, Paphos, combining the best of beaches and historic sites, has risen again as the tourist capital of the Republic of Cyprus. The mosaic floors of the **House of Dionysus,** the **House of Theseus,** and the **House of Aion** are the city's most dazzling ancient remains. To reach the houses, take Sophias Vembo St., off A. Pavlou Ave. (open in summer daily 7:30am-7pm; off-season 7:30am-5pm; £1). The musty **Catacombs of Agia Solomoni,** along the road between Ktima (upper) and Kato (lower) Paphos, include a chapel with deteriorating Byzantine frescoes. A tree with handkerchiefs draped from its branches marks the entrance to the catacombs on A. Pavlos Ave. St. Paul was allegedly whipped for preaching Christianity at **St. Paul's Pillar** (both free and open 24hr.). In the Ktima Paphos, the **Ethnographic Museum,** 1 Exo Vrysi St., just outside of Kennedy Sq., should not be missed (open Mon.-Sat. 9am-5:30pm, Sun. 10am-1pm; £1; English guidebooks £3). Across the way, the **Byzantine Museum,** 26 25th Martiou St., has icons and religious relics. (Open Mon.-Fri. 9am-12:30pm and 4-7pm, Sat. 9am-12:30pm; reduced hours in winter. £0.75.) The **Monastery of Agios Neophytos** lies 9km north near Coral Bay Beach, near a ravine with three rock caves carved by Neophytos and covered with beautiful 12th-century frescoes. Take the bus to Tala (4-6 per day) and walk to the monastery. Bring a flashlight (open daily 7:30am-noon and 3pm-dusk; £0.50).

The **tourist office,** 3 Gladstone St. (tel. (06) 232841), is across from Iris Travel (hours vary). KEMEK **buses** (tel. (06) 234255) run to Limassol (2 per day, £1.25) from the Mitropolis Building, off Thermopylon St. The **HI youth hostel,** 37 Eleftheriou Venizelou Ave. (tel. (06) 232588), is on a residential street northeast of the town center; from the square, follow Pallikaridi to Venizelou, and make a right (£4; sheets £1). The elegant but affordable **Park Mansion Hotel** is off Pavlou Ave. behind the park just outside of Kennedy Sq. (£13). **Peggy's Miranda Café** in Kennedy Sq. serves continental breakfast (£2) and hosts a book swap (open Mon.-Tues. and Thurs.-Fri. 7am-6:30pm, closed Wed. morning), while the classy **Surfcafé,** 1 Gladstone St., provides **Internet access** (£1 per hr.; sandwiches £1-1.50).

Polis ΠΟΛΙΣ

Polis's name means "town," and the simple name suits a simple city: smaller, cheaper, and more relaxed than other coastal towns. Aphrodite came here to bathe in seclusion, but the goddess of beauty no longer bathes alone—Polis has become a popular Cypriot base for budget travel. The road from Polis to the **Baths of Aphrodite,** 10km west, leads past pristine **beaches** and some cheap lodgings, but the beaches to the east are just as beautiful. In town, the church of **Agios Andronikos** was turned into a mosque during Ottoman rule but is currently being converted back. To see its frescoes being recovered from under the plaster, ask for a key from the helpful and enthusiastic **tourist office,** at the end of the winding main street in the *platia* (open Mon.-Sat. 9am-1pm and 2:30-5:45pm). **Minibuses** (tel. (06) 236740 or 236822) from Paphos pass through Polis (5-10 per day, £1), and **taxis** also make the trip. The **Lemon Garden,** past the *platia* to the right, has quality rooms and a restaurant/bar (doubles £14-16). Look for inexpensive rooms in private households down the hill from the Bank of Cyprus, or inquire at a café (£5-6 per person). **The Arsinoe,** across from the church, is run by a fisherman's family and serves the daily catch (swordfish £3.50; open daily 8am-1pm and 7pm-1am).

The Czech Republic (Česká Republika)

US$1	**= 34.20kč (Czech koruny)**	**10kč =**	**US$0.29**
CDN$1	**= 24.73kč**	**10kč =**	**CDN$0.40**
UK£1	**= 54.41kč**	**10kč =**	**UK£0.18**
IR£1	**= 50.14kč**	**10kč =**	**IR£0.20**
AUS$1	**= 24.88kč**	**10kč =**	**AUS$0.40**
NZ$1	**= 21.70kč**	**10kč =**	**NZ$0.46**
SAR1	**= 7.28kč**	**10kč =**	**SAR1.37**

Country Code: 420 **International Dialing Prefix: 00**

In 1945, American troops stood in wait as Soviets "liberated" Prague and consigned it to Communist rule, allowing a land poised on the brink of flourishing to flounder instead. Yet with the waning power of the Soviet Union, the Velvet Revolution of 1989 succeeded where the Prague Spring of 1968 had failed. Freed of Communist rule and its poorer cousin, Slovakia, the Czech economy is the envy of the East. Invasions today are benevolent, led by enamored tourists sweeping in to savor the Czech Republic's magnificent capital, historic towns, and the world's best beer.

Culturally and politically, it has been a decade of rapid change for the Czech people. In November of 1989, following the demise of Communist governments in Hungary and Poland and the fall of the Berlin Wall, Czechs demonstrated in Prague and other cities. Despite half-hearted crackdowns, the Communist government resigned within a month and playwright Václav Havel emerged as the main political leader. He attempted to preserve the Czech-Slovak union, but three years during which ambitious Czechs encouraged Slovak nationalism resulted in the separation of the two nations in 1993. Havel temporarily stepped down during the divorce with Slovakia. Czechs today have much respect for their playwright-president and for the most part are embracing the dizzying pace of the westernization process.

Check out the Czech Republic in further detail in *Let's Go: Eastern Europe 1998.*

GETTING THERE AND GETTING AROUND

U.S. citizens may visit the Czech Republic **visa-free** for up to 30 days; citizens of the U.K. or Canada for up to 180 days, and Ireland for up to 90 days. Australians, New Zealanders, and South Africans need visas, valid for 30 days and available at a Czech embassy or consulate (see **Government Information Offices,** p. 1), or at one of three border crossings: **Rozvadov, Dolní Dvořiště,** or **Hatí.** Single-entry or transit visas cost US$22 (US$60 at the border), double-entry visas US$36, and 90-day multiple-entry visas US$50. They require two photos, a passport, and three days to process (1 day in person). South Africans can get a 30-day, single-entry visa free of charge. Apply for visa extensions of up to six months at the Local Passport and Visa Authorities.

Eastrail is accepted in the Czech Republic, but **Eurail** is valid only with a special supplement. The fastest trains are the *expresný.* The *rychlík* trains cost as much as the express, while the few *spěšný* (semi-fast) trains cost less. Avoid *osobný* (slow) trains. **ČSD,** the national transportation company, publishes the monster *Jízdní řád* (train schedule, 74kč), with a two-page English explanation in front. *Odjezd* (departures) are printed in train stations on yellow posters, *příjezd* (arrivals) on white. If you're heading to Austria or Hungary, it's often less expensive to buy a Czech ticket to the border, then, at the border, buy a separate ticket to your destination. **Seat reservations** (*místenka,* 6kč) are recommended on most express and international trains and for all first-class seating; snag them at the counter with the boxed "R." IC and EC trains require an additional supplement which can double the ticket price.

Buses can be significantly faster and only slightly more expensive than trains. **ČSAD** runs national and international bus lines. From Prague, buses run a few times per week to Munich, Milan, and other transport hubs; buses leave Brno for many destinations in Austria. Consult timetables at stations or buy one (25kč) from a kiosk. **Hitchhiking** remains popular, especially during the morning commute (6-8am).

ESSENTIALS

Čedok, the official state tourist company and relic of the centralized Communist bureaucracy, has been transformed into a travel agency. **CKM,** its junior affiliate, remains helpful for the student and budget traveler, serving as a clearinghouse for youth hostel beds and issuing ISICs and HI cards. The quality of private tourist agencies varies. **Tourist offices** in major cities provide printed materials on sights, cultural events, hotels, and hostels. City maps *(plán města)* are available for 28-60kč. Bookstores sell *Soubor Turistických Map,* a great hiking map with an English key.

Traveler's checks can be exchanged in every town, thanks to the ubiquitous **Komerční banka,** which accept all sorts of checks. **Banks** are generally open weekdays from 9am to 5pm. Czech money is not valid in Slovakia. If you're carrying money with you, beware purse-snatchers and pickpockets in Prague's Old Town Square, on the way to the Castle, and on trams. There is less crime in smaller towns. Lost wallets and purses sometimes appear at embassies with only the cash missing.

The Czech Republic's **postal system** is usually reliable and efficient; letters reach the U.S. in under 10 days. For calls within the country, a **phone card** (150kč for 50 units) is invaluable. It's used in new blue, gray, and green phones—the old blue ones demand coins but usually choke on them. Local calls cost 2kč regardless of length. Use an international long-distance system to avoid the expensive Czech telephone bureaucracy—calls run 31kč per minute to the U.K., 63kč per minute to the U.S., Canada, or Australia, and 94kč per minute to New Zealand. To reach the **AT&T Direct** operator, dial tel. 00 42 00 01 01; **MCI WorldPhone,** 00 42 00 01 12; **Canada Direct,** 00 42 00 01 51; and **BT Direct,** 00 42 00 44 01. In **emergencies,** try contacting your consulate, since police may not be well-versed in English. The number for **police** is 158; for **fire** 150; for **ambulance** 155.

Many Czechs, especially students, speak at least a little English; German phrases go even further, especially in Prague, but might earn you some resentment.

Yes/no	*Ano/Ne*	AH-noh/neh
Please/You're welcome	*Prosím*	PROH-seem
Thank you	*Děkuji*	DYEH-koo-yih
Hello	*Dobrý den*	DOH-bree den
Where is...?	*Kde je...?*	k-DEH YEH
Do you speak English?	*Mluvite anglicky?*	MLOO-vit-eh AHNG-lits-kih
I don't understand.	*Nerozumím*	NEH-roh-zoo-meem
Check, please.	*Prosím, učet*	PRO-seem, OO-chet

Czech festivals enliven the summer. In late May and early June, musicians from around the world congregate for the **Prague Spring Festival.** Cinema bosses spend the first week of July at Karlovy Vary's **international film festival.** In August, Brno hosts the **Czech Grand Prix.** Czechs celebrate: January 1, New Year's Day; Easter (April 12-13); Labor Day (May 1); Liberation Day (May 8); Cyril and Methodius Day (July 5); Jan Hus Day (July 6); Republic Day (Oct. 28); and Christmas.

Accommodations and Camping Converted **university dorms** run through CKM are the cheapest option in July and August. Comfy two- to four-bed rooms go for 200-400kč per person. CKM's **Junior Hotels** (year-round hostels which give discounts to both HI and ISIC holders) are comfortable but often full. Private youth lodgings have broken CKM's monopoly, but may not surpass its reliability. Showers and bedding are usually included, breakfast sometimes too, especially outside Prague.

Across the country, **private homes** have become a legal and feasible lodging option. In Prague, hawkers offer expensive rooms (US$16-30, but don't agree to more than US$20), often including breakfast. Scan train stations for "hostel," *"zimmer,"* or "accommodations" ads. Quality varies widely; *do not* pay in advance. Be prepared for a healthy commute to the center of town. Outside of Prague, **local tourist offices** and **Čedok** handle private room booking, although private agencies are popping up around train and bus stations. If you're sticking to **hotels,** reserve ahead from June to September in Prague and Brno, even if pre-payment is required. In smaller towns, it's easier to find a bed on the spot. **Camping** is available everywhere for 60-100kč per person (most sites open only mid-May to Sept.). The book *Ubytování ČSR,* in decodable Czech, lists accommodations in Bohemia and Moravia.

Food and Drink Anyone in the mood for true Czech cuisine should start learning to pronounce *knedlíky* (k-NED-lee-kee). The thick pasty loaves of dough serve as staples of Czech meals, soaking up *zelí* (sauerkraut) juice and the unbelievably schmaltzy sauces that smother almost any local dish. The Czech national meal is *vepřové* (roast pork), *knedlíky,* and *zelí;* but *guláš* (stew) runs a close second. The main food groups have become *hovězí* (beef), *sekaná pečeně* (meatloaf), and *klobása* (sausage). Meat can be *pečené* (roasted), *vařené* (boiled), or *mleté* (ground). *Ryby* (fish) include *kapr* (carp) and *pstruh* (trout). If you are in a hurry, you can grab a pair of *párky* (frankfurters) or some *sýr* (cheese) at either a *bufet, samoobsluha,* or *občerstvení,* all variations on a diner. Vegetarian restaurants do exist, serving *šopský salat* (mixed salad) and other *bez masa* (no meat) specialties. *Káva* (coffee) is almost always served Turkish-style. A beloved dessert is *koláč,* a tart filled with either poppy-seed jam or sweet cheese. Tipping is uncommon, but patrons often round up the bill.

Prague (Praha)

According to legend, Princess Libuše stood on Vyšehrad above the Vltava and declared, "I see a city whose glory will touch the stars; it shall be called Praha (threshold)." Medieval kings, benefactors, and architects fulfilled the prophecy, as soaring cathedrals and lavish palaces gave notice of Prague's status as the capital of the Holy Roman Empire. But the city's character differed sharply from the holy splendor of

Prague

1 Canadian Consulate
2 Palace Belvedere
3 National Gallery
4 St. Vitus Cathedral
5 Royal Palace
6 Basilica of St. George
7 Lobkovic Palace
8 U.K. Consulate
9 Wallenstein Palace
10 St. Nicholas Church
11 U.S. Consulate
12 Church of Our Lady Victorious
13 Charles Bridge
14 National Theater
15 New Town Hall
16 National Museum
17 Smetana Theater
18 Praha hlavní nádra÷í
19 Church of Our Lady of the Snows
20 Bethlehem Chapel
21 Old Town Hall
22 T§n Church
23 Church of St James
24 Powder Tower
25 Masarykovo nádra÷í

HOSTELS

1 Hostel Sokol
2 CKM
3 Junior Hotel Praha
4 Hotel Juventus

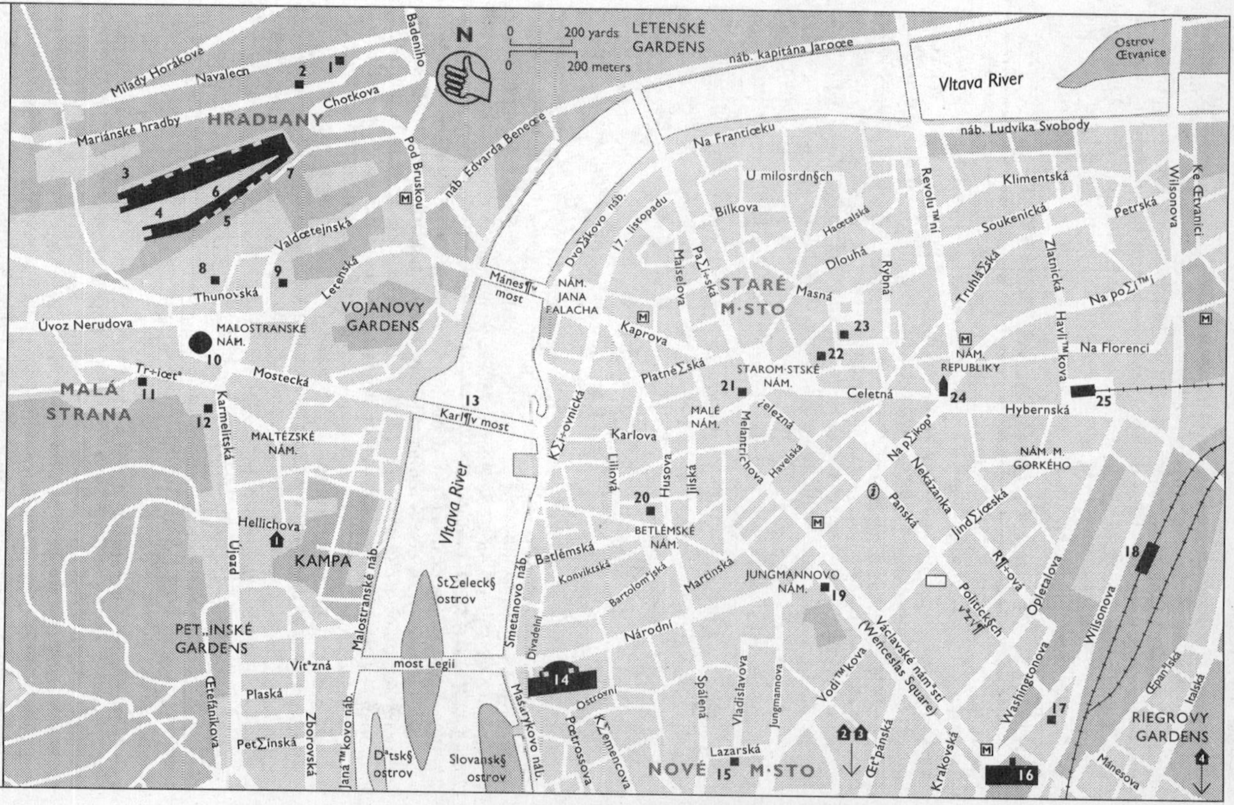

Rome and Constantinople: legends of demons, occult forces, and mazes of shady alleys lent this "city of dreams" a dark side and provided fodder for Franz Kafka's tales of paranoia. Only this century has the spell been broken, as the fall of the Berlin Wall brought hordes of euro-trotting foreigners to the once-isolated capital. Tourists and entrepreneurs have long since explored and exploited every nook and cranny of the city, yet these visitors give Prague a festive air matched by few places in the world.

ORIENTATION AND PRACTICAL INFORMATION

Straddling a bend in the Vltava, Prague is a mess of suburbs and winding streets. **Staré Město** (Old Town) lies along the southeast riverbank; across the Vltava sits the **Hradčany** castle with **Malá Strana** at its south base. Southeast of the Old Town spreads **Nové Město** (New Town), and farther east across **Wilsonova** lie the **Žižkov** and **Vinohrady** districts. **Holešovice** in the north has an international train terminal; **Smíchov,** the southwest end, is the student-dorm suburb. All train and bus terminals are on or near the Metro system. **Metro B: nám. Republiky** is closest to the principal tourist offices and accommodations agencies. Don't just refer to your map: study it. *Tabak* stands and bookstores vend indexed *plán města* (maps). The English-language weekly *The Prague Post* provides news and tips for visitors.

CZECH REPUBLIC

Prague is in the process of carrying out a telephone-system overhaul; throughout 1998 many numbers will change, though the eight-digit ones are less likely to.

Tourist Offices: Signs with "i"s signal tourist agencies that book rooms, arrange tours, and sell maps and guidebooks. Be wary: these private firms didn't just appear in a burst of benevolence. **Prague Information Service** *(Pražská Informační Služba),* Staroměstské nám. 1 (tel. 24 48 25 62 or, in English, 54 44 44), happily sells maps (40kč), arranges tours, and books musical extravaganzas. Open Mon.-Fri. 9am-7pm, Sat.-Sun. 9am-6pm. **Čedok,** Na příkopě 18 (tel. 24 19 71 11), has a formidable institutional memory from 40 years of socialist monopoly, but isn't fully user-friendly yet. Open Mon.-Fri. 8:30am-6pm, Sat. 9am-1pm.

Budget Travel: CKM, Jindřišská 28 (tel. 24 23 02 18; fax 26 86 23), sells budget air tickets and discount cards for students and those under 26 (ISICs and GO25 150kč; Euro26 350kč). Also books rooms in Prague (300kč and up). Open Mon.-Fri. 9am-6pm. The office at Žitná 12 (tel. 24 91 57 67) handles bus, rail, and train tickets. Open Mon.-Fri. 9am-6pm. **KMC,** Karoliny Světlé 30 (tel. 24 23 06 33), sells HI cards (300kč) and can book HI hostels almost anywhere. Open Mon.-Thurs. 9am-noon and 2:30-5pm, Fri. 9am-noon and 2:30-5:30pm.

Passport Office: Foreigner police headquarters at Olšanská 2 (tel. 683 17 39). Metro A: Flora. Walk down Jičinská and turn right onto Olšanská, or take tram 9. Visa extensions. Open Mon.-Tues. and Thurs. 7:30-11:45am and 12:30-2:30pm, Wed. 7:30-11:30am and 12:30-5pm, Fri. 7:30-noon.

Embassies: Travelers from **Australia** and **New Zealand** have honorary consuls (tel. 24 31 00 71 and 25 41 98, respectively) but should contact the British embassy in an emergency. **Canada,** Mickiewiczova 6 (tel. 24 31 11 08). Metro A: Hradčanská. Open Mon.-Fri. 8am-noon and 2-4pm. **Hungary,** Badeniho 1 (tel. 36 50 41). Metro A: Hradčanská. **Ireland,** Tržiště 13 (tel. 53 09 02). Metro A: Malostranská. Open Mon.-Fri. 9:30am-12:30pm and 2:30-4:30pm. **Poland (Consulate),** Václavské nám. 49 (tel. 24 22 87 22). Open Mon.-Fri. 7am-noon. **Russia,** Pod Kaštany 1 (tel. 38 19 45). Metro A: Hradčanská. Open Mon., Wed., and Fri. 9am-1pm. **Slovakia,** Pod Hradbami 1 (tel. 32 05 21). Metro A: Dejvická. Open Mon.-Fri. 8:30am-noon. **South Africa,** Ruská 65 (tel. 67 31 11 14). Metro A: Flora. Open Mon.-Fri. 9am-noon. **U.K.,** Thunovská 14 (tel. 57 32 03 55). Metro A: Malostranská. Open Mon.-Fri. 9am-noon. **U.S.,** Tržiště 15 (tel. 57 32 06 63, after hours tel. 53 12 00). Metro A: Malostranská. From Malostranské nám., head down Karmelitská and take a right onto Tržiště. Open Mon.-Fri. 8am-1pm and 2-4:30pm.

Currency Exchange: The best rates are for AmEx and Thomas Cook's traveler's checks when cashed commission-free at the appropriate office. Exchange counters are everywhere—hotel lobbies, tourist information agencies, and littering the streets—with wildly varying rates. **Chequepoints** are mushrooming around the center of town, and may be the only places open when you need to change cash, but they can cream off a 10% commission. **Komerční Banka,** main branch, Na příkopě 33 (tel. 24 02 11 11; fax 24 24 30 20), exchanges cash and travelers checks for 2% commission. Open Mon.-Fri. 8am-5pm. **ATMs** are all over the place.

American Express: Václavské nám. 5, 113 26 Praha 1 (tel. 24 21 99 92; fax 24 22 11 31). Metro A or C: Muzeum. Mail held. MC and Visa cash advances (3% commission). **ATM.** Exchange office open daily 9am-7pm; travel office May-Sept. Mon.-Fri. 9am-6pm, Sat. 9am-2pm; Oct.-April Mon.-Fri. 9am-5pm, Sat. 9am-noon.

Thomas Cook: Národní tř. 28 (tel. 21 10 52 76; fax 24 23 60 77). Cashes Cook's checks commission-free. MC cash advances. Open Mon.-Sat. 9am-7pm, Sun. 10am-6pm. Also Staroměské nám. 5/934 (tel. 24 81 71 73). Open daily 9am-7pm.

Flights: Ruzyně Airport (tel. 20 11 11 11), 20km northwest of city center. Take bus 119 from Dejvická or the **airport bus** (tel. 20 11 42 96) from nám. Republicky (90kč) or Dejvická (60kč). Taxis to the airport are exorbitant. Many carriers fly into Prague, including **ČSA** (Czech National Airlines; tel. 20 10 43 10).

Trains: (info tel. 24 22 42 00, international fares 24 61 52 49). 4 terminals. **Praha Hlavní Nádraží** (tel. 24 61 72 50; Metro C: Hlavní Nádraží) is the biggest, but most international trains run out of **Holešovice** (tel. 24 61 72 65; Metro C: Nádraží Holešovice). To: Berlin (5 per day, 5hr., 1342kč; Wasteels 1128kč), Budapest (6 per day, 8hr., 1018kč; Wasteels 741kč), Vienna (4 per day, 5hr., 709kč; Wasteels 453kč), and Warsaw (3 per day, 10hr., 722kč; Wasteels 449kč). Domestic trains go from **Masarykovo** (tel. 24 61 72 60; Metro B: nám. Republiky) on the corner of Hybernská and Havličkova, or from **Smíchov** (tel. 24 61 72 55; Metro B: Smíchovské Nádraží), opposite Vyšehrad. **B.I.J. Wasteels:** Office at Hlavní Nádraží (tel. 24 61 74 54; fax 24 22 18 72) sells cheap international tickets to those under 26 and books couchettes. Open Mon. Fri. 8:45am-5:45pm, daily in summer. Wasteels tickets also available from the **Czech Railways Travel Agency** at Holešovice (tel. 80 08 05; fax 80 69 48). Open Mon.-Fri. 8am-5pm, Sat.-Sun. 9am-3pm.

Buses: ČSAD has three *autobusové nádraží* (bus terminals). **Praha-Florenc,** Křižíkova (tel. 24 21 49 90; info 24 21 10 60), behind the Masarykovo Nádraží train station, links to Berlin (1 per day, 6hr., 750kč) and Vienna (6 per week, 8½hr., 330kč). Metro B or C: Florenc. The staff speaks little English and the timetables are tricky; look for the bus-stop number of your destination. Buy tickets at least a day in advance. Students may get a 10% discount. The Tourbus office upstairs (tel. 24 21 02 21) sells **Eurolines** tickets. Open Mon.-Fri. 8am-8pm, Sat.-Sun. 9am-8pm.

Public Transportation: The **metro, tram,** and **bus** services are pretty good and share the same ticket system. Buy tickets from newsstands, machines in stations, or **DP** (*Dopravní Podnik;* transport authority) kiosks. Punch tickets upon first use. Basic 6kč ticket good for one short ride; more useful 10kč ticket valid for 1hr. (90min., 8pm-5am and all day Sat., Sun, and holidays), allowing you to switch from bus to tram to metro and back again. Large bags 5kč each, as are bikes and prams without babies in them (free *with* babies, so don't forget the baby). If a plain-clothes DP inspector issues you a 200kč spot fine for any reason, make sure you see an official badge and get a receipt. The metro's 3 lines run daily 5am-midnight: A is green on the maps, B is yellow, C is red. **Night trams** 51-58 and **buses** run all night after the last metro; look for the dark blue signs at bus stops. DP also sells **tourist passes** valid for the entire network (24hr. 50kč, 3-day 130kč, 1-week 190kč). **DP offices** are by the Jungmannovo nám. exit of Můstek station (tel. 24 22 51 35; open daily 7am-9pm) or by the Palackého nám. exit of Karlovo nám station (tel. 29 46 82; open Mon.-Fri. 7am-6pm).

Taxis: Taxi Praha (tel. 24 91 66 66) and **AAA** (tel. 24 32 24 32) operate 24hr. Reasonable rates are 15-20kč per km on top of a flat charge of 20-30kč. Before entering the cab, make sure the meter has been reset. On shorter trips, check that the meter is running by saying *"Zapněte taximetr";* for longer trips set a price beforehand. Always ask for a receipt *("Prosím, dejte mi paragon")* with distance traveled, price paid, and the driver's signature; if the driver doesn't write the receipt, you aren't obligated to pay. As you may guess, locals strongly distrust cab drivers.

Hitchhiking: Those hitching east take tram 1, 9, or 16 to the last stop. To points south, they walk 100m left from Metro C: Pražskeho povstání, and cross náměstí Hrdinů to 5 Květná (highway D1). To Munich, hitchers take tram 4 or 9 to the intersection of Plzeňská at Kukulova/Bucharova. Those going north take a tram or bus to "Kobyliské nám.," then bus 175 up Horňátecká.

Luggage Storage: Lockers in all train and bus stations take two 5kč coins. If these are full, or if you need to store your pack for longer than 24hr., use the left luggage offices in the basement of **Hlavní nádraží** (15kč per day for first 15kg) and halfway up the stairs at **Florenc** (10kč per day up to 15kg; open daily 5am-11pm).

English Bookstore: The Globe Bookstore, Janovského 14 (tel. 66 71 26 10). Metro C: Vltavská. Many used books, along a big noticeboard and coffeehouse. A legendary (pick-up) center of anglophone Prague. Open daily 9am-5pm.

Laundromat: Laundry Kings, Dejvická 16 (tel. 312 37 43), 1 block from Metro A: Hradčanská. Cross the tram *and* railroad tracks, then turn left onto Dejvická. Wash 60kč. Dry 15kč per 8min. Soap 10-20kč. Beer 11kč (ah, Prague). The note-board aids apartment seekers, English teachers, and friend seekers. Use the spinner to save on drying. Open Mon.-Fri. 6am-10pm, Sat.-Sun. 8am-10pm. In some private apartments, laundry service can be informally arranged.

Pharmacies: At Koněvova 210 (tel. 644 18 95) and Štefánikova 6 (tel. 24 51 11 12). Open 24hr. You may need to ask for *kontrcepční prostředky* (contraceptives), *náplast* (bandages), or *dámské vložky* (tampons).

Emergencies: Na Homolce (hospital for foreigners), Roentgenova 2 (tel. 52 92 21 46, after hours 57 21 11 11). Open Mon.-Fri. 8am-4pm. **American Medical Center** (tel. 80 77 56); **Canadian Medical Centre** (tel. 316 55 19).

Post Office: The main office is at Jindřišská 14. Metro A or B: Můstek. **Poste Restante** at window 28. Open Mon.-Fri. until 8pm. Address mail: "Lara DAY, POSTE RESTANTE, Jindřišská 14, 110 00 Praha 1, Czech Republic." For stamps go to window 16, letters and parcels under 2kg windows 12-14. Open 24hr. Parcels over 2kg can be mailed only at **Celní stanice** (customs office), Plzeňská 139. Take tram 4, 7, or 9 from Metro B: Anděl to "Klamovka." **Postal Code:** 110 00.

Telephones: Everywhere, especially at the main post office. Phonecards sell for 3kč per unit at kiosks, the post office, and some exchange places: don't let kiosks rip you off. **Telephone Code:** 02.

ACCOMMODATIONS AND CAMPING

While hotel prices rise, the hostel market is glutted; prices have stabilized around 200-300kč per night. The smaller hostels are friendly and often full. The Strahov complex and other student dorms bear the brunt of the summer's backpacking crowds. A few bare-bones hotels are still cheap, and growing numbers of residents are renting rooms. Sleeping on Prague's streets is too dangerous to consider.

Accommodations Agencies

Hawkers and agents besiege visitors at the train station with offers of rooms for around US$15-35 (450-1000kč). Arrangements made in this way are generally safe, but if you're wary of bargaining on the street, call around or try one of the agencies listed below. Make sure any room you accept is close to public transportation and that you understand what you're paying for; if you're at all confused, have the staff write it down. Payment is usually accepted in Czech, German, or U.S. currency.

Konvex 91, Ve Smečkách 29 (tel. 96 22 44 44; fax 22 21 15 02). Specializes in apartment rental, 440-590kč per person per night near the TV tower or 590-720kč in Staré Město. Hostels from 340kč per night. English and French spoken.

Ave., Hlavní Nádraží (tel. 24 22 32 26; fax 24 23 07 83), left from the main hall of the train station. The growing firm offers hundreds of rooms (shared and private) starting at 440kč a person and books hostels from 170kč. Open daily 6am-10pm.

Hello Travel Ltd., Senovážné nám. 3, between Na příkopě and Hlavní Nádraží (tel. 24 21 26 47). Arranges every sort of housing imaginable. Singles in pensions from US$23 (low season) or US$35 (high). Doubles US$38-56. Hostels US$10-13. Pay in kč, DM, or by credit card (AmEx, Diners, MC, V). Open daily 10am-9pm.

Hostels

In the Strahov neighborhood, west of the river next to the Olympic stadium, an enormous cluster of dorms/hostels opens up in July and August. These rooms may be best for those who arrive in the middle of the night *sans* clue, but many prefer the smaller, more personable hostels. It's best to phone the night before you arrive or at checkout time around 10am to snag a bed. Staffs generally speak good English.

The Clown and Bard, Bořivojova 102 (tel. 27 24 36). Metro A: Jiřího z Poděbrad. Walk down Slavíkova and take a right onto Ježkova; continue until the intersection with Bořivojova. Prague's newest hostel, in a converted 19th-century Žižkov building, provides beds in the roomy attic dorm for 200kč. Private rooms 250-350kč per person. Apartments from 300kč per person. Wildly popular in summer '97, owing much to the cellar bar, featuring beer and Leonard Cohen (open daily 8am-1am).

Slavoj Wesico (a.k.a. **Hostel Boathouse**), V náklích 1a (tel. 402 10 76). From Holešovice station or Metro A: Staroměstská, take tram 17 south to "Černý Kůň." Descend by the balustrade on the river side and walk to the Vltava. Strikingly clean 3- to 5-bed dorms perched above a working boathouse 250kč (300kč for one night). Big breakfasts 50kč. Laundry 80kč. 50kč key deposit. Call ahead.

V podzámčí, V podzámčí 27 (tel. 472 27 59). From Metro C: Budějovická, take bus 192 to the third stop—ask the driver to stop at "Nad Rybníky." Talking with Eva, the Czech in charge, is a delight. Kitchen, satellite TV, laundry service (100kč), and 2 cats. 2- to 4-person dorms with beds and loft mattresses 240kč per person.

Libra-Q, Senovážné nám. 21 (tel. 24 23 17 54; fax 24 22 15 79). Metro B: nám. Republiky or C: Hlavní Nádraží. Great location, just above the *Elle* and *Bohemian Model* offices, near Staré Město. 8-bed dorms 280kč. Triples and quads 300kč.

Domov Mládeže, Dykova 20 (tel. 25 06 88; fax 25 14 29). From Metro A: nám. Jiřího z Poděbrad, follow Nitranská and turn left on Dykova. Possibly the most enjoyable hostel trek ever. 60 beds in the peaceful, tree-lined Vinohrady district. Clean but not sterile 2- to 7-person dorms 300kč. Breakfast included.

ESTEC Hostel, Vaníčkova 5, blok 5 (tel. 57 21 04 10; fax 57 21 52 63). Take bus 217 or 143 from Metro A: Dejvická to "Koleje Strahov." Hundreds of beds. Try for a double (280kč per person) in the refurbished basement of blok 5. Reception open 24hr. Check-in 2pm. Singles 400kč. Triples 250kč per person. Crowded basement dorms 180kč. Breakfast 50kč. AmEx, Eurocard, MC, V.

Traveller's Hostels, in 8 dorms throughout the city center. The one at **Husova 3** (tel. 24 21 53 26) is the classiest, with dorm beds for 400kč. Smack dab in Staré Město. Take Metro A to Národní třída, turn right onto Spálená (which turns into Na Perštýně after Národní), and then Husova. Brand new outfits at **Dlouhá 33** (tel. 231 13 18), in Staré Město in the same building as the Roxy club (doubles 450kč per person, triples 390kč per person, 6-bed dorms 250kč); and at **Neklanova 32** (tel. 24 91 55 32), Metro C: Vyšehrad; head down Slavojova and it's on the left. No-bunks dorm 270kč. **Střelecký ostrov** (tel. 24 91 01 88), on the island off most Legii (Metro B: Národní třída). 300kč. **Mikulandská 5** (tel. 24 91 07 39). Metro B: Národní třída. 270kč. **Křížovnická 7** (tel. 232 09 87). Metro A: Staroměstská. 230kč. **Růžova 5** (tel. 26 01 11). Metro C: Hlavní nádraží. 220kč. **U lanové dráhy 3** (tel. 53 31 60). Tram 6, 9, 12 to "Újezd" and up the stairs. 200kč.

Welcome Hostel, Zikova 13 (tel. 24 32 02 02; fax 24 32 34 89). Metro A: Dejvická; from escalators, follow Šolinova to Zikova. Check-in 2:30pm. Check-out 9:30am. Singles 350kč. Doubles 480kč. They also run a Strahov dorm, Vaničková 5, blok 3 (tel. 52 71 90; see directions for ESTEC, above). Singles 300kč. Doubles 440kč.

Hotels and Pensions

With so many tourists infiltrating Prague, hotels are upgrading service and appearance, and budget hotels are now scarce. Beware that hotels may try to bill you for a more expensive room than the one in which you stayed. The good and cheap ones require reservations up to a month in advance. Call, then confirm by fax.

Hotel Standart, Přístavní 2 (tel. 87 52 58 or 66 71 04 71; fax 80 67 52). From Metro C: Vltavská, take tram 1, 3, 14, or 25 to "Dělnická." Continue along the street, then make a left. Very quiet neighborhood that gets very dark at night. Spotless hall showers and bathrooms. Singles 595kč. Doubles 750kč. Triples 995kč. Quads 1090kč. All rooms 350kč per person for HI members. Breakfast included.

Pension Unitas, Bartolomějská 9 (tel. 232 77 00; fax 232 77 09), in Staré Město. Metro B: Národní. An old monastery where Beethoven once performed, then a Communist jail where Václav Havel was incarcerated. Havel's basement room (P6) is now a quad outfitted with bunk beds, small windows, and heavy iron doors (1900kč). Singles 1000kč. Doubles 1200kč. Triples 1650kč. The Convent of the Gray Sisters still owns the place, so no smoking or drinking in the rooms.

Hotel Unitour, Senovážné nám. 21 (tel. 24 10 25 36; fax 24 22 15 79). The budget hotel arm of Libra-Q (above). Clean singles 750-890kč. Doubles 810-1250kč. Triples 1200-1480kč. Quads 1400kč.

B&B U Oty (Ota's House), Radlická 188 (tel./fax 57 21 53 23). 400m from Metro B: Radlická, up the slope. Kitchen facilities and free laundry services available after 3 nights. Singles 450kč. Doubles 700kč. Triples 900kč. Quads 1200kč. 100kč extra per person if staying only 1 night.

Camping

Tourist offices sell a guide of campsites near the city (15kč). For a tranquil setting, try **Císařská Louka,** a peninsula on the Vltava. Take Metro B: Smíchovské nádraží, then tram 12 to "Lihovar." Walk toward the river and onto the shaded path, where **Caravan Park** (tel. 54 09 25; fax 54 33 05) and **Caravan Camping** (tel. 54 56 82) charge 95kč per person and 90-140kč per tent. Caravan Park rents two-person (480kč) and four-person (720kč) bungalows. Caravan Camping offers rooms at 310-365kč per person. Reserve bungalows and rooms by fax. Or try **Sokol Troja,** Trojská 171 (tel./fax 688 11 77), north of the center in the Troja district. From Metro C: Nádraží Holešovice, take bus 112 to "Kazanka," the fourth stop, then walk 100m. (90kč per person; 70-150kč per tent. Dorm, bungalow, and flat accommodation at 155kč, 165kč, and 135kč per person respectively.) If full, at least 4 nearly identical places are on the same road. If you've ever felt like crawling into a barrel of *Budvar,* **Na Vlachovce,** Zenklova 217 (tel./fax 688 02 14), provides 2-person barrels (220kč per bed). Take bus 175 or 102 from Nádraží Holešovice toward Okrouhlická, get off, and continue in the same direction. Reserve a week ahead.

FOOD

The general rule is that the nearer you are to the tourist throngs on Staroměstské nám., Karlův most, and Václavské nám., the more you'll spend. Check your bill carefully—you'll pay for anything the waiter brings, including ketchup and bread. In Czech lunch spots, *hotová jídla* (prepared meals) are cheapest. Vegetarian eateries are opening up, but in many restaurants veggie options are limited to fried cheese dishes. Outlying Metro stops become marketplaces in summer. Look for the **vegetable market** at the intersection of Havelská and Melantrichova in the Old Town. For a real bargain, go to the basement level in the **Krone department store,** on Wenceslas Square at the intersection with Jindřišská (open Mon.-Fri. 8am-7pm, Sat. 8am-6pm, Sun. 10am-6pm), or **Kotva department store** (tel. 24 21 54 62) on the corner of Revoluční and nám Republiky (open Mon. 7am-7pm, Tues.-Fri. 7am-8pm, Sat. 8am-6pm).

Restaurants

Lotos, Platnéřská 13 (tel. 232 23 90). Metro A: Staroměstská. Veggie Czech food with a liberal use of leek. Leek soup 15kč. Soy cubes with dumplings 52kč. Wheat-yeast *Pilsner* 22kč for 0.5L. 7-herb tea 19kč. Open daily 11am-10pm.

Klub Architektů, Betlémské nám. 169 (tel. 24 40 12 14). Walk through the gates and descend to the right. A 12th-century cellar thrust into the 20th century with sleek table settings and copper pulley lamps. Veggie options 60-70kč. Meat dishes around 100kč. Chinese cabbage soup 20kč. Open daily 11am-midnight.

U Medvídků, Na Perštýně 7 (tel. 24 22 09 30), outskirts of Staré Město. Metro B: Národní tř. A *restaurace* and a *pivnice;* the latter is cheaper and more fun. Pretty good Czech food at very good prices since 1466. "Bear's Foot toast" 35kč. Beef sirloin with cranberries 71kč. Open Mon.-Sat. 11:30am-11pm, Sun. 11:30am-10pm.

Restaurace U Pravdů, Žitná 15 (tel. 29 95 92). Metro B: Karlovo nám. A deservedly popular Czech lunch spot. Fish dishes 61-76kč. Potato *knedlíky* 15kč. Big glass of *Staropramen* beer 16kč. Open Mon.-Fri. 10am-11pm, Sat.-Sun. 11am-11pm.

Jáma (The Den), V Jámě 7 (tel. 90 00 04 13). Metro A and C: Muzeum. Hidden off Vodičkova. Attracts a diverse but largely non-Czech crowd. Weekend brunches (89-119kč) all come with free coffee refills. Other options include a "super veggie burro" (124kč) and burgers (99-116kč). Open daily 11am-1am.

Bar bar, Všehrdova 17 (tel. 53 29 41). Metro A: Malostranská. Left off Karmelitská walking down from Malostranské nám. A jungle jungle of salads salads with meat, fish, cheese, or just veggies 54-89kč. 40 varieties of whiskey from 41kč. *Velkopopovický kozel* on tap 15kč. Open Mon.-Fri. 11am-midnight, Sat.-Sun. noon-midnight.

Malostranská Hospoda, Karmelitská 25 (tel. 53 20 76), just by Malostranské nám. Metro A: Malostranská. Chairs spill out onto the square from the pub's vaulted interior. Good *guláš* 58kč. Draft *Staropramen* 13kč per 0.5L. English menu. Open Mon.-Sat. 10am-midnight, Sun. 11am-midnight.

Penzion David, Holubova 5. Take tram 14 (catch it by the main post office) to its end at Laurová, take a left off the main street and then a right on Holubova. Caters to gay men, with some of the best food in town. Entrees mostly 45-125kč. Lunch menu a dirt-cheap 45kč. Open Mon.-Fri. 11am-11pm, Sat.-Sun. noon-midnight.

Bohemian Bagel, Újezd 16. Metro A: Malostranská or tram 22 to "Újezd." All the usual bagel flavors, plus some surprising ones. Bagel with cream cheese 35kč. 5 plain ones for 60kč. Open Mon.-Fri. 8am-7:30pm, Sat. 8am-7pm, Sun. 10am-5pm.

Cafés

When Prague journalists are bored, they churn out another "Whatever happened to café life?" feature. Ignore their pessimism, and try some of the places listed below.

U malého Glena, Karmelitská 23 (tel. 535 81 15 or 90 00 39 67), just south off Malostranské nám. Metro A: Malostranská. The "light entree" menu has veggie plates for 70kč and more. Czechs and foreigners here; some descend to the **Maker's Mark bar** for jazz or blues at 9pm (cover 50-70kč). Open daily 7:30am-2am.

U Knihomola, Mánesova 79 (tel. 627 77 68). Metro A: Jiřího z Poděbrad. A living room with comfy couches and coffee-table literature. Coffee 20kč. Carrot cake 75kč. Open Mon.-Thurs. 10am-11pm, Fri.-Sat. 10am-midnight, Sun. 11am-8pm.

The Globe Coffeehouse, Janovského 14 (tel. 66 71 26 10). Metro C: Vltavská. Tasty, bitter black coffee (20kč per cup), a slightly pricey weekend brunch menu (omelette 120kč), and all the expat gossip. Open daily 10am-midnight.

U červeného páva, Kamzíková 6 (tel. 24 23 31 68). Metro A: Staroměstská. Wander down Celetná from the square. Proof that not everything around Staroměstské nám. is over-touristed. Quiet café-bar for gays and straights. Espresso 28kč.

SIGHTS

Orient yourself before tackling the city's many scattered sights. Central Prague is structured by three streets that form a leaning *"T."* The long stem of the *T* is the boulevard **Václavské nám.** (Wenceslas Sq.). The **National Museum** sits at the bottom of this street. Busy and pedestrian **Na příkopě** forms the right arm of the *T* and leads to **nám. Republiky;** on the left, **28. října** becomes **Národní** after a block, leading to the **National Theater** on the river. A maze of small streets leads to Staroměstské nám. two blocks above the *T*. There are two prominent **St. Nicholas churches**—in Malá Strana near the castle and on Starométské nám.

Václavské náměstí (Wenceslas Square) Not so much a square as a broad boulevard, **Václavské nám.** owes its name to the equestrian statue of the Czech ruler and saint **Václav** (Wenceslas), in front of the National Museum. Václav has presided over a century of turmoil and triumph, witnessing no fewer than five revolutions from his pedestal since 1912. The new Czechoslovak state was proclaimed here in 1918, and in 1969, Jan Palach set himself on fire in protest against the 1968 Soviet invasion. Václavské nam. sweeps down from the National Museum past department stores, stately parks, posh hotels, fast-food joints, and trashy casinos. Keep your wits about you: despite frequent police sweeps, the square has become one of the seediest areas in Prague. The **Radio Prague Building,** behind the National Museum, was the scene of a tense battle during Prague Spring between Soviet tanks and Prague citizens trying to protect the radio studios by human barricade. North of the Václav statue, the Art Nouveau style, expressed in everything from lampposts to windowsills, dominates the square. The premier example is the 1903 **Hotel Evropa.**

From the north end of Václavské nám., take a quick detour to Jungmannovo nám. and **Panna Marie Sněžná** (Church of Our Lady of the Snows). The Gothic walls are highest of any church in Prague, but the rest of the structure is still unfinished. Under the arcades halfway down Národní stands a **memorial** honoring the hundreds of Prague's citizens beaten by the police on November 17, 1989. Václav Havel's Civic Forum movement was based at the **Lanterna magika (Magic Lantern)** theater, Národní 4, during the tense days now known as the Velvet Revolution.

Staroměstské náměstí (Old Town Square) A labyrinth of narrow roads and Old World alleys lead to **Staroměstské nám.,** Staré Město's thriving heart. **Jan Hus,** the Czech Republic's most famous martyred theologian, sweeps across the scene in bronze. No less than eight magnificent towers surround the square. The building with a bit blown off is the **Staroměstská radnice** (Old Town Hall), partially demolished by the Nazis in the final week of World War II. **Crosses** on the ground mark the spot where 27 Protestant leaders were executed on June 21, 1621 for staging a rebellion against the Catholic Hapsburgs (open for tours in summer daily 9am-5pm; 30kč, students 20kč). Crowds gather on the hour to watch the wonderful **astronomical clock** *(orloj)* chime with its procession of apostles, a skeleton, and a thwarted Turk. Across from the *radnice,* the spires of **Matka Boží před Týnem** (Týn Church) rise above a huddled mass of medieval homes. The famous astronomer **Tycho Brahe** is buried inside. To the left of the church, the austere **Dům U kamenného zvonu** (House at Stone Bell) shows the Gothic core that lurks beneath many of Prague's Baroque facades (see **Museums,** p. 228). The flowery **Goltz-Kinský palác** on the left is the finest of Prague's Rococo buildings. **Sv. Mikuláš** (Church of St. Nicholas) sits just across Staroměstské nám. (open Tues.-Sun. 10am-5pm). Between Sv. Mikulaš and Maiselova, a plaque marks **Franz Kafka's** former home.

Josefov Prague's historic Jewish neighborhood, Josefov, is located north of Starométstské nám. along Maiselova and several side streets. In 1180, Prague's citizens complied with a pope's decree to avoid Jews by surrounding the area with a 12-foot wall, which stood until 1848. The closed city bred disease but also stories, many focusing on **Rabbi Loew ben Bezalel** (1512-1609) and his legendary *golem,* a creature made from mud that came to life. Hitler's decision to create a "museum of an extinct race" resulted in the preservation of the old cemetery and five synagogues despite the destruction of Prague's Jewish community in the holocaust (open daily 9am-5:30pm; museums and synagogues 450kč, students 330kč). At the 90-degree bend in U Starého hřbitova, **Starý židovský hřbitov** (Old Jewish Cemetery) remains the quarter's most popular attraction. Between the 14th and 18th centuries, 12 layers of 20,000 graves were laid. The 700-year-old **Staronová synagóga** (Old-New Synagogue) is Europe's oldest operating synagogue. The Hebrew clock in exterior of the neighboring **Židovská radnice** (Jewish Town Hall) runs counterclockwise. Walking down Maiselova and turning right on Široka leads you to the **Pinkasova synagóga,** whose walls list the names of victims of Nazi persecution.

Karlův most (Charles Bridge) Head out of Staroměstské nám. on Jilská, and go right onto Karlova. Wandering left down Liliová leads to Bethlémské nám., where the **Betlémská kaple** (Bethlehem Chapel) stands. The present building is a reconstruction of the medieval chapel made famous by Jan Hus, the great Czech religious reformer. Turning back onto Karlova and left toward the river leads to **Karlův most,** which throngs with tourists and people trying to sell them things. At the center of the bridge is the statue of legendary hero **Jan Nepomucký** (John of Nepomuk), confessor to Queen Žofie. Brave Jan was tossed over the side of the Charles for faithfully guarding his queen's confidences from a suspicious King Václav IV. The right-hand rail, where Jan was supposedly ejected, is now marked with a cross and five stars between the fifth and sixth statues. It is said that if you make a wish with a finger on each star you will return to Prague. Climb the Gothic **defense tower** on the Malá Strana side of the bridge or the tower on the Old Town side for a superb view of the city (both towers open daily 10am-5:30pm; 30kč, students 20kč). The stairs on the left side of the bridge (as you face the castle district) lead to **Hroznová,** where a crumbling mural honors John Lennon and the 60s peace movement.

Malá Strana (Lesser Side) The seedy hangout of criminals and counter-revolutionaries for nearly a century, the cobblestone streets of Malá Strana have, in the strange sway of Prague fashion, become the most prized real estate on either side of the Vltava. From Karlův most, continue straight up Mostecká and turn right into **Malostranské nám.** Dominating the square is the magnificent Baroque **Chrám sv. Mikuláše** (Church of St. Nicholas) with its remarkable high dome. Concerts of a narrow range of classical music take place nightly. (Church open daily 9am-4pm; 25kč, students 15kč. Concert tickets 350kč, students 250kč.) Nearby on Karmelitská rises the more modest **Panna Maria Vítězna** (Church of Our Lady Victorious). The famous polished-wax statue of the **Infant Jesus of Prague** resides within (open in summer daily 7am-9pm; off-season 8am-8pm; English mass Sun. 12:15pm). A simple wooden gate just down the street at Letenská 10 opens onto **Valdštejnská zahrada** (Wallenstein Garden), one of Prague's best-kept secrets. This tranquil 17th-century Baroque garden is enclosed by old buildings that glow golden on sunny afternoons.

Pražský Hrad (Prague Castle) Founded 1000 years ago, Pražský Hrad has always been the seat of the Bohemian government. Give the castle a full day—just don't make it Monday. From Metro A: Malostranská, climb up the **Staré Zámecké Schody** (Old Castle Steps), passing between the two armed sentries into the castle. On the left, the **Lobkovický Palác** contains a replica of Bohemia's coronation jewels and a history of the lands the Czech Republic comprises (open Tues.-Sun. 9am-5pm; 40kč, students 20kč). Halfway up Jiřská, the tiny **Zlatá ulička** (Golden Lane) heads off to the right. Once alchemists worked here; later Kafka lived at #22. When Jiřská opens into a courtyard, to the right stands the **Klášter (convent) sv. Jiří,** home to the **National Gallery of Bohemian Art.** (Open Tues.-Sun. 10am-6pm; 50kč, students and seniors 15kč, free first Fri. of each month.) The **basilica sv. Jiří.** next door was first built in 921. (100kč, students 50kč; also good for the cathedral, Old Royal Palace, and Powder Tower. All sights open daily 9am-5pm. Ticket valid for three days.)

Across the courtyard stands Pražský Hrad's centerpiece, the colossal **Chrám sv. Víta** (St. Vitus's Cathedral), finished in 1929—600 years after it was begun. To the right of the high altar lies the **tomb of sv. Jan Nepomucký** of Karlův most fame, 3m of solid, glistening silver, weighing two tons. Look for an angel holding Jan's silvered tongue. The tomb of Emperor Karel IV is in the **Royal Crypt** below the church, along with all four of Karel's wives. Back up the stairs in the main church, the walls of **Svatováclavská kaple** (St. Wenceslas's Chapel) are lined with precious stones and a painting cycle depicting the legend of this saint. The 287 steps of the **Cathedral Tower** lead to a good view of the entire city.

The **Starý královský palác** (Old Royal Palace) houses the lengthy expanse of the **Vladislav Hall;** upstairs is the **Chancellery of Bohemia,** the site of the second Defenestration of Prague. On May 23, 1618, angry Protestants flung two Hapsburg officials (and their secretary) through the windows and into a steaming dungheap, signalling the start of the extraordinarily bloody Thirty Years' War. If you exit the castle though the main gate instead, you'll pass the **Šternberský palác,** home of the National Gallery's European art collection, featuring Goya, Rubens, and Rembrandt (hours same as basilica, above).

Outer Prague The **Petřínské sady,** the largest gardens in central Prague, are topped by a model of the Eiffel Tower and the wacky castle **Bludiště** (castle open

CZECH REPUBLIC

daily 10am-7pm). Take a cable car from just above the intersection of Vítězná and Újezd (6kč; look for *lanová dráha* signs) for spectacular views.

The former haunt of Prague's 19th-century romantics, **Vyšehrad** is clothed in nationalistic myths and the legends of a once-powerful Czech empire. It is here that Princess Libuše adumbrated Prague and embarked on her search for the first king of Bohemia. The 20th century has passed the castle by, and Vyšehrad's elevated pathways now escape the flood of tourists in the city center. Quiet walkways lead between crumbling stone walls to a magnificent **church,** a black Romanesque rotunda, and one of the Czech Republic's most celebrated sites, **Vyšehrad Cemetery,** where Dvořák and other national heroes are laid to rest. To reach the complex, take Metro C: Vyšehrad (complex open 24hr.).

Museums

Národní (National) muzeum, Václavské nám. 68. Metro A or C: Muzeum. Soviet soldiers fired on this landmark, thinking it was a government building. The collection is less interesting. Open daily May-Sept. 10am-6pm; Oct.-April 9am-5pm. Closed first Tues. each month. 40kč, students 15kč, free first Mon. each month.

Národní galérie: Spread around nine locations—the **Šternberský palác** and **Klášter sv. Jiří** are described above in the "Pražský Hrad" section. The other major gallery is the **Klášter sv. Anežky** (St. Agnes's Cloister), where the 19th-century Czech art collection is displayed. Metro A: Staroměstská. These 3 are open Tues.-Sun. 10am-6pm. 50kč, students 15kč. Booklet describing other venues at the cashier.

Bertramka Mozart muzeum, Mozartova 169 (tel. 54 38 93). Metro B: Anděl. Take a left on Plzeňská, and look for a sign pointing up the slope on the left. Mozart dashed off the overture to *Don Giovanni* here the day before it opened in 1787. Open daily 9:30am-6pm. 50kč, students 30kč. Concerts held Wed.-Fri. in summer.

Muzeum hlavního města Prahy (Municipal), Na poříčí 52. Metro B or C: Florenc. Holds the original calendar board from the town hall's astronomical clock and a scale model of old Prague, precise to the last window pane of more than 2000 houses. 100kč deposit for an English guidebook. Open Tues.-Sun. 9am-6pm. 20kč, students 5kč. Other exhibits from the collection reside in the **Dům U kamenného zvonu (House at Stone Bell),** Staroměstské nám., left of Matka Boží před Týnem. Open Tues.-Sun. 10am-6pm. 75kč, students 35kč.

ENTERTAINMENT

For a list of current concerts and performances, consult *The Prague Post, Threshold,* or *Do města-Downtown* (the latter two are free and distributed at most cafés and restaurants). Most shows begin at 7pm; unsold tickets are sometimes available a half-hour before showtime. **Národní Divadlo** (National Theater), Národní třída 2/4 (tel. 24 91 34 37), is perhaps Prague's most famous theater. (Box office open Mon.-Fri. 10am-6pm, Sat.-Sun. 10am-12:30pm and 3-6pm, and 30min. before performances.) Equally impressive is **Stavovské Divadlo** (Estates Theater), Ovocný trh 1 (tel. 24 21 50 01), where Mozart's *Don Giovanni* premiered. (Box office open same hours as National Theater. Earphones available for simultaneous translation.) Most of Prague's theaters shut down in July and return in August with attractions for tourists. Around mid-May to early June, the **Prague Spring Festival** draws musicians from around the world. Tickets (300-2000kč) may sell out a year in advance; try **Bohemia Ticket International,** Salvátorská 6, next to Čedok (tel. 24 22 78 32; open Mon.-Fri. 9am-6pm, Sat. 9am-4pm, Sun. 10am-3pm).

The most authentic way to enjoy Prague at night is through an alcoholic fog; the venues below should satisfy the need for a *pivo* and *takzvaná populární takzvaná hudba*—so-called popular so-called music. Gay bars distribute the linguistically confused *Amigo* (15kč), a guide to gay life in the Czech Republic and Slovakia.

Taz Pub, U Obecního domu 3. Metro B: nám. Republiky, on the street running along the right side of the county house. A somewhat young, mostly Czech crowd comes here to drink, listen to music, and smoke pot (legal, although dealing is not). Imported beers 30-40kč. Open Mon.-Fri. noon-2am, Sat.-Sun. 2pm-2am.

Cafe Gulu Gulu, Betlémské nám. 8. A hangout for the Czech university crowd and summer backpackers. Fun-loving, with impromptu musical jams. By 11pm, people are hanging out of windowsills. *Eggenberg* 25kč. Open daily 10am-1am.

Cafe Marquis de Sade, a.k.a. **Cafe Babylon,** Templová 8, between nám. Republiky and Staroměstské nám. Metro B: nám. Republiky. The band strikes up old pops or mellow jazz for a packed house. Beer 25kč. Open daily until 1am or later.

U Sv. Tomaše, Letenská 12. Metro A: Malostranská. The mighty dungeons echo with boisterous beer songs. The homemade brew is 30kč, as are the other six beers on tap. Live brass band nightly. Open daily 11:30am-midnight.

Agharta, Krakovská 5, just down Krakovská from Václavské nám. The "Jazz Centrum" also operates a CD shop. Nightly live jazz ensembles, starting at 9pm. Beer 40kč. 80kč cover. Open nightly 7pm-1am.

Radost FX, Bělehradská 120. Metro C: I.P. Pavlova. Tourists do come here, but it's still the place where Czechs want to be seen. *Staropramen* 35kč. Cover from 50kč. The vegetarian café upstairs serves chili until 5am (95kč). Open 8pm-dawn.

The Maker's Mark, Karmelitská 23, below "U malého Glena" (see Cafés, above). Jazz or blues nightly. Beer 25kč. Cover 50-70kč. Open daily 8pm-2am.

U Střelce, Karoliny Světlé 12, under the archway on the right. Gay club that pulls a diverse crowd for its Fri. and Sat. night cabarets, when fabulous female impersonators take the stage. Beer 25kč. Cover 80kč. Open nightly 6pm-4am.

L-Club, Lublaňská 48 (tel. 90 00 11 89). Metro C: I. P. Pavlova. Great fun for both the guys and the dolls, with a dancing floor, bar, and café. Blacklights make the white shirts glow. Mostly gay men. Cover 50kč. Open nightly 8pm-4am.

CZECH REPUBLIC

■ Near Prague: Karlštejn, Kutná Hora, and Terezín

The Bohemian hills around Prague contain 14 castles, some built as early as the 13th century. A train ride southwest from Praha-Smíchov (45min., 12kč) brings you to **Karlštejn** (tel. (0311) 846 17), a walled and turreted fortress built by Karel IV to house his crown jewels and holy relics. The **Chapel of the Holy Cross** is decorated with more than 2000 inlaid precious stones and 128 apocalyptic paintings by medieval artist Master Theodorik. (Open Tues.-Sun. 9am-5pm. Admission with English guide 150kč, less for students, with Czech guide, or with no guide.) Ask at the Prague tourist office if they have finished restoring the chapel before setting out.

An hour and a half east of Prague is the former mining town of **Kutná Hora** (Silver Hill). A 13th-century abbot sprinkled soil from Golgotha on the cemetery, which made the rich and superstitious keen to be buried there. In a fit of whimsy, the monk in charge began designing flowers with pelvi and crania. He never finished, but the artist František Rint completed the project in 1870 with flying butt-bones, femur crosses, and a grotesque chandelier made from every bone in the human body. (Open April-Sept. daily 8am-noon and 1-6pm; Oct. 9am-noon and 1-5pm; Nov.-March 9am-noon and 1-4pm. 20kč, students 10kč). The *kostnice* is 2km from the bus station: take a local bus to "Sedlec Tabák" and follow the signs. From Palackého nám., follow 28. října to Havlíčkovo nám. in the old part of the city. Originally a storehouse for Kutná Hora's stash, the imposing **Vlašský Dvůr** (Italian Court) got its name after Václav IV invited the finest Italian architects to refurbish the palace. (Open daily 9am-6pm; tours every 15min.; 20kč, students 10kč; infrequent English tours 50kč, students 25kč.) Pass the ancient **St. James Church** and follow Barborská, which becomes lined with statues and ends at the beautiful Gothic **St. Barbara's Cathedral** (open Tues.-Sun. 9am-5pm; 20kč, students 10kč). **Buses** arrive from Prague's Florenc station (6 per day, 1 per day Sat.-Sun., 1½hr., 44kč) and station 2 at Metro A: Želivského (9 per day, 2 per day Sat.-Sun., 1hr. 40min., 44kč).

In 1940 Hitler's Gestapo set up a prison in the Small Fortress in Theresienstadt, and in 1941 the town itself became a concentration camp known as **Terezín**—by 1942, the civilian population had been evacuated. Some 35,000 Jews died here and 85,000 others were transported to death camps in the east, primarily Auschwitz. Twice, Terezín was beautified in order to deceive delegations from the Red Cross. The **Ghetto Museum,** Komenského (tel. (0416) 78 25 77), displays contemporary documents and harrowing children's art from the ghetto. (Open daily 9am-6pm. 80kč, students 60kč. Including Small Fortress 100kč, students 60kč. Guided tour in English 220kč.) East of the town, the **Small Fortress** is the other major sight (open daily 9am-5:45pm).The Prague-Florenc **bus** (every 1-2hr., 1hr., 43kč) stops by the central square, where the tourist office sells a map (40kč; open until 6pm).

WEST BOHEMIA

Bursting with curative springs, West Bohemia is the Czech mecca for those in search of a good bath. The Czech Republic's two most popular drinks also have their home here—the spicy green *Becherovka* and Plzeň's world-famous *Pilsner.*

Karlovy Vary

Since the Holy Roman Emperor and King of Bohemia Karel IV's hunting dog stumbled upon a fountain here 600 years ago, the spas of Karlovy Vary have attracted such diverse personalities as Sigmund Freud, Peter the Great, and Karl Marx. Therapeutic in its own right, the local brew *Becherovka,* a careful alcoholic synthesis of selected herbs and just the right amount of sugar, also draws visitors.

In the heart of the pedestrian spa area, you're free to drink from the **Pramen svobody** (Freedom Spring) or the half a dozen more spas that cluster along the **Mlýnská kolonáda** (Mill Colonnade). Bring your own cup or buy one for 40-200kč. Across the river, the Baroque dome of the **Church of Mary Magdalene** and the Art Nouveau **Zawojski House** deserve a look. The most potent of the springs, the **Sprudel Fountain** (Vřídlo) spurts thirty liters of 72°C water several meters into the air every second. Follow Stará Louka (Old Meadow) until you reach Mariánská; at the dead end, a **funicular** rises to the **Diana Watchtower.** The tower opens its spiraling staircase daily 10am to 6pm (5kč; funicular runs daily 9am-7pm every 15min; round-trip 30kč). Ogle the **Grandhotel Pupp,** the largest hotel in 19th-century Bohemia, on the way down. In early July, Karlovy Vary hosts an **International Film Festival.**

Practical Information, Accommodations, and Food Many establishments in Karlovy Vary are adding an initial "32" to their **phone numbers.** The town is referred to in German as *Karlsbad,* and prices are often listed in DM. **Trains** arrive from Prague (5 per day, 4hr., 80-100kč). **Buses,** quicker than the train, serve Prague (16 per day, 2½hr., 84kč) and Plzeň (10 per day, 1½hr., 60kč). The white **City-info booth,** Masaryka (tel./fax (017) 233 51), parallel to the city's other main thoroughfare, Bechera, sells maps and brochures and books rooms starting at 330kč per person. Exchange traveler's checks at banks (2% commission) or at **American Express,** Vřídelní 51, for free (AmEx open Mon.-Fri. 9am-5pm, Sat.-Sun. 9am-noon). **Autotourist,** nám. Horákové 18 (tel. (017) 332 28 33), can book a double for 900kč (open Mon.-Fri. 9am-5pm, Sat. 9am-noon; off-season closed noon-1pm). **Pension Kosmos,** Zahradní 39 (tel. (017) 322 31 68), is centrally located (singles 400kč, with bath 700kč; doubles 660kč, with bath 1200kč). The area around **Hotel Adria,** Západní 1 (tel. (017) 322 37 65), can get a bit dangerous at night, but the hotel offers clean rooms and easy nightlife access. (Singles 752kč; doubles 1168kč; triples 1680kč; bathrooms and breakfast included.) Most restaurant fare is aimed at tasteless tourists; try the supermarket **Mwstsuá Tržnice,** Horova 1 (open Mon.-Fri. 6am-7pm, Thurs. until 8pm, Sat. 7am-1pm). The (mostly) **Vegetarian restaurant,** Pavlova 25, has fruit kebab (45kč) and veggie goulash and dumplings (35kč). **E&T,** Zeyera 3, takes in a mixed gay and straight crowd that feeds on meat dishes (80-130kč) and salads (30kč), drowning it all in 20kč beer (open daily 10am-11pm).

Plzeň

Eighty kilometers southwest of Prague, Plzeň's most famous industry centers on the **Prazdroj Brewery,** the home of Pilsner Urquell. Thousands of tourists come here annually just to take the brewery tour and pay homage to a time-honored lager. While you can still see straight, check out the city's other historical sights—many were spruced up for Plzeň's 700th anniversary in 1995. **St. Bartholemew's Church** towers over the market square and offers a vertiginous view of the town from its observation deck (18kč, students 12kč). Inside, a rich collection of Gothic statues and altars bows to the stunning 14th-century **Madonna of Pilsen,** recalling Bohemia's glory days under Charles IV. From the northeast part of nám. Republiky, the short street Pražská takes you to **Masné krámy,** the former slaughterhouse at #16, an impressive late-Gothic building that now features changing art exhibitions (open Mon.-Fri. 10am-6pm, Sat. 10am-1pm, Sun. 9am-5pm; 15kč, students 8kč). Across the street, the 16th-century **Vodárenská věž** (Water Tower) was used to store the water needed for fine beer. Today the tower and the underground cellars *(Plzeňské podzemí)* can be visited on a guided tour that starts at Perlova 4, a building near the tower (tel. (19) 722 52 14; open Tues.-Sun. 9am-4:20pm; 30kč).

Perlova ends at Veleslavínova, where **Pivovarské muzeum** (Brewery Museum), Veleslavínova 6, exhibits beer paraphernalia, gigantic steins, and wacky pub signs (open Tues.-Sun. 10am-6pm; 30kč, students 15kč). The tour of **Měšťanský Pivovar Plzeňský Prazdroj** (Pilsner Urquell Burghers' Brewery; tel. (019) 706 28 88), 300m east of the Old Town, passes the malting area, the old *kellar,* and barrel upon barrel of beer (tour begins 12:30pm on weekdays).

Practical Information, Accommodations, and Food The train station is located east of the Old Town, and the bus station west. **Trains** (info tel. (019) 22 20 79) rumble to Prague (13 per day, 2hr., 48kč), while **buses** (tel. (019) 22 37 04) offer extensive service to Prague and surrounding towns. The MIS **tourist office,** nám. Republiky 41 (tel. (019) 723 65 35; 722 44 73), sells maps (40kč) and arranges rooms from 300kč (open Mon.-Fri. 10am-4:30pm, Sat. 9am-1pm). To get to the fairly institutional **SOU (HI),** Vejprnická 58 (tel. (019) 28 20 12), take tram 2 to "Internáty" (189kč). **Penzion v Solní,** Solní 8 (tel. (019) 723 66 52), has delightful rooms in a renovated 16th-century house. (Reception open daily 9am-6pm. Singles 510kč; doubles 850č; higher in July and Aug. Call ahead.) A young crowd chills over beer (15kč) at **U Dominika,** Dominikanská 3 (pork dishes 5-70kč; open Mon.-Sat. 11am-midnight, Sun. 7pm-midnight). **U bílého lva,** Pražská 15, offers entrees from 35kč (open daily 10am-11pm). The students of West Bohemia University have made Plzeň a boomtown of bars and clubs, and the tourist office's young summer staff gives nightlife advice. **Bílej Mědved,** Prokopova 30, attracts a Budvar (19kč) drinking crowd (open Mon.-Thurs. 6pm-3am, Fri.-Sat. 6pm-4am, Sun. 8pm-2am).

SOUTH BOHEMIA

České Budějovice

No amount of beer can help you correctly pronounce České Budějovice (CHESS-kay BOOD-yay-yov-ee-tzeh). Luckily for pint-guzzlers, the town was known as Budweis in the 19th century when it inspired the name of the popular but pale North American *Budweiser,* which bares little relation to the malty local *Budvar.* But the town has been blessed with more than good beer: mill streams, the Malše, and the Vltava wrap around an amalgam of Gothic, Renaissance, and Baroque houses scattered along medieval alleys and 18th-century streets. The city also serves as a launchpad to South Bohemia's castles and natural wonders.

This Bud's for EU

Many Yankees, having tasted the malty goodness of a Budvar brew, return home to find it conspicuously unavailable. That Budvar was Czech Republic's largest exporter of beer in 1995 makes its absence from American store shelves even stranger. Where's the Budvar? The answer lies in a tale of trademarks and town names. České Budějovice (Budweis in German) had been brewing its own style of lager for centuries when the Anheuser-Busch brewery in St. Louis came out with its Budweiser-style beer in 1876. Not until the 1890s, however, did the Budějovice Pivovar (Brewery) begin producing a beer labeled "Budweiser." International trademark conflicts ensued, and in 1911 the companies signed a non-competition agreement: Budvar got markets in Europe and Anheuser-Busch took North America. But the story continues...

A few years ago, Anheuser-Busch tried to end the confusion by buying a controlling interest in the makers of Budvar. The Czech government replied "nyeh." In response, the following year Anheuser-Busch didn't order its normal one-third of the Czech hop crop. Anheuser-Busch is now suing for trademark infringement in Finland, while Budvar is petitioning the EU to make the moniker "Budweiser" a designation as exclusive as that of "Champagne," meaning that any brand sold in the EU under that name would have to come from the Budweiser region. As long as the battle continues on European fronts, there is little chance that a Budvar in America will be anything but an illegal alien.

Surrounded by Renaissance and Baroque buildings, cobbled **nám. Otakara II** is the largest square in the Czech Republic. In the center, **Samsonova kašna** (Samson's fountain) spews water from anguished looking faces. The *náměstí's* impressive 1555 **radnice** stands a full story above the other buildings on the square and sports a fine set of gargoyles. Near the square's northeast corner, **Černá věž** (Black Tower) looms over the town. Beware: the treacherous stairs rising 72m are difficult even for the sober. (6kč. Open July-Aug. Tues.-Sun. 10am-7pm; Sept.-Nov. 9am-5pm, March-June 10am-6pm.) The tower once served as a belfry for the neighboring 13th-century **Chrám sv. Mikuláše** (Church of St. Nicholas; open daily 7am-6pm). The city's most famous attraction waits a bus ride from the center—the **Budweiser Brewery,** Karoliny Světlé 4, offers tours of the factory for groups of six or more; arrange them at the tourist office (bus 2, 4, or 5).

Practical Information, Accommodations, and Beer The **train** station east of the Old Town welcomes travelers from Prague (2½hr., 72kč), Plzeň (2hr., 56kč), and Brno (4½hr., 100kč). The **tourist office,** nám. Otakara II 2 (tel./fax (038) 594 80), books private rooms (around 350kč) for 10kč (open Mon.-Fri. 9am-5pm, Sat.-Sun. 9-noon). **Pension U Výstaviště,** U Výstaviště 17 (tel. (038) 724 01 48), is a clean, friendly establishment; take bus 1, 13, 14, or 17 from the station to "U parku" and continue 150m along the street that branches right (250kč first night, 200kč thereafter; they may offer you a free lift from the station). The rooms in the more pricey **Hotel Grand,** Nádražní 27 (tel. (038) 565 03; fax 596 23), opposite the train station, come with showers and breakfast included (doubles start at 900kč).

Restaurants pop up everywhere along the Old Town's back streets, but it's hard to find anything but meat and dumplings. A grocery, **Večerka,** awaits at Plachého 10 (entrance on Hroznova; open Mon.-Fri. 7am-8pm, Sat. 7am-1pm, Sun. 8am-8pm). Aid your digestion of Tábor steak (95kč) or veggie dishes (50-70kč) with a tall *Budvar* (19kč per 0.5L) at **U paní Emy,** Široká 25, near the main square. In summer, lakes around the town host open-air **disco concerts** (ask at the tourist office).

Český Krumlov

Winding medieval streets, scenic promenades, and the looming presence of Bohemia's second-largest castle might have earned Český Krumlov its coveted UNESCO-protected status, but the town's wonderful location on the banks of the Vltava also makes it ideal for bicycling, canoeing, and kayaking. Looming high above town, the **castle's** stone courtyard is open to the public for free, and two tours cover the lavish interior, which includes frescoes, a Baroque theater, and crypt galleries. (Open April and Oct. 9am-noon and 1-3pm; May, June, and Sept. 9am-noon and 1-4pm; July-Aug. 9am-noon and 1-5pm. Tours in English 70kč, students 30kč.) Housed in an immense Renaissance building, the **Egon Schiele International Cultural Center,** Široká 70-72, displays hours of browsing material, including works by Picasso and other 20th-century artists (open daily 10am-6pm; 120kč, students 80kč). The **city museum,** Horní 152, features bizarre folk instruments, bone sculptures, and log barges (open May-Sept. daily 10am-12:30pm and 1-5pm; 30kč, students 5kč).

Sixteen kilometers southwest of České Budějovice, the town is best reached by frequent **buses** (10 per day, fewer on weekends, 35min.). The **tourist office,** nám. Svornosti 1 (tel. (0337) 71 11 83), in the town hall, books rooms in pensions starting at 550kč and cheaper private rooms (open Mon.-Sat. 9am-6pm, Sun. 10am-6pm). Mattresses lie among antiques at the **Moldau Hilton,** Parkan 116 (kitchen; 200kč, Czechs 300kč; closed mid-Jan. to mid-May). **U vodnika,** Po vodě 55 (tel. (0337) 71 19 35; email vodnik@ck.bohem-net.cz), has two quads (180kč per bed) and a double (500kč) near the river (**Internet access** 100kč per hr.). Satisfied customers pour onto the cobbled street at **Na louži,** Kájovská 66 (pork, dumplings, and cabbage 54kč; open daily 10am-10pm). The **Cikanská jízba** (Gypsy bar), Dlouhá 31 (tel. 55 85), fills up with English-speaking expats and tourist-friendly locals. *Eggenberg* pours for 16kč per 0.5L (open Mon.-Thurs. 4-11pm, Fri.-Sun. 4pm-1am). To get there, follow Radniční out of the main square, then take a left.

CZECH REPUBLIC

MORAVIA

Wine-making Moravia makes up the easternmost third of the Czech Republic. The home of the country's finest folk-singing tradition and two of its leading universities, it's also the birthplace of a number of Czech notables: Tomáš Masaryk, first president of Czechoslovakia; composer Leoš Janáček; and psychologist Sigmund Freud.

Brno

Second city of the Czech Republic, Brno industrialized early and still attracts keen business interest in its frequent trade fairs—as well as the attention of motorcycling fans fixated on the annual **Grand Prix.** The tourist is likely to enjoy a fine collection of Gothic and Baroque churches, a thriving local arts scene and the lively atmosphere around Masarykova university.

Monks at the **Hrobka Kapucínského Kláštera** (Capuchin Monastery Crypt), just to the left of Masarykova as you come up from the station, developed a revolutionary embalming technique, preserving 100-plus 18th-century monks and assorted worthies. The results are now on display. (Open Tues.-Sat. 9am-noon and 2-4:30pm, Sun. 11-11:45am and 2-4:30pm. 20kč, students 10kč.) At Radnická 8, the tower of the **Stará radnice** (Old Town Hall) looms large over a vegetable market. The dragon hanging on one wall was said to have ravaged the town in medieval times. A knight tricked it into eating quick-lime, and when the dragon tried to quench its thirst, its belly exploded—thus the seam that marks his stomach today (*radnice* open daily 9am-5pm). Towering above Zelný trh on Petrov Hill is the **Katedrála sv. Petr a Pavel** (Cathedral of St. Peter and St. Paul; open Mon.-Sat. 8:15am-6pm, Sun. 7am-6pm), whose bells ring twelve times at 11am to commemorate a ruse which once held off Swedish invaders. Head down Husova and up the hill on the right to reach **Hrad Špilberk,** the mighty Hapsburg fortress-turned-prison where Hungarian, Italian, Polish and Czech patriots and revolutionaries were incarcerated in grim conditions. (Open June-Sept. daily 9am-6pm; Oct.-March 9am-5pm. 20kč, 10kč students. English leaflet available; English-speaking guide 200kč.)

From Šilingrovo nám., a walk along Pekařská leads to the heart of Old Brno, **Mendlovo nám.** The high Gothic **Basilika Nanebevzetí Panny Marie** (Basilica of the Assumption of the Virgin Mary) houses the 13th-century *Black Madonna,* the Czech Republic's oldest wood icon, which purportedly held off the Swedes in 1645 (church open daily 5pm-7:15pm, Sun. also 7am-12:15pm). The Augustinian monastery next door was the home of **Johann Gregor Mendel,** who laid out the fundamental laws of modern genetics. The **Mendelianum,** Mendlovo nám. 1a, documents Mendel's life and works, explaining his remarkable experiments with peas and bees. (Open July-Aug. daily 9am-6pm; Sept.-June 8am-5pm. 8kč, students 4kč. English pamphlet 5kč.) Films and music events are advertised on posters all over town.

Practical Information, Accommodations, and Food The **tourist office,** Radnická 8 (tel./fax (05) 42 21 10 90), in the old town hall, books rooms and sells guidebooks and maps (29kč; open Mon.-Fri. 8am-6pm, Sat.-Sun. 9am-5pm). **Taxatour** at the train station also arranges private rooms. **Trains** (tel. (05) 42 21 48 03) run to Bratislava (2hr., 83kč), České Budějovice (4½hr., 100kč), and Prague (3hr., 110kč). To reach the high-class hostel **Interservis (HI),** Lomená 38 (tel. (05) 45 23 31 65; fax 33 11 65), take tram 9 or 12 from the train station to the end at "Komárov," continue along Hněvkovského, and turn left onto the unmarked Pompova, the penultimate turn before the bridge (220kč per person, without HI or ISIC 265kč; doubles 575kč). **Bulharský Klub,** Česká 9 (tel. (05) 42 21 10 63), has one hall of doubles with a shared shower. (Reception open daily 9am-noon and 5-10pm. Doubles and triples 300kč per person.) A cut-out giraffe presides over a young Czech crowd at **Livingstone,** Starobrněnská 1, on the corner of Zelný trh. (Fine light *kuřeci prsa,* chicken breasts, 45kč; *Krušovice* beer 16.50kč. Open Mon.-Fri. noon-1am, Sat.-Sun. 6pm-1am.) **Sputnik,** Česká 1, just off nám. Svobody, is a self-serve café (grilled chicken 40kč; *Jarošovské* beer 7kč; open Mon.-Fri. 8am-6pm). The microbrewery **Pivnice Minipivovar Pegas,** Jakubská 4, founded in 1992, already has a loyal following. Brews ferment behind the bar (pints 17kč; open daily 9am-midnight). Inside **H46,** Hybešova 46, a mostly gay, partly lesbian, others-welcome bar pours beer (18kč; ring bell if door is locked; open nightly 6pm-4am).

CZECH REPUBLIC

Olomouc

Foreign visitors are by far outnumbered by local students in Olomouc (OH-lo-moats), the historic capital of North Moravia. The imposing spires of **Chrám sv. Václava** (St. Wenceslas Cathedral), tucked away in the northeast corner of the Old Town, features a high-vaulted interior in impeccable condition. Downstairs, the crypt museum exhibits the gold-encased skull of St. Pauline. (Open Mon.-Thurs., Sat. 9am-5pm, Fri. 11am-5pm, Sun. 11am-5pm. Donations accepted.) The massive 1378 **radnice** (town hall) dominates Horní nám.; the saints in its wonderful astronomical clock on the north side were replaced with steel workers in 1954.

Trains connect to Brno (1½hr., 40kč) and Prague (2½-3½hr., 110kč). The **tourist office** (tel. (068) 551 33 85), Horní nám. in the town hall, has tons of info, offers four tours a day, and books rooms from 230kč per person (open daily 9am-7pm). The dorm **Hostel Envelopa,** 17. listopadu 54 (tel. 522 38 41), was recently refurbished. From the train station, take any inbound tram two stops to "Žižkovo nám." and go down the road to the left of Masaryk's statue (singles 183kč; doubles 440-552kč, with ISIC 244-342kč; open summer only). For **Palavecký Stadión,** Legionářská 11 (tel. 41 31 81; fax 541 32 56), at the swimming stadium, take any tram from the train station to "nám. Národních hrdinů," backtrack through the bus park, head left under the airplane, and go around the pool buildings (doubles 380kč, triples 420kč). **U červeného volka,** Dolní nám. 39, serves delicious soy dishes (44kč) and porky plates (48-71kč; open daily 10am-10pm). Classy **Kavárna Terasa,** Křížovského 14 at the Student Center, opens its Renaissance patio in the summer for cappuccino and conversation (open Mon.-Thurs. 10am-midnight, Fri. 10am-2am, Sat. 2pm-2am).

Denmark (Danmark)

US$1 = 6.86kr (Denmark kroner)	**10kr = US$1.46**
CDN$1 = 4.97kr	**10kr = CDN$2.01**
UK£1 = 10.91kr	**10kr = UK£0.92**
IR£1 = 10.19kr	**10kr = IR£0.98**
AUS$1 = 5.01kr	**10kr = AUS$1.99**
NZ$1 = 4.36kr	**10kr = NZ$2.29**
SAR1 = 1.46kr	**10kr = SAR6.83**
Country Code: 45	**International Dialing Prefix: 00**

When a dining Danish woman was arrested in New York for leaving her baby unattended, the world wondered how she could be so cruel. Denmark simply queried, "What's the problem?" This seemingly callous attitude doesn't derive from the Danes' ruthless Viking past but from their 20th-century position as one of the safest, cleanest, and most supportive social states in the world. Babies and tourists alike benefit from the Danish sense of kindness rooted in the national concepts of "Hygge" (meaning 'cozy' or 'warm') and the unofficial "Jante law," which forbids Danes to even *think* they are better than anyone else. As *Jante* and *hygge* abiders, the Danes levy high taxes in order to provide everyone with quality education, health care, and retirement benefits. Danes were also the first to legalize gay and lesbian marriages and have accepted immigrants from around the world. As a result, Denmark is no longer a homogenous blonde, blue-eyed landscape; even the new

Princess Alexandra boasts Austrian and Hong Kong lineage. While Danes are proud of their country of green farmland, beech forests, chalk cliffs, and sand dunes, they are also endowed with a sense of self-criticism reflected in Denmark's more famous voices: Søren Kirkegaard, Hans Christian Andersen, Isak Denisen, and, more recently, Peter Høeg. Contrary to melancholy Hamlet, very little seems to be rotten in the state of Denmark.

Denmark lies at the tip of continental Europe, just west of Sweden, a position which places it physically and culturally between Scandinavia and Europe proper. Well into the 16th century, the Danish crown ruled an empire uniting Norway, Sweden, Iceland, and parts of Germany, and Denmark was the bridge across which Christianity, the Protestant Reformation, and the socialist movements of the late 19th century crossed into Scandinavia. During World War I, Denmark remained neutral, but in 1940 the Danes capitulated to Hitler rather than risking a full invasion, yet smuggled 7000 Danish Jews into neutral Sweden. Since 1972, Queen Margarethe II has been on the throne and is often spotted biking around. Denmark boasts one of the lowest worldwide crime rates, but such a low-key attitude towards safety is unusual. When U.S. President Bill Clinton came to Denmark in 1997, his agents closed the Queen's residence down for weeks before he could pay a visit, in order to subject it to more thorough security checks.

GETTING THERE AND GETTING AROUND

Eurail passes are valid on all state-run **DSB** routes. The *buy-in-Scandinavia* **Scanrail Pass** allows five days within 15 (1300kr, under 26 950kr) or 21 consecutive days (2000kr, under 26 1450kr) of unlimited rail travel through Denmark, Norway, Sweden, and Finland, as well as many free or 20-50% discounted ferry rides. This differs from the *buy-outside-of-Scandinavia* **Scanrail Pass** which offers five out of 15 days (US$176, under 26 US$132), 10 days out of one month (US$284, under 26 US$213), or one month (US$414, under 26 US$311) of unlimited travel.

The **UNG** card (230kr from central stations) offers 20-45% discounts on rail travel in Denmark for those under 26 but rarely pays off; call **Dan Rail** at 33 14 17 01. **Seniors** with ID get 20-45% discounts, and **groups** of three or more adults also enjoy discounts. Seat reservations, compulsory on all IC (20kr) and most international trains (30-45kr), can be made at central stations. Remote towns may be served by **buses** from the nearest train station.

With the completion in 1997 of the **Great Belt Fixed Link,** Zealand is for the first time connected to Funen by an 18km underwater tunnel for trains. A parallel bridge for cars should be completed in 1998, and later phases of this project will link Copenhagen to Malmö, Sweden, and southern Zealand to Germany. These projects are significantly reducing travel time to and in Denmark. Eurail and Scanrail Passes secure discounts on many Scandinavian **ferries** (sometimes free rides) and the free *Ni Rejser* newspaper, available at tourist offices, can help you sort out the dozens of smaller ferries that serve Denmark's outlying islands. See **Ferries,** p. 241.

Flat terrain, bike paths in the countryside, and bike lanes in towns and cities make Denmark a cyclist's dream. Cyclists are required to obey traffic signals; failure to do so will result in fines. You can rent **bicycles** (35-50kr per day) from some tourist offices (not Copenhagen's), ubiquitous bicycle rental shops, and a few railway stations in North Zealand (Copenhagen, Helsingør, Hillerød, Klampenborg, and Lyngby). A 200kr deposit is ordinarily required. The **Dansk Cyklist Førbund** (Danish Cycle Federation), Rømersgade 7, 1362 Copenhagen K (tel. 33 32 31 21; fax 33 32 76 83; http://webhotel.uni-c.dk/def), organizes tours and sells repair and touring products, cycling maps (49-95kr), and helpful literature. You can take your bike on specially marked cars of most trains (12kr; look for the white bicycle sign painted on the doors); consult *Bikes and Trains,* available at most train stations.

ESSENTIALS

Stacks of free brochures in English, available from **tourist offices** and Danish Tourist Boards abroad (see **Government Information Offices,** p. 1), will help you find your way around. The easiest way to get cash is from **ATMs: Cirrus** and **PLUS** cash cards are widely accepted. PIN numbers are four digits long. Most banks charge a commission of 10-35kr per traveler's check, but the **American Express** office in Copenhagen (the only one in Denmark) can exchange checks of smaller denominations for larger ones. Danish **phone** numbers have no city codes. From pay phones, local calls require 2kr. Phone cards are sold at post offices in denominations of 30, 50, and 100kr. Denmark's **emergency** number is 112; no coins are required. For directory information, dial 118 (10kr per min.). For international info, dial 113 (12-35kr). For **collect calls,** dail 141, and for direct international calls, 00 then the country code, etc. For **AT&T Direct** dial 80 01 00 10; **MCI WorldPhone** 80 01 00 22; **SprintExpress** 80 01 08 77; **Canada Direct** 80 01 00 11; **BT Direct** 80 01 04 44; **Australia Direct** 80 01 00 61; **New Zealand Direct** 80 01 00 64; and **South Africa Direct** 80 01 00 27. The country celebrates national **holidays** on Jan. 1, Maundy Thursday (April 9 in 1998), Easter (April 9-13), Great Prayer Day (May 8), Ascension Day (May 21), Whit Sunday and Monday (May 31-June 1), Constitution Day (June 5), Midsummer (June 23-24), Christmas (Dec. 24-26), and New Year's Eve (Dec. 31).

The Danish alphabet adds *æ (*like the "e" in "egg,"*)*, *ø* (like the "i" in "first,"), and *å* (still sometimes written as *aa;* like the "o" in "lord") at the end; thus Århus would follow Viborg in an alphabetical listing of cities. Knowing *ikke* ("not") will help you figure out such signs as "No smoking" *(ikker ryger),* and *åben/lukket* (O-ben/loock-eh, "open/closed") is also useful. Nearly all Danes speak flawless English, but a few Danish words might help break the ice: try *skål* (skoal, "cheers"). Danish has a distinctive glottal stop known as a *stød,* indicated in the chart below as an apostrophe.

Yes/no	*Ja/Nej*	Ya/Ny
Hello/good-bye	*Dav/Farvel*	Dow'/fah-VEL
Hi/bye (informal)	*Hej/Hejhej*	HIGH/HIGH-high
Please	*Vær venlig*	VER VEN-li
Thank you	*Tak*	tak
Excuse me	*Undskyld*	UND-scoold
Do you speak English?	*Taler De engelsk?*	TA' lor dee ENG' elsg
I don't speak Danish.	*Jeg taler ikke dansk.*	Yai TA' lor IG-ge dan'sg
Where is...?	*Hvor er...?*	Vaw' ayr
How much does it cost?	*Hvad koster det?*	Va KOS' tor dey
I would like...a room.	*Jeg vil gerne have...et værelse.*	Yai vil GAYR-ne HAY-ve it VAYR-el-se
Help!	*Hjælp!*	Yel'b

Emergency health care in Denmark is free, but those in less dire straits must pay an initial fee of 200-400kr. **Wheelchairs** and **strollers** are allowed on trains at no additional cost. All Copenhagen buses are equipped for wheelchair access and street lights click slow for "don't walk" and fast for "walk" to help **vision-impaired** pedestrians. For more info, contact the **Danish Association for the Handicapped,** Dansk Handicap Ferbund, Hans Knudsens Plads 1A, 1st Floor, 2100 Copenhagen Ø (tel. 39 29 35 55), and ask for a free copy of *Access in Denmark.* **DSB** publishes *Handicappede,* which details wheelchair access to every train station in the country (tel. 33 14 04 00 or 33 15 19 44). **Women** travelers who take normal precautions should find Denmark safe. **Lesbian, bisexual, and gay** travelers will be amazed at the level of tolerance in Denmark, although more rural areas may still shelter hostility. Contact the **Danish Association for Gays and Lesbians** (see p. 241).

Accommodations and Camping While Denmark's hotels are generally expensive (250-850kr), the country's 120 **HI youth hostels** *(vandrerhjem)* are well run, have no age limit, and generally include rooms for families (150-350kr). All charge 75-90kr per bed; nonmembers pay 25kr extra. Sheets cost about 30kr more. You can generally feast on an unlimited breakfast for 38kr and dinner for 60kr. Kitchen facilities are often available. Reception desks normally take a break between noon and 4pm and close for the day at 9 or 11pm. Because hostels cater primarily to families and school groups, they may be booked far ahead, and may be far from cities. Reservations are required in winter and highly recommended in summer, especially near beaches. They can be made by phone without a deposit, but you will be asked to show up by 5pm or call that day to confirm. Official hostel guides are available at hostels and tourist offices. For more info, contact the **Danish Youth Hostel Association** (tel. 31 31 36 12; fax 31 31 36 26). Many tourist offices book rooms in **private homes** (125-175kr), which are often in suburbs.

Denmark's 525 official **campgrounds** (about 60kr per person) rank from one star (toilets and drinking water) to three (showers and laundry) to five (swimming, restaurants, and stoves). You'll need a **camping pass,** available at all campgrounds and valid for a year (30kr, families 60kr, groups 120kr). One-time guest passes are 10kr (families 18kr), and international passes are accepted. The **Dansk Camping Union,** *Campingrådet,* Hesseløgade 16, DK-2100 Copenhagen Ø (tel. 31 21 06 04), sells a campground handbook (*Camping Denmark;* 100kr by mail-order, 70kr in bookstores) and passes. The free *Camping/Youth and Family Hostels* from the Danish Youth Hostel Association is also adequate. Sleeping in train stations, parks, and streets is illegal, as is camping on private property, beaches, and protected lands.

DENMARK

Food and Drink A "Danish" in Denmark is a *wienerbrød* ("Viennese bread") and can be found in bakeries alongside other flaky treats. Danish ice cream cones are freshly made from thin waffles; Danes love their ice cream. For more substantial fare, Danes favor small, open-faced sandwiches called *smørrebrød.* Look for lunch specials called *dagens ret* and all-you-can-eat buffets *(spis alt du kan* or *tag selv buffet).* Beer *(Øl)* is usually served as a *lille* or *stor fadøl* (.25L or .5L draft), but bottled beer tends to be cheaper. National brews are Carlsberg and Tuborg. Shots of hard liquor like *akvavit* are usually reserved for special occasions. The drinking age in Denmark is 18. Restaurant checks and bar tabs include tax and service. Youth hostels offer hearty breakfasts. For fast food, try a *pølsner* sausage in a bun from a *pølsner vogne* (sausage stand). Many **vegetarian** *(vegetarret)* options are the result of Indian and Mediterranean influences, but salads and vegetables *(grøntsaker)* can be found on most menus. For more info, contact **Dansk Vegetarforening,** Borups Allé 131, 2000 Frederiksberg (tel. 38 34 24 48).

Copenhagen (København)

"Wonderful, wonderful Copenhagen!" sings Danny Kaye in the 1952 film *Hans Christian Andersen,* but despite the swan ponds and cobblestone clichés that Andersen's fairy-tale imagery brings to mind, Denmark's capital is a fast-paced modern city which offers, all at half the cost of Oslo or Stockholm, cafés to rival Paris, nightlife to rival London, and style to rival New York. Some of the most beautiful (and best dressed) people on the planet can be seen walking down Strøget: where else could you find an open-backed, high heeled, *tennis* shoe? Copenhagen today is a cosmopolitan city where mythic blonde children walk to school with their Inuit, Turkish, Greek, Vietnamese, and Ethiopian classmates. But if you are still craving Andersen's Copenhagen, the *Lille Havfrue* (Little Mermaid), *Tivoli,* and *Nyhavn*'s Hanseatic gingerbread houses are also yours to discover. And despite Danny Kaye's penchant for calling the city "CopenhAHgen," most Danes will agree that in English, København is most definitely (and no less wonderfully) "CopenhAYgen."

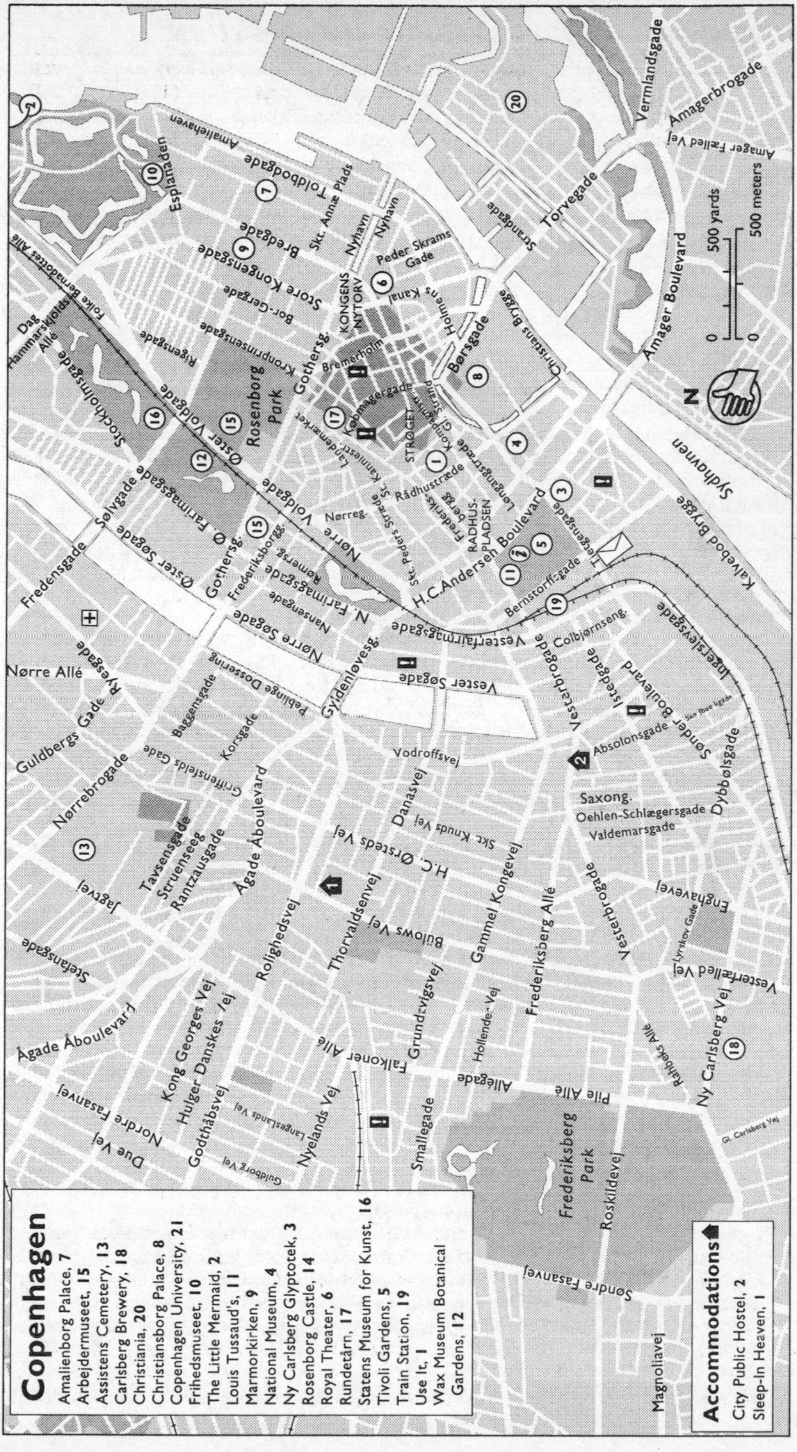
Copenhagen
Amalienborg Palace, 7
Arbejdermuseet, 15
Assistens Cemetery, 13
Carlsberg Brewery, 18
Christiania, 20
Christiansborg Palace, 8
Copenhagen University, 21
Frihedsmuseet, 10
The Little Mermaid, 2
Louis Tussaud's, 11
Marmorkirken, 9
National Museum, 4
Ny Carlsberg Glyptotek, 3
Rosenborg Castle, 14
Royal Theater, 6
Rundetårn, 17
Statens Museum for Kunst, 16
Tivoli Gardens, 5
Train Station, 19
Use It, 1
Wax Museum Botanical Gardens, 12
Accommodations
City Public Hostel, 2
Sleep-In Heaven, 1
500 yards
500 meters
N

ORIENTATION AND PRACTICAL INFORMATION

Copenhagen lies on the east coast of the island of **Zealand** (Sjælland); Malmö, Sweden, is just across the sound (Øresund). Copenhagen's **Hovedbanegården** (Central Station) lies close to the city's heart. One block north of the station, **Vesterbrogade** passes **Tivoli** and **Rådhuspladsen** (the city's central square, where most bus lines originate) and then cuts through the city center as **Strøget** (STROY-yet), the longest pedestrian thoroughfare in the world. Outlying districts fan out from the center: **Østerbro** is known as affluent, while affordable, working-class **Nørrebro** draws students. **Vesterbro** is considered Copenhagen's rougher side because of its red-light district, but the fear may be rooted in an unfair distrust of the area's Muslim population. **Christianshavn** is known as little Amsterdam for its waterways and its hippie-hash artists' colony, **Christiania,** in the district's south-central half.

Tourist Offices: Use It, Rådhusstræde 13 (tel. 33 15 65 18; fax 33 15 75 18; email unginfo@cph96.dk), in the Huset (Danish Youth House) complex. From the station, follow Vesterbrogade, cross Rådhuspladsen onto Strøget then take a right on Rådhusstræde. Free maps, bed-finding (list posted after hours), passport retrieval, mail held, ride and message boards, and free storage (1 day). Offers *Playtime,* a budget guide to the city; *Shortcuts,* for longer stays; and *Use It News,* listing cultural events. Building also houses a bar, café, restaurant, cinema, experimental theater, and housing/job placement office. Open Mon.-Fri. 10am-5:30pm. Less helpful is the **Wonderful Copenhagen Tourist Office,** Bernstorffsgade 1, 1577 København V (tel. 33 11 13 25; fax 33 93 49 69), in a corner of Tivoli. Open May-Sept. 15 daily 9am-9pm; Sept. 16-April Mon.-Fri. 9am-5pm, Sat. 9am-2pm.

Budget Travel: Wasteels Rejser, Skoubogade 6 (tel. 33 14 46 33). Youth fares for trains and planes. Open Mon.-Fri. 9am-6pm, Sat. 10am-5pm, Sun. and holidays 11am-3pm; Oct.-April closed Sun. **Kilroy Travels,** Skindergade 28 (tel. 33 11 00 44). Low ferry and plane fares. Changes dates for CIEE plane tickets. Open Mon. 9am-7pm, Tues.-Fri. 10am-5:30pm; mid-May to mid-Aug. also Sat. 10am-1pm.

Embassies: Australian travelers contact the embassy in Germany at Godesberge Allee 105-7, D-53175 Bonn (tel. (49228) 81 030; fax 373 145). **Canada,** Kristen Bernikowsgade 1 (tel. 33 12 22 99). **Estonia,** Aurehøjvej 19, 2900 Hellerup (tel. 39 40 26 66; fax 39 40 26 30). **Ireland,** Østerbanegade 21 (tel. 31 42 32 33). **Latvia,** Rusbæksvej 17, 2100 Copenhagen Ø (tel. 39 27 60 00; fax 39 27 61 73). **Lithuania,** Bernstorffsvej 214, 2920 Charlottenlund (tel. 39 63 62 07; fax 39 63 65 32). **New Zealanders** contact the British or Kiwi embassy in Brussels. **Poland,** Richelieus allé 10 (tel. 31 62 72 44). **South Africa,** Gammel Vartovvej 8 (tel. 31 18 01 55). **U.K.,** Kastelsvej 36-40 (tel. 35 26 46 00; fax 31 38 10 12). **U.S.,** Dag Hammerskjölds Allé 24 (tel. 31 42 31 44; fax 35 43 02 23).

Currency Exchange: At **Central Station.** 22-30kr commission on cash, 20kr per check with a 40kr min. Open late April-Sept. daily 6:45am-10pm; Oct. to mid-April 7am-9pm. Also at the **Tivoli** office (open in summer daily noon-11pm) or the **airport** (open daily 6:30am-8:30pm). Change counters on Strøget charge up to 10% commission. **Banks** cluster in the pedestrian district and on Vesterbrogade near the train station. Most charge a 20kr commission. Regular banking hours Mon.-Wed. and Fri. 9:30am-4pm, Thurs. 9:30am-6pm. High commissions on traveler's checks (30-35kr min.), except at American Express (see below).

American Express: Amagertorv 18 (tel. 33 12 23 01), on the Strøget. No commission; best exchange rates on traveler's checks. 15kr commission on cash. Mail held for those with AmEx cards or Traveler's Cheques. Open June-Aug. Mon.-Fri. 9am-5pm, Sat. 9am-2pm; Sept.-May Mon.-Fri. 9am-5pm, Sat. 9am-noon.

Flights: tel. 32 47 47 47. Bus 32 and 205S (40min., 17kr) from Rådhuspladsen and the Central Station, and the SAS bus (20min., 35kr) from Central Station both run to and from **Kastrup Airport,** 11km away. SAS buses run daily to the airport 5:40am-9:45pm every 15min., and back 6:30am-11:10pm every 10-15min.

Trains: All trains stop at **Hovedbanegården** (tel. 33 14 17 01). 4-5 per day to Stockholm (9hr., 555kr, under 26 400kr), Oslo (9hr., 710kr, under 26 525kr), Berlin (8hr., 845kr, under 26 625kr). Seat reservations required (20kr). For holders of BIJ, Scanrail, and Eurail passes, the **InterRail Center** in the station is a friendly haven, with a relaxing lounge, telephones, showers (10kr per min.), a stove (no utensils), and a message board for finding and making friends. Open May-Sept. daily 6:30-10:30am and 4-10pm; also open afternoons July-Aug. only.

Public Transportation: For **bus** info, dial 36 45 45 45 (daily 7am-9:30pm); for **train** info, call 33 14 17 01 (daily 6:30am-11pm). Buses and S-trains (subways and suburban trains) operate on a zone system. 3 zones cover central Copenhagen; 11 zones get you to Helsingør. Buy tickets (2 zones 11kr, each additional zone 6kr) or, better, a yellow *rabatkort* (rebate card), which gets you 10 "clips" each good for one journey within a specified number of zones (105kr for a 3-zone/10-clip rebate card). Cards must be clipped in the machines upon beginning a journey. A ticket or clip (available from kiosks or bus drivers) gives 1hr. of transfers. The 24hr. bus and train pass buys use of public transport in greater Copenhagen (70kr from the Tivoli tourist office or any railway station). Railpasses are good on S-trains but not buses. The **Copenhagen Card,** sold in hotels, tourist offices, and train stations, buys unlimited travel in North Zealand, discounts on ferries to Sweden, and free admission to most sights, including Tivoli (140kr for 1 day, 295kr for 3 days). Buses and trains run Mon.-Sat. 5am-12:30am, Sun. 6am-12:30am; **night buses** (20kr extra) run less frequently and on fewer routes.

Ferries: The variety of ferry services from Copenhagen boggles the mind; the tourist office has the details. To **Norway: Scandinavian Seaways** (tel. 33 42 30 00; fax 33 42 30 11) departs daily at 5pm for Oslo. (16hr. 500kr, with berth 720kr. 20% Eurail discount, bigger student discounts through Kilroy Travels.) To **Sweden:** trains cross over the ferry at Helsingør-Helsingborg ferry at no extra charge. **Hydrofoils** (tel. 33 12 80 88) cross hourly between Havnegade (at the end of Nyhavn) and Malmö (40min., 19-49kr). If Hydrofoil is booked, try **Pilen** (tel. 33 32 12 60) or **Flyvebådene** (tel. 33 12 80 88). Bus 999 from the Central Station goes to Lund via ferry at Dragør. To **Poland: Polferries** (tel. 33 11 46 45; fax 33 11 95 78) set out Mon. and Wed.-Fri. at 9:30pm, Sun. at 11am from Nordre Toldbod, 12A off Esplanaden to Świnoujście, where there are rail connections to the rest of Poland (10hr., 375kr, with ISIC 300kr). To **Bornholm** (7hr.) and **Germany,** call **Bornholmstrafikken** (tel. 33 13 18 66; fax 33 93 18 66).

Taxis: tel. 31 35 35 35, 31 22 55 55, or 31 10 10 10. 20kr base, 8kr per km. Central Station to airport 150kr.

Bike Rental: The **City Bike** program lets you borrow bikes for free. Deposit 20kr in any of the 150 bike racks around the city, release the bike, and retrieve the coin upon return at any rack. **Dan Wheel,** Colbjørnsensgade 3 (tel. 31 21 22 27). 35kr per day, 165kr per week; 200kr deposit. Open Mon.-Fri. 9am-5:30pm, Sat.-Sun. 9am-2pm. Also in Central Station near track 13.

Hitchhiking: You have a better chance of ice skating across Egypt in July, and it's illegal on highways. Try Use It's ride boards (see **Tourist Offices,** above) instead. **Interstop,** 54A Vesterbrogade (tel. 33 33 08 25), also connects riders and drivers.

Luggage Storage: Free at Use It and most hostels (but not overnight). At **Central Station,** 20kr per 24hr. Open Mon.-Sat. 5:30am-1am and Sun. 6am-1am. At **DSB Garderobe,** suitcases 25kr, packs 35kr per 24hr. Open daily 6:30am-12:15am.

Lost Property: Police (tel. 38 74 88 22); **bus** (tel. 36 45 45 45); **train** (tel. 36 44 20 10); **planes** (tel. 32 32 32 00). For credit cards: **AmEx** (tel. 80 01 00 21); **MasterCard** and **Visa** (tel. 44 89 25 00).

Bookstores: Atheneum, Nørregade 6, good selection of books in English, but fairly high prices. Open Mon.-Fri. 9am-5pm, Sat. 10am-2pm. The latest English tabloids are at **The British Bookshop,** 8 Badstrustræde (tel. 33 93 11 15). Open Mon.-Fri. 10am-6pm, Sat. 10am-2pm. **Use-It** operates a book swap.

Laundromats: Lots; look for *Vascomat* and *Møntvask* chains. At Borgergade 2, Nansensgade 39, and Istedgade 45. Most open daily 8am-10pm (25-30kr).

Women's Centers: Kvindehuset, Gothersgade 37 (tel. 33 14 28 04), runs a bookstore-café. Open Mon.-Fri. noon-7:30pm. **Kvindecentret Dannerhuset,** Nansensgade 1 (tel. 33 14 16 76). Shelter for battered women. Call 24hr.

Gay and Lesbian Services: National Association for Gay Men and Women, Knabrostræde 3 (tel. 33 13 19 48). Free *Copenhagen Gay and Lesbian Guide.* Small bookstore/library. Open Mon.-Tues. and Thurs.-Fri. 5-7pm, Wed. 5-8pm.

Crisis Hotlines: Den Sociale Døgnvagt (tel. 33 66 33 33) for troubled travelers. **Lifeline** (suicide hotline, tel. 33 32 11 19). **Centre for Sexually Abused** (tel. 33 12 43 03; open Mon.-Thurs. 1-4pm, Wed. also 7-9pm). **AIDS hotline** (tel. 33 91 11 19). **Alcoholics Hotline** (tel. 33 33 06 10).

Pharmacy: Steno Apotek, Vesterbrogade 6c (tel. 33 14 82 66) and **Sønderbro Apoteket,** Amagerbrogade 158 (tel. 31 58 01 40). Open 24hr.; ring for entrance.

Medical Assistance: Doctors on Call (tel. 33 93 63 00), open Mon.-Fri. 9am-4pm; after hours, call 38 88 60 41. Visits 200-400kr. **Emergency rooms** at **Rigshospitalet,** Blegsdamsvej 9 (tel. 35 45 31 93), **Sundby Hospital,** Kastrupvej 63 (tel. 32 34 32 34), and **Bispebjerg Hospital,** Bispebjerg Bakke 23 (tel. 35 31 35 31).

Emergencies: Fire and **ambulance:** tel. 112. No coins needed at public phones.

Police: tel. 112. The **police headquarters** is at Polititorvet (tel. 33 14 14 48).

Internet Access: Free at the **Copenhagen Central Library** *(Hovedbibliotek),* Krystalgade 15 (tel. 33 93 60 60), open Mon.-Fri. 10am-7pm, Sat. 10am-2pm. At the **Wonderful Copenhagen Tourist Office,** with credit card (11kr, plus 2kr per min.). At cafés: **Babel,** Frederiksborggade 33 (tel. 33 33 93 38; open Mon.-Sat. 10am-3am), and **Café@Internet,** Zinnsgade 1 (tel. 31 42 72 02; open 1-11pm).

Post Office: Tietgensgade 37-39, behind Central Station. *Poste Restante.* Open Mon.-Fri. 10am-6pm, Sat. 9am-1pm. Branch office in Central Station open Mon.-Fri. 8am-10pm, Sat. 9am-4pm, Sun. 10am-5pm. *Poste Restante* also at **Use It. Postal Code:** 1500 København V.

Telephones: Telecom Denmark, at Central Station. Call first, pay later (even by credit card). Open Mon.-Fri. 8am-10pm, Sat.-Sun. 9am-9pm. **Faxes** and **telegrams** also sent from here. Phone cards (30, 50, or 100kr) for sale in post office.

ACCOMMODATIONS AND CAMPING

Like all of Scandanavia, Copenhagen is rich in hostels and campgrounds but poor in budget hotels. Because Danish youth hostels are used by families and school groups for cheap country vacations, the HI hostels fill early, despite their remote location (allow 20-30kr for bus fare). Reservations are especially advisable during Karneval (mid-May), the Roskilde Festival (late June), the Copenhagen Jazz Festival (early July), and in early August. If the hostels are booked, consult the **Use It** tourist office. Sleep-Ins are temporary summertime hostels set up by the city to provide cheap and central places to sleep. Slumbering in a park or the station is neither legal nor wise.

Hotel Jørgensen, Rømersgade 11 (tel. 33 13 81 86; fax 33 15 51 05), in a quiet area, 20min. walk from Central Station. Take S-train to "Nørreport," walk along Frederiksborggade, then left on Rømersgade. Large rooms with 6-20 beds. Centrally located and friendly. Reception open daily 8am-midnight. 115kr includes huge breakfast. Sept. 16-June 14 100kr. Singles 350kr. Doubles from 450kr. Quads 520kr. Lockers free with 100kr deposit.

City Public Hostel, Absalonsgade 8 (tel. 31 31 20 70; fax 31 23 51 75), in the Vesterbro Ungdomsgård. From the station, walk away from the Rådhuspladsen on Vesterbrogade. Said to be not the best neighborhood, but possibly just ethnically mixed. 24hr. reception. 120kr includes buffet breakfast. Kitchen. Small unlocked lockers free. Sleeping bags allowed, sheets 30kr. Open early May-late Aug.

Vesterbros Inter Point, Vesterbros KFUM (YMCA), Valdemarsgade 15 (tel. 31 31 15 74), a block from City Public Hostel. Required Inter Point pass (25kr) good through Dec. at YMCAs worldwide. Reception open daily 8am-noon, 3-6pm, and 7:30pm-12:30am. Curfew 12:30am. 65kr. Sheets 20kr. Open July 1-Aug. 9.

Sleep-In, Blegdamsvej 132 (tel. 35 26 50 59; fax 35 43 50 58). From the station, take the S-train to "Østerport," then bus 1, 6, or 14 (night bus 906 or 914) to "Trianglen" or walk 10min. up Hammerskjölds. Centrally located. Clean and spacious converted badminton and tennis courts. No pillows or private showers. Stocked kitchen. 24hr. reception. 70kr. Breakfast 30kr. Sheets 30kr. Open July-Aug.

Sleep-In Green, Ravnsborggade 18, Baghuset (tel. 35 37 77 77). Take bus 16 from the station or walk: turn right on Vesterbrogade, left on H.C. Andersens Blvd., right on Nørre Søgade, left over Dronning Louises Bro, to Ravnsborggade. Central location, just outside city center. 68 beds. 75kr. Breakfast 30kr. Open June-Sept.

Sleep-In Heaven, Peter Bangsvej 30, Frederiksberg (tel. 38 10 44 45). Also outside of the city center in Frederiksberg. Take bus 1 from Central Station or call for directions. 24hr. reception. 70kr includes breakfast. Open June 18-Oct. 31.

København Vandrerhjem Bellahøj (HI), Herbergvejen 8 (tel. 38 28 97 15; fax 38 89 02 10), in Bellahøj. Take bus 2 "Bronshøj" from Rådhuspladsen or night bus 902. In a lakeside park far from the city center. Lockers; optional lock rental 5kr, deposit 20kr. Sheets 30kr. Laundry 28kr. Wheelchair accessible. Open March-Jan.

København Vandrerhjem Amager (HI), Vejlandsallé 200 (tel. 32 52 29 08; fax 32 52 27 08). Take bus 46 (Mon.-Fri. 6am-5pm) from Central Station or the S-train to "Valby" and then bus 37. Night bus 933. Huge, and far from the city center in enormous nature reserve. Lockable 2- and 5-bed rooms. Reception open daily 1pm-10am. Check-in 1-5pm. 80kr, nonmembers 100kr. Kitchen. Free use of safe; no lockers. No sleeping bags. Sheets 30kr. Laundry 25kr. Wheelchair accessible.

Lyngby Vandrehjem (HI), Råduad 1 (tel. 42 80 30 74). Take S-train line A or L from Central Station to "Lyngby" (40 min.), then bus 187 to "Råduad" or 182/183 to "Hjortehaer." Inconveniently far, but in the beautiful Jægersberg Deer Park. Reception open daily 8am-noon and 4-9pm. Curfew 9pm. Dorms 83kr. Doubles 186kr. Triples 289kr. Quads 352kr. Sheets 30kr. Open Easter-Oct. 15.

Mike's Guest House, Kirkevænget 13 (tel. 36 45 65 40). Take the S-train to "Valby," walk to the right on Toftegards Allé, then right again on Valby Langgade. Reception open 24hr. Singles 200kr. Doubles 290kr. Kitchen (15kr).

Bellahøj Camping, Hvidkildevej 66 (tel. 31 10 11 50; fax 38 10 13 32), 5km from the city center. Take bus 11 "Bellahøj" or night bus 902 from Rådhuspladsen. 24hr reception. 50kr. Cabins for two 260kr, for four 375kr. Kitchen, free showers. Bike rental 47kr. Café and market open daily 7am-midnight. Open June-Aug.

Charlottenlund Strandpark, Strandvejen 144B, Charlottenlund (tel. 39 62 36 88), in a park with beach. Take bus 6 from Rådhuspladsen (30min.). Reception 8am-1am. 60kr. Shower 5kr. Laundry 20kr, dryer 5kr per min. Open May 15-Sept. 15.

Absalon Camping, Korsdalsvej 132, Rødovre (tel. 31 41 06 00), 9km from the city center. Take S-train line B or L to Brøndbyøster, then walk 10min. north through the apartment complex (ask for directions at the station). Reception open daily 7am-10pm. 45kr. Cabins 195kr plus 45kr per person. Store, laundry, and kitchen.

DENMARK

FOOD

Copenhagen's fare has much improved since the Vikings slobbered down mutton and salted fish. Stroll down the **Strøget** with peach juice dripping down your chin, munch pickled herring by the waterfront, and sample the goodies in every bakery window. Around **Kongens Nytorv,** elegant cafés serve sandwiches *(smørrebrod)* at lunchtime for around 35kr. All-you-can-eat buffets (40-70kr) are popular, especially at Turkish, Indian, and Italian restaurants. The **Netto** supermarket chain is a budget fantasy; one is located at Fiolstræde 7, a few blocks north of Strøget (open Mon.-Fri. 9am-7pm, Sat. 8am-5pm). Open-air **markets** like the one at Israels Plads near Nørreport Station (open Mon.-Fri. 7am-6pm, Sat. 7am-2pm) provide fresh fruits and veggies; fruit stalls also line Strøget and the side-streets to the North.

Husets Café, Rådhusstræde 13. Grand floor of Huset, next to Use It. Funky bar/café with outdoor seating and good food to the tune of MTV Europe. Brunch 39kr. Salads 25kr. Beer at its cheapest, 15-19kr. Open daily 10am-11:30pm.

Spisehuset, Rådhussetræde 13. Also part of Huset. On the second floor in winter, but in the courtyard off Magstræde (around the corner) during summer. With faux laundry hung across the bright cobblestone courtyard and music and candles at each table. Pasta 35kr. Salads 30kr. Desserts 15-30kr. Open Mon.-Sat. 6-11pm.

Sharen Værtshus, Kampagnistræde 2, off Strøget. This *værtshu* (restaurant, bar, and café) exemplifies *hygge* (coziness). Beer 17-23kr. Danish specialties (served noon-9pm) include *Chèvresalat* (goat cheese salad, 44kr) and *Christiansøsild* (marinaded herring, 42kr). Open Sun.-Thurs. 11am-midnight, Fri.-Sat. 11am-1am.

Restaurant Stedet, Lavendelstræde 13, near Strøget and Rådhuspladsen. Affordable Danish fare. Gay and straight clientele. Lunch specials Tues.-Thurs. 68kr (12:30-7pm). Sunday brunch 58kr (12:30-4pm). Open Tues.-Sun. noon-10:30pm.

Det Lille Apotek, St. Kannike Stræde 15. Dinner entrees include *sild* (pickled herring), *smørrebrod,* and salads (85-120kr). Lunchtime special (59kr; 11:30am-5pm). Open Mon.-Sat. 11am-midnight, Sun. noon-midnight.

Nyhavns Færgekro, Nyhavn 5. Sit along the canal as you lunch on all-you-can-eat herring (65kr). Dinners 135kr. Open daily 11am-4pm and 5-11pm.

Den Grønne Kælder, Pilestraeder, 48. Popular, macrobiotic, ecological, and deliciously vegetarian. Hummus 18-35kr, veggie burgers 28kr. Open daily 11am-9pm.

Southern California, Vester Volgade 87, just south of Rådhuspladsen. The healthiest and cheapest fast food take-out option in town, with excellent burritos, quesadillas, tostadas, and salads (15-45kr). Open Tues.-Thurs. 11:30am-9:30pm, Sat. 5:30pm-midnight, Sun. 5:30-9:30pm.

Cafés

Café Norden, Østergade 61, on Strøget and Nicolaj Plads, in sight of the fountain. A French style café with darkwood interior. Crepes 25-52kr. Sandwiches 16-42kr. Danish and French pastries 14-35kr. The best vantage point on Strøget despite pricey coffee and beer. Open Mon.-Sat. 9am-midnight, Sun. 10am-midnight.

Café Europa, Amagertorv, on Nicolaj Plads opposite Café Norden. As Norden is the place to see, Europa is the place to be seen. Greta Garbo and Marlene Dietrich adorn the walls. Sandwiches and salads 20-45kr. Coffee 15kr. Beer 23-45kr.

Kafe Kys, Læderstræde 7, on a quiet street running to the south of and parallel to Strøget. Minimalist Mediterranean look. Sandwiches 35-42k. Coffee 12kr. Beer 20-32kr. Open Mon.-Fri. 11am-1am, Sat. 11am-2am, Sun. noon-10pm.

Daells Konditori og Bager, Fiolstræde 7, on a small, busy pedestrian street with fruit vendors. All the pastries you've longed to try, like *wienerbrød* (11kr) and *dansk kager* (15kr). Open Mon.-Thurs. 8am-6pm., Fri. 8am-7pm, Sat. 9am-5pm.

SIGHTS

A fairly compact city, Copenhagen is best seen on foot or by bike; the free **city bikes** provide access to the city's stunning architecture (20kr deposit). Ascend the ramp of the **Rundetårn** (Round Tower, built in 1642 by King Christian IV) on Købmagergade for a fantastic panorama of Copenhagen's copper spires and cobbled streets (open April-Aug. Mon.-Sat. 10am-8pm; Sept.-March Mon.-Sat. 10-5pm). **Strøget,** the pedestrian street that transects the entire city center, is lively, especially at its major squares: **Nytorv, Nicolaj Plads,** and **Kungens Nytorv.** Opposite Kungens Nytorv is **Nyhavn,** the "new port" where Hans Christian Andersen wrote his first fairy tale, lined with Hanseatic houses, sailing boats in dock, and **ferries** leaving for tours of Copenhagen's waterways. **Nette-Bådende** tour boats offer the best deal. From their departure at Holmen's Church opposite Nyhavn at Heibergsgade, they make their way past Amalienberg Palace, Christiansborg Palace, and the Lille Havfrue (tours daily 10am-5pm every 20min., 1hr., 20kr).

The varied attractions of the famed 19th-century **Tivoli** amusement park, Vesterbrogade 3, include botanical gardens and marching toy soldiers, as well as the expected rides. On Wednesdays and weekends the night culminates with music and fireworks. (Open late April to mid-Sept. daily 11am-midnight. Children's rides open at 11:30am, others at 1:30pm. 39kr, 9kr discount before 1pm and after 11pm. Single-ride tickets 15kr. Ride-pass 138kr.) Next to Tivoli, the **Ny Carlsberg Glyptoket,** Dante Plads 7, displays Ancient and Impressionist art (open Tues.-Sun. 10am-4pm; 15kr, free with ISIC, Wed. and Sun. free). Nearby, the **National Museum,** Ny Vestergade 10, contains Danish and European archaeological discoveries, including treasures from the Viking Age (open Tues.-Sun. 10am-5pm; 30kr, students 20kr, Wed. free). Across the canals on Slotsholmen Island, the *Folketing* (Parliament) meets at **Christiansborg Palace.** (Tours May-Sept. Wed.-Fri. at 11am and 3pm; Oct.-April Tues.-Thurs. and Sat.-Sun. at 9:30am and 3:30pm.)

The **Royal Theater** is home to the world-famous Royal Danish Ballet. Half-price tickets for theaters are available the day of the performance at the **Arte Nørreport Kiosk,** on the corner of Fiolstræde and Nørrevold opposite the Nørreport Rail Station and in front of the BG bank. (Open Mon.-Fri. noon-7pm, Sat. noon-4pm. Tickets 40-

100kr. Call **Arte,** Hvidkildevej 64, at 38 88 22 22; ask about student discounts. Most post offices also sell tickets.) The changing of the palace guard takes place at noon on the brick plaza of the queen's **Amalienborg Palace.** Although most of the interior is closed to the public, you can view the royal apartments of Christian VII (Open June-Aug. 10am-4pm; May 11am-4pm; Jan.-April Tues.-Sun. 11am-4pm. 35kr.) The western approach to the plaza frames a view of the impressive dome of the 19th-century Romanesque Baroque **Marmorkirken** (marble church). The inside of the dome is almost as elaborate (open Mon.-Sat. 11am-2pm; 20kr).

A few blocks north of Amalienborg is the **Frihedsmuseet** (Resistance Museum), Churchillparken, which chronicles the 1940-45 Nazi occupation. While documenting Denmark's rescue of almost all its Jews, the museum also examines the period of acceptance of German "protection," when the Danish government arrested anti-Nazi saboteurs. (Open May to early Sept. Tues.-Sun. 10am-4pm, Sun. 10am-5pm; mid-Sept. to April Tues.-Sun. 11am-3pm. Free.) Across a bridge is **Kastellet,** a 17th-century fortress-turned-park (open daily 6am-dusk); Edvard Eriksen's statue **Den Lille Havfrue** (The Little Mermaid) honors H. C. Andersen at the harbor's opening.

The area around Øster Voldgade and Sølvgade houses Copenhagen's finest parks and gardens. The **Botanisk Have** (Botanical Gardens), Gothersgade 128, at the corner of Øster Voldgade and Gothersgade, flower daily from 8:30am to 6pm (Sept. to late March 8:30am-4pm; free). Across the street the **Rosenborg Palace and Gardens** *(Rosenborg Slot),* Øster Volgade 4A, houses much of the collection of royal treasures, including the crown jewels. (Open June-Aug. daily 10am-4pm; Sept. to late Oct. and May 11am-3pm; late Oct. to April Tues., Fri., and Sun. 11am-2pm. 40kr.) Nearby, at Rømersgade 22, the gripping **Arbejdermuseet** (Workers' Museum) graphically portrays the lives of the non-royal (open July-Oct. daily 10am-5pm; Nov.-June Tues.-Fri. 10am-3pm, Sat.-Sun. 11am-4pm. 30kr). Three blocks north at Østervoldgade and Sølvgade is the **Statens Museum for Kunst** (State Museum of Fine Arts), Sølvgade 48-50, which displays works by Matisse and Dutch masters (due to reopen in July of 1998).

In the southern Christianshavn district lies **Christiania** (entrances on Prinsessegade). This "free city," founded in 1971 by youthful squatters in abandoned military barracks, still keeps the hippie spirit alive with its young population of artists and "free-thinkers." With visible trash and marijuana, it's not everyone's cup (or pot...) of tea; always ask before taking pictures, never take pictures on the main street, and exercise caution at night. Beer enthusiasts can tour the city's breweries. **Carlsberg,** Ny Carlsbergvej 140, is accessible by taking bus 6 west from Rådhuspladsen to Valby Langgade (tours Mon.-Fri. at 11am and 2pm; meet at Elephant Gate), and **Tuborg,** Strandvejen 54, requires taking bus 6 north from Rådhuspladsen (30min. tours Mon.-Fri. at 10am, 12:30pm, and 2:30pm). Both tours are free and offer beer (about 2 bottles per person) and soda at the end of the tour. If the breweries haven't confused your senses enough, try the **Experimentarium,** Tuborg Havnevej 7 (bus 6 north from Rådhuspladsen), where you can dance in the "reverse disco" or miraculously lose 20kg in seconds. (Open late June-mid-Aug. daily 10am-5pm, late Aug.-early June Mon.-Fri. 9am-5pm, Sat-Sun. 11am-5pm. 69kr, students 55kr.)

The collection of contemporary art in the new **Arken Museum of Modern Art** (in Ishøj Strandpark just south of the city) is as breathtaking as the white marble frigate-shaped building in which it is housed (take S-train to Ishøj and then bus 138; open Tues.-Sun. 10am-5pm; 40kr). To watch exquisite hand-painted porcelain being crafted, tour the **Royal Copenhagen Porcelain Factory** in nearby Frederiksberg. Take bus 1 or 14 from Rådhuspladsen. (15min. Open for tours May-Sept. at 9, 10, 11am, 1, and 2pm; Oct.-April at 9, 10, and 11am. 25kr.)

ENTERTAINMENT

Copenhagen's weekends often begin on Wednesday, and nights rock until 5am. The central pedestrian district reverberates with crowded bars and discos, Kongens Nytorv boasts fancier joints, and Nyhavn exudes salty charisma. A popular option is to buy beer at the supermarket and head to the boats and cafés of Nyhavn. For current events, consult *Copenhagen This Week* (free at hostels and tourist offices) or contact Use It for *Use It News* with (English) listings of concerts and entertainment. The **Scala** complex across the street from Tivoli features a multitude of bars and restaurants. University students liven up the cheaper bars in the Nørrebro area. The **Kul-Kaféen,** Teglgårdsstræde 5 (open Mon.-Sat. 11am-midnight), and **Café Dan Túrell,** Store Regnegade 5 (open Mon.-Sat. 10am-midnight), are great places to meet other young people, see live performers, and get info on music, dance, theater, and bicycling. The **Copenhagen Jazz Festival** draws top musicians from around the globe in early July. Copenhagen's lesbian and gay scene is one of the best in Europe, and gay Danish men and women report equal comfort in straight establishments.

Rust, Guldbergsgade 8, in the Nørreboro. Most popular disco around. A 20-something crowd dances the night away. Open Tues.-Sun. 10pm-5am. Cover 50kr.

Café Pavillionen, Fælleaparken, Borgmester Jensens Allé. Summer only outdoor café features local bands and dance music. Open June-Aug. Tues.-Sat. 8pm-2am.

X-Ray Undergrund/Kitsch, 13 Gothersgade. Techno-dancing rave club. For the hard-core dancing machine in us all. Open Thurs.-Sun. 10pm-3am.

Woodstock, 12 Vestergade, just north of Strøget and Nytorv. Fifties and sixties vintage music attracts a mixed crowd of younger and older couples. A good starter club. Open Tues.-Sat. 6pm-midnight.

Sebastian Bar and Café, 10 Hyskenstræde, off Strøget. The city's best-known gay and lesbian hang-out—get a copy here of *Front* or *Xpansion* for listings of every gay and lesbian establishment in Denmark. Open daily noon-2am. Beer 17-30kr.

PAN Club and Café, Knabrostræde 3. Combination gay café, bar, and disco which publishes *Xpansion.* Café opens Mon.-Sat. 6pm, Sun. 8pm. Disco opens daily 11pm. Both stay open until *late.* No cover before 11pm except Thursday (20kr).

■ Near Copenhagen

Stunning castles, white-sand beaches, and a world-class museum are all within easy reach of Copenhagen by train. Two rail lines go north from the city: a coastal line up to Helsingør (paralleled by the more scenic bus 388) and an S-train line to Hillerød. **Klampenborg** and **Charlottenlund,** close by on the coastal line (and at the end of S-train line C), feature topless beaches. **Bakken,** Dyrehavevej, Klampenborg (tel. 39 63 44), the world's oldest amusement park, though less ornate than Tivoli, delivers more thrills (including untranslated warnings). Just north from the Klampenborg train station, turn left, cross the overpass, and head through the park (open March 25-Aug. 25 daily noon-midnight; rides begin at 2pm; free entry). Bakken borders the **Jægersborg Deer Park,** the royal family's former hunting grounds, and still home to their **Eremitage** summer château, miles of wooded paths, and over 2000 red deer.

Rungsted and Humlebæk The quiet harbor town, **Rungsted,** where Isak Dinesen wrote *Out of Africa,* houses her abode at the **Karen Blixen Museum,** Rungsted Strandvej 111. A path from the gardens leads to Blixen's tree-shaded grave. Trains leave from the courtyard (every 20min.); buy tickets first inside. **Humlebæk,** farther up the coast, distinguishes itself with the spectacular **Louisiana Museum of Modern Art.** Named for the three wives (each named Louisa) of the estate's original owner, the museum contains works by Picasso, Warhol, Lichtenstein, Calder, and other 20th-century masters. Overlooking the Swedish coast, the building and its sculpture-studded grounds are themselves well worth the trip. Follow signs 1.5km north from the Humlebæk station or snag bus 388. Classical music concerts ring out on Wednesday evenings in summer (90kr includes museum); call 42 19 07 19 for info (museum open daily 10am-5pm, Wed. until 10pm; 53kr, with ISIC 45kr).

Helsingør, Hornbæk, and Hillerød Farther north, castles evince the Danish monarchy's fondness for lavish architecture. The most famous of these is undoubtedly **Kronborg Slot** in **Helsingør,** also known as Elsinore, home of Shakespeare's Hamlet. This castle was built in the 15th century to collect tolls from passing merchant ships. Viking chief Holger Danske sleeps in the castle's dungeon; legend has it that he still rises to face any threat to Denmark's safety. The self-guided tour includes a church and impressively furnished royal apartments. The castle also houses the Danish maritime museum. (Open May-Sept. daily 10:30am-5pm; April and Oct. Tues.-Sun. 11am-4pm; Nov.-March Tues.-Sun. 11am-3pm. Combined ticket 45kr.) The **tourist office** (tel. 49 21 13 33; fax 49 21 15 77) in Helsingør is inside **Kulturhuset,** to the left of the train station as you exit. The office books rooms (25kr fee) and provides ferry info. (Open mid-June to late Aug. Mon.-Fri. 9:30am-7pm, Sat. 10am-6pm; Sept. to mid-June Mon.-Fri. 9:30am-5pm, Sat. 10am-1pm.) The **HI youth hostel Villa Moltke,** is at Ndr. Strandvej 24 (tel. 49 21 16 40; fax 49 21 13 99); take bus 340 from the station. (Reception open daily 8am-noon and 4-9pm. 74kr, nonmembers 84kr. Sheets 40kr. Breakfast 40kr. Free showers and kitchen. Open Feb.-Nov.) **Cafeteria San Reno,** Stengade 53, offers a huge menu, or try Kulturhuset's **Kammer Cafeen** (sandwiches 25-30kr) near the train station.

Very near Helsingør, **Hornbæk** is a relaxed beach town about an hour north of Copenhagen. The town comes alive during the summer when city-weary urbanites flock to the beach—see Danes at their most beautiful on display. Wild antics surround the **harbor party** on the fourth weekend in July. Accommodations are generally out of budget reach. Bus 340 runs from Hillerød to Hornbæk (20kr, 20min.).

Moated **Frederiksborg Slot** in **Hillerød** is the most impressive of the castles north of Copenhagen, featuring exquisite gardens, brick ramparts, and the **National Historical Museum,** which displays portraits of prominent Danes. Concerts are given on the famous 1610 **Esaias Compenius organ** in the chapel Sundays at 5pm (free). Call 42 26 04 39 for information. (Castle open May-Sept. daily 10am-5pm; Oct. and April 10am-4pm; Nov.-March 11am-3pm. 40kr, students 10kr.) Along the train line halfway between Hillerød and Helsingør is **Fredensborg Castle,** built in 1722 and still used as the spring and autumn royal residence. The park is free and open year-round (castle open July only daily 1-5pm; 10kr). Peek into the palace gardens from the **Fredensborg Youth Hostel (HI),** Østrupvej 3 (tel. 42 28 03 15; fax 48 48 16 56), 1km from the train station (reception open daily 8am-11pm; 85kr, nonmembers 110kr; sheets 30kr). Hillerød is at the end of S-train lines A and E (40min. via Lyngby, 38kr), and accessible direct from Helsingør by train (30min.).

Roskilde and Lejre West of Copenhagen (25-30min., 35kr or 3 clips on the yellow *rabatkort*), **Roskilde** celebrates its 1000th anniversary in 1998 with a host of special cultural events. Contact **Roskilde 1000 Years,** Skt. Olsgade 15D, DK-4000 (tel. 46 32 09 98) for more info. This millennial city served as Denmark's first capital when King Harald Bluetooth built the first Christian church in Denmark here in 980. Thirty-eight other Danish monarchs repose in the ornate sarcophagi of **Roskilde Domkirke** cathedral. (Open April-June 16 Tues.-Fri. 9am-4:45pm, Sat. 9am-noon, Sun. 12:30-3:45 pm; Oct.-March Tues.-Fri. 10am-3:45pm, Sat. 11:30am-3:45pm. Concerts June-Aug. Thurs. at 8pm, Sun. 12:30pm-3:45pm. 6kr.) The **Viking Ship Museum,** Strandengen on the harbor, houses the dinosaur-like remains of five vessels sunk around 1060 and their less skeletal reconstructions moored in the outside harbor. From June 15 through August you can book a ride on one of these Viking long boats, but be prepared to take an oar—Viking conquest is no spectator sport (open April-Oct. daily 10am-5pm; Nov.-March 10am-4pm; 40kr). A fruit, flea, and flower **market** transforms Roskilde on Wednesdays and Saturdays (open 8am-2pm). From June 25-28 (1998), Roskilde hosts one of northern Europe's largest **music festivals** (tel. 70 10 17 17; http://www.Roskilde-Festival.dk/), drawing over 90,000 fans to see bands such as Beck, U2, Radiohead, Smashing Pumpkins, and David Bowie. The **tourist office** (tel. 46 35 27 00), Gullandsstræde 15, sells festival tickets, books rooms (25kr fee), and offers the 14-day **Roskilde Card** (85kr) which provides admission to 10 sites. (Open Sept.-March Mon.-Thurs. 9am-5pm, Fri. 9am-4pm, Sat. 10am-1pm; April-June Mon.-Fri. 9am-5pm, Sat. 10am-1pm; July-August Mon.-Fri. 9am-6pm, Sat. 9am-3pm, Sun. 10am-2pm.) Roskilde's **HI youth hostel,** Hørhusene 61 (tel. 46 35 21 84; fax 46 32 66 90), has beach access but is booked during the festival. (Bus 601 from train station to Låddenhøj, then walk 0.8km; reception open 9am-noon and 4-8pm. 84kr, nonmembers 109kr. Closed Jan.). Camp by the beach at **Roskilde Camping,** Baunehøjvej 7-9 (tel. 46 75 79 96; fax 46 75 44 26), 4km north; take bus 603 towards Veddelev (reception open daily 7am-10pm; 60kr per person; open early April to mid-Sept.).

Near Roskilde, the **Lejre Research Centre,** Slangealleen 2, reconstructs Viking agrarian life in an open-air museum. Take the S-train from Copenhagen to **Lejre,** then bus 233 to Lejre Experimental Centre. (Open May-June 22 and Aug. 19-Sept. 14 Tues.-Sun. 10am-5pm; June 23-Aug. 17 and Oct. 11-Oct. 19 daily 10am-5pm. 50kr.) Also in Lejre, home of the Holstein-Ledreborgs since 1739 the **Ledreborg Slot,** Ledreborg Allé, displays 18th-century Danish wealth. (From Lejre station take bus 2333. Open June 16-Aug. daily 11am-5pm; May-June 15 and Sept. Sun 11am-5pm. 45kr.)

Møn To see what Andersen called one of the most beautiful spots in Denmark, travel south from Copenhagen two hours to the white cliffs of the isle of **Møn.** Take the train to Vordingborg, bus 62 to Stege, and then bus 852 to Møn Klint. Plan carefully: only three buses go out and back a day; the last often leaves Møn before 4pm. For more info contact the **Møns Turistbureau,** Storegade 2 (tel. 55 81 44 11; fax 55 81 48 46), in Stege. (Open June 15-Aug. Mon.-Fri. 10am-6pm, Sat. 9am-6pm, Sun. 10am-noon; Sept.-June 14 Mon.-Fri. 10am-5pm, Sat. 9am-noon.)

Bornholm

East of Denmark and southwest of Sweden, the gorgeous island of Bornholm lures vacationers to its sand beaches and cozy fishing villages. A dreamland for avid bikers and nature lovers, the red-roofed cliffside villas may remind you of southern Europe, but the flowers and tidy half-timbered houses are undeniably Danish. Walking through Bornholm's tidy capital town, **Rønne,** it's hard to imagine the devastation and rubble left by relentless bombing during World War II.

Bornholmstrafikken offers the most comprehensive and varied means of transport to Bornholm from Denmark, Sweden, and Germany (tel. 56 95 18 66; fax 56 91 07 66; email info@bornholmferries.dk; http://www.bornholmferries.dk). Direct ferries from Copenhagen to Rønne are the slowest route (2 per day, 6½hr., 189kr, 50% Scanrail discount); the combo bus and ferry route via Sweden is faster (160-180kr). If you're in Sweden, a ferry departs daily from Ystad, just one hour from Malmö (2-5 per day, 2½hr., 110kr, 50% Scanrail discount); from Germany, ferries depart from Neu Murkan to Rønne (Mon.-Tues. and Thurs.-Sun. 1-2 per day, 3½hr., 50-100kr).

All ferries run to the harbor in Rønne, where you can rent a **bike** at **Bornholms Cykeludlejning,** Ndr. Kystvej 5, in the center of Rønne (open May-Sept. daily 7am-4pm; 55kr per day, 215kr per week). Bornholm has an efficient local BAT **bus** service. (35kr to Gudhjem or Sandvig-Allinge, 45kr to Svaneke. Unlimited travel for 24hr. 105kr, 5-7 days 350kr. 10-trip discount ticket about 85kr.) There are numerous cycling paths; pick up a guide at the tourist office (see below). Hostel rooms on Bornholm must be reserved in advance.

Rønne, Sandvig-Allinge, Gudhjem, and Svaneke Amid cafés and cobblestoned streets, Rønne, on Bornholm's southwest coast, is the island's principle port of entry. The Rønne **tourist office** (tel. 56 95 95 00; fax 56 95 95 68), a mirrored-glass building behind the Q8 gas station by the Bornholmstraffiken terminal, books rooms in private homes (150-200kr) and provides free copies of the helpful *Turist Bornholm Guide* and *Bornholm This Week.* (Open May Mon.-Fri. 9am-5pm, Sat.-Sun. 11am-3pm; June-Aug. Mon.-Fri. 7am-6pm, Sat. 7am-7pm, Sun. 1-7pm; Sept.-Dec. Mon.-Fri. 9am-4pm, Sat. 11:30am-2:30pm.) The **youth hostel (HI),** Arsenalvej 12 (tel. 56 95 13 40; fax 56 95 01 32), is in a quiet, woodland area; from the ferry terminal, walk along Munch Petersens Vej, turn left up Zahrtmannsvej, and go up the steps to the junction with Skansevej, then follow the signs. (Reception open daily 7am-noon, 4-5pm, and 10-10:30pm. 95kr, nonmembers 130kr. Reserve ahead.) **Galløkken Camping,** Strandvejen 4 (tel. 56 95 23 20; fax 56 95 37 66; open May-Sept.) charges 44kr per person and 40kr per tent. Shop for groceries at **Kvickly,** in the Snellemark

Centret shopping center behind the tourist office, which also has a second-floor cafeteria with affordable sandwiches. (25-35kr. Supermarket open Mon.-Fri 9am-7pm, Sat. 9am-4pm, Sun. 10am-4pm. Cafeteria open Mon.-Fri. 9am-7pm, Sun. 9am-4pm.) The outdoor **Café Hovedvagten,** Søndergade 12, is renowned for its spit-roasted pork dinner (89kr; served Wed. and Sat. after 6pm; café open daily 11am-11pm).

The smaller towns of **Sandvig-Allinge, Gudhjem,** and **Svaneke** anchor Bornholm's spectacular north coast, whose whitesand beaches attract bikers and bathers. The **Nordbornholms Turistbureau,** Kirkegade 4 (tel. 56 48 00 01; fax 56 48 02 26), in Allige, provides free maps, brochures, and accommodation info. Just outside of Sandvig is the **Sandvig Vandrerhjem (HI),** Hammershusvej 94. (Tel. 56 48 03 62; fax 56 48 18 62. Reception open daily 8am-10pm. 90kr. Open June-Oct.) Down the same road and perched above the sea, **Hammershus** is northern Europe's largest castle ruin. **Sandvig Familie Camping,** Sandlinien 5 (tel. 56 48 04 47; fax 56 48 04 57), provides camping sites on the sea (48kr).

Gudhjem's harbor appeared in the Oscar-winning film *Pelle the Conqueror,* based on the novel by Näxo, a native. The **Gudhjem Turistbureau,** Åbogade 7 (tel. 56 48 52 10; fax 56 56 48 52 74), provides free beach and bikepath maps (open June-Aug. Mon.-Fri. 9am-5pm, Sat. 9am-non; Sept. Mon.-Fri. 10am-2pm). The popular **Vandrerhjem Sct. Jørgens Gaard (HI),** Ejner Mikkelsensvej 14 (tel. 56 48 50 35; fax 56 48 56 35), across from the bus stop, has a fantastic view of the sea (reception open daily 8am-6pm; 95kr). Pitch a tent at **Strandlunden Camping,** Melstedsvej 33 (tel./fax 56 48 52 45). A small beach awaits 1km to the right of the harbor.

Svanke's red-tile roofs hover under the town's windmill perched at the top of Storegade. On the harbor, the chimney-capped **Røgeriet** (fish smokery), Fiskergade 12, serves home-made smoked herring (open Mon.-Fri. 9am-6:30pm). The **Svaneke Turistbureau,** Storegade 24 (tel. 56 49 63 50; fax 56 49 70 10), offers maps and the *Svaneke Guide.* (Open June-Aug. Mon.-Fri. 9:30am-4:30pm, Sat. 9am-noon; Sept.-May Mon.-Wed. 10am-4pm, Thurs.-Fri. 11am-5pm.) The **Svaneke Vandrerhjem,** Rebarbanvej 9 (tel. 56 49 62 42; fax 56 49 73 83), has dorms (90kr) while the **Hullehavn Camping,** Sydskovvej 9 (tel./fax 56 49 63 63), offers sites on the beach.

FUNEN (FYN)

Situated between the island of Zealand to the east and the Jutland peninsula to the west, Funen is Denmark's garden. As a new bridge and tunnel connects Zealand to Funen, this remote bread basket is no longer isolated from the rest of Denmark.

Odense

Hans Christian Andersen's birthplace, the old manufacturing metropolis of Odense (OH-n-sa), has become Denmark's third largest city. Unhappy in this mediocre city, Hans left Odense at the earliest opportunity and was not appreciated here until he became famous elsewhere. At **H.C. Andersens Hus,** Hans Jensens Stræde 37-45, learn about the author's eccentricities and see free performances of his work (June 22-Aug. 2 11am, 1, and 3pm) in the garden behind the museum (open June-Aug. daily 9am-6pm; Sept.-May 10am-4pm; 25kr). A few scraps from his ugly duckling childhood are on view in **H.C. Andersens Barndomshjem** (Childhood Home), Munkemøllestræde 3-5 (open June-Aug. daily 10am-4pm; Sept.-March 11am-3pm; 10kr). Don headphones and listen to the classical compositions of another Great Dane at the **Carl Nielsen Museum,** Claus Bergs Gade 11 (open July-Aug. daily 10am-4pm; Sept.-June Tues.-Sun. 10am-4pm; 15kr). At the other end of the pedestrian district, **Brandts Klædefabrik,** Brandts Passage 37-43, (tel. 66 13 78 97), hosts an outstanding modern art gallery (open July-Aug. daily 10am-5pm; Sept.-June Tues.-Sun. 10am-5pm; 20kr). The **Museum of Photographic Art,** Brandt's Passage 37&43, is worth a visit, as is the collection of Danish art featuring Vilhelm Hammershøi in the

Fyns Kunstmuseum (both open July-Aug. daily 10am-4pm; Sept.-June Tues.-Sun. 10am-4pm; 20kr). In southern Odense the **Den Fynske Landsby** (Funen Village), Sejerskovvej 20, is a collection of 18th- and 19th-century buildings brought from around the island. (Take bus 25 or 26. Open June-Aug. daily 10am-7pm; Sept.-Oct. and April-May 10am-4pm; Nov.-March Sun. 11am-3pm. 25kr.) The **H.C. Andersen Garden** and the **Kings Garden** (across from Central Station) are among the many spectacular gardens. The **Odense Eventyrpas,** available at the tourist office, station, youth hostel, and campground, is good for travel on municipal buses and trains and a 75% discount on most museum admissions (1-day pass 50kr). In late June, **Ringe,** 30km away, hosts the **Midtfyn Festival** (tel. 65 96 25 12 or 65 96 25 01 for info, or the Ringe tourist office at 62 62 52 23; http://www.mf.dk), one of the largest rock/folk festivals in Denmark. The Black Crowes, Sting, Jamiroquai, and Sheryl Crowe have all played here (350kr per day, 625kr for Fri.-Sun.; free camping).

Practical Information, Accommodations, and Food The **tourist office,** Rådhuspladsen (tel. 66 12 75 20; fax 66 12 75 86; email otb@odenseturist.dk; http://www.odenseturist.dk), provides free maps, exchanges currency, and books rooms (120kr per person, 25kr fee). From the train station, walk on Nørregade to Vestergade, turn left, and continue to Rådhurpladsen. (Open June 15-Aug. Mon.-Sat. 9am-7pm, Sun. 11am-7pm; Sept. to mid-June Mon.-Fri. 10:30am-4:30pm, Sat. 10am-1pm.) **Buses** depart behind the train station (10kr, pay when you disembark). **Vandrerhjem Kragsbjerggården (HI),** Kragsbjergvej 121 (tel. 09 13 04 25; fax 65 91 28 63), is 2km from the town center; take bus 61 or 62 from the train station. (Reception open daily 8am-noon and 4-8pm. 80kr, nonmembers 105kr. Open mid-Feb. to Nov. Reserve ahead.) You can camp next to the enticing Fruens Boge park at **DCU Camping,** Odensevej 102 (tel. 66 11 47 02; fax 65 91 73 43); hop on bus 41 or 81. (Reception open daily 7am-10pm. 50kr per person. Open late March-Sept.)

Den Grimme Ælling (The Ugly Duckling), across the street from H.C. Andersens Hus, at Hans Jensen Str. 1, serves a huge buffet of "proper Danish food" (lunch 70kr, dinner 100kr; open daily noon-2:30pm and 5:30-10:30pm). **Café Biografen,** Brandt's Passage 39-41, has a daily large brunch (45kr; 11am-1pm), as well as sandwiches and pasta. For veggie fare try the communal kitchen **Kærnehuset,** Nedergade 6 (arrive before 6pm). Groceries are available at **Aktri Super,** corner of Nørregade and Skulkenborg (open Mon.-Fri. 9am-7pm, Sat. 8:30am-4pm).

Egeskov Slot and Svendborg

About 45 minutes south of Odense on the Svendborg rail line is the town of **Kværndup** and its most famous edifice, **Egeskov Slot,** a stunning 16th-century castle that appears to float on the lake that surrounds it—it's actually supported by an entire forest of 12,000 oak piles. The castle's interior features opulent furnishings from the 18th through the 20th centuries and the grounds are a wonderland of formal gardens and a large bamboo labyrinth. On summer Sundays at 5pm, classical concerts resound in the castle's **Knight Hall.** (Castle open April 25-June and Aug.-Sept. daily 10am-5pm; July 10am-7pm. 100kr. Grounds open April 25-May and Sept. daily 10am-5pm, June and Aug. 10am-6pm, July 10am-8pm. 55kr. Combined castle and grounds ticket 100kr.) To get to Egeskov, exit the Svendborg-bound train at Kværndrup; leave the station, and turn right until you reach Bøjdenvej, the main road. You can then wait for the hourly bus 920 (10kr), or turn right and walk the 2km through wheat fields to the castle. The castle has no café, so bring lunch.

On Funen's south coast, an hour from Odense by rail, **Svendborg** is a beautiful harbor town and a major departure point for ferries to the south Funen islands. Retrace Svendborg's nautical history at the **Maritime Museum,** Strangade 1. (Open May-Sept. daily 10am-5pm; Jan.-April and Oct.-Dec. Mon.-Fri. 2-5pm, Sat. 9am-noon. 20kr.) **M/S Helge** (tel. 62 21 09 80) offers cruises (2hr., 50kr) leaving from Jensens Mole which go to the regal 17th-century estate of **Valdemars Slot,** across the bridge on the island of Tåsinge, which was built by Christian IV for his son. The grounds hold a beach which visitors may use and a new Yachting Museum. (Take bus 200. Open March-Sept. daily 10am-5pm; April and Oct. Sat.-Sun. 10am-5pm. 45kr.)

The **tourist office** (tel. 62 21 09 80; fax 62 22 05 53) is on the café-rimmed Centrum Pladsen; the office has a free map of the town and beaches, finds rooms (25kr fee), and has a great 75kr bike map. (Open late June-Aug. Mon.-Fri. 9am-7pm, Sat. 9am-3pm; Sept. to mid-June Mon.-Fri. 9am-5pm, Sat. 9:30am-12:30pm.) On the other side of the train station is the dock for **ferries** to Ærø. The five-star **HI youth hostel,** Vestergade 45 (tel. 62 20 21 66; fax 62 20 29 39), is centrally located. (Reception open daily 8am-9pm; 85kr; breakfast 38kr; sheets 30kr). To get there from the station, take a left onto Jernbanegade, then turn left at Valdemarsgade, which becomes Vestergade (20min.). **Carlsberg Camping,** Sundbrovej 19 (tel. 62 22 53 84; fax 62 22 58 11), is across the sound on Tåsinge (reception open daily 8am-10pm; 50kr; open April to mid-Sept.). Rent a bike from **Hotel Swendborg,** Centrum Pladsen (50kr per day; 200kr deposit; open daily 8am-8pm). **Den Grimme Ælling,** Korsgade 17, serves all-you-can-eat lunch (70kr) and dinner (100kr).

ÆRØ

Ærø's (EH-ruh) wheat fields, busy harbors, and cobblestoned hamlets, quietly preserve an earlier era in Danish history. A small island off the south coast of Funen, Ærø is a place where cows, rather than real estate developers, lay claim to the most beautiful waterfront land. Several **trains** from Odense to Svendborg are timed to meet the ferry from Svendborg to Ærøskøbing. (Ferry 107kr round-trip; buy ticket on board. Departs Svendborg Mon.-Sat. 7:30, 10:30am, 1:30, 4:30, 7:30 and 10:30pm; Sun. 10:30am, 1:30, 4:30, 7:30, and 10:30pm. 70min. Frequent return trips. Call 62 52 10 18 or fax 62 52 20 88.) Bus 990 rides between the main towns of Ærøskøbing, Marstal, and Søby (day pass 44kr), but Ærø is best explored on bike.

DENMARK

In **Ærøskøbing,** ubiquitous rosebushes and half-timbered houses attract yachts from Sweden and Germany. The **tourist office** (tel. 62 52 13 00; fax 62 52 14 36; email Turistar@pust.1.tele.dk), just across from the ferry landing, arranges rooms in private homes. (Singles 110-150kr; doubles 200kr. Open June 15-Aug. Mon.-Fri. 9am-5pm, Sat. 10am-3pm, Sun. 11am-1pm; Sept.-June 14 Mon.-Fri. 9am-4pm, Sat. 10am-1pm.) The gracious **HI youth hostel,** Smedevejen 13 (tel. 62 52 10 44; fax 62 52 16 44), is a 10-minute walk from the ferry; walk left on Smedegade, which becomes Nørregade and then Østergade and Smedevejen. (Reception open daily 8am-noon and 4-8pm; check in by 5pm or call ahead. 80kr, nonmembers 105kr. Breakfast 38kr. Sheets 35kr. Reservations recommended.) **Ærøskøbing Camping,** Sygehusvejen 40b (tel. 62 52 18 54; fax 62 52 14 36), is 10 minutes to the right as you leave the ferry (reception open daily 7am-10pm; 42kr per person; open May to mid-Sept.). You can rent a **bike** at the hostel, the campground (both 40kr for one day), or the gas station at Pilebækken 11. Musicians come to **Café Andelen** at Søndergade 28 to play for appreciative crowds and enjoy the delectable 20kr rhubarb pie. (Music daily 9pm-midnight; 80-150kr. Café open daily 11am-midnight.) Restaurants line Vestergade, the street leading into town from the ferry port. Affordable Danish seafood is available at **Ærøskøbing Røgeri,** Havnen 15. (Open May to mid-June and Aug. daily 10am-6pm; late June-July 10am-8pm; Sept. 10am-4pm.) Thrifty shoppers head to the supermarket **Emerko,** Statene 3 (open Mon.-Fri. 8am-7pm).

Marstal, 13km away on Ærø's east coast, is less pretty but has cheaper restaurants and lodgings. The **tourist office,** Havnegade 5 (tel. 62 53 19 60; fax 62 53 30 35), rents bikes and finds rooms. (Open June-Aug. Mon.-Fri. 9am-5pm, Sat. 10am-3pm, Sun. 10am-noon; Sept.-May Mon.-Fri. 9am-4pm.) The **HI youth hostel,** Færgestræde 29 (tel. 62 53 10 64; fax 62 53 10 67), is by the harbor, a five-minute walk left of the tourist office. (Reception open May-Aug. daily 7am-noon and 4-9pm. 80kr, nonmembers 105kr.) **Marstal Camping,** Egehovedvej 1 (tel. 62 53 36 00), offers waterfront facilities (45kr; open April to mid-Oct.). Grab a bite at **Den Lille Café,** Kirkestræde 15 (open Mon.-Fri. 11am-10pm, Sat. noon-10pm, Sun. noon-8pm).

The sedate **Sørby** is at Ærø's northern end. The **tourist office,** on Havnevejen, provides info on beaches and accommodations (open Mon.-Sat. 10am-4pm). **Sørby Camping** (tel. 62 58 14 70), on Vitsø, has spaces for tents (38kr; open May-mid-Sept.). Rent bikes at **Søby Cykeludlejning,** Langebro 4A (tel. 62 58 18 42).

JUTLAND (JYLLAND)

Homeland of the Jutes who joined the Angles and Saxons in the conquest of England, the Jutland peninsula is Denmark's largest land mass. Beaches and campgrounds mark the peninsula as prime summer vacation territory, while low rolling hills and sparse forests add color and variety. Jutland may not be suitable for a whirlwind tour, but the plentiful supply of hostels will allow you to take a weekend beach fling without denting your budget. To get to **Esbjerg,** on Jutland's west coast, from another Danish city, hop on one of the frequent **trains** that connect the major cities. **Ferries** travel to Norway and Sweden; try **Color Line** (tel. 99 56 19 77), **Stena Line** (tel. 96 20 02 00), and **SeaCat** (tel. 98 42 83 00). Those stuck waiting for connections may try the **HI youth hostel** (tel. 75 12 42 58; 80kr, nonmembers 105k).

Tønder

An hour south of Ribe on the German border lies Tønder (TUH-nuh), the fairy-tale abode for Prince Joachim and his wildly popular new bride, Princess Alexandra. Their primary residence, **Schackenborg Slott,** lies in Slottsgade outside of town in **Møgeltøner** (Old Tønder). A famous lace production center in the 17th century, Tønder carries on the style tradition as the home of **ecco shoes** and the birthplace of famous Danish furniture designer, **H.J. Wegner.** See Wegner's work at the **Tønder Museum of Art,** Kengevej 55, and the **Museum Taver** whose collection also includes work by Christina Jensen and Knud Biehl (open May-Oct. Tues.-Sun. 10am-5pm; Nov.-April Tues.-Sun. 1-5pm; 15kr). Tours of the town's medieval streets (mid-June to Aug. 8; 20kr) leave from the stone sculpture-fountain in front of the tourist office known as "Albert" because the sculpture is quite simply "ein stein" (German for "a stone"). This bit of humor indicates the unique meshing of Danish and German cultures in Tønder, which was part of Germany from 1864 to 1920. The influence can still be seen in details like the Hanseatic door of **Det Gamle Apotek,** Østergade 1, a preserved 17th-century pharmacy (open daily 9:30am-5:30pm; free). **Tønder Krist Kirke** (Christ Church) features Baroque sculpture and spectacular chandeliers (open Mon.-Fri. 11am-4pm, Sat. 10am-4pm, Sun. 10am-3pm; free). In late August, 25,000 people descend on Tønder to hear the best in blues, jazz, gospel, and folk for the **Tønder Festival** (150kr). For info contact **Tønder Festivalen,** Vestergade 80, DK-6270 Tønder (tel. 74 72 10 00 or 74 72 46 10; http://www.tf.dk), or the tourist office.

The **tourist office,** Torvet 1 (tel. 74 72 12 20; fax 74 72 09 00), provides free maps, accommodations booking (20kr fee), tours, and currency exchange. (Open June 16-Aug. 9:30am-5:30pm, Sat. 9:30am-3pm; Sept.-June 15 Mon.-Fri. 9am-4pm, Sat. 9am-noon.) Walk left on Sødergade until you reach Torvet. To get to the **Tønder Vandrerhjem (HI),** Sønderport 4 (tel. 74 72 35 00; fax 74 72 27 97), take a right onto Søndergade, which becomes Søndre Landevej, and take a left onto Sønderport. (Reception open daily 8am-noon and 4-8pm. 85kr, nonmembers 110kr. Bike rental 35kr per day.) **Tønder Camping,** Holmevej 2A (tel. 74 72 18 49), is up the street from the hostel (open daily 8am-7pm; 40kr; bikes 35kr per day). For an affordable lunch buffet (49kr) and sandwiches (20-38kr) try the **Victoria Café,** Storegade 9 (open Mon.-Thurs. 10am-midnight, Fri.-Sat. 10-2am, Sun. noon-10pm). The well-stocked **Krickly supermarket,** Plantagevej, has a cafeteria serving *dagens ret* (30kr; open Mon.-Fri. 10am-7pm, Sat. 9am-7pm, Sun. 9am-5pm). Live music plays between rounds of Danish and Irish beer (25-48kr) at **Hagge's Music Pub,** Vestergade 80.

Ribe

Denmark's oldest town, Ribe gained prominence when the German missionary Ansgar established a cathedral here in 948. After centuries of wrestling with the North Sea, Ribe today is separated from the water by flat salt meadows and boasts migratory seasonal birds, half-timbered medieval houses, and red-tiled roofs. For a great view, climb the 248 steps of the **cathedral** tower. The interior holds a spectacular 16th-century organ. (Open April and Oct. Mon.-Sat. 11am-4pm, Sun. noon-4pm; May and Sept. Mon.-Sat. 10am-5pm, Sun. noon-5pm; June-Aug. Mon.-Sat. 10am-6pm, Sun. noon-6pm; Nov.-March Mon.-Sat. 11am-3pm, Sun. noon-3pm. 7kr.) The **Rådhus** (town hall), Van Støckens Place (tel. 75 42 00 55), a former debtor's prison, houses a small museum on medieval torture (open June-Aug. daily 1-3pm; May and Sept. Mon.-Fri. 1-3pm; 15kr). Follow the **night watchman** on his rounds for an English, Danish, or German tour of town beginning in Torvet, the main square (June-Aug. 8pm and 10pm; May and Sept. 10pm; free). For a taste of all things Viking, visit **Ribe's Vikinger,** Udin Plads 1. (Open April-May and late Sept.-Oct. 10am-4pm; June to mid-Sept. Thurs.-Tues. 10am-5pm, Wed. 10am-9pm; Nov.-March Tues.-Sun. 10am-4pm.) If your appetite is not sated, however, head 2km south to open-air **Ribe Vikingcenter,** Lustrupvej 4, where costumed actors recreate Viking life (open mid-May to Sept. Tues.-Sun. 11am-4pm; 40kr). The **Ribe Kunstmuseum** (Art Museum), Sct. Nicolai Gade 10, has a lovely collection of Danish Golden Age (1800-1850) painting. (Open June 15-Aug. Tues.-Sun. 11am-5pm; Sept.-Dec. and Feb.-June14 Thurs.-Sat. 1-4pm, Sun. 11am-4pm. 20kr.) Opening in spring 1998, the **Vadehavscentret** (the Wadden Sea Center), Okholmvej 5, Vestervedsted (tel. 75 44 61 61), will provide info on and tours of the local marshes, dikes, and sea (open June-Oct. daily 10am-6pm; April-May and Oct.-Nov. 10am-4pm; 30kr), or you can rent a bike and explore on your own.

The **tourist office,** Torvet 3 (tel. 75 42 15 00; fax 75 42 40 78), has free maps and arranges accommodations. (125kr. Open June-Aug. Mon.-Fri. 9am-5:30pm, Sat. 9am-5pm, Sun. 10am-2pm; Sept.-Oct and April-May Mon.-Fri. 9am-5pm, Sat. 10am-1pm; Nov.-March Mon.-Fri. 9:30am-4:30pm, Sat. 10am-1pm.) From the train station, cross Odins Plads, take a left on Dagmarsgade, and at Torvet the office is on your right. The centrally located **Ribe Vandrerhjen (HI),** Sct. Pedersgade 16 (tel. 75 42 06 20; fax 75 42 42 88), has **bike rental** (50kr per day) and view of the flatlands. (Reception open daily 8am-noon and 4-8pm. 85kr, nonmembers 110kr. Sheets 35kr. Open Feb.-Nov.) **Ribe Camping,** 1.5km from the town center, has showers, laundry, a grocery, cafeteria, and campfires (60kr). A number of traditional inns, including **Vægerkælderen,** Hotel Dagmar, Torvet, **Restaurant Sælhunden,** Slabbroen 13, and **Restaurant Backhaus,** Grydergade 12, offer affordable lunch buffets (60-85kr) of Danish seafood, salad, and beer (14-35kr). For groceries head to **Super Nærkøb,** Sønderpo Arsgade 24 (open Mon.-Fri. 8:30am-8pm, Sat. 8am-5pm). At night a young crowd congregates at the **Stenbohus Pub&Bar,** Stenbogade 1, on Torvet, for live music on weekends and every night in the summer (open Sun.-Thurs. 10am-2am, Fri.-Sat 10am-5am).

DENMARK

Århus

Århus (ORE-hoos), Denmark's second largest and many Danes' favorite city, is Jutland's cultural and student center. Queen Margarethe II's summer home here at **Marselisborg Castle** opens its exquisite rose garden to the public. From the train station, take bus 1, 18, or 19. At the town center, the 13th-century **Århus Cathedral (Damkivke)** dominates Bispetorv and the café- and shop-lined pedestrian streets that fan out around its Gothic walls. (Open May-Sept. Mon.-Sat. 9:30am-4pm; Oct.-Dec. 10am-3pm; Jan.-April 10am-3pm. Free.) Two millennia ago, people living near Århus killed some of their own and threw them into nearby bogs, where antiseptic acidity mummified the bodies. Take bus 6 from the train station to the end of the line to reach the **Moesgård Museum of Prehistory,** where Graballe Man, a completely preserved bog body, makes his home (open April-Sept. daily 10am-5pm; Oct.-March Tues.-Sun. 10am-4pm; 35kr). From behind the museum, the **Prehistoric Trail** leads through mock settings to a **sand beach** (3km). Bus 19 (last bus 7:40pm) returns from the beach to the Århus station during the summer. Take bus 3, 14, or 15 to get to **Den Gamle By** (Old Town), Viborgvej 2, a reconstructed 16th-century Jutland village. (Open June-Aug. daily 9am-6pm; May and Sept. 9am-5pm; April, Oct., and Dec. 10am-4pm; Jan.-March and Nov. 11am-3pm. 50kr.) The **Århus Kunstmuseum,** Vennelystparken, has a fine collection of Danish Golden Age painting as well as American and German Realist and Impressionist art (open Tues.-Sun. 10am-5pm; 30kr). Reclaim "herstory" at the **Women's Museum/Café** next door at Domkirkeplads 5 (open June-Sept.15 daily 10am-5pm; Jan.-May and Sept. 15-Dec. 10am-4pm; 15kr). Near the cathedral, just off Domkirkeplads, in former Gestapo headquarters, the Århus **Museet for Besættelsen** (Occupation Museum) has collections of military equipment, propaganda, and items used for sabotage. (Open June-Aug. daily 10am-4pm; Jan.-May and Sept.-Dec. Sat.-Sun. 10am-4pm. 20kr.) The **Århus Festuge,** a rollicking week of theater, dance, and music, begins on the first Saturday in September (tel. 89 31 82 70; fax 86 19 13 36; http://www.aarhusfestuge.dk). In mid-June Århus holds a week-long **Jazz Festival** (tel. 86 12 24 69; fax 86 12 28 89; http://www.musikhuset-aarhus.dk) with Theloneus Monk, Jr. coming in 1998 (tickets free-120kr). You can visit a smaller replica of Tivoli, the **Tivoli Friheden,** at Skovbrynet (open April 25-June 20 and Aug. 4-17 daily 2-10pm; June 21-Aug. 3 1-11pm; 30kr).

Practical Information, Accommodations, and Food The **tourist office** (tel. 86 12 16 00; fax 86 12 95 90; email aarhconv@inet.uni-c.dk) in the town hall, a block down Park Allé from the train station, has free maps and city guides and books accommodations in private homes (120-150kr) for 25kr. (Open June 23-Sept. 14 Mon.-Fri. 9:30am-6pm, Sat. 9:30am-5pm, Sun. 9:30am-1pm; reduced hours off-season.) Århus is walkable, but the tourist office sells one-day bus passes (45kr). Ten minutes from the train station the hip **Århus City Sleep-In,** Havnegade 20 (tel. 86 19 20 55; fax 86 19 18 11), doubles as an unofficial cultural and info center. (Reception open 24hr. 75kr. Breakfast 25kr. Sheets 30kr. Laundry 25-45kr. Bike rental 50kr per day.) The Sleep-In runs in conjunction with the helpful **Kutturgyngen student center,** which has a café/club and offers free psychological counseling. Århus's **HI youth hostel "Pavillonen,"** Marienlundsvej 10 (tel. 86 16 72 98; fax 86 10 55 60) rests 3km from the city center and five minutes from the beach in the Risskov forest. Take bus 1, 6, 9, or 16 to Marienlund (reception open daily 4-11pm; 75kr, nonmembers 100kr; sheets 30kr). Camp at the beautiful **Blommehavenn Camping Århus,** Ørneredevej 35 (tel. 86 27 02 07; fax 86 27 45 22), located near a beach in the Marselisborg forest and near the Royal Family's summer residence. Take bus 19 (summer only) from the rail station directly to the grounds, or bus 6 to Hørhavevej (reception open late March to mid-Sept. daily 7am-11pm; 48kr). **Århus nord camping,** Randersvej 400 (tel. 86 23 11 33; fax 86 23 11 310), is open all year (48kr).

For those on a tight budget, shop at one of the ubiquitous **Føtex Supermarkets** at Frederiks Allé, Brunsgade 55, and Guldsmedgade 3 (all closed Sun.). All-you-can-eat lunch (70kr) and dinner (100kr) buffets are available at **Den Grimme Ælling,** Øutergade 12 (open daily noon-10:30pm). The very hip **Café Knussen,** Mejlgade 24, is a lounge style cigar bar with a great sandwich selection (25-35kr; open daily 10am-10pm). The **Royal Casino Bar,** Store Torr 4, has late night music and dancing (open daily 7pm-4am), and the **Pan Club,** Jægergårdsgade 42, has a café, bar, and largely gay and lesbian dance club. (Café open Sun.-Thurs. 6pm-midnight, Fri.-Sat. 6pm-5am. Dance club open Wed.-Sat. 11pm-4am; Fri.-Sat. 45kr cover.)

■ Near Århus: Legoland and The Bog Man

Billund is renowned as the home of **Legoland**—an amusement park built of 40 million Legos, best seen as a daytrip. More than just baby-babble, "Lego" is an abbreviation of *leg godt* (have fun playing). Don't skip the impressive indoor exhibitions. Unfortunately, private buses and a new price system make Legoland a bit expensive. To get there, take the train from Århus to **Vejle** (1 per hr., 45min.), then bus 912, marked "Legoland." A combined ticket for the bus and park admission (including rides) costs 135-150kr. (Tel. 75 33 13 33. Open late June-Aug. daily 10am-9pm; Sept.-Oct. 10am-6pm; late March-early June 10am-8pm. Rides close at 6pm.)

An hour west of Århus by train (62kr), **Silkeborg** floats in perhaps the most scenic part of Denmark. The Tollund Man, a remarkably preserved 2200-year-old bog man, rests in the **Silkeborg Museum,** Hovedgården (open May-Oct. 18 daily 10am-5pm; Oct.19-April Wed., Sat.-Sun. noon-4pm; 20kr). The **tourist office,** Åhavevej 2A (tel. 86 82 19 11), offers free maps and town guides. From the train station, turn right on Drewsensuej, make a left on Chr. 8 Vej, a right on Rosenørns Allé, and a left on Åhavevej. (Open June 15-Aug. Mon.-Fri. 9am-5pm, Sat. 9am-3pm, Sun. noon-3pm; Sept.-June 14 Mon.-Fri. 9am-4pm, Sat. 9am-noon.)

Aalborg

The site of the first Viking settlement 1300 years ago, Aalborg (OLE-borg) is Denmark's fourth-largest city. Its spotless streets and white church garnered it the title of Europe's Tidiest City in 1990. By contrast, **Lindholm Høje,** Vendilavej 11, in nearby Nørresundby, was filled with unkempt, rowdy Vikings around 700. Today, it's covered with 700 of their gravestones and a museum of Viking life. To reach the site, take bus 6 (11kr) near the tourist office. (Site open daily dawn-dusk. Museum open late March to mid-Oct. daily 10am-5pm; late Oct. to mid-March Tues.-Sun. 10am-4pm. 20kr.) The **Monastery of the Holy Ghost,** C.W. Obelsplads, is Denmark's oldest welfare institution (1431) and houses frescoes (English tours June 23-Aug. 15 Tues. and Thurs. at 2pm; 25kr). The **Budolfi Church** on Algade has a brilliantly colored interior with ringing *carillon.* (Open May-Sept. Mon.-Fri. 9am-4pm, Sat. 9am-2pm; Oct.-April Mon.-Fri. 9am-3pm, Sat. 9am-noon.) The **Nordjyllands Kunstmuseum,** King Christian Allé 50, houses 20th-century painting (open July-Aug. daily 10am-5pm; Sept.-June Tues.-Sun. 10am-5pm; 20kr). For serious rollercoasters visit **Tivoliland,** Karolinelundsvej (open April-Sept. daily noon-10pm; 40kr, full-day "Funcard" 150kr).

The **tourist office,** Østerågade 8 (tel. 98 12 60 22; fax 98 16 69 22), provides free maps and brochures. From the station, cross the street and J.F.K. Plads, turn left on Boulevarden Østerågade, and continue straight for about five minutes. (Open June 15-Aug. 14 Mon.-Fri. 9am-6pm, Sat. 9am-5pm; Jan.-June 14 and Aug. 15-Dec. 9am-4:30pm, Sat. 10am-1pm.) The **Aalborg Vandrerhjem (HI),** Skydebanevej 50 (tel. 98 11 60 44; fax 98 12 47 11), sits on the shore of a beautiful fjord. Take bus 8 ("Fjordparken") to the end. (Reception open Jan. 20-June 19 and Aug. 11-Dec. 15 daily 8am-noon and 4-10pm; June 20-Aug. 10 daily 7:30am-11pm. 85kr, nonmembers 110kr. Camping 45kr. Laundry. Open mid-Jan. to mid.-Dec.) **Jomfru Ane Gade** is lined with bars and restaurants. Head to **Papegøjehaven,** Europa Plads 2, or **Il Mullno,** Bispensgade 31, for grub. Dance all night at **Grand,** Danmarksgade 43.

Frederikshavn

Despite noble efforts to showcase its admittedly charming streets and hospitality, Frederikshavn is most famous for its ferry links. **Stena Line** ferries (tel. 96 20 02 00) leave here for Gothenburg, Sweden (2hr., 50-90kr, round-trip 180kr, 50% off with Scan- or Eurailpass), as well as for Oslo and other points in Norway (150-350kr, round-trip 260-630kr). **SeaCat** (tel. 98 42 83 00) offers speedier and cheaper service to Gothenburg (1¾hr., 110kr). Ferries are less frequent and less expensive off season. Frederikshavn's **tourist office,** Brotorvet 1 (tel. 98 42 32 66; fax 98 42 12 99), is near the Stena Line terminal, south of the rail station and offers a room reservation service (25kr), currency exchange, and free maps and guides. (Open June-Aug.16 Mon.-Sat. 8:30am-8:30pm, Sun. 11am-8:30pm; Jan.-May and Aug.17-Dec. Mon.-Fri. 9am-4pm, Sat. 11am-2pm.) The **HI youth hostel,** Buhlsvej 6 (tel. 98 42 14 75; fax 98 42 65 22), group-oriented and packed, is a 15-minute walk from the station. (Reception open in summer daily 7am-noon and 4-9pm; off-season 4-6pm. Dorms 53kr, nonmembers 78kr. Open Feb. to mid-Dec.) Camp at **Nordstrand Camping,** Apholenvej 40 (tel. 98 42 93 50; fax 98 43 47 85; 48kr; open April-Sept.15).

Skagen

Perched on Denmark's northernmost tip, sunny Skagen (SKAY-en) is a beautiful summer retreat among long stretches of white-sand dunes and sea. The powerful countercurrents of the North Atlantic and Baltic Seas collide at **Grenen.** Do not try to swim amidst these dangerous currents as every year some hapless soul is carried out to sea. To get to Grenen, take bus 99 from the Skagen station to Gammel (10kr) or walk 3.5km down Fyrvej. Bordering the seas are spectacular stretches of sand dunes which reside along the **Råberg Mile.** From here, you can swim along 60km of beaches whose luminescent summer light attracted Denmark's most famous painters in the late 19th century. Their works can be seen in the wonderful **Skagen Museum,** Brøndumsvej 4. (Open June-Aug. daily 10am-6pm; May-Sept. 10am-5pm; April and Oct. Tues.-Sun. 11am-4pm; Nov.-March Wed.-Fri. 1-4pm, Sat. 11am-4pm, Sun. 11am-3pm. 40kr.) You can also tour the artists' homes at **Michael og Anna Archers Hus,** Markvej 2-4, and **Holger Drachmanns Hus,** Hans Baghsvej 21.

The **tourist office** (tel. 98 44 13 77; fax 98 45 02 94; http://www.skagen-tourist.dk) is in the train station. (Open Jan.-April and Oct.-Dec. Mon.-Fri. 9am-4pm, Sat. 10am-1pm; May and Sept. Mon.-Fri. 9am-4pm, Sat.-Sun. 10am-2pm; June 1-20 and Aug. 11-31 Mon.-Sat. 9am-5:30pm, Sun. 10am-2pm; June 21-Aug.10 9am-7pm.) Nordjyllands Trafikselskab runs both **buses** and **private trains** from Frederikshavn to Skagen (1hr., 30kr one way, railpasses not valid). The **Skagen Ny Vandrerhjem,** Rolighedsvej 2 (tel. 98 44 22 00; fax 98 44 22 55), not to be confused with the somewhat inconvenient **Gamel Skagen Vandrerhjemm** (tel. 98 44 13 56; fax 98 45 08 17), 4km west, serves as a springboard for nocturnal forays in town (reception open daily 10am-noon and 4-9pm; 75-85kr, nonmembers 100-110kr). Most **campgrounds** around Skagen are open late April to mid-September (50kr); try **Grenen** (tel. 98 44 25 46; fax 98 44 65 46) or **Østerklit** (tel./fax 98 44 31 23), not far from the city center (50kr). Skagen hosts a large annual folk, brass, and **Dixieland music festival** in late June (50-100kr); contact the tourist office. To sample Skagen's famous seafood try the kiosks lining **Nordkaj** on the harbor, the **Skagen Fiske Restaurant,** Fiskehuskaj 13, or **Pakhuset Fiskerestaurant og Harnecafé,** Rødspættevej 6. Dance the night away at **Hyttefadet,** Jens Bergsvej 2 (disco open daily until 5am).

Vikings Had Grannies Too

While the Viking image may still bring to mind the viciousness of horned helmets, iron mesh, and bad table manners, this ancient people was not alone in their ruthless tactics. Ansgar, the German missionary who is largely credited with the 10th-century Christianization of Viking Scandinavia, was a brutal manager of conversion. Upon arrival in Viking villages, Ansgar immediately accused all the old women of witchcraft and had them burned to death. Old Viking women were the keepers of clan and village lore, and their deaths eliminated generations of Viking history and tradition. And although Denmark today is passionately opposed to capital punishment, Danes still burn witches in effigy in great seaside bonfires during the Midsummer celebrations. The Swedes to the north keep the Viking traditions alive by erecting the phallic Midsummer pole and inserting it into the ground (see **Midsummer Madness,** p. 865).

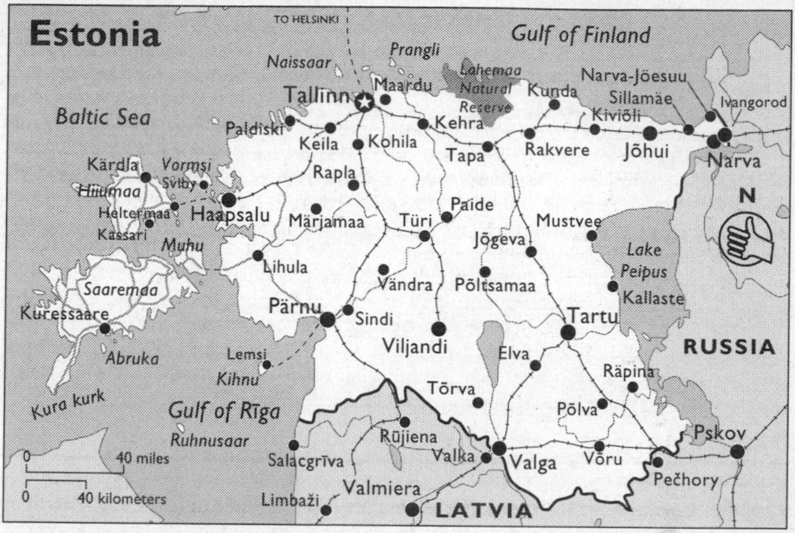

Estonia (Eesti)

US$1	**= 14.55EEK (Estonian Kroons)**	**10EEK =**	**US$0.69**
CDN$1	**= 10.52EEK**	**10EEK =**	**CDN$0.95**
UK£1	**= 23.15EEK**	**10EEK =**	**UK£0.43**
IR£1	**= 21.34EK**	**10EEK =**	**IR£0.47**
AUS$1	**= 10.59EEK**	**10EEK =**	**AUS$0.95**
NZ$1	**= 9.24EEK**	**10EEK =**	**NZ$1.08**
SAR1	**= 3.10EEK**	**10EEK =**	**SAR3.23**

Country Code: 372 **International Dialing Prefix: 800**

Volvos, designer shops, and an ever more stylish young public seem to attest that Estonia is benefiting from its transition to democracy and capitalism, but material trappings mask declining living standards in the face of growing inflation. In the light of these economic troubles, Estonia is redefining its cultural identity to align more with its successful Nordic neighbors, to the chagrin of the 35% of the population who are ethnically Russian. Having been released from successive centuries of domination by the Danes, Swedes, and Russians, the Estonians' serene, patient pragmatism has matured into a dynamic and, some would say, Scandinavian attitude.

More extensive coverage of Estonia is available in *Let's Go: Eastern Europe 1998.*

GETTING THERE AND GETTING AROUND

Citizens of Australia, Canada, Ireland, New Zealand, the U.K., and the U.S. can visit Estonia **visa-free** for up to 90 days. South Africans can obtain a visa at the border for 400EEK, although it is cheaper for South Africans to apply for a visa at an Estonian consulate before departure (30-day single-entry visa US$10).

Several **ferry lines** connect to Tallinn's harbor (info tel. 631 85 50 or 43 12 50). **Tallink** (tel. 640 98 08) sends three boats per day between Helsinki and Tallinn (3½hr., 375-430EEK, students 175EEK). **Tallinn Line Express** (tel. 60 14 55) runs two hydrofoils, making six round-trips per day (1½-2hr.; late spring to late fall only, Mon.-Fri., 360-400EEK). **Estline** (tel. 631 36 36) sails between Stockholm and Tallinn (every other day, 13hr., deck space 500EEK, students 380EEK; cabin space 126EEK). **Silja Line** (tel. 631 83 31) sails two beautiful boats per day between Tallinn and Helsinki

(3½hr., 140mk and up). Reservations for all ferry lines are most easily made through **BalticTours,** in Tallinn (tel. 631 35 55 or 43 06 63). By air, **Finnair** (tel. 631 14 55) connects Tallinn to Helsinki (one way US$142, under 25 US$43), and **SAS** (tel. 631 22 40) flies to Stockholm (US$338).

Three **train** lines cross the Estonian border; one heads from Tallinn through Tartu to Moscow, another goes to Rīga and on to Warsaw, and the third goes through Narva to St. Petersburg. The **Baltic Express** is the only train from Poland that skips Belarus, linking Tallinn to Warsaw via Kaunas, Rīga, and Tartu (one per day; 20hr.; 660EEK, private compartment 1049EEK). Major towns such as Pärnu and Haapsalu are all connected to Tallinn, but trains can be scarce. Diesel trains, as opposed to local electric trains, are express. Estonian rail tickets are the most expensive in the former Soviet Union. **Buses** thoroughly link all towns, often more cheaply and efficiently than the trains. During the school year (Sept. 1-June 25), students receive half-price bus tickets. On the islands, where buses have up to 12-hour gaps between trips, **bike** and **car rentals** can be a relatively inexpensive way of exploring the remote areas. Those who **hitchhike** stretch out an open hand.

ESSENTIALS

Larger towns and cities in Estonia have well-equipped **tourist offices** which often arrange tours and make reservations. Smaller information booths, marked with a green (and sometimes blue) "i," sell maps and give away free brochures. The unit of currency is the **kroon** (EEK), divided into 100 **senti.** Most banks *(pank)* cash **traveler's checks,** and credit card acceptance is increasing, mostly with **Visa** and **MasterCard.** Hotel Viru in Tallinn and many banks across the country provide Visa cash advances. **ATMs** take only local bank cards.

A **letter** sent abroad costs 6.70EEK. To use a pay **phone,** you must insert a digital card, obtainable at any bank or newspaper kiosk. **AT&T Direct** is available in Estonia by dialing 80 08 00 10 01. **International long-distance** calls can be made at post offices. Calls to the Baltic states and Russia cost 8.50EEK per minute (10.50EEK with a card); calls to the U.S. run 30-36EEK per minute (40.80EEK with a card). The system of adding prefixes and codes to Estonian phone numbers proves that the universe tends towards disorder. There are three phone systems (old, new, and cellular), each with its own area codes. In Tallinn, for the **old** system, phone numbers have six digits, and the area code is 22. For the **new** system, in which phone numbers have seven digits (the first of which is a 6 and is often mistakenly placed in parentheses), the area code is 2. For **cellular** phones, the area code is 25. The new (digital) system and the old system can call each other within a given city without the area code. To call Tallinn from outside Estonia on the old system, dial 37 22 before the number; on the digital system, dial 372. To call a cell phone anywhere in Estonia, dial 37 25. To call from Russia with love, dial 014 instead of 372, then the area code. To call out of Estonia on the old system, dial 8, wait for two tones, then dial 00, the country code, and the number. From digital phones, dial 800 without waiting for a tone. From a cell phone, just dial 00 and the number. If you can't figure it out call the English-language **Ekspress Hotline** at 631 32 22 in Tallinn; elsewhere dial 8, then 11 88 after the two tones. In a true **emergency,** dial 01 for fire (001 in Tallinn), 02 for police (002 in Tallinn), and 03 for an ambulance (003 in Tallinn).

Estonians speak the best English in the Baltics; most young people know at least a few phrases. German and Russian are more common among the older set..

Yes/no	*Jaa/Ei*	yah/ay
Hello	*Tere*	TEH-re
Please	*Palun*	PA-lun
Thank you	*Tänan*	TEH-nan
Excuse me	*Vabandage*	vah-pan-TAGE-euh

Do you speak English?	*Kas te räägite inglise keelt?*	Kas te RA-A-gite ING-lise keelt
I don't speak Estonian.	*Ma ei oska eesti keelt.*	Ma ei OS-ka Ees-ti keelt
Where is...?	*Kus on...?*	kuhs on
How much?	*Kui palju?*	Kwee PAL-you
I would like...a single/double.	*Ma sooviksin...ühelist/ kahelist.*	Ma SOO-vik-sin...EW-hel-ist/ KA-hel-ist
Help!	*Appi!*	APP-pi

Tourist offices have listings of all accommodations and prices in their respective towns and can often arrange a place for visitors. A few companies have set up youth hostels and started to arrange stays at private homes. Tallinn's **Baltic Family Hotel,** Mere pst. 6 (tel./fax (2) 44 11 87), **Bed and Breakfast,** Sadama pst. 11 (tel./fax (2) 60 20 91), and **CDS Reisid** (Baltic Bed and Breakfast), Raekoja plats 17 (tel. (2) 44 52 62; fax 31 36 66), offer rooms in homes throughout the Baltic countries. BFH charges US$9-15 per person; CDS is computer-efficient, but charges US$25. Many hotels provide laundry services for an extra charge.

Go into any **restaurant** and you'll see the same assortment of drab sausages, lifeless *schnitzel,* greasy bouillon, and cold fried potatoes that plague the former USSR. But there is more fish on the menus in Estonia, and beer is the national drink for good reason—not only is it inexpensive, it's also delicious and nutritious. The national brand *Saku* is downright excellent, as is the darker *Saku Tume.*

Tallinn

Tallinn's hip cosmopolitan shops and fashionably dressed young crowd complement the ancient beauty and charming serenity of the city; medieval spires climb the skies while vendors below pour glasses of *Saku* and visitors wind their way through the cobblestone streets. The city's proximity to Helsinki accounts for a strong Nordic influence, and a large Russian population brings tension but also vitality to Tallinn's political chambers and coffee shops. Under the clear skies of summer, the sun sets for only two hours and blushes the sky a glowing pink from evening to morning.

ESTONIA

ORIENTATION AND PRACTICAL INFORMATION

Tallinn's **Vanalinn** (Old Town) is ringed by four streets—**Põhja puiestee, Mere puiestee, Pärnu maantee,** and **Toom puiestee.** From the junction of Mere pst. and Pärnu mnt., **Narva maantee** runs east to **Hotel Viru,** the central landmark. The Old Town peaks at the fortress-rock **Toompea,** whose 13th-century streets are level with church steeples in **All-linn** (Lower Town). To reach the Old Town from the ferry terminal, walk along Sadama to Põhja pst., then south on Pikk between the stone towers. From the train station, cross Toom pst. and go straight through the park along **Nunne**—the stairway up **Patkuli trepp** on the right leads to Toompea. In Vanalinn, **Pikk tee** (Long street), the main artery, runs from the seaward gates of All-linn to Toompea via **Pikk Jalg** tower. **Raekoja plats** (Town Hall Square) is the scenic center of the Lower Town. The second-floor shop in Hotel Viru stocks *Tallinn This Week.*

Tourist Office: CDS Travel, Raekoja plats 17 (tel. 44 52 62; fax 631 36 66; email cds@zen.estpak.ee). English walking tours (50EEK; May 15-Sept. 15 daily 2pm). Open Mon.-Fri. 10am-6pm, Sat.-Sun. 10am-4pm. **Tourist Information Center,** Raekoja plats 10. Brochures and useful maps. **Tourist Information Center,** at Sadama 25 (tel. 631 83 21), at Tallinn Harbor (terminal A), has info on smaller hotels.

Embassies: Canada, Toomkooli 13 (tel. (22) 44 90 56; fax (358) 298 11 04; emergencies tel. 630 40 50). Open Mon.-Fri. 9am-4:30pm. **Latvia,** Tõnismägi 10 (tel. 631 13 66; fax 68 16 68). Open Mon.-Fri. 10am-noon. **Russia,** Lai 18 (tel. 60 31 66; visa section fax 646 62 54). Open Mon.-Fri. 9:30am-12:30pm. **U.K.,** Kentmanni 20 (tel.

631 33 53; fax 631 33 54). Open Tues.-Thurs. 10am-noon. **U.S.,** Kentmanni 20 (tel. 631 20 21; fax 631 20 25). Open Mon.-Fri. 8:30am-5:30pm.

Currency Exchange: Five *valuutavahetus* (currency exchange windows) line the inside of the central post office, offering some of the best rates in Tallinn.

American Express: Suur-Karja 15 EE-090 (tel. 631 33 13; fax 631 36 56). Sells and cashes traveler's checks and holds mail for members. Books rooms and transport tickets. Arranges some visas. Open Mon.-Fri. 9am-6pm, Sat. 9am-3pm.

Trains: Toom pst. 35 (tel. 45 68 51); trams 1 and 2 travel to Hotel Viru. Service to St. Petersburg (1 per day, 10hr., 195EEK). Buy same-day international tickets at window 8; domestic tickets at windows 15-18 in the building across the tracks.

Buses: Lastekodu 46 (tel. 42 25 49), just south of Tartu mnt., and 1.5km southeast of Vanalinn. Tram 2 or 4 and bus 22 connect to the city center. Windows 1-9 sell domestic tickets. The *As sebe* window deals with international links. To Rīga (8 per day, 7hr., 114EEK) and St. Petersburg (2 per day, 9hr., 150EEK).

Ferries: At Sadama's end. Terminal A sends ferries to Finland; terminal B to Sweden. Bus 92c runs from the ferry to the center of town; bus 90 to the train station.

Public Transportation: Buses, trams, and trolleybuses cover the suburban area; each category has separate stops marked with symbols. All run daily 6am-midnight. Kiosks sell tickets (4EEK), or you can buy them from the driver (exact change only on the tram and trolley). Tram 2 connects the bus and train stations.

Luggage Storage: Lockers in the train station cost 6EEK. Open daily 5am-12:30pm. Also at the bus station. 2-9EEK per day. Open daily 5am-noon and 12:30-11:40pm.

Pharmacy: RAE Apteek, Pikk 47 (tel. 44 44 08). A broad selection of Scandinavian medical supplies. Open Mon. 11am-6pm, Tues.-Fri. 9am-8pm, Sat.-Sun. 9am-3pm.

Emergencies: Fire: tel. 001. **Ambulance:** 003.

Police: tel. 002.

Internet Access: There is an Internet room at the main **library,** Tõnismägi pst. 2 (tel. 45 25 27); register first. Open Mon.-Tues. and Fri. noon-6pm, Wed.-Thurs. noon-4pm.

Post Office: Narva mnt. 1, 2nd fl., across from Hotel Viru. Open Mon.-Fri. 8am-8pm, Sat. 9am-5pm. **Postal Code:** EE-0001.

Telephones: For all phone services and inquiries go to window #45 at the post office next door. **Fax** services (fax 631 30 88). A 1-page fax to the U.S. costs 50EEK. For phone code info, see **Estonia Essentials,** p. 258.

ACCOMMODATIONS

Inquire at the information desk in the **bus station** about rooms with communal bathrooms (100EEK); no reservations are accepted. **Karol Travel Agency,** Lembitu 4/7 (tel. 45 49 00; fax 31 39 18), sets tourists up in hostels for as low as 100EEK. In summer, make reservations one day ahead (open Mon.-Fri. 9am-6pm).

The Barn, Väike-Karja 1 (tel. 44 34 65), in Vanalinn. The best place for budget travelers. A dormitory bed and pillow 150EEK. Doubles with shared baths 495EEK. HI Members get a 10% discount. Kitchen and laundry services. Call ahead.

Kuramaa 15 Hostel, Vikerlase 15 (tel. 632 77 81; fax 632 77 15). Take bus 67 from across the street from Hotel Viru to the last stop. Go up the stairs and into the first courtyard of the complex. "Hostel" is barely visible in a window to the right. The office is on the first floor (on the left) of the entryway to the right. Each apartment has 2-3 rooms each with 2 beds, full kitchen, and shared bathroom. 140EEK per person, 130EEK with an HI card. Reception open Mon.-Sat. 9am-9pm, but call ahead and someone will wait for you.

Hotel Dorell, Karu 39 (tel. 626 12 00). Rooms have TVs and telephones, and breakfast is included. Small singles 350EEK. Large singles 400EEK. Doubles 460EEK. Shared baths, 5min. from Vanalinn. Cash only.

Hotel Scard, Liivalaia 2 (tel. 44 61 43), left off Pärnu mnt. This place is only open during the summer after June, and is under a transfer of management. Institutional, clean rooms. Central location. No English spoken. 100EEK per person.

FOOD

Although cheaper than in Western Europe, restaurants in Tallinn are becoming increasingly expensive. The most central supermarket is **Kaubahall,** Aia 7, near the Viru Gates (open Mon.-Sat. 9am-8:30pm, Sun. 9am-8pm). The smaller **Kauplus Tallinn,** Narva mnt. 2 (tel. 64 01 10), has lower prices (open daily 9am-10pm).

Paks Margareeta (Fat Margaret's), Pikk 70 (tel. 641 14 13), in the gate tower housing the Maritime museum. Grease and subs that attract many. Chili dog 25EEK. Atomic Fries 40EEK. Small subs 25EEK. Open daily 11am-midnight.

Teater Restoran, Lai 31 (tel. 631 45 18). With jazzy blues in the background, this affordable basement restaurant is romantic and just plain cool. Seafood gumbo 76EEK. Glass of *Saku* 25EEK. Open daily 11am-1am.

Eeslitall, Dunkri 4 (tel. 31 37 55). The "Donkey Stable" is the best place in Tallinn for Balto-Russian cuisine; there's been a restaurant here since the 1300s. Meat and veggie dishes 25-132EEK. Open Sun.-Thurs. 11am-11pm, Fri.-Sat. 11am-1am.

SIGHTS

Get acquainted with **Vanalinn** (Old Town) by starting at Hotel Viru, walking down Narva mnt., then continuing along Viru through the 15th-century **Viru City Gate.** Continue up Viru to **Raekoja plats** (town hall square), where handicrafts are sold on summer evenings, and folk songs and dances are performed on a small stage. The **raekoda** (town hall) was built between 1371-1404 and is guarded by **Vana Toomas** (Old Thomas), a cast-iron figurine of Tallinn's legendary defender. Thomas has done a good job so far; this is the oldest surviving town hall in Europe. Behind the *raekoda,* the medieval town jail, **Raemuuseum,** Raekoja 4/6, now displays early Estonian photography and contemporary Estonian sculpture (open Tues. and Thurs. 11am-5:30pm and Wed. 2-5:30pm; 7EEK, students 3EEK).

For a view of the medieval city's north towers and bastion, go up Vene from Viru, take a right on Olevimägi, and head up Uus. Founded by Dominicans in 1246, **Dominiiklaste Klooster,** Vene 16, across the street and through a courtyard, contains a Gothic limestone courtyard, two Catholic churches, a windmill, stone carvings, and a granary. In the large squat tower known as **Paks Margareeta** (Fat Margaret), a **Meremuuseum** (Maritime Museum), Pikk 70, houses changing exhibits on Tallinn's history as a port (open Wed.-Sun. 10am-6pm; 7EEK, students 3EEK).

Going back down Pikk, **Oleviste kirik** (St. Olav's Church), the tallest church in town, rises to the right. The murals inside the adjoining chapel illustrate the architect's death; he fell from the tower (open Sun. 9am-noon and 5-8pm, Mon. 5-9pm, Thurs. 5-8pm). Go to the end of Pikk and hang a left on Rataskaevu to see the mighty spire of **Niguliste kirik** (St. Nicholas's Church). A fragment of Bernt Notke's medieval masterpiece, *Danse Macabre,* resides inside, and organ concerts are often held in the church (open Wed. 2-9pm, Thurs.-Sun. 11am-6pm). Farther south along Rüütli, the **Kiek in de Kök** (Peek in the Kitchen) tower, Komandandi 2, is aptly named—in the 16th century, it offered voyeuristic views into virtually every home in the area. The museum in the tower maintains six floors of less titillating art and historical exhibits (open Tues.-Fri. 10:30am-5:30pm, Sat.-Sun. 11am-4:30pm; 7EEK, students 3EEK).

Following Lühike jalg uphill onto Toompea from St. Nicholas's Church leads to Lossi plats, a square dominated by **Aleksandr Nevsky katedral,** begun under Tsar Alexander III and finished a few years before the Bolshevik Revolution. A marble marker from 1910 recalls Peter the Great's 1710 victory over Sweden. The exterior renovation is not complete, but the interior is lavish (open daily 8am-7pm). Directly behind the parliament building, an Estonian flag tops **Pikk Hermann,** Tallinn's tallest tower. **Eesti Kunstimuuseum** (Estonian Art Museum), Kiriku plats 1, across from Toomkirik higher up on Toompea, displays Estonian art from the 19th century to the 1940s (open Wed.-Mon. 11am-5:30pm; 10EEK, students 3EEK).

In **Rocca-al-mare,** a peninsula 12km west of Tallinn, the **Vabaõhumuuseumi** (Estonian Open-Air Museum), Vabaõhumuuseumi 12 (tel. 656 02 30; fax 656 02 27), recreates 18th- to 20th-century wooden mills and farmsteads with all the trimmings.

(Open May-Oct. daily 10am-8pm, some buildings close at 6pm. 25EEK, students 10EEK). From Tallinn's train station, take bus 21 (regular 4EEK ticket; ½hr.).

ENTERTAINMENT AND NIGHTLIFE

Estonian Kontserdisaal, Estonia pst. 4 (ticket office tel. 44 31 98; fax 44 53 17; staffed daily 1-7pm), features symphonies almost every night (tickets 40EEK). During the **Organ Festival** (Aug. 1-10 in 1997), St. Nicholas's, Nõmme-Rahu, and Dome churches host recitals. Tickets are sold in St. Nicholas's starting July 1. **Eesti Draamateater,** Pärnu mnt. 5 (tel. 44 33 78), boasts the biggest dramas in town (ticket office open Aug.-June Tues.-Sun. 1-7pm). **Estonia teater,** Estonia pst. 4 (tel. 44 90 40), offers opera, ballet, musicals, and chamber music (ticket office open Aug.-June daily noon-7pm). Check *Tallinn This Week* for wheres and whens. In June or July, **Rock Summer** draws students and bands from around the world for a week-long fest. For info, contact Makarov Music Management (tel. 23 84 03).

Bars have sprouted on almost every street of Vanalinn, and nightclubs are multiplying. By 11pm, the local scene moves from the bars to the clubs.

Von Krahli Teater/Baar, Rataskaevu 10, on the west edge of the lower Old Town. The avant-garde theater showcases talent from Lithuanian jazz to experimental dance. The theater has shows most nights 7-9pm (tickets 35-40EEK). Attached split-level eclectic bar with *Saku* (20EEK) and a dance floor. Tickets for bands in the bar are 35EEK. Open Mon.-Thurs. 7am-2am, Fri.-Sat. 7am-4am.

Nimeta Baar (The Pub with No Name), Suur-Karja 4. Draws a large, boisterous crowd on many nights. Open Sun.-Thurs. 11am-3am, Fri.-Sat. 11am-4am.

Hell Hunt (The Gentle Wolf), Pikk 39. A mellow Irish pub with Guinness and *Kilkenny* on tap. The back room serves cottage pie (49EEK). Open Sun.-Mon. 11am-1am, Tues.-Thurs. 11am-2am, Fri.-Sat. 11am-3am. Occasional live music.

Club Hollywood, Vanna-Posti 8. DJ's spin house and techno. Cover up to 70EEK. Open Wed.-Thurs. 10pm-4am, Fri.-Sat. 10pm-6am, Sun. 10am-3am.

Pärnu

The beach pavilions and grand old summer houses of Pärnu were built in the late 19th century when the city was famed throughout Russia for its therapeutic waters and mud baths. Happily, these curatives continue to soothe its visitors today. The tree-lined street leading south from the **Tallinn Gate,** the only surviving Baltic town wall gate from the 17th century, takes you to a pedestrian zone just behind the **beach.** The famous **mud baths** still function in the Neoclassical bath house at the southern end of Supeluse puistee. (Open daily 8am-3pm; baths stay open until 1am. Mud bath 120EEK, massage 200EEK.) Facing Hotell Pärnu at Rüütli 53 is the **Museum of the City of Pärnu,** a municipal museum full of traditional clothes and arrowheads (open Mon.-Sat. 11am-5pm; 4EEK, students 2EEK). The only other museum, the **Lydia Koidula Museum,** Jannseni 37, across the Pärnu river, commemorates the 19th-century poet who led a revival in Estonian-language verse and drama (open Wed.-Sun. 10am-4pm; 3EEK, students 1EEK). The main street, Rüütli, ends at an **open-air theater,** where music and drama performances are given in summer.

The **tourist office,** Mungu 2 (tel. (244) 406 39; fax 456 33), has maps of the city and other information (open Mon.-Fri. 9am-6pm, Sat. 9am-4pm, Sun. 10am-3pm). The **train station,** east of the city center by the corner of Riia maantee and Raja, serves Tallinn (3½hr., 30EEK). Close to the center of town, **buses** leave the station for Kuressaare (3hr., 70EEK), Rīga (4hr., 76EEK), Tallinn (2-3hr., 50EEK), and Tartu (5hr., 60-68EEK). **Hotell Seedri,** Seedri 4 (tel. (244) 433 50), near the beach, is small and plain, but has a fridge and sink in every room (singles 140EEK, doubles 170-220EEK; reservations recommended). **Hotell Kajakas,** Seedri 2 (tel. (244) 430 98), provides a sauna and old Soviet-style rooms (singles 160EEK, doubles 220EEK). **Villa Marleen,** Seedri 15 (tel. (244) 458 49), a completely refurbished building, offers spotless rooms (singles 250EEK, doubles 350EEK; breakfast included).

A popular spot for a cheap meal is **Georg,** on the corner of Rüütli and Hommiku, a buffet-style restaurant offering *plov* (chicken and rice; 16.50EEK) and salads (5.50EEK; open Mon.-Fri. 7:30am-7:30pm, Sat.-Sun. 9am-7:30pm). A **turg** (market) is at the intersection of Sepa and Karja (open Tues.-Sun. 7am-1pm). **Tallinna Baar,** a small tavern, sits atop the gate (open daily noon-11pm), while **La Pera Vida,** Mere 22, is a disco housed in a sprawling wooden 1930s dancehall (cover 25EEK; open daily 10pm-5am). **Diskoklubi "Hamilton,"** Rüütli 1, boasts different DJs from all over Estonia every night (cover 25-70EEK; open daily 9pm-5am). Around **Jaanipäev** (Midsummer Night), Pärnu hosts the week-long **International Jazz Festival,** along with the **Baltoscandal,** a Baltic and Scandinavian theater extravaganza.

Tartu

Although it is the oldest city in the Baltics, Tartu displays few architectural monuments or medieval relics—the city has burned to the ground 55 times since 1030. However, the 10,000 university students give Tartu an air of collegiate hipness. **Raekoja plats** (Town Hall Square) is the center of the city. Ülikooli runs north-south behind the town hall; to the north, it passes **Tartu Ülikool** (Tartu University), founded in 1632 and key to the development of Estonian nationalism. The **Museum of Classical Art,** a small but interesting gathering of Roman and Greek art, awaits inside (open Mon.-Fri. 11am-4:30pm; 6EEK, students 2EEK). Farther up Ülikooli, the 14th-century **Jaani-kirik** (St. John's Church) is barely standing, but a few hundred *terra cotta* figurines still adorn the outside walls. Across the street, the **Museum of the 19th-Century Tartu Citizen** has displays on life in a particular era we'll leave you to surmise. (Open in summer Wed.-Sun. 11am-6pm; off-season Wed.-Sun. 10am-6pm. 4EEK, students 2EEK.) The **Toomemägi** (Cathedral Hill) dominates Tartu from behind the town hall; on the western hump are majestic remainders of the 15th-century **Toomkirik** (Cathedral of St. Peter and Paul). The **Estonian National Museum,** J. Kuperjanov 9, holds hordes of ethnographic exhibits from across Estonia (open Wed.-Sun. 11am-6pm; 5EEK, students 3EEK).

Everything the traveler needs is located within a square kilometer bordered by the bus and train stations. The **tourist office,** Raekoja plats, 14 provides info and organizes travel and transportation (open Mon.-Fri. 10am-6pm, Sat. 10am-3pm). **Trains** roll out of the station at Vaksali 6, 1.5km from the city center, for Moscow (18hr., 162-363EEK), Rīga (5hr., 95-220.50EEK), and Tallinn (3hr., 67-85EEK). Local buses 5 and 6 shuttle from behind the train station to Raekoja plats, and the bus station. **Buses** run from Turu 2, 300m south of Raekoja plats to Tallinn (2-5hr., 60-70EEK) and Pärnu (4hr., 66-68EEK). **Tartu Võõrastemaja (Hotel Tartu),** Soola 3 (tel. (7) 43 20 91), in the center of town, behind the bus station, has bare rooms with newly tiled communal showers and a sauna (singles 370EEK, doubles 640EEK; breakfast included). **Külalistemaja Tähtvere,** Laulupeo pst. 19 (tel. (7) 42 17 08), northwest of the historic center, in front of the looming beer factory, has singles (150EEK), doubles (250EEK), and a four-person suite with fireplace and fridge (600EEK). A newly redone **market** is on the corner of Va baduse and Vanenmuise, opposite the bus station (open Tues.-Fri. 7am-6pm, Sat. 7am-4pm, Sun. 7am-3pm). A **bistro** at Raekoja plats 9 is good for a quick meal (*karbonada*, pork fried in egg, 27EEK; open daily 9am-11pm).

Haapsalu

In the early 13th-century Haapsalu became the seat of the Saare-Lääne bishopric encompassing most of West Estonia. Today it is a sleepy town known for its sailing and rapid westernization. From Lossiplats, the square just east of the north end of Kavja, you can enter **Lossi Park** (open 7am-11pm), where the limestone **Piiskopilinnus** (Bishop's Castle) stands (adjoining historical museum open daily 10am-6pm; 10EEK, students 5EEK). The **Aafrikarand** (Africa Beach) promenade, northeast of the castle at the end of Rüütli, runs 2km to the yacht club. **Kaluri,** farther east, makes for beautiful walks amid weathered Baltic wooden houses, marsh grasses, and ducks. To get to the **tourist office,** Posti 39 (tel. (247) 332 48), from the bus stop, walk up Tallinna (in the direction the bus drives) and turn right on Posti. The English-speaking staff sells maps (15-25EEK) and hands out helpful brochures like the free *Two Weeks in Haapsalu.* **Buses** run from the defunct train station at Rantee 2 to Pärnu (2-3hr., 40EEK), Tallinn (2hr., 16-30EEK), and Kärdla (3 per day, 3hr., pay 40EEK on the bus). From **Rohuküla,** 9km west of Haapsalu (take bus 1), **ferries** (tel. (247) 336 66) head to Heltermaa on Hiiumaa (port tel. (247) 316 30; 12 per day, 1½hr., 25EEK). The **Hotell Laine,** Sadama 9/11 (tel. (247) 441 91), welcomes visitors on the shores of Väike-viik. Follow Posti north until it ends, go west on Ehte, and then north on Sadama (singles 275EEK, doubles 420EEK). The **Tamme Guest House,** Tamme 10a (tel. (247) 575 50), has clean singles (150EEK). **Rootsituru Kohvik,** Karja 3 (tel. 450 58), a pink building in the castle's shadow on the corner of Ehte, serves unassuming food (open 10am-10pm). One of the few places to hang out at night is the **Cafe Rondo,** Posti 7. It has a café upstairs and a dark bar downstairs. (Café open Mon.-Thurs. 7:30am-7pm, Sat.-Sun. 9am-7pm; bar open Sun.-Thurs. noon-11pm, Fri.-Sat. noon-2am.)

Estonian Islands

Kuressaare Off-limits to outsiders during the Soviet occupation, the island of **Saaremaa** is reckoned to be more Estonian than Estonia itself. Kuressaare, its largest city, was the seat of the Saare-Lääne bishopric from 1358 until the Bishop sold the island to the Danes in the 16th century. It later became a major resort. The **Kuressaare Linnus-Kindlus** (Episcopal Castle), the town's main attraction, lies south of the Raekoja plats (town hall square). Inside the castle, the excellent **Saaremaa Regional Museum** displays a collection of chariots, ceramic masks, and trinkets from the 19th century and the 1918-20 War for Independence (open daily 11am-7pm; last entry 6pm; 20EEK, students 10EEK). Rent a bike at the bus station or behind the city hall, and pedal south to the quiet, clean beaches of **Mändjala** and **Järve,** covering a stretch 8-12km west of Kuressaare.

The **tourist office,** Tallinna 2 (tel. (245) 551 20), inside the town hall, sells maps (6EEK; open Mon.-Fri. 9am-5pm, Sat. 10am-5pm). **Baltic Tours,** Tallinna 1 (tel. (245) 334 80), on Raekoja plats, helps with ferry info and hotels (open Mon.-Fri. 9am-6pm, Sat. 10am-3pm). The **bus station,** Pihtla tee 2 (info tel. (245) 573 80, tickets 562 20), serves Pärnu (3hr., 70-75EEK) and Tallinn (4hr., 96EEK). Clean, institutional **Mardi Öömaja,** Vallimaa 5a (tel. (245) 332 85), has the cheapest rooms in town (hotel: singles 240EEK, doubles 380EEK; hostel: 100EEK per bed; cash only). **Kämping,** Mändjala (tel. (245) 751 93), 11km outside of Kuressaare on the bus to Järve, offers camping near a clean beach and secluded pine woods (tent sites 50EEK per person; 4-bed rooms 160EEK per person; open June-Aug.).

Hiiumaa Because the Soviets closed off Hiiumaa for 50 years, the area's rare plant and animal species, as well as its unhurried local lifestyle, have been preserved. The flat terrain and beautiful, peaceful forests make it ideal for biking. **Kärdla,** the only real city on the island, features a good **tourist office,** Keskväljak 1 (tel. (246) 330 33; email douglas@info.hiiumaa.ee), which has info on hiking and ferry schedules. (Open in summer Mon.-Fri. 9am-6pm, Sat.-Sun. 10am-3pm; off-season Mon.-Fri. 10am-4pm.) Northwest of Kärdla, the **Tahkuna Lighthouse** offers spectacular views. Near the lighthouse stands a **memorial** to the Russian soldiers who were taken as prisoners here during WWII. Gun emplacement and bunkers still stand in the area; bunkers are open, but it's advisable not to enter without a flashlight. **Buses** (tel. (246) 965 02) go from Hiiumaa to Tallinn (4hr., 90EEK), and **ferries** cross to the island from Rohuküla (9-25EEK; call (246) 911 38 for info on schedule info). The food on Hiiumaa is mediocre at best—you may wish to try the grocery store **Tiigi Pood,** Tiigi 5, which stocks western and Estonian foods (open daily 9am-10pm).

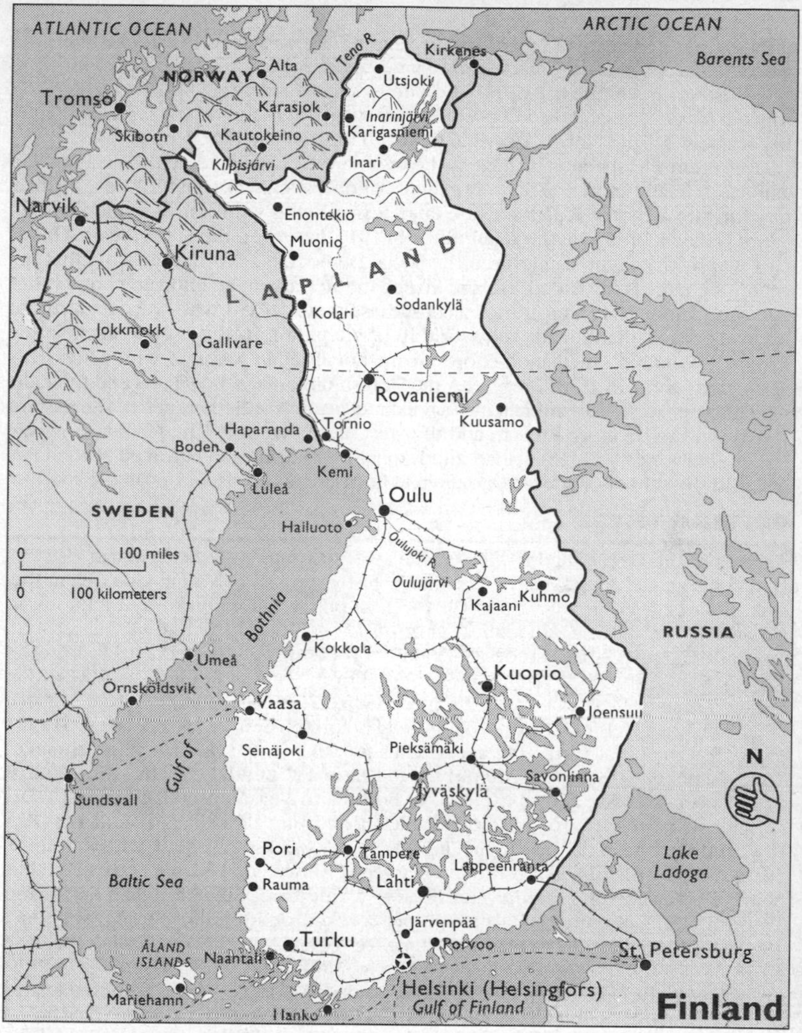

Finland (Suomi)

US$1 = 5.40mk (Finnish markka)
CDN$1= 3.91mk
UK£1 = 8.59mk
IR£1 = 8.03mk
AUS$1 = 3.94mk
NZ$1 = 3.43mk
SAR1 = 1.15mk
Country Code: 358

1mk = US$0.19
1mk = CDN$0.26
1mk = UK£0.12
1mk = IR£0.12
1mk = AUS$0.25
1mk = NZ$0.29
1mk = SAR0.87
International Dialing Prefix: 00

Between the Scandinavian peninsula and the Russian wilderness, Finland is a land of coniferous trees, astounding summer clouds, and five million taciturn souls. Outside the Helsinki metropolitan area, nature reigns. The west coast is dotted with old wooden shacks, and the Swedish-speaking Åland Islands are a biker's paradise. The Lake District in southeast Finland also offers outdoor activities—sailing, skiing, and dance festivals. Lapland, in the north, boasts rugged terrain and rolling fells, boundless wilderness, and Finland's several thousand indigenous Sami people.

After enduring seven centuries in the cross fire of warring Swedish and Russian empires, Finland experienced a romantic nationalistic awakening in the 19th century, nurtured by the *Kalevala* folk epic, Jean Sibelius's rousing symphonies, and Akseli Gallen-Kallela's mythical paintings. In 1917, however, the Finns fought a bitter civil war as the Right slaughtered the Social Democrats. On the principle that my enemy's enemy is my friend, Finland invited in the Nazis in an effort to counter Russian aggression. They later turned against these same "allies" who were reluctant to leave. Today, Finland leads the world in participation in the U.N. Peacekeeping Forces. The nation's mediation efforts are memorialized in Namibia, where hundreds of children are named Ahtisaari after the Finnish diplomat who supervised the independence process. Finland has maintained a delicate Nordic neutrality. The eastern towns tend to be more Russian and the west more Swedish. The Finnish language shares similarities with Hungarian and Estonian. Swedish is an enforced second language in the schools, and signs are often in both languages, especially in the south.

GETTING THERE

Citizens of the U.S., Canada, U.K., Ireland, Australia, and New Zealand can visit Finland **visa-free** for up to 90 days. The titanic, festive vessels of **Viking Line** (tel. in Helsinki (09) 12 135, in Stockholm (08) 452 40 00) steam daily from Stockholm to Helsinki (15hr., 190mk, students 129mk; off-season 109mk), Turku via Mariehamn, on Åland (12hr.,189mk, students 129mk; off-season 69mk), and Turku non-stop (11hr.,189mk, students 129mk; off-season 59mk). Scanrail holders get 50% off on Viking; Eurail holders ride free. The more sedate **Silja Line** (tel. in Finland toll free 9800 745 52, in Helsinki (09) 180 41, in Stockholm (08) 666 35 15, in Vaasa (961) 323 36 30, in Umeå (090) 142 100, in Skellefteå (0910) 141 60) sails from Stockholm to Turku (2 per day, 13hr., 120-240mk) and to Helsinki (1 per day, 14½hr., 250-300mk); from Umeå, Sweden across the Gulf of Bothnia to Vaasa on Finland's west coast (140mk without a cabin); and from Skellefteå and Umeå, Sweden to Kokkola (Karleby) and Pietersaari (Jakobstad) in Finland (3-4 per week, 110-140mk without cabin). Students deduct 25mk on most routes between Sweden and Finland; Scanrail holders enjoy a 50% discount, while Eurail earns a ride free. Silja Line also sails from Travemünde, Germany to Helsinki (3 per week, around 450mk; students deduct 25mk). In Helsinki call **Estonian New Line** (tel. (09) 2282 1277) or **Tallink** (tel. (09) 60 28 22) for info on Estonian ferries. Keep in mind that ferry rates on Friday can be up to twice the weekday rates on some routes. Ask about special summer fares (55mk round-trip to Tallinn). **Finnair** (tel. (09) 818 81 or (800) 950 5000) flies in and out of Finland and offers low youth fares (Copenhagen 1036mk; London 1076mk; St. Petersburg 1023mk). Buses and trains connect Helsinki to St. Petersburg via Lahti.

GETTING AROUND

Efficient **trains** zip as far north as Kolari at the usual painful Nordic prices (Turku to Helsinki 90mk, Helsinki to Rovaniemi 304mk); railpasses are valid and seat reservations (15-30mk) are not required except on the luxurious InterCity trains. Couchettes (in triples) cost 60mk from Monday to Thursday, 90mk from Friday to Sunday. The *buy-outside-of-Scandinavia* **Scanrail Pass** offers five out of 15 days (US$176, under 26 US$132), 10 days out of one month (US$284, under 26 US$213), or one month (US$414, under 26 US$311) of unlimited travel in Finland, Sweden, Denmark, and Norway, as well as free or discounted ferry rides. This differs from the *buy-in-Scandinavia* **Scanrail Pass,** which allows 21 consecutive days (1650mk, under 26 1237mk) or five days within 15 of unlimited rail travel (1080mk, under 26 810mk). A **Finnrail**

Pass offers free rail travel throughout Finland during a one month period (3 days 540mk, 5 days 730mk, 10 days 995mk).

Buses cost about the same as trains, though express buses carry a 10mk surcharge. The **Bussilomalippu** pass offers 1000km of travel over a two-week period for 340mk. For bus information anywhere in Finland, call (09) 692 701. Students often receive a 50% discount for distances over 80km issued at the station to ISIC holders. Railpasses are valid on some buses that follow discontinued train routes.

Finnair gives a discount for those under 25 and has special summer rates that reduce fares by up to 70%. A **Finnair Holiday Ticket,** valid for 30 days, gives you 10 flights for around 2200mk. Steamers link many cities in the lake district. **Hitchhikers** report finding more rides in Finland than elsewhere in Scandinavia, but **cyclists** hanker for Denmark's shorter distances. Some campgrounds, youth hostels, and tourist offices rent bikes. Rates average 45-55mk per day or 190mk per week, plus a deposit.

ESSENTIALS

Most **shops** close at 5pm on weekdays (10pm in Helsinki; Sat. around 1pm), but urban supermarkets may stay open until 8pm (Sat. 4-6pm). **Kiosks,** especially those marked *elintarvikekioski,* sell basic food, snacks, and toiletries until 9 or 10pm. **Banks** are typically open weekdays 9:15am to 4:15pm. Finnish **holidays** include Epiphany (Jan. 6), Good Friday (April 10), May Eve and Day (April 30-May 1), Mayday (May 21), Midsummer (June 20-21), All Saints Day (Nov. 1), and Independence Day (Dec. 6). Many stores and museums, as well as all banks and post offices, are also closed for Easter (April 10-13), Second Easter (May 13), Christmas (Dec. 24-26), and New Year's Day. During Midsummer, when Finns party all night to the light of *kokko* (bonfires) and the midnight sun, virtually the entire country shuts down.

Local and short long-distance calls within Finland usually cost 2mk; most pay **phones** take 1 and 5mk coins. Phone cards (local calls 1mk) are available in 30, 50, 70, and 100mk denominations. "Tele" or "Nonstop" cards work nationwide; other cards only work in the city in which you purchase them. "Nonstop" phones are available at any post office. Call 118 for domestic information, 020 208 for international information, 112 in an **emergency,** and 100 22 for the **police.** For **AT&T Direct,** call 9800 1 0010; **MCI WorldPhone,** 9800 1 0280; **Sprint Access,** 9800 1 0284; **Canada Direct,** 9800 1 0011; **BT Direct,** 9800 1 0440; **Australia Direct,** 9800 1 0610; and **New Zealand Direct,** 9800 1 0640. The mail service is fast and efficient.

The Finnish language, which is not Indo-European, is virtually impenetrable to foreigners. Watch out for town names that modify their form on train schedules due to the lack of prepositions in Finnish. Swedish, often seen on signs, is the official second language; many Finns speak English, but fluency decreases in the north. The stress is always on the first syllable.

Please/ Thank you	*Olkaa hyvä/Kiitos*	AWL-kah HU-va/KEE-tohss
Do you speak English?	*Puhutteko englantia?*	POO-hoot-teh-kaw ENG-lan-ti-ah
I can't understand you.	*En ymmärrä teitä*	EHN ÜM-mar-ra TEH-i-ta
Where is...?	*Missä on...?*	MEESS-ah OWN
I would like...	*Haluaisin...*	HAH-loo-eye-seen
train station	*rautatieasema*	RAO-tah-tee-AH-sehma

Accommodations and Camping Finland has 168 **youth hostels** *(retkeilymaja*; RET-kay-loo-MAH-yah), 62 of which are open year-round. Prices are based on a four-star system and generally range from 45 to 95mk; non-HI-members add 15-35mk. Most include saunas, have laundry facilities, and prohibit sleeping bags. **Hotels** are often exorbitant (over 250mk); *kesähotelli* (summer hotels) offer doubles for around 300mk. **Private room** rental is less common than in Sweden, but local tourist offices will help you find the cheapest accommodations. The **Finnish Youth Hostel Association** (Suomen Retkeilymajajärjestö) is located at Yrjönkatu 38B, Helsinki (tel. (09)

694 03 77). As in much of Scandinavia, you may camp anywhere (except in Åland) as long as you respect flora and fauna and stay a polite distance away from homes. Well-equipped official **campgrounds** dapple the country, some with saunas (tent sites 25-75mk per night, *mökit* (small cottages) 150mk and up).

Food and Drink A *baari* is a café that serves food, coffee, and perhaps beer. *Kahvilat* also serve food and are a bit classier, while *grillit* are fast-food stands. A *ravintola* is a restaurant; some evolve into dance-spots or bars later in the evening (cover 10mk and up; doorkeeper is often tipped 5mk). The standard minimum age is 18, but it can be as high as 25, and alcohol is no bargain. Beer *(olut)* is divided into several groups. Olut IV is the strongest and most expensive (at least 25mk per *iso tuoppi;* 0.5L-liter). Olut III (the best value) is slightly weaker and cheaper. Outside bars and restaurants, all alcohol stronger than Olut III must be purchased at the state-run **Alko** liquor stores. You need not tip servers (the bill is often rounded up).

Among the less expensive supermarkets are **Alepa** and **Antilla.** Many large hotels offer bargain breakfasts open to outsiders. Short of that, lunch is the best deal, often an all-you-can-eat buffet (30-50mk), or pizza buffet with salad, and lasagne for around 39mk. Fish ranges from *silli* (Baltic herring) to *lohi* (salmon). Finnish dietary staples include robust rye bread, potatoes, malodorous cheeses, Karelian pastries, and squirming yogurt-like *viili.* In July and August, the land blossoms with blueberries, cranberries, lingonberries, and—in the far north—Arctic cloudberries.

Helsinki (Helsingfors)

A meeting point of West and East, Helsinki combines the relaxed feeling of Finland with a metropolitan elegance. Lutheran and Russian Orthodox cathedrals stand almost face to face, Red Army uniforms and medals are sold on the street, and St. Petersburg and Tallinn are but a short cruise across the Gulf of Finland. Cobblestone streets, well-tended parks, and boat-thronged coastlines make Helsinki an ideal city for strolling; Mannerheimintie and the Esplanadi offer great people-watching. The southeast corner of the city is a nest of diplomats, elegant mansions, and aggressive traffic, while the area around the train station offers cafés, shops, and street vendors.

ORIENTATION AND PRACTICAL INFORMATION

Helsinki, "daughter of the Baltic" (personified in the harbor's **Havis Amanda** statue), dangles on Finland's southern edge. The central city's layout resembles a "V" with a large, bulbous point and several smaller peninsulas. The train station lies just north of the vertex, from which the **Mannerheimintie** and **Unioninkatu** thoroughfares radiate. The harbor and most sights are southeast of the train station. All street signs have both Finnish and Swedish names. For candid and practical info on what's hot, the free youthful paper *City* is unbeatable, while *Helsinki This Week* provides local information and a list of lodgings, restaurants, and current happenings.

Tourist Offices: City Tourist Office, Pohjoisesplanadi 19 (tel. 169 37 57). From the train station, walk 2 blocks south on Keskuskatu and turn left on Pohjoisesplanadi. Open late May-early Sept. Mon.-Fri. 9am-7pm, Sat.-Sun. 9am-3pm; mid-Sept. to mid-May Mon.-Fri. 9am-5pm, Sat.-Sun. 9am-3pm. **Hotellikeskus** (Hotel Booking Center; tel. 17 11 33), in the train station, has maps and finds rooms (12mk booking fee). Open late May-Aug. Mon.-Sat. 9am-7pm, Sun. 10am-6pm; Sept. to mid-May Mon.-Fri. 9am-5pm. Both offices sell the **Helsinki Card,** offering local transportation and museum discounts (1-day 105mk, 3-day 165mk). The **Finnish Tourist Board,** Eteläesplanadi 4 (tel. 41 76 93 00; fax 41 76 93 01), covers Finland, including transportation routes and campgrounds. Open June-Aug. Mon.-Fri. 8:30am-5pm, Sat. 10am-2pm; Sept.-May Mon.-Fri. 8:30am-4pm. **Finnish Youth Hostel Association,** Yrjönkatu 38B (tel. 694 03 77), on the south side of the bus station, lists hostels and arranges Lapland lodgings. Open Mon.-Fri. 9am-4pm.

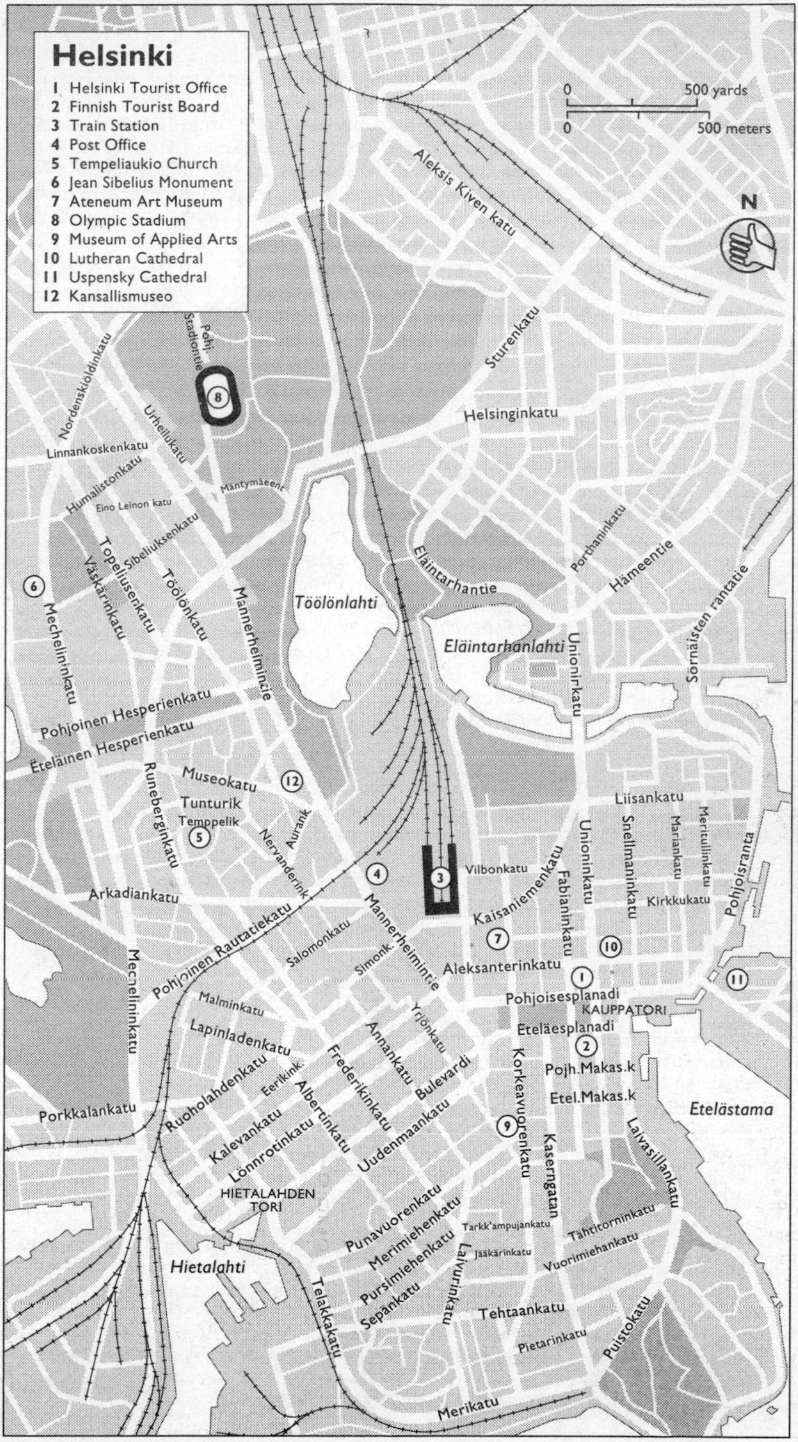
Helsinki
1 Helsinki Tourist Office
2 Finnish Tourist Board
3 Train Station
4 Post Office
5 Tempeliaukio Church
6 Jean Sibelius Monument
7 Ateneum Art Museum
8 Olympic Stadium
9 Museum of Applied Arts
10 Lutheran Cathedral
11 Uspensky Cathedral
12 Kansallismuseo
0 500 yards
0 500 meters
N
Aleksis Kiven katu
Sturenkatu
Helsinginkatu
Pohj. Stadiontie
Nordenskiöldinkatu
Urheilukatu
Linnankoskenkatu
Humalistonkatu
Eino Leinon katu
Mäntymäentie
Sibeliuksenkatu
Topeliuksenkatu
Väskärinkatu
Töölönkatu
Mannerheimintie
Mechelininkatu
Töölönlahti
Eläintarhantie
Eläintarhanlahti
Porthaninkatu
Hämeentie
Sörnäisten rantatie
Unionirkatu
Pohjoinen Hesperienkatu
Eteläinen Hesperienkatu
Runeberginkatu
Museokatu
Tunturik
Temppelik
Aurank
Nervanderink
Arkadiankatu
Vilbonkatu
Kaisaniemenkatu
Fabianinkatu
Unioninkatu
Liisankatu
Snellmaninkatu
Mariankatu
Meritullinkatu
Kirkkokatu
Pohjoisranta
Pohjoinen Rautatiekatu
Salomonkatu
Simonk.
Aleksanterinkatu
Pohjoisesplanadi
KAUPPATORI
Eteläesplanadi
Malminkatu
Lapinladenkatu
Yrjönkatu
Annankatu
Fredrikinkatu
Pojh.Makas.k
Etel.Makas.k
Eteläsatama
Ruoholahdenkatu
Eerikink.
Albertinkatu
Bulevardi
Porkkalankatu
Kalevankatu
Lönnrotinkatu
Uudenmaankatu
Korkeavuorenkatu
Kasarmikatu
Laivasillankatu
HIETALAHDEN TORI
Punavuorenkatu
Merimiehenkatu
Tarkk'ampujankatu
Tähtitorninkatu
Jääkärinkatu
Vuorimiehenkatu
Hietalahti
Pursimiehenkatu
Laivurinkatu
Telakkakatu
Sepänkatu
Tehtaankatu
Pietarinkatu
Puistokatu
Merikatu

FINLAND

Budget Travel: Kilroy Travels, Kaivokatu 100 (tel. 680 78 11). Sells Transalpino tickets, ISIC, and YIEE cards. Open Mon.-Fri. 10am-6pm, Sat. 10am-2pm.

Embassies: In emergencies, **Australians** and **New Zealanders** should contact the British Embassy. **Canada,** Pohjoisesplanadi 25B (tel. 17 11 41). Open Mon.-Thurs. 8:30am-4:30pm, Fri. 8:30am-1:30pm. **Estonia,** Itäinen Puistotie 10 (tel. 62 20 260). **Ireland,** Evottajankatu 7A (tel. 64 60 06). **Latvia,** Armfeltintie 10 (tel. 47 64 72 44). **Lithuania,** Rauhankatu 13A (tel. 60 82 10). **Poland,** Armas Lindgrenin tie 21 (tel. 684 80 77). **Russia,** Tehtaankatu 1B (tel. 66 18 76). **South Africa,** Rahapajankatu 1A (tel. 658 288). **U.K.,** Itäinen Puistotie 17 (tel. 22 86 51 00). **U.S.,** Itäinen Puistotie 14A (tel. 17 19 31). Open Mon.-Fri. 9am-noon.

Currency Exchange: Forex, in the train station, charges a 10mk fee for cash, 10mk per traveler's check, but no fee to exchange markka into foreign currency. Open daily 8am-9pm. Same rates in main post office. Open Mon.-Fri. 7am-9pm, Sat. 9am-6pm, Sun. 11am-9pm. Visa credit card advances available from bank machines.

American Express: Area Travel, Mikonkatu 2D, 2nd floor (tel. 62 87 88). No commission on traveler's checks. Arranges for wiring of money for members. Open Mon.-Fri. 9am-1pm and 2:15-4:30pm.

Flights: For info, call 818 81. Bus 615 runs 2-3 times per hour 5:20am-10:20pm (Mon.-Fri.) between the **Helsinki-Vantaa** airport and the station square (15mk). The Finnair bus shuttles between the airport and the Finnair building at Asema-aukio 3, next to the train station (every 20min. 5am-midnight, 35min., 25mk).

Trains: Dial 101 01 15 for info. Trains chug regularly to Turku (2hr., 90mk), Tampere (2hr., 90mk), and Rovaniemi (10hr., 2304mk). Call 010 01 24 for info on trains to St. Petersburg (7½hr., 265mk, Eurail and Scanrail 148mk) and Moscow (16hr., 506mk, sleeper included). The station has **lockers** and **luggage service** (10mk each; service open daily 6:35am-10pm).

Buses: Call 96 00 40 00 for info. The station with routes throughout Finland and to St. Petersburg via Lahti (3 per day, 8hr., 190-250mk) sits west of the post office, between Salomonkatu and Simonkatu. Buy tickets at the station or on the bus.

Ferries: For details, see **Getting There,** p. 266. **Silja Line,** Mannerheimintie 2 (tel. 180 41). **Viking Line,** Mannerheimintie 14 (tel. 123 51). Viking Line and **Finnjet** (contact Silja Line) ferries leave from Katajanokka island east of Kauppatori (take tram 2 or 4). The departure point for Silja Line, **Polferries** (tel. 980 07 45 52), **Estonian Line** (tel. 66 99 44), and **Tallink** (tel. 22 82 12 77) ferries is south of Kauppatori (take tram 3T). For more info about touring the Baltic, call 63 05 22.

Public Transportation: The metro and most trams and buses run approximately 6am-11pm (certain bus and tram lines, including the indispensable tram 3T, continue to 1:30am). On the weekend, trains run until 2:30am. Within Helsinki, rides cost 9mk; a 10-trip ticket goes for 75mk. Travel between Helsinki, Espoo, and Vantaa costs 15mk; a 10-trip ticket runs 125mk. All tickets are valid for one hour (transfers free) and are available at R-Kiosks and City Transport offices at Simonkatu 1, the Rautatientori metro station, and the Hakaniemi train station. Punch your ticket on board. Ask on trams or at the City Transport office for maps; some routes are more direct than others. The **Tourist Ticket** provides boundless transit in Helsinki, Espoo, and Vantaa (1-day 90mk, 3-day 45mk); the ticket for travel in Helsinki only costs 25mk for 1 day, 50mk for 3 days. You can purchase the tickets at City Transport and tourist offices. For transit information, call 010 01 11.

Bike Rental: Kallio Youth Hostel (tel. 70 99 25 90). 30mk per day. **Töölönlahti Kioski** (tel. 40 40 12), by the Finlandia House. 50mk per day. Open daily 2-6pm.

Bookstore: The Academic Bookstore, Pohjoisesplanadi 39 (tel. 121 41). Dazzling selection of books in English (including travel guides) and classic novels for 15mk. Popular hang-out spot, with café. Open Mon.-Fri. 9am-8pm, Sat. 9am-5pm.

Laundromat: Your best bet is to check for facilities at youth hostels (5-15mk). Otherwise, look for the words *Itsepalvelu Pesula.* Try **Rööperin pesulapalvelut,** Punavuorenkatu 3, with self-serve laundry for 40mk.

Women's Center: The Union of Feminist Women runs **Naisten huone,** Bulevardi 11A (tel. 64 24 61; main switchboard 64 31 58), a cultivated social center and café. Open mid-Aug. to June Mon.-Fri. 5-9pm, Sat. noon-6pm.

Travelers With Disabilities: Rullaten Ry, Pajutie 7 (tel./fax 805 73 93).

Pharmacy: Yliopiston Apteekki, Mannerheimintie 5 (tel. 17 90 92). Open daily 7am-midnight. Also branch at Mannerheimintie 96 (tel. 41 57 78). Open 24hr.

Medical Assistance: Aleksin lääkäriasema, Mannerheimintie 8 (tel. 601 911). Receives and refers foreigners.

Emergencies: tel. 112.

Police: tel. 100 22. Stations at Olavinkatu 1A, Kasarmikatu 25B, 2 Pikku Roobertinkatu 1-3, and the train station near platform 11.

Post Office: Mannerheimintie 11 (tel. 195 51 17). Open Mon.-Fri. 9:30am-5pm. *Poste Restante* office in the same building sells stamps and exchanges money; open Mon.-Fri. 7am-9pm, Sat. 9am-6pm, Sun. 11am-9pm. **Postal Code:** 00100.

Telephones: In the same building as the post office. Open Mon.-Fri. 9am-10pm, Sat.-Sun. 10am-4pm. Get the best rates by using a Tele or Nonstop phone card, which works in all green Nonstop card phones. **Telephone Code:** 09.

ACCOMMODATIONS AND CAMPING

During the summer, it's wise to make reservations, but just showing up is not extraordinarily risky. Most hostels offer laundry facilities, breakfast, and saunas.

Hotel Satakuntatalo (HI), Lapinrinne 1 (tel. 69 58 51; fax 694 22 26), 500m southwest of the train station—turn right on Mannerheimintie, then left up Salomonkatu past the bus station; go down Lapinrinne. Kitchen and baggage storage. Reception open 24hr. Dorms 55mk. Singles 195mk, including breakfast. Doubles 230mk. Nonmembers add 15mk. Sauna 20mk. Laundry 15mk. Open June-Aug.

Stadion Hostel (HI), Pohj. Stadiontie 3B (tel. 49 60 71; fax 49 64 66), in the Olympic Stadium complex. Take tram 3T or 7A from the train station. 200 bed hostel has high ceilings, huge windows, a kitchen, and TV. Reception open June-early Sept. daily 8am-2am; mid-Sept. to May 8-10am and 4pm-2am. Dorms 55mk, nonmembers 70mk. Doubles 160mk. Locked room for luggage. Sheets 20mk.

Academica (HI), Hietaniemenkatu 14 (tel. 13 11 43 34; fax 44 12 01). Just 700m from the train station; walk up Mannerheimintie and turn right, then left onto Arkadiankatu, left on Mechelininkatu, and right onto Hietaniemenkatu. Kitchen. Reception open 24hr. Singles 215mk. Doubles 220mk. Triples 255mk per person. Quads 300mk. Nonmembers add 15mk per person. Open June-Aug.

Kallio Youth Hostel, Porthaninkatu 2 (tel. 70 99 25 90; fax 70 99 25 98). From the train station, walk 15min. north on Unioninkatu, or take the metro to Hakaniemi. Cozy 35-bed hostel. TV room and kitchen. Reception open daily 8am-11pm. 70mk, disposable sheets 10mk. Free lockers and storage room. Open July-Aug.

Finnapartments Fenno, Franzeninkatu 26 (tel. 773 16 61; fax 701 68 89). Home-style apartments in the city center. From the train station, walk north on Unioninkatu (which becomes Siltasaarenkatu), right on Porthaninkatu, left onto Fleminginkatu, then left again. Singles 160-220mk. Doubles 320mk. Also week rentals.

Camping: Rastila Camping (tel. 31 65 51), 14km east of the city center. Take the metro to Itäkeskus and then catch bus 90, 90A, or 96. Vast, cheap, municipal campground with washing and cooking facilities, showers and toilets. Reception open 24hr. One person 40mk. Cabins 210-320mk.

FOOD

In Finland even groceries are expensive; find relief at the **Alepa** chain (the branch under the train station is open Mon.-Sat. 10am-10pm, Sun. noon-10pm). Energetic epicureans can find a variety of wares including fresh fruit, veggies and fish at the **Kauppatori** (Market Square), by the port (open June-Aug. Mon.-Sat. 7am-2pm and 4-8pm; Sept.-May Mon.-Fri. 7am-2pm), and the nearby **Kauppahalli** (Market Hall; open Mon.-Sat. 8am-5pm, Sun. 8am-2pm). If you're not traveling farther east, be sure to try one of Helsinki's many excellent Russian restaurants.

Zetor, Kaivokatu 10. Finnish specialties, a lively crowd, and a real tractor inside make this the essence of Finland: food, drinks, music, dancing, and of course, a sauna. Opens Sun.-Fri. 3pm, Sat. 1pm; closes when the last customer leaves.

Suola Ja Pippuri, Snellmaninkatu 17. On a quiet side street. Lunch 38-44mk. Mainly seafood dinners. Open Mon.-Fri. 11am-midnight, Sat. 1pm-midnight.

Kasvis, Korkeavuorenkatu 3. Serves organically grown vegetable dishes (25-45mk) and amazing homemade bread that they've been perfecting for 20 years. Enjoy your meal outside or inside. Open Mon.-Fri. 11am-10pm, Sat.-Sun. noon-10pm.

Café Engel, Aleksanterinkatu 26. Sip coffee for hours (8.50mk) or try the delicious lingonberry pie (17mk). Open Mon.-Sat. 9am-midnight, Sun. 11am-midnight.

Ravintola Tempura, Mikonkatu 2. Vegetarian restaurant in the heart of the city, down an alley. Lunch special 38mk. *A la carte* around 32mk. Soup 25mk. Open Mon.-Fri. 11am-11pm, Sat. noon-4pm.

Namaskaar, Mannerheimintie 100. Voted best ethnic restaurant in a local magazine. Indian food extraordinaire, but a bit pricey. Daily lunch specials (11am-3pm) 35-55mk. Open Mon.-Fri. 11am-midnight, Sat. 2pm-midnight, Sun. 2pm-11pm.

Kappeli, Eteläesplanadi 1. Victorian Parisian fantasy that has catered to trendies since 1837 (Sibelius had a favorite table here). Warm pies 15mk per slice. Mouth-watering entrees 38-55mk. Lunch 25-37mk. Beer 25mk. Open daily 9am-4am.

University Cafeterias: Fabianinkatu 33; outdoor-terraced Porthania, Hallituskatu 6. Entrees 20mk. Students only. Both open June-Aug. Mon.-Fri. 10am-4pm; Sept.-May Mon.-Fri. 8am-6pm, Sat. 10:30am-2:30pm.

SIGHTS

Tram 3T offers the city's cheapest tour (pick up a free itinerary on board). Better yet, just walk—most sights are packed within 2km of the train station and the city has few hills. The tourist office stocks the booklet *See Helsinki on Foot.* The famed architect Alvar Aalto once said of Finland, "Architecture is our form of expression because our language is so impossible," and the bold 20th-century creations amid slick Neoclassical works that suffuse the region prove him right. Much of the layout and architecture of the old center, however, is the brainchild of a German, Carl Engel. After Helsinki became the capital of the Grand Duchy of Finland in 1812, Engel was chosen to design an appropriate city. In **Senate Square,** on the corner of Unioninkatu and Aleksanterinkatu, his work is well represented by the **Tuomiokirkko** (dome church). After marveling at the Neoclassical exterior, though, you may be disappointed by the austere interior of the Lutheran cathedral, completed in 1852. (Open June-Aug. 9am-6pm, Sun. noon-4pm; Sept.-May Sun.-Fri. 10am-4pm, Sat. 10am-6pm.) A few blocks to the east, on Katajanokka island, the spectacular Byzantine-Slavonic **Uspensky Orthodox Cathedral** guards the island with its red spikes. (Ornate interior open May-Sept. 30 Mon. and Wed.-Fri. 9:30am-4pm, Tues. 9:30am-6pm, Sat. 9am-4pm, Sun. noon-3pm. Oct.-April irregular hours.) Behind the cathedral stretches **Esplanadi.** During the Swedish-Finnish cultural conflict in the 19th century, Finns walked on the south side and Swedes on the north. Today, the cosmopolitan Esplanadi offers a crowded melange of cafés and street entertainment.

Across from the train station sprawls Finland's largest art museum, the **Art Museum of the Ateneum,** Kaivokatu 2, with Finnish and foreign art from the 1700s to the 1960s. (Open Tues. and Fri. 9am-6pm, Wed.-Thurs. 9am-8pm, Sat.-Sun. 11am-5pm. 10mk, students and seniors 5mk; special exhibits 25mk.) The **Kansallismuseo** (National Museum), 500m northwest of the train station at Mannerheimintie 34, displays intriguing bits of Finnish culture, from Gypsy and Sami costumes to *ryijyt* (rugs), along with a splendid history exhibit. (Open June-Aug. Tues. 11am-8pm, Wed.-Sun. 11am-5pm; Sept.-May Tues. 11am-8pm, Wed.-Sun. 11am-4pm. 15mk, students 5mk.) The intriguing **Temppeliaukio Church,** designed in the late 60s by Tuomo and Timo Suomalainen, is built into a hill of rock with only the roof visible from the outside. From the train station, head west on Arkadiankatu and then right on Fredrikinkatu to the square where the church is buried (open Mon.-Fri. 10am-8pm, Sat. 10am-6pm, Sun. between services). The striking **Jean Sibelius Monument,** 750m north of the church in Sibelius Park, on Mechelininkatu, was dedicated to one of the 20th century's greatest composers by sculptor Eila Hiltunen. The monument looks like a cloud of organ pipes blasting into outer space. About one mile north of the city center looms the **Olympiastadion,** the main arena for the 1952 Helsinki Olympics.

The stadium was ready to welcome athletes in 1940, but had to wait after World War II canceled the games that year. It now hosts a hostel and numerous concerts. The stadium tower offers a great view of the city (open Mon.-Fri. 9am-8pm, Sat.-Sun 9am-6pm; 10mk). Outside, check out the nude **statue** of athlete Paavo Nurmi, "The Flying Finn." Although the Finns have no qualms about baring all in the sauna, the unbound statue stirred considerable controversy when it was unveiled. Check out the cacti and palms at the **City Wintergarten,** Hammarskjöldintie 1 (open Mon.-Sat. noon-3pm, Sun noon-4pm, free), or follow the sea gulls to **Market Square** and **Old Market Hall** at the north end of Esplanadi, where fresh fish and souvenirs are sold daily.

Surrounding islands provide a welcome relief from the fast pace of Helsinki's center. Ferries leave hourly from Market Square (round-trip 20mk) for the now-demilitarized fortress island of **Suomenlinna,** built by the Swedes in the 18th century on five interconnected islands to repel attacks on Helsinki. Explore the dark passageways of the old fortress or visit one of the island's museums. Best bets include the model ship collection of the **Ehrensvärd,** the submarine **Vesikko,** and the **Coastal Artillery Museum.** (Open mid-May to Aug. daily 10am-5pm; Sept. 11am-3pm. 10mk, students 5mk. Some museums have additional admission.) If museumed-out, relax on the rocky **beach** or head to **Seurasaari,** linked to the mainland by a walkway, for a picnic, swim, or saunter. Seurasaari's open-air **museum** contains redwood churches and farmsteads transplanted from the countryside. Visit during Midsummer to witness the *kokko* (bonfire) and Finnish tradition in its full splendor. (Open June-Aug. daily 11am-5pm, Wed. until 7pm; May and Sept. Mon.-Fri. 9am-3pm, Sat.-Sun. 11am-5pm. 20mk, students 10mk, Wed. free.) To reach Seurasaari, take bus 24 from Erottaja, outside the Swedish Theater, to the last stop. There's also summer boat service from Market Square. A 15-minute train ride (take R, H, K, or P from the railway station to Tikkurila; 15mk) takes you to the **Heureka Science Center,** with hands-on exhibits, a planetarium, and a fascinating presentation on the Finno-Ugric languages. (Open Fri.-Wed. 10am-6pm, Thurs. 10am-8pm. 75mk, students 45mk; planetarium extra.)

ENTERTAINMENT

Much of Helsinki nods off early, but only because the days are packed. Sway to afternoon street music in the leafy **Esplanadi** or party on warm nights at **Hietaniemi beach.** Open-air concerts take place in **Kaivopuisto park** on Sundays in July. Consult *Helsinki This Week* for current happenings and *City,* printed in English in summer, for popular cafés, bars and nightclubs; both are free. Finland is one of few European countries in which the drinking age—18 for beer and wine, 20 for hard alcohol—is usually enforced. Both bouncers and cover charges usually relax on weeknights; speaking English or German may help you get in. Tickets to some discos sell out before the evening begins; the super-cautious can buy in advance at **Tiketti,** in the Forum mall at the corner of Mannerheimintie and Simonkatu (3rd floor), on the 7th floor of **Stockmans,** or **Lippupalvelu,** Mannerheimintie 5. The cheapest place to buy alcohol is the state-run liquor store **Alko.** (Branches at Eteläesplanadi 22, Mannerheimintie 1, and Salomonkatu 1. Open Mon.-Thurs. 10am-6pm, Fri. 10am-8pm, Sat. 9am-2pm.) Starting in the last week in August, the two-week **Helsinki Festival** brings together a melange of arts events, from ballet to theater to rock concerts.

Manala (i.e. "Hell"), Dagmarinkatu 2, just behind the Parliament building. Live bands, celebrity acts, and a maze-like, mysterious environment draw an international crowd. Rock, disco, and tango. Cover varies. Open daily until 4am.

Happy Days, P. Esplanadi 2, right in the center of the two Esplanadi. Voted "best party place in Helsinki" by locals. Open daily 11am-4am. New adjoining jazz club Royal Cotton Club open daily 11am-4pm, weekend cover 25mk after 10pm.

Old Students' House, Mannerheimintie 3. 19th-century establishment with pubs, dancing, restaurant, and sociable students. Beer 15-20mk. Cover 20-50mk for live bands. Open Mon.-Thurs. 11am-1am, Fri.-Sat. 11am-2am.

Nylon, Kaivokatu 10. Trendy club with women in platform shoes and men up to date on the fashion mags. Open Tues.-Thurs. 11pm-4am, Fri.-Sat. 10pm-4am.

Cantina West, Kasarmikatu 23, off Eteläesplanadi. Popular but fairly expensive Tex-Mex restaurant and bar. Minimum age 22. Cover 35mk on weekends. Open Mon.-Thurs. 11am-3am, Fri. 11am-4am, Sat. noon-4am, Sun. noon-3am.
Storyville, Museokatu 8, near the National Museum. Helsinki's choice jazz club. Live music nightly. Cover varies. Open Mon.-Sat. 8pm-4pm, Sun. 8pm-2am.
Don't Tell Mama, Annankatu 32. Hopping gay dance club with disco, techno, and rock. Open Tues.-Sun 11pm-4am.
$H_2$0, Eerikinkatu 14. Helsinki's crowded gay bar (mostly men). Open daily 4pm-2am.

■ Near Helsinki

The cobblestone streets of **Porvoo,** Finland's second oldest town, lie 50km east of Helsinki along Old King Road, which continues on to Russia. Tsar Alexander I granted Finland its autonomy at the Porvoo **cathedral,** in the old town. (Open May-Sept. Mon.-Fri. 10am-6pm, Sat. 10am-2pm, Sun 2-3pm; Oct.-April Tues.-Sat. 10am-2pm, Sun. 2-4pm.) At **Runeberg's Home,** Aleksanterinkatu 3, poet John Ludvig Runeberg ate his wife's delicious apple pastry, now known as "Runeberg's delight" and served by cafés on Aleksanterinkatu. Check out his wonderful sculpture collection. (House open May-Aug. Mon.-Sat. 10am-4pm, Sun. 11am-5pm; Sept.-April Wed.-Sat. 10am-4pm, Sun. 11am-5pm. 15mk.) The main **tourist office,** Rauhankatu 20 (tel. (015) 85 01 45), can direct you to more attractions (open June-Aug. Mon.-Fri. 8am-4pm, Sat. 10am-2pm; Sept.-May Mon.-Fri. 9am-6pm). **Buses** leave for Porvoo every 30 minutes from Helsinki's bus station (1hr., 40mk). **Porvoo Camping Kokonniemi** (tel. (015) 58 19 67), 1.5km from the center, has tent sites, sauna, showers, laundry, and cooking facilities (call for prices, open May 31-Aug. 8).

Jean Sibelius tormented himself in **Järvenpää,** 40km north of Helsinki. At his home, **Ainola,** the composer drank and brooded, his perfectionism so exacting that he destroyed much of his late work (open May-Sept. Wed.-Sat. 11am-5pm; 20mk). For info contact the **tourist office,** Halinfokatu 2 (tel. 27 19 22 12). **Buses** to Tuusula pass by the home from platforms 9, 11, or 12 in the Helsinki bus station (20mk).

A brief hour and a half train ride southwest of Helsinki leads to a beautiful archipelago that ends with the harbor town of **Hanko,** the southern-most point of Finland, founded in 1874 as a spa. The spectacular residences that line the miles of sandy beaches reflect the splendor and decadence of the now-vanished Russian nobility. At the end of Mannerheimintie, the **House of the Four Winds** sits on Little Pine Island, once owned by the Marshal Mannerheim for whom so many Finnish streets are named; it is now a café. The **Russian Orthodox Church** on Täktomintie celebrated its 100th anniversary in 1995 (open Mon.-Sat. noon-6pm).The best **beaches** are southwest of the town. Paul Feldt/Åke Wiberg's **bicycle shop,** Tarhakatu 4 (tel. (019) 248 18 60), rents bikes (30mk per day; opens around 9am). The helpful **tourist office,** Bulevardi 10 (tel. (019) 220 34 11; fax 248 58 21), has maps. **Villa Doris,** Appelgrenintie 23 (tel. (019) 248 12 28), rents singles (170mk) and doubles (300mk; prices lower off season). **Hanko Camping Silversand,** Hopeahietikko (tel. (019) 248 55 00), is 2.5km northeast of the town center (75mk per tent; open June-Aug.).

ÅLAND ISLANDS (AHVENANMAA)

The Åland (OH-land) Islands have long been a cultural and geographic bridge between Sweden and Finland. Åland became part of Finland in 1807, but since 1921 has sported its own flag, parliament, and postal system as an autonomous territory within the country. Still, Sweden's influence remains strong: all signs are in Swedish, and many islanders work to minimize Finnish influence. Political controversy seems out of place here, though. The gentle landscape more befits leisurely hikes, bike rides, and sun-soaking. Most places accept Swedish and Finnish currencies.

For information on traveling **Viking Line** or **Silja Line** to Mariehamn, see **Getting There,** p. 266. **Birka Lines** (tel. in Mariehamn (018) 270 27, in Stockholm (08) 714 55

20) launches its *Princess* daily from Stockholm to Mariehamn (40mk). **Eckerö Line** (tel. in Mariehamn (018) 280 00, in Grisslehamn (0175) 309 20) travels from Eckerö in Åland, to Grisslehamn, Sweden (36mk, students, railpass holders 18mk) with bus links to both Mariehamn (30min., 22mk) and Stockholm (2hr., 18mk).

Inter-island ferries are free for walk-on and biking passengers; cars cost 30-40mk (45mk entry fee for the Turku archipelago). You can pick up the *Skärgårdstrafiken* **ferry** schedule or the *Ålandstrafiken* **bus** schedule for free at the Mariehamn tourist office. The main island, with its extensive paths and wide roads, is best explored by bike. **RoNo Rent,** facing the ferry terminal in Mariehamn, is the most convenient. (30mk per day, 150mk per week. Mopeds, windsurfers, and boats available. Open June-Aug. daily 9-11:30am and 12:30-7pm; May and Sept. reduced hours.)

Mariehamn

On the south coast of the main island, Mariehamn is the center of activity on Åland and the only town with a significant numbers of shops and restaurants. The only other village is Eckeröon on the western part of the island. The remainder is divided into districts with small campgrounds, beaches, and a few cafés; travelers would do well to stock up on groceries in Mariehamn. Local artwork and history springs to life at the **Åland Museum,** at Stadshusparken off Storagatan. (Open May-Aug. Wed.-Mon. 10am-4pm, Tues. 10am-8pm; Sept.-April Wed.-Sun. 11am-4pm, Tues. 11am-8pm. 15mk.) Just 500m north of the ferry terminal, the **Sjöfartsmuseum** displays navigational instruments in the cleverly constructed land-bound ship **Pommern.** (Open May-June and Aug. daily 9am-5pm; July 9am-7pm; Sept.-Oct. 10am-4pm. 15mk.)

For maps of Åland and an *Åland Islands Guide,* head to the **tourist office** at Storagatan 8 (tel. (018) 240 00), five minutes from the Viking Line terminal (open June-Aug. daily 9am-6pm; July also until 7pm; Sept.-May Mon.-Sat. 10am-4pm). **Botel Alida** (tel. (018) 137 55), on Österleden 2km from the ferry terminal, offers sardine-sized doubles on a ship for 70mk (reception open May-Sept. 24hr.). Otherwise, **Ålandsresor,** Torggatan 2 (tel. (018) 280 40), books accommodations for all the islands. (Reception open Mon.-Fri. 9am-5pm. Singles in private homes 150mk. Doubles 180mk. 30mk booking fee.) **Campground Gröna Udden** (tel. (018) 190 41) relaxes by the water, 10 minutes down Skillnadagatan from the town center (20mk per person; showers, laundry; open mid-May to Aug.). Mariehamn's restaurant prices make **supermarket** food suddenly alluring; try **Fokus** at Torggatan 14 (open Mon.-Fri. 9am-8pm, Sat. 9am-3pm). At **City Mat and Café,** Torggatan 6, lunches run 35mk (open Mon.-Fri. 8:30am-7pm, Sat. 10am-3pm). Bite into *Ålandspannkakor,* covered with marmalade and whipped cream, for 22mk at **Amanda Kaffestuga,** Norragatan 15 (open Mon.-Sat. 10am-6pm, Sun. 11am-7pm), or 10mk at **Café Julius,** Torggatan 10 (open daily 8am-10pm). For a satisfying traditional entrees, try **Cikada,** Norragatan 13, in the Cikada Hotel (35-70mk; open daily 9am-10pm).

Near Mariehamn

The rest of the Åland Islands are very accessible from Mariehamn by a combination of ferries, buses and bikes. To the northeast of Mariehamn lies **Sund,** home to several attractions. Take bus 4 (30min., 18mk) to the Kastelholm stop and follow the sign to the 13th-century **Kastelholm Castle.** (Open May-June and Aug.-Sept. daily 10am-5pm; July 9:30am-8pm. 20mk, students 14mk.) Nearby lurks the **Vita Björn** museum, which features prison cells from various centuries (open May-Sept. daily 10am-5pm; July 10am-8pm), as well as an open-air museum, **Jan Karlsgården.** (Open May-June and Aug.-Sept. daily 9:30am-5pm. 10mk for both museums, students 7mk.) The road from Kastelholm past Bomarsund is worth the trek; it cuts through lush green meadows overflowing with wild flowers and alternating with dense forests, finally opening up into Prästo and the Baltic Sea. **Bomarsund** displays the ruins of an ancient Russian fortress blown up in the Crimean War. In between Kastelholm and Bomarsund, the **Skarpans Gästhem,** Östrasund (tel (018) 459 89), rents singles (180mk) and doubles

(340 mk). **Puttes Camping** (tel. (018) 440 16) at Bomarsund rents bikes and boats and has laundry, showers, and a kitchen (sites 12mk per person). Beyond Bomarsund, **Prästö** also has a campground, **Prästö Stugor & Camping** (tel. (018) 440 45; 15mk per person, bathrooms, laundry, and showers).

From Prästö, a bike-friendly ferry runs to **Lumpo** in northern **Lumparland,** leaving at 12:30pm from June through mid-August, and also 5pm in July only (July ferries cost 30mk, free June-Aug.). From **Langnäs,** Lumparland's east coast, the free ferry leaves to many of the surrounding islands. **Föglo** has a campground with kitchen, showers, and laundry called **C.C Camping** (tel. (018) 514 40; 15mk per person, open June-Aug.). **Kökar's Sandvik Camping,** near Hamno in the southeast (tel. (018) 559 11), charges 40mk for a tent and access to a kitchen, showers, laundry, and bathrooms. Northwest of Sund is **Geta,** the farthest north district of Åland. **Tourist information** may be found near **Västergeta** (tel. (018) 493 70; open June 10-Aug. 9 daily 10am-6:30pm). **Kasvikens Camping** (tel. (018) 414 19), in Geta, has campgrounds for 60mk, laundry, bathrooms, and showers. A free wilderness hut with a wood stove, four bunks, and a portrait of Åland's first prime minister sit proudly atop **Orrdals klint,** Åland's highest peak. Many take the bus to Saltvik-Kvarnbo, between Sund and Geta, and then bike toward Långbergsöda.

Åland's second real town, **Eckerö,** in the west, is also a port for departures to Stockholm. Take bus 1 from Mariehamn to get here. The Eckerö **tourist office,** Storby Centrum (tel. (018) 380 95), has info on island ferries, buses, and campgrounds (open June 9-Aug. 31 daily 10am-7pm). About 4km off the main bus route to Eckerö is **Notvikens Camping,** Överby 57 (tel. (018) 380 20), with tent sites (50mk), a café, showers, laundry, and bathrooms. In **Djurvik,** on the way to Eckerö in the west, affordable but hard-to-reach **Djurviks Gästgård** guesthouse (tel. (018) 324 33) perches on a secluded inlet. Take bus 1 to Gottby (9km), turn left, and walk the 4-5km to the guesthouse; the light traffic makes hitching difficult (1- to 2-person room 130-180mk; call ahead or contact Ålandsresor). Farther west, in Eckerö, **Käringsunds Camping** (tel. (018) 383 09) charges only 35mk per tent; take bus 1 to Storby and walk 1km.

SOUTHWEST FINLAND

Turku (Åbo)

Turku, Finland's oldest city, was once the country's capital. The ascendancy was short-lived, though; in 1812 Tsar Alexander I snatched Finland away from Sweden and declared Helsinki the capital. Shortly thereafter Scandinavia's worst fire devoured Turku's wooden buildings. Despite these losses, Turku remains a flourishing cultural and academic center and serves as a welcome excursion from Helsinki.

Still bearing the Swedish mark, one of Turku's two universities, **Åbo Akademi,** across the river on the hill, operates in Swedish. Nearby, the massive **cathedral** in Tuomiokirkkotori (Cathedral Square), completed in 1300, speaks of the era when Turku was a center for the spiritual and commercial colonization of the Finnish hinterland (open daily 9am-8pm; organ concerts in summer Tues. 8pm; free). Sheltered from the ferry ports by a screen of trees, the 700-year-old **Turku Castle,** along the Aura River about 3km from the city center, tastefully combines sleek lines, medieval artifacts, and a **historical museum.** (Open mid-April to mid-Sept. daily 10am-6pm; mid-Sept. to mid-April Mon. 2pm-7pm, Tues.-Sun. 10am-3pm. 30mk, students 20mk.) **Luostarinmäki,** the only part of Turku to survive the 1827 fire, now stands as an open-air **handicrafts museum.** (Open mid-April to mid-Sept. daily 10am-6pm; mid-Sept. to mid-April Tues.-Sun. 10am-3pm. 20mk, students 15mk.) On Puolalanmäki hill, under the spires of the imperial **Turku Art Museum,** Aurakatu 26, hang some of Akseli Gallen-Kallela's vibrant *Kalevala* paintings. (Open mid-May to Sept. Tues. and Fri.-Sat. 10am-4pm, Wed.-Thurs. 10am-7pm, Sun. 11am-6pm; Oct. to mid-May Tues.-Sat. 10am-4pm, Sun. 11am-6pm. 30mk, students 20mk.) The weekend after Midsummer finds crowds swarming Turku's Ruissalo Island for **Ruisrock** (tel. (02) 251 11 62; email turku.music@tmf.pp.fi; http://ruisrock.weppi.fi), Finland's oldest and largest rock festival, which attracts names like David Bowie and Sting (190mk, 2-day pass 330mk). The **islands** surrounding Turku are best seen on a short cruise through the archipelago. The **S/S Ukkopekka,** Linnankatu 38 (tel. (02) 233 01 23; fax 233 09 23), offers daily cruises (9am, 12:30, 4, and 8pm, 3hr., 90mk).

Practical Information, Accommodations, and Food The **tourist office,** Aurakatu 4 (tel. (02) 233 63 66; fax 233 64 88; http://www.turku.fi), is small but useful (open Mon.-Fri. 8:30am-6pm, Sat.-Sun. 9am-4pm). The **Youth Travel and Information Center, Auran paniino,** Läntinen rautakatu 47 (tel. (02) 253 57 49), on the river 500m from the youth hostel, will store your luggage for free; you can also wash clothes or rent a bike for small fees. The building houses a small café that serves lunch or dinner for an incredible 10mk. **Internet access** is available at the city **library,** Linnankatu 2 (open Mon.-Fri. 10am-7pm). Turku is a two-hour **train** ride from Helsinki (8 per day, 90mk); if you're going to the **ferry** terminal, take the train (3 per day) to Turku *satama* (harbor) or bus 1 from Turku city center (9mk). From there, the Viking and Silja Line ferries ply to Mariehamn in the Åland Islands and beyond to Stockholm (see **Getting There,** p. 266).

Boisterous and amicable, the **Turun Kaupungin Retkeilymaja (HI),** Linnankatu 39 (tel. (02) 231 65 78; fax 231 17 08), is midway between the ferry terminals and the train station. From the station walk west three to four blocks on Ratapihankatu, take a left on Puistokatu to the river, and make a right on Linnankatu, or walk 20 minutes up Linnankatu from the ferry. (Dorms 45mk, nonmembers 60mk; doubles 65mk, nonmembers 80mk. Free laundry.) For immaculate singles (180mk) and doubles (280mk), as well as impeccable hospitality, stay at **St. Birgitta's Convent Guest-house,** Ursininkatu 15A (tel. (02) 250 19 10; reception open daily 8am-9pm; limited kitchen facilities). Nearby, **Matkustaja-Koti Turisti-Aula,** Käsityöläiskatu 11 (tel. (02) 233 44 84), offers 150mk singles and 210mk doubles (reception open 24hr.). **Ruissalo Camping** (tel. (02) 58 92 49) comes with sauna, water slide, and nude beach; take bus 8 (2 per hr., 9mk) from the *Kauppatori* (camping 30mk, families 60mk; open June-Aug.). **Ruissalo Island,** with access to a 20km nature trail, forests, sunbathing, and boat rentals at Saaronniemi Beach, also makes a refreshing daytrip.

Find groceries at **Kauppatori** (Market Square) or walk southwest on Eerikinkatu to the red-brick **Kauppahalli** (Market Hall) for pricey pastries (both closed Sun.) The bakery of **V Supermarket,** Eerikinkatu 19, may be more affordable (open Mon.-Fri 9am-8pm, Sat. 9am-6pm). **Tolmuset,** Hämeenkatu 8, practically gives away hearty meals (22mk daily special; open Mon.-Fri. 7:30am-5pm). **Verso,** upstairs at Linnankatu 3, is a veggie bistro extraordinaire (lunches until 2pm, 34mk;10% student discount; open Mon.-Sat. 11am-5pm). Festive Turku swims in cafés and riverside beer gardens. The hip **Downtown,** 17 Linnankatu, is a nightclub with live music and stamina (open Sun.-Tues. 4pm-4am, Fri.-Sat. 4pm-8am; cover Fri.-Sat. 20mk). **Club 57,** Eerikinkatu 12, and **Cantina West,** Avrakatu 5, join forces during the summer to draw in customers for wild dancing (open Wed. and Fri.-Sat. 10 or 11pm-4am).

■ Near Turku: Naantali (Nådendal)

Naantali, a peaceful enclave of old wooden houses 15km west of Turku, bills itself as the "sunshine town." The town and harbor are scenic, but the hordes of vacationing Finnish families put a strain on Naantali's serenity and make accommodations scarce. The buildings of the **Old Town,** some dating back to the late 18th century, are located south of the **Convent Church,** built in 1462 (open June-Aug. daily noon-6pm; Sept.-May noon-3pm). Try to catch a glimpse of Finland's president lounging in his fortress-like summer home, **Kultaranta,** visible from Naantali's harbor. The tourist office offers daily guided tours of Kultaranta. (By boat from the guest harbor 10am, 45mk. By bus from the tourist office 1pm, 45mk. At the main gate 3pm, 30mk.) Even if you've never read *Finn Family Moomintroll,* you can recapture your youth at

Naked Northerners

True to the stories, the sauna is an integral part of almost every Finn's life. More than simply a place to cleanse oneself thoroughly after a shower, saunas have evolved an entire mystique and are immortalized in *Kalevala,* the Finnish national epic. They are associated with cleanliness, strength, and endurance. The country now boasts over 1.5 million saunas, or one for every 3 people. Modern saunas are found in every hotel, most hostels, and many campgrounds. These wooden rooms reach temperatures around 100°C, so hot that no metal parts may be exposed, or the bathers will be burned. Water thrown on heated stones brings humidity to 100%. Finland's electricity use skyrockets on Friday and Saturday evenings, when hundreds of thousands of saunas are heated.

Moomin Valley, a harborside fantasy land (open Midsummer to mid-Aug. daily 10am-8pm; 80mk, kids 50mk). Mini-trains chug around Naantali daily from Moomin Valley (10mk or free with a Moomin Valley admit ticket). For more info check out the **Moomin shop,** Mannerheiminkatu 21 (tel. (02) 436 51 00; fax 435 61 10), in the center of town. Be warned that on **Sleepyhead Day** (July 27), the residents of Naantali get up at 6am and wake anyone still sleeping. Dressed in carnival costumes, they proceed to crown the year's Sleepyhead and throw him or her into the harbor.

Bus 11 runs to Naantali from the marketplace in Turku every five to 15 minutes (less frequently on weekends, 25min., 15mk). Some buses also pick up at the train station. The helpful **tourist office,** Kaivotori 2 (tel. (02) 435 08 50; fax 435 08 52; http://www.travel.fi/naantali), can book accommodations and arrange tours. From the bus station walk southwest on Tullikatu to Kaivokatu, then go right 300m; the tourist office is on your left (open June to mid-Aug. daily 9am-6pm; mid-Aug. to May Mon.-Fri. 9am-4pm). For tourist info, call the 24-hour hotline (tel. 0600 921 10). There are no youth hostels, but **Naantali camping** (tel. (02) 435 0855; fax 435 46 56), 500m south of town, maintains small huts (180-210mk) and tent sites (40mk per person; open June to mid-Aug.). Another option is the **Spa Hotel,** Opintie 3 (tel. (02) 445 56 60), which has dormitory type rooms (180mk; breakfast, sauna, and pool use included). The best local bargain resides at **Naantalin Klsa,** Tullikatu 6, with its enticing buffet and lovely terrace (43mk; open daily 11am-6pm).

Lahti

Located at the southern tip of the Lake District, Lahti will give you a taste of what lies north: scenic lakeside vistas, an active marketplace, and pleasant bars and pubs, all combined in a modern if uninspired city center. At its prime in the winter, Lahti is no less active in summer. The **Lahti Sports Center** has hosted the Nordic World Ski Championships five times since 1928 and is a candidate for 2001 (open Mon.-Thurs. 6:30am-8pm, Fri. 10am-8pm, Sat.-Sun. 10am-5pm). The **Ski Museum** at the Sports Center has a rather nifty ski-jump simulator (open Mon.-Fri. 10am-5pm, Sat.-Sun. 11am-5pm; 20mk, students 10mk). From the complex radiate 150km of trails through hills cut during the ice age. If you can't get enough of Aalto architecture, visit the towering, macabre **Church of the Cross,** Kirkkokatu 4 (open daily 10am-3pm). Cruise boats go to Jyväskylä at 10am from the passenger dock (207mk).

Lahti serves as a transportation center. **Buses** depart for Jyväskylä (3hr., 110mk) and Savonlinna (4hr., 70mk). **Trains** chug to Helsinki (1½hr., 58mk), Tampere (2hr., 84mk), Jyväskylä (138mk), Savonlinna (76mk), and St. Petersburg, Russia (6hr., 218mk). The **tourist office,** Torikatu 3B (tel. (03) 818 45 68 fax 814 45 64), has transportation and city info. (Open June-Aug. Mon. 8am-6pm, Tues.-Fri. 8am-5pm, Sat. 9am-2pm; Sept.-May Mon. 8am-5pm, Tues.-Fri. 8am-4pm.) A short walk from the train station lies the **Lahti Folk High School Hostel (Lahden Kansanopisto),** Harjukatu 46 (tel. (03) 752 33 44; fax 752 33 22). From the station, go north on Vesijärvenkatu one block and then right on Harjukatu. (Dorms 65mk, nonmembers 80mk; singles 130mk; doubles 95mk. Open June 3-Aug. 15.) On the side of the tracks away from city center is the **Kapungin Retkeilmaja Hostel,** Kirkikatu 1 (tel. (03) 782 63 24; 55mk, nonmembers 70mk). There's a **campground** at the **Mukkula Tourist Center** (tel. (03) 30 67 30; 8mk, tents 40mk; open June-Aug.), accessible by bus 30. **Bellmanni,** Kauppakatu 9, has cheap eats for lunch (25mk) and dinner (25-75mk). **K-Market** on the corner of Vapaudenkatu and Vesijärvenkatu has the usual market fare. For nightlife check out **Open House** in Hotelli Cumulus, Vapaudenkatu 24 (open 9pm-4am), or sample a beer at **Teerenpeli,** Vapaudenkatu 16 (open noon-2am).

Lappeenranta

Lappeenranta was built in the 1600s around a harbor which still thrives today. First ruled by the Swedes, then the Russians, the town's rich culture is reflected in the architecture and the many museums of the old town. A 10-minute walk from the train station up Kauppakatu brings you to **Linnoitus** (the old town) which sits on a small hill. The area has been restored, and the only indicators of the present time are the cafés, museums, and shops occupying the old wood and buildings which once made up the Russian **fortress.** The **South Karelian Museum,** in the fortress at Kristiinankatu 15, has a scale model of the fortress and collections from Vyborg, Russia. Also in the fortress, the **South Karelian Art Museum,** Kristiinankatu 8-10, in the yellow barracks, displays Finnish art along with a small postmodern collection. (Both museums open June-Aug. Mon.-Fri. 10am-6pm, Sat.-Sun. 11am-5pm; Sept.-May Tues.-Thurs., Sat.-Sun. 11am-5pm. 20mk ticket good for all museums in the fortress.) The fortress's **Russian Orthodox Church,** built in 1785, is the oldest in Finland (open Tues.-Sun. noon-4:30pm; free). A Russian serf-turned-merchant family built the **Wolkoff house,** Kauppakatu 26, in 1870, now beautifully decorated with Russian relics. (Open June-Aug. Mon.-Sat. 11am-4pm; Sept.-May Tues.-Thurs. 11am-3pm, Sat.-Sun. 11am-5pm.) Frequent **cruises** navigate the eight locks of the 43km Saimaa canal to Vyborg in Russia; the *M/S Carelia* offers a visa-free trip to Russia for 110mk. Contact the tourist office for info on this and shorter trips. **Karelia Lines** (tel. (05) 453 03 80) operates cruises in the area.

The **tourist office** (tel. (05) 66 77 88) is on Kauppakatu in the bus station (open June-Aug. Mon.-Fri. 9am-6pm; off-season Mon.-Fri. 9:30am-5:30pm). A second tourist office is located by the harbor (open June 2-Aug. 31). Daily **trains** run to St. Petersburg (4hr.), Helsinki (6 per day, 3hr., 130mk), and Savonlinna (5 per day, 2hr., 76mk). Of the two hostels, **Huhtiniemi,** Kuusimäenkatu 18 (tel. (05) 453 18 88), is closer to the town, situated near the water. Take bus 5 or 6 from Valtakatu. (Call ahead in winter. Dorms 40mk, nonmembers 55mk; singles 210mk; doubles 240mk. Camping 75mk.) **Pizza pojat,** Kauppakatu 33, has salads (25mk), lasagne (30mk), and pizza (27-39mk; open Mon.-Sat. 11am-10pm, Sun. noon-10pm). One of the town's many **grocery stores** sits at Kauppakatu 31 (open Mon.-Fri. 9am-9pm, Sat. 9am-6pm).

LAKE DISTRICT

Savonlinna

The tsarist aristocracy turned Savonlinna's sandy beaches and numerous harbors into a fashionable resort 150 years ago, and travelers today come here for the laid-back waterside atmosphere and for the many scenic vestiges of Finland's turbulent history scattered across this part of the Lake District. Go east from the bus and train stations on Olavinkatu and cross the bridge, then hug Linnankatu along the south shore until you reach **Olavinlinna Castle,** a weatherworn medieval fortress, where you can tour the steep defense passages and winding stairways. (Open June to mid-Aug. daily 10am-5pm; mid-Aug. to May 10am-3pm. 25mk, students 15mk.) For peaceful bathing, cross the footbridges north to the pine-covered isle of **Sulosaari.** During the magnificent **Opera Festival** (July 4-Aug. 2 in 1998), divas come from all over the world to perform in the courtyard of the castle. Tickets (300-500mk) should be ordered as early as October. Write to Savonlinna Opera Festival, Olavinkatu 27, SF-57130 Savonlinna (tel. (015) 47 67 50; fax 53 18 66), or contact the tourist office (see below). The few unclaimed tickets are often sold at the ticket booth on Tallisaari (before the castle) at 5pm the day of the show, but individual scalpers often charge less.

Savonlinna is yours by **train** from Helsinki (5 per day, 5hr., 170mk) or **bus** from Pieksämäki (2 per day, 2hr., 57mk) or Kuopio (3 per day, 2½ hr., 88mk, railpass not valid). Most trains to Savonlinna stop at Retretti if you ask; during July, **express trains** shuttle between the city and caves (30min., 20mk, students 10mk, railpasses valid). Once in Savonlinna, the train stops first at Savonlinna-Kauppatori in the center of town and near the tourist office and all lodging, then continues to the Savonlinna stop by the out-of-the-way main train station. **Water travel** provides the best access to the pristine lake regions; vessels cruise between Savonlinna and Kuopio (Tues.-Sun. 9:30am, 11½hr, 280mk). Daily cruises leave from the harbor on the **M/S Timppa** (11:30am, 1:30, 3:30, and 6pm, 30mk) and the **M/S Timppa 2** (9, 11am, 1, 3, and 7pm, 30mk). The friendly **tourist office,** across the bridge from the market at Puistokatu 1 (tel. (015) 27 34 92; fax 51 44 49), will help you find accommodations (reservations 50mk) and changes money when banks are closed (open June and Aug. daily 8am-6pm; July 8am-10pm; Sept.-May Mon.-Fri. 9am-4pm). Despite its location behind the casino, **Vuorilinna Hostel (HI),** Kylpylaitoksentie (tel. (015) 739 54 94), snoozes peacefully on the island 200m across the footbridge from the market. (Reception open June-Aug. daily 7am-11pm. 95mk, nonmembers 115mk. Call ahead.) **Retkeilymaja Malakias (HI),** Pihlajavedenkuja 6 (tel. (015) 232 83), is 1.5km from town. Going up Tulliportinkatu, veer right on Savonkatu, or take bus 1, 2, 3, or 4 (90mk, nonmembers 115mk; kitchen). **Vuohimäki Camping** (tel. (015) 53 73 53) is 7km out of town, but bus 3 runs there twice every hour (33-75mk per person; open early June-late Aug.). Eating and imbibing center on **Olavinkatu.** For lunch, try **Steakhouse San Martin,** Olavinkatu 46. (Salads 28mk; lunch special 28-32mk. Open Mon.-Fri. 11am-9pm, Sat.-Sun. 10am-6pm.) Across Olavinkatu from the market, visitors throw back a few beers at **Happy Time Pub,** Kauppatori 1.

■ Near Savonlinna

The stretch of land and water between Savonlinna and Kuopio includes many worthwhile stops. At the handsome **Valamo Monastery** (tel. (017) 57 01 11), 35km from Heinävesi along the Savonlinna-Kuopio boat route, guests often outnumber monks 20 to one. Take the bus to Heinävesi (100mk) and then the bus to the monastery (30mk). You can stay in the guest house (100mk, breakfast included), and chow at the restaurant (50-60mk). The largest wood church in the world in **Kerimäki,** 24km east of Savonlinna, seats over 3000 people (open Sun.-Fri. 9am-8pm, Sat. 9am-6pm; bus 20mk; church free). A more worldly retreat is **Rauhalinna,** a wooden palace built in the 19th century by a Russian commander for his wife. Cruises to this elegant island leave the market square in Savonlinna daily (30min., 30mk round-trip; open summer Mon.-Sat. 11am-6pm, Sun. 11am-4pm). The 130 islands of the **Linnansaari National Park,** about 50km from Savonlinna, are best seen by canoe; rent them at **Holiday Village Järvisydän** (tel. (015) 44 09 99). Contact the **Forest and Park Service,** P.O. Box 28, SF- 57131, Savonlinna (tel. (015) 57 68 10), to find out about the cooking facilities, camping sites, and huts (4 people 100mk) throughout the park. To get to the park take the bus from Savonlinna to Rantasalmi (25mk) then walk the 4km to the dock; boats go to the park (80mk).

Tampere

When, in 1820, Scotsman James Finlayson harnessed the power of the nearby Tammerkoski rapids for a textile mill, he transformed the provincial town into the country's most industrialized city. Today, though, machines and factories are no longer the centerpieces of "the Manchester of Finland," and the city's energetic nightlife, collection of museums, and pleasant beaches make it well worth a short stay.

Amuri Museum, Makasiininkatu 12, has a fascinating showcase of 25 representative living quarters spanning 1873 to 1973. (Open early May to mid-Sept. Tues.-Fri. 9am-5pm, Sat.-Sun. 11am-6pm. 15mk, students 5mk.) The proletarian spirit burns brightly at the **Lenin Museum,** Hämeenpuisto 28, 3rd floor, established and still managed by the **Finnish-Soviet Friendship Society** also at Hämeenpuisto 28, site of the first conference of Lenin's revolutionary party. It was here that Lenin and Stalin fatefully met (open Mon.-Fri. 9am-5pm, Sat.-Sun. 11am-4pm; 15mk, students 5mk). Round off your Socialist tour with exhibitions on the history of workers' movements at the **Central Museum of Labour in Finland,** Kuninkaankatu 3 (open Tues.-Sun. 11am-6pm; 10mk). Take bus 27 (9mk) to climb up the world's highest *esker* (a glacier-formed ridge) at **Pyynikki** park and catch a view of both Näsijärvi lake and Pyhäjärvi lake from the observation tower (3mk). The **Dammenberg Chocolate Factory,** Multisillankatu 1 (tel. (03) 367 00 80), gives tours. Tampere's **Short Film Festival** (March 4-8 in 1997), featuring contestants from 30 countries (tel. (03) 219 61 49), is rivaled in urbanity only by the **International Theater Festival** (Aug. 11-16 in 1997; tickets 40-80mk; tel. (03) 219 69 58).

The nearby coastal town of **Pori** comes alive during the famous **Pori Jazz Festival** in mid-July (tentatively July 11-19 in 1998), when Bourbon Street is recreated. Cafés, street musicians, and a few free concerts fuel the fun for the masses of people who book rooms a year in advance (tickets 30-240mk; call (02) 550 55 50).

Practical Information, Accommodations, and Food The **tourist office,** Verkatehtaankatu 2 (tel. (03) 212 66 52; fax 219 64 63), is exceptionally helpful and busy. From the train station, walk up Hämeenkatu, turn left just before the bridge, and look for the sign. The office offers two-hour guided tours of Tampere for 40mk, departing at 2pm. (Open June-Aug. Mon.-Fri. 8:30am-8pm, Sat. 8:30am-6pm, Sun. 11am-6pm; Sept.-May Mon.-Fri. 8:30am-5pm.) **Trains** head south to Helsinki (9 per day, 2hr., 84mk) and Turku (7 per day, 2hr., 76mk), and north to Oulu (6 per day, 5hr., 192mk). **Steamers** sail to Ruovesi (Tues., Thurs., and Sat., 4½hr., 164mk) and beyond to Virrat (7½hr., 222mk). For a return trip, your best bet is a package tour that includes traveling one way by bus (Ruovesi 230mk, Virrat 310mk), which leaves from Mustalanti near the amusement park. For info, call (03) 212 48 04.

When you become alienated by the tourism industry, find respite with the masses at the **Domus hostel (HI),** Pellervonkatu 9 (tel. (03) 255 00 00; fax 317 12 00), 2km east of the train station, where every room comes equipped with kitchenette and bathroom (but only one key). The hostel also offers a free sauna, indoor pool (both open daily 7am-10pm), laundry room, and bike rental. From the train station, follow Itsenäisyydenkatu and Sammonkatu and turn left onto Joukahaisenkatu, or take bus 25. (Reception open 24hr. Dorms 60mk, nonmembers 75mk; singles 215mk; doubles 290mk. Open June-Aug.) The alternative is the stark but well-situated **Tampeeren NNKY (YWCA),** Tuomiokirkonkatu 12 (tel. (03) 254 40 20; fax 254 40 22), a block from the train station. (Dorms 55mk; singles 105mk; doubles 90mk. Nonmembers add 15mk. Open June-late Aug.) Five kilometers southwest, **Camping Härmälä** (tel. (03) 265 13 55) overlooks Lake Pyhäjärvi (tents 70-75mk; open mid-May to late Aug.).

Sample *mustamakkara,* a Tampere sausage made with flour and cow's blood, at **Kauppahalli** (Market Hall), Hämeenkatu 19 (open Mon.-Thurs. 8am-5pm, Fri. 8am-5:30pm, Sat. 8am-3pm). At **Kaks Mattia,** Ilmarinkatu 16, load a plate to your heart's content (40mk; open Mon.-Fri. 7am-5pm), or head to **Myllärit,** Åkerlundinkatu 4, for a 40mk all-you-can-eat buffet lunch, served until 2pm (open Mon. 11am-4pm, Tues.-Fri. 11am-midnight, Sat. noon-midnight). A **RIMI supermarket** is located off the main street on Tuomiokirkonkatu 12 (open Mon.-Fri. 8am-8pm, Sat. 8am-6pm). **Papaan Kapakka,** Koskikatu 10, across from the tourist office, has live jazz nightly starting around 9pm (no cover; open Mon.-Sat. noon-2am, Sun. noon-midnight). **Doris,** Aleksanterinkatu 20, is a popular rock club (open daily 10pm-4am), and the **L.A. Garage** offers a lively disco scene (open Tues.-Fri. 9pm-3am). **Mixei,** Otavalankatu 3, becomes a gay disco Friday and Saturday nights from 10pm to 4am.

Jyväskylä

The capital of Finland's lake district, Jyväskylä (YOO-ves-kill-eh) is famous as the home of architect Alvar Aalto. If you like his work, this town's for you. The compact and modern city is sprinkled liberally with buildings designed by Aalto; if you can't pick them out yourself, pick up the guide (10mk) or free map at the **tourist office,** Asemakatu 6 (tel. (014) 62 49 03; fax 21 43 93; email matkailu@jkl.fi), one block up from the train station. (Open June-Aug. Mon.-Fri. 8am-5pm, Sat.-Sun. 9am-4pm; Sept.-May Mon.-Fri. 9am-5pm.) Jyväskylä's museums are all open until 9pm on Wednesdays and are free for students. The **Alvar Aalto Museum,** Alvar Aallon Katu 7, follows the development of his style through furniture, photographs, plans, and models (open Tues.-Sun. 11am-6pm; 10mk, Fri. free). Nearby, the **University of Jyväskylä,** largely designed by you-know-who, occupies an isolated campus in piney woods and lilacs near the museum. The unique **Finnish National Costume Center,** Gummeruksenkatu 3E, displays a changing selection of national costumes that have nothing whatsoever to do with Aalto (open Tues.-Sun. 11am-6pm; 10mk, Fri. free). Jyväskylä keeps a late schedule; many buildings don't open until 11am. Stay out late and sleep in.

In June, Jyväskylä hosts an **arts festival,** with concerts, film screenings, and exhibitions (tel. (014) 62 43 78; fax 21 48 08; tickets 30-110mk; student discounts 25-50%). Two-hour **cruises** on **Lake Päijänne** run 55mk (departing Tues.-Sun. 11:30am and 3pm); the **Blue and White Line** offers more elaborate cruises (June-Aug. 20 Wed.-Sat. leave from the dock 8pm; 70mk). Cruises also sail to and from Lahti (10hr., 207mk).

Trains arrive from Tampere (8 per day, 2hr., 75mk) and Helsinki (8 per day, 3½hr., 140mk), while **buses** arrive from several Lake District towns. Sporty **Laajari (HI),** Laajavuorentie 15 (tel. (014) 25 33 55), has a ski slope with a great view and a free sauna in the basement; take bus 25 (10mk) from stop 6 (reception open daily 6am-3am; dorms 65mk, nonmembers 80mk). Lakeside **Tuomiojärvi Camping** (tel. (014) 62 48 95), 2km north of town, is accessible by bus 8, 22, or 27 (38mk per person, 4-person cabins 200mk; open June-Aug.). **Amarillo,** Puistokatu 2, boasts Tex-Mex delights. (Salads 30-47mk; BBQ57mk; beer 22mk. Open Mon.-Thurs. 10:30-2am, Fri.-Sat. 10:30-3am, Sun. noon-1am.) On Kauppakatu, drop by **Hemingway's** and, staggering out at daybreak, observe that the sun also rises in Jyväskylä (open Mon.-Thurs. 3pm-2am, Fri.-Sat. 3pm-3am). **Club 73,** Vapaudenkatu has a lively disco (open Tues.-Thurs. 11pm-4am, Fri.-Sat. 10pm-4am). For info on gay and lesbian nightlife contact **Pink Club,** Yliopistonkatu 26 (Wed. and Fri. 7-11pm; tel. 310 06 60; email pinkclub@seta.fi.; www.jyu.fi/~juhtolv/pink/).

Kuopio

With nine flea markets and 22 outdoor dining spots, Kuopio lures merchants from the west, chefs from the east, and tourists from all over. Located at the edge of Finland's northern tundra in the Lake District, Kuopio suffers seemingly endless winter darkness but rejoices under the midnight sun when it arrives. The festivities begin in late June when flamenco, bolero, ballet, modern, and Arabian dancers parade into the city for Kuopio's **Dance and Music Festival** (tel. (017) 282 15 41; fax 261 19 90; email kuopio.dance.festival@travel.fi; http://www.travel.fi/kuopiotanssiijasoi). While in Kuopio, don't miss the spectacular Russian icons and textiles at the seat of the archbishop, the **Orthodox Church Museum,** Karjalankatu 1. (Open May-Aug. Tues.-Sun. 10am-4pm; Sept.-April Mon.-Fri. noon-3pm, Sat.-Sun. noon-5pm. 20mk, students 10mk.) On Vajasalo Island, 5km from Passenger Harbor, the **Alahovi Berry Farm** (tel. (017) 362 11 29) produces sweet currant and strawberry wines and offers tours of its winery and samples of its wares (open June-Aug.10 Tues.-Sat. noon-10pm Sun. noon-5pm). Boats leave regularly from Passenger Harbor.

Consult the **tourist office,** Haapaniemenkatu 17 (tel. (017) 18 25 84; fax 261 35 38), on the corner of Market Square, for info on weekly events (open June-Aug. Mon.-Fri. 9am-6pm, Sat. 9am-4pm; Sept.-May Mon.-Fri. 9am-5pm). For enthusiastic help, maps, and brochures, look for tourist advisors dressed in green and white uniforms at the train station, harbor, market place, and at **Puijo,** a tower from which you can view the area (open daily 9am-9pm; 15mk). Kuopio is easily accessible by **train** from Rovaniemi (4 per day, 7hr., 228mk) and Oulu (4 per day, 4hr., 154mk) to the north, and Tampere (7 per day, 4hr., 144mk), Helsinki (9 per day, 5hr.,190mk), and Lahti (8 per day, 4hr.,146mk) to the south. **Hostelli Rauhalahti (HI),** Katiskaniementie 8 (tel. (017) 47 34 73; fax 47 34 70), is less accessible, requiring a long bus ride (100mk, nonmembers 115mk). A tourist bus (15mk) goes directly to the hostel; inquire at the tourist office. The summer hostel **Hermannin Salit** (tel. (017) 364 49 61), while cramped, is the cheapest stay in Kuopio. From the train station, go right on Asemakatu and then left on Haapaniemenkatu. Continue about 1km, veer left at the fork in the road, and turn left on Hermaninaukio (dorms 70mk, singles 120mk; sheets 15mk). **Kuopio Camping Rauhalahti,** Kiviniementie (tel. (017) 361 22 44), has modern facilities but no tent rental (spaces 40mk, cottages 130-260mk; open May-Sept.).

Locals frequent the **Antilla supermarket** in the market place on Puijonkatu, but you can also try **Lounas Veranta,** Savonkatu 17, on the second floor of a furniture store, for a 35mk all-you-can-eat buffet (open Mon.-Fri. 9am-5pm, Sat. 9am-2pm). **Pamukkale Kebab,** across from the marketplace at Puijorikatu 27, offers generous portions of *kebab* (30mk), Greek salad (20mk), and Turkish apple tea. **Amarillo Freetime Bar,** Kirjastokatu 10, serves pricey Tex-Mex and margaritas with a Finnish twist (open Mon.-Thurs. 11am-1am, Fri. 11am-2am, Sat. 11am-3am, Sun. noon-1am).

Kuhmo

The quiet city of Kuhmo near the Russian border draws travelers with its hiking opportunities and *rönttöset* (lingonberry pie). The beautiful paths along Lake Lammasjärvi are approachable from town near the **Arts Center,** Koulakatu 1 (tel. (86) 655 67 50 or 655 67 54; fax 655 67 58; call for a concert schedule). The modern facade of the Arts Center contrasts with the bucolic charm of Kuhmo's **Kalevalakylä Village,** a re-created traditional Finnish village (tel. (08) 655 45 00; fax 655 02 46). Within the complex are various museums. (Open June 6-August daily 9am-6pm. 50mk. 2hr. guided tours 10am, noon, and 3:30pm. 50mk.) To get there take the Lentïra bus (10mk) and ask the driver to drop you at Kalevalakylä Village (buses don't run on weekends). Even the most inexperienced hikers can enjoy the excellent trails around Kuhmo. Buses don't usually go to the trails, but a few are within walking distance. The 2.5km **Kämärä forestpath** winds its way through the hill Pönkävaara and is 10km from Kuhmo's center. Follow the road to Hukkajärvi and look for signs. The must-do12km **Elimyssalo path** meanders through swamps, spruce woods, and wildflowers and is part of the longer **UKK Reitti.** Both these paths begin at the Kuhmo sports center and are dotted with cabins (190mk); call for reservations (tel. (08) 655 04 95). For more hiking info, call the **Finnish Forest and Park Service** (tel. (08) 655 07 16) or the **Kuhmo Recreational Service** (tel. (08) 655 04 95). The **tourist office** (tel. (08) 655 63 82; fax 655 63 84),1km away from town on Kainuuntie after a right at the Shell station, has a few basic hiking maps and info on lodgings. (Open June-Aug. Mon.-Fri. 8am-6pm, Sat. 9am-4pm; Sept.-May Mon.-Fri. 8am-5pm.) Lodging is available in July in the dormitory of the Piilola School at the **Kuhmo Youth Hostel** on Kainuuntie (dorms 70mk, singles 150mk, doubles 90mk; sheets 30mk; sauna 15mk). From the bus station walk right on Koulukatu, then left on to Kainuuntie; it is on the block between Vienantie and Peuranpolku. The **Kuhmo Matkakievari KY Motel,** Vienantie 3 (tel. (08) 655 02 71) is open all year (singles 140-170mk, doubles 190-230mk). To get to the **Kalevala Camping Site** (tel. (08) 655 63 88, in winter 655 63 82; fax 655 63 84), go 4km from the center of town in the direction of Suomussalmi (2-person cabin 150mk; camping 65mk; sauna 60mk; boat rental 20mk per hour). **Lounas Kahvila,** Kainuuntie 85, has the *rönttöset* for 6mk (closed Sun.).

OSTROBOTHNIA

Oulu

A lively university city by Finnish standards, Oulu's flower-bordered streets and well-tended bike paths lend it a Mediterranean grace. See exotic flora in the twin glass pyramids of the **Botanical Gardens,** 7km north of the center along bus routes 4, 6, or 19 (Pyramids closed Sun. 11mk. Open-air gardens open in summer daily 8am-9pm; off-season 7am-5pm. Free.) **Nallikari,** Finland's Côte d'Azur, rims an island 5km northwest of town. Despite its tacky amusement park, the splendid beach is the best place in Northern Finland to enjoy the Bothnian waters. Take the hourly bus 5 (11mk) from Rotuaari in the center of town (11am-6pm). You can stay at nearby **Nallikari Camping** (tel. (08) 554 15 41; 40mk per person; 4-person cabins 320-350mk). Take bus 5 from Kajaanintie outside the hostel heading toward the center of the city.

All **trains** between north and south Finland pass through Oulu; four or five per day leave for Helsinki (240mk) and north to Rovaniemi (105mk). The **tourist office,** Torikatu 10 (tel. (08) 314 12 94), greets visitors with good-natured help. Take Hallituskatu, the broad avenue perpendicular to the train station, for six blocks, then go left on Torikatu (open Mon.-Fri. 9am-4pm). The **library** at Kaavlenväylä 3 has **Internet access** (open Mon.-Fri. 10am-8pm, Sat. 10am-3pm, Sun. noon-4pm). The homey **Välkkylä (HI),** Kajaanintie 36 (tel. (81) 311 80 60; fax 313 67 54), has inexpensive, spacious lodgings (85mk). For a quick bite, go south on Isokatu to the corner of Saaristonkatu, where you'll find **Fantasia,** with all-you-can-eat pizza and salad buffets for around 40mk (open Mon.-Fri. until 10pm, Sat.-Sun. 11pm). The dungeon-like club **45 Special,** Saaristonkatu 12, complete with iron bars and shackles, hosts Finnish bands (open daily 8pm-4am; cover Fri.-Sat. 15-20mk).

LAPLAND (LAPPI)

The sun never sets on Lapland during the pleasant two- to three-month summer. In winter the sun rises for only a few hours a day. Clear sky, moonlight, and white snow produce an eerie blue glow, and the green, red, and yellow streaks of the Northern Lights illuminate a surreal snowscape. In the south you'll find river rapids and whitefish. To the north lies 80km-long **Lake Inari** *(Inarijärvi)* and its countless islands; even farther north, the land rises with the steep tundra slopes of the **Teno River Valley. Skiing** is ideal from February to mid-May, with facilities and rental outlets at almost every tourist center (including **Ounasvaara,** near Rovaniemi). In summer, guides lead **hiking expeditions** from the same places; only experienced groups should undertake independent excursions. Hikers should plan their routes around the mountain huts run by the Finnish Youth Hostel Association. **Etiäinen** (tel. (960) 36 25 26), in Santa Claus's Village (see **Rovaniemi,** below), provides maps, hiking routes, and info about locations of huts and cabins (open July daily 9am-8pm; Aug. 9am-7pm; Sept.-May 10am-6pm). The **Finnish Forest and Park Service** also offers useful info (tel. 329 46 95; open Mon.-Fri.8am-4:15am). The **Ranua Wildlife Park,** one hour from Rovaniemi, has 3km of paths through areas of fenced-in Arctic elk, bears, and wolves (tel. 355 19 21; fax 355 10 34).

Rovaniemi

Tucked 8km south of the Arctic Circle, Rovaniemi is the capital of Finnish Lapland. As a farewell gesture, retreating Germans razed Rovaniemi to the ground in 1944. The city was rebuilt using blueprints conceived in the mind of our friend Aalto, who shaped the layout to resemble reindeer antlers. You can meet the elves and pet the reindeer at **Santa Claus's Village,** if you can fight your way through the hordes of eager tourists. A visit to the brand-new **Arktikum** center, Pohjoisranta 4, is a must; it houses the **Arctic Science Center,** with exhibits on life and culture in the north, as well as the **Provincial Museum of Lapland.** (Open May-June 10am-6pm; July-August 10am-8pm; Sept.-April Tues.-Sun. 10am-6pm. 40mk.)

Buses head to Kuusamo (2 per day, 2½hr., 100mk), Kilpisjärvi (1 per day, 6½hr., 200mk), Muonio (4 per day, 3½hr., 120mk), and north to Ivalo (5hr., 175mk), with connections to Norway. Travel to Sweden by **train** to Kemi, then by bus (railpasses valid) 25km west to the border town of **Tornio.** Some buses continue across the border into Haparanda, Sweden. If you choose that route, check out the Tornio **HI hostel** (tel. (9698) 48 16 82), at Kirkkokatu, 1.6km north of the Finnish customs post. (65mk, nonmembers 80mk). Rovaniemi is easily accessible by trains from Oulu (Helsinki-Rovaniemi 4 per day, 280mk), and by southbound buses from Inari, Muonio, Enontekiö, and Karasjok, Norway. **Finnair** (tel. 98 00 34 66) also flies from Helsinki (youth fare booked 1 week in advance 869mk round-trip).

The **tourist office** at Koskikatu 1 (tel. (016) 34 62 70; fax 342 46 50) dishes up a weekly events listing happily titled *Let's Go.* (Open June-Aug. Mon.-Fri. 8am-6pm, Sat.-Sun. 11:30am-4pm; Sept.-May Mon.-Fri. 8am-4pm.) From the train station, head right on Ratakatu and turn right on Hallituskatu. Follow Hallituskatu to Korkalonkatu, where you go left, then go right on Koskikatu and follow it to the river (about 15min. total). **Lapland Safaris,** Harrikatu 2-4 (tel. (016) 331 12 00), leads groups up the River Ounasjoki to a reindeer farm (6hr., 690mk) and offers cruises (155mk), mountain bike trips (3hr., 240mk), and hiking trips with huskies (3hr., 290mk). Rovaniemi's **HI youth hostel,** Hallituskatu 16 (tel. (016) 34 46 44), is friendly if spartan. Turn right from the station, go up the hill, following the main road, and turn right on Hallituskatu just after the bus station (85mk, nonmembers 100mk; cash only). Across the river from the town center sits **Ounasjoki Camping** (tel. (016) 34 53 04; 90mk; open June-Aug.). **Rinnemarket** is close to the station, with a huge selection of goodies (closed Sun.). The **Panimo and Pub,** Koskikatu 13, has a noisy crowd that starts drinking early (beer 20-30mk; open Sun.-Thurs. 11am-2am, Fri.-Sat. 11am-3am).

Northern Hiking Regions

Finland has preserved large sections of its northern wilderness by turning them into **national parks** which serve as ideal locations for hiking. The **Urho Kekkonen National Park** is one of the nicest areas. Located in northeastern Finland, it is accessible by bus from Rovaniemi or Ivalo. The hiking trail begins between these two cities with an info center at Kiilopää (one-way bus to Kiilopää 160mk). Main points of entry include **Vuotso** on the west side and **Tulppio** on the east. Contact the visitor center at Vuotso (tel. (016) 62 62 41) for more info. **Lemmenjoki National Park,** Finland's largest, is also a popular spot for hikers, and lies just west of Inari. Contact the park service of Ivalo (tel. (9697) 68 77 00) for news about transportation and services in the park. For accommodations in Ivalo try **Montelli Petsamo Hostel,** Petsamontie 16 (tel. (016) 66 11 06; fax 66 16 28; 120-150mk), or for north of Imari in Kaamanen try the **Jokitörmä Hostel,** Lomakylä (tel. (016) 67 27 25; fax 67 27 45; 100-125mk).

More commercial is **Kuusamo,** northeast of Oulu and accessible from there or Rovaniemi. Kuusamo includes the scenic **Oulanka National Park,** suitable for day hikes, and offers such attractions as superb fishing, whitewater rafting, rock climbing at **Ruoppivaara Fell,** and a water park. The Rukatunturi Fell in **Ruka,** one of the leading winter sports centers in Finland, is also the start and finish of the internationally famous 95km **Bear's Ring** hiking route. From the top of the fell (reached by chair lift or on foot), speed demons can shoot down Finland's longest summer toboggan slope (1001m). To get to Rukatunturi Fell take the daily bus from Rovaniemi to Kursamo. Call the Kuusamo **tourist office** (tel. (989) 850 29 10) for info.

France

US$1 = 6.19F (francs)	**1F = US$0.16**
CDN$1 = 4.52F	**1F = CDN$0.22**
UK£1 = 10.1F	**1F = UK£0.099**
IR£1 = 9F	**1F = IR£0.11**
AUS$1 = 4.6F	**1F = AUS$0.22**
NZ$1 = 4.02F	**1F = NZ$0.25**
SAR1 = 1.34F	**1F = SAR 0.75**
Country Code: 33	**International Dialing Prefix: 00**

Temple of culture, cuisine, cheese, and snobbery, France is an extraordinary mosaic of tiny villages, walled medieval cities, and sleazy ports, reigned by the crowded brilliance of Paris. The cliffs and fertile countryside of Normandy posed for the Impressionists and embrace an Anglo-American liberation, while Brittany and Corsica still cling to distinct cultural identities. The Loire Valley blossoms with the architecture of the French Renaissance, while the Alps illustrate the architecture of raw geological force. The Dordogne River Valley shelters 20,000-year-old cave paintings, while the Côte d'Azur is just too glorious for its own good.

Originally home to Neanderthal and Cro-Magnon peoples, France was then inhabited by the Gauls, a Celtic people who fell prey to decentralized turmoil after the fall of the Roman Empire. The coming of Charlemagne in the 8th century, and the feudal lords' consolidation of regions into the "nation" over the next several centuries initiated the spirit of French history: a series of seemingly impossible events that become, inevitably, *faits accomplis.* The Renaissance witnessed mushrooming châteaux in the Loire Valley under the care of François I, and the opulence crescendoed during the reign of Louis XIV, the Sun King. By 1789, the French citizens could no longer support such extravagance; the ensuing years of furious rabble-rousing and violence inspired later revolutions in France and across Europe. In the afterglow of the Revolution, Napoleon's armies gained mastery over Europe. Instability soon followed, however, and the 19th century saw France swap republic for monarchy, for republic, for empire, and for republic again. French and German armies ripped through the countryside in the Franco-Prussian War (1870-71) and both World Wars. Impressionists such as Monet and Renoir redefined painting, and after World War I Paris became the stomping ground of the Lost Generation. President Charles de Gaulle pursued his claims to French Greatness as the foremost public figure of the post-World War II era, and his words still ring in French ears. Today, although France's political scene is still rocky, the country holds its position as a leader in the cultural avant-garde, and its tourist industry, as always, is poised and waiting to receive.

For more detailed fact- and flavor-filled coverage, pick up a copy of *Let's Go: France 1998* or *Let's Go: Paris 1998.*

GETTING THERE AND GETTING AROUND

France does not require **visas** of U.S., Canadian, New Zealand, or EU citizens, but it does of South Africans and Australians (see **Government Information Offices,** p. 1).

The **Société Nationale de Chemins de Fer (SNCF)** manages one of Europe's most extensive rail networks. Timetables are complicated but well-organized, with color-designated periods. Blue periods have lower train traffic, usually Monday afternoon through Friday morning and Saturday afternoon to Sunday afternoon; white periods coincide with heavier train use (most other times). Point-to-point ticket prices vary according to the period. Train tickets are not valid for use until punched in the orange machine at the entrance to the platforms at the *gare* (train station). Seat **reservations,** recommended for international trips, are mandatory on EuroCity (EC), InterCity (IC), and TGV *(train à grande vitesse)* trains. All three require a ticket supplement (US$3-18; railpass holders exempt) and a reservation fee (US$2-3). The

SNCF's premier pass offering, the **France Railpass,** allows 3 days of travel within one month (first-class US$185, second-class US$145), with up to 6 additional days available (US$30 each), and must be bought outside France.

French **buses,** usually affordable, are useful for filling the gaps in the rail network. The bus station, usually near the train station, is called the *gare routière.* **Hitching** in France reportedly requires patience. **Allostop-Provoya** is a service that pairs drivers and riders. It charges 250F for eight trips within a two-year period, or 30-70F for individual trips depending on the distance traveled. Gas and tolls are extra. Their main office at 84, passage Brady, 75010 Paris (tel. within Paris 01 42 46 00 66, outside Paris 01 47 70 02 01), can give you the addresses of offices throughout the country. With a wealth of well-paved minor routes, French roads are terrific for **cycling.** Prime regions include the Loire Valley, Normandy, Provence, the Dordogne River Valley, Alsace-Lorraine, and Burgundy. SNCF's pamphlet *Guide du train et du vélo* offers details on bike-and-rail trips in France. Bike rentals run 100-200F per day; some train stations rent bikes and allow you to drop off at another station.

ESSENTIALS

The extensive French tourism support network revolves around **syndicats d'initiative** and **offices de tourisme** (in the smallest towns, the **Mairie,** the mayor's office, deals with tourist concerns), both of which *Let's Go* labels as "tourist office." Both will help you find accommodations, distribute maps, and suggest excursions to the countryside. The basic unit of currency in France is the franc, subdivided into 100 centimes and issued in both coins and paper notes.

Just about everything snoozes from noon to 2pm and closes on Sundays, and many provincial areas also shut down on Mondays. Museums close at least one day a week, usually Tuesday. The major national **holidays** are: January 1, Easter Monday (April 13 in 1998), Labor Day (May 1), Victory in Europe Day (May 8), Ascension Day (May 21), Whit Monday (June 1), Bastille Day (July 14), Assumption Day (Aug. 15), All Saints' Day (Nov. 1), Armistice Day (Nov. 11), and Christmas (Dec. 25).

Summer brings daytime highs of around 24°C to most of France, although it is cooler in the North and the Alps, and southern France basks in 32°C scorchers every summer. Winters are generally mild, with temperatures rarely dipping below freezing, although frequent rains will dampen more than just spirits.

In 1996 all phone numbers in France changed from eight digits to 10. Phone numbers in Paris and the Ile-de-France acquired an initial 01, in the northwest 02, in the northeast 03, in the southeast and Corsica 04, and in the southwest 05.

Communication To operate payphones, buy a *télécarte* (telephone card). Available at train stations, post offices and *tabacs,* they come in denominations of 41 and 98F. Phone numbers starting with 0 800 are toll-free; those starting with 08 charge high rates. To call collect, tell the operator *"en PCV"* (ahn-PAY-say-VAY). For **AT&T Direct,** dial 99 00 11; **MCI WorldPhone,** 00 00 19; **SprintExpress,** 19 00 87; **Canada Direct,** 19 00 16; **BT Direct,** 19 00 44; **South Africa Direct,** 00 00 27; **New Zealand Direct,** 19 00 64. Anywhere in France, dial 10 for an operator, 12 for directory assistance, and 00 33 11 for an international operator. In an **emergency,** dial 15 for **medical** assistance, 17 for **police,** and 18 for the **fire** department.

Contrary to popular opinion, even flailing efforts to speak French will be appreciated, especially in the countryside. Be lavish with your *Monsieurs, Madames,* and *Mademoiselles,* and greet people with a friendly *bonjour* (*bonsoir* after 6pm).

Yes/no	*Oui/Non*	wee/nohn
Hello	*Bonjour*	bohn-ZHOOR
Please/Thank you	*S'il vous plaît/Merci*	seel voo PLAY/mehr-SEE
Excuse me	*Excusez-moi*	ehks-KOO-ZAY MWAH
Do you speak English (sir, madam)?	*Parlez-vous anglais, (Monsieur, Madame)?*	PAHR-lay VOO zahn-GLAY (muh-SYUR, mah-DAHM)
I don't understand.	*Je ne comprend pas.*	ZHUH NUH kohm-PRAHN pah
I don't speak French.	*Je ne parle pas français.*	zhuh nuh PAHRL pah frahn-SAY
Where is/are...?	*Où est/sont...?*	oo ay/sohn
How much?	*Combien?*	kohm-BYEHN
I would like...	*Je voudrais...*	ZHUH voo-DRAY
I would like a room for one/two.	*Je voudrais une chambre simple/pour deux.*	ZHUH voo-DRAY oon SHAHM-bruh SAM-pluh/poor DEUH
Help!	*Au secour!*	OH suh-COOR

Accommodations and Camping Youth hostels *(auberges de jeunesse)* cover France, ranging from well-kept, centrally located castles to run-down barracks. Most are affiliated with HI and charge nonmembers slightly more. Hostels run 45-80F per person, with breakfast about 15F (usually not obligatory). The quality of **hotels** in France generally matches their standardized rating on the government scale of one to four stars. Expect to pay at least 105F for singles and 130F for doubles. Showers are usually not included and can run 10-25F. Inquire whether the breakfast or meals at the hotel are *obligatoire.* Breakfast (15-25F) usually means bread, jam, and coffee or hot chocolate. Make reservations (confirm with one night's deposit) in summer.

Campgrounds, plentiful in France, are also rated on a four-star system. The *Guide Officiel Camping/Caravaning* is available from the **Fédération Française de Camping et de Caravaning,** 78, rue de Rivoli, 75004 Paris (tel. 01 42 72 84 08). The **Club Alpin Français** maintains mountain huts in upland regions. Contact the office at 24, av. de Lumière, 75019 Paris (tel. 01 53 72 88 00; fax 01 42 02 24 18), for more information. Tourist offices list local *gîtes d'étape* (shelters inaccessible to motorists) and, in many rural areas, *campings à la ferme* (campsites on private farms).

Food and Drink French chefs cook for one of the most finicky clienteles in the world. Traditionally, the complete French dinner includes an *apéritif* (pre-dinner drink), an *entrée* (appetizer), a *plat* (main course), salad, cheese, dessert, fruits, coffee, and a *digestif* (after-dinner drink). The French generally take wine with their meals; *boisson comprise* entitles you to a free drink (usually wine) with your meal. For an occasional 90F spree you can have a marvelous meal.

In restaurants, fixed-price three-course meals (called *menus*) generally begin at 60F. Service is usually included *(service compris)*. Be careful when ordering *à la carte; l'addition* (the check) may exceed your weekly budget. Do as the French do: go from one specialty shop to another to assemble a picnic, or find an outdoor market *(marché)*. Cafés are a forum for long chats, but you pay for the right to sit and watch the world go by: drinks and food are often 10-30% more if served in the dining room *(salle)* or outside *(sur la terrasse)* rather than at the bar *(comptoir)*.

Boulangeries, pâtisseries, and *confiseries* tempt with bread, pastries, and candy, respectively. *Fromageries* and *crémeries* present an astonishing array of cheeses. *Charcuteries* sell meats. For supermarket shopping, look for **Carrefour, Casino, Monoprix, Prisunic, Stoc,** and **Rallye.** The many local markets *(marchés)* are picturesque, animated, and often offer better quality than supermarkets.

Paris

France is sometimes described as *Paris et la Province*—Paris and the provinces, Paris and everything else. Like New York or London, Paris is an island in its own land. Parisians talk faster and dress better than their compatriots, earning a cosmopolitan and loose reputation. The city monopolizes a quarter of France's manufacturing and the bulk of the country's luxury and service trades: fashion, higher education, banking, law, and government. And while the City of Lights may not fulfill every expectation—it is possible to go to Paris and not fall in love; you may not even finish your novel—let yourself be carried away. With attitude, you can get away with anything in Paris.

For dazzling, detailed, definitive coverage of the wonders of Paris and its environs, pick up a copy of *Let's Go: Paris 1998*.

ORIENTATION AND PRACTICAL INFORMATION

Coursing languidly from east to west, the Seine River forms the heart of Paris. Two small islands in the river, the **Ile de la Cité** and **Ile St-Louis,** form the geographical center of the city. The rest of Paris spreads onto the banks—the renowned **Rive Gauche** (Left Bank) to the south, and the **Rive Droite** (Right Bank) to the north. By the time of Louis XIV, the city had grown to 20 *quartiers;* Haussmann's 19th-century reconstructions shifted their boundaries but kept the number, dividing Paris into 20 *arrondissements* (districts) which spiral clockwise like a snail's shell around the **Louvre.** In the majority of *Let's Go* listings, the *arrondissement* is included; thus 8ème signifies the *huitième,* or eighth, *arrondissement. Arrondissements* correspond only roughly to the original neighborhoods. The Right Bank starts with the Louvre-Palais Royal area in the 1er; the northwest 2ème and southwest 9ème comprise the Opéra district. The Marais overlaps the 3ème and the 4ème, while Bastille encompasses the southern 11ème and the eastern 4ème. République refers to the northern 11ème and the western 3ème and 10ème; Montmartre is the 18ème. On the Left Bank, the Latin Quarter takes up the 5ème and 6ème; St-Germain-des-Prés is in the 6ème; and the Champ de Mars-Tour Eiffel area is the 7ème. For further detail, see the **Sights** section.

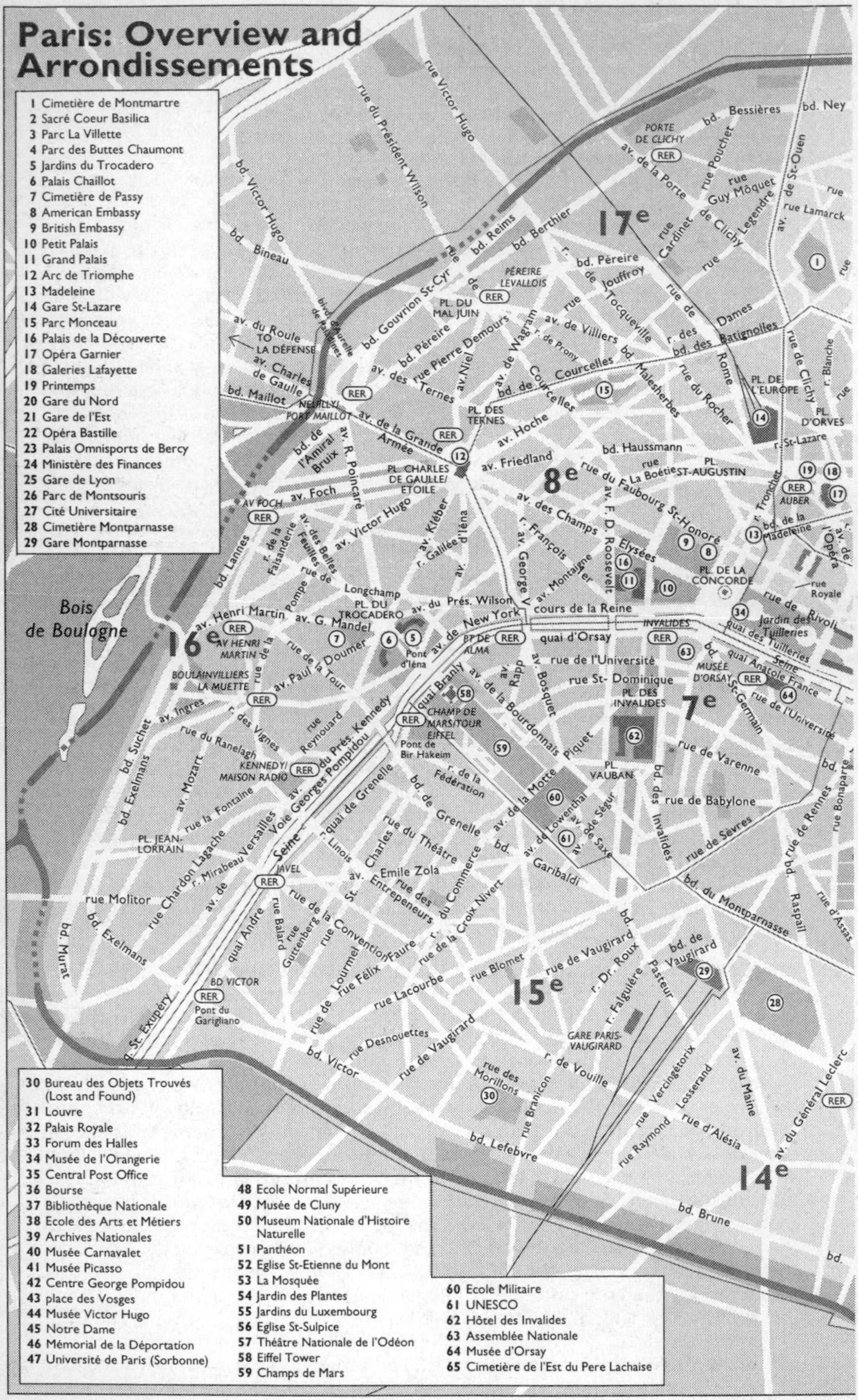
Paris: Overview and Arrondissements
1 Cimetière de Montmartre
2 Sacré Coeur Basilica
3 Parc La Villette
4 Parc des Buttes Chaumont
5 Jardins du Trocadero
6 Palais Chaillot
7 Cimetière de Passy
8 American Embassy
9 British Embassy
10 Petit Palais
11 Grand Palais
12 Arc de Triomphe
13 Madeleine
14 Gare St-Lazare
15 Parc Monceau
16 Palais de la Découverte
17 Opéra Garnier
18 Galeries Lafayette
19 Printemps
20 Gare du Nord
21 Gare de l'Est
22 Opéra Bastille
23 Palais Omnisports de Bercy
24 Ministère des Finances
25 Gare de Lyon
26 Parc de Montsouris
27 Cité Universitaire
28 Cimetière Montparnasse
29 Gare Montparnasse
30 Bureau des Objets Trouvés (Lost and Found)
31 Louvre
32 Palais Royale
33 Forum des Halles
34 Musée de l'Orangerie
35 Central Post Office
36 Bourse
37 Bibliothèque Nationale
38 Ecole des Arts et Métiers
39 Archives Nationales
40 Musée Carnavalet
41 Musée Picasso
42 Centre George Pompidou
43 place des Vosges
44 Musée Victor Hugo
45 Notre Dame
46 Mémorial de la Déportation
47 Université de Paris (Sorbonne)
48 Ecole Normal Supérieure
49 Musée de Cluny
50 Museum Nationale d'Histoire Naturelle
51 Panthéon
52 Eglise St-Etienne du Mont
53 La Mosquée
54 Jardin des Plantes
55 Jardins du Luxembourg
56 Eglise St-Sulpice
57 Théâtre Nationale de l'Odéon
58 Eiffel Tower
59 Champs de Mars
60 Ecole Militaire
61 UNESCO
62 Hôtel des Invalides
63 Assemblée Nationale
64 Musée d'Orsay
65 Cimetière de l'Est du Pere Lachaise
17e
8e
16e
7e
15e
14e
Bois de Boulogne
Seine
PORTE DE CLICHY
PÉREIRE LEVALLOIS
PL. DU MAL JUIN
NEUILLY/ PORT MAILLOT
PL. DES TERNES
PL. CHARLES DE GAULLE/ ETOILE
AV FOCH
PL. DU TROCADERO
AV HENRI MARTIN
BOULAINVILLIERS LA MUETTE
KENNEDY/ MAISON RADIO
PT DE ALMA
CHAMP DE MARS/TOUR EIFFEL
PL. DES INVALIDES
PL. VAUBAN
MUSÉE D'ORSAY
PL. DE LA CONCORDE
PL. ST-AUGUSTIN
PL. DE L'EUROPE
PL. D'ORVES
AUBER
INVALIDES
JAVEL
BD VICTOR
GARE PARIS-VAUGIRARD
PL. JEAN-LORRAIN
Pont d'Iéna
Pont de Bir Hakeim
Pont du Garigliano
TO LA DÉFENSE
RER
bd. Ney
bd. Bessières
bd. Berthier
bd. Péreire
bd. de Courcelles
bd. Haussmann
bd. Malesherbes
bd. des Batignolles
bd. Gouvion St-Cyr
bd. Victor Hugo
bd. Bineau
bd. Maillot
bd. Lannes
bd. Suchet
bd. Exelmans
bd. Murat
bd. de Grenelle
bd. Garibaldi
bd. du Montparnasse
bd. Raspail
bd. Pasteur
bd. de Vaugirard
bd. Victor
bd. Lefebvre
bd. Brune
av. Foch
av. Victor Hugo
av. Kléber
av. d'Iéna
av. de la Grande Armée
av. Friedland
av. Hoche
av. de Wagram
av. des Champs Elysées
av. Montaigne
av. F. D. Roosevelt
av. George V
av. Henri Martin
av. Paul Doumer
av. du Prés. Wilson
av. de New York
av. Rapp
av. Bosquet
av. de la Bourdonnais
av. de la Motte Piquet
av. de Suffren
av. Mozart
av. du Maine
av. du Général Leclerc
cours de la Reine
quai d'Orsay
quai Branly
quai de Grenelle
quai André Citroën
quai Anatole France
Voie Georges Pompidou
rue de Rivoli
rue du Faubourg St-Honoré
rue de l'Université
rue St-Dominique
rue de Varenne
rue de Babylone
rue de Sèvres
rue de Vaugirard
rue de la Convention
rue Lecourbe
rue Blomet
rue de Vouillé
rue d'Alésia
rue Molitor
rue du Ranelagh
rue de la Pompe
rue Lamarck
rue de Rome
rue du Rocher
rue de Clichy
rue Legendre
rue Guy Môquet
rue Cardinet
rue de Tocqueville
av. de Villiers
r. de Prony
rue Pierre Demours
av. Niel
av. de la Porte de Clichy
rue du Président Wilson
rue Victor Hugo
rue Royale
rue Tronchet
r. St-Lazare
Jardin des Tuilleries

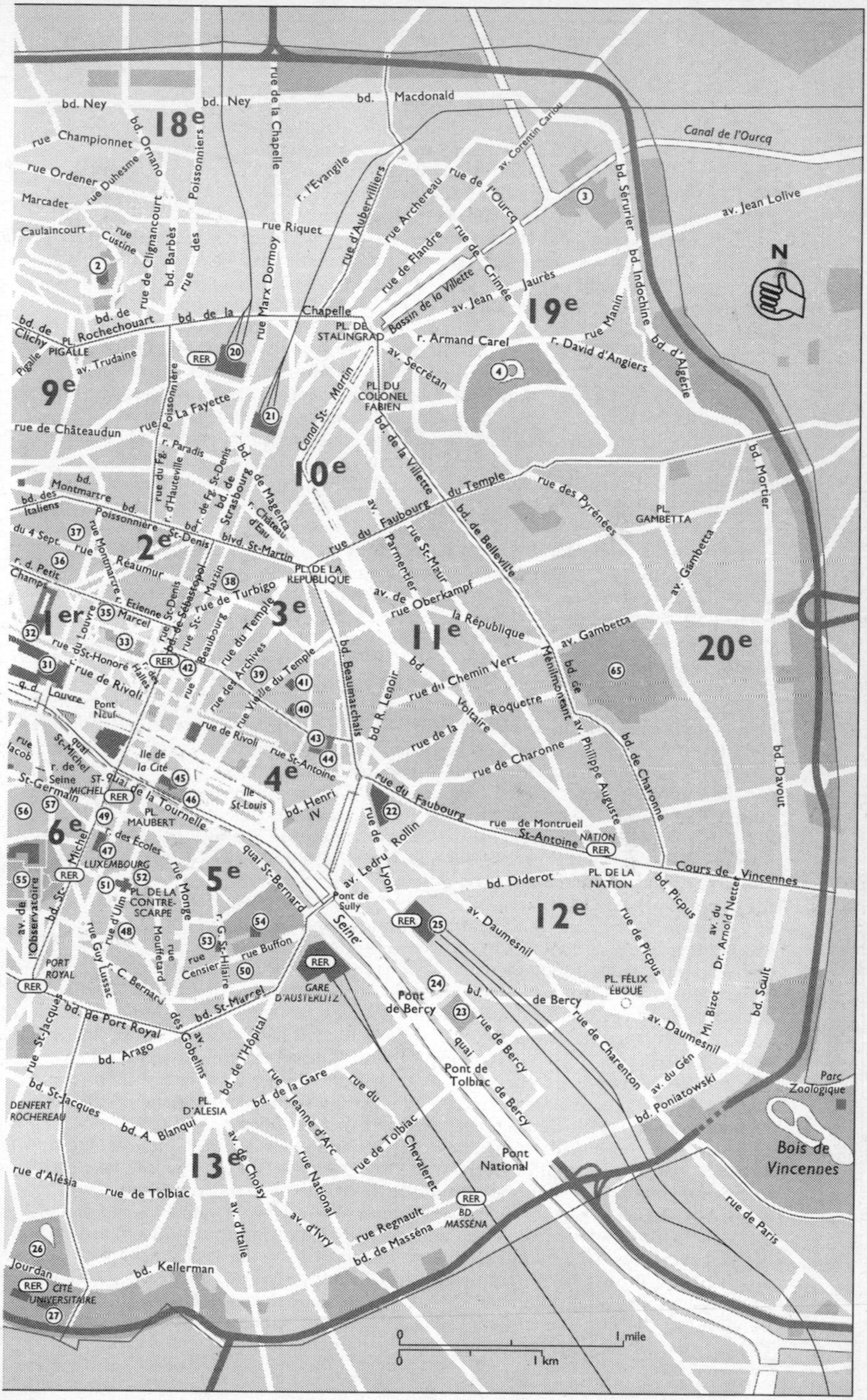

18e
19e
20e
9e
10e
2e
1er
3e
11e
4e
5e
6e
12e
13e
N
bd. Ney
bd. Macdonald
rue de la Chapelle
Canal de l'Ourcq
av. Corentin Cariou
rue Championnet
bd. Ornano
rue Ordener
rue Duhesme
rue des Poissonniers
rue Marcadet
rue Caulaincourt
rue Custine
bd. de Clignancourt
bd. Barbès
r. l'Evangile
rue d'Aubervilliers
rue Archereau
rue de l'Ourcq
bd. Sérurier
av. Jean Lolive
rue Riquet
rue Marx Dormoy
rue de Flandre
rue de Crimée
bd. Indochine
Bassin de la Villette
av. Jean Jaurès
bd. de la Chapelle
bd. de Rochechouart
bd. de Clichy
PL. PIGALLE
Pigalle
av. Trudaine
PL. DE STALINGRAD
r. Armand Carel
rue Manin
r. David d'Angiers
bd. d'Algérie
RER
av. Secrétan
Canal St-Martin
PL. DU COLONEL FABIEN
rue Poissonnière
rue La Fayette
rue de Châteaudun
r. Paradis
rue du Fg. Poissonnière
r. d'Hauteville
r. de Fg. St-Denis
bd. de Strasbourg
bd. de Magenta
r. Château d'Eau
bd. de la Villette
bd. Mortier
bd. Montmartre
bd. des Italiens
bd. Poissonnière
bd. St-Denis
blvd. St-Martin
rue du Faubourg du Temple
rue des Pyrénées
PL. GAMBETTA
av. Gambetta
rue du 4 Sept.
rue Montmartre
rue Réaumur
r. d. Petit Champs
bd. de Sébastopol
rue St-Denis
r. St-Martin
rue de Turbigo
PL. DE LA REPUBLIQUE
av. Parmentier
rue St-Maur
bd. de Belleville
rue Oberkampf
av. de la République
r. Etienne Marcel
rue du Louvre
rue Beaubourg
rue du Temple
rue des Archives
rue Vieille du Temple
rue St-Honoré
rue de Rivoli
r. des Halles
q. d. Louvre
Pont Neuf
bd. Beaumarchais
bd. R. Lenoir
bd. Voltaire
rue du Chemin Vert
rue de la Roquette
Ménilmontant
bd. de
av. Gambetta
rue Jacob
quai St-Michel
r. de Seine
St-Germain
ST-MICHEL
Ile de la Cité
Ile St-Louis
rue St-Antoine
rue de Charonne
av. Philippe Auguste
bd. de Charonne
bd. Davout
quai de la Tournelle
PL. MAUBERT
bd. Henri IV
rue du Faubourg St-Antoine
rue de Rollin
rue de Lyon
rue de Montreuil
NATION
r. des Écoles
LUXEMBOURG
rue Monge
quai St-Bernard
av. Ledru
bd. Diderot
PL. DE LA NATION
Cours de Vincennes
bd. Picpus
av. de l'Observatoire
bd. St-Michel
PL. DE LA CONTRE-SCARPE
Pont de Sully
Seine
av. Daumesnil
rue de Picpus
av. du Dr. Arnold Netter
rue d'Ulm
rue Mouffetard
r. G. St-Hilaire
rue Buffon
rue Censier
PORT ROYAL
rue Guy Lussac
r. C. Bernard
GARE D'AUSTERLITZ
Pont de Bercy
bd. de Bercy
PL. FÉLIX EBOUE
Mi. Bizot
bd. Soult
bd. St-Marcel
bd. de Port Royal
rue St-Jacques
av. des Gobelins
bd. de l'Hôpital
rue de Bercy
quai de Bercy
rue de Charenton
av. du Gén
bd. Poniatowski
bd. Arago
Pont de Tolbiac
Parc Zoologique
bd. St-Jacques
DENFERT ROCHEREAU
PL. D'ALESIA
bd. A. Blanqui
bd. de la Gare
rue Jeanne d'Arc
rue de Tolbiac
rue du Chevaleret
Pont National
Bois de Vincennes
rue d'Alésia
rue de Tolbiac
av. de Choisy
rue National
rue de Paris
av. d'Ivry
rue Regnault
bd. de Masséna
BD. MASSÉNA
av. d'Italie
Jourdan
bd. Kellerman
CITÉ UNIVERSITAIRE
1 mile
1 km

If you get lost while roaming around, remember that Paris metro stops usually have a detailed neighborhood map posted somewhere near the ticket counter.

Tourist Offices: Bureau d'Accueil Central, 127, av. des Champs-Elysées, 8ème (tel. 01 49 52 53 54). M: Charles-de-Gaulle-Etoile. English-speaking and mobbed in summer. Open April-Oct. daily 9am-8pm; Nov.-March Mon.-Sat. 9am-8pm, Sun. 11am-6pm. **Branches** at Gare du Nord (May-Oct.), Gare de Lyon (all year), and the Eiffel Tower (May-Sept.). **Tourist Information:** tel. 01 49 52 53 56 (English), 01 49 52 53 55 (French). Recorded list of the week's big events.

Budget Travel: Accueil des Jeunes en France (AJF), 119, rue St-Martin, 4ème (tel. 01 42 77 87 80), across from the Centre Pompidou. M: Rambuteau. Discount student plane, train, and bus tickets; also ISICs. Staff will book rooms in Paris hotels and hostels (10F fee; 115F per night). Open Mon.-Sat. 10am-6:45pm. Also at 139, bd. St-Michel, 5ème (tel. 01 43 54 95 86). M: Port-Royal. Open Mon.-Thurs. 10am-12:30pm and 1:45-6pm, Fri. 10:30am-12:30pm and 1:45-6pm. **Council Travel,** 16, rue de Vaugirard, 6ème (tel. 01 44 41 89 89). M: Odéon. 22, rue des Pyramides, 1er (tel. 01 44 55 55 65). M: Pyramides. English-speaking budget travel service for those under 26. Books international flights and student train tickets, as well as selling guidebooks, and ISICs. BIJ/Eurotrain tickets. Vaugirard and Pyramides branches both open Mon.-Fri. 9:45am-6:45pm, Sat. 10am-5pm.

Embassies and Consulates: Australia, 4, rue Jean-Rey, 15ème (tel. 01 40 59 33 00). M: Bir-Hakeim. Open Mon.-Fri. 9:15am-noon and 2-4:30pm. **Canada,** 35, av. Montaigne, 8ème (tel. 01 44 43 29 00). M: Franklin-Roosevelt or Alma-Marceau. Open Mon.-Fri. 9am-5pm. **Ireland,** 12, av. Foch, 16ème (tel. 01 44 17 67 00). M: Argentine. Open Mon.-Fri. 9:30am-noon. **New Zealand,** 7ter, rue Léonard-de-Vinci, 16ème (tel. 01 45 00 24 11). M: Victor-Hugo. Open Mon.-Fri. 9am-1pm. **South Africa,** 59, quai d'Orsay, 7ème (tel. 01 53 59 23 23). M: Invalides. Open Mon.-Fri. 9am-noon. **U.K.,** 35, rue du Faubourg-St-Honoré, 8ème (tel. 01 44 51 31 00). M: Concorde or Madeleine. **U.S.,** 2, av. Gabriel, 8ème (tel. 01 43 12 22 22), off pl. de la Concorde. M: Concorde. Open Mon.-Fri. 9am-6pm.

Currency Exchange: Hotels, train stations, and airports offer poor rates but have long hours; Gare de Lyon, Gare du Nord, and both airports are open from 6:30am until 10:30-11:30pm. MC and Visa work in most ATMs; check for stickers saying CB/VISA (Carte Bleue; for Visa) or EC (Eurocard; for MC). AmEx works in ATMs at **Crédit Lyonnais** banks. Cirrus cards work in **Crédit Mutuel** and **Crédit Agricole** ATMs. The PLUS system works in most Visa ATMs. Institutions supporting PLUS are: **Crédit Commercial de France, Banque Populaire, Union de Banque à Paris, Point Argent, Banque Nationale de Paris, Crédit du Nord, Gie Osiris,** and ATMs in many **post offices.**

American Express: 11, rue Scribe, 9ème (tel. 01 47 77 77 07), across from the back of the Opéra. M: Opéra or Auber. Middling rates, long lines. Receives moneygrams and holds mail for cardholders or those with AmEx Traveler's Cheques; otherwise 5F per inquiry. English spoken. Open Mon.-Fri. 9am-6:30pm, Sat. 9am-6:30pm.

Flights: Most transatlantic flights land at **Aéroport Roissy-Charles de Gaulle,** 23km northeast of Paris. As a rule, terminal 2 serves Air France and its affiliates (for 24hr. English language passenger info, call 01 48 62 22 80). The cheapest, fastest way to get to town is by public transportation. Roissy Rail runs to central Paris; take the free shuttle bus from Aérogare 1, gate 28; Aérogare 2A, gate 5; Aérogare 2B, gate 6; or Aérogare 2D, gate 6 to the Roissy train station, and ride the RER B3 to the city (45min., 45F includes transfer to metro). **Aéroport d'Orly** (tel. 01 49 75 15 15), 12km south of Paris, handles charters and many European flights. From Orly Sud, gate H or gate I, platform 1; or Orly Ouest, arrival level gate F, take the free shuttle bus to Orly train station and the RER C2 to central Paris (30min., 30F).

Trains: SNCF (get tickets through travel agencies). Guard your valuables and don't buy tickets from anyone except the uniformed personnel in the booths. **Gare du Nord** covers northern France, Belgium, Britain, the Netherlands, Scandinavia, much of the former USSR, and northern Germany. To: Brussels (2hr., 220F), Amsterdam (5hr., 366F), Cologne (5-6hr., 332F), Copenhagen (16hr., 1343F), and London (by the Eurostar chunnel, 2hr., 360-740F). **Gare de l'Est** for eastern France, Luxembourg, northern Switzerland, southern Germany, Austria, and Hungary. To Zurich (6hr., 412F). **Gare de Lyon** for southern France, parts of Switzerland, Italy, and Greece. To Geneva (3½hr., 498F) and Rome (12hr., 630F). **Gare d'Austerlitz** for the Loire Valley, southwestern France, Spain, and Portugal. To Barcelona (9hr., 600F) and Madrid (12-13hr., 600F). **Gare St-Lazare** for Normandy. To Rouen (1½hr., 102F). **Gare de Montparnasse** for Brittany and the TGV to southwestern France. All train stations are stops on metro lines.

Buses: Most international buses arrive at **Gare Routière Internationale,** 28, av. du Général de Gaulle, Bagnolet (tel. 01 49 72 51 51). M: Gallieni. **Hoverspeed Voyages** runs buses to England (reservations tel. 0800 90 17 77). Its Paris terminal is at 165, av. de Clichy, 17*ème* (tel. 01 40 25 22 00). M: Porte du Clichy.

Public Transportation: The Paris subway, **Métropolitain** or **Métro (M),** is speedy and efficient. Lines are numbered but referred to by their final destinations; connections are called *correspondences.* Tickets to anywhere within the city cost 8F; a *carnet* of 10 is 46F. Ticket windows close as early as 10pm, so keep extras. Special passes include the *Paris Visite* tourist ticket, which is valid for unlimited travel on bus, metro, and RER, and discounts on sightseeing trips, bicycle rentals, etc., but isn't worth it for most (70F for 2 days, 105F for 3 days, 165F for 5). *Formule 1* lasts one day and covers the metro, RER, and bus lines (30F). The weekly *(hebdomadaire)* **Coupon Vert** allows unlimited travel (starting on the first day of the week) but must be accompanied by the ID-style **Carte Orange.** To get your *carte orange,* bring an ID photo to the ticket counter and then buy your swanky *coupon vert* (63F). *Hold onto your ticket* until you exit the metro. If caught without one, you must pay a hefty fine. Changing to and getting *off* the **RER** (Réseau Express Régional—commuter train to the suburbs, express subway within central Paris) require sticking your validated (and uncrumpled) ticket into a turnstile. Watch the signboards next to the RER tracks and check that your stop is lit up before riding. Metro service runs roughly 5:30am-12:30am. The *Principes de Tarification* poster in the center of each station gives each line's last train. **Buses** use the same 8F tickets (which the driver sells), but tickets are only good for one ride and a transfer requires a new ticket. Validate tickets in the machine by the driver. Buses run 7am-8:30pm, *Autobus du Soir* until 12:30am, and *Noctambus* (3-4 tickets) run 1:30-5:30am to the *portes* (city exits) from the Châtelet stop.

Taxis: Cab stands are located near train stations and major bus stops. 3-person max. Taxis are pricey (13F plus 3F23-6F88 per km), and even pricier if you don't speak French and/or are an out-of-towner. The meter starts running when you call (tel. 01 47 39 47 39, 01 45 85 85 85, or 01 41 27 27 27)—i.e., before you're picked up.

Hitchhiking: Traffic at *portes* (city exits) is too heavy for cars to safely stop. **Allostop-Provoya,** 8, rue Rochambeau, 9*ème* (tel. 01 53 20 42 42). M: Cadet. Matches folks with drivers heading in the same direction. Geneva 177F. Frankfurt about 186F. Open Mon.-Fri. 9am-7:30pm, Sat. 9am-1pm and 2-6pm.

Lost Property: Bureau des Objets Trouvés, 36, rue des Morillons, 15*ème* (tel. 01 55 76 20 20). M: Convention. No info given by phone. Open July-Aug. Mon.-Thurs. 8:30am-5pm; Sept.-June Tues. and Thurs. also 5-8pm.

Bookstores: Shakespeare and Co., 37, rue de la Bûcherie, 5*ème*, across the Seine from Notre-Dame. M: St-Michel. No relation to Sylvia Beach's 20s bookstore (which first published James Joyce's *Ulysses*), but a quirky, wide-ranging selection of new and used books. Live poetry most Monday nights. Open daily noon-midnight. **Gibert Jeune,** 5, pl. St-Michel, 5*ème* (tel. 01 43 25 70 07). M: St-Michel. Best bookstore in town; books in all languages for all tastes. Open Mon.-Sat. 9:30am-7:30pm.

Gay and Lesbian Services: Centre Gai et Lesbien, 3, rue Keller, 11*ème* (tel. 01 43 57 21 47 or 01 43 57 75 95). M: Ledru Rollin. Info hub of all gay services and associations in Paris. English spoken. Open Mon.-Sat. noon-8pm, Sun. 2-7pm. **Les Mots à la Bouche,** 6, rue Ste-Croix-de-la-Bretonnerie, 4*ème* (tel. 01 42 78 88 30). M: St-Paul or Hôtel-de-Ville. A gay/lesbian bookstore (some English titles); lists current activities and events. Open Mon.-Sat. 11am-11pm, Sun. 2-8pm.

Public Baths: Beat the high cost of hotel showers at 8, rue des Deux Ponts, 4*ème* (tel. 01 43 54 47 40). M: Pont-Marie. Showers 7F50, with soap and towel around 16F. Clean and popular. Open Thurs. noon-7pm, Fri.-Sat. 8am-7pm, Sun. 8am-noon.

Crises: SOS Friendship (tel. 01 47 23 80 80). For depressed, lonely English-speakers. Open daily 3-11pm. **Rape: SOS Viol** (tel. 0 800 05 95 95). Call free anywhere in France for counseling (medical and legal, too). Open Mon.-Fri. 10am-6pm.

Pharmacy: Pharmacie Dhéry, 84, av. des Champs-Elysées, 8*ème* (tel. 01 45 62 02 41). M: George V. **Grande Pharmacie Daumesnil,** 6, pl. Félix-Eboué, 12*ème* (tel. 01 43 43 19 03). M: Daumesnil. Visible as you exit the metro. Both open 24hr.

Medical Assistance: Hôpital Franco-Britannique de Paris, 3, rue Barbès, in the suburb of Levallois-Perret (tel. 01 46 39 22 22). M: Anatole-France. English-speaking doctors of good repute. **Hôpital Americain,** 63, bd. Victor Hugo, Neuilly (tel. 01 46 41 25 25), also in the 'burbs. M: Porte Maillot, then bus 82 to the end of the line. More expensive. Blue Cross accepted; fill out the forms first. Dental service.

Emergency: Ambulance: tel. 15. **Fire:** tel. 18.

Police: tel. 17. There's a police station in every *arrondissement;* call the operator (tel. 12) to find the closest.

Internet Access: See **Café Orbital** and **Hammam Café** in **Cafés,** p. 301.

Post Office: 52, rue du Louvre, 1*er*. M: Châtelet-les-Halles. *Poste Restante.* Open daily 7:30am-6:30am. For postal info, call 01 40 28 20 40. For urgent telegrams and calls, dial 01 40 28 20 00. **Postal Code:** Formed by adding the *arrondissement* to the number 750 (e.g., the code for 3*ème* is 75003).

Telephones: Paris has as many phones as pigeons. Buy a *télécarte* (40F60 or 97F50) at post offices and most metro stations and *tabacs;* coin-operated phones are scarce. To call to or from anywhere in France, dial the ten digit number. All Paris numbers begin with 01.

ACCOMMODATIONS

If at all possible, make a reservation *before* coming to Paris, but if you haven't yet done so, don't panic. A tourist office on the Champs-Elysées or elsewhere (see **Tourist Offices,** p. 292) can book rooms, although the lines are usually long and the selections are not the cheapest. Try calling around or visit one of these booking services:

La Centrale de Réservations (FUAJ-HI), 4, bd. Jules Ferry, 11*ème* (tel. 01 43 57 02 60; fax 01 40 21 79 92). M: République. Follow the rue du Faubourg du Temple away from pl. de la République until you reach the park-like entity which divides bd. Jules Ferry in two. Cross to the far side and turn right. One of the best ways to secure a cheap bed (113-125F per night per person) in Paris. Same-day reservations. The earlier you show up the better. Open Mon.-Sat. 9am-6pm. If closed, the 24hr. reception at the Jules Ferry Hostel, 2 doors down, may be able to help you.

OTU-Voyage (Office du Tourisme Universitaire), 119, rue St. Martin, 4*ème* (tel. 01 42 77 87 80). Across the pedestrian mall from the Pompidou. Even in the busiest months, OTU-Voyage guarantees "decent and low-cost lodging" in Résidence Bastille and hotels for same-day reservation and immediate use. You must pay the full price of the *foyer* room when making your reservation, even before seeing the room. Employees speak English. 10F service charge. Open Mon.-Sat. 10am-6:30pm.

Hostels and Foyers

Paris's big-city hostels skip many of the restrictions—sleep sheets, curfews, and the like—that the rest of the world has, but they do tend to have (flexible) maximum stays. The hostels below are open daily and include breakfast and showers unless otherwise noted. The six HI hostels in the city proper are for members only. The rest of the dorm-like accommodations in Paris are either private hostels or *foyers* (student dorms that usually are quieter and more private than regular hostels).

CISP "Kellerman," 17, bd. Kellerman, 13*ème* (tel. 01 44 16 37 38; fax 01 44 16 37 39). M: Porte d'Italie. Cross the street and turn right. Ultra-modern and impeccably clean. Laundry. Lockout 1:30-6:30am. Dorms 93F (hallway toilets). Singles 135F-165F. Doubles 270F. 2-4 beds 236F. Reserve ahead. MC, V.

Village Hostel, 20, rue d'Orsel, 18*ème* (tel. 01 42 64 22 02; fax 01 42 64 22 04). M: Anvers. Go up the hill on Steinkerque and turn right. Following renovations in 1997, this should be one of the nicest hostels in Paris. Every room with toilet and shower. Curfew 2am. Dorms 117F. Doubles 127F. Call ahead, even if same day.

Woodstock Hostel, 48, rue Rodier, 9ème (tel. 01 48 78 87 76; fax 01 48 78 87 76). M: Anvers. Walk against traffic on pl. Anvers, go right on ave. Trudaine and then left on rue de Rodier. Conveniently located. Spotless rooms and relatively peaceful atmosphere. Clean hall showers. Summer: dorms 87F; doubles 97F. Off season: 75F; 87F. In summer, call or stop by in the morning; call ahead in winter. MC, V.

Hôtel des Jeunes (MIJE), 6, rue de Le Fourcy, 4ème (tel. 01 42 74 23 45; fax 01 40 27 81 64), books "Le Fourcy," "Le Fauconnier," and "Maubuisson," three small, charming hostels in old Marais aristocratic residences. Ages 18-30. 7-day max. stay. Reception open 7am-10pm. Lockout noon-4pm. Curfew 1am. Quiet after 10pm. Dorms 125F. Singles 198F. Doubles 152F per person. Triples 137F per person. In-room shower, toilet down the hall, sheets and blankets, and breakfast all included.

Auberge de Jeunesse "Jules Ferry" (HI), 8, bd. Jules Ferry, 11ème (tel. 01 43 57 55 60). M: République. Walk east on rue du Faubourg du Temple and turn right on the far side of bd. Jules Ferry. Wonderfully located. Clean, large rooms with bunk beds. Friendly party atmosphere. Flexible 4-night max. stay. Reception open 24hr. Lockout of rooms 10am-2pm. No curfew. Single-sex lodging but can accommodate couples. Dorms 110F. Doubles 118F per person. Wash 20F, dry 10F. No reservations, so arrive by 7am, especially in summer. Lockers 5F. Sheets 5F. MC, V.

Auberge Internationale des Jeunes, 10, rue Trousseau, 11ème (tel. 01 47 00 62 00; fax 01 47 00 33 16). M: Ledru-Rollin. Walk east on rue du Faubourg St-Antoine then turn left. Lively atmosphere, lots of backpackers in the sunny breakfast room. Very clean, cramped rooms. Friendly staff. Common rooms downstairs. Safebox for valuables. Luggage storage. Lockout 10am-3pm. March-Oct. 91F per person; Nov.-Feb. 81F per person. Sheets 5F. Show up by 11:30am to get a room. MC, V.

UCJF (Union Chrétienne de Jeunes Filles, YWCA), 22, rue Naples, 8ème (tel. 01 45 22 23 49; fax 01 42 94 81 24). M: Europe. Take rue de Constantinople and turn left. Organized, homey environment for women only. June-Aug. 2-day min. stay. 30F YWCA membership fee and 50F (for week stays) processing fee. Reception open Mon.-Fri. 8am-12:30am, Sat.-Sun. 9am-12:30pm and 1:30pm-12:30am. Flexible curfew 12:30am. 200F key deposit. Singles 150F. Doubles 260F. Triples 390F. Weekly: singles 900F; doubles 750F. Breakfast and dinner included. Kitchen and laundry. Reserve with deposit. Another location at 168, rue Blomet, 15ème (tel. 01 45 33 48 21; fax 01 45 33 70 32). M: Convention. Men should contact the YMCA *foyer* **Union Chrétienne de Jeunes Gens,** 14, rue de Trévise, 9ème (tel. 01 47 70 90 94).

Centre International de Paris (BVJ) runs a chain of friendly hostels. Reserve well in advance and confirm, especially in summer, or check for available rooms around 9am. **Paris Louvre,** 20, rue J.-J. Rousseau, 1er (tel. 01 53 00 90 90; fax 01 53 00 90 91). M: Louvre. Take rue du Louvre away from river, turn left on rue St-Honoré and then right. *Call if you'll be late.* 120F, no singles. Lunch and dinner 40-60F. **Paris Quartier Latin,** 44, rue des Bernardins, 5ème (tel. 01 43 29 34 80; fax 01 53 00 90 91). M: Maubert-Mutualité. Walk with traffic on bd. St-Germain then turn right. Immense and ultra-modern. Showers in rooms. Reception open 24hr. Check-in by 2:30pm. Dorms 120F. Singles 130F. Lockers 10F.

FIAP Jean-Monnet, 30, rue Cabanis, 14ème (tel. 01 45 89 89 15; fax 01 45 81 63 91). M: Glacière. From metro, turn left off bd. Auguste-Blanqui onto rue de la Santé, then right. A large, fast-moving tourist machine. Well-furnished, impeccably maintained rooms. Laundry room, language institute, and a restaurant. Curfew 2am. Dorms 125F per person. Singles 276F. 2-bed doubles 175F per person. Triples or quads 150F per person. Reserve 2 weeks ahead in summer, more in winter. MC, V.

Centre International du Séjour de Paris: CISP "Ravel," 6, av. Maurice Ravel, 12ème (tel. 01 44 75 60 00; fax 01 43 44 45 30). M: Porte de Vincennes. Walk east on cours de Vincennes, take the first right on bd. Soult, left on rue Jules Lemaître, then right. Large rooms, art exhibits, and access to outdoor pool (25F). Self-serve restaurant. Flexible 3-day max. stay. Reception open daily 6:30am-1:30am. Dorms (shared hall toilet) 118F. Singles 165F. Doubles 270F. Reserve a few days ahead.

Résidence Bastille, 151, av. Ledru-Rollin, 11ème (tel. 01 43 79 53 86; fax 01 43 79 35 63). M: Voltaire. Walk across the pl. Léon Blum and head south onto av. Ledru-Rollin. More subdued than most. Ages 18-35 (flexible). Reception open daily 7am-10pm. Flexible curfew 1am. Lockout noon-2pm. March-Oct.: dorms 120F; singles

171F. Nov.-Feb.: dorms 110F; singles 160F. 10% ISIC and GO25 discount. No phone reservations; write or fax. No credit cards.

Three Ducks Hostel, 6, pl. Etienne Pernet, 15ème (tel. 01 48 42 04 05; fax 01 48 42 99 99). M: Félix Faure. Walk against traffic on the left side of the church. One of Paris's most rowdy summer hangouts for young backpackers, a 15min. walk from the Eiffel Tower. Brand new kitchen, lockers, and renovated dorm-style rooms for 2-8 people. Curfew 2am. March-Oct. 97F; Nov.-Feb. 75F. Sheets 15F. Towels 5F. Breakfast 15F. Reservations with 1 night's credit card deposit. MC, V.

Young and Happy (Y&H) Hostel, 80, rue Mouffetard, 5ème (tel. 01 45 35 09 53; fax 01 47 07 22 24). M: Monge. From the metro, cross rue Gracieuse and take rue Ortolan to rue Mouffetard. Clean, cramped rooms in the heart of a raucous student quarter. Lockout 11am-5pm. Curfew 2am. Doubles 117F. Quads 97F. 600F per week. Rates fall off season. Sheets 15F. Reserve with 1 night's deposit by mail (by phone only on the day you arrive); otherwise show up at 8am. No credit cards.

Aloha Hostel, 1, rue Borromée, 15ème (tel. 01 42 73 03 03; fax 01 42 73 14 14). M: Volontaires. Walk against traffic on rue de Vaugirard, then turn right on rue Borromée. Centrally located and colonized by English-speaking backpackers. Room lockout 11am-5pm. Reception open 8am-2am. Curfew 2am. April-Oct.: 97F; doubles 234F; Nov.-March 75F; doubles 170F. Arrive 8-11:30am for same-day reservations or reserve by phone with a credit card deposit. MC, V.

Hotels

Among Parisian budget accommodations, hotels may be the most practical for the majority of travelers. There are no curfews, no school groups, total privacy, and often concerned managers—features hostels and *foyers* can't offer. Groups of two, three, and four may actually find it more economical to stay in a hotel. Note that Parisian law forbids hanging laundry from windows or over balconies to dry and there are usually rules against bringing food into your room. Expect to pay at the very least 150F for a single, and 200-400 for a one-bed double. Two-bed doubles are rare and more expensive. In inexpensive hotels, few rooms come with private bath. If you book a room without a shower, you will usually have to pay 15-25F for the key to the hall shower.

Rooms disappear quickly after morning checkout (generally 10am-noon), so try to arrive early or reserve well ahead; all hotels accept reservations unless otherwise noted and generally require one night's deposit payable by credit card or check in francs. Instead of parading yourself and your bags around town all morning, call first. For help with directions, check out *Let's Go*'s color maps.

Louvre-Palais Royal (1er and 2ème arrondissements)

This district is central, regal, and cheap; just be careful around rue St-Denis.

Henri IV, 25, pl. Dauphine, 1er (tel. 01 43 54 44 53). M: Cité. Walk toward the Conciergerie, turn right on bd. du Palais, left on quai de l'Horloge, then left at the front of the Conciergerie onto pl. Dauphine. Last outpost of cheap accommodations on Ile de la Cité. Inconvenient first-floor toilets. Singles 120-135F. Doubles 160-260F. Triples 210-230F. Quads 260F. Reserve 2 months ahead with a check for 1 night.

Hôtel Lion d'Or, 5, rue de la Sourdière (tel. 01 42 60 79 04; fax 01 42 60 09 14). M: Tuileries. Walk down rue du 29 Juillet away from the park, right on rue St-Honoré, then left. Quiet, sparsely decorated rooms, some with showers. English-speaking staff. Singles around 230-300F. Doubles around 380-395F. Extra bed 60F. Hall showers 20F. Breakfast 35F. 5% off for stays of more than 3 nights. AmEx, MC, V.

Hôtel Montpensier, 12, rue de Richelieu (tel. 01 42 96 28 50; fax 01 42 86 02 70). M: Palais-Royal. Walk around the left side of the Palais-Royal to rue de Richelieu (directly ahead). Spacious, with clean rooms, most with showers. Singles and doubles 250-450F. Extra bed 70F. Shower 25F. Breakfast 35F. AmEx, MC, V.

Hôtel Vivienne, 40, rue Vivienne (tel. 01 42 33 13 26; fax 01 40 41 98 19). M: Rue Montmartre. Follow the traffic on bd. Montmartre past the Théâtre des Variétés and turn left on rue Vivienne. Gracious living at budget rates. Singles and doubles, all with shower or bath, 350-495F; 3rd person 30% extra. Breakfast 40F. MC, V.

The Marais (3ème and 4ème arrondissements)

With restored 17th century mansions, narrow streets, hidden courtyards, and the old Jewish quarter, all right in the city center, the Marais is an ideal base for tourists.

Hôtel de Roubaix, 6, rue Greneta, 3ème (tel. 01 42 72 89 91; fax 01 42 72 58 79). M: Réaumur-Sébastopol. Walk against traffic on bd. de Sébastopol then turn left. Very clean rooms with shower and toilet, some noisy. Singles 300-330F. 2-bed doubles 390-410F. Triples 415-480F. Quads 500F. Quints 525F. Breakfast included. MC, V.

Grand Hôtel Jeanne d'Arc, 3, rue de Jarente, 4ème (tel. 01 48 87 62 11; fax 01 48 87 37 31). M: St-Paul. Walk against traffic on rue de Rivoli, turn left on rue de Sévigné, then right. Brand-new beds and toilet and shower or bath in all rooms, great views from some. 2 rooms wheelchair accessible. Singles 300-400. Doubles 300-490F. Triples 530F. Quads 550F. Extra bed 75F. Reserve 2 months ahead. MC, V.

Castex Hôtel, 5, rue Castex, 4ème (tel. 01 42 72 31 52; fax 01 42 72 57 91). M: Bastille. Exit on bd. Henri IV and take the 3rd right. Spotless, quiet rooms. Reception open 7am-12pm. Check-in 1pm. Singles 225-275F. Doubles 310-350F. Triples 455F. Extra bed 70F. Breakfast 28F. Reserve 7-8 weeks ahead with deposit. MC, V.

Hôtel du Séjour, 36, rue du Grenier St-Lazare, 3ème (tel. 01 48 87 40 36). M: Etienne Marcel. Follow traffic on rue Etienne Marcel which becomes rue Grenier St-Lazare. Friendly owners, tiny bathrooms. Reception 7am-10:30pm, or call ahead. Singles 150F. Doubles, some with showers, 180-280F; extra bed 120F. Showers 20F.

Hôtel Bellevue et du Chariot d'Or, 39, rue de Turbigo, 3ème (tel. 01 48 87 45 60; fax 01 48 87 95 04). M: Etienne Marcel. Walk against traffic on rue Turbigo. Elegant beyond its price range. All rooms with toilets and bath or shower. Singles 305F. Doubles 330F. Triples 395F. Quads 420F. Breakfast 30F. Reserve 2 weeks ahead; unless reserved by fax, rooms are only guaranteed until 8pm. AmEx, MC, V.

Hôtel Picard, 26, rue de Picardie, 3ème (tel. 01 48 87 53 82; fax 01 48 87 02 56). M: République. Walk down rue du Temple, make your first left on rue Béranger, turn right on rue de Franche-Comté, then turn left. Tasteful, decently sized rooms, some with showers. Singles 200-320F. Doubles 240-390F. Triples 510F. 10% *Let's Go* discount. Hall showers 20F. Breakfast 30F. April-Sept. reserve 1 week ahead. MC, V.

Latin Quarter (5ème and 6ème arrondissements)

Revolving around the **Sorbonne** and the **Ecole des Beaux-Arts,** the *quartier latin* shelters bookstores, art flicks, café-filled squares, markets, and bubbly nightlife.

Stella, 41, rue Monsieur-le-Prince, 6ème (tel. 01 43 26 43 49; fax 01 43 54 97 28). M: Odéon. Down rue Dupuytren then left. Quiet, airy rooms with shower and toilet. Singles 250F. Doubles 300F. Triples 450F. Quads 500F. No credit cards.

Hôtel d'Esmeralda, 4, rue St-Julien-le-Pauvre, 5ème (tel. 01 43 54 19 20; fax 01 40 51 00 68). M: St-Michel. Walk along the Seine on quai St-Michel toward Notre-Dame and turn right at parc Viviani. Friendly staff, homey rooms. Singles 160-320F. Doubles 420-490F. Triples 550F. Quads 600F. Breakfast 40F. No credit cards.

Hôtel des Argonauts, 12, rue de la Huchette, 5ème (tel. 01 43 54 09 82; fax 01 44 07 18 84). M: St-Michel. Walking away from the Seine take the first left off bd. St-Michel. Surprisingly quiet, with clean, spacious, fluorescently lit rooms. Singles 200F. Doubles 250-350F. Triples 350F. Breakfast 25F. AmEx, MC, V.

Hôtel Nesle, 7, rue du Nesle, 6ème (tel. 01 43 54 62 41). M: Odéon. Walk up rue de l'Ancienne Comédie, onto rue Dauphine and take a left. Whimsical, warm management. Laundry available. All rooms have showers. Singles 220F. Doubles 270-400F. Breakfast included. No reservations; arrive between 10am and noon.

Hôtel des Alliés, 20, rue Berthollet, 5ème (tel. 01 43 31 47 52; fax 01 45 35 13 92). M: Censier-Daubenton. Walk south on rue Monge, turn right onto rue Claude Bernard, then left. Clean and comfy rooms, away from the bustle. Singles 200-300F. Doubles 200-300F. Hall showers 15F. Breakfast 28F. MC, V.

Hôtel de Chevreuse, 3, rue de Chevreuse, 6ème (tel. 01 43 20 93 16; fax 01 43 21 43 72). M: Vavin. Walk up bd. Montparnasse away from the Eiffel Tower and take a left. Great neighborhood, elegant rooms. Singles 200F. Doubles 250-380F. Triples 480F. Breakfast 30F. Reserve at least one week in advance with credit card. MC, V.

Hôtel Gerson, 14, rue de la Sorbonne, 5*ème* (tel. 01 43 54 28 40; fax 01 44 07 13 90). M: Cluny-Sorbonne. Left on bd. St-Michel, left on rue des Ecoles, then right. Fairly spacious rooms with excellent beds. Singles 225-306F. Doubles and triples 250-400F. Breakfast 25F. Reserve 3 weeks ahead. MC, V.

Hôtel Gay Lussac, 29, rue Gay-Lussac, 5*ème* (tel. 01 43 54 23 96). M: Luxembourg. Creaky floors and spacious, sunny rooms. Singles and doubles 185-360F. Triples 425F. Quads 550F. Breakfast included. Reserve 2 weeks ahead. No credit cards.

Champ de Mars-Eiffel Tower (7ème arrondissement)

Quieter and more expensive, hotels in this area are indeed close to the Eiffel Tower and other sights, but don't expect a view.

Hôtel de la Paix, 19, rue du Gros Caillou, 7*ème* (tel. 01 45 51 86 17). M: Ecole Militaire. Walk against traffic on av. de la Bourdonnais, turn right on rue de Grenelle, then left. A bit old. Reception open 9am-9pm; key available. Singles 160-230F. Doubles 295-370F. Shower 15F. Breakfast 32F. Call ahead. Deposit (traveler's check in francs) required for arrivals after 3pm. No credit cards.

Grand Hôtel Lévêque, 29, rue Cler, 7*ème* (tel. 01 47 05 49 15; fax 01 45 50 49 36). M: Ecole Militaire. Northeast on av. de la Motte-Picquet then make a left onto the cobblestone pedestrian street. Completely renovated and aiming for luxury. Singles 225F. Doubles 335-380F. Triples 480F. Extra bed 80F. Breakfast 30F. MC, V.

Hôtel Malar, 29, rue Malar, 7*ème* (tel. 01 45 51 38 46; fax 01 45 55 20 19). M: Latour Maubourg. Follow traffic on bd. de la Tour Maubourg, turn left on rue St. Dominique, then right. Provincial family hotel with inner courtyard. Singles 280F-350F. Doubles 330-400F. Triples 380-460F. Extra bed 60F. Breakfast 30F. MC, V.

Bd. Montmartre-Faubourg Montmartre (9ème arrondissement)

The northern part of this district (around Pigalle) is a red-light district, but away from bd. de Clichy it becomes a quiet, diverse residential area near the sights.

Hôtel Beauharnais, 51, rue de la Victoire, 9*ème* (tel. 01 48 74 71 13). M: le Peletier. Follow traffic on rue de la Victoire and look for flower boxes; there is no hotel sign. Each elegant room (with shower) is dressed in a collection of antiques. Singles and doubles 300-350F. Triples 465F. Breakfast free with *Let's Go.* No credit cards.

Résidence Hôtel des Trois Poussins, 15, rue Clauzel, 9*ème* (tel. 01 53 32 81 81; fax 01 53 32 81 82). M: St-Georges. Uphill on rue Notre-Dame-de-Lorette, right on rue H. Monnier, then right. Clean, well-furnished rooms and studios, all with full bath. Rooms start at 320F for singles, 390F for doubles and 470F for triples (extra person 60F). Studio prices drop for longer stays. Reserve 2 weeks ahead. AmEx, V, MC.

Bastille-République (10ème, 11ème, and 12ème arrondissements)

These *arrondissements* offer inexpensive hotels near the Gare de Lyon and the Bastille nightlife. Be careful at night, especially north of the av. de la République.

Mistral Hôtel, 3, rue Chaligny, 12*ème* (tel. 01 46 28 10 20; fax 01 46 28 69 66). M: Reuilly-Diderot. West on bd. Diderot, then left. One of the best deals in Paris. Spectacularly clean. Singles 205-250F. Doubles 235-290F. Triples 310F. Quads 340F. Hall showers 10F. Breakfast 35F. Call to reserve, confirm in writing. AmEx, MC, V.

Hôtel de Nevers, 53, rue de Malte, 11*ème* (tel. 01 47 00 56 18; fax 01 43 57 77 39). M: République. Down av. de la République and right. Spotless rooms. Reception open 24hr. Singles and doubles 170-260F. Triples 310F. Quads 380F. Hall showers 20F. Breakfast 25F. Reserve 2 weeks ahead with 1 night's deposit. MC, V.

Hôtel de Belfort, 37, rue Servan, 11*ème* (tel. 01 47 00 67 33; fax 01 43 57 97 98). M: Père-Lachaise. Left off rue du Chemin Vert. Functional rooms with showers and toilets. *Let's Go* special: 100F a person (rooms for 2, 3, or 4) and 15F breakfast. MC, V.

Montparnasse (14ème arrondissement)

Areas closest to flashy **bd. du Montparnasse** maintain the vitality that drew Picasso, Sartre, and Hemingway, while adjoining neighborhoods are residential and sedate.

Hôtel de Blois, 5, rue des Plantes, 14*ème* (tel. 01 45 40 99 48; fax 01 45 40 45 62). M: Mouton-Duvernet. Left onto rue Mouton Duvernet; left at the end. Unquestionably one of the best deals in Paris. Quality decor. Singles and doubles 230-350F. Triples 360F. Breakfast 27F. Reserve at least 10 days in advance. AmEx, MC, V.

Ouest Hôtel, 27, rue de Gergovie, 14*ème* (tel. 01 45 42 64 99; fax 01 45 42 46 65). M: Pernety. Against traffic on rue Raymond Losserand, then right. Plain, clean and friendly. Singles, doubles 120-230F. Hall showers 20F. Breakfast 20F. MC, V, AmEx.

Champs-Elysées (8ème, 16ème, and 17ème arrondissements)

The neighborhoods of the Champs-Elysées are elegant but not centrally located.

Hôtel d'Artois, 94, rue La Boétie, 8*ème* (tel. 01 43 59 84 12; fax 01 43 59 50 70). M: St-Philippe de Roule. Spacious and clean, but a bit worn. Singles 240-390F. Doubles 270-440F. Extra bed 130F. Hall showers 20F. Breakfast 25F. AmEx, MC, V.

Hôtel Riviera, 55, rue des Acacias, 17*ème* (tel. 01 43 80 45 31; fax 01 40 54 84 08). M: Charles-de-Gaulle-Etoile. North on av. MacMahon, then left. Large, comfy beds. Singles 240-375F. Doubles 350-400F. Triples 460F. Breakfast 27F. AmEx, MC, V.

Hôtel Résidence Chalgrin, 10, rue Chalgrin, 16*ème* (tel. 01 45 00 19 91; fax 01 45 00 95 41). M: Argentine. Down av. de la Grande Armée toward the Arc de Triomphe, right on rue Argentine, then right again. Warm, quiet, and dim. Singles 150-380F. Suites 450F. No hall showers. Extra bed 5F. Breakfast 27F. AmEx, MC, V.

FOOD

With a bakery on every corner and dozens of open-air markets, food is a high-profile, high-quality affair. Affordable and very French breads, cheeses, and pastries appear as standard fare. Catch one of the city's many wonderful and inexpensive Vietnamese, North African, and Middle Eastern restaurants. Or, for a light meal accompanied by excellent wine, hit one the many cozy wine bars. **CROUS (Centre Regional des Oeuvres Universitaires et Scolaires),** 30, av. Georges Bernanos, 5*ème*, has info on university restaurants (tel. 01 40 51 37 10; M: Port-Royal; open Tues.-Sat. 11:30am-1:30pm and 6-8pm). Every *arrondissement* has at least one outdoor market (most are open only mornings); ask at your hotel or hostel for the nearest one. When assembling a picnic, visit some of the many specialty shops; for a concentration of shops selling everything from baguettes to eggs in aspic, head for the **Marché Montorgeuil,** 2*ème*, or **rue Mouffetard,** 5*ème*. Produce overflows at the **Marché Bastille** on bd. Richard-Lenoir (M: Bastille; open Thurs. and Sun. 7am-1:30pm). Beer and soda are cheap in supermarkets. Above all, be bold, be adventurous, and treat yourself at least once: you may never get another chance to slurp snails by the Seine.

Restaurants

Louvre-Palais Royal (1er and 2ème arrondissements)

Near the Palais-Royal and in the inexpensive 2*ème*, small streets teem with traditional restaurants. Cheaper eateries surround Les Halles, which can be sketchy at night.

L'Emile, 76, rue J.-J. Rousseau, 1*er*. M: Les Halles. Walk toward the church St-Eustache, bend right onto rue Coquillère, then turn right. Intimate setting and unusual, heavenly cuisine. 3-course lunch *menu* including wine 71F. Evening *menu* 95F. Open Mon.-Fri. noon-2:30pm and 8pm-midnight, Sat. 8pm-midnight.

Pizza Sicilia, 26, rue de Beaujolais, 1*er*. M: Palais-Royal. On the corner of Montpensier, north of the Palais. Friendly service and absurdly good food. Pastas under 44F. 50F *menu.* Open Mon.-Sat. noon-2:30pm and 7-11:30pm.

La Victoire Suprême du Coeur, 41, rue des Bourdonnais, 1*er*. M: Châtelet. Follow traffic on rue des Halles, then left. Bright, serene veggie restaurant. Lunch *menus* 49-65F. Main dishes 44-78F. Open Mon.-Sat. noon-3:30pm and 6:30-10:30pm.

Le Dénicheur, 4, rue Tiquetonne, 2*ème*. M: Etienne Marcel. Walk against traffic on rue de Turbigo, then turn left. Cozy restaurant/*salon de thé.* Quiche 35F. Large Sunday brunch 75F. Open Tues.-Sun. noon-midnight.

Ile St-Louis and The Marais (3ème and 4ème arrondissements)

The **Ile St-Louis** is charming but not cheap. Budget restaurants in the Marais are as varied as the tightly packed district, ranging from falafel stands to classic (and pricey) sit-down Parisian fare. **Rue de Rosier** is the Marais's traditional Jewish quarter.

Les Fous de l'Isle, 33, rue des Deux-Ponts, on Ile St-Louis. M: Pont Marie. A mellow café-bistro for the young local crowd. Hot main courses 60-98F. Open Tues.-Fri. noon-midnight, Sat. 6pm-midnight, Sun. noon-4pm for brunch (*menus* 100-150F).

Le Hangar, 12, impasse Berthaud, 3*ème*. M: Rambuteau. Tucked away in an alley. *Foie gras de canard poêlé* (fried goose liver) 88F. Open Mon. 6:30pm-midnight, Tues.-Sat. noon-3:30pm and 6:30pm-midnight.

Auberge de Jarente, 7, rue de Jarente, 4*ème*. M: St-Paul. Walk against traffic on rue de Rivoli, turn left on rue de Sévigné, then right. A dim, cottage-like restaurant with Basque specialties. *Cailles* (quail) 68F. *Menu* 77-132F. Open Tues.-Sat. noon-2:30pm and 7:30-10:30pm. Reservations recommended on weekend evenings.

Latin Quarter (5ème and 6ème arrondissements)

French, Greek, and Lebanese restaurants trace **rue Mouffetard.** Budget restaurants also line **rue du Pot-de-Fer.** In the 6*ème*, tiny restaurants with rock-bottom *menus* jostle for customers in the area bounded by bd. St-Germain, bd. St-Michel, and the Seine.

Le Jardin des Pâtes, 4, rue Lacépède, 5*ème*. M: Jussieu. Up rue Linné then right. Organic, gourmet pasta with a host of farm-fresh sauces. Many vegetarian offerings. Main courses 38-73F. Reserve at night. Open Tues.-Sun. noon-2:30pm and 7-11pm.

Le Petit Vatel, 5, rue Lobineau, 6*ème*. M: Mabillon. With traffic on bd. St-Germain, right on rue de Seine, then second right. Delicious. Big Mediterranean influence. 60F lunch *menu.* Take-out available. Open Tues.-Sat. noon-3pm and 7pm-11:30pm.

Orestias, 4, rue Grégoire-de-Tours, 6*ème*. M: Odéon. Go against traffic on bd. St-Germain, then turn left. For 44F, they'll stuff you full. Greek wine. French food. Open Mon.-Sat. noon-2:30pm and 5:30-11:30pm.

Restaurant Perraudin, 157, rue St-Jacques, 5*ème*. M: Luxembourg. Take rue Royer Collard to rue St-Jacques. A slice of classic Paris. 3-course lunch *menu* 63F. Main dishes 56F. Glass of wine 9F. Open Tues.-Sat. noon-2:15pm and 7:30-10:15pm.

Crêperie Saint Germain, 33, rue St-André-des-Arts, 6*ème*. M: St-Michel. Off pl. St-André-des-Arts. Young and funky; specializes in wheat flour *crêpes noires.* Most crepes (20-55F) are unusually filling. Open daily noon-1:00am.

Champ de Mars (7ème arrondissement)

You can't afford the best restaurants in this district. But they're good.

La Varangue, 27, rue Angereau. M: Ecole Militaire. Av. de la Bourdonnais, right on rue de Grenelle, then left. Tiny and close to the Eiffel Tower. Short, varied menu. 77F lunch or dinner *formule.* Open Mon.-Fri. noon-10pm, Sat. 6:30-10pm.

Sifaridi Couscous, 9, rue Surcouf. M: Invalides. Constantinian food, heavy on the couscous. Different *formules* with a generally enormous main dish 60-140F. Fig liqueur and Algerian pastries. Open Mon.-Sat. 11:30am-3pm and 6:45-10:30pm.

Le Club des Poètes, 30, rue de Bourgogne. M: Varenne. Up bd. des Invalides towards the esplanade, right on rue de Grenelle, then left. Established to "make poetry contagious and inevitable." Starting at 10pm, the owner and friends read the great French poets. Dinner 100-150F. Open Mon.-Sat. noon-3pm and 8pm-1am.

Bastille-République (10ème, 11ème, and 12ème arrondissements)

The 10*ème* has a high concentration of ethnic restaurants: **Passage Brady** overflows with Indian eateries. Restaurants in the 11*ème* fill to capacity with young, chic regulars who stay through the night; try to reserve ahead.

Paris-Dakar, 95, rue du Faubourg St-Martin, 10*ème* (tel. 01 42 08 16 64). M: Gare de l'Est. Parisian cuisine blended with flavors of the owner's native Senegal. Lunch *menu* 59F. Dinner *menu* 99F. African *menu* 149F. Open Tues.-Thurs. and Sat.-Sun. noon-3pm and 7pm-2am, Fri. 7pm-2am.

Au Petit Keller, 13, rue Keller, 11*ème* (tel. 01 47 00 12 97). M: Ledru-Rollin. North on av. Ledru Rollin and left. Hip bistro in the heart of the vibrant Bastille district. 50 and 70F *menus* at noon. Open Mon.-Sat. noon-2:30pm and 7pm-midnight.

A la Banane Ivoirienne, 10, rue de la Forge-Royale, 11*ème* (tel. 01 43 70 49 90). M: Faidherbe-Chaligny. West on rue du Faubourg St-Antoine then right. Delicious West African specialties. Main courses 50-75F. 2-course *menus* at 90, 110, and 130F with live pan-African music every Fri. Open Tues.-Sat. 7pm-midnight.

Occitanie, 96, rue Oberkampf, 11*ème* (tel. 01 48 06 46 98). M: St-Maur. Northwest on av. de la République, 1st right onto rue St-Maur, then right. South French. Open Mon.-Fri. noon-2pm and 7-11pm, Sat. 7-11pm. Closed mid-July to mid-Aug.

Montparnasse (14ème arrondissement)

At the turn of the century, Bretons flocked into Montparnasse bringing their speciality crepes and *galettes* (a savory, buckwheat version).

Le Château Poivre, 145, rue du Château. M: Pernety. Walk with the traffic on rue Raymond Losserand, then turn right. Generous portions. Steep *à la carte* prices. 89F *menu.* Open Mon.-Sat. noon-2:30pm and 7-10:30pm.

Phinéas, 99, rue de l'Ouest (tel. 01 45 41 33 50). M: Pernety. Follow the traffic on rue Pernety and turn left. Specializing in *tartes sucrées et salées*—and cartoons. Main dishes 58-80F. Cheaper take-out. Open Tues.-Sat. noon-11:30pm.

Le Colvert, 129, rue du Château (tel. 01 43 27 95 19). M: Pernety. Go with the traffic on rue Raymond Losserand, then turn right. Traditional French food with Mediterranean influences. Lunch *menu* 65F. Dinner *menu* 89F. Open Mon.-Fri. noon-3pm and 7-11:30pm, Sat. 7-11:30pm.

The Champs-Elysées (8ème, 16ème, and 17ème arrondissements)

Vitamine, 20, rue de Bucarest, 8*ème*. M: Liège. Up rue de Moscou to the 1st corner on your right. Straightforward self-serve place with light, low-priced, tasty sandwiches (13-20F) and salads (22-40F). Open Mon.-Fri. 8am-3pm.

Casa Tina, 18, rue Lauriston, 16*ème* (tel. 01 40 67 19 24). M: Charles-de-Gaulle-Etoile. Up av. Victor Hugo 1 block and left. Spanish *tapas* 15-69F. Meal of seven *tapas* 98F. Pitcher of *Sangria* 89F. Open daily 11:30am-3:30pm and Mon.-Fri. 6pm-1am, Sat.-Sun. 7pm-2am. Reservations on weekends.

Le Patio Provençal, 116, rue des Dames, 17*ème* (tel. 01 42 93 73 73). M: Villiers. Rue de Lévis away from the intersection; turn right. Flavors of the south. *Grandes assiettes* 54-65F. Half-portions 34-37F. Open Mon.-Fri. noon-2:30pm and 7-10:30pm, Sat. noon-2:30pm. Reservations recommended.

Joy in Food, 2, rue Truffaut, 17*ème*, on the corner of rue des Dames. M: Rome. Up rue Boursault, right on rue des Dames. Some of the best vegetarian meals in Paris. Main dishes 45F. Two- or 3-course *menus* for 58 and 71F. Open Mon.-Sat. 11:30am-3pm.

Montmartre and environs (9ème and 18ème arrondissements)

Chez les Fondues, 17, rue des Trois Frères, 18*ème*. M: Abbesses. Down rue Yvonne le Tac and left. Raucous. Only two main dishes served: *fondue bourguignonne* (meat fondue) and *fondue savoyarde* (cheese fondue). The wine is served in baby-bottles. *Menu* 97F. Call ahead to reserve or show up early. Open daily 5pm-2am.

Au Grain de Folie, 24, rue la Vieuville, 18*ème*. M: Abbesses. Array of huge veggie dishes, from couscous and hummus to salads and cheese. 100F *menu.* 50F *menu* until 8pm. Open Mon.-Fri. noon-2:30pm and 6-10:30pm, Sat.-Sun. noon-10:30pm.

Hayne's Bar, 3, rue Clauzel, 9*ème*. M: St-Georges. Uphill on rue Notre-Dame-de-Lorette, right on rue H. Monnier, right again. Once the center of the expat African-American crowd (including Louis Armstrong and James Baldwin). Soul food: fried chicken 70F. Jazz piano Fri. nights. Open Tues.-Sat. 7:30pm-1am. Closed early Aug.

Pizzéria King Salomon, 46, rue Richer, 9*ème*. M: Cadet. Down rue Saulner, right. Kosher pizzeria in a Jewish community. Individual pizzas 42-58F. Take-out available. Open Sun.-Thurs. 11:30am-3pm and 6:30pm-midnight, Sat. 6:30pm-midnight.

Cafés and Cyber Cafés

French cafés have long been suffused with the glamor of languid leisure time, conjuring images of writers and long afternoons. Popular café drinks include coffee, wine, *citron pressé* (freshly squeezed lemon juice with sugar and water on the side), soda (which costs lots), and vast selections of spring, mineral, and soda waters. Cafés also serve affordable light lunches and snacks: a *croque monsieur* (grilled ham-and-cheese sandwich) runs about 15-20F. Salads—full meals—cost a bit more. Café prices are two-tiered; it's cheaper at the counter (*comptoir* or *zinc*) than in the seating area.

La Closerie des Lilas, 171, bd. du Montparnasse, 6ème. M: Port-Royal. This flower-ridden café was the one-time favorite of Hemingway (a scene in *The Sun Also Rises* takes place here), and of the Dadaists and Surrealists before him. Picasso came here weekly to hear Paul Fort recite poetry. Enjoy the terrace in summer. Coffee 15F. House wine 26F. *Marquise au chocolat* 65F. Open daily 11am-1am.

La Coupole, 102, bd. du Montparnasse, 14ème (open daily noon-2am, Fri-Sat. with dancing until 4am), and **Le Séléct,** 99, bd. du Montparnasse, 6ème (open weekdays 7am-3am weekdays, weekends 24hr.), across the street. M: Vavin. These vibrant and oh-so-chic spots have served politicos (Lenin, Trotsky), musicians (Stravinsky, Satie), writers (Hemingway, Breton, Cocteau), artists (Picasso), and thinkers (Einstein). So...who are you? Coffee 10-15F. Beer 17-50F.

Les Deux Magots, 6, pl. St-Germain-des-Prés, 6ème (open daily 7am-1:30am), and **Le Flore,** 172, bd. St-Germain, 6ème (open daily 7am-2am), next door. M: St-Germain-des-Prés. In his favorite hangout—Le Flore—Sartre wrote *Being and Nothingness.* In his second choice and Simone de Beauvoir's first—Les Deux Magots, opened in 1875—the couple first spotted each other. Coffee 22-23F. *Café crème* 25-28F.

Café Orbital, 13, rue de Médicis, 6ème. M: Odéon. Access to telnet, newsgroups, and the Web, alongside hot cyberwiches with green salads (45F). **Internet access** 1F per min., but you can create an email account for free. Students may get a *Carte Sidérante:* 200F for 5hr., 300F for 10hr. Open Mon.-Sat. 11am-10pm.

Hammam Café, 4, rue des Rosiers, 4ème (tel. 01 42 78 04 46). M: St-Paul. Replaced an actual *hammam* in 1996; it still has an elegant, bath-house feel. Restaurant has salads, fresh pasta, and grilled fish. Saunter downstairs to hook up (**Internet access** 1F per min.), or upstairs to "hook up" (music nightly at 10:30pm). Cocktails 65F. Open Sun.-Thurs. noon-2am, Fri. noon-4am, Sat. sundown-2am.

Salons de Thé and Wine Bars

Salons de thé provide tea, low-key refinement, and light meals, while wine bars are just the way to sample good French wine by the glass.

Angelina's, 226, rue de Rivoli, 1er. M: Concorde or Tuileries. Return to the "Age of Innocence" in the refined calm of this venerable *salon de thé.* Afternoon tea 33F. Pastries 6-35F. Open Mon.-Fri. 9am-7pm, Sat.-Sun. 9:30am-7:30pm.

Ladurée, 16, rue Royale, 8ème. M: Concorde. Perfection in a *salon de thé:* frescoed ceiling and light green gilt pillars. Macaroons (22F), flavored with chocolate, pistachio, coffee, vanilla, or lemon. Open Mon.-Sat. 8:30am-7pm, Sun. 10am-7pm.

Le Franc Pinot, 1, quai de Bourbon, on the Ile St-Louis. M: Pont Marie. Notorious in the past centuries as a meeting place for enemies of the state. Burgundy wines are a specialty, by the glass 15-36F and up. Bar open Tues.-Sat. 10am-2am, Sun. 2pm-2am. Bistro/jazz club downstairs open Wed.-Sat. 10pm-2am.

Jacques Mélac, 42, rue Léon Frot, 11ème. M: Charonne. *The* Parisian family-owned wine bar and bistro. 16F per glass. 85F per bottle (38F to go). Entrees such as *gigot d'agneau* (69F). Open Sept.-July Mon. 9am-5pm, Tues.-Fri. 9am-10:30pm.

SIGHTS

In a few hours, you can walk from the heart of the Marais in the east to the Eiffel Tower in the west, past almost every monument there is. Try to reserve one day for wandering: you don't have a true sense of Paris until you know how close medieval Notre Dame is to the modern Centre Pompidou, and the *quartier latin* of students to the Louvre of kings. After dark, the glamour increases: spotlights go up over everything from the Panthéon to the Eiffel Tower, Notre Dame to the Obélisque. Until midnight, the city glows like a galaxy of multicolored, glittering chandeliers.

Ile de la Cité and Ile St-Louis If any one location is the heart of Paris, sentimentally as well as physically, the **Ile de la Cité** is it. Since the 3rd century BC, when it was inhabited by the *Parisii,* a Gallic tribe of hunters, sailors, and fisherfolk, the Ile de la Cité has been the administrative center of Paris and the home of kings. In the 12th century work commenced on **Cathédrale de Notre-Dame de Paris** (M: Cité) and Ste-Chapelle under the direction of Bishop Maurice Sully. The cathedral, completed in the 14th century, is one of the most famous and beautiful examples of medieval architecture. After the Revolution, the building fell into disrepair and was even used to shelter livestock, but Victor Hugo's 1831 novel, *Notre-Dame-de-Paris (The Hunchback of Notre Dame)* inspired thousands of citizens to push for restoration. The modifications by the architect Eugène Viollet-le-Duc (including the addition of the spire, the gargoyles, and a statue of himself admiring his work) remain controversial: is it a medieval masterpiece or a 19th-century mock-up? The first thing you see is the intricately carved **facade.** Inside, the soaring light and apparent weightlessness of the walls—Gothic effects produced by brilliant engineering and optical illusions—are inspiring even for the most church-weary. The cathedral's biggest draw is the enormous stained-glass **rose windows** dominating the north and south ends of the transept. A perilous and claustrophobic staircase inside the **towers** emerges onto a spectacular perch, where weather-worn gargoyles survey a stunning view of the city. Once outside again, take a moment to walk around back and scope the spectacular, spidery **flying buttresses,** which support the weight of the structure. (Tours in English Wed. and Thurs. noon; in French Mon.-Fri. noon, Sat. 2:30pm. Free. Towers open April-Sept. daily 10am-6pm; Oct.-March 10am-5pm. Last admission 30min. before closing. 32F, students 12-25 21F. Cathedral open daily 8am-6:45pm. High mass with Gregorian chant Sun. 10am. Confession heard in English.)

The **Palais de Justice** has harbored Paris district courts since the 13th century. Inside its courtyard, the **Ste-Chapelle** is flamboyant Gothic, one of the most beautiful sights in the world, and built by Saint Louis (the IXth) to house his most precious possession, Christ's crown of thorns (now in Notre Dame). Go inside and upstairs, it's worth the price. (Open April.-Sept. daily 9:30am-6:30pm; Oct.-March 10am-5pm. 32F, students and seniors 21F, with the Conciergerie 50F.) The **Conciergerie,** once one of Paris's most infamous prisons, lurks around the corner of the Palais from Ste-Chapelle's entrance. Marie-Antoinette and Robespierre were imprisoned here during the Revolution, but little else besides Robespierre's letters is displayed (open April-Sept. daily 9:30am-6:30pm; Oct.-March 10am-5pm. 28F, students 18F).

A hop, skip, and a jump across the Pont St-Louis is the **Ile St-Louis,** perhaps the city's most charming (and ritzy) neighborhood. Some of the most privileged of Paris's exceedingly privileged elite, like the Rothschilds and Pompidou's widow, now call this home. Check the plaques on the sides of buildings for famous former residents (e.g., Voltaire, Baudelaire, Marie Curie). At night, the Ile St-Louis glows in the light of its cast-iron lamps, outlined against the shadows of the Seine.

The Latin Quarter and St-Germain-des-Prés Home since the 13th century to the famed **Sorbonne,** the Quartier Latin is identified worldwide with bookish (and Latin speaking, hence the name) bohemians scribbling works-in-progress in attic apartments or corner cafés. However, after the violent student riots in protest of the outmoded university system in May of 1968, the University of Paris split into 13 campuses. With decentralization the *quartier* lost many of its youthful, scholarly inhabitants. Many tiny bookstores and cafés have since closed or expanded in response to increased tourism, but a youthful air survives, particularly near the Sorbonne.

The **Panthéon,** its dome visible from anywhere in the Latin Quarter, towers as the highest point on the Left Bank (M: Cardinal Lemoine). In the **crypt** you'll find the tombs of Voltaire, Rousseau, Victor Hugo, Emile Zola, Jean Jaurès, and Louis Braille, which can be seen from behind locked iron gates at each of their niches. The **dome** lavishes you with an up-close view of neoclassical frescoes and a view, but is closed indefinitely for repairs (Panthéon open daily 10am-6:30pm; last admission 5:45pm; 32F, students 21F). The dome will be closed until spring 1997, due to repairs.

Even if an average walk in the park bores you, stroll through the **Jardin des Plantes,** pl. Valhubert (M: Jussieu). Opened in 1640 for the sole purpose of growing medicinal plants for King Louis XIII, it has since sprouted a bunch of museums and a **zoo** which cityfolks raided for food during the siege of 1871. The park is free, but the museums and zoo charge. The **boulevard St-Michel,** flooded with cafés, restaurants, bookstores, and cinemas, is the center of the Latin Quarter and the divider between the 5ème and 6ème. **Place St-Michel,** at the northern tip of this *grand-avenue,* is a microcosm of the neighborhood, attracting tourists, students, and drunken indigents.

West of the Panthéon, the **Jardin du Luxembourg** is one of the world's best parks, fabulous for children, strolling, sunbathing, and dipping fingers in fountains. A block north of the garden is the **Eglise St-Sulpice** (M: St-Sulpice), containing Delacroix frescoes in the front right chapel; the church is a sundial, built to determine the solstices (open daily 7:30am-7:30pm). The **Eglise St-Germain-des-Prés,** pl. St-Germain-des-Prés (M: St-Germain-des-Prés), showing many centuries' wear and whims, is officially the oldest standing church in Paris, dating from 1163 (open daily 9am-7:30pm).

The Faubourg St-Germain The green, tree-lined **Esplanade des Invalides** runs from Pont Alexandre III to the gold-leaf dome crowning the **Hôtel des Invalides** (M: Invalides). The Hôtel, built under Louis XIV for retired and wounded veterans, now houses the **Musée de l'Armée** and **Napoleon's Tomb.** Nearby on rue Varenne is the excellent Musée Rodin (see **Museums,** p. 307).

Of the **Tour Eiffel** (Eiffel Tower; M: Bir-Hakeim), Gustave Eiffel wrote in 1889, "France is the only country in the world with a 300m flagpole." Maupassant liked to eat lunch there because it was the one place in Paris where he didn't have to look at it. Built in 1889 as the centerpiece of the World's Fair (held in Paris for the centennial jubilee of the French Revolution), the structure outlasted criticism and has come to symbolize the city. Don't miss out on one of the most satisfying experiences in Paris, even if it seems tacky or overdone—climb the tower. At night, even the most jaded tourists will be impressed. (Tower open July-Aug. daily 9am-midnight; Sept.-June 9:30am-11pm. Elevator to: 1st floor 20F, 2nd floor 40F, 3rd floor 56F.)

The Louvre, the Opéra, the Marais, and the Bastille Hugging the Seine, the **Louvre**—world-famous art museum and former residence of kings—occupies about one-seventh of the surface area of the 1er *arrondissement* (see p. 306). **Le Jardin des Tuileries** (M: Palais-Royal/Musée du Louvre), at the western foot of the Louvre, was commissioned by Catherine de Médicis in 1564, improved by André Le Nôtre (designer of the gardens at Versailles) in 1649, and has since become one of the most popular open spaces in Paris. The **place Vendôme,** three blocks north along rue de Castiglione, hides 20th-century offices and luxury shops behind 17th-century facades. In the center of the *place* is a column cast from 1250 Austrian and Russian bronze cannon captured in battle by Napoleon (that's him on the top, in the toga). Commissioned in 1632 by Cardinal Richelieu as his Palais Cardinal, the **Palais-Royal,** across rue de Rivoli from the Louvre, became royal when the Cardinal gave it to Louis XIII, a few years before both of them died. In 1784 the elegant buildings enclosing the palace's formal garden become the prototype of a shopping mall; the revolutions of 1789, 1830, and 1848 all began with angry crowds in that same garden. Today, thanks to a late 19th-century revival, the Palais is again a center of luxury commerce.

North of the Louvre, feast your eyes on Charles Garnier's grandiose **Opéra** (M: Opéra), built under Napoleon III in the giddy gaudiness of the Second Empire. The magnificent and eclectic interior is adorned by Gobelin tapestries, gilded mosaics, a 1964 Marc Chagall ceiling, and the six-ton chandelier which fell on the audience in 1896 (open for visits daily 10am-6pm; last admission 5:30pm; 30F). East of the Opéra lie the 3ème and 4ème *arrondissements,* known together as **Le Marais.** With Henri IV's construction of the **place des Vosges** (M: St-Paul) at the beginning of the 17th century, the area became *the* place to live. Several of the many mansions left in the area now house museums. At the meeting point of the 1er, 2ème, 3ème, and 4ème, the **Centre Pompidou** looms like an oversized engine abandoned next to the Seine (closed until Dec. 31, 1999; see p. 306). In afternoon and early evening, the vast cobblestone *place* in front of the complex gathers a mixture of caricature artists, street musicians, monologuists, and more. At night, it gets wild and a little dangerous.

Farther east, Charles V built the **Bastille** prison to guard the eastern entrance to his capital; it became a state prison under Louis XIII, housing religious heretics and political undesirables. On July 14, 1789, revolutionaries stormed the Bastille for its supply of gunpowder; by 1792, nothing was left of the prison but its outline on the *place.* On July 14, 1989, François Mitterrand inaugurated the glittering **Opéra Bastille,** 120, rue de Lyon (M: Bastille) to celebrate the destruction of Charles's fortress. Alas, the ugly Opéra Bastille is almost as hated as its predecessor.

Champs-Elysées, Bois de Boulogne, and La Défense The **place de la Concorde** (M: Concorde), Paris's largest and most infamous public square, is at the western edge of the Tuileries. Constructed between 1757 and 1777 to hold a monument to Louis XV, the vast area soon became the place de la Révolution, site of a guillotine that severed 1343 necks. After the Reign of Terror, the square was optimistically renamed—*concorde* means peace. The huge, rose granite **Obélisque de Louxor** dates from the 13th century BC and depicts the deeds of Ramses II. Given to Charles X by the Viceroy of Egypt in 1829, it's Paris's oldest monument.

Stretching west, the **avenue des Champs-Elysées** is lined with luxury shops, boutiques of *haute couture,* and embassies. The avenue is an example of the work of Baron Haussmann, commissioned by Napolean III's government to level most of the hills of Paris and replace tiny alleys with broad avenues, in an effort to convert the city into a proper capital and strike against Parisian revolutionary ferment by reducing the effectiveness of street barricades. At its western terminus, the **Arc de Triomphe,** pl. Charles de Gaulle, moves every heart not made of stone (M: Charles de Gaulle-Etoile). The world's largest triumphal arch was commissioned in 1806 by Napoleon in honor of his Grande Armée. In 1940, Parisians were brought to tears as the Nazis goose-stepped through the Arc. After four years of Nazi occupation, the city was liberated by British, American, and French troops, who marched through on August 26, 1944, to the roaring cheers of thousands. The terrace at the top has a fabulous view. (Observation deck open April-Sept. Sun.-Mon. 9:30am-11pm, Tues.-Sat. 10am-10:30pm; Oct.-March Sun.-Mon. 10am-6pm, Tues.-Sat. 10am-10:30pm. Last admission 30min. before closing. 35F, students and seniors 23F. Expect lines and buy your ticket before going up to the ground level.)

Avenue Foch, one of Haussmann's finest creations, runs its svelte course from the Arc de Triomphe to the **Bois de Boulogne,** 16*ème* (M: Porte Maillot, Sablons, Pont de Neuilly, Porte Dauphine, or Porte d'Auteuil), a popular place for daytime picnics. Joggers and walkers can find maps at regular intervals on the periphery of the park. Although the police recently cleaned out many of the drug dealers and prostitutes who once did business here, it's still a risky choice for a moonlit stroll.

Outside the city limits, **La Défense** (M: La Défense, zone 2; RER, zone 3) is a techno theme park that exposes the French yen for modernity. A glorified office complex, the area boasts the sleeker-than-thou headquarters of 14 of France's top 20 corporations. The neatest design is that of the **Grande Arche,** inaugurated in 1989, which completes the *axe historique* running through the Louvre, the pl. de la Concorde, and the Arc de Triomphe. There's an unparalleled view from the roof. (Ticket office open daily 10am-7pm; roof closes 8pm. 40F, under 18, students, and seniors 30F.) Shops, galleries, trees, and bizarre sculpture (Miró, Calder) make the pedestrian esplanade a pleasant stroll. Major roads run underneath the esplanade, so you'll feel less oppressed by pollution and cars here than anywhere in central Paris.

Montmartre and Père-Lachaise The **Basilique du Sacré-Coeur** (Basilica of the Sacred Heart), 35, rue du Cheval de la Barre (M: Anvers, Abbesses, or Château-Rouge), crowns the **butte Montmartre** like an enormous white meringue. Its onion dome is visible from almost any corner of the city down below, and its 112m bell tower is the highest point in Paris, with a view that stretches as far as 50km. (Open daily 7am-11pm. Free. Dome and crypt open in summer daily 9am-7pm; off-season 9am-6pm. Dome 15F, students 8F. Crypt 15F, students 8F.)

The **Cimetière Père-Lachaise,** on bd. de Ménilmontant (M: Père-Lachaise), holds the remains of Balzac, Colette, Seurat, Danton, David, Delacroix, La Fontaine, Haussmann, Molière, Sarah Bernhardt, and Proust within its peaceful, winding paths and elaborate sarcophagi. Foreigners buried here include Chopin, Gertrude Stein, Modigliani, and Oscar Wilde, though the most visited grave is **Jim Morrison's,** whose fans' graffiti (as well as flowers, beer, joints, and poetry) fills the cemetery. Oddly, there's a law against filming Morrison's grave. French Leftists make ceremonious pilgrimage to the **Mur des Fédérés** (Wall of the Federals), where 147 *Communards* were executed and buried. (Open March 16-Nov. 5 Mon.-Fri. 8am-6pm, Sat. 8:30am-6pm, Sun. 9am-6pm; Nov.-March 15 Mon.-Fri. 8am-5:30pm, Sat. 8:30am-5:30pm, Sun. 9am-5:30pm. Last admission 15min. before closing.)

MUSEUMS

Every Parisian institution, artistic movement, ethnic group, and custom worth its salt gets its own museum. For listings of temporary exhibits, check the bimonthly *Bulletin des musées et monuments historiques,* available at the tourist office at 127, av. des Champs-Elysées. *Paris Museums and Monuments,* also at the tourist office, has all the information you could want or need (including wheelchair accessibility). *Pariscope* and *L'Officiel des spectacles* also list museum hours and temporary exhibits. Frequent museum-goers, especially those ineligible for student or senior discounts, may want a **Carte Musées et Monuments,** which grants entry to 65 Parisian museums without waiting in line. The card is sold at major museums and metro stops (1 day 70F, 3 consecutive days 140F; 5 consecutive days 200F).

Musée du Louvre, 1er. M: Palais-Royal/Musée du Louvre. The short list of masterpieces includes the Code of Hammurabi, the *Venus de Milo,* the *Winged Victory of Samothrace,* Vermeer's *Lacemaker,* all the David you could want, Ingres's *Odalisque,* Géricault's *Raft of the Medusa,* Delacroix's *Liberty Leading the People,* and that lady with the mysterious smile. (Impressionist works and most late 19th-century art are now at the Musée d'Orsay.) Enter through I.M. Pei's pyramid in the Cour Napoléon, or skip lines by entering directly from the metro. Open Thurs.-Sun. 9am-6pm, Mon. and Wed. 9am-9:45pm. Last admission 45min. before closing. Mon. or Wed. evenings are quiet. Hall Napoléon open Wed.-Sun. until 10pm. 45F before 3pm, 26F after 3pm and Sun., first Sun. of each month free. A 100F Carte Louvre Jeune is good for a year for those under 26. English tours Mon. and Wed.-Sat. at 10, 11:30am, 2, and 3:30pm, 33F. Wheelchair accessible.

Musée d'Orsay, 1, rue de Bellechasse, 7ème. M: Solférino; RER Musée d'Orsay. While works by Monet, Degas, Pissarro, and others have established the Musée d'Orsay as *the* Impressionist museum, this former railway station is dedicated to presenting all of the major artistic movements spanning the period from 1848 until the first World War. Incorporating painting, sculpture, decorative arts, architecture, and photography, the museum's substantial collection juxtaposes revolutionary and conservative artists, sketches and masterpieces. Manet's Olympia is on the ground floor; upstairs, rooms full of Monet (including his stunning series on the Rouen cathedral), Degas, Rodin, Renoir, Cézanne, Van Gogh, Toulouse-Lautrec, Gaugin, and Seurat take your breath away. Open June 20-Sept. 20 Tues.-Wed. and Fri.-Sun. 9am-6pm, Thurs. 9am-9:45pm. Sept. 21-June 19 opens at 10am. Last admission 45min. before closing. 36F, Sun. 24F. Wheelchair access.

Centre National d'Art et de Culture Georges-Pompidou (Palais Beaubourg), 4ème. M: Rambuteau. This inside-out building has inspired passionate debates since its inauguration in 1977—mostly about whether or not it's better than a hole in the ground. Unfortunately, your contribution to this debate must be limited; the Centre Pompidou (including the **Musée National d'Art Moderne** inside) will be closed for major renovations until December 31, 1999. Still, it's a sight from the outside: colored piping and ventilation ducts run up, down, and sideways along the outside (blue for air, green for water, yellow for electricity, red for heating). Framing the building like a cage, huge steel bars support its weight.

Musée Rodin, 77, rue de Varenne, 7ème. M: Varenne. The elegant 18th-century Hôtel Biron holds all the major works of the father of modern sculpture, Auguste Rodin. His bronze sculptures and that of his partner, Camille Claudel, are gentle, gripping, and perfect. Don't miss unfinished *Gates of Hell* (of which *The Thinker* is part), and the *Burghers of Calais,* both outside. Open April-Sept. Tues.-Sun. 9:30am-5:45pm; Oct.-March Tues.-Sun. 9:30am-4:45pm. Last admission 30min. before closing. Grounds alone 5F; museum also 28F, students, seniors, and Sun. 18F.

Musée de l'Orangerie, 1er. M: Concorde. In the southwest corner of the Tuileries. Impressionist collection, smaller and less crowded than the Musée d'Orsay, with works by Renoir, Cézanne, and Mattisse, but featuring Monet's water lilies murals, *Les Nymphéas.* Open Wed.-Mon. 9:45am-5:15pm. 28F, under 25 and Sun. 18F.

Hôtel de Cluny, 6, pl. Paul-Painlevé, 5ème. M: Cluny-Sorbonne. Not only houses one of the world's finest collections of medieval art, but is itself a perfectly preserved medieval manor, built on top of Roman ruins. *La Dame et La Licorne* (The Lady and the Unicorn) is arguably the best extant medieval tapestry series. Open Wed.-Mon. 9:15am-5:45pm. 30F, under 25, over 60, and Sun. 20F, under 18 free.

Musée Salvador Dalí (Espace Montmartre), 11, rue Poulbot, 18ème. M: Anvers or Abbesses. Just off pl. du Tertre, this is chock-full of lithographs and sculptures by the Spanish surrealist, with scads of incarnations of his droopy clocks. It's laid out in "Surrealist surroundings"—i.e. wonderful spacing, interesting lighting, and ridiculous background "space-music." Open daily 10am-6pm. 35F, students 25F.

Musée des Egouts de Paris (Sewer Museum), actually in the sewers at the corner of quai d'Orsay and pl. de la Résistance, 7ème. M: Pont de l'Alma. Explore for yourself the Victor Hugo-esque city beneath the city with a brochure, or follow a guide on an impromptu tour. Open May-Sept. Sat.-Wed. 11am-6pm; Oct-Dec. and Feb.-April Sat.-Wed. 11am-5pm. Last admission 1hr. before closing. 25F, students 20F.

Musée Picasso, 5, rue de Thorigny, 3ème. M: Chemin Vert. Individual works may not be of great significance, but the collection as a whole is superlative, thanks to a good design (with English explanations). Lights by Diego Giacometti (Alberto's bro). Open April-Sept. Wed.-Mon. 9:30am-6pm; Oct.-March 9:30am-5:30pm. Last admission 45min. before closing. 30F, ages 18-25, over 60, and Sun. 20F.

Les Catacombs, 1, pl. Denfert-Rochereau, 14ème. M: Denfert-Rochereau. Contains the bones of 5-6 million Parisians in former limestone mines—including those of a guy who got lost here in 1793 and wasn't found for 9 years. Bring a sweater and a friend. Open Tues.-Fri. 2-4:45pm, Sat.-Sun. 9-11am and 2-4pm. 27F, ages 7-25 19F.

La Villette, 19ème. M: Porte de la Villette or Porte de Pantin. An urban renewal project in the northeastern corner of Paris, previously home to a slaughterhouse compound that provided most of the beef for Paris. Its 55 hectares enclose a landscaped park, a huge science museum (open Tues.-Sat. 10am-6pm, Sun. 10am-7pm, 55F), an Omnimax cinema (57F, Mon.-Fri. students 44F), a conservatory, an exhibition hall, a jazz club, a concert and theater space, and a brand-new high-tech music museum (Tues.-Thurs. noon-7pm, Fri.-Sat. noon-7:30, Sun. 10am-7pm).

Musée d'Art Moderne de la Ville de Paris, 11, av. du Président Wilson, in the Palais de Tokyo, 16ème. M: Iéna. One of the world's foremost collections of 20th-century art. Works by Matisse *(The Dance)* and Picasso *(The Jester)* on permanent display; temporary exhibits vary dramatically. Open Wed.-Mon. 10am-5:30pm. Permanent collection 27F, students and seniors 15F. Temporary exhibits 5-15F extra.

Musée de l'Homme (Man), pl. du Trocadéro, in the Palais de Chaillot. 16ème. M: Trocadéro. A Turkish store, a British Columbian totem pole, and multimedia presentations on cultures worldwide since prehistory. Open Wed.-Mon. 9:45am-5:15pm. 30F, under 27 and seniors 20F. Films Wed. and Sat. at 3 and 4pm.

Musée Marmottan, 2, rue Louis-Boilly, 16ème. M: La Muette. Follow Chausée de la Muette (av. Ranelagh) through the Jardin (park) du Ranelagh. A hunting lodge turned stately mansion and furnished with Empire furniture and primitive German, Flemish, and Italian paintings, Impressionist canvases, and medieval illuminations. Open Tues.-Sun. 10am-5:30pm. Admission 40F, students and seniors 25F.

ENTERTAINMENT

Paris teems with cabarets, discos, and smoky jazz clubs; with U.S. and European cinema; with avant-garde and traditional theater; with rock and classical concerts. Consult the magazine **Pariscope** (3F) and the **Officiel des Spectacles** (2F), both on sale at any newsstand. Even if you don't understand French, you should be able to decipher the listings of times and locations. Or, contact **Info-Loisirs,** a recording that keeps tabs on what's on in Paris (English tel. 01 49 52 53 56, French 01 49 52 53 55).

While it's not London or Berlin, Paris has an open and active gay scene and less visible lesbian and bi scenes. The center of the action is the **Marais** (the 3*ème* and 4*ème* *arrondissements*), sprinkled with clubs, bars, and stores, especially around rue de Ferronerie, rue du Temple, rue des Archives, and rue Vieille du Temple. For the most comprehensive listing of bi, gay, and lesbian establishments, organizations, and services, consult Gai Pied's *Guide Gai 1997* (in English and French, 79F at any kiosk). *Lesbia*'s ads are a good gauge of what's hot, or at least what's open (25F); *Pariscope* also has an English-language section *A Week of Gay Outings.*

Fortunately, the best Parisian entertainment—people-watching—is free. The plaza next to the **Centre Pompidou** fills with fire-eaters, sword-swallowers, Chilean guitar bands, and other performers, but it's rough at night. Around **pl. St-Germain,** throngs of people strut by in the latest fashions, and a few bars offer unlimited jazz for the cost of a drink. By the **Ile St-Louis,** more refined tourists stroll the banks of the Seine two-by-two and gaze meaningfully into each others' eyes. To see a movie or to linger in fashionable cafés, wander around **Montparnasse,** the way-touristed **Champs-Elysées,** and the streets radiating from **bd. St-Michel, bd. St-Germain,** and **bd. Sébastopol.** Don't forget that several sections of Paris have entertainment businesses of a different sort. Prostitutes and drug dealers fill the areas of Pigalle and Gare St-Lazare nightly. After dark, be careful in Montmartre and avoid the Bois de Boulogne entirely.

Theater tickets can run as high as you want, but reduced student rates are nearly always available, and some theaters sell rush tickets an hour or so before curtain. Most theaters close for August. *Pariscope* and *l'Officiel des Spectacles* print complete listings of current shows. The national theater of **La Comédie Française's Salle Richelieu,** 2, rue de Richelieu, 1*er* has an exaggerated style and tends to be heavy on Molière (tel. 01 44 58 15 15; tickets 70-185F, student tickets 60-70F, rush tickets 30F). The other national theater, **Odéon Théâtre de l'Europe,** 1, pl. Odéon, 6*ème*, does the whole range, from classics to avant-garde (tel. 01 44 41 36 36; tickets 50-165F, student rush 60F). The **Théâtre de la Huchette,** 23, rue de la Huchette, 5*ème* (tel. 01 53 32 32 00), has been a bastion of Left Bank intellectualism for years now, playing *La cantatrice chauve* and *La leçon.* (Mon.-Sat. at 7pm and 8pm, respectively. Tickets 100F, students Mon.-Fri. 80F. Both shows 160F, 120F.) Café-Théâtres like **Au Bec Fin,** 6, rue Thérèse, 1*er* (tel. 01 42 96 29 35; tickets 50-80F, with dinner from 178F), perform low-budget, high-energy skits in small settings but require better French to enjoy. Far and away the best place for cut-rate theater tickets is the **Kiosque-Théâtre,** 15, pl. de la Madeleine, 8*ème* (M: Madeleine; also in 1*er*, M: Châtelet-Les Halles), which sells half-price, same-day tickets (16F fee; open Tues.-Sat. 12:30-8pm, Sun. 12:30-4pm). **Alpha FNAC: Spectacles** at 136, rue de Rennes, 6*ème* (tel. 01 49 45 30 00; M: Montparnasse-Bienvenue); Forum des Halles, 1-7, rue Pierre Lescot, 1*er* (tel. 01 40 41 40 00; M: Châtelet-Les Halles); 26-30, av. des Ternes, 17*ème*(tel. 01 44 09 18 00; M: Ternes); and 71, bd. St-Germain, 5*ème* (tel. 01 44 41 31 50), sells tickets for theater, concerts, and festivals (open Mon.-Sat. 10am-7:30pm).

Cinema

Cinema was invented in Paris (by the Lumière brothers, Auguste and Louis), and the first movie premiered at the Grand Café (14, bd. des Capucines) in 1895. Paris, of all the cities in the world, probably plays the greatest number of different films each week. The cinemas offer a range of ticket discounts, especially on Mondays and Wednesdays. Check *Pariscope* for details. The entertainment weeklies list show times and theaters. Film festivals are listed separately. The notation **v.o.** *(version orig-*

inale) after a non-French movie listing means that the film is being shown in its original language with French subtitles; **v.f.** *(version française)* means that it has been dubbed—an increasingly rare phenomenon.

Cinémathèque, Française, pl. du Trocadéro, 16ème. M: Trocadéro. At the Musée du Cinéma in the Palais de Chaillot; enter through the Jardins du Trocadéro. Also 18, rue du Faubourg-du-Temple, 11ème. M: République. Recording (tel. 01 47 04 24 24) lists all shows. A must for film buffs. 2-3 classics, near-classics, or soon-to-be classics per day. Open Wed.-Sun. Shows from 5-9:45pm. 28F, students 18F.

L'Entrepôt, 7-9, rue Francis de Pressensé, 14ème (tel. 01 45 40 78 38). M: Pernety. Off rue Raymond Losserand. An international venue for independent films, this cinema organizes a wide variety of week-long festivals, sometimes with director or actor forums. 3 screens show films in *v.o.* 35F, students and seniors 30F.

La Pagode, 57bis, rue de Babylone, 7ème (tel. 01 36 68 75 07). M: St-François-Xavier. Turn right off bd. des Invalides. Paris's most charming cinema, specializing in contemporary films of the artsy ilk. 44F, students and seniors Mon.-Fri. before 6pm, and everyone on Wed. 37F. Shows in the *Salle Japonaise* a bit more.

Jazz

Aided by a sudden influx of American recordings into post-War France, Paris's status as a jazz hot spot emerged in the late 1940s. Since then, French jazz musicians have themselves become fixtures of international scale. Frequent summer festivals sponsor free or nearly free jazz concerts. French mags *Jazz Hot* (45F), *Jazz Magazine* (35F), and *LYLO* (*Les Yeux, Les Oreilles;* free) have the most complete listings.

Au Duc des Lombards, 42, rue des Lombards, 1er (tel. 01 42 33 22 88). M: Châtelet. The best in French jazz, with occasional American soloists. Packed with regulars. Cover 80-100F, music students 50-80F. Open daily 7:30pm-4am. Music 10pm-2am.

New Morning, 7-9, rue des Petites-Ecuries, 10ème (tel. 01 45 23 51 41). M: Château d'Eau. Halfway between a club and a concert hall, dark, smoky, and crowded. All the greats have played here, from Chet Baker to Miles Davis. Open Sept.-July from 8pm; times vary. Tickets from box office or FNAC 110-140F.

Le Sunset, 60, rue des Lombards, 1er (tel. 01 40 26 46 60). M: Châtelet. An easygoing club with an old and widespread reputation, Le Sunset is where musicians come to jam into the wee hours after their gigs around Paris. Mostly French and European acts. Cover 50-100F. 20% *Let's Go* discount. Open daily 10pm-dawn; hang around past 2am to catch the jam scene.

Dance and Rock Clubs

This ain't Barcelona, Montréal, or Buenos Aires; the streets aren't filled with young people waiting to get into discos. Some clubs here are small, private, and nearly impossible to sniff out unless you're a native. In general, word of mouth is the best guide to the current scene. Many Parisian clubs are officially private, which means they have the right to pick and choose their clientele. Often, people of African or Arab descent find it difficult to get in. Parisians tend to dress up more than Americans for a night on the town; haggard backpackers might want to try a bar instead.

L'Arapaho, 30, av. d'Italie, Centre Commercial Italie 2, 13ème. M: Place d'Italie. The gray door on the right, just past Au Printemps. Some of the best hard-core, rap, pop, and metal bands to come through Paris. Past acts have included Bim Skala Bim and Soul Asylum. Tickets usually around 60-130F. Beer 20F. Cocktails 50F. Open 11pm-dawn; Fri. Asian, Sat. Cuban. Cover 80F, cocktails 50F.

Les Bains, 7, rue de Bourg l'Abbée, 3ème. M: Réaumur-Sébastopol. Ultra-selective and ultra-expensive. Past patrons include Madonna, Mike Tyson, Roman Polanski, and he-who-was-Prince (who gave a surprise free concert here). Cover and 1st drink 100F. Later drinks 100F. Open daily midnight-6am.

La Casbah, 18-20, rue de la Forge Royale, 11ème. M: Faidherbe-Chaligny. This chic dance lair mixes pop and Arabic music. Elegant, with a seriously, honestly, we-mean-it, strict door policy. Dress to impress. Cover Wed. and Thurs. 80F, Fri. and Sat. 120F. Open Wed.-Sat. 9pm-6am.

Le Queen, 102, av. des Champs-Elysées, 8ème. The fiercest funk at the cheapest, most fashionable club in town (and so the toughest to get into). Dress your most (insert adjective): Mon. disco (50F cover, 1 drink); Tues. house, gay men, soap suds (50F cover, 1 drink); Wed. Latin house, free; Thurs. house, free; Fri.-Sat. house (80F cover, 1 drink). Sun. 80s, free. Drinks 50F. Open daily midnight-dawn.

Scala de Paris, 188bis, rue de Rivoli, 1er. M: Palais-Royal. Halfway between a disco and a rollercade, with thumping house and techno. Caters to a sometimes rough-looking 18-24 crowd. Cover Sun.-Thurs. 80F, women free, 1-drink min.; Fri.-Sat. 100F for everyone, 1 drink included. Drinks 45-60F. Open daily 10:30pm-dawn.

Bars

Bars in the 5ème and 6ème often cater to Anglophone students; Bastille and (mostly gay) Marais are young and hip; the rue Vieille du Temple is always hopping. The 11ème and 20ème are working class neighborhoods with fast changing bars. Draft beer is *bière pression; kir royale* mixes champagne with *crème de cassis* (black currant).

Le Bar sans Nom, 49, rue de Lappe, 11ème. M: Bastille. A deep red front distinguishes this bar from the others along the unbelievably lively rue de Lappe. The very hip crowd packs into the bar's two rooms: the first for people-watching, the second is more intimate. Beer 30-40F. Cocktails 50F. Open Mon.-Sat. 7pm-2am.

Café Charbon, 109, rue Oberkampf, 11ème. M: Parmentier or Ménilmontant. Old dance hall now a hidden hotspot for young Parisians. Beer 12-16F at the bar, 14-19F at a table. Surprisingly inexpensive food served noon-5pm. Open daily 9am-2am.

Amnésia Café, 42, rue Vieille-du-Temple, 4ème. M: Hôtel-de-Ville. A classy, relaxed, gay bar (primarily men) where friends gather and gossip. Usually crowded, but without the cruising factor that can make other Marais bars a little overbearing. Beer 17-30F. Open daily 10am-2am. Sun. brunch noon-4pm.

Café Oz, 184, rue St-Jacques, 5ème. M: Luxembourg. Take any street off bd. St-Michel away from the metro; left on rue St-Jacques. Down-to-earth Aussie atmosphere attracts Anglophones and Parisians eager to escape the stress of the city. Beer 22-35F. Cocktails 38-45F. Happy hour daily 6:30-9:30pm. Open daily 11am-1:30am.

Lou Pascalou, 14, rue des Panayaux 20ème. M: Ménilmontant. Left off bd. de Ménilmontant. Out-of-the-way corner in an out-of-the-way *arrondissement;* a *provençal* bar popular with a local artsy crowd. 0.5L of beer 30F. Open daily 10am-2am.

Le Champmeslé, 4, rue Chabanais, 2ème (tel. 01 42 96 85 20). M: Pyramides or Bourse. This intimate lesbian bar is Paris's oldest. Comfortable couches, dim lighting, and a young clientele. No cover. Drinks 25-40F. Open Mon.-Sat. 5pm-dawn.

FRANCE

I'll Trade You My '52 Mantle for Your '88 Gerard Longuet

Anyone in France for any length of time eventually gives up the constant (and futile) search for coin-operated telephones and invests in a *télécarte.* So where are the spent cards? Where is the *télécarte* graveyard? The answer is simple but shocking: collectors' albums. The ads and artwork turn some cards into valuable commodities. So valuable, in fact, that an entire *télécarte* collection business has developed around the credit-card sized *chef d'oeuvres.* Stores and markets may have boxes of common and uncommon cards (for 5-10F each), while the rarities reside under protective covering in binders and acrylic cases. The condition of a card drastically affects its value, while the number of call-enabling *unités* is irrelevant. A 1987-88 carte by Gerard Longuet is one of the gems in the *télécarte* collector's crown. Only 40 exist, and an unblemished one nets 34,000F. But for the real prize, seek out the November 1988 "Les Boxeurs," with artwork by Gilles Chagny. There are 100 out there, but only one is signed by the artist. Maybe it's down at your feet right now as you make your call—it's worth checking, because if it *is* there, you've just stumbled across a cool 60,000F.

■ Near Paris: Versailles, Chartres, and Disneyland Paris

"L'état, c'est moi," (I am the state) declared Louis XIV, who then proceeded to build a royal residence the size of a small nation. Louis gathered the aristocracy of France to this glorified hunting lodge at **Versailles,** keeping an eye on them to prevent any noble insurrections, and giving them little to do but follow him around and vie for his attention. The incredibly lavish building embodies the Old Regime's extravagance, but Versailles was totally sacked during the Revolution and only a smidgen of its original furnishings have been restored. Le Nôtre's geometric **gardens** are studded with unforgettable fountains, which spurt to music every Sunday, May through September. Taking a "best of Versailles" tour (1hr., 25F, leaves from entrance D) is worth it. (Château open May-Sept. Tues.-Sun. 9am-6:30pm; Oct.-April 9am-5:30pm. Last admission 30 min. before closing. Palace 45F; after 3:30pm, ages 18-25, over 60, and Sun. 35F. Gardens open sunrise-sundown. Free, except May-Sept. Sun. 20F.) Take **RER** C5 from M: Invalides to the Versailles Rive Gauche station (every 15min., 35-40 min., round-trip 26F). Any train whose label begins in "V" will do. Buy your RER ticket *before* getting to the platform; though your metro ticket will get you onto the train, it will not get you through the RER turnstiles at Versailles.

The stunning **Cathédrale de Chartres,** spared by bureaucratic inefficiency after being condemned during the Revolution, survives today as one of the most sublime creations of the Middle Ages. Arguably the finest example of early Gothic architecture in the world, the cathedral retains several of its original 12th-century stained-glass windows; the rest of the windows and the magnificent sculptures on the main portals date from the 13th century. Malcolm Miller, an authority on Gothic architecture, leads fantastic English tours of the cathedral. (75min. tours April-Jan. Mon.-Sat. noon and 2:45pm; 30F, students 20F. Cathedral open in summer daily 7:30am-7:30pm; in winter 7:30am-7pm. No casual visits Sat. 5:45-7pm and Sun. 9:15-noon.) The town of **Chartres** celebrates the medieval crafts showcased in its cathedral. The **tourist office** across from the cathedral can give you all the info you need. Frequent **trains** run to Chartres from Gare Montparnasse. (1hr., round-trip 138F, roughly one per hour in summer, but call 08 36 35 35 35 for schedule info.) To reach the cathedral from the station, walk straight to the pl. de Châtelet, turn left into the *place,* turn right onto rue Ste-Même, then go left onto rue Jean Moulin.

It's a small, small world and Disney seems hell-bent on making it even smaller. When EuroDisney opened, it was met by the jeers of French intellectuals and the popular press. Resistance to the park seems to have subsided since Walt & Co. renamed it **Disneyland Paris;** a touch of class goes a long way. Whether you come to mock or celebrate, the park can be whiz-bang fun, even for the budget traveler; every show, attraction, and ride is included in the admission price. For the wildest rides, look for those with the greatest warnings. Warnings directed at pregnant women and people with chronic heart problems are the hallmarks of the real thing. Buy *"passeports"* (tickets) at the 50 windows on Disneyland Hotel's ground floor, at the Paris tourist office, or at any major station on RER line A; buy ahead if you'll be visiting on a weekend. (195F, under 12 150F. Open daily 9am-11pm. Winter hours may change. Reduced prices Oct.-Dec. 22 and Jan. 8-March 31.) To reach Disneyland Paris from Paris, take **RER** A4 "Marne-la-Vallée" to the last stop, "Marne-la-Vallée/Chessy" (every 30min., 45min., round-trip 76F). The last train to Paris leaves Disney at 12:22am but won't reach Paris before the metro closes. **Eurail** holders take notice: the TGV runs from Roissy/Charles de Gaulle to the park in 15 minutes.

THE NORTH (LE NORD)

The Channel Ports

Calais Ever since Richard the Lionheart and his crusaders passed through, **Calais** has been the continent's primary portal to the fairer lands of Britain. **Hoverspeed,** Hoverport (tel. 0 800 90 17 77), zips across to Dover (50min., 240F, with InterRail Pass 172F). **P&O Ferries** (tel. 03 21 46 04 40) and **SeaFrance,** at the Car Ferry Terminal (tel. 03 21 46 80 00), send slower but cheaper ferries to Dover (P&O 200F, SeaFrance 190F; open return P&O and SeaFrance 300F). Free buses connect the hoverport and ferry terminal with the train station at bd. Jacquard (tel. 08 36 35 35 35) during the day. Frequent **trains** leave for Paris (3½hr., 172F; TGV 1¾hr., 224F), Boulogne (30min., 40F), and Dunkerque (1hr., 44F). The **tourist office,** 12, bd. Clemenceau (tel. 03 21 96 62 40; fax 03 21 96 01 92), one block from the train station, provides currency exchange and accommodations help (open Mon.-Sat. 9am-7pm, Sun. 10am-1pm). **Centre Européen de Séjour/Auberge de Jeunesse (HI),** av. Maréchal Delattre de Tassigny (tel. 03 21 34 70 20; fax 03 21 96 87 80), has spiffy doubles (77F, breakfast included; nonmembers 10F extra and 1-night max. stay). **Hotel Bonsaï,** Quai du Danube (tel. 03 21 96 10 10) has two-bed doubles and triples (149F, breakfast 26F; Visa, MC). To fill your stomach, find a **boulangerie** on bd. Gambetta, bd. Jacquard, or rue des Thermes, or go to the **Match supermarket,** pl. d'Armes (open Mon-Fri. 9am-12:30pm and 2:30-7:30pm, Sat. 9am-7:30pm).

Boulogne A pilgrimage site since 636, when a boat aglow with heavenly light carried a statue of the Virgin Mary onto the beach, **Boulogne** today is a mecca of a different sort, ushering thousands of passengers through its ferry terminal daily. **Hoverspeed** (tel. 0 800 90 17 77) shuttles to Folkestone, England (every 3hr., one way or 5-day return 150F). **Trains** leave the station on bd. Voltaire for Paris (3hr., 159F) and Calais (30min., 40F). If your stopover lasts awhile, visit the *vieille ville* atop the city; the towering **Basilique de Notre-Dame** contains precious religious objects and the remains of a Roman temple. (Crypt and treasury open Tues.-Sun. 2-5pm. 10F. Church open Mon.-Sat. 8am-noon and 2-7pm, Sun 8:30am-12:30pm and 2:30-6pm.) The massive **Château-Musée,** rue de Bernet, houses an eclectic and impressive art collection. (Open May 15-Sept. 15 Mon.-Sat. 9:30am-12:30pm and 1:30-6:15pm, Sun. 9:30am-12:30pm and 2:30-6:15pm; Sept. 16-May 14 Mon.-Sat. 10am-12:30pm and 2-5pm, Sun. 10am-12:30pm and 2:30-5:30pm. 20F, students 13F.) To get to the **tourist office,** pl. François Sauvage (tel. 03 21 31 68 38; fax 03 21 33 81 09), exit the train station and go left on bd. Voltaire until you reach the canal. then turn right and follow bd. Diderot past the first bridge on your left. The office has a free accommodations service. (Open June-Sept. Mon.-Sat. 9am-7pm, Sun. 10am-6pm; Oct.-May Mon.-Sat. 9am-7pm, Sun. 10am-12:30pm and 1:30-5pm.) The **auberge de jeunesse (HI)**, 1, pl. de Lisle (tel. 03 21 80 14 50; fax 03 21 80 45 62), across from the Gare-Ville, has a shower and toilet in each room, kitchen, pool table, and bar with TV/VCR. (Members only. Reception open daily 7:30am-1am. Curfew 1am. 80F, breakfast and linen included. Reserve ahead in July-Aug.) Charming **restaurants** cluster on rue de Lille in the *vieille ville,* while cheap food abounds on the waterfront around pl. Gambetta. Enjoy the quiche (27F) at **Joly-Desenclos,** 44, rue de Lille (open Wed.-Mon. 7am-8pm). Bars bustle on pl. Dalton.

Dunkerque The last city in France to be liberated in World War II, the reconstructed Dunkerque holds little charm for visitors. Nevertheless, **Malo-les-Bains** provide an excellent escape whenever the sun is shining. The **Musée d'Art Contemporain,** rue des Bains, has zany modern sculptures in an eccentrically manicured garden (Museum open Wed.-Mon. 10am-noon and 2-6pm. Garden open in summer daily 9:30am-8pm; in spring and fall closes 6:30pm; in winter closes

5:30pm.) More traditional offerings shine at the 15th-century **Eglise St-Eloi,** which shelters Flemish paintings inside its impressive Gothic walls, and in the resonant **belfry** across the street (belfry open July-Aug. Tues.-Sun.; elevators hourly 9:30am-5:30pm; 12F). The **tourist office,** rue Amiral Ronarch (tel. 03 28 66 79 21; fax 03 28 26 27 80), provides currency exchange and excellent maps, and makes hotel reservations (open Mon.-Fri. 9am-12:30pm and 1:30-6:30pm, Sat. 9am-6:30pm). **Trains** roll to Paris (2hr., 209F), Lille (1½hr., 71F), Calais (1hr., 44F), and Boulogne (1½hr., 70F). The **auberge de jeunesse (HI),** pl. Paul-Asseman (tel. 03 28 63 36 34; fax 03 28 69 52), is on the beach 30 minutes from the train station. Take bus 3 to "Piscine"; turn left and walk past the pool and skating rink. (Members only in summer. Curfew 11pm, none July-Aug. 46F. Sheets 17F. Breakfast 19F.) Cafés and bars line the **digue de Allieés** and the **digue de Mer.** Check out **NASA,** 67, digue de Mer, for reggae.

Lille

With a rich Flemish ancestry and exuberant nightlife, the unsullied and largely untouristed Lille flirts its big city charms without the usual accompanying big city hassle. One of France's finest museums, Lille's **Musée des Beaux-Arts,** on pl. de la République, has reopened its galleries, rebuilt and slickly painted, to an eager public (open Mon. 2-6pm, Wed.-Thurs. and Sat.-Sun. noon-6pm; 25F, under 25 20F). To get to the companion **Musée d'Art Moderne,** 1, allée du Musée, which houses an impressive Cubist and postmodern collection, take bus 10 or 41 to "Parc Urbain-Musée" (open Wed.-Mon. 10am-6pm; 25F, students 15F). The Flemish Renaissance **Vieille Bourse** (Old Stock Exchange) at pl. Géneral de Gaulle now houses flower and book markets. Nearby stand two other masterpieces: the **Chamber of Commerce and Industry** and its tower on pl. du Théâtre, and the 14th-century **Eglise St-Maurice.** (M: Rihour. Open Mon.-Sat. 9am-noon and 2-6pm, Sun. 2-6pm, except during mass.) **Charles de Gaulle's birthplace,** 9, rue Princesse, has photographs, newspaper clippings, and the baptismal dress of the Resistance leader and two-time French president (open Wed.-Sun. 10am-noon and 2-5pm; 8F).

The **tourist office,** pl. Rihour (tel. 03 20 21 94 21), occupies a 15th-century castle and offers currency exchange, a free map, and an accommodations service (open Mon.1-6pm, Tues.-Sat. 10am-6pm, Sun. 10am-noon and 2-5pm). **Trains** leave the station on pl. de Gare for Paris (1hr., 203F), Arras (40min., 51F), and Brussels, Belgium (1½hr., 100F). If you're staying in town during the summer, ask **Fédération des Etudiants,** 125, rue Meurein (tel. 03 20 30 60 26), about university housing. **Hôtel Saint-Nicolas,** 11, rue Nicolas Leblanc (tel. 03 20 57 37 26), tucked behind the Musée des Beaux-Arts, offers uniquely decorated singles for 110-170F and doubles for 140-180F (reception closed Sun. noon-8pm). Inexpensive restaurants and cafés pepper the pedestrian zone around rue de Béthune; **Aux Moules,** 34, rue de Béthune, with mussels from 51F, is a local favorite (open daily noon-midnight). Pubs line **rue Sulferino** and **rue Solférino** and the *vieille ville* boasts popular dance clubs and wine bars. Stumble down Jean-Jacques Rousseau to **La Piroge,** or, nearby, try your luck with the bouncer at **Les Visiteurs du Soir** for experimental bands.

Near Lille: Arras and Vimy

Built over the fascinating **Les Boves tunnels** that have sheltered both medieval chalk miners and British World War I soldiers, **Arras** lies 40 minutes by train (51F) from Lille. The friendly folks at the **tourist office** (tel. 03 21 51 26 95), in the 15th-century Hôtel de Ville, find rooms (no charge) and organize tours of the tunnels. (Open May-Sept. Mon.-Sat. 9am-6:30pm, Sun. 10am-12:30pm and 2:30-6:30pm; Oct.-April Mon.-Sat. 9am-noon and 3-6:30pm.) Spend the night at the central **auberge de jeunesse (HI),** 59, Grande Place (tel. 03 21 22 70 02; reception open daily 7:30-noon and 5-11pm; 46F). Elegant **restaurants** are located near the hostel. Ten kilometers northeast of Arras lies the monument of **Vimy,** a memorial to the 66,655 Canadians killed in World War I. The peaceful 11,285 trees planted in the park represent the number of the soldiers whose final resting place is unknown. Stay on marked trails; undetonated mines lie beyond (open daily sunrise-sunset; tours April-Nov. 10am-6pm; free). Frequent **buses** (8F one way) and **trains** (15F) arrive from Arras.

NORMANDY (NORMANDIE)

Inspiration to Impressionists and generals, fertile Normandy is a land of gently undulating fields, tiny fishing villages, and soaring cathedrals. Vikings seized the region in the 9th century, and invasions have twice secured Normandy's place in military history: in 1066, when William of Normandy conquered England, and on D-Day, June 6, 1944, when Allied armies began the liberation of France here.

Normandy supplies much of the country's butter; try the creamy, pungent *camembert* cheese, but be sure it's ripe (soft in the middle). Eating *tripes à la normandaise* (made from cow guts) requires intestinal fortitude. The province's traditional drink *(cidre)* comes both dry *(brut)* and sweet *(doux)*. A harder cousin is *calvados,* aged apple brandy, which ranks with the finest cognacs.

Rouen

Best known as the city where Joan of Arc was burned and Emma Bovary was bored, Rouen is no provincial hayseed town. The city enjoyed prosperity and status from the 10th through the 12th centuries as the capital of the Norman empire, and Victor Hugo later dubbed it "the city of 100 spires." The most famous of these spires emanate from the **Cathédrale de Notre-Dame,** with the tallest tower (151m) in France. The now-grimy Gothic facade so fascinated Monet that he painted it over and over again in varying lights and seasons (open Mon.-Sat. 8am-7pm, Sun. 7:30am-6pm). Behind the cathedral, the flamboyant **Eglise St-Maclou** features an elaborately carved pipe organ. (Open March-Oct. Mon.-Sat. 10am-noon and 2-6pm, Sun. 3-5:30pm; Nov.-Feb. Mon.-Sat. 10am-noon and 2-5:30pm, Sun. 3-5:30pm.) Nearby, at 186, rue de Martainville, **Aitre St-Maclou** served as the church's charnel house and cemetery through the later Middle Ages. Inside, visitors gape at a perfectly preserved cat cadaver, from an unfortunate feline buried alive to exorcise spirits (open daily 8am-8pm; free). From the cathedral, turn onto rue du Gros Horloge to see the charmingly inaccurate, 14th-century **Gros Horloge** (Big Clock).

Joan of Arc died on **place du Vieux Marché,** east of the city center. A cross marks the spot near the unsightly **Eglise Ste-Jeanne d'Arc,** designed to resemble an overturned boat. A block up rue Jeanne d'Arc, the **Musée des Beaux-Arts,** square Verdrel, houses an excellent collection of European masters from the 16th through the 20th centuries (open Wed.-Sun. 10am-6pm; 20F, youth 13F). If you're ill from Monet overdose, be happy that you won't be treated at the **Musée Flaubert et d'Histoire de la Médecine,** 51, rue de Lecat, whose exhibits showcase a gruesome array of pre-anesthesia medical instruments, including gallstone crushers and a battlefield amputation kit (open Tues.-Sat. 10am-noon and 2-6pm; 12F, youth 8F). Possessions of the former occupant, writer Gustave Flaubert, are also on display.

On the way to or from Paris, stop by **Giverny,** where the **Musée Claude Monet** preserves the master's gardens and Japanese prints (open April-Oct. Tues.-Sun 10am-6pm; 35F, students and seniors 25F). Buses run to the museum from **Vernon** (Mon.-Sat. 6 per day, Sun. 3 per day, 10min., 11F), which is 40 minutes from Rouen on the Rouen-Paris-St-Lazare line (every 2hr., 52F).

Practical Information, Accommodations, and Food From Rouen, trains run to Paris (every hr., 1½hr., 104F), Lille (3 per day, 3hr., 160F), Le Havre (every hr., 1hr., 72F), and Caen (via Serguigny, every 2hr., 2hr., 116F). From the station, walk down rue Jeanne d'Arc and turn left onto rue du Gros Horloge to reach pl. de la Cathédrale and the **tourist office** (tel. 02 32 08 32 40; fax 02 32 08 32 44). (Open

April 15-Sept. Mon.-Sat. 9am-7pm, Sun. 9:30am-12:30pm and 2:30-6pm; Oct.-April 14 Mon.-Sat. 9am-12:30pm and 2-6:30pm, Sun. 10am-1pm).

For 24-hour accommodation service, call **Club Hôtel Rouennais** (tel. 02 35 71 76 77). University **CROUS** lodgings are cheap but usually available only on summer weekends (tel. 02 35 15 74 40). **Hôtel Normandya,** 32, rue du Cordier (tel. 02 35 71 46 15), offers hospitality near the train station off rue Donjon (singles and doubles 100-110F, with shower 140-150F). **Hôtel St-Ouen,** 43, rue des Faulx (tel. 02 35 71 46 44), has cheerful rooms and breathtaking views (singles, doubles, and triples 100-200F). **Camping Municipal de Déville** (tel. 02 35 74 07 59) is on rue Jules Ferry in Déville-les-Rouen, 4km from Rouen; take bus 2 from the station to "Mairie" (23F per person, 7F per tent; open May-Sept. for tents).

If you crave *moules* (mussels), **Le Queen Mary,** 1, rue du Cercle, off pl. du Vieux-Marché, is the place for you (44-75F; open July-Aug. daily 11:30am-2pm and 7:30-11pm; Sept.-June closed Mon). **La P'tite Flambée,** 24, rue Cauchoise, off pl. du Vieux-Marché, makes crepes right before your eyes (12-49F; open Tues.-Sat. 11:30am-2:30pm and 6:30-11:30pm). Find tasty organic food at **Natural Gourmand'grain,** 3, rue du Petit Salut, off pl. de la Cathédrale (*menu* 41F or 64F; open Tues.-Sat. noon-6pm). A **market** enlivens pl. du Vieux Marché (open Tues.-Sun. 7am-12:30pm). Packaged foods crinkle at the **Monoprix supermarket,** 73-83, rue du Gros Horloge (open Mon.-Sat. 8:30am-9pm).

Normandy Coast

Dieppe attracts hordes of sun-starved Britons to its long pebbly **beach,** bordered by protective cliffs to the west and the port to the east, which Canadian forces struggled to retake in 1942. The city's **tourist office,** pont Jehan Ango (tel. 02 35 84 11 77; fax 02 35 06 27 66), is on the waterfront in the *centre ville.* (Open July-Aug. daily 9am-1pm and 2-8pm; May-June and Sept. Mon.-Sat. 9am-1pm and 2-7pm, Sun. 10am-1pm and 3-6pm; Oct.-April Mon.-Sat. 9am-noon and 2-6pm.) The **auberge de jeunesse (HI),** 48, rue Louis Fromager (tel. 02 35 84 85 73), has spacious and clean rooms; take bus 2 to "Château Michel" or call ahead for directions for the 30-minute walk (reception open daily 8-10am and 5-10pm; 65F, sheets 16F). Stena **ferries** (tel. 02 35 06 39 00), in the *gare maritime* across the canal at the outer port, chug across the English Channel to Newhaven (3-4 per day, 2-4hr., 100-240F, bikes free).

Fécamp has its own scenic beach and port, as well as two architectural marvels. The magnificent, Renaissance-inspired **Palais Bénédictine,** 110 rue Alexandre Le Grand, houses impressive collections of medieval and Renaissance religious artifacts. The palace is also famous for its after-dinner *liqueur,* originally distilled from 27 plants and spices by the town's monks. (Open May 1-Sept. 14 daily 9:30am-6pm; Sept. 15-Nov. 11 10am-noon and 2-5:30pm; Nov. 12-March 15 at 10:30am and 2-5pm; March 16-April 30 10am-noon and 2-5:30pm. 27F, sample included.) The enormous 11th-century **Abbatiale de la Trinité** houses an even rarer liquid. The relic of the *précieux-sang,* a fig trunk that allegedly carried a few drops of Christ's blood to the shores of Fécamp in the 6th century, rests within the massive nave (open daily 9am-7pm; free). The **train station,** bd. de la République (tel. 02 35 43 50 50), serves Le Havre (5 per day, 45min., 42F), Paris (7 per day, 2½hr., 144F), and Rouen (7 per day, 1¼hr., 67F). The **tourist office,** 113, rue Alexandre Le Grand (tel. 02 35 28 51 01; fax 02 35 27 07 77), books rooms (10F) and dispenses maps. (Open July-Aug. Mon.-Sat. 10am-6pm; Sept.-April Mon.-Fri. 9am-12:15pm and 1:45-6pm, Sat. 10am-12:15pm and 1:45-6pm; May-June Mon.-Fri. 9am-12:15pm and 1:45-6pm, Sat.-Sun. 10am-12:15pm and 1:45-6pm.) The most affordable rooms are located around the Eglise St-Etienne. **Hotel Martin,** 18, pl. St-Etienne (tel. 02 35 28 23 82), offers clean, bright rooms (singles and doubles 140F, with shower 160-190F; breakfast 30F).

Le Havre's value is solely as a stopover *en route* to more enticing places. **Buses** link the city with coastal towns inaccessible by rail; call the station at bd. de Strasbourg (tel. 02 35 26 67 23) for schedules. For travel to England and Ireland call **P&O European Ferries** (tel. 02 35 19 78 50) or **Irish Ferries** (tel. 02 35 19 24 00). If stranded, the **tourist office,** in the Hôtel de Ville (tel. 02 35 21 22 88) can find you accommodations. (Open May-Sept. Mon.-Sat. 8:45am-7pm, Sun. 10am-12:30pm and 2:30-6pm; Oct.-April Mon.-Sat. 8:45am-12:15pm and 1:30-6:30pm, Sun. 10am-1pm.)

Caen

Although Allied bombing leveled three quarters of its buildings, Caen restored its architectural treasures and revitalized its tourist industry. The energy from international voyagers and a chic student population has made the city a major rail, ferry, and party hub. Towering churches and museums draw visitors throughout the year. The city's twin abbeys, **Abbaye-aux-Hommes** and the adjacent **Abbatiale-Saint-Etienne,** both off rue Guillaume le Conquérant, were financed by William the Conqueror as penance for marrying his distant cousin. (Tours of Abbaye-aux-Hommes in French daily 9:30am, 11am, 2:30pm, and 4pm. 10F. Abbatiale-Saint-Etienne open daily 8:15am-noon and 2-7:30pm.) Across the street from the tourist office sprawl the ruins of William's **château** (open May-Sept. daily 6am-9:30pm; Oct.-April 6am-7:30pm). Inside, the **Musée des Beaux-Arts** contains excellent Flemish works and Impressionist paintings (open Wed.-Mon. 10am-6pm; 25F, students 15F). In the shadow of the château, the **Eglise St-Pierre** traces the evolution of the Gothic style in the 13th to 16th centuries (open daily 9am-noon and 2-6pm). Don't miss the powerful **Mémorial: Un Musée pour la Paix,** in the northwest corner of the city, which includes footage from World War II, displays on pre-war Normandy, a tribute to Nobel Peace Prize laureates, and high-tech exhibits. (Open July-Aug. daily 9am-9pm; Feb. 15-June and Sept.-Oct. 9am-7pm; Nov.-Jan. 4 and Jan. 20-Feb. 14 Mon.-Sat. 9am-6pm, Sun. 9am-7pm. 67F, students 59F.)

Accommodations, Practical Information, and Food From pl. de la Gare (tel. 08 36 35 35 35), **trains** leave for Paris (2½hr., 152F), Rouen (2hr., 117F), and Tours (3½hr., 259F). Local **buses** run from the front of the train station (6F) to near the Eglise St-Pierre, where the **tourist office** (tel. 02 31 27 14 14) finds rooms and distributes maps. (Open May-Sept. Mon.-Sat. 9am-7pm, Sun. 9am-1pm and 2-7pm; Oct.-April daily 9am-1pm and 2-7pm.) To find the clean, popular **auberge de jeunesse (HI),** Foyer Robert Reme, 68bis, rue Eustache-Restout (tel. 02 31 52 19 96), walk right from the train station, take a left up the hill at the end of the street, and catch bus 5 or 17 ("Fleury" or "Grâce de Dieu") to "Lycée Fresnel" (reception open daily 5-10pm; 60F, sheets 15F). **University Housing: CROUS,** 23, av. de Bruxelles (tel. 02 31 94 54 50), has adequate singles (reception open Mon.-Fri. 9am-noon and 2-4pm; 46F; open mid-June to mid-Sept.). For recently renovated rooms in the *centre ville,* try **Hôtel de la Paix,** 14, rue Neuve-St-Jean (tel. 02 31 86 18 99; singles 155-200F, doubles 165-210F). **Terrain Municipal,** route de Louvigny (tel. 02 31 73 60 92), has riverside campsites (16F per person, 10F per tent; open May-Sept.).

Ethnic restaurants, *crêperies,* and *brasseries* line the streets of the **quartier Vaugueux** near the château. Nearby, pl. Courtonne stages a colorful morning **market** (Tues.-Sat.). **La Petite Auberge,** 17, rue des Equipes-d'Urgence, offers excellent Norman-style *menus* (68-89F; open Tues.-Sat. noon-2pm and 7-9pm, Sun. noon-2pm). Caen's old streets pulsate in moonlight, especially around **rue de Bras** and **rue St.-Pierre.** Locals head to **Joy's Club,** 10, rue Strasbourg (tel. 02 31 85 40 40), to flail to techno (open daily 10am-5am; 60F cover includes first drink).

Cotentin Peninsula

Bayeux An ideal base for exploring the D-Day beaches, **Bayeux** is renowned for its **Tapisserie de Bayeux** (Bayeux Tapestry), 70m of embroidery depicting the Norman conquest of Britain in 1066. The **Centre Guillaume le Conquérant** on rue de Nesmond displays the tapestry. (Open May-Aug. daily 9am-7pm; Sept.-Oct. 15 and March 15-April 9am-6:30pm; Oct. 16-March 14 9:30am-12:30pm and 2-6pm. 37F, students 15F.) A masterpiece of eclecticism, Bayeux's **Cathédrale Notre-Dame** has Gothic spires and Romanesque towers rising over a small Roman temple. (Open July-Aug. Mon.-Sat. 8am-7pm, Sun. 9am-7pm; Sept.-June Mon.-Sat. 8:30am-noon and 2:30-7pm, Sun. 9am-12:15pm and 2:30-7pm.) The **Musée de la Bataille de Normandie,** bd. Fabian Ware (tel. 02 31 92 93 41), recounts the summer of 1944 with old newspaper clippings, photographs, films, and uniforms. (Open May-Sept. 15 daily 9:30am-6:30pm; Sept. 16-April 10am-12:30pm and 2-6pm. 30F, students 15F.)

Trains roll into pl. de la Gare (tel. 02 31 92 80 50) from Paris (2½hr., 164F) and Caen (20min., 33F). To walk the 10 minutes to the town center, turn left onto the highway (bd. Sadi-Carnot) and then bear right, following the signs to the *centre ville.* Once there continue up rue Larcher to rue St-Martin. On your right, the **tourist office,** pont St-Jean (tel. 02 31 51 28 28; fax 02 31 51 28 29), books rooms. (Open Mon.-Sat. 9am-noon and 2-6pm; July-Sept. 15 also Sun. 9:30am-noon and 2:30-6pm.) **Centre D'Accueil Municipal,** 21, rue des Marettes (tel. 02 31 92 08 19), has small singles, breakfast included, for 90F (reception open 8:30am-noon and 2-7pm). **Hôtel Notre-Dame,** 44, rue des Cuisiniers (tel. 02 31 92 87 24; fax 02 31 92 67 11), across from the cathedral, has comfy rooms with cathedral views (singles and doubles 150-260F; breakfast 30F; shower 20F). *Boulangeries, pâtisseries,* and *charcuteries* line the streets near the intersection of rues Larcher and St-Jean. **Le Table du Terroir,** 42, rue St-Jean, is one of the heartiest restaurants in the region (*menus* 55F-95F; open daily noon-2:30pm and 7-10pm).

D-Day Beaches The record of the 1944 Allied invasion of Normandy can be read in the sobering gravestones and the pockmarked landscape of the D-Day beaches. Ten kilometers north of Bayeux on D514 is **Arromanches,** eastern-most of the beaches, where the British sank old ships to create a harbor. The **Musée du Débarquement** on the beach houses relics and photographs of the Allied landings and explains the logistics of the attack. (Open May 6-Sept. 5 daily 9am-6:30pm; Sept. 6-March 9 11:30am and 2-5:30pm; April-May 5 9-11:30am and 2-6pm; Sept.-May opens 10am on Sun. 32F, students 27F.) At **Omaha Beach,** just east of the Pointe du Hoc, almost 10,000 American graves stretch over a 172.5-acre coastal reserve. A memorial and chapel are dedicated to the fallen Allied troops (open April-Nov. daily 8am-6pm; Dec.-March 9am-5pm). The Canadian Cemetery is located at **Bény-sur-Mer-Reviers;** British cemeteries are at **Hermanville-sur-Mer** and **Ranville. Normandy Tours,** 26, pl. de la Gare (tel. 02 31 92 10 70), runs flexible three- to four-hour tours for 100F. **Bus Fly** (tel. 02 31 22 00 08) will pick you up at the train station, tourist office, or the Bayeux youth hostel. (Tours daily at 8:30am and 1:30pm. 160F, students 140F. Price includes admission to the Musée du Débarquement.)

Cherbourg Northwest of Bayeux at the northern tip of the Cotentin peninsula, **Cherbourg,** World War II's "Port de la Libération," shuttles passengers to and from Ireland and England. Contact **P&O European Ferries** (tel. 02 33 88 65 70) for connections to Portsmouth and **Brittany Ferries** (tel. 02 33 88 44 88) for Poole. **Irish Ferries** (tel. 02 33 23 44 44) runs to Rosslare. The **train station,** a 20-minute walk from the ferry terminal, serves Paris (3½hr., 211F), Rouen (3hr., 181), Caen (1½hr., 96F), and Bayeux (1hr., 78F). The helpful **tourist office** (tel. 02 33 93 52 02), at the northern end of the Bassin du Commerce near the bridge Pont Tournant, has plenty of brochures and books rooms for free (open Mon.-Sat. 9am–6:30pm; off-season Mon.-Fri. 9am-noon and 2-6pm). Opposite the train station, the **Hôtel de la Gare,** 10, pl. Jean Jaurès (tel. 02 33 43 06 81; fax 02 33 43 12 20), sparkles with attractive rooms (singles and doubles 125-210F). Popular restaurants line quai de Caligny. **Les Baladins,** in an inconspicuous courtyard off rue au Blé, offers Norman *menus* for 50-98F (open daily noon-2pm and 7-10pm). Or stock up at **Continent supermarket,** quai de l'Entrepôt, next to the station (open Mon.-Sat. 8:30am-9:30pm).

Mont-St-Michel

Rising abruptly from the sea directly west of Paris, the island of Mont-St-Michel is visible for kilometers. An **abbey** balances precariously on the jutting rock, surrounded by military fortifications and a *ville basse* built to serve medieval pilgrims. Just as overwhelming as the Mont's beauty, though, are its crowds; try to make the trip during the off season or late in the day. Start your visit on the **Porte de l'Avancée,** then walk along the **Porte du Roy** to **Grande Rue,** a winding pedestrian street full of souvenir stands and restaurants. A climb up several flights of stairs places you at the abbey entrance, the departure point for tours. (Open May-Sept. daily 9am-5:30pm; Oct.-April 9:30am-4:30pm. 40F, under 26 25F. Tour times vary; those in French depart more frequently, starting at 10am.) After the tour, escape down the ramparts to the abbey **garden** or the **Porte du Bavole.** Beware the water, though; the tides can rush in at 2m per second. The Mont is stunning at night; view the illumination from the causeway entrance or from across the bay at **Avranches.**

To get to Mont-St-Michel, take a train to **Pontorson;** from Paris, it's a four-hour trip (237F plus 36-90F TGV supplement). From Pontorson, **STN buses** continue on to the Mont (15min., round-trip 22F). The **tourist office,** BP 4 (tel. 02 33 60 14 30; fax 02 33 60 06 75), is behind the wall to your left after you enter the city. You can sometimes rent a **bike** at the train station (70 per day; 1000F deposit). As you near the Mont prices rise higher than the bay's famous tides, but the **Centre Duguesclin (HI),** rue Gén. Patton (tel. 02 33 60 18 65), a 10-minute walk from the Pontorson station, has bright rooms and clean showers. (Reception open daily 8-10am and 6-10pm; 44F; no sheets provided; open June to mid-Sept.) The **Hôtel de l'Arrivée,** 14, rue du Docteur Tizon (tel. 02 33 60 01 57), across from the Pontorson station, has clean, quiet singles and doubles for 90-155F. **Camping Municipal de Pontorson,** chemin des Soupirs (tel. 02 33 68 11 59), off rue Général Patton near the hostel, is 10 minutes from the station (13F per person, 13F per tent; open June-Sept.).

BRITTANY (BRETAGNE)

This rugged peninsula tugs away from mainland France, intent on its own direction. Locals speak lilting *Brezhoneg* (Breton) energetically and claim to be Bretons first, French second. Comic book characters Astérix and Obélix continue to symbolize the Bretons' resistance to outsiders, whether Roman or French. The region's 1800-odd *crêperies* set their tables with the regional specialty, accompanied by the local *cidre* which it shares with Normandy. **Cycling** is the best way to travel. **Hikers** can wander along the long-distance footpaths *(Grandes Randonnées)* GR341, GR37, GR38, GR380, and the spectacular GR34 along the northern coast. Tourist offices can help you coordinate a hiking or biking tour.

Rennes

In 1720, a drunken carpenter knocked over his lamp and set most of Rennes ablaze, but the city survived to become a lively university town and the administrative capital of Brittany. Visit the startlingly green **Jardin du Thabor** behind the Renaissance **Eglise Notre-Dame** and **Cloître Ste-Melanie.** To reach the garden, follow rue Jean Janvier across the river until you see the church on the right. Concerts and art showings are often held within the garden's confines (open June-Sept. daily 7am-9:30pm). On your way, step inside the church to see the magnificent chapel altar and the blazing colors of the *vitraux* (stained-glass windows) of the choir. Church-lovers will revel in the ceiling and chandeliers of the **Cathédrale St-Pierre,** in the *vieille ville* (open daily 9am-noon and 2-5pm). The **Musée de Bretagne** and the **Musée des Beaux-Arts** are housed in the same building at 20, quai Emile Zola. The Musée de Bretagne provides a good introduction to the region's history and traditions; the Musée des Beaux-Arts displays works from the 14th century to the day before yesterday (both open Wed.-Mon. 10am-noon and 2-6pm; to both 25F).

In early July, Rennes holds the **Tombées de la Nuit** festival, nine days of non-stop music, dance, partying, and theater; for info, write the Office de Tourisme, Festival de TN, 8, pl. du Maréchal Juin, 35000 Rennes (tel. 02 99 79 01 98 or 02 99 30 38 01). If you can't make it to the festival, **rue St-Michel** is packed with hopping theme bars, while **rue St-Malo** bops with jazz clubs and boisterous Irish pubs.

Practical Information, Accommodations, and Food The **train station** (tel. 02 99 65 50 50, reservations 02 99 65 18 65), pl. de la Gare, serves Caen (3½hr., 166F) and Paris (2-3½hr., 218F plus 36-90F TGV reservation). **Buses** at 16, pl. de la Gare (tel. 02 99 30 87 80) roll to St-Malo (1½hr., 55F). **Les Courriers Bretons** (tel. 02 99 56 79 09) run to Mont-St-Michel (2½hr., 64F), while **Anjou Bus** (tel. 02 41 69 10 00 in Angers) goes to Angers (3hr., 92F). The **tourist office,** pont de Nemours (tel. 02 99 79 01 98; fax 02 99 79 31 38), has a free map and info (open Mon. 1-6pm, Tues.-Sat. 9am-6pm); there is also an annex in the train station.

To reach the **auberge de jeunesse (HI),** 10-12, Canal St-Martin (tel. 02 99 33 22 33; fax 02 99 59 06 21), walk 30 minutes from the station or take bus 20 ("Centre Commercial Nord"; on weekends, 1 or 18) to "Hôtel Dieu," turn right on St-Malo and follow it to the intersection; the hostel is on the right. (Reception open daily 8-10am and 6-11pm. 80F; singles 130F; doubles 180F. Breakfast included.) **Hôtel Venezia,** 27, rue Dupont des Loges (tel. 02 99 30 36 56; fax 02 99 30 78 78), off quai Richemont, has well-decorated rooms in a great location (singles and doubles 110-190F). Rennes is a *gourmand*'s dream—seek out your fancy on **rue St-Malo, pl. St-Michel,** or **rue St-Georges.** The cheerful staff at **Restaurant la Grolle,** 34-36, rue St-Malo, serves *savoyard* cuisine in unreal portions (open 6:30-10:30pm). The **supermarket** is in the Nouvelles Galeries on quai Duguay-Trouin (open Mon.-Sat. 9am-8pm).

Dinan

Tranquil Dinan boasts proudly of its reputation as the best-preserved medieval town in Brittany. In the *vieille ville,* 15th-century houses line cobblestone streets, and artisans ply their trades as generations before them have done. The **Promenade des Petits-Fossés** begins near the post office and follows the ramparts to the 13th-century **Porte du Guichet,** the entrance to the **Château de la Duchesse Anne.** Inside the oval tower, the **Musée de Dinan** displays old furniture, paintings, and religious statuettes. (Château and museum open June-Oct. 15 daily 10am-6:30pm; Oct. 16-Nov. 15 and March 16-May Wed.-Mon. 10am-noon and 2-6pm; Nov. 16-Dec. and Feb. 7-March 15 Wed.-Mon. 1:30-5:30pm. 26F, students 11F.) In the *vieille ville,* rue Général de Gaulle leads to the Promenade de la Duchesse Anne, at the end of which stands the **Jardin Anglais.** Inside, the facade of the 12th-century **Basilique St-Saveur** depicts the lives (and deaths) of saints. From the port, re-enter the walled city by **rue de Petit Fort,** which becomes **rue du Jerzval,** one of Dinan's prettiest roads.

Trains run to St-Brieuc (1hr., 54F), Rennes (1¼hr., 70F), and Paris (5hr., 294F). **Buses** service Mont-St-Michel (summer only, round-trip 105F). The **tourist office,** 6, rue de l'Horloge (tel. 02 96 39 75 40; fax 02 96 39 01 64), in the *vieille ville,* offers tours (July-Aug. daily 10am and 3pm; 25F) and a guide with a map. (15F. Open June-Sept. Mon.-Sat. 9am-7:30pm, Sun. 10am-noon and 3-5pm; Oct.-May Mon.-Sat. 8:30am-12:30pm and 2-6pm.) The wonderful **auberge de jeunesse (HI),** Moulin du Méen in Vallée de la Fontaine-des-Eaux (tel. 02 96 39 10 83; fax 02 96 39 10 62), has 70 beds in small, clean rooms. Call from the station and the owner may pick you up; if you're walking (30min.), turn left from the station's main exit, then turn left across the tracks, turn right, and follow signs (reception open daily 9-11am and 3-11pm; 49F, sheets 16F; camping 26F). **Hôtel-Restaurant du Théâtre,** 2, rue Ste-Claire (tel. 02 96 39 06 91), across from the tourist office, offers pleasant rooms (singles and doubles 80-150F; breakfast 22F). At 6, rue Ste-Claire, **Le Cantorbery** pleases with a delicious 70F *menu* (open June-Aug. daily noon-2pm and 7-10pm; Sept.-May closed Mon.). Feast on *galettes* and crepes at the **Crêperie des Artisans,** 6, rue du Petit Fort (open June-Aug. daily noon-2:30pm and 7-10:30pm; Sept.-June closed Mon.).

Northern Coast (Côtes d'Armor)

Brittany's northern coast features some of the most spectacular scenery in France. Transportation poses problems, but many tourist offices offer lists of regional bus, train, and boat connections, as well as information on tours and hiking trails.

Côte d'Emeraude and Côte de Granite Rose Between the Côte d'Emeraude and the Côte de Granite Rose, **St-Brieuc** provides a base for trips to the scenic countryside. **Trains** (tel. 02 96 01 61 64) arrive from Rennes (1hr., 83F), Morlaix (1hr., 72F), and Dinan (1hr., 54F); CAT **buses** serve Paimpol (1½hr., 42F) and Cap Fréhel (July-Sept., 1½hr., 42F). To get to **Manoir de la Ville Guyomard (HI)** (tel. 02 96 78 70 70; fax 02 96 78 27 47), take bus 3 ("Les Villages") to "Van Meno" or "Jean Moulin" (6F, last bus 8:15pm; dorms 68F; sheets 20F; camping 26F).

Northeast of St-Brieuc, gorgeous **Cap Fréhel** marks the northern point of the Côte d'Emeraude. The tip of this windswept peninsula drops 70m into the ocean below, while the coastline features the scenic GR34 **hiking trail.** If your spirit is as rugged as the cape's cliffs, you'll love the **Auberge de Jeunesse Cap Fréhel (HI),** la Ville Hadrieux, Kerivet (tel. May to mid-Sept. 02 96 41 48 98; late Sept.-April 02 96 78 70 70), near Plévenon, where many guests choose to camp out. Take a bus to the Cap and walk 30 minutes toward Plévenon on D16 (44F; sheets 20F; camping 25F; open May-Sept.). The hostel also rents **bikes** (25F per half-day); if you ask at St-Brieuc's hostel, you can leave a rented bike at Cap Fréhel and vice-versa.

Paimpol, at the eastern end of the Côte de Granite Rose, offers access to nearby hiking trails, islands, and beaches. **Trains** connect to St-Brieuc (1hr., 60F) via Guincamp (45min., 38F), while CAT **buses** run to St-Brieuc (1¼hr., 42F). The **tourist office** (tel. 02 96 20 83 16) is at pl. de la République (open July-Aug. Mon.-Sat. 9am-7:30pm, Sun. 10am-1pm; shorter hours off-season). The **auberge de jeunesse/gîte d'étape (HI)** (tel. 02 96 20 83 60) is at Château de Kéraoul (47F, sheets 16F; camping 25F).

Finistère Nord Long the naval muscle of the northern peninsula, **Brest** is a lively home to boisterous sailors and students who attend Brittany's second largest university. Brest's **château** was the only building to survive World War II and is now the world's oldest active military institution. **Trains** arrive from Paris (4½hr., 310F plus 36-90F TGV reservation), Morlaix (45min., 53F), Nantes (4hr., 210F), and Rennes (1½hr., 160F). The **tourist office,** pl. de la Liberté (tel. 02 98 44 24 96; fax 02 98 44 53 73), offers a free map and information. (Open July-Sept. Mon.-Sat. 9:30am-12:30pm and 1:30-6:30pm, Sun. 2-6pm; Oct.-June closed Sun.) To get to the **auberge de jeunesse (HI),** rue de Kerbriant (tel. 02 98 41 90 41; fax 02 98 41 82 66), take bus 7 (6F, last bus 8pm) to "Port de Plaisance"; facing the port, take your first right, then another right, and the hostel is on the right. (Reception open Mon.-Fri. 7-9am and 5-8pm, Sat.-Sun. 7-10am and 5-8pm. Curfew midnight; off-season 11pm. 69F.) **Camping du Goulet** (tel. 02 98 45 86 84), is 6km out of Brest and 1km from the sea; take bus 14 to "Le Cosquer" or bus 7, 11, 12, or 26 to "Route de Conquet" (17F per person, 20F per tent; free hot showers). Brest-feed at the **Restaurant l'Hermine,** 9, rue Bois d'Amour (open Tues.-Sun. noon-2:30pm and 7-9:30pm).

Crozon Peninsula To the north and south, Finistère's two larger peninsulas overshadow **Crozon,** a tiny point of land between the profiles of Léon and La Cornouaille. From jagged cliffs, you can gaze across azure pools marred only by the occasional rock formation. Seek out the enchanting, tiny hamlets scattered amongst the larger towns on this peninsula. Bikers may find the terrain challengingly hilly, but hitchers report easy success all over the peninsula. **Boats** sail from Brest's *gare maritime* to Le Fret on the peninsula (56F, with shuttles to Crozon, Morgat, and Camaret 59F). **Buses** connect Brest to Crozon or Camaret (1½hr., 52F). From Quimper, the peninsula is best reached by bus (59F). The bus between Camaret and Crozon or Morgat costs 10F. **ULAMIR,** in Crozon (tel. 02 98 27 10 68), has info on the peninsula's four **gîtes d'étape,** which offer beds for 45F.

Just beyond the edge of **Camaret** on the D8 sit the **Alignements de Lagatjar,** rocky monoliths from 2500 BC. Nearby, the ruins of **Château de St-Pol Roux** afford a magnificent view of the bay. A memorial to the Bretons of the Free French forces stands on the 76m cliff on the **Pointe de Penhir,** just 3.5km away on the D8. Climb out onto the rocks for a blood-boiling view of the isolated rock masses of the **Tas de Pois.** Each Monday in July and August, Camaret hosts **Les Lundis Musicaux** (tel. 02 98 27 90 49), with concerts from classical music recitals to gospel jams. Camaret's **tourist office,** quai Toudouze (tel. 02 98 27 93 05), is in the Gendarmerie next to pl. de Gaulle (open Mon.-Sat. 9:15am-7pm, Sun. 10am-12:30pm and 2:30-5pm).

Surfers and camera-toters flock to **Morgat's** beaches. The **tourist office** faces the beach on bd. de la Plage (tel. 02 98 27 29 49; open Mon.-Sat. 9am-7:30pm, Sun. 4-7:30pm). In the *centre ville,* at pl. de l'Eglise, smilin' Denis rents **mountain bikes,** Morey **boogie boards** (80F per day), and **kayaks** (140-250F per day; open daily 9am-7pm). To make Morgat more than a daytrip, stop at **Camping du Bouis** (tel. 02 98 26 12 53), 1.5km outside town on the way to the Cap. (Gates closed 11pm-8am. 35F, 2 people 62F, each additional person 15F. Showers 5F. Open Easter-Sept.)

Southern Brittany

Quimper Although staunch, half-timbered houses with crooked facades share the *vieille ville's* cobblestone streets with legions of tourists, **Quimper** (kem-PAIR), the capital of La Cornouaille has managed to retain its Breton flavor. During the week preceding the fourth Sunday of July, Quimper recalls its heritage with the **Festival de Cornouaille,** a cavalcade of mirth and music in Breton costume.

Trains leave the station on av. de la Gare for Paris (7½hr., TGV 5hr., 315F, plus 36-90F reservation for TGV), Rennes (3hr., 164F), Nantes (3hr., 165F), and Brest (1½hr., 82F). **Buses** roll from the *gare* next to the train station or across the street. The **tourist office,** 7, rue de la Déesse (tel. 02 98 53 04 05; fax 02 98 53 31 33), has an accommodations service (2F), free maps and *Quimper Magazine,* listing events, and sells bus excursion tickets. (Open July-Aug. Mon.-Sat. 8:30am-8pm, Sun. 9:30am-12:30pm and 3-6pm; Sept.-June Mon.-Sat. 9am-noon and 1:30-6pm.) To reach the **Centre Hebergement de Quimper (HI),** 6, av. des Oiseaux (tel. 02 98 64 97 97; fax 02 98 55 38 37), take bus 1 ("Penhars") to "Chaptal." The *centre* is across the street, 50m to your left. (Reception open daily 9-10am and 4:30-9.30pm. Call ahead if arriving late. 67F. Sheets 17F. Open April-Oct.) Near the train station, the **Hôtel de l'Ouest,** 63, rue le Déan (tel. 02 98 90 28 35), welcomes *Let's Go*ers with open arms and firm mattresses (singles 100-170F, doubles 150-190F, triples 210F, quads 220F). Next to the *centre,* **Camping Municipal,** av. des Oiseaux in the Bois du Séminaire, is clean but crowded. (Reception open Mon.-Tues., Thurs., and Sat. 8-11am and 3-8pm, Wed. and Sun. 9am-noon, Fri. 9-11am and 3-8pm. 17F per person, 4F per tent.) Nearby, the towns of **Locronan** and **Pont-Aven** make beautiful daytrips.

Quiberon All roads in **Quiberon** lead to the smooth, sandy, and wonderfully clean **Grande Plage** at the heart of town. Connected to the mainland by only a narrow strip of land, this *presqu'île* (literally, "almost island") is a great place to relax with an ice cream, check out your neighbor's tan, and make plans for a trip to Belle-Ile. To escape the congested port area, head for the smaller, rockier **Plage du Goviro** near the campgrounds. To get there from the port, follow bd. Chanard east along the water as it becomes bd. de la Mer and then bd. du Goviro.

Trains (tel. 02 97 50 07 07) run to Quiberon in July and August from Auray; TIM **buses** (tel. 02 97 47 29 64) also run to Auray (1hr., 35F) via Carnac (30min., 22F). To find the **tourist office,** 14, rue de Verdun (tel. 02 97 50 07 84; fax 02 97 30 58 22), from the train station, turn left and walk down rue de la Gare. Veer to the right of the church, down rue de Verdun; the tourist office is on the left and has a guide to campsites, B&Bs, and restaurants in the area. (Open July-Aug. Mon.-Sat. 9am-8pm, Sun. 10:30am-noon and 3-7pm; Sept.-June Mon.-Sat. 9am-12:30pm and 2-6:30pm.) To reach the small, centrally located **auberge de jeunesse (HI),** 45, rue du Roch-Priol (tel. 02 97 50 15 54), turn left at the station, then take rue de la Gare through pl. du Repos, take rue de Lille, turn left on rue Roch-Priol (lockout 10am-6pm; 46F; open May-Sept.). **Hôtel de l'Océan,** 7, quai de l'Océan (tel. 02 97 50 07 58; fax 02 97 50 27 81), offers clean rooms on the boardwalk (singles and doubles 160-280F). Spacious **Camping Bois d'Amour** (tel. 02 97 50 13 52; off-season 02 97 30 24 00) has a heated swimming pool (18-35F per person, 2-person tents 32F; open April-Sept.).

Belle-Ile At least five boats depart daily from Quiberon's Port-Maria (45min., 85F per person, 40F per bike round-trip) for **Belle-Ile,** an island that combines high cliffs, narrow creeks, and crashing seas. The massive 16th- to 17th-century **Citadelle Vauban,** now a museum, will catch your eye from the boat (open May-Oct. daily 9am-7pm; Nov.-April 9:30am-noon and 2-6pm; 32F). Boats dock at Le Palais, the island's largest town; the **tourist office** (tel. 02 97 31 81 93; fax 02 97 31 56 17) is on left end of the *quai* as you disembark. (Open July-Aug. Mon.-Sat. 8:30am-8pm, Sun. 9am-12:30pm; Sept.-June Mon.-Sat. 9am-noon and 2-6pm, Sun. 10am-noon.) Rent a bike at **Cyclotour,** quai de Bonnelle (tel. 02 97 31 80 68), near the tourist office. (50-80 per day; passport deposit. Open July-Aug. daily 8:15am-7pm; Sept.-June Mon.-Sat. 9am-noon and 2-7pm.) Bike 6km to **Sauzon,** a tiny picture-book fishing port, and then continue 4km to the **Pointe des Poulains,** at the northernmost tip of the island. Four kilometers southwest on the Côte Sauvage lies the **Apothicairerie** towers over the raging sea. From the grotto, follow D25 south to **Plage de Port-Donnant and** then onward to the rough **Aiguilles de Port-Coton,** which Monet captured in a painting.

A hostel and campsite are located near the citadel, a 10-minute hike from Le Palais' port. Turn right from the port and follow the quay to the footbridge leading to the citadel; cross the bridge, walk diagonally left through the parking lot, follow the street to the left and enter **Camping Les Glacis** (tel. 02 97 31 41 76; 18F per person, 12F per tent, 4F per bike). To reach the **HI youth hostel** (tel. 02 97 31 81 33), continue on, climb another hill, and follow the road through a residential neighborhood (reception open daily 8-10am and 6-8pm; 49F, tents 25F). **La Frégate,** quai de l'Acadie (tel. 02 97 31 54 16), in front of where the ships dock, has rooms above a friendly restaurant and bar (singles and doubles 112-152F; open April-Oct.).

Nantes

While Nantes is part of the Pays de la Loire, most *Nantais* feel a cultural allegiance to Brittany. High-tech industries, 27,000 college students, stately rue Crébillon and pl. Graslin, and bountiful greenery invigorate the city, and while there aren't many must-see sights, its ideal location, year-round festivals, and vibrant nightlife make Nantes a smart stop between Brittany and points south.

Built in the 15th century by François II, Nantes' heavily fortified **Château des Ducs de Bretagne** once held Gilles de Retz (the original Bluebeard). In 1598, Henri IV composed the Edict of Nantes here to soothe national religious tensions. The château has two museums: the **Musée des Arts Populaires Régionaux,** with traditional Breton clothing, and the **Musée des Salorges,** which explores Nantes' colonial and commercial history. (Open July-Aug. daily 10am-7pm; Sept.-June Wed.-Mon. 10am-noon and 2-6pm. Courtyard and ramparts open July-Aug. daily 10am-7pm; Sept.-June 10am-noon and 2-6pm. Château and museums 30F, students 15F.) The **Cathédrale St-Pierre,** pl. St-Pierre, survived bombings and a fire and is now the only cathedral in France with a completely restored interior (open daily 8:45am-7pm). Two blocks away, at 10, rue Georges Clemenceau, is the **Musée des Beaux-Arts,** with fine canvases from the 13th century on, including works by Delacroix, Ingres, Courbet, and Kandinsky. (Take bus 11 or 12 to "Trébuchet." Open Mon. and Wed.-Sat. 10am-6pm, Sun. 11am-6pm. 20F, students 10F.)

The **tourist office,** pl. du Commerce (tel. 02 40 20 60 00; fax 02 40 89 11 99), has good maps and info (open Mon.-Sat. 10am-7pm). The **train** station (tel. 02 40 08 50 50) has two entrances: north (27, bd. de Stalingrad and cours John Kennedy) and south (bus connections at rue de Loumel) across the tracks. Trains run to Paris (3-

4hr., 220-265F; by TGV 2hr., add 36-90F), Bordeaux (4hr., 224F), La Rochelle (2hr., 122F), and Rennes (2hr., 115F). **Cariane Atlantique,** 5, allée Duquesne (tel. 02 40 20 46 99), sends **buses** to Rennes (2hr., 100F) and Vannes (2½hr., 90F).

Nantes has lots of good hotels and, in the summer, student dorm space. Try the **Cité Internationale/Auberge de Jeunesse (HI),** 2, pl. de la Manufacture (June-Aug. tel. 02 40 29 29 20, Sept.-May tel. 02 40 20 57 25; fax 02 40 20 08 94), with rooms for 60F. The hostel **Foyer des Jeunes Travailleurs, Porte Neuve,** 1, pl. Ste-Elisabeth (tel. 02 40 20 63 63), is deluxe (72F). For a more peaceful stay, try **Hôtel du Tourisme,** 5, allée Duquesne (tel. 02 40 47 90 26; fax 02 40 35 57 25; singles and doubles 130-220F). Restaurants on **rue Kervégan** and **rue de la Juiverie,** in the St-Croix quarter, will sautée, boil, skewer, and grill just about anything. **Open-air markets** take place on **pl. du Bouffay** and at the **Marché de Talensac,** along rue de Bel-Air near pl. St-Similien behind the post office (Tues., Fri., and Sun. 9am-1pm). For nightlife listings, check the weekly *Nantes Poche* (6F at any *tabac*). The **rue Scribe** is chock-full of late-night bars and cafés—try **Le Duo, Le Scribe,** or **Le Corneille.**

LOIRE VALLEY (PAYS DE LA LOIRE)

Between Paris and Brittany, the fertile valley of the Loire, France's longest river, practically overflows with châteaux, which run the gamut from dilapidated medieval fortresses to elegant Renaissance homes reflected in pools and surrounded by spectacular gardens. Most châteaux were built in the 16th and 17th centuries, when French monarchs left Paris for countryside around Tours in order to enjoy hunting excursions while attending to their state duties. The history of many of these dignified mansions presents a mixed bag of genius, promiscuity, and dirty dealings.

The hostels in Blois, Saumur, and Orléans are comfortable bases, but pose daunting challenges to the car-less; public transportation routes fan out of the larger cities, but infrequent service can strand you. Tours is the region's best rail hub. Distributed at train stations, *Les Châteaux de la Loire en Train Eté '98* and *Châteaux pour Train et Vélo,* with train schedules and info on bike and car rental, is invaluable.

Orléans

Orléans strikes an uncertain balance between past glories and present hardships, taking pride in the heroic exploits of Joan of Arc but fretting about losing its prominence to more cosmopolitan Tours. Come to Orléans to get better acquainted with feisty St. Joan or to explore the châteaux a daytrip away. The stained glass windows of the stunning **Cathédrale Ste-Croix** depict Joan's dramatic story, from her liberation of the city to the flames that consumed her (open June-Sept. daily 9:15am-7pm, Oct.-May 10am-noon and 2:15-6:45pm). Stepping aside from Ste-Jeanne momentarily, the **Musée des Beaux-Arts** at 1, rue Paul Belmondo, to the right as you exit the cathedral, displays French and Dutch works from the 17th to the 20th centuries (open Wed.-Mon. 10am-noon and 2-6pm; 18F50, students 9F50). The **Maison de Jeanne d'Arc,** 3, pl. de Gaulle, off pl. du Martroi, explores Orléans's obsession with the formidable female fighting machine. (Open May-Oct. daily Tues.-Sun. 10am-noon and 2-6pm; Nov.-April Tues.-Sun. 2-6pm. 13F, students 7F.)

The **tourist office,** pl. Albert 1er (tel. 02 38 24 05 05; fax 02 38 54 49 84), off the mall above the Gare d'Orléans, offers city tours and local info. (Open July-Aug. Mon.-Sat. 9am-7pm, Sun. 9:30am-12:30pm and 3-6:30pm; reduced hours off season.) **Trains** stop at Gare d'Orléans on their way to Paris (1¼hr., 90F), Blois (40min., 51F), and Tours (1¼hr., 88F). A second train station, Gare Les-Aubrais (tel. 02 38 79 91 00), is 30 minutes north of the *centre ville* on rue Pierre Semar; a free and frequent train shuttles between the two stations. The budget accommodation of choice is the **Auberge de jeunesse (HI),** 14, rue du Faubourg Madeleine (tel. 02 38 62 45 75); take bus B ("Paul-Bert") from the Gare d'Orléans. (Reception open daily 7-9:30am and 5:30-

10pm. Members only. 42F. Oct.-May closed Sat.) **Hôtel Sonis,** 46bis, bd. de Châteaudun (tel. 02 38 53 72 36), has pleasant rooms and a family atmosphere. (Call for directions. Singles 102-135F; doubles 118-150F; triples 138-160F. Shower 15F.) Wander **rue de Bourgogne** for inexpensive *brasseries*, restaurants, and bars. **La Brasserie,** 1, rue de Gourville, right off rue de la République, serves salads (44-51F) as well as seafood and vegetarian *tartes flambées* (49-56F; open Tues.-Sat. noon-3pm and 7pm-midnight). **Monoprix,** 46, rue de Fbg. Bannier, stocks the groceries. (Open Mon.-Thurs. 8:30am-12:45pm and 2:30-7:30pm, Fri. 8:30am-8pm, Sat. 8:30am-7pm.)

Blois

Blois relishes its position as gateway to the Loire Valley and welcomes visitors with bucolic charms and nearby châteaux. Home to French monarchs Louis XII and François I, Blois's **château** was the Versailles of the late 15th and early 16th centuries. (Open mid-March to June and Sept. daily 9am-6:30pm; July-Aug. 9am-8pm; Oct. to mid-March 9am-noon and 2-5:30pm. 35F, students 20F.) Rue St-Lubin and rue des Trois Marchands lead to the 12th-century Abbaye St-Laumer, now called **St-Nicolas cathedral,** a towering masterstroke of medieval architecture (open daily 9am-dusk).

The **tourist office,** 3, av. Jean Laigret (tel. 02 54 74 06 49), can direct you to local sights and has complete info on nearby châteaux. (Open May-Sept. Mon.-Sat. 9am-7pm, Sun. 10am-1pm and 4-7pm; Oct.-March Mon.-Sat. 9am-12:30pm and 2-6pm, Sun. 11am-1pm and 3-5pm.) **Point Bus,** 2, pl. Victor Hugo (tel. 02 54 78 15 66), sends buses to Chambord and Cheverny (65F, students 50F; bus passes include reduced admission) and other châteaux. For hot showers and a jovial, countryside atmosphere, make the 5km trip to the **auberge de jeunesse (HI),** 18, rue de l'Hôtel Pasquier (tel. 02 54 78 27 21). Follow Porte Côté then rue Denis Papin to the river, then take bus 4 ("Les Grouets") to "Eglise des Grouets." (Reception open daily 7-10am and 6-10:30pm. 63F, discounts after first night. Open March-Nov. 15. Reserve ahead.) **Le Pavillon,** 2, av. Wilson (tel. 02 54 74 23 27), has clean, bright rooms (singles 100F, doubles 120-150F). **Hôtel du Bellay,** 12, rue des Minimes (tel. 02 54 78 23 62), at the top of porte Chartraine, has clean rooms and spotless bathrooms (singles and doubles 135-185F; breakfast 25F; call ahead).

Blois melts, molds, sculpts, smothers, and indulges its citizens in chocolate. Sumptuous *pavé du roi* (chocolate-almond cookies) and *malices du loup* (orange peels in chocolate) peer invitingly from *pâtisseries* along rue Denis Papin. For those who cling foolishly to the dinner-before-dessert convention, restaurants cluster on **rue St-Lubin** and **pl. Poids du Roi,** near the cathedral, while *boulangeries* and fruit stands line **rue des Jacobins,** below the château. Bathe in sunlight at **Le Marignan,** 5, pl. du Château (3-course dinner for 75F; open daily 8:30am-11pm).

FRANCE

Near Blois: Chambord, Cheverny, and Amboise

Built by François I to satisfy egomania, **Chambord** is the largest and most extravagant of the Loire châteaux. Seven hundred of François I's trademark stone salamanders lurk on Chambord's walls, ceilings, and staircases, and 365 fireplaces are scattered through the 440 rooms. The central staircase is a double helix. (Open July-Aug. daily 9:30am-6:45pm; April-June and Sept. daily 9:30am-5:45pm; Oct.-March 9:30am-4:45pm. 40F, students 25F. Grounds and wildlife preserve free.) By **bike** from Blois, take route D956 south 2-3km, then go left on D33.

Cheverny, accessible by bus or bike from Blois (take D956 south), soothes with manicured grounds and an elegant interior. Watch the castle's 70 foxhounds gulp down entire bins of ground meat in less than a minute. (Feedings April-Aug. Mon.-Sat. 5pm; Sept.-March Mon. and Wed.-Fri. 3pm. Château open June-Sept. 15 9:15am-6:45pm; Sept. 16-Sept. 30 9:30am-noon and 2:15-6pm; Oct. and March 9:30am-noon and 2:15-5:30pm; Nov.-Feb. 9:30am-noon and 2:15-5pm. 80F, students 70F.)

The battlements of the 15th-century château at **Amboise** (tel. 02 47 57 00 98) stretch out across the hill above the town like protective arms: surely an unsettling sight to those who entertained thoughts of attacking the place that four French kings called home. Two of those kings did meet their end here: the four-foot tall Charles VIII bumped his head on a *really* low door and died a few hours later, and the equally clumsy Charles V tripped over a torchbearer and burned himself alive. Today, the jewel of the grounds is the late 15th-century **Chapelle St-Hubert.** A plaque inside marks Leonardo da Vinci's supposed resting place. (Open July-Aug. daily 9am-9:30pm; April-June and Sept.-Oct. 9am-6:30pm; Nov.-March 9am-noon and 2-5pm. 35F, students 24F.) **Trains** pass through on their way to Tours (20min., 28F), Blois (15min. 32F), and Paris (2¼hr., 140F). The **auberge de jeunesse (HI),** Ile d'Or (tel. 02 47 57 06 36), features a beautiful setting along the Loire (reception open Tues.-Sun. 3-9pm; 49F; Nov.-Feb. 35F; call ahead).

Tours

Tours is the urban centerpiece of the Loire region, and its fabulous nightlife, diverse population, and great food will free scenery-imprisoned souls. The one sight you cannot miss is the extraordinary **Musée du Gemmail,** 7, rue du Murier, with its *gemmaux* (layers of illuminated, colored glass shards in a "painting of light") by Picasso. (Open March-Nov. 15 Tues.-Sun. 10am-noon and 2-6:30pm; Nov. 16-Feb. Sat.-Sun. 10am-noon and 2-6:30pm. 30F, students 20F.) **Cathédrale St-Gatien,** rue Jules Simon, may have the most dazzling collection of stained glass in the Loire. (Open Easter-Sept. daily 8:30am-noon and 2-8pm; Oct.-Easter 8:30am-noon and 2-5:30pm.)

Trains run to Amboise (20min., 28F), Paris-Austerlitz (2¼hr., 160F), and Bordeaux (2½hr., 230F). The **tourist office,** 78/82, rue Bernard Palissy (tel. 02 47 70 37 37; fax 02 47 61 14 22), distributes maps, books accommodations, and leads a detailed historical tour on foot. (Open June-Aug. Mon.-Sat. 8:30am-7pm; May and Sept. 8:30am-6:30pm; Oct.-April 9am-12:30pm and 1:30-6pm; also Sun. year-round 10am-12:30pm and 3-6pm.) The **auberge de jeunesse (HI),** av. d'Arsonval, Parc de Grandmont (tel. 02 47 25 14 45), is located 4km from the city. Take bus 1 ("Jotie Blotterie") or bus 6 ("Chambray") from the stop on the right side of av. de Grammont to "Auberge de Jeunesse." The hostel is across the Cher River. (Reception open in summer daily 5-11pm; off-season 5-10pm. 47F. Open Feb.-Dec. 14.) The small **Hôtel St-Eloi,** 79, bd. Béranger (tel. 02 47 37 67 34), has a warm atmosphere (singles 140F, doubles 170F), while **Hôtel Regina,** 2, rue Pimbert (tel. 02 47 05 25 36), and **Le Lys d'Or,** 23, rue de la Vendée (tel. 02 47 05 33 45), offer clean rooms for 55-135F per person. The tourist office has a list of nearby campgrounds. Local favorite **Chez Jean Michel,** 123, rue Colbert, features new culinary creations every day (70F *menu;* open Mon. 7:30-10:30pm, Tues.-Sat. noon-2pm and 7:30-10:30pm).

Near Tours: Chenonceau, Azay-le-Rideau, and Villandry

A series of women created the graceful beauty of **Chenonceau** (tel. 02 47 23 90 07): first the wife of a tax collector distracted by war, then, in succession, the lover (Diane de Poitier) and wife (Catherine de Medici) of Henri II. Its internal bridge over the river Cher marked the border between annexed and Vichy France during World War II. (Open March 16-Sept. 15 daily 9am-7pm; call for off-season hours. 45F, students 30F.) **Trains** roll from the station 2km away to Tours (45min., 34F).

On an island in the Indre River, **Azay-le-Rideau** (tel. 02 47 45 42 04) gazes vainly at its reflection in a purely decorative moat. Azay's 16th-century flamboyance is apparent in the ornate second-floor staircase, complete with the carved faces of 10 kings and queens, including Henri de Navarre and Anne of Brittany. (Open July-Aug. daily 9am-7pm; April-June and Sept. 9:30am-6pm; Oct.-March 9:30am-12:30pm and 2-5:30pm. 32F, students 21F.) The château is a 2km walk from Azay-le-Rideau's train station (1 train per day from Tours, 30min., 28F).

Villandry (tel. 02 47 50 02 09) maintains fantastic gardens with over 120,000 plants, waterfalls, and vine-covered walkways, but the château itself pales before its regal cousins. (Gardens open June-Aug. daily 8:30am-8pm; Sept.-May 9am-nightfall. Château open June to mid-Sept. 9am-6:30pm; mid-Feb. to May and mid-Sept. to Nov. 11 9:30am-5:30pm. Château and garden 45F.) From Tours, take the **train** to Savonnières (10min., 15F) and walk 4km along the Loire. **Cyclists** follow D16.

Saumur

Saumur's 14th-century **château** stands aloof above the city's skyline. Charles V's brother, Louis I of Anjou, built this pre-Renaissance edifice as a country residence. Inside, the **Musée des Arts Décoratifs** features medieval and Renaissance paintings and tapestries, and the **Musée du Cheval** will appeal to even the lukewarm equestrian. (Château and museums open June-Sept. daily 9am-6pm; July-Aug. also Wed. and Sat. 6pm-10pm; Oct.-March Wed.-Mon. 9:30am-noon and 2-5:30pm; April-May Mon.-Sun. 9:30am-noon and 2-5:30pm. 35F, students 25F.) Don't leave Saumur without tasting the region's specialties: *les vins* and *les champignons* (mushrooms). An impressive *cave* is **Gratien et Meyer,** route de Chinon (tel. 02 41 83 13 30). Take bus D from pl. Bilange to "Beaulieu." Check out the bottles of wine in the *cave,* then try some. (Open Sept.-July daily 9am-noon and 2-7pm; Aug. 9am-6pm; Nov.-Feb. Sat.-Sun. 10-11:45am and 3-5:15pm, closed Mon.-Fri. 15F.)

Trains roll out of the station on av. David d'Angers for Tours (45min., 56F) and Angers (30min., 42F). The **tourist office,** pl. Bilange (tel. 02 41 40 20 60; local bus A), next to pont Cessart, books beds (5F) and provides free maps. (Open June 15-Sept. 15 Mon.-Sat. 9:15am-7pm, Sun. 10:30am-12:30pm and 3:30-6:30pm; Sept. 16-June 14 Mon.-Sat. 9:15am-12:30pm and 2-6pm.) The modern **Centre International de Séjour (HI),** rue de Verden (tel. 02 41 40 30 00), on Ile d'Offard, has a superb view of the château (reception open daily 8am-10pm; 8-berth rooms 82F, 2-berth rooms 105F). For an affordable taste of North Africa, try **La Rose des Sables,** 5, rue Bonne Mère (*couscous merguez* 48F; open Tues.-Sun. 11:30am-3pm and 6:30-11pm).

Angers

From behind the massive stone walls of Angers's **château,** the Dukes of Anjou ruled over the surrounding countryside and an island across the Channel; Henry II held court here as often as in London. Inside the 15th-century château, the 14th-century **Tapisserie de l'Apocalypse,** thought to be the largest woven masterpiece anywhere, depicts the Book of Revelations. (Château open June-Sept. 15 daily 9am-7pm; Sept. 16-March 26 9:30am-12:30pm and 2-6pm; March 27-May 9am-12:30pm and 2-6:30pm; Dec.-Feb. 9:30am-12:30am and 2-5:30pm. 35F, students 23F.) The **Galerie David d'Angers,** 37bis, rue Toussaint, houses a collection of the 19th-century sculptor's work, including a scale replica of David's masterwork for the Panthéon facade in Paris. (Open mid-June to mid-Sept. daily 9am-6:30pm; mid-Sept. to mid-June Tues.-Sun. 10am-noon and 2-6pm. 10F.)

The **tourist office,** pl. Kennedy (tel. 02 41 23 51 11; fax 02 41 23 51 66), across the street from the château, organizes tours and reserves rooms. (Open June-Sept. Mon.-Sat. 9am-7pm, Sun. 10am-1pm, 2-6pm; Oct.-May Mon.-Sat. 9am-12:30pm and 2-6:30pm.) **Trains** leave the station on rue de la Gare for Saumur (30min., 42F), Tours (1hr., 84F), Orléans (2¼hr., 143F), and Paris-Austerlitz (2¾hr., 173-229F). **Buses** run to Saumur (1½hr., 44F) and Rennes (3hr., 92F). The **Auberge de Jeunesse Darwin (HI),** 3, rue Darwin (tel. 02 41 72 00 20; fax 02 41 48 51 91), has 320 beds. Take bus 1 ("Belle Baille") to its end (members 60F; kitchen). **Royal Hôtel,** rue d'Iéna (tel. 02 41 88 30 25), off pl. de la Visitation, is a family-run hotel with immaculate rooms (singles 100-210F, doubles 150-225F). The friendly **Hôtel des Lices,** 25, rue des Lices (tel. 02 41 87 44 10), near the cathedral and château, offers clean rooms (115-175F; reserve ahead). For cafés and *pâtisseries,* stroll along rue St-Laud. The **market** in the basement of Les Halles, rue Plantagenêt, sells inexpensive produce and baked goods (open Tues.-Sat. 7am-8pm, Sun. 7am-1:30pm).

La Rochelle

With white sand beaches, refined 14th-century architecture, and annual festivals, La Rochelle is the perfect vacation spot. The **Tour de la Chaîne** presents a model of the old town in Richelieu's day. Climb around the fortifications of the **Tour St-Nicolas,** on the left as you face the harbor. (Tour de la Chaîne open Easter-Sept. daily 10am-7pm; Oct.-Easter 10am-12:30pm and 2-5:30pm. Free. Tour St-Nicolas open April-Oct. daily 10am-7pm; Oct.-March 10am-12:30pm. 25F, students 15F.) From the harbor's *quai,* you can walk along av. Maillac or take bus 10 ("Les Minimes") to the **aquarium,** port des Minimes. (Open July-Aug. daily 9am-11pm; May-June and Sept. 9am-7pm; Sept.-April 10am-noon and 2-7pm. 42F, students 37F.) The **tourist office,** pl. de la Petite Sirène (tel. 05 46 41 14 68; fax 05 46 41 99 85), is in the quartier du Gabut. (Open mid-June to mid-Sept. Mon.-Sat. 9am-7pm, Sun. 11am-5pm; off-season Mon.-Wed. and Fri.-Sat. 10:30am-1:30pm and 4:30-7pm, Sun. 10:30am-12:30pm and 3-5pm.) Take bus 10 ("Port des Minimes") to "Auberge de Jeunesse" to reach **Centre International de Séjour, Auberge de Jeunesse (HI),** av. des Minimes (tel. 05 46 44 43 11; 72F). **Trains** leave daily for Bordeaux (2hr., 130F) and Paris (5hr., 302F).

AQUITAINE

Forested hills, tranquil river valleys, and dramatic cliffs have drawn people to Aquitaine for some 150,000 years. Today, the Dordogne, Vézère, Isle, and Lot rivers wind past limestone caves painted with scenes of Paleolithic life, around 12th-century Romanesque churches and chapels clinging to the rocks of pilgrimage towns, and through *bastides* (fortified mountaintop towns) built during the Hundred Years War. Bus and train connections to smaller towns can be inconvenient, but a bike makes for pleasant touring if a car is not an option.

Bordeaux

Once as darkened with age as its vintages, Bordeaux has found that one of its greatest treasures is the city itself; the buzz-word around town these days is *la conservation.* It takes time to undo the effects of time, however, and restoration work obscures monuments such as the city's Gothic masterpiece, the **Cathédrale St-André.** Two blocks from cours de Maréchal Foch in the Entrepôt Laine gallery at 7, rue Ferrère, the far-out **Musée d'Art Contemporain** and the **Arc en Rêve Centre d'Architecture** exhibit modern painting, sculpture, design and photography. (Open Tues.-Sun. noon-6pm, Wed. noon-10pm. 30F, students 20F, noon-2pm free.) Bordeaux is, of course, famous for wine. You too can swish whites and reds around in a wine-conference room complete with foot-pedal operated spitting sinks. Just take the two-hour "Initiation to Wine Tasting" course given in French and English at the **Maison du Vin/CIVB,** 1, cours du 30 Juillet (tel. 05 56 00 22 66), where they will pour free samples, answer wine questions, and distribute a list of smaller wine-producing chateaux in the area. (Twice weekly July-Aug.; 60F. Maison open May-Oct. Mon.-Fri. 8:30am-6:30pm, Sat. 9am-4pm; Nov.-April Mon.-Thurs. 8:30am-6pm, Fri. 8:30am-5:30pm.) In grape-speak, "château" means "vineyard," but many of the area's châteaux are private homes. It is always best to call ahead and politely ask if they are open to visitors. Approach your meeting as a customer, not tourist. The free *Clubs and Concerts* (at the tourist office) or *Bordeaux Plus* (2F at any *tabac)* gives an overview of nightlife. Sweaty students dance off angst at clubs on **quai Ste-Croix** and **quai de Paludade.**

Practical Information, Accommodations, and Food **Trains** leave from Bordeaux's Gare St-Jean, rue Charles Domercq, for Paris (10-20 per day, 5-8hr., 290F, TGV 330-380F), Toulouse (10 per day, 2½hr., 159F), and Nice (4 per day, 9½hr., 440F). From the train station, take bus 7 or 8 to "Grand Théâtre" and walk toward the Monument des Girondins to reach the **tourist office,** 12, cours du 30 Juillet (tel. 05 56 00 66 00; fax 05 56 00 66 01), which has info on accommodations. (Open May-Sept. Mon.-Sat. 9am-8pm, Sun. 9am-7pm; Oct.-April Mon.-Sat. 9am-7pm, Sun. 9:30am-4:30pm.) An **American Express** office is at 14, cours de l'Intendance (tel. 05 56 00 63 33; open Mon.-Fri. 8:45am-noon and 1:30-6pm).

Relatively inexpensive hotels and an elegant student *maison* highlight the city's abundant budget options. Sidestreets around **pl. Gambetta** and **cours d'Albret** are good places to look for rooms. Reserve a couple of days in advance in June through August. To get to the clean, classy, and central **Maison des Etudiantes,** 50, rue Ligier (tel. 05 56 96 48 30), take bus 7 or 8 from the train station to "Bourse du Travail," and continue in the same direction on cours de la Libération to rue Ligier. Alternatively, walk along cours de la Marne through pl. de la Victoire to cours Aristide Briand, then turn right onto rue Ligier. (Reception open 24hr. Singles 71F, with ISIC 50F; doubles 142F, with ISIC 100F; shower and sheets included.) The **auberge de jeunesse (HI),** 22, cours Barbey (tel. 05 56 91 59 51; fax 05 56 94 02 98), is scheduled to reopen on July 1, 1998; to get there take Cours de la Marne from the right end of the station about five blocks and turn left onto cours Barbey. (Reception open daily 8-10am and 4-11pm. Flexible curfew 11pm. Lockout 10am-2pm. 56F includes breakfast.) For spacious rooms with shower, TV, and mini-bar, consider **Hôtel la Boétie,** 4, rue de la Boétie (tel. 05 56 81 76 68; fax 05 56 81 24 72), off rue Bouffard between pl. Gambetta and the Musée des Beaux-Arts (reception open 24hr.; singles 120F, doubles 135-60F, triples 180F). The same family that runs Boétie also runs 11 other top-notch hotels with good rates in the *centre ville.*

Bordeaux, known as *la Région de Bien Manger et de Bien Vivre* (The Region of Fine Eating and Living), has affordable restaurants in which to do so, especially along and just off **rue Ste-Catherine** and **pl. Gambetta.** Bring a plate and knife and descend into the cool cellar of **Baud et Millet,** 19, rue Huguerie, off pl. Tournu., to consume as much as you can of 200 kinds of *fromage* (cheese plus dessert, 110F; open Mon.-Sat. noon-midnight). Head to the **Taj Mahal,** 24, rue du Parlement Ste-Catherine, to make a mid-day feast of all-you-can-eat Indian and Pakistani (69F; open daily noon-2:30pm and 7:30-9:30pm). The family-run **Pizza Jacomo,** 19, rue de la Devise, offers delicious oven pizza (36-40F) and pasta (from 45F) to happy locals (open Mon. and Wed.-Sat. noon-2pm and 7:30-11:30pm, Sun. 7:30pm-midnight).

Périgueux

Capital of the Périgord region, Périgueux is a good base for visiting local prehistoric caves. The town's *vieille ville* sports Renaissance architecture and the multi-domed **Cathédrale St-Front** combines styles of various eras. (Open daily 8am-12:30pm and 2:30-7:30pm. Free tours in French on request. Cloisters and crypt 10F.) The town sends several **trains** a day to Bordeaux (2½hr., 96F), Paris via Limoges (6-7hr., 265-385F), and Toulouse via Brive (4hr., 171F). Ask the **tourist office,** 26, pl. Francheville (tel. 05 53 53 10 63; fax 05 53 09 02 50), for brochures and a list of accommodations and restaurants. (Open July-Aug. Mon.-Sat. 9am-7pm, Sun. 9:30am-5:30pm; Sept.-June Mon.-Sat. 9am-6pm.) The **Foyer des Jeunes Travailleurs Résidence Lakanal,** (tel. 05 53 53 52 05), off bd. Lakanal, offers comfortable beds. From the tourist office, turn left down cours Fénélon and take a right on bd. Lakanal; when the fire station appears on your left, turn right through the Bridge Club parking lot, go to the left of the building, and through the gate to get to front of the *foyer.* (Reception open daily 9am-11pm. 70-80F. Sheets, showers, and breakfast (Mon.-Sat.) included.) **Hôtel des Barris,** 2, rue Pierre Magne (tel. 05 53 53 04 05), is an immaculate family-run hotel (singles 149F, doubles 169F). Camp 1.5km away in Boulazac at **Barnabé-Plage,** 80, rue des Bains (tel. 05 53 53 41 45). Take city bus D ("Cité Belaire"; 6F, last one about 7:30pm) from cours Montaigne to "rue de Bains" (open 9am-midnight; 16F per person, 15F per tent, 10F per car).

■ Near Périgueux: Les Eyzies-de-Tayac

A perfect daytrip, **Les Eyzies-de-Tayac** is served by five trains a day from Périgueux (40min., 40F). **Prehistoric caves**—bursting with tourists from June to mid-September—house fascinating paintings and carvings, as well as spectacular stalagmites and stalactites. Call at least two weeks in advance to get tickets in summer. The best paintings near town are at the **Grotte de Font-de-Gaume** (tel. 05 53 06 90 80), 1km outside Les Eyzies on D47, where 15,000-year-old horses, bison, reindeer and woolly mammoth cavort along the cave walls. (Open April-Sept. Wed.-Mon. 9am-noon and 2-6pm; March and Oct. Wed.-Mon. 9:30am-noon and 2-5:30pm; Nov.-Feb. Wed.-Mon. 10am-noon and 2-5pm. 35F, ages 12-25 21F, artists and art students free.) Commanding a blistering view of the valley, **Grotte du Grand Roc,** 1.5km northwest of town, contains millions of stalactites, stalagmites, and *eccentriques*—small calcite accretions that grow crookedly. (Open June-Sept. 15 daily 9am-7pm; April-May and Sept. 16-Nov. 11 9:30am-6pm; Feb.-March and Nov. 12-Dec. 10am-5pm. 30min. French guided tour. 35F). About 9km northwest of Les Eyzies on route D66, the **Roque St-Christophe** (tel. 05 53 50 70 45) is the most extensive cave dwelling yet discovered. A 45-minute visit (brochures in English) allows you to examine the cave's tools, ovens, monastic remains, and weapons (open March-Nov. 10 daily 10am-6:30pm; Nov. 11-Feb. 11am-5pm; 31F). At the bridge in Les Eyzies, **Les 3 Drapeaux** (tel. 05 53 06 91 89) rents **canoes.** From June to September, you can paddle downstream and be picked up in a van for the return journey. (2hr.; canoe 60F; kayak 70F. 4hr.; canoe 80F; kayak 90F. All prices per person. Open daily 9am-6pm.) The **tourist office,** pl. de la Mairie (tel. 05 53 06 97 05; fax 05 53 06 90 79), rents bikes, exchanges currency, and has info on hiking. (Open July-Aug. Mon.-Sat. 9am-7pm, Sun. 10am-noon and 2-6pm; March-June and Sept.-Oct. Mon.-Sat. 9am-noon and 2-6pm, Sun. 10am-noon and 2-6pm; Nov.-Feb. Mon.-Fri. 10am-noon and 2-6pm.)

Sarlat and Rocamadour

Even with the dense mobs swarming **Sarlat** each summer, the town's remarkable *vieille ville,* a medieval sculpture of golden sandstone, merits a mosey. Sarlat's movie-set perfection has attracted the gaze of more than a few cameras—*Cyrano de Bergerac* and *Manon of the Springs* were both shot here. The Saturday **market** takes over the entire city (open 7:30am-12:30pm). Stop by the **tourist office,** pl. de la Liberté (tel. 05 53 59 27 67), for a self-serve smorgasbord of info. (Open June-Sept. Mon.-Sat. 9am-7pm, Sun. 10am-noon and 2-6pm; Oct.-May Mon.-Sat. 9am-noon and 2-7pm.) **Trains** run to Bordeaux (2½hr., 119F) and Périgueux (1½hr., 73F) via le Buisson (1hr., 35F). SCETA and STUB **buses** truck to Souillac (35min., 31F), and from there trains chug to Toulouse or Paris. Sarlat's **Auberge de Jeunesse (HI),** 77, av. de Selves (tel. 05 53 59 47 59 or 05 53 30 21 27), is 30 minutes from the train station but only five to 10 minutes from the *vieille ville.* Go straight along rue de la République until it becomes av. Gambetta; follow it for another 100m, then bear left at the fork onto av. de Selves. The hostel will be on your right, behind a gray gate. (Reception open daily 6-8pm or so. 45F. Sheets 16F. Camping 30F. Open March 15-Nov. Reserve ahead.) Stake your tent at **Le Montant** (tel. 05 53 59 18 50 or 05 53 59 37 73), 2.5 km from town on D57 (22.5F per person, 28.5F per tent; open Easter-Sept.).

The sanctity and staggering beauty of historic **Rocamadour** bring pilgrims and tourists to this small town built into the face of a cliff. **Le Grand Escalier** rises steeply beside the town's main street; devotees journey here to kneel at each of its steps. At the top hovers the 12th-century **Cité Réligieuse,** a complex including the **Chapelle de Notre-Dame,** home to the venerated Black Virgin (Cité open July-Aug. daily 9am-6pm and 6:30-10pm; Sept.-June 9am-6pm). Under Notre-Dame lies the **Crypte St-Amadour,** where the saint's body rested until a Protestant tried to set it ablaze during the wars of religion; the relics are now kept in the **Musée d'Art Sacrée.** (Open daily June 15-Sept. 15 10am-7pm; April-June 14 and Sept. 16-Nov. 11 10am-noon and 2-6pm. 27F.) Rocamadour is accessible by **bus** from Brive (45min., 45F) to the north.

From the south (Sarlat or Souillac), catch a bus to St-Denis-Près-Martel (23F), then a train from St-Denis (20F). The main **tourist office** (tel. 05 65 33 62 59; fax 05 65 33 74 14) is in the old Hôtel de Ville, on the pedestrian street of the medieval *cité.* (Open July-Aug. daily 10am-8pm; April-June and Sept. 10am-noon and 1-7pm; Oct.-March 2:30-6pm.) Rocamadour is a great place for your wallet to diet. Call two weeks ahead for rooms in July and August. The **Hôtel du Roc** (tel. 05 65 33 62 43; fax 05 65 33 62 11) is on the main street (singles with shower 170F, doubles with shower 210F; open April-Nov. 3). The closest of the area's four campsites is the **Relais du Campeur** (tel. 05 65 33 63 28) in l'Hospitalet, with a swimming pool. (Reception on rte. de la Cave open daily 8am-10pm. 1 site for 2 people 62F. Showers included. Open Easter-Sept.)

BASQUE COUNTRY (PAYS BASQUE)

Bayonne

A grand port with small-town appeal, Bayonne enjoys a prominent position on the Gulf of Gascony, close to the Spanish border. With its spiny twin steeples biting into the skies, the 13th-century **Cathédrale Ste-Marie** intimidates from afar and impresses from within. (Cloister open daily 9:30am-12:30pm and 2-5pm. 5F. Church open Mon.-Sat. 10am-noon and 3-6pm, Sun. 3:30-6pm.) Highlights of the unbeatable **Musée Bonnat,** 5, rue Jacques Laffitte, in Petit-Bayonne, include the lecherous mythical men in the Rubens room, a ghoulish El Greco, and Goya's grim *La Dernière Communion de San José de Calasanz* (open Wed.-Mon. 10am-noon and 2:30-6:30pm, Fri. until 8:30pm; 20F, students 10F).

Bayonne is linked by **train** to Paris (5½hr., 406-456F), Bordeaux (1½-2½hr., 130-138F), and Biarritz (10min.,12F). The **tourist office** (tel. 05 59 46 01 46; fax 05 59 59 37 55), pl. des Basques, provides a free map and can help find rooms. (Open July-Aug. Mon.-Sat. 9am-7pm, Sun. 10am-1pm; Sept.-June Mon.-Fri. 9am–6:30pm, Sat. 10am-6pm.) In St-Esprit, decent lodgings dot the train station area. The **Hôtel Paris-Madrid,** pl. de la Gare (tel. 05 59 55 13 98), has cheerful rooms. (Reception open July-Sept. 24hr.; Oct.-June daily 6am-12:30am. Singles and doubles 90-165F.) Huge portions of delicious regional cuisine are served in a classy atmosphere at **Le Bistrot Ste-Cluque,** 9, rue Hugues, across from the station (*menu* 55F; duck 55F; *paella* 65F; open daily noon-2pm and 7-11pm).

Anglet

Anglet's *raison d'être* is its nine beaches of fine-grained white sand, from the perfect waves of **Les Cavaliers** to the rocky jetty of the **Chambre d'Amour,** where two legendary lovers perished when the tide came in. All swimmers should beware the strong undertow. The **Rainbow Surfshop,** 18-21, av. Chambre d'Amour (tel. 05 59 03 54 67), rents colorful tools of the trade: bodyboards (100F per day), surfboards (100F per day), and wetsuits (50F per day). Lessons for one or two people cost 170F for the first hour and 150F for each subsequent hour (open daily 9:30am-8pm). The **tourist office,** at 1, av. de Chambre D'Amour (tel. 05 59 03 77 01; fax 05 59 03 55 91), on pl. Leclerc, is exceptionally well-equipped. (Open July-Sept.15 Mon.-Sat. 9am-7pm; Sept.16-June Mon.-Fri. 9am-12:15pm and 1:45-6pm, Sat. 9am-12:15pm.) The only hostel within 100km is in Anglet; the carefree **Auberge de Jeunesse (HI),** 19, rte. de Vignes (tel. 05 59 58 70 00; fax 05 59 58 70 07), lies directly uphill from the beach. From the Hôtel de Ville in Biarritz, take line 4 ("Bayonne Sainsontain"; every 50min.) to Auberge. From pl. de la République or pl. de Réduit in Bayonne, take line 4 to "La Barre," then change to bus 4N ("Mairie Biarritz"). In summer, line 4 runs directly to "Auberge" (reception open daily 8:30am-10pm; 80F; sheets 23F; camping 56F).

Biarritz

Originally a whaling village at the base of the Pyrenees and now home to the "queen of French beaches," Biarritz embodies all that is regal. It's not a budgeteer's dream, but it makes a daytrip *de luxe.* At the **Grande Plage,** you'll find a wealth of surfers and bathers. Just north are the less-crowded **plage Miramar** and **Pointe St-Martin,** where bathers repose *au naturel.* Jutting out from the plateau, the craggy peninsula of the **Rocher de la Vierge** gazes over magical views at sunset. At low tide, the **plage des Basques** boasts the cleanest water and the most open sand.

Trains cruise through **Biarritz-la-Négresse,** 3km out of town (tel. 05 59 33 34 35). To get to the *centre ville,* take blue bus 2 ("Bayonne via Biarritz"; in summer 6:30am-9pm) or green bus 9 ("Biarritz HDV"; in summer 6:30am-7pm). Another option is to get off the train in Bayonne and hop a bus to downtown Biarritz (30min.). All buses cost 7F50. The **tourist office,** 1, sq. d'Ixelles (tel. 05 59 24 20 24), will track down accommodations and dispenses the *Biarritzcope* with events listings (open June-Sept. daily 8am-8pm; Oct.-May 9am-6:45pm). Biarritz hotels have more stars than Cannes in May; commuting from Anglet or Bayonne may be cheapest. **Hôtel Barnetche,** 5bis, rue Charles-Floquet (tel. 05 59 24 22 25; fax 05 59 24 98 71), has dorm accommodations for just 90F (doubles 230-240F, triples and quads 120F per person; open May-Sept.). **Hôtel la Marine,** 1, rue des Goelands (tel. 05 59 24 34 09), offers singles (160F) and doubles (180F).

LANGUEDOC-ROUSSILLON

Languedoc and Roussillon, rugged southern lands where culture and personal origins are as much Spanish as French, have never been comfortable with Parisian authority. Once, an immense region called Occitania (today Languedoc) stretched from the Rhône all the way to the foothills of the Pyrenees, and from the Catalan coastal region of Roussillon in the southeast to Toulouse in the west. Its people spoke the *langue d'oc* as opposed to the *langue d'oïl* spoken in northern France, which evolved into modern French. Independent of France or Spain, the area was ruled by the count of Toulouse. In the mid-12th century, when the Cathar religion was introduced by immigrants from Asia, Occitania's nobles and peasants alike were intrigued. Frustrated by unsuccessful crusades, the Catholic nobility of northern France needed little prodding to turn on their rivals in the south. The region was overwhelmed and integrated into the French kingdom. The *langue d'oc* faded, and in 1539, the Edict of Villiers-Cotterets made the northern *langue d'oïl* official.

Toulouse

From the urban chic of the shopping district to the intimacy of rue St-Rome and the café-swamped rue du Taur, this *"Ville Rose"* caters to virtually every taste and preference. The **Basilique St-Sernin** is the longest Romanesque structure in the world and the seat of St. Dominique's Cathar-hunting inquisition. (Open July-Sept. Mon.-Sat. 9am-6:30pm, Sun. 9am-7:30pm; Oct.-June Mon.-Sat. 8:30-11:45am and 2-5:45pm, Sun. 9am-12:30pm and 2-7:30pm. Tours July-Aug. twice daily; 35F.) The 13th-century **Les Jacobins,** rue Lakanal, is an excellent example of the southern Gothic style. Flamboyant Gothic decorations are tempered by the elegance of the stained glass and serenity of the cloister. A modest crypt inside contains the ashes of St. Thomas Aquinas (open Mon.-Fri. 10am-noon and 2-6pm, Sat.-Sun. 2-6pm; cloister 10F). Housed in the **Palace d'Assézat,** rue de Metz, near the river, the **Foundation Bremberg** displays an impressive collection of Bonnards, Dufys, Pisarros, and Gauguins, supplemented by European pieces spanning five centuries (open Tues. and Thurs.-Sun. 10am-6pm, Wed. 10am-9pm; 25F, groups 15F). Away from the river, the **Musée des Augustins,** 21, rue de Metz, has an unsurpassed collection of Romanesque and Gothic sculptures (open

Thurs.-Mon. 10am-6pm, Wed. 10am-9pm; 12F, students free). For greener pastures, head to **Jardin Royal** and less formal **Jardin des Plantes,** on the outskirts of town, which offer benches and lots of shade. For bicyclists, the **Grand Rond** unfurls into allée Paul Sabatier, which keeps rolling to the Canal du Midi.

Practical Information, Accommodations, and Food To reach the **tourist office** (tel. 05 61 11 02 22; fax 05 61 22 03 63) from the station, turn left along the canal and then right onto the broad allée Jean Jaurès. Walk a third of the way around pl. Wilson (bearing right), then take a right onto rue Lafayette. The office, in a park near the intersection with rue d'Alsace-Lorraine, finds rooms and gives out free maps. (Open May-Sept. Mon.-Sat. 9am-7pm, Sun. 9am-1pm and 2-6:30pm; Oct.-April Mon.-Fri. 9am-6pm, Sat. 9am-12:30pm and 2-6pm, Sun. 10am-12:30pm and 2-5pm.) **Trains,** bd. Pierre Sémard (tel. 08 36 35 35 35), go to Paris (7hr., 425F), Bordeaux (2¼hr., 160F), Lyon (6hr., 295F), and Marseille (4½hr., 234F).

The **Hôtel des Arts,** 1bis, rue Cantegril (tel. 05 61 23 36 21; fax 05 61 12 22 37), at rue des Arts near pl. St-Georges, has spacious, spotless rooms and a friendly staff. Take metro ("Basso Cambo") to "pl. Esquirol" (singles and doubles 80-135F, with shower 125-160F; reserve ahead). New beds and sparkling bathrooms highlight the offerings at **Hôtel Beauséjour,** 4, rue Caffarelli (tel. 05 61 62 77 59), just off allée Jean Jaurès halfway between the train station and pl. Wilson (singles 75-135F, doubles 95-115F; call ahead). **Hôtel du Grand Balcon,** 8, rue Romiguières (tel. 05 61 21 48 08), on the corner of pl. du Capitole, has a wonderful location and bright rooms (singles 110-150F, doubles 130-185F; closed first 3 weeks of Aug.).

Markets line pl. des Carmes, pl. Victor Hugo, and bd. de Strasbourg (open Tues.-Sun. mornings), and inexpensive eateries lie along rue du Taur on the way to the university. The *brasseries* that crowd pl. Wilson offer 50-80F *menus* and ambience. **Salade Gasconne,** 75, rue du Taur, offers tantalizing regional specialties. (Salads 34-49F. 3-course *menu* 55F. Open Mon.-Fri. 11:30am-3pm and 7-10:30pm, Sat. 11:30am-3pm.) **Le Bar à Pâtes,** 8-10, rue Tripière, off rue St-Rome, lets you choose your own pasta and sauce for 39F (open Mon.-Sat. noon-2pm and 7:15-11:30pm, Sun. 7:15-11:30pm). The *salon de thé* **Le Bol Bu,** 8, rue du May, off rue St-Rome, serves whole-wheat crepes with off-the-wall fillings (12-31F) and 80 different kinds of tea (open Mon.-Tues. and Sat. noon-7pm, Wed.-Fri. noon-10pm).

Toulouse has something to please almost any nocturnal whim. Numerous **cafés** flank pl. St. Georges and pl. Capitole, and late-night **bars** line rue St-Rome and rue des Filatiers. The weekly *Flash* (7F) keeps you up to date on the ever-changing bar and club scene. **La Ciguä,** 6, rue de Colombette, just off bd. Lazare Carnot, is a friendly gay bar (open Tues.-Sun. 9pm-2am, Sat. 9pm-4am). From July to September, **Musique d'Eté** brings classical concerts, jazz, and ballet to a variety of outdoor settings, concert halls, and churches (tickets 80-140F at the tourist office and on location).

Carcassonne

The Cité de Carcassonne has had a rough go of it. Attacked at various times by Romans, Visigoths, and Moors, Europe's largest fortress has come to exemplify stalwart opposition in the face of the enemy. Today, the Cité is besieged by equally determined tourists and shop owners. But by simply wandering down a narrow side street, especially when floodlights and music fill the fortress at night, you can experience the charm and impenetrable solitude and of this medieval stronghold.

The Cité perches imperiously above the modern *basse ville,* where shops, hotels, and the train station are located. To reach the fortress, take bus 4 (the black line) from "pl. Gambetta" or the station (5F30), or hike 30 minutes up the hill. Originally constructed as a palace in the 12th century, the **Château Comtal** was transformed into a citadel following Carcassonne's submission to royal control in 1226. (Obligatory guided tour. Open July-Aug. 9am-7:30pm; Sept. and June 9am-7pm; Oct.-May 9:30am-12:30pm and 2-6pm. 32F, ages 18-25 21F.) Visit the torture chamber at the **Exposition Internationale,** 5, rue du Grand Puits, to view the objects of gentle persuasion used by the Catholics to show the Cathars the light (open July-Aug. 9am-11pm; Sept.-June 10am-7pm; 40F, students 30F). At the other end of the Cité, the beautiful **Basilique St-Nazaire** is the coolest place in the fortress on a sultry summer afternoon (open July-Aug. daily 9am-7pm; Sept.-June 9:30am-noon and 2-5:30pm). On Bastille Day (July 14), a lighting effect makes the fortress look as if it's going up in flames when viewed from the *basse ville,* commemorating the villages burned under Carcassonne's stern mandate when the city's *Tour de l'Inquisition* was the seat of the Inquisition's jury. In August, the entire Cité returns to the Middle Ages for the **Spectacles Médiévaux,** complete with daily jousts.

Practical Information, Accommodations, and Food To reach the **tourist office,** 15, bd. Camille Pelletan, pl. Gambetta (tel. 04 68 10 24 30; fax 04 68 10 24 38), from the train station, walk over the canal on rue G. Clemenceau, turn left onto rue de la Liberté, then turn right onto bd. Jean Jaurès. (Open July-Aug. Mon.-Sat. 9am-7pm; Sept.-June Mon.-Sat. 9am-12:15pm and 1:45-6:30pm; Oct.-March Mon.-Sat. 9am-noon and 2-6:30pm.) **Trains** arrive from Toulouse (50min., 72F) on their way to Lyon (5½hr., 258F), Marseille (3hr., 195F), and Nice (6hr., 288F). For **bus** info, check at the tourist office or the station at bd. de Varsovie. In the old, walled Cité, the **auberge de jeunesse (HI),** rue de Vicomte Trencavel (tel. 04 68 25 23 16; fax 04 68 71 14 84), has friendly dorms. (Members only. Reception open Mon.-Fri. 7am-1am, Sat.-Sun. 7am-noon and 5pm-1am. Curfew 1am; off-season 11pm. 70F.) The **Hôtel Astoria,** at the intersection of rue Montpellier and rue Tourtel (tel. 04 68 25 31 38), has spotless rooms in a quiet location. (Reception open daily 7:30am-11pm. Singles 100-155F; doubles 120-180F. Reserve ahead.)

Most restaurants in Carcassonne serve the regional specialty *cassoulet,* a stew of white beans, herbs, and meat. On rue du Plo, 60-70F *menus* abound, but save room for dessert at one of the many outdoor cafés on pl. Marcou. **Les Fontaines du Soleil,** 32, rue du Plo, offers patio dining in a little garden courtyard (open July-Aug. daily 11:30am-2am; Sept.-June 11:30am-3pm and 6pm-2am). Though nightlife is limited, several bars and cafés along rue Omer Sarrant and pl. Verdun offer some excitement. Locals dance the night away at **La Bulle,** 115, rue Barbacane.

PROVENCE: RHONE VALLEY

Avignon

The walled city of Avignon sparkles with artistic brilliance among the lush vineyards of the Rhône Valley. Film festivals, street musicians, and the famed Festival d'Avignon keep this university town shining. The **Palais des Papes,** built in the 14th century when the popes moved from Rome, stands in white granite majesty at the highest point in Avignon. (Open April-Nov.1 daily 9am-7pm, extended hours during festival and through the end of Sept.; Nov. 2-March 9am-12:45pm and 2-6pm. 35F, students 27F. Guided tour 43F, students 35F.) From early July to early August, the **Festival d'Avignon** puts on everything from avant-garde plays to Gregorian chants to all-night readings of the *Odyssey* (some events free; others 50-190F; reservations accepted from mid-June). The cheaper and more experimental **Festival OFF** presents over 400 plays, some in English, from mid-July to early August. For festival information, call the tourist office or the Bureau de Festival (tel. 04 90 82 67 08).

The **tourist office,** 41, cours Jean Jaurès (tel. 04 90 82 65 11; fax 04 90 82 95 03), doles out a free brochure listing rooms, restaurants, and museums. (Open Mon.-Fri. 9am-1pm and 2-7pm, Sat. 9am-1pm and 2-5pm; during festival daily 10am-7pm.) To get to the **Foyer YMCA/UCJG,** 7bis, chemin de la Justice (tel. 04 90 25 46 20; fax 04 90 25 30 64), in Villeneuve, across Pont Daladier, take bus 10 ("Les Angles-Grand Angles") to "Général Leclerc" or bus 11 ("Villeneuve-Grand Terme"; 6F50) to "Pont d'Avignon" (reception open daily 8:30am-8pm; 110F including breakfast). The managers at the **Squash Club,** 32, bd. Limbert (tel. 04 90 85 27 78), will put you up for free if you can beat them at squash (reception open daily 10am-10pm; 58F, sheets 16F). **Camping Municipal: St-Bénezet** (tel. 04 90 82 63 50; fax 04 90 85 22 12), Ile de la Barthélasse, has hot showers, laundry, a restaurant, a supermarket, tennis courts, and clean bathrooms. (Reception open June-Sept. daily 8am-10pm; April-May 8am-8pm; Oct. and March 8am-6pm. 25F per person, 18F per tent. Open March-Oct.)

Buy provisions at the expensive **open-air market** outside the city walls near porte St-Michel (open Sat.-Sun. 7am-noon), or at **Codec supermarket,** 23, rue de la République (open Mon.-Sat. 8:30am-8pm; in winter closes 7:30pm). **Woolloomoolloo,** 16, rue des Teinturiers, has huge portions and a funky, mellow ambiance (entrees 63-79F; open Tues.-Sat. noon-2pm and 8pm-2am). **Gambrinus,** 62, rue Carreterie, 200m down the street from porte St-Lazare and the Squash Club, specializes in *moules.* (Mussels and fries 45F. Draft beer 13F. *Menu* 70F. Open daily 7am-1:30am. Closed Aug. 10-25 and Jan. 1-15.) For the Asian flair in the midst of Avignon, head to **Took Took,** 74 rue de Lices, on the corner of rue de Lices and rue des Teinturiers (salads 25-45F; *plats* Indian 60F; open Tues.-Sun. 10am-2am; daily during the festival).

Arles

Roman grandeur haunts the sun-baked remnants of Arles's amphitheater **arènes** (now used for bullfights) and endures in the **Cloître St-Trophime.** Arles proudly inscribes plaques in the regional tongue and celebrates the **Fête d'Arles** (the last weekend in June and the first in July) in local costume with bonfires blazing. The city's beautiful vistas lured both Picasso and Van Gogh, who spent his final years—and his ear—here. Be sure to get an English copy of *Arles et Vincent,* which explains the markers that now stand where Van Gogh once planted his easel. The mid-July **Rencontres Internationales de la Photographie** (tel. 04 90 96 76 06) courts photographers and agents (20-30F per exhibit, students 10-20F; global ticket 140F, students 70F).

The **tourist office** (tel. 04 90 18 41 20; fax 04 90 18 41 29), in esplanade Charles de Gaulle at bd. des Lices, finds rooms for a 5F fee. (Open April-Sept. Mon.-Sat. 9am-7pm, Sun. 9am-1pm; Oct.-March Mon.-Sat. 9am–6pm, Sun. 10am-noon.) There is also a **branch office** at the train station (tel. 04 90 49 36 90; open Mon.-Sat. 9am-1pm and 2-6pm, reduced hours off season). Frequent **buses** run from the *gare routière* (next to the train station) to the beaches at nearby **Les Stes-Maries-de-la-Mer.** Trains roll from the **train station,** av. P. Talabot, to Avignon (20min., 35F), Marseille (1hr., 71F), Nîmes (25min., 41F), and Aix-en-Provence (1¾hr., 93F). Inexpensive **hotels** cluster around rue de l'Hôtel de Ville and pl. Voltaire, and fill in a flash during the photography festival. The sleek **Auberge de Jeunesse (HI)** is on av. Maréchal Foch (tel. 04 90 96 18 25; fax 04 90 96 31 26), 20 minutes from the station by foot, or by the Fournier stop of bus 8 from pl. Lamartine. (Reception open daily 7-10am and 5pm-midnight. Curfew midnight, later during the festival. 77F 1st night, 65F thereafter. Call ahead April-June.) **Terminus Van Gogh,** 5, pl. Lamartine (tel./fax 04 90 96 12 32), a block from the station, is decorated to match the artist's paintings (doubles 140-200F; breakfast 28F), while **Hôtel Mirador,** 3, rue Voltaire (tel. 04 90 96 28 05; fax 04 90 96 59 89), goes for the modern interior (singles and doubles 190F-255F; extra bed 60F; breakfast 27F). Regional produce fills the **open markets** on bd. Emile Courbes (open Wed. 7am-1pm) and on bd. des Lices (open Sat. 7am-1pm). A **Monoprix supermarket** is on pl. Lamartine. **La Mamma,** 20, rue de l'Amphithéâtre, has delicious pizzas, pastas, and calzones (50-62F; open Tues.-Sun. noon-3pm and 7-10pm or midnight). At the cafés on **pl. du Forum,** everyone knows everyone else by midnight, if they didn't at dusk, while those on **pl. Voltaire** have music on Wednesdays in the summer.

Near Arles: The Camargue

Between Arles and the Mediterranean coast stretches the Camargue. Pink flamingos, black bulls, and the famous white Camargue horses roam freely across this flat expanse of wild marshland, protected by the confines of the natural park. Aspiring botanists and zoologists should stop at the **Centre d'Information de Ginès** (tel. 04 90 97 86 32) along D570, which distributes information on the region's unusual flora and fauna (open April-Sept. daily 9am-6pm; Oct.-March Sat.-Thurs. 9:30am-5pm). Next door, the **Parc Ornithologique de Pont de Gau** (tel. 04 90 97 82 62), on the bus line from Arles to Stes-Maries-de-la-Mer (to "Pont de Gau," 7F from Stes-Maries-de-la-Mer), provides paths through marshland and offers views of marsh birds and grazing bulls. Rarer bird species fly through their aviaries (park open April-Sept. daily 9am-sunset; Oct.-March opens 10am; 33F). The best way to see the Camargue is on **horseback** (70F per hr., 180-200F for 3hr., 320-350F per day; meal included). **Jeep safaris** (100F for 1½hr., 150F for 2½hr.) and **boat trips** (Bateau de Promenade tel. 04 90 97 84 72; 1½hr.; 58F) are also great ways to see this area, and while many trails are only for horseback riders, **bicycle touring** is also an option. Trail maps indicating length, level of difficulty, and danger spots are available from the Stes-Maries-de-la-Mer **tourist office,** 5, av. Van Gogh (tel. 04 90 97 82 55). Frequent **buses** run to the Camargue from Arles' *gare routière* (1hr., 35F50).

Aix-en-Provence

Blessed with plentiful restaurants, elegant cafés, spellbinding museums, and exuberant festivals, Aix (pronounced "Ex") truly marks the spot as the gastronomic and cultural core of Provence. Pass the afternoon sitting in a café on **cours Mirabeau,** or walk the **Chemin de Cézanne,** a walking tour that transforms the city into an open-air museum of the native artist and his work including his studio at 9, av. Paul Cézanne. Pick up the pamphlet *In the Footsteps of Cézanne* and follow the bronze markers in the sidewalk. The **Musée Granet,** pl. St-Jean-Marie-de-Malte, displays bushels of Dutch and French works and several paintings by Cézanne. (Open Sept.-June Wed.-Mon. 10am-noon and 2-6pm; July-Aug. daily same hours. 18F, students 10F.) **Cathédrale St-Sauveur,** rue Gaston de Saporta, on the *place,* is a dramatic melange of 11th-century carvings (open Wed.-Mon. 8am-noon and 2-6pm). Beginning in the second week of June, all of Aix celebrates with **Aix en Musique,** a casual two-week jamboree of big-band jazz and chamber music. Call 04 42 16 11 61 for more info. But those gen-Aix-ers can't get enough: they also host an **International Music Festival** (mid-July to early August), a **Jazz Festival** (early July), and a **Dance Festival** (first two weeks of July). The **Comité Officiel des Fêtes** on cours Gambetta (tel. 04 42 63 06 75), at the corner of bd. du Roi René, can fill you in on festival info. When the sun sets, **Le Scat,** 11, rue Verrerie, is a terrific club with live music nightly (open Mon.-Sat. 11pm-whenever). A little outside town, **La Chimère,** montée d'Avignon, quartier des Plâtrières, attracts a sizeable gay crowd to its bar and disco (open Tues.-Sun. 10pm-6am). **Bistro Aixois,** 37, Cours Sextius, off la Rotonde, packs students and bands in cramped quarters (beer 20F; open daily 6:30am-4am).

The **tourist office,** 2, pl. du Général de Gaulle (tel. 04 42 16 11 61; fax 04 42 16 11 62), books rooms (5F) and has the guides *Le Mois à Aix* and *Aix la Vivante.* From the train station, bear left up av. Victor Hugo for the tourist office and the central bus terminal. (Open June-Aug. daily 8:30am-10pm; May-June and Sept. 8:30am-8pm; Oct.-April 8:30am-7pm.) To get virtually anywhere by **train** from Aix, you must pass through Marseille (1 per hr. until 9:23pm, 40min, 36F) or on the cheaper **bus** (30min., 22F). Four buses a day run to Avignon (1½hr., 70-80F).

The crowded **Auberge de Jeunesse (HI),** 3, av. Marcel Pagnol (tel. 04 42 20 15 99; fax 04 42 59 36 12), quartier du Jas de Bouffan. Follow av. des Belges from la Rotonde and turn right on av. de l'Europe. At the first rotary after the highway overpass, bear left and climb the hill. The hostel is on your left. To avoid the 35-minute walk, take bus 12 (every 15-30min. until 8pm, 7F) from La Rotonde to "Vasarely." (Arrive before noon, or after 4pm. Lockout 10am-4pm. Curfew midnight. 79F 1st night, 68F thereafter. Sheets 11F.) All of the rooms of **Hôtel des Arts,** 69, bd. Carnot (tel. 04 42 38 11 77; fax 04 42 26 12 57), have shower and phone (singles 149-175F, doubles 175-95F).

French decor prevails at the **Hôtel Vigouroux,** 27, rue Cardinale (tel. 04 42 38 26 42), between pl. des Dauphins and Musée Granet.

The streets north of cours Mirabeau are packed with restaurants for all palates and wallets. **Hacienda,** 7, rue Mérindol, in the pl. des Fontêtes, is a good value; the delicious 75F 3-course *menu* includes wine (open Mon.-Sat. noon-2pm and 7-10pm). **Autour d'une Tarte,** 13, rue Gaston de Saporta, off pl. de l'Hôtel de Ville, offers quiches galore (12-40F; open Mon.-Sat. 8:30am-7:30pm). Buy a picnic lunch at the **markets,** on pl. des Prêcheurs, pl. de la Madeleine, and pl. Richelme (open Tues., Thurs., and Sat. 7am-1pm), or stock up at the **Casino supermarkets** at av. de Lattre de Tassigny (open Mon.-Sat. 8:30am-8:30pm) and 3, cours d'Orbitelle (open Mon.-Sat. 8am-1pm and 4-8pm). Be sure to sample Aix's famed almonds, used in cakes and cookies, at one of the *pâtisseries* along rue d'Italie or rue Espariat.

FRENCH RIVIERA (CÔTE D'AZUR)

Paradises are made to be lost. Sparkling between Marseille and the Italian border, the sun-drenched beaches and waters of the Mediterranean form the backdrop for this fabled playground of the rich and famous. But its seductive loveliness has almost been its undoing, as shrewd developers have turned the coast's beauty to profit and its pleasures into big business. Today, the area is as crammed with low-budget tourists as with high-handed millionaires, and many French condemn it as a shameless Fort Lauderdale, a mere shadow of its former self.

The coast is well-served by frequent, inexpensive **trains** and **buses.** Trains for the Côte leave Paris's Gare de Lyon every hour in summer; the trip takes five hours on the TGV to Marseille and eight hours to Nice. Trains and roads are packed in summer; you might want to base yourself in the less expensive coastal towns and take daytrips to the purse-emptying cities. Like western Provence, the Riviera is best visited during early June and in September when the crowds diminish somewhat.

Marseille

France's third largest city, Marseille, is like its famous *bouillabaisse:* steaming hot and spicy. The city enjoys a reputation for roguishness and danger, and a large immigrant population fuels ethnic tensions. Yet colorful and chaotic Marseille remains strangely alluring. The city's daily markets, wild nightclubs, and big-city adventure merit a stopover on the way to Nice or Avignon. Just use caution, and after dark avoid the *vieux port,* the North African quarter, cours Belsunce, and bd. d'Athènes.

To get a sense of *la vraie* Marseille, amble down **rue Paradis, rue St Ferréol, cours Julien,** and the North African **rue des Feuillants.** The majestic 19th-century **Basilique de Notre Dame de la Garde** perches on a hill above the city. To reach the site, take bus 60, or follow rue Breteuil from the *vieux port,* turn right on bd. Vauban, and then right again on rue Fort du Sanctuaire (open in summer daily 7am-8pm; off-season 7am-7pm. Free. No shorts or tank tops). Marseille's public **beaches** are accessible on bus 83 ("Rond pont du Prado") from the *vieux port.* Both **plage du Prado** and **plage de la Corniche** offer wide beaches, clear waters, and scenic views.

The **tourist office,** 4, La Canebière (tel. 04 91 13 89 00; fax 04 91 13 89 20), has a free accommodations service and maps (open July-Aug. daily 9am-8pm; Oct.-June Mon.-Sat. 9am-7pm, Sun. 10am-5pm). **Trains** leave pl. Victor Hugo for Paris (4¾hr., 400F) and Lyon (3½hr., 202F), while **buses** serve Cannes (2¼-3hr., 120F, students 85F), Nice (2¾hr., 133F, students 90F), Avignon (2hr., 89F, round-trip 134F), and Aix-en-Provence (25F). **SNCM,** 61, bd. des Dames (tel. 08 36 67 95 00), runs **ferries** to Corsica (254-286F, students 156-172F), Sardinia, and North Africa. The **Auberge de Jeunesse de Bois-Luzy (HI),** allée des Primevères (tel./fax 04 91 49 06 18), has clean rooms and hot showers. Take bus 6 from cours J. Thierry at the top of La Canebière to "Marius Richard" and follow the signs, or take bus 8 from "La Canebière" to "Bois-

Luzy." At night, take bus T from "La Canebière" to "Marius Richard." (Reception open daily 7:30am-noon and 5-11pm. Curfew 10:30-11pm. 45F. Doubles 50F per person. Call ahead.) The **Auberge de Jeunesse Bonneveine (HI),** impasse Bonfils (tel. 04 91 73 21 81; fax 04 91 73 97 23), a left turn after 47, av. J. Vidal, has a bar, restaurant, and travel agency (members only; reception open daily 7am-11pm; 74-97F; closed Jan.). **Hôtel Gambetta,** 49, allée Léon Gambetta (tel. 04 91 62 07 88), and **Hôtel Béarn,** 63, rue Sylvabelle (tel. 04 91 37 75 83), are both good (singles 99-188F).

The restaurant population soars around the *vieux port;* for a more artsy crowd and cheaper fare, head up to **cours Julien** and the pedestrian mall. **La Manne,** 18, bd. de la Liberté, offers friendly service and a 50F *menu* with a vegetarian option (open Mon.-Sat. noon-3pm and 7-11pm). Nightlife centers on cours Julien, northeast of the harbor, and pl. Thiers near the *vieux port.* **Trolleybus,** 24 quai de Rive Neuve, is a mega-club (cover 64F on Sat. only; open Thurs.-Sat. 11pm-7am).

St-Tropez

Once a fishing hamlet, St. Tropez lured bronzed beauty Brigitte Bardot and her ritzy coterie to this town dubbed *St. Trop d'Aise* (St. Too-Much-Luxury). To reach the **beaches**, take a Sodetrav bus from the *gare routière* on av. Général Leclerc ("St-Tropez-Ramatuelle"; Mon.-Sat. 3 per day, 9F). Or, rent wheels from **Louis Mas,** 3-5, rue Quarenta. (Bikes 50-80F per day, deposit 1000-2000F. Mopeds 110F, deposit 2500-5000F. Open Easter-Oct. 15 Mon.-Sat. 9am-7:30pm, Sun. 9am-1pm and 5-7:30pm.)

To reach St-Tropez take the **bus** (tel. 04 94 97 88 51) from St-Raphaël (1½-2¼hr., 48F). The faster, more scenic boat ride from St-Raphaël is much more suave, but not much more expensive (50min., 100F round-trip, only 80F if you stay at the Fréjus hostel). Call **Gare Maritime de St-Raphaël** at 04 94 95 17 46 for details. **Hitching** is poor—"they'd soil the Porsche's upholstery, dahling."

The **tourist office** (tel. 04 94 97 45 21; fax 04 94 97 82 66), overlooking the frenzied port from quai Jean Jaurès, has transportation and sights info (open in summer daily 9:30am-1;30pm and 3:30-11pm). Budget hotels do not exist in St-Tropez; the closest **HI youth hostel** is in Fréjus. **Camping** is the cheapest option, but make reservations. The tourist office can help you find sites with vacancies. Try the four-star **La Croix du Sud,** route des Plage (tel. 04 94 79 80 84; fax 04 94 79 89 21), in Ramatuelle (85F for 1-2 people, 120F for 3; open Easter-Sept.), or **Kon Tiki** (tel. 04 94 79 80 17; 113F for 2 people, car, and tent). Both lie just behind the Pampelonne beach.

The **Vieux Port** and the narrow cobblestone streets of the hillside *vieille ville* behind the waterfront form the hub of St-Tropez's culinary activity. **Lou Regalé,** 12, rue du Colonel Guichard, next to the Eglise Paroissiale, serves pasta, roast chicken and *ratatouille* on its 50F *menu* (open daily noon-2:30pm and 7-11pm). To create your own ambiance, head to the **Prisunic supermarket,** 7, av. du Général Leclerc (open Mon.-Sat. 8am-10pm; in summer also Sun. 8:30am-1pm and 3-10pm). Dance all night at **Le Pigeonnier,** 13, rue de la Ponche (80F cover includes first drink; drinks 70F; open daily 11:30pm-dawn).

St-Raphaël and Fréjus

Sandwiched between St-Tropez and Cannes, the twin cities of St-Raphaël and Fréjus boast all the wide beaches, seafood restaurants, and coastal charm of their swanky Côte d'Azur cousins at half the cost. Bake in the sun along the long and sandy **Plage Fréjus,** just 10 minutes along the waterfront from the St-Raphaël train station. Ask at the tourist office for info on bullfights and rock concerts at the **Roman amphitheater** on rue Henri Vadon. (Open April-Sept. Wed.-Mon. 9:30am-noon and 2-6:30pm; Oct.-March 9am-noon and 2-4:30pm. Free.) The first weekend in July is the **Compétition Internationale de Jazz New Orleans** in St-Raphaël. Hundreds of musicians face off in the streets and by the port in front of a panel of judges—and the shows are free (ask at the tourist office for more info).

The **tourist office** in St-Raphaël (tel. 04 94 19 52 52; fax 04 94 83 85 40), across the street from the train station, has the scoop on transportation and room availability (open July-Aug. daily 8:30am-7pm; Sept.-June Mon.-Fri. 8:30am-7pm). St-Raphaël sends **trains** to Cannes (25min., 32F) and Nice (1hr., 54F). **Sodetrav buses** connect St-Raphaël to St-Tropez (15 per day, 1½hr.), and **Forum Cars** (tel. 04 94 95 16 71) makes the trip from Cannes to St-Raphaël (70min., 32F50). **Les Bateaux de Saint Raphaël,** at the *vieux port* (tel. 04 94 95 17 46), cruise to St-Tropez four to five times per day in summer (50min., 70-100F round-trip). If you are staying at the youth hostel in Fréjus, ask about ticket discounts. Buses leave from quai 7 for the St-Raphaël-Fréjus voyage every hour (26min., 6F50).

Kind managers run the **Auberge de Jeunesse de St-Raphaël-Fréjus (HI),** chemin du Counillier (tel. 04 94 53 18 75; fax 04 94 53 25 86), 4km from the St-Raphaël train station. A direct shuttle bus runs from quai 7 of the *gare routière* to the hostel at 6pm (6F50); a return shuttle leaves at 8:30am and 6 and 7pm (curfew 11pm; 66F; camping 32; ask about bike rental and boat discounts). **Le Mistral,** 80, rue de la Garonne, (tel. 04 94 95 38 82) is next to the beach and offers discounts for longer stays and *Let's Go*ers. Their restaurant offers 65 and 75F *menus* (singles 120-170F, doubles 150-260F, triples 210-330F, quads 240-360F). Close to the train station, **La Bonne Auberge,** 54, rue de la Garonne (tel. 04 94 95 69 72), has simple rooms (singles 130-170F, doubles 120-200F, triples 210-220F; open March-Oct.).

Cannes

All stereotypes of the French Riviera materialize in Cannes, a favorite stop of the international jet-set. Less reclusive than St-Tropez, Cannes allows even unshaven budget travelers to tan like the stars. In May, Cannes's **Festival International du Film** brings Hollywood's *crème de la crème* from across the sea. None of the festival's 350 screenings are open to the public, but the sidewalk show is free. Most of Cannes's daytime activity (and spending) pulses between rue Félix-Faure and the waterfront. **Rue d'Antibes,** running parallel to the sea, and **boulevard de la Croisette,** passing right along the shore, front high price displays with the familiar names of Christian Dior, Hermès, and Gianni Versace. Further west, the **Castre Cathédrale** and its courtyard stand on the hill on which *vieux* Cannes was built.

Of Cannes's three casinos, the most accessible is **Le Casino Croisette,** 1, jetée Albert Eduoard (tel. 04 93 38 12 11), next to the Palais des Festivals, with slots, blackjack, and roulette. (Gambling daily 5pm-4am; open for slots at 10am. No shorts. Min. age 18. Admission free.) If your luck sours, take to the clubs, but be sure to dress to impress or you may be turned down at the door. From 11pm to dawn, dance at **Jane's,** 38, rue des Serbes, in the Hôtel Gray d'Albion (cover and drink 120F; subsequent drinks 70F). **3 Cloches,** 6, rue Vidal, is a bar/*discothèque* that caters to the gay community (cover 70F; bar opens at 11pm, disco at midnight).

The info-effusive **tourist office** at 1, bd. de la Croisette (tel. 04 93 39 24 53; fax 04 92 99 84 23) has a free accommodations service (open July-Aug. daily 9am-7pm; Sept.-June Mon.-Sat. 9am-6:30pm). Find a **branch office** at the train station. (Open July-Sept. Mon.-Sat. 8:30am-12:30pm and 3-7pm; Oct.-June Mon.-Fri. 9am-12:30pm and 2pm-6:15pm.) On the major coastal **train** line, Cannes's station, 1, rue Jean Jaurès, receives trains from Nice (35min., 31F), Monaco (50min., 44F), and TGV to Paris via Marseille (about 440F; ask for student fares; call regarding prices). **Buses** leave from the *gare routière* (Buz Azur; tel. 04 93 39 18 71) to Antibes (30min., 12F50) Nice (1½hr., 30F), and St-Raphaël (70min., 32F).

A few bargain accommodations lurk near the train station although the area is less than safe at night. Try to book ahead—an absolute must in July and August. From the train station take the stairs leading to a passageway under the station and then follow signs to the **Auberge pour la Jeunese-Le Chalit,** 27, av. Maréchal Galliéni (tel. 04 93 99 22 11; fax 04 93 39 00 28; 90F; sheets 15F). The new **Auberge de la Jeunesse de Cannes,** 35, av. de Vallauris (tel./fax 04 93 99 26 79; follow the signs from under the train station), offers big, comfy beds. (Curfew 1am, 2am on weekends. Reception open daily 8am-noon and 3-10pm. 70-80F.) The best **camping** is the three-star site at **Le Grand Saule,** 24, bd. Jean Moulin (tel. 04 93 90 55 10; fax 04 93 47 24 55), in nearby **Ranguin.** Take bus 9 (7F) from pl. de l'Hôtel de Ville toward Grasse (70F per person, 124F for 2 people and tent; open April-Oct.).

Morning markets tempt you with fresh foodstuffs on the *place* between rue Mimont and av. de la République (open daily 7am-noon). You can also buy your supplies at **Monoprix supermarket,** 9, rue Maréchal Foch, across from the station (open Mon.-Sat. 8:30am-8:30pm), and then picnic in the breezy Jardin de la Croisette. **Le Lion d'Or,** 45, bd. de la République, serves an unbeatable 3-course 67F *menu* (open Sun.-Fri. noon-2pm and 7-9:30pm). **Restaurant des Artistes,** 5, rue Rouguière, and **Pap Nino's,** 15, bd. de la Rèpublique, can tame the hungry beast.

Nice

Cosmopolitan and chic, sun-drenched and spicy, Nice sparkles as the unofficial capital of the Riviera. The city's pumping nightlife, top-notch museums, and bustling beaches enhance the native *provençal* charms: flowery, palm-lined boulevards, casual affluence, and soothing sea breezes. During the **Carnaval** (Feb. 14-March 1 in 1998), the city celebrates spring with wild floral revelry, grotesque costumes, and raucous song and dance. Prepare to have more fun than you'll remember.

ORIENTATION AND PRACTICAL INFORMATION

The **train station,** Gare Nice-Ville, is in the center of town, next to the tourist office on **avenue Thiers.** To the left, **avenue Jean-Médecin** runs toward the water to **place Masséna.** Heading right from the train station, you'll find **boulevard Gambetta,** the other main street running directly to the water. Sweeping along the coast, the **promenade des Anglais** is a noisy people-watching paradise. Cafés, boutiques, and expensive restaurants line the **pedestrian zone** west of pl. Masséna. Women should avoid walking alone after sundown, and everyone should exercise caution around the train station and Vieux Nice. Never leave your belongings unattended.

Tourist Office: (tel. 04 93 87 07 07; fax 04 93 16 85 16; email otc@nice-coteazur.org; http://www.nice-coteazur.org), beside the station. Books a limited number of rooms. Ask for the English-language *Nice: A Practical Guide* and the city map. Open June 15-Sept. 15 daily 8am-8pm; Sept. 16-June 14 8am-7pm.

Currency Exchange: Cambio, 17, av. Thiers (tel. 04 93 88 56 80), across from the station. No commission. Open daily 7am-midnight.

American Express: 11, promenade des Anglais (tel. 04 93 16 53 53), at the corner of rue des Congrès. The office has an **ATM** machine. Open daily 9am-9pm.

Flights: Aéroport Nice-Côte d'Azur (tel. 04 93 21 30 30). Take Sunbus 23 ("St-Laurent") from the train station (every 20min. 6am-9pm, 9F). The airport bus (tel. 04 93 56 35 40) runs from the bus station by pl. Massena every 20min. (21F).

Trains: Gare SNCF Nice-Ville, av. Thiers (tel. 08 36 35 35 35). Trains run frequently to Cannes (40min., 37F), Antibes (25min., 26F), Monaco (25min., 22F), and elsewhere in France, Italy, and Spain. In summer, 11 trains per day connect with the TGV to Paris (7hr., 420-522F plus 20F required reservation). **Lockers** 15-30F. **Luggage storage** 30F per day per piece (open daily 7am-10pm).

Buses: Gare Routière, 5, bd. Jean Jaurès (tel. 04 93 85 61 81). To: Monaco (45min., 17-19F), Antibes (1hr., 25F), Juan-les-Pins (1hr., 27F), and Cannes (1¼hr., 30F).

Public Transportation: Sunbus, 10, av. Félix Faure (tel. 04 93 16 52 10), near pl. Leclerc and pl. Masséna. Tickets 8F. Day pass 22F; *carnet* of 10 tickets 68F; 5-day pass 85F. Buy passes at the agency or kiosk at pl. Leclerc. Bus 12 goes from the train station to pl. Masséna and the beach every 12min. The tourist office's *Guide Infobus* lists other routes.

Ferries: SNCM, quai du Commerce (tel. 04 93 13 66 66; fax 04 93 13 66 81). Take bus 1 or 2 ("Port") from pl. Masséna. To: Bastia (4-5hr., 252-278F, students 191-209F) and Ajaccio (6-7hr., same prices). Open Mon.-Fri. 8am-7pm, Sat. 8am-noon.

Bike Rental: JML Location, 34, av. Thiers. Bikes 60-80F per day. Mopeds 120F per day. Scooters 130-310F per day. Credit card imprint. Open daily 9am-noon and 2-6:30pm. **Cycles Arnaud,** 4, pl. Grimaldi, near the pedestrian zone. Bikes 100F, 2000F credit card deposit. Open Mon.-Fri. 9am-noon and 2-7pm, Sat. 9am-noon.

Laundromat: Laverie Automatique, rue de Suisse, between rue Paganini and rue d'Angleterre. Wash 20F, dry 2F per 5min. Open daily 7am-9pm.

Hospital: St-Roch, 5, rue Pierre Devoluy (tel. 04 92 03 33 75). From av. Jean Médecin, turn left on rue Pastorelli, which turns into rue P. Devoluy.

Emergency: tel. 17. **Medical emergency:** tel. 18.

Police: tel. 04 93 17 22 22; at the opposite end of bd. Maréchal Foch from bd. Jean Médecin.

Post Office: 23, av. Thiers (tel. 04 93 82 65 22 or 04 93 82 65 23). Open Mon.-Fri. 8am-7pm, Sat. 8am-noon. **Telephones** and *Poste Restante.* **Postal Code:** 06000.

ACCOMMODATIONS

Don't make your first *niçois* experience regrettable—come with **reservations.** Affordable places cluster around the train station, but without reservations (made 3-5 days in advance), you'll be forced to join the legions outside the train station, which moonlights as one of the largest and most dangerous bedrooms in France.

Hôtel Les Alizès, 10, rue de Suisse (tel. 04 93 88 85 08), off rue d'Angleterre. From the train station, turn left, walk to av. Jean Médecin and turn right. Friendly owners keep comfortable, spotless rooms, all with showers. Singles 80F. Doubles 200F. Triples 260F. Free breakfast and discounts with *Let's Go.* V, MC.

Hôtel Baccarat, 39, rue d'Angleterre (tel. 04 93 88 35 73; fax 04 93 16 14 25). Turn left from the train station, walk 50m, and turn right. If all hotels were this nice, your mother would backpack around Europe. All rooms and dorms are with bath. Dorms 83F. Singles 153F. Doubles 206F. Breakfast 15F. V, MC.

Hôtel Les Orangiers, 10bis, av. Durante (tel. 04 93 87 51 41; fax 04 93 82 57 82). Walk down the steps by the Thomas Cook agency, cross the street and go down the ramp. The hotel is up on the left. Large, bright dorms and rooms, some with balconies, most with showers. English-speaking owner offers free luggage storage. Dorms 85F. Singles 95F. Doubles 210F. Triples 285F. Quads 360F. V, MC.

Hôtel des Flanders, 6, rue de Belgique (tel. 04 93 88 78 94; fax 04 93 88 74 90). Large, clean rooms with bathrooms and well-worn carpets. Student dorms 90F. Singles 200F. Doubles 250F. Triples 340F. Quads 400F. Breakfast 25F. V, MC.

Hôtel Notre Dame, 22, rue de Russie (tel. 04 93 88 70 44; fax 04 93 82 20 38), corner of rue d'Italie one block west of av. Jean Médecin. Good-sized, quiet rooms. Owners also rent studios. Singles 130F. Doubles 160-240F. Triples 300F. Quads 350F. Apartments (4 people) 350F. Breakfast 20F. Showers 10F. V, MC.

Hôtel Lyonnais, 20, rue de Russie (tel. 04 93 88 70 74; fax 04 93 16 25 56). Singles 110-220F. Doubles 120-220F. Triples 180-290F. Quads 240-344F. *Let's Go*-ers get a 10% off-season discount. Showers 15F. V, MC, AmEx.

Auberge de Jeunesse (HI), route Forestière du Mont-Alban (tel. 04 93 89 23 64; fax 04 92 04 03 10). Worth the commute. Take bus 14 ("Mont Baron") to "l'Auberge" from the *gare routière* off bd. Jean Jaurès (last bus 7:30pm). Otherwise, from the train station, turn left and then right on av. Jean Médecin. Turn left on bd. Jaurès and then right on rue Barla. Reception opens at 5pm. Lockout 10am-5pm. Curfew midnight. 66F, including shower and breakfast. Kitchen.

Relais International de la Jeunesse "Clairvallon," 26, av. Scudéri (tel. 04 93 81 27 63; fax 04 93 53 35 88), in Cimiez, 4km away. Take bus 15 ("Remiez") to "Scudéri" from the train station or pl. Masséna. Call for directions. A large, luxurious hostel in an old villa with a tennis and basketball court. Check-in 5pm. Curfew 11pm. Lockout 9:30am-5pm. Dorms 70F. Breakfast included. Dinner 50F.

Hôtel Belle Meunière, 21, av. Durante (tel. 04 93 88 66 15), near the *gare.* The helpfulness and fluent English of the owner's daughter, Marie-Pierre, make visitors right at home in this well-worn hotel. Dorms 75-100F. Tepid shower 10F for 5min. Doubles 265F. Triples 321F. Quads 400F. Breakfast included.

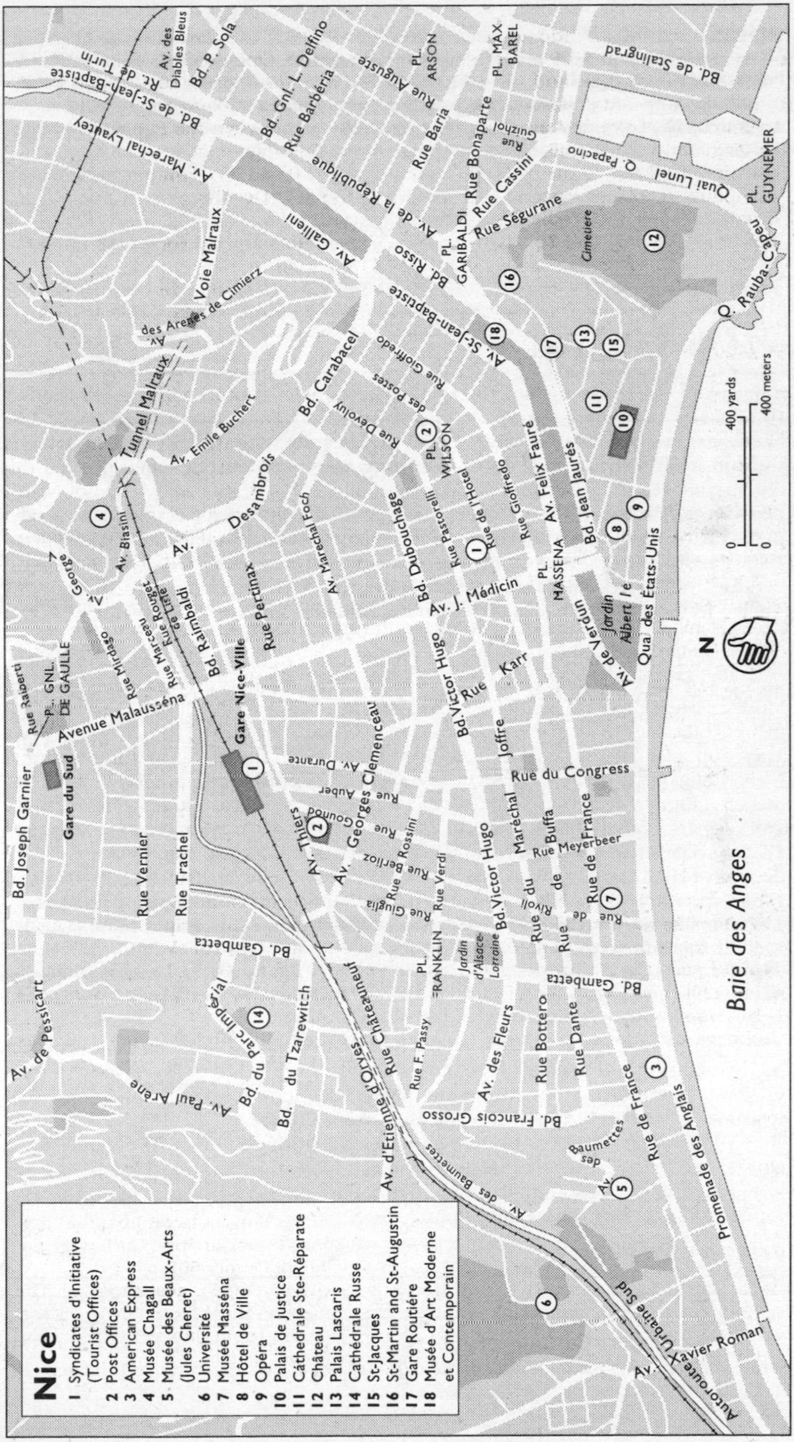
Nice
1 Syndicates d'Initiative (Tourist Offices)
2 Post Offices
3 American Express
4 Musée Chagall
5 Musée des Beaux-Arts (Jules Cheret)
6 Université
7 Musée Masséna
8 Hôtel de Ville
9 Opéra
10 Palais de Justice
11 Cathédrale Ste-Réparate
12 Château
13 Palais Lascaris
14 Cathédrale Russe
15 St-Jacques
16 St-Martin and St-Augustin
17 Gare Routière
18 Musée d'Art Moderne et Contemporain
Baie des Anges
Promenade des Anglais
Quai des États-Unis
Q. Rauba-Capeu
Quai Lunel
Q. Papacino
Bd. de Stalingrad
PL. GUYNEMER
Cimetière
Gare Nice-Ville
Gare du Sud
Avenue Malausséna
Av. Jean Médecin
Bd. Victor Hugo
Rue de France
Rue du Congress
Rue Meyerbeer
Bd. Gambetta
Av. Georges Clemenceau
Av. Thiers
Bd. Dubouchage
Bd. Carabacel
Av. Desambrois
Bd. Raimbaldi
Bd. Jean Jaurès
Av. Félix Fauré
PL. MASSENA
Jardin Albert Ier
Av. de Verdun
Av. St-Jean-Baptiste
Bd. Risso
PL. GARIBALDI
Rue Ségurane
Rue Cassini
Rue Bonaparte
Av. de la République
Av. Gallieni
Av. Maréchal Lyautey
Bd. de St-Jean-Baptiste
Rt. de Turin
Bd. P. Sola
Av. des Diables Bleus
Bd. Gnl. L. Delfino
Rue Barbéria
Rue Auguste
PL. ARSON
Rue Baria
PL. MAX BAREL
Voie Malraux
Tunnel Malraux
Av. des Arènes de Cimiez
Av. Emile Buchert
Av. Biasini
Av. George V
PL. GNL. DE GAULLE
Rue Raiberti
Bd. Joseph Garnier
Rue Vernier
Rue Trachel
Rue Pertinax
Av. Maréchal Foch
Rue Gioffredo
Rue Pastorelli
Rue de l'Hotel des Postes
PL. WILSON
Rue Deyoluy
Rue Alberti
Bd. de Cessole
Av. de Pessicart
Av. Paul Arène
Bd. du Parc Impérial
Bd. du Tzarewitch
Rue Châteauneuf
Av. d'Etienne d'Orves
Rue F. Passy
PL. FRANKLIN
Jardin d'Alsace-Lorraine
Av. des Fleurs
Rue Bottero
Rue Dante
Bd. François Grosso
Av. des Baumettes
Av. Xavier Roman
Autoroute Urbaine Sud
Rue Maréchal Joffre
Rue Buffa
Rue de Rivoli
Rue Rossini
Rue Verdi
Rue Berlioz
Rue Gounod
Rue Auber
Av. Durante
Rue Dalpozzo
Rue Alphonse Karr
Rue Mirdago
Rue Marceau
Rue Rouget de Lisle
Rue Guiglia
Rue Guizhol
400 yards
400 meters
N

FRANCE

FOOD

Nice offers a smorgasbord of seafood and North African, Asian, and Italian gastronomic delights. Avoid the touristy places near the train station in favor of the restaurants that cluster around the *vieux port,* or stock up at the **Prisunic supermarket,** 42, av. Jean Médecin (open Mon.-Sat. 8:30am-8:30pm).

Le Faubourg Montmartre, 39, rue Pertinax, off av. Jean Médecin. Great *niçois* cuisine at low prices. Open daily 11:30am-3pm and 5:30pm-late.

Restaurant de Paris, 28, rue d'Angleterre. Generous *menus* for 38-58F. Open in summer daily 11:30am-3pm and 5:30pm-11pm; reduced hours in winter.

Lou Pilha Leva, 10, rue du Collet, in Vieux Nice. Hustling and bustling order counter will provide a lot for 30F. 15F quiche. 10F *socca.* Open daily 7:30am-1am.

La Petite Biche, 9, rue d'Alsace-Lorraine, has a 63F *menu* of *provençal* specialties. Open 11:45am-3pm and 6:30-10pm.

SIGHTS

Nice's **promenade des Anglais,** which stretches the length of the waterfront, is a sight in itself. Private beaches crowd the water between bd. Gambetta and the Opéra, but plenty of public space remains. Whatever dreams you've had of Nice's beach, the hard reality is an endless stretch of smooth rocks; bring a beach mat. Between av. Verdun and bd. Jaurès off the Promenade des Anglais and quai des Etats-Unis, **Jardin Albert Ier** and **Espace Masséna** offer a break from the heat with benches, plenty of shade, and an ornate 18th-century Triton fountain. Promenade des Anglais leads east to **La Colline du Château,** a flowery hillside park crowned with the remains of an 11th-century cathedral (park open daily 8am-7:30pm).

Even burn-hard sunbathers will have a hard time passing by Nice's excellent museums. The **Musée des Beaux-Arts,** 33, av. Baumettes, exhibits the work of Fragonard, Monet, Sisley, Bonnard, and Degas, and also features sculptures by Rodin and Carpeaux. Take bus 38 from the train station to "Chéret," or bus 12 to "Grosseo" (open Tues.-Sun. 10am-noon and 2-6pm; 25F, students 15F). The elegant **Musée National Marc Chagall,** av. du Dr. Ménard, a 15-minute walk north of the station or a ride on bus 15 ("Rimiez" and "Les Sources"; 8F), stunningly showcases this talented artist's work (open July-Sept. Wed.-Mon. 10am-6pm; Oct.-June 10am-5pm; 28-38F, students 18-28F). The **Musée Matisse,** 164, av. des Arènes de Cimiez, displays the colorful designs of Henri Matisse, who lived and worked in Nice from 1917 until his death in 1954 (open April-Sept. Wed.-Mon. 10am-6pm; Oct.-March 10am-5pm; 25F, students 15F). Finally, the **Musée d'Art Moderne et d'Art Contemporain,** promenade des Arts, at the intersection of av. St-Jean Baptiste and Traverse Garibaldi (bus 5 "St-Charles" from the station), features over 400 French and American avant-garde pieces from 1960 to the present (open Wed.-Thurs. and Sat.-Mon. 11am-6pm, Fri. 11am-10pm; 25F, students 15F).

The gorgeous **Cathédrale Orthodoxe Russe St-Nicolas,** 17, bd. du Tsarévitch, off bd. Gambetta, is a reminder of the days when the Côte d'Azur was a favorite retreat for Russian nobility. (Open June-Aug. daily 9am-noon and 2:30-6pm; Sept.-May 9:30am-noon and 2:30-5pm. 12F.) The **Monastère Cimiez,** pl. du Monastère, housed Nice's Franciscan brethren from the 13th to the 18th centuries. The monastery's cloister, peaceful gardens, cemetery (in which Matisse is buried), and museum are free. Take bus 15 or 17 from the station, or follow the signs from the Musée Matisse (open Mon.-Sat. 10am-noon and 3-6pm).

ENTERTAINMENT

Nice's **Jazz Festival** (tel. 04 93 21 10 00; fax 04 93 18 07 92), in mid-July at the Parc et Arènes de Cimiez near the Musée Matisse, attracts world-famous jazz musicians (40-170F). The **Théâtre du Cours,** 2, rue Poissonnerie, stages traditional drama (75F), while the **Théâtre de Nice** on Promenade des Arts hosts concerts and theater (50-

200F). The **FNAC bookstore,** in the Nice Etoile shopping center, 24, av. Jean Médecin, sells tickets for virtually every performance in town.

Nice guys do finish last—the city's party crowd swings long after the folks in St-Tropez and Antibes have called it a night. The bars and nightclubs around rue Masséna and Vieux Nice rollick with rock, jazz, and pizazz, but the area around Vieux Nice can be dangerous at night. Don't visit clubs in this area alone.

Chez Wayne, 15, rue de la Préfecture. Attracts an English-speaking crowd with live music every summer night and the double whammy of karaoke as well as undubbed *The Simpsons* on Sun. Beers 28-36F. Open daily 2:30pm-midnight.

Master Home, next to Chez Wayne. Too-sexy club where a pint is 28F day or night. Open daily 11am-2:30am.

The Hole in the Wall, 3, rue de l'Abbaye. Tiny but loads of fun. Mellow live music every night. Open daily 8pm-1am.

Cyber Café La Douche, cours Saleya. A dark, black-lit bar/club where you can check your email for 25F (30min.). Open 4pm-2:30am.

■ Near Nice

The narrow streets and pastel houses of **Villefranche-sur-Mer,** only two stops from Nice on the local train, have enchanted Aldous Huxley, Katherine Mansfield, and a bevy of other writers. Strolling from the train station along the quai Ponchardier, a sign to the *vieille ville* points the way to **rue Obscure,** the oldest street in Villefranche. Two excellent museums are located in the 16th-century **Citadelle,** near the waterfront: the **Musée Volti** displays the contemporary art and sculpture of resident Antoniucci Volti, while the **Musée Goetz-Boumeester** traces the work of Villefranche painter Henri Goetz and his wife, Christine Boumeester. (Both open July-Aug. Wed-Mon. 10am-noon and 3-7pm, Sun. 3-7pm; June and Sept. 9am-noon and 3-6pm; Oct.-May 10am-noon and 2-5pm. Free.) **Trains** run from Nice every half-hour (9F). The **tourist office** (tel. 04 93 01 73 68; fax 04 93 76 63 65), on Jardin François Binon, gives out free maps and info on sights. (Open July to mid-Sept. daily 8am-8pm; mid-Sept. to June Mon.-Sat. 8:30am-noon and 2-7pm.)

Antibes has drawn crowds with its beautiful beaches and Picasso museum for years, but the theater and music festivals and seaside youth hostel have made it a new hotspot on the budget itinerary. If you've gotten your share of the sun, retreat to the charming *vieille ville.* Old Antibes, which stretches between bd. Maréchal Foch and the port d'Antibes, is a haven for museums and pricey boutiques. The **Musée Picasso,** in the Château Grimaldi on pl. Mariejol, displays works by the master and his contemporaries. (Open June-Sept. Tues.-Sun. 10am-6pm; Oct.-May 10am-noon and 2-6pm. 30F, students 18F.) Drawings by local artist, Raymond Peyney, can be found in the **Museé Peynet,** pl. Nationale (open daily 10am-noon and 2-6pm; 20F, students 10F).**Trains** connect Antibes with Cannes (10min., 13F), Marseille (2½hr., 135F), Nice (18min., 21F), and Juan-les-Pins. **Buses** go to Nice (1¼hr., 24F50) and Cannes (30min., 12F50). To get to the **tourist office,** 11, pl. de Gaulle (tel. 04 92 90 53 00), exit the train station, turn right onto av. Robert Soleau, and follow signs for the *Maison du Tourisme.* (Open July-Sept. daily 8am-7:30pm; Sept.-June Mon.-Fri. 9am-12:30pm and 2-6pm, Sat. 9am-noon and 2-6pm.) The **Nouvel Hotel,** 1, av. du 24 Août (tel. 04 93 34 44 07; fax 04 93 34 44 08), sits above the bus station (reception open daily 5am-9pm; singles 140-180F, doubles 185-235F, triples 310F). *Vieille* Antibes packs in boulangeries, fruit stands, and restaurants ranging from reasonable to ridiculous. Place Nationale sports great pizzerias including **Restaurant Chez Marguerite,** 31, rue Sade (open daily 7am-11pm). The hamburgers (40-54F) are just as beautiful as the comics at **Comic Strips Café,** 4, rue James Close.

Though joined as one—a city known as Antibes-Juan-les-Pins (pop. 70,000)—Antibes and **Juan-les-Pins** are 3km apart and use separate train stations, post offices, and tourist offices. Juan-les-Pins is the younger, hipper, and more hedonistic of the two. Boutiques remain open until midnight, cafés until 2am, and nightclubs until past sunrise. The streets are packed with seekers of sea, sun, and sex (the order varies), and nightclubs pulse with promises of decadence. The cafés are much cheaper and almost as lively, so even the most miserly traveler can be included in the nightly bash. In winter, Juan-les-Pins becomes a ghost town. *Discothèques* open around 11pm, and their cover charges average 100F (first drink included). Look for advertisements for special events, including the *mega-mousse* party where clubbers dance in a sea of foamy bubbles. Check out the psychedelic **Whiskey à Gogo,** la Pinède, and fluorescent **Voom Voom,** 1, bd. de la Pinède. **Joy's Discotèque,** av. Dautheville, has dance revues as well as a disco. Mingle with chic young locals at **Le Ten's Bar,** 25, av. du Dr. Hochet, off Av. Guy de Maupassant away from the beach (beer 15F), or pay homage to that famous Cuban at **Ché's Café,** 1, bd. de la Pinède, where a beer will liberate your mind for 16F. The dress code at all the clubs is simple: look good.

The **train station** is on av. l'Esterel at av. du Maréchal Joffre. Trains leave every 20 minutes for Nice and Cannes (11F). To get from Antibes's pl. du Général de Gaulle to Juan-les-Pins by foot, follow bd. Wilson (about 1.5km) and turn left on av. Dautheville. Rather than make the post-party trek to Antibes, take a right out of the train station and sack out at **Hotel Trianon,** 14, av. de L'Estérel (tel. 04 93 61 18 11; singles 150-200F, doubles 180-200F, triples 250-280F).

Monaco/Monte-Carlo

Wealth and casual luxury drip from every ornate street lamp and newly-scrubbed sidewalk of sumptuous Monaco. The wealth and mystery of the Monte-Carlo *quartier* revolve around the **Casino,** where Mata Hari shot a Russian spy and Richard Burton wooed Liz Taylor. The interior, ablaze with red velvet curtains, gilded ceilings, and gold and crystal chandeliers, is worth visiting. If you feel lucky, the slot machines open at 10am, while Black Jack, craps, and roulette (25F min.) open at 5pm. These games are also played next door at the **Café de Paris,** where admission to the main room is free (you must be over 21 and can't wear shorts, sneakers, sandals, or jeans), but a peek at the high-stakes *salons privés* costs 50-100F.

After losing your shirt, admire the royal robes at the **Palais Princier,** the sometime home of Prince Rainier and his family. When the flag is down, the prince is away and visitors can tour the lavish palace (open June-Sept. daily 9:30am-6pm; Oct. 10am-5pm; 30F, students 20F). Next door is the stately **Cathédrale de Monaco,** 4, rue Colonel Bellando de Castro, where former Princes of Monaco are buried. Grace Kelly's simple grave is behind the altar (open daily 9am-12:30pm and 1:30-4:30pm; free). Once run by Jacques Cousteau, the **Musée Océanographique,** av. St-Martin, houses thousands of species of marine animals. (Open July-Aug. daily 9am-8pm; April-June and Sept. 9am-7pm; Oct. and March 9:30am-7pm; Nov.-Feb. 10am-6pm. 60F, students 30F.) Naturalists should also visit the new **Jardin Japonais,** av. Princesse Grace (open daily 9am-sunset; free), and the **Jardin Exotique,** bd. du Jardin Exotique. (Open May 15-Sept. 15 daily 9am-7pm; Sept. 16-May 14 9am-6pm or nightfall. 37F, students 18F.) The **Exhibition of H.S.H. the Prince of Monaco's Private Collection of Classic Cars,** les Terraces de Fontvieille, features 105 of the most sexy and stately cars ever made (open daily Dec.-Oct. 10am-6pm; 30F, students 15F).

Practical Information, Accommodations, and Food Monaco is 18km east of Nice and 12km west of the Italian border. The **train station,** av. Prince Pierre (tel. 08 36 35 35 35), connects to Nice (25min., 18F), Antibes (45min., 36F), and Cannes (70min., 44F). When you exit the station, go onto av. du Port, then left onto bd. Albert 1er overlooking the harbor. On the right sits the *quartier* of **Monaco-Ville** with its *vieille ville* and the palace; to the left rises the fabled *quartier* of **Monte-Carlo.** The **tourist office,** 2a, bd. des Moulins (tel. 92 16 61 16; fax 92 16 60 00), near the casino, provides a map and makes room reservations (open Mon.-Sat. 9am-7pm, Sun. 10am-noon). Summertime annexes are set up at the train station and port.

To afford a room in Monaco, you'll need to seduce royalty or win big. Try the **Centre de Jeunesse Princesse Stéphanie,** 24, av. Prince Pierre (tel. 93 50 83 20; fax 93 25 29 82), 100m up the hill from the train station. In summer, arrive before 9am if you want a bed; reservations are accepted during the off season only. (Reception open daily 7am-1am; off-season 7am-midnight. Age limit 26, with student ID 31. 70F, breakfast and sheets included.) Picnickers should stop by the fruit and flower **market** on pl. d'Armes, at the end of av. Prince Pierre (open daily 6am-1pm). The **Carrefour supermarket** is in Fontvieille's *centre commercial* (shopping plaza). From the train station, turn right onto rue de la Colle; at pl. du Canton cross the street and go down one level (open Mon.-Sat. 8:30am-10pm).

CORSICA (CORSE)

Appropriately called *Kallysté,* "the most beautiful," by the Greeks, Corsica combines the mountainous splendor of the Alps with the beaches and crystal-blue Mediterranean waters of the Riviera. Although ferries and other tourist services multiply between June 15 and the end of September, prices soar by 50%. Half the island's one million annual tourists visit then, packing the beaches and hotels along the coast.

Getting There and Getting Around The **Société National Maritime Corse Méditerranée (SNCM)** sends ferries from Marseille and Nice to Bastia, Calvi, Ajaccio, and Propriano on Corsica. About two boats per day travel between Corsica and the mainland in the off season, a few more during summer; the trip usually takes six to 12 hours. Schedules and prices vary, so call ahead. SNCM has offices in Ajaccio, quai L'herminier (tel. 04 95 29 66 88; fax 04 95 29 66 77); Bastia, Nouveau Port (tel. 04 95 54 66 88; fax 04 95 54 66 69); and Calvi, quai Landry (tel. 04 95 65 01 38; fax 04 95 65 09 75). On the mainland, SNCM has offices in Nice, quai du Commerce (tel. 04 93 13 66 99); Marseille, 61, bd. des Dames (tel. 04 91 56 30 10); and Paris, 12, rue Godot-de-Mauroy (tel. 01 49 24 24 24). **Corsica Ferries** cross from the Italian ports of Livorno, Genoa, and La Spezia to Bastia (140-200F). The central reservation office is at 5, bd. Chanoine-Leschi (tel. 04 95 32 95 95), in Bastia.

Air France and **Air Inter** fly to Bastia, Ajaccio, and Calvi from Paris (round-trip 1390F, discounts up to 300F), Nice (653-952F), Marseille (705-1051F), and Lyon (1325-2337F). Phone Air France's offices in Marseille (tel. 04 91 39 36 36) or Paris (tel. 01 45 46 90 00) for more information about flights. Air Inter's offices are at the airports in Ajaccio (tel. 04 95 29 45 45) and Bastia (tel. 04 95 31 79 79).

Trains in Corsica are slow and limited; they don't serve all the major towns (no rail south of Ajaccio) and don't accept any railpasses. **Buses** connect major towns but are neither cheaper nor more frequent. Call **Eurocorse Voyages** (tel. 04 95 21 06 30) for more info. **Car rental** may be convenient for groups of three or four; the least expensive models cost 350-530 per day, plus 2-4F per kilometer. Weekly rentals (1450-1806F) usually include unlimited free mileage. **Hiking** is the best way to explore the island's mountainous interior. The longest marked route, the **GR20,** is a difficult 160km, 13- to 15-day trail going from Calenzana (southeast of Calvi) to Conca (northeast of Porto-Vecchio). Two other popular routes are the **Mare e Monti,** a seven-day trail from Calenzana to Cargèse, and the easier **Da Mare a Mare,** which crosses the southern part of the island between Porto-Vecchio and Propriano (4-6 days). The **Parc Naturel Regional de la Corse,** 2 rue Major Lambrashini, Ajaccio (tel. 04 95 51 79 10), publishes maps and has info on staying at *gîtes d'étapes* near the trails.

Ajaccio and Calvi The urban bustle of **Ajaccio** balances the Mediterranean calm of the city's beachside resort. The **tourist office,** pl. Maréchal Foch (tel. 04 95 51 53 03; fax 04 95 51 53 01), in the Hôtel de Ville, hands out free maps. (Open in summer daily 8:30am-8:30pm; off season Mon.-Fri. 8:30am-6pm, Sat. 8:30am-1pm.) **Hôtel Napoléon,** 4, rue Lorenzo Vero (tel. 04 95 51 54 00), is a more expensive three-star hotel, but rooms on the elevator-inaccessible second floor run 200-250F. **Hôtel Kallysté,** 51, cours Napoléon (tel. 04 95 51 34 45; fax 04 95 21 79 00), has clean rooms with A/C, TV, and bath (singles 200-300F, doubles 235-340F, triples 300-425F).

Hôtel le Dauphin, 11, bd. Sampiero (tel. 04 95 21 12 94; fax 04 95 21 88 69), has clean rooms with TV, shower, and toilet (singles from 202F, doubles 238F), but women may feel uncomfortable at the bars along the street. Bag a baguette at the **Monoprix supermarket,** 31, cours Napoléon (open Mon.-Sat. 8:30am-7:15pm).

With its well-preserved Genoan citadel, stretches of white-sand beaches, and 2400 hours of sunshine a year, **Calvi** is a beautiful but expensive place to soak up the Mediterranean *soleil.* If you tire of the 6km stretch of expensive **public beach,** head to the citadel's rocks to bask in seclusion. Check out the view of the pink and cream Eglise Sainte Marie-Majeure from the **Chapelle de Notre Dame de la Serra** (open daily 9am-noon and 2-7pm; 45F). The **tourist office,** Port de Plaisance (tel. 04 95 65 16 67), distributes *A la découverte de Calvi* and a map. (Open July-Aug. daily 7am-7pm; Sept.-June Mon.-Fri. 7am-noon and 2-6pm.) July and August bring the tourists, and rooms may become prohibitively expensive. The friendly, refreshingly quiet **Relais International de la Jeunesse U Carabellu** (tel. 04 95 65 14 16), rte de Pietra-Maggiore (75F, breakfast included; open May-Sept.), and the clean and airy **BVJ Corsotel,** av. de la République (tel. 04 95 65 14 15; 120F, breakfast included; open late March- Oct.), are good bets. **Hôtel Sole Mare,** rte de St-François (tel. 04 95 65 09 50), 300m from the *centre ville* on a residential street, has quiet, sunny rooms with showers, toilets, and great views (singles 160-180F, doubles 200-350F; open April-Oct.). **Les Tamaris,** rte d'Ajaccio (tel. 04 95 65 00 26), has peaceful, shady camping by a beach (25F per person, 10F per tent). *Boulangeries* and *charcuteries* line rue Clemenceau.

Bastia and Cap Corse Littered with square, graceless buildings, **Bastia** has little in the way of Mediterranean beauty or charm, but offers supplies and a base for excursions to more scenic Cap Corse. Before setting out, meander through pl. de l'Hôtel de Ville and gaze at the immense proportions and gilded domes of the 18th-century **Eglise St-Jean-Baptiste.** The **tourist office,** pl. St-Nicolas (tel. 04 95 55 96 96; fax 04 95 55 96 00), has info on hotels, camping, and transportation in Bastia and Cap Corse (open Mon.-Sat. 8am-6pm, Sun. 8am-noon and 2-6pm). The **Hôtel Central,** 3, rue Miot (tel. 04 95 31 71 12), has many beautifully renovated rooms (singles 180-250F, doubles 200-300F). Camp at **Les Orangiers,** Quartier Licciola-Miomo (tel. 04 95 33 68 02; 22F per person, 12F per tent).

Cap Corse is a 48km peninsula north of Bastia, strung with fishing villages and quiet inlets. From Calvi, **Autocars Mariani** (tel. 04 95 65 05 32) runs tours of the Cap, leaving at 7am and returning at 7:30pm on Fridays (145F; June-Sept.). On Cap Corse, **Macinaggio** is one of the few port towns where you can find services and supplies. Nearby, serene **Rogliano** features the ruins of a Genoan castle and a large 16th-century church. The port of **Centuri,** on the other side of the peninsula 57km from Bastia, is the prototypical picturesque fishing village.

THE ALPS

After countless museum corridors, the Alps come as a refreshing relief. Snow-capped crests and tumbling waterfalls exhilarate the weary soul, and crystal-clear air makes Paris smog seem a distant memory. **Skiing** in the Alps has always been expensive; make arrangements months in advance. The least crowded and cheapest months to go are January, March, and April. Most resorts close in October and November. **FUAJ,** the French Youth Hostel Federation, offers week-long winter skiing and summer sports packages. For more info, contact local FUAJ offices, youth hostels, or the central office at 27, rue Pajol, 75018 Paris (tel. 05 46 07 00 01).

The beauty of the Alps does little good to the traveler who wants to go anywhere quickly or directly. While TGV **train** service will whisk you from Paris to Aix-les-Bains or Annecy at the gateway to the serious mountains, from there it's either slow trains, special mountain trains, or torturously slow **buses**. **Hiking** ranges from simple strolls through mountain meadows to some of the most difficult climbing in the world, including Europe's highest mountain, Mont-Blanc. Many towns maintain chalet dorms, as well as hostels and campgrounds; in less accessible spots, the **Club Alpin Français** runs refuges. Get a list from one of their offices: 136, av. Michel-Croz, Chamonix (tel. 04 50 53 16 03); or 32, av. Félix Vialet, Grenoble (tel. 04 76 87 03 73). *Always* check with local hiking bureaus before setting out on *any* hike; even in summer, you can encounter snowstorms and avalanches.

Grenoble

Stendahl, Grenoble's most famous bookworm, grumbled about his hometown that "at the end of every street, there is a mountain." Few are so rancorous about this lively university city and its majestic surrounding. Take the bubble-shaped cable car (*Téléphérique Grenoble Bastille;* tel. 04 76 44 33 65; round-trip 33F, students 26F) up to the **Bastille** for a view of Grenoble and the landscape that inspired Shelley to ethereal free verse. Several mountain **hikes** begin here. In town are several museums, including the regional **Musée Dauphinois,** 30, rue Maurice Gignoux (open May-Oct. Wed.-Mon. 10am-7pm; Nov.-April 10am-6pm; 15F, students 10F), the art-filled **Musée de Grenoble,** 5, pl. de Lavalette (open Thurs.-Mon. 11am-7pm, Wed. 11am-10pm; 25F, students 15F), and the disturbing **Musée de la Résistance et de la Déportation,** 14, rue Hébert (open Wed.-Mon. 9am-noon and 2-6pm; 20F, students 10F).

The **tourist office,** 14, rue de la République (tel. 04 76 42 41 41), has good maps, accommodations information, and the *Grenoble Magazine,* a guide to events in town (open Mon.-Sat. 9am-12:30pm and 1:30-6pm, Sun. 10am-noon). The *Guide DAHU,* written by hip Grenoble students, is useful for longer stays (15F). To reach the **Auberge de Jeunesse (HI),** 18, av. du Grésivaudan (tel. 04 76 09 33 52; fax 04 76 09 38 99), 4km out of town, take bus 8 ("Pont Rouge") to "La Quinzaine"; the hostel is one block behind the Casino supermarket. (Reception open daily Mon.-Sat. 7:30am-11pm, Sun. 7:30-10am and 5:30-11pm. 68F.) **Le Foyer de l'Etudiante,** 4, rue Ste-Ursule (tel. 04 76 42 00 84, fax 04 76 44 36 85), is a great place to meet friendly students. (Reception open 24hr. 2-night min. stay. Singles 90F; doubles 70F per person. Accepts men and women mid-June to mid-Sept.; off-season only women.) In the center of town, the friendly **Hôtel de la Poste,** 25, rue de la Poste (tel. 04 76 46 67 25), has purple petunias and spacious rooms. (Reception open 24hr. Singles 90-150F; doubles 160-200F; triples 190F; quads 200F.) Cafés and restaurants cluster around **pl. Notre-Dame** and **pl. St-André,** both in the heart of the *vieille ville.* **Le Valgo,** 2, rue St -Hughes, at pl. Notre-Dame, has excellent food (open Tues.-Wed. lunch, Thurs.-Sat. lunch and dinner). The **Prisunic supermarket** sits across from the tourist office.

Chamonix

In other alpine villages, people dip in cold waters that reflect harmless backdrops of distant peaks, but in Chamonix, the Arne river looks like fluid ice, and daggers of mammoth glaciers menace the town. Lying within skiing distance of two countries, Chamonix buzzes with climbers and skiers swapping tall tales of the town's slopes, among the world's toughest. **Mont Blanc,** Europe's highest peak (4807m), reigns just to the east, and the first modern Winter Olympics were held here in 1924.

Reserve a spot on the *téléphérique* in high season (tel. 008 36 68 00 67) or arrive *early.* The simplest trip takes you to **Plan de l'Aiguille** (62F, round-trip 74F), but the **Aiguille du Midi** is much more spectacular (180F; additional 13F to go to the summit). **Balme,** on the southern tip of the valley, is the best slope for intermediates (tel. 04 50 54 00 58; 1-day lift pass 120F). Insane experts ski **Vallée Blanche** (tel. 04 50 53 40 00), a 20km, unmarked, unpatrolled (*téléphérique* 144F). Bring warm clothes, lunch, and your camera, and remember that mountain weather can change rapidly. Special trains run from a small station next to the main train station to the huge **Mer de Glace** glacier (May-Sept. daily 8am-6pm; 50F, round-trip 65F), but you might prefer the two-hour hike. Serious hikers should buy the IGN topographic map, available at the Office de Haute Montagne (see below) and bookstores. Mont Blanc is a two- to three-day expedition for the experienced. Don't do it alone, and get info about storm fronts and avalanches before hiking at high altitudes.

The **tourist office,** pl. du Triangle de l'Amitié (tel. 04 50 53 00 24; fax 04 50 53 58 90), lists hotels, dormitories, and campgrounds. (Open July-Aug. and winter vacation daily 8:30am-7:30pm; off-season 8:30am-12:30pm and 2-7pm.) Next to the church on pl. de l'Eglise, the **Maison de la Montagne** houses the **Compagnie des Guides** (tel. 04 50 53 00 88) and a ski school. Upstairs, the **Office de Haute Montagne** (tel. 04 50 53 22 08) has vital information on trails and mountain refuges.

Mountain chalets with dorm accommodations combine affordability with splendid settings, but many close off season (Oct.-Nov. and May). All hotels and many dorms require reservations (preferably 6 weeks ahead) for school vacations (Dec. and Feb.). For breathtaking views and hordes of schoolchildren, try the **Auberge de Jeunesse (HI)** in Les Pélerins (tel. 04 50 53 14 52; fax 04 50 55 92 34). Take the bus ("Les Houches") from pl. de l'Eglise to "Pélerins Ecole" (7F), and follow signs uphill. By train, get off at "Les Pélerins" and follow the signs. (Reception open daily 8am-noon, 5-8pm, and 9-10pm. 74F; singles 125F; doubles 89-94F per person. Sheets 19F. Breakfast included. Offers winter ski packages.) From the train station, go under the bridge, take a right across the tracks, a left on chemin des Cristalliers, and a right on rte de la Frasse (15min.) at #152 to reach the **Gîte d'Etape La Tapia** (tel. 04 50 53 18 19; fax 04 50 53 67 01), which serves dinners for 75F (reception open daily 10am-noon and 5:30-9pm; dorms 70F). One block away is **Le Chamoniard Volant,** 45, rte de la Frasse (tel. 04 50 53 14 09; fax 04 50 53 23 25; dorms 65F; 5F *Let's Go* discount). The **Gîte le Vagabond,** 365, av. Ravanel-le-Rouge (tel. 04 50 53 15 43; fax 04 50 53 68 21), is a new *gîte* near the center of town (dorms 65F; 100F key deposit).

Straight out of Dublin, **The Jekyll,** 71, rte des Pélerins, provides Guinness (29F) and Irish food favorites (29-49F; open daily 4pm-2am). Get crazy the Aussie way at **Wild Wallabies,** rue de la Tour with excellent BBQ plates (58F; open daily 11am-2am). Frugal folks retreat to **Super U,** 117, rue Joseph Vallot. (Open Mon.-Fri. 8:15am-12:30pm and 2:30-7:30pm, Sat. 8:15am-7:30pm, Sun. 8:30am-12:15pm.)

Annecy

With narrow cobblestone streets, overstuffed flower boxes, and the purest mountain lake in Europe, Annecy is a relentlessly photogenic cataclysm, recalling those high school homecoming queens that everyone resented but fell in love with anyway. Hordes of vacationers enjoy the lakeside beaches and stroll along the flower-dotted canals around the **Palais d'Isle,** a 12th-century fortress rising out of a tiny island. Climb up to the **château,** which doubles as a museum, for a splendid view of the old town's waterways. (Open July-Aug. daily 10am-6pm; Sept.-June Wed.-Mon. 10am-noon and 2-6pm. 30F, students 10F.) Penniless sun-seekers can use the free beach, the **plage des Marquisats.** The **Fête du Lac** enlivens the first Saturday in August with fireworks and water shows (35-270F). Take a train to Lovagny (1-2 per day, 10min., 10F) and then walk 800m to the **Gorges du Fier,** a canyon carved by glaciers. (Open June 15-Sept. 15 daily 9am-6:15pm; March 15-June 14 and Sept. 16-Oct. 15 9am-noon and 2-5:15pm. 23F for the 40min. walk. Call 04 50 46 23 07 for info.)

The **tourist office,** 1, rue Jean Jaurès (tel. 04 50 45 00 33 or 04 50 45 56 66), at pl. de la Libération, dispenses brochures on Annecy and nearby towns. (Open July-Aug. daily 9am-6:30pm; Sept.-June Mon.-Sat. 9am-noon and 1:45-6:30pm, Sun. 3-6pm.) Room reservations are recommended. The **Auberge de Jeunesse "La Grande Jeanne" (HI),** rte de Semnoz (tel. 04 50 45 33 19; fax 04 50 52 77 52), is a super-chalet tucked away in the woods. In summer, take bus 91 ("Semnoz"; last bus 6pm, 7F). From the tourist office, walk down quai Chappuis, turn right on av. de Trésum, and follow D41; after an uphill hike (15min.) the hostel will be on your right (reception open daily 7am-11pm; 69F; sheets 16F). **Hôtel Savoyard,** 41, av. de Cran (tel. 04 50 57 08 08), behind the train station, is hospitable and rustic (singles and doubles 100-180F; breakfast 20F). **Hôtel Plaisance,** 17, rue de Narvik (tel. 04 50 57 30 42), has large rooms (singles 120F, doubles 140-180F, triples 235F, quads 285F). Close to the

HI youth hostel and *busy* is the **camping area,** 8, rte de Semnoz (tel. 04 50 45 48 30; fax 04 50 45 55 56; 260F per tent; open Dec. 15-Oct. 15). Dozens of campgrounds border the lake in **Albigny,** reachable by Voyages Crolard buses or by following av. d'Albigny from the tourist office (1.5km).

Picnics are the only budget options; a **Prisunic supermarket** fills the pl. de Notre-Dame (open Mon.-Sat. 8:30am-7:30pm), and **open-air markets** are held on pl. Ste-Claire (Tues., Fri., and Sun. mornings) and bd. Taine (Sat. mornings). **Tartes à la Folie,** 7, rue Vaugelas, redefines the art of tarts (10-15F).

CENTRAL FRANCE

Lyon

France's second-largest city shines in its own right. With spectacular industrial and culinary *savoir faire,* Lyon has firmly established itself as an economic and cultural alternative to the capital. Quaint sidewalk cafés coexist with giant skyscrapers; modern transport systems pass quiet, flowering parks; and prestigious concert halls and flashy discos share the musical spotlight with summer festivals and street performers. Lyon is a must-see (and must-taste) on any French itinerary.

ORIENTATION AND PRACTICAL INFORMATION

The Saône and the Rhône rivers cradle the city in a huge "Y." East of the Rhône resides the **Part-Dieu** train station, its commercial complex, and most of the city's population. Between the two rivers, the *centre ville* is home to the **Perrache** train station, **pl. Bellecour,** the main tourist office, and the old Terraux neighborhood. Farther west, the **Fourvière hill** and its basilica overlook the city as **Vieux Lyon** unfolds below to the banks of the Saône. Lyon is divided into nine *arrondissements;* the first, second, and fourth lie between the rivers, the third includes Part-Dieu, the fifth encompasses *Vieux Lyon* and Fourvière, and the sixth is to the north.

Tourist Office: pl. Bellecour, 2*ème* (tel. 04 72 77 69 69; fax 04 78 42 04 32). M: Bellecour. Smorgasbord of info. Ask about the "key to the city" (90F) which allows admission to 7 museums. Open mid-June to mid-Sept. Mon.-Fri. 9am-7pm, Sat. 9am-6pm; mid-Sept. to mid-June Mon.-Fri. 9am-6pm, Sat. 9am-5pm. If you're arriving at the **Perrache station,** pick up a map at the annex in the Centre d'Echanges. Open Mon.-Fri. 9am-1pm and 2-6pm, Sat. 9am-5pm.

Budget Travel: Wasteels (tel. 04 78 37 80 17), in the Perrache's Galerie Marchande. BIJ tickets. Long lines. Open Mon.-Fri. 9am-6:30pm, Sat. 9am-5pm.

Currency Exchange: AOC, in the tourist offices on pl. Bellecour and Perrache. **Thomas Cook** (tel. 04 72 33 48 55), in the Part-Dieu train station. Open 24hr.

American Express: 6, rue Childebert, 2*ème* (tel. 04 72 77 74 50). Open May-Sept. Mon.-Fri. 9am-noon and 2-6:15pm, Sat. 9am-noon; Oct.-April closed Sat. Currency exchange closes at 5:30pm.

Flights: Aéroport Lyon-Satolas (tel. 04 72 22 72 21), 25km east of Lyon. **Buses** leave from Perrache via Part-Dieu until 9pm (every 20min., 46F).

Trains: TGV trains to Paris pass through both the Part-Dieu and Perrache stations. Check schedule posters about other destinations. **Perrache,** between the Saône and Rhône rivers, is more central. SNCF info and reservation desk open Mon.-Sat. 8am-7:30pm. **Part-Dieu** is in the business district on the east bank of the Rhône. SNCF info desk open Mon.-Fri. 9am-7pm, Sat. 9am-6:30pm. To Paris (most are TGV, 2-5hr., 262F), Dijon (2hr., 130F), Grenoble (1¼hr., 92F), Strasbourg (6hr., 246F), Geneva (2hr., 112F), Marseille (3hr., 197F), and Nice (6hr., 288F).

Buses: in the Perrache train station. Open July-Aug. Mon.-Sat. 7:30am-6:30pm; Sept.-June Mon.-Sat. 6:30am-5pm. To Annecy and Grenoble. **Philbert** (tel. 04 78 98 56 00) handles many domestic routes. **Eurolines** (tel. 04 72 41 09 09) runs throughout Europe. **Iberbus** (tel. 04 72 41 72 27) goes to Spain.

Public Transportation: TCL (tel. 04 78 71 80 80). Info offices at both train stations and major metro stops. The **Metro (M)** operates 5am-midnight. Tickets, good for 1hr. in 1 direction, bus and trolley connections included, are 8F each (*carnet* of 10 tickets 68F, students 55F). *Ticket Liberté* (20F) offers 1 day of unlimited travel—buy at tourist and TCL offices, not in stations. **Trolleys** *(funiculaires)* operate until 10pm and run from pl. St-Jean to St-Just and the top of Fourvière. **Buses** run 5am-9pm (a few until midnight), later on theater performance nights.

Taxis: Taxi Radio de Lyon (tel. 04 72 10 86 86). 24hr. service. 200F to the airport.

Hitchhiking: Some report that the *autoroute* ramps to Paris are hard places to find rides; it's reputedly easier to take bus 2, 5, 19, 21, 22, or 31 and stand past pont Monton at the intersection with N6. Those heading to Grenoble take bus 39 to the rotary at bd. Mermoz Pinel. This is a big city—big-city weirdos abound.

English Bookstore: Eton, 1, rue du Plat, 2*ème* (tel. 04 78 92 92 36), 1 street west of pl. Bellecour. Open Mon. 2-7pm, Tues.-Sat. 10am-12:30pm and 1:30-7pm.

Laundromat: Lavadou, 19, rue Ste-Hélène. Open 7:30am-8:30pm.

Crisis Lines: CISL (tel. 04 78 01 23 45), an international center for visitors to Lyon. **SOS Racisme** (tel. 04 78 39 24 44). Open Mon.-Fri. 6:30-8:30pm. **AIDS Lyon Rhône-Alps,** 21, pl. Tolozan, 3*ème* (tel. 04 78 28 61 32).

Medical Assistance: Hôpital Edouard Herriot, 5, pl. Arsonval (tel. 04 72 11 73 00). M: Grange Blanche. Well-equipped for serious emergencies, but far from the city center. For non-emergencies, go to **Hôpital Hôtel-Dieu,** 1, pl. de l'Hôpital, 2*ème* (tel. 04 72 41 30 00), near quai du Rhône.

Emergencies: tel. 17. **Medical emergency:** tel. 15.

Police: 47, rue de la Charité (tel. 04 78 42 26 56).

Post Office: pl. Antonin Poncet (tel. 04 72 40 65 22), next to pl. Bellecour. Open Mon.-Fri. 8am-7pm, Sat. 8am-noon. **Postal Code:** 69000-69009; main post office and *centre ville* is 69002. The last digit indicates *arrondissement.*

ACCOMMODATIONS AND CAMPING

As a financial center, Lyon has few empty beds during the work week but openings on the weekends. "Low season" is actually considered to be July and August. If the hotels near Perrache are full, rooms should be available near pl. des Terreaux.

Auberge de Jeunesse (HI), 51, rue Roger Salengro, Vénissieux (tel. 04 78 76 39 23). Take bus 35 ("St-Priest") from pl. Bellecour to "George Lévy" (last bus 9pm); alternatively, take either bus 48 express or 36 ("Minguettes") from Part-Dieu or bus 32 ("Etats-Unis-Vivani") from Perrache to "Etats-Unis-Vivani," then continue walking on bd. des Etats-Unis and follow the footpath to the right after the Peugeot dealership. Friendly modern hostel with kitchen, bar, and TV. Reception open daily 7:30-11am and 5pm-midnight. 68F. Sheets 17F. Laundry 30F.

Centre International de Séjour, 46, rue du Commandant Pegoud, 8*ème* (tel. 04 78 01 23 45; fax 04 78 77 96 95), near the youth hostel. From Perrache, take bus 53 ("St-Priest") to "Etats-Unis-Beauvisage" (last bus 11:30pm). From Part-Dieu, take bus 36 ("Minquettes"; last bus 11:15pm). Small, modern rooms with shower. Reception open 24hr. Singles 133F. Doubles 106F. Triples 90F. Reserve ahead.

Résidence Benjamin Delessert, 145, av. Jean Jaurès, 7*ème* (tel. 04 78 61 41 41; fax 04 78 61 40 24). From Perrache, take any bus going to "J. Macé," walk under the train tracks, and look left after 2½ blocks. From Part-Dieu, take the metro to "Macé." Bright, clean dorms, all with phones. TV room and laundry service. Reception open 24hr. 70-75F; mid-Sept. to mid-June 90-95F. Reserve ahead.

Hôtel Vaubecour, 28, rue Vaubecour, 2*ème* (tel. 04 78 37 44 91; fax 04 78 42 90 17). M: Ampère-Victor Hugo. Spacious, elegant rooms. Singles 99-110F, with shower 140F. Doubles 130F, with shower 160F. Breakfast 25F.

Camping: Dardilly (tel. 04 78 35 64 55). From the Hôtel de Ville, take bus 19 ("Ecully-Dardilly") to "Parc d'Affaires." Hot showers, swimming pool, grocery store, bar, and restaurant. Reception open mid-June to mid-Sept. 8am-noon and 4-9pm; mid-Sept. to mid-June 8am-11pm. 53F per tent and car. Open year-round.

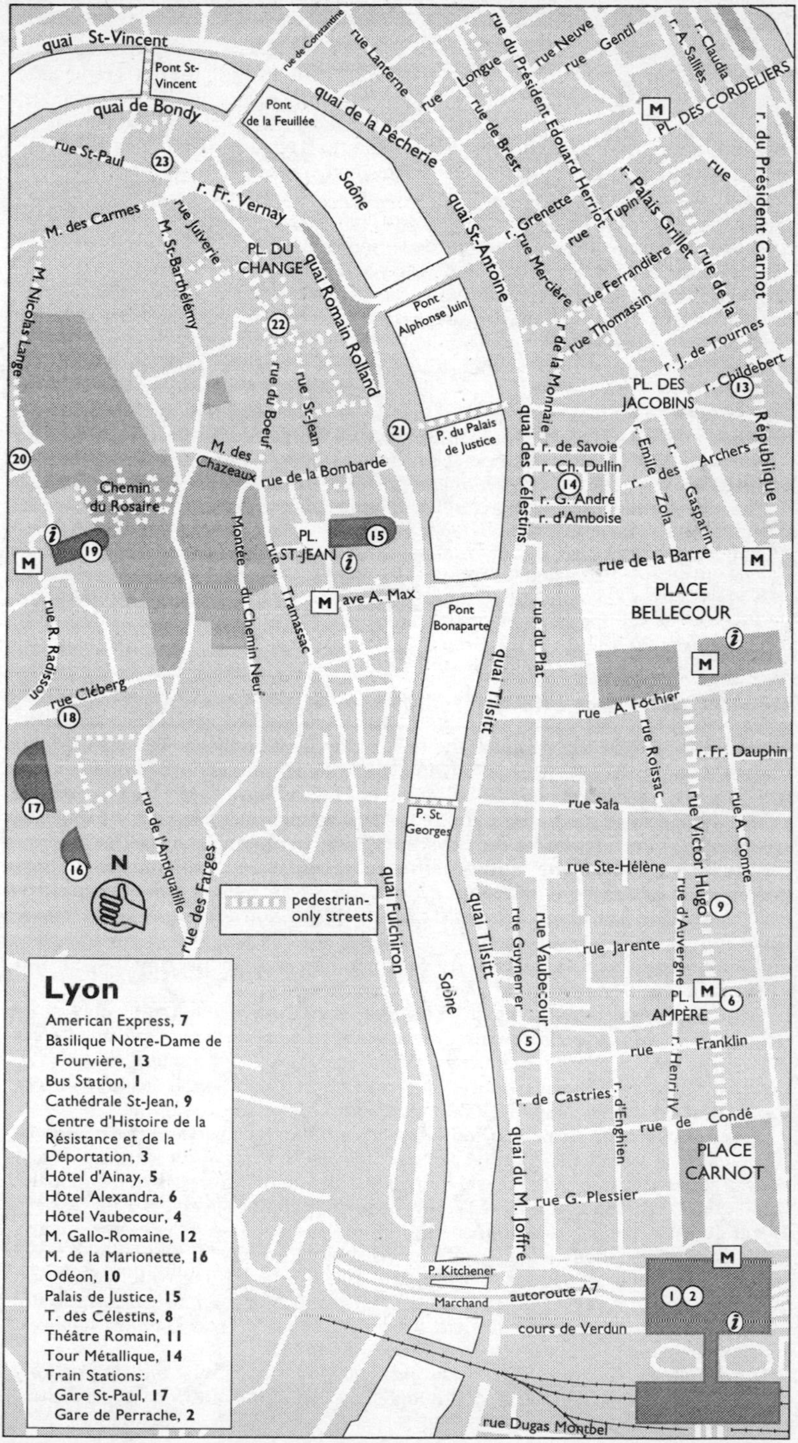

Lyon
American Express, 7
Basilique Notre-Dame de Fourvière, 13
Bus Station, 1
Cathédrale St-Jean, 9
Centre d'Histoire de la Résistance et de la Déportation, 3
Hôtel d'Ainay, 5
Hôtel Alexandra, 6
Hôtel Vaubecour, 4
M. Gallo-Romaine, 12
M. de la Marionette, 16
Odéon, 10
Palais de Justice, 15
T. des Célestins, 8
Théâtre Romain, 11
Tour Métallique, 14
Train Stations:
Gare St-Paul, 17
Gare de Perrache, 2
pedestrian-only streets
N
quai St-Vincent
Pont St-Vincent
quai de Bondy
rue St-Paul
rue de Constantine
Pont de la Feuillée
quai de la Pêcherie
Saône
rue Lanterne
rue Longue
rue de Brest
rue du Président Edouard Herriot
rue Neuve
rue Gentil
r. A. Salliès
r. Claudia
PL. DES CORDELIERS
r. du Président Carnot
r. Fr. Vernay
M. des Carmes
rue Juiverie
M. St-Barthélémy
PL. DU CHANGE
quai Romain Rolland
quai St-Antoine
r. Grenette
rue Tupin
r. Palais Grillet
rue de la République
rue Mercière
rue Ferrandière
rue Thomassin
Pont Alphonse Juin
M. Nicolas Lange
rue du Boeuf
rue St-Jean
r. de la Monnaie
r. J. de Tournes
PL. DES JACOBINS
r. Childebert
P. du Palais de Justice
quai des Célestins
r. de Savoie
r. Ch. Dullin
r. G. André
r. d'Amboise
r. Emile Zola
r. des Archers
r. Gasparin
M. des Chazeaux
rue de la Bombarde
Chemin du Rosaire
PL. ST-JEAN
Montée du Chemin Neuf
rue Tramassac
rue de la Barre
ave A. Max
Pont Bonaparte
PLACE BELLECOUR
rue R. Radisson
rue du Plat
quai Tilsitt
rue Cléberg
rue A. Fochier
rue Roissac
r. Fr. Dauphin
rue Sala
rue de l'Antiquaille
P. St. Georges
rue Ste-Hélène
rue Victor Hugo
rue A. Comte
rue des Farges
quai Fulchiron
rue Guynemer
rue Vaubecour
rue d'Auvergne
rue Jarente
PL. AMPÈRE
rue Franklin
r. Henri IV
r. de Castries
r. d'Enghien
rue de Condé
PLACE CARNOT
quai du M. Joffre
rue G. Plessier
P. Kitchener
Marchand
autoroute A7
cours de Verdun
rue Dugas Montbel

FOOD

The galaxy of *Michelin* stars adorning Lyon's restaurants confirm the city's reputation as the culinary capital of Western civilization. There are plenty of options for budget travelers. Cozy *bouchons,* descendants of inns, serve *andouillettes* (sausages made of cow intestines—yum) and other local treats in the Terreaux district and along rue Mercière in the second *arrondissement.* Finish off your dinner with *Torte Tatin,* an upside-down apple pie *à la mode,* or *cocons,* chocolates wrapped in marzipan. Chocolate lovers swoon at **Bernachon,** 42, cours Franklin Roosevelt, 6*ème*. Ethnic restaurants congregate on the streets off **rue de la République** (2*ème*).

The market at **Les Halles,** 102, cours Lafayette, 3*ème*, counts Paul Bocuse, the culinary king, as well as mere mortals among its patrons (open Tues.-Sat. 7:30am-noon and 3-7pm, Sun. 7:30am-noon). **Open markets** are held at quai St-Antoine and on bd. de la Croix Rousse (open Tues.-Sun. 7:30am-12:30pm). The **Carrefour Supermarché,** one of the largest in France, looms across the highway from the hostel.

Le Sud, 11, pl. Antonin Porcet, 2*ème* (tel. 04 72 77 80 00), off pl. Bellecour. Highly praised. Provençal and Italian cuisine with Mediterranean ambiance. 78F *plat du jour* and 120F *menu.* Open noon-2pm and 7-11:30pm. Reserve 2 days in advance.

Chez Mounier, 3, rue des Marrioniers, 2*ème*. Just around the corner from Le Sud. Generous portions of traditional specialties on a four-course *menu* starting at 59F. Open daily noon-2pm and 7-10:30pm.

Chabert et Fils, 11 rue des Marroniers, 2*ème*. Familiar favorites on the 97F *menu.* Open daily noon-2pm and 7-11pm.

La Mère Vittet, 26, cours de Verdun, 3*ème*, near Perrache. Authentic *lyonnais* cuisine. *Menus* starting at 100F. Open Thurs.-Sat. 24hr., Sun.-Wed. 7am-2am.

Chez Carlo, 22, rue du Palais Grillet, 2*ème*. Locals call it the best pasta and pizza (46F) in Lyon. Open Tues.-Sat. noon-2pm and 7-11pm, Sun. noon-2pm.

SIGHTS AND ENTERTAINMENT

A good place to start your tour of the city is atop the **Fourvière Hill,** admiring the landscape and the last vestiges of Roman Lyon. It's quite a walk up from **Vieux Lyon;** most prefer to take the *funiculaire* from the head of av. Max, off pl. St-Jean, in the old town. When you've reached the top of the hill, admire the view on the **Esplanade Fourvière,** where a model of the cityscape points out local landmarks. Behind the Esplanade is the **Basilique Notre-Dame de la Fourvière.** Multicolored mosaics, gilded pillars, and elaborate carvings adorn every square inch of the interior. If you walk down the hill making a left as you exit the church, you'll see signs for the **Musée Gallo-Romain,** 17, rue Cléberg, 5*ème*, which displays mosaics, helmets, swords, jewelry, and tablet inscribed with a speech by Emperor Claudius (open Wed.-Sun. 9:30am-noon and 2-6pm; 20F, students 10F).

Nestled up against the Saône at the bottom of the Fourvière hill, the cobblestone streets of *Vieux Lyon* are lined with lively cafés and magnificent medieval and Renaissance townhouses. The 12th-century **Cathédrale St-Jean,** at the south end of *Vieux Lyon,* towers over pl. St-Jean. Henri IV met and married Marie de Médici here in 1600 (open Mon.-Fri. 8am-noon and 2-7:30pm, Sat.-Sun. 2-5pm; free).

Monumental squares, statues, and fountains are the trademarks of the **presqu'île,** the lively area between the Rhône and the Saône. The heart of the area is **pl. Bellecour,** a barren expanse of red gravel fringed by shops and flower stalls and dominated by an equestrian statue of Louis XIV. Across the square, the spectacular Renaissance **Hôtel de Ville** stands guard opposite the **Musée des Beaux-Arts,** which includes a small but distinguished collection of French painting, works by Spanish and Dutch masters, an Italian Renaissance wing, and a sculpture garden (open Wed.-Sun. 10:30am-6pm; 20F, students 10F). A few blocks north of the museum on rue Burdeau, 1*er*, lie the ruins of the Roman **Amphithéâtre des Trois Gaulles,** where an unfortunate band of Christians met their demise in 177.

Historically Lyon dominated the European silk industry, and by the 18th century, 28,000 looms operated in the city. Although the silk industry is now based elsewhere, an extraordinary collection of silk and embroidery remains at the **Musée Historique des Tissus,** 34, rue de la Charité (open Tues.-Sun. 10am-5:30pm; 26F, students 13F, Wed. free). Weave through the **Musée Lyonnais des Arts Décoratifs,** down the street at 30, rue de la Charité, 2ème, which displays 17th and 18th century furniture, porcelain, silver, and tapestries (open Tues.-Sun. 10am-5:30pm; free with Musée des Tissus ticket). **La Maison des Canuts,** 10-12, rue d'Ivry, 4ème, demonstrates the actual weaving techniques of the *canuts lyonnais* (open Mon.-Fri. 8:30am-noon and 2-6:30pm, Sat. 9am-noon and 2-6pm; 15F).

The **Centre d'Histoire de la Résistance et de la Déportation,** 14, av. Bertholet, 7ème, has assembled documents and photos of the Lyon-based resistance to the Nazis (open Wed.-Sun. 9am-5:30pm; 20F, students 10F). The **Musée d'Art Contemporain,** in the futuristic *Cité Internationale de Lyon* on quai Charles de Gaulle, 6ème (M: Masséna), has an extensive collection of modern art. The *Cité* is a sight itself—the super-modern complex houses offices, shops, theaters, and the Interpol world headquarters (don't jaywalk to get there). Nearby is the massive **Parc de la Tête d'Or,** a 259-acre park with a zoo, botanical garden, and beautiful rose garden (park open April-Sept. daily 6am-11pm; Oct.-March 6am-9pm).

Lyon's major theater is the **Théâtre des Célestins,** 4, rue Charles Pullin, 2ème (tel. 04 78 42 17 67; 70-200F). The **Opéra,** pl. de la Comédie, 1er (tel. 04 72 00 45 45), has 70F standing room only tickets the evening of the show. In the summer, Lyon bursts with festivals and special events nearly every week. Highlights include the **Fête de la Musique** in early June, when performers take over the city streets, and the **Bastille Day** celebration on July 14. The **Biennale de la Danse Lyon,** slated for 1998, draws modern dance performers from around the world. (Tickets 40-240F. Reserve at the Maison de Lyon, pl. Bellecour, 2ème; tel. 04 72 41 00 00.) Lyon, considered by some to be the birthplace of cinema, shows silver screen classics. The **Cinéma Opéra,** 6, rue J. Serlin (tel. 04 78 28 80 08), and **Le Cinéma,** 18, impasse St-Polycarpe (tel. 04 78 39 09 72), show black-and-white oldies, all in *v.o.* (original language; 30-40F).

Local students spend their nights at Lyon's *"Pubs Anglais."* Exercise your British accent at **Albion,** 12, rue Ste-Cathérine, 1er (open Mon.-Thurs. 6pm-2am, Fri.-Sat. until 3am, Sun. until 1am). A mixed gay and lesbian crowd gathers for a drink at **Le Verre à Soi,** 25, rue des Capucins, 1er (open Mon.-Fri. 11am-3am, Sat. 5pm-3am). **Le Mylord,** 112, quai Pierre Scize, 5ème, is a hard-core half-gay, half-straight dance mecca (cover 60F; Tues.-Sun. free; open Tues.-Sun. 10:30pm-7am). The **nightclub** scene centers on quai Romain Rolland, quai de Bondy, and quai Pierre Scize in the old city. Rattle the rafters and enjoy 15F beers at **Road 66,** 8, pl. des Terraux, 1er, just off highway 66 in the *centre ville* (open daily 2pm-4am).

BURGUNDY (BOURGOGNE)

Burgundy's best ambassadors to the world are its annual 40 million bottles of wine, which graciously represent a grand landscape splashed with vineyards and peppered by monasteries, cathedrals, and châteaux.

Dijon

Dijon's prospects looked bleak in 1513, as a Swiss siege gripped the city. Negotiations faltered until the *Dijonnais* sent wine casks across enemy lines — the foes, with inebriated generosity, retreated. Today, Dijon is famous for its wine-based mustards, and the city, with myriad museums and a lively international student population, is almost as spicy as its Grey Poupon. Should you visit Dijon? But of course.

A 20F card admits you to all of Dijon's museums, including the **Musée des Beaux-Arts,** occupying a wing of the colossal **Palais des Ducs de Bourgogne.** The palace's **Salle des Gardes** gallery is dominated by the huge sarcophagi of Philippe le Hardi and Jean sans Peur (open Wed.-Mon. 10am-6pm; 18F, students and Sun. free). With a facade of gargoyles, the **Eglise de Notre-Dame** exemplifies the Burgundian Gothic style, while the **Eglise St-Michel** on pl. St-Michel is a melange of Gothic and Renaissance artistry. On pl. St-Bénigne, the elegant **Cathédrale St-Bénigne** memorializes the 2nd-century missionary priest whose martyred remains were exhumed near Dijon. Nearby, the **Musée Archéologique,** 5, rue Docteur Maret, unearths Gallo-Roman sculpture, jewelry, and weapons. (Open June-Sept. Wed-Mon 9:30am-6pm; Oct.-May Wed.-Mon. 9am-noon and 2-6pm. 12F, students and Sun. free.) A trip to the **Grey Poupon store,** 32, rue de la Liberté, where *moutarde au vin* has been made since 1777, should not be considered a mere condiment to your Dijon excursion.

In June, Dijon's **Eté Musical** (tel. 03 80 30 61 00) stages many of the world's best symphony orchestras and chamber groups. From mid-June to mid-August, **Estivade** (tel. 03 80 67 23 23) brings dance, music, and theater to the streets. Operas and classical music concerts are performed at the 18th-century **Théâtre de Dijon,** pl. du Théâtre (tel. 03 80 67 20 21; mid-Oct. to late April; 110-240F, student rush 50F). Evenings, try **Atmosphère,** 7, rue Audra, a combination bar, pool hall, nightclub, and disco (no cover; open daily 2pm-3am), or **Le Kilkenny,** 1, rue Auguste Perdix, an authentic Irish pub (pint of Guinness 34F; open Mon.-Sat. 6pm-3am, Sun. 7pm-3am).

Practical Information, Accommodations, and Food **Trains** chug steadily to the station at cours de la Gare, at the end of av. Maréchal Foch, from Paris by TGV (2hr., 250-270F), Lyon (1½hr., 130F), and Nice (7-8hr., 380F). The **tourist office,** pl. Darcy (tel. 03 80 49 11 44), a 5-min. walk from the train station along av. Maréchal Foch, finds accommodations (15F) and gives out info on sights and events (open May to mid-Oct. daily 9am-9pm; mid-Oct. to April 9am-7pm).

Reservations for accommodations are advised in summer. The **Foyer International d'Etudiants,** 6, rue Maréchal Leclerc (tel. 03 80 71 70 00; fax 03 80 71 60 48), has TV rooms and a kitchen; from pl. Darcy take bus 4 ("St-Apollinaire") to "Parc des Sports" (Reception open 24hr.; singles 75F). The enormous **auberge de jeunesse (HI),** 1, bd. Champollion (tel. 03 80 72 95 20; fax 03 80 70 00 61), offers a laundry facility, bar, and disco. Take bus 5 ("Epirey") from pl. Grangier to the end of the line (dorms 68-76F, singles 138-144F). Find spotless, air-conditioned rooms at **Hôtel Montchapet,** 26-28, rue Jacques Cellerier (tel. 03 80 55 33 31), north of av. Première Armée Française (singles 140-185F, doubles 210-245F, triples 320F). **Hôtel Monge,** 20, rue Monge (tel. 03 80 30 55 41; fax 03 80 30 63 87), has cozy rooms and friendly owners (singles 120-130F, doubles 130-170F). Take bus 12 ("Fontaine d'Ouche") to "Hôpital des Chartreux" for the lakeside **Camping Municipal du Lac,** 3 bd. Kir (tel. 03 80 43 54 72; 14F per person, 12F per tent; open April-Oct. 15).

Pick up supplies at the supermarket in the basement of the **Galeries Lafayette,** 41, rue de la Liberté (open Mon.-Sat. 9am-7:15pm), or at **Prisunic,** 11, rue Piron, off pl. J. Mace (open Mon.-Sat. 8:30am-8pm). University cafeterias stay open all summer; **R.U. Maret,** 3, rue Docteur Maret, has an all-you-can-eat dinner for 12F with student ID. (Open Mon.-Fri. 11:30am-1:30pm and 6:30-8pm, Sat.-Sun. 11:40am-1:15pm and 6:40-7:45pm.) Find sandwiches or a date at the **Pick-Up Café,** 9, rue Mably, or for a square meal, try a restaurant on rue Berbisey or rue Monge such as **Le Rapido,** 102 rue Berbisey, with generous entrees and salads (around 30F), as well as *plats* (49-59F). Vegetarians and vegans will enjoy **La Vie Saine,** 27-29, rue Musette, off pl. Grangier (salad and dessert bar 55F; open Mon.-Sat. 11:45am-2:30am).

■ Near Dijon: Beaune and the Côte d'Or

The well-touristed town of **Beaune,** a half-hour south of Dijon on the Lyon rail line (36F), has disgorged wine for centuries. Surrounded by the famous **Côte de Beaune** vineyards, the town itself is packed with wineries offering free *dégustations.* Try the **Marché aux Vins,** near the Hôtel-Dieu, where you can descend into a candle-lit cellar and follow a trail of 20 wine kegs, each with a different Burgundian vintage for your sampling delight (50F; open Mon.-Thurs. 9:30am-noon and 2-6:30pm, Fri.-Sun. 9:30am-7pm). The town's biggest non-potable attraction is the **Hôtel-Dieu.** Built in the 15th century as a hospital for the poor, it is a regional architectural icon. (Open

March 22-Nov. 16 daily 9am-6:30pm; Nov. 17-March 21 9-11:30am and 2-5:30pm. 32F, students 25F.) The **tourist office,** rue de l'Hôtel-Dieu (tel. 03 80 26 21 30), lists *caves* in the region offering tours. (Open June 15-Sept. 15 Mon.-Sat. 9am-8pm, Sat. 9am-7pm; Sept. 16-June 14 closes Sun. at 6pm.)

The 60km **Côte d'Or,** with its rolling vineyards, has produced some of the world's best wines. Tour the 10th-century **Château de Gevrey-Chambertin** (tel. 03 80 34 36 13), 10km south of Dijon, before visiting its *cave* with favorites of Napoleon I and Louis XIV. (Open April-Oct. daily 10am-noon and 2-6pm; Nov.-March Mon.-Sat. 10am-noon and 2-5pm, Sun. 11am-noon and 2-5pm. 30min. tour 20F.)

ALSACE-LORRAINE

Strasbourg

Sitting just a few kilometers from the Franco-German border, Strasbourg has spent much of its history being annexed by one side or the other, but today the city is seen as a symbol of the French-German détente. Covered bridges, half-timbered houses, and breweries reflect Germanic influence, while wide boulevards, spacious squares, and a Gothic cathedral have a distinctly French flavor. Several European Union offices, including the European Parliament, add to its cosmopolitan credentials.

Constructed between the 11th and 15th centuries, the ornate deep-red Gothic **Cathédrale de Strasbourg** thrusts its heaven-tickling tower 142m into the sky. Inside, the **Horloge Astronomique** demonstrates the wizardry of 16th-century Swiss clockmakers; each day at 12:30pm, the apostles troop out of the face while a cock crows to greet St. Peter. While you wait, take a gander at the **Pilier des Anges** (Angels' Pillar), a masterpiece of Gothic sculpture. (Cathedral open Mon.-Sat. 7-11:40am and 12:45-7pm, Sun. 12:45-6pm. *Horloge* tickets go on sale at 11:50am at the cathedral entrance. 5F.) Across the way, the **Maison de l'Oeuvre Notre-Dame** houses some of the cathedral's statues and reconstructed stained glass (closed Mon.). Also across from the cathedral, the **Musée d'Art Moderne** has an excellent collection but will not reopen until at least September 1998 (guided tour 40F; closed Tues.). The **Château des Rohan,** 2, pl. du Château, houses a trio of small, noteworthy museums: the **Musée des Beaux-Arts,** the **Musée des Arts Décoratifs,** and the **Musée Archéologique** (admission to all three 40F, students 20F).

Practical Information, Accommodations, and Food Strasbourg is a major European rail junction. **Trains** (tel. 03 88 22 50 50) run to Paris (4hr., 210F), Luxembourg (2½hr., 153F), Zurich (2½hr., 226F), Frankfurt (3hr., 307F), and Milan (7hr., 491F). **Tourist offices** across from the station (tel. 03 88 32 51 49) and next to the cathedral (tel. 03 88 52 28 28) dispense maps (3F) and give out accommodation listings as well as the free *Shows and Events* and *Strasbourg Actualités* (open June-Sept. Mon.-Sat. 8:30am-7pm, Sun. 9am-6pm; Oct.-May daily 9am-6pm).

Everyone stays the night in Strasbourg, so make reservations or arrive early. **CIARUS (Centre International d'Accueil de Strasbourg),** 7, rue Finkmatt (tel. 03 88 15 27 88; fax 03 88 15 27 89), boasts sparkling rooms and a central location. From the train station, take rue du Maire-Kuss to the canal, turn left, follow quais St-Jean, Kléber, and Finkmatt, and take a left onto rue Finkmatt. (Reception open daily 6:30am-1am. Dorms 86-98F; singles 177F; doubles 116F. Breakfast included.) At the **Auberge de Jeunesse René Cassin (HI),** 9, rue de l'Auberge de Jeunesse (tel. 03 88 30 26 46; fax 03 88 30 35 16), 2km from the station, you can find clean, slightly worn rooms and **Internet access.** Take bus 3 ("Holtzheim-Entzheim Ouest") or 23 ("Illkirch"; every 30min., 7F) from rue du Marché-aux-Vins. (Members only. Reception open daily 7am-1am. Curfew 1am. Dorms 69-99F; singles 149F. Sheets 17F. Camping 41F. Breakfast and shower included. Closed Jan.-Feb. 10.) **Hôtel Patricia,**

1a, rue du Puits (tel. 03 88 32 14 60), in thc *vieille ville* by Eglise St-Thomas, is spacious (reception open daily 7:30am-8pm; singles 145-170F, doubles from 200F).

Strasbourgeois restaurants are known for delicious *choucroute garnie,* spiced sauerkraut with meat. *Winstubs* are informal joints traditionally affiliated with wineries. Don't miss the triple-decker **Au Pont St-Martin,** 13-15, rue des Moulins, where you can gaze on the canal locks and savor huge servings of seafood, salads, and *choucroute* (lunch *menu* Mon.-Fri. 56F; open daily noon-11pm). For French-Carribean and African fare, head to **La case de l'Ile Bourbon,** 34, Grand Rue. (49-78F *à la carte.* Open Sun.-Mon. 11:30am-2pm and 6:30pm midnight, Sat. 11:30am-2pm.)

Metz

In the neighboring region of Lorraine, attractive Metz boasts over 21km of trails, sculptured gardens, sinuous canals, and golden cobblestone streets. In pl. d'Armes, marvel at the stained-glass windows of the **Cathédrale St-Etienne,** built between the 13th and 16th centuries. The 6500 square meters of glass, including windows by Chagall, have earned the cathedral the moniker "Lantern to God." (Info office open May-Sept. Mon.-Sat. 9am-7pm, Sun. noon-7pm; Oct.-April Mon.-Sat. 9am-noon and 2-5:30pm, Sun. 2-5:30pm.) Nearby, the **Musée d'Art et d'Histoire,** 2, rue du Haut-Poirier, built atop Roman baths, reconstructs medieval and Renaissance home interiors (open daily 10am-noon and 2-6pm; 30F, under 25 15F, Wed. and Sun. mornings free).

Trains run to Paris (3hr., 203F), Strasbourg (1½hr., 110F), and Lyon (5hr., 255F). The **tourist office,** pl. d'Armes (tel. 03 87 55 53 78), has maps and listings. (Open July-Aug. Mon.-Sat. 9am-9pm, Sun. 10am-1pm and 2-5pm; Sept.-Oct. and April-June Mon.-Sat. 9am-7pm, Sun. 10am-1pm and 3-5pm; Nov.-March Mon.-Sat. 9am-7pm, Sun. 10am-1pm.) The **Foyer Carrefour (HI),** 6, rue Marchant (tel. 03 87 75 07 26; fax 03 87 36 71 44), offers superb facilities; from the station take bus 3 ("Metz-Nord") or bus 11 ("St-Eloy") to "St-Georges" (members only; dorms 68F, singles and doubles 78-80F). The same two buses also pass the Pontiffroy stop, where the **auberge de jeunesse (HI),** 1, allée de Metz Plage (tel. 03 87 30 44 02; fax 03 87 33 19 80), attracts many budget travelers (members only; reception open daily 7-10pm; dorms 46F). **Le Beverly,** 2, pl. St-Jacques, serves big salads for 30-50F (open daily 7am-2am).

CHAMPAGNE

Champagne, the region between Lorraine and Paris, is under French law the only source of real champagne, which must be aged according to the rigorous *méthode champenoise.* The best way to see and taste the results is to visit the underground *caves* of Reims and Epernay, both a little over an hour from Paris's Gare de l'Est.

Reims

Though most travelers put Reims on their maps for its fabulous *caves,* the city's other sights—most notably the Cathédrale de Notre-Dame and the Basilique St-Remi—should not be overlooked. The **cathedral,** ornamented with dreamlike Chagall windows, was built with blocks of golden limestone quarried in the Champagne *caves* beginning in 1211 (open Mon.-Sat. 7:30am-7:30pm, Sun. 8:30am-7:30pm). The **Palais du Tau** next door contains wonderful treasures, including Charlemagne's 9th-century talisman and the extravagant gold and velvet coronation vestments of Charles X. (Open March 16-Nov. 14 daily 9:30am-12:30pm and 2-6pm; Nov. 15-March 15 Mon.-Fri. 10am-noon and 2-5pm, Sat.-Sun. 10am-noon and 2-6pm. 26F, students 17F.) South of the cathedral area stands the **Basilique St-Remi,** a Gothic renovation of a Carolingian Romanesque church believed to contain the tombs of many of France's earliest kings. Behind the altar lies the tomb of St. Remi himself, whose baptism of Clovis brought Catholicism to the French people. (Open Mon.-Wed., Fri., and Sun. 8am-7pm or dusk, Thurs. and Sat. 7am-7pm or dusk.) The **Musée des Beaux-Arts,** 8, rue Chazny, houses an eclectic collection. (Open Mon. and Wed.-Fri. 10:30am-noon and 2-6pm, Sat.-Sun. 10am-noon and 2-6pm. 10F, students free.) The **Salle de Reddition,** 12, rue Franklin Roosevelt, houses the simple schoolroom where the Germans surrendered to the Allies on May 8, 1945. A film and several galleries lead up to the room itself. (Open April-Oct. Wed.-Mon. 10am-noon and 2-6pm; Nov.-March open only by appointment with the Musée des Beaux-Arts. 10F, students free.)

Four hundred kilometers of *crayères* (Roman chalk quarries) wind underground through the countryside around Reims. Today, they shelter bottles emblazoned with the great names of Champagne—Pommery, Piper-Heidsieck, Mumm, and Taittinger. The tourist office has a map with a list of the **caves** open to the public. Many houses give tours by appointment only, so call ahead. The most engaging *caves* and great wines belong to **Pommery,** 5, pl. du Général Gouraud (tel. 03 26 61 62 55), set in a magnificent group of 19th-century English-style buildings. (Tours by appointment April-Oct. daily 10am-5:30pm; Nov.-March Mon.-Fri. 10am-5:30pm. 30F, students 15F.) For an affordable taste of the bubbly, order a *coupe de champagne* at any bar in town (25-30F) or look for sales at wineshops (from 70F per bottle).

Practical Information, Accommodations, and Food The **train station,** bd. Joffre (tel. 08 36 35 35 35), serves Paris (1½hr., 113F). The **tourist office,** 2, rue Guillaume de Machault (tel. 03 26 77 45 25), near the cathedral, has a free map and books rooms for free. For local events pick up *Les Rendez-vous Remois.* (Open July-Aug. Mon.-Sat. 9am-8pm, Sun. 9:30am-7pm; Easter-June and Sept. Mon.-Sat. 9am-7:30pm, Sun. 9:30am-6:30pm; Oct.-Easter Mon.-Sat. 9am-6:30pm, Sun. 9:30am-5:30pm.) The **Centre International de Séjour/ Auberge de Jeunesse (HI),** chaussée Bocquaine (tel. 03 26 40 52 60; fax 03 26 47 35 70), is a 15-minute walk from the station. Continue straight through the park (1 block), then turn right onto bd. Général Leclerc. Follow it to the canal and cross the first bridge (pont de Vesle); chaussée Boc quaine is your first left. The hostel has attractive rooms and great facilities (reception open daily 7am-midnight; singles 83F, doubles 65F). **Ardenn' Hôtel,** 6, rue Caqué (tel. 03 26 47 42 38), is vividly decorated (reception open 24hr.; singles 160-200F, doubles 200-260F). **Hôtel Thillois,** 17, rue de Thillois (tel. 03 26 40 65 65), is a charming hotel with bright rooms and a central location (reception open daily 7am-10pm; singles 120-140F, doubles 140-160F). Fast-food joints, cafés, and bars abound on pl. Drouet-Erlon. **Le Petit Basque,** 13, rue de Colonel Fabien, serves five varieties of paella (65-90F, lunch *menu* 55F). **Monoprix supermarket** is housed in a graceful 19th-century building on the corner of rue de Vesle and rue de Talleyrand (open Mon.-Sat. 8:30am-9pm). Beer drinkers crowd the popular **An Bureau,** 40, pl. d'Erlon., while the club fiends turn to **Le Curtayn Club,** 7, blvd. Général Leclerc.

No Preservatifs Added

Having invented the French kiss and the French tickler, the speakers of the language of love have long had *savoir faire* in all things sexual—safety included. In the age of responsibility, French pharmacies (those flashing green crosses) provide 24-hour condom *(preservatif)* dispensers. They aren't hidden in dark, smoky bar bathrooms; instead, in typical French style, they unabashedly adorn the public streets. But don't ask for foods *sans preservatifs.*

Germany (Deutschland)

US$1 = DM1.84 (Deutschmarks)	**DM1 = US$0.54**
CDN$1= DM1.32	**DM1 = CDN$0.76**
UK£1 = DM2.95	**DM1 = UK£0.33**
IR£1 = DM2.70	**DM1 = IR£ 0.37**
AUS$1 = DM1.36	**DM1 = AUS$0.73**
NZ$1 = DM1.19	**DM1 = NZ$0.84**
SAR1 = DM0.39	**DM1 = SAR2.55**
Country Code: 49	**International Dialing Prefix: 00**

It seems somehow appropriate that as the world reinvents itself, Germany once again stands at the center of it all. Despite its history of reactionary governments, Germany has always been a wellspring of revolutionaries and innovators. One of the greatest heroes of German history, Karl der Große (Charlemagne), was the first to unify post-Roman Europe. Martin Luther stands as one of the most influential figures in Western history for the forces of change unleashed when he triggered the Protestant Reformation. Lessing, Bach, and Beethoven turned the worlds of drama and music upside-down. Socialist pioneers Karl Marx and Friedrich Engels equipped the revolutionary groundswell of 19th-century Europe with an ideology and a goal whose power has only been blunted and redirected, but never defused. Adolf Hitler, one of the most loathsome figures in Western history, organized in this country the capacity to perform deeds—the seizure of power, the conquest of Europe, the Holocaust—that elude explanation. This last image, of course, indelibly colors all subsequent German history. Germans must grapple with the fact that the cradle of Goethe and Beethoven also created Dachau and Buchenwald. Although burdened with the memory of the Third Reich, Germany is also blessed with an incomparable cultural tradition. No major European artistic movement of the last 500 years is entirely without debt to Germans, and quite a few would be unthinkable without German influence.

While the historical truths underlying popular stereotypes do provide some insight into what it means to be German, the nation that has finally emerged from World War II and the bipolarism of the Cold War is decidedly non-stereotypical. There are, to be sure, certain "German" characteristics—industriousness, efficiency, and a mystifying refusal to cross the street against the light, even in the absence of traffic—but the broad social and political range of the nation comprises defies easy categorization.

As tensions continue to simmer between the two cultures east and west of the old Wall, Germany's global influence continues to grow. In the wake of Europe's most recent wave of revolution, Germany's pivotal position between East and West is even more important than it was during the Cold War. As the troubles of reunification are slowly overcome, the country is emerging as the dominant economic power on the Continent. Forced to face the moral bankruptcy of its nationalism, Germany brings a unique perspective and motivation to recent nationalist conflicts as well as to the project of an integrated Europe. The legacy represented by the wealth of artistic, historical, and cultural treasures that Germany has managed to accumulate throughout centuries of war and division defines a healthy chunk of Western civilization's collective past, and may conceal more than just a glimpse into the future.

For more comprehensive and stimulating coverage of the country, treat yourself to *Let's Go: Germany 1998.*

GETTING THERE AND GETTING AROUND

German Train Systems and Railpasses The **Deutsche Bahn** integrated the **Deutsche Bundesbahn (DB)** and old eastern **Reichsbahn (DR).** Integration is still taking place; many connections are as of yet incomplete. Moving from west to east,

there are significant differences in quality and service. The DB network is one of Europe's finest (and most expensive) systems, averaging over 120km per hour with stops. Commuter trains, marked "City-Bahn" (CB) are fairly slow. "S-Bahn" trains are commuter rail lines that run through the city center and may be integrated with the local subway or streetcar system; "D" trains are slightly faster. "RE" or "RB" trains run between neighboring cities. "Interregio" (IR) trains cover larger networks between cities quickly and comfortably, while "IC" (intercity) trains zoom along between major cities every hour. You must purchase a supplementary "IC Zuschlag" to ride an IC or EC train (DM6 when bought in the station, DM8 on the train). The pricey, futuristic **InterCity Express** (ICE) zips as fast as 174mph. For these, railpass users do not usually pay a *Zuschlag* unless the seat requires a reservation.

Non-Germans can purchase the **German Railpass** in their home countries. The pass allows a selected number of days of rail travel within a one-month period on all DB trains. The second-class version costs US$188 for five days, US$304 for 10 days, and US$410 for 15 days in a month; the first-class version costs US$276, US$434, and US$562, respectively. Children 4-11 pay half of adult rates; those under 4 travel free. The **German Rail Youth Pass,** available to non-Germans aged 12-25, offers second-class passage only at US$146 for five days, US$200 for 10, and US$252 for 15. For anyone under age 27, the **Tramper-Ticket** allows 10 days of unlimited second-class rail travel in a month on all DB trains, the railroad-run buses *(Bahnbusse),* and the local S-Bahns in cities—all for DM369. This pass, available between June 15 and October 15, may be purchased *only* in Germany. Also available only in Germany, the **BahnCard** is valid for one year and secures a 50% discount on all rail tickets, including the ICE. Students under 27 and anyone under 23 or over 60 can get a second-class pass for DM120; first-class cards are DM240. Normal rates are DM240 second-class, DM480 first-class. These passes require a passport-sized photo.

Buses, Flights, Bikes, and Eurail Buses between cities and to small, outlying towns usually run from the **Zentral Omnibus Bahnhof (ZOB),** which is often near the train station. Buses are usually slightly more expensive than the train for comparable distances. Check university bulletin boards or the classified pages of local magazines for occasional deals. Railpasses are not valid on any buses other than those (relatively few) run by the DB. Although more than 100 international **airlines** serve Germany, flying across the country is generally expensive and unnecessary.

Bikes are sight-seeing power tools; Germany makes it easy with its wealth of trails and bike tours. Cities and towns usually have designated bike lanes. German rail's **Fahrrad am Bahnhof** ("bikes at the station") program offers cycle rentals throughout the country for DM6-10 per day. Usually bikes can be rented from one station and returned at another for a small deposit. For information about bike routes, regulations, and maps, contact **Allgemeiner Deutscher Fahrrad-Club,** Postfach 10 77 47, 28077 Bremen. A bike tour guidebook, including extensive maps, is available from **Deutsches Jugendherbergswerk (DJH)** (tel. (05231) 740 10).

Although *Let's Go* does not recommend **hitchhiking** as a safe means of transportation, it is permitted and quite common on the German *Autobahnen* (expressways). Hitchers may stand only at *Raststätten* (rest stops), *Tankstellen* (gas stations), and in front of the *Autobahn* signs at on-ramps. **Mitfahrzentralen** offices in many cities pair drivers and riders, with a fee to the agency (about US$20) and to the driver (per km).

Eurail is valid in Germany and provides free passage on S-Bahns in cities and DB bus lines but not on the U-Bahn. Urban **public transit** is excellent in the western and decent in the eastern regions. You'll see four types: the **Straßenbahn** (streetcar), **S-Bahn** (commuter rail), **U-Bahn** (subway), and regular **buses.** Consider purchasing a day card *(Tagesnetzkarte)* or multiple-ride ticket *(Mehrfahrkarte);* they usually pay for themselves by the third ride. Public transportation tickets must be validated.

ESSENTIALS

Although violent crime is relatively uncommon in Germany, homosexuals and foreigners, particularly non-whites and members of certain religious groups, may feel threatened by local residents in certain regions. Neo-Nazi skinheads are most active in large cities of the former East Germany. Skinheads subscribe to a "shoelace code" with white supremacists and neo-Nazis wearing white laces and anti-gay skinheads lacing with pink. Anti-Nazi skinheads favor red laces.

Every city in western Germany has a **tourist office,** usually located near the main train station *(Hauptbahnhof)* or central market square *(Marktplatz).* They go by a bewildering variety of names (often *Verkehrsamt* or *Verkehrsverein*), but they are all marked by a thick lowercase **"i"** sign. The offices provide city maps and info on cycling routes and local sights, and often book rooms (usually for DM5 fee or less).

The **Deutschmark** (abbreviated DM, or occasionally M) and **Pfennig** (Pf) are the primary units of currency in Germany. One DM equals 100Pf. Coins come in 1, 2, 5, 10, and 50Pf, and DM1, 2, and 5 amounts. Bills come in DM5, 10, 20, 50, 100, 200,

500, and 1000 denominations. **Currency exchange** *(Wechsel)* is available in all large train stations, banks, and kiosks; banks generally offer the best rates. **Credit card** acceptance is markedly less common in Germany than in the U.S. or U.K., but **ATMs,** especially linked to Cirrus and Plus, are widespread. Most locals carry large wads of hard cash, but for tourists, **traveler's checks** are probably the best option. **Bank hours** are often quite bizarre; typical would be Monday through Wednesday and Friday 9am to 12:30pm and 2:30 to 4pm, Thursday 9am to 12:30pm and 2:30 to 5pm.

Store hours are usually Monday through Friday 9am to 6:30pm, Saturday 9am to 2pm. Some stores remain open until 8:30pm on Thursday and until 4pm on the first Saturday of each month. In larger cities, shops inside train stations are open longer. Many smaller shops take a mid-day break from noon to 2pm. Germany celebrates the following public **holidays:** January 1, Easter (April 10-13 in 1998), May 1, Ascension Day (May 21), Whit Monday (June 1), October 3, and December 25-26.

Communication The main **post office** in a town generally has the longest hours; all accept *Poste Restante,* known as *Postlagernde Briefe.* Local calls should be made with a *Telefonkarte.* This is by far the best option available; cards are sold in all post offices in DM12, DM20, and DM50 denominations. In the booth, pick up the receiver, deposit coins (even if your call is toll-free) and dial. **Local calls** cost 30Pf. Phones accept 10Pf, DM1, and DM5 coins, but not DM2 or 50Pf. Sometimes you can also pay by credit card. The **national information** number is 011 88. For information within the EU, call 00 11 88. Pay phones marked with a bell allow you to receive calls. From anywhere in Germany, the number for the **AT&T Direct** operator is 0130 00 10; for **SprintExpress,** 0130 00 13; **Canada Direct,** 0130 00 14; **BT Direct,** 0130 80 00 44; and **New Zealand Direct,** 0130 80 00 64. You must pay for the local connection time to the operator; if you don't have a phone card, be sure to have 30Pf in change. In case of an **emergency,** call the police at 110; fire 112; ambulance 115.

English **language** ability is common in the west, but far less so in the east. Keep in mind that the letter ß is equivalent to double *s.* To make more friends, try:

Yes/No	*Ja/Nein*	ya/nine
Good day/evening	*Guten Tag/Abend*	GOO-ten tahg/AH-bend
Please	*Bitte*	BIT-teh
Thank you	*Danke*	DAHN-keh
Excuse me	*Entschuldigung*	ent-SHUL-di-gung
Do you speak English?	*Sprechen Sie englisch?*	SHPREK-en zee AYN-glish
I don't understand.	*Ich verstehe nicht.*	ikh fair-SHTAY-uh nikht
Where is...?	*Wo ist...?*	Vo ist
How much does that cost?	*Wieviel kostet das?*	vee-feel KOHS-tet das
I would like...	*Ich möchte...*	ikh MURKH-tch
I would like a room for one/two	*Ich möchte ein Zimmer für ein/zwei*	ikh MURKH-teh ine TZIM-mehr feer INE/TSVIY
Bill, please.	*Zahlen, bitte*	TZAHL-en, BIT-tuh
Help!	*Hilfe!*	HIL-feh

Accommodations and Camping A German schoolteacher founded the world's first youth hostel in 1908, and there are now more than 600 *Jugendherbergen* throughout the country. **Deutsches Jugendherbergswerk (DJH)** (tel. (05231) 740 10; fax 74 01 49) oversees hosteling in Germany. Rates range around US$8-20. The DJH has, in recent years, initiated a growing number of **Jugendgästehäuser** (youth guest houses); with higher prices (around DM32 for a bed in a four person dorm) and additional facilities, these cater more to young adults than schoolchildren. Keep in mind that hostels in Bavaria do not accept guests over the age of 26. DJH publishes *Deutsches Jugendherbergsverzeichnis* (DM14.80), which details all federated German hostels; it is available at all German bookstores and many newsstands, or by writing DJH-Hauptverband, Postfach 1455, 32704 Detmold, Germany.

There are about 2600 **campgrounds** in Germany, about 400 of which are open in the winter. Prices run about DM4-5 per tent with additional charge for tent and vehicles. Most tourist offices have lists of nearby sites.

Food and Drink Though German cuisine is neither as sophisticated as French cooking nor as sultry as Italian or Hungarian food, it is far from taste bud torture. *Deutsche* delights often include *Schnitzel* (a lightly fried veal cutlet), *Spätzle* (a southern noodle), and tasty seafood. However, pork and potatoes are the more steady staples of the family table. Most notable is Germany's broad palette of breads and cheeses that puts baguettes to shame. The fresh rolls (*Brötchen* or *Semmeln*) sold in any bakery will satisfy even the most discriminating of dough connoisseurs.

German breakfasts *(Frühstück)* consist of coffee or tea, rolls, butter, marmalade, slices of bread, cheese, and *Wurst* (cold sausage). The main meal, *Mittagsessen,* is served at noon. Around 4pm, many Germans head to the *Konditorei* for *Kaffee und Kuchen* (coffee and cake). The evening meal, *Abendbrot* or *Abendessen,* is traditionally a reprise of breakfast, but with beer instead of coffee. Restaurant prices include tax and service *(Mehrwertsteuer und Bedienung),* but it is customary to round up the bill. For inexpensive food, try a department-store cafeteria or, with a student ID, a *Mensa* (university dining hall). Stop at an *Imbiß* for anything fast.

The average German beer is, very generally, relatively malty and "bread-like." From the south comes *Weißbier,* a smooth, refreshing, richly brown brew. Sampling local brews numbers among the finest of Germany's pleasures. On hot summer days, lightweight drinkers prefer *Radler,* a Bavarian mix containing half beer and half lemon-lime soda. Also try the largely overlooked German wines, particularly the sweet (*lieblich* or *süß*) whites of the Rhine and Mosel Valleys.

Berlin

Contemporary Berlin is an inchoate tangle of experiences in search of an identity. Long recognized as the cultural capital of Germany, Berlin is not yet the political capital, as the parliament continues to meet in Bonn. Split into eastern and western sectors as a result of divisions among the one-time Allies, the city acted as the focal point of the Cold War in Europe, then symbolized its end when the Wall came down in 1989. Even as money is finally allocated to rebuild the eastern sectors, the disparity between east and west is troubling to residents of both. Raised in the shadow of global conflict, Berliners respond with a glorious storm of cultural activity and the nightlife you might expect from a population that has its back against the wall. A kaleidoscope of GDR apartment blocks and designer boutiques, decaying buildings and gleaming modern office complexes, Berlin's gritty melancholy is balanced by the exhilaration of being on the cutting edge.

ORIENTATION AND PRACTICAL INFORMATION

Berlin surveys the Prussian plain in the northeast corner of reunited Germany, about four hours southeast of Hamburg by rail and eight hours north of Munich. Berlin is well connected to other European cities as well— Prague is five hours by rail, Warsaw six hours. For now, western Berlin's **Bahnhof Zoologischer Garten (Bahnhof Zoo)** remains Berlin's major train station and the focus of the city's subway and surface rail systems. The situation is changing, though, as the eastern **Berlin Hauptbahnhof** surpasses the space-constricted Zoo Station. **Friedrichstraße, Alexanderplatz,** and **Berlin-Lichtenberg** are other important subway and rail stations.

The city is immense. Berlin's historic east half and commercial west half are connected by the grand tree-lined boulevard, **Straße des 17 Juni,** which runs through the massive **Tiergarten** park. The commercial district of west Berlin centers on Zoo Station and **Breitscheidplatz.** The district is marked by the bombed-out Kaiser-Wilhelm-Gedächtniskirche and the boxy tower of Europa Center. A star of streets radi-

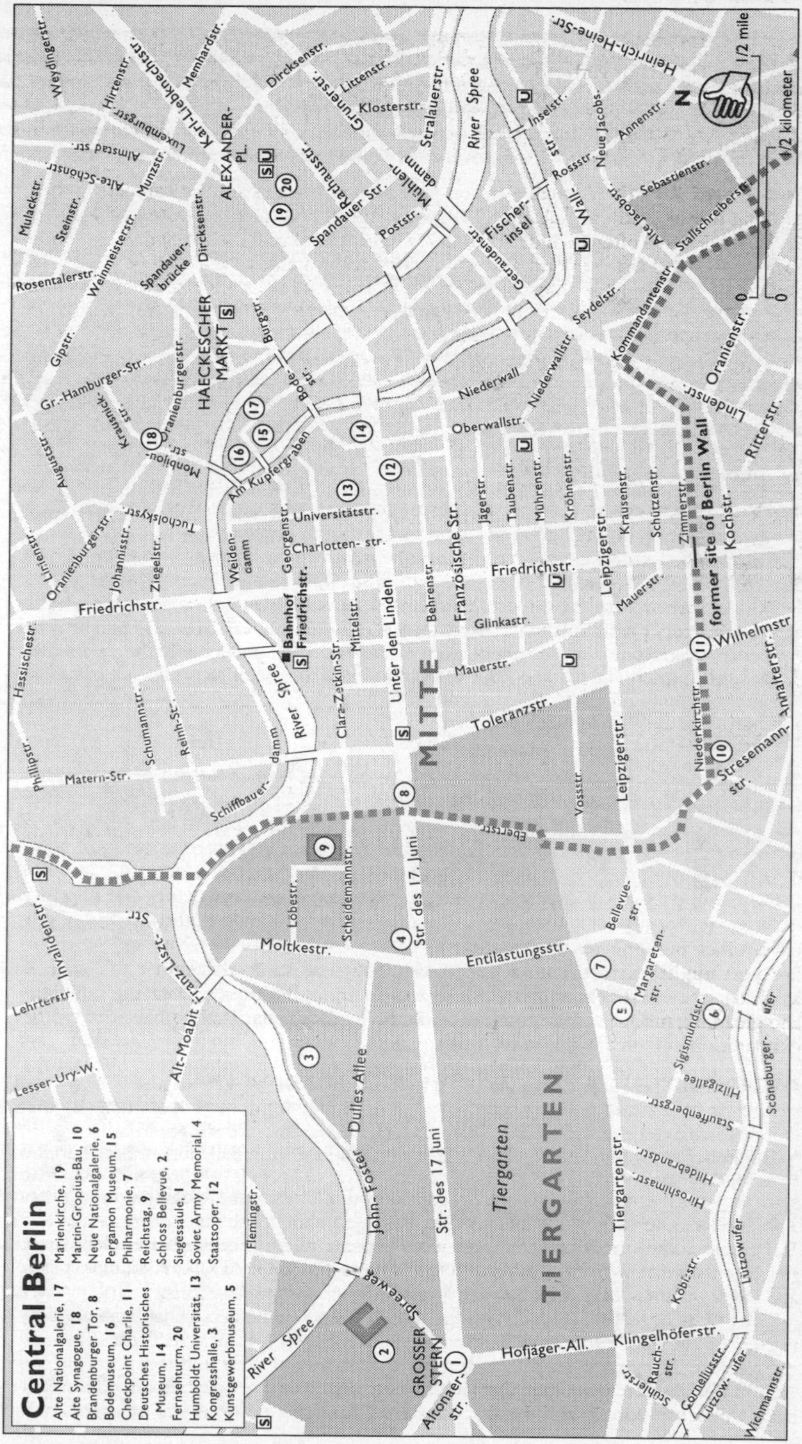
Central Berlin
Alte Nationalgalerie, 17
Alte Synagogue, 18
Brandenburger Tor, 8
Bodemuseum, 16
Checkpoint Charlie, 11
Deutsches Historisches Museum, 14
Fernsehturm, 20
Humboldt Universität, 13
Kongresshalle, 3
Kunstgewerbmuseum, 5
Marienkirche, 19
Martin-Gropius-Bau, 10
Neue Nationalgalerie, 6
Pergamon Museum, 15
Philharmonie, 7
Reichstag, 9
Schloss Bellevue, 2
Siegessäule, 1
Soviet Army Memorial, 4
Staatsoper, 12
TIERGARTEN
Tiergarten
MITTE
ALEXANDER-PL.
HAECKESCHER MARKT
Bahnhof Friedrichstr.
GROSSER STERN
Fischer-insel
River Spree
former site of Berlin Wall
Unter den Linden
Str. des 17. Juni
Friedrichstr.
Leipzigerstr.
Wilhelmstr.
Oranienstr.
Karl-Liebknechtstr.
0 1/2 mile
0 1/2 kilometer
N

GERMANY

ates from Breitscheidpl. Toward the west run **Hardenbergstraße, Kantstraße,** and the great commercial boulevard **Kurfürstendamm,** or **Ku'damm.** Down Hardenbergstr. are **Steinplatz** and the enormous Berlin Technical University. Down Kantstr., **Savignyplatz** is lined with cafés, restaurants, and pensions.

The newly asphalted **Ebert Straße** runs along the path of the deconstructed Berlin Wall from the Reichstag to **Potsdamer Platz.** The landmark **Brandenburg Gate** and surrounding Pariser Paviserpl., reconstructed with the aid of EU funds, open onto **Unter den Linden,** which leads to the historic heart of Berlin around **Lustgarten.** Farther east is **Alexanderplatz,** the east's growing commercial district. The alternative **Kreuzberg** and **Mitte,** for 45 years the fringe neighborhoods of the West and East, are again at the city's heart. If you're planning to stay more than a few days in Berlin, the blue and yellow **Falk Plan** (DM11), available at kiosks, is a useful map.

> Although neo-Nazis represent a tiny minority of Berliners, conspicuously non-German individuals should be on guard in less-touristed areas of eastern Berlin.

Tourist Offices: For tourist info, call 25 00 25. **Berlin-Touristen-Information, Europa Center,** Budapesterstr. 45. From Bahnhof Zoo, walk along Budapesterstr. past the Kaiser-Wilhelm-Gedächtniskirche (5min). Free copies of city magazines *030* and *Serge* (for gays and lesbians) which have entertainment listings. *Tip* and *Zitty* are better, but in German (DM4). Open Mon.-Sat. 8am-10pm, Sun. 9am-9pm. Branches in the main hall of **Tegel Airport.** Open daily 5:15am-10pm. Also inside the **Brandenburger Gate,** south wing. Open daily 9:30am-6pm. All offices provide a simple city map (DM1) and book rooms for a DM5 fee.

Tours: Berlin Walks (tel. 301 91 94) offers a range of English-language walking tours, including their famous Discover Berlin tour. Tours last about 2½hr. and meet at 9:15am, 10am, and 2:30pm in front of the Zoo station. DM14, under 26 DM10.

Budget Travel: The **Insider Tour** of Berlin hits all the major sights and enjoys a very good reputation. Tours last 3hr. and leave from the McDonald's by the Zoo station May-Nov. at 10am and 2:30pm. DM10.

Embassies and Consulates: Australia: Uhlandstr. 181-183 (tel. 880 08 80). Open Mon.-Fri. 9am-noon. **Canada:** Friedrichstr. 95 (tel. 261 11 61; fax 262 92 06). Open Mon.-Fri. 8:30am-12:30pm and 1:30-5pm. **Ireland:** Ernst-Reuter-Pl. 10 (tel. 34 80 08 22; fax 34 80 08 63). Open Mon.-Fri. 10am-1pm. **New Zealanders** contact the embassy in Bonn (Bundeskanzlerpl. 2-10; tel. (0228) 22 80 70). **South African:** Douglasstr. 9 (tel. 82 50 11; fax 826 65 43). Open Mon.-Fri. 9am-noon. **U.K.:** Unter den Linden 32 (tel. 20 18 40; fax 20 18 41 58). Open Mon.-Fri. 9am-noon and 2-4pm. **U.S.:** 170 Clayallee (tel. 832 92 33; fax 831 49 26). U-Bahn 1: "Oskar Helene Heim." Open Mon.-Fri. 9am-noon. Phone advice Mon.-Fri. 9am-5pm; after hours, recorded emergency instructions.

Currency Exchange: Deutsche Verkehrs-Kredit Bank (tel. 881 71 17), Bahnhof Zoo on Hardenbergstr. 1% commission on traveler's checks (DM7.50 min. fee). Open daily 7:30am-10pm. The **Reisebank** at the *Hauptbahnhof* (tel. 296 43 93) changes traveler's checks for DM7.50. Open Mon.-Fri. 7am-10pm, Sat.-Sun. 7am-4pm. **Berliner Bank** in Tegel Airport is open daily 8am-10pm.

American Express: Uhlandstr. 173, 10719 (tel. 884 58 80). Members only. Mail held; all banking services. Open Mon.-Fri. 9am-5:30pm, Sat. 9am-noon. **Branch office,** Bayreutherstr. 37 (tel. 21 49 83 63). Open Mon.-Fri. 9am-6pm.

Flights: Flughafen Tegel (tel. 41 01 23 06). Berlin's main airport. From "Bahnhof Zoo" or "Jakob-Kaiser-Pl." stations, take bus 109 to "Tegel." **Flughafen Tempelhof** (tel. 69 51 22 88). Bus 119 to "Pl. der Luftbrücke." **Flughafen Schönefeld** (tel. 60 91 51 66), in eastern Berlin, is connected by S-Bahn 3 to the city center.

Trains: Bahnhof Zoo sends trains to the west, while the **Hauptbahnhof** serves lines to the south and east, with many exceptions. The stations are connected by S-Bahn. Trains from the east also arrive at **Berlin-Lichtenberg.** To reach **Deutsche Bahn Information,** dial 194 19; be prepared for a long wait. Similarly long lines at offices in Bahnhof Zoo (open daily 5:30am-10:30pm) and the *Hauptbahnhof.*

Buses: ZOB, the central bus station (tel. 301 80 28), is by the *Funkturm.* U-Bahn 2: "Kaiserdamm." *Zitty* and *Tip* list deals on long-distance buses, cheaper than trains.

Public Transportation: Construction will affect S- and U-Bahn service for the next few years. **Max,** a bespectacled mole, appears on posters and signs announcing usually minor disruptions to service. Info and tickets available at the **BVG Pavillon,** Bahnhof Zoo (tel. 25 62 25 62). Open daily 8am-8pm. A single ticket *(Einzelfahrschein Normaltarif)* costs DM3.90 and is good for 2hr. after validation. An *Einzelfahrschein Kurzstreckentarif* (short-trip fare, DM2.50) allows travel through up to 6 bus stations (no transfers; not valid on airport bus lines) or 3 U- or S-Bahn stops (unlimited transfers). A 4-trip *Sammelkarte* (multiple ticket) costs DM13; each "click" is good for 2hr. A short-trip 4-ride *Kurzstreckensammelkarte* is also available for DM8.50. Buy tickets from machines, bus drivers, or ticket windows in the U- and S-Bahn stations. The **Berlin Tagesticket** (DM13) is a 24hr. pass for the bus and U- and S-Bahn. A **7-Day Ticket** runs DM40. A calendar-month **Umweltkarte** costs DM93. AB tickets cover nearly all of Berlin. Validate tickets in the red box marked *"hier entwerten"* before boarding. Tickets bought on board a bus are automatically valid. The U- and S-Bahn do not run 1-4am, except for the **U-9** and **U-12,** covering parts of U-1 and U-2, which run all night Fri.-Sat. An extensive system of **night buses,** centered on Bahnhof Zoo, runs every 15min. Pick up the free *Nachtliniennetz* map. All-night bus numbers are preceded by **N.**

Bike Rental: Bahnhof Zoo, next to the lost and found. DM13-23 per day. DM60 for 3 days. DM120 per week. Open daily 6am-11pm. **Herr Beck,** at Goethestr. 7 (tel. 312 19 25), near Ernst-Reuter-Pl. DM12 per day. Mountain bikes DM20 per day. Call for selection and deposit information. Bring passport. No English spoken.

Hitchhiking: Those who hitch west and south take S-Bahn 1 or 3 to "Wannsee," then bus 211 to the *Autobahn* entrance ramp. Those headed north take U-Bahn 6 to "Tegel," then bus 224, and ask the driver to be let out at the *Trampenplatz.* **City Netz,** Joachimstalerstr. 17 (tel. 194 44 or 882 76 04; fax 882 44 20), in the Ku'Dorf Mall, has a **ride-share** database. U-Bahn 1 or 9: "Kurfürstendamm." To Hamburg (DM11 fee for info, DM18 paid to driver) and Vienna (DM18, DM39). Open daily 8am-9pm. **Mitzfahrzentrale Alex,** in the Alexanderpl. U-Bahn station (tel. 241 58 20), specializes in the East. Open Mon.-Fri. 8am-8pm, Sat. 8am-6pm, Sun. 10am-6pm. Many smaller *Mitzfahrzentralen;* check *Zitty, Tip,* or *030* magazines.

Luggage Storage: In the **Bahnhof Zoo** station. Lockers DM2 per day, larger ones DM4; 3-day max. At the **Hauptbahnhof,** lockers DM2, larger ones DM4. At Bahnhof **Lichtenberg** and S-Bahnhof **Alexanderplatz,** lockers cost DM2; 24hr. max.

Lost Property: Zentrales Fundbüro, Platz der Luftbrücke 8 (tel. 69 95). **BVG Fundbüro,** Lorenzweg 5 (tel. 256 230 40). U-Bahn 6: "Ullsteinstr." For items lost on the bus or U-Bahn. Open Mon.-Tues., Thurs. 9am-3pm, Wed. 9am-6pm, Fri. 9am-2pm. **Fundbüro Berlin,** Mittelstr. 20 (tel. 29 72 96 12), at the Schönefeld train station.

Bookstores: Marga Schoeler Bücherstube, Knesebeckstr. 34 (tel. 881 11 12). Many books in English. Open Mon.-Wed. 9:30am-7pm, Thurs.-Fri. 9:30am-8pm, Sat. 9am-4pm. **British Bookshop,** Mauerstr. 83-83 (tel. 238 46 80), has English newspapers and magazines. Open Mon.-Fri. 9am-6pm, Sat. 10am-4pm.

Laundromat: Wasch Centers are at Leibnizstr. 72 in Charlottenburg; Wexstr. 34 in Schöneberg; Bergmannstr. 61 in Kreuzberg; Behmstr. 12 in Mitte; and Jablonskistr. 21 in Prenzlauer Berg. Wash DM6 per 6kg. Dry DM2 for 30min. Soap included. All open daily 6am-10pm.

Crisis Lines: Sexual Assault Hotline: tel. 251 28 28. Open Tues. and Thurs. 6-9pm, Sun. noon-2pm. **Schwüles Überfall** hotline and legal help for gays: tel. 216 33 36. Open daily 6-9pm. **Drug Crisis:** tel. 192 37. **Frauenkrisentelefon,** a women's crisis line: tel. 615 42 43. Open Mon. and Thurs. 10am-noon, Tues., Wed., and Fri. 7-9pm, Sat.-Sun. 5-7pm. English speakers staff all lines.

Pharmacies: Europa-Apotheke, Tauentzienstr. 9-12 (tel. 261 42 44), by Europa Center (close to Bahnhof Zoo). Open daily 9am-9pm. Closed *Apotheken* post signs direct you to the nearest one open, or call 011 41.

Medical Assistance: The American and British embassies have a list of English-speaking doctors. **Emergency Doctor:** tel. 31 00 31. **Emergency Dentist:** tel. 841 91 00. English-speaking dentists available.

Emergencies: Ambulance and **Fire:** tel. 112.

Police: Pl. der Luftbrücke 6 (tel. 110 or 69 90).

Internet Access: Cyberb@r Zoo, Joachimtalerstr. 5-6 (tel. 88 02 40; email cyberbarzoo@hotmail.com), in the Karstadt Sport Megastore. DM5 for 30min. Open Mon.-Fri. 10am-8pm, Sat. 9am-4pm. Also in **Cybermind's Virtuality Café,** Lewishamstr. 1 (tel. 327 51 43). DM7 for 15min. Open daily from 2pm.

Post Offices: In the **Bahnhof Zoo.** Open Mon.-Fri. 6am-midnight, Sat.-Sun. 8am-midnight. *Poste Restante,* held at window 7, should be addressed: Poste Restante/ Hauptpostlagernd, Postamt Bahnhof Zoo, 10612 Berlin. Branch office at **Tegel Airport** (tel. 430 85 23) open daily 6:30am-9pm. **Postamt Berlin 17,** Str. der Pariser Kommune 8-10, 10243 Berlin, around the corner from the *Hauptbahnhof.* Open Mon.-Fri. 7am-9pm, Sat. 8am-8pm.

Telephone Code: 030.

ACCOMMODATIONS AND CAMPING

Even though tourists mob Berlin during the summer, same-day accommodations are easy to find. As always, it's best to call ahead, particularly during the Love Parade. For a DM5 fee, **tourist offices** will find you a room: be prepared to pay DM70 for singles and DM100 for doubles. There are also over 4000 private rooms *(Privatzimmer)* available; the majority are controlled by the tourist offices. Expect to pay DM80 for singles, DM100 for doubles, plus a single-night surcharge of DM5.

For longer visits (over 4 days) the various **Mitwohnzentralen** can arrange for you to housesit or sublet someone's apartment. Prices start at DM40 per night, plus a commission of 20-25%. The **Mitwohnzentrale,** Joachimtalerstr. 17 (tel. 88 30 51; fax 882 66 94), in the Ku'Dorf mall, is the biggest (open Mon.-Fri. 9am-7pm, Sat. 11am-3pm).

Hostels and Dormitory-Style Accommodations

Hostels fill quickly with German school groups (especially in summer and on weekends)—always call ahead. All HI-affiliated hostels are for members only, but for an extra DM4, some will let nonmembers spend the night. Head to Tempelhofer Ufer 32, 10963 Berlin (tel. 264 95 20; fax 262 04 37) to buy an HI card (open Mon., Wed., and Fri. 10am-4pm, Tues.-Thurs. 1-6pm). For non-Germans, membership cards cost DM36. HI hostels have strict curfews. Many accept written or faxed reservations.

The Backpacker, Köthenerstr. 44, 10963 Berlin (tel. 262 51 40; email ante@aol.com). U-Bahn 2: "Potsdamerpl."; from the Stresemannstr. exit, turn right on Stresemannstr., then right again. Close to Mitte's action. One of the best budget options, with a kitchen and a hip staff that updates you on nightlife. Reception open 7am-11pm, but check-in easiest 9-11am. No curfew. First night DM30, subsequent nights DM25. Sheets DM3. Laundry facilities DM5. On January 15, 1998, a **second location** will open in Mitte at Chausseestr. 102 (tel. 251 52 02). U-Bahn 6: "Zinnowitzerstr." or S-Bahn 1 or 2: "Nordbahnhof." Discounted public transportation tickets and **Internet access.** DM25-30. Sheets DM4. Breakfast DM5-10.

Die Fabrik, Schlesischestr. 18, 10997 Berlin (tel. 611 71 16; fax 618 29 74). U-Bahn 1: "Schlesisches Tor." Beautifully converted factory within walking distance of Kreuzberg's nightlife. **Bikes** DM16 per day. Reception open 24hr. No curfew. Surprisingly comfortable 16-bed room DM30. Singles DM66. Doubles DM94 (honeymoon suite DM110). Triples DM120. Quads 144. Breakfast DM10. Call ahead.

Circus, Am Zirkus 2-3, 10117 Berlin (tel. 28 39 14 33; email circus@mind.de), near Alexanderpl. Brand new and trying for hostel hipness, offering **Internet access,** laundry machines, and a disco ball in the lobby. No curfew. Dorms DM25. Singles DM38. Doubles DM60. Triples DM84. Sheets DM3.

Jugendgästehaus (HI), Kluckstr. 3, 10785 Berlin (tel. 261 10 97; fax 265 03 83), in the Schöneberg/Wilmersdorf area. From Ku'damm, bus 129 ("Hermannpl.") to "Gedenkstätte," or U-Bahn 1: "Kurfürstenstr.," then walk up Potsdamerstr., go left on Pohlstr., then right. Clean and modern. Reception open 1pm-midnight with 30min. breaks; ring the bell. Curfew midnight; door opened at 12:30 and 1am. Lockout 9am-1pm. DM32, over 26 DM41. Sheets and breakfast included. Key deposit DM10. Lockers and laundry facilities available. Call at least 2 weeks ahead.

Jugendgästehaus am Zoo, Hardenbergstr. 9a, 10623 Berlin, 5th floor (tel. 312 94 10; fax 401 52 83), opposite the Technical University *Mensa.* Bus 145, or walk from *Bahnhof* Zoo: take the back exit onto Hardenbergstr. Well-located but spartan and poorly lit. Reception open 24hr. Check-out 9am. No curfew. Dorms DM35. Singles DM47. Doubles DM85. Over 26 DM5 extra. No reservations.

Jugendgästehaus Nordufer, Nordufer 28, 13351 Berlin (tel. 451 70 30; fax 452 41 00). U-Bahn 9: "Westhafen," left over the bridge and left onto Nordufer for about 15min. Away from the center, but on the pretty, swimmable Plötzensee Lake. Reception open 7am-midnight. No curfew. DM38. Breakfast and sheets included.

Jugendgästehaus am Wannsee (HI), Badeweg 1, 14129 Berlin (tel. 803 20 35; fax 803 59 08). S-Bahn 1 or 3: "Nikolassee," turn left at the main exit, cross the bridge, and head left for 5min. Far from the center, but Wannsee has its own charm. Building reminiscent of a municipal swimming pool. Book 2 weeks ahead. DM31, over 26 DM40. Breakfast and sheets included. Key deposit DM20.

Hotels and Pensionen

Many small *Pensionen* and hotels are within the means of budget travelers, particularly since most establishments listed in *Let's Go* are amenable to *Mehrbettzimmer,* where extra beds are moved into a large double or triple. Most affordable hotels are in western Berlin; the hotels in Mitte are ridiculously expensive. The best places to find cheap hotel rooms are around Savignypl. and along Wilmersdorfstr.

Hotelpension Cortina, Kantstr. 140, 10623 Berlin (tel. 313 90 59; fax 31 73 96). S-Bahn 3, 5, 7, or 9 or bus 149 ("Savignypl"). Bright, convenient, and hospitable. Reception open 24hr. Dinky singles DM70. Doubles DM120, with shower DM130. *Mehrbettzimmer* DM45-50 per person. Breakfast included.

Pension Knesebeck, Knesebeckstr. 86, 10623 Berlin (tel. 312 72 55; fax 313 34 86). S-Bahn 3, 5, 7, or 9: "Savignypl." Just north of the park. Large *Alt-Berliner* rooms, many with couches and sinks. Hearty buffet breakfast. Reception open 24hr. Singles with showers DM85. Doubles DM120-140. Big *Mehrbettzimmer* DM50-60 per person. Laundry DM2.50. Phone reservations must be confirmed by fax or letter.

Hotel-Pension München, Güntzelstr. 62 (tel. 857 91 20; fax 85 79 12 22). U-Bahn 9. "Güntzelstr." *Pension-cum-*gallery with art by contemporary Berlin artists and sculptures by the owner. Superclean rooms with TVs. Singles DM60-110. Doubles DM80-125. Breakfast DM9. Written reservations are best, or call before 2pm.

Hotel Sachsenhof, Motzstr. 7, 10777 Berlin (tel. 216 20 74; fax 215 82 20). Small, plain rooms but clean and well-furnished. Reception open 24hr. Singles DM57-65. Doubles DM99-156. Extra beds DM30. Breakfast DM10.

Frauenhotel Artemesia, Brandenburgischestr. 18, 10707 Berlin (tel. 873 89 05; fax 861 86 53). U-Bahn 7: "Konstanzerstr." An immaculate, elegant (if pricey) hotel for women only. The **Artemesia Café** serves an all-female (straight and lesbian) crowd that digs Tracy Chapman. Reception open 7am-10pm. Singles DM99-149. Doubles DM169-200. Extra beds DM45. Breakfast included. "Last-minute, same-day" specials: singles from DM79 and doubles from DM129 (without breakfast).

Pension Kreuzberg, Grossbeerenstr. 64, 10963 Berlin (tel. 251 13 62; fax 251 06 38). U-Bahn 6 or 7: "Mehringdamm" or bus 119. Small but well-decorated rooms in an old, grand building near the Kreuzberg scene. Reception open 8am-10pm. Singles DM70. Doubles DM95. *Mehrbettzimmer* DM42 per person. Breakfast DM5.

Hotel Transit, Hagelbergerstr. 53-54, 10965 Berlin (tel. 785 50 51; fax 785 96 19). U-Bahn 6 or 7: "Mehringdamm," or bus 119 or night bus N19. Party hard and crash gently. Singles DM90. Doubles DM152. Triples DM140. Quads DM180. With "Sleep-In," share a *Mehrbettzimmer* (DM34). Breakfast included.

Hotel-Pension Hansablick, Flotowstr. 6 (tel. 390 48 00; fax 392 69 37). S-Bahn 3, 5, 7, 75, or 9: "Tiergarten." An absolute *Jugendstil* pearl, from the decorative ceilings to the marble entrance. Reception open 24hr. Singles DM125-150. Doubles DM150-215. Extra bed in the doubles DM55. 5% *Let's Go* discount. July-Aug. same-day specials are available but without the *Let's Go* discount. Reserve ahead.

Camping

Deutscher Camping-Club runs two of the major campgrounds in Berlin; both are adjacent to the site of the former Berlin Wall. Rreservations can be made by writing the Deutscher Camping-Club Berlin, Geisbergstr. 11, 10777 Berlin. DM9.50 per person, DM7 for a tent. **Dreilinden** (tel. 805 12 01). U-Bahn 1: "Oskar-Helene-Heim," then bus 118 to "Kätchenweg"; follow Kremnitzufer to Albrechts-Teergfen (about 20min.). City campsite surrounded by the vestiges of the Wall. Open March-Oct. **Kladow,** Krampnitzer Weg 111/117 (tel. 365 27 97). U-Bahn 7: "Rathaus Spandau," then take bus 135 to "Alt-Kladow" (last stop). Switch to bus 234 to "Krampnitzer Weg/Selbitzerstr.," and follow Krampnitzer Weg 200m. Open year-round.

Internationales Jugendcamp Fließtal, Ziekowstr. 161 (tel. 433 86 40). U-Bahn 6: "Tegel," then bus 222 or night bus N22 to "Titusweg." Next to Jugendgästehaus Tegel. Blanket and mattress under a big tent with free showers DM10. Campfire every night. Officially under 27 only, but rules are made for conformists, and they aren't into that sort of thing here. No reservations. Open July-Aug.

FOOD

Berlin's restaurant scene is as international as its population; typically German food and drink should be a second priority here. One exception is the smooth, sweet *Berliner Weiße mit Schuß,* a concoction of local beer with a shot of syrup. Much Berlin food is Turkish: almost every street has its own Turkish *Imbiß* or restaurant. The *Imbiß* stands are a vital lifeline for the late-night partier; some are open 24 hours. The *Döner Kebab,* a sandwich of lamb and salad, has cornered the fast food market, with falafel running a close second. For DM3-5, either makes a small meal; ask for *außer Haus* (take-out) to save 2DM at many an *Imbiß.* A second wave of immigration has brought quality Indian restaurants to Berlin, and Italian is always a safe choice.

A gloriously civilized tradition in Berlin cafés is *Frühstück,* breakfast served well into the day. New cafés in **Mitte** and **Prenzlauer Berg** provide stiff competition for their western counterparts; prices tend to be lower and portions larger. In addition, street vendors with all sorts of cheap eats fill **Alexanderplatz** every day.

Aldi, Bolle, and **Penny Markt** are the cheapest **supermarket** chains, along with the many **Plus** stores in Wilmersdorf, Schönberg, and Kreuzberg. Supermarkets are usually open Monday through Friday 9am to 8pm, and Saturday 9am to 4pm. The best **open-air market** fires up Saturday mornings in Winterfeldpl., though almost every neighborhood has one. There's a kaleidoscopic **Turkish market** in Kreuzberg on the banks of the Landwehrkanal (near U-Bahn 1: "Kottbusser Tor") every Friday.

Mensa TU, Hardenbergstr. 34. Bus 145 to "Steinpl.," or walk 10-min. from Bahnhof Zoo. The mightiest of Berlin's mensae, serving rather good vegetarian *(Bio Essen)* dishes. Meals DM4-6. *Mensa* open Mon.-Fri. 11:15am-2:30pm.

Café Hardenberg, Hardenbergstr. 10. Big *Belle Epoque* spot. Funky music, artsy interior, lots of students. Breakfast (9am-5pm) DM4-8. Most entrees under DM13. Also good for a drink—grog DM4. Open Sun.-Thurs. 9am-1am, Fri.-Sat. 9am-2am.

Restaurant Marché, Kurfürstendamm 15, a couple of blocks down from Bahnhof Zoo and the *Gedächtniskirche.* Probably the most affordable lunch on the Ku'damm. The colorful cafeteria area is full of fresh produce, salads, grilled meats, pour-it-yourself wines, and hot pastries (DM12-25). Open daily 8am-midnight.

Schwarzes Café, Kantstr. 148, near Savignypl. Dark walls, big-band music, and dapper waiters. A bit pricey, but they have breakfast at all hours (DM7-13). Open 24hr., except for Tues., when closed early morning-6pm.

Mexico Lindo, Kantstr. 134, on the corner of Wielandstr. S-Bahn: "Savignypl." One of the cheaper Mexican restaurants around. Lunch specials DM9-13. Quesadillas DM3.50 at the *Imbiß* stand (open Mon.-Fri. noon-7pm). Open daily 5pm-midnight.

Baharat Falafel, Winterfeldtstr. 37. U-Bahn 1 or 2: "Nollendorfpl." Perhaps the best falafel in Berlin (DM6). Open Mon.-Sat. 10am-3am, Sun. 11am-3am.

Rani, Goltzstr. 32, behind the church on Winterfeldtpl. U-Bahn 1 or 2: "Nollendorfpl." Very casual and cheap Indian restaurant popular with students. Most dishes DM6-10. Generous portions. Open daily 11am-2am.

Kurdistan, Uhlandstr. 161. U-Bahn 15: "Uhlandstr." One of Berlin's most exotic and most appetizing offerings. Fabulous *Yekawe* (meat with rice, raisins, and cinnamon) DM15. Most entrees DM15-20. Open Mon.–Sat. 5pm-late.

Morena, Wiener Str. 60. U-Bahn 1 or 12: "Görlitzer Bahnhof." A gracious, roomy café with some of Kreuzberg's best *Frühstück* (DM5-8.50, served 9am-5pm). Open Sun.-Thurs. 9am-4am, Fri.-Sat. 9am-5am.

Die Rote Harfe, Oranienstr. 13, in Heinrichpl., the center of Kreuzberg. U-Bahn 8: "Moritzpl." or U-Bahn 1: "Kottbusser Tor." Leftists and grizzled types eating solid German food are bound to spark the radical in you. Daily 3-course lunch menu DM15. Open Sun.-Thurs. 10am-2am, Fri.-Sat. 10am-3am.

Humboldt University Mensa, Unter den Linden 6. Full meals from DM1.50. Student ID required. Open Mon.-Fri. 11:30am-2:30pm.

Taba, Chausseestr. 106. U-Bahn 6: "Zinnowitzerstr." Big portions of great Mexican and Brazilian food. Occasional live salsa music. Most entrees DM15-20. On Wed., all entrees are DM10 and all cocktails DM8. Open Tues.-Sat. 6pm-late, Sun. 6pm-late.

SIGHTS

Between Eastern and Western Berlin

For decades a barricaded gateway to nowhere, the **Brandenburger Tor** (Brandenburg Gate) symbolizes the reunited Berlin, ushering you onto Unter den Linden (S-Bahn: "Unter den Linden" or bus 100). Built during the reign of Friedrich Wilhelm II as an emblem of peace, the gate embedded in the Berlin Wall wasn't unlocked until December 22, 1989, over a month after the Wall came down. The **Berlin Wall** itself is a dinosaur with only fossil remains. Fenced in overnight on August 13, 1961, the 160km long wall separated families and friends, sometimes running through homes. Portions of it are preserved near the *Hauptbahnhof* and the Reichstag. The longest remaining bit is the brightly painted **East Side Gallery** (S-Bahn: "Hauptbahnhof").

The demolished Wall has left an incompletely healed scar across the city center. From the west side, trees have been planted extending the Tiergarten park a few meters more. But on the east side, a grassy, cinder block strewn no-man's-land awaits construction. **Potsdamer Platz,** cut off by the Wall, was once a major transportation hub designed under Frederick Wilhelm I to approximate Parisian boulevards.

Just south of Potsdamer Platz stands the **Martin-Gropius-Bau,** at Stresemanstr. 110. The decorous edifice was designed by Martin Gropius, a pupil of Schinkel and uncle of Bauhausmeister Walter Gropius. The **Haus am Checkpoint Charlie,** Friedrichstr. 44 (U-bahn: "Kochstr." or bus 129), narrates the history of the Wall through film and photo. Upstairs there are exhibits on human rights, as well as artistic renderings of the Wall (open daily 9am-10pm; DM7.50, students DM4.50).

Western Berlin

The Reichstag and Tiergarten

Just to the north of the Brandenburg Gate sits the imposing, stone-gray **Reichstag** building, former seat of the parliaments of the German Empire and the Weimar Republic, and future home of Germany's governing body, the *Bundestag.* In 1918 Philipp Scheidemann proclaimed a German republic from one of its balconies. His move turned out to be wise, since two hours later Karl Liebknecht, in the Imperial Palace a few kilometers away on Unter den Linden, announced a German Socialist Republic, ironically on the site that later supported the parliament of the GDR. As the Republic declined, Nazi members showed up to sessions in uniform, and on February 28, 1933, a month after Hitler became Chancellor, fire mysteriously broke out in the building. The fire provided a pretext for Hitler to declare a state of emergency, giving the Nazis broad powers to arrest and intimidate opponents before the upcoming elections. The infamous end result was the Enabling Act, which established Hitler as legal dictator and abolished democracy. In the summer of 1995, the Reichstag metamorphosed into an artsy parcel, when husband-and-wife team **Christo** and **Jeanne-Claude** wrapped the dignified building in 120,000 yards of shimmery metallic fabric. The government held a massive design competition for the building's new dome. The current plans call for a huge glass dome but will likely change, since a scale model of the design fried the miniature model ministers inside. The lush **Tiergarten** in the northwest corner of western Berlin is a relief from the neon lights of the Ku'damm to the west and the din and dust of construction work to the east. In the heart of the Tiergarten, the slender 70m **Siegessäule** (victory column), topped by a gilded statue of winged victory (where Bruno Ganz hung out in *Wings of Desire*), commemorates Prussia's humiliating defeat of France in 1870. Climb the 285 steps to the top for a panorama of the city (open April-Nov. Mon. 1-6pm, Tues.-Sun. 9am-6pm; DM2). The **Soviet Army Memorial** (yes, you're still in western Berlin) stands at the end of Str. des 17 Juni, flanked by a pair of giant toy tanks.

Ku'damm, Schöneberg, and Charlottenburg

A sobering reminder of the devastation caused by World War II, the shattered **Kaiser-Wilhelm-Gedächtniskirche** now houses an exhibit dedicated to peace (open Tues.-Sat. 10am-4pm). The exhibit, however, has lost some of its didactic force amid the giddy neon of the **Ku'damm** and the Europa Center. The renowned **Zoo,** with entrances across from the train station and at Budapesterstr. 34 (the famous Elephant Gate), houses an exotic collection of fauna. (Open May-Sept. daily 9am-6:30pm; Oct.-Feb. 9am-5pm; March-April 9am-5:30pm. DM11, students DM9.) Next door at Budapesterstr. 32 stands the spectacular **Aquarium.** (Open daily 9am-6pm. DM8, students DM5. Zoo and aquarium DM17, students DM14.)

South of Nollendorfpl. is the **Rathaus Schöneberg,** where West Berlin's city government met in the 60s. On June 26, 1963, 1.5 million Berliners swarmed beneath the *Rathaus* to hear John F. Kennedy reassure them of the Allies' continued commitment to the city 15 years after the Berlin Airlift. Kennedy's speech ended with the now-famous "All free men, wherever they may live, are citizens of Berlin. And therefore, as a free man, I take pride in the words *Ich bin ein Berliner*" ("I am a jelly doughnut").

Schloß Charlottenburg (U-Bahn: "Sophie-Charlotte-Pl." or bus 145 from Bahnhof Zoo), the vast Baroque palace built by Friedrich I for his second wife, presides over a carefully landscaped Baroque park. The *Schloß*'s many buildings include **Neringbau,** the palace proper, which contains rooms filled with historical furnishings. (Castle open Tues.-Fri. 9am-5pm, Sat.-Sun. 10am-5pm. Entire palace complex *Tageskarte* DM15, students DM10.) Seek out the **Palace Gardens,** with their carefully planted rows of trees, footbridges, and fountains which surround the **Royal Mausoleum, Belvedere,** an 18th-century residence housing a porcelain exhibit and the **Schinkel Pavilion,** with furniture designed by Schinkel (open Tues.-Sun. 6am-9pm; free).

Kreuzberg

Indispensable for a sense of Berlin's famous *alternative Szene,* or counter-culture, is a visit to **Kreuzberg.** Much of the area was occupied by *Hausbesetzer* (squatters) during the 60s and 70s, who were forcibly evicted in the early 1980s, provoking riots and throwing the city into upheaval. For a look at the district's more respectable face, take U-Bahn 6 or 7: "Mehringdamm" and wander. At night, many bohemian cafés and punk clubs spill onto **Gneisenaustraße,** which heads west from the intersection with Mehringdamm. The cafés and bars on Oranienstr. boast a more radical element; the May Day parades always start on Oranienpl. (U-Bahn 1 or 8: "Kottbusser Tor.") The **Landwehrkanal,** a channel bisecting Kreuzberg, is where Rosa Luxemburg's body was thrown after her murder in 1919. The tree-dotted strip of the canal near Hallesches Tor, **Paul-Linke Ufer,** may be the most beautiful street in Berlin, with its shady terraces and old facades. The east end of Kreuzberg near the old Wall is home to Turkish and Balkan neighborhoods, with a wealth of ethnic restaurants popular with radicals, students, and shabby genteel gourmets. From the "Schlesisches Tor" U-Bahn stop, a three-minute walk takes you across the **Oberbaumbrücke,** through a fragment of the Wall and into the Friedrichshain district of the former East.

Eastern Berlin

Unter den Linden and Gendarmenmarkt

The Brandenburg Gate opens eastward onto **Unter den Linden,** once one of Europe's best-known boulevards and the spine of old Berlin. All but the most famous buildings have been destroyed, but farther down many 18th-century structures have been restored to their original Prussian splendor. Past Friedrichstr., the first massive building on your left is the **Deutsche Staatsbibliothek** (library), with a pleasant café inside. Beyond the library is **Humboldt Universität,** once one of the finest in the world. Next door, the old **Neue Wache** (New Guard House), designed by the renowned Prussian architect Friedrich Schinkel, is today the somber **Monument to the Victims of Fascism and Militarism.** Buried inside are urns filled with earth from the Nazi concentration camps of Buchenwald and Mauthausen and from the battlefields of Stalingrad, El Alamein, and Normandy. Across the way is **Bebelplatz,** the site of Nazi book-burning. The square houses a monument to the book-burning, consisting of a hallowed-out chamber lined with illuminated empty white bookshelves. The impressive building with the curved facade is the **Alte Bibliothek.** The most striking of the monumental houses is the **Zeughaus,** now the **Museum of German History.** From the museum, you can enter the courtyard and see the tormented faces of Andreas Schlüter's *Dying Warriors.*

Berlin's most striking ensemble of 18th-century buildings is a few blocks south of Unter den Linden at **Gendarmenmarkt,** graced by the twin cathedrals of the **Deutscher Dom** and the **Französischer Dom,** built for the French Huguenot community. Enclosing the far end of the square, the classical **Schauspielhaus** is Berlin's most elegant concert space and hosts many international orchestras and classical performers.

Lustgarten, the Museumsinsel, and Alexanderplatz

As it crosses the bridge, Unter den Linden opens out onto the **Museumsinsel** (Museum Island). To the left is the **Altes Museum,** with a big polished granite bowl in front, and the poly-domed **Berliner Dom.** Severely damaged by an air raid in 1944, the cathedral emerged from 20 years of restoration in 1993; the interior is ornately gaudy (open Mon.-Sat. 9am-8pm, Sun. noon-8pm; DM5, students DM3). Behind the Altes Museum lie three other enormous museums and the reconstructed **Neues Museum.** The cobblestone square in front of the Altes Museum is known as the **Lustgarten.** Once a small park, it became a military parade ground under the Nazis. Across the street, the Lustgarten turns into Marx-Engels-Pl. under the amber-colored **Palast der Republik,** where the GDR parliament once met.

Across the Liebknecht Brücke, in the park, stands the "conceptual memorial" consisting of steel tablets engraved with images of worker struggle and protest surrounding a twin statue of Marx and Engels. The park and the street behind it used to be known as the **Marx-Engels Forum;** the street is now called **Rathausstraße.**

On the other side of the Museumsinsel, Unter den Linden leads to teeming, concrete **Alexanderplatz.** Its landmark is the **Fernsehturm** (television tower), the city's tallest structure (open March-Oct. daily 9am-1am; Nov.-Feb. 10am-midnight; DM8).

Nikolaiviertel and Scheuenviertel-Oranienburger Str.

The graceful 15th-century **Marienkirche** stands on the open plaza behind the *Fernsehturm.* Nearby is the gabled **Rotes Rathaus,** Old Berlin's famous red-brick town hall. Behind the *Rathaus,* the twin spires of the **Nikolaikirche** mark Berlin's oldest building. Inside the 13th-century structure, a small museum documents the early history of the city (open Tues.-Sun. 10am-6pm; DM3, students DM1). The church gives the surrounding **Nikolaiviertel,** a carefully reconstructed *Altstadt,* its name.

Northwest of Alexanderpl. lies the **Scheunenviertel,** once the center of Berlin's Orthodox Jewish community (U- or S-Bahn: "Alexanderpl." or S-Bahn 1 or 2: "Oranienbergerstr."). Prior to World War II, wealthier and more assimilated Jews tended to live in western Berlin, while more Orthodox Jews from Eastern Europe settled in the Scheunenviertel. The shell of the **Neues Synagoge** stands at Oranienburgerstr. 30. This huge, "oriental-style" building was designed by the famous Berlin architect Knoblauch. The temple's beautiful gold-laced domes and some of the sumptuous interior have been reconstructed. **The New Synagogue 1866-1995,** chronicling the synagogue's history, and **Jewish History in Berlin,** documenting the history of Jews in Berlin since the 1660s are housed here (open Sun.-Thurs. 10am-6pm, Fri.

10am-2pm; DM5, students DM3). **Oranienburgerstraße** has become a center of the squatter and artist communities, with a correspondingly rich cultural and café life.

Prenzlauer Berg and Treptow

East of Oranienburgerstr. is **Prenzlauer Berg,** a former working-class district largely neglected by East Germany's reconstruction efforts. Many of its old buildings are falling apart; others still have shell holes and embedded bullets from World War II. The result is an aged charm and graceful decay. Home to cafés, restaurants, and a few museums, restored **Husemannstraße** is worthy of a stroll. The area's population belies the aging architecture; there are heaps of students, artists, clubs, and communes, but the city government's anti-commune policy is in danger of destroying this counter-cultural renaissance. The scene around **Kollwitzplatz** is especially vibrant.

The powerful **Sowjetische Ehrenmal** (Soviet War Memorial) is a mammoth promenade built with marble taken from Hitler's Chancellery (S-Bahn: "Treptower Park"). The Soviets dedicated the site in 1948, honoring the soldiers of the Red Army who fell in the "Great Patriotic War." The memorial sits in the middle of **Treptower Park,** a spacious wood ideal for morbid picnics. The neighborhood adjoining the park is known for its pleasant waterside cafés and handsome suburban mansions.

Museums

Berlin is one of the world's great museum cities, with collections of art and artifacts encompassing all subjects and eras. The National Prussian Cultural Foundation *(Staatliche Museen Preußischer Kulturbesitz)* runs the four major complexes—Charlottenburg, Dahlem, Museumsinsel, and Tiergarten—that form the hub of the city's museum culture. Their prices and hours are standardized: Tues.-Fri. 9am-5pm, Sat.-Sun. 10am-5pm; DM4, students DM2. A *Tageskarte* (good for all of the national museums, including the 4 above, except the Altes Museum) is DM8, students DM4. All national museums and most of the private ones close on Monday; on the first Sunday of each month admission to the national museums is free.

Pergamonmuseum, Kupfergraben, in Museumsinsel. One of the world's great ancient history museums. The scale is mind-boggling: the Babylonian Ishtar Gate (575 BC), the Roman Market Gate of Miletus, and the majestic Pergamon Altar of Zeus (180 BC). Extensive collection of Greek, Islamic, and Far Eastern art. Last admission 30min. before closing.

Alte Nationalgalerie, Bodestr. 19th-century art, mostly German but includes a sizable collection of French Impressionist paintings.

Bodemuseum, Monbijoubrücke. A world-class exhibit of Egyptian art as well as late Gothic wood sculptures, early Christian art, 15th- to 18th-century paintings, and an exhibit on ancient history. Open Tues.-Sun. 9am-5pm.

Altes Museum, Lustgarten. Converted into a special-exhibit museum, it has recently showcased powerhouse exhibitions of 20th-century avant-garde and political art. A SMPK *Tageskarte* is not valid here. Exhibits run up to DM10, students DM5. Open Tues.-Sun. 10am-5pm; during major exhibitions Thurs. to 8pm.

Dahlem Museum, Arnimallee 23-27 and Lansstr. 8. U-Bahn: "Dahlem-Dorf." Huge complex of 7 museums, each worth a half-day. Particularly superb are the **Gemäldegalerie** (Painting Gallery), a collection of Italian, German, Dutch, and Flemish Old Masters (including 26 Rembrandts), and the **Museum für Indische und Islamische Kunst,** extensive collections of Indian and Islam culture.

Schloß Charlottenburg, Spandauer Damm (U-Bahn 2: "Sophie-Charlotte-Pl." or bus 145) contains several museums. The **Ägyptisches Museum,** across Spandauer Damm from the castle's main entrance, houses a fascinating collection of ancient Egyptian art, including the 3300-year-old bust of Queen Nefertiti. Also check out the **Sammlung Berggruen** and the **Galerie der Romantik.** *Tageskarte* for the non-SMPK parts of the *Schloß* costs DM15, students DM10.

Neue Nationalgalerie, Potsdamerstr. 50. Bus 129 from the Ku'damm or S-Bahn 1 or 2 or U-Bahn 2: "Potsdamer Pl." Part of the Tiergarten complex. This sleek building, gives quantity its own quality in a collection devoted to large art displays. Permanent collection includes works by Kokoschka, Barlach, Kirchner, and Beckmann.

The Love Parade

Every year during the second weekend in July, the Love Parade brings Berlin to its knees—the trains run late, the streets fill with litter, and the otherwise sedate and productive populace dye their hair, drop ecstasy, and get down *en masse.* What started off in 1989 with 150 people celebrating a DJ's birthday has mutated into an annual techno Woodstock, the world's only million-man rave, and a massive corporate event. A huge "parade" takes place on Saturday afternoon, involving a snail-paced procession of tractor-trailers loaded with blasting speakers and people dancing on top. The city-wide party turns Str. des 17 Juni into a raving dance-floor, and the Tiergarten into a garden of original—indeed, sometimes quite creative—sin. Club prices skyrocket for a frantic weekend of parties and dancing. While the Love Parade has been held in the Tiergarten in the past, the authorities may move it next year.

Martin-Gropius Bau, Stresemannstr. 110 (tel. 25 48 60). S-Bahn or U-Bahn: "Anhalter Bahnhof." The **Berlinische Galerie,** on the second floor, is devoted to rotating exhibits of contemporary art, much of it very famous. On the top floor, the **Jüdisches Museum** hosts extremely varied exhibits of painting, sculpture, and design related to Jews in Germany. Most exhibits in both are open Tues.-Sun. 10am-8pm. DM12, students DM6. Adjacent to the museums, built on top of the ruins of a Gestapo kitchen, the **Topographie des Terrors** details the development of Nazi-ism in Germany. Open Tues.-Sun. 10am-6pm. Free. The adjacent **Prinz-Albrecht-Gelände** contains the ruins of most of the Gestapo buildings. Signs describe what once took place. Open during daylight hours. Free.

Bauhaus Archiv-Museum für Gestaltung, Klingenhöferstr. 13-14. Take bus 129 to "Lützowpl." Designed by Walter Gropius, this building displays a permanent exhibit devoted to the development of *Bauhaus.* Open Wed.-Mon. 10am-5pm.

Brücke Museum, Bussardsteig 9. From the Zoo, take bus 249 a few stops to "Güntzelstr.," then take bus 115 to "Pücklerstr." at Clayallee. *The* Expressionist museum in Berlin, with works by the Brücke school that flourished in Dresden and Berlin from 1909 to 1913. DM7, students DM3. Open Wed.-Mon. 11am-5pm.

Deutsches Historisches Museum (Museum of German History), Unter den Linden 2, in the former arsenal. Across from the Museumsinsel. Permanent exhibits trace German history from the Neanderthal period to the Nazis, while rotating exhibitions examine the last 50 years. Open Thurs.-Tues. 10am-6pm. Free.

ENTERTAINMENT

Berlin is *wild,* all night, every night. The best guides to theater, cinema, nightlife, and the extremely active music scene are the biweekly magazines *Tip* and *Zitty* (both DM4 and in German). The main English language mag, *Berlin* (DM3.50), is largely limited to opera and classical music. The monthly *Berlin Program* lists more "cultural" events and includes good theater info. The free magazines *Serge* (from the tourist office) and *Siegessäule (*available in gay bars and bookstores) detail gay events. Berlin has **de-criminalized marijuana possession** of up to eight grams. Smoking in public, however, has not been officially accepted. *Let's Go* does not recommend puffing clouds of hash smoke into the face of police officers.

Concerts, Opera, and Dance

Berlin reaches its musical zenith during the fabulous **Berliner Festwochen,** lasting almost the entire month of September and drawing the world's best orchestras and soloists, and the **Berliner Jazztage** in November. For more information on these events (and tickets, which sell out far in advance), write to Berliner Festspiele, Budapesterstr. 48-50, 10787 Berlin 30 (tel. 25 48 92 50; open daily noon-6pm). In mid-July, **Bachtage** (Bach Days) offer an intense week of classical music. Every Saturday night in August, **Sommer Festspiele** turns the Ku'damm into a multifaceted concert hall with punk, steel drum, and folk groups competing for attention.

In the monthly pamphlets *Kultur in Berlin, Metropolis,* and *Berliner Programm,* as well as the biweekly magazines *Tip* and *Zitty,* you'll find notice of concerts in the courtyard of the old Arsenal, on the **Schloßinsel Köpenick** (Castle Island), or in the parks. Tickets for the *Philharmonie* and the *Oper* are often impossible to acquire through conventional channels. Instead, try standing out in front before performances with a small sign saying, *"Suche Karte"* (I seek a ticket).

Berliner Philharmonisches Orchester, Matthäikirchstr. 1 (tel. 25 48 81 32; fax 25 48 81 35). Bus 129 from Ku'damm to "Potsdamerstr." and walk 3 blocks north; or S-Bahn 2: "Potsdamerpl." The *Berliner Philharmoniker,* led for decades by the late Herbert von Karajan and currently under the baton of Claudio Abbado, is perhaps the finest orchestra in the world. Check an hour before concert time for seats or write at least eight weeks in advance. The *Philharmonie* is often closed during the summer months. Tickets around DM30. Box office open Mon.-Fri. 3:30-6pm, Sat.-Sun. and holidays 11am-2pm. Send a fax or write to: Kartenbüro, Berliner Philharmonisches Orchester, Matthäikirchstr. 1, 10785 Berlin.

Deutsche Oper Berlin, Bismarckstr. 34-37 (tel. 341 02 49 or 343 84 01 for tickets). U-Bahn 2 or 12: "Deutsche Oper." Berlin's best opera. Main box office open Mon.-Sat. 11am-1hr. before performance, Sun. 10am-2pm. Within a week of performances, you can get student discounts of up to 50%. Tickets DM15-125.

Deutsche Staatsoper, Unter den Linden 7 (tel. 20 35 44 94; fax 20 35 44 83). U-Bahn 6: "Friedrichstr." East Berlin's leading opera company. Ballet and classical music, too. Box office open Mon.-Fri. noon-6pm, Sat.-Sun. 2-6pm. Tickets DM18-35. 50% student discounts. Backstage tours daily at 11am.

Theater and Film

Berlin has a lively English-language theater scene; look for listings in *Tip* or *Zitty* that say *"in englischer Sprache"* next to them or the separate list in *Metropolis.* On any night in Berlin, you can also choose from 100 different films, many in the original language. (*"O.F."* next to a movie listing means "original version;" *"O.m.U."* means original with German subtitles. Everything else is dubbed.) Check *Tip, Zitty, Metropolis,* or subway posters for information on films. There is an international **Film Festival** (late Feb.-March) and a **Theater Festival** (May).

Deutsches Theater, Schumannstr. 13a (tel. 287 12 25). U-6 or S-Bahn 1-3, 5, 6, or 9: "Friedrichstr." The best theater in the country. Innovative productions of both classics and newer works. The **Kammerspiel des Deutschen Theaters** (tel. 28 44 12 26) has smaller productions. Tickets DM15-40. 50% student discount often available. Box office open Mon.-Sat. noon-6pm, Sun. 3-6pm.

Hebbel Theater, Stresemannstr. 29 (tel. 25 90 04 27). U-Bahn 1 or 6: "Hallesches Tor." The most *avant* of the *avant-garde* theaters in Berlin, drawing talent from all over. Watch for tomato-throwers in the audience. Box office open daily 4pm-7pm.

Maxim Gorki Theater, Unter Den Linden 2 (tel. 20 22 11 29). U-Bahn 6 or S-Bahn 2, 3, 5, 6, or 9: "Friedrichstr." Excellent contemporary theater. Tickets DM5-25. Box office open Mon.-Sat. 1-6:30pm, Sun. 3-6:30pm.

Nightlife

In western Berlin, the best places to look are the **Savignyplatz, Schöneberg, Wilmersdorf,** and **Kreuzberg** districts. Mainstream activity centers around two areas to the north and south of the Ku'damm. Ku'damm is best avoided. The north is a bit more inviting; the middle point is **Savignyplatz.** South of the Ku'damm, the area between Uhlandstr. and Olivaerpl. is littered with crowded late-night cafés. Traditionally, the social nexus of bisexual, gay, and lesbian life has centered around **Nollendorfplatz,** encompassing Winterfeldpl., Goltzstr, and Kleiststr. The *Szene* in **Kreuzberg** clusters around Gneisenaustr. and becomes more intense along Oranienstr, between U-Bahn 1: "Kottbusser Tor" and U-Bahn 1: "Görlitzer Bahnhof."

Despite Kreuzberg's funky appeal, the center of gravity of the *Szene* is shifting inexorably eastward. Low rents and a fascinating new "alternative" population give the east an edge in nurturing new spots that the west can't match. Its cafés and bars have a grittier, more vital feel and attract an exciting mix of people. Some of the more interesting bars abound in the **Scheuenviertel,** especially along Oranienburgerstr. (not to be confused with Kreuzberg's Oranienstr.) near the old synagogue. The **Prenzlauer Berg** area also boasts some interesting places along Schönhauser Allee, Kastanienallee, and especially the area around the Water Tower. Streetlights are sparse on many of the residential streets of the east: avoid empty areas and travel in groups.

Quasimodo, Kantstr. 12a (tel. 312 80 86). S-Bahn 3, 5, 7, or 9: "Savignypl." This unassuming basement pub with attached *Biergarten* is one of Berlin's most crucial jazz venues, drawing in big names and lively crowds. Cover depends on performance, ranging from free to DM30. Concert tickets available from 5pm or at Kant Kasse ticket service (tel. 313 45 54; fax 312 64 40). Open daily from 8pm.

M, Goltzstr. 33. U-Bahn 7: "Eisenacherstr." One of the more interesting Schöneberg bars, stark and neon-lit, and slightly wild late at night. Black is eternally in. "Karlheinz, you are beautiful and angular." Open daily 8am-whenever.

Yaam, Eichenstr. 4. U-Bahn 1: "Schlesisches Tor." Neither club nor bar, but rather *the place* to chill on weekends. African and Caribbean food market Sun. and Berlin's largest pick-up basketball league. Open Fri.-Sun. 2pm-10pm. Cover DM5.

SO 36, Oranienstr. 190 (http://www.SO36.de). U-Bahn 1: "Görlitzer Bahnhof." A mish-mash of wild oeuvres: Sun. is ballroom dancing, Wed. means gay and lesbian disco night, Thurs. keeps heads banging with ska, metal, punk, and hardcore. Fri.-Sat., the crowd gets younger for the slightly raucous parties. Open Sun. after 7pm, Mon. after 11pm, Wed.-Thurs. after 10pm, Fri.-Sat. 11pm-late.

KitKat Club, Glogauerstr. 2 (tel. 611 38 33). People with varying degrees of clothing; leave your inhibitions outside. Jaw-dropping, fluorescent interior. Open Tues.-Sun. after 11pm. Cover DM10. The popular Sunday after-hours party (8am-7pm) is free and more fully clothed. On Thursdays, the **Crisco Club** sees some serious homoerotics (men only!). Not for the faint of heart.

Tresor, Leipzigerstr. 8. U-Bahn 2: "Mohrenstr." or "Potsdamer Platz." One of the most rocking techno venues in Berlin, packed from wall to wall with enthusiastic ravers. Open Wed. and Fri.-Sun. after 11pm. Cover DM5 on Wed., DM12 on weekends. The garden stays open all day Sat. with free entry after 7am.

Tacheles, Oranienburgerstr. 53-56 (tel. 282 61 85). U-Bahn 6: "Oranienburger Tor." Perhaps the greatest source of artistic pretense in all of Berlin. The art commune has decorated the interior with graffiti, collages, and exhibits. Bands, films, raves, and three bars serve up nightly entertainment. Open 24hr.

Franz-Klub, Schönhauser Allee 36-39 (tel. 442 82 03). U-Bahn 2: "Eberswalderstr." The east's most reliable rock venue. Cover varies. Live music every night, including world music acts, local ska bands, blues, and rock. Bands usually start around 10pm, followed by dance and a DJ until late.

Insel der Jugend, Alt Treptow 6. S-Bahn 8,9. or 10: "Treptower Park," then bus 265 or N65: "Alt-Treptow." Located on an island in the middle of the park. Top 2 floors spin reggae, hip-hop, ska, and house; basement has a frantic techno scene. Hipsters chill in the café. Café open daily 2-9pm. Club open after 9pm on Thurs., after 10pm on Fri., after 11pm on Sat. Cover for club DM5-15.

Rose's, Oranienstr. 182, U-Bahn 1 or 8: "Kottbusser Tor." Popular and energetic gay and lesbian bar. Open daily 10pm-6am.

90°, Dennewitzstr. 37. U-Bahn 1: "Kurfürstenstr." Exceptionally popular gay and lesbian techno dance scene for the sartorially splendiferous (dress sleekly!) on Thurs. and Sun. Open Thurs.-Sun. after 11pm.

BRANDENBURG

Surrounding Berlin on all sides, the province of Brandenburg is overshadowed by the sprawling metropolis within it. Many believe that Brandenburg, now an agrarian hinterland, will unite with Berlin in the future, to form a single federal state, Berlin-Brandenburg. Brandenburg's lakes and forests are all easily accessible from Berlin, and provide a soul-saving break from the overloaded circuits of the capital.

Potsdam

Visitors discomfited by Berlin's sprawling urban demeanor could do no better than to catch the S-Bahn to nearby Potsdam, the glittering city of Frederick the Great. The 600-acre **Sanssouci Park** will make you sing the praises of absolutism, with its countless marble fountains, exotic pavilions, and Baroque castles. Inside the largest of the castles, the **Neues Palais,** is the 19th-century *Grottensaal,* a glittering reception room. (Open April-Oct. daily 9am-5pm; Feb.-March 9am-4pm; Nov.-Jan. Wed.-Mon. 9am-3pm. Closed 1st and 3rd Mon. of each month.) At the opposite end of the park stands **Schloß Sanssouci,** which Frederick used to escape his wife and other troubles (open April-Oct. Tues.-Sun. 9am-5pm; Feb.-March 9am-4pm; Nov.-Jan. 9am-3pm). Romantic **Schloß Charlottenhof** melts into its landscaped gardens and grape arbors at the south end. The most bizarre of the park's pavilions is the **Chinesisches Teehaus,** a gold-plated opium dream, complete with a parasol-toting rooftop Buddha. (Compulsory German tours of Sanssouci, Neue Kammern, Schloß Charlottenhof. Neue Kammern DM5, students DM3; other palaces each DM8, students DM4. Pavilions each about DM4, students DM2.) Try to arrive at the park early.

Potsdam's second park, the **Neuer Garten,** contains several former royal residences; the most interesting is the **Schloß Cecilienhof,** where the Potsdam Treaty was signed in 1945. To get there, take tram 96 to "Pl. der Einheit" then take tram 95 to "Alleestr." (open Tues.-Sun. 9am-noon and 12:30-5pm; DM3, students DM2). Take tram 93-95 to "Burgstr." for the **Glienicker Brücke** ("The James Bond Bridge"), which was used until 1989 to exchange spies between the GDR and West Berlin.

The **tourist office,** Friedrich-Ebert-Str. 5 (tel. (0331) 27 55 80, accommodations info 275 58 16), is between the "Alter Markt" and "Pl. der Einheit" streetcar stops. The office provides a city map as well as info on local events and private rooms. Rooms run DM20-40, and the office charges a DM5 booking fee. (Open April-Oct. Mon.-Fri. 9am-8pm, Sat. 10am-6pm, Sun. 10am-4pm; Nov.-March Mon.-Fri. 10am-6pm, Sat.-Sun. 10am-2pm.) The S-Bahn 7 **public transportation** routes run directly from Berlin's Bahnhof Zoo to Potsdam-Stadt, the center of town (just under 30min.). Berlin rapid transit tickets are valid on the S-Bahn and for regular public transportation, but are not valid for the bus lines to the tourist areas; a surcharge of around DM3 is levied.

SAXONY (SACHSEN)

Saxony is known to foreigners primarily for Leipzig and Dresden, but the entire region reveals a great deal about life in the former East. The castles around Dresden attest to the bombastic history of Saxony's prince-electors, while the socialist monuments of Chemnitz depict the colorless world of the GDR. On the eastern edge, Sächsische Schweiz and the Zittauer Gebirge provide a respite from the aesthetic violence of GDR's city planners with hiking trails that march through a land of escapism to the borders of the Czech Republic and Poland.

Dresden

Dresden pulses with an intensity that is both sublime and vicious, an emblem of everything that was and is East Germany. Allied bombings shattered the "Baroque Jewel" in 1945, and the city still houses spectacular ruins. As palaces and churches burst forth from the rubble left uncleared throughout the GDR years, Dresden acts as a focal point for Germany's reunification; a skyline of over 200 cranes steadily assists the reconstruction, scheduled for completion by 2006, the city's 800-year anniversary. While you'll hear tourists everywhere waxing pretentious about "the hope of tomorrow," the raw Dresden of today offers a vitality that goes beyond the process of reincarnation. Rather than a phoenix from ashes, it might well be a phoenix of ashes.

ORIENTATION AND PRACTICAL INFORMATION

The capital of Saxony, Dresden stands magnificently on the Elbe River 80km northwest of the Czech border and 180km south of Berlin. The **Altstadt** lies on the same side of the river as the **Hauptbahnhof** (main train station); the **Neustadt** to the north, having escaped most of the bombing, is now paradoxically one of the oldest parts of the city. Many of Dresden's tourist attractions are located between the *Altmarkt* and the Elbe, a mere five-minute walk from the *Neustadt.* For longer outings, public transportation offers rides for DM1.30 and day passes for DM8.

Tourist Office: Dresden Information, Pragerstr. (tel. 49 19 20; fax 495 12 76). Exit the *Hauptbahnhof* from the Wienerpl. exit, cross the *Straßenbahn* tracks and head toward the main square ahead. Finds rooms in hotels or private rooms (DM35 and up, plus a DM5 fee). Open Mon.-Fri. 9am-8pm, Sat. 9am-4pm, Sun. 10am-2pm.

Currency Exchange: ReiseBank, in the main hall of the train station. DM3 for cash exchange, DM7.50 for traveler's checks. Open Mon.-Fri. 7:30am-7:30pm, Sat. 8am-noon, 12:30-4pm, Sun. 9am-1pm. There are also a number of banks on Pragerstr.

American Express: Hoyerzwalderstr. 20 (tel. 80 70 30), in front of the Frauenkirche. Standard AmEx offerings. Open Mon.-Fri. 7:30am-6pm.

Trains: For info, call 194 19, or use the computerized schedule center in the main hall of the *Hauptbahnhof.* To: Warsaw (10hr.), Paris (10-13hr.), Prague (3hr.), Berlin-Lichtenberg (1½-2½hr.), Budapest (11hr.), Munich (7½-9hr.), Frankfurt am Main (5hr.), and Leipzig (1½hr.). **Bahnhof Dresden Neustadt** sits on the other bank of the Elbe; trains leave from here to Weimar and other eastern cities.

Bike Rental: (tel. 461 32 85) in the *Hauptbahnhof* near the luggage storage. DM10 per day. Open Mon.-Fri. 6am-10pm, Sat. 6am-9pm.

Hitchhiking: Hitchers stand in front of the *"Autobahn"* signs at on-ramps. To Berlin: streetcar 3 or 6 to "Liststr.," then bus 81 to "Olter." To Prague or Frankfurt am Main: bus 72 or 76 to their last stops ("Lockwitz" or "Luga," respectively). **Mitfahrzentrale,** Martin-Luther-Str. 23 (tel. 801 05 48). Prices are DM0.03 per km plus a finder's fee. Berlin DM18. Call one day in advance. Open Mon.-Fri. 10am-6pm.

Gay and Lesbian Organizations: Gerede-Dresdner Lesben, Schwule und alle Anderen, in Haus der Jugend, Wienerstr. 41 (tel. 464 02 20), near the station.

Laundromat: Groove Station, Katharinenstr. 11/13. DM5-6. Open Sun.-Fri. 11am-2am, Sat. 10am-late. **Jugendherberge Rudi Arndt,** in the cellar. DM3-4.

Women's Center: Frauenzentrum "sowieso," Dornblüthstr. 18 (tel. 33 77 09). Phone line (tel. 281 77 88) for confidential crisis counseling. Office open Mon. 10am-noon, Tues. 10am-6pm, Fri. 9am-noon.

Emergencies: Ambulance: tel. 115. **Fire:** tel. 112.

Police: tel. 110.

Internet Access: Spiel-In, Königsbrücke 56 (tel. 804 47 28). 30min. and one drink DM5. Open Mon.-Fri. 6am-11pm, Sat.-Sun. 8am-11pm.

Post Office: Hauptpostamt (tel. 444 10), in Dresden-Neustadt, Königbrückerstr. 21/29, 01099 Dresden. Open Mon.-Fri. 8am-6pm and Sat. 8am-noon.

Telephone Code: 0351.

ACCOMMODATIONS, CAMPING, AND FOOD

Dresden is prepared for a convergence of all the citizens of the world, if need be. A 110-bed **riverboat hostel (HI)** is due to open on the Elbe (DM20-30). Ask the tourist offices or the Hostel Rudi Arndt (below) to find out if its rooms are ready.

Jugendgästehaus Dresden (HI), Maternistr. 22 (tel. 49 26 20; fax 492 62 99). Turn left out of the Pragerstr. exit of the *Hauptbahnhof,* following the streetcar tracks along Annonstr. to Freibergerstr. Turn right then take another quick right. Over 400 beds; singles and family rooms available. Reception open 4-10pm. DM33, over 26 DM38. Nonmembers DM5 extra. Breakfast and sheets included.

Mondpalast Backpacker, Katharinenstr. 11-13 (tel./fax 804 60 61), a 5-minute walk from *Bahnhof-Neustadt,* above DownTown and Groove Station. A brand-new backpacker's paradise. Reception open 24hr. Dorms DM29. Doubles DM35 per person. Sheets included.

Jugendherberge Dresden Rudi Arndt (HI), Hübnerstr. 11 (tel. 471 06 67; fax 472 89 59). From the *Hauptbahnhof,* walk down Fritz-Löffler-Str., bear right onto Münchenerstr., turn right onto Nürnbergerstr. Walk 1 block and turn left. HI members only. Central and laid-back. Crowded rooms for 3-5 don't detract from the convenience. Check-in 3-10pm. Curfew 1am. Lockout 10am-3pm. DM22, over 26 DM27. Mandatory one-time linen fee DM5. Reserve ahead March-Aug.

City-Herberge, Lignerallee 3 (tel. 485 99 00; fax 485 99 01). From the Pragerstr. exit of the *Hauptbahnhof,* right on Wienerstr., left on J.-v.-Goethe-Str., which becomes Blüherstr., then left. Central location. Well-kept if sterile rooms of hotel-caliber. Shared bathrooms. Singles DM70. Doubles DM100. Breakfast included.

Camping: Campingplatz Altfranken, Altfranken (tel. 410 24 00), 7km outside of Dresden. Take streetcar 7 to "Julius-Valdrecht," then bus 70 to the end. Reception open Mon.-Fri. 7am-9pm, Sat.-Sun. 8:30am-4pm. DM10 per tent.

The surge in Dresden tourism has also meant a surge in food prices. The cheapest eats are at **supermarkets** or *Imbiß* stands on Pragerstr. **Raskolnikow,** Böhmischestr. 34, beneath a sign for Galerie Erhard, is a Dostoevskian haunt serving Russian and Afghan fare for DM8-15 (open daily 7pm-2am). **Café Aha,** Kreuzstr. 7, opposite the Kreuzkirche, celebrates things indigenous and detests things meaty (entrees DM6.50-DM14; open Tues.-Sat. 11am-midnight, Sun.-Mon. 11am-10pm). **City Center,** across from the *Hauptbahnhof* on the Bayerischestr. side, houses an **Aldi supermarket** and a cafeteria-style **Fleischerei** (butcher shop) that dishes out huge portions at itsy-bitsy prices (most shops open Mon.-Fri. 8am-8pm, Sat. 8am-4pm).

SIGHTS AND ENTERTAINMENT

From the banks of the Elbe, the **Electors of Saxony** once ruled almost all of central Europe. The extravagant art collection of Emperor Augustus the Strong and the incredible palace he built to house it, the **Zwinger,** once rivaled the Louvre. The northern wing of the palace was designed by Gottfried Semper, whose Opera House, the **Semper-Oper,** reverberates with the same robustness. The interior opens for tours every few weeks (DM8, students DM5; ask at the tourist office for times). Across from the Zwinger lies the nearly restored **Dresdnerschloß** (Dresden Palace), featuring a display on the Renaissance and Baroque eras of the palace and the history of its reconstruction (open Tues.-Sun. 10am-6pm; DM5, students DM3). The nearby **Katholische Hofkirche** (Catholic Cathedral), was built to hide the ruling family's Catholic pageantry from Protestant subjects. From the Cathedral, the 16th-century **Brühlsche Terrasse** offers a prime photo opportunity of the Elbe. Turn right at the end to reach the **Albertinum,** another fabulous museum complex. The **Gemäldegalerie der Neuen Meister** has one of the world's premier collections of painting from 1500 to 1800 (open Fri.-Wed. 10am-6pm; DM7, students DM3.50). From the Albertinum, a walk to the *Neumarkt* leads to the shell of the **Frauenkirche,** once Germany's most splendid Protestant church.

A cobblestone, tree-lined pedestrian avenue of shops and restaurants, **Hauptstraße** (Main Street) stretches from the magnificent **Augustus Brücke** over the Elbe past the **Goldener Reiter,** a gold-plated vision of Frederick August II (a.k.a. Augustus the Strong). At the other end of Hauptstr., **Albertplatz** (formerly Pl. der Einheit) is surrounded by handsome 19th-century mansions.

Dresden's sprawling nightlife provides ample entertainment. Much of the hustle and bustle takes place around Albertpl. in the *Neustadt,* with the big time bar and hard-core scene on Alaunstr. The local magazine *Blitz* (free at the tourist office) runs down the city's cultural calendar, but *SAX* (DM2.50) is more complete. At **Scheune,** Alaunstr. 36-40 (tel. 802 66 19), you can eat Indian food in the garden or candlelit pool hall, then disco to Baltic or Yiddish music (club opens at 8pm; call for a schedule of events). **DownTown and Groove Station,** Katharinenstr. 11-13, is the place to shake your booty and indulge in Dresden's neon techno scene with straight, gay, and lesbian co-revelers (cover up to DM5; open Thurs.-Mon. 9pm-5am). **Studentenklub Bärenzwinger,** Brühlscher Garten 1, features cheap drinks and varied disco action (open Tues.-Thurs. and Sun. 8pm-midnight, Fri.-Sat. 9pm-3am).

Leipzig

Leipzig gained fame for its role as the crucible of *die Wende,* the sudden toppling of the GDR in 1989. The city currently jumps out from the calm Eastern German landscape in a fiery blaze of nowNowNOW. The glitzy nightlife and glassy skyscrapers set amidst concrete blights cast a decidedly Western flavor, while the *Uni*-culture spawned by over 20,000 students harkens back to the days when Goethe, Nietzsche, and Leibniz stalked these ivory (well...gray) towers.

ORIENTATION AND PRACTICAL INFORMATION

Most of sights dwell in the ringed *Innenstadt.* It's a 10-minute walk from the main train station on the north edge of the *Innenstadt* to the **Augustus Platz,** the center surrounded by the *Gewandhaus,* the university, and the main post office.

Tourist Office: Leipzig Information, Richard-Wagner-Str. 1, across Willy-Brandt-Pl. from the station (tel. 710 42 60; fax 710 42 76). Brochures, a free map, and accommodations service (Mon.-Sat. only). *Kreuzer* (DM2.50) is the best guide to nightlife. Open Mon.-Fri. 9am-7pm, Sat.-Sun. 9:30am-2pm.

Currency Exchange: Dresdner Bank, on Goethestr. between the station and Augustuspl. Open Mon.-Thurs. 8:30am-7:30pm, Fri. 8:30am-4pm. Several **ATMs.**

American Express: Dorotheenpl. 224 (tel. 96 70 00). On the far side of the central city from the station. Head down Schillerstr. from Dittrichring about a block; it's on the left. All AmEx services. Open Mon.-Fri. 9:30am-6pm, Sat. 9am-noon.

Trains: tel. 194 19. Leipzig lies on the Berlin-Munich line with regular IC service to Frankfurt am Main. Information counter on the platform near track 15.

Public Transportation: Streetcars and **buses** cover the city; the hub is on Pl. der Republik, in front of the train station. Tickets are DM2 for 1hr. (with line changes); day pass DM7. Streetcars and S-Bahn run daily approximately 5:30am-3am.

Pharmacies: Löwen Apotheke, Grimmaischestr. 19 (tel. 960 50 27). Open Mon.-Fri. 8am-8pm, Sat. 9am-4pm. After hours, push the button for emergency service.

Emergencies: Ambulance: tel. 115. **Fire:** tel. 112.

Police: tel. 110.

Post Office: Hauptpostamt 1, across from Augustuspl. on Grimmaischestr. Open Mon.-Fri. 8am-8pm, Sat. 9am-4pm. **Postal Code:** 04109.

Telephone Code: 0341.

ACCOMMODATIONS AND FOOD

Leipzig does not have many rooms for budget travelers; be sure to book ahead, especially during the summer. Private rooms are reasonable at around DM35 a person, but the tourist office charges a DM10 booking fee per night. The **Jugendherberge Leipzig Centrum (HI),** at Käthe-Kollwitz-Str. 64 in 1997 (tel. 47 05 30; fax 47 58 88), is scheduled to move to Volksgarten 24 (cell phone (0172) 910 41 66, check with tourist office) in January 1998 (new prices DM24, over 26 DM29).

The **Jugendherberge Grethen (HI),** in Grethen (tel. (03437) 76 34 49), is 30 minutes away by train ("Groß Steinberg") to "Grethen." Call to be picked up (DM20, over 26 DM26.50). **Am Auensee,** Gustav-Esche-Str. 5 (tel. 461 19 00), can be reached from the train station by taking streetcar 10, 28, or 30 ("Wahren") to "Rathaus Wahren." Turn left at the city hall and then make a right at the end of the street. (Camping DM6-10 per tent. Small 2-bed bungalows DM50-55. Two person huts with bath DM90.) You can also camp at **Campingplatz am Kulkwitzer See,** Seestr. in Markrandstadt (tel. 941 13 15); take streetcar 8 ("Lausen") to the last stop and bear right (reception open daily 7am-5pm; open April 15-Oct. 15).

The **Innenstadt** is well supplied with *Imbiß* (snack joints), bistros, and restaurants, although an ever-increasing number are not exactly of the budget variety. The Brühl, running in front of Sachsenpl., offers a lifesaver in the form of **Kaiser's Supermarket.** Sachsenpl. also offers a **market** on Tuesdays and Fridays. **Maître,** Karl-Liebknecht-Str. 62, treads the fine line between bar, café, and restaurant. (Sun. breakfast buffet Sun. 10am-3pm. DM11.80. Generous slices of quiche and onion tart DM4. Open Mon.-Fri. 9am-1am, Sat. 2pm-1am, Sun. 10am-midnight.)

SIGHTS AND ENTERTAINMENT

The heart of the city beats in the **Marktplatz,** a colorful square guarded by the 16th-century **Altes Rathaus.** Inside the *Rathaus,* the **Stadtgeschichtliches Museum Leipzig** offers entrancing temporary exhibits and a straightforward look at Leipzig's history (open Tues.-Fri. 10am-6pm, Sat.-Sun. 10am-4pm; DM4, students DM2). Behind the *Altes Rathaus,* on Nikolaistr., the 800-year-old **Nikolaikirche** witnessed the birth of Bach's *Johannes Passion* as well as the GDR's peaceful revolution (open Mon.-Sat. 10am-6pm, Sun. after services; free). Continuing away from the *Marktplatz,* take Universitätsstr. to the former Karl Marx University, now rechristened **Universität Leipzig.** The **Museum der Bildenden Künste** (Museum of Fine Arts), Georg-Dimitroff-Pl. 1, chronicles German art from the 18th century to the present (open Tues. and Thurs.-Sun. 9am-5pm, Wed. 1-9:30pm; DM5, students DM2.50).

Just north of the *Neues Rathaus* and close to the *Marktplatz* is the **Thomaskirche,** where Bach served as cantor. Mozart and Mendelssohn also performed in this church, and Wagner was baptized here in 1813. (Open in summer daily 8am-6pm; off-season 9am-5pm; services Sun. 9:30am and 6pm.) Across the street, the **Johann-Sebastian-Bach-Museum,** Thomaskirchhof 16, chronicles Bach's activities in Leipzig from 1723-1750 (open daily 10am-5pm; last admission 4:30pm; DM4, students DM2.50). North of the Thomaskirche lies Leipzig's most fascinating museum, the **Museum der "Runden Ecke,"** Dittrichring 24. Once the headquarters of the feared East German Ministry for State Security or *Stasi,* the building is now home to an exhibit on the *Stasi*'s activities and overthrow (open Wed.-Sun. 2-6pm; free).

The tourist office has info on **Bach festivals** in July and August and performances by the famous **Gewandhaus Orchestra** and Leipzig's **Opera** (tel. 126 10; tickets DM8-50; student discounts available). **Moritzbastei,** Universitätsstr. 9 (tel. 960 51 91 or 960 51 92), right next to the university tower, is one of the more fascinating sights in Leipzig. A place of execution in the 16th century, it now houses the largest student club in Europe, with underground bars and dance floors, a café, and open-air movie theater. Things kick off after 9pm (cover DM4-10, discount with student ID). **Barfußgäschen,** a street just off the *Markt,* is the "see and be seen" bar venue in town. **Markt Neun** and **Spizz** fill up by 10pm and remain packed into the wee hours. **Karl-Liebknecht-Straße** is as *Szene*-ic without being quite so claustrophobic as Barfußgäschen. Streetcar 10 or 11 to "Arndtstr." At night, bars along the street pour drinks for Irish lovers (**Killiwilly** at #44), Francophiles (**Maître** at #62), tough art-house film types (**nato** at #46), caffeine addicts (**KAHWE** at the corner of Arndtstr. and Karl-Liebknecht-Str.), and everyone else (**Weisses Rössel,** next door).

THURINGIA (THÜRINGEN)

Affectionately dubbed the "Green Heart of Germany," Thuringia is certainly the most beautiful of the new Federal States. Echoes of Thuringia are heard throughout Europe's cultural canon: Bach, Goethe, Schiller, Luther, and Wagner all left their mark on this landscape. Relatively unexplored by foreign tourists, Thuringia is the perfect destination for an authentic German experience—are you experienced?

Weimar

Chosen as Europe's Cultural Capital of 1999, Weimar is cocooning itself in plastic and scaffolding to emerge renewed for the impending hoopla. But the new facades can't hide the importance of Weimar's old historical foundations. A city of daring cultural achievement and spectacular political failure, Weimar epitomizes the contradictions of German history. Home to a strong humanist tradition and birthplace of the remarkably liberal Constitution of 1919, Weimar also became the site of Buchenwald. Modern Weimar looks backwards for answers and inspiration, towards the intellectual ghosts who dominate the setting.

One hundred and fifty years after their deaths, Goethe and Schiller still loom large. The **Goethehaus,** on Frauenplan 1, has flawless original manuscripts and letters (open Tues.-Sun. 9am-5pm; DM8, students DM5). Between the Frauenplan and the **Marktplatz** is the beginning of **Schillerstraße,** a vivacious shop-lined pedestrian zone. Nearby, the **Schillerhaus,** at Schillerstr. 12, displays original drafts and early editions of plays (open March-Oct. Wed.-Mon. 9am-5pm; Nov.-Feb. 9am-4pm; DM5, students DM3). One block away on Hummelstr., Schiller and Goethe are memorialized in bronze before the **Deutsches Nationaltheater,** which first breathed life into their stage works and where the Weimar Constitution emerged in 1919 (tickets DM9-44; 50% student discounts). Directly across from the theater is the slick new **Bauhaus-Museum** featuring works produced by the Bauhaus School of Design and Architecture (open Tues.-Sun. 10am-6pm; DM5, DM3).

Steps away from the **Bauhaus Universität** on Marienstr. (connected to the Bauhaus of the 1920s in name only) is the **Franz Liszt Haus,** where the composer spent his last years (open Tues.-Sun. 9am-1pm and 2-5pm; DM4, students DM3). The **Nietzsche-Archiv,** Humboldtstr. 36, was founded by Nietzsche's sister Elisabeth, who helped the Nazis distort her brother's philosophy. (Open March-Oct. daily 9am-1pm and 2-5pm; Nov.-Feb daily 9am-1pm and 2-4pm. DM4, students DM3.) **Park an der Ilm** on the river, landscaped by Goethe, sports 18th-century pavilions. Of particular note are the fake ruins built by the Weimar shooting club and the eerie Soviet war memorial. Perched on the far slopes is Goethe's **Gartenhaus,** Corona-Schöfer-Str., the poet's first home in Weimar and his retreat from the city. (Open March-Oct. Tues.-Sun. 9am-noon and 1-5pm; Nov.-Feb. 9am-noon and 1-4pm. DM4, students DM3.) South of the town center, Goethe and Schiller lie in rest together at the **Historischer Friedhof** cemetery (open March-Sept. 8am-9pm; Oct.-Feb. 8am-6pm).

Practical Information, Accommodations, and Food Weimar is on the Dresden-Frankfurt and Berlin-Frankfurt rail lines; call (03643) 33 30 for schedules and prices. **Weimar Information,** Marktstr. 10 (tel. (03643) 240 00 or 656 90; fax 24 00 40), within view of the *Rathaus,* offers maps and books rooms for DM5. (Open March-Oct. Mon.-Fri. 9am-6pm, Sat. 9am-4pm, Sun. 10am-4pm; Nov.-Feb. Mon.-Fri. 9am-6pm, Sat. 9am-1pm.) Finding a cheap place to stay in town is not difficult. **Jugendhotel Hababusch,** Geleitstr. 4 (tel. 85 07 37; email yh@larry.scc.uniweimar.de), smack in the middle of the sights and run by a bunch of architecture students, is the best-located and coolest place to stay. From Goethepl., turn left on Geleitstr. and follow its rightward twist to the clearing with the statue on the left (reception open 24hr.; DM15). **Jugendherberge Germania (HI),** Carl-August-Allee 13 (tel. 85 04 90; fax 85 04 91) offers newly renovated facilities. Arriving at the train station, head straight down the hill for two minutes; it's on your right (reception open 24hr.; DM22, over 26 DM26, breakfast included; sheets DM7).

Weimar is best at cooking for the wealthy; the light of pocket should try the daily **produce market** in the Marktplatz or the **Rewe grocery store** at the corner of Frauenplan and Wielandpl. (open Mon.-Fri. 7am-8pm, Sat. 7am-4pm). **C-Keller-Galerie,** Markt 21, has tasty and cheap vegetarian dishes (open Tues.-Sun. noon-11pm), while **Da Toni Ristorante Pizzeria,** Windsichenstr. 12 (tel. 50 27 19), serves delicious, no-foolin' Italian food close to Schiller's house—so Italian they hardly understand German (pizzas from DM5.50; open daily 10am-1am).

■ Near Weimar: Buchenwald

It is especially tragic that a city which reached such heights in humanistic and artistic expression also witnessed one of the greatest failures of human reason and conscience. From 1937 to 1945, the concentration camp at Buchenwald, overlooking Weimar, held over 250,000 Jews, political prisoners, gypsies, and gays. Most did not survive the Holocaust. What remains is the **Nationale Mahn-und Gedenkstätte Buchenwald** (National Buchenwald Memorial). At the memorial, signs point to two destinations: the **KZ Lager** and the **Gedenkstätte.** The former refers to the camp, while the latter is a monument overlooking a valley, 20 minutes away. The camp is now a vast, flat, gravel plain. In the large storehouse building, a **museum** documents the history of Buchenwald and Nazism. **Memorial stones** near the former children's barracks read in English, German, and Hebrew: "So that the generation to come might know; that the children, yet to be born, may rise and declare to their children." (Camp open May-Sept. Tues.-Sun. 9:45am-5:15pm; Oct.-April Tues.-Sun. 8:45am-4:15pm.) To reach the camp, take bus 6 from the station or downtown Weimar (the bus schedule puts a "B" (Buchenwald) *not* "EB" after departure times).

Erfurt

The capital of Thuringia, Erfurt surprises its guests with an exquisitely renovated and quirky *Altstadt,* many cosmopolitan cafés, and an abundance of verdant parks. A lot of money has been funneled into Erfurt recently, allowing the cultural offerings to flourish and creating a strikingly picturesque look all too rare in the cities of the east. Dominating the view from the Marktplatz atop its perch on Domhügel Hill, the mammoth Erfurt **Dom** is one of Germany's most impressive cathedrals. Martin Luther was invested as a priest here and interrupted his first mass by hurling his Bible across the altar. He claimed the target was the devil himself, impressing his audience if not the Bishop. The *Dom* is further enriched by the adjacent **Church of St. Severi.** (Both open May-Oct. Mon.-Fri. 9-11:30am and 12:30-5pm, Sat. 9-11:30am and 12:30-4:30pm, Sun. 2-4pm; Nov.-April Mon.-Sat. 10-11:30am, Sun. 2-4pm. Mass Sun. 11am and 6pm.) From the *Domplatz,* Marktstr. leads down to the breezy, open **Fischmarkt,** bordered by restored guild houses sporting wildly decorated facades. Overlooking the space is the brazenly neo-Gothic **Rathaus,** whose bonanza of paintings depicting mythical sequences is open for public gawking (open Mon. and Wed.-Thurs. 9am-4pm, Tues. 9am-6pm, Fri. 9am-2pm; free). Farther down Markstr., the Gera River is spanned by the **Krämerbrücke,** a medieval bridge covered by small shops some of which date from the 12th century. From the far side of the bridge, follow Gotthardtstr. and cut left through Kirchengasse to reach the **Augustinerkloster,** where Martin Luther spent 10 years as a Catholic priest and Augustine monk. He ultimately had the last laugh—the cloister now functions as a Protestant college (ask for times of tours; DM4.50, students DM3).

From Erfurt's *Hauptbahnhof,* **trains** shoot off to Leipzig (3hr.), Würzburg (2½hr.), Frankfurt (2½hr.), and Dresden. The **tourist office,** Schlösserstr. 37 (tel. (0361) 562 62 67; fax 562 33 55), next to the *Rathaus* (follow signs from the station), offers maps and books rooms (singles DM30-50) for a DM5 fee (open Mon.-Fri. 10am-6pm, Sat. 10am-1pm). The best bet for budget beds is the **Jugendherberge Karl Reiman (HI),** Hochheimerstr. 12 (tel. (0361) 562 67 05), an old mansion a fair distance from the city center. From the station, take streetcar 5 ("Steigerstr.") to the last stop, then backtrack a little, and turn left onto Hochheimserstr. (reception open daily 6-9am and 3-10pm; curfew midnight; DM24, over 26 DM28). In a pinch, Weimar's hostels are a 15-minute train ride away. Sample the succulent regional specialty *Thüringer Bratwurst* at markets, street corners, and train stations throughout the city (DM2-3). **Internet Café,** across from the *Hauptbahnhof* at Willi-Brandt-Pl. 1, has pricey but super-fast access (DM12 for 1hr.; open Mon.-Fri. 7am-7pm, Sat.-Sun. 10am-6pm).

Eisenach

Birthplace of Johann Sebastian Bach and home-in-exile to Martin Luther, Eisenach boasts impressive humanist credentials. High above Eisenach's half-timbered houses, the **Wartburg Fortress** sheltered the excommunicated Luther in 1521 while he worked on his German translation of the Bible. Check out the amazing view of the Thuringian Forest from the walls of the courtyard. A plethora of city-sponsored **tourist buses** runs from the city center up the enormous hill to the castle (round-trip DM2.50); for the more adventurous, there are several well-cleared **footpaths** leading up the steep incline. From the train station, a stroll down **Wartburger Allee** leads to the foot of the hill. (Castle open March-Oct. daily 8:30am-5pm; Nov.-Feb. 9am-3:30pm. DM11, students DM6, seniors and disabled DM8.)

Back at the base of the mountain, the **Bachhaus,** Frauenplan 21, where Johann Sebastian stormed into the world in 1685, recreates the family's living quarters with period instruments. Turn off Wartburger Allee down Grimmelgasse to reach the house. (Open April-Sept. Mon. noon-5:45pm, Tues.-Sun. 9am-5:45pm; Oct.-March Mon. 1-4:45pm, Tues.-Sun. 9am-4:45pm. DM5, students and seniors DM4.) Town life centers on the pastel **Markt,** bounded by the **Rathaus** and the latticed **Lutherhaus,** Lutherpl. 8, where young Martin lived from 1498 to 1501. (Open May-Sept. daily 9am-5pm; Oct.-April Mon.-Sat. 9am-5pm, Sun. 2-5pm. DM5, students DM2.)

Eisenach's **tourist office,** Bahnhofstr. 3-5 (tel. (03691) 67 02 60 or 67 02 61), a short walk from the train station, has plenty of info on the castle and books rooms (DM30-40) in private homes (open Mon. 10am-6pm, Tues.-Fri. 9am-6pm, Sat. 10am-2pm). Frequent **train** connections link Eisenach to Erfurt (1hr.) and Weimar (1¼hr.). If you arrive by train, Eisenach's *Bahnhof* provides many services for travelers, including luggage storage, an ATM, a grocery store open until 8pm, and a bakery. **Jugendherberge Artur Becker (HI),** Mariental 24 (tel. (03691) 74 32 59), fills a comfortable villa near the castle. From the station, take Bahnhofstr. to Wartburger Allee, which runs into Mariental, or grab bus 3 ("Mariental") to "Lilienstr." (reception open daily 7am-11pm; DM22, over 26 DM26; breakfast included). The nearest **camping** is at **Am Altenberger See** (tel./fax (03691) 21 56 37) about 10km away; from the Eisenach station, take a bus toward Bad Liebenstein and tell the driver your destination (reception open until 10pm; DM6 per person, DM5 per tent).

Thuringian Forest

Stretching south of Eisenach, Erfurt, and Weimar to the border with Bavaria, the time-worn mountains and peaceful pine woods of the Thuringian Forest fostered and inspired many of Germany's composers, philosophers, and poets: Bach, Goethe, Schiller, and Wagner each left their mark on the landscape. The **Rennsteig,** a 168km scenic hiking trail, snakes from Hörschel near Eisenach right into Bavaria.

Arnstadt Founded in 704, the stately **Arnstadt** is the oldest town in Thuringia and lies at the fringe of the forest just beyond Erfurt. In what is now the **Bachkirche,** J.S. Bach began his career as an organist (open March-Sept. Tues.-Sat. 10am-noon and 2-4pm, Sun. 2-4pm). Nearby, the **Liebfrauenkirche** makes up for a less glamorous past with its 14th-century stained glass windows. (Open March-Sept. Tues.-Sat. 10:30am-12:30pm and 2-4pm, Sun. 2-4pm; call the tourist office for off-season hours.) The **Neues Palais** (New Palace), Schloßpl. 1, houses the fascinating **Mon Plaisir,** a museum where more than 400 dolls and 24 dollhouses offer a miniature panorama of the mid-18th century. (Open May-Oct. Tues.-Sun. 8:30am-noon and 1-4:30pm; Nov.-April Tues.-Sun. 9:30am-4pm. DM3.50, students and seniors DM2.50.) Arnstadt is best reached by **train** from Erfurt or Ilmenau (20-40min.). The **tourist office,** Markt 3 (tel. (03628) 60 20 49), finds rooms (DM25-40) for DM3 and has info on hiking trails and bus connections to the **Drei Gleichen** (three castles). To reach the office, turn left from the station, then right on Bahnhofstr., and bear right across Ledermarkt (open Mon.-Fri. 10am–6pm, Sat. 9am-noon).

Ilmenau and the Goethe Trail Johann Wolfgang Goethe, by far Thuringia's favorite son, first worked in **Ilmenau** reorganizing the area mining industry as a government bureaucrat, only to return later in life as a soul-searching poet. South of the city center, parallel to Waldstr., the 18.5km **Goethe Trail** *(Goethewanderweg)* is marked by Goethe's over-flourished "G" monogram. About 4km into the hike, in the hut on the **Kickelhahn,** you can read the poetry he scratched on the walls as a young man. A year before his death at age 83, Goethe himself returned to the hut on a tour of his past. The trail ends in **Stützerbach,** where the local glass-works magnate hosted the poet. The house is now a **Goethe Memorial,** with demonstrations of traditional **glass-blowing.** (Open May-Oct. Tues.-Sun. 9am-noon and 1-5pm; Nov.-April Wed.-Sun. 9am-noon and 1-4pm. DM3, students DM2.) Ilmenau also makes a good starting point for a hike along the **Rennsteig** (take the train to Schmiedefeld).

Ilmenau's **tourist office,** Lindenstr. 12 (tel. (03677) 20 23 58; fax 20 25 02), provides maps and hiking brochures and books private rooms (from DM20) for a DM2 fee per person. From the *Hauptbahnhof,* walk on Bahnhofstr. to Wetzlarerpl. and follow the pedestrian zone until it becomes Lindenstr.; from the Ilmenau-Bad station, turn left on Waldstr. across the river and continue straight on Lindenstr. (open Mon.-Fri. 9am-6pm, Sat. 9am-noon). The brand new **Jugendherberge,** Am Stollen 49 (tel. (03677) 88 46 81; fax 88 46 82), offers a shower and a bathroom for each spacious four-bed room. Leaving the *Hauptbahnhof* to the left, take another left at the dead end, cross the tracks and follow the path to the right. After the sharp curve, cross the bridge on your left (10min.; DM20, over 26 DM24; breakfast included).

SAXONY-ANHALT (SACHSEN-ANHALT)

Saxony-Anhalt's endless, mesmerizing grass plains offer one of the more tranquil landscapes in Eastern Germany. Once serving as the stronghold of the Holy Roman Empire, the region today suffers from high unemployment rates and pollution. Yet the area is cleaning up its act. The grand cathedrals filling the skyline attest to the region's former importance, and, with the help of Western tourist dollars, the many construction sites mushrooming across the *Land* point toward the future.

Wittenberg and Dessau

The Protestant Reformation, which initiated centuries of religious conflict, began quietly in Wittenberg on October 13, 1517, when local professor and priest Martin Luther nailed his 95 theses to the wooden door of the Schloßkirche (castle church). All the major attractions are accessible from **Collegienstr.** At #54 lies Luther's home, **Lutherhaus,** where he lived from 1508. The museum inside features an original Gutenberg Bible and follows the course of the Reformation from Luther's first misgivings about papal indulgences to his fiery refusal to recant before the Pope. (Open April-Oct. Tues.-Sun. 9am-6pm; Oct.-April Tues.-Sun. 10am-5pm. DM6, students DM3.) Turning right on leaving Lutherhaus brings you to the sickly **elm tree** by Lutherstr. under which Luther defiantly burned a papal decree of excommunication. **Stadt-Kirche-St. Marienkirche** (St. Mary's Church), known for its dazzling altar, awaits at the end of Mittelstr. near Collegienstr., at the Marktplatz (open Mon.-Sat. 9am-noon and 2-5pm, Sun. 11am-noon and 2-5pm). Near the church towers the **Rathaus** (city hall), with its imposing facade and 16th-century portal frame. Matching statues of Luther and philosopher-humanist Melanchthon share the square with the 16th-century **Jungfernröhrwasser** (fountain of virginity), whose original wooden pipes still course with potable water. Farther down Collegienstr., the **Schloßkirche** holds a copy of Luther's theses. (Open May-Oct. Mon. 2-5pm, Tues.-Sat. 10am–5pm, Sun. 11:30am-5pm; Nov.-April Mon. 2-4pm, Tues.-Sat.10am-4pm, Sun. 11am-4pm.)

Wittenberg, a mere hour and a half by **train** from Berlin, Halle, and Leipzig, is an excellent daytrip. Instead of disembarking at the *Hauptbahnhof,* get off at the more central *"Haltepunkt Lutherstadt Wittenberg-Elbtor."* Walk straight down Elbstr., to the second intersection. To the right lies Collegienstr. Turn left here instead onto Schloßstr., and walk five minutes to the *Schloß.* Directly across the street, the new **Wittenberg Information,** Schloßpl. 2 (tel. (03491) 49 86 10; fax 49 86 11), caters to all your info, map, and room (for a DM3 fee) needs (open Mon.-Fri. 9am-6pm, Sat. 10am-2pm, Sun. 11am-3pm). Expect to pay DM25-75 for a **private room** with breakfast. The **Jugendherberge (HI)** (tel./fax (03491) 40 32 55) is located in the castle. Newly renovated but often filled with schoolkids, the hostel features some two- to four-bed rooms and many spacious 10- to 18-bed rooms. (Reception open daily 7am-

10pm. DM20, over 26 DM25. Breakfast included. Sheets DM6.) Cheap yet delectable food is found along the Collegienstr.-Schloßstr. strip.

Some 30km west of Wittenberg, **Dessau** is worth a daytrip for those interested in the *Bauhaus* school or native son musician Kurt Weill. Although concrete Communist blocks predominate, a number of buildings reflect the *Bauhaus* aesthetic. The school began in Weimar in 1919 but moved to Dessau from 1925 to 1932, before its exile by the Nazis. American skyscrapers were the highpoint of *Bauhaus,* whose teachers were intrigued by the possibilities of glass and steel. Contact the **tourist office,** Zerbsterstr. 2c (tel. (0340) 204 14 12), for more info. Every year the **Kurt Weill Festival** alienates a new generation of fans (Feb. 28-March 3 in 1998; tel. (0810) 321 35 35; fax (0340) 250 54 10).

SCHLESWIG-HOLSTEIN

Between Schleswig-Holstein's twin coastlines lies a flat, green countryside populated primarily by cows. Scenic cycling paths wind from the North Sea beaches, across the cobblestone hills of Lübeck, and on to the vivaciously gritty port of Kiel. Schleswig-Hostein became a Prussian province in 1867 as step one of Bismarck's unification plan, and chose, after World War I, to remain part of Germany, but the state retains close cultural and commercial ties with Scandinavia, and the major ports send ferries to Danish, Swedish, and Norwegian docks.

Hamburg

With a fiercely activist population and a licentious, reckless sex industry, modern Hamburg is a crazy coupling of the progressive and the perverse. A proud tradition of autonomy dates back to 1618, when Hamburg gained the status of Free Imperial City, and even today the city is a politically autonomous *Land.* Restoration and riots determined the post-World War II landscape, but recently Hamburg, the largest port town in Germany, has become a harbor for lonesome sailors, contemporary artists, and revelling party-goers who absorb Germany's self-declared "capital of lust."

ORIENTATION AND PRACTICAL INFORMATION

Hamburg's harbor is 100km inland on the north bank of the **Elbe River,** but most major sights lie between the **St. Pauli Landungsbrücken** ferry terminal in the west and the *Hauptbahnhof* (main train station) in the east.

Tourist Offices: Hamburg's 2 tourist offices supply free maps and pamphlets. The **Hauptbahnhof office,** Kirchenallee exit (tel. 30 05 12 01; fax 30 05 13 33), books rooms for a fee of DM5 (open daily 7am-11pm). Information is also available at the **St. Pauli Landungsbrücken office** (tel. 30 05 12 00), between piers 4 and 5 (open April-Oct. 10am-7pm; Nov.-March 9:30am-5:30pm).

Consulates: Ireland: Feldbrunnenstr. 43 (tel. 44 18 62 13). U-Bahn: "Hallerstr." Open 9am-noon. **New Zealand:** Heimhuderstr. (tel. 442 55 50). **U.K.:** Harvestehuder 8a (tel./fax 448 03 20), near the "Hallestr." U-Bahn station. Open 9am-noon and 2-4pm. **U.S.:** Alsterufer 27 (tel. 41 17 13 51), on the west side of the Außenalster. Open Mon.-Fri. 9am-noon.

Currency Exchange: Although the train station bank is convenient and has long hours, better rates are available at downtown banks. Most banks are open Mon.-Wed. and Fri. 9am-1pm and 2:30-4pm, Thurs. 9am-1pm and 2:30-6pm.

American Express: Ballindamm 39, 20095 Hamburg (tel. 30 90 80; refund service (0130) 85 31 00; fax 30 90 81 30). Mail held for cardmembers (no charge). All banking services. Open Mon.-Fri. 9am-5:30pm, Sat. 10am-1pm.

Flights: For info, call 507 50. **Lufthansa** (tel. (01803) 80 38 03) and **Air France** (tel. 50 75 24 59) are the two heavy-hitters that fly to Hamburg. Buses zoom to **Fuhlsbüttel Airport** from the Kirchenallee exit of the *Hauptbahnhof* (every 20min.

5:00am-9:20pm, 30min.). Or take the U-Bahn to "Ohlsdorf" and catch the bus to the airport. In the other direction, buses leave the airport from Terminal 4 for the *Hauptbahnhof* (every 20min. 6:30am-11pm).

Trains: For train info, call 194 19. The **Hauptbahnhof** handles most traffic, with connections to: Berlin (3½hr.), Bremen (1hr.), Munich (5½hr.), Copenhagen (6hr.), and Zurich (9½hr.). **Dammtor** station is across the Kennedy/Lombards bridge; **Altona,** the end station for most intercity trains, is in the west.

Buses: The **bus station** is around the corner of the *Hauptbahnhof* on Adenauerallee; buses go to Berlin (3½hr., one way DM39, round-trip DM62) and beyond.

Public Transportation: Buses, the U-Bahn, and the S-Bahn cost DM2.50-15, depending on distance. All public transit shuts down from midnight to 4:30am. While regular **day tickets,** *Ganztageskarte* (DM9.20-13.90; 3-day tickets DM22.30), for the U-Bahn and the S-Bahn are available, the **Hamburg Card** (DM12.50, 3-day DM24.50) is a better deal with free travel on all public transportation and a discount of up to 50% at museums and tours. The **9-Uhr-Tageskarte** (9hr. ticket), costs DM7.70-12.40. A **family day ticket** (DM13.20-17.70) is good for up to 4 adults and 3 children under 12. All cards available at tourist offices; day tickets can also be bought at orange *Automaten* (automated machines).

Ferries: Scandinavian Seaways, Van-der-Smissenstr. 4 (tel. 38 90 30; fax 38 90 31 41), about 1km west of the *Fischmarkt* (U-Bahn: "Königstr."), runs ferries every other day to England and elsewhere. Tickets begin at DM183; students DM147.

Bike Rental: O'Niel Bikes, Beethovenstr. 37 (tel. 531 177 44), offers German-language bike tours of the city and environs (DM49 for 3hr., DM129 per day). They also rent bikes (DM19 per day).

Hitchhiking: Those headed to Berlin, Lübeck, or Copenhagen take U-Bahn 3 to "Rauhes Haus," then walk up Hammerstr. to Hamburg Horn. Hitchers aiming for points south take S-Bahn to "Wilhelmsburg" and wait at Raststatte Stillhorn.. Instead of hitchhiking, try **City Netz Mitfahrzentrale,** Gotenstr. 19 (tel. 194 44), U-Bahn 3: "Berliner Tor." DM0.10 per km. Open daily 9am-7pm.

Lesbian and Gay Services: Magnus Hirschfeld Centrum, Borgweg 8 (tel. 279 00 69). U-Bahn 3 or bus 108 to "Borgweg." Daily films and counseling sessions. Café open daily 5pm-midnight; women only Wed.-Thurs. 3-7pm. Center open Mon.-Fri. 9:30am-1pm. **Hein und Fiete Gay & Lesbian Information Center** (tel. 24 03 33), Kleiner Pulverteich 17-21, open Mon-Fri. 4-9pm, Sat. 4-7pm.

Laundromat: Schnell und Sauber, Grindelallee 158. S-Bahn 21 or 31: "Dammtor." Wash DM6; dry DM1 per 15min. Open daily 6am-11pm.

Rape Crisis Line: tel. 25 55 66. Phones staffed Mon. and Thurs. 9:30am-1pm and 3-7pm, Tues.-Wed. 9:30am-1pm and 3-4pm, Fri. 9:30am-1pm.

Emergencies: Ambulance: tel. 112.

Police: Kirchenallee 46, opposite the train station (tel. 110).

Internet Access: In the **Regionales Rechenzentrum der Universität Hamburg,** Schlüterstr. 70 (tel. 412 31).

Post Office: At the Kirchenallee exit of the train station. Open Mon.-Fri. 8am-8pm, Sat. 8am-6pm, Sun. 10am-4pm. *Poste Restante,* Gr. Burstah 3, 20097 Hamburg, at main branch. Open Mon.-Fri. 8am-6pm, Sat. 8am-noon.

Telephones: Make international calls (with German phone card) at the post office in the train station. Phone cards are available in denominations of DM12 or DM50. **Telephone Code:** 040.

ACCOMMODATIONS AND CAMPING

It is expensive to stay in Hamburg: single rooms start at around DM60, doubles at DM75. A slew of small, relatively cheap *Pensionen* line **Steindamm, Bremer Weg,** and **Bremer Reihe** to the north of the *Hauptbahnhof.* Check out your hotel before you accept a room, or let the tourist office's *Hotelführer* (DM1) help steer you clear. For longer stays, try the **Mitwohnzentrale** at Lobuschstr. 22 (tel. 194 45).

Jugendherberge auf dem Stintfang (HI), Alfred-Wegener-Weg 5 (tel. 31 34 88; fax 31 54 07). Take S-Bahn 1, 2, or 3, or U-Bahn 3 from the main station to "Landungsbrücke"; hike up the steps to the hill above. Harbor view and Fantasy Island chess-

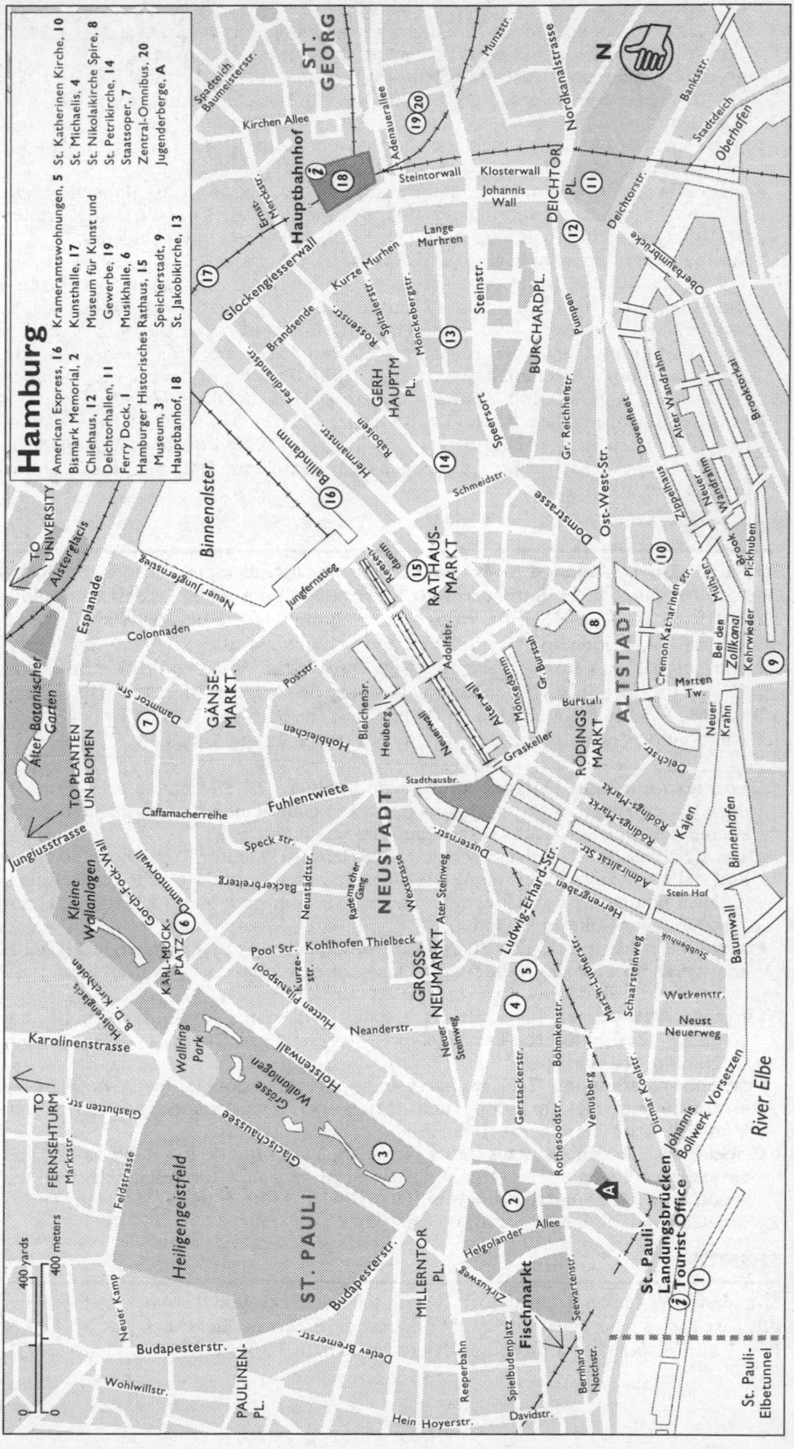
Hamburg
American Express, 16
Bismark Memorial, 2
Chilehaus, 12
Deichtorhallen, 11
Ferry Dock, 1
Hamburger Historisches Museum, 3
Hauptbanhof, 18
Krameramtswohnungen, 5
Kunsthalle, 17
Museum für Kunst und Gewerbe, 19
Musikhalle, 6
Rathaus, 15
Speicherstadt, 9
St. Jakobikirche, 13
St. Katherinen Kirche, 10
St. Michaelis, 4
St. Nikolaikirche Spire, 8
St. Petrikirche, 14
Staatsoper, 7
Zentral-Omnibus, 20
Jugenderberge, A
N
ST. GEORG
Hauptbahnhof
Binnenalster
TO UNIVERSITY
TO PLANTEN UN BLOMEN
Alter Botanischer Garten
Kleine Wallanlagen
Grosse Wallanlagen
Heiligengeistfeld
ST. PAULI
TO FERNSEHTURM
NEUSTADT
ALTSTADT
RATHAUS-MARKT
GÄNSE-MARKT
GROSS-NEUMARKT
RÖDINGS MARKT
BURCHARDPL.
DEICHTOR PL.
GERH HAUPTM PL.
KARL-MUCK-PLATZ
MILLERNTOR PL.
PAULINEN-PL.
Fischmarkt
St. Pauli Landungsbrücken
Tourist Office
St. Pauli-Elbetunnel
River Elbe
Binnenhafen
Oberhafen
Zollkanal
400 yards
400 meters

board. Reception open noon-1am. Curfew 1am. Stragglers admitted at 2am. DM24, over 26 DM29. Sheets and breakfast included. Reservations essential.

Jugendgästehaus-und-Gästehaus Horner-Rennbahn (HI), Rennbahnstr. 100 (tel. 651 16 71; fax 655 65 16). Take U-Bahn 3 to "Horner-Rennbahn," turn right, and walk 10min. Very clean and peaceful, if a bit far. Reception open 7:30-9am and 1pm-1am. Curfew 1am. Stragglers admitted until 2am. DM26, over 27 DM24.50, nonmembers DM36. Sheets and excellent breakfast buffet included.

Pension Sarah Peterson, Lange Reihe 50 and 98 (tel./fax 24 98 26). Bohemian *Pension* in a historic building. Singles DM60. Doubles for 2 or 3 people DM85. Triples DM180. Quads DM240. Rooms have TV and phones. Breakfast included.

Schanzenstern Übernachtungs-und-Gasthaus, Bartelsstr. 12 (tel. 439 84 41; fax 439 34 13). U- and S-Bahn: "Sternschanze," turn left onto Schanzenstr., right on Susannenstr., left to Bartelsstr. In the student district. Very friendly staff. Dorms DM35. Singles DM60. Doubles DM90. Triples DM110. Breakfast buffet DM10.

Hotel Terminus Garni, Steindamm 5 (tel. 280 31 44; fax 24 15 18). From the *Hauptbahnhof*'s Kirchenallee exit, turn right. Reception open 24hr. Doubles DM45, with shower DM60. Triples with bath DM165. Breakfast included.

Camping: Campingplatz Buchholz, Kielerstr. 374 (tel. 540 45 32). S-Bahn 3 ("Pinneberg") or S-Bahn 21 ("Elbgaustr") to "Stellingren." Walk straight on Volksparkstr. and turn right on Kielstr. Reception open daily 7am-10pm. DM7 per person. Showers DM1.50. Call ahead.

FOOD

St. Pauli's Quai, Landungsbrücke, has seafood restaurants and fry stands. Less fishy fare can be found at the **Rathausmarkt,** serving all things edible at easy-to-swallow prices. Better deals reside in the cafés and restaurants of the university area around **Renteelstraße, Grindelhof, Grindelallee,** and **Schanzenstraße.** The *Fußgangerzone* (pedestrian mall) in **Altona** leading up to the train station is packed with ethnic food stands and produce shops. The **Safeway Grocery Store** in the Mercado Mall, Altona, offers basic foodstuffs (open Mon-Fri. 10am-8pm, Sat. 9am-4pm). Don't let your stomach miss out on *Labskau,* the city's greasy but delicious specialty stew.

Geo Pizza aus dem Holzbackofen, Beim Schlump 27. Delectable pizza from an oven hot enough to make steel glow (DM8-15) complements a formidable vegetarian menu. Open Sun.-Thurs. 11am-1am, Fri.-Sat. 11am-2am.

Mensa, Schlüterstr. 7. University cafeteria. S-Bahn: "Dammtor," then head north on Rothenbaumchaussee, left on Moorweidenstr., then right onto Schlüterstr. Check bulletin boards for special events. Student ID required. Meals DM1.70-6. Open Mon.-Fri. 11am-2pm and 4-7pm.

Machwitz, Schanzenstr. 121. Student crowd munches croque sandwiches (DM10) and works up a sweat on the foosball tables. Occasional concerts from local musicians. Open daily 10am until everyone gets tired.

Libresso Antiquariat, Binderstr. 24. U-Bahn: "Hallerstr.," south on Rothenbaumchaussee, then right onto Binderstr. Bookstore and café attract a student crowd. Open Mon.-Fri. 9am-6pm.

Frauenbuchladen und Café, Bismarckstr. 98. U-Bahn: "Hoheluftbr." A women-only establishment. Pick up the German *Hamburger Frauenzeitung* (DM6). Open Mon.-Fri. 10am-7:30pm, Sat. 10am-2pm.

Gorki Park, 2 locations: Hans Henry Jahn Weg (take bus 106 to "Muhlenweg") and Grindelallee 1. Amid red velvet and socialist propaganda, the restaurants feed the revolution with Sunday brunch buffets (DM16, 11am-3pm). Open Mon.-Thurs. 5pm-2am, Fri. 5pm-3am, Sat. 6pm-3am, Sun. 11am-3pm.

SIGHTS

The **Hamburg Hafen** lights up nightly with ships from around the world. After sailing the East Indies, the 19th-century **Windjammer Rickmer Rickmers** was docked at Pier 1 and restored as a museum (open daily 10am-5:30pm; DM5, students DM3).

Inside the building behind Pier 6 resides the elevator to the **Old Elbe Tunnel.** With all its machinery exposed, the building looks like a nautilus machine for the gods.

The copper spire of the **Rathaus,** a richly ornamented 19th-century monstrosity, rises above the city center. For English tours (every 30min.; Mon.-Thurs. 10:15am-3:15pm, Fri.-Sun. 10:15am-1:15pm) call 36 81 24 70. Built in 1932, the **column** to the left of the *Rathaus* stands in memorial to the 40,000 Hamburg men who died in World War I. Hamburgers continuously try to bring a smile to the long face on the statue of poet **Heinrich Heine** in the square. To the north of the *Rathaus* are the two **Alster lakes** bordered by arbored paths, elegant promenades, commercial facades, and water sport fiends. To the west, the **Planten un Blomen** park extends almost down to the harbor and flaunts flowers and fountains.

Just south of the *Rathaus,* off Ost-Weststr., stand the somber ruins of the **St. Nikolaikirche.** An early example of neo-Gothic architecture, the church was flattened by Allied bombing in 1943. Just east of the *Rathaus* are two more churches: the 12th-century **St. Petrikirche** (open Mon.-Fri. 9am-6pm, Sat. 9am-5pm, Sun. 9am-noon and 1-5pm) and **St. Jacobikirche,** known for its 14th-century **Arp-Schnittger organ** (open daily 10am-5pm). But the grandaddy of them all is the gargantuan 18th-century **Große Michaelskirche.** The church's Baroque tower is the official emblem of Hamburg. (Open April-Sept. Mon.-Sat. 9am-6pm, Sun. 11:30am-5:30pm; Oct.-March Mon.-Sat. 10am-4:30pm., Sun. 11:30am-4:30pm. Church DM1; tower DM4, students DM2. Organ music April-Aug. daily at noon and 5pm.)

The dozens of museums in Hamburg range from the erotic to the Victorian. **Hamburger Kunsthalle,** Glockengiesserwall 1 (tel. 24 86 24 82), one block north of the *Hauptbahnhof,* holds an extensive and dazzling collection of art from the medieval to the modern (open Tues.-Sun. 10am-6pm, Thurs. 10am-9pm; DM10, students DM5). Hamburg's contemporary art scene resides at **Deichtorhallen Hamburg,** Deichtorstr. 1-2, with mind-boggling architecture (U-Bahn: "Steinstr."; open Tues.-Sun. 11am-6pm; DM10, students DM8). The **Erotic Art Museum,** Nobistor 12, has a stimulating collection of art and porn. (S-Bahn: "Reeperbahn" or U-Bahn: "St. Pauli." Open Tues.-Sun. 10am-midnight. DM15, students DM10.) The **Museum für Kunst und Gewerbe,** Steintorpl. 1, one block south of the *Hauptbahnhof,* has exhibits of Egyptian, Roman, and Asian handicrafts, china, and furnishings as well as a Lego reconstruction of the life and times of the ancient Egyptians. (Open Tues.-Wed. and Fri-Sun. 10am-6pm, Thurs. 10am-9pm. DM10, students and seniors DM5.)

ENTERTAINMENT AND NIGHTLIFE

The cultural capital of the North, Hamburg patronizes the arts generously with both money and attention, keeping ticket prices down. The **Staatsoper,** Dammtorstr. 28 (tel. 35 17 21; S-Bahn 28: "Dammtor"), houses one of the best opera companies in Germany, and the associated **ballet** company is the acknowledged dance power house of the nation. **Orchestras** abound—the **Philharmonie,** the **Hamburg Symphony,** and the **Nord-Deutscher-Rundfunk** are the big three. Lighter music, popular musicals, and transvestite cabarets play at the **Operettenhaus Hamburg,** the **Neue Flora Theater,** and other smaller venues. Call the tourist office for info. Traditional jazz can be found at the **Cotton Club,** Alter Steinweg 10 (tel. 34 38 78), and on Sunday mornings at the Fish Auction Hall of the **Fischmarkt.** International rock groups play at **Docks,** Spielbudenpl. 19 (tel. 319 43 78). The renowned **Fabrik,** Barnerstr. 36 (tel. 39 10 70), in Altona, features everything from funk to punk. Pick up a copy of *Szene, Oxmox,* or *Prinz* (free at hostels) for the latest info on the music scene.

The heart of Hamburg's nightlife lies in St. Pauli on the **Reeperbahn,** featuring the best clubs and bars, as well as porn theaters and sex shops to satisfy the naval libido. **Mojo Club,** Reeperbahn 1, has more attitude than it knows what to do with and was labeled "Germany's Best Club" by MTV. The attached **Jazz Café** also attracts the trendy. (Club open Fri.-Sat. from 11pm; cover DM10. Café open Wed.-Sat. from 10pm; no cover.) **Große Freiheit 36/Kaiser Keller,** Große Freiheit 36 (tel. 31 42 63), featured the Beatles back in the day downstairs and today showcases the Wu-Tang Clan upstairs (open daily; call for info). **Molotow,** Spielbudenpl. 5, parallel to the Reeperbahn, has rump-shaking funk (opens Wed. at 10pm, Thurs.-Sat. at 11pm, Sun. at 9pm; cover DM5-10). **Herbertstraße,** south of the Reeperbahn off Davidstr., is a legalized prostitution strip, open only to men over 18. If you're female and out late in the area, take a cab.

Students avoiding the debauchery of the Reeperbahn head north to the spiffy streets of **Sternschanze** and **Altona.** Unlike St. Pauli, these areas are centered around cafés and weekend extravaganzas of the alternative flavor. **Rote Flora,** Schulterblatt 71, a café during the week and a night club during the weekend is the nucleus of the Sternschanze scene (café open Mon.-Fri. 5pm-10pm; weekend parties DM6-8.) Much of the Hamburg gay scene is located in the **St. Georg** area of the city, near the *Hauptbahnhof.* **Front,** Heidencampsweg 32, is a jungle and house haven for both the gay and lesbian scene and for straight people just trying to stay hip (U-Bahn 3: "Berliner Tor"; opens Wed and Fri.-Sat. 11pm; cover DM10-12), while **Frauenkneipe,** Stresemannstr. 60, is a bar for gay and straight women (S-Bahn: "Altona"; open Mon.-Fri. 8pm-1am, Sat. 9pm-3am, Sun. 8pm-1am).

Lübeck

With a prickly skyline of green medieval spires, each of them giving a defiant *Stinkefinger* to the ugly cement and ribbonglass face of modernity, Lübeck is easily Schleswig-Holstein's most beautiful city. As boys, local heroes Heinrich and Thomas Mann ran through its labyrinth of cobblestone streets, garnering reflections on the German bourgeoisie for literary *Stinkefinger* of their own. The **Buddenbrooks House,** Mengstr. 4, is a museum dedicated to the life and work of the Mann brothers (open daily 10am-4pm; DM5, students DM3). The centerpiece of Lübeck's *Altstadt* is the **Rathaus,** a 13th-century structure of glazed black and red bricks (tours Mon.-Fri. at 11am, noon, and 3pm; DM4, students DM2). Behind the Marktplatz, the North-German Gothic **Marienkirche** boasts the largest mechanical organ in the world (concerts Sat. 6:30pm) and a reproduction of its famous **Totentanzbild,** a mural depicting the era of the plague (open in summer daily 10am-6pm; off-season 10am-4pm; free). Between the inner city and the train station is the massive **Holstentor,** one of the four gates built in the 15th century to guard the entrance to Lübeck. Inside, the **Museum Holstentor** features exhibits on ship construction, trade, and quaint local implements of torture. (Open April-Sept. Tues.-Sun. 10am-5pm; Oct.-March 10am-4pm. DM5, students DM3.) On Schmiederstr., the steeple of the 750-year-old **Petrikirche** gives a sweeping view. (Church open Tues.-Sun. 11am-4pm. Tower open April-Oct. 9am-6pm. DM3, students DM1.50.)

Frequent **trains** serve Lübeck from Hamburg (40min.), Berlin (4hr.), Munich (9hr.), Copenhagen (5½hr.), and Amsterdam (6½hr.). At the **tourist office** in the train station (tel. (0451) 86 46 75; fax 86 30 24; open Mon.-Sat. 9am-6pm), grab a free map and make for the larger **main office** at Breitestr. 62 (tel. (0451) 122 81 06), in back of the Marienkirche (open Mon.-Fri. 9:30am-6pm, Sat.-Sun. 10am-2pm). **Jugendgästehaus Lübeck (HI),** Mengstr. 33 (tel. (0451) 702 03 99; fax 770 12), is a superb hostel (DM26.50-40; call ahead). **Sleep-In (CVJM),** Große Petersgrube 11 (tel. (0451) 719 20), near the Petrikirche, is a clean, laid back YMCA. (Reception open July-Aug. daily 8am-noon and 5-10pm; Sept.-June Mon.-Fri. 9am-noon and 5-10pm., Sat.-Sun. 9-10am and 5-10pm. Dorms DM15; doubles DM40. Sheets DM5.) The Wulfs welcome you to their friendly **Rucksack Hotel,** Kanalstr. 70 (tel. (0451) 70 68 92), in the *Altstadt* by the canal (reception open daily 9am-10pm; dorms DM22-25, doubles DM80, quads DM122). **Café Affenbrot,** Kandstr. 70, serves veggie dishes (open daily 9am-midnight). Don't miss Lübeck's famous marzipan from **I. G. Niederegger,** Breitestr. 89, opposite the *Rathaus* (open daily 9am-7pm). For entertainment listings, pick up *Piste, Zentrum,* or *Zimtzicke* (for women) from the tourist office. Enjoy a drink at **Finnegan,** 42 Mengstr., or raucous local music and the occasional tattooing and piercing fiesta at **In Bad Taste,** An der Untertrave 3A.

Kiel

Site of the 1936 and 1972 Olympic sailing events, the waters around industrial Kiel swim ceaselessly with brightly colored sails and shipping vessels of every kind, and the city boasts the largest **canal locks** in the world. Take the tour to get the full effect. Take bus 4 north to "Kanal," then the free ferry that runs every 15min. Walk right 10min. on Kanalstr. from dock to the *Schleuseninsel* or Lock Island. Alternatively, take bus 1 or 41 to "Schleuse." (30min. Obligatory tours daily 9am-3pm, every 2hr. DM3, students DM1, 50% off with *Kieler Karte.*) The end of June sees the annual **Kieler Woche,** an internationally renowned regatta that enlivens the harbor and fills the town with people, music, food, and beer, particularly around the Olympia Zentrum (bus 44 north). Near the **St. Nicolaskirche** (open Mon.-Fri. 10am-1pm and 2-6pm, Sat. 10am-1pm; free) stands Barlach's haunting statue, the **Geistkämpfer** (ghost-fighter). The **tourist office** (tel. (0431) 67 91 00), in the Sophienhof mall across from the train station, has maps (DM1) and info on local events, and helps find rooms for a DM3.50 fee. (Open May-Sept. Mon.-Sat. 9am-6:30pm, Sun. 9am-1pm; Oct.-April Mon.-Fri. 9am-6:30pm, Sat, 9am-1pm.) To route fiscal bloodletting, invest in a discount garnering *Kieler Karte* (1-day DM12, 3-day DM17). **Buses** run to Hamburg airport from the *ZOB* around the corner from the train station (every 2hr., 1½hr., DM20). From the wharf on the west bank, **Baltic Line** (tel. (0431) 98 20 00) goes to Sweden (1 per week, 60hr., DM430), **Color Line** (tel. (0431) 97 40 90) journeys to Oslo, Norway (1 per day, 18hr., DM150, students 50% off selected sailings), and **Langeland-Kiel** (tel. (0431) 97 41 50; fax 945 15) will take you to Bagenkop, Denmark (1 per day, 18hr., DM150, students 50% off selected sailings). To find the **Jugendherberge (HI),** Johannesstr. 1 (tel. (0431) 73 14 88; fax 73 57 23), take bus 4 to Kielerstr., backtrack a block, and go right on Johannesstr. (reception open daily 7am-11:30am; DM24, over 26 DM29).

LOWER-SAXONY (NIEDERSACHSEN)

Extending from the Ems River to the Harz Mountains and from the North Sea to the hills of central Germany, Lower-Saxony has two distinct flavors. Along the northern coast, descendants of the Frisians run their fishing boats from ports built on foggy marshland. The vast remainder of the *Land* is a broad plain which supports agricultural communities. Since the Middle Ages, the region has been the seat of intense individualism and unbridled innovation. Christianity found a foothold here in the wake of Charlemagne's march through the fringe of the deep-purple Lüneburger Heath. A pocket of its area belongs to Bremen and Bremerhaven, two seafaring cities united in a unique case of state federalism to form Germany's smallest *Land.*

Bremen

Bremen's cultural flair, liberal politics, and strong desire to remain an independent *Land* have caused Germans to coin the adjective *bremisch,* which simply means something unusual. Close to the *Altstadt,* artists create murals with charcoal and paint as musicians provide accompaniment. The *Altstadt* revolves around the ornate **Rathaus,** which was spared during World War II by a pilot who could not bear to bomb it. (Tours usually Mon.-Fri. 10, 11am, and noon, Sat.-Sun. 11am and noon. Ask at the tourist office.) The **St. Petri Dom,** Sandstr. 10-12, next to the *Rathaus,* has a mosaic interior of orange, gold, and gray stone arches (open Mon.-Fri. 10am-5pm, Sat. 10am-1:45pm, Sun. 2-5pm; free). If you can't resist the yeasty smell of brewing beer, head across the Weser to **Beck's Brewery** for tours (DM5).

Bremen lies below the mouth of the Weser River at the North Sea, just over an hour from Hamburg and Hanover by train. The **tourist office** (tel. (0421) 308 00 51; fax 308 00 30), across from the train station, offers info and books rooms for a DM3 fee plus a DM10-20 deposit (open Mon.-Wed. 9:30am-6:30pm, Thurs.-Fri. 9:30am-8pm, Sat. 9:30am-4pm). Inexpensive hotels fill fast in Bremen, so call ahead. To reach the sleek **Jugendgästehaus Bremen (HI),** Kalkstr. 6 (tel. (0421) 17 13 69; fax 17 11 02), take bus 26 or streetcar 6 to "Am Brill," then walk along Bürgermeister-Smidt-Str. to the river, turn right, and walk two blocks (reception open 24hr.; DM27, over 26 DM32). Take bus 24 to "Am Neuenmark," then turn right to get to the spacious and plaid **Hotel Enzensperger,** Braustr. 9 (tel. (0421) 53 32 24; singles DM48-49; doubles DM70-92. Breakfast included.) In the *Rathaus,* Bremen's renowned **Ratskeller** is one of the oldest wine bars in Germany. (From DM4.40 per glass; meals DM40. Open daily 11am-midnight; kitchen open noon-2:30pm and 6-11pm.) For a cheap meal, try the open-air **market** nearby (open daily 8am-2pm).

Hanover (Hannover)

Despite its relatively small size, Hanover puts on a magical display of cultural and cosmopolitan charm. With great economic vigor, a wealth of museums, an unmatched concert hall, and a tradition of outdoor festivals, the city reigns as the political and cultural capital of Lower Saxony. The spectacular **Neues Rathaus,** recreated after the war, offers an amazing tower view. (Tower open daily 10am-5pm; elevator open April-Oct. daily 10am-12:15pm and 1:30-4:15pm. DM3, students DM2.) While wandering through the wild and ambitious landscaping of the **Herrenhausen Gardens** you'll pass exotic vegetation, Europe's highest garden fountain, and the 18th- century **Herrenhausen Palace** in the center. Take U-Bahn 4 or 5 to "Stöcken." (Gardens open in summer Mon.-Tues. 8am-8pm, Wed.-Sun. 8am-11pm; DM3. Tickets for Palace concerts available in advance at the tourist office.) The **Sprengel Museum,** Kurt-Schwitters-Pl., is a modern art lover's dream— Turrell, Dalí, Picasso, Magritte, and Antes highlight the impressive collection (open Tues. 10am-8pm, Wed.-Sun. 10am-6pm; DM8.50, students DM4.50). To completely experience Hanover, follow the **Red Thread,** a walking tour connecting major sites.

The **tourist office,** Ernst-August Pl. 2 (tel. (0511) 30 14 22; fax 30 14 14), near the train station, dispenses maps and info and finds rooms (DM10; open Mon.-Fri. 9am-7pm, Sat. 9:30am-3pm). The **Jugendherberge Hannover (HI),** Ferdinand-Wilhelm-Fricke-Weg 1 (tel. (0511) 131 76 74; fax 185 55), is cramped, but the scenic location and affordable prices make for a pleasant stay. Take U-Bahn 3 or 7 ("Mühlenberg") to "Fischerhof/Fachhochschule"; cross the tracks and walk to the left of the school. Follow the bike path and turn right; the hostel is 50m down on the right (Reception open daily 7:30-9am and 2-11:30pm. Curfew 11:30pm. DM22, over 26 DM27. Camping sites DM13.25, over 26 DM15.50. Breakfast included.) **Naturfreundehaus Misburg,** Am Fahrhorstfelde 50 (tel. (0511) 58 05 37; fax 958 58 36), is on a beautiful lake. Take U-Bahn 4 ("Roderbruch") to "Misburger Straße," then take bus 631 to "Misburg Waltfriedhof," and follow Am Fahrhorstfelde to the end. (Reception open Tues.-Fri. 3-10pm, Sat.-Sun. 10am-10pm. DM14-24. Sheets DM7.50. Reservations needed.) The **Kröpcke,** a world-renowned café/food court in the center of the pedestrian zone, can provide ample eats. Check the *Prinz* (DM4.50) or the *Schädelspalter* (DM5) for a guide to nightlife, or head to **The Capitol,** Schwarzer Bär 2 (tel. (0511) 929 880; call for a schedule).

Harz Mountains

Heinrich Heine wrote that even Mephistopheles trembled when he approached the Harz, the devil's dearest mountains. It's easy to see why Heine—as well as Goethe, Bismarck, and a host of others—fell in love with the mist-shrouded woodlands, which stretch from the western **Oberharz** to the eastern **Ostharz** and to sun-sheltered health resorts in the south. Spring thaws turn ski slopes into webs of hidden hiking trails. The **Harzerquerbahn** and **Brockenbahn,** antique narrow-gauge railways, steam through gorgeous Harz scenery from Nordhausen to Wernigerode. The Harzer Verkehrsverband **regional tourist office,** Markstr. 45 (tel. (05321) 340 40), inside the Industrie und Handels Kammer building, sells the indispensable *Grüner Faden fur den Harz-Gast* pamphlet (DM5), which lists nearby attractions. Also pick up *Jugend und Freizeitheime im Harz und im Harzvorland,* a complete compilation of youth hostels and student centers in the area (open Mon.-Fri. 8am-4pm).

Goslar Forty minutes by train from Hanover, **Goslar's** *Altstadt* is congested with immaculate half-timbered houses and winding narrow streets, encircled by the divinely lush, green Harz Mountains. In addition, as the hub of an extensive bus network, Goslar spins you to any part of the region. **Kaiserpfalz,** at Kaiserbleek 6, is a massive Romanesque palace that served as the ruling seat for 11th- and 12th-century emperors. (Open April-Oct. daily 10am-5pm; Nov.-March 10am-4pm. DM3.50, students DM2.) Each day at 9am, noon, 3, and 6pm, mechanical figures of court nobles and the miners whose work made the region prosperous dance to the chime of the **Glocken- und Figurenspiel,** opposite the *Rathaus.* Unfortunately for Goslar—but fortunately for modern tourists—Goslar lost mining rights in the area in the 16th century and has changed little since. The **Mönchehaus,** Mönchestr. 3, exhibits a grand modern art collection including the works of Miró and Calder (open Tues.-Sat. 10am-1pm and 3-5pm, Sun. 10am-1pm; donations requested).

The **tourist office,** Markt 7 (tel. (05321) 780 60; fax 230 05), across from the *Rathaus,* finds rooms (from DM30) for free. To get there from the station, turn left and walk to the end of Rosentorstr., which becomes Hokenstr. (Open May-Oct. Mon.-Fri. 8am-6pm, Sat. 9am-2:30pm; Nov.-April Mon.-Fri. 9am-5pm, Sat. 9am-1pm.) The **Jugendherberge (HI),** Rammelsbergerstr. 25 (tel. (05321) 222 40), wins the prize for most confusing location, but there's a shortcut: from the Marktplatz, take Bergstr. southwest until it ends at Clausthalerstr. Directly across the street, follow the stairway between the trees, head right at the fork halfway up, and you'll be there in 5 minutes. (Members only. Reception open 8:30am-10pm. Check-in after 3pm. Curfew 11:30pm. DM20, over 26 DM25. Breakfast included.) **Campingplatz Sennhütte,** Clausthalerstr. 28 (tel. (05321) 224 98), 3km from town along the B241, has a restaurant and sauna (DM5.50 per person, DM4 per tent; showers DM1).

Bad Harzburg and Torfhaus The train from Hanover to the mountains ends at **Bad Harzburg,** gateway to the **Harz National Park,** 10 minutes past Goslar. By the station, the **tourist office** (tel. (05322) 29 27) finds rooms (DM30-50) for a DM5 fee (open Mon.-Fri. 9am-1pm and 3-6pm, Sat. 10am-1pm). **Torfhaus,** a humble crossroads 3km from the former inter-German border, offers an airy mountain hostel, near-perfect hiking trails, and the Harz's highest mountain, the 1142m **Brocken. Buses** arrive in town from Bad Harzburg (20min.; DM4.70) and Braunlage (20min.; DM4.50; both Mon.-Fri. 7:45am-9pm). Turn left at the "Altenau-8km" sign for the **Goethe Weg** and the 16km trail to Brocken's peak. Along the way it hops the stream that once divided the two Germanies; look for the **electronic warfare post** of the former East German state security service. Turn right at the same sign for the **Jugendherberge (HI),** Torfhaus 3. (Tel. (05320) 242. Members only. Reception 8:15-9am, 12:15-1pm and 6:15-7pm. Curfew 10pm. DM22.30, over 26 DM27.30.)

Wernigerode One of Goethe's secret spots in the hills, and now a stop on the Harzquerbahn route, **Wernigerode** still charms with half-timbered houses and a magnificent hilltop **castle.** The Kaiser came to the *Schloß* for hunting; his room is wildly brocaded green and gold. From the flower-trimmed terrace, you can see straight to the peak of Brocken. (Open May-Oct. daily 10am-6pm; Nov. Sat.-Sun. 10am-6pm; Dec.-April Tues.-Sun. 10am-6pm. Last entry 5pm. DM7, students DM6; tour DM1 extra.) Wernigerode's busy **tourist office,** on Breitstr. (tel. (03943) 330 35), around the corner from the *Rathaus,* books rooms (DM30-40) for a 10% commission. (Open May-Oct. Mon.-Fri. 9am-7pm, Sat.-Sun. 9am-3pm; Oct.-April Mon.-Fri. 9am-6pm, Sat.-Sun. 9am-3pm.) To reach the **Jugendgästehaus,** Friedrichstr. 53 (tel. (03943) 63 20 61), walk from Westerntor station right on Unter den Zindeln, then turn right on

Friedrichstr. (25min.); or, take bus 1, 5, or 7 to "Kirchstr." (Reception open 8am-10pm. DM15. Sheets DM5. Meals DM6-7. You must buy one meal.)

Thale Behind the dramatic front of **Thale's** jagged cliffs lurks a region of myths and witches. Legend dates Thale's cultic past back to prehistoric times, when a sorceress named **Watelinde** led pagan rituals to indoctrinate young witches-to-be. A few thousand years later a whirlwind threw a startled Watelinde into some rocks which now comprise the **Hexentanzplatz** (witches' dance place). Adjacent to Hexentanzpl. is the **Walpurgishalle,** a museum commemorating the Harz history of witchcraft (open May-Sept. daily 9am-5pm; Oct.-April 9am-1pm; DM3, students DM1). Also located on the Hexentanzpl. is **Harzer Bergtheater Thale** (tel. (03947) 23 24), a huge outdoor amphitheater with performances ranging from broadway musicals and operas to Goethe's *Faust* and the *Hexenkonzerts* (witches' concerts; shows run sporadically May-Sept.; 30% discount for students). One can ascend to the Hexentanzpl. either by following the **trail** that begins by the hostel (30min.) or by **cable car** (May-Sept. daily 9:30am-6pm; Oct.-April 10am-4:30pm; DM8, students DM5).

Trains leave every hour for Thale from Halberstadt (30min.) and Quedlinburg (7min.). Across from the train station, the **tourist office,** Rathausstr. 1 (tel. (03947) 25 97 or 22 77; fax 22 77), books rooms (DM25-40 per person) at no charge. (Open Dec.-Oct. Mon.-Fri. 9am-6pm; May-Aug. also Sat.-Sun. 9am-4pm; Nov. Mon.-Fri. 9am-4pm only.) The cavernous rooms of the **Jugendherberge,** Bodetal Waldkater 1 (tel. (03947) 28 81), look out into the mountains and the running river below. From the train station, cut diagonally through the park, go past the *Opfer des Fascismus* statue on the right and the cathedral on the left; then turn right and continue walking along the river. (Reception open 7am-10pm. DM22, over 26 DM27. Breakfast buffet included. Sheets DM6.) The hostel's cafeteria has lunch and dinner specials (DM7.50-9). Otherwise, check out the many food stands by Hexentanzpl. Thale explodes in nuptial bliss and revelry every year on April 30 (the wedding anniversary of Nordic gods of the seasons Wodan and Freja) for the **Walpurgisnacht.**

NORTH RHINE-WESTPHALIA

In 1946, the victorious Allies attempted to speed Germany's recovery by merging the traditionally distinct regions of Westphalia, Lippe, and the Rhineland to unify the economic nucleus of post-war Germany. The resulting *Land,* North Rhine-Westphalia, meets no typical German stereotype. With its 17 million inhabitants and the mighty Ruhr Valley, North Rhine-Westphalia is the most heavily populated and economically powerful area in Germany. Despite downturns in heavy industry and high unemployment, the great industrial wealth of the region continues to support a multitude of cultural offerings. While the region's squalor may have inspired the philosophy of Karl Marx and Friedrich Engels, the area's natural beauty and intellectual energy of Cologne and Düsseldorf have spurred the muses of Goethe, Heine, and Böll.

Cologne (Köln)

Founded by Romans in 48 AD, Cologne gained fame and fortune in the Middle Ages as an elite university town and the center of important trade routes. While most of the inner city was destroyed during World War II, the Gothic cathedral survived no less than 14 bombings. Today, tourists come to see this symbol of Cologne's rebirth, participate in libatious celebrations, and indulge in the burgeoning fine arts scene.

PRACTICAL INFORMATION

Tourist Office: Verkehrsamt, Unter Fettenhennen 19 (tel. 221 33 45; fax 221 33 20), across from the cathedral. Free maps. Books rooms (DM5). Pick up *Monats-*

vorschau (DM2), with info and events schedule. Open May-Oct. Mon.-Sat. 8am-10:30pm, Sun. 9am-10:30pm; Nov.-April Mon.-Sat. 8am-9pm, Sun. 9:30am-7pm.

Currency Exchange: You can exchange money at the train station (open daily 7am-9pm), but the service charges are lower at the post office.

American Express: Burgmauerstr. 14 (tel. 925 90 10), near the cathedral. **ATM.** Cardholders' mail held for free. Open Mon.-Fri. 9am-5:30pm, Sat. 9am-noon.

Flights: info tel. (02203) 40 25 38. Bus 170 runs from stop 4 of the *Hauptbahnhof* to the **Köln-Bonn Airport** (15min., DM8.20, children DM4.50).

Public Transportation: VRS (Verkehrsverbund Rhein-Seig) offices carry plans of the S- and U-Bahn lines, as well as maps of city bus and streetcar lines. One office is located downstairs in the train station. Tickets priced by distance: 1-ride tickets DM1.55-13.50; day cards DM11-33. The DM11 card gets you anywhere in Cologne.

Hitchhiking: Hitchers take bus 132 to the last stop for all destinations. **Citynetz Mitfahrzentrale,** Maximistr. 2 (tel. 194 40), to the left of the train station, lists rides. Open Mon.-Fri. 9am-6pm, Sat. 9am-2pm.

Laundry: Öko-Express, Neue Weyerstr. 1. Wash DM6, dry DM1 per 10min. Soap included. Open Mon.-Sat. 6am-11pm. Also at Zülpicher Wall 2.

Pharmacy: Dom Apotheke, Komodienstr. 5 (tel. 257 67 54), near the station. Their *Pharmacie-Internationale* advises in English. Open Mon.-Fri. 8am-6:30pm, Sat. 8:30am-4pm. List of after-hours pharmacies posted outside.

Emergency: Police: tel. 110. **Hospital:** 112.

Post Office: Main office, WDR Arkaden. From the *Dom* exits of the train station, head down Breitestr., then An den Ruhr. Open Mon.-Fri. 8am-6pm, Sat. 8am-6pm, Sun. 8am-1pm. **Postal Code:** 50667.

Telephone Code: 0221.

ACCOMMODATIONS AND FOOD

Most hotels fill up in the spring and fall when conventions come to town, and the two hostels are both filled to the beams from June to September. Call ahead.

Jugendherberge Köln-Deutz (HI), Siegesstr. 5a (tel. 81 47 11; fax 88 44 25), just over the Hohenzollern Bridge. From the station, take S-Bahn 6, 11, or 12 to "Köln-Deutz." Cramped, but prime location and free laundry. Reception open daily 6-9am and 12:30pm-12:30am. DM27, over 26 DM32. Sheets included.

Jugendgästehaus Köln-Riehl (HI), An der Schanz 14 (tel. 76 70 81; fax 76 15 55), on the Rhine north of the zoo. From the station, take U-Bahn 16 or 18 ("Ebertpl./Mülheim") to "Boltensternstr." Posher but less central than Köln-Deutz. Reception open 24hr. DM37. Sheets and breakfast included.

Hotel Im Kupferkessel, Probsteigasse 6 (tel. 13 53 38; fax 12 51 21). From the station bear right; follow the street as it changes names (eventually becoming Christophstr.), then turn right on Probsteigasse. Elegant. Reception open daily 7am-9pm, or call. Singles DM44-78. Doubles DM125. Breakfast included.

Camping: Campingplatz Poll (tel. 83 19 66), southeast of the *Altstadt* on the Rhine. U-Bahn 16 to "Marienburg," then cross Roddenkirchener Bridge. Reception open daily 8am-noon and 3-10pm. DM6 per person. DM5 per tent.

Students pack cafés and diners from Zülpicherstr. into the university complex; the mid-priced restaurants and ethnic eateries center on the *Altstadt.* Don't leave Cologne without trying the city's smooth **Kölsch beer.** Put away pizzas for under DM10 at **Café Rendezvous,** Heinsberg 11a, at the corner of Heinsberg and Zülpicherstr. (open Sun.-Thurs. 8am-8pm, Fri.-Sat. 8am-3am). **Schlotzky's Deli,** at the corner of Hohenzollern Ring and Edro Palmstr., serves up classic deli items with veggie options (open Mon.-Thurs. and Sun. 11am-1am, Fri.-Sat. 11am-3am). For great Japanese food without the financial bite, try **Momotaro,** Benesisstr. 56 (sushi from DM24; entrees DM12-15; open Mon.-Sat. noon-3pm and 6-10pm).

SIGHTS AND ENTERTAINMENT

Cologne will be celebrating **Gothic Year in Köln** in 1998 to honor the 750th anniversary of the **Dom** (cathedral). Visitors exiting Cologne's *Bahnhof* are immediately confronted by the building, overwhelming in both intricacy and scale. Inside, the stained-glass windows cast an intense play of colored light over a gilded altarpiece, magnificent woodcuts, and other treasures. Look for the 976 **Gero Crucifix,** the oldest intact sculpture of Christus patiens. A mere 509 steps lead to the top of the **Südturm** (south tower); catch your breath 400 steps up at the *Glockenstübe,* where the 24-ton **Der große Peter,** the world's heaviest swinging bell, roosts. (Cathedral open daily 6am-7pm. English tours Sun.-Fri. 2pm, Sat. 10:30am. DM6. Free organ concerts mid-June to Sept. Tues. 8pm. Tower open May-Sept. daily 9am-6pm; March-April and Oct. 9am-5pm; Nov.-Feb. 9am-4pm. DM3, students DM1.50.)

The 12th-century **Groß St. Martin** rises like a medieval castle beside the *Dom* despite extensive wartime damage. (Open Mon.-Sat. 11am-6pm, Sat. 10am-6pm, Sun. 2-4pm. Crypt DM1, students DM0.50.) Farther on, the squares and crooked streets of the old **Fischmarkt** district open onto paths along the Rhine, and crowded cafés give way to riverside stretches of grass. If you've skimped on hostel showers, stop by the famous **house #4711,** Glockengasse, where a small fountain dispenses the fragrant liquid that made Cologne a household word.

A three-day pass for entry into all of the city's museums, the DM15 **Köln Bonbon** cannot be eaten, but it can get you into the chocolate museum, **Das Museum (Imhoff-Stollwerk Museum),** Rheinauhafen 1a, to writhe in ecstasy at the sight of the gold fountain spurting streams of chocolaty goo. The **Römische-Germanisches Museum,** Roncallipl. 4, was built over Roman ruins. (Open Tues., Wed., and Fri. 10am-5pm, Thurs. 10am-8pm, Sat.-Sun. 11am-5pm. DM7, students DM4.) The **Heinrich-Böll-Platz,** Bischofsgartenstr. 1, behind the Römische-Germanisches Museum, houses three museums: the **Wallraf-Richartz Museum** has pieces from the 13th to 19th centuries; the **Museum Ludwig** starts with Picasso, Dalí, and Klee, and ends with art fresh off the easel; and the **Agfa Foto-Historama** chronicles chemical art of the last 150 years. (All open Tues. 10am-8pm, Wed.-Fri. 10am-6pm, Sat.-Sun. 11am-6pm. DM13 for all three, students DM7.) Take U-bahn 12, 16, or 18 to "Barbarossaplatz" to find **The Beatles Museum,** Heinsbergstr. 13, which is crammed with Fab Four memorabilia (open Sept.-July Wed.-Sat. 10am-7pm; DM5).

Cologne becomes a living spectacle during **Karneval,** a week-long pre-Lenten festival. The weekend builds up to a bacchanalian parade on **Rosenmontag,** the last Monday before Lent (Feb. 23 in 1998). Everyone's in costume and gets and gives a couple dozen *Bützchen* (kisses on a stranger's cheek). For info and tickets to events, ask at the **Festkomitee des Kölner Karnevals,** Antwerpenerstr. 55 (tel. 57 40 00). The *Köln, Karneval* booklet at the tourist office also has helpful tips.

Students congregate in the **Quartier Lateng,** the area bounded by Zülpicherstr., Zülpicherpl., Roonstr., and Luxemburgstr. Gay nightlife runs up Matthiasstr. to Möhlenbach, Hohe Pforte, Marienpl., and up to Heumarkt by the Deutzer Brücke. The only science going on at **Museum,** Zülpicherpl. 9, is blood alcohol level experiments, under the watchful eye of the local dinosaur (open Sun.-Thurs. 6am-1am, Fri.-Sat. 6pm-3am). **MTC,** Zülpicherstr. 10, has varied musical offerings (cover DM6; open Mon.-Thurs. and Sun. 9pm-2am, Fri.-Sat. 9pm-3am). At **Päffgen Brauhaus,** Friesenstr. 64-66, *Kölsch* is brewed on the premises and consumed in cave-like halls and the *Biergarten* (0.2L shot DM2.20; open daily 10am-midnight). An unforgettable transvestite cabaret resides in the pink building at **Star-Treff,** Alte Wallgasse (tel. 25 50 63; tickets DM35, call ahead). At **Gloria,** Apostelnstr. 11, a gay and lesbian café fronts a popular disco. (Disco DM10; call 25 44 33 for days and times. Café open Sun.-Thurs. 9am-1am, Fri.-Sat. 9am-3am.)

Bonn

Derisively called the *"Hauptdorf"* (capital village), Bonn has been Germany's whipping boy for 50 years simply because it's not Berlin. Unimportant for most of its 2000 years, Bonn made it big by chance: since Konrad Adenauer, the postwar chancellor, had a house in the suburbs, the ever-considerate occupying powers promoted humble Bonn to capital status. Since reunification, the city lost the seat of government to

Berlin but remains a worthy destination with a spread of museums, bustling *Altstadt*, and respected university.

Baby Ludwig wailed his first notes in the **Beethoven Geburtshaus** (Birthplace), Bonngasse 20, now a museum. Take U-Bahn 62, 64, or 66 to "Bertha-von-Suttner-Pl.," or follow the signs from the pedestrian zone. (Open Mon.-Sat. 10am-5pm, Sun. 11am-4pm; DM8, students DM4. Call (0228) 63 51 88 for English tours.) The castles, palaces, and museums lie just outside the inner city. The **Kurfürstliches Schloß,** an 18th-century palace, was later converted into the central building of Bonn's university. Down the Poppelsdorfer Allee promenade, the 18th-century **Poppelsdorfer Schloß** sports a French facade and Italian courtyard, with the manicured **Botanical Gardens** nearby. (Gardens open May-Sept. Mon.-Fri. 9am-6pm, Sun. 9am-1pm; Oct.-April Mon.-Fri. 9am-4pm. Free.) A **Bonncard** (DM12), available at the tourist office, provides public transportation and admission to the museums of **Museum Mile** (U-Bahn 16, 63, or 66 to "Heussallee"). The **Kunstmuseum Bonn,** Friedrich-Ebert Allee, has superb Expressionist and contemporary art (open Tues.-Sun. 10am-6pm; DM5, students DM3), while the art in the **Kunst- und Ausstellungshalle der BRD** is so new that you can smell the glue (open Tues.-Wed. 10am-9pm, Thurs.-Sun. 10am-7pm; DM8, students DM4). The futuristic **Haus der Geschichte** offers an interactive look at German history (open Tues.-Sun. 9am-7pm; free).

Practical Information, Accommodations, and Food Bonn's **tourist office,** Münsterstr. 20 (tel. (0228) 77 34 66 or 19 44 33; fax 77 31 00), books hotels (DM3-5 fee). Take the "Stadtmitte" exit from the station, walk up Poststr., and turn left (open Mon.-Fri. 9am-6:30pm, Sat. 9am-5pm, Sun. 10am-2pm). For the first-rate **Jugendgästehaus Bonn-Venusberg (HI),** Haager Weg 42 (tel. (0228) 28 99 70; fax 289 97 14), take bus 621 ("Ippendorf Altenheim") to "Jugendherberge" (reception open daily 9am-1am; DM37; sheets and breakfast included). **Jugendgästehaus Bonn-Bad Godesberg (HI),** Horionstr. 60 (tel. (0228) 31 75 16; fax 31 45 37), is even farther from downtown but has tidy, modern rooms. To get there, ride U-Bahn 16 or 63 from the main station to "Rhein Allee," then hop on bus 615 ("Stadtwald/Evangelische Krankenhaus") to Venner-Str. (Reception open daily 8am-5pm and 8pm-1am. DM34.50. Sheets and breakfast included.)

Münsterpl. features several fast-food counters, small cafés, and an open-air market (open Mon.-Sat. 9am-6pm). The **University Mensa,** Nassestr. 11, a 15-minute walk from the train station along Kaiserstr., also offers cheap, tasty meals. (DM2-5. Open for lunch Mon.-Thurs. 11:30am-2:15pm, Fri. 11:30am-2pm, Sat. noon-1:45pm. Open for dinner Mon.-Fri. 5:30-8pm. Closed mid-July to late Aug.) Fulfill your wildest vegetarian fantasies at **Cassius Garten,** Maximilianstr. 28d, at the edge of the *Altstadt* (DM2.58 per 100g; open Mon.-Fri. 9am-8pm, Sat. 9am-4pm). For cultural and entertainment listings, check out the *Schnüss* guide, or hang at the *über*-hip **Café Blan,** Franziskanerstr. (beer DM3.50-6; desserts DM5-8; open daily 9am-1am).

Aachen

Charlemagne sang the mantra of multiculturalism when he made Aachen the capital of his Frankish empire in the 8th century, and the tunes are still heard today—Aachen jives day and night in four different languages, and a flux of students and international travelers continually renew the city's vibrant atmosphere. The neo-Byzantine **cathedral,** in the center of the city circle, is one of the world's best-known cathedrals. Stained glass rings the 15th-century Gothic choir, and beneath the chancel lie the bones of Charlemagne himself (open daily 7am-7pm). The 14th-century stone **Rathaus** looms over the wide Marktplatz beside the cathedral. On the northern facade stand 50 statues of former German sovereigns, 31 of whom were crowned in Aachen (open daily 10am-1pm and 2-5pm; DM3, students DM1.50). The **Ludwig Forum für Internationales Kunst,** Jülicherstr. 97-109, in a converted *Bauhaus* umbrella factory, showcases modern masters from Warhol to Barbara Kruger. The Eastern European collection is especially impressive. (Open Tues. and Thurs. 10am-

5pm, Wed. and Fri. 10am-8pm, Sat.-Sun. 11am-5pm. Last entrance 30min. before closing. DM6, students DM3. Free tour Wed. at 8pm.)

Aachen sits at the crossroads between Germany, Belgium, and the Netherlands, and is one hour from Cologne by **train.** The **tourist office** (tel. (0241) 180 29 60; fax 180 29 31), in the Atrium Eliserbrunnen on Friedrich-Wilhelm-Pl., books rooms for a DM3 fee. From the train station, head up Bahnhofstr., turn left on Theaterstr., and then right onto Kapuzinergraben, which becomes Friedrich-Wilhelm-Pl. (open Mon.-Fri. 9am-6:30pm, Sat. 9am-2pm). The **Jugendherberge (HI),** Maria-Theresia-Allee 260 (tel. (0241) 711 01; fax 70 82 19), has old rooms but a friendly atmosphere. From the station, walk left on Lagerhausstr. until it intersects Kareliterstr. and Mozartstr. From here, take bus 2 ("Preusswald") to "Ronheide" or bus 12 ("Diepenbendem") to "Colynshof" (reception open daily until 10pm; curfew 11:30pm; DM25, over 26 DM30). To get to **Hotel Marx,** Hubertusstr. 33-35 (tel. (0241) 375 41; fax 267 05), commune on Lagerhausstr. (which becomes Boxgarden), take a right on Stephanstr., and be won over to the left on Hubertusstr. (singles DM60-85, doubles DM100-130; breakfast included).

Pontstraße is lined with restaurants and pubs. At **Van Den Daele,** Büchel 18, off the Markt, treat yourself to the fine baked goods (open Mon.-Fri. 9am-6:30pm, Sat. 9am-6pm, Sun. noon-6pm). Eat and drink in Charlemagne's shadow at **Egmont,** Pontstr.1 (open daily 9am-1am). **Tam-phat,** Pontstr. 100, offers Chinese and Thai dishes (DM7-14; open Mon.-Fri. 11am-3pm and 5pm-11pm, Sat.-Sun. noon-11pm).

Düsseldorf

As the capital of North Rhine-Westphalia and the headquarters of Germany's largest corporations and mod fashion, Düsseldorf radiates the confidence and glamour of a blue-blooded aristocrat. The city has rebounded from war-time destruction with resilience and fierce pride. By day, crowds line the runways and promenades; by night, propriety and sobriety are cast aside in the 500 pubs of the *Altstadt.*

ORIENTATION AND PRACTICAL INFORMATION

Tourist Office: Main office, Konrad-Adenauer-Pl. (tel. 17 20 20; fax 35 04 04). Up and to the right from the station. Pick up the free *Düsseldorf Monatsprogram.* Open Mon.-Fri. 8:30am-6pm, Sat. 9am-12:30pm; open for hotel reservations (DM5) Mon.-Sat. 8am-8pm, Sun. 4-10pm. The **branch office,** Heinrich-Heine-Allee 24 (tel. 899 23 46), specializes in cultural listings. Open Mon.-Fri. 9am-5pm.

Currency Exchange: Deutsche Verkehrs Credit Bank, in the *Hauptbahnhof* and airport. Open Mon.-Sat. 7am-9pm, Sun. 8am-9pm.

American Express: Neusserstr. 111 (tel. 90 13 50). Mail held for card holders. All financial services. Open Mon.-Fri. 9am-5:30pm, Sat. 8:30am-noon.

Flights: Call 421 22 23 for flight info. 24hr. emergency service tel. 421 66 37. Frequent S-Bahns and a Lufthansa shuttle travel from the station to the international **Flughafen Düsseldorf.** Open 5am-12:30am.

Trains: All trains arrive at **Düsseldorf Hauptbahnhof** (tel. 194 19).

Public Transportation: Call 582 28 for schedule info. The **Rheinbahn** includes subways, streetcars, buses, and the S-Bahn. Single tickets DM1.90-11.70. Closes by 1am. The *Tagesticket* (from DM10) is the best value around—up to 5 people can travel 24hr. on any line. Tickets sold at vending machines; pick up the *Fahrausweis* brochure in system, which connects surrounding areas.

Laundromat: Wasch Center, Friedrichstr. 92, near the Kirchpl. S-Bahn. Wash DM6, dry DM1 per 15min. Soap included. Open daily 6am-11pm.

Pharmacy: In the *Hauptbahnhof.* Closed pharmacies post lists of nearby open ones. **Emergency pharmacy:** tel. 115 00.

Emergency: Ambulance and **Fire:** tel. 112. **Emergency Doctor:** tel. 192 92.

Police: tel. 110.

Internet Access: g@rden, Rathausufer 8. DM5 per 30min. Open daily 11am-1am. Also **Café InterNezzo,** Fichtenstr. 40, in the "zakk." DM5 per hr. Open Mon.-Thurs. 6-11pm.

Post Office: Hauptpostamt, Konrad-Adenauer-Pl., to right of the tourist office. Open for most services Mon.-Fri. 8am-6pm, Sat. 9am-2pm; Sun. noon-1pm. A **branch office** is located in the *Hauptbahnhof.* **Postal Code:** 40210.

Telephone Code: 0211.

ACCOMMODATIONS, CAMPING, AND FOOD

Düsseldorf is a convention city where corporate crowds make rooms scarce and costly; it's imperative that you call as far in advance as possible. Most rooms go for at least DM50 per person even in the off season. Check around the train station.

Jugendgästehaus Düsseldorf (HI), Düsseldorferstr. 1 (tel. 55 73 10; fax 57 25 13), just over the Rheinkniebrücke bridge from the *Altstadt.* Take U-Bahn 70, 74, 75, 76, or 77 to "Luegpl.," then walk 500m down Kaiser-Wilhelm-Ring. Unbeatable location. Reception open daily 7am-1am. Curfew 1am, but doors open every hour on the hour 2-6am. DM33.50, over 26 DM37. Private lockers.

Jugendherberge Duisburg-Wedau, Kalkweg 148E (tel. (0203) 72 41 64; fax 72 08 34). Take S-Bahn 1 or 21 to "Duisburg Hauptbahnhof," then bus 934 to "Jugendherberge." Old but clean rooms. Reception open daily 8:30-9am, 12:30-1pm, and 6:30-7pm. DM22.50, over 26 DM27.50. Open mid.-Jan. to mid-Dec.

Hotel Diana, Jahnstr. 31 (tel. 37 50 71; fax 36 49 43), 5 blocks from the station. Head left down Graf-Adolf-Str., turn left on Hüttenstr., and head right onto Jahnstr. Small but comfortable rooms with phone and TV. Reception open daily 8am-7pm. Singles DM55. Doubles DM85-125. Breakfast included.

CVJM-Hotel, Graf-Adolf-Str. 102 (tel. 17 28 50; fax 361 31 60), down the street to the left of the train station. Clean, spacious rooms with hot water and inspirational messages on the walls. Reception open 24hr. Singles DM62. Doubles DM101. Noisier streetside rooms DM65, DM111. Breakfast DM8. No credit cards.

Camping: Kleiner Torfbruch (tel. 899 20 38). S-Bahn to "Düsseldorf Geresheim," then bus 735 ("Stamesberg") to "Seeweg." DM6 per person. DM9 per tent.

The streets of the *Altstadt* are lined with restaurants and fast-food joints. The **Markt** on Karlspl. offers shoppers foreign fruits and a local favorite, *Sauerbraten* (pickled beef). Dine with the glitzy in the *Biergarten* at **Galerie Burghof,** Burgallee 1-3 (open daily 11am-1am), or peruse a periodical while eating at **Heine Geburtshaus,** Bolkerstr. 53, Heinrich Heine's birthplace (open daily noon-midnight). Try the *Blutwurst* (blood pudding; DM3.50) or *Mainzer* (Mainz cheese; DM4) at **Zum Uerige,** Bergerstr. 1 (open daily 10am-midnight). **Marché,** Königsalle 60, may be your only hope to dine in the **Kö** (see below) and save some marks for later (entrees from DM8.60; café-bar open daily 7:30am-11pm, restaurant 8am-11pm).

SIGHTS AND ENTERTAINMENT

The **Königsallee** ("the Kö"), the fashionable shopping district outside the *Altstadt,* embodies the vitality and glamour of Düsseldorf. If you can resist the chi-chi shops, the **Hofgarten** park adds an oasis of green and culture at the upper end of the promenade. West of the Hofgarten is the mirror-glass **Kunstsammlung Nordrhein-Westfalen,** Grabbepl. 5, an exceptional modern art museum with the definitive Paul Klee collection. Take U-Bahn 70 or 75-79 to Heinrich-Heine-Allee and walk north two blocks (open Tues.-Thurs., Sat.-Sun. 10am-6pm, Fri. 10am-8pm; DM5, students DM3). Beloved poet's Heinrich Heine manuscripts are on display at **The Heinrich Heine Institut,** Bilkerstr. 12-14 (open Tues.-Fri. and Sun. 11am-5pm, Sat. 1-5pm; DM4, students DM2). **Burgplatz** was once the site of a glorious castle, but tired citizens rebuilt only one tower after the castle was destroyed in World War II for the fourth time. Farther from the city center, in **Kaiserwerth,** are the ruins of Emperor Friedrich's **palace.** Take U-Bahn 79 to "Klemenspl.," follow Kaiserwerther Markt to the Rhine, and walk left (open daily 8am-12:30pm; free).

Prinz magazine (DM4.50, often free at the youth hostel) is Düsseldorf's fashion cop and scene detective; the free cultural guides *Coolibri* and *Biograph* are less complete but still helpful. The gay and lesbian nightlife magazine, *Facolte,* is available at most newsstands. **Das Kommödchen** (tel. 32 94 43) is a tiny, extraordinarily popular theater behind the Kunsthalle at Grabbepl. (Box office open Mon.-Sat. 1-8pm, Sun. 3-8pm.Tickets DM33, students DM23. Call at least two days ahead.) Purchase ballet and opera tickets at the **Opernhaus** (tel. 890 82 11), on Heinrich-Heine-Allee (open Mon.-Fri. 11am-6:30pm, Sat. 11am-1pm, and 1hr. before performances).

Folklore holds that Düsseldorf's 500 pubs make up *die längste Theke der Welt,* the longest bar in the world. The cool and bizarre alike frequent **Stahlwerk,** Ronsdorfer 134 (U-Bahn 75 to "Ronsdorferstr."), with a beer patio and multi-floor dance hall (cover DM10; open Fri.-Sat. and last Sun. of every month at 10pm). A watering hole with a Latin feel, **Poco Loco,** Mortengasse 2, packs in a few hundred horny Germans (open Tues.-Thurs. 7pm-3am, Fri.-Sun. 7pm-5am). Plan transport home from **Tor 3,** Ronsdorferstr. 143, across from Stahlwerk—the public transportation will stop long before you leave (cover DM15; open Fri.-Sat. 10pm-5am). Düsseldorf's oldest brewery, **Brauerei Schumacher,** Bolkerstr. 44, draws a multi-generational crowd (open Mon.-Thurs. and Sun. 10am-midnight, Fri.-Sat. 10am-1am). **Café Rosa,** Oberbilker Allee 310, is the mecca of Düsseldorf's gay community, offering a café, bar, and disco. (Tues., Thurs., and most Sat. mixed, Fri. lesbians only, last Sat. of each month gay men only. Call 77 52 42 for a gay male hotline and 54 42 for a lesbian hotline. Call hotlines for daytime hours; evenings usually Tues.-Sat. 8pm-1am.)

HESSE

Prior to the 20th century, Hesse was known for exporting mercenary soldiers to rulers such as King George III, who sent them off to put down an unruly gang of colonial hicks in 1776. Today, Hesse has exchanged its guns for briefcases and is the busiest commercial center in the country. Fortunately, the medieval delights and Baroque elegance of areas outside Frankfurt attract little attention from tourists.

Frankfurt am Main

Martin Luther once remarked that Frankfurt resembled a pot of silver and gold, and today the pot has become a thriving financial and commercial center, one of the most Americanized cities in Europe, and, perhaps not coincidentally, the notorious crime capital of Germany. Anne Frank, Goethe, and the social theorists of the Frankfurt School enriched the city's cultural treasury, and the *Kulturszene* retains both hipness and gravity. But if that isn't enough to make you come to Frankfurt, the immense likelihood of arriving in Germany at the Rhein-Main Airport probably is.

Almost all of Frankfurt was destroyed by Allied bombings during World War II—what's left of the old city is in the **Römerberg** area. The towering **Dom** served as the coronation site for German emperors between 1562 and 1792, and the view from its tower is well worth the punishing climb. (Cathedral open June-Aug. daily 9am-noon and 2:30-5pm; Sept.-May 9am-noon and 2:30-5:30pm. Tower closed in winter; DM3.) Frankfurt's city hall since 1405, the red sandstone **Römer** stands at the west end of the *Römerberg.* The upper floors contain the **Kaisersaal,** adorned with portraits of the 52 German emperors from Charlemagne to Franz II (open daily 10am-1pm and 2-5pm; obligatory tour 3DM). Near the Römer at Saalgasse 19, the **Historisches Museum** presents first-rate exhibitions on Frankfurt's history (open Tues. and Thurs.-Sun. 10am-5pm, Wed. 10am-8pm; DM5, students DM2.50). A few blocks northwest of the *Römer* stands the **Goethe Haus,** Großer Hirschgraben 23-25, birthplace of the great poet. (Open April-Sept. Mon.-Sat. 9am-6pm, Sun. 10am-1pm; Oct.-March Mon.-Sat. 9am-4pm, Sun. 10am-1pm. Tours Mon.-Sat. 10:30am and 2pm, Sun. 10:30am. DM4, students DM3.)

From Römerberg, walk across the Eiserner Steg footbridge to the **Museumsufer,** home to seven museums and the **flea market.** (Most museums open Tues. and

Thurs.-Sun. 10am-5pm, Wed. 10am-8pm. Market open Sat. 9am-2pm.) Enjoy animal antics at the world-famous **zoo.** (U-Bahn 6 or 7. Open mid-March to Sept. Mon.-Fri. 9am-7pm, Sat.-Sun. 8am-7pm; Oct. to mid-March daily 9am-5pm. DM11, students DM5.) The *Journal Frankfurt* (DM2.80), *Fritz,* or *Strandgut* (both free) have info on Frankfurt's **theatrical performances.**

Practical Information, Accommodations, and Food From the **airport,** S-Bahn 8 and 5 travel to the train station (DM5.80; Eurail valid). Frequent **trains** service major cities including Berlin (5-6hr.), Munich (3½-4½hr.), and Paris (6-7hr.); call (069) 194 19. The **tourist office,** in the station (tel. (069) 21 23 88 49, room reservation 21 23 08 08), books rooms for a DM5 fee and sells the **Frankfurt Card,** which gives two days of unlimited public transportation as well as a 50% discount to museums and the zoo (DM15; open Mon.-Fri. 8am-9pm, Sat.-Sun. 9am-6pm). **Currency exchange** is available in the station, Airport Hall B, or at the **main post office,** Zeil 110 (open Mon.-Fri. 9am-6pm, Sat. 9am.-1pm).

Hotel prices in Frankfurt rise as high as the skyscrapers. For affordable, convenient rooms, try the **Jugendherberge (HI),** Deutschherrnufer 12 (tel. (069) 61 90 58; fax 61 82 57). To reach the hostel, take bus 46 to "Frankensteinerpl." and walk 50m west; after 7:30pm, take S-Bahn 2-6 or tram 16 to "Lokalbahnof," walk north on Darmstädter Landstr. (which becomes Dreieichstr.), and turn left. (Reception open 24hr. Curfew midnight. DM24, over 20 DM29.50. Required sheet deposit DM10.) **Pension Bruns,** Mendelssohnstr. 42 (tel. (069) 74 88 96; fax 74 88 46), has sunny rooms with TVs. From the train station, take a left onto Düsseldorferstr., and after two blocks veer right on Beethovenstr. At the small circle, go right (doubles DM79, triples DM105; showers DM2; breakfast included). Farther along, **Pension Backer,** Mendelssohnstr. 92 (tel. (069) 74 79 92), is bright and clean (singles DM50, doubles DM60, triples DM68; showers DM3; breakfast included).

Frankfurt is famous for its *Äpfelwein* (apple wine), but a glance at the portly clientele in **Zum Gemalten Haus,** Schweizerstr. 67, lets you know that the food is good too (*Äpfelwein* DM2.50 for .3L; open Wed.-Sun. 10am-midnight). Log on at the **CybeRyder Internet Cafe,** Töngesgasse 31, for Internet access (6DM per 30min.; Mon.-Fri. 10am-9pm, Sat. 10am-10pm). The **HL Markt,** Dreieichstr. 56, is a grocery store near the youth hostel (open Mon.-Fri. 8am-8pm, Sat. 8am-9pm). For pubs and taverns, try the **Alt Sachsenhausen** district, between Brückenstr. and Dreieichstr. Gay nightlife bustles around Zeil and Bleichstr., while the renowned jazz scene centers on Kleine Bockenheimer Str., also known as **Jazzgasse** (Jazz Alley). The most famous venue is **Der Jazzkeller,** Kleine Bockenheimer Str. 18a (tel. (069) 28 85 37; cover varies; open Tues.-Sun. 9pm-3am).

Marburg

The Brothers Grimm spun their fairy tales in Marburg's rolling hills, and from a distance, the city seems more like their world than ours. Tough terrain and dense forests surround the town, and the *Oberstadt* is still a maze of tiring staircases and narrow alleys. Founded in the heart of Marburg in 1527, the world's first Protestant **university** boasts alumni Martin Heidegger, Boris Pasternak, and T.S. Eliot. Climb 250 steps or take bus 16 from Rudolphspl. to the exalted **Landgrafenschloß,** former haunt of the Teutonic knights. The castle now houses the university's **Museum für Kulturgeschichte** (Cultural Museum), with exhibits on Hessian history and religious art. (Open April-Oct. Tues.-Sun. 10am-6pm; Nov.-March Tues.-Sun. 11am-5pm. DM3, students DM2.) To reach the 13th-century **Elisabethkirche,** the oldest Gothic church in Germany, cross the bridge opposite the train station and take a left at Elisabethstr. (Open April-Sept. daily 9am-6pm; Oct. 9am-5pm; Nov.-March 10am-4pm, Sun. after 11am. Church free. Reliquary DM3, students DM2.) The church is the starting point for free tours of the town (April-Oct. Sat. at 3pm).

The **tourist office,** Pilgrimsteinstr. 26 (tel. (06421) 991 20; fax 99 12 12), sells maps and hotel lists (DM0.50-1.50) and books rooms for free. Take buses 1-6 to

"Rudolphspl." and exit to the north along Pilgrimsteinstr.; the office is on the left (open Mon.-Fri. 9am-6pm, Sat. 9am-1pm). If the tourist office is closed, call **hotel info** at (06421) 194 14. Marburg is served by frequent **trains** from Frankfurt (1hr.) and Kassel (1hr.). The riverside **Jugendherberge (HI),** Jahnstr. 1 (tel. (06421) 234 61; fax 121 91), features beautiful rooms, some with bath. From Rudolphspl., cross the bridge and follow the riverside path until you reach the small wooden bridge (reception open daily 9am-noon and 1:30-11:30pm; DM28, over 26 DM33). **Camping Lahnaue** (tel. (06421) 213 31) is on the Lahn River; to reach the campsite, follow directions to the Jugendherberge and continue downriver (DM6 per person, DM6 per tent). **Café Barfuß,** Barfüßerstr. 33, serves big breakfasts until 3pm (under DM12) and beer (DM2-5.50; open daily 10am-1am).

Kassel

When Napoleon III was captured by Prussian troops and brought to the Schloß Wilhelmshöhe prison in 1870, Aacheners jeered *"Ab nach Kassel"* ("off to Kassel"). Today, hordes answer the call to see the ultra-sophisticated metropolis. **Schloß Wilhelmshöhe** was the home of the local rulers. (Open March-Oct. Tues.-Sun. 10am-5pm; Nov.-Feb. Tues.-Sun. 10am-4pm. Tours DM6, students DM4.) All paths lead up to the large **Riesenschloß,** an amphitheater topped by the figure of **Herkules,** Kassel's emblem. Spectacular summertime fountain displays start at 2:30pm on Sundays and Wednesdays (access to top of statue March-Nov. Tues.-Sun. 10am-5pm; DM2, students DM1). Hordes of art-lovers and curiosity seekers descend on Kassel every five years to take part in **documenta,** the world's preeminent contemporary art exhibition, scheduled next for 2002. The remainders of previous exhibitions sprawl across the city—even the *Hauptbahnhof* gets a piece of the action. The **Fridericianum,** Friedrichspl. 18, shows items related to past *documentas.*

The **Wilhelmshöhe station,** an ICE hub, is the point of entry to Kassel's ancient castles on the west side; the older **Hauptbahnhof** is the gateway to the *Altstadt.* Kassel is accessible by **trains** from Hanover (1hr.) and Frankfurt (1½-2hr.). The **tourist office,** Königspl. 53, 2nd fl. (tel. (0561) 707 71 62; fax 707 71 69), gives out free maps, a hotel list (DM0.50; rooms from DM45), and brochures in English (open Mon.-Thurs. 9:15am-6pm, Fri. 9:15am-4:30pm). The **Jugendherberge am Tannenwäldchen,** Schenkendorfstr. 18 (tel. (0561) 77 64 55; fax 77 68 32), offers huge common areas and eight-bed rooms. From the *Hauptbahnhof,* go out the *Südausgang* (south exit), turn right on Kölnischestr., and then right again. (Reception open until 11pm. DM24, over 26 DM29. Breakfast included. Sheets DM6. No phone reservations.) **Hotel-Restaurant Palmenbad,** Kurhausstr. 27 (tel./fax (0561) 326 91), is comfortable and clean. Take streetcar 3 or 4 to "Wiganstr." and walk 5min. uphill. (Reception open Mon. 5:30-11pm, Tues.-Sat. 9am-11pm, Sun. 9am-2pm. Singles DM49-58; doubles DM86-99.) Cheap meals await in the **university complex** on Arnold-Bode-Str. (open Mon.-Fri. noon-2pm and 5-9pm; DM4.80-5.50, students DM2.60-3.30). Nightlife flourishes on the stretch along Ebertstr. and Goethestr.

RHINELAND-PALATINATE

A trip to the Rheinland-Pfalz to see the castles and wine towns along the Rhine is an obligatory tourist tromp. The region is a visual feast—the Mosel River curls downstream to the Rhine Gorge, a soft shore of castle-backed hills. Trier is a millennia-old collage of sights, while medieval Speyer bows down around glorious cathedrals.

The Rhine: Mainz to Koblenz

The Rhine River may run from Switzerland to the North Sea, but in the popular imagination it exists only in the 80km of the **Rhine Gorge** that stretches from Mainz to

Bonn. This is the Rhine of legend: a sailor's nightmare, a poet's dream, and often the center of rhetorical storms of nationalism. From the Lorelei Cliffs, poet Heinrich Heine's legendary siren lured passing sailors to their deaths on the sharp rocks below. The vineyards along the hillsides have inspired many a lesser illusion.

The best way to see the sights is probably by **boat,** if you're willing to put up with lots of tourists. The **Köln-Düsseldorfer line** (tel. (0211) 258 30 11) sails to 40 Rhine landings between Cologne and Mainz, including the cliffs and waterfalls at **Königswinter,** and offers connections to Mosel ferries. (Round-trip DM40. Seniors half-price on Mon. and Fri. Students half-price. Trips between Cologne and Mainz are covered by both Eurail and German Railpasses.)

Mainz and Bacharach The capital of the Rhineland-Palatinate region, vibrant **Mainz** successfully combines modernity and antiquity. Concrete and cobblestone mesh seamlessly to carry people of every stamp through the city proper. It also makes a convenient starting point for Rhine tours. **Köln-Düsseldorfer ferries** depart from the docks across from the ultramodern *Rathaus.* Across Liebfrauenpl. stands the colossal **Martinsdom,** the final resting place of several Archbishops of Mainz, whose extravagant tombs line the walls. (Open April-Sept. Mon.-Fri. 9am-6:30pm, Sat. 9am-4pm, Sun. 12:45-3pm and 4-6:30pm; Oct.-March Mon.-Fri. 9am-5pm, Sat. 9am-4pm, Sun. 12:45-3pm. Free.) The adjacent **Dom Museum** houses sculptural artifacts from the early years of the Holy Roman Empire (open Mon.-Wed. and Fri. 10am-4pm, Thurs. 10am-5pm, Sat. 10am-2pm; free). Mainz's favorite son and the father of movable type, Johannes Gutenberg, is immortalized along with his creations in the marvelous **Gutenberg Museum** on Liebfrauenpl (open Tues.-Sat. 10am-6pm, Sun. 10am-1pm; DM5, students DM2.50, Sun. free). On a hill several blocks to the south, in the opposite direction from the river, the **Stephanskirche** is noted for its stunning stained-glass windows created by Marc Chagall in the eight years prior to his death in 1984 (open daily 10am-noon and 2-5pm).

To make the maze of Mainz more maneuverable, streets running parallel to the Rhine have blue nameplates; those running towards it have red ones. The **tourist office,** Bahnhofstr. 15 (tel. (06131) 28 62 10; fax 286 21 55), on the *Brückenturm* of the *Rathaus,* reserves mostly expensive rooms for a DM5 fee (open Mon.-Fri. 9am-6pm, Sat. 9am-1pm). Mainz's well-run **Jugendgästehaus (HI),** Otto-Brunsfels-Schneise 4 (tel. (06131) 853 32; fax 824 22), is in the *Volkspark* in Weisenau; take bus 1 to "Jugendherberge" or bus 22 to "Viktorstift." (Reception open daily 5-10pm. DM21, over 26 DM26.20. Doubles DM48.40, over 26 DM53.20.) At the *Universität,* the **Taverne Academica** serves cheap food and drinks (open Mon.-Fri. 11am-midnight, Sat. 11:30am-3pm and 6-11pm).

On the west bank of the Rhine between Mainz and Koblenz, **Bacharach's** many *Weinkeller* (wine cellars) and *Weinstuben* (wine pubs) do their best to live up to the town's name—"altar to Bacchus." From the Gothic **Peterskirche** in the center of town, stairs lead up to the **Wernerkapelle,** the red sandstone frame of a chapel that took 140 years to build (1294-1434) but only a few hours to destroy during the War of Palatine Succession in 1689. The **tourist office,** Overstr. 1 (tel. (06743) 12 97; fax 31 55), has maps of hiking trails and a list of wine cellars and pubs (open Mon.-Fri. 10am-noon and 3-5:15pm, Sat. 10am-1pm). Hostels get no better than the **Jugendherberge Stahleck (HI)** (tel. (06743) 12 66; fax 26 84), a gorgeous 12th-century castle with an unbeatable panoramic view. The painful 20-minute hike is worth every step (curfew 10pm; DM23.50; call ahead).

Koblenz The beauty of Koblenz—not to mention its strategic value at the confluence of the Rhine and the Mosel—has attracted Roman, French, Prussian, and German conquerors over the past 2000 years. Before reunification the city served as a large munitions dump, but now the only pyrotechnics are during the **Rhein in Flammen** (Rhine in Flames) fireworks festival, held each August.

The focal point of the city is the **Deutsches Eck** (German Corner), the peninsula that purportedly saw the birth of the German nation when the Teutonic Order of

Knights settled here in 1216. The tremendous **Mahnmal der Deutschen Einheit** (Monument to German Unity), erected in 1897 in honor of Kaiser Wilhelm I, now dominates the peninsula. Most of the nearby *Altstadt* was flattened during World War II, but several attractive churches have been carefully restored. The **Florinskirche** towers (open daily 11am-5pm; free) shine with bursts of vibrant color, while the **Liebfrauenkirche** features oval Baroque towers, emerald and sapphire stained glass, and intricate ceiling latticework. Across the river, the **Festung Ehrenbreitstein** was the largest fortress in Europe in Prussian days. There are several ways to reach the fortress; the easiest is to take bus 8, 9, or 10 from the main station to the Ehrenbreitstein Bahnhof (DM3), then take the *Sesselbahn* (chairlift; DM6 round-trip).

The **tourist office** (tel. (0261) 313 04 or 331 34; fax 129 38 00), across from the train station, has boat schedules and city maps complete with hotel, restaurant, and pub listings (open May-Sept. Mon.-Fri. 9am-8pm, Sat.-Sun. 10am-8pm). The **Jugendherberge Koblenz (HI)** (tel. (0261) 97 28 70; fax 972 87 30), inside the fortress, has standard four- to six-bed rooms, but boasts arguably the best location of any German hostel (DM23.50; breakfast included). **Campingplatz Rhein-Mosel** (tel. (0261) 827 19) is across the Mosel from the *Deutsches Eck;* a ferry crosses the river during the day. (Reception open daily 8am-noon and 2-8pm. DM5.50 per person, DM4.60-6 per tent. Open April-Oct. 15.) A 10-minute walk to the left of the station, turning right immediately after the Herz-Jesu-Kirche, **Restaurant-Café Dubrovnik,** Obere Löhrstr. 91, has inexpensive daily specials from noon-3pm (soup and entree DM10-18) and pricier evening dining (open daily 9am-midnight). **Altes Brauhaus,** Braugasse 4, has hearty, traditional dishes for around DM15 (open Mon.-Sat. 10:30am-10pm; kitchen open 11:30am-2:30pm and 5:30-10pm).

The Mosel Valley (Moseltal)

As if trying to avoid its inevitable surrender to the Rhine at Koblenz, the Mosel meanders slowly past the sun-drenched hills, pretty towns, and ancient castles of the softly cut Mosel Valley. The valley's slopes aren't as steep as the Rhine's narrow gorge, but the arresting landscape, ancient castles, and vineyards easily compensate.

See the splendid scenery by boat, bus, or bicycle; the **train** line between Koblenz and Trier often strays from the river into unremarkable countryside. Some train stations will rent you a sturdy three-speed **bike** for DM11 if you have a ticket or railpass. Although passenger **boats** no longer make the Koblenz-Trier run, several companies still run summer trips along shorter stretches; inquire at local tourist offices.

Cochem and Beilstein Like so many precious German wine-making villages, the hamlet of **Cochem** has become a repository of German nostalgia, its quintessential quaintness eaten up voraciously by busloads of city-dwellers. Yet the impressive vineyard-covered hills and majestic **Reichsburg** castle, perched high on a hill above town, simply can't be cheapened. The 11th-century castle was destroyed in 1689 by French troops led by Louis XIV, but was rebuilt in 1868 and is now open to the public for frequent 40-minute tours. (Written English translations available. Open March 15-Oct. daily 9am-5pm. DM6, students DM5.)

The **tourist office** (tel. (02671) 39 71 or 39 72; fax 84 10) is on Endertpl. right next to the bridge; from the train station, head to the river and turn right. The office reserves rooms for free (open May-Nov. 15 Mon.-Fri. 10am-1pm and 2-5pm, Sat. 10am-3pm). Cochem's friendly but unadorned **Jugendherberge (HI),** Klottenerstr. 9 (tel. (02671) 86 33; fax 85 68), is 10 to 15 minutes from the station on the opposite shore. (Reception open daily noon-1pm and 5-10pm; late arrivals ring the bell. Curfew 10pm. DM21; breakfast included.) **Campingplatz am Freizeitzentrum** (tel. (02671) 44 09) is on Stadionstr. just below the youth hostel (reception open daily 8am-9pm; DM6.50 per person, DM6-12 per tent).

Ten kilometers upstream from Cochem lies tiny **Beilstein,** with its half-timbered houses and crooked cobblestone streets. The ruins of **Burg Metternich,** another casualty of French troops in 1689, offer a sweeping view of the valley (open April-

Oct. daily 9am-5pm; DM2, students DM1.50). The Baroque **Karmelitenkirche** has an intricate wooden altar and famous 16th-century sculpture. **Buses** to Beilstein depart about once an hour from both the *Endertplatz* and train station in Cochem (DM3.50). The **passenger boats** of Personnenschiffahrt Kolb (tel. (02673) 15 15) also travel between the two towns (May-Oct. 4 per day, 1hr., round-trip DM19).

Trier The oldest town in Germany, **Trier** was founded by the Romans during the reign of Augustus, and reached its heyday in the 4th century as the capital of the western Roman Empire and the residence of Emperor Constantine. Today, the city preserves several Roman ruins and a beautiful and dignified *Altstadt.* The natural point of departure for any tour of the city is the 2nd-century **Porta Nigra** (Black Gate), named for the centuries of grime that have turned its sandstone face varying shades of gray (DM4, students DM2). From here, stroll down Simeonstr. to the **Hauptmarkt,** a shopping district packed with fruit stalls and lined with architecturally diverse buildings. The masses may want to make a pilgrimage to **Karl-Marx-Haus,** Brückenstr. 10, where young Karl first walked, talked, and dreamed of labor alienation. (Open April-Oct. Mon. 1-6pm, Tues.-Sun. 10am-6pm; Nov.-March Mon. 3-6pm, Tues.-Sun. 10am-1pm and 3-6pm. DM3, students DM2.) Make a left onto Sternstr. and explore the impressive interior of the 11th-century **Dom.** (Open April-Oct. daily 6:30am-6pm; Nov.-March 6:30am-5:30pm. Daily tours at 2pm. Free.) A walk down Liebfrauenstr. and uphill along Olewigerstr. brings you to the remains of the 2nd-century **amphitheater,** an enormous 20,000-seat venue.

Trier's **tourist office** (tel. (0651) 97 80 80; fax 447 59), in the shadow of the Porta Nigra, hands out free maps, books rooms, and offers **tours** in English daily at 1:30pm (DM9). (Open April-Nov. 15 Mon.-Sat. 9am-6:30pm, Sun. 9am-3:30pm; Nov. to 16-Dec. Mon.-Sat. 9am-6pm, Sun. 9am-1pm; Jan.-Feb. Mon.-Fri. 9am-5pm, Sat. 9am-1pm; March Mon.-Sat. 9am-6pm, Sun. 9am-3:30pm.) Frequent **trains** go to Koblenz (1½hr.) and nearby Luxembourg (45min., day excursion DM12.80). **Personnenschiffahrt ferries** (tel. (0651) 15 15) mosey along the Mosel from beside Kaiser-Wilhelm Brücke (May-Oct. 9:15am, round-trip DM44).

Trier's **Jugendgästehaus (HI),** An der Jugendherberge 4 (tel. (0651) 14 66 20; fax 14 66 230), has an extensive array of vending machines and ping-pong tables. Take bus 2 or 8 ("Trierweilerweg" or "Pfalzel/Quint") to "Moselbrücke," and walk 10 minutes downstream on the path along the river. (Reception open daily 7pm-midnight. Quads with toilet and shower DM26.50. Breakfast and sheets included.) The well-located **Jugendhotel Kolpinghaus,** Dietrichstr. 42 (tel. (0651) 97 52 50; fax 975 25 40), is one block off the Hauptmarkt. (Reception open daily 8am-11pm. 4-bed dorms DM25; singles DM37; doubles DM74. Breakfast included. Call ahead.) To reach **Trier City Campingplatz,** Luxemburgerstr. 81 (tel. (0651) 869 21), from the Hauptmarkt, follow Fleischstr. to Bruckenstr. to Karl-Marx-Str. to the Römerbrücke; from here, cross the bridge and head left. If you end up in Luxembourg, you've gone too far. (Reception open daily 8-11am and 6-10pm in Gortätle Kranich, up from the river. DM7 per person.) **Astarix,** Karl-Marx-Str. 11, is a relaxed student hangout with wonderfully inexpensive meals (open Mon.-Thurs. 11am-1am, Fri.-Sat. 11am-2am, Sun. 6pm-1am). The **wine information office,** Konstantinpl. 11 (tel. (0651) 736 90), will help you make decisions about wine tasting in the Mosel region (open Mon.-Fri. 10:15am-6:30pm, Sat. 10am-4pm, Sun. 1-5pm).

Saarbrücken

For centuries, Saarbrücken's proximity to the French border has made it a center of one violent conflict after another, leaving virtually none of the *Altstadt* intact. One of the last undiscovered centers of the modern European cultural scene, Saarbrücken's focus is on the future, and today's shambles are products only of the creation of a slick DM500-million rail transit system, scheduled for completion by 2000. The figures on the bronze doors of the **Basilika St. Johann** are either writhing in hell-fire or heavenly bliss (opens Mon., Wed., and Fri. at 8:30am, Tues., Thurs., and Sun. 9:30am,

Sat. 9am). A walk along Am Stadtgarten with the river on the right leads you to the **Saarland Museum,** Bismarckstr. 11-19, which displays Picasso, Matisse, and Beckmann. Across the street at **Alte Sammlung,** Karlstr. 1, medieval Madonnas repose. (Both open Tues. and Thurs.-Sun. 10am-6pm, Wed. noon-8pm. Joint admission DM3, students DM1.50.) The 9th-century **Saarbrücker Schloß,** on the other side of the Saar river, has tall sparkling glass columns (tours in German Wed.-Sun. 4pm; free). Around the Schloßpl., the **Historisches Museum** includes a disturbing collection of war propaganda (open Tues.-Sun. 10am-6pm; free).

The **tourist office,** Am Hauptbahnhof 4 (tel. (0681) 365 15; fax 905 33 00), to the left of the train station, finds rooms (DM3) and gives out free maps (open Mon.-Fri. 9am-6pm, Sat. 9am-3pm). Trains chug to Trier (1hr.), Frankfurt (2hr.), and Koblenz. The **Jugendherberge,** Meerwiesertalweg 31 (tel. (0681) 330 40), is a 25-minute walk from the station, or you can take bus 19 to "Prinzenweiher" and backtrack (reception open 4-11pm; curfew 11:30pm; DM26.30; breakfast included). **Gästehaus Weller,** Neugrabenweg 8 (tel. (0681) 37 19 03; fax 37 55 65), offers huge rooms with bath, phone, and TV. Go down Ursulinenstr., right on Mozartstr., on to Schumannstr., left on Fichtestr., and cross the bridge. (Reception open Mon.-Sat. 8am-11pm, Sun. 6-11pm. Singles DM59-69. Doubles DM79-98.) For **Campingplatz Saarbrücken,** Am Spicherer Berg (tel. (0681) 517 80), take bus 42 to "Spicherer Weg," cross Untertürkheimstr., and head uphill (DM6 per person, DM8 per tent; open April-Sept.). The streets around **St. Johannis Markt** brim with bistros and beer gardens. **Hela,** at the end of Ursulinenstr., is a supermarket-drugstore-hair salon rolled into one (open Mon.-Fri. 8:30am-6:30pm, Sat. 8:30am-2pm).

BADEN-WÜRTTEMBERG

Two of the most prominent German stereotypes—the Brothers Grimm and the Mercedes-Benz—shake hands in Baden-Württemberg. Rural custom and tradition are still widely evident in the scenic, foreboding hinterlands of the Black Forest and the Swabian Jura, while the modern capital city of Stuttgart is rooted in the latter-day ascendancy of the German industrial machine. The province is also the home of the snooty millionaires' resort of Baden-Baden, the vacation getaways of Lake Constance, and the ancient university towns of Freiburg, Tübingen, and Heidelberg.

Stuttgart

Visiting Stuttgart is like stepping into a little piece of the archetypal utopian fantasy. Completely destroyed in World War II, the city had nowhere to move but the future, and that it did, with an unmitigated sense of optimism. Despite the rampant modernization, the home of Porsche and Daimler-Benz and the capital of Baden-Württemberg gloats in one of the most verdant settings of any major German city.

At the heart of Stuttgart lies an enormous pedestrian zone where shops and restaurants stretch as far as the eye can see. **Königstraße** and **Lautenschlagerstraße** are the main thoroughfares. The **Schloßgarten,** Stuttgart's main municipal park, runs south from the train station to the elegant Baroque **Neues Schloß.** The north end of the park contains the **Rosensteinpark** and **Wilhelma,** Stuttgart's famous zoo and botanical garden. (Open March-Oct. daily 8:15am-5:30pm; Nov.-Feb. 8:15am-4pm. DM11, students DM5.) Across from the Schloßgarten at Konrad-Adenauer-Str. 30 is the superb **Staatsgalerie Stuttgart,** containing works by Picasso, Kandinsky, Beckmann, and Dalí. (Open Wed. and Fri.-Sun. 10am-5pm, Tues., Thurs. 10am-8pm. DM5, students DM3.) For artistry of a different sort, the **Mercedes-Benz Museum** covers the history of the luxury automobile from its creation to modern experimental models. (S-Bahn 1 to "Neckarstadion," walk left under the bridge, then left at the next intersection. Open Tues.-Sun. 9am-5pm. Free.) The **Porsche Museum** tells basically the same story about different cars (S-Bahn 6 to "Neuwirtshaus"; open Mon.-Fri. 9am-

4pm, Sat-Sun. 9am-5pm; free). The **Staatstheater** (tel. (0711) 22 17 95), across the plaza from the Neues Schloß, is Stuttgart's most famous theater (box office open Mon.-Fri. 10am-6pm, Sat. 9am-1pm; tickets DM16-90). Other local theaters are usually much cheaper (DM10-25, students DM5-15); the tourist office has info and tickets.

Practical Information, Accommodations, and Food The **tourist office, I-Punkt,** Königstr. 1 (tel. (0711) 222 80), directly in front of the escalator down to the Klett-Passage, books rooms for free and sells the *Monatsspiegel* (DM3.20, in German), a guide to museums, events, restaurants, and nightlife. (Open Mon.-Fri. 9:30am-8:30pm, Sat. 9:30am-6pm, Sun. 11am-6pm; Nov.-April opens 1pm on Sun.) As a transportation hub of southwest Germany, Stuttgart has direct **trains** to most major cities, including Munich (2½hr.), Berlin (6hr.), Frankfurt (1½hr.), and Paris (6hr.); dial (0711) 194 19 for 24-hour schedule info. The **American Express** office, Lautenschlagerstr. 3 (tel. (0711) 187 50), is one block south of the station (open Mon.-Fri. 9:30am-6pm, Sat. 9:30am-12:30pm). Stuttgart's **public transportation** system offers single-ride tickets for buses, streetcars, U-Bahns, and S-Bahns ranging from DM3.20-9.60. The *Tageskarte,* not valid for night buses, is DM18.50.

Most of Stuttgart's budget beds are on the two ridges surrounding the downtown area and are easily accessible by streetcar. The busy **Jugendherberge Stuttgart (HI),** Haußmannstr. 27 (tel. (0711) 24 15 83; fax 236 10 41), is out the "ZOB" exit of the Klett-Passage, through the Schloßgarten, and past the signs leading uphill via the paved path. Or take U-Bahn 15 ("Heumaden") to "Eugenspl.," go down the hill, bear left, and enter on Kernerstr. (Reception open daily 7-8:45am and noon-11pm. DM22, over 26 DM27. Sheets DM5.50. Reserve by mail or fax.) The **Jugendgästehaus Stuttgart,** Richard-Wagner-Str. 2 (tel. (0711) 24 11 32), is less centrally located in a quiet residential neighborhood. Take Strassenbahn 15 ("Heumaden") to "Bubenbad." (Reception open Mon.-Fri. 9am-8pm, Sat.-Sun. 11am-8pm. Singles DM35-50; doubles DM70-90. Breakfast and lockers included.)

At the **University Mensa,** Holzgartenstr. 11, quantity compensates for quality. (Meals DM4-5. Open mid-April to late July and mid-Oct. to mid-Feb. Mon.-Fri. 11:15am-2pm; the rest of the year, Mon.-Fri. 11:15am-1:30pm.) **Iden,** Eberhardstr. 1 (U-Bahn: "Rathaus"), serves good cafeteria-style vegetarian fare (salads DM2.65 per 100g; open Mon.-Fri. 11am-9pm, Sat. 10am-5pm). When you're full, take in one of Stuttgart's **mineral baths.** The **Mineralbad Leuze,** Am Leuzebad 2-6 (tel. (0711) 216 42 10), has spectacular facilities and soothing waters (open daily 6am-9pm; DM15.50, students DM10.50). Once refreshed, join the crowd for drinks at **Palast der Republik,** Friedrichstr. 27 (beer DM4-6; open in summer daily 10am-3am; off-season 11am-3am), or dancing at **The Buddha,** Schwabenzentrum. (Open Tues.-Wed. 9pm-2:30am, Thurs. 9pm-3am, Fri. 9pm-5am, Sat. 8pm-6am, Sun. 8pm-3am.) **King's Club,** Calverstr. 21 (tel. (0711) 22 45 58), and **Laura's,** Lautenschlagerstr. 20 (tel. (0711) 29 01 60), are Stuttgart's premiere gay and lesbian locales, respectively.

Heidelberg

Believe the tourist propaganda—Heidelberg is surrounded by magnificence that truly shines. In 1386, the sages of Heidelberg turned from illuminating manuscripts to illuminating young German minds, and in the process founded Germany's first and greatest university. Set against a backdrop of wooded hills along an ancient river, the crumbling edifices of the once-majestic *Schloß* and the *Altstadt*'s lively nightlife exert a magnetism that draws thousands of shutter-clicking tourists daily.

ORIENTATION AND PRACTICAL INFORMATION

Heidelberg occupies both sides of the Neckar River about 20km east of the river's convergence with the Rhine, but most of its attractions are clustered on the southern shore. To reach the *Altstadt* from the train station, take any bus or streetcar going to "Bismarckpl.," where the **Hauptstraße,** known as the longest shopping street in Germany, runs straight down the middle of the heart of the city.

Tourist Office: (tel. 277 35; fax 16 73 18). Directly in front of the train station. The office sells maps (DM1) and reserves rooms (7% down payment), but the staff steers guests towards pricier places. *Meier* (DM2) and *Fritz* (free) list local events and attractions. Open Mon.-Sat. 9am-7pm, Sun. 10am-6pm; Jan-Feb. closed Sun.

Currency Exchange: If banks and the post office are closed, try the *Hauptbahnhof*, where the exchange office stays open later.

American Express: Brückenkopfstr. 1 (tel. 450 50; fax 41 03 33), at the end of Theodor-Heuss Bridge. Mail held for members and those with AmEx traveler's checks. All banking services. Open Mon.-Fri. 10am-6pm, Sat. 10am-1pm.

Trains: Frequent trains run from Stuttgart (45min.) and Frankfurt (1hr.); Mannheim is less than 10min. away. Trains also serve towns in the Neckar Valley.

Public Transportation: To get to, out of, and around Heidelberg, buy a 24hr. pass good on all streetcars and buses (DM10). The pass is available at the tourist office or from any bus or streetcar conductor. Single-ride tickets cost DM3.

Bike Rental: Per Bike, Bergheimerstr. 125 (tel. 16 11 48). DM25 per day. Open Mon.-Fri. 9am-6pm, Sat. 9am-1pm; Nov.-March closed Sat.

Hitchhiking: Hitchers walk to the western end of Bergheimerstr. for all directions. The **Mitfahrzentrale,** Bergheimerstr. 125 (tel. 246 46; fax 14 59 59), matches drivers and riders. Paris about DM51. Köln DM28. Hamburg DM54. Open Mon.-Fri. 9am-5pm, Sat. 9am-noon; Nov.-March closed Sat.

Laundromat: Wasch Salon SB, Poststr. 49, next to Kurfürst Hotel. Wash DM7, dry DM1 per 20min. Open Mon.-Sat. 7am-11pm, Sun. 9am-8pm.

Emergencies: tel. 110. **Women's Emergency Hotline:** tel. 18 36 43.

Police: Römerstr. 2-4 (tel. 990).

Post Office: The main office is on Belfortstr., diagonally to the right across from the train station. Held mail can be picked up at counters 15-17. Open Mon.-Fri. 8am-6pm, Sat. 8am-noon. Limited services Mon.-Fri. 6-8pm. **Postal Code:** 69115.

Telephone Code: 06221.

ACCOMMODATIONS, CAMPING, AND FOOD

Finding accommodations in Heidelberg (even expensive ones) can be a nightmare. In the summer, call ahead or arrive early in the day. Those with a railpass might try the little towns and villages scattered short distances from Heidelberg. Many Neckar Valley towns with youth hostels lie along the reliable Heidelberg-Heilbronn railroad.

Jeske Hotel, Mittelbadgasse 2 (tel. 237 33). From the train station, take bus 33 ("Köpfel") or 11 ("Karlstor") to "Bergbahn," then follow Zwingerstr. west back toward the *Hauptbahnhof;* Mittelbachgasse is the first right after Oberbadgasse. An unbeatable location at a great price draws students to this quiet overnighter. DM24. Open Feb. to mid-Nov.; at other times call ahead.

Jugendherberge (HI), Tiergartenstr. 5 (tel. 41 20 66). From the station or Bismarckpl., take bus 33 ("Zoo-Sportzentrum") to "Jugendherberge." Somewhat cramped and noisy, but still popular. Members only. Small disco open nightly. Lockout 9am-1pm. Flexible curfew 11:30pm. DM22, over 26 DM27. Sheets DM5.50. Partial wheelchair access. Reserve a week ahead or forget it.

Hotel-Pension Elite, Bunsenstr. 15 (tel. 257 33). From Bismarckpl., follow Rohrbacherstr. away from the river and turn right onto Bunsenstr. High ceilings, Victorian decor, and pastoral views. Bath and TV in each room. Doubles DM100. DM15 per extra person. Breakfast included. Reserve by mail or phone.

Camping: Haide (tel. (06223) 21 11), between Ziegelhausen and Kleingemünd. Take bus 35 to "Orthopedisches Klinik," then cross the river. DM8 per person, DM6 per tent. Cabins DM14-16. Open April-Oct. Camp on the other side of the river at **Camping Heidelberg-Schlierbach** (tel. 80 25 06); take bus 35 ("Neckargmünd") to "Im Grund." DM10 per person, DM4-12 per tent. DM2 per car.

Eating out is costly in Heidelberg, especially around Hauptstr. Student pubs and restaurants beyond the pedestrian zone offer better value. Buy groceries at **Handelshof,** Kurfürsten-Anlage 60, 200m in front of the train station on the right (open Mon.-Wed. and Fri. 7:30am-8pm, Sat. 7:30am-4pm).

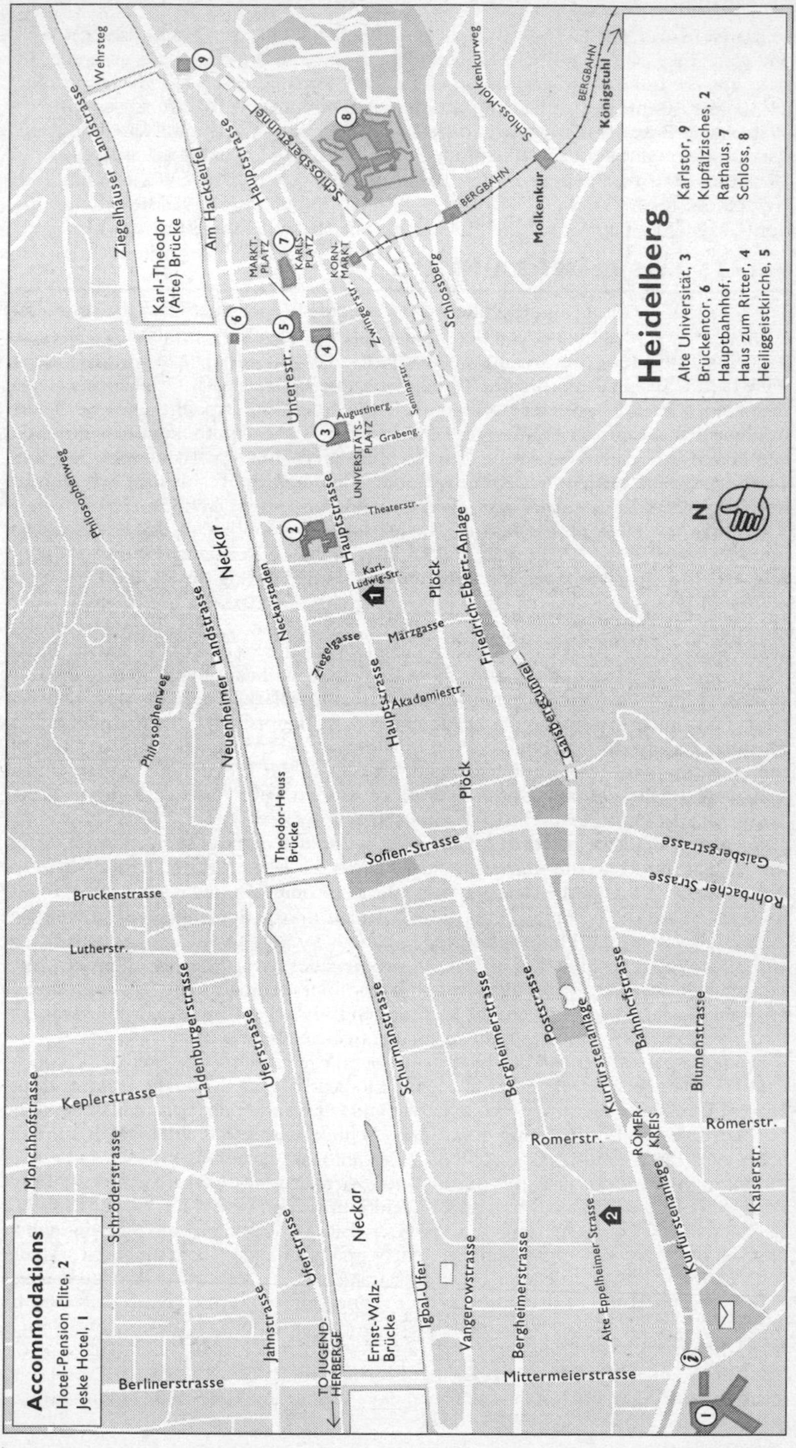
Heidelberg
Alte Universität, 3
Brückentor, 6
Hauptbahnhof, 1
Haus zum Ritter, 4
Heiliggeistkirche, 5
Karlstor, 9
Kupfälzisches, 2
Rathaus, 7
Schloss, 8
Accommodations
Hotel-Pension Elite, 2
Jeske Hotel, 1
N
Neckar
Karl-Theodor (Alte) Brücke
Theodor-Heuss Brücke
Ernst-Walz-Brücke
Ziegelhäuser Landstrasse
Neuenheimer Landstrasse
Philosophenweg
Am Hackteufel
Hauptstrasse
Schlossbergtunnel
Neckarstaden
Untere Str.
Zwingerstr.
Seminarstr.
Augustinerg.
Grabeng.
UNIVERSITÄTS-PLATZ
MARKT-PLATZ
KARLS-PLATZ
KORN-MARKT
Theaterstr.
Karl-Ludwig-Str.
Plöck
Friedrich-Ebert-Anlage
Schlossberg
Schloss-Molkenkurweg
Molkenkur
BERGBAHN
Königstuhl
Ziegelgasse
Märzgasse
Akademiestr.
Gaisbergtunnel
Sofien-Strasse
Gaisbergstrasse
Rohrbacher Strasse
Bruckenstrasse
Lutherstr.
Ladenburgerstrasse
Uferstrasse
Schurmanstrasse
Bergheimerstrasse
Poststrasse
Kurfürstenanlage
Bahnhofstrasse
Blumenstrasse
Römerstr.
Romerstr.
RÖMER-KREIS
Kaiserstr.
Monchhofstrasse
Keplerstrasse
Schröderstrasse
Jahnstrasse
Vangerowstrasse
Igbal-Ufer
Alte Eppelheimer Strasse
Berlinerstrasse
Mittermeierstrasse
Wehrsteg
TO JUGEND-HERBERGE

GERMANY

The **Mensa** on Marstallstr. serves cheap food and beer in a state-subsidized cafeteria and café. Take bus 35 to "Marstallstr.," or from the Alte Brücke take a left along the river; it's the huge stone installation on the left. (Open Mon.-Fri. 11:30am-2pm, Sat. 11:30am-1:30pm. During vacations, alternates hours with the *Mensa* on Universitätspl.) At **Gastätte Essighaus,** Plöck 97 (tel. 224 96), tasty specials include soup, salad, and an entree for DM10-12 (open daily 11:30am-12:30am, food available until 11:30pm). **Zum Schwarzen Wal,** Bahnhofstr. 27 (tel. 201 85), is *the* place in Heidelberg for big, delicious breakfasts (DM6-15) but also serves lunch and dinner (DM10-20; open Mon.-Fri. 7:30am-1am, Sat. 8:30am-1am, Sun. 9am-1am).

SIGHTS AND ENTERTAINMENT

The remarkable Gothic and High Renaissance **Heidelberger Schloß,** at the southeast corner of town, was built over a period of 400 years, beginning in the early 13th century. The obligatory tour includes a visit to the **Faß,** reputedly the world's largest wine barrel. Also in the castle, the **Apothekenmuseum** features a 17th-century alchemist's lab. (Grounds open daily 8am-dusk; before 5pm DM3, students DM1.50. Tours in English and German 11am-3pm. DM4, students DM2. Apothekenmuseum open late March-Oct. daily 10am-5pm; Nov. to mid-March Mon.-Fri. 10am-5pm, Sat.-Sun. 11am-5pm.) The castle is accessible by foot or by *Bergbahn* (cable car), which runs from the "Bergbahn/Rathaus" stop (bus 11 or 33; round-trip DM4.50).

In town, several sights cluster near the **Marktplatz,** a cobbled square that holds an open-air market every Wednesday and Saturday. In the center stands **Hercules' Fountain,** where accused witches and heretics were burned during the Middle Ages. Two of the oldest structures in the city border the Marktplatz: the 14th-century **Heiliggeistkirche,** a Gothic church with an ancient library, and the 16th-century **Hotel zum Ritter.** The stately **Rathaus** presides over the far end of the square. From the square, take Hauptstr. west for more Heidelbergian beauty; five blocks down, a stone-lion fountain oversees activities on **Universitätsplatz,** where the **Alte Universität** (Old University) was once headquartered. At Hauptstr. 97, the **Kurpfälzisches Museum** features the jawbone of *Homo heidelbergensis* ("Heidelberg Man," one of the oldest humans unearthed), works of art by Van der Weyden and Dürer, and a spectacular 15th-century Gothic altarpiece. (Open Tues.-Sun. 10am-5pm, Wed. 10am-9pm. DM5, students DM3, discounts on Sun.)

No trip to Heidelberg would be complete without a visit to the northern bank of the Neckar, opposite the *Altstadt.* A stroll across the elegant **Karl-Theodor-Brücke** finds a statue of the Prince-Elector himself; Brücke commissioned it as a symbol of his modesty. From the far end of the bridge, clamber up the **Schlangenweg,** a winding stone stairway, to the **Philosophenweg,** a famous pedestrian walkway where Hegel and Max Weber indulged in afternoon promenades. Atop the **Heiligenberg,** the mountain traversed by the *Philosophenweg,* lie the ruins of the 9th-century **St. Michael Basilika,** the 13th-century **St. Stephen Kloster,** and an **amphitheater,** built under Hitler's order, on the site of an ancient Celtic gathering place.

Heidelberg's **Faschings Parade** struts through town the day before Ash Wednesday. The two-week **Spring Festival** begins at the end of May, while the **Heidelberger Herbst** takes over the town with a market and fair on the third Saturday of September. For five weeks beginning in late July, **Schloßfestspiele Heidelberg** features a series of concerts and plays; call 58 35 21 for info and tickets. For drinks and entertainment year-round, visit the popular **historical student taverns;** the two best-known are **Roter Ochsen,** Haupstr. 217, and **Zum Sepp'l** next door. (Meals DM8-31. Beer DM4.50-5. Roter Ochsen open April-Oct. daily 11:30am-2pm and 5pm-midnight; Nov.-March Mon.-Sat. 5pm-midnight. Zum Sepp'l open daily 10am-midnight.) Much of Heidelberg's nightlife centers on Hauptstraße and the Marktplatz. **Little Heaven,** Fahrtgasse 18, is the local outpost of Euro-dance music culture (open daily 10pm-3am), while **Blue Note,** Neckarstaden 24, in the basement of the *Kongresshaus,* hosts theme nights that range from "Havana" to the oh-so-unusual "beer" (open Wed.-Sat. 10pm-3am). **Mata Hari,** on Zwingerstr. near the corner of Oberbadgasse, is a small, subdued gay and lesbian bar (open daily 10pm-3am; Tues. nights men only).

Near Heidelberg: Speyer and Neckar Valley

The **Neckar Valley,** a scenic stretch of narrow, thickly wooded ridges along the Neckar River, encompasses several medieval castles and untouristed small towns. At the north end of the valley, 14km upstream from Heidelberg, **Neckarsteinach** is notable for its four medieval castles, all within 3km of one another along the north bank of the river. Set against the ruins of a Roman imperial castle on a ridge high above the Neckar, **Bad Wimpfen** is one of the best-kept secrets in Southwest Germany. It lies along the alternate rail route Heilbronn-Heidelberg—that and another **train** line from Heidelberg pass through the many smaller towns along both sides of the valley on their way to Heilbronn. One of the best ways to explore the valley is along the 85km **bike** route. Alternatively, the **Rhein-Neckar Fahrgastschiffahrt** (tel. (06221) 201 81 or (06229) 526) runs boat tours from Easter through late October beginning in front of the *Stadthalle* in Heidelberg (DM16.50-22.50).

Just into Rhineland-Palatinate, **Speyer** is most easily accessed from Heidelberg. Spared during the two world wars and, until recently, well off the beaten path of mass tourism, the city boasts a gracefully ramshackle *Altstadt* and several glorious churches. Since its construction in the 12th century, the enormous **Kaiserdom** (Imperial Cathedral) has been the symbol of Speyer. The crypt under the east end holds the remains of eight Holy Roman Emperors and their wives (open April-Oct. daily 9am-7pm; Nov.-March 9am-5pm). Just south of the *Dom,* the **Historisches Museum der Pfalz** displays ancient artifacts, cathedral treasures, and the oldest bottle of wine in the world (open Tues.-Sun. 10am-6pm, Wed. 10am-8pm; DM8, students DM6). Speyer's **tourist office,** Maximilianstr. 11 (tel. (06232) 143 92), is two blocks from the cathedral's main entrance (open Mon.-Fri. 9am-5pm, Sat. 10am-4pm). Get here by **rail** (1-1½hr.) or by **bus** 7007 (1½hr.) from Heidelberg.

Tübingen

Situated on the willow-lined Neckar River near the Black Forest, Tübingen has gracefully retained the aloofness of its intellectual origins. Nearly half the city's residents are affiliated with the 500-year-old university, and students energize the city center. The 15th-century **Stiftskirche,** the focal point of the *Altstadt,* houses the tombs of 14 members of the former House of Württemberg in the chancel. The church's tower affords an amazing view of the city. (Church open daily 9am-5pm. Chancel and tower open Aug.-Sept. daily 10:30am-5pm; April-July and Oct. Fri.-Sun. 10:30am-5pm. Chancel and tower DM2, students DM1.) Just down the road from the Stiftskirche is the **Tübingen Evangelischer Stift.** Built as an Augustinian monastery, it later became a seminary which housed such academic luminaries as Kepler, Hölderlin, Hegel, Schelling, and Mörike. Alas, the historical interest of this building outweighs its aesthetic appeal. The ornate, painted facade of the **Rathaus** faces the old market square in the middle of the *Altstadt.* On top of the hill that separates the university from most of the city stands the **Schloß Hohentübingen,** a castle with a rough stone balcony overlooking the old town. On the north riverbank is the **Hölderlinturm,** a tower where 18th-century poet Friedrich Hölderlin lived out the final 36 years of his life. The tower now houses a memorial museum. (Open Tues.-Fri. 10am-noon and 3-5pm, Sat.-Sun. 2-5pm. Tours Sat.-Sun. 5pm. DM3, students DM2.)

Practical Information, Accommodations, and Food Tübingen's **tourist office,** Neckarbrücke (tel. (07071) 913 60; fax 350 70), books hotel or private rooms for a DM5 fee (DM30-100). From the front of the train station, turn right and walk to Karlstr., turn left, and walk to the river (open Mon.-Fri. 9am-7pm, Sat. 9am-5pm, Sun. 2-5pm). The large, worn **Jugendherberge (HI),** Gartenstr. 22/2 (tel. (07071) 230 02; fax 250 61), overlooks the Neckar and has a great breakfast but cramped rooms. Take bus 11 (DM2.50) from the station to "Jugendherberge." (Reception open daily 5-8pm and 10-10:15pm. Curfew midnight. Members only. DM22, over 26 DM27. Breakfast included.) Camp at **Rappernberghalde** (tel. (07071)

431 45) on the river. Go upstream from the old town or left from the station, cross the river on the Alleenbrücke, and turn left again (20min.). Follow the blue camping signs. (Reception open daily 8am-12:30pm and 2:30-10pm. DM9.50 per person, DM5.50-7 per tent. Open April to mid-Oct.)

Tübingen's students keep a number of superb yet inexpensive restaurants busy. **Marquardtei,** Herrenbergstr. 34, serves whole-wheat pizza and a vast selection of vegetarian and meat dishes (entrees DM10-14; open Mon.-Sat. 11:30am-1am, Sun. 10am-10pm). **Mensa,** on Wilhelmstr. between Gmelinstr. and Keplerstr. offers generic fare for the severely budget-conscious. (Meals under DM8.80. Open late Aug.-late July Mon.-Thurs. 11:30am-2pm and 6-8:15pm, Fri. noon-2pm, Sat. 11:45pm-1:15pm.) The *Altstadt*'s zig-zagging streets are lined with excellent pubs and cafés. **Tangente-Night,** Pfleghofstr., is a premier Tübingen student hangout; during the school year, a DJ spins house, acid jazz, hip-hop, and techno Thursday through Sunday nights (open daily 10am-3am). **Marktschenke,** Am Markt 11, and **Neckarmüller,** Gartenstr. 4, are popular with young folks.

Freiburg im Breisgau

Freiburg may be the "metropolis" of the Schwarzwald, but it has not succumbed to the hectic rhythms of city life. The palpable unhurriedness may result from the surrounding hills. The pride of Freiburg is the **Münster,** a tremendous stone cathedral with a 116m spire built at intervals between the 13th and 16th centuries. (Cathedral open Mon.-Sat. 10am-7pm, Sun. 1-6pm. Tower open May-Oct. Mon. and Wed.-Sat. 9:30am-5pm, Sun. 1-5pm; Nov.-April Wed.-Sat. 9:30am-5pm. DM2, students DM1.) A stroll through the surrounding *Altstadt* will uncover several **Bächle,** narrow streams of swiftly flowing water that run through the city. In medieval times, these open gutters were used to water cattle and protect against fires; today, they exist only to soak the shoes of unwary tourists. Two medieval gates—the **Schwabentor** and the **Martinstor**—still stand within a few blocks of one another in the southeast corner of the *Altstadt.* From the Schwabentor, take the pedestrian overpass across the heavily trafficked Schloßbergring and climb the **Schloßberg** for an excellent view of the city.

Freiburg's museums cater to a variety of interests. The **Augustiner Museum,** housed in a former monastery on Augustinerpl., has a large collection of mostly medieval artifacts (open Tues.-Sun. 10am-5pm; DM4, students DM2). Farther south, the **Museum für Neuekunst** (Museum of Modern Art), Marienstr. 10a, displays the work of 20th-century German artists such as Otto Dix (open Tues.-Sun. 10am-5pm; free).

Practical Information, Accommodations, and Food The **tourist office,** Rotteckring 14 (tel. (0761) 388 18 80; fax 370 03), two blocks down Eisenbahnstr. from the train station, distributes the comprehensive *Freiburg Official Guide* (in German or English, DM6) and finds rooms for DM5. (Open June-Sept. Mon.-Fri. 9:30am-5pm, Sat. 9:30am-6pm, Sun. 10am-noon; Oct.-May Mon.-Fri. 9:30am-6pm, Sat. 9:30am-2pm, Sun. 10am-noon.) The **Jugendherberge (HI),** Kartäuserstr. 151 (tel. (0761) 676 56; fax 603 67), provides rooms in an arboreal setting. Take S-Bahn 1 ("Littenweiler") to "Römerhof," walk down Fritz-Geiges-Str., cross the stream, and turn right. (Reception open daily 7am-11:30pm. Curfew 11:30pm. Members only. DM22, over 26 DM27.) **Hotel Zum Löwen,** Breisgauerstr. 62 (tel. (0761) 846 61; fax 840 23), doesn't feel like a budget hotel. Take S-Bahn 1 to "Padua-Allee" and walk down Breigauerstr. for 5 minutes; the entrance is in the court (singles DM45-50, doubles DM80-130). To find the attractive **Haus Lydia Kalchtaler,** Peterhof 11 (tel. (0761) 671 19), take S-Bahn 1 ("Littenweiler") to "Lassbergstr.," then hop on bus 17 to "Kleintalstr.," and follow Peterhof up to the wooden farmhouse (DM20-25).

Freiburger Salatstuben, Löwenstr. 1, offers imaginative salads and health foods, while **Milano,** Schusterstr. 7, dishes up tasty and inexpensive pizza and pasta. The brewery **Brauerei Ganter,** Schwarzwaldstr. 43 (tel. (0761) 218 51 81), conducts one-hour tours tracking the production process of the malt beverage; the grand finale consists of food and lots of beer atop one of the factory buildings (free). For less structured entertainment, Freiburg's nightlife revolves around the Martinstor. **Jazzhaus,** Schnewlingstr. 1, features live performances almost every night, while **Greiffenegg-Schlößle,** Schloßbergring 3, offers beer (DM5-7) on a hillside terrace.

Black Forest (Schwarzwald)

Throughout its rocky development, the German cultural consciousness dreamed of the dark, from the earliest fairy tales to Franz Kafka's disturbing fiction. Nowhere are such nightmarish thoughts more at home than in the southwest corner of Baden-Württemberg—the Black Forest, so named because of the eerie gloom that prevails under its canopy of evergreens. Inspiration for *Hänsel and Gretel,* the Black Forest draws travelers and skiers to its trails, now marked by more than bread crumbs.

The main entry points to the Black Forest are Freiburg at its center; Baden-Baden to the northwest; Stuttgart to the east; and Basel, Switzerland to the southwest. The **Freiburg tourist office** is the best place to gather info about the Black Forest. The longest slope is at Feldberg (near Titisee), and the most scenic route is the stretch from northern Waldkirch to southeastern Hinterzarten. **Rail lines** run along the perimeter from Baden-Baden to Freiburg and east from Freiburg to Donaueschingen and Stuttgart, but many of the innermost regions are accessible only by infrequent **buses.** Check return connections in advance before setting off on daytrips. Many bus lines are privately owned, rendering railpasses invalid.

Titisee and Schluchsee The touristed town of **Titisee,** 30km east of Freiburg, is set against dark pine-forested ridges and a lake of the same name. Hourly **trains** connect Freiburg to Titisee. The **tourist office** is in the *Kurhaus,* Strandbadstr. 4 (tel. (07651) 980 40; fax 98 04 40). To reach the building, turn right in front of the train station, walk to the first intersection, and turn right before the entrances to the pedestrian zone. The office books rooms (DM3) and sells maps of the 130km of hiking trails surrounding the lake. (DM1-15. Open May-Oct. Mon.-Fri. 8am-6pm, Sat. 10am-noon and 3-5pm, Sun. 10am-noon; Nov.-April Mon.-Fri. 8am-noon and 1:30-5:30pm.) **Paddleboats** can be rented from several vendors along Seestr. for DM11-15 per hour. Guided **boat tours** of the lake (25min., DM6) depart from the same area. **Jugendherberge Veltishof (HI),** Bruderhalde 27 (tel. (07652) 238; fax 756), is beautifully if inconveniently located at the far end of the lake. From the train station, take Südbaden bus 7300 to "Feuerwehrheim" (every 1-3hr., DM3). By foot, it's a 30-minute walk along the main road from the *Kurhaus.* (Members only. Reception open daily 5-8pm. Curfew 10pm. DM22, over 26 DM26. Resort tax DM2.10.) Several campgrounds lie along the same road; **Naturcamping Weiherhof,** Bruderholde 26 (tel. (07652) 14 68 or 14 78), has laundry facilities and great, tree-shaded places to pitch a tent (DM8 per person, DM6.50 per tent; *Kurtaxe* DM2.10; open mid-May to Sept.).

South of Titisee is the comparably picturesque, less-touristed **Schluchsee.** Hourly **trains** make the 30-minute jaunt from Titisee. The **tourist office** (tel. (07656) 77 32; fax 77 59), a block into the pedestrian zone in the *Kurhaus,* sells hiking maps and finds rooms. (Open July-Aug. Mon.-Fri. 8am-6pm, Sat. 10am-noon and 4-6pm, Sun. 10am-noon; Sept.-Oct. and May-June Mon.-Fri. 8am-noon and 2-6pm, Sat. 10am-noon.; Nov.-April closed Sat.) The **Jugendherberge Schluchsee-Wolfsgrund (HI)** (tel. (07656) 329; fax 92 37) is situated on the shore; from the station, cross the tracks, hop the fence and then follow the path right, over the bridge parallel to the tracks (reception closed daily 2-5pm; curfew 11pm; DM22, over 26 DM27).

St. Peter, St. Märgen, and Triberg North of Titisee and about 15km east of Freiburg, the twin villages of **St. Peter** and **St. Märgen** lie within the High Black Forest. **Bus** 7216 runs occasionally from Freiburg to St. Märgen via St. Peter; the more timely route requires a train ride on the Freiburg-Neustadt line to "Kirchzarten," where bus 7216 stops on the way to St. Peter's. **St. Peter's,** designed by architect Peter Thumb, appears where a halo of green farmland breaks through the dark crust of pine forests. The abbey's **Klosterkirche** is aflutter with Baroque angels inside (sporadic tours; call the tourist office). From the "Zähringer Eck" bus stop, the **tourist office** (tel. (07660) 91 02 24; fax 91 02 44) is about 100m up the street (open Mon.-Fri. 8am-noon and 2-5pm; June-Oct. also Sat. 11am-1pm). Well-marked **trails** cover the surrounding area; an 8km trail from the abbey leads to St. Märgen.

Nestled in a valley 800m above sea level and 1½ hours by train from Konstanz, the touristy whistle stop of **Triberg** has Germany's highest **waterfalls,** a series of white cascades tumbling over mossy rocks for 162 vertical meters (park admission DM2.50, students DM2). **Hiking trails** abound throughout the outskirts of town, including a portion of the Pforzheim-Basel *Westweg.* Triberg's **tourist office** (tel. (07722) 95 32 30; fax 95 32 36), on the ground floor of the local *Kurhaus,* dishes out brochures, sells town maps (DM1; not good enough for hiking) and hiking maps (DM5.50), and dispenses a catalog of all accommodations in the region (open Mon.-Fri. 9am-5pm; May-Sept. also Sat. 10am-noon). The town's sparkling, modern **Jugendherberge (HI),** Rohrbacherstr. 35 (tel. (07722) 41 10; fax 66 62), requires a grueling 30-minute climb up Friedrichstr. (which turns into Rohrbacherstr.) from the tourist office. (Reception open 5-7pm and at 9:45pm. DM22, over 26 DM27. Sheets DM5.50. Call ahead.) For those avoiding the climb, the **Hotel Zum Bären,** Hauptstr. 10 (tel. (07722) 44 93), offers worn-in rooms, most with showers, closer to the town center. The jolly staff has been dealing with American students for 25 years (singles DM46, doubles DM86).

Baden-Baden

If you're fabulously wealthy, Baden-Baden can be a lot of fun. Minor royalty and the like convene here to bathe in the curative mineral spas and drop fat sums of money in the casino. Students with shorts and backpacks may feel a bit out of place, but with a little grooming and diplomacy even humble tourists can bask in the opulence of this pampering and relaxed resort town.

Baden-Baden's history as a resort goes back nearly two millennia, when the Romans built the first **thermal baths** here. The **Friedrichsbad,** Römerpl. 1, is a palatial 19th-century bathing palace where you can enjoy a three-hour Roman-Irish Bath. No clothing is permitted. (Open Mon.-Sat. 9am-10pm; last entry 7:30pm. Baths are co-ed Tues. and Fri. 4-10pm and all day Wed., Sat., and Sun. DM36, with soap and brush massage DM48.) More modest and budget-minded cure-seekers should try next door at the beautiful **Caracalla-Thermen,** Römerpl. 11, which offers placid soaking—in bathing suits (DM19 for 2hr., with youth hostel coupon DM15.50; open daily 8am-10pm). When not getting wrinkled at the baths, Baden-Baden's affluent guests head to the **Casino,** whose lavish decor, modeled on Versailles, can be viewed during guided tours. (Open April-Sept. daily 9:30am-noon; Oct.-March 9:30am-noon. Last tour at 11:30am. DM3.) To enter during gaming hours (Sun.-Thurs. 2pm-2am, Fri.-Sat. 2pm-3am), you must be 21, pay DM5, and wear semi-formal attire.

For a sumptuous view of the Black Forest, mount the 668m **Merkur** peak east of town. Take bus 4 or 5 from Leopoldspl. to "Merkurwald," then take the railway to the top (round-trip DM10). On the hill, the **Neues Schloß** houses a museum of the town's history. (Open Tues.-Sun. 10am-12:30pm and 2-5pm. DM2, students DM1. Tours Mon.-Fri. 3pm.) From the neighboring garden, Baden-Baden lies at your feet. The 12th-century ruins of the **Altes Schloß** in the upper hills, a few kilometers from the Neues Schloß, afford a view extending all the way to France. Take bus 15 from Augustapl. (open Tues.-Sun. 10am-10pm; free).

Practical Information, Accommodations, and Food The **tourist office** is at Augustapl. 8 (tel. (07221) 275 20; fax 27 52 02), in the building next to the Kongreßhaus (open daily 9:30am-6pm). Baden-Baden's **train station** is 7km northwest of town. To avoid the 90-minute walk, take bus 201 ("Lichtental/Oberbeuren") to "Augustapl." (DM3, 24hr. pass DM8). The **post office** on Leopoldpl. has phones and changes money, as does the casino. The cheapest bed in town is at the modern **Jugendherberge (HI),** Hardbergstr. 34 (tel. (07221) 522 23; fax 600 12), halfway between the station and the town center; take bus 201 to "Große-Dollen-Straße" and follow the signs uphill. (Reception open daily 5-6pm and briefly at 8pm and 10pm. Curfew 11:30pm. Members only. DM22, over 26 DM27. Wheelchair accessible.) Most rooms in the center of town are ritzy and overpriced, but the **Hotel am Markt,** Marktpl. 18 (tel. (07221) 227 47 or 227 43; fax 39 18 87), offers reasonable prices and a great location uphill from the main pedestrian area. (Reception open daily 7am-10pm. Singles DM54-60, with shower DM80; doubles DM100-105, with shower DM135. Breakfast included.) Most restaurant prices aren't compatible with budget travel, but daily specials often run for under DM12. Another option is to fill up a picnic basket at **Pennymarkt** at the Große-Dollenstr. bus stop.

Lake Constance (Bodensee)

The third-largest lake in Europe, Lake Constance forms a graceful three-cornered border at the conjunction of Austria, Switzerland, and Germany. Ancient castles, manicured islands, and great sunbathing provide an excellent escape during the summer.

Spanning the Rhine's exit from the lake, the elegant university city of **Konstanz** is among the few German cities to have escaped Allied bombing. Narrow streets wind around painted Baroque and Renaissance facades in the town's center. Particularly inspiring is the **Münster;** don't miss the view from the top of its Gothic spire. (Cathedral open daily 8am-5:30pm; free. Tower open Mon.-Sat. 10am-6pm, Sun. 1-6pm; DM2, students DM1.) Konstanz's free **beaches** are packed in good weather. **Strandbad Horn** is the largest and most popular (take bus 5). Twenty-somethings frolic on the beach at the university; take bus 4 to "Egg" and walk past the playing fields.

The **tourist office,** Bahnhofspl. 13 (tel. (07531) 13 30 30; fax 13 30 60), in the arcade to the right of the train station, provides an excellent walking map. (Open May-Sept. Mon.-Fri. 9am-6:30pm, Sat. 9am-1pm; Oct.-April Mon.-Fri. 9am-noon and 2-6pm; April and Oct. also Sat. 9am-1pm.) The top-rate **Jugendherberge Kreuzlingen (HI),** Promenadenstr. 7 (tel. in Switzerland (071) 688 26 65; from Germany (0041) 71 688 26 63), is in an old manor south of the border in Kreuzlingen, Switzerland. (Call for directions. Reception open daily 8-9am and 5-9pm. First night 21.20SFr/DM26.50, then 18.70SFr/DM23.40. Open March-Nov.) The hostel in Konstanz, **Jugendherberge "Otto-Moericke-Turm" (HI),** Zur Allmannshöhe 18 (tel. (07531) 322 60), has rooms in a former water tower. Take bus 4 from "Marktstätte" (around the corner from the post office in front of the station) to "Jugendherberge." (Reception open daily 3-7:10pm. Curfew 10pm. DM21.50, over 26 DM26.50. Members only. Call ahead.) The **University Mensa** dishes out the city's cheapest food; take bus 9 from the station to "Universität" (open Mon.-Fri. 8am-6pm; Aug. 11am-2pm). **Sedir,** Hofhaldestr. 11, serves delectable vegetarian noodles for DM9.50 (open Mon.-Fri. 11:30am-2pm and 6pm-1am, Sat.-Sun. noon-2:30pm and 6pm-1am).

Lindau im Bodensee Connected to the lake shore by a narrow causeway, the romantic medieval city of **Lindau** looks out across the Bodensee, where the aquamarine waters and the small detachment from the mainland contribute to the resort-like ambience. The **Städtische Kunstsammlung** (town art museum) is in **Cavazzen-Haus,** an ornate Baroque mansion (open April-Oct. Tues.-Sun. 10am-noon and 2-5pm; DM4, students DM1). The harbor is framed by a 19th-century **Bavarian Lion** and the **New Lighthouse,** the latter offering an illuminating overview of the neighborhood (open daily 10am-7pm; DM2, students DM1). For those over 21 and well-dressed, the **casino** on the island can be fun (open 3pm-2am; admission DM5 and a passport). Lindau has three **beaches.** (All open June to mid-Aug. and weekends year-round daily 10am-8pm; other times 10:30am-7:30pm. Last admission 1hr. before closing.) **Römerbad,** left of the harbor, is the smallest and most familial (DM5, students DM3).

The **tourist office,** Am Hauptbahnhof (tel. (08382) 26 00 30; fax 26 00 26), across from the station, finds rooms for a DM5 fee and leads tours daily at 10am (DM3-5; open Mon.-Sat. 9am-1pm and 2-7pm). **Ferries** chug to Konztanz (5-7 per day, 3hr., DM18). The **train** takes two hours (DM13). Rent **boats** (tel. 55 14) 50m to the left of the casino, right next to the bridge. (Open mid.-March to mid.-Sept. daily 9am-9pm.

Paddleboats DM12-15 per hr. Power boat DM45 per hr.) One-hour excursions on a boat leave from the dock behind the casino at 11:30am, 1, 2:30, and 6pm (DM12).

The spectacular **Jugendherberge,** Herbergsweg 11 (tel. (08382) 967 10), lies across the Seebrücke off of Bregenzerstr. (Reception open 9am-midnight. Curfew midnight. Under 27 and families with small children only. DM27.50. Breakfast, sheets, and *Kurtaxe* included.) **Campingplatz Lindau-Zech,** Frauenhoferstr. 20 (tel. (08382) 722 36), is 3km south of the island on the mainland. Take bus 1 or 2 from the station to "Anheggerstr.," then bus 3 ("Zech"). (DM9.50 per person, DM4 per tent. *Kurtaxe* DM1.50. Showers included. Open April-Oct.) Sit down for Greek at **Taverna Pita Gyros,** Paradiespl. 16, which offers big platters (DM6-15; open daily 10am-9pm).

BAVARIA (BAYERN)

Bavaria is the Germany of Teutonic myth, Wagnerian opera, and fairy tales. From the Baroque cities along the Danube to the turreted castles perched high in the Alps, the region draws more tourists than any other part of the country. Indeed, when most foreigners conjure up images of Germany, they imagine Bavaria, land of beer halls, oom-pah-pah bands, and *Lederhosen.* Though mostly rural, Catholic, and conservative, this largest of Germany's federal states nurtures flourishing commerce and industry, including Bayerische Motor Werke (BMW). The region's independent residents have always been Bavarians first and Germans second.

Reminder: HI-affiliated hostels in Bavaria do not admit guests over age 26.

Munich (München)

As Germany's second city, Munich's sensual air of merriment—most obvious during the wild *Fasching* and the legendary *Oktoberfest*—contrasts with Berlin's starker, more cutting-edge energy. But despite the brilliance of Munich's postwar economic glory, the modern city emerges from a powerful and troubled history. The Bavarian Golden Age of the 18th and 19th centuries, characterized by the wildly extravagant castles of Ludwig II, ended abruptly with Germany's defeat in World War I. Munich was home to Adolf Hitler's squashed Beer Hall Putsch in 1923. After Chamberlain's Munich Agreement sold the Sudetenland to Hitler but failed to buy "peace in our time," World War II shattered the city, leaving less than 3% of the city center intact. Efforts to redeem Munich's reputation by hosting the 1972 Olympics failed when Palestinian terrorists attacked Israeli athletes during the Games. Munich has become a sprawling, relatively liberal metropolis in the midst of solidly conservative southern Germany, but beneath the good spirits lurk the memories of a darker time.

ORIENTATION AND PRACTICAL INFORMATION

A map of Munich's center looks like a skewed circle quartered by one horizontal and one vertical line. The circle is the main traffic **Ring,** within which lies the lion's share of Munich's sights. The east-west and north-south thoroughfares cross at Munich's epicenter, the **Marienplatz** (home to the **Neues Rathaus**), and meet the traffic ring at **Karlsplatz** in the west, **Isartorplatz** in the east, **Odeonsplatz** in the north, and **Sendlinger Tor** in the south. The **Hauptbahnhof** (main train station) is just beyond Karlspl. outside the Ring in the west. To get to Marienpl. from the train station, go straight on Schützenstr. to Karlspl., then continue through Karlstor to Neuhauserstr., which becomes Kaufingerstr. before it reaches Marienpl. (15-20min.). Or take S-Bahn 1-8 two stops from the main train station to "Marienpl."

At Odeonspl., the **Residenz** palace sprawls, and **Ludwigstraße** stretches north to the university district. **Leopoldstraße,** Ludwigstr.'s continuation, reaches farther into the student area **Schwabing** ("Schwabylon"). To the west is the **Olympiazentrum;** even farther west sits the posh **Nymphenburg,** built around the **Nymphenburg Pal-**

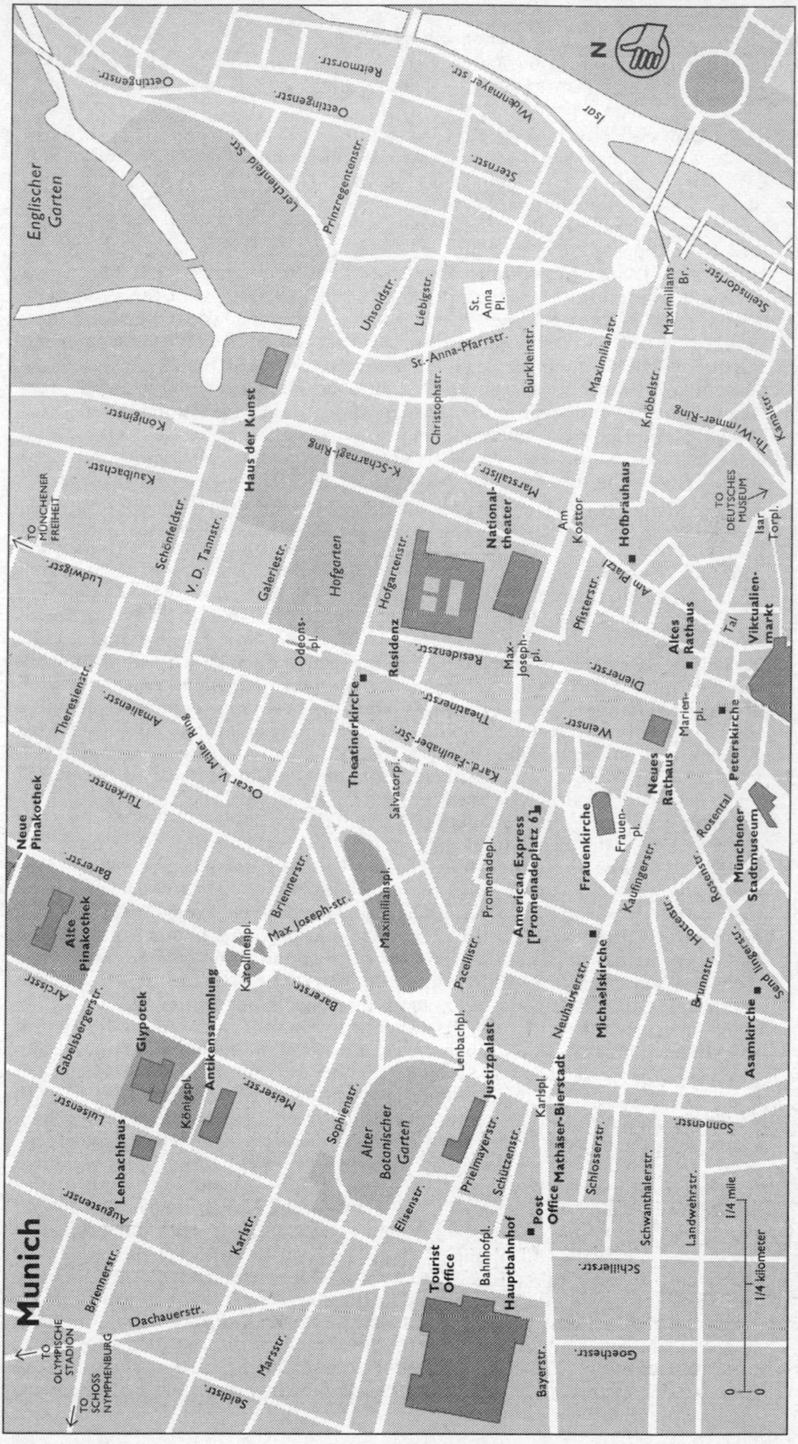
Munich
TO OLYMPISCHE STADION
TO SCHOSS NYMPHENBURG
Briennerstr.
Dachauerstr.
Marsstr.
Seidlstr.
Augustenstr.
Lenbachhaus
Luisenstr.
Königspl.
Glypotek
Antikensammlung
Gabelsbergerstr.
Arcisstr.
Alte Pinakothek
Neue Pinakothek
Barerstr.
Türkenstr.
Theresienstr.
Amalienstr.
Karlstr.
Meiserstr.
Sophienstr.
Alter Botanischer Garten
Elisenstr.
Prielmayerstr.
Justizpalast
Lenbachpl.
Karolinenpl.
Max Joseph-str.
Briennerstr.
Maximilianspl.
Oscar V. Miller Ring
Pacellistr.
Promenadepl.
Salvatorpl.
Theatinerkirche
Kard.-Faulhaber-Str.
Theatinerstr.
Residenzstr.
Residenz
Odeons-pl.
Hofgarten
Galeriestr.
Hofgartenstr.
V. D. Tannstr.
Schönfeldstr.
Ludwigstr.
TO MÜNCHENER FREIHEIT
Kaulbachstr.
Königinstr.
Haus der Kunst
K.-Scharnagl-Ring
Englischer Garten
Lerchenfeld Str.
Oettingenstr.
Oettingenstr.
Reitmorstr.
Prinzregentenstr.
Unsoldstr.
Liebigstr.
Christophstr.
St.-Anna-Pfarrstr.
St. Anna Pl.
Bürkleinstr.
Maximilianstr.
Widenmayer str.
Isar
Sternstr.
N
Maximilians Br.
Steinsdorfstr.
Knöbelstr.
Th.-Wimmer-Ring
Kanalstr.
Marstallstr.
National-theater
Max-Joseph-pl.
Am Kosttor
Hofbräuhaus
Am Platzl
Pfisterstr.
TO DEUTSCHES MUSEUM
Isar Torpl.
Tal
Viktualien-markt
Altes Rathaus
Dienerstr.
Weinstr.
Marien-pl.
Peterskirche
Neues Rathaus
Frauenkirche
Frauen-pl.
Kaufingerstr.
Rosental
Rosenstr.
Münchener Stadtmuseum
Hotterstr.
Sendlingerstr.
Brunnstr.
Asamkirche
Sonnenstr.
Neuhauserstr.
Michaelskirche
American Express [Promenadeplatz 6]
Karlspl.
Mathäser-Bierstadt
Schlosserstr.
Schwanthalerstr.
Landwehrstr.
1/4 mile
1/4 kilometer
0
0
Schillerstr.
Goethestr.
Bayerstr.
Hauptbahnhof
Bahnhofpl.
Tourist Office
Post Office
Schützenstr.

GERMANY

ace. Southwest of Marienpl., **Sendlingerstraße** leads past shops to the Sendlinger Tor. From there, Lindwurmstr. proceeds to Goethepl., from which Mozartstr. leads to **Thereslenwiese,** site of the annual beer extravaganza—*Oktoberfest.*

Tourist Offices: Fremdenverkehrsamt (tel. 23 33 02 56 or 23 33 02 57; fax 23 33 02 33). On the main train station's east side. Books rooms (DM5 per room, plus DM3-9 deposit), sells accommodations lists (DM0.50), and gives out excellent free city maps. *München Infopool* (DM1) is aimed at young tourists. Open Mon.-Fri. 10am-1pm. A **branch office** (tel. 97 59 28 15), at the airport in the *Zentralgebäude,* provides general info, but no room bookings. Open Mon.-Sat. 8:30am-10pm, Sun. 1-9pm. **EurAide in English** (tel. 59 38 89; fax 550 39 65; http://www.cube.net/kmu/euraide.html), along Track 11 (room 3) of the *Hauptbahnhof,* is good for transportation needs. Room reservations DM6. Open from June-Oktoberfest daily 7:45am-noon and 1-6pm; Oct.-April. Mon.-Fri. 7:45am-noon and 1-4pm, Sat. 7:45am-noon; May daily 7:45am-noon and 1:4:30pm.

Tours: Mike's Bike Tours (tel. 651 42 750). 4-6hr. tours leave 1-4 times daily from March through October from the *Altes Rathaus*; DM33-45. **Munich Walks** (tel. 017 72 27 59 01). 2½hr. guided tours provide a general historical overview (1-2 times daily), or emphasize Nazi history (2-4 times weekly). DM10-15.

Budget Travel: Council Travel, Adalbertstr. 32, 80799 München (tel. 39 50 22; fax 39 70 04), near the university, sells ISICs. Open Mon.-Fri. 10am-1pm and 2-6:30pm.

Consulates: Australians contact the consulate in Bonn (Godesberger Allee 105-107; tel. (0228) 81 30). **Canada,** Tal 29 (tel. 219 95 70). Open Mon.-Thurs. 9am-noon and 2-5pm, Fri. 9am-noon and 2-3:30pm. **Ireland,** Mauerkircherstr. 1a (tel. 98 57 23). Open Mon.-Thurs. 9am-noon and 2-4pm, Fri. 9am-noon. **New Zealanders** head to the consulate in Bonn (Bundeskanzlerpl. 2-10; tel. (0228) 22 80 70). **South Africa,** Sendlinger-Tor-Pl. 5 (tel. 231 16 30). Open Mon.-Fri. 9am-noon. **U.K.** Bürkleinstr. 10 (tel. 21 10 90), 4th fl. Consular section open Mon.-Fri. 8:45-11:30am and 1-3:15pm. **U.S.** Königinstr. 5 (tel. 288 80). Open Mon.-Fri. 8-11am.

Currency Exchange: American Express offers the best rates; otherwise pick up a copy of EurAide's free publication *Inside Track* and take it to the Reise Bank for a 50% discount on commission (regularly DM3-10) if cashing US$50 or more in U.S. traveler's checks. At the main station in front of the main entrance on Bahnhofpl. (open daily 6am-11pm) and at track 11 (open Mon.-Sat. 7:30am-7pm).

American Express: Promenadepl. 6 (tel. 29 09 00; fax 29 09 01 18; 24hr. hotline (0130) 85 31 00), in the Hotel Bayerischer Hof. Holds mail, cashes traveler's checks, no *kiquebaque.* Open Mon.-Fri. 9am-5:30pm, Sat. 9:30am-12:30pm.

Flights: For flight info, call 97 52 13 13. **Flughafen München** is accessible from the train station by S-Bahn 8, which runs daily 3:22am-12:42am, every 20min.

Trains: *Hauptbahnhof* (tel. 22 33 12 56). The transportation hub of southern Germany. To: Frankfurt (3½hr.), Berlin (7½hr.), Hamburg (6hr.), Prague (6-7½hr.), Vienna (4-5hr.), Paris (9½-10hr.), and Amsterdam (9hr.). Call for schedules, fare information (tel. 194 19), and reservations (in German only, tel. 13 08 23 33).

Public Transportation: The **MVV** system runs 5am-12:30am (until 1:30am on weekends. A few lines run through the night every hour. Eurail, InterRail, and German railpasses are valid on any S-Bahn (commuter rail) but *not* on the U-Bahn (subway), *Straßenbahn,* or buses. Single ride tickets (with transfers) are DM3.40 within the *Innenraum* (city center). A *Streifenkarte* (11-strip ticket) costs DM15. Cancel 2 strips per person. Single-day tickets give one person unlimited travel (city center DM8). Stamp your ticket in the boxes marked with an "E" *before you go to the platform* (or on board a bus). If you cheat, the fine is DM60.

Bike Rental: Radius Touristik (tel. 59 61 13), in the rear of the *Hauptbahnhof* near tracks 30-31. DM10-15 for 2hr. DM30-45 for 24hr. DM100-200 deposit. 10% discounts for students and Eurailpass. Open daily April-early Oct. 10am-6pm.

Hitchhiking: Those offering rides post info in the **Mensa,** on Leopoldstr. 13. Otherwise, hitchers try *Autobahn* on-ramps. Hitchers heading to E11 towards Salzburg-Vienna-Italy, take U-Bahn 1 or 2 to "Karl-Preis-Pl." For E11 in the other direction (towards Stuttgart/France), they take U-Bahn 1 to "Rotkreuzpl.," then streetcar 12 to "Amalienburgstr." Those aiming for the E6 interchange north to Berlin take U-Bahn 6 to "Studentenstadt" and walk 500m to the Frankfurter Ring. A safer bet is

McShare Treffpunkt Zentrale, Klenzestr. 57b and Lämmerstr. 4 (tel. 59 45 61; DM54 to Berlin; open daily 8am-8pm). **Frauenmitfahrzentrale,** Klenzestr. 57b, is for women only. U-Bahn 1 or 2 to "Fraunhoferstr.," then walk up Fraunhoferstr. away from the river, and turn right. Open Mon.-Fri. 8am-8pm.

Laundromat: The **Waschsalon Prinz,** Paul-Heyse-Str. 21, near the station; wash and soap DM7. Open daily 6am-10pm. **Münz Waschsalon,** Amalienstr. 61, near the university. Wash DM5.20. Open Mon.-Fri. 8am-6:30pm, Sat. 8am-1pm.

Crisis Lines: Rape Crisis: Frauennotruf München, Güllstr. 3 (tel. 76 37 37). **AIDS Hotline:** tel. 520 73 87 or 520 74 12 (Mon.-Thurs. 8am-3pm, Fri. 8am-noon) or 194 11 (Mon.-Sat. 7-10pm).

Pharmacy: Bahnhof Apotheke, Bahnhofpl. 2 (tel. 59 41 19 or 59 81 19), outside the station. Open Mon.-Fri. 8am-6:30pm, Sat. 8am-2pm. 24hr. service rotates—call 59 44 75 for info in German, or get a schedule at the tourist office or EurAide.

Medical Assistance: Clinic across the river on Ismaningerstr. U.S. and British consulates carry a list of English-speaking doctors.

Emergency: Police: tel. 110. **Ambulance:** tel. 192 22. **Emergency medical service:** tel. 55 77 55. **Poison Control:** tel. 192 40. **Fire:** tel. 112.

Internet Access: Internetcafé (see **Food,** p. 421). **Hotel Kurpfalz** (guests only; see **Accommodations and Camping,** p. 420).

Post Office: Post/Telegrafenamt, Arnulfstr. 32., 80074 München (tel. 54 54 23 36). *Poste Restante* and money exchange. Go out of the train station and turn left onto Arnulfstr.; the post office will be on your right. Open Mon.-Fri. 8am-8pm, Sat. 8am-noon. EurAide offers a "message-forwarding service."

Telephone Code: 089.

ACCOMMODATIONS AND CAMPING

Munich's accommodations fall into one of three categories: seedy, expensive, or booked. Reserve in advance in summer and during *Oktoberfest,* when all three often apply. Sleeping in the *Englischer Garten* or train station is unsafe and illegal. Augsburg's hostel (40min. by train) is an option, but mind the 1am curfew. HI hostels are not supposed to accept solo travelers over 26, although families may book rooms.

Hostels and Camping

Jugendherberge München (HI), Wendl-Dietrich-Str. 20. (tel. 13 11 56). U-Bahn 1 to "Rotkreuzpl." then cross Rotkreuzpl. towards the Kaufhof store. Reception open 24hr. Check-in begins at 10:30am, but lines start before 9. Dorms DM23-25.50. Breakfast and sheets included. Key deposit DM20. Safes with DM50 deposit.

Jugendlager Kapuzinerhölzl ("The Tent"), In den Kirschen 30 (tel. 141 43 00). Streetcar 17 ("Amalienburgstr.") from the *Hauptbahnhof* to "Botanischer Garten," go straight on Franz-Schrank-Str., then turn left. Under 24 only (under 27 if there's room). Sleep with 400 others on a foam pad under a circus tent. Reception open 5pm-9am. DM13 with breakfast. Actual "beds" DM17. Lockers provided; bring a lock. Group reservations only. Open mid-June to early-Sept.

Jugendherberge Pullach Burg Schwaneck (HI), Burgweg 4-6 (tel. 793 06 43; fax 793 79 22). S-Bahn 7 ("Wolfratshausen") to "Pullach." Romantic, but swarming with schoolchildren. Reception open 4-11pm. Curfew 11:30pm. Dorms DM18.50-22.50. Breakfast included. Sheets DM5. Try to make reservations 7:30-10am.

Jugendgästehaus Thalkirchen, Miesingstr. 4 (tel. 723 65 50). U-Bahn 1 or 2 to "Sendlinger Tor," then 3 ("Fürstenrieder West") to "Thalkirchen" (Zoo). Follow Schäftlarnstr. toward Innsbruck and bear right, follow Frauenbergstr., then left on Münchnerstr. Reception open 7am-1am. Curfew 1am. Dorms DM27.50. Singles DM35.50. Doubles DM63. Triples and quads DM29.50 per person. Sheets and breakfast included.

4 you münchen (ökologisches Jugendgästehaus), Hirtenstr. 18 (tel. 55 21 660; fax 55 21 66 66), 200m from the *Hauptbahnhof.* Beautiful and ecological. Reception open daily 7am-noon, 3-7pm, and 7:30-10pm. Dorms DM24-29. Singles DM54. Doubles DM76. Over 27 15% surcharge. Sheets DM5. Key deposit DM20. Breakfast DM7.50. In adjoining hotel, singles DM69; doubles DM99; breakfast included.

Jugendhotel Marienberge, Goethestr. 9, 80336 München (tel. 55 58 05), less than a block south of the train station, staffed by jolly nuns. Open only to women under

26. Kitchen and laundry facilities. Wash DM2, dry DM2. Reception open 8am-midnight. Curfew midnight. 6-bed rooms DM30 per person. Singles DM40. Doubles DM70. Triples DM105. Showers and breakfast included.

CVJM (YMCA) Jugendgästehaus, Landwehrstr. 13 (tel. 552 14 10; fax 550 42 82; email muenchen@cvjm.org). Take the Bayerstr. exit from the station, and go straight down Goethestr. Spic'n'span rooms. Reception open 8am-12:30am. Curfew 12:30am. Over 27 add 15%. Singles DM50. Doubles DM86. Coed rooms for married couples only. Breakfast included. Closed Easter and Dec.20-Jan. 7.

Haus International, Elisabethstr. 87 (tel. 12 00 60). U-Bahn 2 ("Feldmoching") to "Hohenzollernpl.," then streetcar 12 ("Romanpl.") or bus 33 ("Aidenbachstr.") to"Barbarastr." It's the 5-story beige building behind the BP gas station. Reception open 24hr. Singles DM55-85. Doubles DM104-144. Larger rooms DM138-200.

Camping: Campingplatz Thalkirchen, Zentralländstr. 49 (tel. 723 17 07; fax 724 31 77). U-Bahn 1 or 2 to "Sendlinger Tor," then 3 to"Thalkirchen," and change to bus 57. Laundry facilities and a restaurant (meals DM3-8). Curfew 11pm. DM7.80 per person. Tent DM5.50-7. Showers DM2. Open mid-March to late Oct.

Hotels and Pensions

When the city is full, finding clean singles under DM55-65 and doubles under DM80-100 in a safe area is nearly impossible. Reserving weeks ahead is particularly important during *Oktoberfest.* The tourist office and EurAide find rooms for a DM5-6 fee.

Hotel Helvetia, Schillerstr. 6 (tel. 55 47 45; fax 55 02 381), to the right as you exit the station. Recently renovated. Singles DM53-62. Doubles DM68-115. Triples DM99-120. Showers, breakfast included. Hostel-like dorms DM19-24. Shower included. Breakfast DM7. Sheets DM4. Laundry service DM8.50.

Pension Locarno, Bahnhofpl. 5 (tel. 55 51 64; fax 59 50 45), right outside the train station. Plain rooms with TVs. Reception open 7:30am-midnight. Singles DM55-75. Doubles DM90. Triples DM135. Quads DM160. Hall showers, breakfast included.

Hotel Kurpfalz, Schwanthalerstr. 121 (tel. 540 98 60; fax 54 09 88 11; email hotel-kurpfalz@munich-online.de). Exit the station onto Bayerstr., turn right down Bayerstr., and veer left onto Holzapfelstr. Reception open 24hr. Singles DM89. Doubles DM129, with extra cot DM165. Breakfast included. Free **internet access.**

Hotel Central, Bayerstr. 55 (tel. 453 98 46; fax 54 39 84 70), 5min. to the right from the Bayerstr. exit of the train station. Spacious, plain rooms. Reception open 24hr. Singles DM50-60. Doubles DM85-95, with bath DM100-120.

Pension Schillerhof, Schillerstr. 21 (tel. 59 42 70; fax 550 18 35). Two blocks right from the Bahnhofspl. train station exit. Non-descript rooms floating in a sea of neighborhood sex shops and kinos. Singles DM60-75. Doubles DM80-110. Extra bed DM20. *Oktoberfest* surcharge DM25-40 per person. Breakfast included.

Pension Frank, Schellingstr. 24 (tel. 28 14 51; fax 280 09 10). Take U-Bahn 4 or 5 to "Odeonspl.," then U-Bahn 3 or 6 to "Universität." Reception open 7:30am-10pm. Dorms DM35. Singles DM55-65. Doubles DM78-85. During *Oktoberfest* add DM5. Shower and breakfast included. No credit cards.

Pension am Kaiserplatz, Kaiserpl. 12 (tel. 34 91 90), close to the nightlife. U-Bahn 3 or 6 to "Münchener Freiheit." Exit onto Herzogstr., turn left onto Viktoriastr. and walk to the end. Elegantly decorated rooms. Reception open daily 7am-9pm. Singles DM49-59. Doubles DM82-89. Larger rooms DM30-35 each. Breakfast included.

Hotel-Pension am Markt, Heiliggeiststr. 6 (tel. 22 50 14; fax 22 40 17), right in the city center. S-Bahn 1-8 to "Marienpl.," walk through the *Altes Rathaus,* and turn right. Singles DM62-110. Doubles DM110-160. Triples DM165-205. Breakfast, showers included. Reserve rooms at least 3-4 weeks in advance. No credit cards.

FOOD

Munich's gastronomic center is the vibrant **Viktualienmarkt,** two minutes south of Marienpl., with a rainbow of bread, fruit, meat, pastry, cheese, wine, vegetable, and sandwich shops (open Mon.-Fri. 9am-6:30pm, Sat. 9am-2pm). Otherwise, look for cheap meals in the **university district** off Ludwigstr. **Tengelmann,** Schützenstr. 7, near the train station, satisfies grocery needs quickly and conveniently (open Mon.-Wed. and Fri. 8:30am-6:30pm, Thurs. 8:30am-8:30pm, Sat. 9am-2pm).

Türkenhof, Türkenstr. 78. Smoky and buzzing at night. Creative entrees (*Schnitzel,* omelettes, soups) DM7-14. Open Sun.-Thurs. 11am-1am, Fri.-Sat. 11am-3am.

Café Puck, Türkenstr. 33. Spacious café/bar with a young and energetic attitude. Breakfast DM5-16. Veggie specials DM11-16. Open daily 9am-1am.

La Bohème, Türkenstr. 79. Pastas DM7-11. Pizzas DM7-11. Salads DM5-13. At dinner add DM1 to all dishes. Beer DM3.50 (0.4L).

News Bar, Amalienstr. 55, at the corner of Schellingstr. Bustling, trendy, and youthful new café. Crepes DM6-11. Sandwiches DM7-11. Open daily 7:30am-2am.

Shoya, Orlandostr. 5, across from the Hofbräuhaus. Japanese restaurant/take-out. *Teriyaki* DM8-16. Sushi DM5-30. Open daily 10:30am-midnight.

buxs, Frauenstr. 9, on the Viktualienmarkt. Vegetarian café/restaurant with salads (DM3 per 100g) and tasty pastas. Open Mon.-Fri. 11am-8:30pm, Sat. 11am-3:30pm.

Beim Sendlmayr, Westenriederstr. 6, off the Viktualienmarkt. A slice of Little Bavaria. Specials DM7-25. Beer DM5.30 for 0.5L. Open daily 11am-11pm.

Internetcafé, Nymphenburgerstr. 145 (http://www.icafe.spacenet.de). U-Bahn 1 to "Rotkreuzpl." Unlimited free **Internet access** with an order of pasta (DM9.50), pizza (DM7.50-10), or beer (DM4.90 for 0.5L). Open daily 11am-4am.

SIGHTS

The **Marienplatz** serves as an interchange for major S-Bahn and U-Bahn lines as well as the social nexus of the city. On the square, the onion-domed towers of the 15th-century **Frauenkirche** have long been one of Munich's most notable landmarks (towers open April-Oct. Mon.-Sat. 10am-5pm; DM4, students DM2). At the neo-Gothic **Neues Rathaus,** the **Glockenspiel** marks the hour at 11am, noon, 5, and 9pm with jousting knights and dancing barrel-makers. At 9pm, a mechanical watchman marches out and a Guardian Angel escorts the *Münchner Kindl* ("Munich Child," the city's symbol) to bed (tower open Mon.-Fri. 9am-7pm, Sat.-Sun. 10am-7pm, DM3).

The 11th-century **Peterskirche** is at Rindermarkt and Peterspl.; 302 steps scale the saintly tower, christened *Alter Peter* (Old Peter) by locals (tower open Mon.-Sat. 9am-6pm, Sun. 10am-6pm; DM2.50, students DM1.50). Nearby, Ludwig II of Bavaria rests in peace in a crypt of the 16th-century Jesuit **Michaelskirche,** on Neuhauserstr. (crypt DM0.50). A Bavarian Rococo masterpiece, the **Asamkirche,** Sendlingerstr. 32, is named after the brothers, Cosmas and Egid, who vowed to build it if they survived a shipwreck. The magnificent **Residenz,** Max-Joseph-Pl. 3, boasts richly decorated rooms built with the wealth of the Wittelsbach dynasty, Bavaria's ruling family from the 12th to the early 20th century. The grounds now house several museums, and the **treasury** *(Schatzkammer)* contains jeweled baubles, crowns, swords, and ivory from as early as the 10th century (treasury open Tues.-Sun. 10am-4:30pm; DM5, students DM2.50). To reach the *Residenz,* take U-Bahn 3, 4, 5, or 6 to "Odeonspl."

Ludwig I's summer residence, **Schloß Nymphenburg,** is worth the trip northwest of town; take streetcar 17 ("Amalienburgstr."). A Baroque wonder set in a winsome park, the palace hides treasures including a two-story granite marble hall seasoned with stucco, frescoes, and a Chinese lacquer cabinet. Check out Ludwig's "Gallery of Beauties"—whenever a woman caught his fancy, he would have her portrait painted. (*Schloß* open April-Sept. Tues.-Sun. 9am-noon and 1-5pm; Oct.-March 10am-12:30pm and 1:30-4pm. Main palace DM6, students DM4; entire complex DM8, students DM5. Grounds free.) Next door is the immense **Botanischer Garten,** where greenhouses shelter rare flora from around the world. (Garden open daily 9am-7pm. Greenhouses open 9-11:45am and 1-6:30pm. DM3, students DM1.50.) Abutting the city center is the **Englischer Garten,** one of Europe's oldest landscaped parks.

Museums Munich is a supreme museum city. Take a break from Monet et al. at the **Deutsches Museum,** on the Museumsinsel (Museum Island) in the Isar River (S-Bahn 1-8 to "Isartor"), one of the world's largest, most exciting museums of science and technology. Particularly interesting are the mining exhibit, which winds through a labyrinth of recreated subterranean tunnels, the planetarium (DM3), and the daily electrical show (museum open daily 9am-5pm; DM10, students DM4). The **Neue Pinakothek,** Barerstr. 29, exhibits the work of 18th- to 20th-century masters such as Van Gogh and Klimt. (Open Tues. and Thurs. 10am-8pm, Wed. and Fri.-Sun. 10am-5pm. DM7, students DM4.) **Lenbachhaus,** Luisenstr. 33, houses Munich cityscapes, along with works by Kandinsky, Klee, and the *Blaue Reiter* school, which forged the modernist abstract aesthetic (open Tues.-Sun. 10am-6pm; DM8, students DM4). Between them, **Glyptohek,** Königspl. 3, and **Antikensammlung,** Königspl. 1, hold Munich's finest collection of ancient art. (Glyptohek open Tues.-Wed. and Fri.-Sun. 10am-5pm, Thurs. 10am-8pm. Antikensammlung open Tues. and Thurs.-Sun. 10am-5pm, Wed. 10am-8pm. Joint admission DM10, students DM5.) **Staatsgalerie moderner Kunst,** Prinzregentenstr. 1, in the **Haus der Kunst,** has a sterling 20th-century collection that includes Klee, Picasso, and Dalí. The Haus der Kunst was built by Nazis and opened with the famous exhibit on "degenerate art." (Open Tues.-Wed. and Fri.-Sun. 10am-5pm, Thurs. 10am-8pm. DM6, students DM3.50.) The **ZAM: Zentrum für Außergewöhnliche Museen** (Center for Unusual Museums), Westenriederstr. 26, includes favorites like the Corkscrew Museum, Museum of Easter Bunnies, and the Chamberpot Museum (open daily 10am-6pm; DM8, students DM5). If you're looking for the kinky rather than the quirky, try the **Museum für erotische Kunst** (Museum of Erotic Art), Odeonspl. 8 (U-Bahn 3-6: "Odeonspl." or bus 53).

ENTERTAINMENT

Munich's streets erupt with bawdy beer halls, rowdy discos, and cliquish cafés every night. Pick up *Munich Found* (DM4), *In München* (free), or the hip and hefty *Prinz* (DM5) at any newsstand to find out what's up.

Beer To most visitors, Munich means beer. The six great city labels are *Augustiner, Hacker-Pschorr, Hofbräu, Löwenbräu, Paulaner-Thomasbräu,* and *Spaten-Franzinskaner;* each brand supplies its own beer halls. Beer is served by the *Maß* (about a liter, DM8-11). The biggest keg party in the world, Munich's **Oktoberfest** (Sept. 19-Oct. 4 in 1998) features speeches, a parade of horse-drawn beer wagons, and the mayor tapping the first ceremonial barrel. The Hofbräu tent is the rowdiest (for more info on the Oktoberfest see http://www.munich-tourist.de). Most *Müncheners* claim that **Augustiner Keller,** Arnulfstr. 52 (S-Bahn 1-8 to "Hackerbrücke"), is the finest beer garden in town, with lush grounds and 100-year-old chestnut trees. (*Maß* DM9-10. Open daily 10am-1am; beer garden open 10:30am-midnight. Food served until 10pm.) The world-famous **Hofbräuhaus,** Am Platzl 9, two blocks from Marienpl., has been tapping barrels for the commoners since 1897 and now seems reserved for drunken tourists; 15,000-30,000L of beer are sold each day (*Maß* DM10.40; 2 *Weiwurst* sausages DM7.50; open daily 10am-midnight). The new **Augustiner Bräustuben,** Landsbergerstr. 19 (S-Bahn 1-8 to "Hackerbrücke"), in the Augustiner Brewery's former horse stalls, offers delicious Bavarian food at excellent prices (DM6-20; open daily until 11pm). The largest beer garden in Europe, **Hirschgarten,** Hirschgartenallee 1 (U-Bahn 1 to "Rotkreuzpl.," then streetcar 12 to "Romanpl."), is boisterous and verdant (*Maß* DM8.60; open daily 11am-11pm; restaurant open Nov.-Feb. Tues.-Sun.). **Chinesischer Turm,** in the **Englischer Garten** next to the pagoda (U-Bahn 3 or 6 to "Giselastr.") is a fair-weather tourist favorite with lots of kids (*Maß* DM9.50; salads DM7-13.50; open daily in good weather 10:30am-11pm).

Theater, Music, and Nightlife Stages sprinkled throughout the city span styles and tastes from dramatic classics at the **Residenztheater** and **Volkstheater** to comic opera at the **Staatstheater am Gärtnerplatz** to experimental works at the **Theater im Marstall** in Nymphenburg. The tourist office's *Monatsprogramm* (DM2.50) lists schedules for all Munich's stages. Leftover tickets sell for about DM10. Munich's **Opera Festival** (in July) is held in the **Bayerische Staatsoper** (tel. 21 85 19 20), accompanied by a concert series in the Nymphenburg and Schleissheim palaces. (Regular season standing-room and student tickets DM15-20. Box office open Mon.-Fri. 10am-6pm, Sat. 10am-1pm.) **Gasteig,** Rosenheimerstr. 5 (tel. 48 09 80, box office

54 89 89), hosts diverse musical performances on the former site of the *Bürgerbräukeller* where Adolf Hitler launched his abortive Beer Hall Putsch. (Box office open Mon.-Fri. 10:30am-2pm and 3-6pm, Sat. 10:30am-2pm, and 1hr. before curtain.) The **Muffathalle,** Zellerstr. 4 (tel. 45 87 50 00), in Haidhausen, a former power plant, still generates energy with techno, hip-hop, jazz, and dance performances (DM30).

Munich's nightlife is a curious mix of Bavarian *Gemütlichkeit* and trendy cliquishness, so dress well. **Münchener Freiheit** is the most famous and touristy bar/café district. More low-key is the southwestern section of **Schwabing,** directly behind the university on Amalienstr. The center of Munich's homosexual scene lies within the "Golden Triangle" defined by Sendlinger Tor, the Viktualienmarkt/Gärtnerpl. area, and Isartor. Mingle with an English speaking crowd at **Günther Murphy's,** Nikolaistr. 9a, (Guinness DM6; open Mon.-Fri. 5pm-1am, Sat.-Sun. 11am-1am). **Reitschule,** Konigstr. 34, is more relaxed (*Weißbier* DM6). Live music at **Shamrock,** Trautenwolfstr. 6, runs the gamut from blues and soul to Irish fiddling to rock (Guinness DM6.20; open Mon.-Thurs. 5pm-1am, Fri.-Sat. 5pm-3am, Sun. 2pm-1am). Things get rolling late at **Nachtcafé,** Maximilianspl. 5, with live jazz, funk, soul, and blues until the wee hours (beer DM8 for .3L). Dance clubs include the huge complex **Kunstpark Ost,** Grafingerstr. 6 (Hours, cover, and themes vary—call 49 00 29 28 for info and tickets) and **Nachtwerk and Club,** Landesbergerstr. 185, twin clubs spinning mainstream dance tunes for sweaty crowds (beer DM6; cover DM10; open daily 10pm-4am). **Club Morizz,** Klenzestr. 43, reminiscent of *Casablanca* scenes, is frequented by gay men and a few lesbians (open Sun.-Thurs. 7pm-2am, Fri.-Sat. 7pm-3am).

■ Near Munich: Dachau

"Once they burn books, they'll end up burning people," wrote the 19th-century German poet Heinrich Heine. This eerily prophetic statement is posted at **Konzentrationslager-Gedenkstätte,** the concentration camp at **Dachau,** next to a photograph of one of Hitler's book burnings. Though most of the buildings had fallen apart by 1962, the walls, gates, and crematoria were restored. The terrifying legacy of Dachau lives on in the several memorials and chapels on the grounds, and in photographs and letters housed in the Dachau **museum.** Take S-Bahn 2 ("Petershausen") to "Dachau," then catch bus 724 ("Kräutgarten") or 726 ("Kopernikusstr."; either one DM2) in front of the station to the *KZ Gedenkstätte,* a 20-minute ride (grounds open Tues.-Sun. 9am-5pm). The state offers free two-hour tours in English leaving the museum daily at 12:30pm. Call (08131) 17 41 for more info.

The Chiemsee

For almost 2000 years, artists and musicians have marveled at the picturesque islands, mountains, and forests of the Chiemsee region. The main attractions are the two inhabited islands on Lake Chiem, the largest lake in Bavaria. Ferries ply the waters from the port in Prien to the **Herreninsel** (Gentlemen's Island), the **Fraueninsel** (Ladies' Island), and towns on the other side of the lake (DM10-14). On Herreninsel, the architecture of **Königsschloß Herrenchiemsee,** King Ludwig II's third and last "fairy-tale castle," is fabulously overwrought. Candlelit concerts are given in the **Hall of Mirrors** throughout the summer. (Open April-Sept. daily 9am-5pm; Oct.-March 10am-4pm. Obligatory guided tour DM7, students DM4.) Fraueninsel offers subtler pleasures. Its miniature world has no room for cars; only footpaths wander through this village of fishermen and nuns. The **abbey** dates back to at least 866. Various artifacts, including the impressive 8th-century Merovingian **Cross of Bischofhofen,** are on display in the room above the Torhalle, the oldest surviving part of the cloister (open daily 11am-6pm; Oct. to mid-June closed Sun; DM4, students DM1.50).

The town of **Prien** works as a base for excursions on the lake. The **tourist office,** Alte Rathaus 11 (tel. (08051) 690 50 or 69 05 55), offers free maps and brochures, and finds rooms in private houses (DM20-40) for no fee (open Mon.-Fri. 8:30am-6pm, Sat. 9am-noon). The cheapest beds in town are at the raucous **Jugendherberge (HI),**

Carl-Braun-Str. 66 (tel. (08051) 687 70; fax 68 77 15), a 10-minute walk from the lake. (Reception open daily 8-9am, 5-7pm, and 9:30-10pm. Curfew 10pm. DM22.80. Sheets DM5.50. Open Jan.-Oct.) **Campingplatz Hofbauer** is at Bernauerstr. 110 (tel. (08051) 41 36; fax 626 57); walk right from the station, turn left at Seestr., then left again at the next intersection and follow Bernauerstr. out of town (DM8.20 per person, DM9 per tent; open late March-Oct.). Munch on a hearty meal at **Scherer SB Restaurant,** Alte Rathausstr. 1 (DM9-20; open Mon.-Fri. 8am-8pm, Sat. 8am-3pm), or grab groceries from **HL Markt,** Seestr. 11 (open Mon.-Fri. 8am-6pm, Sat. 8am-4pm).

Nuremberg (Nürnberg)

Although few visible scars remain and historical landmarks shine in splendor, Nuremberg is a city inextricably bound to its troubled past. The very mention of Nuremberg, backdrop of the massive annual Nazi party rallies from 1933-1938 and namesake of the 1935 racial purity laws that paved the way for the Holocaust, still conjures up totalitarian imagery of the sort immortalized in Leni Riefenstahl's film *Triumph des Willens* (Triumph of the Will). For these reasons, the 1949 war criminal trials were held here to reestablish justice in a world of horror. Thanks largely to the Marshall Plan, the city today is a model of postwar prosperity, known for its connection to Albrecht Dürer, its toy-fair and Christmas-Markt, and its sausages and gingerbread.

Allied bombing reduced 90% of Nuremberg to rubble in 1945, but restoration projects have recaptured some of the city's charm and majesty. The **Lorenzkirche** on St. Lorenzpl., destroyed during the war, has now been completely restored and once again displays its priceless works of art. Of particular interest is the 20m high tabernacle, with delicate stone tendrils curling up into the roof vaulting (open Mon.-Sat. 9am-5pm, Sun. 1-4pm). Across the river on Hauptmarktpl. is the **Frauenkirche** (Church of Our Lady), Catholic since 1916, and the **Schöner Brunnen** (Beautiful Fountain), with 40 imaginatively carved figures. Walk uphill from the fountain to find the **Rathaus,** built between 1616 and 1622 in early Baroque style with a little Renaissance Classicism thrown in. Beneath the building are the **Lochgefängnisse** (dungeons), containing an exhibit of medieval torture instruments. (Obligatory 30min. tour every 30min. Open Mon.-Fri. 10am-4:30pm, Sat.-Sun. 10am-1pm. DM4, students DM2.) Across from the *Rathaus* is the **Sebalduskirche,** a Protestant Church. The Catholic congregation celebrates the feast day of St. Sebaldus by parading through town with his relics. During the other 364 days, his bits rest in his gilded cast bronze tomb in front of the altar. (Open June-Aug. daily 9:30am-8pm; Nov. and Jan-Feb. 9:30am-4pm; March-May 9:30am-6pm.) Up the hill is a three-part castle: the **Kaiserburg** (Emperor's fortress), the **Burggrafenburg** (fortress count's fortress), and the **Stadtburg** (city fortress). (Open April-Sept. daily 9am-noon and 12:45-5pm; Oct.-March 9:30am-noon and 12:45-4pm. Last tour April-Sept. 4:30pm; Oct.-March 3:30pm. DM5.) The **Albrecht Dürer Haus,** Albrecht-Dürer-Str. 29, was the last residence of Nuremberg's favorite son. The *Fachwerk* house contains period furniture along with Dürer etchings and copies of his paintings (open Tues.-Sun. 10am-5pm; DM5, students DM3).

The ruins of **Dutzendteich Park,** site of the Nazi *Parteitage* (Party Convention) rallies in the 1930s, remind visitors of a darker time in German history. To reach the park, take S-Bahn 2 to "Dutzendteich," then walk left as you exit the station until you come to the long building to the right. **Zeppelin Field** sits on the far side of the lake near the massive marble platform from which Hitler addressed throngs. The exhibit *Faszination und Gewalt* (Fascination and Terror), located inside the **Zeppelin Tribune** in the Golden Hall, attests to the emotional power of these events (open mid-May to Oct. Tues.-Sun. 10am-6pm; DM2, students DM1).

Practical Information, Accommodations, and Food Nuremberg's **tourist office** (tel. (0911) 233 61 32), in the *Hauptbahnhof,* finds rooms for a DM5 fee (open Mon.-Sat. 9am-7pm). **Trains** (tel. (0911) 194 19) leave the station frequently for Munich (2hr.), Berlin (6hr.), and Würzburg (1hr.). The comfortable and well-run **Jugendgästehaus (HI),** Burg 2 (tel. (0911) 230 93 60; fax 23 09 36 11), was once a grain storage house of the imperial castle. From the train station, take the escalator down into the tunnel passage and walk straight, then left up to the sloping exit. Follow Königstr. to the marketplace, then head toward the golden fountain on the left and bear right on Burgstr., up the hill (reception open daily 7am-1am; curfew 1am; DM29; reserve ahead). **Jugend-Hotel Nürnberg,** Rathsbergstr. 300 (tel. (0911) 521 60 92), is rustic and cheerful but far from the city center; take streetcar 3 to "Ziegelstein" or bus 41 to "Felsenkeller" (dorms DM22-25, singles DM35, doubles DM70; breakfast DM7.50; call ahead). **Campingplatz im Volkspark Dutzenteich,** Hans-Kalb-Str. 56 (tel. (0911) 81 11 22), is behind the soccer stadium; take the U-Bahn South to "Messe Zentrum" (DM8 per person, DM5 per tent; open May-Sept.; call ahead).

Nuremberg is famous for its *Rostbratwurst* (grilled sausage). The place to try some is beneath the crowded, popular **Bratwurst Häusle,** Rathauspl. 1, next to St. Sebaldus Church. (6 *Rostbratwürste* with sauerkraut or spiced potato salad DM9-15.50. Open Mon.-Sat. 9:30am-10pm.) The crowded **Internetcafé Falkens Maze,** Färberstr. 11, on the third floor of the *Maximum* complex, invites you to grab a cup of coffee (DM3), then email or chat the night away. (Open Mon.-Sat. noon-midnight, Sun. 4pm-midnight. DM5 for 30min., DM5-8 for 1hr.) **Café Mohr,** Färberstr. 3, is a fun place to meet people and enjoy crepes (DM5-8.50) and salads. (DM6.50-11.50. Open Mon.-Thurs. 9am-midnight, Fri.-Sat. 9am-1am, Sun. 2pm-midnight.) Pick up the weekly *Plärrer* (DM4) for listings of musical events, bars, and discos. **Cince Citta,** Gewerbemuseumpl. 3 (tel. (0911) 20 66 60), packs seven cafés, 12 movie theaters, and a disco into an eight-story, multimedia mega-complex (open daily until 3am or later).

Romantic Road (Romantische Straße)

Between Würzburg and Füssen, at the foothills of the Alps, lies a beautiful countryside of castles, walled cities, elaborate churches, and dense forest. Sensing opportunity, the German tourist industry christened these bucolic backwaters the Romantic Road in 1950. The world has responded—this is the most visited region in Germany, so be prepared for a group experience. Deutsche Bahn's **Europabus** runs during April to October daily from Frankfurt to Munich (12hr.; change at Dinkelsbühl for Füssen) and back, stopping at most towns in the area along the way. Eurail and German Railpass holders ride free after a DM10 registration fee, but otherwise the service is fairly slow and costly (Frankfurt to Rothenburg DM58; to Dinkelsbühl DM69; to Munich DM113). A more economical way to see the region for those without railpasses is to use the faster and more frequent **trains,** which run to every town except Dinkelsbühl. Tourist offices can provide maps and info to the many travelers who **bike** the route. For general information, contact the **Romantische Straße Arbeitgemeinschaft,** Marktpl., 91550 Dinkelsbühl (tel. (09851) 902 71).

Würzburg Surrounded by vineyard slopes and bisected by the Main River, **Würzburg** is the bustling center of the Franconian wine region. The imposing 13th-century **Marienburg Fortress,** the striking symbol of the city, all but overshadows the town from across the river. Inside, German paintings and furniture grace the **Fürstenbau Museum.** (Open April-Sept. Tues.-Sun. 9-12:30am and 1-5pm; Oct.-March Tues.-Sun. 10-12:30am and 1-4pm. DM4, students DM3.) The fortress also houses the **Mainfränkisches Museum,** with statues by Würzburg's native son, Tilman Riemenschneider. (Open April-Oct. Tues.-Sun. 10am-5pm; Nov.-March Tues.-Sun. 10am-4pm. DM3.50, students DM2.) Climb to the fortress or take bus 9 from "Spitäle" (DM2). The **Residenz** palace, a Baroque masterpiece containing the largest ceiling fresco in the world, stands over the sweeping Residenzpl. (Open April-Oct. Tues.-Sun. 9am-5pm; Nov.-March Tues.-Sun. 10am-4pm. Last admission 30min. before closing. DM5, students and seniors DM3.50.) Also in town, the **Residenzhofkirche** is simply astounding: the gilded moldings, pink marble, and frescoes place this little church at the apex of Baroque fantasy. (Open April-Oct. Tues.-Sun. 9am-noon and 1-5pm; Nov.-March Tues.-Sun. 10am-noon and 1-4pm. Free.)

Trains (tel. (0931) 344 25) roll to Frankfurt (1hr.), Munich (2½hr.), Hamburg (3½hr.), and Rothenburg (1hr.); **buses** head to Rothenburg (DM26) and Munich (DM82). In front of the train station, the **tourist office** (tel. (0931) 374 36) provides a hotel list (DM0.50) and free map, and finds rooms for a DM5 fee (open Mon.-Sat. 10am-6pm). The 24-hour **accommodations hotline** is (0931) 194 14. Würzburg's **Jugendgästehaus (HI),** Burkarderstr. 44 (tel. (0931) 425 90; fax 41 68 62), is across the river; take tram 3 ("Heidingsfeld") or 5 ("Heuchelhof") from the station to "Löwenbrücke." (Reception open daily 8am-10pm. Check-in 2-5:15pm and 6:30-10pm. Under 27 only. DM25-29. Breakfast included.) **Uni Café,** Neubaustr. 2, has a relaxed student atmosphere and outdoor seating (baguettes and salads DM3.50-9.50; open Mon.-Sat. 8am-1am, Sun. 9am-1pm). To sample the region's distinctive wines try **Haus des Frankenweins Fränkischer Weinverband,** Krankenkai 1 (tel. (0931) 120 93), or stop by during the **Wine Festival** (early June and late Sept.-early Oct.).

Rothenburg to Augsburg Although **Rothenburg ob der Tauber** has got to be the most touristed spot in Germany, it may be your only chance to see a walled medieval city without a single modern building. The **tourist office,** Marktpl. 1 (tel. (09861) 404 92), supplies handy maps and books rooms (DM35-60); from the station, bear right on Ansbacherstr. and follow it to the *Marktplatz* (open Mon.-Fri. 9am-12:30pm and 2-6pm, Sat. 9am-noon and 2-4pm). **Trains** run every hour from major cities to Steinach, where you can transfer for a quick trip to Rothenburg (15min.). *"Zimmer frei"* signs mark private rooms for rent (DM20-45). To reach the exemplary **Jugendherberge Rossmühle (HI),** Mühlacker 1 (tel. (09861) 45 10; fax 57 62), from the *Marktplatz,* make a left onto Obere Schmiedgasse and go straight until you see the sign to the right (reception open daily 7-9am, 5-7pm, and 8-10pm; under 27 only; DM22). Not as pre-packaged as Rothenburg, **Dinkelsbühl,** 40km south, maintains a full complement of medieval half-timbered houses. The walled city of **Nördlingen im Ries,** 35km south of Dinkelsbühl, sits on the plain where a kilometer-wide meteorite smashed into the earth with the power of 250,000 atomic bombs 15 million years ago. You can view the crater from **Der Daniel,** the tower of the 15th-century **St. Georgskirche** (tower open Mon.-Fri. 9am-noon and 2-5pm, Sat.-Sun. 9am-5pm).

Founded by Caesar Augustus in 15 BC, **Augsburg** was the financial center of the Holy Roman Empire and a major commercial city by the end of the 15th century. Jakob Fugger the Rich, personal financier to the Hapsburg Emperors, founded the **Fuggerei** quarter in 1519 as the first welfare housing project in the world. The **Fuggerei Museum** documents this classic piece of urban planning, as well as the financial adventures of its patrons (open March-Oct. daily 9am-6pm; DM1, students DM0.70). Augsburg's medieval past unfolds at the brightly frescoed **Guildhaus,** down Bürgermeister-Fischer-Str.; from here, a left down Maximilianstr. leads to the huge Renaissance **Rathaus** (open daily 10am-6pm; free). The **Bertolt Brecht Haus** on Auf dem Raim is scheduled to reopen on February 10, 1998. (Open May-Sept. Tues.-Sun. 10am-5pm; Oct.-April 10am-4pm. DM2.50, students DM1.50.)

Augsburg's **tourist office,** Bahnhofstr. 7 (tel. (0821) 50 20 70; fax 502 07 45), about 300m in front of the station, books rooms for a DM3 fee (open Mon.-Fri. 9am-6pm). There's also an office at Rathauspl. (tel. (0821) 502 07 24; also open Sat.-Sun. 10am-4pm). The **Jugendherberge (HI),** Beim Pfaffenkeller 3 (tel. (0821) 339 03; fax 151 11 49), is cramped but well-located. (Reception open daily 7-9am, 5-10pm. DM20. Open late Jan. to early Dec. Call ahead.)

Bavarian Alps (Bayerische Alpen)

South of Munich, the land buckles into dramatic peaks and valleys which stretch through Austria into Italy. Mountain villages, glacial lakes, icy waterfalls, and ski resorts dot the landscape. Rail lines are scarce, but buses fill in the gaps. For regional information, contact the **Fremdenverkehrsverband Oberbayern,** Bodenseestr. 113 (tel. (089) 829 21 80), in Munich (open Mon.-Fri. 9am-4:30pm, Sat. 9am-noon).

Insults for Sale

The concept of free speech in Germany does not imply *kostenlos* (cost-free) speech. While doling out compliments requires no budget, dropping insults will unload your wallet in no time. Public humiliation in Germany carries such destructive and belittling force that officials have created an insult price list. Angry, offended, or drunk budget travelers should beware. The heaviest fines will be incurred by mouth-flappers who put down a female police officer's respectability: belting out *Trottel in Uniform* (slut in uniform) costs DM3000, while the lesser insult *Dumme Kuh* (dumb cow) requires a mere DM1200 payoff. Call any uniformed official *Idioten* (idiot), and you'll be out a whopping DM3000. If you give another driver the *Stinkefinger* (middle finger) and he or she can round up witnesses, you'll be DM2200 poorer. Equivalent insults in English are not exempt; stories abound of policemen who've doled out thousands of *Marks* in fines to tourists who think that Germans don't understand what "asshole" means. We tell you this merely as a warning—prices are, of course, subject to change, you idiot.

Füssen and the Royal Castles Curled up at the toes of the Alpine foothills and at the southern end of the Romantic Road, **Füssen** provides easy access to Mad King Ludwig's famed **Königsschlösser** (royal castles). The town also boasts impressive architectural monuments of its own. The inner walls of the **Hohes Schloß** (High Castle) courtyard are decorated with arresting *trompe l'oeil* windows and towers; the **Staatsgalerie** inside displays regional late Gothic and Renaissance art. (Open April-Oct. Tues.-Sun. 11am-5pm; Nov.-March Tues.-Sun. 2-4pm. DM3, students DM2.) Just below the castle rests the 8th-century Baroque basilica **St. Mangkirche** and its abbey. An ancient fresco discovered during 1950 renovations lights up the church's 10th-century subterranean crypt (tours Sat. 10:30am; call (08362) 48 44 for more info).

The **tourist office,** Kaiser-Maximilian-Pl. 1 (tel. (08362) 70 77; fax 391 81), dispenses maps (under DM8), advises on hikes, and finds rooms (open Mon.-Fri. 8am-noon and 1:30-7pm, Sat. 9am-noon, Sun. 10am-noon). Budget singles in *Gästhäuser* run DM35-40. The **Jugendherberge (HI),** Mariahilferstr. 5 (tel. (08362) 77 54; fax 27 70), is often packed; turn right from the station and follow the train tracks. (Reception open daily 7-9am, 5-7pm, and 8-10pm. Under 27 only. DM20.50, plus DM1.40 resort tax. Closed Nov. Reserve ahead.) Stock up on groceries at **Plus,** on the corner of Bahnhofstr. and Luitpoldstr. (open Mon.-Fri. 8:30am-7pm, Sat. 8am-1pm).

The *Königsschlösser* lie 5km across the Lech River in the village of **Hohenschwangau.** Ludwig II's building spree culminated with the construction of the **Schloß Neuschwanstein;** the palace castle was the inspiration for DisneyWorld's "Fantasyland" castle and now draws lines just as long as its American counterpart. Consider taking the tour early in the morning and spending the afternoon hiking around the spectacular **Pöllat Gorge** behind the castle. (Castles open April-Sept. daily 8:30am-5:30pm; Oct.-March 10am-4pm. DM10, students, seniors, and disabled DM7.) From Füssen, take the "Königsschlösser" **bus,** which departs from the train station hourly (DM2.40). Buses also run from the Garmisch-Partenkirchen train station (daily at 8:05am, 1:05, 4:15, and 5:05pm; Mon.-Fri. also at 9:35 and 11:15am); the two-hour journey costs DM13 round-trip with a *Tagesticket.* From Munich, take a **train** to Buchloe and transfer to the regional train to Füssen (2hr., DM30).

Berchtesgaden At the easternmost point of the Bavarian Alps, Berchtesgaden profits from a sinister and overtouristed attraction—Hitler's **Kehlsteinhaus,** a mountaintop retreat christened "Eagle's Nest" by occupying American troops, and now a restaurant. The best reason to visit the Kehlsteinhaus is for the stunning view from the 1834m mountain peak. On your way back down, inspect the remains of the **Berghof;** here in 1938 Hitler browbeat Austrian Chancellor Kurt von Schuschnigg into giving over control of the Austrian police, paving the way for the *Anschluss.* The Berchtesgaden **Schloß,** a monastic priory until Bavarian rulers appropriated the property, now houses a mixture of art and weaponry. (Open Sun.-Fri. 10am-1pm and 2-5pm; Oct.-Easter closed Sun. Last admission 4pm. DM7, students DM3.50.)

The **tourist office,** Kurdirektion (tel. (08652) 96 70), opposite the train station on Königsseerstr., sells hiking passes (DM5) with tips on trails. (Open June-Oct. Mon.-Fri. 8am-6pm, Sat. 9am-5pm, Sun. 9am-3pm; Nov.-May Mon.-Fri. 8am-5pm, Sat. 9am-noon.) Hourly **trains** (tel. (08652) 50 74) run to Munich (2½hr.) and Salzburg (1hr.); change at Freilassing for both. The **Jugendherberge (HI)** is at Gebirgsjägerstr. 52 (tel. (08652) 943 70; fax 94 37 37); from the station, take bus 9539 ("Strub Kaserne," DM2.40) to "Jugendherberge." (Reception open daily 8am-noon and 5-7pm. Check-in until 10pm. DM23 with tax. Sheets DM5.50. Breakfast included. Open Dec. 27-Oct.) Pick up a *Wurst* from vendors or groceries at **Edeka Markt,** Dr.-Imhof-Str. near Griesstätterstr. (open Mon.-Fri. 8am-12:30pm and 1:30-6pm, Sat. 8am-2pm).

The Danube

The Danube Valley, with Baroque Passau and Gothic Regensburg, is every bit as inviting as the Romantic Road. Northeast of Munich, the valley's rolling hills and lovely riverscapes attract Germans and international tourists year-round.

Regensburg and the Bavarian Forest Once the capital of Bavaria, **Regensburg** later became the administrative seat of the Holy Roman Empire and then the site of the first German parliament. The (Holy Roman) Imperial Parliament met in the **Reichstags Museum,** housed in the Gothic **Altes Rathaus.** The different heights of the chairs reflect the political hierarchy of the legislators. (English tours May-Sept. Mon.-Sat. 3:15pm. German tours daily year-round. DM5, students DM2.50.) The splendid high-Gothic **St. Peter's Cathedral** towers over the city (open April-Oct. daily 6:30am-6pm; Nov.-March 6:30am-4pm; DM4, students DM2).

The **tourist office,** Altes Rathaus on Rathauspl. (tel. (0941) 507 44 10; fax 507 44 19), finds rooms (DM1.50) and provides a free map. From the train station, walk down Maximilianstr. to Grasgasse and take a left. Follow it as it turns into Obermünsterstr., then turn right at the end to Obere Bachgasse, and walk straight to Rathauspl. **Trains** chug to Munich via Landshut (1½hr.), Nuremburg (1hr.), and Passau (1-1½hr.). The **Jugendherberge (HI),** Wöhrdstr. 60 (tel. (0941) 574 02), offers pleasant but sterile rooms. (Reception open daily 7am-11:30pm. DM20. Under 27 only. Partial wheelchair access. Closed mid-Nov. to mid-Jan.) Campers should head for the **Azur-Camping,** Am Weinweg 40 (tel. (0941) 27 00 25); take bus 11 ("West Bad") to "Westheim" from Albertstr. (DM10 per person, DM7 per tent). The beer garden **Goldene Ente,** Badstr. 32, serves steaks, spare-ribs, *Würstchen,* and *Schnitzel* grill for wallet-friendly prices (DM9-14; open Mon.-Sat. 11am-2pm and 5pm-1am, Sun. 10am-1am). A grocery store, **Tengelmann,** is on Ernst-Reuter-Pl., off Maximilianstr.

Northeast of Regensburg and Passau along the Austrian and Czech borders, the **Bavarian Forest** *(Bayerischer Wald)* is Central Europe's largest range of wooded mountains. The **Bavarian Forest National Park** is strictly protected from any activities that may alter the forest ecosystem. Clearly marked trails lace 20,000 sylvan acres. You can hoof it alone, or sign up for guided walking, botanical, and natural history tours. For information and schedules, contact the **Nationalparkverwaltung Bayerischer Wald,** Freyunstr. 94481 Grafenau (tel. (08552) 427 43; fax 46 90). The **Tourismusverband Ostbayern,** Luitpoldstr. (tel. (0941) 58 53 90; fax 585 39 39), in Regensburg, gives news on the rest of the forest. The park's thick woods hide palaces and 17 **HI youth hostels.** Regensburg's tourist office has an omniscient brochure.

Passau Poised on two peninsulas forged by the confluence of the Danube, Inn, and Ilz Rivers, **Passau** embodies the ideal Old World European city. The city's Baroque architecture reaches its apex in the sublime **Stephansdom** (St. Stephen's Cathedral). Hundreds of cherubs are sprawled across the ceiling, and the world's largest **church organ** looms above the choir. (Cathedral open Mon.-Sat. 8-11am and 12:30-6pm. Free. Organ concerts May-Oct. Mon.-Sat. noon. DM4, students DM2. Concerts also held Thurs. 7:30pm. DM10, students DM5.) The **Domschatz** (cathedral treasury) within the **Residenz** behind the cathedral houses an extravagant collection of gold and tapestries (open May-Oct., Mon.-Fri. 10am-4pm; DM2). Nearby is the gilded **St. Michael,** built by the Jesuits. (Open April-Oct. Tues.-Sun. 9am-5pm; Nov.-Jan. and March 10am-4pm. DM3, students DM1.50.) The 13th-century **Rathaus** is less opulent but still stunning. (Open May 16-Sept. 30 daily 10am-5pm; Easter-May 15 10am-4pm; Oct. Mon.-Fri. 10am–4pm. DM2, students DM1.)

The **tourist office,** Rathauspl. 3 (tel. (0851) 95 59 80), has free maps and books rooms (DM5. Open April-Oct. Mon.-Fri. 8:30am-6pm, Sat.-Sun. 10am-2pm; Nov.-March Mon.-Thurs. 8:30am-5pm, Fri. 8:30am-4pm.) The **train station** (tel. (0851) 194 19), west of downtown on Bahnhofstr., serves Regensburg (1-2hr.), Nuremburg (2hr.), Munich (2hr.), and Vienna (3¼hr.). **Rotel Inn** (tel. (0851) 951 60; fax 951 61 00) has wide beds in tiny rooms overlooking the Danube. To get there, go through the tunnel in front of the station toward the blue head of this hotel built in the shape of a sleeping man (reception open 24hr.; singles DM30, doubles DM50). **Pension Rößner,** Bräugasse 19 (tel. (0851) 93 13 50; fax 931 35 55), has homey rooms on the Danube (singles DM60-85, doubles DM80-100; breakfast included). The **Jugendherberge (HI),** Veste Oberhaus 125 (tel. (0851) 413 51; fax 437 09), is a long walk for adequate facilities. (Reception open 7am-11:30am and 4-11:30pm; new arrivals after 6pm only. Curfew 11:30. DM16.50, breakfast included. Sheets DM5.50.)

The **Mensa,** Innstr. 29, offers cafeteria meals for DM2.40-4.50; any student ID will do. From Ludwigspl., follow Nikolastr. and turn right. (Open July-Aug. Mon.-Thurs. 8am-3:30pm, Fri. 8am-3pm; Sept.-June Mon.-Thurs. 8am-4pm, Fri. 8am-3pm.) The popular **Innsteg,** Innstr. 13, is one block from Nikolastr. (menu DM5-21; open daily 10am-1am). **Ratskeller,** Rathauspl. 2, a bustling restaurant in the back of the *Rathaus* overlooking the Danube, serves salads (DM4) and daily "local cuisine" specials (DM8-17; open daily 10am-11pm).

Bamberg and Bayreuth

Bamberg Packed with sights but largely overlooked by travelers, this little city on the Regnitz River boasts a history spanning a thousand years. The 15th-century **Altes Rathaus** guards the middle of the river like an anchored ship. Stand on one of the two bridges to gaze at the half-timbered, half-Baroque facade with a Rococo tower in between. Across the river and up the hill is the **Dom** (cathedral), dating from the early 11th century. The most famous object inside is the 13th-century equestrian statue the **Bamberger Reiter** (Bamberg Knight), embodying the chivalric ideal of the medieval warrior-king. (Open April-Oct. daily 8am-6pm; Nov.-March 8am-5pm; closed during services. 30min. organ concerts May-Oct. Sat. at noon. Free.) Across the square, the **Neue Residenz,** Dompl. 8, boasts a prim rose garden outside and lavish furnishings inside. (Open April-Sept. daily 9am-noon and 1:30-5pm; Oct.-March 9am-noon and 1:30-4pm. Last entry 30min. before closing. DM4, students DM3.)

The **tourist office,** Geyerwörthstr. 3 (tel. (0951) 87 11 61; fax 87 19 60), on an island in the Regnitz River, offers a free hotel list and booklet with a map (open Mon.-Fri. 9am-6pm, Sat. 9am-3pm). The **train station** on Ludwigstr. (tel. (0951) 194 19) serves Nuremberg (30min.-1hr.), Würzburg (1hr.), and Munich (2½-4hr.). Though far away, **Jugendherberge Wolfsschlucht (HI),** Oberer Leintritt 70 (tel. (0951) 560 02; fax 552 11), is clean and pleasant; take bus 18 from the Zentral Omnibus Bahnhof to "Am Regnitzufer." (Reception open 4-10pm. Curfew 10pm. Under 27 only. DM20. Sheets DM5.50. Breakfast included. Open Feb. to mid-Dec. Reserve well in advance.) Rooms in the **Maisel-Bräu-Stübl,** Obere Königstr. 38 (tel./fax (0951) 255 03), overlook a serene courtyard 10 minutes from the station. (Reception open daily 9am-midnight. Singles DM39; doubles DM70-80. Breakfast included.) Also convenient is **Hospiz,** Promenadestr. 3 (tel. (0951) 98 12 60), off Schönleinspl. (reception open daily 7am-10pm; singles DM50-66, doubles DM80-98; call ahead). The **University Mensa,** Austr. 37, off Obstmarkt, serves cheap meals (DM5 with any student ID; open daily 11:30am-2pm). **Café Müller,** Austr. 23, has a French feel. (Crepes DM4.80-8. Open Mon.-Thurs. 9am-11pm, Fri.-Sat. 9am-1am, Sun. 11am-10pm.) The **Jazzclub,** Obere Sandstr. 18, plays a funky mix (cover DM8-10; live jazz Fri.-Sat. 9pm-1am).

Bayreuth Once you've turned off Tristanstr. onto Isoldenstr. and passed Walküregasse, there will be little doubt that you're in Bayreuth, the adopted home of Richard Wagner. Every summer from July 25 to August 28, thousands of visitors pour in for the **Bayreuth Festspiele,** a vast, bombastic celebration of Wagner's works. Tickets go on sale three years in advance and sell out almost immediately (write to Bayreuther Festspiele, 95402 Bayreuth). The avid fan can tour Wagner's house (Haus Wahnfried), now the **Richard Wagner Museum,** Richard-Wagner-Str. 48. (Open Mon., Wed. and Fri. 9am-5pm, Tues. and Thurs. 9am-8:30pm. DM4-5, students DM2.) Bayreuth is an easy daytrip by hourly **trains** from Nuremberg. The **tourist office,** Luitpoldpl. 9 (tel. (0921) 885 88), to the left and about four blocks from the station, provides maps and hotel listings (open Mon.-Fri. 9am-6pm, Sat. 9:30am-12:30pm). You'll need the map to reach the friendly but regimented **Jugendherberge (HI),** Universitätsstr. 28 (tel. (0921) 252 62), near the university. (Under 27 only. Reception open daily 7am-noon and 5-10pm. Strict curfew 10pm. DM20. Open March to mid-Dec.)

Greece Ελλας

US$1 = 290dr (Greek Drachmae) — **100dr = US$0.35**
CDN$1 = 208dr — **100dr = CDN$0.48**
UK£1 = 462dr — **100dr = UK£0.22**
IR£1 = 418dr — **100dr = IR£0.24**
AUS$1 = 215dr — **100dr = AUS$0.46**
NZ$1 = 186dr — **100dr = NZ$0.54**
SAR1 = 61dr — **100dr = SAR1.63**
Country Code: 30 — **International Dialing Prefix: 00**

Even before Odysseus made his epic voyage, Greece was a place for wanderers. Today, countless backpackers travel through the country's classical remains and modern cities every day. Some areas are plowed over by the heaviest tourist industry in Europe; the West's oldest, most sacred monuments cringe amid tacky tourist strips. Yet many smaller towns proudly retain their heritage, and many cities have successfully blended popular and ethnic influences. There is a good chance of finding a heavenly piece of solitary Greece amid the tour buses and flashing cameras.

In some ways, Greece is an aggressively Western country whose capital rivals London, Paris, and Rome. As proud guardians of the classical inheritance, Greeks consider western civilization a homespun export. But to step into Greece is to walk east—into a whirl of Byzantine icons, Orthodox priests trailing long dark robes, and air spiced with the strains of *bouzouki* music. Greece's eastern flavor is the result of four centuries of Ottoman rule. Thanks mostly to the integrity of the Orthodox Church, the Greek identity survived Turkish captivity. Memories of the 1821 War of Independence still excite Greek nationalism; 400 years are not easily forgotten.

Socialist Andreas Papandreou has been the major figure in recent politics. As Prime Minister in the early 1980s, Papandreou oversaw advances in civil liberties, but drew criticism at home and abroad for economic austerity policies and heated anti-NATO rhetoric. After Papandreou's government was linked to embezzlement, a series of elections left Constantine Mitsotakis of the conservative New Democracy Party as Prime Minister in 1990. In an attempt to bring Greece's huge debt under control, Mitsotakis imposed his own austerity program which lost him his narrow majority and returned Papandreou to power. In January 1996, Papandreou finally stepped down due to persisting health problems. His Socialist Party (PASOK) named Constantinos Simitis as its new Prime Minister. Elections in September 1996 maintained the Socialists in power with Simitis still as prime minister.

For coverage of Greece rivaling that of Pausanias (the 2nd century's equivalent of a *Let's Go* researcher), grab a copy of *Let's Go: Greece and Turkey 1998.*

GETTING THERE

Greece is served by a number of relatively cheap international **train** routes that connect Athens, Thessaloniki, and Larissa to most European cities, but count on at least a three-day journey from Trieste or Vienna to Athens. Buses are even cheaper, but a real marathon. **Eurolines,** 4 Cardiff Rd., Luton LU1 1PP,; tel. (01582) 40 45 11), is Europe's largest operator of Europe-wide coach services.

Certainly the most popular way of getting to Greece is by **ferry** from Italy. Boats travel primarily from Italy (Ancona and Brindisi) to Corfu (10hr.), Igoumenitsa (12hr.), and Patras (20hr.). Seats run L50,000-105,000 (US$31-66; in low season L22,000-45,000 or US$13-29). Rhodes is connected by ferry to Marmaris, Turkey; Limassol, Cyprus; and Haifa, Israel (10,000-32,000dr in low season). If you plan to travel from Brindisi in the summer, make reservations and arrive at the port well before your departure time. ISIC holders can often get student fares, and Eurail passholders get many reductions and free trips. Everyone pays the port tax (L10,000, or US$6.25, in Brindisi) and, in high season, a supplementary fee of L19,000 (US$12).

Flying from northern European cities is also a popular way of getting to Greece. From North America, an indirect flight through Brussels or Luxembourg may cost less than a flight going directly to Athens. **Olympic Airways,** 96-100 Syngrou Ave., 11741 Athens (tel. (01) 929 21 11), serves many large cities and islands within Greece.

GETTING AROUND

Train service in Greece is limited and sometimes uncomfortable, and no lines go to the western coast. The new express air-conditioned intercity trains, though slightly more expensive and rare, are well worth the price. **Eurailpasses** are valid on Greek trains. **Hellenic Railways Organization (OSE)** connects Athens to other major Greek cities. In Greece, call 145 or 147 for schedules and prices.

Faster, more extensive, and reasonably priced, **buses** are a good alternative to train travel; most are run through **KTEL.** Smaller towns may use cafés as bus stops; ask for a schedule. Confirm your destination with the driver; signs may be wrong. Along the road, little blue signs marked with white buses or the word "ΣΤΑΣΗ" indicate stops, but drivers usually stop anywhere if you flag them down. Let the driver know ahead of time where you want to get off; if your stop is passed, yell "Stasi!"

Greeks are not eager to pick up foreigners. Sparsely populated areas have little or no traffic. Visitors who do choose to **hitchhike** write their destination on a sign in both Greek and English, and hitch from turn-offs rather than along long stretches of straight road. Women should *never* hitch alone. The mountainous terrain and unpaved roads make **cycling** in Greece difficult. **Mopeds** can be great for exploring, but they also make you extremely vulnerable to the carelessness of other drivers. The majority of tourist-related accidents each year occur on mopeds.

There is frequent **ferry** service to the Greek islands, but schedules are irregular and exasperating; misinformation is common. In some places, fierce competition will keep one ferry agent silent about another ferry line's schedule; the government tourist office should provide complete, or at least unbiased, ferry info. To avoid hassles, go to **limenarheio** (port police)—every port has one, and they all carry ferry schedules. **Flying dolphins** (hydrofoils) are a speedier but more expensive alternative to ferry transport. Finally, if you're planning a trip to Turkey, keep in mind that information about Turkey is sketchy in Greece; plan your trip outside of Greece.

The national airline, **Olympic Airways** (tel. (01) 929 21 11), operates efficient and reasonably priced flights between many islands. Note that these flights are often booked weeks in advance in summer. Coverage to remote areas is spotty.

ESSENTIALS

Tourism in Greece is overseen by two national organizations: the **Greek National Tourist Organization (GNTO)** and the **tourist police** *(touristiki astinomia)*. The GNTO can supply general information about sights and accommodations throughout the country. The main office is at 2 Amerikis St., Athens (tel. (01) 322 41 28). Remember that the GNTO is known as **EOT** in Greek. The **tourist police** (tel. in Athens 171 in Athens, elsewhere in Greece 922 77 77) deal with more local and immediate problems: where to find a room, what the bus schedule is, or what to do when you've lost your passport. They are open long hours and are willing to help, although their English is often limited. For tourist info (in English) 24 hours a day, call 171 in Athens or 922 77 77 elsewhere in Greece. The **emergency** number for **police** is 100 in most of Greece; for **first aid,** 166; for **U.S. citizens emergency aid,** (01) 722 36 52.

Women traveling in Greece, as in other Mediterranean countries, are likely to experience verbal harassment. Ignore it, or turn to an older woman for help. In an emergency, call out "vo-EE-thee-a" ("help"). Modest dress (no shorts, short skirts, or revealing tops) is likely to reduce unwanted attention, and is required of both sexes at monasteries and churches. Normal **business hours** in Greece include a break from about 2pm until 6pm or so. Hours vary from place to place. Banks are normally open Monday through Friday 8am to 1:30pm, and also 3:30-6pm in some larger cities. The major **national holidays**—during which all banks and shops are closed—are New Year's Day, Epiphany (Jan. 6), days commemorating Greek independence (March 25 and Oct. 28), Good Friday (April 10), Easter (April 12), Labor Day (May 1), The Assumption of the Virgin Mary (Aug. 15), and Christmas (Dec. 25).

Communication Greece's **telephone** company is **OTE.** Their offices are usually open 7:30am to 3pm in villages, 7:30am to 10pm in towns, and 24 hours in larger cities. For **AT&T Direct,** dial 00 800 1311; **MCI WorldPhone,** 00 800 12 11; **Sprint Access,** 00 800 14 11; **Canada Direct,** 00 800 16 11; **BT Direct,** 00 800 44 11; and **Ireland Direct,** 155 11 74. **Post offices** are generally open Monday through Friday 7:30am to 2pm. A letter to the U.S. costs 120dr and usually takes 4-14 days.

Although many Greeks in Athens and other heavily touristed areas speak English—particularly young people—those living off the beaten path are unlikely to. The following transliteration table should help you decipher things, although prepare for some exceptions (for instance, Φ and φ are often spelled *ph*).

Greek	Roman	Greek	Roman	Greek	Roman
Α, α	A, a	Ι, ι	I, i	Ρ, ρ	R, r
Β, β	V, v	Κ, κ	K, k	Σ, σ, ς	S, s
Γ, γ	G, g; Y, y	Λ, λ	L, l	Τ, τ	T, t
Δ, δ	D, d	Μ, μ	M, m	Υ, υ	Y, y; I, i
Ε, ε	E, e	Ν, ν	N, n	Φ, φ	F, f
Ζ, ζ	Z, z	Ξ, ξ	X, x	Χ, χ	Ch, ch; H, h
Η, η	I, i; Ē, ē	Ο, ο	O, o	Ψ, ψ	Ps, ps
Θ, θ	Th, th	Π, π	P, p	Ω, ω	O, o; Ō, ō

To avoid misunderstandings, it is also important to know Greek body language. To say no, Greeks lift their heads back abruptly while raising their eyebrows. To indicate a yes, they emphatically nod once. A hand waving up and down that seems to say "stay there" actually means "come."

Yes/No	ΝΑΙ/ΟΧΙ	NEH /OH-hee
Hello	ΓΕΙΑ ΣΑΣ	YAH-sas
Excuse me.	ΣΥΓΓΝΩΜΗ	seeg-NO-mee
Do you speak English?	ΜΙΛΑΣ ΑΓΓΛΙΚΑ	mee-LAHS ahn-glee-KAH
I don't speak Greek.	ΔΕΝ ΜΙΛΑΩ ΕΛΛΗΝΙΚΑ	dhen mee-LAHO el-leen-ee-KAH
Where is...?	ΠΟΥ ΕΙΝΑΙ	pou EE-neh
How much?	ΠΟΣΟ ΚΑΝΕΙ	PO-so KAH-nee
I would like...	ΘΑ ΗΘΕΛΑ	thah EE-the-lah
Can I see a room?	ΜΠΟΡΩ ΝΑ ΔΩ ΕΝΑ ΔΩΜΑΤΙΟ	bo-RO nah DHO E-nah dho-MAH-tee-o
Help!	ΒΟΗΘΕΙΑ	vo-EE-thee-ah

Accommodations and Camping Lodging in Greece is a bargain. At time of publication, Hostelling International (HI) had yet to reach an agreement with Greek hostels, and they endorse only one hostel in the entire country (in Athens). Nevertheless, hostels that are not currently endorsed by HI are in most cases still safe and reputable. Curfews in hostels are strict, and they may leave you on the street. Hotel prices are regulated, but proprietors may try to push you to take the most expensive room. Check your bill carefully, and threaten to contact the tourist police if you think you are being cheated. GNTO offices usually have a list of inexpensive accommodations with prices. In many areas, *dhomatia* (rooms to let) are an attractive and perfectly dependable option. Although you may sacrifice some amenities, the possibility of sharing coffee or some intriguing conversation with your proprietor is worth it. Often you'll be approached by locals as you enter town or disembark from your boat; Greek tourist officials consider this illegal. Greece hosts plenty of official **campgrounds,** and discreet freelance camping—though illegal—is common in July and August, but may not be the safest way to spend the night.

Food and Drink Greek food is simple and healthy. Most restaurants in Greece work from the same culinary palette, but create original masterpieces with subtle shadings. A restaurant is known as either a *taverna* or *estiatorio,* while a grill is a *psistaria.* Breakfast can be bread, *tiropita* (cheese pie), or a pastry with *marmelada* (jam) or *meli* (honey), and a cup of coffee *(elliniko* is Turkish style and *frappe* is a frothy iced drink). Lunch, the largest meal of the day, is eaten in the mid to late afternoon. The evening meal is a leisurely affair; usually served after 8 or 9pm, and as late as 11pm-1am during the summer in the larger cities. A few *drachmae* as tip is customary in restaurants. Greek restaurants divide food into two categories: *magiremeno,* meaning cooked, and *tis oras,* to indicate grilled meat. The former is generally cheaper. *Tis oras* includes grilled *moskari* (veal), *arni* (lamb), or *kotopoulo* (chicken), served with *tiganites patates* (french fries), *rizi* (rice), or *fasolia* (beans). Popular *magiremeno* dishes include *mousaka* (chopped meat and eggplant mixed with a cheese and tomato paste), *pastitsio* (a lasagna-like dish of thick noodles covered with a rich cream sauce), *yemista* (stuffed tomatoes and peppers), *dolmadhes* (stuffed grape leaves) and *youvrelakia* (meatballs in egg and lemon sauce). You can hardly avoid *souvlaki,* a large skewer of steak, generally pork or lamb. A *souvlaki pita,* known as "the budget food of the masses," is a pita crammed full of skewered meat and fillings (about 300dr). *Gyros* also abound in street vendor fast-food stands (approximately 300dr). A favorite Greek snack combination is *ouzo* with *mezes,* tidbits of cheese, sausage, cakes, and octopus. *Ouzo* is a distilled spirit to which anise is added, giving it a licorice taste. Mixed with water, it's sweet but not overwhelming.

One of the great arts in Greece is wine-making, and every region has its own specialty. Long ago, the Greeks discovered that when wine was stored in pine pitch-sealed goatskins, it developed a fresh, sappy flavor. After much deduction, they discovered that adding pine resin in varying amounts during fermentation achieved the same result. The resulting wine became known as *retsina*. Resinated wines now come in three varieties: white, rosé, and red *(kokkineli)*.

Athens ΑΘΗΝΑ

Visitors harboring mental images of togas and philosophers may be disappointed to find that Athens is a 20th-century city in every sense of the word—crowded, noisy and polluted. The Neoclassical mansions of 30 years ago have largely been replaced by white monolith towers to accommodate a booming population. The Plaka neighborhood, which borders the Acropolis, is one of the few remnants of the ancient grandeur; column-bound temples stand as proud reminders of the faith of the ancient Athenians. But modernity cannot rest on teetering ruins: the city still needs a comprehensive subway system, a manageable communications system, and space for its citizens to live. Nevertheless, the city center is a mosaic of Byzantine churches, ancient ruins, traditional outdoor *tavernas*, and shopping centers.

ORIENTATION AND PRACTICAL INFORMATION

Syntagma Square, with transportation terminals and subway construction sites, is the tourist's focal point. The **Greek National Tourist Office (EOT), post office, American Express office, transportation terminals,** and a number of **travel agencies** and **banks** surround the square. **Filellinon Street** and **Nikis Street,** which run parallel from Syntagma toward the Plaka, contain the city's budget travel offices, cheap hotels, and dance clubs. The **Plaka,** between Syntagma and the **Acropolis,** is the oldest section of the city and now brims with shops, restaurants, and hotels. Northwest of Syntagma, **Omonia Square** is the site of the city's central subway station. Cheap shops and lodgings abound, but in recent years, this cosmopolitan area has become increasingly unsafe. *Do not travel alone at night in Omonia Sq.*

Athens is impossible to negotiate without a map. Make use of the free maps from the tourist office: the city map is clear and includes bus and trolley routes, while the magazine *Greece-Athens-Attica* has a more detailed street plan. Cultural listings appear in the English newspaper *Athens News* (300dr). Be alert when crossing streets, and remember that Athenian streets often have multiple spellings.

Tourist Office: Info window at the **National Bank of Greece,** 2 Karageorgi Servias, Syntagma Sq. (tel. 322 25 45). Transportation schedules and prices, lists of museums and banks, and info on travel in Greece. Open Mon.-Fri. 9am-6:30pm, Sat. 9am-2pm. Another office is in the **East Terminal** of the airport (tel. 969 45 00). Open same hours. The **central office** is at 2 Amerikis St., off Stadiou St. (tel. 322 41 28). Open in summer Mon.-Fri. 11am-2pm; off-season 11:30am-2:30pm.

Budget Travel: The only discounts on domestic travel for foreign students are for domestic air fares, often available to the more popular islands. **Magic Travel Agency** (formerly **Magic Bus**), 20 Filellinon St. (tel. 323 74 71, -4; fax 322 02 19), has a very competent, English-speaking staff. Open Mon.-Fri. 9am-7pm, Sat. 9am-2:30pm. **Consolas Travel,** 100 Aiolou St. (tel. 325 49 31; fax 321 09 07), next to the post office has a second office on 18 Filellinon St. (tel. 323 28 12).

Embassies: Australia, 37 D. Soutsou St. (tel. 644 73 03). Open Mon.-Fri. 8:30am-12:30pm. **Canada,** 4 Ioannou Genadiou St. (tel. 725 40 11). Open Mon.-Fri. 8:30am-12:30pm. **Ireland,** 7 Vas. Konstantinou Ave. (tel. 723 27 71). Open Mon.-Fri. 9am-3pm. **South Africa,** 60 Kifissias St. (tel. 680 66 45). Open Mon.-Fri. 8am-1pm. **U.K.,** 1 Ploutarchou St. (tel. 723 62 11), at Ypsilantou St. Open for visas Mon.-Fri. 8:30am-1pm. **U.S.,** 91 Vasilissis Sofias (tel. 721 29 51; fax 645 62 82). Open Mon.-Fri. 8:30am-5pm. Visas 8-11am.

Currency Exchange: National Bank of Greece, 2 Karageorgi Servias St., Syntagma Sq. (tel. 322 27 38, -7). Open Mon.-Thurs. 8am-2pm, Fri. 8am-1:30pm. Also open for currency exchange only Mon.-Thurs. 3:30-6:30pm, Fri. 3-6:30pm, Sat. 9am-3pm, Sun 9am-1pm. Also try AmEx, the post office, hotels, and other banks.

American Express: 2 Ermou St., P.O. Box 3325, above McDonald's in Syntagma Sq. (tel. 324 49 75, -9). Cashes Traveler's Cheques with no commission, runs travel agency, holds mail, and provides special services for cardholders. Open Mon.-Fri. 8:30am-4pm; also open Sat. 8:30am-1:30pm for travel and mail service only.

Flights: East Terminal, foreign airlines and some charters; **West Terminal,** Olympic Airways domestic and international service; **New Charter Terminal,** most charters. From Athens, take the Express bus 090 and 091 from either Syntagma Sq., in front of McDonald's, or Stadiou St. near Omonia Sq. (091 goes only to East and West terminals). Buses run roughly every half-hour from 6am to 9pm (160dr); every 40min. from 9pm to 11:30pm (160dr); and every hr. on the half-hour from 11:30pm to 5:30am (200dr). A taxi costs 1500-2000dr, plus luggage charge.

Trains: Larissis Train Station (tel. 524 06 01) serves northern Greece (Thessaloniki 3720dr) and Europe. Take trolley 1 from El. Venizelou (also called Panepistimiou St.) in Syntagma (every 10min. 5am-midnight, 75dr). **Peloponnese Railroad Station** (tel. 513 16 01) serves Patras (1580dr) and major Peloponnesian towns. Also has OSE buses to Bulgaria, Albania, and Turkey. To reach the station from Larissis, exit to your right and cross the foot-bridge, or catch bus 057 from El. Venizelou (every 15min. 5:30am-11:30pm, 75dr). For info, try **Hellenic Railways (OSE)** (tel. 323 62 73). Call 145, 146, or 147 for timetables.

Buses: Terminal A, 100 Kifissou St. (tel. 512 49 10), serves most of Greece, including the Peloponnese, and can be reached by blue bus 051 at the corner of Zinonos and Menandrou near Omonia Sq. **Terminal B,** 260 Liossion St. (tel. 831 71 81), sends buses to central Greece. Take blue bus 024 at El. Venizelou (Panepistimiou St.). Buy a ticket at a kiosk and stamp it at the orange machine on board.

Ferries: Most dock at **Piraeus.** Boats to Andros, Tinos, and Mykonos leave from **Rafina,** a port suburb east of Athens. Always check ferry schedules available at the tourist office or in the *Athens News* just prior to departure, with the **Port Authority of Piraeus** (tel. 422 60 00), or any travel agency.

Hydrofoils: Ceres' Flying Dolphins (tel. 428 00 01) and **Ilios Lines' Dolphins** (tel. 322 51 39) are the main companies. Both open Mon.-Sat. 8am-6:30pm, Sun. 8am-1pm. Hydrofoils, roughly twice as fast and twice as expensive as ferries, leave from **Zea Port** near Piraeus, Agios Konstantinos, and Volos and serve the mainland and the Argosaronic, Sporades, and Cyclades islands.

Public Transportation: Blue buses, designated by 3-digit numbers, and yellow trolley rides (1-2 digits) cost 75dr. Money is not accepted on trolleys; buy tickets ahead of time at a kiosk. The **subway** runs from Piraeus harbor to Kifissia in north Athens with stops along the way (every 10min. 5am-midnight, 75-100dr).

Luggage Storage: At the airport for 700dr per piece per day; keep your ticket stub. Several offices on Nikis and Filellinon St. charge 300dr per piece per day.

English Bookstores: Eleftheroudakis Book Store, 4 Nikis St. (tel. 322 93 88), is bliss for bibliophiles. Open Mon.-Fri. 9am-8:30pm, Sat. 9am-3pm.

Laundromats: The Greek word for laundry is *plinitirio.* At 10 Angelou Geronta St. in Plaka and 41 Kolokinthous and Leonidou St. (tel. 522 62 33), near the train stations. One load (wash, dry, and detergent) costs about 2000dr.

Pharmacies: Indicated by a red or green cross extending out over the street. The daily *Athens News* (300dr) lists each day's emergency pharmacies and their hours in its "useful information" section. For pharmacy info, dial 107 or 102.

Medical Assistance: Near Kolonaki is a **public hospital** at 45-47 Evangelismou (tel. 722 0101; fax 729 1808). In Greek, "hospital" is *nosokomio.*

Emergencies: Ambulance: tel. 166. **Police:** tel. 100. Broken English spoken. **Tourist Police:** 77 Dimitrakopoulou St. (tel. 171). Open 24hr.

Post Offices: 100 Aiolou St., Omonia Sq. (tel. 321 60 23). **Postal Code:** 10200. **Syntagma Sq.,** on the corner of Mitropolis (tel. 322 62 53). **Postal Code:** 10300. **60 Mitropoleos,** a few blocks from Syntagma Sq. (tel. 321 81 43). All offices open Mon.-Fri. 7:30am-8pm, Sat. 7:30am-2pm, Sun. 9am-1:30pm.

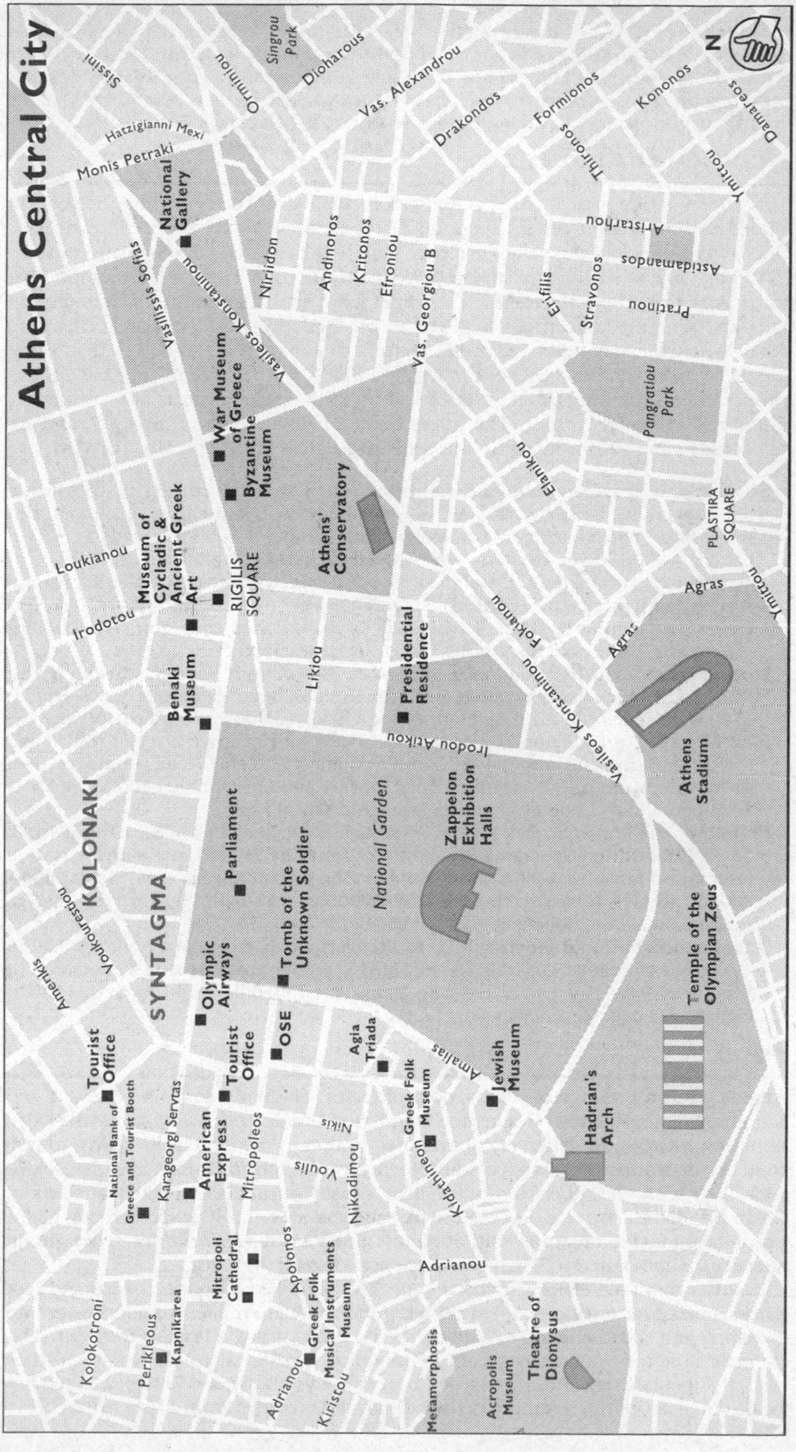
Athens Central City
N
Sissini
Hatzigianni Mexi
Monis Petraki
Orminiou
Singrou Park
Dioharous
Vas. Alexandrou
Drakondos
Formionos
Kononos
Damareos
Thironos
Ymittou
National Gallery
Vasilissis Sofias
Vasileos Konstaninou
Niriidon
Andinoros
Kritonos
Efroniou
Vas. Georgiou B
Aristarhou
Astidamandos
Pratinou
Erifilis
Stravonos
War Museum of Greece
Byzantine Museum
Athens' Conservatory
Pangratiou Park
Elanikou
PLASTIRA SQUARE
Loukianou
Museum of Cycladic & Ancient Greek Art
Irodotou
RIGILIS SQUARE
Likiou
Presidential Residence
Fokianou
Agras
Benaki Museum
Irodou Atikou
Vasileos Konstaninou
Athens Stadium
KOLONAKI
Voukourestiou
Amerikis
SYNTAGMA
Parliament
National Garden
Zappeion Exhibition Halls
Tomb of the Unknown Soldier
Olympic Airways
Temple of the Olympian Zeus
Tourist Office
OSE
Agia Triada
Amalias
Jewish Museum
National Bank of Greece and Tourist Booth
Karageorgi Servtas
American Express
Mitropoleos
Niki
Greek Folk Museum
Voulis
Nikodimou
Kidathineon
Hadrian's Arch
Mitropoli Cathedral
Apolonos
Adrianou
Kolokotroni
Perikleous
Kapnikarea
Greek Folk Musical Instruments Museum
Adrianou
Kiristou
Metamorphosis
Acropolis Museum
Theatre of Dionysus

Telephones: OTE, 15 Stadiou St. (tel. 330 21 21). Open 24hr. for all communication needs. **Telephone cards** for local phone booths are sold for 1500, 6500, or 12,000dr. Push the "i" button on the phones for English-language instructions. For telephone info, call 134; for info on overseas calls, dial 161; for complaints 135; for a domestic operator speaking English 151 or 152. **Telephone Code:** 01.

ACCOMMODATIONS

Many hotel hawkers meet trains at the station. Some distribute pamphlets for decent places near the station, others lure tourists to expensive dumps far from town. Have the hawker point out the place on a large map of the city and set a firm price, ideally in writing, *before* leaving the station. When you arrive at a hotel, ask for a room that faces away from noisy streets. Men arriving by bus should be aware of "friendly barkeepers" who may deceitfully lead you to brothels. Most budget hotels cluster in Plaka-Syntagma; stay here if nightlife matters to you. If you stay fewer than three nights, an Athenian hotel owner can legally add a 10% surcharge to your bill. Athens proper has **no camping** facilities. Do not sleep in the parks, even as a last resort; it's illegal and extremely unsafe. The prices quoted below are from mid-1997, and are expected to rise 10-20% in 1998. Prices are 20-40% less from September to May.

Student and Travelers Inn, 16 Kidathineon (tel. 324 48 08; fax 321 00 65). Pricey but convenient with a great staff, outdoor courtyard, and hardwood floors. Hot water 24hr. Singles 6500dr. Doubles 8000dr. Triples 10,000dr. Quads 11,500dr. Breakfast 800-1000dr. 10% Discount with student ID or Youth Card.

Thisseos Inn, 10 Thisseos St. (tel. 324 59 60). From Syntagma Sq., take Karageorgi Servias (which becomes Perikleous), and Thisseos St. is on the right. Near Syntagma but far from its noise. Communal TV and kitchen, common showers (hot water 24hr.). Curfew 2am. Dorms 2500dr. Doubles 5500dr.

Hotel Phaedra, 16 Herefondos St. (tel. 322 77 95). From Hadrian's Arch on Vas. Sofias, go 1 block up Lysikrateus St. to Herefondos. Some Acropolis views. Singles 6500dr. Doubles 8000dr. Triples 10,000dr. Quads 12,000dr. Breakfast 1500dr.

Hotel Festos, 18 Filellinon St. (tel. 323 24 55). A bit run-down but still festive and fun; reservations often needed. Come as a guest and stay as an employee. Hot showers mornings and evenings only. Dorms 3000dr. Doubles 7000dr. Triples 10,500dr. Quads 14,000dr. Luggage storage 200dr per day.

Pella Inn, 104 Ermou St. (tel. 325 05 98 or 321 22 29; fax 325 05 98), a 10min. walk down Ermou from Syntagma Sq., 2 blocks from the Monastiraki subway station (entrance on Karaiskaki St.). Lounge and terrace with Acropolis view. Singles 5000-7000dr, with bath 9000dr. Doubles 7000-9000dr, with bath 9000dr. Free luggage storage. Breakfast 1000dr.

Athens International Hostel (HI), 16 Victor Hugo St. (tel. 523 41 70; fax 523 40 15). From Omonoia Sq., walk down Third Sept. St., take a left on Veranzerou; it becomes Victor Hugo after crossing Marni St. HI membership required. 1500dr, including sheets. Reserve ahead.

FOOD

Athens offers a melange of stands, open-air cafés, outdoor sidestreet *tavernas,* and intriguing dim restaurants frequented by grizzled Greek men. *Souvlaki* (250-400dr), either on a *kalamaki* (skewer) or wrapped in *pita,* is the Greek alternative to fast-food. A *tost,* a grilled sandwich of variable ingredients (normally ham and cheese) for 250-500dr is another portable option. Beer, usually Amstel or Heineken, runs about 200dr per bottle. *Tiropita* (hot cheese pie) and *spanakopita* (hot spinach pie) go for around 300dr. Ice cream is sold at almost every kiosk. A *koulouri,* a doughnut-shaped, sesame-coated roll, makes a quick breakfast for 50-100dr.

Tourists eat in the Plaka. Crowded in peak season, the outdoor *tavernas* and roof gardens make for terrific people-watching, and there are numerous good places up Adrianou and Kidatheneon St. Women should know that the Plaka is frequented by *kamakia* (literally, "octopus spears") who enjoy making catcalls at women as they walk by. Ignore them and they should pose no physical danger. Restaurants tend to be deserted at 6pm, near-empty before 10pm, and crowded from 11pm to 1am.

Eden Vegetarian Restaurant, 12 Lissiou St. On the corner of Minissikleous on the western side of Plaka. Airy, secluded, and popular. Spinach special 1700dr.

Zorbas, 15 Lissiou St., right across the street from Eden, is one of the cheapest places around. Most entrees around 1800dr. Lamb Zorbas 1900dr. Pumpkin balls 700dr.

Souvlaki ee Lievadia, 7 Gladstonos St. Walk along Patissan St. and take the first left away from Omonia Sq. Cheap and delicious. They've been making *souvlaki* (230dr) for 32 years. All-you-can-eat free bread.

Restaurant of Konstantinos Athanasias Velly, Varnava Sq., Plastira. Take trolley 2, 4, 11, or 12 to Plastira Sq., walk 3 blocks up Proklou St. to far right corner of Varnava Sq. No English spoken. Tomato salad 500dr. *Keftedes* (Greek meatballs) with potatoes 900dr. *Fasolia* (bean soup) 400dr.

Cafe Plaka, 1 Tripodon. A dessert lover's haven. French crepes loaded with ham, mushrooms, chicken or cheese for a meal, or the sinful chocolate-banana option. Take-out crepes are identical but half the price (500dr compared to 1000dr).

SIGHTS

The **Acropolis,** or "high city," with its strategic position overlooking the Aegean Sea and Attic Plains, has served throughout history as both a military fortress and a religious center. Today, the hilltop's remarkable (if scaffolded) ruins grace otherwise rubble-strewn grounds. The ramp that led to the Acropolis in classical times no longer exists: today's visitors make the five-minute climb to the ticket-window, enter through the crumbling **Beulé Gate** (added by the Romans), and continue through the **Propylaea,** the ancient entrance. The site is not wheelchair accessible. The marble can be slippery, so wear appropriate shoes. At the cliff's edge, the tiny **Temple of Athena Nike** was built during a respite from the Peloponnesian War, the so-called Peace of Nikias (421-415 BC). Looming over the hillside, the **Parthenon,** or "Virgin's Apartment," keeps vigil over Athens. The temple features many almost imperceptible intentional irregularities; the Doric columns bulge in the middle, and the stylobate (pedestal) of the building bows slightly upward in order to compensate for the optical illusion in which straight lines, viewed from a distance, appear to bend. The **Erechtheum,** to the left of the Parthenon as you face it, was completed in 406 BC, just prior to Athens's defeat by Sparta. This unique two-leveled structure housed a number of cults. On the south side of the Erechtheum, facing the Parthenon, are the **caryatids,** six columns sculpted in the shape of women. (Acropolis open in summer Mon.-Fri. 8am-6:30pm, Sat.-Sun. and holidays 8:30am-2:30pm; off-season 8:30am-4:30pm. 2000dr, students 1000dr.) The **Acropolis Museum** (tel. 323 66 65), footsteps away from the Parthenon, contains a superb collection of sculpture, including five of the original caryatids of the Erechtheum. (Open Mon.-Sat. 8am-6:30pm, Sun. 8:30am-2:30pm. Admission included in Acropolis ticket.)

The **Athenian Agora,** at the foot of the Acropolis, was the administrative center and marketplace of Athens from the 6th century BC through the late Roman Period (5th and 6th centuries AD). The **Temple of Hephaestos,** on a hill in the northwest corner, is the best-preserved Classical temple in Greece. Built around 440 BC, it is notable for its friezes depicting the labors of Hercules and the adventures of Theseus. To the south, the elongated **Stoa of Attalos,** a multi-purpose building for shops, shelter, and informal gatherings, was rebuilt between 1953 and 1956 and now houses the **Agora Museum.** The museum contains a number of relics from the site and offers sanctuary from the sweltering summer sun. There are several entrances to the Agora, including one at the edge of Monastiraki, one on Thission Sq., and one on Adrianou St. (Agora and museum open Tues.-Sun. 8:30am-3pm; 1200dr, students 600dr). Fifteen majestic columns are all that remain of the **Temple of Olympian Zeus,** Vas. Olgas and Amalias Ave., the largest temple ever built in Greece (open Tues.-Sun. 8:30am-3pm; 500dr, students 300dr). Next to the Temple, **Hadrian's Arch** marked the 2nd-century boundary between the ancient city of Thisseos and the new city built by Hadrian. One of the world's finest selections of classical sculpture, ceramics, and bronzework is found in the **National Archeological Museum,** 44 Patission St.

Pieces that would shine elsewhere seem almost unremarkable amid the general magnificence. The "Mask of Agamemnon," from Heinrich Schliemann's Mycenae digs, is a must-see. (Open Mon. 12:30-7pm, Tues.-Fri. 8am-7pm, Sat.-Sun. 8:30am-3pm. 2000dr, students 1000dr, Sun. and holidays free. No flash photography.) The **Chapel of St. George,** on top of **Lycabettos Hill,** offers a beautiful view of the city. The **National Gallery** (Alexander Soutzos Museum), 50 Vasileos Konstandinou, exhibits Greek artists' works supplemented by periodic international displays. Consult *This Week in Athens* or call for info on exhibits (open Mon. and Wed.-Sat. 9am-3pm, Sun. 10am-2pm; free). Walk along the tranquil paths and visit the duck pond and zoo of the pleasant **National Garden,** adjacent to Syntagma Square. Women should avoid strolling alone (open daily sunrise to sunset). Don't miss the changing of the guard every hour on the hour in front of the **Parliament** building. Unlike the British equivalents, *evzones* occasionally wink or even smile. Every Sunday at 10:45am, the pomp-filled ceremony occurs with the full troop of guards and a band. Byzantine churches in Athens include the **Agia Apostoli,** at the east edge of the Agora; **Metamorphosis,** in Plaka near Pritaniou St.; **Agia Triada,** on Filellinon St., a few blocks from Syntagma; and **Agios Eleftherios,** next to the **Mitropoli Cathedral,** on Mitropoleos St. Viewing hours are at the discretion of each church's priest. Mornings are the best bet. Dress appropriately: skirts for women, pants for men, and sleeved shirts for everyone.

ENTERTAINMENT

During the summer, hip Athenians head to the numerous seaside clubs on Poseidons Ave. in **Glyfada** (past the airport). Many do not admit anyone in shorts. Covers range 2000-3000dr, and beers run as high as 1000-2000dr (cocktails 1500-3000dr). Nearby, off the water, on Vouliagmenis St. in Glyfada, the best bars are all lined up. Some good hotspots include **La Mamounia at La Playa** and **Amphitheatro** for dance beat, **Wild Rose** for rock, and **Prinz** for people watching. You will wait in line on Friday and Saturday for the current hot spots, **Privilege** and **Empire.** Cover charges are roughly 3000kr, and taxi fare to and from the city center is 1500-2500dr each way. Other parts of the city have good clubs as well. Try venturing to the posh **Kolonaki** district, where a coffee or beer at any of the outdoor *tavernas* is manageable. **Jazz Club 1920,** 10 Ploutarchou St., up from the British Embassy, is nearby. In **Kifissia,** a hip residential area north of Athens, there are many slick *tavernas* and discos. For gay (primarily male) clubs, try **Lembessi St.** off Singrou.

The **Athens Festival** runs annually from June until September, featuring classical theater groups performing in the Odeon of Herodes Atticus, the Lycabettos Theater at the top of Lycabettos Hill, and in Epidavros. The Greek Orchestra plays during this festival regularly; visiting artists have ranged from the Bolshoy to B. B. King. The **Festival Office** (tel. 322 14 59, -31 11, ext. 240) is in the arcade at 4 Stadiou St. Student tickets are generally affordable. (Tickets 3000-5000dr. Open Mon.-Fri. 8:30am-2pm and 5-7pm, Sat. 8:30am-1pm, Sun. 10am-1pm.)

The bazaar-like **Athens Flea Market,** adjacent to Monastiraki Sq., offers a potpourri of the second-hand, the costly, and everything in between (market open Mon., Wed., and Sat.-Sun. 8am-3pm, Tues. and Thurs.-Fri. 8am-8pm). Sunday is the grand bazaar: the flea market overflows the square and Fillis Athinas St. A huge indoor-outdoor **food market** lines the sides of Athinas St. between Evripidou and Sofokleous St. The **meat market** is huge, but not for the faint of heart.

■ Near Athens

The view of the Aegean from the **Temple of Poseidon** makes a visit here a sublime experience. The remaining Doric columns of the sanctuary, built by Pericles in 440 BC, sit on a promontory above the coast at **Cape Sounion,** 70km from Athens (open daily 9am-sunset; 800dr, students 400dr, EU students free). Two **buses** go to Cape Sounion. One travels the Apollo Coast, leaving every hour on the half-hour from Mavromateon St. (6:30am-6:30pm, 2hr., 1200dr). The other bus, on a less scenic route, leaves from Areos Park (every hr. on the hr. 6am-6pm, 2¼hr., 1200dr). Bring water and a lunch. Check return schedules at the bus station upon arrival.

The serene **Monastery of Kesariani** near the top of Mt. Hymettus will let you view all of Athens and keep its noise and congestion at a safe distance. Now housing splendid 17th-century frescoes, the site was originally a temple to Dimitra, goddess of agriculture and nature (open Tues.-Sun. 8:30am-3pm; 800dr, students 400dr, EU students free). To get there, take blue bus 224 from the ΚΗΠΟΣ stop two blocks up Vas. Sofias from Syntagma Sq. to the last stop (every 15min., 20min., 75dr). Follow the left-hand road uphill, and when you reach the overpass, bear right under it. Bear right again when the road forks and finally take the stone path that branches from the road to the monastery. The walk is 45 minutes; bring water.

Troubled denizens of the ancient world journeyed to the Oracle of Apollo at **Delphi,** where the *Pythia* (priestess of Apollo) gave them profound, if cryptic, advice. If modern Delphi is the center of anything, it's of the tour-bus circuit—try to visit early in the morning. **Buses** leave Athens for Delphi from the 260 Liossion St. station (5 per day, 3½hr., 2700dr). If you have a railpass, take the **train** to Levadia and catch the Delphi bus there (700dr).

NORTHERN GREECE

The northern provinces of Macedonia, Thessaly, Thrace, and Epirus seldom find their way onto postcards, but not for lack of beauty. Greece's forgotten half is graced with pine-filled mountains and winding trails that lead to some of the country's most precious Byzantine treasures, graceful springs, and breathtaking scenery. Robust and unpretentious, the region waits to be discovered by adventurous travelers.

Thessaloniki ΘΕΣΣΑΛΟΝΙΚΗ

Cosmopolitan and energetic, Thessaloniki is at its best in the markets that fringe busy squares, its thick-walled ruins, splendid mansions, and Roman monuments. The old city's winding, castlebound streets surprise the wayfarer with their charms and panoramic views. Few foreigners make it this far north, but those who do discover the pleasant anomaly of this Cultural Capital of Europe in 1997—a Greek urban center that shows off its history without being overshadowed by it.

ORIENTATION AND PRACTICAL INFORMATION

Running parallel to the water, the main streets are **Nikis, Mitropoleos, Tsimiski, Ermou,** and **Egnatia.** Cheaper hotels dwell on Egnatia and waterfront bars and cafés are on Nikis. Facing inland, head left on Mitropoleos to reach the **Ladadika** district. Roughly 15 blocks inland, north of Athinas St. and flanked by ancient castle walls, wind the streets of the **old town.**

Tourist Offices: EOT (tel. 27 18 88 or 22 29 35), off Aristotelous Sq. at #8, one block from the water. Take any bus on Egnatia st. to Aristotelous Sq. Free city maps, hotel listings, and transportation schedules. Inquire about Thessaloniki's **festivals** (Sept.-Nov.). Open Mon.-Fri. 8am-8pm, Sat. 8:30am-2pm. **United Travel System,** 28 Mitropoleos St. (tel. 28 67 56; fax 28 31 56), near Aristotelous Sq. Ask for English-speaking Liza and carry *Let's Go.* Open Mon.-Fri. 9:30am-5pm. Other offices at the port (tel. 59 35 78) and the airport (tel. 42 50 11, ext. 215).

Currency Exchange: National Bank, 11 Tsimiski St. (tel. 53 86 21). Open for exchange Mon.-Fri. 8am-2pm and 6-8pm, Sat. 9am-1pm, Sun. 9:30am-12:15pm. Smaller banks charge slightly higher commissions. Many line Tsimiski.

American Express: Northern Greece representative at **Memphis Travel,** 23 Nikis St. (tel. 22 27 96), on the waterfront. Open Mon.-Fri. 10am-4pm, Sat. 9am-2pm.

Flights: The airport (tel. 47 39 77) is 16km from town. Take bus 78 (110dr) or a taxi (1800dr). **Olympic Airways Office,** 3 Koundouriotou St. (tel. 23 02 40). Open

Mon.-Sat. 8am-3:30pm. Call 28 18 80 for reservations Mon.-Sat. 7am-9pm. To: Athens (21,700dr), Lesvos (17,500dr), Crete (29,600dr), Rhodes (31,600dr), and elsewhere in Europe.

Trains: The Main Terminal (tel. 51 75 17) is on Monastiriou St., in the western part of the city. Take any bus down Egnatia St. (75dr). To: Athens (50 per day, 8hr., 3800dr), Kalambaka (6 per day, 5hr., 2300dr), Istanbul (1 per day, 20hr., 11,900dr), and Sofia (1 per day, 7hr., 5110dr). A **ticketing office** is at the corner of Aristotelous and Ermou. Open Tues.-Fri. 8am-8pm, Sat. and Mon. 8am-3pm.

Buses: KTEL has dozens of stations. Departure times posted above ticket counters. To Athens (10 per day, 7hr., 7700dr). Call 142 for Greek language info.

Public Transportation: An office across from the EOT gives limited scheduling info. Buses 8, 10, 11, and 31 run along Egnatia St. Buy your ticket on the bus (75dr).

Ferries: Ticketing at **Karacharisis Travel and Shipping Agency,** 8 Kountourioti St. (tel. 52 45 44; fax 53 22 89). Open Mon.-Fri. 9am-9pm, Sat. 9am-3pm. To: Crete (24hr., 10,700dr), Santorini (17hr., 9100dr), and Mykonos (13hr., 8000dr). Ferries travel twice a week to Lesvos (9hr., 7700dr.), Chios (12hr. 7800dr), Rhodes (20hr., 13,200dr), and Kos (18hr., 11,500dr). In July and August, reserve 2-3 days in advance. Ferry service is reduced significantly in the winter.

Hydrofoils: Flying Dolphins travel daily (June-Sept. only) to Skiathos (3hr.), Skopelos (4hr.), and Alonissos (5hr.). Buy tickets (average 10,000dr) at **Crete Air Travel,** 1 Dragoumi St. (tel. 54 74 07 or 53 43 76), across from the main port. Open Mon.-Fri. 9am-9pm, Sat. 9am-3pm.

Laundromat: Bianca, 3 L. Antoniadou St. (tel. 20 96 02). 1400dr per load includes wash, dry, and soap. Open Mon.-Fri. 8am-8:30pm, Sat. 8am-3pm.

Hospital: Ippokration Public Hospital, 50 A. Papanastasiou (tel. 83 79 20), some doctors speak English. **Red Cross First Aid Hospital,** 6 Kountourioti St. (tel. 53 05 30), located at the entrance to the main port. Free minor medical care.

Post Office: 45 Tsimiski St., between Agia Sophias St. and Aristotelous St. Open Mon.-Fri. 7:30am-8pm, Sat. 7:30am-2pm, Sun. 9am-1:30pm. **Postal Code:** 54101.

Telephones: OTE: 27 Karolou Diehl St., at the corner of Ermou, 1 block east of Aristotelous Sq. Open 24hr. **Telephone Code:** 031.

ACCOMMODATIONS AND FOOD

Many hotels sit along the western end of Egnatia St., between Vardari Sq. (500m east of the train station) and Dikastirion Sq. Egnatia is loud at all hours. Prices may rise 25% between September and November. Single women should avoid offers for cheap rooms from English-speaking "tourist officials" at the train station.

Hotel Argo, 11 Egnatia St. (tel. 51 97 70). Old rooms, good bargains, and classical music. Singles 4000dr, with bath 5500dr. Doubles 5000dr, with bath 7000dr.

Hotel Kastoria (tel. 53 62 80; fax 53 62 50), at the intersection of Egnatia St. 24 and L. Sofou St. 17. Tidy, dark rooms with baths. Singles 5000dr. Doubles 6000dr.

Hotel Averof, at the intersection of Egnatia St. and L. Sofia St. 24 (tel. 53 88 40; fax 54 31 94). New furniture but old floors. Communal living room with TV. Singles 5500dr, with bath 7500dr. Doubles 7500dr, with bath 9500dr.

Hotel Tourist, 21 Mitropoleos St. (tel. 27 63 35; fax 22 68 65), 1 block from Aristotelous Sq. High ceilings and an old-fashioned salon and elevator. Singles 7500dr, with bath 9000dr. Doubles with bath 10,000dr. Triples with bath 17,000dr.

Youth Hostel, 44 Alex. Svolou St. (tel. 22 59 46; fax 26 22 08). Tram 8, 10, 11, or 31 from Egnatia St. to the Arch of Galerius. Walk toward the water; 2 blocks later turn left onto Svolou St. You'll want to wear your shoes everywhere. Lockout 11am-6:30pm. 2000dr. Shower included. 3-night max. stay, 1-night without membership.

Thessaloniki is known throughout Greece for its excellent *mezedes.* **Open-air markets** line Vati Kioutou St. just off Aristotelous Sq. The Aretsou Area, along the bay about 4km toward the airport, boasts excellent seafood. Explore the old town and Ladadika district for inexpensive, family-oriented *tavernas.* **The Brothers,** Navarino Sq. (full meal 1500dr; open daily noon-midnight) and **To Palati,** 3 Platcia Morichovou (meals 1300-1600dr), offer traditional Greek meals. **Ta Spata,** 28 Aristotelous, has a wide selection of tasty entrees (1500dr; open daily 11am-midnight).

SIGHTS AND ENTERTAINMENT

The superlative **Archaeological Museum** unearths a collection of Macedonian treasures, including gold *larnakes* (burial caskets) that once contained the cremated royal family of Vergina. Take bus 3 from the railway station to Hanth Sq. (Open Mon. 12:30-7pm, Tues.-Fri. 8am-7pm, Sat.-Sun. 8:30am-3pm; off-season Mon. 10:30am-5pm, Tues.-Fri. 8am-5pm, Sat.-Sun. 8:30am-3pm. 1500dr, students 800dr, EU students free.) The **International Fairgrounds,** across from the museum, hold a variety of **festivals** in the fall, including the International Trade Fair in September (for info call 23 92 21). The fairgrounds also house the **Macedonian Museum of Contemporary Art** (open Tues.-Sat. 10am-2pm and 6-9pm, Sun. 11am-2pm; 500dr, students 300dr). On the other side of the park looms the **Lefkos Pirgos,** all that remains of a 16th-century Venetian seawall whose blood-stained walls were painted white to obliterate wartime memories. The tower houses a museum of early Christian art (same hours as archaeological museum; 800dr, students 400dr, EU students free). The ruins of the **Eptapirgion Walls,** erected during the reign of Theodosius the Great, stretch along the north edge of the old city. Take bus 22 from Eleftherias Sq. on the waterfront.

The celebrated but scaffolded **Arch of Galerius** stands at the end of Egnatia St. at the corner of Gounari St. For further historical pursuits, head north of Dikastirion Sq. to the **Roman Market** between Filippou and Olibou St. The centerpiece of the remains of the **Palace of Galerius,** near Navarino Sq., is the octagonal hall. Over the centuries, earthquakes and fire have severely damaged most churches in this region. The churches of **Panagia Ahiropitos, Panagia Halkeon,** and **Agios Nikolaos Orfanos,** however, still feature some brilliant mosaic work and frescoes from the late Byzantine era. For a glimpse of the former glory, visit the **Crypt of Agios Dimitrios** (open Mon. 12:30-7pm, Tues.-Sat. 8am-8pm, and Sun. 10:30am-8pm; free). You can also visit the beautiful **Old Synagogue** at 35 Sigrou St.; the caretaker at the **Jewish Community Center,** 24 Tsimiski St., will let you in.

The king of café-hangouts for bohemian locals is the **Milos** district, accessible by taxi. On weekend evenings, mingle with Greeks along **Plaza Dhimitrio Gounari.** Fashion-conscious couples promenade from the waterfront to the Arch of Galerius. A grungier crowd mellows out in the park and at **Navarinou Square,** one block west of D. Gounari. Lesbian and gay revelers head to **Taboo** on Kastritsiou St., one block from Egnatia St. Turn to the water on Mitropolitou Genadiou and take your first left. The Ladadika district has clubs and live Greek music (beers 1000dr; cocktails 1800dr). All the nightclubs that boom to the techno-beat are near the airport, accessible only by taxi (2000-2500dr). Most clubs have a cover of about 2000dr including the first drink. The beloved **Ab Fab** is past the turn-off for the airport.

Mount Olympus and Meteora

Greece's loftiest peak, **Mt. Olympus** (ΟΛΥΜΠΟΣ, 2917m), rises from the coastal plain 90km southwest of Thessaloniki. This summit of the gods requires two days of challenging hiking (May-Oct. only) but no special equipment. To reach the small village of **Litohoro,** the gateway to Olympus, take the train from Thessaloniki to Katerini, then walk 1km to catch the bus that will take you the remaining 5km into town. From the main square, follow signs to the **EOS Greek Mountaineering Club** (tel. (0352) 845 44) and the **SEO Mountaineering Club** which provide maps and have **refuges** on the mountain. (EOS open June-Aug. Mon.-Fri. 9am-12:30pm and 6:30-8:30pm, Sat.-Sun. 9am-noon.) The **tourist office** (tel. (0352) 831 00) offers free maps (open mid-June to Sept. daily 9am-8pm). The **Hotel Aphroditi** (tel. (0352) 814 15; fax 221 23) is uphill from the main square (singles 8000dr, doubles 12,000dr; prices differ off season). Do not freelance camp on the north side of the road connecting the town and the highway: this is training ground for the armored units of the Greek army.

Southwest of Olympus lies **Meteora** (ΜΕΤΕΩΡΑ), where several exquisite Byzantine monasteries grip the tops of mysterious black rock formations. The **Grand Meteoron Monastery** is the oldest and largest of the monasteries and has brilliant frescoes of the Roman persecution of Christians. The **Varlaam Monastery** has 16th-century frescoes in its chapel, including a particularly disturbing rendition of the Apocalypse. (Most monasteries open 9am-1pm and 3:30-5pm. 400dr. No picture-taking or revealing dress.) The most popular base for exploring Meteora is the town of **Kalambaka** (ΚΑΛΑΜΠΑΚΑ). **Trains** arrive from Athens (7hr., 2700dr) and Thessaloniki (6hr., 2220dr); when you arrive in Kalambaka, take the bus to Meteora (Mon.-Fri. 9am and 1:20pm, Sat.-Sun. 8:20am; 20min., 190dr). Most people walk the 6km back to town, visiting the monasteries along the way. **Koka Roka** (tel. (0432) 245 54) is up from the bus station in Kalambaka (singles 3000dr, doubles 6000dr).

THE PELOPONNESE

Separated from the rest of the mainland by the Corinth Canal, the fertile Peloponnese unites human achievement with natural beauty. The ancient theater at Epidavros, the shell of a medieval city at Mystra, and Agamemnon's palace at Mycenae are all impressive architectural and artistic masterpieces. Beyond these ruins and a few scattered cities, however, the Peloponnese's rocky mountains reveal only undeveloped sandy beaches and wondrous mountain fields and villages.

Corinth Most visitors to the Peloponnese stop first at Corinth (ΚΟΡΙΝΘΟΣ), where a green bus drives 7km to the ruins of **Ancient Corinth** (every hr. 6:10am-9:10pm, 210dr), where the **Ministry of Culture Archaeological Museum** houses artifacts from the archaeological site. To the left as you exit the museum is the 6th-century BC **Temple of Apollo.** (Both open in summer daily 8am-7pm; in winter 8am-5pm. 1200dr, students 600dr, Sun. free.) The lower peak of the **Acrocorinth** is the site of an ancient fortress; the upper summit once held a **Temple to Aphrodite.** Until pollution took over, you could see all the way to the Acropolis from here. The walk up is 1½ hours, or a taxi can take you round-trip (2500dr; tel. (0741) 31 464).

Back in New Corinth, **trains** arrive on Demokratia St. from Athens (15 per day, 2hr., 800dr) and connect to all major Peloponnesian towns. The luxurious **Ephira Hotel,** 52 Ethnikis Antistasis St. (tel. (0741) 24 021), two blocks inland from the park (singles 7500dr, doubles 10,000dr), and the more modest **Hotel Acti,** 3 Ethnikis Antistasis St. (tel. (0741) 23 337; singles 3000dr, doubles 6000dr), comfort the weary. **Kanita,** on Damaskinov, is the best harbor eatery (open 24hr.), and at night motorcycling teenagers and vacationing families alike head down to the cafés and bars of **Kalami beach.** In the ancient city, go right at the fork behind the bus stop (away from the entrance to the ruins) to reach **Rooms Marinos** (tel. (0741) 31 209; singles 7500dr, doubles 11,000), or try **Taverna Tassos,** on the road to Corinth (tel. (0741) 31 225), with crisp white rooms (singles 4000dr, doubles 5000dr).

Argolis and Corinthia ΑΡΓΟΛΙΔΑ ΚΑΙ ΚΟΝΙΝΘΟΑ

Chronicled in the pages of ancient writers, the 100-eyed Argos once roamed the northern Peloponnese, subduing unruly satyrs and rampaging bulls. Today, the greatest threat comes from heat and crowds: try to visit early in the day.

Nauplion Old **Nauplion** (ΝΑΥΠΛΙΟ) is a soothing antidote to the bustle of Corinth and the hordes of island sun-worshippers, and it serves as an ideal base for exploring nearby ruins. The town itself boasts impressive monuments, most notably the **Palamidi Fortress.** Visitors can travel a 3km road or walk up 999 steps to the fortress, with its well-preserved walls and stunning views. (Open in summer Mon.-Fri. 7:45am-

7pm, Sat.-Sun. 8:30am-3pm; off-season daily 8:30am-3pm. 800dr, students 400dr, EU students free.) The **bus station,** at the base of the hill on Singrou St., serves Athens (3hr., 2350dr), Corinth (2hr., 1050dr), Mycenae (45min., 550dr), and Epidavros (1hr., 550dr). **Hotel Economou** (tel. (0752) 239 55), on Argonafton, a 15-minute walk from the station, offers balconies and pleasant company for 2000dr per person. To get to **Dimitris Beka's Domatia** (tel. (0752) 245 94), turn up the stairs onto Kokinou and follow the sign for rooms off of Staikopoulou. Climb to the top, turn left, and climb another 50 steps. The beautiful view compensates for the trek (doubles 4500dr). Dining options cluster around Syntagma Sq. **Taverna O Vasiles,** on Staikopoulou, serves fresh fish and rabbit in onion (1400dr). **Ellas,** in the square, is the cheapest restaurant around (entrees 950-1250dr).

Mycenae and Epidavros Greece's supreme city from 1600 to 1100 BC, **Mycenae** (ΜΥΚΗΝΑΙ) was once ruled by Agamemnon, leader of the Greek forces during the Trojan War. Find the gory details in Homer's *Iliad* and Aeschylus' *Oresteia.* Most of the treasures from the excavation are in Athens, but the **Lion's Gate** and the **Treasury of Atreus** are among the most celebrated modern archaeological finds. (Site open April-Sept. daily 8am-7pm; Oct.-March 8am-5pm. Citadel and tomb of Agamemnon 1500dr, students 800dr, EU students free. Keep your ticket or pay twice.) The **Belle Helene Hotel** (tel. (0751) 762 25) serves as a bus stop on the main road (singles 5000dr, doubles 6000dr, triples 9000dr). **Buses,** which stop right in front of the hotel, arrive daily from Nauplion (40min., 550dr) and Argos (30min., 260dr).

Try to visit **Epidavros** (ΕπΙΔΑΥΡΟΣ) on Friday or Saturday night from late June to mid-August, when the **National Theater of Greece** and visiting companies perform plays from the classical Greek canon (in Greek). Performances start at 9pm, and you can buy tickets (3000-4500dr, students 2000dr) at the site (open Sun.-Thurs. 9am-5pm, Fri.-Sat. until 9pm). Contact the **Athens Festival Box Office** (tel. (01) 322 14 59) for advance ticket sales. The **theater** itself, built in the 4th century BC, is remarkable. Henry Miller wrote that he heard "the great heart of the world" beat here; at the very least, you can still stand on the top row of seats and hear a *drachma* dropped on stage. Near the theater and other classical ruins, Epidavros's **museum** houses painted decorations from the ruins and huge stones with inscriptions of hymns to Apollo (Theater, site, and museum open in summer Tues.-Sun. 8am-7pm and Mon. noon-7pm; off-season closes 5pm. 1500dr, students 800dr, EU students free.) **Buses** connect to Nauplion (6 per day, 1hr., 550dr).

Patras ΠΑΤΡΑΣ

Sprawling Patras, Greece's third largest city, is mostly known as a transportation hub, but try to pass through during **Carnival** (mid-Jan. to Ash Wednesday), when the Greeks get groovy and the port becomes one vast dance floor. At other times, visitors spend time exploring the 13th-century Venetian **castle** and park (follow Ag. Nikolaou St. inland from town) or the largest Orthodox cathedral in Greece, the **Agios Andreas,** which holds magnificently colored frescoes and an unusual relic—St. Andrew's head. To get there, follow the water to the west end of town (open daily 9am-dusk). Sweet black grapes produce *Mavrodaphne* wine at the **Achaïa Clauss winery.** (Take bus 7 from the intersection of Kolokotroni and Kanakari St. Tours in summer daily 9am-7:30pm; off-season 9am-5pm. Free.)

The **tourist office** (tel. (061) 62 22 49), on the waterfront at the entrance to the customs complex, helps secure accommodations and gives out free maps and timetables (open Mon.-Sat. 7am-9:30pm). **Trains** (tel. (061) 27 36 94) depart from Othonos Amalias St. for Athens (8 per day, 2600dr) via Corinth (1000dr). The **bus terminal** (tel. (061) 62 38 86), on Othonos Amalias between Aratou and Zaïmi, regularly serves Athens (3hr., 3350dr), Thessaloniki (3hr., 7500dr), Tripolis (2hr., 2850dr), and other cities. **Ferries** go to Cephalonia, Ithaka, and Corfu, as well as Italy's Brindisi, Bari, and Ancona (prices fluctuate). If you have a railpass, go to **HML** (tel. (061) 45 25 21) on Iroon Politechinou. For ferries to the Ionian islands contact **Strintzis Tours,** 14 Othonas Amalias St. (tel. (061) 62 26 02; open daily 9am-10pm).

Cheap accommodations are scattered around Ag. Andreas St., a block up and parallel to the waterfront. The cramped but convenient **youth hostel,** 68 Iroon Polytechniou St. (tel. (061) 42 72 78; 1700dr; sheets 150dr; breakfast 600dr) is planning to move; inquire at the tourist office. **Pension Nikos,** 3 Patreos St. (tel. (061) 22 16 43), has clean rooms (singles 3500dr, doubles 6000dr, triples 8000dr). A good pick for vegetarians and omnivores alike is the traditional **Taverna Nicolaras,** three blocks inland on Ag. Nikolarou (entrees 800-1100dr).

Olympia ΟΛΥΜΠΙΑ

Beginning in 776 BC, leaders of rival city-states in ancient Greece shed their armor and congregated to enjoy the Olympic games and make offerings to their gods in Olympia. Today, the remains of a gymnasium, wrestling school, workshop, and other monuments are scattered around **Ancient Olympia,** although they are not particularly well-preserved or labeled. The gigantic **Temple of Zeus,** which once held a statue of the god so beautiful it was one of the seven wonders of the ancient world, dominates the site. On the north edge of the Altis are the remains of the 7th-century BC **Temple of Hera,** now one of the best-preserved local monuments. Atlanta's 1996 **Olympic flame** was lit at this temple. The **New Museum,** across the street from the site, houses Praxiteles' statue of Baby Dionysus, the famous **Little Man with the Big Erection,** and other ancient works. (Site open daily 8am-7pm. 1200dr, students 600dr, EU students free. Museum open Tues.-Fri. 8am-7pm, Sat.-Mon. 8:30am-3pm. 1200dr, students 600dr. Extra charge for flash and video cameras.)

In new Olympia, the **tourist office,** Kondili Ave. (tel. (0624) 231 00), on the east side of town, provides essential maps (open April-Sept. daily 9am-9pm; Oct.-March 11am-5pm). **Buses** run to Tripoli (3½hr., 2200dr) and Pirgos (40min., 360dr). The **youth hostel,** 18 Kondili Ave. (tel. (0624) 225 80), charges 1500dr per person. **Camping Diana** (tel. (0624) 223 14), uphill from the Sports Museum, has a clean pool and hot water (1300dr per person, 900-1200dr per tent). A walk toward the railroad station and away from the hungry busloads of tourists reveals some charming *tavernas* and inexpensive restaurants.

Arcadia and Messenia ΑΡΚΑΔΙΑ ΚΑΙ ΜΕΣΣΗΝΙΑ

Poets since Theocritus have fancied Arcadia as the archetypal scene of pastoral pleasure. Tripoli and a few other towns now rumble with buses and other traffic, but rural serenity persists among the hidden bays, dramatic mountains, and vast fir forests in this area. In adjacent Messenia, olives, figs, and grapes spring from the rich soil along the coastline, and towns like Pylos and Methoni offer easy access to the region's sparkling beaches and turquoise waters.

Arcadia Urban **Tripoli** (ΤΡΙΠΟΛΙΗ) intimidates with crowded sidewalks and perilous streets, but the town provides pleasant squares and cafés for those awaiting transportation to other points in Arcadia. For overnight stays, your best bet is **Hotel Anactoricon** (tel. (071) 22 25 45), along Ethnikis Antistasis two blocks before the park (singles 6000dr, doubles 9000dr). The new **Archaeological Museum,** Evangelistrias St., has pottery from the Paleokastro tombs (open Tues.-Sun. 8:30am-2:30pm; 500dr, students free). Westward, the little villages of **Dimitsana** (ΔΗΜΗΤΣΑΝΑ) and **Stemnitsa** (ΣΤΕΜΝΙΤΣΑ) are good bases for hiking and walking excursions, and will entice you to stay awhile with their chalet-like houses and natural beauty. Monks also dug the area; off the road from Dimitsana to Stemnitsa are several **monasteries,** some built right into the mountain (open daily until dusk; free). In Dimitsana, the **Enoikiazomena Domatia,** off the main square, affords great views of the town's copper-roofed chapels (singles 5000dr, doubles 7000dr). In Stemnitsa, enjoy a comfy night at the gorgeous **Hotel Triokolonion** (tel. (0795) 812 97), on the main road (singles 6000dr, doubles 8000dr; bath included).

Messenia The second largest city in the Peloponnese, **Kalamata** (ΚΑΛΑΜΑΤΑ) serves as a fine base for exploring the southwestern coast. **Trains** (tel. (0721) 950 56) leave the station at the end of Sideromikou Stathmou St. for Athens (7hr., 2400dr) via Tripoli (2½hr., 840dr), Patras (5½hr., 1500dr), Corinth (5¼hr., 1700dr), and other cities. **Buses** (tel. (0721) 285 81) run to Athens (4hr., 3950dr), Sparta (2hr., 1000dr), and Tripoli (2hr., 1450dr). **Hotel Nevada,** 9 Santa Rosa (tel. (0721) 824 29), has clean rooms and countless potted plants; take bus 1 and get off when it turns left along the water (singles 3000dr, doubles 4000dr, triples 6000dr). A short bus ride west of Kalamata (1½hr., 850dr), somnolent **Pylos** (ΠΥΛΟΣ) offers sandy beaches and tanned bodies. Buses continue to **Methoni** (ΜΕΘΩΝΗ, 15min., 210dr), where hibiscus-lined streets wind around the impressive 13th-century **Venetian fortress.** In the beachside square, **Hotel Giota** (tel. (0723) 312 90 or 312 91), offers clean rooms (singles 5000dr, doubles 7000dr). **Camping Methoni** (tel. (0723) 312 28) is crowded but offers attractive sites along the beach (950dr per person, 650-850dr per tent).

Laconia ΛΑΚΩΝΙΑ

Although Laconia boasts three of the Peloponnese's most popular sights—Mani's Pirgos Dirou caves, the Byzantine ruins at Mystra, and Monemvassia's "rock"—the region remains low key; even the tourist industry here is far less businesslike than on the islands or in Athens. As a result, Laconia's friendly villages are a welcome break from the urban atmosphere of other, more touristed areas in Greece.

Sparta and Mystra Although **Sparta** (ΣΠΑΡΤΗ) has been immortalized in the annals of military history, the modern city is noted mostly for its olive oil and orange trees and serves best as a base for visits to more impressive **Mystra** (ΜΥΣΤΡΑΣ), just 6km away. Mystra overflows with Byzantine churches and well-labeled castle ruins. Don't miss the **Metropolis of St. Demetrios** in the lower tier, with its sanctuary and museum of architectural fragments. The **Church of Perivleptos** is perhaps Mystra's most stunning relic—every inch of the church is covered in exquisitely detailed paintings of religious scenes and figures (site open daily 8am-7pm, off-season 8:30am-3pm; 1200dr, students 600dr). Back in Sparta, the **tourist office** (tel. (0731) 248 52), to the left of the town hall in the square, helps with bus schedules and hotels (maps 400dr; open daily 8am-2pm). **Buses** (tel. (0731) 264 41) head to Athens (3hr., 3450dr), Pirgos Dirou and the caves (1½hr., 1350dr), and many other towns. For buses to Mystra (190dr), head to the station at the corner of Leonidou and Kythoni-

A Hard-Knock Life

A young Spartan's training for a life of war began early, even before conception. Lycurgus believed two fit parents produced stronger offspring, so he ordered all Spartan women to undergo the same rigorous training endured by men. Furthermore, newlyweds were permitted only an occasional tryst on the theory that the heightened desire of the parents would produce more robust children. If they weren't winnowed out as weak or deformed, boys began a severe regimen of training under an adult Spartan. The young were forced to walk barefoot to toughen their feet and wore only a simple piece of clothing in both summer and winter to expose them to drastic weather changes. The Spartan creed dictated that young men be guarded against temptations of any kind—strict laws forbidding everything from drinking to sodomy governed Spartans' actions. Moreover, young Spartans were given the plainest and simplest foods for fear that rich delicacies would stunt their growth. One visitor to Sparta, upon sampling the fare, allegedly quipped, "Now I know why they do not fear death."

gou, two blocks past the town hall; call the tourist office to verify departures. Decent rooms are available at **Hotel Panellinion** (tel. (0731) 280 31), past the Lykourgou intersection (singles 4000dr, doubles 6000dr), and **Hotel Cecil** (tel. (0731) 249 80), on the corner of Paleologou and Thermopilion St. (singles 5000dr, doubles 8000dr).

Mani Once known for violent family feuds and savage piracy, sparsely settled **Mani** (MANH) remains a stark and rugged place, where bald mountains provide the backdrop for a jagged coast and austere settlements, and forbidding towers add muted greys and greens to the landscape. The port town of **Gythion** (ΓΥΘΕΙΟ), the self-proclaimed "Gateway to Mani," offers easy access to Areopolis and the rest of the coast. The **bus station,** on the north end of the waterfront, serves Athens (4150dr) via Sparta (1hr., 750dr), Kalamata via Itilo (1hr., 650dr), Areopolis (1hr., 450dr), and the caves near Pirgos Dirou (1¼hr., 450dr). **Ferries** depart from the quay to the right of Mavromichali Sq. for Kythera (1 per day, 1535dr) and Crete (2 per week, 4560dr). In Gythion, you can rent **motorbikes** to explore the hard-to-reach Mani. In town, try the spacious and clean rooms of **Xenia Karlafti's** (tel. (0733) 227 19), near the port police (doubles 5000dr, triples 6000dr). The most luxurious campgrounds are **Meltemi** (tel. (0733) 228 33; 1180dr per person, 1000dr per tent) and **Gytheio Bay Campgrounds** (tel. (0733) 225 22; 1200dr per person, 800dr per tent). Also try **Mani Beach** (tel. (0733) 234 50; 1050dr per person, 750-950dr per tent). The campgrounds are south of town and accessible by bus. **Mavromichali Sq.** is the perfect place for lunch or a cheap dinner, and the **grill** that is inland from the plastic chairs serves delicious gyros for 300dr. For a drink try **Statos** on the main strip.

From **Areopolis** (ΑΡΕΟΠΟΛΗ), along the western coast, you can make daytrips to the spectacular **Glyfatha Lake Cave** (also known as Spilia Dirou or Pirgos Dirou). The boat ride down the subterranean river passes a forest of stalactites and stalagmites (30min.). After the boat trip, you can walk through more of the caves at your own pace (open June-Sept. daily 8am-4pm; Oct.-May 8am-2:30pm; 3500dr). There is a beautiful pebble beach and a cafeteria near the caves. From Areopolis, **buses** drive to the caves (3 per day, 210dr), Sparta (1½hr., 1150dr) via Gythion (30min., 450dr), and other towns. For a bed in Areopolis, find **Tsimova** (tel. (0733) 513 01), off Kapetan Matapan St. (singles 5000dr, doubles 6000dr). Very cheap and small rooms reside above the restaurant **O Barba Petros** (tel. (0733) 512 05; singles 3000dr, doubles 4000dr). Rooms also line the road from Pirgos Dirou to the caves.

Monemvassia The ancient Byzantine city of **Monemvassia** (MONEMBAΣIA) is dominated by a huge rock with vertical cliffs. The narrow streets of this wonderfully preserved city, replete with child-sized doorways, stairways, and flowered courtyards, should be explored. **Buses** connect to Sparta (2½hr., 1700dr), Tripoli (4hr., 2600dr), and Corinth (5hr., 3850dr) via Molai; the express bus to Athens costs 3550dr. **Flying dolphins** leave for Kythera (1¼hr., 4465dr). Rooms in the medieval village are scarce and expensive; there are many *domatia* along the waterfront. **Kritikos Domatia** (tel. (0732) 614 39), about 200m away from the bus stop, has suites with kitchen and bathroom for 6000dr. Pitch a tent at **Camping Paradise** (tel. (0732) 611 23), 3½km along the water on the mainland (1100dr per person, 800-1100dr per tent; prices lower off season).

IONIAN ISLANDS
ΝΗΣΙΑ ΤΟΥ ΙΟΝΙΟΥ

Situated on Greece's western edge, the Ionian islands escaped Turkish occupation during the Middle Ages only to be overrun by the Venetians, British, French, and Russians. These uninvited visitors left a lasting cultural, commercial, and architectural imprint, and today this legacy complements an equally impressive array of beaches, flowers and trees, and hiking trails around the islands.

Corfu (Kerkyra) ΚΕΡΚΥΡΑ

Since Odysseus washed ashore and praised the lush beauty of **Corfu,** the seas have brought Franks, Venetians, and the French to this verdant Ionian Island. Today, international visitors ramble through the shuttered alleys of an *ersatz* Venice, stroll along a Parisian esplanade, and sip tea on the grounds of a British imperial palace. And as if to fulfill the budget traveler's every wish, prices in Corfu have temporarily dropped because its trendiness as a resort has been exhausted.

All ferries and most buses originate in **Corfu Town,** the logical base for touring the island. **Ferries** travel to and from Brindisi (8hr., 4500-8000dr), Bari (10hr., 10,000dr), Ancona (23hr., 16,000dr), and Venice (26hr., 18,000dr) in Italy, as well as Patras (9hr., 5600dr) and several other Greek towns and islands. The **National Tourist Office** (tel. (0661) 375 20), on the second floor of the building at Rizospaston Voulefton and Iak. Polila, dishes out info in several languages. Keep in mind that the office has moved since the publication of the map dispensed around town (open Mon.-Fri. 8:30am-1:30pm; Sept.-May also from 5-8pm). **Tourist agencies** along Arseniou and Stratigou St. find single rooms from 3000dr, doubles from 4000dr, and triples from 5000dr. **Hotel Hermes,** 14 Rue G. Markora (tel. (0661) 392 68; fax 317 47), and **Hotel Ionina,** 46 Xen. Stratigou (tel. (0661) 399 15), at the New Port, offer accommodations (singles 5000-6000dr, doubles 7000-8000dr).

The premier restaurant areas are at the two ends of **N. Theotoki Street,** near the Spianada and by the Old Port. For a visual treat and inexpensive fresh produce head to the open-air **market** on Dessila St. near the base of the New Fortress (open daily 6am-2pm). Try the delicious feta and tomato sandwiches (500dr) at the **Art Café** in a garden behind the palace of St. Michael and St. George. Below the palace on a small pier reside the **En Plo Café** and the **Faliraki Restaurant.**

KTEL **buses** leave frequently from Corfu Town's New Fortress for most of the island's major spots; other buses leave from Sanrocco Sq. A trip west takes you to **Paleokastritsa beach** and its white mountaintop monastery, **Panagia Theotokos.** The monastery houses a collection of Byzantine icons and a skeleton of a sea monster. Buses run to Paleokastritsa from behind the new fortress (45min., 400dr). South of Paleokastritsa is **Pelekas,** a base town with access to beaches. **Pelekas beach** is a 30-minute downhill walk from town. The **Glyfada Beach,** 5km up the coast from Pelekas Town, is served directly by bus from behind the New Fortress. The isolated beach of **Moni Myrtidon** and the unofficial nude beach **Myrtiotissa** are also nearby.

Agios Gordios, accessible by bus 7 (45min., 260dr), with its steep cliffs and impressive rock formations, is the setting for the **Pink Palace** (tel. (0661) 530 24; fax 530 25). The resort has legendary status among English-speaking hedonists for weekly toga parties, which groove all night as pink *ouzo* flows. Rooms vary significantly in quality (5000dr per person; breakfast, dinner, and nightclub included).

Cephalonia ΚΕΦΑΛΛΩΝΙΑ

Dubbed "The Island of Peculiarities" for its disparate but beautiful sandy beaches, subterranean caves, rugged mountains, and shady forests, Cephalonia is ideal for a week-long stay, but an inconvenient bus network and multiple ports will frustrate the budget traveler or island hopper. Bustling **Argostoli** is the capital and transportation center. The surprisingly interesting **Historical and Folk Museum** shows pictures and relics of the city before it was destroyed by a 1953 earthquake (open Mon.-Sat. 9am-2pm; 500dr). The **tourist office** (tel. (0671) 22 248 or 22 466), at the port, gives out maps and advice on accommodations and beaches (open Mon.-Fri. 8am-10pm). **Buses** (tel. (0671) 22 281) leave from the station at the south end of the waterfront. Check schedules carefully or risk being stranded; service is reduced on Saturday and non-existent on Sunday. **Hotel Allegro** (tel. (0671) 28 684), up from the water on Andrea Choïda, has private baths (singles 4000dr, doubles 5500dr).

A small town on a harbor surrounded by verdant hills, **Sami** is more tranquil than Argostoli and boasts an ethereal pebble beach. **Buses** run from Argostoli (450dr).

From the port, **ferries** travel to Ithaka (daily at 3:30pm, 1350dr), Patras (daily at 8:30am, 3095dr), and Astakos (daily at 8:45am, 1948dr), as well as Bari and Brindisi in Italy. Many of the rooms at **Hotel Kyma** (tel. (0674) 22 064), in the town square, offer spectacular views (singles 6000dr, doubles 10,000dr).

Ithaka (Ithaki) ΙΘΑΚΗ

As she did for Odysseus, Athena blesses those lucky souls who wash up on the islets of Ithaka's twisted coastline. The buildings of the main town, **Vathi,** cluster around a horseshoe harbor. Those of a poetic bent and sturdy footwear may want to climb to the **Cave of the Nymphs,** where Odysseus hid the treasure the Phoenicians gave him; bring a flashlight (200dr). Back in Vathi, **ferries** go to Sami on Cephalonia (1hr., 950dr), and Astakos on the mainland (2½hr., 1850dr). **Delas Tours** (tel. (0674) 321 04; fax 330 31), in the main square, can help you find a room and decipher mercurial fares and schedules. The proprietors of private *domatias* may meet the ferry (3000-4000dr), and **camping** is tolerated on the nearby beach.

The island's only **bus** runs north from Vathi, passing through the scenic villages of Lefki, Stavros, Platrithiai, Frikes, and Kioni. Schedules are erratic, but in high season the bus usually runs three times daily; check return times before you go (1hr., 350dr to Frikes). The road skirts both sides of the isthmus, and offers stunning views of the strait. In **Stavros,** the highest point on the island, classicists will enjoy the alleged site of **Odysseus's Palace,** which overlooks three bays just as Homer related. Close to Vathi is **Daxa beach,** Odysseus's mythical landing point and still a sunning spot.

CYCLADES ΚΥΚΛΑΔΕΣ

When people wax rhapsodic about the Greek islands, chances are they're talking about the Cyclades. Whatever your idea of Greece—whitewashed houses, *ouzo* sipped outside during warm sunsets, inebriated revelry—you can find it here. Most of the islands are practically international colonies during the summer, when countless hippies, backpackers, and businesspeople convene for the post-Eurailpass party.

Mykonos ΜΙΚΟΝΟΣ

Coveted by pirates in the 18th century for its blonde beaches, chic Mykonos is still lusted after by those seeking drunken revelry and Bacchanalian excess amidst the charm of a rich history. Social life, both gay and straight, may abound, but it's not cheap on this choicest of the Cyclades—you'll need a wallet thicker than your *Let's Go* to afford all the festivities. Mingle with the *kosmopolitikos*, and then savor the beaches and labyrinthine streets of Mykonos Town and the surrounding coastline.

During the day, the beaches are the island's main attraction. **Megali Ammos,** 1km past the windmills on the southwest corner of the harbor, the unspectacular but central **St. Stefanos Beach,** and crowded **Psarou Beach** are all close to Mykonos Town. All beaches on Mykonos are technically nudist, but the degree of bareness is as varied as the specimens you'll inevitably see. Take a bus to **Plati Yialos** (210dr), not a bad beach in its own right, and a *caïque* from there to join the crowds at **Paradise** (300dr) and **Super Paradise** (380dr), the most popular of the gay beaches. At night, *everyone* passes through the **Skandinavian Bar,** near the waterfront, where mellowness becomes madness around midnight (beer 700dr; cocktails 1500dr; open nightly 7:30pm-3am, Sat. until 4am). At **Pierro's,** on Matogianni St., the mainly gay crowd spills out into the square with dancing and music (beers 1000dr; cocktails 2000dr). Step into a Toulouse-Lautrec and sip a glass of wine (800dr) at **Montparnasse,** Agion Anargyron St., in the Little Venice district (open nightly 7pm-3am).

Everything you'll need is near the waterfront—banks, travel agencies, shops, cafés, and bars. If you still have questions, the **tourist police** (tel. (0289) 224 82), in an office at the ferry landing, have English speakers (daily 8am-9pm). North Station, uphill from the ferry dock, sends **buses** to the northern and eastern beaches; at the opposite end of town, South Station, oddly enough, serves the south (tel. for both (0289) 233 60). **Ferries** travel to Paros (2hr., 1800dr), Naxos (3hr., 1810dr), Santorini (6½hr., 3290dr), Ios (4hr., 3100dr), and many other islands.

Accommodations-hawking is a full-blown industry on Mykonos; if you're aggressive and undaunted, you may find a good deal. Otherwise, push past the solicitors at the ferry port and bear right 10m along the water; you can't miss the offices for **hotels** (tel. (0289) 245 40), **rooms-to-let** (tel. (0289) 248 60), and **camping** (tel. (0289) 235 67), which have plenty of info and will telephone proprietors on your behalf. **Chez Maria Pension,** 27 N. Kalogera St. (tel. (0289) 224 80), off Matogianni St., is above Chez Maria Restaurant (doubles 12,000dr, triples 15,000dr). The **campground** on Paradise Beach (tel. (0289) 221 29 or 228 52; fax 243 50) often feels crowded and has the occasional nude bather traipsing through (1500dr per person, 800-1000dr per tent). On Mykonos, self-consciously trendy food is the rule, but several affordable options remain. **Niko's Taverna** (tel. (0289) 243 20), inland from the excursion boat docks, hops with traditional Greek cuisine (baked *kalamari* 2000dr; open daily noon-2am). **Klimataria,** on Florov Zouganeli St., has tasty *moussaka* (1100dr) and rabbit stew (1700dr; open daily 9am-1am), while **Alexi** will put on a show as he cooks up your *gyro*-pita (350dr) at his eponymous restaurant at the back of Taxi Sq. (open daily 22hr.—closed 7am-9am for clean up).

Paros ΠΑΡΟΣ

The geographical center of the Cyclades and a convenient base for excursions to the other Cyclades, Paros gracefully absorbs its hordes of summer tourists with its golden beaches and tangled whitewashed villages. **Paroikia,** the island's main port, at first presents a shallow commercial facade, but further inland redeems itself with the stuff of substance—windmills, basilica, and an *agora.* Byzantine architecture buffs will be enraptured by the **Panagia Ekatontapiliani** (Church of Our Lady of 100 Gates), an imposing 6th-century edifice that houses three adjacent churches, cloisters, and a large peaceful courtyard (open daily 8am-9pm). Ten kilometers south of town is the cool, spring-fed **Valley of the Butterflies,** home to an enormous spawning swarm of the winged creatures. Take the bus from Paroikia to Aliki (10min., 200dr), ask to be let off at the butterflies *(petaloudes),* and follow the signs (open Mon.-Sat. 9am-8pm, Sun. 9am-1pm and 4-8pm; 230dr). You can also take a tour from one of the various travel agents (2500dr).

The **tourist office** (tel. (0284) 245 28), to the right of the windmill, facing inland, offers currency exchange, free maps, and info on buses, sights, and beaches (open daily 8:30am-midnight). **Ferries** sail to countless islands in the area, including Naxos (1hr., 1470dr), Ios (2½hr., 246dr), Santorini (3½hr., 2655dr), Mykonos (2hr., 1760dr), Rhodes (16hr., 6520dr), and Crete (8hr., 4660dr). Many hotels and private rooms are located near the waterfront and in the old town, but a slew of cheaper accommodations have opened up behind the town beach. Rooms may still be scarce in summer. **Festos Pension** (tel. (0284) 216 35; fax 241 93) has a friendly staff; at the steps of the waterfront church, turn right, then left at the side street marked with a "the Festos" sign (2500-4500dr per person; call ahead). **Parasporas Camping** (tel. (0284) 222 68 or 211 00), 1500m south of the port with frequent shuttle bus service, has showers, laundry, and kitchen (1000dr per person, 500dr per tent). **Koula Camping** (tel. (0284) 220 81 or 220 82), 400m north of town on the beach boasts a market in addition (1000dr per person, 500dr per tent). The psychedelic **Happy Green Cow** has delicious vegetarian food (open daily noon-1am).

Naxos ΝΑΞΟΣ

After Ariadne, daughter of King Minos of Crete, saved Theseus from her father's labyrinth, the young prince expressed his gratitude by abandoning her on Naxos. Today, rocky promontories, squat windmills, and demure villages tucked between rolling hills dot this largest and most fertile island of the Cyclades. The streets of **Naxos Town** offer glimpses of the brilliant blue sea as they wind around stone archways and gardens. Be sure to stroll around the old **Venetian Castle,** a series of mansions still inhabited by the descendants of Frankish and Venetian nobility. The **Portara,** a marble archway on the hilltop peninsula near the port, is one of the best star-watching and picnic spots in town. Writer Nikos Kazantzakis once studied at the **Archaeological Museum,** which displays Cycladic artifacts, Mycenaean jewels, and Geometric chamber tombs (open Tues.-Sun. 8:30am-3pm; 500dr, students 300dr, Sun. free).

Ferries travel to Paros (1hr., 1400dr), Ios (1½hr., 2100dr), Santorini (3hr., 2650dr), and many other islands; **buses** run to Chalki (30min., 300dr) and other towns on the island. Offices, stores, and agencies meet travelers' needs along the waterfront in Naxos Town. There is a privately owned tourist office directly on the dock, but you should continue on to find the public **tourist office** (tel. (0285) 243 58; fax 252 00), which offers advice on accommodations, bus and ferry schedules, currency exchange, and luggage storage (open daily 8am-midnight). People who meet ferries offer singles for 3000-4500dr and doubles for 4000-8000dr; it's virtually assured you can get a better deal if you haggle. Or, follow signs to the clean and welcoming **Hotel Panorama** (tel. (0285) 244 04), in Old Naxos with a—surprise, surprise—panoramic view of the harbor and town (singles 8000dr, doubles with bath 10,000; breakfast 800dr). If you have a few extra *drachmae,* try the sparkling **Hotel Anixis** (tel./fax (0285) 221 12 or 229 32; 11,000-13,000dr; breakfast 1600dr), or the nurturing **Hotel Chateau Zevgoli** (tel. (0285) 229 93); light blue signs point the way from the old town (doubles 15,000dr, triples 18,000dr). Basically a youth hostel, **Hotel Dionysos** (tel. (0285) 223 31), in Old Naxos is a bit run-down but social (1500-5000dr, illegal roof space 1500dr). **Naxos Camping** (tel. (0285) 235 00), 1500m along St. George's beach, has a swimming pool (1000dr per person, 300dr per tent; *Let's Go* discount).

Restaurants in the old town are more scenic and have traditional, tasty food; those near the waterfront are a bit more pricey. The exceptional fish taverna **Galini,** 500m down the inland road past Hotel Hermes, is the best-kept secret in Naxos. To try it all order the *peekeelia,* an assortment of bite-size morsels (1500-2000dr; open daily noon-2am). High up in the old city, **Koutouki** serves huge entrees with veggies, fries, and rice (*souvlaki* and stuffed peppers 1300dr each). Naxos's nightlife isn't as frenetic as some of the other islands; try **The Rocks** or **The Jam** behind the OTE.

Naxos's bewitching **interior** features rolling hills, staggering rock formations, tranquil villages, and herds of sheep and goats. The ideal way to appreciate the landscape is on foot; you can also traverse the terrain by bus or, with some difficulty, by moped. The main road across the island passes through the resplendent **Tragea,** a vast arcadian olive grove. Stop in **Chalki's** parish church, **Panayia Protothonis,** where renovations have uncovered wall paintings from the 11th through the 13th centuries. If the church is closed, find a local priest to admit you. Drive from Naxos Town via Melanes to **Flerio,** where one of the **kouroi** (colossal statues of nude males dating from as early as the 7th century BC) sleeps in a woman's garden.

Ios ΙΟΣ

There is little to do in Ios but sleep late, sunbathe in the afternoon, and join the cavorting at night. The town is your mother's worst nightmare—people swilling from wine bottles at 3pm, condoms scattered on dirt roads, people dancing naked in bars, and oh so much more. Ios's wild and famous bar scene centers on the old village area. **Sweet Irish Dream** is in a large building near the "donkey steps." Come here to dance on the tables after 2am (beers 500-600dr; cocktails 700-800dr). Across the street, **Dubliner** has a pub-like wooden section and a large outdoor terrace (beers 500dr; cocktails 1000dr). **The Slammer Bar,** just uphill from the main square in the village, serves tequila slammers to a full house (600dr), while **Kalimera,** lower down off the main strip, features jazz and reggae (beers 500-800dr; cocktails 1000-1200dr). If you can still stand up straight, **Scorpion Disco,** outside of town on the way to the beach, is a dance emporium, and one of the craziest spots on the island (1000dr cover after 2am includes first drink).

The **Tourist Information Center** (tel. (0286) 911 35), right next to the bus stop, sells ferry and flying dolphin tickets, provides currency exchange, helps with accommodations, and offers free maps, luggage storage, and safety deposit boxes (open daily 8am-midnight). Also next to the bus stop is the **Medical Center** (tel. (0286) 912 27; open daily 10am-1pm and 6-7pm). Along the road heading to Kolitsani Beach are the English-speaking **police** (tel. (0286) 922 22; open 24hr.). **Buses** shuttle continuously between the ferry landing and the village (service ends 2am, 210dr). **Ferries** travel to Naxos (1½hr., 2295dr), Mykonos (4-5hr., 3190dr), Santorini (1¼hr., 1170dr), Paros (2½hr., 2605dr), and many other islands.

It helps to arrive on Ios sober, so you can bargain intelligently with the swarm of room hawkers that will meet you at the port. Depending on how the season is going, prices fluctuate between 2000-7000dr for singles and 2500-10,000dr for doubles. The owner of **Francesco's** (tel./fax (0286) 912 23), uphill from the National Bank, will do his best to see that you enjoy Ios (doubles 5000dr, with bath 8000dr; triples 6000-9000dr; reservations encouraged). To get to the friendly **Pension Markos** (tel. (0286) 910 59; fax 910 60) from the bus stop, take the right (uphill) just before the supermarket, and watch for a sign which directs you to a sidestreet (doubles 8000dr, triples 10,000dr; reserve a few days in advance). You won't be roughing it at **Far Out Camping** (tel. (0286) 923 01, -2; fax 923 03), at the far end of Mylopotas beach: the site has a restaurant, bar, swimming pool, and water slides (1000dr per person; tent rental 400dr; open April-Sept.). If you arrive late, go to **Camping Ios** at the port (1000dr per person; open June-Sept.). For divine Greek cuisine look for **Lord Byron,** uphill from the National Bank on the street below the main drag (Greek omelette 1000dr; fava bean dip 900dr; open daily 7pm-midnight).

Santorini ΣΑΝΤΟΡΙΝΗ

Santorini's landscape is as dramatic as the cataclysm that carved it—a massive volcanic eruption that gave rise to the Atlantis legend and is believed by many to have destroyed the Minoan civilization on Crete. In **Thira** (ΘΗΡΑ), the island's capital, the **Archaeological Museum** holds an impressive collection of vases, most from the site of ancient Thira (open Tues.-Sun. 8am-3pm; 800dr, students 400dr). More fascinating are the excavations at **Akrotiri,** a late Minoan city preserved virtually intact under layers of volcanic rock (open Tues.-Sun. 8:30am-3pm; 1200dr, students 600dr). Breeze through on your own or join a guided tour. Bus tours (4000-4500dr) are often coupled with a visit to the **Profitias Ilias Monastery** and a local wine-tasting. From Profitias Ilias, it's an hour's hike to **ancient Thira,** where the ancient theater, church, and forum of the island's old capital are visible (open Tues.-Sun. 8am-3:30pm; free). The most frequented black sand beaches are **Perissa** and **Kamari,** both accessible by bus.

Ferries leave Santorini for Piraeus (10hr., 5825dr), Ios (1½hr., 1588dr), Paros (5hr., 3100dr), Mykonos (7hr., 3380dr), Thessaloniki (9300dr), and many other ports. Most ferries land at **Athinios** harbor, where you can strike a deal for a room with the dock hawks. Try for one of the small towns near Thira. **Thira Youth Hostel** (tel. (0286) 223 87), about 300m north of the square, offers clean mixed-gender and women-only dorm rooms. Hot showers are available 24 hours, but bring toilet paper. (Reception open 24hr. Quiet after 11pm enforced. Dorms 1500dr; doubles 6000-8000dr. Open April-Oct.) **Kontohori Youth Hostel** (tel. (0286) 227 22; in summer 225 77) is down a slope about 400m north of the square (reception open 24hr.; dorms 1200dr, doubles 7500dr; 10% discount after 5 days). Nearby **Kamares Youth Hostel** (tel. (0286) 244 72) has some beds on a canopied roof. (Reception open daily 8am-1pm and 5-9pm. Dorms 1000dr; roof 900dr. Hot showers 5-9pm.) Follow blue "camping" signs to **Santorini Camping** (tel. (0286) 229 44; 1300dr per person, 800dr per tent).

THE SPORADES ΣΠΟΡΑΔΕΣ

Lush islands of fragrant pines, luxurious beaches, and abundant fruit orchards, the Sporades offer travelers a smorgasbord of earthly delights. Tourism is on the rise, but there are spots on this archipelago that remain relatively quiet and inexpensive.

Skiathos ΣΚΙΑΘΟΣ

Although less beautiful than the other Sporades, cosmopolitan Skiathos compensates by hosting the archipelago's largest social scene. Tourists pack the streets of **Skiathos Town,** but in the residential neighborhoods, balconies still burst with white gardenias over undisturbed terraces. A bus leaves the harbor in Skiathos Town (every 15-20min., 7:15am-1am, 280dr) and stops at beaches along its southern route, including **Megali Ammos, Nostros, Platanias,** and **Vromolimnos.** The bus route and the road end where more secluded beaches begin, such as Koukounaries, Banana Beach and the nude Little Banana Beach. No comment.

Back in town, the **tourist police** (tel. (0427) 231 72), on the right side of Papadiamanti St., have brochures with a map. They can also help you arrange *domatia* rooms (open daily 8am-9pm). **Ferries** arrive from Agios, Skopelos and Alonissos; if you're coming from Athens, take the bus from the station at 260 Liossion St. to Agios Konstantinos (2½hr., 2650dr), and then the ferry (3½hr., 3500dr). Most tourists book accommodations ahead; if you are having trouble locating a room, contact **Rooms to Let** (tel. (0427) 229 90 or 222 60; fax 238 52) in the wooden kiosk by the port (open daily 8:30am-midnight). **Pension Anglea** (tel. (0427) 229 62), to the left at the end of Papadiamanti St., offers clean doubles with bath (6000-10,000dr). **Camping Koukounaries** (tel. (0427) 492 25) lies close to the beach on the bus route between stops 19 and 20, and has a restaurant and minimarket (1500dr per person, 1000dr per tent). The cheapest dining option is to hit the *gyros/souvlaki* stands (350dr) which line Papadiamanti and the waterfront, or forage in the numerous **supermarkets.** Bars cluster on Polytechniou St., Evangelistra St., and Papadiamantis Sq., and dance clubs line the far right side of the coast. The gay-friendly **Kalypso,** on the water above the restaurant of the same name, guides you through a journey of classical, traditional, and jazz music (beer 600dr; cocktails 1200-1400dr).

Skopelos ΣΚΟΠΕΛΟΣ

Looming cliffs rise from the coastline of Skopelos, but inland acres of pine, olive, and plum trees blanket the hills and temper the mountains' starkness. Roads and hiking paths wind through the terrain and lead to monasteries and beaches. Except for the inevitable front line of tourist offices and *tavernas,* **Skopelos Town** is a complex and delightful cobblestone maze stacked up against the hillside. The Thalpos **tourist agency** (tel. (0424) 229 47; fax 230 57), past the Commercial Bank, is on the second floor (open daily 9am-2pm and 6-8pm; extended hours July-Aug.). **Ferries** connect to Skiathos (1½hr., 1490dr) and other islands. Wander around the narrow streets behind the waterfront to find lodging, or try asking friendly faces for *dhomatia.* **Hotel Eleni** (tel. (0424) 223 93) is on the far right side of the waterfront (singles 6500-8500dr, doubles 8500-13,500dr). Platanos Sq. is home to the 350dr gyro, but **Greca's Crêperie** may well be the highlight of Skopelos (crepes 800-1200dr).

Alonissos and Skyros ΑΛΟΝΝΗΣΟΣ ΚΑΙ ΣΚΥΡΟΣ

Alonissos Though it lacks polished beauty, **Alonissos** is one of the friendliest and least touristed islands in Greece. A **National Marine Park** protects its unruffled atmosphere. All boats dock at **Patitiri,** but a trip to the island is not complete without a visit to rebuilt **Chora** (old town), set high on the hillside to ward off pirate attacks. Exploring the town feels like discovering the ruins of a castle, and nearly every building commands a fabulous view of the bay, the mountains, and the town below. Buses run between Chora and Patitiri hourly in the summer (9am-3pm and 7-11pm, 10min., 250dr). A 30-minute downhill walk from town leads to four sandy **beaches. Ferries** arrive from Athens via Agios Konstantinos (5½hr., 4100dr), Skiathos (2hr., 1800dr), and Skopelos (30min., 1200dr). In Patitiri, **Alonissas Travel** (tel. (0424) 651 88; fax 655 11) helps you find rooms, change money, book excursions, and buy ferry tickets (open daily 9am-10pm). A **"Rooms to Let" office** helps with accommodations (tel./fax (0424) 655 77; open daily 9:30am-3pm and 6-10pm), although it may be cheaper to negotiate with locals and look for EOT signs on inland streets. Inquire at Boutique Mary, on the right side of Pelsagon, for rooms at **Dimakis Pension** (tel. (0424) 652 94; singles 5000-7000dr, doubles 8000-10,000dr).

Skyros Rolling purple hills, sandy beaches, fragrant pine groves, and gnarled cliffs form the spectacular backdrop for daily life on **Skyros.** Tourism is beginning to encroach, but the island remains the quietest and most isolated of the Sporades. In **Skyros Town,** visit the **Monastery of St. George** and the ruins of the Byzantine **Castle of Licomidus.** Both afford spectacular views of the eastern coast. Down the steps and to the left of the statue of English poet Rupert Brooke, the fascinating **Faltaits Museum** has a superior folk art collection (open daily 10am-1pm and 5:30-8pm; free). **Skyros Travel,** Agoras St. (tel. (0222) 911 23 or 916 00), organizes boat and bus excursions, rents mopeds (3000dr), helps find rooms, and sells maps (500dr; open daily 9:15am-2:15pm and 6:30-10:30pm). There are no ferries to the rest of the Sporades, but expensive **Flying Dolphins** travel to Alonissos (1¼hr., 6760dr), Skopelos (1¾hr., 7040dr), and Skiathos (2¼hr., 8125dr). Marble-floored **doubles** (tel. (0222) 914 59), below the National Bank of Greece, go for 5000-7000dr.

CRETE ΚΡΗΤΗ

Greece's largest island embraces an infinite store of mosques and monasteries, mountain villages, gorges, grottoes, and beaches. Since 3000 BC, Crete has had a distinct identity expressed in the language, script, and architecture of the ancient Minoans.

Most travelers arrive in Crete by **ferry.** From Iraklion, boats connect to Athens (12hr., 6500dr), Paros and Naxos (each 4800dr), Rhodes (12hr., 6190dr), Santorini (4hr.), and several other islands. Ferries also dock at Chania, Rethymnon, and Agios Nikolaos. If you prefer to fly, **Olympic Airways** sends planes from the island to Athens (45min., 21,600dr), Rhodes (30min., 21,600), and other destinations; **Air Greece** has less frequent but less expensive service to the island as well.

Iraklion (Heraklion) ΗΡΑΚΛΙΟΝ

As Crete's capital, **Iraklion** sports a chic native population, a nightlife more diverse than those of nearby beach resorts, and an ideal location as the base for a cultural tour of Crete. The phenomenal **Archaeological Museum,** off Eleftherias Sq., has appropriated the major finds from all over the island and comprehensively presents the island's history from the Neolithic period to Roman times. The highlight is the **Hall of the Minoan Frescoes,** which depicts aspects of ancient Minoan life. (Open Mon. 12:30-7pm, Tues.-Sun. 8am-7pm. 1500dr, students 800dr, EU students free.)

Across from the Archaeological Museum, the **tourist office,** 1 Xanthoudidou St. (tel. (081) 22 82 03 or 24 46 62), has maps, hotel lists, and transportation schedules (open Mon.-Fri. 8am-2:30pm, Sat. 10am-2:30pm). The **tourist police,** 10 Dikeosinis St. (tel. (081) 28 31 90), provide info for those who arrive late (open daily 7am-11pm). Inquire at **Travel Hall Travel Agency,** 13 Hatzimihali Yiannari St. (tel. (081) 34 18 62; fax 28 33 09), for **Olympic Airways** and **Air Greece** tickets (open daily 8am-9pm).

There are several **bus terminals** in town. Terminal A, between the old city walls and the harbor near the waterfront, serves Ag. Nikolaos (1½hr., 1300dr) and Malia (1hr., 700dr); Terminal B serves Matala (2hr., 1400dr) and other towns. A third terminal sends buses to Chania (2500dr) and Rethymnon (1400dr); walk down 25th Augustou Ave. to the waterfront, turn right, and walk about 500m. The **youth hostel,** 5 Kyronos St. (tel. (081) 28 62 81 or 22 29 47), off 25th Augustou Ave., has standard, quiet hostel rooms (open for late arrivals; 1400dr per person, doubles 3800-4000dr). **Rent a Room Hellas** is at 24 Handakos St. (tel. (081) 28 08 58; dorms 1500dr, singles 4000dr, doubles 5000dr). Rave and disco pulses at **Factory** (Thurs.-Sat.) and Greek music wafts from **Café Aman.**

■ Near Iraklion: Knossos

Knossos is undoubtedly the most famous archaeological site in Crete—few visitors escape the island without at least a quick visit. Excavations here revealed remains of a Minoan city that thrived 3500 years ago. Dr. Arthur Evans, who financed and supervised the excavations, eventually restored large parts of the **palace** in Knossos; his work often crossed the line from preservation to artistic interpretation, but the site is still impressive nonetheless (open daily 8am-7pm; 1500dr, students 800dr, Sun. free). To reach Knossos from Iraklion, take bus 2 at 25th Augustou Ave. (every 20min. 7am-10:30pm, 210dr); look for the signposts on the west side of the street.

Western Crete

While the resort towns of Crete's eastern half seem to have sprung spontaneously from the brains of U.K. booking agents, the vacation spots of Western Crete have grown naturally around towns with rich histories and distinctive characters.

Rethymnon and Chania The Turkish and Venetian influences that pervade the northern Crete's towns are best appreciated at the scenic harbor of **Rethymnon** (ΡΕΘΥΜΝΟ). Arabic inscriptions lace the walls of the town's narrow, arched streets, and minarets highlight the old city's skyline. Keeping watch over the harbor's west end, the walls of the 16th-century **Venetian Fortezza** are in excellent condition (open daily 8am-8pm; 500dr), and now protect a lively **Renaissance Festival** (July and August). The **Wine Festival** (August or July) is a crowded all-you-can-drink fest. (First night admission 1000d; required souvenir glass 150dr.) The **tourist office** (tel. (0831) 291 48), on the waterfront, supplies maps and bus and ferry schedules (open Mon.-Fri. 8am-5:30pm, Sat. 9am-2pm). The cheerful **youth hostel,** 41-45 Tombazi St. (tel. (0831) 228 48), at the center of the old town, teems with international youngsters in the summer. (Reception open in summer daily 8am-noon and 5-10pm; off-season closes 9:30pm. 1200dr.) **Olga's Pension** is at 57 Souliou St. (tel. (0831) 298 51), off Ethnikis Antistaseos (singles 4500dr, doubles 5000dr, triples 7000dr). Pitch tents at **Elizabeth Camping** (tel. (0831) 286 94), 3km east of town. The staff lends kitchen and camping supplies (3600dr for 2 people and a tent; open May-Oct.).

Narrow, four-story Venetian buildings and Ottoman domes mingle in the lively harbor town of **Chania** (ΧΑΝΙΑ). The **tourist office,** on the first floor of the Megaro Pantheon, Platia 1866 (tel./fax (0821) 926 24), behind the Greek Agricultural Bank, has info on ferries, buses, and hotels in town (open Mon.-Fri. 7:30am-2:30pm, Sat.-Sun. 8am-3pm). To get to **Hotel Fidias,** 6 Sarpaki St. (tel. (0821) 524 94), from Halidon St., turn right at the cathedral on Athinagora St., which becomes Sarapaki St. (Dorms 1700dr, singles 3000-3500dr, doubles 3800-4000dr, triples 5000dr). For a truly Cretan experience, replete with mustachioed old men dancing to traditional music, head east to **Café Kriti,** 22 Kalergon St. (beer 500dr; open daily 7pm-late; not recommended for women traveling alone).

Samaria Gorge The most popular excursion from Chania, Rethymnon, or Iraklion is the five- to six-hour hike down the 16km **Samaria Gorge,** a spectacular ravine that cuts through heavy forests and sheer granite cliffs. Be sure to bring lots of water and good hiking boots (open May-Oct. 15 daily 6am-4pm; 1200dr). For gorge info call **Chania Forest Service** (tel. (0821) 922 87). Buses run from Chania to **Xyloskalo** (1½hr.) at the start of the trail. The trail ends in **Agia Roumeli** on the south coast; from here, take a boat to Chora Sfakion and then a bus back to Chania.

Eastern Crete

The endlessly winding main highway joining Malia and Hersonissos to Agios Nikolaos, Ierapetra, and Sitia is spectacular—it grips the side of the mountains, ascending and descending deep valleys. Destinations along this highway are equally impressive. The white villages along the coast are colored by small green gardens, olive plains, and an astonishingly blue sea.

Hersonissos and Malia Twenty-six kilometers east of Iraklion, the port town of **Hersonissos** (ΧΕΡΣΟΝΗΣΟΣ) is free of ancient ruins and monasteries. The most famous monuments here are the bars, discos, and clubs that cluster near the beach. As night progresses, visitors head to Main St., the Paraliakos, and the waterfront. The dance floors of **Disco 99** (open daily 9pm-4:30am) and **La Luna** (open daily 10:30pm-5am) are large and crowded with tourists. The hottest club in town is the **Camelot Dancing Club,** featuring international rave and house (open daily 10pm-5:30am). **The Hard Rock Café** offers live British rock (open 12:30pm-5am).

Malia (ΜΑΛΙΑ) has been increasingly encroached upon by self-aggrandizing hotels, neon signs, and billboard advertisements. Nonetheless, the palatial Minoan site at Malia merits a visit. The **Minoan Palace** lacks the labyrinthine architecture and magnificent interior decoration of Knossos, but is still imposing. Northwest of the main site slumbers the **Hypostyle Crypt,** which may have been a social center for Malia's intelligentsia. To reach this area, follow the road to Agios Nikolaos 3km to the east and turn left toward the sea, or walk along the beach and then 1km through the fields (open Tues.-Sun. 8:30am-3pm; 800dr, Sun. free). In Malia, **Pension Aspasia** (tel. (0897) 312 90), and **Pension Menios** (tel. (0897) 313 61), both on 25th Martiou St., have clean doubles (5000-6000dr) and triples (6000dr).

Agios Nikolaos An intense nightlife, diverse selection of glamorous shops, and remnants of an indigenous Cretan culture make Agios Nikolaos (ΑΓΙΟΣ ΝΙΚΟΛΑΟΣ) an appealing mix of humility and pretension. The **tourist office** (tel. (0841) 223 57), at the bridge between the lake and the port, changes money, finds rooms, has a free brochure with map, and provides boat and bus schedules (open April-Oct. daily 8:30am-9:45pm). From the tourist office, walk up 25th Martiou St. and go left onto Manousogianaki. After four blocks, go right onto Solonos to find **Argiro Pension,** 1 Solonos St. (tel. (0841) 287 07), with its jasmine-scented garden (doubles 5000-5500dr, triples 6600-7000dr). For nocturnal pursuits, stroll around the harbor on I. Koundourou St., or go up 25th Martiou St.

NORTHEAST AEGEAN ISLANDS

The intricate, rocky coastlines of the Northeast Aegean Islands enclose thickly wooded mountains and isolated valleys. Proximity to Turkey explains the presence of guns, camouflage, and large numbers of young soldiers.

Samos ΣΑΜΟΣ

With its sultry landscape and engrossing archaeological remains, quiet Samos is perhaps the most beautiful and certainly the most touristed island in the Northeast Aegean. The waterfront of **Samos Town** is a snarl of tourist shops and cafés, but the town itself has wide sidewalks, garden-laced residential lanes, and picturesque red-roofed houses nestled against the mountainside. The **tourist office** (tel. (0273) 285 30 or 285 82), is on a side street one block before Pythagoras Sq. (open July-Aug. Mon.-Sat. 8:30am-2pm). **Olympic Airways** (tel. (0273) 272 37) flies to Athens (1hr., 17,100dr) from Samos's airport (2500dr by taxi from Samos Town). **Ferries** travel to Naxos (6hr., 3925dr), Paros (6hr., 4020dr), Chios (5½hr., 2720dr), Lesvos (8hr., 3700dr), and other islands. Ferries also go daily to **Kuşadası,** Turkey. (8am and 5pm, 2hr., 5000dr. Greek port tax 5000dr. Turkish port tax 3000dr. Americans and Brits pay US$20 for entrance visa.) To get to **Pension Ionia,** 5 Manoli Kalomiri St. (tel. (0273) 287 82), turn right at the end of the ferry dock, take a left onto E. Stamatiadou St. before the Hotel Aiolis on the waterfront, and then take the second left (singles 2500dr, doubles 4000dr). **Hotel Artemis,** Pythagoras Sq. (tel. (0273) 277 92), offers clean rooms and helpful service (doubles 4000dr, with bath 5000dr).

Buses from Samos Town and boats from Patmos and points south arrive at **Pythagorion,** the former capital of Samos. Near the town, you can see the magnificent remains of Polykrates's 6th-century BC engineering projects: the **Tunnel of Eupalinos,** which diverted water form a natural spring to the city, a 40m deep **harbor mole,** and the **Temple of Hera,** one of the seven wonders of the ancient world (temple open Tues.-Sun. 8:30am-3pm; 800dr, students 400dr).

Lesvos and Chios ΛΕΣΒΟΣ ΚΑΙ ΧΙΟΣ

Lesvos Once home of the sensual poet Sappho, Lesvos is still something of a mecca for lesbians. The island mixes horsebreeding, serious *ouzo* drinking, and leftist politics. Most travelers pass through crumbling but picturesque **Mitilini,** the capital and central port city. Ubiquitous signs point tourists to various sights. The enormous **Church of St. Therapon** presides benignly over the fish market, while the **Archaeological Museum,** 7 Argiri Eftalioti St., expected to open in 1998, has an impressive collection of the island's historical finds. (Open Tues.-Sun. 8:30am-3pm. 500dr, students 300dr, EU students free; Nov.-March Sun. free.) The **tourist office,** 6 James Aristarchou (tel. (0251) 425 11; fax 425 12), has info, free brochures, and maps (open Mon.-Fri. 8:30am-3pm). **NEL Lines,** 67 Pavlou Koudoutrioti St. (tel. (0251) 222 20), runs ferries to Peiraias (12hr., 6570dr), Chios (3hr., 3088dr), Thessaloniki (12hr., 7800dr), Çesme, Turkey, and elsewhere. The **Rooms to Let Office,** one block inland from the center of the waterfront, can secure singles for 4000-5000dr and doubles for 7000dr (open Mon.-Sun. 9am-1pm). The towns of **Petras** and **Molyvos** are also frequently touristed. The red-tiled stone houses of Molyvos cluster at the base of the castle-peaked hill, conveying picture-perfect charm, while Petra stretches along a fine sand beach and presses into the fertile plain behind. Just up from the Mylvos bus stop, the **tourist office** (tel. (0253) 713 47) will help you find a room. In Petra, contact the **Women's Cooperative** (tel. (0253) 34 12 38) to find rooms.

Chios When the mythical hunter Orion drove the wild beasts off **Chios** (ΧΙΟΣ), grand pine and cypress trees sprouted on the vast mountainsides. Chios has only recently been opened to tourism, but as its striking volcanic beaches and medieval villages become more accessible, the island may become a new vacation hotspot. In **Chios Town,** the tourist office, 18 Kanari St. (tel. (0271) 443 89), will get you started by answering questions and providing brochures and an accommodations list. **Ferries** travel to Samos (4½hr., 24800dr), other islands, and the Turkish coast.

THE DODECANESE ISLANDS

An endless succession of conquerors and explorers, from the Turks and Knights of St. John in the Middle Ages to the Italians and Germans of this century, has left an indelible imprint on the Dodecanese Islands. The landscape is dotted with classical ruins, Italian buildings, and restored medieval homes. Rhodes in particular endures frenzied tourism, tempered by the islands' distance from the mainland.

Rhodes ΡΟΔΟΣ

While the resort towns of Rhodes suffer from the maladies brought on by crowds and commercialism, the interior regions and the smaller coastal towns retain a sense of serenity and dignity. Beaches stretch along the east coast, jagged cliffs skirt the west, and green mountain views fill the interior, where villagers continue in the centuries-old traditions. At the northern tip of the island, the **City of Rhodes** welcomes visitors with tourist amenities as well as medieval turrets and archways, decaying mosques and minarets, and soothing palm trees. The **Old Town** features an incredible array of medieval castles and fortresses left by the Knights of St. John. The best place to begin exploring this quarter is at **Symi Square,** inside **Eleftherias Gate** at the base of the Mandraki. Nearby, in **Museum Square,** the beautiful halls and courtyards of the former **Hospital of the Knights** now house the **Archaeological Museum,** where most of the island's archaeological treasures are located. (Open Tues.-Fri. 8am-7pm, Sat.-Sun. 8:30am-3pm. 800dr, EU students free, other students 400dr.) At the top of the hill, an archway leads to Kleovoulou Sq.; to the right sits the pride of the city, the **Palace of the Knights of St. John** (Palace of the Grand Masters), a complex of 300 rooms, moats, drawbridges, watch towers, and colossal battlements (open Tues.-Fri. 8am-7pm, Sat.-Sun. 8:30am-3pm; 1200dr, students 600dr).

Rhodes is the most accessible island in the Dodecanese. Regular **ferries** connect to Kos (3257dr), Patmos (5208dr), Crete (5969dr), and virtually every other major island and coastal city in the area. **Hydrofoils** travel to the Northeast Aegean islands, Turkey, and the other Dodecanese islands; schedules vary from day to day and should be checked at travel agencies. **Planes** soar to Athens (24,600dr), Kos (11,000dr), Karpathos (12,500dr), and other cities. The airport (tel. (0241) 917 71) is on the west coast, 17km from town near the city of Paradisi; public buses run hourly (daily 7am-midnight, 300dr). The **City of Rhodes tourist office** (tel. (0241) 359 45), in Rimini Sq., helps with accommodations and changes money (open Mon.-Sat. 8am-9pm, Sun. 8am-3pm). The **Greek tourist office** (tel. (0241) 232 55 or 236 55) is several blocks up Papagou St. (open Mon.-Fri. 7:30am-3pm). In the Old Town, stay at **Hotel Andreas,** 28 Omirou St. (tel. (0241) 341 56; fax 742 85; doubles 6000-8000dr, triples 10,000, quads 12,000dr), or the spotless **Pension Olympos,** 56 Ag. Fanouriou St. (tel./fax (0241) 335 67; doubles 8000dr, triples 10,000dr). In a quiet area of the New Town, **Hotel Capitol,** 65-67 Dilberaki St. (tel. (0241) 620 16), has private showers in all rooms (singles 7000dr, doubles 8000dr, triples 12,000dr; breakfast included).

Excursion boats follow the coast from Rhodes to Lindos, making several stops along the way. Schedules and prices are posted at the dock along the lower end of the Mandraki; most cost roughly 3500dr round-trip. **Buses** also connect to smaller towns on the island. Ten kilometers south of the city lies **Kalithea,** site of a deserted spa for European aristocrats. Another 5km south, **Faliraki** is a popular resort with a sandy beach and rocking nightlife. About halfway down the eastern coast, **Lindos** is perhaps the most picturesque town on Rhodes. Beautiful whitewashed houses cluster beneath a soaring castle-capped acropolis, but the town's charms are no secret; in summer the population and prices skyrocket. If you make it to the island's southwestern tip, you can see the impressive ruins of the **Castle of Monolithos,** which crumble at the summit of a 160m rock pillar.

Kos ΚΩΣ

In summer, visitors to Kos throng to the classical and Hellenic ruins, fill the beaches, and frisk about booming bars and nightclubs. In **Kos Town,** minarets from Turkish mosques stand alongside grand Italian mansions and the massive walls of a Crusader's fortress. Brilliantly colored flowers and date palms embellish the streets, squares, and ancient monuments. The **tourist office** (tel. (0242) 287 24), at the meeting point of Akri Miaouli, Hippokratous St., and Vas. Georgiou, has info on accommodations and ferry schedules (open Mon.-Fri. 7:30am-9pm, Sat. 7:30am-3pm). **Ferries** travel to Rhodes (4hr., 3300dr), Patmos (4hr., 2700dr), and the usual set of islands in the area.

The room hawkers in Kos are notorious; it's best to seek out your own room unless you arrive very late. **Pension Alexis,** 9 Herodotou St. (tel. (0242) 287 98), the first right off Meg. Alexandrou, has incomparable hospitality and a jasmine-vined patio (doubles 5500-6500dr, triples 7500dr; breakfast 800dr). **Hotel Afendoulis,** 1 Evripolou St. (tel. (0242) 253 21; tel./fax 257 97), has well-kept rooms in a quiet part of town near the beach; go down Vas. Georgiou and look for Evripolou on the right (doubles with private bath 7500-8500dr). **Rooms to Let Nitsa,** 47 Averof St. (tel. (0242) 258 10), near the beach north of town, has super-clean rooms with baths and kitchenettes (doubles 6500dr, triples 8000dr). The nightlife in Kos can be heard pounding all over the Dodecanese. The **Exarhia** area is packed with bars. The other party zone is on **Porfiriou St.** in the north, near the beach. Beers (500dr) at **Pub Cuckoo's Nest** and **Crazy Horse Saloon** are often accompanied by free shots. The most popular island discos, **Kahlua** and **Heaven,** both on the beach, reside here.

The **Asclepion,** an ancient sanctuary dedicated to the god of healing, lies 4km west of Kos Town. In the 5th century BC, Hippocrates opened the world's first medical school here. The most interesting remains are in the three central terraced planes, called "andirons." These contain the **School of Medicine,** statues of deities, and a figure of Pan. Climb the 30 steps to the second andiron to see the best preserved remains of the Asclepion—the elegant white columns of the **Temple of Apollo** and the **Minor Temple of Asclepios.** The climb to the third andiron leads to the **Main Temple of Asclepios** and affords a view of the whole site, Kos Town, and the Turkish coast (open June-Sept. Tues.-Sun. 8:30am-3pm; 800dr, students 400dr). Sixteen **buses** a day make the short schlepp to the Asclepion during the summer.

Patmos Solemn **Patmos** (ΠΑΤΜΟΣ), imbued with a weighty sense of its religious past, is where St. John is said to have written the Book of Revelation. The sprawling monastery dedicated to him, just above the charming and labyrinthine hilltop village of **Chora,** presides over the island. **Ferries** depart from the port town of **Skala** for Kos (4hr., 2721dr), Rhodes (10hr., 5305dr), and nearby islands. If you prefer not to haggle for a room at the dock, contact **Maria Paschalidis** (tel. (0247) 321 52) or **Pension Sofia** (tel. (0247) 315 01). Both have clean doubles for 6000-8000dr. To get to **Flower Camping at Meloi** (tel. (0247) 318 21), follow the waterfront road all the way to the right, facing inland, and look for the signs (1200dr per person, 750dr per tent).

Karpathos Friendly **Karpathos** (ΚΑΡΠΑΘΟΣ) boasts a charming port town and some of the most beautiful, non-touristed beaches in Greece. **Karpathos Town** is the island's administrative and transportation center; from here, **Olympic Airways** (tel. (0245) 221 50) flies to Athens (25,700dr) and elsewhere, and **ferries** ply to Paros (17hr., 4700dr), Rhodes (5hr., 4050dr), and Santorini (12hr., 4500dr). In town, **Mertonas Studios** (tel. (0245) 226 22 or 230 79), two blocks to the left and uphill from the bus station, rents gorgeous, furnished studios (doubles 5000-7000dr).

Hungary (Magyarország)

US$1 = 198Ft (Hungarian forints)	**100Ft = US$0.51**
CDN$1 = 143Ft	**100Ft = CDN$0.70**
UK£1 = 314Ft	**100Ft = UK£0.32**
IR£1 = 290Ft	**100Ft = IR£0.35**
AUS$1 = 144Ft	**100Ft = AUS$0.70**
NZ$1 = 125Ft	**100Ft = NZ$0.80**
SAR1 = 42Ft	**100Ft = SAR2.38**
Country Code: 36	**International Dialing Prefix: 00**

As of summer 1997, inflation was running high in Hungary. Prices listed in this section may change but should give you a relative idea of cost.

Forty-five years of isolation and relative powerlessness under Soviet rule are a mere blip in Hungary's 1100-year history, and traces of socialism are evaporating with each passing iron-free day. Budapest dominates the country, though by no means has a monopoly on cultural attractions. To forsake the beauty of the countryside for a whirlwind tour of the capital is to see the heart of the country while missing its soul.

The Magyars, as Hungarians call themselves, arrived from Central Asia in the 9th century. Over the course of the next millennium, a succession of tribes, royal houses, and countries laid claim to part or all of the country. Mongols invaded in the 13th century, while the 16th and 17th centuries saw the arrival of the Turks, then Hapsburgs. World War I redistributed two thirds of Hungary's territory, and during World War II the Nazis occupied the country until the two-month Soviet siege of 1945. A short-lived Hungarian republic gave way in 1949 to the Communist People's Republic, under which the country became strongly tied to the USSR. In 1956, Imre Nagy declared a neutral, non-Warsaw-Pact government during a violent uprising. Soviet troops crushed the revolt. In fall 1989 the Hungarian people fulfilled the dreams of the previous generation and at last broke away from the Soviet orbit in a bloodless revolution. The 1990 elections transferred power to the center-right Hungarian Democratic Forum, led by Prime Minister József Antall and President Árpád Göncz, a former Soviet political prisoner. The renamed and revamped Socialists were again entrusted with power in 1994. Hungarians have adapted well since the last Soviet troops departed in 1991, but are deeply troubled by high inflation—18% in 1997 was an improvement from 1996. Hungarian culture has flourished throughout the country's tumultuous history: musical contributors, heavily influenced by folk and particularly Gypsy music, include Ferenc (Franz) Liszt and Béla Bartók. György Konrád (1933-) is among this century's most influential writers, and his work has been critical in defining dissident movements all over Eastern Europe.

For superbly detailed and exciting coverage of Hungary, procure a copy of *Let's Go: Eastern Europe 1998.*

GETTING THERE AND GETTING AROUND

Citizens of the U.S., Canada, and Ireland can travel to Hungary **visa-free** with a valid passport for 90 days; citizens of the U.K. for 6 months; and citizens of South Africa for 30 days. Australians and New Zealanders must obtain 90-day tourist visas from their Hungarian embassy or consulate (see **Government Information Offices,** p. 1); no border-control posts issue visas. For U.S. residents with a green card, visas cost US$40 (single-entry), US$75 (double-entry), US$180 (multiple-entry), or US$38 (48hr. transit visa). Nonresidents pay US$65, US$100, US$200, and US$50, respectively. Obtaining a visa takes one day and requires proof of means of transportation (such as a plane ticket), a valid passport, three photographs (5 for double-entry), payment by cash or money order, and a self-addressed, stamped (certified mail) envelope. Visa extensions are rare, but can be applied for at police stations in Hungary.

Budapest's **Ferihegy airport** handles all international traffic, including **Malév,** the national airline. Hungarian **trains** *(vonat),* many of which pass through the capital, are reliable and inexpensive; Eurail and EastRail are valid. *Személyvonat* are excruciatingly slow; *gyorsvonat* trains (listed on schedules in red) cost the same and move at least twice as fast. Air conditioned InterCity trains are the fastest. Large provincial towns are accessible by the blue *expressz* rail lines. Seat reservations are required on trains marked with an "R" on schedules. Travelers under 26 are eligible for a 33% discount on some domestic train fares, and an ISIC earns 30% discounts on international tickets from IBUSZ, Express, and station ticket counters. Flash your card and state "DEE-ahk" (*diák,* student)—sometimes you need to be persistent. Other important words to know include *érkezés* (arrival), *indulás* (departure), *vágány* (track), and *állomás* or *pályaudvar* (station, abbreviated *pu.*).

The extensive **bus** system is cheap but crowded; it links many towns whose only rail connection is to Budapest. Buy inter-city bus tickets on board (get there early if you want a seat); purchase **public transportation** tickets in advance from a newsstand and punch them on board. There is a fine if you're caught ticketless. The Danube **hydrofoil** goes to Vienna via Bratislava (11,000Ft); Eurailpass holders get 50% off. Either IBUSZ or Tourinform can provide a brochure about **cycling** in Hungary which includes all the details you'll need to plan an excursion. Write the **Hungarian Tourist Board** (MTSZ), 1065 Budapest, Bajcsy-Zsilinszky út 31, or the **Hungarian Cycling Federation,** 1146 Budapest, Szabó J. u. 3, for more info.

ESSENTIALS

IBUSZ offices throughout the country will find rooms, change money, sell train tickets, and charter tours. Snare the pamphlet *Tourist Information: Hungary* and the monthly entertainment guides *Programme in Hungary* and *Budapest Panorama* (all free and in English). **Express,** the former national student travel bureau, handles youth hostels and changes money. Regional travel agencies are helpful in outlying areas; knowledgeable **Tourinform** has branches in every county.

Change money only as you need it, and keep some dollars in cash on hand. **American Express** offices in Budapest and IBUSZ, OTP banks, and Postabank offices cash traveler's checks. Cash advances on credit cards are available at all major OTP branches, and major credit cards are accepted at more expensive hotels and at many shops and restaurants. New Zealand dollars cannot be exchanged here, so pack another currency. At the few exchange offices with extended hours, the rates are generally poor. Hungary swarms with **ATMs,** which have great rates.

Business hours in Hungary are continuing to expand slowly; right now, shops are typically open Monday through Friday 9am to 5pm (7am-7pm for food stores). Banks close around 3pm on Friday. Tourist bureaus are usually open Monday through Saturday 8am to 8pm in summer (some are open until noon on Sun.); off-season these hours shrink to Monday through Friday 10am to 4pm. Museums are usually open Tuesday through Sunday 10am to 6pm, with occasional free days on Tuesday. With an ISIC you can often get in free or pay 50%. Nothing is open on Christian and national **holidays,** including May 1, June 1 (Whit Monday), August 20, and Oct. 23.

Over 600 street names in Budapest alone have changed since the 1989 revolution, but maps in tourist offices are generally up to date. Hungarian addresses usually involve one of the following: *utca,* abbreviated *u.* (street); *út,* or *útja* (avenue); *tér,* or *tere* (square, but may be a park, plaza, or boulevard); *híd* (bridge); and *körút,* abbreviated *krt.* (ring-boulevard). Some streets are numbered odd on one side and even on the other, while others are numbered up one side and down the other.

COMMUNICATION

Hungarian belongs to the Finno-Ugric family of languages. English is the country's very distant third language after Hungarian and German—much of Hungary is accustomed to German-speaking tourists. A few starters for pronunciation: *c* is pronounced "ts" as in ca*ts*; *cs* is "ch" as in *ch*urch; *gy* is "dy" as in fri*dg*e; *ly* is "y" as in *y*am, *s* is "sh" as in *sh*ovel; *sz* is "s" as in "*S*amantha"; *zs* is "jh" as in plea*s*ure, and *a* is "a" as in *a*lways. The first syllable always gets the emphasis.

Yes/No	*Igen/Nem*	EE-gen/nem
Hello/Goodbye	*Jó napot/Szia*	YOH naw-pot/SEE-ya
Please	*Kérem*	KAY-rem
Thank you	*Köszönöm*	KUR-sur-num
Excuse me	*Sajnálom*	shoy-na-lawm
Do you speak English/German?	*Beszél angolul/németül?*	BES–el AWN-gohlul/NAY-met-yuhl
I don't understand.	*Nem értem*	NEM AYR-tem
Where is...?	*Hol van...?*	hawl von
How much does this cost?	*Mennyibe kerül?*	menyeebeh keh rewl
Do you have a vacancy?	*Van szabad szobájuk?*	von sub-od soh-bah-yook
Bill, please.	*Kérem a számlát*	KAY-rem o SAAM-laat
Men/Women	*Férfi/Női*	FAIR-fee/NOY-ee
Help!	*Segítség!*	SHEH-gheet-shayg

Almost all phone numbers in the countryside have six digits and begin with "3." For inter-city calls, wait for the tone and dial slowly; a "06" goes before the city code. **International calls** require red phones or new, digital-display blue ones, found at large post offices, on the street, and in metro stations. Though the blue phones are more handsome than their red brethren, they tend to cut you off after three to nine minutes. Pay phones devour coins so fast you may need a companion to feed them. Half of the public phones throughout the country require **phone cards,** available at kiosks, train stations, and post offices in units of 750 or 1500Ft. Direct calls can also be made from Budapest's phone office. To call collect, dial 09 for the international operator. To make a direct call, put in a 10 or 20Ft coin (which you'll get back), dial 00, wait for the second dial tone, then for **AT&T Direct** dial 80 00 11 11; **MCI WorldPhone,** 80 00 14 11; **Sprint Access,** 80 00 18 77; **Canada Direct,** 80 00 12 11; **BT Direct,** 80 04 40 11; **Mercury Call UK,** 80 00 44 12; **Ireland Direct,** 80 00 35 31; **Australia Direct,** 80 00 61 11; **New Zealand Direct,** 80 00 64 11. For **ambulance** call 104, **police** call 107, and **fire** call 105.

The **mail** service is perfectly reliable; airmail *(légiposta)* to the U.S. takes five to 10 days. Hungarians put the family name first; hence *Poste Restante* or a phone directory would list "Gabor Zsa Zsa." When using hand signals for numbers, remember to start with the thumb for "1"—holding up your index finger means "wait."

ACCOMMODATIONS AND CAMPING

Most travelers stay in **private homes** (look for "Zimmer Frei" or "Kiadó Szoba" signs) booked in person or through a tourist agency. Singles are scarce; it's worth finding a roommate, because solo travelers often must pay for a double room. Agencies may initially try to foist off their more costly quarters. Outside Budapest, the best and cheapest office is usually the regional one (such as Eger-Tourist in Eger). These agencies will often call ahead to make reservations at your next stop. Making arrangements with the owner directly avoids the tourist agencies' 20-30% commission.

Some towns have cheap **hotels,** but most are disappearing. As the hotel system develops and room prices rise, **hostels** become more attractive, although year-round hostels are rare outside of Budapest. Many can be booked at Express or sometimes the regional tourist office after you arrive. From late June through August, **university dorms** change into hostels. Locations change annually; book with an Express office in the off-season, at the dorm itself during the summer. The staff at Express generally speaks German, sometimes English. Over 300 **campgrounds** are sprinkled throughout Hungary. If you rent bungalows, you must pay for unfilled spaces. Most sites are open May-September. Tourist offices offer the annual *Camping Hungary.* For more info and maps, contact **Tourinform** in Budapest.

FOOD AND DRINK

Paprika, Hungary's chief agricultural export, colors most dishes red. In Hungarian restaurants, called *étterem,* you may begin with *gulyásleves,* a delicious and hearty beef soup seasoned with paprika. *Borjúpaprikás* is a veal dish with paprika, often accompanied by small potato-dumpling pasta. Vegetarians can find the tasty *rántott sajt* (fried cheese) and *gombapörkölt* (mushroom stew) on most menus. *Túrós rétes* is a chewy pastry pocket filled with sweetened cottage cheese.

Finding a genuine, "local" eatery is hard. Gypsy music often spells tourist trap. A 10% gratuity has become standard, even if the bill includes a service charge (which goes to the management). Tip as you pay—leaving it on the table is rude. A gypsy musician expects about 150Ft from your table, depending on the number of listeners. A *csárda* is a traditional inn, a *bisztró* an inexpensive restaurant, and an *önkiszolgáló étterem* a cheap cafeteria. Since few menus outside Budapest are written in English, a dictionary can spare you from a point-and-pray meal. *Salátabárs* vend deli concoctions. Fresh fruit and vegetables abound on stands and in produce markets. For pastry and coffee, look for a *cukrászda,* where you can fulfill relentless sweet-tooth desires for dangerously few forints. *Kávé* means espresso. Hungarians are justly proud of their wines. Most famous are the red *Egri Bikavér* ("Bull's Blood of Eger") and the sweet white *Tokaji.* Fruit schnapps *(pálinka)* are a national specialty. Local beers are good; the most common is *Dreher.*

Budapest

At once a cosmopolitan European capital and the stronghold of Magyar nationalism, Budapest awakened from its Communist-era cocoon with the same pride that rebuilt the city from the rubble of World War II and endured the Soviet invasion of 1956. Endowed with an architectural majesty befitting the Hapsburg Empire's number two city, Budapest is huge and yet fragile, as puzzling as that elusive "shhhh" at the end of its name. Today, the city maintains its charm and a vibrant spirit—neon lights and hordes of tourists have added a new twist to the Budapest rhapsody, but below it all the main theme is still expertly played by the genuine, unspoiled Magyar strings.

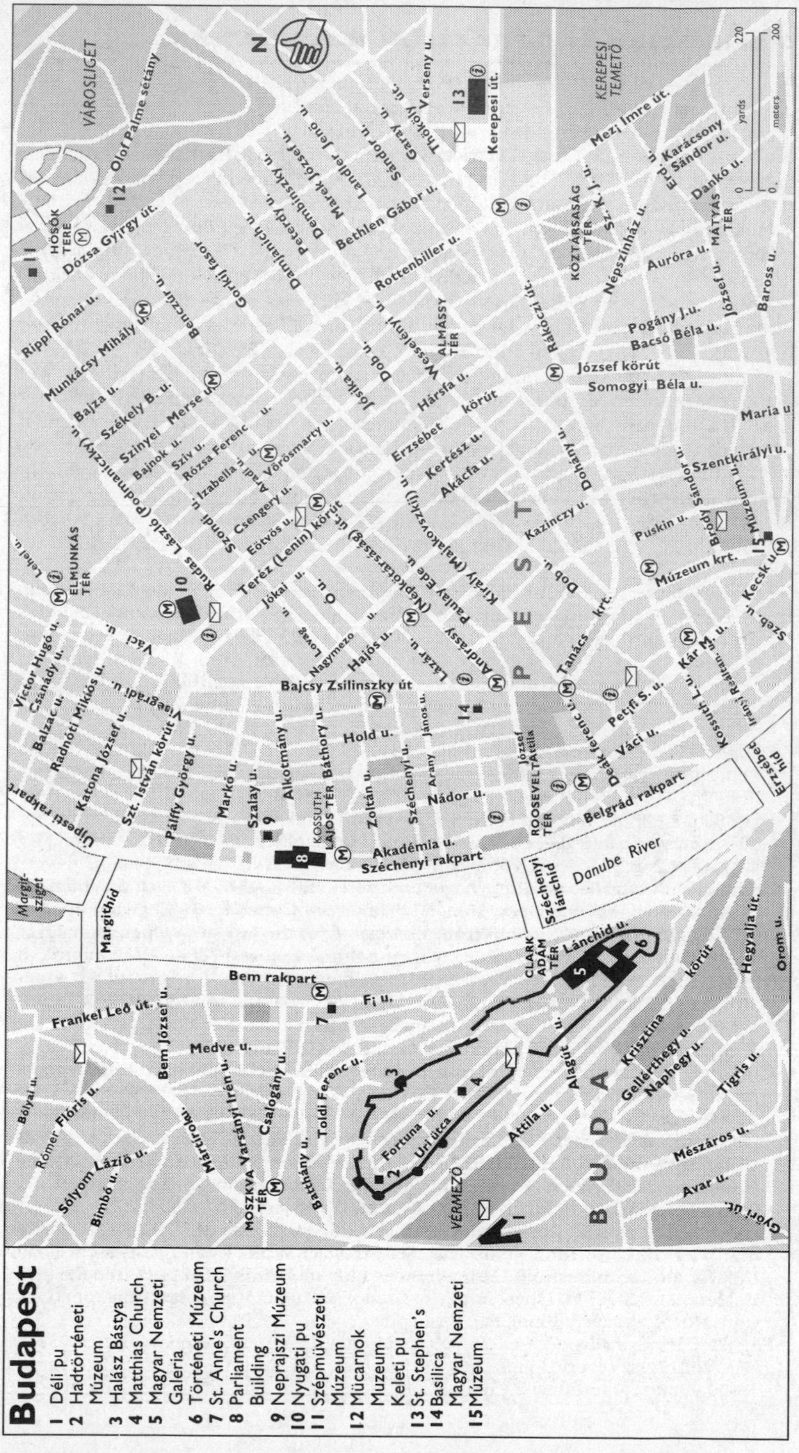
Budapest
1 Déli pu
2 Hadtörténeti Múzeum
3 Halász Bástya
4 Matthias Church
5 Magyar Nemzeti Galeria
6 Történeti Múzeum
7 St. Anne's Church
8 Parliament Building
9 Neprajszi Múzeum
10 Nyugati pu
11 Szépmüvészeti Múzeum
12 Mücarnok Muzeum
13 Keleti pu
14 St. Stephen's Basilica
15 Magyar Nemzeti Múzeum
BUDA
PEST
Danube River
VÁROSLIGET
KEREPESI TEMETŐ
Margit-sziget
Margithíd
Széchenyi lánchíd
Erzsébet híd
VÉRMEZŐ
HŐSÖK TERE
ELMUNKÁS TÉR
KOSSUTH LAJOS TÉR
ROOSEVELT TÉR
CLARK ADÁM TÉR
MOSZKVA TÉR
KÖZTÁRSASÁG TÉR
MÁTYÁS TÉR
ALMÁSSY TÉR
N
yards
meters
0
220
200

ORIENTATION AND PRACTICAL INFORMATION

Previously two cities, Buda and Pest (PESHT), separated by the **Duna** (Danube), modern Budapest straddles the river in north-central Hungary 250km downstream from Vienna. On the west bank, **Buda** inspires countless artists with its hilltop citadel, trees, and cobblestone **Castle District,** while on the east side **Pest** pulses as the heart of the modern city. Three bridges bind the two halves together: **Széchenyi lánchíd,** slender, white **Erzsébet híd,** and green **Szabadság híd.**

Moszkva tér (Moscow Square), just down the north slope of the Castle District, is where virtually all trams and buses start or end their routes. One Metro stop away in the direction of Örs vezér tere, **Batthyány tér** lies opposite the Parliament building on the west bank; this is the starting node of the **HÉV commuter railway.** Budapest's three Metro lines converge at **Deák tér,** at the core of Pest's loosely concentric ring boulevards, next to the main international bus terminal at **Erzsébet tér.**

Many street names occur more than once in town; always check the district as well as the type of street. Moreover, streets arbitrarily change names from one block to the next. Because many have shed their Communist labels, an up-to-date **map** is essential. To check if your map of Budapest is useful, look at the avenue leading from Pest toward the City Park (Városliget) in the east: the name should be Andrássy út. The **American Express** and **Tourinform** offices have reliable and free tourist maps, while *Belváros Idegenforgalmi Térképe* is available at any Metro stop (150Ft). Anyone planning a long visit should look at András Török's *Budapest: A Critical Guide.*

Tourist Offices: All tourist offices have *Budapest Kártya,* which buys 3 days of public transportation use, entrance to all museums, and other discounts (2900Ft). **Tourinform,** V, Sütő u. 2 (tel. 117 98 00; fax 117 95 78), off Deák tér just behind McDonald's. M1, 2, or 3: Deák tér. Busy and multilingual. Open Mon.-Fri. 9am-7pm, Sat.-Sun. 9am-4pm. Accommodation bookings available at **IBUSZ** and **Budapest Tourist** (offices in train stations and tourist centers). The 24hr. IBUSZ central office is at V, Apácsai Csere J. u. 1 (tel. 118 57 76; fax 117 90 00).

Budget Travel: Express, V, Szbadság tér 16 (tel. 131 77 77). Some reduced international air and rail fares for the under-26 crowd (reductions also available at train stations). ISIC for 700Ft. Open Mon. and Wed.-Thurs. 8am-4:30pm, Tues. 8am-6pm, Fri. 8am-2:30pm. Amazing discounts for **youth** (under 26) as well as **standby** (purchase 2 days before flight) available at the **Malév office,** V, Dorottya u. 2 (tel. 266 56 16; fax 266 27 84), on Vörösmarty tér. Open Mon.-Fri. 7:30am-5pm.

Embassies: Australia, XII, Királyhágó tér 8/9 (tel. 201 88 99). M2: Déli pu., then bus 21 to "Királyhágó tér." Open Mon.-Fri. 9am-noon. **Canada,** XII, Zugligeti út 51-53 (tel. 275 12 00). Take bus 158 from Moszkva tér to the last stop. Open Mon.-Fri. 9-11am. **New Zealanders** should contact the British embassy. **U.K.,** V, Harmincad u. 6 (tel. 266 28 88), off the corner of Vörösmarty tér. M1: Vörösmarty tér. Open Mon.-Fri. 9:30am-noon and 2:30-4pm. **U.S.,** V, Szabadság tér 12 (tel. 267 44 00). M2: Kossuth Lajos; walk down Akademia and turn left on Zoltán. Open Mon. and Wed. 8:30am-11am; Tues., Thurs., and Fri. 8:30-10:30am.

Currency Exchange: The bureaus with longer hours generally have less favorable rates. **General Banking and Trust Co. Ltd.,** Váci u. 19/21 (tel. 118 96 88; fax 118 82 30), has excellent rates. Open Mon.-Fri. 9am-4:30pm. **IBUSZ,** V, Petőfi tér 3, just north of Erzsébet híd. Cash advances on Visa and ATM machine for Cirrus. Open 24hr. **GWK Tours** (tel. 322 90 11), in the Keleti Station. Good rates and convenient for rail travelers. Open daily 6am-9pm. **Citibank,** Vörösmarty tér 4 (tel. 138 26 66; fax 266 98 45). Efficient and pleasant. Open Mon.-Fri. 9am-4pm.

American Express: V, Deák Ferenc u. 10 (tel. 266 86 80; fax 267 20 28). M1: Vörösmarty tér, next to Hotel Kempinski. Sells traveler's checks and cashes checks in US$ for a 6% commission. Cash advances only in forints. Mail held free for cardholders. AmEx **ATM.** Open July-Sept. Mon.-Fri. 9am-6:30pm, Sat. 9am-2pm; Oct.-June Mon.-Fri. 9am-5:30pm, Sat. 9am-1pm.

Flights: Ferihegy Airport (tel. 267 43 33, info tel. 157 71 55, reservations tel. 157 91 23). Volánbusz (every 30min. between 5:30am and 9pm) takes 30min. to terminal 1 and 40min. to terminal 2 (300Ft) from Erzsébet tér. The **airport shuttle bus** (tel.

296 85 55) will pick you up anywhere in the city, or take you anywhere from the airport (1000Ft). Call for pick-up a few hours in advance. Youth and stand-by discounts available at the **Malév office** (see **Budget Travel,** above).

Trains: For domestic info, call 322 78 60; for international 142 91 50. The word for train station is *pályaudvar,* often abbreviated "pu." Those under 26 get a 33% discount on international tickets. Show your ISIC and tell the clerk *"diák"* (*DEE-ak*, student). The three main stations—**Keleti pu., Nyugati pu.,** and **Déli pu.**—are also Metro stops. Each station has schedules for the others. To: Belgrade (6½hr., 6350Ft), Berlin (12½hr., 16,200Ft), Prague (7½hr., 8230Ft), Vienna (3½hr., 5100Ft), and Warsaw (10hr., 8430Ft). The daily **Orient Express** arrives from Berlin and continues on to Bucharest. **Luggage storage** at Keleti pu. (80Ft).

Buses: Volánbusz main station, V, Erzsébet tér (tel. 117 25 62). M1, 2, 3: Deák tér. To: Berlin (14½hr., 13,800Ft), Bratislava (3½hr., 1450Ft), Prague (8½hr., 3100Ft), and Vienna (3hr., 3150Ft). Buses to the Czech Republic, Slovakia, Poland, Romania, Turkey, and Ukraine depart from the **Népstadion** terminal on Hungária körút 48/52, as do most domestic buses to eastern Hungary. M2: Népstadion. Buses to the Danube Bend leave from the **Árpád híd** station.

Public Transportation: The **Metro (M)** is rapid and punctual. There are 3 lines—M1 is yellow, M2 is red, and M3 is blue. "M" indicates a stop, but you won't always find the sign on the street; look for stairs leading down. Most public transportation stops about 11:30pm. The subway, buses, and trams all use the same yellow **tickets** which are sold in Metro stations, *Trafik* shops, and by some sidewalk vendors. A single-trip ticket costs 60Ft; punch it in the orange boxes at the gate of the Metro or on board buses and trams (10-trip *tíz jegy* 540Ft, 1-day pass 500Ft, 3-day pass 1000Ft). The **HÉV commuter rail** runs between Batthyány tér in Buda and Szentendre, 40min. north on the Danube Bend, every 15min.

Hydrofoils: MAHART International Boat Station, VI, Belgrád rakpart (tel. 118 15 86; fax 118 77 40), on the Duna near Erzsébet híd, has information and tickets. Open Mon.-Fri. 8am-4pm. Or try **IBUSZ,** VII, Dob u. (tel. 322 16 56; fax 322 72 64). M2: Astoria. Open Mon.-Fri. 8am-4pm. Arrive at the docks 1hr. before departure for customs and passport control. Eurailpass holders receive a 50% discount. To Vienna (6hr., 12,100Ft, students 9000Ft).

Taxis: Főtaxi, tel. 222 22 22. **Budataxi,** tel. 233 33 33. 100Ft base fare plus 80Ft per km. Stay away from other companies and especially avoid the Mercedes-Benz taxis, which charge double the jalopy fee. Taxis are more expensive at night.

English Bookstore: Bestsellers KFT, V, Október 6 u. 11, near Arany János u. M: Deák tér or M1: Vörösmarty tér. Open Mon.-Fri. 9am-6:30pm, Sat. 10am-6pm.

Gay and Lesbian Organizations: Cruise Victory Co., II Váci u., 9 (tel./fax 267 38 05). Eponymous free brochure with gay listings. Open Mon.-Fri. 9am-6pm.

Laundromats: Irisz Szalon, VII, Rákóczi út 8b. M2: Astoria. Wash 350Ft per 5kg. Dry 120Ft per 15min. Pay the cashier before you start. Open Mon.-Fri. 7am-7pm, Sat. 7am-1pm. Many youth hostels have washing machines for a fee.

Pharmacies: I, Széna tér 1 (tel. 202 18 16); VI, Teréz krt. 41 (tel. 111 44 39); IX, Boráros tér 3 (tel. 117 07 43); and IX, Üllői út 121 (tel. 133 89 47). Open 24hr. At night, call the number on the door or ring the bell; there is a small fee.

Medical Assistance: tel. 204 55 00 or 204 55 01. English spoken. Open 24hr.

Emergencies: Ambulance: tel. 104. **Fire:** tel. 105.

Police: tel. 107. For tourist police, call 112 15 37.

Post Office: *Poste Restante* at V, Városház u. 18 (tel. 118 48 11). Open Mon.-Fri. 8am-8pm, Sat. 8am-3pm. 24hr. **branches** at Nyugati station, VI, Teréz krt. 105-107, and Keleti station, VIII, Baross tér 11c. English generally spoken. Sending mail via American Express may be better. **Postal Code:** 1052.

Telephones: V, Petőfi Sándor u. 17. English-speaker usually on hand. Fax service. Open Mon.-Fri. 8am-8pm, Sat.-Sun. 8am-2pm. Or try the post office. Many public phones use **phone cards,** available at newsstands, post offices, and Metro stations. 50-unit card 750Ft. 120-unit card 1750Ft. **Card phones** are better than coin phones for **international calls,** but both will probably cut you off. **Telephone Code:** 1.

ACCOMMODATIONS AND CAMPING

Travelers arriving in Keleti station enter a frenzy of hostel hucksters. Always ask that a solicitor show you on a map where the lodging is located, and inspect your room before you pay. It may be wiser to head directly to an accommodation agency, hostel, or guesthouse. Whatever approach you choose, make sure that the room is easily accessible by public transportation, preferably by Metro, which arrives more frequently than buses. The area around Keleti station is a favorite of thieves.

Accommodations Agencies

Accommodation services are overrunning Budapest. The rates (1200-5000Ft per person) depend on location and bathroom quality. Haggle stubbornly. Arrive around 8am and you may get a single for 1400Ft or a double for 1800Ft. Travelers who stay for more than four nights can obtain a somewhat better rate. Most agencies allow travelers to see rooms before accepting them.

To-Ma Tour, V, Október 6. u. 22 (tel. 153 08 19; fax 269 57 15), promises to find you a central room, even if only for one night. Doubles 2100-4000Ft, with private bathroom 3200Ft. 20% off if you stay more than a month. Open Mon.-Fri. 9am-noon and 1-8pm, Sat.-Sun. 9am-5pm.

Budapest Tourist, V, Roosevelt tér 5 (tel. 117 35 55; fax 118 16 58), near Hotel Forum, 10min. from Deák tér on the Pest end of Széchenyi lánchíd. A well-established enterprise. Singles 2000-2800Ft. Doubles 4800Ft. Open Mon.-Thurs. 9am-5pm, Fri. 9am-3pm. Same hours at branches throughout the city.

IBUSZ, at all train stations and tourist centers. **24hr. accommodation office,** V, Apáczai Csere J. u. 1 (tel. 118 39 25; fax 117 90 99). An established service offering the most rooms in Budapest. Private rooms 1800-3600Ft per person. Swarms of people outside IBUSZ offices push "bargains"; quality varies, but they're legal. Old women asking *"Privatzimmer?"* are vending private rooms.

Pension Centrum, XII, Szarvas Gábor út 24 (tel. 201 93 86 or 176 00 57). A non-profit group that makes reservations in private rooms. Open daily 10am-7pm.

Duna Tours, Bajcsy-Zsilinszky út 17 (tel. 131 45 33 or 111 56 30; fax 111 68 27), next to Cooptourist. The English-speaking staff administers rooms in districts V and VI. Doubles from 2400Ft. Open Mon.-Fri. 9:30am-noon and 12:30-5pm.

Hostels

Most hostel-type accommodations, including university dorms, are under the aegis of **Express.** Try their office at V, Semmelweis u. 4 (tel. 117 66 34 or 117 86 00); leave Deák tér on Tanács krt., head right on Gerlóczy u., then take the first left. Or try the branch at V, Szabadság tér 16 (tel. 131 77 77), between M3: Arany János and M2: Kossuth tér. Again, be cautious when accepting a room at the train station.

Open year-round

Backpack Guesthouse, XI, Takács Menyhért u. 33 (tel. 185 50 89). From Keleti pu. or the city center, take bus 1, 7, or 7A (black numbers) heading toward Buda and disembark at "Tétényi u.," after the rail bridge. Go back under the bridge, turn left, and follow the street parallel to the train tracks for 3 blocks. Look for the small green signs. Carpeted rooms, clean bathrooms, and humor in every niche. 1000-1100Ft. Hot showers, private locker, and use of kitchen, TV, and VCR.

Nicholas's Budget Hostel, XI, Takács Menyhért u. 12 (tel. 185 48 70). Follow the directions to the Backpack Guesthouse (see above), then continue a half block down the road. Spacious, clean hostel with TV, garden, kitchen. Dorms 1000Ft. Doubles 3200Ft. Bedding 500Ft. Laundry 600Ft per 5 kg. Reservations accepted.

Summer Hostels

Almost all dorms of the **Technical University** (Műegyetem) become youth hostels in July and August; they are conveniently located in district XI, around Móricz Zsigmond Körtér. From M3: Kálvin tér, ride tram 47 or 49 across the river to "M. Zsigmond." For more information, call the **International Student Center** (tel. 166 77 58 or 166 50 11, ext. 1469). In summer, the center also has an office in Schönherz.

Martos, XI, Stoczek u. 5/7 (tel. 463 37 76; tel./fax 463 36 51), near the Technical University. The cheapest rooms in town, independent and student-run. Free use of washers, dryers, and kitchens. **Internet access.** Hall bathrooms. Check-out 9am. Singles 1800Ft. Doubles 2400Ft. 6-person apartment 9000Ft.

Strawberry Youth Hostels, IX, Ráday u. 43/45 (tel. 218 47 66), and Kinizsi u. 2/6 (tel. 217 30 33). M3: Kálvin tér. Two converted university dorms within a block of one another in Pest, off Kálvin tér. Check-out 10am. Spacious rooms with refrigerators and sinks. No bunk beds. Doubles 4060Ft. Triples 5760Ft. Quads 7680Ft. Old washing machines free; new ones 160Ft. 10% off with HI card.

Universitas, XI, Irinyi József u. 9/11 (tel. 463 38 25 or 463 38 26). First stop after crossing the river on tram 4 or 6. Check-out 9am. In-room fridges. Communal bathrooms. Doubles 4320Ft. Laundry 200Ft. Satellite TV, active nightlife in the disco and bar on weekends. HI members 10% off. Fine cafeteria with 540Ft *menü*.

Guest Houses

Guest houses and rooms for rent in private homes include a personal touch for about the same as an anonymous hostel bed. Proprietors carry cellular telephones so they can always be reached for reservations. In stations, bypass the pushier hostel representatives and look for the quieter ones hanging around in the background.

Caterina, V, Andrássy út 47, III. 48 (tel. 291 95 38, cellular tel. 06 20 34 63 98). Take M1 or tram 4 or 6 to "Oktogon." A century-old building only a few min. from downtown Pest. Two guest bathrooms. 1000Ft. Owners speak only some English.

Weisses Haus, III, Erdőalja u. 11 (cellular tel. 06 20 34 36 31). Take bus 137 from Flórián tér to "Iskola." On a hillside in residential Óbuda. Panoramic view of northern Pest across the Danube. 4000Ft per room. Breakfast included.

"Townhouser's" International Guesthouse, XVI, Attila u. 123 (cellular tel. 06 30 44 23 31; fax 342 07 95). M2: Örs Vezér tere, then 5 stops on bus 31 to Diófa u. A quiet residential area 30min. from downtown. Five spacious guest rooms, with two or three beds each, and two clean bathrooms. Kitchen available for guests' use. Owners transport guests to and from the train station. 1200Ft per person.

Ms. Vali Németh, VIII, Osztály u. 20/24 A11 (tel. 113 88 46, cellular tel. 06 30 47 53 48), 400m east of M2: Népstadion. Two doubles, one triple, and one bathroom close to the bus station, grocery stores, and a restaurant. 1500Ft per person.

Hotels

Budapest's few affordable hotels are frequently clogged with groups, so call ahead. Proprietors often speak English. All hotels should be registered with Tourinform.

Hotel Góliát, XIII, Kerekes út 12-20 (tel. 270 14 55; fax 149 49 85). M1: Árpád híd, then take the tram away from the river and get off before the overpass. Walk down Reitler Ferere ut. until you see the 10-story yellow building on the left. Clean, spacious rooms. Singles 2000Ft. Doubles 2500Ft.

Hotel Citadella, Citadella Sétány (tel. 166 57 94; fax 186 05 05), atop Gellért Hill. Take tram 47 or 49 three stops into Buda to "Móricz Zsigmond Körtér," then catch bus 27 to "Citadella." Perfect location and spacious rooms. Doubles, triples, and quads US$40-58. Usually packed, so write or fax to reserve.

Camping

Camping Hungary, available at tourist offices, describes Budapest's campgrounds.

Római Camping, III, Szentendrei út 189 (tel. 168 62 60; fax 250 04 26). M2: Batthyány tér, then take the HÉV commuter rail to "Római fürdő," and walk 100m toward the river. Tip-top security with grocery, swimming pool, and huge park on the site. Common showers. Reception open 24hr. 650Ft per person, students 500Ft; 780Ft per tent, students 600Ft. Bungalows 1800-6000Ft.

Hárs-hegyi, II, Hárs-hegyi út 5/7 (tel./fax 200 88 03). From "Moszkva tér," bus 22 to "Dénes u." Currency exchange and restaurant. 600Ft per tent, students 550Ft.

Riviera Camping, III, Királyok u. 257/259 (tel. 160 82 18). Take the HÉV commuter rail from Batthyány tér to "Romai fürdö," then bus 34 until you see the campground (10min.). Restaurant. 500Ft per tent. Bungalows 2300Ft. Open year-round.

FOOD

Most restaurants in Budapest will fit your budget, though the food at family eateries may be cheaper and yummier. An average meal runs 700-900Ft, and a 10% tip is usual, plus another 10% for live music. Seek out a *kifőzde* or *vendéglő* for a taste of Hungarian life. Cafeterias lurk under **Önkiszolgáló Étterem** signs (vegetarian entrees 180Ft; meat entrees 300-400Ft). Travelers may also rely on grocery stores and markets. The king of them all is the **Central Market,** V, Kőzraktár tér u. 1 (M3: Kelvin tér; open Mon. 6am-4pm, Tues.-Fri. 6am-6pm, Sat. 6am-2pm). You can also shop at the **produce market,** IX, Vámház krt. 1/3, at Fővám tér (open Mon. 6am-3pm); the **ABC Food Hall,** I, Batthyány tér 5/7 (open Sun. 7am-1pm); or the **Non-Stops** at V, Október 6. u. 5 and V, Régi Posta u., off Váci u. past McDonald's.

Fatâl Restaurant, V, Váci u. 67. One of the most popular restaurants in Budapest. Large, hearty, and delicious Hungarian meals in pleasant, rustic surroundings. Entrees 450-1000Ft. Open daily 11am-11pm.

Paprika, V, Varosáz u. 10. Cafeteria food from 260Ft, but come here for the bakery. Tasty snacks 50-80Ft. Open Mon.-Fri. 11am-4pm, Sat. 11am-3pm.

Marxim, II, Kis Rókus u. 23. M2: Moszkva tér. With your back to the Lego-like castle, walk along Margit krt. KGB pizza (300Ft) and Lenin salad (120-200Ft) are prepared by the staff according to their abilities, consumed by the patrons according to their needs. Open Mon.-Thurs. noon-1am, Fri.-Sat. noon-2am, Sun. 6pm-1am.

Vegetárium, V, Cukor u. 3. 1½ blocks from M3: Ferenciek tere. Walk up Ferenciek tere (once Károlyi M. u.) to Irány u. on the right, and take a quick left. Elaborate, imaginative veggie dishes 500-900Ft. 15% off with ISIC. Open daily noon-10pm.

Remiz, II, Budakeszi út 8 (tel. 275 13 96). Take bus 158 from "Moszkva tér" to "Szépilona" (about 10min.), and walk three stores past the stop. Traditional and tasty Hungarian cuisine in a fancy setting. Entrees 720-1400Ft. Outdoor seating in warm weather. Live music. Open daily 9am-1am. Call for reservations.

Alföldi Kisvendéglő, V, Kecskeméti u. 4. M3: Kálvin tér, past Best Western. Traditional folk cuisine—even the booths are paprika-red. The spicy, sumptuous rolls (60Ft) are reason enough to come. Entrees 400-800Ft. Open daily 11am-midnight.

Picasso Point Kávéház, VI, Hajós u. 31. Make a right onto Hajós u. two blocks north of M3: Arany János. A Bohemian hang-out with Hungarian, French, Tex-Mex offerings. Dance club downstairs. Open daily noon-4am.

New York Bagels (The Sequel), VI, Bajcsy-Zsilinszky út 21. M3: Arany János u. Assorted bagels baked hourly, freshly made spreads, sandwiches, salads, and cookies. Bagel sandwich specials 500Ft, or design your own. Open daily 7am-10pm.

Marquis de Salade, VI, Hajós u. 43, corner of Bajcsy-Zsilinszky út two blocks north of M3: Arany János. Self-service mix of salads, Middle Eastern, and Bengali food in a tiny, cozy storefront. Most dishes 500-730Ft. Open daily noon-midnight.

Cafés

These amazing establishments were once the pretentious haunts of Budapest's literary, intellectual, and cultural elite. A café repose is a must for every visitor; the absurdly ornate pastries are inexpensive, even in the most genteel establishments.

Café Mozart, VII Erzsébet krt 36. M2: Blaha Lujza Tér. Newly opened café serves 75 different coffee drinks (120Ft-310Ft) and almost as many ice cream creations. Shiny, glitzy environment and some of the best drinks in town.

Művész Kávéház, VI, Andrássy út 29, diagonally across the street from the State Opera House. M1: Opera. Golden period wood panelling and gilded ceilings. One of Budapest's most elegant. Open daily 10am-midnight.

Café New York, VII, Erzsébet krt. 9/11. M2: Blaha Lujza tér. One of the most beautiful cafés in Budapest, with plenty of velvet, gold, and marble. Cappuccino 200Ft. Ice cream and coffee delights 30-500Ft. Filling Hungarian entrees from 920Ft served downstairs noon-10pm. Open daily 9am-midnight.

Café Pierrot, I, Fortuna u. 14. Antique clown dolls hang from the curvaceous walls. Espresso 120Ft. Fabulous crepes *(palacsinta)* 350Ft. Open daily 11am-1am. Live piano music daily from 8:30pm.

SIGHTS

Buda The **Castle District** rests 100m above the Duna, atop the 2km mound called **Várhegy** (Castle Hill). Find a path up the hill, or cross the **Széchenyi lánchíd** (Széchenyi Chain Bridge) from Pest and ride the *sikló* (cable car) to the top (operates daily 7:30am-10pm; closed 2nd and 4th Mon. of each month; 150Ft). Built in the 13th century, the hilltop castle was leveled in sieges by Mongols then Ottoman Turks. Christian Hapsburg forces razed the rebuilt castle while ousting the Turks after a 145-year occupation. A reconstruction was completed just in time to be destroyed by the Germans in 1945. Determined Hungarians pasted the castle together once more, only to face the new Soviet menace—bullet holes in the palace facade recall the tanks of 1956. The current **Budavári palota** (Royal Palace) houses several notable museums. During recent reconstruction, excavations revealed artifacts from the earliest castle here; they are now displayed in Wing E in the **Budapesti Történeti.** (Budapest History Museum. Open March-Oct. daily 10am-6pm; Nov.-Dec. 10am-5pm; Jan.-Feb. Tues.-Sun. 10am-4pm. 100Ft, students 50Ft, Wed. free.) Wing A contains the **Kortárs Művészeti Múzeum** (Museum of Contemporary Art) and the **Ludwig Museum,** a collection of international modern art (open Tues.-Sun. 10am-6pm; 100Ft, students 50Ft, Tues. free). Wings B-D hold the **Magyar Nemzeti Galéria** (Hungarian National Gallery), a vast hoard of the best Hungarian painting and sculpture. (Open Tues.-Sun. 10am-6pm. 150Ft, students 40Ft, for all 3 wings. English tour 200Ft.)

From the castle, stroll down Színház u. and Tárnok u. to **Szentháromság tér** (Trinity Square), site of the Disney-esque **Fisherman's Bastion.** This arcaded stone wall supports a squat, fairy-tale tower, but you'll have to pay for the magnificent view across the Danube (50Ft). Behind the tower stands the delicate, neo-Gothic **Mátyás templom** (Matthias Church); it served as a mosque for 145 years after the Turks seized Buda. These days, high mass is celebrated Sundays at 10am with orchestra and choir. On summer Fridays at 8pm, organ concerts reverberate in the resplendent interior (open daily 7am-7pm). Intricate door-knockers and balconies adorn the Castle District's other historic buildings; ramble through **Úri u.** (Gentlemen's Street) among Baroque townhouses, or **Táncsics Mihály u.** in the old Jewish quarter. Enjoy a tremendous view of Buda from the Castle District's west walls.

The **Szabadság Szobor** (Liberation Monument) crowns neighboring **Gellért-hegy,** just south of the castle. This 30m bronze woman honors Soviet soldiers who died while liberating Hungary from the Nazis. The hill itself is named for the 11th-century bishop sent by the Pope to help King Stephen convert the Magyars. Unconvinced Magyars hurled poor St. Gellért to his death from atop the hill. His statue overlooks the **Erzsébet híd** (Elizabeth Bridge). The **Citadella,** adjacent to the Liberation Monument, was built as a symbol of Hapsburg power after the 1848 revolution; climb the hill to it from Hotel Gellért (bus 27 also drives up).

North of the castle, the **Margit híd** spans the Danube and connects to the **Margitsziget** (Margaret Island). Off-limits to private cars, the island offers capacious thermal baths, luxurious garden pathways, and numerous shaded terraces. According to legend, the *sziget* is named after King Béla IV's daughter; he vowed to rear young Margit as a nun if the nation survived the Mongol invasion of 1241. The Mongols decimated Hungary but did not destroyed it, and Margaret was confined to the island convent. Take bus 26 from "Szt. István krt." to the island.

Pest Across the Danube lies Pest, the capital's throbbing commercial and administrative center. The old **Inner City,** rooted in the pedestrian zone of Váci u. and Vörösmarty tér, is a tourist haven. On the riverbank, a string of modern luxury hotels leads up to the magnificent neo-Gothic **Ovszágház** (Parliament) in Kossuth tér (arrange 1500Ft tours at IBUSZ and Budapest Tourist). Nearby, at Kossuth tér 12 in the former Hungarian Supreme Court, the **Néprajzi múzeum** (Museum of Ethnography) hosts an outstanding exhibit of pre-World War I Hungarian folk culture. (Open March-Nov. Tues.-Sun. 10am-5:45pm; Dec.-Feb. Tues.-Sun. 10am-4pm. 200Ft, students 60Ft.)

Sz. István Bazilika (St. Stephen's Basilica), two blocks north of Deák tér, is by far the city's largest church, with room for 8500 worshippers. Climb 302 spiraling steps to the Panorama tower for a 360-degree view of the city (open April-Oct. daily 10am-6:30pm; 200Ft, students 100Ft). St. Stephen's holy **right hand,** one of Hungary's most revered religious relics, is displayed in the **Basilica museum.** (Basilica open Mon.-Sat. 9am-5pm, Sun. 1-5pm. 120Ft, students 60Ft. Museum open April-Sept. Mon.-Sat. 9am-4:30pm, Sun. 1-4:30pm; Oct.-March Mon.-Sat. 10am-4pm, Sun. 1-4pm.) At the corner of Dohány u. and Wesselényi u., the **Zsinagóga** (Synagogue) is the largest active temple in Europe and the second largest in the world (open Mon.-Sat. 10am-2:30pm, Sun. 10am-1:30pm; 400Ft, students 200Ft). Next door, the **Jewish Museum** juxtaposes magnificent exhibits dating back to the Middle Ages with haunting documentation of the Holocaust (open April-Oct. Mon.-Fri. 10am-3pm, Sun. 10am-1pm; 150Ft.).

To the east of the basilica, **Andrássy út,** Hungary's grandest boulevard, extends from the edge of Belváros in downtown Pest to **Hősök tere** (Heroes' Square), some 2km away. The **Magyar Állami Operaház** (Hungarian State Opera House), VI, Andrássy út 22 (M1: Opera), is laden with sculptures and paintings in the ornate Empire style of the 1880s. If you can't actually see an opera, at least take a tour (daily at 3 and 4pm; 400Ft, students 200Ft). The **Millenniumi emlékmű** (Millennium Monument), commemorating the nation's most prominent leaders and national heroes from 896 to 1896, dominates Hősök tere. The **Szépművészeti Múzeum** (Museum of Fine Arts) on the square maintains a splendid collection; highlights include an entire room devoted to El Greco and an exhaustive display of Renaissance works. (Open Tues.-Sun. 10am-5:30pm. 200Ft, with ISIC 100Ft. Tours for up to 5 people 1500Ft.)

Behind the monument, the **Városliget** (City Park) is home to a circus, an amusement park, a zoo, a castle, and the impressive **Széchenyi Baths.** The **Vajdahunyad Vára** (Castle), created for the Millenary Exhibition of 1896, incorporates Romanesque, Gothic, Renaissance, and Baroque styles. Outside the castle broods the hooded statue of **Anonymous,** the secretive scribe to whom we owe much of our knowledge of medieval Hungary. Rent a **rowboat** (June to mid-Sept. daily 9am-8pm) or **ice skates** (Nov.-March daily 9am-1pm and 4-8pm; 80Ft) on the lake by the castle.

The ruins of the north Budapest garrison town of **Aquincum** crumble in the outer regions of the third district. To reach the area, take M2: Batthyány tér, then the HÉV to "Aquincum"; the site is about 100m south of the HÉV stop. Here are the most impressive vestiges of the Roman occupation which spanned the first four centuries AD. The **museum** on the grounds contains a model of the ancient city, musical instruments, and other household items (open March-Oct. 10am-6pm, Nov.-Feb. 10am-4pm; 100Ft, students 50Ft). The remains of the **Roman Military Baths** are visible to the south of the Roman encampment, beside the overpass at Flórián tér near the "Árpád híd" HÉV station. From the stop, follow the main road away from the river.

ENTERTAINMENT AND NIGHTLIFE

Budapest hosts cultural events year-round. Pick up a copy of the English-language monthly *Programme in Hungary, Budapest Panorama,* or *Pestiest,* all available free at tourist offices; they contain daily listings of all concerts, operas, and theater performances in the city. The "Style" section of the weekly English-language *Budapest Sun* is another excellent source for schedules of entertainment happenings.

The **Central Theater Booking Office,** VI, Andrassy út 18 (tel. 112 00 07), next to the Opera House, and the branch at Moszkva tér 3 (tel. 212 56 78; both open Mon.-Fri. 10am-5pm), sell commission-free tickets to almost every performance in the city. An extravaganza at the gilded, neo-Renaissance **State Opera House,** VI, Andrássy út 22 (tel. 332 81 97; M1: Opera), costs only US$4-5; the box office (tel. 153 01 70), on the left side of the building, sells unclaimed tickets at even better prices 30min. before showtime (open Tues.-Sat. 11am-1:45pm and 2:30-7pm, Sun. 10am-1pm and 4-7pm). The **Philharmonic Orchestra** is also world-renowned; concerts thunder through town almost every evening September to June. The ticket office (tel. 117 62

Like a Troubled Bridge over Water...

The citizens of Budapest are justly proud of the bridges that bind Buda to Pest. The four great lions that have guarded the **Széchenyi lánchíd** (Széchenyi Chain Bridge) since 1849 make the bridge one of the most recognizable. These beasts were created by János Marschalkó in a naturalistic style, with the tongues resting far back in their gaping mouths. The anatomical correctness of their new mascots did not impress Budapestians—distraught by public laughter over the seemingly missing tongues, Marschalkó jumped from the bridge to his death. Another version of the story has the king reprimanding Marschalkó, with the same result. *Let's Go* does not recommend sculpting lions without visible tongues.

22) is located at Vörösmarty tér 1. (Open Mon.-Fri. 10am-6pm, Sat.-Sun. 10am-2pm. Tickets 1000-1500Ft; 400Ft more on the day of performance.)

In late summer, the Philharmonic and Opera take sabbaticals, but summer theaters and concert halls are ready to pick up the slack. In July, classical music and opera are performed at 8:30pm in the **Hilton Hotel Courtyard,** I, Hess András tér 1/3 (tel. 214 30 00), next to Mátyás templom in the Castle District. The **Margitsziget Theater,** XIII, Margitsziget (tel. 111 24 96), features opera and Hungarian-music concerts on its open-air stage. Take tram 4 or 6 to "Margitsziget." Try **Zichy Mansion Courtyard,** III, Fő tér 1, for orchestral concerts, or the **Pest Concert Hall** (Vigadó), V, Vigadó tér 2 (tel. 118 99 03; fax 175 62 22), on the Danube bank near Vörösmarty tér, for operettas (cashier open Mon.-Sat. 10am-6pm; tickets 3200Ft). Folk-dancers stomp across the stage at the **Buda Park Theater,** XI, Kosztolányi Dezső tér (tel. 117 62 22); brochures and concert tickets flood from the ticket office at Vörösmarty tér 1 (open Mon.-Fri. 11am-6pm; tickets 200-300Ft). For a psychedelic evening, try the laser shows at the **Planetarium** (tel. 134 11 61; M3: Népliget). The multi-media sorcery even reunites the Beatles on occasion, with perhaps more tuneful results than "Free as a Bird." (Wed.-Thurs. and Sat. 6:30, 8, and 9:30pm; Mon. and Fri. 8 and 9:30pm; Tues. 6:30 and 9:30pm.) The **Budapest Spring Festival** in late March and the **Budapest Arts Weeks** each fall showcase Hungarian art and music. Check with **Music Mix 33 Ticket Service,** V, Vaci u. 33 (tel. 266 70 70), for pop concerts.

A virtually unenforced drinking age and cheap drinks draw old and young alike to Budapest's clubs and bars. As clubs become more and more sophisticated, the cover prices are rising—a night of techno may soon cost the same as an opera ticket.

Old Man's Pub, VII, Akácfa u. 13 (tel. 322 76 45). M2: Blaha Lujza tér. Live blues and jazz in a classy and upscale environment. Kitchen serves pizza, spaghetti, and salads. Occasional free samples of beer. Open Mon.-Sat. 3pm-dawn.

Morrison's Music Pub, VI, Révay u. 25, left of the State Opera House. M1: Opera. Pub and dance club with a young, international crowd. Beer 240Ft. Junc-Aug. cover 400Ft. Open daily 8:30am-4pm.

Angel Bar, VII, Rákóczi út 51. M2: Blaha Lujza tér. Bar, popular disco for the city's gay community. Transvestite shows Fri.-Sun. at 11pm. Open nightly 10pm-dawn.

Made-Inn Music Club, VI, Andrassy út 112. M1: Bajza u. Crowds come for the frequent live bands in this cavernous club. Cover varies. Open Wed.-Sun. 8pm-5am.

Véndiák (Former Student), V, Egyetem tér 5. M2: Kálvin tér. Walk up Kecskeméti u. Late-night bar with a lively dance floor after midnight. Popular with local students during the school year. Open Mon. 9pm-2am, Tues.-Sat. 9pm-5am.

Bahnhof, on the north side of Nyugati train station. M3: Nyugati pu. One of the most popular dance clubs and with good reason; guaranteed no techno and two superb dance floors. Well ventilated. Cover 400Ft. Open Mon.-Sat. 6pm-4am.

E-Play Cyberclub, VI, Terez krt. 55, by the McDonald's in the station. M3: Nyugati pu. More fog and lights per person than any other dance club. Cover 600Ft.

Danube Bend (Dunakanyar)

On its way from Vienna along the Slovak border, the Danube sweeps south in a dramatic arc known as the Danube Bend *(Dunakanyar)* before reaching Budapest. This lush and relaxed region is deservedly one of the great tourist attractions in Hungary.

Szentendre By far the most tourist-thronged of the Danube bend cities, Szentendre's proximity to Budapest, narrow cobblestone streets, and wealth of art galleries keep the visitors coming. On Szentendre's **Templomdomb** (Church Hill), above Fő tér, sits the 13th-century Roman Catholic **parish church.** Facing it, the **Czóbel Museum** exhibits works of Hungary's foremost Impressionist, Béla Czóbel. (Open March 15-Oct. 31 Tues.-Sun. 10am-4pm; off-season Fri.-Sun. 10am-4pm. 90Ft, students 50Ft.) To the north across Alkotmány u., the Baroque **Serbian Orthodox Church** displays Serbian religious art (open Wed.-Sun. 10am-4pm; 60Ft). Szentendre's most impressive museum, **Kovács Margit Múzeum,** Vastagh György u. 1, exhibits brilliant ceramic sculptures and tiles by the 20th-century Hungarian artist Margit Kovács. (Open March 15-Oct. 31 Tues.-Sun. 10am-6pm; Nov.1-March 14 Tues.-Sun. 10am-4pm. 250Ft, students 150Ft.) **Szabó Marcipán Múzeum,** Dumtsa Jenő u. 7 (tel. (26) 31 14 84), chronicles marzipan's history and production with clever and tasty displays (open daily 10am-6pm; 100Ft, students and seniors 50Ft).

The HÉV, train, and bus station is south of the Old Town; to get to Fő tér, use the underpass, and head up Kossuth u. The HÉV **commuter rail** leaves for Budapest's Batthyány tér (every 20min., 45min., 168Ft). **Buses** run from Budapest's Árpád bridge station (every 10-40min., 30min.-1hr., 126Ft), many continuing past Szentendre to Visegrád (45min. farther) and Esztergom (1½hr from Szentendre). The **MAHART boat pier** is a 10-minute walk north of Fő tér (3 per day to Budapest, 420Ft, students 295Ft; May 17-Aug. 31 only). The helpful staff of **Tourinform,** Dumsta Jenő u. 22 (tel. (26) 31 79 65 or 31 79 66), provides 50Ft maps and brochures (open Mon.-Fri. 10am-4pm, Sat.-Sun. 10am-2pm). **IBUSZ,** Bogdányi u. 4 (tel. (26) 31 03 33), changes money and finds private doubles (2000-3000F; open Mon.-Fri. 9am-4pm; June 15-Sept. 30 also Sat.-Sun. 10am-2pm). **Ilona Panzió,** Rákóczi Ferenc u. 11 (tel. (26) 31 35 99), near the center of town, has clean doubles with private baths (3500Ft, 2500Ft for one person; breakfast included). **Pap-szigeti Camping** (tel. (26) 31 06 97) is 1km north of the town center on Pap-sziget island and has rooms with three beds (2 people 2500Ft, 1 person 1000Ft), bungalows (triples 3000Ft), and tent sites (600Ft per person).

Esztergom If you can't find the Esztergom **cathedral,** you're either too close or in the wrong town; step back and look up. Hungary's largest church, consecrated in 1856, is responsible for the town's nickname "The Hungarian Rome." On a smaller scale, the red marble **Bakócz Chapel** on the south side of the cathedral is a masterwork of Renaissance Tuscan stone-carving. Climb to the 71.5m high **cupola** for a view of Slovakia (50Ft), or descend into the **crypt** to honor the remains of Hungary's archbishops (open daily 9am-5pm). The **cathedral treasury** (Kincstár), on the north side of the main altar, protects Hungary's most extensive ecclesiastical collection. The jewel-studded cross labeled #78 in the case facing the entrance to the main collection is the **Coronation Cross,** on which Hungary's rulers pledged their oaths until 1916 (open daily 9am-4:30pm; 130Ft, students 65Ft). Nearby stands the restored 12th-century **Esztergom Palace.** (Open in summer Tues.-Sun. 9am-4:30pm; off-season 10am-3:30pm. 80Ft, students 20Ft, free with ISIC.) For an extra 10Ft, you can ascend to the roof to survey the kingdom. At the foot of the hill, **Keresztény Múzeum** (Christian Museum), Berenyi Zsigmond u. 2, houses exceptional Renaissance religious artwork (open Tues.-Sun. 10am-6pm; 100Ft, students 50Ft).

Trains connect to Budapest (1½hr., 278Ft). Catch **buses** a few blocks south of Rákóczi tér—take Simor János u. straight up—to Budapest (1½hr., 292Ft) and Szentendre (1hr., 214Ft). Three times a day, **MAHART boats** depart from the pier (tel. (33) 31 35 31) at the end of Gőzhajó u., on Primas Sziget island in the south, for Visegrád (1½hr., 420Ft) and Szentendre (3½hr., 880Ft) on the way to Budapest (5hr.,

1218Ft). Twice a day on weekends a **hydrofoil** leaves from the same pier and scoots directly to Budapest (1hr.) and Visegrád (40min.). To reach the central Rákóczi tér from the train station, walk up Baross Gábor út, make a right onto Kiss János Altábornagy út, and keep going straight as it becomes Kossuth Lajos u. **Gran Tours,** Széchenyi tér 25 (tel./ fax (33) 41 37 56), at the edge of Rákóczi tér, provides maps and arranges 1400Ft singles or 2500Ft doubles (open Mon.-Fri. 8am-4pm, Sat. 8am-noon; off-season closed Sat.). One of several centrally located pensions, **Platán Panzió,** Kis-Duna Sétány 11 (tel. (33) 31 13 55), between Rákóczi tér and Primas Sziget, rents singles (1120Ft) and doubles (2464Ft) with shared bath. **Gran Camping,** Nagy-Duna Sétány (tel. (33) 31 13 27), is in the middle of Primas Sziget. Closed in 1997 due to floods, it may reopen in 1998. **Vadászkert Vendeglő,** Széchenyi tér, serves *sertés* (schnitzel) starting at 510Ft (open daily 11am-9pm). **Szalma Csárda,** in the middle of Primas Sziget near the pier at the end of Cőzhajó 4, cooks up fish straight from the Danube for 400Ft (open daily noon-midnight).

Eger

In 1552, Captain Dobó István and his tiny army held off the invading Ottomans for an entire month in Eger. Credit for their fortitude is given to the potent *Egri Bikavér* ("Bull's Blood" wine) they quaffed before battle. Today, Dobó's name and likeness appear throughout the city, and the sweet red *Bikavér* still flows copiously and cheaply. With good company or sheer determination, you can spend an entire afternoon and evening in the wine cellars of **Szépasszonyvölgy,** the Valley of the Beautiful Women. The valley is lined with the doors of cellars dug into the hills; 25 are open for wine tasting. Most open after 10am and begin to close around 6-7pm; some stay open as late as 10pm. The best time to go is late afternoon. Little glasses for tasting are free; 100mL glasses run 30-50Ft. One liter of the wine costs 300Ft. To reach the wine cellars, walk west from Deák u. down Telekessy u., which with a quick jog to the left takes you to Király u. and then Szépasszonyvölgy u.

Wander back to Eszterházy tér to explore the wealth of Baroque architecture around town. The yellow **basilica** here, the second-largest church in Hungary, was built in 1837 by Joseph Hild, who also built Hungary's largest—the Esztergom cathedral. Organ concerts are held here May to mid-October (Mon.-Sat. 11:30am, Sun. 12:45pm; 200Ft, students 60Ft). Opposite the cathedral is the Rococo **Lyceum.** The fresco in the magnificent library on the first floor depicts an ant's-eye view of the Council of Trent (open Tues.-Fri. 9:30am-1pm, Sat.-Sun. 9:30am-noon; 120Ft). On the south side of Dobó tér stands the luxuriously Baroque **Minorite Church,** which overlooks a statue of Captain Dobó and two co-defenders, one of them a woman poised to hurl a rock at an unfortunate Turk. Hungarians revere medieval **Eger Castle;** it was here that Dobó István and his 2000 men held off the unified Ottoman army, halting their advance for another 44 years (grounds open daily 8am-7:30pm; 50Ft, students 20Ft). A 200Ft ticket (students 100Ft) buys admission to the **picture gallery,** the **Dobó István Castle museum,** which displays excavated artifacts and an impressive array of weapons, and the **Dungeon Exhibition,** a collection of torture equipment to inspire sadists and masochists alike (museums open Tues.-Sun. 9am-5pm). Climb the nearby **Turkish minaret** for a great view, but be careful on the steep, narrow staircase (open daily in summer 10am-6pm; 30Ft). The 18th-century **Serbian Orthodox Church,** Vitkovics u., at the town center's north end, displays magnificent murals and an impressive altar (open daily 10am-4pm; free).

Eger revels in its heritage during the **Baroque Festival** held throughout August. Nightly performances of operas and operettas and medieval and Renaissance court music are held in the courtyard of the Franciscan church, the cathedral, and in Dobó tér. An international folk-dance festival called **Eger Vintage Days** is held daily in the end of June. Check at the Tourinform office for schedules and tickets.

Practical Information, Accommodations, and Food The **Tourinform** office at Dobó tér 2 (tel./fax (36) 32 18 07) has brochures, English newspapers, and maps (60Ft), as well as accommodations info. (Open in summer Mon.-Fri. 9am-

6pm, Sat.-Sun. 9am-2pm; off-season Mon.-Fri. 9am-6pm, Sat.-Sun. 10am-4pm.) The **bus station** (tel. (36) 41 05 52), five minutes west of Dobó tér, provides transport to Budapest (2hr., 820Ft) and Aggtelek (3hr., 690Ft). **Trains** bound for Budapest's Keleti station (2hr., 800Ft) split in Hatvan; make sure you're in the right car.

The best and friendliest accommodations are private rooms; look for *"Zimmer Frei"* signs outside the city center. Several are on Almagyar u. and Mekcsey u., near the castle. **Eger Tourist,** Bajcsy-Zsilinszky u. 9 (tel. (36) 41 17 24), can arrange private rooms for about 1400Ft per person. (Open June-Sept. Mon.-Fri. 10am-6pm, Sat. 9am-noon; Oct.-May Mon.-Fri. 8:30am-5pm.) Eger Tourist operates the very basic **Tourist Motel,** Mekcsey u. 2 (doubles 2400-3200Ft, triples 3000-3900Ft, quads 3200-4400Ft). **Eszterházi Károly Kollégiuma,** Leányka u. 2/6 (tel. (36) 41 23 99), just up the hill behind the castle, charges 800Ft per person in triples and quads (open July-early Sept.; call ahead). Eger Tourist also runs **Autós Caravan Camping,** Rákóczi u. 79, 20 minutes north of the city center. Buses 5, 10, 11, and 12 go there (320Ft per person, 250Ft per tent; open April 15-Oct. 15).

For quick gourmet food, go to the **HBH Bajor Söház,** Bajcsy-Zsilinszky u. 19, off Dobó tér, a Bavarian beer house that serves Hungarian specialties. (Entrees 450-100Ft. English menu. Open daily 10am-10pm; Nov.-March closed Sun.) **Gyros Étterem,** Széchenyi u. 10, serves gyros (585Ft), souvlaki (555Ft), and Greek salads (299Ft), while **Kulacs Csárda Borozó,** in the Valley of the Beautiful Women, specializes in goulash and other fine dishes (open Tues.-Sun. noon-10pm).

Near Eger

Just 70 minutes away from Eger by **train** (140Ft) or 45 minutes away by **bus** (130Ft), **Szilvásvárad** is beloved for its 400-year-old race of Lipizzaner horses and surrounding national parks. **Horse shows** kick into action on weekends usually at 2 and 4pm in the arena across from Tourinform on Szalajka u. (300Ft). If you prefer more active participation, **Péter Kovács,** Egri út 62 (tel. (36) 35 53 43), lends horses for 1500Ft per hour, or horse-drawn carriages for 2000-3500Ft per hour. The nearby **Bükk mountains** (45min. walking, 20min. by train) entices hikers with the **Fátyol waterfalls** and the **Istálósk cave,** which housed a bear cult in the Stone Age.

The **Baradla caves** (tel./fax (48) 35 00 06) are a 25km long system of limestone tunnels that wind between Hungary and Slovakia. Each chamber is a forest of dripping stalactites and stalagmites and fantastically shaped stone formations. Cave **tours** begin from the town of **Aggtelek.** A large chamber with perfect acoustics has been converted into an auditorium, and the tours pause here for a dazzling light-and-sound show. (Bring a jacket. Hour-long tours leave daily 10am, 1, 3, and 5pm. 300Fr, students 150Ft.) The daily **bus** from Eger (400Ft) leaves at 8:40am, wizzes through Szilvásvárad at 9:20am, arriving in Aggtelek at 11:20am in the front of Hotel Cseppkő, 200m uphill from the cave entrance. The bus back to Eger leaves at 3pm.

Tokaj

Locals say that King Louis XIV called Tokaj (toke-EYE) wine "the wine of kings and the king of wines." While Tokaj is just one of the 28 villages that take advantage of the local volcanic yellow soil and sunny climate to produce unique whites, it lends its name to the entire class of wine. Signs reading *"Bor Pince"* herald **private wine cellars.** Owners are generally pleased to let visitors sample their wares (50mL 90-300Ft, depending on the cellar)—walk on in, or ring the bell if the cellar looks shut. Explore the less touristy side streets for higher-quality wines. Serious **tasting** takes place at the best-respected and largest of the lot: **Rákóczi Pince,** Kossuth tér 15 (tel. (47) 35 20 09), a 1.5km long system of 24 tunnels dug from volcanic rock in 1502. In 1526, János Szapohjai was elected king of Hungary in the elegant and surprisingly large hall; the tunnel served as the imperial wine cellar for two centuries, until the end of World War I. A jacket is a good idea down here, even in summer. **Wine-tastings** and **group tours** of the cellar are usually held on the hour, but can be pre-empted by tour groups. **Individual tours** can also be arranged. (English-speaking guides available July-

Aug. 200Ft for the 15-20min. tour; 300Ft for the tour and a glass of wine. 700Ft for 6 glasses. Open daily 10am-7pm.)

Trains, Baross G. u. 18 (tel. (47) 35 20 20), puff to Miskolc (1hr., 266Ft), which connects Tokaj to the rest of the country. The only **bus** service is to local towns. The train station sits 15 minutes southwest of town; with your back to the station, walk left along the railroad embankment until you reach an underpass, then turn left on Bajcsy-Zsilinszky u. At the Hotel Tokaj fork, stay on the left road. Some pensions' brochures include primitive street **maps. Tokaj Tours,** Serház u. 1 (tel./fax (47) 35 22 59), at Rákóczi u., arranges private and hotel rooms (no fee) and organizes tours of the region and wine-tastings (open Mon.-Sat. 9am-4pm). *"Zimmer Frei"* and *"Szoba Kiadó"* signs abound—your best bet is to walk along Rákóczi u. (singles generally 1200Ft-1400Ft, doubles 2750Ft). **Graf Széchenyi István Students Hostel,** Bajcsy-Zsilinszky u. 15-17 (tel. (47) 35 23 55), between the train station and the center, is the best hotel deal around, with fresh, recently renovated doubles (3800Ft with bath) and sparse but clean quads (3000Ft; open July-Aug. only). **Makk-Marci Panzió-Pizzéria,** Liget Köz 1 (tel. (47) 35 23 36; fax 35 30 88), facing Rákóczi u., provides relaxing, bright rooms with bath. (Singles 2464Ft; doubles 3584Ft; triples 4816Ft; quads 6048Ft. Breakfast included. Reserve ahead.) **Camping Tisza** is on the right as you cross the river (tents 470Ft per person; tiny bungalows 450Ft per person). **Gödör,** in the Tisza Vízisport complex, cooks up heavy meat dishes and some veggie ones (meals 200-400Ft; open Mon.-Fri. 9am-11pm, Sat.-Sun. 7am-11pm).

HUNGARY

Kecskemét

Nestled amid vineyards, fruit trees, and the sandy *puszta* (plains), Kecskemét (CATCH-keh-MATE) lures tourists with museums and its famous *barack pálinka* (apricot brandy). The salmon-colored **town hall,** Kossuth tér 1, built in 1897 during the height of the Hungarian Art Nouveau movement, is Kossuth tér's most impressive building. (Tours by appointment daily 7:30am-6pm; call (76) 48 36 83 and ask for Földi Margit. 50Ft, in English 300Ft.) You can brave the rickety wooden floors and wobbly stairs of the Neoclassical **Roman Catholic Big Church** on Széchenyi tér for a superb view at the top of the tower (tower open June-Aug. daily 10am-8pm; 200Ft). If you're not going to the *puszta,* visit the **Magyar Népi Iparművészet Múzeuma** (Museum of Hungarian Folk Art), Serfőző u. 19/a. In addition to clothes, furniture, and ceramics, the museum has an impressive collection of horse whips and Easter eggs (open in summer Wed.-Sun. 10am-6pm; off-season 9am-5pm; 80Ft, students 50Ft). The Art Nouveau **Kecskeméti Galéria,** Rákóczi út 1, displays the works of local artists (open Tues.-Sun. 10am-5pm; 100Ft, students 60Ft, Thurs. free). The **Katona József Színház** (Theater), Katona tér 5 (tel. (76) 48 32 83), not only puts on excellent drama, but is located in a magnificent 1896 building (off-season operettas 400-500Ft).

Trains run from the station at the end of Rákóczi út (tel. (76) 32 24 60) to Budapest (1¼hr., 600Ft). The station around the corner (tel. (76) 32 17 77) sends **buses** to Budapest (1½hr., 560Ft), Eger (2½hr., 1010Ft), and Pécs (5hr., 1260Ft). **Local buses** head into town from the train station (63Ft).**Tourinform,** Kossuth tér 1 (tel./fax (76) 48 10 65), in the town hall, has maps and lots of info on the *puszta.* (Open in summer Mon.-Fri. 8am-6pm, Sat.-Sun. 9am-1pm; off-season Mon.-Fri. 8am-5pm, Sat. 9am-1pm.) **Cooptourist,** Kettemplom köz 9 (tel. (76) 48 14 72), rents singles and doubles (2000Ft for two people), with a 30% additional fee on the first day for stays of less than 3 days. **Hotel Pálma,** Hornyik János u. 4 (tel. (76) 32 10 45 or 32 30 94), is as close to the heart of the city as possible, with newly redone and super-clean rooms (dorms 2000Ft, doubles 3500Ft, triples 4000Ft, quads 4800Ft).**Tanitóképzo Kollégiuma,** Piaristák tér 4 (tel. (76) 48 69 77 or 48 73 48), 2min. from Kossuth tér, offers beds in spacious doubles, triples, and quads (1000Ft per person; washing machine 150Ft; open July-Aug., but try off-season). Enjoy Greek food at **Göröd Udvar Étterem,** Hornyik J. 1 (veggie dishes 510Ft; open daily 11am-11pm). **Kilele Music Cafe,** Jokai 34, offers a mellow good time. (Beer 160Ft. Cover 100-150Ft. Open Mon.-Fri. noon-2am, Sat. 6pm-4am, Sun. 6pm-1am.)

HUNGARY

Szeged

Szeged straddles the Tisza River about 10km north of the Yugoslav border. The town's easygoing charm belies its status as Hungary's only planned city; after an 1879 flood wiped out the town, streets were laid out and lined with row after row of colorful neo-Renaissance and Art Nouveau buildings. Street names recall the many cities which helped Szeged rebuild. Walk east to the river to find the **Móra Ferenc Múzeum,** Roosevelt tér 1/3, which boasts an exhibit of folk art from the 18th century to the present (open Tues.-Sun. 10am-5pm; 80Ft, students 20Ft). On Dóm tér, the red brick **Votive Church** pierces the city's skyline with its twin 91m towers (open Mon.-Sat. 9am-6pm, Sun. 12:30-6pm; sometimes closes early). Beside the church is the 12th-century **Demetrius Tower.** Smaller and brighter than the Votive Church is the 1778 **Serbian Orthodox Church** across the street, home to 60 gilt-framed paintings (open whenever there's someone around to collect the 50Ft admission fee). At the corner of Hajnóczi u. and Jósika u. stands the beautiful and eclectic **Great Synagogue,** built in 1903. English-speaking guides explain every detail of the building, used now mainly for concerts and memorials (open May-Sept. Sun.-Fri. 9am-noon and 1-6pm; 100Ft, students 50Ft). The Szeged **Open-Air Theater Festival** (mid-July to mid-Aug.) is the country's largest outdoor theatrical festival. Traveling troupes perform folk dances, operas, and musicals in the amphitheater in Dóm tér. Tickets (400-1500Ft) are sold at Déak u. 28/30 (tel. (62) 47 14 66; fax 47 13 22).

Practical Information, Accommodations, and Food **Szeged Tourist,** Klauzál tér 7 (tel. (62) 32 18 00; fax 31 29 28), has maps and arranges bus and boat tours of the town in July and August (bus tours 450Ft). The English-speaking staff also sells international bus tickets with a 10% student discount (open Mon.-Fri. 9am-5pm; in summer also Sat. 9am-1pm). **Trains** chug to Budapest (2½hr., 100Ft). **Buses** leave the terminal on Mars tér just west of Londoni krt., a 10-minute walk west of the center, for Budapest (3½hr., 1200Ft) and Pécs (4½hr., 1260Ft). In July and August only, Szeged Tourist finds bargain private rooms, 900-1800Ft for singles and 2400Ft for doubles. **Fortuna Panzió,** Pécskai u. 8 (tel./fax (62) 43 15 85), across Belvárosihíd bridge to the northeast, is a bit tricky to find but boasts spacious rooms and sparkling bathrooms (doubles with bath 4500Ft). **Apáthy Kollégium,** Apáthy u. (tel. (62) 45 40 00; fax 45 57 29), is a centrally located dorm (singles 1800Ft; doubles 2400Ft; triples 3000Ft; open July-Aug.). **Napfény,** Dorozsmai u. 4 (tel./fax (62) 32 45 73), is both a hotel and a campground. Take tram 1 to the last stop, then ascend the overpass behind you and walk ten minutes (300Ft per person, 200Ft per tent; bungalow doubles 1900Ft; open year-round).

Aranykorona Étterem, Déak Ferenc u. 29, at the corner of Victor Hugo u., offers mouth-watering Hungarian dishes that are the cheapest of their kind. (Red wine and fish with tomato sauce 370Ft. Open Mon.-Thurs. 11am-11pm, Fri.-Sat. 11am-2am, Sun. 11am-10pm.) **Roosevelt téri Halászcsárda (Sótartá Étterem),** Roosevelt tér 14, on the square's southeast side next to the river, is the place to sample the spicy fish soup for which Szeged is famous. Try any of the *"hallé"* (fish soup) dishes (550-900Ft; other meals 350-1500Ft; open daily 11am-11pm). Enjoy excellent pastries (50-90Ft), including regional specialty *Somlói galuska* (98Ft), and ice cream (35Ft per scoop) at **Kisvirág Cukrásda,** Klauzál tér (open daily 8am-10pm).

Pécs

Two thousand years of history and a lively student population make Pécs (PAYTCH) one of Hungary's most interesting and energetic cities. In streetside cafés and bars around town, students and locals enjoy drinks and people-watching while planning evening activities. Towering above them, buildings and monuments recall the city's more turbulent years under Roman, Ottoman, Hapsburg, and Nazi rule.

Ornate buildings surround Széchenyi tér, centered on the **Gazi Khasim Pase Belvarosi templom** (Gazi Khasim Pasha Inner City Parish Church), a converted Turkish mosque. On the southwest corner of the square, the **Patika Múzeum** (Pharmacy Museum), Apáca u. 1, tries to convince visitors that leeches and blood-letting were sound techniques to cure anything from stubbornness to political incorrectness (open Mon.-Fri. 7:30am-4:30pm). Stroll along Ferencesek u. until you reach the quasi-Baroque **Franciscan Church;** nearby, Szent István tér is surrounded by trees and offers a welcome rest during a hot summer afternoon. On the square's east side, 4th-century **Roman ruins** slowly crumble in the shadow of the Romanesque **cathedral,** Pécs's centerpiece. Below the ruins lie the largest known burial site in Hungary (open Tues.-Sun. 10am-6pm). East of the Old Town, **Várostörténeti Múzeum** (History Museum), Felsőmalom u. 9, chronicles Pécs's subordination under foreign rule from the Middle Ages through the 20th century. The exhibit on the local industrial revolution showcases Pécs determination to turn out elegance—porcelain, musical instruments, and champagne—in an age of conveyor belts and smokestacks (open Tues.-Sun. 10am-4pm; 100Ft, students 50Ft).

Practical Information, Accommodations, and Food Pécs sits on the knees of the Mecsek mountain range; north and south correspond to up and down the hillside. The middle of the inner city is **Széchenyi tér,** where most of the tourist offices are located. **Tourinform,** Széchenyi tér 9 (tel. (72) 21 33 15), sells tourist maps (250Ft) and an informative historical guide (60Ft; open June-Aug. daily 9am-2pm; Sept.-May 8am-4pm). The Pécs **train station** is located just beyond the bottom of the city's historic district, a 10-minute bus ride (30 or 34) from the center of town. **Trains** (tel. (72) 31 24 43) run to Budapest (2½-3hr., 1112Ft, plus 200Ft for IC trains only).

Private accommodations can be arranged at the Old Town's tourist offices. For stays of less than three nights, a 30% fee is added to the first night's price. **Mecsek Tours,** Széchenyi tér 1 (tel. (72) 21 33 00; fax 21 20 44), seeks out singles (1100Ft) and doubles (1800Ft). **Szent Mór Kollégium,** 48-es tér 4 (tel. (72) 31 11 99), offers doubles in a gorgeous old building for 700Ft; take bus 21 to "48-es tér." From the train station, take bus 34 to **Hotel-Camping Mandulás,** Angyán János u. 2 (tel. (72) 31 59 81), in the hills above the city. The one-star hotel offers tent sites (12DM for 2 people), three-bed bungalows (35DM), and doubles with breakfast (45DM) at the entrance to **hiking trails** into the Mecsek Hills (open mid-April to mid-Oct.).

Low prices, choice beers, and local students lurk in a cellar at **Liceum Söröző,** off Király u. 35 opposite the Liceum church (entrees from 330Ft; open Mon.-Thurs. 11am-10pm, Fri.-Sat. 11am-11pm). **Kolping,** Szent István tér 9, just north of Ferencesek u., serves good *borda* (cutlet) and a rainbow of colorful veggies, with a heavy emphasis on German food (main courses 420-840Ft; 0.5L *Gösser* beer 280Ft; open daily 11am-10pm). Nightlife centers around Széchenyi tér, especially on the first two blocks of Király u. **Rózsakert Sörkert/Rosengarten Biergarten,** Janus Pannonius u., east of the cathedral, features live music in an outdoor setting (open daily 11am-11pm). **Kioszk Eszpresszo,** opposite Janus Pannonius 1 next to Dóm tér, is a popular café/beer garden with a mixed gay and straight crowd (open daily 11am-11:45pm).

Lake Balaton

Balaton is the largest lake in Central Europe and one of the region's most coveted vacation spots. Villas first sprouted along its shores during the Roman Empire, and in the 1860s, rail connections transformed the lake into a favored summer playground. Today, the region's rich scenery and relatively low prices draw mobs of German, Austrian, and Hungarian vacationers. Be aware, though, that storms roll in over Lake Balaton quickly. Amber lights on tall buildings give storm warnings: 60 revolutions per minute means swimmers must be within 100m of shore.

Siófok The largest town on Lake Balaton, Siófok attracts countless surf-starved Germans and Austrians each summer. All attractions pale in comparison with the **Strand,** which is not a beach but a series of park-like lawns running to the concrete shoreline. There are public and private sections, with some private spots charging at least 80Ft per person. Nightclubs of varying seediness line the lakefront, while amphibious boppers revel on the **Disco Boat** from July 9 to August 21 (leaves harbor at 9:30pm; 500Ft). If boats aren't your thing, dance at **Flört Disco,** Sió u. 4 (open nightly 9pm-5am), or the **Kajman Pub Disco,** Fő u. 212 (cover 200Ft; open nightly 10pm-4am).

The **bus** and **train stations** are next to each other off the town's main drag, **Fő u.** A *gyorsjárat* (fast bus) leaves for Budapest four times a day (2½hr., 718Ft); seven trains go every day to Budapest (3hr., 540Ft). **Tourinform** (tel. (84) 31 53 55), inside the base of the water tower at Fő u. 41, will find rooms for you commission-free (open July-Aug. Mon.-Sat. 8am-8pm, Sun. 8am-1pm; Sept.-June Mon.-Fri. 9am-4pm). **IBUSZ,** Fő u. 174 (tel. (84) 31 14 81), has doubles for 2000Ft in July and August. (30% surcharge for stays of less than 4 nights. Open June-Aug. Mon.-Sat. 8am-6pm, Sun. 9am-1pm; Sept.-May Mon.-Fri. 8am-4pm.) **Tuja Panzió,** Szent László u. 74 (tel. (84) 31 49 96), has well-equipped rooms with shower and TV (2600Ft per person; discounts off-season). **Hunguest Hotel Azúr,** Vitorlás u. 11 (tel. (84) 31 20 33), off Erkel Ferenc u., offers bright doubles with bathrooms (2000Ft). The **Csárdás Restaurant,** Fő u. 105, offers Hungarian dishes in a friendly atmosphere (600-900Ft; open daily 11am-11pm).

Keszthely The pride of **Keszthely** (KESS-tay), on the southern tip of Balaton, is the Helikon Kastélymúzeum, the **Festetics Kastély** (palace). Built by a powerful Austro-Hungarian family, it contains 360 rooms (only the central wing is open to tourists), including the 90,000-volume **Helikon Library.** Concerts are held in the mirrored ballroom hall during summer (palace open Tues.-Sun. 9am-6pm; 560Ft, students 230Ft). The surrounding park is a vast and well-kept strolling ground. The **Georgikon Majormuzeum** (Georgikon Farm Museum), Bercsényi u. 67, presents an amusing tribute to György Festetics, who founded Europe's oldest agricultural university here in 1797 (open April-Oct. Tues.-Sat. 10am-5pm, Sun. 10am-6pm; 60Ft, students 30Ft).

The **train station** and **bus terminal** are adjacent to each other, near the water. **Trains** head to Budapest (3hr., 920Ft), while **buses** zip to Pécs (3hr., 560). To reach the main square, Fő tér, walk up Mátirok u. and turn right on Kossuth Lajos u. **Tourinform**, Kossuth Lajos u. 28 (tel./fax (83) 31 41 44), arranges apartments for four (7000Ft; open Mon.-Fri. 9am-5pm, Sat.-Sun. 9am-1pm), while **IBUSZ,** Kossuth Lajos 27 (tel. (83) 31 29 51), finds doubles for 2500Ft. (Open June-Aug. Mon.-Sat. 8am-6pm, Sun. 9am-1pm; Sept.-May Mon.-Thurs. 8am-4pm, Fri. 8am-3pm.) **Mr. Athla Lukic's** cozy *panzió,* Jókai Mór u. 16 (tel. (83) 31 12 32), has doubles for 6400Ft. **Castrum Camping,** Móra Ferenc u. 48 (tel. 31 21 20), has four-person bungalows (4000Ft) and tent sites (400Ft per person, 400Ft per tent; open May-Sept.). **Gösser Restaurant,** Erzsébet Királyné u. 23, north of the Strand, creates culinary delights out of the rich fish stocks of Lake Balaton (carp and trout 400-900Ft; open Mon.-Sat. 11am-10pm).

Tihany With its lush vegetation, luxurious homes, and great views, **Tihany** (TEE-hawn) is the pearl of Lake Balaton. Lording over the peninsula, the 1754 **Abbey Church** features Baroque altars, pulpit, and organ (open daily 9am-6pm; 120Ft, students 60Ft). Next door, an 18th-century monastery now houses the **Tihany Museum,** with psychedelic dreamscapes, colorized etchings, and Roman inscriptions (open March-Oct. Tues.-Sun. 10am-6pm; 60Ft). The promenade behind the church leads to the **beach** (follow the "strand" signs; open daily 7am-7pm; 80Ft). Frequent **buses** pass by the beaches at both Tihany and the more popular Tihanyi-rév. If you're enchanted by the town, **Balatontourist,** Kossuth u. 12 (tel. (86) 44 85 19), arranges private rooms (2800-3800Ft; open Mon.-Sat. 8:30am-6:30pm, Sun. 8:30am-1pm).

Győr

Usually associated with the Rába truck factory, Győr (DYUR) nonetheless maintains a certain charm. Some of the finest 17th- and 18th-century buildings in all of Hungary crowd the inner city, and the occasional horse-drawn cart still plods through rush-hour traffic. The **city hall,** a few steps from the train station, is the most magnificent building in Győr. Most sights, however, lie within a rough triangle between Bécsi

Kapu tér, Káptalandomb, and Széchenyi tér. Bécsi Kapu tér is the site of the yellow **Carmelite church** and the remains of a medieval **castle** built to defend Győr against the Turks. At the top of Káptalandomb is the **Székesegyház** (Episcopal Cathedral), originally built in 1030. Generations of embellishments have resulted in a hybrid of architectural styles. The miraculous **Weeping Madonna of Győr** in the altar in the north nave, brought from Ireland in the 1650s, is rumored to have spontaneously wept blood and tears for three hours on St. Patrick's Day, 1697. The **Kovács Margit Gyűjtemény** (Margit Kovács Museum), Rózsa Ferenc u. 1, a block north of Széchenyi tér, is one of Győr's hidden treasures, displaying the artist's distinctive ceramic sculptures and tiles (open April-Oct. Tues.-Sun. 10am-6pm; Nov.-March 10am-5pm; 100Ft, students 50Ft). The marketplace on the river erupts into a **bazaar** on Wednesday, Friday, and Saturday mornings. Győr frolics in June and July during **Győri Nyár,** a festival of daily concerts, theater, and ballet. Buy tickets at the box office on Baross Gábor út, or at the performance venues. Schedules are available at Tourinform and IBUSZ.

HUNGARY

Practical Information, Accommodations, and Food From the station south of the inner city, **trains** roll to Budapest (2½hr., 700Ft) and Vienna (2hr., 3618Ft). **Buses** depart from the terminal beside the train station for Budapest (2½hr., 670Ft). Packed with free **maps** and brochures, a **Tourinform kiosk** awaits at Árpád u. 32 (tel. (96) 31 17 71), one block north of the train station. (Books private singles for 1800Ft and up; doubles 2200Ft; 30% surcharge for stays of under 4 nights. Open Mon.-Sat. 8am-8pm, Sun. 9am-1pm.) A few blocks north, **IBUSZ,** Kazinczy u. 3 (tel. (96) 31 17 00), is bigger but less oriented toward Győr. The office books only doubles. (2000Ft and up; same surcharge as Tourinform. Open Mon.-Tues. and Thurs. 8am-3:30pm, Wed. and Fri. 8am-3pm.) **Hotel Szárnyaskerék,** Révai Miklós u. 5 (tel. (96) 31 46 29), is right outside the train station; it's clean and the staff speaks English (doubles 2750Ft, with private bath 4200Ft). For hostel-type accommodation, try **2sz. Fiú Kollégium** (Boy's Dormitory No. 2), Damjanich u. 58 (tel. (96) 31 10 08), just north of the Mosoni-Duna River (600Ft; open weekends and mid-July to Aug.). **Széchenyi Istvan Főiskola Kollégiuma,** Hédevári út 3, entrance K4 (tel. (96) 42 97 22 or 42 93 48), also north of the river, has beds in triples (600Ft, students 550Ft; open mid-July to Aug.). **Kiskút-ligeti Camping,** Kiskút liget (tel. (96) 31 89 86), has a motel open year-round (triples 3300Ft). Camping and bungalows are available April to mid-Oct. (400Ft per person, 400Ft per tent; 4-person bungalows 2800Ft).

Napoleon Pince, Munkácsy Mihály u. 6, just south of the Petőfi Bridge, is a slightly upscale French restaurant with an English menu (entrees 480-1000Ft; open daily noon-midnight). **Sárkányluk** (Dragon's Hole), Arany János u. 27, is a popular little bistro (entrees 320-900Ft; open Mon.-Sat. 11am-9pm, Sun. 11am-3pm). **Paradiso,** Kazinczy u. 20, offers huge, tasty *menűs* (500Ft) and transforms into a bar at night (open daily 9am-1am). A first-rate **Julius Meinl grocery store** is located at the corner of Baross Gábor and Árpád (open Mon.-Fri. 6am-8pm, Sat. 6am-1pm).

Sopron

In 1920, the Swabians of Ödenburg (as they called Sopron) voted to remain part of Hungary instead of joining their linguistic brethren in Austria. The disappointed Austrians were left with no choice but friendly invasion: Sopron today is deluged daily by Austrians drawn by low prices for medical care and sausage—especially sausage. The **Tűz Torony** (Fire Tower), on the north side of Fő tér, consists of a 17th-century spire atop a 16th-century tower, sitting on a 12th-century base that straddles a Roman gate (open Tues.-Sat. 10am-6pm; 100Ft, students 50Ft). Across the square is the **Bencés Templom** (a.k.a. Goat Church), built in the 13th century with funds from a happy herder whose goats found gold. The **Chapter's Hall** in the small **monastery** next door is a room of textbook Gothic architecture enriched by 10 sculptures of human sins and taped Gregorian chants (church and hall open daily 10am-noon and 2-5pm).

At Fő tér 8, the **Storno-ház** (Storno House) is the best museum in town. The Stornos were 19th-century Swiss-Italian restorers of monuments and cathedrals; their taste in churches is often less than impressive, but their home and personal collection of furniture and artwork are exquisite. (Open Tues.-Sun. 10am-6pm. Compulsory pre-recorded tour; English fact sheet. 100Ft, students 50Ft.) For a brief but enchanting tour of Old Sopron, walk down Templom u. to the **Evangelical Church** and admire the late Baroque interior, especially the organ. Return to Fő tér via Szent György u. and peek inside **Szent György Templom** (St. George's Cathedral). The church's plain exterior conceals an exquisite blend of Gothic and Baroque ornamentation.

Practical Information, Accommodations, and Food Frequent **trains** run to Vienna (1hr., 2578Ft), Budapest (3-4hr., 1140Ft), and Győr (1hr., 440Ft). The train station is a 10-minute walk south of the center of town on Mátyás Király út, and the **bus station** is two blocks northwest from the old town, on Lackner Kristóf. **Ciklámen Tourist,** Ógabona tér 8 (tel. (99) 31 20 40), offers maps and advice (in German or Hungarian) and finds private rooms (singles 1600Ft, doubles 2000Ft; open Mon.-Fri. 8am-4:30pm, Sat. 8am-1pm). **Locomotiv Tourist,** Új u. 1 near Fő tér, arranges singles (1400Ft) and doubles (1900-3200Ft; open Mon.-Sat. 9am-5pm). **Talizmán Panzió,** Táncsics u. 15 (tel. (99) 31 16 20), offers small, tidy doubles with shower (but shared toilet) for 2350Ft. About 1km west of the inner city, **Galéria Szálló,** Baross Gábor u. 4-6 (tel. (99) 31 11 50), is open all year and often full, and charges 750Ft per night (no reservations). **Lővér Campground** is at the south end of town on Kőszegi u. (tel. (99) 31 17 15; 500Ft per person, 300Ft per tent; open April 15-Oct. 15).

Várkerület Restaurant, Várkerület 38 near Széchenyi tér, serves tasty *sertés pörkölt* (stews), home-made dumplings, and vegetarian entrees (440-800Ft; ½ liter of *Zipfer* or *Steffl* beer 300Ft; open daily 10am-midnight). **Pince Csárda,** Széchenyi tér 4, upholds its good reputation with a tremendous array of chicken, venison, and veal dishes (450-900Ft; open Mon.-Thurs. 10am-11pm, Fri.-Sat. 10am-midnight). **Julius Meinl grocery,** Várkerület 100-102, is one of the town's best-stocked groceries (open Mon.-Fri. 6:30am-8pm, Sat. 6:30am-3pm).

■ Near Sopron: Fertőd

Twenty-seven kilometers east of Sopron in tiny **Fertőd** stands the magnificent Baroque **Eszterházy Palace,** Bartók Béla u. 2 (tel. (99) 37 04 71). Miklós Eszterházy, known as Miklós the Sumptuous before he squandered his family's vast fortune, ordered the palace built in 1766 to hold his multi-day orgiastic feasts. (Open mid-April to mid-Dec. Tues.-Sun. 9am-5pm; mid-Dec. to mid-April Tues.-Sun. 9am-4pm. 500Ft, students 100Ft.) Josef Haydn composed and conducted here, and stellar concerts still resound within. **Buses** leave hourly for Fertőd from stage 11 of Sopron's Lackner Kristóf station (45min., 190Ft). They continue on to Győr every two hours (2hr., 440Ft). Book rooms in Fertőd with Ciklámen Tourist in Sopron.

Iceland (Ísland)

US$1 = 72.06Ikr (Icelandic krónur) — **100Ikr = US$1.39**
CDN$1= 52.17Ikr — **100Ikr = CDN$1.91**
UK£1 = 114.56Ikr — **100Ikr = UK£0.87**
IR£1 = 107.01Ikr — **100Ikr = IR£0.93**
AUS$1 = 52.60Ikr — **100Ikr = AUS$0.19**
NZ$1 = 45.80Ikr — **100Ikr = NZ$2.18**
SAR1 = 15.37Ikr — **100Ikr = SAR6.51**
Country Code: 354 — **International Dialing Prefix: 00**

Perpetually rent asunder and forged anew by volcanoes, gorged and scarred by the glaciers that continue to advance tiny tendrils, and whipped by seemingly never-ending wind, rain, and snow, Iceland is contorted and warped into a landscape unique to the world. Nature, in its primeval fury, is the greatest attraction: desolate moonscapes, thundering waterfalls, spouting geysers, and smothering icecaps dominate the territory. Vegetation stands little chance, and the twisted shadows of the few existing trees provide mute evidence of the environment's brutality.

Surprisingly, humans have survived here and bent nature to their will. Geothermal power provides hot water and electricity to Iceland's settlements, roads are carved through the inhospitable terrain, and planes battle the whipping winds or wait for better weather. Yet much of Iceland remains in a rugged, unspoiled state. Several major roads are not paved, and the combination of strict immigration laws and the interior's inaccessibility has kept Iceland's entire population to 267,000.

Icelanders may not disembowel enemies over slander anymore, but much of the strong Viking heritage that inspired the world's first democracy still exists today. A language committee systematically banishes foreign words, and, instead of surnames, people follow the patronymic custom of identifying themselves as the sons or daughters of their fathers (the phone book is ordered by first name). The determination and work ethic that led Leif Ericsson to discover North America persists as well—all Icelandic children are expected to work summer jobs from the age of 13. The deep sense of community, strong economy, booming tourist industry, and pollution-free environment ensures one of the highest standards of living in the world.

GETTING THERE

Icelandair (tel. (800) 223-5500) flies to Reykjavík from Baltimore, Boston, Halifax, Ft. Lauderdale (not in summer), New York, and Orlando. The planes often continue to other European cities: Amsterdam, Copenhagen, Glasgow, Hamburg, London, Luxembourg, Oslo, Stockholm, and, in summer only, Frankfurt and Paris. **SAS** from Copenhagen and **Lufthansa** from Frankfurt also fly to Iceland.

The best way to feel the sea wind off Iceland's rugged shores is on the ferry *Norröna,* which circles the North Atlantic via Seyðisfjörður, East Iceland; Tórshavn in the Faroe Islands; Bergen, Norway; and Esbjerg, Denmark; for more information, see **East Iceland,** p. 500. **Eimskip** (tel. 569 9300) offers more expensive ferry rides on cargo ships from Reykjavík to Immingham, Rotterdam, and Hamburg.

GETTING AROUND

Buses Iceland has no trains, and although flying is more comfortable, **buses** are often cheaper and offer a close-up look at the terrain. Within Iceland, one tour company, **BSÍ** (tel. 552 2300), in the Reykjavík bus terminal, coordinates all schedules and prices. Free schedules are available at hostels and tourist offices. The *Iceland 1998* brochure lists selected bus schedules as well as tours and ferry routes; the *Leiðabók* lists all bus schedules. Land travel focuses on the 1411km **Highway 1,** completed in 1974, which circles the island (only 30% paved: the going is slow). Plan on at least 10 days if you want to circle the country on the Ring Road; buses do it in several five- to nine-hour stages (Reykjavík to Akureyri to Egilsstaðir to Höfn and back to Reykjavík, and vice versa), with daily service on each leg from mid-June through August. Frequency drops dramatically off season. You can buy tickets in the stations *(umferðarmiðstöð)* in Reykjavík and Akureyri, or from the driver.

BSÍ sells passes that simplify bus travel greatly. The **Full Circle Passport** (14,100Ikr) allows you to circle the island at your own pace on the Ring Road, although no backtracking is allowed (available mid-May to Sept.). For an additional 6,300Ikr, the pass allows you to visit the West Fjords. If you don't complete the circle you can finish it on your next trip to Iceland. The **Omnibus Passport** (available all year) entitles you to a period of unlimited travel on all scheduled bus routes including non-Ring roads (1 week 15,700Ikr, 2 weeks 22,700Ikr, 3 weeks 29,700Ikr, 4 weeks 33,200Ikr). All passes entitle you to 10% discounts on many ferries, campgrounds, farms, *Hótel Edda* sleeping-bag accommodations, and guided bus tours. Unless you're on the whirlwind tour and plan to go off the Ring Road or do some backtracking, the Full Circle passes are best. During the off season, Omnibus passes prices drop because fewer routes are available. Keep in mind that neither pass covers the interior bus routes. BSÍ does offer a **Highland Pass** for hardy inland explorers (see **The Interior,** p. 502). Although they are often quite expensive, Iceland's guided bus tours are considered by many well-seasoned travelers to be exceptional.

Flights The only quick way to travel in Iceland is by air; flights are on propeller planes with occasional views of glaciers, mountains, and lava fields, though more often of dark and brooding storm clouds. **Flugleiðir** (Icelandair's domestic service) flies between Reykjavík and major towns, **Flugfélag Norðurlands** out of Akureyri, and **Flugfélag Austurlands** among towns in the east. The two available air packages may be cheaper than the bus. The **Air Rover,** sold at Icelandair offices, offers four stops from Reykjavík, Ísafjördur, Akureyri, Egilsstaðir, and the Vestmann Islands for 21,890Ikr. The **Four Sector Icelandair Pass,** allows three destinations from Reykjavík (US$190). Both are also valid on the regional airlines. Another option is the **Air/Bus Rover** (fly one way, bus the other), offered by Icelandair and BSÍ Travel (June 1-Sept. 30, Reykjavík to Akureyri US$212). Icelandair offers some student discounts, including half-price on standby flights. Iceland's dicey weather can ground flights, so *do not* plan to fly back to Reykjavík the day before your plane leaves Iceland.

Driving, Biking, and Hiking Seeing the country by **car** (preferably 4-wheel-drive) allows you the most freedom. Car rental *(bílaleiga)* starts at about 3700Ikr per day and 30Ikr per km after the first 100km (ask about special package deals). Determined **hitchers** try the roads in summer, but sparse traffic and harsh weather exacerbate the inherent risks of hitching. Nevertheless, for those who last, the ride does come (easily between Reykjavík and Akureyri; harder in the east and the south). **Cycling** is becoming increasingly popular, but ferocious winds, driving rain, and nonexistent road shoulders make the going difficult. You can put the bike on the bus for 500Ikr. **Trekking** is even more arduous; well-marked trails are rare, but several suitable areas await the truly ambitious (see **The Interior,** p. 502).

ESSENTIALS

The tourist season in Iceland doesn't start until mid-June, and it isn't truly high season until July when the interior opens up, the snow has almost disappeared, and all the bus lines are running. Except for the intensely hard-core, winter is not a time to visit; virtually all tourist services are closed, and it's perpetually night. In the summer, the sun dips below the horizon for a few hours each night, but it never gets really dark and it's warm enough to camp and hike. An eye-shade may make sleeping easier. The Gulf Stream keeps temperatures moderate: the mercury rarely rises above 60°F (16°C) in summer, or dips below 20°F (-6°C) in winter. Bring watertight, windproof, lightweight clothing that can be layered. A rain jacket, woolen sweaters, ski gloves, a wool hat, and sturdy shoes are musts any time of the year since the weather is very capricious. Stormclouds are a common evil. It *will* rain. Iceland's geothermal springs spawn an outdoor bathing culture, so pack a swimsuit. Every town has comfortable pools with special hot pools on the side. Film is expensive; bring plenty with you.

Seek out the **tourist offices** in large towns for schedules, maps, and brochures; check at hotel reception desks in smaller towns for local info. Must-haves are the free brochures *Around Iceland,* with accommodation, restaurant, and museum listings for every town, and *The Complete Iceland Map.* The Icelandic language has changed little from Old Norse. Icelandic has two extra letters: Þ (lowercase þ) as in *th*orn; Ð (lowercase ð) as in *th*em. All young people and most adults speak English proficiently, but knowing a few phrases may endear you to Icelanders.

Thank you	Takk fyrir	tahk FIH-rihr
Yes / No	Já / Nei	yow / nei
Excuse me	Afsakið	ahf-sahk-ith
Where is...?	Hvar er...?	hvahr air
How much does it cost?	Hvað kostar það?	hvath koh-star thath
Do you speak English?	Talar þú ensku?	tah-lar thoo EN-skoo
Can you help me please?	Getur þú hjálpað mér?	geh-tur thoo HYOWL-pohth myehr
Goodbye	Bless	bless
Help!	Hjálþ!	Hyoulth

On June 17, Independence Day festivals are held all over Iceland, with the best of them in Reykjavík. Other legal **holidays** in 1998, when most everything closes, include Jan. 1, Easter (April 9-13), Labor Day (May 1), Ascension Day (May 21), Whit Sunday and Monday (May 31-June 1), Bank Holiday Monday (Aug. 4), and Christmas (Dec. 24-26). Regular business hours are weekdays from 9am to 5pm, 6pm in summer. **Banks** open weekdays from 9:15am to 4pm. Currency exchange commissions vary only slightly between banks (except at the airport), and the government sets the rates. **Post offices** *(póstur)* are generally open weekdays from 8:30am to 4:30pm, as are **telephone** *(sími)* offices (often in the same building). Post offices and hostels normally hold mail. Pay phones take 5, 10, and 50Ikr pieces; local calls cost 10Ikr. For the best prices and connections, make calls from the telephone offices or, second best, with prepaid phone cards. For assisted international calls, dial 09. For **AT&T Direct** dial 800 9001; **MCI WorldPhone** 800 9002; **Canada Direct** 999 010; **New Zealand Direct** 800 9064; **Sprint Access** 999 003; and **BT Direct** 800 9044. In case of **emergency,** dial 112. Iceland does not observe daylight savings time—the time is even with London in winter but an hour behind in summer.

Accommodations and Camping Iceland has 28 **HI youth hostels** which are invariably clean, with kitchens and common rooms (1000Ikr, nonmembers 1250Ikr, sheet rental not included). Pick up the free *Hostelling in Iceland* brochure at tourist offices for a complete listing. **Sleeping-bag accommodations** *(svefnpokapláss),* widely available on farms, at summer hotels, and in guesthouses *(gistiheimili),* are viable and competitively priced (most often you get at least a mattress); consult the free *Around Iceland* and *Icelandic Farm Holidays* brochures (the latter lists about 100 farms nationwide). Starting in early June, many schoolhouses become *Hótel Eddas,* which offer sleeping-bag accommodations from 850Ikr (no kitchens, 10% discount for bus pass holders). Most of these places also offer breakfast and made-up beds (both *quite* expensive). Be warned: while staying in a tiny farm or hostel may be the highlight of your Iceland trip, the nearest bus may be 20km away and run once a week. Check the bus schedules carefully and try not to hurry through your trip. Many remote lodgings offer to pick up tourists at the nearest town for a small fee.

In cities and nature reserves, **camping** is permitted only at designated campsites. Outside of official sites, camping is free but discouraged; watch out for *Tjaldstæði bönnuð* (No Camping) signs, and *always* ask at the nearest farm before you pitch tent. Use gas burners; Iceland has no firewood, and it is illegal to burn the sparse vegetation. Always bring your waste with you to the nearest disposal. **Official campsites** (summer only) range from rocky fields with cold water taps to the sumptuous facilities in Reykjavík. Upper-crust sites may cost 500Ikr per person; more basic ones start at about 250Ikr. Many offer discounts for students and bus pass holders.

Food and Drink Icelandic cuisine celebrates animals you might normally envision in a zoo or at your local aquarium. Traditional foods include *lundar* (puffin), *rjúpa* (ptarmigan), and *selshreifar* (seal flippers). You can stick to fish and lamb, or bust out and try *svið* (singed and boiled sheep's head), *hrútspungur* (ram's testicles), or *hákarl* (rotten, years-old shark). Icelanders usually limit their consumption of these delicacies to a four-week period beginning in mid-January, preferring Italian, American, and Chinese food for much of the year. If you just can't get that last bite of puffin down, rejoice: Iceland has some of the purest water in Europe. Beer, which was legalized in 1989, costs 300-600Ikr at most pubs and is consumed mostly on weekends. The national drink is *Brennivín,* a type of schnapps known as "the Black Death." Alcohol is sold only in a few state-run outlets and in pubs and restaurants. The rarely-enforced drinking age is 20. Drunk driving is severely punished.

Grocery stores are the basic hunting grounds for travelers in Iceland; virtually every town has a **Kaupfélag** (cooperative store) and usually a fast-food kiosk. Gas stations (usually open from 9am until 10 or 11pm) sell snacks too. Groceries often close for an hour at noon. Larger towns commonly have supermarkets: **Bonus** and **Netto** are cheaper alternatives to the omnipresent **Hagkaup.** Some supermarkets stay open until 11pm. Food is extremely expensive in Iceland; a *cheap* restaurant meal will cost you no less than 600Ikr. Tipping is not customary.

Reykjavík

"To ill purpose we crossed good land to settle this spit," lamented Reykjavík's founder, the Norwegian Ingólfur Arnarson, upon arriving at the land the gods had chosen for him. Three years earlier, he had heaved his high seat pillars overboard into the North Atlantic and promised to settle wherever the gods washed the pillars ashore. In 874, he landed in the desolate Bay of Smoke. Today, that "smoke" (geothermal steam) heats all houses in the Reykjavík area, and the city has "spit" evolved into the country's capital, with two-thirds of Icelanders living in its greater metropolitan area. Although the urban planning might remind you of a Lego city, Reykjavík's charm more than makes up for its size. Its bold, modern architecture complements the backdrop of snow-dusted purple mountains, and the air is refreshingly sweet, thanks to the legions of youngsters who are out sweeping the streets by 7am. Reykjavík's inhabitants are particularly proud of how "with it" they are: black-clad bohemians brood in cafés while weekend Vikings thrash their skateboards outside. On Friday nights, the staid city busts out on the *runtur,* a bout of bar-hopping and parties. Inviting and virtually crime-free, Reykjavík's only weakness is the often blustery weather.

ORIENTATION AND PRACTICAL INFORMATION

Lækjartorg, the main square of old Reykjavík, sits on the northern side of a peninsula on Iceland's southwest coast. To the north, across the harbor, looms Mount Esja. South of Lækjartorg are the lake, the long-distance bus station, and the Reykjavík Airport on the shore. Extending east and west from Lækjartorg is the pedestrian thoroughfare which forms the axis of the city; the street name changes from **Austurstræti** in the west to **Bankastræti** to the east and finally to **Laugavegur.**

All international flights arrive at **Keflavík Airport,** 55km from Reykjavík. Forty-five minutes after each arrival, a "Flybus" (tel. 562 10 11; 600Ikr) shuttles passengers to the domestic **Reykjavík Airport** and the adjacent Hótel Loftleiðir, from which bus 1 (100Ikr) leaves every 30 minutes for Lækjartorg downtown. Outgoing Flybuses leave the Grand Hotel Reykjavík two and a half hours and Hótel Loftleiðir two hours before each departure from Keflavík; buses also leave the youth hostel at 4:45am from June 1 to September 10. Many flights depart before city buses run, so allow time for walking to the Flybus stops or book a cab in advance. It is reportedly quite easy to hitch from the airport. If purchasing or picking up an Omnibus Pass from BSÍ Travel, be aware that the Flybus fare is covered by the pass and can be refunded at either BSÍ Travel or the Reykjavík Excursions desk in the Hotel Loftleiðir (open 24hr.). This is not true of the Full Circle Passport. Pick up free copies of *What's On in Reykjavík* and *Around Reykjavík* almost anywhere.

Tourist Office: Upplýsingamiðstöð Ferðamála í Íslandi, Bankastræti 2 (tel. 562 30 45), at the end of a courtyard on the corner of Lækjartorg and Bankastræti. Free maps and information galore. Open May 15-Sept. 15 daily 8:30am-7pm; Sept. 15-May 15 Mon.-Fri. 8:20am-6pm, Sat. and Sun. noon-6pm. A **small tourist office** (tel. 563 20 05; http://www.arctic.is) is in the new city hall on Vonarstræti. Open in summer Mon.-Fri. 8:20am-6pm, Sat.-Sun. noon-6pm.

Budget Travel: Ferðaskrifstofa Stúdenta, Hringbraut (tel. 561 56 56; fax 551 91 13), next to National Museum. Sells ISIC, InterRail, Eurobus, Explorer, Euroline, and Greyhound passes. Open Mon.-Fri. 9am-5pm.

Embassies and Consulates: Canada: Suðurlandsbraut 10, 3rd fl. (tel. 568 08 20; fax 568 08 99; email kristbj@mmedia.is). Open Mon.-Fri. 8am-4pm. **Ireland:** Kringlan 7 (tel. 588 66 66; fax 588 65 64; email mottaka@chamber.is). Open Mon.-Fri. 8am-4pm. **South Africa:** Hafnarstræti 7 (tel. 562 95 22, after hours 561 71 81). Open Mon.-Fri. 9am-5pm. **U.K.:** Laufásvegur 31 (tel. 550 51 00; fax 550 51 05). Open Mon.-Fri. 9am-noon; phones staffed until 4pm. **U.S.:** Laufásvegur 21 (tel. 562 91 00; fax 562 91 10; email amemb@iin.is). Open Mon.-Fri. 8am-12:30pm and 1:30-5pm. Open for visas and passports Mon., Wed., and Fri. 9am-noon.

Currency Exchange: Banks open Mon.-Fri. 9:15am-4pm; many are located on Austurstræti and Laugavegur. **Landsbanki Íslands** branches have the best rates and charge no commission. Other banks charge a 90-100Ikr commission for cash and 165Ikr for traveler's checks. After hours, try the tourist office until 8pm and the **Salvation Army** (open May-Oct.) or the **McDonald's** on Austurstræti until 11pm.

American Express: Úrval-Útsýn Travel, Lágmúli 4, P.O. Box 8650, 128 Reykjavík (tel. 569 93 00; fax 588 02 02). Open Mon.-Fri. 9am-5pm. Mail held for members. No wired money accepted.

Flights: Keflavík Airport, for international flights (see above). Icelandair is at Laugavegur 7 (info tel. 505 01 00; staffed Mon.-Fri. 9am-5pm). Domestic **Reykjavík Airport,** just south of town, has two halves. On the *west* side of the runways, **Flugleiðir** (Icelandair; tel. 505 02 00) has regular flights all over Iceland, Greenland, and the Faroe Islands. Take bus 5 from Lækjartorg or Sundlaugavegur, or walk 15min. along the dirt road near the bus station, at the junction of Hringbraut and Vatnsmýrarvegur. From the *east* side of the airport, next to Hótel Loftleiðir, **Íslandsflug** (tel. 561 60 60) flies to several small towns in Iceland, including Vestmannaeyjar. Take bus 1 or walk 15min. from the bus station.

Buses: Umferðarmiðstöð, Vatnsmýrarvegur 10 (tel. 552 23 00), off Hringbraut near the Reykjavík Airport. Terminal open 7am-11:30pm; tickets sold from 7:30am. Upstairs, **BSÍ Travel** has bus passes and schedules, as well as bike rentals. Open June-Aug. Sun.-Fri. 7:30am-7pm, Sat. 7:30am-2pm.

Ferries: HF Skallagrimur (tel. 551 60 50) goes to and from Akranes (4 per day, 1hr., one way 700Ikr) from the main harbor by Geirsgata. Another runs to Viðey Island (2-8 per day, 5min., round-trip 400Ikr).

Public Transportation: Strætisvagnar Reykjavíkur (SVR) (tel. 551 27 00) runs yellow city buses (120Ikr). Ask the driver for a free transfer ticket *(skiptimiði),* good for 30-45min. Kiosks at 4 terminals sell tickets; the 2 main ones are at Lækjartorg (in the building on the north side of the square) and at Hlemmur (in the building between Hverfisgata and Laugavegur at Rauðarárstígur). A map and schedule are printed in *Around Reykjavík,* and maps of routes are available at the tourist office. Buses run at 20-30min. intervals Mon.-Sat. 7am-midnight, Sun. and holidays 10am-midnight. Night buses with limited routes run until 4am on weekends.

Taxis: BSR, Skolatröð 18 (tel. 561 00 00). 24hr. service. The ride costs about 500Ikr from Lækjartorg to Hótel Loftleiðir, but rates are slightly higher at night.

Bike Rental: BSÍ Travel. Mountain bikes 1100Ikr per day, 6500Ikr per week. Omnibus Passport holders receive a 50% discount; Full Circle Passport holders 20%. Reservations required. The youth hostel also rents bikes (1000Ikr per day).

Camping Equipment: Sport Leigan (tel. 551 30 72), next to the bus station. Open Mon.-Fri. 9am-6pm, Sat. 10am-3pm. **Skátabúðin,** Snorrabraut 60 (tel. 561 20 45). Try Hagkaup groceries for gas ovens, sleeping pads, and basic supplies.

Hitchhiking: Those hitching take buses 15, 10, or 110 to the east edge of town, then stand on Vesturlandsvegur for the north, Suðurlandsvegur to go southeast.

Luggage Storage: At the HI hostel. 50Ikr per day, 300Ikr per week, even for non-guests. Also at the BSÍ terminal. 150Ikr per day, 400Ikr per week.

English Language Bookstore: Mál og Menning, Laugavegur 18 (tel. 552 42 40). Stationery, books on Iceland, and a phenomenal selection of fiction, non-fiction, and poetry. Open Mon.-Fri. 9am-10pm, Sat.-Sun. 10am-10pm.

Gay/Lesbian Organizations: SAMTÖKIN 78, in a yellow house at Lindargata 49 (tel. 552 85 39; fax 552 75 25). Small café and large library. Information office open Mon.-Fri. 11am-noon; house open Mon. and Tues. 8-11:30pm, Sat. 8pm-late.

Disabled Services: Icelandic Association of the Disabled (tel. 581 49 99).

Laundromat: Many hostels have arrangements with nearby cleaners. Otherwise, visit **Þvoið Sjálf,** Barónsstígur 3, below Hverfisgata (tel. 552 74 99). Wash 400Ikr, dry 300Ikr; student discount. Open Mon.-Fri. 8am-7pm, Sat. 10am-6pm.

Weather Conditions: Tune to 92.4FM or 93.5FM at 8:55am (summer only) for a report in English. Also try the tourist office or call 515 36 90 for a recording.

Crisis Lines: Women's Hotline (tel. 800 62 05) has English-speaking operators.

Pharmacies: Lyfia Apótek, Lágmúli 5 (tel. 533 23 00). Open daily 9am-10pm. Or just look for *apótek* signs. To find a 24hr. pharmacy, call 551 88 88.

Medical Assistance: Borgarspítalinn (City Hospital), on Sléttuvegur (tel. 525 17 00; staffed 24hr.). Take bus 6, 7, 8, or 9. **The Medical Center:** Barónsstígur 47 (tel. 552 12 30). Open Mon.-Fri. 5pm-8am, Sat.-Sun. and holidays 24hr.

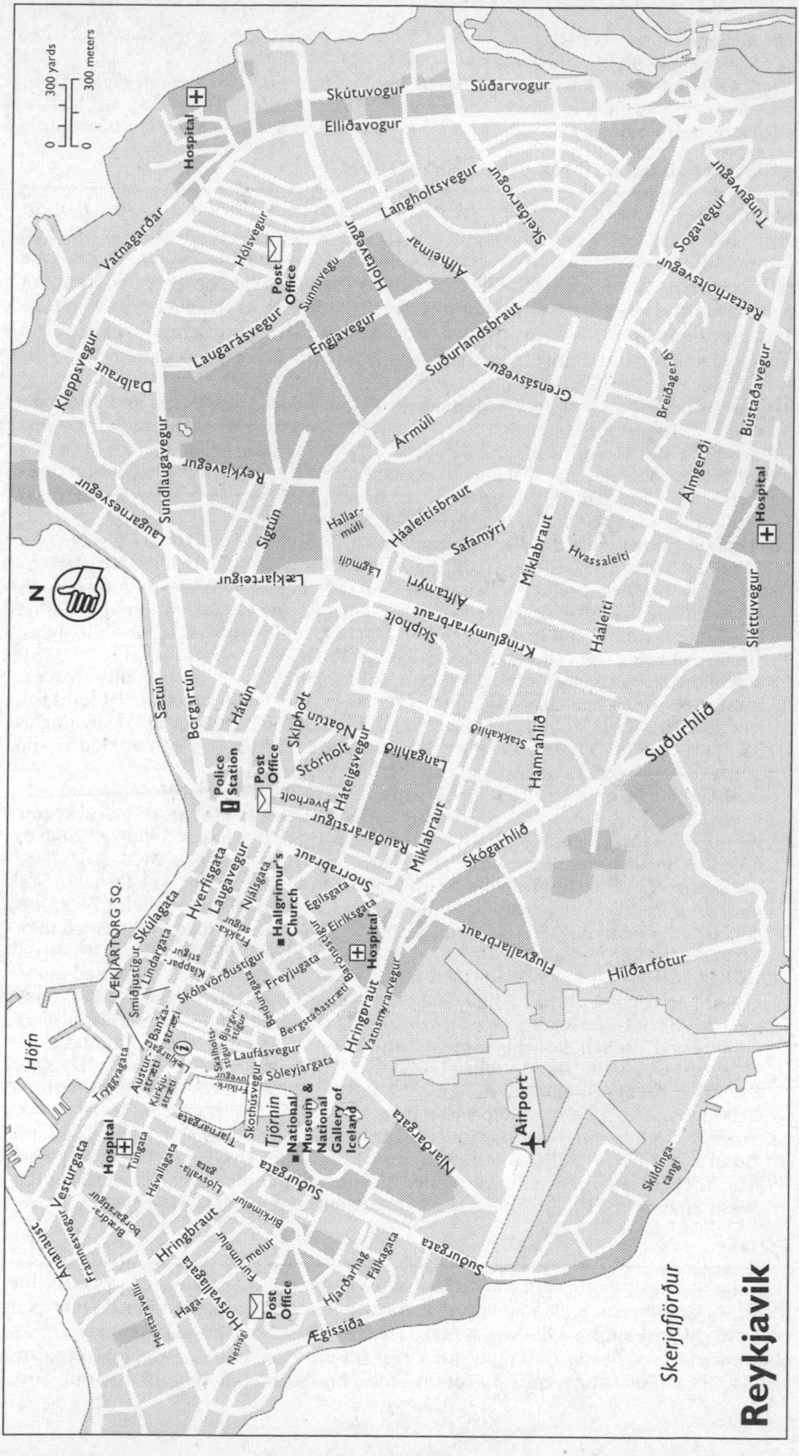
Reykjavik
N
0 300 yards
0 300 meters
Skerjafjörður
Höfn
Tjörnin
Airport
Hospital
Post Office
Police Station
Hallgrímur's Church
National Museum & National Gallery of Iceland
LÆKJARTORG SQ.
Vesturgata
Hringbraut
Hofsvallagata
Ægissíða
Suðurgata
Njarðargata
Tryggvagata
Skúlagata
Hverfisgata
Laugavegur
Skólavörðustígur
Laufásvegur
Sóleyjargata
Tjarnargata
Fríkirkjuvegur
Bergstaðastræti
Barónsstígur
Eiríksgata
Egilsgata
Snorrabraut
Miklabraut
Flugvallarbraut
Hildarfótur
Skógarhlíð
Suðurhlíð
Rauðarárstígur
Háteigsvegur
Stórholt
Skipholt
Nóatún
Hátún
Borgartún
Sætún
Laugarnesvegur
Sundlaugavegur
Reykjavegur
Kleppsvegur
Dalbraut
Laugarásvegur
Vatnagarðar
Hólsvegur
Sunnuvegur
Engjavegur
Holtavegur
Langholtsvegur
Elliðavogur
Skútuvogur
Súðarvogur
Skeiðarvogur
Álfheimar
Suðurlandsbraut
Ármúli
Grensásvegur
Sigtún
Lækjarteigur
Hallarmúli
Háaleitisbraut
Safamýri
Álftamýri
Kringlumýrarbraut
Hvassaleiti
Háaleiti
Langahlíð
Stakkahlíð
Hamrahlíð
Sogavegur
Réttarholtsvegur
Tunguvegur
Breiðagerði
Bústaðavegur
Álmgerði
Sléttuvegur
Vatnsmýrarvegur
Freyjugata
Hjarðarhagi
Fálkagata
Birkimelur
Furumelur
Neshagi
Melstravellir
Framnesvegur
Ánanaust
Túngata
Hávallagata
Ljósvallagata
Skothúsvegur
Skildinganes

ICELAND

Emergencies: tel. 112.
Police: tel. 569 90 00, after hours 369 90 11.
Post Office: Póstur, Pósthússtræti 5 (tel. 550 70 10). *Poste Restante.* Open Mon.-Fri. 8am-4:30pm; June-Aug. also Sat. 10am-2pm. **Postal Code:** 101.
Telephones: Póstur og Sími, across from Kirkjustræti 8. Open Mon.-Fri. 9am-6pm.

ACCOMMODATIONS AND CAMPING

The city has dozens of guesthouses that offer sleeping-bag accommodations. In most cases, this means you get a nice room with a nice bed, *sans* sheets and blanket. Rooms range from doubles to rooms with six people; bunkbeds and double beds are most common. A cheap hotel will cost no less than 4000Ikr; breakfast is often not included in the price. Virtually all of Reykjavík's lodgings are packed from mid-June through August, so reserve in advance and ask about student discounts. Prices drop in the off season. The tourist office has loads of info on all accommodations.

Hjálpræðisherinn Gisti-og Sjómannaheimili (Salvation Army Guest and Seamen's Home), Kirkjustræti 2 (tel. 561 32 03), in a pale yellow house. Located in the center of the old town, near the Tjörnin pond. Young people, adults, and grizzled sailor-types all enjoy the spacious rooms and free soap and towels. Reception open daily 7am-1am; use the doorbell after hours. Sleeping-bag accommodations 1100Ikr. Singles 2200Ikr. Doubles 4000Ikr. Sheets 200Ikr.

Reykjavík Youth Hostel (HI), Sundlaugavegur 34 (tel. 553 81 10; fax 580 92 01). Take bus 5 from Lækjargata to Sundlaugavegur. Spiffy hardwood floors are saved by the strict no-shoe policy. Sells bus and air tickets and rents bikes for 1000Ikr. Kitchen. Luggage storage 50Ikr per day, 300Ikr per week. Reception open Mon.-Fri. 8am-midnight; ring bell after hours. 1000Ikr, nonmembers 1250Ikr. Breakfast 500Ikr. Sleeping bags allowed; sheets 250Ikr. V, MC.

Baldursbrá, Laufásvegur 41 (tel. 552 66 46; fax 562 66 47; email heijfisch@centrum.is). Located in a nice residential neighborhood 5-7min. from the BSÍ terminal. Sleeping-bag room 1600Ikr. Singles 5000Ikr. Doubles 7000Ikr. Sept.-Oct. singles 3500Ikr; doubles 500Ikr. Nov.-Mar. singles 2250Ikr; doubles 4500Ikr. Jacuzzi and sauna ($7 per week). Well-stocked kitchen. V, MC.

Hótel Garður, Hringbraut (tel. 551 56 56), next to the National Museum and relatively close to downtown. A student dorm during the school year. Laundry. Reception open 24hr. Sleeping-bag accommodations 1950Ikr. Singles 5480Ikr. Doubles 6450Ikr. Breakfast and sheets included. Open June-Aug. V, AmEx, MC.

Guesthouse Smárar, Snorrabraut 52 (tel. 562 33 30; fax 562 33 31). Spacious singles; doubles have refrigerators. TV lounge and kitchen. Laundry 400Ikr. Sleeping-bag accommodations 1500Ikr. Singles 3600Ikr. Doubles 4900Ikr. Triples 6400Ikr. Breakfast 600Ikr. V, Euro.

Gistihemlð Flókagata 1, Flókagata 1 (tel. 552 11 55; fax 562 03 55; email guesthouse@skyrr.is), with an entrance on Snorrabraut. Take bus 1 from the BSÍ terminal. Spotless rooms with cable TV, coffeemakers, tea bags, and fridges. Free laundry and kitchen. Reception open 8am-11:30pm. Sleeping-bag accommodations on mattresses in the attic 1300Ikr, 1900Ikr with breakfast. Singles 4200Ikr. Doubles 6100Ikr. Breakfast included. Sept. 15-May 1: sleeping-bag accommodations 1100Ikr; singles 2500Ikr; doubles 4000Ikr. V, Euro, MC, AmEx.

Camping: Right behind the Sundlaugavegur hostel (tel. 568 69 44); take bus 5 from Hotel Loftleiðir or a Flybus. An exceptional campsite. Grocery store nearby. Toilets, kitchen, and barbeque. 250Ikr per person and per tent. 2-bed cabins 2800Ikr. Wash 200Ikr; dry 100Ikr. Showers 50Ikr. Call ahead. Open May 15-Sept. 15.

FOOD

Hunting down affordable cuisine in Reykjavík can be quite a challenge, especially for those seeking typical Icelandic fare. A real experience of traditional foods (centered on seafood and lamb) will cost at least 1000Ikr. Fast food restaurants and kiosks abound; most sell *pylsur* (hot dogs) for about 120Ikr. **Hagkaup** is a supermarket giant with a branch at Laugavegur 59 (open Mon.- Fri. 9am-9pm, Sat. 10am-6pm, Sun.

noon-6pm). Other major chains are **Bonus,** at Faxafen 14 (open Mon.-Thurs. noon-6:30pm, Fri. noon-7:30pm, and Sat. 10am-4pm), and **10/11** (open daily 10am-11pm). Smaller convenience stores throughout the city stay open until 10pm.

Restaurants

Jómfrúin, Laekjargata 4. Danish restaurant serving filling open-faced sandwiches and Icelandic specialties for 700Ikr. Open 11:30am-11:30pm.

One Woman Restaurant, Laugavegur 20B, at the intersection with Klapparstígur. One flight up, this colorful veggie restaurant is as soothing as its food. Small combo platter 600Ikr. Soup 320Ikr. Hot buffet on Saturday night for 900Ikr. Open Mon.-Fri. 11:30am-2pm and 6-10pm, Sat. 11:30am-9pm, Sun. 5-9pm.

The Gallery Restaurant, Bergstaðastræti 37, at the Hotel Holt. Ritzy eating features delicious cuisine and the owner's art collection, with local painters such as Kjarval and Stefánsson. Entrees 1200-1500Ikr. Open daily noon-2:30pm and 6-10:30pm.

Við Tjörnina, Templarasund 3, around the corner from the parliament. Nostalgic knick-knacks, bric-a-brac, and ancient paper dolls adorn the walls. Entrees 1000-1500Ikr. Open daily noon-midnight.

Devito's Pizza, in a parking lot off Rauðarastigur, across from the Hlemmur bus station. A take-out stand with a great lunch special—9in. pizza with 3 toppings and soda 390Ikr. Slices 180Ikr. Open Sun.-Thurs. 11:30am-1am, Fri.-Sat. 11:30am-5am.

Grænn Kostur, Skólavörðustígur 8B, through the parking lot off Bergstaðstræti. Vegetarian fare free of sugar, yeast, and white flour. Dishes 275-650Ikr. Cake 250Ikr. Open Mon.-Sat. 11:30am-9pm, Sun. 4-9pm.

Þrír Frakkar Hjá Úlfari, Baldursgötu 14. Some of the best Icelandic food in town. Try butter-fried monkfish chins and filets of stingray. Even better, ask for whale pepper steak served the traditional style, raw (1420Ikr). Lunch 750-920Ikr, dinner from 1000Ikr. Open Mon.-Fri. 11am-2:30pm, Sun.-Thurs. 6-10pm, Fri-Sat. 6-11pm.

Cafés

The cafés of Reykjavík transform from quiet places for an early breakfast by day to boisterous coffeehouses and bars at night. At marble tables or in smoke-filled dives, the hard working locals kick back and indulge their bohemian alter-egos. Here you can try the light, creamy Icelandic ice cream, grab a quick lunch, enjoy a beer, or even have a cup of coffee. Pick up a copy of *Efst á Baugi,* with listings of live shows.

Sólon Íslandus, Bankastræti 7a. Sophisticated students and literati congregate in this hip café/art gallery to read and drink the bottomless coffee. Live jazz upstairs. No cover. Soup 300Ikr. Children cake (made from chocolate) 280Ikr.

Cafe Paris, across the street from the Parliament. One of the few places where you can eat outside on a sunny day: Icelanders wait in line to shiver over their coffee.

Cafe au Lait, Hafnarstræti 11. Park your skateboard at the counter and hang with the younger crowd in this intimate, smoky café. Huge chocolate cake (200Ikr). Beer (400Ikr). Open Mon.-Fri. 10am-1am, Sat.-Sun. 10am-3am.

xnet.is, Nóatún 17 (http://www.xnet.is), in a shopping complex at the intersection with Laugavegur. This brand new computer center/café features high-tech equipment and a wide selection of computer magazines for the digiterati. 400Ikr buys you an hour of **email** and **Internet access.** The only pillaging and havoc since the Vikings takes place in the daily game tournaments. Open daily 10am-1am.

SIGHTS AND ENTERTAINMENT

Your best deal for sights is the **Reykjavík Card,** which allows free and unlimited use of public transportation and admission to the swimming pool, the Farm Animal Zoo, the Sculpture Museum, and other sites. Buy the card at the tourist office (600Ikr for one day, 800Ikr for two, 1000Ikr for three). For a phenomenal view, hike up Skólavörðustígur to **Hallgrímskirkja** (Hallgrímur's Church) which rises high above the city. The church's design was inspired by Iceland's ubiquitous basalt columns, but its steeple better resembles a rocket ship preparing to lift off. (Open in summer Mon.-Fri. 9am-6pm, Sat.-Sun. 10am-6pm; in winter daily 10am-6pm. 200Ikr.)

The **Þjóðminjasafn Íslands** (National Museum of Iceland), at Hringbraut and Suðurgata beside the university, packs a millennium of history into a few well-arranged rooms, with everything from disintegrating 10th-century swords to models of 19th-century fishing boats. Exhibits are in Icelandic, but a catalogue in English will help you. (Open mid-May to mid-Sept. Tues.-Sun. 11am-5pm; mid-Sept. to mid-May Tues., Thurs., and Sat.-Sun. noon-5pm. 300Ikr.) Across the street is the **National and University Library of Iceland,** whose exterior is shaped like a giant book. A wide selection of magazines is available. Although you can sign up at the information desk for a free hour of **web surfing,** there is no telnet access. (Open June-Aug. Mon.-Fri. 9am-5pm, Sat. 1-5pm; Sept.-May Mon.-Fri. 8:15am-7pm, Sat. 10am-5pm.)

The **Árni Magnússon Institute,** Árnagarður-Suðurgata, located on the university campus, contains a prized collection of old Icelandic illuminated books, histories, and sagas, some dating as far back as 1200. Many Icelanders can trace their families back to people named in these brittle books. The vellum manuscripts, which had resided in Copenhagen since the 17th century, began to be repatriated to an overjoyed Iceland in 1971. The last books arrived home on May 6, 1997. (Open June-Aug. daily 1-5pm; Sept. mid-Dec. and Jan. 6-May 15 Tues.-Thurs. 2-4pm; 300Ikr includes a color catalogue in English.) For a relaxing break, lounge on one of the benches next to **Tjörnin pond** in the center of the old city—you can admire the neat rows of blue, white, and green houses, or just feed the ducks.

On the east shore of the pond, the bright **Listasafn Íslands** (National Gallery of Iceland), at Fríkirkjuvegur 7 (entrance on Skálholtsstígur), shows Icelandic paintings and hosts international exhibits. The building itself, a stunning construction of glass marble and stainless steel, outdoes the paintings inside (open Jan. to mid-Dec. Tues.-Sun. 11am-5pm; 300Ikr). The **Ásmundur Sveinsson Sculpture Museum,** Sigtún, has huge concrete monuments to the working man (open June-Sept. daily 10am-4pm; Oct.-May 1-4pm; 200Ikr). Bus 5 stops at the museum and also runs to the **Farmland Animal Zoo** and **Family Park** in Lavgardalur (open in summer daily 10am-6pm; in winter Mon.-Fri. 1-5pm, Sat.-Sun. 10am-6pm; 300Ikr), where the **Botanical Gardens** are located. (Open in summer Mon.-Fri. 8am-10pm, Sat.-Sun. 10am-10pm; in winter 8am-3pm, Sat.-Sun. 10am-6pm. Free.) The outdoor **Laugardalslaug,** on Sundlaugavegur next to the campground, is the largest of Reykjavík's geothermally heated pools (open Mon.-Fri. 7am-9:30pm, Sat. 8am-7:30pm, Sun. 8am-7:30pm; 200Ikr).

Further east is the **Árbaer Open-Air Folk Museum,** which depicts life in Iceland through the ages. Take bus 10 or 110 to reach the museum (open Tues.-Sun. 10am-6pm; 300Ikr, students 150Ikr). Well-marked trails lead to the salmon-filled Elliðaár river. If you follow the river to **Lake Elliðavatn,** you will find the popular picnic spot and photo stop, **Heiðmörk reserve.** On a sunny, warm, and non-windy day (it could happen), **Viðey Island** provides an excellent opportunity for hiking and picnicking. The island has been inhabited since the 10th century and boasts Iceland's second-oldest church. Ferries run to the island regularly.

If you have the idea that Icelanders are austere and staid people, visit as the work week winds down. Reykjavík nightlife breaks out during the Friday night *runtur,* as alcohol and music flow in bars and clubs around the city. Unfortunately, a fat wad of *krónur* is needed; cover charges run 300-1000Ikr, and beers can cost 550Ikr. **22,** Laugavegur 22, is an artsy hangout that attracts a large gay crowd over the weekend with its disco upstairs (open daily noon-1am, Fri.-Sat. until 3am). Iceland's first pub, **Gaukur á Stöng,** Tryggvagata 22, has live music (food served until 10pm; open Sun.-Thurs. 6pm-1am, Fri.-Sat. until 3am). **Astró,** Austurstræti 22, is the most exclusive and popular club in town—dress to impress (open daily 6pm-1am, Fri.-Sat. until 3am). A younger punk crowd jams at **Bíóbarinn,** Klapparstig 26, on the corner of Hverfisgata (open daily 4pm-1am, Fri.-Sat. until 3am).

■ Near Reykjavík

Some of Iceland's stellar attractions lie within an hour or two from downtown Reykjavík. BSÍ runs many tours of the area; the "Golden Circle" bus tour departs from BSÍ

Travel in Reykjavík (see p. 488) daily at 8:45am (daily except Tues. and Thurs. Oct.-April) for an 8 hour tour of Hveragerði, Kerið, Skálholt, Gullfoss, and Þingvellir National Park ($US73; book in advance). Scheduled buses can also get you around.

Þingvellir National Park, 50km east of Reykjavík, commemorates the world's first democracy and Iceland's ancient parliament, the Alþing. For almost nine centuries, Icelanders gathered once a year in the shadow of **Lögberg** (Law Rock) to discuss matters of blood, money, and justice. The geology of the area is equally interesting. Straddling the junction of the European and North American tectonic plates, the park spreads 2cm apart every year, and massive rifts abound. The river Öxará slices through the lumpy lava fields and jagged fissures on its way to the **Drekkingarhylur** (Drowning Pool), where convicted witches were drowned, and to **Lake Þingvallavatn,** the largest lake in Iceland. The river, according to legend, portends doom by changing into blood, and changes mysteriously into wine for one hour every year. Buses run from Reykjavík (May 15-Sept. 15 at 1:30pm, returning at 5pm; 550Ikr one way). The **tourist office** (tel. 482 26 60), a 20-minute walk north, sells a brochure and hiking map for 100Ikr (open in summer daily 9am-10pm). **Campgrounds** are located by the info center and the lake (450Ikr per person, no showers); the grounds farther north are cheaper but have no bathrooms (300Ikr).

The bus from Reykjavík traverses lush green valleys and bright red clay paths to **Geysir,** a favorite attraction. The Geysir area is a rocky, rugged tundra, with steaming pools of hot water every few meters. Most are small and content to bubble away, but two of them are more fickle and ferocious. Granddaddy of them all, the Geysir itself is the etymological parent of geysers and one of the largest such natural wonders in the world. It used to spray water almost 80m into the air, but now sits and simmers quietly, unless large quantities of soap are added to break the surface tension and make it erupt. These eruptions are announced in the papers and at tourist offices. Just a few steps away, the smaller **Strokkur** makes up for its size with the energetic frequency of its eruptions (every 5-10min.). Look for the water beginning to swell, and then take cover. You can also find azure and rust-colored boiling mud baths near the geysers—at over 120°C they're too hot for a dip. Across the road, **Hotel Geysir** (tel. 486 89 15; fax 486 87 15) provides sleeping-bag accommodations, hotel rooms, breakfast (700Ikr), and a pool with a panoramic view of the valley. (Sleeping-bag dorms 600Ikr, rooms 1100-1300Ikr; singles 2900Ikr; doubles 4000Ikr. V, MC.) The hotel also runs the nearby **campsite,** where falling water serenades you on a soft, grassy field close to the action (350Ikr per person; bus pass discounts). A **tourist shop,** which runs a snack bar, grocery store, gas station, and bus stop, sells all the supplies you'll need (open daily 10am-7pm).

Nine kilometers further along on the same road roars the torrential **Gullfoss** (Golden Falls), named for the hue the fall acquires as it carries mud downstream. The glacial river drops 30m in two stages through a gorge, sending billowing mist high into the air—get as near as you dare, but bring raingear. Nearby, a small museum/info shack details the geology and history of the falls. **Buses** leave for Geysir (1210Ikr) and Gullfoss (1290Ikr) May-Sept. at 9am, June 15-Aug. also 11:30am, and Oct.-April Fri. 4:45pm. They return from Gullfoss May-Sept. at 12:45pm, June 15-Aug. also at 4:15pm, from Geysir at 8am, May-Sept. also at 2:30pm, and June 15-Aug. also 5pm.

VESTMANN ISLANDS (VESTMANNAEYJAR)

Vaulting boldly and majestically from the icy blue depths of the North Atlantic, the precipitous black cliffs off the Vestmann Islands (named after the Irish slaves of the first Viking settlers) are the newest product of the volcanic fury that created Iceland. Forged in fire and baptized in the salty sea water, these 16 jagged monoliths fascinate visitors and welcome thousands of seabirds from all over the north. The newest island, Surtsey, was created during an underwater volcanic explosion in 1963.

Heimaey The town of **Vestmannaeyjar,** on island of **Heimaey,** is one of the most important fishing ports in the country. The islanders have had far from an easy life—in the early 17th century, pirates from North Africa rampaged through the town, killing most of the men and forcing many others to become slaves in Algiers. The town was repopulated and continued to thrive until 1973, when a fiery volcanic fault tore through the northern sector of the island, spewing forth glowing lava and hot ash in a five-month eruption. Though the encroaching lava threatened to close off the natural harbor, a bit of ingenuity probably saved the island's commercial viability, as a massive effort was undertaken to spray sea water on the advancing lava front, slowing and redirecting its flow. The harbor was preserved and actually improved. When the eruption of the volcano **Eldfell** finally ceased, the town was 20% smaller, and the island was 20% larger. Today, the town is rebuilt and modernized, framed by still-cooling lava and the black and green mountains that shelter its harbor, but the chilling remnants of buildings half-crushed by the lava still stand.

Hiking is encouraged; the tourist office distributes a free map with hiking trails outlined. The most spectacular spot is on the cliff's edge at **Há.** Creep close to the sheer edge and you can spy the tents of the campground scores of meters down, past the multitude of nesting seabirds hugging the cliff face and clowning around in the powerful updrafts. Admire the stunning view of the town below, the twin volcanic peaks across, and the snow-covered mainland afar. Both volcanic peaks await the intrepid hiker, but beware the biting winds that howl over their summits. If you head over to one of the country's two **aquariums,** near the gas station on the second floor, you can ogle strange and wonderful creatures without getting your feet wet (open in summer daily 11am-5pm; 200Ikr). The **Volcanic Film Show,** Heiðarvegur 12 (tel. 481 10 45), at the corner of Faxastígur and Heiðarvegur, shows two documentaries in English: one on the exploits of an Icelandic sailor and the other on the eruption. Both include plenty of blood and violence, especially against puffins (June-Aug. at 12:45pm and 4pm, July-Aug. also 9pm; 500Ikr).

Despite its insular reputation, getting to and from Vestmannaeyjar is relatively easy. Four to five Flugleiðir flights per day arrive from Reykjavík (20min., 9130Ikr round-trip), but cancellations abound in bad weather. The **airport** sits below Eldfell's twin peak **Helgafell,** a 20-minute uphill walk from town. A slower but much cheaper option is the **ferry** (tel. 481 28 00), a potentially stomach-churning two- or three-hour ride that leaves from Þorlákshöfn. (Ferries leave daily at noon, Fri., Sun. also at 7pm; June-July also Thurs. at 7pm. 1500Ikr. Buses from Reykjavík connect to the dock and leave 1½hr. before the ferry sails. 550Ikr. Ferries return at 8:15am, Fri, Sun. also at 3:30pm, June-July also Thurs. at 3:30pm.) Vestmannaeyjar's **tourist office** is at Vestmannabraut 38 (tel. 481 15 72), in the Samvinnuferðir-Landsýn travel agency (open June-Sept. Mon.-Fri. 9am-5pm, Sat.-Sun. 1-5pm). Ask there about island bus tours (2 per day, 1300Ikr) and whale watching. The **HI hostel,** Faxastígur 38 (tel. 481 29 15), is a typical Icelandic hostel: meticulously clean, warm and friendly, with a TV that gets two channels. (Sleeping bags allowed. 1000Ikr, nonmembers 1250Ikr. Sheets 250Ikr. Open June to mid-Sept.) The **campground,** 10 minutes west of town on Dalvegur, near the golf course, has showers and cooking facilities (200Ikr per tent and per person). The **K.A. supermarket** is on Strandvegur (open Mon.-Sat. 9am-7pm, Sun. 10am-6pm).

SNÆFELLSNES AND THE WEST FJORDS

Nowhere in Iceland is the awesome power of the Ice Age glaciers more vividly expressed than in the deeply striated northwest. Raking through the Greenland Sea like the curved talons of a hawk, the Snæfellsnes Peninsula and the Vestfirðir (West Fjords) are Iceland's most isolated coastal landscapes. With mossy, snow-covered cliffs rising high above the sea, the West Fjords allow little permanent settlement. Towns are few and far between. Amid this desolation beats the heart of Iceland's vital fishing industry; fishermen prowl the waters night and day, trawling for cod and herring. At the tip of Snæfellsnes, the extinct glacier-capped volcano **Snæfellsjökull** provides the dramatic entrance to the mysterious, subterranean world of Jules Verne's *Journey to the Center of the Earth.* To the north, **Breiðafjörður,** a bay of some thousand islands, separates Snæfellsnes from the **West Fjords,** whose ever-changing terrain lends a stunning backdrop to myriad glacier-carved valleys and waterfalls.

Snæfellsnes is served by **bus** (from Reykjavík all year Mon.-Fri. 9am, Sat. 1pm, and Fri.-Sat. 7pm; June-Aug. also Mon., Wed., Fri., and Sat. 7pm), but the West Fjords are not so easily accessible. To reach Stykkishólmur (3hr., 1950Ikr, round-trip 3450Ikr), transfer buses near the end of the trip. To see Snæfellsjökull, disembark at Ólafsvík (3¼hr., 2150Ikr, round-trip 3750Ikr) or Hellisandur (3½hr., 2250Ikr, round-trip 3900Ikr). Ask at the Reykjavík tourist office about glacier **snowmobile** tours. On the rare clear day, you can hike out for a view of the mountains of ice. Buses return daily to Reykjavík from Ólafsvík (Sun.-Fri. 5pm, Mon. and Sat. 8pm) and Stykkishólmur (Sun.-Fri. 5:20pm, Mon. and Sat. 8:20am, and Mon.-Wed. and Fri.-Sat. 4pm). Be sure to check schedules in advance, and expect many hours on unpaved roads.

ICELAND

Stykkishólmur

Stykkishólmur, the peninsula's largest town and principle port, is a tiny but attractive fishing community with a bustling harbor. It is rich in folk history and home to the mysterious **Helgafell,** the Holy Mountain. According to legend, anyone who climbs this hill for the first time will be granted one wish, as long as the wisher doesn't look back on the way up the hill, faces east while silently making the wish (bring a compass), and never reveals the wish to anyone else. The turn-off to Helgafell is 5km south of town off the main highway; a round-trip hike to the mountain takes at least four hours. Stykkishólmur's modern **church,** which resembles a giant praying mantis, commands a hill above the town (open daily 1-5pm; free). Summer concerts, held on every second Monday (1500Ikr), take advantage of the church's great acoustics. The **Norwegian House,** Hafnargata 5, hosts exhibits from local artists as well as historical displays (open June-Sept. daily 11am-5pm; 200Ikr). For an awe-inspiring view of the sun's descent over Breiðafjörður, whose deep blue expanse is framed by the peninsula's jagged backbone of mountains, take the short climb up to the top of **Súgandisey,** a former island now connected to the harbor by a narrow walkway.

The **tourist office,** Aðalgata 2 (tel. 438 14 50), in a parking lot near the gas station, books private rooms in local houses and also runs a **campground** next door (230Ikr, bathrooms and showers on site; office open June-Aug. 20 9am-9pm). To get there, follow Aðalgata (the main street and continuation of the intercity road) up the hill, and watch for the big parking lot on your left. To get to the **HI hostel,** Höfðagata 1 (tel. 438 10 95), continue on Aðalgata around to the left, and then take another left up the hill on the dirt road. (Sleeping bags allowed. 1000Ikr, nonmembers 1250Ikr. Sheets 250Ikr. Open June-Sept. Reserve ahead.) The hostel also runs a **fishing tour** (2000Ikr, 2½hr.)—hungry backpackers can fry their catch on the grill or use the kitchen. The **pool** near the tourist office costs 100Ikr, including a shower. Feed yourself at the gas station grill, the **Stykkiskaup** supermarket, or the bakery across from the gas station. Ask at the tourist office about **tours** of Breiðafjörður on the speedboat *Eyjaferðir* (3 per day, 2½hr., 2200Ikr, 20% off with student ID).

Your link to the West Fjords is the car-ferry *Baldur* (tel. 438 11 20), which chugs across the bay to the tiny settlement of **Brjánslækur,** to the south of the fjords. The ride is cheap, scenic, and generally calm. (June-Aug. leaves Stykkishólmur 10am and 4:30pm, returns 1 and 7:30pm. 1400Ikr one way, student and bus pass discounts. Cars 1400-2100Ikr; book in advance.) Buses run from Ísafjörður to Brjánslækur and back (mid-June to Aug. Mon., Wed., Fri., and Sat. 3hr. one way), connecting to the *Baldur* at 1pm. The *Baldur* stops briefly (too short to disembark unless you want to wait for the later ferry) at the small, rocky island of **Flatey,** once home to a monastery where many of Iceland's great works of literature were composed. Today, a few beautifully preserved houses are clustered near a bird sanctuary of puffins, ducks, and

Eider geese. The island's remote, magical aura draws summer residents from Reykjavík, but the winter population hovers around ten. The **Café Vogur** (tel. 438 14 13), inside a big blue farmhouse in "town," stocks food, serves hearty meals, and offers sleeping-bag accommodations (1000Ikr).

Ísafjörður

As you approach Isafjörður by car, the high walls of the fjord that flank the harbor might give the impression that you have entered a fortified town. The tiny houses and friendly inhabitants dispel any fears of an immanent invasion; the only thing that the cliffs keep out is the sun, which fails to rise over them for a month during the winter. A sense of the frontier is particularly keen here—the ocean stretches uninterrupted all the way to Greenland and the North Pole. In the highlands above the fjord, awesome vistas of snow-covered mountains and vast, glacial valleys extend on either side of the narrow road. Isafjörður offers an array of activities and excursions; just pray for good weather. For an exceptional view of the West Fjords, **Jórvik** (tel. 456 51 11) offers affordable flightseeing excursions (2½-3hr., 5500Ikr). The **Westfjords Folk Museum and Maritime Exhibit,** in a restored 18th-century house at the end of the spit on Suðurtangi, which displays a bewildering collection of old nautical equipment (open May 15-June daily 1-5pm; July 10am-5pm; Aug.-Sept. 1-5pm; 200Ikr). For a glimpse of Isafjörður's **old cottages** fronted with bright corrugated iron, take a stroll down Njarðarsund and its surrounding streets near the tip of the harbor's horn.

ICELAND

The main part of Ísafjörður rests on a narrow sliver of land that curves out into **Skutulsfjörður,** forming a natural harbor. **Flugfélag Islands** flies 2-3 times daily from Reykjavík, and regular service is available between Isafjörður and the many small communities of the West Fjords (call the tourist office for details). All **buses** to Hólmavík (Tues., Fri., and in summer Sun. 11:45am, Wed. and Sat. 1:30pm; 2500Ikr) easily connect with buses to Reykjavík (5500Ikr) and Akureyri. The **tourist office** is at Aðalstræti 7 in a big green house (tel. 456 5121; open Mon.-Fri. 8am-6pm, Sat.-Sun. 10am-2pm). The **bank** at Hafnarstræti 1-3 has an **ATM.** The excellent **summer hotel** (tel. 456 44 85), the *Framhalosskói á Ísafirði,* on Skutulsfjarðarbraut (the main highway), has a helpful management and sleeping-bag accommodations ranging from a well-equipped double to a mattress on the floor (900Ikr-1500Ikr; open mid-June to Aug.). Next to the hotel is a small, quiet **campsite** (tel. 456 41 11; 400Ikr for 1 tent and 1 person; 10% bus pass discount). There is also one unnamed **guest house** (tel. 456 36 59; fax 456 46 59) in town; find it above a little flower shop at Mjallargötu 5 (sleeping-bag accommodations 1200Ikr, made-up beds 1700Ikr; V, AmEx, MC). The café-restaurant **Gallery Pizza,** on Hafnarstræti at the main intersection, is the most affordable in town (meals from 700Ikr). The **Hotel Ísafjörður** has a relatively cheap tourist menu (lunches 800-1000Ikr, dinner 1100-1700Ikr). The light-of-pocket should visit the supermarket **Björnsbuð,** on Silfurgata, just off Hafnarstræti (open Mon.-Fri. 9am-9pm, Sat. 10am-6pm, Sun. 1-6pm).

NORTH ICELAND (NORÐURLAND)

Dipping its toes into the Arctic Circle and basking in the glow of the midnight sun, North Iceland has a surprisingly mild climate, thanks to well-placed mountains and warm southern currents. Roads connecting the north to the west are lined with hillside fields where the long-haired sheep and sturdy Iceland horses tramp past black stone walls. Wispy birch trees thrive amidst the volcanic melee of steam and stone.

Akureyri

Set against the snowy banks of Eyjafjörður, Akureyri's forested hills make it a soothing oasis in rocky environs. Despite a size that would hardly make it a midsized town elsewhere in the world, Akureyri is the nerve center of northern Iceland. Galleries, museums, and coffee shops provide a dose of bohemian culture that contrasts with the region's hearty fishing tradition. On weekend nights, bands of revelers don their skimpiest and brave the northern exposure in search of a good time.

ORIENTATION AND PRACTICAL INFORMATION

Snow-capped mountains, expansive fjords, and tall trees make Akureyri seem large, but the town of 15,000 people is quite manageable by foot. City bus 3a (100Ikr) takes those arriving by plane 2½km north to the town center, **Ráðhústorg.** Buses from Reykjavík and Egilsstaðir stop at the bus station on **Hafnarstræti,** where the tourist office is located. Pick up a copy of *Akureyri: Tourist Information and Map* at the tourist office or at hotels and guesthouses around town.

Tourist Office: Hafnarstræti 82 (tel. 462 77 33; fax 461 17 18; email tourinfo@ismennt.is), also serves as the BSÍ station. Free guides, maps, brochures, and **luggage storage.** English-speaking staff will book accommodations and sightseeing excursions. Open Mon.-Fri. 7:30am-9pm, Sat.-Sun. 7:30-10:30am and 2-5pm.

Currency Exchange: Landsbanki Íslands is in the main square at Strandgata 1; **Íslandsbanki** is on a street parallel to Hafnarstræti, closer to the water at Skipagata 14. Most banks are open Mon.-Fri. 9:15am-4pm and have 24hr. **ATMs.**

American Express: Úrval-Útsýn Travel, Ráðhústorg 3 (tel. 462 50 00), on the south side of the town center. Same services as in Reykjavík.

Telephones: Postur og Simi, Hafnarstræti 102. Open Mon.-Fri. 9am-4:30pm, Sat. 10am-1pm.

Flights: Flugeiðir Íslands (tel. 461 22 00) flies to and from Reykjavík (5-8 per day, 1 hr., 7085Ikr). Local flights are available to Grímsey, Isafjörður (both Sun.-Fri., 9000Ikr each), and Húsavík (Tues., Sat., and Sun., 4600Ikr). Sightseeing planes also fly to Grímsey (2¼hr., Sun.-Fri., 12,000Ikr).

Buses: BSÍ, Hafnarstræti 82 (tel. 462 44 42), in the same building as the tourist office. The local bus terminal is at the eastern end of Ráðhústorg Square. A schedule *(leiðabok)* can be found at the tourist office.

Ferries: FMN Saefari (tel. 461 15 22) sends ferries to Grímsey from the neighboring village of Dalvik at 11pm on Mon. and Thurs. A connecting bus leaves from the BSÍ station on Hafnarstræti at 10am, and the bus from Dalvik returns to Akureyri at 9:30pm (round-trip 3200Ikr, bus included). **Saevar** (tel. 853 22 11) runs boats to Hrísey from Árskógssandur (round-trip 462Ikr). The bus from Akureyri to Árskógssandur is 450Ikr each way.

Taxis: BSO leigubílar, Strandgata (tel. 461 10 10). About 500Ikr to the airport.

Bike Rental: Ás guesthouse (tel. 461 22 49) rents mountain bikes (800Ikr per day), as does the youth hostel.

Boat Rental: To cruise the fjord on a jetski, call 896 53 32.

Laundromat: Höfði Þvottahús, Hafnarstræti 34 (tel. 462 25 80). 600Ikr per load.

Crisis Lines: Women's Hotline: Tel. 463 08 00 (at hospital). English-speaking.

Pharmacy: Stjörnu apótek, Hafnarstræti 97 (tel. 463 04 52).

Medical Assistance: Hospital: tel. 463 01 00. **Doctor:** tel. 852 32 21.

Emergency: tel. 112.

Post Office: Hafnarstræti 102 (tel. 463 06 00). Open Mon.-Fri. 9am-4:30pm, Sat. 10am-1pm.

ACCOMMODATIONS, CAMPING, AND FOOD

Akureyri has 14 guesthouses which work as cooperatives, sharing profits and customers. While some are nice and convenient, most are not the best place for solo travelers, refusing to play dorm-matchmaker. You might want to make a few friends at the bus station and arrive as a group. Prices for sleeping-bag accommodations in the nicer guesthouses are uniform: singles cost 1900Ikr, doubles 2800Ikr, triples 3900Ikr, and quads 4800Ikr. The tourist office has a list of accommodations with phone numbers and prices. Reserve whenever possible.

Salka, Skipgata1 (tel. 461 23 40; fax 462 26 97). The best option for groups. Each of the 3 reasonably priced rooms (a double, triple, and a quad) is spacious and filled with books, magazines, and games. Soap, towels, and earplugs available.

Farfuglah Youth Hostel (HI), Storholt 1 (tel. 462 36 57; fax 461 45 29), is a bit far. From the tourist center, go through the heart of town and down Gleragata; Storholt is the right after the river. If you're tired, take a bus or call to see if the owner can pick you up. Reception open daily 8am-midnight. Sleeping-bag accommodations 1000Ikr, non-members 1400Ikr. Family-sized room 1000Ikr per person. Doubles 4200Ikr. Breakfast 600Ikr. Sheets 250Ikr. Wheelchair access.

Solgarðar (tel. 461 11 33). African masks and pictures of Hong Kong add an international flair to the spacious rooms. Sleeping-bag accommodations 1200Ikr. Singles 2500Ikr. Doubles 3700Ikr. Triples 4700Ikr. TV in each room. Kitchen.

Brekkukot, Brekkugata 8, (tel. 461 25 65; fax 461 18 67). Flower boxes and family portraits will make you feel right at home. Sleeping-bag accommodations. Singles 1500Ikr. Doubles 2800Ikr. Quads 5000Ikr. Laundry 500Ikr. Kitchen.

Ás, 2 locations. The first is Hafnarstræti 77 (tel. 461 22 49; fax 461 38 10). Sleeping-bag accommodations 2800kr. Kitchen. Free laundry. The other is Skipgata 4 (tel. 461 22 48; fax 461 38 10). Singles 2900Ikr. Doubles 4200Ikr, 5400Ikr with bath.

Camping: (tel. 462 33 79; fax 461 20 30) Between the swimming pool and grocery store, across the street from the Hótel Edda. 400Ikr per person. Showers at the pool 160Ikr. Laundry.

Akureyri's food prices are as steep as its mountains—your best bet is to visit a supermarket. **KEA Nettó,** on Óseyri and Krossanesbraut, is the cheapest. Slightly closer to town is the giant **Hagkaup** at Furuvellir 17, just off Krossanesbraut. The pedestrian street in the heart of town has snack kiosks and a **bakery.** The less expensive restaurants in town tend to be American in style. **Bautinn,** Hafnarstræti 92, is slightly touristy but sometimes offers daily specials of fish and meat starting at 1050Ikr, including soup and salad (open daily until 11:30pm). For lunch specials from 1000Ikr, try **Súlnaberg,** Hafnarstræti 89, across the street from Bautin at the Hotel KEA (open daily 8am-10pm). The hotel also has a restaurant with good breakfast deals. **Café Karólína,** Kaupvangsstræti 600, is a hangout for artists and students, with delicious desserts and the cheapest wine in town (450Ikr).

SIGHTS AND ENTERTAINMENT

A stroll down **Aðalstræti** gives visitors a good introduction to the layout and character of the city. The 3.6 hectares of the **Lystigarður Akureyrar botanical garden** flaunt Iceland's finest flora (open in summer Mon.-Fri. 8am-10pm, Sat.-Sun. 9am-10pm; free). Below the park in a birch grove, the **Akureyri Museum,** Aðalstræti 58, chronicles local history. (Open daily in summer 11am-5pm; July-Aug. 28 also 8-11pm; winter Sun. 2-4 pm. 200Ikr.) The museum organizes free **guided tours** of Akureyri every other Sunday in July and August (tel. 462 41 62; English tours available). Traditional Icelandic music is performed in the **church** next to the museum (July-Aug. 28 Tues. and Thurs. 9pm; 600Ikr includes museum admission). Also nearby is **Nonnahús,** the 19th-century abode of Jón Sveinnson, author of the Nonni children's books (open daily June-Sept. 15 10am-5pm).The **galleries** at Kaupvangsstræti 12 display contemporary Icelandic work (open Tues.-Fri. 2-6pm).

If you're after a more strenuous afternoon, **Mt. Súlur** offers a spectacular view of the Eyafjorður region; to access the one-way 5km trail, take any bus except 3a to Súluvegur and walk up the road 1.5km. **Kjarnaskógur,** 5km out of town on bus 3a, is ideal for jogging and picnicking. **Golf** enthusiasts can tee off into the midnight sun at the world's northernmost 18-hole golf course (tel. 462 29 74), on the hills above town (club rental and 18 holes under 2500Ikr). The last weekend in June brings pros and amateurs from all over for the 36-hole **Arctic Open.** If your muscles need relaxing after your taxing golf activities, take a dip in the **swimming pool,** Pingvallastræti 7, adjacent to a small amusement park replete with waterslides, electric cars, and minigolf (open Mon.-Fri. 7am-7pm, Sat. and Sun. 9am-7pm; 150Ikr).

Besides the riveting world of golf, Akureyri's other passion is music. During the summer, free **jazz** concerts are held every Tuesday night on Kaupvangsstræti. After the show, musicians and fans move to **Café Karólína** to continue the merriment. On Friday and Saturday nights bands play at the nightclubs and bars around town where the dance floors seethe with Akureyrites. **Sjallinn,** Geislagata 14, with bars on three floors, is popular with beautiful people of all ages. A slightly older crowd hits **Oddvitinn** and **Pollinn** on Strandgata. Bars stay open until 3am on Friday and Saturday (1am other nights). Popular bands mean cover charges (about 1200Ikr).

■ Near Akureyri: Hrísey and Grímsey

An island nestled inside a fjord, **Hrísey** is famous for its bird preserve, lush, green walking trails, and quarantined cattle (many come for the great steaks). In Hrísey, the restaurant **Brekka** (tel. 466 17 51; fax 466 30 51) also offers accommodations (sleeping-bag accommodations 1200Ikr, singles 2500Ikr, doubles 4400Ikr). Call **Saevar** (tel. 853 22 11) for ferry information. Besides its Arctic circle location, **Grímsey** is well-known for its bird population and, surprisingly enough, chess players. The American philanthropist Willard Fiske donated chess sets, money, and a library in the late 19th century, thereby establishing himself as something of the island's patron saint. **Básar Guesthouse** offers meals and accommodations (tel. 467 31 03). **Ferries** run from Dalvik, near Akureyri: call **FMN Saefsari** (tel. 461 15 22) for info. Ask at the tourist office in Akureyri about hikes, river rafting, and other activities. A word of caution: the local fowl, having taken a cue from Hitchcock's *The Birds,* are in the habit of divebombing pedestrians. While these "attacks" present no real danger, a sturdy cap is advised.

ICELAND

Mývatn

The beauty and fury of Iceland's fiery past, present, and future explode into view in the area surrounding Mývatn, a shallow volcanic lake 100km east of Akureyri. Like Þingvellir in the south, Mývatn straddles the juncture of European and American tectonic plates. Although the continental bump and grind has produced jagged fissures, bizarre lava formations, and boiling springs, the lake itself sits placidly amid the tumult. Its marshy shores are home to dozens of bird species, some rare, making the protected nesting area on the north-west side a birder's paradise. Directly east, the gnarled lava towers of **Dimmuborgir** disappear over the hills. Nearby, inside the lip of a deep fissure, the underground pool **Grjótagja** simmers with geothermal heat. To the north, plumes of steam rise from dark red lava fields, still warm from the most recent eruption, and an extremely odiferous, luminous blue lagoon surrounds the geothermal power plant. The surface at Vindbelgur on the south end of the lake is pockmarked by **pseudo-craters** created 2300 years ago when a lava flow was cooled by the lake water. The **Krafla** volcanic region, 13km from Reykjahlið, smolders from subterranean activity and holds the explosion crater **Viti** (Hell).

Two towns lie on the edge of lake Mývatn, **Reykjahlið** to the north and the smaller, southern **Skútustaðir**. On foot you'll need several days to appreciate the area's sights, but renting a bike will speed your progress. In Reykjahlið, **mountain bike rental** is located at the gas station in front of the Hótel Reynihlíð (700Ikr per ½day, 1100Ikr per day) or for the same prices at Eldá on route 1. One-day **bus tours** (tel. 462 44 42 35 10) leave daily from Akureyri (mid-May to Sept. 8:15am, 10hr., 4700Ikr, 500Ikr bus pass discount). Eldá also runs regional tours from their guesthouse at 8:45am (3½-4½hr., 3800Ikr). **Buses** run to Reykjahlið from Egilsstaðir (Mon., Wed., and Fri. 6pm) and Akureyri (daily in summer 8:15am and 8pm, around 2hr.). In Reykjahlið the **tourist office** (tel. 464 43 90) is located about a kilometer from town down Hliðarvegur (open June 10-Aug. 25 daily 9am-10pm), and sleeping-bag accommodations are available at the **Gistiheimilið Bjarg** (also called Eldá; tel. 464 42 20; 1100-1300Ikr) with camping available on premises (450Ikr; showers and bathrooms). **Hlið** (tel. 464 41 03), north past Hotel Reynihlið at the edge of a lichen-stained lava flow, also offers camping (450Ikr; 405Ikr with bus pass) and sleeping-bag accommodations (1300Ikr; showers; laundry 800Ikr). In Skútustaðir, **Sel Mývatn** (tel. 464 41 64; fax 464 43 65) has sleeping-bag accommodations and **campsites** with showers (tel. 464 42 12).

EAST ICELAND (AUSTURLAND)

Crossing the inland road to East Iceland from Akureyri, you may think vegetation has made a dash for friendlier fjords. Flat planes of barren earth stretch their way to the horizon, and only jagged lava flows and hills of unbroken beige color the landscape. Suddenly, though, across gravel fields and blasted heaths, glacial rivers carve their way to the coast, where small ports and fishing villages dot the mighty fjords.

Egilsstaðir The main town in this area is landlocked Egilsstaðir, at the northern tip of the narrow lake **Lögurinn** (actually just a widening of the river Lagarfljót). The town is principally a transportation hub, and everything of use to the tourist is in the center. From mid-June to August, **buses** head to Akureyri (daily 3pm, 4½hr., 3500Ikr), and Höfn (Mon.-Sat. 3pm, 4-5hr., 3500Ikr), departing from the **campground/tourist office** (tel. 471 23 20; open June-Aug. 7am-11pm). Shell out 450Ikr (10% off with bus pass) to camp. The campground also offers sleeping-bag accommodation in a small thatch-roofed **guesthouse** with warm, tidy rooms and a small kitchen (1000Ikr, 3000Ikr to rent the whole house). Across the parking lot from the campground, a **supermarket** stocks the basics (open Mon.-Thurs. 9am-6pm, Fri. 9am-7pm, Sat. 10am-2pm). Facing the supermarket, the gas station offers late-night groceries and a grill (open daily 8am-11:30pm).

Seyðisfjörður Cradled between the massive cliffs of a winding fjord lies Seyðisfjörður, 26km over a snowy mountain pass from Egilsstaðir. This tiny town gets very big on Thursdays when the **Norröna** (tel. 472 11 11; in Reykjavík 562 63 62), Iceland's only international car and passenger ferry, calls at the port. The ship departs on the same day (June-Aug.) for Tórshavn in the Faroe Islands (16hr., US$205, 25% student discount), and continues to Esbjerg, Denmark (28hr. from Tórshavn, US$350). Those continuing on to Bergen, Norway, have a three-day layover in the Faroe islands (36hr., US$285). Find the **tourist office** at Vesturvegur 8 (tel. 472 15 51; open mid-June to August Thurs.-Tues. 9am-6pm, Wed. 7am-midnight). Seyðisfjörður was settled by Danes who came for the herring but stayed for the ambience; modern day travelers might also feel tempted to linger, enticed by the sight of ribbon-thin waterfalls cascading down the sheer mountainside. The excellent **HI Hostel** (tel. 472 14 10; fax 472 16 10; email Thora@eldhorn.is) is in the mauve house on the north shore of the fjord and fills quickly on Wednesdays (sleeping-bag accommodations 1000Ikr, nonmembers 1250Ikr). **Snaefell** (tel. 472 14 60l; fax 472 15 70), in the blue house on Austurvegur, has live music on Wednesday nights and is good for family stays. (Sleeping-bag accommodations 2000Ikr; singles 5490Ikr; doubles 7490Ikr. Breakfast included.) The **campground** next to the tourist office is 350Ikr per person.

The Eastern Coast The road from Egilsstaðir to Höfn meanders in and out of fjords, past tiny villages and brightly painted fishing boats. The scenery is some of Iceland's finest, with high rocky cliffs descending into the vast, shimmering Atlantic. Buses from Egilsstaðir stop at **Reyðarfjörður** along Highway 96, which winds through small fjord villages before joining Highway 1 at **Breiðdalsvík.** There are two isolated **HI hostels** along the way, at **Berunes** (tel. 478 89 88; off Highway 1) and at Stafafell (tel. 478 17 17). From Berunes there are a number of daytrip options, including walking trips through bird colonies (2500Ikr), jeep safari tours (2700Ikr), and self-guided hikes (free). The Berunes hostel also runs a **campsite** (400Ikr).

SOUTHERN ICELAND (SUÐURLAND)

Throughout southern Iceland, a flat strip of land of varying width, formed from the silt of snow and glacial outwash, skirts the jagged cliffs and glaciers of the Icelandic interior. Dozens of torrential waterfalls cascade over cliff faces where sea birds glide and elves and trolls dwell. The occasional farm appears, lost in the sea of green and humbled by the towering cliffs. Blessed with good weather, the journey from Höfn to Selfoss is arguably the most stunning in Iceland.

Höfn

The small fishing town of **Höfn** (pronounced *huh*-bin) spreads out on a flat spit of land a few kilometers in front of the icy tendrils of **Vatnajökull**, Europe's largest glacier. A good base for exploring Vatnajökull and the surrounding mountains, Höfn is the link between the south coast and the eastern fjords and the terminus for buses to and from Egilsstaðir (to Egilsstaðir mornings and returning afternoons; 4-5hr., 3300Ikr one way) and Reykjavík (1 per day, 8½hr., 4500Ikr). The **campsite** (tel. 478 10 00; fax 478 19 01) is on your left as you come into town (450Ikr per person; 10% bus pass discount) and doubles as a **tourist info center** (open daily 7:30am-11:30pm). Showers (150Ikr), washers (250Ikr), and dryers (300Ikr) are available. Most establishments are located on Víkurbraut and Hafnarbraut, which form a ring that passes by the harbor. The **HI youth hostel,** Hafnarbraut 8 (tel. 478 17 36), can be a bit claustrophobic. (Reception open daily 7:30-11:30am and 5-11:30pm. 1000Ikr, nonmembers 1250Ikr. Open May-Sept.) There is a **pool** with hot tubs across the street (190Ikr). The **Gistihus Asgarður,** Ránarslóð 3 (tel. 478 13 65), has dorm-style sleeping-bag accommodations (900Ikr), sleeping-bag doubles (1600Ikr), made up singles and doubles with showers and bathrooms (5700Ikr and 7600Ikr respectively, both with breakfast), big lounges, a TV room, and laundry (400Ikr). If arriving the first weekend of July, get stuffed at the **Lobster Festival;** if not, head for the **grocery store** on the corner of Álaugareyjarvegur and Víkurbraut (open Mon.-Fri. 8am-11:30pm, Sat.-Sun. 10am-11:30pm). **Osinn,** on Hafnarbraut past the intersection with Víkurbraut, serves as a gas station, convenience store, and restaurant (9in. pizza 550Ikr). **Restaurant Víkin,** next to the grocery store, dishes up fresh fish for 980Ikr, lamb for 1280Ikr, and beer for 350Ikr (open 11am-11pm).

Skaftafell National Park

Perched between two icy tongues of the Vatnajökull ice cap are the numerous hiking paths and birch forests of **Skaftafell National Park.** The park is ideal for day-hikes, offering well-marked trails and spectacular views of the nearby glacier-capped mountains, the flat, fan-like alluvial plain which reaches toward the sea, and many cascading waterfalls. The most impressive of these is **Svartifoss** (Black Falls), where glacial water pours out over vaulting basalt columns (1-2hr. round-trip by foot from the campground). To the east, **Sjónarnípa** (1hr. one way) and **Gláma** (3hr. one way) offer fantastic views of the glacier, and **Sjonarsker** is also worthy of a roll of film or two. A map with all the hiking routes is available at the info center (100Ikr, free for those staying at the campsite). The traveler with time and money can choose between many guided treks and climbs. **Icelandic Mountain Guides** (tel. 854 29 59; fax 551 13 92) offers guided hikes (1900Ikr) and climbing instruction.

The park is just off Highway 1, three hours west of Höfn. **Buses** run from Reykjavík (3000Ikr) and from Höfn (1300Ikr). Skaftafell becomes a swarming hive of frenzied activity as foreigners and Icelanders alike descend during July and the first half of August. Plan carefully, especially for the weekends. The often crowded **campsite** (tel. 478 16 27; 500Ikr per person, children under 16 free, showers 200Ikr) serves as base for exploration and houses a well-stocked **info center** and **restaurant/grocery store** (open 11am-10pm). Following the main road out of the campsite and then turning right for 30-minute uphill hike brings you to the farmhouse **Bolti** (tel. 478 16 26), which offers all the comforts of home and fantastic views over the vast sandy plains. (Sleeping-bag accommodations 1300Ikr, cabins 2000Ikr per person; dinner 1200Ikr.)

Between Skaftafell and Höfn, buses stop for 20 minutes at the glacial lake **Jökulsárlón,** where large chunks of calved glacial ice ground themselves in the shallow bay on their inexorable journey to the sea. Surreal, natural sculptures appear as the sun does its thing, and the blue "bergs" slowly melt away. **Fjölnir Torfason** (tel. 478 1065; fax 478 1065) offers boat tours from the lagoon (30min., 1300Ikr), but the timing only works if you take a bus from Höfn in the morning and continue on to **Kirkjubæjarklaustur** (Klaustur) to spend the night, as there is nowhere to sleep at Jökulsárlón. More convenient (and more expensive) is a **glacier tour** of the area which leaves the info center in Höfn at 9am and returns at 6pm (9200Ikr).

Vík in Mýrdalur

Situated at the bottom of a green valley beneath the Mýrdalsjökull glacier, Vík is Iceland's southern-most village. The long strand of its black volcanic beach was hailed by *Island Magazine* as one of the top ten island beaches in the world—unfortunately, the water temperature precludes anything beyond cautious toe-dipping in the surf. Just offshore, the jagged rock columns of **Reynisdranger** tower above the churning water, where hundreds of birds (allegedly a band of magical "little people") make their homes. Further west, the natural rock arch of **Dyrhólaey** forms the southern tip of Iceland. **Hiking** trails lead from Vík to the 120m cliffs above the ocean, as well as to inland waterfalls and views of the hulking glacier. **Mýrdaelingur Ltd** (tel. 487 13 34) leads tours to **Reynisdranger** and **Dyrhólaey** in amphibious boats-on-wheels (1500Ikr for one hour, 2400Ikr for two), as well as jeep tours into the mountains.

The **tourist office** (tel. 487 13 95), located inside the main service center/bus station, provides information on the area and on private lodgings, as well as three hiking maps (open June 15-Aug. 15). The **Youth Hostel (HI),** Reynisbrekka (tel. 487 11 06; fax 487 13 03), 9km from the bus station, is perched high up in a breathtaking valley where the sheep roam. The owner doubles as the local police chief and can pick guests up at the bus station in his squad car. Breakfast is 550Ikr, and guests are advised to bring their own food due to the hostel's inaccessibility (1000Ikr, nonmembers 1250Ikr). The newly opened **Hotel Lundi,** Víkurbrant 12 (tel. 487 12 12; fax 487 14 04), has spacious, red-carpeted rooms with shower and telephone (singles 5050Ikr, doubles 7100Ikr; breakfast 700Ikr; V, Euro). The hotel offers sleeping-bag accommodations in an annex next door, which has a kitchen (1200-1400Ikr; open June 1-Sept. 15). The **campground** at the foot of mossy cliffs, 200m from the bus station, has an airy indoor pagoda with a kitchen, big windows, and plenty of seats (400Ikr per person; showers 50Ikr). Outside of hotels, the only place to eat in Vík is the restaurant/snack bar inside the bus station (open daily 9am-10pm). In summer, two Austurleið hf. **buses** shuttle between Reykjavík and Vík every day (in winter 4 per week, 3-4 hr., 1800Ikr) and between Vík and Höfn once every day (in winter 3 per week, 5-6 hr., 2700Ikr).

THE INTERIOR

The abode of elves and outlaws, Iceland's interior is the most forbidding and desolate wilderness in Europe. Today, as 1000 years ago, it remains completely uninhabited; the truly adventurous, or lost, can tramp for leagues without glimpsing another soul. No paved roads, bridges, or gas stations—just limitless stretches of sand rising into mountains, peaked with glaciers, which unleash tumbling waterfalls that evolve into rivers. Four-wheel-drive buses trundle through the emptiness, plow through rivers, and are overtaken by jeeps sporting balloon-like tires and 9m antennas. At times obscured by swirling clouds of red dust, the landscape is so other worldly that Apollo astronauts trained here for their rendezvous with the moon.

Tour buses traverse the interior routes in July and August; they are listed in the ubiquitous *Iceland '98* brochure. BSÍ Travel (tel. 552 23 00) offers the **Highland Pass** (19,700Ikr), consisting of highland units used to "pay" for the interior bus routes (each assigned a value in units). The pass, valid all summer, is highly uneconomical for a one-time visit, although there is a discount for Omnibus Pass holders.

The two most popular destinations, **Þórsmörk** (Thor's Forest) and **Landmannalaugar,** lie within easy striking distance of Reykjavík. In both, the forest-clad valley of Þórsmörk and the technicolor rhyolite mountains of Landmannalaugar have **campgrounds** (500Ikr per person) and bunkrooms with **sleeping bag accommodation** (1200Ikr per person). Both lodgings are run by the Icelandic Touring Club (see below). The four-day trek between Þórsmörk and Landmannalaugar is Iceland's most magnificent. Past Laudmannalaugar, is the **Eldgjá** volcanic fissure, a 40km gash that once produced some 750 square kilometers of lava. On the western side, a spectacular double-waterfall cut a land bridge out of the stone until a flood in 1993 washed it away. Other attractions are the volcano **Hekla** (once thought to be the entrance to Hell) and the summer-skiing at **Kerlingarfjöll,** west of Mýrdalsjökull. From Mývatn, the mud-filled volcanic crater **Askja** is a popular destination.

Interior routes from Reykjavík to Akureyri are available; some are "guided tours." Consult BSÍ Travel in Reykjavík for reservations and more info. (Buses to Þórsmörk run June-Sept. 15 daily at 8:30am, Mon.-Thurs. also at 5pm; buses return to Reykjavík at 3:30pm, Mon.-Thurs. also at 8am. 3½hr. Round-trip 4500Ikr. To Landmannalaugar at 8:30am, return to Reykjavík at 2:30pm. 4½hr. Round-trip 5800Ikr. To Eldgjá passing through Landmannalaugar and continuing to Skaftafell; from Reykjavík at 8:30am, return from Skaftafell at 8am. 11hr. One way 5100Ikr, discounts of around 30% for Full Circle pass holders.) BSÍ operates a **guided tour** from Reykjavík to Lake Mývatn across the interior. (Departs from the BSÍ terminal Wed. and Sat. at 8am, returning from Mývatn Thurs. and Sun. at 8:30am. 12 hr. US$108 one way, US$185 round-trip. Reservations recommended.) Hardcore highlanders can take the "Highland Special," a five-day guided tour of the interior that loops through Mývatn, Akureyri, and the Southern "golden circle" (leaves BSÍ terminal in Reykjavík June 30-Aug.11 Mon. 10am). US$605 includes sleeping-bag accommodations and food. BSÍ also organizes **self-guided trekking** tours of the interior for those with their own gear who want only to be dropped off and picked up several days later. Sleeping-bag accommodations are available in huts along the way.

You *must* pack all food and gas needed for your trip since there are *no* places to buy anything. Anyone driving in the interior should get a free copy of *Mountain Roads* (available at most tourist offices), which details all the "cans" and "cannots" of interior driving. Never venture out without a detailed map, an all-season sleeping bag, a sturdy windproof tent, and a compass. The **Ferðafélag Íslands** (Icelandic Touring Club), Mörkinni 6, 108 Reykjavík (tel. 568 25 33; fax 568 25 35), organizes a variety of interior tours or can help you plan your own (open Mon.-Fri. 9am-6pm). The club also runs numerous huts in the interior and can make reservations for some of them (recommended for popular sites like Þórsmörk and Landmannalaugar). If undertaking a truly hard-core interior journey, leave an itinerary with the **Association of Icelandic Rescue Teams,** Stangarhylur 1 (tel. 587 40 40; fax 587 40 10), in Reykjavík. Topographic maps of the entire interior are available from **Landmælingar Íslands** (the Iceland Geodetic Survey) at their well-organized and well-stocked store at Laugavegur 178 (tel. 533 40 00; fax 533 40 10) in Reykjavík (open Mon.-Fri. 9am-6pm).

Ireland (Éire and Northern Ireland)

US$1 = Irish Pounds IR£0.69 | **IR£1 = US$1.45**
CDN$1 = IR£0.50 | **IR£1 = CDN$1.99**
UK£1 = IR£0.89 | **IR£1 = UK£1.13**
AUS$1 = IR£0.51 | **IR£1 = AUS$1.95**
NZ$1 = IR£0.45 | **IR£1 = NZ$2.23**
SAR = IR£0.15 | **IR£1 = SAR6.68**
Country Code: Republic of Ireland: 353 | **International Dialing Prefix: 00**
Northern Ireland (UK): 44

It can be hard to see Ireland through the mist of stereotypes that surrounds the island even on the clearest of days. Much of the country is rural, religious, and deeply conservative (abortion is illegal here, and divorce was legalized only in 1995), although there is also a developing urban culture with links to Great Britain and the Continent. Traditional musicians roam Western pubs, while rockers try hard in Dublin, Cork, and Galway. The Irish language lives in coastal villages and, for patriotic reasons, in magazines. Long hiking trails, roads, and cliff walks make a chain of windy, watery, spectacular scenery around the coast from Wexford all the way up to Inishowen, while Dublin diffuses its uniquely Irish modernity and sophistication to all in its orbit.

Current tensions and conflicts in Ireland continue centuries-old disputes. In 1171, Henry II claimed the Emerald Isle for the English throne in a less-than-decisive victory, and both English feudal and Gaelic Irish influences split Ireland during the Middle Ages. Following the Reformation in England, the defiant Catholic population was ruthlessly suppressed by the English. The Potato Famine of the late 1840s resulted in the death or emigration of one third of the population, and the malicious negligence of the English government during those years exacerbated tensions while creating an American base of support for Irish nationalism. Turn of the century Fenians agitated passionately for home rule, then following the abortive proclamation of the Irish Republic on Easter 1916, fighting degenerated into civil war. The island was provisionally partitioned into the Irish Free State and Northern Ireland, which remained part of the United Kingdom. In 1949, the Free State officially proclaimed itself the Republic of Ireland (*Éire* in Irish), an independent country that still stakes a territorial claim over the six counties that remain under British rule.

By the end of the 1960s, the tension between Catholic Nationalists and Protestant Unionists in Northern Ireland again erupted into violence. For years, the British and Irish governments' attempts to defuse the situation only led to indiscriminate sectarian attacks by paramilitaries on both sides of the debate. A cease-fire was proclaimed by the Irish Republican Army in 1994, an act which led to the abandonment of many border checkpoints and raised hopes for lasting peace, but permanent solutions have not yet been found. Sporadic violence confirms that radicals on both sides are distrustful and uncertain. Ordinary citizens continue to pray for peace.

For more detailed coverage of Ireland, snag a copy of *Let's Go: Ireland 1998* or *Let's Go: Britain & Ireland 1998.*

GETTING THERE

Be aware that the **ferry** prices listed below exclude an IR£5 government travel tax. **Irish Ferries** sail between Rosslare Harbour and Pembroke, Wales (4hr., IR£20-29, students IR£18-26), and between Dublin (tel. (01) 661 05 11) and Holyhead, North Wales (4hr., IR£25-34; bikes free). Inquire about HI member discounts. **Stena Sealink ferries** (tel. (01) 280 88 44) sail from Holyhead to Dún Laoghaire, a Dublin suburb (IR£26-32), and serve Fishguard Harbor, South Wales, from Rosslare Harbour (UK£20-30, students UK£18-26; bikes free). **Cork-Swansea Ferries** (tel. (021) 27 11

66) run between Swansea, Wales, and Cork (IR£25-30; bikes IR£7). The **Hoverspeed SeaCat** (tel. (0345) 52 35 23, outside the U.K. (01232) 31 35 43) leaves from Stranraer, Scotland for Belfast. (UK£25-32, students UK£16-22; bikes free.) **Stena-Sealink ferries** (in Larne tel. (01574) 27 36 16, in Stranraer (01776) 22 62) also run from Stranraer to Belfast, Northern Ireland (2¾hr., UK£22-26, students £16-19; bikes free). **Supabus** connects Dublin with London (where Supabus connects with Eurolines) in a combination bus/ferry deal for UK£10-25 (students IR£8-23). Book tickets at any Bus Éireann or National Express office in Britain (tel. (0990) 80 80 80).

En route to France? Sail between Cork and Roscoff, France with **Brittany Ferries,** Tourist House, 42 Grand Parade, Cork (tel. (021) 27 78 01; March-Sept. 1 per week, 14hr., IR£51-66). **Irish Ferries** also sail from Cork (tel. (021) 55 19 95) and Rosslare Harbour (tel. (053) 331 58) to Le Havre (20-22hr.), Cherbourg (approx. 16hr.), and Roscoff (22hr.), France (fares IR£40-65, students IR£35-60). Eurailpasses grant passage (no seats) on ferry service between Rosslare and Cherbourg/Le Havre.

You can combine a ferry across the Irish Sea with a stopover on the Isle of Man, which also allows you to ferry into Dublin and ferry out of Belfast at no extra charge. The **Isle of Man Steam Packet Co.** (Douglas info tel. (01624) 64 56 45, reservations 66 16 61; fax 66 10 65; http://www.steam-packet.com) uses Heysham and Liverpool as its principal ports (UK£23-33 one way, students £16-33, bikes free).

British Airways, British Midlands, and **Manx Air** offer **flights** from Britain (including Gatwick, Stansted, Heathrow, Luton, Manchester, Birmingham, Liverpool, and Glasgow) to Dublin, Shannon, Cork, Kerry, Galway, Knock, Sligo, Waterford, Belfast, and Derry. The **Air Travel Advisory Bureau,** 28 Charles Square, London N16ST, England (tel. (0171) 636 50 00) can point out the cheapest carriers out of London.

GETTING AROUND

Trains run by **Iarnród Éireann (Irish Rail)** branch out from Dublin to larger cities, but there is limited service. For schedule information, pick up an *InterCity Rail Traveler's Guide* (50p), available at most train stations. By far the most useful student travel pass in Ireland is the **TravelSave stamp,** available from USIT (see **Dublin,** p. 508) with an ISIC and IR£8. Affixed to your ISIC, this stamp decreases single fares by about 50% on national rail lines and 15% on bus services in Ireland (except fares less than IR£1). The **Eurailpass** is valid on trains (but not buses) in Ireland.

Buses in the Republic of Ireland reach more destinations than trains, but are less frequent, less comfortable, and slower. **Bus Éireann,** the national bus company, operates **Expressway** buses, which link larger cities, and **Local** buses, which serve the countryside and smaller towns. The bus timetable book (80p) is available at Busáras Station in Dublin and many tourist offices. Ireland has **Rambler** tickets, offering unlimited bus travel in Ireland for three out of eight days (IR£28), eight out of 15 days (IR£68), or 15 out of 30 days (IR£98)—you have to move fast to make them pay off.

Northern Ireland Railways (tel. (01232) 89 94 11) service isn't extensive, but covers the northeast coastal region well. The major line connects Dublin to Belfast (UK£15, return UK£22.50), where lines run to Bangor and Larne. There is a **Travelsave stamp** (UK£5.50) in Northern Ireland similar to the one offered in the Republic of Ireland. Find it at the **Student Travel Office,** 13b The Fountain Centre, College St., Belfast, offers 50% off all trains and 15% off bus fares over UK£1 within Northern Ireland. The **Freedom of Northern Ireland** ticket allows unlimited travel by train and Ulsterbus for seven consecutive days (UK£32) or a single day (£9).

Much of Ireland and Northern Ireland's countrysides are well suited for **cycling. Irish Cycle Hire,** Mayoralty St., Drogheda, Co. Louth (tel. (041) 410 67; fax 353 69), with offices in Dublin, Cork, Killarney, Dingle, Galway, and Donegal, rents bikes for IR£6 per day, IR£30 per week (deposit IR£30, one-way rental IR£7 extra; 10% off with ISIC). Ireland offers rugged hills and small mountains to its **hikers.** The best hiking maps are the **Ordnance Survey** series (IR£3.70 each), available at tourist offices.

ESSENTIALS

Bord Fáilte (the Irish Tourist Board) operates a nationwide network of offices, selling maps and local guidebooks. Most tourist offices will book a room for an IR£1-3 fee and 10% deposit, but many fine hostels and B&Bs are not "approved," so the tourist office can't tell you about them. **Weather** in Ireland is temperate (summer averages 15-18°C, 60-65°F) yet temperamental. Keep a poncho or umbrella handy, and carry a sweater, as sunshine often yields suddenly to chilly rain.

Banks are open Monday to Friday 9am-4pm, sometimes later on Thursdays. Dial 114 for an **international operator.** For **Australia Direct,** call (1800) 550 061 in the Republic and (0800) 890 061 in the North; **British Telecom** (1800) 550 144 in Ireland; **Ireland Direct** (0800) 890 353 in the North; **Telecom New Zealand** (1800) 550 064 in the Republic and (0800) 890 064 in the North; **Telekom South Africa** (1800) 550 027 in the Republic and (0800) 890 027 up North; **AT&T Direct** (1800) 550 000 in the Republic and (0800) 890 011 in the U.K.; **MCI World Phone** (1800) 551 001 in Ireland and (0800) 890 222 in the North. Dial 190 for the operator; for directory inquiries 1190 in the South and 192 in the North. In an **emergency,** dial 999.

Much of the Southern Ireland closes for **holidays** on Jan. 1, St. Patrick's Day (March 17), Easter (April 10-13 in 1998), June 1, Aug. 3, Oct. 26, and Christmas (Dec. 25-26). Northern Ireland celebrates Jan. 1, St. Patrick's Day, Easter, May Day (May 4 in 1998), Spring or Whitsun Holiday (May 25), Orange Day (June 12), Aug. 31, and Christmas.

Accommodations, Camping, and Food Hosteling is the way to go in Ireland. **An Óige,** the Irish Hostelling International affiliate, runs 37 hostels which are often relatively bare and somewhat out of the way. The *An Óige Handbook* (IR£1.50) lists and details these hostels; its standard pricing system isn't always followed by every hostel listed. The North's HI affiliate is **YHANI** (Youth Hostel Association of Northern Ireland). It operates nine nicer hostels. A number of hostels in Ireland belong to the **Independent Holiday Hostels (IHH).** These hostels have no lockout or curfew (with a few exceptions), accept all ages, require no membership card, and have a comfortable atmosphere; all are Bord Fáilte-approved. **B&Bs** provide a luxurious break from hosteling. Expect to pay IR£12-20 for singles and IR£20-36 for doubles. "Full Irish breakfasts" are often filling enough to get you through to dinner.

Camping in Irish State Forests and National Parks is not allowed; camping on public land is permissible only if there is no official campsite in the area. Most caravan and camping parks are open April through October, though some stay open year-round. The *Caravan and Camping Ireland,* available from any Bord Fáilte office (IR£4), lists all approved campgrounds in the Republic.

Food in Ireland is expensive. The basics are simple and filling. "Take-away" (take-out) fish and chips shops are quick, greasy, and very popular. Many pubs serve food as well as drink; typical pub grub includes Irish stew, burgers, soup, and sandwiches. Soda bread is delicious and keeps well, and Irish dairy products are addictive. Pubs in Ireland are the forum for banter, singing, and *craic* meaning "a good time." In the evening, many pubs play impromptu or organized traditional music (trad); there's quite a bit of variety to these watering holes. Guinness, a rich, dark stout, is the most revered brew in Ireland. Irish whiskey is sweeter and more stinging than its Scotch counterpart. Pubs are usually open Monday to Saturday 10:30am to 11 or 11:30pm, Sunday 12:30 to 2pm and 4 to 11pm (in the North Sun. 12:30-2:30pm and 7-10pm).

Dublin

In a country known for its quiet and lackadaisical pace, Dublin is fast, urban, and energized. The city and its suburbs, home to one-third of Ireland's population, are at the vanguard of the country's rapid social change: countercultures flourish here in a way the rest of the Emerald Isle would summarily reject, and cutting-edge, world-renowned music bursts from within the city's pub doors. Yet, despite Dublin's progressive pace and rocking nightlife, the old Ireland still courses through its citified veins. Statues of writers like Joyce, Swift, Burke, and Beckett pepper the streets with literary landmarks, and beneath the urban bustle, majestic cathedrals and quaint pubs welcome visitors with Ireland's trademark friendliness and zeal.

ORIENTATION AND PRACTICAL INFORMATION

The **River Liffey** cuts central Dublin in half. Better food and the more famous sights reside on the **South Side,** though hostels and the bus station inhabit the grittier **North Side.** When streets split into "Upper" and "Lower" sections, "Lower" is closer to the Liffey's mouth (east). Most attractions are in the area circumscribed by North and South Circular Rd. **Trinity College Dublin (TCD)** functions as the nerve center of Dublin's activity. Heading west on Dame St., **Temple Bar** is a lively nightspot area. The **North Side** should perhaps be avoided at night. Streets change names often; get a good map with an index. Dundrum's *Handy Map of Dublin* (IR£4) is superb.

Tourist Offices: Main office on Suffolk St. (tel. (1550) 11 22 33, 58p per min.; fax 605 77 87). From Connolly Station, walk left down Amiens St. to the Quay, turn right past Busáras, and make a left over O'Connell Bridge. Go past TCD; Suffolk St. is on the right. Accommodations service (IR£1 and 10% booking deposit). *Map of Greater Dublin* (IR£4.10). Open mid-June to mid-Sept. Mon.-Sat. 8:30am-7:30pm, Sun. 11-5pm; mid-Sept. to mid-June Mon.-Sat. 9am-5:30pm, Tues. opens at 9:30am.

Budget Travel: USIT (Irish Student Travel Agency), 19-21 Aston Quay (tel. 679 88 33), near O'Connell Bridge. ISICs, HI cards. TravelSave stamps IR£7. Many discounts, especially for those under 26. Open Mon.-Fri. 9am-6pm, Sat. 11am-4pm.

Embassies: Australia, Fitzwilton House, Wilton Terrace (tel. 676 15 17). Open Mon.-Thurs. 10am-12:30pm and 2-3:30pm, Fri. 9am-noon. **Canada,** 65 St. Stephen's Green South (tel. 478 19 88, emergencies 285 12 46). Open Mon.-Fri. 10am-noon and 2-4pm. **New Zealanders** should contact the London embassy. **South Africa,** 2nd fl., Alexander House, Earlsford Centre (tel. 661 55 53; fax 661 55 90). **U.K.,** 29 Merrion Rd. (tel. 269 52 11). Open Mon.-Fri. 9am-1pm and 2-5pm. **U.S.,** 42 Elgin Rd., Ballsbridge (tel. 668 87 77). Open Mon.-Fri. 8:30am-4:30pm.

Currency Exchange: Best rates at banks; try the **Bank of Ireland** and **AIB** on Lower O'Connell St. Also in the General Post Office and at the AmEx office.

American Express: 116 Grafton St. (tel. 677 28 74). Currency exchange. Client mail held. Open Mon.-Sat. 9am-5pm; June-Sept. also Sun. 11am-4pm.

Flights: Dublin Airport (tel. 844 49 00). Catch Dublin bus 41, 41A, or 41C (every 20min., IR£1.30) to Eden Quay in the city center, or try **Airport Express** buses (tel. 704 42 22; IR£2.50), which go to Busáras and sometimes Heuston stations.

Trains: Most intercity trains arrive at **Heuston Station** (tel. 703 21 32), just south of Victoria Quay. Buses 26, 51, and 79 go to the city center. The other main terminus is **Connolly Station** (tel. 836 33 33), centrally located on Amiens St. **Pearse Station,** on Pearse St. and Westland Row, is served by fewer trains. **Irish Rail Information,** 35 Lower Abbey St. (tel. 836 62 22). Open Mon.-Fri. 9am-5pm, Sat. 9am-1pm; phones staffed Mon.-Sat. 9am-6pm, Sun. 10am-6pm.

Buses: Busáras, Store St. (tel. 836 61 11), next door to Connolly Station, is the central station for inter-city buses. **Luggage storage** IR£1.50-2 per day.

Public Transportation: Dublin Bus (Bus Átha Cliath). Distressingly lime green. Fares 55p-IR£1.25. Buses run daily 6am-11:30pm. **Dublin Area Rapid Transportation (DART)** serves coastal suburbs from Howth to Bray; fares 75p-IR£2. DART runs daily 6am-midnight. **NiteLink** service runs express routes to the suburbs (Thurs.-Sat. midnight-3am 1 per hr., IR£2.50, no passes valid). Among passes, the **One Day Travel Wide** (IR£3.30; Dublin buses only), the **One Day Bus/Rail** (IR£4.50; valid on buses, DART, and rail service between Kilcoole, Balbriggan, and Maynooth), and the **Four Day Explorer** (IR£10; like a One Day Bus/Rail plus 3 days) are good bets. Insert your pass into the scanner near the bus entrance as you get on.

Ferries: Stena Sealink ferries arrive in Dún Laoghaire, where the DART shuttles to the city center (IR£1.30). **B&I** ferries dock at the mouth of the Liffey; from there, buses 53 and 53A run along Alexandra Rd. (80p). **Irish Rail,** 35 Lower Abbey St. (tel. 836 62 22), handles bookings. Open Mon.-Fri. 9:15am-5pm, Sat. until 12:45pm; phones staffed Mon.-Sat. 9am-6pm, Sun. 10am-6pm.

Car Rental: Argus, 59 Terenure Rd. E. (tel. 490 44 44; fax 490 63 28). Also at the O'Connell St. tourist office and the airport. IR£8 per day, IR£225 per week. Ages 26-64 can rent. Special arrangements for drivers aged 23-26 or 64-70.

Bike Rental: C. Harding, 30 Bachelor's Walk (tel. 873 24 55; fax 873 36 22). Bikes IR£7 per day, IR£30 per week. Deposit IR£30. For IR£12, return your bike to other depots. Bike repair. Open Mon.-Sat. 8:45am-5:45pm.

Laundromat: The Laundry Shop, 191 Parnell St. (tel. 872 35 41). Wash IR£2.20, dry IR£1.30. Soap 50p. Open Mon.-Sat. 8:30am-7pm, Sun. 10am-6pm.

Gay and Lesbian Information: Gay Switchboard Dublin, Carmichael House, North Brunswick St., Dublin 7 (tel. 872 10 55). Open Sun.-Fri. 8-10pm. **Lesbian Line:** tel. 872 99 11; Thurs. 7-9pm. Get *Gay Community News,* covering Ireland, from the **National Gay and Lesbian Federation,** Hirschfeld Centre, 10 Fownes St.

Crisis Lines: Samaritans, 112 Marlborough St. (tel. (1850) 60 90 90 or 872 77 00), for the depressed or suicidal. 24hr. **Rape Crisis Centre,** 70 Lower Leeson St. (tel.

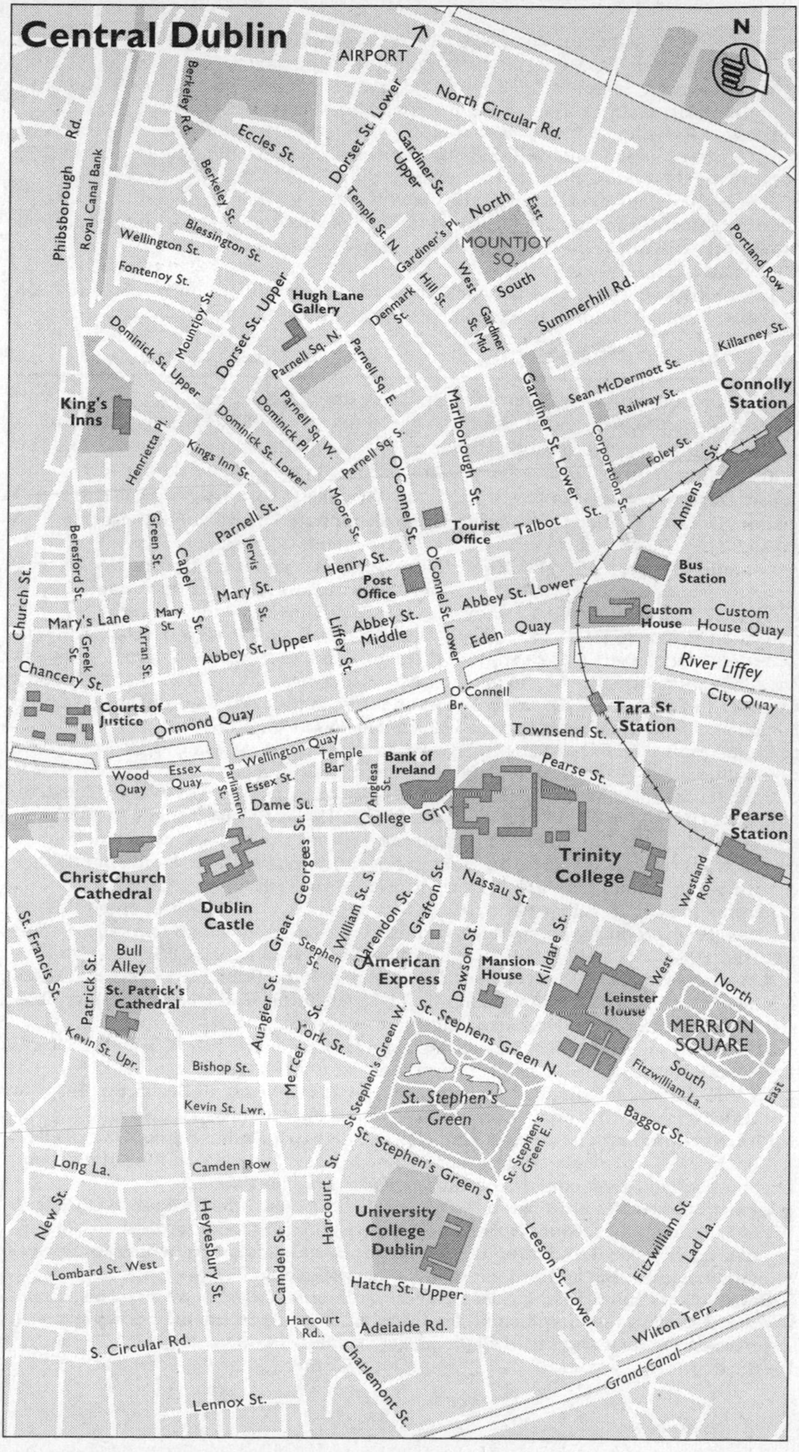
Central Dublin
AIRPORT
N
North Circular Rd.
Berkeley Rd.
Eccles St.
Dorset St. Lower
Gardiner St. Upper
Phibsborough Rd.
Royal Canal Bank
Berkeley St.
Temple St. N.
North
East
Blessington St.
Wellington St.
Gardiner's Pl.
MOUNTJOY SQ.
Portland Row
Fontenoy St.
Hugh Lane Gallery
Dorset St. Upper
Denmark St.
Hill St.
West
South
Summerhill Rd.
Mountjoy St.
Gardiner St. Mid
Killarney St.
Dominick St. Upper
Parnell Sq. N.
Parnell Sq. E.
Sean McDermott St.
Connolly Station
King's Inns
Parnell Sq. W.
Dominick Pl.
Marlborough St.
Gardiner St. Lower
Railway St.
Dominick St. Lower
Henrietta Pl.
Kings Inn St.
Parnell Sq. S.
Corporation St.
Foley St.
Amiens St.
O'Connell St.
Moore St.
Tourist Office
Talbot St.
Parnell St.
Green St.
Beresford St.
Capel St.
Jervis St.
Henry St.
Bus Station
Post Office
O'Connell St. Lower
Abbey St. Lower
Church St.
Mary's Lane
Mary St.
Custom House
Custom House Quay
Abbey St. Middle
Greek St.
Arran St.
Liffey St.
Eden Quay
Abbey St. Upper
River Liffey
Chancery St.
O'Connell Br.
City Quay
Courts of Justice
Ormond Quay
Tara St Station
Townsend St.
Wellington Quay
Temple Bar
Bank of Ireland
Pearse St.
Wood Quay
Essex Quay
Parliament St.
Essex St.
Anglesea St.
Dame St.
College Grn.
Pearse Station
Trinity College
ChristChurch Cathedral
Dublin Castle
Great Georges St.
William St. S.
Grafton St.
Nassau St.
Westland Row
St. Francis St.
Clarendon St.
Bull Alley
Stephen St.
American Express
Dawson St.
Mansion House
Kildare St.
West
North
Patrick St.
St. Patrick's Cathedral
Aungier St.
Leinster House
MERRION SQUARE
Kevin St. Upr.
York St.
St. Stephens Green N.
Mercer St.
St. Stephen's Green W.
Bishop St.
Fitzwilliam La.
South
East
St. Stephen's Green
Kevin St. Lwr.
Baggot St.
St. Stephen's Green E.
Long La.
Camden Row
St. Stephen's Green S.
New St.
Heytesbury St.
Camden St.
Harcourt St.
University College Dublin
Leeson St. Lower
Fitzwilliam St.
Lad La.
Lombard St. West
Hatch St. Upper
Harcourt Rd.
Adelaide Rd.
Wilton Terr.
S. Circular Rd.
Charlemont St.
Grand Canal
Lennox St.

IRELAND

661 49 11; freephone 1 800 77 88 88). **Women's Aid:** tel. (1800) 34 19 00 or 860 00 33. Lines staffed Mon.-Fri. 10am-10pm, Sat. 10am-6pm.

Pharmacy: O'Connell's, 55 Lower O'Connell St. (tel. 873 04 27). Convenient to bus routes. Open Mon.-Sat. 8:30am-10pm, Sun. 10am-10pm.

Medical Assistance: Meath Hospital, Heytesbury St. (tel. 453 65 55, 453 60 00, or 453 66 94). Open 24hr. **AIDS Resource Center,** 14 Haddington Rd. (tel. 660 21 49). Advice, counseling, and HIV testing.

Emergency: Dial 999 for police, fire, or ambulance; no coins required.

Post Office: General Post Office, O'Connell St. (tel. 705 70 00), on the left from the Liffey. *Poste Restante* at *bureau de change* window. Open Mon.-Sat. 8am-8pm. **Postal Code:** Dublin 1.

Telephones: In the **General Post Office.** Public pay phones open Mon.-Sat. 8am-8pm, Sun. and holidays 10:30am-6:30pm. **Telephone Code:** 01.

ACCOMMODATIONS

Dublin's accommodations overflow, especially during Easter, holidays, and July and August—reserve well ahead. Summertime singles in B&Bs are especially hard to come by. Dorms range from £7-12 per night. Quality **B&Bs** blanket Dublin and the surrounding suburbs; most charge IR£12-25, and many cluster along Upper and Lower Gardiner St., on Sherriff St., and near the Parnell Sq. area. Bord Fáilte's annual *Dublin Accommodation Guide* (IR£3) lists all approved B&Bs.

IRELAND

Ashfield House, 19/20 D'Olier St. (tel. 679 77 34). You can't beat the location or the condition of the bright, airy rooms, all with bath. Kitchen open 24hr. Dorms IR£7.70-13. Doubles IR£30-36. Triples IR£33-39. Wheelchair accessible.

Avalon House (IHH), 55 Aungier St. (tel. 475 00 01; fax 475 03 03). From Dame St., take South Great Georges St. until it becomes Aungier St. Groovy comforters and terra-cotta decor. Coed showers, toilets, and dorms. Dorms IR£7.50-12. Doubles IR£12-14. Wheelchair-accessible rooms IR£13.50. Breakfast and luggage storage included. Café, all meals under £5 (open daily noon-10pm).

Kinlay House (IHH), 2-12 Lord Edward St. (tel. 679 66 44; fax 679 74 37), on the continuation of Dame St. Comfy beds and excellent security. Dorms IR£7.50-11. Singles IR£15.50-16.50. Doubles IR£25-28. Breakfast and luggage storage included.

Isaac's (IHH), 2-4 Frenchman's Ln. (tel. 855 62 15; fax 855 65 74), the first right on Lower Gardiner St. walking up from the Custom House. Attractively decorated rooms. Everyone meets in the ground floor café. Bed lockout 11am-5pm. Dorms IR£8-9.25. Triples IR£14.50. Sheets included. Towels IR£1.

Jacob's Inn, 21-28 Talbot Place (tel. 874 93 21; fax 874 15 74), just behind Busáras bus. Bright rooms with sly safety deposit boxes. Bed lockout 11am-3pm. Dorms IR£10.95-14.50. Doubles IR£18.50. Triples IR£15.50. Nov.-May IR£2 less. Café.

Abraham House, 82 Lower Gardiner St. (tel. 855 06 00; fax 855 05 98). Dorms IR£7-11. Singles IR£13-20. Doubles IR£11-15.50. Quads IR£11-13.50. Laundry IR£4. Light breakfast and towels included.

Mrs. M. Ryan, 10 Distillery Rd. (tel. 837 41 47), off Clonliffe Rd. With mercurial hair coloring and firm beds, the proprietor welcomes all. IR£13. Singles IR£15.

Mrs. R. Casey, Villa Jude, 2 Church Ave. (tel. 668 49 82), off Beach Rd. Bus 3 or DART ("Lansdowne Rd."). Every room is immaculate and has a TV. IR£13.

Mrs. Bermingham, 8 Dromard Terr. (tel. 668 38 61). Take bus 3 from O'Connell St. or the DART to Sandymount. Old-fashioned rooms and a TV in the sitting room. Soft beds and great comforters. Singles IR£15. Doubles IR£26-28.

Leitrim House, 34 Blessington St. (tel. 830 87 28), on the final stretch of O'Connell St., after it crosses Mountjoy St. One block past the false teeth repair shop. Alternatively, take bus 10 to the top of Mountjoy St. Lilac walls in the bedrooms, flowers on the windowsill, and reliquaries in the parlor. IR£15.

Backpackers EuroHostel, 80/81 Lower Gardiner St. (tel. 836 49 00). This "campsite" is really a big room behind the hostel of the same name. IR£4 gets you a mattress on the floor and use of all the hostel facilities.

FOOD

Dublin's open-air **Moore St. Market,** which runs between Henry St. and Parnell St., provides fresh, cheap fixings (open Mon.-Sat. 9am-5pm). **Dunnes Stores** offer cheap wares at three locations: St. Stephen's Green Shopping Center, the ILAC Center off Henry St., and on North Earl St. off O'Connell St. (all open Mon.-Wed. and Fri.-Sat. 9am-6pm, Thurs. 9am-8pm). Cheap, creative eateries fill the Temple Bar area.

La Mezza Luna, 1 Temple Ln., corner of Dame St. The food *is* celestial. *Paglia* IR£5.50. Lunch special IR£5. Open Mon.-Sat. 12:30-11pm, Sun. 4-10:30pm.

Bad Ass Café, Crown Alley, off Temple Bar. Colorful, exuberant atmosphere. Sinéad O'Connor once worked here; the food fits right in. Lunch IR£3-5. Pizza IR£5.75-7.75. Student menu (with ISIC) IR£5.75. Open daily 9am to past midnight.

The Well Fed Café, 6 Crow St., off Dame St. Veggie dishes from a worker's co-op. Bread and soup IR£1. Main courses IR£2.40-2.70. Open Mon.-Sat. noon-8pm.

Marks Bros., 7 South Great Georges St., off Dame St. Thick sandwiches (IR£1.30-1.70) and salads for starving artists and punks. Popular gay hang-out. Legendary cinnamon buns 40p. Open daily 11am until "late."

Chez Jules, 16a D'Olier St. Fun atmosphere amidst pasta and seafood consumption. 3-course lunch IR£5. 3-course dinner IR£10. Garlic mussels IR£5. Open Mon.-Fri. noon-3pm and 6-11pm, Sat. 1-4pm and 6-11pm, Sun. 5-10pm.

Leo Burdock's, 2 Werburgh St., uphill from Christ Church Cathedral. Take-out fish and chips are divine. Haddock or cod IR£3. Large chips 95p. Open Mon.-Fri. 11am-11pm, Sat. 2-11pm. Branches at Westmoreland St. and O'Connell St.

Bewley's Cafés, A Dublin institution: delightful crowd, dark wood paneling, marble table tops, and mirrored walls. Wildly complex pastries (IR£1), superb coffee, and plain but cheap meals. Largest branch at 78 Grafton St. (open Sun.-Thurs. 7:30am-1am, Fri.-Sat. 7:30am-2am). James Joyce frequented 12 Westmoreland St. (open Mon.-Sat. 7:30am-9pm, Sun. 9:30am-8pm). Also at 13 South Great Georges St. (open Mon.-Sat. 7:45am-6pm) and at Mary St., past Henry St. (open Mon.-Wed. 7am-9pm, Thurs.-Sat. 7am-2am, Sun. 10am-10pm).

SIGHTS

Dublin is a walkable city; most of the sights lie less than 1 mi. from O'Connell Bridge. The tourist office sells *Visitor Attractions in Dublin* (IR£2) outlining the main sights. The **Historical Walking Tour** (tel. 845 02 41) inundates you with Dublin's history from the Celts to the present. (June-Sept. Mon.-Sat. 11am, noon, and 3pm, Sun. also at 2pm; Oct.-May Sat.-Sun. noon. 2hr. IR£5, students IR£4.) The irreverent **Trinity College Walking Tour** covers Dublin's history but concentrates on university lore (June-Sept. daily every 15min. from 10am-4pm; 30min.; IR£5, students IR£4).

Sprawling at the center of Dublin, **Trinity College,** *alma mater* of Swift, Moore, Beckett, and Wilde, houses the *Book of Kells* (from about 800 AD) in its **Old Library,** built in 1712 (open Mon.-Sat. 9:30am-5pm, Sun. noon-4:30pm; IR£3.50, students IR£3). South of the city, on the block between Kildare St. and Upper Merrion St., Irish history and culture reign. The **National Museum** protects the Ardagh Chalice and the Tara brooch. Down the street on Merrion Sq., portraits of Lady Gregory, Eliza O'Neill, Joyce, Shaw, and Yeats line the **National Gallery's** staircase (open Mon.-Sat. 10am-5:30pm, Thurs. 10am-8:30pm, Sun. 2-5pm; free).

Kildare, Dawson, and Grafton St. all lead from Trinity south to **St. Stephen's Green.** Bequeathed to the city by the Guinness clan, this 22-acre park boasts arched bridges, a lake, fountains, gazebos, swans, and waterfalls. On summer days, half of Dublin fills the lawns, in various stages of undress, and outdoor theatrical productions are held near the old bandstand (open Mon.-Sat. 8am-dusk, Sun. 10am-dusk).

West of Trinity College, between Dame St. and the Liffey, the **Temple Bar** neighborhood bustles with cheap cafés, hole-in-the-wall theaters, rock venues, and used clothing and record stores. New to this hipster scene is the **Dublin Viking Adventure,** Essex St. West, where you can walk through the recreated Dublin of the 9th and 10th centuries (open Thurs.-Mon. 9:30am-4pm; IR£4.75, students IR£3.95).

At the west end of Dame St., where it meets Parliament and Castle St., hovers **Dublin Castle.** Built in 1204 by King John, the castle was the seat of English rule in Ireland for more than 700 years. (State Apartments open Mon.-Fri. 10am-12:15pm and 2-5pm, Sat.-Sun. 2-5pm. IR£2, students IR£1; rest of castle free.) Strangely, Dublin's two official cathedrals, **Christ Church Cathedral** on Dame St. and **St. Patrick's Cathedral** down Nicholas St., are owned by the Church of Ireland, not the Catholic Church. (Christ Church open daily 10am-5pm except during services; choral evensong Sept.-May Thurs. 6pm. IR£1. St. Patrick's open Mon.-Fri. 9am-6pm, Sat. 9am-5pm, Sun. 10-11am and 12:45-4:30pm. IR£1.20). Christ Church hosts **Dublinia,** a life-size recreation of parts of medieval Dublin (open April-Oct. daily 10am-5pm; Nov.-March 11am-4pm; IR£3.95, students IR£2.90).

Those craving alcoholic ambrosia are drawn to the giant **Guinness Brewery,** St. James Gate. To get there from Christ Church, follow High St. west as it becomes Cornmarket, Thomas and then James St. The **Hop Store,** on Crane St. off James St., perpetuates the Guinness mystique and gives complimentary beer with tours. (Take bus 68A or 78A from Ashton Quay or bus 123 from O'Connell St. Open April-Sept. Mon.-Sat. 9:30am-5pm (last admission), Sun. 10:30am-4:30pm; Oct.-March Mon.-Sat. 9:30am-4pm, Sun. noon-4pm. IR£2, students IR£1.) On the North Side, the **Dublin Writer's Museum,** 18 Parnell Sq. North, introduces visitors to the city's rich literary legacy with manuscripts, memorabilia, and caricatures of pen-wielding Dubliners. (Open June-Aug. Mon.-Fri. 10am-7pm, Sat. 10am-5pm, Sun 11:30am-6pm; Jan.-Dec. Mon.-Sat. 10am-5pm, Sun. 11:30am-6pm. IR£2.90, students IR£2.40.)

ENTERTAINMENT

The *Dublin Event Guide* (free at Temple Bar restaurants) and *In Dublin* (IR£1.50) detail a smorgasbord of events. Hostel workers are also a good, if sometimes biased, source of information on entertainment options.

Music, Theater, and Festivals

Hot Press (IR£1.50) has the most up-to-date listings for Dublin's music scene. Traditional music (trad) is a vibrant component of the musical offerings. Pubs in the city center resound with clapping, the drone of a pipe, and roll of a *bodhrán* drum. **Whelan's,** 25 Wexford St. (tel. 478 07 66), is one of the hottest spots in Dublin. Excellent bands frequent the **Baggot Inn,** 143 Baggot St. (tel. 676 14 30)—U2 played here in the early 80s. The **National Concert Hall,** Earl's Fort Terrace (tel. 671 15 33), is the venue for classical music (concerts July-Aug. at 8pm; IR£8-15, students half-price).

Part of the National Theater, the **Abbey Theatre,** 26 Lower Abbey St. (tel. 878 72 22), was founded in 1904 by Yeats and Lady Gregory to promote Irish culture and Modernist theater. (Box office open Mon.-Sat. 10:30am-7pm. Tickets IR£8.50-20; student standby IR£6 1hr. before Mon. and Thurs. shows.) The **Gate Theatre,** 1 Cavendish Row (tel. 874 40 45), produces everything from Restoration comedies to Irish classics. (Box office open Mon.-Sat. 10am-7pm. Tickets IR£10-12; student standby IR£6 Mon.-Thurs. at curtain.)

The city returns to 1904 on **Bloomsday,** June 16, the day on which the action of Joyce's *Ulysses* takes place. The festivities begin about a week earlier. The **Joyce Center** (tel. 873 19 84) sponsors a mock funeral and wake, a lunch at Davy Byrne's, and a breakfast with Guinness as part of its Bloomstime program. On the day itself, a Messenger Bike Rally culminates in St. Stephen's Green with drink and food and readings from *Ulysses.* To find Joyce's works head to Dublin's premier bookdealer, **Fred Hanna's,** 27-29 Nassau St. (open Mon.-Sat. 9am-5:30pm).

Pubs and Clubs

Clubs open at 10:30 or 11pm, but the action gets moving after 11:30pm when pubs close. Most clubs close at 3 or 4am. Covers run IR£4-8, pints IR£3-4. The **Dublin Literary Pub Crawl** (tel. 454 02 28) traces Dublin's liquid history in reference to its literary one. Meet at **The Duke,** 2 Duke St. (June-Aug. Mon.-Sun. 7:30pm, Mon.-Sat. 3pm, and Sun. noon; May and Sept. Mon.-Sun. 7:30pm; Oct.-April Fri.-Sat. 7:30pm, Sun.

noon. IR£6, students IR£5.) *Let's Go* recommends beginning your personal journey at Trinity College Gates, moving onto Grafton Street, stumbling onto Camden, teetering down South Great Georges St., and crawling (triumphantly) into the Temple Bar area.

The Bleeding Horse, 24 Upper Camden St. Mellow, wood-paneled pub with lots of cozy nooks for chats with the friendly crowd. Open until Thurs.-Fri. 1:30am, Sat. 12:30am, Sun.-Wed. 11:30pm.

Whelan's, 25 Wexford St., continue down South Great Georges St. Nightly music makes it one of the hot spots for live rock in Dublin. They know it, and have a "21 and over" policy. Nightly Irish indie rock or blues (cover £2-4).

The George, 89 South Great Georges St. (tel. 478 2983). Dublin's first gay bar. Young, fashion-conscious crowd. Mostly gay men. Lesbians welcome any time but most come Wed. nights. Late bar Wed.-Sat. until 2am. Upstairs, **The Block** is a bar and nightclub for gay men (Fri.-Sat.).

Mulligan's, 8 Poolbeg St., behind Burgh Quay off Tara St. *Let's Go* pick for the best pint of Dublin Guinness. This low-key favorite is your typical Irish pub: smoke and chat with mellow middle-aged men.

The Chocolate Bar, Hatch St., corner of Harcourt St. Hugely popular. Young, lively group of clubbers drink here until **The Pod,** the attached nightclub (Naomi Campbell's favorite), opens.

McDaid's, 3 Harry St., off Grafton St., across from Anne St. Books adorn the walls, inspiring conversations of love and honor among young Dubliners. Crowded downstairs, spacious upstairs areas; occasional rock gigs.

Slattery's, 129 Capel St. Famous for trad and set dancing. Rock and blues, too. Music nightly 9pm: trad downstairs (free), rock and blues upstairs (cover £2-4).

Oliver St. John Gogarty, corner of Fleet St. and Anglesea St. Lively and convivial. Named for Joyce's nemesis and roommate, who appears in *Ulysses* as Buck Mulligan. Trad sessions nightly 7:30pm (no cover) and good food. Always crowded. Open Thurs.- Fri. until 1am, Sat. until midnight.

The Porter House [17], 16-18 Parliament St. Dublin's only microbrewery brews 6 different kinds of porter, stout, and ale, including Wrasslers 4X Stout. If you're up for it, try *An Brainblásta*—7% alcohol by volume.

The White Horse, 1 Georges Quay. For the early morning urge, the White Horse opens at 7:30am. Small, simple, frequented by regulars who come for the trad and rock (starts around 9:30pm; no cover). Low-key—yet to be invaded by tourists.

■ Near Dublin: Howth and Boyne Valley

Nine miles north of Dublin and easily accessible by DART trains (30min., IR£1.10) and buses, Howth provides a bit of countryside—scenic paths, a castle, and great pubs—near the capital city. Orient yourself with the *Guide to Howth Peninsula,* posted at the harbor entrance across from the St. Lawrence Hotel. Howth's primary attraction is the **Howth Castle** on the outskirts of town; take a right on Harbour Rd. as you leave the DART station. A patchwork of architectural styles give it an awkward charm. Farther up the hill, follow the path to the right around the Deer Park Hotel to reach the fabulous **Rhododendron Gardens.** A one-hour **cliff walk** rings the peninsula; the slope's views and springtime blooms are amazing. To get to the trail head, turn left at the station and follow Harbour Rd. around the corner and up the hill. Howth's **B&Bs** make a fine base for hopping to Dublin. **Glenn Na Smol** (tel. (01) 832 29 36), at the end of Nashville Rd., off Thormanby Rd., and **Highfield** (tel. (01) 832 39 36), a 20-minute walk up Thormanby Rd., offer convenient bases (IR£16-17.50). **Ye Olde Abbey Tavern,** Abbey St., pumps out trad (Tues.-Sun. at 9pm).

Among the towns, highways, back lanes, and furrows of the **Boyne Valley** are the richest sets of **archaeological remains** anywhere in Ireland. **Slane** and **Trim** have some of the best-preserved medieval castles, while the **Celtic Hill of Tara** and the Neolithic tomb-mounds of **Newgrange, Knowth,** and **Dowth** puzzle professionals and amaze more casual visitors. Newgrange, the most spectacular, is the prime example of a passage-tomb. Built over 5000 years ago, using stones believed to have been carted from Wicklow 40 mi. away, Newgrange is covered with elaborate patterns and symbols mystifying to archaeologists. **Buses** from Dublin hit the major Boyne towns, but service between towns is spotty (£3-6 return). **Bikers** will find the terrain between the sights welcomingly gentle. Several tours herd visitors through the circuit of sites. **Celtic Twilight** (tel. (088) 547 87) offers a full sight-seeing "Tour of the Royal Meath" (June-Aug. Sun.; £12). The coach leaves the Nassau St. entrance to Trinity College Dublin at 10am and returns to Dublin at 5:30pm. **Sightseeing Tours** (tel. (01) 283 99 73) visits Newgrange and Knowth on its Boyne Valley tour. The bus leaves the Dublin Tourist Office (June-Sept. daily at 1:20pm, return at 6pm; £14).

SOUTHEAST IRELAND

The Wicklow Mountains Over 2000 ft. high and laced with scenic trails, the Wicklow Mountains provide a perfect opportunity to earn that tall drink back in Dublin. The 70 mi. **Wicklow Way** hiking trail starts near Dublin and jogs south all the way to Clonegal in Co. Carlow. Although the path is well-posted with yellow arrows, you should get the *Wicklow Way Map Guide* (IR£5), available at tourist offices, bookstores, and mountaineering stores. **Glendalough** (GLEN-da-lock), a spectacularly uninhabited valley in the midst of the mountains, cradles two lakes, a pine forest, and the remains of a medieval monastic settlement. Stay at **Glendalough Hostel (HI)** (tel. (0404) 453 42; IR£6; Oct.-May IR£5), or in nearby **Laragh** at **Gleannailbhe B&B,** Main St. (tel. (0404) 452 36; IR£14-16) or the **Wicklow Way Hostel** (tel. (0404) 453 98; co-ed dorms IR£6.50-7). **St. Kevin's Bus Service** (tel. (01) 281 81 19) runs to Laragh from Dublin (IR£5, return IR£8) and from the Bray town hall (return IR£6).

Rosslare Harbour Jutting out along St. George's Channel in southeast Ireland, **Rosslare Harbour** offers little in the way of Irish charm, but serves as an important transportation link to Wales, France, and the Irish coast. Rosslare has two **tourist offices:** the overworked one in the ferry terminal (tel. (053) 336 23) and the more sedate one in Kilrane (tel. (053) 332 32), on Wexford Rd. (Ferry office open daily 6:30-9:30am and 11am-8:30pm or 1-8:30pm, depending on ferry arrivals. Kilrane open daily May to mid-Sept. 11am-8pm.) **Irish Ferries** (tel. (053) 331 58) chug to Cherbourg and Le Havre in France (to Cherbourg 19hr., Le Havre 22hr.; IR£35-65). **Buses** run to Cork (IR£12), Limerick (IR£12), Dublin (3hr., IR£10), Waterford (IR£6), and Wexford (20min., IR£3.50). The quicker **trains** have similar prices. If you have to stay in town, try the **Rosslare Harbour Youth Hostel (HI),** Goulding St. (tel. (053) 333 99; fax 336 24; IR£7, Sept.-May IR£5.50). The quiet, thatched fishing town of **Kilmore Quay,** 13 mi. southwest of Rosslare on Forlorn Point, has beautiful beaches; for info call the **Stella Maris Community Center** at (053) 299 22.

Kilkenny Touted as the best preserved medieval town in Ireland, Kilkenny offers rocking nightlife too—nine churches line the same street as 78 pubs. Thirteenth-century **Kilkenny Castle** evokes images of flowing robes and clashing swords. (Open daily June-Sept. 10am-7pm; Oct.-March Tues.-Sat. 10:30am-5pm, Sun. 11am-5pm; April-May daily 10:30am-5pm. IR£3, students IR£1.) **St. Canice's Cathedral** has medieval tombstones embedded in the floor and walls (open daily 10am-6pm, except during services). The **tourist office,** Rose Inn St. (tel. (056) 515 00), offers a free map and city guide and has info on B&Bs. (Open June-Sept. Mon.-Sat. 9am-6pm, Sun. 11am-5pm; shorter hours and closed Sun. off season.) **Trains** (tel. (056) 220 24) and **buses** (tel. (056) 649 33) stop at **McDonagh Station,** Dublin Rd. **Kilkenny Town Hostel (IHH),** 35 Parliament St. (tel. (056) 635 41), is always brimming with activity (IR£7). **Foulksrath Castle (An Óige/HI),** Jenkinstown (tel. (056) 676 74), may be far, but it's one of the nicest hostels in Ireland (curfew 10:30pm; IR£5.50). Throbbing rock music spills into the street from the **Pump House Bar,** 26 Parliament St.

Enniscorthy Extremely proud of its Republican history, **Enniscorthy** is worth a visit in 1998 because it is celebrating the bicentennial anniversary of the local rebels' 12-day stand against British troops. On June13-14, in a fit of national confusion, the **Tour de France** wheels its way through Enniscorthy. The annual **Strawberry Fair,** beginning the last weekend in June, reddens the city for eight days. Musical strains fill the city in mid-September for the **Blues Festival.** For more info contact Maura Flannery (tel. (054) 368 00), who also gives **walking tours.** The **tourist office** is in the castle off Castle Hill Rd. (tel. (054) 346 99; open mid-June to mid-Sept. Mon.-Sat. 10am-6pm, Sun. 2-5:30pm). **Trains** running between Dublin (2hr., IR£10) and Rosslare (50min., IR£7) stop in Enniscorthy. **Buses** go to Dublin (IR£7). Small rooms and a downstairs pub can be found at **P.J. Murphy's,** Main St. (tel. (054) 335 22; IR£14-20).

Cashel Magical when seen from a distance or when lit at night, the commanding **Rock of Cashel** rises above the town. The dark limestone hill bristles with an elaborate complex of medieval buildings 300 ft. above the plain. **Cormac's Chapel,** a majestic, dual-towered structure, was consecrated in 1134. The interior displays gorgeous Romanesque carvings and a richly decorated sarcophagus. The 13th-century **Cashel Cathedral** overshadows all the other ruins in grandeur. The museum at the entrance to the complex preserves the 12th-century **St. Patrick's Cross;** Kings of Munster were crowned on the site marked by the *croix faux.* (Complex open mid-June to mid-Sept. daily 9:30am-7:30pm; mid-March to mid-June 9:30am-5:30pm; mid-Sept. to mid-March 9:30am-4:30pm. Last admission 40min. before closing. IR£2.50, students IR£1.) The superb **Cashel Holiday Hostel (IHH),** 6 John St. (tel. (062) 623 30), off Main St., features comfortable rooms and friendly management (IR£7-8, private rooms IR£10). The stunning **O'Brien's Farmhouse Hostel** (tel. (062) 610 03), off Dundrum Rd., is on the way to **Hore Abbey** (IR£8, private rooms IR£10; camping IR£4 per person). Bushels of *craic* entice locals to **Feehan's,** Main St.

SOUTHWEST IRELAND

Traveling west from Cork City means moving from a bustling, 20th-century landscape into one that often seems untouched: the hills are rugged, the sheep numerous, and the roads lousy. The derelict monuments that once had spiritual significance to ancient civilizations now bestow a sense of timelessness. Yet as the area grows in popularity among tourists, it is becoming increasingly cosmopolitan.

Cork City

Though Cork City dates back to the 7th century, there are few historical traces of its existence before the 20th century: the old city burned down in 1622, an 1853 flood washed away the town, and the British torched the city again in 1920 during the Irish War of Independence. In between these depredations, industry somehow thrived, and the town is now a center for commerce, culture, and nightlife.

Downtown Cork is the tip of an arrow-shaped island in the River Lee; bridges link the island to Cork's residential south side and less affluent north side. **St. Finbarr's Cathedral,** south of the Lee on Bishop St., reflects the Victorian ideal of Gothic bombast (open April-Sept. daily 10am-5:30pm; Oct.-March 10am-1pm and 2-5pm; free). The dynamic **Triskel Arts Centre,** Tobin St. (tel. (021) 27 20 22), maintains a small gallery, runs an excellent café, and organizes many cultural events (open Mon.-Wed. and Fri.-Sat. 10am-5:30pm; free). On the other side of the river, **St. Anne's Church** is Cork's most famous landmark. The church earned the nickname of "the four-faced liar" because the four tower clocks are notoriously out of sync with each other (open in summer Mon.-Sat. 10am-5pm; off-season Mon.-Sat. 10am-4pm). The **Crawford Municipal Art Gallery,** Emmet Pl., boasts an exceptional collection of Irish art and features many traveling exhibits (open Mon.-Sat. 10am-5pm; free).

Practical Information, Accommodations, and Food Pick up the *Tourist Trail* (IR£1) at the **tourist office** (tel. (021) 27 32 51), Tourist House, Grand Parade (open in summer Mon.-Sat. 9am-6pm; off-season Mon.-Sat. 9:30am-5pm). **Trains** leave from Kent Station, Lower Glanmire Rd. (tel. (021) 50 67 66), for Dublin (3hr., IR£32, students IR£13.50), Limerick (1½hr., IR£15.50, students IR£5.50), and Killarney (2hr., IR£13.50, students IR£6). **Buses** drive from Parnell Pl. (tel. (021) 50 81 88), two blocks from Patrick's Bridge on Merchants' Quay, to Dublin (4½hr., IR£12, students IR£8.50), Belfast (7½hr., IR£17, students IR£13), and other cities. **Ferries** to France and England dock at Ringaskiddy Terminal, nine mi. south.

The **Cork City Independent Hostel,** 100 Lower Glanmire Rd. (tel. (021) 50 90 89), is super-relaxed and entertaining (dorms IR£6, doubles IR£14). Positively packed with perks, **Sheila's Budget Accommodation Centre (IHH),** 3 Belgrave Pl. (tel. (021) 50 55 62), lures visitors with a huge kitchen, free **Internet stations,** and a sauna (24hr. reception; dorms IR£6.50-7.50, singles IR£15, doubles IR£19). For true Irish hospitality, try the **Aran House Tourist Hostel** on Lower Glanmire Rd. (021) 55 15 66), a family-run enterprise (dorms IR£6.50, doubles IR£15), or prepare to be pampered at **Garnish House,** Western Rd. (tel. (021) 27 51 11; singles from IR£20, doubles from IR£36). **Bienvenue Ferry Camping** (tel. (021) 31 27 11), very near the airport, is located 5 mi. south of town on Kinslade Rd. (Take the airport bus from the bus station. 1-person tent IR£3, multiple-person tent IR£5 plus IR£1 per person.)

Restaurants and cafés cluster near the city center. **Kafka's,** 7 Maylor St., has cheap but delicious Euro-American hybrid cuisine (open Mon.-Sat. 8am-6pm). Sink into cool jazz and heavenly breads at the **Gingerbread House,** Paul St. (Open in summer Mon.-Thurs. 8am-10:30pm, Fri.-Sat. 8am-11pm, Sun. 8am-6pm; off-season Mon.-Thurs. 8am-9:30pm, Fri.-Sat. 8am-10:30pm, Sun. 8am-6pm.) The creative vegetarian entrees and blissful desserts at **Café Paradiso,** Western Rd., are worth the splurge (open Tues.-Sat. 10:30am-10:30pm). **Quinnsworth Supermarket** on Paul St. and **Quay Co-op,** 24 Sullivan's Quay, offer grocery store wares.

Cork is the proud producer of both **Murphy's** and **Beamish,** which you can enjoy in the pubs along Oliver Plunkett St., Union Quay, and South Main St. **An Spailpín Fánach,** 28 South Main St., is one of Cork's most popular (live music Sun.-Fri.; meals served Mon.-Fri. noon-3pm). **The Lobby,** 1 Union Quay (tel. (021) 31 11 13), arguably the most famous venue in Cork, has given some of Ireland's biggest folk acts their starts (cover IR£3-5). The hardwood floors and stained glass cathedral ceilings strain to contain the crowd in **The Old Oak,** Oliver Plunkett St. **Loafer's,** 26 Douglas St., is Cork's sole gay and lesbian pub. Steps away from campus, **The Thirsty Scholar,** Western Rd., proves that students will walk no farther for a pint than they absolutely have to. Nightclubs fill up when the pubs close. The twin clubs **Club FX** and **The Grapevine,** Gravel Ln., draw students. **Sir Henry's,** South Main St., is crowded and intense (open Wed.-Sat.; cover IR£2-11).

■ Near Cork City: Blarney

Busloads of tourists travel five mi. northwest of Cork to see **Blarney Castle** and its overrated **Blarney Stone.** But the view from the top of the castle, if you get one, makes up for all the tour groups. (Open Mon.-Sat. May 9am-6:30pm; June-Aug. 9am-7pm; Sept. 9am-6:30pm; Oct.-April 9am-sundown. Sundays: summer 9:30am-5:30pm; off-season 9:30am-sundown. IR£3, students IR£2.) Adjacent to the castle lies the **Rock Close,** a beautiful and relatively quiet rock-and-plant garden. **Bus Éireann** runs buses from Cork to Blarney (10-16 per day, round-trip IR£2.60).

Southwest Coast

Kinsale A half-hour drive southwest of Cork lies the ritzy seaside town of Kinsale. **Charles Fort** (tel. (021) 77 22 63), 2 mi. east of town, offers spectacular views of the town and its watery surroundings. (Open mid-June to mid-Sept. daily 9am-6pm; mid-April to mid-June and mid-Sept. to mid-Oct. Mon.-Sat. 9am-5pm, Sun. 9:30am-5:30pm.

IR£2, students IR£1.) Reach the fort by following the sylvan, coastal **Scilly Walk.** Across the harbor, the ruins of **James Fort** delight with secret passageways and panoramic views of Kinsale (open 24hr.; free). Near James Fort, the **Castlepark Marina Centre** (tel. (021) 77 49 59) has rooms with beautiful marina views (IR£8; open March-Nov.). Closer to town, stay at **Dempsey's Hostel (IHH),** Cork Road (tel. (021) 77 21 24; IR£5). Kinsale is Ireland's gourmet food capital with its renowned eateries of the **Good Food Circle.** From the hills on Scilly Peninsula, **Spaniard** (tel. (021) 77 24 36), on the road to Charles Fort, rules over the Kinsale pub scene.

Beara Peninsula Most visitors to Ireland's southwest coast skip Beara altogether, giving it a more profound sense of tranquility than the Ring of Kerry. For unspoiled scenery and great cycling Beara can't be beat. **Bantry** is an ideal base for exploring natural wonders. **Buses** connect with Cork (IR£9). The **tourist office** is in Wolfe Tone Sq. (tel. (027) 502 29; open June-Sept. Mon.-Sat. 9am-6pm). The **Bantry Independent Hostel (IHH),** Bishop Lucey Pl. (tel. (027) 510 50), provides a friendly place to stay (dorms IR£6.50, private rooms IR£9; open mid-March to Oct.).

The largest town on Beara, the fishing center of **Castletownbere** reverberates with the sounds of ferry engines, cars, children, and wind. **Buses** link the town to Killarney in summer (IR£8.80, students IR£5). On the Allihies Rd. two mi. west of town, enjoy comfortable beds in a pleasant rural setting at the **Beara Hostel** (tel. (027) 701 84; dorms IR£6, private rooms IR£7.50; camping IR£3.50). Four miles farther is the luxurious, intimate **Garranes Farmhouse Hostel** (tel. (027) 731 47; dorms IR£6, doubles IR£16; call ahead). On Main St., gorge on seafood at **Jack Patrick's** or **Niki's,** or guzzle a beer at **MacCarthy's.** On the route between Beara, the ring of Kerry, and Cork, **Kenmare** retains its charm despite a fast flow of tourists. Stay at **Fáilte Hostel (IHH),** Henry and Shelbourne St. (tel. (064) 410 83; dorms IR£6.50, doubles IR£18).

Ring of Kerry The Ring of Kerry once embodied the tough, romantic spirit of Ireland, but today it is the epitome of package tourism. **Killarney** is lively and a good base for exploring the spectacular national park nearby. B&Bs are easy to come by, and good hostels reside in town. Try **Neptune's (IHH),** Bishop's Lane (tel. (064) 352 55), the first walkway off New St. on the right (dorms IR£8.50, doubles IR£16; 10% discount with ISIC), or the **Bunrower House Hostel (IHH)** (tel. (064) 339 14), right next to the park (dorms IR£7, doubles IR£19; camping IR£3.50). **Atlas House,** Park Rd. (the extension of College St.; tel. (064) 361 44), is a 10-minute walk from town (dorms IR£9, doubles IR£30, triples IR£37.50; breakfast included). **Yer Mans,** Plunkett St., is the unequivocal best pub in town and the only bar in Ireland licensed to sell Guinness in jam jars. From June through September, buses leave Killarney for the **Ring of Kerry Circuit,** which stops in Killorglin, Cahirsiveen, Caherdaniel, and other towns (IR£8 if booked in a hostel).

The spectacular **National Park** offers some respite from the crowds. Get a decent map from the Killarney **tourist office,** Beach St. (tel. (064) 316 33), off New St., or the **Information Centre** behind Muckross House, a 19th-century manor lying 3 mi. south of Killarney on Kenmare Rd. (tel. (064) 314 40; open daily 9am-7pm). You can bike to the hallowed **Gap of Dunloe,** which divides the epic **Macgillycuddy's Reeks** (Ireland's tallest mountain range) from the **Purple Mountains.** Take a **motorboat** to the head of the Gap (£7.50; £6.50 if booked at the tourist office or a hostel), which will leave you and your bike at **Lord Brandon's Cottage.** The 1½ mi. stretch before arriving at the head of the Gap is a steep climb well-rewarded by the 7 mi. downhill coast through the park's most breathtaking scenery. At the foot of the Gap, you'll pass **Kate Kearney's Cottage** and droves of tourists (open daily 9am-midnight; food until 9pm; frequent live trad). The 8 mi. ride back to Killarney (bear right after Kate's, turn left on the road to Fossa, then right on Killorglin Rd.) passes the ruined **Dunloe Castle,** an Anglo-Norman stronghold which Cromwell's armies demolished.

What tiny **Caherdaniel** lacks in excitement it makes up for with the 2 mi. of white sand in **Derrynane Strand** and the 19th-century patriot Daniel O'Connell's **Derrynane House** (IR£2, students IR£1). The new **Traveller's Rest Hostel** (tel. (066)

751 75) sits near the crossroads (IR£6.50; call ahead). The town of **Cahersiveen** is worth a stop for the extraordinarily friendly **Sive Hostel (IHH),** 15 East End, Main St. (tel. (066) 727 17; IR£6.50-16), and the very Irish **Anchor Bar** and **Mike Murt's** pubs. In **Killorglin,** the **Laune Valley Farm Hostel** (tel. (066) 614 88), 1½ mi. from town off the Tralee road, shares its land with a barnyard full of cats, dogs, and chickens (IR£6, doubles from IR£16; camping IR£3).

Dingle Peninsula Touristy Dingle Peninsula, County Kerry's northernmost, has one of Ireland's few surviving Irish-speaking communities. Base yourself in **Dingle Town,** rich in traditional culture and famous for **Fungi the dolphin,** permanent resident of Dingle Bay. While the town is well-connected to Killarney and Tralee, public transport on the peninsula is scarce. **Buses** run daily in July and August, but only two or three times per week the rest of the year. For info, call the Tralee **bus station** (tel. (066) 235 66) or stop in the Dingle town **tourist office** (tel. (066) 511 88), at the corner of Main and Dykegate St. (open April-Oct. Mon.-Sun. 9am-6pm). The **Grapevine Hostel** (tel. (066) 514 34), on Dykegate St. just off Main St., offers comfortable dorm rooms. The common room has a peat fire, cushy chairs, and a CD player (IR£7). Try **An Droichead Beag** on Lower Main St. for drinks and the best trad in town. For tasty food and Irish patriotism, go to the bookstore/café **An Café Liteartha,** on Dykegate St. (open Mon.-Fri. 10am-5:30pm, Sat.-Sun. 11am-5:30pm).

No matter how tight your schedule is, you will inevitably be waylaid by glorious **Slea Head.** *Ryan's Daughter* and parts of *Far and Away* were filmed amid the green hills, sheep, and jagged cliffs of this area. The scattered settlement of **Dunquin** has stone houses and plenty of spoken Irish. **Kruger's** (tel. (066) 561 27) features pub grub, music sessions, and fantastic views. The adjacent **B&B** has basic but comfortable rooms (IR£15 per person). Just outside of "town" on the road to Ballyferriter, the **Blasket Centre** recreates life on the isolated Blasket Islands with writings and photographs of the Great Blasket authors. (Open July-Aug. daily 10am-7pm; Easter-June and Sept. 10am-6pm. IR£2.50, students IR£1.) A winding cliffside road runs northward from Dingle via the **Connor Pass** and affords tremendous views of bays and valleys.

Tralee While tourists see Killarney as the core of Kerry, residents correctly identify Tralee as the county's economic center. **Kerry the Kingdom,** Ashe Memorial Hall, Denny St., uses amazing modern technology to chronicle the history of Co. Kerry from 8000 BC to the present. (Open April-June and Sept.-Oct. daily 9am-6pm; July-Aug. 9am-7pm; Nov.-March 9am-5:30pm. IR£5.50, students IR£4.75.) Near the museum, the radiant **Roses of Tralee** in the town park and the famous **Siamsa Tíre Theatre** (tel. (066) 230 55), Ireland's national folk theater, draw many visitors. (Productions July-Aug. Mon.-Sat. at 8:30pm; May-June and Sept. Mon.-Thurs. and Sat. at 8:30pm. IR£9, students IR£8.) During the last week of August, the **Rose of Tralee International Festival** (info tel. (066) 213 22) brings a maelstrom of entertainment to the town, as young women of Irish ancestry compete for the title "Rose of Tralee."

It's not difficult to get to Tralee. **Trains** zoom to Cork (2½hr., IR£17, students IR£7), Killarney (40min., IR£5.50, students IR£3.50), and Dublin (4hr., IR£33.50, students IR£12.50). **Buses** run to Cork (2½hr., IR£10, students IR£6), Dingle (1¼hr., IR£6, students IR£4), Killarney (40min., IR£4.40, students IR£3), and Limerick (2¼hr., IR£9, students IR£5). The kind **tourist office** (tel. (066) 212 88) is in Ashe Memorial Hall on Denny St. (Open in summer Mon.-Sat. 9am-7pm, Sun. 9am-6pm; off-season Tues.-Sat. 9am-5pm.) **Finnegan's Hostel (IHH),** 17 Denny St. (tel. (066) 276 10), is in a majestic 19th-century townhouse (IR£6.50, doubles IR£18).

WESTERN IRELAND

The West was hardest hit by the potato famine in the 19th century; entire villages emigrated or died, and the population is still less than half of what it was in 1841. The rugged land also limited foreign influence, preserving spoken Irish in the Connemara and the untamed mountainous landscapes that draw hikers and nature lovers. Booming Galway City remains an enclave of carousing in this otherwise staid country.

Limerick

Although high unemployment and grimy industry have long kept it sagging, **Limerick City** is completing a multi-year facelift. Attractive Georgian architecture and **King John's Castle,** Nicholas St., with pre-Norman excavations and scale models of battle machinery, are worth exploring (castle open daily 9:30am-6pm; IR£3.80, students IR£2.10). Visit the **tourist office,** Arthurs Quay (tel. (061) 31 75 22), for free city maps. (Open July-Aug. Mon.-Fri. 9am-7pm, Sat.-Sun. 9am-6pm; March-June and Sept.-Oct. Mon.-Sat. 9:30am-5:30pm; Nov.-Feb. Mon.-Fri. 9:30am-5:30pm, Sat. 9:30am-1pm.) **Trains** (tel. (061) 31 55 55) leave Colbert Station, just off Parnell St., for Dublin (2hr., IR£25, students IR£10), Cork (2½hr., IR£13.50, students IR£6), Killarney (2½hr., IR£15, students IR£6.50), and Tralee (2¼hr., IR£14, students IR£6.50). **Buses** (tel. (061) 31 33 33) also leave from Colbert Station. From the station, walk down Davis St. and turn left onto Pery Sq. to reach the hostel **Finnegan's (IHH),** 6 Pery Sq. (tel. (061) 31 03 08; dorms IR£7.50; private rooms IR£10 per person; laundry IR£4). Or try the pleasant rooms at **St. Anthony's,** 8 Coolraine Terrace, Ennis Rd. (tel. (061) 45 26 07; *Let's Go* readers IR£14.50-16). Dine at **The Green Onion Café,** Evlen St. (open daily noon-10pm). Trad music is played nightly around town.

Eight miles northwest of Limerick along Ennis Rd. (N18), **Bunratty Castle** claims to be Ireland's most complete medieval castle, with superbly restored furniture, tapestry, and stained-glass windows. Farther west off Ennis Rd., **Shannon Airport** (tel. (061) 47 14 44; Aer Lingus info (061) 47 16 66) sends jets to North America and Europe. The airport also provides ground transport direct to Dublin, and through Limerick to Ennis, Galway, Westport, Tralee, and Killarney.

Clare Coast

Gorgeous high cliffs rise above eroded islands, and meadows freckled with wildflowers and golf courses roll down to the sea along Clare Coast from Kilkee in the south to Doolin in the north. **Bus Éireann** (tel. (065) 241 77) offers daily routes between Limerick and Ennis and also serves the many small coastal towns.

Halfway up the coast, past Lahinch, are the extraordinary **Cliffs of Moher.** Standing 700 ft above the Atlantic's angry spray, you'll peer onto gulls circling below amid limestone spires. Vaguely marked paths cut the cliffs; tourist traffic diminishes after the first curve. They've most likely biked the 3 mi.on the Burren Way north to **Doolin,** sometimes called **Fisherstreet.** Doolin has near-legendary status as the trad capital of Ireland. The town's three pubs boast world-class music and tasty food. **McGann's,** in the Upper Village, and **O'Connor's,** in the Lower, have won awards for the best trad in Ireland. **McDermott's,** in the Upper Village, is also highly recommended. The ambient **Aille River Hostel (IHH)** (tel. (065) 742 60) sits only a ¼ mi. downhill from the Upper Village. (IR£6-6.50 per person; private rooms IR£8. Camping IR£3.50. Free laundry. Open mid-March to mid-Nov.) The **Westwind B&B,** Upper Village (tel. (065) 742 27), advises amateur explorers (rooms IR£11). The **campsite** (tel. (065) 744 58) near the harbor has a kitchen and a view of the Cliffs of Moher (IR£4 per tent, IR£1 per person; showers 50p; laundry IR£3).Wherever you stay, always book ahead. The Doolin Bike Store (tel. (065) 742 60) rents **bikes** for IR£6 per day.

Lisdoonvarna hosts one of Ireland's last remaining **Matchmaking Festivals.** At these traditional fêtes, farmboys, their crops safely harvested (but with wild oats left to sow), gather to pick their girls. Every September, Irish women stay home and mock the amorous bachelors and foreign women who fill the town for the five-week festival. The **Tourist Information Centre** (tel. (065) 746 30) is buried in the Spa Wells Shop (open July-Sept. daily 10am-6pm). The **Burren Holiday Tourist Hostel (IHH),** Doolin Rd. (tel. (065) 743 00), looks like a palace with a cheery pub downstairs (dorms IR£6.50-7, doubles IR£16-17; stew IR£5; bike rental IR£6).

The Burren

As you travel east from Lisdoonvarna, bare limestone pops up amid the grasses and sheep. This region, encompassing 100 sq. mi., is the Burren, where an elaborate moonscape includes rare wildflowers, flat stone pedestals, and jagged hills. The best way to see the area is to walk or bike the **Burren Way,** a 26 mi. trail marked with yellow arrows. A small town 5 mi. southeast of Lisdoonvarna along R478, **Kilfenora** calls itself "the heart of the Burren." Biking tourists stop here for a pint, some grub, and a peek at the **Burren Centre,** which explains the formation of the Burren. The center also shows an excellent film on the biology of the area, which may help in recognizing the unique species you'll see. (Open June-Sept. daily 9:30am-6pm; March-May and Oct. 10am-5pm. Lecture and film IR£2.20, students IR£1.60.) The **tourist office** (tel. (065) 881 98) in the Tea Shop building sells the helpful *Burren Rambler* map series (IR£2; open June-Sept. daily 9:30am-6pm). **Ms. Mary Murphy,** Main St. (tel. (065) 880 40), runs a comfortable B&B (£14 per person; open June-Sept.).

Galway City

Galway's prestigious university and relative wealth encourage sophisticated theater and literary activity, but high culture doesn't dominate the city. The streets bustle with conversation and carousing, and people discuss poetry over a pint. Before staking out a bar stool or theater seat, check out the impressive interior of Galway's **cathedral,** across the river at the intersection of Gaol and University Rd. (tours Mon.-Fri. 9:30am-4:30pm; also Sun. for mass). Closer to the town center, the **Nora Barnacle House,** 8 Bowling Green, displays letters and photos of James Joyce and his wife (open mid-May to mid-Sept. Mon-Sat. 10am-1pm and 2-5pm; IR£1). The 16th-century **Lynch's Castle** now houses the Allied Irish Bank and an exhibit on the castle's architecture and heraldry (open Mon.-Wed. and Fri. 10am-4pm, Thurs. 10am-5pm; free).

The challenge in Galway is choosing among the city's countless pubs, clubs, and cultural events. There is an average of five pubs on every block. Fast-paced trad usually blazes from several each night. Generally speaking, Quay St. pubs cater to the holiday crowd, while patrons of Dominick St. pubs are more local. The second floor of **The Crane,** 2 Sea Rd., just off Dominick St., is the place to hear trad in Galway. **Seaghan Ua Neachtain** (a.k.a. Knockton's), Quay St., is one of the most traditional pubs in Co. Galway, featuring trad nightly. **The Blue Note,** William St. West, pulsates every night with acid jazz. **Roisín Dubh,** Dominick St., and **The King's Head,** High St., both attract fans with Irish and international music. *The Advertiser* and *Galway Guide* are free and provide listings of other events and performances.

Practical Information, Accommodations, and Food From the Eyre Square Station (tel. (091) 56 14 44; open Mon.-Sat. 7:40am-6pm), **trains** run to Dublin (3hr., IR£14-17, students IR£9) and many smaller cities. **Buses** (tel. (091) 56 20 00) leave for Dublin (IR£8, students IR£7), Cork (IR£12, students IR£8), Belfast (IR£16.30, students IR£12.30), and many more. The main **tourist office,** Victoria Pl. (tel. (091) 56 30 81), southeast of Eyre Sq., offers piles of pamphlets and information on ferries and planes to the Aran Islands (open daily 9am-5:45pm). Another office (tel. (091) 52 05 00) is visible from the main beach at Salthill.

Galway boasts excellent hostels. The **Great Western House,** Eyre Sq. (tel. (091) 56 11 50), offers luxurious living with sauna, pool room, and satellite TV (dorms IR£8-12.50, doubles with bath IR£28-31). **Galway City Hostel,** 25-27 Dominick St. (tel. 56 63 67), has acquired a cult-like following among backpackers with its quirky alternative style (dorms £6-8; laundry £2.50; sheets provided). Also on Eyre Sq., **The Galway Hostel** (tel. (091) 56 69 59) has attractive, airy rooms and spotless bathrooms (dorms IR£6.50-13, doubles with bath IR£26-28). B&Bs also offer reasonable rates. **St. Martin's,** 2 Nuns' Island (tel. (091) 56 82 86), has a gorgeous location on the west bank of the river at the end of Dominick St. (singles IR£18, doubles IR£32). For affordable eats, stay east of the river near Quay St., High St., Shop St., and Abbeygate St. **The Home Plate,** Mary St., dishes up colossal servings (veggie fajita IR£3.50; sandwiches IR£2.50; open Mon.-Sat. 10am-8pm). The supermarket **Roches Stores** is on Eyre St. (open Mon.-Thurs. and Sat. 9am-5:30pm, Fri. 9am-9pm).

Aran Islands (Oileáin Árann)

Fifteen miles off the coast of Galway, the Irish-speaking Aran Islands—Inishmore, Inishmaan, and Inisheer—color Galway Bay with stunning limestone landscapes. The local lifestyle remain traditional, down to its fashion and fishing. Two **ferry** companies—**Island Ferries** (tel. (091) 56 17 67, after hours 722 73; based in the Galway tourist office), and **O'Brien Shipping/Doolin Ferries** (tel. (065) 744 55, after hours 717 10)—send boats to the Arans from Galway and Doolin (return IR£10-20). For **flight** info, call **Aer Árann** (tel. (091) 930 34), or make reservations in person at the Galway tourist office (return IR£35, students IR£29).

Dozens of ruins, forts, churches, and holy wells rise from the stark, stony terrain of **Inishmore** (Inis Mór), the largest island. Ferries land at the pier in **Kilronan,** the island's main harbor. The thick walls of the first-century **Dún Aengus Fort** (Dún Aonghasa), 4 mi. west of the pier, guard Inishmore's northwest quarter and the strangely brilliant turquoise waves that hollow the base of the surrounding cliffs. The **tourist office** (tel. (099) 612 63), at the pier, sells maps, holds bags (75p), and changes money (open May to mid-Sept. daily 10am-7pm). To get to **Mainistir House (IHH)** (tel. (099) 611 69) from the pier, go up the hill and turn right after the supermarket (dorms IR£8, doubles IR£20). The **Spar Market,** past the hostel in Kilronan, is the island's social center (open Mon.-Sat. 9am-8pm, Sun. 10am-6pm).

On the smaller islands of **Inishmaan** (Inis Meáin) and **Inisheer** (Inis Oírr) you can admire the scenery and meet the locals who construct *curraghs,* small boats made of curved wicker rods tied with string. Inisheer's **Brú Hostel (IHH)** (tel. (099) 750 24) organizes *curragh* trips (dorms IR£6.50, private rooms IR£9-10; breakfast IR£2-3.50).

Connemara

Flexing west from Galway City to the Atlantic, rugged Connemara comprises a lacy net of inlets and islands along the coast and a rough gang of inland mountains. Like much of the western coast, the most rewarding way to see Connemara is on a bike. The three-hour public bus from Galway to Clifden via Cong also passes through the some of the most spectacular areas. You can use Galway as a base or camp along Connemara's southern coast, home to Ireland's largest Gaelic-speaking population. If you are without tent, stay at the **Indreabhán Youth Hostel (An Óige/HI)** (tel. (091) 59 31 54), 7 mi. from Spiddal (IR£5.50-6.50). The coastal bus from Galway stops outside.

Clifden (An Clochán) Connemara's western outpost is the region's only community approaching town status. Cheery Clifden has become a miniature Killarney, with five hostels and tour buses by the ton. The **tourist office** (tel. (095) 211 63), at the end of Market St., has plenty of info (open Mon.-Sat. 9am-6pm; July-Aug. also Sun. noon-4pm). If you hunger for more knowledge, **Connemara Heritage Tours,** Market St. (tel. (095) 213 79), forays into local history, folklore, and archaeology (Easter-Oct. daily 9, 11am, 2, and 7pm; 4hr.; IR£10, students IR£8). **Buses** run to Clifden from Galway through Oughterard (June-Aug. 2-6 per day; fewer off-season; 1½hr.; IR£6.50). **Mannion's,** Bridge St. (tel. (095) 211 60), rents bikes. (IR£5 per day, IR£30 per week. IR£10 deposit. Open Mon.-Sat. 9:30am-6:30pm, Sun. 10am-1pm and 5-7pm.)

The well-located **Clifden Town Hostel,** Market St. (tel. (095) 210 76), has clean rooms and is friendly yet quiet (dorms IR£7, private room IR£9 per person; sheets IR£1; bikes IR£5 per day). **Leo's Hostel (IHH),** Sea View (tel. (095) 214 29), is beginning to show its age, but a turf fire and good location more than compensate (July-Aug. dorms IR£7, private rooms IR£8; **camping** IR£3; bikes IR£5 per day). At **Derryclare Restaurant,** enjoy a lunch special (half-dozen oysters IR£3.50) or slightly higher-priced dinner (pesto tagliantelle IR£6.20) The Square (open daily 8am-10:30pm), then relax with a drink at **The Central,** Main St.

Cleggan and the Twelve Bens Ten miles northwest of Clifden, tiny **Cleggan,** the center of Connemara's fishing industry, offers the charms of Clifden without the tourists. Explore the rolling sandhills and minor ruins of **Omey Island.** Just offshore due south, it is accessible by foot at low tide. People remain for days at the **Master House Hostel** (tel. (095) 447 46); the bathrooms are not extremely clean, but the hostel is full of plants and bright wood. (IR£6; private rooms IR£8. **Camping** IR£3. Sheets IR£1. Breakfast IR£2.50. Bikes IR£5 per day.) The Master House Hostel arranges bareback rides along the strand (IR£12 per hour).

IRELAND

The **Twelve Bens** (*Na Benna Beola,* Twelve Pins) soar 2400 ft. in the heart of boggy **Connemara National Park** (tel. (095) 410 54). Experienced hikers (note the plural—don't go alone) prepare for the climb with a stay at the **12 Bens Youth Hostel (An Óige/HI)** (tel. (095) 511 36) in Ballinafad, 8 mi. east of Clifden, west on Roundstone Rd. from N59 (June-Aug. IR£6.50; Easter-May and Sept. IR£5.50). Visitors are asked not to ascend Diamond Hill due to soil erosion. Farther east along N59, **Killary Harbour,** Ireland's only fjord, breaks through the mountains to the town of **Leenane,** which wraps itself in the skirts of the **Devilsmother Mountain.**

Westport A pleasant town with a more-than-satisfactory pub life and plenty of good cafés, Westport's location at the elbow-crook of **Clew Bay,** with Connemara to its south and Co. Mayo's islands a short jaunt northwest, makes it a likely stop. **Croagh Patrick's** perfect cone of a mountain rises 2510 ft. over Clew Bay. The summit has been considered holy for thousands of years. Most climbers start from the village of **Murrisk,** west of Westport on R395, and continue on to Louisburgh; **buses** go all year, though a **cab** is cheaper for three. The **tourist office** (tel. (098) 257 11) in Westport occupies the North Mall by the river (open Mon.-Fri. 9am-6pm, Sat. 10am-6pm). Find **bike rental** at **Breheny & Sons,** Castlebar St. (tel. (098) 250 20). **Trains** (tel. (098) 252 53 or 253 29) arrive from Dublin (IR£15, Fri. and Sun. IR£20) at the Altamont St. Station. **Buses** leave from the Octagon for Galway (IR£9.70).

The **Old Mill Holiday Hostel (IHH),** James St. (tel. (098) 270 45), between the Octagon and the tourist office, offers firm beds in a renovated mill and brewery (IR£6.50; laundry IR£4). **Club Atlantic (IHH),** Altamont St. (tel. (098) 266 44 or 267 17), a five-minute walk from North or South Mall, is a massive 140-bed complex with a huge kitchen, pool table, and video games (dorms IR£5.50-6.50, singles IR£9, doubles IR£11.80-13.80; rates vary). Bop down Bridge St. for a night of drinking and carousing. **McCormack's,** Bridge St., is praised as the exemplary teahouse. Join the crowds at **Matt Molloy's,** owned by the Chieftains' flautist, or enjoy live rock with Westport youths at **The West,** at the corner of Bridge St. and South Mall.

NORTHWEST IRELAND

The strips of farmland interrupted by monasteries and islands in the upper Shannon are a gradual windup to the punch of Sligo, a bay town close to the heart of poet William Butler Yeats. Donegal is the most remote and foreign of the Republic's counties, with its windy mountains and winding coasts. From the inspiring Inishowen Peninsula, it's easy to cross into Derry, a Northern city filled with nervous energy.

Sligo Town, Donegal Town, and the Donegal Coast Childhood haunt of W.B. Yeats, **Sligo Town** is a convenient stopover for northern wanderers and has a happening pub life. In **Drumcliff churchyard,** 4 mi. northwest of Sligo on N15 Bundoran Rd., Yeats is buried. By his command, his headstone reads: "Cast a cold eye/On life, on death./Horseman, pass by!" A few miles northeast of Drumcliff is spectacular **Glencar Lake,** mentioned in Yeats's "The Stolen Child." Back in Sligo, the **tourist office,** Temple St. (tel. (071) 612 01), on the corner of Charles St., is a regional office. (Open June Mon.-Sat. 9am-6pm; July-Aug. Mon.-Sat. 9am-8pm, Sun. 9am-2pm; Sept. Mon.-Fri. 9am-8pm, Sun. 9am-1pm; Oct.-May Mon.-Fri. 9am-5pm.) The **bus/train station** sends trains to Dublin (£12.50, students £9.50) and buses to Belfast (4hr; IR£12.10, students IR£8.50), Derry (3hr.; IR£10, students £6), and Galway (2½hr.; IR£10.50, IR£6.50). Reserve ahead for rooms: the awesome **Harbour House,** Finisklin Rd. (tel. (071) 715 47), and the hip **White House Hostel (IHH),** Markievicz Rd. (tel. (071) 451 60 or 423 98), offer accommodations for IR£6.50-10. **Hargadon Bros.,** O'Connell St., and **Shoot the Crows,** Castle St., are two popular pubs. **McLynn's,** Old Market St., features great music on Friday nights.

Gateway to the splendor of the north and west, **Donegal Town** features an energetic nightlife. Be sure to stop at the superb **tourist office,** Quay St. (tel. (073) 211 48), for brochures and advice before heading north. (Open July-Aug. Mon.-Sat. 9am-8pm, Sun. 9am-5pm; Sept.-Oct. and Easter-June Mon.-Fri. 9am-6pm, Sat. 9am-5pm.) **Buses** travel to Galway (4hr., IR£13) via Sligo (1hr., IR£7.30) and also go to Dublin (4hr., IR£10). The **Donegal Town Hostel (IHH),** Killybegs Rd. (tel. (073) 228 05), presents a great community for the road-weary backpacker (IR£6, doubles IR£15; camping IR£3.50; owners will pick you up in town). **The Blueberry Tea Room,** Castle St., and **Errigal Restaurant,** Main St., serve popular, affordable meals.

Donegal puts on a good show by night. **Schooner's,** upper Main St., has the best trad sessions in town in the summer, while **Charlie's Star Bar,** Main St., offers live rock, country, and blues. **The Voyager Bar,** The Diamond, draws crowds with "contemporary bands" and copious *craic.* During the last weekend of June, the **International Arts Festival** features drama, storytelling, traditional music, and parachuting.

The road west along Donegal's southern edge, the N56, snakes along the Atlantic coast, then inland around weather-beaten cliffs and tiny villages. Although not very appealing, the fishing harbor of **Killybegs** has some of the only services in the area. Farther up the coast, between Kilcar and Carrick, **Dun Ulun House** (tel. (073) 381 37) is a luxurious alternative to hostel life (IR£5-IR£8.50). Nearby, the **Derrylahan Hostel (IHH)** (tel. (073) 380 79) welcomes guests with hot showers and an amiable staff (IR£6, private rooms IR£8; camping IR£3). Still farther north, the small town of **Carrick** offers great fishing and access to **Slieve League,** a 2000 ft. mountain which drops precipitously into Donegal Bay. For info, contact the **tourist info desk** at the Tweed Factory Craft Shop and Tea Room (tel. (073) 380 02), in Kilcar (open Mon.-Fri. 9am-7pm, Sat. 10am-6pm, Sun. 2-4pm). Just south of Carrick, **Teelin Bay House** (tel. (073) 390 43) is deservedly famous for its hospitality (IR£13; book ahead).

Derryveagh Mountains and Letterkenny The imposing **Derryveagh Mountains** isolate the northwest corner of Donegal, the country's largest Irish-speaking area. The **Chamber of Commerce Visitors Information Centre,** 40 Port Rd. (tel. (074) 248 66 or 255 05), doles out pamphlets and friendly advice (open Mon.-Fri. 9am-5pm). **The Manse Hostel (IHH),** High Rd. (tel. (074) 252 38), has kitschy decor in a central location (IR£6). Fourteen miles northwest of Letterkenny stretches the **Glenveagh National Park** (tel. (074) 370 88)—37 sq. mi. of glens, mountains, and nature walks, plus a castle. (Both open April-Sept. daily 10am-6:30pm; June-Sept. also Sun. until Sun.7:30pm; Oct. Sat.-Thurs. 10am-6:30pm. Each IR£2, students IR£1.)

Letterkenny is Donegal's commercial center and one of the fastest growing towns in Europe. Stop here between peninsular jaunts, or on your way to Glenveagh

National Park or Donegal. The **Chamber of Commerce Visitors Information Centre,** 40 Port Rd. (tel. (074) 248 66 or 255 05), doles out pamphlets and friendly advice (open Mon.-Fri. 9am-5pm). **The Manse Hostel (IHH),** High Rd. (tel. (074) 252 38), is clean, tidy, and in a central location (3- or 4-bed dorms, some with sinks, IR£6).

Donegal Peninsulas Between Lough Swilly and Mulroy Bay, the **Fanad Peninsula** juts into the Atlantic, somewhat in the shadow of its larger neighbor, the Inishowen. North of Rathmullan, a dozen slow brooks cross the road as the land rises over the Knockalla Mountains and Glenvar. Beyond this stretch of road, the coast arcs dramatically between mountain and shore. Follow the signs to the peaceful **Bunnaton Hostel,** Glenvar (tel. (074) 501 22; IR£6.50, private rooms IR£8.50 per person).

A mosaic of rugged mountains, lush forests, and sumptuous beaches, the **Inishowen Peninsula** is a microcosm of Ireland. A logical place to begin is the 4000-year-old cultural center of the peninsula, the hilltop ringfort of **Grianán of Aileach,** which was originally a Druidic temple of sun worship. **Buncrana,** on the west side of the peninsula along the shores of Lough Swilly, is an energetic resort where sweeping beaches repose in the long shadow of **Slieve Snacht,** a 2019 ft. peak. About 6 mi. north of Buncrana and 800 ft. above sea level, the **Mamore Gap** offers a view over the mountains to the Atlantic. From **Malin Head,** the northernmost point in Ireland, you can see across to the Paps of Jura, Scotland, on a clear day. A path to the left of the car park leads to **Hell's Hole,** a 250 ft. chasm which roars with the incoming tide.

Situated on a lovely estuary, the village of **Culdaff** exudes a warmth from its beaches. **McGrory's Pub** (tel. (077) 791 04) offers renowned trad as well as B&B accommodations (IR£15). Glorious **Culdaff Strand,** best seen in sunrise or sunset, is a short walk from McGrory's. Nearby **Kinnagoe Bay,** site of the 1588 wreckage of the Spanish Armada, offers breathtaking views. On the southeast coast of the Inishowen Peninsula, 5 mi. over the border from Derry, **Muff Hostel (IHH)** (tel. (077) 841 88) provides a base for exploring Inishowen and Derry (IR£6; open March-Oct.).

NORTHERN IRELAND

International media coverage of political unrest and violence has contributed greatly to Northern Ireland's notoriety. The area is, in fact, divided—Protestants and Catholics often live in separate neighborhoods and go to different stores and pubs, and unemployment and lousy housing has exacerbated class tensions in many cities. Yet the tenor of life in the North is surprisingly calm and peaceful, and the natural beauty some of the best in Ireland. Lively Belfast is the center of the area's commercial and cultural activity. East of the city, the North features the string of beautiful seaside villages on the Ards Peninsula; to the north, the Glens of Antrim and one of the world's strangest geological sights, the Giant's Causeway; and to the southwest, the beautiful Fermanagh Lake District and an amazing folk park in Omagh.

Money in Northern Ireland is in British pounds ("pounds sterling"). Notes printed Northern Ireland have the same value as those printed in England and Scotland, but are *not* accepted in the rest of the U.K. English, Scottish, and Manx notes, however, *are* accepted in Northern Ireland and on the border. Most towns have shops that take "punt for pound" or the other way around.

Border check-points have recently been removed, and armed soldiers are less common in Belfast and Derry; still, it's especially unwise to hitch in South Armagh. Do not take photographs of soldiers or of military installations or vehicles; if you do, your film will be confiscated, and you may be detained for questioning. Some urban areas have "control zones," where there's no parking due to fear of car bombs. Since unattended luggage can also conceal a bomb, it's viewed with suspicion.

Belfast

The second-largest city on the island, Belfast is in some ways more cosmopolitan than Dublin. The Troubles are not forgotten: unemployment and the "peace line," a wall separating the Catholic Falls Rd. and Protestant Shankill Rd., are clearly visible, but so are vibrant art scenes, a charming university, and prosperous shopping zones. The Troubles may have even had unintended benefits, from the brilliantly grim irony of the literati to the ban on cars downtown.

ORIENTATION AND PRACTICAL INFORMATION

Belfast is loosely centered on **City Hall** in **Donegall Square,** six blocks west of the River Lagan and the harbor. To the north lies the city's snazzy shopping district, while two blocks west of the center the **Golden Mile** follows Great Victoria St. from Shaftesbury Sq. to the Opera House. South of Donegall Square, **University Road** and **Botanic Ave.** lead to Queen's University and a neighborhood of B&Bs, pubs, and cafés. Divided from the rest of the city by the Westlink Motorway, **West Belfast** is both poorer and more politically volatile than the city center. If you plan on visiting the docks for the nightlife, it is best to travel to and from there in a taxi.

> Tourists should avoid Belfast around **July 12,** when the Protestant Orangemen hold their parades. These days have seen riots and violence, and tourists hold no special amnesty when passions are high. It is also prohibited to take **photographs** of soldiers or any sort of military item year-round; this rule *is* enforced.

Tourist Office: St. Anne's Court, 59 North St. (tel. 24 66 09). Free map with bus schedules. Books rooms. 24hr. info computer outside. Open July-Aug. Mon.-Fri. 9am-7pm, Sat. 9am-5:15pm, Sun. noon-4pm; Sept.-June Mon.-Sat. 9am-5:15pm.

Budget Travel Office: USIT, 13b The Fountain Centre, College St. (tel. 32 40 73), near Royal Ave. Open Mon. and Wed.-Fri. 9:30am-5:30pm, Tues. 10am-5:30pm, Sat. 10am-1pm. Also at Queen's University Student Union (tel. 24 18 30).

Consulates: None for **Australia, Canada,** and **Republic of Ireland. U.S.:** Consulate General, Queens House, Queen St. (tel. 22 82 39). Open Mon.-Fri. 1-5pm.

Currency Exchange: Thomas Cook, 22/24 Lombard St. (tel. 23 60 44). Cashes traveler's checks. Open Mon.-Fri. 9am-5:30pm. Most banks and post offices provide *bureau de change* and traveler's check cashing for a minimal fee.

American Express: Royal Ave. (tel. 24 23 41).

Flights: Belfast International Airport, Aldee Grove (tel. 42 28 88). Bus runs to Europa/Glengall Station and Central Station (every 30min., Sun. every hr., UK£4).

Trains: Belfast Central Station, East Bridge St. (tel. 89 94 11 or 23 06 71). From Dublin (2½hr., UK£15, return UK£24) and Derry (2¼hr., UK£5.50, return UK£9.50). Some also stop at **Botanic Station** or the **Great Victoria Station.**

Buses: Europa/Glengall St. Station (tel. 32 00 11). Buses arrive from Dublin (UK£10, return UK£12.50) and Derry (UK£6.10, return UK£10.70). Buses from Ireland's east coast arrive at the **Laganside Station** (tel. 33 30 00). **Leaping Leprechaun** (tel. (015047) 42 65 55) goes to hostels on the Antrim coast (UK£18).

Taxis: Huge, very partisan **black cabs** run set routes to West and North Belfast (standard 60p charge). Cabs heading to Catholic neighborhoods are marked with a Falls Rd., Andersontown, or Irish-language sign; those going to Protestant neighborhood are marked with a Shankil sign or a red poppy. Or try **City Cab** (tel. 24 20 00).

Bisexual, Gay, and Lesbian Information: Rainbow Project N.I. (tel. 31 90 30).

Crisis Lines: Samaritans, tel. 66 44 22. Open 24hr. **Rape Crisis Center,** 29 Donegall St. (tel. 32 18 30). Open Mon.-Fri. 10am-6pm, Sat. 11am-5pm.

Medical Assistance: Belfast City Hospital, Lisburn Rd. (tel. 32 92 41).

Emergency: Dial 999; no coins required.

Police: 65 Knock Rd. (tel. 65 02 22).

Internet Access: Revelations Internet Café, 27 Shaftesbury Sq. UK£5 per hr. ISIC discounts. Open Mon.-Fri. 10am-10pm, Sat. 10am-8pm, Sun. noon-10pm.

Post Office: 25 Castle Pl. (tel. 32 37 40). Open Mon.-Fri. 9am-5:30pm, Sat. 9am-1pm. *Poste Restante* mail arrives here. **Postal Code:** BT1 1NB.

Telephone Code: 01232.

ACCOMMODATIONS AND FOOD

Look for safe and convenient lodgings near Queen's University, south of the city center. Buses 59, 69-71, 84, and 85 run from Donegall Sq. East to areas farther south. From the bus station, it's a 15-minute walk to accommodations.

Arnie's Backpackers (IHH), 63 Fitzwilliam St. (tel. 24 28 67). Relaxed, friendly atmosphere. 24hr. kitchen. Luggage storage. UK£7.50.
The Ark, 18 University St. (tel. 32 96 26). New and hip, with that college co-op feel. Kitchen. Dorms UK£7.50-9.50. Doubles UK£28. Luggage storage.
YHANI Belfast Hostel (HI), 22 Donegall Rd. (tel. 32 47 33). Clean, spacious, modern dorms, some with bath. UK£8-10. Wheelchair accessible.
Mrs. Davidson's East-Sheen Guest House, 81 Eglantine Ave. (tel. 66 71 49). The best deal in Belfast, if you can get a room. Enormous breakfast included. UK£18.50.
The George, 9 Eglantine Ave. (tel. 68 32 12). Spotless rooms, each with shower and TV. Singles UK£19. Doubles UK£36-38.

Dublin Rd., Botanic Rd., and the **Golden Mile** (Great Victoria St.) have the highest concentration of places to eat. The **Mace Supermarket** on the corner of Castle and Queen St. offers cheap groceries (open Mon.-Wed. and Fri.-Sat. 9am-6pm, Thurs. 9am-9pm). **Bookfinders,** 47 University Rd., a smoky bookstore/café, offers soup and bread (UK£1.40) amid stacks of old books (open Mon.-Sat. 10am-5:30pm). **Maggie May's Belfast Café,** 50 Botanic Ave., the preferred hangout of young intellectuals, has great food and homemade ice cream (open Mon.-Sat. 8am-10:30pm, Sun. opens 10am). Chill with travelers and expats at **Spuds,** 23 Bradbury Pl. (open Mon.-Thurs. and Sat. 11am-3am, Fri. 11am-4am, Sun. 11am-1am). **The Daily Sandwich,** 60 Lower Donegall St., has big, fresh sandwiches (UK£1.30; open Mon.-Fri. 10am-4pm).

SIGHTS AND ENTERTAINMENT

Belfast's **City Hall,** Donegall Sq., is the administrative and geographical center of the city, regally set apart from the crowded streets by a grassy square. Its 173-ft.-high green copper dome can be seen from anywhere in the city. (Tours June-Sept. Mon.-Fri. 10:30, 11:30am, and 2:30pm, Sat. 2:30pm; Oct.-May Mon.-Fri. 2:30pm, Wed. also 10:30am. Free.) At the northwest corner of Donegall Square, the **Linen Hall Library** is famous for its comprehensive collection of political materials relating to the Troubles (open Mon.-Wed. and Fri. 9:30am-5:30pm, Thurs. 9:30am-8:30pm, Sat. 9:30am-4pm). West of City Hall, the **Golden Mile** (Great Victoria St.) passes Belfast's pride and joy, the oft-bombed and restored **Grand Opera House.** Follow Great Victoria St. south from City Hall to **Queen's University,** whose attractive Tudor buildings overlook the meticulously groomed **Botanic Gardens.** Amid the gardens off Stranmillis Rd., the **Ulster Museum** exhibits Irish art and an astounding collection of silver and gold looted from the *Girona,* a Spanish Armada ship wrecked off the Giant's Causeway in 1588 (open Mon.-Fri. 10am-5pm, Sat. 1-5pm, Sun. 2-5pm; free).

North of the city center at the bottom of the hills that rise over the city's valley, **Belfast Castle** rests in perfect condition. An interpretive center has opened there (open Mon.-Fri. 10am-4pm). You can walk though the grounds and climb higher to **McArt's Fort,** which offers a breathtaking view of the city. The fascinating **Ulster Folk and Transport Museum,** 7mi. east of the city center on A2 Bangor Rd. in Cultra, stretches over 176 acres. The Folk Museum is the best part: over 25 buildings from the past three centuries have been moved from their original locations all over Ulster and reconstructed here. (Open July-Aug. Mon.-Sat. 10:30am-6pm, Sun. noon-6pm; April-June and Sept. Mon.-Fri. 9:30am-5pm, Sat. 10:30am-6pm, Sun. noon-6pm; Oct.-March Mon.-Fri. 9:30am-4pm, Sat.-Sun. 12:30-4:30pm. UK£4, students UK£2.50.)

The best sources of info on Belfast's many arts and entertainment offerings are the *Arts Council Artslink,* Thursday's *Irish News,* and the daily *Belfast Telegraph.* The **Grand Opera House** (tel. 24 19 19) boasts a mix of opera, ballet, and drama (UK£8-160, 50% student discount Mon.-Thurs. after noon on performance days). For other events stop by the box office at 2-4 Great Victoria St. (Open Mon.-Wed. 8:30am-8pm,

The Yard of Ale Challenge

Chugging a "yard" of ale is a bibulous experience shared almost exclusively by the already "half-pissed," easily bullied set. According to a sign in **The Fly** pub in Belfast, this English tradition is supposed to "separate the men from the boys" as they down those 2½ pints of ale. The trick, says Fly manager Billy McGlade, is to rotate the yard-long glass as you chug; that way, once you get to the last bits in the bulb at the bottom, you won't get a rush of beer all at once (if you don't rotate the stem, you're likely to end up covered in ale—or sick in the loo). Bass Ale is the beverage of choice for many challengers, but the brand is up to you. Just don't ask for Guinness, which is never meant to be chugged. If you need to, take your time: one 72-year-old man is said to have spent three months—including three falls into his glass, for he was a short little thing—to complete the task.

Thurs. 8:30am-9pm, Fri. closes 6:30pm, Sat. closes 5:30pm.) In November, Queen's University hosts the **Belfast Festival at Queen's,** a three-week extravaganza of drama, music, and art. (Contact the Festival House, 25 College Gardens, Belfast BT9 6BS, by Aug. Ticket sales by mail begin Sept. 15; after Oct. 14 call 66 76 87.) Pubs cluster around Great Victoria St., the city center, and the university. The rather unattractive **Lavery's Gin Palace,** 12 Bradbury Pl., is one of the hottest spots in town. **The Fly,** 5 Lower Crescent, is a truly traditional bar with great trad most nights. **Crown Liquor Saloon,** 46 Great Victoria St., has gilt ceilings and "snugs" (booths) for that special drink. The friendly **Queens Bar,** 4 Queen's Arcade, draws a gay and straight crowd, and **The Crow's Nest,** 26 Skipper St., off High St., is a popular gay and lesbian bar.

Derry (Londonderry)

Despite a history of conflict and the shadow of "Bloody Sunday," Derry is now engaged in a determined effort to cast off the legacy of the Troubles. New growth and a thriving rock scene attract young tourists. Built between 1625 and 1633, **St. Columb's Cathedral,** Bishop St., was the first Protestant cathedral in Ireland. (Open April-Oct. daily 9am-1pm and 2-5pm; Nov.-March until 4pm. UK£1 donation suggested.) The stellar **Tower Museum,** just inside Magazine Gate, offers an unbiased city history. (Open July-Aug. Mon.-Sat. 10am-5pm, Sun. 2-5pm; Sept.-June Tues.-Sat. 10am-5pm. Last entrance 4:30pm. UK£3.25, students UK£1.) Political **murals** in both Protestant and Catholic neighborhoods also illustrate the turbulent past.

Derry has a turbulent present as well: avoid the city on and around **Marching Day** (July 12). The **tourist office,** 44 Foyle St. (tel. (01504) 26 72 84), distributes a city guide and free maps. (Open July-Sept. Mon.-Sat. 9am-8pm, Sun. 10am-6pm; Oct.-June Mon.-Fri. 9am-5:15pm.) **Ulsterbus** (tel. (01504) 26 22 61) serves all destinations in Northern Ireland and some in the Republic, including Belfast (1½-3hr., UK£5.80), Galway (5½hr.), and Dublin (UK£10). **Oakgrove Manor (YHANI/HI),** Magazine St. (tel. (01504) 37 22 73), is centrally located (dorms UK£7.50-8, singles UK£15). To get to the friendly **Steve's Backpacker's,** 78 Marlborough St. (tel. (01504) 37 78 98), follow William St. across from the supermarket uphill, past St. Euan's Cathedral; Marlborough St. is on the left (UK£7.50). **The Sandwich Co.,** on the corner of Ferryquay and Bishop St., offers tasty sandwiches (UK£1.45; open Mon.-Sat. 8:30am-5pm). **The Dungloe,** 41-43 Waterloo St., is a popular pub with a disco upstairs (cover UK£1-2).

Causeway Coast

As the Northern Irish coast rounds Torr Head, between Ballycastle in the east and Portstewart in the west, 600 ft. cliffs plummet into the restless surf. The scenic **A2,** suitable for cycling, connects the main towns along the Causeway. **Ulsterbus** 172 also runs along the coast from Ballycastle to Portrush with connections to Portstewart (1hr.; UK£2.90). In good summer weather, take the open-topped **Bushmills Bus** (tel. (01265) 433 34), which follows the coast between Coleraine, 5 mi. south of Portrush, and the Giant's Causeway (Mon.-Sat. 4 per day, Sun. 2 per day).

The Glens of Antrim and the Causeway Coast meet at L-shaped **Ballycastle,** a bubbly seaside town with a popular beach. The **tourist office,** 7 Mary St. (tel. (012657) 620 24), is in Sheskburn House. (Open July-Aug. Mon.-Fri. 9:30am-7pm, Sat. 10am-6pm, Sun. 2-6pm; Sept.-June Mon.-Fri. 9:30am-5pm.) The **Castle Hostel (IHH),** 62 Quay Rd. (tel. (012657) 623 37), has a central location and cozy bunk room (UK£6-7.50; laundry UK£1). The new **Ballycastle Backpackers Hostel,** 4 North St. (tel. (012657) 636 12 or 694 58), is spacious and extra-friendly (UK£6; free laundry). From Ballycastle, a ferry runs to **Rathlin Island,** the ultimate in escapism for 20,000 puffins, one golden eagle, and about 100 people. Five miles west of Ballycastle, the village of **Ballintoy** features a picturesque church and a tiny harbor. Crossing the flimsy bridge that connects the mainland to **Carrick-a-rede Island** (over a dizzying 80 ft. drop to rocks and sea) is a popular tourist activity. Take the sign-posted turnoff from the coast road ½ mi. east of Ballintoy. Three miles south of Ballycastle, **Fair Head** draws international hikers to its majestic basalt cliffs.

Advertised as the eighth natural wonder of the world, the **Giant's Causeway** is Northern Ireland's most famous sight. Two miles west of Ballintoy, the 40,000 hexagonal columns of basalt form a honeycomb path from the foot of the cliffs into the sea. The **Causeway Visitors Centre** (tel. (012657) 318 55) has tourist info, a *bureau de change,* and a post office (open July-Aug. daily 10am-7pm; Sept.-June 10am-5pm). Two miles farther west, **Bushmills** is the home of the oldest functioning whiskey distillery in the world. (Open Mon.-Sat. 9:30am-5:30pm. Tours, with free sample, every 15min. April-Oct. 9:30am-4pm; Nov.-March 6 per day. UK£2.50, students UK£2.).

Glens of Antrim

Between Belfast and the Causeway Coast, the rolling green hills and moors of County Antrim drop through nine lush valleys—the Glens of Antrim—down to the rocky coast. Scant **bus** lines serve the area: the Ulsterbus 162 starts at Belfast and sometimes continues to Waterfoot, Cushendall, and Cushendun, while the Antrim Coaster runs in summer from Belfast to Coleraine (June-Sept. Mon.-Sat. 2 per day; July-Sept. Sun. 2 per day). Most rides within the Glens average UK£2-5. Call **Ulsterbus** in Belfast (tel. (01232) 32 00 11) for details. Many also bike or hitch a ride along these lovely roads.

Tiny **Ballygally** is an excellent gateway to the Glens. The only accommodation in town is **Cairnview,** 13 Croft Heights (tel. (01574) 58 32 69), located off Croft Rd., the left branch of the street perpendicular to the castle (UK£16-18 per person). Two miles outside Ballygally on the way to Larne, the **Carnfunnock Country Park** (tel. (01574) 27 84 65 or 27 05 41) provides **campsites** (UK£5). In the park, paths lead from the sundials in the garden to a hedge maze shaped like Northern Ireland.

Five miles down the coast, the village of **Waterfoot** guards Antrim's broadest glen, part of the **Glenariff Forest Park,** 4 mi. south of the village along Glenariff Rd. There waterfalls feed the River Glenariff among steep, tree-shaded hills. Camp at **Glenariff Forest Park Camping,** 98 Glenariff Rd. (tel. (012667) 582 32; tents UK£5-7.50), or find a farmer who welcomes campers (ask in town). The Ballymena-Cushendun **bus** (Mon.-Fri. 5 per day, Sat. 3 per day) stops at the park entrance.

Two miles north of Waterfoot, **Cushendall** offers plenty of rooms and practical convenience for the glen explorer. The **HI youth hostel** (tel. (012667) 713 44) is a 10-minute walk from town on Layde Rd. (UK£7-12.50; open March-Dec.). You'll receive an amazingly warm welcome from Mrs. O'Neill at the **Glendale B&B,** 46 Coast Rd. (tel. (012667) 714 95; UK£16 per person). **Bikes** can be rented from **Ardclinis Activity Center,** 11 High St. (tel. (012667) 713 40; UK£10 per day).

Farther north via an inland road that rises through the moors, the National Trust preserves the tiny seaside village of **Cushendun.** Vast sandy beaches and amazing stone sea caves make the village a terrific afternoon stopover. The town's most popular attraction is **Mary McBride's,** 2 Main St., with slightly unusual pub grub (mac and cheese UK£3.50) and spontaneous trad sessions. One mile toward Cushendall is **Sleepy Hollow B&B,** 107 Knocknacarry Rd. (tel. (01266) 76 12 54; UK£18).

Italy (Italia)

US$1	**= L1793 (lire)**	**L1000 =**	**US$0.56**
CDN$1	**= L1309**	**L1000 =**	**CDN$0.76**
UK£1	**= L2927**	**L1000 =**	**UK£0.34**
IR£1	**= L2608**	**L1000 =**	**IR£0.38**
AUS$1	**= L1333**	**L1000 =**	**AUS$0.75**
NZ$1	**= L1164**	**L1000 =**	**NZ$0.86**
SAR1	**= L389**	**L1000 =**	**SAR2.57**

Country Code: 39 **International Dialing Prefix: 00**

Italy is more than your average boot. Throughout the centuries, natural barriers as well as hand-made medieval stone walls have insulated communities, nurturing local dialects and customs. Only unified in 1870, Italy's regional and city bonds often prove stronger than nationalist sentiment. The split is particularly pronounced between the wealthy, industrial north and the poorer, agrarian south. The political scene is equally varied: since the fall of Mussolini and the fascists, Italy has seen no fewer than 50 governments, the result of an electoral system that gives power to even the smallest of parties and necessitates unwieldy, tenuous coalitions. In the midst of this volatile political system and even in the face of the still powerful mafia, however, Italy perseveres, with all of its pleasures and laid-back elegance intact.

A trip through the history of Italy begins beneath the grassy hills of Tarquinia, in the brightly painted tombs of the Etruscans; this highly developed civilization ruled central Italy centuries before the birth of Christ. Meanwhile, in Sicily, the Greeks honored their gods with soaring temples in white marble. Traces of the vast Roman Empire define the landscape, from the monumental amphitheaters of Rome and Verona to the volcanically embalmed towns of Pompeii and Herculaneum. Early Christian churches sparkling with Byzantine frescoes distinguish Ravenna as a treasure house of early medieval culture, while San Gimignano bristles with the forbidding towers of the later Middle Ages. In Florence the Italian Renaissance continues to make its intoxicating presence known.

Glean fistfuls of informative tips by reading the other-worldly *Let's Go: Italy 1998.*

GETTING THERE AND GETTING AROUND

Alitalia (tel. (800) 223-5730) is Italy's national airline and may offer off-season youth fares. **Ferry** services in the port towns of Bari, Brindisi, and Ancona connect Italy to Greece. Unless you have a Eurailpass (only honored at Brindisi), Bari and Ancona services are cheaper, and they don't involve Brindisi's chaotic hordes of tourists.

The **Ferrovie dello Stato (FS),** the Italian State Railway, runs more or less on time and its network is comprehensive. A *locale* train stops at nearly every station; the *diretto* goes faster but serves fewer stations, while the *espresso* stops only at major stations. The *rapido,* an InterCity (IC) train, zips along but costs a bit more. If you plan to travel extensively in Italy and are under 26, the **Cartaverde** (L40,000, valid for 1 year) should be your first purchase. Showing this card entitles you to a 20% discount on any state rail fare. When traveling in groups, sleep in shifts, and always keep documents and valuables concealed on your person.

Intercity **buses** are often more convenient for shorter hauls off the main rail lines, and they serve countryside points inaccessible by train. For **city buses,** buy tickets in *tabacchi,* newsstands, or kiosks, and validate them on board. An *Autostrada* (superhighway) is a worthy successor to the Appian Way, but gas and tolls are prohibitive, and Italian driving frightens some foreigners. **Mopeds** (L40,000-60,000 per day) can be a great way to see the islands and the more scenic areas of Italy, but are potentially disastrous in the rain and on rough roads or gravel. **Bicycling** is a popular national sport, but bike trails are rare, drivers often reckless, and, except in the Po Valley, the terrain challenges even the fittest. Although hitchhiking is relatively common, *Let's Go* urges travelers to consider the safety risks. Women should never hitchhike alone.

ESSENTIALS

The **Ente Nazionale Italiano di Turismo (ENIT)** is a national tourist office with bureaus in Rome (on Via Marghera, 2) and abroad. In provincial capitals, look for a branch of the **Ente Provinciale per il Turismo (EPT)** with info on the entire province. The city tourist board, **Azienda Autonoma di Soggiorno e Turismo (AST)** is generally the most useful. A new brand of tourist office, the **Azienda di Promozione Turismo (APT),** is allowed to present you with a list of only those hotels that have paid to be listed; some of the hotels we recommend may not be on the list. Keep an eye out for the **Centro Turistico Studentesco e Giovanile (CTS)** and **Compagnia Italiana Turismo (CIT).**

Italy closes on the following **holidays:** January 1 (New Year's Day); January 6 (Epiphany); Easter Monday (April 13, 1998); April 25 (Liberation Day); May 2-4 (May

Day); August 15 (Assumption of the Virgin); November 1 (All Saints' Day); December 8 (Immaculate Conception); December 25 (Christmas Day); and December 26 (Santo Stefano). August, especially the weeks around the 15th, is vacation month for Italians; the cities shut down and empty out. At other times of the year, nearly everything closes from around 1 to 3 or 4pm for *siesta.* Most museums open from 9am to 1pm and some again from 4 to 7pm; Monday is often their *giorno di chiusura* (day of closure). Banks are usually open from 8:30am to 1:30pm and 3 to 4pm. Food shops have a different *giorno di chiusura* from province to province.

Summers are humid and hot in the north, drier and hotter in the south. Winters are ferocious in the Alps and cold and damp in Venice and Florence, but Sicilian waters are swimmable year-round. Italy's cathedrals and churches are religious institutions and not museums. Don't visit during mass, and *cover your legs and shoulders;* the more conservative your appearance, the more likely you are to see what you came for. Italian men, generally speaking, have earned their tarnished reputation. For tips on handling unwanted attention and harassment, see **Women Travelers,** p. 33.

Communication **Fermo Posta** is Italian for *Poste Restante.* There are four types of phones in Italy. Some phones take only coins—put more in than you think you'll need, or risk getting cut off. *Scatti* calls (often available only from telephone offices) are made from a phone run by an operator. A meter records the cost of the call, and you pay when you finish. Check first for a service fee. The most common type of phone accepts either coins or **phone cards** (L5000, L10,000, or L15,000 from *tabacchi,* newsstands, bars, post offices, and the occasional machine). A fourth kind of phone accepts only phone cards. A collect call is a *contassa a carico del destinatario* or *chiamata collect.* The English-speaking **operator** in Italy (dial 170) can put through collect calls. For **AT&T Direct,** dial 172 10 11; **MCI WorldPhone** 172 10 22; **Sprint Access** 172 18 77; **Canada Direct** 172 10 01; **BT Direct** 172 00 44; **Ireland Direct** 172 03 53; **Australia Direct** 172 10 61; **NZ Direct** 172 10 64; **South Africa Direct** 172 10 27. In an **emergency,** call the state **police** at 112, **fire** department at 115, and **medical** help at 113.

Any knowledge of Spanish, French, Portuguese, or Latin will help you understand Italian. Pig Latin will *not* help. Most tourist office staff speak at least some English.

Yes/No	*Sì/No*	see/no
Hi/Bye	*Ciao*	chow
Please	*Per favore*	pehr fah-VOH-ray
Thank you	*Grazie*	GRAHT-syeh
Excuse me	*Scusi?*	SKOO-zee
You're welcome.	*Prego.*	PRAY-go
Do you speak English?	*Parla (Parli) inglese?*	par-LA (par-LEE) in-GLAYZ-ay
I don't speak Italian.	*Non parlo italiano*	nohn PAR-loh ee-tahl-YAHN-o
Where is...?	*Dov'è...?*	doh-VAYY
I would like...	*Vorrei...*	vohr-RAY
I would like a room (with single bed) (with double bed) (with two beds).	*Vorrei una camera (singola) (matrimoniale) (doppia).*	vohr-RAY oo-NA ka-MEHR-ah (seen-GO-la) (mah-tri-moh-nee-o-NAHL-ay) (doh-PEE-uh)
Help!	*Aiuto!*	ah-YOO-toh

Accommodations and Camping **Associazione Italiana Alberghi per la Gioventù (AIG),** the Italian **hostel** federation, operates dozens of youth hostels *(ostelli Italiani)* across the country, especially in the north. A complete list is available from most **EPT** and **CTS** offices and from many hostels. Prices average about L20,000 per night, including breakfast. Hostels are the best option for solo travelers

ITALY

(single rooms are relatively scarce in hotels), but curfews, lockouts, out-of-the-way locations, and less than perfect security detract from their appeal.

Italian hotel rates are set not by private owners but by the state. Under Italian law all guests must be registered by passport on a special form; check the room *first,* and then don't be afraid to hand the passport over for a while (usually overnight), but ask for it as soon as you think you will need it. One-star *pensioni* are the best budget option. Prices fluctuate by region, but singles usually start around L30,000, doubles L50,000. By law, the price must be posted behind the door of each room; if it isn't, get it in writing. Always check to see if breakfast and shower privileges are included and/or mandatory. A private bath *(con bagno)* usually costs 30-50% more. **Affitta camere** (rooms to let in private residences) can be significantly less.

An even better value in most large cities are the **Protezione della Giovane,** dorms run by religious orders for women travelers only. Quality is high, but the curfew is generally early. Try to reach your destination and begin looking for accommodations before noon, especially in summer. If you must arrive late, call and reserve a day ahead. **Monasteries** are an alternative to hostels; for more info contact the province's archdiocese or tourist board. **Camping** sites tend to be loud and modern and average around L8000 per person (or tent) plus L7000 per car, much higher near big cities. A free map and list of sites is available from **Federcampeggio,** Via V. Emanuele, 11, Casella Postale 23, 50041 Calenzano, Florence (tel./fax (055) 88 23 91).

Food and Drink *"Mangia, mangia!"* The production, preparation, and loving consumption of food are all close to the core of Italian culture. For simple, hearty, and inexpensive eating, try *alimentari* stores; they often prepare *panini* (sandwiches) with fresh local cold cuts and slices of excellent Italian cheese: *Bel Paese, provolone, La Fontina,* or *mozzarella. Rosticcerie* sell hot food to take out and are often the cheapest option for a filling dinner. A *tavola calda* is a cheap, sit-down option. The student *mensa* in every university town is a great deal but not always accessible by foreigners. *Osterie, trattorie,* and *ristoranti* are, in ascending order, fancier and more expensive. They are usually open 12:30 to 2pm and 7 to 11pm (later in the south). Pizza can be sold by the *etto* (100g) or the *fetta* (slice) in a *pizza a taglio* place, although you can order a whole round pizza at a sit-down pizzeria. Menus in smaller restaurants are often incomplete or nonexistent; ask for the *piatti del giorno* (daily specials). A *menù turistico,* when offered, might run only L14,000-18,000 for a full meal, but variety is limited. Sit-down establishments often charge *pane e coperto* (a bread and cover charge), usually not much more than L2000. Check whether service is included *(servizio compreso).*

A full meal consists of an *antipasto* (appetizer), a *primo piatto* (pasta or soup), a *secondo piatto* (meat or fish) occasionally with a *contorno* (vegetable), and usually salad, fruit, and/or cheese. In the north, butter and cream sauces dominate. Rome and central Italy are notoriously spicy regions. As one travels south, tomatoes play an increasingly significant role. Pastries also become progressively sweeter toward the south, reaching an all-time glucose high in the sinfully sugary *marzipan* of Sicily.

Coffee is another rich and varied focus of Italian life. Espresso is meant to be quaffed quickly. *Cappuccino,* a mixture of espresso and hot, frothy milk, is the normal breakfast beverage. Order it after 11:30am and expect sneers of *"turista." Caffè macchiato* ("spotted") is espresso with a touch of milk, while *latte macchiato* is milk with a splash of coffee. Perhaps the best finish to a meal is a *caffè corretto* ("corrected"), espresso spiked with your favorite liqueur. When you order at a *caffè* or *bar* (both "cafés" in Italy), you'll get a receipt, which you should then give to the bartender who makes your coffee.

Wines from the north of Italy, such as the Piedmont's *Asti Spumante* or Verona's *Soave,* tend to be heavy and full-bodies; stronger, fruitier wines come from the hotter climate of south Italy and the islands. Moretti and Peroni are popular beers, although many Italians prefer Guinness or German imports. Those who do drink Italian beer reportedly order *Peroni.* Bars are good places to sample wines, eat breakfast, stop for snacks, or watch locals socializing. They also serve a wide collection of Italian liqueurs. Try *grappa,* a gut-wrenching liqueur often flavored with various fruits, and

Roman *sambuca,* a sweet anise concoction served flaming, with coffee beans floating on top. Sitting down at a table generally doubles the price of anything you order.

In almost every Italian town you can find numerous shops selling Italy's greatest contribution to civilization: *gelato* (ice cream). Look for the *produzione propria* (homemade) sign. Also delicious on hot summer days are *granite* ("Italian ices") and *frullati* (cool fruit shakes), both guaranteed to please.

Rome (Roma)

To the question *"Bella Roma, no?"* there can be only one answer. Even amidst today's flip historical and artistic scepticism, Rome's glory is not dimmed, its head not bowed, its ruins not—well, ruined. Augustus boasted that he found Rome a city of brick and left it one of marble, but his work was only the start. For two thousand years, Caesars and popes built forums, churches, temples, palaces, and *piazze,* all testifying to monumental ambitions and egos. Although today the Colosseum crumbles from pollution and the screech of maniacal scooters precludes any semblance of tranquility, Romans revel in their city rather than letting it stagnate as a museum. Concerts animate monuments, kids play soccer around the Pantheon, and august *piazze* serve as movie theaters. Decline and fall seems ridiculous here; all of Rome's empires live on and leave the city undefined by any single epoch. The millions of pilgrims who try to conquer Rome every year may find themselves wearied by its twisting, hot alleyways, and multi-layered design. But why worry about what has been missed? Everything in sight is sweet, everything tastes good, and the eternal city isn't going anywhere. *Bella Roma?* No. *Bellissima.*

For more detailed information about Rome (or for steamy gossip about its former inhabitants), curl up with a copy of *Let's Go: Rome 1998.*

ORIENTATION AND PRACTICAL INFORMATION

Livy once concluded that "the layout of Rome is more like a squatter's settlement than a properly planned city." Two thousand years of city-planning later, Rome is still a splendid sea of one-way streets, dead ends, clandestine *piazze,* incongruous monuments, and incurable traffic. Getting lost is inevitable, but not necessarily undesirable.

Rome is divided into nine neighborhoods, used as headings throughout the chapter. Most visitors arrive by train in **Termini** and the area of **San Lorenzo.** The central artery, **Via Nazionale,** connects Termini to **Piazza Venezia,** the endpoint of all major city roads. To the east lie the Roman ruins of the **Ancient City.** The west claims the **Centro Storico,** home to Piazza Navona, the Pantheon, and countless museums. Just north of Piazza Venezia, the trendy **Piazza di Spagna** and the Spanish Steps border on the urban museum-park, **Villa Borghese.** South of Piazza Venezia, find the blue-collar **Testaccio** and **Aventino** as well as Mussolini's project, **EUR.** The far south is home to the outlying **Monti** and the **Appian Way.** West of the Centro Storico, across the Tiber, expats create art in **Trastevere.** To its north, **Vatican City** is a country in itself.

Rome's circuitous streets make **maps** indispensable. Use the detailed **Tax Free For Tourists** map (available at tourist offices), or try the one published by **AmEx.** Those shopping for retro cool clothing pick up a free **Diesel** map at Via del Corso, 186, and get a well-labeled plan of the Centro Storico. The **Metro/Bus/Tram** map is free from tourist offices or the info office at Stazione Termini. If you are willing to pay for a map, **Roma: Nuova Pianta della Città** is for you.

For a major city, Rome is relatively safe. Exercise common sense and be especially aware around the Forum and the Colosseum, where people are blindly admiring the architecture, and on the crowded buses such as 64 and 492. At night women and men will generally feel safe walking through the historic center of town, but use caution beyond these well-lit, crowded areas. The area around Termini and to its south (especially near P. Vittorio Emanuele and the Oppian Hill) and Testaccio deserve special care, as do the streets around the Olympic Village in the north.

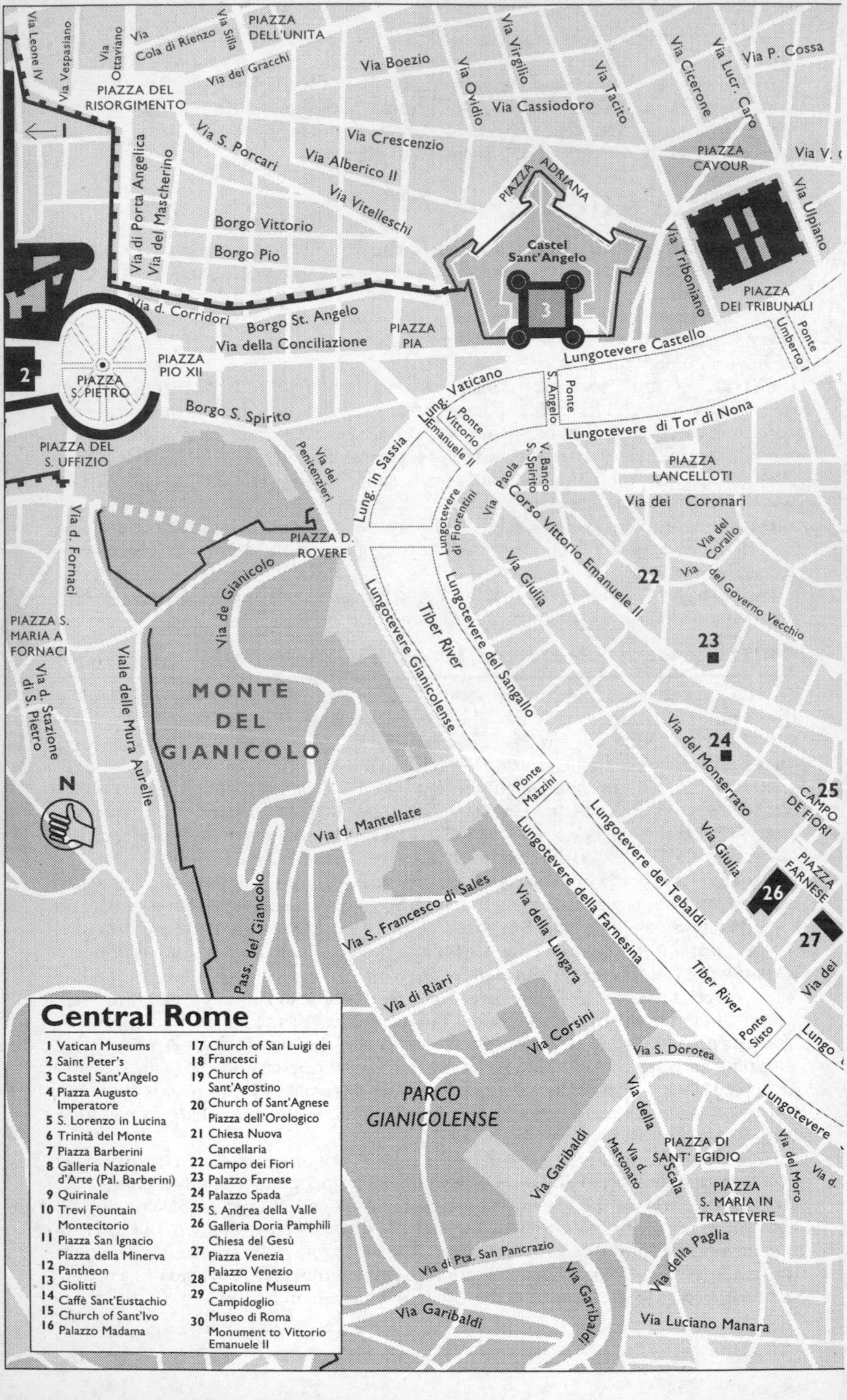
Central Rome
1 Vatican Museums
2 Saint Peter's
3 Castel Sant'Angelo
4 Piazza Augusto Imperatore
5 S. Lorenzo in Lucina
6 Trinità del Monte
7 Piazza Barberini
8 Galleria Nazionale d'Arte (Pal. Barberini)
9 Quirinale
10 Trevi Fountain
Montecitorio
11 Piazza San Ignacio
Piazza della Minerva
12 Pantheon
13 Giolitti
14 Caffè Sant'Eustachio
15 Church of Sant'Ivo
16 Palazzo Madama
17 Church of San Luigi dei
18 Francesci
19 Church of Sant'Agostino
20 Church of Sant'Agnese
Piazza dell'Orologico
21 Chiesa Nuova
Cancellaria
22 Campo dei Fiori
23 Palazzo Farnese
24 Palazzo Spada
25 S. Andrea della Valle
26 Galleria Doria Pamphili
Chiesa del Gesù
27 Piazza Venezia
28 Palazzo Venezio
29 Capitoline Museum
Campidoglio
30 Museo di Roma
Monument to Vittorio Emanuele II
Via Leone IV
Via Vespasiano
Via Ottaviano
Via Cola di Rienzo
Via Silla
PIAZZA DELL'UNITA
Via dei Gracchi
Via Boezio
Via Virgilio
Via Ovidio
Via Cassiodoro
Via Tacito
Via Cicerone
Via Lucr. Caro
Via P. Cossa
PIAZZA DEL RISORGIMENTO
Via S. Porcari
Via Crescenzio
Via Alberico II
Via Vitelleschi
PIAZZA CAVOUR
Via V.
Via di Porta Angelica
Via del Mascherino
Borgo Vittorio
Borgo Pio
PIAZZA ADRIANA
Castel Sant'Angelo
Via Triboniano
Via Ulpiano
PIAZZA DEI TRIBUNALI
Via d. Corridori
Borgo St. Angelo
Via della Conciliazione
PIAZZA PIA
Lungotevere Castello
Ponte Umberto
PIAZZA PIO XII
PIAZZA S. PIETRO
Lung. Vaticano
Ponte S. Angelo
Borgo S. Spirito
Ponte Vittorio Emanuele II
Lungotevere di Tor di Nona
PIAZZA DEL S. UFFIZIO
Via dei Penitenzieri
Lung. in Sassia
V. Banco S. Spirito
PIAZZA LANCELLOTI
Via dei Coronari
Via d. Fornaci
Via Paola
Corso Vittorio Emanuele II
Lungotevere di Fiorentini
PIAZZA D. ROVERE
Via del Corallo
Via del Governo Vecchio
Via Giulia
Via de Gianicolo
PIAZZA S. MARIA A FORNACI
Lungotevere Gianicolense
Tiber River
Lungotevere del Sangallo
Viale delle Mura Aurelie
Via d. Stazione di S. Pietro
MONTE DEL GIANICOLO
Via del Monserrato
N
Ponte Mazzini
CAMPO DE FIORI
Via d. Mantellate
Lungotevere dei Tebaldi
Lungotevere della Farnesina
PIAZZA FARNESE
Via S. Francesco di Sales
Via della Lungara
Pass. del Giancolo
Via di Riari
Via Corsini
Ponte Sisto
Lungo
Via del
Via S. Dorotea
PARCO GIANICOLENSE
Via della Scala
Via d. Mattonato
Lungotevere
PIAZZA DI SANT' EGIDIO
Via Garibaldi
Via del Moro
Via d.
PIAZZA S. MARIA IN TRASTEVERE
Via della Paglia
Via di Pta. San Pancrazio
Via Luciano Manara

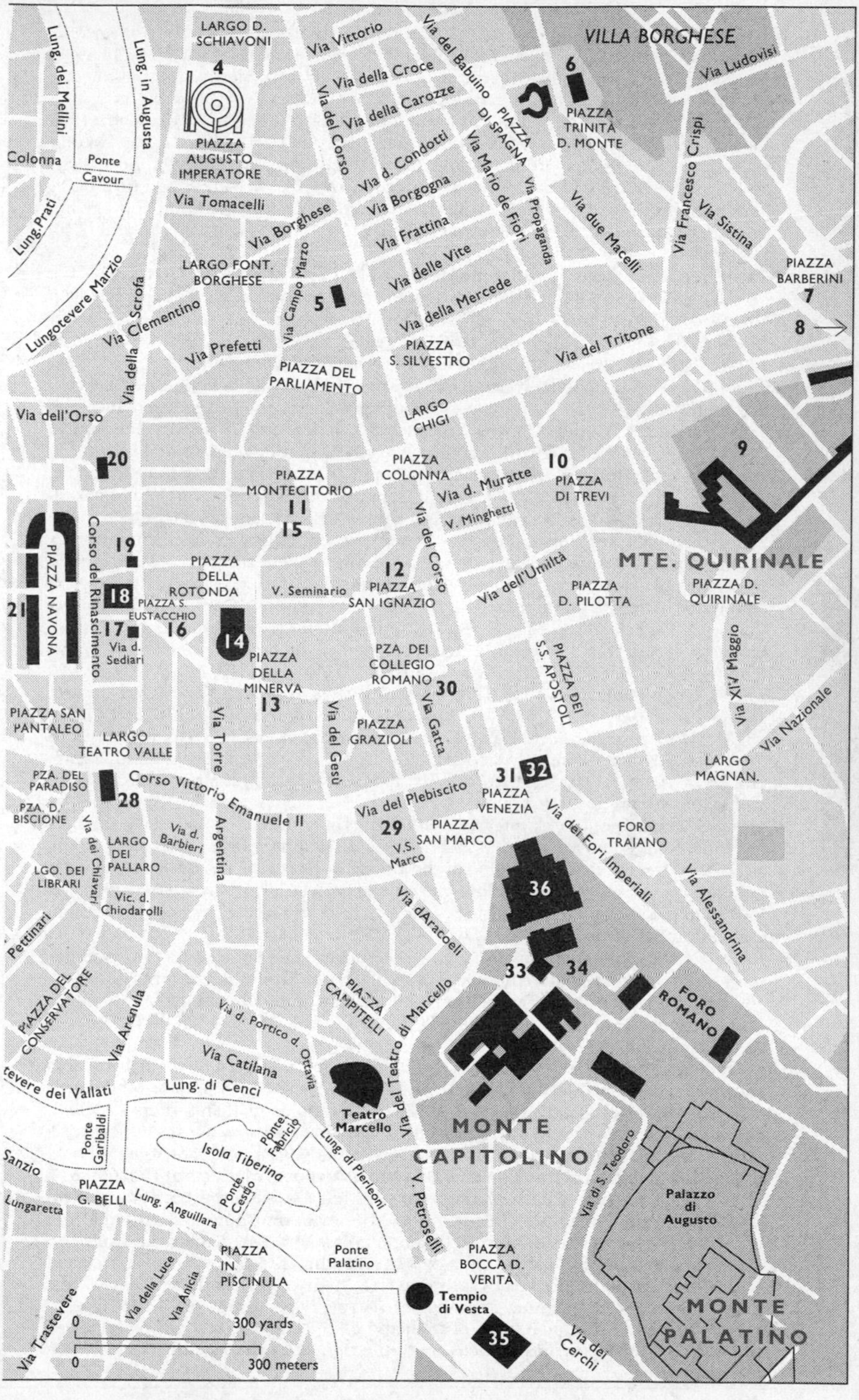
LARGO D. SCHIAVONI
Lung. dei Mellini
Lung. in Augusta
4
PIAZZA AUGUSTO IMPERATORE
Colonna
Ponte Cavour
Lung. Prati
Via Tomacelli
Via Vittorio
Via della Croce
Via della Carozze
Via del Corso
Via del Babuino
VILLA BORGHESE
6
PIAZZA DI SPAGNA
PIAZZA TRINITÀ D. MONTE
Via Ludovisi
Via Mario de Fiori
Via Propaganda
Via d. Condotti
Via Borgogna
Via Frattina
Via delle Vite
Via della Mercede
Via Borghese
Via due Macelli
Via Francesco Crispi
Via Sistina
PIAZZA BARBERINI
7
8
LARGO FONT. BORGHESE
Via Campo Marzo
5
Lungotevere Marzio
Via Clementino
Via della Scrofa
Via Prefetti
PIAZZA S. SILVESTRO
Via del Tritone
PIAZZA DEL PARLIAMENTO
LARGO CHIGI
Via dell'Orso
20
PIAZZA MONTECITORIO
11
15
PIAZZA COLONNA
Via d. Muratte
V. Minghetti
10
PIAZZA DI TREVI
9
MTE. QUIRINALE
PIAZZA NAVONA
Corso del Rinascimento
19
18
21
17
Via d. Sediari
PIAZZA S. EUSTACCHIO
16
PIAZZA DELLA ROTONDA
14
V. Seminario
12
PIAZZA SAN IGNAZIO
Via dell'Umiltà
PIAZZA D. PILOTTA
PIAZZA D. QUIRINALE
PIAZZA DELLA MINERVA
13
PZA. DEI COLLEGIO ROMANO
30
Via Gatta
PIAZZA DEI S.S. APOSTOLI
Via XX Maggio
Via Nazionale
PIAZZA SAN PANTALEO
LARGO TEATRO VALLE
Via Torre Argentina
Via del Gesù
PIAZZA GRAZIOLI
LARGO MAGNAN.
PZA. DEL PARADISO
28
Corso Vittorio Emanuele II
31
32
Via del Plebiscito
PIAZZA VENEZIA
Via dei Fori Imperiali
FORO TRAIANO
PZA. D. BISCIONE
Via dei Chiavari
LARGO DEI PALLARO
Via d. Barbieri
29
PIAZZA SAN MARCO
V.S. Marco
LGO. DEI LIBRARI
Vic. d. Chiodarolli
Via dAracoeli
36
Via Alessandrina
Pettinari
33
34
PIAZZA DEL CONSERVATORE
Via Arenula
Via d. Portico d. Ottavia
PIAZZA CAMPITELLI
Via del Teatro di Marcello
FORO ROMANO
Via Catilana
Lungotevere dei Vallati
Lung. di Cenci
Teatro Marcello
MONTE CAPITOLINO
Ponte Garibaldi
Isola Tiberina
Ponte Fabricio
Ponte Cestio
Lung. di Pierleoni
Via di S. Teodoro
Palazzo di Augusto
Sanzio
PIAZZA G. BELLI
Lung. Anguillara
Lungaretta
V. Petroselli
PIAZZA IN PISCINULA
Ponte Palatino
PIAZZA BOCCA D. VERITÀ
Via della Luce
Via Anicia
Tempio di Vesta
MONTE PALATINO
Via Trastevere
0
300 yards
0
300 meters
35
Via dei Cerchi

Tourist Offices: EPT: (tel. 482 40 70) in the Termini Station in front of track 2. Lines can be horrendous. **Central Office,** Via Parigi, 5 (tel. 48 89 92 55 or 48 89 92 53; fax 48 89 92 50). Walk from the station diagonally to the left across bus-filled P. Cinquecento and go straight across P. della Repubblica. Via Parigi starts on the other side of the church. Offices open Mon.-Sat. 8:15am-7pm. **Enjoy Rome:** Via Varese, 39 (tel. 445 18 43; fax 445 07 34; http://dbweb.agora.stm.it/markets/magenta39/enjoy.htm). From Termini station with trains behind you, head right and cross Via Marsala. Head 3 blocks on Via Milazzo to Via Varese and turn right. Hotel accommodations and short-term lodging. Books 3hr. walking and cycling tours and shuttle service to Pompeii. Open Mon.-Fri. 8:30am-1:30pm and 3:30-6:30pm, Sat. 8:30am-1:30pm.

Budget Travel: Centro Turistico Studentesco (CTS): Via Genova, 16 (tel. 467 91), off Via Nazionale, about halfway between P. della Repubblica and P. Venezia. Open Mon.-Fri. 9am-1pm and 3-7pm, Sat. 9am-1pm. **Branch** office at Via degli Ausoni, 5 (tel. 445 01 41). Free accommodations service.Open Mon.-Fri. 9:30am-1pm and 2:30-6:30pm, Sat. 10am-1pm. Other offices throughout the city.

Budget Travel: Compagnia Italiana di Turismo (CIT), P. della Repubblica, 64 (tel. 474 65 55; fax 481 82 77). Books discount train tickets and tours. Open Mon.-Fri. 9am-1pm and 2-5:30pm. **Centro Turistico Studentesco (CTS),** Via Genova, 16 (tel. 467 91), off Via Nazionale, about halfway between P. della Repubblica and P. Venezia. Open Mon.-Fri. 9am-1pm and 3-7pm, Sat. 9am-1pm. **Branch** office at Via degli Ausoni, 5 (tel. 445 01 41). Free accommodations service, including out-of-town reservations. Boards with notices for rides, special services, etc. Open Mon.-Fri. 9:30am-1pm and 2:30-6:30pm, Sat. 10am-1pm. Other offices throughout Rome.

Embassies and Consulates: Australia: Via Alessandria, 215 (tel. 85 27 21; fax 85 27 23 00). Consular and passport services around the corner at Corso Trieste, 25. Open Mon.-Thurs. 9am-noon and 1:30-5pm, Fri. 9am-noon. **Canada:** Consulate at Via Zara, 30, 5th fl. (tel. 44 59 84 21). Open Mon.-Fri. 10am-noon and 2-4pm. Embassy at Via G.B. De Rossi, 27 (tel. 44 59 81). **Ireland:** Consulate at Piazza Campitelli, 3 (tel. 697 91 21). **New Zealand:** Via Zara, 28 (tel. 440 29 28; fax 440 29 84). Open Mon.-Fri. 8:30am-12:45pm and 1:45-5pm. **South Africa:** Via Tenaro, 14 (tel. 841 97 94; fax 85 25 43 00). **U.K.:** Via XX Settembre 80a (tel. 482 54 41; fax 48 90 30 73), near the Porta Pia and the corner with Via Palestro. Open mid-July to Aug. Mon.-Fri. 8am-1pm; Sept. to mid-July Mon.-Fri. 9:15am-1:30pm and 2-4pm. **U.S.:** Via Veneto, 119a (tel. 467 41; fax 46 74 22 17). Open Mon.-Fri. 8:30-noon and 1:30-3:30pm.

Currency Exchange: Check rates at *cambio* booths, but banks often have the best rates. Banking hours are often Mon.-Fri. 8:30am-1:30pm with an extra hour in the afternoon. Decent deals are found at the **Banca di Roma** or the **Banca Nazionale del Lavoro.** Or, **Numismatica Internazionale,** P. del Cinquecento, 57/58 (tel. 488 50 05), in the arcade on the left side of the Piazza as you face away from the station. Open Mon.-Sat. 8am-7pm. **ACITOUR,** Via Marsala, 14a (tel. 446 99 20), inside the Galleria Caracciolo shopping arcade. L1000 flat traveler's check fee; no commission. Open Mon.-Fri. 9am-1pm and 2-6pm. **Thomas Cook,** P. Barberini, 21a (tel. 482 80 82/3). Open Mon.-Sat. 8:30am-5:30pm, Sun. 9am-1:30pm. Also at Via della Conciliazione, 23/25 (tel. 68 30 04 35), Via del Corso, 23 (tel. 323 00 67), and P. della Repubblica, 65 (tel. 48 64 95).

American Express, P. di Spagna, 38 (tel. 676 41; fax 67 64 24 99). For lost cards and/or checks issued in the U.S. call toll-free 24hr. 167 87 43 33. For other cards call 722 81. Perfect English is spoken. The office holds mail and offers excellent free maps, but it's wiser to change checks at the small *cambio* booths. Open April-Sept. Sat. 9am-12:30pm; Oct.-March Mon.-Fri. 9am-5:30pm, Sat. 9am-3pm.

Flights: Most flights arrive at **Leonardo da Vinci Airport (Fiumicino)** (tel. 659 51). After leaving customs, follow the signs to your left for **Stazione FS/Railway Station.** The Termini line goes directly to the city's main transportation station (1 per hr. at 8min. past the hr. 8:08am-10:08pm, 30min., L15,000). Trains run from Termini Station to the airport from track 22 (every hr., L15,000). Most charter and some domestic flights arrive at **Ciampino** (tel. 79 49 41). From here take the blue COTRAL bus to the Anagnina stop on Metro A (every hr. 6am-11pm, L1500).

Trains: Termini, is the focal point of train and Metro lines. Be wary of pickpockets and con-artists. **Railway info** offices are to the right at as you face the tracks. Open daily 7am-11pm. **Luggage storage,** by tracks 1 and 22, costs L5000 per bag for 12hr. Open daily 5:15am-12:20pm. To: Florence (2-3hr., L38,500), Naples (2-2½hr., L28,500), Milan (5-6hr., L68,000), Bologna (3¼-4hr., L50,000), Venice (5hr., L63,500), Genoa (5-5½hr., L49,500), and Palermo (11-12hr., L92,600).

Public Transportation: Efficient and extensive. The network of routes may seem daunting at first, but the **ATAC** *(Aziende Tramvie Autobus Comunali)* intra-city bus company (tel. 469 51) has a myriad of booths. Each stop *(fermata)* is marked by yellow signs listing all routes that stop there and key stops on these routes. Tickets, good for 75min. of travel on a bus or one ride on the Metro, cost L1500; buy them at newsstands, *tabacchi,* and machines in stations. Daily (L6000) and weekly bus/metro passes (L24,000) are valid everywhere in the *Commune di Roma,* including Ostia but not Fiumicino. You must board buses from the back door and immediately stamp your ticket in the yellow machine. Most buses run daily 5 or 6am-midnight. Night routes are indicated by black shields or by the letter "N" following the number. The two lines of the **Metropolitana (M)** subway intersect at Termini. **Linea A** runs from Ottaviano, near the Vatican, through Lepatano, Flaminio, P. di Spagna, P. Barberini, P. della Repubblica, and the Termini, before terminating in Anagnina. **Linea B** runs from the suburbs through the university to Termini, then to the Colosseum, Piramide, and Magliana (change for trains to Ostia and the beach), ending at Laurentina. The subway runs daily 5:30am-11:30pm.

Taxis: Ride only in yellow or white taxis with meters. Meter starts at L4500. Night surcharge L5000. Sun. surcharge L2000. Airport surcharge L11,500-14,000. Luggage L2000.

Bike and Moped Rental: Rent-a-Scooter, Via F. Turati, 50 (tel. 446 92 92), near Termini, has great prices. Scooters from L30,000 per day. 24hr. roadside assistance. Open Sun.-Fri. 9am-7pm. **I Bike Rome,** Via Veneto, 156 (tel. 322 52 40), in Villa Borghese's underground parking garage; entrance near the intersection of Via di S. Paolo del Brasile and Via della Magnolie. Bikes L10,000-18,000 per day, L35,000-54,000 per week. Mopeds L45,000 per day. Open daily 9am-8pm.

Bookstore: Economy Book and Video Center, Via Torino, 136 (tel. 474 68 77), off Via Nazionale. Enormous selection of books in English. Open June-Aug. Mon.-Fri. 9am-8pm, Sat. 9am-2pm; Sept.-May Mon. 3-8pm, Tues.-Fri. 9am-8pm, Sat. 9am-2pm.

Laundromat: OndaBlu, Via Principe Amedeo, 70b, off Via Cavour 2 blocks south of Termini. Also at Via Milazzo, 20, and Via Vespasiano, 50 (M: Ottaviano). Wash L6000 per 6.5kg. Dry L6000. Open daily 8am-10pm.

Crisis Line: Samaritans, Via San Giovanni in Laterano, 250 (tel. 70 45 44 44). Helpful English speakers. Open for calls daily 1-10pm; call ahead before visiting.

24-Hour Pharmacies: Farmacia Internazionale, P. Barberini, 49 (tel. 48 54 56) near Via Nazionale. MC, V. **Farmacia Piram,** Via Nazionale, 228 (tel. 488 07 54). MC, V.

Medical Assistance: Policlinico Umberto I, Viale di Policlinico, 155 (tel. 49 97 21 01or 499 71), near Termini. Take Metro B to the Policlinico stop. Free first aid. Open 24hr. **Rome-American Hospital,** Via E. Longoni, 69 (tel. 225 33 33 or 225 52 90). Private emergency and lab services. English-speaking physician on call 24hr. **International Medical Center,** Via G. Amendola, 7 (tel. 488 23 71, nights, Sun. 488 40 51). Staffed 24hr. English doctor referral. L100,000-170,000 per visit.

Emergency: First Aid: tel. 118. **Fire:** tel. 115. **Ambulance (Red Cross):** tel. 55 10.

Police: tel. 113 (English interpreter). **Carabinieri** (tel. 112). **Ufficio Stranieri (Foreigners' Office),** Via San Vitale, 15 (tel. 46 86 27 11). English spoken. Open 24hr. **Headquarters (Questura),** Via San Vitale, 15 (tel. 468 61). Report thefts in person.

Internet Access: C.T.S. Interpoint, Via Genova, 16, (tel. 467 91), off Via Nazionale. L5000 per 30min. Open Mon.-Fri. 9am-1pm and 3-7pm, Sat. 9am-1pm.

Post Office: Main office at P. San Silvestro, 19, south of P. di Spagna. Stamps at booths 23-25. *Fermo Posta* at booth 72. Currency exchange at booth 9. Open Mon.-Fri. 9am-6pm, Sat. 9am-2pm. **Postal Code:** 00187 for *Fermo Posta* at the post office and AmEx office. The generic code for Rome is 00100.

Telephones: Telecom, in the main gallery of Termini. 2 metered phones; tell the manager you're calling, dial direct, and pay afterwards. Open daily 8am-9:45pm. Booths are located throughout Rome. **Phone cards** are available in L5000, L10,000, and L15,000 denominations at *tabacchi,* newsstands, bars, and post offices. **Telephone Code:** 06.

ACCOMMODATIONS AND CAMPING

A huge quantity of rooms meets the tourist demand, but quality varies significantly and hotel prices are often astronomical. Although reservations help, large groups take precedence over a reserved double in the minds of some proprietors. Once you find a room, make sure the hotel charges you no more than the price posted on the back of your room's door; it's the law. The **tourist offices** in Rome will scrounge (sometimes reluctantly) to find you a room, as will the **Enjoy Rome** agency (see above) and the **Centro Turistico Studentesco (CTS).** Termini is full of "officials" swarming around to find you a place. Many are genuine and have photo IDs issued by the tourist office. Ask for maps and directions (real officials will always have maps), and always insist on seeing a room first. It is illegal and stupid to "rough it" in public areas of Rome. Be careful even at designated campgrounds.

Institutional Accommodations

If you are looking for a raucous time in Rome, institutional accommodations are not the place to go. While they provide affordable accommodations, most are inconveniently located and the curfews may keep you locked away from *la dolce vita.*

Ostello del Foro Italico (HI), Viale delle Olimpiadi, 61 (tel. 323 62 67; fax 323 62 79). Metro A: Ottaviano, and then exit onto Via Barletta and take bus 32 (in the middle of the street) to "Cadorna." Get off at the 5th stop; the entrance is in the back. Huge red lockers, but you supply the lock. Bring earplugs. Reception open noon-11pm. Lockout 9am-2pm. Curfew midnight. L23,000 with HI card. HI cards L30,000. Breakfast and showers included. Wheelchair accessible.

YWCA, Via Cesare Balbo, 4 (tel. 488 04 60 or 488 39 17; fax 487 10 28), off Via Torino, west of Termini. A fantastic place for women who enjoy safety in numbers. Cheerful atmosphere. Men accompanying their wives are allowed. Curfew midnight. Singles L50,000-70,000. Doubles L80,000-100,000. Triples L99,000. Quads L132,000. Showers and breakfast included, Mon.-Sat. 7:30-8:15am.

ITALY

Hotels and Pensions

North of Termini

There are clusters of clean *pensioni* and hotels awaiting within five to 15 minutes of Termini. The area has recently become a trendy haven for budget travelers.

Pensione Fawlty Towers, Via Magenta, 39 (tel. 445 03 74). Exit Termini to the right and cross Via Marsala to Via Marghera. Walk a block up Via Marghera, turn right on Via Magenta, and look for the yellow sign. Lovely, English-speaking staff has useful info. Communal fridge and microwave. No curfew. Dorms L25,000. Singles L50,000-65,000. Doubles L75,000-100,000. Triples L100,000-110,000.

Pensione Papa Germano, Via Calatafimi, 14a (tel. 48 69 19). With the trains behind you, exit the station to your right and turn left on Via Marsala, which becomes Via Volturno; Via Calatafimi is on the right. Papa Gino and Mamma Pina exude pure charm. Gino will often help you find a place if he's booked. Check-out 11am. No curfew. Singles L40,000. Doubles L65,000, with bath L80,000. Triples L85,000, with bath L90,000. Quads L100,000. 10% reduction Nov.-March. AmEx, MC, V.

Hotel Virginia, Via Montebello, 94 (tel. 488 17 86 or 445 76 89). Exit Termini to the right onto Via Marsala, turn left, and follow the street until it becomes Via Volturno; Via Montebello is on the right. Singles L35,000, with shower L45,000. Doubles with shower L50,000-65,000, with full bath L75,000-80,000. Triples L75,000-90,000. Prices vary by the season. Washing machine L5000 per load.

Pensione Tizi, Via Collina, 48 (tel. 482 01 28; fax 474 32 66). Take Via XX Settembre onto Via Piave, then take the first left onto Via Flavia, which leads to Via Collina (15min.). This family *pensione* has welcomed students for years. Pristine condition. Check-out 11am. Singles L50,000. Doubles L70,000, with bath L90,000. Triples L105,000. Quads L140,000, with bath L160,000. Breakfast L9000.

Hotel Matilde, Via Villafranca, 20 (tel. 445 43 65; fax 446 23 68). From Termini Station, make a left onto Via Marsala and a right onto Via Vicenza; the hotel is on the fifth cross-street, to the left. Spotless rooms. No curfew. Singles L60,000. Doubles L90,000. Triples L120,000. Quads L140,000. Breakfast L5000. AmEx, MC, V.

Pensione Piave, Via Piave, 14 (tel. 474 34 47; fax 487 33 60). Off Via XX Settembre past the Ministry of Finance. Rooms have private bath, telephone, and carpeted floors. Singles have double beds. English spoken. Check-in noon. Check-out 10:30am. No curfew. Singles L50,000, with bath L65,000. Doubles with bath L90,000. Triples with bath L120,000. V, MC.

Pensione Alessandro, Via Vicenza, 42 (tel. 446 19 58), near the corner of Via Palestro. 4, 6, or 8 to a large room. Kitchen with microwave. Reception open 6:30am-11pm. Check-out 9am. No curfew. April-Sept. L25,000; Oct.-March L20,000.

Hotel Lachea and **Hotel Pensione Dolomiti,** Via San Martino della Battaglia, 11 (tel. 495 72 56 or 49 10 58; fax 445 46 65), off P. dell'Indipendenza. *Let's Go*'s biggest fan, the warm-hearted owner will ensure every comfort. 3 balconied rooms. Check-out 11am. Singles L45,000-50,000. Doubles L60,000-65,000, with bath L80,000-85,000. Triples L80,000-115,000. Quads available; bargaining possible.

Hotel Galli, Via Milazzo, 20 (tel. 445 68 59; fax 446 85 01), off Via Marsala. Room renovation continues. Singles L50,000, with bath L75,000. Doubles L75,000-120,000. Triples L90,000. Quads L120,000-160,000. MC, V.

South of Termini

The area south of Termini is often portrayed as busier, noisier, and seedier than other parts of central Rome, but lately the neighborhood has started to clean up its act. Nevertheless, exercise caution, especially at night. Prices tend to be very flexible in this area; they depend on the season, length of stay, and how many people are in your group. Many of the prices listed below are in the form of ranges; expect to pay the maximum during the peak season and closer to the minimum off season.

Pensione di Rienzo, Via Principe Amedeo, 79a (tel. 446 71 31 and 446 69 80). Tranquil retreat. Spacious, newly renovated rooms. Warm, friendly, English-speaking staff. No curfew. Singles L50,000-90,000. Doubles L70,000-95,000. MC, V.

Pensione Cortorillo, Via Principe Amedeo, 79a (tel. 446 69 34), at Via Gioberti. Five flights upstairs. Charming rooms; a little tight, but fun. Singles with bath L30,000-50,000. Doubles L50,000-70,000. Triples L75,000-90,000. Small breakfast included.

Hotel Kennedy, Via Filippo Turati, 64 (tel. 446 53 73; fax 446 54 17). Comfy rooms with private bath, satellite TV, phone, and even A/C. English spoken. Young staff. 10% discount to *Let's Go* travelers under 29. Singles L60,000-109,000. Doubles L80,000-169,000. Triples L110,000-199,000. Great breakfast. AmEx, MC, V.

Hotel Orlanda, Via Principe Amedeo, 76, 3rd fl. (tel. 488 06 37; fax 488 01 83), at Via Gioberti. Tidy rooms, with TV, phone, and shower. Singles with bath L70,000-110,000. Doubles L90,000-180,000. Breakfast L8000. AmEx, Diner's, MC, V.

Hotel Il Castello, Via Vittorio Amedeo II, 9 (tel. 77 20 40 36 or 77 20 60 51; fax 70 49 00 68). Take Metro A: Manzoni (don't try to walk from Termini), go 1 block down Via San Quintino, and take the first left. Friendly management. Lounge with bar and TV. No curfew. Dorms L25,000. Singles L50,000. Doubles L80,000-L100,000. Triples from L120,000. Breakfast L6000. MC, V.

West of Termini

The area west and southwest of Termini, though close to the action, has managed to preserve an authentic Roman atmosphere. Here you'll find cobblestone alleyways with family-run businesses as well as hip wine shops and Irish pubs.

Pensione Sandy, Via Cavour, 136, 4th fl. (tel. 488 45 85), near Santa Maria Maggiore. No sign; look for the Hotel Valle next door. Buzz to be let in. Run by peppy English speakers and a native Roman, Slim, who claims to have learned his English from "Beavis and Butthead." Shared rooms. L25,000 in summer; off-season L20,000 (no heat, but lots of blankets). Showers included. Lockers available.

Hotel San Paolo, Via Panisperna, 95 (tel. 474 52 13; fax 474 52 18), follow Via S. Maria Maggiore, just off Via Cavour to your right. Clean hall baths. English spoken. Singles L40,000-65,000. Doubles L55,000-90,000, with bath L80,000-120,000. Triples L80-000-120,000. Breakfast L10,000. Reservations accepted. AmEx, MC, V.

Hotel Giugiu, Via del Viminale, 8 (tel./fax 482 77 34). Steps away from the Termini. Friendly, English-speaking family runs the joint. Show them your recent *Let's Go* for special rates. Singles L55,000-60,000. Doubles L80,000-90,000. Breakfast L8000.

Centro Storico: Near Piazza Navona and Campo dei Fiori

Il Centro Storico (the Historic Center) is the ideal, if expensive, base for living as the Romans do. From Stazione Termini, take bus 64, 170, or 75 to Largo Argentina, the transportation hub of the historic center.

Hotel Mimosa, Via Santa Chiara, 61 (tel. 68 80 17 53; fax 683 35 57), off P. della Minerva behind the Pantheon. A family-run, kitschy abode. English spoken. Drunkenness not tolerated. Singles L70,000. Doubles L100,000, with bath L130,000. Triples L150,000. Quads L195,000. Breakfast L8000. 10% price reduction in winter.

Hotel Navona, Via dei Sediari, 8 (tel. 686 42 03; fax 68 80 38 02, call before faxing). Take Via dei Canestrari, off the southern end of P. Navona, cross over Corso del Rinascimento, and continue straight. Upstairs, restored rooms supposedly housed Keats and Shelley. Checkout 10am. Singles L85,000-95,000. Doubles L120,000-140,000. Triples L170,000-180,000. Breakfast included.

Albergo della Lunetta, P. del Paradiso, 68 (tel. 686 10 80 or 687 76 30; fax 689 20 28). Take Via dei Chiavari off Corso Vittorio Emanuele II, then the first right off Via dei Chiavari. Eden in the heart of Rome. Singles L60,000-80,000. Doubles L100,000-140,000. Triples L135,000-180,000. Reserve with V or MC.

Albergo Pomezia, Via dei Chiavari, 12 (tel./fax 686 13 71). Renovated 1st floor section with baths is nicer than the old part. Singles L80,000-120,000. Doubles L110,000-170,000. Triples L132,000-200,000. Prices drop Nov.-Feb., except at Christmas. Breakfast included. AmEx, Diner's, MC, V.

Hotel Piccolo, Via dei Chiavari, 32 (tel. 689 23 30 or 68 80 25 60), off Corso Vittorio Emanuele II, behind Sant'Andrea della Valle. Clean, comfy rooms. English spoken. Curfew 1:30am. Singles L80,000-100,000. Doubles L100,000-130,000. Triples L120,000-140,000. Quads L160,000. Breakfast L7000. Reserve ahead. AmEx, MC, V.

Piazza di Spagna

In this neighborhood of designer silk suits, leather loafers, and mini-skirts, inexpensive accommodations are scarce. However, it may be worthwhile to spend a few extra bucks to sleep in the hippest part of town.

Pensione Panda, Via della Croce, 35 (tel. 678 01 79; fax 69 94 21 51), between P. di Spagna and Via del Corso. Modern rooms with wrought-iron accoutrements. No curfew. Singles L65,000-80,000. Doubles L95,000-130,000. Triples and quads available; additional beds L25,000. Reserve ahead. AmEx, MC, V.

Pensione Parlamento, Via delle Convertite, 5 (tel./fax 679 20 82, for reservations 69 94 16 97). Off Via del Corso, on the street leading to P. San Silvestro. Glamorous roof-top flowered terrace. Safes, hairdryers, telephones, and TVs in every room. A/C L20,000. Singles with bath L120,000. Doubles L150,000-160,000. Each additional person L35,000. Breakfast included. Reserve ahead. AmEx, MC, V.

Pensione Fiorella, Via del Babuino, 196 (tel. 361 05 97), just off P. del Popolo. Cheerful breakfast room and large, sparkling bedrooms. Curfew 1am. Singles L65,000. Doubles L105,000. Breakfast included. Advance reservations require one-night's deposit; otherwise, call within 24 hours of your arrival.

Pensione Jonella, Via della Croce, 41 (tel. 679 79 66), between P. di Spagna and Via del Corso. Attractive rooms. Singles L60,000. Doubles L90,000. Reserve ahead.

Across the Tiber: Borgo and Prati

The *pensioni* on the other side of the Tiber are fairly expensive but also tend to be comfortable, clean, and friendly. Those in **Prati,** near the Vatican, are attractive for their proximity to popular sights and a safer residential area. Bus 64 from Termini ends right near St. Peter's and Metro A runs to Ottaviano, the Metro stop in the area.

Pensione Ottaviano, Via Ottaviano, 6 (tel. 39 73 72 53 or 39 73 81 38), off P. del Risorgimento north of P. San Pietro. Near Metro A and St. Peter's. 3-6 beds per room. Satellite TV, individual lockers, fridges, and microwave. No curfew. L20,000-25,000. 2 doubles in summer L70,000; off-season L45,000.

Residence Giuggioli, Via Germanico, 198, 1st fl. (tel. 324 36 97 or 324 21 13), at Via Paolo Emilia. Antiques adorn pristine rooms. Gleaming common bath. Room 6 is superb. Doubles L100,000. Double-bed suite with private bath L130,000.

Pensione Lady, Via Germanico, 198, 4th fl. (tel. 324 21 12). Renovations have restored the building to its original charm; bathrooms are blissful. Closed a few weeks yearly; call ahead. Singles L100,000. Doubles L120,000, with bath L150,000.

Hotel Florida, Via Cola di Rienzo, 243, 2nd and 3rd fl. (tel. 324 18 72 or 324 16 08; fax 324 18 57). Great rooms flaunt their recent renovation. Phones and hairdryers in each room. Singles L70,000, with bath L90,000. Doubles L100,000-145,000. Triples with bath L180,000. 10% off-season discount. AmEx, MC, V.

Camping

Several campgrounds around Rome are downright luxurious, with everything from swimming pools to campground bars. In August, arrive well before 11am.

Seven Hills, Via Cassia, 1216 (tel. 30 36 27 51 or 303 31 08 26; fax 303 31 00 39), 8km north of Rome. Take bus 907 from P. Risorgimento to Via Cassia, or bus 201 from Flaminio. Ask where to get off, then follow the country road about 1km. Houses a bar, market, restaurant, pizzeria, and disco. Daily Vatican shuttle (L6000 round-trip). Reception open daily 7am-11pm. L12,000 per person, L8000 per tent, L6000 per car. Bungalows L70,000-110,000. Open late May-late Oct.

Flaminio, Via Flaminia Nuova, 821 (tel. 333 14 31), about 8km outside of Rome. Take bus 910 from Termini to Piazza Mancini, then transfer to bus 200. Get off on Via Flaminia Nuova when you see the "Philips" or EUCLID building on your right. The landscaping is a bit rough around the edges, but they're outfitted with a pool, market, restaurant, bar, and disco. L13,000 per person, L8000 per tent. Bungalows L38,000. Doubles L64,000. Triples L102,000. Quads L128,000. Open March-Oct.

FOOD

Meals in Rome are prolonged affairs, each course often continuing for hours on end. When you're ready to indulge, stay away from the area near the train station; "bargain" restaurants are often tourist snares. Instead, hop on the bus to reach the nearby university district of **San Lorenzo** or the **Testaccio,** the last truly untouristed neighborhoods in Rome. Closer to the city center, the **Piazza Navona** and **Campo dei Fiori** boast some romantic *trattorie,* and **Trastevere** harbors the best *pizzerie* in the city. Romans generally eat late, around 8 or 9pm; set out early to avoid the rush.

Get a taste of local produce and local haggling techniques at Rome's many outdoor **markets.** The largest markets are at P. Campo de' Fiori, P. Vittorio Emanuele II, and in P. San Cosimato in Trastevere. Smaller markets can be found on Via Montebello and P. della Pace off Piazza Navona. **Supermarket STANDA** offers a huge selection of foodstuffs, produce, toiletries, kitchen supplies, cheap clothing, and anything else you can think of. There is one located on Viale Trastevere, 62, a few blocks from Piazza Sidney Sonnino, and one on Via Cola di Rienzo, 173, near the Vatican.

Restaurants

Pizzeria Baffetto, Via del Governo Vecchio, 114, on the corner of Via Sora. Once a meeting place for 60s radicals, now just radically crowded. Outdoor seating. Pizzas L5000-9000. Cover L1000. Open daily 10am-noon and 7pm-1am.

Palladini, Via del Governo Vecchio, 29. No sign or place to sit; but brimming with a *panini* munching lunch crowd. Favorites include *prosciutto e fiche* (ham and figs) or *bresaola e rughetta* (cured beef and arugula). Veggie options. Sandwiches L2500-5000. Open in summer Mon.-Fri. 8am-2pm and 5-8pm, Sat. 8am-2pm; off-season closed Thurs. afternoons.

Hostaria Grappolo d'Oro, P. della Cancelleria, 80-81, on Via Cancelleria off Corso Vittorio Emanuele II. Owner Andrea d'Angelo creates gastronomic ecstasy in his neighborhood *trattoria.* Words are too cheap for his *antipasti* (L10,000-12,000) and *penne all'arrabbiata* (L10,000). House white wine L9000. Cover L2000. Open Mon.-Sat. noon-3pm and 7-11:30pm.

Margherita, P. delle Cinque Scole, 30, right next to the S. Maria del Pianto church. Behind the simple green door (don't look for a sign), locals and students fight over politics. On Thursday, try homemade *gnocchi* for L10,000. *Fettuccine* L10,000. *Baccalà* (fried cod) L11,000. Cover L1000. Open Mon.-Fri. noon-3pm.

La Capricciosa, Largo dei Lombardi, 8. Right off Via del Corso, across from its intersection with Via della Croce. *Capricciosa* pizza, divided into four sections of ham, egg, artichoke, and a topping of your choice L9000. *Primi* L8000-11,000. Cover L2000. Open Wed.-Mon. 12:30-3pm and 6:30pm-12:30am.

Trattoria da Settimio all'Arancio, Via dell'Arancio, 50-52. Take Via dei Condotti from P. di Spagna, cross Via del Corso, and continue on Via della Fontanella Borghese; take the first right, then the first left. Excellent meals from L27,000. *Ossobuco* (braised veal shank) L15,000. *Ravioli all'arancia* (with orange) L10,000. Cover L2000. Open Mon.-Sat. 12:30-3pm and 7:30-11:30pm.

Pizzeria al Leoncino, Via del Leoncino, 28. Take Via Condotti from P. di Spagna, cross Via del Corso, continue on Via della Fontana Borghese. Take the first right onto Via del Leoncino. Fast and cheap. Pizza L8000-13,000. Wine L5000 per liter. Open Mon.-Tues. and Thurs.-Fri. 1-3pm and 7pm-midnight, Sat.-Sun. 7pm-midnight.

Taverna dei Quaranta, Via Claudia, 24. Cool, tree-shaded outdoor dining. Outstanding *bruschetta al pomodoro* L3000. *Gnocchi al pomodoro e basilico* L9000. Beer on tap L6000. Open daily noon-3pm and 8pm-midnight.

Hostaria da Nerone, Via delle Terme di Tito, 96. Near the Colosseum. Outdoor dining. Feast on *fettuccine alla Nerone* (with salami, ham, beans, and mushrooms) L8000. *Fritto di cervello* (fried, buttered brain with mushrooms) L14,000. Cover L2500. 10% service charge. Open Mon.-Sat. noon-3pm and 7:30-11pm.

Pizzeria Panattoni, Viale Trastevere, 53-59. Waiters race around an entire block of tables, serving superb crispy pizzas (L9000-11,000). Fantastic appetizers include *ascolane* olives (stuffed with meat and breaded) L6800. Open daily 6pm-2:30am.

Pizzeria Ivo, Via di San Francesco a Ripa, 158. Take a right on Via delle Fratte di Trastevere off Viale Trastevere and a right on Via S. Francesco a Ripa. Alas, tourists have finally discovered this Trastevere legend. Pizzas L8000-16,000. Open Sept.-July Wed.-Mon. 5pm-2am.

Il Tulipano Nero, Via Roma Libera, in P. San Cosimato. Friendly, rowdy pizzeria. Very spicy *pennette all'elettroshock* L10,000. Innovative pizza combos. *Pizza tonno, mais, e rughetta* (tuna, corn, and arugula) L10,000. Open daily 6pm-2am.

Ristorante Max, P. dell'Unità, 26/27, just east of P. del Risorgimento at Via dei Gracchi and Via C. Mario. Small and cozy. Heaping portions of pasta L6,000-10,000. Delicious *bruschetta* with olive spread L2000. *Secondi* L7000-16,000. Open May-Aug. Wed.-Mon. noon-3pm and 7-11pm; Sept.-April Mon.-Sat.

L'Archetto, Via Germanico, 105. Nice staff. Pizzas L7000-12,000. Salmon *bruschetta* L4000. Open Tues.-Sun. 7pm-midnight. Closed for part of Aug.

Da Giggetto, Via Alessandria, 43, near the Porta Pia. Claims to be "the king of pizza." Savory *bruschetta* with tomatoes and mozzarella (L4000) is just a prelude to the pizza (L7200-13,000). Open Mon.-Sat. 7pm-1am. Closed in Aug.

Osteria da Luciano, Via Giovanni Amendola, 73/75. Head south on Via Cavour from Termini and turn left after one block onto Via G. Amendola. Hearty, generous pasta dishes L3900-5000. Tourist menu a steal at L15,000. Wine L4500 per liter. Cover L1000. Service 10%. Open Mon.-Fri. 11:30am-9pm, Sat. 11:30am-5pm.

Il Pulcino Ballerino, Via degli Equi, 66/68, off Via Tiburtina. Artsy atmosphere with cuisine to match. *Tagliolini al limone* (pasta in a lemon cream sauce) L9000. *Risotto* (various types) L10,000-12,000. Cover L1000. Open Mon.-Sat. 12:30-2:30pm and 8pm-midnight. Closed first 2 weeks of Aug.

Desserts and Caffè

Creamy and flaky pastries and *gelato* rainbows taunt passersby from countless bakery windows; if you can't resist any longer, try one of the revered places listed below. When you need a few minutes to recover from your travels, relax at one of the city's many *caffè*. Many cluster around Campo dei Fiori and Trastevere, the neighborhood around Piazza Cavour, and the areas near Via della Scrofa and Via Cola di Rienzo.

Keep in mind that you'll pay one price to stand and drink at the bar, and a higher price (as much as double) if you sit down at a table.

Giolitti, Via degli Uffici del Vicario, 40. From the Pantheon, follow Via del Pantheon (at the northern end of the *piazza*) to its end, then take Via della Maddelena to its end; Via degli Uffici del Vicario is on the right. A Roman institution as venerable as the Vatican, Giolitti is revered by many as the mecca of *gelato.* Cones L2500-4000. Open daily 7am-2am; Nov.-April closed Mon.

Grattachecca da Bruno, on Viale Giulio Cesare, near the corner of Via Vespasiano (MetroA: Ottaviano). Yummiest Italian ice you'll ever have. Pick from a variety of fresh fruit. *Grattaceccha* L3000. Open daily until the wee hours.

Palazzo del Freddo Giovanni Fassi, Via Principe Eugenio, 65/67, off P. Vittorio Emanuele, southeast of Termini. Another location at V. Vespasiano, 57, near the Vatican. Century-old *gelato* factory is a confectionery altar. Cones L2000-3000. Open Tues.-Sun. noon-midnight; in summer also Mon. 6pm-midnight.

Tre Scalini, P. Navona, 30. Famous for its *tartufo,* a menacing hunk of chocolate ice cream rolled in chocolate shavings (L11,000, at the bar L5000). Bar open Thurs.-Tues. 8am-1am. Restaurant open Thurs.-Tues. 12:30-3:30pm and 7:30-9pm.

Sant'Eustachio, Il Caffè, P. Sant'Eustachio, 82, in the *piazza* southwest of the Pantheon. Take Via Monterone off Corso Vittorio Emanuele. Rome's "coffee empire." Cool blue industrial decor. Tremendous *gran caffè speciale* L5000, at the bar L3000. Open Tues.-Fri. and Sun. 8:30am-1am, Sat. 8:30am-1:30am.

Bar San Calisto, P. S. Calisto, 4, in Trastevere. Truly incredible cappuccino (L1200 sitting or standing) and *granita di limone* (L2000). Exciting, crowded bar. Open Mon.-Sat. 6am-1:30am, Sun. 4pm-1:30am; off-season closed Sun.

Tazza d'Oro, Via degli Orfani, 84/86, off the northeast corner of P. della Rotonda. No sit-down but great brews. *Caffè* L1200. Open Mon.-Sat. 7am-8:20pm.

SIGHTS

Rome wasn't built in a day, and it's not likely that you'll see any substantial portion of it in 24 hours either. The city is layered with monuments—ancient temples, medieval fortresses, Baroque confections of marble, and rushing water—crowding next to each other on every interwoven street. No other city in the Western world can lay claim to so many masterpieces of architecture from so many different eras of history, not to mention the treasures of painting and sculpture found inside each of them. It may be impossible to see everything, but don't be afraid to try.

It's best to explore Rome for yourself, but if you're on a tight schedule or have difficulty walking for long, you might opt for a city tour. **Carrani Tours,** Via V.E. Orlando, 95 (tel. 474 25 01), runs 11 different bus tours of the city; they range from a simple three-hour tour for L45,000 to a nighttime ride with all the fixings for L100,000. **Walk Thru the Centuries,** Via Varese, 39 (tel. 445 18 43, toll free 167 27 48 19), offers two walking tours, one which focuses on the historic center and another which explores the Vatican Museums (2 per day, 3hr., L25,000-40,000).

The Ancient City Across the Tiber, the ancient city of Rome centered on the Capitoline and Palatine Hills in the southern part of the modern city center. To reach the Capitoline Hill, head down Via dei Fori Imperiali from the "Colosseo" Metro stop, and walk around the Vittorio Emanuele II monument. The ancient city is also accessible on any of the buses that stop at Piazza Venezia. The original capitol and one of the most sacred parts of the city, the **Campidoglio** (Capitoline Hill) still serves as the seat of the city's government, perched in a spectacular *piazza* designed by Michelangelo. Here you can also enjoy unforgettable views of the Forum and Palatine, as well as several superb museums. The **Musei Capitolini,** in the twin *palazzi* on either side of the *piazza,* display one of the largest collections of ancient sculpture in the world, including the Capitoline Wolf, the centuries-old symbol of Rome (open Tues.-Sun. 9am-5pm; L10,000, students L5000, last Sun. of the month free).

The **Roman Forum** and **Palatine** mark the geographical and commercial center of the ancient city. For nearly a thousand years, these few acres of dusty valley were the most beautiful in existence, the pattern for the ideal European city, and the center of the Western world. From the entrance gate on Via dei Fori Imperiali (across from the end of Via Cavour), a ramp descends past the Temple of Antoninus and Faustina on the left and the remains of the **Basilica Aemilia** on the right. The **Curia,** or Senate House, to the right of the Basilica Aemilia as you exit, was one of the oldest buildings in the Forum, although the present structure dates from the time of Diocletian (303 AD). The broad space in front of the Curia was the **Comitium,** or assembly place, where male citizens came to vote and representatives of the people gathered for public discussions. The brick platform to the left of the arch was the **Rostra,** or speaker's platform, erected by Caesar in 44 BC, which any citizen could mount to voice his opinion. Cicero's head and hands were displayed here after his assassination, and Augustus' rebellious daughter Julia allegedly engaged in amorous activities with some of her father's greatest enemies on this platform. Proceed along Via Sacra, the main thoroughfare of the Forum and oldest street in Rome. At the end, the **Arch of Septimius Severus** (203 AD) commemorates the emperor's victories in the Middle East.

This part of the Forum also has several shrines and sacred precincts. The three great temples of the lower Forum have been closed for restorations, but the eight columns of the **Temple of Saturn** have at last shed their scaffolding. This was the site of the public treasury and an underground stash of sacred treasures. Around the corner to the left, justice was administered at Caesar's **Basilica Julia** (54 BC). Look for inscribed grids and circles in the steps where Romans awaiting judgement distracted themselves with a form of tic-tac-toe. At the east end of the Basilica Julia, the **Temple of Castor and Pollux** celebrates the Roman rebellion against the Etruscan king.

The flowering sculptured gardens and broad grassy expanses of the **Palatine Hill** make for a refreshing change from the dusty Forum. The best way to reach this area is by the stairs to the right after the street turns at the Arch of Titus. When you're ready to tackle the ruins again, check out the **Domus Augustana,** the imperial palace built by Domitian (81-96 AD) and used subsequently as the empire headquarters. Also on the hill, a walkway offers a sweeping view of the grassy **Circus Maximus,** where chariot races were once held. (Forum and Palatine open in summer Mon.-Sat. 9am-7pm, Sun. 9am-1pm; off-season Mon.-Fri. 9am-1hr. before sunset. Sun. and holidays 9am-noon. Last admission 1hr. before closing. L12,000.)

Across the street from the old Forum Romanum sprawl the **Fori Imperiali,** a vast conglomeration of temples, basilicas, and public squares. Caesar, Augustus, Vespasian, Nerva, and Trajan all built capacious monuments in this area to glorify the city and, more often, themselves. The **Forum of Trajan** (107-113 AD), the largest and most impressive of the lot, spreads across Via dei Fori Imperiali below two Baroque churches at the eastern end of Piazza Venezia. The complex includes the famous **Trajan's Column,** which narrates the Emperor's victorious campaigns against the Dacians and now stands as the greatest specimen of Roman relief-sculpture ever carved. Down the street, with an entrance on Via IV Novembre, 94, the three-floors of the fascinating **Markets of Trajan** once sheltered dozens of single-room stores along cobblestone streets. (Open in summer Tues.-Sat. 9am-6:30pm, Sun. 9am-1:30pm; off-season closes sunset. L3750, students L2500.)

The **Colosseum,** Metro: "Colosseo," stands as the city's grandest symbol. At its opening in 80 AD, the Colosseum could hold as many as 50,000 spectators; its first 100 days saw some 5000 wild beasts perish in the bloody arena, and the slaughter of animals and people continued for three centuries. The outside of the arena is well-preserved around three-quarters of its circumference. Inside, the missing floor reveals a labyrinth of underground cells, corridors, ramps, and elevators used for transporting animals up to the arena level. (Ground level open in summer Mon.-Tues. and Thurs.-Sat. 9am-7pm, Wed. and Sun. 9am-2pm; off-season closes 1hr. before sunset. Free. Upper level closes 1hr. before the ground level. L8000.) Built to commemorate Constantine's victory over his rival Maxentius in 312, the amazingly preserved **Arch of Constantine** lies between the Colosseum and the Palatine Hill.

West of the Capitoline Hill, the **Church of Santa Maria in Cosmedin** harbors some of Rome's most beautiful medieval decoration and the famed **Bocca della Verità** in the portico. Originally a drain cover, the relief was credited with supernatural powers in the Middle Ages. It's said that the hoary face will chomp on the hand of a liar, severing his fingers (portico open 9am-5pm; church open 9am-noon and 3-5pm).

From P. di Porta Capena at the east end of the Circus Maximus, Via delle Terme di Caracalla passes the hulking remains of the **Baths of Caracalla,** the largest and best-preserved baths in the city. (Open in summer Mon. 9am-2pm, Tues.-Sat. 9am-7pm; off-season closes 1hr. before sunset. Last admission 1hr. before closing. L8000.) Outside the city proper lie the **catacombs,** mysterious multi-story condos for the dead. Of the 60 such tunnels around Rome, the most notable are those of **San Sebastiano, San Callisto,** and **Santa Domitilla,** next door to one another on Via Appia Antica south of the city. Buses 218 and 660 provide service to this part of the city. San Sebastiano is perhaps the most impressive of the three: the tunnels here run for 7 mi. on three levels and accommodate 174,000 bodies, and the passageways are eerily decorated with animal mosaics, disintegrating skulls, and fantastic symbols of early Christian iconography. (Catacombs open 8:30am-noon and 2:30-5:30pm; off-season they close at 5pm. San Sebastiano is closed Thurs. and Nov., Santa Domitilla is closed Tues. and Jan., San Callisto is closed Wed. and Feb. Each L8000.)

Pantheon and Piazza Navona Between Via del Corso and Piazza Navona, in the *centro storico,* the **Pantheon** has stood for nearly 2000 years: the marble columns (brought whole from Egypt in the 2nd century AD), bronze doors, and soaring domed interior remain largely unchanged from the day the building was erected by Hadrian. (Pantheon open June Mon.-Sat. 9am-6pm, Sun. 9am-1pm; July-Aug. Mon.-Sat. 9am-6:30pm, Sun. 9am-1pm; Oct.-May Mon.-Sat. 9am-4pm, Sun. 9am-1pm. Free.) Around the left side of the Pantheon, an obelisk supported by Bernini's winsome elephant statue marks the center of **Piazza Minerva.** In back, the unassuming facade of the **Church of Santa Maria Sopra Minerva** hides Renaissance masterpieces, including a brilliant fresco cycle by Filippino Lippi. Michelangelo's great *Christ Bearing the Cross* stands guard near the altar (open daily 7am-noon and 4-7pm). North of the P. della Rotonda, stands the **Church of San Luigi dei Francesi,** the French national church in Rome and home to three of Caravaggio's most famous ecclesiastical paintings (open Fri.-Wed. 7:30am-12:30pm and 3:30-7pm, Thurs. 7:30am-12:30pm).

Once the site of an ancient racetrack, the **Piazza Navona,** a few blocks west across Corso del Rinascimento, evolved into a glorious Baroque *piazza* as the result of a century of one-upmanship. Innocent X, who came to the papal throne in 1644, was only too eager to distract the Roman people from the achievements of his predecessor, the ubiquitous Urban VIII Barberini. He therefore cleared out the stadium on the site and constructed a new *piazza* and palace to rival those of the Barberini across town. The towering, rippling bodies in Bernini's **Fountain of the Four Rivers** command the center of the *piazza* with the grandeur that Innocent intended. Of course, Bernini himself was competing with a rival as well; one story holds that he designed the Nile and Plata statues on the fountain to block the view of the nearby **Church of Sant'Agnese in Agony,** designed by Bernini's great rival Borromini.

Off Via del Corso, Via Lata leads into Piazza del Collegio Romano and to another stunning *palazzo* and museum. The **Palazzo Doria Pamphilj** hides the Rococo frivolity of the stunning **Galleria Doria Pamphilj,** Piazza del Collegio Romano, 2 (open Fri.-Wed. 10am-5pm; L12,000, students and seniors L9000).

Campo dei Fiori to Via Giulia Across Corso Vittorio Emanuele II from Piazza Navona, down Via della Cancelleria, the **Campo dei Fiori** saw countless executions during papal rule; now the only carcasses that litter the *piazza* are those of the fish in the colorful **market** that springs up (Mon.-Sat. 6am-2pm). Continuing southwest, away from Piazza Navona, you'll reach **Piazza Farnese,** where two amazing palaces merit a visit. Towering over the *piazza* is the huge, stately **Palazzo Farnese,** begun in 1514 with an elaborate cornice by Michelangelo (interior not open to the public). To the east, the **Palazzo Spada** represents a masterpiece of Baroque stucco. Inside, the palace houses paintings in the **Galleria Spada;** Room 2 has works by Tintoretto and Titian (Galleria open Tues.-Sat. 9am-6:30pm, Sun. 9am-12:30pm; L8000).

South of Piazza Farnese and these palaces begins **Via Giulia,** commissioned by Pope Julius II in the early 16th century as a straight road leading directly to the Vatican. Throughout the 16th century, this luxurious expanse remained a refined neighborhood, and today it is one of the most peaceful and exclusive roads in Rome, with well-maintained *palazzi,* antique stores, and art galleries.

Piazza del Popolo, Villa Borghese, and the Spanish Steps The traditional northern entrance to the city, **Piazza del Popolo** (the people's square) is a favorite arena for communal antics. Masked revelers once filled the square for the torch-lit festivities of the Roman carnival; today, the *piazza* bustles with tourists during the summer and resounds with music and celebration after soccer victories and other notable events. Tucked away on the north side of the *piazza* near the Porta del Popolo, the small **Church of Santa Maria del Popolo** contains two exquisite canvases by Caravaggio, the *Conversion of St. Paul* and the *Crucifixion of St. Peter,* among other notable works (open daily 7am-noon and 4-7pm).

Immediately north of the Spanish Steps and northeast of the Piazza del Popolo, the park of the **Villa Borghese** features cool, shady paths, countless fountains and statues, and three major museums. To get to Villa Borghese, take Metro A to "Flaminia." In the park, the **Galleria Borghese** has reopened its marvellous doors and brims with gold, crystal, and marble. Inside are Bernini's greatest early sculptures, including *Apollo and Daphne,* the *Rape of Proserpina,* and *David.* (Open Tues.-Sat. 9am-7pm, Sun. and holidays 9am-1pm. Last admission 30min. before closing. L10,000.) The **Galleria Nazionale d'Arte Moderna** is filled with the best Italian and European art of the 19th and 20th centuries (open Tues.-Sat. 9am-7pm, Sun. 9am-1pm; L8000).

Designed by an Italian, paid for by the French, occupied by the British, and now under the sway of American ambassador-at-large Ronald McDonald, the **Spanish Steps** (Scalinata di Spagna) exude a truly international atmosphere as a tourist attraction and hangout for foreigners and Italians alike. Today, you're more likely to see con artists, but in its day the area attracted Stendhal, Balzac, Wagner, and Liszt; Henry James and the Brownings lived on Via Bocca di Leone, a small sidestreet in the area. A small plaque on the side of Piazza di Spagna, 26, marks the place where Keats died in 1821. The second floor of the house now features the charming **Keats-Shelley Memorial Museum,** full of curious relics from the poets' lives. (Open May-Sept. Mon.-Fri. 9am-1pm and 3-6pm; Oct.-April Mon.-Fri. 9am-1pm and 2:30-5:30pm; closed 2nd and 3rd weeks of Aug. L5000.) Despite its simple design (by Carlo Maderno), the rosy facade of the **Church of Santa Trinità dei Monti** provides a worthy climax to the steps' grand curves, not to mention a sweeping view of the city (open daily 9:30am-12:30pm and 4-7pm; upper half open Tues. and Thurs. 4-6pm).

Trevi Fountain to Piazza Barberini Nicola Salvi's famed and now sparkling-clean **Fontana di Trevi** (Trevi Fountain) emerges from the back wall of Palazzo Poli, dwarfing the already narrow *piazza.* In the foreground of the fountain, two enormous Tritons struggle out of the rough-hewn stone and guide the winged chariot of Neptune. **Piazza del Quirinale,** southeast of Trevi Fountain at the end of Via del Quirinale, occupies the summit of the tallest of Rome's seven hills. In the middle of the *piazza,* the heroic statues of **Castor and Pollux** flank yet another of Rome's many obelisks. Nearby, the President of the Italian Republic officially resides in the **Palazzo del Quirinale,** a Baroque architectural collaboration by Bernini, Carlo Maderno, and Domenico Fontana. Along Via del Quirinale is the undulating facade of Borromini's **Church of San Carlo alle Quattro Fontane,** also called San Carlino (open Mon.-Fri. 9:30am-12:30pm and 4-6pm, Sat. 9am-12:30pm).

Just north of Trevi Fountain and a few blocks north of Piazza del Quirinale, Via del Tritone runs east to **Piazza Barberini.** Bernini's **Fontana del Tritone** (Triton Fountain) spouts a stream of water high into the air over the bustling traffic circle of this *piazza.* Follow Via Veneto from the *piazza* to reach the **Church of Santa Maria della Concezione,** a mausoleum built in 1626 as part of the Counter-Reformation. In the **Capuchin Crypt** downstairs, the arranged bones of 4000 Capuchin friars make this one of the most bizarre and elaborately macabre settings in Rome (church and crypt open Fri.-Wed. 9am-noon and 3-6pm; donation L1000). On the side of Piazza Barberini opposite the church, up Via delle Quattro Fontane, Palazzo Barberini's **Galleria Nazionale d'Arte Antica** houses a superb collection of paintings from the 12th to 17th centuries (open Tues.-Fri. 9am-7pm, Sat. 9am-2pm, Sun. 9am-1pm; L8000).

East of the Ancient City The grandiose **Church of San Giovanni in Laterano,** the cathedral of the diocese of Rome, lies east of the Colosseum at the end of Via San Giovanni in Laterano, in the *piazza* of the same name. The traditional pilgrimage route from St. Peter's ends here, at the city's oldest Christian basilica. (Metro A: San Giovanni. Open in summer daily 7am-6:45pm; off-season 7am-6pm. Dress appropriately.) Four blocks down Via Cavour from Termini, the Basilica of **Santa Maria Maggiore** occupies the summit of the Esquiline Hill. Both the front and rear facades are Rococo works, but the interior is the best-preserved example of a paleo-Christian basilica in the city. To the right of the altar, a simple slab marks the **tomb of Bernini.** A L5000 ticket allows you to see the 14th-century mosaics in the church's *loggia* (church open daily 7am-7pm; *loggia* open daily 9:30am-5:40pm). Down Via Cavour, away from the station, steps on the left lead you through the narrow archway of Via San Francesco di Paola to the **Church of San Pietro in Vincoli,** home to Michelangelo's masterful statue of Moses (open daily 7am-12:30pm and 3:30-7pm).

Trastevere Across the river, Trastevere boasts a proud, independent vitality, giving the neighborhood a character and atmosphere unlike that of the rest of central Rome. To reach Trastevere, take bus 75 or 170 from Termini, or bus 56 or 60 from Via Claudio in front of Piazza San Silvestro, near the Spanish Steps. Buses to Trastevere stop at **Piazza Sonnino,** which is close to most attractions in the historic center. The *piazza* itself draws crowds of tourists for its restaurants, pizzerias, and bars, although the buses and bus terminals here diminish some of the charm. Near the *piazza,* Via dei Genovesi runs toward the river to the intersection with Via di Santa Cecilia; turn right here to find the **Basilica of Santa Cecilia in Trastevere,** up ahead on the right. Stefano Maderno's famous statue of Santa Cecilia reclines under the high altar (open Tues. and Thurs. 10-11:30am). From Viale di Trastevere take Via della Lungaretta to P. di Santa Maria in Trastevere, home to the grandiose 4th-century **Church of Santa Maria in Trastevere.** Although the church is being restored, the 12th-century mosaics in the apse and the chancel arch still glimmer in their full splendor (open daily 7am-7pm). Villa della Lungara leads north to the **Renaissance Villa Farnesina,** the jewel of the Trastevere. Baldassare Peruzzi built the magnificent villa for the Sienese banker and philanthropist Agostino Chigi ("il Magnifico"). The walls are covered in frescoes (open Mon.-Sat. 9am-1pm; L6000).

To ascend **Janiculan Hill (Gianicolo),** where the beautiful **Botanical Gardens** lie, take Via della Scala in Trastevere up to Via Garibaldi (about 10min.). Atop the hill sits the **Church of San Pietro in Montorio,** built on the spot once believed to be the site of St. Peter's upside-down crucifixion (open daily 9am-noon and 4-6:30pm).

Vatican City Occupying 108.5 acres entirely within the boundaries of Rome, Vatican City is the last toehold of a church that once wheeled and dealed as a mighty European power. Under the Lateran Treaty of 1929, the pope exercises all legislative, judicial, and executive powers over this tiny theocracy, but must remain neutral in Italian national politics and Roman municipal administration. On the western bank of the Tiber, the Vatican can be reached from Rome's center by Metro A to "Ottaviano"; after leaving the station, walk south on Via Ottaviano toward the distant colonnade. You can also take buses 64 and 492 from Termini and Largo Argentina, bus 62 from P. Barberini, bus 23 from Testaccio, or bus 19 from San Lorenzo.

The **Basilica di San Pietro** (St. Peter's Basilica) rests on the reputed site of St. Peter's tomb. In 1506, Pope Julius II called on Donato Bramante to improve on the aging brick basilica on the site, and through the years Bramante, Sangallo, Michelangelo, and Raphael had a hand in designing the church. Today, Michelangelo's sorrowful **Pietà** greets visitors to the basilica, though unfortunately from behind bullet-proof glass. Further down the nave on the right, toward the intersection of the two arms of the church, a medieval bronze **statue of St. Peter** presides over the crossing. In the center of the crossing of the two arms, Bernini's **baldacchino** rises on spiraling solomonic columns over the plain marble altar, which only the Pope may use. Steps at the crossing, below Bernini's spear-wielding statue of St. Longinus, lead down to the **Vatican Grottoes,** the final resting place of countless popes and saints. The grottoes lead to the stairs that climb to the **cupola;** at the top, you will find perhaps the most expansive and breathtaking view of Rome. (Basilica open April-Sept. daily 7am-6pm; Oct.-March 7am-7pm. Free. Cupola closes one hr. before the church. L5000 by stairs, L6000 by elevator and stairs. Proper dress must be worn.)

When in town, the Pope grants **public audiences** in P. San Pietro on Wednesdays, usually at 10:30am. To attend an audience, apply in writing to the **Prefettura della Casa Pontificia,** 00120 Città del Vaticano, specifying the number of tickets desired and the preferred date. Otherwise, stop by the office on the Monday or Tuesday before the audience you wish to attend and see if tickets are available. The office is beyond the bronze doors to the right of the basilica at the beginning of the colonnade, past the Swiss guards (open Mon.-Wed. 9am-1pm; tickets free).

A 10-minute walk around the Vatican City walls or bus ride from the *piazza* brings you to the extraordinary **Vatican Museums.** Of the four color-coded paths through the museums, Tour A hits only the barest essentials, while Tour D covers absolutely everything. Several of the greatest extant works of classical sculpture adorn the **Pio-Clementine Museum,** including the sublime *Apollo Belvedere,* the evocative *Laocoön,* and the sarcophagus of St. Helen. A floor above, the remarkable **Etruscan Museum** displays artifacts from Tuscany and northern Lazio. Several routes lead through the breathtakingly frescoed **Raphael Rooms,** the sumptuous papal apartments built by Pope Julius II in the 16th century. The **Stanza della Segnatura** contains Raphael's splendid *School of Athens,* in which Plato and Aristotle stroll through an airy architectural fantasy as other famous scholars and artists converse around them. The climax of any tour of the Vatican Museums is the **Sistine Chapel.** The barrel vault of the ceiling, some 70 feet above the floor, gleams with the undaunted genius, brave simplicity, and brilliant coloring of Michelangelo's unquestioned masterpiece. The altar wall is covered by Michelangelo's restored *The Last Judgment.* Refrain from taking flash photos; it's detrimental to the frescoes and you can buy much better shots on postcards. Once out of the Sistine Chapel, explore several more masterpieces at the **Pinacoteca.** Room 8 houses three important works by Raphael, including the exquisite *Transfiguration.* (Major galleries are open Mon.-Fri. 8:45am-1pm. Easter week, April-May, and Sept.-Oct. museums are open Mon.-Fri. 8:45am-4pm, Sat. 8:45am-1pm. The last Sun. of every month museums are open 8:45am-1pm, though the Cistene Chapel remains closed. Last entrance is 45min. before closing. L15,000, under 26 and with ISIC L10,000, last Sun. of the month free.)

A short walk down Via della Conciliazione from St. Peter's stands the massive **Castel Sant'Angelo.** Built by the Emperor Hadrian (117-138 AD), the edifice has served the popes as a fortress, prison, and palace. The enormous complex now contains a museum of arms and artillery, but the papal apartments and the incomparable views of Rome are the real reasons to visit. (Open in summer daily 9am-7pm; off-season 9am-2pm; closed 2nd and 4th Tues. of each month. L8000.) The marble **Ponte Sant'Angelo,** lined with Bernini's angels, leads back across the river.

ENTERTAINMENT

Since the days of bread and circuses, Roman entertainment has been a public affair; concerts under the stars, street fairs with acrobats and fire-eaters, Fellini-esque crowds of slick Romeos, modern-day minstrels and maestros, and enchanted foreigners flooding *piazze* and *caffè* are all part of a normal evening. Organized entertainment requires a little research; in addition to the listings below, check out **Roma C'è,** with its comprehensive English language section, available at newsstands for L1500.

Music, Theater, and Dancing

The classical music scene in Rome goes wild in the summer. It all starts with the **Festa Europea della Musica,** a weekend of non-stop music at the end of June. In July, the **Accademia Nazionale di Santa Cecilia** (tel. 361 28 73 or 679 36 17) holds concerts in the **Villa Giulia,** Piazzale della Villa Giulia, 9. All kinds of classical music are represented here, from Scarlatti to Gershwin. Buy tickets at Villa Giulia or from the Agenzia Tartaglia in P. di Spagna, 12 (678 45 65). The **Theater of Marcellus,** at Via del Teatro di Marcello, 44, near Piazza Venezia, hosts summer evening concerts organized by the **Associazione Il Tempietto.** Tickets are L26,000 including entrance to the otherwise inaccessible ancient theater. During the opera season (Sept.-June), look for performances and tickets at the **Teatro dell'Opera** in P. Beniamino Gigli (tel. 48 16 01). Summer performances usually take place in Piazza di Siena in the Villa Borghese. Most big-time pop and rock performers play at the **Palazzo dello Sport** in EUR or at the **Foro Italico.** Head out to **Testaccio Village,** at Via di Monte Testaccio, 16 (tel. 57 28 76 61), for live music of all kinds every night at 9pm from mid-June to mid-September. You can usually buy tickets from **Orbis,** Piazza Esquilino, 37 (tel. 474 47 76 or 482 74 03). For theater offerings, check with the tourist office or call the **Teatro Ghione,** Via delle Fornaci, 37 (tel./fax 637 22 94).

Rome's music clubs attract a hip Italian crowd; some have dancing and most are cheaper than discos. The city's discos and dance clubs, by contrast, are often flashy and require high cover charges. **Alexanderplatz Jazz Club,** Via Ostia, 9 (tel. 39 74 21 71), near the Vatican, is the best jazz venue in the city. Take Metro A to "Ottaviano"; from there, go west on Viale Giulio Cesare, take the second right onto Via Leone IV, and the first left. (open Sept.-June nightly 10pm-1:15am; shows start at 10:30pm). In late July they organize the **Jazz & Image Festival** (tel. 580 68 76 or 77 20 13 11) in Villa Celimontana. **The Groove,** Vicolo Savelli, 10, off Via del Governo Vecchio near Piazza Pasquino, has some of the grooviest dancing in Rome (no cover; open Tues.-Sun. 10pm-2am or later; closed most of Aug.). The best gay club is **L'Alibi,** Via Monte di Testaccio, 39-40, in Testaccio near the "Piramide" Metro stop (L15,000 cover includes first drink; Thurs. no cover; open Tues.-Sun. 11pm-4am).

Pubs

There are many pubs in Rome, quite a few with some sort of Irish theme. Drinks often go up in price after 9pm, so imbibe accordingly. The pubs and *birrerie* in Trastevere offer the best mix of foreigners and Romans.

Jonathan's Angels, Via della Fossa, 16. West of P. Navona. Take Vicolo Savelli Parione Pace off Via Governo Vecchio. The pub boasts live music and a hip, young crowd enjoying the campy, candlelit ambience. Check out the bathroom. Medium beer on tap L10,000. Cocktails/long drinks L15,000. Open nightly 9pm-2am.

Julius Caesar, Via Castelfidardo, 49, just north of Termini near Piazza dell'Indipendenza. Backpackers, tourists, and Italian men flock here for live music, cheap drinks, and crazy fun. During happy hour (9-10pm), a beer and pizza run L10,000. Pitchers L15,000. Cocktails L10,000. Inquire about the *Let's Go* discount. Open daily 9pm-3am. Live music Mon.-Sat.

The Drunken Ship, Campo dei Fiori, 20/21. This slick establishment warmly welcomes backpackers with special reduced prices on drinks. The DJ spins American favorites, and all of the staff speaks English. Pint of beer L5000. Pitcher L15,000. Sandwiches L8000. Open in summer daily noon-2am; off-season 6pm-2am.

Vineria, Campo dei Fiori, 15. Chic spot for young Romans to sip wine and swap phone numbers. In summer the crowd merges with thousands of *piazza* partiers. Chardonnay L2000. Gin and tonic L6000. Open Mon.-Sat. 10am-2pm and 6pm-2am.

■ Near Rome

In **Tivoli,** water is the inspiration and principal attraction. Ancient Roman glitterati such as Catullus and Horace enjoyed the delicious cold of the cascades. From Largo Garibaldi, the gardens of the 16th-century **Villa d'Este** spill over watery terraces from the entrance in Piazza Trento (open May-Aug. daily 9am-6:45pm; Sept.-April 9am-1hr.

before sunset; L8000). Just outside of Tivoli is the **Villa Adriana,** where Emperor Hadrian reconstructed the architectural wonders of his far-flung empire (open May-Aug. daily 9am-7:30pm; Sept.-April 9am-dusk; L8000). **COTRAL buses** depart from the "Rebibbia" metro stop for Tivoli (every 30min., L4100). To get to Villa Adriana, get off the COTRAL bus headed for Giudonia from Largo S. Angelo (every hr., L2000) or take bus 4 (L1500) from Largo Garibaldi in Tivoli.

The remains of **Ostia Antica** offer a cooler, closer, and cheaper alternative to the more famous ruins at Pompeii and Herculaneum. You'll have no trouble finding a spot for a picnic. Take Metro B to "Magliana," change to the Lido train, and get off at Ostia Antica (25min., same metro ticket for both legs of trip). Cross the overpass, go left when the road ends, and follow the signs. (Open in summer daily 9am-7pm; off-season 9am-5pm. Last admission 1hr. before closing. L8000.)

THE VENETO

The Veneto encompasses a wide range of geographical terrains, from the rocky foothills of the Dolomites and the Alps to the fertile valleys of the Po River. These territories were linked only loosely under the Venetian Empire, and regional dialects testify to the relative isolation in which the towns developed. The sense of local culture and custom that remains quite strong in each town may surprise visitors lured to Italy's most-touristed region primarily by Venice, the *bella* of the north.

Venice (Venezia)

It is with good reason that Venetians call their city *La Serenissima*—the most serene. Venice awakes each morning with a refreshing absence of the cars and mopeds that infest other Italian cities; her citizens make their way on foot or by boat through an ancient maze of narrow streets and winding canals. The serenity is broken only by tourists, who swarm in the *campi* (squares) and thoroughfares of the city, searching out its wealth of museums and landmarks. As you follow the crowds to Venice's many architectural and artistic attractions, be sure to save some time to explore the quiet backstreets and lively residential quarters of the city as well.

ORIENTATION AND PRACTICAL INFORMATION

At the northern tip of the Adriatic, Venice is linked by ferry to Greece and the Middle East, and by rail to major European cities. The **Santa Lucia train station** lies on the northwest edge of the city; the bus terminals are across the Grand Canal in nearby **Piazzale Roma.** If you're in a rush to get to **Piazza San Marco** and the central tourist office, take *vaporetto* (canal boat) 82 from the station or Piazzale Roma. If you prefer to walk to San Marco (about 40min.), head left from the station onto Lista di Spagna, and follow the signs and crowds.

The main part of Venice is divided into *sestieri* (districts): **San Marco, Castello, San Polo, Santa Croce, Santa Elena, Cannaregio,** and **Dorsoduro.** Within each section, there are no individual street numbers, but one long sequence of numbers (roughly 6000 per *sestiere*) that winds its way haphazardly through the district. Every building is located on a "street"—*fondamenta, salizzada, calle, campo, canale, rio, ponte,* and *rio terrà. Let's Go* lists these wherever possible. Always be sure you're in the proper *sestiere;* some street names are duplicated and no *sestiere* boundaries are marked. Yellow signs posted all over town will direct you to and from Piazza San Marco (at the border of San Marco and Castello), the **Rialto Bridge** (linking San Marco to San Polo), the **train station** (in Cannaregio), Piazzale Roma (in Santa Croce), and the **Accademia** (in Dorsoduro). If you haven't figured it out already, you're going to need a detailed map to navigate Venice successfully. The color-coded *Storti Edizioni* map-guide (L5000) shows all the major streets, has an invaluable street index, and is more useful than anything you'd get for free.

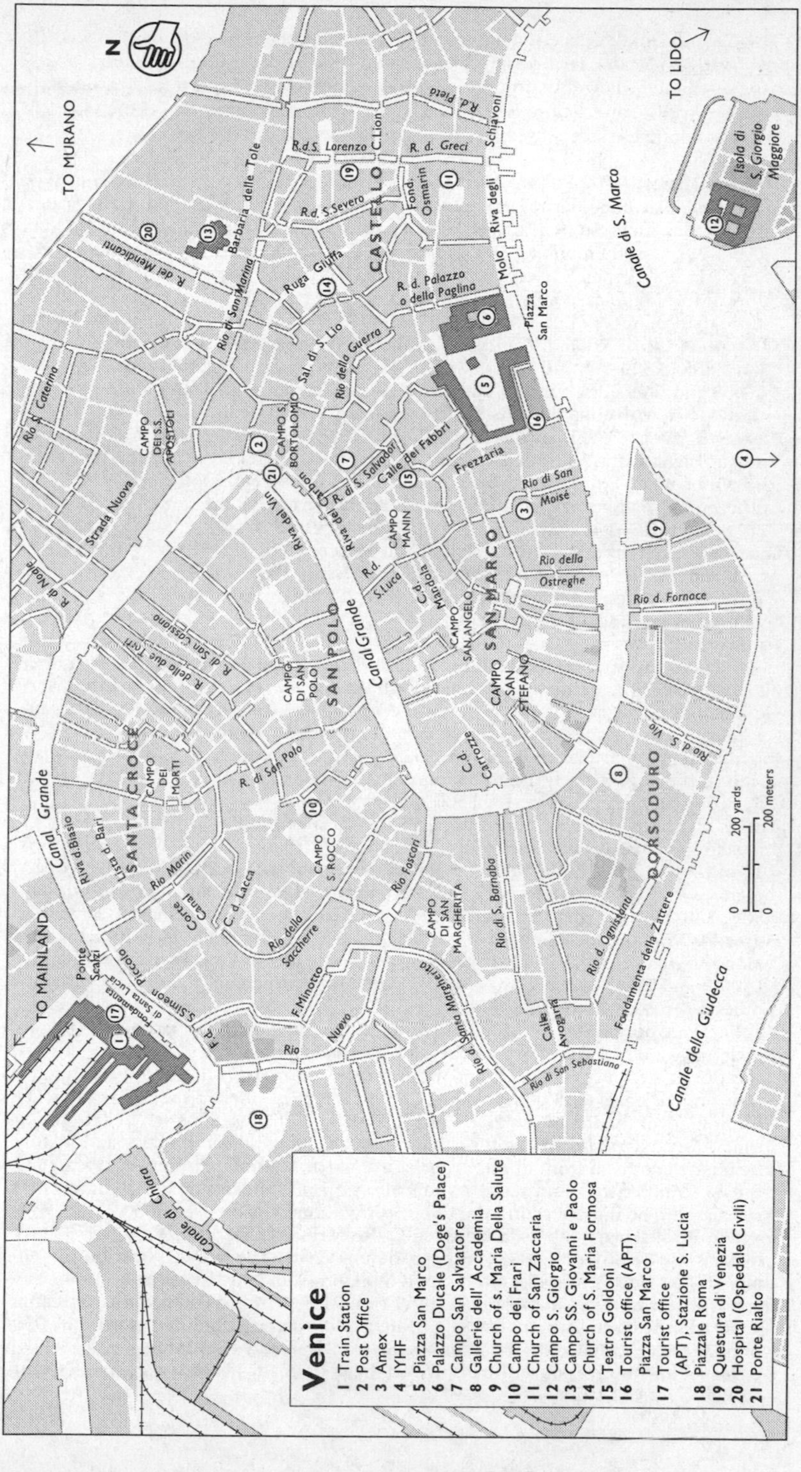
Venice
1 Train Station
2 Post Office
3 Amex
4 IYHF
5 Piazza San Marco
6 Palazzo Ducale (Doge's Palace)
7 Campo San Salvaatore
8 Gallerie dell' Accademia
9 Church of s. Maria Della Salute
10 Campo dei Frari
11 Church of San Zaccaria
12 Campo S. Giorgio
13 Campo SS. Giovanni e Paolo
14 Church of S. Maria Formosa
15 Teatro Goldoni
16 Tourist office (APT), Piazza San Marco
17 Tourist office (APT), Stazione S. Lucia
18 Piazzale Roma
19 Questura di Venezia
20 Hospital (Ospedale Civili)
21 Ponte Rialto
TO MAINLAND
TO MURANO
TO LIDO
N
Canal Grande
Canale di S. Marco
Canale della Giudecca
Canale di Chiara
SANTA CROCE
SAN POLO
SAN MARCO
CASTELLO
DORSODURO
Isola di S. Giorgio Maggiore
Piazza San Marco
CAMPO S. BORTOLOMIO
CAMPO DEI S.S. APOSTOLI
CAMPO MANIN
CAMPO SAN ANGELO
CAMPO SAN STEFANO
CAMPO DI SAN POLO
CAMPO DEI MORTI
CAMPO S. ROCCO
CAMPO DI SAN MARGHERITA
Ponte Scalzi
Strada Nuova
Barbaria delle Tole
Ruga Giuffa
Frezzaria
Calle dei Fabbri
Riva degli Schiavoni
Molo
200 yards
200 meters

ITALY

The **Grand Canal,** the central artery of Venice, can be crossed on foot only at the **ponti** (bridges) **Scalzi, Rialto,** and **Accademia.** *Traghetti* (gondola-like ferry boats) cross the canal fairly frequently where there is no bridge. High tides (particularly from Nov.-April) cause *acque alte,* periodic floods that swamp parts of the city. San Marco is sometimes under three feet of water for two or three hours.

Tourist Offices: APT, Palazzetto Selva (tel. 522 63 56; fax 52 98 87 30), just past the park. Exit P. S. Marco between the columns and turn right along the waterfront. Open Mon.-Sat. 9:40am-3:20pm. Another office at the **train station** (tel./fax 71 90 78). Usually mobbed. Get in line at the left side of the booth. Open Tues.-Sun. 7:15am-9:15pm. The office at the **Lido,** Gran Viale 6/A (tel. 526 57 21), is open during the high season only (open Mon.-Sat. 9am-2pm). If you're in Venice for more than a couple of days and are between 14 and 29 years old, check out **Youth Discount Card: Rolling Venice,** Comune di Venezia, Assessorato alla Gioventù, San Marco, 1529 (tel. 270 76 50; fax 270 76 42), on Corte Contarina. The card costs L5000 and offers discounts at many hotels, restaurants, shops, and museums. The card comes with a map that lists participating establishments.

Budget Travel: CTS, Dorsoduro, 3252 (tel. 520 56 60; fax 523 69 46), on Fondamenta Tagliapietra. Off the Dorsoduro-to-San Marco route, near Campo S. Margherita. Open Mon.-Fri. 9am-12:30pm and 2:30-6:30pm. **Transalpino** (tel./fax 71 66 00), for international train tickets, is to the right as you exit the station. Open Mon.-Fri. 8:30am-12:30pm and 3-7pm, Sat. 8:30am-12:30pm.

Currency Exchange: Banco di Sicilia, San Marco, 5051 (tel. 521 97 30). Changes cash and traveler's checks (open Mon.-Fri. 8:30am-1:30pm and 2:35-3:35pm). Many automatic change machines located next to **ATMs** outside banks offer 24hr. service, low commission, and decent rates.

American Express: San Marco, Sal. S. Moise, 1471 (tel. 167 87 20 00), between S. Marco and the Accademia (look for the AmEx directional mosaic underfoot). Free mail service for members or those with AmEx Traveler's Cheques. Mediocre exchange rates; no commission. Office open Mon.-Fri. 9am-5:30pm, Sat. 9am-12:30pm. Exchange service open in summer Mon.-Sat. 8am-8pm.

Flights: Aeroporto Marco Polo, tel. 541 54 91. ACTV (tel. 528 78 86) local bus 5 runs to the airport every 1½hr. (30min., L1200), or take the ATVO coach (tel. 520 55 30), with luggage space, for L5000.

Trains: Stazione di Santa Lucia, tel. 71 55 55 (lost and found 71 61 22). Info office in station across from tourist office. Open daily 7:15am-9:20pm. To: Padua (every 15min., 30min., L3500), Bologna (every 30min., 1½hr., L20,000), Milan (every 30min., 3hr., L34,000), Florence (12 per day, 3hr., L32,000), and Rome (6 per day, 5hr., L48,000). **Luggage Storage:** L1500 per 12hr. Open daily 3:45am-1:20am.

Buses: ACTV, the local line for buses and boats (tel. 528 78 86) in P. Roma. Open Mon.-Sat. 8am-2:30pm. **ATP** is the long distance carrier. To Padua (every 30min., L5000) and Treviso (every hr., L3800). Ticket office open daily 7am-11:30pm. Info office open Mon.-Sat. 7am-8pm.

Public Transportation: The alternative to walking is taking the *vaporetti* (motorboat buses), which cruise waterways. Most principal boats run 24hr. but frequency is reduced after 11pm. The 24hr. or 3-day *biglietto turistico* is good for unlimited travel on all boats (L15,000-30,000). The ACTV office offers a special 3-day ticket for holders of the Rolling Venice Card (L20,000). Not all stations sell tickets all the time—buy extras and get the type that can be machine-validated at any station. Buy tickets at booths in front of *vaporetti* stops and at self-serve dispensers (located at the ACTV office in P. Roma and at the Rialto stop). Buy tickets on board for an L800 surcharge. The fine for riding the *vaporetti* without a ticket is L24,000.

English Bookstores: Libreria Editrice Cafoscarina, Dorsoduro, 3259 (tel. 523 89 69; fax 522 81 86), on Cà Foscari near the university. The largest selection in Venice. 10% Rolling Venice discount. Open Mon.-Fri. 9am-7pm, Sat. 9am-12:30pm.

Laundromat: Lavaget, Cannaregio, 1269 (tel. 71 59 76), on Fondamenta Pescaria. Take a left from the station, cross 1 bridge, and turn left along the canal. L15,000 per 3kg, soap included. Open Mon.-Fri. 8:30am-1pm and 4-6:30pm.

24-Hour Pharmacy: Look at the display on the door of any pharmacy, check *A Guest in Venice* or call 192.

Hospital: Ospedale Civili, Campo SS. Giovanni e Paolo (tel. 529 45 17). **Boat Ambulance/Medical Assistance:** tel. 523 00 00.

Emergency: tel. 113.

Police: Carabinieri, P. Roma (tel. 523 53 33 or 112 in an emergency).

Post Office: San Marco, 5554 (tel. 522 06 06), on Salizzada Fontego dei Tedeschi near the eastern end of the Rialto bridge off Campo San Bartolomeo. *Fermo posta* at desk 4. Stamps are available at desk 12 or any *tabacco* in town. Open Mon.-Sat. 8:15am-6:45pm. **Branch office** through the arcades at the end of P. San Marco. Open Mon.-Fri. 8:15am-1:30pm, Sat. 8:15am-12:10pm. **Postal Code:** 30124.

Telephones: San Marco, Fontego dei Tedeschi, 5550, next to the main post office. Open Mon.-Fri. 8am-12:30pm and 4-7pm. **Telephone Code:** 041.

ACCOMMODATIONS AND CAMPING

Plan to spend slightly more for rooms here than elsewhere in Italy. Reservations, ideally made as much as a month in advance, will preserve your sanity in the summer. If your plans are more uncertain, dormitory-type accommodations are sometimes available in Venice without reservations, even during August and September. Such accommodations often have irregular operating seasons, so check with the tourist offices to see which are open. In *pensioni,* be wary of L12,000 breakfasts and other forms of bill-padding, and always agree on what you'll pay before surrendering your passport. In a pinch, you might want to visit Venice while based in one of the nearby towns; Padua is just 30 minutes away and a good place to secure a room.

Hostels and Dormitories

Ostello Venezia (HI), Fondamenta di Zitelle, 86 (tel. 523 82 11; fax 523 56 89), on Giudecca. Take *vaporetto* 82 from the station (25min., L4000) or 82 or 85 from San Zaccharia near San Marco (5min., L4000); get off at Zitelle and walk right. A renovated warehouse on the canal. Members only; HI cards sold. Check-in 7-9:30am and 1-10:30pm. Lockout 9:30am-1pm. Curfew 11:30pm. L24,000 per person. Sheets and breakfast included. Full meals L14,000. No phone reservations.

Foresteria Valdese, Castello, 5170 (tel. 528 67 97). Take *vaporetto* 82 to San Zachariaor 1 to Rialto, then go to Campo Santa Maria Formosa. From the *campo,* take Calle Lunga S. M. Formosa, just over the 1st bridge. 18th-century building with frescoed ceilings in many rooms. Reception open Mon.-Sat. 9am-1pm and 6-8pm, Sun. 9am-1pm. Lockout 10am-1pm. Dorms L28,000. Doubles L76,000. Breakfast included. Phone reservations strongly suggested. Closed 15 days in Nov.

Domus Civica, ACISJF, San Polo, 3082 (tel. 72 11 03), on the corner of Calle Chiovere, Calle Campazzo, and S. Rocco, between the Basilica dei Frari and P. Roma. Follow the yellow arrows between P. Roma and the Rialto. Ping-pong tables, TV room, and piano. Curfew 11:30pm. Singles L38,000. Doubles L64,000. 20% discount with Rolling Venice or ISIC. Open June to mid-Oct.

Suore Cannosiano, Fondamenta del Ponte Piccolo, 428 (tel. 522 21 57). Take *vaporetto* 82 to the Guidecca/Palanca, and walk left over the bridge. Run by nuns. Women only. Check-out 7:30-8:30am. Strict curfew 10:30pm. Dorms L19,000.

Hotels

Casa Gerotto, Campo S. Germia, 283 (tel./fax 71 53 61). Make a left after leaving the station and walk along Main St. to Campo S. Germia (2min.). The city's best bargain. Wonderful owner is justly proud of her huge, bright rooms. Clean bathrooms/showers on each floor for rooms without their own. Owner matches solo travelers and puts them into larger rooms for L25,000-30,000 each. Singles L35,000-40,000. Doubles L55,000-100,000. Triples L75,000-120,000. Discounts for longer stays.

Albergo Adua, Cannaregio, 233a (tel. 71 61 84), on Lista di Spagna. Amiable owner will tell you that he has the best showers in Europe. Singles L40,000-45,000. Doubles L55,000-75,000, with bath L85,000-130,000. Nine new rooms in an adjacent building. L80,000-85,000 for 2-3 people. Breakfast L7500.

Hotel Calderan, Cannaregio, 283 (tel. 71 55 62), in P. San Geremia at the end of Lista di Spagna, a short walk from the station. Friendly, family-run hotel with big rooms, but no private baths. Some rooms overlook a park or square. No English spoken. No curfew. Singles L35,000-40,000. Doubles L60,000-70,000. Triples L28,000 per person. Breakfast L6000. Reserve ahead Aug.-Oct. V, MC.

Locanda Montin, Dorsoduro, 1147 (tel. 522 71 51), near Accademia. Take *vaporetto* 1 to Cà Rezzonico, walk straight ahead to Campo San Barnaba, and go south through the *sottoportego* Casin dei Nobili. Cross the bridge, turn right on the Fondamenta Lombardo, and walk around the corner onto Fondamenta di Borgo. Modern paintings, restored antiques, and enthusiastic owners. Singles L55,000. Doubles L80,000, with shower L90,000. Reserve with 1 night's deposit. Closed 20 days in Jan. and 10 days in Aug. V, MC, AmEx.

Hotel Noemi, Calle dei Fabbri, 909 (tel. 523 81 44). Leave P. San Marco through the bell towers, turn left on Calle Fiubra, and turn left again on Calle dei Fabbri. Clean rooms in an unbeatable locale. Singles L60,000. Doubles L80,000. Triples L100,000. Breakfast L10,000.

Hotel Riva, Ponte dell'Angelo, 5310 (tel. 522 70 34; fax 528 55 51). From P. S. Marco, walk under the clock tower and take a right on Calle Larga S. Marco; turn left on Calle Angelo and go over the bridge. Gorgeous rooms overlook a canal. Curfew 1am. Singles with bath L120,000. Doubles L120,000-L150,000. Triples L220,000. Breakfast included. Reserve 2 weeks ahead. Open Feb.-Oct.

Locanda Corona, Calle Corona, 4464 (tel. 522 91 74). *Vaporetto:* San Zaccharia. Head north on Sacrestia from Campo SS. Filippo e Giacomo; take the first right, then a left on Calle Corona. Fine rooms. Limited hot water. Singles L50,000. Doubles L70,000. Triples L90,000. Breakfast included. Showers L3000.

Camping

Litorale del Cavallino, on the Adriatic side of the Lido, east of Venice. From San Marco, take *vaporetto* 14 to Punta Sabbioni (40min.). Many beachfront campgrounds.

Camping Miramare, Punta Sabbioni (tel. 96 61 50; fax 530 11 50), about 700m along the beach to your right as you descend from the Punta Sabbioni *vaporetto* stop. L8000 per person, L17,600 per tent in high season. 4-person bungalows L50,000. 5-person bungalows L75,000. Open Feb.-Nov.

FOOD

It is becoming difficult to sit down to a good meal in Venice without emptying your wallet. To avoid paying a fortune, visit any bar or *osteria* in town and make a meal from the vast display of meat- and cheese-filled pastries, tidbits of seafood, rice, and meat, and *tramezzini,* triangular slices of soft white bread with every imaginable filling. Good deals on tourist *menù* abound in the university area, **Dorsoduro.**

Located in the area surrounding the Rialto (San Polo side), the city's most famous **market** was once the center of trade and merchandise for the old Venetian Republic. Fruit stands line the Ruga degli Orefici, and on the right are the vegetable and fish markets. Locals shop around **Campo Beccarie** in San Polo near the Rialto. In Cannaregio, **STANDA,** on Strada Nuova, 3660, near Campo S. Felice, has groceries in the back (open daily 8:30am-7:15pm). In Castello near San Marco, stock up on the basics at **Su. Ve.,** 5816, on Calle del Mondo Novo, off Campo Santa Maria Formosa (open Mon.-Tues. and Thurs.-Sat. 8:30am-1pm and 4-7:30pm, Wed. 8:30am-1pm). **Kosher food** is served in Europe's oldest Jewish quarter, the **Ghetto Vecchio.**

Ai Promessi Sposi, Cannaregio, 4367. From Strada Nuova, take a left on Calle del Duca just before Campo SS. Apostoli, then the first left. Mellow music, outdoor seating, and lots of locals. *Primi* L7000-10,000. *Secondi* L14,000-18,000. Cover L1500. Open Thurs.-Tues. 10am-3pm and 6-11pm.

Trattoria/Pizzeria All'Anfora, Santa Croce, 1223, on Lista dei Bari. From the station, cross the Grand Canal, go straight, and then cross the first bridge on the left. Walk around Chiesa di S. Simeon onto Lista dei Bari. A hearty eatery with a vine-covered patio. *Primi* L8000-15,000. *Secondi* L9000-23,000. Pizza L7000-13,000. Cover L3000, service 12%. Open Wed.-Mon. 9am-11pm.

Crepizza, Dorsoduro, 3760, on Calle San Pantalon. From Campo S. Margherita, walk across Rio di Cà Foscari and around the right side of Chiesa di S. Pantalon. Pizzas L4000-10,000. *Primi* L6000-12,000. *Secondi* L9000-17,000. Cover L1500. Service 10%. *Menù* L14,500. Open Wed.-Mon. noon-2:30pm and 7-10:30pm.

Ai Pugni, Dorsoduro, 2839, along Rio di S. Barnaba and Fondamenta Gherardini, off Campo S. Barnaba. Take *vaporetto* 1 to Cà Rezzonico. Sandwiches, salads, and huge, tasty pizzas. *Primi* L7000-8000. *Secondi* L13,000. Pizzas L5500-8000. *Menù* L20,000. No cover. Open for drinks Tues.-Sun. 11am-1am.

Vino, Vino, San Marco, 2007a, on Calle del Sartor da Veste, off Calle Larga XXII Marzo along the S. Marco to Accademia route. An ambient oasis in this tourist-infested area. Delicious, aromatic food and varied wines. *Primi* L8000, *secondi* L15,000. Cover L1000. 10% Rolling Venice discount on food. Open for food Wed.-Mon. noon-2:30pm and 7-11pm.

Bora Bora, San Marco, 5251. From the Rialto, walk along Salizzada Pio X, turn right on Merceria 2 Aprile, then left on Calle Stranieri. Huge pizzas. Pizzas and *primi* L8000-13,000. *Secondi* from L9000. 10% Rolling Venice discount.

La Boutique del Gelato, Castello 5727, on Sal. S. Lio, off Campo S. Lio. *The* Venetian *gelateria*. Join the locals packing some home. Open daily 9am-9:15pm.

Gelati Nico, Dorsoduro, 922, near the Zattere *vaporetto* stop. Venice's pride. *Gianduiotto,* chocolate-hazelnut ice cream dunked in whipped cream L3800. Cones from L2000. Open in summer Fri.-Wed. 7am-11pm; mid-Jan. to mid-Dec. 7am-9pm.

SIGHTS

In Venetian churches a strict dress code applies. No shorts, sleeveless shirts, or miniskirts are allowed. Also, be aware that many of the sights have student, youth, senior, and group discounts; don't be afraid to ask if policies aren't posted.

San Marco and Environs

Piazza San Marco is the city's pigeon-infested, *campanile*-punctuated nucleus. In contrast to the narrow, maze-like streets that cover most of Venice, San Marco is an expanse of light and space, framed all around by museums and medieval buildings. Construction of the **Basilica of San Marco** began in the 9th century, when two Venetian merchants stole St. Mark's remains from Alexandria by hiding them in a barrel of pork to hoodwink Arab officials. The basilica's main treasure is the **Pala d'Oro,** a Veneto-Byzantine gold bas-relief encrusted with precious gems. The ticket to this area will also get you into the small **treasury,** with a hoard of gold and relics from the Fourth Crusade. (Basilica open daily 9:45am-7:30pm. Free. Pala d'oro open Mon.-Sat. 10am-5pm, Sun. 1-5pm. L3000.) The 15th-century **Torre dell'Orologio** (clock tower), left of San Marco, is a florid arrangement of sculpture and sundials, but is closed for renovations.

Next to San Marco stands the **Palazzo Ducale** (Doge's Palace). Rebuilt in the 14th century after a fire, the palace epitomizes the Venetian Gothic with elegant arcades and light-colored stone cladding. Facing the palace are Sansovino's masterpieces, the elegant **Libreria** and the **Zecca** (coin mint). Farther north, Calle Lunga and Calle Cicogna lead to Campo **SS. Giovanni e Paolo** and to the church of the same name. This grandiose Gothic structure, built by the Dominican order from the mid-13th to mid-15th centuries, has a wonderful polyptych by Bellini and several marvelous paintings. If you cross the Ponte Rosso and go straight, you'll come to the Lombardos' masterpiece, the **Chuch of Santa Maria dei Miracoli.**

To the east of San Marco, off the Riva degli Schiavoni, stands the beautiful, 15th-century **Church of San Zaccaria.** Inside, the second altar on the left houses Bellini's masterpiece, *The Madonna and Saints* (open daily 10am-noon and 4-6pm). Around the corner on the waterfront is Massari's **Church of the Pietà,** containing celebrated Tiepolo frescoes. Vivaldi was concertmaster here at the beginning of the 18th century, and concerts are held in the church throughout the summer. (Open in summer daily 9:30am-12:30pm and 3-6pm; off-season only for masses and concerts.)

Art Galleries and Museums

The **Accademia** in Dorsoduro, southwest of San Marco across the Ponte dell'Accademia, displays the best of Venetian painting. The world-class collection includes the superb Bellini *Pala di San Giobbe,* Giorgione's enigmatic *La Tempesta,* and Titian's last work, a brooding *Pietà.* Go early to get your money's worth (open Mon.-Sat. 9am-7pm, Sun. 9am-2pm; off-season Mon.-Sat. 9am-1pm; L12,000). For art of a different flavor, visit the **Collezione Peggy Guggenheim,**

Dorsoduro, 701, housed in the late Ms. Guggenheim's Palazzo Venier dei Leoni. All the major names in modern art are here, shown in glorious surroundings. (Open Wed.-Mon. 11am-6pm. L12,000, students with ISIC or Rolling Venice L8000.) Another art-filled area surrounds the Gothic **Basilica dei Frari** in San Polo across the Rialto. The basilica houses a moving wooden sculpture of St. John by Donatello, Bellini's *Madonna and Saints,* and Titian's famous *Assumption* (open Mon.-Sat. 9am-noon and 2:30-6pm, Sun. 3-6pm; L2000, holidays free). The *scuole* of Venice, a cross between guilds and religious fraternities, erected ornate "clubhouses" throughout the city. The richest is the **Scuola Grande di San Rocco,** across the *campo* at the end of the Frari, which boasts 56 Tintorettos. To see the paintings in chronological order, start on the second floor in the Sala dell'Albergo and follow the cycle downstairs. (Open in summer daily 9am-5:30pm; off-season Mon.-Fri. 10am-1pm, Sat.-Sun. 10am-4pm. L8000, with Rolling Venice L6000.)

The Lagoon and Outlying Sights Many of Venice's most beautiful churches are a short boat ride away from San Marco. Two of Palladio's most famous churches are visible in the distance from the *piazza.* The **Church of San Giorgio Maggiore,** across the lagoon (take boat 52 or 82; L4500), graces the island of the same name. The church houses Tintoretto's famous *Last Supper* (open daily 10am-12:30pm and 2:30-5pm; L2000). A bit farther out on the next island, Giudecca, is Palladio's famous **Church of Il Redentore.** During the pestilence of 1576, the Venetian Senate swore that they would build this devotional church and make a yearly pilgrimage here if the plague would leave the city. To make your own pilgrimage, take *vaporetto* 82 from S. Zaccharia (open daily 8am-noon and 3-7pm).

North of Venice stretches the **lagoon.** With a *vaporetto* ticket you can visit the island of **Murano** (*vaporetto* 52), famous for its glass since 1292, the fishing village of **Burano,** and **Torcello** (both *vaporetto* 12), an island with an enchanting Byzantine cathedral and some of the finest mosaics in Italy. Accessible by *vaporetto* 1, 6, 14, or 52 is the **Lido,** the setting for Thomas Mann's *Death in Venice.*

ENTERTAINMENT

Mark Twain may have called the **gondola** "an inky, rusty canoe," but tourists still pay top dollar for a leisurely trip along the Grand Canal. Unfortunately, gondolas aren't very romantic for budget travelers—at L80,000-100,000 for 50 minutes, the ride is only affordable if you and your significant other squeeze on with two or three strangers. If you can't afford a long trip, there are several points along the canal where *gondole* operate a one- or two-minute cross-canal service for locals (L2000).

The weekly booklet *A Guest in Venice* (free at hotels) lists current festivals, concerts, and gallery shows. For theatrical entertainment, **Commedia in Campo** performs outdoors in various *campi* throughout the city; contact Teatro Goldoni (tel. 520 54 22; fax 520 52 41) for more info (tickets L30,000). The famed **Venice Beinnale** (tel. 521 87 11; fax 521 00 38), centered in the Giardini di Castello, takes place every odd-numbered year, with a gala exhibit of international modern art (admission to all exhibits L16,000). Contact the tourist office for info on Venice's several **movie theaters** and the Venice International Film Festival in late August and early September. Venice's selection of **nightclubs** is rather paltry, but several cluster around San Marco. The principal after-midnight stop is **Fondamenta della Misericordia,** in Cannaregio, just past the "Ghetto."

Padua (Padova)

It took the prosperous Roman city of Padua over five centuries to recover from the Lombardic invasion of 602, but when it did, luminaries like Dante, Petrarch, Galileo, and Mantegna helped transform the city into an intellectual and artistic power. Today Padua still bustles with students and commercial activity, providing an excellent base for trips to Venice and the surrounding area.

You can buy a ticket good at most of the museums in Padua for L15,000 (students L10,000), valid for one year. The **Cappella degli Scrovegni** (Arena Chapel) contains Giotto's breathtaking floor-to-ceiling fresco cycle, illustrating the lives of Mary and Jesus. The adjoining **Museo Civico,** where you buy tickets for both sights, features Giorgione's *Leda and the Swan* and a restored Giotto crucifix. (Open Feb.-Oct. daily 9am-7pm; Nov.-Jan. 9am-6pm. L10,000, students L7000. The museum is closed on Mon., but the chapel remains open.) Next door, the 13th-century **Church of the Eremitani** boasts an imposing exterior and a beautifully carved wooden ceiling that was restored after a devastating 1944 bombing. (Open April-Sept. Mon.-Sat. 8:15am-noon, Sun. 9am-noon and 3:30-6:30pm; Oct.-March Mon.-Sat. 8:15am-noon, Sun. 9am-noon and 3:30-5:30pm. Free.) Thousands of pilgrims are drawn to see St. Anthony's jawbone and well-preserved tongue at the **Basilica di Sant'Antonio,** where he is entombed (open daily 7:30am-7pm).

Practical Information, Accommodations, and Food The **tourist office** is in the train station (tel. (049) 875 20 77; open Mon.-Sat. 9:15am-5:45pm, Sun. 9am-noon). Pick up a map and a copy of the free *Padua Today*. **Trains** depart from P. Stazione for Venice (30min., L3500), Verona (1hr., L7400), Milan (2½hr., L20,000-31,500), and Bologna (2hr., L10,500). The **bus station,** Via Trieste, 42 (tel. (049) 820 68 44), offers rides to Venice (every 30min., 45min., L4800).

Cheap lodgings abound in Padua, but they tend to fill up quickly. If you can't get into the places listed below, try any of the hotels near **Piazza del Santo,** or call the **APT local tourist board** (tel. (049) 875 20 77) or the **provincial tourist board** (tel. (049) 820 15 54) for private rooms in a local home. For summer housing at the university, call or write **Centro Universitario,** Via Zabarella, 82 (tel. (049) 65 42 99). The **Ostello Città di Padova (HI),** Via Aleardi, 30 (tel. (049) 875 22 19; fax 65 42 10), near Prato della Valle, has an English-speaking staff. Take bus 3, 8, 12, or 18 from the station. (Reception open daily 8-9:30am and 5-11pm. Lockout 9am-5pm. Curfew 11pm. L20,000. Hot showers and breakfast included.) **Albergo Verdi,** Via Dondi dall'Orologio, 7 (tel. (049) 875 57 44), has large, comfortable rooms in the center of town (singles L40,000, doubles L56,000; reserve ahead), while **Albergo Pavia,** Via dei Papafava, 11 (tel. (049) 66 15 58), features newly renovated rooms and a kitchen (singles L40,000, doubles L54,000).

Prepare for culinary bliss at **Trattoria da Paccagnella,** Via del Santo, 113 (*primi* L7000-11,000, *secondi* L15,000; open daily 7:30am-11pm), or serve yourself at **Brek,** P. Cavour, 20. (*Primi* L4000-6000, *secondi* L6100-7200. Open Sat.-Thurs. 11:30am-3pm and 6:30-10:30pm.) Supermarket wares are available at **PAM,** on Via Cavour in P. della Garzeria (open Mon.–Sat. 8:30am-8pm).

Verona

In July and August, the tranquil Verona, backdrop to Shakespeare's *Romeo and Juliet,* resounds with music, as tourists and singers from around the world descend for the annual **Opera Festival.** The performances, staged in the majestic first-century **Arena** in P. Brà, are unforgettable. (Arena open Tues.-Sun. 8am-6:30pm; during opera season 8am-3:30pm. L6000, students L4000, free on the 1st Sun. of the month. For opera info, call (045) 59 01 09 or 59 07 26; for tickets call (045) 800 51 51.) The heart of the city lies on the southern side of the **Adige River,** between Piazza delle Erbe and the Arena. From P. Brà, Via Mazzini leads to **Piazza delle Erbe,** the former Roman Forum. Today the *piazza* offers views of a fountain, several medieval buildings, and countless fruit vendors. The della Scala fortress, the **Castelvecchio,** at the end of Via Roma from P. Brà, is decked out with walkways, parapets, and an extensive collection of art including Pisanello's *Madonna and Child* and Luca di Leyda's *Crucifixion.* (Open Tues.-Sun. 8am-6:30pm. L5000, students L1500, free on the 1st Sun. of each month.) At **Casa di Giulietta** (Juliet's House), Via Cappello, 23, you too can stand on a diminutive balcony and have your photo snapped by camera-happy tourists only to find out that the dal Capello (Capulet) family never lived here (open Tues.-Sun. 9am-

6:30pm; L5000, students L1500). The **Casa di Romeo** is around the corner from P. dei Signori at Via Arche Scaligeri, 2. Much more interesting is the **Museo Africano,** Vicolo Pozzo, 1, which celebrates the arts and traditions of African peoples (open Tues.-Sat. 9am-noon and 3-6pm, Sun. 3-7pm; L5000, students L3000).

Practical Information, Accommodations, and Food The **tourist office,** Via Leoncino, 61 (tel. (045) 59 28 28; fax 800 36 38), in P. Brà, has an English-speaking staff that will help you find a room. (Open July 15-Aug. Mon.-Sat. 8am-8pm, Sun. 8:30am-1pm; Sept.-July 14 Mon.-Sat. 9am-7:30pm.) The **train station** at P. XXV Aprile (tel. (045) 59 06 88 or (1478) 880 88), linked with P. Brà by Corso Porta Nuova, serves Venice (2hr., L10,000), Milan (2hr., L12,100), Bologna (2hr., L10,100), and other cities. **Buses** leave from P. XXV Aprile (tel. (045) 800 41 29) for Riva del Garda (L9300), Sirmione (L4800), and Brescia (L10,000).

To reach the unbeatable **Ostello Verona (HI), "Villa Francescatti,"** Salita Fontana del Ferro, 15 (tel. (045) 59 03 60; fax 800 91 27), from the station, hop on bus 73 or night bus 90 to "P. Isolo." The hostel is located in a renovated 16th-century villa with gorgeous gardens, where you may **camp** for L8000. (Rooms open at 5pm, but you may register and drop off bags as early as 7am. 5-day max. stay. Curfew 11:30pm, flexible for opera-goers. L20,000. Hot showers, breakfast, and sheets included. Reservations accepted from groups and families only.) Women should also try the beautiful **Casa della Giovane (ACISJF),** Via Pigna, 7 (tel. (045) 59 68 80), in the historic center of town. (Curfew 11pm, extended for opera-goers. Dorms L22,000; singles L32,000; doubles L25,000. Call ahead.) To get to **Locanda Catullo,** Vicolo Catullo, 1 (tel. (045) 800 27 86), walk along Via Mazzini until you reach #40, turn onto Via Catullo, and then left onto Vicolo Catullo (2- or 3-day min. stay; singles L50,000, doubles L70,000, with bath L90,000).

Vendors in Piazza Isolo sell Verona's famous wines: *soave* (dry white), *valpolicella,* and *bardolino* (both red). For a large sampling, try **Oreste dal Zovo,** Via S. Marco in Foro, 7/5, off Corso Porta Borsari (open Tues.-Sun. 8:30am-1:30pm and 2:30-10pm). **Ristorante Brek,** P. Brà, has a prime location (no cover; open Mon.-Fri. and Sun. 11:30am-3pm and 6:30pm-midnight). The **METÁ supermarket** is at Via XX Settembre, 81 (open Thurs.-Tues. 8:30am-12:45pm and 3:45-7:30pm).

FRIULI-VENEZIA GIULIA

Triest (Trieste)

Evidence of Triest's multinational history lingers in the numerous buildings and monuments of Hapsburg origin and the Slavic influence on local cuisine. The 15th-century Venetian **Castle of San Giusto** presides over **Capitoline Hill,** the city's historic center. Take bus 24 (L1200) from the station to the last stop at the fortress, and ascend the hill by way of the daunting **Scala dei Giganti** (Steps of the Giants—all 265 of them). Take a right on Via Capitalina, which will take you to **Piazza della Cattedrale,** with a great view of the sea and downtown. Directly below are the remains of the old Roman city center, and across the street is the restored **Cathedral of San Giusto.** Down the other side of the hill lies the **Museo di Storia de Arte** and **Orto Lapidario,** Via Cattedrale, 15, in P. Cattedrale. The museum provides exhibits on Triest's ancient history and boasts a growing collection of Egyptian art as well as artifacts from southern Italy (open Tues.-Sun. 9am-1pm; L2000, students L1000).

Triest is a departure point for many travelers to Eastern Europe. Pick up travel info at the **tourist office** in the train station (tel. (040) 42 01 82; open Mon.-Sat. 9am-7pm, Sun. 10am-1pm and 4-7pm). **Trains** (tel. (040) 41 82 07) depart from P. della Libertà for Venice (2hr., L14,000), Milan (7½hr., L33,400), and Ljubljana (3½hr., L16,000). **Agemar Viaggi,** P. Duca degli Abruzzi, 1/A (tel. (040) 36 37 37), arranges ferries to the former Yugoslavia and other locales. The **Ostello Tegeste (HI),** Viale Miramare,

331 (tel. (040) 22 41 02), stacks only HI members in its bunks; take bus 36 (L1200) from the station. (Reception open daily noon-11:30pm. Curfew 11:30pm. L18,000. Shower and breakfast included.) **Rino,** Via Boccardi, 5 (tel. (040) 30 06 08), offers decent rooms by the sea (singles L25,000, doubles L35,000), while **Gianni,** Via Razaretto Vecchio, 22 (tel. (040) 30 07 38), has singles for L40,000 and doubles L70,000.

THE LAKES AND THE DOLOMITES

When Italy's monuments and museums all start to blur together, explore the natural beauty of the country's lakes and mountains. The Dolomites dominate the landscape in the province of Trentino-Alto Adige, rising from Austrian-influenced valley communities to lofty peaks equipped for skiing, hiking, and awestruck admiration. The Lake Country lends itself to relaxation by the lakeside or in nightclubs, and windsurfing and water sports are also popular throughout the region.

The Lakes

With its romantic shores and inexpensive hostels, **Lake Como** (Lago di Como) is one hour north of Milan by train (L7800) near the Swiss border. Situated at the southwest tip of the lake, **Como** is the largest urban outpost. A multitude of luxurious *ville* overlook the sparkling lakes and shoreside parks and gardens, while the stately **duomo,** a harmonious combination of Gothic and Renaissance elements, presides over the town near P. Cavour. For excellent hiking and stunning views, take the *funicolare* up to **Brunate;** the cars leave from the far end of Lungo Lario Triest, in front of P. Cavour (round-trip L7100, at the hostel L5000). Como's **tourist office,** P. Cavour, 16 (tel. (031) 26 20 91), near the waterfront, has maps and currency exchange and reserves rooms (open Mon.-Sat. 9am-12:30pm and 2:30-6pm, Sun. 9am-12:30pm). **Ostello Villa Olmo (HI),** Via Bellinzona, 6 (tel. (031) 57 38 00), offers clean rooms and discounts on various attractions in Como; from the station, it's a 20-minute walk left down Via Borgovico, which becomes Bellinzona. (Reception open March-Nov. daily 7:30-10am and 4-11pm; Dec.-Feb. open to groups by reservation only. L15,000 per person, breakfast included. Call ahead.) In nearby Menaggio, **Ostello La Prinula (HI),** Via IV Novembre, 86 (tel./fax (0344) 323 56), is one of the jollier and better-kept hostels around (lockout 10am-5pm; curfew 11:30pm; L17,000; open mid-March to early Nov.). The laid back **hostel (HI)** in Domaso, 50km (2hr.) from Como by bus and also accessible by boat, comforts backpackers and windsurfers at Via Case Sparse, 12 (tel. (0344) 960 94; L14,000; open March-Oct.). The tourist office in Como has info on the many **campsites** that dot the region.

Lake Garda (Lago di Garda) is one of the grandest and most popular of the lakes. To explore the region, travel to **Desenzano** along the Milan-Venice train line; from there, the lake towns are easily accessible by buses, hydrofoils, and ferries. You can also reach the lake by bus from Brescia (1hr., L5400) and Verona (1hr., L4600). Along the southern edge of the lake, near most bus and rail lines, **Sirmione** boasts extensive Roman ruins and a beautifully situated medieval **castle.** Sleep right next to the castle at **Albergo Grifone,** Via Bocchio, 5 (tel. (030) 91 61 57; singles L50,000, doubles L78,000), or pick up info on other accommodations at the **tourist office** (tel. (030) 91 61 14). In **Gardonne Riviera,** the **Il Vittoriale,** sight of poet, novelist, and latter-day Cassanova, Gabriele D'Annunzio's villa, is Lake Garda's famous sight. At the north end of the lake, secluded **Riva** offers splendid hiking, swimming, and windsurfing.

The Dolomites

An hour north of Verona on the Bologna-Brenner train line, beautiful **Trent** (Trento, Trient) balances Germanic and Mediterranean flavors. Italian prevails culturally and linguistically, but you'll taste Austrian culinary influences and notice interest in all things mountainous. For an introduction to Trent's history, take a right at the end of Via Belenzani onto Via Roma and head to the **Castello del Buonconsiglio.** The castle features beautiful gardens and an impressive art museum, while the towers offer a panoramic view of the city. (Open April-Sept. Tues.-Sun. 9am-noon and 2-5:30pm; Oct.-March closes at 5pm. L7000.) The pointed dome of Trent's Gothic-Romanesque *duomo,* the **Cathedral of Saint Vigilio,** rises in modest emulation of the looming Alps. The famed Council of Trent's decrees, the Roman Catholic church's response to the Protestant Reformation, were delivered in front of the huge cross in the Chapel of the Holy Crucifix (open daily 6:40am-12:15pm and 2:30-7:30pm). The Azienda Autonoma **tourist office** is across the park from the train station at Via Alfieri, 4 (tel. (0461) 98 38 80; fax 98 45 08). **Ostello Giovane Europa (HI),** Via Manzoni, 17 (tel. (0461) 23 45 67), has sparkling rooms and a friendly staff (L20,000). **Hotel Venezia,** P. Duomo, 45 (tel. (0461) 23 41 14), deserves more than its one star (singles L44,000-59,000, doubles L65,000-85,000). **Monte Bondone** rises majestically over Trent and begs for pleasant excursions. Check at the **tourist office** (tel. (0461) 94 71 28; fax 94 71 88) in **Vanzene,** halfway up the mountain, about accommodations, ski lifts, and maps. The cable car from Ponte di San Lorenzo, between the train tracks and the river, will take you to **Sardagna,** a great picnic spot (L1300 round-trip).

Only 45 minutes by train from Trent (14 per day, L1500) and *en route* to the Brenner Pass, **Bolzano's** (Bozen) bilingual street signs and mandatory instruction in both Italian and German betray the city's true Austrian bent. The historic center is a combination of spacious *Plätze/piazze* and arcaded alleys, and is an ideal place to stock up on essentials for excursions to the Dolomites. The **tourist office,** P. Walther, 8 (tel. (0471) 97 56 56 or 97 06 60; fax 98 01 28), offers hiking and accommodations advice (open Mon.-Fri. 9am-6pm, Sat. 9am-12:30pm). To prep for serious mountaineering, go to the **Provincial Tourist Office for South Tyrol,** P. Parrocchia, 11 (tel. (0471) 99 38 08), just down from P. Walther across from the *duomo.* **Schwarze Katz,** Sta. Maddalena di Sotto, 2 (tel. (0471) 97 54 17), has clean rooms and a garden restaurant (doubles L70,000), while the spacious **Croce Bianca,** P. del Grano (Kornplatz), 3 (tel. (0471) 97 75 52), has old-style charm (L40,000-90,000).

LOMBARDY (LOMBARDIA)

Although urbane Milan looms largest in foreigners' image of Lombardy, Mantua and smaller regional towns offer their own artistic and culinary treasures. The foothills of the Alps are close by, mixing an Italian climate with Swiss and Austrian culture, and the region has become a magnet for North African and Middle Eastern immigrants

Milan (Milano)

Once the capital of the western half of the Roman Empire, modern Milan retains few reminders of its distinguished pedigree. The city has forged toward modernity with more force than any other major Italian city, creating a fast paced life where even the requisite *siesta* is shortened. Although success has also brought petty crime and drugs, Milan remains a vibrant city on the cutting edge of high finance and fashion.

ORIENTATION AND PRACTICAL INFORMATION

The layout of Milan resembles a giant target, encircled by concentric ancient city walls. The **duomo** and **Galleria Vittorio Emanuele II** comprise the bull's-eye, roughly at the center of the downtown circle. From the train station, a scenic ride on bus 60 or quick commute on metro line 3 takes you to the downtown hub.

Tourist Office: APT, Via Marconi, 1 (tel. 252 43 01; fax 72 52 43 50), in the Palazzo di Turismo in P. del Duomo, to the right as you face the *duomo.* Comprehensive local and regional info, a useful map, and a museum guide. Doesn't reserve rooms,

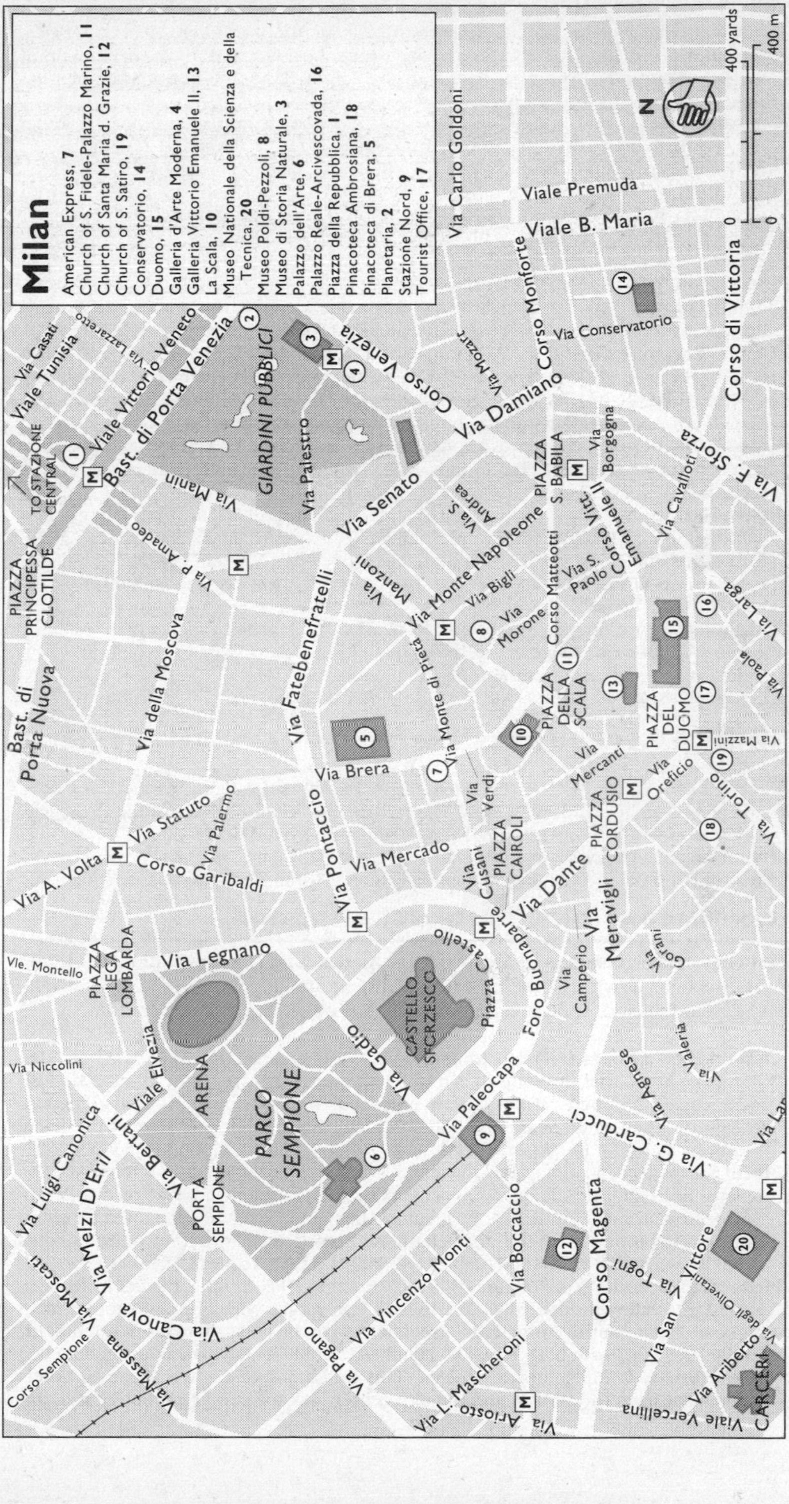
Milan
American Express, 7
Church of S. Fidele-Palazzo Marino, 11
Church of Santa Maria d. Grazie, 12
Church of S. Satiro, 19
Conservatorio, 14
Duomo, 15
Galleria d'Arte Moderna, 4
Galleria Vittorio Emanuele II, 13
La Scala, 10
Museo Nationale della Scienza e della Tecnica, 20
Museo Poldi-Pezzoli, 8
Museo di Storia Naturale, 3
Palazzo dell'Arte, 6
Palazzo Reale-Arcivescovada, 16
Piazza della Repubblica, 1
Pinacoteca Ambrosiana, 18
Pinacoteca di Brera, 5
Planetaria, 2
Stazione Nord, 9
Tourist Office, 17
N
0
400 yards
400 m
Via Carlo Goldoni
Viale Premuda
Viale B. Maria
Corso Monforte
Via Conservatorio
Corso di Vittoria
Via Mozart
Corso Venezia
Via Damiano
Via Senato
GIARDINI PUBBLICI
Via Palestro
Bast. di Porta Venezia
Viale Vittorio Veneto
Viale Tunisia
Via Casati
Via Lazzaretto
TO STAZIONE CENTRALE
Via Manin
Via P. Amadeo
PIAZZA PRINCIPESSA CLOTILDE
Bast. di Porta Nuova
Via della Moscova
Via Fatebenefratelli
Via Manzoni
Via Monte Napoleone
Via S. Andrea
Via Bigli
Via Morone
PIAZZA S. BABILA
Via Borgogna
Corso Vitt. Emanuele II
Via S. Paolo
Corso Matteotti
Via Cavallotti
Via F. Sforza
Via Larga
Via Paola
Via Mazzini
PIAZZA DEL DUOMO
PIAZZA DELLA SCALA
Via Monte di Pietà
Via Brera
Via Verdi
Via Mercanti
Via Orefici
Via Torino
PIAZZA CORDUSIO
PIAZZA CAIROLI
Via Cusani
Via Dante
Via Meravigli
Via Mercado
Via Pontaccio
Via Statuto
Via Palermo
Corso Garibaldi
Via A. Volta
PIAZZA LEGA LOMBARDA
Vle. Montello
Via Legnano
Via Niccolini
ARENA
Viale Elvezia
PARCO SEMPIONE
CASTELLO SFORZESCO
Piazza Castello
Foro Buonaparte
Via Camperio
Via Gorani
Via Valeria
Via Agnese
Via Gadio
Via Paleocapa
Via G. Carducci
PORTA SEMPIONE
Via Bertani
Via Luigi Canonica
Via Melzi D'Eril
Via Moscati
Corso Sempione
Via Canova
Via Massena
Via Vincenzo Monti
Via Boccaccio
Corso Magenta
Via Togni
Via San Vittore
Via degli Olivetani
Via Pagano
Via L. Mascheroni
Via Ariosto
Viale Vercellina
Via Aribert
CARCERI

but will check for vacancies. Be sure to pick up *Milano: Where, When, How* as well as *Milano Mese* for info on activities and clubs. Open Mon.-Fri. 8:30am-8pm, Sat. 9am-1pm and 2-7pm, Sun. 9am-1pm and 2-5pm. **Branch office** at Stazione Centrale (tel. 72 52 43 70). Open Mon.-Sat. 8am-7pm.

Currency Exchange: Banca Nazionale delle Comunicazioni, at Stazione Centrale, has standard rates. L6000 fee. Open Mon.-Sat. 8:30am-12:30pm and 2-7:30pm.

American Express: Via Brera, 3 (tel. 72 00 36 93), on the corner of Via dell'Orso. Mail held free for AmEx members, otherwise US$5 per inquiry. Accepts wired money (L2500 fee if over US$100). Open Mon.-Thurs. 9am-5:30, Fri. 9am-5pm.

Flights: For flight information, call 74 85 22 00. **Malpensa Airport,** 45km from town, handles intercontinental flights. Buses connect to the airport from P. Luigi di Savoia, on the east side of Stazione Centrale (1-2 per hr., L13,000). **Linate Airport,** 7km from town, covers domestic and European routes. The cheapest trip to this airport is on bus 73 from MM1: P. San Babila (L1500).

Trains: Stazione Centrale, P. Duca d'Aosta (tel. 67 50 01). To: Genoa and Turin (each 1½-2hr., L22,000), Venice (3hr., L36,000), Florence (2½hr., L38,000), Rome (4½hr., L68,000, IC L79,500). Info office open daily 7am-9:30pm. Eurailpasses and *Cartaverde* available outside the building. **Luggage storage** L500. Open 24hr.

Buses: Many buses leave from Stazione Centrale. Intercity buses are often less convenient and more expensive than trains. **SAL, SIA, Autostradale,** and other carriers leave from P. Castello and nearby. MM: Cairoli.

Public Transportation: ATM (tel. 669 70 32 or 89 01 07 970), in P. del Duomo MM station. Municipal buses require pre-purchased tickets (L1500). Day passes L5000. Info office open Mon.-Sat. 8am-8pm; ticket office open 7:45am-7:15pm.

Laundromat: Onda Blu, Via Scarlatti, 19. Self-service wash or dry L6000 for 6.5kg. Soap L1500. Open daily 8am-10pm.

Pharmacy: In Stazione Centrale (tel. 669 07 35 or 669 09 35). Open 24hr.

Hospital: Ospedale Maggiore di Milano, Via Francesco Sforza, 35 (tel. 550 31), 5min. from the *duomo* on the inner ring road.

Emergencies: tel. 113. **First Aid:** tel. 38 83. **Ambulance:** tel. 77 33. **Police:** tel. 772 71 or 112.

Internet Access: Hard Disk Café, down Corso Sempione, 44 (tel. 33 10 10 38). Open Mon.-Sat. 7am-2am. L6000 per hour.

Post Office: Via Cordusio, 4 (tel. 869 20 69), near P. del Duomo toward the castle. For stamps, go to windows 1 and 2; for *fermo posta* the CAI-POST office to the left. Open Mon.-Fri. 8:30am-7:30pm, Sat. 8:30am-1pm. **Postal Code:** 20100.

Telephones: In Galleria Vittorio Emanuele. Open daily 8am-7:30pm. Phones are also available in Stazione Centrale. Open daily 8am-9:30pm. **Telephone Code:** 02.

ACCOMMODATIONS, CAMPING, AND FOOD

Every season is high season in Milan, except August when locals vacation and much of the city shuts down. For the best deals, hang around the area east of the train station or go to the city's southern periphery. When possible, make reservations.

Ostello Pietra Rotta (HI), Via Salmoiraghi, 1 (tel. 39 26 70 95). Take MM1 to QT8, and go right (so that the church is to the left, across the street) for 10min. Modern facilities and 350 beds. Rules strictly enforced. Members only; HI cards L30,000. Reception open daily 7-9am and 5pm-midnight, but no morning check-in. Curfew 11:30pm. L23,000. Breakfast, sheets, and lockers included. Open Jan. 13-Dec. 20.

Hotel San Marco, Via Piccinni, 25 (tel. 29 51 64 14; fax 29 51 32 43). From MM1-2: Loreto, head left on P. Luigi di Savoia. Take a right at the post office on Via Pergolesi, which crosses P. Caiazzo, C. Buenos Aires, and finally becomes Via Piccinni. Comfy retro rooms with TV and telephone compensate for street noise. Singles L62,000, with bath L80,000. Doubles L82,000-105,000. Triples L135,000.

Hotel Ca' Grande, Via Porpora, 87 (tel. 26 14 40 01), about 7 blocks in from P. Loreto in a yellow house. MM1-2: Loreto. Clean rooms with phones, simple, plain beds, and a wonderful proprietor. Street below can be noisy. Reception open 24hr. Singles L53,000, with bath L70,000. Doubles L78,000-93,000. Breakfast included.

Viale Tunisia, 6. MM1: Porta Venezia. This building houses two separate hotels equidistant from the station and the city center. Ask for keys if going out at night.

Hotel Kennedy (tel. 29 40 09 34), 6th fl. Pristine rooms with light blue dreamscape decor. Some English spoken. Check-out 11am. Singles L50,000-70,000. Doubles L70,000-130,000. Triples L40,000 per person; quads L35,000 per person. Breakfast L6000. Reserve ahead. **Hotel San Tommaso** (tel./fax 29 51 47 47), 3rd fl. Large, clean, renovated, tile-floored rooms, some overlooking a courtyard. English spoken. Singles L45,000. Doubles L70,000. Prices may fluctuate.

Hotel Aurora, C. Buenos Aires, 18 (tel. 204 79 60; fax 204 92 85). MM1: Lima. Spotless rooms with TV. English-speaking owner. Reception open 24hr. Singles L70,000-75,000, with bath L75,000-80,000. Doubles with bath L110,000-120,000.

Camping di Monza (tel. (039) 38 77 71), in the park of the Villa Reale in Monza. Take a train or bus from Stazione Centrale to Monza, then a city bus. Restaurant/bar nearby. L5000 (L8000 in Sept.) per person and per tent. Open April-Sept.

Like its fine *couture,* Milanese cuisine is sophisticated and overpriced. **Markets** open around Via Fauché and Viale Papiniano on Saturday, Viale Papiniano on Tuesday, and along P. Mirabello on Thursday. On Saturday, join the **Fiera di Sinigallia,** a 400-year-old extravaganza, on Via Calatafimi. Splurge on a local pastry at **Sant'Ambroeus,** under the arcades at Corso Matteotti, 7 (open 8am-8pm), or pick up groceries at **Pam,** Via Piccinni, 2, off Corso Buenos Aires (open daily 9am-7pm).

For a balanced meal, try one of the self-service restaurants that cater to city professionals. **Ciao,** on the second floor of the Duomo Center, is particularly convenient (*secondi* L8000; open daily 11:30am-3pm and 6:30-11pm). **Brek,** Via Lepetit, 20, by Stazione Centrale, is a popular and more elegant self-service restaurant (*secondi* around L7500; open Mon.-Sat. 11:30am-3pm and 6:30-10:30pm). Both the very busy **Pizzeria Grand'Italia,** Via Palermo, 5 (open Wed.-Mon. 12:15-2:45pm and 7pm-1;15am; August also Wed.) and **Tarantella,** Viale Abruzzi, 35, just north of Via Plinio (open Mon.-Fri. noon-2:30pm and 7-11:30pm, Sun. 7-11:30pm; closed Aug.) offer salads for L10,000. The neighborhood **Ristorante "La Colubrina,"** Via Felice Casati, 5 (MM1: Porta Venezia) has mosaic-style stone floors. (Cover L2000. Pizza L6000-9000. Open Sept.-July Tues. 7-11:30pm, Wed.-Sat. noon-2:30pm and 7-11:30pm, Sun. 7-11:30pm.) The Islamic **Il Fondaco dei Mori,** Via Solferino, 33, offers a delicious buffet (L16,000) with the option of eating under a richly furnished tent (no alcohol; open Tues.-Sun.; closed Fri. morning). **Viel,** Via Marconi, 3E, next to the tourist office, vends fresh fruit *gelati* (L2500-6000) and *frullati* (whipped fruit drinks; L2500-8000).

SIGHTS AND ENTERTAINMENT

The **Piazza del Duomo** marks the geographical focus of Milan, and makes a good starting point for a walking tour of the city. The **duomo,** a looming Gothic creation, presides over the *piazza.* More than 3400 statues, 135 spires, and 96 gargoyles grace this third-largest church in the world. (Open June-Sept. daily 7am-5pm; Oct.-May 9am-4pm. Free. Tower L6000, with elevator L8000. Proper dress required.) Beside the *duomo* is the entrance to the **Galleria Vittorio Emanuele II,** a four-story arcade of *caffè* and shops. Those in the know here rub the bull's balls in the center for good luck. Meander through this beautiful gallery to the **Teatro alla Scala (La Scala),** the world's premier opera house where Maria Callas, among other opera titans, became a legend. Enter the lavish hall through the **Museo Teatrale alla Scala,** which includes opera memorabilia such as Verdi's famous top hat. (Open Mon.-Sat. 9am-12:30pm and 2-5:30pm, Sun. 9:30am-12:30pm and 2:30-6pm; Oct.-May closed Sun. L5000.)

Via Verdi leads to Via Brera and the 17th-century **Pinacoteca di Brera,** which features works by Caravaggio, Bellini, and Raphael (open Tues.-Sat. 9am-5:30pm, Sun. 9am-12:30pm; L8000). The **Museo Poldi-Pezzoli,** at Via Manzoni, 12, houses a superb private collection; the museum's signature piece is Antonio Pollaiolo's *Portrait of a Young Woman.* (Open Tues.-Fri. 9am-12:30pm and 2:30-6pm, Sat. 9:30am-12:30pm and 2:30-7:30pm, Sun. 9:30am-12:30pm; Oct.-March also open Sun. 2:30-6pm. L10,000.) For a taste of Italian sculpture, visit the enormous **Castello Sforzesco** (MM1: Cairoli), a 15th-century castle which houses Michelangelo's unfinished *Pietà Rondanini* and other excellent works (open Tues.-Sun. 9:30am-5:30pm; free).

Finally, marvel at Leonardo Da Vinci's immensely famous *Last Supper* on the refectory wall of the **Church of Santa Maria delle Grazie** (MM1: Cairoli; open Tues.-Sun. 8am-2pm; L12,000). The **Museo Nazionale della Scienza e della Tecnica "Leonardo da Vinci,"** Via San Vittore, 21 (MM1: San Ambrogio, or bus 50 or 54), off V. Carducci, fills an entire room with models of Leonardo's most ingenious and visionary inventions (open Tues.-Fri. 9:30am-4:50pm, Sat.-Sun. 9:30am-6:30pm; L10,000). Following Via Spadari off Via Tornio and then making a right onto Via Cantú will take you to the **Pinacoteca Ambrosiana,** P. Pio XI, 2, with exquisite works from the 15th through 17th centuries by Botticelli, Leonardo, Raphael, and others (re-opens Dec. 1997).

Populism and posh converge for the **Musica in Metro,** a series of summer concerts performed in subway stations. More renowned singers and dancers perform at the famed **La Scala** (box office tel. 72 00 37 44; open daily noon-7pm), where gallery seats go for as little as L30,000 about 30 minutes before curtain (opera season Dec. 7-June; fewer shows July-Sept.). If you've come to Milan to (window) **shop,** as many do, the city's most elegant boutiques are between the *duomo* and P. S. Babila, especially on the glamorous **Via Monte Napoleone** and off P. Babila at Via Spiga.

At night excellent people-watching resides through the Neoclassical Arco di Porta Ticinese at the Venice of Lombardy, the **navigli district.** Young *Milanese* migrate to the areas near **Porta Ticinese** and **Piazza Vetra** to sip a beer at one of the many *birrerie* (pubs). An older crowd heads to the safe, chic area around **Via Brera.** Most clubs charge a cover of around L20,000. For rock music, hit the trendy **Hollywood,** Corso Como, 15 (open Tues.-Sun. 10:30pm-4am), or **Plastic,** Viale Umbria, 120, Milan's premier disco-pub (open Tues.-Sun. 11pm-4am). The city's best jazz spot is **Le Scimmie,** Via Ascanio Sforza, 49 (open Wed.-Mon. 8pm-2am). For disco, head to **City Square,** Via Castelbarco, 11, with some of the biggest dance floors in Milan and occasional live music (open nightly until 4am). **Grand Café Fashion,** Corso di Porta Ticinese, on the corner of Via Vatere, sports the requisite beautiful people and good music (mandatory first drink L15,000; open daily 10am-4am). For gay and lesbian nightlife, women head to **Cicip e Ciciap,** Via Gorani, 9 (open Tues.-Sun. 7pm-2am); men frequent **Nuova Idea,** Via de Castilla, 30 (MM2: Gioia; women welcome Sat.), and a mixed crowd fills **Uitibar,** Via Monvisa, 14 (open Tues.-Sun. 8:30pm-2am).

Mantua (Mantova)

Although Mantua's first claim to fame was as the hometown of the great poet Virgil, the city enjoyed its heyday as the court of the extravagant, 400-year Gonzaga dynasty. Beginning in 1328, the Gonzagas loaded Mantua with palaces, churches, and towers, and lured some of the most important Renaissance artists to their court. While industry and commercial agriculture now rule the city, the historic center preserves much of the rustic flavor and artistic flair of this earlier age.

The cobblestone **Piazza Sordello** forms the center of a vast complex built by the Gonzaga. Towering over the *piazza,* **Palazzo Ducale** is one of the largest and most sumptuously decorated palaces in Europe, with no less than 500 rooms and 15 courtyards. In the palace's **Hall of Dukes,** marvel at Antonio Pisanelli's frescoes, discovered in 1969 under thick layers of plaster. (Open Tues.-Sat. 9am-1pm and 2:30-6pm, Sun.-Mon. 9am-1pm. L12,000 for the entire palace.) A trek through P. Veneto and down Largo Patri leads to the opulent **Palazzo del Tè,** widely regarded as the finest building of the Mannerist period. Once the Gonzaga family's suburban villa, the palace now exhibits works by modern Italian artists and a collection of Egyptian art (open Tues.-Sun. 9am-6pm; L12,000, students L5000). Near Piazza delle Erbe, south of P. Sordello, the **Church of Sant'Andrea** is acclaimed as the crowning achievement of Florentine architect Leon Battista Alberti.

Trains pass through the station at P. Don Leoni, southwest of town, for Verona (40min., L3400) and Milan (2hr., L30,600). The **bus station** at P. Mondadori serves Brescia (1½hr., L9300). The **tourist office,** P. Mantegna, 6 (tel. (0376) 32 82 53; fax 36 32 92), adjacent to the church of Sant'Andrea, offers the invaluable *Mantova: Directions for Use* (open Mon.-Sat. 9am-noon and 3-6pm, Sun. 8:30am-12:30pm). Mantua's

youth hostel (near the water on Via Leguago, east of the city) and **campsite** have been under renovation for three years, so visitors in 1998 should find them polished to perfection. We hope. Contact the tourist office for reservations at either one. **Hotel ABC Moderno,** P. Don Leoni, 25 (tel./fax (0376) 32 50 02), right across from the train station, offers beautiful singles (L80,000) and doubles with bath (L105,000). Ask at the tourist office about **agriturismo** lodgings (around L20,000) if rooms are scarce. Gorge on *real* pizza, salami, and something from the sea all in one sitting at **4 Stagioni,** Via Verdi, 5, off P. Mantegna (*primi* from L6000 and *secondi* from L10,000). **Antica Osteria ai Ranari,** Via Trieste, 11 (tel. 32 84 31), near Porto Catena, specializes in regional dishes. (*Primi* L8000, *secondi* L9000-14,000. Cover L2000. Closed for 3 weeks in late July and early Aug. Call for reservations.)

Bergamo

Glimmering in the distance, an entire medieval city is nestled in the hills over Bergamo, complete with palaces, churches, and a huge stone fortification. **Via Pignolo** connects the *città bassa* (lower city) with the upper, winding past a succession of handsome 16th- to 18th-century palaces. Turning right on Via San Tommaso brings you to the astounding **Galleria dell'Accademia Carrara,** with works by virtually every Italian notable, as well as Breughel, van Dyck, and El Greco (open Wed.-Mon. 9:30am-12:30pm and 2:30-5:30pm; L5000, Sun. free). The *città alta,* perched above the modern city and accessible by funicular from **Viale Vittorio Emanuele II** (every 7min., L1400), is a wonderfully preserved medieval town. Via Gambito ends in **Piazza Vecchia,** a majestic mix of medieval and Renaissance buildings. Through an archway, **Piazza del Duomo** is the multicolored marble facade of the 1476 **Colleoni Chapel,** designed for the Venetian mercenary Bartolomeo Colleoni. (Open April-Oct. daily 9am-noon and 2-6:30pm; Nov.-March 9am-noon and 2:30-4:30pm.)

The train station, bus station, and numerous budget hotels are in the *città bassa.* Take bus 1a to the funicular, then follow Via Gambito to the P. Vecchiahe to find the **tourist office,** Vicolo Aquila Nera, 2 (tel. (035) 23 27 30), in the *città alta* (open daily 9am-12:30pm and 2:30-5:30pm). **Trains** run from P. Marconi to Milan (1hr., L5100) and Brescia (1hr., L4300). **Buses** leave from across the train station for Milan (L7200) and local cities. Take bus 14 from Porto Nuova to "Leonardo da Vinci" to reach **Ostello Città di Bergamo (HI),** Via G. Ferraris, 1 (tel./fax (035) 36 17 24), with mint-condition rooms. (L23,000 per person, including breakfast. Private singles L30,000; doubles L60,000. Members only.) **Albergo S. Giorgio,** Via S. Giorgio, 10 (tel. (035) 21 20 43; fax 31 00 72), is nearer the train station, with neat, modern rooms. Go left on Via Pietro Paleocopa, which becomes Via S. Giorgio after a few blocks (15min.) or take bus 7 (singles L35,000-55,000, doubles L65,000-90,000). **Ristorante Self-Service Pastimbaldo,** Via Taramelli, 23b, draws students and business types with satisfying dishes. From the station, walk down Viale Papa Giovanni XXIII, right on Via San Francesco d'Assisi, then left onto V. Taramelli. (*Primi* from L4500, *secondi* from L6500. Open Mon.-Fri. 11:45am-3pm, Sun. 11:45am-3pm and 6:30-11pm.) **Trattoria Bernabò,** Via Colleoni, 31, is the quintessential *trattoria* (entrees start at L15,000; open Sept.-June Fri.-Wed. noon-2:30pm and 7-11pm).

ITALIAN RIVIERA (LIGURIA)

Liguria is the Italian Riviera, with lemon trees, almond blossoms, and turquoise water. Genoa divides the area neatly in half—**Riviera di Ponente** (setting sun) and the more splendid **Riviera di Levante** (rising sun) lie to the west and east respectively. This crescent-shaped coastal stretch differs greatly from its hyped French counterpart; here you'll find elegance, not arrogance. Especially lovely are the **Portofino peninsula** (about 30min. by train from Genoa) and the **Cinque Terre** area (immediately west of La Spezia). In July and August, only reservations will get you a place for the night.

Genoa (Genova)

Genoa's leading families began prospering in the 13th century, when the port town's international trade flourished. The sudden riches went to furnish the city with parks, palaces, and countless works of art. Genoa's financial glory was matched by intellectual brilliance: native sons include Chistopher Columbus, Giuseppe Mazzini, and Nicolò Paganini. After falling into decline in the 18th century, modern Genoa has turned its attentions to restoring the city to its former grandeur.

Via Garibaldi, the most impressive street in Genoa, is bedecked with elegant *palazzi.* Approaching from the west from Via Cairoli, you'll first see the **Palazzo Bianco,** which houses Ligurian, Dutch, and Flemish art. Across the street, the **Palazzo Rosso** features magnificent furnishings and lavish frescoes. (Both *palazzi* open Tues., Thurs.-Fri., and Sun. 9am-1pm, Wed. Sat. 9am-7pm, Sun. 10am-6pm.) Farther along Via Garibaldi, the **Palazzo Tursi** now serves as the city hall (open Mon.-Fri. 8:30am-noon and 1-4:30pm; free), while the **Palazzo Podestà** and **Palazzo Parodi** boast beautiful courtyards and doorways. Near P. Corvetto, **Villetta di Negro** spreads over the hill with grottoes, waterfalls, and terraced gardens. On the summit, the **Museo d'Arte Orientale** displays impressive sculptures. (Open Tues. and Thurs.-Sat. 9am-1pm, 1st and 3rd Sun. of the month 9am-1pm. L6000.)

From P. Corvetto, Via Roma leads to the **Palazzo Ducale,** P. Matteotti, where the city's rulers once lived; on the opposite corner stands the ornate **Church of the Gesù,** which holds two Rubens. The historical center of town *(centro storico),* south and west of Via Garibaldi, is safe for tourists only during the day. There the **Duomo San Lorenzo** features a Gothic facade, carved central portal, and statues of Adam and Eve (open Mon.-Sat. 8am-noon and 3-6:30pm, Sun. noon-6:30pm; free). On the eastern side of town, Via San Luca leads past the **Church of San Siro,** Genoa's first cathedral (open Mon.-Fri. 4-6pm; free). **Palazzo Spinola,** P. di Pellicceria 1, demonstrates Genoa's mercantile wealth with its lavish rooms adorned with art (open Mon. 9am-1pm, Tues.-Sat. 10am-7pm, Sun. 2-7pm; L8000).

Practical Information, Accommodations, and Food Genoa is easily accessible by rail from Rome (6hr., L38,000) and Turin (2hr., L14,600). There are two train stations: **Stazione Principe,** P. Acquaverde, and **Stazione Brignole,** P. Verdi. Call (010) 167 88 80 88 for train info (daily 7am-9pm). Buses 37 and 40 connect the stations. Bus 40 from Brignole and bus 41 from Principe run to the center of town. **Via Balbi** extends from Stazione Principe to the central **Piazza de Ferrari,** while **Via XX Settembre** runs east towards Stazione Brignole. Procure a decent map in the train station (about L6000) or at any newsstand to make sense of the tangled streets. The **tourist office** is at Porto Antico, P. Santa Maria (tel. (010) 248 71; open Mon.-Fri. 8am-1:15pm and 2-6:30pm, Sat. 8am-1:30pm). There is a **branch** (tel. (010) 246 26 33) at the Principe train station (open Mon.-Fri. 8am-8pm).

For accommodations, head for the hostel or stick to the safer areas around Stazione Brignole. **Ostello per la Gioventù (HI),** Via Costanzi, 120 (tel./fax (010) 242 24 57), offers panoramic views and incredible facilities. Take bus 35 five stops from Stazione Principe, then transfer to bus 40 (which goes directly from Brignole) and ride to the end. (Members only. Reception open daily 7-9am and 3:30pm-midnight. L22,000. Wheelchair accessible.) **Pensione Mirella,** Via Gropallo, 4/4 (tel. (010) 839 37 22), is in a beautifully maintained and secure building (singles L37,000, doubles L65,000). Genoa is famous for its *pesto* and *focaccia.* **Trattoria da Maria,** Vico Testadoro, 14r, off Via XXV Aprile, serves great, quintessential Genovese cuisine (*menù* L13,000; open Mon. noon-2pm, Tues.–Fri. and Sun. noon-2pm and 4:30-10pm).

Riviera di Ponente and Riviera di Levante

Finale Ligure Eschewing the glamor and arrogance of other Riviera towns, Finale Ligure welcomes weary backpackers with soft sands and luxurious flora. The city is divided into the three sections. **Finalborgo** (the old village), to the west, is enclosed within solid ancient walls. **Finalpia** is to the east, while **Finalmarina,** in the center, includes the train station and most other sights. Follow your nose to the Genovese Baroque **Basilica di San Giovanni Battista,** in the beautiful, gardenia-filled *piazza* of the same name. The best free beach is on Via Aurelia.

From P. Vittorio Veneto, **trains** (tel. (019) 69 27 77) offer frequent service to Genoa (1hr.). **SAR buses,** near the train station (tel. (019) 69 22 75), travel to neighboring beachside towns. The **IAT tourist office,** Via San Pietro, 14 (tel. (019) 69 25 81; fax 68 00 50), offers a great map and can arrange rooms in private homes (open Mon.-Sat. 8:30am-12:30pm and 3:30-7:30pm; in summer also Sun. 9am-noon). **Castello Wuillerman (HI),** Via Generale Caviglia (tel. (019) 69 05 15), is worth the tough uphill hike from the station. From the station, take a left onto Via Mazzini, which turns into Via Torino, turn left onto Via degli Ulivi when you hit a gas station, and climb the Gradinata delle Rose. (Reception open daily 7-10am and 5-10pm. Curfew 11:30pm. HI members L18,000. No phone reservations. Open March 15-Oct. 15.) **Albergo San Marco,** Via della Concezione, 22 (tel. (019) 69 25 33), offers singles for L40,000. Camp at **Del Mulino** (tel. (019) 60 16 69; L9000 per person, L7000-12,000 per tent; open April-Sept.). From the station take the bus for Calviso from "P. Vittorio Veneto" and get off at the **Boncardo Hotel,** Corso Europa, 4. Turn left at P. Guglielmo Oberdanm, right onto Via Porra, and left onto Via Castelli. Take the stairs up to the right and follow signs. *Trattorie* and *pizzerie* line the streets closest to the beach, but you'll pay less farther inland along Via Rossi and Via Roma.

Camogli A small, peaceful resort town, **Camogli** takes great pride in its ancient maritime traditions. The name is a contraction of "Casa Mogli," meaning "Wives' House," from the women who ran the town while their husbands manned its once-huge fishing fleet. **Trains** arrive from Genoa (20min., L2000) and Santa Margherita (10min., L1500); **Tigullio buses** (tel. (0185) 167 01 48 08) depart from P. Schiaffino to nearby towns. The **tourist office** is at Via XX Settembre, 33 (tel. (0185) 77 10 66), to your right as you leave the station. (Open June-Sept. daily 9:30am-12:30pm and 4-7pm; Oct.-May Mon.-Sat. 8:30am-noon and 3:30-6pm, Sun. 9:30am-12:30pm.) Your best bet for accommodations is unquestionably **Albergo La Camogliese,** Via Garibaldi, 55. (Tel. (0185) 77 14 02. Singles with bath L50,000-70,000. Doubles L80,000-100,000. 10% discount for cash-paying *Let's Go* readers.) The pleasant **Pensione Augusta,** Via Schiaffino, 100 (tel./fax (0185) 77 05 92), and **Albergo Selene,** Via Cuneo, 16 (tel. (0185) 77 01 49), also offer singles for L50,000-65,000 and doubles for L65,000-100,000. For an affordable meal, the restaurants on Via Repubblica should suffice, or try the **Picasso Supermercato,** Via XX Settembre, 35 (open Mon.-Sat. 8am-12:30pm and 4:30-7:30pm; closed Wed. afternoons).

Santa Margherita Ligure Once accessible only to wealthy vacationers, **Santa Margherita Ligure** now welcomes budget travelers and provides an ideal, serene base for exploring the rest of the Italian Riviera. There are two main squares that cover the waterfront: **Piazza Martiri della Libertà** and the smaller **Piazza Vittorio Veneto.** Both are lovely parks lined with palm trees. **Trains** arrive at P. Federico Raoul Nobili, at the summit of Via Roma, from Genoa (L2800). **Buses** depart from P. Vittorio Veneto for Camogli (L2000) and Portofino (L1700). The **tourist office,** Via XXV Aprile, 2b (tel. (0185) 28 74 85), gives a town map and has an accommodations service. Turn right from the train station onto Via Roma, then right on Via XXV Aprile (open Mon.-Sat. 9am-12:30pm and 2:30-7pm, Sun. 9:30am-12:30pm).

When looking for a room, sacrifice a waterfront view for peace, quiet, and an extra L20,000-30,000 in your pocket. The proprietor of **Hotel Terminus,** P. Nobili, 4 (tel. (0185) 28 61 21; fax 28 25 46), is dedicated to the comfort of his guests (singles L65,000-75,000; doubles L90,000-110,000). **Hotel Conte Verde,** Via Zara, 1 (tel. (0185) 28 71 39), on your right as you come down Via Roma, has clean, functional rooms (singles L45,000-75,000, doubles L80,000-130,000). Supermarkets, bakeries, fruit vendors, and butcher shops line Corso Matteotti. **Trattoria Baicin,** Via Algeria, 9, off P. Martiri della Libertà near the water, and **Rosticceria Revelant,** Via Gramsci, 15, east of P. Martiri della Libertà, offer hearty and scrumptious meals.

Portofino and San Fruttuoso Scenic yacht- and boutique-filled **Portofino** merits a daytrip from Santa Margherita. Trek up to the **Chiesa di San Giorgio** or the **castle** for enchanting vistas of the bay, or follow the "Al faro" signs to reach the **light-house.** There's no train to Portofino, but Tigullio **buses** run along the coastline to and from Santa Margherita (L1700; take the bus to Portofino Mare, not Portofino Vetta). The gorgeous but expensive **San Fruttuoso** is set in a natural amphitheater of pines, olive trees, and green oaks. Boats make the trip every hour from Camogli (round-trip L12,000), or you can walk from Portofino (1½hr.). Be sure to visit the **Abbazia di San Fruttuoso di Capo di Monte,** for which the town is named.

Cinque Terre and La Spezia A group of five connected villages clinging to the cliffs above the sea, **Cinque Terre** is justly famed for impressive vistas, clear waters, and the sweet *sciacchetrà* wine. The towns, in order of increasing distance from Genoa, are **Monterosso, Vernazza, Corniglia, Manarola,** and **Riomaggiore,** of which Monterosso is the biggest, easiest to reach, and least charming. Enjoy the best views from the narrow goat paths that link the towns; the best and most challenging **hike** lies between Monterosso and Vernazza (1½hr.), while the trail between Vernazza and Corniglia passes through some of the area's most gorgeous scenery. Cinque Terre's two public **beaches** reside on the south side of Monterosso and on the long strip of pebbles between Corniglia and Manarola. You can reserve parts of Monterosso's beach (L2500), or head to Guvano Beach to chill with nudist hippies. To get to Guvano for free, hike down off the road between Corniglia and Vernazza. Tiny trails off the road to Vernazza lead to hidden coves popular among the locals.

The **tourist office** (tel. (0187) 81 75 06) in Monterosso below the train station, provides an accommodations service and currency exchange (open April-Oct. Mon.-Sat. 10:30am-noon and 3-7pm, Sun. 10am-noon). In Riomaggiore, sack out at sign-less **Hostel Mamma Rosa,** P. Unità, 2 (tel. (0187) 92 00 50), across from the train station (L25,000), or check out the *affitta camere* (private rooms) throughout the Cinque Terre. **Albergo Barbara,** P. Marconi, 21 (tel. (0187) 81 22 01), at the port in Vernazza offers bright, airy rooms with fantastic views of the port (singles L50,000, doubles L70,000-80,000, triples L10,000, quads L120,000). **Hotel Souvenie,** Via Gioberti, 24 (tel. (0187) 81 75 95), in Monterosso, is a quiet family-run hotel (L40,000). Cinque Terre's seafood is swimmingly fresh, and *sciacchetrà,* the sweet local white wine, complements it deliciously. To get to **Ristorante Cecio** (tel. (0187) 81 20 43), in Corniglia on the small road that leads to Vernazza, follow the signs at the top of the stairs that lead to town from the train station (cover L3000; *primi* from L8000; try the *spaghetti alla scogliera*). Spend the night here, too (doubles L80,000).

La Spezia, more commercial and less pleasant than the smaller towns of the surrounding coast, serves as a departure point to Corsica. **Corsica Ferries** (tel. (0187) 77 80 97), at the Molo Italia dock, serve Bastia, Corsica (5hr., L36,000-48,000). **Tirrenia** sends ferries to Olbia, Sardinia (5½hr., L110,000). The **tourist office** (tel. (0187) 77 09 00) sits beside the port at Viale Mazzini, 45; a branch office is in the train station (tel. (0187) 71 89 97). If you must stay here, **Albergo Terminus,** Via Paleocapa, 21 (tel. (0187) 70 34 36; fax 71 49 35), has singles and doubles for L32,000-65,000.

EMILIA-ROMAGNA

Come to Emilia-Romagna to eat. Italy's wealthiest wheat- and dairy-producing region covers the fertile plains of the Po river valley and fosters the finest in culinary traditions. Here, enjoy Parmesan cheese and *prosciutto,* Bolognese fresh pasta and *mortadella,* and the region's sparkling red wines, such as *lambrusco.*

Bologna

With one forkful of Bologna's *tortellini,* it becomes clear that this city appreciates the better things in life. The city founded the first university in Europe 900 years ago, and the **Università di Bologna** has since graduated the likes of Dante, Petrarch, Copernicus, and Tasso. Scholarly wisdom and general opulence have made Bologna particularly open-minded. Social tolerance and student energy fan both local nightlife and strong political activism.

Bologna's most remarkable sights are its endless series of porticoed buildings, a 14th-century solution to the housing crisis of a growing city. The tranquil expanse of **Piazza Maggiore** is the heart of the city. It adjoins the **Piazza del Nettuno,** which features the Romanesque **Palazzo del Podestà** and the famous 16th-century *Neptune and Attendants* statue and fountain. Behind the fountain of Neptune are displayed the photos of those who lost their lives fighting for Italian freedom from Germany; also remembered are those who lost their lives in the right-extremist attacks of 1974, 1980, 1984. Nearby, the **Basilica di San Petronio** was going to be larger than St. Peter's in Rome until jealous Church officials diverted the funds to a different project (open daily 7:15am-1pm and 2-6pm). Via Rizzoli leads from P. Nettuno to **Piazza Porta Ravegnana,** where seven streets converge in Bologna's medieval quarter. The two towers here are the emblem of the city; climb the **Torre degli Asinelli** for an amazing view of the city (open in summer daily 9am-6pm; off-season 9am-5pm; L3000). From the two towers, the Strada Maggiore leads east past the **Basilica of San Bartolomeo.** Stop here and see the exquisite *Madonna* by Guido Reni before proceeding to the **Church of Santa Maria dei Servi** (open daily 6:30-noon and 3:30-8pm). Down Via Santo Stefano, the triangular **Piazza Santo Stefano** opens onto a complex of beautiful Romanesque churches. Under the pulpit of the **Chiesa del San Sepolcro,** in the center of the group, is buried San Petronio, patron saint of Bologna. The **Museo Civico Archeologico,** Via Archiginnasio, 2, has a fascinating collection of antiquities. (Open Tues.-Fri. 9am-2pm, Sat.-Sun. 9am-1pm and 3:30-7pm. L8000, students L4000.)

ITALY

Practical Information, Accommodations, and Food Bologna sends **trains** to Florence (1½hr., L8200), Venice (2hr., L14,000), Milan (3hr., L18,000-28,000), Rome (4hr., L34,000-50,000), and other cities. Buses 25 and 30 shuttle between the train station and P. Maggiore (L1500). The **tourist office** in Palazzo Comunale, P. Maggiore, 6 (tel. (051) 23 96 60), is modern, genial, and efficient (open Mon.-Sat. 9am-12:30pm and 2:30-7pm). Prices are high and rooms scarce in Bologna. The clean, new **Ostello di San Sisto (HI),** Via Viadagola, 5 and 14 (tel./fax (051) 50 18 10), is in the Località di San Sisto 6km northeast of the center of town, off Via San Donato; ask at the tourist office for a map with directions. (Reception open daily 7-9am and 3:30-11:30pm. Lockout 9am-5pm. L20,000, nonmembers L22,000.) **Albergo Apollo,** Via Drapperie, 5 (tel. (051) 22 39 55), couldn't be closer to the center of town (singles L49,000, doubles L84,000; closed in Aug.), while **Albergo Minerva,** Via de' Monari, 3 (tel. (051) 23 96 52), has nice, breezy rooms (singles L52,000, doubles L86,000-112,000, triples L115,000-152,000). **Pensione Marconi,** Via Marconi, 22 (tel. (051) 26 28 32), has clean rooms and a desk monitored all night (singles L48,000-60,000, doubles L75,000-92,000) while **Hotel Pderini,** Strada Maggiore, 79 (tel. (051)

30 00 81), has many conveniences and handicap access (singles L65,000-90,000, doubles L100,000-120,000; prices reduced off season).

Don't miss Bologna's namesake dish, *spaghetti alla bolognese,* pasta with a hefty meat and tomato sauce. The areas around Via Augusto Righi and Via Piella, as well as the neighborhood of Via Saragozza, are good for *trattorie.* **Mensa Universitaria Irnerio,** Via Zamboni, 47, is amazingly cheap for students (open Tues.-Fri. 11:45am-3pm and 7-10pm, Sat.-Sun. 11:45am-3pm). **Trattoria De Marro,** Via Broccaindosso, 71/D, offers *tortellini.* (L8000. Cover L1500. Open Mon.-Fri. noon-3pm and 8-10:15pm, Sat.-Sun. noon-3pm.) **Pizzeria La Mamma "Self-Service,"** Via Zamboni, 16, caters to boisterous students (pizza L5000-9000; open daily noon-2:30pm and 7-10pm). At **Ristorante Clorofilla,** Strada Maggiore, 64, the food is innovative and almost exclusively vegetarian (open Sept.-July Mon.-Sat. 12:15-3pm and 7:30-midnight).

Bologna's huge university population makes for lively nighttime diversion during the academic year. To reach **Made in Bo,** an open-air disco held in July and August in Parco Nord, take bus 25 or 91A from the station (free; starts 10pm). Look for posters about **Bepop,** a free festival in July and August with events ranging from poetry reading to raves (bus 38 or 91A to "Fiera"). **Discoteca**, near the Two Towers, offers alternative music and gay and lesbian night on Saturday (cover L25,000-40,000). To get drunk with the locals head to **Irish Times Pub,** Via Paradiso, 1d (open daily 7:30pm until no one is left standing). From September through June on Sunday afternoons, the Bolognese **soccer team** plays in the **Stadio Comunale,** Via Adrea Costa, 174 (tel. (051) 614 53 91). Take bus 21 from the station or 14 from Porta Isaia.

Parma

ITALY

Parma enjoys a rich history and robust cultural activity, but the city is best known for its incomparable delicacies: luscious *prosciutto* ham, sharp *parmigiano* cheese, and the sparkling white wine *Malvasia.* Try to arrive in Parma famished. The **duomo** contains masterpieces like the moving *Descent from the Cross* by Benedetto Antelami, Correggio's *Virgin,* and the Episcopal Throne supported by piers in the apse (open daily 9am-noon and 3-7pm). The **baptistery** features sculpted portals by Antelami and stunning 13th-century frescoes (open daily 9am-12:30pm and 3-6pm; L3000, students L1000). Behind the *duomo* on P. San Giovanni, the **Church of San Giovanni Evangelista** features frescoes by Correggio and Parmigianino (open daily 6:30am-noon and 3:30-8pm; free). A few blocks from the *duomo,* the **Palazzo della Pilotta** houses the **Galleria Nazionale,** with works by da Vinci and Correggio (open daily 9am-1:45pm; L12,000). Make sure to see the premier opera house of Parma, the **Teatro Regio,** Via Garibaldi 16 (tel. (0521) 21 89 10), next to P. della Place. If you can't afford a ticket, people-watch nearby at **Piazza Garibaldi.**

Trains connect Parma to Milan (1½hr., L11,700), Bologna (1hr., L7200), and Florence (3hr., L15,500). The **train station** is located on P. Carlo Alberto della Chiesa. The **tourist office,** Via Melloni, 1b (tel. (0521) 21 88 89; tel./fax. 23 47 35), off Strada Pisacane, has info on nearby towns (open Mon.-Sat. 9am-7pm, Sun. 9am-1pm). The **Ostello Cittadella (HI),** Via Passo Buole (tel. (0521) 96 14 34), occupies a 15th-century fortress. To reach the hostel, get on bus 9 in front of the station or snag bus 2 from P. Garibaldi. (Members only, but sometimes accepts students with ID. Lockout 9:30am-5pm. 3-day max. stay. Strict curfew 11pm. L15,000.) **Casa Della Giovane,** Via del Conservatorio, 11 (tel. (0521) 28 32 29), offers first-class rooms for women only (L20,000-35,000). There's a restaurant downstairs at the comfortable **Locanda Lazzaro,** Borgo XX Marzo, 14 (tel. (0521) 20 89 44), off Via della Repubblica (singles L45,000, doubles L65,000). The cuisine of Parma is wonderfully affordable. An **open-air market** can be found at P. Ghiaia, off Viale Mariotti (open daily 8am-1pm and 3-7pm). Local specialties fill the windows of many *salumerie* along Via Garibaldi. For dinner, try **Trattoria Corrieri,** Via Conservatorio, 3 (cover L3000; open Mon.-Sat. noon-2:30pm and 7:30-10:30pm). **Le Sorelle Pachini,** Strada Farini, 27, is a traditional *salumeria* which hides one of the best *trattorie* in town in back. (*Trattoria* open Mon.-Sat. noon-3pm. *Salumeria* open 8:30am-1pm and 4-7pm for picnic fixings.)

TUSCANY (TOSCANA)

Tuscany is the stuff Italian dreams (and more than one romantic Brits-in-Italy movie) are made of. With rolling hills covered with olives and grapevines, bright yellow fields of sunflowers, and inviting cobblestone streets, it's hard not to wax poetic. Tuscany's Renaissance culture, an unprecedented explosion of art, architecture, and humanist scholarship, became the culture of Italy, while Tuscan, the language of Dante, Petrarch, and Machiavelli, is today's textbook Italian. The region has only one drawback: it's too popular. An extensive and convenient transportation system makes it easy to tour the countryside. The state railroad serves all major towns and many smaller ones, though in the hill-towns the incredible vistas that bus travel affords more than compensate for the infrequent service and changeovers.

Florence (Firenze)

Although Dante Alighieri bitterly bemoaned his hometown's greed and materialism in the 13th century, nearly every visitor to walk Florence's cobblestone streets since then has fallen in love with the city. Henry James, Albert Camus, and even cranky Mark Twain were all won over by its beauty. Stimulated by an innovative banking system, the city evolved from a booming, 13th-century wool- and silk-trading town into the archetype of political experimentation and artistic rebirth. Periodic civil wars thwarted the city's highest ambitions during these years, but soon the Medici clan rose to power and Lorenzo the Magnificent established peace in the 15th century. Florence became the unchallenged Renaissance capital of art, architecture, science, commerce, and political thought.

ORIENTATION AND PRACTICAL INFORMATION

Florence is easily accessible by train from major cities in Italy. From **Stazione Santa Maria Novella,** it's a short walk on Via de' Panzani and then left on Via de' Cerrentari to the center of Florence. This area is bounded by the *duomo* on the north, the Arno River on the south, and the Bargello and Palazzo Strozzi on the east and west.

Major arteries radiate from the *duomo* and its two *piazze:* **Piazza San Giovanni** encircling the baptistery and **Piazza del Duomo** around the cathedral. A lively pedestrian walkway, **Via dei Calzaiuoli** runs from the *duomo* to **Piazza Signoria** toward the river. Parallel to Via dei Calzaiuoli on the west, **Via Roma** leads from P. S. Giovanni through **Piazza della Repubblica** (the city's largest open space) to the **Ponte Vecchio,** which spans the Arno to the district called the **Oltrarno.**

Florence has two entirely independent sequences of street numbers: red indicates a commercial building (noted here with an "r"), and blue or black a residential one (including most sights and hotels); always note which color you're after. For guidance through Florence's tangled center, pick up a free map (ask for one with a street index) from one of the tourist offices.

Tourist Offices: Consorzio ITA (tel. 28 28 93 or 21 95 37), in the train station by track 16, next to the pharmacy. Come in person and they'll find you a room for a L3000-10,000 commission. Open daily 8:30am-9pm. **Informazione Turistica** (tel. 21 22 45 or 238 12 26), inside the round glass-and-concrete building outside the train station (exit by track 16). No booking service, but plenty of up-to-date info on entertainment and cultural events. Open April-Oct. daily 8:15am-7:15pm; Nov.-March 8:15am-1:45pm. The **branch office** is at Chiasso dei Baroncelli, 17r.

Budget Travel: S.T.S., Via Zanetti, 18r (tel. 28 41 83). Student discounts on bus and train tickets. Open Mon.-Fri. 9:30am-1pm and 1:30-7pm, Sat. 9:30am-12:30pm. **CTS,** Via Ginori, 25r (tel. 28 95 70). No Eurailpasses, but just about everything else. Get there early. Open Mon.-Fri. 9am-1pm and 2:30-6pm, Sat. 9am-noon.

Consulates: Australians, Canadians, and **New Zealanders** should contact their consulates in Rome or Milan. **U.K.,** Lungarno Corsini, 2 (tel. 28 41 33). Open Mon.-

Fri. 9:30am-12:30pm and 2:30-4:30pm. **U.S.,** Lungarno Vespucci, 38 (tel. 239 82 76), near the station. Open Mon.-Fri. 8:30am-noon and 2-4pm.

Currency Exchange: Banks have the best rates. Most open Mon.-Fri. 8:20am-1:20pm and 2:45-3:45pm; some open Sat. morning. **Cassa di Risparmio di Firenze** has 24hr. **ATMs** for changing money at several locations: Via de' Bardi, 73r; Via Nazionale, 93; Via de' Tornabuoni, 23r; Via degli Speziali, 16r; and Via dei Servi, 40r.

American Express: Via Dante Alighieri, 20-22r (tel. 509 81). From the *duomo,* walk down Via dei Calzaiuoli and turn left onto Via dei Tavolini. AmEx is on the little *piazza* at its end. Holds mail. Open Mon.-Fri. 9am-5:30pm, Sat. 9am-12:30pm.

Trains: Santa Maria Novella Station, near the center of town. Info office (tel. 27 87 85) open daily 7am-9pm; after hours go to ticket window 20. The yellow computers outside the office can help you plan. To: Bologna (1hr., L13,200), Milan (3½hr., L36,200), Rome (2½hr., L36,2000 for IC trains), and Venice (3hr., L31,600).

Buses: SITA, Via Santa Caterina da Siena, 15r (tel. 48 36 51). Frequent buses to Siena (2hr., L10,500) and San Gimignano (1½hr., L9400). **LAZZI,** P. Adua, 1-4r (tel. 21 51 55), sends buses to Pisa (L10,600) and Rome (L24,000).

Public Transportation: ATAF buses generally run 6am-1am; schedules vary by line. Tickets must be bought before boarding and validated by the punch-machine on board, or you'll pay a L70,000 fine. Tickets cost L1400 for 1hr. or L1900 for 2hr.; a 24hr. pass runs L5000. Get a bus map at the ATAF office outside the station.

Bike and Moped Rental: MotoRent, Via S. Zanobi, 9r (tel. 49 01 13). Bikes start at L3000 per hr., L20,000 per day; mopeds begin at L9000 per hr., L40,000 per day, L200,000 per week. Min. age 18.

Hitchhiking: Hitchers take the A-1 to Bologna and Milan or the A-11 to the Riviera and Genoa, or they take bus 29, 30, or 35 to the feeder near Peretola. For the A-1 to Rome and the Siena extension, they take bus 31 or 32 from the station to exit 23. The **International Lift Center,** Borgo dei Greci, 40r (tel. 28 06 21), matches passengers with drivers for a fee. Open daily 10am-7pm. Call 1 week in advance.

Bookstores: After Dark, Via de' Ginori, 47r (tel. 29 42 03). New English books and magazines. Open Mon.-Fri. 10am-1:30pm and 3-7pm, Sat. 10am-1:30pm.

Laundromat: Launderette, Via Guelfa, 55r. Wash and dry L10,000. Open daily 8am-10pm. **Wash and Dry Lavarapido,** Via dei Servi, 105r, 2 blocks from the *duomo.* Wash and dry L12,000. Open daily 8am-10pm; last wash 9pm.

Public Baths: Bagno S. Agostino, Via S. Agostino, 8, off P. Santo Spirito. Bath L3000. Soap and towel L2000. Open Tues. and Thurs. 3-6pm, Fri.-Sat. 8am-noon.

Pharmacy: Farmacia Comunale (tel. 28 94 35), by track 16 in the station. **Molteni,** Via dei Calzaiuoli, 7r (tel. 28 94 90). Both open 24hr.

Medical Assistance: Misericordia, P. del Duomo, 20 (tel. 21 22 22 or 21 95 55). **Tourist Medical Service,** Via Lorenzo il Magnifico, 59 (tel. 47 54 11). On call 24hr.

Emergency: tel. 113.

Police: Questura (headquarters), Via Zara, 2 (tel. 497 71). Also at P. del Duomo, 5. Open Mon.-Fri. 8am-8pm, Sat. 8am-2pm.

Internet Access: Internet Train, Via dell'Orvio, 25r (tel. 234 53 22; email info@fionline.it; http://www/fionline.it). L6000 per 30min., L12,000 per hr. Open Mon.-Fri. 10am-7:30pm, Sat. 10am-2pm.

Post Office: The main office is on Via Pellicceria (tel. 21 61 22), off P. della Repubblica. *Fermo Posta* at window 24. Open Mon.-Fri. 8:15am-7pm, Sat. 8:15am-12:30pm. The **telegram** office in front is open 24hr. **Postal Code:** 50100.

Telephones: Via Cavour, 21r. Open daily 8am-9:45pm. **Telephone Code:** 055.

ACCOMMODATIONS AND CAMPING

Florence abounds with one-star *pensioni* and private *affitta camere.* If you arrive late in the day, check with the train station's accommodations service for available rooms and going rates. Sleeping in train stations, streets, or parks is a poor idea—police actively discourage it. Make reservations *(prenotazioni)* in advance, at least 10 days if you plan to visit at Easter or in summer. The vast majority of *pensioni* prefer to take reservations in the form of a letter with at least one night's deposit by postal money order. If you have any complaints, talk first to the proprietor and then, if necessary, to the **Ufficio Controllo Alberghi,** Via Cavour, 37 (tel. 276 01). The municipal govern-

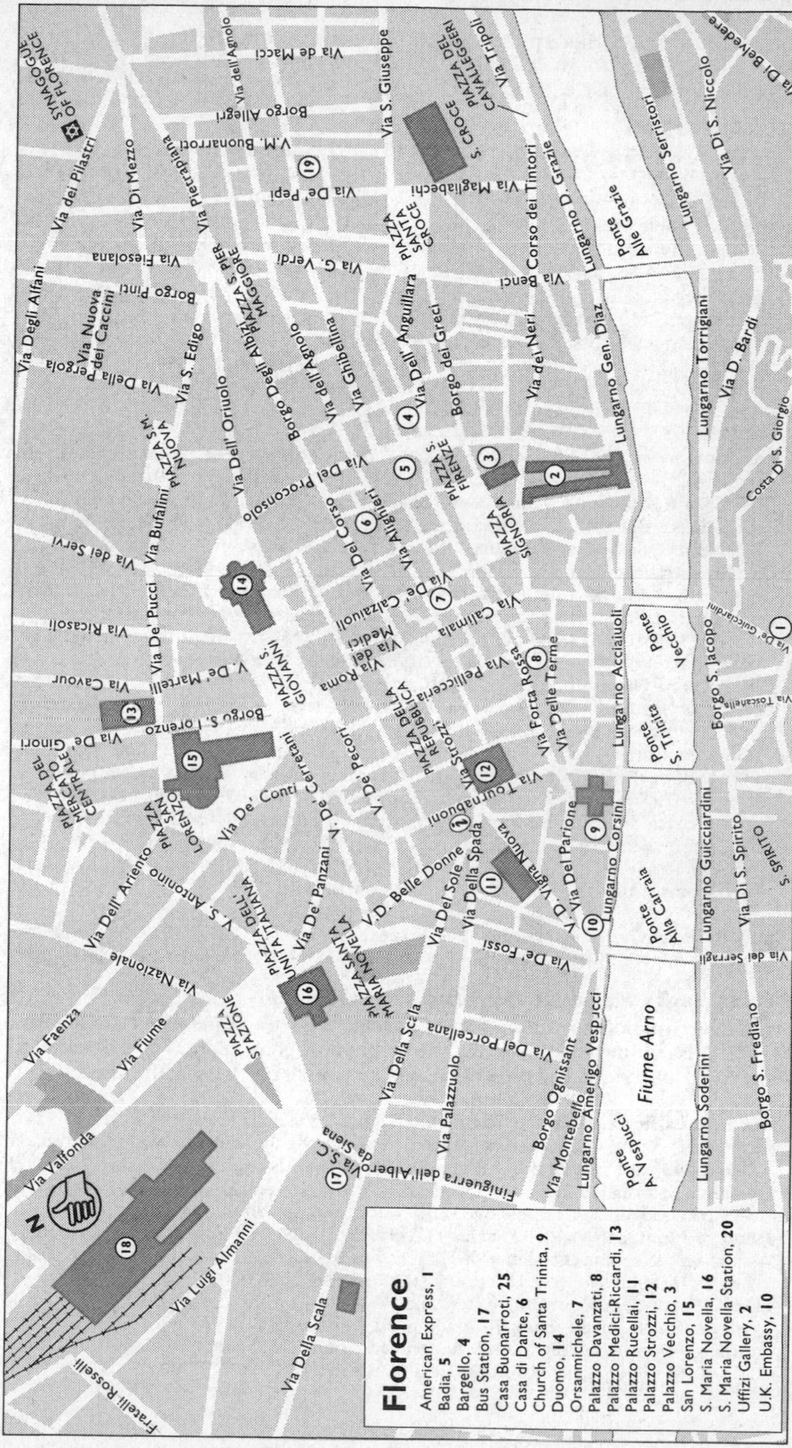
Florence
American Express, 1
Badia, 5
Bargello, 4
Bus Station, 17
Casa Buonarroti, 25
Casa di Dante, 6
Church of Santa Trinita, 9
Duomo, 14
Orsanmichele, 7
Palazzo Davanzati, 8
Palazzo Medici-Riccardi, 13
Palazzo Rucellai, 11
Palazzo Strozzi, 12
Palazzo Vecchio, 3
San Lorenzo, 15
S. Maria Novella, 16
S. Maria Novella Station, 20
Uffizi Gallery, 2
U.K. Embassy, 10
N
SYNAGOGUE OF FLORENCE
PIAZZA S. CROCE
PIAZZA SANTA CROCE
PIAZZA DEL CAVALLEGGERI
PIAZZA SIGNORIA
PIAZZA S. FIRENZE
PIAZZA S. GIOVANNI
PIAZZA DELLA REPUBBLICA
PIAZZA SAN LORENZO
PIAZZA DEL MERCATO CENTRALE
PIAZZA SANTA MARIA NOVELLA
PIAZZA DELL' UNITÀ ITALIANA
PIAZZA STAZIONE
PIAZZA S. PIER MAGGIORE
Fiume Arno
Ponte Vecchio
Ponte S. Trinita
Ponte Alla Carraia
Ponte A. Vespucci
Ponte Alle Grazie
Lungarno Gen. Diaz
Lungarno Acciaiuoli
Lungarno Corsini
Lungarno Amerigo Vespucci
Lungarno Guicciardini
Lungarno Torrigiani
Lungarno Serristori
Lungarno Soderini
Lungarno D. Grazie
Via Nazionale
Via Faenza
Via Fiume
Via Valfonda
Via Luigi Alamanni
Via Della Scala
Fratelli Rosselli
Via Cavour
Via Ricasoli
Via dei Servi
Via Del Proconsolo
Via Del Corso
Via Dante Alighieri
Via Ghibellina
Borgo Degli Albizi
Via G. Verdi
Via dei Neri
Via Calzaiuoli
Via Roma
Via Tornabuoni
Via Por Santa Maria
Via de' Guicciardini
Borgo S. Jacopo
Via Maggio
Via Di S. Spirito
Via dei Serragli
Borgo S. Frediano
Via Dei Benci
Corso dei Tintori
Via de' Pepi
Via de Macci
Borgo Allegri
Via dei Pilastri
Via Di Mezzo
Via Pietrapiana
Via Fiesolana
Borgo Pinti
Via Degli Alfani
Via Della Pergola
Via Bufalini
Via De' Pucci
Via De' Martelli
Via De' Ginori
Borgo S. Lorenzo
Via De' Cerretani
Via De' Panzani
Via Dell' Ariento
Via S. Antonino
Via De' Fossi
Via Del Sole
Via Della Spada
Via Vigna Nuova
Via Del Parione
Via Strozzi
Via De' Pecori
Via Pellicceria
Via Porta Rossa
Via Delle Terme
Via Del Porcellana
Via Palazzuolo
Borgo Ognissanti
Via Montebello
Via Di Belvedere
Via Di S. Niccolo
Via D. Bardi
Costa Di S. Giorgio
Via Tripoli
Via Magliabechi
Via S. Giuseppe
Via Dell' Anguillara
Borgo dei Greci
Via Toscanella
Via dell' Oriuolo
Borgo Degli Albizi

ITALY

ment strictly regulates hotel prices; proprietors can charge neither more nor less than the approved range for their category. Rates uniformly increase by 5% or so every year; the new rates take effect in March or April.

Hostels

Ostello Archi Rossi, Via Faenza, 94r (tel. 29 08 04; fax 230 26 01), 2 blocks from the train station. Exit left from the station onto Via Nazionale and turn left at Via Faenza. Look for the blue neon *"ostello"* sign. A funky hostel with floor-to-ceiling graffiti. Room lockout 9:30am, hostel lockout 11am. Curfew 12:30am. L20,000-26,000. Laundry L10,000. Arrive by 11am in summer. Wheelchair accessible.

Istituto Gould, Via dei Serragli, 49 (tel. 21 25 76), in the Oltrarno. Take bus 36 or 37 from the station to the 1st stop across the river. One of the best lodgings in Florence: the staff is welcoming and the sunny rooms are spotless. All profits fund social services for local children. No check-in or out Sat. afternoons and Sun. No curfew and no lock-out. Office open Mon.-Fri. 9am-1pm and 3-7pm, Sat. 9am-1pm. Singles L45,000, with bath L50,000. Doubles L66,000, with bath L70,000. Triples L90,000, with bath L96,000. Quads with bath L120,000. Quints with bath L125,000.

Pensionato Pio X, Via dei Serragli, 106 (tel./fax 22 50 44). Follow the directions to the Istituto Gould (above), then walk a few blocks farther down the street. Clean rooms and bathrooms. Four comfortable lounges. 2-night min. stay, 5-night max. stay. Check-out 9am. Curfew midnight. L22,000 per person, showers included; L3000 more for a room with bath. No reservations. Arrive before 9am.

Ostello Santa Monaca, Via S. Monaca, 6 (tel. 26 83 38; fax 28 01 85), off Via dei Serragli in the Oltrarno. Kitchen facilities. Self-service laundry L12,000 per 5kg. Reception open daily 6-9:30am and 2pm-12:30am. Check-in 9:30am-1pm and after 2pm. Curfew 12:30am. L21,000 per person. Sheets and immaculate showers included. 7-night max. stay. Written reservations must arrive at least 3 days in advance.

Ostello della Gioventù Europa Villa Camerata (HI), Viale Augusto Righi, 2-4 (tel. 60 14 51; fax 61 03 00), northeast of town. Take bus 17 from P. dell'Unità across from the train station or from P. del Duomo (20-30min.). In a gorgeous villa. Reception open daily 1-11pm. Check-out 7-9:30am. Curfew midnight. L23,000. Nonmembers L5000 extra. Sheets and breakfast included. Laundry. Reserve by letter or fax. If they're full, you can sleep in an outdoor tent for L16,000. Breakfast L2000.

Suore Oblate dello Spirito Santo, Via Nazionale, 8 (tel. 239 82 02), across from the Apollo Theater. Exit left from the station onto Via Nazionale and walk 100m. The nuns welcome women, married couples, and families. Huge rooms with modern bathrooms. Curfew 11pm sharp. Doubles with bath L75,000. Triples and quads L28,000 per person, with bath L30,000. Open July-Oct. 15.

Suore Oblate dell'Assunzione, Via Borgo Pinti 15 (tel. 248 05 83). Nun-run and open to all. Midnight curfew. Singles L40,000. Doubles L60,000. Closed in Aug.

Piazza Santa Maria Novella and Environs

Standing in front of the station, you'll be facing the back of the Basilica of S. Maria Novella. Beyond the church are budget accommodations galore. You'll be close to the *duomo,* the *centro,* and the station. Ask for a room overlooking the *piazza.*

Locanda La Romagnola and **Soggiorno Gigliola,** Via della Scala, 40 (tel. 21 15 97 or 28 79 81). Leave the station by track 5, walk across the street to Via S. Caterina da Siena, and turn right a block later. Simple, spacious rooms; some have frescoed ceilings or ornately carved beds. Curfew midnight. Singles L39,000-48,000. Doubles L66,000-80,000. Triples L90,000-99,000. May be closed Jan.-Feb.

Albergo Montreal, Via della Scala, 43 (tel./fax 238 23 31). Cozy hotel with friendly staff. Ample rooms get plenty of light and noise. Little TV lounge. Curfew 1:30am. Singles L60,000. Doubles L80,000-90,000. Triples L130,000. Quads L150,000.

Hotel Visconti, P. Ottaviani, 1 (tel./fax 21 38 77), on the corner diagonally across the *piazza* from the church. Attempted Neoclassical decor with huge Grecian nudes. Friendly management. Reception open 24hr. Singles L45,000. Doubles L63,000-83,000. Triples L80,000-105,000. Quads L94,000-114,000.

Soggiorno Abaco, Via dei Banchi, 1 (tel./fax 238 19 19). With S. Maria Novella behind you, walk to the end of the *piazza* onto Via dei Banchi. Medieval feel and polished wood-beamed ceilings. All rooms have fans and TVs. No curfew. Singles L65,000. Doubles L90,000-120,000. Triples L120,000-140,000. Laundry washed and dried for L5000 per load. Kitchen facilities L6000. V, MC, AmEx.

Old City (Near the Duomo)

Tourists flood this area, but budget accommodations are usually available. Many provide great views of Florence's monuments; others lie hidden in Renaissance *palazzi.*

Locanda Orchidea, Borgo degli Albizi, 11 (tel. 248 03 46), a left off Via Proconsolo, which begins behind the *duomo.* Dante's wife was born in this 12th-century *palazzo* built around a still-intact tower. Singles L48,000. Doubles L70,000. Triples L110,000. Reserve ahead. Closed 2 weeks in Aug.

Soggiorno Bavaria, Borgo degli Albizi, 26 (tel./fax 234 03 13). Newly renovated rooms, some with balconies and frescoed ceilings, in a cool, quiet 15th-century *palazzo.* Singles L50,000. Doubles L80,000-90,000. Triples L90,000-100,000.

Soggiorno Panerai, Via dei Servi, 36 (tel./fax 26 41 03). Via dei Servi radiates out from the side of the cathedral opposite the *campanile.* Every 2 rooms share a bath. Refrigerator available to guests. Doubles L60,000. Triples L94,000. Quads 90,000.

Hotel Il Perseo, Via Cerretani, 1 (tel. 21 25 04), a block from the *duomo.* Bright, immaculate rooms, all with fans and many with breathtaking views. If they're full, the owners will call around to find you a room. Singles L60,000-70,000. Doubles L95,000-110,000. Triples L125,000-140,000. Quads L140,000-175,000. Ample breakfast included. V, MC, AmEx with 3% surcharge.

Via Nazionale and Environs

If you can't avoid this quarter, at least walk away from its center. As you leave the station, take a left onto Via Nazionale to find budget hotels. Cheap establishments abound on **Via Nazionale, Via Faenza, Via Fiume,** and **Via Guelfa.**

Via Faenza, 56 houses 6 separate *pensioni,* among the best budget lodgings in the city. From the station, Via Faenza is the 2nd intersection on Via Nazionale. **Pensione Azzi** (tel. 21 38 06) styles itself as the *locanda degli artisti* (the artists' inn), but anyone will enjoy the friendly management, large, immaculate rooms, and elegant dining room and terrace. No curfew. Singles L45,000. Doubles L75,000-85,000. Triples L90,000-100,000. Quads L115,000-125,000. Breakfast L5000. AmEx, MC, V. **Albergo Merlini** (tel. 21 28 48; fax 28 39 39). Curfew 1:30am. Singles L50,000. Doubles L75,000-90,000. Triples L95,000-110,000. Quads L105,000-120,000. Breakfast L10,000. **Albergo Marini** (tel. 28 48 24). Polished wood hallway leads to spotless rooms. Curfew 1am. Singles L50,000-70,000. Doubles L70,000-90,000. Triples L100,000-130,000. Quads L120,000-140,000. Breakfast L7000. **Albergo Anna** (tel. 239 83 22). Lovely rooms. Management and prices the same as the Pensione Azzi. **Albergo Armonia** (tel. 21 11 46). Posters of American films bedeck the clean rooms. Singles L55,000. Doubles L85,000. Triples L110,000. Quads L140,000. **Locanda Paola** (tel. 21 36 82). Standard rooms. Curfew 2am. Doubles L80,000-90,000. Triples L90,000-100,000.

Hotel Nazionale, Via Nazionale, 22 (tel. 238 22 03), near P. Indipendenza. Sunny rooms with comfy beds. Breakfast included. Door locks at midnight, so ask for a key. Singles L55,000-67,000. Doubles L79,000-98,000. Triples L104,000-139,000.

Via Faenza, 69, also has a slew of affordable rooms. **Hotel Soggiorno d'Erico,** 4th fl. (tel./fax 21 55 31). Small rooms with nice views of the hills around Florence. Free kitchen use. Laundry washed for L6000 per load (no dryer). Singles L50,000. Doubles L72,000. Triples L92,000. Quads L102,000. **Locanda Giovanna.** Basic, well-kept rooms, some with garden views. Singles L50,000. Doubles L75,000. **Locanda Pina** and **Albergo Nella** (tel. 21 22 31), on the 1st and 2nd floors. Twin establishments offering standard rooms at a good price. Singles L40,000. Doubles L70,000. Quads L100,000. Free kitchen use. Laundry L5000 per load; no dryer.

Near Piazza San Marco and the University Quarter

This area is considerably calmer and less tourist-ridden than its proximity to the center might suggest. Follow Via Nazionale from the station and take a right on Via Guelfa, which intersects with Via San Gallo and Via Cavour.

Hotel Tina, Via San Gallo, 31 (tel. 48 35 19 or 48 35 93). Small *pensione* with new furniture. Amicable owners will find you another place if they're full. Singles L50,000-60,000. Doubles L75,000-95,000. Triples L110,000. Quads L130,000.

La Colomba, Via Cavour, 21 (tel. 28 43 23). Friendly Italo-Austrian proprietor rents out immaculate rooms. Windows peer across the Florentine roofscape. Singles L70,000. Doubles L105,000-125,000. Breakfast included. V, MC.

Albergo Sampaoli, Via San Gallo, 14 (tel. 28 48 34). A little faded, but renovations should brighten things up. Singles L50,000. Doubles L70,000-90,000. Triples L105,000. Quads L120,000-140,000. No written reservations; call the night before.

Hotel Sofia, Via Cavour, 21 (tel. 28 39 30), just upstairs from La Colomba. Rooms with floral borders and new furniture. Curfew 1am. Singles L50,000. Doubles L80,000. Triples L120,000. Quads L140,000. Large American breakfast included.

Camping

Michelangelo, Viale Michelangelo, 80 (tel. 681 19 77), near P. Michelangelo. Take bus 13 from the station (15min., last bus 11:25pm). Extremely crowded, but offers a spectacular panorama of Florence. Fantastic facilities. If you show up without a vehicle they will often let you in. L10,000 per person, L8000 per tent, L6000 per car, L4000 per motorcycle. Open April-Nov. daily 6am-midnight.

Villa Camerata, Viale A. Righi, 2-4 (tel. 60 03 15), outside the HI youth hostel on the bus 17 route. Catch the bus at P. dell'Unità or P. del Duomo. Reception open daily 1pm-midnight; if the office is closed, stake your site and return later (before midnight) to register and pay. L7000 per person. L8000 per small tent.

FOOD

White beans and olive oil are two main staples of the hearty local cuisine. Popular specialties include *bruschetta* and *ribollita* (a thick bean, bread, and vegetable stew). *Bistecca alla fiorentina* is usually served *al sangue* (rare, literally "bloody"), often accompanied by a red *chianti classico.* To finish up a meal, try some *cantuccini* (hard almond cookies) dipped in *vinsanto,* a sweet, strong wine made from raisins.

For lunch, visit a *rosticceria gastronomica,* peruse the pushcarts, or stop by the **students' mensa,** Via dei Servi, 52 (meals L12,000; open Mon.-Sat. noon-12:15pm and 6:45-8:45pm; closed mid-July to Aug.). Buy supplies at the **Mercato Centrale,** between Via Nazionale and the back of San Lorenzo (open Mon.-Sat. 7am-2pm; Oct.-May Sat. 7am-2pm and 4-8pm), or at the **STANDA supermarket,** Via Pietrapiana, 1r (tel. 24 08 09; open Tues.-Sat. 8:30am-8pm, Sun. 8:30am-1:30pm). The two best **health-food/vegetarian** stores are named after the American book **Sugar Blues:** Via XXVII Aprile, 46r, near the *duomo* (open Mon.-Fri. 9am-1:30pm and 4-7:30pm, Sat. 9am-1pm), and Via dei Serragli, 57r, in the Oltrarno next to the Institute Gould. (Open Mon.-Sat. 9am-1:30pm and 4:30-8pm. Closed Sat. mornings and Wed. afternoons.) **Il Cuscussù,** Via Farini, 2, by the synagogue, serves **kosher** meals. (Open Sun.-Thurs. 12:30-2:30pm and 7:30-9:30pm. Fri. dinner and Sat. lunch by reservation only. March 16-Sept. 30 no Sat. dinner. Oct.-March no Sun. dinner.)

Trattoria Contadino, Via Palazzuolo, 71r. Filling, home-style meals for weary travelers. Lunch and dinner *menù* (L14,000 and L17,000). Feast on *pollo cacciatore* or the *vitello con vino.* Open Mon.-Sat. noon-2:30pm and 6-9:45pm.

Trattoria da Giorgio, Via Palazzuolo, 100r. Short on atmosphere, long on quantity. *Menù* L15,000. Dishes change daily, but try the *fettucine alfredo* if it's available. Expect to wait. Open Mon.-Sat. 11am-3pm and 7pm-midnight.

Trattoria da Zà-Zà, P. del Mercato Centrale, 26r (tel. 21 54 11). Hopping *trattoria.* Cover L2000. Open Mon.-Sat. noon-3pm and 7-11pm. Reservations suggested.

Ristorante Il Vegetariano, Via delle Ruote, 30, off Via San Gallo. Self-service restaurant offers fresh meat-free dishes (refreshingly not all cheese-dependent) to be consumed either indoors or in their peaceful bamboo garden. *Primi* L6000-7000. *Secondi* L9000-12,000. Amazing desserts L5000. Cover L2000. Open Tues.-Fri. 12:30am-3pm and 7:30pm-midnight, Sat.-Sun. 8pm-midnight.

I Latini, Via Palchetti, 6r. From the Ponte alla Carraia, walk up Via del Moro; Via Palchetti is on the right. Be prepared to wait. *Ribollita* L8000. *Stracotto alla fiorentina* L15,000. Cover L2500. Open Tues.-Sun. 12:30-2:30pm and 7:30-10:30pm.

Aquerello, Via Ghibbelina, 156r. Pseudo-Memphis 80s chic decor. Superb, offbeat food includes *tarteglione con tartufo nero* (L10,000). Lunch *menù* L15,000. Cover L3000. Open Fri.-Wed. 11am-3pm and 7pm-1am. AmEx.

Il Borgo Antico, P. Santo Spirito, 61 (tel. 21 04 37). An array of creative dishes. *Primi* L10,000. *Secondi* L15,000-25,000. Cover L3000. Reservations advised. Open Mon.-Sat. 1-2:30pm and 8-11pm; *pizzeria* until 12:30am.

Osteria Santo Spirito, P. Santo Spirito, 16r. Outdoor tables under the stars. Lively at night. Rustic, tasty *casalinga* dishes and very good wines. *Spaghetti al pesto* L8000. Open daily noon-2:30pm and 8pm-midnight.

SIGHTS

Piazza del Duomo

The red-brick dome of Florence's **duomo** is visible from virtually every part of the city. Brunelleschi directed the construction of this dome, the largest in Europe, using a revolutionary double shell with interlocking bricks that would support itself during construction. The church also boasts the world's third-longest nave, after St. Peter's in Rome and St. Paul's in London. The unique **orologio** on the cathedral's back wall, a 24-hour counter-clockwise clock designed by Paolo Uccello, runs on medieval Florentine time: midnight is set at dusk. Climb the 463 steps around the inside of the dome to the external gallery of the lantern for a fantastic view of the city. (Lantern open Mon.-Sat. 8:30am-7pm; L8000. *Duomo* open Mon.-Fri. 10am-5pm, Sat. 10am-4:45pm, Sun. 1-5pm; first Sat. of every month closes 3:30pm.)

The much older **baptistery,** just in front of the *duomo,* contains mosaics of Hell that inspired Dante, who was baptized here (open Mon.-Sat. 1:30-6pm, Sun. 9am-12:30pm; admission L3000). Florentine artists competed fiercely for the commissions to execute the baptistery's famous **bronze doors.** In 1330 Andrea Pisano left Pisa to cast the first set of doors, which now guard the south entrance. Brunelleschi (then 23 years old) and Ghiberti (then 20) were asked to work together on the doors, but Brunelleschi left in a huff shortly thereafter. Ghiberti's doors, now on the north side, use Pisano's quatrefoil frames, but he endowed his figures with more detail, depth, and movement. When Ghiberti finished these doors, after 22 years of labor, he immediately received the commission to forge the last set of doors, the **"Gates of Paradise,"** which abandon the 28-panel design for 10 large, gilded squares, each incorporating mathematical perspective to create the illusion of deep space. The *Gates of Paradise* took 28 years to complete, but the doors currently in place are only copies, as the originals have been under restoration since the 1966 flood.

Next to the *duomo* rises the 82m **campanile,** whose 414-step climb is worth the view (open April-Oct. daily 9am-6:50pm; Nov.-March 9am-5:30pm; L8000). Most of the art from inside, outside, and around the *duomo* resides in the **Museo dell'Opera di S. Maria del Fiore,** P. del Duomo, 9. Up the first flight of stairs is a late *Pietà* by Michelangelo. According to legend, in a fit of frustration he severed Christ's left arm with a hammer. The sculpture that once covered the bell tower's exterior includes Donatello's prophets and Andrea Pisano's *Progress of Man* cycle. The museum also holds four of the frames from the baptistery's *Gates of Paradise* and will eventually house the entire collection. (Open in summer Mon.-Sat. 9am-7:30pm; off-season Mon.-Sat. 9am-6pm. L8000. Look for the English tours in summer Wed.-Thurs. 4pm.)

Piazza della Signoria

Via dei Calzaiuoli, one of Florence's oldest streets, leads south from the Duomo to the intriguing **Orsanmichele** (tel. 28 47 15), built in 1337 as a granary and later converted into a church. Secular and spiritual concerns mingle in the statues along the facade. Inside, a Gothic tabernacle designed by Andrea Orcagna encases Bernardo Daddi's miraculous *Virgin* (open daily 9am-noon; free).

At the end of Via dei Calzaiuoli, in **Piazza della Signoria,** the fortress-like **Palazzo Vecchio** marks the city's civic center (open Mon.-Wed. and Fri.-Sat. 9am-7pm, Sun. 8am-1pm; L15,000). The square came into being in the 13th century with the destruction of the homes of the city's powerful Ghibelline families. In 1497, the religious leader and social critic Savonarola convinced Florentines to light the **Bonfire of the Vanities** here, a grand roast that consumed some of Florence's best art. A year later, disillusioned citizens sent Savonarola up in smoke on the same spot. Michelangelo's **David** used to stand here in self-assured perfection, but it now keeps four unfinished **Prisoners** company in the **Accademia,** Via Ricasoli, 60, northeast of the *duomo* (open Tues.-Sat. 8:30am-6:15pm, Sun. 8:30am-2pm. L12,000).

The heart of medieval Florence lies east of P. della Signoria, around the 13th-century **Bargello** in Piazza San Firenze. Once the chief magistrate's residence and then a brutal prison, the restored fortress now houses a sculpture museum, with Donatello's *David* and *Sacrifice of Isaac* panels by Ghiberti and Brunelleschi. (Open daily 9am-2pm; closed the 1st, 3rd, and 5th Sun. and 2nd and 4th Mon. of each month. L8000.)

The **Badia,** across Via del Proconsolo from the Bargello, was the site of medieval Florence's richest monastery. Note Filippo Lippi's *Apparition of the Virgin to St. Bernard,* one of the most famous paintings of the late 15th century, on the left as you enter (open Mon.-Sat. 5-7pm, Sun. 7:30-11:30am). Around the corner in Via S. Margherita is the **Casa di Dante,** a museum dedicated to the poet (open Mon.-Wed. and Sat. 10am-6pm, Sun. 10am-2pm; L5000).

The Uffizi

In May of 1993, terrorists set off a bomb in the **Uffizi** (tel. 21 83 41), killing five people and destroying priceless works of art. Some rooms are closed for security and restoration, but the museum continues to display an unparalleled collection of Renaissance works. For an extra L1600, save yourself hours by purchasing advance tickets; call 47 19 60 (credit card required) or visit the **Informazioni Turistiche Alberghiere** office, Viale Gramsci, 9a. They have another branch at the **Informazione Turistica** in the train station. (Both open Mon.-Fri. 8am-6:30pm. Uffizi open Tues.-Sat. 8:30am-6:50pm, Sun. 8:30am-1:50pm. L12,000.)

Vasari designed the Uffizi palace in 1554 for Cosimo I, Grand Duke of Tuscany, and included a **secret corridor** between Palazzo Vecchio and the Medici's Palazzo Pitti in the design. It runs through the Uffizi and over the Ponte Vecchio and houses more art. Among the masterpieces in the Uffizi are Botticelli's *Primavera* and *Birth of Venus,* Leonardo da Vinci's brilliant *Annunciation* and the equally remarkable unfinished *Adoration of the Magi,* Michelangelo's only oil painting (the *Doni Tondo*), and a clutch of Caravaggios, including both his *Sacrifice of Isaac* and a *Bacchus.*

Piazza della Repubblica and Santa Maria Novella

The starkly Neoclassical **Piazza della Repubblica** replaced the Mercato Vecchio as the site of the town market in 1890. The inscription *"Antico centro della città, da secolare squalore, a vita nuova restituito"* ("The ancient center of the city, squalid for centuries, restored to new life") epitomizes that determinedly progressive age. The statue in the center is a pillar erected by Donatello with a later statue representing *Abundance,* sculpted by a lesser artist, crowning its top. The pricey **Gilli,** perhaps Florence's most famous coffeehouse, was established in this area in 1733.

As Florence's 15th-century economy expanded, its bankers and merchants showed off their new wealth by erecting palaces grander than any seen before. The great Quattrocento boom commenced with the construction of the **Palazzo Davanzati,** Via Porta Rossa, 13. Today the palazzo has been reincarnated as the **Museo della Casa**

Fiorentina Antica (tel. 21 65 18) and illustrates the lives of affluent 15th-century merchants (due to reopen in 1998, so call ahead; L5000).

The Medici staked out an entire portion of the city north of the *duomo* in which to build their own church, the spacious **Basilica of San Lorenzo,** and the **Palazzo Medici.** San Lorenzo was designed by Brunelleschi in 1419. Michelangelo designed the church's exterior but moved to Rome instead of finishing it, so the facade stands bare. Inside the basilica, two massive bronze pulpits by Donatello command the nave (church open daily 8am-noon and 5:30-6pm). To reach the **Chapels of the Medici,** walk around to the back entrance on P. Madonna degli Aldobrandini. Michelangelo's **New Sacristy** (1524) is a starkly simple architectural design reflecting the master's study of Brunelleschi. (Open daily 9am-2pm; closed the 2nd and 4th Sun. and 1st, 3rd, and 5th Mon. each month. L10,000.)

Frescoes covered the interior of the **Church of Santa Maria Novella,** near the train station, until the Medici commissioned Vasari to paint some in their honor and then ordered the other walls whitewashed so their rivals would not be remembered. The **Cappella di Filippo Strozzi,** to the right of the high altar, contains frescoes by Filippo Lippi, including an excruciatingly accurate *Torture of St. John the Evangelist.*

Oltrarno

Historically disdained by downtown Florentines, the far side of the Arno remains a lively, unpretentious quarter. Start your tour a few blocks west of P. Santo Spirito at the **Church of Santa Maria del Carmine.** Inside, the **Brancacci Chapel** houses a group of 15th-century frescoes that were declared masterpieces even in their own time. Note especially the *Expulsion from Paradise* and *The Tribute Money* (open Mon. and Wed.-Sat. 10am-4:30pm, Sun. 1-4:30pm; L5000).

Brunelleschi originally planned an exciting four-aisled nave encircled by hollow chapels for the **Church of Santo Spirito.** However, he died before the project was completed, and the plans were altered to make the building more conventional. Nonetheless, it remains a masterpiece of Renaissance harmony, similar to but less busy than San Lorenzo (open daily 8am-noon and 4-6pm).

Luca Pitti, a *nouveau-riche* banker of the 15th century, built his *palazzo* east of Santo Spirito. Today, the **Pitti Palace** houses no fewer than seven museums. The **Museo degli Argenti** on the ground floor displays Medici's gems, ivories, silver pieces, and Lorenzo's famous collection of vases. (Open daily 9am-2pm; closed the 1st, 3rd, and 5th Mon. and 2nd and 4th Sun. of each month.) The **Museum of Costumes** displays more items from the Medici fortune (same hours as Museo degli Argenti; L8000 gets you into both). The **Royal Apartments** on the main floor preserve the furnishings from the residence of the Royal House of Savoy, together with a few Medici treasures (open Tues.-Sat. 8:30am-7pm, Sun. 8:30am-2pm; L12,000). The amazingly ornate **Galleria Palatina** was one of only a handful of galleries when it opened in 1833. Today its eclectic collection includes a number of Raphaels and works by Titian, Andrea del Sarto, Rosso, Caravaggio, and Rubens (open Tues.-Sat. 8:30am-7pm, Sun. 8:30am-2pm; L12,000). Inside the **Galleria d'Arte Moderna** hides one of the big surprises of Italian art: the early 19th-century proto-Impressionist works of the Macchiaioli school (same hours as Museo degli Argenti; L4000).

The elaborately landscaped **Boboli Gardens** behind the palace stretch to the hilltop **Forte del Belvedere,** once the Medici fortress and treasury. Ascend Via di Costa San Giorgio (off P. Santa Felicità, to the left after crossing Ponte Vecchio) to reach the fort, an unusual construction with a central *loggia* designed by Ammannati. (Gardens open June-July daily 9am-7:30pm; April-May and Sept.-Oct. 9am-6:30pm; Nov.-Feb. 9am-4:30pm; March 9am-5:30pm. Closed the first and last Mon. of each month. L4000. Fort open in summer daily 9am-10pm; off-season 9am-5pm.)

ENTERTAINMENT

For reliable information on what's hot and what's not, consult the monthly *Firenze Spettacolo* (L2700). The area around P. Santo Spirito hops with a good selection of bars and cafés, while locals strut their stuff along Via dei Calzaiuoli.

Lo Sfizzio, Lungarno Cellini, 1. Watering hole of the bombed and the beautiful, who carouse over colossal drinks on the outdoor terrace. Open daily 8pm-1am.

The Red Garter, Via dei Benci, 33r. A raucous mix of American students, Italian youth, flying peanut shells, and classic American rock. If you have what it takes, they might even let you on stage. Open nightly, happy hour 8:30pm.

Auditorium Flog, Via Mercati, 24. *The* hottest place in Florence for live rock and jazz. Come in your skin-tight metallic blue catsuit.

Angie's Pub, Via dei Neri, 35r. Caters mostly to students, remaining generally uncrowded in summer. Imported beer and cider on tap start at L4000 per glass. Sandwiches anytime of day. Open Tues.-Sat. 12:30-3pm and 7pm-1am.

Betty Boop, Via Alfani, 26r. Live jazz and rock give way to cabaret on Thurs. and Sun. You'll need to get a "membership" at the door. It's not annoyingly exclusive—just leave the sneakers at home. Closed Mon.

Tabasco Gay Club, P. Santa Cecilia, 3r, in a tiny alleyway across P. della Signoria from the Palazzo Vecchio. Popular gay disco. Min. age 18. Cover L15,000-25,000. Open Tues.-Sun. 10pm-3am.

Festivals

Every June, the various *quartieri* of the city turn out in costume to play the city's medieval version of soccer, **Calcio Storico.** Two teams of 27 players face off over a wooden ball in one of the city's *piazze.* Tickets start at L20,000 and are sold at the Chiosco degli Sportivi (tel. 29 23 63), Via dei Anselmi. Real games occur at the **stadio,** north of the city center. Buy tickets (from L20,000) from the bar opposite the stadium. May welcomes the classical festival **Maggio Musicale.** On June 24, the festival of **St. John the Baptist** features a fireworks display from P. Michelangelo. The **Estate Fiesolana** (June-Aug.) fills the Roman theater in nearby Fiesole with concerts, opera, theater, ballet, and film. *Funghi*-lovers should check out the annual **Festa dei Porcini,** a three-day long mushroom festival in August. The **Festa del Grillo** (Festival of the Cricket) is held the first Sunday after Ascension Day—crickets in tiny wooden cages are hawked in the Cascine park to be released into the grass. In September, Florence hosts the **Festa dell'Unità,** an organized music and concert series at Campi Bisenzio (take bus 30). The **Florence Film Festival** is generally held in December.

Siena

After centuries of often violent rivalry with its neighbors, especially the Florentines, Siena today shines peacefully amidst its more touristed sibling cities. The city lingers complacently as a living masterpiece. Even in Italy, few places are as aesthetically harmonious. The salmon-colored, shell-shaped **Piazza del Campo** is the focus of Sienese life. At the bottom of the shell is the **Palazzo Pubblico,** a graceful Gothic palace over which soars the **Torre del Mangia** clock tower, named for the gluttonous bellringer Mangiaguadagni (literally, "eat the profits"). Inside, the **Museo Civico** contains excellent Gothic painting; the **Sala del Mappamondo** and the **Sala della Pace** have particularly stellar works. (Palazzo and museum open March-Oct. Mon.-Sat. 9am-6:15pm, Sun. 9am-12:45pm; Nov.-Feb. daily 9am-12:45pm. L6000, students L5000. Torre del Mangia open July-Aug. daily 9:30am-7:30pm; May and Sept. 10am-6pm; April and Oct. to mid-Nov. 10am-5pm; March and Nov.-Dec. 10am-6pm. L5000.)

The construction of Siena's **duomo** spanned two architectural eras, incorporating Romanesque arches and Gothic pinnacles. The **pulpit** is one of Andrea Pisano's best, with allegorical and biblical reliefs, and the **baptistery** has carvings by some of greatest of Italian sculptors. The lavish **Libreria Piccolomini,** off the left aisle, holds frescoes by Pinturicchio and 15th-century illuminated musical scores. (Duomo open mid-March to Oct. 7:30am-7:30pm; Nov. to mid-March 7:30am-1:30pm and 2:30-5pm. Library open mid-March to Oct. 9am-7:30pm; Nov. to mid-March 10am-1pm and 2:30-5pm. L2000. Proper dress required.) The **Museo dell'Opera della Metropolitana,** next to the cathedral, displays the foremost Gothic statuary of Italy by Giovanni Pisano, as well as Duccio di Buoninsegna's splendid Maestà, and an exhilarating view of Siena and Tuscany from the parapet. (Open mid-March to early Nov. 9am-7:30pm; Nov. to mid-March 9am-1:30pm. L5000.)

All day during the **Palio di Siena,** July 2 and August 16, Sienese parade around in 15th-century costume. The central event is a traditional bare-back horse race around the packed P. del Campo. Get there three days early to watch the rambunctious horse selection in the *campo* (10am) and to pick a *contrada* (neighborhood) to root for. The night before the race everyone revels until 3am or so, strutting and chanting their way around the city, pausing only to eat and drink. You can stand in the "infield" of the *piazza* for free, but access closes early, so stake out a spot early in the day. For tickets and a list of rooms-to-let write to the tourist office by March; arrive without a reservation and you'll be sleeping on the streets.

Practical Information, Accommodations, and Food Siena lies off the main Florence-Rome **rail line.** Direct trains run from Florence (L8000), but from Rome you must change at Chiusi (L20,800). Take any bus passing across the street from the station to the center of town (L1400), or prepare for a 45-minute uphill trek. Express TRA-IN/SITA **buses,** faster than the train, link Siena with Florence (L10,500) and other Tuscan destinations. The **tourist office,** Il Campo, 56 (tel. (0577) 28 05 51), provides info on local sights, hotels, and other Tuscan towns. (Open in summer Mon.-Sat. 8:30am-7:30pm, Sun. 8am-2pm; off-season Mon.-Sat. 8:30am-1:30pm and 3:30-7pm.) Finding a room in Siena is usually simple, but call a few days ahead during July and August and months ahead for either Palio. The rather inconveniently located **Ostello della Gioventù "Guidoriccio" (HI),** Via Fiorentina, 89 (tel. (0577) 522 12; fax 561 72), in Località Lo Stellino, is a 20-minute ride on bus 15 across from the station at P. Gramsci; if coming from Florence by bus, get off at the stop just after the large black-and-white sign announcing entry into Siena (curfew 11:30pm; L20,000; breakfast included). **Alma Domus,** Via Camporegio, 37 (tel. (0577) 441 77; fax 476 01), behind San Domenico, is a spotless establishment with fantastic views of the *duomo.* (Reception open daily from 7:30am. Curfew 11:30pm. Doubles L60,000-80,000; triples L100,000; quads L125,000.) **Locanda Garibaldi,** Via Giovanni Dupré, 18 (tel. (0577) 28 42 04), behind the Palazzo Publico and P. del Campo, is homey (curfew midnight; doubles L75,000, triples L90,000).

Siena specializes in rich pastries, most notably *panforte,* a concoction of honey, almonds, and citron. Sample it at **Bar/Pasticceria Nannini,** Via Banchi di Sopra, 22-24. Pick up supplies at the **Consortio Agrario supermarket,** Via Pianigiani, 5, off P. Salimberi (open Mon.-Fri. 7:45am-1pm and 4:30-8pm, Sat. 7:45am-1pm). **Mensa Universitaria,** Via Sant' Agata, 1, has full meals for L10,000 and pasta for L4000-7000 (open Mon.-Sun. noon-2pm and 6;45-9pm; closed Aug.). **La Nuova del Gallo Nero,** Via del Porrione, 65-7, serves medieval Tuscan dishes in a *menú assaggio,* which allows varied sampling (from L25,000; open Tues.-Sun. noon-2:30pm and 7pm-1am).

■ Near Siena

Only an hour from Siena by bus (L7900), the medieval towers of **San Gimignano** reach skyward. The towers and the walled *centro* testify to a 13th-century building competition between San Gimignano's wealthiest families. Of the original 72 edifices, 14 remain. Scale the **Torre Grossa,** the tallest of the remaining towers, attached to **Palazzo del Popolo,** for a panorama of Tuscany. (Torre open March-Oct. daily 9:30am-7:30pm; Nov.-Feb. Tues.-Sun. 9:30am-1:30pm and 2:30-4:30pm. L6000-8000. Palazzo open Tues.-Sun. 9am-7:30pm.) In Torre Grossa's shadow, the **Museo Civico** houses an amazing collection of Sienese and Florentine works, most notably Lippi's *Annunciation* (open same hours as the tower; L5000-7000). The hostel, **Ostello di San Gimignano,** P. Repubblica, 1 (tel. (0577) 94 19 91), is refreshingly peaceful. (Reception open daily 7-9am and 5-11:30pm. L20,000-22,000. Sheets and breakfast included.) *Affitte camere* (singles around L60,000) are another alternative to overpriced hotels. Get a list from either the **tourist office,** P. del Duomo, 1 (tel. (0577) 94 00 08), or the **Associazione Strutture Extralberghiere,** P. della Cisterna, 6 (tel.

(0577) 94 31 90; open daily 9am-8pm). **Albergo/Ristorante Il Pino,** Via S. Matteo, 102 (tel. (0577) 94 04 15), offers simple rooms in a quiet quarter near the convent (doubles L70,000). Pitch a tent at **Il Boschetto,** at Santa Lucia (tel. (0577) 94 03 52), 2½km downhill from Porta San Giovanni. Buses run from town to the site (L1400), but it's not a bad hike. (Reception open daily 8am-1pm, 3-8pm, and 9-11pm. L7500 per person, L7000 per small tent. Open April-Oct. 15.) Find take-out fare at the **market,** Via S. Matteo, 19 (open Mon.-Sat. 8am-1:30pm and 4-8pm).

If you've had it with city-hopping, soak in a few days of sun and swimming just off the coast of Tuscany on the island of **Elba,** where Napoleon spent his exile. Take the train to **Piombino Marittima,** where you can hop on one of the frequent Toremar or Navarma **ferries** (about 16 per day, 1hr., L9000-18,000). Talk directly to Toremar (tel. (0565) 91 80 80) or Navarma (tel. (0565) 22 12 12) at Piazzale Premuda, 13, in Piombino. The **APT tourist office** is at Calata Italia, 26 (tel. (0565) 91 46 71), across from the Toremar boat landing (open in summer daily 8am-8pm; off-season Mon.-Sat. 8am-1pm and 3-6pm). Avoid over-crowded Elba in July and August.

Pisa

Tourism wasn't always Pisa's prime industry: throughout the Middle Ages this city was a major port with an empire extending to Corsica, Sardinia, and the Balearics. But when the Arno River silted up, the city's power and wealth declined accordingly. Today, the city resigns itself to welcoming tourists and countless t-shirt and ice cream vendors to the **Piazza del Duomo,** also known as the **Campo dei Miracoli** (Field of Miracles), a grassy expanse on the northern side of the Arno where most of the major attractions are located. A L17,000 ticket admits you to the Campo's sights.

The famous **Leaning Tower** continues to slip 1-2mm every year. Although many tourists come to Pisa simply to marvel at the tower's odd appearance, more perceptive visitors also note that it is a prime example of the innovative architecture of the Pisan Romanesque period. Unfortunately, visitors are no longer allowed to enter the tower. Also on the Campo, the dazzling **duomo** is a treasury of fine art, including Giovanni Pisano's greatest pulpit (open Mon.-Sat. 10am-7:45pm and Sun. 1-7:45pm; L2000). Next door is the **baptistery,** where precision acoustics allow an unamplified choir to be heard 20km away (open in summer daily 8am-7:30pm; off-season 9am-4:40pm). The adjoining **Camposanto,** a long, white-walled cemetery, has many classical sarcophagi and a series of haunting frescoes by an unidentified 14th-century artist known only as the "Master of the Triumph of Death" (open daily 9am-5:40pm; off-season 9am-4:40pm). The **Museo delle Sinopie,** across the square from the Camposanto, displays *sinopie* (preliminary fresco sketches) discovered during restoration after World War II (open daily 8am-7:30pm; off-season 9am-12:30pm and 3-4:30pm), while the **Museo dell'Opera del Duomo,** behind the Tower, displays artworks from three buildings of the P. del Duomo (open daily 8am-7:30pm; off-season 9am-12:30pm and 3-4:30pm). One hidden treasure in town is the Gothic church of **Santa Maria della Spina,** which faces Lungarno Gambacorti against the river. Its bell tower allegedly holds a thorn from Christ's crown.

Practical Information, Accommodations, and Food The **tourist office,** P. della Stazione (tel. (050) 422 91), to your left as you exit the station, doles out maps (open Mon.-Sat. 8am-8pm, Sun. 9am-1pm). There's a **branch office** (tel. (050) 56 04 64) at P. del Duomo in the Museo dell'Opera (open April-Oct. daily 8am-8pm; Nov.-March 9am-5:30pm). **Trains** run to Florence every hour (1hr., L7200) from P. della Stazione (tel. (050) 413 85), in the southern part of town; the main coastal line links Pisa to Genoa and Rome.

The **Centro Turistico Madonna dell'Acqua** hostel, Via Pietrasantina, 15 (tel. (050) 89 06 22), awaits beneath an old sanctuary. Take bus 3 from the station and ask to be let off at the *ostello* (reception open daily 6-11pm; singles L30,000, doubles L40,000). The **Albergo Gronchi,** P. Archivescovado, 1 (tel. (050) 56 18 23), just off P. del Duomo, has frescoed ceilings and a pretty garden (singles L32,000, doubles L52,000, triples L70,000). The **Casa della Giovane (ACISG),** Via F. Corridoni, 29 (tel. (050) 430 61), a 10-minute walk from the station (turn right immediately), offers beds to women only (curfew 10pm; doubles and triples L25,000; bath included). **Campeggio Torre Pendente,** Viale delle Cascine, 86, is 1km away. Follow the signs from P. Manin (L10,000 per person, L3500-6000 per tent; open Easter-Oct. 15).

For more authentic restaurants than those by the touristy *duomo,* head to the river or university area. Pisans prefer the **open-air market** in P. Vettovaglie. At **Trattoria da Matteo,** Via l'Aroncio, 46, off Via S. Maria, *ravioli* goes for L7000 and pizza starts at L6500 (open Sun.-Fri. noon-3pm and 7-10:30pm). Walk between the legs of the Palazzo d'Orlogio and turn right to reach the **Mensa Universitaria,** Via Martiri; one ticket (L5400) buys two filling meals (open daily noon-2pm and 7-9pm).

UMBRIA

Christened the "Green Heart of Italy," Umbria has enjoyed renown since ancient times for its wooded hills, valleys, and riverbanks. Often shrouded in an ethereal silvery haze, the landscape has enticed mystics from St. Benedict to Umbria's most famous visionary, the nature-adoring ascetic St. Francis. Generations of visual artists also clambered about these hills, among them Giotto, Signorelli, and Perugino.

Perugia

The extremely polite residents of Perugia may be trying to make up for two millennia of excessive nastiness, during which Perugians regularly stoned each other and even threw tree-hugging St. Francis of Assisi into a dungeon. The city earns more dubious fame as the birthplace of the Flagellants, who wandered Europe whipping themselves, and as the site of two popes' death by poisoning. But Perugia now attracts visitors with steep medieval streets and mellow university atmosphere, a world-class jazz festival in July, and irresistible chocolate *baci* (kisses).

The city's most noteworthy sights frame **Piazza IV Novembre.** The **Fontant Maggiore,** in the center is adorned with sculptures and bas-reliefs by Nicolà and Giovanni Pisano. The 13th-century **Palazzo dei Priori** presides over the *piazza* and shelters the **Galleria Nazionale dell'Umbria,** Corso Vannucci, 19. Inside, the immense collection includes fine works by Fra Angelico, Piero della Francesca, and a definitive collection of Umbrian art. Perugino's *Adoration of the Magi* is the gallery's premiere piece (open Mon.-Sat. 9am-7pm, Sun. 9am-1pm; L8000). Perugia's austere Gothic **duomo** looms at the end of the *piazza;* its facade was never completed because the *Perugini* were forced to return the marble they had stolen to build it. At the far end of Corso Vannucci, the well-tended **Giardini Carducci** offer a broad view of the Umbrian countryside. Around the gardens and down Via Marzia, stands the 16th-century fortress, the **Rocca Paolina,** built by Sangallo.

Practical Information, Accommodations, and Food The **tourist office,** P. IV Novembre (tel. (075) 572 53 41 or 572 33 27), offers info on accommodations and the jazz festival (open Mon.-Sat. 8:30am-1:30pm and 3:30-6:30pm, Sun. 9am-1pm). The **train station,** P. Veneto, serves Assisi (25min., L3400), Rome via Terontola (3hr., L25,400), and Florence (2½hr., L20,700). From the station, city buses 28, 29, 36 and 42 make the trip to town (L1000). To get to the **Ostello della Gioventù/Centro Internazionale di Accoglienza per la Gioventù,** Via Bontempi, 13 (tel. (075) 572 28 80), from Pl. Italia, walk to Pl. IV Novembre, continue through Pl. Dante, taking the furthest street to the right through pl. Piccinio, and right again onto Via Bontempi. (Curfew midnight. L15,000. Showers included. Sheets L2000. Open mid-Jan. to mid-Dec.) The clean, cool rooms in **Albergo Anna,** Via dei Priori, 48, 4th fl. (tel. (075) 573 63 04), off Corso Vannucci, offer great views of the city (singles L37,000-56,000, doubles L56,000-75,000). **Paradis d'Ete** (tel. (075) 517 21 17), 5km away in Colle della Trinità, has hot showers and a pool at no extra charge. Take bus 36 from the station (L7000 per person, L6000 per tent).

Trattoria Dal Mi Cocco, Corso Garibaldi, 12, writes its menu in a Perugian dialect, but enjoys well-deserved popularity (L24,000 *menù;* open Tues.-Sun. 1-2:30pm and 8:15-10:30pm). **L'Oca Nera,** Via dei Priori, 78/82, serves everything from *gnocchi* to burgers (around L6500; open Thurs.-Tues. 7:30pm-1am). Though renowned for chocolate, Perugia also serves up a variety of delectable breads and pastries; try **Ceccarani,** P. Matteotti, 16 (open Mon.-Sat. 7:30am-2pm and 4:30-8pm), or the **Co.Fa.Pa.** bakery two doors down (open Mon.-Sat. 7:30am-1pm and 5-7:30pm). **Pasticceria Sandri,** Corso Vannucci, 32, serves local confections amid old-world elegance (open Mon.-Sat. 7:30am-8pm).

Assisi

Assisi's serenity originates with the legacy of St. Francis, the eco-friendly monk who preached poverty, obedience, and love eight centuries ago. After his death in 1226, Florentine and Sienese painters decorated the **Basilica di San Francesco** with a spectacular ensemble of frescoes illustrating his life. The upper level is elaborate and sumptuously decorated, while the lower level, built around the crypt housing the saint's tomb, is more modest. The walls of the church are almost completely covered with Giotto's *Life of St. Francis* fresco cycle. (Open daily sunrise to sunset; closed on Holy Days. English-language Mass Sat. and Sun. 6:30pm. English tours Mon.-Sat. 10am and 3pm. Modest dress. No photography.) Towering above town, the restored fortress **Rocca Maggiore** overwhelms with huge proportions and tremendous views. (Open in summer daily 10am-dusk; off-season 10am-4pm; closed in bad weather. L5000, students L3500.) On the other side of Assisi stands the **Basilica of Santa Chiara,** where St. Francis attended school and St. Clare now rests (open Mon.-Sat. 6:30am-noon and 2-7pm; in winter closes 6pm).

ITALY

Assisi is on the Foligno-Terontola **rail** line; trains go to Perugia (L2900), Florence, Rome (direct at 6:04pm, L25,500, also via Foligno), and Ancona (via Foligno, L12,000). **Buses** run to Perugia (L4900) and other Umbrian towns. The **tourist office,** P. del Comune, 12 (tel. (075) 81 25 34), offers an accommodations service and posts train and bus schedules outside. (Open Mon.-Fri. 8am-2pm and 3:30-6:30pm, Sat. 9am-1pm and 3:30-6:30pm, Sun. 9am-1pm.) The tremendous **Ostello della Pace (HI),** Via San Pietro Campagna (tel./fax (075) 81 67 67), has large rooms and spotless bathrooms (reception open daily 7-9:15am and 3:30-11:30pm; L20,000). From the top of P. Matteotti, Via Eremo leads to the Porta Cappuccini and the superb **Ostello Fontemaggio,** Via per l'Eremo delle Carceri. (Tel. (075) 81 36 36. L17,000. Breakfast L5000. Camping L7000 per person, L6000 per tent.) **Albergo Anfiteatro Romano,** Via Anfiteatro Romano, 4 (tel. (075) 81 30 25), and **Albergo Italia,** Vicolo della Fortezza (tel. (075) 81 26 25), both offer comfortable singles for L28,000-35,000 and doubles for L49,000-50,000. **Pizzeria Otello,** Via Sant'Antonio, 1, off P. del Comune, is a great deal (open 7:30am-11pm).

THE MARCHES (LE MARCHE)

Urbino

With humble stone dwellings huddled around an immense turreted palace, Urbino's fairy tale skyline has changed little over the past 500 years. The city's most remarkable monument is the Renaissance **Palazzo Ducale** (Ducal Palace), celebrated in Italy as "the most beautiful in the world." The interior **courtyard** testifies to the Renaissance interest in balance and proportion; to the left, a monumental staircase leads to the private apartments of the Duke, which now house the **National Gallery of the Marches.** Among the works here are Piero della Francesca's *Flagellation of Christ,*

Berruguete's famous portrait of Duke Federico, Raphael's *Portrait of a Lady,* and Paolo Uccello's tiny, strange *Profanation of the Host.* The most intriguing room of the palace is the Duke's study on the second floor, where inlaid wooden panels give the illusion of real books and shelves covered with astronomical and musical instruments. Don't leave the palace without heading underground to see the well-documented "works" of the *palazzo.* The meandering maze includes the Duke's baths, kitchen, washroom, and freezer (entire palace open daily 9am-2pm; L8000).

At the end of Via Barocci lies the 14th-century **Oratorio di San Giovanni Battista,** decorated with brightly colored Gothic frescoes representing events from the life of St. John. (Open Mon.-Sat. 10am-noon and 3-5pm, Sun. 10am-12:30pm. L3000, but you will be obliged to see S. Giuseppe next door for another L2000.) **Raphael's house,** Via Raffaello, 57, is now a vast and delightful museum with period furnishings. His earliest work, a fresco entitled *Madonna e Bambino,* hangs in the *sala* (open March-Oct. Mon.-Sat. 9am-1pm and 3-7pm, Sun.10am-1pm; L5000).

Practical Information, Accommodations, and Food The SAPUM **bus** from Pesaro (on the main Bologna-Lecce line along the Adriatic coast) to Urbino is cheap and direct (1hr., L3700). After winding up steep hills, the bus will deposit you at Borgo Mercatale; from here, a short uphill walk leads to **Piazza della Repubblica,** the heart of the city. The **tourist office,** P. Rinascimento, 1 (tel. (0722) 26 13; fax 24 41), across from the palace, distributes a list of hotels and a map. (Open Mon.-Sat. 9am-1pm and 3-6pm, Sun. 9am-1pm; off-season Mon.-Sat. 8:30am-2pm.)

Cheap lodging is rare in Urbino, so reservations are essential. **Pensione Fosca,** Via Raffaello, 67 (tel. (0722) 32 96 22 or 25 42), has charming rooms with high ceilings (singles L35,000-39,000, doubles L50,000-55,000). **Hotel San Giovanni,** Via Barocci, 13 (tel. (0722) 28 27), has a restaurant downstairs (singles L35,000-53,000, doubles L50,000-80,000; closed July). Pitch your tent 2km from the city walls at **Camping Pineta,** Via San Donato (tel./fax (0722) 47 10), in Cesane; take bus 7 from Borgo Mercatale and tell the driver your destination (L8500 per person, L16,500 per tent; open April to mid-Sept.). Many *paninoteche, gelaterie,* and burger joints cluster around P. della Repubblica. **Morgana,** Via Nuova, 3 (open daily noon-3pm and 7pm-12:30am), and **Pizzeria Le Tre Piante,** Via Foro Posterula, 1, off Via Budassi (open daily noon-3pm and 7pm-2am), serves delicious pizzas (L5000-10,000) and other dishes. Shop for supplies at the supermarket **Margherita,** Via Raffaello, 37 (open Mon.-Sat. 7am-2pm and 4:30-8pm). At night, students enjoy music and drinks at the **University ACLI,** Via Santa Chiona.

ADRIATIC PORTS

Ancona, Bari, and Brindisi—all on the Bologna-Lecce train line—are Italy's principal departure points for Greece, Cyprus, and Israel.

Ancona Roman Emperor Trajan recognized Ancona's value as a trade center in the first century AD. History has proven him right, although today's cargo consists of tired, ferry-borne tourists, not spices and silks. **Trains** arrive at P. Rosseli from Rome and all points along the Bologna-Lecce rail line. From the station, take bus 1 to P. Cavour in the center of town (10min., L1200); from here, Corso Garibaldi and Corso Mazzini lead to the port. Detailed **ferry** schedules are available at the **Stazione Marittima,** on the waterfront just off P. Kennedy. All the ferry lines operate ticket and information booths. Make reservations for travel in July or August, and always arrive at the station at least two hours before departure. The main lines are: **Marlines** (tel. (071) 20 25 66; fax 411 77 80), **Minoan/Strintzis** (tel. (071) 20 17 08; fax 56 00 09), **ANEK** (tel. (071) 207 32 22; fax 546 08), **Jadrolinija** (tel. (071) 20 45 16; fax 562 56), **SEM Maritime Co.** (tel. (071) 552 18; fax 20 26 18), **Superfast** (tel. (071) 20 20 33; fax 20 22 19), and **Adriatica** (tel. (071) 20 49 15; fax 20 22 96).

In summer, people waiting for ferries often spend the night at the Stazione Marittima, but you'll find lots of reasonably priced hotels past the train station in the town center. Make reservations or arrive early in the summer. **Pensione Centrale,** Via Marsala, 10 (tel. (071) 543 88), one block from P. Roma, is a quick 10-minute stroll from the Stazione Marittima (singles L35,000; doubles L50,000, with bath L80,000). **Hotel Cavour,** Viale della Vittoria, 7 (tel. (071) 20 03 74), one block from P. Cavour, has large singles for L40,000 and doubles from L70,000. The supermarket **SIDIS,** Via Matteotti, 115, offers the best grocery deals around. (Open Mon.-Wed. and Fri.-Sat. 8:15am-12:45pm and 5-7:30pm, Thurs. 8:15am-12:45pm.)

Bari The capital of Apulia, Bari is a vibrant modern city, home to a university, historic sights, and the world's friendliest backpacker welcoming committee. **Stop-Over in Bari** (summer hotline (080) 577 23 49) lures backpackers by doling out irresistible amounts of **free stuff,** including city bus passes, bicycle rentals, luggage storage, hotel reservations, campsites with tents and showers, excursions, seminars and concerts, and **Internet access.** At their dapper **information bus** outside the train station, hip, multilingual gen-Xers will tell you everything known about city sights and attractions. Be especially careful of pickpockets and petty thieves in the old city. Bari is connected by **train** to Rome (8hr., L37,000), Milan (10hr., L65,400), and Brindisi (2hr., L9800). There are no discounts for Eurailpass holders, but **Ventouris Ferries** (tel. (080) 524 43 88) has student rates.

To party in Bari, Brits chat with the expat owners of **Bohémian,** Via de Napoli, 17, Americans drink up with a 10-foot Statue of Liberty at the **Charles Wells,** Via Caroulli, 56, Irish enjoy Guinness stout on tap at **Joy's Shop,** Corso Sonino, 118, and Aussies head to **Castelmaine,** Via DeFarraris, 49b, where the bar is a 15-foot boomerang. Local students cram into **Largo Adua** and the other *piazzas* along the Lunomare, where the **Kyb Cafe** hosts a Spanish party every Tuesday. Most bars are open from around 8pm until 1 or 2am, 3am on Saturdays, and close down during the August holidays. Near Bari, **Alberobello's** famous *trulli* (mortarless conical roofs) and the **Castellana Grotte** are worth a daytrip (by train 1hr., L5700).

ITALY

Brindisi Every year, about a million Eurailers get off the train at Brindisi, walk to the port, and catch a boat to Greece. If you're one of them, arrive at the station in the afternoon, as the ferries leave in the evening. **Trains** journey from Naples (6hr., L47,900), Rome via Barletta (7hr., L47,700), and Milan via Ancona and Bologna (12hr., L72,400). **Corso Umberto,** a frenetic jumble of ferry offices and tourist restaurants, runs straight out from the station 1km to the port, turning into **Corso Garibaldi** midway. The *stazione marittima* is on the right at the end, the **tourist office** a block to the left, at Via Regina Margherita, 5 (open Mon.-Fri. 8am-2pm, Tues. also 3-6:30pm). For Eurailers, **Adriatica,** Via Regina Margherita, 13 (tel. (0831) 59 04 71) and **Hellenic Mediterranean Lines,** Corso Garibaldi, 8 (tel. (0831) 52 85 31), offer free deck passage on a space-available basis to Corfu (10hr.), Patras (20hr.), and Igoumenitsa (12hr.). At their offices on the main drag, pay the L29,000 **port tax** (L10,000 Sept. 11-June 9), pick up your ticket, and be sure to clear your passport with the police at the port before you leave. Non-Eurailers can buy tickets from one of the many competing lines—expect to pay L40,000-80,000 and check for departures outside the **American Express Office** at Corso Umberto, 1 (tel. (0831) 56 38 34). Stock up at the **Sidis** supermarket on C. Garibaldi near the port. Bring warm clothes or a sleeping bag and check the weather—deck passage loses its appeal when it's pouring. During August, consider arriving early or buying a reservation in another city. Board the ferry two hours in advance.

Brindisi quiets down two blocks from the frenzied C. Umberto. A pleasant walk along the water to the left of C. Garibaldi leads to a staircase with a column marking the end of the **Appian way;** ascending the stairs and continuing straight takes you to P. del Duomo and Brindisi's **archaeological museum** (open Mon.-Fri. 9:30am-1:30pm, Tues. also 3:30-6:30pm; free). Or, call **Ostello della Gioventù "Brindisi"** (tel. (0831) 41 31 23), 3km away in Casale, where you can get a room for the day

(L9,000). After they've picked you up, you can leave luggage, do laundry, nap, check email, and take the shuttle to the beach before getting a ride back to the port. Stay the night for L18,000 with breakfast and sheets. In town, try **Albergo Venezia,** Via Pisanelli (tel. (0831) 52 75 11; L25,000). At **Pub La Tortuga,** Via C. Colombo, 55, you can eat cheap pizza in an ivy-covered garden amid Roman ruins, or in a dungeon under the city walls (open daily noon-4am). If stuck in Brindisi, make a daytrip by train to **Lecce,** with its distinctive Baroque architecture made from soft local stone (every 30min., 30min., L3400).

SOUTHERN ITALY

South of Rome, the sun gets brighter, the meals longer, and the passions more intense. Though long subject to the negative stereotypes and prejudices of the more industrialized North, the so-called "Mezzogiorno" (midday) region remains justly proud of its open-hearted and generous populace, strong traditions, classical ruins, and enchanting, relatively untouristed beaches.

Naples (Napoli)

Naples has gotten a bad rap. True, mopeds race down sidewalks like they were streets, stoplights are taken as mere suggestions, and markets are mile-long hordes of shoppers and shouting merchants. Yet somehow the Neapolitans thrive on this chaos. The city has an almost palpable vitality; you can see it at the street markets off Piazza Dante, and taste it in the world's best pizza. If you're patient with Naples' rough edges, and there are many, you will be rewarded with great food, superb museums, and wonderful Renaissance and Baroque churches.

ORIENTATION AND PRACTICAL INFORMATION

Naples is on the west coast of Italy, two hours south of Rome. The main train and bus terminals cram immense **Piazza Garibaldi,** on the east side of Naples. Broad **Corso Umberto I** leads southwest ending at **P. Bovio.** From here Via Depretis leads left to **P. Municipio,** the city center, and **Molo Beverello** ferry port. **Via Toledo** leads up from regal **P. Plebiscito** through the picturesque Spanish quarter and **Piazza Dante,** to **P. Museo.** The narrow streets in the historical area between P. Garibaldi and Via Toledo— densely packed with *piazze,* churches, and monuments, are the best place to start a tour. Along the coast past P. Plebiscito, you'll find the **Santa Lucia** and **Mergellina** districts and the public gardens, **Villa Comunale.**

While violence is rare in Naples, petty theft is relatively common (unless you're in the mafia, in which case the opposite is true). Always be careful. Young women walking alone or in groups are harassed; travel in mixed company whenever possible.

Tourist Office: EPT (tel. 26 87 79), at the central train station. English spoken. Helps with hotels and ferries. Pick up *Qui Napoli* and a free city map. Open Mon.-Sat. 8am-8pm. **Main office,** P. Martiri, 58 (tel. 40 53 11). Open Mon.-Fri. 8:30am-8pm, Sun. 8am-2pm. **AAST information office,** P. Gesù Nuovo (tel. 552 33 28); on the R1 bus line. Open Mon.-Sat. 9am-8pm, Sun. 9am-2pm.

Consulates: U.K., Via Crispi, 122 (tel. 66 35 110). Metro: P. Amedeo. Open Mon.-Fri. 8am-1:30pm. **U.S.,** P. della Repubblica (tel. 583 81 11 or 761 43 03, 24hr. emergency (0337) 79 32 84). Open Mon.-Fri. 8am-noon.

Currency Exchange: Closest to the train station is **Banca Nazionale del Lavoro,** P. Garibaldi (tel. 799 71 13). Open Mon.-Fri. 8:30am-1:30pm and 2:45-4pm.

Trains: FS (tel. 147 88 80 88). To: Milan (8hr., L64,000-91,000), Rome (2½hr., L18,000-28,5000), and Brindisi (6½hr., L34,500). **Circumvesuviana** (tel. 772 21 44) runs to Pompeii, Ercolano, and Sorrento.

ITALY

Public Transportation: L1500 ticket works for buses, metropolitana, trams, and funiculars; one-day pass L5000. R1, R2, and R3 buses connect the center to Mergellina, P. Garibaldi, and Voremo respectively.

Ferries: Caremar, Molo Beverello (tel. 761 36 88). To Capri (4 per day, 1¼hr., L8800) and Ischia (9 per day, 1¼hr., L8800). **Tirrenia,** Molo Angioino (tel. 720 11 11). To Palermo (11hr., L69,100) and Cagliari (Oct.-May Thurs. 7:15pm; June-Sept. 5:30pm; late June to mid-Sept. also Sat. 5:30pm; 16hr., L65,000).

Emergencies: tel. 113. **Ambulance:** tel. 752 06 96. **Hospital: Cardarelli** (tel. 747 28 41), north of town on the red line.

Police: tel. 794 11 11 or 113. English speakers always available.

Internet Access: Internet Bar, Piazza Bellini. L10,000 per hr. Open daily 10am-3am.

Post Office: P. Matteotti (tel. 551 14 56), on Via Diaz (R2 line). Also in Galleria Umberto and Stazione Centrale. All open Mon.-Fri. 8:15am-7:15pm, Sat. 8:15am-noon. **Postal Code:** 80100.

Telephone Code: 081.

ACCOMMODATIONS AND FOOD

The shoddy area around P. Garibaldi is packed with hotels, many of which solicit customers at the station. Following a hawker is usually safe as long as you don't give up your passport before seeing the room and you always agree on a price before unpacking. Try bargaining. The **ACISJF** (tel. 28 19 93), at the Stazione Centrale, helps women find safe and inexpensive rooms. (Supposedly open Mon. and Wed.-Thurs. 3-7pm, Tues. and Fri.-Sat. 9:30am-1pm and 3-7pm.)

Ostello Mergellina (HI), Salita della Grotta, 23 (tel./fax 761 23 46). Make two sharp rights onto Via Piedigrotta from M: Mergellina. 2- to 6-bed rooms vary in quality. Curfew 12:30am. Lockout 9:30am-4pm. Dorms L23,000. Doubles L52,000.

Casanova Hotel, Via Venezia, 2 (tel./fax 26 82 87). Take Via Milano right from P. Garibaldi and turn left at its end. Clean, airy rooms and a rooftop terrace. Prices for *Let's Go* users: singles L25,000; doubles L54,000, with bath L68,000.

Hotel Eden, Corso Novara, 9 (tel. 28 53 44), right from the station. Well-maintained rooms on a noisy thoroughfare. All rooms with bath. With *Let's Go:* singles L42,000; doubles L66,000; triples L90,000; quads L104,000.

Soggiorno Imperia, P. Miraglia, 386 (tel. 45 93 47). Up Via Mezzaconnane from C. Umberto near P. Bovio. Brand new rooms, all with private shower. Singles L70,000. Doubles L100,000. Triples L130,000. Quads L160,000.

Hotel Ideal, P. Garibaldi, 99 (tel. 26 92 37 or 20 22 23), to the left of the station. Well-furnished rooms are modern and secure. With *Let's Go 1998:* singles L40,000-50,000; doubles L60,000, with bath L90,000.

Pizza-making is an art born in Naples. **Antica Pizzeria da Michele,** nine blocks to the right off C. Umberto from P. Garibaldi, is the city's most venerable *pizzeria* (open Mon.-Sat. 8am-11pm), while **Trianon da Ciro,** across the street, offers more variety. **Pizzeria Port'Alba,** Via Port'Alba, 18, is the oldest *pizzeria* in town (cover L2000; open Thurs.-Tues. 9am-2am). *Pizza margherita* (L5000), the most common pizza in Italy, was invented in 1889 at **Pizzeria Brandi,** Salita S. Anna di Palazzo, 1. A cult following of students flocks to **Di Matteo,** Via Tribunali, 94, for spectacular pies.

SIGHTS AND ENTERTAINMENT

Although the region around the train station is unpleasant, further searching reveals a wealth of treasures in Naples' museums and galleries. The renowned **Museo Nazionale Archeologico,** near the "Cavour" metro stop, houses a stunning collection of mosaics, frescoes, and jewelry excavated from Pompeii. Look for the tender *Portrait of a Woman,* and the famous wall-sized Alexander Mosaic, which portrays a young and fearless Alexander routing the Persians (open Wed.-Mon. 9am-7pm; hours subject to change; L12,000). Take bus 24 to the **Museo e Gallerie di Capodimonte,** a newly restored museum in an 18th-century royal palace in the northern hills (open Tues.-Sat. 9am-6pm, Sun. 9am-2pm; L8000). You can also tour the Royal Apartments and the San Carlo Theater in the **Palazzo Reale,** commissioned by the Bourbon King Charles III to imitate Versailles (open Sun.-Tues. 9am-1pm, Thurs.-Sat. 9am-6pm, also summer evenings; L8000). Up the funicular to Voremo's villas, the **Museo Nazionale di San Martino** documents the art and history of Naples (open Tues.-Sun. 9am-2pm; L8000), while the parks of **Villa Floridiana** are on a hill overlooking the bay.

Walk along the bay of Naples in the late afternoon or early evening to see the **Villa Comunale,** a waterfront park with the oldest aquarium in Europe, fill with locals taking their *passeggiata.* Nicer walks await in the hills of Posillipoto to the west. A fascinating alternative is to see Naples from beneath; **Laes** (tel. 40 02 56) offers tours of subterranean Naples on weekend mornings (L10,000).

The hippest downtown area is **Piazza Bellini,** near P. Dante, while the small streets off **Piazza Amedeo** beckon with nightlife and a night bus returning to P. Garibaldi after the Metro stops running. The city's hotspots include **Piazza di Spagna,** Via Petrarca, 101; **Chez Moi,** Parco Margherita, 13 (Metro: P. Amedeo); and the larger **Madison Street,** Via Sgambati, 47, in Voremo. They feature dancing Friday through Sunday starting at 10pm and charge a L15,000-20,000 cover (Madison Street open Mon.-Thurs. also; all open Sept.-July). **ARCI-Gay/Lesbica** (tel. 551 82 93) has free advice on gay and lesbian goings-on about town.

■ Near Naples: Pompeii and Herculaneum

Immense **Mount Vesuvius** looms indomitably over the area east of Naples, the only active volcano on the European continent. Its infamous eruption in 79 AD buried the nearby Roman city of Herculaneum (Ercolano) in mud, and its neighbor Pompeii (Pompei) in ashes. Excavations, beginning in 1784, have unearthed a stunningly well-preserved picture of Roman daily life. The frescoed houses, colonnaded forum, wide roads, and small brothels haven't changed much since then. Neither have the victims, some of whose ghastly remains were preserved by plaster casts in the hardened ash.

Take the Circumvesuviana **train** from Naples, Salerno, or Sorrento to the Pompeii Scavi station (about L3000; Eurail not valid). To reach the archaeological site, head downhill and take your first left to the west entrance. Before you enter, consider buying the informative **How to Visit Pompeii** (L8000) available outside all site entrances. Guided tours are expensive, but some sneaky folks have been known to successfully freeload. You'll want a **map** of the site; free ones are available at the **tourist office** at the bottom of the hill outside the western entrance. Pack a lunch and a water bottle, as the cafeteria is hideously expensive.

The west entrance to Pompeii leads past the Antiquarium (permanently closed since the 1980 earthquake) to the **Forum,** the commercial, civic, and religious center of the city. Showcases along the western side display some of the gruesome body casts of the volcano's victims. At the **Forum Baths** on Via di Terme, parts of the body casts here have chipped away to reveal the teeth and bones underneath. The **House of the Vettii** is home to some of the most vivid frescoes in Pompeii. In the vestibule is a depiction of Priapus (the god of fertility) displaying his colossal member. Phalli were believed to scare off evil spirits in ancient times, but now they seem only to invite hordes of tittering tourists. On Vico di Vetti there is a small **brothel** with several bed-stalls. Above each of the stalls a pornographic painting depicts with unabashed precision the specialty of the stall's occupant (or so archaeologists fantasize). The **amphitheater,** the oldest in the world still standing (80 BC), held 12,000 spectators. (Entrances to Pompeii open daily 9am until 1hr. before sunset; June-July until 8pm; Nov.-Dec. until 3:45pm. L12,000.)

Herculeneum is 500m downhill of the Ercolano stop on the Circumvesuviana Line (15min. from Naples). Stop at the **tourist office** on the way for a **map.** Less of the city has been excavated, but the 15 or so houses open to the public were so neatly dug up that the tour feels like an invasion of privacy (L12,000).

Amalfi Coast

The bold, arresting bluffs and picturesque towns scattered into the ravines of the **Amalfi coast** merit every tourist brochure superlative. A calm sea, delicious seafood, and sumptuous fruits temper the rugged shore, while the tiny towns exude rustic character. The **Monte Lattari** above the peninsula is wonderful for hiking expeditions inland and between towns; pick up the Club Alpino Italiano map. **Trains** connect Naples to Sorrento on the northwestern side of the peninsula (1hr., L4300) and Salerno at its southeastern base (1hr., L5100), but the coastal towns can only be reached by ferry journeys and the more tortuous (and torturous) bus rides. The **SITA bus** (tel. (089) 22 66 04) runs from Corso Garibaldi, 117 in Salerno to the Circumvesuviana station in Sorrento and back, stopping in Vietri, Maiori, Minori, Atrani, Amalfi, Praiano, and Positano. A bus to inland Ravello runs from Amalfi. Buy tickets at the tabac, and don't go after lunch. Frequent, inexpensive **ferries** connect Salerno, Amalfi, Positano, and Sorrento.

Paestum Forty-five minutes south of Salerno by train (L4300), **Paestum** boasts three spectacularly preserved Doric temples and rare examples of Greek wall painting. Once a flourishing mercantile center, epidemics and attacks forced out its population by the 10th century, and the ruins have been lying in the grass ever since (L8000 for the ruins, L8000 for the museum).

Salerno, Vietri sul Mare, Maiori, and Minori Industrial **Salerno** has few worthwhile sights, but it's a good base for daytime excursions to nearby towns, and the **bayside promenade** is perfect for an evening stroll. Pick up a map and the MEMO entertainment guide at the **tourist office** in the *piazza* outside the station (tel. (089) 23 14 32). The **Ostello della Gioventù "Irno" (HI),** Via Luigi Guercia, 112 (tel. (089) 79 02 51), is the cheapest sleep in town (L15,500 with breakfast and sheets). Closer to the station is **Albergo Santa Rosa,** Corso Vittorio Emanuele 14 (tel. (089) 25 53 46), a safe *pensione* with a grandmotherly proprietor (singles L40,000, doubles L60,000). Head to the restaurant row on the western end of Via Roma for **food,** or check your email at **Mailboxes, Etc.,** Via Diaz, 19 (tel. (089) 23 12 95). West of Salerno, **Vietri sul Mare** is a charming seaside resort. **Maiori**'s half-mile beach partly makes up for its ugly postwar concrete, while nearby **Minori** has a smaller beach and generic family atmosphere.

Amalfi and Atrani Seemingly a sleepy seaside town, **Amalfi** has white homes snuggled into a small coastal town ravine and a quaint port. But in its heyday, Amalfi ruled the neighboring coast as the first Sea Republic of Italy, and it retains the noise, life, and chaos of a city many times its size. Visitors indulge in swims off its pebbly beach, strolls on bayside promenades, forays into the hills of the surrounding coast, and visits to the elegant, Moorish-influenced 9th-century **duomo,** rebuilt in the 19th century. **Villa Graf** (tel. (335) 45 58 74) will set *Let's Go* readers up in a nice apartment in town (L50,000, less for longer stays and groups over 3). The cheapest double runs L80,000 at **Pensione Proto** (tel. (089) 87 10 03). The **Shahrazad Club** on the left of the *duomo* offers an abbreviated tourist *menù,* including wine (L10,000). A 10-minute walk around the bend from Amalfi is **Atrani,** a tiny ravine town which tourism hasn't changed a bit. The delightful **Piazza Umberto** is under the arch from Atrani's sandy beach. There, **A Scalinatella** (tel. (089) 87 19 30) hosts travelers (L30,000-35,000 per person, including breakfast and dinner).

Ravello Capping a promontory a thousand feet above Amalfi, **Ravello** is an ideal spot for an afternoon stroll or quiet contemplation. Its tranquil setting and exquisite gardens have attracted a long list of great writers and celebrities. The Moorish cloister and meandering gardens of **Villa Rudolfo** inspired Boccaccio's *Decameron* and Wagner's *Parsifal* (off P. Duomo, open 9am-8pm; L5000). On the small road passing to the right, signposts lead to the more impressive **Villa Cimbrone.** Its floral walkways and gardens hide temples and statued grottos. Ravello hosts numerous acclaimed classical music festivals, shattering the tranquility with pompous Wagnerian operatics. The two-hour hike up to Ravello from Amalfi is spectacular, but a bus carries the weary and lazy (35min., L1500). With bath, balcony, and breakfast, the best rooms are at **Villa Amore** (tel. (089) 85 71 35; doubles L112,000).

Praiano Halfway between Amalfi and Positano, **Praiano** is a small residential community with hearty food and an active nightlife. **La Tranquillità,** Via Roma, 10 (tel. (089) 87 40 84), has wonderful views, campsites (L20,000 per person), and bungalows with bath (with *Let's Go* singles L52,000, doubles L80,000; open Easter-Nov.). Around the bend towards Amalfi is **Marina di Praia,** a 400-year-old fishing village turned local hot spot. At **Africana,** fish swim under the glass dance floor as the nightly live music echoes off the dimly lit cave above (cover L30,000; women free on Wed.). **Boats** connect to Amalfi and Salerno in August (tel. (089) 87 40 42). Farther on, the SITA **bus** services the spectacular **Grotto dello Smeraldo** (Emerald Grotto), which rivals Capri's azure equivalent (admission and tour L5000).

Positano The idyllic setting, cliffside homes, and idiosyncratic locals of **Positano** began to lure writers, artists, painters, and actors in the beginning of the century. Soon afterwards, its artsy cachet made it a popular destination for high rollers. It's best enjoyed by those who have money to throw around, but budget travelers can also rub elbows with the jet set here. Positano's nearby majestic mountains are good for hiking, its sandy beaches are always crowded, and its window shopping is almost as satisfying as the real thing. The **tourist office** (tel. (089) 87 50 67) in the pink building below the *duomo* has maps and useful info. For lodgings, take the local bus to Fornillio, the west part of town. **Villa Maria,** Via Fornillio, 40 (tel. (089) 87 50 23), has seaside terraces and the jolliest owner in Italy (singles L50,000, doubles 85,000). **Casa Guadagno** (tel. (089) 87 50 42), next door, earns praise for spotless rooms and sublime views (doubles L90,000). For delicious pastries on a charming patio, try **La Zagara,** in town, at Via dei Moullini, 6. The **Music on the Rocks** disco off Spiaggia Grande is expensive but classy.

Sorrento The largest, most touristy town on the peninsula, **Sorrento** is charming despite its reputation as a retirement home for Neopolitan grandparents. The old town is lively, and the trilingual locals make it easy for English- and German-speaking tourists. **Ferries** from Marina Piccola go to Capri (L7000), and a local bus shuttles between P. Tasso and the port. **Ostello Le Sirene,** Via Degli Aranci, 160 (tel. (081) 807 29 25), has clean six-bed rooms right behind the train station (sheets, bed, and breakfast for L25,000). Halfway to the free beach at Punta del Capo on the "A" bus, **Hotel Elios,** Via Capo, 33 (tel. (081) 878 18 12), has clean rooms in a tranquil area (singles L35,000, doubles L60,000). **Terlizzi,** Corso Italia, 30, is the only **laundromat** in the area (L16,000 for detergent, wash, and dry). In Sorrento, good, affordable food is easy to find. At the pretty Marina Grande, **Taverna Azzura** has fresh sea food and pasta cooked to perfection. Off C. Italia two blocks from P. Tasso, **Davide,** Via Giuliani, 39, makes divine gelato and masterful mousse (55-80 flavors daily). At **Ristorante Giardiniello,** Via Accademia, 7, off V. Giuliani, Mamma Luisa's *gnocchi* is served in a peaceful garden (L6000; cover L1500). At night, a crowd gathers upstairs in the rooftop lemon grove above **The English Inn,** C. Italia, 55.

Bay of Naples Islands

Capri The sheer bluffs, divine landscapes, and azure waters of **Capri** have beckoned wayfarers from the Italian mainland since Imperial times. The **Grotta Azzurra** (Blue Grotto) is a must-see—light enters the cavern though a hole in the rock under the water, causing the whole grotto to glow a fantastic neon blue. Boat tours (L15,000 plus tip) barely last long enough to let your eyes adjust; locals say it's better to swim to the grotto with a friend when the waters are calm and the boats aren't running (after 6pm and before 9am). To appreciate Capri's Mediterranean beauty from higher ground, take the **chairlift** up Monte Solaro from P. Vittoria (L7500 round-trip) or Via Longano from P. Umberto in Capri center and make the trek up to the left on Via Tiberio to **Villa Jovis** (1hr.), the most magnificent of the 12 villas that Tiberius scattered about (L4000). From Piazza Umberto, Via Roma leads to **Anacapri** after winding up the mountain; buses also make the trip. Up the stairs from P. Vittoria in Anacapri, **Villa San Michele** houses remarkable classical sculptures retrieved from the sea bottom (open in summer daily 9am-6pm; in winter 10am-3pm; L6000).

Caremar **ferries** run to Marina Grande from Naples' Beverello port (last return 6pm; L9500) and from Sorrento (last return 6:45pm; L6500), Ischia (L12,000), and the Amalfi coast; **hydrofoils** are faster, costlier, and more frequent. There's a **tourist office** on the dock and in P. Umberto (tel. (081) 837 06 34) in Capri. In Anacapri, the **tourist office** is to the right from the P. Vittoria bus stop at Via Orlandi, 19/A. (Tel. (081) 837 15 24. Both open Mon.-Sat. 9am-1:30pm and 3:30-6:45pm; longer in summer.) With its luxurious gardens, elegant pool, and beautiful rooms, **Villa Eva,** Via della Fabbrica, 8 (tel. (081) 837 15 49 or 837 20 40), is the island paradise you came for. Call from the dock, take the bus to P. Vittoria in Anacapri, and wait for Eva's car (L25,000-40,000; reserve early and confirm often; open March-Oct.). The deluxe **Hotel Caesar Augustus,** Via Orlandi, 4 (tel. (081) 837 14 21), has the most spectacular view of the island. (*Let's Go* prices: singles L60,000; doubles L80,000 with breakfast. Seaside rooms start at L120,000. Open Easter-Oct.) **Hotel Loreley** (tel. (081) 837 14 40), off P. Vittoria towards Capri, is a cute hotel with bright rooms and private baths (doubles L100,000), and **Il Girasole** (tel. (081) 837 23 51) also has a pool and some renovated rooms (L25,000-40,000). Dine in style in Anacapri at **Ristorante Il Cucciolo,** Via Fabbrica, 52, on the way to the Blue Grotto (cover L28000; *Let's Go* discounts), or **Trattoria Pizzeria il Solitario,** Via Orlandi, 96, in an ivy-covered garden. At night, droves of beautiful Italians come out for Capri's *passegiatta,* and the bars and discos lining the streets around P. Umberto keep the music pumping late. They're expensive, but women can often get in free. **Buses** return to Anacapri until 1:45am, and **taxis** (tel. (081) 837 05 43) gather at the bus stop.

Ischia Across the bay from overrun Capri, larger, less glamorous Ischia (EES-kee-yah) offers a variety of landscapes, including beautiful beaches, natural hot springs, ruins, forests, and vineyards. Bus 1 follows the coast in a counterclockwise direction from **Ischia Porto,** a port formed by the crater of an extinct volcano. Along the way, you can stop at **Casamicciola Terme,** with its overcrowded beach, or **Lacco Ameno,** known for the island's cleanest boardwalk. The bus continues to **Forio,** the hippest area on Ischia thanks to its tree-lined streets and popular bars.

Caremar **ferries** (tel. (081) 99 17 81) arrive from Naples every hour (8am-7pm, L9500). **Linee Lauro** (tel. (081) 837 75 77) runs from Sorrento to Ischia (L16,000) and connect the island to Capri with a **hydrofoil** (1 per day, L18,000). SEPSA **buses** run from P. Trieste to destinations all over the islands (one-way tickets L1500, full-day L5400). Reserve a room at least a month in advance. In Forio, try floral **Pensione Di Lustro,** Via Filippo di Lustro, 9 (tel. (081) 99 71 63), a short walk from the beach. (With *Let's Go* June L90,000 doubles with bath; July-Aug. L100,000; prices lower off season.) **Eurocamping dei Pini** is at Via delle Ginestre, 28 (tel. (081) 98 20 69), 20 minutes from the port. Take Via del Porto to Via Alfredo de Luca, walk uphill, turn right on Via delle Terme, and follow the arrow (L12,000 per person, L7000 per tent). **Camping Internazionale,** (tel. (081) 99 14 49) Via M. Mazzella, is 15 minutes from the port; take Via Alfredo de Luca from Via del Porto and bear right at P. degli Eroi (L14,000 per person, L10,000 per tent; open May-Oct. 15).

SICILY (SICILIA)

Every great Mediterranean civilization of the past 2500 years has left its mark on Sicily: the ancient Greeks scattered temples and theaters; the Romans, bridges and aqueducts; the Saracens, mosques and towers; and the Normans, churches and castles.

Sicilians, however, don't revel in their island's traditions. Today, they speed unabated toward the future, installing condom-vending machines in front of medieval cathedrals and demonstrating against their most well known institution, the Mafia. The tempestuousness of Sicilian history and political life is matched only by the island's dramatic landscapes and climate. The countryside is dominated by sheer, rock-strewn crags, and Europe's highest volcano, Mt. Etna, serves as an uneasy reminder that Sicily rests on the edge of the European geologic plate

Tirrenia, in Palermo (tel. (091) 33 33 00), the largest private ferry service in Italy, is the most extensive and reliable, though you should still beware the summer tourist rush and strikes. Prices and schedules vary according to specific dates; approximations are given below. Listings are for Tirrenia and include low- to high-season prices for *poltrone* (reserved reclining deck chairs). Tickets can often be purchased at travel agencies, either in foreign countries or within Italy.**Tirrenia** (tel. (091) 33 33 00), in Palermo, runs the most extensive ferry service to Sicily. From Rome, first take a train to Reggio di Calabria on the southern tip of Italy, and then the ferry to Messina on Sicily's northeast coast (ferry L42,000). Ferries also offer direct service to Palermo from Genoa (24hr., L50,000-70,000) and Naples (11hr., L53,600-69,100). Call Tirrenia for departure times and other routes. Once on the island, two bus companies, the private, air-conditioned **SAIS** and the public, often steamy **AST,** serve many destinations inaccessible by train. Expect delays and confusion. **Hitchhiking** is difficult and very risky, especially for long trips.

Palermo

As Sicily's capital, Palermo is notorious as the cradle of Italian organized crime. Since the election of Palermo's first avowedly anti-mafia mayor in 1993, however, the city has begun cleaning up its politics and revitalizing its historic district, much of which was destroyed in World War II. Although Palermo has its share of sketchy neighborhoods, it is also sports the attractions of a modern metropolis.

Venturing from the Quattro Canti onto Corso Vittorio Emanuele, heading away from the harbor, you will confront the striking exuberance of Palermo's **cattedrale.** Begun by the Normans in 1185, it absorbed elements of every architectural style from the 13th through 18th centuries (open daily 7am-noon and 4-6pm). Nearby, the **Palazzo dei Normanni** contains the **Cappella Palatina,** which features a carved wooden stalactite ceiling and an outstanding cycle of golden Byzantine mosaics. Next to the statue of Philip III in the Quattro Canti, the dismal gray facade of the **Church of San Giuseppe dei Teatini** belies its dazzling Baroque interior. Perhaps the most romantic spot in Palermo is the garden of the **Church of San Giovanni degli Eremiti,** Via dei Benedettini, 3, with fountains, vines, and stone archways. To get there from the station, take bus 122 and get off before P. Indipendenza (open Mon. and Wed. 3-6pm, Tues. and Thurs.-Sun. 9am-1pm; free).

The **tourist office,** P. Castelnuovo, 34 (tel. (091) 605 83 51 or 605 81 11), is 2km up Via Maqueda; turn right on Via Maqueda from the station or take bus 101 or 107 going toward Teatro Politeama (open Mon-Fri. 9am-1pm and 4-8pm, Sat. 8am-2pm). **Hotel Luigi,** Salita Santa Caterina, 1 (tel. (091) 58 50 85), is well located and has simple rooms (singles L25,000, doubles L50,000). **Hotel Lampedusa,** Via Roma, 111 (tel./fax (091) 617 14 09), has great prices on the main drag (singles L40,000, doubles L60,000). The quiet and clean **Petit Hotel,** Via Principe di Belmonte, 84 (tel. (091) 32 36 16), is to the left off Via Roma, three blocks after Via Cavour from the station (singles L35,000, doubles L60,000). Camp at **Trinacria,** Via Barcarello, 25 (tel. (091) 53 05 90); take bus 101 to "Gasperifour Teatro Politeama," then 628 to "Sferracavallo" (L7000-8000 per person and per tent).

Palermo is famous for its *pasta con le sarde* (with sardines and fennel) and *rigatoni alla palermitana* (with a sauce of meat and peas). **Antica Focacceria S. Francesco,** Via Alessandra Paternostro, 58, off Corso Vittorio Emanuele, is a 161-year-old *pizzeria* (open Tues.-Fri. 9:30am-10pm, Sat.-Sun. 9:30am-midnight). Award-winning Italian and North African cuisine awaits at **Hostaria al Duar,** Via Ammiraglio

Gravina, 31, off Via Roma three blocks north toward the port (open Tues.-Sun. 1-3pm and 7pm-midnight). The 92-year-old **Osterio Lo Bianco,** Via E. Amari, 104, off Via Roma heading toward the port, has delectable fare (*calamari* L9000; pasta from L5000; open Mon.-Sat. noon-3pm and 7-11pm).

■ Near Palermo

About 10km southwest of Palermo, **Monreale's** magnificent Norman-Saracen cathedral, **Santa Maria la Nuova** (c. 1174), was the largest cathedral in Europe at the time of its construction. The church features incredible mosaics and intricate arches, and the **cloister** next door houses a renowned collection of Sicilian sculpture. (Cathedral open daily 8am-noon and 3:30-6pm. Cloister open July-Sept. Mon.-Sat. 9am-1pm; Mon., Wed., and Fri. also 3-6pm, Sun. 9am-12:30pm; Oct.-June ask at cathedral. Cloister L2000.) **Buses** 389 and 309 drive here from Palermo's Piazza Indipendenza.

An hour from Palermo by train (L5700), **Cefalù** guards a cache of Arab, Norman, and medieval architecture. In P. Duomo off Corso Ruggero you'll find the town's 11th-century Norman **cathedral.** Inside, 16 Byzantine and Roman columns support superb capitals, and the elegant horseshoe arches exemplify the Saracen influence on Norman architecture in Sicily (open 8:30am-noon and 3:30-6:30pm; proper dress required). For a bird's-eye view of the city, make the half-hour haul up the **Rocca** by way of the Salita Saraceni, which begins near P. Garibaldi off Corso Ruggero. Follow the brown signs for *"pedonale Rocca."* On the mountain, walkways lined with ancient stone walls lead to the **Tempio di Diana** (Temple of Diana), dating from the 4th century BC. The **tourist office,** C. Ruggero, 77 (tel. (0921) 210 50; fax 223 86), in the old city, has maps and finds rooms. (Open June-Sept. Mon-Sat. 8am-8:30pm, Sun. 8am-2pm; Oct.-May Mon.-Fri. 8am-2pm and 4-7pm, Sat. 8am-2pm.)

■ Agrigento

Among Sicily's classical remains, the **Valle di Templi** at Agrigento shares top honors with those at Syracuse. Take bus 1, 2, or 2/ from the train station (L1000) and ask to be dropped off at the *quartiere ellenistico-romano.* The **Tempio della Concordia,** one of the world's best-preserved Greek temples, owes its survival to consecration by St. Gregory of the Turnips (we kid you not). On the road to the archaeological park from the city center, the **Museo Nazionale Archeologico di San Nicola** contains a notable collection of artifacts, especially vases from all over central Sicily (open Mon.-Sat. 8am-12:30pm; free). Revisit modern fashion and convenience at the **centro storico,** a cobblestone web of welcoming streets and shops.

Trains arrive from Palermo (1½hr., L12,100). The staff of the **tourist office,** Via Atenea, 123 (tel. (0922) 204 54), will happily give you an adequate map (open in summer daily 8:30am-1:30pm and 4:30-7:30pm). **Hotel Bella Napoli,** P. Lena, 6 (tel./fax (0922) 204 35 or 205 92), off Via Bac Bac, has clean rooms and a terrace overlooking the valley (singles L25,000-40,000, doubles L55,000-75,000). Take your first left off Via Imera and follow signs up the hill to **Hotel Concordia,** Via San Francesco, 11 (tel. (0922) 59 62 66; singles L25,000-35,000, doubles L50,000-70,000). **Trattoria Atenea,** Via Ficani, 32, the 4th right off Via Atenea from P. Moro, has a quiet courtyard and seafood offerings (squid L9000; open Mon.-Sat. noon-3pm and 7pm-midnight).

■ Syracuse (Siracusa)

Founded in 734 BC by Greeks who fancied the splendid harbor, ancient Syracuse cultivated such luminaries as Pindar, Archimedes, and Theocritus. The city just hasn't been the same since the Romans sacked it in 211 BC, but several ancient monuments still remain. Cross the bridge on Corso Umberto to the island of **Ortigia** to pay homage to the Temples of **Apollo** and **Athena.** The latter, now part of the city's cathedral, has a richly embellished facade added in the 18th century. From P. del Duomo, a trip down Via Picherale leads to the ancient **Fonte Aretusa,** a freshwater spring by the sea. Syracuse's larger monuments are in or near the **Archaeological Park** on the north side of town; follow Corso Gelone until it meets Viale Teocrito, then walk down Via Augusto to the left. The park contains an enormous ancient **Greek theater** where Aeschylus premiered his *Persians* (park open daily 9am until 2hr. before sunset; L2000). Check out the **Orecchio di Dionigi** (Ear of Dionysius), a giant artificial grotto with exceptional acoustics and an earlobe-shaped entrance. The tyrant Dionysius reputedly put all his prisoners here so he could eavesdrop on their conversations. Nearby, the **Altar of Hieron II** (241-215 BC) is the largest known altar, while the **Roman amphitheater,** constructed in the 2nd century AD, is stunningly well-preserved. If you prefer tans to temples, bus the 18km to **Fontane Bianche** (bus 21, 22, or 24; L600), a silken beach frequented by the jet-set crowd.

Near the **Catacombe di San Giovanni** (open March 15-Nov. 14 daily 9am-6pm; Nov. 15-March 14 9am-1pm; L2000), the **tourist office,** Via San Sebastiano, 43 (tel. (0931) 46 14 77), distributes maps and brochures (open Mon.-Sat. 8:30am-1:30pm and 3:30-6:30pm). **Trains** arrive from Taormina (2¼hr., L11,700) and Messina (4hr., L15,500), while **buses** pull into town from Palermo (4hr., L20,000, round-trip L30,000). **Pensione Bel Sit,** Via Oglio, 5 (tel. (0931) 602 45), is close to the train station and has modern, basic rooms (singles L35,000-65,000, doubles L45,000-55,000). **Albergo Aretusa,** Via F. Crispi, 73 (tel. (0931) 242 11), just down the street from the station, offers large rooms and friendly management (singles L40,000-47,000, doubles L60,000-70,000). Budget eateries center on Ortigia, or try the **market** on Via Trento, near the Temple of Apollo (open Mon.-Sat. 8am-early afternoon). For staples, try the **Linguanti** supermarket, Corso Umberto I, 174, a block from the train station (open Mon.-Tues. and Thurs.-Sat. 5:30am-8:30pm, Wed. 5:30am-1:30pm). **Spaghetteria do Scugghiu,** Via D. Sciná, 11, off P. Archimede, serves up 18 delicious kinds of spaghetti (most L6000; open Tues.-Sun. noon-3pm and 5pm-midnight).

Taormina

Taormina is and has always been a place of unsurpassed beauty—a cliff-top city of mansions, pine trees, and purple flowers, with a hazy-blue coastline stretching out below. The 3rd-century **Greek theater,** at the very edge of the cliff, is arguably the most dramatically situated theater on earth. To get there, walk up Via Teatro Greco, off Corso Umberto I at P. Vittorio Emanuele (open daily 9am-7pm; L2000). On the other side of P. Vittorio Emanuele, is the **Roman Odeon,** a small theater now partly covered by the Church of Santa Caterina next door. A small set of steep steps snake up the mountainside to the **piccolo castello.** A short trip away lies **Gole Alcantara,** a haven of gorgeous gorges, freezing waterfalls, and crystal rapids. SAIS runs a **bus** there and back (leaves 9:15am, 12:15, and 2pm; returns 2:20pm; round-trip L7300).

Reach Taormina by **bus** from Messina or Catania (L5100). **Trains** are more frequent and only L4200, but the train station is far below town with access controlled by buses (L1500) that make the climb every 15 to 75 minutes until 10:20pm. A helpful and well-organized **tourist office** waits on P. Santa Caterina (tel. (0942) 232 43; fax 249 41), in Palazzo Corvaia off Corso Umberto (open Mon.-Sat. 8am-2pm and 4-7pm; may be open Sun. July-Aug.). Accommodations can be hard to come by in August, so call ahead in July. The **Villa Pompei,** Via Bagnoli Croci, 88 (tel. (0942) 238 12), is across from the public gardens (singles L35,000, doubles L52,000-60,000). In two buildings overlooking the sea, **Inn Piero,** Via Pirandello, 20 (tel. (0942) 231 39), has recently renovated rooms (singles L50,000, doubles L70,000; breakfast included). Dining can be expensive; consider stocking up at the **STANDA supermarket** on Via Apollo Arcageta, at the end of Corso Umberto (open Mon.-Sat. 8:30am-1pm and 5-9pm). The sign in front of **Trattoria da Nino,** Via Pirandello, 37, reads "Stop, you have found the best homemade cooking and pasta in Taormina." It may well be correct (open daily noon-3:30pm and 6-11:30pm; closed Fri. off-season).

Aeolian Islands (Isole Eolie)

Home of the wind god Aeolu and the Sirens, the Aeolian (or Lipari) Islands comprise one of the last areas of unspoiled seashore in Italy, with its fiery volcanos and long, rocky beaches. To reach the archipelago from Sicily, first travel to the town of **Milazzo** on the Messina-Palermo train line (from Messina 1hr., L3400; from Palermo 3hr., L15,500). From the Milazzo train station, take the orange bus (L600) to the port. From there, **Siremar** (tel. (090) 928 32 42) and **Navigazione Generale Italiana** (tel./fax (090) 92 24 01) run reliable ferries to the islands. The increasingly popular **hydrofoils** make the trip in half the time but cost twice as much.

Lipari On Lipari, the largest and most developed of the islands, pastel-colored houses dot a small promontory crowned by the walls of a medieval *castello,* the site of an ancient Greek acropolis. Many of the artifacts found here decorate the exterior of the superb **Museo Archeologico Eoliano,** in the two buildings flanking the cathedral (open Mon.-Fri. 9am-2pm and 4-7pm; free). Farther from town, the island features everything from nude beaches to churches to pumice mines; rent a bike or moped and explore at your own pace. The **tourist office,** C. Vittorio Emanuele, 202 (tel. (090) 988 00 95), is up the street from the ferry dock. (Open July-Aug. Mon.-Sat. 8am-2pm and 4:30-10pm, Sun. 8am-2pm; Sept.-June Mon.-Sat. 8am-2pm and 5:30-7:30pm. Closed Sat. afternoons.) Next to the cathedral, the **Ostello Lipari (HI),** Via Castello, 17 (tel. (090) 981 15 40, off-season 981 25 27), is one of the best deals on the islands. (Reception open daily 7:30-9am and 6pm-midnight. Strict 11:30pm curfew. L12,000. Showers L1000. Open March-Oct.) A few steps up from the hydrofoil port, **Locanda Salina,** Via Garibaldi, 18 (tel. (090) 981 23 32), has beautiful rooms overlooking the water (singles L35,000, doubles L60,000). **Hotel Europeo,** C. Vittorio Emanuele, 98 (tel. (090) 981 15 89), boasts an awesome location on the bustling *corso* (singles L40,000-45,000, doubles L85,000-90,000; showers L2000).

Vulcano and Stromboli The island of **Vulcano** offers an intriguing daytrip of thermal springs and bubbling mud baths. A good way to start your visit is to tackle the challenging one-hour hike to the **Gran Cratere** (Great Crater) along the snaking footpath beside the crater's fumaroles. On a clear day you'll be able to see all the other islands from the top. Just up Via Provinciale from the port sits the **Laghetto di Fanghi** (mud pool); you can't miss the smell. If you would prefer not to bathe in dirt, wade in the nearby waters of the **acquacalda** just behind the *laghetto.* Here, underwater volcanic outlets make the sea percolate like a jacuzzi. For cooler pleasures, visit the crowded beach and crystal-clear waters of **Sabbie Nere,** just down the road from the *acquacalda* (follow the signs off Via Ponente through the black sand). Stop by the **tourist office,** Via Provinciale (tel. (090) 985 20 28; July-Aug. only), for more info on these sights. **Ferries** make the trip to Vulcano from Lipari (L4500) and Milazzo (L9900); **hydrofoils** cost L4500 and L21,000, respectively.

Viewed from Lipari or Vulcano, **Stromboli** looks like a giant iceberg jutting out of the water. In reality, the island is a volcano, and an active one at that. **Società Navigazione Pippo** (tel. (090) 98 61 35) operates daily tours of the island (10:10am-1:10pm and 3:10-6:10pm; L20,000). Hiking the volcano is illegal and dangerous, but that hasn't seemed to stop people. If you decide to go, be sure to bring sturdy shoes, a flashlight, warm clothes, and water. Reaching the summit (about 3hr.) around dusk allows adventurers to camp out and see the brilliant lava bursts by night. The **ferry** from Lipari to Stromboli runs L13,900.

SARDINIA (SARDEGNA)

Sardinia is the perfect antidote to Italy-overdose. Inspired by the island's mountainous terrain and rustic villages, D. H. Lawrence declared that Sardinia, like Russia, had "escaped the net of European civilization." Much of the area south of over-touristed **Costa Smeralda** persists in its untamed state, and Sardinia's beaches rival Europe's finest. Ancient civilizations that settled in Sardinia some 3500 years ago built **nuraghe,** cone-shaped fortified tower-houses. Constructed of huge blocks of stone and assembled without the aid of mortar, over 7000 *nuraghe* survive today.

Tirrenia runs the most extensive ferry network, including service to Cagliari from Genoa (L54,000-96,000) and Palermo (L35,000-60,000). For info, call the Cagliari *Stazione Marittima* (tel. (070) 66 60 65). **Flights** are quicker but much more expensive; check with local tourist offices for details. On the island, **ARST** buses link villages while **PANI** buses connect only major cities. Bus and train service has improved the last few years, but **car rental** is still the only way to reach many locations (L50,000-175,000 per day). Ask at tourist offices for the comprehensive and semi-reliable *Alberghi e Campeggi,* which lists prices for all hotels, pensions, and campsites. Decent singles go for L35,000, but rooms are scarce in August.

Cagliari, Alghero, and Oristano At the southern tip of the island, **Cagliari** gracefully combines the vigor of a bustling city, the rich history of a medieval town, and natural panoramic splendor. The cramped medieval quarter and impressive **duomo,** with dazzling gold mosaics atop each entryway, rest on a hill above the modern port. If you prefer to worship the sun, take city bus P, PQ, or PF to **Il Poetto,** Cagliari's most popular beach (20min., L1300). The **tourist office,** P. Matteotti (tel. (070) 66 92 55 or 66 49 23), aids in finding rooms and offers info on local sites (open in summer Mon.-Fri. 8am-8pm, Sat. 8am-2pm; off-season Mon.-Sat. 8am-2pm). **Allogio Firenze,** Viale Trieste, 56, on the 5th floor (tel. (070) 65 36 78 or 65 52 22), has large singles (L38,000-40,000) and doubles (L50,000-54,000). **Pensione Vittoria,** Via Roma, 75 (tel. (070) 65 79 70), is an elegant *pensione* with mosaic floors (singles L50,000, with bath L58,000; doubles L80,000, with bath L95,000).

The sea breezes and twisting streets of **Alghero** grant a respite from the sun's glare. The FS bus brings visitors to the nearby **Grotte di Nettuno,** an eerie cavern complex. (Round-trip bus ticket L5700. Grottoes open April-Sept. daily 9am-7pm; Oct. 10am-5pm; Nov.-March 9am-2pm. L10,000.) The **tourist office** in Alghero, P. Porta Terra, 9 (tel. (079) 97 90 54), is the most organized in Sardinia (open May-Aug. Mon.-Sat. 8am-8pm, Sun. 9am-noon; reduced hours off-season). **Ostello dei Giuliani (HI),** Via Zara, 3 (tel./fax (079) 93 03 53), 7km from the city center (take the orange AF city bus from Via La Marmora), is close to the beach (L14,000; reserve ahead).

Situated on the western coast, **Oristano** is a quiet base for excursions to stunning beaches and archaeological sites. The **tourist office** is at Via Cagliari, 278. (Tel. (0783) 731 91. Open Mon. and Thurs.-Fri. 8am-2pm, Tues.-Wed. 8am-2pm and 4-8pm.) The nearby **Sinis Peninsula** and **Costa Verde** offer everything that the better-known resorts do—except the crowds and concrete. At the tip of the peninsula, 17km west of Oristano, lie the ruins of the ancient city of **Tharros.**

Latvia (Latvija)

US$1 = 0.59Ls (Lats)	**1Ls = US$1.71**
CDN$1= 0.42Ls	**1Ls = CDN$2.36**
UK£1 = 0.93Ls	**1Ls = UK£1.07**
IR£1 = 0.86Ls	**1Ls = IR£1.16**
AUS$1 = 0.43Ls	**1Ls = AUS$2.34**
NZ$1 = 0.37Ls	**1Ls = NZ$2.69**
SAR1 = 0.13Ls	**1Ls = SAR8.01**
Country Code: 371	**International Dialing Prefix: 810**

Except for 20 years of independence that ended with the 1939 Molotov-Ribbentrop Pact, Latvia was ruled by Germans, Swedes, and Russians from the 13th century until 1991. The country is now rebuilding after almost 50 years of Soviet occupation but remains less affluent and developed than Estonia, its Baltic neighbor to the north. Attitudes toward the Russians who still live in the country are softening: Latvians speak Russian well and are willing to use it more often than Estonians. But evidence of national pride abounds. Street names have been changed to honor national heroes, crimson-and-white flags adorn countless buildings throughout the country, and national holidays predating even the Christian invasions have reemerged. Rīga, the only large city, is an impressively Westernized capital that serves as the base of operations for many Baltic corporations. Beyond Rīga awaits a peaceful expanse of deep green hills, dairy pastures, quiet settlements, and unbelievably fresh air.

Latvia is covered in delightful detail in *Let's Go: Eastern Europe 1998*.

GETTING THERE AND GETTING AROUND

Irish, U.K., and U.S. citizens can visit Latvia visa-free for up to 90 days. Citizens of Australia, Canada, New Zealand, and South Africa require 90-day visas, obtainable at a Latvian consular office (see **Government Information Offices,** p. 1) or at Rīga's airport. Single-entry visas cost US$15, multiple-entry US$30, and 24-hour rush processing US$60 (single-entry) or US$90 (multiple-entry). Multiple-entry visas are issued only if an official invitation from a Latvian government agency or an officially registered organization is submitted with the visa application. Allow 10 days for standard processing. With the application, send your passport, one photograph, and payment by check or money order. Visa extensions are difficult to get; start by contacting the Dept. of Immigration and Citizenship, Raina iela 5 (tel. 721 91 81) in Rīga.

Latvia is well-connected by **train** to Moscow, St. Petersburg, Vilnius, Tallinn, and even Berlin; efficient long-distance **buses** travel to Tallinn, Vilnius, Prague, and Warsaw. **Ferries** run to Rīga from Stockholm and Kiel, but from Stockholm the train through Tallinn is cheaper, and from Germany a bus passes through Klaipėda on its way to Rīga. **Flights** to Latvia use the overworked Rīga Airport. Once in Latvia, buses and trains run everywhere; getting from town to town is rarely a problem. The suburban train system centered in Rīga stretches to the Lithuanian and Estonian borders.

ESSENTIALS

Look for the big green "i" marking some tourist offices. The **Tourist Club of Latvia,** in Rīga, is invaluable. Stores often close between noon and 3pm, and restaurants may break from 5 to 7pm. **Homosexuality,** though legal, may not be tolerated.

The Latvian currency unit is the **Lats** (100 santīmu = 1 Lats, abbreviated Ls). There are a few **ATM** machines in Rīga linked to Cirrus and MasterCard, and in most towns there are a few establishments that accept **Visa** and **MasterCard.** It's difficult to cash **traveler's checks,** but AmEx and Thomas Cook checks can be converted in Rīga.

Buy slick **phone cards** for the newly digitalized telephones at the local post office and anywhere sporting a phone-card sticker (lowest denomination 2Ls). For **interna-**

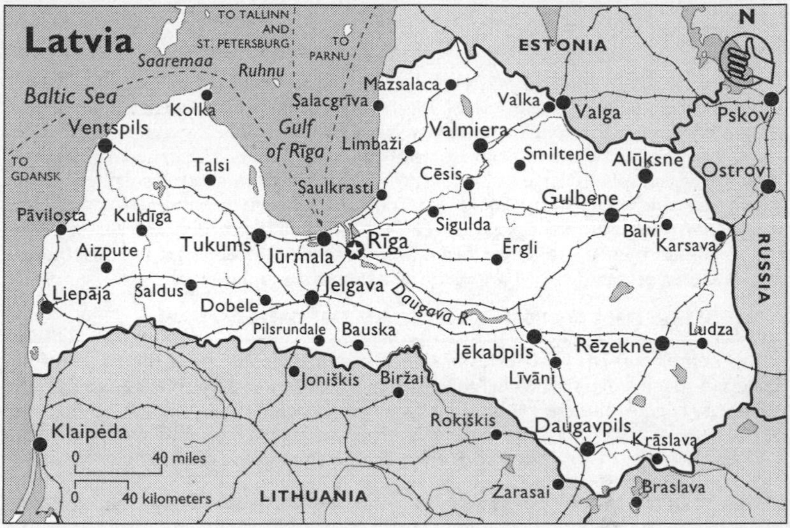

tional calls, the only reliable places are the post office or your hotel room. The **AT&T Direct** number in Latvia is 700 70 07; it's not a free call, but it's your best option for an English speaking operator. The gradual switch to digital phones has left some travelers feeling like safecrackers—sometimes you must dial a 2 before a number to make a connection, sometimes a 7, sometimes other assorted digits. Check a phone office or *Rīga in Your Pocket* for the latest in digit disaster. In an **emergency,** dial 01 for **fire,** 02 for **police,** and 03 for an **ambulance.**

Many young Latvians study English, while the older set knows some German. Latvians speak Russian, although the language may inspire some hostility.

Yes/No	*Jā/Nē*	yah/ney
Hello	*Labdien*	LAHB-dyen
Please	*Lūdzu*	LOOD-zuh
Thank you	*Paldies*	PAHL-dee-yes
Where is...?	*Kur ir...?*	kuhr ihr
How much does this cost?	*Cik maksā?*	sikh MAHK-sah
I don't understand	*Es nesaprotu*	ehs NEH-sah-proh-too
Help!	*Palīdzājiet!*	PAH-leedz-ah-yee-eht

Heavy and filling, Latvian **food** tries to fatten you for winter. National specialties, simple and tasty on the whole, include smoked *sprats* (once the fame of Rīga), the holiday dish *zirņi* (gray peas with onions and smoked fat), *maizes zupa* (bread soup usually made from cornbread and full of currants, cream, and other goodies), and the warming *Rīgas balzams* (a sweet black liquor great on ice cream or in coffee). Dark rye bread is an essential staple of the Latvian table, and homemade bread and pastries are deliciously worth asking for. Try the *speķa rauoi,* a warm pastry, or *biezpienmaize,* bread with sweet curds. Beer is quite good, plentiful, and inexpensive; standouts include the Aldaris brewery's *Porteris* labels.

June 23 brings the amorous Midsummer's Eve Festival (Līgo) to Rīga, while November 18 sees feasts on Latvian National Day.

Rīga

Founded in 1201 by the Teutonic Order of the Knights of the Sword as a base for conquering Livonian and Latvian tribes, Rīga soon became the seat of a bishopric that fought the knights for control of the city. Later ruled by Poles, Swedes, and then Russians, Rīga grew to be the most prosperous city in the Baltics. The famed Art Nouveau architecture reveals German influences, while the population and atmosphere reflect the inescapable legacy of the Soviet era. Tensions between disenfranchised Russians, *nouveau-riche* businesspeople with cellular phones, and returning Latvians who fled in the 40s after Stalin's takeover make Rīga a hotbed of post-Soviet politics. But the city's eclectic attractions cast a spell on all its residents and visitors.

ORIENTATION AND PRACTICAL INFORMATION

Rīga's center consists of a series of concentric half-circles along the banks of the **Daugava** River, engulfing **Vecrīga** (Old Riga). The train and bus stations sit on the southeast edge of the city. With the train station behind you, walk left on the busy Marijas iela; once you pass the canal's terminus, you are in the Old Town. A city map (1Ls) and *Rīga in Your Pocket* (0.50Ls) will help you out the rest of the way.

Tourist Office: Balta Tourist Agency, Elizabetas iela 63 (tel. 728 63 49; fax 724 30 99), gives out maps and pamphlets. Open Mon.-Fri. 9am-6pm, Sat. 10am-2pm. The English-speaking **Tourist Club of Latvia,** Skārņu iela 22 (tel. 722 17 31; fax 722 76 80), behind St. Peter's Church, arranges Russian visas and has many brochures. English tours of Rīga 17.40Ls. Open 24hr. **Latvijas Universitātes Tūristu Klubs,** Raiņa bulv. 19, #127 (tel. 722 52 98; fax 782 01 13; email mountain@com.latnet.lv), organizes hiking and canoeing trips. Open Mon.-Fri. 9am-6pm.

Embassies: Canada, Doma laukums 4 (tel. 722 63 15, emergency 755 11 81). Open Mon.-Fri. 10am-1pm. **Russia,** Antonijas iela 2 (tel. 22 06 93). Open Mon.-Fri. 10am-1pm. Citizens of **Ireland** should contact the **U.K.** embassy, Alunāna 5 (tel. 733 81 26). Open Mon.-Fri. 9:30am-noon. **U.S.,** Raiņa bulv. 7 (tel. 721 00 05). Open Mon.-Fri. 9am-noon and 2-5pm.

Currency Exchange: At any of the *Valutos Maiņa* kiosks or shops in the city. **Unibanka,** Kaļķu iela 13 (tel. 722 83 51), has long hours, gives MC and Visa cash advances, and cashes traveler's checks. Open Mon.-Fri. 9am-9pm, Sat. 9am-6pm.

American Express: Latvia Tours, Grēcinieku iela 22/24 (tel. 721 63 06). The Latvian AmEx representative. *Doesn't* cash traveler's checks; try Unibanka (listed above) instead. Mail held. Open Mon.-Fri. 9am-6pm, Sat. 10am-2pm.

Flights: For flight info, call 20 70 09. **Lidosta Rīga** (Rīga Airport) is 8km southwest of the Old Town. Take bus 22 from Gogol iela.

Trains: The **station** (info tel. 007) is east of the Old Town and north of the canal. To: Moscow (2 per day, 17hr., *coupé* 23.53Ls), St. Petersburg (1 per day, 15hr., *coupé* 19.69Ls), Tallinn (1-2 per day, 8½hr., *coupé* 13.98Ls), Berlin (1 per day, 31hr., *coupé* 46.28Ls), and other cities.

Buses: The **station** (tel. 21 36 11) lies 200m south of the train station along Prāgas iela, across the canal from the Central Market. To Vilnius (6hr., 6Ls) and Tallinn (6hr., 5-6Ls). **Eurolines,** to the right of the ticket window, serves Prague (30hr., 38Ls) and Warsaw (14hr., 14.50Ls).

Public Transportation: Buses, trams, and trolleybuses require 14-santīmi tickets available at kiosks, post offices, and sometimes on board. Punch tickets on board.

Ferries: Transline Balt Tour, Eksporta iela 1a (tel. 232 99 03), 1km north of the castle at the passenger port. Service to Stockholm, Sweden (Mon., Wed., and Fri. 6pm, 16hr., 10-25Ls).

Gay and Lesbian Center: Latvian Association for Sexual Equality, Puškina 1a (tel./fax 722 70 50; http://dspace.dial.pipex.com/town/parade/gf96).

Laundromat: Miele, Elizabetes iela 85a (tel. 271 76 96). The wash takes about 2hr. Wash 1.89Ls. Dry 0.63Ls. Open 24hr.

Internet Access: Latnet, Raiņa 29 (tel. 721 12 41; http://www.latnet.lv). 1.60Ls per hr. Open Mon.-Thurs. 9am-6pm, Fri. 9am-5pm. **Bilteks,** Jēkaba 20 (tel. 732 22 08),

2Ls per hour, open daily 10am-9pm. **Internet Café Audalūzijas Suns,** Elizabetes iela 83/85 (tel. 724 28 26). 1.50Ls per hr. Open daily noon-10pm.

Post Office: Stacijas laukums 1 (tel. 721 32 57), near the train station. *Poste Restante* at window 1. Open Mon.-Fri. 8am-8pm, Sat. 8am-4pm, Sun. 10am-4pm. **Postal Code:** LV-1050.

Emergencies: Ambulance: tel. 03. **Fire:** tel. 01.

Police: tel. 02.

Telephones: Office at Brīvības bulv. 21. Open daily 8am-10pm. **Telephone Code:** 2 (8 for digital lines).

ACCOMMODATIONS

Rīga's prices for decent rooms are generally the highest in the Baltics. However, there are a number of very cheap, if grim, places to stay in town.

Arena, Palasta iela 5 (tel. 722 85 83), in the heart of Vecrīga. Hall shower and communal kitchen. 3Ls per person. Open April-Oct.

Saulite, Merķela iela 12 (tel. 22 45 46), across from train station. Clean halls, rooms, and communal showers and toilets. Singles 5.40Ls. Doubles 7.8Ls.

Studentu Kopmītne (Student Dormitories), Basteja bulvarīs 10 (tel. 721 62 21), above the Europcar Interrent office, on the edge of Vecrīga. Clean and well-maintained. Mostly new communal bathrooms. 2-3Ls, with private bath and refrigerator 5-6Ls. Call ahead—this place is popular!

Viktorija, Čaka iela 55 (tel. 27 23 05), 8 blocks from the train station on Marijas iela (which becomes Čaka iela), or 2 stops on trolleybus 11 or 18. Grim common toilets. Singles from 10Ls. Doubles from 14Ls.

Aurora, Marijas iela 5 (tel. 722 44 79), across from the train station. Rooms are old and the toilets, most of which don't have seats, smell. Hall bathrooms. All rooms have sinks with hot water. Singles 3.50-3.70Ls. Doubles 5.80-6.20Ls. Cash only.

Patricia, Elizabetes iela 22-26, 3rd fl. (tel. 28 48 68; fax 28 66 50), 2 blocks from the train station, arranges US$15 homestays in Vecrīga. Reception open Mon.-Fri. 9am-7pm, Sun. 9am-1pm. Doubles US$30. Breakfast US$5.

FOOD

Bleary-eyed women tend an insomniac's daydream: 24-hour food and liquor stores. Pricey **Interpegro,** Elizabetes iela 18 (tel. 287 190), is just one example, selling mostly packaged foods, fruits, and vegetables (open Mon.-Sat. 10am-10pm, Sun. 10am-7pm). In five immense zeppelin hangars behind the bus station, **Centrālais Tirgus** (Central Market), one of the largest in Europe, has by far the best selection at the cheapest prices. Shop around and haggle, as vendors' prices vary quite a bit (open Mon.-Sat. 8am-5pm, Sun. 8am-3pm). **McDonald's** is at Basteja bulv. 18.

Lido Bistro-Piceria, Elizabetes iela 65. Very popular fast-food. Spaghetti 1.40Ls. Shish kebab and rice 1.95Ls. Salad 0.50Ls. Open daily 8am-11pm.

Rozamunde, Mazā Smilšu iela 8, 1 block off Filharmonija laukums. An upscale pub run by the Rīga Jazz Company. Good beef tenderloin stuffed with champignons and cheese 3.80Ls. Lamb curry 3.95Ls. Open daily 11am-11pm.

Fredis Café, Audēju iela 5. Decent tunes, smoky air, and carefully dressed, consciously cool patrons. Small subs 0.90-1.30Ls. Spaghetti with mushrooms 2.20Ls. 0.5L *Aldaris* 0.65Ls. Open daily 9am-midnight.

Arve Restaurant, Aldaru iela 12, next to the Swedish Arch. Relatively fancy place with outdoor seating. Passable *fettucine alfredo* with chicken filet 2.60Ls. Tomato, eggplant, and feta cheese 3.15Ls. Open daily noon-11pm.

LuLu Pizza, Ģertrūdes iela 27. Best thin-crust pizza in town. Hip new interior. Large pizzas enough for 3 moderately hungry people 2.99-3.99Ls. Slices 0.69-0.95Ls. *Aldaris* 0.85Ls. Open daily 8am-midnight.

Hotel Latvija Express Bar, Elizabetes iela 55, at the corner of Brīvības bulv. past the Freedom Monument. Renowned breakfast joint. Small portions of pancakes with jam 0.96Ls. 23 varieties of omelettes 0.81-3.04Ls. Big windows overlook the Orthodox Cathedral's park. Open daily 7am-11pm. Cash only.

SIGHTS AND ENTERTAINMENT

While most of Rīga's monuments are located in the Old Town, the **New Town** merits a visit; one good route is to turn left onto Elizabetes iela from Marijas and walk the length of the street. In Verīga, at the end of Audēju iela, **Sv. Pētera baznīca** (St. Peter's Church) prods the clouds with a dark spire visible throughout the city. First built in 1209, the church now standing dates from 1408. From the top of the 103m tower, you can see the Baltic Sea (open Tues.-Sun. 10am-6pm; church 0.30Ls; tower 1Ls, students 0.70Ls). Just behind at Skārņu iela 10/20 stands the 1208 **Juras Kirik** (St. George's Church), the oldest stone edifice in Rīga. Constructed for the German Knights of the Sword, the church was secularized in the 1500s and divided into warehouses by German merchants. It now houses the magnificent **Museum of Applied Arts,** showcasing Latvian ceramics, jewelry, and tapestries. (Open Tues.-Sun. 11am-5pm. Museum 0.50Ls, students 0.20Ls. Exhibition 0.40Ls, students 0.20Ls.)

Farther right on Skārņu iela at the corner with Jāņa iela stands **Sv. Jāņa baznīca** (St. John's Church), a small 13th-century chapel embellished as late as the 1830s in a medley of architectural styles, from Gothic to Baroque to Neoclassical (open Tues.-Sun. 10am-1pm). Through a tiny alleyway to the left, **Jāņa Sēta** (St. John's Courtyard) is the oldest site in Rīga, where the first city castle stood. Part of the old city wall is preserved here, and in summer a beer garden toasts the city's history. Nearby rise the ominous black walls of the **Occupation Museum Fund,** Strēlnieku laukums 1, one of Rīga's finest museums. The initial Soviet occupation is depicted so vividly you can almost hear the Red Army marching, and a model gulag helps explain why the Germans were welcomed as liberators.

Down Zirgu iela, between the two guild houses, the cobblestone expanse of **Doma laukums,** Vecrīga's central square, remains timelessly serene despite several vast new outdoor bars that serve tourists and Rīga's *nouveau riche.* Rīga's centerpiece, **Doma Baznīca** (Dome Cathedral), begun in 1226, stands on one side of the square. Inside, an immense pipe organ is one of Europe's largest and reputedly finest. (Open Tues.-Fri. 1-5pm, Sat. 10am-2pm. 0.50Ls, students 0.20Ls. Concerts Wed. and Fri. 7pm.) Behind the cathedral, at Palasta iela 4, the **History and Maritime Museum** thoroughly explores Rīga's complex history (open Wed.-Sun. 11am-5pm; 1Ls, students 0.40Ls). **Rīga Pils** (Rīga Castle), Pils laukums 2, at the street's end, houses three modest museums (art, history, and literature) labeled in Latvian only.

At Jēkaba iela 11, Latvia's **Saeima** (Parliament) was barricaded with trucks, barbed wire, sandbags, and nationalism during the 1991 struggle for independence. A couple blocks away and though the **Swedish Gate,** Torņa iela leads to **Pulvertornis** (Powder Tower), one of Rīga's oldest landmarks and the only city tower left. Nine cannonballs are still lodged in its 14th-century walls; it's not clear why they're on the side facing *into* the city. Inside, the **Latvian Museum of War** (Latvijas Kara Muzejs), Smilšu iela 20, explores the Latvian resistance to Soviet rule (open Tues.-Sun. 10am-6pm; 0.40Ls, students 0.20Ls).

At the north end of the park, on Kr. Valdemāra iela, lies the **National Theater,** where Latvia first declared its independence on November 18, 1918 (open Mon.-Fri. 10am-7pm, Sat.-Sun. 11am-6pm). In the park, Kaļķu iela widens to become Brīvības bulv., where the beloved **Brīvības Piemineklis** (Freedom Monument), nicknamed "Milda," was dedicated in 1935 while Latvia was an independent republic.

Birthplace of Mikhail Baryshnikov, Rīga is home to the excellent **Rīga Ballet** and the **Latvian National Opera.** The theaters are closed during the summer, but during the rest of the year, get tickets at Teātra 10/12 (tel. 722 57 47; open daily 11am-3pm and 4-6pm). At the Doma Baznīca, **Ērģeļmūzikas koncerts** (organ concerts) feature the third-largest organ in the world. Purchase tickets at Doma laukums 1 (tel. 721 34 98), opposite the main entrance at *koncertzāles kase* (open daily noon-3pm and 4-7pm). A prime evening plan is to hop from dinner to the beer gardens in Doma laukums and then to a dance club. At **Paddy Whelan's,** Grēcineku iela 4, fast-flowing beer satisfies a noisy, friendly crowd of local students and backpackers (beers 1.20Ls; open nightly 5pm-midnight; food served until 8pm). **Pulkuedim Neviens Neraksta,**

Peldu 26/28, is a restaurant by day and a trendy bar at night (cover 1Ls after 8pm; open Sun.-Thurs. noon-3am, Fri.-Sat. noon-5pm). **Underground,** Slokas 1, is perhaps Rīga's most popular dance club (cover 1Ls; open Tues.-Sun. 9am-6pm). **Purrs,** Matisa 60/62, and **808,** Kalmiņa 8, are two gay nightspots.

Jūrmala

Since the late 19th century, Rīgans have spent their summers on this narrow spit of sand between the Gulf of Rīga and the Lielupe River. Public **buses** string together the towns of Jūrmala, each connecting two to four towns. The Rīga **commuter rail** runs one train every half hour from 5am to 11:30pm.

On the side facing the gulf, **Lielupe** (30min., 0.23Ls) has access to a beach and impressive sand dunes. The stops between **Bulduri** and **Dubulti,** however, are the most popular spots for sunning and swimming. In 1987, authorities claimed the Gulf water was polluted, but since then swimming has made an unsanctioned comeback. In **Majori** (35min., 0.32Ls), trainloads of people enjoy the beach in the morning and the relaxing cafés and restaurants in the afternoon and evening. The **tourist office,** Jomas iela 42 (tel. 642 76), has maps and brochures (open Mon.-Fri. 9am-5pm). The cheapest place to stay, **Sanatoriaja Marienbāde,** Meijerovica Prospekt 43 (tel. 625 18; fax 614 64), is surprisingly nice, with clean rooms and private baths (7Ls).

At the end of Jūrmala, **Ķemeri** was once the top health resort of the Russian Empire. In town, the aging but impressive **Sanatorium,** Jomas iela 5, features a restored library complete with period furniture, tapestries, and acres of gardens (US$25-30 for up to 3 people). To reach the Sanatorium, take bus 6 to Sanitorija Latvia, then walk along the paved road next to the bus stop.

Sigulda

As the gateway to the Gauja National Park and Gauja gorge, Sigulda rewards adventurers with hiking trails, castles, a bobsled run, bungee jumping, a funicular, and hot-air ballooning. Perched on a ridge to the right of Gauja iela on the near side of the gorge is the **Siguldas dome,** the new "castle." Behind it, the **Siguldas pilsdrupas** (Siguldas Castle), now in ruins, was constructed by the German Knights of the Sword between 1207 and 1226 and destroyed in the Great Northern War. Down the slope and to the left along Turaidas iela about 500m, the chiseled maw of **Gūtmaņa ala** (Gūtman's Cave) continues to erode, inscribed with coats of arms and phrases by generations of Latvians and other visitors since the 16th century. The wooden building up the hill to the right is the 1750 **Turaida Church,** now home to a small archaeological museum (open daily 9:30am-6pm). Farther out rise the towers and walls of **Turaidas pils** (Turaidas Castle). Restored earlier in this century, the red tower is home to the **Sigulda History Museum,** Turaidas iela 10 (0.80Ls).

Hiking options here are numerous. One excellent 2km walk follows the Gauja River to the steep **Piķenes Slopes,** where two more caves merit a look. Another good hike goes from the Sigulda castle down to the Gauja, then upstream to cross **Vējupite creek.** Another 100m upstream on Vējupite, stairs rise to **Paradīzes Kalns** (Paradise Hill), where 19th-century Latvian painter Jānis Rozentāls made the valley view famous. Visible from the commuter rail, the Olympic-size **bobsled and luge run** plummets from Sveices iela 13 (tel. (29) 739 44; fax 790 16 67). From October to March, you can take the plunge for 1Ls (open Sat.-Sun. 10am-8pm). **Vade Mecum,** Pusas iela 12 (tel. (29) 61 16 14), offers rides in a **hot-air balloon** (0.50Ls).

Trains roll to Sigulda from Rīga (1hr., 0.53Ls). From the train and bus stations, walk up **Raiņa iela** to the town center. For affordable lodging, take bus 12 to **Hotel Senleja,** Turaidas iela 4 (tel. (29) 721 62; fax 790 16 11; doubles 9Ls). If you can brave the cold, you can also rent a double-occupancy **cottage** near the river (4Ls). **Kafejuīca/Bistro,** Raiņa iela 1, next to the bank, a cafeteria-style eatery, has salads, chicken shish kebabs, and rice, all sold by weight. (Meals about 1.5Ls. *Aldaris* beer 0.35Ls. Open Mon.-Fri. 7am-10pm, Sat.-Sun. 7am-midnight.)

Liechtenstein

Famous chiefly for its wines, royal family, and yes, postage stamps, Liechtenstein's minute size (160 sq. km) and population (30,629) make the principality itself more of an attraction than any sight it contains. With the only German-speaking monarchy in the world, Liechtenstein remains the last vestige of the Holy Roman Empire. Although the official language is German, many residents also speak English and French; the **currency** is the Swiss franc. **Biking** is a dream in flatter areas, and an efficient and cheap **postal-bus** system links all 11 villages (most trips 2.40SFr, 1-month pass 20SFr; Swisspass valid). To enter the principality, catch a postal bus from Sargans or Buchs in Switzerland, or Feldkirch just across the Austrian border (each 3.60SFr). The **postal code** is FL-9490. The **telephone code** for all of Liechtenstein is 075. For international calls, use the Swiss **country code** (41) and **international dialing prefix** (00). For the **police,** call 117, and for **medical emergencies,** call 144. For a map of Liechtenstein, see the Switzerland map.

Vaduz

More a hamlet than a national capital, Vaduz is not a budget-friendly place. Above the town sits the 12th-century **Schloß Vaduz,** regal home to Hans-Adam II, Prince of Liechtenstein. The **Staatliche Kunstsammlung** (State Art Museum), Städtle 37, is next to the tourist office (5SFr, students 3SFr). Nearby, philatelists salivate over (not on) the collection in the **Briefmarkenmuseum.** (Stamp Museum. Free. Both museums open daily 10am-noon and 1:30-5:30pm; Nov.-March closes 5pm.)

Liechtenstein's **national tourist office,** Städtle 37 (tel. 392 11 11), up the hill and to the right from the Vaduz-Post bus stop, stamps passports (2SFr), finds rooms, and advises on hiking, cycling, and skiing. (Open June-Oct. Mon.-Fri. 8am-noon and 1:30-5:30pm, Sat. 9am-noon and 1-4pm, Sun. 10am-noon and 1-4pm; Nov.-May closed weekends). Liechtenstein's lone **Jugendherberge (HI),** Untere Rütigasse 6 (tel. 232 50 22; fax 232 58 56), is in nearby **Schaan.** Take the bus to "Mühleholz" and turn down Marianumstr. (Members only. Reception open Mon.-Sat. 5-10pm, Sun. 6-10pm. Curfew 10pm. 26.30SFr. Open March-Nov. 15.) If the hostel is full, walk 10 minutes back toward Vaduz to **Hotel Falknis** (tel. 232 63 77; singles 50SFr). Buy groceries at **Denner Superdiscount,** Äulestr. 20 (closed Sun.).

Upper Liechtenstein

With gorgeous views and great hiking, the villages in the upper country are far more rewarding to visitors than Vaduz. **Triesenberg,** the principal town, was founded in the 13th century by the Walsers, a group of Swiss immigrants fleeing poverty and oppression. The **Walser Heimatmuseum** chronicles their customs and crafts. (Open June-Aug. Tues.-Fri. 1:30-5:30pm, Sat. 1:30-5pm, Sun. 2-5pm; Sept.-May Tues.-Fri. 1:30-5:30pm, Sat. 1:30-5pm. 2SFr.) The **tourist office** (tel. 262 19 26) is in the same building and has the same hours. **Pension Alpenblick,** Neudorf 383 (tel. 262 35 77), offers spacious rooms 10 minutes (downhill) from the tourist office (singles 40SFr, doubles 70SFr). **Camping Mittagspitze** (tel. 392 36 77 or 392 26 86) is between Triesen and Balzers on the road to Aargans (reception open daily 7am-noon and 2-10pm; 8SFr per person, 5SFr per tent).

Malbun, on the other side of the mountain from Triesenberg, offers great skiing (day pass 33SFr; week pass 142SFr) and hiking: contact Malbun's **tourist office** (tel. 263 65 77) for more info (open June-Oct. and mid-Dec. to mid-April Mon.-Wed. and Fri. 9am-noon and 1:30-5pm, Sat. 9am-noon and 1:30-4pm). The superb duo of chalet-*cum*-hotels **Hotel Alpen** (tel. 263 11 81; fax 263 96 46) and **Hotel Galina** are the accommodations of choice. (Reception at Hotel Alpen for both. Singles and doubles 40-65SFr per person. Open mid-May to Oct. and Dec. 15-April 15.)

Lithuania (Lietuva)

US$1 = 4.00Lt (Litai)	**1Lt = US$0.25**
CDN$1= 2.89Lt	**1Lt = CDN$0.35**
UK£1 = 636Lt	**1Lt = UK£0.16**
IR£1 = 5.86Lt	**1Lt = IR£0.17**
AUS$1 = 2.91Lt	**1Lt = AUS$0.35**
NZ$1 = 2.54Lt	**1Lt = NZ$0.39**
SAR1 = 0.85Lt	**1Lt = SAR1.18**
Country Phone Code: 370	**International Dialing Prefix: 810**

Lithuania once thrashed through Central Europe—repelling proselytizing Teutonic knights, joining up with Poland to rule modern Belarus and Ukraine, and generally stirring up trouble. Ruined castles and fortifications stand as mute reminders of these glory days, while ancient and beautiful Vilnius welcomes visitors with green parks and relaxed cafés. Sun, fun, and the Baltic's best beaches can be found where the mighty Baltic Sea washes up at Palanga and Kuršių Nerija (Curonian Spit). Lithuania occupies a bizarre niche in the annals of modern culture; their Olympic basketball team was sponsored by the Grateful Dead, and busts of the likes of Frank Zappa now fill the void left by Lenin's drop in the Billboard charts.

Get the full scoop on Lithuania in the 1998 edition of *Let's Go: Eastern Europe.*

GETTING THERE AND GETTING AROUND

Citizens of the U.S., Canada, the U.K., Ireland, and Australia can visit Lithuania **visa-free** for up to 90 days. New Zealand, and South African citizens without visas for Estonia or Latvia need a 90-day visa. Border posts don't issue visas. Send a photo, passport, and check or money order (single-entry US$20, multiple-entry US$40, transit visa US$10) to the nearest embassy or consulate (see **Government Information Offices,** p. 1). Regular service takes two weeks; rush costs US$20 extra. For visa extensions, contact the **Migration Dept.** at Šaltoniškų 19, Vilnius (tel. (222) 72 58 53).

Trains are slow, noisy, and often crowded. Two major rail lines cross Lithuania: one runs north-south from Latvia through Šiauliai and Kaunas to Poland; the other runs east-west from Belarus through Vilnius and Kaunas to Kaliningrad, or on a branch line from Vilnius through Šiauliai to Klaipėda. Slightly more expensive and faster **buses,** however, radiate from all the cities of Lithuania.

Klaipėda, Kaunas, and Vilnius are accessible by **train** or **bus** from Belarus, Estonia, Latvia, Poland, and Russia. Most trains from Poland to Vilnius go through Belarus, requiring a transit visa (US$30). The *Baltic Express* chugs from Warsaw to Tallinn daily, departing Warsaw at 2:30pm, passing through Kaunas at 11:55pm, and arriving in Tallinn the next day at 1:10pm. There is also one overnight train running between Warsaw and Šeštokai, Lithuania; it arrives at 6:30pm, two hours before a Šeštokai-Kaunas-Vilnius train departs. These two trains, as well as buses from Poland to Lithuania, do not go through Belarus. **Planes** fly to Vilnius from Warsaw, Berlin, Stockholm, and Moscow. **Ferries** connect Klaipėda with Kiel and Muhkran in Germany.

ESSENTIALS

Litinterp offices arrange private accommodations, rent cars, and stock city information. The three big Lithuanian cities have helpful guidebooks. *Vilnius in Your Pocket,* thoroughly updated every two months and available at newsstands (4Lt), is a best-seller, as are sister guides *Kaunas in Your Pocket* and *Klaipėda in Your Pocket.*

The unit of **currency** is the Litas (Lt); 1 Lt equals 100 centų. Since March 1994, Litai have been tied to the U.S. dollar (4Lt=US$1). Traveler's checks can be cashed at most banks (usually for a 2-3% fee). Cash advances on a **Visa** card can usually be obtained with a minimum of hassle in banks; **Vilniaus Bankas,** with outlets in major Lithuanian cities, accepts all major credit cards and traveler's checks and charges no higher than a 0.5% commission. Some cities have 24-hour **ATMs**.

Lithuania's Independence Day falls on February 16. Other **holidays** include St. Kazimieras's Day on March 4, and Midsummer Night (Rasos), the night of June 23, a beer-drinking, folk-dancing, song-singing, countryside party. The following day is Jonines (St. John's Day). Mindaugas's Day, July 6, commemorates the day the first King of Lithuania was crowned. On this day, Kaunas is the place to be.

Accommodations and Food

Be sure to take advantage of the eight **Lithuanian Youth Hostels (LJNN/HI).** HI membership is nominally required, but an LJNN guest card (US$3 at any of the hostels) will suffice. The LJNN main office is in Vilnius at Filaretų g. 17 (tel./fax 26 26 60). Grab a copy of their *Hostel Guide,* a handy booklet with info on bike and car rentals, advance booking, and maps.

Lithuanian **cuisine** is generally heavy, filling, and sometimes very greasy. Many restaurants serve various types of *blynai* (pancakes) with *misa* (meat) or *varške* (cheese). *Cepelinai* are heavy, potato-dough missiles stuffed with meat, cheese, and mushrooms, most prominent in West Lithuania. *Šaltibarščiai* is a beet and cucumber soup prevalent in the eastern half of the country. *Karbonadas* is fried breaded pork fillet. Most restaurants and shops stock the Lithuanian **beer** *Kalnapilis,* which is passable. *Baltijos,* brewed in Klaipėda, has several good varieties, including *Utenos.*

Communication

Local **phones** in Lithuania cost 20 centų. Long-distance calls can be made from some of the old gray public phones with the wide-grooved gold *žetonai* sold at post offices (0.24Lt). For international calls, it is often best to use the

Norwegian card phones which have been installed at main phone offices and large railway terminals; cards are sold at the phone offices in denominations of 3.54, 7.08 and 28.32Lt. Rates for international calls to the U.S. are 10.50Lt per minute, to Estonia and Latvia 1.65Lt per minute, to Europe 3.54Lt. You can ring only some countries directly. Dial 8, wait for the second tone, and dial 10 followed by the country code and number. Calls to cities within the former Soviet Union can be placed by dialing 8, followed by the old Soviet city code. For countries to which direct dialing is not available, dial 8, wait for the second tone, and dial 194 or 195 (English-speaking operators available). To reach the **AT&T Direct** operator, dial (8) 196; **Sprint Access,** (8) 197.

English-language **books** are cheap but rare. The Tallinn-based *Baltic Independent* and Rīga's *Baltic Observer* are both available in Vilnius, Kaunas, and Klaipėda. In Vilnius, pick up Voice of America **radio** at 105.6 FM, broadcasting 24 hours. Lithuanians pride themselves on the fact that their national language is the most archaic among the spoken Indo-European tongues, and one of only two surviving languages in the Baltic branch (Latvian is the other). All "r"s are trilled. Nearly all Lithuanians speak Russian, but a few Lithuanian words and phrases will secure instant goodwill.

Yes/No	*Taip/Ne*	TAYE-p/neh
Hello	Labądien	Lah-bah-DEE-yen
Please/You're welcome	*Prašau*	prah-SHAU
Thank you	*Ačiu*	AH-chyoo
Excuse me	*Atsiprašau*	ahtsy-i-prah-SHAoo
Do you speak English?	*Ar Jūs kalbate angliškai?*	ahr yoos KAHL-bah-te AHNGL-ish-kī
I don't understand.	*Aš nesuprantu*	AHSH neh-soo-PRAHN-too
Where is...?	*Kur yra....?*	Koor EE-rah
How much does this cost?	*Kiek kainuoja?*	KEE-yek KYE-new-oh-yah
I'd like a room.	*Aš norėčiau kambario.*	ahsh no-RYEH-chi-aoo KAHM-bah-ri-o
I'd like to pay.	Aš *norėčiau užmokėti*	ahsh no-RYEH-chi-aoo ush-moh-KYEH-TI
Help!	*Gelbfkite*	GYEL-beh-kyi-te

Vilnius

Although Catholicism has replaced Judaism as its dominant religion, Vilnius continues to draw energy from the cosmopolitan mix of its citizenry. One synagogue remains of pre-war Wilno's 400, but Orthodox churches still co-mingle with Baroque cathedrals, pagan temples, and medieval castles, reflecting the Russian-Polish-Lithuanian party that takes place on the city's sidewalks and squares. The foreign investment that has started to pour in recently keeps reinvigorating this "next Prague." See it for yourself, before everyone else gets in on the secret.

ORIENTATION AND PRACTICAL INFORMATION

From the **train** or **bus stations,** directly across from each other, walk east on **Geležinkelio g.** (to your right as you exit the train station), and turn left at its end. **Aušros Vartų g.** leads north from here through the south gates of **Senamiestis** (the Old Town). At the north end, **Arkikatedros aikštė** (Cathedral Sq.) and the **Castle Hill** loom over the banks of the river **Neris. Gedimino pr.,** the commercial artery, leads west from the square in front of the cathedral. Pick up a copy of *Vilnius in Your Pocket* at any self-respecting kiosk or hotel (4Lt).

Tourist Offices: The **Tourist Information Centre,** Gedimino pr. 14 (tel. 61 68 67; fax 22 61 18), finds rooms for free and sells *Vilnius in Your Pocket.* Open Mon.-Fri. 9am-6pm, Sat. 10am-3pm. **Lithuanian Youth Hostels Head Office,** Filaretų g. 17

(tel./fax 26 26 60; email lyh@jnakv.vno.soros.lt), at the Filaretai Hostel (see below). ISICs and worldwide hostel reservations. Open daily 8am-6pm.

Passport Office: Imigracijos Taryba, Verkių 3, #3, (tel. 75 64 53), 2km north of Senamiestis. Extends visas for 61Lt. Open Mon.-Fri. 9am-4:30pm.

Embassies: Belarus, P. Klimo g. 8 (tel./fax 26 34 43). Visa services at Muitinės g. 41 (tel. 63 06 26). Open Mon.-Tues. and Thurs.-Fri. 10am-4:30pm. **Canada,** Gedimino pr. 64 (tel. 22 08 98). Open Mon.-Fri. 10am-1pm. **Estonia,** Tilto g. 29 (tel. 22 04 86, visa info 62 20 30). Open Mon.-Thurs. 10am-noon and 2-4 pm. **Latvia,** M.K. Čiurlionio g. 76 (tel. 23 12 60, visa info 23 12 20). Open Mon.-Thurs. 10am-noon and 2-4pm, Fri. 10am-1pm. **Poland,** Smėlio g. 20a (tel. 70 90 01). Open Mon.-Fri. 9am-1pm. **Russia,** Latvių g. 53/54 (tel. 72 17 63, visa info 72 38 93). Open Mon.-Tues. and Thurs.-Fri. 10am-1pm. **Ukraine,** Turniškių g. 22 (tel./fax 76 36 26). Visa services on Kalvarijų 159, 2nd fl. (tel. 77 84 13). Open Mon.-Tues. and Thurs.-Fri. 10am-1pm. **U.K.,** Antakalnio g. 2 (tel. 22 20 70). Open Mon.-Fri. 9:30am-12:30pm. **U.S.,** Akmenų g. 6 (tel. 22 30 31; fax 670 60 84). Open Mon.-Thurs. 9-11:30am.

Currency Exchange: Vilniaus Bankas, Gedimino pr. 12 (tel. 61 07 23). Cash advances with no commission from Diners Club, MC, or Visa. Cashes traveler's checks. Open Mon.-Thurs. 9am-1:30pm and 2:30-4:30pm, Fri. 9am-4pm. Visa-linked **ATM. Litimpeks Bankas,** Geležinkelio g. 6 (tel. 23 54 54), under the red Valiutos Keitykla sign. Cashes traveler's checks (2.5% commission). Open 24hr.

Flights: Aerouostas (airport; tel. 63 55 60), Rodūnės Kelias 2, 5km south of town. Take bus 1 from the train station, or bus 2 from the "Sparta" stop of trolley bus 16 on Kauno g. **LOT** (tel. 26 08 19) flies to Warsaw; **SAS** (tel. 23 60 00) to Copenhagen. **Estonian Air** (tel. 26 15 59) to Tallinn (1 per day, 1½hr.). **Lithuanian Airlines** (tel. 75 25 88) to Berlin, Kiev, London, and Moscow.

Trains: Geležinkelio g. 16 (tel. 63 00 86 or 63 00 88). Tickets for **local** trains sold in a separate building to the left on the main (pink) building. Tickets for international trains in the yellow addition also to the left of the main station. **Reservation Bureau** (tel. 62 39 27), in the station hall (open daily 6am-midnight). To: Berlin via Belarus (transit visa a must—19½hr., 309Lt), Kaliningrad, Russia (7hr., 40Lt, *coupé* 65Lt), Minsk (5hr., 32Lt, *coupé* 52Lt), Moscow via Belarus (transit visa; 17hr., 80Lt, *coupé* 128Lt), Rīga (7½hr., 41Lt, *coupé* 67Lt), St. Petersburg (18hr., 64Lt, *coupé* 108Lt), Warsaw via Belarus (transit visa; 12hr., 60Lt, *coupé* 115Lt).

Buses: Autobusų Stotis, Sodų g. 22 (info tel. 26 24 82, reservations 26 29 77 or 63 52 77), opposite the train station. **Priemiestinė Salė,** is for local destinations; **Tarpmiestinė Salė** covers long-distance and has an info booth open daily 7am-8pm. To: Kaliningrad (8hr., 34-40Lt), Minsk (4hr., 19Lt), Rīga (5-6hr., 25-40Lt), Tallinn (10hr., 81Lt), and Warsaw (10hr., 60-65Lt).

Public Transportation: Buses and **trolleys** don't run in Senamiestis but link Vilnius's train and bus stations, its suburbs, and Senamiestis's edges (daily 6am-midnight). Buy tickets at any kiosk (0.60Lt; 0.75Lt from the driver; punch on board).

Taxis: Former State Taxis (tel. 22 88 88) or **Flast Rollo** (tel. 44 44 44). 1Lt to start, plus 1Lt per km (double after 10pm). **Private taxis** show a green light in the windshield; debate the fare before you go.

Gay Information Line: tel. 63 30 31. Info about organizations, events, and accommodations for gay men. **Lithuanian Gay and Lesbian Homepage** (http://cs.ektaco.ee/~forter) lists gay and lesbian establishments in Lithuania.

Laundromat: Slayana, Latvių g. 31 (tel. 75 31 12), in Žvėrynas. Wash and dry 10Lt. Detergent 3Lt. Open Mon.-Fri. 8am-8pm.

Pharmacy: Vokiečių Vaistinė, Didžioji g. 13 (tel. 22 42 32), in Senamiestis. Open Mon.-Fri. 9am-8pm, Sat. 10am-8pm, Sun. 11am-3pm. **Gedimino Vaistinė,** Gedimino pr. 27 (tel. 61 01 35 or 62 49 30). Open Mon.-Fri. 24hr., Sat. 9am-8pm.

Medical Services: Baltic-American Medical & Surgical Clinic, Antakalnio g. 124 (tel. 74 20 20), at Vilnius University Hospital. Open Mon.-Fri. 9am-5pm.

Emergencies: Police: 02. **Ambulance:** 03.

Internet Access: Send free email from the offices of the **Soros Foundation,** Šv. Jono g. 3/5 (tel. 22 38 06; call 22 37 to reserve a terminal). Open Mon.-Fri. noon-8pm.

Post Office: Centrinis Paštas, Gedimino pr. 7 (tel. 61 67 59), west of Arkikatedros aikštė. *Poste Restante* at the window that says *"iki pareikalavimo."* 0.30Lt to pick up mail. Open Mon.-Fri. 8am-8pm, Sat. 10am-5pm. **Postal Code:** LT-2001.

Telephones: In the main post office (info. tel. 62 55 11). Norwegian phones take phone cards (3.54Lt and up) and allow direct dialing abroad. Open Mon.-Fri. 8am-8pm, Sat. 10am-5pm. **Telephone Code:** 02.

ACCOMMODATIONS

Few of the accommodations in Vilnius cater to budget travelers. **Litinterp,** Bernardinų 7, #2 (tel. 22 38 50; fax 22 35 59; email litinterp@post.omnitel.net), arranges homestays. (Reserve ahead. Singles 60-100Lt. Doubles 100-140Lt. Open Mon.-Fri. 9am-6pm, Sat. 9am-4pm.) In a pinch, head to the overnight office in the main train station (tel. 69 24 72), to the left of the ticket info office, for **a couchette in a non-working stationary train** (check-in after 8pm; check-out 8am; 15Lt).

Filaretai Youth Hostel (HI), Filaretų g. 17 (tel. 69 66 27; fax 22 01 49; email filareta@vno.osf.lt). Take bus 34, leaving from the right of the station to the 7th stop. Clean kitchen, St. Petersburg visa invitations (20Lt), and oodles of Vilnius info. Curfew midnight. Reception open 7am-midnight. Dorms 20-24Lt. Doubles 56-64Lt.

Žaliasis tiltas (The Green Bridge), in the center of downtown at 2 different locations around the corner from each other. **Gedimino pr. 12** (tel. 61 54 50; fax 22 17 16) has sumptuous rooms. Singles 90Lt. Doubles 130Lt. **Vilniaus g. 2, #15** (tel. 61 54 60, info and reservations tel./fax 22 17 16). Small but clean singles 60Lt. Doubles 120Lt. Breakfast included. AmEx, Diners Club, MC, and V.

Šauni Vietelė, Pranciškonų g. 316 (tel./fax 22 41 10), in a former monastery. Excellent location and extremely comfortable. Rooms 100Lt per person. Reserve ahead.

Vilnius Pedagogical University Dormitory, A. Vivulskio g. 36 (tel. 23 07 04; fax 26 22 91). Take trolleybus 7, 15, or 16 from the station and switch to trolleybus 10, 13, or 17. Shared toilets. Singles 28Lt, students 23Lt. Doubles 54Lt, students 46Lt.

FOOD

The four French **Iki** supermarkets are stocked with foreign foods. The most convenient one lies at Žirmūnu g. 68, 1.5km north across the Neris. Trendy yet inexpensive restaurants are popping up everywhere. A full meal can be as cheap as US$4-6, but the more English words on the menu, the more you'll pay.

Ritos Slėptuvė (Rita's Hideaway), A. Goštauto g. 8, west of Senamiestis along the Neris. *The* place to go. Pasta 5-10Lt. Transforms into a **bar** by night with live music and disco on Fri and Sat. Open Sun.-Thurs. 7:30am-2am, Fri.-Sat. 7:30am-4am.

Ritos Smuklė (Rita's Tavern), Žirmūnų g. 68. Rita's newest creation is this traditional Lithuanian restaurant. Take trolley bus 12, 13, or 17. Homemade *kvass* (gyros) 2Lt. Live folk music Fri. and Sat. 8-10pm. Open daily 11am-2am.

Literatų Svetainė, Gedimino pr. 1. Full of dark wood and velvet. English menu. Superb Lithuanian main dishes 5-9Lt. Open daily 8:30am-midnight.

Café Afrika, Pilies g. 28, smack in the center of it all. Look for the yellow-and-blue zebra. Soup, salad, and gourmet cup of coffee in this mellow yellow establishment for less than 11Lt. Open daily 10am-11pm.

SIGHTS

Through the gates to the Old Town, the first door on the right leads to the 17th-century **Aušros Vartų Koplyčia** (Chapel of the Gates of Dawn). The miraculous reputation of the icon inside fuels Catholic pilgrimages. Farther along, the crown-topped **Šv. Kazimiero bažnyčia** (St. Casimir's Church) has an oh-so-very Lithuanian history: in 1832, the church gained a Russian Orthodox dome; in World War I, the Germans made it Lutheran; after World War II, the Soviets turned it into a museum of atheism; and it was restored as a church in 1989 (open Mon.-Sat. 4pm-6:30pm, Sun. 8am-2pm).

Didžioji g. broadens into **Rotušės aikštė,** the ancient marketplace dominated by the 18th-century **town hall.** Inside, the **Lietuvos Dailės Muziejus** (State Art Museum) has a rich collection of Lithuanian paintings. Now under restoration, its art resides in a former palace at Didžioji g. 4—the **Vilniaus Paveikslu Gallerija Lietuvos Dailė** (open Tues.-Sun. noon-6pm; 2Lt, students 1Lt, Sept.-May Wed. free). As Didžioji g. continues north, it passes **Šv. Mikalojaus bažnyčia** (St. Nicholas's Church), Lithuania's oldest. A bit farther, Didžioji g. widens into a triangular square and merges with the pedestrian **Pilies g.,** lined with souvenir shops and cafés. At the corner of Pilies and Šv. Jono g. stands the **University of Vilnius.** Founded in 1579, the Jesuit university was a major player in the Counter-Reformation. Through the arches opposite St. John's Church waits the remarkable 17th-century **Astronomical Observatory.**

North on Pilies g. (or Universiteto g.), the picturesque **Arkikatedros aikštė** (Cathedral Square) has had a church here since 1387; the present 18th-century **Arkikatedra** resembles a Greek temple. Gedimino pr. leads west from here; at its far end sits the **parliament.** In January 1991, the world watched as Lithuanians raised barricades to protect their parliament from the Soviet army. On the other side of the Cathedral, up on Castle Hill, **Gedimino Tower** affords a great view of Vilnius's spires. Descending the hill, meander through the park to the south to Mairionio g., which leads south to the Gothic **Šv. Onos ir Bernardinų b.s** (St. Anne's Church and Bernadine Monastery), so beautiful that Napoleon wanted to carry it back to France. One final must-see is the high Baroque **St. Peter and Paul Church,** on Antakalnio g., northeast of Cathedral Square. On the ceiling, two thousand carved figures dance and sing.

ENTERTAINMENT

Vilnius's breakneck economic development has opened the gates for a fast and furious arts scene. For a list of performances, check *Vilnius in Your Pocket* or the paper *Lietuvos Rytas.* Consult the tourist office at Gedimino pr. 14 (tel. 61 68 67; fax 22 61 18) for ticket info. Check out posters in Senamiestis or Prie Parlamento's bulletin board. Lithuanian hipsters Eduardas and Vladimiras organize a **gay disco** every Saturday night at a different venue. Call them (tel. 63 30 31) for more info (cover 15Lt).

The Pub (Prie Universiteto), Dominikonų g. 9, is an immensely popular traditional English pub (pint of *Pilsner Urquell* 10Lt; open daily 11am-2am). In an unassuming white building on Etmonų g. 6, **BIX** is surrealist to the nth degree, with crazy rhythms and a young, cutting-edge crowd (open daily noon-4am). The fanciest disco in town is **Indigo Klubas,** Trakų g. 312. (Cover 10-15Lt. Wed. is ladies' night, Sun. jazz. Open Sun.-Thurs. 8pm-3am, Fri.-Sat. 8pm-5am.) Communist kitsch and the reputed best singles scene lurk at **Naktinis Vilkas** (Night Wolf), Lukiškių g. 3 (cover 5Lt; open daily 5pm-5am), while **Bočiu Baras,** Šv. Ignoto g. 413, is a dim-lit lair of teenage sin (beer 3-4Lt; disco starts at 9pm; open daily noon-3am).

■ Near Vilnius: Trakai

The capital of the Grand Duchy of Lithuania in the 14th and 15th centuries, Trakai, 28km west from Vilnius, is a lakeside village full of intricate wooden cottages, castles, and ruins. Eight **trains** to run to Trakai from Vilnius every day (30min., 2Lt), as well as 26 **buses** (45min., 2Lt). Trakai's train station is on Vilniaus g., 500m south of the bus station; follow the crowd into town. The exquisite **Trakai Castle** sits on an island in Lake Galvė, accessible by a footbridge on Karaimų g. The 30m high watchtower is stocked with historical displays.

Kaunas

Burnt to the ground 13 times, Kaunas, Lithuania's second-largest city, has been repeatedly reincarnated and is still considered to embody Lithuania's true heart and soul. This was the capital city from 1918 until 1940, but is now a serene place whose unhurried pace has been little changed by the growing number of bars, restaurants, and shops. Where Laisvės al. ends, Kaunas's Old Town begins; follow Vilniaus g. through an underpass and you'll be inside the medieval city walls. The **Kauno Arkikatedra Bažnyčia** is a shockingly large 15th-century cathedral with a Gothic and

Renaissance interior. Wander up Karaliaus dvaro off the north end of the square and you'll arrive at **Santakos Parkas,** a tree-dotted chunk of land where the Neris and Nemunas rivers meet and site of Kaunas's 13th-century **castle.**

The massive **St. Michael the Archangel Church** commands the east end of Laisvės al., a 2km pedestrian avenue. The church's sumptuous neo-Byzantine exterior is a feast for the eyes, though the recently redone interior is strangely unattractive. (Open Mon.-Fri. 8am-5pm, Sat.-Sun. 9am-4pm; services Mon.-Fri. noon, Sat. 10am, Sun. 10am and noon.) Two blocks down Laisvės al. and right on Daukanto g. lies **Vienybės aikštė** (Unity Sq.), depicted in etched glory on the back of the 20Lt note. Surrounding the square are several museums. The **M. K. Čiurlionis Museum,** Putvinskio g. 55, honors the avant-garde artist who sought to combine image and music to express an idea without words (open Tues.-Sun. noon-6pm, closed last Tues. of every month; 3Lt, students 1.50Lt). Across the street, the hellish **Velnių muziejus** (Devil Museum), Putvinskio g. 64, houses a collection of nearly 2000 devils, most of them folk carvings. Don't miss Devil Hitler and Devil Stalin chasing each other across bone-covered Lithuania (open Tues.-Sun. noon-6pm, closed last Tues. of every month; 4Lt, students 2Lt).

The **Pažaislis Monastery and Church,** a vibrant Baroque ensemble with rich frescoes, sits on the Nemunas's right bank 10km east of central Kaunas. Used as a KGB-run "psychiatric hospital," the monastery was returned to the Catholic Church in 1990 (open Mon.-Sat. 10am-5pm, Sun. 10am-6pm). Take trolleybus 5 from the train station to the end of the line; then walk 1km down the road.

Practical Information, Accommodations, and Food **Delta/Tourist Information,** Laisvės al. 88 (tel. (27) 20 49 11), sells maps (8Lt) and gives info on accommodations and sights (open Mon.-Fri. 9am-6pm, Sat. 10am-2pm). **Litinterp,** Kumelių 15, apt. 4 (tel./fax (27) 22 87 18), in the Old Town, find private rooms (singles 60Lt, doubles 100Lt) and rents bikes (20Lt per day, US$100 deposit; open Mon.-Sat. 9am-6pm, Sat. 9am-4pm). **Trains** arrive at Čiurlionio g. 16 (tel. (27) 29 22 60) on their way to Rīga (6hr., 25-55.50Lt) and Vilnius (1½-2hr., 7.30-8.70Lt). The **bus station,** Vytauto pr. 24/26 (tel. (27) 22 19 42), services cities including Vilnius (2hr., 9.40Lt). In summer, a daily **hydrofoil** leaves Raudondvario pl. 107 for Nida (4hr., 49Lt). The **Svečių Namai,** Prancūzų g. 59 (tel. (27) 74 89 72; fax 22 41 85), offers excellent facilities a bit far from town. From the train station, cross the tracks, and head left at the end of the bridge to Prancūzų g. (doubles 124Lt, triples 111Lt; singles 40Lt with IYH card). **Hotel Baltijos,** Vytauto pr. 71 (tel. 28 32 02), offers basic accommodations near the end of Laisvės al. Its aging rooms can be had for 70Lt per single and 104-58Lt per double. At **Liepaitė,** Donelaičio 66, the food is decent and service, impeccable. (Veal with salmon in olive oil 25Lt. Open Sun.-Thurs. noon-midnight, Fri.-Sat. noon-3am.) **Pieno Baras,** Laisvės al. at S. Daukanto, serves up *blyneliai* (3Lt) and whipped milk (1.56Lt; open Mon.-Fri. 9am-7pm, Sat. 10am-6pm).

■ Near Kaunas

On a sunny morning in 1236, German Knights of the Sword, returning after a campaign to Christianize Lithuania, were ambushed and massacred. To commemorate the bloodshed, people began a tradition of placing crosses on eerie **Kryžių Kalnas** (Hill of Crosses), 10km northwest of the city. After uprisings in 1831 and 1863, Lithuanians brought crosses to remember the dead and the deported. Under the Soviets, more crosses appeared and the hill became a mound of anti-Russian sentiment, with crosses replaced despite the best effort of Soviet bulldozers. Since independence, crosses have been placed by or in honor of emigrated Lithuanians. **Trains** shuttle from Kaunas (2hr., 6Lt). From the station, walk left on Dubijos g., right on Višinskio and left on Stoties to the bus station, Tilžės 109. From there, **buses** running north to Joniškis, Meškuičiai, Rīga, or Tallinn pass by at Kryžių Kalnas; ask the driver to stop. From where the bus drops you, a marked road leads down for about 2km.

"You hear the murmur of the pines, so solemn, as if they were trying to tell you something," avant-garde artist, composer, mystic, and native son Mikolojus Konstantinas Čiurlionis wrote of **Druskininkaiin** 1905. The artist's unique works are kept alive at **M. K. Čiurlionio Memorialinis Muziejus,** Čiurlionio g. 41 (open Tues.-Sun. noon-6pm, closed last Tues. of the month; 1Lt, students 0.50Lt). **Piano concerts** on Sunday evenings in summer feature Čiurlionis's own compositions, as well as those of Bach, Debussy, and Beethoven (5pm, 1hr., 5Lt). Poles used to flock to Druskininkai to bathe in its natural spring waters; after World War II, the town became a favorite vacation resort among Russians. These days, the Russians are gone, and the Poles are returning in droves. **Buses** head from the station at Gardino g. 1 (tel. (233) 513 33) to Vilnius (2½hr., 12-14Lt) and Kaunas (3hr., 12-14Lt). To get to town, make a left after exiting the station and walk down Gardino g. The **tourist office,** Laisvės al. 18 (tel. (233) 517 77; fax 553 76), is at the corner of Vilniaus g. (open Mon.-Fri. 9am-6pm). **Druskininkai Hotel,** Kudirkos g. 43 (tel. (233) 525 66; fax 522 66), on the corner of Taikos g., offers spartan, clean rooms and balconies (singles 40Lt, doubles 30-46Lt, triples 45Lt). Even if you're not hungry, stop by the **Baltoji Astra,** Vilniaus g. 10, to ogle its architecture (salads 4Lt; main courses 10Lt; open daily noon-midnight).

Palanga

Every summer, Lithuanians flock to Palanga, one of the former Soviet Union's prime beach resorts, to crowd its streets and brave the icy Baltic. Visitors enjoy sandy beaches, extensive botanical gardens, mineral springs, and a relaxing small-town feel. The best way to spend a day here is at the **beach,** which runs from Girkeliai, 5km south of town, all the way to the border, 18km north. **Nude bathing** is allowed—women control the section starting 200m north of the pier, men head south. At the end of Basanazičiaus g., a fountain-bedecked plaza opens onto the boardwalk which stretches behind the dunes for the length of the town. Its cafés and bars let you sip away the evening and dance away the weekends. Alternatively, wander through the **Botanical Park** at Palanga's south end. Well-marked paths and flowering trails make for romantic walks around sunset. In the park, Count Tiškevičius's **palace** contains the glittering **Amber Museum,** a gargantuan collection of more than 35,000 pieces of amber (open Tues.-Sun. 11am-7pm; 3Lt, students 1Lt). For candle-lit entertainment, **Kavinė Fontanas,** Basanazičiaus g. 46, tempts with good beer (6Lt), snacks (around 6-15Lt), and live music in summer.

Buses run from the corner of Kretingos and Vytauto g. to Klaipėda (40min., 2.80Lt), Kaunas (4hr., 26Lt), and Vilnius (6hr., 30Lt). A 24-hour **tourist booth** (tel. (236) 543 68) outside the bus station sells maps and helps with accommodations. The sunny **Lithuanian Youth Hostel,** S. Nėries g. 23 (tel. (236) 570 76), off the path between #17 and 21, shelters rooms reminiscent of lakeside cabins (20Lt per person). Klaipėda's **Litinterp** (tel. (26) 21 69 62) arranges **homestays** in and around Palanga starting at 60Lt for singles, and 100Lt for doubles (reserve in Klaipėda). **Basanavičiaus gavė,** is lined with bars and outside eateries. The food at **Daisa,** Basanavičiaus g.7a, is a little better than the usual fare, and includes salads (4.10Lt), steak (18.40Lt), and *pilmeni* (4.50Lt). The popular **Elnio Ragas,** Basanavičiaus g. 25, has low prices, but the food might be a little greasy and bland (pancakes with bananas 8Lt; 0.5L Czech *Budvar* 7Lt; open daily 11am-midnight).

Klaipėda

This busy port was always the apple of Lithuania's eye, and centuries of foreign control could not shake the country's hopes of one day having Klaipėda all for its very own. Now that the dream has come true, proud Lithuanians are adding comfortable cafés, elegant restaurants, and bars throughout the city. Before settling in for the evening, check out the **Klaipėda Theater** in the Old Town center, Teatro aikštė. Built in 1857, the theater is famous as one of Wagner's favorite haunts and infamous for the *Anschluss* (annexation) speech Hitler gave from its balcony in 1939. For tickets, call (026) 21 25 89 (open Tues.-Sun. 11am-2pm and 4:30-7pm). In front stands the **Simon Dach Fountain,** at the center of which is the symbol of Klaipėda, a statue of Ännchen von Tharau. On **Smiltynė**, the **Ethnografinė Pajūrio Žvejo Sodyba** (Ethnographic Coastal Fishermen's Village) reconstructs a 17th-century settlement (open 24hr.; free). Forest paths lead west about 500m to the **beaches.** Signs mark gender-restricted areas for **nude bathing**—*moterų* is women, *vyrų* men. Bars in the Old Town are a staple of Klaipėda nightlife, and a growing number of discos provide evening fun. **Nova,** Janonino 27, a neon palace of a disco, is the most popular place in town (cover 10-20Lt; open Tues.-Sun. 10pm-5am).

The **Danė River** divides the city into the southern **Senamiestis** (Old Town) and northern **Naujamiestis** (New Town), while a lagoon cuts off **Smiltynė,** Klaipėda's Curonian Spit quarter. The Litinterp **tourist office,** S. Šimkaus g. 21/8 (tel. (026) 21 98 62; fax 21 69 62), arranges private rooms in and around Klaipėda (doubles 100Lt), rents bikes (20Lt per day with US$100 deposit), and sells maps and guidebooks (open Mon.-Fri. 9am-6pm, Sat. 10am-4pm). **Trains** roll from Priestočio g. 7 (tel. (026) 21 46 14, reservations 29 63 56) to Vilnius (5hr., 27Lt) and Kaunas (7½hr., 27Lt). **Buses** also serve Kaunas (4hr., 20Lt), Nida (2hr., 7.40Lt), and Vilnius (7½hr., 30Lt) from Butkų Juzės 9 (tel. (026) 21 48 63, reservations 21 14 34). Frequent **ferries** go to Smiltynė (1Lt round-trip). **Hotel Viktorija,** S. Šimkaus g. 2 (tel. (026) 21 36 70), offers the best location at the best price (singles 120Lt, doubles 70Lt; private bath 120Lt). The central **market** on Turgaus aikštė, at the south end of *Senamiestis,* is open 8am to 6pm daily. **Skandalas,** Kanto 44, is a change from most Lithuanian food; tasty grilled steaks are 20Lt before 6pm, 28Lt after (live jazz at night; open daily noon-3am). **Restoranas Luiza,** Puodžių 40, opposite the Hotel Klaipėda, has a pleasant outside bar (stuffed squid 22Lt; open daily noon-midnight).

Nida

If you're watching the sunrise from a high white dune as the crisp smell of smoked fish rises into the air, you must be in Nida. The town lies on the **Curonian Spit** (Kuršiçe Nerija), a 3km wide strip of dunes, unspoiled beaches, and thick pine and birch forests. The **Drifting Dunes of Parnidis** rise south of town. You can hike out and climb the 60m high dune for a spectacular, desert-like view. All of the **wooden houses** clustered along Naglių g. and Lotmiškio g. are classified historic monuments. From the center of town, walk north on Pamario or along the waterfront promenade to reach the **Thomas Mann House** at #17 (open Tues.-Sun. 11am-6pm; 1Lt), where Mann wrote *Joseph and his Brother.* **Buses** from Klaipėda (2hr., 7Lt) and Vilnius (4hr., 35Lt) run to Naglių 2, just north of Taikos g. Another option is to go by **hydrofoil** from Kaunas to Nida (4hr., 49Lt). The **tourist office,** Taikos g. 4 (tel. (0259) 52 34 59), opposite the bus and ferry stations, sells maps (3Lt) and arranges accommodations (20-40Lt per person). **Urbo Kalnas,** Taikos g. 32 (tel. (0259) 524 28 or 529 53), will accommodate you in big, balconied rooms with hot showers (37Lt per person; breakfast included). **Laumē,** Pamario 24 (tel. (0259) 523 35), has clean rooms with small beds (40-50Lt per person), as well as shoddier rooms in another building (20Lt). The local specialty is *rūkyta žuvis* (smoked fish); selection varies from nondescript "fish" to eel and perch. **Seklyčia,** Lotmiško 1, is considered to be the best restaurant in town (tomato salad 4Lt; open daily 9am-3pm). **Ešerinė,** Naglių 2, is a wacky thatched-roofed collection of glass-wall huts (pork chops 16.50Lt).

Luxembourg

US$1= 37.51LF (francs, or LUF)	**10LF =US$0.27**
CDN$1= 27.16LF	**10LF =CDN$0.37**
UK£1= 59.63LF	**10LF =UK£0.17**
IR£1= 55.70LF	**10LF =IR£0.18**
AUS$1= 27.38LF	**10LF =AUS$0.37**
NZ$1= 23.84LF	**10LF =NZ$0.42**
SAR1= 8.00F	**10LF =SAR1.25**
Country Code: 352	**International Dialing Prefix: 00**

Founded in 963, the Grand Duchy of Luxembourg was first named *Luclinburhuc,* or "little castle." By the time successive waves of Burgundians, Spaniards, French, Austrians, and Germans had receded, the little castle had become a bristling armored mountain, and the countryside was saturated with fortresses. Only after the last French soldier returned home in 1867 and the Treaty of London restored its neutrality did Luxembourg begin to cultivate its current image of peacefulness. Today Luxembourg is an independent constitutional monarchy, a member of the European Union, and a tax-haven for investors world-wide. The Grand Duke and his Cabinet of 12 ministers still wield supreme executive power over the country's 400,000 residents and 2600 sq. km. From the wooded and hilly Ardennes in the north to the fertile vineyards of the Moselle Valley in the south, the country's unspoiled rural landscapes provide a sharp contrast to the high-powered banking of the capital city.

ESSENTIALS

The tiny territory is split into even smaller travel zones, and the price of a trip is calculated according to the number of zones crossed. A *billet courte distance* (short distance ticket) costs 40LF and allows you to traverse up to six zones (10 tickets 320LF). Most intercity trips require at least two or three tickets. Undoubtedly the best deals are **Billets Réseau** (160LF), which allow a day's unlimited second-class travel on any train or national bus. A **Benelux Tourrail Pass,** good for unlimited travel any five days in a month-long period in Belgium, the Netherlands, and Luxembourg, costs 4400LF (under 26 3300LF). **Bicycles** are permitted on many trains for a 40LF fee. **Hitchhiking** has mixed results, as traffic is light and safety is never guaranteed.

The many **tourist offices** are skilled at finding cheap rooms. Hostels frequently give discounts on tours, and the hostel association maintains trails marked with white triangles between each of their houses. Luxembourg francs are worth the same as Belgian francs; you can use Belgian money in Luxembourg, and vice versa. Most **banks** are open Monday through Friday 8:30am to 4:30pm; most shops are open Monday 2 to 6pm and Tuesday through Saturday 9:30am to 6pm. Many shops close at noon for two hours, especially in the countryside, where only taverns may be open after 6pm.

Luxembourg's official **languages** are French and German, but the most common is Letzebuergesch, a German dialect with French loanwords. French is often preferred to German; English is heard nearly everywhere. For **AT&T Direct,** call 08 00 01 11; **MCI WorldPhone** 08 00 01 12; **Sprint Access** 08 00 01 15; **Canada Direct** 08 00 01 19; **BT Direct** 08 00 00 44; **Australia Direct** 08 00 00 61; and **NZ Direct** 08 00 00 64.

Accommodations, Camping, and Food The 13 **HI youth hostels** in Luxembourg charge between 340 and 650LF, ages over 26 425-780LF; nonmembers pay 100LF extra. Breakfasts are included, packed lunches cost 125LF, and dinners are 260LF; eating a meal in the hostel earns a 15LF discount. Sheets are 120LF. Lockers require 500LF or your passport deposit. All but three of the hostels have kitchens. Many hostels also close during December and January; phone ahead to verify hours. Luxembourg **hotels** advertise 800-1500LF per night but often try to persuade tourists to take more expensive rooms. **Campgrounds** abound, and almost all have hot show-

ers. Two people with a tent will pay 250-300LF. Restaurant prices will devour your budget. Luxembourg cuisine is closely linked to that of the neighboring Lorraine region of France, and sliced Ardennes ham is the national specialty.

Luxembourg City (Ville de Luxembourg)

Rising triumphantly from the lush valleys of the Pétrusse and Alzette Rivers, the city of Luxembourg is one of the most attractive and dramatic capitals in Europe. It is at once testimony to Europe's war-torn history and a symbol of the hope for peace. Visitors can see not only the many defenses that shielded the city's inhabitants for centuries, but also the forested parks that now lie in the place of dismantled fortifications. Four or five languages are always within earshot, as Luxembourg's international banking firms draw professionals from all over Europe, but it is the natural beauty that makes Luxembourg both a restful locale and a fascinating destination.

PRACTICAL INFORMATION

Tourist Offices: Grand Duchy National Tourist Office, in the train station (tel. 48 11 99; fax 40 47 48; touristinfo@luxembourg-city.lu; http://www.luxembourg-city.lu/touristinfo/). Free map and reservations service (no fee). Open 9am-noon and 2pm-6:30pm. The **Municipal Tourist Office,** pl. d'Armes (tel. 22 28 09; fax 47 48 18), in the center of town, offers more specific city info. Open Mon.-Sat. 9am-7pm, Sun. 10am-6pm. At either location grab *La Semaine à Luxembourg* (free).

Budget Travel: SOTOUR, 15, pl. du Théâtre (tel. 46 15 14). BIJ and other discount tickets. Open Mon.-Fri. 9am-6pm, Sat. 9am-noon.

Embassies: Travelers from **Australia, Canada, New Zealand,** and **South Africa** should contact their embassies in France or Belgium. **Ireland,** 28, rue d'Arlon (tel. 45 06 10; fax 45 88 20). Open Mon.-Fri. 9am-12:30pm and 2-5pm. **U.K.,** 14, bd. Roosevelt (tel. 22 98 64; fax 22 98 67). Same hours as Ireland. **U.S.,** 22, bd. E. Servais (tel. 46 01 23). Open Mon.-Fri. 8am-5pm.

Currency Exchange: Mediocre rates at the train station *bureau de change.* Open Mon.-Sat. 8:30am-9pm, Sun. 9am-9pm. Banks have similar rates. An automatic **currency exchange machine** is across from the station at Banque UCL.

American Express: 34, av. de la Porte-Neuve (tel. 22 85 55). Mail held. Traveler's checks cashed, sold, and replaced; wired money accepted. Exchange rates similar to banks. Open Mon.-Fri. 9am-5:30pm, Sat. 9:30am-noon.

Flights: Bus 9 to the airport (40LF plus a rarely enforced 40LF charge for baggage) is cheaper than the Luxair bus (120LF) and runs the same airport-hostel-train station route more frequently (every 20min, 20min.).

Trains: Gare CFL, av. de la Gare (tel. 49 24 24), near the foot of av. de la Liberté in the southern part of the city (10min. from the city center). Bus 9 runs between the railway station, the hostel, and the airport. Pick it up on your right as you leave the station, in front of the Luxair office. To: Amsterdam (5¾hr., 16,342LF), Brussels (2¾hr., 890LF, under 26 520LF), and Milan (9hr., 3612LF).

Buses: Buy tickets from the driver (40LF; valid 1hr. or 160LF for full day), or get a package of 10 (320LF) at banks.

Luggage Storage: At the station. Check and insure your bags for up to 1 month (60LF per day; open daily 6am-10pm) or use lockers (60-100LF, good for 2 days). Hotels and hostels will often hold bags for the day free of charge.

Laundromat: Quick Wash, 31, rue de Strasbourg, near the station. Wash 290LF, dry 90LF. Open Mon.-Fri. 8:30am-7pm, Sat. 8am-6pm. Cheaper at the hostel.

Taxis: (tel. 48 22 33). 32LF per km. 10% more 9pm-6am. 25% more on Sundays. 600LF from city center to airport.

Crisis Lines: tel. 54 16 16; Mon.-Fri. 9am-5pm. **SOS Distress:** tel. 45 45 45. Staffed daily 3-11pm. **SOS Drogue:** tel. 49 60 99, for drug problems. Staffed 24hr.

Pharmacy: Pharmacie du Globe, 12, rue Jean Origier (tel. 48 70 09), off av. de la Gare. Open Mon.-Fri. 7:40am-6pm. Dial 112 on weekends to find a pharmacy, or look in any pharmacy window for the address of the current *pharmacie de garde.*

Medical Emergencies: tel. 112. English spoken. Open 24hr.

Police: tel. 113. The station is at 58-60, rue Glesner (tel. 40 94 01).

Post Office: Main office, 38, pl. de la Gare, across the street and to the left of the train station. Open Mon.-Fri. 6am-7pm, Sat. 6am-noon. **Branch office** at 25, rue Aldringern, 2 blocks from pl. d'Armes. Open Mon.-Fri. 7am-8pm, Sat. 7am-6pm. *Poste Restante* available at both offices. **Postal Code:** For *Poste Restante,* address mail L-1009 for main office and L-1118 for the branch office in the center.

Telephones: Outside both post offices and in two locations at the train station. 50 units (50 short calls in the city), 250LF. Coin phones are only in hostels and hotels.

ACCOMMODATIONS, CAMPING, AND FOOD

Inexpensive hotels jam the streets near the train station, but hotels become increasingly pricey and posh as you move north of the ravine. Both the main and branch tourist offices will help you find cheap rooms.

Auberge de Jeunesse (HI), 2, rue du Fort Olisy (tel. 22 68 89). Take bus 9 from the airport or train station to Vallée d'Alzette below rue Sigefroi. From the stop walk back under the bridge and turn right down the path (35min. total). Can be noisy, with lots of students. Bar, pool table, and laundry. Clean dorms and rooms for groups. Reception open 7am-10pm. Lockout 10am-1:30pm. Curfew 2am. Dorms 415-465LF, over 26 500-560F. Singles 630LF, over 26 730LF. Doubles 1100LF, over 26 1120LF. Nonmembers add 110LF. Sheets 125LF. Breakfast included.

Hotel Carlton, 9, rue de Strasbourg (tel. 48 48 02). From the station, walk up av. de la Liberté and turn left on rue de Strasbourg (2min.). Beautiful hotel complete with

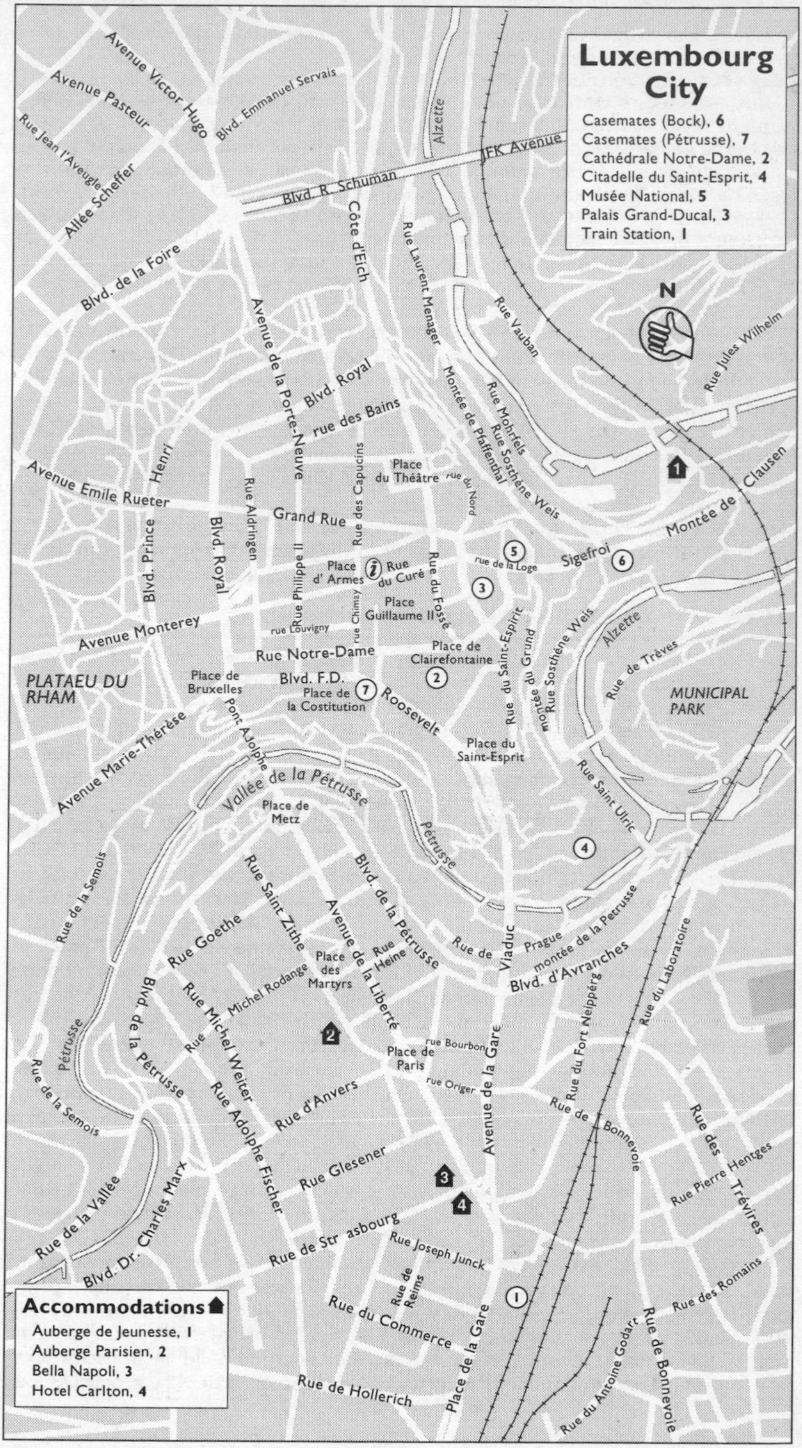
Luxembourg City
Casemates (Bock), 6
Casemates (Pétrusse), 7
Cathédrale Notre-Dame, 2
Citadelle du Saint-Esprit, 4
Musée National, 5
Palais Grand-Ducal, 3
Train Station, 1
N
Accommodations
Auberge de Jeunesse, 1
Auberge Parisien, 2
Bella Napoli, 3
Hotel Carlton, 4
Avenue Victor Hugo
Avenue Pasteur
Rue Jean l'Aveugle
Allée Scheffer
Blvd. Emmanuel Servais
Alzette
JFK Avenue
Blvd. R. Schuman
Blvd. de la Foire
Côte d'Eich
Rue Laurent Menager
Rue Vauban
Rue Jules Wilhelm
Avenue de la Porte-Neuve
Blvd. Royal
rue des Bains
Montée de Pfaffenthal
Rue Mohrfels
Rue Sosthène Weis
Avenue Emile Rueter
Blvd. Prince Henri
Rue Aldringen
Rue des Capucins
Place du Théâtre
rue du Nord
Grand Rue
Montée de Clausen
Rue Philippe II
Place d' Armes
Rue du Curé
Rue du Fossé
rue de la Loge
Sigefroi
Avenue Monterey
rue Louvigny
rue Chimay
Place Guillaume II
Rue Notre-Dame
Place de Clairefontaine
Rue du Saint-Esprit
montée du Grund
Rue Sosthène Weis
Alzette
Rue de Trèves
MUNICIPAL PARK
PLATAEU DU RHAM
Place de Bruxelles
Blvd. F.D. Roosevelt
Place de la Costitution
Pont Adolphe
Avenue Marie-Thérèse
Place du Saint-Esprit
Rue Saint Ulric
Vallée de la Pétrusse
Place de Metz
Pétrusse
Rue de la Semois
Rue Saint Zithe
Blvd. de la Pétrusse
Avenue de la Liberté
Rue Goethe
Place des Martyrs
Rue Heine
Rue de Prague
Viaduc
montée de la Petrusse
Blvd. d'Avranches
Rue du Laboratoire
Rue Michel Rodange
Rue Michel Weiter
Rue du Fort Neipperg
rue Bourbon
Place de Paris
rue Origer
Avenue de la Gare
Rue de Bonnevoie
Rue d'Anvers
Rue Adolphe Fischer
Rue des Trévires
Rue Pierre Hentges
Rue Glesener
Rue de la Vallée
Blvd. Dr. Charles Marx
Rue de Strasbourg
Rue Joseph Junck
Rue de Reims
Rue des Romains
Rue du Commerce
Place de la Gare
Rue du Antoine Godart
Rue de Hollerich

stained-glass windows. Friendly staff. Reception open 24hr. Singles 750LF. Doubles 1400LF, with bath 1700LF. Breakfast included.

Bella Napoli, 4, rue de Strasbourg, opposite Hotel Carlton. (tel. 48 46 29; fax 48 64 80). Plain rooms with TV. Singles 950LF, with bath 1200LF. Doubles 1500LF. Triples 1900LF. Quads 2300LF. Breakfast included.

Auberge Le Parisien, 46, rue Ste-Zithe (tel. 49 23 97; fax 40 20 92). From the station walk down av. de la Liberté to pl. de Paris (5min.). Small, clean rooms, all with a TV and a sunny Provençal feel. Reception open 24hr. Singles 1200LF, with shower 1350LF. Doubles 1700LF, with shower 1850LF. Triples 2150LF, with shower 2300LF. Breakfast included. Open Jan. 9-Dec. 22.

Camping: Kockelscheuer (tel. 47 18 15). Bus 2 from the station. 110LF, children 50LF, tents 120LF. Showers included. Wheelchair accessible. Open Easter-Oct.

Most restaurants are crowded by Luxembourgeois with cash to spare, but with a little searching, you can actually afford to eat. The area around **Place d'Armes,** with its covering of outdoor terraces and frequent live music, is great for dining. **Bella Napoli,** 4, rue de Strasbourg, has an extensive classical Italian menu: 200LF for a pizza, and dinner-size pastas start at 250LF. For a touch of high class without high prices, try **Restaurant Bacchus,** 32, Marché-aux-Herbes, down the street from the Grand-Ducal palace (pizza 340LF; open Tues.-Sun. noon-10pm). **Girogio,** 11, rue du Nord, has veggie options (330LF), while **Maybe Not Bob's,** 107, rue de la Tour Jacob, complements its veggie fare (340-425LF) with burgers (305LF) and spare ribs (355LF). Gather up the fixings for a picnic in the parks by the ravine at the subterranean supermarket **Nobilis,** 47, av. de la Gare (open Mon.-Fri. 9am-7:30pm, Sat. 9am-7pm).

SIGHTS AND ENTERTAINMENT

The tourist office provides free leaflets for a self-guided tour through the historical city center. Guided tours of the **city promenade** are available (Easter-Oct. daily at 2:30pm; meet at Municipal tourist office; 2hr.; 200LF). The **Wenzel walk** takes you through 1000 years of history in 100 minutes as it winds around the walls of the old city and down into the casemates. Tours are held every Saturday at 3pm, beginning at the **Bock-Casemates.** Looming imposingly over the Alzette River valley, this fortress (part of Luxembourg's original castle, dating back to the 10th century) sheltered 35,000 people while the rest of the city was pounded during World War II. (Entrance on rue Sigefroi near the bridge that leads to the hostel. Open March-Oct. daily 10am-5pm. 70LF.) If that isn't enough, follow up by descending into the **Pétrusse Casemates,** on the place de la Constitution. Dating back to the 1600s, these fortifications were built by the Spanish and later improved by the Austrians (open July-Sept. daily 11am-4pm; 70LF). Back above ground, check out the imposing medieval **Citadel of the Holy Ghost,** midway up the side of a cliff. You won't find Quasimodo lumbering around the eaves of the **Notre Dame Cathedral** off bd. F.D.R., but a visit to this three-towered 17th-century centerpiece is still worthwhile. (Free. Open Easter-Oct. Mon.-Fri. 10am-5pm, Sat. 8am-6pm, Sun. 10am-6pm; Nov.-Easter Mon.-Fri. 10-11:30am and 2-5pm, Sat. 8-11:30am and 2-5pm, Sun. 10am-5pm.) The **Musée National d'Histoire et d'Art** houses a curious mix of local art (mostly modern), ancient ruins, and all sorts of rocks, minerals, and scientific equipment. Most importantly, it's free (open Tues.-Fri. 10am-4:45pm, Sat. 2-4:45pm, Sun. 10-11:45am and 2-5:45pm). The city's most beautiful and impressive sights may well be in the many parks lining the valleys. Walk along twisting, shady paths to many splendid viewpoints. *La Semaine à Luxembourg,* available free at the city tourist office, provides a guide to the week's events.

Luxembourg has a relatively quiet nightlife, Wednesdays being the most raging night. A series of bars line the **Bisserweg** and **rue Münster** down in the valley. **Chiggeri,** 11, rue de Nord, is always crowded (open daily noon-1am; **Internet access** noon-5pm), and the rocking **Scott's Pub,** 4, Bisserweg, is packed with students (open daily noon-12:45am). Drink in the caves of a Romanesque building at **Yesterday's Bar,** rue de la Loge, and then meander around the corner to the **Playground,** 8, rue

Sigefroi to chill with a younger crowd. Across the valley lie the clubs. Mosh in Morocco or dance to techno in Tunisia at the **The Pulp,** 36, bd. d'Avranches (cover 200-300LF; open Wed., Fri., and Sat. 11pm-3am). **Melusina,** 145, rue Tour Jacob, is more of a student's dance club (cover 250LF; open Fri.-Sat. 10pm-3am).

THE COUNTRYSIDE

In 1944 the Battle of the Bulge raged through Luxembourg, mashing the Ardennes into slime and mud. Now, 50 years later, the forest is verdant again, its thick greenery broken only by the many small, shallow rivers. The valleys and castles draw thousands of Deutsch and Dutch tourists as well as travelers from around the world.

Miles of hiking trails cut through dark wooded areas up mountainsides and past waterfalls. A web of **bus** and **train** routes blanket the countryside, especially in July and August when extra routes are added. The one-day *Billet Réseau* pass (160LF) makes it possible to visit many towns in one day. Take a bus from the city to **Grevenmacher** (35min.), continue on to **Echternach** (40min.) and then to **Diekirch** (25min.) All buses going to **Vianden** stop in Diekirch (15min.). To complete this loop, go to **Ettelbrück** (10min.), where you can catch a train back to the city (1hr., 50LF). You can also head north from Ettelbrück to **Clervaux** (30min.). Stay in the **HI hostel** (tel. 980 18) across from the train station in **Troisvierges.** (10min. by train from Clervaux. 480LF, under 26 125LF. Excellent breakfast included.)

Echternach

Best known for its impressive 9th-century Benedictine monastery, Echternach is a beautiful town next to the German border in an area known as **Petite Suisse Luxembourgeoise** (Little Switzerland in Luxembourg). Turn left at the marketplace on av. de la Gare and walk past the church to see the **Abbaye,** whose museum provides a short but interesting history of the monastery. Echternach also serves as a base for hiking, mountain biking, windsurfing, and spelunking. Walk down av. de la Gare and follow signs to your left to find the **tourist office,** which offers information on outdoor activities (open Mon.-Fri. 9:30am-noon and 2-5pm, Sat. 10am-noon and 2-4pm). To reach the **youth hostel,** 9, rue André Drechscher (tel. 721 58), make a right just before the market on av. de la Gare, where the road curves sharply to the left (10min.; 425LF, under 26 345LF; dinner 260LF; sheets 125LF). Cheap **eateries** line the central av. de la Gare, including a little *friture* that serves German *bratwurst* with Belgian *frites.*

The Moselle and Sûre Valleys

The **Moselle Valley,** with its sunny weather and abundance of water, was discovered by French winemakers as a suitable substitute for the Champagne region of France. Now, the valley is itself renowned for its still wines, like *Riesling* and *Pinot Gris,* and for its sparkling wines (often marked *méthode champenoise*). The village of **Grevenmacher,** once home to a training ground for the *greven* (a second-class form of nobility), is right in the center of this wine culture and makes an excellent base for exploring the famous vineyards. Begin with a tour of the **Bernard-Massard winery,** rue du Vin, right next to the bridge. You'll learn all about the Champagne method, but more importantly, you'll indulge in a glass at the end of the tour (open April-Oct. daily 9:30am-6pm; 80LF). A **Jardin des Papillons** (butterfly garden), resides nearby (open April to mid-Oct. daily 9:30am-5pm; 180LF, with winery 240LF).

The **HI youth hostel** at Grevenmacher, 15 Gruewereck (tel. 752 22), is an excellent facility; the rooms are clean and intimate, and the management makes you feel at home. Turn left from the bus stop and walk through the pedestrian district to the fountain, then turn right and follow that road to the end. At the "T" turn right, and 10m away a staircase will take you up to the hostel (reception open daily 5-9pm; no curfew; 425LF, under 26 345LF). Few buses or trains run through this secluded valley, but **riverboats** glide along regularly on the placid Moselle (Grevenmacher-Remich 240LF, round-trip 370LF). Pick up a schedule at the hostel. **Buses** run to Grevenmacher from Echternach throughout the day (40min., 105LF).

If you tire of the Moselle, tackle the **Sûre River,** where kayaking is readily available. The **Outdoor Center,** 34, av de la Gare, by the station in **Diekirch** (a 20min. ride from Ettelbrück), has everything you'll need. The shop will pick up kayaks but not people at the final destination (200LF; about 4-6hr. away paddling). In Diekirch, the **Historical Museum,** 10, Bamental, around the corner from the tourist office, presents a powerful exhibition of relics from World War II's Battle of the Bulge. Around the corner from the 15th-century **Eglise Saint-Laurent,** the **Municipal Museum,** Place Guillaume, houses three wonderful Roman mosaics. (Church open April-Oct. Tues.-Sun. 10am-noon and 2-6pm. Free. Musuem open Easter-Oct. Fri.-Wed. 10am-noon and 2-6pm. 90LF). The **tourist office,** 1, Esplanade (tel. 80 30 23), across from the church, provides information on museums and makes hotel reservations (open Mon.-Sat. 9am-6pm). There is no hostel here, so stay in Echternach or Luxembourg City.

Vianden

Victor Hugo found Vianden "consoling and magnificent." There's no arguing with the man that the city, nestled within rocky cliffs and the dense Ardennes woods, has more than its share of beauty. Just across the river from Germany, Vianden was the ancestral home of the Orange-Nassau dynasty, rulers of Holland and (in the person of William III) England as well. The village spills down a steep hill beneath a renovated 9th-century **château.** (Open April-Sept. daily 10am-6pm.; March and Oct. 10am-5pm; Nov.-Feb. 10am-4pm. 120LF, students 100LF.) For a great view of the château, ride Vianden's **télésiège** (chairlift) from rue de Sanatorium, 500m upstream from the tourist office, down rue de Victor Hugo. (Open in spring and summer daily 10am-5pm. Round-trip 160LF, one-way with easy hike down 90LF.) With a small hike, the ascent also affords a view of Europe's largest hydroelectric plant, the **Barrage.**

Buses arrive from Echternach and Ettelbrück, via Diekirch about once every hour. The **tourist office** (tel. 842 57; fax 84 90 81) is in the **Victor Hugo House,** on rue de la Gare, beside the bridge over the River Our (open Easter-Sept. daily 9:30am-noon and 2-6pm; Oct.-Easter Mon.-Sat. same hours). The **HI youth hostel,** 3, Montée du Château (tel. 841 77), sits atop a large hill beneath the castle; cross the bridge from the tourist office and follow the Grande Rue until it curves to the left and ends. In early summer the hostel accepts many groups and is closed December through February except for groups. (Reception open daily 5-9pm or later if you call ahead. 425LF, under 26 345LF. Sheets 125LF.) Halfway up Grand-Rue at #10 lies the **Auberge Café de la Poste** (tel. 84 92 64), a simple, clean hotel. (Reception open 8am-midnight. Singles 900LF; doubles 1400LF; triples 2000LF; quads 2400LF. Breakfast included.) Numerous cheap hotels litter Grand-Rue. The tourist office lists rooms in private homes (singles from 800LF, doubles 1000LF). **Camp op dem Deich** (tel. 843 75), a five-minute hike downstream from the tourist office, offers campsites in the shadows of the château (130LF per person and per tent; open Easter-Aug.).

Food in Vianden is good, cheap, and plentiful, with a strong Germanic influence. Try one of the local **grasseries** for a full meal of soup, salad, meat (like *entrecôte* or *Wiener Schnitzel*), and dessert for 400LF, or head to one of the many smoked meat shops on Grand-Rue, such as **Charcuterie Jacobsen.** Get groceries at **Economart,** 1, rue de la Gare (open Mon.-Sat. 8am-6pm and Sun. 10am-noon).

Near Vianden, nestled in the northern town of **Clervaux,** the **château** houses the striking **Family of Man exhibition**. This collection of over 500 pictures from 68 countries depicts all aspects of human life and emotions. It was compiled in 1955 by Edward Steichen, a photographer born in Luxembourg, and has been displayed around the world (open March-Dec. Tues.-Sun. 10am-6pm; 150LF).

Malta

Malta is something of a fairy-tale island, in whose crowded past lurk knights in shining armor, pirates, and the salvation of Christian Europe. The archipelago, consisting of the islands of Malta, Gozo, and Comino, as well as the uninhabited islets of Cominotto in the north and Fifla to the south, has developed into a major tourist destination. Maltese is the official language, but everyone knows English. The Maltese **lira** (Lm) is divided into 100 **cents.** One U.S. dollar is worth about 0.4Lm; one U.K. pound is worth about 0.64Lm. Visitors must declare foreign currency upon arrival, and may take no more than Lm25 in unspent Maltese currency out of the country. Dial 190 for **telephone assistance.** The **emergency** number is 196. Malta's **country code** is 356.

Citizens of Australia, Canada, EU countries, New Zealand, and the U.S. can stay in Malta visa-free for up to three months. South African citizens need to obtain a visa. **Island Seaway** runs from Catania in Sicily and Reggio Calabria in Italy to Valletta. **Virtu Ferries** sends speedy catamarans to Catania and Syracuse (each round-trip Lm36). Reach Reggio Calabria by **train** from Naples (5hr., L37,000), Catania from Syracuse (1¾hr., L7400). **Flights** leave from Rome (round-trip about Lm130) on **Air Malta** (tel. 69 08 90) and **Alitalia** (tel. 24 67 82). In Valletta, **NSTS** travel service, 220 St. Paul's St. (tel. 24 49 83), has discount plane fares. Buses 8 and 39 run between the airport and Valletta (6am-8pm, 11¢). If taking a **taxi,** agree on a price in advance.

MALTA

Valletta

Capital of the nation, Valletta is located on a narrow finger of land on Malta's southeast side. **Republic Street,** the city's backbone, has shops and restaurants, and most of the important sights are not far away. The **National Museum of Archaeology** is an excellent introduction to the temple sites scattered across the islands. One block beyond the museum to the right, **St. John's Co-Cathedral** (1573-1577) vaunts an absurdly ornate Baroque interior and contains Caravaggio's two final masterpieces. The historical residence of Malta's rulers since 1574, the opulent **Grand Master's Palace** is just beyond the cathedral. **The Malta Experience,** at the Mediterranean Conference Center along the Grand Harbor, gives an introduction to the islands (shows Mon.-Fri. every hr., 11am-4pm, Sat.-Sun. 11am-1pm; Lm2.50, students Lm1.50).

The **tourist office** (tel. 23 77 47) is just inside City Gate. (Open June 16-Sept. Mon.-Sat. 9am-7pm, Sun. 9am-2pm; Oct.-June 15 Mon.-Sat. 8:30am-12:30pm and 1:15-6pm, Sun. 9am-2pm.) There is another office at the airport. The **Asti Guest House,** 18 St. Ursula St. (tel. 23 95 06; Lm5.25), and **Coronation Guest House,** 10 E.M.A. Vassalli St. (tel. 23 76 52; Lm4-5), are in Valletta. The suburbs of **Sliema, St. Julian's,** and **Paceville** offer better nightlife (take bus 62, 64, 67, 68, 667, 662, or 671 from the fountain outside Valletta's main gate; 5:30am-11pm). Reserve ahead through NSTS for Sliema's **Hibernia House,** Depiro St. (tel. 33 38 59; Lm2.70-3.70). **Agius Pastizzeria,** 273 St. Paul's St. in Valletta, has cheap take-out. **Axis** is Paceville's best disco.

Near Valletta

Once the island's capital, **Mdina** (em-DEE-nah) hasn't changed much since its glory days. **St. Paul's Catacombs** and **St. Agatha's Catacombs** offer Christian and Jewish relics. Inside Mdina's 9th-century Saracen fortifications lies a preserved 17th-century Baroque world. Take bus 80 or 81 to Mdina from Valletta, or bus 65 from Sliema.

The popular **Blue Grotto** hides near the end of bus route 38. Boats leave the harbor for the phosphorescent wonder (call 82 99 25 in advance; Lm2.50). The astonishing megalithic temples of **Hagar Qim** and **Mnajdra** are a 20-minute walk away.

The best bet for **beaches** is the west coast, where crowded **Golden Bay** (bus 47 from Valletta, 652 from Sliema) leads to quieter **Gnejna Bay.** Try the **Marfa** peninsula in the northwest, or take bus 11 to **Pretty Bay** in the east.

The Netherlands (Nederland)

US$1 = f2.03 (guilders)	**f1 = US$0.49**
CDN$1= f1.47	**f1 = CDN$0.68**
UK£1 = f3.23	**f1 = UK£0.31**
IR£1 = f3.01	**f1 = IR£0.33**
AUS$1 = f1.48	**f1 = AUS$0.67**
NZ$1 = f1.29	**f1 = NZ$0.78**
SAR1 = f0.43	**f1 = SAR2.31**
Country Code: 31	**International Dialing Prefix: 00**

The Dutch say that God created the rest of the world but that they created the Netherlands. This country, often called Holland, is truly a masterful feat of engineering. Since most of the country is below sea level, vigorous pumping and a series of dikes were used to create thousands of square kilometers of land (including Amsterdam). What was once the domain of seaweed and cod is now sprinkled with windmills, cheese, tulips, and the occasional wooden shoe.

During the Age of Exploration, Dutch conquerors fanned out over the globe, as the Dutch East and West India companies traded as far afield as Java, the Caribbean, and Africa. The wealth flowing into the country from these commercial ventures contributed to the Dutch Golden Age in the seventeenth century. During this time, Holland also served as a sanctuary for Europe's religious and political dissidents, and this atmosphere of freedom and tolerance spawned the masterpieces of Rembrandt and Vermeer as well as the philosophies of Descartes and Spinoza.

The Dutch have continued to race ahead and push the boundaries of social frontiers. Recovering from the devastating effects of two world wars, residents rebuilt their cities with the stark, modernistic influence of Mondriaan's De Stijl school and the architecture of Mies van der Rohe. Now, where rubble once lay, modern buildings gleam and tower. Yet the country has by no means abandoned its medieval and Renaissance heritage; ancient canals wind through the countryside and centuries old buildings and cathedrals still grace small towns.

GETTING THERE AND GETTING AROUND

Trains, Buses, and Trams **NS,** the efficient rail authority, runs up to four trains an hour between major cities. Intercity trains generally cruise nonstop, *sneltreins* trace the fastest route, and *stoptreins* pause in most of the villages along the way. **Eurail** is valid throughout the country. A round-trip ticket is valid only on the day of issue. **Day Trip** (or **Rail Idee**) programs, available at train stations in spring and summer, allow you to pay an all-inclusive, reduced price for a round-trip train ticket, entrance fees for attractions, and often, connecting transport and a snack.

The **Euro Domino Holland** card allows three days (f92, under 26 f77), five days (f144, under 26 f100), or 10 days (f256, under 26 f179) of unlimited rail travel in a period of one month. If you're traveling with a group, consider the **Meerman's kaart,** which grants one day of unlimited travel for two to six people (f100-174). Conversely, if you're alone and under 19, a **tourtime** pass gives three days of unlimited travel in any 10-day period (f49). Many passes offer a "plus" package, with use of trams and other services for f15-20 extra.

A nationalized fare system covers city buses, trams, and long-distance buses. The country is divided into zones; you need a certain number of *strippenkaart* (strip tickets) depending on the number of zones through which you travel. The base charge is two strips, and travel to some smaller towns can exceed 20 strips. Bus and tram drivers sell two-strip (f3), three-strip (f4.50), and eight-strip tickets (f12). Tickets are

much cheaper (15-strip ticket f11.25, 45-strip ticket f33) from public transportation counters, post offices, and some tobacco shops and newsstands. Alternatively, *daskaartan* (day tickets) are available for one to nine days. The one-day ticket (f10), is worth it, but each additional day adds only f4. Riding without a ticket can result in a f60 fine plus the original cost of the ticket.

Cycling and Hitchhiking **Cycling** is the way to go in the Netherlands. Distances between cities are short, the countryside is flat, and most streets have separate bike lanes. You can rent one-speed bikes for about f8 per day or f32 per week (deposit f50-200, discount with railpass); the flatness of the terrain (except near the coast) renders three-speeds unnecessary. Many train stations rent bikes upon presentation of your ticket or railpass. Call the station a day ahead to reserve; phone numbers are listed in the free booklet *Fiets en Trein.* Purchasing a used bike (about f140) at a station and then reselling it may prove more thrifty. However, you must take care to secure your bike, especially in cities. **HEMA,** a large, fairly ubiquitous department store, sells locks from f25. **Hitchhiking** is risky but fairly effective in many areas, although competition on roads out of Amsterdam is cutthroat. The **International Lift Center,** Nieuwezijds Voorburgwal 256, 1st fl. Amsterdam (tel. (020) 622 43 42), matches riders and drivers for destinations all over Europe (f10 membership, plus gas money; open Mon.-Fri. 10am-6pm, Sat. 10am-2pm).

ESSENTIALS

The **VVV** tourist information offices are marked by blue triangular signs. These offices, along with museums themselves, sell passes which cover admission to most of the hundreds of museums in the Netherlands.

Dutch **currency** includes the *stuiver* (5¢), *dubbeltje* (10¢), *kwartje* (25¢), and *rijksdaalder* (f2.50). Post offices, generally open weekdays from 9am to 5pm, offer currency exchange at reasonable rates for a commission. **Banks** are usually open weekdays from 10am to 4pm and often Thursdays from 6 to 8pm or 7 to 9pm. **GWK** often offers the best exchange rates and does not change a commission to ISIC holders. Otherwise, expect to pay a flat fee of about f2-5 and a 1-2% commission. **Quick Change** exchange centers are open later than banks, but commissions are often 8-10%. You can make international **calls** from pay phones, which take 25¢ and f1 coins. A **phone card** (in denominations of f10) is more economical than change (overseas calling around 25¢ for 15 seconds). For directory assistance, dial 06 80 08 within the Netherlands or 06 04 18 from outside the country; for collect calls, dial 06 04 10. To reach an **AT&T Direct** operator, call 06 022 91 11; **MCI WorldPhone,** 06 022 91 22; **Sprint Access,** 06 022 91 19; **Canada Direct,** 06 022 91 16; **BT Direct,** 06 022 99 44; **Australia Direct,** 06 022 00 61; **New Zealand Direct,** 06 022 44 64; and **South Africa Direct,** 06 022 02 27.

Although most Dutch speak English extremely well, do try out their native tongue. The language of food is essential: *dagschotel* means "dinner special," *broodje* means "bread," *bier* is "beer," and *kaas* is "cheese." Eventually you'll need directions to the *wissel kantor* meaning "money exchange" or *toiletten,* "bathroom."

Yes/No	*Ja/Nee*	Ya/nay
Hello	*Hallo* or *das*	hallo
Please	*Als't u blieft*	ALST oo bleeft
Thank you	*Dank u wel*	Dank oo vel
How much does it cost?	*Wat kost dit?*	Vat kost dit
Where is...?	*Waar is....?*	Vahr ees
What can you recommend?	*Wat kunt u aanbevelen?*	Wat kunt oo ahn-bev-ay-len
Are there rooms available?	*Zijn er nog kamers vrij?*	Zij-n er nock kamers vrij
Do you speak English?	*Sprecht u engels?*	Sprect oo engels

Accommodations and Camping The VVV offices which supply accommodations lists can nearly always find a room, and will make reservations in other cities (f4 fee). Rooms in private homes cost about two-thirds as much as hotels but are hard to find; check with the VVV. During July and August many cities add a f2.50 "tourist tax" to the price of all rooms. The country's best values are the 38 **HI youth hostels** run by the **NJHC (Dutch Youth Hostel Federation),** divided into three price categories based on quality. Most cost f20-23 for bed and breakfast, plus high-season and prime-location supplements. The VVV has a hostel list, and the useful *Jeugdherbergen* brochure describes each one (both free). For more info, contact the NJHC at Prof. Tupelstraat 2, Amsterdam (tel. (020) 551 31 55; open Mon.-Fri. 9am-5pm). Youth hostel cards are available at hostels (f27.50; bring a passport photo). **Camping** is available country-wide, but many sites are crowded and trailer-ridden in summer.

Food and Drink Dutch food is hearty and simple: plenty of meat, potatoes, vegetables, bread, cheese, and milk. Pancakes, salted herring, and pea soup are national specialties. Dutch cheeses transcend *gouda* and *edam;* nibble *leiden,* the mild *belegen,* and the creamy *kernhem,* too. Cold meat and cheese on bread with a soft-boiled egg are a typical breakfast. For a hearty brunch, order an *uitsmijter,* which packs in the salad, ham, cheese, and eggs. At dinner, reap the benefits of Dutch imperialism: *rijsttafel* is an Indonesian specialty comprising up to 25 different dishes, including curried chicken or lamb with pineapple, served on a mountain of rice. Or try *pan-*

nekoeken, the traditional Dutch supper of buttery, sugary, golden brown pancakes. Wash it all down with a foamy mug of hometown beers Heineken and Amstel (f2-2.50 per glass, f5-6 per pint), or try *jenever* (usually f3), a strong gin made from juniper berries and traditionally accompanied by eel. In the many university towns, you can eat cheaply and plentifully at student *mensas* when school is in.

Despite what you may see, hear, and smell, drugs are illegal in this country. Although police largely ignore the soft drug scene, possession of up to 30g of hashish can incur hefty fines, and possession of more than this amount is a serious offense. Police consider hard drugs (acid, cocaine, heroin, ecstasy, etc.) a different category altogether and punish offenders accordingly. Avoid pot milkshakes and space cakes; the government cannot control their contents and they have been known to cause serious damage, including paralysis. Never buy anything from street pushers; ignore them and keep walking.

Amsterdam

Amsterdam is your fairy godmother embodied—she caters to lucky boys' and girls' whims and, to spread the wealth, even throws in a bit of fairy dust. After enduring both Spanish and French rule, Amsterdam now has the last laugh as it lures nationals of every country to its never-never land of bacchanalian excess. The aroma of cannabis wafts from coffeeshops, and the city's infamous sex scene swathes itself in red light. However, one need not be naughty to enjoy Amsterdam. Art enthusiasts will delight in the troves of Rembrandts, Vermeers, and Van Goghs, and romantics can stroll along the endless cobbled streets and canals which sparkle with the reflected city lights.

ORIENTATION AND PRACTICAL INFORMATION

Amsterdam is a major hub for budget flights from around the world (especially southeast Asia) and train service throughout Europe. Emerging from the train station, you'll hit **Damrak,** a key thoroughfare that leads to the **Dam,** the main square. Concentric canals ripple out around the Dam and **Centraal Station,** so that the city resembles a horseshoe with the station at the open north end. Radiating from the station, the canals lined by streets of the same name are **Singel, Herengracht, Keizergracht,** and **Prinsengracht.** The names of streets change capriciously; buy a good **map** of the city (f3.50) at the VVV or from most magazine stands. *Use It* (f2.50) includes a map, info on cheap accommodations, an index of youth agencies, and city news.

The areas around the train station and up Damrak are the easiest places to "lose" valuables: pickpockets abound here. Do not head immediately left of the train station, into the **red-light district,** until you've locked up your bags either at the train station or where you'll be staying. Lone travelers should be wary of the train station at night. The police are extremely helpful, so report all thefts. While illegal, marijuana and hashish are tolerated and readily available at cafés and coffeeshops. For info on the legal ins and outs of the Amsterdam drug scene, call the Jellinek clinic at 570 22 22. Anyone with **drug-related health problems** should call 555 55 55.

Tourist Office: VVV, Stationsplein 10 (tel. (06) 34 03 40 66; fax 625 28 69), to the left and in front of Centraal Station. Charges a hefty f5 fee plus a f5 deposit for room booking. Sells maps (f3.50), tickets, changes money (poor rates), and plans excursions. Get *What's On,* a fabulous listing of events (f3.50). Go early to skirt long lines. **Branch offices:** at Centraal station (open daily 8am-8pm), Leidseplein 1, Stadionplein (both open daily 9am-5pm), and Schiphol Plaza (airport; open daily 7am-10pm). Buy phone cards and *strippenkaart* here.

Budget Travel: NBBS, Rokin 38 (tel. 624 09 89 or 620 50 71). Budget student flights. Open mid-May to mid-Aug. Mon.-Fri. 9:30am-5:30pm, Sat. 10am-4pm; mid-Aug. to mid-May closes Sat. at 3pm. No credit cards. **Budget Bus/Eurolines,** Rokin 10 (tel. 627 51 51), has Euroline bus deals. Open Mon.-Fri. 9:30am-5:30pm, Sat. 10am-4pm. **Wasteels,** on Rokin as well, has cheap plane tickets.

Consulates: Australian, Canadian, New Zealand, and **South African** embassies are in The Hague. **U.K.,** Koningslaan 44 (tel. 676 43 43). Open Mon.-Fri. 9am-noon and 2-3:30pm. **U.S.,** Museumplein 19 (tel. 664 56 61). Open Mon.-Fri. 8:30am-noon and 1:30-4:30pm.

Currency Exchange: Best rates at the American Express office (see below). The **GWK** offices at Centraal Station and Schipol have good rates, and no commission for traveler's checks with ISIC or student ID (open 24hr). **Change Express,** Kalverstr. 150 (open daily 8am-8pm) or Leidestr. 106 (open daily 8am-midnight) has good rates and a 3% commission. Avoid **Chequepoint's** outrageous commissions.

American Express: Damrak 66 (tel. 520 77 77; fax 504 87 07). Excellent rates and no commission on any traveler's checks. Open Mon.-Fri. 9am-5pm, Sat. 9am-noon. Cash machine for cardholders. Be careful; the area's thieves are notorious. **Branch office,** Van Baerlestr. 28 (tel. 671 41 41). Safer area and much less crowded. Both cash checks, but only Damrak holds mail. Open Mon.-Fri. 9am-5pm, Sat. 9am-noon.

Flights: Schiphol Airport (tel. (06) 350 33 08 for charters, 350 34 05 for other flights). Trains connect to Centraal Station (every 20min., 20min., f6).

Trains: Centraal Station, Stationsplein 1, at the Damrak's end, opposite the tourist office. For international info and reservations, get a number at the booth, then wait until you're called. In summer, expect waits as long as 1hr. Open for info Mon.-Fri. 8am-10pm, Sat.-Sun. 9am-8pm; reservations Mon.-Fri. 8am-8pm, Sat.-Sun. 9am-5pm. For info, call (06) 92 96 (international) or (06) 92 92 (domestic). **Lockers** f4-6.

Buses: Trains are quicker. The **GVB** (see Public Transportation, below) will direct you to a bus departure point if your destination isn't on a rail line. **Muiderpoort** (2 blocks east of Oosterpark) goes east; **Marnixstation** (at the corner of Marnixstr. and Kinkerstr.), west; and **Stationsplein depot,** north and south.

Public Transportation: Trams, buses, *nachtbussen* (night buses), and 2 subway lines. Most tram and bus lines radiate from Centraal Station and stop running at midnight; get a separate *nachtbussen* schedule. Don't buy your *strippenkaart* and *dagkaart* (Amsterdam day passes, f12) on the bus; you'll pay dearly. The 15-strip card (f11.25) is the best deal for light travel over several days. The **GVB,** Stationsplein, public transportation company (tel. (06) 92 92 for info) sells tickets and distributes the *Public Transport* flyer. Open daily 8am-10:30pm.

Taxis: tel. 677 77 77. Fares start at f5.80 plus f2.80 per km or min.; more at night.

Bike Rental: All **train stations** rent plain ol' bikes for f8 per day, f30-40 per week with a train ticket. **Damstraat Rent-a-Bike,** Pieter Jacobstr. 11 (tel. 625 50 29), just off Damstr. near the Dam, charges f10 per day or f50 per week (deposit f50 and passport); used bikes are sold for f140-200. **Yellow Bike Tours,** N.Z. Voorburgwal 66 (tel. 620 69 40), offers 3hr. city (f29) and 6½hr. countryside (f42.50).

Hitchhiking: Those hitching to Utrecht, central and southern Germany, and Belgium take tram 25 to the end and start at the bridge. Those heading to Groningen and northern Germany take bus 56 to Prins Bernhardplein or the metro to Amstel and start along Gooiseweg. Those going to the airport, Leiden, and The Hague take tram 16 or 24 to Stadionplein and start on the other side of the canal on Amstelveenseweg. Those going to Haarlem, Alkmaar, and Noord Holland take bus 22 to Haarlemmerweg and start from Westerpark. (For a rider/driver matching service contact, see **International Lift Center,** p. 623)

Bookstores: Mountains of paperbacks at the **American Discount Book Center,** 185 Kalverstr. 10% student discount. Open Mon.-Wed. and Fri.-Sat. 10am-8pm, Thurs. 10am-10pm, Sun. 11am-6pm. **Ako,** Regulierbreestraat 19. Extensive collection and international newspapers. Open Mon.-Sat. 9am-10pm, Sun. 9:30am-8pm.

Laundry: Look for a *Wasserette* sign. **Enzo Clean,** Jorge Roelensteeg Ya., between Nieuwezijds Voolburgwal and Spuistraat. f10 wash and dry. Open daily 9am-7pm.

Condoms: Find the widest variety of colors, flavors, and styles at the **Condomerie,** Warmoesstraat 141. Next to the red-light district. Open Mon.-Sat. 11am-6pm.

Gay and Lesbian Services: COC, Rozenstr. 14 (tel. 623 40 79 or 626 30 87), is the main info source. Open Wed.-Sat. 1-5pm. Coffee shop open Tues. and Sat. 1-5pm. *Best Guide to Amsterdam & The Benelux* is reliable. **Intermale,** Spuistr. 251 (tel. 625 00 09), is a gay bookstore. Open Mon. noon-6pm, Tues.-Sat. 10am-6pm. **Gay and Lesbian Switchboard** (tel. 623 65 65) is answered daily 10am-10pm.

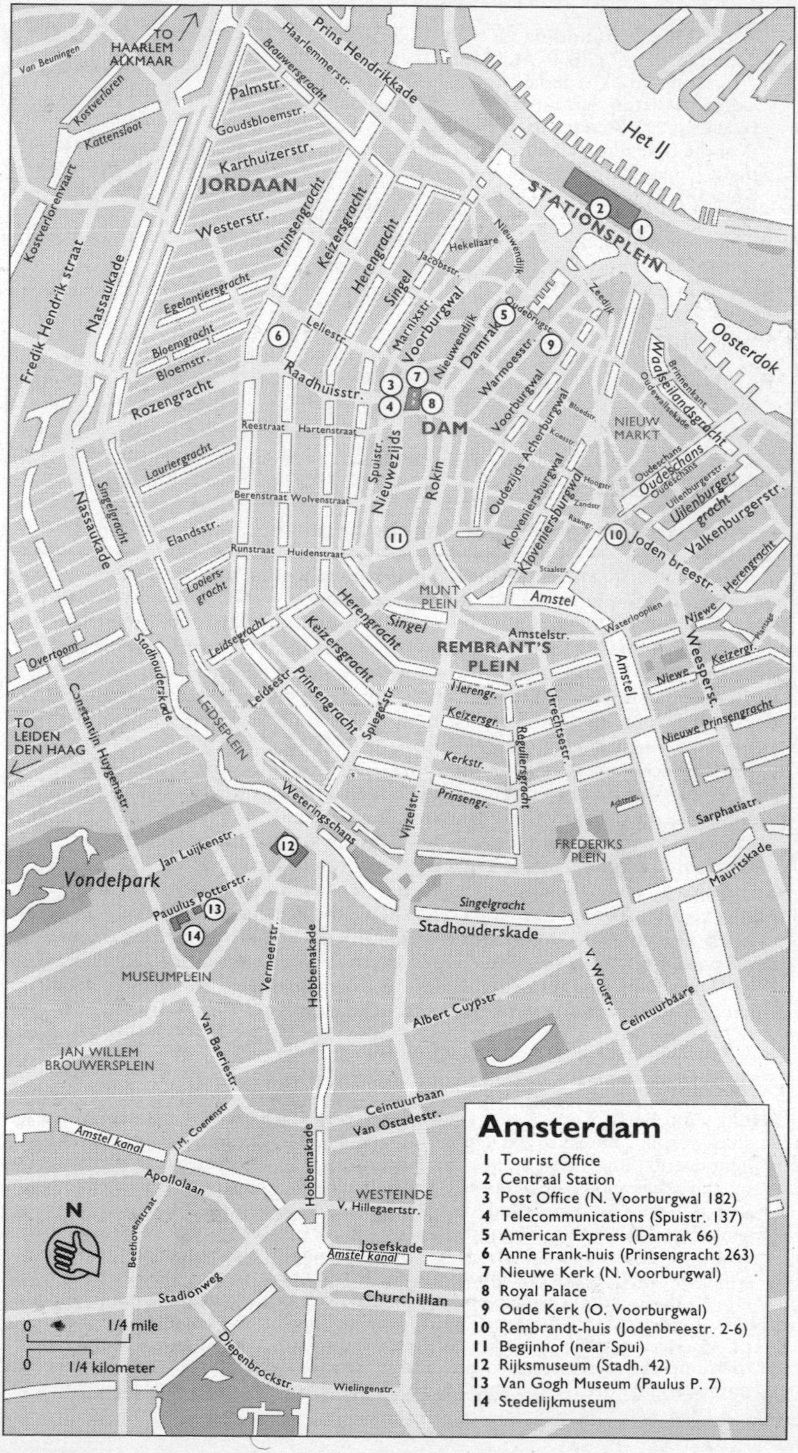

NETHERLANDS

Crises: Rape crisis hotline for both sexes, tel. 612 75 76; staffed Mon.-Fri. 10:30am-11:30pm, Sat.-Sun. 3:30-11:30pm. **Drug counseling,** Binnenkant 46 (tel. 624 47 75), 10min. from Centraal Station, near the Oosterdok.

Medical Assistance: Tourist Medical Service, tel. 695 56 38. Open 24hr. For hospital care, call **Academisch Medisch Centrum,** Meibergdreef 9 (tel. 566 91 11), near the Holendrecht Metro stop. For free emergency medical care, visit the **Kruispost,** Oudezijds Voorburgwal 129 (tel. 624 90 31). Open Mon.-Fri. 6:45am-11pm. **Sexually Transmitted Disease Clinic** at Groenburgwal 44 (tel. 622 37 77); free and confidential. Open daily 8-10:30am. **STD Line,** tel. 623 22 52.

Pharmacies: Most are open Mon.-Fri. 8:30am-5pm. When closed, each *apotheek* (pharmacy) posts a sign directing you to the nearest open one.

Emergencies: tel. 06 11.

Police: Headquarters, Elandsgracht 117 (tel. 559 91 11).

Internet Access: Cybercafé, Nieuwendijk 19 (tel. 020 623 51 46; email cyber@cybercafe.euronet.nl). f3 per min. Open Mon.-Sat. 10am-10pm.

Post Office: Singel 250-256 (tel. 556 33 11), at Raadhuisstr. behind the Dam. *Poste Restante.* Open Mon.-Fri. 9am-6pm, Sat. 10am-1:30pm. **Postal Code:** 1016 AB.

Telephones: Public phones are outside Centraal Station or at the post office. Call first and pay afterward at **Telehouse,** Raadhuisstr. 48-50, near the Dam (open 24hr.), or **TeleTalk Center,** Leidsestr. 101, near the Leidseplein (open daily 10am-midnight). Both handle faxes. **Telephone Code:** 020.

THE NETHERLANDS

ACCOMMODATIONS AND CAMPING

Amsterdam is packed from late June to mid-September, but several enormous hostels help accommodate most visitors. Reserve in advance for private rooms. For HI hostels, book (and pay for) rooms in advance from any other HI hostel (free within the Netherlands, f4 outside). Many hostels do not accept reservations for dorms; arrive between 9-10am in the summer. The Christian hostels' single-sex dorms are safer, less wild, and easily the best bargain in town. Private hostels generally charge more, set later curfews (or none at all), and have more laid-back atmospheres. Almost all places are about f2.50 cheaper in the off season. At the station and tourist office you'll be accosted by accommodations pushers; many are from reputable hostels, but be cautious. The legitimate ones often carry printed cards with their hostel's address and prices; ask to see the card. Carry your own luggage, and never pay before you look. If you arrive at night and can't find a room, consider staying in a neighboring city.

Staying in a hotel or hostel in a quieter part of town, such as near the Leidseplein or in the Jordaan, may be enjoyable. "Quieter" relative to Amsterdam standards, these areas have their share of bars and coffeeshops, but accommodations here are found on safer, peaceful side street. The red-light district and city center are about a 15-minute walk from these areas. Accommodations closer to the station often take good security measures. If you need to buy your own padlock (f7-25), stop by **HEMA,** a department store behind the Damrak American Express.

Red-light District and Rembrandtsplein

Private Hostels

Nelly's Inn B&B, Warmoesstr. 115/117 (tel. 638 01 25). From Centraal Station, it's an easy walk 2 blocks to the left of the Damrak. New, comfortable hostel in the red-light district. Reception open 24hr. Dorms f25-35. Arrive as close to 9am as possible, no reservations. Breakfast and sheets included. Connected to **Dirty Nelly's,** a Irish pub with live bands and lots of, guess what...Guinness.

Flying Pig: Downtown, Nieuwendijk 100 (tel. 421 05 83; fax 421 08 02). All rooms with bath. Crowded but clean. Lively bar. TV lounge. 26-person dorm f24.50-36.50. 6-person f33. Doubles f55. Quads f36.50. Blanket f4.50, deposit for sheets and key f15. 5% discount on cash payments. No curfew. Free lockers. Breakfast included.

NJHC-herberg Stadsdoelen (HI), Kloveniersburgwal 97 (tel. 624 68 32; fax 639 01 35), between Nieuwmarkt and Rembrandtsplein. Take tram 4, 9, 16, 24, or 25 to Muntplein. Walk down Amstel and cross the bridge on your left. Large, clean dorms. Lounge area with cable TV. Lively bar sells diners (f8); daily happy hour (8-

9pm). Reception open daily 8am-12:30am. Curfew 2am. f29, nonmembers add f5. July-Aug. f2.50 surcharge. Breakfast included. Free lockers. Open mid-March to Jan. Reservations accepted, but you must arrive by 4pm.

BA Hostel, Martelaarsgracht 18 (tel. 638 71 19; fax 638 88 03). Staff goes out of their way to accommodate the needs of weary backpackers. Price includes showers, sheets, towels, breakfast, luggage storage, and a locker/safety-deposit box. Mention at check-in that *Let's Go* sent you to get a free beer in the downstairs **café** (meals f8.50-f22; happy hour 6-7pm). Reception open 8:30am-midnight. Bright and airy 8-12 bed dorms f35. Sept. 16-May f25. Weekends in May and in June f30.

Meeting Point, Warmoesstr. 14 (tel./fax 02 06 27 74 99). Dark and crowded in the heart of the red-light district. Reception open 24hr. Female-only dorm on request. No curfew. Beds f20-5. 4-bed dorms f30-35. f20 key deposit. No credit cards.

The Last Waterhole, Oudezigds Arusteeg 12 (tel. 624 48 14; fax (023) 42 47 89). From Centraal Station walk down Damrak, take a left on Brugsteeg, and then a left on Warmoesstr; the 3rd block on the right is Oudezijds Armsteeg. 3 pool tables, big-screen TV, games, darts, and live music nightly. Bar open until 2am, Fri.-Sat. until 4am. Beds f30. Blankets and sheets f2.50. Breakfast included.

Hotel Kabul, Warmoesstr. 38-42 (tel. 623 71 58), 5min. from Centraal Station, on the edge of the red-light district. Two bars; live bands Thurs.-Sat. Pool table. Reception open 24hr. Dorms f37-45. Singles f92. Doubles f125-135. Triples f150.

Bob's Youth Hostel, Nieuwezijds Voorburgwal 92 (tel. 623 00 63; fax 675 64 46), near Centraal Station and the police station. Take tram 1, 2, 5, 13, or 17. No smoking in rooms; you'll inhale enough on the stairs. This place keeps the Amsterdam myths going. Reception open daily 8am-3am. Dorms f23. Mattress on floor f19. f25 deposit for key and locker. Breakfast included. No reservations, no credit cards.

Hotel Crown, Oudezijds Voorburgwal 21 (tel. 626 96 64). Simple accommodations in the red light district. Clean and comparatively safe. Attached bar stays open until 5am nightly. Dorms f35. Quads f40. Reception open 8am-midnight. No curfew.

Christian Youth Hostel "The Shelter," Barndesteeg 21-25 (tel. 625 32 30), off the Nieuwmarkt. Virtue amid the red lights. Snack bar, cozy courtyard, and religious slogans. Reception 7:30am-midnight. Enforced midnight curfew, Fri.-Sat. 1am. Ages 16-35 f25. Showers, sheets, and breakfast included. Lockers f10; f1 deposit.

Hotels

Hotel Brian, Singel 69 (tel. 624 46 61). Nothing fancy, but clean, friendly, and comfortable. TV lounge. All-you-can-eat breakfast included—with eggs cooked to order. Reception open 24hr. No curfew. 2-4 bed rooms April-Aug. f40; Sept. f35; Oct.-March f25. Sheets, towels, and luggage storage included. No credit cards.

Old Nickel, Niemuebrugsteeg 11 (tel. 624 19 12; fax 620 76 83). Quiet hotel assures a friendly welcome. Reception open 8am-midnight. No curfew. Singles f50-65. Doubles f80-100. Luggage storage, sheets, and towels included. No credit cards.

Hotel Monopole, Amstel 60 (tel. 624 62 71; fax 624 58 97). Gay-friendly hotel overlooking the canal near Rembrandtsplein. Spacious rooms with bath. Doubles f125. Triples f180. AmEx, MC, and V.

International Student Center, Keizersgracht 15-17 (tel. 625 13 64; fax 624 70 12). Classy rooms, beds with thick mattresses. Peaceful hotel, overlooking a canal, is just 10min. from Centraal Station. Reception 7am-3am. Flexible 3am curfew. Singles f60-75. Doubles f95-120. Triples f105-128. Quads f128-160. All with shower.

Leidseplein/Museumplein

Private Hostels

The Flying Pig: Vondelpark, Vossiusstr. 46-47 (tel. 400 41 87; fax 400 41 05). Tram 1, 2, 5, or 11 to the Leidseplein. Cross the street and canal; at the Marriot turn left. Vossiusstraat is the first street on the right. New, clean, and comfortable. Kitchen and bar. Dorms from f23.50. Sheets and lockers for f15 deposit. Breakfast included.

International Budget Hotel, Leidsegracht 76 (tel. 624 27 84; fax 626 18 39). Take tram 1, 2, or 5 to Prinsengracht. Turn right down the next street, cross the bridge, and turn left on Leidsegracht. Beautiful location, friendly staff. Addictive cartoon network in TV lounge. Reception open 8am-11pm. 4-bed dorms f35. Breakfast f2.50-6. Reservations recommended. AmEx, MC, V.

NJHC City Hostel Vondelpark (HI), Zandpad 5 (tel. 683 17 44), bordering Vondelpark. Take tram 1, 2, or 5 to Leidesplein. Head toward the Mariott and turn left on Stafhouderskade. Turn right at the 2nd street before the park entrance. Newly renovated. Clean, spacious rooms with full baths. Reception open 7am-12:30am. No curfew. Dorms f29. Singles f70. Doubles f90. Quads f150. Nonmembers add f5. Sheets f6.25. Avoid the park at night.

The Arena, 's-Gravesandestr. 51-53 (tel. 694 74 44; fax 663 26 49). Take trams 3, 6, 7 or 10 from Leidseplein, 9 from Centraal Station, or 14 from the Dam to Mauritskade; take the right after the "Weesperplein" Metro stop. Palatial hostel has marble columns, art deco staircases, concert hall, and art gallery. Crowded and crazy. **Bike rental** (f10 per day) open daily 10am-noon and 7-8pm. DJ Thurs.-Sat.; f5 cover. Reception open daily 9am-1pm and 4-9pm. Dorms f25. Doubles f105. Triples f140. Quads f180. Blankets and sheets f5. Free lockers.No dorm reservations.

Euphemia Budget Hotel, Fokke Simonszstr. 1-9 (tel. 622 90 45; fax 622 90 45), 10min. walk from Leidseplein. Take tram 16, 24, or 25 to 6th stop, near the Heineken Brewery. Relatively safe and comfy. Reception open daily 8am-11pm. Dorms f25-40. Singles f45-12. Doubles f70-150. Triples f105-180. Sheets included.

Hans Brinker, Kerkstraat 136 (tel. 622 06 87; fax 638 20 60). Take trams 1, 2, 5, or 11 to Prinsengracht and walk one block back towards the city center. Clean and comparatively safe, but a bit pricey at f40 for a dorm bed.

Hotels

Hotel Museumzicht, Jan Luykenstraat 22 (tel. 671 29 54; fax 671 35 97). A lovely little hotel in a quiet neighborhood across the street from the Rijksmuseum. Singles f65. Doubles f130, with shower f140. Triples f150. Breakfast included.

Hotel Bema, Concertgebouwplein (tel. 679 13 96; fax 662 36 88), across from the Concertgebouw. Take tram 5 or 16 to Museumplein. Showing its age a bit, but still spacious and spotless rooms in a posh area. Reception open 24hr. Singles f65-70. Doubles f95-125. Triples f150. Quads f175. Breakfast included. No credit cards.

Liliane's Home, Sarphatistraat 119 (tel./fax 627 40 06). Trams 3, 6, 9, 14. A classy guesthouse for women, about a 10min. ride from Leidseplein. Color TV in all rooms. Minimum stay on weekends 2 nights. Singles f65-70. Doubles f120-150. Triples 155-170. Quads f220. Breakfast included. Tea and coffee free. No credit cards.

Greenwich Village, Kerkstraat 25 (tel. 626 97 46 or 625 40 81). Gay-friendly hotel not far from Leidseplein. All rooms with bath and cable TV. Bar with pool table. Reception 8am-midnight. 4-6 bed rooms f60 per person. Singles f100. Doubles f125. Breakfast included. MC, V, AmEx.

Casa Cara, Emmastraat 24 (tel. 662 31 35), 10min. behind Rijksmuseum; from Concertegebouwplein walk down Verhulststr and take the 4th right. Simple rooms in a quiet area. Singles f60. Doubles f75. Triples f130. Quads f150. Breakfast included. f10-20 cheaper in winter, but breakfast not included. Call ahead.

The Jordaan

Christian Youth Hostel Eben Haëzer, Bloemstr. 179 (tel. 624 47 17; fax 627 61 37), 1 street from Rozengracht in the Jordaan (tram 13 or 17 to Marnixstr.). Pristine bargain with clean-cut, cheery staff. Huge single-sex dorms with a few showers. Midnight curfew; Fri.-Sat. 1am. f20-5. Showers, sheets, and breakfast included. Lockers f1; f10 deposit. Free luggage storage.

Hotel van Onna, Bloemgracht 104 (tel. 626 58 01), in Jordaan. Tram 13 or 17 from Centraal Station. Sparkling, newly renovated. *Twice a Woman* was filmed in room 24. Reception open daily 8am-midnight. f60-70 per person. Breakfast included.

Hotel Arrivé, Haarlemmerstr 65 (tel. 622 14 39; fax 622 19 83). Convenient location between the Jordaan and Central Station. Clean rooms, newly renovated. 4-bed dorms f40 per person. Singles f50-75. Doubles f70-100. Triples 120-180. No curfew. Reception open 24hr. AmEx, DC, MC, and V.

Hotel Hortus, Plantage Parklaan 8 (tel. 625 99 96). Take tram 9 to the zoo (7 stops). Comfy rooms and free rein over the VCR and CD player. Reception open daily 8am-midnight. f45 per person. Book 1 week in ahead in summer.

Pensions and Private Accommodations

Roommate's snoring keeping you up all night? Hate being part of the masses (or Bible-reading sessions) at the local hostels? Head out to the cheap and wonderful pensions surrounding the city; it's well worth the travel time.

Ursula Schoniau, 134 Jan Evertstr. (tel. 612 25 27). Take tram 13 to "Mercatorplein." Staying with Ursula can be an adventure. Husband Henry cooks a great egg, provided you say "Good Morning." Clean rooms, shower, and a great breakfast (f25). Only for stays of more than one night. Reserve only one day in advance.

Gerda Rikker-Kouwenhoren, Iepenlaan 16 (tel. (02993) 639 33). About 35min. by bus in beautiful downtown Volendam. Knowledgeable, friendly owner. Central to Edam, Hoorn, and Zaanse Schaus for all you windmill lovers. f29.50 per person.

Pension Kil, Volendammerpad 19 (tel. (0299) 37 18 27). Take the NZH bus to Edam. Violently verdant, eclectically eccentric; living room was transformed into a replica of the jungle, complete with aviary of songbirds. Doubles f70, breakfast included. Reserve 1-2 weeks ahead June-Sept.

Camping

Camping Zeeburg, Zuider-Ijdijk 20 (tel. 694 44 30), next to the Amsterdam Rijncanal. Direct ferry from Centraal Station, or take buses 22, or 37, or night bus 170. Backpacker-oriented. Live music regularly. Reception open July daily 8am-11pm; April-June and Sept.-Aug. 9am-1pm and 5-9pm. Campsites f6.75 per person, f3.50 per tent. f12.25 for 2 people and tent. Showers f1.50.

Gaaspercamping, Loosdrechtdreef 7, (tel. 696 73 26; fax 696 93 69) in Gaasper Park. 20min. from Centraal Station by metro ("Gaasperplas") to the end; or night bus 75. Vast and fully rigged. Reception open daily 9am-12:30pm and 1:30-9pm. f6 per person, f7 per tent. Showers f1.50. Laundry f11. Open mid-March to Dec.

FOOD

Dutch food ranges from the hopelessly bland to the oddly tasty. The closest you'll come to Dutch cuisine is the local **FEBO,** reasonably priced self-service fast food stands. *Frikandel* (fried sausage) usually costs as little as f1.50. Sample Surinamian, Indonesian, Chinese, and Indian food in the red-light district around the Nieuwmarkt and off the Dam, on streets such as Hartenstr. Indonesian *rijsttafel* (a collection of rice, noodles, and spices) here is bliss. Many cheap restaurants cluster around the Leidseplein and the Rembrantsplein. *Eetcafés,* especially in the Jordaan, purvey good meat-and-potatoes fare for f12-20. Bakeries selling inexpensive cheese croissants and magnificent breads congregate along Utrechtsestr. south of Prinsengracht. Some restaurants close during school vacations.

Fruit, cheese, flowers, and sometimes even live chickens populate the **markets** on Albert Cuypstr., behind the Heineken brewery (open Mon.-Sat. 10am-4:30pm). The cheapest groceries are found at **Aldi Supermarket,** Nieue Weteringstr., off of Vijizelgracht, near the Heineken brewery (closed Sun.). **De Eenhoorn,** Warmoesstr. 16, adds a touch of class with its fresh meats and cheeses and broad selection of wines. Health food addicts rejoice at **De Natuurwinkel,** Weteringschans 135.

Red Light/Rembrandtsplein

Atrium, Oudezijds Achterburgwal 237, at Binnengasthuisstr. A huge, spotless university trough on the fringe of the red-light district. Dinners f7.75. Meals served Mon.-Fri. noon-2pm and 5-7pm. Snack bar open 9am-7pm. Closed July.

Say Saté, Amstelstr. 26. Specializes in *rijsttafel* and its signature *Saté* (skewered meat). Delicious meals (f18-25). Open Sun.-Thurs. 5-11pm, Fri.-Sat. 5pm-2:30am.

Keuhen Van 1870, Spuistr. 4. Traditional Dutch food at the cheapest prices around. Open Mon.-Fri. noon-8pm, Sat.-Sun. 4pm-9pm.

Bolhoed, 60-62 Prinsengracht, across the canal from the Anne Frank house. Specializes in organic vegetarian food (f10-20). Open daily noon-10pm.

Kam Yin, 6 Warmoesstr. This Chinese/Surinamese landmark serves cheap, heaping portions. Meals f7.50-15. Open daily noon-midnight.

Vishandel de Kreeft, Vijzelstr. 3, near Muntplein. Stand-up seafood counter that satisfies your salty, wet desires cheaply. Open Mon.-Sat. 10am-6pm.

La Place, on Rokin near Muntplein, and at Vroom Dreesman, Kalverstraat 201. Make up for your vegetable and fresh meat deficiency at this buffet-style restaurant. Meals around f10. Open daily 10am-9pm.

Cybercafé, Nieuwendijk 19. Munch on sandwiches (f3-7) and sip coffee as you log on. f3 per 15min. Open Mon.-Sat. 10am-10pm.

Café de Jaren, Nieuwe Dodenstraat 20-22. A great place to chill with your favorite magazine/newspaper—which you can borrow from their collection. Meals f12-20, served until 10pm. Open daily 10am-midnight, Fri. until 1am, Sat. until 2am.

Café Restaurant Turquoise, Wolvenstr. 30. Turkish cuisine with unbeatable prices. Sandwiches and crepes f3.50. Most meals f5-15. Open daily noon-11pm.

C.O.C. Koffieshop, Rozenstr. 14. Find out what's happening in Amsterdam's gay community as you lunch. Most items f1.50-4. Open Tue.-Sat. 1pm-5pm.

Downtown, Reguleersdwarsstr. 21. Brighten your day amidst the yellow walls and gay-friendly crowd. Sandwiches and simple meals f2.50. Open daily 10am-8pm.

Museum District

Dionysos, Overtoom 176 (tel. 689 44 41). From Leidseplein, walk right on the Stadhouderskade (past the Marriott); Overtoom is on the left. Tasty Greek dishes served daily from 5am-1am. Call ahead if you arrive after 12:30am on a weekday.

Paviljoen de Carrousel, Weteringschans. Feast on scrumptious pancakes (f5.50) after your Heineken tour. Open daily 10am-10pm.

Café 't Hoekje, Frans Hals Str., corner of Eerst Jacob Can Campen Str. Chill with the locals on your way from the Rijksmuseum to the Heineken brewery. Sandwiches f3.50-4.75. Open daily 10am-10pm.

Brasserie van Gogh, Hoofstraat 28. Pleasant spot down from the Rijksmuseum towards Leidseplein. Salads f17.50-22.50. Lasagna f19.50. Open daily 10am-7pm.

Petite Bordeaux, Keizersgracht 594, corner of Nieuwe Spiegel. Classy restaurant with reasonable prices. Lasagna f16.50. Pancakes f10. Sandwiches and burgers f5.80. Open daily 11am-9pm.

SIGHTS

Although bike theft is very common in Amsterdam, many people prefer to manipulate the city with a **bike** rented from the train station. **Circle Tram 20** stops at 30 attractions throughout the city (buy tickets on the tram or at VVV offices; runs daily 9am-7pm, every 10min). A more peaceful way to explore is on the **canal bus** which allows you to hop on or off (departs every 45min., f19.75 per day), or you can rent a **canal bike** and power your own way through the canals. (2 people f19.50 per hour; 4 people f29.50; f50 deposit) Pick up and drop off points for both the bus and bikes are at Rijksmuseum, Anne Frank Huis, Leidseplein Central Station, and City Hall/ Rembrandt House. **Mike's Bike Tours** provides an entertaining introduction to the city's sites and the surrounding countryside. Meet at the west entrance of the Rijkmuseum (June-Aug. daily 11:30pm and 4pm; Sept.-Oct. 12:30pm; 4hr.; f37). The economical **Museumkaart** (f33.60), gives discounts or admission to museums and transportation.

Amsterdam's former town hall, **Koninklijk Palace,** in the Dam, may be a symbol of the city's 17th-century commercialism, but its majesty is topped by the nearby **Magna Plaza,** today's homage to commercialism (open Mon. 11am-6pm, Tues.-Sat. 9:30am-6pm, Sun. 11am-5pm). A visit to Amsterdam would be sinful without seeing the **Rijksmuseum,** and that's precisely why you'll have to use guerrilla fighting skills to get past the crowds to Rembrandt's famed militia portrait *The Night Watch.* Slide shows every 25 minutes make it possible to handle such an art overload (open daily 10am-5pm; f12.50). The 14th-century **Oude Kerk,** 23 Oudekerksplein, has three 16th-century stained glass windows depicting scenes from Maria's life and hides a self-portrait of the organ's creator in the marblework. **Rembrandthuis,** Jodenbreestr. 4-6, at the corner of the Oude Schans Canal, is where the master lived, worked, and taught until the house was confiscated by the city for taxes. It holds 250 of Rembrandt's etchings and dry points, as well as many of his tools and plates (open Mon.-

Sat. 10am-5pm, Tues. until 9:30pm, Sun. 1-5pm; f7.50). See how a painter can fall deeper and deeper into insanity while his art gets better at the renowned **Van Gogh Museum,** where over 200 of the master's paintings are on display (open daily 10am-5pm; f12.50). The interesting **Tropenmuseum** (Museum of the Tropics), Linnaeusstr. 2, is a center devoted to the emergence and problems of developing countries (open Mon.-Fri. 10am-5pm, Tues. until 9:30pm; Sat.-Sun. noon-5pm; f10). **newMetropolis,** Oosterdok 2, houses interactive science and technology exhibits (open July-Aug. daily 10am-9pm; Sept.-June Sun.-Thurs. 10am-6pm, Fri.-Sat. 10am-9pm).

See the tiny space where the young journal keeper hid with her family from the Nazis until their capture in 1944 at the **Anne Frank Huis,** Prinsengracht 263. (Lines often 35-45min. Open Mon.-Sat. 9am-6:45pm, Sun. 10am-6:45pm; Sept.-May closes daily at 5pm. f10.) While you're there check out the **Homomonument,** a memorial to those who have been persecuted for their sexual orientation. The **Verzetsmuseum Amsterdam,** Lekstr. 63, tells the poignant story of the Nazi resistance in the Netherlands. To reach the museum, take trams 4 and 25. (Open Tues.-Fri. 10am-5pm, Sat.-Sun. and holidays 1-5pm. f5, free with Museumkaart.) A handsome 17th-century building, the **Joods-Portuguese Synagogue** at Jonas Daniël Meijerplein, near Waterlooplein, was founded by Portuguese Jews expelled from their country (open Sun.-Fri. 10am-4pm; f2). Next door at Jonas Daniël Meijerplein 2-4 is the **Joods Historisch Museum,** with exhibits on Jewish history and culture (open daily 11am-5pm; f8). The **Museum Amstelkring "Ons' Lieve Heer op Solder"** ("Our Lord in the Attic"), O.Z. Voorburgwal 40, in the red-light district, dates from Reformation days, when Catholics were forbidden to practice their faith publicly. The former Catholic priest's house hides an attic church (open Mon.-Sat. 10am-5pm, Sun. 1-5pm; f7, students f5).

Probably the best f2 you can spend in Amsterdam is on a visit to the retired **Heineken Brewery,** Stadhouderskade 78 (free beer *and* the f2 goes to charity). The presentation is super slick, and at the end uniformed servers give out samples. (Tours Mon.-Fri. Buy tickets at 9am for the 9:30am and 11am tours; at 11:15am for the 1pm and 2:30pm tours.) See sex in every way you dreamed possible (and many you didn't) to the tune of tasteful porno music at the **Amsterdam Sex Museum,** Damrak 18, near Centraal Station (open daily 10am-11:30pm; f4; under 17 not admitted).

To continue your "Only in Amsterdam" tour, visit the **Hash Marijuana Hemp Museum,** Oudezijds Achterburgwal 148, where, "if you come on the right day, you will see fat ripe buds glistening with the rich resin and smell air heavy with the fragrance of the crop. What an experience!" If you come on the wrong day, you may be subject to one of the frequent police raids. (Open in summer daily 11am-10pm; off-season Sun.-Wed. 11am-6pm, Thurs.-Sat. 11am-10pm. f6.)

Lose the invading hordes in the artsy narrow streets of the **Jordaan.** Bounded roughly by Prinsengracht, Brouwersgracht, Marnixstr., and Lauriersgracht, the Jordaan holds small cafés, unique shops, and vine-laden buildings. Built as an artisan district in the Golden Age, the streets still reflect times past. You can also take refuge from Amsterdam's mobbed sights and seamy streets in **Begijnhof,** a beautifully maintained, grassy courtyard surrounded by 18th-century buildings. To get there, walk down Kalverstr. and turn onto Begijnensteeg, a small side street between Kalverstr. 130 and 132. Spend a day people-watching in the grassy **Vondelpark.**

Amsterdam's art scene is not confined to musty galleries filled with the same dusty "old masters" you've seen a hundred times already. Some of the most exciting stuff in Amsterdam is free—painted on doors, walls, and trams. Graffiti and psychedelic murals dot the facades of several of the area's buildings. Check out the **Vrankrijk** building, Spuistr. 216, for some angry anarchistic menages surrounded by rampaging dragons, idiotic tourists, and angst-ridden youths. At the neck of Vondelpark, where it widens, a bridge displays more of the trippy kaleidoscope of wacked-out bodies and swirling colors. The area around **Mr. Visserplein,** near Waterlooplein and the Hortus Botannicus, yields further evidence that graffiti is much more than names and vulgar phrases. Continue your psychedelic survey at the **3D Hologram Store,** Grimburgwal 2 (open Tues.-Fri. noon-6pm, Sat. noon-5:30pm, Sun. 1-5:30pm).

The **red-light district,** bounded by Warmoestr., Gelderskade, and Oude Doelenstr., is the vice sink of Europe; it will either repulse you or fulfill your wildest dreams. Pushers, porn shops, and live sex theaters do a brisk business. **Sex shows** (f10-50) usually consist of costumed, disaffected couples repeatedly acting out your "wildest" (choreographed) dreams. Red neon marks houses of legal ill repute. Unlike the illegal streetwalkers, these prostitutes have regular gynecological exams—but keep in mind that HIV/AIDS takes six months to detect. During the day, the red-light district is comparatively flaccid, with tourists milling about, consulting their maps, and even bringing their children. As the sun goes down, the people get braver, and the area much more stimulating. Cops patrol the district until midnight, and there's a police station on Warmoestr. Women may feel uncomfortable walking through this area.

To round off your tour of Amsterdam, pet a stray cat at the **Poezenboot** (the Cat Boat), moored off Singel 40, home to cuddly pussies and the movement to keep them from multiplying (open daily 1-3pm; free, but donations accepted).

ENTERTAINMENT

Cafés and Bars

Amsterdam's finest cafés are the old, dark, wood-paneled *bruine kroegen* (brown cafés) of the **Jordaan,** where denizens gather under the nicotine-stained ceilings and dim brass lamps. **Leidseplein** is the liveliest nightspot, with coffeeshops and clubs galore. **Rembrandtsplein** is the place to watch soccer and sing with drunk revelers; just pretend you know the words (think German surfer trying to talk like a Valley girl—"*uitstekend* (excellent), dude"). Gay bars line **Reguliersdwarsstr,** which connects Muntplein and Rembrandtsplein, and Kerkstraat, five blocks north of Leidseplein. Most cafés open at 10 or 11am and close at 1am on Fridays and 2am Saturdays.

Café II Prinsen, Prisenstr. 27, on edge of the Jordaan. Filled with upscale Dutch partygoers. Beer from f2.75. Open Sun.-Thurs. 11am-1am, Fri.-Sat. 11am-2am.

Café de Tuin, Tweede Tuindwarsstr. 13 (open Mon.-Thurs. 10am-1am, Fri.-Sat. 10am-2am, Sun. 11am-1am), and **de Reiger,** Nieuwe Leliestr. 34 (open Mon.-Thurs. 11am-1am, Fri.-Sat. 11am-3am, Sun. 10am-1am), attract a young, artsy set.

't Gasthuys, Grimburgwal 7. Popular with students. Outdoor seating overlooking a canal at O.Z. Achterburgwal's end. Open nightly 11am-1am, Fri and Sat. until 2am.

Saarein, Elandstr. 119, is a hip bar in the Jordaan. Women (gay and straight) only. Open Mon. 8pm-1am, Tues.-Thurs. and Sun. 3pm-1am, Fri.-Sat. 3pm-2am.

Grand Café Dulac, Haarlemserstr. 118. A fantasy from "1001 Nights," with erotic statues jumping out of every metallic corner. Open daily 4pm-1am or 2am.

De Prins, Prinsengracht 124. A very lively student bar located in the Jordaan. Open 11am-1am, Fri. and Sat. until 2am.

The Sound Garden, Marnixstr. 164. Grunge café near the Christian Youth Hostel where you can recharge on angst before entering happyland. Open Mon.-Fri. 1pm-1am, Sat.-Sun. 1pm-2am.

Café D'Oude Herbergh, Handboogstr. 19 at the end of N.Z. Voorburgwal. Dutch 20-somethings come here to drink, drink, drink. Open nightly 8pm until late.

April, Reguliersdwarsstr. 37, **Havana,** Reguliersdwarsstr. 17-19, **Downtown,** Reguliersdwarsstr. 31, and **The Other Side,** Reguliersdwarsstr. 6, are gay bars all open from 3 or 4pm until 1am weekdays and 2am weekends.

Coffeeshops

Yes, the rumors are true: marijuana and hashish, though technically illegal, are so decriminalized that coffeeshops don't just sell coffee (unless one counts the green leafy coffee like "mother's milk" and "super skunk"). Shops are listed in the *Mellow Pages.* In general, hash is more common than marijuana here and comes in two varieties, black—like Afghan and Nepal—and blonde—like Moroccan. Black tends to be heavier and hits harder (f10-24 per gram). Dutch marijuana is the most common and costs f10-15 per gram. You can buy a bag for f25; the smaller the quantity, the smoother and more potent. Dutch tend to mix tobacco with their pot, so joints are harsher on your lungs. Most places will also supply rolling papers and filter tips. Steer away from milkshakes and cakes ("space cakes") made with grass: their marijuana content cannot be controlled, and ingestion has caused illness and paralysis.

Self-proclaimed cannabis experts and casual experimenters alike can find their niche among the hundreds of unique coffeeshops. The farther you travel from the touristed spots, the better and cheaper the establishments. People at shops are neither exceptionally welcoming nor unfriendly; they are simply...mellow. Acceptance of tourists depends on how much they blend in. Only tourists smoke from pipes; locals roll burnt, powdered has into cigarettes with tobacco. Joints can also be bought for f7.50. Do not to take pictures inside coffeehouses. Whatever approach you take, don't get too caught up in Amsterdam's narcotic quirk: use common sense, and remember that any experiment with drugs can be dangerous.

Dutch Flowers, 1012 Prinsengracht, is the winner of the coveted "Highlife" cup. **La Tertulia,** Prinsengracht 312, in the Jordaan, defies any of your coffeeshop preconceptions; in this bright shop plants and flowers surround an indoor pond and waterfall. Gloat about your Amsterdam experience to friends back home over email sent from **Tops,** Prinsengracht 480, near Leidseplein (f3 for 15min.; open daily 11pm-1am daily, until 3am Fri.-Sat.). The most famous and touristy coffeeshops are **The Grasshopper,** Nieuwezijds Voorburgwal 57 (open Sun.-Thurs. 9am-midnight, Fri.-Sat. 9am-1am), and **The Bulldog,** Oudezijds Voorburgwal 90 and on Leidseplein (open Sun.-Thurs. 9am-1am, Fri.-Sat. 9am-2am). **Barney's Coffeeshop,** Haarlemmerstr 102, serves great meals (f7.50-12.50; open daily 7am-8pm).

Live Music

While Amsterdam lacks a thriving music scene, it does offer a great deal of variety and occasionally headlines some mainstream groups. The **Jazzlijn** (tel. 626 77 64) provides info on local concerts. Many clubs avoid a cover charge by inflating beer prices.

Melkweg, Lijnbaasgracht 234a (tel. 624 17 77), in an old factory off Leidseplein, across from the police station. Amsterdam's legendary nightspot retains a cutting-edge aura despite the crowds. Live bands, theater, films, an art gallery, and a snack bar contribute to the multimedia sensory overload. "Tearoom" that sells Amsterdam's leaves of choice. Cover for the bar f5 plus membership fee (f4, good for 1 month). Open Wed.-Thurs. and Sun. 7pm-2am, Fri.-Sat. 7pm-4am. Box office open Mon.-Fri. noon-5pm, Sat.-Sun. 4-7pm, and while the club is open.

Paradiso, Weteringschans 6-8 (tel. 626 45 21). Some of the foremost international punk, new-wave, and reggae bands play here. Cover f10-27 depending on the band. Shows start daily at 10pm.

Alto, Korte Leidsedwarsstraat 115, is a lively jazz bar off Leidseplein with music nightly. Open 9pm-3 or 4am.

PH31, Prins Hendriklaan 31. Hosts hard-core, punk, and new-wave bands on Thursday and jazz and blues on Sundays. Open daily 8pm to between 2 and 4am.

De Kroeg, Lijnbaansgracht 163. Vibrant crowds writhe to reggae, salsa, rock, and blues. f5 cover on live music nights, f2.50 on DJ night (Fri.), periodic jam sessions (Mon. and Wed.) free. Open Sun.-Thurs. 8pm-3am, Fri.-Sat. Music starts at 10pm.

The Bimhuis, Oude Schans 73-77, near Waterlooplein. The hub of Dutch jazz. More than 200 concerts held yearly. Cover f10, students f7.50. Sun.-Tues. jazz workshops. Wed.-Sat. concerts after 9pm.

Winston Kingdom, Warmoesstraat 127. Bands and themes change nightly. Cover f5-10. Open Sun.-Wed. 8pm-2am, Thurs.-Sat. until 3am.

Odeon Jazz Kelder, Singel 460, near Leidsestr. Men in sharp suits and women in heels come here to groove. Cover f7.50, weekends f12.50. Bar opens daily at 4pm. Shows from 6-10pm. Open until 4am on Fri. and Sat. for dancing.

Dancing

Many nightclubs in Amsterdam charge a membership fee in addition to the normal cover, so the tab can be obscene. Be prepared for arrogant, cocky doormen who live to turn away tourists: be a beautiful woman or show up early. If you're really desperate, a f10-20 tip to the doorman may make him overlook your imperfections. There are expensive discos aplenty on Prinsengracht, near Leidsestr., and on Lange Leidsedwarsstr. Gay discos line Amstelstr.

MAZZO, Rozengracht 114, in the Jordaan. Artsy disco that is constantly revolving its DJs, music styles, display, and slideshow. Live music Tues. Cover f7.50, weekends f10. Open Sun.-Thurs. 11pm-4am, Fri.-Sat. 11pm-5am. No dress code.

Dansen bij Jansen, Handboogstr. 11, near Spui. Near the university and popular among students (student ID officially required). Cover f4-5. Happy hour Sun.-Wed. 11pm-midnight. Open Sun.-Thurs. 11pm-4am, Fri.-Sat. 11pm-5am.

C.O.C., Rogenstraat 14 (tel. 623 40 79). Cultural center for gay men and women that sponsors weekly events. Friday night disco 11pm-4am. Sat. night is the girls' café (8pm-midnight) and disco (11pm-3am). Sun. is Arabian disco night (8pm-12:30am).

RoXY, Singel 465. The hippest crowd in town busts a move to house. Obvious tourist attire rebuffed. Cover Wed. and Sun. f7.50, Thurs. f10, Fri.-Sat. f12.50. Open Wed.-Thurs. around 11am-4am, Fri.-Sun. 11am-5am.

iT, Amstelstr. 24, near Waterlooplein. Clients tout this as one of the best and most decadent gay discos in Europe. Free to members, otherwise f15. Difficult to get into. Gay only on Sat. Open Thurs. and Sun. 11pm-4am, Fri.-Sat. 11pm-5am.

Ministry, Reguliersdwarsstr. 12. The most popular gay disco, Sat. excluded. Expect to pay f15 cover. Open nightly 11pm-5am.

Theater, Dance, and Music

The VVV puts out *What's On* (f3.50) monthly, with comprehensive cultural listings. Also check out Boom Chicago's mini-magazine, available for free at restaurants and cafés around the city or the free monthly *UITKRANT*. The monthly *Culture and Camp* (f5) gives info on gay venues and events. In summer, there are free performances Wednesday through Sunday at the **Vondelpark Openluchttheater** (tel. 673 14 99); jazz and folk concerts dominate, but children's theater, rock bands, political music, and mime also grab the limelight. Check posters at park entrances. While you're in the park, see what's playing at **The Vertigo** movie theater and café. The sparkling new **Muziektheater,** perched over the junction of the Amstel and the Oude Schans (tel. 625 54 55), hosts the **Netherlands Opera** and the **National Ballet.** The **Royal Concertgebouw Orchestra** at the Concertgebouw on Van Baerlestr. is one of the world's finest (tickets f25). Frequent English-language performances and cabarets are given at the theater/café **Suikerhof,** Prinsengracht 381 (tel. 22 75 71; open daily from 5pm, Sun. from 2pm). Make reservations for any cultural event at the **Amsterdams Uit Buro** (AUB) ticketshop (tel. 621 12 11; open daily 10am-6pm) or at the VVV's theater desk, Stationsplein 10 (open Mon.-Sat. 10am-5pm).

Organ concerts resound during the summer at **Westerkerk,** Prinsengracht 281 (Wed. 8:15pm), where Rembrandt is buried. Concerts resonate at **Nieuwe Kerk,** on the Dam (f5-12.50) where Dutch monarchs are sworn in (they're not crowned). The June **Holland Festival** of dance, drama, and music is closely followed by the **Summer Festival** of small theater companies in July. (Contact the Balie Theatre on Kleine cannabis at 623 29 04. Tickets f10-15.) On the first weekend in August, gay pride abounds in street parties along Reuliersdwarsshaat, Amstel, Kerkstraat, and Raguliersdwursstr. Call 625 83 75 for more info (staffed daily 5am-midnight).

There's no escaping **Boom Chicago;** their *Boom Paper* is ubiquitous. Here American actors perform improvised sketches taking cues from the audience (shows nightly at 8:15pm, doors open at 7pm). It's also chock full of tourist info the VVV only wishes it had. Boom will be closed for renovations from January to March 1998, but will reopen in April at **Boom,** Leideplein 12. Reserve tickets (tickets f25, f20 with Boom Paper) by calling 639 27 07 (box office open 10am-6pm). The restaurant serves American-style meals from noon to 11pm (f12-30) and is the only Amsterdam haunt to snag pitchers of beer (f19).

■ Near Amsterdam: Alkmaar, Edam, and Hoorn

When you tire of free-living (morally, not monetarily) Amsterdam, explore the surrounding countryside. Trains are expensive, so buy a cheap day-return or get a oneday bus pass (f18.10). **Alkmaar,** 45 minutes away by regular train, holds a large open-air **cheese market** every Friday from 10am to noon (mid-April to mid-Sept.). When the market is over, there is still plenty to buy along the narrow, canal-lined streets. Fanatical windmill fans should blow over to **Zaanse Schaanz,** a traditional (and touristy) town alongside a river. Five windmills are accompanied by a cheese-making facility and traditional crafts (from Amsterdam 15min., round-trip f6).

Discover quaint cottages, peaceful parks and canals, and lots of cheese and clogs in **Edam.** Holland's sleeping beauty lies just outside Amsterdam, accessible by NZH bus from Centraal Station (7 strips). The 15th-century **Grote Kerk,** or St. Nicholaaskerk, is the largest three-ridged church in Europe and has 30 entrancing stained-glass windows (open April-Oct. daily 2-4:30pm). Farmers still bring their famed cheese to market by horse and boat on Wednesdays in July and August (10am-12:30pm). Rent a bike at **Ronald Schot,** Kleine Kerkstraat 9-11 (f10 per day), and head to the source yourself. At **Alida Hoeve,** Zeddewed 1, a traditional cheese factory across the street from the bike path as you head toward Volendam (pass the first touristy cheese factory you see), Edam cheese is still made by hand and the generous samples are free (open daily 9am-6pm). Farther down the path stands a towering **windmill.** For f1, you can climb the steep ladder to the top while it's turning (open April-Aug. daily 9am-4pm). If you decide to crash for the night, **Pension Kil,** Volendammerpad, 19 (tel. 229 37 18 27) near the bus stop, has comfortable doubles with breakfast for f70.

A little farther from Amsterdam, **Hoorn** awaits on the edge of the **Ijsselmeer,** an inlet of the Atlantic that the ever-enterprising Dutch diked off in 1932 to form a fresh-water sea. The town itself is charming, with frequent open-air markets and a picturesque harbor. If the weather cooperates, **swimming** and **sailing** in the Ijsselmeer can be the perfect tranquilizer after the frenzy of Amsterdam. The **tourist office,** Veemerkt 4, organizes comprehensive walking tours. From the station, go right and take your first left; cross the bridge and follow signs to get there (open Mon.-Fri. 9-11:30am and 12:30-4pm). **De Toorts (HI)** (tel. (229) 21 42 56) has rooms right on the water. To reach the hostel, take buses 153, 137, or 147 to the Julianaplaen stop (dorms f23.85, nonmembers f28.85; open July-Aug.).

Haarlem

Haarlem is home to the Renaissance facades and placid canals that inspired the Golden Age Dutch artists. The local 17th- and 18th-century *hofjes* (almshouses for elderly women) feature elegant brickwork and grassy courtyards; notable among them are the secluded **Hofje van Bakenes,** Wijde Appelaarsteeg 11, near the Teylers Museum, and the **Hofje van Oirschot,** at the end of Kuisstr. where it becomes Barteljorisstr. These are inhabited private properties, so be respectful. From the station, Kruisweg leads to the **Grote Markt** and the glorious medieval **Stadhuis** (Town Hall), originally the hunting lodge of the Count of Holland. When the Hall of Counts is not in use, sneak a peek at the lavish interior; ask at the reception desk. The **Grote Kerk** graces the opposite end of the Grote Markt and houses the Müller organ, which Mozart played at the age of 11. (Church open Mon.-Sat. 10am-4pm. f2, students f1. Free recitals May-Oct. Tues. 8:15pm; July-Aug. also Thurs. 3pm.)

From the church, walk down Damstr. to the Netherlands' oldest museum, the **Teylers Museum,** Spaarne 16. Looking like something out of an H.G. Wells novel, the museum lets you see what people in 1788 thought a museum should be: a blend of scientific instruments, fossils, coins, paintings, and drawings, including works by Raphael and Michelangelo (open Tues.-Sat. 10am-5pm, Sun. noon-5pm; f6.50). The legacy of Haarlem's brash portraitist Frans Hals lives on in the **Frans Hals Museum,** Groot Heiligland 62. Housed in a charming 17th-century almshouse, the collection includes Hals's lively group portraits and a permanent collection of modern art (open Mon.-Sat. 11am-5pm, Sun. 1-5pm; f7.50). The **Corrie Ten Boomhuis,** better known as The Hiding Place, Barteljorisstr. 19, is where Corrie Ten Boom and her family hid Jewish refugees during World War II. The refugees were never discovered, but the entire Ten Boom family was removed to concentration camps. Corrie was the only survivor. (Tours every hour on the half hour April-Oct. Tues.-Sat. 10am-3pm; Nov.-

March Tues.-Sat. 11am-3pm. Free.) On Saturdays, a technicolor **flower and fruit market** fills the Grote Markt (open 9am-4pm).

Practical Information, Accommodations, and Food The **VVV Tourist Office,** Stationsplein 1 (tel. (0900) 616 16 00, f1 per min.; fax (023) 534 05 37), sells an excellent map (f3), offers the informative *Holiday Magazine* (f2), and books rooms for f4.50. (Open April-Sept. Mon.-Sat. 9am-5:30pm; Oct.-March Mon.-Fri. 9am-5:30pm, Sat. 9am-4pm.) Haarlem is easily accessible from Amsterdam by **train** (f5.25) or by **bus** 80 from Marnixstr., near Leidseplein (2 per hr., 6 strips). Five night buses (86) cruise from Amsterdam's Leidseplein to Haarlem (12:42-3:20am).

A welcoming staff keeps the **NJHC-herberg Jan Gijzen (HI),** Jan Gijzenpad 3 (tel. (023) 537 37 93), clean and comfortable. Bus 2 ("Haarlem-Nord") will drive you the 3km from the station to the hostel; tell the driver your destination. (Reception open daily 7am-midnight. Flexible midnight curfew. f25.75, nonmembers f30.75. Sheets f6.25. Open March-Oct.) Haarlem has apparently not heard of budget hotels, but the VVV can find you a private room for a f9 fee (from f28). **Hotel Carillon,** Grote Markt 27 (tel. (023) 531 05 91), is ideally located if not ideally priced. (Reception and bar open daily 7:30am-1am. Singles f52.50-87.50; doubles f110. Breakfast included.) The **Stads Café,** Zijlstr. 56-58 (tel. (023) 532 52 02), offers Dutch cuisine (*dagschotel* f9.75) and sleeping quarters. (Singles f60-80; doubles f75-100; triples f130. Breakfast f8.50. Café open Mon.-Thurs. 8:30am-11pm, Fri.-Sat. 8:30am-1:30am, Sun. 2-11pm.) Cheap pensions are located in nearby Zandvoort (see **Near Haarlem,** below). A campground awaits at **De Liede,** Liewegje 17 (tel. (023) 33 23 60). Take bus 2 ("Zuiderpolder") and walk 10 minutes (f4.50 per person and per tent; f2.50 tax per person in summer). **Pannekoekhuis De Smikkel,** Kruisweg 57, serves plump buttery pancakes (f9.25-16.00) with anything from bananas to seafood (open Mon.-Sat. noon-10pm, Sun. 2-10pm). For healthier fare, try out **Eko Eetcafé,** Zijlstr. 39, which serves a vegetarian plate for f17 and pizzas for f12-16.50 (open daily 5:30-9:30pm). The **De Gouth Café,** Botermarket 19, has meals for f17-21 (open daily 11am-10pm).

Near Haarlem

Haarlem is only 10 minutes by train (round-trip f3.50) from **Zandvoort,** a seaside town that boasts seven **nude beaches** along with more modest sands for the bashful (for more info call (023) 571 82 31). Cheap pensions and hotels populate Zandvoort, and the **VVV,** Schoolplein 1 (tel. (023) 571 79 47), in the village center, a downhill walk from the beach and the station, sells a lodgings guide for f3.50. (Open April-Sept. Mon.-Sat. 10am-12:30pm and 1:30pm-5pm; Oct.-March Tues.-Fri. 10am-12:30pm and 1:30-4:30pm, Sat. 10am-12:30pm and 1:30-3:30pm.) **Hotel-Pension Noordzee,** Hogeweg 15 (tel. (023) 571 31 27), is only 100m from the beach (singles f45, doubles f80). **Hotel van der Aar,** Brederodestr. 44 (tel. (023) 571 48 02), is a good second choice (reception open daily 8am-midnight; singles f32.50, doubles f65). **Guest House Corper,** Koninginneweg 21 (tel./fax (023) 571 34 49), is 10 minutes from the beach (singles f40-60, doubles f60-90, triples f90-120).

Bloemendaal, a less revealing beach, accessible by bus 81 from the Haarlem train station (15min.), is famous for its stately mansions, peaceful sand dunes, and acres of woods. An international flower auction is held year-round in the nearby town of **Aalsmeer.** From Haarlem, take bus 140 (auction open Mon.-Fri. 7:30-11am). The **Frans Roozen Gardens** bloom with 500 different types of flowers and plants; summer flower shows are free. Bus 90 ("Den Haag") stops in front of the gardens (open July-Oct. Mon.-Fri. 9am-5pm; tulip shows April-May daily 8am-6pm). Bus 50 or 51 runs past some of Holland's famous flower fields. Daffodils blossom in early to late April, hyacinths in mid- to late April, and tulips from late April to mid-May.

Leiden

Rembrandt's birthplace and the site of the first Dutch tulips, Leiden has long been a cradle of national culture. In the 16th century, Leiden's residents threw open dikes to flood the surrounding plain and thwart invading Spanish armies. William of Orange rewarded the city by founding the University of Leiden in 1574, and now Leiden is the archetypal Dutch college town, brimming with bookstores, cafés, bicycles, museums, and a few requisite windmills. The **Rijksmuseum voor Volkenkunde** (National Museum of Ethnology), Steenstr. 1, one of the world's oldest anthropological museums, boasts a collection of fantastic artifacts from the Dutch East Indies (open Tues.-Fri. 10am-5pm, Sat.-Sun. noon-5pm; f7, students f5). The **Rijksmuseum van Oudheden** (National Antiquities Museum), Rapenburg 28, harbors Egyptian mummies, exhibits on ancient Dutch history, and the lovingly restored Egyptian Temple of Taffeh, removed from the reservoir basin of the Aswan Dam (open Tues.-Sat. 10am-5pm, Sun. noon-5pm; f5). The university's 400-year-old garden, the **Hortus Botanicus,** Rapenburg 73, has a vast range of plants from all around the world. (Garden open April-Sept. Mon.-Sat. 9am-5pm, Sun. 10am-5pm; Oct.-March Mon.-Fri. 9am-5pm. Some greenhouses close at 4:30pm. f5.) Inspect the mechanical innards of a functioning windmill at the **Molenmuseum "De Valk,"** 2e Binnenvestgracht 1 (open Tues.-Sat. 10am-5pm, Sun. 1-5pm; f5, free with Museumkaart). The **Museum De Lakenhal,** Oude Singel 32, exhibits works by Rembrandt and Jan Steen and displays pewter, silver, and glass collections, while the **Boerhaave Museum,** Lange St. Agnietenstraat 10, traces scientific development (both open Tues.-Sat. 10am-5pm, Sun. noon-5pm; f5).

THE NETHERLANDS

Practical Information, Accommodations, and Food Leiden makes a good **rail** daytrip from Amsterdam (30min., f11.50) or the Hague (20min., f4.50). The **VVV Tourist Office,** Stationsplein 210 (tel. (071) 51 14 68 46), across the street and to the right of the train station, doles out maps (f1.25), and locates rooms in private homes (f3.50 fee). Their *Rembrandt Tour* (f3.50) and *Pilgrim Tour* (f1) brochures offer creative ways to see the town on foot and their city guide has a long list of accommodations (open Mon.-Sat. 9am-5:30pm, Sun. 10am-2pm). Due to a student housing crunch, finding inexpensive rooms may be difficult. Idyllic **NJHC-herberg De Duinark (HI),** Langevelderlaan 45 (tel. (0252) 37 29 20), is 18km from Leiden in Noordwijk, a five-minute walk from beautiful white sand beaches. Take bus 60 or 61 to "Kappellebosiaan" or bus 61 to "Sancta Maria," and walk 15 minutes (reception open daily 8am-1am; f28.50, nonmembers f33.50; sheets f6.25). The **Hotel Pension Witte Singel,** Witte Singel 80 (tel. (071) 12 45 92), offers immaculate rooms overlooking gardens and canals (singles f60, doubles f85). Enjoy a comfy night at **Pension In de Goede Hoek,** Diefsteeg 19a (tel. (071) 12 10 31), near the *Stadhuis* (reception open daily 7am–10pm; singles f45, doubles f75; no credit cards).

For Leiden's cheapest eats, try the university *mensas:* **Augustinus,** Rapenburg 24 (open Sept.-June Mon.-Fri. 5:30-7:15pm), and **De Bak,** Kaiserstr. 23-25 (open mid-Aug. to late July Mon.-Fri. noon-2pm and 5-7pm). Both start at f5. **Café de Illegale,** Hooigracht 72, draws an intellectual crowd with vegetarian and Dutch cuisine (f15-22; open daily 5pm-midnight; kitchen closes at 10pm). The **Bruin Boon,** Stationsweg 1, is a convivial pub serving cheap snacks and lunches. (Under f10. Open Mon.-Fri. 8am-11:30pm, Sat. 9:30am-11:30pm, Sun. 10:30am-6:30pm.) The **Edan** supermarket, just across from the station has the basics (open Mon.-Fri. 8am-8pm, Sat. 8am-5pm). The **Duke,** Oude Singel 2, rounds up live jazz nightly at 9:30pm and open jam sessions on Sundays (open Sun.-Fri. 7pm-1am, Sat. 2pm-2am).

■ Near Leiden: Lisse

Arriving in Lisse, you'll feel as Dorothy did when she landed in technicolor Oz. From late March to May, the **Keukenhof** garden (f15) blooms into a colorful kaleidoscope as over five million bulbs explode into life. Chronicle the history and science of tulip raising at the **Museum Voor de Bloembollenstreek** (open Tues.-Sun. 1-5pm; f4). Take bus 50 or 51 toward Lisse from the Haarlem train station; a combination bus and admission ticket bought at Centraal Station (f21) saves money. The **VVV Tourist Office** (tel. (02522) 41 42 62) is at Grachtweg 53 (open Mon. noon-5pm, Tues.-Fri. 9am-5pm, Sat. 9am-4pm). Look for petals in motion at the April **flower parade.**

The Hague (Den Haag)

Centuries of wealth have bestowed The Hague, the Dutch seat of government, with many beautiful buildings, fine museums, and parks. But, most of the attractions can be seen in one day, and wandering the streets at night may not be a good idea. Consider making The Hague a daytrip, or stay in the nearby beachfront **Scheveningen** (a town so difficult to pronounce correctly, it was used as a code word by the Dutch in World War II), where beaches, casinos, and a boardwalk make for fine weekend getaways. For titillating snippets of Dutch politics visit The Hague's **Binnenhof,** the complex of Parliament. Guided tours (leaving from Binnenhof 8a) move on to the 13th-century **Ridderzaal** (Hall of Knights), and usually one or both of the chambers of the States General (open Mon.-Sat. 10am-4pm, last tour at 3:45pm; f5). Just outside the north entrance of the Binnenhof, the 17th-century **Mauritshuis** features an impressive collection of Dutch paintings, including Rembrandt's *The Anatomy Lesson* and Vermeer's *Lady with a Turban* (open Tues.-Sat. 10am-5pm, Sun. 11am-5pm; f10).

The opulent home of the International Court of Justice, the **Peace Palace,** Carnegieplein, 10 minutes from the Binnenhof, was donated by Andrew Carnegie as he suffered a bout of Robber Baron guilt. The palace is usually closed when the Court is in session; call ahead to check if it's open. (Tel. (070) 302 42 42. Tours Mon.-Fri. 10, 11am, 2, 3, and 4pm; Oct.-May last tour leaves at 3pm. f5.) The interesting **Madurodam** has miniatures of Dutch sites (open April-Sept. daily 9am-10pm; f19.50).

Den Haags Filmhuis, Spui 191, features oldies and the best of current movies; all films are shown in their original language with Dutch subtitles (f11-15, students f8.50-12.50; screenings nightly at 7:30pm and 9:45pm). **Muziekcafé La Valletta,** Nwe. Schoolstr. 13a, is a jazz café that features live shows Thursday nights at 10pm (open daily 5pm-1am). In mid-June the beach hosts the **Nationale Nederlanden Kite Festival** and the **International Sandcastle Festival. Parkpop,** the last weekend in June, is the largest free mainstream rock concert in Europe. In July, the annual **North Sea Jazz Festival** brings four incredible days of the world's best jazz to The Hague. For a smurfy good time, check out the unbelievably tacky **Smurf Festival** in Scheveningen in early July, or peruse the weekly brochure *Over Uit,* free from the VVV.

Practical Information, Accommodations, and Food For **trains** (tel. (06) 92 92) which serve Amsterdam (1hr., f28.25) and Rotterdam (30min., f12.25) use **Holland Spoor;** most others come and go at **Centraal Station.** Both have **lockers** (f4-6). *Stoptrein* and trams 9 and 12 run from Holland Spoor to Centraal Station and the **VVV Tourist Office,** Kon. Julianaplein 30 (info tel. (06) 34 03 50 51, .75f per min.), in front of Centraal Station under the Hotel Sofitel, which distributes brochures (f4) and maps (f2.75), books rooms (f4 fee), and publishes events listings (open Mon.-Sat. 9am-5pm; July-Aug. also Sun. 10am-5pm).

The **Australian** embassy is at Carnegielaan 4 (tel. 310 82 00; open Mon.-Fri. 9am-12:30pm and 2-5:30pm; visas mornings only). The **Canadian** embassy is at Sophialaan 7 (tel. 361 41 11; open Mon.-Fri. 9am-1pm and 2-5:30pm). Kiwis head to the **New Zealand Immigration Service,** Carnegielaan 10 (tel. 365 80 37; open Mon.-Fri. 9am-12:30pm and 1:30-5:30pm; Fri. closes at 5pm). The **South African Consulate** is at Wassenarseweg 36 (tel. 392 45 01; open daily 9am-noon). The **U.K.** embassy sits at Lange Voorhout 10 (tel. 364 58 00; open Mon.-Fri. 9am-1pm and 2:15-5:30pm). Citizens of the U.S. call the consulate in Amsterdam (tel. (020) 664 56 61).

The Hague is home to one of the nicest Dutch hostels, the **NJHC-herberg,** Scheepmakerstr. 27 (tel. (070) 397 00 11; fax 397 22 51), which boasts fluffy comforters, a bar, and free info packets. From Centraal Station take tram 1, 9, or 12 to "Rijswijkse." (Dorms f28-30; doubles f82.50-90; triples f110-120; quads f130-145. Nonmembers add f5. Sheets f6.25.) Even more alluring quarters wait in nearby Scheveningen, where the **VVV Tourist Office,** Gevers Deynootweg 1134 (tel. (06) 354 350 51), can give you an accommodations guide. (Open July-Aug. Mon.-Sat. 9am-noon, Sun. 10am-5pm; Sept.-June Mon.-Sat. 9am-5:30pm, Sun. 10am-5pm.) Five minutes from a sublime beach and huge casino is **Hotel Pension Lobèl,** Haagsestr. 53 (tel. (06) 354 58

03). Take tram 1, 7, or 9 ("Scheveningen") from the station (3 strips), and tell the driver your destination (singles f50, doubles f110). Or rest at **Hotel Scheveningen,** Gevers Deynootweg 2 (tel. (06) 354 70 03), with a shower and a TV in each room (singles f50, larger rooms f35 per person). To reach the beachside campground **Recreatiecentrum Kijuduinpark,** Wijndaelerweg 25 (tel. (06) 325 23 64), take tram 3 from Centraal Station (f7.55 per person, f10 per tent; open April-Sept.).

The bike ride from The Hague to Scheveningen is pleasant; **bike rental** for f8 per day and f32 per week is available at both Holland Spoor (tel. (070) 389 08 30) and the Centraal Station (tel. (070) 385 32 35). The VVV sells cycling maps (f8) but routes and nearby towns are clearly marked along paths. Cheap cafés line **Korte Poten,** a pedestrian section of the street that connects Centraal Station with the Binnenhof complex. Tasty pizza and pasta (f10-15) are available at **Donatello's,** Molenstr. 8-10 (open daily 11am-10pm). **Muziekcafé La Valletta,** Nwe. Schoolstr. 13a, is a jazz café that features live shows Thursday nights at 10pm (no cover; open daily 5pm-1am).

THE NETHERLANDS

Delft

To gaze out over Delft's lilied canals from one of its stone footbridges is to behold the very images that local master Jan Vermeer immortalized on canvas over 300 years ago. The city has not lost its charm. A stroll down Delft's tree-lined canals and many-hued *markts* alone justifies the jaunt south from The Hague. Mondays and Thursdays, when townspeople flood to the bustling marketplace, are the best days to visit. While meandering amidst merchants, those with a sweet tooth should sample a warm *stroopwafel* or the more daring may try the local specialty of raw fish *Karp.*

Delft is renowned for its **Delftware,** the blue-on-white china developed in the 16th century to compete with the newly imported Chinese porcelain. You can gawk at the precious platters in the main boutique at **De Porceleyne Fles,** Rotterdamseweg 196, in south Delft, where there are hourly demonstrations. To get to the boutique, take bus 129 or 63 from the station. (Open April-Oct. Mon.-Sat. 9am-5pm, Sun. 9:30am-5pm; Nov.-March Mon.-Sat. 9am-5pm. f5.) For more in-depth study, tour the factory at **De Delftse Pauw,** Delftweg 133, in the northern reaches of the city, where artisans still painstakingly hand-paint the porcelain. Daily tours explain the process. Take tram 1 from the station to "Vrijenbanselaan." (Open April to mid-Oct. daily 9am-5:30pm; late-Oct. to March Mon.-Fri. 9am-5:30pm, Sat.-Sun. 11am-1pm. Free.)

Built in 1381, the **Nieuwe Kerk** looms over the central **Markt** and holds the mausoleum of Dutch liberator William of Orange, flanked by a statue of his dog, who starved to death out of despair after his master died (church open April-Oct. Mon.-Sat. 9am-6pm; Nov.-March 11am-4pm; f4). Ascend the church tower, as caretakers of the 48-bell *carillon* have done for six centuries, for a view of old Delft (tower closes 30min. earlier than the church; f2.50). Built in the 15th century as a nun's cloister, **Het Prinsenhof** at Sint Agathaplein was William's abode until a crazed Spanish sympathizer assassinated him in 1584. Today it exhibits paintings, tapestries, pottery, and contemporary art (open Tues.-Sat. 10am-5pm, Sun. 1-5pm; f3.50).

Practical Information, Accommodations, and Food Delft is one hour southwest of Amsterdam by **train,** with connections to The Hague (15min., f4) and Leiden (30min., f6.25). For train or **bus** info, call (06) 92 92. The **VVV Tourist Office,** Markt 85 (tel. (015) 212 61 00), has a city pamphlet (f3.50) and hiking and cycling maps (f4-10). They book rooms for a 10% deposit. (Open Mon.-Fri. 9am-6pm, Sat. 9am-5:30pm, Sun. 10am-3pm; Oct.-March closed Sun.) **Rondvaart Delft,** Koormkt 113 (tel. 212 63 85), offers canal rides (April-Oct. 10:30am-5:30pm; f8). Delft has few budget accommodations. The sage's choice is a cozy but unmarked **Van Leeuwen,** Achterom 143 (tel. (015) 212 37 16), overlooking a canal (ring the bell; singles f35, doubles f70; breakfast included). A few hotels dotting the Markt offer spiffy rooms at decent prices, including the nearby **Pension Van Domburg,** Volderstracht 24 (tel. (015) 212 30 29; doubles f65). If you still haven't found a room, ask for help from **Let Krakeelhof,** Jacoba von Bierernlaan. The guys in room 39 will try to find you a place to stay, although technically their services are reserved for Delft university students. Expect to pay about f20. Delft also has a **campground** on Korftlaan (tel. (015) 13 00 40) in the Delftse Hout recreation area. (Reception open May to mid-Sept. daily 9am-10pm; mid-Sept. to April 9am-6pm. f3.50 per person, f17.50 per tent. Laundry facilities available.) Take bus 60 or 64 from the station to "Korftlaan."

Many inexpensive restaurants line **Volderstraat** and **Oude Delft,** so skip the tourists traps in the *Markt.* For f7, you can savor any one of the sandwiches voted the best *broodje* in the Netherlands at **Kleyweg's Stads-Koffyhuis,** Oude Delft 133-135 (omelettes and salads from f8.25; open Mon.-Fri. 9am-7pm, Sat. 9am-6pm). **Stads Pan,** down the street, has multitudes of savory pancakes (f5-17; open March-Oct. daily 11am-9pm; Nov.-Feb. Mon.-Sat. 11am-9pm). The immense café **Verderop,** Westuest 9, near the station, has inexpensive drinks and live music (open Mon.-Fri. 10am-1am, Sat.-Sun. 2pm-2am; July-Aug.opens daily at 3pm). The **Straattheater festival** (2nd week in June) summons street performers from the city's every nook and cranny. The **Oude Stijl Jazz Festival** swings into Delft in the third week in August.

Rotterdam

Although a barrage of German bombs obliterated Rotterdam's center in 1940, the city's modern architectural marvels, such as the famed cube houses, and a vibrant student population are proof that Rotterdammers are looking ahead. Those seeking shelter from the commercialized drug scene and crowds of Amsterdam may appreciate the mellower, friendlier aura of Rotterdam.

PRACTICAL INFORMATION

Rotterdam sprawls over a vast area, but the touristed area is quite small. The borders are roughly defined as **Centraal Station** to the north, **Blaak Station** to the east, **'s Gravendijkwal** to the west, and the river **Maas** to the south. Most sights are within walking distance. Most museums and shops are closed Mondays.

Tourist Offices: VVV, Coolsingel 67 (tel. (063) 403 40 65), just across the street from the *Stadhuis.* Cross the square and the road in front of the station and follow Weenastraat until the fountain, then turn right onto Coolsingel (15min.). Decent map and guide book f3. Large map f4. Books rooms (f2.50), makes theater and concert reservations, and offers tours. Open Mon.-Thurs. 9am-7pm, Fri. 9am-9pm.

Budget Travel: NBBS, Meent 126 (tel. 414 94 85), near the *Stadhuis.* Open Mon.-Thurs. 9:30am-5:30pm, Fri. 9:30am-8:30pm, Sat. 10am-4pm.

American Express: Office on Meent 92 cashes checks and holds mail (f2.50 without AmEx card or checks). Good exchange rates. Open Mon.-Thurs. 9am-5pm, Fri. 9:30am-8:30pm, Sat. 10am-4pm.

Trains and Buses: All trains pass through **Centraal Station,** and some also stop at **Blaak Station.** Buses also use Centraal Station as a hub. Call 06 92 92 for train information, 411 71 00 for buses. Daily connections to The Hague (20min., f7.25), Amsterdam (1hr., f22.25), and Utrecht (45min., f14.50).

Luggage Storage: Lockers at the train stations. Small f4 per 24hr. Large f6 per 24hr.

Public Transportation: Fast and efficient metro (most rides2 strips). Metro and trams spread over the entire city and run daily 6am-midnight. Night buses also run Fri. and Sat. nights. *Strippenkaarten* are f11 for 15 strips.

Emergencies: tel. (06) 112; connects to a general emergency switchboard.

Internet access: Use-it, Mathenesserlaan 173 (tel. (010) 436 57 30).

Post Office: Delftsplein 31, across the street from the VVV. Cardphones, fax, and photocopy machine. Open Mon. 11am-6pm, Tues.-Thurs. 9am-6pm, Fri. 9am-8:30pm, Sat. 10am-4pm.

Telephones: In post office; fax available. **Telephone Code:** 010 for the city center.

ACCOMMODATIONS AND FOOD

The possibilities for sleeping cheaply are limited, but the two budget accommodations are centrally located. Your best bet is the **NJHC City-Hostel Rotterdam (HI),** Rochussenstr. 107-109 (tel. 436 57 63; fax 436 55 69); take the metro to "Dijkzigt," or ride tram 4. The hostel is in the process of being redone, but remains comfy with a cheerful staff, TV room and kitchen, and laundry (Reception open daily 7am-midnight. Dorms f25-28.50, nonmembers f5 extra; doubles with bath f75. Shower and breakfast included. Lockers f3.50 per 24hr. Sheets f6.25. Laundry f17.) For even cheaper accommodations, there's always the student-run **Sleep-In,** hidden away at Mauritsweg 29 (tel. 412 14 20; fax 414 32 56). No sheets, blankets, or pillows, but if you take advantage of the cheap downstairs bar (beer f1.50) you probably won't notice. (Reception open daily 8am-10am and 4pm-1am. f15. Breakfast and showers included. Sheets f3. Open mid-June to mid-Aug.) To get to the **Hotel Bienvenue** (tel. 466 93 94) from the Centraal Station's back entrance, walk straight for five minutes; the hostel is on the right (reception open daily 7am-11pm; singles f65, doubles f100).

Most eating options cluster around **Nieuwe Binnenweg** or in the **Oude Haven. Congo Bongo,** 's Gravendijkwal 136a, is home to Caribbean cuisine (menu f5-25; open Tues.-Sun. 6-11pm). Linger over coffee at **Dudok,** Meent (sandwiches f6-9, spaghetti f12.50; open Sun.-Fri. 8am-11pm, Sat. until midnight). **De Consul,** Westeringracht 28, is the best choice for dinner (f12-15) and features a large university crowd (open Sun.-Tues. 3pm-1am, Wed.-Sat. 3pm-4am). Buy groceries at **A&P,** Nieuwe Binneweg 30 (open Mon.-Thurs. 9am-8pm, Fri. 9am-9pm, Sun. 9am-6pm).

SIGHTS AND ENTERTAINMENT

Much of Rotterdam's appeal lies in its futuristic, abstract architecture heavily influenced by the de Stijl school. The city is in a state of constant construction; what has been completed, however, should not be missed. For a dramatic example of the eccentric approach of some recent architecture, check out the freaky 1984 **cube houses** (Kijks-Kubus), designed by Piet Blom. Looking like something out of *Alice in Wonderland,* the inhabitants must either defy gravity or live upside down. You can tour one (#70) if you like. To find them, take the metro to "Blaak," turn left, and look up (open March-Oct. daily 11am-5pm; Nov.-Feb. Fri.-Sun. 11am-5pm; f3.50). Such modern architecture strikes a strange contrast with nearby **Oude Haven** (old harbor), home to classy restaurants with views of the ships going by.

As the largest grossing port in the world, Rotterdam attracts some magnificent ships, best viewed from a **watertaxi** (Mon.-Fri. 8am-midnight, Sat.-Sun. 9am-midnight; f3) that crosses the harbor from the **Mariteim Museum** to the romantic New York Café. The museum has a collection of sailing memorabilia (open Tues.-Sat. 10am-5pm, Sun. 11am-6pm; f6). Perhaps the most powerful monument in the city is Ossip Zadkine's incredible **Monument for the Destroyed City,** a statue of an anguished man, his arms raised in self-defense. This vision vividly embodies the pain and terror of the 1940 bombing raid. Take the Metro to "Churchillplein," walk toward the Blaak, and the statue is directly behind the Mariteim Museum on your right.

To the north, across from the Mariteim Museum, the stately **Schielandshuis** (Historical Museum), Korte Hoogstr. 31, recounts the history of Rotterdam through painting, sculpture, and other artifacts (open Tues.-Fri. 10am-5pm, Sat.-Sun. 11am-5pm; f6). For an astoundingly comprehensive collection of art, check out the **Museum Bogmans-van Bogningen,** Museumpark 18-20. Take the Metro to "Eendractsplein" or tram 5. The vast museum includes a row of Rubens, a vault of Van Gogh, and a mix of Magritte (open Tues.-Sat. 10am-5pm, Sun. 11am-5pm; f7.50).

Mellow **coffee shops** line Oude Binneweg and Nieuwe Binnenweg, but avoid the area west of **Dijkzigt.** A slightly older crowd chills at **LeVagabond,** Nieuwe Binnenweg 99A (open Mon.-Sat. 12pm-2am, Sun. 2pm-2am). For less talk and more sweat, check out one of Rotterdam's dance clubs. The most active spot, **Night Town,** West Kruiskade 28, hosts alternative and indie bands. Expect a f5 "membership fee" and f10-35 cover (open Fri.-Sat. 11pm-late). **Rotown,** Nieuwe Binnenweg 19, draws a large crowd with techno music and the occasional live band (band cover f10; open daily 11am-1am, Fri.-Sat. until 3am). Gay men and women disco at **Gay Palace,** Schiedamsesingel 139, (cover f5-10; open Fri. and Sat. 10pm-late).

Near Rotterdam: Gouda

Gouda ("HOW-da") is the quintessential Dutch town, complete with windmill, cheese, and canals. The **VVV Tourist Office** (tel. (0182) 51 36 66) is in the *Markt* (open Mon.-Fri. 9am-5pm, Sat. 10am-4pm; June-August also Sun. 1-4pm). Gouda's late Gothic splendor centers on the monstrous **St. John's Church.** Ravaged by everything from lightning to Reformation iconoclasts, it has managed to maintain a stunning collection of 16th-century stained-glass windows. (Open April-Oct. Mon.-Sat. 9am-5pm; Nov.-March Mon.-Sat. 10am-4pm. f3, students f2.) Across the street **The Catharina Hospital and The Blackamoor** holds an enormous collection of early and contemporary Flemish art, period rooms (including a torture cell), and early surgical instruments (open Mon.-Sat. 10am-5pm, Sun. noon-5pm; f4.25, students f2.25). You can also climb inside a working windmill, **De Roode Leeuw** as it turns (open Thurs. 9am-2pm, Sat. 9am-4pm). The **Goudse Pottenbakkerij,** Peperstr. 76, has been producing clay pipes since the 17th century (open Mon.-Fri. 9am-5pm, Sat. 11am-5pm; free). Behind the factory, the **Het Trefpunt Hotel,** Westhaven 46 (tel. (01825) 128 79), has clean rooms. (Reception open Mon.-Sat. 8am-11pm, Sun. 8am-7pm. Singles f85. Doubles f110. Triples f135.) Great Dutch pancakes are served at **Het Goudse Winkeltje,** Achter de Kerk 9a, across from the church (f6-18; open Tues.-Sat. 9am-5pm).

Utrecht

At the geographical center of the Netherlands, Utrecht is defined by its pretty canals, grandiose cathedral, and leftist university whose students support a dynamic cultural scene. If you arrive by train, you'll find yourself trapped in the middle of an ultramodern mall, the **Hoog Catharijne.** Its storefronts wait to devour wallets whole, but if you escape, Utrecht's old town lies only blocks away. At Utrecht's center rises the **Domkerk,** begun in 1254 and finished 250 years later. The church's statues were defaced in the early 16th century by Calvinists who considered artistic representations of biblical figures to be sacrilegious. (Open June-Sept. Mon.-Fri. 10am-5pm, Sat.-Sun. 10am-3:30pm; Oct.-May Mon.-Fri. 11am-4pm. Free.) The **Domtoren,** originally attached to the cathedral but freestanding since a malevolent medieval tornado blew away the church nave, is the highest tower in the Netherlands—on a clear day you can see to Amsterdam. (Tower open April-Oct. Mon.-Fri. 10am-5pm, Sat.-Sun. noon-5pm; Nov.-March Sat.-Sun. noon-5pm. Obligatory guided tours on the hour. f5.50.) The **Pandhof,** the church's 15th-century cloister garden, has been converted into a rustic herb garden (open same hours as Domtoren; free). At the **Centraal Museum,** Agnietenstr. 1, you can marvel at a 9th-century Viking ship and paintings of the Utrecht school (open Tues.-Sat. 10am-5pm, Sun. noon-5pm; f6). **Het Catharijneconvent,** Nieuwe Gracht 63, documents the progress of Christianity in the Netherlands with a collection of Dutch religious artwork (open Tues.-Fri. 10am-5pm, Sat.-Sun. 11am-5pm; f7). **Van Speelklok tot Pierement,** Buurkerhof 10, displays musical instruments from the 18th century to the present (open Tues.-Sat. 10am-5pm, Sun. 1-5pm; f7.50).

Practical Information, Accommodations, and Food Utrecht has a lamentable dearth of cheap hotels. The VVV **tourist office,** Vredenburg 90, (tel. (090) 04 14 14 14, 50¢ per min.; fax (030) 233 14 17), at the end of the shopping mall, charges f4.50 to locate lodgings, but they can secure special discounts. Follow signs from the train station. (Open Mon.-Fri. 9am-6pm, Sat. 9am-4pm. A machine outside spews a map and info (f2) after hours.) Set in a majestic medieval manor house surrounded by country canals and a medieval fortress, **Jeugdherberg Ridderhofstad (HI),** Rhijnauwenselaan 14 (tel. (030) 656 12 77; fax 691 31 14), offers a peaceful retreat. Take bus 40, 41 or 43 from Centraal Station (3 strips; tell the driver your destination), and walk 5 minutes. (Reception open daily 8am-12:30am. Bar open 4pm-12:30am. f26, nonmembers f31. Showers and breakfast included.) **Pension Memory,** Pr. Magrietstraat 5 (tel. (030) 242 07 37; fax 242 07 37), is closer to the city center (singles f49-65, doubles f76). **Camping De Berekuil,** Ariënslaan 5-7 (tel. (030) 271 38 70), is not far from the center of town; take bus 57 (2 strips) from the station to the "Veemarkt" stop (f7 per person, f8 per tent; open April-Oct.).

Café De Baas, Lijnmarkt 8, across the canal from the Domtoren, features yummy vegetarian dishes (from f12.50) with occasional live music. (Open Wed. 5pm-3am, Thurs.-Sat. 5pm-3am, Sun. 5pm-10pm. Kitchen closes at 8:30pm.) The two main student *mensas,* open to all, are **Veritas,** Kromme Nieuwe Gracht 54, and **Unitas,** Lucasbolwerk 8 (meals f6-10; both open mid-Aug. to late June Mon.-Fri. 5-7:30pm). The restaurants on the Oude Gracht are atmospheric but costly. For traditional Dutch fare, try the **Pancake Bakery "de oude muntkelder,"** #112 on the Oude Gracht (pancakes f8.50-13.95; omelette f10-15; open daily noon-9:30pm). The hip **Toque Toque,** Oude Gracht 138, at Vinkenburgstr. serves up generous pasta dishes (f16.50; open Mon.-Fri. 10am-midnight, Sat. 9am-midnight, Sun. noon-midnight).

Utrecht presents ample opportunity to get wild and let loose. Pick up a free copy of the Vitagenda for info in weekly shows. **De Winkel van Sinkel,** Oude Gracht 158, combines a café, restaurant, bar, and dance hall in an 18th-century building by the water's edge (salads f10.50-15.50, sandwiches f8.50; food served 11am-10pm) and **Café Flitz,** Rozenstraat 15, is a lively place to drink and dance (open daily 8:30pm-late). A slightly mellower crowd chills at **Zeezicht,** Nobelstraat 2 (open daily 9am-2am) while the theater-café **De Bastaard,** Jansveld 17, serves up flavored coffees and liqueurs. **De Rose Wolk,** Jacobskerkhof, on the corner of Oude Gracht, and the **Homocafé Bodytalk,** Oude Gracht 64 (open Mon.-Thurs. 8pm-3am, Fri-Sat. 8pm-5am, Sun. 4pm-4am) are popular gay hangouts. For more info on the gay scene, contact the **C.O.C.,** Oude Gracht 300 (tel. (030) 231 88 41; open Mon.-Fri. noon-5pm).

Arnhem and Hoge Veluwe

Rebuilt after savage World War II bombings, **Arnhem,** 100km southeast of Amsterdam (70min.), is the self-proclaimed representative of "culture and nature." Let the rumpus begin as you check out where the wild things are at the contiguous **Hoge Veluwe National Park,** a 13,000-acre preserve of woods, heath, dunes, red deer, wild boars which shelters one of the finest modern art museums in all of Europe. This may well prove one of your trip's highlights. Take one of the free white **bikes** from the Koperen Kop **visitor center** to explore over 20 mi. of paths which wind through woods, alongside ponds, and amidst sand dunes. (Park open June-Aug. daily 8am-10pm; Sept. 9am-8pm; Oct. 9am-7pm; Jan.-March 9am-5pm; April 8am-8pm; May 8am-9pm. Free.) Tucked deep within the park and a 35-minute walk from the nearest entrance, the **Rijksmuseum Kröller-Müller** has 276 Van Goghs and superb paintings by Seurat, Mondriaan, and many others. The paths behind the museum harbor (often bizarre) sculptures nestled in the trees. (Museum open Tues.-Sun. 10am-5pm. Sculpture garden closes at 4:30pm. f8.50 includes Museonder.) The **Museonder,** at the visitor center, is the world's first underground museum, dedicated to the study of the subterranean ecosystem (open May-Oct. daily 9am-5pm; Nov.-April 10am-4pm). The **Burger's Zoo** has recreated spacious tropical and safari environments and rescued animals from tiny cubicles at other zoos (open in summer daily 9am-7pm; off-season 9am-sunset; f22.50). Take bus 13 from the station to reach this alterna-zoo.

The park is equally accessible from Arnhem and Apeldoorn (15km, 9mi. from both). From March through October bus 12 (f7.50 or 5 strips) leaves from Arnhem train station, and stops at the museum or Koperen Kop. After hours bus 2 can also be taken to the Schaarvbergen stop to pick up bicycles. From Apeldoorn train station, take bus 110 (f6.75 or 4 strips); buses leave regularly between 9:40am and 4:10pm.

In Arnhem, the VVV **tourist office** (tel. (090) 02 02 40 75; fax 02 64 42 26 44), to the left of the station on Stationsplein, finds accommodations and distributes info about the park (open Mon.-Fri. 9am-5:30pm, Sat. 9am-4pm). The placid **Jeugdher-**

berg Alteveer (HI), Diepenbroeklaan 27 (tel. (026) 442 01 14), in a rural setting offers basketball, volleyball, badminton, ping-pong, pool, and air-hockey and facilities. Take bus 3 toward Alteveer from the station (3 strips), ask the driver to let you off at the hostel, and follow the signs. (Reception open daily 7am-12:30am. Curfew 12:30am. f26.75, nonmembers f31.75; July-Aug. add f2 tourist tax. Sheets f6.25. Breakfast included.) **Hotel-Pension Parkzicht,** Apeldoornsestr. 16 (tel. (026) 442 06 98), is a 15-minute walk from the station (singles f47.50, doubles f90-95, triples f135; breakfast included). Camp at **Kampeercentrum Arnhem,** Kemperbergerweg 771 (tel. (026) 44 56 100), accessible by bus 2 "Haedaveld" (20min., 3 strips; f23.50 per site, includes 2 people and tent; open March-Sept.). **The Old Inn,** Stationsplein 39a (tel. (026) 442 06 49), is a café and restaurant with a f13.50 *dagschotel* (open daily 11am-11pm). The **Luxor theater,** at Willensplein 10, heats up with concerts (cover up to f20; open Thurs.-Sun. 10pm-5am).

Near Arnhem: Apeldoorn

In addition to providing access to De Hoge Veluwe, **Apeldoorn** is home to the **Museum Paleis Het Loo,** a magnificent palace from the 17th century (open Tues.-Sun. 10am-5pm. f12.50). From Apeldoorn station, take bus 102 or 104 (2 strips, 10min.). In Apeldoorn, the **VVV tourist office** sits next to the station at Stationstr. 72 (tel. (0900) 01 68 16 36; fax (055) 521 12 90). The staff books accommodations and has biking maps. (f7. Open Sept.-April 25 Mon.-Fri. 9am-5:30pm, Sat. 9am-1pm; April 26-Sept. Mon.-Fri. 9am-6pm, Sat. 9am-5pm.) **De Grote Beer (HI),** Asselsestr. 330 (tel. (055) 355 31 18; fax 355 38 11), is hidden in a quiet area of town but has a lively atmosphere. Ask for swimming, biking, and skating info (reception open 8am-midnight; dorms f28-31; breakfast included). Take bus 4 or 7 from the station.

Maastricht

Situated on the narrow strip of land between Belgium and Germany, Maastricht has seen its share of interstate rivalries, and centuries of foreign threats have inspired an innovative defense system combining natural resources and hand-built fortifications. Shedding its armor, the city has since become the symbol of a hopeful European unity with the passage of the 1991 Maastricht Treaty. The **Saint Peter Caves,** a maze of more than 20,000 passages, were used during siege times, including World War II, as shelter. (1hr. tours July-Aug. daily every hour from 10:45am to 3:45pm, and in English at 2:15pm; April-June and Sept.-Oct. daily at 12:30, 2, and 3pm; Jan.-March and Oct.-Dec. Wed., Fri., Sat., and Sun. at 2pm. f5.50.) The **Kazematten,** 10km of underground passageways constructed between 1575 and 1825, enabled locals to detect enemies and to carry out surprise attacks. From Vrijtmarkt head west towards Tongerseplein and follow signs for the Waldeck Bastion (mostly Dutch tours June 28-Aug. daily 12:30 and 2pm; Sept.-June 27 Sun. at 2pm). Maastricht's above ground marvels include the beautiful **Basilica of Saint Servatius,** Keizer Karelplein, which contains 11th-century crypts and the largest bell in the Netherlands. (Open Dec.-March daily 10am-4pm; Sept.-Nov. until 5pm; July-Aug. until 6pm. f4.) The **Onze Lieve Vrouwe Basiliek,** O.L. Vrouweplein, is a medieval basilica with ecclesiastical arts and crafts (open Easter-Oct. Mon.-Sat. 11am-5pm, Sun. 1-5pm; f3.50).

Arriving in Maastricht's Centraal Station, you'll end up on the eastern side, across the river from all the action. Buses run frequently from the station across the river to the Markt. Most sights, bars, and restaurants are located in the pedestrian zone connecting the **Markt** to **Vrijthof Square** and **O.L. Vrouweplein.** The VVV **tourist office** is about a block south of the Markt at Het Dinghuis, Kleine Staat 1 (tel. (043) 325 21 21). The office books rooms for free, dispenses a map, and sells a useful brochure. (f1.75. Open May-Oct. Mon.-Sat. 9am-6pm, Sun. 11am-3pm; Nov.-April Mon.-Fri. 9am-6pm, Sat. 9am-5pm.) With a pool and recreation park, the **HI Hostel Sportel de Dousberg,** Dousbergweg 4 (tel. (043) 346 67 77; fax 346 67 55), is 10 minutes from the station by bus 57 to "De Dousberg" (Sun. bus 28 toward Pottenberg; tell the driver your destination. (2 strips or f3. Strict 1am curfew. Dorms f29.50-32.59; triples f120; quads f140. Breakfast included. Key deposit f10.) Sleep on the Maas River at **de Hotelboot,** moored at Maasbouleverd 95 (tel. (043) 321 90 23; singles f55-65, doubles f75-85; breakfast included). **Tilly,** Coxstr. 42 (tel. (043) 325 23 05), offers rooms in a quiet area about 15min. from the station (singles f40, doubles f65; call ahead).

Eat to your heart's content at **Stap in,** Kesselskade 61, where a three-course meal is only f15-18.50 (open daily 10am-9pm). **De Bobbel,** Wolfstr. 32, is a fun café not far from the Vrijthof (meals from f10; open Mon.-Sat. 10am-midnight). On Platielstr., off Vrijthof, **Pourquoi Pas** serves simple meals during the day (f15-f12) and then becomes a booming nightspot. On Brusselstr., **Oase** features house music while **Kommel** offers live jazz (both open 8pm-late). A gay crowd mingles at **Trait d'Union** and **Rembrandt,** cafés located at Mkt. 32 and 38 respectively (both open daily 8pm-2am). The **C.O.C.** (tel. (043) 321 83 36) has more info on Maastricht's **gay scene.**

Groningen

Groningen, about two hours northeast of Amsterdam, boasts a brash flamboyancy that attracts the bold and the beautiful from all over the Netherlands. Principally a college with a city built around it, Groningen is home to all the bars, bookstores, and bistros you would expect from a college town. While World War II bombing left most of the city in ruins, one building that survived is the **Martinitoren,** a 97m tower that weathered everything from German attacks to a victory celebration that got out of hand (open Easter-Sept. daily noon-5pm; Oct.-Easter Sat.-Sun. noon-5pm; f2.50). Groningen's newest building is the 1994 **Groninger Museum,** a quirky pastel assemblage of squares, cylinders, and slag metal. The art—ranging from ancient Chinese to cutting-edge modern work—is quite unique, as reflected in exhibition titles such as "Mutant Materials in Contemporary Design" (f10; open Tues.-Sun. 10am-5pm). Groningen is also within easy biking distance from surrounding lakes and forests; rent a **bike** at the station (f8 per day) and buy a map at the VVV (f7). **Shiermonnikoog,** a peaceful island with bike paths and nature trails is two hours away. Take bus 63 (3 per day, 10 strips) to the ferry (10min, f20; in summer f35 for bus and ferry).

To get to the VVV **tourist office,** Ged. Kattendiep 6 (tel. (0900) 20 23 30 50, 50¢ per minute; fax (050) 311 02 58), turn right out of the station and follow the signs. (Open Mon. 1-6pm, Tues.-Fri. 9:30am-6pm, Sat. 9am-5pm. Machine outside has f2.50 maps.) The city's vitality is reflected in the perky **Simplon Youth Hotel,** Boteidiep 73 (tel. (050) 318 41 50), with funky ceiling art, laundry facilities, and a weight room. To get there, take bus 1 or 2 from the station (dorms f19.50; breakfast f6; lockers f5; linen f4.50). The mellow café **Ugly Duck,** 28 Zwanestr., will set you back only f12-15 for a meal. (Open Mon. 4pm-2am, Tues.-Fri. noon-2am, Sat. 11am-2am, Sun. 3pm-2am. Kitchen closes 9pm.) At the corner of Markt and Poelestr., **Spring's Restaurant** on the top floor of the "Body Café" overlooks the Grote Mkt. (meal f17.50; open July-Aug. daily 11am-11pm; Sept.-June 5-11pm).

Groningen's nightlife would make a metropolis twice its size proud. The hotspots are Poelstr. and Peperstr. (off the Groete Markt) and Zwanestr. (by the University). Dance till dawn at **The Palace,** Gelkingestr. 1, on the corner of the Markt (f6 cover; open Mon.-Sat. 11pm-5am), or head to **Jazz Café de Spieghel,** Peperstr. 11, for live music (open daily until 5am). **El Rubio,** Zwanestr. 26, welcomes gay men and women with a cozy atmosphere (open daily 4pm-3am).

Wadden Islands (Waddeneilanden)

Wadden means "mudflat" in Dutch. In summer, however, sand rather than mud defines the islands; sand beaches hide behind dune ridges with windblown manes of golden grass. Tulip-lined bike trails carve through the natural preserves that are home to over 300 species of birds. The Wadden Islands are an idyllic retreat, especially from May to early July, before they are overrun by hordes of German and Dutch tourists.

Texel With a little planning, you can visit **Texel,** the southernmost and largest island, on a daytrip from Amsterdam. The island is a voyeur's paradise with two popular **nude beaches** (south of Den Hoorn and off De Cocksdorp at paal 28) and fine **bird watching.** You can visit the **nature reserves** only on a guided tour (2hr., f7.50). Book in advance from **Ecomare,** Ruyslaan 92 (tel. (0222) 31 77 41), in De Koog, and specify English-speaking tours not requiring rubber boots. Rent a **bike** at **Verhuurbedrijf Heijne,** across from the ferry stop at 't Horntje (f7.50 per day; open Apr.-Oct. daily 9am-9pm; Nov.-March 9am-6pm) and peddle between the island's three major villages: the central **Den Burg,** the beach-front **De Koog,** and the more isolated, northern **De Cocksdrop.** Alternatively, a **Texel Ticket** allows unlimited one-day travel on the excellent bus system (mid-June to mid-Sept.; f6).

To get to Texel from Amsterdam, take the train to Den Helder (70min., f20), then bus 3 from the station to the ferry. Boats leave at 35 minutes past the hour, every hour from 6am to 9pm daily (20min., last boat back 9:05pm, round-trip f10). The VVV **tourist office,** Den Burg, Emmaln 66 (tel. (0222) 31 47 41; fax 31 00 54; http://www.texel.net), gives camping and accommodations info and sells excellent hiking and walking maps (f6) as well as a birdwatcher's booklet (f5.50; open Mon.-Fri. 9am-6pm, Sat. 9am-5pm; July-Aug. also Sun. 10am-1:30pm). Both of Texel's **HI youth hostels** are immaculate and easily accessible from the ferry; grab bus 27 or 28 from the ferry landing to reach either one (tell the driver your destination). **Panorama,** Schansweg 7 (tel. (0222) 01 54 51; fax 01 38 89), snuggles in a nature reserve 7km from the ferry and 3km from Den Burg center. (Curfew midnight, but night key available. f50 deposit. f24, nonmembers f29. f1.50 tourist tax July-Aug. Sheets f6.25.) The three-star **Hotel de Merel,** Warmoestr. 22 (tel. (0222) 31 31 32), is around the corner from the main square in Den Burg (f45-50 per person; add f10 for stays under 3 nights and f15 for singles). Numerous **campgrounds** cluster in De Koog (f4-7).

Sample the local seafood at **Theodorahoeve,** Kogerstr. 26 in Den Burg (open daily 11am-9pm). **De 12 Balcken Tavern,** Weverstr. 20 in Den Burg, is a snug and dimly lit pub that specializes in *'t Jutterje,* the island's wildly popular alcohol, blended from herbs and wheat (beer f2.75; open Mon.-Sat. 10am-2am, Sun. noon-2am). The second weekend in June, brings **RondeVan Texel,** the largest catamaran race in Europe and the culmination of a week-long **jazz festival** in Den Burg. Sate yourself with sea creatures during the last weekend in August at the **Tropical Sea Festival.**

The Friese Islands The four other islands (the Friese Islands) all have extensive dunes and wildlife sanctuaries. **Schiermonnikoog** and **Vlieland** are quiet, while **Terschelling** and **Ameland** offer more nightlife. On boat excursions to Vlieland from Texel, you must return the same day. Schiermonnikoog's VVV **tourist office,** Reeweg (tel. (05195) 312 33), finds private rooms for about f35 (open Mon.-Fri. 9am-1pm and 2-6:30pm). Reserve ahead, even in the off season. You can stay at the **Terschelling Hostel (HI),** van Heusdenweg 39. (Tel. (05620) 23 38. Reception open daily 8am-midnight; midnight curfew; f32, nonmembers f37. Breakfast included. Sheets f6.25.) For Terschelling or Vlieland, take the main train line from Amsterdam to **Leeuwarden** (2½hr.), then continue to Harlingen (3hr., f35), where you can catch the ferry to either island (2hr., round-trip f41.25; bikes f17). To reach Ameland, take bus 66 from Leeuwarden (50min., 6 strips) to Holwerd and then the ferry (45min., round-trip f17.20). To reach Schiermonnikoog take bus 51 from Lauwersoog where you catch the ferry (40min., round-trip f17.50). From May to September, ferries run among some of the islands, making it possible to see several in a few days. For more info, call the Ameland VVV tourist office (tel. (0519) 54 20 20; open Mon.-Sat. 9am-5pm).

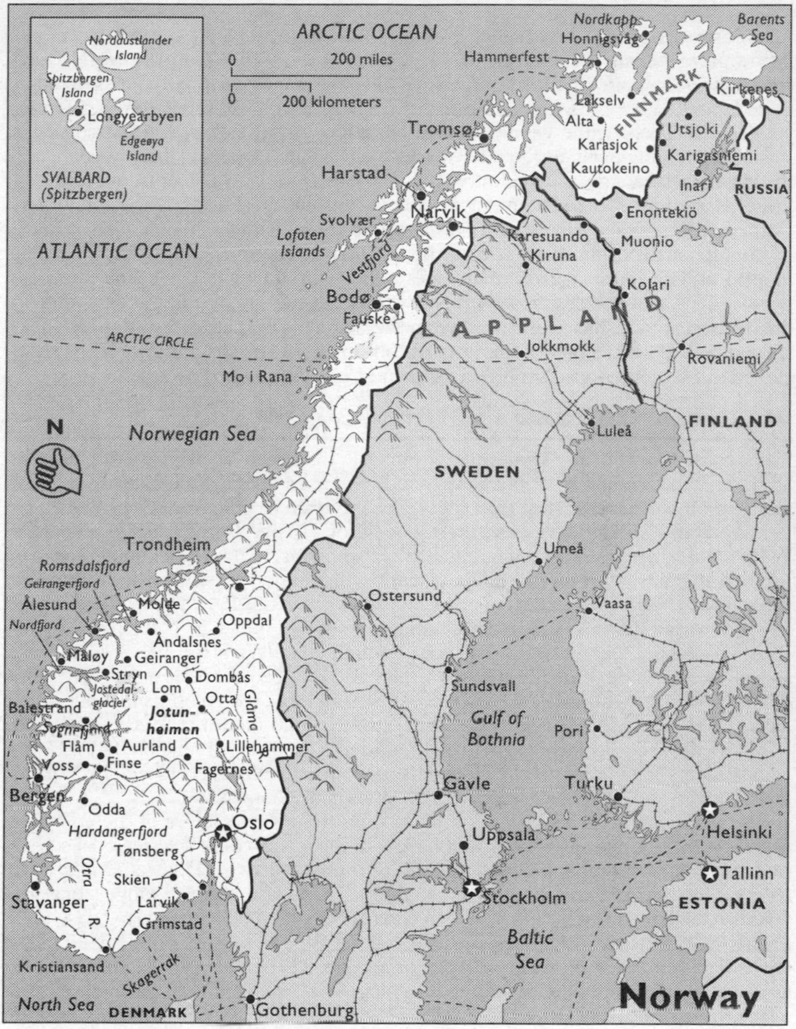

Norway (Norge)

US$1	=7.41kr (Norwegian kroner)	1kr =	US$0.14
CDN$1	= 5.36kr	1kr =	CDN$0.19
UK£1	= 11.77kr	1kr =	UK£0.08
IR£1	= 11.00kr	1kr =	IR£0.09
AUS$1	= 5.41kr	1kr =	AUS$0.19
NZ$1	= 4.71kr	1kr =	NZ$0.21
SAR1	= 1.58kr	1kr =	SAR0.63

Country Code: 47 **International Dialing Prefix: 095**

Norway is fjords, mountains, pastures, and rivers extending to the northernmost point in Europe. From these rugged shores, fierce Norsemen spread across the

Atlantic and "settled" communities in England, Ireland, and France. Their pagan pillaging party subsided, however, in the 10th century, when King Harald Hårfagre (Harold the Fair-haired) unified the realm and Olav Haraldsson imported Christianity. Rune stones, stave churches, and preserved Viking ships still survive from this age, while sagas chronicle the Vikings' adventures and myths in rich poetry and epics.

After the Viking twilight, Norway was annexed first to Denmark, then Sweden, but the closing years of the 19th century spawned great luminaries of art from Munch to Ibsen, Hamsun to Grieg. Independent once again only after 1905, Norway endured German occupation during World War II, but developed into a modern welfare state in the aftermath of the war. Today, the country is one of the most expensive in Europe, and citizens pay gargantuan taxes to maintain their social net. However progressive its social policies, however, Norway's doggedly pro-whaling stance attracts disapproval abroad. Most residents live in the bulge of southern Norway, which also sprouts Scandinavia's highest mountains, but intrepid farmers and fishermen have carved out settlements as far north as Kirkeness on the Russian border.

GETTING THERE AND GETTING AROUND

Every coastal town of any significance from Oslo to Bergen has **ferry** service to Denmark, England, Germany, or the Netherlands (more frequent and expensive in summer and on weekends). Most foreigners take the **train** to Oslo from Copenhagen (3 per day, 10hr., 710kr, under 25 525kr) or Stockholm (3 per day, 6hr., 621kr, under 25 435kr), but Norway's northern rail lines can also be reached via Stockholm. **Eurail** is valid on all trains. The **Norway Railpass** grants unlimited travel within the country for three days (US$135), seven days (US$190), or 14 days (US$255). The *buy-in-Scandinavia* **Scanrail Pass** allows five days within 15 (1380kr, under 26 1040kr) or 21 consecutive days (2130kr, under 26 1600kr) of unlimited rail travel through Scandanavia, as well as many free or discounted ferry rides and reduced bus fares in Norway. This differs from the *buy-outside-Scandinavia* **Scanrail Pass,** which offers five out of 15 days (US$176, under 26 US$132), 10 days out of one month (US$284, under 26 US$213), or 30 consecutive days (US$414, under 26 US$311) of unlimited travel. Foreign students sometimes get the discounts on domestic rail travel enjoyed by Norwegian students too. Off-peak green trains are always discounted.

No free brochure gives you a complete, comprehensive picture of the complex domestic transportation scene; you'll have to collect sheaves of free regional schedules, or ask at travel agencies, train stations, or tourist offices for a look at *Rutebok for Norge.* Norwegian trains run only up to Bodø. Trains farther north move along the Swedish rail line through Kiruna, which ends at Narvik on the Norwegian coast, on a line from Murmansk in Russia. Seat reservations are compulsory on many long-distance trains and all night trains (20kr). For a price, sleeping cars and couchettes are available on all night trains, including the spiffy new Trondheim-Oslo sleepers.

For those under 25 or students under 32, special youth fares make **flying** a viable option, often cheaper than the train. **Braathens SAFE** (tel. 67 58 60 00) and **SAS** (tel. 81 00 33 00) are the main airlines, and both offer domestic standby tickets *(chance billet).* Any trip which does not pass Trondheim but stays either north or south of it costs 400kr one way (800kr if the trip involves both the northern and southern zones). A 71kr tax is added for trips to the south. Tickets bought in the U.S. through the "Visit Norway Pass" from **Scanam World Tours** (tel. (800) 545-2204) should cost US$85 per short journey and US$170 per long, but the service may change in 1998. **Widerøe** (tel. 67 11 14 60) offers refundable tickets to Norway's smaller airports (375kr for each segment of journey). Open date ticket with stopovers in many airports along the coast allow flexibility at a reasonable price.

Buses are quite expensive (about 1kr per km), but are the only firm surface option north of Bodø and in the fjords. **Norway Bussekspress** (tel. 23 00 24 40) operates 75% of the domestic bus routes. They publish a free, easy-to-follow book schedules and prices. Scanrail and InterRail pass holders are entitled to a 50% discount on most bus routes, and students are entitled to a 25-50% discount on most routes—be insistent and follow the rules listed in the Norway Bussekspress booklet. Seats are guaranteed on routes operated by Norway Bussekspress. Bus passes valid for one (1375kr) or two (2200kr) weeks are a good deal for travelers exploring the fjords or the north.

Car ferries *(ferjer)* are usually much cheaper (and slower) than the many **hydrofoils** *(hurtigbåte)* that cruise the coasts and fjords; both often have student, Scanrail, and/or InterRail discounts. The **Hurtigruten** (the famed Coastal Steamer) takes six days for its fantastic voyage from Bergen to Kirkenes; each of the 25 stops en route have one northbound and one southbound departure per day. The *Hurtigruten* often have a free sleeping-bag room; cabins run from 100kr per night (50% off during the off-season). No student or railpass discounts are offered, and generally buses and trains will be more affordable. In Norway, all vehicles are required to drive with dipped headlights during the daytime. **Hitching** is notoriously difficult throughout Scandanavia. Many Norwegians hitch beyond the rail lines in northern Norway and the fjord areas of the west. Hitchers should bring several layers, rain gear, and a warm sleeping bag. Those using a sign have better odds, and many attempt to find a ride before or during a ferry trip to avoid getting stuck at the landing.

ESSENTIALS

Virtually every town, village, and pit stop in Norway has a **Turistinformasjon** office; look for a black lower-case **"i"** on a green sign. Try to go the night before you're planning to head out of town, as buses often leave early in the morning. Throughout July and the first half of August all tourist offices are open daily; most have reduced hours the rest of the year. Most businesses, including travel agents and ticket offices, close early during the summer, especially on Fridays and during August when Norwegians vacation. If a store closes at 3pm, get there by 2:45pm. **Banks** are open Monday through Friday from 8:15am to 3pm (during the winter until 3:30pm), Thursday until 5pm. Large post offices **exchange money,** usually charging a small commission and offering the best rates. Offices are generally open Monday through Friday 8am-5pm, Saturday 8am-1pm. Legal **holidays** include New Year's Day, Easter (April 9-13, 1998), Labor Day (May 1), Ascension Day (May 21, 1998), Constitution Day (May 17), Whit Monday (June 1), Christmas (Dec. 24-26), and New Year's Eve.

For a few weeks around the summer solstice (June 21), Norway north of Bodø basks in the midnight sun. You stand the best chance of seeing the Northern Lights between November and February above the Arctic Circle (although they are occasionally visible in the south). Skiing is best just before Easter, when the winter has slackened, and the sun returns after months of darkness. Oslo averages 63°F (18°C) in July, 24°F (-4°C) in January; up north, average summer temperatures dip to about 50°F (10°C) while winter temperatures are much the same as in the south. The north and the fjord country are wetter than south and east.

Domestic and international **telephone** calls can butcher the budget in Norway. Pay phones take 1, 5, 10 and 20kr coins, and local calls require at least 3kr; buying a *telekort* (available in 22, 65, and 150kr denominations) card is more economical in the long-run. Calls from pay phones costs twice as much as from private lines, and between 10pm and 8am calls are 15-20% cheaper. To make collect international calls, dial 115, within Norway 117. **AT&T Direct's** number is 800 19 011; **MCI WorldPhone,** 800 19 912; **Sprint Access,** 80 01 98 77; **Canada Direct,** 800 19 111; **BT Direct,** 800 19 044; **Ireland Direct,** 800 19 353; **Australia Direct,** 800 19 961; **New Zealand Direct,** 800 19 964; and **South Africa Direct,** 800 19 927.

Norway is officially bilingual. The Danish-influenced *bokmål* Norwegian used in Oslo and a standardized language *(nynorsk)* based on dialects of rural western Norway are both taught in schools. Most Norwegians speak fluent English.

Yes/No	*Ja/Ikke* or *Ne*	yah/IK-eh, nay
Hello	*Hallo*	hah-LOH
Thank you	*Takk*	tak
Excuse me	*Unnskyld*	oon-SKILT
Do you speak English?	*Kan du tale engelsk?*	kan doo TA-leh ENG-elsk

NORWAY

I don't understand.	*Jeg forstår iike..*	yay foh-STOH IK-eh
Help!	*hjelpe!*	YELP-eh

Accommodations and Camping When in Norway, camp. Norwegian law allows you to camp for free anywhere you want on public land for two nights, provided you keep 150m from all buildings and fences and leave no traces of your frolicking. **Den Norske Turistforening** (DNT, the Norwegian Mountain Touring Association) sells excellent maps, offers hiking trips, and maintains 300-plus mountain huts *(hytter)* throughout the country. (70-145kr per night. Open to nonmembers for a 50kr surcharge. Membership 315kr, under 25 160kr.) Staffed huts serve full meals and are akin to hostels, but have a more attractive ambience and more Norwegian guests. Get the entrance key for unattended huts (100kr deposit required) from a DNT or tourist office. Staffed DNT huts are open during Easter and from late June to early September; unstaffed huts are open from late February until mid-October. Their Oslo (see p. 654) and Bergen (see p. 664) offices are particularly helpful.

The indispensable *Vandrerhjem i Norge* brochure lists prices, phone numbers, and more for Norway's 98 **HI youth hostels** *(vandrerhjem)*. Beds run 70-165kr; breakfasts (45-60kr) are included in the price if mandatory (often the case). Usually only rural or smaller hostels have curfews. Only a few are open year-round. Most tourist offices in Norway can book you a room in a private home (roughly 190kr for singles, 330kr for doubles). Official **campgrounds** charge 90-100kr per tent. Many also have two- to four-person cabins (450-800kr). Hot showers almost always cost extra.

Food and Drink Eating in Norway can be hazardous to your wallet; markets and bakeries will be your best company. The nationwide discount **REMA 1000** supermarkets generally have the best prices (usually open Mon.-Fri. 9am-8pm, Sat. 9am-6pm). Join Norwegians at outdoor markets for good buys on fresh seafood and fruit. Many restaurants have inexpensive *dagens ret* (dish of the day) specials (60-70kr for a full meal); otherwise you're doing well to escape for less than 100kr. **Tips** are included. All-you-can-eat restaurant buffets abound in major cities and towns (pizza 47-69kr). Self-service *kafeterias* are a less expensive option. Fish in Norway—cod, salmon, and herring—is fresh, good, and cheap. National specialties include cheese (*ost;* try *Jarlsberg* and the brown goat cheese *geitost*), pork and veal meatballs *(kjøtkaker)* with boiled potatoes, and (for lusty carnivores) reindeer and controversial *kval* (whale meat). Pick berries of all colors, sizes, and flavors yourself, or sample a vendor's offerings. Come during the winter and delight in dried fish *(lutefisk)*. In most Norwegian restaurants, alcohol is served only after 3pm and never on Sundays, although this is beginning to change, especially in the cities. Beer is *very* expensive (45kr for 0.5L is average in a bar). Alcohol is cheapest in supermarkets, but few towns permit the sale of alcohol outside of government operated liquor stores.

Oslo

The all-too-often bypassed Oslo redefines sophistication. Not simply a quality bestowed on chic café-goers, Oslo's sophistication requires a savvy appreciation of the numerous forests, islands, rivers, and lakes within the city limits. Perhaps the extraordinary reflected blue light in winter and the sleep-cycle-stumping Midnight Sun in summer inspire the Osloenseres' vibrance and physical vigor despite the gloomy shadows of natives Edvard Munch and Henrik Ibsen. Unexpectedly welcoming to a new wave of immigrants, Oslo also tries to make the notoriously expensive city affordable to those lucky, wayward Eurailers who stop here.

ORIENTATION AND PRACTICAL INFORMATION

Running from *Sentralstasjon* (train station) to the *Slottet* (Royal Palace), **Karl Johans gate** is Oslo's main boulevard. Virtually everything of interest to visitors clusters in the center of the city, easily accessible by foot. Oslo centers on the **National Theater,**

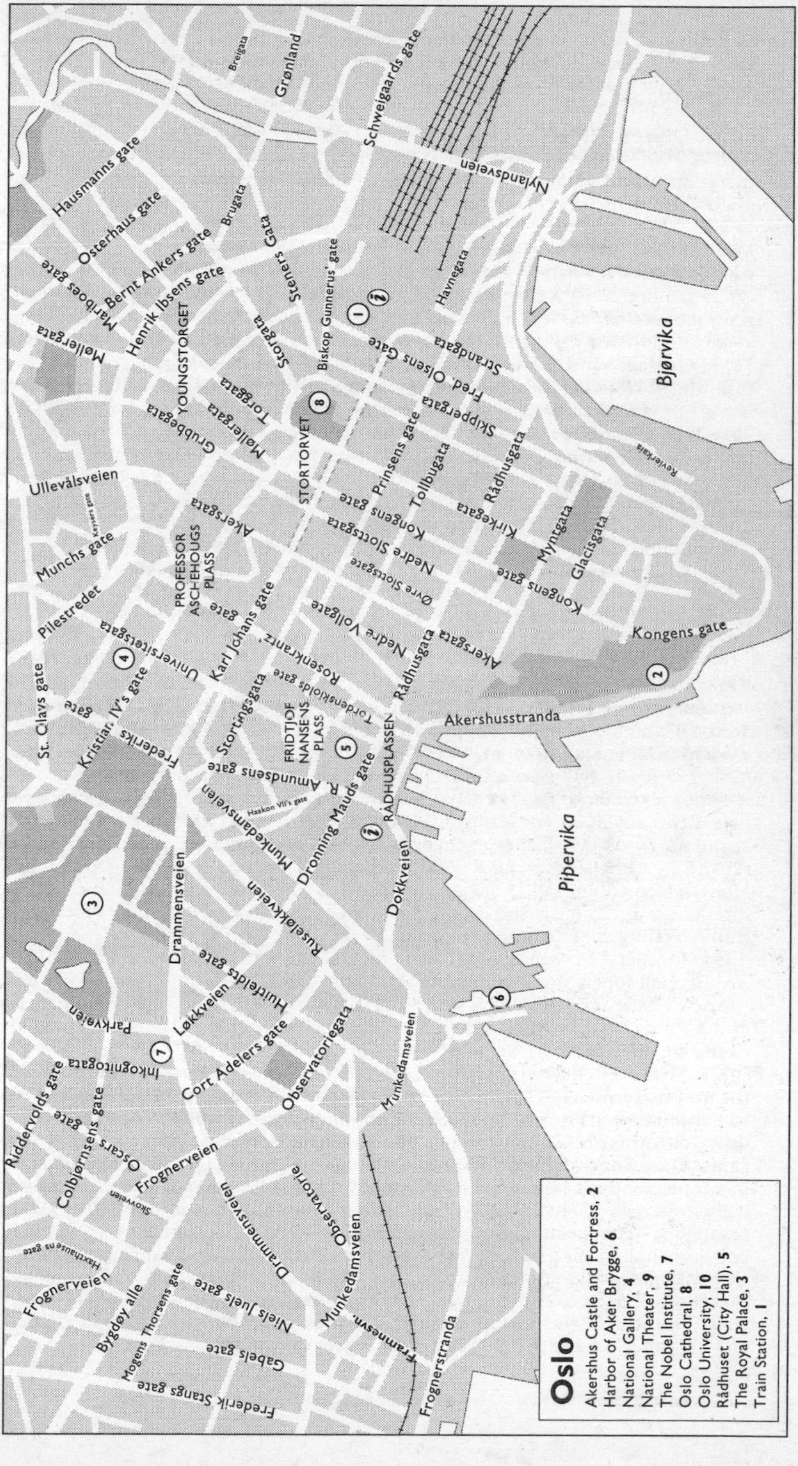
Oslo
Akershus Castle and Fortress, 2
Harbor of Aker Brygge, 6
National Gallery, 4
National Theater, 9
The Nobel Institute, 7
Oslo Cathedral, 8
Oslo University, 10
Rådhuset (City Hall), 5
The Royal Palace, 3
Train Station, 1
Bjørvika
Pipervika
Akershusstranda
Kongens gate
Schweigaards gate
Nylandsveien
Grønland
Brugata
Hausmanns gate
Osterhaus gate
Maridoes gate
Bernt Ankers gate
Henrik Ibsens gate
Møllergata
YOUNGSTORGET
Storgata
Steners Gata
Biskop Gunnerus' gate
Havnegata
Strandgata
Fred. Olsens Gate
Skippergata
Prinsens gate
Tollbugata
Rådhusgata
Kirkegata
Myntgata
Glacisgata
Revierkaia
STORTORVET
Torggata
Grubbegata
Ullevålsveien
Akersgata
PROFESSOR ASCHEHOUGS PLASS
Nedre Slottsgate
Øvre Slottsgate
Nedre Vollgate
Karl Johans gate
Rosenkrantz gate
Munchs gate
Pilestredet
Universitetsgata
St. Olavs gate
Kristian IV's gate
Frederiks gate
Stortingsgata
Tordenskiolds gate
FRIDTJOF NANSENS PLASS
RÅDHUSPLASSEN
R. Amundsens gate
Haakon VII's gate
Dronning Mauds gate
Munkedamsveien
Drammensveien
Dokkveien
Ruseløkkveien
Hulfeldts gate
Løkkveien
Parkveien
Inkognitogata
Cort Adelers gate
Observatoriegata
Riddervolds gate
Colbjørnsens gate
Oscars gate
Frognerveien
Skovveien
Observatorie
Bygdøy alle
Mogens Thorsens gate
Niels Juels gate
Gabels gate
Frederik Stangs gate
Frognerstranda
Framnesvn.

at the far end of the fountained **Spikersuppa Park** and midway between the station and the palace. For the few not-so-nearby sights and for weary travelers, Oslo has an excellent public transport system of subways, trams, buses, and ferries.

Tourist Offices: The **Main Tourist Office,** Vestbaneplassen 1 (tel. outside Norway 22 83 00 50; inside Norway 82 06 01 00; fax 22 83 81 50; http://www.oslopro.no), in a yellow former train station behind the Rådhus. Free maps and guides. Sells the **Oslo Card,** which covers public transit and admission to nearly all sights for 1 day (130kr), 2 days (200kr), or 3 days (240kr). Open June-Aug. daily 9am-8pm; Sept.-May Mon.-Fri. 9am-4pm. Branch at **Sentralstasjon,** an Oslo-only info center, books rooms (open daily 8am-11pm). **Den Norske Turistforening,** Storgata 28 (tel. 22 83 25 50; fax 22 83 24 78), with an entrance around the corner on Olav V gate, rents mountain huts, sells trail maps, and has Norway-wide hiking info. Open Mon.-Wed. and Fri. 10am-4pm, Thurs. 10am-6pm, Sat. 10am-2pm. Youth-oriented **USE IT,** Møllergata 3 (tel. 22 41 51 32; fax 22 42 63 71), 4 blocks up Karl Johans gate from the station and then right, offers listings of cheap lodgings and restaurants, travel tips, and the invaluable *Streetwise* guide. Books rooms. Open June 17-Aug. 8 Mon.-Fri. 7:30am-6pm, Sat. 9am-2pm; Sept.-May Mon.-Fri. 11am-5pm.

Budget Travel: Kilroy Travels, Nedre Slottsgate 23 (tel. 22 42 01 20; fax 22 11 13 48), and also at Universitetssenteret (tel. 22 85 32 40; fax 22 85 32 39; http://www.kilroytravels.com), has student and youth airline bargains. Open Mon.-Fri. 10am-6pm, Sat. 10am-3pm. **Khan Travels Ltd.,** Brugate 3C (tel. 22 17 14 91; fax 22 17 12 48), offers competitive rates, especially on international flights.

Embassies: Australian citizens should contact the Canadian embassy or the Australian Government Information Office (tel. 22 41 44 33; fax 22 42 26 83). **Canada**, Oscarsgate 20, 2nd fl. (tel. 22 46 69 55; fax 22 69 34 67), near Bislett Stadium. Take tram 11 or 13. Open Mon.-Fri. 8am-3:30pm; consular services open 8:30am-12:30pm. **Ireland,** Holenkollvej 120B (tel. 22 92 00 80; fax 22 92 00 30). **New Zealand** (General Consul), Drammensveien 230 (tel. 22 13 20 00). **South Africa**, Drammensveien 88c (tel. 22 44 79 10; fax 22 44 39 75); consular service open Mon.-Fri. 9am-noon. **U.K.**, Thomas Heftyesgate 8 (tel. 22 55 24 00; fax 22 55 10 41). Open Mon.-Fri. 9am-4pm. **U.S.**, Drammensveien 18 (tel. 22 44 85 50; fax 22 43 07 77). Open Mon.-Fri. 9am-3pm; consular services mornings only.

Currency Exchange: Banks charge fees per check exchanged, so bring checks in large denominations. For changing small amounts (up to US$100), the best deal is at the AmEx offices. Larger exchanges are best accomplished at the post offices (20kr for cash, 10kr per check; 20kr minimum). The rates in the rail station (open Mon.-Fri. 7am-6pm, Sat. 9am-2pm) are not as good as offices outside the station. After-hours exchange at the central post office, the tourist and AmEx offices, or in **Bankveksling,** next to the post office in the station (20kr per traveler's check; open Mon.-Sat. 7am-9pm, Sun. 10am-5pm) and at **Fornebu Airport,** International Arrivals Hall (open Mon.-Sat. 6:30am-8pm, Sun. 7am-8pm).

American Express: Karl Johans gate 33, N-0121 Oslo (tel. 22 86 13 50, emergencies 80 03 32 44). All services. Open Mon.-Fri. 9am-6pm, Sat. 10am-3pm; currency exchange open Mon.-Fri. 9am-9pm, Sat. 9am-7pm, Sun. 2-7pm.

Flights: White SAS buses (35kr) run every 15min. between **Fornebu Airport** and the Air Bus Terminal (tel. 67 59 62 20) at Galleri Oslo behind the train station. Oslo to Fornebu Mon.-Fri. and Sun. 9am-10:40pm, Sat. 6am-7:40pm. Fornebu to Oslo daily 7:30am-11pm. The slower bus 31 also runs to Fornebu (18kr).

Trains: Oslo Sentralstasjon (Central Station; tel. 22 36 80 00). Book at least 1 day in advance and get reduced *minipriser* any day but Fri. or Sun. Several trains run daily to Bergen (7-8hr., 500kr), Trondheim (7-8hr., 570kr, *minipris* 380kr), Bodø (change at Trondheim; 17hr., 950kr, *minipris* 530kr), Lillehammer (2hr., 225kr), and Stockholm (7hr., 584kr). A **green card** (260kr) offers 50% off tickets during off-peak, green-zone times (usually Tues.-Thurs. in the mornings and evenings). Ticket office open daily 6am-11pm; terminal open daily 4:30am-1:15am. The **Inter-Rail Center** near the station entrance has **showers** (10kr per 5min.), a kitchen, and **luggage storage** (free). Open mid-June to Aug. daily 7am-11pm.

Buses: Norway Bussekspress, Schweigårdsgate 8 (tel. 23 00 24 40), in the Oslo Galleri Mall, behind and to the right as you exit the train station, sends buses scurrying throughout Norway (Bergen 550kr) and across Europe.

Public Transportation: Info at **Trafikanten** (tel. in Oslo 177), in front of the station. All forms (bus, tram, subway, and ferry) 18kr per trip. Fines for traveling without a valid ticket over 300kr. 24hr. **Dagskort** (day pass) 40kr. **7-day card** 120kr. A **flexicard** allows 8 separate trips (105kr). Many buses, trams, and subways have late night schedules midnight to 5am. Ferries tend to stop service around 7-8pm.

Ferries: Passenger ferries arrive at 2 different ports, one (Color Line) a 20min. walk from the center, the other a 15min. walk due south of the center. Fares vary greatly with time, season, age, and cabin. **Color Line** (bookings tel. 22 94 44 44; fax 22 83 20 96) has daily ferries year-round to Kiel, Germany (20hr., high season 540-690kr) and Hirtshals, Denmark (12½hr., high season 450-580kr). Eurail, InterRail, and Scanrail passes offer 50% off. **DFDS Scandinavian Seaways** (tel. 22 41 90 90; fax 22 41 3838) sails to Helsingborg, Sweden, and Copenhagen daily (1 per day; 16hr. to Helvingberg, 18hr. to Copenhagen; 425-530kr in summer, higher Thurs.-Sat.). **Stena Lines** (tel. 22 33 50 00 or 22 41 22 10) has 1 daily run to Frederikshavn, Denmark (high season 390-450kr; 50% off with Eurail, InterRail, or Scanrail).

Bike Rental: Den Rustne Eike, Vestbaneplassen 2 (tel. 22 83 72 31), behind the tourist office. 7-speed 120kr per 24hr., 495kr per week. Mountain bike 150kr per day, 835kr per week. Deposit 500-1000kr or passport. Open June-Sept. daily 10am-6:30pm; Oct.-May 10am-3pm. 15% discount with Oslo card. For more info on cycling in Norway contact the **Syklistenes Landsforening** (tel. 2241 50 80).

Hitchhiking: Oslo is not a hitchhiker's paradise; the diligent reportedly go to gas stations and ask everyone stopping. Those heading southwest (E-18 to Kristiansand and Stavanger) take bus 31 or 32 to "Maritime." Hitchers to Bergen ride bus 161 "Skui" to the last stop. Hitchers heading for Trondheim hop on bus 32, 321, or Metro 5 to "Grorudkrysset" or bus 31 or 32 to "Aker Sykehus." Those going to Sweden take bus 81, 83, 85 to "Bekkeleget" or a local train "Ski" to "Nordstrand."

Luggage Storage: Train station lockers are 10-20kr for 24hr. Free storage for multiple days at the InterRail Center in the station.

Bookstore: Tanum Libris, Karl Johans gate 43 (in Paléet). English paperbacks. Open Mon.-Fri. 10am-8pm, Sat. 10am-4pm. **Pocket Bøker,** Storgata 37 (tel. 22 11 48 64), buys and sells used books. Open Mon.-Fri. 10am-5pm, Sat. 10am-2pm.

Laundromat: Look for the word *Myntvaskeri.* **Selvbetjent Vask,** Ullevålsveien 15. Wash 30kr per 6kg, dry 20kr. Soap included. Open daily 8am-9pm.

Gay and Lesbian Services: The **Landsforeningen for Lesbiskog Homofil fri gjøring (LLH),** Oslo lag, St. Olavs plass 2 (tel. 22 11 05 09; fax 22 20 24 05), provides an array of essential services and copies of *Blick* (30kr), a monthly gay and lesbian newspaper with daytime and nightlife listings (open Mon.-Fri. 10am-5pm).

Travelers with Disabilities: The **Norwegian Association of the Physically Challenged,** P.O. Box 9217 Vaterland, N-0134 Oslo (tel. 22 17 02 55; fax 22 17 61 77), has general info. Most museums are wheelchair accessible and buses and trams can be used with a little help. From the tourist office get the essential *"Welcome to/ Velammantil Oslo,"* a free, comprehensive guide for disabled visitors.

Crisis Lines: Rape Crisis Line: tel. 22 11 70 80 and 22 37 47 00. **AIDS info:** tel. 80 03 40 00. **Emotional Crisis Line:** tel. 22 11 70 80. **AA:** tel. 22 11 72 00.

24-Hour Pharmacy: Jernbanetorvets Apotek (tel. 22 41 24 82), near the station.

Medical Assistance: Oslo Kommunale Legevakt, Storgata 40 (tel. 22 11 70 70). 24hr. emergency care.

Emergencies: Ambulance: tel. 113. **Fire** and **Accidents:** tel. 110.

Police: tel. 112.

Internet Access: Velvet, Nedre Slottsgate 2. 10kr per 30min. Open Mon.-Fri. 10am-6pm, Sat. 10am-3pm. **Oslo Internet Café,** Østbanehallen. 25kr per 30min. Open Mon.-Fri. 9am-8pm, Sat. noon-2pm.

Post Office: Dronningens gate 15 (tel. 22 40 78 10); enter at Prinsens gate. *Poste Restante.* Open Mon.-Fri. 8am-8pm, Sat. 8am-3pm. **Postal Code:** 0101 Oslo 1.

Telephones and Faxes: Kongens gate 21; enter at Prinsens gate. Fax service to North America or Europe 10kr plus 10kr per page. Open Mon.-Fri. 8:30am-8pm, Sat.-Sun. 10am-5pm. Phone cards sold at kiosks and post offices.

ACCOMMODATIONS AND CAMPING

There are a dearth of budget accommodations in Oslo. **USE IT** (see above) offers one of the best deals in town—private rooms, accessible by public transportation, though the later in the day you appear, the farther the trek from downtown (125kr, with sleeping bag 100kr). If you plan on a stay of a week or more, you may be able to sublet a university student dorm room (around 360kr per week plus deposit). For more info call **SiO** (tel. 22 85 33 76) or **OAS** (tel. 22 46 39 90). *Pensjonater* (pensions) are usually less expensive versions of hotels; call for reservations. Some hotels offer cheaper "last minute" prices on vacant rooms through the tourist office. In principle the Norwegian *allmansvett* gives you the right to camp anywhere, but effectively no one really camps on private lawns. You can camp in Oslo's forests for free.

Albertine Hostel, Storgata 55 (tel. 22 99 72 00; fax 22 99 72 20). 10min. from the train station. Brand new and beautifully furnished. Reception open 7am-1am. From 1am-7am the front door is locked, but opened every hour, on the hour by night watchmen. 95kr. Sheets 35kr. Buffet breakfast 45kr. Kitchen.

Oslo YMCA (KFUM) Sleep Inn, Møllergata 1 (tel. 22 20 83 79; fax 22 42 39 56); enter on parallel Grubbegata. Central location. Toss your sleeping bag (required) on 1 of 60 mats in 3 dorms. High-pressure showers. Reception open daily 8-11am and 5pm-midnight. 100kr. Kitchen and baggage storage. Open July 7 to Aug. 20.

Oslo Vineyard, Lillogata 5 (tel. 22 15 20 99). Take tram 11, 12, 17 or bus 56 to "Grefsenveien," then walk for 5min. Bare bones, dare we say "monastic," church hostel with simple breakfast. Reception open 8am-11am and 5pm-12am. Sleeping-bag accommodations 95kr. Groups of 15 or more 80kr each. Open July 7-Aug. 17.

NORWAY

Oslo Vandrerhjem Haraldsheim (HI), Haraldsheimveien 4 (tel. 22 15 50 43 or 22 22 29 65; fax 22 71 34 97). Take tram 10, 11, or 17 or bus 31 or 32 to "Sinsenkrysset," and follow the signs across the field and up the hill. Pristine lounges with cable TV. Kitchen. No sleeping bags. Reception open 24hr. Dorms 155kr, nonmembers 180kr. Singles 260kr. Doubles 370kr. Breakfast included. Lunch 70kr. Dinner 90kr. Sheets 35kr. Laundry 40kr (soap included).

Oslo Vandrerhjem Holtekilen (HI), Michelets vei 55 (tel. 67 53 38 53; fax 67 59 12 30) Take bus 151/161, 251/252, or 261 to "Kveldsroveien." Popular, if somewhat far. Dorms 145kr. Bed in a 4-person room 155kr. Nonmembers 25kr extra. Breakfast included. Open May 16-Aug. 17. Reserve ahead.

Cochs Pensjonat, Parkveien 25 (tel. 22 60 48 36; fax 22 46 54 02), at Hegdehaugsveien by the royal park. 15min. from train station. Singles 310kr, with bath and kitchenette 390kr. Doubles 420kr, with bath and kitchenette 530kr.

Ellingsens Pensjonat, Holtegata 25 (tel. 22 60 03 59; fax 22 60 99 21). Take tram 19 "Majorstuen," or walk 3km from the city center. Huge, sign-less gray building is hard to spot but popular with backpackers. Showers in the corridor. Reception open daily 7:30am-11pm. Singles 230kr. Doubles 360kr; extra bed 100kr.

OSI-Chalet, Kjellerberget (tel. 22 49 90 36). Students in sleeping bags snooze in forest cottages. Take bus 41 to Sørhedalen School (30min.), and then walk 45min. Call for directions, or pick up a needed map from USE IT; pack some food. 120kr.

Camping: Ekeberg Camping, Ekebergveien 65 (tel. 22 19 85 68), about 3km from town. Take bus 24, 24A or B, or 46 from the train station. Marvelous view. Tent and 2 people 110kr, showers included. Tent and 4 people 160kr. Open June-Aug. Camping on the island of Langøyene (take boat 94), at **Langøyene Camping** (tel. 22 36 37 98), is cheaper and on the beach (tent and two people 60kr, extra person 30kr). Open June-Aug. **Bogstad Camping,** Ankerveien 117 (tel. 22 50 76 80), on Bogstand Lake is beautiful, if a bit far. Take bus 32 from the station (30min.) Tent and 2 people 115kr. Tent and 4 people 160kr. Extra person 30kr. **Free camping** in the forest north of town as long as you avoid public areas. Recommended are the woods and lake at the end of the Sognsvann line (yes, those are naked Norwegians). Fires are not allowed. As always, exercise caution.

FOOD

For many, filling one's belly in Oslo consists of forming a cosmic union with grocery stores. Some of the most central are the **Rema 1000** at Torggata 2-G (open Mon.-Fri. 9am-7pm, Sat. 9am-6pm) and the **Kiwi Supermarket** on Storgata (open Mon.-Sat. 8am-11pm). One must be a culinary strategist in Norway: take full advantage of your hostel's breakfast buffet. Vietnamese and Pakistani influences have multiplied veggie options in Oslo. **Seafood** offerings include freshly caught and boiled shrimp (25kr for 0.5kg) from the fishing boats docked in the harbor behind the Rådhus.

Café Suit, Thorrald Meyersgate 26, in the trendy 'hood of **Løka** north of the station. Norwegian salmon with feta salads (50-160kr). Open daily 11:30am-2:30am.

Primo Piano, Kristian IV gate 7. Filling pasta dishes with a fishy flare (59-86kr). Open daily 11am-11pm. Bar open Mon.-Sat. until 2am, Sun. until midnight.

Vegeta Vertshus, Munkedamsveien 3b, off Stortings gate. A vegetarian feast. Eco/bio beer 44kr. All-you-can-strategically-engineer-onto-a-plate 79kr, unlimited refills 108kr. 10% student discount. Buffet available daily 11am-10pm.

Coco Chalet, Øvre Slottsgade 8. Charming, *hyggelig* (cozy), and therefore very popular. Lunch soup menu 30-40kr. Salads 30-48kr. Sandwiches 40-70kr.

Stortorvets Gjæstgiveru, Grensen 1. One of Oslo's oldest restaurant-pubs with live music on Fridays and Saturdays. Lunch specials featuring salmon, herring, and mackerel 85-120kr. Open Mon.-Thurs. 10am-midnight, Fri.-Sat. 10am-1am.

Børsen Café Stock Exchange, Nedre Vollgate 19. Drink prices change according to supply and demand. Watch for the rush when the "stock exchange" crashes. **Internet access** 20kr. Open Wed.-Thurs. 8pm-3:30am, Fri.-Sat. 8pm-5am.

Sikamikanico, Møllergate. *The* hip coffee bar in Oslo. Live music on weekends. Open Mon.-Wed. 11am-1am, Thurs. 11am-2am, Fri.-Sat. 11am-4am.

Ett Glass, Rosenkrantz 11. The latest in chic. To keep your cool as well as your budget don't try for more than coffee (18kr) or a beer (40kr). Open Sun.-Tues. noon-1am, Wed.-Sat. noon-3am.

SIGHTS

The **Munch Museum,** Tøyengata 53, has an outstanding collection of Edvard Munch's unsettling paintings, lithographs, and photographs. (Open June to late Sept. daily 10am-6pm; mid-Sept. to May Tues.-Wed. and Fri.-Sat. 10am-4pm, Thurs. and Sun. 10am-6pm. 40kr, students 15kr. Take bus 20 or the subway to "Tøyen," or walk 10min. from the train station.) Another of Munch's copies of "The Scream" is at the **Nasjonal Galleriet,** Universitetsgaten 13. (Open Mon., Wed., and Fri.-Sat. 10am-4pm, Thurs. 10am-8pm, Sun. 11am-3pm. Free.) Next door at the **University** you can see Munch's enormous mural "Sun" paintings (open Mon.-Fri. 9am-4pm; free). **The Museet for Samtidskunst,** Bankplassen 4, houses contemporary Norwegian art. (Open Tues., Wed., Fri. 10am-5pm, Thurs. 10am-8pm, Sat. 11am-4pm, Sun. 11am-5pm. Free.) Gustav Vigeland's powerful, masculine sculptures at **Vigeland Park (Frognerpark)** depict each stage of the human life cycle; the park is a playground of grassy knolls, duck ponds, and tennis courts (open 24hr.; free). To reach the park, take tram 12 or 15 from "Nationaltheatret" or walk 20 minutes.

South of the **National Theater** on Fridtjof Nansens plass stands the towering **Rådhus.** The artists who painted the interior earned the pride of their compatriots by defying the Nazi occupiers; they were punished by deportation to prison camps. The Nobel Peace Prize ceremony takes place here each December 10. (Open Sept.-April 20 Mon.-Sat. 9am-4pm, Sun. noon-5pm. May-Aug. 20kr, Sept.-April free. Free tours Mon.-Fri. at 10am, noon, and 2pm.) See the changing of the guard (daily at 1:30pm) at the beautiful **Slottsparken,** the royal garden. The 17th-century **Oslo Damkirke** (Cathedral) has stained glass windows designed by Emmanuel Vigeland (open daily 10am-4pm; free). **Akershus Castle and Fortress** was built in 1299 and transformed into a Renaissance palace by Christian IV. Explore the castle's underground passages, banquet halls, and dungeons and enjoy concerts on summer Sundays in the church at 2pm. (Open mid-April to Oct. 15-30 Sun. 12:30-4pm; May to mid-Sept. also Mon.-Sat.

10am-4pm. 20kr, students 10kr. English tours in summer at 11am, 1, and 3pm; spring and fall at 1 and 3pm.) The poignant **Hjemmefrontmuseet** (Resistance Museum) in the fortress documents Norway's efforts to subvert Nazi occupation. (Open April 15-June 14 and Sept. Mon.-Sat. 10am-4pm, Sun. 11am-4pm; June 15-Aug. Mon.-Sat. 10am-5pm, Sun. 11am-5pm; Oct. to mid-April Mon.-Fri. 10am-3pm, Sun. 11am-4pm. 20kr.)

The peninsula of **Bygdøy** is reached by the commuter ferry Bygdøyfergene (tel. 22 20 07 15) from pier 3 (every 20min., 25kr) or bus 30 from Nationaltheatret. The 30kr museum shuttle is unnecessary as all museums are within an easy 2km radius. The **Folkemuseum** is a massive outdoor museum with houses and other structures from all over Norway and from various eras. (Open mid-May to mid-June and early to mid-Sept. daily 10am-5pm; mid-June to Aug. 9am-6pm; Jan. to mid-May and mid-Sept. to Dec. Mon.-Sat. 11am-3pm, Sun. 11am-4pm.) The three vessels of the **Viking Ship Museum** include the 9th-century ring-prowed, dragon-keeled *Oseberg* burial barge. (Open May-Aug. daily 9am-6pm; Sept. 11am-5pm; April and Oct. 11am-4pm; Nov.-March 11am-3pm. 20kr, students 10kr.) At the ferry's second stop, Bygdøynes, the **Polar Ship "Fram"** chronicles the Arctic and Antarctic explorations of two of Norway's most famous, Fridtjof Nansen and Roald Amundsen. (Open in summer daily 9am-5:45pm; off-season reduced hours. 20kr, students 10kr.) The ethnologist **Thor Heyerdahl's** crafts *Kon-Tiki, Ra I,* and *Ra II* have their own museum, featuring the original *Kon-Tiki,* which set out in 1947 to prove that the first Polynesian settlers could have sailed from pre-Inca Peru. (Open June-Aug. daily 9:30am-5:45pm; Sept.-May 10:30am-5pm; Jan.-March 10:30am-6pm. 25kr, students 15kr.) Dive into bracing water off the popular **Huk Beach,** about 1km from the Viking Ship Museum. Or, weather permitting, go bare at **nude Paradisbukten,** across the inlet.

Other islands in the inner Oslofjord also offer delightful, inexpensive daytrips. In summer, you can visit the ruins of a monastery on **Hovedøya; Langøyene** has Oslo's best beach. Boats leave from **Vippetangen,** reached by bus 29 (round-trip 36kr). Kayaks and canoes can be rented on the Akerselva river (ask at the tourist office).

For a great panorama of **Oslofjord** and the city, take subway 15 to the last stop on the Frognerseteren line, and walk to the ski jump **Holmenkollen.** The **Ski Museum,** which chronicles the history of skiing, has its only entrance to the jump's top. (Open July-Aug. daily 9am-10pm; June 9am-8pm; April-May and Sept. 10am-5pm; Oct. and March 10am-4pm. 50kr, students 35kr.) A **simulator** outside recreates the adrenaline rush of a four-minute, 130km-per-hour downhill ski run—hold on tight! (same hours as museum; 35kr, with the Oslo card 25kr). To bask in Norway's natural grandeur, take the Sognsvann subway from Nationaltheatret to the end of the line. USE IT provides free trail maps; in winter, ask the tourist office about cross-country ski rental.

ENTERTAINMENT

What's on in Oslo, free at the tourist offices, details Oslo's "high-culture," including the opera, Philharmonic, and theater. The hipper culture rag, *Natt og Dag,* free at USE IT and cafés, lists concerts and events. From late June to early September the **Norwegian Folklore Show** features all things folksy (100kr; call 22 83 45 10). **Filmenshus,** Dronningsgate 16, is the center of Oslo's artsy film scene while more Hollywood type flicks are screened at **Saga Cinema,** Stortingsgata 28. Immigrant and minority Norwegians at **Nordic Black Theater,** Olaf Ryes plass 11 (tel. 22 38 12 62), stage socially critical productions in English. Big-name rock concerts take place at the **Rockefeller Music Hall,** Torggata (tel. 22 20 32 32; tickets 50-350kr).

In addition to the countless bars along **Karl Johans gate** and the **Aker Brygge** harbor complex, Oslo boasts a number of nightclubs with busy DJs and live music. Dance to the house, rock, and funk of **Barock,** Univeritetsgate 6 (50kr weekend cover; open Wed.-Sun. 9pm-3:30am) or the hippy and loungy retro favorites of **Broadway,** Karl Johans gate 17 (weekend cover 45kr; open daily 9pm-3:30am). **So What!,** Grensen 9, is popular with a young, indie and beer-loving crowd (open Mon.-Thurs. 2pm-2am, Fri.-Sat. 11pm-3:30am, Sun. 4pm-1am). Oslo's gay and lesbian scene takes cocktails at the elegant **Chairs** piano bar, Pilestredet 9 (open Mon.-Fri. 3pm-midnight, Fri.-Sat. 3pm-4am), before heading to the new 3-floor dance club **Castro,** Kristian IV gate 7, arguably the coolest bar, gay or straight, in Oslo (45kr weekend cover; open Tues.-Sat. 9pm-3:30am, Sat. 5pm-3:30am).

■ Near Oslo: Tønsberg

Two and a half hours from Oslo, **Tønsberg** attracts daytrippers with its sand beaches at **Skallevold** and **Ringshuag.** Trains run from Oslo 10 to 15 times daily (170kr). Once in Tønsberg, alight bus 116 at the station on Jernbauegate (18kr; last bus leaves beach at 10:40pm). The **tourist office,** Nedre Langgate 36B, on Tønsberg Brygge (tel. 33 31 02 20) provides free maps and town guides. (Open June Mon.-Sat. 10am-5pm; July daily 10am-8pm; Aug. Mon.-Sat. 10am-5pm; Sept.-May Mon.-Fri. 10am-3:30pm.) Cafés on **Øvre Langgate** offer affordable options for a famished sunbather.

SOUTHERN NORWAY

Norway's southern coast substitutes serenity for drama. *Skjærgård,* archipelagos of water-worn rock hugging the shore, stretch from Oslo south and smooth to endless white beaches past Kristiansand. This coast is the country's premier summer holiday resort for Norwegians. Inland, green woods cover the high cliffs: fishing, hiking, rafting, and canoeing are popular summer options, and cross-country skiing reigns in winter. Two inland **train** lines with a beautiful view run south from Oslo. The main branch extends through Kristiansand around to Stavanger; the other loops through Tønsberg to Skien before reconnecting with the main line at Nordagutu.

■ Kristiansand

Kristiansand, the town in Norway closest to the equator, attracts many glacier- and winter-weary Norwegian tourists to its beaches. The open-air **Vest-Agder Fylkesmuseum,** Vigeveien 22b, showcases 17th-century Southern Norwegian farmhouses and traditional folk dancing. (Open June 20-Aug. 20 Mon.-Sat. 10am-6pm; May 19-Sept. 14 also Sun. noon-6pm; Sept. 21-May 18 also Sun. noon-5pm. 20kr.) The remains of the Nazi's well-equipped bunker can be seen at the **Kristiansand Kanonenmuseum.** (Open May 2-June 11 and Sept. Thurs.-Sun. 11am-6pm; June 12-Aug. 31 daily 11am-6pm. 40kr.) During the first weekend in July, Kristiansand hosts the **Quart Festival,** with hip-hop, rock, pop, house, and techno. For more info, check with the **tourist office** on Dronningensgate 2 (tel. 38 12 13 14), a five-block walk from the train station along Vestre Strandgate; turn right as you leave the station and make a left on Dronningensgate. (Open June 1-June 21 Mon.-Fri. 8am-7:30pm, Sat. 8am-3pm; June 22-Aug. 10 Mon.-Sat. 8am-7:30pm, Sun. noon-7:30pm; Sept.-May Mon.-Fri. 8am-4pm.) The **Kristiansand Youth Hostel (HI),** Skansen 8 (tel. 38 02 83 10; fax 38 01 75 05), is a 15-minute walk from the station (reception open 24hr.; 150kr, nonmembers 175kr; breakfast included). Buses drop guests off 400m from the big hostel. The **campground,** a 45min. walk from town, calls itself *Roligheden* (Quiet Place), but this misnomer predated the motor homes and trailers (20kr per person, 100kr per tent; showers 5kr per 3min.; open June to mid-Sept.). The area around **Markensgata** is full of affordable bars, cafés, and restaurants; **Munch,** Kristian IV gate 1, is a lively pub. **Color Line ferries** (bookings tel. 38 07 88 88 or 81 00 08 11) float to Hirsthals, Denmark (5 per day, 2½-4¼hr., 155-378kr). Daily **trains** chug to Oslo (4½-5½hr., 400kr).

■ Stavanger

Stavanger is a delightful port town with colorful Bergen-esque wooden fishing houses lining a busy pier and daily fish market. On the other side of the picture-perfect harbor, is **Gamle Stavanger,** a restored neighborhood recalling 19th-century prosperity. Built by King Sigurd Jorsalfar the Crusader in 1125, the Gothic **cathedral** broods in medieval solemnity amid Stavanger's modern center. (Open mid-May to mid-Sept. Mon.-Sat. 9am-6pm, Sun. 1-6pm; late Sept. to early May Mon.-Fri. 9-11:30am and noon-2pm. Free.) To find the genealogical skinny on your Norwegian ancestors check out the **Norwegian Emigration Centre,** Bergjelandsgate 30 (tel. 51 50 12 67; open Mon.-Fri. 9am-3pm). The **Norsk Hermetikkmuseum** (Canning Museum), Østre Strandgate 88 in Gamle Stavanger, chronicles Stavanger's fishing history and features sardine smoking and free samples. (Open mid-June to mid-August Tues. and Thurs.; late Aug. to early June first Sun. of each month.) Feel like a Norse god, command your sea-minions, opiate the masses, but don't tumble over the edge of **Preikestolen** (Pulpit Rock), one of Norway's postcard sweethearts in nearby **Lysefjord.** To climb the pulpit yourself, pilgrim, take the 8:20 or 9:15am ferry to Tau (June 22-Sept. 7, 40min., 25kr), plant yourself on the waiting bus (40kr), and power up for two hours of serious hiking on the marked paths (return bus 4:15pm).

The main **tourist office,** Roskildetorget 1 (tel. 51 85 92 00; fax 51 85 92 02), on the harbor next to the fish market, offers free maps, a town guide, and currency exchange (open June-Aug. daily 9am-8pm; Sept.-May Mon.-Fri. 9am-5pm, Sat. 9am-2pm). **Flaggruten Catamarans** run daily to **Bergen** (4hr., 450kr, students 255kr, 50% off with Scanrail). **Color Line** (tel. 51 89 50 90) runs ships five times weekly to **Newcastle,** England (18hr., July-Aug. 810-1130kr; Sept.-June 310-710kr). **Trains** pull out of the station four times a day for Oslo (8hr., 620kr). The **Mosvangen Youth Hostel (HI),** Ibsensgate 21 (tel. 51 87 29 00; fax 51 87 06 30), has doubles, a kitchen, and free laundry (125kr, nonmembers 150kr; breakfast 45kr). Next door sprawls **Mosvangen camping** (tel. 51 53 29 71; 65kr per tent, 20kr per person; open late May to mid-August). Take bus 93 (116kr) and ask to be dropped at the hostel or campground. The retro-hip **Café M,** Øvre Holegate 20, serves coffee (14kr) and affordable dishes (59kr) while **Armadillo,** across the street, has great music (open Sun.-Thurs. 6pm-midnight, Fri.-Sat. 6pm-1:30am). **Dickens Pub,** Skagenkaien 6, serves all-you-can-eat crab for 82kr (open daily 11am-1:30am; live blues band Sun. nights). The daily **fish and fruit market** opposite the cathedral may also satisfy your seafood fantasies.

NORWAY

EASTERN NORWAY

Gudbrandsdalen, Rondane, and Dovrefjell

Two train lines shoot north from Oslo to Trondheim: the slower goes east through the Østerdalen valley and Røros, the faster one through the **Gudbrandsdalen** valley that runs from Lillehammer northwest through Otta and Dombås. Gudbrandsdalen is famous for its skiing, hiking, and canoeing, for its old churches and wooden houses, and for being the birthplace of the brown *Gudbrandsdalsost* cheese. Lillehammer is the largest town and marks the southern edge of the region. Farther up the valley, the old, soft slopes of the mountain ranges of **Rondane** and **Dovrefjell** provide easy access to hiking and the more stellar ranges farther west. Both areas have national parks.

Lillehammer In February 1994, the world learned that reindeer really do exist when Norway's second winter Olympic Games were hosted in Lillehammer and the neighboring towns of Kvitfjell, Faberg, Hunder, Hamar, and Gjøvik. Despite the construction of several billion kroner's worth of infrastructure, Lillehammer maintains a natural atmosphere; all the sports facilities were designed to be environmentally friendly, and the Olympic housing has been recycled for use by the army. In the **Olypmic Park,** the famous egg from the opening ceremonies incubates inside **Håkons Hall,** which once housed the Olympic ice hockey rink (open daily 10am-7pm; 15kr). The hall also features one of the most advanced **climbing walls** in the world (tel. 61 26 93 70; 60kr per hour does not include supervision and equipment).

The **Norwegian Olympic Museum** inside the hall gives the opportunity to relive Norway's athletic past. In the square outside the hall, a **bobsled simulator** (35kr) gives your spinal cord a what-for. On the course itself, 15km north at Hunderfossen (tel. 61 27 75 50), you can reach speeds of up to 65mph in a wheeled bobsled (125kr).

Most of Lillehammer's shops and restaurants are located on **Storgata,** which runs parallel to the hillside, two blocks uphill from the bus and train stations. The main **tourist office,** Elvegata 19 (tel. 61 25 92 99), is at the end of a side street projecting off Storgata. (Open June-Aug. Mon.-Fri. 9am-7pm, Sat. 9am-7pm, Sun. 11am-6pm; Sept.-May Mon.-Fri. 9am-5pm, Sat. 10am-2pm.) Daily **trains** run to Oslo (2½hr., 225kr), Åndalsnes (4hr., 330kr), and Trondheim (4½hr., 410kr). **Gjeste Bu,** Gamleveien 110 (tel. 61 25 43 21; fax 61 25 43 21), one block north of Storgata, has three kitchens, free tea and coffee, and a non-smoking floor. (Reception open Mon.-Sat. 9am-11pm, Sun. 11am-11pm. Sleeping bag accommodations 60kr, singles 175kr, doubles 250kr, triples 375kr. Sheets 40kr.) The **Lillehammer Youth Hostel (HI)** (tel. 61 26 25 66) is on the top floor of the bus station, which adjoins the train station. Each modern, clean four-bed room has its own bathroom (165kr, 140kr with Scanrail; breakfast 20kr). Ingest some pasta from the 79kr buffet (Mon.-Fri. noon-7pm) at **Pipa Pub and Kro Kafé,** a half block down Elvegata from the tourist office (open daily noon-1am).

Otta and Dombås The mountains of Rondane are most accessible from **Otta,** 1½ hours north of Lillehammer. The **tourist office** (tel. 61 23 02 44), in the station, explains white water rafting on the Sjoa River and the Rondane hiking trails at nearby **Mysuseter** and **Høvringen.** (Open late June-early Aug. Mon.-Fri. 8:30am-7:30pm, Sat.-Sun. 10am-6pm; mid-Aug. to mid-June Mon.-Fri. 8:30am-4pm.) The nearest **youth hostel** (tel. 61 23 62 00; fax 61 23 60 14) is in Sjoa, 15km south on the rail line (reception open 8am-11pm; 70kr, nonmembers 95kr). Buses leave weekdays from Otta (30kr) to Sjoa. In town, **Guesthouse Sagatun,** Ottekra (tel. 61 23 08 14), offers singles (160kr), doubles (250kr), and triples (375kr). Otta is a springboard for the train-deficient fjord country. Spectacular **bus** routes snake from Otta across the Jotunheimen mountains to **Sogndal** on Sognefjord (4 per day, 5hr., 220kr) via **Lom** (7 per day, 59kr) and **Stryn** on Nordfjord (2 per day, 3½hr., 205kr).

The slightly more challenging **Dovrefjell** range is best reached from **Dombås.** The train station perches on a hill above town. From there, go with gravity, and then cross the highway to enter the **tourist office** (tel. 61 24 14 44; fax 61 24 11 90; open mid-June to mid-Aug. daily 9am-8pm). The **Dombås Youth Hostel (HI)** (tel. 61 24 10 45), though near the train station, is accessible by slogging up the road behind the massive parking lot from town. (Reception open daily 8-10am and 4-11pm. Lockout 10am-4pm. 100kr, nonmembers 125kr. Reserve in summer. Open mid-June to mid-Aug.) **Dombås Gård Hyltetun og Caravancamp** (tel. 61 24 10 26), 300m behind the tourist office, has four-person cabins (from 280kr) and tent sites (70kr; open May-Sept.).

Valdres and Jotunheimen

The **Valdres** valley, running parallel and to the west of Gudbrandsdalen, has six of Norway's 25 medieval wooden stave churches. The valley terminates in the highest mountain range in Europe north of the Alps, the jagged, reindeer-inhabited **Jotunheimen** massif. Even though only two of the several hundred peaks require technical gear to climb, the weather can be harsh and it snows even in July. The DNT offices in Bergen and Oslo and tourist offices in the region overflow with maps and tips on trails and huts. **Gjendesheim,** an hour north of Fagernes by bus, is a stellar hiking base. The DNT **hut** here provides a sleeping bag and lodging. Buses also run to Gjendesheim from the Oslo-Trondheim train line at Otta, 30km downvalley from Vågåmo. From Gjendesheim, you can hike across the **Besseggen,** a spectacular ridge with a deep blue lake at 1200m and an emerald green one at 984m.

Fagernes Within the valley, Fagernes holds a central location. Reach the town by **bus** from Gol on the Oslo-Bergen rail line (70min., 45kr, students 33% off), from Lillehammer (2hr., 95kr, students 33% off), or by *Valdresekspressen* bus from Oslo (3hr., 185kr). The **tourist office** (tel. 61 36 04 00), by the bus station, will gladly hand over the comprehensive *Valdres Summer Guide* or *Winter Guide.* (Open July to mid-Aug. Mon.-Fri. 8am-7pm, Sat. 9am-6pm, Sun. 11am-6pm; late Aug.-June Mon.-Fri. 8am-4pm.) Ask at the tourist office about the riot of nearby **stave churches** (20-30kr each) and the large **folkmuseum.** The more rough 'n' tumble should request a map and further info about the *Vardevandring* (watchtower hike), which winds through most of the valley. The **Leira Youth Hostel (HI),** Valdres Folkehøjskole (tel. 61 36 20 25), is 4km south of town (85kr, nonmembers 105kr; open June to mid-Aug.).

Lom, Bøverdalen, Spiterstulen, and Turtagrø The northwest approach entails a phenomenal bus ride over the main massif of Jotunheimen, between Otta on the rail line and Sogndal on Sognefjord (5hr., 205kr). Sixty-two kilometers out of Otta, the bus stops in **Lom** (63kr), north of Jotunheimen and the branching point for buses to Stryn in Nordfjord. Lom's **tourist office** (tel. 61 21 12 86) is uphill and across the street from the bus stop. Pick up a copy of the brochure *Lom* and ask here about hiking in the nearby Jotunheimeu Mountains. (Open June-Aug. Mon.-Sat. 9am-8pm, Sun. 10am-6pm; Sept.-May Mon.-Fri. 7:30am-3:30pm.) While in Lom, visit the wonderful **wooden statue-church,** the oldest part of which dates from 1170 (open June 15-Aug.15 daily 9am-9pm; Sept.-May 10am-4pm; 20kr). Below the church, the grey waters of glacier-fed **Bøvra River** churn past. The two daily buses to Sogndal stop at **Bøverdalen,** 20km from Lom. There, stay at the **HI youth hostel** (tel. 61 21 20 64; 75kr, nonmembers 100kr; open June-Nov.). Both **Galdhøpiggen** (2469m) and **Glittertinden** (2464m), the highest points in Norway, can be reached without technical gear. About 18km off Route 55, the **tourist chalet** (tel. 61 21 14 80) at **Spiterstulen** provides better access to Glittertinden (200kr, DNT members 150kr; camping 50kr). A **bus** runs daily from Lom at 8:30am and 4:25pm, returning from Spiterstulen at 10:30am and 5:25pm (round-trip102kr). Southwest of Bøverdalen, the plateau between **Krossbu** and **Sognefjellhytta** is strewn with rock cairns tracing the way between snow-covered lakes; cross-country skiing is possible throughout the summer. Near **Turtagrø,** just above the tip of the Sognefjord system, is one of Norway's premier rock-climbing areas. From Sognefjellhytta, a steep four-hour path leads to **Fannaråkhytta** (2069m), the highest hut in the DNT system.

THE FJORDS AND WEST COUNTRY

Ten thousand years ago during the last Ice Age, glaciers scoured out huge valleys at the edge of Norway, and when they melted, the sea rushed in, creating fjords. So goes the history of west Norway, which stretches from south of Bergen to Ålesund. Buses and ferries wind through the scenic coastal region. Approaches to the fjords are infinite, and routes through them are plentiful; it is worthwhile to consult the tourist office in Oslo to plan your itinerary. Keep in mind that except for a small stretch on the Oslo-Bergen line, seeing the fjords from a train is impossible.

Bergen

Vaunted as the "Gateway to the Fjords," Bergen is surrounded by unblemished, forested mountains. In the Middle Ages, when cod was king, Bergen boomed as Hanseatic merchants set up shop and dominated the local economy. The city still interacts with the sea via an excellent daily fish market and the touristy Bryggen wharf. The real heart of Bergen, however, lies outside of its touristed spots; it is a city that begs visitors to bypass the hype and hike a nearby mountain, cruise a fjord, or explore the backstreet neighborhoods that thrive amidst a lively student population.

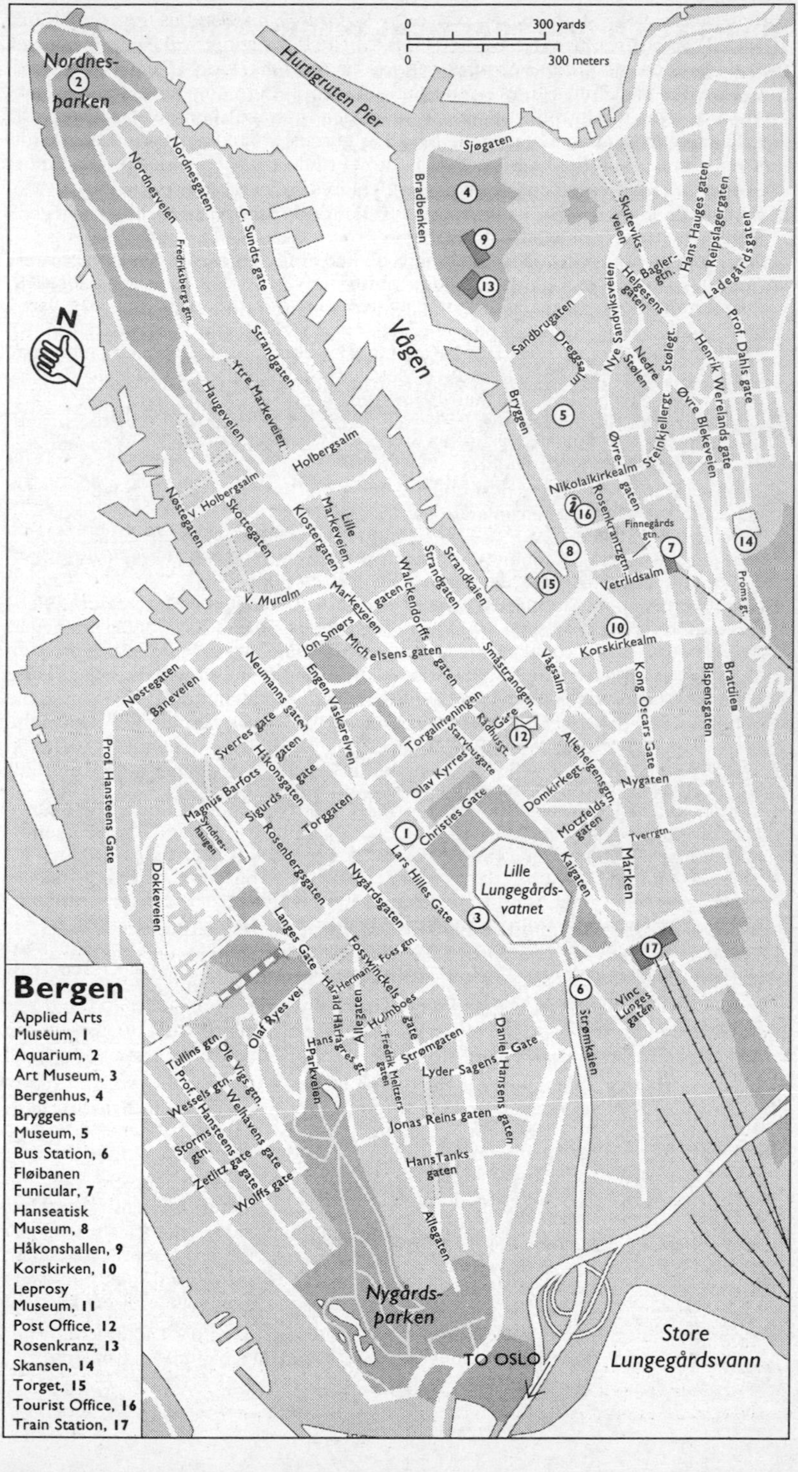
Bergen
Applied Arts Museum, 1
Aquarium, 2
Art Museum, 3
Bergenhus, 4
Bryggens Museum, 5
Bus Station, 6
Fløibanen Funicular, 7
Hanseatisk Museum, 8
Håkonshallen, 9
Korskirken, 10
Leprosy Museum, 11
Post Office, 12
Rosenkranz, 13
Skansen, 14
Torget, 15
Tourist Office, 16
Train Station, 17
0 300 yards
0 300 meters
N
Nordnes-parken
Hurtigruten Pier
Vågen
Sjøgaten
Bradbenken
Nordnesveien
Nordnesgaten
C. Sundts gate
Fredriksbergs gtn.
Strandgaten
Ytre Markeveien
Haugeveien
Holbergsalm
V. Holbergsalm
Skottegaten
Nøstegaten
Klostergaten
Lille Markeveien
V. Muralm
Markeveien
Walckendorffs gaten
Strandgaten
Strandkaien
Bryggen
Sandbrugaten
Dreggsalm
Nikolaikirkealm
Rosenkrantzgtn.
Øvre-gaten
Vetrlidsalm
Finnegårds gtn.
Skuteviks-veien
Nye Sandviksveien
Helgesens gaten
Bagler-gtn.
Hans Hauges gaten
Reipslagergaten
Ladegårdsgaten
Prof. Dahls gate
Henrik Werelands gate
Øvre Blekeveien
Steinkjellergt.
Nedre Stølen
Stølegt.
Proms gt.
Korskirkealm
Vågsalm
Kong Oscars Gate
Bispengaten
Brattliea
Smastrandgtn.
Jon Smørs gaten
Michelsens gaten
Neumanns gaten
Engen
Vaskerelven
Sverres gate
Nøstegaten
Baneveien
Håkonsgaten
Magnus Barfots gaten
Sigurds gate
Torggaten
Torgalmenningen
Starvhusgate
Rådhusgt.
Gate
Olav Kyrres
Christies Gate
Allehelgensgtn.
Domkirkegt.
Nygaten
Motzfelds gaten
Tverrgtn.
Kaigaten
Marken
Lille Lungegårdsvatnet
Prof. Hansteens Gate
Syndnes-haugen
Dokkeveien
Rosenberggaten
Lars Hilles Gate
Nygårdsgaten
Langes Gate
Fosswinckels gate
Foss gtn.
Herman
Harald Hårfagres gt.
Allegaten
Humboes gate
Olaf Ryes vei
Hans
Parkveien
Fredrik Meltzers gaten
Strømgaten
Lyder Sagens Gate
Daniel Hansens gaten
Vinc. Lunges gaten
Strømkaien
Jonas Reins gaten
HansTanks gaten
Allegaten
Tullins gtn.
Ole Vigs gtn.
Prof. Wessels gtn.
Hansteens gate
Welhavens gate
Storms gtn.
Zetlitz gate
Wolffs gate
Nygårds-parken
TO OSLO
Store Lungegårdsvann

ORIENTATION AND PRACTICAL INFORMATION

Bergen's train station lies several blocks above the gleaming harbor, at the top of the city center. Looking towards the water, **Bryggen** (the extension of Kong Oscars gate) and the town's most imposing mountain are to your right; most of the main buildings are to the left. **Torget**—an outdoor market—is at the harbor's tip.

Tourist Office: Bryggen 7 (tel. 55 32 14 80; fax 55 32 14 64), on the harbor's right side, just past the Torget. Books rooms, exchanges currency, and sells the **Bergen Card** which gets you admission to most of the museums plus other discounts (1-day 120kr, 2-day 190kr). Pick up the free, all-knowing *Bergen Guide.* Luggage storage 10kr per piece per day. Ask for a photocopy of their suggested itineraries through the fjords. Open May-Sept. daily 8:30am-9pm; Oct.-April Mon.-Sat. 9am-4pm. Train station branch open daily 7am-11pm. **DNT,** Tverrgaten 4-6 (tel. 55 32 22 30), off Marken, a pedestrian thoroughfare beginning at the railroad station and leading to the harbor, has info and sells detailed topological maps for all of Norway. Open Mon.-Wed. and Fri. and Sun. 10am-4pm, Thurs. 10am-6pm.

Budget Travel: Kilroy Travels, Parkveien 1 (tel. 55 32 64 00), in the Studentsentret. Sells ISIC and InterRail. Finds travel discounts for students and those under 26. Open Mon.-Fri. 8:30am-4:30pm.

Currency Exchange: At the post office. After hours both tourist offices will change currency at 4% below the bank rate. No commission.

Trains: tel. 81 50 08 88 or 55 96 69 00. 3 trains head daily to Oslo (6½-7½hr., 500kr, 20kr seat reservations compulsory) via Voss (1hr., 110kr) and Myrdal (1¾-2½hr., 165kr). **Luggage storage** 20kr. Open daily 7am-11:50pm.

Buses: Bystasjonen, Strømgaten 8 (tel. 177). Service to neighboring areas, the Hardangerfjord district, Ålesund (455kr, students 25% off), and Oslo (560kr, students 25% off). Ticket office and information open Mon.-Fri. 7am-6pm, Sat. 7am-2pm.

Public Transportation: Yellow and red buses chauffeur you around the city (5-15kr per ride; free from the bus station into the center of town on bus 100).

Ferries: To Stavanger and fjords: from the train station, boats leave from the left side of the harbor. International ships leave from Skoltegrunnskaien, a 20min. walk past Bryggen along the right side of the harbor. **Fjord Line,** Rosenkrautz Gate 3 (tel. 55 54 88 00), runs ferries to Hanstholm, Denmark that depart Mon., Wed. and Fri. at 4:30pm and arrive at 8am the next morning. (560-640kr; off season 440kr-540kr. Round-trip 10% discount; Aug.18-June 20 50% student discount.) **Smyril Line,** with offices in Slottsgaten 1 (tel. 55 32 09 70; fax 55 96 02 72), departs June-Aug. Tues. at 3pm for the Faroe Islands (24hr., 560-1750kr one way), Shetland Islands (12hr., 450-1430kr one way), and Iceland (40hr., 1190-3220kr one way). Student discount are available. **Color Line,** Skuteviksboder 1-2 (tel. 55 54 86 00; fax 55 54 86 01), sails year-round to Newcastle via Stavanger and Haugesund (3 per week in summer, 25hr., US$82-364, 50% off with student ID in winter). **P & O Scottish Ferries** sails June-Aug. to the Shetland Islands (14hr., 600kr, 25% student discount) and on to Aberdeen, Scotland (30hr., 1000kr, 20% student discount); reserve through Color Line. The **Hurtigruten,** which travels from Bergen to Kirkenes, leaves daily at 10:30pm (full trip 3578kr; 50% student discount; cheaper Oct.-April) from a separate harbor; inquire at the tourist office.

Gay and Lesbian Services: Gay Movement, in the **Café Fincken,** Nygårdsgaten 2a (tel. 55 31 21 39). Open Mon.-Sat. noon-2:30am, Sun. 3pm-12:30am.

Pharmacy: Apoteket Nordstjernen (tel. 55 31 68 84). Second floor of the bus station. Open Mon.-Sat. 7:30am-midnight, Sun. 8:30am-midnight.

Medical Assistance: Accident Clinic, Vestre Strømkai 19 (tel. 55 32 11 20). Open 24hr.

Emergencies: Ambulance: tel. 113. **Fire:** tel. 110.

Police: tel. 112.

Post Office: tel. 55 54 15 00. A green building with a clock on Småstrand gate. Open Mon.-Wed. 8am-5pm, Thurs.-Fri. 8am-6pm, Sat. 9am-3pm. **Postal Code:** N-5002.

Telephones and Faxes: Tele Building, Starvhusegate 4, across Rådhusgate from the post office. Fax service (10kr fee; 10kr per page). Open Mon.-Fri. 8am-4pm.

ACCOMMODATIONS AND CAMPING

The tourist office books rooms (some with bathrooms) in private homes, for a 15kr fee (20kr for 2 people; singles 160-180kr, doubles 250-320kr).

Intermission, Kalfarveien 8 (tel. 55 31 32 75), 5min. walk from the train station. Head right from the exit, and right again on Kong Oscars gate, which mystically becomes Kalfarveien. Friendly staff, co-ed dorm with free sheets, blankets, tea and cookies, and laundry. Make free waffles Mon. and Thurs. nights. Reception open daily 7-11am and 5pm-midnight, until 1am on Fri. and Sat. nights. Lockout 11am-5pm. Curfew 1am. 95kr. Breakfast 25kr. Pack your own lunch for 15kr. Open mid-June to mid-Aug. Reserve ahead, or leave your name at the tourist office.

YMCA InterRail Center, Nedre Korskirkealmenningen 4 (tel. 55 31 72 52; fax 55 31 35 77). Single-sex and co-ed dorms. Kitchen, laundry, piano, and free sauna. Reception open daily 7am-1am. Lockout noon-4pm. 100kr. Open June 15-Sept. 15.

Montana Youth Hostel (HI), Johan Blyttsvei 30 (tel. 55 29 04 75; fax 55 29 29 00), halfway up Mt. Ulriken, 5km from the city center. Take bus 4 ("Lægdene") to "Montana" (15kr). Big dorms with bunk beds. Reception open 24hr. Flexible lockout 10am-3pm. Dorms 130-160kr. Doubles with shower and bathroom 450kr. Sheets 40kr. Dinner 70kr. Wash and dry each 20kr.

Camping: Bergenshallen Camping, Vilhelm Bjerknesvei 24 (tel. 55 27 01 80; fax 55 27 15 51), in the city. Take bus 90 to "Bergenshallen" (15kr, 20min.). Free showers. 10kr per person, 50kr per tent. Reception open 24hr. Open mid-June to mid-Aug. **Bergen Camping Park,** Haukås om Åsane (tel. 55 24 88 08). 10kr per person, 60kr per tent. **Free camping** on the far side of the hills above town. Pick up a map and ask for further info at the DNT office in town.

FOOD

Bergen's culinary centerpiece is the **fish market** that springs up on Torget by the water (open Mon.-Fri. 7am-4pm, Thurs. until 7pm, Sat. until 3pm). **Pasta Sentral,** Vestre Strømkai 6, behind the bus station, is inexpensive and popular with local students. (Daily special 44kr, drink included. Open Mon.-Sat. 11am-midnight, Sun. 1pm-midnight.) **Fellini,** Tverrgate, just off Marken, serves up Italian specialties (pizzas from 69kr; open daily 2pm-midnight). Be at one with Norwegian cuisine and the older Bergen set at **Kaffistova til Ervingen,** Strandkaien 2B, on the second floor next to the harbor; it's cafeteria-style with a heavy emphasis on fish (*Dagens ret* 60-70kr; open Mon.-Fri. 8am-7pm, Sat. 8am-5pm, Sun. 11am-6pm). **Den Gode Klode,** Fosswinckelsgate 18, satisfies vegetarians in an elegant establishment with outdoor seating. (Salads from 30kr, daily special 60-70kr; 10% student discount. Open Mon.-Fri. 11:30am-7pm, Sat. noon-5pm.) The discount supermarket **Mekka** sprouts clones throughout the city; one lurks at Marken 3.

SIGHTS AND ENTERTAINMENT

Bergen, like the rest of Norway, is best seen on foot. The tourist office and bookstores sell *Round Bergen on Foot,* which details three walking tours with pictures, history, and anecdotes (29kr). As you gaze at the right side of the harbor from the Torget, you will see the pointed gables of **Bryggen,** a row of medieval buildings that's survived half a dozen disastrous fires and the explosion of a Nazi munitions ship in 1944. Listed by UNESCO as one of the world's most significant showcases of the Middle Ages, Bryggen also features restaurants and artsy-craftsy workshops. **Bryggens Museum,** behind a small park at the end of the rows of Bryggen houses, displays old costumes, runic inscriptions, and scenes from life in old Norway (open daily 10am-5pm; 20kr). At the end of Bryggen stands the **Hanseatic Museum,** a preserved wooden house replete with secret compartments, mummified hanging fish, and an aura of affluent gloom from the days when German merchants controlled trade through Europe (open daily 9am-5pm; 35kr; guided tour of both museums 60kr). The former city fortress, **Bergenhus,** teeters at the end of the quay, and the **Rosenkrantz Tower** stands in late medieval splendor. **Håkonshallen,** built by Håkon Håkonsson in the 13th century, is what is left of the original castle. (Open late May-early Sept. daily 10am-4pm; mid-Sept. to mid-May noon-3pm; closed during the Festival. 15kr.)

Lose your head over the **Leprosy Museum,** Kong Oscars gate 59. Since 1970, the university has tastefully documented the history of the disease in a 19th-century hospital (open mid-May to Aug. daily 11am-3pm; 15kr, students 6kr). On the east shore of **Lille Lungegårdsvatnet,** a shimmering pond in the middle of town, the **Rasmus Meyer's Collection** provides a extensive overview of Norwegian Naturalists, Impressionists, and Expressionists. Two buildings down the street, it is joined by the **Stenersens Collection,** with works by Munch and Picasso, at the **Municipal Art Museum.** (Both open late May-early Sept. Mon.-Sat. 11am-4pm, Sun. noon-3pm; mid-Sept. to mid-May Tues.-Sun. noon-3pm. 35kr for both museums and the Bergen Museum of Art, students 20kr.) Down the street the immaculate **West Norway Museum of Applied Arts Museum** highlights stunning 20th-century Norwegian design developments. (Open mid-May to mid-Sept. Tues.-Sun. 11am-4pm; mid-Sept. to mid-May Tues.-Sat. noon-3pm, Thurs. until 6pm, Sun. until 4pm. 20kr, students 10kr.) A quick bus trip from downtown is **Gamle Bergen** (Old Bergen), a rather touristy "village" and open-air museum of wooden buildings from the last century. Take city bus 20, 21, 22, 70, 71, 80, or 90 to the first stop past the second tunnel and then walk under the overpass, following the signs. (Houses open mid-May to Aug. 10am-4pm. Obligatory guided tours 40kr, students 20kr.) Get wall-eyed with the sea-life at the **Bergen Aquarium,** Nordnesparken 2, on the tip of the peninsula near the harbor entrance; take bus 4, or walk 15 minutes from the center (open May-Sept. daily 9am-8pm; Oct.-April 10am-6pm; 50kr). To experience an authentic taste of the city, stroll through Bergen's quieter, more residential neighborhoods. Good areas to explore are the steep streets between **Korskirken** and the **Skansen** tower, and the **Sydneskleiben** and **Dragefjellsbarker** neighborhoods near the university campus.

A vast archipelago lies to the west and towering mountains encroach on all other sides. Trails surrounding the city are sure to inspire awe. The **Fløibanen funicular** takes you to the top of Mount Fløyen, looming above the city. (Mon.-Fri. 7:30am-11pm, Sat. from 8am, Sun. from 9am; until midnight May-Aug. One-way 15kr.) At the summit you can enjoy the spectacular views, munch at the restaurant, or join up with one of the many **hiking trails** that lead both to the bottom or up to the top of **Mt. Ulriken** (4hr. one way), the highest peak above Bergen. A cable car also runs to the top of Mt. Ulriken (daily 9am-9pm; round-trip 50kr). Pick up a map of the hills above Bergen at the DNT office. Take any bus leaving from platforms 19, 20, or 21 from the Bergen bus station to "Hopsbroen", turn right, walk about 200m, then turn left, and walk for about 20 minutes to reach **Troldhaugen** (Troll Hill), Edvard Grieg's summer villa. The house still contains many of the composer's belongings, including his Steinway piano, which is used at summer concerts in Troldsalen Hall next door (tel. 55 91 17 91; open May-Sept. 9:30am-5:30pm; 40kr).

Virtually all of the **fjords** of western Norway are accessible by daytripping ferries from Bergen. Most leave from the **Strandkaiterminalen** on the opposite side of the harbor from Bryggen. **Flaggruten** (tel. 55 23 87 80) arranges daily boat and ferry excursions to **Hardangerfjord** (round-trip 180-410kr), while **Fylkesbaatane** (tel. 55 32 40 15) sends boats to towns on the **Sognefjord** (one way 300-410kr) and up to **Nordfjord** (one way 450kr) with 50% student discounts. They also give day tours of Sognefjord and the Flåm valley (520-540kr). **M/S Bruvik** (tel.56 59 66 22) tours of nearby **Osterfjord** depart daily from Bradbenken on the Bryggen Wharf (9hr., 290kr). One of the most popular and affordable day trips of the fjords is the **Norway in a Nutshell** which includes train, bus, and boat rides amidst the scenery. (470kr round-trip from Bergen, 890kr from Oslo, 660kr between Bergen and Oslo.)

All stops are pulled out for the annual **Bergen International Festival** (tel. 55 21 61 50), a 12-day program of music, ballet, folklore, and drama in late May. The **Garage Bar,** at the corner of Nygårdsgaten and Christies gate, has live bands Fridays and Saturdays (cover 50-100kr). Wednesdays and Thursdays, check out the psychedelic dungeon (open daily until 3am). The milder scene is on at **Café Opera,** Engen 18, a mellow café/restaurant (try the reindeer roast with mountain cranberries, 89kr). It gets funky on Fridays with DJ dance music, and surprise live concerts and "Club Eliassen" on Saturday nights. (No cover. Open Mon.-Thurs. noon-2am, Fri. noon-3am, Sat. 11:30am-3am, Sun. 1pm-2am.) **Miles Ahead,** Olevull Sq., hosts a popular disco (cover 50kr; opens around 9pm), while **Rick's,** Veiten 3, combines the best of both worlds with a great bar and a disco upstairs (cover 50kr after 10:30pm; open 10pm-4am).

Hardangerfjord

Slicing through one of Norway's fruit growing regions, the steep banks of the Hardangerfjord are lined with orchards and small farms. **Odda,** on the tip of Sørfjord, a slender branch of the main fjord, is the only "town" in the region. Odda's **tourist office** (tel. 53 64 12 97) distributes the free *Hardanger Guide.* (Open in summer Mon.-Fri. 10am-8pm, Sat. 10am-5pm, Sun. 11am-6pm; mid-Aug. to mid-June Mon.-Fri. 9am-3pm.) The comfortable **Odda Youth Hostel** is at Bustetungata 2 (tel. 53 64 14 11; reception open 24hr.; 130kr, nonmembers 155kr). The area south of Odda on RV13 harbors many natural marvels including the twin waterfalls of **Låtefoss.** For extended stays on the Hardangerfjord check out the towns of **Utne** or **Jondal.** The thunder of stampeding hikers can be heard in beautiful **Eidfjord,** on the main road RV13, 45km southeast of Voss, as they pass through this main gateway to **Hardangervidda,** Norway's largest national park. Duck into the **tourist office** (tel. 53 66 51 77) for an information refill. (Open high season Mon.-Fri. 9am-8pm, Sat. 9am-6pm, Sun. noon-8pm; reduced hours off season.) Vikings from 400-800 AD decay at the **Viking Burial Place** in Hereid, while the waterfall **Vøringstossen,** one of Norway's most famous waterfalls, plummets 182m nearby (hikes to both 1hr. round-trip from the tourist office). Ask the tourist office to find a guest house (singles about 200kr) or try **Saebø Camping** (tel. 53 66 59 27; 10kr per person, 30kr per tent, 220kr per cabin).

Sognefjord

The longest of the fjords (200km), Sognefjord's deep, slender fingers penetrate all the way to the foot of the Jotunheimen mountains. A short ride north of the stunning Oslo-Bergen rail line, Sognefjord is ideal for those seeing Norway by train. A natural starting point deep in Sognefjord, **Flåm** is the only fjord town accessible by rail (connecting to the Oslo-Bergen line through **Myrdal;** 11-13 per day, 50min., 80kr, 50kr for railpass holders). If your legs can manage, you can also walk down to Flåm from Mydral and linger over the rainbow-capped waterfalls and snowy mountain vistas (around 4hr.) Express boats also run between Flåm and Bergen (2 per day, 5hr., 410kr, 50% off with InterRail or ISIC), traveling through **Aurland** and on to **Balestrand.** The post office, café, and train ticket office in Flåm coexist in the large building by the train station. The **tourist office** (tel. 57 63 21 06) dwells inside as well (open June to mid-Aug. daily 8:30am-8:30pm). You can buy a fishing license (150kr per 24hr.) at **Flåm Camping and Hostel (HI)** (tel. 57 63 21 21; fax 57 63 23 80). To get there, cross to the side of the river opposite the train station and follow the road into the valley (80kr, nonmembers 105kr; tent and 1 person 45kr, 2 people 80kr; open May-Sept.). The **Heimly Pensjonat** (tel. 57 63 23 00) on the right bank of the fjord, offers sleeping bag accommodations for 125kr (reception open 24hr.)

Wilderness junkies hop off the Oslo-Bergen train at **Finse,** just east of Myrdal, and hike for three or four stunning days down the Aurlandsdalen Valley to **Aurland,** 10km from Flåm. You can sleep warmly all the way in evenly spaced DNT *hytter.* For maps, prices, and reservations, inquire at DNT in Oslo or Bergen. One of the most popular day **hikes** (8-10hr. one way) in Norway begins in Østerbø and runs through the Aurlandsdal Valley to Vassbydgi. Both endpoints can be reached by bus (4 per day, 30kr) from Aurland or Flam. Buses also connect Aurland and Flåm (20kr). There is a fantastic view of the Aurland fjord a short hike up from **Otternes Bygdetun** (tel. 57 63 33 00), a unique cluster of 27 17th-century houses between the two towns (open mid-June to mid-Aug. 11am-6pm; 20kr). The **Aurland tourist office** (tel. 57 63 33 13), at the highway junction, serves Flåm in the winter (open May-Aug. Mon.-Fri. 8am-

7pm, Sat.-Sun. 10am-5pm; Sept.-April Mon.-Fri. 8am-3:30pm). **Lunde Camping** (tel. 57 63 34 12), 1km from town along the river, sprouts its quota of tents and caravans (15kr per person, 30kr per tent). Five hundred meters up the road, a trail branches to the left and offers a scenic, lung-searing four-hour hike to the top of **Prest** (1360m).

On the north side of Sognefjord, **Balestrand** is a groovy mid-way point between Flåm and Bergen or Nordfjord. Express boats whiz up the **Fjærland fjord** to Mundal (3 per day, round-trip 278kr). Buses (75kr) whisk passengers to two off-shoots of the **Jostedal glacier,** where guides await novices and experts (ask at any tourist office north of Bergen for schedules and prices). Buses stop en route at the new **Glacier Museum** (60kr), and return in time for riders to catch the boat back to Balestrand (bus fare included in express boat price). Those headed to Stryn from Mundal must plod 3km to the main highway and coordinate with the Sogndal-Skei buses (to Stryn 113kr, 50% ISIC discount). In Balestrand, the **tourist office** (tel. 57 69 12 55), near the quay, can help (open Mon.-Fri. 7:30am-9pm, Sat. 7:30am-6:30pm, Sun. 8am-5:30pm). The Bergen **hydrofoils** serve Balestrand twice a day (3½hr., one way 300kr, railpasses and ISIC 50% off). The gorgeous fjord-side **Kringsjå Hotel and Youth Hostel (HI)** (tel. 57 69 13 03) is up the hill behind town. (145kr, nonmembers 170kr. Doubles 190-210kr, nonmembers 200-240kr. Breakfast included.) **Sjøtun camping** (tel. 57 69 12 23), 1km down the coastal road, provides tent sites and huts. (Reception 9-10am, 6-7, and 9-10pm.15kr per person. 25kr per tent. 2-person hut 125kr.)

Ferries run from Flåm and Aurland west through narrow fjords to **Gudvangen** (4 per day, 2½hr., 115kr from Flåm or Aurland, 50% discount for InterRail and ISIC). From Gudvangen, buses (5-8 per day, 70min., 58kr, 50% ISIC discount) run up to **Voss,** birthplace of the canonized American football figure Knute Rockne, east of Bergen on the Oslo rail line. By train get to Voss from Oslo (6 daily, 430kr) or Bergen (over 12 daily, 110kr). Voss is boss when it comes to winter sports and the **Voss Adventure Center** (tel. 56 51 36 30) in a mini-golf hut behind the Park Hotel, books horsetrekking (80kr per day), white-water rafting (590kr), and paragliding (600kr per hr.) From the train station, turn left when you face the lake and bear right at the fork by the church to reach the **tourist office,** Hestavangen 10 (tel. 56 51 00 51; fax 56 51 08 37), which has info on accommodations and outdoor activities in the area (open June-Aug. Mon.-Sat. 9am-7pm, Sun. 2-7pm; Sept.-May Mon.-Fri. 9am-4pm). Turning right from the station and trudging along the lakeside road brings you to Voss's large, modern **HI youth hostel** (tel. 56 51 20 17), where you can rent canoes and rowboats (20kr per hr., 75kr per day) or bikes (20kr per hour, 75kr per day) or relax in the sauna (reception open 24hr.,155kr, nonmembers 180kr; open mid-Jan. to Oct.). To reach the central **Voss Camping** (tel. 56 51 15 97), head left from the station, stick to the lake shore, and follow the avenue of trees that projects off towards the water (tents 60kr; bike rental 30kr per hour, 150kr per day; canoe and row boat rental).

Nordfjord

Twisting over 100km inland to the foot of the **Jostedal glacier,** Nordfjord probably has an inferiority complex brought on by its more stunning neighbors to the north and south. Wedged between the mountains near the inner end of the fjord, **Stryn** attracts (rich) skiers going through winter withdrawal with **summer skiing** (lift ticket 200kr) at Strynefjellet (1hr. by bus, round-trip 70kr). In Stryn, buses stop at the edge of town; walk past the Esso station and veer right to find the main street, Tonningsgata, where the **tourist office** (tel. 57 87 23 33) awaits on the corner of the paved square (open July daily 10am-8pm; June and Aug. 10am-6pm). The **HI youth hostel** (tel. 57 87 11 06; fax 57 87 11 06) is an arduous hike up the hill behind the town; see if the owners can pick you up in their van. (Reception open daily 8-11am and 4-11pm. 140kr includes breakfast, 170kr nonmembers. Wash and dry 30kr. Open June to mid-Sept.) **Stryn Camping** (tel. 57 87 11 36) blooms in the center of town with caravans and tents (reception open 8am-11pm;10kr per person, 60kr per tent). Take a bus to **Briksdalsbreen** (daily at 10am, 1hr., round-trip 88kr) to probe the crevasses of the Jostedal glacier. Be warned: glaciers can be extremely dangerous so never walk on them without a guide or supervision. **Olden Aktiv** (tel. 57 87 38 88) organizes icy excursions while **Stryn Fjell-og Breførarlay** (tel. 57 87 76 59) runs trips to the Bødal glacier (4-5hr., 250kr per person). Stryn is a cosmically ordained convergence for **buses** from Otta on the Oslo-Trondheim rail line via Lom and Jotunheimen (Otta-Stryn 205kr, students 25% off; Lom-Stryn 140kr, students 25% off), from Hellesylt in Geirangerfjord (59kr), and from Fjærland in Sognefjord (119kr).

Geirangerfjord

The most southern inland arm of the fjord system that begins at Ålesund, the sublime Geirangerfjord's 16km of green-blue water reflect stunning cliffs and waterfalls. Watch the drama of the **Seven Sisters,** the spurting and gushing of the **Suitor,** and the **Bridal Veil's** mist. **Hiking** opportunities abound in this charmed country—especially notable is the path behind the **Storseter waterfall,** Flydalsjuvet Cliff, Skageflå farm, and Dalsnibba Mountain (which can be reached by bus daily at 10am, 75kr). Many of the tiny, now abandoned farms clinging to these cliffs could be reached only by ladders which were artfully yanked up when tax collectors passed by. From June through August, 10 daily **ferries** (1hr., 30kr) connect the tiny towns of Hellesylt and Geiranger, at opposite ends of the fjord. From the south or southeast, go through Stryn to Hellesylt (2 per day, 59kr, students 43kr); from the north, start from Åndalsnes or Ålesund. The **Golden Route** is an 85km trail over the Eagle's road and Trollstigen beginning in Geiranger and ending in Åndalsnes; enjoy the scenery aboard one of the two daily buses to Åndalsnes (250kr, 50% discount for railpass holders).

Over 3000 tourists trample the streets of **Geiranger** every day, and an armada of ocean liners maintains a steady presence off-shore. The ferry to and from Hellesylt is the cheapest way to cruise the fjord, but there are also organized sight-seeing trips (1½hr., 67kr; call Geiranger Fjordservice 94 66 05 02). The Geiranger **tourist office** (tel. 70 26 30 99), up from the landing, finds private rooms (from 200kr) for a 20kr fee (open June-Aug. daily 9am-7pm). **Geiranger Camping** (tel. 70 26 31 20) is by the water 500m to the right of the ferry dock (wheelchair accessible; 15kr per person, 40kr per tent; showers 5kr per 3min.). To get to the palatial **Vinjebakken Hostel** with its wonderful views, follow the main road up the steep hillside behind town. (15min; reception open 8-11am and 2pm-midnight; 115kr).

At the less spectacular east end of the fjord, tiny, unspoiled **Hellesylt** is a base for mountain hiking and home to some of the wildest and woolliest scenery in Norway. Hikers head for the **Briksdal glacier** and the **Troll's Path.** The **tourist office** (tel. 70 26 50 52), right on the ferry landing, rents fishing equipment (15kr per hr.), provides hiking maps (20kr), and is the departure point for out-bound buses (open June to mid-Aug. daily 9am-5pm). The **Hellesylt Youth Hostel (HI)** (tel. 70 26 51 28), up the steep hill along the road to Stranda (if coming by bus ask the driver to let you off in front of the hostel), has a great view; take the path up the right side of the waterfall that thunders through town, and hang a right at the top (100kr, nonmembers 125kr). Walk 1km across the bridge from the dock and to the left to find **Hellesylt Camping** (tel. 70 26 51 04; 10kr per person, 35kr per tent).

Åndalsnes and Ålesund

The mountains around Åndalsnes draw mountaineers, rock climbers, and casual hikers. Daily trains that split off the Oslo-Trondheim line at Dombås end at Åndalsnes (from Oslo 6½hr., 490kr), taking off onto the roller-coaster **Rauma Line** which passes over stunning bridges before making a U-turn in the 1340-m Stavems tunnel. The train passes Norway's ultimate mountaineering challenge, **Trollveggen**—the highest vertical rock wall in Europe—and the most notable peak in the area, **Romsdalshorn.** The Dombås-Åndalsnes buses parallel the train. An equally awesome approach is the dizzying road down **Trollstigen,** traversed by the bus to and from Geiranger.

Åndalsnes At the mouth of the Rauma River and surrounded by a ring of serrated mountain peaks, Åndalsenes is a paradise for mountaineers. The local **tourist office** (tel. 71 22 16 22; fax 71 22 16 82) is next to the train station. (Open June to mid-Aug. Mon.-Sat. 9:30am-6:30pm, Sun. 12:30-6:30pm; late Aug. to May Mon.-Fri. 9am-3pm.) Get a list of **private accommodations** from the tourist office and call yourself to avoid the booking fee (doubles from 250kr). To get to the **Åndalsnes Youth Hostel Setnes (HI)** (tel. 71 22 13 82), walk up Jernbanegata, take a left onto Storgata when the road ends, proceed to the traffic circle, stay right, pass the gas stations, and cross the river (30min.). The hostel is on the left; you can see it from the road. (Reception open 4-11pm. Dorms 160kr, singles 260kr, doubles 395. Enormous breakfast included. Open mid-May to mid-Sept.) En route to the hostel, would-be campers turn left after crossing the bridge and check in at the amazingly scenic **Åndalsnes Camping.** (Tel. 71 22 16 29; 15kr per person, 45kr per tent, 4-bed huts 150-600kr. Bikes 90kr per day.) Between the hostel and campground, the **Norsk Tindemuseum** houses legendary mountaineer Arne Randers Heen's collection of expedition paraphernalia, as well as exhibits on the few folk warped enough to parachute off Trollveggen. Arne climbed Romsdalshorn for the 233rd time when he was 80 years old (open mid-June to mid-Aug. daily 1-5pm; other times on request; 30kr). Ask about paragliding at the tourist office. To hit the mountains, contact **Aak** (tel. 71 22 71 00), 4km east of town on the E9 back toward Dombås; they have beds (190kr) with showers and a fireplace and organize climbing clinics. Cheap shopping is found at the **Raumaullvare Fabrink** factory outside town. Call in advance (tel. 71 22 10 33).

NORWAY

Ålesund The largest city between Bergen and Trondheim, Ålesund enjoys a beautiful cliffside location and is renowned for its Art Nouveau architecture. For a view of the splendid city, the distant mountains, and the coastal ferries inching their ways between islands, gasp up the 418 steps to **Aksla.** The **Summøre Museum,** Borgundgavlen (10min. by bus 13, 14, 18, or 24; 15kr), displays local fishing boats from days of yore and a reconstructed Viking ship (open Mon.-Fri. 10am-5pm, Sat.-Sun. noon-5pm; 35kr, students 20kr). Commune with the fishes of the North Sea at the **Ålesund Akvarium,** Nedre Strandgate 4 (open Mon.-Fri. 10am-5pm, Sat. 10am-3pm, Sun. noon-4pm; 30kr). There's an old Viking site and 12th-century marble church on **Giske,** a short bus ride from Ålesund (route 64, 12 per day, 35kr). Ornithusiasts flock to the island of **Runde,** sanctuary to over 500,000 of our fine feathered friends. A hydrofoil links Ålesund and Hareid; a *Soreid* bus leaves from there (1-3 per day, 94kr).

The **tourist office** (tel. 70 12 12 02), on Keiser Wilhelms gate, is across from the bus station in the city hall. (Open June-Aug. Mon.-Fri. 8:30am-7pm, Sat. 9am-5pm, Sun. 11am-5pm; Sept.-May Mon.-Fri. 9am-4pm.) **Hansen Gaarden,** Kongensgate 14 (tel./fax 70 12 10 29), has spotless, spacious rooms, but may be closed in 1998 for renovations (reception open 8am-9pm; singles 200kr, doubles 280-300kr). **Annecy,** Kirkegata 1B (tel. 70 12 96 80, after hours 90 53 60 05), has big airy rooms and a kitchen (reception open 9am-9pm; doubles from 290kr; open June 15-Aug. 15). **Volsdalen Camping** (tel./fax 70 12 58 90) has the closest sites to town, 2km out along the main highway next to a beach. Take bus 13, 14, 18, or 24 (11kr), turn right off the highway, and follow the downhill road to the bottom of the stairs. Cross the road, turn right and cross the overpass, then turn left and walk 200m. (Reception open 9am-9pm. Tents 90kr, 10kr per person; cabins 290-490kr. Laundry 60kr. Open May to mid-Sept.) Ålesund is accessible by **bus** (3 per day from Åndalsnes, 138kr, 50% railpass discount), or by **Hurtigruten,** which docks here daily.

Trondheim

Viking kings turned Trondheim into one of the most influential cities in Norway, but it's the slightly better-mannered 20,000 students who now light the city's flare. Fresh from celebrating its 1000th birthday, Trondheim hopes to keep the good times rolling for the millennium to come. Olav Tryggvason founded Trondheim in 997; his image presides over an outdoor market from a column in the main town square, **Tor-**

vet. Local boy King Olav Haraldsson became Norway's patron saint after he fought to introduce Christianity. A steady stream of pilgrims prompted the construction of **Nidaros Cathedral,** Scandinavia's largest medieval structure, built over a holy well that sprang up beside St. Olav's grave. Site of all Norwegian coronations, it holds the crown jewels. (Open mid-June to Aug. Mon.-Fri. 9am-6:15pm, Sat. 9am-2pm, Sun. 1-4pm; reduced hours off season. 20kr.) The view from the top of the 172-step spiral staircase in the tower is worth the 5kr (admission every 30min.). The church (1150-1320) is at the tail end of a renovation that began in 1869. Among the buildings that surround the church is the **Archbishop's Palace** and **War Museum** (Palace open mid-June to Aug. Mon.-Fri. 10am-3pm, Sat. 10am-2pm, Sun. 12:30-3:30pm. 20kr. Museum open June-Aug. Mon.-Fri. 9am-3pm, Sat.-Sun. 11am-4pm; Feb.-May and Sept.-Nov. Sat. and Sun. 11am-4pm. 5kr.) Cross the **Gamle Bybro** (Old Town Bridge) and visit the old district on Innherredsveien, parallel to the river, for a taste of Trondheim of yore. On the hill across the river roosts the white 1681 **Kristiansten Fortress.** Some of Norway's bizarre and excellent art works are displayed at the **Trondhjems Kunst-Forening,** next to the cathedral. A whole hallway is devoted to Edvard Munch, highlighted by the woodcuts *Lust* and *Jealousy* (open June-Aug. daily 10am-4pm; Sept.-May Tues.-Sun. noon-4pm; 20kr, students 10kr). Bus 4 "Lade" will take you to the intriguing **Ringve Museum of Musical History.** Displays (with demonstrations) range from a one-stringed Ethiopian violin to the ornate Mozart Room. (Tours, the only way in, in English at 11am, 12:30, 2:30, and 4:30pm from July to mid-Aug. 50kr, students 30kr.) Ferry over to **Munkholmen,** an island monastery that became a prison fortress and then a quiet beach and picnic spot (round-trip 30kr; fortress 14kr).

Practical Information, Accommodations, and Food The **train station** faces the center of town, which is circled by the Nid River. From the station, walk across the bridge, then six blocks on Søndregate, turn right on Kongensgate, and continue to the main square and the **tourist office,** Munkegata 19 (tel. 73 92 94 05). The office gives out the comprehensive *Trondheim Guide* and rents bikes. (100kr per day; 300kr deposit. Open June to mid-Aug. Mon.-Fri. 8:30am-10pm, Sat. 8:30am-8pm, Sun. 10am-8pm; late Aug. to May Mon.-Fri. 9am-4pm, Sat. 9am-1pm.) **Trondheim's Turistforening,** Munkegata 64, 2nd fl. (tel. 73 52 38 08), above Paul's Tandoori Restaurant, describes huts and trails to the north and south (open Mon.-Wed. and Fri. 9am-4pm, Thurs. 9am-6pm). All **city buses** leave from the Munkegata-Dronningensgate intersection and require exact change (16kr). **Trains** arrive from Oslo (4 per day, 7-8hr., 510kr), Stockholm via Storlien (3 per day, 13hr.), and Bodø (2 per day, 10-11hr., 650kr, 360kr *minipriser*). **Long-distance buses** leave from the train station. The **airport** is 45km out of town and accessible via *flybussen* (45kr).

Trondheim has a wide variety of budget lodgings. The invaluable **InterRail Center,** Elgesetergate 1 (tel. 73 89 95 38; email tirc@stud.ntnu.no), resides in the Studentersenter, a huge, red and round building. From the station, cross the bridge, turn right on Olav Tryggvasonsgate, and left on Prinsensgate; it's across the next bridge on the left. Alternatively, take bus 41, 42, 48, 49, 52, or 63 (10kr) to "Samfundet." Ask for a smaller room if you want to avoid noisy groups (90kr, breakfast included; open July to late Aug.). The student-run center also offers free **Internet access** and serves the cheapest meal in town (35kr for the daily special; beer 25kr). To reach the generic **Trondheim Vandrerhjem (HI),** Weidemannsvei 41 (tel. 73 53 04 90), walk 15 minutes from the city center or ride bus 63 from the train station (160kr, nonmembers 185kr; breakfast included; sheets 45kr). Walk up Lillegårdsballken to reach the student-run **Singsaker Sommerhotell,** Rogertsgate 1 (tel. 73 89 31 00; fax 73 89 32 00), which perches above town near the Kristiansten Fortress and includes a grill and TV room. (Sleeping-bag accommodations 125kr. Singles 240kr. Doubles 370kr. Triples 480kr. Sheets 30kr. Breakfast included. Open June-Aug.) **Sandmoen Camping** (tel. 72 88 61 35), 10km south of town, is the closest campsite; take bus 44 or 45 from the bus station to Sandbakken (reception open 8am-11pm; 80kr per tent). At **Café Gåsa,** Øvre Baklande 36, live peacocks glut the already over-loaded atmosphere (dinners from 50kr). Award-winning marzipan and pastries at **Erichsens**, Nordre Gate 8, can liquidate your savings. The **Rema 1000** store across from the tourist office offers groceries and supplies (open Mon.-Fri. 9am-8pm, Sat. 9am-6pm). A **market** is outside the tourist office. Nightlife centers around on Nordre Gate and along Bratlørgata.

NORTHERN NORWAY

Bodø

Its provincial charm obliterated in World War II, Bodø (BUD-dha) is the northern terminus of the Norwegian rail line and the starting point for buses and boats to the Arctic. Travelers generally flee quickly to their true destinations. The strongest maelstrom in the world, **Saltstraumen,** is only 33km from Bodø; pick up a tidal timetable from the tourist office to ensure you won't be disappointed (Mon.-Fri. 9-10 buses per day, Sat. 5 buses per day, Sun. 2 buses; 40kr). For those under 25, daily stand-by **flights** to northern Norway from Oslo cost only 800kr. From Bodø they run 400kr. By **train,** Bodø is 10 hours north of Trondheim (650kr, 50% student fare). Two **buses** per day run from Bodø north to Narvik (7hr., 305kr, 50% railpass discount). The **tourist office,** Sjøgata 21 (tel. 75 52 60 00; fax 75 52 21 77), about five blocks toward the center from the train station, doles out the all-encompassing *Bodø Guide,* rents bicycles (70k per 24hr.), and books private accommodations for a 20kr fee (15-200kr. Open June-Aug. Mon.-Fri. 9am-9pm, Sat. 10am-7pm, Sun. noon-3pm and 7-9pm; Sept.-May Mon.-Fri. 9am-4pm.) The **youth hostel,** Sjøgata 55 (tel. 75 52 11 22), is directly above the train station on the third floor. (Reception open 24hr. Sleeping bags allowed. 140kr, nonmembers 165kr. Sheets 35kr. Breakfast 45kr. Laundry 60kr.) Cheap Norwegian victuals await in **Lövold's Kafeteria,** Tollbugata 9 (closed Sun.).

NORWAY

Narvik

Undoubtedly, the most glorious aspects of Narvik are the approach and departure—from a distance, the city's metal buildings flicker beneath the awesome, looming mountains. In World War II, the city was the site of vicious early fighting and the Allies' first victory over the Nazis (May 28, 1940). Cemeteries east of the train station silently testify to the war's brutality. The **Nordland Red Cross War Museum,** on the main square, tells the story behind the gravestones. (Open early June to late Aug. Mon.-Sat. 10am-10pm, Sun. 11am-5pm; late Aug. to mid-Sept. and early March to early June Mon.-Fri. 10am-4pm. 25kr.) The daily tour at 1pm that leaves from the LKAB guardhouse on Havnegata offers an up-close and personal view of Narvik's industrial innards (20kr). In winter (mid-Dec. to April), Narvik becomes a **skiing** center; slopes run from above tree level to sea level. The Narvik Ski Center (tel. 76 94 16 05) operates the lifts and dispense info. Nordic nature in its untamed magnificence is yours on the **bus** north to Tromsø (3 per day, 5hr., 270kr; 50% off with Scanrail) or south to Bodø (2 per day, 7hr., 305kr), the **hydrofoil** to Svolvær (3½hr., 255kr; 50% off with Scanrail), or the **train** to Kiruna in the Swedish Lappland (2per day, 3hr., 90kr).

Answers to all your questions await at the **tourist office,** Kongensgate 66 (tel. 76 94 60 33; fax 76 94 74 05), uphill from the **bus station** and **train station.** The office also books private rooms. (Singles 150kr, doubles 250kr; 20-25kr fee. Open mid-June to mid-Aug. Mon.-Fri. 9am-7pm, Sat. 10am-6pm, and Sun. 2-7pm.) Turn left from the tourist office, and walk about 1.4km down Kongensgate to reach the **youth hostel (HI),** Havnegata 3 (tel. 76 94 25 98; fax 76 94 29 99), housed in a big yellow building. (Reception open 7:30am-11pm. Dorms 150kr. Singles 240kr. Doubles 360kr. Nonmembers add extra 25kr. Kitchen availible.)**Narvik Camping** (tel. 76 94 58 10) is 2km north of town along the main road (80kr per tent; 4-person hut 425kr; showers 5kr for 5min.; kitchen available). There is a **Mini 1000** grocery store on the main square (open Mon.-Fri. 9am-8pm, Sat. 10am-6pm).

Lofoten Islands

Made luscious by the Gulf Stream, the Lofoten Islands' jagged, green-gray mountains shelter fishing villages, farms, bird colonies, and happy sheep. The crystal clear water and mild climate make the Lofotens a magical place to spend a few days or weeks. Rugged hikers and mountaineers will enjoy the network of trails covering the archipelago, but much of the Lofoten's charm can be easily appreciated from a deck chair or cozy fireplace. As late as the 1950s, fisherfolk lived in the small *rorbuer,* yellow and red wooden shacks which cluster along the coast. Today, tourists book the *rorbuer* solid (75-125kr per person in a group of 4 or more). The indispensable brochure *Nordland 1998*—available at any tourist office from Bodø north—lists them, along with other accommodations, while the *Lofoten Info-Guide 1998,* available at tourist offices in the Lofotens, also furnishes information on ferries, buses, and sights.

Highway E10 binds the four largest of the Lofotens—Vågen, Vestvågøy, Flakstad, and Moskenes—which point toward the tiny outlying isles of craggy **Værøy** and flat, puffin-thronged **Røst.** Both outlying islands have HI **hostels** (on Røst, tel. 76 09 61 09, 95kr, nonmembers 100kr; on Værøy, tel. 76 09 53 52, 85kr, nonmembers 110kr). Frequent bus and ferry connections are available from Bodø and Narvik, the two best mainland springboards to the Lofotens. Bus service runs daily from Narvik to Svolvær (7hr., 316kr, 50% railpass a discount) and from Bodø, to Svolvær (10½hr., 371kr, 50% railpass discount). By **boat,** your best and cheapest bet is a car ferry from Bodø to Moskenes (4-5 per day, 4hr., 104kr), which stops four times per week at Røst (110kr) and Værøy (92kr). Hydrofoils skim to Svolvær from Bodø (daily except Sat., 218kr) and from Narvik (Tues.-Fri. and Sun., 255kr; 50% railpass discount). A final approach is the *Hurtigruten,* which connects Bodø with Stamsund (4½hr., 216kr) and Svolvær (6hr., 232kr) daily. **Bus** service between the four major islands is frequent, but can be expensive. Only an InterRail pass grants a 50% discount on *internal* routes on the Lofotens, but a Scanrail will get you a discount if your destination town has a rail connection. A student ID will get up to 50% off *any* route. Finally, many long routes in the Lofotens are broken into several segments with connecting buses; for the best deal always ask for a ticket to your final destination and not a connecting stop.

NORWAY

Moskenes and Flakstad Ferries to **Moskenes,** the southernmost of the larger Lofotens, dock at the town of the same name. The **tourist office** (tel. 76 09 15 99) in Moskenes, by the ferry landing, gives advice on rooms and sights. (Open June 1-18 Mon.-Fri. 10am-5pm, June 19-Aug. 13 daily 10am-7pm, Aug. 14-31 Mon.-Fri. 10am-5pm.) A local bus whisks incoming ferry passengers 5km south to **Å** (pronounced Oh), a tiny fishing village at the end of Highway E10. The **Å tourist office** is located at the end of the bus station parking lot (open daily 10am-5pm). Half of Å's buildings make up the **Norsk Fiskeværsmuseum,** an open-air museum documenting life in the old fishing days (open mid-June to mid-Aug. daily 10am-6pm; mid-Aug. to mid-June Mon.-Fri. 10am-3:30pm. Guided tours at 11:30am and 2pm. 55kr, students 30kr). The **HI youth hostel** (tel. 76 09 11 21; fax 76 09 12 82) bunks travelers in mid- to late-19th-century buildings (95kr, nonmembers 120kr; laundry 25kr; reservations essential; open May-Sept.). The hostel also rents *rorbuer,* which are affordable for groups of four or more (360-950kr). Follow the path into town from the tourist office, then turn right along the path to reach **Moskenes-Straumen Camping** (tel. 76 09 11 48) overlooking the sea (tent 50kr, 10kr per person, showers 5kr). **Camp** free on the shores of the snow-fed lake behind town (read: soggy ground); heading toward town on the E10, hop out before the tunnel, and follow the paths on your right for five to 10 minutes. The enticing aroma of freshly baked cinnamon rolls (7kr) may draw you to the wood-fired **bakery** in the center of town (open daily 7am-4pm).

Moving north, the next large island is **Flakstad,** centered on the hamlet of **Ramberg.** Flakstad has perhaps the best hiking trails on the islands; get maps at the **tourist office** (tel. 76 09 34 50), which also books doubles from 100kr. (Open June 16-30 Mon.-Fri. 10am-5pm, July- Aug. 15 daily 10am-7pm; Aug. 15-31 Mon.-Fri. 10am-5pm.)

Vestvågøy and Austvågøy The mountain-backed hamlet of **Stamsund** on **Vestvågøy,** the next island north, is also home to an **HI youth hostel** (tel. 76 08 93 34; fax 76 08 97 39) where travelers from all over the world come for a night and remain for weeks. The benevolent ruler of this island utopia, Roar Justad, provides guests with fishing gear (100kr deposit), rowboats (free), mopeds (80kr per day plus 0.50kr per km), and mountain bikes (75kr per day). More sedate types enjoy the TV/VCR and cooking on the wood-burning stoves. (75kr per night. Laundry 50kr. *Rorbuer* 400-600kr. Handicapped accessible. Open mid-Dec. to mid.-Oct.) A **tourist office** (tel. 76 08 97 92) is 1km down the main road (open mid-June to mid-Aug. Mon.-Sat. 6-9:30pm). Buses run daily from Å (88kr, 50% off with railpass) and Svolvær (75kr, 50% off with railpass) via Leknes. On the bus route between Leknes and Svolvær lies **Borg,** the site of the largest Viking building ever found. The reconstructed longhouse holds a Viking museum staffed by costumed Norse folk (open daily 10am-7pm; 70kr).

Svolvær, on the northernmost island of **Austvågøy,** is the bland hub of beautiful Lofoten. The **tourist office** (tel. 76 07 30 00), inside the large red building by the ferry dock, dishes up healthy servings of info (open Mon.-Fri. 9am-10pm, Sat. 10am-8pm, Sun. 11am-10pm). **Svolvær Sjøhuscamping** (tel./fax 76 07 03 36) offers rooms in a structure on stilts above the harbor near the center; take the third right from Torget on Vestfjordgata going north from the tourist office (reception open 24hr.; 120kr, double 300kr). A bit more distant and even more interesting is the friendly **Marinepollen Sjøhus** (tel. 76 07 18 33), north along the E10 for 15 minutes until *Jektveien* on the right. (100kr, double 300kr. Free use of rowboat and fishing gear. Kitchen. Fridge in every room.) Call, and the owners may pick you up. Shop for groceries at **Rimi** on the corner of Torggata and Storgata (open Mon.-Fri. 9am-8pm, Sat. 9am-6pm).

Tromsø

Norway's fastest growing city, Tromsø, population 58,000, makes many claims about its importance and uniqueness: "Gateway to the Arctic," "Paris of the North," "world's northernmost university city." After two winter months of perpetual darkness, it's necessary to feel good about *something.* Still, Tromsø is the last city of note for those trudging even farther north. The bizarre, some might even say hideous, modern **Arctic Cathedral** on the mainland has one of the largest stained glass windows in Europe as well as clean white lines designed to blend with ice and snow. (Open May daily 3-6pm; June to mid-Aug. daily 10am-8pm, Sun. 1-8pm; mid-Aug.to mid-Sept. 3-6pm. 10kr. Organ concerts Wed., Thurs., Fri. at 3pm. 10kr.) The **Tromsø Museum,** Lars Thøringsvei 10, features exhibits on the region's natural history, and ethnographic displays on Sami culture. (Open June-Aug. daily 9am-9pm; Sept.-May Mon.-Fri. 8:30am-3:30pm, Sat. noon-3pm, Sun. 11am-4pm. 20kr, students 10kr.) To reach the museum, take bus 21 or 27 to the south end of the island (15kr). The **Polar Museum,** Søndre Tollbugata 11b, residing in a red warehouse on the wharf, details the history of hunting, exploration, and research in the high Arctic with musk ox, polar bears, seals, and countless pelts. (Open late May-early Sept. daily 11am-8pm; mid-Sept. to mid-May 11am-3pm. 25kr.) For a magnificent view of the city in the midnight sun (roughly May 20-July 22), take the **cable car** to the top of Tromsdalstind (daily 10am-5pm; in summer, weather permitting, 1am; 50kr); reach the cable car station on bus 28, or by walking across the enormous bridge over to the mainland.

To sample the nightlife, wander down the west end of **Storgata** and its sidestreets. **Blå Rock Café,** Strandgata 14, features three floors of posters and rock paraphernalia. (0.5L-beer 35kr in summer. Large pizza 90kr, small 85kr. 20kr cover Fri. and Sat. nights. Open Mon.-Thurs. 11:30am-2am, Fri. and Sat. 11:30am-4am, Sun. 2pm-2am.) **Middags Kjelleren,** Strandgata 22, in a basement grotto on the corner of Strandskillet, has live rock or blues bands virtually every night. (40-50kr cover after 11pm. Open Mon.-Thurs. 3pm-2am, Fri.-Sat. 3pm-4am, Sun. 6pm-2am.)

Practical Information, Accommodations, and Food Three to four **buses** per day cruise south to Narvik (4½hr., 276kr), while two daily buses head to

Alta for 305kr (not including ferries, 41kr). Buses leave from the parking lot below Roald Amundsens *plass,* near the water. All these buses merit a 50% discount with a Scanrail pass. The northbound *Hurtigruten* leaves daily at 6:30pm; the southbound at 1:30am (to Honningsvåg 702kr, Bodø 758kr.) A standby **flight** from Oslo costs 800kr. The **tourist office,** Storgata 61/63 (tel. 77 61 00 00; fax 77 61 00 10), books rooms in private homes for a 25kr fee (singles from 170kr, doubles from 200kr), and will smother you with facts. From the bus station, walk up Kirkegata away from the water, and turn left on Storgata. (Open June to early Aug. Mon.-Fri. 8:30am-6pm, Sat.-Sun. 10am-5pm; mid-Aug. to May Mon.-Fri. 8:30am-4pm.)

The **Elverhøy Youth Hostel (HI),** Gitta Jønnsons vei 4 (tel. 77 68 53 19), is a large student dorm, whose rooms have kitchenettes; board bus 24 at Storgata and Franz Langes gate downtown. (Reception open daily 8-11am and 5-11pm. 100kr, nonmembers 125kr; 200kr deposit mandatory for keys. Open mid-June to mid-Aug.) To reach **Tromsdalen Camping** (tel. 08 33 80 37), walk across the river to Tromsdalen, 30 minutes from the town center, or spend 15kr and hop on bus 36. (Reception open 8am-11pm. 90kr plus 10kr per person. 2- to 4-person huts 250-400kr.) The unique and special dishes available at the arctic restaurant at **Vertshuset Skarven,** Strandtorget 1 (whale, seal, reindeer, and fresh arctic seafood), explain the priciness. (Beer 45kr. Appetizers from 50kr. Dinner from 115kr. Restaurant open daily 5-10:30pm; pub/café open daily noon-12:30am. Reservations a must.) Unique to Tromsø is the atmosphere and pancakes of **Paletten,** Storgata 51. Next to the open-air market, **Domus** sells traditional supermarket wares (open Mon.-Fri. 9am-8pm, Sat. 9am-6pm).

Finnmark

On most maps, Finnmark appears about as inviting as a walk-in freezer. The sun takes a permanent vacation from late November until late January, and only the exquisite colors of the *aurora borealis* (Northern Lights) illuminate the frigid countryside. But in summer the snow-capped peaks, vast stretches of coastal tundra, and inland forest bask under the midnight sun, and the landscape becomes an arctic wonderland (beware the mosquitoes that have countless fiestas on the unprotected skin of mesmerized tourists). The wilderness of **Finnsmarksvidda** that spreads east from Tromsø is Europe's largest, a highly popular hiking area spotted with tourist huts. Consult the DNT offices in Oslo or Bergen for maps, prices, and other info.

Buses run once or twice per day along the E6, the main highway around the top of Norway; spur lines branch south to Sweden and Finland. Both buses and the *Hurtigruten* are *very* expensive. Scanrailers get 50% off on *Nord-Norge Ekspressen* buses from Bodø to Kirkenes and reductions on some buses run by **FFR.** Some travelers find **hitchhiking** surprisingly successful, though traffic is light and distances are long. Thumbers bring a tent, a warm sleeping bag, and patience. If you're under 25, **flying** is the cheapest way to get to Finnmark. SAS offers 800kr standby *(Superhaik)* to Alta from any SAS destination south of Bodø. In summer, Widerøe Airlines will fly all ages between any two cities north of and including Tromsø for 400kr (make reservations); for those under 21, last-minute fares in Sweden (310 Swedish kr from Stockholm to Kiruna in Swedish Lapland) can be an even better option.

Alta and Hammerfest Slate-gray mountains, towering cliffs, and an icy green sea make the road from Tromsø north to **Alta,** Finnmark's largest town, a spectacular bus route. The town stretches along several kilometers of the main highway with two distinct centers. Arriving from the south, the first sign of approaching civilization is the **Alta Museum,** winner of "European Museum of the Year Award 1993," which displays Scandinavia's only prehistoric UNESCO World Heritage site: spectacular rock carvings 2500-6200 years old. A network of wooden boardwalks leads you to exposed boulders, on which red-painted figures hunt reindeer, boats navigate the fjords, and cows copulate. (Open in summer daily 8am-11pm; off season reduced hours. 40kr, students 35kr; in winter 35kr, students 30kr.) Two kilometers farther along E6 is the old center, Bossekap, which the **tourist office** (tel. 78 43 77 70) calls home, sharing a building with a **Domus** supermarket. (Open July to mid-Aug. Mon.-Fri. 9am-7pm, Sat. 9am-5pm, Sun. 1-6pm; June and late Aug. Mon.-Fri. 9am-5pm.) Ask about the daily four-hour tours to the nearby **Alta river canyon** (280kr; 5-person minimum), Europe's longest. The **bus station** awaits 2km farther on the E6. The **Frikirkens Elevheim (HI)** (tel. 78 43 44 09) mellows another 1km up the road; hang a left at the first traffic circle past the new center on E6, and follow the signs (reception open daily 8-11am and 5-11pm; 3 kitchens; 105kr, nonmembers 130kr). **Alta River Camping** (tel. 78 43 43 53) is 4km out of town on Route 94, accessible only by the twice-daily bus to Kautokeino or an hour-long hike. (Reception open daily 9am-11pm. 15kr per person, 40-50kr per tent. 4-bed huts 300-350kr. Open mid-June to mid-Aug.) Or try **Alta Strand Camping** (tel. 78 43 40 22) or **Wisløff Camping** (tel. 78 43 43 03). A city bus route (16kr) binds all of far-flung Alta, running along E6 from the Alta Museum to the **airport,** 3km east of the new center. One or two **buses** per day run to Tromsø (7-8hr., 298kr, not including 41kr ferries), Hammerfest (3hr., 152kr), Honnigsvåg (5hr., 215kr with ferry), Kautokeino (3hr., 146kr), and Karasjok (4hr., 259kr), all 50% off with Scanrail discount.

At **Hammerfest,** the world's northernmost town (only the tiny village of **Honningsvåg** is farther north), you can become a member of the Royal and Ancient Polar Bear Society (est. 1963; 125kr) against the backdrop of parading fishing trawlers in the harbor and grazing reindeer in the streets. The *Hurtigruten* stops here for 1½ hours. Daily **buses** head south to Alta and north to Honningsvåg (4hr., 169kr). An express **boat** plies the waters to Honningsvåg twice daily (260kr). Contemplate the midnight sun from **Salen,** a short, steep hike up the hill from the **tourist office** (tel. 78 41 21 85), on Storgata across from the Hammerfest Hotel (open Mon.-Fri. 9am-6pm, Sat.-Sun. 9am-5pm; mid-Aug. to May Mon.-Fri. 10am-3pm). Arriving from the bus station, walk into town and then follow the near lakeshore to reach the **youth hostel** (tel. 78 41 36 67; 100kr, nonmembers 125kr).

Nordkapp and Honningsvåg Looming above the Arctic Ocean from the island of Magerøy, the famed **Nordkapp** is much ado about less than you might have hoped. Not even continental Europe's northernmost point (a title held by Knivskjellodden, a peninsula to the west), Nordkapp is an expensive tourist mecca (ticket not including bus 175kr). Perched on and inside the rock is the **Nordkapp Complex,** with a bank, post office, telephones, cafeteria, and a gold-enameled Thai Museum commemorating King Chulalongkorn's visit in 1907. No joke. Around the complex is rough landscape, open ocean basking beneath the midnight sun (mid-May to July), and a cliff-side champagne bar. Be warned: the complex closes at 2am, and the only rooms are in Honningsvåg (last bus leaves at 1:10am).

Buses complete the sojourn to Nordkapp via **Honningsvåg,** 33km south (4 per day, round-trip 100kr). They leave from the parking lot by the main pier in town, passing by the ferry dock 2km east. The **tourist office** (tel. 78 47 25 99; fax 78 47 35 43) is next door to the bus station. (Open June-Aug. Mon.-Fri. 8:30am-7pm, Sat.-Sun. noon-6pm; Sept.-May Mon.-Fri. 8:30am-4pm.) The **Nordkapp Museum,** upstairs, chronicles the history of the region and has a giant pinwheel of fish skins (open Mon.-Sat. 9am-8pm, Sun. 1-8pm; 20kr, students 10kr). The 33-km trip to Nordkapp can be made by bus (4 per day, round-trip 100kr); some thumb it, but get the weather forecast first—Nordkapp is dullsville in the mist. The recently renovated **Nordkapp Youth Hostel and Camping (HI)** (tel. 78 47 33 77) is 8km up the road to Nordkapp (bus 17kr). The toilets are outside, but otherwise the facilities are fine. (110kr, nonmembers 135kr. Camping 20kr per tent plus 20kr per person. Open mid-May to Sept. Reserve ahead.) Due to the fragility of the tundra, it is illegal to **camp** outside of designated sites on the island. The **bus** to Honningsvåg from Alta (1-2 per day, 6hr., 200kr with ferry) or Hammerfest (1-2 per day, 4½hr., 230kr) is cheaper than the *Hurtigruten* (from Kirkenes 635kr, Tromsø 655kr, Hammerfest 255kr).

Poland (Polska)

US$1	**= 3.50zł (Polish złoty)**	**1zł =**	**US$0.29**
CDN$1	**= 2.53zł**	**1zł =**	**CDN$0.40**
UK£1	**= 5.57zł**	**1zł =**	**UK£0.18**
IR£1	**= 5.14zł**	**1zł =**	**IR£0.20**
AUS$1	**= 2.55zł**	**1zł =**	**AUS$0.39**
NZ$1	**= 2.22zł**	**1zł =**	**NZ$0.45**
SAR1	**= 0.75zł**	**1zł =**	**SAR1.34**

Country Code: 48 **International Dialing Prefix: 00**

From the amber-strewn shores of the Baltic in the north to the snow-capped peaks of the Tatra range in the south, Poland is shaking off the last remnants of Communism and reclaiming its heritage as one of the world's oldest democracies. After centuries of foreign intervention, occasional non-existence (notably from 1795 to 1918), and the devastation of World War II, a new, headstrong generation is emerging, determined to rebuild the country in its own image. Resilient, these Poles have drawn strength from the Catholic Church and a rich intellectual tradition.

The choice of Karol Wojtyła (John Paul II) as the first Polish pope in 1978 helped unify Polish Catholics and lent strength to the nascent Solidarity, the first independent worker's union in Eastern Europe, which was organized in 1980. The first and most gracious of the 1989 Eastern European shakedowns unfolded in Poland; after political imprisonments failed to conquer Solidarity's charismatic leader Lech Wałęsa, the Central Committee met with him and other Solidarity leaders for several weeks of round-table discussions. In return for Solidarity's pledge to end strikes, the government legalized the union, amended the constitution, and held free elections. Solidarity members swept into all but one of the contested seats in June, and Tadeusz Mazowiecki became Eastern Europe's first non-Communist premier in 40 years.

Today Poland, one of the largest and most populous of the newly liberated Eastern European nations, is gritting its teeth in a determined attempt to rejoin the modern world. In 1990, the Solidarity government opted to take the bitter dose of capitalism in one gulp. In an effort to attract investment, the government eliminated subsidies, froze wages, and devalued currency, throwing the antiquated economy into recession and producing the first unemployment in 45 years. Despite setbacks, however, Poland continues to move toward economic prosperity and political stability.

Even the pope sometimes kicks back with a copy of *Let's Go: Eastern Europe 1998* for the more detailed coverage of Poland therewithin.

GETTING THERE

Citizens of the U.S. and Ireland can visit Poland **visa-free** for up to 90 days; citizens of the U.K. can stay up to six months. Australians, Canadians, New Zealanders, and South Africans need **visas.** Single-entry visas (valid 90 days) are US$40 (students under 26 US$30), double-entry visas cost US$55 (students US$42), and 48-hour transit visas run US$20 (students US$15). If you need a visa, contact a Polish embassy (see **Government Information Offices,** p. 1). Processing takes 4 days (24hr. rush US$35).

LOT, British Airways, and Delta offer **flights** to Warsaw and Kraków from London, New York, Chicago, Toronto, and other cities. **Trains** and **buses** connect to all the neighboring countries, but **Eurail** is not valid in Poland. ALMATUR offers ISIC holders 25% off international fares for the Polish portion of the trip, sells **InterRail** passes, and, for those under 26, provides **Wasteels** tickets and **Eurotrain** passes that give 40% off international train travel. Discount tickets for those under 26 are also sold at major train stations and ORBIS offices. Thefts are a major problem on international overnight trains. **Ferries** run from Sweden and Denmark to Świnoujście and Gdańsk.

GETTING AROUND

PKP trains zip to most towns at bargain prices. In station *Odjazdy* (departures) are posted in yellow and *przyjazdy* (arrivals) are in white. InterCity and *Ekspresowy* (express) trains are listed in red and "IC" or "Ex." *Pośpieszny* (direct, in red), are almost as fast. *Osobowy* (in black), the slowest, are 35% cheaper. All *ekspresowy* and some *pośpieszny* need reservations; if you see a boxed R on the schedule, ask the clerk for a *miejscówka* ("myay-SOOV-ka"). Buy your ticket aboard the train for a surcharge, but find the *konduktor* before he or she finds you or risk a fine. Tickets are only valid on the day for which they are issued.

PKS buses are cheapest and fastest for short trips. As with trains, red means fast and black means slow. Purchase advance tickets at the bus station. In the countryside, PKS markers (like yellow Mercedes-Benz symbols) indicate bus stops, but drivers will often halt wherever you flag them down. Though legal, **hitching** is becoming increasingly dangerous for foreigners. *The Hitchhike Book,* sold by PTTK, includes an insurance policy, an ID card, and vouchers that qualify drivers for compensation.

ESSENTIALS

ORBIS, the Polish state travel bureau, sells international and domestic train tickets and international bus, plane, and ferry tickets. **ALMATUR,** the Polish student travel organization, sells ISIC cards and helps find university dorm rooms in summer. Both provide maps and brochures, as do **PTTK** and **IT** bureaus in every town. While private **tourist agencies**'s prices are competitive, you should watch out for scams.

The Polish currency, **złoty** (plural *złote*), is fully convertible. For cash, private **kantor** offices (except those at the airport and train stations) offer better exchange rates than banks. **Bank PKO S.A.** accepts traveler's checks and gives MasterCard and Visa cash advances all over Poland. In 1995 the National Bank issued a new currency; only the new currency is valid. Learn the difference between old and new (posters at the airport and train stations show both), and never accept old currency.

Holidays include: January 1; Epiphany (Jan. 6); Ash Wednesday (March 6); Holy Week and Catholic Easter (April 9-13); Labor Day (May 1); Constitution Day (May 3); Ascension Day (May 21); Corpus Christi (June 11); Assumption Day (Aug. 15); All Saints' Day (Nov. 1); Independence Day (Nov. 11); and December 25-26.

Communication **Mail** is becoming increasingly efficient, though still plagued by theft. Airmail usually takes seven to 10 days to the U.S. For *Poste Restante,* put a "1" after the city name to ensure it goes to the main post office. Older pay **phones** use tokens (*żetony;* "A" for local calls and "C" for intercity calls); newer phones use **phone cards.** These phones have card slots and instructions in English. Both tokens and phone cards are available at any *poczta* (post office) as well as some kiosks. To reach an **AT&T Direct** operator, dial 010 480 01 11 (from outside Warsaw dial 0 and wait for a tone first); **MCI WorldPhone,** 010 480 02 22; **Sprint Access,** 010 480 01 15; **Canada Direct,** 010 480 01 18; and **BT Direct,** 044 00 99 48. To make a **collect call,** write the name of the city or country and the number plus *"Rozmowa 'R'"* on a slip of paper, hand it to a post office clerk, and be patient.

Many Poles speak at least a little English, German, or French. Polish spelling is phonetic and has some letters which don't belong to the Latin alphabet: *"ł"* sounds like a "w," *"ą"* is a nasal "o"; *"ę"* is a nasal "eh"; *"ó"* and *"u"* are equivalent to a short "oo"; and *"ż"* and *"rz"* are both like the "s" in pleasure. A dash above a consonant softens it. The language also has consonantal clusters: *"sz"* is "sh," *"cz"* is "ch," *"ch"* and *"h"* are equivalent to each other. When addressing a man, use the formal *"Pan,"* with a woman, use *"Pani."* The following chart lists important words and phrases in Polish:

Yes/No	*Tak/Nie*	tak/nyeh
Hello	*Cześć*	tcheshch
Please/You're welcome	*Proszę*	PROH-sheh
Thank you	*Dziękuję*	jeng-KOO-yeh
Where is...?	*Gdzie jest...?*	g-jeh yehst
Excuse me	*Przepraszam*	Soho-PRAH-sham
Do you speak English?	*Cozy mow Pan(i) po Ewangelisty?*	tcheh MOO-vee PAHN (-ee) poh an-GHEL-skoo
I don't understand	*Nie rozumiem*	nyeh roh-ZOO-myem
How much does this cost?	*Ile to kosztuje?*	EE-leh toh kosh-TOO-yeh
I'd like a...	*Chciał(a) bym...*	HTSHAH-w(ah) bim
Check, please.	*Proszę rachunek*	PROH-sheh rah-HOON-ehk
Help!	*Na pomoc!*	nah POH-motz

Accommodations and Camping Grandmotherly **private room** owners smother travelers at train stations or outside tourist offices. Private rooms are usually safe, clean, and convenient, but sometimes far from city centers. Expect to pay about US$10 per person. **PTSM** is the national hostel organization. **HI youth hostels** *(schronisko młodzieżowe)* run from basic to divine; they're everywhere and average US$3 per night (less for "juniors" under 18 or 26, more for nonmembers). Hot water is standard. **University dorms** transform into spartan but cheap housing in July and August. Ask at ALMATUR; the Warsaw office can arrange stays in all major cities. **PTTK** runs a number of hotels called **Dom Turysty,** where you can stay in multi-bed rooms for US$2-5, as well as budget singles and doubles. Many towns have a **Biuro Zakwaterowań,** which arranges stays in private homes. Rooms come in three categories based on location and hot-water availability; category 1 is the best.

Campsites average US$2 per person, US$4 with a car. **Bungalows** are often available; a bed costs about US$5. *Polska Mapa Campingów* lists all campsites. ALMATUR also runs a number of sites in summer; ask for a list at one of their offices.

Food and Drink Monks, merchants, invaders, and dynastic unions have all flavored Polish cuisine—a blend of hearty dishes drawing from French, Italian, and Jewish traditions. And while Polish food is often loaded with cholesterol, it is less starchy than Czech cuisine, and less fiery than that of Hungary or Bulgaria.

A Polish meal always starts with a soup. From a typical menu, you should be able to choose between *barszcz* (beet broth), *chłodnik* (a cold beet soup with buttermilk and hard-boiled eggs), *kapuśniak* (sauerkraut soup), *krupnik* (barley soup), and *żurek* (barley-flour soup loaded with eggs and sausage). *Bigos* (sauerkraut cooked with beef and mushrooms) and *flaczki* (tripe) can be eaten either as soup or entree.

More filling main courses include *gołąbki* (cabbage rolls stuffed with meat and rice), *kotlet schabowy* (pork chops), *kopytka* (potato dumplings topped with buttered bread crumbs), *naleśniki* (cream-topped pancakes filled with cottage cheese or jam), and *pierogi* (dumplings with various fillings—meat, potato, blueberry...).

Poland is bathed in beer, vodka, and spiced liquor. *Żywiec* is the favorite strong brew, and *EB* is its excellent, gentler brother. *Wódka* ranges from wheat to potato: *Wyborowa, Żytnia,* and *Polonez* usually decorate private bars, though the so-called *Kosher* is rumored to be top-notch. The herbal *Żubrówka* vodka comes with a blade of grass from the region where the bison roam. *Miód* and *krupnik*—two kinds of mead—were best loved by the gentry, and most idle grandmas make *nalewka na porzeczce* (black currant vodka).

Warsaw (Warszawa)

Warsaw's motto, *contemnire procellas* (to defy the storms), has been put to the test too often during this capital city's history. According to legend, Warsaw was created when the fisherman Wars netted a mermaid who pledged to protect his new town in return for her release. Warsaw has needed all the protection it can get; centuries of invaders have taken a shot at this bastion of Polish pride. WWII saw two-thirds of the population killed and 83% of the city destroyed, but the city has been revitalized. Warsaw today is an international business center, and tourists are drawn to the rebuilt city. The mermaid appears to have kept her promise.

ORIENTATION AND PRACTICAL INFORMATION

Warsaw, the country's principal air and rail hub, spreads out in east-central Poland, about 150km from the Belarusian border. The **Śródmieście** (city center) and most points of interest lie on the west bank of the **Wisła River,** which bisects the city. To the right of the **Warszawa Centralna** train station, the intersection of **ul. Marszałkowska** and **Aleje Jerozolimskie** forms the center of the modern downtown and serves as a major bus and tram stop. Beyond, Al. Jerozolimskie extends east to **rondo Charles de Gaulle.** To the left, **ul. Nowy Świat** runs north and then becomes **ul. Krakowskie Przedmieście,** which leads to the Old Town. A right at rondo Charles de Gaulle puts you on **Al. Ujazdowskie,** which leads down embassy row to the Łazienki Palace. A good **map** of the whole city with bus, tram, and metro routes is essential.

Tourist Offices: Warszawskie Centrum Informacji Turystycznej (WCIT), pl. Zamkowy 1B (tel. 635 18 81; fax 831 04 64), at the entrance to the Old Town. The friendly, busy staff runs an information line and provides maps, guidebooks, and listings of hotels and restaurants. The office also changes currency and helps with hotel reservations. Pick up the *Warsaw Insider* (4zł), an excellent publication jammed packed with info, listings, and reviews. Open Mon.-Fri. 9am-6pm, Sat. 10am-6pm, Sun. 11am-6pm. **ORBIS,** ul. Bracka 16 (tel. 827 45 16 or 827 76 03), with an entrance on Al. Jerozolimskie near Nowy Świat, sells train, plane, and bus tickets. Open Mon.-Fri. 8am-7pm, Sat. 9am-2pm.

Budget Travel: ALMATUR, ul. Kopernika 23 (tel. 826 35 12 or 826 26 39; fax 826 35 07), off ul. Nowy Świat. ISICs, as well as bus, ferry, and plane tickets, and vouchers to ALMATUR hotels in major Polish cities (US$15, students US$12). Often busy, so be patient. Open Mon.-Fri. 9am-6pm, Sat. 10am-2pm. **Room 3,** ul. Krakowskie Przedmieście 24 (tel. 826 99 80; fax 826 47 57), is ALMATUR's train ticket depart-

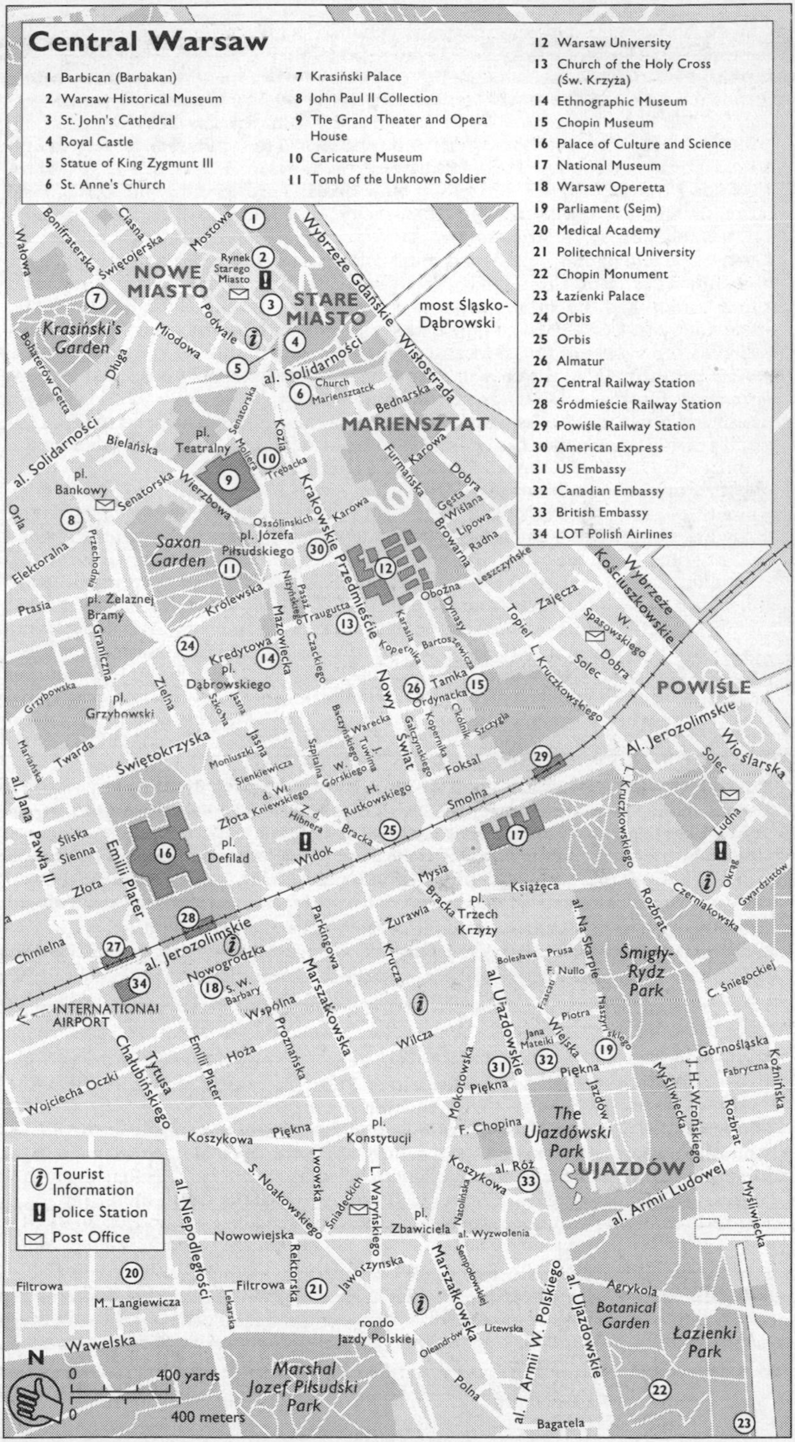
Central Warsaw
1 Barbican (Barbakan)
2 Warsaw Historical Museum
3 St. John's Cathedral
4 Royal Castle
5 Statue of King Zygmunt III
6 St. Anne's Church
7 Krasiński Palace
8 John Paul II Collection
9 The Grand Theater and Opera House
10 Caricature Museum
11 Tomb of the Unknown Soldier
12 Warsaw University
13 Church of the Holy Cross (Św. Krzyża)
14 Ethnographic Museum
15 Chopin Museum
16 Palace of Culture and Science
17 National Museum
18 Warsaw Operetta
19 Parliament (Sejm)
20 Medical Academy
21 Politechnical University
22 Chopin Monument
23 Łazienki Palace
24 Orbis
25 Orbis
26 Almatur
27 Central Railway Station
28 Śródmieście Railway Station
29 Powiśle Railway Station
30 American Express
31 US Embassy
32 Canadian Embassy
33 British Embassy
34 LOT Polish Airlines
NOWE MIASTO
STARE MIASTO
MARIENSZTAT
POWIŚLE
UJAZDÓW
Krasiński's Garden
Saxon Garden
Śmigły-Rydz Park
The Ujazdówski Park
Botanical Garden
Łazienki Park
Marshal Jozef Piłsudski Park
most Śląsko-Dąbrowski
INTERNATIONAL AIRPORT
Tourist Information
Police Station
Post Office
N
0
400 yards
0
400 meters

POLAND

ment. Go through the main university entrance to the first building on the right. InterRail and Eurotrain tickets sold here. Open Mon.-Fri. 10am-5:30pm.

Embassies: Australia, ul. Estońska 3/5 (tel. 617 60 81). Open Mon.-Thurs. 8:30am-1pm and 2-5pm. **Belarus,** ul. Ateńska 67 (tel. 617 39 54). **Canada,** ul. Matejki 1/5 (tel. 629 80 51). Open Mon.-Fri. 9am-1pm and 2-4pm. **Russia,** ul. Belwederska 49, bldg. C (tel. 621 34 53). Open Wed. and Fri. 8am-1pm. **South Africa,** ul. Koszykowa 54 (tel. 625 62 28). **Ukraine,** al. Ujazdowskie 13 (tel. 629 32 01). **U.K.,** Al. Róż 1 (tel. 628 10 01). Citizens of **New Zealand** are served at the **U.K.** consulate, ul. Emilii Plater 28 (tel. 625 30 30). **U.S.,** Al. Ujazdowskie 29/31 (tel. 628 30 41). Open Mon.-Fri. 8:30am-5pm.

Currency Exchange: Hotels, banks, tourist offices, and private *kantors* (which have slightly better rates) throughout the city exchange cash. The counters at the main train station and the airport departures area are open 24hr. **Bank PKO S.A.,** pl. Bankowy 2 (tel. 637 10 61), in the blue skyscraper, cashes AmEx and Visa traveler's checks for a 1% commission and gives MasterCard and Visa cash advances. Branches throughout the city; all open Mon.-Fri. 8am-6pm. **ATMs** abound.

American Express: ul. Krakowskie Przedmieście 11 (tel. 635 20 02). Exchanges cash and traveler's checks with no commission. Also holds mail (send to box 159) and provides emergency cash advances for card members. The **postal code** for the AmEx office is 00-950. Open Mon.-Fri. 9am-6pm.

Flights: Port Lotniczy Warszawa-Okęcie, ul. Żwirki i Wigury (tel. 650 30 00), commonly referred to as Terminal 1. Take bus 175 to the center (after 11pm, bus 611); buy bus tickets at the Ruch kiosk in the departure hall or at the *kantor* outside (1.40zł plus 1.40zł for every large suitcase or backpack). **Airport-City Bus** (5.60zł, with ISIC 2zł; luggage free) is a faster way to the center and back (every 20-30min. 5:30am-11pm). Buy tickets from the driver. **LOT,** Al. Jerozolimskie 65/79 (tel. 952 or 953), in Hotel Marriott, has regular flights to London and New York. **British Airways** has an office at ul. Krucza 49 (tel. 628 94 31), off Al. Jerozolimskie.

Trains: Warszawa Centralna, ul. Jerozolimskie 54 (tel. 25 50 00), in the center of town, is the most convenient stop. Most employees speak only Polish; write down where and when you want to go, and ask *"Który peron?"* to find your platform. To: Berlin (7-8hr., 97zł), Budapest (10hr., 170zł), Kiev (22-24hr., 88zł), Minsk (12hr., 50zł), Moscow (27-30hr., 160zł), Prague (12-14hr., 94zł), and Polish cities.

POLAND

Buses: PKS Warszawa Zachodnia, Al. Jerozolimskie 144 (tel. 23 64 94 or 23 64 95), sends buses north and west of the city. Buses from **PKS Warszawa Stadion,** on the other side of the river, head to the east and south. Both stations are easily reached by taking the commuter train from the Warszawa Śródmiescie station (next to Warszawa Centralna; 1.60zł). **Polski Express,** Al. Jana Pawła II (tel. 630 29 67), offers fast and comfortable bus service to Gdańsk (2 per day, 6hr.), Kraków (3 per day, 6hr.), Lublin (6 per day, 4hr.), and Szczecin (9½hr.).

Public Transportation: Bus and **tram** lines are marked on some city maps. Day trams and buses (including express lines) cost 1.40zł, night buses 3zł; large baggage costs 1.40zł per piece. Buy tickets at a Ruch kiosk or street vendor, and punch the end marked by the arrow in the machines on board. Warsaw's **metro** only connects the southern border of town with the center (1zł).

Taxis: Stands are marked by blue-and-white signs. For relatively cheap 24hr. taxi service, call 919 or 96 22. Taxi usually start at 3.60zł plus 1.20zł per km. At night, the rates are about 50% higher. Cabs frequently overcharge.

Hitchhiking: Thumbers usually pick up a hitchhiker's guide available at the **PTTK office,** Podwale 23 (tel. 635 27 25), in the Old Town. Open Mon.-Fri. 9am-3pm.

Luggage Storage: At the main train station, below the main hall. Lockers come in 3 sizes: "A" (5zł per day), "B" (7zł per day), and "C" (12zł per day). Open 24hr.

Bookstores: American Bookstore, ul. Krakowskie Przedmieście 45 (tel. 26 01 61). Lots of fiction and reference books, as well as periodicals. Open in summer Mon.-Sat. 11am-7pm, Sun. 11am-4pm; off-season Mon.-Sat. 10am-6pm, Sun. 11am-4pm.

Gay and Lesbian Organizations: tel. 628 52 22. The **Lambda Center Information Line** runs two weekly phone sessions: Wed. 6-9pm for women, Fri. 3-9pm for men. Both sessions are in English or Polish. They'll tell you what's up and where.

Laundromat: ul. Karmelicka 17 (tel. 31 73 17; call to reserve). Take bus 180 north from ul. Marszałkowska towards Żoliborz and get off at ul. Anielewicza. Bring your own detergent. Wash and dry 13zł. Open Mon.-Fri. 9am-5pm, Sat. 9am-1pm.

Crisis Lines: Women's hotline: tel. 635 47 91; staffed Mon.-Fri. 4-8pm. **AIDS:** tel. 628 03 36; staffed Mon.-Fri. 10am-10pm; or call 958. **Mental health:** tel. 29 58 13.
24-Hour Pharmacy: Apteka Grabowski (tel. 25 69 84), at the central train station.
Medical Assistance: Medical Information Line, ul. Smolna 34/22 (tel. 827 89 62). Directs callers to private doctors and dentists. Open Mon.-Fri. 8am-8pm, Sat. 8am-3pm. **24hr. service** and **ambulance,** ul. Hoża 56 (tel. 999 or 628 24 24).
Emergencies: Fire: tel. 998. **Ambulance:** tel. 999.
Police: tel. 997.
Internet Access: Cyberia Internet Cafe, ul. Krakowskie Przedmieście 4/6 (http://www.cyberia.com.pl). Telnet and Netscape 9zł per hr. Open daily 9am-midnight.
Post Office: ul. Świętokrzyska 31/33 (tel. 826 60 01). Take your ticket and await your turn. For stamps and letters, press "D." For packages, press "F." For *Poste Restante,* press "C" and head to *kasa* 12 or 13. Open 24hr. **Postal Code:** 00-001.
Telephones: at the post office. Tokens and **phone cards** available. **Telephone Code:** 022 for 6-digit numbers; 02 for 7-digit numbers.

ACCOMMODATIONS AND CAMPING

Prices rise and rooms become scarce in July and August; call ahead. Differences in hotel prices often do not reflect differences in quality. For help finding private rooms, check in with **Syrena,** ul. Krucza 17 (tel. 628 75 40), off Al. Jerozolimskie (open Mon.-Sat. 9am-7pm, Sun. 9am-5pm). Singles start at 45zł and doubles at 65zł. WCIT (see **Practical Information,** above) can help find rooms.

Schronisko Młodzieżowe (HI), ul. Smolna 30, top floor (tel. 827 89 52), across from the National Museum. You can make the short walk from the train station, or take any tram headed east 3 stops to Nowy Świat. Price and location can't be beat. Regulations are enforced. Kitchen and baggage room. Only two showers. 3-day max. stay. Lockout 10am-4pm. Curfew 11pm. 12zł, nonmembers 15zł. Sheets 2.50zł.

Schronisko Młodzieżowe (HI), ul. Karolkowa 53a (tel. 632 88 29). Take tram 22 or 24 west from Al. Jerozolimskie or the train station; get off at "Okopowa." Go left on al. Solidarności, then right onto ul. Karolkowa. Excellently maintained and not crowded. Kitchen. Great showers. Lockout 10am-5pm. Curfew 11pm. Dorms 16zł, nonmembers 18zł. Doubles 40zł. Triples 72zł. Sheets 3.50zł.

Schronisko Młodzieżowe, ul. Międzyparkowa 4/6 (tel. 31 17 66), close to the river, between two parks. Take tram 2, 6, or 18 northbound from ul. Marszałkowska to "K.K.S. Polonia." The hostel is across the street as you continue down the road. The least formal of the hostels in town. 14.50zł. Sheets 3zł. Open April 15-Oct. 15.

Hotel Metalowiec, ul. Długa 29 (tel. 831 40 20; fax 635 31 38), 3 blocks away from the Old Town near the "Arsenał" stop. Very affordable and in a great location. Comfortable rooms. Singles 30zł. Doubles 55zł. Quads 81zł. Private bath 10zł.

Dom Literata, ul. Krakowskie Przedmieście 87/89 (tel. 635 04 04), at the entrance to the Old Town, over a café. Lacks a sign or real reception desk, but worth hunting for. Spacious rooms and sparkling shared bathrooms. 60zł per person.

Hotel Aldona, ul. Wybrzeże Kościuszkowskie (tel. 628 58 53). From the train station, take any tram east to Most Poniatowskiego, then go north along Wisłostrada, which becomes Wybrzeże Kościuszkowskie. On a ship floating in the Wisła. A great budget option, unless the thought of sleeping on a boat makes you queasy. 4 communal bathrooms. Singles 40zł. Doubles (bunk beds) 50zł.

Hotel Belfer, Wybrzeże Kościuszkowskie 31/33 (tel. 625 05 71; fax 625 26 00). Same directions as for Hotel Aldona. Overlooks a park, river, highway, and electric plant. Singles 64zł, with bath 94zł. Doubles 84zł, with bath 126zł.

Hotel Garnizonowy, ul. Mazowiecka 10 (tel. 682 20 69). Over a block from ul. Krakowskie Przedmieście off ul. Świętokrzyska. One of the most affordable downtown hotels: nice for the price. Singles 70zł. Doubles 100zł. Triples 120zł.

Camping "123", ul. Bitwy Warszawskiej 1920r. 15/17 (tel. 23 37 48), down the road from the rotary by the main bus station. Take bus 127 to "Zachodnia" and cross the street. Close to downtown, shady, not too crowded, and near a popular swimming pool. 8.56zł per person, 6-8zł per tent. Open year-round.

POLAND

FOOD

Food stands line ul. Marszałkowska. You can blow your budget on roast duck or grilled salmon at any of Warsaw's finest bunched around **Rynek Starego Miasta,** but proletarian cafeterias are much cheaper and more colorful. There is a **24-hour grocery** at the central train station; you can also do late-night shopping at **Delikatesy,** ul. Nowy Świat 53. Fish, poultry, and meat is often sold by weight in restaurants.

Restaurants

Bar Uniwersytecki, ul. Krakowskie Przedmieście 16/18, next to the university. under a yellow awning. As Polish as it gets. Rice with apples 1.20zł. Soups 1.30zł. Pork chops 3.50zł. English menu. Open Mon.-Fri. 7am-8pm, Sat.-Sun. 9am-5pm.

Bar Pod Barbakanem, ul. Mostowa 27/29, entrance on ul. Freta. A popular cafeteria-style eatery between Stare and Nowe Miasto. A full meal runs only 6zł. English menu. Open Mon.-Fri. 8am-6pm, Sat.-Sun. 9am-5pm.

Bar Familijny, ul. Nowy Świat 39. More traditional (fat) Polish (plentiful) food for the lighter-than-air wallet, in a great location. Open Mon.-Fri. 7am-8pm, Sat.-Sun. 9am-5pm.

Zapiecek, ul. Piwna 34/36, at the corner of ul. Zapiecek in the Old Town. German ambiance and Polish cuisine. Veal 10zł. Outdoor dining. Open daily 11am-11pm.

Restauracja Boruta, ul. Freta 38, on Rynek Nowego Miasta. Dine outdoors or in. Roasted duck 7zł. Vegetarian menu. Open daily 11am until the last guest leaves.

Pod Samsonem, ul. Freta 3/5. Cheap eats on the way from Stare Miasto to Nowe, opposite Maria Skłodowska-Curie's museum. Polish-Jewish cuisine to make you big and strong like Samson. *Cymes* salad 3zł. Open daily 10am-10pm.

Restauracja-Kawiarnia "Chmielna," at the corner of ul. Chmielna and ul. Zgoda. Real bargains. Seasonal salad 2.70zł. *Penne* with mushroom sauce 4zł. Pizza 3zł. Outdoor dining on a lively, pedestrianized street. Open Mon.-Sat. 11am-10pm.

Cafés

Kawiarnia Bazyliszek, Rynek Starego Miasta 3/9. A relaxing outdoor café amid the splendor of the Old Town. Tortes 3.50zł. Coffee 2.50zł. Open daily noon-midnight.

Gwiazdeczka, ul. Piwna 40/42, in the Old Town. The menu is full of snacks and coffees (3-6zł); beer and cocktails are also tempting. Open daily 9am-10pm.

Lody W. Hoduń, ul. Nowomiejska 9, in the Old Town. The best selection of ice cream in the city. Large scoops 0.70zł. Open daily 10am-7pm.

SIGHTS

Razed beyond recognition during World War II, Warsaw was rebuilt from rubble by defiant and proud survivors. The city requires quite a bit of time to fully explore, since a few important sights are quite distant from the downtown area.

Stare Miasto, Nowe Miasto, and Trakt Królewski Warsaw's postwar reconstruction shows its finest face in the narrow, cobbled streets and colorful facades of the **Stare Miasto** (Old Town), at the end of ul. Krakowskie Przedmieście. At the right side of the entrance to the Old Town stands the impressive **Zamek Królewski** (Royal Castle), burned down in 1939 but masterfully restored in the 1970s. Many residents of Warsaw risked their lives hiding the castle's priceless artworks here during Nazi plundering, and the castle has since become a symbol of Polish patriotism. Past the Royal Castle, turn onto ul. Świętojańska to reach the 14th-century **Katedra Św. Jana** (Cathedral of St. John), the oldest church in Warsaw (open daylight hours). From here, Ul. Świętojańska takes you straight to the wonderfully restored Renaissance and Baroque houses of **Rynek Starego Miasta** (Old Town Square). Although most of the houses surrounding the *rynek* were razed to their foundations during the Warsaw Uprising, a few managed to survive WWII; the **house at #31** dates back to the 14th century. The square now oozes with cafés, kitschy art, and tourists. Many of the buildings on the north side of the square comprise the **Muzeum Historyczne Miasta Warszawy** (the Historical Museum of the City of Warsaw), with the entrance at #28. (Open Tues. and Thurs. noon-7pm, Wed. and Fri. 10am-3:30pm, Sat.-Sun. 10:30am-4:30pm. 3zł, students 1.50zł, Sun. free.)

Ul. Krzywe Koło leads from the square to **Barbakan** (Barbican), a rare example of 16th-century Polish fortifications, where street performers now sing folk music to entertain the crowds. Near the Barbican is a statue of the **Warszawska Syrenka** (mermaid). Through the Barbican Gate, ul. Freta marks the edge of the **Nowe Miasto** (New Town), which, in spite of its name, is actually the second-oldest district in the city. At ul. Freta 16, the great physicist and chemist **Maria Skłodowska-Curie,** winner of two Nobel prizes, was born in 1867; the house is now a museum chronicling her life (open Tues.-Sat. 10am-4:30pm, Sun. 10am-2:30pm; 2zł, students 1zł).

Lined with palaces and churches as well as hordes of tourists, the 4km **Trakt Królewski** (Royal Route) is the city's most attractive thoroughfare. The route begins on **Plac Zamkowy** (Castle Square) in the Old Town and continues along **ul. Krakowskie Przedmieście.** Fryderyk Chopin gave his first public concert in the **Pałac Radziwiłłów** (a.k.a. **Pałac Namiestnikowski**) at #46/48, which is now the Polish White House. The Chopin theme continues at **Kościół Wizytek** (Church of the Visitation Nuns), one block down the street, where he was an organist. Much of his composing was done in the **Czapski-Krasiński Palace,** which now houses the Academy of Fine Arts and the **Salonik Chopinów** (The Chopins' Drawing Room; open Mon.-Fri. 10am-2pm; 1zł, students 0.50zł). If you really can't get enough of the mop-topped composer, waltz over to the **Muzeum Fryderyka Chopina** in Zamek Ostrogskich, ul. Okólnik 1; to get there, walk a few blocks down the street from the Academy, turn left onto ul. Ordynacka, and follow it to ul. Okólnik (open Mon.-Wed. and Fri.-Sat. 10am-2pm, Thurs. noon-6pm; 3zł, students 2zł).

Back on the Royal Route, the **Mikołaj Kopernik Monument,** a permanent seat for the image of the famous astronomer, marks the end of ul. Krakowskie Przedmieście. The Royal Route, however, continues along **ulica Nowy Świat** (New World St.), a glorious street named for a working-class settlement of the 17th century. The street ends at the **Botanical Gardens** (open daily 9am-4pm; 3zł, students 1zł), on the left side of Al. Ujazdowskie, and the **Park Łazienkowski,** summer residence of the last Polish king. Al. Ujazdowskie then becomes ul. Belwederska, which leads to Łazienki, setting for the striking Neoclassical **Pałac Łazienkowski,** also called **Pałac na Wodzie** (Palace on the Water). The building harbors galleries of 17th- and 18th-century art (open Tues.-Sun. 9:30am-4pm barring rain; 3.50zł, students 2zł; English tours 20zł).

POLAND

Commercial District, the Ghetto, and Wilanów Warsaw's commercial district lies southwest of the Old Town along ul. Marszałkowska. Here, at Al. Jerozolimskie 3, is the **Muzeum Narodowe** (National Museum), Poland's largest museum. The galleries illustrate the evolution of Polish art over the centuries, and also showcase medieval art and the works of German, Italian, and Dutch painters. (Open May-Sept. Tues.-Wed. and Fri.-Sun. 10am-4pm, Thurs. 11am-6pm; Oct.-April Tues.-Wed. and Fri.-Sun. 10am-4pm, Thurs. 11am-6pm. 5zł, students 2.50zł, Thurs. free.) Also in this part of town, the 70-story "Stalinist Gothic" **Pałac Kultury i Nauki** (Palace of Culture and Science), ul. Marszałkowska, is a fitting monument to Stalin—larger than life, omnipresent, and tacky. Locals say the view from the top is exceptional, in large part because it doesn't include the palace (open daily 9am-6pm; 7.50zł). Below, **plac Defilad** (Parade Square) is the largest square in all of Europe, even bigger than Moscow's Red Square.

The modern Muranów (literally "walled") neighborhood of Warsaw holds few vestiges of what was once a community numbering nearly 400,000 Jews. At **Umschlagplatz,** a monument marks the spot where Nazis gathered 300,000 Jews for transport to death camps. A small section of the **original ghetto wall** still stands between two apartment buildings in the courtyard at ul. Sienna 55, just west of al. Jana Pawła II. The beautifully reconstructed **Nożyk Synagogue,** ul. Twarda 6, lies just north of the Pałac Kultury i Nauki. On ul. Zamenhofa, look for the **Pomnik Bohaterów Ghetta** (Monument of the Ghetto Heroes). The **Cmentarz Żydowski** (Jewish Cemetery), in the western corner of the district, is a forest-covered treasure of gravestone art (open Mon.-Thurs. 9am-3pm, Fri. 9am-1pm).

After his coronation in 1677, King Jan III Sobieski bought the village of Milanowo, had its existing mansion rebuilt into a Baroque-style palace, and named the new residence Villa Nova (in Polish *Wilanów*). The grounds were opened to visitors in 1805. Since then the **Palac Wilanowski** has functioned both as a museum and as a residence for the highest-ranking guests of the Polish state. (Palace open Wed.-Mon. 9:30am-2:30pm. 3zł, students 1zł. Gardens open Wed.-Mon. 9:30am-2:30pm. 1.50zł, students 0.70zł.) **Muzeum Plakatu** (Poster Museum), next to the palace, displays 50,000 posters from the last 100 years (open Tues.-Sun. 10am-4pm; 2zł, students 1zł). To get here, take bus 180 or express bus B from ul. Marszałkowska to the end.

ENTERTAINMENT

Don't be fooled by people who tell you Warsaw doesn't have much nightlife outside of the cafés of the Old Town and ul. Nowy Świat. Concerts fill the city year-round, and students energize several excellent clubs and bars on weekends.

Performances

Classical concerts fill the Gallery of Sculptures in **Stara Pomarańczarnia** near Pałac Łazienkowski on Sundays in June and July. Inquire about concerts at **Warszawskie Towarzystwo Muzyczne** (Warsaw Music Society), ul. Morskie Oko 2 (tel. 49 68 56; tickets available Mon.-Fri. 9am-3pm and before concerts). **Pomnik Chopina** (Chopin Monument), nearby in Park Łazienkowski, hosts free Sunday performances by classical pianists (May-Oct. noon and 4pm). **Teatr Wielki,** pl. Teatralny 1 (tel. 826 32 87), Warsaw's main opera and ballet hall, offers performances almost daily. **Filharmonia Narodowa,** ul. Jasna 5 (tel. 826 72 81), gives regular concerts but is closed in summer. Classical music is also played in Zamek Królewski's **Sala Koncertowa,** pl. Zamkowy 4 (tel. 657 21 70; tickets sold Tues.-Sun. 10am-3pm). The **Mozart festival** is held every summer to rave reviews. Jazz, live-rock, and blues fans have quite a few options as well, especially in summer. **Sala Kongresowa** (tel. 620 49 80), in the Palace of Culture and Science, hosts excellent jazz and rock concerts.

POLAND

Pubs and Nightclubs

Warsaw's pubs are popular with both trendy locals and visitors. Drinks are expensive, but many pubs compensate by offering live music. The nightclub and dance scene shifts frequently; posters around town are the best source for the latest info. Gay life is a bit underground here; the gay and lesbian hotline (tel. 628 52 22; Fri. 6-9pm) has the latest info. Magazines *Inaczej* and *Filo* list gay establishments.

The Irish Pub, ul. Miodowa 3. Irish in the sense that the name, decor, and beer are Irish; the clientele, however, is local. Guinness 11.50zł for 0.5L. 23zł 1L. Free folk and country music concerts nightly at 7:30pm. Open daily 9am-11pm.

Morgan's, ul. Okólnik 1 (entrance on ul. Tamka), under the Chopin Museum. Irish in the sense that you may find that you're the only one not speaking with an Irish accent (unless, of course, you are). Guinness 10zł for 0.4L. Open daily 3pm-late.

Harenda Pub, ul. Krakowskie Przedmieście 4/6, at Hotel Harenda. Decorated like a British social club, complete with pictures of the owners doing chummy things. Friendly crowd; don't go to learn Polish. 0.5L *Żywiec* 6.50zł. Open daily 8am-3am.

Park, Al. Niepodległości 196. This international disco is one of the more popular student hangouts in Warsaw. Open Tues.-Thurs. 8pm-2am; cover 6zł, students 3zł. Fri.-Sat. 9pm-3am; cover 12zł, students 6zł. Sun. 10pm-2am; cover 6zł, students 3zł.

Club Giovanni, ul. Krakowskie Przedmieście 24, at Warsaw University to the right and down the steps as you enter the main gate. Draws the low-key student crowd. Beers 5zł. Veggie pizza 12zł. Open Mon.-Fri. from 10am, Sat.-Sun. from 1pm.

Jazz Club Akwarium, ul. Emilii Plater 49. An older crowd enjoys the best live jazz in town. Schedule posted. Open daily 11am-11pm or later, Fri.-Sat. until 3am.

Stara Dziekanka, ul. Krakowskie Przedmieście 56. This outdoor club has a permanent awning that protects revelers from the elements. A great place to meet both locals and foreigners. Cover Sun.-Thurs. 5zł, Fri.-Sat. 10zł. Open daily 7pm-2am.

Między nami, ul. Bracka 20, left off al. Jerozolimskie coming from the Pałac Kultury. Look for the outside seating area. Mixed during the day, mostly gay in the evening. Open Mon.-Thurs. 10am-10pm, Fri.-Sat. 10am-midnight, Sun. 4-10pm.

Koźla, ul. Koźla 10/12. One block left from Rynek Nowego Miasta, when walking away from the Old Town. No sign outside, but it's the only club on Koźla. Ring the buzzer to be let in. A narrow staircase leads down to a small space that manages to combine the qualities of a beerhouse, lounge, and cruise bar. Open daily 5pm-2am.

Szczecin

Settled in the 8th century, Szczecin (SHCHEH-cheen) has a tightly packed downtown area as its core, where magnificent historic structures provide the backdrop for the daily life of a busy shipping center. A relic of the Prussian settlement, the Baroque **Brama Portowa** (Port Gate) marks the downtown area. It features a Latin inscription commemorating Frederich Wilhelm I, King of Prussia, and a panoramic view of 18th-century Szczecin. The 870-year-old **Kościół św. Piotra i Pawla** (Church of St. Peter and Paul) has photo collages inside, including shots of the pope's visit. On ul. Korsarzy, the giant, newly restored **Zamek Książąt Pomerańskich** (Castle of Pomeranian Princes) now houses an opera and theater group (open daily 10am-6pm). Check at the castle for upcoming events. While you're at it, climb the tall *wieża* (tower; 2zł) for an amazing view. The 15th-century **ratusz** (town hall) now houses part of the city's **Muzeum Narodowe** (National Museum); this branch illustrates Szczecin's history. The rest of the museum, chronicling Pomeranian art from the medieval to the modern, is located in the Baroque **Pomeranian Parliament,** ul. Staromłyńska 27/28, north of Castle Hill. (All three branches open Tues. and Thurs. 10am-5pm, Wed. and Fri. 9am-3:30pm, Sat.-Sun. 10am-4pm. One ticket gets you into all three galleries.)

From the station at the end of ul. 3-go Maja, **trains** leave for Poznań (3hr., 13.80zł) and Berlin (2½hr., 70.20zł). The **bus station** is at pl. Tobrucki, northeast of the train station. **CIT (Centrum Informacji Turystycznej),** ul. Wyszyńskiego 26 (tel. (091) 34 04 40), is a great source for maps (4.50zł), brochures, and room-finding tips (open Mon.-Fri. 9am-5pm, Sat. 10am-2pm). To get to the **youth hostel,** ul. Monte Cassino 19a (tel. (091) 22 47 61; fax 22 54 01), take tram 1 from the train station or the center of town to ul. Felczarka. Hike through downtown Szczecin along ul. Wojska Polskiego, take a right on ul. Zygmunta Felczarka, and then a left onto ul. Monte Cassino. (Lockout 10am-5pm. Curfew 11pm. Dorms 6.90zł, nonmembers 14.60zł; singles 14.70zł, nonmembers 18.60zł.) In a scenic downtown location resides **Hotel Piast,** pl. Zwycięstwa 3 (tel. (091) 33 66 22; singles 46-54.05zł, doubles 71-92zł). The **supermarket Extra** is centrally located at ul. Niepodległości 27 (open 24hr.).

POLAND

Świnoujście

Visitors flock to the shady parks of Świnoujście's Baltic shoreline and its grassy dunes and relaxed beach combing. The **beach** and the **promenade**, along ul. Żeromskiego, are sights in their own right. Kiosks, selling delicious *gofry* (Belgium waffles) and *kiełbasa* by day transform into places for good times and cheap beer by night (2.50zł for 0.5L). In the main part of town, be sure to stop at **Bar "Neptune,"** ul. Bema 1, where you can feast on cheap Polish delectables and meet the charismatic and multilingual Mr. Tomasz Strybel—*Let's Go's* pick for one of the coolest guys in Central Europe. College-age revelers move onto the nearby **nightclubs.** For a real culture shock check out **Manhattan** nightclub, ul. Zeromskiego 1, with its New York City decor (cover 6zł; open nightly 9pm-6pm).

Świnoujście occupies parts of two islands that are linked by a ferry across the Świna River. The train and bus stations and the international ferry terminal are located on the east bank. **Trains** travel to Szczecin (2hr.,11.60zl) and Warsaw (8½hr., 38zl), while **Polferries,** ul. Dworciwa 1 (tel. (97) 321 30 06), sends ferries to Copenhagen (10:30am and 10:30pm, 9hr., 159zl) and Malmö, Sweden (11am and 11pm, 10hr., 159zl). To get to the main part of town, hop on the free **car ferry** (5am-11pm, every 20min.; hourly at night) across the street from the stations. **PTTK,** ul. Paderewskiego 24 (tel. (97) 321 26 13), sells maps (3-4zł; open Mon.-Tues. and Thurs.-Fri. 7am-3pm, Wed. 9am-5pm). Two kilometers west of town on Wojska Polskiego, there is a pedestrian and bicycles only **border crossing** to Seebad Ahlbeck, Germany. **Hotel Wisus,** ul. Żeromskiego 17 (tel. (97) 321 58 50), has comfortable rooms near the beach (25-30zł per person). **Dom Rybaka** (Fisherman's Inn), ul. Wybrzeże Władysława IV 22 (tel. (97) 321 29 43), is a budget option near the car ferry (singles 32zł-50zł, doubles 56zł-97zł). A short hike from the town center and beach, the **Youth Hostel (HI),** ul. Gdyńska 26 (tel. 327 06 13; reception open 6-10am and 5-10pm), has free luggage storage and clean rooms (14-17zł per person, members 8.50-11zł). At **Camping Relax,** ul. Słowackiego 1 (tel. (97) 321 39 12, for reservations 321 47 00), tents and sites cost 9zł, or relax in cozy cabins (triples 60-125zł, quads 100-165zł).

Gdańsk

A port city strategically located on the Baltic coast and the mouth of the Wisła River, Gdańsk (gh-DA-neesk) was annexed by Prussia in 1793 and established as a free city by the Treaty of Versailles in 1919. There was little time to enjoy this freedom, though, as the city witnessed the first deaths of WWII just two decades later. Yet despite centuries of conflict, the city has flourished architecturally and culturally, and the birth of Solidarity here under the leadership of Lech Wałęsa, an electrician in the shipyards, was critical in restoring pride to all of Poland. Beautiful cathedrals tower over ornately decorated houses and works of art along the streets, and post-war reconstruction efforts have restored all but a few landmarks to their former majesty.

ORIENTATION AND PRACTICAL INFORMATION

Gdańsk dips its toes in the Baltic Sea, serving as Poland's principal port. From the Gdańsk-Główny **train station,** the Old Town center lies a few blocks south, bordered on the west by **Wały Jagiellońskie** and on the east by **Stara Motława,** one of the Wisła's tributaries.

Tourist Offices: IT Gdańsk, uł. Dluga 45 (tel. 31 93 27; fax 31 30 08), has info about sites and accommodations. Open daily 9am-6pm. **ORBIS,** ul. Heweliusza 22 (tel. 31 44 25), sells ferry, train, and plane tickets, and doubles as an **American Express** branch office. Open Mon.-Fri. 9am-5pm, Sat. 10am-2pm.

Budget Travel: ALMATUR, Długi Targ 11, 2nd fl. (tel. 31 29 31; fax 31 78 18), in the Old Town center. The office sells ISICs and has youth and student hostel information. Open Mon.-Fri. 9am-5pm, Sat. 10am-2pm.

Currency Exchange: At hotels, banks, *kantors,* and certain post offices throughout the city. 24hr. *kantor* at the train station. **Bank Gdański,** Wały Jagiellońskie 14/16 (tel. 37 92 22), cashes traveler's checks for 1% commission. AmEx, Eurocard, MasterCard, and Visa advances without commission. Another branch located at the train station. Open Mon.-Fri. 8am-6pm.

Flights: Planes arrive at **Rebiechowo airport** (tel. 31 40 26), 22km south of the city. Bus B runs to the train station.

Trains: Gdańsk-Główny station (tel. 31 11 12). To: Warsaw (4hr., 23zł), Kraków (33zł), Prague (15hr., 120zł), St. Petersburg (36hr., 250zł), and Berlin (7hr., 85zł). **Commuter trains** run every 6-12min. to Gdynia (40min., 2.90zł) and Sopot (15min., 2.10zł). Punch your ticket at one of the *kasownik* machines before boarding. Commuter train schedule posted separately from main one.

Buses: The station (tel. 32 15 32) is behind the train station through the underground passageway. To Toruń (4hr., 17zł) and Malbork (1hr., 4.70złŶ

Ferries: Take the commuter rail to the Nowy Port terminal. To Oxelösund, near Stockholm (17hr., 170.20zł). Book through **Polferries Travel Office** (tel. 43 18 87; fax 43 65 74) or the **ORBIS** travel office (see above).

Public Transportation: Gdańsk has an extensive bus and tram system. 1.32zł for 30min. 2.64zł at night. Pay for large baggage as you would for yourself.

Taxis: Radio taxi: tel. 91 95. **Hallo Taxi:** tel. 91 97. **Super Hallo Taxi:** tel. 91 91.

Luggage Storage: At the train station. 0.50zł plus 1% of baggage value. Open 24hr.
English Bookstore: English Books Unlimited, ul. Podmłyńska 10 (tel. 31 33 73). Look for the black and gold sign. Open Mon.-Fri. 10am-6pm, Sat. 10am-3pm.
Pharmacy: At the train station. Open 24hr.
Medical Assistance: Ambulance service, ul. Nowe Ogrody 1/7 (tel. 41 10 00). Emergency doctors available at al. Zwycięstwa 49 (tel. 32 39 29 or 32 39 24) and ul. Pilotów 21 (tel. 47 82 51 or 56 69 95), in Gdańsk Zaspa. These 24hr. facilities treat foreigners. 25zl per visit. For general info on health emergencies, call 32 39 44.
Emergencies: Fire: tel. 998. **Ambulance:** tel. 999. **AIDS:** 958.
Police: tel. 997.
Post Office: ul. Długa 22/25 (tel. 38 91 39). **Fax** bureau. *Poste Restante* two doors down. Open Mon.-Fri. 8am-8pm, Sat. 9am-1pm. **Postal Code:** 80-800.
Telephones: Inside and outside the post office. Open daily 7am-9pm. **Telephone Code:** 058.

ACCOMMODATIONS AND FOOD

Gdańsk and the resort town of Sopot up the coast are home to Poland's most popular beaches, and Gdańsk is growing in popularity among international tourists. Reserve rooms well in advance. **Gdańsk Tourist (Biuro Usług Turystycznych),** ul. Heweliusza 8 (tel. 31 26 34; fax 31 63 01), across from the train station, arranges stays in private rooms (singles about 30zł, doubles 50zł; open Mon.-Sat. 9am-5pm). **ALMATUR,** Długi Targ 11 (tel. 31 29 31), directs travelers to student dorms in July and August (25zł þēŗ þēŗśōń).

Schronisko Młodzieżowe (HI), ul. Wałowa 21 (tel. 31 23 13). Cross the street in front of the train station, go up ul. Heweliusza, and turn left at ul. Łagiewniki. Most convenient of the hostels. Reception open daily July-Aug. 8am-7pm. Lockout 10am-5pm. Curfew 10pm. 12-16zł, students 10-14zł. Sheets 2zł. Luggage storage 1zł.
Schronisko Młodzieżowe (HI), ul. Grunwaldzka 244 (tel. 411 660). Take tram 6 to the end of the line or 12 north from in front of the train station to where the tracks form a jug-handle (30min.). Cross the tracks and follow the path to ul. Grunwaldzka. Immaculate and efficiently run. Reception open daily 5pm-9pm. Lockout 10am-5pm. Curfew 10pm. 12-17zł per bed. Sheets 2.50zł. Luggage storage 1zł.
Hotel Zaułek, ul. Ogarna 107/108 (tel. 31 41 69). A good bet if hostels are full or you want more privacy. The hotel is a bit noisy, but well-located and clean, with comfortable beds. Singles 40zł. Doubles 55zł. Triples 60zł. Quads 70zł.

For fresh food, try the **Hala Targowa market** on ul. Pańska, in the shadows of St. Catherine's Church just off of Podwale Staromiejskie (open Mon.-Fri. 9am-6pm, first and last Sat. of the month 9am-3pm). **Bar "Neptun,"** ul. Długa 33/34, serves hearty, homestyle meat dishes alongside vegetarian entrees in a cafeteria setting (meals 4zł; open Mon.-Fri. 7am-6pm, Sat. 9am-5pm). **Pizzeria Napoli,** ul. Długa 62/63, lives up to its "Best in Town" sign, with 30 varieties of tasty pizza (6-20złŶ ǎńð spaghetti (12-17złŶ and its prime people-watching location (open daily 11am-10pm). **Royal,** ul. Długa 40/42, is a wonderful pastry shop that also serves coffee and drinks (fried apple pastry 1zł; open Mon.-Fri. 10am-9pm, Sat. 11am-9pm, Sun. noon-6pm).

SIGHTS AND ENTERTAINMENT

Gdańsk was one of the first Polish cities to undergo an exhaustive postwar facelift. The handsome market square, **Długi Targ,** forms the physical and social center of the Old Town, where the original 16th-century facade of the **Dwór Artusa** looks out onto the **Fontanna Neptuna** (Neptune Fountain). Artists, musicians, and vendors now fill the square. Next to the fountain, the 14th-century **ratusz** (town hall) houses the **Muzeum Historii Gdańska** (Gdańsk Historical Museum); don't miss the fantastic Red Chamber with a ceiling covered with allegorical paintings by Baroque masters (open Tues.-Thurs. 10am-4pm, Sun. 11am-4pm; 4zł, students 2zł).

One block north of Długi Targ is Gdańsk's grandest house of worship, the 14th-century **Kościół Najświętszej Marii Panny** (St. Mary's). Almost completely rebuilt after

WWII, the church reigns as Poland's largest brick cathedral; trudge the 405 steps up the steeple (open May to mid-Oct. daily 9am-5:30pm; 2zł). **Ul. Mariacka,** behind the church, is perhaps Gdańsk's most beautiful street. If you follow this tree-shaded lane and pass through the **Mariacka Gate,** the river will appear in front of you. From here, head left along ul. Dugie Pobrzeże to reach the **Gothic Harbor Crane,** which set the masts on medieval ships.

On Plac Obrońców Poczty Polskiej, the **Old Post Office** was a rallying point for Polish resistance to the German invasion, and has since become a symbol of the city. Patriotism also runs high at the **Gdańsk Shipyard** and at the **monument to the 1970 uprising,** pl. Solidarności, just north of the center at the end of ul. Wały Piastowskie. Take a ferry to the island of **Westerplatte** to visit the site of the first shots of WWII; boats (tel. 31 49 26) leave from outside the Green Gate at the end of Długi Targ (March 20-Nov. 15 9 per day, 1hr., round-trip 18zł, students 11.50zł).

Along the left bank of the Stara Motława, a handful of pubs offer good beer and company after sunset. The turreted mansion at ul. Wały Jagiellońskie 1 is home to the student club **Żak,** your best bet on any weekend night. It has a movie theater (4-5zł), a pub downstairs (open daily 2pm-2am), and a fashionably downtrodden café upstairs (open daily 2pm-2am). For billiards and jazz (or at least a jazzy atmosphere), head to the **Cotton Club** on ul. Złotników 25/29 (no cover; open daily 4pm-late). **Bar Kubicki,** ul. Wartka 5, on the Motława off the north end of Długie Pobrzeże, has good music and beer (open daily noon-late). Follow the signs from near the Golden Gate on ul. Długa to **Irish Pub "Piwnica,"** ul. Podgarbary. The brick and wood setting of this cellar pub is perfect for a bowl of Irish stew (9zł) followed by a glass of "snake mix" (Guinness and cider, 6zł; open daily 1pm-midnight).

■ Near Gdańsk

Malbork Castle, in the unassuming town of the same name, became the focal point of the state established by the Teutonic Knights in the early 14th century. The castle withstood several sieges by the Prussians during this period, and for the next 300 years served as one of the major arsenals and strongholds in the Kingdom of Poland. After sustaining heavy damage during WWII, the castle is currently being restored. (Castle open May-Sept. Tues.-Sun. 8:30am-5pm; Oct.-April 9am-2:30pm. Admission with 2½hr. guided tour in Polish 9.50zł, students 6zł. English-speaking tour guide 78zł extra.) Malbork is 40 minutes from Gdańsk by **train** (25 per day, 7zł) and an hour away by **bus** (7 per day, 4.20zł). With your back to Malbork's train station, head right on ul. Dworcowa, then go left at the fork (direction "Elbląg" on the sign) up and around the corner to a traffic circle. Nearby is the **tourist office,** ul. Sienkiewicza 15 (tel. (055) 72 26 14; open Mon.-Fri. 10am-4:30pm, Sat. 10am-2pm). A **youth hostel** is at ul. Żeromskiego 45 (tel. (055) 72 25 11); buy a bus ticket at a train station kiosk, and ride bus 6, 7, or 8 one stop or bus 1 or 9 two stops to Wielbark (reception open daily 8am-10am and 5-9pm; 11zł). **Café Zamkowa,** next to the castle entrance, prepares a regal feast (entrees 12-20zł; open daily 7am-midnight).

Little **Frombork** is closely associated with the astronomer Mikołaj Kopernik (Copernicus), who lived and worked here from 1510 until his death in 1543. Follow the signs from the bus stop; once you cross the wooden bridge, the *kasa* on the left sells tickets to **Muzeum Kopernika,** the **cathedral,** and the **wieża** (tower). The museum houses copies of his revolutionary book, *De Revolutionibus Orbium Coelestium.* (Open May-Sept. Tues.-Sun. 10am-5:30pm; Oct.-April Tues.-Sun. 9am-3:30pm. 1.20zł, students 0.70zł) The 17th-century organ in the **cathedral** next door has a seven-second echo (opens Tues.-Sat. 9:30am-5pm; 1.80zł, students 0.90zł). A climb up the tower provides a phenomenal view of the cathedral, the town, and the Wisła lagoon (open Mon. 9:30am-5pm, Tues.-Sat. 9:30am-7:30pm; 2zł, students 1.20zł). Frombork is best reached by **bus** from Gdańsk (5 per day, 2hr., 6.80zł). The main **tourist office,** ul. Elbląska 2 (tel./fax (055) 73 54), sits in the *rynek,* at the end of the path from the bus stop on ul. Dworcowa (open daily 9am-7pm). To reach the **Youth Hostel Copernicus,** ul. Elbląska 11 (tel. (055) 74 53), follow the blue and white signs from the bus stop (8zł per bed, over 26 10zł; camping 4zł). **Dom Wyciec-**

zkowy **PTTK,** ul. Krasickiego 2 (tel. (055) 72 52), offers dorms (12zł), singles (18-25.60zł), doubles (40zł), and a **restaurant** (open daily 7am-9pm).

Just 15 minutes north of Gdańsk by commuter train (1.80zł), **Sopot** features miles of white beaches, the longest pier on the Baltic (512m), a casino, and a growing number of cafés, pubs, and discos. The most popular and extensive sands spread along the end of ul. Monte Cassino. **ORBIS,** ul. Monte Cassino 49 (tel. (058) 51 41 42), sells train, plane, and ferry tickets, as well as tickets to the **Opera Leśna,** which hosts a summer rock and pop music festival (ORBIS open Mon.-Fri. 10am-6pm, Sat. 10am-2pm). The **IT tourist office,** ul. Dworcowa 4 (tel. (058) 51 26 17), sells maps and helps find rooms (open Mon.-Fri. 8:30am-6pm, Sat.-Sun. 9am-2pm). **Pub FM,** ul. Monte Cassino 36, offers beer, food, and good company (open daily 12:30pm-2am), while new discos and clubs like **Non-Stop** and **Fantom** rage by the pier.

Toruń

Toruń extols itself as the birthplace and childhood home of Mikołaj Kopernik, a.k.a. Copernicus, who argued that the earth revolves around the sun. The **Stare Miasto** (Old Town), commanding the right bank of the Wisła River, was constructed by the Teutonic Knights in the 13th century. Copernicus's birthplace, **Dom Kopernika,** ul. Kopernika 15/17, has been meticulously restored (open Tues.-Sun. 10am-4pm; 3zł, students 2zł). The **ratusz** (town hall), Rynek Staromiejski 1, in the center of the tourist district, houses the **Muzeum Okręgowe** (Regional Museum), with a famous 16th-century portrait of Copernicus and works by modern Polish artists. For an additional 3zł (students 2zł), you can climb the 13th-century tower to survey the city (museum open Tues.-Sun. 10am-6pm; 3zł, students 2zł). **Kamienica Pod Gwiazdą** (House Under the Star), Rynek Staromiejski 35, features a finely modeled facade with floral and fruit festoons (open Tues.-Sun. 10am-4pm; 3zł, students 1zł).

A city-wide burghers' revolt in 1454 lead to the destruction of the **Teutonic Knights' Castle,** but the ruins on ul. Przedzamcze are still impressive. The 50 ft. **Leaning Tower,** Pod Krzywą Wieżą 17, built in 1271 by a Teutonic knight as punishment for falling in love with a peasant girl, now deviates 5 ft. from the center at its top. Among the tall Gothic churches that dot the skyline, the **Cathedral of St. John the Baptist and St. John the Evangelist** is the most impressive. Built in the 13th through 15th centuries, the church mixes Gothic, Baroque, and Rococo elements, and houses Poland's second-largest bell, cast in 1500, in its tower. At the end of a long day, stroll along **Bulwar Filadelfijski,** named for Toruń's sister city, Philadelphia, where fishermen and couples line the stone steps to the river.

The Toruń Główny **train station,** across the Wisła River from the city center, serves Warsaw (3hr., 20.40zł), Poznań (2hr., 15.60zł), Szczecin (5hr., 23.10zł), and Gdańsk (2½hr., 18.75zł). The **IT tourist office,** ul. Piekary 37/39 (tel. (056) 62 10 93), offers helpful advice in English. Take city bus 22 or 27 (0.95zł; punch both ends; baggage requires its own ticket) to plac Rapackiego, the first stop across the river, and head through the little park area. (Open Mon. and Sat. 9am-4pm, Tues.-Fri. 9am-6pm, Sun. 9am-1pm; Sept.-April closed Sun.) To reach **Dom Wycieczkowy,** ul. Legionów 24 (tel. (056) 238 55), take bus 10 outside the Old Town gate away from the river to the third stop (singles 34zł, doubles 42zł, triples 57zł). For large beds and rooms, stay at the **Hotel Polonia,** pl. Teatralny 5 (tel. (056) 230 28), opposite the municipal theater (singles 33zł, with bath 50zł; doubles 42zł). **Campground "Tramp,"** ul. Kujawska 14 (tel. (056) 241 87), is across from the train station (tent sites 5zł, tent rental 5-7zł; 3-person cabins 30zł, 4-person bungalows 35zł).

Toruń's centuries-old calling card, sometimes covered with chocolate and even shaped like old Copernicus himself, is *pierniki* (gingerbread), sold at **Serdelek,** ul. Szeroka 19 (open daily 8am-7pm), and other grocery stores throughout the city. **Bar Mleczny,** ul. Różana 1, serves up primarily vegetarian traditional Polish dishes. *Naleśniki,* the house specialty, come with a multitude of fillings. Try them with blueberries and cream (*z jagodami i śmietaną,* 2.80zł; open Mon.-Fri. 9am-7pm, Sat. 9am-4pm). **Pizzeria Muzyczna "Vir,"** ul. Browarna 1, may have the best pizza in town for under 10zł (open daily 11am-midnight).

Poznań

The provincial feel of Poznan (POSE-nine) belies the city's cosmopolitan offerings: the annual Trade Fair lures hundreds of businesspeople, international musicians contribute to the city's lively music scene, and tourists are seduced with culinary and architectural marvels. Downtown, in the **Stary Rynek,** opulent 15th-century merchant homes surround the multi-colored **ratusz** (town hall). Considered the finest secular monument of the Renaissance north of the Alps, the town hall now houses the **Muzeum Historii Poznania.** (Open Mon.-Tues. and Thurs.-Fri. 10am-4pm, Wed. 11am-6pm, and Sun. 10am-3pm. 1zł, students 0.60zł, Fri. free.) Behind the town hall, on the northeast corner of the *rynek,* starts **ul. Żydowska** (Jewish Street), the center of the pre-war Jewish district. On the opposite side of the square, the **Kościół Farny Marii Magdaleny** (Parish Church), resplendent with frescoes and pink marble, blesses the end of ul. Świętosławska and offers organ concerts (Sat. 12:15pm). In the *rynek* itself, the **Museum of Historic Musical Instruments,** Stary Rynek 45/47, stars Chopin's piano and instruments from Polynesia and Africa. (Open Tues. and Sat. 11am-5pm, Wed. and Fri. 10am-4pm, Sun. 10am-3pm. 1zł, students 0.60zł.)

The main **train station,** in the Old Town's southwest corner, serves Warsaw (3½hr., 29.40zł), Szczecin (3hr., 18.75zł), Kraków (6hr., 24.60zł), and Berlin (3hr., 93.40zł). The **bus station** is just 500m down the street. If you're not up for the 20-minute walk to the city center from the train station, take any tram heading down Św. Marcin (to the right) from the end of ul. Dworcowa, and get off at the corner of ul. Św. Marcin and al. Marcinkowskiego. The Glob-Tour **tourist office** (tel./fax (0618) 66 06 67), in the train station, offers maps, tourist info in English, and currency exchange (open 24hr.). **Centrum Informacji Turystycznej (IT),** Stary Ryenk 59 (tel. (0618) 852 61 56), sells maps (5zł) and provides info on budget accommodations (open Mon.-Sat. 9am-5pm). The **youth hostel (HI),** ul. Berwińskiego 2/3 (tel. (0618) 66 36 80), has clean rooms; from the train station, turn left on ul. Głogowska, walk about two blocks, and turn right. (Reception open daily 5-10:30pm. Lockout 10am-5pm. Curfew 11pm. 10zł, nonmembers 13.50zł.) **Wojewódzki Ośrodek Metodyczny,** ul. Niepodległości 34 (tel. (0618) 53 22 51), has spacious rooms on a tree-shaded street just a short walk from ul. Św Marcin and the Old Town (17zł, students 10zł).

For traditional Polish food at unbeatable prices, try **Bar Mleczny Pod Kuchcikiem,** ul. Św. Marcin 37 (open Mon.-Fri. 8am-7pm, Sat. 8am-4pm, Sun. 10am-4pm), while **Cara Mia,** Stary Rynek 51, can satisfy both your Polish and Italian cravings (open daily noon-11pm). Pick up groceries at **Prospero,** ul. Wielka 18 (open 24hr.). Aptly named, **The Dubliner,** ul. Św. Marcin 80/82, with an entrance on al. Niepodległości, is a true Irish Pub (pint o' Guinness 9zł; open daily 11am-1am).

Kraków

Once tucked away behind the Iron Curtain, Kraków, recently chosen as a cultural capital of Europe, is now a trendy, international city. Although the city suffered little damage during World War II, the specter of destruction is never far removed: the notorious Nowa Huta steelworks in Kraków's eastern suburb are a grim reminder of the Stalinist era, and the Auschwitz-Birkenau death camp lies only 70km to the west. Yet it is also perhaps precisely this combination of vitality and darkness that gives Kraków its uniquely dynamic atmosphere.

ORIENTATION AND PRACTICAL INFORMATION

The city fans outward in roughly concentric circles from the **Rynek Główny** (Main Market Square), at the heart of **Stare Miasto** (Old Town). The green belt of the **Planty** gardens rings Stare Miasto, and the **Wisła River** skims the southwest corner of **Wzgórze Wawelskie** (Wawel Hill). The **bus** and **train stations** are adjacent to each other, 10 minutes northeast of the *rynek.* From the stations, head toward Hotel Europejski; the underpass leads diagonally across the street to the Planty. Across the gardens, follow **ul. Szpitalna** to the cathedral, then turn right to get to the *rynek.*

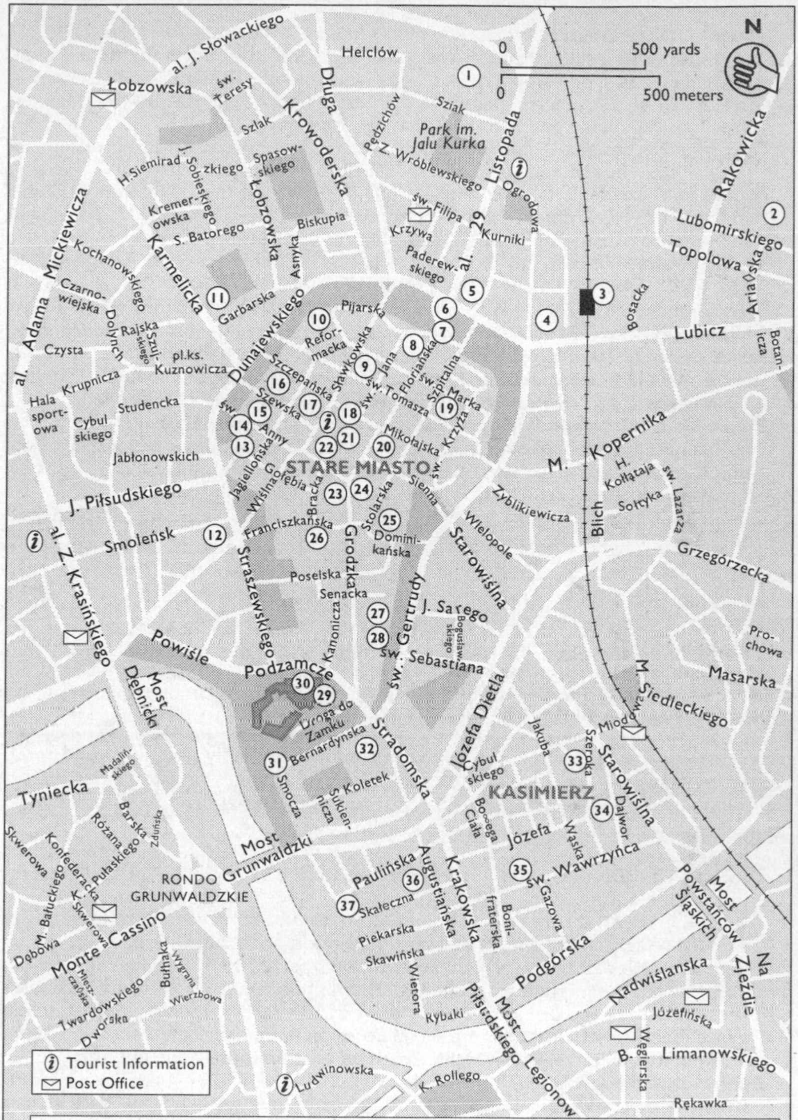

Central Kraków

Akademia Ekonomiczna, **2**
Almatur Office, **24**
Barbican, **6**
Bernardine Church, **32**
Bus Station, **4**
Carmelite Church, **11**
Cartoon Gallery, **9**
City Historical Museum, **17**
Collegium Maius, **14**
Corpus Christi Church, **35**
Czartoryski Art Museum, **8**
Dominican Church, **25**
Dragon Statue, **31**
Filharmonia, **12**
Franciscan Church, **26**
Grunwald Memorial, **5**
Jewish Cemetery, **33**
Jewish Museum, **34**
Kraków Głowny Station, **3**
Monastery of the Reformed Franciscans, **10**
Muzeum Historii Fotografii, **23**
Orbis Office, **19**
Pauline Church, **37**
Police Station, **18**
Politechnika Krakowska, **1**
St. Andrew's Church, **28**
St. Anne's Church, **15**
St. Catherine's Church, **36**
St. Florian's Gate, **7**
St. Mary's Church, **20**
St. Peter and Paul Church, **27**
Stary Teatr (Old Theater), **16**
Sukiennice (Cloth Hall), **21**
Town Hall, **22**
University Museum, **13**
Wawel Castle, **29**
Wawel Cathedral, **30**

POLAND

Tourist Offices: Dexter, Rynek Główny 1/3 (tel. 21 77 06 or 21 30 51; fax 21 30 36). English-speaking staff organizes tours and offers free pamphlets on the town and cultural events. Open Mon.-Fri. 9am-6pm, Sat. 9am-1pm. **ORBIS,** Rynek Główny 41 (tel. 22 40 35), sells ferry, plane, bus, and train tickets. Open April-Oct. Mon.-Fri. 8am-7pm, Sat. 8am-3pm; Nov.-May Mon.-Fri. 9am-6pm.

Currency Exchange: At *kantor*s, ORBIS offices, and hotels. *Kantor*s, except the ones around the train and bus stations, usually have the best rates.

American Express: Rynek Główny 41 (tel. 22 91 80), in the ORBIS office. Cashes and sells traveler's checks with no commission, replaces lost checks, holds mail, and accepts wired money. Open same hours as ORBIS (see above).

Trains: Kraków Główny, pl. Kolejowy (tel. 22 41 82, info tel. 933). **Luggage storage.** To: Warsaw (2½-4½hr., 20zł, express 35zł), Vienna (9hr., 141zł), Kiev (22hr., 52zł), Budapest (11hr., 147zł), Prague (8½hr., 120zł), and Berlin (8hr., 106zł). **Kraków Plaszów** is a suburban station; take bus 198 into the city if stranded there.

Buses: ul. Worcella (info tel. 936), opposite the train station. **Sindbad** (tel. 22 12 38), in the main hall, sells tickets to Western European cities. Open Mon.-Fri. 9am-5pm. To: Warsaw (6hr., 28zł), Prague (11hr., 190zł), and Budapest (11hr., 45zł).

Public Transportation: Buy tickets at kiosks and tram stops (1zł) and punch them on board. Large backpacks require their own tickets. Slight surcharge for tickets purchased on board. Express buses A, B, and C 1.30zł; night buses 2zł. Day passes 5zł; weekly passes 12zł. The fine for violating the system is 36zł.

Laundromat: ul. Piastowska 47, on the 2nd floor of Hotel Piast. 2hr. drop-off available. Wash 4zł; dry 4zł. Open daily 10am-7pm.

Emergency: Fire: tel. 998. **Ambulance:** tel. 999.

Police: tel. 997.

Post Office: ul. Westerplatte 20 (tel. 22 51 63 or 22 86 48; fax 22 36 06). Open Mon.-Fri. 7:30am-8:30pm, Sat. 9am-2pm, Sun. 9-11am. **Postal Code:** 31-045.

Telephones: 24hr. phones at the main post office and at the office opposite the train station, ul. Lubicz 4 (tel. 22 14 85 or 22 86 35). **Telephone Code:** 012.

ACCOMMODATIONS AND CAMPING

Reservations are highly recommended in summer. Friendly neighborhood room-retriever **Waweltur,** ul. Pawia 8 (tel./fax 22 19 21), arranges private singles for 43zł and doubles for 75zł (open Mon.-Fri. 8am-8pm, Sat. 8am-2pm). Other locals gladly rent rooms; watch for signs or solicitors in the train station.

Jan-Pol PTTK Dom Turysty, ul. Westerplatte 15 (tel. 22 95 66; fax 21 27 26), by the post office and near the *rynek.* The place to meet young travelers (and rowdy schoolchildren). Dorms remain unlocked, so use the hotel vault. You may only be allowed to arrange for a night at a time. Reception open 24hr. 23zł.

Schronisko Młodzieżowe (HI), ul. Kościuszki 88 (tel. 22 19 51), inside the gates of a convent, a 20min. walk from the Old Town. Take tram 2 ("Salwator") from ul. Westerplatte to the last stop. Run by nuns in a heavenly setting, although school groups may detract from the serenity. Reception open daily 8am-2pm and 5-11pm. Lockout 10am-5pm. Curfew 11pm. 7.50zł, nonmembers 9zł. Sheets 2.50zł.

Schronisko Młodzieżowe (HI), ul. Oleandry 4 (tel. 33 88 22). Take bus 119 north from the train station, and get off once the main drag turns into ul. Mickiewicza. Oleandry is parallel to Mickiewicza outside the Old Town. Cheap but dingy. Flexible lockout 10am-5pm. Curfew 11pm. Dorms 13-15zł. Doubles 16zł per person.

Pensjonat "Rycerska," pl. Na Groblach 22 (tel. 22 60 82 or 23 18 43; fax 22 33 99), in the shadow of the castle between ul. Straszewskiego and Powiśle. A clean and charming establishment with a quiet courtyard. Doubles 85zł, with bath 120zł.

Hotel Wycieczkowy, ul. Poselska 22 (tel. 22 67 65; fax 22 04 39), 3 blocks south of the *rynek* off ul. Grodzka. Small, quiet rooms and clean hall bathrooms. Singles 100zł. Doubles 90zł, with bath 140zł. Quads 160zł.

Hotel Piast, ul. Piastowska 47 (tel. 37 49 33 or 37 21 76). Take bus 139, 159, 173, 208, 238, or 258 westbound to ul. Piastowska. Popular with young foreigners who come to study Polish. Singles 32.10zł. Doubles 42.80zł, with bath 60zł. Triples with bath 60.90zł. Coin-operated laundry. Discounts after the first night.

Hotel Saski, ul. Sławkowska 3 (tel. 21 42 22; fax 21 48 30), close to the *rynek*. Popular among students; also caters to ministers of state and VIPs. Singles 64zł, with bath 90zł. Doubles 99zł, with bath 140zł. Triples 112zł, with bath 160zł.

Camping Krak, ul. Radzikowskiego 99 (tel. 37 21 22 or 37 21 71; fax 37 25 32). Take tram 4, 8, 12, or 40 to "Fizyków" and walk north. 9zł per person. Caravans 13zł. Open May 15-Sept. 15.

FOOD

There are 24-hour. grocery stores in town including **Społem,** pl. Kolejowy, across from the train station. *Obwarzanki* (soft pretzels with poppy seeds), Kraków's street-stand specialty, sell for just 0.50zł. The eateries listed are near Rynek Główny.

Chimera, ul. Św. Anny 3. Popular with students between classes. Huge plate of creative, delicious salads 7zł. Smaller plate 5zł. Open daily 9am-10 or 11pm.

Różowy Słoń (Pink Elephant), ul. Straszewskiego 24. Funky pop art decor and delicious salads. Bowls 1.30zł per 100g. Rice dishes 2.50-3zł. Huge plates of spaghetti 2.70-3.40zł. Open Mon.-Sat. 9am-9pm, Sun. 11am-9pm.

Jadłodajnia u Stasi, ul. Mikołajska 16. A one-man show. Budget meals. Famous for its Polish dishes, such as *pierogi z serem* (cheese dumplings) and *pierogi z truskawkami* (strawberry dumplings). Open Mon.-Fri. 12:45-around 5pm.

Bar Mleczny Barcelona, ul. Piłsudskiego 1, across from Planty on the west side of Stare Miasto. A bastion of proletarian dining—a full meal for under 3zł. *Ryż z jabłkami* (rice with apples) 0.91zł. Open daily 8am-7pm or 8pm.

Cechowa, ul. Jagiellońska 11, a block west of the *rynek*. Crowded tables and chairs give a homey feel. Try their specialty, *śledź po krakowsku* (Kraków herring) for 3.80zł. Other traditional Polish dishes 3.50-17zł. Open daily 11am-10pm.

Café and Gallery Krzysztofory, ul. Szczepańska, in the smoked-filled cellars of the Krzysztofory House. The gallery exhibits every 2-3 weeks; the café hosts avant-garde theater. *Żywiec* beer 3.30zł. Open daily 11am-midnight.

Kawiarnia Jama Michalika, Floriańska 45. Over a century old, this is one of Kraków's most famous cafés, the former haunt of Polish intellectuals. Sip espresso (3.10zł), nibble on pastries, and attack elaborate ice cream specialties.

SIGHTS

At the center of the Stare Miasto (Old Town) spreads **Rynek Główny,** one of the largest medieval market squares in Europe. In its northeast corner rise the asymmetrical towers of the **Kościół Mariacki** (Cathedral of St. Mary). An interrupted *hejnał* (trumpet call) each hour from one tower recalls the death of a watchman warning the city of invading Tatars in 1241. The call has become Kraków's emblem and is broadcast on national radio daily at noon. The richly decorated interior holds a 500-year-old carved wood altarpiece (open daily noon-6pm; altar 1.50zł, students 1zł). Diagonally across the square stands the **Wieża Ratuszowa** (Town Hall Tower), the lone remnant of the old town hall (open Mon.-Fri. 10am-4:30pm, Sat.-Sun. 10am-3:30pm; 1.50-3zł). Dividing the square in half, the yellow Italianate **Sukiennice** (Cloth Hall) is as mercantile now as it was in guild times; the ground floor contains an enormous trinket market. Upstairs, **Muzeum Narodowe** (National Museum) houses a gallery of 18th- and 19th-century Polish classics (open Tues.-Sun. 10am-3:30pm, Thurs. until 6pm; 3zł, students 1.50zł). Kraków's **Uniwersytet Jagielloński** is the second-oldest university in Eastern Europe and names Copernicus among its alumni. The university's 15th-century **Collegium Maius,** west of the *rynek* on ul. Jagiellońska 15, has a Gothic courtyard and vaulted walkway (open Mon.-Fri. 11am-2:30pm, Sat. 11am-1:30pm).

Zamek Wawelski (Wawel Castle) is one of the finest surviving pieces of Renaissance architecture in Poland. Begun in the 10th century, the castle contains 71 chambers, a magnificent sequence of 16th-century tapestries commissioned by the royal family, and a series of eight tapestries from Arras depicting the story of Noah's Ark. The **Crown Treasury** inside the castle features the sword long used in the coronations of Polish kings. Also inside, the **Oriental Collection** boasts vases and an enormous and elaborately decorated 17th-century Turkish tent. The castle is undergoing renovations—not all the chambers are open to the public. A visitor's office sells English guidebooks. (Office open Mon.-Sat. 8:45am-4pm, Sun. 10am-3pm. Royal Chambers (5zł, students 2.50zł) and Oriental Collection (3 zł, students 1.50zł) and Treasury open Tues.-Fri. 9:30am-4:30pm, Sun. 9:30am-3pm, Sun. 10am-3pm. Admission free on Wed. Oct.-March exhibits close at 3pm and are free Sat.) Poland's monarchs were crowned and buried in the **Katedra** (Cathedral) next door to the castle. Its former archbishop, Cardinal Karol Wojtyła, is now Pope John Paul II (open May-Sept. daily 9am-5pm; Oct.-April 9am-3pm; 4zł).

South of the Old Town lies **Kazimierz,** the 600-year-old Jewish quarter. You can still see the remnants of what was once a large and vital community, including the beautiful **Remuh Cemetery,** ul. Szeroka 40 (open Mon.-Fri. 9am-4pm), and Kraków's only operating synagogue. In 1860-62, the Association of Progressive Israelis founded **Templ,** ul. Miodowa 24, with its 36 splendid stained-glass windows. Poland's oldest synagogue, **Stara Synagoga,** ul. Szeroka 24, houses a small **museum** (open Wed.-Thurs. and Sat.-Sun. 9am-3pm, Fri. 11am-6pm; 4zł, students 2zł). Close to the synagogue, the **Jewish bookstore Jordan,** ul. Szeroka 2, organizes tours of Kazimierz which trace the sites of *Schindler's List.* (Open Mon.-Fri. 9am-6pm, Sat.-Sun. 10am-6pm. English tours depart from the bookstore. 2-6hr. 30-60zł.)

ENTERTAINMENT

See the Dexter tourist office for cultural activities. Classical music buffs will appreciate **Filharmonia Krakowska** (tel. 22 09 58), which performs regularly at ul. Zwierzyniecka 1. Student clubs romp from 8pm to midnight or 1am with a small cover.

U Louisa, Rynek Głowny 13. Live jazz and blues on weekends. **Internet access** 3-5zł per hr. Beer 4-8zł. Open Mon.-Fri. 11am-2am, Sat.-Sun. 11am-late.

Pub Pod Papugami (Under the Parrots), ul. Św. Jana 18. A quiet student crowd gathers around low tables. Guinness 7zł. Open daily 4pm-2am.

Jazz Club "U Muniaka," ul. Floriańska 3. Well-known jazzman invites his friends to jam. Weekend concerts with 15zł cover. Open daily 5pm-midnight or 1am.

Student Club, Rynek Główny 8. Very cheap, very laid back. Jazz on Tuesdays and disco on weekends. Usually open around 9am-2am.

Hadi, ul. Starowiślna 6, in Kazimierz. Mixed gay club open daily. Disco Fri.-Sat.

■ Near Kraków: Auschwitz-Birkenau and Wieliczka

An estimated 1.5 million people were murdered and thousands more suffered in the Nazi concentration camps at **Auschwitz** (Oświęcim) and **Birkenau** (Brzezinka). Prisoners were originally kept at the smaller **Konzentrationslager Auschwitz I,** within the city limits. The camp itself is now a museum; barracks and crematoria hold displays detailing Nazi atrocities, and many nations have erected their own exhibits or memorials. An English guidebook is sold at the entrance for 2zł. Begin your visit with the horrifying film, shot here by the Soviet Army on January 27, 1945. (Film shown daily. 1zł. Museum open June-Aug. daily 8am-7pm; May and Sept. 8am-6pm; April and Oct. 8am-5pm; March and Nov.-Dec. 15 8am-4pm; Dec. 16-Feb. 8am-3pm. Free. Children discouraged from visiting the museum.) The starker **Konzentrationslager Auschwitz II-Birkenau,** in the countryside 3km from the original camp, is a well-marked half-hour walk. From April 15 to September 31, a bus shuttles to this site from the parking lot of the Auschwitz museum (7 per day, 1zł). In the central watchtower, you can listen to recorded commentaries in 12 languages while getting a view of the immensity of the camp, which was mostly destroyed by the retreating Nazis—rows of chimneys, a few barracks, watchtowers, and, at the far end of the train tracks, gas chambers and crematoria. A pond in the far right corner is still slightly gray from the ashes deposited there half a century ago.

Buses run to Auschwitz-Birkenau from Kraków's central bus station (11 per day, 1½hr., 5.40zł); get off at "Muzeum Oświęcim." **Trains** leave from Kraków Główny (4 per day, 1¾hr., 5zł), although times are not particularly convenient. More trains run from Kraków's suburban Płaszów station. Tourist offices in Kraków also offer tours including transportation and knowledgeable guides. From the train station in the town, buses 2, 3, 4, and 5 drop visitors off at the Museum Oświęcim bus stop, outside the driveway. By foot, turn right as you exit the station, go one block and turn left; the road stretches 1.6km to Auschwitz, which will be on the right.

Thirteen kilometers southeast of Kraków lies the 1000-year-old salt mine at **Wieliczka,** where Poles carved a 20-chapel complex in salt 100m underground. The most spectacular is **St. Kinga's Chapel.** The Wieliczka salt mine has been declared by UNESCO one of the 12 most priceless monuments in the world. (Open April 15-Oct. 15 daily 7:30am-6:30pm; Oct.16-April 14 8am-4pm. Separate obligatory guided tours of salt sculptures and of historical museum. 17zł, students 8.50zł; in English 1-5 per day, 21zł.) **Trains** travel to Wieliczka from Kraków (1 per hr., 25min., 1.50zł) and private **mini buses** depart from the little road between the train and bus stations (every 15min., 1.50zł). Once in Wieliczka, follow the tracks' former path and then the *"do kopalni"* (to the mine) signs. Local kiosks sell guidebooks in English.

Mrągowo

Tiny orange-roofed houses speckle the endless lakes and rivers (once part of a Scandinavian glacier) of **Mrągowo** (mrawn-GOH-voh), where Germans and other tourists come to frolic in the water and ride horses. The main **beaches**—Plaża Orbisu, packed with canoeists, and Plaża Miejska—are both on Jezioro Czos. To cap off your beach day, **Miejski Dom Kultury "Zodiak"** (House of Culture), ul. Warszawska 26 (tel. (08984) 30 63), features weekend concerts at 6pm.

Regional trains are painfully slow, but **buses** run to Gdańsk (daily at 9:30am, 5hr., 40zł), Warsaw (7 per day, 4[hr., 20.40zł), and Olsztyn (21 per day, 1½hr., 5.40zł; switch here for 5 daily buses to Kaliningrad, Russia). The bus station separates ul. Warszawska, a leg of Mrągowo's main thoroughfare, from ul. Wojska Polskicgo, which leads out of town. The staff of **Eco-Travel,** Mały Rynek 6 (tel./fax (08948) 36 67; open Mon.-Fri. 8am-5pm, Sat. 9am-2pm), books rooms (no fee) and changes money. The clean **Hotel Meltur,** ul. Sienkiewicza 16 (tel. (08948) 29 00), rents out doubles only (37.45zł, with shower 42.80zł). From the bus station, turn left on ul. Wojska Polskiego, follow it down for 0.5km, and turn right onto ul. Sienkiewicza (10min.). You may want to take a taxi after dark (3zł). Mrągowo's other hotels are on **ul. Jaszczurcza Góra.** To get there, turn right from the bus station and head through town until you come to ul. Gizycka, which hugs the lake and eventually leads to ul. Jaszczurcza Góra (50min.). **Restauracja Fregata,** just left of ul. Ratuszowa near ul. Dolny Zaułek, serves both international *plats* and local dishes (open daily 9am-9pm). Locals gather until the wee hours to eat spaghetti (4zł) or *kiełbasa* (2zł) and indulge in Polish beer (3zł) at **Bar Lasagna,** ul. Warszawska 7a (bar open daily 11am-1am). **Milano,** ul. Królewiecka 53, is a disco that plays pop, rock, and—yes, oh yes—Polish hip-hop. Every July 29th to August 1st, an amphitheater on the shore of Jezioro Czos holds a **Country Picnic Festival** with country tunes galore, cowboy.

Częstochowa

Częstochowa (CHEN-sto-HO-va) is the Catholic Mecca of Poland. Every year thousands make the pilgrimage to **Klasztor Paulinów** (Paulite Monastery) on top of Jasna Góra to catch glimpse of the miraculous **Czarna Madonna** (Black Madonna), the most sacred of Polish icons. The monastery also houses a large **treasury** containing invaluable works of art, many of them donations of previous pilgrims: monstrances, chalices, crosses, liturgical vestments, and jewelry. (Chapel open daily 5am-9:30pm. The icon is displayed Mon.-Fri. 6am-noon and 1-9:30pm, Sat.-Sun. 6am-1pm and 2-9:30pm. Treasury open daily 9-11:30am and 3:30-5:30pm. Donations appreciated.)

Częstochowa is accessible by **train** from Kraków (2hr., 19.60zł), Warsaw (3hr., express 18.50zł), or Wrocław (3½hr., 11zł). The WCIT **tourist office,** al. NMP 65 (tel.

(034) 24 13 60; fax 24 34 12), provides a free map and hotel info (open Mon.-Fri. 9am-6pm, Sat.-Sun. 10am-6pm). The popular **Dom Pielgrzyma im. Jana Pawla,** ul. Wyszyńskiego 1/31 (tel. (034) 24 70 11; fax 65 18 70), just outside the west gate of the monastery, has spacious rooms (singles with bath 42zł, doubles 47zł). Across the parking lot from the west gate of the monastery, **Camping Oleńka,** ul. Oleńki 10/30 (tel. (034) 24 74 95; fax 25 14 79), is a clean, sprawling complex (tent sites 6zł; bungalows 15-18zł per person). Students gather around the wax-dripping candles and salad-laden tables of **Pod Gruszką,** al. NMP 37 (open daily 10am-10pm). **Solidom,** al. NMP 75, offers grocery store wares (open Mon.-Sat. 6am-9pm, Sun. noon-8pm).

Between Częstochowa and Kraków, the fantastic **Trail of Eagles' Nests** runs along a narrow 100km chain of crags tipped with the ruins of fortifications from the 12th century onwards. A **hiking trail** dotted by villages runs along the entire length, while bus 58 or 58bis from near the Częstochowa train station provides access to **Olsztyn Castle.** In Kraków or Częstochowa, **PTTK** can provide **hiking maps.**

Lublin

A center for religious and social movements since it acted as the catalyst of the Polish Reformation and Counter-Reformation, Lublin was silenced during World War II. But the city regained a vibrant, bohemian flair after the war, when its Catholic university was the only institute of higher learning in Poland to maintain independence from the Communist government. The 19th-century facades of **ul. Krakowskie Przedmieście** introduce the medieval **Stare Miasto** (Old Town). A stroll east from pl. Litewski leads to pl. Łokietka and the1827 **Nowy Ratusz** (New Town Hall), seat of Lublin's government. To the right starts ul. Królewska with the grand, 16th-century **Katedra Św. Jana Chrzciciela i Jana Ewangelisty** (Cathedral of St. John the Baptist and St. John the Evangelist), with frescoes and a gilded altar. To the left of the Nowy Ratusz runs **ul. Lubartowska,** the main artery of pre-war Lublin's Jewish district. **Plac Ofiar Getta** (Victims of the Ghetto Square), on the left of the street, centers around the **monument to the Murdered Jews.** Ul. Krakowskie Przedmieście travels straight through pl. Łokietka to the **Brama Krakowska** (Kraków Gate), which houses **Oddział Historyczny Muzeum Lubelskiego** (Historical Division of the Lublin Museum), pl. Łokietka 3 (open Wed.-Sat. 9am-4pm, Sun. 9am-5pm). Across the gate, ul. Bramowa leads to the **rynek,** lined with early Renaissance houses. In the middle of the *rynek* stands the Neoclassical **Stary Ratusz** (Old Town Hall). A walk along ul. Grodzka leads through the 15th-century **Brama Grodzka** (Grodzka Gate) to ul. Zamkowa, which runs to the massive **Zamek Lubelski** (Lublin Castle). Most of the structure was built in the 14th century, but was restored in the 19th century with a neo-Gothic exterior.

The Lublin Główny **train station,** pl. Dworcowy 1 (tel. (081) 202 19, info 933), south of the Old Town, sends trains to Warsaw (2½hr., 16.65zł) and Kraków (4hr., 23zł); **buses** leave the station at ul. Tysiąclecia 4 (tel. (081) 77 66 49, info 934), near the Old Town, for Warsaw (3hr., 12zł). The **IT tourist office,** ul. Krakowskie Przedmieście 78 (tel. (081) 534 12), carries regional maps (4zł) and brochures (open Mon.-Fri. 9am-6pm, Sat. 10am-2pm). **ORBIS,** ul. Narutowicza 31/33 (tel. (081) 532 56; fax 532 15 30), handles plane, train, and bus tickets, and books hotel rooms (open May-July Mon.-Fri. 9am-5pm, Sat. 10am-2pm; Aug.-April Mon.-Fri. 9am-5pm). In summer, **university dorms** provide inexpensive rooms, although many are far from the city center; ask at the tourist offices. To get to **Schronisko Młodzieżowe (HI),** ul. Długosza 6a (tel. (081) 533 06 28), walk to the end of the Saxon Gardens and turn right onto ul. Długosza. (Lockout 10am-5pm. Curfew 10pm. Dorms 8zł; triples 10zł per person. Sheets 3.50zł.) **Hotel Lublinianka** (tel. (081) 532 42 61) is centrally located at ul. Krakowskie Przedmieście 56 (singles 33-40zł, doubles 54zł).

Jazz Pizza, ul. Krakowskie Przedmieście 55, serves delicious pizzas (5.50-7zł; open Mon.-Sat. 11am-midnight, Sun. 3-10pm), and **Bar Staromiejski,** ul. Jezuicka 1, in the Old Town, has cheap cafeteria-style food (soups 1zł, *pierogi* 2.50zł; open Mon.-Fri. 8am-5pm, Sat.-Sun. 8am-4pm). A few **grocery stores** line ul. Krakowskie Przedmieście. Thanks to a student crowd, Lublin has an impressive number of pubs and an active music scene. The **Old Pub,** ul. Grodzka 8, serves drinks downstairs, and has a disco upstairs (open Sun.-Thurs. 11am-10pm, Fri.-Sat. 11am-11pm).

■ Near Lublin: Majdanek

The largest concentration camp after Auschwitz, **Majdanek** lies only 4km from Lublin's city center. Because the Nazis did not have time to destroy the camp, **Państwowe Muzeum na Majdanku** (The Majdanek State Museum) contains original structures and houses chilling piles of ashes and prisoners' shoes. (Open May-Sept. Tues.-Sun. 8am-6pm; Oct.-Nov. and March-April daily 8am-3pm. Free. Under 14 not admitted.) Walking through the camp takes approximately two hours. The **information center** (tel. (081) 744 26 47 or 744 19 55) shows a 15-minute documentary. To get to Majdanek from Lublin take eastbound bus 28 from the train station, tram 153 or 158 from Al. Racławickie, or the southbound tram 156 from ul. Królewska.

Zakopane

Set in a valley surrounded by sky-high jagged peaks and soul-stirring alpine meadows, Zakopane buzzes with hikers and skiers clambering to be a part of the great outdoors. Short mountain hikes are a specialty of **Tatrzański Park Narodowy** (Tatran National Park). Entrances to the park lie at the head of each trail (1zł, students 0.50zł). **Dolina Kościeliska** offers an easy hike and biking route in a valley along a stream; a bus shuttles from Zakopane west to Kiry (1.50-2zł), where the green trail begins. For more dramatic vistas, catch a bus to **Kuźnice** (1zł), 20 minutes south of central Zakopane, and hop on the **Kasprowy Wierch** cable car (round-trip 17zł, students 11zł). To conquer **Czerwone Wierchy** (Red Peaks), follow the red trail that leads west from the top of the cable car route along the ridge that separates Poland and Slovakia. If you tire, four of the seven peaks along the way have paths descending to Zakopane.

The mountain lake **Morskie Oko** dazzles herds of tourists in the summer; to get there, take a bus from Zakopane's bus station (45min., 3zł) to Polana Palenica, then hike an easy 8km along the road. The **Dolina Pięciu Stawów Polskich** (Five-Lake Valley) hike, a 14-hour summer-only option starting from Kuźnice, and the **Rysy** hike to Poland's highest peak, are extremely demanding, but compensate with incredible views and plenty of self-satisfaction. Before setting out, buy the map *Tatrzański Park Narodowy: Mapa turystyczna* at local kiosks and bookstores.

Practical Information, Accommodations, and Food The **train** and **bus stations** are across ul. Jagiellonska from each other, right next to the street's intersection with ul. Kosciuszki. Trains go to Kraków (3½hr., 9.60-14.50zł) and Warsaw (8hr., 15.40-23zł); buses travel to Kraków (2½hr., 9zł), Warsaw (8hr., 24-60zł), Budapest (8hr., 30-35zł), and Poprad, Slovakia (2½hr., 8zł). The **IT tourist office,** ul. Kościuszki 17 (tel. (0165) 122 11; fax 660 51), at the intersection with ul. Sienkiewicza, sells maps and brochures and arrange private rooms (20-40zł per person; open daily 7am-9pm). **ORBIS,** ul. Krupówki 22 (tel./fax (0165) 122 38), cashes traveler's checks and sells plane and bus tickets (open Mon.-Fri. 9am-5pm, Sat. 9am-3pm).

The tourist office will help you find a room, or you can prowl around looking for *"pokój"* (private room) signs (10-15zł). To reach **Schronisko Młodzieżowe (HI),** ul. Nowotarska 45 (tel. (0165) 662 03), walk down ul. Kościuszki toward town, then take the second right onto ul. Sienkiewicza and walk two blocks (curfew 11pm; dorms 13-17zł per person, doubles 46zł; HI card US$2 per night). **PTTK Dom Wycieczkowy,** ul. Zaruskiego 5 (tel. (0165) 632 81), a large chalet in the town center, has spacious rooms and 24-hour hot water (16-20zł). If you make it to the Morskie Oko lake, **Schronisko Morskie Oko** (tel. (0165) 776 09) is a gorgeous hostel in an ideal location (28zł; reserve ahead). Pitch a tent at **Camping Pod Krokwią,** ul. Żeromskiego (tel. (0165) 122 56; tents 7-9zł plus 7zł per person, students 6zł; bungalows 22-25zł). **U Wandy,** ul. Sienkiewicza 10, off Kościuszki, has immense, tasty servings (chicken cutlet 8zł; open Tues.-Sun. 2-6pm). **Grocery stores** line ul. Krupówki.

Wrocław

After decades of elaborate postwar rebuilding, only photographs recall the destruction of Wrocław (VROTS-wahv) during World War II. Now, the city charms visitors with bridges, lush parks, and restored 19th-century buildings. The oldest neighborhood, **Ostrów Tumski** (Cathedral Island) ages peacefully across the river from the center next to the **Botanical Gardens,** ul. Sienkiewicza 23 (open Mon.-Fri. 8am-6pm, Sat.-Sun. 10am-6pm; 3zł; students 2zł). The stately **Katedra Św. Jana Chrzciciela** (Cathedral of St. John the Baptist) gives this section its dignified character. Inside, a nun will show you the amazing marble **Kaplica Św. Elżbiety** (Chapel of St. Elizabeth). Climb up the tower for a phenomenal view (open daily 10am-3pm; 2zł, students 1zł). The modern heart of the city, *Stare Miasto,* showcases the Renaissance and Gothic **ratusz** (town hall) on **Rynek Główny** (Main Market Square) and contains the **Historical Museum.** One exhibit entirely focuses on ul. Świdnicka, a street in central Wrocław so beautiful that the Germans tried to have its stones moved to their soil. (Open Wed.-Fri. 10am-4pm, Sat. 11am-5pm, Sun. 10am-6pm; cashier closes 30min. earlier. 3zł, students 1.5zł, Wed. free.) **Aula Leopoldina,** pl. Uniwersytecki 1, on the second floor of the main University building, is an 18th-century lecture hall with magnificent ceiling frescoes (open Thurs.-Tues. 10am-3:30pm; 2.50zł, students 1zł).

The well-stocked **IT tourist office,** ul. Rynek 14 (tel. (071) 44 31 11 or 44 11 09; fax 44 29 62), has handy maps (2.50zł; open in summer Mon.-Fri. 9am-6pm, Sat. 10am-4pm). **ALMATUR,** ul. Kościuszki 34 (tel. (071) 44 30 03 or 44 72 56; fax 44 39 51), in the student center "Pałacyk," has info on hostels, ISICs, and youth fare bus tickets (open Mon.-Fri. 9am-5pm, Sat. 10am-2pm). **Trains** arrive at ul. Piłsudskiego from Warsaw (5hr., 24zł), Kraków (4hr., 21zł), Prague (6½hr., 52zł), Budapest (12hr., 101zł), and Berlin (5½hr., 58zł). The **bus** station, ul. Sucha 1, behind the train station serves Warsaw (8hr., 29.60zł), Kraków (7hr., 26zł), and Poznań (3hr., 16zł). Speak with the tourist office staff about private rooms. The clean, safe **youth hostel (HI),** ul. Kołłątaja 20 (tel. (071) 343 88 56), is opposite the train station (lockout 10am-5pm; curfew 10pm; 7-13zł). **Hotel Piast,** ul. Piłsudskiego 98 (tel. (071) 343 00 33), near the train station, has sinks in all rooms (singles 38zł, doubles 70zł, triples 81zł, quads 100zł).

Bar Vega, Rynek Ratusz 27a, serves tasty vegetarian dishes for less than 5zł (open Mon.-Fri. 8am-7pm, Sat.-Sun. 9am-5pm), while **Bar Miś,** ul. Kuźnicza 48, offers cafeteria-style meals for 4-5zł (open Mon.-Fri. 7am-6pm, Sat. 8am-5pm). There are several 24-hour grocery stores: **U Pana Jana,** pl. Solny 8/9, is convenient to the *rynek*. For up to the nano-second cultural info pick up *Co jest grane* free at the tourist office. With its Marilyn Monroe plastered walls and barstools/saddles, **Pałacyk,** ul. Kościuszki 34, is blissfully bad-ass. Next to the decadent artist's corner, **Kawiarnia "Pod Kalamburem,"** ul. Kuźnica 29a, the **Cyberkawiarnia** gives you a cup of coffee and an hour of **Internet access** for 8zł (open daily 10am-10pm).

Portugal

US $1 = 187.64$ (Portuguese escudos)	**100$ = US $0.53**
CDN $1 = 134.63$	**100$ = CDN $0.74**
UK £1 = 298.65$	**100$ = UK £0.33**
IR £1 = 271.02$	**100$ = IR £0.37**
AUS $1 = 140.05$	**100$ = AUS $0.71**
NZ $1 = 120.11$	**100$ = NZ $0.83**
SAR 1 = 50.03$	**100$ = SAR 1.99**
Country Code: 351	**International Dialing Prefix: 00**

Centuries ago, Portuguese explorers noticed that the Atlantic Ocean didn't swallow the sun every evening. Their ensuing revolutionary navigational and shipbuilding techniques allowed Vasco da Gama to sail around the Cape of Good Hope and Magellan to sail around the world. These discoveries also fed the country's prosperity, transforming art and architecture into the ornate and sometimes eccentric Manueline style. Following the Age of Discovery a period of decline set in, imbuing the culture with a nostalgia still reflected in the folk ballads of *fado*—fate. By 1580, Portugal had exhausted both its resources and its royal line, and after minimal resistance, the Spanish Hapsburg Philip II claimed the Portuguese throne. Independence wasn't regained until 1640, when the royal house of Bragança established itself by hooking up with England. An earthquake in 1755 reduced much of Lisbon to rubble, shaking the country's faith and economy so much that when Napoleon invaded in 1807, King Pedro III moved the court of his crumbling empire to Brazil.

Events in Portugal this century have proven no less turbulent. A parliamentary republic emerged in 1910, only to be overthrown by a 1926 military coup. Strongman António Salazar, an economist-turned-dictator, and his successor, Marcelo Caetano, ruled the country for the next 50 years, exploiting the domestic peasantry and African laborers under colonial rule. In 1974, a bloodless coup toppled the regime, prompting mass rejoicing—every Portuguese town now has its Rua 25 de Abril to honor the day. The new junta finally granted independence to Portugal's African holdings, but the ensuing civil wars in Mozambique and Angola set off a rush of immigration into an already unstable Portugal. In 1986, President Mario Soares and Prime Minister Cavaco Silva supervised Portugal's entry into the European Economic Community, and initiated a sometimes painful modernization drive. Portugal remains quite poor by European standards but is striving to catch up and should enter the European Monetary Union in 1999. Expo '98 is being held in Lisbon from May to September of 1998, and has prompted one of largest urban renewals, transforming a decaying industrial center into a thriving, beautified waterfront. All told, prospects for the future are especially bright given the influx in industry and vastly improved educational system. But some things seem destined never to change—the pristine beaches along the Atlantic seaboard, the plush landscape in the north, the wines of Porto, and the character and traditions which evolved over Portugal's rich history.

For more detailed, energetic, and sunny information on Portugal, grab a copy of *Let's Go: Spain & Portugal 1998.*

GETTING THERE AND GETTING AROUND

Citizens of the U.S., Canada, the U.K., and New Zealand can visit Portugal **visa-free** for up to 90 days. Citizens of Australia need only a passport as well, but must have a visa to cross into Spanish territory. Citizens of South Africa need a visa; contact the consulate at 701 Van Erkom Building, 217 Pretorius St., Pretoria (tel. (012) 262 141).

The **airports** in Lisbon serves major European and North American cities; Lisbon and Porto are also accessible by daily **trains** from Madrid and Paris. **Eurail** is valid on the Portuguese national train system, but if you're planning to stay within the country, the reasonable fares and short distances may make a pass unnecessary. Be aware that posted schedules for trains and buses may be wrong, and that unless you have a Eurail pass, the return on round-trip tickets must be used by 3pm the next day. **Caminhos de Ferro Portugueses,** Portugal's national railway, operates throughout the country, but aside from the Braga-Porto-Coimbra-Lisbon line, the bus is better. **Rodoviária,** the national bus company, has recently been privatized and divided by region. These buses link just about every town, while private regional companies cover the more obscure routes. Express coach service *(expressos)* between major cities is especially quick and convenient. **Hitchhiking** in Portugal is not reliable or safe enough to serve as a means of transportation, particularly as automobiles are relatively unsafe in Portugal, with its ill-kept smaller roads and reckless drivers.

ESSENTIALS

The national tourist board is the **Direcção Geral do Turismo (DGT).** Their offices are in virtually every city; look for the **"Turismo"** sign. Services offered are similar to those in Spain. Finding an English speaker at bigger offices is usually no problem. The principal student travel agency is **TAGUS-Youth Student Travel.**

Portuguese **currency** is the escudo ($). Normal banking hours are weekdays from 8:30am to 3pm, but many close for lunch from around 11:45am to 1pm. Travelers checks are readily convertible. There are a decent number of **ATMs** throughout the country, and many establishments accept major credit cards.

A strongly Catholic country, Portugal recognizes many religious **holidays** and observances. Every town has its patron saint; their feast days are local holidays, accompanied by pilgrimages, village fairs, makeshift amusement parks, and closed shops. National festivals and holidays include *Semanta Santa* (March 6-12 in 1998), Liberty Day (April 25), Labor Day (May 1), Corpus Christi (June 11), Feast of the Assumption (Aug. 15), Republic Day (Oct. 5), All Saints' Day (Nov. 1), Feast of the Immaculate Conception (Dec. 8), and Christmas (Dec. 24-25).

Communication **Airmail** usually takes 8-10 business days to reach North America. If you're sending a letter to Portugal, *Poste Restante* is available in nearly early town and costs 60$ per piece picked up. The **phone system** in Portugal is currently being updated, and many numbers are gaining an extra digit. *Let's Go* lists all the known changes, but undoubtedly some numbers will change after the publication of this book. For a time, at least, you will probably be re-routed if you call the old number. **Phone booths** marked by "Credifone" signs are located at phone offices, on the street, and in some post offices. Few pay phones accept coins; the Credifone system uses magnetic cards that are sold at locations posted on the phone booth. For **directory assistance,** dial 118; for an **international operator,** dial 099 for Europe, 098 for intercontinental calls. For MCI's **WorldPhone,** dial 05 017 12 34; **AT&T Direct** 05 017 12 88; **Sprint Access** 05 017 18 77; **Canada Direct** 05 017 12 26; **BT Direct** 05 05 00 44; **Australia Direct** 05 017 61 10; **New Zealand Direct** 05 017 64 00; and **SA Direct** 05 017 27 00. In an **emergency,** dial 112.

Portuguese is a Romance language similar to Spanish, but also accessible to those who know French or Italian. English, Spanish, and French are also widely spoken.

Yes/No	*sim/não*	seeng / now
Hello	*Olá*	oh-LAH
Please	*por favor*	poor fah-VOR
Thank you	*obrigado*	oh-bree-GAH-doo
Sorry	*desculpe*	dish-KOOL-peh
Do you speak English?	*Fala inglês?*	FAH-lah een-GLAYSH
I don't understand.	*Não compreendo*	now kohm-pree-AYN-doo
Where is...?	*Onde é que é...*	OHN-deh eh keh eh
How much does this cost?	*Quanto custa?*	KWAHN-too KOOSH-tah
Do you have a single/double room?	*Tem um quarto individual/ duple?*	tem oom KWAR-toe een-DE-vee-DU-ahl/DOO-play
Help!	*Socorro!*	so-ko-RO

Accommodations and Camping **Movijovem,** Av. Duque D'Avila, 137, 1050 Lisbon (tel. (1) 355 90 81 or 355 90 87; fax 352 14 66), the Portuguese Hostelling International affiliate, looks over the country's HI hostels. All bookings may be made here. To stay in a hostel, you must have an HI card (3000$); buy one in your home country or at Movijovem's office in Lisbon. A bargain bed in a *pousada de juventude* (not to be confused with plush *pousadas*) costs 1100-2340$ per night, slightly less off season (breakfast and sheets included). Lunch or dinner usually costs 900$. Rates may be slightly higher for guests 26 or older. Check-in hours are 9am to noon and 6pm to midnight; some have lockouts from 10:30am to 6pm, and early curfews might cramp your style if you're planning a late night of club-hopping.

Pensões, also called *residencias,* will likely be your mainstay in Portugal; they're cheaper than hotels, and far more common than crowded hostels. All are rated by the government on a five-star scale, and are required to clearly display their category and legal price limits. During high season, it helps to book rooms at least a month in advance, although travelers planning a week ahead will likely find a room.

Quartos are rooms in private residences, sometimes the only choice in small or less touristed towns, particularly in southern Portugal. The tourist office can usually help you find them, and restaurant proprietors and bartenders often supply names and directions. A **pousada** (literally, resting place) is a castle, palace, or monastery converted into an expensive and luxurious government-run hotel (Portugal's version of the Spanish *parador nacional*). For information contact **ENATUR,** Av. Santa Joana Princesa, 10-A, 1749 Lisbon (tel. (1) 848 90 78; fax 80 58 46).

In Portugal, locals regard **camping** as a social activity more than anything else. Over 150 official campgrounds *(parques de campismo)* feature countless amenities and comforts; most have a supermarket and café, and many are beach-accessible or near rivers and pools. Given the facilities' quality and popularity, happy campers arrive early; urban and coastal parks may require reservations. Police have been cracking down on illegal camping, so don't try it, especially near official campgrounds. Big tourist offices stock the free *Portugal: Camping and Caravan Sites,* a handy guide to official campgrounds. Otherwise, write the **Federação Portuguesa de Campismo e Caravanismo,** Av. 5 de Outubro, 15-3, 950 Lisbon (tel. (1) 315 27 15; fax 315 54 93 72; open 9:30am-12:30pm and 1:30-6:30pm).

Food and Drink Olive oil, garlic, herbs, and sea salt routinely season local specialties. The aromatic Portuguese cuisine is heavy on herbs and light on spices. Main dishes run a delectable gamut. Seafood lovers get their fix from *chocos grelhado* (grilled cuttlefish), *lulas grelhado* (grilled squid), *linguado grelhado* (grilled sole), *polvo* (boiled or grilled octopus), and *mexilhões* (mussels). Pork fiends indulge in *bife de porco à alentejana,* made with clams in a coriander sauce. Those who prefer chicken fork into *frango assado* (roasted on a spit) and *frango no churrasco* (grilled). The entire country feeds on *cozida à portuguesa* (boiled beef, pork, sausage, and vegetables) in winter. Portugal's favorite dessert is *pudim,* a rich caramel custard. Portuguese *vinho* (wine) costs a pittance by North American standards. Sparkling *vinho verde* (literally "green wine") comes in red and white versions. Excellent local table wines include Colares, Dão, Borba, Bairrada, Bucelas, and Periquita. Port, pressed (by feet) from the red grapes of the Douro Valley and fermented with a bit of brandy, is a fortified dessert in itself. A unique heating process gives Madeira wines their odd "cooked" flavor.

The Portuguese eat their main meal between noon and 2pm and supper between 7:30 and 10pm. A good meal costs 1000-2000$ just about anywhere; oddly, prices don't vary much between ritzy and economy restaurants. Half portions *(meia dose)* cost more than half-price but are often more than adequate. The ubiquitous *prato do dia* (special of the day) and *menú* (appetizer, bread, entree, and dessert) satisfy hungry folks; the *ementa turistica* (tourist menu) is usually a way to rip off foreigners. Vegetarians will find a **mercado municipal** (open-air produce market) and at least one **supermercado** (supermarket) in every town. Most restaurants will add a 10% service charge to your bill, and couples typically leave around 150$ as a tip.

Lisbon (Lisboa)

Over 400 years ago, Lisbon was the home of renowned explorers and the center of the world's richest and most far-reaching empire. Although the glory days of the Age of Discovery are long gone, Lisbon's continual renovation of its mosaic sidewalks, pastel facades, and cobbled alleys will pay off this year, when it hosts **Expo '98,** just in time to commemorate the 500th anniversary of Vasco da Gama's voyage to India. Nine million visitors are expected to arrive in Lisbon for the event and make their own exploration of the New World that $565 million *escudos* can construct.

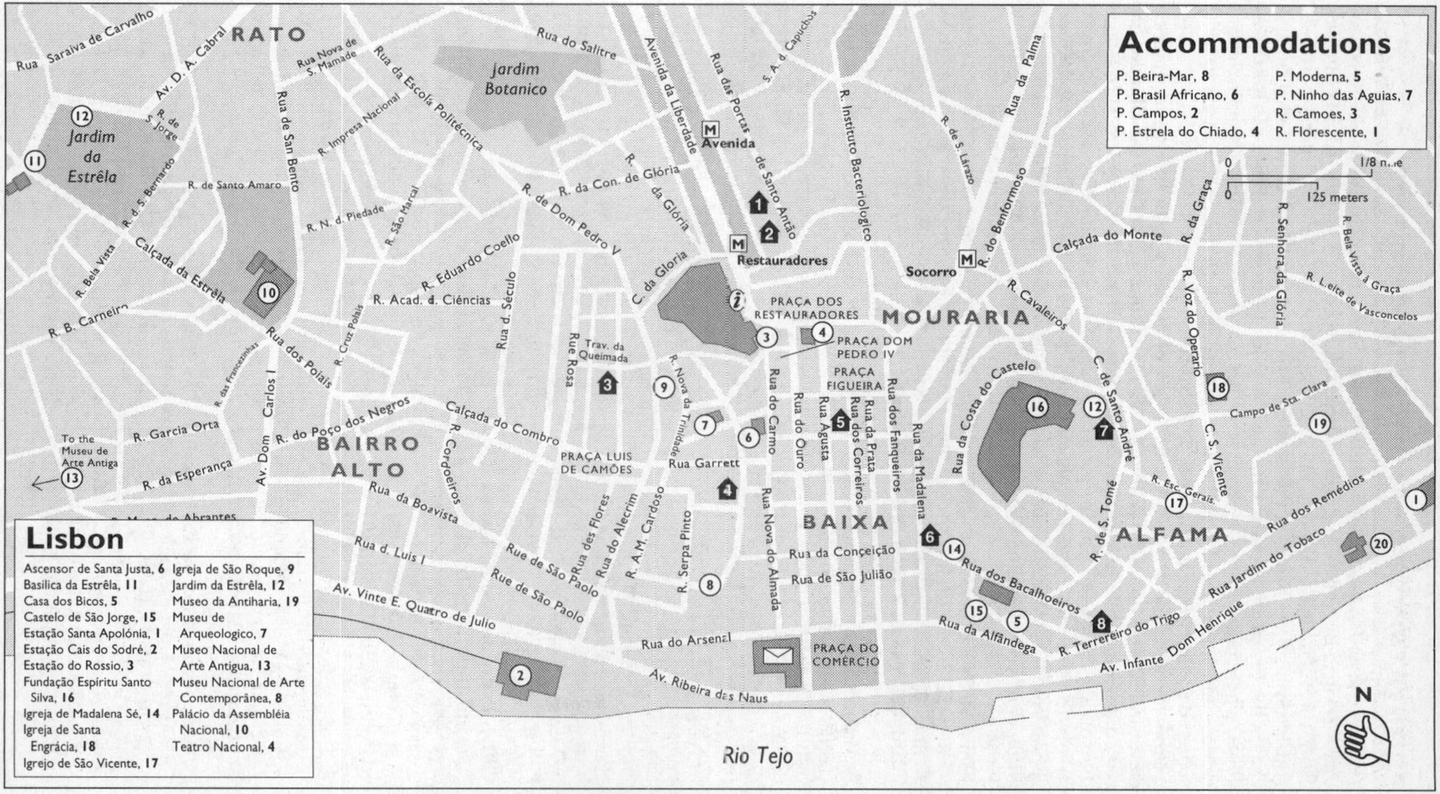
Accommodations
P. Beira-Mar, 8
P. Brasil Africano, 6
P. Campos, 2
P. Estrela do Chiado, 4
P. Moderna, 5
P. Ninho das Aguias, 7
R. Camoes, 3
R. Florescente, 1
Lisbon
Ascensor de Santa Justa, 6
Basilica da Estrêla, 11
Casa dos Bicos, 5
Castelo de São Jorge, 15
Estação Santa Apolónia, 1
Estação Cais do Sodré, 2
Estação do Rossio, 3
Fundação Espíritu Santo Silva, 16
Igreja de Madalena Sé, 14
Igreja de Santa Engrácia, 18
Igrejo de São Vicente, 17
Igreja de São Roque, 9
Jardim da Estrêla, 12
Museo da Antiharia, 19
Museu de Arqueologico, 7
Museo Nacional de Arte Antigua, 13
Museu Nacional de Arte Contemporânea, 8
Palácio da Assembléia Nacional, 10
Teatro Nacional, 4
125 meters
RATO
BAIRRO ALTO
MOURARIA
BAIXA
ALFAMA
Jardim Botanico
Jardim da Estrêla
Rio Tejo
PRAÇA DOS RESTAURADORES
PRAÇA DOM PEDRO IV
PRAÇA FIGUEIRA
PRAÇA LUIS DE CAMÕES
PRAÇA DO COMÉRCIO
Avenida
Restauradores
Socorro
To the Museu de Arte Antiga
Avenida da Liberdade
Rua das Portas de Santo Antão
R. Instituto Bacteriologico
Rua da Palma
Rua do Salitre
Rua da Escola Politécnica
Rua de San Bento
Calçada da Estrêla
Rua dos Poiais
Calçada do Combro
Rua Garrett
Rua do Carmo
Rua do Ouro
Rua Agusta
Rua da Prata
Rua dos Correiros
Rua dos Fanqueiros
Rua da Madalena
Rua Nova do Almada
Rua da Conçeição
Rua de São Julião
Rua dos Bacalhoeiros
Rua da Alfândega
Rua do Arsenal
Av. Ribeira das Naus
Av. Infante Dom Henrique
Rua Jardim do Tobaco
Rua dos Remédios
Calçada do Monte
R. Voz do Operario
C. S. Vicente
C. de Santo André
Rua da Costa do Castelo
R. Cavaleiros
R. do Benformoso
Av. Vinte E. Quatro de Julio
Rue de São Paolo
Rua da Boavista
Rua d. Luis I
Rue Rosa
R. de Dom Pedro V
R. Eduardo Coello
R. Acad. d. Ciências
Rua d. Seculo
Av. Dom Carlos I
R. do Poço dos Negros
R. Garcia Orta
R. da Esperança
R. B. Carneiro
R. Bela Vista
R. d. S. Bernardo
R. de Santo Amaro
Av. D. A. Cabral
Rua Saraiva de Carvalho
Rua Nova de S. Mamade
R. Impresa Nacional
R. N. d. Piedade
R. São Marcal
R. Cruz Polais
R. das Francezinhas
R. Cordoeiros
Rua des Flores
Rua do Alecrim
R. A.M. Cardoso
R. Serpa Pinto
R. Nova da Trinidade
Trav. da Queimada
C. da Glória
R. da Con. de Glória
R. da Glória
R. de S. Lárazo
R. da Graça
R. Senhora da Glória
R. Bela Vista à Graça
R. Leite de Vasconcelos
Campo de Sta. Clara
R. Esc. Gerais
R. de S. Tomé
R. Terreiro do Trigo
N

PORTUGAL

ORIENTATION AND PRACTICAL INFORMATION

The three main *bairros* (neighborhoods) of the city center are the **Baixa** ("low" district, resting in the valley), the **Bairro Alto** ("high district"), and the **Alfama** (the oldest district). The Baixa, Lisbon's old business district, sits in the center of town. Its grid of small streets begins at the **Rossio** (also called the **Praça dom Pedro IV**) and ends at the **Praça do Comércio,** on the **Rio Tejo** (Tagus River). **Praça dos Restauradores,** where buses from the airport stop, lies just above the Baixa. From Pr. Restauradores, tree-lined **Avenida da Liberdade** runs uphill to the new business district, centered around **Praça do Marquês de Pombal.**

From the west side of the Baixa, the **Ascensor de Santa Justa,** an elegant, outdoor elevator, lifts you up to the **Bairro Alto's** ritzy shopping district, the **Chiado,** traversed by fashionable **Rua do Carmo** and **Rua Garrett.** Most of Bairro Alto, where the young Portuguese come to party, is a populous, working-class area of narrow streets, tropical parks, and Baroque churches. To the east of the Baixa, the **Alfama,** Lisbon's medieval Moorish quarter, has tiny whitewashed houses stacked along a labyrinth of narrow alleys and stairways beneath the **Castelo de São Jorge.**

Tourist Office: Palácio da Foz, Pr. Restauradores (tel. 346 63 07 or 346 33 14). M: Restauradores. English spoken. Bus schedules, free map. Open Mon.-Sun. 9am-8pm. **Branch office** at the airport (tel. 849 36 89). Open daily 6am-2am.

Budget Travel: Tagus (Youth Branch), Pr. Londres, 9B (tel. 849 15 31). M: Alameda. From the Metro, walk up Av. Guer. Junqueiro. English spoken. **Tagus (Main Office),** R. Camilo Castelo Branco, 20 (tel. 352 59 86). M: Rotunda. Both offices open Mon.-Fri. 9am-1pm and 2:30-5:30pm.

Embassies: Australians should turn to the Australian Embassy in Paris. **Canada,** Av. Liberdade, 144, 4th fl., #4 (tel. 347 48 92). **South Africa,** Av. Luis Bivar, 10 (tel. 353 50 41; fax 353 57 13). **U.K.,** R. São Bernardo, 33 (tel. 392 40 00; fax 392 41 86). Also handles **New Zealand** affairs. **U.S.,** Av. das Forças Armadas (tel. 727 33 00; fax 726 91 09).

Currency Exchange: For a low commission and decent rates, try **Cota Cámbio,** R. Áurea, 283, one block off Pr. Dom Pedro IV in the Baixa. Higher commission at the Santa Apolónia train station; open 24hr. **Banks** open Mon.-Fri. 8:30-11:45am and 1-2:45pm. **ATMs** line the streets of Baixa and offer the best exchange rates.

American Express: Top Tours, Av. Duque de Loulé, 108 (tel. 315 58 85). M: Rotunda. Exit toward R. Rodrigo Sampaio and walk up Av. da Liberdade toward the Marquês de Pombal Statue, then turn right. This office handles all AmEx services; expect long lines. Traveler's checks sold and cashed. Mail held. English spoken. Open Mon.-Fri. 9:30am-1pm and 2:30-6:30pm.

Flights: Aeroporto de Lisboa (tel. 840 20 60 or 849 63 50), on the northern outskirts of the city. Local buses 44 and 45 connect to the tourist office (20min., 150$); the express bus (AeroBus or 91; 430$) is faster. Taxis run 1300$, plus a 300$ flat fee for luggage. **TAP Air Portugal,** Pr. Marques de Pombal, 3 (tel. 386 40 80), **Iberia,** Rua Rosa Araújo, 2 (tel. 355 81 19), and the domestic **Portugália Airlines,** Av. Almirante Gago Coutinho, 88 (tel. 848 66 93) are major airlines.

Trains: For info, call 888 40 25. **Estação Rossio,** between Pr. Restauradores and Pr. Dom Pedro IV, serves Sintra (185$) and western cities. **Estação Santa Apolónia,** Av. Infante D. Henrique, handles international, northern, and eastern lines. To: Coimbra (1300$), Madrid (8200$), Paris (24,000$). **Estação Cais do Sodré,** just beyond the south end of R. Alecrim, serves Estoril and Cascais (180$) and a few other cities. **Estação Barreiro,** on the south bank of the Tejo (accessible by ferry), covers southern lines.

Buses: Rodoviária da Estremadeira, Av. Casal Ribeiro, 18 (tel. 55 77 15). M: Saldanha. From the metro station, walk to the Pr. Duque de Saldantia. To: Coimbra (2½hr., 1350$), Lagos (5hr., 2200$), Porto (4hr., 1900$). **Caima,** R. Bacalhoeiros, 16 (tel. 887 50 61), runs to the Algarve, Porto, (2000$), and Lagos (2400$).

Public Transportation: CARRIS buses (tel. 363 93 43 or 363 20 44) will take you virtually anywhere in the city for 150$ per ride. **Metro (M)** tickets cost 70$; a book of 10 tickets runs 550$. The *bilhete de assinatura turístico* (tourist pass), good for unlimited public transportation travel, costs 430$ for 1 day, 1600$ for 4 days, or 2265$ for a week. The passes are sold in CARRIS booths (open daily 8am-8pm), located in most network train stations, and the busier metro stations. **Trams** are old and ubiquitous, offering beautiful views of the harbor and older neighborhoods. Line 28 is good for sightseeing (stops in Pr. Comércio; 150$).

Taxis: Rádio Táxis de Lisboa (tel. 815 50 61), **Autocoope** (tel. 793 27 56), and **Teletáxi** (tel. 815 20 16) cover the city. Available 24hr. 300$ luggage fee.

Luggage Storage: At **Estações Rossio** and **Santa Apolónia**. Lockers 450-600$ for up to 48hr. At the **bus station,** storage runs 150$ per bag per day.

English Bookstore: Livraria Bertrand, R. Garrett, 73. Best-sellers, magazines, and maps. Open Mon.-Fri. 9am-7pm, Sat. 9am-1pm.

Laundromat: Lavatax, R. Francisco Sanches, 65A (tel. 812 33 92). M: Arroios. Wash and dry 1180$ per 5kg. Open Sun.-Fri. 9am-1pm and 3-7pm, Sat. 9am-noon.

Medical Assistance: British Hospital, R. Saraiva de Carvalho, 49 (tel. 395 50 67, for direct appointments 397 63 29).

Emergencies: tel. 115 anywhere in Portugal. **Fire:** tel. 342 22 22.

Police: R. Capelo, 3 (tel. 346 61 41 or 347 47 30).

Post Office: Correio, Pr. Comércio (tel. 346 32 31). Open for *Poste Restante,* telephones, and faxes Mon.-Fri. 8:30am-6:30pm. The **branch office** at Pr. Restauradores has the same services. Open Mon.-Fri. 8am-10pm, Sat.-Sun. 9am-6pm. **Postal Code:** 1100.

Telephones: Everywhere. **Portugal Telecom,** Pr. Dom Pedro IV, 68, has a bank of pay phones and booths for international calls. **Phone cards** come in 50 units (875$) or 120 units (2100$); local calls cost at least 1 unit. **Telephone Code:** 01.

ACCOMMODATIONS AND CAMPING

Expect to pay about 3000$ for a single and 5000$ for a double: if the fee seems padded, request the printed price list. Most hotels are located in the center of town on **Av. da Liberdade,** while convenient budget *pensões* are in the **Baixa** along the **Rossio** and on **Ruas da Prata, dos Correeiros,** and **do Ouro.** Lodgings near the **Castelo de São Jorge** or in the **Bairro Alto** are quieter, closer to the sights, and more expensive. If the central accommodations are full, head east to the *pensões* along **Av. Almirante Reis.** Be cautious in the isolated and poorly lit streets of Bairro Alto, the Alfama, and the Baixa after dark.

Pousada de Juventude de Lisboa (HI), R. Andrade Corvo, 46 (tel. 353 26 96; fax 353 75 41). M: Picoas. Exit the Metro station facing south, turn right, and walk one block. Huge, ultra-clean youth haven. Members only. Reception open 8am-midnight. Check-out by 10:30am. Dorms 1900-2350$. Doubles with bath 4800-5700$. Breakfast included. Lockers 250$. Wheelchair access.

Pousada de Juventude de Catalazete (HI), Estrada Marginal (tel. 443 06 38). Take a train from Estação Cais do Sodré to the costal town **Oeiras** (20min., 155$). Exit through the underpass from the side of the train coming *from* Lisbon, cross the street, and follow signs to Lisboa and Cascais. At the intersection across from a bus stop, turn left and go downhill along R. Filipa de Lencastre. At underpass, go straight and follow HI signs to the INATEL complex. Reception open daily 8am-midnight. Curfew midnight. Dorms 1700$. Doubles 4100$. Prices lower off season. Breakfast included. Reservations recommended.

Pensão Beira-Mar, Largo Terreiro do Trigo, 16, 4th fl. (tel. 886 99 33, for reservations 09 31 64 63 09; fax 887 15 28). In a small square off Av. Infante Dom Henrique (the road that runs parallel to the river) between the Estação Santa Apolónia and the ferry station. Clean, spacious rooms and friendly owners. 2000$; off-season 1500$. Laundry 1000$. Reservations recommended.

Pensão Campos, R. Jardim do Regedor, 24 (tel. 346 28 64), between Pr. Restauradores and R. Portas de Santo Antão. Comfortable rooms run by a cool polyglot owner. Singles 2500$. Doubles 4000$, with shower 5000$. Triples 5300$.

Pensão Brasil Africano, Tr. Pedras Negras, 8, 3rd fl. (tel. 886 92 66), off R. Madalena. A homey *pensão* with friendly management, large rooms, and balconies. Singles 2000$. Doubles 3500$, with bath 4000$. Triples 5000$.

Pensão Moderna, R. Correeiros, 205, 4th fl. (tel. 346 08 18), 1 block from the south side of Pr. Figueira. Antique-fitted rooms have large windows and balconies. Singles 3000$. Doubles 3500-5000$.

Residêncial Florescente, R. Portas de Santo Antão, 99 (tel. 342 66 09; fax 342 77 33), 1 block from Pr. Restauradores. Luxurious by budget standards. Singles and doubles 3500-5000$, with shower 6500$, with full bath and A/C 8500$.

Pensão Ninho das Águias, R. Costa do Castelo, 74 (tel. 886 70 08). Spectacular views of Lisbon are worth the long hike. Singles 4500-5500$. Doubles 6000-7000$. Triples 6500-7000$. Reserve ahead.

Residêncial Camões, Tr. do Poço da Cidade, 38, 1st fl. (tel. 367 75 10; fax 346 40 48), off R. Misericórdia. A pristine set of rooms in the heart of the Bairro Alto party district. Singles 2500-3500$, with bath 6000$. Triples 6000$, with bath 7000$. English spoken. Breakfast included. Reservations essential.

Pensão Estrêla do Chiado, R. Garrett, 29, 4th fl. (tel. 342 61 10). The 12 spotless rooms, hot water, and large well-furnished singles entice. Recent renovations. Singles 2500$, with shower 3500$. Doubles 4500$, with shower 5000$.

Camping: *Portugal: Camping and Caravan Sites* is free from the tourist office. **Parque de Campismo Municipal de Lisboa** (tel. 760 20 61; fax 760 74 74) is on the road to Benfica. Take bus 43 from the Rossio to the Parque Florestal Monsanto. Swimming pool and supermarket. 420$ per person. 355$ or more per tent (depending on size). Prices lower during winter.

FOOD

Lisbon has some of the least expensive restaurants and best wine of any European capital. A full dinner costs about 1800$ per person, and the *prato do dia* (special of the day) is often a great deal. Try the areas near the end of the port and bordering the Alfama in Baixa, or find the smaller eateries in the Bairro Alto. Lisbon reels with seafood specialties such as the local classic, *bacalhau cozido com grão e batatas* (cod with chick-peas and boiled potatoes). Bus 40 runs to **Mercado Ribeira,** a market complex on Av. 24 de Julho, outside Cais do Sodré (open Mon.-Sat. sunrise-2pm). The smaller **Supermercado Celeiro,** Rua 1 de Dezembro, 65, is centrally located (open Mon.-Fri. 8:30am-8pm, Sat. 8:30am-7pm).

Restaurante João do Grão, R. dos Correeiros, 222. Chow down at one of Lisbon's most highly recommended eateries. House wine 295$. Entrees from 850$.

Restaurante Bonjardim, Tr. de Santo Antão, 11, off Pr. Restauradores. Tasty roast chicken 1100$. Entrees 1000-2500$. Open daily noon-11pm.

Rio Coura, R. Augusto Rosa, 30, up the hill from the Igreja da Sé. Fresh fish every day. Entrees 800-1300$. Open daily 1-4pm and 7-10:30pm.

Cervejaria da Trindade, R. Nova Trindade, 20C. Two blocks down a side street that begins in front of the Igreja do São Roqua and parallels R. Misericórdia. Part beer hall, part restaurant; altogether, a local favorite. Daily *sugestões do chefe* (chef's suggestions) are budget finds. Open Mon.-Sat. noon-2am.

Hua Ta Li, R. dos Bacalhoeiros, 109-115A, near the Pr. Comércio. Great Chinese vegetarian options. *Menú* 1400$. Open daily noon-3:30pm and 6:30-11pm.

Celeiro, Rua 1 de Dezembro, 65, take a right off the Rossio. Beneath a health food supermarket. Cafeteria-style salads, souffles, and sandwiches satisfy hungry herbivores. Entrees 200-570$. Open Mon.-Fri. 8:30am-8pm, Sat. 8:30am-7pm.

Confeitaria Nacional, Praça da Figueira 18B. Succumb to sweet temptation with the *austríaca* (120$) at this famous *pastelaría.* Open Mon.-Sat. 10am-5pm.

SIGHTS

The **Rossio,** or **Praça Dom Pedro IV,** is the city's main square and the domain of drink-sipping tourists and heart-stopping traffic. At the north end of the *praça,* the **Teatro Nacional** marks the former site of the Palace of the Inquisition. Further north, in **Praça dos Restauradores,** an obelisk and a bronze sculpture of the Spirit of Independence commemorate the 1640 "restoration" of Portugal's independence from Spain. The **Avenida da Liberdade,** one of the city's most elegant promenades, begins

World Expo '98: The Chronicles of Nautica

All eyes turn seaward as Lisbon prepares the century's biggest World Expo fair with the theme of "The Oceans: A Heritage for the Future." The fair itself runs May 22-September 30, but the events kicks off 100 days before the official opening with a festival showcasing operas by Phillip Glass and native son António Pinto Vargas. Make your reservations yesterday, or head to the youth hostels at Oeiras, Sintra, and Setúbal to find rooms amidst the nautically hungry hordes. The Expo grounds stretch along Av. Marechal Gomes da Costa on the industrial northern bank of the Tejo. Take buses departing from Terreiro do Io or Estaçao Santa Apolónia. You can purchase individual tickets for the Expo for 1 or 3 days, 1 night, or a 3-month pass. For more information, email info@expo98.pt, or check out their bubbly web page at http://www.expo98.pt.

here and extends to the **Praça do Marquês do Pombal** in the center of a bustling commercial district. South of the Rossio, a grid of streets connects the town center and the river. This area, known as the **Baixa,** is crowded with pedestrians, upscale shops, and ice cream vendors.

Although you can get from the Baixa to the **Bairrio Alto** by walking up the hill, the **Ascensor de Santa Justa,** an elevator built in 1902 inside a fanciful Gothic tower, offers a more memorable trip (75$ one way). At the top, turn left and walk one block to Rua Garrett, the heart of the chic **Chiado** neighborhood. Nearby, on R. da Misericórdia, the **Igreja de São Roque** is noted for its **Capela de São João Baptista** (fourth from the left), a chapel ablaze with precious gems and metals. Continue up R. da Misericórdia, which becomes R. São Pedro de Alcântara, to reach Lisbon's most beautiful park, the **Parque de São Pedro de Alcântara.**

A half-hour walk down Av. Infante Santo leads to the **Museu Nacional de Arte Antiga,** R. Janelas Verdes, home to a representative collection of European paintings ranging from Gothic to 18th-century French masterpieces (open Tues. 2-6pm, Wed.-Sun. 10am-6pm; 500$, students 250$). Buses 40 and 60 stop to the right of the museum exit and head back to the Baixa.

The **Alfama,** Lisbon's medieval quarter, was the lone neighborhood to survive the 1755 earthquake intact. Between the Alfama and the Baixa is the **Mouraria** (Moorish quarter), established after Dom Alfonso Henriques and the Crusaders expelled the Moors in 1147. Climb along the R. da Madalena (which runs north-south) to Largo Santo António da Sé, which changes names several times as you follow the tram tracks to the delicate **Igreja de Santo António da Sé.** The church was built in 1812 over the saint's alleged birthplace (open daily 7:30am-7:30pm). From here, follow the signs for a winding uphill walk to the restored, luxurious **Castelo de São Jorge,** which offers spectacular views of Lisbon and the ocean. Built in the 5th century by the Visigoths, this castle was the royal family's palace from the 14th to the 16th centuries (open April-Sept. daily 9am-9pm; Oct.-March 9am-7pm; free).

Belém is more of a suburb than a neighborhood of Lisbon. To get there, take tram 15 from Pr. do Comércio (20min., 150$) or the train from Estação Cais do Sodré (10min., 110$). From the train station, cross the tracks and street to get into town. Rising from the banks of the Tagus, **Mosteiro dos Jerónimos** celebrates the Age of Discovery and showcases Portugal's own Manueline style, combining Gothic forms with early Renaissance details. (Open Tues.-Sun. 10am-5pm. June-Sept. 400$, students 200$; Oct.-May 250$, students free.) Within the monastery complex is the **Museu da Marinha,** an intriguing ship museum (open Tues.-Sun. 10am-6pm; 400$, students 200$, free Sun. 10am-2pm). A 10-minute walk along the coast from the monastery, the **Torre de Belém,** built to protect the seaward entrance of the Portuguese capital, rises from the Tagus's north bank and has a magnificent view of the coast (open Tues.-Sun. 10am–5pm; June-Sept. 400$, Oct.-May 250$; students 200$). Contemporary art buffs will bask in the glow of the gigantic, luminous **Centro Cultural de Belém** (http://www.fdescccb.pt), with four pavilions, several art galleries, and a huge auditorium for performances (open daily 11am-8pm).

ENTERTAINMENT

The *Agenda Cultura* (also at http://www.consiste.pt/agenda) and *Lisboa em,* available free from kiosks in the Rossio and at the tourist office, publish listings of concerts, movies, plays, exhibits, and bullfights. Lisbon's trademark is the heart-wrenching *fado,* an expressive art which combines elements of singing and narrative poetry. *Fadistas* perform sensational tales of lost loves and faded glory; their melancholy wailing is expressive of *saudade,* nostalgia and yearning. The Bairro Alto has many *fado* joints off **R. Misericórdia,** particularly on sidestreets radiating from the Museu de São Roque. Feel the knife twisting in your heart at **Adega Machado,** R. do Norte, 91 (2500$ cover includes 2 drinks; open nightly 8pm-3am in summer; Nov.-May closed Mon.) or **O Faia,** R. Baroca, 54 (cover 2500$; open Mon.-Sat. 8pm-2am). Afterwards, cheer up at the many bars and clubs around **Rua do Norte, Rua Diário Notícias,** and **Rua da Atalaia.** Most places open around midnight.

Termas D'Atalaia Bar, R. da Atalaia, 108. One of the best, featuring drinks such as *orgasmo* and *sangue dos deuses* (blood of the gods; 400$). A waterfall flows down the front window. Open Mon.-Sat. 10pm-3:30am.

Memorial, R. Gustavo de Matos Sequeira, 42A, 1 block south of R. Escola Politécnica in the Bairro Alto. This hip gay and lesbian disco-bar is far-out—in all senses. Europop blasts from 10pm, but the fun starts after midnight. 1000$ cover (except Mon. or Thurs.) includes 2 beers or 1 mixed drink. Open Tues.-Sun. 10pm-4am.

Frágil, R. da Atalaia, 126/8, on the corner of R. da Atalaia and Tr. Queimada. A mixed gay/straight (but uniformly beautiful) crowd. Beer 600$. Hard liquor could empty your wallet. Open Mon.-Sat. 10:30pm-3:30am.

Os Três Pastorinhos, R. da Barroca, 111-113. Funk, pop, soul, and disco merge into a dancing frenzy. Open Tues.-Sun. 11pm-4am.

Solar do Vinho do Porto, R. São Pedro de Alcãntara, 45. Port-tasting in a mature setting. Glasses 130-2800$. Open Mon.-Fri. 10am-11:30pm, Sat. 11am-10:30pm.

Portas Largas, R. da Atalaia, 105. Scrawl on the walls and hang with the locals. Opens at 10am, closes around 2:30am.

Pé Sujo, Largo de St. Martinho, 6-7, in the Alfama. Live Brazilian music nightly from 11:30pm-2am. Try the killer Brazilian *caipirinha* (from sugarcane alcohol, 700$), or, for the truly brave, a *caipirosca* (700$). Open Tues.-Sun. 10pm-2am.

■ Near Lisbon: Sintra, Mafra, Estoril, and Cascais

After Lord Byron dubbed it "glorious Eden" in the epic poem *Childe Harold,* **Sintra** became a must for 19th-century aristocrats on the Grand Tour. Twentieth-century romantics trek 3km uphill to the architectural potpourri of the **Palácio da Pena,** a Bavarian castle embellished with Arab minarets, Gothic turrets, Manueline windows, and a Renaissance dome. (Open in summer Tues.-Sun. 10am-6pm; in winter Tues.-Sun. 2-4:30pm. 600$, students 400$; in winter 200$.) Signs point to the ruins of the **Castelo dos Mouros** (Moorish Castle), perched on the boulder-studded peaks towering over Sintra. Below, between the train station and the town center, looms the **Palácio Nacional de Sintra,** formally the summer residence of Moorish sultans and their harems (open Thurs.-Tues. 10am-1pm and 2-5pm; 400$, students 200$). North of Sintra, the otherwise unremarkable town of **Mafra** is home to one of Portugal's most impressive sites, the **Palácio Nacional** complex, which incorporates a palace, royal library, Baroque church, and hospital (open Wed.-Mon. 10am-1pm and 2-5pm; 300$, students free). Reach Mafra from Sintra by train (1hr., 350$).

Sintra is accessible by **train** from Lisbon's Rossio station (40min., 180$). The **tourist office** (tel. (01) 923 11 57; fax 923 51 76) is at Pr. República (open June-Sept. daily 9am-8pm; Oct.-May 9am-7pm). Hike 3km uphill for the gorgeously situated **Pousada da Juventude de Sintra (HI),** Sta. Eufémia. (Tel./fax (01) 924 12 10. Reception open daily 9am-noon and 6pm-midnight. 1300-1600$.) The recently renovated **Pensão Nova Sintra,** Largo Afonso de Albuquerque, 25 (tel. (01) 923 02 20) is closer (call for prices; reservations necessary).

The reputation of **Estoril** and **Cascais,** 30 minutes west of Lisbon, as playgrounds for the rich and famous, shouldn't deter you from spending a day at the beach, although on weekends the bronzed-flesh to bronzed-sand ratio skyrockets. From Cascais you can take bus 403 to the westernmost point on the European continent, **Cabo da Roca,** with spectacular views of the ocean (1hr., 300$). **Trains** to Estoril leave from the Estação do Sodré in Lisbon (30min., 180$). If you're traveling from Sintra, Rodoviária **buses** run from Av. Dr. Miguel Bombarda, across the street from the train station, to both towns (Cascais 1hr., 550$; Estoril 40min., 320$). The Estoril **tourist office,** Arcadas do Parque (tel. (01) 466 38 13; fax 467 22 80), across from the train station, offers detailed maps and schedules of events in the area (open Mon.-Sat. 9am-7pm, Sun. 10am-6pm). Its swanky counterpart in Cascais (tel. (01) 486 82 04) is on Av. Combatentes da Grande Guerra at R. Visconde da Luz (open June-Sept. 15 daily 9am-8pm; Sept. 16-May 9am-7pm).

In Estoril, **Residencial Smart,** R. Maestro Lacerda, 6 (tel. (01) 468 21 64), has gorgeously cultivated grounds. To get there, follow Av. Marginal toward Lisbon past the Paris Hotel to the corner of Av. Bombeiros Voluntários, and make a left. Walk three blocks uphill to R. Maestro Lacerda and follow this street for three blocks (doubles 5000-8000$; breakfast included). The Cascais tourist office will call around to find you a room (5000$). In Estorial, try the **Yate Restaurante-Snack Bar** (a.k.a. Yacht Bar), Arcados do Parque, for simple entrees (800-1400$; open daily 7am-2:30am), or save your appetite for the better options in Cascais.

CENTRAL PORTUGAL

The meadowed **Ribatejo** is a fertile region that fills most of the basin of the Tejo (Tagus) and its main tributary, the Zêzere. Although farmed intensely—yielding vegetables, olives, and citrus fruits—the area is best known in Portugal as a breeding ground for Arabian horses and black bulls. Stretching beyond the Tagus, the **Alentejo** region covers almost one-third of the Portuguese land mass. With barely over half a million residents, it remains the country's least populous region. Aside from the mountainous west, the region is a vast granary.

Tomar

For centuries the arcane Knights Templar—part monks, part Crusaders—schemed and plotted from Tomar, a small town straddling the Rio Nabão. It's worth trekking in from all corners of Portugal to explore the mysterious **Convento de Cristo** grounds, established in 1320 as a refuge for the disbanded Knights. An ornate octagonal canopy protects the high altar of the **Templo dos Templares,** modeled after the Holy Sepulchre in Jerusalem. The Knights supposedly attended mass here on horseback, each under one of the arches. Below two great stained glass windows stands the **Janela do Capítulo** (chapter window), a tribute to the Golden Age of Discoveries. The **Claustro dos Felipes,** one of Europe's masterpieces of Renaissance architecture, honors King Felipe II of Castille, crowned in Tomar as Felipe I of Portugal during Iberia's unification (1580-1640). To reach the complex, walk from the tourist office and take the second right, bear left at the fork, and follow the steep dirt path on the left (open daily 9:30am-12:30pm and 2-5:30pm; 400$, students 600$).

The **Museu Luso-Hebraíco,** in the 15th-century **Sinagoga do Arco** at R. Dr. Joaquim Jaquinto, 73, is Portugal's most significant reminder of what was once one of Europe's great Jewish communities of the 15th century (open Thurs.-Tues. 9:30am-12:30pm and 2-6pm). Europe's largest matchbox collection lies in the **Museo dos Fósforos** in the Convento São Francisco (open Sun.-Fri. 2-5pm; free).

Practical Information, Accommodations, and Food The **Rio Nabão** divides Tomar, but most accommodations and sights, as well as the train and bus stations, lie on the west bank. Tomar's **tourist office,** Av. Dr. Cândido Madureira (tel. (049) 32 34 27), offers a map and accommodations list. To reach the office from the

PORTUGAL

train and bus stations, go through the small square onto Av. General Bernardo Raria. Continue for four blocks and turn left (open Mon.-Fri. 9:30am-6pm, Sat.-Sun. 10am-1pm and 3-6pm). The **train station,** on Av. Combatentes da Grande Guerra (tel. (049) 31 28 15), serves Lisbon, Coimbra, and Porto. Most destinations require a transfer at Entrocamento; you can buy tickets for both parts of your trip here. **Buses** (tel. (049) 31 27 38) leave for Lisbon (2hr., 1200$), Coimbra (2½hr., 1150$), Porto (4hr., 1400$), and Lagos (11hr., 2300$).

Accommodations are fairly plentiful in Tomar, so try bargaining. **Residencial União,** R. Serpa Pinto, 94 (tel. (049) 32 31 61; fax 32 12 99), halfway between Pr. República and the bridge, has bright, plush rooms, each with a shower or full bath, telephone, and TV. (Singles 3500-4500$; doubles 6000-6500$; triples 7500$. Breakfast included. Reserve ahead.) Camp at the thickly forested **Parque Municipal de Campismo** (tel. (049) 32 26 07; fax 32 10 26), on the river, across Ponte Velha near the stadium. (Reception open in summer daily 8am-8pm; off-season 9am-5pm. 380$ per person, 200$ per tent. Free showers.) Tomar is the picnic capital of Portugal—a section of the lush Parque Mouchão is set aside for just that purpose. The **market** on the corner of Av. Norton de Matos and R. Santa Iria, across the river, provides all the fixings (open Mon.-Sat. 8am-2pm). **Restaurante Tabuleiro,** R. Serpa Pinto, serves mouth-watering *bitoque de porco* (675$; open Mon.-Sat. 11am-10pm).

Santarém

The capital of the Ribatejo province, Santarém was once a flourishing medieval center of 15 convents, and is known today as the centerpiece of Portugal's Gothic style. The austere facade of the **Igreja do Seminário dos Jesuítas** dominates Praça Sá da Bandeira, the main square. Stone friezes carved like ropes separate each of the church's three stories, and Latin mottos embellish the lintels and doorways. The church is under renovations. If it is closed, enter the door to the right of the main entrance and ask Sr. Domingos to unlock it. In the chapel to the right of the severe **Igreja da Graça** is the tomb of Pedro Alvares Cabral, who discovered Brazil and was one of the few *conquistadores* who lived long enough to be buried in his homeland.

The main exhibit in the **Museu Arqueológico de São João do Alporão,** off R. São Martinho, is the elaborate Gothic tomb of Dom Duarte de Meneses, who was hacked apart while fighting the Muslims. The tomb contains all that his comrades could salvage from the battlefield—one tooth. (Open June-Sept. Tues.-Sun. 10am-12:30pm and 2-6pm; Oct.-May Tues.-Sun. 9am-12:30pm and 2-5:30pm. Free.) **Portas Do Sol,** at the end of Av. 5 de Outubro, is a garden paradise with fountains surrounded by old Moorish walls. Climb up the remaining steps of the citadel for an awe-inspiring view.

The **train station,** 2km outside town, serves Lisbon (1hr., 520$) and Tomar (1hr., 370$). The **bus station,** Av. Brasil, also serves Lisbon (1½hr., 1000$; *expressos* 1hr., 1450$) and major cities. The **tourist office,** R. Capelo Ivêns, 63 (tel. (043) 39 15 12), elucidates bus and train schedules and finds rooms. (Open Mon. 9am-12:30pm and 2-6pm, Tues.-Fri. 9am-7pm, Sat.-Sun. 10am-12:30pm and 2:30-5:30pm.) Room prices increase 10-40% during the Ribatejo Fair. **Residencial Abidis,** R. Guilherme de Azevedo, 4 (tel. (043) 220 17 or 220 18), around the corner from the tourist office, has soothing rooms (singles 2500-4500$, doubles 4500-7000$; breakfast included). Cramped rooms and medieval windows await travelers at the **Pensão do José** (a.k.a. Pensão da Dona Arminda), Trav. Froes, 14 and 18 (tel. (043) 230 88). Go left as you exit Turismo, and take the first right (singles 2000$, doubles 3000-3500$). Santarém's **sweets fair** ruins thousands of diets the last Wednesday to Sunday in April. Starting the first Friday in June, people flock for the 10-day orgy of bullfighting and horseracing at the **Feira Nacional de Agricultura (Ribatejo Fair).**

Évora

From a rolling plain of cork tree groves and sunflower fields, Évora rises like a megalith on a hill. Considered Portugal's foremost showpiece of medieval architecture, the town is also home to the famous Roman Temple to Diana, several Moorish arches, and a 16th-century university. Amid these monuments and museums, marble-floored shops display their wares and attract a steady (though not overwhelming) stream of tourists from Lisbon and the Algarve. The U.N. has taken notice as well, and has granted the city World Heritage status for its cultural and architectural achievements.

ORIENTATION AND PRACTICAL INFORMATION

Évora is easily accessible by train from Lisbon, about 140km to the west. Near the edge of town, R. Dr. Baronha turns into **Rua República,** which leads to **Praça do Giraldo,** the main square, and home to most monuments and lodgings. From the train station, it might be best to hail a taxi (400$) to reach the center; from the bus station, simply proceed uphill to the *praça.*

Tourist Office: Pr. Giraldo, 73 (tel. 226 71). Helpful multilingual staff compensates for the illegible map by calling around until you have a room. Open June-Sept. Mon.-Fri. 9am-7pm, Sat.-Sun. 9am-12:30pm and 2-5:30pm; Oct.-May Mon.-Fri. 9am-12:30pm and 2-6pm, Sat.-Sun. 9am-12:30pm and 2-5:30pm.

Currency Exchange: There is a 24hr. exchange machine near the tourist office.

Trains: From the *praça,* walk down R. República until it turns into R. Dr. Baronha; the **station** (tel. 221 25) is at the end of the road, 1½km from town. To Lisbon (6 per day, 3hr., 810$) and Faro (2 per day, 6hr., 1430$).

Buses: R. República (tel. 221 21), 5min. downhill from Praça Giraldo, opposite the Igreja de São Francisco. To: Lisbon (5 per day, 3hr., 1120$), Faro (5hr., 1470$), and Porto (7hr., 2300$). **Luggage storage** in the basement. 110$ per bag per day.

Laundromat: Lavandaria Lavévora, Largo D'Alvaro Velho, 6 (tel. 238 83), off R. Miguel Bombardo. 370$ per kg. Open Mon.-Fri. 9am-1pm and 3-7pm.

Hospital: Largo Senhor da Pobreza (tel. 250 01), close to the city wall and the intersection with R. D. Augusto Eduardo Nunes.

Emergency: tel. 112.

Police: R. Francisco Soares Lusitano (tel. 220 22), near the Temple of Diana.

Post Office: R. Olivença (tel. 264 39), 2 blocks north of Pr. Giraldo. Walk up R. João de Deus, pass under the aqueduct, and turn right. Open for *Poste Restante,* mail, telephones, and faxes Mon.-Fri. 8:30am-6:30pm. **Postal Code:** 7000.

Telephone Code: 066.

ACCOMMODATIONS, CAMPING, AND FOOD

Most *pensões* are located near the **Praça do Giraldo.** *Quartos,* rooms in private houses from 2000-4000$ per person, are pleasant alternatives to crowded *pensões* in the summer. Ask the tourist office to call around to find you a room.

Pensão Os Manueis, R. Raimundo, 35 (tel. 228 61). Marble stairs lead to homey rooms lining a sun-roofed courtyard. Singles 3000-5000$. Doubles 4000-6000$.

Pensão Giraldo, R. Mercadores, 27 (tel. 258 33). From the tourist office, take a left, and then left 2 blocks later. Rooms have TV, winter heat, and either a sink, shower, or full bath. Singles 3900$. Doubles 4800-7800$. Reserve ahead for the best rooms.

Casa Palma, R. Bernardo Mato 29-A (tel. 235 60); 3 blocks to the right from the tourist office. Pink frilly bedspreads in bright, well-furnished doubles. The singles are cheaper but dimmer. Singles 3000$. Doubles 4000$. Prices lower off season.

Orbitur's Parque de Campismo de Évora (tel. 251 90; fax 298 30). 3-star park on Estrada das Alcáçovas, which branches off the bottom of R. Raimundo. 40min. walk to town; 1 bus runs daily. Washing machines, market. Reception open daily 8am-10pm. 500$ per person, 400$ per tent. Showers 50$. Discounts Oct.-March.

Many passable budget restaurants cluster around the **Praça do Giraldo.** The **public market** sets up in the small square in front of Igreja de São Francisco and the public gardens, selling produce and cheeses. For other supplies, try **Maxigrula,** R. João de Deus, 130 (open Mon.-Sat. 9am-7pm). **Restaurante A Choupana,** R. Mercadores, 16-20, off Pr. Giraldo, has a snack bar on the left for a quick budget lunch. Avoid the astronomical cover charge by refusing the various sundries placed on the table (entrees 900-1300$; half-portions 600$; open daily 10am-2pm and 7-10pm). **Restaurante A Gruta,** Av. General Humberto Delgado, 2, serves barbecued chicken buried under a heap of fries (half-chicken 650$). Exit Pr. Giraldo and pass by the bus station, follow R. República toward the train station, and turn right at the end of the park (open Sun.-Fri. 11am-3pm and 5-10pm).

SIGHTS AND ENTERTAINMENT

Off the east side of the *praça,* R. 5 de Outubro leads to the colossal 12th-century **cathedral.** The 12 Apostles adorning the doorway are masterpieces of medieval Portuguese sculpture; inside, the **Museu de Arte Sacra** houses the cathedral's treasury and stunning 13th-century ivory *virgem do paraíso* (open Tues.-Sun. 9am-noon and 2-5pm; cathedral free, cloister and museum 350$). Nearby, housed above Roman, Visigoth,a nd moorish ruins, the **Museu de Évora** showcases a collection ranging from Roman tombs to 17th-century Virgin Mary polyptychs (open Tues.-Sun. 10am-noon and 2-5pm; 250$, under 25 and seniors 125$). Across from the museum stands Évora's most famous monument, the 2nd-century **Templo de Diana,** honoring the Roman goddess of the moon, purity, and the hunt. The temple was used as a slaughterhouse for centuries, but now only a platform and 14 Corinthian columns remains.

Évora's best-kept secret is the 15th-century **Igreja de São João Evangelista,** facing the temple. The interior is covered with dazzling *azulejos,* but you must ask to see the church's hidden chambers (open Tues.-Sun. 10am-noon and 2-5pm; 250$). Another standout is the **Igreja Real de São Francisco,** in its own square downhill from Pr. Giraldo. You might pause to admire the art, but the real show-stopper is the perverse **Capela de Ossos** (Chapel of Bones). Three tireless Franciscan monks ransacked assorted local graveyards for the remains of 4000 people to construct it. Enormous femurs and baby tibias neatly panel every inch of the walls, while rows of skulls line the capitals and ceiling vaults. (Open Mon.-Sat. 8:30am-1pm and 2:30-6pm, Sun. 10-11:30am and 2:30-6pm. Chapel closed during mass. Chapel 50$. Photos 100$.)

Although most of Évora tucks itself in with the sun, **Xeque-Mate,** R. Valdevinos, 21, the second right off R. 5 de Outubro from the *praça,* and **Discoteca Slide,** R. Serpa Pinto, 135, keep the music blaring until 2am. Only couples and single women need apply (cover 1000$). Évora's festival, the **Feira de São João,** keeps the town up all night with a huge Portuguese-style country fair during the last week of June.

ALGARVE

Once a quiet fishing backwater, Portugal's southern coast has now embraced commercial capitalism. In July and August, hordes of foreigners are lured by the Algarve's gorgeous sands, topless sunbathing, and exhilarating (and exhausting) nightlife. If you haven't reserved a room, ask at tourist offices and bars, keep your eyes peeled for signs, or take your chances with the room-pushers who accost incoming travelers at bus and train stations. **Faro,** the Algarve's capital, is at once a transportation hub and a provincial Portuguese city, to which trains chug from Lisbon (6 per day, 5hr., 2060$). In addition to the towns described here, plenty of villages welcome budget travelers; notable among them are **Salema, Burgau, Sagres,** and the region between **Olhão** and the Spanish border. Reaching more remote towns and beaches is a snap, as EVA has extensive bus services with convenient schedules and low fares. The train costs less than the bus but only connects major coastal cities, and in some towns the station is a hike from the center.

Lagos

There isn't much more than beaches and bars in Lagos, but nobody's complaining. Whether soaking in the view from the cliffs, soaking in the sun on the beach, or simply soaking themselves in beers and cocktails, tourists here enjoy one of the backpacker party centers of Europe. To the west, rock tunnels through sheer cliffs connect sandy coves, while to the east, a 4km long beach spreads along the coast.

ORIENTATION AND PRACTICAL INFORMATION

Running the length of the river, **Avenida dos Descobrimentos** carries traffic in and out of the city. **Rua das Portas de Portugal** marks the gateway leading into **Praça Gil Eanes** and the town's glitzy tourist center. Most restaurants, accommodations, and services hover about the *praça* and **Rua 25 de Abril;** they are usually mobbed.

Tourist Office: Largo Marquês de Pombal (tel. 76 30 31). Take the sidestreet R. Lina Leitão (off Pr. Gil Eanes), which leads to the Largo. A 20min. walk from the train station, 15min. from the bus station. Brochures, maps, transportation info, and a list of *quartos.* Open daily 9:30am-12:30pm and 2-5:30pm.

Currency Exchange: Commission-free exchange is available at the youth hostel.

Trains: For info, call 76 29 87. The **station** is on the east edge of town, across the river from the bus station. To: Lisbon (6½hr., 2000$), Évora (6hr., 1740$).

Buses: EVA (tel. 76 29 44), on the east edge of town, off. Av. dos Descobrimentos. To: Lisbon (5hr., 2000-2500$), Sagres (1hr., 445$), Faro (2½hr., 670$).

Laundromat: Lavandaria Miele, Av. dos Descobrimentos, 27. Wash and dry 1000$ per 5kg. Open Mon.-Fri. 9am-8pm, Sat. 9am-7:30pm.

Medical Assistance: Hospital, R. Castelo dos Governadores (tel. 76 30 34), next to Igreja Santa María. **Ambulance:** tel. 76 01 81.

Emergency: tel. 115.

Police: General Alberto Silva (tel. 76 26 30).

Post Office: R. Portas de Portugal (tel. 76 30 67), between Pr. Gil Eanes and the river. Open Mon.-Fri. 9am-6pm. For *Poste Restante,* make sure to label all letters "Estação Portas de Portugal." **Postal Code:** 8600.

Telephone Code: 082.

ACCOMMODATIONS, CAMPING, AND FOOD

The youth hostel and most pensions fill up in summer, so reserve ahead. Rooms in *casa particulares* (private homes) go for 1000-2000$—try haggling.

Pousada de Juventude de Lagos (HI), R. Lançarote de Freitas, 50 (tel./fax 76 19 70). From the train and bus stations, walk into town on Av. República and turn right up R. Portos de Portugal. Head into Pr. Gil Eanes and turn right up R. Garrett into Pr. Luis de Camões, then take a left on R. Cândido dos Reis. At the bottom of the hill, take a left. *Hostal* heaven: comfy beds and beautiful grounds. Kitchen. Reception open 9am-2am. No curfew. Dorms 1900$. Doubles with bath 4500$. Lower prices off season. Breakfast included. Reserve ahead.

Residencial Rubi Mar, R. Barroca, 70 (tel. 76 31 65, ask for David; fax 76 77 49), down R. 25 de Abril, then left on Senhora da Graça. Centrally located and comfortable—the 8 rooms go fast. Doubles 5500-6500$. Quads 7500-9000$. Lower prices off season. Breakfast included.

Residencial Caravela, R. 25 de Abril, 8 (tel. 76 33 61), has small but well-located rooms surrounding a courtyard. Singles 3500$. Doubles 5200$, with bath 5800$. Lower prices off season. Breakfast included.

Camping: Parque de Campismo do Imulagos (tel. 76 00 31) is annoyingly far away but linked to Lagos by a free shuttle bus. Reception open daily 8am-10pm. 900$ per person, 640$ per tent, 370$ per car. Closer by, **Camping Trindade** charges 400$ per person with tent, 800$ without tent. Follow Av. dos Descobrimentos towards Sagres.

Casa Rosa, R. do Ferrador, 22, has dozens of vegetarian dishes and all-you-can-eat specials; Mondays and Wednesdays have spaghetti and garlic bread for 850$ (open daily 9am-2pm and 7pm-3am). **Mullin's,** R. Cândido dos Reis, 86, is a Lagos hot spot. Servers dance to the tables with huge portions of spicy food (chicken *piri-piri* smothered in hot sauce 1200$; open daily noon-2am). For supplies, hit the **mercado,** Av. dos Descobrimentos, five minutes from the town center, or **Supermercado São Toque,** R. Portas de Portugal, across from the post office (open July-Sept. daily 9am-5pm; Oct.-June Mon.-Fri. 9am-8pm, Sat. 9am-2pm).

ENTERTAINMENT

Lagos's beaches are beautiful any way you look at them. Flat, smooth sands (crowded during the summer, pristine in the off season) stretch along the 4km long **Meia Praia,** across the river from town. For beautiful cliffs that hide less crowded beaches and caves (perfect to swim in and around), follow Av. Descobrimentos west until you reach the sign for **Praia do Pinhão.** From the beach, continue further on the paths and choose your own cove. The sculpted cliffs and grottoes of **Praia Dona Ana** appear on at least half of all Algarve postcards. For even more picturesque (and thinly populated) stretches, bike or hike your way west to **Praia do Camilo** and the grotto-speckled cliffs of **Ponta da Piedade.** There are relatively uncrowded sands between Lagos and Albufeira—try making **Portimão** your hub to explore them (by bus 30min., 350$).

The streets of Lagos pick up as soon as the sun dips down. The area between Pr. Gil Eanes and Pr. Luis de Camões bursts with cafés. The area around R. Marreiros Netto, north of Pr. Gil Eanes and R. 25 de Abril, off the *praça,* forms the center of nightlife—bars and clubs runneth over until well past 5am, and club-hopping is more a profession than a pastime. North of the *praça,* **Garagem de José** (Joe's Garage), opposite Mullin's restaurant at R. 1 de Maio, 78, will keep you on your toes from happy hour to early-morning tabletop-dancing. **Bad Moon Rising,** R. Marreiros Neto, 50, jams to grunge and indie rock from 8pm to 4am, with a lively scam scene on the side. Stop by **Shots in the Dark,** R. 1 de Maio, 16, to hang out with a younger backpacking crowd. Another hot watering hole is the **Calypso Bar,** R. 1 de Maio, 22. Closer to the water, bars scatter along R. 25 de Abril and its extension, R. Silva Lopes. **Sins,** R. Silva Lopes, has a friendly frat party atmosphere, with beer funneling and the infamous nine deadly sins (nine shots 4000$). A hopping gay bar, **The Last Resort,** is along R. Lançarote de Freitas and has live entertainment every Thursday night. Half a block up the street, the British pub **Taverna Velha** (The Old Tavern) hosts jolly happy hours with televised soccer matches.

■ Near Lagos: Sagres

Marooned atop a bleak, scrub-desert promontory on the barren southwest corner of Europe, Sagres's dramatic, desolate location discourages tour groups and upscale travelers—all the better for the town, which remains one of the most unspoiled destinations in the Algarve. Empty beaches, several open for nude bathing, fringe the peninsula. **Mareta** is at the bottom of the road from the center of town. Rock formations jut out into the ocean on both sides of the sandy crescent. The less popular **Tonel** is along the road east of town. Prince Henry the Navigator's polygonal **stone fortress** dominates the town in regal fashion. From this cliff-top outpost, Vasco da Gama, Magellan, Columbus, Diaz, and Cabral apprenticed in Henry's school of navigation. Six kilometers further west, the **Cabo de São Vicente,** once thought to be the end of the world, hangs onto the southwest tip of continental Europe.

The privately run **Turinfo** (tel. (082) 62 00 03; fax 62 00 04), on Pr. República in the main square, is versatile—they recommend accommodations and events, rent **bikes** (2000$ per day), have bus and trains schedules, and do laundry. There you can also take a **jeep tour** of the natural preserve (6500$, including lunch) and soak up **scuba** advice (open daily 10am-7pm). Down the road, the **Quiosque do Papa** kiosk station rents **bikes** (1000$ per day) and **mopeds** (2500$ per day) and offers commission-free **currency exchange** (open daily 9am-10pm). Rodoviária **buses** (tel. (082) 76 29 44) run from Lagos (4 per day, 1hr., 445$). The **market** is off R. Comandante Matoso; turn left off the main street at R. do Correio (open Mon.-Sat. 10am-8pm).

Albufeira

Those who come to Albufeira, the largest seaside resort in the Algarve, are hell-bent on relaxation. Of course, relaxation does not have to mean beaches and alcohol; Albufeira has preserved its graceful Moorish architecture in the old quarters of town, and a stroll out from the frenzied center affords a taste of genuine Portuguese culture. But who are we trying to kid? Albufeira's spectacular **beaches** range from the popular **Galé** and **São Rafael** west of town, to the central **Baleeira, Inatel,** and **Oura,** to the very chic **Falésia,** 10km east of town. Many small and relatively uncrowded beaches lie scattered among the praiasq—it pays to explore. The hottest clubs in town, **Disco Silvia's** and **Qué Pasa?,** face off on R. São Gonçalo de Lagos, near the east side of the beach. Other dandy mingling spots include the **Fastnet Bar** on R. Cândido dos Reis and the **Classic Bar** down the street. For more mellow nightlife, head east along the coast into the old town, where salsa tunes complement a stunning seaside view at **Café Latino,** on R. Latino Coelho.

The **tourist office,** R. 5 de Outubro, 5 (tel. (089) 58 52 79), has maps, brochures, and a list of *quartos* (3000-5000$; open daily 9:30am-noon and 2-7pm; Sat.-Sun. until 5:30pm). The **train station** (tel. (089) 57 16 16), 6km inland, is accessible from town by bus (every hr., 180$). Albufeira is on the Lagos-Vila Real de Santo António line, with frequent departures to Faro (45min., 300$) and Lagos (1½hr., 480$). The **bus station** (tel. (089) 58 97 55) is at the entrance to town, up Av. Liberdade; walk downhill to reach the center. EVA buses head to Faro (1hr., 570$) and Lagos (1½hr., 850$) as well. Many accommodations are booked from the last week in June through mid-September; if you can't find a room, ask for *quartos* around town or choose wisely among renters who meet you at the stations. **Pensão Silva,** R. 5 de Outubro (tel. (089) 51 26 69), near the tourist office, is in an old building with wood floors and chandeliers (singles 3000$, doubles 5000$; Oct.-May 2500$ and 4000$, respectively). The modern **Pensão Albufeirense,** R. Liberdade, 18 (tel. (089) 51 20 79), one block downhill from the bus station, has comfortable rooms and a TV lounge (singles 3500$, doubles 5000$; closed Oct.-April). **Parque de Campismo de Albufeira** (tel. (089) 58 98 70; fax 58 76 33) is a few km outside town on the road to Ferreiras. The place boasts swimming pools, restaurants, tennis courts, a supermarket, and a hefty price tag (850$ per person, per car, and per tent). Budget restaurants spill across the old fishing harbor east of the main beach. Locals recommend **Tasca do Viegas,** R. Cais Herculano, 2, where meat and fish dishes start at 750$ (open daily 11am-11pm).

Tavira

White houses and palm trees fringe the banks of the slow Gilão River and Baroque churches glorify the hills above one of the loveliest communities in the Algarve. Most of Tavira's sights are planted along the side streets leading off Pr. República. Steps from the *praça* lead past the tourist office to the **Igreja da Misericórdia,** whose superb Renaissance doorway glowers with heads sprouting from twisting vines and candelabra. Just beyond, the remains of the city's **Castelo Mouro** (Moorish Castle) enclose a handsome garden (open Mon.-Fri. 8am-5:30pm, Sat.-Sun. 10am-7:30pm) and the adjacent church **Santa Maria do Castelo** (open daily 9am-8pm). Local beaches, including **Pedras do Rei,** are close to town and accessible year-round. To reach Tavira's excellent beach on **Ilha da Tavira,** an island 2km away, take the Tavira-Quatro Águas bus from Pr. República to the ferry (daily 8am-midnight, 13 per day, 10min., round-trip100$; keep ticket stub for the return).

Tavira is easily reached from Faro by **bus** (1hr., 405$) and **train** (30min., 300$). The **tourist office,** R. Galeria, 9 (tel. (089) 32 25 11), off Pr. República, has maps and recommends accommodations. (Open in summer daily 9:30am-7pm; off-season Mon.-Fri. 9:30am-7pm, Sat.-Sun. 9:30am-12:30pm and 2-5:30pm.) Tavira has plenty of *pensões* and *quartos.* **Pensão Residencial Lagôas Bica,** R. Almirante Cândido dos Reis, 24 (tel. (089) 222 52), on the far side of the river, has nicely furnished rooms, an outdoor patio, and a rooftop picnic area. From Pr. República, cross the bridge and continue straight down R. A. Cabreira; turn right and go down one block (singles 2500$, doubles 3500-5000$; less in winter). **Ilha de Tavira campground** (tel. (089) 32 35 05) sprawls on the beach of the island 2km from the *praça.* (Reception open 24hr. 340$ per person, 510$ per tent. Showers 100$. Open Feb.-Sept.) Seek and ye shall find reasonably priced cafés and restaurants on Pr. República and opposite the garden on R. José Pires Padinha. **Churrasqueira "O Manuel,"** R. Almirante Cândido dos Reis, 6, has food *pronto a comer* (ready to eat) and serves up *febres na brasa* (pork chops) and *entrecostos* (baby back ribs) for700$ (open Wed.-Mon. 4pm-midnight).

NORTHERN PORTUGAL

Although their landscapes and shared Celtic past invite comparison with neighboring Galicia, the **Douro** and **Minho** regions are more populated and faster developing. South of the Rio Minho lies **Braga,** a busy commercial city whose concentration of religious architecture has earned it the title of "Portuguese Rome." Braga's people are considered by some the most pious, by others the most fanatic, and by all the most conservative in Portugal. Buses travel between Braga and Porto (2hr., 600$).

Farther inland rises the rugged region of **Trás-os-Montes.** Train service is slow and rickety here, but hiking opportunities, especially in the natural reserves of the Parque Natural de Alvão, abound. Southward lies the region of the **Three Beiras. Beiras Litoral** to the west is swiftly modernizing and rests on the beautiful "Silver Coast." Farther east, however, the mountainous **Beira Alta** and **Beira Baixa** are among the least developed areas in Portugal. Throughout the Beiras, farmers cultivate grapes and while silvery olive trees cloud the horizon.

Coimbra

Portugal's former capital, Coimbra regained importance in the late 16th century as a center of the Inquisition. Centuries later, António Salazar (Portugal's longtime Fascist dictator) attended the city's renowned university. Today, crew races, rowdy cafeteria halls, and swinging bars may make Coimbra noisy, grimy, and chaotic to some. Yet its youthful energy, medieval churches, and refreshing degree of diversity make it popular with more open-minded visitors.

ORIENTATION AND PRACTICAL INFORMATION

Coimbra has two train stations, connected by bus 5: **Coimbra-A,** in the lower town center, and **Coimbra-B,** 3km northwest of town. The lower town lies between the triangle formed by the river, **Largo da Portagem,** and **Praça 8 de Maio.** The university district perches atop the steep hill overlooking the lower town. Downhill, on the other side of the university, the **Praça da República** plays host to cafés, a shopping district, and the youth hostel.

Tourist Office: Largo Portagem (tel. 286 86 or 330 19; fax 255 76), 2 blocks east of Coimbra-A in a yellowish building off the square. The skilled staff offers free maps and accommodations info. Open July-Oct. Mon.-Fri. 9am-7pm, Sat.-Sun. 9am-1pm and 2:30-5:30pm; Oct.-April Mon.-Fri. 9am-6pm, Sat.-Sun. 10am-1pm.

Currency Exchange: Montepio Geral, C. Estrela. Decent rates. No charge for transactions less than 10,000$. Open Mon.-Fri. 8:30am-3pm. **Hotel Astória,** across from the tourist office (1000$ per transaction; open 24hr). **ATMs** line Pr. República and Largo Portagem.

Trains: For info on either **station,** call 246 32, 349 98, or 341 27. Trains arriving in Coimbra will stop in Coimbra-B first and Coimbra-A second; bus 5 connects the two. To: Figueira da Foz (every hr., 1hr., 280$), Porto (13 per day, 3hr., 900$), Lisbon (15 per day, 3hr., 1300$), and Paris (1 per day, 22hr., 23,000$).

Buses: Av. Fernão Magalhães (tel. 48 40 45 or 48 40 46), on the river's university side, 10min. out of town. To: Lisbon (15 per day, 3hr., 1250$), Porto (5 per day, 6hr., 1200$), Évora (5 per day, 6hr., 1850$), and Faro (4 per day, 12hr., 2800$).
Public Transportation: Buses and street cars handle inner-city traffic. Single tickets bought on board run 190$; a book of 10 costs 600$. Special tourist passes are also available. Tickets are sold in kiosks at Largo da Portagem and Pr. República.
Hospital: Hospital da Universidade de Coimbra (tel. 40 05 00 or 40 04 00). Near the Cruz de Celas stop on line 29.
Emergency: tel. 112.
Police: R. Olímpio Nicolau Rui Fernandes (tel. 220 22), facing the post office. Special division for foreigners on R. Venâncio Rodrigues 25 (tel. 240 45).
Post Office: R. Olímpio Nicolau Rui Fernandes (tel. 243 56), across from the police station. Open for *Poste Restante,* telephone, fax, and telegrams Mon.-Fri. 8:30am-6:30pm, Sat. 9am-12:30pm. **Postal Code:** 3000.
Telephones: In post offices and at Largo Portagem, 1. **Telephone Code:** 039.

ACCOMMODATIONS, CAMPING, AND FOOD

Somewhat seedy *pensões* line **Rua da Sota** and the surrounding streets across from Coimbra-A; **Av. Fernão Magalhães** and a few other streets offer nicer doubles for around 3500$. The hostel is an excellent choice if you have an HI card.

Pousada de Juventude (HI), R. Henriques Seco, 14 (tel./fax 229 55). From either Coimbra-A or Largo Portagem, take bus 7, 8, 29, or 46 to República, walk up R. Lourenço Azevedo to the left of the park, and take the 2nd right. Comfortable, friendly place. Reception open daily 9-10:30am and 6pm-midnight. Bag drop-off all day. Lockout 10:30am-6pm. Curfew midnight. 1300-1500$. Doubles 3000-4000$. Breakfast included. Prices may rise due to renovations.
Residencial Internacional de Coimbra, Av. Emídio Navarro, 4 (tel. 255 03), in front of Coimbra-A. The fluorescent lighting and lumpy pillows may annoy, but the location is very convenient. Singles 2000-2500$. Doubles 3000-4000$.
Pensão Rivoli, Pr. Comércio, 27 (tel. 255 50), in a mercifully quiet pedestrian plaza 1 block downhill from R. Ferreira Borges. Well-furnished rooms are comfortably worn. Singles 2000$. Doubles 4500$, with shower 5000$. Triples 6500$.
Camping: Municipal Campground (tel. 70 14 97), in a recreation complex ringed by noisy streets. Take bus 1 or 5 from Largo Portagem; enter the campground at the arch off Pr. 25 de Abril. Reception open April-Sept. daily 9am-10pm; Oct.-March 9am-6pm. 231$ per person, 163-174$ per tent. Showers included.

PORTUGAL

For cheap eats, scout out **Rua Direita,** west off Pr. 8 de Maio, the side streets to the west of Pr. Comércio and Largo da Portagem, and the university district around **Praça da República.** Perhaps the best budget meal deal in the country awaits at the **UC Cantina,** the university's cafeteria. The cafeteria is located on the right side of R. Oliveiro Matos, about a half block downhill from the base of the steps leading from the university to Pr. República. An international student ID is (theoretically) needed to partake of meals for as little as 270$. **Churrasqueria do Mondego,** R. Sargento Mor, 25, off R. Sota, frequented by truck drivers and students serves a half-chicken for 350$ (open daily noon-3pm and 6-10:30pm). The **Supermarcado Minipreço** is in the lower town on R. António Granjo, 6C; go left out of Coimbra-A, and make another left (open Mon.-Sat. 9am-8pm). **Café Santa Cruz,** Pr. 8 de Maio, has seen better days, but it's still the most popular café in town (open daily 7am-2am).

SIGHTS AND ENTERTAINMENT

The best way to take in Coimbra's old town sights is to climb from the river up to the university—and quite a climb it is. Begin the ascent at the decrepit **Arco de Almedina,** the remnant of a Moorish-era town wall. Up a narrow stone stairway looms the hulking 12th-century Romanesque **Sé Velha** (Old Cathedral). Tours leaving around noon explore the principal tombs and friezes while Gregorian chants echo in the background (open daily 9:30am-12:30pm and 2-5:30pm; cloisters 100$).

Enter the center of the university complex through the **Porta Férrea** (Iron Gate) off R. São Pedro. These buildings were Portugal's de facto royal palace when Coimbra was the capital of the kingdom. The staircase at the right leads up to the **Sala dos Capelos,** where portraits of Portugal's kings hang below a beautifully painted 17th-century ceiling (open daily 9:30am-noon and 2-5pm; free). Past the Baroque clock tower are the **university chapel** and the 18th-century **university library.** The library holds 300,000 books from the 12th to 19th centuries in three gilded halls (open daily 10am-noon and 2-5pm; 300$, students with ID free).

The **Igreja de Santa Cruz** (Church of the Holy Cross) on Pr. 8 de Maio, at the far end of R. Ferreira Borges in the lower town, is a 12th-century church with a splendid barrel-vaulted **sacristía** (sacristy) and ornate **túmulos reals** (royal tombs) where the first two kings of Portugal lie buried (open daily 9am-noon and 3-6pm). Crossing the bridge in front of the other side of the river, you'll find the **Convento de Santa Clara-a-Velha**—smack on top of a swamp. The convent sinks a little deeper each year and today is more than half underground, but the **Convento de Santa Clara-a-Nova** (1649-1677), where Queen Isabel's 14th-century Gothic tomb and a new silver one rest, is standing firm (open daily 8:30am-12:30pm and 2-6:30pm; free). Swallow your pride and mingle with the minors at **Portugal dos Pequenitos,** between the new convent and the river bridge, with scaled-down reproductions of famous castles and monuments (open Mon.-Sat. 10am-5pm; 500$).

Nightlife gets highest honors in student-rich Coimbra. After free beer with dinner in the **UC Cantina,** enjoy a few bottles with the crowd at outdoor cafés around **Praça República,** which buzzes from midnight to 4am. Around the corner uphill is the disco **Via Latina,** R. Almeida Garret, 1, near the Santa Cruz garden. Free-form *fado* singing resonates from **Bar 1910,** above a gymnasium on R. Simões Castro (beers about 200$; open until 4am).

Figueira da Foz

Halfway between Lisbon and Porto and only an hour from Coimbra, Figueira is one of the biggest (and seediest) party towns in Portugal. Those exhausted by their nights of debauchery collapse on Figueira's beach, which, at 1km by 3km, seems roomy even when packed. Nightlife takes off between 10pm and 2am, depending on the disco or bar, and continues all night. Jumping joints line **Avenida 25 de Abril** next to and above the tourist office, as well as **Buarcos,** a 30-minute walk along the waterfront to the other side of the cove. A lively student crowd gathers at **Bergantim,** R. Dr. António Lopes Guimarães, inland from the train station. Disco at **CC Café,** just off the water at the end of the ramp. A happenin' crowd frequents **Bar 31,** a block away from the beach on R. Cândido dos Reis. The **casino** complex on R. Bernardo Lopes (tel. (033) 220 41) also contains a **nightclub** (1500$ cover charge), **cinema** (500$), and **arcade.** Entry to the slot machine and bingo is free; you must be over 18 and show ID to gamble. (casino open July-Aug. daily 4pm-4am; Sept.-June 3pm-3am). Figueira's party mode shifts from high gear to warp speed during the **Festa de São João** (June 6-July 9), as free public concerts ring the town every night.

Trains connect Figueira da Foz with Coimbra (1hr., 280$), Lisbon (3½hr., 1400$), and Porto (3hr., 1120$). The **tourist office** (tel. (033) 226 10; fax 285 49), Av. 25 de Abril, next to the Aparthotel Atlântico, has a map and temporary luggage storage (open June-Sept. daily 9am-11pm; Oct.-May Mon.-Fri. 9am-12:30pm and 2-5:30pm). **Pensão Central,** R. Bernardo Lopes, 36 (tel. (033) 223 08), down the street from the casino, has comfy rooms (singles 4500$, doubles 6000$, triples 7000$). On a street perpendicular to R. Bernardo Lopes, **Pensão Residencial Rio-Mar,** R. Dr. António Dinis, 90 (tel. (033) 230 53), has rooms with their own baths (2500$) and doubles (4000-6000$). **Parque Municipal de Campismo** (tel. (033) 327 42 or 330 33) beckons with an Olympic-size pool, tennis courts, and market. With the beach to your left, walk up Av. 25 de Abril and turn right at the roundabout on R. Alexandre Herculano. Then turn left at Parque Santa Catarina going up R. Joaquim Sotto-Mayor past Palácio Sotto-Mayor. A taxi from the station costs about 500$. (Reception open June-Sept.

daily 8am-8pm; Oct.-May 8am-7pm. Quiet time midnight-7am. June-Sept. each party must be at least 2 people. 400$ per person, 300$ per tent and per car. Showers 100$.) For a great meal, try **Restaurante Rancho,** R. Miguel Bombarda, 40-44, two blocks up from the tourist office (entrees 650-1100$; open Mon.-Sat. 11am-10pm).

Porto (Oporto)

Situated on a dramatic gorge cut by the Rio Douro, 6km from the Atlantic, Porto, Portugal's second-largest city, is an attractive harbor town and the industrial and commercial center of the north. Granite church towers pierce the skyline, closely packed orange-tiled houses tumble down to the river, and three of Europe's most graceful bridges span the gorge above. For Henry the Navigator's 1415 invasion of Ceuta, residents here slaughtered their cattle, gave the meat to the Portuguese fleet, and kept only the entrails for themselves. The tasty dish *tripas à moda do Porto* commemorates this culinary self-sacrifice. Porto's real fame, however, springs from the taste of its *vinho.* Developed by English merchants in the early 18th century, the port wine industry across the River Douro in Vila Nova de Gaia drives the economy.

ORIENTATION AND PRACTICAL INFORMATION

Constant traffic and a chaotic maze of one-way streets disorient even veteran travelers; arm yourself with a map. At the heart of Porto is **Praça da Liberdade.** The **Estação São Bento** lies smack in the middle of town, just off Pr. Liberdade. The **Ribeira,** or Esplanade, district is a few blocks to the south, directly across the bridge from **Vila Nova de Gaia,** the wine house area.

Tourist Office: R. Clube dos Fenianos, 25 (tel. 31 27 40), just off the top of Pr. Liberdade. The polyglot staff doles out maps. Open July-Sept. Mon.-Fri. 9am-7pm, Sat. 9am-4pm, Sun. 10am-1pm; Oct.-June Mon.-Fri. 9:30am-5:30pm, Sat. 9am-4pm.

Currency Exchange: ATMs line Pr. Liberdade, and are omnipresent throughout the city. Most banks on **Pr. Liberdade** offer currency exchange (open Mon.-Fri. 8:30am-3pm), and some have automatic currency exchange machines outside.

American Express: Top Tours, R. Alferes Malheiro, 96 (tel. 208 27 85), up R. do Almada from the tourist office. Open Mon.-Fri. 9am-12:30pm and 2:30-6:30pm.

Flights: Aeroporto Francisco de Sá Carneiro (tel. 94132 60 or 941 32 70). Take bus 44 and 56 from Pr. Lisboa. **TAP Air Portugal,** Pr. Mouzinho de Albuquerque, 105 (tel. 948 22 91), flies to Lisbon and Madrid.

Trains: Estação de Campanhã (tel. 57 41 61), the main station, is east of the city center. To: Coimbra (2½hr., 910$), Lisbon (4½hr., 1950$), Braga, via Nine (2hr., 450$), Madrid via Entroncamento (12-13hr., 9100$), and Paris (28hr., 24,000$). **Estação de São Bento** (tel. 200 27 22), 1 block off Pr. Liberdade, receives local and regional trains. Buses run to Pr. Liberdade and beyond (every 30min., 170$).

Buses: If you know your destination, ask at Turismo and they'll direct you to a particular company as there is no central station. **Garagem Atlântico,** R. Alexandre Herculano (tel. 200 69 54), serves Coimbra (1½hr., 1200$) and Lisbon (5½hr., 1900$). **Internorte,** Pr. Graliza, 96 (tel. 69 32 20 or 48 75), makes trips to Spain, France, Belgium, Switzerland, Germany, and Luxembourg.

Public Transportation: A *Passe Turístico* discount pass is available for Porto's trolleys and buses for 160$. A 4-day pass costs 1600$, a 7-day pass 2150$.

24-Hour Pharmacy: tel. 118 for information on which pharmacy is open.

Medical Assistance: Hospital de Santo António, R. Prof. Vicente José de Carvalho (tel. 200 52 41 or 200 73 54).

Emergency: tel. 112.

Police: R. Alexandre Herculano (tel. 200 68 21).

Post Office: Pr. General Humberto Delgado (tel. 31 98 77), next to the town hall. Open for *Poste Restante* (60$ per item), fax, phones, and stamps Mon.-Fri. 8am-9pm, Sat.-Sun. 9am-6pm. **Postal Code:** 4000.

Telephones: Pr. Liberdade, 62. Open daily 8am-11:30pm. Also at the post office. **Telephone Code:** 02.

ACCOMMODATIONS, CAMPING, AND FOOD

Most *pensões* lie west of Av. Aliados and on Rua de Fernandes Tomás and Rua Formosa, perpendicular to the Aliados Square. Rates for singles can be criminal; shop around for a reasonable deal.

Pousada de Juventude do Porto (HI), Paulo da Gama, 551 (tel. 617 72 47). Take bus 3, 20, or 52 (10min., 160$) from the stop on the lower west end of Pr. Liberdade. After a right onto R. Júlio Dinis, get off at the 2nd traffic light. Cross the street and walk 1 block uphill; hang a left at the billboard. Lively social scene. Reception open daily 9-11am and 6pm-midnight. 1750$ per person. Doubles with bath 5000$. Reduced prices in winter. Reservations highly recommended.

Pensão São Marino, Pr. Carlos Alberto, 59 (tel. 32 54 99). Facing town hall, go up the street on the left and take 1st left onto R. Dr. Ricardo Jorge, which becomes R. Conceição; turn left onto R. Oliveiras, and make a quick right onto Pr. Carlos Alberto. Singles 3000-4000$. Doubles 4000-6500$. Triples 4500-7000$. Off-season 500$ less. Breakfast included.

Residencial Paris, R. da Fábrica, 29 (tel. 32 14 12). Across Pr. Liberdade from the train station, make a left onto R. do Dr. Artur de Magalhães Basto, which quickly turns into R. Fábrica. Rooms are large and clean, and the manager has maps and train schedules to help you plan your trip. TV room, breakfast room, and garden. Singles 2500$, with bath 4000$. Doubles with bath 5500$. Reserve ahead.

Camping: Prelada, R. Monte dos Burgos, Quinta da Prelada (tel. 81 26 16), 5km from the beach. Take bus 6 from Pr. Liberdade. 550$ per person, 475$ per tent, 475$ per car. **Salgueiros** (tel. 781 05 00), near Praia de Salgueiros in Vila Nova de Gaia, is harder to reach and has fewer amenities, but is closer to the surf. 200$ per person and per tent, 100$ per car. Open May-Sept.

Restaurant food costs more in Porto than in any other Portuguese city. Pick up produce and supplies at the **markets** that line Cais de Ribeira (open daily 8am-8pm), or at the **Mercado de Bolhão,** on the corner of R. Formosa and R. Sá de Bandeira (open Mon.-Fri. 8am-6pm, Sat. 7am-1pm). If you can afford something more elegant, colorful, expensive restaurants border the river in the Ribeira district, particularly on **Cais da Ribeira, Rua Reboleira,** and **Rua de Cima do Muro.** Cheaper eateries surround the **Hospital de Santo António** and **Praça de Gomes Teixeira.** On a street parallel to Av. Aliados,**Churrasqueira Moura,** R. Almada, 219, has dirt-cheap, solid meals (half portions 850$; full portions less than 1300$; open Mon.-Sat. 9am-10pm).

SIGHTS AND ENTERTAINMENT

Fortified on the hilltop south of the train station is Porto's pride and joy, the **cathedral,** situated in one of the city's oldest residential districts. It was built in the 12th and 13th centuries, and the Gothic, *azulejo*-covered cloister was added in the 14th century. The **Capela do Santíssimo Sacramento** to the left of the altar shines with solid silver and plated gold (open daily 9am-12:30pm and 2:30-6pm; cloister 200$).

Cash acquires cachet at the **Palácio da Bolsa** (Stock Exchange), R. Ferreira Borges, the epitome of 19th-century elegance. Although tours are pricey, get a feel for its opulence by popping in to peer at the ornate courtyard ceiling. (Open April-Oct. Tues.-Sat. 2-8pm, Sat.-Sun. 10am-8pm; Nov.-March Tues.-Sun. 2-7pm. Tours 700$, students 50$. Main courtyard free.) To get to the Bolsa, turn left out of the cathedral and follow the winding streets straight ahead to Travessa da Bainharia and Largo de Santo Domingos; the Bolsa is downhill on the right. From in front of the train station, follow R. Mouzinho da Silveira to the square. Next door to the Bolsa, the Gothic **Igreja de São Francisco** glitters with one of the most elaborate gilded wood interiors in Portugal. Under the floor, thousands of human bones have been stored in the *osseria* in preparation for Judgement Day. (Museum and church open April-Oct. Mon.-Fri. 9am-6pm, Sun. 9am-5pm; Nov.-March Mon.-Sat. 9am-5pm. 500$, students and seniors 250$.)

Fine Wine, Port Gratis

Woe to the backpacker who has spent her last ducats on that pint of pissy ale! Let her dock her parched mouth and empty pockets in Porto where the fine and bounteous port wines are completely *gratuito* (free). As you'll learn while waiting impatiently for the tours to terminate and the toasting to begin, port was discovered when some enterprising English wine dealers added a strong brandy to cheap Portuguese wine to prevent it from souring *en route* to England. Nowadays, wine from grapes grown in the Douro Valley 100km west of Porto is mixed with 170 proof brandy and aged in barrels to yield port. The lodges are across the river in Vila Nova da Gaia— cross the lower level of the large bridge. A good starter is **Sandeman** with costumed guides and high quality port. **Cálem,** next door, has a less stilted tour, and the port's almost as good. At **Ferreira,** down the road from Sandeman, you'll learn about the famed *senhora* who built the Ferreira empire in the late 19th century. And finally, **Taylor's** wins the highly unscientific *Let's Go* poll for best port in Porto.

To get to Porto's rocky but popular **beach** in the ritzy Foz district, take bus 78 from P. Liberdade (160$ one way) and jump off wherever you fancy. At the bottom of the hill on R. Alfândega, the **Ribeira** (Esplanade) skirts past a marvelous quay filled with shops and restaurants.

Back uphill rises the 82m **Torre dos Clérigos** (Tower of Clerics). Built in the mid-18th century and the city's most prominent landmark, its granite bell tower glimmers like a grand processional candle. Mount the 200 steps to view Porto and the Rio Douro Valley (open daily 10:30am-noon and 2-5pm; church free; tower 130$). For modern art in a lovely setting, visit the **Fundação Casa de Serralves (Museu de Arte Moderna),** a contemporary museum west of the town center on the way to the beach. The building crowns an impressive 44 acres of sculptured gardens, fountains, and even old farmland tumbling down toward the Douro River. (Museum open Tues.-Fri. 2-8pm, Sat.-Sun. 10am-8pm. 300$, students 150$, Thurs. free.) Bus 78 leaves for the museum from Pr. Dom João I—ask the driver for the museum stop (about 30min. to R. Serralves; 160$ one way; buses return until midnight).

Mellow **bars** keep the lights on until 2am on the waterfront in **Pr. da Ribeira, M. dos Bacalhoeiros,** and **R. Alfândega.** Try **Pub O Muro,** Muro dos Bacalhoeiros, 87-88, right above the riverside near the bridge going to the port wine houses. **Discoteca Swing,** on R. Júlio Dinis near the youth hostel, caters to a mixed gay-straight crowd (cover about 1000$). The Beautiful People party in the Foz beach district. Try discos **Industria, Twins,** and **Dona Urraca.**

Romania (România)

US$1	**= 7450 lei**	**1000 lei =**	**US$0.13**
CDN$1	**= 5386 lei**	**1000 lei =**	**CDN$0.19**
UK£1	**= 11,851 lei**	**1000 lei =**	**UK£0.08**
IR£1	**= 10,921 lei**	**1000 lei =**	**IR£0.09**
AUS$1	**= 5420 lei**	**1000 lei =**	**AUS$0.19**
NZ$1	**= 4728 lei**	**1000 lei =**	**NZ$0.21**
SAR1	**= 1585 lei**	**1000 lei =**	**SAR0.63**

Country Code: 40 **International Dialing Prefixes: EU: 00; USA: 011**

Ensconced within the mysterious Carpathian Mountains, Romanians preserve folk traditions abandoned in the rest of Europe centuries ago. The fortified towns of Transylvania still look like an array of medieval woodcuts, and the green hills of Moldavia remain as serene as the frescoes on their monastery walls. Sadly, more recent developments have come to overshadow the picturesque charm of these rural retreats: the country was the poorest and most totalitarian in the Soviet Bloc earlier this century, and industrial soot still tarnishes Bucharest and several other cities. The hospitality of the Romanian people, however, has not wavered through these difficult times, and many beautiful buildings and untamed natural wonders ensure a memorable visit.

Romanians suffered terribly in the aftermath of World War II. The Communist regime was responsible for the deaths of 200,000 people in purges in the 1950s. In 1965, Nicolae Ceauşescu became the leader of the Party, and his rule deprived Romanians of such basic needs as food, heat, and electric power. By the 1980s, Romania was a police state, but in 1989, the country erupted in a revolution as ruthless as the man it pulled down. The revolt started the arrest in Timişoara of a popular Hungarian priest by the *Securitate* (secret police). Riots ripped across the city, then around the country. On December 21-22, clashes with security forces in Bucharest brought hundreds of thousands of protesters into the streets. Ceauşescu and his wife were captured, summarily tried, and executed on Christmas Day. Power was quickly seized by Ion Iliescu's National Salvation Front, accused by many of being a continuation of the Communist Party. Nonetheless, Iliescu won the 1990 presidential elections with 70% of the vote, and his government began to reform the system, albeit slowly.

In the first democratic transfer of power in Romania's history, President Emil Constantinescu replaced Iliescu in November 1996. Constantinescu hopes to repair the economy by opening Romania up to capital markets and by lifting barriers on international investment, and promises to bring to trial those responsible for the numerous bouts of political violence that marred Romania's first post-Communist years. Prosperity, however, may still be far away; ragged beggars in front of flashy shop windows remind visitors that Romania has a long climb ahead. France supports admitting Romania into NATO, but has not yet overcome American resistance.

For more thorough coverage of Romania, brave *Let's Go: Eastern Europe 1998.*

GETTING THERE

Citizens of the U.S. can visit Romania **visa-free** for up to 30 days, but citizens of the Canada, the U.K., Ireland, Australia, New Zealand, and South Africa all need visas. Single-entry (US$22) and multiple-entry (US$68) visas allow two- and six-month stays, respectively; a transit visa (US$22) is valid for four days. You can obtain a visa at the border with no additional fee. If you prefer to prepare in advance, contact an **embassy** or **consulate** (see **Government Information Offices,** p. 1).

You can **fly** into Bucharest on Air France, Alitalia, AUA, British Airways, Delta, Lufthansa, and Swissair. **TAROM** (Romanian Airlines) is currently renewing its aging fleet and also flies to most major European cities. Daily **trains** head from Bucharest via Budapest to Vienna and Munich. There are also direct trains to and from Moscow, Prague, Sofia, and Warsaw. To buy international tickets in Romania, go to the **CFR**

office in larger towns. An ISIC will occasionally get you 50% off on domestic tickets, but technically the discount applies only to Romanian students. **Buses** connect major cities in Romania to Athens, Istanbul, Prague, Varna, and various cities in Western Europe. Buses are typically slow but fairly inexpensive.

GETTING AROUND

CFR sells domestic **train** tickets up to 24 hours before the train's departure. After that, only train stations will sell tickets, generally only an hour before the train leaves. There is an info desk at all stations (staffers sometimes speak English), where you can inquire which counter sells tickets to your destination. The train timetable *Mersul Trenurilor* is incredibly useful in forming your plans (5000 lei; instructions in English and French). **InterRail** is accepted, but **Eurail** is not. There are four types of trains: *InterCity* (IC), *rapid* or *expres* (in green), *accelerat* (red), and *de persoane* (black or blue). *InterCity* trains stop only at major cities. *Rapid* trains are the next fastest. *De persoane* are slow, dirty, and stop at nearly every station. If taking an overnight train, opt for first class in a *vagon de dormir* (sleeping carriage). During holidays and in July and August, try to buy train tickets to the beach five days in advance. Use the extensive local **bus** system only when trains are not available; they are usually packed and poorly ventilated. Look for signs for the bus station *(autogară)* in each town. Hitchers report success, but consider the safety risks. A wave of the hand is the recognized sign; drivers generally expect a payment similar to the price of a train ticket.

ESSENTIALS

ONT (National Tourist Office) doesn't always give reliable information about the price and availability of cheap rooms. Branches in expensive hotels are often more useful than the main offices. Many ONT offices have been replaced by private **travel agencies,** but they aren't always helpful either. The most common banknotes are 500, 1000, 5000, 10,000, and 50,000 **lei.** Pay for everything in lei; whenever someone offers to take U.S. dollars directly, it's usually at a disadvantageous rate. Private **exchange bureaus** litter the country, but few take credit cards and traveler's checks. German and U.S. currencies are preferred, though others can be exchanged in some places. Whatever currency you have, know the going rates and commissions before exchanging anywhere. Unofficial currency exchange is illegal, but getting cheated is more of a risk than getting jailed; train stations demand special wariness. Don't hand over your money before you get your lei.

Many banks and businesses close on Friday afternoons. National **holidays** include New Year's Day (Jan. 1-3), Orthodox Easter (3-4 days, a week later than Roman Catholic Easter), May Day (May 1), Union Day (Dec. 1), and Christmas (some businesses may be closed Dec. 25-31).

Many Romanians hold conservative attitudes about sexuality; these attitudes may translate into harassment of gay and bisexual travelers, but affection is not uncommon between Romanian women. Homosexuality was only recently legalized in Romania. Be aware also that public **hygiene** in Romania will challenge Westerners. Most public restrooms lack soap, towels, and toilet paper, and even "privatized" public bathrooms that charge 300-500 lei may give you only a square of toilet paper. Feminine hygiene products are available in large cities. If you have to buy medicines in Romania, know what you're purchasing: *antinevralgic* for headaches, *piramidon* for colds and the flu, and *saprosan* for diarrhea. Condoms, available at drugstores and many vending kiosks, are called *prezervative.*

Communication Orange **phones** take phone cards; blue and all non-orange phones take coins. Unless you like the idea of carrying around a kilogram of coins, use a phone card, available at post and telephone offices in denominations of 20,000 and 40,000 lei. Rates per minute run around 6500 lei to most of Europe, and 11,900 lei to the U.S. For **AT&T Direct,** dial 018 00 42 88; **MCI WorldPhone,** 018 00 18 00; **Sprint,** 018 00 08 77; **Canada Direct,** 018 00 50 00; **BT Direct,** 018 00 44 44. Some pay phones will cut off calling card calls after two or five minutes. **Local calls** cost 300-400 lei and can be made from any phone; **intercity** calls can be made from the new digital phones (orange and blue) or from old phones marked *telefon interurban.* Dial several times before giving up; a busy signal can just indicate a bad connection. In a small town, it may be necessary to a make a call with the help of an operator in a telephone office. It's no easy task, but it may be the only option. At the phone office, write down the destination, duration, and phone number for your call. Pay up front, and always ask for the rate per minute.

Romanian is a Romance language; travelers familiar with French, Italian, Spanish, or Portuguese can usually decipher public signs. Young Romanians often speak some English, and French or Russian are widely spoken by the older generation.

Yes/No	*Da/Nu*	dah/noo
Hello	*Bună ziua*	BOO-nuh zee-wah
Please	*Vă rog*	vuh rohg
Thank you	*Mulţumesc*	mool-tsoo-MESK
Excuse me	*Scuzaţi-mă*	skoo-ZAH-tz muh
Do you speak English?	*Vorbiţi englezeşţē?*	vor-BEE-tz ehng-leh-ZESH-teh
I don't understand	*Nu înţeleg*	noo ihn-TZEH-lehg
Where is...?	*Unde...?*	OON-deh

How much does this cost?	*Cît costă?*	kiht KOH-stuh
Do you have a vacancy?	*Aveţi camere libere?*	a-VETS CA-mer-eh LEE-ber-e
Check, please.	*Plata, vă rog*	PLAH-tah, VUH rohg
Help!	*Ajutor!*	AH-zhoot-or

Accommodations, Camping, Food, and Drink In general, **hotels** charge foreigners two to three times the price for Romanians. One-star hotels are iffy, corresponding to a mediocre youth hostel, two-star are decent, and three-star are good but expensive. If you go to the ONT office and ask for a room, you may get a price up to 50% lower than that quoted directly at the hotel. **Private accommodations** are a good idea; rooms run 40,000-50,000 lei, breakfast included. Hosts rarely speak English, and renting a room with someone else generally means sharing a bed. Always see the room and fix a price before you accept. Many towns reserve **university dorms** for foreign students at insanely low prices; ask local university officials or the ONT. **Campgrounds** are crowded, and their bathrooms are very often foul.

An average homemade dish is probably better than the similar dish cooked at Romanian restaurants, so try to get an invitation. Lunch usually starts with a tasty soup, called *supă* or *ciorbă* (the latter is saltier and usually better), followed by a main dish (usually grilled pork, beef, or chicken) and dessert. Pork comes in several varieties, of which *muşchi* and *cotlet* are the best quality. Restaurants often quote prices for meats in lei per 100g and charge for every side order, including bread. Vegetarians will probably want to stick to salads. For dessert, *clătite* (crepes) or *papanaşi* (donuts with jam and sour cream) can be fantastic when they're fresh. Local specialties include *mămăligă* (cornmeal served with butter, cheese, and sour cream) and delicious *sarmale* (ground meat wrapped in grape or cabbage leaves). If you have to fend for yourself, private bakeries sell the best *pîine* (bread), and street vendors offer cheap *mititei* (garlicky barbecued ground meat; make sure the meat is fresh).

Bucharest (Bucureşti)

Bucharest bears the scars of Romania's political struggles. The city was known in the 19th century as "Little Paris" and "Pearl of the Balkans" for its beautiful boulevards, parks, and fine Neoclassical architecture. Ceauşescu's government demolished historic neighborhoods in the area and replaced them with concrete housing, and today Bucharest is a somber ghost of its former self.

ORIENTATION AND PRACTICAL INFORMATION

Trains connect Bucharest, 60km north of the Danube, with most Eastern European capitals. From the main train station, take a left then a right onto **Calea Griviţei,** heading east, then take another right onto **Calea Victoriei** to reach the sights. Or walk another four blocks on strada Biserica Amzei, the continuation of Griviţei, to **bulevardul Magheru** (which becomes Bd. Bălcescu, then Bd. Brătianu), the main artery in Bucharest. The Metro and trolley 79 lead to Piaţa Romană, where Bd. Magheru starts.

Tourist Offices: For decent help, head to the **ONT** office, Bd. Magheru 7 (tel. 614 07 59). From Piaţa Romană, walk down Magheru; ONT is on the right. The staff offers maps (2000 lei), tours, and accommodations across Romania. Their private rooms run US$20 per person in the center. Open Mon.-Fri. 8am-8pm, Sat. 8am-3pm, Sun. 8am-1pm. Major hotels also have ONT desks or private tourist offices.

Embassies: Canada, Str. Nicolae Iorga 36 (tel. 222 31 78), near Piaţa Romană. Open Mon.-Thurs. 8:30am-1pm and 2-5pm, Fri. 8:30am-1pm. Citizens of **Australia, Ireland,** and **New Zealand** should contact the **U.K.** embassy, Str. Jules Michelet 24 (tel. 312 03 03; fax 312 02 29). Open Mon.-Thurs. 8:30am-1pm and 2-5pm, Fri. 8:30am-1:30pm. **Russia,** şos. Kiseleff 6 (tel. 617 13 19). Open Mon., Wed., and Fri. 9am-1pm. **South Africa,** Str. Grigore Alexandrescu 86 (tel. 746 85 81). Open Mon.-Fri. 9am-2pm. **U.S.,** Str. Snagov 26 (tel. 210 40 42, after-hours 210 01 49; fax 211 33 60). Open Mon.-Thurs. 8am-11:30am and 1-3pm, Fri. 8-11:30am.

Currency Exchange: Use currency exchange offices instead of the black market. Banks often charge high commissions. For a better rate, try the **O.K. exchange bureaus,** 16 N. Bălcescu (open "non-stop"; traveler's checks 7% commission), and Bd. Magheru 33 (open Mon.-Fri. 8:30am-9:30pm, Sat. 8:30am-8pm; traveler's checks 4% commission). **ATMs** are at major banks.

American Express: Bd. Magheru 43, 1st fl., #1 (tel. 223 12 04). Replaces lost cards and Cheques. Doesn't cash Cheques. Open Mon.-Fri. 9am-5pm, Sat. 10am-noon.

Flights: Otopeni Airport (tel. 230 00 22), 16km from the city, handles international traffic. Bus 783 leaves for the airport from Piaţa Unirii every 1-2hr. (3000 lei). From Otopeni, buses stop near the Hotel Intercontinental on Bd. Magheru. **Băneasa Airport** (tel. 232 00 20), linked with Piaţa Romană by bus 131 (1000 lei) and the train station by bus 205, handles domestic flights. Buy international tickets at the **CFR/TAROM office,** Str. Domniţa Anastasia 10 (tel. 646 33 46). The **domestic** TAROM office, Piaţa Victoriei (tel. 659 41 85), sells domestic and international tickets. Both open Mon.-Fri. 7am-7pm, Sat. 7:30am-1pm.

Trains: Gara de Nord (tel. 57 76) is the principal station. **Obor** (tel. 152), accessible by trolley 85 from Gara de Nord or 69 from Piaţă Universităţii, and **Băneasa** (tel. 48 27), accessible by bus 301 from Piaţă Romană, serve the Black Sea Coast. **Tickets** can be purchased at **CFR,** Domniţa Anastasia 10 (tel. 614 55 28). Open Mon.-Fri. 8am-7pm, Sat. 8am-noon. One or more trains per day serve Budapest (13hr., 220,000 lei), Istanbul (18hr., 215,000 lei), Kiev (17hr., 300,000 lei), and Sofia (10hr., 160,000 lei). Also to: Berlin, Moscow, Munich, Prague, and Vienna.

Buses: Filaret, Piaţa Gării Filaret 1 (tel. 336 06 92), and **Rahova,** Şos. Alexandriei 164 (tel. 220 44 10), are in the south suburbs; **Obor** and **Băneasa** train stations also host bus stations. For international buses, the **Toros** bus line (tel. 638 24 24), outside Gara de Nord, sells tickets to Istanbul leaving from Gara de Nord (12-15hr.; 200,000 lei). For buses to Athens, try **Liotsikas,** Bd. Cantemir 25 (tel. 330 46 46; 3 per week, 20hr., US$50). Bus offices for destinations in the West cluster around Piaţă Dorobanţilor along Str. Sofia. International buses tend to be better than trains.

Public Transportation: Bus, trolley, and tram rides cost 800 lei. Tickets, which must be punched, are sold at kiosks near most stops or on some buses. Buses are packed on busy routes—mind your valuables. The **Metro** runs daily 5am-midnight.

Luggage Storage: At Gara de Nord. 1800-4000 lei. Open 24hr.

24-Hour Pharmacy: Şos. Colentina 1 (tel. 635 50 10), by the Bucur Obor Metro stop, and in Gara de Nord (tel. 222 91 55). Ring the bell at night. Info tel. 065.

Medical Assistance: Spitalul de Urgenţă, Calea Floreasca 8 (tel. 230 01 06). Near the Ştefan cel Mare Metro station.

Emergencies: Fire: tel. 981. **Ambulance:** tel. 961.

Police: tel. 955.

Internet Access: Raffles, Calea Victoriei 25, just south of Bd. Carol I. L6500 lei per 30min. Open Mon.-Fri. 10am-6pm, Sat. 10am-2pm.

Post Office: Str. Matei Millo 10, off Calea Victoriei. Open Mon.-Fri. 7:30am-8pm, Sat. 7:30am-2pm. *Poste Restante* next to Hotel Carpati. **Postal Code:** 70154.

Telephones: Orange card phones for international calls are available throughout the city center, in the train station, and near the telephone office, Calea Victoriei 37 (open 24hr.). You can also order collect or operator-assisted calls. For directory assistance, dial 930. **Telephone Code:** 01.

ACCOMMODATIONS

The ONT office on Bd. Magheru can arrange private rooms or hotel accommodations. Men hanging out by the hotels in front of Gara de Nord offer rooms at 40,000-50,000 lei per person. During the school year, Romanian students will often share their drab rooms; try the **Polytechnic Institute** near the Semănătoarea Metro stop. It's hard to find a decent hotel room for less than 100,000-200,000 lei per person.

Hotel Cerna, Str. Golescu 29 (tel. 637 40 87). A surprisingly nice hotel next to Gara de Nord; exit the station and turn right. Singles 48,000 lei, with bath 120,000 lei. Doubles 85,000 lei, with bath 160,000 lei. Apartments 250,000 lei.

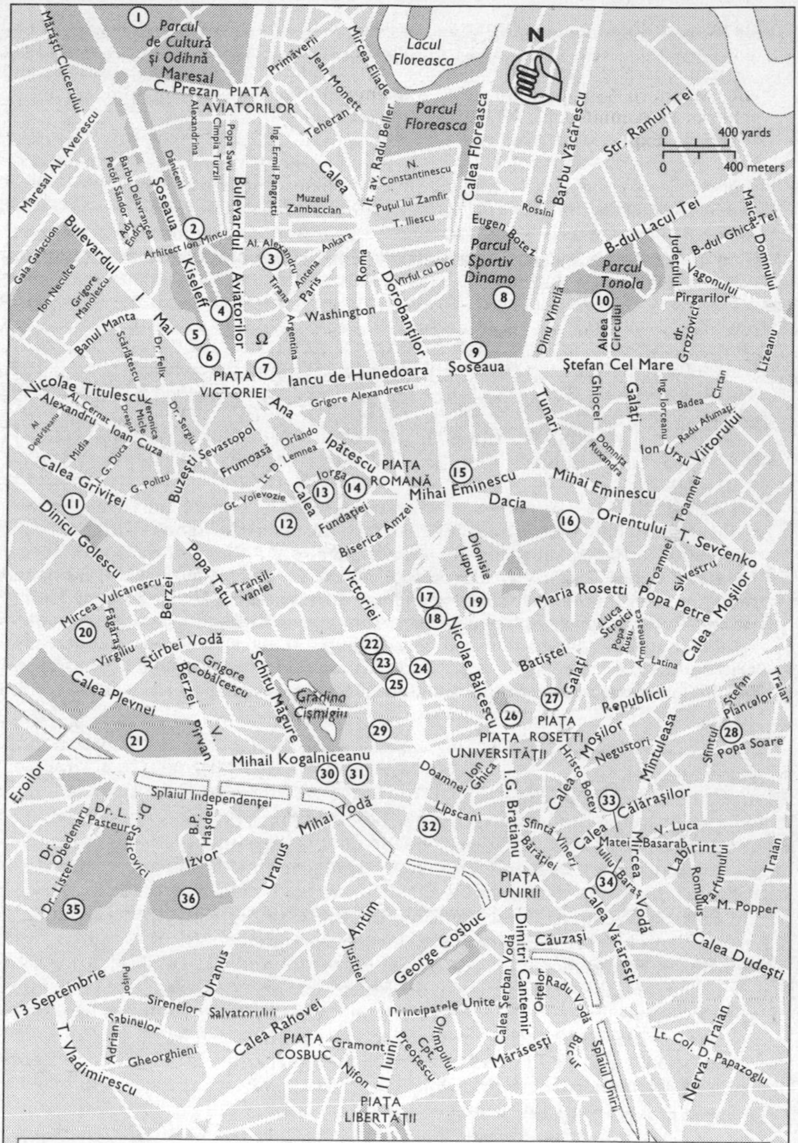

Bucharest

1 Village Museum
2 Russian Embassy
3 Ministry of Foreign Affairs
4 Geological Museum
5 Romanian Peasant Museum
6 Museum of Natural History
7 Government of Romania
8 Dynamo Stadium
9 Emergency Hospital
10 Bucharest Circus
11 North Railway Station
12 Art Collections Museum
13 Goethe Institute
14 Canadian Embassy
15 British Council
16 French Library
17 Romanian Development Agency
18 Romanian Atheneum
19 State Ownership Fund
20 National Military Museum
21 Opera House
22 National Art Gallery
23 Great Palace Hall
24 Senate
25 Natl. Agcy. for Privatization
26 National Theatre
27 American Library
28 Italian Library
29 Palas
30 Ministry of Justice
31 City Hall
32 National History Museum
33 Caritas
34 Jewish Theatre
35 Progresul Arena
36 Casa Republicii

Villa Helga Youth Hostel, Str. Salcămilor 2 (tel. 610 22 14). Meet staffers at Gara de Nord or take bus 86, 79, or 133 from Piaţă Romană to Piaţă Galaţi (east along Bd. Dacia), then turn right on Str. V. Lascăr, a hard left on Str. Viitorului, and right on Str. Salcămilor. Friendly and funny staff provides beds in dormitory rooms, free laundry, and free use of the kitchen. English spoken. US$12 per bed.

Hotel Triumpf, Şos. Kiseleff 12 (tel. 222 31 72; fax 223 24 11). Take bus or trolley 131, 205, 301, or 331 (from Piaţa Lahovari) to Arcul de Triumf and walk south on Şos. Kiseleff. In the heart of embassy country. Singles 250,000-270,000 lei. Doubles 360,000-390,000 lei. Breakfast included. Laundry service available.

Hotel Bucegi, Str. Witing 2 (tel. 637 52 25), across the street from Hotel Cerna and Gara de Nord. Small, dark rooms with middling bathrooms. Singles with shower L40,000. Doubles 70,000-80,000 lei. Triples 90,000 lei. Quads 90,000 lei.

FOOD

Daily **open-air markets** offering all manner of veggies, fruits, meats, and cheese abound in Bucharest—good ones are at Piaţa Amzei, Piaţa Matache, and Piaţa Latina. **Vox Maris Supermarket,** at Piaţa Victoriei, is open 24 hours. When dining in a restaurant, be sure you are not being ripped off; check the math. Eating in fast-food restaurants like McDonald's is usually more expensive than a quality restaurant.

Cafe de la Joie, Str. Lipscani 80-82. From Piaţa Universităţii, walk down Bd. I.C. Babtianu and turn right on Str. Lipscani, then take the next left. French-style bistro. Salads 10,000 lei. Open Mon.-Sat. 6pm-2am or 3am.

Club Art Papillon, Str. Matei Voievod 66A, off Bd. Pache Protopopescu. Artsy hangout with music during the school year. Meat dishes under 10,000 lei. Open 24hr.

Salt and Pepper, Ion Cimpinanu 2. Super-modern, with art to match, serves spicy food to the Mexican food-deprived. Meals 20,000-30,000 lei. Open daily 10am-1am.

Carul cu Bere, Str. Stavropoleos 5. Chicken soup *à la greque* 4500 lei. Meals up to 40,000 lei. Folklore performances nightly at 8pm. Open daily 10am-1am.

SIGHTS

In the heart of downtown is **Piaţa Universităţii,** home to the **National Theater.** Demonstrators fought Ceauşescu's forces here on December 21, 1989, the day before his fall; the confrontations left casualties. In spring 1990, students declared the square a "Neo-Communist-free zone," and for almost two months their daily meetings here gathered tens of thousands of people. The government brought in miners to brutally end the demonstration in June. Today, crosses commemorate the martyrs.

On **Piaţa Unirii,** up from Bd. Brătianu, the inside of the 18th-century **St. John's Church** is chiseled in rock. Ceauşescu drastically rearranged the square here, but spared **Dealul Mitropoliei,** the small hill on the southwest side. Head up Str. Dealul Mitropoliei to find the headquarters of the Romanian Orthodox Church in one of the largest **cathedrals** in Romania (open Mon.-Sun. 8am-7pm). The cathedral flanks the Communist **parliament building,** now owned by the church. A left down Bd. Unirii from the Dealul is the world's second-largest building after the Pentagon, the **Palatul Parlamentului,** formerly **Casa Poporului** (People's House). Ceauşescu spent billions of dollars and destroyed historic neighborhoods in favor of this private palace.

The oldest buildings in Bucharest are northwest of Piaţa Unirii, in the triangle between the river, Bd. Brătianu, and Bd. Kogălniceanu. Behind Hanul Manuc, in Piaţa Unirii, are the ruins of the old princely court, **Curtea Veche.** In the old town at the corner of Str. Stavropoleus and Calea Victoriei is the **Muzeul National de Istorie a României** (History Museum of Romania),Calea Victoriei 12; the Romanian treasures here include the famed *cloşca cu pui de aur* (golden hen and chicks; open Wed.-Sun. 10am-5pm). North of Piaţa Universitaţii, along Bd. N. Bălcescu, is the elegant **Ateneul Român,** the country's premier music hall and acoustically the continent's second best (after Milan). The concert hall's fresco depicts Romanian history from Dacia to World War I, but restoration work unfortunately prevents access to the interior. To the north, **Muzeul Colecţiilor de Artă,** Calea Victoriei 111, near Bd. Dacia, displays private collections of Romanian painting and temporary exhibits (open Wed.-Sun. 10am-6pm; 3000 lei, students 1500 lei, Wed. free). Next door, **Muzeul Ţăranului Român** (Peasant Museum) displays religious objects as well as textiles and folk crafts (open Tues.-Sun. 10am-6pm; 3000 lei, students 1000 lei).

On the other side of town, **Muzeul Naţional Cotroceni** (tel. 221 12 00) offers a tour of royal apartments. Originally built as a monastery, Cotroceni became home to Romania's crown prince Ferdinand. Call ahead to join a mandatory tour. (Open Mon.-Fri. 9am-4pm. 20,000 lei, temporary exhibits 8000 lei. English book 20,000 lei; English pamphlet 1000 lei.) The **Muzeul de Istorie a Comunitaţilor Evreieşti din România** (Jewish History Museum of Romania), Str. Mămulari 3, has displays on Jewish cultural contributions and the history of Romania's Jewish community (open Wed. and Sun. 9am-1pm; 2000 lei; photos 1000 lei). Bucharest is replete with parks, which compensate in part for its urban wastescape. Well-groomed **Cişmigiu Park** is, along with Herăstrău Park, the focal point for much of the city's social life. Elderly pensioners, young couples, chess whizzes, and football players abound.

ENTERTAINMENT

The magnificent **Ateneul** concert hall in Piaţa Revoluţiei (tel. 615 00 26) often hosts excellent concerts at affordable prices. Also check out the **Opera Română** (tel. 613 18 57) and the **Teatrul de Operetă** (tel. 613 63 48) near the **Teatrul Naţional** (tel. 613 91 75). Most shows are in Romanian. Some tickets are available one hour before show times, and managers may provide house seats. Bucharest hosts some of the biggest rock festivals this side of Berlin; inquire at the tourist office and keep your eyes peeled for posters detailing upcoming events. Whatever you do in the evening, pack a map and cab fare; the streets are poorly lit and buses are unreliable.

Dubliner Irish Pub, Bd. N. Titulescu 18. Pricey, but has Guinness, English-speakers, and celebrations of Irish holidays. Open daily noon-2am.

Club A, Str. Blanari 14. The Architecture College's established club, now open to the public. Tues. jazz, Wed. blues, Thurs. alternative, Fri.-Sat. disco, Sun. oldies. Cover 4000-6000 lei, weekdays women free. Open Tues.-Sun. 9pm-5am. Closed summers.

Martin, at the intersection of Calea Dorobanţilor and Bd. Iancu de Hunedoara. Reputed to be the best disco in town. Cover Fri.-Sat. 10,000 lei. Open Thurs. and Sun. 9:30pm-5am, Fri.-Sat. 10pm-5am.

Laptărie, at the National Theater; take the elevator to the top. Entertains the cool crowd. Winter jazz concerts 10,000-25,000 lei; summer movies 2500 lei. Terrace open in summer daily 9:30pm-2am or 4am; bar open 10am-2am off season.

Cafe Indigo, Str. Eforie 2. off Culea Victoriei. Jazz and blues make noise here every weekend during the school year, while a movie theater showing classic films operates during the day. Light meals around L10,000. Open 24hr.

■ Near Bucharest

When Bucharest has gotten the better of you, take a daytrip to **Snagov,** a tiny village 30 minutes north. In summer, hordes invade **Snagov Park,** 5km west, where people swim or rent a rowboat and navigate to **Snagov Monastery** (30min. row; 5000 lei). Here lies (probably) the grave of Vlad Ţepeş (Count Dracula). **Villa Helga Youth Hostel's tours** (tel. (01) 610 22 14; US$9) make the island far more accessible.

Flanked by the Bucegi mountains and less than two hours from Bucharest by train (11,000 lei), **Sinaia** is Romania's most celebrated year-round alpine resort. The town's **Peleş castle** and **monastery** still draw scholars and religious pilgrims, but the serious tourists are far outnumbered by athletes and daredevils. From the station, cross the street, climb the stairs, and bear left onto a cobblestone ramp at the first landing. Climb the first steps, and take two left turns to reach **Bd. Carol I,** the main street. Larger hotels provide **tourist information.** Locals in the station offer private rooms for US$5-10; when hiking, stay in mountain *cabana* (250,000 lei).

TRANSYLVANIA

Although the name evokes images of black magic and vampires, Transylvania *(Ardeal)* is a region of green hills descending gently from the Carpathians to the Hungarian Plain. This is Romania's cleanest and most western-oriented region.

Cluj-Napoca

Transylvania's unofficial capital and largest student center, Cluj is over 70% Romanian with a vocal Hungarian minority. To reach the center of town take bus 3 or 4, left and across the street from the train station, to Piața Mihai Viteazul (round-trip 1700 lei); continue along the road and turn right on Bd. 21 Decembrie 1989. By foot, cross the street and head down Str. Horea, which changes to Str. Gh. Doja after crossing the river. At the end of Str. Gh. Doja spreads the main drag, **Piața Unirii,** where the 80m Gothic steeple of the Catholic **Church of St. Michael** offers a magnificent city view. The fanciest of the square's palaces built by Hungarian nobles is **Bánffy Palace,** Piața Unirii 30, home to the **Art Museum** (one hall open Wed.-Sun. 10am-5pm; 3000 lei). From Piața Unirii, head to **Piața Avram Iancu,** along either busy Str. 21 Dec. 1989 (commemorating the victims of the 1989 revolution) or Bd. Eroilor. Tickets to the **National Theater and Opera** in the square are affordable (best seats 5000 lei, students 2500 lei). Buy tickets at Piața Ștefan cel Mare 14 (tel. 19 53 63; open Mon.-Fri. 11am-5pm). Museums to see include the **History Museum,** Str. Constantin Daicoviciu 2 (open Tues.-Sun. 10am-4pm; 1000 lei), and the **Ethnographic Museum,** Str. Memorandumului 21 (open Tues.-Sun. 9am-5pm; 1500 lei, students 1000 lei).

Cluj-Napoca is accessible by **train** from Brașov (4 per day, 4hr., 21,800 lei), Bucharest via Sighișoara and Brașov (4 per day, 7hr., 27,700 lei), Budapest (3 per day, 5-7hr., 161,000 lei), and Iași via Suceava (4 per day, 9hr., 27,700 lei). The **tourist office,** Piața Unirii 10 (tel. (064) 19 11 14), changes money and may be able to find you a room (US$7-18; open Mon.-Fri. 8am-6pm, Sat. 10am-2pm). **OJT Feleacul,** Str. Memorandumului (tel. (064) 19 69 55), three blocks from Unirii, offers similar services (open Mon.-Fri. 8am–8pm, Sat.-Sun. 9am-1pm). Private rooms are hard to come by in Cluj. The **Hotel Central-Melody,** Piața Unirii 29 (tel. (064) 11 75 65), has its own restaurant (singles 72,000 lei, doubles 120,000-164,000 lei, triples 165,000-210,000 lei). **Hotel Piccolia Italia,** Str. Racoviță 20 (tel. (064) 13 61 10), has singles for 120,000 lei and doubles for 140,000 lei (reserve ahead). **Camping Fbget** (tel. (064) 11 62 27) is 7km from the city towards Bucharest (campsites 11,000 lei; bungalows 60,000-90,000 lei; open May-Nov.). A **market** sprawls over Piața Mihai Viteazul during daylight. Take a special someone to **Mary's,** Str. Pavlov 27 (tel. (064) 19 19 47), the continuation of Str. Gh. Barițiu, which takes music requests (bring tapes) and serves excellent meals. (Meat entrees under 17,000 lei. Open daily noon-midnight. Reservations encouraged.) Relax at **Diesel,** Piața Unirii 15, a stylish jazz bar near St. Michael's Church (open 24hr.). **Hali Gali,** Calea Florenți is a new and popular club. (Cover 5000 lei, women 3000 lei and free on Sun. Open Thurs.-Fri. and Sun. 10pm-3am).

Sighișoara

Of all the medieval towns in Transylvania, Sighișoara (see-ghee-SHWAH-rah) is perhaps the least spoiled and the most enchanting. Surrounded by mountains and crowning a green hill on the railroad line between Cluj and Brașov, Sighișoara's gilded steeples, old clock tower, and irregular tile roofs have survived centuries of attacks and natural disaster. You can enter the **Cetate** (Citadel) through the **clock tower** off Str. O. Goga. A **history museum** inside offers an outstanding view of the area and a peek into the clock's mechanism (open Tues.-Fri. 9am-5:30pm, Sat.-Sun. 9am-3:30pm; 3000 lei, students 1500 lei). From the clock tower, walk straight past Vlad Dracul's house and take a left at Str. Școlii to reach the 175-step **covered wooden staircase,** leading to the old Saxon **church** (closed for renovations) and graveyard (open May-Oct. daily 8am-8pm; Nov.-April 9am-4pm). On the riverbank of the lower town is the 1937 Orthodox **cathedral** (open for services Tues.-Sat. 8-10am and 5-6pm, Sun. 8:30-noon).

Trains run to Bucharest (13 per day, 4½hr., 19,300 lei), Cluj-Napoca (4 per day, 2½-3hr., 18,000 lei), and Brasov. To reach the center, take a right on Str. Libertaţii, a left on Str. Gării, veer left at the Russian cemetery, cross the footbridge over the river, and walk down street behind Sigma. A right at the fork leads to the *Cetate,* a left to main Str. 1 Decembrie 1918. The **tourist office,** Str. 1 Decembrie 1918 10 (tel. (065) 77 10 72), helps find rooms, organizes tours, and sells English maps (3000 lei; open Mon.-Fri. 9am-5pm, Sat. 9am-2pm). At the train station, a man may offer you a room at the new summer **Bobby's Hostel,** Str. Tache Ionescu 18 (tel. (065) 77 22 32); the hostel needs improvement, but young people from all over stop here. Ask about hot water availability (dorms 35,000 lei, double 80,000 lei). **Hotel-Restaurant Non-Stop** (tel. (065) 77 95 01), near the train station, has well-kept rooms and bathrooms (doubles 70,000 lei; breakfast included). In the *Cetate,* **Restaurant Cetate,** Piaţa Cositorarilor 5, boasts that the father of "Count Dracula" might have lived there (main dishes 20,000-30,000 lei; open daily noon-7pm).

Braşov

One of Romania's most beautifully restored cities, Braşov rises from the foot of Muntele Tâmpa, providing a base for trips to the Carpathian mountains. Piaţa Sfatului and Str. Republicii in the Old Town are good places to begin an afternoon walking tour. The **Orthodox Cathedral** in the central *piaţa* was built in 1896 of marble and delicate gold. The **History Museum,** in the middle of the square, used to be a courthouse; legend holds that the condemned had to jump from its tower to their deaths (open Tues.-Sun. 10am-6pm; 4000 lei, students 1000 lei). Uphill from the square along Str. Gh. Baritiu looms the Lutheran **Biserica Neagră** (Black Church), Romania's most celebrated Gothic building (open Mon.-Sat. 10am-3:30pm; 1000 lei). Str. Prundului behind the *poarta* leads to Piaţa Unirii's **Prima Şcoala Românească** (Romania's First School) and the black-towered, icon-filled **Biserica Sfintu Nicolae.**

Hotel Aro-Palace, Bd. Eroilor 9, offers **city maps** (3000 lei). From Piaţa Sfatului, walk on Str. Mureşenilor until it intersects Bd. Eroilor at the park, and turn right. All Budapest-Bucharest **trains** stop in Braşov; the ride to Bucharest takes about three hours. To get to the town from the station, ride bus 4 ("Piaţa Unirii"; 1600 lei) to the main Piaţa Sfatului (10min.). The **bus station,** near the Hotel Aro-Palace, offers service to most major cities (open Mon.-Fri. 5:30am-11:30pm, Sat.-Sun. 6:30am-10:30pm). If you have no luck with the private room hawkers at the train station, visit **EXO,** Str. Postăvarului 6 (tel. (068) 14 45 91). From Piaţa Sfatului, walk 15m on Str. Republicii, go right on Diaconu Coresi, and take the next left (rooms starting at 20,000 lei; open Mon.-Sat. 11am-8pm, Sun. 11am-2pm). If you insist on staying in a hotel, **Coroana,** Str. Republicii 62 (tel. (068) 14 43 30), will strain but not break your budget (doubles 310,000 lei, with bath 360,000 lei). A daily outdoor **market** on Str. Nicolae Bălescu provides famished hikers with tasty bread, cheese, and veggies. **Crama,** Piaţa Sfatului 12, in the 16th-century Hirschner house, welcomes guests with traditional dancing (entrees from 9000 lei; open Tues.-Sun. 7pm-2am).

Near Brasov: Bran

Bran, 23km southwest of Braşov, is a picturesque town housing the famed **Castle of Vlad Ţepeş,** ostensibly home to the count who inspired Bram Stoker's novel *Dracula.* Actually, Count Dracula had nothing at all to do with this castle, but Bram Stoker traveled in Transylvania and based the bat-filled fortress in his novel on this model (open Tues.-Sun. 9am-5pm; 15,000 lei, students 10,000 lei). To get to Bran from Braşov, take bus 28 ("IAR Caminul") to "Gară Bartolomeu" (1600 lei), where the **bus** to Bran departs (45min., 4500 lei). To get to the castle, head down the main road (Str. Principal) back towards Barşov and take the first right. To find the Bran Imex **tourist office,** 395 Dr. Aurel Stoian (tel. (068) 23 66 42), follow the main road away from Braşov and take a right (open daily 8am-6pm).

ROMANIAN MOLDOVA AND BUCOVINA

Eastern Romania, which before World War II included the neighboring Republic of Moldova, extends from the Carpathians to the Prut River. The northern landscape of green, gentle hills shelters some of Romania's most beautiful churches and villages.

Iași

The intoxicating perfume of lindens floats among the famous churches and monuments of Iași, Romania's cultural center in the late 19th century. In those years, Iași's writers, nobles, and intellectuals filled the city with Neoclassical homes and palaces, and a century later tourists still enjoy the clean, picturesque streets and homes. The massive neo-Gothic **Palatul Culturii** dominates monument-lined Bd. Ștefan cel Mare, which runs from Piața Unirii to Piața Ștefan cel Mare. The palace houses several museums. **Sala Voivozilor** (Voivodes' Hall), in the **Art Museum,** displays portraits of all Romanian rulers from Trajan (the Roman emperor) to King Carol II; also featured is the wall-sized *Execution of Horea.* The archaeological section of the **Muzeul de Istorie** contains a rich and valuable display of the 5000-year-old Neolithic Cucuteni culture. The rest of the museum examines the more recent history of the region, but comes to a grinding halt at the end of World War II instead of assessing Communism (museums open Tues.-Sun. 10am-4:30pm; 2000-3000 lei each; students half-price). A few meters up Bd. Ștefan cel Mare on the left stands the gorgeous **Trei Ierarhi** church, whose exterior walls display Moldavian, Romanian, and Turkish patterns in raised relief (open daily 9am-noon and 3-7pm).

Frequent **trains** from Bucharest (6hr., 27,400 lei) deliver visitors to the station on Str. Silvestru. The **tourist office** is located at Piața Unirii 9/11 (tel. (032) 11 46 64; open Mon.-Fri. 10am-6pm). A favorite among Americans, **Hotel Traian,** Piața Unirii 1 (tel. (032) 14 33 30), is Rococo and comfortable (singles with shower 88,000 lei, doubles with bath 140,000 lei; breakfast included). **Hotel Continental,** Str. Cuza Vodă 4. (tel. (032) 11 43 20), has more modest rooms but is cheaper and very convenient; some rooms have TV, phone, and fridge (singles 56,000-76,000 lei, doubles 96,000-130,000 lei, triples 144,000 lei). Head to the basement of **Bolta Rece** (Cold Ceiling), Str. Rece 10, for the renown pub in which great writers used to get sloshy (tasty meals up to 20,000-30,000 lei). Cheap food is also available at the **market** at Piața Mihai Viteazul near the intersection of Str. Copou and Bd. Independenței.

Suceava

Suceava has few monuments of its own, but serves as a useful base for exploring Bucovina's monasteries. The ruins of **Cetatea de Scaun** (Royal Fortress) spread in **Parcul Cetății,** east from Piața 22 Decembrie. Take a left on Bd. Ipătescu, a right on Str. Cetății, walk down the hill, and go up the path. The fortress was built around 1388, and withstood several sieges before falling to the Ottomans in 1675 (open daily 8am-9pm; 2000 lei). The **History Museum,** Str. Ștefan cel Mare 33, fulfills your prehistoric yearnings (open Tues.-Sun. 10am-6pm; 8000 lei).

Suceava lies 100km northwest of Iași near the foothills of the Carpathians. There are two train stations: **Suceava,** Str. Lorga 7, Cart. Burdujeni (tel. (30) 21 38 97), and **Suceava Nord,** Str. Gării 4 Cart. Ițcani. **Trains** run to Bucharest (8 per day, 6hr., 27,700 lei), Iași (4 per day, 2½hr., 1150 lei), and Timișoara (4 per day, 12-13hr., 37,100 lei). Buy tickets at **CFR,** Str. Bălcescu 8 (tel. (30) 21 43 35; open Mon.-Fri. 7am-8pm). The **bus station,** Str. Alecsandri 2 (tel. (30) 21 60 89), also serves Iași (1 per day, 3hr., 22,000 lei). Ask at **Bucovina Estur,** Str. Ștefan cel Mare 24 (tel. (30) 22 32 59), across the *piața* from the tourist office, for private rooms in the area (US$15). **Hotel Autoară,** above the bus station (tel. (30) 21 60 89), has sunny new doubles with private bathrooms (35,000 lei for a bed, doubles 70,000 lei).

■ Near Suceava: Bukovina Monasteries

Bukovina's painted monasteries are hidden away among green hills and forests, near rustic farming villages. Built 500 years ago by Ștefan cel Mare and his successors, the small structures serenely mix Moldovan and Byzantine architecture, Romanian soul, and Christian dogma. When visiting, wear long sleeves and a long skirt or pants.

The 15th-century **Voroneț** monastery is among the most famous in the area. The monastery's frescoes are stupendous, and the *Last Judgment* mural a masterpiece. To get here from Suceava, go to Gura Humorului by train (4 per day, 1hr., 5300 lei) or bus (2 per day, 1hr., 6000 lei), and then take a bus to Voroneț (4 per day Mon.-Fri., 10min., 1500 lei) from near the train station. **Humor,** which dates from 1530, is also impressive, decorated with a fresco of the Virgin Mary at war with the Persians (open daily 8am-8pm; 5000 lei). To get there, walk to the heart of Gura Humorului on Ștefan cel Mare from the train or bus station. At the fork, near a park on the right, follow the soft left 6km to the monastery. Beautiful in its simplicity, the 15th-century **Putna** monastery features the marble-canopied tomb of Ștefan cel Mare and sells tapes of music of the monastery, somewhat similar to Gregorian chant (open daily 9am-7pm). It's also probably the best-kept and easiest to access of the monasteries. For the scenic ride to Putna, catch a train from Suceava, 75km southeast (6 per day, 2½hr., 5600 lei). The last train leaves Putna in late afternoon. The monastery lies 2km from the station; exiting the platform, take a right, then a left at the first intersection, and keep walking. Quiet **lodging** can be found along the main road in two-bed bungalows (25,000-40,000 lei); or at **Cabana Putna** off the main road (doubles 100,000 lei; breakfast included), which is also a bar-restaurant (meals under 21,000 lei).

BLACK SEA COAST

From Constanța, roads lead south along the coast past dry valleys, rocky hills, and Roman, Greek, and early Christian ruins. To the south await several popular resort towns. Prices here are too high (especially in July and August) for many Romanians, but tourists crowd this area for the attractive beaches and delicious wines.

Constanța

Starting out as the Greek harbor Tomis some 2500 years ago, Constanța, due to Ceaușescu's megalomania, has became one of Europe's largest ports. Escape the city's innumerable gray apartment blocks by exploring the Old Town. In Piața Ovidiu, behold the **Statue of Ovid,** commemorating the Roman who wrote his most famous poems in exile here. On the same street, the **Archaeology Museum** has several Roman artifacts and depicts the War of Independence from Turkey with a particular flair (open in summer daily 9am-8pm; off-season Tues.-Sun. 9am-5pm; 5000 lei). To the left of the museum, excavations have unearthed the world's largest floor mosaic, preserved from the 4th century, while the **mosque,** one of the few reminders of Turkish domination, boasts one of the largest oriental carpets in Europe (open June-Sept. daily 9:30am-5:30pm; 2000 lei). Near Lacul Tăbăcăriei at Bd. Mamaia 255 (tel. 64 70 55), a **planetarium** and a **delfinarium** (dolphin show) coexist. Take trolley 40 or 41 from Bd. Ferdinand and get off after crossing the tram tracks at the "Delfinariu" stop (5 shows daily in summer 11am-7pm; off-season 11am-4pm; 4000 lei).

Trains from Constanța pass through Bucharest (2¾hr., *accelerant* 17,000 lei) and continue on to virtually every corner of the country. Constanța's main **train** and **bus stations** are near each other, but northbound buses leave from **Autogară Tomis Nord** (from the train station, ride 5 stops on tram 100, then head left). To get downtown from the train station, take trolley 40 or 43 and get off where Bd. Tomis intersects Bd. Ferdinand ("Stație Continental"; 4 stops). Although there is no official tourist office, **Trans Danubis,** Bd. Ferdinand 36 (tel. (041) 61 31 03), is a travel agency which caters to foreigners and can also rent cars (open Mon.-Sat. 9am-7:30pm, Sun. 9:30am-

1pm). **Cazare la Particulari,** Str. Lăpuşneanu (tel. 64 28 31), can find you singles (70,000 lei) or doubles (100,000 lei). Take tram 100 to the end of the line from the train station, and look for Restaurant Nord on the right (open mid-June to mid-Sept. Mon.-Sat. 8:30am-5:30pm, Sun. 8:30am-1pm). The seaside **Hotel Palace,** Str. Remus Opreanu 5 (tel. (041) 61 46 96), offers ritzy rooms, all with bath, TV, and phone (singles 128,800 lei, doubles 182,000 lei). The restaurant in the Hotel Palace has an English menu and a beautiful view of the sea (open daily 7am-midnight). At the corner of Bd. Tomis and Bd. Ferdinand, the **Grand supermarket** has it all.

■ Near Constanţa: Black Sea Resorts and Histria

The coast south of Constanţa is lined with sandy beaches and 70s tourist resorts. **Buses** run south from Constanţa's train station about every 30 minutes in the direction of **Mangalia** (40km, 3500 lei); more comfortable private buses have variable fares (5000-10,000 lei). **Minivans** connect the constellation of resorts near Mangalia late into the night (2000 lei). The first resorts to the south are **Eforie Nord** and **Eforie Sud,** renowned for the mud baths near **Lake Techirghiol.** Its water is so salty you can't sink. From here, head straight to **Costineşti,** a seaside hotspot brimming with young'ns. If you take the train, get off at Costineşti Tabără and circle right around the lake to the entrance. **Albatros** (tel. (041) 73 40 15), straight ahead, provides decent doubles overlooking the sea (32,000 lei with bath). **Disco Ring** is one of the largest outdoor dance clubs in Eastern Europe (cover 5000 lei; open nightly 8pm-4am).

Heading south, you'll pass through **Neptun, Jupiter, Venus,** and **Saturn** before reaching Mangalia. Neptun and its northern neighbor, **Olimp,** have some of the best beaches in the area. The Dispecerat de Cazare **housing office** in Neptun (tel. (041) 73 13 10; open May-Sept. 24hr.) helps find rooms; their prices often beat those at hotels. Local women near Tokapî can find you a room for 50,000-60,000 lei for 10% commission; two-star doubles run 240,000 lei. Probably least spoiled by the tourist industry, **2 Mai** and **Vama Veche** are located on the coast's southern end of the coast. Many young people camp at the southern end of the villages, on the nude beach (7000 lei per tent; parking 10,000 lei).

A Hellenic colony mentioned by Greek historian Strabo in the 5th century BC, **Histria** was rediscovered this century by Romanian archaeologist Vasile Pârvan. Several walls and a few columns still stand, and the **museum** has carved stones, statue fragments, and amphorae. Most explanations are in Romanian, French, and German (museum open daily 10am-6pm; 1000 lei). The excavations are about 30km north of Constanţa, on the shore of Lake Sinoe. **Buses** leave from the Tomis Nord station in Constanţa (6:30am-4:10pm; 1-1½hr., 7400 lei), but drop you off 7km from the site.

Russia (Россия)

US$1	**= 5843R (Russian rubles)**	**1000R =**	**US$0.17**
CDN$1	**= 4224R**	**1000R =**	**CDN$0.24**
UK£1	**= 9295R**	**1000R =**	**UK£0.11**
IR£1	**= 8566R**	**1000R =**	**IR£0.12**
AUS$1	**= 4251R**	**1000R =**	**AUS$0.24**
NZ$1	**= 3608R**	**1000R =**	**NZ$0.27**
SAR1	**= 1243R**	**1000R =**	**SAR0.81**

Country Phone Code: 7 **International Dialing Prefix: 810**

In Russia's unstable economy, expect prices to have changed dramatically. On January 1998 the **ruble** will be redenominated. The exchange rate for new bills was predicated at approximately six rubles to the U.S. dollar, so in effect three zeros will be lopped off the end. The change will occur over the next two years, as old bills are gradually removed from circulation.

"It is a riddle wrapped in a mystery inside an enigma," said Winston Churchill about Russia in 1939. Immense changes have occurred in Russia in this decade, and Churchill is as right today as he was over a half-century ago. Though considered a superpower, Russia is more a chaotic bazaar with ever-changing rules and frustrations. Rapid economic change and the collapse of a legal infrastructure have led to rising poverty and growing discontent with the new system of government. As a result, many Russians have started to lend political support to old Communist leaders, making restructuring the system even more difficult. The collapse of the Soviet Union has allowed Russia's vast patchwork of autonomous regions and minority nationalities, assembled over hundreds of years, to fray and tear apart.

The Eastern Slavs, ancestors of the Russians, started migrating to present-day Russia in the 6th century. The Mongol invasion of the 13th century isolated Russia from the rest of the world until the 17th-century, when Peter the Great dragged the country into Europe and precipitated a permanent crisis of cultural identity between the "Westerners" and "Slavophiles." Revolutions hit hard and heavy in the 20th century, adding ideological strife; Lenin's October 1917 coup ushered the specter of Communism into the world in the form of the Soviet Union. Under Stalin, Russia experienced a boom in industrialization and political executions. Khrushchev emerged as leader for a brief political and cultural "thaw," only to be ousted by Brezhnev. Andropov and Chernyenko followed in humorously quick succession, resulting in Gorbachev's tenure and the beginning of political and economic reform for the Soviet Union. But what began as *glasnost* (openness) and *perestroika* (rebuilding) gradually turned into semi-anarchy, economic crisis, and cynicism. Despite Gorbachev's Western popularity and Nobel Peace Prize, discontent and a failed right-wing coup in 1991 brought about his resignation, the dissolution of the Union, and Boris Yeltsin's election as President of Russia.

Russia's future is uncertain. Yeltsin, trying to construct a new Russian economy, is continually engaged in a power struggle with the Russian Parliament, which includes right-wing nationalist Vladimir Zhirinovsky. The war in Chechnya, the president's unstable health, and the admission of Poland, Hungary, and the Czech Republic to NATO in the face of strong Russian opposition have whittled away at the national morale. Still, the Russians themselves manage to endure with unique resourcefulness, a heavy dose of black humor, and a good amount of vodka.

Satiate your curiosity about Russia in *Let's Go: Eastern Europe 1998*.

GETTING THERE

Russian **visas** require an invitation stating itinerary and dates of travel, and thus are inherently difficult to get without a contact in Russia. Fortunately, several organizations specialize in supplying invitations and/or visas for individual tourists. **Traveler's Guest House,** Bolshaya Pereyaslavskaya 50, 10th fl., 129401 Moscow, Russia (tel. (095) 971 40 59 or 280 85 62; fax 280 76 86; email tgh@glas.apc.org), arranges visa invitations, will register you once you arrive, makes reservations, and gets train tickets. With offices in the U.S. and Russia, **Russia House,** Leningradsky Prospekt 17, 125040 Moscow, Russia (tel. (095) 250 01 43; fax 250 25 03), provides invitations and visas for all countries of the former Soviet Union. In the U.S., their address is 1800 Connecticut Ave. NW, Washington, D.C. 20009, attn: Chris Poor (tel. (202) 986-6010; fax 667-4244). **Red Bear Tours/Russian Passport,** also known as **Russia-Rail Internet Travel Service,** Ste. 11A, 401 St. Kilda Rd., Melbourne 30004, Australia (tel. (3) 98 67 38 88, toll-free in Australia (800) 33 30 31; fax 98 67 10 55), provides invitations on the condition that you book accommodations with them. They also sell rail tickets for the Trans-Siberian/Manchurian/Mongolian and Silk routes and arranges assorted tours (email passport@werple.net.au; http://www.travelcentre.com.au or http://www.russia-rail.com). Also try **Host Families Association, HOFA,** Tavricheskaya 5-25, 193015 St. Petersburg, Russia (tel./fax 812 275 1992; email hofa@usa.net), for homestays in more than 20 cities of the former Soviet Union (US$30-50). Visa invitations are also available through HOFA. Finally, **IBV Bed&Breakfast Systems,** 13113 Ideal Dr., Silver Spring, MD 20906, USA (tel. (031) 942-3770; fax 933-0024), offers visa invitations and accommodations booking.

If you have received an invitation, apply for a visa at a Russian **embassy** or **consulate** (see **Government Information Offices,** p. 1). Send a photocopy of your invitation and the front pages of your passport, a completed application (contact the embassy or a travel agent for blanks), three photographs, a cover letter (with your name, arrival and departure dates, planned itinerary, birth date, and passport number), and the visa fee (2-week service US$40, 1-week US$50, same-day US$120) to the embassy or consulate. Include a return envelope with postage. If you have even tentative plans to visit a city, have it put on your visa, and get a visa for longer than you actually plan to stay. Most organizations will register your visa for you on arrival, but if not, go down to the central OVIR (ОВИР) office (in Moscow called УВИР) to register. This is also where you should attempt to extend your visa—a bureaucratic hassle.

Flying on British Airways to St. Petersburg or Moscow is the most direct way to reach Russia. **Rail travel** from European capitals to Moscow and St. Petersburg is cheaper. Check to see if you are going through Belarus, for which you need a transit visa; sometimes you can get by with just a Russian visa. The Warsaw-Tallinn express goes through Lithuania instead. Finnord **buses** leave for St. Petersburg from Lahti, Finland (4 per day) and are cheaper than the trains.

Customs enforcement is arbitrary and unpredictable; one day they'll tear your pack apart, the next they'll just nod and dismiss you. At the border, politely answer the officials, but *do not* offer any information they don't specifically ask for. You will be given a **Customs Declaration Form** at the border on which to declare all your valuables and foreign currency. *Don't* lose it. Everything listed on the customs form must be on your person when you leave the country.

GETTING AROUND

As of summer 1996, the U.S. State Department had issued a warning about the overnight train between Moscow and St. Petersburg, a popular route for tourists. Check http://travel.state.gov/travel_warnings.html for more info.

Foreigners are officially required to buy internal plane and train tickets at inflated Intourist prices. You must show your *dokumenty* (документы, i.e. passport) at the time of purchase, which makes it impossible to get the Russian rate. You can buy train tickets originating in a different city, but it is best to use Moscow or St. Petersburg as a base and make a series of round-trip journeys from there.

Russia boasts an extensive **rail** and **bus** network and a vast, not-so-reliable air system monopolized by the aging **Aeroflot.** Nascent Aeroflot alternative, **Transair** services only select cities. Train cars are divided into many classes: luxury two-bed "*ess-veh*" (СВ) compartments, four-bed cozy *"koupé"* (К), and open-car *platskarty* (П). *Let's Go* recommends the *koupé* class. *Elektrichka* (the commuter rail, marked on train station signs as пригородные поезда; *prigorodnye poezda*) has its own platforms; buy tickets from the *kassa* (касса; ticket counter). These trains are often packed; you may have to stand in line for an hour or more. Buses, a good option for shorter trips, are slightly more expensive and therefore less crowded than trains. On the Hungarian **Ikarus** buses, you'll get a fairly comfy reclining seat. You can often store luggage under the bus for a fee (5000-25,000R).

Within Russian cities, overcrowded **buses, trams, trolleys,** and (in major metropoles) unbelievably efficient **metro** systems ferry citizens quickly and cheaply. In the metro, buy *zhetony* (жетоны; tokens) at the *kassa* and drop them into machines that let you onto escalators. Magnetic strip cards have recently been introduced on the metro; you can buy one for 10 rides or more. There are regular buses and more comfortable express buses (marked with "Э"). On the express buses, pay the driver (usually 2500R); otherwise, buy bus tickets at newsstands or in special kiosks and punch them on board. *Do not* buy them from the *babushki* at metro stations (they may be fake or invalid). Don't try to ride for free, especially in city centers; the system is very energetic in searching out free riders, particularly during the last week of the month, and fines are high (8900-25,000R). Metro stations are labeled only in Cyrillic; if you don't read Russian, you can usually recognize stations by memorizing the first and last letters. When two lines intersect, there is often a different station name for each line. You'll want to know the words *vkhod* (вход; entrance), *vykhod* (выход; exit), *vykhod v gorod* (выход в город; exit to the city), and *perekhod* (переход; transfer to another line). Metro stations are marked above ground by a capital "M." Acquire the newest city map possible—names have been changing wildly in recent years.

Hailing a **taxi** is indistinguishable from hitchhiking. Almost all of those who stop will be private citizens trying make a little extra cash. Those seeking a ride stand off the curb and hold out a hand; when a car stops, riders tell the driver the destination before getting in. The driver will either refuse the destination and speed off, or nod his head, at which point haggling begins. Meters are non-operational. Keep in mind that hitching is very risky, and that non-Russian speakers *will* get ripped off.

ESSENTIALS

Be flexible. Expect airport delays, tour cancellations, hotel changes, cold showers, and bathrooms *sans* toilet paper. The rules have changed so often no one really knows what they are anymore. Travel in Russia requires ample preparation. Pack carefully; bring your sense of humor and any Western goods you'll need. Most toiletries and such are available in Moscow and St. Petersburg for a price. Plastic bags and packs of tissue are indispensable. Roach traps can be a godsend in a dormitory.

Russia celebrates: Jan. 1, Orthodox Christmas (Jan. 7), Defenders of the Motherland (Feb. 23), International Women's Day (March 8); Orthodox Easter (March/April); Labor Day (May1-2); Victory Day (May 9); Independence Day (June 12); Great October Socialist Revolution (Nov. 7).

Currency exchange in Russia is now easy—just find an *Obmen Valyuty* (Обмен Валюты; currency exchange) sign. Besides U.S. dollars, many will change Deutschmarks, and some francs and British pounds, but few besides main branches will change traveler's checks or give cash advances on credit cards. Changing rubles back at the end of your trip is no problem, but the unstable exchange rate makes it best not to change large sums of money at once. Do *not* exchange money on the street.

Communication There is neither rhyme nor reason to Russia's **mail service.** Delivery can take anywhere from two weeks to eternity. **AmEx** card- and Traveler's Cheque-holders can receive letters at their travel service bureaus in Moscow and St. Petersburg; this is usually more reliable than Russian mail. **DHL** has offices in Moscow, St. Petersburg, and Nizhny Novgorod; they are expensive but reliable.

Local **telephones** in Moscow take special tokens, sold at Metro station *kassy;* in St. Petersburg they take metro tokens. In most small towns, payphones are free for local calls. You can make **intercity calls** from *mezhdugorodnye* (междугородные) phone booths. It will take a while, but you can usually get through. Dial 8, wait for the tone, then dial the city code. Direct **international calls** are possible from telephone offices and hotel rooms: dial 8, wait for the tone, then dial 10 and the country code. You *cannot* call collect, unless using AT&T service (listed below), which will cost your party dearly. To make calls from the telephone office, buy tokens and use a *mezhdugorodny* (междугородный) telephone; press the *otvet* (ответ) button when your party answers or you will not be heard. If there are no automatic phones, you must pay for your call at the counter. Several hotels in Moscow now have direct-dial booths operated by a special card or credit card. The cost is astronomical (at least US$6 per min. to the U.S.). For **AT&T Direct,** dial in Moscow 755 50 42, in St. Petersburg 325 50 42; **Sprint Access,** 155 61 33 in Moscow. Dial 8-095 first when calling from another city; you will pay for the phone call to Moscow in addition to the international connection. For **Canada Direct,** dial 810 80 04 97 72 33 (Moscow and St. Petersburg only); **New Zealand Direct,** 81 08 00 47 70 64. Calling into the country can be equally frustrating. Most countries have direct dial to Moscow and St. Petersburg. For other cities, go through the international operator. In **emergencies,** call 01 for **fire,** 02 for **police,** and 03 for an **ambulance.**

Language Though more and more people speak English in Russia, take some time to look over the Cyrillic alphabet. It's not as difficult as it looks and will make getting around and getting by immeasurably easier. The "r" in Russian is trilled.

Cyrillic	English	Pronunciation	Cyrillic	English	Pronunciation
А, а	a	St*a*lin	Р, р	r	*R*achel
Б, б	b	*B*yzantine	С, с	s	*C*ircuit board
В, в	v	The *V*illage People	Т, т	t	*T*itrate
Г, г	g	*G*oats	У, у	u	P*oo*dle
Д, д	d	*D*eliverance	Ф, ф	f	*F*abulous
Е, е	ye or e	*Ye*sterday	Х, х	kh	*Ch*utzpah (*hkh*)
Ё, ё	yo	*Yaw*n	Ц, ц	ts	Le*t's* Go
Ж, ж	zh	*Zh*irinovsky	Ч, ч	ch	Mun*ch*ies
З, з	z	*Z*ohra	Ш, ш	sh	*Ch*ivalry
И, и	i	Kathl*ee*n	Щ, щ	shch	Khru*shch*ev
Й, й	y	*Y*ak	Ъ, ъ	(hard)	(no sound)
К, к	k	*C*atharine	Ы, ы	y	P*i*t
Л, л	l	*L*onging	Ь, ь	(soft)	(no sound)
М, м	m	*M*ara	Э, э	eh	Al*e*ksander
Н, н	n	*N*eanderthal	Ю, ю	yoo	*You*
О, о	o	L*aw*	Я, я	yah	*Ya*hoo!
П, п	p	*P*avement			

In the Slavic world, plurals of words are usually formed by adding "ы" or "и" at the end, so the plural of *matryoshka* is *matryoshki.* Note that улица (*ulitsa;* abbreviated ул.) means "street"; проспект (*prospekt;* пр.) means "avenue"; площадь (*ploshchad;* пл.) means "square"; and бульвар (*bulvar;* бул.) is "boulevard." Once you get the hang of the alphabet, you can pronounce most Russian words.

Yes/No	Да/Нет	dah/nyet
Hello	Добрый день	DOH-brih DYEN
Thank you	Спасибо	spa-SEE-bah
Please/You're welcome	Пожалуйста	pa-ZHOW-a-sta
Excuse me.	Извините	eez-vee-NEET-yeh
Where is...?	Где...?	g-dyeh...?
How much does this cost?	Сколько стоит?	SKOHL-ka STOH-yeet?
I don't understand.	Я не понимаю	ya nee pa-nee-MAH-yoo
Do you speak English?	Вы говорите по-английски?	vih go-vo-REE-tyeh po ahn-GLEE-skee?
Do you have a vacancy?	У вас есть свободный номер?	oo vahss yehst svah-BOD-niy NOH-meer
Help!	Поможите!	pah-mah-ZHEE-tyeh

Accommodations Western-style **youth hostels** have begun to appear in Russia; some arrange visas for your stay. Reserve well in advance, especially in summer. **Hotels** offer several classes of rooms. *Lux,* usually a two-room double with TV, phone, fridge, and bath, is most expensive. *Pol-lux* is a one-room single or double with TV, phone, and bath. Rooms with bath and no TV, if they exist, are cheaper. The lowest price rooms are *bez udobstv* (без удобств), which means one room with a sink. Many hotels have restaurants, often the best eatery in town; all have at least a buffet or cafeteria—probably the worst food in town. Hot water—even all water—is sometimes turned off for pipe repair and conservation, and water only gets turned on once every two weeks due to shortages in parts of south Russia. Another cheap option can be staying in a **university dorm;** many take in foreign students for US$10 per night. The rooms are livable, but don't expect sparkling bathrooms or reliable hot water. Make arrangements with an institute from your home country.

Food and Drink Russians look upon food principally for nourishment. The standard hotel dinner menu includes *salat* (салат), usually cucumbers or beets and potatoes with mayonnaise and sour cream; *soup* (суп), meat or cabbage; and *kuritsa* (курица; chicken) or *myaso* (мясо; meat), often called *kutlyety* (кутлеты) or *beefshteak* (бифштек). Ordering a number of *zakusky* (закуски; Russian appetizers) instead of a main dish can save money and add variety to your diet. Dessert is *morozhenoye* (мороженое; ice cream) and *coffye* (кофе) or *chai* (чай; tea). Russian cafés (кафе) offer similar-quality food more cheaply; often the tables have no chairs. A *stolovaya* (столовая; cafeteria) will likely be unsanitary.

In Russia, you can buy food on the street, from a store, or at a market. A *dieta* (Диета) sells goods for special diets (e.g. diabetics); *produkty* (Продукты) offer a variety of meats, cheeses, breads, and packaged goods; a *gastronom* (Гастроном) carries a smaller range of meat and dairy products; and an *universam* (Универсам) has the variety of a supermarket. The market (рынок; *rynok)* has abundant fruits and vegetables, meat, fresh milk, butter, honey, and cheese. Wash and dry everything before you eat it—Russian farmers use pesticides liberally. Bring bags; containers are not provided. The ubiquitous kiosks are mini-convenience stores; just point at what you want. Buy your booze in a foreign grocery store. *Zolotoye koltso, Russkaya,* and *Zubrovka* are the best vodkas; *Stolichnaya* and *Moskovskaya* are well-known names, and generic brands get the job done.

Travelers are generally advised not to drink the water in Russia. While often potable in limited doses, its cleanliness is on the decrease. It is recommended that you boil your water for at least 10 minutes. A gamma globulin shot will lower your risk of hepatitis. For **medical emergencies,** leave the country or get to a St. Petersburg or Moscow clinic for foreigners.

Moscow Москва

Moscow is huge, apocalyptic, and compelling. Home to one in 15 Russians, the city is full of contrasts. The colors of churches and monasteries splash against the backdrop of gray Stalinist edifices, while on the street awaits a haphazard and anarchic conglomerate of peasant villages. Careerists sell Japanese televisions from the back of a truck next to grandmothers offering the potatoes and dill they've been growing at their *dachas* for the past 30 years. Anything and everything is possible; after enough time, the contradictions begin to seem normal. Russia's center of change, Moscow provides the visitor with a dizzying view of the country's possibilities. You may not love it—you may even hate it—but you won't regret you came.

ORIENTATION AND PRACTICAL INFORMATION

A series of concentric rings emanates from the **kremlin** (кремль). The outermost ring road forms the city boundary, but most sights lie within the inner **Sadovoe koltso** (Садовое кольцо; Garden Ring). **Red Square** (Красная площадь; **Krasnaya Ploshchad**) and the kremlin mark the city center. Nearby begin the popular shopping streets: **Novy Arbat** (Новый Арбат), running west parallel to the Metro's blue lines, and **ul. Tverskaya** (Тверская), extending north along the green line. Ul. Tverskaya was formerly called ul. Gorkovo (Горкого); the upper half, which leads to the Garden Ring, is now known as ul. Pervaya Tverskaya-Yamskaya (1-я Тверская-Ямская). An extensive **map,** including all public transportation routes and a street index, is sold at many kiosks for around 25,000R. Many are outdated; check that a recent year is marked. See this book's **color maps** of the **Metro** and the city. *Let's Go* lists Metro stops in their transliterated form; refer to the color maps for Cyrillic.

Tourist Offices: Intourservice Central Excursion Bureau, Nikitsky per. 4A (Никитский пер.; tel. 203 75 85 or 203 80 16; fax 200 12 43 or 203 56 19). M1: Okhotny Ryad. Open daily 9am-7:30pm. **Moskovsky Sputnik** (Московский спутник), Maly Ivanovsky per. 6, kor. 2 (Малый Ивановский; tel. 924 03 17 or 925 92 78). M5, 6: Kitai Gorod. Student travel, visas, and tickets. Open Mon.-Fri. 9am-1pm and 2-6pm, Sat. 9am-1pm and 2-5pm.

Budget Travel: Student Travel Agency Russia (S.T.A.R.), 50 Bolshaya Pereyaslavskaya, 10th fl. (tel. 913 59 52; fax 280 90 30). Open Mon.-Fri. 10am-6pm.

Embassies: Most open Mon.-Fri. 9 or 9:30am-noon or 1pm; some also 1-5 or 6pm. **Australia,** Kropotkinsky per. 13 (Кропоткинский; tel. 956 60 70 or 246 50 12). M3: Smolenskaya. **Belarus,** ul. Maroseyka 1716 (Маросейка; tel. 924 70 31; fax 928 64 03). **Canada,** Starokonyushenny per. 23 (Староконюшенный; tel. 241 50 70). M1: Kropotkinskaya. Closed Wed. **Ireland,** Grokholsky per. 5 (Грохольский; tel. 288 41 01). M4,5: Prospekt Mira. **Lithuania,** Borisoglebsky per. 10 (Борисоглебский; tel. 291 15 01; fax 202 35 16). M3: Arbatskaya. **New Zealand,** ul. Povarskaya 44 (Поварская; tel. 956 35 78). M4,6: Krasnopresnenskaya. **South Africa,** Bolshoy Strochinovsky per. 22/25 (Большой Строчиновский; tel. 230 68 69). **U.K.,** nab. Sofiskaya 14 (Софиская; tel. 956 72 00; fax 956 74 20). M1,3,8: Borovitskaya. Open Mon.-Fri. 9am-5pm. **U.S.,** Novinsky 19/23 (Новинский; tel. 252 24 51). M6: Krasnopresnenskaya. **Ukraine,** Leontevsky per. 18 (Леонтевский; formerly ul. Stanislavskovo), off ul. Tverskaya (tel. 229 10 79, visa inquiries 229 69 22). M3: Tverskaya.

Currency Exchange: Banks at almost every corner; check ads in English-language newspapers. The pamphlet *Moscow Express Directory,* updated biweekly and free in most luxury hotels, lists the addresses and phone numbers of many banks, as well as places to buy and cash traveler's checks. Nearly every bank and hotel has an **ATM;** a particularly useful and reliable ATM stands in the lobby of the Central Telegraph building (Visa/MC/Cirrus/Plus/Unioncard).

American Express: ul. Sadovaya-Kudrinskaya 21a (Садовая-Кудринская; tel. 755 90 00 or 755 90 04). M2: Mayakovskaya. Take a left onto ul. Bolshaya Sadovaya (Большая Садовая), which becomes ul. Sadovaya-Kudrinskaya. Travel assistance, mail, and banking services for members. **ATM** in lobby exchanges money 24hr. Office open Mon.-Fri. 9am-5pm, Sat. 9am-1pm.

Flights: International flights arrive at **Sheremetyevo-2** (Шереметьево-2; tel. 956 46 66). M2: Rechnoy Vokzal. The van under the sign "автолайн" on the street in front of the train station picks up passengers every 10min. 7am-10pm for a 20min. ride to Sheremetyevo-2 (10,000R). 24hr. Visa ATM and MC cash advances on the 1st fl. Most flights to within the former USSR originate at **Vnukovo** (Внуково; tel. 436 21 09), **Bikovo** (Биково; tel. 558 47 38), **Domodedovo** (Домодедово; tel. 323 85 65), or **Sheremetyevo-1** (tel. 578 23 72). Buy tickets in *kassy* at the **Tsentralny Aerovokzal** (Центральный Аэровокзал; Central Airport Station), a 2-stop tram (23) or trolley (12 or 70) ride from M2: Aeroport. Express bus schedules are posted outside the station. Taxis will rip you off like you've never dreamed possible.

Trains: tel. 266 93 33; for tickets tel. 266 83 33. Bring your passport and purchase tickets at the *Tsentralnoe Zhelezhnodorozhnoe Agenstvo* (Центральное Жележнодорожное Агенщтво; Central Train Agency), by Yaroslavsky Vokzal (M4: Komsomolskaya), window 10 or 11 (complete schedules posted; *kassy* open daily 8am-1pm and 2-7pm). After hours, try the 24hr. Intourist *kassy* on the 2nd floor of Leningradsky Vokzal (entrance 3, windows 20 and 21). Your ticket will tell you at which *vokzal* (вокзал; station) to catch your train. Tickets for local *elektrickas* (local trains) should be bought at the local ticket booths (Пригородные Кассы) in each station. Moscow's nine train stations are arranged around the metro's circle line (M4). Trains to St. Petersburg depart from **Leningradsky Vokzal** (Ленинградский), Komsomolskaya pl. 3 (Комсомольская). M1,4: Komsomolskaya. **Kazansky Vokzal** (Казанский), Komsomolskaya pl. 2, opposite Leningradsky Vokzal, services the east and southeast, including Volgograd and Central Asia. **Yaroslavsky Vokzal** (Ярославский) Komsomolskaya pl. 5, sends trains to Siberia and the Far East (the Trans-Siberian Railroad; buy tickets 1-2 days in advance). **Paveletsky Vokzal** (Павелетский) Paveletskaya pl. 1 and **Kursky Vokzal** (Курский) ul. Zemlyenoy Val 29, 1, serve Crimea, eastern Ukraine, Georgia, Azerbaijan, and Armenia. **Rizhsky Vokzal,** (Рижский) Rizhkaya pl. To Rīga (16hr.) and Estonia. **Belorussky Vokzal** (Белорусский), pl. Tverskaya Zastava. To Warsaw (24hr.), Minsk (9-13hr.), and Kaliningrad. **Kievsky Vokzal** (Киевский), pl. Kievskovo Vokzala (Киевского Вокзала), sends trains to Bulgaria, Romania, Slovakia, and Ukraine.

Public Transportation: The **Metro** is large, fast, and efficient—a work of art in urban planning. Passages between lines or stations are shown by a sign of a man walking up stairs. A station that serves more than one line will generally have more

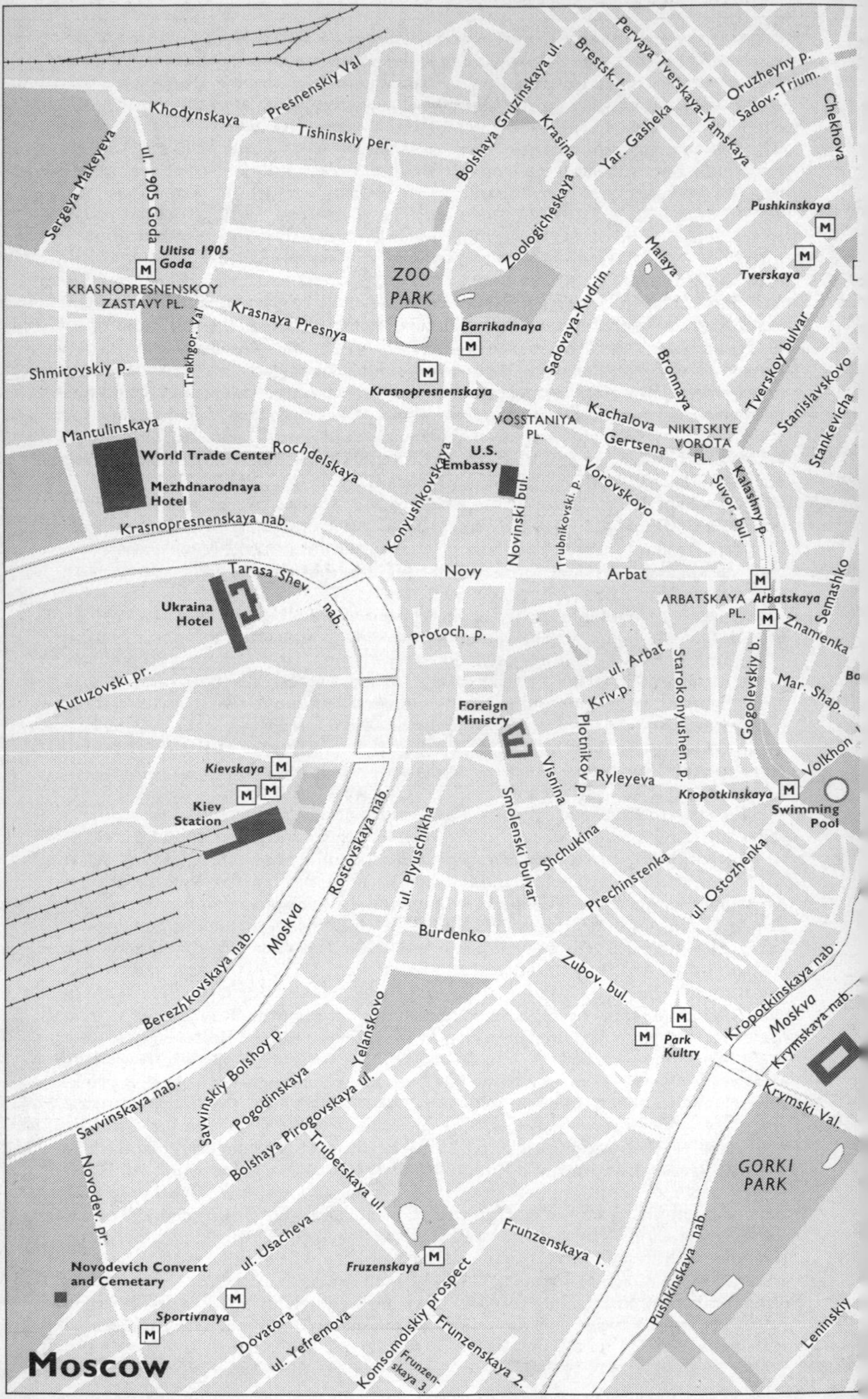
Moscow
Presnenskiy Val
Khodynskaya
Tishinskiy per.
Sergeya Makeyeva
ul. 1905 Goda
Ultisa 1905 Goda
KRASNOPRESNENSKOY ZASTAVY PL.
Krasnaya Presnya
Trekhgor. Val
Shmitovskiy p.
Mantulinskaya
World Trade Center
Mezhdnarodnaya Hotel
Rochdelskaya
Krasnopresnenskaya nab.
ZOO PARK
Barrikadnaya
Krasnopresnenskaya
Bolshaya Gruzinskaya ul.
Brestsk. I.
Pervaya Tverskaya-Yamskaya
Oruzheyny p.
Sadov.-Trium.
Chekhova
Krasina
Yar. Gasheka
Zoologicheskaya
Pushkinskaya
Tverskaya
Malaya
Sadovaya-Kudrin.
Bronnaya
Tverskoy bulvar
Stanislavskovo
Stankevicha
Kachalova
VOSSTANIYA PL.
Gertsena
NIKITSKIYE VOROTA PL.
U.S. Embassy
Konyushkovskaya
Novinski bul.
Trubnikovski. p.
Vorovskovo
Suvor. bul.
Kalashny p.
Novy
Arbat
Tarasa Shev. nab.
Ukraina Hotel
ARBATSKAYA PL.
Arbatskaya
Semashko
Znamenka
Protoch. p.
ul. Arbat
Starokonyushen. p.
Gogolevskiy b.
Mar. Shap.
Kutuzovski pr.
Kriv. p.
Foreign Ministry
Plotnikov p.
Volkhon
Kievskaya
Kiev Station
Vishnina
Ryleyeva
Kropotkinskaya
Swimming Pool
Smolenski bulvar
Rostovskaya nab.
ul. Plyuschikha
Shchukina
Prechinstenka
ul. Ostozhenka
Moskva
Burdenko
Berezhkovskaya nab.
Zubov. bul.
Kropotkinskaya nab.
Krymskaya nab.
Park Kultry
Yelanskovo
Savvinskiy Bolshoy P.
Pogodinskaya
Savvinskaya nab.
Bolshaya Pirogovskaya ul.
Krymski Val.
Trubetskaya ul.
GORKI PARK
Novodev. pr.
ul. Usacheva
Frunzenskaya 1.
Fruzenskaya
Novodevich Convent and Cemetary
Sportivnaya
Komsomolskiy prospect
Pushkinskaya nab.
Dovatora
ul. Yefremova
Frunzenskaya 2.
Frunzenskaya 3.
Leninskiy

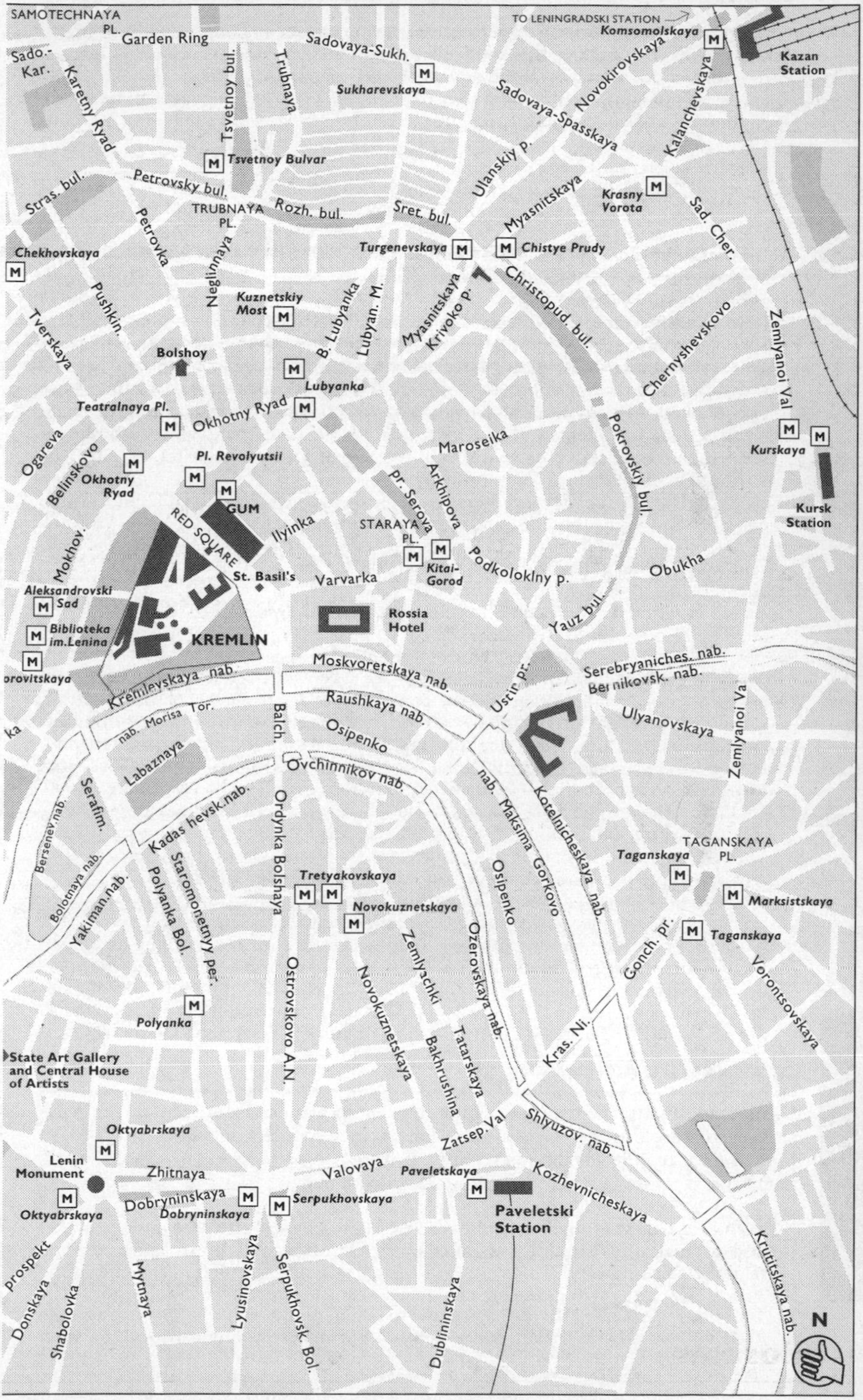
SAMOTECHNAYA PL.
Garden Ring
Sado.- Kar.
Karetny Ryad
Tsvetnoy bul.
Trubnaya
Sadovaya-Sukh.
Sukharevskaya
Sadovaya-Spasskaya
Novokirovskaya
Komsomolskaya
TO LENINGRADSKI STATION
Kazan Station
Kalanchevskaya
Tsvetnoy Bulvar
Petrovsky bul.
Stras. bul.
TRUBNAYA PL.
Rozh. bul.
Sret. bul.
Ulanskiy p.
Myasnitskaya
Krasny Vorota
Sad. Cher.
Chekhovskaya
Petrovka
Neglinnaya
Turgenevskaya
Chistye Prudy
Christopud. bul.
Pushkin.
Tverskaya
Kuznetskiy Most
B. Lubyanka
Lubyan. M.
Myasnitskaya
Krivoko p.
Chernyshevskovo
Zemlyanoi Val
Bolshoy
Lubyanka
Teatralnaya Pl.
Okhotny Ryad
Maroseika
Pokrovskiy bul.
Kurskaya
Ogareva
Belinskovo
Okhotny Ryad
Pl. Revolyutsii
pr. Serova
Arkhipova
Kursk Station
GUM
RED SQUARE
Ilyinka
STARAYA PL.
Mokhov.
Kitai-Gorod
Podkolokny p.
Obukha
Aleksandrovski Sad
St. Basil's
Varvarka
Rossia Hotel
Biblioteka im.Lenina
KREMLIN
Yauz bul.
orovitskaya
Moskvoretskaya nab.
Ustin pr.
Serebryaniches. nab.
Bernikovsk. nab.
Kremlevskaya nab.
Raushkaya nab.
Ulyanovskaya
Zemlyanoi Va
nab. Morisa Tor.
Balch.
Osipenko
Labaznaya
Ovchinnikov nab.
nab. Maksima Gorkovo
Kotelnicheskaya nab.
Serafim.
Bersenev.nab.
Kadas hevsk.nab.
Ordynka Bolshaya
TAGANSKAYA PL.
Taganskaya
Bolotnaya nab.
Staromonetny per.
Polyanka Bol.
Tretyakovskaya
Osipenko
Marksistskaya
Yakiman.nab.
Novokuznetskaya
Taganskaya
Zemlyachki
Ozerovskaya nab.
Gonch. pr.
Ostrovskovo A.N.
Novokuznetskaya
Vorontsovskaya
Polyanka
Bakhrushina
Tatarskaya
Kras. Ni.
State Art Gallery and Central House of Artists
Zatsep. Val
Shlyuzov. nab.
Oktyabrskaya
Lenin Monument
Zhitnaya
Valovaya
Paveletskaya
Kozhevnicheskaya
Dobryninskaya
Dobryninskaya
Serpukhovskaya
Paveletski Station
Oktyabrskaya
prospekt
Donskaya
Shabolovka
Mytnaya
Lysinovskaya
Serpukhovsk. Bol.
Dubininskaya
Krutitskaya nab.
N

than one name. Trains run daily 6am-1am. Buy light green tokens (2000R) from the *kassy* inside the stations. **Bus** and **trolley** tickets are available in gray kiosks labeled "проездные билеты" and from the driver (1500R). Be sure to punch your ticket upon boarding—the fine for not doing so is 10,000R. *Edinye bilety* (единые билеты; calendar month passes) let you ride on any form of transportation (180,000R). Monthly Metro passes are 90,000R. Purchase either from the *kassy*. Metro maps (in Latin and Cyrillic) are in the front or back of this book.

Taxis: Call 927 00 00. Look for a round sign with a green "T." If you don't speak Russian, you'll get taken for a ride in more ways than one. Ask around for the going rate and agree on a price before you get in. Be sure the meter is turned on.

Laundromat: Traveler's Guest House (see p. 746) will do your laundry for 25,000R per load. **California Cleaners,** Leninsky pr. 113/1 (tel. 956 52 84). Free pickup and delivery (tel. 497 00 05 or 497 00 11). Wash and dry 20,000R per kg.

24-Hour Pharmacies: Leningradsky pr. 74 (Ленингадский; tel. 151 45 70). M2: Sokol. Also at Kutuzovsky pr. 14 (Кутузовский; tel. 243 16 01). M3: Kutuzovskaya.

Medical Assistance: American Medical Center, Vtoroy Tverskoy-Yamskoy per. 10 (2-ой Тверской-Ямской; tel. 956 33 66; fax 956 23 06). M2: Mayakovskaya. Most experienced Western medical clinic in Moscow (US$215 per visit). Monthly membership US$55, students US$45. Open Mon.-Sat. 9:30am-7pm; call for after-hours service. Also **Mediclub Moscow,** Michurinsky pr. 56 (Мичуринский; tel. 931 50 18 or 931 53 18). M1: Prospekt Vernadskovo.

Emergencies: Try the above centers for medical emergencies, call your embassy for passport and visa problems, and give up on legal retaliation. Call 299 11 80 to report offenses by the police (no coins needed from pay phones), or try the **U.S. embassy's emergency number,** tel. 230 20 01. **Fire:** tel. 01.

Police: tel. 02.

Express Mail: DHL: Radisson-Slavyanskaya, Berezhkovskaya nab. 2 (Бережковсая; tel. 941 87 40). M3: Kievskaya. **GUM** (ГУМ) business center (бизнес-центр), 2nd fl. (tel. 921 09 11; fax 921 46 09). Open Mon.-Sat. 8am-8pm.

Post Offices: Moscow Central Telegraph, ul. Tverskaya 7, a few blocks from the kremlin. Look for the globe and the digital clock out front. M1: Okhotny Ryad. Unreliable **international mail** service open Mon.-Fri. 8am-2pm and 3-9pm, Sat. 8am-2pm and 3-7pm, Sun. 9am-2pm and 3-7pm. Address mail: "Москва 103009, POSTE RESTANTE, McLOUGHLIN, Lucille." *Poste Restante* also at the **Gostinitsa Intourist post office,** ul. Tverskaya 3/5. Address mail "До Востребования, К-600, Гостиница Интурист, ул. Тверская 3/5 Москва, Russia." To mail **packages,** bring them unwrapped to the Intourist post office (open Mon.-Fri. 9am-noon and 1-7pm, Sat. 9am-noon and 1-5pm) or to Myasnitskaya 26 (Мясницкая, formerly Kirova); they will be wrapped and mailed while you wait. **Postal Code:** 103009.

Telephones: Moscow Central Telegraph (see Post Offices, below). Open 24hr. Prepay at the counter. Calls to the U.S. and Australia cost approximately 14,700R per min., to Europe 6300R per min. Do not call collect or use a calling card here; use the **international telephone cabinets** (международные телефоны; *mezhdunarodnye telefony*). Major hotels have direct-dial international phone booths at exorbitant prices (1min. to the U.S. US$6-15). **Local calls** require a plastic *zheton* (жетонь Є%%Р), sold at some Metro stations or kiosks. **Telephone Code:** 095.

ACCOMMODATIONS

Suffice it to say that the concept of budget accommodations for student travelers has yet to arrive in Moscow. Options are slim, so in summer reservations are a must. *Babushki* at major rail stations will rent private rooms (сдаю комнату) and apartments (сдаю квартиру) for as low as 30,000R if you haggle.

Traveler's Guest House, ul. Bolshaya Pereyaslavskaya 50 (tel. 971 40 59; fax 280 76 86; email tgh@glas.apc.org). M4,5: Prospekt Mira, walk north along pr. Mira, take the third right on Banny pere. (Банный пере.), and turn left at the end of the street. TGH is the white, 12-story building across the street; take the elevator to the 10th floor. If you are arriving in Moscow speaking no Russian and knowing no one, TGH will be all you'll ever need. Helpful, enthusiastic, English-speaking staff.

RUSSIA

Kitchen facilities, a laundry service, and a common room with TV and phone. *Moscow Times* free. Dorms 105,300R. Singles 210,000R. Doubles 280,000R. Reserve 1 week ahead. Retain copies of reservation forms and receipts.

Galina's Flat, ul. Chaplygina 8, #35 (Чаплыгина; tel. 921 60 38). M1: Chistye Prudy. Head down bul. Chistoprudny (Чистопрудный) past the statue of Griboyedov (Грибоедов), take the first left onto Bol. Kharytonyevsky per. (Бол. Харитоньевский) just after the blue Kazakh Embassy, then the second right. Go through the courtyard, turn right, and enter by the "Уникум" sign; the flat is on the 5th floor on the right-hand side. Friendly Galina and her sidekick Sergei welcome you to their homey apartment. Hot showers. Kitchen facilities. Safe location. The best deal in Moscow. Only 7 beds and a cot, so call ahead. 5-bed dorm US$8. Doubles US$10 per person.

Gostinitsa Tsentralnaya (Гостиница Центральная), ul. Tverskaya 10 (tel. 229 89 57), next to Pizza Hut. M2,6,8: Pushkinskaya. Standard Russian hotel with downstairs guard and floor women to keep your key. Much cheaper than other centrally located hotels. All rooms have sinks; bath and toilet off the hall. Singles US$37. Doubles US$50 (prices listed in US$, but you still pay in rubles). MC, V.

American Academy of Foreign Languages, ul. Bolshaya Cheryomushkinskaya 17a (Большая Черемушкинская; tel. 129 43 00; fax 123 15 00). M5: Akademicheskaya. From the Metro station, turn left at the Ho Chi Minh sculpture and walk 15min. on ul. Dmitriya Ulyanova (Дмитрия Ульянова), then turn left on Bolshaya Cheryomushkinskaya. Trolley 26 also runs to the hotel from M5: Shabolovskaya; get off at "Shveinaya Fabrika Moskva" (15min., 1500R). Beds 55,000-75,000R. 2-room "lux" suites 400,000R. "Half-lux" suites 300,000-340,000R. Cash only.

Prakash Guesthouse, ul. Profsoyuznaya 83, kor. 1, 3rd fl. (Профсоюзная; tel. 334 82 01; fax 334 25 98). M5: Belyaevo. From the Metro, take the exit nearest the last car of the train and go all the way to the right of the *perekhod* (tunnel), exiting from the last stairway on the left-hand side. The guest house is a 16-story structure; enter through the second entrance. Friendly if far. Reception open daily 7am-11pm or call; they'll meet you at the Metro. Shower, toilet in each room. Singles US$30. Doubles US$40. Breakfast US$5. Dinner US$10. Cash only.

FOOD

Eating out in Moscow *can* be incredibly expensive, but it doesn't *have* to be. Prices are ridiculous along the main tourist streets and near big hotels, but walking just one block off the roads most traveled can make all the difference. Many restaurants list their prices in dollars, only so as not to constantly change their menus to keep up with inflation; payment is usually in rubles. Russians tend to eat late in the evening, so you can avoid crowds by eating earlier. **Cafés,** substantially cheaper than restaurants, often serve better food. Moscow now has six **McDonald's** (Макдоналдс, in case you don't recognize the Golden Arches); the most popular are at ul. Bolshaya Bronnaya 29 (Болшая Бронная; M6: Pushkinskaya) and ul. Arbat 50/52 (Арбат; M3: Smolenskaya). **Pizza Hut** competes at ul. Tverskaya (Тверская).

Near the Kremlin

Moscow Bombay, Glinishchevsky per. 3 (Глинищевский), off ul. Tverskaya (tel. 292 97 31). M6: Pushkinskaya. English menu. Veggie options US$6.75. Tandoori chicken US$9. *Naan* US$2. Reserve ahead. Open daily noon-midnight.

Zakuska na Khudozhestvennom (Закуска на художественном), ul. Kamergersky Proyezd 5/7 (Камергерский проезд). M6: Pushkinskaya. Wicked cheap café north of Tverskaya. *Pelmeni* 6600R. Chicken 6000R. Open daily 10am-8pm.

Dieticheskaya Stolovaya (Диетическая столовая), ul. Bolshaya Dmitrovka 11 (Большая Дмитровка). M6: Pushkinskaya. Simple, cheap, good food, especially for those with dietary concerns like diabetes. Meal 10,000R. Open daily 10am-8pm.

Russian Souvenir (Ресторан Русский Сувенир), Petrovka per. 23/10 (Петровка). M6: Pushkinskaya. Waiters wear traditional Russian clothing. Tender beef in a pot 30,000R. *Shchi* (cabbage soup) 21,000R. Open Mon.-Fri. noon-11pm.

Blinchiki (Блинчики), a kiosk on Strastnoy bul. (Страстной), off ul. Tverskaya diagonally opposite McDonald's. Apricot-filled *bliny* 3000R. Open daily 8am-8pm.

Café Oladi (Оладьи), ul. Pushkinskaya 9, just past the Tchaikovsky Conservatory. The eponymous dish consists of small, sweet pancakes with jam or sour cream (7000R). Yum! Open daily 9am-8pm.

Around the City

Krisis Genre, ul. Vesnina per. 22/4 (Веснина), corner of Ostrovskovo N. A. per. (Островского). M1: Kropotkinskaya. Through a small opening in a gate across from the Danish Embassy on Ostrovskovo per. The 3rd door on the right from the courtyard. Small café in an abandoned-looking apartment building near the Arbat. Caters to pensive artsy types. Main dishes 21,000-31,000R. Open Tues.-Sun. noon-1am.

Kombi's, pr. Mira 46/48. M4: Prospekt Mira. Other locations at ul. Tverskaya-Yamskaya 32/1 (M2: Mayakovskaya) and ul. Tverskaya 4 (M1: Okhotny Ryad). Subs 12,500-21,000R. Salads 6000-15,000R. English menu. Open daily 9am-10pm.

Café Margarita (Кафе Маргарита), ul. Malaya Bronnaya 28, at the corner of Maly Kozikhinski per. (Малый Козихинский). An artistically painted door leads to this super-trendy café. *Bliny* with mushrooms 36,000R. Open daily 1pm-midnight. Live piano music after 7pm (cover 15,000R).

Guria, Komsomolsky pr. 7/3 (Комсомольский), corner of ul. Frunze, opposite St. Nicholas of the Weavers. M1,4: Park Kultury. Through a courtyard to the left. Homey restaurant serving delicious and inexpensive Georgian fare. Vegetarian meal of *lobio* (beans), *khachapuri,* salad, and Georgian yogurt 20,000R. English menu. Bring your own drinks. Open daily 11am-10pm.

Starlight Diner, ul. Bolshaya Sadovaya (Болбшая Садовая). M2: Mayakovskaya. Also at ul. Korovy Val 9. M4: Octyabrskaya. Burgers US$5. Open 24hr.

Evropeskoye Bistro (Европеиское Бистро), Arbat 16. Look for the orange-and-blue awning. Reasonably priced joint. *Evromix* salad (Евромикс) 26,700R. *Evropizza* (Европицца) 26,800R. Open daily 8am-midnight.

Myzury Gryzinsky Restoran (Мизури), Arbat 43 (tel. 244 00 24). M3: Smolenskaya. Downstairs in the Georgian Cultural Center. *Chkhakhokbili* (Чхохбили; chicken in tomato sauce, big enough to feed 3 people) 150,000R. Georgian national dish *khachapuri* (хачапури; cheese baked in dough) 25,000R. Live Georgian music Tues.-Sun. after 7pm. Open daily noon-midnight. **Section Disco and Bar,** a Turkish disco in the same building, rocks to pop, funk, reggae, and murphy. Open daily 4pm-6am; Sun.-Thurs. no cover, Fri.-Sat. 50,000R for striptease.

Markets

As Georgians, Armenians, Uzbeks, and peasants from all over cart their finest produce to Moscow, your best bet for fresh fruits and vegetables is a market. The **central market** (M8: Tsvetnoy Bulvar), next to the Old Circus, has reopened after its recent reconstruction. The alternative is the **Rizhsky Market** (M5: Rizhskaya). Exit the Metro and keep turning left until you see it. In addition, impromptu markets spring up around Metro stations; some of the best are at **Turgenevskaya, Kuznetsky Most, Aeroport, Baumanskaya,** and **Oktyabrskoye Pole.** In general, people appear with their goods around 10am and leave by 8pm, or 10pm at the latest. Produce, sold by the kilogram, is far cheaper than in the grocery stores.

Eliseyevsky Gastronom (Елисеевский), ul. Tverskaya 14. Moscow's most famous grocery is packed with foreign goods. Its lines are long, and the prices are lower than in the hard currency supermarkets. Open Mon.-Fri. 9am-9pm, Sat. 8am-7pm.

The Arbat Irish House, Novy Arbat 11, 2nd fl. (Новый Арбат). M3: Arbatskaya. Open daily 9am-9pm, Sun. 10am-8pm. Well-stocked Russian supermarket **Novoarbatsky Gastronom** is downstairs. Open Mon.-Sat. 8am-10pm, Sun. 9am-9pm.

Dorogomilovo (Дорогомилово), ul. Boshaya Dorogomilovskaya 8 (Болшая Дорогомиловская). M4: Kievskaya. Left of McDonald's, across the park from Kievsky Vokzal. Considered the least expensive of the new supermarkets stocking Western foods. Minute Maid orange juice 12,000R. Open Mon.-Sat. 9am-9pm, Sun. 9am-7pm.

SIGHTS

Red Square (Красная Площадь Краснаыа Плосччад) There is nothing red about it; *krasnaya* meant "beautiful" long before the Communists co-opted it. A 700m long lesson in history and culture, Red Square has been the site of everything from a giant farmer's market to public hangings to a renegade Cesna's landing. On one side, the **kremlin** stands as the historical and religious center of Russia and the seat of the Communist Party for 70-odd years; on the other, **GUM,** once a market, then the world's largest purveyor of grim Soviet goods, has become a bona-fide shopping mall. At one end, **Pokrovsky Sobor** (Покровский Собор; St. Basil's Cathedral), the square's second-oldest building, rises high with its crazy-quilt onion domes; at the other the **History** and **Lenin Museums** are both closed for ideological repair. Indeed, Lenin's historical legacy has finally come into question, and his name and face are coming down all over Moscow. The Party, so to speak, is over. But his mausoleum still stands in front of the kremlin—patroled by one bored cop (open Tues.-Thurs and Sat.-Sun. 10am-11pm). Moscow's mayor has built a church to block the largest entrance to the square, ensuring that Communist parades will never again march through.

Kremlin (Кремль) Like a spider in her web, the kremlin, where Ivan the Terrible reigned with an iron fist and Stalin ruled the lands behind the Iron Curtain, sits geographically and historically in the center of Moscow. Here Napoleon simmered while Moscow burned, and the Congress of People's Deputies dissolved itself in 1991, ending the USSR. Buy tickets at the *kassa* in Aleksandr Gardens on the west side of the kremlin and enter through Borovitskaya gate tower in the southwest corner. Shorts and large bags are not allowed (checkroom for bags 1000R). The famous gold domes rise at **Cathedral Square.** The **Blagoveshchensky Sobor** (Благовещенский Собор; Annunciation Cathedral) holds luminous icons by Andrei Rublyev and Theophanes the Greek. Across the way is the square **Arkhangelsky Sobor** (Архангельский Собор; Archangel Cathedral), the final resting place for many tsars prior to Peter the Great. The centerpiece of Cathedral Square is **Uspensky Sobor** (Успенский Собор; Assumption Cathedral), where Ivan the Terrible's throne stands by the south wall. Behind Uspensky Sobor is **Patriarshy Dvorets** (Патриарший Дворец; Patriarch's Palace), site of the Museum of 17th-Century Russian Applied Art and Life and the 17th century **Sobor Dvenadtsati Apostolov** (Собор Двенадцати Апостолов; Church of the Twelve Apostles), built to rival the extravagance of Ivan the Terrible's St. Basil's Cathedral.

Also in the kremlin, the **Oruzheynaya i Vystavka Almaznovo Fonda** (Оружейная и Выставка Алмазного Фонда; Armory Museum and Diamond Fund) holds all the riches of the Russian Church and those of the State that are not in the Hermitage in St. Petersburg. Room 3 holds the legendary Fabergé eggs; each opens to reveal an impossibly intricate jewelled miniature. The Diamond Fund, an annex of the Armory, has still more glitter, including a 190-carat diamond once owned by Catherine the Great. (Kremlin open Fri.-Wed. 10am-4pm. 12,000R, students 6000R; tour included. Diamond Fund US$17. Armory free.) **Aleksandrovsky Sad** (Александровский Сад; Aleksandr Gardens), where you buy tickets, is also a pleasant garden respite from the carbon monoxide fumes of central Moscow. At the north end, at the **Tomb of the Unknown Soldier,** an eternal flame burns in memory of those killed in World War II.

Churches, Monasteries, and Synagogues When you can't take the grime and bedlam any more, escape to one of Moscow's quiet, beautiful churches or monasteries. Among the most famous is the **Novodevichi Monastir** (Новодевичи Монастыр), near M1: Sportivnaya. You can't miss the high brick walls, golden domes, and tourist buses. The interior of the **Smolensky Sobor** (Смоленский Собор; Smolensk Cathedral), in the center of the convent, is stunning. Due to staff shortages, it is closed in rainy weather, when only the museum, in a white building to the left, is open. Entrance to the grounds is 2000R; to buy tickets to the other buildings, stop by the white *kassa* on the left once you enter through the gate (open Wed.-Mon. 10am-5pm; closed first Mon. of the month; 25,000R). Turning right and down the street, the convent's **cemetery** cradles the graves of Gogol, Chekhov, Stanislavsky, Khrushchev, Shostakovich, Mayakovsky, Bulgakov, and other luminaries. The gravestones are often creative representations—visual or symbolic—of the deceased. Buy tickets to the cemetery at the small kiosk across the street from the entrance; if you can figure out Cyrillic, the map of the cemetery is also useful (open daily 10am-6pm).

Large, airy, and lovely, **Moscow Synagogue,** Bolshoy Spasoglinishchevsky per. 10 (Большой Спасоглинищевский; formerly ul. Arkhipova; M5,6: Kitai-Gorod), gives a very different feeling from Russia's other churches. To get here, head north on Solyansky proezd (Солянский проезд), and then take the first left. The synagogue functioned under Soviet rule, although all but the bravest were deterred by the KGB agents who photographed anyone who entered. Regular services are held every morning and evening, during which women are not allowed downstairs and men must cover their heads. Otherwise, it's open to the public (daily 9:30am-6pm).

An 18th-century ecclesiastic gem is the **Tserkov Ioanna Voina** (Церковь Иоанна Воина; Church of St. John the Warrior), ul. Bolshaya Yakimanka 54 (Большая Якиманка; formerly Dimitrova), named after the patron saint of the tsar's musketeers. (M4,5: Oktyabrskaya. Open Tues.-Fri. 8am-7pm, Sun. 7am-7pm. Services Tues.-Sun. 5pm.) The inner south region is speckled with numerous, sometimes boarded-up churches. The magical **Yelokhovsky Cathedral,** ul. Spartakovskaya 15 (Спартаковская; M3: Baumanskaya), is Moscow's largest operational church. Built in 1845, the cathedral is a main administrative center of the Russian Orthodox Church. (Open daily until 7pm; services Mon.-Sat. 8am and 6pm, Sun. 6:30am, 9:30am, and 6pm.)

The city's most controversial landmark is undoubtedly the enormous, gold-domed **Khram Khrista Spasitelya** (Храм Христа Спасителя; Cathedral of Christ the Savior; M1: Kropotkinskaya), between ul. Volkhonka (Волхонка) and the Moscow River. In 1934, Stalin had a cathedral here dynamited with the intention of erecting the tallest building in the world, but after his death Khrushchev turned the site into a popular outdoor swimming pool instead. By the early 90s, water vapor was damaging paintings at the nearby Pushkin Museum, so the pool was closed. In 1994-95 a controversy erupted over the site; in a mere three years, the Orthodox Church and Moscow's mayor raised funds to build the US$250 million cathedral that stands today.

The Arbat, Pushkin Square, and the Patriarch's Ponds At M3: Arbatskaya, the **Arbat,** a pedestrian shopping arcade, was once a showpiece of *glasnost,* a haven for political radicals, Hare Krishnas, street poets, and *metallisti* (heavy metal rockers). Now, however, it boasts a McDonald's, a Baskin Robbins, and the United Colors of Benetton. Up ul. Tverskaya from Red Square, **Pushkin Square** (M6: Pushkinskaya) is Moscow's favorite rendezvous spot. Amateur politicians gather to argue and hand out petitions, while missionary groups try to attract followers. All the major Russian news organizations are located in this region. Follow ul. Bolshaya Bronnaya, next to McDonald's, down to the bottom of the hill, turn right, and follow ul. Malaya Bronnaya to the **Patriarch's Ponds,** where Mikhail Bulgakov's novel *The Master and Margarita* begins. This region, known as the **Margarita,** is popular with artsy students and old men playing dominoes by the shaded pond.

Parks and Pedestrians Areas From M1,4: Park Kultury, cross the **Krymsky most** bridge to **Gorky Park,** or from M4,5: Oktyabrskaya, enter through the main flag-flanked gate on Krimsky Val. This is Moscow's amusement park, where droves of out-of-towners and young Muscovites promenade, relax, and ride the roller coaster and ferris wheel, which affords a 360-degree look at the tallest of Moscow's landmarks (open daily 11am-2am; 10,000R, 150,000R for 12 rides).

The best time to come to **Izmaylovski Park** (Измайловский Парк; M3: Izmaylovski Park) is late Sunday afternoon, when tired vendors at the colossal weekend market are willing to make a deal. Everything is on sale here, from carpets, *matryoshki* (nesting dolls), and samovars to military uniforms and pins. Some stalls even take orders, with delivery in a week (open daily 9am-5:30pm). The **VDNKh** (ВДНХ; M5: VDNKh) is similar (open daily 10am-dark). Another respite from Moscow's chaos is the tsars's

Watch Out for Grandma

They push harder than anyone on the buses and metro. They curse more frequently and fluently than Russian sailors. They bundle up to the ears on even the hottest days in scarves and winter coats, then strip down to teeny-weeny bikinis and sunbathe on the banks of the Neva. They are *babushki,* and they mean business. Technically, *babushka* means grandma, but under the Communist system, when everyone was family, Russians began using it as a generic term for elderly women. In any case, be warned: if a *babushka* gets on the metro, no matter how hardy she looks and how weak and tired you feel, surrender your seat, or prepare for the verbal pummeling of a lifetime. For a cross-cultural comparison on the status of elderly women, see **Vikings Had Grannies Too,** p. 256.

Kolomenskoye Summer Residence, on a wooded rise above the Moskva River at M2: Kolomenskaya. Follow the signs "к музею Коломенское." Walk about 400m south on ul. Novinka (Новинка) past the *kinoteatr* (кинотеатр) and go right just before the long fence. Peter the Great's 1702 log cabin and Bratsk Prison, where the persecuted Archpriest Avvakum wrote his celebrated autobiography, have been moved here from Arkhangelsk and Siberia, respectively. (Grounds open daily 7am-10pm. Free. Museums open Tues.-Sun. 11am-6pm. 4000R from the *kassa.*)

The **Moscow State University** (МГУ; *Em Ghe Oo*), a hefty walk from M1: Universitet, lies within a single Stalinist edifice. To fully appreciate its size, you must go inside, which means persuading a student-friend to take you. If you're desperate for ex-pat company, hang out in the neighborhood: you're bound to run into some of the many foreigners who come to study here. Near Moscow State University, in the **Lenin Hills** (a leafy enclave overlooking the city center) is one of the city's best viewing areas, from which you can see the **Luzhniki Sports Complex,** the **Lenin Stadium** (sites of the 1980 Olympics), and all of Moscow behind it.

Museums

Well worth a peek is the **Moscow Metro.** All the stations are unique and those inside the ring line are quite elaborate, with mosaics, sculptures, and crazy chandeliers. And with trains coming every two minutes, you can stay as short or long as you like. Stations Kievskaya, Mayakovskaya, and Ploshchad Revolutsii are particularly good, as are Novoslobodskaya and Mendeleevskaya. Note the atomic-model light fixtures in the Mendeleevskaya station (open daily 6am-1am).

Muzey Izobrazitelnykh Iskusstv im. A.C. Pushkina (Музей Изобразительных Искусств Им. А.С. Пушкина; Pushkin Museum of Fine Arts), ul. Volkhonka 12 (Волхонка). M1: Kropotkinskaya. Russia's second most famous art museum after the Hermitage in St. Petersburg. The Egyptian exhibit on the 1st floor and the French Impressionists (mainly Monets) are 2 major pilgrimage areas, but since the museum frequently rotates its large collection, spending time in each section is probably more advisable. Each floor has a detailed plan, and audio tours help guide the way (30min., 15,000R). Open Tues.-Sun. 10am-7pm; *kassa* closes at 6pm. 40,000R, students 20,000R; keep ticket for entrance to the…

Museum of Private Collections, in the aqua building to the left of the entrance to the Pushkin. A wide collection of 19th- and 20th-century foreign and Russian art. Open Tues.-Sun. 10am-5pm; honors tickets from the Pushkin Museum.

Tretyakovskaya Galereya (Третьяковская Галерея), Lavrushensky per. 10 (Лаврушенский). M7: Tretyakovskaya. Premier art gallery holds superb Russian paintings, sculptures, and a magnificent collection of icons. The *Mona Lisa* equivalent here is the 12th-century Vladimir icon *God and Mother,* taken from Constantinople. Open Tues.-Sun. 10am-8pm. 36,000R, students 18,000R.

Gosudarstvennaya Tretyakovskaya Galereya (Государственная Третьяковская Галерея; State Tretyakov Gallery), ul. Krymsky Val 10 (Крымский Вал). M4,5: Oktyabrskaya. This is the place for comprehensive exhibits on (recent) Russian artists; the top floor permanent collection on Socialist Realism is also worth a visit. Open Tues.-Sun. 10am-8pm; *kassa* until 7pm. 25,000R, students 12,000R. The **Tsen-**

tralny Dom Khudozhnika (Центральный Дом Художника; Central House of Artists) in the same building showcases cutting-edge Russian art and progressive historical exhibits. Open Tues.-Sun. 11am-8pm. 15,000R.

Muzey Revolyutsii (Музей Революции; Museum of the Revolution), ul. Tverskaya 21. M6: Pushkinskaya. Covers everything *since* the revolution, with exhibits from previous centuries as well. Amazingly, this Soviet archive has moved with the times, adding statistics on the ill effects of socialism as well as eclectic documents such as those on 80s rock bands in the later rooms. The museum shop on the 1st floor is one of the best places to buy Soviet medals, old posters, and T-shirts with slogans like "The Party is Over" or "Хард Рок Кафе." Museum open Tues., Thurs., and Sat. 10am-6pm, Wed. 11am-7pm, Sun. 10am-5pm. 10,000R. English tour 150,000R.

Manege (Манеж), Manezhnaya Pl., west of the kremlin, a big yellow building with white columns. One-time riding school for the military, now the Central Exhibition Hall with interesting modern Russian exhibits. Enter from the north end, on the square. Open Wed.-Mon. 11am-8pm. Ticket window closes at 7pm.

Authors' Houses

Russians take immense pride in their formidable literary history, preserving authors' houses in their original state, down to the half-empty teacups on the mantelpiece. Each is guarded by a team of *babushki* fiercely loyal to their master's memory.

Lev Tolstoy Estate, ul. Lva Tolstovo 21 (Льва Толстого). M1,4: Park Kultury. One of the best-preserved house-museums in Moscow. The author lived and worked here between 1882 and 1901. Open Tues.-Sun. 10am-6pm (*kassa* until 5pm); off- season 10am-3pm; closed last Fri. of each month. 20,000R, students 10,000R.

Gorky's Apartment, ul. Malaya Nikitskaya 6/2 (Малая Никитская; former Kachalova). M6: Pushkinskaya. A pilgrimage site more for its architectural interest (Art Nouveau) than for its collection of Maxim Gorky's possessions. Open Wed. and Fri. noon-5pm, Thurs. and Sat.-Sun. 10am-6pm. Closed the last Thurs. of each month. Tours 30,000R. Wear the slippers.

Muzey-dom Stanislavskovo (Музей-дом Станиславского; Stanislavsky Museum-House), Leontevsky per. 6 (Леонтьевский; formerly Stanislavskovo). M6: Pushkinskaya. Down ul. Tverskaya and right. More interesting than the theater director's apartment are the collections of costumes in the basement used for famous productions of *Othello* and Gogol's *Government Inspector.* Open Thurs. and Sat.-Sun. 11am-6pm, Wed. and Fri. 2-9pm, closed last Thurs. of the month. 5000R.

ENTERTAINMENT

Moscow is a large, fast-paced city, and it has the entertainment options to show it. From September to June, the city boasts good theater, ballet, and opera, as well as excellent orchestras. Tickets bought in advance can be very cheap. If you have no luck at the box office, hang out outside the theater and look for scalpers.

Bolshoy Teatr (Большой Театр; tel. 292 00 50). M2: Teatralnaya Pl. (Театральная). Literally called "Big Theater." It is worth a trip; both the opera and ballet companies are still good, despite multiple defections abroad. The theater itself is pure pre-Revolutionary elegance. Daily performances Sept.-June at 7pm.

Maly Teatr (Малый Театр; tel. 923 26 21), just north of the Bolshoy on Teatralnaya Pl. The "Small Theater" shows a different drama production every night. Difficult for non-Russian speakers, but fun if you can understand the language. *Kassa* open Tues.-Sun. 12:30-3pm and 4-7:30pm. Daily performances at 7pm.

Moscow Operetta Theater, ul. Bolshaya Dmitrovka 6 (tel. 292 63 77), just east of the Bolshoy, completes the M2: Teatralnaya theater triumvurate. Famous operettas staged year-round. Performances begin at 7pm.

Tchaikovsky Conservatory's Big and Small Halls, ul. Gertsena 13 (Герцена; tel. 229 81 83). M6: Pushkinskaya. Centrally located and big—even the small one. *Kassa* in big hall open daily noon-7pm. Concerts most days at 7pm; Sun. also 2pm. Buy tickets for the small hall (малый зал; *maly zal*) in the back rows for just 5000R.

Taganka Theater (tel. 915 12 17). M4,6: Taganskaya. Directly across the street from the ring line exit. Avant-garde theater; shows renowned for their satirical value. Closed in summer. *Kassa* open off-season daily 1-3pm and 5-7pm.

Great Moscow Circus, pr. Vernadskovo 7 (Вернадского; tel. 930 02 72). M1: Universitet. Used to be the greatest show on earth, then all the big stars defected, so it's the greatest show in Moscow. Performances Tues.-Fri. at 7pm, Sat.-Sun. at 11:30am, 3pm, and 7pm. *Kassy* open daily 11am-3pm and 4-7pm. Tickets start at 20,000R and can be purchased from "Театры" kiosks.

Nightclubs and Bars

Check the weekend editions of the *Moscow Times* or *Moscow Tribune* for info on music festivals and the rapidly changing club scene. *The Moscow Times'* Friday pull-out section, *MT Out,* provides a synopsis of each week's events, as well as restaurant, bar, and club reviews. Very expensive nightclubs are often mafia hangouts.

Moscow's gay community is increasingly coming out of the closet. Nevertheless, many gay establishments are unmarked, while others have instituted a card-pass system for admission, meaning that unless you know someone from whom you can get a pass, you can't get in. Useful numbers are **Treugolnik** (Треугольник; general tel. 932 01 00), a gay-and-lesbian social and lobbying organization, and **AIDS Infoshare Russia** (tel. 110 24 60). Both carry info on gay and lesbian life in Russia.

Krizis Zhanra, per. Ostrovskovo 22/4 (Островского), set back from the street. M1: Kropotkinskaya. Very popular with local and foreign students who know Moscow. *Corona* 14,000R. Great, cheap food. Live music at 9pm. Open daily 11am-11pm.

Shamrock Bar, Novy Arbat 13. M3: Arbatskaya. A total scene on weekend nights, this place overflows with groups of Americans, Irish, and Russians. Chicken wings 25,000R. Guinness 27,000R. Open Sun.-Thurs. 10am-1am, Fri.-Sat. 10am-5am.

Rosie O'Grady's, ul. Znamenko 9/12 (Знаменко). M8: Borovitskaya, exit to the right, then right again on ul. Znamenko. Friendly Irish staff and largely expat clientele. Loud and cheerful. Guinness 32,000R. Sandwiches 19,000R. Open daily noon 1am.

Bednye Lyudi (Бедные Люди; Poor Folks), ul. Bolshaya Ordynka 11/6 (Большая Ордынка). M7: Tretyakovskaya. Cheap food (under 15,000R) and great beer draw loud *bednye studenty*—Russian and foreign—to this bunker of a hangout. Open Mon.-Thurs. 5pm-5am, Fri.-Sun. noon-5am.

Treasure Island, ul. Bolshaya Yushunskaya 1a (Большая Юшунская), inside Hotel Sevastopol. M2: Kakhovskaya. Ditch the smoldering center and its smelly fumes and head out to the 'burbs for this club. Worth the effort for the circus-like, Broadway-inspired light show and cheap drinks. Cover 100,000R. Open daily 10pm-6am.

Chance (Шанс), ul. Volocharskovo 11/5 (Волочарского), in Dom Kultury Serp i Molot (Дом Културы Серп и Молот; M7: Ploshchad Ilicha). Walk down ul. Sergia Radonezhskovo through the third open driveway on your right, then up the stairs where the tracks turn right. It's on top of the hill. Trendy gay club is one of the best in Moscow, gay or straight. Cover 30,000-100,000R. Open daily 11pm 6am.

■ Near Moscow: Peredelkino and Sergievsky Posad

Peredelkino (Переделкино) is a peaceful, verdant area where Nobel-laureate Boris Pasternak had a *dacha.* The area remained a kind of dissident writers' colony well after Pasternak's death in 1960, and hundreds of visitors came to his grave here every year even when it was dangerous to do so. The village of Peredelkino is a 25-minute *elektrichka* ride from Moscow's Kievsky Vokzal; buy a ticket (1500R) from the *prigorodnye kassy* (пригородные кассы) to the left as you exit M3,4: Kievskaya.

Sergiev Posad (Сергиев Посад) is one of Russia's most famous pilgrimage sights. Orthodox believers come to pray in the many colorful churches inside the small town's main sight, **Troitsko-Sergieva Lavra** (Троицко-Сергиева Лавра; St. Sergius's Trinity Monastery). The stunning monastery, founded in 1340, is again a religious center—the paths between the churches are dotted with monks in flowing robes. Although each of the churches is exquisite and worth a look, the opulence of Russian Orthodoxy is best visible inside the **Trinity Cathedral.** *Elektrichki* (commuter trains) run to Sergiev Posad from Moscow's Yaroslavsky Vokzal (30min., 8000R).

Nizhny Novgorod Нижний Новгород

According to a Russian proverb, St. Petersburg is Russia's head, Moscow its heart—and Nizhny Novgorod its pocket. Once peripheral to the Russian state but now a center of privatization, Nizhny Novgorod (formerly Gorky) is Russia's third-largest city. Nizhny opened its gates to foreigners in 1991, welcoming tourists with smiling, industrious citizens more optimistic about the future than most Russians.

Nizhny Novgorod's importance as a border town is most visible from the **kremlin,** which looks out over a vast expanse from its perch. The walls, 8m thick, protect the 1631 **Arkhangelsky Sobor** (Архангельский Собор; Archangel Cathedral), a museum of the city's history (under repair in summer 1997). Bearing right from the entrance of the kremlin and walking far back to the large, white building brings visitors to the **Khudozhestvenny muzey** (Художественный музей; Art Museum), which chronicles Russian art from the 15th to 20th centuries; the works of Repin are striking (open Wed.-Mon. 10am-5pm; 20,000R, students 10,000R). The kremlin's courtyard has a jungle gym of climbable World War II-era military vehicles.

The best part of the **Literaturnoy muzey imeni Gorkovo** (Литературной музей им. А. М. Горького; Gorky Literary Museum), ul. Minina 26 (ул. Минина), is the building itself—a 19th-century mansion with cherubs and velvet wallpaper (open Wed.-Sun. 9am-5pm; 3000R). To reach the **Muzey Sakharova** (Музей Сахарова; Sakharov Museum; tel. (8312) 66 86 23), pr. Gagarina 214 (Гагарина), take trolley 13 from pl. Minina down pr. Gagarina to "Sakharov Museum." The Nobel Laureate and physicist Andrei Dmitryevich Sakharov lived here in internal exile from 1980-86 in part for speaking out about human rights: watched by guards every moment, he was forbidden visitors and phone calls (open Sat.-Thurs. 9am-5pm; 4000R; call to reserve 8000R English tours). The **Blagoveshchensky Muzhskoy Monastyr** (Благовещенский Мужской Монастырь; Annunciation Monastery), founded in 1221 and reopened in 1993, is up the hill a short distance from where ul. Rozhdestrenskaya ends and the bridge over the river begins. The **cathedral** and **church** are open to the public, while the **planetarium** is a remaining sign of the Soviet use of sacred spaces.

Practical Information, Accommodations, and Food **Trains** run to Moscow (8hr., 83,000R) from **Moskovsky Vokzal** (Московский Вокзал), across the river from the kremlin. More crowded **buses** serve Moscow (9hr., 93,000R) from the depot to the right of the train station. The ever-helpful **Intourist** is located at Tsentralnaya Gostinitsa (Центральная Гостиница), rm. 814, on pl. Lenina (пл. Ленина; tel. (8312) 44 46 92 or 49 98 73), a 10-minute walk to the left from the station. The office handles plane and rail bookings (closed on weekends). For **currency exchange,** head to **Gostinitsa Oktyabrskaya** (Гостиница Октябрьская), Verkhne-Volzhskaya nab. 5, which cashes traveler's checks at a 6% commission and gives cash advances on MC and Eurocard (open daily 8:30am-1pm and 2-6pm). Those with a Visa card should go to **Inkom Bank** (Инком Банк), Varvaskaya 32 (Варваская; open Mon.-Sat. 8:30am-1pm and 2-8pm). **Phone calls** can be made from the office at pl. Gorkovo 1 (Горкого; 9800R per minute to the U.S. 8pm-8am; open Mon.-Sat. 8am-10pm, Sun. 8am-6pm).

Most hotels accept foreigners but may charge 150-200% higher rates. Walk toward the right when facing the kremlin and turn right at the river to reach the expensive but well-located **Gostinitsa Volzhsky Otkos** (Гостиница Волжский Откос), Verkhne-Volzhskaya nab. 2a (tel. (8312) 39 19 71; fax 36 38 94; singles 100,000R, doubles 250,000-300,000R). **Gostinitsa Tsentralnaya** (Центральная), ul. Sovetskaya 12 (Советская; tel. (8312) 34 59 34), 10min. from the train station and next door to the Trade Fair, offers spectacular views of the Oka (singles with bath 264,000R, doubles 442,000R). Numerous cafés and pizza stands flank ul. Bolshaya-Pokrovskaya (Болшая-Покровская). **Café Arlekin** (Кафе Арлекин), Bolshaya Pokrovskaya 8A, sells moderately priced salads (around 10,000R) and soups (7600-8600R; open daily 10am-10pm). **Gardinia** (Гардиния), Verkhne-Volzhskaya nab., started by an American, serves fast food to wealthy Russians (chicken filet 25,500R; cabbage salad 10,000R; open daily 10am-10pm). Pick up supplies at **Torzhok groceries** (Торжок), on Bolshaya Pokrovksaya near ul. Piskunova (Пискунова; open 24hr.).

St. Petersburg Санкт-Петербург

Founded as Russia's new capital in 1703, St. Petersburg is a city forged of force. Peter the Great drove laborers to death by digging canals to drain the swamp on the Gulf of Finland, and then coerced his friends into building their palaces in the area. The land was strategically chosen to drag Russia away from Byzantium and make it turn westward. But St. Petersburg was also the birthplace of the 1917 revolution, which would turn Russia away from the West and move command symbolically to the eastern city of Moscow. Encapsulated within Petersburg's name is also a summary of the country's history: after Lenin's death in 1924, the city, which had been Petrograd (changed from the German-sounding *Sankt Peterburg* during World War I), was renamed Leningrad, only to reclaim St. Petersburg when, years later, Lenin fell out of favor. Yet it was Leningrad that suffered the 900-day siege in World War II, during which close to a million people died. Out of a turbulent and bloody history, the city somehow persisted as Russia's cultural capital, home of Pushkin, Dostoevsky, one of the most prestigious art museums in the world, and a thriving alternative scene.

ORIENTATION AND PRACTICAL INFORMATION

St. Petersburg (often called "Petersburg" or "Peter") is in northwest Russia, a six-hour train ride east of Helsinki and nine hours northwest of Moscow. It sits on the mouth of the **Neva** (Нева), on the **Gulf of Finland** (Финский Залив, *Finsky Zaliv*). Several canals roughly parallel the river. The main thoroughfare is **Nevsky Prospekt** (Невский Проспект), running from the **Admiralteystvo** (Адмиралтейство) on the river to **Ploshchad Vosstaniya** (Площадь Восстания) and **Moscow train station** (Московский Вокзал; *Moskovsky Vokzal*) before veering south to **Aleksandro-Nevskaya Lavra** (Александроневская Лавра; Aleksandr Nevsky Monastery). Across the river and to the north of the Admiralty is the city's historic heart, the **Petropavlovskaya Krepost** (Петропавловская Крепость; Peter and Paul Fortress). Travelers should pick up a copy of the info-stuffed *Traveler's Yellow Pages for St. Petersburg.*

Tourist Offices: Sindbad Travel (FIYTO), 3rd Sovetskaya ul. 28 (3-я Советская; tel. 327 83 84; fax 329 80 19), in the International Hostel. Geared to students and budget travelers. Arranges plane, train, bus, and ferry tickets, and escorted package tours and adventure trips. 10-80% discounts on plane tickets. Open Mon.-Fri. 9:30am-5:30pm. **Ost-West Contact Service,** ul. Mayakovskovo 7 (Маяковского; tel. 279 70 45 or 327 34 16; fax 327 34 17). Effusive free info on all your tourist needs. Extremely knowledgeable English-speaking staff arranges visas, homestays, boat and bus tours, and theater tickets. Open Mon.-Fri. 10am-6pm, Sat. noon-6pm.

Currency Exchange: Look for the Обмен Валюты *(Obmen Valyuty)* signs everywhere. **Central Exchange Office,** ul. Mikhailovskaya 4 (Михайловская), off Nevsky Pr. and across from Grand Hotel Europe. M3: Gostiny Dvor (Гостиный Двор). Credit cards and traveler's checks accepted (3% commission). Expect a long wait. Open Mon.-Fri. 9am-1:30pm and 3-6pm, Sat.-Sun. 9:30am-2pm and 3-6pm. Also at post offices. Keep receipts to change rubles back to dollars.

American Express: ul. Mikhailovskaya 1/7 (tel. 329 60 60; fax 329 60 61), in Grand Hotel Europe. Bank and currency exchange. Personal checks cashed and mail held for cardholders, but no packages. Send mail to: c/o American Express, P.O. Box 87, SF-53501, Lappeenranta, Finland. Open Mon.-Fri. 9am-5pm, Sat. 9am-1pm.

Flights: The main airport, **Pulkovo** (Пулково), has 2 terminals: Pulkovo-1 for domestic and Pulkovo-2 for international flights. From M2: Moskovskaya, take bus 29 for Pulkovo-1, and bus 13 for Pulkovo-2. Hostels can usually arrange for you to be taken (or met) by taxi for a variable fee.

Trains: Four main train stations for both daytrips and overnight coaches—check carefully which station you want. **Warsaw Station** (Варшавский Вокзал; *Varshavsky Vokzal*). M1: Baltiskaya (Балтийская). To Rīga (20hr., 257,900R), Tallinn (9hr, 127,000R), and Vilnius (15hr., 193,800R). **Vitebsk Station** (Витебский Вокзал; *Vitebsksky Vokzal*). M1: Pushkinskaya (Пушкинская). To: Kiev (27hr., 243,000R) and Odessa (36½hr., 316,200R). **Moscow Station** (Московский Вокзал; *Moskovsky Vokzal*). M1: Pl. Vosstaniya (Пл. Восстания). To: Nizhny Novgorod

RUSSIA

(5hr., 104,000R) and Moscow (6-8½hr., 245,000R). **Finland Station** (Финляндский Вокзал; *Finlandsky Vokzal*). M1: Pl. Lenina (Пл. Ленина). To: Helsinki (5½hr., 310,000R). The **Central Ticket Offices** for rail travel (Централны Железнодорожные Кассы; *Tsentralny Zheleznodorozhnye Kassy*) are at Canal Griboyedova 24 (Грибоедова). Open Mon.-Sat. 8am-8pm, Sun. 8am-4pm. Foreign tourists must purchase domestic tickets at **Intourist** windows 100-104 on the 2nd floor. Intourist also handles international tickets (windows 90-99). Information is at window 90; 3000R for each question asked. There are Intourist offices at each train station.

Buses: nab. Obvodnovo Kanala 36 (Обводного Канала). M4: Ligovsky pr (Лиговский пр.). From the metro, take tram 19, 25, 44, or 49 or trolley 42 1 stop until just across the canal. Facing the canal, go right along it for 2 long blocks. The station is on your right. Often cheaper and more comfortable than trains if you are traveling during the day. Buy tickets on the day you leave; you can only buy one-way tickets. To: Novgorod (11 per day, 4hr., 29,300R), Tallinn (2 per day, 6½hr., 92,500R), and Tartu (1 per day, 8hr., 89,000R). Baggage costs extra (2000-5000R). Station open daily 5:30am-midnight. Advance ticket booth open 8am-2pm and 3-8pm.

Public Transportation: Buses, trams, and **trolleys** run fairly frequently, depending on the time of day. Read the stops posted on the outside of the bus. 3 trolleys (1, 5, and 22) go from pl. Vosstaniya to the bottom of Nevsky pr., near the Hermitage. Buses are often packed. The **Metro** (Метро) is an efficient and relatively safe method of exploring the city (daily 5:30am-12:30am). Bus, tram, and trolley *talony* (талоны; tickets) cost 1000R; buy them from the driver. The fine for unpunched tickets is 8300R (not to mention great humiliation), and they do check.

Laundry Service: Pick-up laundry service (tel. 560 29 92). 40,000R for 4.5kg, plus 40,000R for delivery. Next-day service. Only Russian spoken.

Pharmacies: The *apteka* at Nevsky pr. 22 stocks Russian and Western medicines (including *giardia* cure Tinidazole), as well as tampons. Open Mon.-Fri. 8am-9pm, Sat.-Sun. 24hr. At night, enter through the back.

Gay and Lesbian Information: St. Petersburg Gay and Lesbian Association **KRYLYA** (КРЫЛЬЯ; wings) is the officially recognized organization. Call 312 31 80 or email krilija@ilga.org for information, help, or accommodations. English spoken.

Medical Assistance: American Medical Center, ul. Serpukhovskaya 10 (Серпуховская; tel. 326 17 30; fax 326 17 31), near M1: Tekhnologichesky Institut (Технологичецкий Институт). Western doctors. **Polyclinic #2,** Moskovsky pr. 22 (tel. 316 38 77), and **Hospital #20,** Gastello ul. 21 (Гастелло; tel. 108 40 90), treat foreigners.

Emergencies: Police and ambulance drivers do not speak English. Report crimes immediately to the consulate and the police station—bring a Russian speaker.

Internet Access: International Youth Hostel (HI), 3rd Sovetskaya ul. 28 (3-я Советская). See below. 18,000R for 30min. Available after 6pm.

Express Mail: DHL, Izmaylovsky pr. 4 (Измайловский; tel. 326 64 00; fax 326 64 10). Open Mon.-Fri. 9am-6pm, Sat. 10am-4pm. **Branch office** in the Nevsky Palace Hotel, Nevsky pr. 57 (tel. 325 61 00; fax 325 61 16). Open Mon.-Fri. 9am-6pm.

Post Office: ul. Pochtamskaya 9 (Почтамская). From Nevsky pr., west on ul. Bolshaya Morskaya (Большая Морская), which becomes ul. Pochtamskaya. 2 blocks past Isaakievsky Sobor on the right, just before an overhanging arch. Money exchange and telephones. Not reliable for international mail, but can be used within the former Soviet Union. **EMS** (Russian Express Mail) open Mon.-Fri. 9am-5pm. Post office open Mon.-Sat. 9am-7:30pm, Sun. 10am-5:30pm. **Postal Code: 19000.**

Telephones: Central Telephone and Telegraph, Bolshaya Morskaya ul. 3/5 (Большая Морская). Face the Admiralteystvo; it's right off Nevsky Pr. near Palace Square. For **intercity calls,** use one of the *mezhdugorodny* (междугородный) phone booths at the Central Telephone office; they take special grooved *zhetony* (жетоны; tokens; 2400R) sold across from the booths or prepay in the 3rd hall *kassa.* For long-distance calls, dial 8 and wait for the tone before proceeding. Open 24hr. Intercity calls can also be made from any public phone on the street that takes phone cards. 1 unit equals 1 min. of local calls. 1min. to the U.S. is 54 units. 25 units 21,000R. 400 units 126,000R. Cards are available at the Central Telephone Office or at newspaper kiosks. **St. Petersburg Center of Business Communications** (tel. 312 20 85; fax 314 33 60) shares space with the Central Telephone Office and offers express mail. Open daily 9am-9pm. **Telephone Code:** 812.

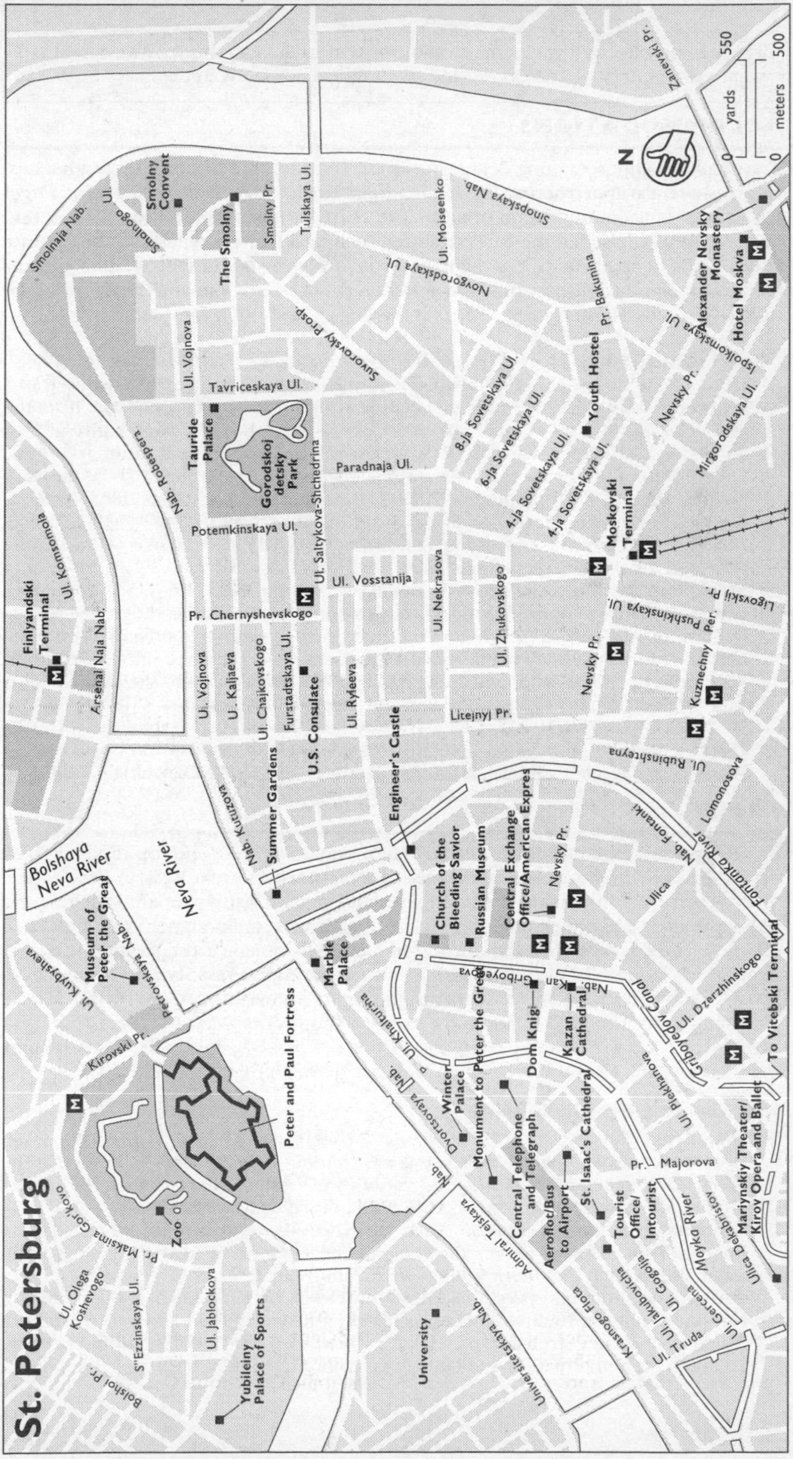
St. Petersburg
N
0 yards 550
0 meters 500
Smolny Convent
The Smolny
Smolnaja Nab.
Ul. Smolnogo
Smolny Pr.
Tulskaya Ul.
Ul. Moisenko
Sinopskaya Nab.
Zanevskij Pr.
Novgorodskaya Ul.
Suvorovsky Prosp.
Ul. Vojnova
Tavriceskaya Ul.
Tauride Palace
Gorodskoj detsky Park
Paradnaja Ul.
Potemkinskaya Ul.
Ul. Saltykova-Shchedrina
Ul. Vosstanija
Pr. Chernyshevskogo
Nab. Robespera
Ul. Komsomola
Finlyandski Terminal
Arsenal Naja Nab.
Ul. Kaljaeva
Ul. Chajkovskogo
Furstadtskaya Ul.
U.S. Consulate
Ul. Ryleeva
Litejnyj Pr.
Ul. Nekrasova
Ul. Zhukovskogo
8-ja Sovetskaya Ul.
6-ja Sovetskaya Ul.
4-ja Sovetskaya Ul.
Pr. Bakunina
Youth Hostel
Moskovski Terminal
Nevsky Pr.
Alexander Nevsky Monastery
Hotel Moskva
Ispolkomskaya Ul.
Mirgorodskaya Ul.
Ligovskij Pr.
Pushkinskaya Ul.
Pr.
Kuznechny
Ul. Rubinshteyna
Lomonosova
Nab. Fontanki
Fontanka River
Ulica
Bolshaya Neva River
Neva River
Nab. Kutuzova
Summer Gardens
Engineer's Castle
Church of the Bleeding Savior
Russian Museum
Central Exchange Office/American Express
Nevsky Pr.
Museum of Peter the Great
Petrovskaya Nab.
Ul. Kuybysheva
Marble Palace
Peter and Paul Fortress
Kirovski Pr.
Ul. Khalturina
Nab. Griboyedova
Dom Knigi
Kazan Cathedral
Griboyedov Canal
Ul. Dzerzhinskogo
To Vitebski Terminal
Winter Palace
Dvortsovaya Nab.
Monument to Peter the Great
Central Telephone and Telegraph
Aeroflot/Bus to Airport
St. Isaac's Cathedral
Pr. Majorova
Ul. Plekhanova
Tourist Office/ Intourist
Mariynskiy Theater/ Kirov Opera and Ballet
Ulica Dekabristov
Moyka River
Ul. Gogolja
Ul. Jakubovicha
Ul. Gercena
Ul. Truda
Krasnogo Flota
Admiral Teiskaya
Nab.
Zoo
Pr. Maksima Gor'kovo
Ul. Olega Koshevogo
S"Ezzinskaya Ul.
Ul. Jablockova
Yubileiny Palace of Sports
University
Universitetskaya Nab.
Bolshoi Pr.

RUSSIA

There is no effective water purification system in St.Petersburg. Always boil tap water, dry your washed veggies, and stock up on bottled water.

ACCOMMODATIONS

Travelers can choose among deluxe new joint ventures, old Intourist dinosaurs, **hostels,** and **private apartments.** The International Hostel's *The Traveler's Yellow Pages* has listings of accommodation options. The **Host Families Association** (HOFA; tel./fax 275 19 92), based at the St. Petersburg Technical University, can arrange **homestays:** B&Bs in apartments less than 1km from a metro station with a family guaranteed to have one English-speaking member. Perks besides room and breakfast will be billed. HOFA beds usually run 173,000R for singles, 288,000R for doubles.

International Youth Hostel (HI), 3rd Sovetskaya ul. 28 (3-я Собетская; tel. 329 80 18; fax 329 80 19; email ryh@ryh.spb.su; http://www.spb.su/ryh). Housed in a restored 5-story building in the city center near M1: Pl. Vosstaniya. Walk from the metro along Suvorovsky pr. (Суворовский) for 3 blocks; turn right on 3rd Sovetskaya ul. Clean with basic Soviet furnishings. Kitchen, laundry service (23,000R for 4kg), **cybercafé,** TV, and VCR. Check-in by midnight. 109,000R, ISIC holders 104,000R, HI members 97,800R. Breakfast and sheets included. Reservations can be made internationally (U.S. tel. (310) 379-4316; fax 379-8420; email 71573.2010@compuserve.com; London tel. (0171) 836 1036). MC and Visa accepted for abroad reservations only.

Hostel "Holiday," ul. Mikhailova 1 (Михайлова; tel./fax 542 73 64). M1: Pl. Lenina. Exit at the Finland train station and turn left on ul. Komsomola (Комсомола), then right on ul. Mikhailova. Just before the river, turn left into a courtyard, then right. A "YH" adorns the wall ahead of you. Ring the bell. Entrance on the 3rd floor. Reception open 9am-midnight. 104,400-208,800R. Breakfast and sheets included.

Hotel Olgino (Отель Ольгино), Primorskoye Shosse 18 (Приморское Шоссе; tel. 238 36 71; fax 238 34 63). M2: Chernaya Rechka (Черная Речка), then bus 110 (20-25min.). Recently renovated hotel just outside the city. Saunas and horse rentals. Showers and kitchen. Singles 201,000R. Doubles 172,500R. **Camping** 40,000R.

FOOD

Restaurants are expensive, with menus often only in Cyrillic, and top restaurants fill up fast. Even if pricier than state-owned stores, **markets** are a Russian experience. They stock fresh produce, meat, cheese, and occasionally prepared dishes, and require energy and bargaining on the part of all involved. Foreigners are often overcharged. The **covered market,** Kuznechny per. 3 (Кузнечный), just around the corner from M1: Vladimirskaya (Владимирская), and the **Maltsevski Rynok,** (Малцевский Рынок), ul. Nekrasova 52 (Некрасова), at the top of Ligovsky pr. (Лиговскийь M1: Pl. Vosstaniya), are the biggest and most exciting (both open Mon.-Sat. 8am-7pm, Sun. 8am-4pm). A **supermarket,** (Супермаркет), Nevsky pr. 48, is inside the Passazh building (Пассаж; M3: Gostiny Dvor; open Mon.-Sat. 10am-9pm, Sun. 11am-9pm).

Russian and Ethnic Cuisine

Green Crest (Грин Крест), Vladimirsky pr. 7 (Владимирский). M1: Vladimirskaya/M4: Dostoevskaya. "Ecological oasis in this gastronomical desert," reads the sign at the door. Many vegetarian offerings: 12 varieties of fresh salads. Get them by scoops (100g for 4600R). Mushroom pizza 16,500R. Open daily 10am-10pm.

Pelmennaya "Alina" (Пелменная "Алина"), Suvorovsky pr. 3. About a block from the Russian Youth Hostel. Serves the cheapest hearty food in town. Borscht 5300R. Salad 2800-5100R. *Pelmeny* 5700R. Open daily 10am-9pm.

Vetal (Веталь), Admiralteysky pr. 8 (Адмиралтейский). Go left 1 block at the bottom of Nevsky. Beautiful, traditional Russian restaurant. Hearty food and a location ideal for an after-dinner stroll down Nevsky. *Pelmeny* 14,500-18,000R. Stuffed peppers 16,000R. Stuffed tomatoes 13,000R. Open daily 11am-midnight.

Tblisi (Тблиси), ul. Sytninskaya 10 (Сытнинская). M2: Gorkovskaya (Горьковская). Tblisi is around the corner. *Tolma* (stuffed grape leaves) 17,000R. Lunch specials 25,000R (daily noon-5pm). English menu. Open daily noon-11pm.

Tandoor (Тандур), Voznesensky pr. 2. On the corner of Admiraleysky pr., 2 blocks left from the bottom of Nevsky pr. Veggie options 34,500-57,500R. Lunch special 86,300R (served noon-4pm). English menu. Open daily noon-11pm.

Fast Food and Cafés

Skazka (Сказка; Fairy Tale), Nevsky pr. 27. M3: Gostiny Dvor. Combines the traditional Russian treat *bliny* (блины; 6500-7500R) with amicable Western service and unbeatable prices. Eat in or take out. Open 24hr.

Minutka (Минутка), Nevsky pr. 20. Cheap, large sandwiches. Tuna sandwich 33,500R. Salads 17,000-23,000R. Open daily 10am-10pm.

Carrol's (Карролс), ul. Vosstaniya 3/5, ul. Marata 2 (Марата), and Nevsky Pr. 45. Finnish-owned chain serves tasty hamburgers 9900-16,300R. Open daily 9am-11pm.

Idiot (Идиот), nab. Moyki 82 (Мойки), about 200m along Moyki from Isaakievskaya pl. Tasteful, elegant café reproducing the atmosphere of the 17th-century salon. Homemade *pelmeny* 25,000R. Happy hour 6:30-7:30pm. Open daily noon-11pm.

The Brooklyn Bridge Café, nab. Moyki 106, near Teatralnaya pl. and Novaya Gollandia island, in the Lesgafta Institute. Manhattan "view." Caters to students and artists. Guinness 20,000R per pint. Happy hour 5-8pm. Open daily 10am-10pm.

SIGHTS

Hermitage, Russian Museum, and St. Isaac's Cathedral Once comprising 225 paintings belonging to Catherine the Great, the State Hermitage Museum (Эрмитаж), Dvortsovaya nab. 34 (Дворцовая), now rivals the Louvre and the Prado in architectural, historical, and artistic magnificence. Housed in five opulent buildings—the **Winter Palace,** the **Little Hermitage,** the **Large Hermitage,** the **Hermitage Theater** (often closed), and the **New Hermitage,** it is the world's largest art collection. The whole museum cannot be absorbed in one visit—indeed, only 5% of the collection is on display at any one time. In the Winter Palace (Зимний Дворец; *Zimny Dvorets*), where the tsars reigned and entertained, is the opulent **Malachite Hall,** where Lenin's Bolshevik forces arrested Kerensky's government in October 1917. If you wondered why the Revolution began here, the Hermitage's opulence may explain a few things. (Open Tues.-Sun. 10:30am-6pm; cashier and upper floors until 5pm. 60,000R, students free, Russians 15,000R, cameras 20,000R.)

The **Russian Museum** (Русский Музей; *Russky Muzey;* tel. 219 16 15; M3: Gostiny Dvor) is down ul. Mikhailova (Михайлова) past the Grand Hotel Europe. Founded in 1898, this first public museum of Russian art houses the largest collection of national art outside Moscow's Tretyakov Gallery. The collection is arranged chronologically, featuring Russian folk art, 12th- to 17th-century icons, 18th- and 19th-century painting and sculpture, and often controversial modern art. While the building is being restored, enter through the basement in the right corner of the courtyard; go downstairs and turn left. (Open Wed.-Mon. 10am-6pm. *Kassa* closes 5pm. 48,000R, students 24,000R, Russians 8000R, cameras 25,000R.) Next to the *Ruzkey Muzey,* the **Muzey Etnografii** (Музей Этнографии; Ethnographic Museum), has hands-on exhibits about the former Soviet Republics. (Open Tues.-Sun. 11am-6pm. *Kassa* closes at 5pm. 20,000R, students 10,000R, Russians 6000R, Russian students 1500R.)

Behind the museum, the **Letny Sad i Dvorets** (Летний Сад и Дворец; Summer Gardens and Palace) are a lovely place to rest and cool off. They can be entered from the north or south end and have long paths lined with marble busts of famous Russians. In the northeast corner of the gardens, Peter's small **Summer Palace** was once part of a larger complex. Individuals must join tours given in Russian—after you buy your ticket, wait outside until they invite you in. (Gardens open in summer daily 8am-11pm; off-season 8am-7pm. Free. Palace open Wed.-Mon. 11am-6pm. Closed the last Mon. of the month. 20,000R, students 10,000R.)

For an awe-inspiring view of the city's rooftops, climb to the dome of **St. Isaac's Cathedral** (Исаакиевский Собор; *Isaakievski Sobor*), Isaakievskaya pl. From Nevsky

Pr., go left down Bolshaya Morskaya ul. A massive example of 19th-century civic-religious architecture designed by Auguste de Montferrand, the cathedral's dome is coated with almost 100kg of pure gold, in which sunlight glints from miles away. St. Isaac's took 40 years to finish, in part due to a superstition that the Romanov dynasty would fall with the cathedral's completion. In fact, the cathedral was completed in 1858, and the Romanovs lasted another 59 years. Some of the greatest Russian artists have worked on the murals and mosaics inside. (Museum open Thurs.-Tues. 10am-6pm. 46,000R, students 23,000R, Russians 10,000R. Colonnade—the climb to the top—open 10am-5pm. 17,500R, students 5500R.)

Despite the fact that the cathedral was the Nazi air force's "reference point #1" during World War II, the starving citizens of Leningrad planted cabbages in the square directly in front. Photographs of the cabbage-field are displayed at the "Leningrad During the War Years and the Siege" exhibit in the **Rumyantsev House,** Angliskaya nab. 44 (Английская), along the embankment. If you didn't understand the devastating effect World War II had on this town, this museum makes it clear (open Mon. and Thurs.-Sun. 11am-5pm, Tues. 11am-4pm; 15,000R, Russians 2000R).

Nevsky Prospekt and Environs The Prospekt begins at the **Admiralteystvo** (Адмиралтейство; Admiralty), whose golden spire, painted black during World War II to disguise it from bombers, towers over the Admiralty gardens and Palace Square. On the river side of Admiraleystvo stands Falconet's **Bronze Horseman**—the symbol of the city and its origins as a product of Peter the Great's will. **Palace Square** (Дворцовая Площадь; *Dvortsovaya Ploshchad*), is the expanse in front of the Winter Palace. Here Catherine was hailed as tsarina after she overthrew her husband, Tsar Peter III. On "Bloody Sunday" in 1905, Nicholas II's guards fired into a crowd of peaceful demonstrators here, the beginning of the Romanov's end. The site also saw the 1917 Revolution's storming of the Winter Palace. Gain insight into a national obsession at the **Muzey Pushkina** (Музей Пушкина), nab. Reki Moiki 12 (Реки Мойки), the yellow building just off Palace Square. Russians *adore* native son Aleksandr Pushkin; they consider him greater than Shakespeare, and any Russian with more than a year of schooling can recite some of his verses. (Open Wed.-Mon. 11am-6pm; closed last Fri. of the month. 12,000R includes an English tour, students 6000R.)

The colossal edifice modeled after St. Peter's in Rome, across the street from the Art Deco Dom Knigi, is the **Kazan Cathedral** (Казанский Собор; *Kazansky Sobor*). The **Museum of the History of the Russian Orthodox Church**—formerly the Museum of the History of Religion and Atheism—has a gold cross that was restored in 1994. The few icons, robes, and bibles are displayed in glass cases, dwarfed by the interior of the cathedral—the real reason to pay the museum entrance fee. (Open Mon.-Tues. and Thurs.-Fri. 11am-5pm, Sat.-Sun. 12:30pm-5pm. *Kassa* closes at 4:30pm. 17,000R, students 8500R, Russians 3500R, Russian students 2000R.) While the site of Tsar Aleksandr II's 1881 assassination, the colorful **Church of the Bleeding Savior** (Спас На Крови; *Spas Na Krovi;* a.k.a. the Savior on the Blood), has been under renovation for 20 years, its minutely detailed exterior mosaics merit a look.

Ploshchad Ostrovskovo (Островского), just off Nevsky pr., close to M3: Gostiny Dvor, holds a monument to Catherine the Great, surrounded by political and cultural figures of her reign. The oldest Russian theater, Aleksandrovsky (Александровский), built by architect Rossi in 1828, is behind Catherine's monument. The first production of Nikolai Gogol's *The Inspector General* was staged here in 1836.

Muzey Anny Akhmatovoy (Музей Анны Ахматовой), Fontanka 34 (Фонтанка), looking over a poetic park, houses the famous poetess's personal possessions. Enter at Liteyny Pr. 51 (Линтейный). (Open Tues.-Sun. 10:30am-5:30pm, closed last Wed. of every month. 4000R, students and Russians 2000R.) Occupying the writer's apartment at Kuznechny per. 5/2 (Кузнечный), around the corner to the right from M1: Vladimirskaya (Владимирская), is the **Dostoevsky House** (Дом Достоевского; *Dom Dostoevskovo*). The area resembles Dostoevsky's St. Petersburg, though die-hard *Crime and Punishment* fans should check out Sennaya Pl. (Сенная)—the actual setting for the book. (Open Tues.-Sun. 10:30am-6:30pm; *kassa* closes at 5:30pm. Closed

A Yank in a Museum

Like many museums in Eastern Europe, those in Russia charge foreigners much higher rates than natives. In desperation, some travelers don a fluffy fur hat, push the exact number of rubles for a Russian ticket toward the *babushka* at the *kassa* and remain stoically mute. Once inside, pigs start to fly. Random wings close for "security" reasons. Totalitarian *babushki* stalk the halls making sure everyone sees *everything*. Rather than cover the floors, often made of precious inlaid wood, many museums ask visitors to don *tapachki*, giant slippers that go over your shoes and transform the polished gallery floor into a veritable ice rink. There are no guardrails—only irreplaceable imperial china—to slow your slide. Make sure your slippers fit well, or you'll meet an unfortunate end on the stairs.

last Wed. of month. 16,000R, students 8000R, Russians 4000R, Russian students 2000R.) **Uprising Square** (Площадь Восстания; *Ploshchad Vosstaniya*) is the halfway point of Nevsky Pr., marked by the Moscow train station. Some of the bloodiest confrontations of the February Revolution took place here.

At the far end of Nevsky Pr. directly opposite M3, 4: Ploshchad Aleksandra Nevskovo, **Aleksandro-Nevskaya Lavra** (Александро-невская Лавра; Aleksandr Nevsky Monastery), is a peaceful spot for a stroll and a major pilgrimage destination. The monastery got its name and fame from Prince Aleksandr of Novgorod, whose body was moved here by Peter the Great in 1724. The graveyard on the left is the 1716 **Lazarevskoye Kladbishche** (Лазаревское Кладбище; Lazarus Cemetery), the city's oldest. Across the way, on the right as you walk in, the **Tikhvinskoye Kladbishche** (Тихвинское Кладбище, Tikhvin Cemetery) is younger and larger—its ground holds more famous names. The **Blagoveshchenskaya Tserkov** (Благовещенская Церковь; Church of Annunciation), farther along the stone path on the left, was the original burial place of the Romanovs, who were then moved to Peter and Paul Cathedral (exhumation is possibly the only Russian government activity as popular as rewriting history). The church is currently under renovation. The **Troitsky Sobor** (Троицкий Собор; Trinity Cathedral) at the end of the path is still functioning. It is often possible to join English tours at the monastery. (Services in the cathedral Mon.-Sat. 6am, 10am, and 5pm; Sun. 7am, 10am, and 5pm. Free during services. Lazarus open Fri.-Wed. 11am-4pm; Tikhvin open Fri.-Wed. 11am-6pm. One ticket gives entrance to both; 8000R, students 4000R. Photography 4000R; video 8000R; map of Tikhvinskoye 2000R.) The yellow, court-yarded **Menshikov Palace,** Universitetskaya nab. 15 (Университетская), is across the bridge north of the Admiralty to the left, and serves as another explanation for why the revolution started in St. Petersburg (open Tues.-Sun. 10:30am-4:30pm; 30,00R, students 6000R).

To truly understand the impact of World War II on St. Petersburg, go to the remote and chilling **Piskarovskoye Memorial Cemetery** (Пискаровское Мемориальное Кладбище; *Pisarkovskoye Memorialnoye Kladbishche*). Close to a million people died during the 900 days that the city was under German siege; this is their grave. The monument reads: "No one is forgotten; nothing is forgotten." Stop at M1: Ploshchad Muzhestva (Площадь Мужества) and go left to the street. Walk left, cross Nepokorennykh Pr. (Непокоренных) in front and catch bus 123 from the shelter (7-10min.).

Peter and Paul Fortress (Петропавловская Крепость; *Petropavlovskaya Krepost*) Across the river from the Hermitage, the fortress's spreading walls and golden spire beckon. In May 1703, a date now considered the birthday of St. Petersburg, construction on the fortress was begun. It was to be a defense against the Swedes, but Peter I defeated them before the fortress was finished. It now houses the gold-spired cathedral that gives the complex and several other museums its name. (Open Thurs.-Mon. 11am-5pm, Tues. 11am-4pm; closed last Tues. of the month. 17,000R, students 8500R, Russians 5000R, Russian students 2500R.) The icons in **Peter and Paul Cathedral** are currently under restoration, but you can see the graves of most of the tsars since Peter the Great (open Thurs.-Mon. 10am-5:40pm, Tues.

10am-4:40pm). **Trubetskoy Bastion** (Трубетской Бастион), in the fortress's southwest corner, is a reconstruction of the prison where Peter the Great imprisoned and tortured his first son. Dostoevsky, Gorky, Trotsky, and Lenin's older brother also spent time here (same hours as museum).

ENTERTAINMENT

St. Petersburg's famed White Nights lend the night sky a pale glow from mid-June to early July. During the third week in June, the city holds a series of outdoor evening concerts as part of the **White Nights Festival.** Check kiosks and posters for more info. If you walk through the city during the White Nights (never do it alone!) and watch the bridges over the Neva go up at 1:30am, remember to walk on the same side of the river as your hotel—the bridges don't go back down until 3 or 4am. **Marinsky Teatr** (Марийнский Театр), Teatralnaya pl. 1 (Театральная; tel. 114 43 44; M4: Sadovaya (Садовсая), then along canal Griboyedova and right), is one of the most famous theaters for ballet in the world. Pavlova, Nureyev, Nizhinsky, and Baryshnikov all started here. For two weeks in June, the theater hosts the White Nights Festival; tickets (8000-50,000R) start selling 10 days in advance (*kassa* open Wed.-Sun. 11am-3pm and 4-7pm). Second to the Marinsky for opera and ballet, the **Maly Teatr** (Малый Театр), pl. Iskusstv 1 (Искусств; tel. 219 19 78), has the advantage of being open July and August when the Marinsky is closed (*kassa* open daily 11am-3pm and 4-8pm). **Shostakovich Philharmonic Hall,** Mikhailovskaya ul. 2 (tel. 311 73 33), is a large concert hall with classical and modern concerts.

During the pre-Gorbachev era, Petersburg was always the heart of the underground music scene, and this is still evident today. Be careful going home late at night, especially if you've been drinking—loud, drunk foreigners might as well be carrying neon signs saying "rob me!" Clubs last shorter than the fleeting life of a college relationship; both hostels can recommend the newest places. Or check the *St. Petersburg Times* and *Pulse* for ads. Soviet rock superstars like Kino and Igry got their starts at **St. Petersburg Rock Club** (Рок Клуб), ul. Rubinshtayna 13 (Рубинштайна; M4: Dostoevskaya; cover 15,000-30,000R). The place for techno and dancing is **Tunnel,** in an old bomb shelter on Lyubyansky per (Любянский) between ul. Blokhina (Блохина) and Zverinskaya (Зверинская; cover 30,000R). **Fish Fabrique,** ul. Pushkinskaya 10 (Пушкинская; M3: Mayakovskaya), recreates that bomb shelter ambience for its bohemian crowd (cover 20,000R), while the signless **Jungle,** (tel. 238 80 33), ul. Blokhina 8 (Блохина), with its aquamarine door, is the city's newest gay club. Admission is based on membership; call ahead (cover 20,000-50,000R). **The Shamrock,** ul. Dekrabristov 27 (Декрабристов), across from the Marinsky, serves pints of Guinness and Kilkenny (28,000R) to prove its Irish mettle in the heart of Eastern Europe.

■ Near St. Petersburg

Ride the suburban *electrichka* trains any spring or summer weekend day and you will witness the Russian love of the countryside. Most Russians own or share a *dacha* outside the city. The tsars were no different; they, too, built country houses, and several of these places have been restored for tourists. They make particularly good daytrips from St. Petersburg. Do as the Russians do and bring a picnic lunch.

Peterhof (Петергоф), also known as Petrodvorets (Петродворец), is the most thoroughly restored of the palaces. The entire complex is 300 years old, and many of the tsars added to it or expanded existing palaces. The **Bolshoy Dvorets** (Большой Дворец; Grand Palace; tel. 427 95 27) was Peter's first residence here. From the **Lower Gardens,** more extensive but less well-kept than the upper ones, the view up the cascade is stunning. Activated by one misstep and located by shrieking kiddies are the **joke fountains,** which splash unwitting victims. On the other side of the gardens stands **Monplaisir,** the graceful and elegant house in which Peter actually lived. (Parks open daily 9am-9:30pm. 22,000R. Palace open Tues.-Sun. noon-12:30pm, 1-2:30pm, and 4:15-5pm; closed last Tues. of every month. 46,000R, students 23,000R; mandatory bag check 500R. Most museums open variable days 10:30am-5pm. Each of the other sites about 17,000R, students 8500R.) It's an easy trip by *electrichka* (every 15min., 40min., 4000R) from the Warsaw Station; M1: Baltiskaya (Балтийская). Buy round-trip tickets from the ticket office (Биллетные Кассы) in the main courtyard. Get off at Novy Peterhof (Новый Петергоф); walk left down the road for 15 minutes or take any bus from the station to the stop after the cathedral (1000R).

South of the city 25km, **Tsarskoye Selo** (Царское Село; Tsar's Village) surrounds Catherine the Great's summer residence, a gorgeous azure, white, and gold Baroque palace. The area was renamed "Pushkin" during the Soviet era. Catherine's far-reaching artistic taste is visible throughout the palace, **Ekaterinsky Dvorets.** (Open Wed.-Mon. 10am-5pm, closed last Mon. of every month. 40,000R, students 20,000R.) Take any *electrichka* from Vitebsk Station; M1: Pushkinskaya (Пушкинская). Ask for "Detskoe Selo" or "Pushkin" (one way 3000R). Once at the station, it is a 15-minute walk, or ride on bus 371 or 382 (10min., 1000R). An easy bus ride from Tsarkoye Selo, **Pavlovsk** (Павловск) is a modest Classical contrast to Peterhof. One of the largest landscaped **parks** in the world is Pavlovsk's biggest draw. (Park open May-Oct. daily 8am-11pm; Nov.-April 8am-6pm. Closed the first Mon. of each month. 3000R.) From St. Petersburg, take an *electrichka* from Vitesbsk Station (M1: Pushkinskaya) to Pavlovsk (4000R). Any train on platform 1, 2, or 3 is fine. Then take bus 370, 383A, 383, or 493 (1000R) to the palace (5 stops).

Rostov-na-Donu

Having served as a trade hub for millenia, Rostov-na-Donu (Ростов-на-Дону) today has little to offer the visitor beside its importance as a transportation hub. If you're interested in exploring, **Gostinitsa Intourist,** ul. Bolshaya Sadovaya 115 (Большая Садовая; tel. (8632) 65 90 66; fax 65 90 07), organizes tours and sells brochures (5000-10,000R; open daily 9am-5pm). The **Passport Office (ОВИР)** is at ul. Abaroni 8 (Абарони; tel. 39 23 70; open Wed. and Fri., 11am-noon). Registration is not compulsory if you've registered elsewhere in Russia. Tourist hotels automatically register you, and bus and train station hotels will give you a card that proves you're staying there. The **vokzal** (train station; tel. (8632) 67 02 10) is at the westernmost stop of tram 1 and bus 12. Trains go to Kiev (1 per day, 23hr., 210,000R), Moscow (1 per day, 25hr., 160,000R), and Volgograd (1 per day, 15½hr., 60,000R). Unless you have a Ukranian transit visa, make sure your train is *"pro Rossii,"* meaning it does not enter Ukraine. **Buses** leave from pr. Siversa 1 (Сиверса), opposite the trains (tel. (8632) 32 32 83), for Volgograd (10-12hr., 100,000R). The **airport** (tel. (8632) 54 88 01) is east of the town center. **Aeroflot** flies to Moscow-Vnuknovo (3 per day, 614,000R) and Volgograd (3 per week, 375,000R). From the train station and ul. Bolshaya Sadovaya, take bus 7, express bus 62 or 93, or trolley 9. Tickets can be purchased at ul. Bolshaya Sanovaya 135 (tel. (8632) 65 34 78; open Mon.-Sat. 9am-6pm). If you have to spend the night, the best budget options are the **hostels** at the train (80,0000R per person) and bus stations (tel. (8632) 32 66 63; 70,000R per person).

Slovakia (Slovensko)

US$1	= 35Sk (Slovakian koruny)	10Sk =	US$0.29
CDN$1	= 25Sk	10Sk =	CDN$0.39
UK£1	= 56Sk	10Sk =	UK£0.18
IR£1	= 52Sk	10Sk =	IR£0.19
AUS$1	= 26Sk	10Sk =	AUS$0.39
NZ$1	= 22Sk	10Sk =	NZ$0.45
SAR1	= 7.48Sk	10Sk =	SAR1.34

Country Code: 421 **International Dialing Prefix: 00**

Survivor of centuries of Tartar invasions, Hungarian domination, and Soviet industrialization, Slovakia has emerged as an independent country. Natural wonders blanket the map: the forested northern mountains provide the backdrop for the gentler hills of central Slovakia, and many areas offer excellent hiking and skiing. The countryside is also dotted with the ruins of castles once used as defenses against the Tartars and Turks. Bratislava, an easy trip east from Vienna, is settling into its role as the political and cultural capital and provides access to the rest of the country. In the smaller towns, suburban factories have not destroyed the old-time atmosphere. Take a deep swig of Slovak wine, lace up your hiking boots, and enjoy the freedom.

For more comprehensive coverage of Slovakia and surrounding countries, look for a copy of *Let's Go: Eastern Europe 1998*.

GETTING THERE AND GETTING AROUND

Citizens of the U.S. and South Africa can visit Slovakia **visa-free** for up to 30 days; citizens of Ireland and Canada, 90 days; and citizens of the U.K., 180 days. Australians and New Zealanders need a 30-day, single-entry or transit visa (US$21), double-entry visa (US$32). For the Slovak embassy in your country, see **Government Information Offices,** p. 1. Submit your passport, cash or money order, as many visa applications as planned entries, and twice the number of photographs; processing takes two days.

International bus and rail links connect Slovakia to all of its neighbors. Many train stations operate **BIJ-Wasteels** offices, which offer 20-50% off tickets to European cities (but not Prague) for those under 26. **EastRail** is valid in Slovakia, but **Eurail** is not. A *miestenka* (reservation, 7Sk) is required for international trips (including the Czech Republic). Buy tickets at windows marked with a boxed "R."

ŽSR is the national train company; every information desk has a copy of **Cestovný poriadok** (58Sk), the master schedule. *Odchody* (departures) and *príchody* (arrivals) are on the left and right of schedules, respectively, but be sure to check revolving timetables. A reservation is needed for *expresný* trains and first-class seats, but not for *rychlík* (fast), *spešný* (semi-fast), or *osobný* (local) trains. In many hilly regions, **ČSAD** or **SAD buses** are the best and sometimes the only way to get around. Except for very long trips, buy tickets on the bus. Schedules have many complicated footnotes: "X" means weekdays only, "a" indicates Saturdays and Sundays only, and "r" and "k" exclude holidays. Numbers refer to days of the week on which the bus travels a given route—1 is Monday, 2 is Tuesday, and so forth. *Premava* means "including," and *nepremava* is equivalent to "except."

ESSENTIALS

Access has opened up tourist services in major towns. They generally sell good maps and book inexpensive rooms. After 1993, Slovakia hastily designed its own currency which is now the country's only legal tender. One hundred **halérs** make up one **koruna** (Sk). Keep your exchange receipts to change Slovak korunas back into hard currency. **Všeobecná Úverová Banka (VÚB)** operates offices in even the smallest towns and cashes AmEx Traveler's Cheques for a 1% fee. Most offices give Master-

Card cash advances, and have Cirrus, Eurocard, MC, and Visa **ATMs.** Many **Slovenská Sporitel'ňa** bureaus handle Visa cash advances and have Visa ATMs.

The **mail** service in the Slovak Republic is efficient and modern. Almost every *pošta* (post office) provides **Express Mail Services,** but a trip to a *colnice* (customs office) is in order to send a package abroad. *Poste Restante* mail with a "1" after the city name will arrive at the main post office. Local **telephone** calls cost 2Sk; drop the coin in after being connected. Throughout Slovakia, phone cards (100Sk) are common; though sometimes frustrating, they are better than coin phones. To contact an **AT&T Direct** operator, dial 004 210 01 01; for **MCI WorldPhone,** 004 210 01 12; for **Sprint Access,** 004 218 71 87; for **Canada Direct,** 004 210 01 51; and for **BT Direct,** 004 210 44 01. In an **emergency,** dial 150 for **fire,** 158 for **police,** and 155 for an **ambulance.**

Slovak resembles Czech closely but the languages are not identical. The younger generation typically knows some English, but German is more widely understood.

Yes/no	*Áno/Nie*	AA-no/nyieh
Hello	*Dobrý deň*	DOH-bree dyeny
Please	*Prosím*	PROH-seem
Thank you	*Dakujem*	dyak-uh-yem
Do you speak English?	*Hovoríte po anglicky?*	HO-voh-ree-tyeh poh ahn-glits-kih
I don't understand.	*Nerozumiem*	nyeh-ro-zuh-miehm
Where is...?	*Kde je...?*	gdyeh yeh
How much does this cost?	*Coto stojí?*	KOH-to STOH-yee
I would like...	*Prosím si...*	PROH-seem sih
I'd like a (single room) (double room)	*Potrebujem (jednolužkovú izbu) (izbu pre dve osoby)*	poh-tre-buh-yem (yed-noh-loozh-koh-voo iz-buh) (iz-buh preh dveh oh-soh-bih)
Help!	*Pomoc!*	po-mots

Tap **water** is heavily chlorinated and may occasionally cause abdominal discomfort. Bottled water is available in grocery stores. A reciprocal Health Agreement between Slovakia and the U.K. entitles Brits to free medical care here.

Accommodations, Camping, Food, and Drink Cheap housing may be difficult to come by in Bratislava before student dorms open up in July. **Juniorhotels (HI),** though uncommon, are a step above the usual brand of hostel. In the mountains, **chaty** (mountain huts/chalets) range from plush quarters for 400Sk per night to a friendly bunk and outhouse for 100Sk. **Hotel** prices fall dramatically outside Bratislava and the High Tatras. **Pensions** are generally less expensive then hotels and, especially when family run, often nicer. **Campgrounds** lurk on the outskirts of most towns, and for travelers without tents, many offer bungalows. Sites range from basic to deluxe, and give good value for money. Camping in national parks is illegal.

Slovakia rose out of its 1000 year Hungarian captivity with a taste for paprika, spicy *gulaš,* and fine wines. The national dish, *bryndzove halušky,* knocks stomachs out with heavy dumplings smothered in a thick sauce of goat cheese. In fact, dumplings *(knedliky)* come with everything—fruit, gravy, and fried pork steak. If dumplings are not for you, most restaurants also serve potatoes *(zemiaky)* and french fries *(hranolky).* Slovakia's second favorite dish is *pirohy,* a pasta-pocket usually filled with potato or *bryndza* cheese, with bits of bacon on top. *Pstruh* (trout) is also popular. Fine white wines are produced in the Small Carpathians northeast of Bratislava, especially around the town of Pezinok. *Riesling* and *Müller-Thurgau* grapes are typically used; quality varies greatly. You can enjoy these at a *vináreň* (wine hall). *Pivo* (beer) is served at a *pivnica* or *piváreň* (beer hall). Most **tip** by rounding up.

Bratislava

After 80 years of playing second fiddle to starlet Prague, Bratislava, a burgeoning city of half a million, has been thrust into a new role as the capital of Slovakia. Although much of the population lives in the grim housing projects, the compact historic center—where the Austrian Empress held court during the 18th century and the rulers of Hungary were crowned—is where visitors spend much of their time. Lightly touristed, the city still merits a visit, if only to catch a train to flashier destinations.

ORIENTATION AND PRACTICAL INFORMATION

Bratislava lies on the banks of the Danube, a proverbial stone's throw from the Austrian and Hungarian borders. Avoid getting off at the **Nové Mesto** train station, which is much farther from the center than **Hlavná stanica** (the main station). To get to the downtown area from Hlavná stanica, take tram 1 to **nám. SNP.** Uršulínska leads to the tourist office. From the bus station, take bus 107 to **nám. J. Štúra** by the river. Walk up Mostova, cross Hviezdoslavovo nám. onto Rybárska brána, then turn right at Hlavné nám. onto Kostolná—the tourist office is across Primaciálne nám.

Tourist Offices: Bratislavská Informačná Služba (BIS), Klobučnicka 2 (tel. 533 37 15). Sells maps (30Sk), gives city tours, and books rooms. Open Mon.-Fri. 8am-7pm, Sat.-Sun. 8:30am-1:30pm. **Branch** in train station annex open daily 8am-6pm.

Embassies: Canada, Kolárska 4 (tel. 36 12 77). **South Africa,** Jančova 8 (tel. 531 15 82). Open Mon.-Fri. 9am-noon. **Irish** citizens and **Commonwealth** nationals should contact the embassy of the **U.K.,** Panská 16 (tel. 531 96 32; fax 531 00 02). **U.S.,** Hviezdoslavovo nám. 4 (tel. 533 08 61). Open Mon.-Fri. 8am-4:40pm.

Currency Exchange: Všeobecná Úverová Banka (VÚB), Gorkého 9 (tel. 515 79 76), cashes traveler's checks and handles MC and Visa cash advances. Open Mon.-Wed. and Fri. 8am-4:30pm, Thurs. 8am-3pm. An outdoor machine at Mostová 6 changes US$, DM, and UK£ into Sk for a 3% commission.

American Express: At **Tatratour,** Františkánske nám. 3, Bratislava 81101 (tel. 533 55 36). Cashes (2% commission) and sells (1% commission) traveler's checks and holds mail. Open Mon.-Fri. 10am-6pm, Sat. 9am-noon.

Trains: Bratislava Hlavná stanica (tel. 469 45), north of town at the end of Štefánikova. To: Berlin (11hr., 2699Sk; Wasteels 1993Sk), Budapest (3hr., 378Sk; Wasteels 435Sk), Prague (5hr., 228Sk), Vienna (1hr., 200Sk), Kiev (26hr., 1287Sk), Kraków (8hr., 1022Sk; Wasteels 527Sk), and Warsaw (8hr., 1284Sk; Wasteels 742Sk). International tickets at counters 9-16. **Wasteels** office at front of station offers discounts to those under 26 (open Mon.-Fri. 8:30am-4pm). **Lockers** 5Sk.

Buses: Mlynské nivy 31 (tel. 542 22 22), east of the Old Town. To: Budapest (5hr., 330Sk), Prague (4½hr., 240Sk), and Vienna (1½hr., 320Sk). Check your ticket for the bus number; several different buses may depart simultaneously. **Lockers** 5Sk.

Hydrofoils: Lodná osobná doprava, Fajnorovo nábr. 2 (tel. 36 35 22; fax 536 22 31), in summer along the river. To: Vienna (1½hr.; one way 210AS, round-trip 330AS) and Budapest (4hr.; one way 680AS, round-trip 1000AS, book at least 48hr. in advance). Ask about 30% student discounts.

Public Transportation: All daytime trips on **trams** and **buses** require a 7Sk ticket, available at kiosks and orange automats found at most stops. Night buses have black and orange numbers in the 500s and cost 14Sk. Most trams pass by nám. SNP, and a majority of buses stop at the SNP bridge's north base.

Hitchhiking: Those hitching to Vienna or to Hungary (via Győr) cross the SNP bridge and walk down Viedenská cesta. Those headed to Prague take bus 104 from the center up Pražská to the "Patronka" stop. Hitching is legal and common.

Pharmacy: At the corner of Gorkého and Lavrinská. Open 24hr.

Post Office: Main office at nám. SNP 35. *Poste Restante* at counter 6. Open Mon.-Fri. 7am-8pm, Sat. 7am-6pm, Sun. 9am-2pm. **Postal Code:** 81000 Bratislava 1.

Telephones: Kolárska 12. Open 24hr. **Telephone Code:** 07.

ACCOMMODATIONS AND CAMPING

In July and August, dorms open up for backpackers on their way to Vienna. Cheap rooms and beds are harder to come by in June, so call ahead. The **BIS** offices (see above) find rooms on a moment's notice; singles run 400Sk and doubles 600Sk.

Pension Gremium, Gorkého 11 (tel. 32 18 18; fax 533 06 53). Sterling showers and stuffed chairs in the heart of the Old Town. English spoken. Reception open daily until 2am. One single 800Sk. Doubles 1300Sk. Breakfast included. A popular café will feed you downstairs. There are only a few rooms, so call ahead.

Youth Hostel Bernolak, Bernolákova 1 (tel. 39 77 23). From the train station, take bus 22, 23, or 210, or tram 3; from the bus station take bus 37 or 210 to "Račianské Mýto." Friendliest hostel in town with the best English. Spacious singles 440Sk. Doubles 520Sk. Triples 600Sk. All with showers and toilets. 10% discount for those with a Euro26, ISIC, or HI card. Open July-Aug.

YMCA na Slovenska, Karpatská 2 (tel. 39 80 05), only 500m from the train station. Walk the long lane out of the station and turn left on Šancova. Sterile, spacious rooms with less sterile showers. Bar and movie theater. Check-out 9am. Doubles, triples, and quints 200Sk per person.

Youth Hostel, Wilsonova 6 (tel. 39 77 35). On the street parallel to Bernolákova (see YH Bernolak above). Rooms remarkable only for being cheap. Dorms 150Sk. 30% discount with Euro26, HI, or ISIC. Open July-Aug.

Camping: Autocamping Zlaté Piesky, Senecká cesta 2 (tel. 25 73 73), in suburban Trnávka by the lakeside. Take tram 2 or 4 to the last stop, or bus 118 from Trnavské Mýto to the last stop. 90Sk per person, 80Sk per tent. Bungalows 650-900Sk.

FOOD

Besides burgers, Bratislava's restaurants serve the region's spicy meat mixtures with West Slovakia's celebrated **Modra** wine. There's a **market** at Žilinská 5, near the train station (open Mon.-Sat. 6am-4pm), and a **non-stop deli** at Špitalská 45. For groceries, head to **Tesco's Potraviny,** Kamenné nám. 1. (Open Mon.-Wed. 8am-7pm, Thurs. 8am-8pm, Fri. 8am-9pm, Sat. 8am-5pm, Sun. 9am-5pm.)

Bratislavaburg

The only thing more incomprehensible than a Slovak menu is a Bratislava menu at one of the city's ubiquitous burger stands. A cheeseburger costs less than a *hamburger so syrom* (hamburger with cheese) because, as the stand owner will explain with humiliating logic, a cheeseburger is made of cheese. A *pressburger* consists of bologna on a bun, and hamburgers are actually ham. Everything comes boiled (except the cheese) on a roll with cabbage, onions, and sauce.

Prašná Bašta, Zámočnícka 11, off Michalská. Weird mannequin statues and wooden beams frame the vaulted interior. Sheep cheese *gnocchi* 49Sk. Fine onion soup 22Sk. Generous glasses of wine 9Sk. English menu. Open daily 11am-11pm.

Vel'kí Františkání, Františkánske nám. 10. Dishes range from bean soup (25Sk) to plates of roast duck that fly off into Sk infinity. The candle-lit wine cellar is the restaurant's focus. Music nightly; 25Sk cover. Open daily 10am-10:30pm.

Cafe London, Panská 17, in the British Council's courtyard. Serves up Anglophile nostalgia to expats. Generous portions of quiche 63Sk. Chicken salad, tuna, and roast beef sandwiches 39-72Sk. Open Mon.-Fri. 9am-9pm.

Corleone's, Hviezdoslavovo nám., on the north side. Italian *trattoria,* a little expensive—except for delicious pizzas 69-139Sk. Open daily until midnight.

SIGHTS AND ENTERTAINMENT

From **nám. SNP,** which commemorates the bloody Slovak National Uprising against the fascist Slovak state, a walk down Uršulínska leads to **Primaciálné nám.** The Neoclassical **Primaciálny Palác** (Primate's Palace) dates from 1781. Napoleon and Austrian Emperor Franz I signed the Peace of Pressburg here in 1805. The **Múzeum Histórie Mesta** (Town History Museum) is in the **Stará Radnica** (Old Town Hall), accessible from Primaciálné nám. Inside, past a 1:500 model of Bratislava, galleries display exhibits on the city's history (open Tues.-Sun. 10am-5pm; 25Sk, students 10Sk). Stará Radnica fronts onto **Hlavné nám.,** where brass bands play on summer evenings. South of the square on Panská is the **Dóm sv. Martina** (St. Martin's Cathedral), where the kings of Hungary were crowned for three centuries.

Another block to the south, long, wooded **Hviezdoslavovo nám.** is dominated at its eastern end by the 1886 **Slovenské Národné Divadlo** (Slovak National Theater). Down by the river, the **Slovenské Národné Múzeum** (Slovak National Museum), Vajanského nábr. 2, houses local archaeological finds, including casts of Neanderthal skeletons (open Tues.-Sun. 9am-5pm; 20Sk). Also on the river, the **Slovak National Gallery,** Rázusovo nábr. 2, displays Slovak Gothic and Baroque art (open Tues.-Sun. 10am-5pm; 25Sk, students 5Sk). The SNP suspension bridge spans the Dunaj, its reins held by a giant flying saucer (10Sk). On the northern side of the bridge, the road zooms over what used to be **Schlossberg,** the old Jewish quarter. Over the road from the cathedral, the **Múzeum Židovskej Kultúry** (Museum of Jewish Culture), Židovská 17, preserves valuable fragments of a vanished population (open Sun.-Fri. 11am-5pm; 30Sk). From the cathedral, go down Kapitulská, right onto Prepoštská, and left onto Michalská, a busy pedestrian street guarded by the **Michalská Brána** at the north end. Trot up to the top (open Wed.-Mon. 10am-5pm; 20Sk).

From the banks of the Danube to the center's historic squares, the four-towered Bratislavský hrad (castle) is a visible landmark. Of strategic importance for more than a millennium, the castle's heyday was in the 18th century, when Maria Theresa held court here. The castle was burned down in 1811 and bombed during World War II, so what the visitor sees today is largely Communist-era restoration. There's also a **Historické Múzeum** (open Tues.-Fri. 9am-5pm, Sat.-Sun. 10am-6pm; 30Sk).

For concert and theater schedules, pick up a copy of *Kám* at BIS. It's not in English, but the info is easy to decipher. Unfortunately, the Filharmonia and many theaters take their vacations in July and August. **Slovenská Filharmonia** plays regularly at Palackého 2, which fronts onto Mostova; buy tickets (approx. 600-700Sk) at the box office around the corner on Medená (tel. 533 33 51; open Mon.-Fri. 1-5pm). **Slovenské Narodné Divaldo** (National Theater) tickets are sold at the box office at Laurinská 20 (around 50Sk; open Mon.-Fri.noon-6pm). Tickets for the **Bohdan Warchal Quartet** are also available here.

Bratislavans prefer the conversation and carousing of wine pubs, beer halls, and cafés to the thumping of dance clubs. The mammoth **Stará Sladovňa,** Cintorínska 32, serves up 20Sk pints of *Budvar* to over a thousand patrons every night in one of Europe's largest beer-hall complexes (open daily 10am-midnight). **Dubliner,** Sedlarsná, just of Hlavné nám., Bratislava's *ersatz* Irish pub, has wobbly wooden tables, a leaky roof, and a tremendously lively atmosphere as it fills up after dinner (open Mon.-Sat. 10am-11am, Sun. noon-midnight).

VYSOKÉ TATRY (THE HIGH TATRAS)

Slovaks take great pride in Vysoké Tatry, a mountainous mecca for hikers, skiers, and nature-lovers. The jagged **High Tatras** are one of the most compact mountain ranges in the world, and feature sky-scraping peaks, beautiful glacial lakes, and many excellent hiking trails. Electric trains and buses connect all the towns in the area.

Starý Smokovec

Starý Smokovec is the Vysoké Tatry's most central resort town and one of the oldest. The neighboring hamlet Horný Smokovec offers cheap sleeps making Starý Smokovec easily accessible to the budget traveler. The real draw, however, is the network of **hiking** trails that lead to the quiet, rugged slopes of the Tatras. The funicular to **Hrebienok** (1285m) takes you to the hiking country's heart, and an easy 20-minute walk from there leads to the foaming **Cold Waterfall** *(Studenovodské vodopády).* The eastward blue trail descends from the waterfall through the towering pines to **Tatranská Lomnica** (1½hr.). The long, red *"Tatranská magistrála"* trail travels west from Hrebienok through the chalet **Sliezsky dom** (1670m), to **Chata kapitána Moravku** ashore **Popradské pleso.** From here, descend to **Štrbské Pleso.** The truly ambitious can climb the stony, 2450m **Slavkovský štít** (about 8hr.).

The resort is easily reached from Poprad by TEŽ **trains** (every 30min.-1hr., 30min., 10Sk). **Buses** to many mountain resorts stop in a parking lot east of the main train station along the road to Horný Smokovec. **VKÚ map 113** (65-85Sk; essential for hiking) and weather info are cheerfully offered at the **Tatranská Informačná Kancelária** (tel. (0969) 34 40), in Dom Služieb, near the west end of the town's artery (open Mon.-Fri. 8am-noon and 12:30-6pm, Sat.-Sun. 8am-noon and 12:30-4pm).

The suburb Horný Smokovec, 1km east along Starý's main street, offers affordable rooms and is home to **Slovakotourist** (tel. (0969) 42 30 31), whose English-speaking staff books mountain *chaty* (350-450Sk) and private rooms (250-300Sk). Further along the road (2 TEŽ stops toward Tatranská Lomnica), **Hotel Junior Vysoké Tatry** (tel. (0969) 42 26 61) has clean, basic rooms and a disco club. (Singles 320Sk; doubles 610Sk; triples 760Sk; with ISIC or HI 200Sk per person, including breakfast.) Other decent rooms are available at **Hotel Šport** (tel. (0969) 23 61), also in Horný Smokovec but almost within sight of Starý Smokovec (singles 490Sk, doubles 790Sk; discounts off season). In Starý Smokovec itself, **Hotel Plesnivec** (tel. (0969) 25 35; fax 29 93), near the lift station, rents aging but cheap rooms with common bathrooms (370Sk per person). Near the train station, a first-rate **grocery store** has abundant supplies and an outdoor terrace (open Mon.-Sat. 7:45am-7pm, Sat. 8am-3pm).

Levoča

The medieval "Law of Storage" forced passing merchants to stay in Levoča 14 days and sell their goods at wholesale prices. To this commercial prosperity was added artistic distinction in the early 16th century, when Majster Pavol's workshop pioneered an expressive style of wood-carving and erected the world's tallest Gothic altar in **Chrám sv. Jakuba** (St. James's Church; open Sun.-Mon. 1-6pm, Tues.-Sat. 9am-6pm; 20Sk, students 10Sk). Branches of the **Spišské Múzeum** are dotted around the main square. The best is in **Dom Majstra Pavla,** at #20, which now contains high quality copies of the Master's best work for a closer view than in the Chrám sv. Jakuba (all museums open Tues.-Sun. 9am-5pm; 10Sk, students 5Sk). The architecture of the Gothic **town hall** is more exciting than its exhibit of armor and local crafts.

Buses for Košice (2hr., 62Sk), Poprad (30min., 18Sk), and Prešov (2hr., 128Sk) leave hourly. Turn right out of the bus station, right again along the main road, and duck under the arch that appears on the left to walk up to **nám. Majstra Pavla.** The helpful **tourist office,** nám. Majstra Pavla 58 (tel. (0966) 37 63), has lots of info about

Majster Pavel and the town. They book *penzión* rooms for 300Sk (open Mon. 9am-5pm, Tues.-Fri. 9am-6pm, Sat.-Sun. 9:30am-5:30pm). For the modern hostel **Hotel Texon,** Francisciho 45 (tel. (0966) 51 44 93), catch the local bus and hop off when you see the white Obchodné centrum Texon building. Majster Pavol pictures adorn every wall. Every two rooms share a bathroom (180Sk per person; 150Sk for 3 or more nights). **Hotel Faix,** Probstnerova cesta 22 (tel. (0966) 51 23 35), lies by the town wall, an easy walk from the bus station. The aging doubles (480-720Sk) are a better value than the singles (440-680Sk). Two floors share one bathroom.

Poprad

Poprad was born when Czechoslovakia glued together four sleepy mountain villages with drab apartment blocks. Although not pretty, it acts as the "gateway to the Tatras," as well as to the towns of the Spiš region. If you have extra time, **Námestie sv. Egídia,** down Mnohemova from the bus station, boasts medieval buildings. The most eye-catching is the fortified **St. Egídius Church,** erected by Saxons in the 13th century. A 15-minute walk east on Štefánikova, and then a left on unmarked Kežmarská, leads to **Spišská Sobota,** a tiny historic village centered on **Sobotské nám.**

Poprad Information Agency *(Popradská Informačná Agentúra),* nám. sv. Egídia 114 (tel. (092) 72 17 00; fax 72 13 94), provides info on the Tatras and find rooms in Poprad (DM10-15) and the Tatras (open Mon.-Fri. 8am-7pm, Sat. 9am-1pm). **Trains** (tel. (092) 72 18 30) leave from the north edge of town for Košice (1¼hr., 70Sk) and other cities; *Tatranská Električka Železnica* (TEŽ) trains connect Poprad with the Tatran resorts (up to 18Sk depending on the destination). Buses are generally quicker, more frequent, and less fun. For info on **bus** connections, call (092) 233 90. Poprad eagerly accommodates the annual tourist hordes with booking agencies on every block and pensions around every corner. **Domov Mládeže,** Karpatská 9 (tel. (092) 634 14), off Alžbetina which runs from the station, is a large workers' hostel that doubles as a tourist hostel in summer, basic and cheap (130Sk, 200Sk for one-night stays). Very close to the train station, **Hotel Európa,** Wolkerova 3 (tel. (092) 72 18 83), has old but well-groomed rooms and communal toilets and baths (singles 400Sk, doubles 550Sk, triples 850Sk). **Panorama Pizzeria** on the eighth floor of Hotel Gerlach, on Hviezdoslavovo, has a fine view of the Tatras and serves heavily cauliflowered veggie dishes (19-35Sk), and Tatran beer (17Sk; open daily 7am-11pm).

ŠARIŠ

Šariš once served as a borderland against Turkish and Saracen invasions, but now rests quietly tucked in the hills of East Slovakia. English is spoken widely here, but tourism has yet to make a significant appearance in these sleepy, religious towns.

Košice

Košice's Gothic and Renaissance center has managed to survive fires, revolutions, an Ottoman invasion, and the city's intense industrial development. **Hlavná** marks the heart of the Old Town. At its widest point is the towering **Dom sv. Alžbety** (Cathedral of St. Elizabeth), a conglomeration of nearly every style known to Western architecture and the final resting place of Rakóczi Ferenc II, Hungary's anti-Hapsburg national hero. Built from stones discarded by the cathedral, the 19th-century **Jakabov Palác,** Mlynská 30, off Hlavná, was home to Czechoslovakia's president in the spring of 1945. **Rákóczi's House,** Hrnčiarska 7, is a shrine to Rakóczi, containing an entire room from his home in Turkey. Hlavná ends at Hviezdoslavova between the buildings of the **Východnoslovenské Múzeum** (East Slovak Museum). The museum has exhibits on the early inhabitants of the area, examples of the region's folk and religious art, and thousands of gold coins (open Mon.-Sat. 9am-5pm, Sun. 9am-1pm).

Košice's main **train station** is on Predstaničné nám. Trains run west to Bratislava (5hr., 226Sk) and Prague (9hr., 403Sk); eastbound trains travel to Lviv (6-8hr., 800Sk) and Kiev (12hr., 818Sk). North-south trains run to Kraków (6hr., 543Sk) and Budapest (4hr., 470Sk). The **tourist office,** Hlavná 8 (tel. (95) 186; fax 622 69 38), near the station, greets visitors with maps and a booking service. (Open June-Sept. Mon.-Fri. 8am-6pm, Sat. 9am-1pm; Oct.-May Mon.-Fri. 9am-5pm, Sat. 9am-1pm.) **Hotel Európa,** Protifašistických Bojovníkov 1 (tel. (95) 622 38 97), across the park in front of the train station, is a 19th-century hotel with communal toilets and showers (singles 330Sk, doubles 570Sk). **Pension Rozália,** Oravská 14 (tel. (95) 633 97 14), has small rooms overlooking a garden. From the station, take tram 6 to Amfitéater and walk up Stará spišská cesta (200Sk per person). Recently renovated and spotless, **Hotel Strojár,** Južná Trieda 93 (tel. (95) 544 06; fax 544 07), is accessible on tram 3 from the train station (singles 210-350Sk, doubles 600Sk). **Ajvega,** Orlia 10, off Mlynská, offers veggie pasta, pizza, and salads (open daily 11am-11pm). **Lampáreň,** Hlavná, serves solid, tasty dishes (50-116Sk) and becomes a disco after 10pm (open Mon.-Tues., Thurs., and Sun. 11am-1am, Wed. and Fri.-Sat. 11am-2am).

Prešov

Magyars, Gypsies, and Rusins maintain their diverse traditions in Prešov, and clean-cut couples, black-clad widows, and Catholics flaunting their Sunday best complete the cultural mix. As **Hlavná** splits into two main branches, **Kostol sv. Mikuláša** (St. Nicholas's Cathedral) captures tourists' attention. The Gothic cathedral's distinctive turrets attest to the Saxon influence in Prešov during the late Middle Ages (open irregular hours). Beside the church at Hlavná 86, the 16th-century **Rákóczi Palace** now houses the eclectic **Vlastivedné múzeum** (City Museum), with exhibits on lace work and old fire trucks (open Tues.-Fri. 10am-5pm, Sat.-Sun. 11am-3pm; 20Sk, students 10Sk). On the west side of Hlavná, the restored **Šarišská galéria** (Šariš Gallery) features exhibits of Slovak art. (Open Tues., Wed., and Fri. 9am-5pm, Thurs. 9am-6pm, Sat. 9am-1pm, Sun. 1:30-5:30pm. 6Sk, students 2Sk, Sun. free.) Heading west from Hlavná, the narrow medieval street **Floriánova** leads to **Brána sv. Floriána** (St. Florian's Gate), a remnant of the town's early Renaissance fortification. In the northwest of the Old Town at Švermova 56 is an ornate **synagogue;** a monument outside commemorates the Jewish victims of fascist regimes.

Trains (tel. (91) 73 10 43) leave regularly for Košice (50min., 18Sk); **buses** (tel. (91) 72 45 91) run to Košice (30-45min., 24Sk), Poprad (1½hr., 65Sk), and many smaller towns. The **tourist office,** Hlavná 67 (tel. (91) 186 73 11 13), provides town and hotel information (open Mon.-Sat. 7am-5pm, Sun. 7am-noon). Inexpensive rooms hide in Prešov's southwest suburb, and vacancies are common.**Turistická Ubytovaňa Sen,** Vajanského 65 (tel. (91) 73 31 70), offers a few rooms for 140Sk per person; call in advance. From the station, walk towards the town center, take the first left on Škultétyho, and a left again at Budovatelská to reach **Penzion Lineas,** Budovatelská 14 (tel. (91) 72 33 25, ext. 28), whose clean doubles include toilets and baths (430Sk). **Florianka,** Baštová 32, sits next to Slovakia's best hotel and restaurant management school, which explains the excellent food and service (meals 30-200Sk; open Mon.-Fri. 11am-9:30pm). **Bagetéria,** Hlavné 36, serves delicious baguette sandwiches (15-90Sk; open Min.-Fri. 6am-10pm, Sat.-Sun. 7:30am-10pm).

Slovenia (Slovenija)

US$1	= 170Slt (Slovenian Tolar)	100Slt =	US$0.59
CDN$1	= 123Slt	100Slt =	CAD$0.81
UK£1	= 270Slt	100Slt =	UK£0.37
IR£1	= 249Slt	100Slt =	IR£0.40
AUS$1	= 124Slt	100Slt =	AUS$0.81
NZ$1	= 108Slt	100Slt =	NZ$0.93
SAR1	= 36Slt	100Slt =	SAR2.77
DM1	= 93Slt	100Slt =	DM1.07

Country Phone Code: 386 **International Dialing Prefix: 00**

Slovenia, the most prosperous of Yugoslavia's breakaway republics, revels in its independence, modernizing rapidly as it turns a hungry eye toward the West. For a country half Switzerland's size, Slovenia, on the "sunny side of the Alps," is extraordinarily diverse: in a day, you can breakfast on an Alpine peak, lunch under the Adriatic sun, and dine in a vineyard on the Pannonian plains. Painters, bring extra green and white: Slovenia's pine-covered hills and mountains, which irresistibly lure hikers in the summer and skiers in the winter, won't disappoint you.

For more detailed coverage of Slovenia, check out *Let's Go: Eastern Europe 1998.*

GETTING THERE AND GETTING AROUND

Australian, Canadian, Irish, New Zealand, U.K., and U.S. citizens can visit visa-free for up to 90 days. South Africans need **visas** (US$35 for 3-month single-entry and transit; US$70 for 3-month multiple-entry). Apply by mail or in person to the embassy in your home country (see p. 1) with your passport and the fee in the form of a money order.

Slovenia is easily accessible by car, train, or plane. Ljubljana has frequent and reliable international **train** connections, and discounts are sometimes available for travelers under 26; check at the Ljubljana station (look for the **BIJ-Wasteels** logo). Say *"vlak"* for train, *"prihodi vlakov"* for arrivals, and *"odhodi vlakov"* for departures. **Buses** are about 25% more expensive and usually slower, but run to some otherwise inaccessible places. Tickets are sold at the station or on board; put your luggage in the passenger compartment if possible. There are several international **airports:** commercial flights arrive at the **Ljubljana Airport** in Brnik, with regular bus service to the city center 25km away. The reformed national carrier— **Adria Airways—** flies to European capitals and Tel Aviv. Some **hitchers** report success in the countryside and near cities, but they advise avoiding December to January and July to August.

ESSENTIALS

Tourist offices are located in most major cities and tourist spots. The staff are generally helpful, speak English, provide basic information, and assist in finding accommodations. The national **currency** is the Slovenian tolar (Slt). Hard currency prices tend to be stable, but are usually set in Deutschmarks (DM) rather than US$. **Exchange offices** abound. **Banks** are usually open Monday to Friday 8am to 5pm and Saturday 8 to 11am. Rates vary, but tend to be better in cities. Some establishments charge no commission (a fact reflected in the rates). Major **credit cards** are widely accepted, particularly MasterCard/Eurocard and Visa. **ATMs** exist only in major cities.

Postal services are reliable. At the post office, buy a **phone card** (750Slt per 50 impulses, which yields 50 local calls or 16min. to the U.S.). For **MCI WorldPhone,** call 080 88 08. Services from other carriers may become available in 1998. Operators will assist in connecting calls if you dial 90 in Ljubljana, Kranj, Maribor, and Nova Gorica, 900 elsewhere. Calling the U.S. is expensive (over US$6 per min.).

Most young people speak at least some English, but older folk are more likely to understand German or Italian. Slovene resembles other Slavic languages; *"č," "š,"* and *"ž"* are pronounced as in Czech. The following phrases should get you started.

Yes/No	*Ja/Ne*	yah/neh
Hello	*Idravo*	ee-drah-voh
Thank you	*Hvala*	HVAA-lah
I am sorry	*oprostite*	oh-proh-stee-teh
Do you speak English?	*Govorite angleško?*	go-vo-REE-te ang-LEH-shko
I don't understand	*Ne razumem*	neh rah-ZOO-mehm
Where is...?	*Kje je...?*	kyeh ye
How much does this cost?	*Koliko to stane?*	koh-lee-koh toh stah-neh
I (feminine) would like a (single) (double) room.	*Rad (Rada) bi (enopostel-jno) (dvoposteljo)sobo*	rat (RAA-da) bi (e-no-POHS-tel-yno) (dvo-POHS-tel-yno) so-bo
Help!	*Na pomoč!*	nah poh-MOHCH

Accommodations, Camping, Food, and Drink At the height of tourist season, prices are steep and rooms scarce. Tourists tend to swarm in the mountains around July and August, but student rooms are generally available late June to early September. **Hotels** fall into five categories (L (deluxe), A, B, C, and D) and tend to be expensive. **Youth hostels** and **student dormitories** are cheap, but generally open only during summer. Usually, the best option is to rent **private rooms;** prices depend on location, but rarely exceed US$30. They're advertised on the street with *"sobe"* or *"Zimmer"* signs, or you can inquire at the tourist office. **Campgrounds** can also be crowded, but they are generally in excellent condition.

Self-serve fast food places have mushroomed in Slovenia, especially in the larger, more touristed cities. Traditional Slovene cuisine is becoming increasingly hard to find; a *gostilna* or *gostišče* (both words for a restaurant with a country flavor) are the best bet for mouth-watering, home-style cooking. A good national dish to start with is *jota*—a potato, bean, and sauerkraut soup. Vegetarians should look for *śtruklji,* large dumplings that are eaten as a main dish. The country's wine tradition dates from antiquity. *Renski Rizling* and *Śipon* are popular whites. Slovenia produces many unique red wines including the light *Cvićek* from the center of the country and the potent *Teran* bottled on the coast. The art of brewing is also centuries old in Slovenia; not surprisingly, there are several good beers. The ubiquitous red shield of Ljubljana-based *Union Pivo* testifies to its popularity. For a potent dark beer, swig a stein of *Črni Baron.* For something stronger, try *Žganje,* a strong fruit brandy.

Ljubljana

Legend has it that Jason the Argonaut, Golden Fleece in tow, fled across the Black Sea and up the Danube to escape King Aietes. Trapped by the Barje marshlands, he founded a city on the banks of the Ljubljanica River. In reality, Ljubljana (lyoob-LYAH-nah) was settled by Romans and later became the capital of the Austrian duchy of Carniola. By the 19th century, the city stood at the center of a Slovene nationalist movement. Today, the small but prosperous capital features an attractive Old Town with well-preserved Baroque and Art Nouveau facades. Perhaps because the name of the city is only one vowel away from the word for "beloved" *(ljubljena),* even monuments are said to fall in love here.

ORIENTATION AND PRACTICAL INFORMATION

The **train** and **bus stations** are on **Trg Osvobodilne Fronte (Trg OF),** north of **Stari Grad** (Old Town). To reach the central square, proceed perpendicular to Trg OF along **Resljeva cesta,** bear right on **Trubarjeva cesta,** which leads to **Prešernov Trg.** After crossing the **Tromostovje** (Triple Bridge), Stari Grad emerges at the castle hill's base; the tourist office is the first building on your right.

Tourist Office: Tourist Information Center (TIC), Stritarjeva 1 (tel. 133 01 11; fax 133 02 44). Free maps. Open Mon.-Fri. 8am-7pm, Sat.-Sun. 9am-5pm.

Embassies and Consulates: Australia, Trg Republike 3 (tel. 125 42 52; fax 126 47 21). **U.K.,** Trg Republike 3 (tel. 125 71 91; fax 125 01 74). **U.S.,** Pražakova 4 (tel. 30 14 27; fax 30 14 01). Open Mon., Wed., and Fri. 9am-noon.

Currency Exchange: Currency exchanges *(menjalnićna)* abound. **Ljubljanska Bank,** Beethovnova 7, at the corner of Cankarjeva, cashes traveler's checks for no commission. Open Mon.-Fri. 8:30am-noon and 2-4pm, Sat. 9am-noon. **Publikun,** Miklošićeva 38, is also good. Open Mon.-Fri. 7am-8:30pm, Sat. 7am-1pm.

American Express: Atlas, Trubarjeva cesta 50, 1000 Ljubljana (tel. 131 90 20). Holds mail; doesn't do traveler's checks. Open Mon.-Fri. 8am-4pm, Sat. 8am-noon.

Flights: The airport is in Brnik, 26km away (tel. (064) 22 27 00). Buses regularly run to the airport from the central bus station (500Slt).

Trains: The **station** (tel. 131 51 67) is on Trg OF. To: Budapest (2 per day, 10hr., 5370Slt), Munich (2 per day, 6hr., 8468Slt), Venice (2 per day, 6hr., 3000Slt), and Vienna (1 per day, 6hr., 6300Slt).

Buses: The **station** (tel. 133 61 36) neighbors the train station. To Budapest (3 per week, 8hr., 4350Slt) and Munich (1-3 most days, 6hr., 5250Slt).

Public Transportation: Buses run until midnight and cost 100Slt or one 65Slt token, available at post offices and newsstands. Passes are sold at **Ljubljanski Potniški Promet,** Celovška 160 (tel. 159 41 14).

Laundromat: Alba, Wolfova 12 (tel. 21 44 04). Open Mon.-Fri. 8am-6pm.

Emergencies: Fire: tel. 112. **Ambulance:** tel. 94.

Police: tel. 113.

Post Office: Slovenska 32. Open Mon.-Fri. 7am-8pm, Sat. 7am-1pm. *Poste Restante* at Pražakova 3 (tel. 31 45 84), 3 blocks south of the train station in a yellow building; enter in back. Open Mon.-Fri. 7am-8pm, Sat. 7am-1pm. **Postal Code:** 1106.

Telephone Code: 061.

ACCOMMODATIONS, CAMPING, AND FOOD

Don't expect Eastern European prices here. Room prices are often quoted in DM. Keep in mind that a nightly tourist tax is added to the bill (approx. 2DM). **TIC** (see **Practical Information,** above) finds private singles (DM20) and doubles (DM30-50).

Dijaški Dom Tabor, Vidovdanska 7 (tel./fax 32 10 60), from the stations, go south on Resljeva, then east on Komenskega. Athletic facilities make up for common bathrooms. DM26, with ISIC DM22. Breakfast included. Open June 25-Aug 25.
Hotel Tivoli, Tivolska 30 (tel. 131 43 59; fax 30 26 71). Well-kept and just renovated. Singles 5500Slt, with extra bed 6800Slt. Doubles 7720Slt. Breakfast included.
Dijaški Dom Ivana Cankarja, Poljanska 260-28 (tel. 133 52 74), south along Resljeva, then east on Poljanska from the stations. Close to civilization, but further from transportation. DM20 per person. Open June 25-Aug. 25.
Park Hotel, Tabor 9 (tel. 133 13 06; fax 32 13 52), near Dijaški Dom Tabor. Cheap Socialist look. Poorly maintained. Most rooms have showers and toilets. Singles 4930-6130Slt. Doubles 6260-7660Slt. 20% student discount. Breakfast included.
Autocamp Ježica, Dunajska 270 (tel. 168 39 13; fax 168 39 12). Take bus 6 from Slovenska northbound. Campers greeted by tall trees and green grass. Swimming and tennis. 920Slt per person plus 160Slt per night. Open year-round.

Facing the Old Town and the three bridges, turn right for bargain, river-front restaurants. Popular cafés line Mestni Trg and Stari Trg. **Vodnikov hram,** Vodnikov Trg 2, serves traditional fare amid stained wood and antiques. (*Golaž,* stew, 480Slt; *pasulj z meson,* beans with meat, 500Slt. Open Mon.-Fri. 5:30am-8pm, Sat. 5:30am-3pm.) At **Gostilna Pri Pavli,** at the corner of Stari and Levstikov Trg, the daily *menü kosilo* includes soup, salad, and an entree (800Slt; open Mon.-Fri. 9am-10pm, Sat. 9am-3pm). Vodnikov Trg, near the cathedral, hosts a **market** (open Mon.-Sat. until 2pm).

SIGHTS AND ENTERTAINMENT

Prešernov Trg, Ljubljana's main square, boasts the Neoclassical **Franciscan Church** and the **Trimostovje** (Triple Bridge). In the 1930s, architect Jože Plečnik transform the old bridge here into one of Ljubljana's most admired architectural marvels. To the left is the 1901 **Zmajski Most** (Dragon Bridge), adorned with many dragon decorations. Near the Triple Bridge, a fantastic fountain embellished with allegorical sculptures spurts in front of the **rotovž** (city hall). Free two-hour walking tours of many of the town's major sights begin here; guides speak English and Slovene (June-Sept. daily 5pm; Oct.-May Sun. 11am). Across the bridges, the **cathedral** has an impressive 15th-century Gothic Pietà, triple organ, and ubiquitous gold trim. From virtually anywhere in the Old Town, **Ljubljanski Grad** (Ljubljana Castle) is a short hike up the hill. The 12th-century castle may not stun, but the views of the city surely will.

Trg Francoske Revolucije (French Revolution Square) and its immediate surroundings were once occupied by Teutonic Knights; the neighborhood is still called **Križanke,** the Slovene translation of their title. In the square, the Knights built a monastery which now hosts musical, theatrical, and dance performances during the **Ljubljana International Summer Festival** (mid-July to late Sept.). Ljubljana's museums cluster around the Slovene parliament buildings near Trg Republike. The **Narodni Muzej** (National Museum), Muzejska 1, has exhibits on archaeology, ethnography, and history, while the **Moderna Galerija** (Museum of Modern Art) displays works of 20th-century Slovenian artists. To the left of Moderna Galerija stands the **Narodna Galerija** (National Gallery), Cankarjeva 20, with Slovene art from the Middle Ages to the present. (Most museums are open Tues.-Sat. 10am-6pm, Sun. 10am-1pm. 500Slt, students 300Slt.) Near the museums, **Tivoli park** offers some of the prettiest strolling grounds in the city.

Cankarjev Dom hosts the **Slovene Symphony Orchestra** and well-known jazz musicians from around the world, while **Tivoli Hall** is the venue for rock concerts. For more info grab a copy of the monthly *Where To?/Events* brochure, available at tourist offices. Cafés and bars line the streets of Old Town. The ever-popular **K-4,** Kersnikova 4, remodeled every year, features a different music program every night; Sunday is gay night (**Internet access** 9am-10pm; cover 200-1000Slt; open daily 10pm-4am). **Eldorado,** Nazorjeva 6, is a Mexican restaurant by day and flashy club by night (cover Fri.-Sat. 500Slt; open daily 11pm-4am). **Jazz Club Gaj,** Slovenska 36, alternates live music with jazz (open Mon.-Fri. 10am-2am, Sat.-Sun. 6pm-midnight).

■ Near Ljublijana: Postojna Caves

Like a poodle guarding the gates of heaven, the town of Postojna is a proud keeper of the natural wonder, the two-million-year-old **Postojnaska jama.** Follow the signs out of the center of town or ask anyone; the *jama* (cave), Jamska cesta 30 (tel. (061) 250 41), is 15 minutes northwest of the town. The tour (1½hr.) passes through only 20% of the 27km cave, but that's enough time to captivate most with plant-like columns, curtains of stone, gorges, rivers, and multi-colored stalactites. (Tours leave May-Sept. on the hr.; Oct.-April on even hours. 1960Slt, students 800Slt.) Bring a jacket to the chilly caves, or rent a cloak for 100Slt. You can reach the town of Postojna via **bus** (1hr., 650Slt) or **train** (1hr., 550Slt) from Ljubljana.

JULIJSKE ALPE (JULIAN ALPS)

The Southern Alps are not as high as their Austrian or Swiss counterparts, but they are no less beautiful. The mountains cover the northwest of Slovenia, peaking at 2864 meters on Mt. Triglav in the heart of the Triglav National Park. This mountain range is also the source of one of the region's largest rivers, the Sava.

Bled

Green alpine hills, snow-covered peaks in the distance, an opaque lake, and a stately castle make Bled one of the most striking destinations in all Slovenia. Having drawn visitors for centuries, the present-day town is a resort of international renown. A stroll around the lake's 6km perimeter takes about two hours. On the island in the middle, a **church,** largely rebuilt in the 17th century, retains a pre-Romanesque apse. To get there, you can rent a boat for 1000Slt per hour, travel by **gondola** (round-trip 900Slt), or even swim. High above the water perches the picture-perfect medieval **castle.** The admission price also grants entry into an excellent **museum,** housing art, furniture, and weaponry (open Feb.-Nov. daily 8am-7pm; Dec.-Jan. 8am-4pm; 300Slt). Numerous **paths** lead from the lake into the neighboring hills. The best one can be found by walking around the lake until the castle and the island are aligned—the path across the street takes about 45 minutes to climb.

For **tourist info** or to rent **mountain bikes** (1300Slt per day), visit **Kompas Bled,** Ljubljanska cesta 4 (tel. (064) 741 515); pick up a copy of the *Bled Tourist News* for the latest on hiking and skiing (open Mon.-Sat. 8am-8pm, Sun. 9:30am-6:30pm). **Trains** stop in Lesce, 5km from Bled on the Ljubljana-Salzburg-Munich line (1hr., 420Slt). From there, commuter buses (160Slt) run to Bled. You can travel directly to Bled by **bus** from Ljubljana (every hr., 1½hr., 800Slt). Accommodations prices are generally quoted in DM, but can be paid in Slt. Kompas Bled seeks out **private** singles (DM20-31) and doubles (DM34-52; tourist tax DM1.50 per night). Stays of less than three nights cost 30% more. Finding a room yourself may save money; look for *"sobe"* signs on Pre ernova cesta. The newly renovated **youth hostel,** Grajska cesta 17 (tel. 782 30), is a jewel up the hill of Grajska cesta from the bus station (DM24, with student ID DM20; meals DM6). **Camping Zaka-Bled,** Cesta Svobode 13 (tel. (064) 74 11 17), asks DM12 per person (open April-Oct.). **P-hram,** Cesta Svobode 19a, serves delicious Slovenian entrees for 650-900Slt (open daily 9am-9pm). Locals justly recommend **Gostilna pri Planincu,** Grajska cesta 8 (tel. (064) 74 16 13), visible from the bus station. This 1903 restaurant serves main dishes (900-1200Slt) until 10pm, pizzas (600-850Slt) until 10:30pm, and drinks until midnight. If all else fails, try **minimarket Špecerija,** Ljubljanska 4 (open Mon.-Sat. 7am-8pm, Sun. 9am-noon).

Lake Bohinj (Bohinjsko Jezero)

Surrounded by the Triglav National Park and windy peaks, Bohinjsko Jezero is Slovenia's center for alpine tourism. There's plentiful **hiking** around the area—trips from the shores of the lake range from the casual to the nearly impossible. **Triglav,** the highest point in Slovenia, is a challenging two-day journey from town. The 2865m ascent may not seem extraordinary, but on a clear day the sea is visible from the summit. The most popular and accessible destination is **Slap Savica** (Savica Waterfall). The hike is only 20 minutes from the trailhead; just follow the signs and the people. Trails throughout Slovenia are well-marked with a white circle inside a red circle; look for the blaze on trees and rocks. *An Alpine Guide* is free at the tourist office, but for more in-depth coverage, pick up maps of *Triglavski Narodni Park* and *Gorenjska* (around 1200Slt). **Śport Klub Alpinum,** Ribčev Laz 50 (tel. (064) 723 441; fax 723 446), near a church, has gear for biking and water sports (open daily 9am-7pm).

Five **trains** per day arrive in **Bohinjska Bistrica,** 6km from the water, from Ljubljana, most via Jesenice where you may have to change trains (2hr. direct). From there, take the bus from the post office to the lake. You can also reach the lake directly by **bus** from Bled (every hr., 1½hr., 380Slt) or Ljubljana (every hr., 3hr., 850Slt). Buses to "Bohinjsko Jezero" generally finish their routes in **Ribčev Laz;** the stop after the sign is most central. Buses marked "Bohinj Zlatorog" take you through Ribčev Laz to the village on the lake's west end, and a few buses climb all the way to the trailhead for the Savica waterfall. You should find anything you need on **Ribčev Laz** by the water's edge. The **tourist office,** Ribčev Laz 48 (tel. (064) 72 33 70; fax 72 33 30), has singles for DM13-19 and doubles for DM22-32, plus a DM2 tax, with higher rates for stays of under three days. Prices rise by 25% in late July and August (open July-Aug. daily 7am-9pm; Sept.-June Mon.-Sat. 8am-8pm, Sun. 9am-3pm). **Autokamp Zlatorog,** on the west side of the lake, has spaces for DM10 (May-June and Aug.-Sept.) and DM16 (July-Aug.). The smell of fish grilling entices visitors into **Restaurant Triglav,** Stara Fužina 23, for an affordable daily *menü* with main course, soup, and salad for 1100Slt. To find it, cross the bridge by the church and walk 10 minutes to the next village (open daily 11am-11pm). Stock up at the **Mercator supermarket** next to the tourist office (open Mon.-Sat. 7am-9pm, Sun. 7am-1pm).

Hey, Numbnutz!

The English word "numbnutz" makes no reference to the tactile abilities of certain organs, but rather is derived from the Slavic word *"nemec,"* which originally meant "stupid" or "mute." The Slavs used this word as a moniker for the Germans and their tongue, as the foreigners seemed unable to communicate in a sensible Slavic way, but rather spoke in gibberish: *nemecký.* The Germans took this rather personally, resulting in a whole series of wars in which much of Eastern Europe was invaded, occupied, otherwise slapped around, and, eventually, touristed by the Germans. As a result, that crazy cacophony is no longer so inscrutable, and *niemiecki* makes perfect sense to many modern-day Slavs.

Spain (España)

US$1	**= 156.53ptas (pesetas)**	**100ptas =**	**US$0.64**
CDN$1	**= 112.3ptas**	**100ptas =**	**CDN$0.89**
UK£1	**= 249.15ptas**	**100ptas =**	**UK£0.40**
IR£1	**= 226.16ptas**	**100ptas =**	**IR£0.44**
AUS$1	**= 116.83ptas**	**100ptas =**	**AUS$0.85**
NZ$1	**= 100.20ptas**	**100ptas =**	**NZ$0.99**
SAR1	**= 41.74ptas**	**100ptas =**	**SAR2.40**

Country Code: 34 **International Dialing Prefix: 07**

With a history that spans over 50 constitutions, an endless array of amorphous kingdoms controlled by Arabs, Visigoths, Germans, French, Celts, and indigenous peoples, Spain can be described only imprecisely—as a *mestizo* culture. Nine centuries of Roman rule left the empire's imprint in irrigation techniques, architecture, language, and its trademark use of olives and grapes. The Muslim invasion of 711 ushered in centuries of general religious toleration and the cultivation of classical Greek science and Eastern artistic traditions. Following the marriage of Fernando de Aragón and Isabel de Castilla and the fall of the Moorish Granada, Spain became a Catholic dominion. Soon after, Columbus, among others, was dispatched to the New World, as the country's Jews and Moors were cruelly expelled. Through savvy royal matchmaking, the Spanish Empire by the 16th century had become Europe's most powerful, encompassing modern-day Belgium and the Netherlands, as well as parts of Germany, Austria, Spain, and the Americas.

Eventual Napoleonic occupation and incompetent government inspired Spanish-American colonies to declare their independence and ushered in an era of nationalism and political unrest in Spain itself. Tensions arising from rapid industrialization in some areas and increasingly mounting nationalism were sparked by international depression, and erupted in the Spanish Civil War (1936-1939). Aided by Hitler and Mussolini, Francisco Franco emerged as the country's dictator and ruled until his death in 1975. Under King Juan Carlos I, Franco's hand-picked successor, Spain has become a modern, stable, and democratic constitutional monarchy.

Still scintillating with noble flamenco dancers, graceful bullfighters, and five different spoken languages Spain doubles its population of 40 million yearly with an influx of tourists. Much of the crunch comes in July and August. This fact—and Andalusia's searing heat—counsel against traveling in summer in southern Spain.

For more detailed coverage of Spain, grab *Let's Go: Spain & Portugal 1998.*

GETTING THERE AND GETTING AROUND

Travelers need legal **passports** or **visas** to enter and leave Spain. A passport allows U.S., Canadian, British, and New Zealand citizens to remain for 90 days. Australian and South African citizens need a visa to enter Spanish territory.

Airports in Madrid, Barcelona, and Málaga handle most of Spain's international air traffic. **Trains** chug over the border into France and connect with most major European cities. Spanish trains are clean, punctual, and reasonably priced, although they ignore many small towns. The centralized rail network radiates from Madrid. **RENFE,** the Spanish national rail system, offers many types of services with a corresponding variety of prices. AVE trains are the fastest but currently run only between Madrid and Seville (via Córdoba). *Talgos* are elegant low-slung trains that zip passengers in air-conditioned compartments. *Electros* are very comfortable and quick, but stop more often than *Talgos. Talgo 200s* are *Talgo* trains on AVE rails and offer some services out of Madrid. Talgo's long neglected cousin, *Intercity,* is cheaper, a bit dowdier, and operates some lines form Madrid. *Estrellas* are slow night trains with bunks. The commuter trains, *Cercanías,* radiate from cities to suburbs and nearby *pueblos.* Don't bother with the ludicrously slow *tranvía, semidirecto,* or *correo* trains.

Unfortunately, no official youth railpass exists, but a **Tarjeta Turística** (a.k.a. the Spanish Flexipass) permits unmitigated travel for three to 10 days (US$144-368). The RENFE calendar divides into **blue days** (almost every day) and **red days** (holidays and some Friday and Saturday afternoons). Red days up your fare by 10%. Buy tickets within 60 days of departure at RENFE travel offices, train stations, and authorized travel agencies. Reservations are strongly advised. The only other train company in Spain is **FEVE,** a conglomeration of private companies which, sluggishly but dependably, run trains between northern towns not served by RENFE.

More exhaustive, cheaper, sometimes even faster than the rail network, **buses** are the only public transportation to isolated areas. Spain has a multitude of private companies rather than one national bus line, which makes trip planning an ordeal. **Transmediterránea** ferries (Barcelona tel. (93) 443 25 32; fax 443 27 51) frequently shuttle back and forth between Tangier, Morocco and Málaga, Gibraltar, and Algeciras. They also service the Balearic Islands and the Canary Islands.

Rental cars cost considerably less than in other European countries, but you must be over 21, have had a driver's license for at least one year, and be prepared to pay for expensive fuel. Renting from abroad is significantly less expensive than doing so once you have arrived in Spain. **Hitchhiking** is supposedly slow and can be dangerous; it's reportedly best in the north, northwest, and along the Mediterranean coast.

ESSENTIALS

Most towns have a centrally located **Oficina de Turismo** (tourist office, fondly called *Turismo*) that distributes information on sights, lodgings, and events, plus a free map here and there. Although most don't book accommodations, many *Turismos* keep a list of approved establishments or can point you to a *casa particular* (private room). **Viajes TIVE,** the national chain of student travel agencies, dispenses transportation info and peddles discount travel tickets, ISICs, and HI cards.

Spanish workers get started around 9am, close down the shop at 1:30 or 2pm for a loooong lunch, and go back around 4:30 or 5pm until 8pm. On Saturday, shops are usually open only in the morning, and Sunday is a day of rest for everyone except a few indispensables (tourist offices are not considered indispensable). **Banking** hours in Spain are Monday through Friday 9am to 2pm; from October 1 to May 31, banks are also open Saturday 9am to 1pm. Some banks are open in the afternoon as well. Banks charge a minimum commission for currency exchange. **Banco Central Hispano,** marked by blue signs with a yellow seashell symbol, do not charge commission and offer the best rates for exchange.

Spain levies a **Value-Added Tax** (VAT, in Spain IVA) on all goods and services. The standard rate is 7%. Foreigners (non-EU) who have stayed in the EU less than 180 days can claim back the VAT paid on purchases which exceed 15ptas at the airport (ask shops to supply you with a tax return form). The tax on accommodations and other "services" is not refundable. Stores, restaurants, and lodgings include the IVA in their prices, unless otherwise noted. Most restaurants add a service charge to your bill. It's customary to round off the bill and leave the change as a **tip.** You should generally tip 5-10% more if the service is exceptional. Porters can be tipped 100-150ptas per bag, taxi drivers 10% of the meter fare (if they're nice).

SPAIN

The northwest is rightly called "wet" or "green" Spain, with a humid, temperate climate open to the sea and a lush, often thickly wooded landscape resembling the mountain areas of the south and east, where ranges are high enough to catch moisture. The interior's climate resembles that of Central Europe—long winters and, in the lowlands, torrid summers. The east and south coasts enjoy a Mediterranean climate. The northeast coast can be humid, but the southwest is the most sweltering, especially the Guadalquivir river basin (including Seville and Córdoba).

Spanish men sometimes dole out pickup lines and even rude gestures toward women. It is extremely rare that this should be more than simply annoying, but women should memorize the Spanish **emergency** phone number, 091 or 092. For additional travel tips, see **Women Travelers,** p. 33.

Holidays in Spain include: New Year's Day, Epiphany (Jan. 6), *Semana Santa* (April 6-12), May Day (May 1), Corpus Christi (June 11), July 25, Aug. 15, Oct. 12, Nov. 1, Dec. 6, Dec. 8, and Christmas. Some of these religious celebrations are no longer legal holidays, but business slows anyway and sometimes stops altogether. *Semana Santa* (Holy Week), the week before Easter, sees much celebration, especially in Andalusia. Cities and towns strive to outdo one another with ardent displays of adoration. Bullfights are featured in most festivals from May to October.

Communication An airmail letter *(por avión)* takes four to seven business days to reach the U.S. and Canada; service is faster to the U.K. and Ireland, slower to Australia and New Zealand. Standard postage is 87ptas. The Spanish version of *Poste Restante* is **Lista de Correos.** Most post offices also have fax service. Local calls cost 20ptas; an international connection is 500ptas. Phone cards, sold in kiosks and *estancos* in 1000 and 2000ptas denominations, are more convenient than feeding coins into a payphone. Collect calls *(cobro revertido)* are billed according to pricier person-to-person *(persona a persona)* rates, but may still be cheaper than calls from hotels. Useful numbers include the **local operator,** 009; **directory assistance,** 003; **national police,** 091; and local **police emergency,** 092. For **AT&T Direct,** dial 900 99 00 11; **MCI WorldPhone,** 900 99 00 14; **Sprint Access,** 900 99 00 13; **Canada Direct,** 900 99 00 15; **BT Direct,** 900 99 00 44; and **NZ Direct,** 900 99 00 64. When dialing a Spanish town from outside of Spain, drop the "9" from the **city code.**

There are five **languages** in Spain, plus plenty of dialects, such as the Mallorquín of the Balearic Islands. Catalan is the language of choice in Catalonia, Valencian in Valencia. The non-Indo-European Basque (Euskera) language is spoken in north central Spain, and Galician (related to Portuguese) is spoken in the once-Celtic northwest, though both are minority languages even in their own dominions. Spanish (Castilian, or *castellano*) is spoken everywhere. In Spanish, "ll" is pronounced like the English "y," "j" and soft "g" (before "e" or "i") like the English "h," and "z" and soft "c" like "th." "H" is not pronounced. The following chart is in Castilian:

Yes/no	*Sí/no*	see/no
Hello	*Hola*	OH-la
Please	*Por favor*	pohr fah-VOHR
Thank you	*Gracias*	GRAH-see-as
Excuse me	*Con permiso*	con pehr-MEE-so
Do you speak English?	*¿Habla usted inglés?*	AH-blah oos-TED in-GLEHS
I don't understand.	*No entiendo*	no en-tee-EN-doh
I don't speak Spanish.	*No hablo español*	no AH-bloh es-pahn-YOL
Where is...?	*¿Dónde está...?*	DOHN-deh es-TAH
How much does this cost?	*¿Cuánto cuesta?*	KWAHN-toh KWES-tah
I'd like...	*Quisiera...*	kee-see-EHR-ah
I would like a room.	*Quisiera un cuarto*	kee-see-EHR-ah oon KWAHR-toh
Help!	*¡Socorro!*	soh-KOHR-roh

Accommodations and Camping **REAJ,** the Spanish Hostelling International (HI) affiliate, runs 165 youth hostels year-round. **HI cards** are required and are available for 1800ptas at youth hostels and from Spain's main national youth/travel company, TIVE. Reservations can be made through the central REAJ office (tel. (91) 347 76 29 or 347 76 30; fax 401 81 60) or by direct calls to specific hostels.

Accommodations have many an alias in Spain; each name indicates a specific type of establishment. Cheapest and barest are *hospedajes* and *casas de huéspedes.* Higher in quality are *pensiones* and *fondas,* then *hostales,* then *hostal-residencias;* all three levels offer similar amenities and are budget travel staples. The highest priced accommodations are *hoteles,* often far beyond the reach of budget travelers.

Campgrounds are government-regulated and on a three-class system, rated and priced by the quality of amenities. Tourist offices stock the *Guía de Campings,* a fat guide to all official campgrounds in Spain. Alternate types of accommodations include *casas particulares* (private residences), *casas rurales* (rural cottages), *casas rústicas* (farmhouses), *refugios* (rustic huts in the mountains), *colegios mayores* (state university student dorms), and monasteries or convents.

Food and Drink Spaniards start their day with a breakfast of coffee or hot chocolate and *bollos* (rolls) or *churros* (lightly fried fritters). Dinner ("lunch" to Americans) is served between 2 and 3pm, and traditionally consists of several courses. Supper at home is light and eaten around 8pm. Supper out—also a light meal—begins later, usually around 10pm.

Some restaurants are "open" from 8am until 1 or 2am, but most only serve meals from 1 or 2 to 4pm and from 8pm until midnight. Each city's tourist office rates its restaurants with a row of forks, five forks indicating luxury. *Cafeterías* are rated by a row of up to three cups. Prices for a full meal start at about 800ptas in the cheapest bar-restaurants. Many places offer *platos combinados* (combination platter—includes a main course and side dishes, plus bread—500-1000ptas) or a *menú del día* (two or three dishes, bread, beverage, and dessert—800-1500ptas).

Tasty *tapas* are ever so conducive to convivial good spirits. A *tasca,* or *taberna,* serves *tapas* at a counter; *mesones* bring them to the table. *Pinchos* are the north's equivalent of *tapas. Raciones* may equal an entree in size. *Bocadillos* are *tapas* served as a sandwich on a hunk of thick bread—often a viable substitute for lunch. Your fork may find its way into *champiñones al ajillo* (mushrooms in garlic sauce), *jamón serrano* (smoked ham), *atún* or *bonito* (tuna), *calamares fritos* (fried squid), *chorizo* (spicy sausage), *gambas* (shrimp), *ternera* (veal), and *lomo* (pork).

The most sophisticated and varied cuisines on the peninsula were developed in the Basque Country, Navarre, Catalonia, and Galicia. Other regions make a good showing, though—Valencia claims *paella* (steamed saffron rice with chicken stock and an assortment of seafood), Andalusia presides over *gazpacho* (cold tomato-based soup), and Castile cooks a mean *tortilla de patata* (potato omelette).

Food is almost always washed down with alcohol, whether a glass of wine (*vino blanco* is white, *tinto* is red) or beer *(cerveza)*. Beer is served in bottles or on draft. Aguila, Estrella, and San Miguel are fine national brands; Volldamm (Catalonia) and Alhambra (Andalusia) are fine regional brews. Rioja is a world-renowned grape-growing region, with especially good red wines; there are innumerable fine regional wines. *Sangría* is made of red wine, sugar, brandy, seltzer, and fruit. Another native beverage is *jerez* (sherry), from the city of the same name.

Madrid

The stately grandeur of Old Madrid's royal palaces and majestic museums rapidly dissipates as one enters the smaller avenues and encounters the libertarian *joie-de-vivre* of its transplanted citizens. After decades of totalitarian repression under Franco, Madrid's youth burst out laughing and crying in the 1980s during an era known as *la Movida* ("Shift" or "Movement"), exemplified by filmmaker Pedro Almodóvar's cinematic models of frenetic lives and passionate colors. Madrid's cultural renaissance has been led by its 200,000-strong student population, who have taken over the streets, shed the decorous reserve of their predecessors, and captured the present. Too young to recall the Franco years, Madrid's chosen generation seems neither cognizant of their city's historic landmarks nor preoccupied with the future, despite unemployment rates of over thirty percent. Bright lights and a perpetual stream of automobile and pedestrian traffic blur the distinction between 4pm and 4am, and infinitely energized *madrileños* crowd bars and discos until dawn. Unlike much of the world, Madrid still works to live, not the reverse.

ORIENTATION AND PRACTICAL INFORMATION

The "Kilometro 0" marker in front of the police station signals the city's epicenter at **Puerta del Sol.** Sol is *the* transportation hub of the city: below ground, three Metro lines (blue 1, red 2, yellow 3) converge here and transport people to within walking distance of any point in the city; above ground, buses and taxis swarm.

Madrid is divided into distinct neighborhoods. **Old Madrid,** the nucleus of neighborhoods clustered around Sol, is bordered by the **Palacio Real** to the west, **Gran Vía** to the north, the **Museo del Prado** to the east, and fades away in the south around **Atocha** (the older train station). Within this nucleus, to the west of Sol, lie the two royal Madrids: red brick Madrid de los Austrias around **Plaza de la Villa** and **Plaza Mayor,** and granite Madrid de los Borbones around **Ópera.** Both neighborhoods feature churches and historical houses; *hostales* mingle with the monuments. Continuing clockwise, the segment north of Sol is a shopper's paradise—a web of pedestrian-only streets leads past **El Corte Inglés** to Gran Vía (bright lights and big movie theaters). East from Sol, the majestic **Calle de Alcalá** leads out of Old Madrid toward broader avenues, passing by **Cibeles** and the **Parque del Retiro.** Alcalá borders the north end of **Huertas,** Madrid's erstwhile literary district, crowded with some of the best-value hostels, bars, and cafés and centered on **Plaza Santa Ana.** Fewer tourists venture south into the area around **La Latina** and **Tirso de Molina** Metro stops.

The newer parts of Madrid that are of interest to travelers lie mainly to the east and north of the old city. In the northwest, Gran Vía runs up to **Plaza de España,** its tall Torre de Madrid the pride of 50s Spain. From the Plaza, Gran Vía turns into **Calle de la Princesa,** a bustling shopping avenue leading to **Moncloa** and **Argüelles,** two upscale student neighborhoods near the **Ciudad Universitaria.** East of Argüelles, and connected to Gran Vía by **Calle de Fuencarral,** are the two club- and bar-ridden districts of **Malasaña** and **Bilbao. Chueca,** basically Bilbao in black and chains, is the

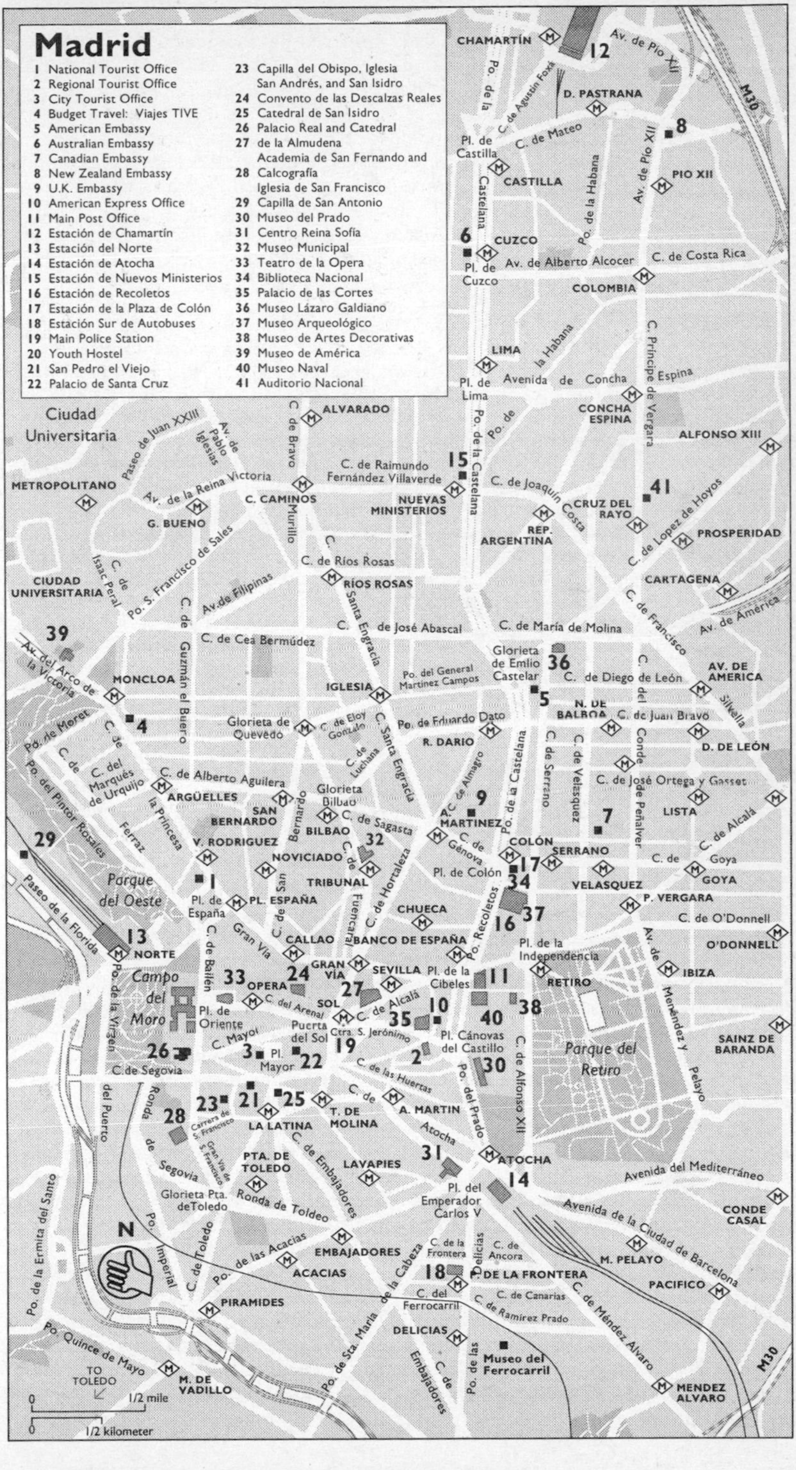
Madrid
1 National Tourist Office
2 Regional Tourist Office
3 City Tourist Office
4 Budget Travel: Viajes TIVE
5 American Embassy
6 Australian Embassy
7 Canadian Embassy
8 New Zealand Embassy
9 U.K. Embassy
10 American Express Office
11 Main Post Office
12 Estación de Chamartín
13 Estación del Norte
14 Estación de Atocha
15 Estación de Nuevos Ministerios
16 Estación de Recoletos
17 Estación de la Plaza de Colón
18 Estación Sur de Autobuses
19 Main Police Station
20 Youth Hostel
21 San Pedro el Viejo
22 Palacio de Santa Cruz
23 Capilla del Obispo, Iglesia
San Andrés, and San Isidro
24 Convento de las Descalzas Reales
25 Catedral de San Isidro
26 Palacio Real and Catedral
27 de la Almudena
Academia de San Fernando and
28 Calcografía
Iglesia de San Francisco
29 Capilla de San Antonio
30 Museo del Prado
31 Centro Reina Sofía
32 Museo Municipal
33 Teatro de la Opera
34 Biblioteca Nacional
35 Palacio de las Cortes
36 Museo Lázaro Galdiano
37 Museo Arqueológico
38 Museo de Artes Decorativas
39 Museo de América
40 Museo Naval
41 Auditorio Nacional
CHAMARTÍN
Av. de Pio XII
D. PASTRANA
M30
C. de Mateo
Pl. de Castilla
CASTILLA
PIO XII
Po. de la Habana
Po. de la Castellana
CUZCO
Pl. de Cuzco
Av. de Alberto Alcocer
C. de Costa Rica
COLOMBIA
LIMA
Pl. de Lima
Avenida de Concha Espina
C. Principe de Vergara
CONCHA ESPINA
ALFONSO XIII
Ciudad Universitaria
ALVARADO
C. de Bravo Murillo
C. de Raimundo Fernández Villaverde
NUEVAS MINISTERIOS
Paseo de Juan XXIII
Av. de Pablo Iglesias
METROPOLITANO
Av. de la Reina Victoria
C. CAMINOS
G. BUENO
C. de Joaquín Costa
CRUZ DEL RAYO
REP. ARGENTINA
C. de Lopez de Hoyos
PROSPERIDAD
Po. S. Francisco de Sales
C. de Isaac Peral
CIUDAD UNIVERSITARIA
Av. de Filipinas
C. de Ríos Rosas
RÍOS ROSAS
CARTAGENA
Av. de América
C. de José Abascal
C. de María de Molina
C. de Cea Bermúdez
Santa Engracia
C. de Francisco Silvela
Av. del Arco de la Victoria
MONCLOA
Glorieta de Emilio Castelar
C. de Diego de León
AV. DE AMERICA
Po. del General Martinez Campos
IGLESIA
C. de Guzmán el Bueno
Glorieta de Quevedo
C. de Eloy Gonzalo
Po. de Eduardo Dato
N. DE BALBOA
C. de Juan Bravo
Po. de Moret
R. DARIO
D. DE LEÓN
C. de Luchana
C. de Serrano
C. de Velasquez
C. de José Ortega y Gasset
C. del Marqués de Urquijo
C. de Alberto Aguilera
Glorieta Bilbao
C. de Almagro
ARGÜELLES
SAN BERNARDO
Po. del Pintor Rosales
la Princesa
Ferraz
V. RODRIGUEZ
BILBAO
C. de Sagasta
MARTINEZ
C. de Génova
Conde de Peñalver
LISTA
C. de Alcalá
NOVICIADO
TRIBUNAL
C. de Hortaleza
COLÓN
SERRANO
C. de Goya
GOYA
Pl. de Colón
VELASQUEZ
Parque del Oeste
Pl. de España
PL. ESPAÑA
C. de San Bernardo
C. de Fuencarral
CHUECA
P. VERGARA
C. de O'Donnell
Paseo de la Florida
Gran Via
Po. Recoletos
Pl. de la Independencia
O'DONNELL
NORTE
CALLAO
BANCO DE ESPAÑA
C. de Bailén
Campo del Moro
OPERA
GRAN VIA
SEVILLA
Pl. de la Cibeles
RETIRO
IBIZA
Po. de la Virgen del Puerto
C. del Arenal
SOL
Av. de Menéndez y Pelayo
Pl. de Oriente
C. Mayor
Puerta del Sol
Ctra. S. Jerónimo
Pl. Cánovas del Castillo
SAINZ DE BARANDA
Parque del Retiro
Pl. Mayor
C. de Alfonso XII
C.de Segovia
C. de las Huertas
Po. del Prado
Ronda de Segovia
Carrera de S. Francisco
Gran Via de S. Francisco
LA LATINA
T. DE MOLINA
A. MARTIN
C. de Atocha
C. de Embajadores
ATOCHA
PTA. DE TOLEDO
LAVAPIES
Avenida del Mediterráneo
Glorieta Pta. deToledo
Ronda de Toldeo
Pl. del Emperador Carlos V
Po. de la Ermita del Santo
Avenida de la Ciudad de Barcelona
CONDE CASAL
N
Po. Imperial
C. de Toledo
Po. de las Acacias
EMBAJADORES
C. de la Frontera
C. de Ancora
M. PELAYO
ACACIAS
Po. de las Delicias
P. DE LA FRONTERA
PACIFICO
PIRAMIDES
C. del Ferrocarril
C. de Canarias
C. de Ramírez Prado
C. de Méndez Alvaro
Po. de Sta. María de la Cabeza
DELICIAS
Po. Quince de Mayo
Museo del Ferrocarril
TO TOLEDO
M. DE VADILLO
MENDEZ ALVARO
1/2 mile
1/2 kilometer

next neighborhood to the east. Chueca is bordered by the great north-south thoroughfare **Paseo de la Castellana-Paseo de Recoletos-Paseo del Prado,** which runs from Atocha in the south to **Plaza Castilla** in the north, passing the Prado, the fountains at Cibeles and **Colón,** and the skyscrapers past Colón. East of Po. Castellana, the **Barrio de Salamanca** offers posh shopping for the heavy of wallet.

The *Plano de Madrid,* free at tourist offices, is useful but index-less. For a comprehensive **map,** get the *Almax* at a newsstand (375ptas). Madrid is extremely safe compared to other major European cities, but the Puerta del Sol, Pl. 2 de Mayo in Malasaña, Pl. de Chueca, and Pl. España are particularly intimidating late at night. Generally, avoid the parks and quiet residential areas after dark. Watch out for thieves and con artists in the Metro and on crowded city streets.

Tourist Offices: Municipal, Pl. Mayor, 3 (tel. 366 54 77 or 588 16 36; fax 366 54 77). M: Sol. Open Mon.-Fri. 10am-8pm, Sat. 10am-2pm. **Oficinas de Información,** C. Princesa, 1 (tel. 541 23 25), off Pl. España. M: Pl. España. **Regional/Provincial Office of the Comunidad de Madrid,** Mercado Pta. de Toledo, Ronda de Toledo 1, stand #3134 (tel. 364 18 76). M: Pta. de Toledo. Open Mon.-Fri. 9am-7pm, Sat. 9:30am-1:30pm. A **second office** is at C. Duque Medinaceli, 2 (tel. 429 49 51, 429 31 71, or 429 37 05), just off Pl. Cortes. M: Sol. Open Mon.-Fri. 9am-7pm, Sat. 9am-1pm. Other offices at **Estación Chamartín** (tel. 315 99 76) and the **airport** (tel. 305 86 56). Both open Mon.-Fri. 8am-8pm, Sat. 9am-1pm.

Embassies: Australia, Po. Castellana, 143 (tel. 579 04 28; fax 570 02 04). M: Cuzco. **Canada,** C. Núñez de Balboa, 35 (tel. 431 43 00; fax 577 98 11; http://info.ic.gc.ca/Tourism). M: Velázquez. **New Zealand,** Pl. Lealtad, 2 (tel. 523 02 26; fax 523 01 71). M: Banco de España. **South Africa,** C. Claudio Coello, 91, 6th fl. (tel. 435 66 88; fax 577 74 14). **U.K.,** C. Fernando el Santo, 16 (tel. 319 02 00; fax 308 10 33). M: Colón. **U.S.,** C. Serrano, 75 (tel. 587 22 00; fax 587 23 03). M: Rubén Darío. Embassies open Mon.-Fri.; call for hours.

Currency Exchange: Banco Central Hispano charges no commission on traveler's checks and cash and offers the best rates on AmEx traveler's checks. Open in summer Mon.-Fri. 8:30am-2:30pm; off-season Mon.-Thurs. 8:30am-4:30pm, Fri.-Sat. 8:30am-1pm. **ATMs** are plentiful; use only the first 4 digits of your PIN code.

American Express: Pl. Cortes, 2 (tel. 322 55 00 or 572 03 03 for main info). M: Sevilla. Currency exchange. 1% cash and 2% traveler's check commission. No commission on AmEx traveler's checks. No min. charge. Mail held for 30 days and money wired. Open Mon.-Fri. 9am-5:30pm, Sat. 9am-noon.

Flights: Aeropuerto Internacional de Barajas, 15km northeast of Madrid. **Bus** to Pl. Colón (every 15min., 370ptas). **Iberia,** C. Goya, 29 (tel. 587 81 09), is a major carrier. For reservations, call (900) 400 500 (24hr.).

Trains: For general info, call 328 90 20. Madrid has two *Largo Recorrido* (long distance) and two intermediate stations. **Estación Chamartín,** Agustín de Foxá (tel. 328 90 20). M: Chamartín. Bus 5 departs from just beyond the lockers and runs to and from Sol (45min.). Chamartín serves Spain, Lisbon, and Paris. Ticket windows open daily 8:30am-10:30pm. The other long-distance station is **Estación Atocha.** M: Atocha-Renfe. Trains head to the provinces Castilla La Mancha, Andalusia, and Valencia, as well as Salamanca, El Escorial, Portugal, and other areas. Also AVE (high-speed train) service to Seville via Córdoba (tel. 534 05 05). Ticket windows open daily 6:30am-11:30pm. The **RENFE Main Office,** C. Alcalá, 44, where Gran Vía hits C. Alcalá, has schedules, national and international tickets, and plenty of info. M: Banco de España. Open Mon.-Fri. 9:30am-8pm.

Buses: Numerous private companies serve Madrid, each with its own station, but buses usually pass through the large **Estación Sur de Autobuses,** C. Méndez Alvaro, s/n (tel. 468 42 00 or 468 45 11). Companies include: **Estación Auto Res,** Pl. Conde de Casal, 6 (tel. 551 72 00). M: Conde de Casal. To Salamanca (3¼hr., 1690ptas) and Cuenca (2½hr., 1300ptas). **Estación Empresa Larrea,** P. Florida, 11 (tel. 530 48 00). M: Cercedilla. To Ávila (2hr., 910ptas).

Luggage Storage: Estaciones de Chamartín and **Atocha.** Lockers 300-600ptas per day. Open daily 6:30am-12:30pm. **Estación Sur de Autobuses.** 800ptas.

Public Transportation: The **Metro** is clean and efficient. Rides cost 130ptas; a 10-ride ticket runs 660ptas. Trains operate roughly 6am-1:30am. The free *Plano del Metro* deciphers train schedules; wall maps abound in the stations. The more unwieldy *Plano de Transportes* (200ptas) and the free *Madrid en autobus* elucidate the city's **bus** system (bus fare 130ptas; 10-ride *bonobus* pass 660ptas). Buses run daily 6am-midnight. Night buses travel from Sol and Pl. Cibeles as far as the outskirts every 30min. from midnight to 3am, every hr. from 3 to 6am. Night buses (numbered with N) are explained in a special section of the *Plano*. There are N stops all along the marked routes, not just in Sol and Pl. Cibeles. **Information:** Empresa Municipal de Transportes (tel. 401 99 00; Spanish only).

Hitchhiking: Neither popular nor safe. Hitchhiking is legal only on minor routes; the Guardia Civil de Tráfico picks up would-be highway hitchers and deposits them at nearby towns or on a bus. Try the message boards at HI hostels.

Taxi: (tel. 445 90 08 or 447 51 80). Base fare is 170ptas, plus 50-75ptas per km and supplements. From city center to airport about 2500ptas.

Car Rental: Don't do it unless you're planning to zoom out of Madrid. **Autos Viaducto:** C. Segovia, 26 (tel. 548 48 48); C. Martín de los Heros, 23 (tel. 541 55 41); and Av. Mediterráneo, 4 (tel. 433 12 33 or 552 10 44). Base price 6400ptas per day. First 100km free, then 15ptas per km. Open Mon.-Fri. 9am-1pm and 4-7:30pm.

Bookstores: FNAC, C. Preciados, 28 (tel. 595 62 00). M: Callao. Open Mon.-Sat. 10am-10pm. **Librería Turner,** C. Genova, 3 (tel. 319 09 26), sells English-language books. M: Alonzo Martínez. Open Mon.-Fri. 10am-8pm, Sat. 10am-2pm.

Laundromat: Lavandería Donoso Cortés, C. Donoso Cortés, 17 (tel. 446 96 90). M: Quevedo. Self-service wash 600ptas. Open Mon.-Fri. 9am-2pm and 3:30-7:45pm, Sat. 9am-1:30pm. **Lavomatique,** C. León at C. Cervantes (tel. 448 40 02). M: Antón Martín. Self-service wash 600ptas. Open daily 9am-2pm and 4:30-8pm.

Gay and Lesbian Services: Colectivo de Gais y Lesbianas de Madrid (COGAM), C. Fuencarral, 37 (tel./fax 523 00 70). M: Gran Vía. Wide range of services and activities. Reception open Mon.-Fri. 5-9pm; library open 7-9pm. **GAI-INFORM** (tel. 523 00 70), provides information in Spanish about gay associations, leisure-time activities, and health issues. Line staffed daily 5-9pm.

Crisis Lines: Rape Hotline: tel. 574 01 10. **AIDS Information:** tel. 445 23 28; Mon.-Fri. 9am-2pm. **English-Language Help:** tel. 559 13 93, daily 7-11pm.

Medical Assistance: Anglo-American Medical Unit, Conde de Aranda, 1, 1st fl. (tel. 435 18 23), to the left. M: Retiro. Not an emergency clinic.

Emergency: tel. 091 or 092. **Ambulance:** tel. 061.

Police: C. Luna, 29 (tel. 521 12 36). M: Callao.

Post Office: Palacio de Tele-Comunicaciones, Pl. Cibeles (tel. 396 24 43). M: Banco de España. Information open Mon.-Fri. 8am-10pm or call 537 64 94. Open for stamps and certified mail Mon.-Fri. 8am-10pm, Sat. 8:30am-8:30pm, Sun. 9:30am-1:30pm; for *Lista de Correos* Mon.-Fri. 8am-9:30pm, Sat. 8:30am-2pm. English and French spoken at information desk. **Postal Code:** 28070.

Telephones: Telefónica, Gran Vía, 30, at C. Valverde. M: Gran Vía. **Telephone Code:** 91.

ACCOMMODATIONS AND CAMPING

Demand for rooms rises dramatically in summer, so make reservations. Expect to pay 2400ptas per person for a typical *hostal* room, slightly less for a bed in a *pensión*. The centrally located **Puerta del Sol** zone crawls with tourists and hostels. The **Gran Vía** has *hostales* in a slightly louder and rougher part of town, while **Calle de Fuencarral** is less expensive and closer to the nightlife of Malasaña and Chueca. For 300ptas, **Viajes Brújula,** Torre de Madrid, 6th fl., #14 (tel. 559 97 04 or 559 97 05; fax 548 46 24; M: Pl. España), will book you a room, but you must go in person to specify desired prices and locations. (Youth hostels excluded. English spoken. Open Mon.-Fri. 9am-2pm and 4:30-7pm, Sat. 9am-2pm.) **Branch offices** are located at Estación Atocha at the AVE terminal (tel. 539 11 73; open daily 8am-10pm); Estación Chamartín (tel. 315 78 94; open daily 7:15am-11:30pm); and the airport bus terminal in Pl. Colón (tel. 575 96 80; open daily 8am-10pm).

Albergue Juvenil Santa Cruz de Marcenado (HI), C. Santa Cruz de Marcenado, 28 (tel. 547 45 32; fax 548 11 96). M: Argüelles. Exit Metro at C. Alberto Aguilera, and walk down C. Alberto Aguilera away from C. Princesa for a block. Turn right on C. Serrano de Jóver and take the first left on C. Santa Cruz de Marcenado. Mem-

SPAIN

bers only, or buy an HI card (1800 ptas). Recently renovated facilities. 3-day max. stay. Reception open daily 9am-9:30pm. Strict curfew 1:30am, lights out at 2:30am. 950ptas, over 26 1300ptas. Breakfast included. Reserve in writing 15 days in advance, or arrive early. If you can't get a bed at Santa Cruz, **Hostal-Residencia La Montaña,** C. Juan Álvarez Mendizábal, 44, 4th fl. (tel. 547 10 88), and the 4 other *pensiones* in the same building are a short jaunt away. From the HI, cross the busy C. Princesa, turn left, go right on C. Rey Fancisco, then left on C. J. A. Mendizábal. Singles 1800-2000ptas. Doubles 3400-3700ptas. Triples 5800ptas.

Hostal-Residencia Paz, C. Flora, 4, 1st and 2nd fl. (tel. 547 30 47). M: Ópera. On a quiet street parallel to C. Arenal, off C. Donados or C. Hileras. Firm beds in 10 recently renovated, brilliant rooms. Singles 2300ptas. Doubles 3500-4100ptas. Triples 5100ptas. Laundry 1000ptas. Reservations encouraged. MC, V.

La Pensión Luz, C. Fuentes, 10, 3rd fl. (tel. 542 07 59). M: Sol. Sunny, inviting rooms in an elegant old building off C. Arenal. The bathrooms sparkle so much you won't mind sharing. Singles 2500ptas. Doubles 3700ptas, made into triples for 5300ptas.

Hostal Cruz-Sol, Pl. Santa Cruz, 6, 3rd fl. (tel. 532 71 97). M: Sol. Pleasant, ample rooms, many of which overlook the plaza. Singles 2000ptas. Doubles 2500-4000ptas. Triples 3000-5000ptas. Showers 200ptas per person, free for singles.

Hostal R. Rodríguez, C. Nuñez de Arce, 9, 3rd fl. (tel. 522 44 31), off Pl. Santa Ana. M: Sol. Alluring rooms. Shared baths only. English spoken. Reception open 24hr. Singles 2300ptas. Doubles 3300ptas. Triples 4300ptas.

Hostal Aguilar, C. San Jerónimo, 32, 2nd fl. (tel. 429 59 26). M: Sol. More than 50 modern rooms, all with shower. Singles 3200-3500ptas. Doubles 4400-5500ptas. Quads with bath 8000ptas. 1500ptas more for each extra person. MC, V.

Hostal Lauria, Gran Vía, 50, 5th fl. (tel./fax 547 35 49). M: Callao. Ultra-comfortable rooms have oriental rugs and random artwork. Use of kitchen and refrigerator. English spoken. All rooms with shower. Singles 3700ptas. Doubles 4500-4700ptas. Triples 6000ptas. Laundry 1200ptas. MC, V.

Hostal Margarita, Gran Vía, 50, 4th fl. (tel. 541 91 82; fax 541 91 88). M: Callao. Stucco walls, light wood shutters and baby-blue beds create an airy feel. Rooms are tastefully sparse, with big windows, pretty little bathrooms, and TVs. Show the owner your *Let's Go.* Singles 3500-3800ptas. Doubles 5000ptas. Triples 6500ptas.

Hostal Palacios and Hostal Ribadavia, C. Fuencarral, 25, 1st-3rd fl. (tel. 531 10 58 or 531 48 47). M: Gran Vía. Both *hostales* are run by the same cheerful family. **Ribadavia** (3rd fl.) has pleasant, bright rooms with old furniture. **Palacios** (1st and 2nd fl.) flaunts brand-new rooms, all with baths. Singles 2400-2800ptas. Doubles 3800ptas-4400ptas. Triples 6400ptas. Quads 7500ptas.

Hostal Medieval, C. Fuencarral, 46, 2nd fl. (tel. 522 25 49), at C. Augusto Figueroa. M: Tribunal. Don't think Dark Ages, think pink. Singles 3000ptas. Doubles 4000ptas-5000ptas. Triples 6000ptas.

Hostal-Residencia Abril, C. Fuencarral, 39, 4th fl. (tel. 531 53 38). M: Tribunal or Gran Vía. Nice and simple—light wood, low prices, and random baby posters. Singles 1900ptas-2500ptas. Doubles 2900-3400ptas. Triples 3100-4300ptas.

Hostal Greco, C. las Infantas, 3, 2nd fl. (tel. 522 46 32 or 522 46 31; fax 523 23 61). M: Gran Vía or Chueca. You get lots of bang for your buck at this Art Nouveau *hostal.* Enormous rooms with large bathrooms, telephones, TVs, and personal safes (100ptas). Singles 3400ptas. Doubles 5600ptas. Triples 7500ptas. MC, V.

Tourist offices can provide details about the 13 or so **campsites** within 50km of Madrid. For further info, contact the Consejería de Educación de Juventud, C. Fernando el Católico (tel. 522 29 41 or 521 44 27). **Camping Osuna** (tel. 741 05 10; fax 320 63 65) is located on Av. Logroño Vicálvaro (8km). Take the Metro to Canillejas, cross the pedestrian overpass, walk through the parking lot, and turn right along the freeway (600ptas per person, per tent, and per car). **Camping Alpha** (tel. 695 80 69) hides on a shady site 12.4km down Ctra. de Andalucía in Getafe. From the M: Legazpi station take bus 447, which stops next to the Nissan dealership (every 30min. until 10pm, 10min). Ask the driver to let you off at the pedestrian overpass near the Amper building. Cross the bridge and walk 1.5km back toward Madrid along the highway (590ptas per person, 640ptas per tent). Both campgrounds have phones, showers, laundry, currency exchange, medical care, a bar, and a restaurant.

FOOD

In Madrid, it's not hard to fork it down without forking over too much; you can't walk a block without tripping over at least five *cafeterías,* where a sandwich, coffee, and dessert sell for around 600ptas. **Chueca** is the none-too-closeted gay/glam district, where scenesters crowd the chic gourmet joints and stalk the streets in platform shoes. **Calles Echegaray, Ventura de la Vega,** and **Manuel Fernández González** are its budget boulevards. **Argüelles** is full of moderately priced eateries.

In the following listings and in Madrid generally, a *restaurante* is open from 1 to 4pm and 8pm to midnight unless otherwise noted. Establishments such as *mesones, cafeterías, bares, cafés, terrazas,* and *tabernas* include a bar and serve drinks and *tapas* all day until midnight. Some close on Sundays. Keep in mind the following buzz words for quicker, cheaper *madrileño* fare: *bocadillo* (350-400ptas), a sandwich on a french roll; *sandwich* (about 300ptas), a sandwich on sliced bread, usually grilled; *croissant* (250ptas), a croissant sandwich; *ración* (300-600ptas), a plate of meat, cheese, or some other finger food served with bread; and *empanada* (200-300ptas), a puff pastry generally filled with tuna.

Fresh produce in the center of Madrid is scarce—your best bet is to walk around a residential area like Argüelles for neighborhood markets. Vegetarians may shrink a size. For **groceries,** the **Mercado de San Miguel,** on Pl. San Miguel, just off the northwest corner of Pl. Mayor, is a spectacle (open Mon.-Fri. 9am-2pm and 5:30-8pm, Sat. 9am-3pm), but **%Dia,** right behind the Mercado de San Miguel, is cheap. Excellent pastry shops and delis line the streets. The sublime **Horno La Santiaguesa,** C. Mayor, 73, sells everything from *empanadas* to chocolate and candy.

SPAIN

Museo del Jamón, C. San Jerónimo, 6. M: Sol. Five other locations throughout the city. Succulent Iberian ham served up in any and every form your piggish little heart could possibly desire. Open Mon.-Sat. 9am-12:30am, Sun. 10am-12:30am.

El Estragón, Costanilla de S. Andrés, 10, Pl. Raja. M: La Latina. Uphill off C. Segovia, facing La Capilla del Obispo. Vegetarian food that will make die-hard meat-eaters reconsider. *Menú* 1000ptas.

Casa Botín, C. Cuchilleros, 17 (tel. 366 42 17). M: Sol. The best restaurant in Madrid, and maybe all of Spain, and worth the ducats. Founded in 1725, it's the oldest restaurant in the world, according to Guinness. Hemingway, a patron, wrote about it in *A Clean, Well-lighted Place.* Reservations recommended.

Mesón La Caserola, C. Echegaray, 3, off C. San Jerónimo. M: Sol. Bustling, crowded joint serves a solid *menú* (975-1500ptas) to ravenous locals. Many entrees around 900ptas. Open Tues.-Sun. until 1:30am, Mon. opens at noon.

Restaurante Integral Artemisa, C. Ventura de la Vega, 4, off C. San Jerónimo. M: Sol. Tasty veggie food unspoiled by nicotine (no smoking). All proceeds from Wed. dinners go to humanitarian organizations. Salads 800-1100ptas. Entrees 995-1350ptas. *Menú* 1200ptas. Non-vegetarian entrees 1150-1350ptas.

El Granero de Lavapiés, C. Argumosa, 10. M: Lavapiés. Old-World charm. Gazpacho 475ptas. Vegetarian *menú* 1200ptas. Open for lunch Sun.-Fri. 1-4pm.

Cáscaras, C. Ventura Rodríguez, 7 (tel. 542 83 36). M: Ventura Rodríguez. Sleek interior that kind of looks like a *tortilla,* which is also what they serve (725-955ptas). Vegetarian dishes 675-975ptas. Breakfast and non-vegetarian fare as well.

La Farfalla, C. Santa María, 17. M: Antón Martín, 1 block south following C. Huertas. La Farfalla's specialty is Argentine-style grilled meat (1100-1750ptas), but true love is one unforgettable mouthful of their thin-crust pizza: *erótica* or *exquisita* 700ptas. Open Sun.-Thurs. until 3am, Fri.-Sat. until 4am.

Costa Del Sol, opposite C. Valverde. M: Gran Vía. A well-kept secret. Deliciously inexpensive meat and loads of it. Salads 250-450ptas. *Carnes* 400-875ptas. Lunchtime *menú* 1000ptas.

Nabucco, C. Hortaleza, 108, a few blocks off Pl. Santa Bárbara. M: Alonso Martínez or Chueca. Upscale clientele, excellent food, and affordable prices. Pizzas 640-870ptas. Pasta 690-910ptas. Salads 370-755ptas.

La Gata Flora, C. Dos de Mayo, 1, and across the street at C. San Vicente Ferrer, 33. M: Noviciado or Tribunal. Huge servings. Pizzas and pastas 825-1000ptas. Salads 550-700ptas. Open Sun.-Thurs. 2-4pm and 8:30-midnight, Fri.-Sat. until 1am.

SIGHTS

Madrid, large as it may seem at first, is a walker's city. A lounger's city, too—when panting for a break from the museums or a retreat from the summer's scorching heat, head for the shade at the Parque del Retiro or any sidewalk café.

From Plaza Mayor to Puerta de Toledo Hapsburgs' elegant black-slate roofs and spindly, pagoda-like towers top the arcaded **Plaza Mayor,** which was completed in 1620 for Felipe III; his statue dates from the 17th century, though it took the city until 1847 to install it. The days of public executions and bullfights are now past, but ghosts haunt the plaza's lively cafés. Not far from this most picturesque part of Old Madrid is the smaller and quieter **Plaza de la Villa,** where the 15th-century **Torre de los Lujanes** on the eastern side is the sole remnant of the once lavish residence of the Lujanes family. The characteristically Hapsburg 17th-century **Ayuntamiento** (or Casa de la Villa) on the plaza was both the mayor's home and the city jail. South of Pl. Mayor on C. Toledo looms **Iglesia de San Isidro** (M: Latina), a 17th-century church dedicated to Madrid's patron saint and designed by the famed Pedro Sánchez and Francisco Bautista. The remains of San Isidro landed here after being passed from church to church. The church served as the cathedral of Madrid from the late 19th century until 1993, when a new cathedral was consecrated (open for mass only).

Between Sol and Paseo del Prado Masterpieces in the collection of the **Museo de la Real Academia de Bellas Artes de San Fernando,** C. Alcalá, 13 (M: Sol or Sevilla), include Velázquez's portraits of Felipe IV and Mariana de Austria and Goya's *La Tirana.* (Open Tues.-Fri. 9am-7pm, Sat.-Mon. 9am-2:30pm. 300ptas, students 150ptas, free on Sat.-Sun.) The **Círculo de Bellas Artes,** C. Alcalá, 42, has undergone a recent resurgence and is again the gathering place of Madrid's high society of the arts. Designed by Antonio Palacios, the building encloses two stages and several salons and studios for lectures and workshops run by prominent artists. Exhibition galleries for all media are open to the public.

The Retiro and Jerónimos **Parque del Retiro,** Madrid's top picnic and suntanning zone, was originally intended to be a *buen retiro* (nice retreat) for Felipe IV. The palace burned down, but the **Museo del Ejército** remains, featuring interesting military paraphernalia. The **Estanque Grande,** a rectangular lake in the middle of the park, has become the social center of the Retiro. Ricardo Velázquez built the steel and glass **Palacio de Cristal,** south of the lake by the boat rental center, to exhibit Philippine flowers; it now hosts a variety of art shows. A few steps away, the **Palacio de Velázquez** (named after the Ricardo; tel. 573 62 45), north of the *estanque,* exhibits works in conjunction with the Museo de Arte Reina Sofía. Fernando and Isabel were crowned and King Alfonso XIII married at the **Iglesia de San Jerónimo** (open daily 6am-1pm and 6-8pm).

Triángulo de Arte Don't miss the **Paseo del Arte** ticket that grants patrons unlimited access to the Museo del Prado, Colección Thyssen-Bornemisza, and Centro de Arte Reina Sofía for 1050ptas. Spain's premier museum, and one of Europe's finest, the **Museo del Prado** is on Po. Prado at Pl. Cánovas del Castillo (M: Banco de España or Atocha). This Neoclassical building has sheltered the royal painting collection since the time of Fernando VII, who cared precious little for art and plenty about making an impression at home and abroad. Over 3000 paintings, many collected by Spanish monarchs between 1400 and 1700, include Spanish and foreign masterpieces, with particular strengths in the Flemish and Venetian Schools. The museum is laid out in a fairly logical fashion, and rooms are numbered, but it can be easy to lose sight of the forest for the groves of Goyas once within. Guides to the Prado can be helpful and informative; they vary in size and detail, ranging from 150ptas "greatest hits" brochures to weighty 2000ptas tomes packed with serious art criticism.

The second floor presents Spanish works from the 16th and 17th centuries, highlighted by the collection of Diego Velázquez, including *Las meninas* (The Maids of Honor)—widely considered Velázquez's masterpiece. Goya is represented by *La maja vestida* (Clothed Maja), *La maja desnuda* (Nude Maja), the sarcastic and unflattering *La familia de Carlos IV,* and the famous *Executions of May 3rd*. Don't miss the large room devoted to Goya's *Pinturas negras* (Black Paintings)—works dating from the end of his life, when the artist was in poor health and living in a small country house outside Madrid. Goya painted these chillingly macabre scenes on the walls of his house; years after his death they were placed on canvas and restored. Among the El Grecos are *La trinidad* (The Trinity) and *La adoración de los pastores* (The Adoration of the Pastors). The Prado also has a formidable stash of Italian works by greats including Titian, Raphael, Tintoretto, and Botticelli. The Spanish Hapsburgs' long reign over the Netherlands resulted in the strong Flemish collection, with Van Dyck, Roger van der Weyden, Albrecht Dürer, Peter Breughel the Elder, and Rubens leading the way. Look for Bosch's decadent *Garden of Earthly Delights* (open Tues.-Sat. 9am-7pm, Sun. 9am-2pm; 500ptas, students 250ptas).

Your ticket to the Prado also admits you to the nearby **Casón del Buen Retiro,** C. Alfonso XII, 28, facing the Parque del Retiro (M: Retiro or Banco de España). Once part of Felipe IV's Palacio del Buen Retiro, it was destroyed in the war against Napoleon. The rebuilt version has a superb collection of 19th-century Spanish paintings (open Tues.-Sat. 9am-6:45pm, Sun. 9am-1:45pm).

Picasso's *Guernica* is the centerpiece of the **Museo Nacional Centro de Arte Reina Sofía,** a collection of 20th-century art at C. Santa Isabel, 52, near the south end of Po. Prado (M: Atocha). When Germans bombed the Basque town of Guernica for the Fascists in Spain's Civil War, Picasso painted this huge work of distorted figures in agony to denounce the bloodshed. When asked by Nazi officials if he was responsible for the painting, Picasso answered "No, you are." He gave the canvas to New York's Museum of Modern Art on condition that it return to Spain when democracy was restored. Works by Miró, Julio González, Juan Gris, Picasso, and Dalí illustrate the essential role of Spanish artists in the Cubist and Surrealist movements. (Open Mon. and Wed.-Sat. 10am-9pm, Sun. 10am-2:30pm. 500ptas, students 250ptas, free Sat. after 2:30pm and Sun. all day.)

The **Museo Thyssen-Bornemizsa,** on the corner of Po. Prado and C. San Jerónimo (M: Banco de España), is an 18th-century palace with a collection of art ranging from the Old Masters to major 20th-century names (open Tues.-Sun. 10am-7pm; last admission 6:30pm; 600ptas, with ISIC 350ptas).

The Palacio Real and Environs With 20 sq. km of tapestry and a huge candelabra, the luxurious **Palacio Real** was built for the first Bourbon King Felipe V to replace the burned-down Alcázar (M: Ópera). The shell of the palace took 40 years to complete, and interior decoration of its 2000 rooms dragged on for a century. To see the collection of porcelain, tapestries, furniture, armor, and art, take a guided tour or stroll around. (Palace open Mon.-Sat. 9am-6pm, Sun. 9am-3pm. 950ptas, students 350ptas; arrive early to avoid waiting.) The palace faces the **Plaza de Oriente,** a square with statues of monarchs nearby. To the northwest are the serene **Jardines de Sabatini,** the park of choice for romantics. The view of the **Campo del Moro** is straight out of a fairy tale. In the heart of downtown, the **Convento de las Descalzas Reales,** Pl. Descalzas, between Pl. Callao and Sol (M: Callao or Sol), sheltered royal widows for a few centuries and acquired an exceptional collection of religious artwork. (Mandatory tour in Spanish. Open Tues.-Thurs. and Sat. 10:30am-12:45pm and 4-6pm, Fri. 10:30am-12:45pm, Sun. 11am-1:45pm. 650ptas, students 250ptas.)

Casa de Campo Catch the *teleférico* (cable car; 345ptas one way) down to the city's largest park, the **Casa de Campo.** Woods, a municipal pool, zoo, and an amusement park all conspire to leave the city far behind. Don't attempt to explore the entire park on foot; it's so large it makes Madrid's center look like a clearing in the woods. (M: Lago or Batán. Park open daily 11am-9pm; off-season Sat.-Sun. reduced to noon-8pm.) The Madrid **zoo** is a five-minute walk from the amusement park (open in summer daily 10am-9pm; off-season 10am-6:30pm; 1560ptas).

El Pardo Built as a hunting lodge for Carlos I in 1547, El Pardo was subsequently enlarged by generations of Hapsburg and Bourbon royalty into the magnificent country palace that stands today. Renowned for its collection of tapestries—several of which were designed by Goya—El Pardo also holds a little-known Velázquez depicting a deer slain by Felipe IV. Franco resided here from 1940-1975, and the palace is still the official reception site for distinguished foreign visitors. (Mandatory 45min. tour in Spanish. Open Mon.-Sat. 9:30am-6pm, Sun. 9:30am-2pm. 650ptas, student 250ptas, Wed. free for EU citizens.) To reach the palace, take bus 601 from the stop in front of the Ejército del Aire building above M: Moncloa (15min., 150ptas each way). The palace's **chapel** and the nearby **Casita del Príncipe** are free.

ENTERTAINMENT

Enormously proud of their nightlife, residents of Madrid will tell you with a straight face that they were bored in Paris and New York. The weekly *Guía del Ocio* (125ptas) carries comprehensive entertainment listings; the free municipal tourist office's *En Madrid* is less thorough, but still helpful.

Nightlife Spaniards get on average one less hour of sleep then other Europeans, and people in Madrid claim to need even less than that. Some clubs don't even bother opening until 4 or 5am; warm up for the night's activities at one of Madrid's many **classic cafés.** Ceiling frescoes and a marble nude add style to the **Café Circulo de Bellas Artes,** C. Alcalá, 42 (M: Banco de España; cover 100ptas; coffee 200ptas). **Café Gijón,** Po. Recoletos, 21 (M: Colón), has both a breezy terrace and a smoky bar-restaurant. Long a favorite of the literati, this café has become an official historic site (coffee 300ptas; open daily 9am-1:30am).

As the sun sets and bathes the streets in gold, **terrazas** and **chiringuitos** (outdoor cafés/bars) spill across sidewalks all over Madrid. Enjoy a glass of wine at **Plaza Mayor** while digesting the tourist office's brochures. **Calle Bailén,** by the Viaducto, has spectacular views of flaming sunsets and couples equally aflame. **Paseo Castellana, Paseo Recoletos,** and **Paseo Prado** are fashionable areas, hence a bit pricey. **El Viso,** between Po. Castellana and C. María de Molina, is a pre-war garden city within the city. Villas, walled gardens, and winding streets exude a charming village-like aura. Hippies, intellectuals, bohemians, street musicians, and junkies quaff drinks in the shade of umbrellas and trees at **Plaza 2 de Mayo** and **Plaza Olavide**, the main spots of *Malasaña.* **Chueca** is home to an outrageous, mostly male, gay scene.

For **clubs and discos,** life begins at 3am. Many discos have "afternoon" sessions (cover 250-1000ptas; usually 7-10pm) for teens; but the "night" sessions (lasting until dawn) are when to really let your hair down. Don't be surprised if at 5:30am there's still a line of people waiting to get in. Really. Cover *(entrada)* can get as high as 2000ptas; men may be charged up to 500ptas more than women. The cover charge often includes a drink. The hippest clubs change quickly, so consult the *Guía del Ocio* or ask around.

Kapital, C. Atocha, 125 (tel. 420 29 06). M: Atocha. A block off Po. Prado. One of the most extreme results of *La Movida,* this place tries really hard to impress. Two dance floors, a sky-light lounge, and tons of bars amount to a total of 7 floors. Cover 1200ptas. Includes 2 drinks if you have their invite from the tourist office, 1 drink without. Don't lose your ticket or they'll fine you 5000ptas when you leave. Drinks 800-1000ptas. Open Thurs. 12:30-6am, Fri.-Sun. 6-11pm and 12:30-6am.

Mogador, C. Magallanes, 1 (tel. 448 94 65). M: Quevedo. Mature crowd gets down and dirty to salsa Tues.-Thurs. Free salsa classes Tues. 11pm-midnight. Open Mon.

9:30pm-5:30am, Tues.-Thurs. 11pm-5am, Fri.-Sat. midnight-5am, Sun. 7:30pm-3am. Cover 1000ptas includes 1 drink, 1200ptas for 2 drinks.

Las Noches de Babel, Ronda de Toledo, 1 (tel. 366 49 23). M: Puerta de Toledo. *Pijolandia*—where sleek young "beautiful people" wiggle around in tight clothes to funk and house. Vegetable decor a quirky surprise. Open daily 11pm-6am.

Refugio, C. Dr. Cortezo, 1. M: Tirso de Molina. The most outrageous gay men's scene in the…you decide. Cover 1000ptas. Open Tues.-Sun. midnight-morning.

Joy Eslava, C. Arenal, 11 (tel. 366 37 33). M: Sol or Ópera. A 3-tiered theater turned disco. Young crowd of all types grooves to disco. Cover 2000ptas includes one drink. Open Mon.-Thurs. 11:30pm on, Fri.-Sat. 7-10:15pm and 11:30pm-5:30am.

Tierra, Cabarello de Gracia, 20 (tel. 532 72 71). M: Gran Vía. Off C. Montera, but best to go over 1 block to C. Peligios. Black interior with psychedelic glow-in-the-dark design plays host to house. Open Thurs.-Sat. midnight-4:30am. Beer 500ptas.

Angels of Xenon, C. Atocha, 38 (tel. 369 38 81). M: Antón Martín. Threatening black walls enclose a mostly gay crowd, dancing hard. Cover 1000-1500ptas.

Naturbier, Pl. Santa Ana, 9 (tel. 429 39 18). M: Antón Martín. Locally brewed *bier*. Superior lager 225-500ptas. Open Sun.-Thurs. 11:30am-1am, Fri.-Sat. 11am-3am.

Viva Madrid, C. Manuel Fernández González, 7 (tel. 429 36 40), next to Pl. Santa Ana. M: Antón Martín. Tiled and classy U.S. expat hangout. Packed. Beer 300-400ptas. Mixed drinks 700-800ptas. Open 1pm-7am.

Kasbah, C. Santa Maria, 17. M: Antón Martín. Dazed aliens and other funked out decorations look on as house DJs spin some of the best jungle and techno in Madrid. On Sun., amateurs are invited to give it a whirl. Beer 300ptas. No cover.

Black & White, C. Libertad, 34 (tel. 531 11 41). M: Chueca. Upstairs a more mature crowd mingles and downstairs the young ones whoop it up on the dance floor. Gays and lesbians, but not exclusively. Beer 500ptas. Open daily 8pm-5am.

Film, Theater, and Music The **Parque del Retiro** sometimes shows free movies at 11pm. The state-subsidized *filmoteca,* in the renovated Art Deco **Cine Doré,** C. Santa Isabel, 3 (tel. 369 11 25, M: Antón Martín), is the best for repertory cinema (tickets 200-400ptas). Subtitled films are shown in many private theaters, including **Alphaville** and **Renoir 1** and **2**—check the V.O. (for *versión original*) listings in entertainment guides. **Huertas,** east of Sol, is the theater district. In July and August, **Plaza Mayor, Plaza de Lavapiés,** and **Plaza Villa de París** host frequent plays. Theater goers can consult magazines published by state-sponsored theaters, such as **Teatro Español, Teatro de la Comedia,** and the city's superb **Teatro María Guerrero.** The **Centro Cultural de la Villa,** Pl. Colón (tel. 575 60 80; M: Colón or Serrano), is a major performance center (tickets 2000ptas). The **Auditorio Nacional,** C. Príncipe de Vergara, 136 (tel. 337 01 00; M: Cruz del Rayo), hosts the finest classical performances (800-4200ptas). **Flamenco** is tourist-oriented and expensive. If you must, try **Casa Patas,** C. Cañizares, 10 (tel. 369 04 96; flamenco starts at midnight Thurs.-Sat.).

Sports Spanish sports fans go ballistic for **fútbol** (soccer)! Every Sunday and some Saturdays between September and June, one of two local teams plays at home. "Real Madrid" plays at Estadio Santiago Bernabeu, Po. Castellana, 104 (tel. 457 11 12; M: Lima). "Atlético de Madrid" plays at Estadio Vicente Calderón, C. Virgen del Puerto, 67 (tel. 366 47 07; M: Pirámides or Marqués de Vadillos). **Corridas** (bullfights) are held during the Festival of San Isidro and every Sunday in summer, less frequently the rest of the year. The season lasts from March to October, signalled by posters in bars and cafés (especially on C. Victoria, off C. San Jerónimo). **Plaza de las Ventas,** C. Alcalá, 237 (tel. 356 22 00), east of central Madrid, is the biggest ring in Spain (M: Ventas). Tickets are 450-15,200ptas.

■ Near Madrid: El Escorial, El Valle de los Caídos, Aranjuez

They called **El Escorial** the eighth wonder of the world, and they were right. The fascinating complex includes a monastery, two palaces, a church, two pantheons, a magnificent library, and innumerable artistic treasures. El Escorial is located near the charming town of **San Lorenzo,** within easy striking distance of Madrid. *Don't* come on Monday, when the complex and the town shut down.

The first two stops on tours of the complex are the **Museo de Arquitectura** and the **Museo de Pintura.** The former has an outstanding exhibition on the construction of El Escorial, with some wooden models of 16th-century machinery and the buildings themselves. The Museo de Pintura holds a collection of masterpieces by Bosch, Dürer, El Greco, Titian, Tintoretto, Velázquez, Zurbarán, Van Dyck, Rubens, and others. The **Monasterio de San Lorenzo del Escorial** was a gift from Felipe II to God, the people, and himself, commemorating his victory over the French at the battle of San Quintín in 1557. The **Palacio Real** includes the *Salón del Trono* (Throne Room) and two dwellings in one—Felipe II's spartan 16th-century apartments and the more luxurious 18th-century rooms of Carlos III and Carlos IV. The astonishing **Panteón Real** (known affectionately as *el pudridero,* the rotting chamber) was another brainchild of Felipe II. Although he didn't live to see it finished, he's buried here with Carlos V and most of their royal descendants. (Entire El Escorial complex open April-Sept. Tues.-Sun. 10am-7pm; Oct.-March 10am-6pm. Last admission 1hr. or 30min. before closing. Monastery 850ptas, students 350ptas, Wed. free for EU citizens.)

The easiest way to travel between El Escorial and Madrid is by bus. Autocarres Herranz **buses** pull right up to the kiosk outside the M: Moncha station (buy a ticket here) and whisk travelers to El Escorial's **Plaza Virgen de Gracia.** Plaza Virgen is in the center of town, close to the **tourist office,** C. Floridablanca, 10 (tel. (91) 890 15 54; open Mon.-Fri. 10am-2pm and 3-5pm, Sat. 10am-1:45pm). Confirm your return ticket before boarding the bus for Madrid at the **bar/casino,** C. Rey, 3 (tel. (91) 890 41 00), around the corner from Pl. Virgen de Gracia. **Trains** arrive at Ctra. Estación, 2km from town, and shuttle buses run frequently to Pl. Virgen. Trains run to Madrid's Atocha and Chamartín stations (1hr., round-trip 750ptas).

Built by war prisoners on Franco's command, the overpowering monument of **Santa Cruz del Valle de los Caídos** was created as a memorial to those who died "serving God and Spain"—Franco's Nationalists. The eerie combination of medieval and Neoclassical aesthetics illustrates the fascists' attempts to claim Spain's past glories as their own. Although the tourist literature does not point it out, Franco lies buried underneath. (Open in summer daily 9:30am-7pm; off-season 10am-6pm. 650ptas, students 250ptas, free Wed. for EU citizens. Funicular ride up to the cross 350ptas.) El Valle de los Caídos is accessible only via El Escorial. Autocares Herranz runs one bus to the monument. (Leaves El Escorial Tues.-Sun. at 3:15pm and returns at 5:30pm, 15min., round-trip plus admission 870ptas. Funicular not included.)

Aranjuez's stately **Palacio Real** warrants a daytrip from Madrid. The white brick marvel features finely worked Vatican mosaics in marble, chandeliers and mirrors from the La Granja crystal factory, Buen Retiro porcelain, Flemish tapestries, and ornate French clocks. (Open June-Sept. Wed.-Mon. 10am-6:15pm; Oct.-May Wed.-Mon. 10am-5:15pm. Compulsory tour in Spanish 500ptas, students 250ptas, Wed. free for EU citizens.) The city is famed for its strawberries and asparagus, and for its beautiful, humid gardens. River walkways run from the **Jardín de la Isla,** with its banana trees and mythological statuary, to the huge **Jardín del Príncipe** (gardens open June-Sept. daily 8am-8:30pm; Oct.-May 8am-6:30pm; free). The **tourist office** (tel. (91) 891 04 27) in Pl. San Antonio, provides a brochure and a map of Aranjuez (open Mon.-Fri. 10am-2pm and 4-6pm). The **train station** (tel. (91) 891 02 02) is a pleasant 10-minute walk from the center of town and serves Madrid (45min., round-trip 740ptas) and Toledo (3 per day, 30min.). Frequent **buses** run to Madrid (1hr., 355-390ptas) from the station at C. las Infantas, 8 (tel. (91) 891 01 83 or 530 46 06).

CASTILLA LA MANCHA

Cuenca

Perched atop a hill, tall Cuenca overlooks the two rivers that confine it and the stunning rock formations they created. The enchanting old city safeguards Cuenca's **casas colgadas** (hanging houses). Down C. Obispo, they dangle over the riverbanks as precariously today as they did six centuries ago. Inside one of the *casas* at Pl. Ciudad de Ronda, the **Museo de Arte Abstracto Español** displays important works by recent Spanish artists. (Open Mon.-Fri. 11am-2pm and 4-6pm, Sat. 11am-2pm and 4-8pm, Sun. 11am-1:30pm. 500ptas, students 150ptas.) Nearby on C. Obispo Valero, the **Museo Municipal** is a treasure-trove of archaeological finds, including Visigoth jewelry. (Open Tues.-Sat. 9am-2pm and 4-6pm, Sun. 11am-2pm. 200ptas, students 100ptas.) Perhaps the most beautiful of the museums along this street is the **Museo Diocesano.** Exhibits are imaginatively displayed and include Juan de Borgoña's *retablo* from local Convento de San Pablo and two El Grecos. (Open Tues.-Fri. 11am-2pm and 4-6pm, Sat. 11am-2pm and 4-8pm, Sun. 11am-2pm. 200ptas.) Cuenca's **cathedral** is the only Anglo-Norman Gothic cathedral in Spain. A 1724 fire cut short the latest attempt to build a front, leaving the current exterior incomplete. (Open in summer daily 8:45am-2pm and 4-7pm; off-season 8:45am-2pm and 4-6pm. Free.)

Trains chug from Po. Ferrocarril (tel. (969) 22 07 20) to Madrid (2½-3hr., 1325ptas) and Valencia (2¾-3¾hr., 1455ptas). **Buses** roll from C. Fermín Caballero (tel. (969) 22 70 87), down the street from the train station, to Madrid (2½hr., 1305-1600ptas) and Toledo (Mon.-Fri. at 5:30am, 3hr., 1600ptas). To get to **Plaza Mayor** in the old city from either station, go left until you hit the first bus shelter and take bus 1 or 2 to the last stop. The **Municipal Tourist Office,** C. San Pedro, 6 (tel. (969) 23 21 19), next to the cathedral in Pl. Mayor, has maps, listings of accommodations, and hiking and excursion routes (open daily 9:30am-2pm and 4-7pm). Cheap, adequate rooms collect in the new city, while rooms on the hill exact a bit more money. **Hostal-Residencia Posada de San José,** C. Julián Romero, 4 (tel. (969) 21 13 00; fax 23 03 65), just up the street from the cathedral, gives deluxe treatment with cushy beds, historic echoes, and gorgeous views. (Singles 2600ptas, with shower 4300ptas; doubles 4300-8400ptas; triples 5800-11,000ptas; one quad 13,200ptas; prices may vary. Reserve 2-3 weeks in advance.) **Pensión Cuenca,** Av. República Argentina, 8 (tel. (969) 21 25 74), along Hurtado de Mendoza from the train or bus station (singles 1600-1900ptas, doubles 2300-3500ptas), and **Pensión Central,** C. Alonso Chirino, 9 (tel. (969) 21 15 11), off C. Carretería (singles 1400ptas, doubles 2100-2500ptas, triples 3450ptas), provide decent accommodations at good prices. Budget eateries line **C. Cervantes** and **C. República Argentina.** A Communist hangout during the Civil War, **El Mesón,** C. Colón, off Av. República Argentina, still attracts workers of all stripes with its *manchego* cuisine at decent prices.

Toledo

Cervantes called Toledo a "rocky gravity, glory of Spain and light of her cities." Successively a Roman settlement, capital of the Visigothic kingdom, stronghold of the Emirate of Córdoba, and imperial city under Carlos V, medieval Toledo became the European capital for the study of natural sciences, the Bible, and languages. Synonymous with the notion of cultural tolerance, the city exemplified the Spanish *convivencia* (co-existence of Christian, Islamic, and Jewish cultures), as represented in the pervasive churches, synagogues, and mosques. The arts continue to flourish, and the city is famous for *damascene* swords and knives (black steel inlaid with gold) and *mazapán* (marzipan). Toledo's cultural tolerance is tried today by tacky gift shops and busloads of tourists, but the nighttime lull brings quiet to the streets.

ORIENTATION AND PRACTICAL INFORMATION

To get to **Plaza de Zocodóver** in the center of town, take bus 5 or 6 (110ptas) from the bus or train station. Toledo could not be more labyrinthine if it contained a real Minotaur. Streets are well-labeled and the tourist office distributes a fairly detailed map, but it's virtually impossible not to get lost frequently. Many major sights are near or atop the central hill, which is basically circular.

Tourist Office: The **main office** (tel. 22 08 43; fax 25 26 48) is outside the Puerta Nueva de Bisagra on Po. Merchán, on the north side of town. Maps and info. From the train station, turn right and take the right-hand fork across the bridge; follow the city walls until the gateway. The office is on the road, outside the walls. Open Mon.-Fri. 9am-6pm, until 7pm in the summer, Sat. 9am-7pm, Sun. 9am-3pm. For a map without the walk, visit the **information booth,** Pl. Zocodóver. Open Mon.-Fri. 10am-6pm, Sat. 10am-7pm, Sun. 10am-3pm.

Trains: Po. Rosa (tel. 22 30 99), opposite the Puente de Azarquiel. Trains to Madrid's Estación de Atocha (1½hr., 575ptas), pass through Aranjuez (35min., 290ptas). To get anywhere else, transfer in Madrid or Aranjuez.

Buses: (tel. 21 58 50) in Zona Safón, 5min. from the city gate and tourist office (from Pl. Zocodóver, take C. Armas). To Madrid (1½hr., 575ptas) and Cuenca (3hr., 1565ptas).

Medical Services: Hospital Virgen de la Salud (tel. 26 92 00), Av. de Barber, toward Avila highway.

Emergency: tel. 091 or 092.

Police: Municipal: tel. 236 97 13. **Local:** Ayuntamiento, 1 (tel. 21 34 00 or 092).

Post Office: C. Plata, 1 (tel. 22 36 11 or 25 10 66), off Pl. Zocodóver via C. Comercio and then C. Toledo. Open Mon-Fri. 8am-9pm, Sat. 9am-2pm. **Postal Code:** 45001.

Telephone Code: 925.

ACCOMMODATIONS, CAMPING, AND FOOD

Finding a bed during the summer, especially on weekends, can be a hassle. The tourist office provides an invaluable list of hotels, *hostales,* and *pensiones*.

Residencia Juvenil "San Servando" (HI), Castillo San Servando (tel. 22 45 54), uphill from the train station (15min.). From the train station, turn left and immediately right up Callejón del Hospital. When the steps reach a road, turn right, then right again, following signs to the Hospital Provincial. Pass a castle on your steep walk uphill. Anyone returning alone at night should take a cab. Pool and TV room. Reception open daily 7am-11:50pm. Curfew around 11:50pm. 1100ptas, over 26 1350ptas. Laundry service around 500ptas. Closed mid-Aug. to mid-Sept.

Pensión Nuncio Viejo, C. Nuncio Viejo, 19, 3rd fl. (tel. 22 81 78), on a street leading from the cathedral. Familial ambience; only 6 rooms. A bit cramped, but your new mom is a great cook. TV room. Singles 1300ptas. Doubles 2900ptas, with bath 3200ptas. Breakfast 190ptas. Lunch and dinner 750ptas each.

La Belviseña, Cuesta del Can, 7 (tel. 22 00 67). From Zocodóver, walk down Cuesta Carlos V (a.k.a. Cuesta del Alcázar) through the small plaza beyond it. Take C. Soledad and go left on C. San Miguel. Make another left on C. San Justo. Turn left and go uphill. Cuesta del Can is on the right. Singles 1000ptas. Doubles 2000ptas.

Pensión Lumbreras, C. Juan Labrador, 9 (tel. 22 15 71), 2 blocks from Pl. Zocodóver, near Hostal-Residencia Labrador. Simple rooms, some with a skyline view. Singles 1700ptas. Doubles 3000ptas. One triple 4200ptas. IVA not included.

Pensión Descalzos, C. Descalzos, 30 (tel. 22 28 88), down the steps off Po. San Cristóbal or down the Bajada Descalzos near the Casa del Greco. Rooms with bath also have music and TV. High season 2500ptas. Doubles 3500ptas, with bath or shower 5600ptas. Cheaper off season. IVA not included. Closed Feb.

Camping: Camping El Greco (tel. 22 00 90), 1½km from town on the road away from Madrid (C-401). Bus 7 (from Pl. Zocodóver), stops just up the hill and to the left. Wooded and shady first-class site between the Tajo and an olive grove. 650ptas per person, 570ptas per tent. 550ptas per car. IVA.

Toledo grinds almonds into marzipan delights of every shape and size, from colorful fruity nuggets to half-moon cookies. If the pocket allows, dining out in Toledo could be an ecstatic culinary experience; *menús* hover between 1400 and 1600ptas. Regional specialties include *perdiz* (fowl), *venado* (venison), and *carcamusas* (mystery meat). **Pastucci,** C. Sinagoga, 10, is a colorful Italian eatery tucked away from touristy sites. (Pizzas 900-2150ptas; pasta 850-950ptas; salads 600-950ptas. Open Mon.-Fri. noon-4pm and 7pm-midnight, Sat. 8pm-1am.) **Restaurante El Zoco,** C. Bacrio Rey, 1, is reasonably priced and attractive (*menús* 800, 900, and 1500ptas; open daily 1-4pm and 8-11pm). Pick up groceries at **Frutería-Pan,** C. Real Arrabal, inside the Puertas de Bisagra (open Mon.-Fri. 9am-10pm), or try the **market** in Pl. Mayor, behind the cathedral (open Mon.-Fri. 8:30am-2pm, Sat. 8:30-2pm).

SIGHTS AND ENTERTAINMENT

South and uphill from Pl. Zocodóver is the **Alcázar,** Toledo's most formidable landmark. The site was a stronghold of Visigoths, Muslims, and Christians, each rebuilding it in their own style. Little remains of the 16th-century structure built by Carlos V; the building was largely reduced to rubble during the Civil War, as besieged Fascist troops held out against heavy Republican bombardment. The rooms above ground are now a military museum, housing armor, swords, guns, knives, and dried plants. (Open July-Aug. open Tues.-Sun. 9:30am-2:30pm; Sept.-June Tues.-Sat. 10am-2pm and 4-6pm, Sun. 10am-1:30pm and 4-6:30pm. 125ptas, Wed. free for EU citizens.) To the west, the grandiose **cathedral,** with five naves, delicate stained glass, and ostentation throughout, soars from the city center. Noteworthy features of the cathedral are the 14th-century Gothic *Virgen Blanca* (White Virgin) by the entrance and, above all, Narciso Tomés's 1732 *Transparente,* a whirlpool of Spanish Baroque architecture, sculpture, and painting. The **Sacristía** hoards 18 El Grecos and two Van Dycks. (Cathedral open July-Aug. Mon.-Sat. 10:30am-1pm and 3:30-7pm, Sun. 10:30am-1:30pm and 4-7pm; Sept.-June closes 1hr. earlier. 500ptas.)

El Greco ("The Greek"), the artist formerly known as Domenico Theotocopuli, lived most of his life in Toledo, and locales throughout town display his work. The **Iglesia de San Tomé** houses El Greco's amazing *El entierro del Conde de Orgaz* (The Burial of Count Orgaz. Open in summer Tues.-Sat. 10am-2pm and 3:30-6:45pm, Sun. 10am-2pm; off-season Tues.-Sat. 10am-2pm and 3:30-5:45pm, Sun. 10am-2pm. 150ptas.) El Greco is also found at the **Casa Museo de El Greco,** C. Levi, 3, down the hill from the Ayuntamiento. The museum has a copy of the *Vista y mapa de Toledo* (View and Map of Toledo) and several portraits of saints (1200ptas, students free).

Two synagogues, both in the **Judería** on the west side, are all that remain of what was once Spain's largest Jewish community. The 1366 **Sinagoga del Tránsito** is a simple building with Mudéjar plasterwork and an ornately designed wood ceiling. Inside, the **Museo Sefardí** is packed with artifacts including a *torá.* (Open Tues.-Sat. 10am-1:45pm and 4-5:45pm, Sun. 10am-1:45pm. 400ptas, students 200ptas, Sat. after 4pm and Sun. free.) **Sinagoga de Santa María la Blanca,** down the street, was built in 1180 and became the city's main synagogue, but was later converted to a church. (Open daily 10am-1:45pm and 3:45-6:45pm; off-season until 5:45pm. 400ptas, students 200ptas.) Less touristed arc the remnants of the city's Islamic past, near the Puerta del Sol off C. Real de Arrabal. Both a Muslim and a Christian house of worship at different times, the striking **Mezquita del Cristo de la Luz** is the only surviving building in Toledo built before the Christian *Reconquista.*

Toledo loves **Corps Christi,** celebrated the eighth Sunday after Easter. During the rest of the year, nightlife thrives at **Calle de Santa Fe,** east of Pl. Zocodóver and **Calle de la Sillería,** west of Pl. Zocodóver. **Zaida,** in the Centro Comercial Miradero, downhill from Pl. Zocodóver, is a hotspot for dancing. **El Café de Louise,** on Chainería, is a popular rock 'n roll hangout (open until 2:30am).

CASTILLA Y LEÓN

Segovia

Legend has it that Segovia's famed 813m aqueduct was built in only a day by the Devil trying to win the heart of a Segovian water-seller named Juanilla. In fact, it was built by the Romans around 50 BC to pipe in water from the Río Frío, and neither it nor the Romans' home town was built in a day, you know. The **acueducto romano** is constructed out of great blocks of granite with no mortar. View it at its maximum height (28.9m) from Plaza del Azoguejo, or catch its profile from the steps on the left side of the plaza. Amazingly, the Romans' feat of engineering, restored by the Catholic Monarchs in the 15th century, was still in use until 10 years ago.

In addition to the aqueduct, Segovia boasts amazing churches and palaces, beautiful views, and twisting alleyways. The **Alcázar,** an archetypal late-medieval castle and site of Isabel's coronation in 1474, occupies the north end of the old quarter. The castle is filled with trappings of its royal and bloody past. The **Sala de Armas** holds a veritable arsenal of medieval weaponry, while the **Sala de Reyes** is adorned with wood and gold inlay sculptures of the monarchs of Asturias, Castile, and León. (Alcázar open April-Sept. daily 10am-7pm; Oct.-March 10am-6pm. 375ptas, seniors 275ptas.) Commissioned by Carlos I in 1525, the **cathedral** towers above Pl. Mayor in the center of town. Inside, the **Sala Capitular** (chapter house), hung with well-preserved tapestries, also displays a silver and gold chariot and various crucifixes and chalices. The **museum** collection includes Claudio Coello's *La duda de Santo Tomás,* and a series of Francisco de Solis's 17th-century paintings on marble depicting the Passion of Christ (open daily 9:30am-7pm; off-season 9am-6pm; 250ptas).

Practical Information, Accommodations, and Food Rail lines to Segovia are limited, but **trains** do run frequently from the station on Po. Obispo Quesada to Madrid (15 per day, 6 on Sun., 2hr., 750ptas). From Po. Ezequiel González, 10, **buses** trek to Ávila (1hr., 555ptas), Madrid (1¾hr., 765ptas), and Salamanca (3hr., 1400ptas). The helpful **tourist office,** Pl. Mayor 10 (tel (921) 46 03 34), is in front of the bus stop; take any bus from the station (200ptas). (Open Mon.-Fri. 10am-2pm and 5-8pm, Sat. 10am-2pm and 4:30-8:30pm, Sun. 11am-2pm and 4:30-8:30pm.)

During the summer, finding an *hostal* room can be a nightmare; book ahead and be prepared to pay at least 2500ptas. The **regional tourist office,** Pl. Azoguejo (tel. (921) 44 03 02), helps with reservations (open Mon.-Sat. 10am-8pm, Sun. 10am-2pm). The **Residencia Juvenil "Emperador Teodosio" (HI),** Av. Conde de Sepúlveda (tel. (921) 44 11 11), is only open to travelers in July and August, when its hotel-like doubles and triples, all with private baths, make it extremely popular. From the bus station, turn right on C. Ezequiel González, which becomes Av. Conde Sepúlveda (1450ptas, under 26 1050ptas). **Hostal Juan Bravo,** C. Juan Bravo, 12, 2nd fl. (tel. (921) 46 34 13), on the main thoroughfare in the old town, has bright rooms that stay cool in the summer (doubles 3500-4400ptas, triples 5000-6300ptas). Centrally located **Pensión Ferri,** C. Escuderos, 10 (tel. (921) 46 09 57), off Pl. Mayor, has clean rooms but no sinks. (Singles 1350ptas; doubles 2300ptas; converted into triples 3300ptas. Shower 300ptas.) **Camping Acueducto,** Ctra. Nacional, 601 (tel. (921) 42 50 00), 2km toward La Granja, is an adequate site in the shadow of the Sierra de Guadarrama (450ptas per person and per tent; open April-Sept.).

Segovia is famed for sublimely tender roast suckling pig *(cochinillo)* and lamb, but steer clear of pricey Pl. Mayor and Pl. Azoguejo. **Bar-Mesón Cueva de San Estéban,** C. La Victoria, 9, off the top of Pl. San Estéban, reached via C. Escuderos, serves a 900ptas *menú.* Pl. Mayor and its tributaries reign at night, crammed with **cafés** and **bars.** Pl. Azogejo and C. Carmen, down near the aqueduct, are filled with bars as well; for **clubs,** head off Pl. Azoguejo to C. Ruiz de Alda.

SPAIN

■ Near Segovia: La Granja de San Ildefonso

The royal palace and grounds of La Granja, 9km southeast of Segovia, were commissioned by Felipe V, the first Bourbon King in Spain, who detested the Hapsburgs' austere El Escorial. The "Versailles of Spain," La Granja was one of four royal summer retreats (with El Pardo, El Escorial, and Aranjuez), and far and away the most extravagant. Marble, lace curtains, and lavish crystal chandeliers—made in San Ildefonso's renowned crystal factory—liven up the palace. (Open June-Sept. Tues.-Sun. 10am-6pm; Oct.-March Tues.-Sat. 10am-1:30pm and 3-5pm, Sun. 10am-2pm; April-May Tues.-Fri. 10am-1:30pm and 3-5pm, Sat.-Sun. 10am-6pm. 650ptas, students 250ptas.) Frequent **buses** arrive at La Granja from Segovia (20min., 200ptas round-trip).

Ávila

Ávila's fame is forever ensured by St. Teresa of Ávila (1515-1582). This mystic, writer, and reformer of monastic life founded the Order of the Discalced Carmelites, whose raptures were immortalized in marble by Bernini. Less crowded and tourist-oriented than Toledo or Cuenca, Ávila offers nearly as many sights and keeps cool on its rocky escarpment in the summer while the plain swelters below.

Construction of the **murallas medievales,** the oldest and best preserved medieval walls in Spain, began in 1090. Eighty-two massive towers reinforce the 3m thick *murallas.* To walk on the walls, head to Puerta del Alcázar. (Open in summer Tues.-Sun. 11am-1:30pm and 5-7:30pm; off-season Tues.-Sun. 10:30am-3:30pm. 100ptas.) Some believe that the profile of the **cathedral** looming over the watchtowers inspired St. Teresa's metaphor of the soul as a diamond castle. Begun in the late 12th century, the cathedral participated in Ávila's defense system and recalls the long, turbulent centuries of the *Reconquista.* (Cathedral open May-Sept. daily 10am-1:30pm and 3:30-6pm; Oct.-April 10am-1:30pm and 3:30-5:30pm. 250ptas.)

St. Teresa's admirers built the 17th-century **Convento de Santa Teresa** on the site of her childhood home. Next door, the **Sala de Reliquias** holds relics, including her forefinger, the sole of her sandal, and her flagellation cord. (Convent open May-Sept. daily 9:30am-1:30pm and 3:30-9pm; Oct.-April 9:30am-1:30pm and 3:30-8:30pm. Sala de Reliquias open daily 9:30am-1:30pm and 3:30-7:30pm. Free.) Most of St. Teresa's mystical experiences took place during the 30 years she spent in the **Monasterio de la Encarnación,** a short way outside the city walls. The mandatory guided tour (in Spanish, 10-15min.) reveals her tiny cell. (Open in summer daily 10am-1pm and 4-7pm; off-season 10am-1pm and 3:30-6pm. 150ptas.)

Practical Information, Accommodations, and Food Ávila's **tourist office** is at Pl. Catedral, 4 (tel. (920) 21 13 87); from Pl. Santa Teresa, walk through the main gate and turn right up C. Cruz Vieja. (Open Mon.-Fri. 10am-2pm and 4-7pm, Sat. 9:30am-2pm and 4-7pm, Sun. 9:30am-2pm and 4:30-8:30pm; off-season Mon.-Fri. 10am-2pm and 5-8pm, Sat. 9:30am-2pm.) The **bus station,** Av. Madrid, 2 (tel. (920) 22 01 54), on the northeast side of town, serves Segovia (1hr., 555ptas), Salamanca (1½hr., 820ptas), and Madrid (2hr., 915ptas). To reach Pl. Santa Teresa from the station, cross the street and walk down C. Duque de Alba. **Trains** leave the station at Av. José Antonio, 40 (tel. (920) 25 02 02), for Medina del Campo (1hr., 480-1400ptas; change here for Segovia), Salamanca (2hr., 805ptas), and Madrid (2hr., 805-1800ptas). To reach Pl. Santa Teresa from the train station, follow Av. José Antonio to C. Isaac Peral, which leads to C. Duque de Alba; turn left and continue.

Lodgings in Ávila are plentiful and reasonably priced. Attractive, comfortable **Pensión Continental,** Pl. Catedral, 6 (tel. (920) 21 15 02; fax 25 16 91), is right next to the tourist office. (Singles 2200-3900ptas; doubles 3700-4500ptas; triples 5200-6300ptas. IVA not included.) **Hostal Casa Felipe,** Po. Victoria, 12 (tel. (920) 21 39 24), has standard rooms (singles 2200ptas, doubles with shower 4000ptas). **Residencia Juvenil "Duperier" (HI),** Av. Juventud (tel. (920) 22 17 16), only has six to eight beds reserved for HI purposes; call ahead to see if there's an opening and to get directions for the fairly long hike from the center of town (curfew 11pm; 1050ptas, over 26 1450ptas; meals available; open July-Aug.).

The city won fame for its *ternera de Ávila* (veal) and *mollejas* (sweetbread). The *yemas de Santa Teresa* or *yemas de Ávila,* local confections made of egg yolks and honey, and *vino de Cebreros,* the smooth regional wine, are delectable. Every Friday (9am-2pm), a **market** in Pl. Victoria sells fruits, vegetables, meat, and other meal basics. **Plaza de la Victoria** is a center of budget dining. **Restaurante El Grande,** Pl. Santa Teresa, 8, is a big, popular family-style restaurant with outdoor seating on the plaza (*raciones* 350-850ptas; *menú* 1100ptas). **El Arbol,** C. Alfonso de Montalvo, 1, off Pl. Santa Ana, is a decent supermarket. (Open Mon.-Sat. 9:30am-2pm and 5:30-8:30pm; off-season Mon.-Sat. 9:30am-2pm and 5-8pm.)

SPAIN

Salamanca

For centuries the "hand of Salamanca," the brass knocker on the doors of the city, has welcomed students, scholars, rogues, royals, and saints. Bustling Salamanca is famed for its 13th-century university—the oldest in Spain—and for its architecture of warm golden sandstone. Nowhere is this more apparent than in **Plaza Mayor,** in which all styles—Roman, Gothic, Renaissance, and Baroque—are in the characteristic stone. Between the almost 100 arches hang medallions with bas-reliefs of famous Spaniards, from El Cid to Franco. The 15th-century **Casa de las Conchas** (House of Shells) is adorned by rows of scallop shells chiseled in sandstone. The house is now a public library, but the courtyard is open to tourists. (Open Mon.-Fri. 9am-9pm, Sat. 9am-2pm and 4-7pm, Sun. 10am-2pm and 4-7pm. Free.)

Enter the **Universidad,** founded in 1218, from the Patio de las Escuelas, off C. Libreros. The university's **entryway** is one of the best examples of Spanish Plateresque, a style named for the filigree work of *plateros* (silversmiths). The smallish frog carved on a skull is said to represent the dankness of prison life and to bring good luck on exams. If you spot the frog without help, you'll be married within the year. The walls are marked by students' initials in bold red, painted in an ink of bull's blood, olive oil, and herbs. Inside the **Escuelas Menores,** the *Cielo de Salamanca,* a 15th-century fresco of the zodiac, is preserved in the **University Museum.** (Open Mon.-Fri. 9:30am-1:30pm and 4-7:30pm, Sat. 9:30am-1:30pm and 4-7pm, Sun. 10am-1:30pm. Free.)

Follow Rúa Mayor south from Pl. Mayor; the *vieja* (old) and *nueva* (new) cathedrals sit together just past Pl. Anaya. Begun in 1513 to accommodate the growing tide of Catholics, the spindly spires of the Late Gothic **catedral nueva** weren't finished until 1733. The Romanesque **catedral vieja** (1140) has a striking cupola with depictions of apocalyptic angels separating the sinners from the saved. The cathedral **museum** houses a Mudéjar Salinas organ, one of the oldest organs in Europe. (Cathedrals open April-Sept. daily 10am-1:30pm and 4-7:30pm; Oct.-March 9am-1pm and 4-6pm. *Vieja,* cloister, and museum 300ptas. *Nueva* free.)

Practical Information, Accommodations, and Food Most sights and budget accommodations lie south of **Plaza Mayor.** To get to the city center from the train station, catch bus 1; from the bus station, take bus 4. Both buses go to Gran Vía, a block from Pl. Mercado (next to Pl. Mayor). The helpful **tourist office** is at Pl. Mayor, 13-14. (Tel. (923) 21 83 42. Open Mon.-Sat. 9am-2pm and 4:30-6:30pm, Sun. 10am-2pm and 4:30-6:30.) During the summer, students sometimes offer maps and accommodations listings at **information booths** in Pl. Anaya and both stations. **Trains** chug from Po. Estación Ferrocarril (tel. (923) 12 02 02) to Madrid (3½hr., 1590ptas), Barcelona (12hr., 6500ptas), Ávila (2hr., 820ptas), and transfer center Valladolid (805ptas). **Buses** run to Ávila (1-2hr., 820ptas), Segovia (2hr., 1340ptas), Madrid (2½-3hr., 1690-2210ptas), and León (3hr., 1675ptas).

The abundance of students means many rooms. Cheap *pensiones* abound on the side streets off Pl. Mayor, especially on **Calle Meléndez,** just south of the plaza. One of the best bargains for travelers going two-by-two, **Pensión Marina,** C. Doctrinos, 4, 3rd fl. (tel. (923) 21 65 69), between C. Compañía and C. Prado, boasts mammoth TV lounges (doubles 2500ptas, showers 200ptas). **Pensión Las Vegas,** C. Meléndez, 13 (tel. (923) 21 87 49), has comfy beds and lots of plants. (Singles 1000-1500ptas; doubles 2200-3000ptas; triples 3600-4000ptas. Showers 150ptas). For camping, head 4km toward Madrid to reach **Regio** (tel. (923) 13 88 88), on the Ctra. Salamanca (425ptas per person, 375-425ptas per tent).

Every clique has its favorite café in Plaza Mayor; each hangout serves the same moderately good food at a standard, slightly inflated price. A slew of bar-restaurants line the streets between the plaza and the university, where a full meal costs no more than 1000ptas. **Restaurante El Bardo,** C. Compañía, 8, between the Casa de Conchas and the Clerecía, is a traditional Spanish restaurant with a lively bar downstairs (entrees 900-1700ptas; closed Mon.). **Bocata World Company,** C. Rua Mayor, 26, will teach you the Spanish word for "fast food" as you chow down on their tasty bocadillos, including some vegetarian (340-475ptas). **Simago,** C. Toro, 82, has a downstairs **supermarket** (open Mon.-Sat. 9:30am-8:30pm).

Lugares, a free pamphlet at the tourist office and some bars, lists everything from movies to bus schedules. **Plaza Mayor** is the social center of town; people overflow from the plaza as far west as San Vicente. Student nightlife also concentrates on **Calle Bordedores,** the **Gran Vía,** and side streets. **Camelot,** C. Bordedores, is a monastery-turned-club, packed with converts looking to be defrocked. **El Corrillo Café,** C. Meléndez, has live jazz for the ultra-hip in a neon setting (cover 1000ptas for performances). For a more relaxed setting, **Birdland,** on C. Azafranal, 57, by Pl. España, has jazz greats. A gay and straight clientele grooves under black lights at **De Laval Genoves,** C. San Justo, built in an old submarine.

SPAIN

■ Near Salamanca: Ciudad Rodrigo

A medieval town characterized by fabulous masonry and honey-colored stone, Ciudad Rodrigo rises from the plains near the Portuguese border. The **cathedral** is the town's masterpiece. The cloister alone, with biblical and mythological scenes illustrated in fascinating stonework, justifies the trip from Salamanca. Fascinating figures festoon the columns—making love, playing peek-a-boo, or nibbling body parts. The cathedral's **museum** is filled with strange and thrilling old pieces, including an ancient clavichord, the ornate "ballot box" used to determine the cathedral's hierarchy, and Velázquez's *Llanto de Adán y Eva por Ariel muerto.* (Cathedral open daily 10:30am-1:30pm and 4-8pm. Free. Cloister and museum open daily 10:30am-1:30pm and 4-6pm. 200ptas, students 100ptas. Mandatory guided tour in Spanish.) Eight **buses** per day (3-5 on weekends) arrive from Salamanca (1½hr., 710ptas).

León

The name León derives from *legio,* after the Seventh Roman Legion which founded the city in 68 AD. Proud *leoneses* ("lions") roar that their cathedral, La Pulchra Leonina, is the finest in all of Spain. Its blue stained-glass windows have earned the city the nickname *La Ciudad Azul* (Blue City). The 13th-century Gothic **cathedral** features a glorious rose window with spiralling saints, and a fanciful garden of tiny faces (open daily 8:30am-1:30pm and 4-8pm; 700ptas). The cathedral's **museo** includes gruesome Renaissance wonders. (Open Mon.-Fri. 9:30am-2pm and 4-7:30pm, Sat. 9:30am-2pm; off-season closes 30min. earlier. 450ptas.)

The **Basílica de San Isidoro** was dedicated in the 11th century to San Isidoro of Sevilla, whose remains were brought to León while Muslims ruled the south. The corpses of León's royal family rest in the Basilica's **Panteón Real,** with vibrant frescoes covering two crypt ceilings. (Open July-Aug. 9am-2pm and 3-8pm; Sept.-June 10am-1:30pm and 4-6:30pm. 350ptas.) The **Museo de León,** Pl. San Marcos, holds an extensive archaeological collection with pieces dating back to the Paleolithic era, including Isabel II's chest of drawers. (Open Tues.-Sat. 10am-2pm and 5-8:30pm, Sun. 10am-2pm. 200ptas; students, seniors, and weekends free.)

For the "early" part of the night, the *barrio húmedo* (drinker's neighborhood) around **Plaza San Martín** sweats with bars, discos, and techno-pop. After 2am, the crowds stagger to **Calles Lancia** and **Conde de Guillén,** both heavily populated with discos and bars. **Fiestas** commemorating St. John and St. Peter enliven a week-long celebration (June 21-30) including *la corrida de toros* (bullfight).

Practical Information, Accommodations, and Food León's **tourist office** is at Pl. Regla, 3 (tel. (987) 23 70 82; fax 27 33 91), in front of the cathedral. (Open Mon.-Fri. 10am-2pm and 5-7:30pm, Sat. 10am-2pm and 4:30-8:30pm, Sun. 10am-2pm.) **Trains** leave from Av. Astorga, 2 (tel. (987) 27 02 02), across the river from Pl. Guzmán el Bueno, for La Coruña (7hr., 3200-4400ptas), Madrid (4½-5½hr., 3190-3500ptas), and other locales. The ticket office is at C. Carmen, 4 (tel. (987) 22 05 25). **Buses** (tel. (987) 21 10 00) depart from the Estación de Autobuses, Po. Ingeniero Saenz de Miera, for Madrid (4½hr., 2550ptas). For lodging, look on Avenida de Roma, Avenida de Ordoño II, and Avenida de la República Argentina, which lead into the new town from Pl. Guzmán el Bueno. The **Consejo de Europa (HI),** Po. Parque, 2 (tel. (987) 20 02 06), behind P. Toros, was recently renovated (850ptas, over 26 1000ptas; breakfast 300ptas; open July-Aug.; call ahead). The chatty proprietors of **Hostal Oviedo,** Av. Roma, 26 (tel. (987) 22 22 36), offer huge rooms, many with sinks and terraces (singles 1900ptas, doubles 3000ptas, triples 4500ptas). Downstairs from the Oviedo, the spotless **Hostal Europa** (tel. (987) 22 22 38) is also a good bet (singles 1600ptas, doubles 2700ptas, triples 3500ptas).

Eateries cluster by the cathedral, on the small streets off Av. Generalísimo Franco, and at Pl. San Martín. The **Cafetería-Restaurante Catedral,** by the cathedral at C. Mariano Dominguez Berrueta, 17, serves monumental portions (*menú* 1100ptas; open daily 1-4pm and 8-11pm, closed Tues. and Wed. afternoon). **Lleras, 38,** C. Burgos Nuevo, 38, is a jazzy restaurant with a 1050ptas *menú* (open daily 1-5pm and after 8pm). Gourmet and vegetarian dishes abound at **Calle Ancha,** C. Generalísimo Franco, between C. General Mola and C. Conde Luna (*menú* 900ptas; open daily 8am-1:30am). You can also find fresh produce at **Mercado Municipal del Conde,** Pl. Conde, off C. General Mola (open Mon.-Sat. 9am-3:30pm).

Burgos

Despite its small size, the chestnut-colored city of Burgos has figured prominently in Spain's history, first through the exploits of native son Rodrigo Díaz de Vivar (El Cid) and later as the capital of the Castile kingdom in the 15th century. The hard-line politics that justified El Cid's expulsion were revived in the 20th century when General Franco stationed his Nationalist headquarters here during the Civil War, but today the city hosts international brigades of pilgrims and enjoys peaceful riverside games, a nightly *paseo,* and a notable nightlife invigorated by the university.

The magnificent **cathedral** dominates the city. The 13th-century Gothic north facade is stark in comparison to the intricate 15th-century towers and 16th-century *Puerta de la Pellejería.* Beneath the glass skylight of the **Capilla Mayor,** El Cid's bones and those of his wife Jimena lie side by side in marmoreal serenity. Before leaving the cathedral, look for the fly catcher high up near the main door. As the hour strikes, the strange creature imitates the gawking crowds below (open daily 9:30am-1:30pm and 4-7pm; 400ptas, students 200ptas). The ruins of a **medieval castle** crown the hilltop behind the cathedral. If you're not already panting from the climb, the view will take your breath away.

After the cathedral, the **Estatua del Cid** in Pl. General Primo de Rivera is Burgos's most venerated landmark. El Cid won his fame in battle against the Moors, and the medieval poem celebrating his life, *El Cantar de Mio Cid,* is considered the first great work in the Castilian language. Burgos tradition compels its youth to climb the statue and fondle the testicles of El Cid's horse to ensure their own strength, courage, and fame. Just up C. Santander on the other side of the statue, the restored **Casa del Cordón,** where Columbus met Ferdinand and Isabel after his second trip to America, glows in the sunshine. Nearby, the **Museo de Pintura Marceliano Santa María** (a.k.a. the **Monasterio de San Juan**) features landscapes and portraits by Marceliano Santa María, a 20th-century local artist (open Tues.-Sat. 10am-2pm and 5-8pm, Sun. 10am-2pm; 25ptas, students free).

Practical Information, Accommodations, and Food Lying 240km north of Madrid, Burgos is divided by **Río Arlanzón.** The train and bus stations are on the south side, while the cathedral and sights are to the north. The **tourist office,** Pl. Alonso Martínez, 7 (tel. (947) 20 18 46), opposite the Capitanía General building, can be reached from the train or bus station by crossing the river and turning right onto Avenida del Generalísimo Franco (which becomes Paseo del Espolón), then following C. Santander (open Mon.-Fri. 9am-2pm and 5-7pm, Sat.-Sun. 10am-2pm and 5-7pm). **Trains** (tel. (947) 20 35 60) roll into the station at the end of Av. Conde Guadalhorce, across the river from Pl. Castilla, from San Sebastián (4hr., 2000-2300ptas), Madrid (3½hr., 2515-2885ptas), Barcelona (8hr., 4800-5170ptas), and Santiago (8hr., 4400-5500ptas). **RENFE,** C. Moneda, 21 (tel. (947) 20 91 31), sells tickets. **Buses** go from C. Miranda, 4 (tel. (947) 28 88 55), just off Pl. Vega, to Madrid (3hr., 1920ptas), Barcelona (7½hr., 4960ptas), and Pamplona (3hr., 1850ptas).

Reservations are crucial during late June and early July. Scout the streets near **Plaza Alonso Martínez** and **Calle San Juan** for a room. **Pensión Peña,** C. Puebla, 18 (tel. (947) 20 63 23), has small, elegant rooms (singles 1300-1400ptas, doubles 2500-2600ptas). **Hostal Hidalgo,** C. Almirante Bonifaz, 14 (tel. (947) 20 34 81), one block from Pl. Alonso Martínez off C. San Juan, is warm and friendly (singles 1700ptas, doubles 2800ptas). For camping, take the "Fuentes Blancas" bus from Pl. España (July to mid-Sept. 9:30am, 12:30, 4:15, and 7:15pm; 75ptas) to **Camping Fuentes Blancas** (450ptas per person and per tent; open April-Sept.). **Gaia Comedor Vegetariano,** C. San Francisco, 31, offers New Age ambiance (open Mon.-Fri. 1:30-4pm), while **La Riojana,** C. Arellanos 10, is a haven for the famished (*menú* 900ptas; open daily in summer 11:30am-2pm; winter noon-5pm). **Mercado de Abastos (Norte),** near Pl. España, and **Mercado de Abstos,** on C. Miranda near the bus station, have pungent market wares (open Mon.-Sat. 7am-3pm; Mercado Norte also Fri. 5:30-8pm).

After dinner, bars on C. San Juan and C. Puebla fill up with merrymakers aiming for an early start (try **Marmedi** on C. Puebla). By 11pm a steady hum rises up from **Las Llamas** (a series of plazas and streets in the shadow of the cathedral), where startling numbers of teenagers swarm. When the "early" bars close at 4 or 5am, head to **Las Bernardas,** the general area circumscribed by C. Las Calzadas, C. Belorado, and Av. General Yagüe, for "la penúltima"—the perpetual second-to-last drink. From June 24 to July 9, Burgos celebrates its patron saints Peter and Paul with concerts, parades, fireworks, bullfights, and dances.

GALICIA

Santiago de Compostela

Embraced by the Ríos Tambre and Ulla, Santiago was founded in 813 when, according to legend, a tomb containing the remains of the apostle St. James was found in the area. The city soon became one of Christianity's great holy sites. Many believed that the arduous journey to Santiago's glorious cathedral would halve their time in purgatory; in time, the volume of visitors was so great that monks built monasteries to host the pilgrims on their way, thus giving rise to Europe's first large-scale travel industry. Today, sunburnt pilgrims, smiling nuns, musicians, and tourists fill the granite streets, awed by Santiago's magnificence.

ORIENTATION AND PRACTICAL INFORMATION

The **cathedral** marks the center of the old city, which sits higher than the new city. Three streets lead directly to the cathedral from the south side of town, where the train station is located: **Rúa do Franco** (Calle del Franco), **Rúa do Vilar** (Calle del Vilar) and **Rúa Nova** (Calle Nueva). From the train station, turn right at the top of the stairs and take C. Hórreo to **Praza de Galiza** (do *not* take Avenida de Lugo). One block ahead is **C. Bautizatos,** from which the three cathedral-bound streets spring. From the bus station, take bus 10 to Pr. Galiza (every 10-15min., 85ptas).

Tourist Office: R. Vilar (tel. 58 40 81), in the old town. Open Mon.-Fri. 10am-2pm and 4-7pm, Sat. 11am-2pm. Also in the Modernist structure in the center island of Pr. Galizia. Open Mon.-Fri. 10am-2pm and 5-8pm; in summer also Sat. 11am-2pm.
Budget Travel: TIVE, Plazuela del Matadero (tel. 57 24 26). Turn right up R. Fonte Santo Antonio from Pr. Galiza. Train, bus, and plane tickets for international destinations. ISIC 700ptas. HI cards 500ptas. Open Mon.-Fri. 9am-2pm.
American Express: Ultratur Viajes, Av. Figueroa, 6 (tel. 58 70 00). Open Mon.-Fri. 9:30am-2pm and 4:30-7:30pm, Sat. 10am-12:30pm.
Trains: R. General Franco (tel. 52 02 02). Open Mon.-Sat. 7am-9pm, Sun. 7am-1pm. To: Madrid (8hr., 4700-5500ptas), La Coruña (1hr., 490-565ptas), León (6½hr., 2800-3300ptas), and Porto, Portugal (through Vigo, 4½hr., 2415-2530ptas).
Buses: Estación Central de Autobuses, C. San Cayetano (tel. 58 77 00). Nothing central about it, but bus 10 leaves every 15min. from the R. Montero Río side of Pr. Galiza for the station (35ptas). Info open daily 6am-10pm. **ALSA** (tel. 58 61 33) runs to Madrid (8-9hr., 5010ptas), Bilbao (9½hr., 6170-6340ptas), and San Sebastián (6hr., 6910ptas). **Castromil** (tel. 58 90 90) serves La Coruña (1½hr., 650-800ptas) and Pontevedra (1½hr., 600ptas), among others.
Luggage Storage: At the train station. Lockers 400ptas. Open daily 7:30am-11pm. Also at the bus station. 75ptas per bag. Open daily 8am-10pm.
Laundromat: Lavandería Lobato, C. Santiago de Chile, 7 (tel. 59 99 54).
Medical Assistance: Hospital Xeral, C. Galeras (tel. 54 00 00).
Emergency: tel. 091 or 092.
Police: Guardia Civil: tel. 58 22 66 or 58 16 11.
Post Office: Travesa de Fonseca (tel. 58 12 52; fax 56 32 88), on the corner of R. Franco. Open for stamps, faxes, and *Lista de Correos* Mon.-Fri. 8:30am-8:30pm, Sat. 9:30am-2pm. **Postal Code:** 15080.
Telephone Code: 981.

ACCOMMODATIONS, CAMPING, AND FOOD

Hospedajes and *pensiones* multiply around **Rúa do Vilar** and **Calle Raíña,** and hand-drawn *"habitaciones"* signs are just about everywhere else.

Hospedaje Ramos, C. Raíña, 18, 2nd fl. (tel. 58 18 59), above a restaurant. Spacious rooms in a great location. Singles 1600-1750ptas. Doubles 3000-3500ptas.
Hospedaje Viño, Pr. Mazarelos, 7 (tel. 58 51 85). At Pr. Galiza, take a right onto R. Fonte San Antonio, then the first left up a diagonal granite street. Well-furnished rooms overlook a peaceful plaza. Singles 1500ptas. Doubles 3000ptas.
Hospedaje Sofía, C. Cardenal Paya, 16 (tel. 58 51 50). Enter the restaurant on the ground floor and head upstairs. Spic 'n' span rooms ensure a comfortable stay. Singles 2500ptas. Doubles 3600-4000ptas. Less in winter.
Hospedaje Santa Cruz, R. Vilar, 42, 2nd fl. (tel. 58 28 15). Newly renovated rooms have big windows overlooking the most popular street in Santiago. Singles 2000ptas. Doubles 2500ptas. Off-season: 1500ptas; 3000ptas.
Camping: Camping As Cancelas, R. 25 de Xullo, 35 (tel. 58 02 66), 2km from the cathedral on the north edge of town. Take bus 6 or 9. Laundry, a supermarket, and a pool on the site. 425ptas per person, car, and tent. Open year-round.

Santiago is a budget diner's dream. The city's open-air **market** is a sight in its own right; produce carts, meat stalls, and baskets of cheeses line the streets from Pr. San Felix to Convento de San Augustín (open Mon.-Sat. 7:30am-2pm). Most restaurants in the old town lie south of the cathedral, on **Rúa do Villar, Rúa Franco,** and **Calle Raíña.** Near the market and Pl. San Augustín, **Casa Manolo,** R. Traviesa, 27, offers the best deal in town (*menú* 650ptas; open Mon.-Fri. 1-4pm and 8pm-midnight).

SIGHTS AND ENTERTAINMENT

The entire old town has been designated a national monument, but the centerpiece is the **cathedral.** Modern pilgrims congregate around the altar, and every candle is lit and every pew filled to bursting during mass. Consecrated in 1211, the cathedral later acquired Gothic chapels in the apse and transept, a 15th-century dome, a 16th-century cloister, and a Baroque facade called the **Obradoiro,** which sends two exquisitely ornate towers soaring above the city. Encased in the Obradoiro, the **Pórtico de la Gloria** is considered the crowning achievement of Spanish Romanesque sculpture. Inside, St. James's revered remains lie beneath the high altar in a silver coffer, while his bejeweled bust sits above. The cathedral's four entrances open onto four plazas: Platerías, Quintana, Obradoiro, and Azabaxería. Across Pr. Obradoiro, the long facade of the former **Pazo de Raxoi** (Royal Palace) shines with gold-accented balconies and Neoclassical columns. On the other side of the cathedral, the **Mosteiro de San Pelayo** has a striking statue of Mary holding Jesus and clubbing a demon (open Mon.-Sat. 10am-1pm and 4-8pm, Sun. 10am-2pm; 200ptas).

Santiago offers an eclectic mix of entertainment. The newspaper *El Correo Gallego* (125ptas) lists art exhibits and concert info. Ten minutes from the old town, the **Auditorio** features mostly classical music (concerts Oct.-June; check at the tourist office). On the streets of the old town, various student troupes called **tunas** dress in medieval garb, sing ribald songs, and serenade selected victims. After enjoying a tune, head to one of the packed bars on **Rúas Nova, Vilar,** and **Franco.** (Cover for men 500-800ptas; women generally free. Most open 11pm-4am, action starts well after midnight.) Santiago's **fiestas** (July 18-31) enliven the city.

Rías Altas

If Galicia is the forgotten corner of Spain, then the small *rías* of the Costa de la Muerte are the forgotten corner of Galicia. Beaches here are arguably the emptiest, cleanest, and loveliest in all of Spain. Bus service to the smaller towns and isolated beaches is infrequent or nonexistent.

La Coruña and Environs North of Santiago, the Rías Altas stretch their watery fingers into the land from the province of Lugo down to Cabo Finisterre. In the misty mountains of Galicia the weather is anything but predictable, but views are spectacular year-round. Thanks to a healthy burst of summer tourism, the Rías Altas have modern conveniences to complement a relatively unspoiled coastline.

La Coruña (A Coruña), an ideal base for exploration of the region, boasts a stellar nightlife, a historic old town, and pleasant beaches. The **tourist office,** Dársena de la Marina (tel. (981) 22 18 22), near the waterfront, is full of tips on trips to the Rías Altas (open Mon.-Fri. 9am-2pm and 4:30-6:30pm, Sat. 10:30am-1pm). **Trains** leave from Pr. San Cristóbal (tel (981) 15 02 02) for Vigo (3hr., 1195-1370ptas) and Santiago (1¼hr, 490-565ptas). **Buses** serve the Rías Altas and surrounding area from C. Caballeros (tel. (981) 23 96 44), across Av. Alcalde Molina from the train station. Buses 1 (100ptas) and 1A (110ptas) run from the train and bus stations to the tourist office. The best place to look for a room is one block back from Av. Marina, near the tourist office. Calle Riego de Agua and the surrounding area always have rooms. **Hospedaje María Pita,** C. Riego de Agua, 38, 3rd fl. (tel. (981) 22 11 87), has cheery rooms and pristine bathrooms (doubles 2200-2700ptas).

The Rías Altas beckon with their relatively unspoiled coastline. Where buses and trains seldom tread, hitching is futile, and ferny rain forests give way to soft, empty beaches lie the **Rías de Cedeira** and **Viveiro.** Buses and a few FEVE trains run inland

SPAIN

to Viveiro from El Ferrol, but the sporadic coastal bus from is preferable—you can always hop off if you see a place you like.

PICOS DE EUROPA

Intrepid mountaineers, novice trekkers, and even idle admirers flock to the Picos, the most notable section of the **Cordillera Cantábrica** mountain range, which extends across northern Spain. Other European ranges may be higher, but few match the beauty of the Picos de Europa's abrupt and jagged profile.

Most trails in the Picos traverse the region's north-south axis between **Arenas de Cabrales** and **Fuente Dé.** The bus company **ALSA,** and its subsidiary **Económicos,** are the best way to get around. The Oviedo (tel. (98) 521 33 85) and Cangas de Onís (tel. (98) 584 80 05) tourist offices stock schedules. Often only campers can find beds during July and August, and even this endeavor can be touch and go—many campgrounds and **refugios** (cabins with bunks but not blankets) fill up in high season. **Albergues** are ancient, non-heated buildings with bunks and access to cold water. **Casas** have hot water and wood stoves. In any case, you should bring a sleeping bag. Make reservations at *hostales* or *pensiones* in June or earlier. In a jam, tourist offices can help you find a bed in a private residence. Small towns often do not have an ATM machine or a supermarket, so stock up in Oviedo. If you set off the bus alone (not recommended), leave a copy of your planned route so a rescue squad can be alerted if you don't return or call by a certain time. Always pack **warm clothes** and **rain gear.** If a heavy mist descends *en route* (as often happens), don't continue unless you know exactly where you're going. Just be patient and wait for the mist to clear.

Gray, urban **Oviedo** is a good base for excursions to the Picos de Europa. **Trains** run from C. Uría (tel. (98) 524 33 64 or 525 02 02), at the junction with Av. Santander, to León (2½hr., 850-1470ptas), Madrid (6½-8hr., 4200ptas), and Barcelona (13hr., 6000ptas). **ALSA** sends **buses** from Pl. General Primo de Rivera, 1 (tel. (98) 528 12 00; unmarked, on the lower level of a shopping arcade), to Barcelona (12hr., 4850ptas), Burgos (4hr., 1630ptas), León (2hr., 1005ptas), and Madrid (6hr., 3655-5800ptas). **Económicos (EASA),** C. Jerónimo Ibrán, 1 (tel. (98) 529 00 39), sends buses to Cangas de Onís (1½hr., 670ptas), Covadonga (1¾hr., 785ptas), and Arenas de Cabrales (2¼hr., 945ptas), all near the Picos. Significantly fewer buses run on weekends.The English speaking **tourist office** at Pl. Alfonso II (tel. (98) 521 33 85) has maps and advice on Picos treks (open Mon.-Fri. 9:30am-1:30pm and 4:30-6:30pm, Sat. 9am-2pm, Sun. 11am-2pm). Robin Walker's *Picos de Europa* is a good **English guidebook** to the trails and towns of the area. Organizations devoted to activities and accommodations in the Picos include **TIVE** travel agency, C. Calvo Sotelo, 5 (tel. (98) 523 60 58; open Mon.-Fri. 8am-3pm); **Dirección Regional de la Juventud,** C. Calvo Sotelo, 5 (tel. (98) 523 11 12; open Mon.-Fri. 10am-1pm); **ICONA,** C. Arquitecto Reguera, 13, 2nd fl. (tel. (98) 524 14 12); **Dirección Regional de Deportes,** Pl. España (tel. (98) 527 23 47); and **Oxígeno,** C. Manuel Pedregal (tel. (98) 522 79 75).

A plethora of *pensiones* pack Oviedo's new city near the transport stations. Try **Calle Uría, C. Campoamor** (1 block east), and **C. Nueve de Mayo** (a continuation of C. Manuel Pedregal, 1 block farther east). Near the cathedral, try C. Jovellanos. Across from the hospital, **Residencia Juvenil Ramón Menéndez Pidal,** C. Julián Clavería, 14 (tel. (98) 523 20 54), has a few rooms for 720ptas per person (over 26 1000ptas). Call first, then take bus 2 from C. Uría. **Pensión Pomar,** C. Jovellanos, 7 (tel. (98) 522 27 91), provides super-clean, airy rooms (singles 1500-2000ptas, doubles 3000-3500ptas, triples 4500ptas). **Pensión Martinez,** C. Jovellanos, 5 (tel. (98) 521 53 44), has clean rooms with sinks and communal bathrooms (singles 1500ptas, doubles 3000ptas, triples 3000ptas). **Pensión Riesgo,** C. Nueve de Mayo, 16, 1st fl. (tel. (98) 521 89 45), has smallish, clean, and unglamorous rooms (singles 1800ptas, doubles 3500ptas). A posh indoor **market** with an **ATM** is on C. Fontán, off Pl. Mayor (open Mon.-Sat. 8am-

8pm). For groceries, try **El Corte Inglés** at C. General Alorza, opposite the ALSA station, and C. Uría (open Mon.-Sat. 10am-9:30pm).

BASQUE COUNTRY (PAÍS VASCO, EUSKADI)

Bilbao (Bilbo)

Bilbao defines bourgeois. Industrial engine of the Basque Country, Bilbao has practiced making men wealthy since the 16th century, when its ports served as the key shipping link between Castile and Flanders. But Bilbao doesn't rest on its economic laurels; the city has bought itself respectability by investing heavily in the arts, and the new Guggenheim museum, scheduled to open in October of 1997, promises to provide Bilbao with the cultural esteem for which it yearns.

The **Museo de Bellas Artes,** boasts aesthetic riches from 12th- to 19th-centuries Spanish and Flemish holdings, to numerous canvases by Basque painters and a sizeable abstract art collection. From Pl. Federico Moyúa (with Pl. España behind you), angle right on C. Elcano and follow it to Pl. Museo, 2 (open Tues.-Sat. 10am-1:30pm and 4-7:30pm, Sun. 10am-2pm; free). A shimmering structure of multiple levels and unexpected curves, the new **Guggenheim museum** will attract visitors as much for its striking architecture as its important collection of modern and contemporary art. Designed by American Frank Gehry, it is built around a light-filled atrium and contains the largest single gallery in the world (expected admission 600ptas). The **Museo Arqueológico, Etnográfico, e Histórico de Vizcaya,** C. Cruz, 4, housed in a beautiful old cloister, has displays on Basque hand-weaving, blacksmithing, and life on the sea. The museum is in the old city; walk past Pensión de la Fuente away from C. Correo to Pl. Miguel de Unamuno, then to C. Cruz (open Tues.-Sat. 10am-1:30pm and 4-7pm, Sun. 10:30am-1:30pm; free).

In Bilbao's **casco viejo** (old town) people spill out into the streets to tipple *chiquitos,* small glasses of regional beer or wine. Youngsters jam **Calle Licenciado Poza** and **Calle Barrencalle;** with 200 bars within 200m, **Calle Ledesma** exerts a similar pull. The most radical bar in town is **Herriko Taberna** (The People's Tavern), C. Ronda, 20, with political posters and photos of Basque detainees papering the walls. For afternoon entertainment, hop on a train to reach the **beaches** at **Plencia** or at **Sopelana,** north of the city. **Getxo** also lies near the waves; its suspension bridge fords the river, leading to a spate of all-night bars. **Buses** go here from Pl. Ensanche in Bilbao, near the market (150ptas; taxi home for late-night revelers 2000-2500ptas). Beginning the weekend after August 15, the city explodes for two weeks with music, theater, bullfights, and fireworks for its **Semana Grande** *fiesta.*

What the Devil Are They Txpeaking?

Linguists still cannot pinpoint the origin of *euskera,* an agglutinate non-Indo-European language spoken by half a million natives in País Vasco regions. Its commonalties with Caucasian and African tongues regarding root structures suggest that prehistoric Basques may have migrated from the Caucasus through Africa. Historically referred to by other Spaniards as *la lengua del diablo* (the devil's tongue), *euskera* has come to symbolize cultural self-determination and is promoted in part by Basque nationalists who want separation from Spain. Franco banned *euskera* and forbid parents to give their children Basque names, but nowadays usage spreads through *ikastolas* (all-Basque schools), TV, and Basque publications. The younger generations listen to rock music in *euskera,* conduct normal conversations in the language, and give their kids traditional names such as Iñaki, Idoya, and Estibaliz.

Practical Information, Accommodations, and Food Bilbao has six **train stations. RENFE, Estación de Abando/del Noret,** Pl. España (info tel. 423 86 23, reservations 423 86 36), serves Madrid (6-9hr., 4100ptas), Barcelona (10¾-11½hr., 4800-5400ptas), Seville (14hr., 12,900ptas), and Salamanca (6¼hr., 3400ptas). The **bus** system is even more confusing; the tourist office details companies and stations serving San Sebastián (1¼hr., 1060ptas), Burgos (2hr., 1390ptas), and Madrid (5hr., 3185ptas). Mercifully, in 1997 the city should have opened its **Estácion Intermodal,** which will house all major bus and train lines under one roof. From any of the stations, navigate toward the Gran Vía, leading to Pl. España and the **Puente del Arenal** bridge, which links the new town with the *casco viejo.* Across the bridge, the **tourist office** (tel. (94) 416 00 22; fax 416 81 68) offers a free booklet on Bilbao (open Mon.-Fri. 9am-2pm and 4-7:30pm, Sat. 9am-2pm, Sun. 10am-2pm).

Plaza Arriaga and nearby **Calle Arenal** are good starting points for hunting budget pensions. The tourist office has a list of budget *pensiones.* To find **Pensión de la Fuente,** C. Sombrería, 2 (tel. (94) 416 99 89), from C. Arenal, turn left on C. Correo and walk one block, then turn left. The pension offers spacious rooms and a TV room (singles 1500-2000ptas, doubles 2500-3000ptas). From the bridge, turn right on C. Bidebarrieta and right again to reach **Pensión Mardones,** C. Jardines, 4, 3rd fl. (tel. (94) 415 31 05), which features gorgeous rooms, some with balconies. (Singles 2000-2700ptas; doubles 3000ptas; triples 4500-5500ptas; quads 6000-7000ptas.) Restaurants and bars in the *casco viejo* are crowded but offer hearty local dishes. Dining spots in the modern quarter offer more variety and comfort, but not nearly as much flavor. **Mercado de la Ribera,** on the bank of the river heading left from the tourist office, is the biggest indoor market in Europe. It's worth a trip even if you're not eating (open Mon.-Thurs. and Sat. 8am-2pm, Fri. 7:45am-2pm and 4:30-7:30pm).

SPAIN

San Sebastián (Donostia)

Think Rita Hayworth. In the 1940s the glamorous American movie star visited San Sebastian, and the city fell so in love with her that it named a *pincho* (a local specialty) after one of her movies. City and star were a perfect fit, both of them coolly elegant and extravagantly beautiful. Glittering on the shores of the Cantabrian Sea, San Sebastián is a city of broad boulevards, ornate buildings, and lovely beaches.

ORIENTATION AND PRACTICAL INFORMATION

The **Río Urumea** splits San Sebastián in two. The city center, many monuments, and the two most popular beaches are on the west side of the river, on a peninsula. Inland on the peninsula is the **parte vieja** (old city), where the nightlife rages, and budget accommodations and restaurants cluster. To the south is the **Catedral del Buen Pastor.** East of the river lies the **RENFE station,** the **Barrio de Gros,** and **Playa de la Zurriola.** The west and east are connected by three bridges.

To get to the *parte vieja* from the station, head straight to Puente María Cristina, cross the bridge, and then turn right and walk four blocks north to Av. Libertad. Turn left and follow it to the port; the *parte vieja* fans out to the right. To get to the **tourist office** from the station, turn right after crossing Puente María Cristina (the southern bridge) and continue past Puente Santa Catalina; Calle Reina Regente will be on the left. The **bus station** is in the south of the city in Plaza de Pío XII.

Tourist Office: Centro de Atracción y Turismo, C. Reina Regente (tel. 48 11 66; fax 48 11 72), in the Teatro Victoria Eugenia. Open June-Sept. Mon.-Sat. 8am-8pm, Sun. 10am-1pm; Oct.-May Mon.-Fri. 9am-2pm and 3:30-7pm, Sat. 8am-8pm.

Currency Exchange: Banco Central Hispano sits on Av. Sancho el Sabio as you exit the bus station to the right.

Trains: RENFE, Estación del Norte, Po. Francia (tel. 28 30 89; info tel. 28 35 99), on the east side of Puente María Cristina. To: Burgos (3-4hr., 2570ptas), Madrid (6-9hr., 4300-5800ptas), Barcelona (9½-11hr., 4600-6000ptas), and Paris (10,800ptas;

change at Hendaye, France). **RENFE office,** C. Camino, 1, on the corner with C. Oquendo. Open Mon.-Fri. 9am-1pm and 4-7pm, Sat. 9am-1pm.

Buses: Several private companies run from different points in the city; most pass through the station on Pl. Pío XII. **Continental Auto,** Av. Sancho el Sabio, 31 (tel. 46 90 74). To: Madrid (6hr., 3620ptas) and Burgos (3¼hr., 1800ptas). **Irbarsa,** Po. Vizcaya, 16 (tel. 45 75 00), sends buses to Barcelona (7hr., 2450ptas). **La Roncalesa,** Po. Vizcaya (tel. 46 10 64), runs to Pamplona (1½hr., 750ptas).

Public Transportation: Tickets are 100ptas; a 10-ride pass available at *estancos* runs 570ptas. Call 28 71 00 or check at the tourist office for routes.

Luggage Storage: At RENFE station. 400ptas per day. Open daily 7am-11pm.

Laundromat: Lavomatique, C. Iñigo, 13 off C. San Juan. Open Mon.-Fri. 10am-1pm and 4-7pm, Sat.-Sun. 10am-1pm.

Medical Assistance: Casa de Socorro, C. Pedro Egaño, 8 (tel. 46 63 19). **Red Cross Hospital,** C. Matías, 7 (tel. 21 46 00).

Emergencies: tel. 091 or 092. **Ambulance:** tel. 28 40 00.

Police: C. Larramendi, 10 (tel. 45 00 00).

Post Office: C. Urdaneta (tel. 46 49 14; fax 45 07 94), just south of the cathedral. Open Mon.-Fri. 8:30am-8:30pm, Sat. 9:30am-2pm. **Postal Code:** 20007.

Telephone Code: 943.

SPAIN

ACCOMMODATIONS AND CAMPING

Rooms are scarce in July and August—particularly during *Sanfermines* (July 6-14) and *Semana Grande* (the week of Aug. 15). Consider 3000ptas per night to be a good deal. Prices are also higher during *Semana Santa.* Budget options congregate both in the **parte vieja** and around the **cathedral.** The tourist office has lists of rooms, and most *pensión* owners know *casas particulares* that take in guests.

Albergue Juvenil la Sirena (HI), Po. Igueldo, 25 (tel. 31 02 68; fax 21 40 90), near the beach at the far west end of the city (1st stop after the tunnel). Bus 5 takes you one street past the hostel on C. Matia. Bus 24 runs from train and bus stations to Av. Zumalacárregui (stop in front of the San Sebastián Hotel); from there, turn left at the end of the street that angles toward the mountain (Av. Brunei). Luggage storage, laundry facilities, and kitchen. Members or ISIC holders only. Reception closed 11am-3pm. Summer curfew 2am; off-season midnight, weekends 2am. 1850ptas, over 26 2100ptas. Off-season prices 250-325ptas cheaper. Breakfast included. Sheets 375ptas.

Pensión Loinaz, C. San Lorenzo, 17 (tel. 42 67 14). Attentive, English-speaking owners have bright rooms that will make you want to stay—forever. Doubles 3200-4700ptas. Triples 4500-6200ptas. *Let's Go* discount. Laundry 800ptas.

Pensión Amaiur, C. 31 de Agosto, 44, 2nd fl. (tel. 42 96 54). From Alameda del Boulevard, go up C. San Jerónimo and turn left. Stunning floral rooms and delightful owner. Doubles 2800-4800ptas. Triples 3600-6300. *Let's Go* discount 300ptas.

Pensión San Lorenzo, C. San Lorenzo, 2 (tel. 42 55 16), a right off C. Narrica from Alameda del Boulevard, on the corner of C. San Juan. Cozy rooms. Use the kitchen, which serves as a chatty community center. 1000-1250ptas per person.

Pensión Larrea, C. Narrica, 21, 1st fl. (tel. 42 26 94). Simple rooms. Spotless bathrooms. Singles 2000-2500ptas. Doubles 3000-4500ptas. *Let's Go* discount.

Pensión Urkia, C. Urbieta, 12, 3rd. fl. (tel. 42 44 36), bordering the cathedral on the west side. Upscale and lovely. Singles 3000-3500ptas. Doubles 3500-5000ptas.

Pensión La Perla, C. Loyola, 10, 2nd fl. (tel. 42 81 23), the street directly ahead of the cathedral. Attractive rooms. Singles 3000ptas. Doubles 3500-5000ptas.

FOOD

Pinchos (*pintxos* in Basque; bite-size snacks) are a religion here, usually chased with the fizzy regional wine *txacoli.* Worship at the *pincho* altar and you will surely be rewarded in the afterlife. Bars in the lively old city spread an array of enticing tidbits on toothpicks or bread. Vendors also sell *gambas* (shrimp) and *caracolillos* (periwinkles) for 100-200ptas.

Close to 40 restaurants and bars line **Calle Fermín Calbetón.** The least expensive hunting ground for a full meal at a restaurant (*jatetxea* in Basque) is the **Gros** neighborhood. For history's greatest *pinchos* tour, start at **Bar La Cepa,** C. 31 de Agosto, 7-9, which has exquisite peppers and a host of other delicacies (*pinchos* 150-250ptas, *menú del día* 1500ptas). Then continue to **Gastelv,** C. 31 de Agosto, 22, for exquisite seafood confections (*pinchos* 150ptas, lunch *menú* 950ptas). **Bar Juantxo,** C. Embeltrán, 6, in the *parte vieja,* sells 1000 *bocadillos* a day (270-465ptas; open daily 9am-3pm and 7-11:30pm). Near the cathedral, **Zakusan** and **Cachón,** C. San Marcial 52 and 40, are perfect stops on the tour (*pinchos* 140-180ptas). For groceries near the hostel, try **Todo Todo 3,** C. Serrano Anguta, between C. Zumalacárregui and C. Matia (open Mon.-Fri. 9am-1pm and 4-8pm, Sat. 9am-1pm). In the *parte vieja,* shop at **Iñigo Saski,** C. Iñigo, 7 (open Mon.-Fri. 9am-1:30pm and 4:45-7:30pm; Sat. 9am-1:30pm).

SPAIN

SIGHTS AND ENTERTAINMENT

The view of the bay is spectacular on weekends after dark, when the base of Isla Santa Clara is lit by banks of floodlights. The top of **Monte Igueldo,** at the bay's far side, provides the best view. For the **funicular** to the top, take hourly bus 16 ("Igueldo") from Alameda del Boulevard or walk along the beach and turn left just before the tennis courts. (Funicular runs June 25-Sept. 25 Mon.-Fri. 10am-9pm, Sat.-Sun. 10am-10pm; Sept. 26-June 24 11am-8pm. 100ptas one way.) At the other end of the bay, paths wind through the cool, shady woods of **Monte Urgull.** The overgrown **Castillo de Santa Cruz de la Mota** crowns the summit with cannons and a chapel (castle open in summer daily 8am-8pm; off-season 8am-6pm). **Paseo Nuevo,** starting at the end of the port, circles the base of Monte Urgull, bringing you close enough to the waves to feel the spray. At one end of the road, the **Museo de San Telmo,** housed in a former Dominican monastery, has an array of Basque funerary artifacts, a couple of dinosaur skeletons, some El Grecos, and contemporary art. (Open Tues.-Sat. 10:30am-1:30pm and 4-8pm, Sun. 10am-2pm. 350ptas, students 200ptas.)

Movie stars and directors own the streets for a week in September during the **Festival Internacional de Cine,** deemed among the four most important in the world. For info about this year's film festival, call 48 12 12, fax 48 12 12, or write to Apartados de Correos, 397, San Sebastián 20080. San Sebastián's five-day **Festival de Jazz** is also one of Europe's most ambitious. For information on the 1998 festival, contact the Oficina del Festival de Jazz (tel. 48 11 79) at C. Reina Regente, 20003 San Sebastián (beneath the tourist office). The week of August 15, **Semana Grande** (Big Week) is ablaze with concerts, movies, and an international fireworks festival.

The **parte vieja** pulls out all the stops after dark. The **Bar Uraitz** and **Bar Eibartarra,** C. Mayor, 26, are human zoos, while another pair, **Bar Sariketa** and **Bar Txalupa,** C. Fermín Calbetón, 23 and 3, feature sonic-boom music and sweltering climate. Techno fans head to the sleek, black bars of **Akerbeltz and Etxe Kalte,** on C. Mari near the port. The city's small but mighty disco scene starts thumping at **Ku,** atop Monte Igueldo (opens nightly 8pm). Many crowd along the beach at **Bataplán,** Po la Concha (cover with drink 2000ptas; opens nightly midnight).

NAVARRE (NAVARRA)

Pamplona (Iruña)

At Pamplona's bullring, a statue of Ernest Hemingway welcomes *aficionados* and rowdy partiers to eight days of dancing, drinking, and dashing. **Los San Fermines** (July 6-14)—known to English speakers as "The Running of the Bulls"—celebrates the patron saint San Fermín, who was martyred when bulls dragged him through the streets. The mayor kicks off the craziness by lighting the first rocket, the *chupinazao,* from the Ayuntamiento's balcony. A barbaric howl explodes from eager *sanfermini-*

stas below, and within minutes the *casco antiguo* is flooded with singing and dancing. The *peñas,* societies more concerned with beer than bulls, lead the brouhaha.

The **encierro** (the actual running of the bulls) takes place at 8am every morning; hyper-adrenalized and hung-over men flee from not-so-innocuous herbivores that charge 825m down the streets to the bull ring *(Plaza de Toros).* The race lasts less than three minutes when the bulls stay together; isolated bulls are equally dangerous, since they run into the crowds. *Let's Go* strongly recommends that you enjoy the festivities only as a spectator. In recent years, surging numbers of inexperienced foreigners have joined the run and crowded the course, increasing the risks for everyone involved. Travelers who decide to participate should watch an *encierro* first and avoid running with the dangerous, enormous weekend bunch. It is not wise to cower in a doorway; you can be trapped and killed. Many more runners are injured at the end of the course, where a narrow opening rudely interrupts the bravado. If you fall, stay down and protect yourself by curling up into a fetal position. Runners must get to the course by 7:30am; many recommend getting there at 6am. Those not confident in their running ability line up by the Plaza de Toros before 7:30am, run in before the bulls are even in sight, then "play" with the bulls in a mass of people. Bullfight spectators should arrive around 6:45am to experience the crowd heating up for the *encierro.* Buying tickets for the **Grada** section of the bull ring may be a good idea (arrive before 7am; 450ptas).

After the taurine track meet, the hoopla moves into the streets with dancing in the alleys, wild parades, and a no-holds-barred party on **Plaza Castillo.** At the corner of C. Navarría and C. Carmen, in front of Casa Santa Cecilia, a number of people die each year jumping from a fountain. Nearby towns sponsor *encierros* too: **Tudela** during the week surrounding July 24, **Estella** the Friday before the first Sunday in August, **Tafalla** the week of August 15, and **Sangüesa** the week of September 11.

During the other 51 weeks of the year, a different but no less enchanting side of Pamplona emerges. A center of Basque nationalist activity, Pamplona's impassioned politics and active bar scene are nicely offset by acres of tranquil parks and a well-regarded university. The pentagonal **Ciudadela,** featuring a duck pond, deer park, and gravel paths, sprawls next to the delicious **Jardines de la Taconera.** Throughout the year, Pl. Castillo is the city's social heart, with people of all ages congregating in and around its bars and cafés. Hemingway's favorite was **Café-Bar Iruña**—the backdrop for *The Sun Also Rises.*

Practical Information, Accommodations, and Food Pamplona is miserably connected by rail. Although **trains** do run to Madrid (5-6hr., 2750-4200ptas) and Barcelona (7-9hr., 3800-5400ptas), it is better to take **buses** from the station on C. Conde Oliveto, at the corner of C. Yanguas y Miranda. Over 20 companies compete to fill their buses to Barcelona (6hr., 3245ptas), San Sebastián (1½hr., 750ptas), and Bilbao (2¼hr., 1510ptas). The **tourist office,** C. Duque de Ahumada, 3 (tel. (948) 22 07 41; fax 21 14 62), offers a map, bus info, and a guide to the festivities. To find the office from Pl. Castillo, take Av. Carlos III one block, turn left on C. Duque de Ahumada, and cross C. Espoz y Mina (open daily 10am-5pm, Sat. 10am-2pm; during *San Fermines* daily 10am-5pm).

And now for an economics lesson in supply and demand. Diehard *sanferministas* book their rooms up to a year in advance; in most cases, you must reserve at least two months ahead and pay up-front rates two to four times higher than those listed here. Check newspapers *(Diario de Navarra)* for **private rooms,** but be wary of people at the train and bus stations offering couches and floor space. Many who can't find rooms take quick naps during the day or sleep outside on the lawns of the Ciudadela and the Pl. Fueros; do this only if you can sleep in a group and protect your belongings. **Luggage storage** is available at the stations.

When the bulls stop running, follow C. Estafeta to its end in Mercaderea and turn right and then left at a 30° angle for **Casa Santa Cecilia,** C. Navarrería, 17 (tel. (948) 22 22 30), for good prices during *San Fermines* (singles 2000-4000ptas, doubles 3000-8000ptas). **Hostal Bearán,** C. San Nicolás, 25 (tel./fax (948) 22 34 28), has clean

SPAIN

rooms with TV and bath. (Singles 4500-5500ptas, doubles 5500-6500ptas; *San Fermines* 13,000ptas, 15,000ptas.) Use Hostal Bearán's reception desk to secure a more spartan room at **Fonda La Aragonesa** (singles 2500-3000ptas, doubles 3000-3500ptas; *Sanfermines* 8000ptas, 9000ptas). The rooms may feel like cells in the former prison **Hostal Otano,** C. San Nicolás, 5 (tel. (948) 22 50 95; singles 1700-2000ptas, doubles 2000-3500ptas). A La Montañesa bus runs from Pl. Toros four times a day to **Camping Ezcaba** (tel. (948) 33 16 65; 450ptas per person and per tent; open June-Oct.). Look on Calle Navarrería, the neighborhood of Casa de Huéspedes Santa Cecilia, around Pl. San Fransisco, and C. Descalzos near Po. Ronda for frenzied feeding. At C. San Nicolás, 19-21, **Restaurante Sarasate** has scrumptious vegetarian food (*menú* 1200ptas; open Mon.-Thurs. 1:15-4pm, Fri.-Sat. 1:15-4pm and 9-11pm). The supermarket **Autoservicio Montserrat** is located at the corner of C. Hilarión Eslava and C. Mayor. (Open Mon.-Fri. 9am-2pm and 5-7:30pm, Sat. 9am-2pm; *Sanfermines* Mon.-Thurs. and Sat. 8am-2pm, Fri. 8am-2pm and 4:30-7:30pm.)

■ Near Pamplona: Olite

Only 42km south of Pamplona, Olite is an enchanting Spanish town. Intrigue and sabotage have lurked about the **Palacio Real** of the kings of Navarre for centuries. In the 15th century King Carlos III made this sumptuous palace with flowery courtyards the focus of Navarrese courtly life. The 1937 restoration was not exactly subtle—the castle now resembles Disneyland, complete with screaming children. (Open April-Sept. daily 10am-2pm and 4-8pm; Oct.-March 10am-6pm. 300ptas, students 200ptas.)

Trains (tel. (948) 70 06 28) run to Pamplona (45min., 450ptas) and other destinations. **Conda** (tel. (948) 82 03 42) and **La Tafallesa** (tel. (948) 70 09 79) run **buses** to Pamplona (50min., 220ptas) and nearby Tudela (45min.). To reach the helpful **tourist office** (tel./fax (948) 71 23 43), follow the metal staircase in the middle of Pl. Carlos III (open April-Sept. Mon.-Fri. 10am-2pm and 4-7pm, Sat.-Sun. 10am-2pm). Affordable lodgings include the **Fonda Gambarte,** R. Seco, 13, 2nd fl. (tel. (948) 74 01 39), off Pl. Carlos III (doubles 3500ptas), and the bright rooms of **Pensión Cesareo Vidaurre,** Pl. Carlos III, 22, 1st fl. (tel. (948) 74 05 97; doubles 3000ptas). Try **Restaurante Gambarte,** downstairs from the Fonda Gambarte, for a royal three-course *menú* for 1100ptas (open Mon.-Fri. 1-3:30pm and 8-11pm).

ARAGÓN

Jaca

For centuries, pilgrims bound for Santiago crossed the Pyrenees into Spain, then crashed in Jaca for the night. By sunrise, they were probably gone. They had the right idea. Today's travelers still get a good night's sleep here on their way to the hiking and skiing trails of the Aragonese Pyrenees. The **tourist office,** Av. Regimiento Galicia, 2 (tel. (974) 36 00 98), left off C. Mayor, has a useful map and hiking advice. (Open July to mid-Sept. Mon.-Fri. 9am-2pm and 4:30-8pm, Sat. 10am-1:30pm and 5-8pm, Sun. 10am-1:30pm; mid-Sept. to June Mon.-Fri. 9am-1:30pm and 4:30-7pm, Sat. 10am-1pm and 5-7pm.) Shuttle buses run from downtown to the train station 30 minutes before each train leaves; the buses stop at the Ayuntamiento on C. Mayor or (if closed) at the taxi stop, and at the bus station. The **train station,** at C. de la Estación, serves Zaragoza (3hr., 1325-1900ptas) and Madrid (6½hr., 4100ptas). **La Oscense** (tel. (974) 35 50 60) sends **buses** to Pamplona (2hr., 855ptas), Zaragoza (2¼hr., 1450ptas) and elsewhere.

Jaca's *hostales* and *pensiones* are mainly grouped around C. Mayor and the cathedral. The **Albergue Juvenil Escuelas Pias (HI)** is at Av. Perimetral, 6 (tel. (974) 36 05 36; fax 36 03 92). From C. Mayor, make a left on Regimento de Galicia and another left on C. Perimetral. Go down the road to the left of the metal sculpture to the bungalows. (Midnight curfew. 1300ptas, over 26 1800ptas; nonmembers 100ptas more. Sheets 300ptas.) **Hostal Paris,** Pl. San Pedro, 4 (tel. (974) 36 10 20), a left off Av. Jacetania as you face *ciudadela,* has doubles for 3300ptas (Sept.-June 3000ptas). Camp at **Peña Oroel** (tel. (974) 36 02 15), 3.5km down the road to Sabiñánigo. (525ptas per person, 550ptas per tent. Open Holy Week and mid-June to mid-Sept.)

■ Near Jaca

Once you've rested up in Jaca, head for the mountains and valleys that surround the city. Getting to **Parque Nacional de Ordesa y Monte Perdido** can mean riding with the mail for an hour and then hiking 9km, but the park more than compensates with primeval majesty, cascades, rivers, and miles of trails crossing sheer, poplar-covered mountain faces. If you only have a day to spend in Ordesa, the **Soaso Circle** is the most practical hike, especially for novice mountaineers. If you prefer a private mountain climb to a communal, multilingual parade, try the **Circo Cotatuero** or **Circo Carriata** hikes. Both are two- to three-hour hikes that can be combined into a single five-hour hike. More experienced hikers brave the **Torla-Gavarnie** trail, a six-hour haul (one way) all the way to Gavarnie, France, or the 10-hour **Ordesa-Gavarnie** trail. For any of these, the **Editorial Alpina** guide is a must; buy it at the souvenir shop by the parking lot (675ptas) or the supermarket down the street (600ptas). Get trail maps (400ptas) and info about the park from the **ICONA office,** in Torla on Ctra. Ordesa just beyond C. Francia (tel. (974) 48 63 48; open July-Sept. Mon.-Fri. 10am-2pm and 5-7pm), or in Huesca (tel. (974) 24 33 61). The **Visitors' Center** at the park entrance has info on local fauna (open July 15-Dec. 15 daily 10am-2pm and 5-7pm).

Buses go only as far as **Torla,** a stone village 9km short of the park. A mail-delivery bus leaves **Sabiñánigo** Monday through Saturday at 10am, stopping in Torla at 11:55am before continuing to Aínsa. The bus passes through Torla again at 3:30pm on its way back to Sabiñánigo (arrives 4:30pm). Sabiñánigo connects by bus or train to Jaca (2-5 per day, 15min., 160ptas). From Torla, the park is accessible only by foot or car; hitchhiking is common, though not recommended. In the park, you can **camp** for only one night, and only at heights over 2200m and above the Soaso Steps, but several *refugios* facilitate overnight stays. The 120-bed **Refugio Góriz** (tel. (974) 48 63 79), about four hours from the parking lot, has winter heating and meager hot showers (950ptas per person). Get a preview of the *refugio* feel in Torla in the 21-bunk room at the **Refugio L'Atalaya,** C. Francia, 45 (tel. (974) 48 60 22; 900ptas per person). The newer **Refugio Briet** (tel. (974) 48 62 21), across the street, has similar facilities, but its bunks are dispersed through a few rooms (1000ptas). **Camping Río Ara** (tel. (974) 48 62 48) is about 1km down the path from its sign off Ctra. Ordesa (400ptas per person and per tent; open April-Oct.). The more upscale **Camping Ordesa** (tel. (974) 48 61 46), is 750m farther along Ctra. Ordesa. (550ptas per person, tent 550ptas; tax not included; 30% discount off season. Open April-Oct.)

CATALONIA (CATALUNYA, CATALUÑA)

Barcelona

While Europe's tourist-reliant cities stagnate behind sandblasted facades, busily preserving a past glory, Barcelona has dropped its cultural baggage to embrace contemporaneity. After the suffocating years of Franco's regime, Barcelona, it seemed, took only a millisecond to reclaim its role as the world's premier showcase of avant-garde architecture. On a single block known as the *Manzana de la Discordia* (Block of Discord), works by Cadafalch, Gaudí, and Montaner battle each other for attention. Their disparate colors and flamboyance assert Barcelona's identity as a 20th-century city. While Paris, New York, and London have been described as *noir* cities, better captured in black and white, Barcelona must be seen in vibrant color.

ORIENTATION AND PRACTICAL INFORMATION

On Spain's Mediterranean coast 200km from the French border, Barcelona slopes gently upward from the harbor to the mountains. From the harbor, **Las Ramblas** proceeds directly to **Pl. Catalunya,** the city's center, site of the **new tourist office** and **El Corte Inglés** department store (both dispense El Corte Inglés's **free map**). To the right of Las Ramblas lies **Barri Gòtic,** enclosed on the other side by **Vía Laietana.** Beyond Vía Laietana lies the **Ribera,** which touches **Parc de la Ciutadella** and **Estació de França.** Past Parc de la Ciutadella is the **Vila Olímpica,** with its two new towers and a shiny assortment of malls and hotels. On the left side of Las Ramblas rises **Montjuïc,** a picturesque hill crammed with tourist attractions.

From Pl. Catalunya, fanning up toward the mountains away from Las Ramblas, the **Eixample** is bordered along its lower edge by the **Gran Vía de les Corts Catalanes** and bisected by **Passeig de Gràcia,** with its numerous shops and cafés. **Avinguda Diagonal** marks the upper limit of the grid-planned neighborhoods, separating the Eixample from **Gràcia,** an older neighborhood in the foothills of the mountains that encircle Barcelona. In this mountain range, the peak of **Tibidabo,** the highest point in Barcelona, provides the best view of the city.

Pickpocketing is the only common crime in Barcelona. **El Raval,** on your left side while ascending Las Ramblas, is not safe for lone walkers at night; you should also watch your belongings in **Plaça Reial,** on the opposite side of Las Ramblas.

SPAIN

Tourist Offices: For city info dial 010 (110ptas), for tourist info 412 20 01. Brand-new **Centre D'Informaciá,** Pl. Catalunya (tel. 304 31 34; fax 304 31 55). Multilingual advice, a slew of maps and pamphlets, and currency exchange. **Estació Central de Barcelona-Sants,** Pl. Països Catalans (tel. 491 44 31). M: Sants-Estació. Barcelona info only. Open in summer daily 8am-8pm; off-season Mon.-Fri. 8am-8pm, Sat.-Sun. 8am-2pm. **Gran Vía de les Corts Catalanes,** 658 (tel. 301 74 43). M: Urquinaona or Pl. Catalunya. Two blocks from the Pg. Gràcia. Open Mon.-Fri. 9am-7pm, Sat. 9am-2pm. **Airport branch,** International Terminal, to the left of customs. Open Mon.-Sat. 9:30am-8:30pm, Sun. 9:30am-3pm.

Budget Travel: Wasteels, Pl. Catalunya-Estació RENFE (tel. 301 18 81; fax 301 18 53). M: Catalunya. In the Metro/RENFE terminal. Air and train discounts for students. Open Mon.-Fri. 8:30am-8:30pm, Sat. 10am-1pm. **Centre d'Informació: Assesorament per a Joves,** C. Ferrán 32 (tel. 402 78 01). Free advice, a travel library, and an events bulletin board. Open Mon.-Fri. 10am-2pm and 4-8pm.

Consulates: Australia, Gran Vía Carlos III, 98 (tel. 330 94 96; fax 411 09 04). **Canada,** Pg. de Gracia, 77-30 (tel. 215 07 04; fax 487 91 17). **New Zealand,** Traversa de Gracia 64, 4th fl. (tel. 209 03 99; fax 202 08 90). **South Africa,** Teodora Lamadrid, 7-11. **U.K.,** Av. Diagonal, 477, 13th fl. (tel. 419 90 44; fax 405 24 11). **U.S.,** Pg. Reina Elisenda, 23 (tel. 280 22 27; fax 205 52 06). All open Mon.-Fri.

American Express: Pg. Gràcia 101 (tel. 415 23 71, 24hr. service line (91) 572 03 03; fax 415 37 00). M: Diagonal. Enter on C. Rosselló, around the corner. Mail held. 24hr. **ATM** outside. Open Mon.-Fri. 9:30am-6pm, Sat. 10am-noon.

Currency Exchange: Find the best rates at **banks** (open Mon.-Fri. 8:30am-2pm). **Banco Central Hispano,** Las Ramblas at C. Boqueria, is best for AmEx traveler's checks. **Banco de Espanya** and **El Corte Inglés,** both in Pl. Catalunya, and the AmEx office charge no commission. On Sun., try **Estació de Sants** (tel. 490 77 70). Open daily 8am-10pm.

Airport: El Prat de Llobregat (tel. 478 50 00), 12km southwest of Barcelona. RENFE trains run from the airport (6:13am-10:13pm, every 30min., 300-345ptas) to Estació Central-Sants and Pl. Catalunya in town, then return to the airport. A late-night bus (marked "EN") travels from the airport to Pl. Espanya from 6:20am-2:40am; the bus returns to the airport from Pl. Espanya (at Av. Reina María Cristina and the Gran Vía) from 7am-3:15am. A **taxi** costs 2500-3500ptas. **Iberia,** Pg. Gràcia, 30 (tel. 412 56 67, reservations (902) 40 05 00), flies in, around, and out of Spain.

Trains: Call **RENFE** (tel. 490 02 02, international 490 11 22) for train info. Open daily 7:30am-10:30pm. **Estació Sants,** Pl. Països Catalans (tel. 490 24 00), is the main station. M: Sants-Estació. To: Madrid (7hr., 5000-7000ptas), Valencia (4hr.,

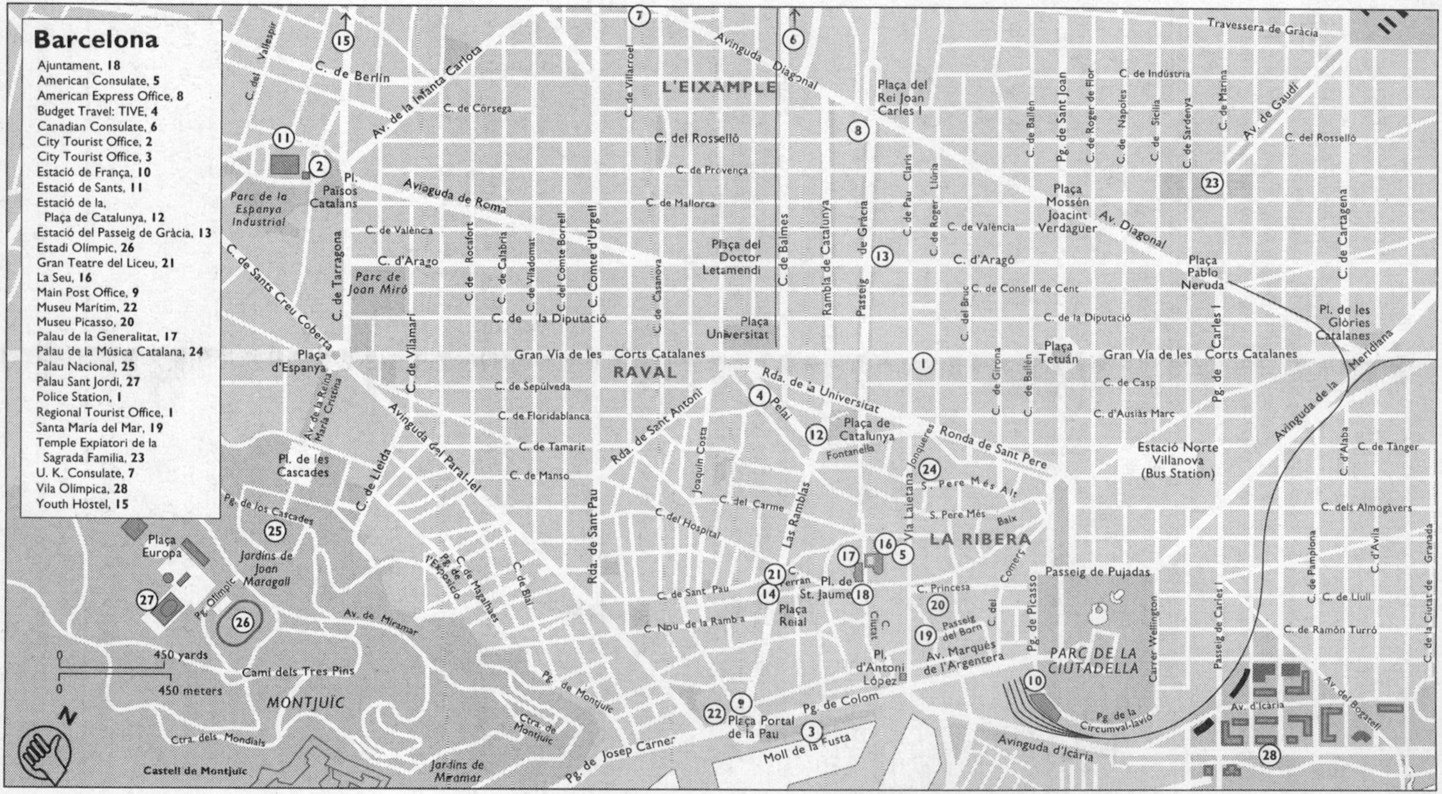
Barcelona
Ajuntament, 18
American Consulate, 5
American Express Office, 8
Budget Travel: TIVE, 4
Canadian Consulate, 6
City Tourist Office, 2
City Tourist Office, 3
Estació de França, 10
Estació de Sants, 11
Estació de la, Plaça de Catalunya, 12
Estació del Passeig de Gràcia, 13
Estadi Olímpic, 26
Gran Teatre del Liceu, 21
La Seu, 16
Main Post Office, 9
Museu Marítim, 22
Museu Picasso, 20
Palau de la Generalitat, 17
Palau de la Música Catalana, 24
Palau Nacional, 25
Palau Sant Jordi, 27
Police Station, 1
Regional Tourist Office, 1
Santa María del Mar, 19
Temple Expiatori de la Sagrada Família, 23
U. K. Consulate, 7
Vila Olímpica, 28
Youth Hostel, 15
L'EIXAMPLE
RAVAL
LA RIBERA
MONTJUÏC
PARC DE LA CIUTADELLA
Avinguda Diagonal
Gran Vía de les Corts Catalanes
Plaça d'Espanya
Plaça de Catalunya
Las Ramblas
Via Laietana
Passeig de Gràcia
Rambla de Catalunya
Avinguda del Paral·lel
Estació Norte Villanova (Bus Station)
Plaça Portal de la Pau
Moll de la Fusta
Pg. de Colom
Pg. de Josep Carner
Avinguda d'Icària
Avinguda de la Meridiana
Pl. de les Glòries Catalanes
Plaça Europa
Jardins de Joan Maragall
Jardins de Mramar
Castell de Montjuïc
Parc de la Espanya Industrial
Parc de Joan Miró
Travessera de Gràcia
450 yards
450 meters
N

3200-3900ptas), Seville (12hr., 6400-7300ptas), Milan (18hr., students 10,500ptas), and Paris (11hr., 12,7000ptas). Open daily 4:30am-12:30am. **Estació França**, Av. Marqués de L'Argentera. M: Barceloneta. Open daily 7am-10pm.

Buses: Most buses arrive at the **Estació del Nord,** C. Ali-bei, 80 (tel. 265 65 08). M: Arc de Triomf. **Enatcar** (tel. 245 25 28) serves Madrid (8hr., 2690ptas) and Valencia (4½hr., 2690ptas). **Linebús** (tel. 265 07 00) travels to London (25hr., 13,450ptas) and Paris (14hr., 11,450ptas). 10% discount for travelers under 26. **Sarfa** (tel. 265 11 58) sends buses to Costa Brava beach towns. **Julià Vía,** C. Viriato (tel. 490 40 00), to the right of Estació-Sants, connects to: Marseille (10hr., 6100ptas), Paris (15hr., 11,125ptas), and Frankfurt (19hr., 14,550ptas).

Ferries: Transmediterránea, Estació Marítima-Moll Barcelona (tel. 443 25 32). M: Drassanes. From Las Ramblas, Columbus points the way. Open Mon.-Fri. 9am-1:30pm and 4:30-7pm, Sat. 9am-1pm. In summer there are voyages most days to: Mallorca (8hr.), Menorca (8hr.), and Ibiza (8hr.). A *butaca* seat is 6650ptas.

Public Transportation: tel. 412 00 00, for handicapped transportation 412 44 44. *Guía del Transport Públic,* free at tourist offices and the info booth in Pl. Catalunya, maps out the city's **Metro** (M) lines and **bus** routes. Rides cost 135ptas; 10-ride T2 Metro pass 720ptas; 10-ride T1 combo pass 740ptas. Riding without a receipt incurs a hefty 5000ptas **fine.** Metro open Mon.-Thurs. 5am-11pm, Fri.-Sun. 6am-midnight. Day buses usually run daily 5am-10pm; night buses 11pm-4am.

Taxis: tel. 330 03 00 or 300 11 00. Base rate 235ptas, then 100ptas per km.

Car Rental: Docar, C. Montnegre, 18 (24hr. tel. 322 90 08; fax 439 81 19). Free delivery and pickup. Base price 1900ptas per day, 19ptas each additional km. Insurance 1100ptas. Open Mon.-Fri. 9am-2pm and 4-8pm, Sat. 9am-2pm.

Hitchhiking: Hitching on *autopistas* (toll roads, marked by an "A") is illegal; on national highways (N), it's legal. Those hitching to France take the Metro to Fabra i Puig, then Av. Meridiana to reach A-7. Those en route to Valencia take bus 7 from Rambla Catalunya at Gran Vía. **Barnastop,** C. Sant Ramon 29 (tel. 443 06 32), at Non de Rambla. M: Liceu. Matches drivers with riders. Driver's fee is 3ptas per km in Spain, 4ptas per km outside Spain. 1000ptas first-time commission for domestic travel is 1000ptas; international travel 2000ptas; commission 1pta per km thereafter. Open Mon.-Fri. 11am-2pm and 5-7pm, Sat. noon-2pm.

Luggage Storage: Estació Sants, lockers 400-600ptas. Open daily 6:30am-11pm. **Estació França,** lockers 300-500ptas. Open daily 7am-10pm. **Estació del Nord,** lockers 300ptas. Open 24hr.

English Bookstores: LAIE, Av. Pau Claris, 85 (tel. 318 17 39), a block from the Gran Vía. M: Urquinaona or Pl. Catalunya. Rooftop café and an extensive collection. Open Mon.-Sat. 10am-9pm.

Laundromat: Tintoreria San Pablo, C. San Pau, 105 (tel. 329 42 49). Wash, dry, and fold 1600ptas, do-it-yourself for 1200ptas. Open Mon.-Fri. 9am-1pm and 4-8pm.

Gay and Lesbian Organization: Coordinadora Gay Lesbiana, C. Les Carolines, 13 (tel. 237 08 69, toll free tel. 900 60 16 01). Line staffed daily 6-10pm.

Medical Assistance: Médicos de Urgencia, C. Pelai 40 (tel. 412 12 12). M: Catalunya. For an **ambulance,** dial 061.

Emergency: tel. 092 or 091.

Police: Las Ramblas, 43 (tel. 301 90 60), across from Pl. Real, next to C. Nou de la Rambla. M: Liceu. English spoken.

Internet Access: El Café de Internet, Gran Vía de les Corts Catalanes, 656 (tel. 412 19 15; http://www.cafeinternet.es). M: Pg. Gràcian, exit to the tourist office. 600ptas per hr. 800ptas per hr. with student ID. Open Mon.-Fri. 10am-midnight.

Post Office: Pl. Antoni López (tel. 318 38 31), at the foot of Vía Laietana. M: Jaume I or Barceloneta. Open for stamps Mon.-Fri. 8am-10pm, Sat. 8am-2pm; for *Lista de Correos* (general delivery) Mon.-Fri. 8am-9pm, Sat. 9am-2pm. **Postal Code:** 08002.

Telephones: Phones and **fax** service at Estació Sants (tel./fax 490 76 50). M: Sants-Estació. Open daily 9am-10:15pm. **Directory assistance** tel. 003. **Telephone Code:** (9)3.

ACCOMMODATIONS AND CAMPING

Although *hostales* and *pensiones* abound, visitors may face a scramble in July and August when tourists flood every corner of the city. Room quality varies tremendously—your night-time refuge could be a paper-thin mattress near the train tracks or a ritzy, antique-filled room with a view. Barcelona's *albergues* offer basic accommodations at low prices, but ask to see your room before you sign your night away.

Ciutat Vella: Barri Gòtic and Las Ramblas

Barcelona's *ciutat vella* (old quarter) has a wealth of affordable rooms. Police patrol the area, but be aware of your possessions and surroundings on Las Ramblas.

Alberg Juvenil Palau (HI), C. Palau 6 (tel. 412 50 80). M: Jaume I. One block from Pl. Sant Jaume; take C. Ciutat to C. Templaris, then take the 2nd left. Full kitchen. 5-night max. stay. Reception open daily 7am-3am. Curfew 3am. 1300ptas. Sheets 150ptas. Showers available 8-11am and 4-10pm. Breakfast included.

Albergue de Juventud Kabul, Pl. Reial 17 (tel. 318 51 90). M: Liceu. Head toward the port on Las Ramblas, and turn left after C. Ferrán to enter Pl. Reial. Kabul is at the near right corner. Social atmosphere—beer vending machines and satellite TV. 5-night max. stay. Reception open 24hr. 1500ptas. Sheets 200ptas. Laundry 800ptas. Free lockers. The area is relatively safe, but police urge caution at night.

Pensión Fernando, C. Ferrán, 31 (tel. 301 79 93). M: Liceu. From Las Ramblas, take the 4th left off C. Ferrán. Recent renovations have completely transformed the appearance (but not the price) of this *pensión.* Winter heating. Most rooms have bunks. 1300ptas per person, 1500ptas with shower.

Pensión Francia, C. Reva Palau, 4 (tel. 319 03 76). From Estación França, cross the main avenue and go left; C. Reva Palau is the 5th right. New wooden furniture and a mini-library. Keys for 24hr. entry. Singles 1400ptas. Doubles 2500ptas-4600ptas. Triples with shower 3600ptas. Quads with shower 4300ptas.

Hostal Levante, Baixada de San Miguel, 2 (tel. 317 95 65). M: Liceu. Walk down C. Ferrán and turn right on C. Avinyó; Bda. San Miguel is the first left. Despite a slightly shabby entrance, an oasis awaits inside. Reception open 24hr. Singles 2500ptas. Doubles 4000ptas, with bath 5000ptas. Book ahead July-Aug.

Casa de Huéspedes Mari-Luz, C. Palau 4 (tel. 317 34 63), 1 bl. from Pl. Sant Jaume; take C. Ciutat to C. Templaris, then take the 2nd left. M: Jaume I or Liceu. Basic rooms with 2-8 beds. Public phone, kitchen use with permission, and keys for 24hr. entry. 1300ptas per person, in room with shower 1500ptas.

Hotel Call, Arco San Ramón del Call, 4 (tel. 302 11 23; fax 301 34 86). M: Liceu. Take C. Boqueria to the end and veer left onto C. Call. All the amenities: phone, A/C, and bathroom in every room. Reception/key drop open 24hr. Singles 3200ptas. Doubles 4500ptas. Triples 5700ptas. Quads 6400ptas. Credit cards accepted.

Hostal Layetana, Pl. Ramón Berenguer el Gran, 2 (tel. 319 20 12). M: Jaume I. Less than a block from the Metro, on your left as you walk away from the ocean. Bedrooms with terraces. Living Room. Singles 2300ptas. Doubles 3700ptas, with bath 5200ptas. Exterior shower 200ptas each. Call ahead July-Aug. V, MC.

Hostal Terrassa, Junta de Comerç 11 (tel. 302 51 74; fax 301 21 88). Descending Las Ramblas, turn right on C. Hospital, then turn left after Teatre Romea. M: Liceu Social courtyard. Singles 2000ptas, with shower 2500ptas. Doubles 3400-4000ptas. Triples 4400ptas-5000. Call ahead. Credit cards accepted.

Citat Vella: Near Plaça de Catalunya

A bit pricier than in the Barri Gòtic, accommodations here are safer, more modern, and close to the action (and rumble) of Las Ramblas. The Metro stop is Pl. Catalunya.

Hostal Fontanella, Vía Laietana, 71 (tel./fax 317 59 43). Go 3 blocks past El Corte Inglés and hang a right. Rooms with soft lighting, floral bouquets, lace curtains, and logo-endowed towels. Singles 2700ptas, with bath 3500ptas. Doubles 4800ptas, with bath 5900ptas. Reservations with deposit accepted. V, MC, AmEx.

Hostal Residencia Lausanne, Av. Portal de L'Angel 24 (tel. 302 11 39). Elegant interior lives up to imperial facade. TV lounge. Singles 2000ptas. Doubles 3000ptas, with shower 4500ptas. Triples with shower 5000ptas, with bath 6000ptas.

Hotel Toledano (Hostal Residencia Capitol), Las Ramblas 138 (tel. 301 08 72; fax 412 31 42). 50m away on the left from Pl. Catalunya. Hotel-*hostal* has been making tourists happy for 78 years. Cable TV (4 English channels). Keys for 24hr. entry.

Singles 2900ptas. Doubles 4600-5200ptas. Triples 5900-6500ptas. Quads 6800-7400ptas. Prices don't include IVA. Reservations and credit cards accepted.

Residencia Australia, Ronda Universitat, 11 (tel. 317 41 77). Ceiling fans and embroidered sheets. Winter heating. English-speaking owner. Singles 2600ptas. Doubles 3800ptas, with bath 4600ptas. IVA not included.

Pensión Nevada, Av. Portal de L'Angel, 16 (tel. 302 31 01), just past Hostal Lausanne. Cozy bedrooms with throw pillows, firm beds, and flowers on the balcony. Keys for 24hr. entry. Singles 3500ptas. Doubles 5200ptas. Call ahead.

Residencia Victoria, C. Comtal, 9 (tel. 317 45 97). From Pl. Catalunya, take the first left off Av. Portal de L'Angel. Full kitchen, TV, washer/dryer (100ptas), iron, and open-air dining room. Singles 2000ptas. Doubles 4000ptas.

Pensión Santa Anna, C. Santa Anna, 23 (tel. 301 22 46). What this place lacks in size and ambience, it makes up for with clean bathrooms and firm beds. Singles 2500ptas. Doubles 4000ptas, with bath 5000ptas. Triples 5000ptas.

SPAIN

The Eixample

The most beautiful and safest *hostales* are located along wide, safe *avingudas* in the newer part of town. Most have elevators and huge entryways with colorful tiles.

Hostal Residencia Oliva, Pg. Gràcia, 32, 4th fl. (tel. 488 01 62 or 488 17 89), at C. Disputació. M: Pg. Gràcia. The Aerobus drops you off in the lap of luxury. New bathrooms, frilly curtains, and bedspreads. Some doubles are cramped. Singles 3000ptas. Doubles 5500ptas, with bath 6500ptas.

Hostal Residencia Windsor, Rambla Catalunya, 84 (tel. 215 11 98). M: Pg. Gràcia. Aristocratic *hostal* lives up to its name with crimson carpets, palatial quarters, and a price to match. Singles 3300-4100ptas. Doubles 5700-6800ptas. Laundry 600ptas.

Hostal Girona, Girona, 24, 1st fl. (tel. 265 02 59), between C. Casp and C. Ausias Marc. M: Urquinaona. Carpeted hallways, large wooden doors, and affordable prices. Directly above a branch of the University. Winter heating. Singles 2000ptas. Doubles with shower 4500ptas, with bath 5000ptas. Breakfast 200ptas.

Gràcia

Berlitz Spanish won't help in this Catalan-dominated area five to ten minutes north of Av. Diagonal. The accommodations listed here are small and well-kept, and neighborhood bars and *pastelerías* remain relatively undiscovered.

Pensión San Medín, C. Gran de Gràcia 125 (tel. 217 30 68; fax 415 44 10). M: Fontana. Family-run *pensión.* Each room has new furniture and a phone. Winter heating. Singles 2500-3500ptas. Double 4500-5600ptas. Breakfast 250ptas. V, MC.

Pensión Norma, C. Gran de Gràcia, 87 (tel. 237 44 78). M: Fontana. Newly renovated and fully approved by Mr. Clean. Singles 2000ptas. Doubles 3000-4000ptas.

Camping

Although there is no camping in Barcelona, intercity buses (190ptas) run to these locations in 20 to 45 minutes: **El Toro Bravo** (tel. 637 34 62), 11km south of Barcelona, accessible by buses L94 (summer only) and L95 from Pl. Catalunya or Pl. Espanya (650ptas per person, 700ptas per tent); and **Filipinas** (24hr. tel. 658 28 95; 650ptas per person, 700ptas per tent), 1km down the road from El Toro Bravo.

FOOD

For the cheapest meals, be on the lookout for 850-1000ptas *menús* posted in the restaurants in the Barri Gòtic. Small, family owned eateries serve basic but satisfying dishes. Closer to the port, bars and cafés get more crowded and harried, whereas on Rbla. Catalunya leisurely *al fresco* meals are an expensive excuse for people-watching. *Patisserías* often sell budget-friendly *bocadillos* (sandwiches). Catalan specialities include *mariluz a la romana* (white fish in tomato sauce), *butifarra con judias blancas* (sausage with white beans), and *crema catalana* (Catalan pudding). Consult the weekly *Guía del Ocio* (available at most newsstands; 125ptas) for more dining options. **La Boqueria** (officially the Mercat de Sant Josep), off Rambla Sant Josep 89, vends fresh fish and produce (open Mon.-Sat. 7am-8pm). Be aware that food options shrink drastically in August, when restauranteurs and bar owners close up shop and take their vacations.

Restaurante Pollo Rico, C. Sant Pau, 31. C. Sant Pau breaks directly off Las Ramblas one street down from C. Hospital. M: Liceu. Take home your very own chicken (800ptas). Half chicken, fries, and bread 675ptas. Baked whole artichokes 150ptas. Afternoon *menú* 900ptas. Open Thurs.-Tues. 10am-midnight.

Irati, C. Cardenal Casañas, 17. Barcelona's most popular *tapas* bar. *Tapas* 125ptas each. Try the *turutu* (fried chicken, bacon, ham, and cheese) or *anchoas rellenas* (stuffed anchovies). Open Tues.-Sat. noon-midnight, Sun. noon-5pm.

La Morera, Pl. Sant Augustí, 1. M: Liceu. Take C. Hospital to Pl. Sant Augustí. Friendly establishment near La Boqueria that specializes in *comida del mercado* (fresh market food). Argentine and Catalan dishes 600-1000ptas. Afternoon *menú* 995ptas. Open Mon.-Sat. 1-3:30pm and 8:30-11:45pm.

La Fonda, C. Escudellers, 10. M: Drassanes or Liceu. C. Escudellers enters Barri Gòtic between Liceu and Drassanes. Meals 475-1200ptas. Try the *postre de tirentos* (pineapple, truffles, strawberry ice cream, and cookies atop *creama catalana*). Open Sept.-June 9am-1:30pm and 8:30-11:30pm.

El Gallo Kirko, C. Avinyó, 19. M: Liceu. Walk down C. Ferrán; it's the 4th right. Fill up on Pakistani rice by a 4th-century stone wall. Most dishes under 500ptas. Several vegetarian options. 5% ISIC discount. Open daily noon-midnight.

Restaurante Bidasoa, C. Serra, 21. M: Drassanes. Take the 3rd left off C. Josep Anselm Clavé heading from Las Ramblas. Locals greet the owner with hugs and kisses, with good reason. Soups, salads, and meat and fish items under 550ptas. Full meals under 1000ptas. Open Tues.-Sun. noon-midnight. Closed Aug.

Botiga Restaurant Corts Catalanes, Gran Vía de les Corts Catalanes, 603, just off Rambla Catalunya. M: Catalunya. Groceries in front; food and drink in back. Imaginative vegetarian dishes. Salads 525-645ptas. Pastas around 1000ptas. Restaurant open daily 1-4pm and 8:30-11pm. Store open daily 9am-midnight.

Can Conesa, C. Llibreteria, 1, at Pl. Sant Jaume. Delicious *bocadillos* 250-500ptas. Open Mon.-Sat. 8am-9:30pm. Closed first half of Aug.

Les Quinze Nits, Pl. Reial, 6. Streams of locals and foreigners wait in line every night to try this Catalan restaurant's contemporary and traditional dishes. *Menú* 950ptas. Braised rabbit 690ptas, octopus with onions and mushrooms 756ptas. Entrees 540-1185ptas. Open 1-3:45pm and 8:30-11:45pm.

Els Quatre Gats, C. Montsió, 3bis. Walk down Av. Portal de L'Angel. M: Catalunya. Once the hangout of Picasso, who designed the menu cover. Live music 9pm-1am. *Menú* (1500ptas) served Mon.-Fri. 1-4pm. Entrees 1100-2600ptas. Open Mon.-Sat. 8am-2am, Sun. 5pm-2am.

SIGHTS

Ruta del Modernisme passes (1200ptas, students 750ptas) allow privileged and economical access to Barcelona's architectural masterpieces. The pass allows entrance, over a 9-day period, to Casa Batlló, Casa Amatller, Casa Lleó Morera (inaccessible without pass), Palau Guell, Sagrada Familia, Casa Milá, Palau de la Música, Casa-Museu Gaudí, Fundació Antoni Tápies, and Museu d'Art Modern. Passes are sold in the Palau Güell (see below) or at Casa Lleó Morera on Pg. Grácia. During the summer, the air conditioned **Bus Turístic** (marked #100) stops at 15 points of interest; a 1400ptas full-day pass allows you to get on and off freely. Las Ramblas and Barri Gòtic are the traditional tourist areas, and the Eixample is the showcase of Gaudí and *modernisme.*

Ciutat Vella: Las Ramblas and Barri Gòtic The broad pedestrian lane of **Las Ramblas** is a veritable urban carnival: street performers dance flamenco, fortune-tellers survey palms, and merchants hawk their wares. The tree-lined lane runs from Pl. Catalunya to the Monument de Colom at the port. Half-way down, **Joan Miro's** pavement mosaic brightens Pl. Boqueria. At #61, the **Gran Teatre del Liceu** was one of Europe's leading stages before a fire gutted it in 1994. It will reopen in October 1994. The newly-restored **Palau Güell,** C. Nou de la Rambla, 3, two streets down from Teatre Liceu on the right, attracts visitors with its fascinating architecture. At the port end of Las Ramblas, the **Monument a Colom** towers over the city. (Elevator to the top open June-Sept. daily 9am-8:30pm; Oct.-April Mon.-Fri. 10am-6:30pm, Sat.-Sun. 10am-6:30pm; May Mon.-Fri. 10am-7:30pm, Sat.-Sun. 10am-7pm. 250ptas.)

Palaces, cathedrals, and Roman ruins make the **Barri Gòtic** (located between Las Ramblas and Vía Laietana) a monument to Barcelona's past. Countless souvenir stands and bars now diminish the medieval charm, but also give the area a liveliness that it would otherwise lack. Since Roman times, the handsome **Plaça de Sant Jaume** has been the city's political center. The *plaça* is dominated by two of Catalonia's most important buildings: the **Palau de la Generalitat** (seat of Catalonia's autonomous government) and the **Ajuntament** (city hall; tel. 402 72 62 to visit). The Gothic **Església Catedral de la Santa Creu** is in Plaça de la Seu, up C. Bisbe next to the Generalitat (look for the cathedrals's high-flying jagged spires). The cathedral's cloister has magnolias growing in the middle and geese waddling around the periphery. (Cathedral open daily 8am-1:30pm and 4-7:30pm. Cloister open daily 8:45am-1:15pm and 4-6pm. Entrance to choral chamber 100ptas.) On the opposite side of the cathedral, on C. Comtes, is the **Palau Reial** (Royal Palace). Inside, the **Museu Frederic Marès** holds the sculptor's idiosyncratic personal collection, and the **Museu d'Historia de la Ciutat** displays the ruins of a Roman colony. (Marès museum open Tues.-Sat. 10am-5pm, Sun. 10am-2pm. 300ptas, students 150ptas. History museum open July-Sept. Tues.-Sat. 10am-8pm, Sun. 10am-2pm; Oct.-June Tues.-Sat. 10am-2pm and 4-8pm, Sun. 10am-2pm. 500ptas, students 250ptas.)

SPAIN

Barri de la Ribera and Parc de la Ciutadella The venerated **Barri de la Ribera** section of the old city grew with Barcelona's development as a major sea power during the Middle Ages. During the "Bourbon Tyranny" (as it is known locally), Felipe V burned much of the neighborhood. The Gothic **Església Santa María del Mar,** on Pl. Santa María, survived the era and today represents the pinnacle of Catalan Gothic design. Off Pg. Born, #15 C. Montcada features the famous **Museu Picasso,** housed in the medieval **Palau Berenguer d'Agüilar.** It is the most comprehensive exhibition of Picasso's early works; the two rooms devoted to studies and renditions of Velázquez's *Las Meninas* is the *museu*'s centerpiece (open Tues.-Sat. 10am-8pm, Sun. 10am-3pm; 500ptas, students 250ptas). At #25, the **Galeria Maeght** (tel. 310 42 45) is Catalonia's most prestigious art gallery and a former medieval palace (open Tues.-Sat. 10am-2pm and 4-8pm; free).

The **Parc de la Ciutadella,** where Felipe incarcerated Barcelona's influential citizens and later the site of the 1888 Universal Exposition, now harbors a lake with rowboats for rent, Gaudí and friends' **Cascada** fountains, several museums, and a zoo. On Pl. Armes, outside the park, the **Museu d'Art Modern** showcases 20th-century Catalan artists (open Tues.-Sun. 10am-7pm; 300ptas, students 200ptas).

The Eixample The 1859 demolition of Barcelona's medieval walls symbolically ushered in a *Renaixença* (Renaissance) of Catalan culture. Catalan architect Ildefons Cerdà's design for a new Barcelona included a grid of squares softened by the cropped corners of streets, forming octagonal intersections. Meanwhile, the flourishing bourgeoisie commissioned a new wave of architects to build their houses, reshaping the face of the Eixample with *modernista* architecture. The best way to approach this macro-museum of Catalan architecture is with the *Ruta del modernisme* pass (see p. 817). Two handy guides are available free at the tourist office: *Discovering Modernist Art in Catalonia* and *Gaudí*. The odd-numbered side of Pg. Gràcia is popularly known as *la manzana de la discordia* (block of discord), referring to the aesthetic competition of the buildings on the block. Situated between C. Aragò and Consell de Cent, it offers an overview of the peak of the modernist movement. The bottom two floors of the facade of **Casa Lleó i Morera,** by Domènech i Montaner, were destroyed to house a store, but the upper floors sprout flowers and winged monsters. Puig i Cadafalch opted for a cubical pattern on the facade of **Casa Amatller** at #41. Gaudí's balconies ripple and tiles sparkle on **Casa Batlló,** #43. The rooftop is a scaly representation of Catalunya's patron Sant Jordi slaying a dragon. Although the central hallway and variegated blue-tiled stairway are open to the public, only the privileged holders of the *Route to Modernisme* pass (available two doors down at Casa Lleó Morera) can enter the *casa principal* (main apartment).

Many modernist buffs argue that the **Casa Milà** apartment building (popularly known as **La Pedrera**—Stone Quarry), Pg. Gràcia, 92, is architect Antoni Gaudí's masterpiece, with intricate ironwork around the balconies and egg-shaped window panes in the front gate. (Rooftop tours and a multi-media presentation on the hour Tues.-Sat. 10am-8pm, Sun. 10am-3pm. Same-day reservations accepted in the morning. 500ptas.) Only Gaudí's genius could draw tourists to a half-finished church, the **Temple Expiatori de la Sagrada Família,** on C. Marina between C. Mallorca and C. Provença (M: Sagrada Familia). The church's three planned facades symbolize Jesus' nativity, passion, and glory; only the first is finished. Elevators and symmetrical staircases lead to its towers, bridges, and crannies. (Open April-Aug. daily 9am-8pm; Sept. and March 9am-7pm; Jan., Feb., and Oct.-Dec. 9am-6pm. 750ptas.)

Montjuïc With a harbor view and a Jewish cemetery buried underneath, **Montjuïc** (mountain of the Jews) and its **fortress** served as strategic posts for Barcelona's ruling classes for centuries before Franco made it one of his "interrogation" headquarters. Bus 61 (every 10min.) leaves for the *mont* from Pl. Espanya (M: Espanya) at Av. Reina María Cristina. The **Fonts Luminoses** (Illuminated Fountains) lining Av. Reina María Cristina put on a dazzling show in the evening. About midway up and tucked off to the right-hand side is the **Pavelló Mies van der Rohe,** an import from the 1929 Expo in Germany. Just across the hillside, **Poble Espanyol** features replicas of famous sights from every Spanish region: a Plaza Mayor (with a self-service cafeteria), a Plazuela de la Iglesia, and so on. (Town open Mon. 9am-8pm, Tues.-Thurs. 9am-2am, Fri.-Sat. 9am-4am, Sun. 9am-midnight. 750ptas.)

In 1929, Barcelona inaugurated the **Estadi Olímpic de Montjuïc** in its bid for the 1932 Olympic games. Over 50 years later, Catalan architects Federic Correa and Alfons Milá and Italian Vittorio Gregotti renovated the shell and lowered the playing field to maximize seating for the 1992 Games (open daily 10am-8pm; free). **Palau d'Esports Sant Jordi** (tel. 426 20 89; call in advance for visits), the most technologically sophisticated of the Olympic structures, hosts concerts and other spectacles. About 100m down the road from the Olympic stadium is the **Fundació Joan Miró,** with works from all periods of Miró's career. (Open Tues.-Sat. 10am-8pm, Thurs. 10am-9:30pm, Sun. 10:30am-2:30pm. 700ptas, students 400ptas.)

Parc Güell and Tibidabo Gaudí intended **Parc Güell** (after Eusebi Güell, its commissioner) to be a garden city, its multicolored dwarfish houses and sparkling ceramic-mosaic stairways to house the city's elite. When only two people signed on, it became a park. Inside, an elegant white staircase adorned with patterned tiles and a multicolored salamander leads to a pavilion supported by 86 pillars. In the back of the park, sweeping elevated paths, supported by columns shaped like palm trees, swerve through large hedges and prehistoric plants. The **Casa-Museu Gaudí** displays an eclectic collection of designs, sensual furniture, and portraits. (Park open May-Aug. daily 10am-9pm; April and Sept. 10am-8pm; March and Oct. 10am-7pm; Nov.-Feb. 10am-6pm. Free. Museum open Sun.-Fri. 10am-2pm and 4-7pm. 250ptas.) Bus 24 from Pg. Gràcia reaches the upper park entrance.

You can survey the Pyrenees and the ocean blue from atop **Tibidabo,** Barcelona's highest point. It derives its odd name from the devil's promise to Jesus, "All this I will give to you (*tibi dabo* in Latin) if you fall down and worship me." Tibidabo's huge **Temple del Sagrat Cor** has received little artistic but all too much touristic attention. The view of Montserrat and the Pyrenees from the bust of Jesus is worth the elevator ride (75ptas). **Torre de Collserola,** a communications tower built 560m above sea level, offers excellent views as well (500ptas). To reach the mountain top, either wait 15 minutes for the *tramvia blau* streetcar (Tramvia runs 9:05am-9:35pm; Oct.-May Sat.-Sun.; 275ptas) or walk up Av. Tibidabo in almost the same time. At the top of the street, you have to take a funicular (300ptas).

ENTERTAINMENT

Every evening around 5pm, people stroll along Las Ramblas, Pg. Gràcia, and the sea—nightlife in Barcelona starts then and there, and winds down about 14 hours later. The best source of information on fun things to do in the city is the weekly *Guía del Ocio* (125ptas, available at newsstands). Although listings are in Castilian, they are comprehensible even if you don't speak the language. The *Cine* section designates subtitled films with *V.O. subtitulada;* other films are dubbed. Other sections are *Arte* (exhibitions), *Tarde/Noche* (nightlife), and *Música* (live music).

Music and Film The **Gran Teatre del Liceu** (see **Sights,** p. 817), Rambla de Caputxins, 61, will reopen in October 1998 with Puccini's *Turandant.* Rock and pop stars play at the **Palau d'Esports Sant Jordi** (tel. 426 20 89). At the **Palau de la Música Catalana,** an extraordinary brick *modernista* building on C. Francesc de Paula 2 (tel. 268 10 00), off Vía Laietana near Pl. Urquinaona, concerts cover all varieties of symphonic and choral music. Ask about free winter concerts (Tues. nights) and the October music festival. (Tickets 800-1500ptas. Box office open Mon.-Fri. 10am-9pm, Sat. 3-9pm, Sun. from 1hr. prior to the concert. Tours are offered daily around 2 and 3pm. 300ptas, free with a *Ruta del Modernisme* pass.) **Teatre Grec** turns Barcelona into a theater, musical, and dance extravaganza from June to mid-August. Some of the major venues (the Teatro Grec itself and the **Convent de Sant Augusti**) are open-air theaters. Tickets can be purchased through **TelEntrades** (tel. 310 12 12).

Films are popular in Barcelona; besides Spanish and Catalan features, you should be able to find a Hollywood classic or the hot recent flick in English. Check the schedule of the **Filmoteca,** Av. Sarrià 33 (tel. 410 75 90; M: Hospital Clínic), run by the Generalitat, for classic, cult, exotic, and otherwise exceptional films (always subtitled if not a Castilian- or Catalan-language film; 400ptas).

Discos and Bars The evening *passeig* (stroll) is divided into two shifts: the post-siesta burst (around 5-7pm), then a second wave after dinner (perhaps 9-11pm), fueled by alcohol. After the bars wind down around 2am, crowds flood the discos until morning. Bouncers can be finicky, and what's hip varies from day to day.

Eixample: Velodrom, C. Muntaner, 213. M: Diagonal. Pre-party crowd. Students drink in cushioned booths and shoot pool in a weatherworn hangout with ceiling fans, monstrous windows, and a loft. *Jarras* (mugs) of beer 275ptas. Mon.-Sat. 6pm-2am. **Otto Zutz,** C. Lincoln, 15, near Pl. Molina where C. Balmes intersects Vía Augusta. M: FFCC Muntaner. Large, flashy club. Three floors and 6 bars. Cover 2000ptas, drink included. Open Tues.-Sat. midnight-5am.

Ciutat Vella: L'Ovella Negra, C. Sitges, 5. M: Catalunya. From Pl. Catalunya, down Las Ramblas and the first right at C. Tallers; C. Sitges is the first left. Smoky tavern where locals and travelers mix freely over pool and foosball. Beer 325ptas. Open Mon.-Thurs. 9pm-3am, Fri.-Sat. 9pm-3am, Sun. 5pm-3am. **Café d l'Opera,** Ramblas, 74. M: Liceu. A drink at this café was once a post-opera tradition for bourgeois *barcelonenses.* Despite Liceu's recent fire, a scaled-up crowd still fills its indoor and outdoor tables. Open daily 8am-12:30pm.

La Ribera: Xampanyet, C. Montcado, 15, off Pg. Borne near Museu Picasso. Sophisticated relaxation: *cava* and anchovies are served up at a history-laden champagne bar. Open Tues.-Sat. noon-4pm and 6:30-11:30pm, Sun. 6:30-11:30pm.

Montjuïc: Poble Espanyol, Av. Marqués de Comillas. M: Pl. Espanya. 15 bars, 3 *bares-musicales,* and 1 large late-night *discoteca,* where dancing starts at 1:30am and usually doesn't end until 9am. Open Thurs.-Sat.

Port Olímpic (M: Ciutadella-Vila Olímpica): **Panini,** Moll de Mestral, 11. A classy pizzeria by day, a strobe light beast by night. Pop and dance mixes with lots of bass. One of the larger spots on the port. Open midnight-6am.

■ Near Barcelona: Montserrat and Sitges

An hour northwest of Barcelona, the **Montserrat** mountain range—legendary site of the Holy Grail and inspiration of Wagner's *Parsifal*—juts out from the flat Río Llobregat valley. In the 10th century, a wandering mountaineer had a blinding vision of the Virgin Mary here, and the site is now a major pilgrimage center, second in Spain only to Santiago de Compostela. The **basílica** stands above Pl. Creu and looks out onto Pl. Santa Noría (open Mon.-Fri. 8-10:30am and noon-6:30pm, Sat. 7:30-8:30pm). Plaça Santa María also boasts the **Museu de Montserrat,** which exhibits a sweeping range of art—from Israeli Torahs to paintings by El Greco, Caravaggio, and Picasso (open Mon.-Fri.10am-6pm, Sat.-Sun. 9:30am-6:30pm; 500ptas, students 300ptas). A visit to Montserrat without a meditative walk along the ridge of what Maragall called "the mountain of a hundred peaks" would be a sin. From Pl. Creu, the Santa Cova **funicular** descends to paths winding along the sides of the mountain to ancient hermitages (every 20min., 340ptas). Take the St. Joan funicular up for more inspirational views of Montserrat (every 20min, 835ptas). The dilapidated **St. Joan monastery** and **shrine** are only a 20-minute tromp away, but the real prize is **Sant Jerónim,** with its mystical views of Montserrat's celebrated rock formations.

For details on daily religious services and navigating your way through the mountains, go to the **info booth** in **Plaça Creu** (tel. 835 02 51, ext. 586). **Trains** to Montserrat leave from Barcelona's Pl. Espanya stop (every hr., 9:10am-5:10pm; round-trip 1720ptas). Odd-hour trains are direct on the Manresa line. Even-hour trains are destined for Igualada; you must transfer at the Martorell-Enllaç stop (for info call 205 15 15). Be sure to get off at "Aeri de Montserrat." The trains stop at the base of the mountain, where a funicular (included in train fare) carries you up the slope. Upon exiting the upper funicular station, turn left and walk up 100m to reach Pl. Creu. If you choose to spend the night, apartments for up to ten are available through **Administació de les Cel.les** (tel. 835 02 01; fax 835 06 59), to your right with your back to the corner of Pl. Creu and Pl. Santa María. The office runs three *hostales* (2965-3750ptas); **Abat Marcet** is the newest and nicest of the lot.

Long considered a watered down version of the raging Ibiza, **Sitges,** 40km from Barcelona, is developing its own radical identity with an international gay community and wired nightlife. The **beach** is a 10-minute walk from the train station. On C. Fonollar, the **Museu Cau Ferrat** houses a veritable shrine to Modernist art. (Open June 22-Sept. 10 Tues.-Sat. 9:30am-2pm and 4-9pm, Sun. closes at 2pm; off-season reduced hours. 700ptas, students 350ptas.) Late night bacchanalia clusters around **C. primer de Maig,** which runs directly from the beach. The wild things are at **Atlántida,** Scetor Terramar and **Pachá,** Pg. Sant Didac, in nearby Vallipenda. Buses run from C. Primer de Maig to the two (midnight and 4am).

Sitges celebrates its holidays with style. On June 1, for the **Festa de Corpus Christi,** the city overflows with intricate carpets weaved of hundreds of thousand of flowers. Papier-mâché creatures dance in the streets on August 23-25 for the **Festa Major.** Yet nothing compares to the **Carnaval** during the first week of Lent, when Spaniards of every ilk crash town for a frenzy of dancing, outrageous costumes, and vats of alcohol. Ask the tourist office about other Sitges revelries.

Trains (tel. (93) 894 98 89) link Sitges to Barcelona-Sants and M:Gràcia (every 15min., 40min. 305ptas). To get to the **tourist office,** Pg. Vilafranca (tel. (93) 894 50 04; fax 894 43 05), from the station, turn right on C. Salvador Mirabent Pareta and go downhill (open mid-Sept. to June Mon.-Fri. 9am-2pm and 4-6:30pm, Sat. 10am-1pm). They have a super map and plenty of info. Accommodations are expensive in Sitges: it is best to make it a daytrip form Barcelona. If you must stay, however, **Hostal Parelladas,** C. Parelladas, 11 (tel. (93) 894 08 01), is one block from beach (singles 2300ptas, doubles 4700ptas).

Girona (Gerona)

A world-class city waiting patiently for the world to notice, Girona rules its namesake province from the banks of the gorgeous Riu Onyar. The city is really two in one: a hushed medieval masterpiece of stone alleyways on one river bank, and a thriving modern city on the other. Girona was founded by the Romans, but owes more to the renowned *cabalistas de Girona,* who for centuries spread the teachings of Kabbalah (mystical Judaism) in the West. Still a center of culture and home to a large university, the city is a magnet for artists, intellectuals, and activists.

Most of Girona's sights are in the old city across the coffee-colored Riu Onyar from the train station. The **Pont de Pedra** connects the two banks and leads directly into the old quarter by way of Carreras Ciutadans, Peralta, and Força. **El Call,** a medieval Jewish neighborhood, begins at C. Sant Llorenç, a right off C. Força onto a narrow alleyway. A thriving community during the Middle Ages, it was virtually wiped out by the 1492 expulsion, mass emigration, conversion, and the Inquisition. The entrance to **Casa de Isaac el Cec,** the probable site of the last synagogue in Girona, is off C. Sant Llorenç about halfway up the hill. The Casa now serves as a museum linking the baths, butcher shop, and synagogue, all of which surround a serene patio. (Open June-Oct. Mon.-Sat. 10am-9pm, Sun. 10am-2pm; Nov.-May Mon.-Sat. 10am-6pm, Sun. 10am-2pm. Free.) Farther uphill on C. Força and around the corner to the right, Girona's Gothic **cathedral** rises up a record-breaking 90 Rococo steps from its *plaça.* The northern **Torre de Charlemany** is the only structure which remains from the 11th century; the cavernous interior has one rather than the customary three naves, making it the world's widest Gothic vault at 22m. In the trapezoidal cloister, the **Museu del Claustre** hoards some of Girona's most precious possessions, including the intricate and animated **Tapis de la Creació,** which takes up the entire wall of Room IV. Woven in the 11th or 12th century, its illustrations depict the cycle of creation and biblical scenes. (Cathedral and museum open July-Aug. Tues.-Sun. 10am-2pm and 4-7pm; Sept.-June Tues.-Sat. 10am-2pm and 4-6pm, Sun. 10am-2pm. Museum 300ptas.)

Practical Information, Accommodations, and Food Girona is the Costa Brava's transport center: all trains on the Barcelona-Portbou-Cerbère line stop here, scores of buses travel daily to the Costa Brava and nearby cities. Girona is also an ideal base for exploring the Catalan Pyrenees. The RENFE and bus terminals are off **Carrer de Barcelona** on the modern side of town. **Trains** (tel. (972) 20 70 93) chug to Figueres (26-52min., 310ptas), Barcelona (1-2hr., 735-1650ptas), Zaragoza (3-4hr., 3400-3800ptas), Valencia (8hr., 3115ptas), and Madrid (9hr., 6000-7100ptas). **Buses** (tel. (972) 21 23 19) depart from around the corner from the train station. **Sarfa** (tel. (972) 20 17 96) travels to Tossa de Mar (1hr., 475ptas). The **tourist office,** Rambla de la Llibertat, 1 (tel. (972) 22 65 75; fax 22 66 12), directly on the left as you cross Pont de Pedra from the new town, is an oasis for the directionally dehydrated (open Mon.-Fri. 8am-8pm, Sat. 8am-2pm and 4-8pm, Sun. 9am-2pm). There is also a **branch office** at the train station (tel. (972) 21 62 96; open July-Aug. Mon.-Fri. 9am-2pm).

Rooms are hardest to find in June and August. **Alberg-Residència Cerverí de Girona (HI),** C. Ciutadans, 9 (tel. (972) 21 81 21; fax 21 20 23), lies in the heart of the old quarter on the street running left after Pont de Pedra. A college dorm most of the year, the building is ultra-modern inside. (Curfew 11pm, but door opens every 30min. until 1am. 1600ptas per person, over 25 2200ptas. Breakfast included. Sheets 350ptas. Closed Aug. 21-Sept. 21.) **Pensió Viladomat,** C. Ciutadans, 5 (tel. (972) 20 31 76), is on the same street and features sparkling rooms and bathrooms (singles 1850ptas, doubles 3600ptas, triples 4200ptas). **Café Le Bistrot,** Pujada Sant Domènec, 4, packs in the locals and young lovers for a lunchtime 3-course *menú* (1200ptas) as well as pizzas and crepes. (450-625ptas. Open Tues.-Thurs. 11am-2am, Fri.-Sat. 11am-1am, Sun. 11am-4pm, Mon. 7pm-1am.) Enjoy *torradas* (delectable toasts with toppings; 500-1300ptas for 2 or 3) with the local student crowd at **Café la**

Torrada, C. Ciutadans, 18, a block from the youth hostel (open Mon.-Fri. 9am-4pm and 7pm-1am, Sat. 7pm-midnight).

Girona takes its evening *passeig* seriously. The **Rambla** is the place to see and be seen, gossip, politic, flirt, and dance. Most summer Fridays see spontaneous *sardanas,* traditional Catalan dances involving 10-12 musicians, who serenade a ring of dancers. After the *passeig* there's dinner, and after dinner there's bar-hopping, when the throngs move to the newer part of the city. Bars near **Pl. Ferrán el Catòlic** draw big crowds, but during the summer, **Parc de la Devesa,** across the river from the old town and several blocks to the left, has all the cachet, and often live music as well. Of Girona's four discos, the mightiest is **La Sala de Cel,** C. Pedret, 118, off Pl. Sant Pere in the northern quarter of the city (cover 2000ptas, includes 2 drinks; open Sept.-July Thurs.-Sun. nights). Artsy folk mill around bars and cafés in the old quarter.

SPAIN

■ Near Girona

Tossa de Mar is a touristy resort on the lower part of the Costa Brava, about 40km north of Barcelona. All four of Tossa's **beaches** are worth a visit, as are the **calas** (small bays) accessible by foot. Beaches aside, inside the **Vila Vella** (old town), a spiral of medieval alleys leads to the remains of a Gothic church, the **Església de Sant Vincenç** reposes above a cliff. **Bus** service is frequent in summer from Barcelona (6-8 per day) and Girona (3 per day), but is so limited during low- and mid-season that travelers may wish to head for **Lloret de Mar** (8km south) and catch the bus (15min.) from there to Tossa. The **tourist office** (tel. (972) 34 01 08; fax 34 07 12), in the bus terminal at the corner of Av. Ferran Agulló and Av. Pelegrí, has a well-indexed city map (open Mon.-Sat. 9am-9pm, Sun. 10am-1pm). **Fonda Lluna,** C. Roqueta, 20 (tel. (972) 34 03 65), is an amazing budget find: immaculate rooms with private baths and a rooftop terrace with a heart-stopping view of Tossa (1600-1800ptas; breakfast included; open March-Oct.). Camping is available at **Can Martí** (tel. (972) 34 08 51; fax 34 24 61), at the end of Rbla. Pau Casals. (June 20-Aug. 725ptas per person, 750ptas per tent; off-season 575ptas per person, 625ptas per tent. Open May-Sept.) The *paella* at **Restaurant Marina,** C. Tarull, 6, is as good as it gets (*menú* 950ptas, *paella menú* 1250ptas). **Ely,** C. Bernats, 2 and Av. Costa Brava, 5, is a fashionable disco, and **Bar La Pinta,** C. Portal, 32, has outdoor seating overlooking the sea.

In 1974 Salvador Dalí built a museum for his works in his native, beachless **Figueres,** 36km north of Girona. Ever since, melting clocks have meant fast bucks. Transformed from an old municipal theater, the **Teatre-Museu Dalí,** in Pl. Gala i S. Dalí, parades the artist's capricious projects: erotically nightmarish drawings, extraterrestrial landscapes, and even a personal rock collection. (Open July-Sept. daily 9am-8pm; Oct.-June 11:30am-5pm. 1000ptas, students 800ptas; Oct.-June 800ptas, 600ptas.) The **tourist office** (tel. (972) 50 31 55) on Pl. Sol offers a good city map, list of accommodations, and ranking of restaurants. (Open July-Aug. Mon.-Sat. 9am-9pm; Easter-June and Oct. Mon.-Fri. 8:30am-3pm and 4:30-8pm, Sat. 9:30am-1:30pm and 3:30-6:30pm; Sept. and Nov.-Easter Mon.-Fri. 8:30am-3pm.) **Barcelona Bus** (tel. (972) 50 50 29) connects Figueres with Girona (1hr., 415ptas) and Barcelona (2¼hr., 1375ptas). **Trains** (tel. (972) 20 70 93) run to Girona (25min.-1hr., 370ptas) and Barcelona (1½-2hr., 1100ptas). **Alberg Tramuntana (HI),** C. Anicet de Pagès, 2 (tel. (972) 50 12 13; fax 67 38 08), provides hot showers, a VCR, vegetarian meals, and friendly hosts. (Members only, but they sell HI cards. Curfew midnight, but opens briefly on the hr. until 4am. Lockout 10am-4pm, Sat.-Sun. 10am-5pm. May-Sept. 1600ptas, over 25 2200ptas; Oct.-April 1375ptas, 1875ptas. Reserve 1 month ahead through Barcelona office at (93) 403 83 63, or call the hostel 2-3 days before arrival.)

■ Catalan Pyrenees

So far, only the discerning few have made it to the Catalan Pyrenees: hikers, skiers, Romanesque-church lovers, and small-town buffs will be in good company. The Department of Commerce and Tourism distributes pamphlets on local winter sports and areas of scenic grandeur. Skiers will find the *Snow in Catalonia* guide (free at tourist offices) especially useful. Cyclists should ask for *Valles Superiores del Segre/ Ariège,* which covers the Alt Urgell, Cerdanya, and the Val de Ribas. **Editorial Alpina** publishes indispensable topographical maps bound in red booklets.

Núria A Club Med-type resort area, **Núria** has carved a market niche for itself with year-round, right-at-your-doorstep skiing and hiking. The mountains around Núria are inaccessible by train or car, but the old Cremallera **cable car** zips from the "Ribas de Freser" stop on the Ripoll-Puigcerdá line. The 45-minute ride scales 800m through virgin mountain faces where stubborn sheep, goats, and pine trees cling (6-11 per day, 8:15am-9pm, round-trip 2150ptas). Climbers prefer the **hike** to **Puigmal** (4hr., 2913m) and **Eina.** The less ambitious may follow the path to neighboring Quelrabs (1½-2½hr.) which passes along waterfalls and gorges carpeted with wildflowers (the return trip is significantly harder). Ten **ski trails** range from *molt facil* (very easy) to *molt difficil* (very difficult or expert) at **Estació de la Vall de Núria.**

From Núria, a modern cable line (included in the price of Cremallera ticket) whisks passengers straight to **Alberg de Joventut Pic de l'Aliga** (tel. (972) 73 00 48), the alternative being an arduous 20-minute climb. The modern three-story youth hostel loyally maintains Núria's training-camp atmosphere with ping-pong, volleyball, and basketball. (1600ptas per person, over 25 2200ptas. Hot showers. Breakfast included. Closed Nov.) For reservations, especially in July, August, and (if there's snow) January through March, call the Barcelona office at (93) 483 83 63. The **Bar Finistrelles,** downstairs from the souvenir store in the main complex, vends tortilla sandwiches (400ptas) and a whole roast chicken with potatoes (975ptas).

SPAIN

BALEARIC ISLANDS (ILLES BALEARES)

Discos, ancient history, and beaches—especially beaches—draw 1.7 million almost exclusively European tourists to the Baleares, 100km off the east coast of Spain, each year. Mallorca is home to the province's capital, Palma, as well as limestone cliffs, countless orchards, and clear turquoise waters. Ibiza, southwest of Mallorca, successfully plays the role of entertainment capital of the islands and has an active gay community. The smaller, less-touristed islands offer empty white beaches, hidden coves, and mysterious Bronze Age megaliths.

Getting There and Getting Around **Charters** are the cheapest and quickest means of round-trip travel to the islands; check newspaper ads or through travel agencies. **Scheduled flights** are easier to book. Frequent departures soar from cities throughout Europe. On **Iberia/Aviaco Airlines** (tel. (902) 40 05 00; call six months ahead), round-trip student fares from Barcelona to Palma, Menorca, or Ibiza run 17,250-20,050ptas. From Madrid to Ibiza, Palma, or Menorca, flights costs 25,500-28,750ptas. *Tarifa-mini* round-trip tickets, with 50% discounts, are sporadically available. **Transmediterránea ships** depart from Barcelona, Est. Marítima (tel. (93) 443 25 32), and Valencia, Est. Marítima, Pta. de Valencia (tel. (96) 367 65 12). Any travel agent in Spain can book seats to Palma, Mahón, and Ibiza; high-season prices run 3325-7875ptas one way. **Flebasa** (toll-free tel. (900) 177 177), sends ferries to Ibiza (1 per day, 3½hr.) and to San Antonio (2 per day, 4hr.) from Denia, on the FEVE rail line between Valencia and Alicante. In summer, the ferry ticket can be supplemented with a bus connection from Valencia, Alicante, or Madrid for 350ptas extra. A ferry from Ibiza connects to Palma. All one-way trips cost 5475ptas.

Flying is the best way to island-hop. **Iberia** flies from Palma to Ibiza (3-4 per day, 20min., 5900ptas) and Mahón, Menorca (2-3 per day, 20min., 5800ptas). Iberia also flies from Menorca to Ibiza (2-3 per day, 11,700ptas), but the stopover in Palma can last up to four hours. Planes fill a couple of days in advance in summer, so make reservations. If flying round-trip, ask if the *tarifa-mini* fare is applicable. Seafarers between the islands sail Transmediterránea, whose **ships** connect Palma with Ibiza (1-2 per week, 4½hr., 3325ptas) and Mahón (1 per week, 6½hr., 3325ptas). Flebasa **ferries** connect Palma and Ibiza (1 per day, 2-4½hr., 3245ptas), and Mallorca and Menorca (14-35 per week, 1-3½hr., 3150ptas). **Bus** fares between cities in Mallorca and Ibiza range from 100-700ptas each way. **Car** rental runs 5200ptas, **moped** rental 2300ptas, and **bike** rental 900ptas per day.

Mallorca **Mallorca** subscribes to a simple theorem—more hotels, more tourists, more money. Yet amid the tourism, jagged cliffs line the north coast, while lazy calm bays and caves scoop into the rest of the coast. The capital of the province, **Palma** is a showy Balearic upstart; its streets hustle with conspicuously consuming shoppers, and the town boasts a swinging nightlife. Though better **beaches** spread throughout the expanse of the island, decent ones are a short bus ride from Palma. The beach at **El Arenal** (Platja de Palma, bus 15), 11km to the southeast, is popular. The equally crowded **Palma Nova** and **Illetes** beaches (buses 21 and 3, respectively) are 15 and 9km southwest. Every Friday, *El Día de Mundo* newspaper (125ptas) includes numerous listings of bars and discos all over Mallorca. Palma nightlife centers in the **El Terreno** area, with nightclubs on Pl. Gomilia and along C. Joan Miró. Good drinks complement elegant furniture and piles of fresh fruit at **ABACO,** C. Sant Joan, 1, in the Barri Gòtic near the waterfront (fruit nectars 1100ptas; potent cocktails 1700-2100ptas). The divine **Baccus,** on C. Lluis Fábregas, 2, attracts lively lesbian and gay hedonists (open nightly until 3am). **BCM** in nearby **Magaluf** is supposedly the biggest nightclub in Europe. (Playa-Sol bus company sends last bus at 8pm; return on bus 10 at 6:45am. Taxi from Palma 1800ptas. Cover 1800-2500ptas. Open 11pm-6am.)

In Palma, the **tourist office,** Pl. Reina 2 (tel. (971) 71 22 16), offers island info, a city map, and bus and train schedules (open Mon.-Fri. 9am-8pm, Sat. 9am-1:30pm). The **Albergue Residencia de Estudiantes (HI)**, C. Costa Brava, 13 (tel. (971) 26 08 92), new furniture, showers, and a TV lounge; take bus 15 from Pl. Espanya (every 8min., 170ptas) and ask to get off at Hotel Acapulco. (Reception open daily 8am-3am. Curfew Sun.-Thurs. midnight, Fri.-Sat. 3am. Members only. 1200ptas. Open July-Aug.) **Hostal Bonany,** C. Almirante Cerevera, 5 (tel. (971) 73 79 24), **Hostal Apuntadores,** C. Apuntadores, 8 (tel. (971) 71 34 91), and **Hostal Cuba,** C. San Magín, 1 (tel. (971) 73 81 59), all offer clean rooms (singles 2000-2400ptas, doubles 3500-4200ptas).

Ibiza Once a hippie enclave, **Ibiza** (Eivissa) is now a summer camp for disco maniacs, high-fashion posers, and self-marginalized youths. Although its thriving gay community lends credence to Ibiza's self-image as a "tolerant" center, the island's high cost of touring precludes true diversity. No beach is within quick walking distance, but **Platja de Talamanca, Platja des Duros, Platja de Ses Figures,** and **Platja Figueredes** are no farther than 20 minutes away by bike. At nightfall, even the clothing stores (open until 1am) dazzle with throbbing music and flashing lights. Jazz wails through the smoky air of **Arteca,** on C. Bisbe Azara. **Capricios,** on C. de la Virgen, has an outdoor terrace, while **Bar Galerie** and **Exis** are a bit livelier. Gay nightlife hovers around **C.Virgen** and the part of Dalt Vila closest to the port. Ibiza's **disco** scene is world famous and ever changing. **Incognito** and **Angelo's** on Alfonso XII, break up the nightly exodus to the gay scene at **Discoteca Anfora** in Dalt Alta. **Privelege,** Urbanización San Rafael, draws a mixed crowd (open June-Sept. daily midnight-9am), while **Pachá,** Pg. Perimetral, a 20-minute walk from the port, features a playful atmosphere with palm trees and terraces (open daily midnight-6:30am). **El Divino,** Puerto Ibiza Nueva, hosts extravagant parties, earning it the title *"un lugar de locuras"* (cover 3000ptas; open mid-June to mid-Sept. daily 1:30-6:30am). The **Discobús** runs to and from the major hotspots (midnight-6:30am, 225ptas).

The **tourist office,** Av. España, 49 (tel. (971) 30 19 00), has good maps and bus schedules (open Mon.-Fri. 9:30am-1:30pm and 5-7pm, Sat. 10:30am-1pm). Decent, cheap accommodations in Ibiza are rare. "CH," which stands for **casa de huéspedes,** marks many doorways, but often the owner must be reached through the phone number tacked on the door. The sun and breeze have done wonders for the **Hostal**

Residencia Sol y Brisa, Av. Bartomeu v. Ramón, 15 (tel. (971) 31 08 18; fax 30 30 32), parallel to Pg. Vara de Rey (singles 1800-2200ptas, doubles 3000-4000ptas). **Hostal La Marina,** C. Andenes del Puerto, 4 (tel. (971) 31 01 72), across from Estació Marítima, is conveniently located (singles 1800ptas, doubles 3300-4800ptas).

VALENCIA

Valencia's rich soil has earned it the nickname "Huerta de España," or orchard of Spain. Miles of geometrically-laid fruit trees suggest an Eden xeroxed, and lovely fountains and pools grace carefully landscaped public gardens in many cities. Local *fiestas* amplify Valencia's enchantment with fire, water, and love into hyperbolic proportions, with every little coastal town erupting in its own pyrotechnic celebration.

Valencia

Valencia is a stylish, cosmopolitan nerve center, a striking contrast to the surrounding orchards and brown-speckled mountain ranges. Fountainous parks and gardens soothe the city's high-powered business environment, while soft-sanded beaches complement its kinetic nightlife. Graffiti that "corrects" Castilian road signs into *valenciá* reflects a recent surge in regionalism, but these sentiments are rarely seen or heard beyond a few spray-painted expressions. The legions of university students who invigorate the city still favor *castellano.*

ORIENTATION AND PRACTICAL INFORMATION

The train station is close to city center. **Avenida Márquez de Sotelo** runs from the train station to **Plaza del Ayuntamiento,** where the city tourist office is located. The avenue then splits into **Avenida Maria Cristina,** which leads to the Central Market, and **Carrer de Sant Vicent,** which leads to **Plaza de la Reina** and the cathedral.

Tourist Offices: Regional office, Estación del Nord, C. Xàtiva, 24 (tel. 352 85 73), on the train station's right as you exit. Pamphlets and maps. Open Mon.-Fri. 9am-6:30pm. **City office,** Pl. Ayuntamiento, 1 (tel. 351 04 17). Dedicated staff, useful lists of hostels. Open Mon.-Fri. 8:30am-2:15pm and 4:15-6pm, Sat. 9am-12:45pm.

Currency Exchange: El Corte Inglés, C. Pintor Sorolla, 26 (tel. 351 24 44). From Pl. Ayuntamiento, walk down C. Bareas as it turns into a pedestrian walk; El Corte Inglés sits on the left. Awesome **map.** Open daily 10am-9pm. **Citibank** is in Pl. Ayuntamiento on the corner of C. San Vicente Mártir. **Banco Central Hispano,** which offers the best exchange rates, is across the street.

American Express: Duna Viajes, C. Cirilo Amorós, 88 (tel. 374 15 62; fax 334 57 00), next to Pl. América on the edge of Río Turia. No commission on AmEx Traveler's Cheques. Mail held. Open in summer Mon.-Fri. 10am-2pm and 5-8pm, Sat. 10am-2pm; off-season Mon.-Fri. 9:30am-1:30pm and 4:30-7:30pm.

Flights: The airport is 15km southwest of the city (tel. 370 95 00). *Cercanías* trains run between the airport and train station from 7am-10pm (32min., 145ptas). For international and national reservations call **Servilberia** (tel. 902 40 05 00).

Trains: Estación del Nord, C. Xàtiva, 24 (tel. 351 36 12). Info office open daily 8am-9pm. Ticket windows open daily 6:30am-10pm. **RENFE** (tel. 352 02 02) serves Barcelona (4-6hr., 3100ptas), Madrid (5-7½hr., 3800ptas), and Seville (8½-9½hr., 5600ptas).

Buses: Estación Terminal d'Autobuses, Av. Menéndez Pidal, 13 (tel. 349 72 22), across the river. Take bus 8 (100ptas) from Pl. Ayuntamiento, 22, or walk northwest from the center. To: Madrid (4-5hr., 2845-3145ptas) and Barcelona (4½hr., 2650ptas). Eurolines also runs international service from here.

Public Transportation: EMT Buses (tel. 352 83 99). Half leave from Pl. Ayuntamiento, 22. Buy tickets aboard or at newsstands (105ptas, 10-ride 675ptas).

Ferries: Transmediterránea, Estació Maritima (tel. 367 65 12). Service to Palma (Mon.-Sat., 9hr., 6350ptas). Advance tickets Mon.-Fri. 9:30am-2pm and 5-11pm, Sat.

9:30am-2pm; or buy tickets on the day of departure at the port office. Take bus 4 from Pl. Ayuntamiento. Ask a travel agent for the **Flebasa** schedule to Ibiza.

Pharmacies: Check listing in local paper *Levante* (135ptas) or the *farmacias de guardia* schedule posted outside any pharmacy for 24hr. pharmacies.

Medical Assistance: Hospital Clínico Universitario, Av. Blasco Ibáñez, 17 (tel. 386 26 00), at the corner of C. Dr. Ferrer. Take bus 70 or 81 from Pl. Ayuntamiento. An English-speaking doctor is often on duty.

Emergency: tel. 091 or 092. **Ambulance:** tel. 085.

Police: Guardia Civil: tel. 333 11 00 or 602. **Policía Local:** tel. 362 10 12.

Post Office: Pl. Ajuntament, 24 (tel. 351 67 50). Open Mon.-Fri. 8:30am-8:30pm, Sat. 9:30am-2pm. **Postal Code:** 46080.

Telephones: Estación del Nord, C. Xàtiva, 24, near the RENFE info booth. Open daily 8am-10pm. Faxes (fax 394 27 44) sent and received. **Telephone Code:** 96.

ACCOMMODATIONS

The business of Valencia is business, not tourism, so rooms are plentiful during the summer. The best options cluster around **Plaza del Ayuntamiento** and **Plaza del Mercado.** Avoid the areas by the *barrio chino* (red-light district) around Pl. Pilar.

Alberg Colegio "La Paz" (HI), Av. Puerto, 69 (tel. 369 01 52). Take bus 19 from Pl. Ayuntamiento; it's the 2nd stop on Av. del Puerto. Forbidding fortress safeguards peace and quiet. 2-4 beds and a bathroom in each room. Members only. Reception open daily 9:30am-1pm and 5pm-1am. Lockout 10am-5pm. Curfew midnight. 1000ptas, over 26 1500ptas. Breakfast included. Open July-Sept. 15.

Pensión Paris, C. Salvá, 12 (tel. 352 67 66). From Pl. Ayuntamiento turn right at C. Barcas, left at C. Poeta Querol, and right onto C. Salvá. 13 spotless rooms with angelic white curtains and balconies. A real bargain. Singles 2000ptas. Doubles 3000ptas, with shower 3600ptas, with bath 4000ptas. Triples 4500ptas.

Hostal-Residencia El Cid, C. Cerrajeros, 13 (tel. 392 23 23), off C. Vicente Mártir after Pl. Ayuntamiento (and before Pl. Reina). Homey feel and heating in winter. Singles 1380ptas. Doubles 2600ptas, with shower 3000ptas. *Let's Go* discount.

Hostal del Rincón, C. Carda, 11 (tel. 391 60 83). From Pl. Ayuntamiento, Pl. Mercado extends past the market building; its continuation is C. Carda. First 2 floors are newly renovated. Rooms cleaned daily. Singles 1500ptas, with bath 2000ptas. Doubles 2800ptas, with bath 3600ptas.

FOOD

Celebrated as the birthplace of *paella,* Valencia boasts 200 rice specialties. Another regional favorite is *horchata,* a sweet, milky-white drink pressed from local *chufas* (earth almonds). Fresh fish, meat, and fruit sell at the **Mercado Central** on Pl. Mercado (open Mon.-Thurs. 7am-2pm, Fri. 7am-2pm and 5-8:30pm, Sat. 7am-3pm).

Restaurante La Utielana, Pl. Picadero Dos Aguas, 3. Take C. Barcelonina off Pl. Ayuntamiento, turn left at its end, then make a sharp right onto C. Procida. Ideal service, and not a plate on the menu over 750ptas. Scrumptious seafood *paella* a shocking 325ptas. *Gambas a la plancha* 475ptas. Afternoon *menú* 800ptas. A/C. Open Sept.-July Mon.-Fri. 1:15-4pm and 9-11pm, Sat. 1:15-4pm.

La Lluna, C. Sant Ramón, in El Carme district near IVAM. A veggie restaurant to moon over. 4-course *menú* and whole-grain bread served weekday afternoons 850ptas. Open Mon.-Sat. 1:30-4:30pm and 8pm-midnight.

La Pappardella, C. Bordadores, 5. Stand in front of the doors to the Cathedral (Pl. Reina) and look left. Delicious pasta dishes. *Penne i gambi con vodka* 850ptas. Open Wed.-Mon. noon-4:30pm and 8pm-midnight.

SIGHTS AND ENTERTAINMENT

Most of the sights line the **Río Turia** or cluster near **Plaza de la Reina.** The Aragonese began the **cathedral** in Pl. Reina shortly after the *Reconquista.* Seized by a fit of Romantic hyperbole, or maybe just vertigo, French novelist Victor Hugo counted 300 bell towers in the city from the **Micalet** (cathedral tower)—actually there are about 100. (Tower open Mon.-Fri. 10am-12:30pm and 4:30-7:30pm, Sat.-Sun. 10am-1pm and 5-7:30pm. Reduced hours off season. 100ptas. Cathedral open daily 7:30am-1pm and 4:30-8:30pm. Free.) The **Museo de la Catedral** squeezes many treasures into very little space. Check out a Holy Grail, two Goyas, and an tabernacle made from 1200kg of gold, silver, platinum, emeralds, and sapphires. (Open March-Nov. Mon.-Sat. 10am-1pm and 4:30-6pm; Dec.-Feb. 10am-1pm. 100ptas.) In Pl. Mercado, the old **Lonja de la Seda** (Silk Exchange) is a foremost example of Valencian Gothic architecture (open Tues.-Fri. 9am-2pm and 5-9pm, Sat.-Sun. 9am-1:30pm; free).

For diversion from its concrete center, the city maintains impressive **parks** on the outskirts of the historic district. Taxonomists marvel at the **Jardín Botánico,** C. Beato Gaspar Bono, a university-maintained open-air botanical garden that cultivates 43,000 plants from around the world (open Tues.-Sun. 10am-9pm). A series of pillared public recreation areas mark the banks of the now diverted Río Turia; on one end, hundreds of children climb on a gigantic version of Jonathan Swift's "Gulliver" (open July-Aug. daily 10am-8pm; Sept.-June 10am-dusk).

On C. Sant Pius V, the **Museu Provincial de Belles Artes** displays superb 14th- to 16th-century Valencian primitives and works by later Spanish and foreign masters—a Hieronymous Bosch triptych, El Greco's *San Juan Bautista,* Velázquez's self-portrait, and a slew of Goyas. (Open Oct.-July Tues.-Sat. 10am-2pm and 4-6pm, Sun. 10am-2pm; Aug. Tues.-Sun. 10am-2pm. Free.) Across the river and to the west, the **Instituto València de Arte Moderno (IVAM),** C. Guillem de Castro, 118, has a modern art collection (open Tues.-Sun. 11am-8pm; 350ptas, students 175ptas).

Bars and pubs around the **El Carme** district, just beyond the market, pick up around 11:30pm. West of Gran Vía Fernando El Católico, popular bars line **Calle Juan Llorens** between San José la Montaña and Angel Guimera. Discos near the university, especially on **Avenide Blasco Ibañez,** don't draw a crowd until 3am. **Caballito de Mar,** C. Eugenia Viñes, 22, at Playa de Malvarrosa, remixes recent favorites and *bacalao* (Spanish techno) while artfully mimicking a cruise ship (open in summer daily until 2am). **Distrito 10,** C. General Elío, 10, has mirrors, three floors of balconies, and a huge video screen. (Open Sept.-July Thurs.-Sat. 6-9:30pm and midnight-7am, Sun. 6-9:30pm. Early session 400ptas, late 1500ptas.) Gay men congregate at **Balkiss,** C. Dr. Monserrat, 23; lesbians favor **Carnaby Club,** Poeta Liern, 17.

Valencia's most illustrious traditional event is undoubtedly **Las Fallas,** March 12-19. The city's neighborhoods compete to build the most elaborate and satirical papier-mâché effigy; over 300 such *ninots* spring up in the streets. Parades, bullfights, fireworks, and dancing add to the festivities, and on the final day—*la nit del foc* (fire night)—all the *ninots* burn together in one last, clamorous release.

■ Near Valencia: Gandía

Before everyone became so fascinated by beaches, **Gandía** was best known as the hangout of the refined and powerful Borjas family. The **train station,** on Marqués de Campo, serves Valencia (every 30min., 1hr., 480ptas). The **tourist office** (tel. (96) 287 77 88), across from the station, offers a detailed map and accommodations listings. (Open in summer Mon.-Fri. 10am-2pm and 4:30-7:30pm, Sat. 10am-1:30pm; off-season Mon.-Fri. 10am-2pm and 4-7:30pm.) A branch is at the beach at Pg. Marítim (tel. (96) 284 24 07). Flattery does not do justice to **Alberg Mar i Vent (HI),** C. Doctor Fleming (tel. (96) 283 17 48), a hostel/beachfront resort in Platja de Piles 10km south of Gandía. Take the **La Amistad bus** (tel. (96) 287 44 10) from the right of the train station (100ptas). Water laps at the door, and the hostel offers an outdoor patio, basketball court, and bike and windsurfer rental. (Alcohol prohibited. 5-day max. stay. Curfew midnight, 2am, or 4am. 800ptas, with breakfast 900ptas; over 26 1100ptas, 1400ptas. Open Feb. 15-Dec. 15.)

Alicante (Alacant)

It's hard to imagine today that Alicante (pop. 250,000) once had to earn its city status—Fernando only relented when *alicantinos* helped reconquer the last Muslim outpost in Granada. Now confident in its urbanity, Alicante boasts what its bigger sibling Valencia cannot: a beautiful beach at its front door. Above the bastion of bronzing bodies, a *castillo,* spared by Franco when Alicante was the last Republican city to fall in the Civil War, guards a tangle of antiquated sheets in the *casco antiguo.*

ORIENTATION AND PRACTICAL INFORMATION

Avenida la Estación runs from the train station and becomes **Avenida Alfonso X el Sabio** after passing through **Plaza de los Luceros. Esplanada d'Espanya** stretches along the waterfront between **Rambla Méndez Núñez** and **Avenida Federico Soto,** which reach back up to Av. Alfonso X el Sabio, forming a box of streets where nearly all services cluster.

Tourist Office: Regional office, Esplanada d'Espanya, 2 (tel. 520 00 00; fax 520 02 43). Info on the entire coast and city. Open Mon.-Fri. 10am-8pm, Sat. 10am-2pm and 38pm. A **branch office** is located at the airport (tel. 691 93 67).

Budget Travel: TIVE, Av. Aguilera, 1 (tel. 590 07 70), near the train station off Av. Oscar Esplá. ISIC 700ptas. HI card 1800ptas. Open Mon.-Fri. 9am-1:30pm.

Currency Exchange: El Corte Inglés, Maisonnave, 53 (tel. 511 30 01). No commission. The office also has maps, novels, and guidebooks in English, and features a cafeteria, restaurant, and telephones. Open Mon.-Sat. 10am-9:30pm.

Flights: Aeroport Internacional El Altet (tel. 691 90 00), 10km from town. **Alcoyana** (tel. 513 01 04) sends buses (line C-6) every 40min. between the airport and the bus station and Pl. Luceros (from town 6:30am-10:20pm, from airport 6:55am-11:10pm; 100ptas).

Trains: RENFE, Estació Término, Av. Salamanca (tel. 592 02 02), west of the city center. Info open daily 7am-midnight. To: Murcia (1½hr., 525-560ptas), Valencia (2hr., 1325-2800ptas), Madrid (4hr., 3200-4700ptas), and Barcelona (6hr., 4300-6300ptas). **Ferrocarriles de la Generalitat Valenciana, Estació de la Marina,** Av. Villajoyosa, 2 (tel. 526 27 31), is a 15min. walk down Esplanada d'Espanya, away from Rambla Méndez Núñez; or, take bus G from the bus station and Corte Inglés. Local service along the Costa Blanca.

Buses: C. Portugal, 17 (tel. 513 07 00). To reach Esplanada d'Espanya, turn left onto Carrer d'Italia and right on Av. Dr. Gadea; follow Dr. Gadea to the park, then turn left. **UBESA** (tel. 513 01 43) runs to Valencia (1875ptas). **Enatcar** (tel. 513 06 73) serves Madrid (5½hr., 2895ptas), Granada (6hr., 3325ptas), Málaga (8hr., 4435ptas), Seville (10hr., 5740ptas), and Barcelona (8hr., 4590ptas).

Ferries: Flebasa, Estació Marítima, Puerto de Denia (tel. 578 40 11). Service from Denia to Ibiza (3 per day, 3½hr., 5740ptas). Open Mon.-Fri. 9am-1pm and 4:30-8pm, Sat. 9am-noon. **Pitra** (tel. 642 31 20) offers the same price with 2 trips daily to Ibiza. Also from Denia.

Medical Services: Hospital General, Maestro Alonzo, 109 (tel. 590 83 00).

Emergency: tel. 091 or 112.

Police: Comisaría, C. Médico Pascual Pérez, 27 (tel. 514 22 22).

Post Office: Pl. Gabriel Miró (tel. 521 99 84), off C. Sant Ferran. *Lista de Correos* arrives here. Open Mon.-Fri. 8:30am-8:30pm, Sat. 9am-2pm. **Postal Code:** 03000.

Telephone Code: 96.

ACCOMMODATIONS, CAMPING, AND FOOD

Although *pensiones* and *casas de huéspedes* are everywhere, stay away from places along **C. Sant Ferran,** where theft and prostitution are common, and around the **Església de Santa María.** Opt instead for the newer section of town. Arrive early or call ahead for a good room. The tourist office has accommodations listings.

SPAIN

Residencia Universitaria (HI), Av. Orihuela, 59 (tel. 511 30 44). Take bus G (100ptas) to the last stop, directly behind the large *residencia.* Individual rooms, private bath, and A/C. Members only. 3-day max. stay. 800ptas per person, with breakfast 900ptas; over 26 1100ptas, 1400ptas. Few rooms available Sept.-June.

Pensión Les Monges, C. Monjas, 2 (tel. 521 50 46). Behind the Ayuntamiento. In the center of the historic district, only a few blocks from the beach. A budget traveler's dream. Winter heating. Laundry service. Singles 1700-2800ptas. Doubles 3000-4500ptas. Triples 5000-5500ptas.

Habitaciones México, C. General Primo de Rivera, 10 (tel. 520 93 07), off the end of Av. Alfonso X El Sabio. Pristine rooms. Laundry service 800ptas per load. Singles 1900ptas. Doubles 3200-3800ptas. Triples 4500ptas. 15% cheaper in winter.

Camping: Playa Muchavista (tel. 565 45 26), 2nd class site near the beach. Take bus C-1. 520ptas per person and per tent. Open year-round.

Small family-run joints in the old city (between the cathedral and steps to the castle) are quieter and often cheaper than the restaurants on the pedestrian thoroughfare. The most popular *terrazas* stuff **C. San Francisco** locals with cheap *menús* and *tapas;* natives also devour *tapas* in the **Calle Mayor. Capitol,** C. Bazan, 45, between Alfonso El Sabio and the Esplanada, serves an appetizing 1150ptas *menú* (day and night; open Mon.-Fri. 1-4:30pm and 8-11pm, Sat. 1-4:30pm). For some of the best *tapas* in town, head to **La Taberna del Gormet,** C. San Fernando, 10. The ham (*"pata negra"* 975ptas) is the most *riquísimo* in all of Spain (open daily noon-midnight). **Restaurante Mixto Vegetariano,** Pl. Santa María, 2, has creative vegetarian fare as well as some meat dishes. (*Menú* 1100ptas; salad bar 395ptas. Open Tues.-Sun. 1:30-4:30pm and 8pm-midnight. Reduced hours off season.) The **market** near Av. Alfonso X El Sabio sells picnic materials (open Mon.-Sat. 8am-2pm).

SIGHTS AND ENTERTAINMENT

Built by the Carthaginians and recently reconstructed, the 200m high **Castell de Santa Bárbara** has a dry moat, a dungeon, an ammunition storeroom, and an amazing view of Alicante. A paved road from the old section of Alicante leads to the top; most people take the elevator (300ptas) from a hidden entrance on Av. Jovellanos, across the street from the beach (castle open April-Sept. daily 10am-7:30pm; Oct.-March 9am-6:30pm; free). Bronze Age dowries and Roman statues mingle in the **Museu Arqueológic de la Diputación,** Av. Estación, 6 (open Mon.-Fri. 9am-6pm; free). Skipping ahead a few centuries, a crowd of Valencian Modernist pieces, along with Mirós, Picassos, Kandinskys, and Calders, fraternize in the **Museu de Arte del Siglo XX La Asegurada,** at the east end of C. Mayor. (Open Oct.-April Tues.-Sat. 10am-1pm and 5-8pm; May.-Sept. Tues.-Sat. 10:30am-1pm and 6-9pm. Free.) If Alicante's beach doesn't suit you, hop on bus C-1 in Pl. Espanya and bus S from either Pl. Espanya or Pl. Mar (100ptas) or board the Alicante-Denia train (20min., 100ptas) for 6km long **Playa de San Juan.** For more privacy and even more flesh visit **Platja del Saladar** in Urbanova. Buses from the Alicante bus station (line C-7) run to Urbanova (35min., 100ptas).

Warm-weather nightlife centers on the **Platja de Sant Joan.** In July and August, **Ferrocarriles de la Generalitat Valenciana** runs special **Trensnochador** night trains from Estació de la Marina to several points along the beach (every hr. 9pm-7am, 100-700ptas). Pick up a schedule (including cover charge discounts) at the tourist office. **Voy Voy,** on Av. Niza at the "Discotecas" night train stop, swings with outdoor bars, loud music, and dancing (beers 350ptas; open daily until 6am). **Copity** is another popular disco, along Av. Condomina, a long walk or short taxi ride away from the "Condomina" night train stop. Get off at the second **Benidorm** stop (650ptas roundtrip) for hard-core *discotecas* like **Penélope, Pachá, KM,** and, for those who don't stop even when the sun rises, **Insomnia** (cover 1500ptas and up).

For those in search of parties closer to home, Alicante itself offers popular *discotecas* and bars. In the old section of town, **El Barne,** students hop from one bar-musical to the next. Popular with both gay and straight dancers is **Celestial Copas** on C. San

Pascual. **Rosé** on C. San. Juan Bosco also attracts a gay crowd, while lesbians head to **Paripe,** C. Baron de Finestront. **Desdén** on C. Santo Tomás attracts an astronomical number of Americans. On the Esplanada, at Pl. Canelejas, **Pachá** welcomes those who do not brave the bigger brother in Benidorm.

From June 20 to 24, the city bursts with hedonistic celebrations for the **Festival de Sant Joan,** as *fogueres* (symbolic or satiric effigies) are paraded around town. The figures burn in a *cremá* on the 24th, but the revelry continues with breathtaking and hazardous nightly fireworks and decorations along the streets. Ask at the tourist office about concerts and performances held throughout the summer to honor Alicante's patron saint, Virgen del Demedio.

ANDALUSIA (ANDALUCÍA)

Andalusia derives its spirit from a mix of cultures. Greeks, Phoenicians, and Romans colonized and traded in the region, but the most enduring influences were left by Arabs, who arrived in 711. Under Moorish rule, which lasted until 1492, Seville and Granada reached the pinnacle of Islamic arts, and Córdoba matured into the most culturally influential Islamic city of the western Caliphet. The Moors perfected a distinctive architectural style marked by cool patios and the alternation of red brick and white stone and sparked the European Renaissance by reintroducing the wisdom and science of Classical Greece and the Near East. The dark legacy of Andalusia is its failure to progress economically; stagnant industrialization and severe drought have mired the region in indefinite recession. Even so, residents believe the good life is possible with good food, good drink, and spirited company.

Seville (Sevilla)

Site of a Roman acropolis, seat of Moorish culture, focal point of the Spanish Renaissance, and guardian angel of traditional Andalusian culture, Seville has never failed to spark the imagination. Jean Cocteau included it with Venice and Beijing in his trio of magical cities, and Bizet, Mozart, and Rossini wrote operas inspired by the metropolis. The 16th-century maxim *"Qui non ha visto Sevilla non ha visto maravilla"*—one who has not seen Seville has not seen a marvel—remains true today.

ORIENTATION AND PRACTICAL INFORMATION

Río Guadalquivir flows roughly north-south through Seville. Most of the city, including the alleyways of the old **Barrio de Santa Cruz,** is on the east bank; the historic and proud **Barrio de Triana** and the modern, middle-class **Barrio de los Remedios** occupy the west bank. The **cathedral,** next to Barrio de Santa Cruz, is Seville's centerpiece. **Avenida de la Constitución,** home of the tourist office and other agencies, runs alongside the cathedral. **El Centro,** a busy commercial pedestrian zone, lies north of the cathedral where Av. Constitución hits **Plaza Nueva.**

To reach El Centro from **Estación Santa Justa,** catch bus 27, which heads to **Plaza de la Encarnacíon.** To get to Barrio Santa Cruz and the cathedral, first take bus C1, C2, or 70 to Santa Justa and the main bus station at Prado de San Sebastián. Beware; Seville is the Spanish capital of pickpocketing and car theft. The city has become safer in recent years, but if you value your stuff, don't leave it unattended or in a locked car.

Tourist Offices: Junta de Andalucía, Av. Constitución, 21B (tel. 422 14 04; fax 422 97 53), 1 block south of the cathedral. An absolute must. Open Mon.-Sat. 9am-7pm, Sat. 10am-2pm. **Municipal office,** Po. Delicias, 9 (tel. 423 44 65), across from Parque de María Luísa by Puente del Generalísimo. Open Mon.-Fri. 9am-6:30pm.

Budget Travel: Viajes TIVE, C. Jesús de Veracruz, 27 (tel. 490 60 22). Downtown near El Corte Inglés. Sells HI cards (800ptas), ISICs (700ptas), BIJ tickets and Inter-Rail Passes. Also offers language courses and excursions. Open Mon.-Fri. 9am-1pm.

Currency Exchange: Banco Central Hispano, C. Sierpes, 55 (tel. 456 26 84), exchanges cash without commission. Good rates. Open Mon.-Fri. 8:30am-2:30pm.
American Express: Pl. Nueva 7 (tel. 421 16 17), changes cash and AmEx Traveler's Cheques without commission, holds mail, and offers emergency services for cardmembers. Open Mon.-Fri. 9:30am-1:30pm and 4:30-7:30pm, Sat. 10am-1pm.
Flights: Aeropuerto San Pablo (tel. 467 29 81 or 467 52 10), 12km from town on Ctra. Madrid. A taxi to the airport from the center of town costs about 2000ptas. **Los Amarillos** runs a bus (750ptas) from outside the Hotel Alfonso XIII in the Puerta de Jerez (approx. hourly 6:15am-10:30pm; call 441 52 01 for schedule).
Trains: Estación Santa Justa, Av. Kansas City (tel. 454 03 03, reservations 454 02 02). Buses C1 and C2 link this station to the Prado de San Sebastián bus station, stopping on Av. Kansas City, left as you exit the train station. **RENFE,** C. Zaragoza, 29 (tel. 422 26 93), near Pl. Nueva. Open Mon.-Fri. 9am-1:15pm and 4-7pm. To: Madrid (on AVE 2½hr., 8000-9600ptas), Cádiz (2hr., 1195ptas), Córdoba (on AVE 45min., 2100-2200ptas), Málaga (3hr., 1850ptas), and Granada (4hr., 2280ptas).
Buses: The older **Prado de San Sebastián,** C. José María Osborne, 11 (tel. 441 71 11), serves mainly Andalusia. **Transportes Alsina Graells** (tel. 441 88 11). To: Córdoba (2hr., 1200ptas), Granada (3hr., 2700ptas), and Málaga (2½hr., 2245ptas). **Transportes Comes** (tel. 441 68 58). To: Cádiz (2hr., 1300ptas), Jerez de la Frontera (1¾hr., 875ptas), and Algeciras (3½hr., 2100ptas). **Enatcar-Bacoma** (tel. 441 46 60). To Barcelona (14hr., 8360 ptas). **Los Amarillos** (tel. 441 52 01). To Arcos de la Frontera (2hr., 905ptas) and Marbella (3hr., 1820ptas). The newer bus station at **Plaza de Armas** (tel. 490 80 40), on the riverbank where Puente Cristo de la Expiración meets C. Arjona, serves destinations outside Andalusia and Spain. **Socibus** (tel. 490 11 60; fax 490 16 92) runs to Madrid from there (6hr., 2715ptas).
Luggage Storage: At the Prado de San Sebastián bus station, 250ptas. Open daily 6:30am-10pm. At the newer bus station at Plaza de Armas. 30ptas first day, then 85ptas per day; lockers 300ptas. Also at Santa Justa train station.
Laundromat: Lavandería Robledo, C. F. Sánchez Bedoya, 18 (tel. 421 81 32), 1 block west of the cathedral, across Av. Constitución. 5 kg 950ptas. Open Mon.-Fri. 10am-2pm and 5-8pm.
24-Hour Pharmacy: 5-6 pharmacies open each night, all night, on a rotating basis. Check list posted at any pharmacy in the city.
Medical Assistance: Ambulatorio Esperanza Macarena (tel. 442 01 05). **Hospital Universitario Virgen Macareno,** Av. Dr. Fedriani (tel. 424 81 81). English spoken.
Emergency: tel. 091 or 092.
Police: Av. Paseo de las Delicias (tel. 461 54 50).
Internet Access: Bar Metro Internet (tel. 434 14 01), C. Betis. 300ptas per 15min. 600ptas per hour. Open Mon.-Sat. 10pm-late, Sun. 6:30pm-late.
Post Office: Av. Constitución, 32 (tel. 421 95 85), across from the cathedral. Open for stamps, *Lista de Correos,* and faxes Mon.-Fri. 8:30am-8:30pm, Sat. 9:30am-2pm. **Postal Code:** 41808.
Telephones: C. Sierpes, 11, in a small alley. Open Mon.-Fri. 10am-2pm and 5:30-9:30pm, Sat. 10am-2:30pm. **Faxes** 100ptas plus cost of call. **Telephone Code:** 95.

ACCOMMODATIONS AND CAMPING

During *Semana Santa* and the *Feria de Abril,* rooms vanish and prices soar; make reservations well in advance. Look in the **Barrio de Santa Cruz,** especially on C. Fabiola and C. Archeros, and around the quiet backstreets near the Plaza de Armas. Also try the *casco viejo* of **El Centro,** a disorienting array of narrow, winding streets radiating from the Plaza de la Encarnación.

Sevilla Youth Hostel (HI), C. Isaac Peral, 2 (tel. 461 31 50). Take bus 34 from Prado de San Sebastían, which stops behind the hostel just after Po. Delicias. Newly renovated, bright, white, and disinfected. Wheelchair accessible. 1300ptas, over 28 1600ptas. Nonmembers 300ptas extra for six nights to become members.
Hostal Sánchez Sabariego, C. Corral del Rey, 23 (tel. 421 44 70), on the continuation of C. Argote de Molina, northeast of the cathedral. Follow signs to Hostel Sierpes.

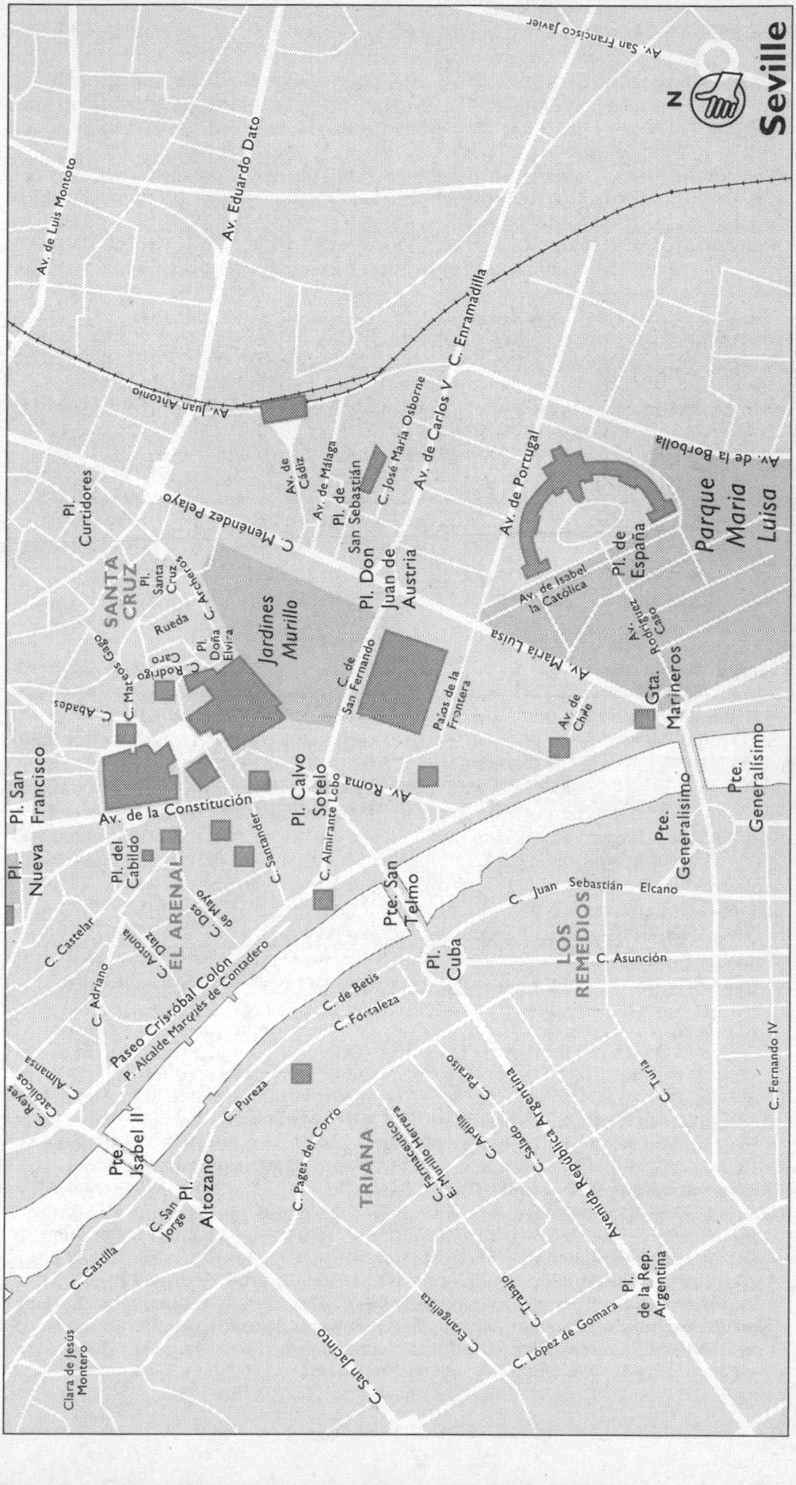
Seville
N
Av. San Francisco Javier
Av. de Luis Montoto
Av. Eduardo Dato
C. Enramadilla
Av. Juan Antonio
Av. de Cádiz
Av. de Málaga
Pl. de San Sebastián
C. José María Osborne
Av. de Carlos V
Av. de Portugal
Av. de la Borbolla
Parque María Luisa
Pl. de España
Av. de Isabel la Católica
Av. Rodríguez Caso
Av. María Luisa
Gta. Marineros
Pte. Generalísimo
Pte. Generalísimo
Av. de Chile
Pasos de la Frontera
C. de San Fernando
Pl. Don Juan de Austria
C. Menendez Pelayo
Pl. Curtidores
SANTA CRUZ
Pl. Santa Cruz
C. Archeros
Rueda
Pl. Doña Elvira
C. Rodrigo Caro
C. Mateos Gago
C. Abades
Jardines Murillo
Pl. San Francisco
Pl. Nueva
Av. de la Constitución
Pl. del Cabildo
Av. Roma
Pl. Calvo Sotelo
C. Almirante Lobo
C. Santander
C. Dos de Mayo
EL ARENAL
C. Castelar
C. Antonia Díaz
C. Adriano
Paseo Cristóbal Colón
P. Alcalde Marqués de Contadero
C. Almansa
C. Reyes Católicos
Pte. Isabel II
Pte. San Telmo
Pl. Cuba
C. Juan Sebastián Elcano
LOS REMEDIOS
C. Asunción
C. de Betis
C. Fortaleza
C. Pureza
C. Pages del Corro
TRIANA
C. Farmaceutico E. Murillo Herrera
C. Paraíso
C. Ardilla
C. Salado
Avenida República Argentina
C. Turia
C. Fernando IV
Pl. Altozano
C. San Jorge
C. Castilla
Clara de Jesús Montero
C. San Jacinto
C. Evangelista
C. Trabajo
C. López de Gomara
Pl. de la Rep. Argentina

SPAIN

Friendly little hostel with antique furniture and spacious rooms. A/C upstairs. You get your own key. Singles 2000ptas. Doubles 4000-6000ptas.

Hostal Santa María La Blanca, C. Sta. María La Blanca, 28 (tel. 442 11 74). Gregarious owner offers one of the few bargains in the Sta. Cruz district. *Torrero*-friendly decor. Each room has a fan. Singles 2000ptas. Doubles and triples 1500ptas per person, 2000ptas with bath.

Pensión Archero, C. Archeros, 23 (tel. 441 84 65). Relaxed, friendly owner oversees pleasant rooms facing a wide-open fern-laden patio. Singles 1700ptas. Doubles 3200ptas, with shower 3700ptas.

Pensión Hostal Nevada, C. Gamazo, 28 (tel. 422 53 40), in El Arenal. From Pl. Nueva, take C. Barcelona and turn right on C. Gamazo. Naturally cool courtyard. Sleek leather sofas and large collection of *abanicos* (fans). Dark, tapestry-laden rooms. Singles 2300-2500ptas, with bath 3200ptas. Doubles 5000ptas.

Hostal Lis, C. Escarpín, 10 (tel. 421 30 88), on an alley just east of Pl. Encarnación. Eye-bugging entry and patio with psychedelic Sevillian tiles. Large, decorative rooms, all with showers. Singles 2000ptas. Doubles 3500ptas. Triples 5000ptas.

Hostal Paris, C. San Pedro Mártir, 14 (tel. 422 98 61; fax 421 96 45), off C. Gravina. New, clean, and classy. Bath, A/C, phone, TV. For comforts, one of the best values in town. Singles 3500ptas. Doubles 5000-6000ptas. Ask about student discounts.

Hostal Toledo, C. Santa Teresa, 15 (tel. 421 53 35), off C. Ximénez de Enciso, which is perpendicular to C. Sta. María la Blanca. Just west of Jardines de Murillo. Quiet, comfortable hostel houses researchers using the Archivo de Indios. Private baths. Curfew 1am. Singles 2675-3180ptas, depending on bath size. Doubles 5350ptas.

Camping Sevilla, Ctra. Madrid-Cádiz, km 534 (tel. 451 43 79), 12km out of town near the airport. From Est. Prado de San Sebastián, take bus 70, which stops 800m away at Parque Alcosa. Grassy sites, hot showers, supermarket, and swimming pool. 460ptas per person, per car, and per tent. Children 375ptas.

FOOD

Sevillians offset the merciless midday sun by keeping their cuisine light—the town claims to be the birthplace of *tapas.* Popular venues for *el tapeo* (*tapas*-bar hopping) hide out in **Triana** and in **Barrio Santa Cruza** and **El Arenal** around the bullring. More casual still are Sevilla's bountiful markets. Buy renowned jams, pastries, and candies from convent kitchens or the stores in **Plaza Cabildo** off Av. Constitución. **Mercado del Arenal,** near the bullring on C. Pastor y Leandro, between C. Almansa and C. Arenal, has fresh produce, *toro de lidia* (fresh bull meat), and screaming vendors. Merchants also hawk excellent fresh produce, fish, meat, and baked goods at **Mercadillo de la Encarnación** (both open Mon.-Sat. 9am-2pm). **El Corte Inglés,** Pl. Duque de la Victoria, 7, has a huge basement supermarket (open Mon.-Sat. 10am-9:30pm). For better prices, try **%Día,** C. San Juan de Ávila, on Pl. Gravídia, around the corner from El Corte Inglés (open Mon.-Fri. 9:30am-2pm and 6:30-9pm, Sat. 9am-1pm).

Jalea Real, Sor Angela de la Cruz, 37. From Pl. Encarnación, head 150m east on C. Laraña, and turn left just before Iglesia de San Pedro. Young, hip vegetarian restaurant with interesting salads and homemade desserts. Delectable spinach crepe 675ptas. Lunch *menú* 1200ptas. Open Mon.-Sat. 1:30-5pm and 8:30-11:30pm.

Bodega Santa Cruz, C. Rodrigo Caro, 1. Take C. Mateos Gago from the fountain by the cathedral to the 1st corner on the right. Casual and crowded. Varied and tasty *tapas* 175-200ptas. Beer 125ptas. Mega-watt A/C. Open daily 8am-midnight.

Restaurante-Bar El Baratillo/Casa Chari, C. Pavia, 12 (tel. 422 96 51), on a tiny street off C. Dos de Mayo. Friendly owner, early 80s posters, and rock-bottom prices. *Menú* 500ptas. *Platos combinados* 450-750ptas. Call ahead for homemade *paella* and drinks (2500ptas for two). Meals Mon.-Fri. 8am-10pm, Sat. noon-5pm.

La Ortiga, C. Procurador, 19, off C. Castilla. Health food bar/patio in a theater. *Tapas ecológicas.* All organic. Open Mon.-Fri. from 7:30pm; off-season until 6pm.

Bodega Sierpes, C. Azofaifo, 9, off C. Sierpes. Specializes in cheap, enormous portions of chicken eaten outside in a *terraza. Gazpacho* in a glass 150ptas. Half-chicken, bread, salad, and beverage 650ptas. Meals served daily 11am-midnight.

Casa Cuesta, C. Castilla, 3-5, north of Puerte Isabel II, 1 block inland. A bit expensive, but recommended by locals. *Pescado* 900-1700ptas. *Cola de toro* (bull's tail) 1700ptas. Open for lunch and dinner, especially popular on weekends.

Café-Bar Jerusalem, C. Salado, 6, at C. Virgen de las Huertas. Meat and cheese *shoarma* called a *bocadillo hebreo* (bread, lettuce, roast pork, holland cheese, hebrew spices) isn't kosher but sure is tasty (500ptas). Open Wed.-Mon. 8pm-3am.

SIGHTS

Christians razed an Almohad mosque to clear space for Seville's cathedral in 1401, leaving only the famed **La Giralda** minaret. The tower and its twins in Marrakech and Rabat are the oldest and largest surviving Almohad minarets. The **cathedral,** which took over a century to complete and stands as the largest Gothic edifice in the world, is by far Seville's most impressive sight. To demonstrate their religious fervor, the conquerors constructed a church so great that, in their own words, "those who come after us will take us for madmen." The **retablo mayor** (altarpiece), the largest in the world, is the golden wall of intricately wrought figurines, depicting 36 biblical scenes. By encircling the choir, you will approach a monument to **Cristóbol Colón** (Christopher Columbus). His black and gold coffin-bearers represent the eternally grateful kings of Castilla, León, Aragón, and Navarra. Farther on and to the right stands the cathedral's most precious museum, the **Sacristía Mayor,** which holds Riberas, Murillos, and a glittering Corpus Christi icon, **la Custodia processional.** Outside the cathedral proper, on the north end, the **Patio de Los Naranjos** (orange trees) evokes the bygone days of the Arab Caliphate. (Cathedral complex and Giralda open Mon.-Sat. 10:30am-5pm, Sun. 2-4pm; Giralda Sun. 10:30am-1:30pm. Tickets sold until 1hr. before closing. 600ptas, students and senior citizens 200ptas, under 12 free.)

The 9th-century walls of the **Alcázar**—the oldest palace still used by European royalty—face the south side of the cathedral. Within, the **Patio de las Muñecas** (Courtyard of the Dolls) remains from the Moorish era. Of later Christian additions to the palace, the most exceptional are the **Patio de las Doncellas** (Maids' Court), with foliated archways, glistening tilework, and a central fountain, and the golden-domed **Salón de los Embajadores** where Fernando and Isabel welcomed Columbus upon his return from America. (Open Tues.-Sat. 9:30am-4pm., Sun. 10am-1pm. 600ptas, students, seniors, and under 12 free.) The 16th-century **Casa Lonja,** between the cathedral and the Alcázar, was built by Felipe II as a commercial exchange for American trade. In 1785 it was turned into the Archive of the Indies, a collection of over 44,000 documents relating to the conquest of the "New World." Highlights include letters from Columbus to Fernando and Isabel. (Access to documents restricted to scholars. Exhibits open Mon.-Fri. 10am-2pm. Free). Next door, the **Museo de Arte Contemporáneo,** C. Santo Tomaso, 5, has some celebrated Mirós on the top floor (open Tues.-Sun. 10am-2pm; 250ptas, free for EU students).

King Fernando III forced Jews fleeing Toledo to live in the **Barrio de Santa Cruz,** now a neighborhood of winding alleys, wrought-iron gates, and fountained courtyards. Northeast of Barrio Santa Cruz off Pl. Pilatos, the **Casa de Pilatos** is a palace of plenty—Roman antiques, Renaissance and Baroque paintings, period furniture, and several courtyards (open daily 9am-7pm; 1000ptas). The **Museo Provincial de Bellas Artes,** Pl. Museo, 9, houses Spain's finest collection of Seville School painters (especially Murillo, Leal, and Zurbarán) as well as works by El Greco and Dutch master Jan Breughel (open Wed.-Sat. 9am-8pm, Tues. 3-8pm, Sun. 9am-3pm; 250ptas, EU citizens free). Flanking the west end of the twelfth century walls in the northeast of the city, the **Basílica Macarena** houses the venerated *La Virgen de la Macarena,* which is featured in Holy Week processions (open daily 9:30am-1pm and 5-9pm).

ENTERTAINMENT

The tourist office distributes *El Giraldillo,* a free monthly magazine with complete entertainment listings. Popular bars cluster around **Plaza Alfalfa** and **Plaza Salvador** in el Centro, **Calle Mateos Gago** near the cathedral, **Calle Adriano** by the bullring, and **Calle Betis** across the river in Triana. Summer crowds sweep towards the river in hopes of a pleasant breeze. A trio of bars (popular with exchange students) line C. Betis: **Alambique, Múdáqui,** and **Big Ben.** On the other bank and downstream on Po. Dlicias, near Parque María Luisa, **Alfonso, Libano,** and **Chile** are popular *chiringuitos* (beach bars). Upstream, there's always a crowd at **Bar Capote,** Po. Cristóbal Colón, beside Puente Isabel II. (Open Mon.-Thurs. until 4:30am, later Fri.-Sat. Live music, DJs Wed.-Thurs. Beer 200ptas.) A number of sandy summer dance floors open up in **Puerta Triana,** upstream from Triana on the old Expo '92 grounds. There is usually no cover (crowds build around 3am). In winter time, bar-hoppers stick to El Centro around Pl. Alfalfa and Pl. Salvador. The most popular disco is the ultra-chic **Catedral,** Cuesta Rosario off of Pl. Salvador (expect a cover charge). Other popular spots congregate on **Avenida de la Raza,** parallel to the river off Puente de las Delicias.

The gay scene is coming out strong in Seville: popular disco-bars include **Isbiliyya,** Po. de Colón, 2, and **To Ca Me,** C. Reyes Católicos, 25 (both open nightly until 4am). The liveliest gay disco in town is **Itaca,** C. Amor de Dios in El Centro. (Show Wed. at 1am; open until 5am weeknights, later on weekends; knock on the door to be let in.)

On the west edge of Barrio Santa Cruz, **Los Gallos,** Pl. Santa Cruz, 11 (tel. 421 69 81), performs the flashiest flamenco in town. To get a ticket (much less a good seat) arrive early (cover and drink 3000ptas). Several booths on C. Sierpes, C. Velázquez, and Pl. Toros sell **bullfight** tickets (anywhere from 1500-10,000ptas). For current information on dates and prices, call 422 35 06. Seville's world-famous **Semana Santa** (Holy Week) festival lasts from Palm Sunday to Good Friday (April 5-10, 1998). Penitents in hoods guide bejeweled floats lit by hundreds of candles through the streets. The city explodes during the six-day **Feria de Abril** (April Fair), which began as a 19th-century popular revolt against foreign influence. The party rages through the night with circuses, bullfights, and flamenco shows.

■ Near Seville

Located on the southeast corner of the Iberian peninsula, **Cádiz** claims to be the oldest city in Western Europe—and one of Spain's most progressive. Cádiz's inhabitants drafted a liberal (although ignored) constitution in 1812 and fought fiercely against the Fascists in the 1936-39 Civil War. Socially, the city rocks: summer nightlife centers on the **beach,** while the **Carnaval** (Feb. 6-16) makes New Orleans's Mardi Gras look like Thursday night bingo. The **tourist office,** Pl. San Juan de Dios, 11 (tel. (956) 24 10 01), provides a free map (open Mon.-Fri. 9am-2pm and 5-8pm, Sat. 10am-2pm). *Hostales* huddle around the harbor, in Pl. San Juan de Dios, and behind it on C. Marqués de Cádiz. The **Hostal Colón,** C. Marqués de Cádiz, 6 (tel. (956) 28 53 51), is squeaky clean and colorful (singles 2000ptas). The manager of **Hostal Cádiz,** C. Feduchy, 20 (tel. (956) 28 58 01), has tips on restaurants and nightlife (1500-1700ptas per person).

Unremarkable in appearance, **Jerez de la Frontera** is the cradle of three staples of Andalusian culture: flamenco, Carthusian horses, and above all, *vino de jerez*—known in English as sherry. You can visit *bodegas* (wine cellars) throughout Jerez de la Frontera. **Williams and Humbert, Ltd.** (tel. (956) 34 65 39; 300 ptas), **Harvey's of Bristol** (tel. (956) 15 10 02; 300ptas), and **B. Domecq** (tel. (956) 15 15 00; 350ptas) have multilingual tour guides who distill the complete sherry-making process as you sip free samples (call ahead for tour hours; reservations often required). Avoid visiting the town in August, when many *bodegas* close down for the annual hangover. The **Fiestas de la Bulería** in September celebrates the town's *flamenco* tradition. The **tourist office,** C. Larga, 39 (tel. (956) 33 11 50), has info on *bodegas* tours and festivals. (Open Mon.-Fri. 9am-2pm and 5-8pm, Sat. 9am-2pm and 5-7pm; off-season Mon.-Sat. 8am-3pm and 5-7pm.) **Trains** roll to Seville (1½hr., 735ptas) and Cádiz (45min., 365ptas). Finding a bed in Jerez is as easy as finding sherry. Look along **Calle Medina,** near the bus station, and **Calle Arcos,** which intersects C. Medina at Pl. Romero Martínez. The **Albergue Juvenil (HI)** is at Av. Carrero Blanco, 30 (tel. (956) 14 39 01); walk 25 minutes from downtown, or take bus L-8 near the bus station (every 15min., 125ptas) or bus L-1 from Pl. Arenal. The hostel has spacious doubles, pool, tennis and basketball courts, library, and a TV room (900-1300ptas, over 26 1300-1600ptas; non-members 300ptas extra). *Tapas*-hoppers bounce all around **Plaza del Arenal,** and northeast on Av. Alcalde Alvaro Domecq around **Plaza del Caballo.**

The road to **Arcos de la Frontera** snakes through fields of sunflowers and sherry-grape vines; the city itself is a maze of little white houses, alleyways, medieval ruins, and stone arches. The most beautiful sight might just be the view from **Plaza Cabildo.** In this square stands the **Iglesia de Santa María,** built in 1553, with its well-preserved wall painting from the 14th century (open daily 10am-1pm and 3:30-6pm; 150ptas). The **tourist office** at Pl. Cabildo (tel. (956) 70 22 64) offers a detailed map of the old city and essential info. (Open in summer Mon.-Sat. 10am-2pm and 5-8pm, Sun. 11am-2pm; off-season Mon.-Sat. 9am-2pm and 5-7pm.) **Hostal Callejón de las Monjas,** C. Dean Espinoza, 4 (tel. (956) 70 23 02), offers roomy, cool accommodations (singles 2500-3000ptas, doubles 3500-4500ptas). T.G. Comes **buses** (tel. (956) 70 20 15) travel to Cádiz (1½hr., 670ptas) and Jerez (280ptas), while Los Amarillos (tel. (956) 70 02 57) jaunts to Seville (2hr., 905ptas) and Jerez (15min., 295ptas).

SPAIN

Córdoba

A Spaniard well versed in regional subtleties once made the following distinction between Córdoba and her more flamboyant Andalusian sister to the west: "Seville is a young girl, gay, laughing, provoking—but Córdoba...Córdoba is a dear old lady." Córdoba does indeed show a dignity and refinement befitting a city known less for joviality than for breadth of mind. Romanization brought the incomparable playwright and philosopher Seneca here. During Islamic rule (711-1263) the city emerged as an intellectual powerhouse and the capital of the Western Caliphate. No where else in Spain are remnants of Islamic, Jewish, and Catholic civilizations so well mixed.

ORIENTATION AND PRACTICAL INFORMATION

Córdoba sits atop the Andalusian triangle (north of Seville and Granada), about halfway between Madrid and Gibraltar. The city's more modern and commercial northern half extends from the train station on **Avenida de América** down to **Plaza de las Tendillas** in the center of the city. The older (touristy), maze-like southern half, known as the **Judería** (old Jewish quarter), extends from Pl. Tendillas down to the banks of the Guadalquivir, winding past the Mezquita and Alcázar.

Tourist Office: Junta de Andalucía, Pl. Judá Leví (tel./fax 20 05 22), next to the youth hostel. The office provides free maps, schedules, and guide to cultural events. Open April-Sept. Mon.-Sat. 9:30am-8pm; Oct.-March Mon.-Sat. 9:30am-6pm.

Trains: Av. América (tel. 49 02 02). To: Seville (45min.-1¼hr, 890-2500ptas), Málaga (2¼hr., 2000-2200ptas), Madrid (2-6½hr., 3500-9600ptas), Cádiz (2½-3hr., 2020-4865ptas), Granada via Bobadilla, and Algeciras (5hr., 2220-3270ptas). For international tickets, contact **RENFE,** Ronda de los Tejares, 10 (tel. 47 58 84).

Buses: The main bus station is at C. Diego Serrano, 14. **Alsina-Graells Sur** (tel. 23 64 74), off C. Noguer, covers most of Andalusia. To: Seville (2hr., 1200ptas), Málaga (3-3½hr., 1510ptas), Granada (2¾hr., 1765ptas), and Marbella (4hr., 2085ptas). **Bacoma** (tel. 45 65 14), off Av. de Cervantes, travels to Valencia, Murcia, and Barcelona (1 per day). **Socibus** (tel. (902) 22 92 92) provides exceptionally cheap service to Madrid (4½hr., 1540ptas), departing from Camino de los Sastres in front of Hotel Melia. **Autocares Priego** (tel. 29 01 58) runs anywhere on the Sierra Cordobesa; **Empresa Carrera** (tel. 23 14 01) serves the Campiña Cordobesa; and **Empresa Ramírez** (tel. 41 01 00) runs buses to nearby towns and camping sites.

Luggage Storage: At the train station and main bus station. 300ptas per locker.

Medical Assistance: Red Cross Hospital, Po. de la Victoria (tel. 29 34 11).

Emergency: tel. 091 or 092. **Ambulance:** tel. 061.

Post Office: C. Cruz Conde, 15, just north of Pl. Tendillas. Open for *Lista de Correos* Mon.-Fri. 8:30am-8:30pm, Sat. 9:30am-2pm. **Postal Code:** 14070.

Telephone Code: 957.

ACCOMMODATIONS AND CAMPING

Accommodations cluster near the train station, in and around the Judería, and off the Plaza de las Tendillas. Most are crowded during *Semana Santa* and in summer.

Residencia Juvenil Córdoba (HI), Pl. Judá Leví (tel. 29 01 66; fax 29 05 00), next to the municipal tourist office. Huge, recently renovated, modern, and antiseptic. No curfew. 1300ptas, over 26 1600ptas; nonmembers 300ptas extra. Call ahead in the summer, and confirm a day before arriving. Expect prices to rise.

Hostal-Residencia Séneca, C. Conde y Luque, 7 (tel. 47 32 34), 2 blocks north of the Mezquita. Impeccably maintained by vivacious English-speaking owner. All rooms have fans; 1000ptas extra for A/C. Singles 2400ptas. Doubles 4400ptas, with bath 5400ptas. Breakfast included. Expect prices to rise.

Huéspedes Martínez Rücker, Martínez Rücker, 14 (tel. 47 25 62), just east of the Mezquita. Gregarious young owner displays his antiques on the comfortable patio and smallish rooms. All rooms have quiet fans. Singles 1500ptas. Doubles 3000-3500ptas. Larger rooms 1500ptas per person.

Camping: Municipal, Av. Brillante (tel. 28 21 65). From the train station, turn left on Av. América, left again at Av. Brillante, and then walk 2km uphill. Alternatively, take bus 10 or 11, both of which leave from Av. Cervantes near the station and run to the campsite. Public pool. 550ptas per person, per tent, and per car.

FOOD

The famous Mezquita attracts nearly as many high-priced eateries as Muhammad does followers, but a five-minute walk north, west, or east yields local specialities at reasonable prices. **Calle Doctor Fleming,** demarcating the west side of the Judería, is sprinkled with little *mesones* dispatching *platos combinados* for a moderate 600ptas. Student-priced eateries await in **Barrio Cruz Conde,** around Av. de Menéndez Pidal. Join locals at the outdoor cafés around **Plaza Tendillas,** or pick up snacks and groceries downstairs at supermercado **Simago,** C. Jesús María, half a block south of Plaza Tendillas (open Mon.-Sat. 9am-9pm).

Sociedad de Plateros, C. San Francisco, 6, between C. San Francisco and the top end of Pl. Potro. Casual and tasty. *Tapas* 150-200ptas. Fresh fish every day. Bar open Mon.-Sat. 8am-4pm and 7pm-1am. Meals served 1-4pm and 8pm-midnight.

Taberna San Miguel, Pl. San Miguel, 1, one block north of Pl. Tendillas. Classic *tapas* joint with bullfighting decor. *Tapas* 230-265ptas, *raciones* 750-1500ptas. Open Mon.-Sat. noon-4pm and 8pm-midnight. Closed Aug.

El Pincantón, C. F. Ruano, 19, one block east of the top of C. Judíos. A perennial favorite among young locals, with nothing above 300ptas. Specializes in *salsas picantes.* Beer 100ptas. Open daily 10am-2pm and 8pm-midnight.

SIGHTS AND ENTERTAINMENT

Begun in 784, the **Mezquita** was intended to surpass all other mosques in grandeur. Over the next two centuries the spectacular building was gradually enlarged, making it for a time the largest mosque in the world. Inside, past the impressive **Patio de los Naranjos,** 850 pink and blue marble, alabaster, and stone columns support hundreds of red and white striped two-tiered arches. At the far end of the Mezquita lies the **Capilla Villaviciosa,** where Caliphal vaulting, greatly influential in later Spanish architecture, appears for the first time. Intricate gold, pink, and blue marble Byzantine mosaics given by Emperor Constantine VII shimmer across the arches of the **Mihrab,** the dome where the Muslims guarded the Koran. Additions such as the church transept and choir dome were added after the mosque became a church in 1236. (Open April-Sept. Mon.-Sat. 10am-7pm, Sun. 3:30-7pm; Oct.-March Mon.-Sat. 10am-6:30pm, Sun. 3:30-5:30pm. 750ptas. Mass weekdays 8:30-10am; Sun. 9:30am-1:30pm.)

The area known as **Judería,** just north of the Mezquita, is the historically Jewish quarter of the city. Tucked away on C. Judíos, the small **Sinagoga** is one of only three synagogues remaining in Spain. (Open Tues.-Sat. 10am-2pm and 3:30-5:30pm, Sun.

10am-1:30pm. 50ptas; EU citizens free.) Just west of the Mezquita and closer to the river lies the **Alcázar.** The palace was constructed for the Catholic monarchs in 1328 during the conquest of Granada, and later served as headquarters for the Inquisition. The walls of the Alcázar enclose a manicured hedge garden and a museum displaying Roman mosaics. (Open May-Sept. Tues.-Sat. 10am-2pm and 6-8pm, Sun. 9:30am-3pm; Oct.-April Tues.-Sat. 10am-2pm and 4:30-6:30pm, Sun. 9:30am-3pm. Illuminated gardens open 8pm-midnight. 425ptas. Fri. free.) The **Museo Taurino y de Arte Cordobés,** Pl. Maimonides, displays the heads of bulls who killed matadors and other unfortunates. (Open May-Sept. Tues.-Sat. 10am-2pm and 6-8pm, Sun. 9:30am-3pm; Oct.-April Mon.-Sat. 10am-2pm and 5-7pm, Sun. 9:30am-3pm. 425ptas, Fri. free.)

For flamenco, try the **Tablao Cardenal,** C. Torrijos, 10 (tel. 48 33 20), facing the Mezquita (shows Tues.-Sat. 10:30pm; 2800ptas, including one drink). During the **Festival de los Patios** in early May, the city erupts with classical music concerts, *flamenco* dances, and a city-wide decorated *patio* contest. Late May brings the **Feria de Nuestra Señora de la Salud,** with lively dancing and non-stop drinking for an entire week. A **Concurso Nacional de Arte Flamenco** (National Flamenco Contest) will be held in May of 1998. From the first weekend in June until the heat subsides, the **Brillante** barrio (uphill from and north of Av. América or a 500-900ptas cab ride) is the place to be: the Sierra is cool, the beer cold, and the prices low. Around 4am, Cordoban youth head to **Kachao,** a huge disco and *terraza* outside the city along Ctra. Santa María de Trassierra. In winter, pubs around **Plaza de las Tendillas** are a safe bet.

SPAIN

■ Near Córdoba: Medina Azahara

Built in the Sierra Morena by Abderramán III for his favorite wife, the 10th-century **Medina Azahara** (tel. 32 91 30) was considered one of the greatest palaces of its time. Before excavations in 1944, the existence of the site had been mere rumor; today the *medina* is one of Spain's most impressive archaeological finds. (Open May-June 14 Tues.-Sat. 10am-2pm and 6-8:30pm, Sun. 10am-2pm; June 15-Sept. 15 Mon.-Sat. 10am-1:30pm and 6-8:30pm, Sun. 10am-1:30pm; Sept. 16-April Mon.-Sat. 10am-2pm and 4-6:30pm, Sun. 10am-2pm. 250ptas, EU citizens free.) Reaching Medina Azahara takes some effort; first call ahead to make sure it's open. The O-1 **bus** (info tel. 25 57 00) leaves from Av. República Argentina for Cruce Medina Azahara (about every hr., 6:30am-10:30pm, 100ptas); from there it's a 35-minute walk mostly uphill.

Úbeda

As a stop on the crucial trade route linking Castile to Andalucía in the 16th century, Úbeda fattened on American gold shipped up from Seville. The **Hospital de Santiago** lists cultural events and houses a modern art museum (museum open Mon.-Fri. 8am-3pm and 3:30-10pm, Sat. 8am-3pm; 225ptas). The **barrio antiguo,** stretching downhill from Pl. Andalucía and centered at the **Plaza Vázquez de Molina,** holds well-preserved Spanish Renaissance architecture. Two stone lions guard the **Palacio de las Cadenas,** now the city hall, and across the pathway is the Gothic **Colegiata de Santa María de los Reales Alcázares,** whose chapels are embellished by wrought iron grilles. The **Sacra Capilla del Salvador** sits at the far end of the plaza (open Mon.-Fri. 7:30-8:30pm). Uphill, the **Museo Arqueológico,** C. Cervantes, 6, narrates Úbeda's history through prehistoric, Roman, Moorish and Castilian times (open Tues.-Sun. 10am-2pm, 5-7pm; free). A walk all the way downhill leads to a stunning view of the olive-laden **Guadalquivir valley** and the ruins of the **muralla,** built by the Moors.

The **tourist office** in the **Centro Cultural Hospital de Santiago,** Obispo Cobos (tel. (953) 75 08 97), between the bus station and Pl. Andalucía, offers a 100ptas map (open Mon.-Sat. 8am-3pm). There is no train service to Úbeda. **Buses** leave from C. San José, 6 (tel. (953) 75 21 57) for Granada (8 per day, 2-3hr., 1400ptas), Córdoba (3 per day, 2½hr., 1305ptas) and Seville (3 per day, 5hr., 2555ptas). The **Hostal Sevilla,** Av. Ramón y Cajal, 7 (tel. (953) 75 06 12), has private baths and A/C (singles 2100ptas, doubles 4000ptas; try bargaining). Calle Rastro leading from Pl. Andalucía has *terrazas* with entrees around 600ptas. **Pizzeria Restaurante Venecia,** C. Huelva, 2, near the bus station, serves great homemade pasta (600-900ptas) and a huge *ensalata mixta* (425ptas; open daily 1-4:30pm and 8pm-12:30am). The **market** is down C. San Fernando from Pl. Andalucía (open Mon.-Sat. 7am-2:30pm).

Granada

"There is nothing crueler in life than to be blind in Granada," proclaims an inscription above the majestic red-clay Alhambra, the fortress which the Moors held until 1492, when ruler Boabdil lost the city to Catholic monarchs Fernando and Isabel. The last Muslim stronghold in Spain, Granada's mosques were destroyed, but the Albaicín, a maze of Moorish houses and twisting alleys, remains Spain's best-preserved Arab settlement. Not to be outdone by artistry of the Alhambra, Fernando and Isabel built their own magnificent Renaissance cathedral and royal chapel in the city. Today the Moors and Christians still vie with each other—for visitors' attention.

ORIENTATION AND PRACTICAL INFORMATION

From RENFE and all bus stations except Alsina Graells, follow Av. Constitución to Gran Vía de Colón, turn right, and walk 15-20 minutes into town. The **Gran Vía de Colón** intersects with **Calle Reyes Católicos** at **Plaza de Isabel la Católica,** the geographical center of the city. Two blocks north is **Plaza Nueva,** framed by Renaissance buildings and many hotels and restaurants. To the northeast is the **Alhambra.** If alone, avoid the streets at the foot of the **Albaicín,** northeast of Pl. Nueva, after dark.

Tourist Office: Pl. Mariana Pineda, 10 (tel. 22 66 88; fax 22 89 16). From Pta. Real turn right onto C. Angel Ganivet, and right three blocks later. Helpful staff has free maps. Open Mon.-Fri. 9:30am-7pm, Sat. 10am-2pm. **Branch office** at C. Mariana Pineda (tel. 22 10 22; fax 22 39 27). Open Mon.-Sat. 9am-7pm, Sun. 10am-2pm.

Budget Travel: Viajes TIVE, C. Martínez Campos, 21 (tel. 25 02 11), off C. Recogidos. BIJ tickets. Open Mon.-Fri. 9am-1:30pm.

Currency Exchange: Banco Central Hispano, Gran Vía de Colón, 3, exchanges money and traveler's checks without commission (open Mon.-Fri. 8am-3pm).

American Express: C. Reyes Católicos, 31 (tel. 22 45 12). Holds mail. Open Mon.-Fri. 9:30am-1:30pm and 4:30-7:30pm, Sat. 9am-2pm.

Trains: RENFE Station, Av. Andaluces (tel. 27 12 72). From Pl. Isabel la Católica, follow Gran Vía de Colón to the end, then bear left on Av. Constitución. Turn left on Av. Andaluces. To: Madrid (5hr., 1900ptas), Barcelona (12-13hr., 6300ptas), Seville (4-5hr., 2280ptas), and Cádiz (7hr., 2885ptas).

Buses: A new bus station sits on the outskirts of Granada on Ctra. de Madrid. **Bacoma** (tel. 15 75 57) serves Alicante (6hr., 3335ptas), Valencia (8hr., 4855ptas), and Barcelona (14hr., 7830ptas). **Alsina Graells** (tel. 18 50 10) sends buses to Algeciras (5hr., 2500ptas), Cádiz (4hr., 4010ptas), Córdoba (3hr., 1765ptas), Madrid (5hr., 1900ptas), and Seville (3hr., 2710ptas). Bus 3 goes from the station to Av. Constitución, Gran Vía, and Pl. Isabel la Católica.

Luggage Storage: At the train and bus stations. 400ptas. Open 4-9pm.

Laundromat, C. La Paz, 19. Wash 400ptas; dry 100ptas per 15min. Open Mon.-Fri. 9:30am-2pm and 4:30-8:30pm, Sat. 9am-2pm.

Red Cross: C. Escorianza, 8 (tel. 22 22 22, 22 20 24, or 22 21 66).

Medical Services: Clínica de San Cecilio, C. Doctor Oloriz, 16 (tel. 28 02 00).

Police: C. Duquesa, 21 (tel. 24 81 00).

Internet Access: Net, C. Santa Ecolástica, 13. 150ptas per 15min. 400ptas per hr. Open 9am-2:30pm and 4-11:30pm.

Post Office: Puerta Real (tel. 22 48 35; fax 22 36 41), on the corner between Acera de Darro and C. Angel Ganivet. Open for stamps and *Lista de Correos* Mon.-Fri. 8:30am-8:30pm, Sat. 9:30am-2pm. **Faxes** sent and received. **Postal Code:** 18009.

Telephone Code: 958.

ACCOMMODATIONS, CAMPING, AND FOOD

Granada has even more cheap accommodations than shoe stores. Lodgings pose a problem only during *Semana Santa* (Holy Week), when you should call ahead.

Albergue Juvenil Granada (HI), Ramón y Cajal, 2 (tel. 27 26 38 or 28 43 06; fax 28 52 85). Take the bus 11 from the center or bus 10 from the bus station and ask the driver to stop at "El Estadio de la Juventud." Tiny windows and winter heating. 1300ptas, over 26 1600ptas. Nonmembers add 300ptas. Limited wheelchair access.

Hostal Residencia Britz, Cuesta de Gomérez, 1 (tel. 22 36 52). On the corner of Pl. Nueva. Large rooms with luxurious beds and green-tiled bathrooms. Reception open 24hr. Singles with bath 2100ptas. Doubles 3300ptas, with bath 4700ptas. 6% discount for *Let's Go* readers if you pay in cash and are courteous. V, MC.

Hostal Navarro-Ramos, Cuesta de Gomérez, 21 (tel. 25 05 55). Quarters are comfortable and cool in the evening. Singles 1375ptas. Doubles 2200ptas, with bath 3500ptas. Triples with bath 4700ptas. Shower 150ptas.

Hostal Gomérez, Cuesta de Gomérez, 10 (tel. 22 44 37). Clean rooms with firm beds. Singles 1400ptas. Doubles 2500ptas. Triples 3200ptas. Offers a 100-200ptas discount to *Let's Go*ers during off-season.

Hospedaje Almohada, C. Postigo de Zarate, 4 (tel. 20 74 46). Walk a block from Pl. Trinidad along C. Duquesa; it's at the top of C. Málaga and has no sign. A successful experiment in communal living. Singles 1800ptas. Doubles 3500ptas. Longer stays 30,000-33,000ptas per month. Laundry 500ptas per load.

Pensión Romero, C. Sillería de Mesones, 1 (tel. 26 60 79), off Pl. Trinidad. Bright, cozy rooms, but not quiet. Singles 1500ptas. Doubles 2200ptas.

Hostal Gran Vía, Gran Vía de Colón, 17 (tel. 27 92 12), about 4 blocks from Pl. Isabel la Católica. Clean rooms with a pristine shower in each single 2500ptas. Doubles 3000ptas, with full bath 3500ptas. Triples with bath 4500ptas.

Sierra Nevada, Av. Madrid, 107 (tel. 15 00 62); take bus 3 or 10. Shady trees, modern facilities, and free showers. 535ptas per person and per tent. Open March-Oct.

Cheap, tasty, and healthy Middle Eastern cuisine is available in and around the Albaicín. Near Pl. Nueva, the usual fare of *menús* awaits. Picnickers and vegetarians can collect fresh fruit and veggies at the **market** on C. San Augustín. Pick up groceries at **Supermercado T. Mariscal,** C. Genil (open Mon.-Sat. 9:30am-2pm and 5-8:30pm).

La Nueva Bodega, C. Cetti-Meriem, 3, on a small side street off C. Elvira out of Pl. Nueva, is popular with locals and tourists (*menús* 825-1400ptas; *bocadillos* 300ptas; open daily noon-midnight). **Bodega Mancha** and **Bodega Castañeda,** both in the alleyways left of C. Reyes Católicos leading from Pl. Nueva, offer *bocadillos* and *tapas* (under 300ptas), and lots of wine and sherry (125-200ptas; open daily 11am-4pm and 6pm-1am). **El Ladrillo II,** C. Panaderos, near the Iglesia El Salvador, is a thunderous evening hangout with large rations of fresh seafood (open daily 2:30pm-1:30am).

SIGHTS AND ENTERTAINMENT

Against the silvery backdrop of the Sierra Nevada, the Christians drove the first Nazarite King Alhamar from the Albaicín to a more strategic location on the hill that overlooks Granada. The **Alhambra** is the name for this hill and the sprawling palace-fortress atop it. Here King Alhamar built a fortress called the **Alcazaba,** the oldest section of the complex, and the great Moorish rulers Yusuf I (1333-1354) and Mohammed V (1354-1391) constructed the **Alcázar** (Royal Palace). After the Christian *Reconquista* drove the Moors from Spain, Fernando and Isabel respectfully restored the Alcázar, never suspecting that, two generations later, Emperor Carlos V would demolish part of it to make way for his **Palacio de Carlos V.** Although it's glaringly incongruous amidst all the Moorish splendor, many experts agree that the Palacio is one of the most beautiful Renaissance buildings in Spain. Up the hill past the Alhambra's main entrance is the lush palace greenery of the **Generalife,** the spacious summer retreat of the sultans. Canals, fountains, and water jets criss-cross the gardens. To reach the complex, follow Cuesta de Gomérez from Pl. Nueva. (Alhambra open April-

Sept. Mon.-Sat. 9am-8pm, Sun. 9am-6pm; Oct.-March daily 9am-5:45pm. 725ptas, Sun. after 3pm free. Entry limited to 8000 visitors daily, so go early. Open in summer also Tues., Thurs., and Sat. 10pm-midnight; off-season Sat. 8-10pm. 725ptas.)

Back down from heaven, in the town proper, is the **Capilla Real** (Royal Chapel), Fernando and Isabel's private chapel. Isabel's private **colección de arte,** including royal jewels and Flemish and German masterpieces of the 15th century, is exhibited next door in the sacristy. (Open April-Sept. Mon.-Sat. 10:30am-1pm and 4-7pm; Oct.-March Mon.-Sat. 10:30am-1pm and 3:30-6:30pm, Sun. 11am-1pm. 250ptas.) The adjacent **cathedral** dwarfs the Capilla Real. The first purely Renaissance cathedral in Spain boasts massive Corinthian pillars supporting an astonishingly high vaulted nave. (Open April-Sept. daily 10am-1:30pm and 4-7pm; Oct.-March 10am-1:30pm and 3:30-6:30pm. Closed Sun. mornings. 250ptas includes admission to the museum.) Don't miss the **Albaicín,** the old Arab quarter, where the Moors built their first fortresses. The best way to explore the maze is to proceed along Carrera del Darro off Pl. Nueva, climb up Cuesta del Chapiz on the left, and then wander through Muslim ramparts, cisterns, and gates. Be fairly cautious here at night.

Entertainment listings are near the back of the daily paper, the *Ideal* (120ptas), under the heading *Cine y Espectáculos;* the Friday supplement lists even more bars, concerts, and special events. The *Guía del Ocio,* sold at newsstands (100ptas), lists the city's clubs, pubs, and cafés. **Eschavira,** C. Postigo de la Cuna (tel. 20 32 62), in an alley off C. Azacayes, is *the* place to go for flamenco, jazz, and flamenco-jazz fusion (call for a schedule). Pubs and bars cluster in three areas: Campo de Príncipe, the Albaicín, and the small streets off C. Pedro Antonio de Alarcón. Outside **El 22,** close to Pl. Nueva, at the top of Calderería Nueva, a young throng of vacationers with beer bottles lounge on the steps of Placeta San Gregorio. Higher up, in the Albacín, patrons of the refined **Casa de Yanguas** sip beer (200ptas) to classical tunes amidst contemporary art in fountained Moorish patios (open 8pm-3am). **Babylon,** Placeta Sillería, 5, off C. Reyes Católicos before Pl. Nueva, pumps reggae, hip-hop, and funk. Avoid the **Cuevas Gitanas de Sacromonte** (gypsy caves), a snare for gullible tourists.

■ Near Granada: La Cartuja

On the outskirts of Granada stands **La Cartuja** (tel. 16 19 32), a Carthusian monastery and pinnacle of Baroque artistry. Marble with rich brown tones and swirling forms (a stone unique to nearby Lanjarón) marks the sacristy of Saint Bruno. To reach the monastery, take bus 8 (115ptas) from the cathedral. (Open April-Sept. Mon.-Sat. 10am-1pm and 4-8pm; Oct.-March 10am-1pm and 3:30-6pm. Free Sun. 10am-noon.)

Costa del Sol

Costa del Sol has sold its soul to the Devil, and now he's starting to collect. Artifice covers its once-natural charms as chic promenades, and hotels seal off small towns from the shoreline. Although the Costa del Sol officially extends from Tarifa in the southwest to Cabo de Gata east of Almería, the name most often refers to the resorts from Marbella to Motril (directly south of Granada). Post-industrial Málaga divides the Costa in two. To the southeast, the Costa is built up and water washes against concrete, while to the northeast, the hills dip straight to the ocean, resulting in less popular beaches. Nothing can take away the major attraction: eight months of spring and four of summer each year. Prices double in high season, and visitors should make reservations or be ready to search. Ask around for *casas particulares.* June is the best time to visit, when summer weather has come to town but most vacationers haven't.

Málaga Birthplace of Picasso, and once celebrated by Hans Christian Andersen, and native poet Vicente Aleixandre, **Málaga** has lost some of its gleam. While dinginess and petty thievery have soured the city, Málaga is a critical Andalusian transportation hub. The 11th-century **Alcazaba,** built as a palace for Moorish kings and its attached **Museo Arqueológico** are both closed for renovations. The **Museo de Bellas**

Artes, C. San Agustín, 8, displays works by Andalusian artists including Picasso (open Tues.-Fri. 10am-1:30pm and 5-8pm, Sat.-Sun. 10am-1:30pm; 250ptas).

The **tourist office,** Pasaje de Chinitas, 4 (tel. (95) 221 34 45), provides the basics. (Open July-Sept. Mon.-Sat. 9am-7pm, Sun. 9am-1pm; Oct.-June Mon.-Fri. 9am-2pm, Sat. 9am-1pm.) **Trains** (tel. (95) 236 02 02) roll to Córdoba (3hr., 1500ptas), Seville (3hr., 1800ptas), Barcelona (14hr., 7500ptas), and Madrid (9hr., 5000ptas). To get to the station, take bus 3 at Po. Parque or bus 4 at Pl. Marina. Nearby on Po. Tilos, **buses** (tel. (95) 235 00 61) leave the station for Marbella (1hr., 545ptas), Madrid (8hr., 2745ptas), Granada (2hr., 1135ptas), Seville (3hr., 2245ptas), and many other cities.

Head to the downtown area between **Plaza Marina** and **Plaza de la Constitución** for a good night's sleep. After dark, be particularly wary of Alameda de Colón, El Perchel (towards the river from the stations), Cruz de Molnillo (near the market), and La Esperanza/Santo Domingo (up the river from El Corte Inglés). **Pension Córdoba,** C. Bolsa, 11, 2nd fl. (tel. (95) 221 44 69), off C. Molina Lario, has antique furniture and spotless common bathrooms (singles 1300ptas, doubles 2500ptas). **Hostal Residencia Chinitas,** Pasaje Chinitas, 2, 2nd fl. (tel. (95) 221 46 83), off Pl. Constitución, is run by a warm family (singles 1800-2000ptas, doubles 3400-4000ptas). Seafood restaurants cluster in the beachfront district **El Pedregalejo** (a 35min. walk or bus 11 from Pl. La Marina, 115ptas). In summer the boardwalk bars of **El Pedregalejo** overflow, while year-round the bars between C. Comedias and C. Granada, are hopping.

SPAIN

Marbella Glamorous Marbella, the jewel of the Costa del Sol, extorts *pesetas* quickly, efficiently, and in many different languages from hordes of the flashy and the famous. The **Museo del Grabado Español Contemporáneo,** C. Hospital Bazán, displays works by Miró and Picasso (open Mon.-Fri. 10:15am-2pm and 5:30-8:30pm; 300ptas). With 22km of beach, Marbella offers a variety of sizzling settings, from below the chic promenade to **Playa de las Chapas,** 10km east via the Fuengirola bus. The sand is generally gritty and scorching but the human landscape is scenic, to say the least. Because of the towering mountains nearby, Marbella's winter temperatures tend to be warmer than Malaga's, and beach season goes on and on. Take buses from along Av. Richard Soriano to "San Pedro" (125ptas) to reach the opulent and trendy **Puerto Banús.** Buffered by imposing white yachts and rows of boutiques and fancy restaurants, *this* is where the Beautiful People are. The port is frequented by the likes of Sean Connery, Richard Gere, Elton John, and King Fahd of Saudi Arabia, and throngs of Eurochicks roaming the marina in hopes of landing a rich husband. Gawk at the toys of the rich (Ferraris, Rolls Royces), or kick back at **Sinatra Bar,** on the first row, and drink it all in. The Moroccan coast is visible on exceptionally clear days.

Back in town, Marbella's nightlife is unrivaled; beaches don't fill up until three in the afternoon because people are just waking up. In the *casco antiguo* (old town), actions brews along C. Peral. A international crowd socializes in **Planet,** C. Aduar, 22, and **Kashmir,** C. Rafina, 8, off C. Aduar. Their smoky lounges upstairs might remind Amsterdam natives of home. Toward morning, the young population swarms to the **Puerto Deportivo** ("The Port"), an amusement park of disco-bars and clubs.

From the new station atop Avenida Trapiche, s/n (tel. (95) 276 44 00), **buses** leave for Málaga (1½hr., 545ptas), Seville (3¾hr., 1805ptas), and Granada (4hr., 1680ptas). To get to the town center, walk left, make the first right onto Av. Trapiche, and follow any downhill route to **Avenida Ramón y Cajal.** Calle Peral curves up from here and around the **carco antiguo** (old town). The **tourist office** is at C. Glorieta de la Fontanilla (tel. (95) 277 14 42), fronting the shore (open Mon.-Fri. 9:30am-8pm, Sat. 9:30am-2pm). Another office is located in Pl. Naranjos (tel. (95) 282 35 50; open same hours). The casco antiguo around Pl. Naranjos (Orange Square) is loaded with little *hostales.* Several cheap guest houses line **Calles Ancha, San Francisco, Aduar,** and **de los Caballeros,** all of which are uphill off C. Huerta Chica. The **Albergue Juvenil (HI),** Av. Trapiche, 2 (tel. (95) 277 14 91), is just downhill from the station and only slightly removed from the action. Facilities include a TV room, basketball court, and pool (900-1300ptas, over 26 1200-1600ptas). **Hostal del Pilar,** C. Mesoncillo, 4 (tel. (95) 282 99 36), the second left off C. Pera when coming form Av. Ramón y

Cajal, an extension of C. Huerta Chica, is run by a Scottish woman and three multilingual countrymen who love to party with their guests (mattresses on the roof in warm months from 1000ptas; otherwise 1500-2000ptas). **Bar El Gallo,** C. Lobatas, 44, has a loud TV, louder locals, and cheap, tasty food (open daily 9am-midnight). Stock up at the 24-hour **minimarket** at the corner of C. Pablo Casals and Av. Fontanilla.

Gibraltar

The gateway to the Atlantic, **Gibraltar** soothes homesick Brits with fish 'n' chips, while all the other expats go batty over the tax-free cigarettes (80p per pack). Britain and Spain have long hotly contested the enclave, but despite the peninsula's history, Gibraltar pales in comparison with the picturesque Spanish coast. At best, the grimy tourist trap is a daytrip—stand on the Rock to say that you've done it. From the northern tip of the massif known as **Top of the Rock,** there's a remarkable view of Iberia and the Straits of Gibraltar. Cable cars carry visitors from the southern end of Main St. to the Top of the Rock, making a stop at **Apes' Den,** where a colony of monkeys clamber lithely about the sides of rocks. The ruins of a Moorish wall crumble down the road from the cable car station to the south, where the spooky chambers of **St. Michael's Cave** cut into the rock. (Cable car Mon.-Sat. 9:30am-5:45pm. Last tickets sold 5:15pm. Round-trip £4.90.) From the southern tip of Gibraltar, **Europa Point** commands a view of the straits; on a clear day you can see all the way to Morocco. Take buses 3 or 1b from Line Wall Rd., off Main St., to the end (every 15min., 45p).

Main St. is dotted with lively **pubs.** Busybodies enjoy people-watching (and occasional live music) at the **Angry Friar,** also known as **The Convent,** 287 Main St. across from the Governor's Residence (open daily 10am-midnight). **Smith's Fish and Chips,** 295 Main St., dishes out hardy servings of guess what (from £3; open Mon.-Thurs. 11am-6pm, Fri. until 9pm, Sat. noon-3pm).

From Spain, dial 9567 (from the Cádiz province 7) to access **telephone** numbers in Gibraltar. From Britain dial (00) 350; from the US (011) 350. The **USA Direct** number is 88 00. Although *pesetas* are accepted everywhere (except in pay phones), the pound sterling is clearly preferred. **Buses** run to **La Línea,** the nearest Spanish town on the border, from Málaga (4hr., 1225ptas), Algeciras (30min., 220ptas), Seville (6hr., 1440ptas), and Granada (6hr., 2390ptas). The main **tourist office** is at 18-20 Bomb House Lane (tel. 748 05; open Mon.-Fri. 10am-6pm, Sat. 10am-2pm). If you must stay, try **Emille Youth Hostel Gibraltar,** Line Wall Rd. (tel. 511 06; dorms £10) or **Queen's Hotel,** 1 Boyd St. (tel. 740 00; £12-20; ask about *Let's Go* discounts).

Algeciras

On the Spanish side of the Bahía de Algeciras, Algeciras has some pleasant older areas, but most tourists see only the dingy port, which offers easy access to Gibraltar and Morocco. The **tourist office,** C. Juan de la Cierva (tel. (956) 57 26 36), is the tube-shaped pink and red building (open Mon.-Fri. 9am-2pm). The Empresa Portillo **bus station,** Av. Virgen del Carmen, 15 (tel. (956) 65 10 55), serves Marbella (1½hr., 760ptas), Granada (5hr., 2455ptas), Málaga (3hr., 1290ptas), and other cities; **trains** chug to Granada (5½hr., 2300ptas) from the station on Ctra. Cádiz. During the summer, **ferries** leave hourly for Ceuta (35-90min., 1884-3000ptas) and Tangier (2½hr., 2960ptas per person, 9300ptas per car). Ferry passengers with Eurail get a 20% discount. Convenient lodgings bunch around **Calle José Santacana,** parallel to Av. Marina and one block inland, and **Calle Duque de Almodóvar,** two blocks farther from the water. Follow C. Santacana into the small market square, bear left and continue up C. Rafael del Muro to the quiet and cool **Hostal Rif** at #11 (tel. (956) 65 49 53; 1200ptas per person), or try **Hostal Residencia González,** C. Santacana, 7 (tel. (956) 65 28 43), close to the port (singles 1500-1750ptas, doubles 3000-3500ptas).

Sweden (Sverige)

US$1	**= 7.77kr (Swedish kronor)**	**1kr =**	**US$0.13**
CDN$1	**= 5.62kr**	**1kr =**	**CDN$0.18**
UK£1	**= 12.35kr**	**1kr =**	**UK£0.08**
IR£1	**= 11.54kr**	**1kr =**	**IR£0.09**
AUS$1	**= 5.67kr**	**1kr =**	**AUS$0.18**
NZ$1	**= 4.94kr**	**1kr =**	**NZ$0.20**
SAR1	**= 1.66kr**	**1kr =**	**SAR0.60**

Country Code: 46 **International Dialing Prefix: 009**

When the celebrated Swedish entertainer Jonas Gardell named his last hit show *På besök i Mellanjmjölks Land* (On Tour in the Land of 2% Milk), he was poking fun at the Swedish concept of *lagom* (moderation). The idea implies that life should be lived somewhere between wealth and poverty, ecstasy and depression, whole milk and skim. The reputation of the *lagom* Swede runs anywhere from the complaint that Swedes are sober, boring, unemotional folk to praise for Volvo's sleek designs and Swedes' skill in international conflict resolution. Yet Sweden is, in fact, a country of dramatic extremes: even the Scandinavian weather silently defies the *lagom* stereotype; while the summer sun never sets, it seems to disappears almost entirely in the winter. Over 2400km long, Sweden stretches from the mountainous arctic reaches of Kiruna down to the flat, temperate farmland and white-sand beaches of the southern Skåne and Småland. While Dalarna, Värmland, and Norrland counties invoke images of quiet woods, folk music, and rustic country Midsummer celebration, the capital city of Stockholm shines as a thoroughly cosmopolitan center.

The contrast of natural and geographical extremes is reflected also in Sweden's social and cultural landscape. Sweden's mythic early history of violent Viking conflict and conquest stands in contrast to its 20th-century succession of international peacekeepers, from Alfred Nobel, who established his prizes for peaceful contributions to humanity, to Raoul Wallenberg, who clambered over the roofs of Nazi trains to hand out Swedish passports that saved thousands of Jews from concentration camps, to Prime Minister Olof Palme who marched against the Vietnam war, sheltered American draft resisters, and was later assassinated for his peace efforts. Culturally, Sweden is thought of as the land of Oompa-Loompa folk-fiddlers and hurdy-gurdy accordions, but playwright August Strindberg and film director Ingmar Berman gained fame for their dark sophistication, and Lasse Hallström's films, like *My Life as a Dog,* show a range of Swedish humor and drama. Even its population of nearly 9 million shows the range of modern Sweden's extremes, from blond and blue-eyed Nordic types to the darker beauty of immigrants who have made Sweden home. Sweden offers unlimited possibilities for the curious traveler, ensuring that even in the *lagom* land of mellanmjölk, the milk is never sour.

GETTING THERE AND GETTING AROUND

Sweden is easily accessible by boat or train from Denmark and Germany, by ferry from Poland and Finland, and by train and bus from Norway and Finland. Trains are reliable in the southern half of Sweden; in the north, long-distance buses are often a better option. The *buy-in-Scandinavia* **Scanrail Pass** allows five days within 15 (1550kr, under 26 1150kr, seniors 1350kr) or 21 consecutive days (2350kr, under 26 1750kr, seniors 2050kr) of unlimited rail travel through Sweden, Norway, Denmark, and Finland, as well as free or discounted ferry rides. This differs from the *buy-outside-of-Scandinavia* **Scanrail Pass** offering five out of 15 days (US$176, under 26 US$132), 10 out of 21 days (US$284, under 26 US$213), or 30 consecutive days (US$414, under 26 US$311) of unlimited travel. For **Reslust** cardholders (150kr, seniors 50kr; valid for owner and companion), fares are reduced 25% on rail journeys over 50km on Tuesdays, Wednesdays, Thursdays, and Saturdays. From June to August, Reslust cardholders receive half off every ticket bought within seven days before departure. One-way second-class tickets can be bought at half-price for trains marked with a red circle in the timetable. **Eurail** is valid in Sweden, but reservations are required for some journeys, such as those on express trains.

For travelers under 21, **SAS** offers a special standby fare of 300kr (one way) on **flights** between Stockholm and other Swedish cities (tel. (020) 91 01 50; outside Sweden (08) 797 40 00). **Hitching** can be slow near major cities but picks up in the north. All must wear seatbelts, and headlights must always be on. Sweden is a biker's heaven: paths cover most of the country, particularly in the south, and you can complete a trip of Sweden on the hostel-spotted **Sverigeleden bike route.** Contact the Svenska Turistföreningen (STF, see **Essentials,** below) for more info.

ESSENTIALS

Throughout Sweden, **tourist offices** will help you find rooms and provide information on local activities. Most **banks** are open weekdays until 3pm (sometimes later in Stockholm); exchange rates are constant, but commissions vary. Exchange checks in large denominations, as there is often a 35-50kr commission per check. Many **post offices** double as banks (open Mon.-Fri. 9am-6pm, Sat. 10am-1pm). **Phones** require at least 2kr, but almost all only accept Telefonkort cards, available at newsstands and post offices. For **AT&T Direct,** dial 020 79 56 11; **MCI WorldPhone** 020 79 59 22; **Sprint Access** 020 79 90 11; **Canada Direct** 020 79 90 15; **BT Direct** 020 79 51 44; **Australia Direct** 020 79 90 61; **NZ Direct** 020 79 90 64. For **emergency help,** dial 112. Almost all Swedes speak some English, and those under 50 are usually fluent. Sweden leads the world in facilities for people with disabilities.

Sweden's public **holidays** include January 1, Epiphany (Jan. 6), Easter (April 10-13), Labor Day (May 1), Ascension Day (May 21), Whit Sunday and Monday (May 31-June 1), Midsummer Day (June 20), All Saints Day (Nov. 1), Christmas (Dec. 24-26), and December 31. **Midsummer** incites family frolicking and bacchanalian dancing around maypoles. July and August bring two special festivals, the *surströmming* (herring) and eel parties. *Surströmming* is prepared by letting fish ferment (or rot), after which it is tinned and sold. In mid-August, the **Stockholm Water Festival** features fireworks, market stalls, and outdoor cafés. Plan ahead for holidays, especially around Midsummer, as many transportation lines shut down and some hotels close.

Yes/No	*Ja/Nej*	yaa/ney
Hello	*Goddag/Hallå*	goo-DAAG
Thank you	*Tack*	TUCK
Excuse me.	*Ursäkta*	ur-SAK-ta
Do you speak English?	*Pratar du Engelska?*	PRAH-tar du en-GELL-ska
I don't speak Swedish.	*Jag pratar inte Svanska.*	yaag PRAH-tar IN-te SVAN-ska
I would like a single/double.	*Jag will haen enkel/dubbel.*	yaag vill HAA-ain EN-kel/DUB-bel
Help!	*Hjälp!*	YELP

Accommodations and Camping Sweden's top-notch **youth hostels** *(vandrarhem),* at 110kr for HI members and an additional 40kr for nonmembers, are the only budget option in Sweden; hotels cost at least 400kr. If you arrive in the off season and the local hostel is closed (a problem in the north and in smaller towns), staying in private homes is a bearable alternative (150-250kr). Book through the local *turistbyrå* (tourist office). In some Swedish hostels sheets are paper disposables, so you may want to bring your own (or pay 35kr extra for cotton sheets). The **Svenska Turistföreningen (STF)** runs Sweden's hostels, which fill up quickly in the summer; reserve in advance (tel. (08) 463 21 00; fax 678 19 38). Most hostels have kitchen facilities, laundry, and TV, and receptions are usually open 8 to 10am and 5 to 9 or 10pm (shorter hours in winter). *Vandrarhem* are often used by Swedish families, so beware of screaming children. STF sells **Hostelling International (HI)** membership for 170kr or gives HI cards valid in Sweden that will make you a member after paying full price six times in Swedish hostels. STF also distributes the free *Swedish Youth and Family Hostels,* listing all hostels with phone and fax numbers, and a map. The STF manages mountain huts in the northern wilds with 10-80 beds which cost 130-195kr in high season (nonmembers 180-145kr). Huts are very popular; plan ahead.

Many **campgrounds** (80-100kr per site) also offer *stugor* (cottages) for around 85-175kr per person. If you don't have an International Camping Card, you'll need a Swedish one (90kr), available with the free booklet *Camping i Sverige.* Get these from **Sveriges Campingvärdars Riksförbund (SCR),** Box 255, 451 17 Uddevalla (fax (0522) 393 45). You may walk or camp for one or two nights anywhere on privately owned land—except gardens—as long as you respect the flora, fauna, and the owner's privacy. Pick up the brochure *The Common Right of Access (Allemansrätten)* at the STF. Summer days are pleasant—around 20°C (68°F) in the south, 16°C (61°F) in the north—but nights can get chilly, around 10°C (50°F) in the south, 5°C (41°F) in the north. Winters last nine months, and are frequently below -5°C (23°F).

Food and Drink Food is unbelievably expensive in restaurants and not much cheaper in grocery stores. Rely on supermarkets and outdoor fruit and vegetable markets. Ubiquitous stands provide the most kebabs for your kronor (25-35kr for meat, rice, and veggies). Potatoes are the national staple. These and other dishes are invariably smothered with dill. Try tasty milk products like *messmör* (spreadable whey cheese) and *fil,* a fluid yogurt. When you tire of groceries, seek out restaurants that offer an affordable **dagens rätt** (40-60kr), a daily special including an entree, salad, bread, and drink, usually available only at lunch. A real beer *(starköl)* usually costs at least 15kr in stores and 30-45kr in city pubs. The cheaper, weaker, and lousier low-alcohol alternative is *lättöl* (8-12kr). Note that the drinking age in bars is 18, but you must be 20 to buy alcohol from the state-run Systembolaget stores, which monopolize the sale of booze (open Mon.-Fri.; expect long lines on Fri.).

Stockholm

"Water! Stockholm's full of water!" beam the words of a popular Swedish tune. Situated on a series of archipelago islands, Stockholm—the Venice of the North, the Jewel of Scandanavia, the Queen of the Baltic—lives up to its monikers. Waterways wend through the city that launched ABBA and the Cardigans, and the relentless summer sun allows Stockholm's cobblestoned streets, world-class museums, chic cafés, and nightclubs to shine around the clock. In 1998, Stockholm proudly wears its tiara as the Cultural Capital of Europe. With *Absolut* vodka absolutely everywhere and founts of cultural options, Stockholm flows with so much more than water.

ORIENTATION AND PRACTICAL INFORMATION

Stockholm is built on five islands at the junction of **Lake Mälaren,** to the west, and the **Baltic Sea,** to the east. The northen island is divided into two sections: **Norrmalm**—home to the Central Station, the tourist office on the central park, **Kungsträdgården,** and the shopping district on Drottningg.—and **Östermalm,** home to the elegant waterfront **Strandvägen** and much of the nightlife fanning out from **Stureplan Square.** The largely residential western island, **Kungsholmen,** is home to the **Stadshuset** (city hall) and grassy beaches. The southern island **Södermalm,** formerly Stockholm's slum, hosts cafés, artists, and the extensive gay scene. Södermalm's little sister-island, **Långholmen,** is a nature preserve, while **Djurgården,** in the heart of the city, is a veritable nature-playground and site of the Nordiska Museet and the Vasamuseet. At the center of these four islands is **Gamla Stan** (Old Town) island, which fans out from the main thoroughfare, **Västerlånggatan.** Gamla Stan's neighboring island **Skeppsholmen** (best reached via Normalm), harbors the **Moderna Museet.** The extensive and efficient **tunnelbana** (subway) links the islands together (14kr), though you can easily walk between the sites that cluster around the center.

Tourist Offices: Tourist Information (tel. 789 24 90; fax 789 24 91; email info@stoinfo.se; http://www.stoinfo.se), in the northeast corner of Kungsträdgården at Hamng. From Centralstation, walk up Klarabergsg. to Sergels Torg (T-bana: T-Centralen), then bear right on Hamng. Books hostels (20kr) and hotels (40kr). Distributes the free *Stockholm this Week,* maps, and the **Stockholmskortet,** which provides free museum entrance and public transportation (one-day, 185kr; two-day, 350kr; three-day, 470kr). Tourist info open June-Aug. Mon.-Fri. 8am-6pm, Sat.-Sun. 9am-5pm; Sept.-May Mon.-Fri. 9am-6pm, Sat.-Sun. 10am-3pm. **Hotellcentralen** (tel. 789 24 25; fax 791 86 66; email hotels@stoinfo.se). At the train station. Secures hotels (40kr) and hostels (20kr). No charge if reserved in

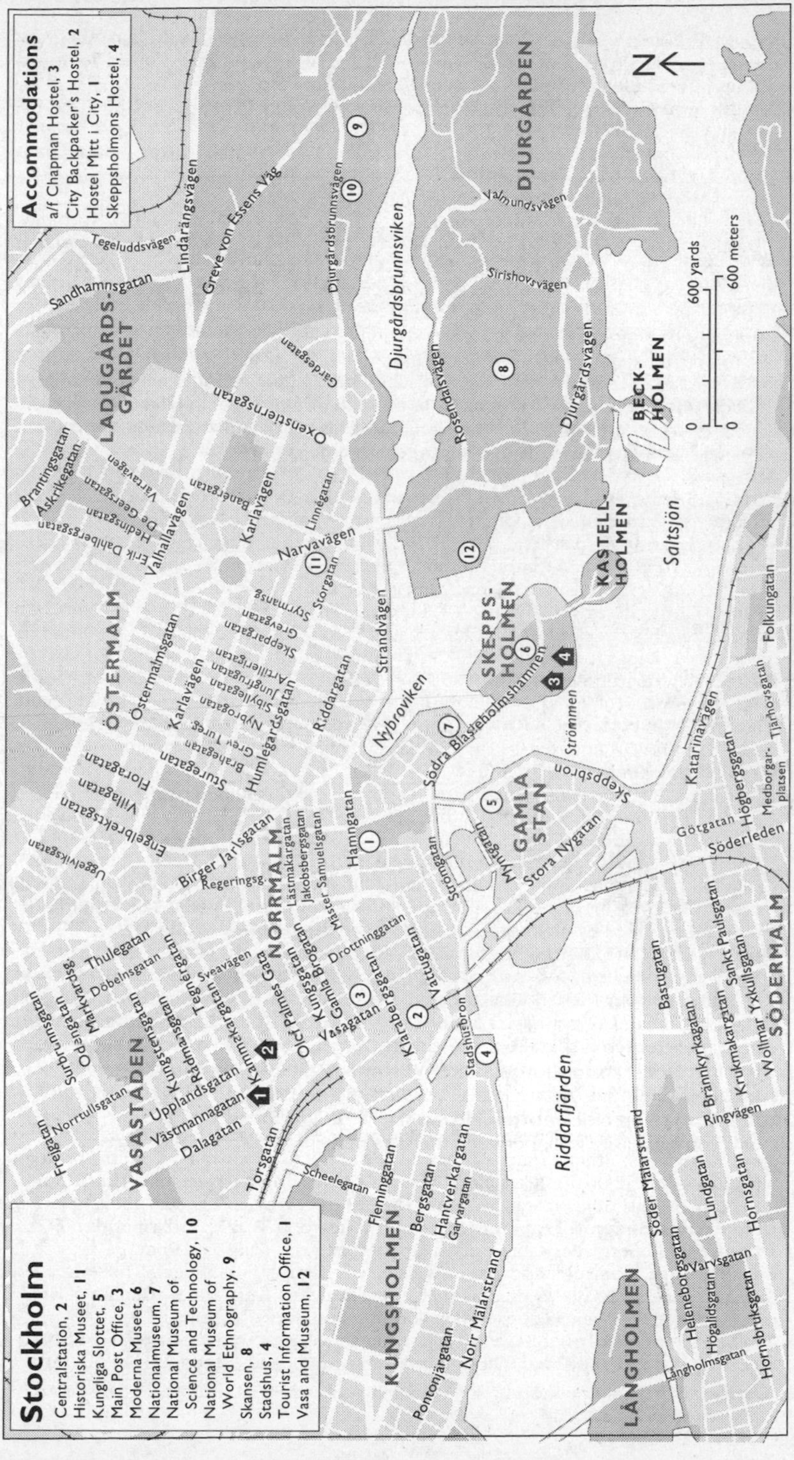
Stockholm
Centralstation, 2
Historiska Museet, 11
Kungliga Slottet, 5
Main Post Office, 3
Moderna Museet, 6
Nationalmuseum, 7
National Museum of Science and Technology, 10
National Museum of World Ethnography, 9
Skansen, 8
Stadshus, 4
Tourist Information Office, 1
Vasa and Museum, 12
Accommodations
af Chapman Hostel, 3
City Backpacker's Hostel, 2
Hostel Mitt i City, 1
Skeppsholmens Hostel, 4
ÖSTERMALM
LADUGÅRDS-GÄRDET
DJURGÅRDEN
VASASTADEN
NORRMALM
KUNGSHOLMEN
GAMLA STAN
SKEPPS-HOLMEN
KASTELL-HOLMEN
BECK-HOLMEN
SÖDERMALM
LÅNGHOLMEN
Riddarfjärden
Saltsjön
Nybroviken
Djurgårdsbrunnsviken
600 yards
600 meters

advance. Comprehensive color city map 20kr. Open June-Aug. daily 7am-9pm; May and Sept. 8am-7pm; Oct.-April 9am-6pm. Tune into Kathy Riley on Radio Stockholm International (89.6 FM) for daily tourist info in English.

Budget Travel: Kilroy Travels Sweden, Kungsg. 4 (tel. 23 45 15; fax 10 16 93; T-bana: Östermalmstorg). Student flight tickets. Open Mon.-Fri. 10am-6pm. Also at Frescati, Universitetsv. 9, (tel. 16 05 15; fax 15 33 21; T-bana: Universitetet). Open Mon.-Fri. 10am-4pm. **Transalpino,** Birger Jarlsg. 13 (tel. 679 98 70; fax 611 09 95). Open Mon.-Fri. 10am-5:30pm. T-bana: Östermalmstorg.

Embassies: Australia, Sergels Torg 12 (tel. 613 29 00; fax 24 74 14). **Canada,** Tegelbacken 4 (tel. 453 30 00, 24hr. line (070) 549 34 63; fax 24 24 91). **Ireland,** Östermalmsg. 97 (tel. 661 80 05). **South Africa,** Linnég. 76 (tel. 24 39 50; fax. 660 71 36). **U.K.,** Skarpög. 6-8 (tel. 671 90 00; fax 662 99 89). **U.S.,** Strandv. 101 (tel. 783 53 00, 24hr. line (071)24 02 00; fax 660 58 79).

Currency Exchange: Forex in Centralstation (tel. 411 67 34; open daily 7am-9pm), in Cityterminalen (tel. 21 42 80; open Mon.-Fri. 8am-7pm, Sat. 8am-5pm), and in the tourist office in Sverigehuset (tel. 20 03 89). 20kr commission on traveler's check transactions. 30kr commission on cash. **Valutaspecialisten,** Kungsg. 30 (tel. 10 30 00; open Mon.-Fri. 8am-7pm, Sat. 9am-4pm), and at Arlanda Airport (tel. 797 85 57; open daily 5:30am-8:30pm) charges no commission.

American Express: Birger Jarlsg. 1 (tel. 679 78 80, 24hr. refund assistance (020) 79 51 55). T-bana: Östermalmstorg. No fee for cashing AmEx Traveler's Cheques; 20kr charge for cash exchange. Open Mon.-Fri. 9am-5pm, Sat. 10am-1pm.

Flights: Arlanda Airport (tel. 797 60 00), 45km north of the city. **Flygbussar** buses (tel. 600 10 00.; every 15min., 40min., 60kr) run between the airport and Cityterminalen. Buses run daily 4:30am-10pm; public transportation passes not valid.

Trains: Centralstation. T-bana: T-Centralen. **Train info:** tel. (020) 75 75 75. To Copenhagen (4 per day, 8½hr., 560kr) and Oslo (3 per day, 6hr., 621kr). Reservations 30kr. Luggage storage 40kr per day. **Lockers** 20-30kr. **Showers** 25kr.

Buses: City terminalen (tel. 440 85 70 or 762 59 97), upstairs from Centralstation. To: the airport (60kr), the Gotland ferries (50kr), the Poland ferries (120kr, every other day on even dates), Gothenburg (2 per day, 7-8hr., 190kr, under 25 140kr), and Malmö (2-3 per day, 10-11hr., 250kr, under 25 180kr).

Public Transportation: SL office in Sergelstorg (tel. 600 10 00). Open Mon.-Fri. 7am-9pm, Sat.-Sun. 8am-9pm. T-bana: T-Centralen. Walk-in office open Mon.-Thurs. 8:30am-6:30pm, Fri. 8:30am-5:30pm. Most in-town destinations cost 2 coupons (14kr, 1hr. unlimited bus/subway transfer). **Rabattkuponger** (95kr), sold at *Pressbyrån* news agents, are valid for 10 trips. **SL Tourist Card (Turistkort),** valid on buses, subways, commuter trains, and the trams and ferries to Djurgården, costs 60kr for 24hr. or 120kr for 3 days. Subway runs roughly 5am-2am. After hours they are replaced by night buses. Check schedules on bus-stop kiosks.

Ferries: Silja Line, Kungsg. 2 (tel. 22 21 40), sails overnight to Helsinki (1 per day, 14hr, 450-550kr, 50% off with Scanrail, free with Eurail; book ahead), Mariehamn (1 per day, 19hr., 430-580kr, 50% off with Scanrail, free with Eurail), and Åbo (Turku), Finland (2 per day, 12-13hr., 200-335kr, 50% off with rail passes). To get to Silja's ferry terminal, take the T-bana to "Gärdet" and walk toward the water, or take the Silja bus (14kr) from City terminalen. **Viking Line** also sails to Helsinki (1 per day, 15hr., 440-575kr, 50% off with Scanrail, free with Eurail), Mariehamn (1 per day, 19hr., 432-600kr, same rail pass discounts), and Åbo (1 per day, 12hr., 192-228kr, same rail pass discounts). The Viking Line terminal is at Stadsgården on the northeast coast of Södermalm (F-bana: "Slussen"). **Gotlandslinjen,** Skeppsbron 34 (booking tel. 52 06 40 00), sails to Visby, Gotland from Nynäshamn, 1hr. south of the city by bus (50kr) from City terminalen (3 per week, 18hr., 328-420kr).

Bike Rental: Skepp & Hoj on Djurgårdsbron (tel. 660 57 57). 150kr per day, 500kr per week. Rollerblades same prices. Open April-Sept. daily 9am-9pm.

Hitchhiking: Laborious and risky. Waiting on highways is illegal. Those headed south take the T-bana to the gas station on Kungens Kurva in Skärholmen. Those going north take bus 52 to Sveaplan and stand on Sveav. at Nortull.

Taxis: Extraordinarily high fares. 345kr from the airport to the center. **Taxi Stockholm** (tel. 15 00 00), **Taxi 020** (tel. (020) 93 93 93), and **Alltaxi** (tel. 14 00 00).

Bookstore: Akademibokhandeln, at Mäster Samuelsg. 32 (tel. 613 61 00), Sergels Torg 12 (tel. 411 59 90), and at the university campus's Allhuset Student Union, Universitetsv. (tel. 15 18 65), next to Kilroy Travels. Open June-Aug. Mon.-Fri. 9:30am-6pm, Sat. 10am-3pm; Sept.-May Mon.-Fri. 10am-4pm, Sat. 10am-4pm.

Gay and Lesbian Services: RFSL, the Riksförbundet för Sexuellt Likaberättigande (Swedish Federation for Sexual Equality), Sveav. 57 (tel. 736 02 19). T-bana: Rådmansg. Organizes support services. Features a bookstore, **Rosa Rummet,** a café, **Divan,** and distributes *Queer Xtra (QX),* with bar, club, and events guide. Open Mon.-Thurs. noon-8pm, Fri. noon-6pm, Sat.-Sun. 1-4pm.

Services for the Disabled: DHR, or **De Handikappades Riksförbund (The Swedish Federation for the Handicapped),** Katrinebergsv. 6 (tel. 18 91 00; fax 645 65 41; TTD 18 85 01), provides info on deaf, blind, and wheelchair services and access in Sweden, as does the tourist office.

Crisis Lines: Suicide and Crisis Hotline: tel. 463 91 00. **Rape and Reproductive Health: RFSU,** the **Riksförbundet för Sexuell Upplysningen (Swedish Federation for Sexual Education),** Drottningholmsv. 37 (tel. 692 07 00 or 692 07 70). **Womens' Helpline:** Kvinnojouren (tel. 644 09 25). Also contact the **Womens' Center,** Kvinnchuset, Snickarbacken 10 (tel. 10 76 56).

Pharmacy: Apotek C. W. Scheele, Klarabergsg. 64, under the green-and-white "Apotek" signs at the overpass over Vasag. T-bana: T-Centralen. Open 24hr.

Medical Assistance: Call 644 92 00 for a referral to the nearest hospital. **AIDS Info: AIDS-Jouren,** tel. (020) 78 44 40.

Emergencies: Ambulance and **fire:** tel. 112.

Police: tel. 112. The local police station is at Bryggarg. 19, north of Centralstation (tel. 454 81 30). Police headquarters are at Agneg. 33-37 (tel. 401 00 00).

Post Office: In Centralstation (tel. 781 20 41). Open Mon.-Fri. 7am-10pm, Sat.-Sun. 10am-7pm. Also at Drottningg. 53 (tel. 781 46 82). Open Mon.-Fri. 9am-6pm, Sat. 10am-1pm. **Postal Code:** 101 10 Stockholm 1.

Telephones: Telecenter, at Centralstation, assists with international calls and sells phone cards for 30, 55, and 95kr. Open Mon.-Sat. 8am-9pm, Sun. 10am-5pm. You can also buy phone cards at **Pressbyrån** stores (especially at T-bana stations) or at **Telia Butiker,** Kungsg. 36, behind Hötorget.**Telephone Code:** 08.

SWEDEN

ACCOMMODATIONS AND CAMPING

Hostels (Vandrarhem)

Summer demands reservations, and most hostels limit stays to five nights. If you haven't booked ahead, arrive early—around 7am. Check-out time is usually 10am.

a/f Chapman (HI) (tel. 679 50 15; fax 611 98 75), a full-rigger sailing ship majestically moored off Skeppsholmen, to the right as you cross the bridge. Take bus 65 from T-Centralen. Reception open daily 7am-noon and 3pm-2am. Lockout noon-3pm. Curfew 2am. 110kr, nonmembers 150kr. Open April to mid-Dec. V, MC.

Skeppsholmens Vandrarhem (HI) (tel. 679 50 17; fax 611 71 55), in the Hantverkshuset, on the shore behind the a/f Chapman. Less mythic and more institutional, but bigger, plusher rooms. Reception open 24hr. 110kr, nonmembers 150kr. Breakfast 45kr. Lockers 10kr. Open Jan. to mid-Dec. V, MC.

Långholmens Vandrarhem (HI), Gamla Kronohäktet (tel. 668 05 10; fax 720 85 75, on Långholmen Island. From T-bana: "Hornstull," march north on Långholmsg., turn left (before the bridge) onto Högalidsg., then right on Bergsundsg. over the bridge onto Långholmen, then follow the "Kronohäktet" signs. Plush cells in a transmogrified prison, most with TV, phone, and private shower. Think Alcatraz. Very cool. Reception open 24hr. No curfew or lockout. 140kr, nonmembers 180kr. Kitchen. Wheelchair accessible. Open late June-early Oct.

Gustaf af Klint, Stadsgårdskajen 153 (tel. 640 40 77; fax 640 64 16). A former Navy ship moored 200m east of T-bana: "Slussen." Reception open in summer 24hr. No curfew. 14-bed dorms 110kr. Cabins 130kr per person. Doubles 155kr. Breakfast 40kr. Free lockers. Laundry 25kr. Open all year. V, MC.

City Backpackers' Vandrarhem, Barnhusg. 16 (tel. 20 69 20; fax 10 04 64). Exit Centralstation, walk left on Vasag. to Norra Bantorget. Barhusg. is the 1st street on your right after you cross the square (5min.). Reception open Mon.-Fri. 8am-8pm, Sat.-Sun. 8am-7pm. 130kr. Breakfast 4kr. Sheets 45 kr.

Hostel Mitt i City, Västmannag. 13 (tel. 21 76 30, fax 21 76 90), near City Backpackers' Hostel. Västmannag. is the continuation of Vasag. on the other side of Norra Bantorget, behind the "LO" building. Reception open 24 hr. 130kr.

Backpackers' Inn (HI), Banērg. 56 (tel. 660 75 15; fax. 665 40 39). T-bana: "Karlaplan"; exit station, walk right on Banērg. 200m. Has beds to spare when the others are fully booked. Reception open 7-11am and 4pm-2am. Curfew 2am. 90kr, nonmembers 130kr. Breakfast 40kr. Sheets 35kr. Open late June-early Oct.

Zinkensdamm Vandrarhem (HI), Zinkens Väg 20 (tel. 616 81 00; fax 616 81 20). From T-bana: "Zinkensdamm," head south on Ringv. 3 blocks, then turn right on Zinkens Väg. Peaceful, comfortable hostel in the heart of Södermalm, frequented more by families than by youths. Kitchen, TV, sauna, restaurant, and pub. No lockout. No curfew. 120kr, nonmembers 160kr. Lockers in rooms.

Columbus Hotell-Vandrarhem, Tjärhovsg. 11 (tel. 644 17 17; fax 702 07 64). Three blocks east of T-bana: "Medborgarplatsen" on Södermalm. A former brewery, prison, and plague hospital. Kitchen facility. Reception open 24hr. No curfew. 130kr. Hostel singles 290kr. Hotel singles 420kr. Lockers 5kr. Open Jan.-late Dec.

Brygghuset, Norrtullsg. 12N (tel. 31 24 24; fax 31 02 06). Two blocks north of T-bana: "Odenplan." Small kitchen. Ping-pong and TV area. Reception open daily 8am-noon and 3-10pm. Lockout noon-3pm. Hostel closes at 2am, but get a key (20kr deposit). Dorms 125kr. Doubles 155kr per person. Open June to mid-Sept.

SWEDEN

Camping

Be sure to bring insect repellant to ward off the infamous Swedish mosquitoes.

Ängby Camping, Blackebergsv. 24 (tel. 37 04 20; fax 37 82 26). Wooded campground on Lake Mäloren. T-bana: Ängbyplan. Reception open daily 7am-11pm. 110kr. Open Sept.-April.

Bredäng Camping (tel. 97 70 71; fax 708 72 62), 10km southwest of the city center near Lake Mälaren. T-bana: Bredäng. You can also take the ferry from nearby Mälarhöjdsbadet to Stockholm City Hall or Drottningholm. Follow signs down stairs, past the large apartment complex, and parallel to the train tracks along Stora Sällskapets väg to the campsite (7-10min.). Store, laundry, and running water. Reception open March-April and Oct. 7am-9pm. 130kr per tent. 4-bed cabins 400kr.

Vårberg Camping (tel. 710 63 70 or 710 13 30; fax 710 88 68), 12km southwest of city center, 1km from Lake Mälaren. T-bana: Vårberg. Follow signs to Vårbergs Idrottsplats (sports ground). Reception open daily 8am-10pm. 60kr per tent. Hot water included. Open late June to mid-Aug.

FOOD

In the past few years, Stockholm's restaurant scene has doubled, due to the culinary imports of the influx of the immigrants to Sweden. The cheapest options are the *dagens rätt* lunch specials (45-80kr) that many restaurants offer between 11:30am and 3pm. For groceries, look for the ubiquitous green signs of the **Konsum Supermarket** chain, at Odeng. 65, Sveav. 70, Vasag. 22, and in Gamla Stan at Järntorget 80 (all open daily 10am-9pm.) **Hötorget** square hosts an open-air fruit **market** (Mon.-Sat. 10am-5pm). The 3-story **Kungshallen food court,** across the street at Kungsg. 44, offers cafés, delis, and fast-food (lunch or dinner 25-85kr; open daily 11am-11pm).

Collage, Smålandsg. 2. T-bana: Östermalmstorg. The ultimate budget place for dinner. Extensive buffet (6:30-9:30pm) 28kr. Obligatory coat and backpack check (10kr). Get discount tickets for all kinds of alcohol. Show up early. Dance off your dinner at the disco after 10:30pm (see **Entertainment,** p. 854).

Pauli's Café, Dramaten 2 trappen, Nybroplan (T-bana: Kungsträdgården). Fantastic café restaurant on the terrace-level, second floor of Dramaten, the National Theater. Daily summer lunch buffet of Swedish delicacies (11:30am-2:30pm) 65kr.

Lantis, Gulla Villau, Frescativ. 6. T-bana: Universitet. Student cafeteria housed in a Viking-inspired building. Filling and varied *dagens rätt* (42-48kr). Open Mon.-Fri. 8am-5pm, Sat. 10am-4pm.

Café Art, Västerlångg. 60, in Gamla Stan. Former medieval wine cellar; one of the oldest and hippest cafés in the old town. Sandwiches 35-42kr. Salads 20-40kr. Great Swedish pastries 10-22kr. Open daily 11am-11pm.

Café Gråmunken, Västerlångg. 18, in Gamla Stan. Funky, candle-lit vaulted atmosphere. Sandwiches 20-44kr. Salads 30-42kr. Open daily 9am-10pm.

Sandy's, Drottningg. 2. In the shadow of the *Riksdag* (Parliament). Wide selection of submarine and baguette sandwiches 34-45kr. Great coffee and chocolate chip cookie deal 10kr. Open Mon.-Fri. 10am-7pm, Sat.-Sun. 11am-5pm.

Herman's Hermitage, Stora Nyg. 11, in Gamla Stan; **Herman's Höjdare,** Fjällg. 23A, in Söder. Best deals in town for the budget vegan or vegetarian. Generous servings from your choice of green cuisine (55kr at lunch, 65kr at dinner). 10% *Let's Go* discount. Open Mon.-Fri. 11am-8pm, Sat. noon-8pm, Sun. 1-7pm.

SIGHTS

Towering above Stockholm's skyline is the regal **Stadshuset** (City Hall), Handverkarg. 1 (T-bana: Rådhuset). Emblematic of 1920s Swedish architecture and the symbol of Stockholm, its exterior tower provides the best aerial view of the city. The interior boasts municipal Viking chambers, the marbled **Blå Hallen** (Blue Hall), where the annual Nobel Prize Celebration is held, and the glittering mosaic-tiled **Gyllene Halen** (Gold Hall), where the Nobels, nobles, and other notables dance the rest of the night away. (Open for guided tours only: June.-Aug. 10am, 11am, noon, and 2pm; May-Oct. and April 10am and noon; Sept. 10am, noon, and 2pm. Tower open May-Sept. 10am-4:30pm. Tower 15kr, with tour 30kr.) To cool off, take the plunge into the water off Stadshuset lawn; the water downtown is clean enough to swim and even fish in.

Across Stadshuset is **Gamla Stan,** the medieval center of Stockholm, whose winding, catacombed streets on Västerlångg., Stora Nyg., and Österlångg. are packed with cafés, shops, and restaurants. Gamla Stan is home to the commanding **Kungliga Slottet,** winter home of the Swedish royal family, and site of the daily changing of the guard (Mon.-Sat. 12:15pm, Sun. 1:15pm; free). Tours of the Versailles-like interiors reveal the royal chambers. (Open June-Aug., daily 10am-4pm; May and Sept.-April Tues.-Sun. noon-3pm. 45kr, students 25kr.) The palace's **Skattkammaren** (Royal Treasury) houses the crown jewels, including the sword of Sweden's first king, the legendary Gustav Vasa, who established a unified Swedish kingdom in 1523 (same hours as palace; 40kr, students 25kr; combined ticket 80kr, students 50kr).

At the top of Gamla Stan's winding streets is **Stortorget Square,** where the annual **Julmarknad** (Christmas Fair) serves hot *glögg* (spiced wine) and Swedish handicrafts for your Christmas list. Behind the square towers the 700-year-old **Storkyrkan** (cathedral), site of royal weddings and home of the dramatic medieval sculpture of Stockholm's patron Staint Göran slaying the dragon (open mid-May to Aug. daily 9am-6pm; Sept.-April 9am-4pm; 10kr). For more info on Gamla Stan, visit **Turistbyrå,** in the *Passagen* (off-street gallery) at Västerlångg. 66 (tel. 20 00 68), or take one of their daily English **tours** which leave from behind the Storkyrkan (7pm; 40kr).

Stockholm's many museums are far from dusty collections of Scando-esoterica. On the lush island of Djurgården resides **Skansen,** an open-air museum with historical buildings from all over Sweden, and a great way to survey Sweden's history and architecture. There area also daily folk music concerts and folk dancing shows in colorful *folkdräkt* (folk costumes) as well as seasonal events such as the annual *Julmarknad* (Christmas Market), *Luciafest* (Dec. 13th; St. Lucia Day, the beginning of Swedish Christmas), and *Midsummmar* (June 23rd; Midsummer jubilation). From the corner of Drottningg. and Klarabergsg. in Sergels Torg square (T-bana: T-Centralen), take bus 44 or 47. (Open May daily 9am-8pm; June-Aug. daily 9am-10pm; Sept.-Oct. daily 9am-5pm; Nov.-Dec. daily 9am-6pm. 55kr). Across from Skansen, on Djurgården, the extraordinary **Vasa Museet** houses a mammoth wooden Vasa warship that sunk on its maiden voyage in 1628. (Open late Aug.-early June, Mon.-Tues. and Thurs.-Sun. 10am-5pm, Wed. 10am-8pm; late June to mid-Aug. 9:30am-7pm. 50kr, students 35kr.) Next door, the castle-like **Nordiska Museet** (Nordic Museum) presents an innovative exhibit on Swedish history from the Viking age to the modern era of Volvo, ABBA.

SWEDEN

and Electrolux. (Open June-Aug., Tues. 11am-9pm, Wed.-Fri. 11am-5pm, Sat.-Sun. 10am-5pm; Sept.-May Tues.-Wed. and Fri-Sun. 11am-5pm, Thurs. 11am-9pm. 60kr, students 30kr.) The **National Museet,** Blarieholmskajen (T-bana: Kungsträdgården), houses an impressive collection of paintings and sculpture with some of Sweden's most famous works, including Carl Larsson's 19th-century Nationalist Viking murals and paintings by Anders Zorn, Prins Eugen, Eugen Jansson, and Edvard Munch. (Open May-June 5th Tues. 11am-8pm, Wed.-Sun. 11am-5pm; June 6th-May, Tues. and Thurs. 11am-8pm, Wed. and Fri.-Sun. 11am-5pm. 60kr, students 30kr.) Just across the Skeppsholmsbron on Skeppsholmen and behind the af Chapman 1888 frigate youth hostel is the hip **Moderna Museet,** whose permanent collection includes a fabulous Andy Warhol *Marilyn* series. In February 1998 the museum will open a completely new space on the island of Skeppsholmen. (New hours may vary slightly. Open Tues.-Thurs. 11am-7pm, Fri.-Sun. 11am-5pm. 60kr, students 30kr.) Former home of 19th-century painter Prince Eugen, the **Prins Eugens Waldemarsudde** is now a museum with more Larssons, Janssons, Zorns, and of course, Eugens. (Open Sept.-May Tues.-Sun. 11am-4pm; June-Aug., Tues. and Thurs. 11am-8pm, Wed. and Fri.-Sun. 11am-5pm. 50kr, students 30kr.) For literary pilgrims, the **Strindbergsmuseet,** Drottningg. 85 (T-bana: Rådmang.), sponsors exhibitions, films, and lectures in the dramatist August Strindberg's (1908-1912) home (open Tues.-Fri. 11am-4pm, Sat.-Sun. noon-4pm; 30kr, students 20kr).

ENTERTAINMENT

For up-to-date info on the latest events, check out *Stockholm this Week, N&D* (Night and Day), or *Dagens Nyheter*'s weekly Swedish-language supplement, *DN Påstan* (all free at the tourist office). **Östermalm** is home to most of Stockholm's straight nightlife, while **Södermalm** hosts a wide selection of queer cafés, bars, clubs, and *restaux.* See the informative monthly *QX (Queer Extra)* for a last-minute guide to gay entertainment and nightlife. The national theater, **Dramaten,** Nybroplan (tel. 667 0680), stages Swedish- and English-language performances of Strindberg and other Scandinavian and international playwrights (80-350kr), while the **Operan** (tel. 24 82 40) offers opera and ballet (70-350kr). Ask for the cheaper student and rush seats. The **Konserthuset** at Hötorget (tel. 10 21 10) features classical music concerts from the Stockholm Philharmoniker (symphony orchestra), while concerts are held at the **Globen** arena (tel. 60 034 00; 50-300kr). Pop music venues include **Skansen** (tel. 57 89 00 05) and the stage at **Gröna Lund** (tel. 670 76 00), Djurgården's huge outdoor *Tivoli* amusement park. (Open late April-early Sept., Sun. noon-10pm, Mon. noon-11pm, Tues.-Sat. noon-midnight. 40kr for park. 125-300kr for concert tickets.) Catch a film at the 18-theater **Sergel Filmstaden** (tel. 789 60 60) on Hötorget (70kr), or for smaller art-house releases, head to the **Röda Lilla Kvarn** cinema, Biblioteksg. 5 (tel. 789 60 60; T-bana: Östermalmtorget, exit "Stureplan").

Stockholm's festivals include: the world-class **Jazz and Blues Festsival** at Skansen (early July); the **Stockholm Water Festival,** a week-long aqua party and carnival (mid-August; tel. 10 23 03); the two-week **Strindberg Festival** (early Sept.; tel. 34 14 01); the annual gay pride **Homo Festival** (late July; tel. 736 02 10); and the annual Lollopalooza-inspired 3-day **Lollipop Music Festival** (late July), which draws international stars such as David Bowie, De La Sol, Primal Scream, and Jamiroquai (tel. 457 02 20; http://www.lollipop.se). Skansen and Gamla Stan also host celebrations for many national holidays, including Nobel Dagen (Dec. 10), St. Lucia Dagen (Dec. 13), Christmas, Midsummer (June 20), and Flag Day (June 6).

Alcohol is very expensive (45-55kr per beer) but available at one of the ubiquitous **Systembolaget** state liquor stores (open Mon.-Fri. 9am-5pm).

Styrecompagniet, Stureg. 4. T-bana: Östermalmstorg. In the center of Stureplan square, the heart of Östermalm's nightlife. Ultra-chic 3-level restaurant, bar, and disco. Cover 50kr. Open Mon.-Wed. noon-midnight, Thurs.-Sat. noon-5am.

Stockholm: Cultural Capital of Europe 1998

With over 600 programs and events, Stockholm will reign in 1998 as Europe's Cultural Capital. Some of the special events on the cultural itinerary include **Art-Genda,** a celebration of young new artists, musicians, actors, and dancers, **Järgardes Nya Rum,** a multi-venue highlight of modern and contemporary art, and **Diva '98,** a series of saucy concerts and performances. For info on the celebrations, contact **Stockholm-Europas Kulturhuvudstad '98,** Box 163 98, 10327 Stockholm (tel. 698 1998; fax 698 1999; email info@kultur98.stockhom.se; www.kultur98.stockholm.se). The Cultural Capital divas will be joined by thousands of Europe's other Dancing Queens during **EuroPride '98,** the largest Gay and Lesbian PrideFest in the world (July 18-26). The separately organized festival will culminate in a Pride Parade through Stockholm. For more info, contact the **EuroPride office**, box 3444, S-103 69 Stockholm (tel. 33 59 55; fax 30 47 30; email europride98@bahnhof.se; http://www.europride98.se).

Riche, Birger jarlsg. 4. T-bana: Östermalmsturg. A Stockholm institution since 1893. Fortunately, you don't need to be *riche* to attend. Beer 48kr. Cover Fri.-Sat. 40kr. Open Mon.-Thurs. noon-2am, Fri.-Sun. noon-5am.

Collage, Smålandsg. T-bana: Östermalmstorg. Great dance floor with techno-pop. Cover Fri.-Sat. 30kr. Disco open Mon.-Thurs. 10:30-3am, Fri.-Sun. 10:30-5am.

Fasching, Kungsg. 3. T-bana: T-Centralen. One of the best jazz clubs in Europe. Live jazz, Latin, blues, funk, fusion, and world music from Swedish and international groups in a funky loft-like space with a refreshingly non-neon, non-laser, non-strobe light dance floor. Leave your neon club-kid synthetics at home and think black. Cover 60kr. Open Mon.-Thurs. and Sun. 8pm-2am, Fri.-Sat. 8pm-5am.

Berns, Berzelii Park. T-bana: Östermalmstorg or Kungsträdgården. Bar-restaurant (and now disco) that August Strindberg and other Swedish literati frequented. Today, the glitterati dance after surviving the long line on weekends. Cover Wed.-Sat. 70kr. Open Mon.-Tues. 11am-1am, Wed.-Thurs. 11am-3am, Fri.-Sat. 11am-4am.

Patricia, Stadsgården. T-bana: Slussen. A floating bar-restaurant-nightclub aboard a former luxury yacht. Fantastic techno disco below decks, and open-air bars on deck. Sunday is the popular queer night. Cover 50kr. Open Wed.-Sun. 7pm-5am.

Baren 2 Lika, Wollmar Yxkullsg. 7. T-bana: Mariatorget. Across from the T-bana entrance. Popular gay bar. No cover. Open daily 8pm-1am.

Bangcock, in the Chinateaterns Foajé, Berzeliiparken next to Berns. T-bana: Kungsträdgården. More than just some Orientalist fantasy, Bangcock is currently the hottest gay club in Stockholm. Cover 50kr. Open Fri.-Sat. 10pm-5am.

Squeeze, St. Eriksplan 9. T-bana: St. Eriksplan. New gay club on Sat. nights. Dancing on two floors and a young, beautiful crowd. Cover 40kr. Open Sat. 10pm-3am.

Bitch Girl Club Stockholm's rotating lesbian club with a mixed crowd of lipstick lesbians and baby butch women with attitude. Call **Lesbisk Nu** (Föreningen LN), Kocksg. 28 (tel. 641 86 16) in Södermalm for more information.

SWEDEN

■ Near Stockholm

The peninsulas and islands of Stockholm's surrounding *skärgård* (Share-gourd; archipelago) offer myriad opportunities to beach, swim, sail, fish, and explore. To the west, **Björkö** was a Viking Age trade center whose capital, Birka, had the first Sweden encounter with Christianity on the arrival of the German missionary Ansgar in 829. Today you can visit the excavation sites, burial mounds, and a Viking museum. **Strömma Kanalbolaget ferries** (tel. 23 33 75), leave from Stadshusbron near the Stadshuset at 10am and return at 3:45pm (round-trip 195kr). Built by King Gustav Vasa, **Vaxholm**'s mighty 16th-century fortress and museum are closer to central Stockholm; contact Strömma Kanalbolaget or **Waxholmsbolaget** (tel. 679 58 30) about trips out (1½hr., round-trip 90kr) from both ferries terminals on Strömkajen on Nybroplan in central Stockholm. Contact Waxholmsbolaget or Strömma Kanalbolaget for more info on the islands of the **outer skärgård.** The Waxholmsbolaget **Båtluffarkortet** card (250kr) pays for 16 days of sailings around the archipelago.

Just 45 minutes away by ferry, the Swedish royal family makes their summer home at the exquisite Versailles-inspired palace of **Drottningholm.** Lush Baroque gardens and extravagant Rococo interiors echo with the ghosts of elegant Drottning (Queen) Larisa Ulrika, for whom the palace was a wedding gift. Catch the free half-hourly English tour of the palace's **theater** and watch the original stage machinery produce thunderstorm effects (tel. 759 04 06). Enjoy a ballet or opera for 85-410kr (tel. 660 82 25). **Kina Slott,** Drottningholm's Chinese pavilion, was an 18th-century royal summer cottage. (Palace open May daily 11am-4:30pm; June-Aug. daily 10am-4:30pm, Sept. daily noon-3:30pm. 40kr, students 20kr. Theater tours 40kr, students 10kr. Kina Slott open May-Aug. daily 11am-4:30pm; Sept. noon-3:30pm; Oct. 1-3:30pm. 40kr, students 200kr.) Get to Drottningholm via hourly **Strömma Kanalbolaget ferries** (May-Sept. daily 10am-6pm) from Stadshusbron (round-trip 70kr), or on far less palatial **buses** 301-323 from T-bana: Brommaplan.

Once the home of Swedish sculptor Carl Milles, **Millesgården** is now a beautiful, marble-facaded museum nestled in the suburb of **Lidingö,** with an extensive collection of classical sculpture from Rome, Greece, and medieval Europe. The most intriguing works, however, are Milles' own, perched on garden terraces throughout the grounds. (Open May-Sept. daily 10am-5pm; Oct.-April Tues.-Sun. noon-4pm. 50kr, students and seniors 35kr.) Take T-bana to "Ropsten" (14kr) and then bus 201, 202, 204, 205, 206, or 212 (21kr) to "Torsviks" and follow the signs.

Built in 1380 on Lake Mälarens by the Lord High Chancellor Bo Jonsson Grip, **Gripsholm Castle** majestically looms over the bucolic hamlet of **Mariefred.** The interior of the castle is adorned with portraits and its original Renaissance wall paintings and furniture. (Open May-Aug. daily 10am-8pm; Sept. Tues.-Sat. 10am-3pm; Oct.-April Sat.-Sun. noon-3pm. 40kr, students 20kr.) A short walk from the castle is the old royal barn, now a print-making workshop, **Grafikeus Hus** (open daily 11am-5pm; 40kr, students 20kr). Take the train to Läggesta, then hop on bus 303 (15kr) to Mariefred (1hr. total). Ask the driver to drop you off at the castle. The M/S Mariefred steamboat (tel. (0152) 296 86; fax 296 85), from Klara Mälarstrand in Stockholm, also goes to Mariefred (mid-June to mid-Aug. 10am, 3hr., 140kr).

GOTLAND

Three hundred kilometers from Stockholm, Gotland's green meadows, light-house bedecked cliffs, white-sand beaches, and cobble-stoned, medieval capital, **Visby,** make this one of the most popular summer destinations for vacationing Swedes. First a Viking, and then Hanseatic trading center, Visby now hosts the annual **Medieval Festival** every August. Locals don authentic Dark Age (and we don't mean the seventies) fashions, Strandg. transforms into a medieval market, and Danish king Valdemar Atterdag's invasion of Visby and a dramatic jousting tournament are re-enacted.

All year long, **Visby's** ancient wall—the oldest medieval monument in Scandinavia—encloses winding streets, ruined churches, and a wealth of petite squares and rose gardens. At the **Gotlands Fornsal** history museum, Strandg. 14, you'll discover that in 1361 this wall sheltered the town's privileged merchants while peasants were massacred outside the gates. Exhibits cover the Viking Age, ancient burial rituals, and the town's 15th-century sewage system. (Open mid-May to Aug. daily 11am-6pm; Sept. to mid-May Tues.-Sun. noon-4pm. 30kr, students 20kr.)

Examine the mystical monoliths on **Fårö,** off the northern tip of Gotland (bus 21; 2hr.), the blazing beaches of **Tofta**, about 15km south of Visby (bus 31, 21 min.), or the calcified cliffs of **Hoburgen** at the island's southernmost tip (bus 11, 2½hr.). **Cycling** is the best way to explore Gotland's flat terrain with its extensive paths and bike-friendly motorways. Rent wheels at **O'Hoj Cykeluthyrning,** across the street from the ferry terminal. (55-100kr per day, 275-500kr per week; open daily 7am-6pm). Contact the Turistcenter (see below) for more info on biking. Do not be alarmed if you see men and women in military fatigues marching by; part of northern Gotland is a military area closed to the public.

Practical Information, Accommodations, and Food **Gotlandslinjen ferries** sail to Visby from Nynäshamn (south of Stockholm, 5-6hr.) or Oskarshamn (north of Kalmar, 4-6hr.). Fares are highest on weekends (175kr one-way) and cheapest during the week (135kr, students 88kr). During the winter (Oct.-May) there is one ferry per day, in summer (June-Sept.), 2 per day. A Scanrail earns 50% off. Nynäshamn is linked to Stockholm by **bus** from Cityterminalen (1hr.,60kr) and by *pendeltåg* (commuter train) from Centralstation (1hr., 60kr; *rabattkuponger* valid). Oskarshamn is linked to Kalmar by bus (1½hr., 75kr). To book ferry transport or to get regional tourist info in Stockholm, contact Gotland's satellite tourist center, **Gotland City,** Kungsg. 57A (tel. (08) 23 61 70, fax 411 19 65; open Mon.-Fri. 9:30am-6pm, Sat. 10am-2pm). Once you reach Gotland, find the helpful **tourist office,** Hamng. 4 (tel. (0498) 20 17 00; fax 20 17 17), a 10-minute walk left from the ferry terminal. (Open June-Aug. Mon.-Fri. 7am-7pm, Sat.-Sun. 7am-6pm; March-April Mon.-Fri. 10am-noon and 1-3pm; May Mon.-Fri. 8am-5pm, Sat.-Sun. 10am-4pm.) The office changes money before and after banking hours and offers detailed maps of Gotland and Visby (20-50kr) and the helpful *Gotlands Guiden* (free). They also give guided tours of Visby (80kr) and Fåro (200kr). Pick up a bus timetable at the ferry terminal or at the Visby bus station, Kung Magnusväg 1 (tel. (0498) 21 41 12).

Gotlands Turistcenter, Korsg. 2 (tel. (0498) 27 90 95; fax 21 29 20) will help you find a room. (Open May-Sept. Mon.-Fri. 9am-6pm, Sat.-Sun. 10am-6pm; Oct.-April Mon.-Fri. 9am-5pm.) Private rooms inside Visby's walls cost 285kr for singles and 425kr for doubles (outside the city walls 240kr and 380kr). The more affordable **STF Vandrarhem Visby** is at Gamla A7 området (tel. (0498) 26 98 42; fax 20 35 51). From the bus station, head east along the southern edge of the walled sports complex to Artillerig.; the hostel is on the right. (15min. Reception open daily 8-10am and 5-8pm. 100kr. Breakfast 45kr. Open early June-early Aug. Book ahead.) For a more rural setting, try **Västerhejde Vandrarhem,** 5km south of the center (tel. (0498) 26 49 95; fax 29 62 60); take bus 31 from the bus station, and ask the bus driver to drop you off (reception open 24hr.; 100kr; breakfast 45kr; kitchen, TV room, cafeteria). More centrally located, the **Soldathemmet Wisborg** hostel, Längs väg 2 (tel. (0498) 29 55 83; fax 27 15 02), offers a more expensive, but affordable alternative (reception open 8:30am-3:30pm; 130kr). **Campgrounds** abound on Gotland. **Kneippbyns Campingplats** (tel. (0498) 26 43 65; fax 29 62 95), 4km south of Visby, the home of Pippi Longstocking's Villa Villekulla, mini-golf, and a water park, dips its toes in the sea and is accessible by tourist buses from the center (95kr per tent; 2- to 4-bed cabins with breakfast 250kr per person; open May-Sept.).

If you'd like to pack a picnic lunch for the beach or for a bike-tour, head to the **Rimi supermarket,** Stenkumlav. 36 (open daily 8am-10pm). **Trossen,** Skeppsbron 14, offers large pasta (65-120kr) and Gotländska fish specialities (50-146kr), right on the marina (open daily 11:30am-1am). **Snäck!,** Gustavsviksv., is a combo lounge-nightclub that offers live bands (tickets 185kr) and a disco (open Thurs.-Sun. 8pm-2am). Take one of the frequent and free shuttle buses from Östercentrum.

SOUTHERN SWEDEN

Islands and skerries line both the east and west coasts of Sweden; the southwest **Småland** coastline, between Västervik and Kalmar, is particularly scenic, while the western **Halland** coast between Gothenburg and Helsingborg is scattered with small resort towns like **Båstad, Falkenberg,** and **Varberg,** whose beaches entice many sun-worshipping Swedes. Inland, clear lakes and limitless woods abound. The island of **Öland,** accessible from Kalmar via Europe's longest bridge, supports a nature reserve and has its share of archaeological sites. **Skåne** (the stub of Sweden across from Copenhagen) and **Blekinge** (around Karlskrona) are Sweden's southernmost provinces; Blekinge is known as Sweden's garden and Skåne as its breadbasket. *Pågatågen* (local trains, railpasses valid) run to most of Skåne (tel. (020) 61 61 61).

From **Helsingborg** in northern Skåne, trains bound for Copenhagen cross on ferries to Helsingør in Denmark; reach Helsingborg by SJ train or by *pågatåg* (from Malmö or Lund 65kr). **Trelleborg,** in southern Skåne, sees several ferries per day off to Saßnitz (railpasses valid) and Travemünde in Germany; take an SJ train or bus from Malmö (48kr). From **Ystad,** also in southern Skåne, ferries serve Bornholm. Reach Ystad by *pågatåg* (from Malmö 63kr).

Kalmar

Nesting on the deep blue Baltic waters, Kalmar is home to the stunning 12th- to 14th-century castle **Kalmar Slott,** the site of the inception of 1397 Kalmar Union, an attempt to unite the kingdoms of Denmark, Norway, Sweden, and Finland. (Open April-May and Sept. daily 10am-4pm; June-Aug. daily 10am-6pm; Oct.-March Sat.-Sun. 10am-4pm. 60kr, students 30kr.) The equally impressive **Kalmar Domkyrka,** in the center of town on Stortorget, enjoys all the splendor of a major cathedral, but, alas, is *sans* bishop (open daily 9am-6pm; free organ concerts Wed. at noon). The **Kalmar Läns Museum,** Skeppsbrog. 51, houses the salvaged wreckage of the 17th-century warship, **Krohan,** which sank during the 1676 Battle of Öland against the Danish (open June-Aug. daily 10am-6pm; Sept.-May 10am-4pm; 40kr). The **Kalmar Canstmuseum,** Slottsv. 1D, houses a collection of Scandinavian art with an emphasis on local masters (open Mon.-Fri. 10am-5pm, Sat.-Sun. noon-5pm; 30kr). In the nearby towns, collectively dubbed **Glasriket** (Kingdom of Crystal), exquisite hand-blown crystal, such as **Orreforas** (tel. (0481) 341 95) and **Kosta Boda** (tel. (0481) 240 30), are produced by the artisans depicted in *My Life as a Dog.* Take bus 138 (1hr., 70kr) from Kalmar's train station (both open Mon.-Fri. 9am-6pm, Sat. 10am-4pm).

Kalmar's **train station** and **bus terminal** lie just south of town, across the bay from the castle. From the train station, go right on Stationsg. and at the small park make a left onto Ölandsg. to reach the helpful **tourist office,** Larmg. 6 (tel. (0480) 153 50; fax 174 53). They provide free maps and book private rooms (190kr. Open Jan.-April Mon.-Fri. 9am-5pm; May and Sept. Mon.-Fri. 9am-5pm, Sat. 10am-1pm; June-Aug. Mon.-Fri. 9am-8pm, Sat. 9am-5pm, Sun. 1-6pm.) Rent **bikes** at **Team Sportia,** Södrav. 2 (40kr per day; open Mon.-Fri. 10am-4pm, Sat. noon-3pm). To get to the **Kalmar Vandrarhem (HI),** Rappeg. 1 (tel. (0480) 129 28; fax 882 93), on the island of Angö, walk from the tourist office north on Lamng., go right on Fiskareg. until it becomes Angöleden; cross the bridge and cruise—the hostel is on the right (reception open daily 7:30-10:30am and 4:30-9pm; 120kr). **Stensö Camping** (tel. (0480) 888 03), 2km south of Kalmar, has a grocery (100kr; open May-Aug.). Restaurants cluster around Larmorget. Do the Copacabana thing at the nightclub **Havanna,** Gästhamnen (open Thurs.-Sat. 8pm-2am, Sun. 8pm-midnight).

In view of Kalmar's coast, the vacation island of **Öland** stretches over 100km of green fields, white sand beaches, and lakes. The royal family roosts here on holiday, and Crown Princess Victoria's birthday, **Victoriadagen** (July 14), is celebrated island-wide. Commoners flock to the beaches of **Löttorp** and **Böda** in the north and **Grönhögen** and **Ottenby** in the south. The best way to get to Öland from Kalmar is to bicycle, but **Kalmar Läns Trafik buses** 101 and 105 leave from in front of the train station (60-100kr). Öland's **tourist office** (tel. (0485) 386 21) is in Färjestaden. If you stay here, **Vandrarhem Borgholm,** Reosenfors (tel. (0485) 107 56), and **Vandrarhem Böda** on Melböda in Löttorp (tel. (0485) 220 38) await.

Malmö

Malmö (mahl-MER), the country's third-largest city, is often used a gateway through which travelers pass without pause, but Malmö, with its beautiful squares **Stortorget** and **Lilla Torg,** has its attractions. Both the **Rooseum,** Gasverksg. 22 (30kr), and the **Malmö Konsthall,** St. Johannesg. 7 (free), house modern art exhibits. The **Form**

Design Center, in an old yellow building at Lilla Torg 9, highlights the Swedish design work that has become famous through IKEA, Volvo, Saab, and Electrolux (open Tues.-Fri. 11am-5pm, Sat. 10am-4pm; free). In Malmö's west end, the green **Slottsparken** (Castle Park) is home to **Malmöhus,** a collection of museums housed in the castle at the park's center (open daily 10am-4pm; 40kr).

The **train station** and **harbor** lie just north of the Old Town. Pilen (tel. (040) 23 44 11) has **ferry** service to Copenhagen (45min., 30-50kr); **trains** arrive from Gothenburg (318kr) and Stockholm (494kr). The **tourist office** in the train station has free maps and the useful *Malmö this Month.* (Open June-Aug. Mon.-Fri. 9am-7pm, Sat. 10am-2pm, Sun. 10am-2pm; Jan.-May and Sept.-Dec. Mon.-Fri. 9am-5pm, Sat. 10am-2pm.) Exchange money and cash traveler's checks at **Forex,** next to the tourist office (open daily 8am-9pm). **Fridhem Cykelaffär,** Tessinsväg 13 (tel. (040) 26 03 35), offers affordable bike rental (45kr per day; open daily 9am-noon and 1-6pm).

From the train station or boat terminal, cross Mälarbran bridge and take a right on Västerg. to the hostel **City Vandrarhem,** Västerg. 9. (Tel./fax (040) 23 56 40. Reception open 10-11am and 5pm-midnight. 150kr. Open June-Aug.) The **KFUM Interpoint Malmö,** Betaniaplan 4 (tel. (040) 769 30), is a comfortable summer hostel. Walk 15 minutes from the station or take bus 11 to the "Kanserthuset" (reception open 8am-midnight; 65kr; open June-Aug.). The **HI hostel,** Södergården, Backav. 18 (tel. (040) 822 20; fax (040) 51 06 59), offers clean, cheap rooms; take bus 21A to Vandrarhemmet, cross the main street, and follow the youth hostel signs. (Reception open daily 8-10am and 4-8pm. 150kr, nonmembers 180kr. Open mid-Jan. to mid-Dec.) **Sibbarp Camping,** Strandg. 101 (tel. (040) 15 51 65; fax 15 97 77), is at the end of bus route 12B (tents 100kr).

While Lilla Torg is filled with trendy cafés, your wallet will thank you for feasting at **Café Siesta,** Hjorttackeg. 1, on soups (45kr) and pasta (69kr; open Mon.-Fri. 10am-midnight, Sun. noon-midnight). A very hip crowd gets interactive at the **Cyberspace C@fé,** Engelbrecksg. 13 (30min. for 20kr; open daily 10am-10pm). **Spår 14,** in the station, is a lively bar all week and a disco on the weekends, while **Indigo,** Monbijoug. 15, hosts a hopping gay and lesbian café and disco. The **Malmö Festival,** held every year in late August sponsors a week of international cultural events. For more info call (040) 34 10 00 or check their web site at http://www.malmo.se.

Lund

What Oxford and Cambridge are to England, Uppsala and Lund are to Sweden. Lund University's antagonism with its scholarly northern neighbors in Uppsala has inspired countless pranks, drag shows, and drinkfests in Lund's bright streets. To see the last 400 years of Lund's antics, check out the comical **Studentmuseet Arkivet,** Sandg. 2 (open Tues. 4-8pm, Wed. 4-6pm; 20kr). For more information on student life contact **Student Info** on the ground floor of the student union (*akademiska föreningen* or AF; Sept.-May Mon.-Fri. 10am-4pm). The university campus is north of the town's ancient **cathedral,** an impressive 900-year-old remnant of the time when Lund was the religious epicenter of Scandinavia. (Open Mon.-Tues. and Fri. 8am-6pm, Wed.-Thurs. 8am-7pm, Sat. 10am-5pm, Sun. 10am-6pm. Guided English tours Mon.-Sat. 3pm. Free organ concerts Sun. 10am.) **Kulturen,** Tegnérplatsen, is an open-air museum with 17th- and 18th- century Swedish houses and history displays. (Open mid-Aug. to mid-June daily 11am-5pm; mid-June to mid-Aug. daily 11am-9pm. 40kr.)

Most intercity **SJ trains** from Malmö stop at Lund; the cities are also connected by *pågatågen* (15min., 30kr, railpasses valid). Lund's **tourist office,** Kyrkog. 11 (tel. (046) 35 50 40; fax 12 59 63), near the cathedral, books rooms. (130-200kr, 50kr fee. Open June-Aug. Mon.-Fri. 10am-6pm, Sat.-Sun. 10am-2pm; Sept. and May Mon.-Fri. 10am-5pm, Sat. 10am-2pm; Oct.-April Mon.-Fri. 10am-5pm.) Rest your tired limbs at the delightful **HI Hostel Tåget** (The Train), Vävareg. 22 (tel. (046) 14 28 20; fax 32 05 68), with authentic sleeping cars from the 1940s. Follow the signs from the central station. (Reception open daily 8-10am and 5-8pm. 100kr, nonmembers 140kr. Open Jan. to mid-Dec.) If you've missed the train, **Lastrada Vandrarhem,** Brunnhögsv. (tel.

(046) 32 32 51; fax 104 27) has reserve beds (reception open daily 8-10am and 5-8pm; 130kr; open June-Aug.). To pitch your tent, take bus 1 ("Klostergården") and ask to be let off at **Källby Camping** (tel. (046) 35 51 88; 40kr; open mid-June to Aug.).

Mårtenstorget features a fresh fruit and vegetable **market** (open Mon.-Sat. 7am-2:30pm); for more standard groceries, try the **Vivo Mat,** Stora Söderg. (open Mon.-Fri. 9am-7pm, Sat. 9am-4pm, Sun. 9am-5pm). **Govindas,** Bredg. 28, has a variety of veggie and vegan options (30-65kr; open Mon.-Thurs. 11:30am-5pm, Fri.-Sat. 11:30am-3pm). The tragically hip **Stortorget Bar, Café, och Restaurant,** Stortorget 1, is the place to chill on weekend nights. (*Dagens rätt* 54kr;pasta 50kr. Open Mon. 10am-midnight, Tues.-Thurs. 10am-1am, Fri.-Sat. 10am-2am, Sun. 10am-11pm.)

Varberg

Located in Halland county between Gothenburg and Malmö, coastal Varberg beckons with expansive white sand beaches and a spectacular fortress. The **Varberg Fortress** looks out onto the sky-blue waters of the Kattegatt. Although you can't explore the castle on your own, tours are offered (open daily Sept.-May 10am-5pm; June-Aug. daily 10am-7pm; 20kr, children 5kr). In the second week of August, the fortress hosts a **Medieval festival.** Get to the gorgeous **beaches** on the island of Getterön or the southern Apelviken peninsula by peddling on a **bike** rented from **Cykel och Barnvagnhuset,** Lindbersv. 2 (open Mon.-Fri. 11am-6pm, Sat. noon-4pm; 70kr per day).

Trains arrive from Gothenburg (1hr., 90kr, under 25 65kr) and from Malmö (3hr., 290kr, under 25 205kr). The **tourist office,** in Brunnsparken (tel. (0340) 887 70; fax 61 11 95), offers maps of the Halland region (30kr), an invaluable town guide, and a guide detailing handicap accessibility. It also books rooms in private homes. (Singles 140kr, doubles 120kr per person; 25kr fee. Open Mon.-Sat. 9am-7pm, Sun. 3-7pm; early June and late August, Mon.-Fri. 9am-6pm, Sat. 10am-3pm; April-May and Sept. Mon.-Fri. 9am-5pm, Sat. 10am-1pm; in winter Mon.-Fri. 9am-5pm.)

The bright rooms of **Varbergs Fästning Vandrarhem,** inside the fortress itself (tel. (0340) 887 88) will make you forget it was used as the **Crown Jail** from 1852-1931. Being locked up was never this fun (unless you're into that), nor this popular; book ahead (reception open daily 8-10am and 5-9pm; 125kr; open June-Aug.). If you're acquitted, there's usually room at **Skeppsgårdens Vanrarhem,** Krabbesväg (tel. (0340) 130 35; fax 103 95), in the center of town (open daily 8am-noon and 3-7pm; 150kr, includes breakfast). Located on a small bay, **Apelvikens Camping** (tel. (0340) 141 78; fax 104 22) is a 3km waterfront bike ride away, or take bus 8 to the end of the line and follow the signs (140kr per day, off-season 113kr; open late April to mid-Sept.). The **Mignan Café,** Drottningg. 23, and **Majas Café** and **Nyfiken,** on Kungsg., all offer fantastic breakfasts (around 40kr) and daily lunch specials (around 47kr). **Sophia och Uscars** and their second floor disco **Gustavs,** Norrg. 16, offer live jazz, rock, and stand-up comedy as well as dancing (open Thurs.-Sun. 9pm-2am).

Gothenburg (Göteborg)

Sweden's second-largest city, Gothenburg, or Göteborg (YUH-ta-boy), dominates the west coast. Identifying more with their closer northern neighbor Oslo, *Göteborgare* refer contemptuously to Stockholmers as *Nollåttor* (zero-eights) after Stockholm's area code, and when asked why there are street-level trams as opposed to Stockholm's underground subway, Göteborgare explain, "because we have nothing to hide." In fact, Gothenburg has a great deal to show, including an exciting port, a vibrant university, a huge theater scene, and the largest art museum in Scandinavia.

Standing at the very top of **Kungsportsavenyn,** Gothenburg's main avenue, which extends from Kungsportsplats and the tourist office all the way up to Götaplatsen, the regal **Konstmuseet** is flanked by the **Stadstatern** and the **Konserthuset**. At the center of Götaplatsen, in front of the museum, theater, and concert hall is Carl Milles' famous **sculpture-fountain** of Poseidon. Gothenburg's more conservative citizens were uncomfortable with Milles's original design, which featured a more virile Poseidon wielding his member like a mighty trident. Milles compromised by replacing the trident with a large fish, squirming out of Posiedon's hand. The **Konstmuseet** houses the largest collection of Nordic art in Scandinavia. (Open May-Aug. Mon.-Fri., 11am-4pm, Sat.-Sun. 11am-5pm; Sept.-April closed Mon. 35kr.)

The **Stadsteatern** (tel. (031) 81 99 60) and the **Konserthuset** (tel. (031) 16 70 00) host a full schedule of theater, musicals, classical, and popular concerts (tickets 50-250kr). Check the tourist office's free *What's on in Göteborg* for events. The **Göteborgs Operan,** Lilla Bommen (tel. tickets (031) 13 13 00; tours 10 80 50), emulates a ship at full mast. Even for the opera-allergic, this trademark building is worth a look on your way to the **Göteborg Maritime Centrum,** which features a large number of docked ships and sailing vessels which you can board and tour. (Open April to mid-Sept. Mon.-Fri. 9am-4pm, Sat.-Sun. 11am-5pm; late Sept.-March closed Mon. 35kr.) For vehicles of another ilk, stop at the **Volvo Museum,** on Götaverken in nearby Arendal, which houses some of Volvo's most famous designs from 1927 to 1997. From Eketräg., take bus 28 ("Sörred") and get off at Götaverken Arendal, then follow the signs (open Tues.-Fri. 10am-5pm, Sat. 11am-4pm; 30kr).

Göteborgs Skärgård (Archipelago) is a summer paradise for beach-goers and sailors. Pick up a free copy of the *Skärgårds Guiden* at the tourist office. For a simple one-day excursion to the Skärgården, **Vrångö** island offers a secluded and serene beach; take tram 4 to Saltholmen, then a ferry to the island. Call **Styrsöbolaget Ferry Line** (tel. (031) 69 64 00) for info. To rise above it all, climb the bell tower of **Masthuggskyrkan,** a 20th-century church with the best view of the city. (Bus 85 from Lilla Torget, or tram 4 to Fjällg. Open Mon.-Fri. 9am-3pm, Sat. 9:30am-1:30pm.)

Practical Information, Accommodations, and Food The main **tourist office,** Kungsportsplatsen (tel. (031) 10 07 40; fax 13 21 84; http://www.gbg-co.se), provides free maps, copies of the *Göteborg Guide* and *What's on in Göteborg,* and **Göteborg Cards,** which grant free public transportation and free entry or discounts for many attractions (1 day 125kr, 2 days 225kr, 3 days 275kr). Exit right from the train station, cross Drottningtarget to Norra Hamng., take a left on Östra Hamng. to Kungsportsplatsen. (Open late June-early Aug. daily 9am-8pm; early June and late Aug. 9am-6pm; May Mon.-Fri. 9am-6pm, Sat.-Sun. 10am-2pm; Jan.-April and Sept.-Dec. Mon.-Fri. 9am-5pm, Sat. 10am-2pm.) **Currency exchange** is available at the Forex shops at Centralstation (20kr commission per traveler's check, 30kr for cash; open daily 8am-9pm). Financial services are also available at **American Express,** c/o Ticket Östra Hamng. 35 (tel. (031) 13 07 12; open Mon.-Fri. 10am-6pm).

Trains arrive at Centralstation on their way to Oslo (5hr., 428kr, under 25 305kr), Stockholm (3½-5hr., 505kr, under 25 355kr), and Malmö (3½hr., 395kr, under 25 275kr). The station also offers **lockers** (20kr for 24hr.) and **showers** (25kr; open Mon.-Sat. 7am-9pm, Sun. 8am-9pm). **Stena Line ferries** (tel. (031) 704 00 00; fax 85 85 95) sail to Frederikshavn, Denmark (3hr.) and to Kiel, Germany (14hr.). **SeaCat hydrofoils** (tel. (031) 775 08 00; fax 12 60 90) whisk to Frederikshavn (1¾hr., 60-100kr). **Scandinavian Seaways** (tel. (031) 65 06 66) **ships** sail to Newcastle, England (22hr.; 1095kr, mid-June to early Aug.), Harwich, England (23hr., 495-995kr), and Copenhagen (1 per week, 14hr., 95kr). Gothenburg is a compact city, but the weary may ride **Stadstrafiken trams** and **buses** (16kr; one-day pass 40kr).

Docked among the ships of the Maritime Museum and in view of the opera house is the **M/S Seaside** (tel. (031) 10 59 70), a floating youth hostel centrally located at Packhuskajen harbor, with newly renovated cabins in a former Norwegian motorship well worth the 100kr—if you don't get seasick. (Reception open daily 8am-11pm. Private cabins 175kr; 10-bed dorms 100kr. Check-in 4pm-9pm. No curfew or phone reservations.) From the train station, take tram 5 to Lilla Bommen and then walk left along the pier. The landlocked **Masthuggs Terrassens Vandrarhjem** (tel. (031) 42 48 20) is a new hostel located minutes from the main ferry terminal. From the train station, take tram 3 or 4 to Masthuggstorget and then the lift (reception open 8-10am and 5-8pm; 125kr). Farther inland resides the new **City Vandrarhem,** Södrav. 60 (tel. (031) 20 89 77). Take tram 4 or 5 to Korsv. and walk 200m (reception open daily

10am-7pm, call after 7pm; 150kr; breakfast 25kr). The cheapest option is at **Nordengården,** Stockholmsg. 16 (tel. (031) 19 66 31). Take tram 3 to Stockholmsg. and walk downhill to Stockholmsg. (Reception open mid-Sept. to May daily 3-4pm; June to mid-Sept. 8-10am and 4-9pm. Breakfast 45kr.) Pitch your tent at **Kärralund Camping,** Olbersg. (tel. (031) 840 200; fax 84 05 00). Take tram 5 to Wellangerg. and walk east on Olbersg. (rooms 110kr, nonmembers 150kr; tents 120-170kr).

The best place in Gothenburg to sample this port city's fruits of the sea is at **Kajskjul 8,** on Parkhuskajen, next to the Maritime Centrum (open June 28-Aug. 6 daily noon-1am). **Café Kalori,** Magasinsg. 13, near Kungsportsplats, off of Vallg., turns a reverent eye towards protein and carbohydrates without the fat (entrees 45kr). The straight crowd discos at **Park Lane,** in the Radisson SAS Park Avenue Hotel, Kungsportsavenyn 1 (open Wed.-Thurs. 11pm-3am, Fri.-Sat. 11pm-5am), while the queer set heads to **Café Hellman** (open Mon., Thurs., and Sun. 7pm-midnight) and **Disco Touch** (open Wed. 9pm-1am, Fri. 9pm-2am, Sat. 9pm-3am), both located at **RFSL Göteberg** (the Gothenburg Gay Center), Esperantoplatsen 7.

CENTRAL SWEDEN

Uppsala

Once a hotbed of pagan spirituality and the cradle of Swedish civilization, Uppsala is now a Nordic Oxbridge, sheltering the 20,000 students of Sweden's oldest university. Scandinavia's largest cathedral, the magnificent **Domkyrka,** where Swedish monarchs were crowned, looms just over the river (open daily 8am-6pm; free; for tours call (018) 18 71 77). The **Gustavianum,** across from the Cathedral, lodges the **Anatomical Theater**—the site of 18th-century public human dissections (open June-Aug. daily 11am-3pm; Sept.-May noon-3pm; 10kr). For university events, scope the bulletin board at the home of the Silver Bible, the **Carolina Rediviva Library,** Övre Slottsg. at Drottningg. (open Mon.-Fri. 8:30am-8pm). A glorious pagan temple once dominated the landscape of **Gamla Uppsala** (Old Uppsala), 4km north of the city center. Little remains save huge burial mounds of monarchs and **Gamla Uppsala Kyrka,** one of Sweden's oldest churches. (Open Mon. 8:30am-5pm, Tues.-Sat. 8:30am-7pm, Sun. 10am-7pm. Closes at dusk Sept.-March. Free. Take bus 2, 20, 24, or 54 (16kr) north from Dragarbrunnsg. Return within 1½hr. to re-use ticket.) Science buffs can visit **Linnaeus' house** and the gardens he designed at Svartbäcksg. 27. After exhausting Uppsala, you can hop the boat to **Skokloster,** a dazzling Baroque palace built between 1654-1676 (open in summer daily 7am-5pm; 60kr, students 40kr). The boat departs in summer Tues.-Sun. at 11:45am and returns at 5:30pm from Islandsbron on Östra Åg. and Munkg. (round-trip 105kr).

The **tourist office,** Fyris Torg 8 (tel. (018) 27 48 00; fax 13 28 95), is near the west bank of the River Fyris. From the train station, walk right on Kungsg., left on St. Persg., and cross the bridge (open Mon.-Fri. 10am-6pm, Sat. 10am-3pm). **Trains** from Stockholm's Centralstation run to Uppsala about hourly (50min., 60kr, students 50kr). The **Uppsala English Bookshop AB,** Svartbäcksg. 30, has an extensive English-language collection (open Mon.-Fri. 11am-6pm, Sat.11am-3pm, Sun. noon-3pm). **Plantan Apartment and Youth Hostel,** Dragarbrunnsg. 18 (tel. (018) 10 43 00; fax 10 43 10), is a 10-minute walk from the central train station. Go right on Kungsg., then left on St. Persg., and a left on Dragarbrunnsg. (reception open Mon.-Fri. 8am-10pm, Sat.-Sun. 9am-9pm; dorms 125-150kr). For pleasing rooms and swimming in Lake Mälar, try **Sunnersta Herrgård (HI),** Sunnerstav. 24 (tel. (018) 32 42 20), 6km south of town. Take bus 20 or 50 from Dragarbrunnsg. to Herrgårdsv. (15kr), then walk two blocks behind the kiosk, turn left, and walk 50m. (Reception open daily 8-10am and 5-9pm. 100kr, nonmembers 145kr. Open May-Aug.) **Fyrishov Camping,** Idrottsg. 2 (tel. (018) 27 49 60; fax 24 83 14), off Svartbäcksg., is 2km from the city center. Take bus 4 to "Fyrishov." (Reception open daily 7am-10pm. Tents 75kr; 4-5 bed huts June 1-Aug 8 400kr; Sept. 9-Dec. 31 290kr. Reserve ahead.)

All Uppsala university students belong to refined fraternities called *nationer,* which practically give away food and drink (meals average 40kr, beer 30kr) and throw flamboyant fests. If you are a university student, bring your ID (not an ISIC) and your passport to the student union office, Övre Slottsg. 7 (tel. (018) 10 59 54; open Thurs. only 5-7pm), at Åsgränd, for a one-week student card (30kr, each additional week 10kr extra), and ask about events at and locations of the *nations,* as nightlife revolves around them. Grab a quick bite at **Landings,** Kungsängg. 5 (Sandwiches 20-40kr. Open Mon.-Fri. 8:30am-6:30pm, Sat. 8:30am-4pm, Sun. in summer only 11am-4pm.) For veggie options from 25kr, try **Stadsoasen,** Drottningg. 7 (open Sun.-Fri. 11am-3pm, Sat. noon-3pm). Good bets after dark are **Katalin,** Svartbäcksg. 19, which has live music (open daily 4pm-1am), and **Fellini,** Svartbäcksg. 7, a loud student rock and blues bar (open Mon.-Sat. 11am-1am).

Gävle

A survivor of three major fires in its 550-year history, the city of Gävle bursts with lilacs and pansies in summer and thrives year-round amidst the charm of old-world cobblestone and enchanting gardens. Gävle centers on the **Gavleån River,** with **Gamla Gefle** (old city) on the south bank. A 17th-century church, the **Heliga Trefaldighetskyrkan's** leaning tower throws the greenery along the river into relief. The **Galleri Gunnar Cyrén,** Nedre Bergsg. 11 (open Sept.-June Tues.-Sat. noon-5pm; free), holds work by Gunnar Cyrén, who designed the 1991 Nobel Peace prize plates. The **Länsmusset Gävleborg,** S. Strandg. 20, contains art by Cyrén and other Swedes (open Tues. and Thurs.-Fri. 10am-4pm, Wed. 10am-9pm, Sat.-Sun. 1-5pm; 25kr).

The **tourist office,** Kyrkog. 14 (tel. (026) 14 74 30), is set in Berggrenska Gården (open Mon.-Fri. 10am-6pm, Sat. 10am-2pm). From the train station, go up Kyrkog. to the yellow building on the left; enter through the courtyard. **Trains** run from Stockholm through Uppsala (2hr.). The **Vandrarhem Gävle (STF),** S. Rådmansg 1 (tel. (026) 62 17 45), with immaculate rooms and a friendly owner, is located at the south end of Gamla Gefle. (Reception open daily 8-10am and 5-7pm. 110kr, nonmembers 150kr; singles 185kr, nonmembers 225kr. Sheets 50kr. Kitchen and laundry.) The **Vandrarhem Engeltofta (STF)** on the water (tel. (960) 63 14 69 75) is accessible by taking bus 5 or 20 to "Engeltofta" (110kr, nonmembers 150kr; sheets 40kr). Get to **Engesberg Camping** (tel. (960) 990 25) by taking bus 5 (40min.) to "Engesberg." (Reception open daily 8am-10pm. Tents 75kr, nonmembers 85kr. Open June15-Sept. 1.) The **library** at Slottstorget 1 has **Internet access** (open Mon.-Thurs. 10am-5pm, Fri. 10am-5pm, and Sat. 10am-2pm). The open-air **market** in the Stortorget sells fresh fruit and vegetables and is surrounded by cafés and restaurants. Good, cheap grub can be found at **Tennstopet,** Nyg. 38 (salads 49-50kr, cheeseburger 29kr; open Mon.-Sat. 9am-10pm, Sun. noon-10pm). At night, the best places to hit are on S. Kungsg.

Hiking, swimming, and fishing are a ferry-ride away from Gälve on the island of **Limon.** Ferries leave from the tourist boat dock on S. Skeppsboron May 17-June 6 and August 18-31 at 9:30am, returning from Limon at 3pm, and July 7-August 17 at 9:30, 11:30am, and 4:25pm, returning at 10:30am, 3, and 5:15pm (30kr, children 20kr). Local smoked herring can be eaten straight from the curing barrels at **Böna,** a fishing village north-east of Gälve. Take bus 5 from Gälve (20min., 20kr).

Dalarna

Swedes get dreamy-eyed just talking about Dalarna, close to southern Sweden and yet part of the northern wilderness. This popular vacation spot is Sweden's *Smultronstället*—a secret spot where one goes to commune with nature, one's self, and one's significant other. Scores of Swedes summer here in tidy red and white farmhouses in the woods. The **Siljansleden,** a 340km cycling and hiking trail, winds its way through forests and over mountains around Lake Siljan which is enjoyed for its swimming, boating, and fishing. **Trains** run from Stockholm via Uppsala to Borlänge, and from there either northeast to Falun or northwest to Leksand, Rättvik, and Mora. If you wish to be near Lake Siljan around **Midsummer** (June 20), reserve a bed months in advance and know that many bus and train lines shut down.

Leksand More than 20,000 people flock to this small town above the lake to take part in the Midsummer festivities, featuring a maypole, folk music, and the **Siljansrodden,** a two-week series of churchboat competitions on Lake Siljan to revive the tradition of rowing to church. The annual **Musik vid Siljan** festival in Leksand and Rättvik (the first week of July) has music from all over the earth (30-200kr; tel. (0701) 27 27 69; fax (0248) 519 17; http://www.siljan.se). The **tourist office** (tel. (0247) 803 00; fax (0248) 516 17), attached to the Leksand train station, has more details. (Open mid-June to mid-Aug. Mon.-Fri. 9am-8pm, Sat. 10am-8pm, Sun. 11am-8pm; mid-Aug. to mid-June Mon.-Fri. 9am-5pm, Sat. 10am-1pm.) From Leksand's quay there are breezy **cruises** on the M/S Gustaf Wasa a few times a day to Rättvik and Mora (tel. (010) 252 32 92 or 204 77 24; June 14-Aug. 17, 2-4hr., 80-120kr).

Accommodations are often crowded (packed for Midsummer), but the tourist office can find you a private room for a 25kr fee (doubles from 265kr). Try the **Ungdomsgården** (tel. (0247) 100 90), on Rättviksv. near Tällbergsv., a few minutes from the station. A combination campground, lodge, and country kitchen, the main building is a red farmhouse. (Reception open daily 7:30am-9:30pm. 100kr per bed, tents 80kr. Open mid-June to mid-Aug.) With new facilities and lots of common space, Leksand's **HI hostel** (tel. (0247) 152 50) is 2.5km from the train station; cross the bridge near the tourist office and head left on Insjöv. (Reception open daily 9-10am and 5-8pm; May and Sept. 5-7pm.; Oct.-April call before you arrive. 120kr, nonmembers 150k. Laundry 30kr.) A 20-minute walk along the road toward Tällberg brings you to swimming and camping (tel./fax (0247) 803 13) at **Camping Stugby** (100kr per tent, 150kr with camper). Hit **Leksands Kebab & Pizza,** Norsg. 23, for substantial pizza (from 30kr; open Mon.-Sat. 11am-11pm, Sun. noon-11pm). Delicatessen items can be found at **Mårtas** (open daily until 7pm).

Mora Head north by bus to **Mora,** perhaps the nicest of the Siljan villages and home to artist Anders Zorn (1860-1920), famous for painting large, naked women. See his collection and house at the **Zornmuseet,** Vasag. 36. (Open June-Aug. Mon-Sat. 9am-5pm, Sun. 11am-5pm; Sept.-May Mon.-Sat. 10am-5pm, Sun. 1-5pm. 25kr, students 20kr.) **Nusnäs,** 10km east of Mora (bus 108, 20min., 13kr), is the home of the red wooden *dalahäst* horses, the Swedish equivalent of American baseball and apple pie. Tour the factory at **Nils Olsson Hemslöjd** (tel. (0250) 372 00) for free; ask the bus driver to stop at the factory. (Open June to mid-Aug. Mon.-Fri. 8am-6pm, Sat.-Sun. 9am-5pm; mid-Aug. to May Mon.-Fri. 8am-5pm, Sat. 10am-1pm.) Santa Claus's humble abode (or one of them; every snowy village claims the title) is called **Tomteland** and is in nearby **Gesunda;** take bus 107 (13kr) from Mora (tel. (0250) 290 00; open June-Aug. daily 10am-5pm; 95kr). The chairlift in Gesunda takes you 514 meters above sea-level and affords a beautiful view of Lake Siljan (25kr). **Vasaloppsmuseet,** on Vasag., houses exhibits on the world's premiere cross-country skiing race, the Vasaloppet, whose 14,000 skiers finish yearly in Mora to commemorate King Gustav Vasa's snowy trek from Sälen to Mora in 1520 (open daily 10am-6pm; 30kr, students 25kr).

Mora's "central" train station is a hike from civilization; get off at the Morastrand (second) stop instead. The **Inlandsbanan** train route (see **Lappland,** p. 866) begins in Mora, with a train leaving at 8am and arriving at Östersund at 1:45pm; another train leaves Östersund at 7:05am and arrives at Gällivare at 2:30pm (Midsummer to early August only; 4kr per 10km, whole trip 300kr). The **tourist office** (tel. (0250) 265 50), on the lakefront by Morastrand, on the left after getting off the train, books beds in private homes. (200kr; 25kr fee. Open mid-June to mid-Aug. Mon.-Fri. 9am-8pm, Sat. 10am-8pm, Sun. 11am-8pm; mid-Aug. to mid-June Mon.-Fri. 9am-5pm, Sat. 10am-1pm.) Mora's **youth hostel (HI)** (tel. (0250) 381 96; fax 381 95) is 500m from the Morastrand station; go right on the main road and cross the street when you see the sign for "Målkull Ann's." The redwood hostel is behind the inexpensive Ann's Café. (Reception open daily 8-10am and 5-8pm. 100kr, nonmembers 135kr. Phone reserva-

Midsummer Madness

For Midsummer (June 20) Swedes emerge from the woodwork to welcome the sun after a long and dark winter. Groups of families, villages, and amorous youngsters erect and dance around the **Midsommarstång,** a cross-shaped pole with two rings dangling from the ends. Its phallic construction symbolizes the fertilization of the soil it is staked in, and thoughts of other fertilization abound as girls place flowers under their pillows to induce dreams of their future spouses. The largest celebrations are in Dalarna, where alcohol and pickled herring flow freely and people flood the city for a two-day party. Keep Midsummer in mind while planning a trip—most transportation lines and establishments are closed. For more on Midsummer celebrations, see **Vikings Had Grannies Too,** p. 256.

tions mornings only.) For cheap grub, browse the bakeries on **Kyrkogatan,** or load up on supplies at the **ICA supermarket,** also on Kyrkog. (Mon.-Sat. 9am-8pm). **Lilla Björn Restaurant and Pizzeria** at the south end of Kyrkog. offers sit-down meals.

Östersund

At the edge of the serene Lake Storsjön, right where the Inlandsbanan crosses to Trondheim, Norway, Östersund is a natural stopover (5½hr. to Trondheim, 300kr; 6hr. to Stockholm, 497kr). The patriots of Jämtland county boisterously boost their region with dancing in the streets during the **Storsjöyran,** in the last weekend in July or first weekend in August. **Lake Storsjön** is home to a cousin of the Loch Ness monster, which King Oscar II and a crew of Norwegian whalers tried unsuccessfully to capture in 1894. See their harpoons at **Jamtli,** an indoor and open-air museum, north of the city center on Kyrkg. The museum features Sami photography, crafts, Viking Age paintings, and people dressed in traditional clothing "living" in the buildings. (Open June-Aug. daily 11am-5pm; Sept.-May Tues. 11am-8pm, Wed.-Sun. 11am-5pm. 60kr.) Rent a bike at **Cykelogen,** Kyrkg. 45 (tel. (063) 12 20 80), for 100kr per day (open Mon.-Fri. 10am-1pm and 2-6pm, Sat. 10am-2pm), and let gravity draw you over the footbridge to **Fröson Island,** once home to the Viking Æsir gods. Climb the **Fröson Tower** (10kr) for the ultimate view of the area. (Open May 10-June 20 11am-6pm; June 21-Aug. 10 9am-9pm; Aug. 11-Sept. 7 noon-6pm.)

The **tourist office,** Rådhusg. 44 (tel. (063) 14 40 01), has city maps (free-55kr), and books rooms for a 40kr fee. (135-180kr. Open June-Aug. Mon.-Sat. 9am-9pm, Sun. 10am-7pm; Sept.-May Mon.-Fri. 8am-5pm.) From the train station, walk up the hill on your left and continue down Prästg.; hang a right up Postgränd one block. Östersund's splendid **HI youth hostel** (tel. (063) 13 91 00) is 600m from the railroad station on Södra Gröng. (Call for directions. Reception open daily 8-10am and 5-9pm. 95kr, nonmembers 130kr. Kitchen and TVs.) Wild strawberries grow on the thatched roof of **Frösötornets Härbärge hostel** (tel. (063) 51 57 67), at the top of a 176m ski slope overlooking the city. Take bus 5 from the city center (last one 8:22pm; no buses Sunday) or endure a hellish climb. (Reception open daily 9am-9pm. 115kr; showers 1kr per 2min. Open mid-June to mid-Aug.) Take bus 2, 6, or 9 to **Östersunds Camping** (tel. (063) 14 46 15) at Fritidsbyn (camping spaces 90-100kr). You'll find Mexican and Creole cuisine in the old-fashioned Swedish interior of **Brunkullans Café/Restaurang,** Postgränd 5, with its 55kr lunch buffet (café open Mon.-Sat. noon-5pm; bar open daily until midnight). An even cheaper option is the supermarket **Hemköp** at 56 Kyrkg. (open Mon.-Fri. 9am-7pm, Sat. 9am-4pm, Sun. noon-5pm).

Örnsköldsvik

Off the beaten track and main train route is Örnsköldsvik (Ö-vik to the locals), surrounded by mountains with ski jumps and a harbor filled with tiny islands waiting to be explored. Several day hikes are conveniently near—the **Yellow Trail** loops an easy 6km. **Gene Fornby,** a 2000-year-old settlement discovered 6km from Ö-vik, has been rebuilt to look as it did as an Iron Age village in the year 500 (50kr; open June 21-Aug. 10 daily 11am-5pm; tours on the hour from 1-4pm). A journey to **Ulvön Islands** is an easy excursion to the land of fermented Baltic herring. Throughout the north island are **hiking trails,** the toughest leading to the peak of Lotsberget Mountain. The M/S Otila leaves Örnsköldsvik at 9:30am and returns at 3pm (2½hr., round-trip 100kr). The island of **Trysunda** also has beautiful biking trails and a beach in Björnviken. A bus timed to meet the boat (departing from Köpmanholmen, 30km to the south) leaves Örnsköldvik at 9am. The 45-minute boat ride continues to Ulvöhamn (40kr).

Örnsköldsvik's **tourist office,** Nyg. 18 (tel. (0660) 125 37; fax 881 23), off Fabriksg., has maps and info about hiking and daytrips to nearby islands. It also books private rooms (150kr) and cottages (200kr) for a 50kr fee (open mid-June to mid-Aug Mon.-Fri. 9am-7pm, Sat.-Sun. 9am-3pm; mid-Aug. to mid-June Mon.-Fri. 9am-5pm, Sat. 9am-1pm). **Buses** run to Örnsköldsvik from Umeå (2½hr., 88kr) and Östersund (5hr., 205kr). The youth hostel **STF Vandrahem Örnsköldsvik,** Högsnäsgården pl. 1980 (tel. (0660) 702 44), is a 15-minute ride into the cow-pie-scented countryside. (Bus 4, 19kr; last bus leaves from near the tourist office at 9pm. Reception open in summer 9-10am and 5-7pm; off-season 9-10am. Members 110kr, nonmembers 150kr.) **Arnströms Bageri and Kondtori,** Storatorget, has sandwiches for 14kr or coffee and pastry for 20kr (open Mon.-Fri. 7:30am-5pm, Sat. 10am-3pm).

SWEDEN

Umeå

Return to the sunnier coast in Umeå (OOM-eh-oh), a fast growing university town at the mouth of the Ume Älv. To get there, take a connecting bus or train (30min., 25kr) from Vännäs, on the main train route. **Silja Line** ferries (tel. (090) 71 44 00) sail to Vaasa, Finland from Umeå (165kr.; 50% off with Eurail or Scanrail.) On weekends younger passengers stay on board to enjoy the cheap booze and slot machines. Brave the **rapids** of Vindelälven in a rubber raft navigated by the staff of **Sotarns Forsränning** (tel. (090) 77 33 55). Take bus 15 to Vännäs (reservations required; 130kr).

Trains run to Umeå from Boden (5hr.), Luleå (6hr.), and Stockholm (11hr., 444kr), but the faster route north is by **bus** (to Luleå 4½hr., 149kr.) To get to the **tourist office,** Renmarkstorget 15 (tel. (090) 16 34 39), stroll down Rådhusesplanaden across from the train station and turn right on Skolg. They have a list of contacts for private rooms. (150kr. Open June-Aug. Mon.-Fri. 8am-8pm, Sat. 10am-5pm, Sun. 11am-5pm; Sept.-May Mon.-Fri. 9am-6pm, Sat. 10am-2pm.) The new **HI youth hostel,** V. Esplanaden 10 (tel. (090) 77 16 50; fax 77 16 95), is a short walk from the train station; go straight up Rådhusesplanaden, take a right on Skolg., then left on V. Esplanaden. (Reception open daily 8am-noon and 4-10pm. 110kr, nonmembers 135kr. Breakfast 45kr. Laundry 10kr.) Camp at **Nydala Lake** (tel. (090) 16 16 60); bus 81 goes straight to the campgrounds in summer (bus 13kr; 2-person cabins 175kr). **Oves Cykelservice,** Storg. 86 (tel. (090) 12 61 91), rents bikes (40kr per day; open Mon.-Fri. 8am-5pm) to adventurous souls who head for the 30km **Umeleden** bike trail. Along the Umeleden await old hydropower stations, gardens, restaurants, and **Baggböle Herrgård,** a delightful café in a 19th-century mansion (open Tues.-Sun. noon-8pm).

Collegiate types eat at vegetarian-friendly **Teater Café,** Vasaplan, where lunch specials run 38-49kr (open Mon.-Thurs. 11am-midnight, Fri. 11am-1am, Sat. noon-1am, Sun. 5-11pm). Nearby, students congregate at the lively **Mucky Duck Pub,** also across the street from the Teater Café, on Skolg. An ICA **supermarket** waits on Storg., as does a library with **Internet access** at Rådhusplanaden 6A (open Mon.-Fri. 11am-7pm, Sat. 11am-3pm; Aug. 15-June 15 also Mon.-Fri 8-11am).

LAPPLAND

Those "Southerners" living south of the Arctic Circle correctly imagine that Lappland consists of reindeer herds roaming through dense forest, thick snow, unrelenting darkness, and bitter cold for half the year and perpetual light for the other half. While mining has encroached upon previously virgin land, the lure here is still nature, from swampy birch and pine forests in the vast lowlands to the spectacular rounded mountains that rise to meet the Norwegian border. The wilderness is comprised of several national parks good for hiking. The summer's mosquitoes are vicious, but many eco-unfriendly bug repellents are banned; buy your repellent (75kr) in Lappland.

Swedish Lappland is home to 17,000 reindeer-tending **Sami** ("Lapps" is derogatory), descendants of the prehistoric inhabitants of Scandinavia. Jokkmokk, Gällivare, and Kiruna are the main settlements north of the Arctic Circle. All make good stopovers on the way to mountain stations such as Kvikkjokk and Abisko, or the national parks Muddus, Padjelanta, Sarek, and Stora Sjöfallet. Flying north is a good time-saver; enjoy youth standby fares on **Transwede** (tel. (020) 22 52 25; under 24 only; Stockholm-Gällivare 340kr) or **SAS** (tel. (020) 91 01 50; outside Sweden (08) 797 40 00; under 21 only; Stockholm-Kiruna 500kr). There are two **rail routes** to Lappland. The **coastal route** runs from Stockholm through Boden, Gällivare, and Kiruna to Narvik, Norway, along the **Malmbanan** (2 per day in either direction, 18hr., 623kr, reservations necessary). The touristy **Inlandsbanan** (inland railway) stops for reindeer and souvenirs, and to let you touch the ground of the Arctic Circle. Traveling the entire length requires overnight stopovers in Östersund. (One per day. Mora-Gällivare June-Aug. 700kr, Sept.-May 600kr. 50% discount with Eurail and Scanrail. 14-day unlimited travel 995kr. Runs June 23 to mid-Aug.) Connections between the parallel inland and coastal train routes can be made at Uppsala-Mora, Sundsvall-Östersund, and Luleå-Boden-Gällivare. **Buses,** most of which do not accept railpasses, are the only way to smaller towns and often the easiest way to larger ones; get a copy of the *Länstrafiken i Norrbotten* company schedule. The **Norrlandskortet** allows unlimited travel on all SJ trains (second-class, excluding Inlandsbanan) and Länstrafikens buses in Sweden north of Sundsvall, as well as trains to Narvik, Trondheim, and Mo i Rana in Norway (890kr, under 19 445kr). The brochure *Follow the Summer Light to Sweden's North Country* (at tourist offices) supplies routes and trails. Ask tourist offices for help with transportation routes and for hiking and biking trail maps.

Transportation out of Lappland can be challenging. Those heading farther north can take the most scenic train ride in Sweden to Narvik on the Norwegian coast (stop at Abisko Turiststation or lonelier Låktatjåkka for dramatic mountain trails). Two daily trains go from Luleå to Narvik (7½hr.) stopping in Gällivare, Kiruna, and Abisko. One bus a day (100kr) links Kiruna to **Karesuando** on the Finnish border. From there you can continue to Skibotn, Norway, or Kilpisjärvi and Muonio, Finland. Finland is also accessible by bus from **Boden.** Railpasses are valid on all **buses** from Boden to **Haparanda,** on the Finnish border. At Haparanda, stay at the **HI youth hostel,** Strandg. 26 (tel. (0922) 111 71). Remember that Finland is one time zone ahead.

Luleå

At the mouth of the **Lule Älv** (Lule River) lies Luleå (LOOL-eh-oh), a small university town with a laid-back atmosphere and plenty of natural beauty. Take bus 8, 9, 10, or 32 (20kr) to reach the 15th-century church (open in summer daily 10am-6pm; 18kr) in **Gammelstad** (Old Luleå). Return to the 20th century with the techno-toys at the **Teknikens Hus** (Technology Museum), Högskolan. (Open mid-June to late Aug. Tues.-Sun. 11am-5pm; late Aug. to mid-June Tues., Thurs., and Fri. 9am-4pm, Wed. 9am-8pm, Sat.-Sun. noon-5pm. Free.) Info on the hundreds of uninhabited islands of the **Luleå Archipelago** is available at the **tourist office,** Storg. 43 (tel. (0920) 29 35 00 or 29 35 05; fax (0920) 29 41 38), which also rents rooms (150-200kr per person plus a 25kr booking fee). From the train station, cross Prästg., walk diagonally across the park, cross Hermalingsg., and tromp up Storg. (Open in summer Mon.-Fri. 9am-7pm, Sat.-Sun. 10am-4pm; off-season Mon.-Fri. 10am-7pm, Sat. 10am-4pm.) The library, Kyrkog. 15, has **Internet access.** (Open May-Aug. Mon.-Thurs. 10am-7pm; Sept.-April Mon.-Thurs. 10am-8pm, Sat. 11am-3pm.)

Ogle exotic birds and farm animals at the high-tech **Örnviks Youth Hostel (HI),** Örnviksv. 87 (tel. (0920) 523 25), 6km from the city center. Take bus 6 (20kr) and ask the driver to drop you off after the bridge, then cross the road, walk back towards the bridge, and follow the path into the field on your right. At night, buses go to the front door. A bit closer is **Vandrarhem Kronan,** Kronan House 7 (tel. (0920) 608 00; fax 608 60). To get there exit the train station, make a right, and cross the train tracks. Continue to the left around the water's edge, cross the bridge on the right, and wind around the water. Follow the bike path left up the hill. (Reception open daily 8-10:30am. Singles 200kr. Other rooms 150kr. Laundry 30kr. Breakfast 30kr.) **EFS Sundet** (tel. (0920) 520 74) is the closest campground; take bus 6 (50kr per tent, 2-bed cabins 120kr). Grab a sandwich (18-28kr) at **Börje Olssons Konditori,** Storg. 61 (open Mon.-Fri. 8am-9pm, Sat. 10am-6pm, Sun. noon-9pm), or feast at affordable **Café Pimpinella,** Storg. 40, which is a bar at night (*dagens rätt* 57kr; closed Sun.). Summer nightlife revolves around **Sommarmix.** (Cover Sun.-Fri. 40kr, before 10:30pm 20kr; Sat. 60kr, before 10:30pm 40kr. Open Tues.-Sat. 7pm-3am.)

Jokkmokk and Gällivare

One of the only reasons to stop in **Jokkmokk** is its outstanding museum of indigenous Sami culture, **Ájtte,** with a new alpine flower garden (Oct.-April closed Mon; 25kr). Ask the **tourist office,** Stortorget 4 (tel. (0971) 121 40), about hikes and tours of the reconstructed Stone Age village of **Vuollerim,** 45km east of Jokkmokk. The office keeps a list of private rooms (100-150kr per person), stores luggage (15kr), rents bikes (50kr per day), and sells mountain maps (open June-Aug. daily 9am-7pm; Sept.-May Mon.-Fri. 8:30am-3:30pm). The **HI youth hostel** (tel. (0971) 559 77), which has a kitchen, sauna, and laundry facilities, is across from the tourist office on Åsg. (reception open daily 7-10am and 5-8pm; 100kr, nonmembers 135kr). The **Skogskojan** hostel is open mid-June to August (tel. (0971) 103 97; fax 108 31). The **campsite,** which rents boats and bikes, is 3km outside town at **Jokkmokks Turistcenter** (tel. (0971) 123 70). To get there, hike east on Storg. (tents 60kr, 4-bed cabins 540kr). **Buses** to Jokkmokk run from Gällivare (5 per day, Sat.-Sun. 1 per day, 1½hr., 73kr) and from Boden (2hr., 120kr) in the south. From Jokkmok, buses run to **Kvikkjokk,** a good place to enter the vast western wilderness (2hr., 100kr). **Sarek,** just north of Kvikkjokk, is a dramatic national park *sans* trails or huts to which Europe's expert hikers come (see **Northwest Hiking Regions,** p. 869).

Spend some time underground in the mining town of **Gällivare** (YELL-i-var-ay). Geological amusements abound, and you can tour the **copper and iron mines** in summer. From June 23 to August 8, tours to the copper mines leave from the tourist office at 2pm (140kr; children under 15 excluded). Iron mine tours leave from the tourist office at 10am (160kr, children under 12 excluded; open July 7-Aug. 8). Or take a gentle day hike up 820m **Dundret mountain.** The **tourist office** (tel. (0970) 166 60) is at Storg. 16; from the train station, turn right onto the main road, walk up the hill and cross through the parking lot (open mid-June to mid-Aug. daily 9am-8pm; mid-Aug. to May Mon.-Fri. 9am-4pm). The **HI youth hostel** (tel. (0970) 143 80; fax 165 86) is a five-minute walk from the station. Cross the bridge over the tracks heading away from town, then take the one over the river (reception open daily 8-10am and 5-7pm; 100kr, nonmembers 140kr; call ahead). **Gällivare Camping** (tel. (0970) 165 75) is 1.5km from the station (95kr per tent; open early June-early Sept.).

Kiruna

Kiruna bills itself as the "City of the Future," but it's a rather dystopian vision of mining, missile launching, and satellites. The town's major claim to fame is that the first satellite pictures of Chernobyl were taken here, but you can also see the world's largest **underground iron ore mine.** (Sign up at **Kiruna Guidetour,** across from the tourist office. Tours early June to mid-Sept. 10am, noon, 2pm. 85kr.) You can satisfy your regional yearnings by staying in a **Lappish sod hut** on reindeer-fur beds, eating Lappish specialities, and riding a rapid of the Torne; meet at the tourist office at 6pm and return the next day at 9am (495kr). Book all tours in advance at the tourist office or with Guidetour (tel. (0980) 811 10). The **midnight sun** lasts from May 28 to July 15.

To get to the **tourist office,** Lars Janssonsgatan 17 (tel. (0980) 188 80; fax 182 86), walk up the hill from the station on the path through Järnvägsparken to Lars Janssongatan. (Open early June to mid-Sept. Mon.-Fri. 9am-8pm, Sat.-Sun. 9am-6pm; mid-Sept. to March Mon.-Fri. 9am-4pm; April-early June Mon.-Fri. 9am-5pm, Sat. 10am-1pm.) The **HI youth hostel,** Skyttegatan 16a (tel. (0980) 171 95), is a hike from the train station. (Reception open daily 8-9:30am and 4-9:30pm. 100kr, nonmembers 130kr. Open mid-June to mid-Aug.) Camping is available at **Radhusbyn Ripan** (tel. (0980) 630 00), a 20-minute walk up the hill from the train station (75kr per tent; 4-person cabins 500kr in summer). **Buses** leave across from the city hall on Hjalmar Lundbohmsvägen and go, among other places, south to Gällivare. Load up on groceries at the **ICA Supermarket** near the town center (closed Sun.).

Northwest Hiking Regions

Beginning in snow-melting July, northwest Sweden attracts hikers from all over Europe to its impeccably preserved national parks. The most popular trail is the **Kungsleden,** stretching from Abisko on the Norwegian border south for 500km to Hemavan. The marked trails have cabins, usually 10-20km apart. Good for novices, the **Padjelanta** trail, which runs from Kvikkjokk west through Staloluokta, up into the mountains, and ends in Ritsem, is the way into Sweden's largest national park. There are six principal points of entry from which to access these trails: Abisko, Nikkaluokta, Ritsem, Saltoluokta, and Kvikkjokk in Sweden, and Sulitelma in Norway. If you're coming from Sweden, take a bus from Jokkmokk to Kvikkjokk (2hr., 100kr), or from Kereine to Abisko or Nikkaluokta for the easiest access.

Organized **day trips** leave from the Abisko **Turistation** (tel. (0980) 402 00; fax 401 40). Excursions include a hike through Kårsavagge and the surrounding waterfalls (4hr., 60kr), a tour of the Stordalen blossoming wetland (7hr., 100kr), a tour of Klövjetur on Siberian huskies (90kr), and an exploration of the Kåppasjåkka caves (6hr., 140kr). All **trains** between Kiruna and Narvik stop in Abisko.

This is rugged country, and there may be snow as late as July. Bring food, maps, raingear, and warm clothing, and leave a copy of your route with someone in town. Contact **STF (Svenska Turistföreningen)** before heading north (see p. 847). STF runs most of the mountain stations and huts and publishes essential hiking guides. Many sections of trails, in particular from Abisko to Kvikkjokk, have HI-staffed **cabins** 8-21km apart (170-195kr, nonmembers 220-245kr).

To climb Sweden's highest peak, **Kebnekaise** (2117m), take a bus from Kiruna to Nikkaluokta (53kr) and hike 19km to the mountain cabin. From there, you can reach the summit in a day. You can connect back to the Kungsleden Trail via Singisturgorna from the bottom of Kebnekaise. The most dangerous and difficult of the area trails, **Sarek,** offers an expansive wilderness without trails or huts and is touted as Europe's last virgin wilderness. It is also accessible from Kvikkjokk, Saltoluokta, and Ritsem. Pick up *Sarek—Myth and Reality* at any northern tourist office. Before leaving on any hike, be sure to grab maps and vital info—and some strong mosquito repellent.

Storuman is a stop on both the **Inlandsbanan** train route and the **Blå Vägan** (Blue Way). A steep 2km-walk up to **Utsikten** affords a view of the town and the **Lusphol-marna** island and peninsula connected to the mainland by suspension bridges. **Buses** run to Umeå (3½hr., 155kr); after June 23, the Inlandsbanen train runs from Östersund to Storuman (3hr.). The **tourist office,** Järnvägsg. (tel. (0951) 333 70), has hiking info. To get to the **Vandrarhem Storuman (STF),** exit the train station, go left on Järnvägsg. and make a right on Centralg. (Tel. (0951) 777 30. Reception open 8-10am and 5-9pm. 100kr, nonmembers 135kr. Open June 6-Aug. 4.) **Storumans Camping** (tel. (0951) 106 96) is five minutes behind the train station (tents 60kr; bikes 16kr per hr.).

Switzerland (Svizzera, Suisse, Die Schweiz)

US$1 = 1.53SFr (Swiss francs)	**1SFr = US$0.66**
CDN$1 = 1.11SFr	**1SFr = CDN$0.90**
UK£ = 2.48SFr	**1SFr = UK£0.40**
IR£1 = 2.22SFr	**1SFr = IR£0.45**
AUS$1 = 1.14SFr	**1SFr = AUS$0.88**
NZ$1 = 0.99SFr	**1SFr = NZ$1.01**
SAR1 = 0.33SFr	**1SFr = SAR3.01**
Country Code: 41	**International Dialing Prefix: 00**

Divided by impassable Alpine giants and united by neither language nor religion, Switzerland at first seems a strange agglomeration. What is now a confederation of 23 cantons (and three sub-cantons) was first created out of only three cantons in 1291. Swiss politics have an old fashioned feel; approximately 3000 local communes retain a great deal of power, and major policy disputes are routinely settled by national referenda. Official neutrality since 1815 has kept the ravages of war away from this postcard-perfect haven, but recent news suggests that Swiss bankers may have been a little too neutral in accepting gold and money from all sources in the 1930s and 1940s. For good and for ill, placidity has nurtured the growth of Big Money in the staid banking centers of Geneva and Zurich.

One aspect of Switzerland will likely always overshadow whatever internal divisions exist: the majestic Alps. Keats, Shelley, and Byron glorified the mountains in their Romantic poetry, while others have fallen silent against a landscape that defies words. Snow-capped peaks lord over half the country's area, enticing hikers, skiers, bikers, and paragliders from around the globe to one of the most finely tuned tourist industries in the world. Victorian scholar John Ruskin called the Alps "the great cathedrals of the earth." You're welcome to worship here—if you can spare the cash.

Poetry in its own right, *Let's Go: Austria and Switzerland 1998* provides updated and comprehensive info on indoor and outdoor activities throughout the country.

GETTING THERE AND GETTING AROUND

Getting around Switzerland is gleefully easy. Federal (SBB, CFF) and private **railways** connect most towns and villages, and yellow post buses (Swisspass often valid, but not Eurailpasses) pick up the slack in rural areas. Although **Eurail** passes are valid for the state-run railways that connect cities, private companies exert control on Alpine rail routes, particularly in the Berner Oberland—special passes are needed here.

To beat ruinous transportation costs, those planning to spend much time in the country should consider the myriad rail options. The **Swisspass** entitles you to unlimited free travel on government-operated trains, ferries, buses in 30 Swiss cities, and private railways, and a 25-50% discount on many mountain railways and cable cars. Second-class prices are US$176 for four days, US$220 for eight days, and US$256 for 15 days. The pass is sold abroad through Rail Europe and major travel agencies; in major train stations in Switzerland it may be cheaper depending on the exchange rate. The **Swiss Flexipass,** valid for any three days of second-class travel within 15 days, costs US$176 and may not be worth it. **Regional Passes** (50-175SFr), available in eight different regions, are available in major tourist offices for holders of Eurailpasses. The **Swiss Card,** sold only abroad, offers 50% off most trains and buses in Switzerland for one month (US$96). For national rail info, dial 157 22 22.

Postal buses, a barrage of banana-colored coaches run by the Swiss government, take care of transport in rural areas. Swisspasses are valid on many buses, although pass holders pay 5-10SFr on the faster buses. **Steamers** traverse many of the larger lakes. Fares are no bargain, but a Eurailpass sometimes gets you free passage, and a Swisspass almost

always wins a free ride. **Cycling,** though strenuous, is a splendid way to see the country; rental at most stations is 22-23SFr or slightly more per day (return to any station). With sufficient stamina, overland **walking and hiking** can be the most enjoyable ways to see Switzerland. **Hitching** is difficult and risky as always.

ESSENTIALS

Switzerland is quadrilingual: French is spoken in the west, Italian in the south, Romansch (a relative of Latin and Etruscan) in parts of the canton of Graubünden, and Swiss German (*Schwyzerdütsch,* a dialect nearly incomprehensible to other German speakers) everywhere else. Most people know at least three languages, including English. **Tourist offices** (*Verkehrsbüro* or *Kurverein*) in every Swiss city locate rooms, distribute maps, and suggest hiking and biking routes. A fat green **"i"** marks all official tourist offices. The **Anglo-phone** (tel. 157 50 14) provides info and English-speaking doctor referrals (1.40SFr per min.).

Currency exchange at its easiest is available in train stations; rates are comparable to those at banks. Switzerland is in the process of updating its **phone system;** some of the numbers that *Let's Go* lists have not yet been updated and may be incorrect. **Local calls** cost 60 centimes. Post offices provide the easiest way to make collect **calls abroad.** Ask for a *Zurückrufen,* or return call, and you will receive a card with a number on it. Make the call and tell your party to call you back at that number; at the end of the conversation, you pay just for the original call. Dial 191 or 114 for English-friendly assistance. For **AT&T Direct,** dial 0 800 89 00 11; **MCI WorldPhone** 0800 89 02 22; **Sprint Access** 155 97 77; **Canada Direct** 155 83 30; **BT Direct** 155 24 44; **Ireland Direct** 155 11 74; **Australia Direct** 155 11 74; **New Zealand Direct** 155 64 11; **South Africa Direct** 155 85 35. Dial 111 for **information** (including directory assistance and train schedules), and 191 or 114 for an English-speaking **international operator.** The **police** emergency number is 117, **fire** emergency is 118, **medical** emergency is 144.

Most stores are open Monday through Friday from 8am to 6:30pm with a break from noon to 2pm, and Saturday mornings. In cities, shops also close Monday mornings. Museums close on Mondays. The country closes down for **national holidays** on Jan. 1, Good Friday (April 10 in 1998), Easter Monday (April 13), Ascension (May 21), Whit Monday (June 1), Aug. 1, and Christmas (Dec. 25-26).

Switzerland is justifiably proud of its reputation for great **skiing** and **hiking.** Contrary to popular belief, skiing in Switzerland is often less expensive than in the U.S., if you avoid the pricey resorts. Ski passes (valid for transportation to, from, and on lifts) run 30-50SFr per day and 100-300SFr per week. A week of lift tickets, equipment rental, lessons, lodging, and *demi-pension* (half-pension, breakfast plus one other meal, usually dinner) averages 475SFr. Summer skiing is no longer as prevalent as it once was, but it's still available in Zermatt, Saas Fee, Les Diablerets, and on the Diavolezza in Pontresina. Over 30,000 miles of hiking trails lace the entire country. Trails are marked by bands of white-red-white; yellow signs give directions and traveling times. Tourist offices offer maps and info on hiking preparation and safety.

Accommodations, Camping, Food, and Drink True to legend, all things Swiss are meticulous, orderly, efficient, and expensive. The uniformly cheery **HI Jugendherbergen** are bright, clean, and open to all ages (US$5-25, breakfast and sheets included). **Hotels** are generally pretty pricey. In smaller towns, *Zimmer frei* (private rooms) abound; the tourist office can supply a list and make reservations. Wherever you stay, be sure to ask for a **guest card,** which often grants discounts to local attractions and transportation. As befits a country so blessed by Mother Nature, Switzerland blossoms with over 1200 **campgrounds.** Prices average 6-9SFr per person and 4-10SFr per tent, a rare treat in such an expensive country. You must obtain permission from landowners to camp on private property; camping along roads and in public areas is forbidden. **Swiss Alpine Club (SAC) huts** are modest and extremely practical for those interested in trekking in higher, more remote areas. Bunk rooms sleep 10 to 20 weary hikers, with blankets provided. SAC huts are open to all, but SAC members get discounts. An average one-night stay is 20-25SFr, 30SFr for non-members. Those serious about conquering the summits should contact SAC, Sektion Zermatt, Haus Dolomite, CH-3920 Zermatt, Switzerland (tel. (028) 67 26 10).

The Swiss are hardly culinary daredevils, but they're very good at what they do. In French Switzerland, try the cheese specialties; *fondue* is always excellent, as is *raclette* (melted cheese with pickled onions and boiled new potatoes). Swiss-German food is heartier. Try *Züricher Geschnetzeltes* (veal strips in a delicious cream sauce) and *Rösti* (hashbrowned potato with onion). Of course, *Lindt* chocolate is a perennial favorite, especially in its home city of Zurich. **Migros** supermarket cafeterias and **Co-op** centers are the budgeteer's choices for self-service dining.

GERMAN SWITZERLAND

Zurich (Zürich)

Switzerland has a bank for every 1200 people, and about half of them are in Zurich, where battalions of ballyhooed and Bally-shoed executives charge daily to the world's fourth-largest stock exchange and preeminent gold exchange. Yet there is more to Zurich than money. A radical spirit has been apparent since the firebrand Ulrich Zwingli led the Swiss Protestant Reformation in the 16th century. Revolution brewed again in 1916, when artistic and philosophical radicalism shook the town's institutions: James Joyce toiled away on *Ulysses*, the Dadaists pushed the limits of the ridiculous at the Cabaret Voltaire, and Russian exile Vladimir Lenin, unhappily situated next door to the raucous cabaret, read Marx and bided his time.

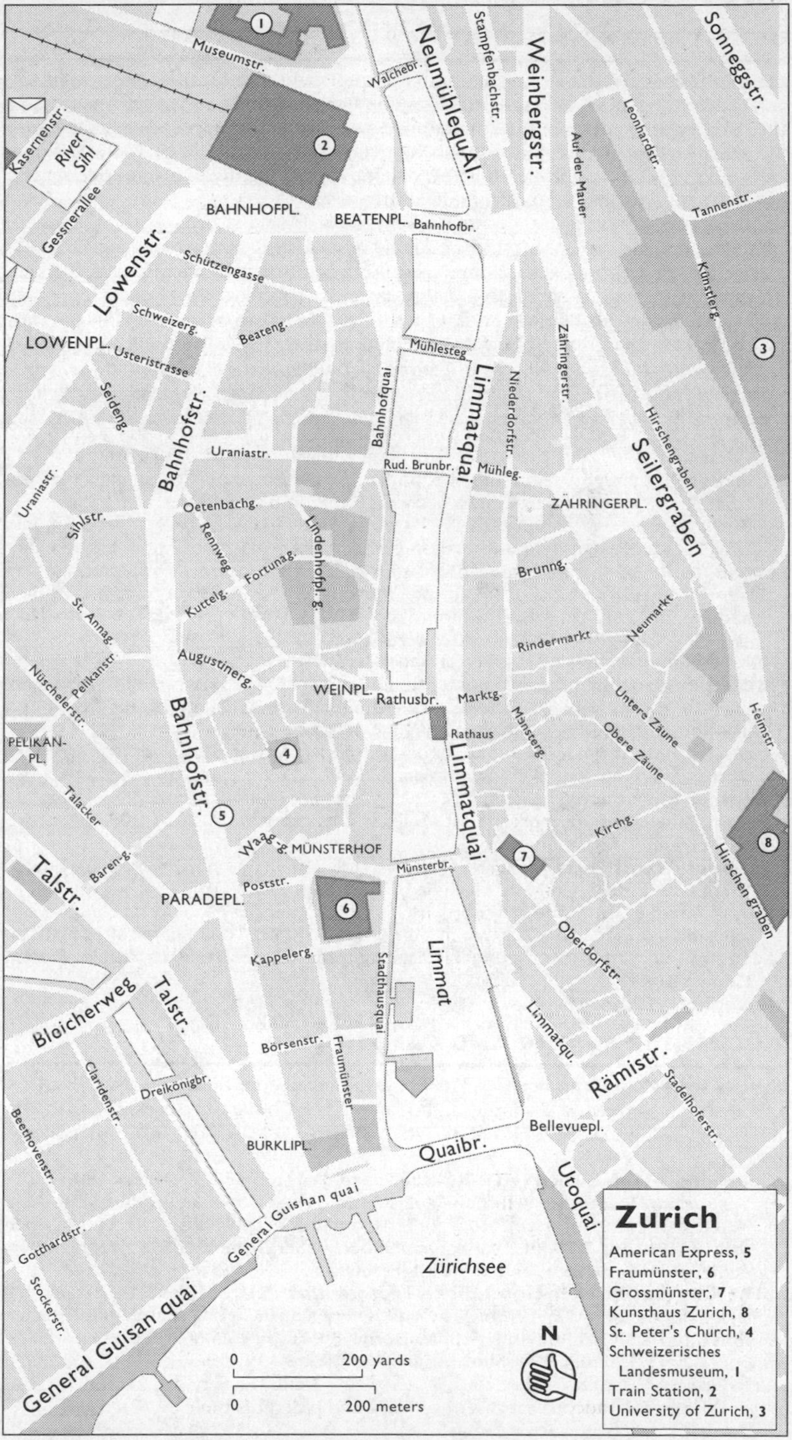

SWITZERLAND

ORIENTATION AND PRACTICAL INFORMATION

Zurich sits smack in the middle of northern Switzerland. The **Limmat River** splits the city down the middle. From the train station, **Bahnhofstraße** runs south, parallel to the river, through much of the **Altstadt** and past countless banks and shops. Most of the activity in Zurich is confined to this relatively small, walkable area. For weary travelers, trams criss-cross the city; buy the 24-hour *Tageskarte* if you plan to ride several times (7.20SFr), or pay 2.20SFr for individual rides.

Tourist Offices: Bahnhofpl. 15 (tel. 211 40 00, hotel reservation service 211 11 31; fax 211 39 81; email zhtourismus@access.ch; http://www.zurichtourism.ch); exit the train station to Bahnhofpl. and walk to the left. The reservation desk finds rooms. Wade through the crowd for copies of *Zürich News* and *Zürich Next.* Open April-Oct. Mon.-Fri. 8:30am-9:30pm, Sat.-Sun. 8:30am-8:30pm; Nov.-March Mon.-Fri. 8:30am-7:30pm, Sat.-Sun. 8:30am-6:30pm.

Consulates: Australians, Canadians, and **Irish** citizens should contact the embassies in Bern. **New Zealand's** consulate is in Geneva. **U.K.,** Dufourstr. 56 (tel. 261 15 20). Open Mon.-Fri. 9am-noon and 2-4pm. **U.S.,** Zollikerstr. 141 (tel. 422 25 66). Open Mon.-Tues. and Thurs.- Fri. 9am-noon and 2-4pm, Wed. 1:30-4:30pm.

Currency Exchange: The **train station** has competitive rates. Open daily 6:30am-10:45pm. Also try **Credit Suisse** or **Swiss Bank** on Bahnhofstr.

American Express: Bahnhofstr. 20, P.O. Box 5231, CH-8022 (tel. 211 83 70), just after Paradepl. Mail held and checks cashed. Open May-Sept. Mon.-Fri. 8:30am-6:30pm, Sat. 9am-1pm; Oct.-April Mon.-Fri. 8:30am-5:30pm, Sat. 9am-noon.

Trains: The *Hauptbahnhof* (main train station), at the northern terminus of Bahnhofstr., has connections to Geneva (3hr., 77SFr), Basel (1hr., 32SFr), Bern (1hr., 45SFr), Lugano (3hr., 62SFr), and Lucerne (1hr., 22SFr).

Hitchhiking: Hitchers take streetcar 4 to "Werdhölzli."

Bike Rental: At the baggage counter in the train station. 23SFr per day. Open daily 6am-7:40pm. Bikes are available at Werdmühlepl. and Theaterpl. for free, but a passport and 20SFr deposit are required. Open daily 7:30am-9:30pm.

Laundromat: At the train station, under the tracks. Wash 8-10SFr per 6kg. Dry 5SFr for 1hr. Soap included. Open daily 6am-midnight.

24-Hour Pharmacy: Theaterstr. 14 (tel. 252 56 00), on Bellevuepl.

Emergency: Ambulance: tel. 144. **Medical Emergency:** tel. 261 61 00.

Police: tel. 117.

Internet Access: Internet Café, Uraniastr. (tel. 210 33 11), above a parking garage. 5SFr per 20min. Open Mon. 10am-6pm, Tues.-Sun. 10am-11pm.

Post Office: Main office at Kasernenstr. 95/97. Open for *Poste Restante* Mon.-Fri. 6:30am-10:30pm, Sat. 6:30am-8pm, Sun. 11am-10:30pm. 1SFr charge after 6:30pm. Address to: Sihlpost, Kasernenstr., Postlagernde Briefe, CH-8021 Zürich. **Postal Code:** CH-8021.

Telephone Code: 01.

ACCOMMODATIONS AND CAMPING

Expensive as Zurich can be, there are a few budget accommodations available. Hostels are often somewhat distant from the town center, but easily accessible with Zurich's extensive public transportation system. Reserve at least a day in advance.

Jugendherberge Zürich (HI), Mutschellenstr. 114 (tel. 482 35 44; fax 480 17 27). Take train S1 or S8 to "Bahnhof Wollishofen," walk 3 blocks up the hill to Mutschellenstr., and turn right. Huge, orderly, and impeccably clean. Reception open daily 6-10am and 2-10pm. 29SFr, nonmembers 34SFr. Doubles 88SFr, nonmembers 98SFr. Showers, sheets, and breakfast included.

The City Backpacker-Hotel Biber, Niederdorfstr. 5 (tel. 251 90 15; fax 251 90 24), in the heart of the *Altstadt.* The staff is very helpful at this central hotel. Reception open daily 8-11am and 3-10pm. Dorms 30SFr. Singles 65SFr. Doubles 85SFr. Sheets 3SFr. Laundry 9SFr. Showers included.

Justinhaus heim Zürich, Freudenberg 146 (tel. 361 38 06; fax 362 29 82). Take tram 9 or 10 to "Seilbahn Rigiblick," and then take the tram up the hill to "Rigiblick." Recently renovated hotel with spectacular views. Reception open daily 8am-5pm and 7-8pm. Singles 50-60SFr. Doubles 75-90SFr. Breakfast included.

Martahaus, Zähringerstr. 36 (tel. 251 45 50; fax 251 45 40). Take a left from the station, cross the Balinkofbrücke, and take the second right after Limmatquai. Simple but comfy. Reception open daily 7am-11pm (ring the bell after hours). Dorms 34SFr. Singles 65SFr. Doubles 96SFr. Triples 114SFr. Prices lower off season. Showers and breakfast included.

Studenthaus, Rötelstr. 100 (tel. 361 23 13). Take tram 11 to "Bucheggpl." and walk downhill on Rötelstr. Singles 45SFr. Doubles 60SFr. Open July 15-Oct. 15.

Foyer Hottingen, Hottingenstr. 31 (tel. 261 93 15; fax 261 93 19); take streetcar 3 ("Kluspl.") to "Hottingerpl." Usually admits only women. Reception open daily 6am-midnight. Dorms 25SFr. Singles 55SFr. Doubles 85Sfr. Breakfast included.

Camping Seebucht, Seestr. 559 (tel. 482 16 12; fax 482 16 60). Take tram 7 to "Wollishofen," and then walk 15min. along the shore to the right, or take bus 161 or 165 from Bürgklipl. to "Grenzsteig." Reception open daily 7:30am-noon and 4-8pm. 6SFr per person. 10SFr per tent. Open early May to late Sept.

FOOD

Zurich boasts over 1300 restaurants, but few cater to budget travelers. The cheapest meals can be found at *Würstli* or fruit and vegetable stands. **Co-op Super Center** is a super-huge market stretching from the Limmat River all the way to the train station (open Mon.-Fri. 7am-6:30pm, Thurs. 7am-9pm, Sat. 7am-4pm).

Mensa der Universität Zürich, Rämistr. 71. Take streetcar 6 from Bahnhofpl. to "ETH Zentrum" for stunningly edible food. Meals 6-7SFr with ISIC, salads 6SFr. Open July 15-Oct. 21 Mon.-Fri. 11am-2pm; Oct. 22-July 14 Mon.-Fri. 11am-2:30pm and 5-7:30pm. Self-service cafeteria open Oct. 22-July 14 Mon.-Sat. 8am-4:30pm. **Mensa Polyterrasse,** just down the street, has the same food and prices.

Zeughauskeller, Bahnhofstr. 28a, near Paradepl. Handsome *Biergarten* serving Swiss specialties. *Rösti* 10-30SFr. Open Mon.-Sat. 11:30am-11pm.

Restaurant Raclette-Stube, Zähringerstr. 16. Fondues at their richest, largest, and cheapest (20SFr). Open Sat.-Fri. 6-11:30pm, Fri. also 11am-2pm.

Hiltl Vegi, Sihlstr. 28. Trade carrot sticks with the swanky vegetarian elite. Huge salad buffet (10SFr per 0.5kg). Open Mon.-Sat. 7am-11pm, Sun. 11am-11pm.

Rheinfelder Bierhalle, Niederdorfstr. 76. Local crowd enjoys the self-proclaimed "cheapest beer in town" for 4.10SFr. Entrees 11-30SFr. Open daily 9am-12:30am.

Sprüngli Confiserie Café, Paradepl. A Zurich landmark, founded by one of the original makers of Lindt chocolate. Absolutely exquisite confections. Café open Mon.-Fri. 6am-midnight, Sat. 7:30am-midnight. Confectionary open Mon.-Fri. 7:30am-6:30pm, Sat. 8am-4pm.

SIGHTS AND ENTERTAINMENT

Stately and colorful, the **Bahnhofstraße** runs from the station to the Zürichsee; trees lining each side of the street shade shoppers in this causeway of capitalism. **Paradeplatz,** about halfway down Bahnhofstr., marks the center of the city. Two giant cathedrals face each other from opposite sides of the river in the *Altstadt.* To the east loom the twin towers of the **Grossmünster,** a Romanesque cathedral financed by Charlemagne. Zwingli spearheaded the Swiss Reformation with tirades from the pulpit here. (Open March 14-Oct. daily 9am-6pm; Nov.-March 13 Tues.-Wed., Fri.-Sat., and Sun. 10am-6pm, Mon. and Thurs. 10am-5pm.) On the left bank rises the 13th-century **Fraumünster,** with stained-glass art by Marc Chagall. The nearby **St. Peter's Church** has the largest clockface in Europe—and appropriately loud bells.

Yes I said yes I said take tram 6, 9, or 10 to "ETH" uphill from the university to reach the grave of author **James Joyce,** in the Fluntern Cemetery. (Open May-Aug. daily 7am-8pm; March-April and Sept.-Oct. 7am-7pm; Nov.-Feb. 8am-5pm. Free.) Next door, the **Zurich Zoo,** Zürichbergstr. 221, features over 2000 species. (Take tram 5 or

6. Open March-Oct. daily 8am-6pm; Nov.-Feb. 8am-5pm. 12SFr, students 6SFr.) The **Kunsthaus Zürich,** Heimpl. 1 at Rämistr., houses a stunning collection of 15th- and 20th-century art. (Open Tues.-Thurs. 10am-9pm, Fri.-Sun. 10am-5pm. 4SFr, students 3SFr., Sun. free.) **The Lindt and Sprüngli Chocolate Factory,** Seestr. 204, has a museum and free samples (open Wed.-Fri. 10am-noon and 1-4pm; free).

Nightlife revolves around Niederdorfstraße, Münstergasse, and Limmatquai, where cafés and bars overflow with people until the wee hours of the morning. Women may be uncomfortable walking alone near the strip clubs of Niederdorfstraße. **Casa Bar,** Münstergasse 30, is a tiny, crowded pub with first-rate live jazz (beers from 9.50SFr; open daily 7pm-2am). Thornton Wilder and Lenin used to get sloshed at the posh **Bar Odeon,** Limmatquai 2, near the Quaibrück (beers from 6SFr). **Emilio's Bagpiper Bar,** Zähringerstr. 11, is a popular gay bar with occasional male strip shows (open daily 3pm-midnight).

St. Gallen

St. Gall, a 7th-century Irish missionary attempting a quick tour of the Alps, fell into a bier near the Bodensee and decided to stay. Thirteen centuries later, book lovers gasp at the sight of St. Gallen's main attraction, the **Stiftsbibliotek** (Abbey Library), with a collection of 2000 manuscripts. Even these are over-shadowed by the breathtaking **Baroque reading room.** (Open April and June-Aug. Mon.-Sat. 9am-noon and 1:30-5pm, Sun. 10:30am-noon and 1:30-4pm; May and Sept.-Oct. closed Sun. afternoon; Dec.-March open Tues.-Sat. 9am-noon and 1:30-4pm. 7SFr, students 5SFr.) The Abbey's **Kathedrale St. Gallen** was founded in the 8th century but took its present form in the mid-18th century. **Museumstraße** has several museums of interest. The **Historical Museum** at #50 displays artifacts from Switzerland and outside Europe (open Tues.-Sat. 10am-noon and 2-5pm, Sun. 10am-5pm; 6SFr, students 2SFr). **Kirchofer House Museum,** #27, showcases an impressive array of coins, Russian imperial silver, and the Appenzeller cave bear skeletons (open Tues.-Sat. 10am-noon and 2-5pm; 6SFr, students 2SFr). In late June arrives the **Open Air St. Gallen Music Festival** (tickets 135SFr; info tel. (071) 223 41 01).

SWITZERLAND

The **tourist office,** Bahnhofpl. 1a (tel. (071) 227 37 37; fax 227 37 67), makes free hotel reservations and provides a **city tour.** From the train station, cross straight through the bus stop and past the fountain on the left. (Tours June 12-Sept. Mon., Wed., and Fri. 2:30pm. 15SFr. Office open Mon.-Fri. 9am-noon and 1-6pm, Sat. 9am-noon.) **Trains** run from Bahnhofpl. to Zurich (1hr., 26SFr), Bern (2½hr., 59SFr), and Munich (3hr., 60SFr, under 26 49SFr). Find **Internet access** at **Media Lounge,** Marktpl. (12SFr for 1hr. Open Mon. 11:30am-9pm, Tues.-Fri. 10am-9pm, Sun. 9:30am-9pm.) Perched on a hill overlooking St. Gallen, the **Jugendherberge St. Gallen (HI),** Jüchstr. 25 (tel. (071) 245 47 77), is clean and quiet. From the train station, take the *Trogenerbahn* from the smaller Appenzeller/Trogener station to the right. (Reception open Mon.-Sat. 5-10:30pm, Sun. 6-10:30pm. Dorms 20.50-23SFr; singles 54.50-57SFr; doubles 59-64SFr. Closed Dec. 15-March 7.) **Hotel Elite,** Metzgergasse 9-11 (tel. (071) 222 12 36), has simple, airy rooms (singles 54-100SFr, doubles 108-150SFr; breakfast included). **Restaurant Spitalkeller,** Spitalgasse 10, down Marktgasse from Marktpl., serves hearty Alpine food (from 13SFr; open Tues.-Sat. 8am-midnight). **Christina's,** Webergasse 9, is an indigo-tinted bar/restaurant with exotic veggie specialties from 16SFr. (Open Tues.-Thurs. 9:30am-11:30pm, Fri.- Sat. 9:30am-12:30am, Sun.-Mon. 3-11:30pm.)

Lucerne (Luzern)

The sunrise over Lucerne's most acclaimed peak, the 2132 ft. **Mount Pilatus,** has hypnotized hikers and artists for centuries. Wagner composed his masterful *Die Meistersänger* and *Siegfried* here. When clouds obscure the mountain peak, Lucerne's extraordinary museums, medieval streets, and painted bridges provide an equally rewarding afternoon of sightseeing and exploration. Much of Lucerne's tourist cul-

Photo: R. Olken

Greetings from Let's Go Publications

The book in your hand is the work of hundreds of student researcher-writers, editors, cartographers, and designers. Each summer we brave monsoons, revolutions, and marriage proposals to bring you a fully updated, completely revised travel guide series, as we've done every year for the past 38 years.

This is a collection of our best finds, our cheapest deals, our most evocative description, and, as always, our wit, humor, and irreverence. Let's Go is filled with all the information on anything you could possibly need to know to have a successful trip, and we try to make it as much a companion as a guide.

We believe that budget travel is not the last recourse of the destitute, but rather the only way to travel; living simply and cheaply brings you closer to the people and places you've been saving up to visit. We also believe that the best adventures and discoveries are the ones you find yourself. So put us down every once in while and head out on your own. And when you find something to share, drop us a line. We're **Let's Go Publications,** 67 Mount Auburn St., Cambridge, MA 02138, USA (email: fanmail@letsgo.com; http://www.letsgo.com). And let us know if you want a free subscription to ***The Yellowjacket,*** the new Let's Go Newsletter.

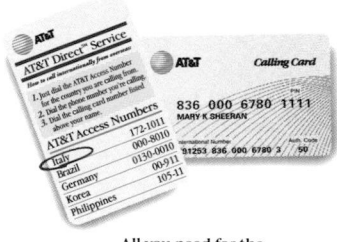

ture thrives on the Vierwaldstättersee and the cobblestone streets lining the Reuss River in the **Altstadt** (Old Town). The area is famous for its frescoed houses and *oriel* windows. The 660-year-old **Kapellbrücke,** a famous wooden-roofed bridge running from the train station to the *Altstadt,* is ornately decorated with scenes from Swiss history. Down the river, cross the covered **Spreuerbrücke,** adorned with Kaspar Meglinger's eerie *Totentanz* (Dance of Death) paintings. For a magnificent view of Lucerne, climb the ramparts of the medieval city. At the base of the cliff on Denkmalstr., the melancholy **Lion of Lucerne** honors the Swiss Guard who died defending Marie Antoinette in Revolutionary Paris, and was described by Mark Twain as "the saddest and most moving piece of rock in the world."

Lucerne's outstanding museums include the **Verkehrshaus der Schweiz** (Transport Museum), Lidostr. 5, which features a planetarium, Imax shows (9-12SFr), and a virtual reality exhibit (open April 4-Oct. daily 9am-6pm; Nov.-March 10am-5pm; 16SFr, students 14SFr). The **Picasso Museum,** Am Rhyn Haus, Furrengasse 21, chronicles the artist's life in photos. (Open April-Oct. daily 10am-6pm; Nov.-March 11am-1pm and 2-4pm. 6SFr, students 3SFr.) The **Natur-Museum,** Kasernenpl. 6, details Lucerne's pre-history and offers "hands-on" exhibits (open Tues.-Sat. 10am-noon and 2-5pm, Sun. 10am-5pm; 4SFr, students 3SFr). The **Richard Wagner Museum,** Wagnerweg 27, set in Wagner's secluded sylvan home, displays the composer's letters, scores, and instruments. (Open April 15-Oct. Tues.-Sun. 10am-noon and 2-5pm; Feb.-April 14 Tues., Thurs., and Sat.-Sun. 10am-noon and 2-5pm. 5SFr, students 4SFr.)

To gaze down from Mt. Pilatus, get a boat to Alpenachstad and ascend by the steepest **cogwheel train** in the world. On a clear day you can see to Italy. Return by cable car to Kriens and bus to Lucerne (round-trip 75.40SFr, with Eurail 40SFr). Though banned until the 17th century for fear of angry ghosts, it is now legal to climb Mt. Pilatus. The trails require sturdy hiking boots and at least five hours. The **Seepark,** 15 minutes to the right of the train station, allows a lakeside dip.

SWITZERLAND

Practical Information, Accommodations, and Food The **tourist office,** Frankenstr. 1 (tel. (041) 410 71 71; fax 410 73 34), leads walking tours of the city, and sojourns to the top of Mt. Pilatus. (Open April-Oct. Mon.-Fri. 8:30am-6pm, Sat. 9am-5pm, Sun. 9am-1pm; Nov.-March Mon.-Fri. 8:30am-noon and 2-6pm, Sat. 9am-1pm.) Lucerne sends **trains** to Basel (1¼hr., 30SFr), Bern (1¼hr., 33SFr), Geneva (3¼hr., 65SFr), Interlaken (2hr., 25SFr), Lausanne (1¾hr., 55SFr), and Zurich (50min., 22SFr). The train station also **rents bikes** (22SFr).

Backpackers, at Alpenquai 42, across the concrete bridge from Inseli-Quai (tel. (041) 360 04 20; fax 360 04 42), has rooms with balconies (reception open daily 7-10am and 4pm-midnight; 21.50-26.50SFr, sheets 2SFr). Hop on bus 18 ("Goplismoos") to get to the **Jugendherberge (HI),** Sedelstr. 12 (tel. (041) 420 88 00; fax 420 56 16). After 7:30pm, take bus 1 ("Schlossberg") and walk 15 minutes down Friedentalstr. (Reception open daily 7-9:30am and 2pm-midnight. Dorms 29.50SFr. Lockers, sheets, shower, and breakfast included.) The **Touristen Hotel Luzern,** St. Karliquai 12 (tel. (041) 410 24 74; fax 410 84 14), is by the river. From the station, go underground, exit the complex to the *Altstadt,* walk left along the river and cross the second covered bridge. (Reception open daily 7am-10pm. Dorms 31-36SFr, students 28-33SFr; doubles 98-108SFr.) **Privatpension Panorama,** Kapuzinerweg 9 (tel. (041) 420 67 01; fax 420 67 30), overlooks the *Altstadt* (singles 45SFr, doubles 70-90SFr; breakfast included). Take bus 2 ("Würzenbach") to "Verkehrshaus" to **Camping Lido,** Lidostr. 8. (Tel. (041) 370 21 46. Fax 370 21 45. Reception open daily 8am-6pm. 6.50SFr per person, 3SFr per tent. Open March 15-Oct.)

Saturday morning markets along the river offer fresh goods for an inexpensive picnic. **Krone,** Rössligasse 15, serves good food cafeteria-style (all sandwiches under 8SFr; food served 10am-9pm; bar open until midnight). The city's nightlife revolves around the crowded corridors of the *Altstadt.* The riverfront **Mr. Pickwick's** is a popular pub (open Mon.-Sat. 11am-12:30am, Sun. 4pm-12:30am).

Bern (Berne)

Although Bern has been Switzerland's capital since 1848, do not expect fast tracks and screeching cars. Parliament is in session only four times a year, and politics is considered part-time work. Indeed, you'll probably see more suitors than suits in Bern: the city is known for chocolate and flowers, and its design is decidedly romantic.

PRACTICAL INFORMATION

Stately Bern awaits at the juncture of the French- and German-speaking areas of the country. Most of medieval Bern lies in front of the train station and nestled along the Aare River. Drug users may lurk around the Parliament park and terraces at night, but **Bundesgasse** bypasses that area.

Tourist Office: Verkehrsbüro (tel. 311 66 11; fax 312 12 33), in the train station. Distributes maps and *This Week in Bern.* Room reservations 3SFr. Open June-Sept. daily 9am-8:30pm; Oct.-May Mon.-Sat. 9am-6:30pm, Sun. 10am-5pm.

Budget Travel: SSR, Rathausgasse 64 (tel. 312 07 24); take bus 12 to "Rathaus." BIJ tickets. Open Mon.-Wed. and Fri. 9:30am-6pm, Thurs. 9:30am-8pm.

Embassies: Australia, Alpenstr. 29 (tel. 351 01 43). Open Mon.-Thurs. 10am-12:30pm and 1:30-3pm, Fri. 10am-12:30pm. **Canada,** Kirchenfeldstr. 88 (tel. 352 63 81). Open Mon.-Fri. 8am-noon and 1-4:30pm. **Ireland,** Kirchenfeldstr. 68 (tel. 352 14 42). Open Mon.-Fri. 9:15am-12:30pm and 2-5:30pm. **U.K.,** Thunstr. 50 (tel. 352 50 21). Open Mon.-Fri. 9am-12:30pm and 2-6pm. **U.S.,** Jubiläumsstr. 93 (tel. 357 70 11). Open Mon.-Fri. 9am-12:30pm and 1:30-4pm.

Currency Exchange: Downstairs in the train station. Open June to mid-Oct. daily 6:15am-9:45pm; mid-Oct. to May 6:15am-8:45pm.

American Express: In **Kehrli and Oeler,** Bubenbergpl. 9 (tel. 311 00 22). From the train station, walk to the bus area across Bahnhofplatz. Mail held. All banking services. Open Mon.-Fri. 8:30am-5:30pm, Sat. 9am-noon.

Trains: The **Hauptbahnhof** (train info 157 22 22) serves Geneva (2hr., 48SFr), Lucerne (1¼hr., 31SFr), Interlaken (1hr., 24SFr), Zurich (1½hr., 42SFr), Paris (4½hr., 76SFr), Prague (12hr., 190SFr), Munich (5½hr., 115SFr), and Venice (7hr., 78SFr).

Public Transportation: For all **SVB** buses and trams (tel. 321 88 88), buy a visitor's card from ticket offices downstairs at the train station or at Bubenbergpl. 5. 24hr. ticket 6SFr. Swisspass valid. Buses run 5:45am-11:45pm. **Nightbuses** leave the train station at 12:40, 1:40, and 3:15am on Fri. and Sat. nights, and cost 5SFr (no passes valid). SVB offices in the train station open Mon.-Wed. and Fri. 6:30am-7:30pm, Thurs. 6:30am-9:30pm, Sat. 6:30am-6:30pm.

Bike Rental: At the station (tel. 680 34 61). 23SFr per day. 88-120SFr per week. Reserve ahead—bikes disappear quickly. Open daily 6:15am-11:45pm.

Pharmacy: In train station, open daily 6:30am-8pm. Pharmacies cluster near the clock tower. Call 311 22 11 for 24hr. pharmacy info, or 111 for general info.

Emergencies: Ambulance: tel. 144. **Doctor's night service:** tel. 311 22 11.

Police: tel. 117.

Post Office: Schanzenpost 1, next to the train station. Open Mon.-Fri. 7:30am-6:30pm, Sat. 7:30-11. Send *Poste Restante* to Schanzenpost 3000, Bern 1. **Postal Code:** CH-3000 to 3030.

Telephone Code: 031.

ACCOMMODATIONS AND CAMPING

Bern's shortage of inexpensive hotels thwarts budget travelers. Even outside the city itself, cheap accommodations are rare. Reserve ahead.

Jugendherberge (HI), Weihergasse 4 (tel. 311 63 16; fax 312 52 40). From the station, walk across Bubenbergpl., past the tram lines toward your left, and then onto Christoffelgasse Turn left on Bundesgasse, which turns into Kochergasse and empties into Casinopl. Follow signs after going down Münzrain. 3-night max. Reception

SWITZERLAND

open in summer daily 7-9:30am and 3pm-midnight; off-season 7-9:30am and 5pm-midnight. Curfew midnight. 18SFr. Laundry 4SFr.

Pension Martahaus, Wyttenbachstr. 22a (tel. 332 41 35; fax 333 33 86). Take bus 20 to "Gewerbeschule," then turn right onto Wyttenbachstr. Calm, comfortable pension in a quiet suburb. Reception open daily 7am-9pm, live-in night-porter. Singles 55-90SFr. Doubles 85-120SFr. Triples 110-150SFr. Breakfast included. Laundry 7SFr.

Hotel Goldener Schlüssel, Rathausgasse 72 (tel. 311 02 16; fax 311 56 88). Tram 9 or 12 to "Zytglogge." A newly renovated, central hotel, with a popular restaurant-café downstairs. Reception daily 7am-midnight. Singles 75-95SFr. Doubles 110-135SFr. Breakfast included. Reserve ahead May-Oct. V, MC.

Camping: Camping Eichholz, Strandweg 49 (tel. 961 26 02). Ride streetcar 9 to "Wabern" (last stop). 5.50SFr per person, 4.30SFr per student, 4-9SFr per tent. A few doubles for 13SFr plus 5.50SFr per person. Shower 15SFr. Open May-Sept.

FOOD

The **Bärenplatz** is a lively square overflowing with cafés and restaurants, most with *menus* and lighter fare in the 9-17SFr range. The sidewalk arcades that line Bern's main drags are a treasure trove of potential culinary curiosities, including Bern's specialties: *Gschnätzltes* (fried veal, beef, or pork) and *sur chabis* (a sauerkraut). Sweet teeth will enjoy the world-renowned **Toblerone chocolate.** Pick up a snack at the daily **fruit and vegetable market** at Bärenpl. (open May-Oct. 8am-6pm); Tuesdays and Saturdays year-round it sprawls into Bundesplatz. For a sit-down meal, **Manora,** Bubenbergpl. 5a, features tasty salads, fruits, and entrees (open Mon.-Sat. 7am-10:45pm, Sun. 9am-10:45pm). **Zähringerhof,** Hallerstr. 19, at Gesellschaftstr., cooks up great Swiss dishes (*menus* 17-19SFr; open daily 9am-midnight). **Café des Pyrenées,** Kornhauspl., has inventive sandwiches (calamari 6.50SFr; open Mon.-Fri. 9am-12:30am, Sat. 8am-5pm).

SIGHTS AND ENTERTAINMENT

The massive **Bundeshaus** dominates the Aare river and hides the politicians in the **Parlamentsgebäude.** (45min. tour every hr. 9am-noon and 2-4pm. Free. Watch the parliament in session from the galleries.) From the state house, Kockergasse and Herrengasse lead to the 15th-century Protestant **Münster.** The imagination of the late-Gothic period runs riot in the portal sculpture of the Last Judgment. (Open Easter-Oct. Tues.-Sat. 10am-5pm, Sun. 11am-5pm; Nov.-Easter Tues.-Fri. 10am-noon and 2-4pm, Sat. 10am-noon and 2-5pm, Sun. 11am-2pm. Tower closes 30min. before the church. 3SFr.) Head down Münstergasse and take a right and then the first left to find the 13th-century **Zytglogge** (clock tower), which performs four minutes before the hour. Bärengrabenbrücke leads to the **Bärengraben** (bear pits), which have held bears since the 15th century (open April-Sept. daily 8am-6pm; Oct.-March 9am-4pm). The **Botanical Gardens** of the University of Bern sprawl down the river at Lorrainebrücke. (Park open March-Sept. Mon.-Fri. 7am-6pm, Sat.-Sun. 8am-5pm. Greenhouse open 8-11:30am and 2-5pm. Free.) A walk south along the Aare (or bus 19 to "Tierpark") leads to the **Dählhölzli Städtischer Tierpark** (Zoo), Tierparkweg 1 (open daily in summer 8am-6pm; off-season 9am-4:30pm; 6SFr, students 4SFr).

Several **museums** cluster at **Helvetiaplatz** across the **Kirchenfeldbrücke** (take tram 3 or 5); ask the tourist office or the museum cashier for a day ticket (*Tageskarte,* good at many but not all museums; 7SFr, students 5SFr). The **Kunstmuseum,** Hodlerstr. 8-12, near the Lorrainebrücke, presents the largest Klee collection anywhere (over 2500 works), plus Kandinsky, Braque, Picasso, Matisse, and Delacroix. (Open Tues. 10am-9pm, Wed.-Sun. 10am-5pm. 6SFr, students 4SFr, *Tageskarte* not valid.) The **Swiss Alpine Museum,** Helvetiapl. 4, has spell-binding models of Swiss mountains and geology. (Open mid-May to mid-Oct. Mon. 2-5pm, Tues.-Sun. 10am-5pm; mid-Oct. to mid-May Mon. 2-5pm, Tues.-Sun. 10am-noon and 2-5pm. 5SFr, students 3SFr.) **Albert Einstein's House,** Kramgasse 49, is a small apartment good for a relatively brief visit. (Open Feb.-Nov. Tues.-Fri. 10am-5pm, Sat. 10am-4pm. 3SFr, *Tageskarte* not valid.) **Bernisches Historische Museum,** Helvetiapl. 5, exhibits everything from a hilarious Dance of Death to an astonishing Islamic collection (open Tues.-Sun. 10am-5pm; 5SFr, students 3SFr, Sat. free).

The **Berner Altstadtsommer** comes to life in July and August with dance and music concerts in the squares of the *Altstadt.* July's **Gurten Festival** attracts big names to its stage (contact the tourist office or check http://www.gurtenfestival.ch). At night, head to the bars and cafés along the Bärenplatz, or to Bern's oldest wine cellar: the **Klötzlikeller Weine Stube,** Gerechtigkeitsgasse 62, which resounds with the songs of patrons (open Tues.-Sat. 4pm-12:30am). A block away, the **Art Café,** Gurtengasse 3, is a bar for the cigarette-smoking, gesticulating set at night. (Open Mon.-Thurs. 7am-12:30pm, Fri.-Sat. 7am-7pm and 8pm-2:30am, Sun. 6pm-12:30am.)

Interlaken

Less than an hour by train from Bern, Interlaken provides access to the mountains, the Brienzersee and Thunersee lakes, and trains throughout Switzerland. But with few tourist attractions, the town functions better as a base than as a destination. Sign up at Balmer's (see below) for activities run by **Adventure World,** Kirchgasse 18 (tel. (033) 826 77 11), Interlaken's main "adventure coordinator." On the water, there's **river rafting** (half-day 85SFr) and **canyoning** down waterfalls (half-day 85-125SFr). On land, **rock climbing** (half-day 75SFr) affords the opportunity to grapple with the Alps. In the air, enjoy **tandem paragliding** (half-day 140-200SFr) or experience **bungee jumping** from Schilthorn (100m 129SFr; 180m 259SFr, one previous jump required). Combination packages are available (150-350SFr).

Practical Information, Accommodations, and Food Interlaken has two train stations. The **Westbahnhof** (tel. (033) 826 47 50) borders the Thunersee in the center of town, while the **Ostbahnhof** (tel. (033) 822 27 92) is on the Brienzersee. Trains arrive from Bern (24SFr), Basel (54SFr), Zurich (60SFr), and Geneva (60SFr). Each station houses a tourist office that changes currency. The main **tourist office,** Höheweg 37 (tel. (033) 822 21 21), in the Hotel Metropole near Westbahnhof, provides free maps and schedules. (Open July-Aug. Mon.-Fri. 8am-noon and 1:30-6:30pm, Sat. 8am-noon and 1:30-5pm, Sun. 5-7pm; Sept.-June Mon.-Fri. 8am-noon and 2-6pm, Sat. 8am-noon.) **Bicycles** can be rented at the train stations (22-29SFr per day).

Finding a place to sleep is easy. Take the hourly shuttle or walk 15 minutes from either station to **Balmer's Herberge,** Haupstr. 23 (tel. (033) 822 19 61; fax 823 32 61), which draws a primarily American crowd with its frat-party atmosphere. From Westbahnhof go left, veer right onto Bahnhofstr., turn right on Centralstr., and follow the signs. Sign in and return at 5pm, when beds are assigned (no reservations). The hostel provides bike rental, laundry (8SFr per load), a mini department store, and other amenities. (Reception open in summer daily 6:30am-noon and 4:30-11pm; off-season 6:30-9am and 4:30-11pm. Dorms 17-19SFr; doubles 56SFr; triples 72SFr; quads 96SFr. Breakfast included.) **Jugendherberge Bönigen (HI),** Aareweg 21 (tel. (033) 822 43 53; fax 823 20 58), farther from town, compensates with a tranquil setting and large rooms. Take bus 1 ("Bönigen") to "Lütschinenbrücke." (Reception open daily 6-10am and 4-11pm. Dorms 18.30-22.30SFr first night, then 15.80-19.80SFr; doubles 62.60SFr.) **Heidi's Garni-Hotel Beyeler,** Bernastr. 37 (tel./fax (033) 822 90 30), is a friendly, family-run hotel on a quiet and convenient street (doubles 75SFr, triples 93SFr, quads 124SFr). Just across the river from Ostbahnhof is **Camping Sackgut** (tel. (033) 824 44 34; 7.60SFr per person, 6.50-14SFr per tent; open May-Sept.). **Camping Jungfraublick** (tel. (033) 822 44 14; fax 822 16 19) is five minutes past Balmer's on Gsteigstr. (7-12SFr per person; open May-Sept.).

Interlaken is filled with overpriced restaurants, but some in old Interlaken across the river are cheaper. The Balmer's Herberge crowd tends to eat at Balmer's (fondue, bratwurst, and burgers all under 10SFr), while the hostel crowd eats at the Jugendherberge (11SFr). Stock up for hikes at the **Migros supermarket** across from Westbahnhof (open Mon.-Thurs. 7:30am-6:30pm, Fri. 7:30-9pm, Sat. 7:30am-4pm).

Most Americans start at Balmer's (beer 3SFr). When the staff clears the patio at 11pm, revelers head to **Buddy's,** Höheweg 33, for beer (3.20-5.30SFr) and **email** (15min for 6SFr; bar open daily 10am-12:30am). Some then stumble to **Johnny's Dancing Club,** Höheweg 92, in the Hotel Carlton (Sat. cover 7SFr; open Dec.-Oct. Tues.-Sun. 9:30pm-2:30am). Every summer Interlaken performs Schiller's *Wilhelm Tell.* The cast of hundreds includes children and livestock. (Late June to mid-July Thurs. 8pm; mid-July to early Sept. also Sat. 8pm. 12-32SFr. Tickets at Tellbüro, Bahnhofstr. 5; tel. (033) 822 37 23.)

■ Near Interlaken: Thunersee and Brienzersee

You can appreciate Berner Oberland's calm waters and stark mountain peaks by cruising on Interlaken's lakes, the **Thunersee** (to the west) and the **Brienzersee** (to the east). Ferries on Thunersee are free with Eurail, Swisspass, and Berner Oberland passes, while day passes for area ferry, bus, and train travel can be bought at Interlaken's station (July-Aug. 42SF; June and Sept. 32SFr).

The **Beatushöhlen,** caves with stalactites, waterfalls, and the ancient cell of St. Beatus, are reachable by bus 21 from Interlaken to Thun (caves open April-Oct. daily 9:30am-5pm; 12SFr, students 10SFr). The walk back to Interlaken takes two hours. Across the lake in Spiez, **Spiez Castle** features fabulous woodwork, a stunning tower view, and a rose garden. (Open July-Aug. Mon. 2-6pm, Tues.-Sun. 10am-6pm; April-June and Sept.-Oct. Mon. 2-5pm, Tues.-Sun. 10am-5pm. 4SFr, students 1SFr.) Accommodations on the lake are difficult to find; ask at the tourist offices about private rooms. Get there by **boat** to Thun and Interlaken or by **train** to Bern, Thun, and Interlaken West (6-18SFr). The towns of **Spiez** and **Thun** have offices adjacent to the train stations (Spiez tel. (033) 654 21 38; Thun tel. (033) 222 83 23). The tourist office in Spiez can help you find private rooms for 27-40SFr per person. Campgrounds are numerous; take the bus to Mustermattli to reach **Panorama Rossen** (tel. (033) 654 43 77), in Aeschi (6.40SFr per person, 6-7SFr per tent; open May-Sept.).

The **Brienzersee** is more rugged and less developed. The town of **Brienz** has escaped tourism and makes a serene daytrip (from Interlaken1¼hr. and 10.60SFr by boat or 20min. by train). On the outskirts of town, the **Ballenberg Swiss Open-Air Museum** is a 50-hectare park which displays traditional rural dwellings from every region of Switzerland. The park is an hour's walk from the train station, but a **bus** (round-trip 5.60SFr) connects the two every hour (open mid-April to Oct. daily 10am-5pm; 12SFr, students 10SFr). The **tourist office** (tel. (033) 952 80 80; fax 952 80 88), across from the train station, gives tips to hikers of all experience levels. (Open July-Aug. Mon.-Fri. 8am-6:30pm, Sat. 9am-noon and 4-6pm; Sept.-June Mon.-Fri. 8am-noon and 2-6pm, Sat. 8am-noon.) From the tourist office, cross the tracks, face the lake, turn left, and trace the lake for 15 minutes to reach the rustic **Brienz Jugendherberge (HI),** Strandweg 10 (tel. (033) 951 11 52; fax 951 22 60). The hostel rents **bikes** (10SFr for 1 day, 15SFr for 2) to its guests. (Reception open daily 8-10am and 5-10pm. First night 23SFr, then 20.50SFr; doubles 28SFr, then 25.50SFr.) Along the same stretch sprawl **Camping Seegärtli** (tel. (033) 951 13 51; 7SFr per person, 5-7SFr per tent; open April-Oct.) and **Camping Aaregg** (tel. (033) 951 18 43; fax 951 43 24; 9SFr per person, 16SFr per tent; open April-Oct.).

SWITZERLAND

Jungfrau Region

The most famous (and most visited) region of the Berner Oberland, the Jungfrau area has attracted tourists for hundreds of years with glorious hiking trails and perennially snow-capped peaks. As the birthplace of skiing (or so they claim), the area offers some of the most challenging slopes in Switzerland. Transportation throughout the area, unfortunately, is scandalously expensive. **Berner Oberland Bahn,** which runs mountain trains linking Interlaken to the valleys, often grants only minor price reductions to Swiss- and Eurailpass holders. Of uncertain value is the 15-day **Berner Oberland Regional Pass** (190SFr, with Swisspass or Half-Fare Card 155SFr), which gives free travel for five days on many railways and cable cars (e.g. Rothorn, Schynige Platte, First, Niesen) and half-price travel on the remaining 10 days, but only a 25% discount on the Schilthorn and Kleine Scheidegg-Jungfraujoch. A seven-day variation is also available with three free days and four half-priced days (150SFr, with Swisspass or Half-Fare Card 120SFr). Both are available at train stations or any tourist office.

The best way to see the Alps, of course, is to **hike.** Maps for hikers are available from nearly every tourist office. Trails are clearly marked by bright yellow signs indicating the estimated time to nearby destinations ("Std." is short for *Stunden,* or hours). Climbers should pack sunglasses, water, raingear, and a sweater, and follow standard safety procedures; the Alps are not kind to the unprepared. There are several types of **ski passes** for the Oberland; the **Kleine Scheidegg/Männlichen** pass is 52SFr for one day, 95SFr for two. All passes include transportation to and from the lifts, and can be purchased at tourist offices or at chair lifts. **Balmer's Herberge** in Interlaken (see above) offers expert advice on skiing in the area, as well as ski rental (40-42SFr per day). Call or ask at the desk for more details. Ski rental is available throughout the valleys. The **ski schools** in **Wengen** (tel. (033) 855 20 22) and **Mürren** (tel. (033) 855 12 47) supply information on classes. Call (033) 855 10 22 for **weather information,** and check out conditions on the TVs in tourist offices and large hotels.

Grindelwald **Grindelwald** is a skier's and climber's dream. Ride Europe's longest chairlift up the **First** mountain for awesome scenery (27SFr, round-trip 43SFr; free with Regional Pass). Gondola rides to the **Männlichen** mountain start from the Grindelwald-Grund station (27SFr, round-trip 43SFr, 25-50% off with Eurail or Swissrail); the summit affords a glorious glance at the Oberland's three main peaks: Eiger, Mönch, and Jungfrau. The **tourist office** (tel. (036) 854 12 12; fax 854 12 10) in the Sport-Zentrum provides hiking and skiing maps and finds rooms in private homes. (25-50SFr. Open July-Aug. Mon.-Fri. 8am-7pm, Sat. 8am-5pm, Sun. 9-11am; Sept.-June Mon.-Fri. 8am-noon and 2-6pm, Sat. 8am-noon and 2-5pm.) For **hiking** info, try the **Bergführerbüro** (Mountain Guide Office; tel. (036) 853 52 00) on Hauptstr. (Open June-Oct. Mon.-Fri. 9am-noon and 3-6pm, Sat. 9am-noon and 3-6pm, Sun. 4-6pm.)

The Jugendherberge (HI) (tel. (036) 853 10 09; fax 853 50 29) is undoubtedly one of the best hostels in Switzerland. Go left from the station (5-7min.), turn right at the tiny brown sign, and go up the hill (29.50SFr first night, thereafter 27SFr; doubles and quads 32-45SFr). The newly renovated **Mountain Hostel** (tel. (036) 853 39 00; fax 853 47 30), at the Grund station, simply gleams (dorms 29-34SFr, doubles 78-88SFr; breakfast included). **Gletscherdorf** (tel. (036) 853 14 29; fax 853 31 29) is the closest campsite. From the station, turn right, take first right after the tourist office, and then the third left (9SFr per person, 4-9SFr per tent). Or try **Camping Eigernordwand** (tel. (036) 853 42 27), across the river and to the left of the Grund station (9.50SFr per person, 7-8SFr per tent). The budget-minded buy provisions at the **Co-op** across from the tourist office (open Mon.-Thurs. 8am-6:30pm, Fri. 8am-9pm, Sat. 8am-5pm).

Lauterbrunnen Valley **Lauterbrunnen** village feels small, dwarfed by sheer rock cliffs and beautiful glacier-cut valleys of the **Lauterbrunnen valley.** The **tourist office** (tel. (033) 855 19 55) is 200m left of the station on the main street. (Open Mon.-Fri. 8am-noon and 2-6pm; July-Aug. also Sat.-Sun. 10am-noon and 2-5pm.) A delightful farmhouse-turned-hostel, the **Matratzenlager Stocki** (tel. (033) 855 17 54) offers a mellow atmosphere and a full kitchen stacked with spices. From the back of the station, descend the steps, cross the river, turn right, and walk 200m. The sign on the house reads "Massenlager" (check-in by 6pm; 10SFr per person; open Jan.-Oct.). **Camping Jungfrau** (tel. (033) 856 20 10; fax 856 20 20), up the main street from the station toward the large waterfall, provides cheap beds, kitchens, showers, lounges, and a grocery store (8.20-9.60SFr per person, 6-15SFr per tent; dorms 18SFr). **Camping Schützenbach** (tel. (033) 855 12 68; fax 855 12 75), on the Panorama walkway to the falls, has communal bathrooms, laundry and kitchen facilities (4.60SFr per person, 11SFr per tent; dorms 14-16SFr). Follow the signs toward Trümmelbach from the station (15min.). Lauterbrunnen's **Co-op** roosts next to the post office.

When you're ready to move on, an easy 40-minute hike leads to the fabulous **Trümmelbach Falls,** 10 consecutive glacier-bed chutes that gush up to 20,000L of water per second and generate mighty winds. Explore via tunnels, footbridges, and underground funiculars (open July-Aug. daily 8am-6pm; April-June and Sept.-Nov. 9am-5pm; 12SFr). Follow signs along the river to **Stechelberg,** where cable cars leave for Gimmelwald (7.20SFr), Mürren (14SFr), Birg (32.20SFr), and Schilthorn (46SFr). Rides are 25% off with Swisspass. If you stop at **Mürren,** ask at the **tourist office** (tel. (036) 856 86 86; fax 856 86 96) in the sports center (10min. from the Schilthorn cable car station, 5min. from the railway station) about private rooms, hiking trails, and skiing prices (open Mon.-Fri. 8:30am-noon and 1:30-5:30pm, Sat. 8:30am-noon and 1:30-4pm). The single hostel in the valley rewards those who trek to **Gimmelwald** on the steep Stechelberg trail; the **Mountain Hostel** (tel. (036) 85 17 04) is rustic, inexpensive, friendly (and shares a name with the one in Grindenwald). Don't arrive without food—there are cooking facilities but no restaurants in this microscopic burg (15SFr). If this hostel is full, *Let's Go* recommends heading back to the hostels in Lauterbrunnen or Mürren.

Zermatt and the Matterhorn

A trick of the valley blocks out the great Alpine summits surrounding **Zermatt,** allowing the **Matterhorn** (4478m), orange at dawn and cloud-shrouded much of the time, to rise alone above the town. To climb this beast, you need a mountain of money, rock climbing experience, and a courageous heart; the hike takes two days and hiring a guide costs over 670SFr. Fortunately, you can hike miles of sign-posted paths around Zermatt without grave danger to life or wallet. Find out more at the **Bergführerbüro** (Mountaineering Office; tel. (027) 966 24 60), five minutes from the train station up Bahnhofstr. (Open July-Sept. Mon.-Fri. 8:30am-noon and 4-7pm, Sat. 4-7pm, Sun. 10am-noon and 4-7pm.) The **tourist office** (tel. (027) 967 01 81; fax 967 01 85), adjacent to the station, provides skiing and hiking maps. (Open mid-June to mid-Oct. Mon.-Fri. 8:30am-6pm, Sat. 8:30am-7pm, Sun. 9:30am-noon and 4-7pm; mid-Oct. to mid-June Mon.-Fri. 8:30am-noon and 1:30-6:30pm, Sat. 8:30am-noon.) Sturdy boots, warm clothing, and raingear are essential. For a spectacular glimpse of the Matterhorn and its splendid valleys, climb to **Hörnlihütte,** the base camp for ascents of the Matterhorn, a grueling 4-5 hour hike past the bathtub-sized lake **Schwarzsee** from Zermatt. The less zealous can take a cable car to Schwarzsee (round-trip 29.50SFr). Zermatt has more summer **ski trails** than any other Alpine resort—36 sq. km of year-round runs between 3900m and 2900m. During the winter, downhill ski passes cost 60SFr for a day, and discounts are available for longer stays. For more time on the slopes, rent equipment in town a day ahead. Most ski shops are open Monday through Saturday 8am to noon and 2 to 7pm and charge about 43SFr (10% discount for hostelers at ROC Sport on Kirchstr.). For **alpine rescue,** call (027) 967 20 00.

The **Jugendherberge (HI),** Winkelmatten (tel. (027) 967 23 20; fax 967 53 06), provides a view of The Mountain from the bedroom windows, but it's a 15-minute trek. From the train station, walk to the right down the main street, turn left at the church, cross the river, and take the second street to the right. (Reception open in summer daily 7:30-9am and 4pm-midnight; off-season 6:30-9am and 3pm-midnight. Curfew 11:30pm. 37.50-40SFr.) Closer to the station, **Hotel Bahnhof** (tel. (027) 967 24 06; fax 967 72 16), on Bahnhofstr. just past the Gornergratbahn, feels like a rustic cabin (dorms 26-28SFr, singles 40-50SFr, doubles 71-79SFr). The lone campground is **Camping Matterhorn Zermatt** (tel. (027) 967 39 21), a five-minute walk down Bahnhofstr. from the station (reception open May-Sept. daily 8:30-10am and 5:20-7pm; 8SFr, showers included). **Walliser Kanne** on Bahnhofstr. serves inventive Swiss food (open daily 10am-midnight). Zermatt's oldest restaurant, the **Café du Pont,** at the end of Bahnhofstr., serves hearty Alpine fare (open daily 9am-midnight; food served 11am-3pm and 5-10pm; closed Nov. and May). Cars are not permitted in Zermatt.

Saas Fee

Nicknamed "the pearl of the Alps," Saas Fee is situated in a hanging valley above the Saastal and snuggles among 13 4000m peaks. One of the peaks is the **Dom** (4545m), the second highest mountain in Switzerland. Summer **skiers** can enjoy 20km of runs and a stupendous Alpine view, but in winter an immense network of lifts opens (day ski passes 56SFr). Stores in the **Swiss Rentasport System** offer good rates (skis or snowboard and boots 43SFr per day). In summer, turn to **hiking:** the **Alpine Guide's office** (tel. (027) 957 44 64) by the church has a selection of climbs for both amateurs and experts (open Mon.-Sat. 9:30am-noon and 3-6pm).

The staff of the **tourist office** (tel. (027) 957 14 57; fax 957 18 60), across from the bus station, reserves rooms (5SFr) and dispenses seasonal information and hiking advice. (Open July-Sept. and Dec.-April Mon. and Wed.-Fri. 8:30am-noon and 2-6:30pm, Tues. 8:30am-noon and 3-6:30pm, Sat. 8am-7pm, Sun. 9am-noon and 3-6pm; reduced hours off season.) A **post bus** runs every hour to **Visp** (1hr., 13.20SFr), which connects to Lausanne and elsewhere, and **Stalden Saas** (35min., 10.40SFr), which connects to Zermatt for another 30SFr. You must reserve a place on all buses starting at Saas Fee at least two hours before departure (call (027) 957 19 45 or stop by the station). The best budget accommodations are at **Hotel Feehof Garni** (tel. (027) 957 23 08; fax 957 23 09). From the bus station, head down to the main street left of the tourist office, turn left, and pass the church (49-69SFr per person). One of the town's better values is **Pension Garni Mascotte** and its two sister chalets (tel. (027) 957 27 24; fax 957 12 16). With your back to the station, head down the road opposite you just left of the tourist office. At the main street, turn right and continue up the hill for 200m (dorms 27-55SFr; breakfast included; open mid-Dec. to April and July-Sept.). **Spaghetteria da Rasso,** two minutes to the left of the pharmacy, has 14 variations on spaghetti (13-24SFr; open Dec.-April and July-Oct. daily 11:30am-10:30pm).

FRENCH SWITZERLAND

Basel (Bâle)

Perched on the Rhine a stone's throw from France and Germany, Basel (rhymes with "nozzle") exemplifies the cultural dimorphism of Northern Switzerland; it is neither French nor German, but takes from both to create a distinct character all its own. A beautiful city with a charming cobblestone *Altstadt,* Basel's medieval image subtly masks the vibrancy of a modern university town.

ORIENTATION AND PRACTICAL INFORMATION

The **Gross-Basel** part of town, where most sights are located, lies on the left bank of the Rhine on two hills separated by the valley of the Birsig; on the right bank lies **Klein-Basel.** Be sure to pick up a city **map** (0.50SFr) at either tourist office.

Tourist Office, Schifflände 5 (tel. 268 68 68; fax 268 68 70). Take tram 1 (from the SBB station) to "Schifflände"; the office is on the river, near the Mittlere Bridge. Open Mon.-Fri. 8:30am-6pm, Sat. 10am-4pm. Grab lists of museums, cultural events, and suggested walking tours. Hotel reservations here, or at the **branch office** (10SFr), located at the SBB station (tel. 271 36 84; fax 272 93 42). Open June-Sept. Mon.-Fri. 8:30am-7pm, Sat. 8:30am-12:30pm and 1:30-6pm, Sun 10am-2pm; Oct.-May Mon.-Fri. 8:30am-6pm, Sat. 8:30am-noon.

Currency Exchange: Rates uniform city-wide; SBB station open daily 6am-9pm.

Trains: Three stations. The **French** (**SNCF;** tel. 00 33 36 35 35 36) and **Swiss** (**SBB;** tel. 157 22 22) stations are in Centralbahnpl., near the *Altstadt;* trains from Germany arrive at the **DB** station across the Rhine down Riehenstr. (tel. 690 11 11).

To: Zurich (1hr., 30SFr), Geneva (3hr., 67SFr), Lausanne (2½hr., 57SFr), Bern (1hr., 34SFr), Vienna (10hr., 154SFr), Paris (5hr., 675SFr), and Rome (7hr., 1195SFr).

Buses: The DB station sends buses to Germany, while the SBB and SNCF stations run to Germany and France.

Public Transportation: Trams and buses operate from 5:45am-11:45pm. Most sights are within zone 10. One-zone tickets cost 2.60SFr, day ticket 7.40SFr.

Bike Rental: In the train station. 22SFr per day. Open Mon.-Sun. 7am-9pm.

Hotlines: Helping Hand: tel. 143. **Rape Crisis Hotline:** tel. 261 89 89.

Emergency: Medical Assistance: tel. 144. All lines have English speakers.

Police: tel. 117.

Post Office: Freiestr. 12, at the intersection with Rudengasse. Ride streetcar 1, 8, or 15 to "Marktplatz"; go 1 block up Gerbergasse to Rudengasse. Open Mon.-Fri. 7:30am-noon and 1:30-6pm, Sat. 8-11am. **Postal Code:** CH-4000 to CH-4060.

Telephone Code: 061.

ACCOMMODATIONS AND CAMPING

Only one crowded hostel and very few hotels even remotely approach budget status; reserve a room ahead of time. A service books private rooms in and around the city for 20SFr (tel./fax 702 21 51 between 10am and noon or 2pm and 6pm; rooms 50-100SFr). The truly desperate can try **Stadhof,** Gerbergasse 84 (tel. 261 87 11), which has showerless rooms in extremely limited numbers (singles 60-75SFr).

Jugendherberge (HI), St. Alban-Kirchrain 10 (tel. 272 05 72; fax 272 08 33). Take streetcar 1 to "Aeschenplatz," then streetcar 3 to "St. Alban-Tor"; or walk 10-15min. from the SBB station down Aeschengraben, then St. Alban Anlage. Near the river in a calm, verdant stretch. Reception open 7-10am and 2pm-midnight. Midnight curfew. First night 26.80SFr, each subsequent night 24.30SFr. Doubles 37.80SFr, then 35.30SFr. Showers and breakfast included. Laundry 8SFr.

Hotel-Pension Steinenschanze, Steinengraben 69 (tel. 272 53 53; fax 272 45 73). From the SBB station, turn left on Centralbahnstr., toward Heuwage-Viadukt, and walk straight ahead. Amenities make up for the higher price. 3-day max. stay. Singles from 100SFr, under 25 with ISIC 50SFr. Doubles 150SFr and up; under 25 with ISIC 100SFr and up. Breakfast and shower included. Free luggage storage.

Hecht am Rhein, Rheingasse 8 (tel. 691 22 20; fax 681 07 88). Reception open 7am-6pm. Singles 70-80SFr. Doubles 120-130SFr. Breakfast included.

Camping: Camp Waldhort, Heideweg 16, 4153 Reinach (tel. 711 64 29). Streetcar 1 to "Aeschenplatz," then streetcar 11 to "Landhof." Reception open daily 8am-12:15pm and 2:30-10pm. 6.50SFr per person, 4SFr per tent. Open March-Oct.

FOOD

Basel is a university town, so relatively cheap eateries are fairly numerous, even in the heart of the city. Check out cafés and weekday morning fruit, vegetable, and baked goods stalls on the **Marktplatz.** Shop for groceries at **Migros,** Claraplatz or Sternengasse 17, or at the **Co-op** center opposite the train station.

Hirscheneck, Lindenberg 23. Cross the Wettsteinbrücke and take the first left. A left-of-center restaurant/bar where dreadlocks and piercings prevail. Features vegetarian dishes. *Menu* 13SFr. Open Mon. 5pm-midnight, Tues.-Thurs. 8am-midnight, Fri. 8am-1am, Sat. 2pm-1am, Sun. 10am-midnight.

Zum Schnabel, Trillengässlein 2. Take streetcar 1 or 8 to Marktplatz; walk a block on Hutgasse, then left onto Schnabelgasse. Comfy restaurant serves well-prepared German dishes. 12.80SFr meal will fill you up. Open Mon.-Sat. 8am-midnight.

Topas Kosher Restaurant, Leimenstrasse 24 (tel. 271 87 00). Entrees 18.50-28SFr. Open Sun., Tues., and Thurs. 11:30am-2pm and 6:30-9pm, Fri. 11:30am-2pm. Call a day ahead for Sat. lunch and Fri. dinner.

SIGHTS AND ENTERTAINMENT

The **Münster,** the crown jewel of Basel's medieval buildings, was built on the site of a Celtic town and Roman Fort. The church holds Erasmus's tomb, but the red sandstone facade steals the show with hundreds of figures in pious acts ranging from trumpet-playing to dragon-slaying. The Münster **tower** boasts the best view of **Klein Basel,** the Rhine, and the Black Forest. (Cathedral open in summer Mon.-Fri. 10am-5pm, Sat. 10am-noon and 2-5pm, Sun. 1-5pm; off-season Mon.-Sat. 11am-4pm, Sun. 2-4pm. Free. Tower 2SFr.) Toward Barfüsserpl. on Steinenberg, the **Jean Tinguely Fountain** contrasts with the medieval *Altstadt.* Nearby Freiestr., the main shopping avenue, leads to the Marktplatz and the **Rathaus** (City Hall). This gaudy building was erected in the early 1500s to celebrate Basel's entry into the Confederation.

Off Marktplatz, Sattlegasse marks the beginning of the **artisan's district,** with street names such as Schneidergasse (Tailor's Street). Find the **Lane of 11,000 Virgins** (Elftausendjungfern-Gässlein) in this area. Legend has it that St. Ursula's pilgrimage of girls to the Holy Land during the Children's Crusade passed through here. **St. Alban-Tor** by the hostel is one of the three remaining towers of the **Old City Wall.**

Basel's 30 **museums** feature everything from medieval medicine to Monteverdi cars. Deservedly the best known is the **Kunstmuseum** (Museum of Fine Arts), St. Alban-Graben 16 (tel. 271 08 28; streetcar 2 from the station), established in the 17th century, with works by Matisse, Chagall, Picasso, and Dalí (open Tues.-Sun. 10am-5pm, Wed. until 9pm; 7SFr, students 5SFr, Sun. free). For more modern works, try the **Museum für Gegenwartskunst** (Museum of Contemporary Art), St. Alban-Rheinweg 60, by the youth hostel (open Tues.-Sun. 11am-5pm; 7SFr, students 5SFr). The **Museum der Kulturen Basel** (Museum of Ethnology), Augustinergasse 2, just off Munsterpl., contains an off-beat gathering of exotic art (open Tues.-Sun. 10am-5pm, Wed. until 9pm Mar.-Aug.; 6SFr, students 4SFr).

Barfüsserplatz is a good place to start bar-hopping, though drinks just about everywhere are quite expensive. **Atlantis,** Klosterburg 13, is a large bar that sways to salsa, reggae, blues, and rock (cover 5-7SFr; open Sun.-Thurs. 10am-midnight, Fri.-Sat. 10am-1am). **Brauerei Fischerstube,** Rheingasse 45, Basel's smallest brewery, brews four of the best beers in town (open Mon.-Thurs. 10am-midnight, Fri.-Sat. 10am-1am, Sun. 5pm-midnight). **Caveau Mövenpick Wine Pub,** Grünpfahlgasse 4, by the post office, is a sophisticated change from the bar scene (wine glasses 6-10SFr; open Mon.-Sat. 11am-midnight). The annual Basel blow-out is **Fasnacht** carnival, the week of Feb. 30 in 1998, when revelers wear masks to scare away winter.

Neuchâtel

Perhaps at a loss for words, Alexandre Dumas once likened Neuchâtel to a city carved out of a block of butter. Although he was obviously referring to the unique yellow stone that makes up a large part of the city's architecture, Dumas could easily be mistaken these days as an overly appreciative fan of the calorie-laden treats in the local *pâtisseries.* But even after the visual and gastronomical novelty has worn off, Neuchâtel possesses a remarkable medieval beauty. The **château** and neighboring **Eglise Collégiale,** featuring a 1372 **Cenotaph,** dominate the town from their hilltop perches. (Free guided tours in English of the complex April-Sept. Mon.-Fri. every hr. 10am-4pm, Sat. 10-11am and 2-4pm, Sun. 2-4pm. Church open daily 8am-6pm.) The wonderful **Tour des Prisons** is just an arrow-shot away on rue de Château. Lock your traveling companion in one of the tiny wooden cells used in 1848 (0.50SFr). The **tower** provides a magnificent view (tower open April 1-Oct. 1). The **Musée d'Art et d'Histoire,** Esplanade Léopold-Robert, 1, offers an eclectic look at the history of Neuchâtel and features Renoir, pre-dot Seurat, pre-island Gauguin, and a *Balzac* by Rodin (open Tues.-Sun. 10am-5pm; 7Sfr, students 4SFr).

Trains connect Neuchâtel to Basel (1½hr., 35SFr), Bern (40min., 16.60SFr), Interlaken (2hr., 39SFr), and Geneva (1½hr., 41SFr). The helpful **tourist office** (tel. (032) 889 68 90; email neuchatel@tourisme.ch; http://www.etatne.ch), Hôtel des Postes, is two blocks to the left if you're facing the lake. (Open July-Aug. Mon.-Sat. 9am-7pm, Sun. 9am-7pm; Sept.-June Mon.-Fri. 9am-noon and 1:30-5:30pm, Sat. 9am-noon.) The ecologically friendly **Oasis Neuchâtel,** rue de Suchiez, 35 (tel. (032) 731 31 90; fax 730 37 09), boasts a view of the lake. From the station, take bus 6 to pl. Pury, walk in front of the kiosk, and take bus 1 ("Cormondrèche") to "Vauseyon." From there, head uphill (reception open daily 8-9am and 5-9pm; curfew 10:30pm; 22.50SFr). Closer to town, **Hotel Terminus** (tel. (032) 723 19 19) is just across from the train station (reception open daily 7:30am-10pm; singles 50SFr, doubles 90SFr).

The student hang-out **Crêperie Bach et Buck,** 50 yards from the university toward pl. Plury along av. du Premier-Mars, offers crepes (and only crepes) for under 10SFr. (Open Mon.-Thurs. 7:30am-10:30pm, Fri. 7:30am-midnight, Sat. 11am-midnight, Sun. 5-10:30pm.) If you hanker for something else, **A.R. Knect Boulangerie, Patisserie,** Place des Halles, serves up meaty sandwiches and flaky pastries for a pittance. Keep on keepin' on until 4am at **Le Garage,** rue de l'Hôpital, 4, which features the ever popular "sex night" and other special themes.

Geneva (Genève)

"I detest Geneva," muttered Napoleon Bonaparte in 1798, "they know English too well." They still do. Two-thirds of Geneva's population are foreign-born or transplants from other regions of Switzerland, and the city is a hybrid of many cultures. The large concentration of international banks and multinational organizations preserves the intricate melange—quite a contrast to Switzerland's other, mostly homogeneous towns. Yet modern internationalism contrasts with past isolationism. Geneva's citizens have a long and belligerent tradition of doing battle to protect their political and religious independence, and it wasn't until the Enlightenment that Madame de Staël's salons won out over Calvinist intolerance.

SWITZERLAND

ORIENTATION AND PRACTICAL INFORMATION

Genevois sun themselves on the western shore of **Lac Léman** (Lake Geneva), in southwestern Switzerland. In the city's *vieille ville,* cobbled streets and quiet squares surround the **Cathédrale de St-Pierre** and the **university.** Heading north, banks, bistros, and boutiques line the **river Rhône.** The United Nations, the Red Cross, and other international bodies overlook the city in a northern suburb. Carry your passport with you at all times; the French border is close and regional buses often cross it.

Tourist Offices: Must-haves are the city map, *Info Jeunes* (budget accommodations and activity info), and *Genève pratique* (detailed city info). **Main office,** rue du Mont-Blanc 3 (tel. 909 70 00; fax 929 70 11; http://www.geneve-tourisme.ch), 5min. to the right of the station. Books hotel rooms (5SFr fee) and offers **walking tours.** Open June 15-Sept. 15 Mon.-Fri. 8am-7pm, Sat.-Sun. 9am-6pm; Sept. 16-June 14 Mon.-Sat. 9am-6pm. **Office du Tourisme,** pl. du Molard 4 (tel. 311 98 27; fax 311 80 52), across the river. Same services, friendlier staff. Open Mon. 12:30-6:30pm, Tues.-Fri. 9am-6:30pm, Sat. 10:30am-4:30pm. Mobile, backpacker-oriented **Centre d'Accueil et de Renseignements (CAR)** (tel. 731 46 47), parks during the summer at the top of rue du Mont-Blanc after the pedestrian underpass beneath Gare Cornavin. Open June 16-Sept. 6 daily 9:30am-11pm. Last resort—**Anglo-phone** (tel. 157 50 14), a 24hr. hotline (in English; 2.13SFr per min.).

Currency Exchange: In Gare Cornavin. Good rates, no commission on traveler's checks. Will advance cash on major credit cards. Open daily 6:45am-9:30pm.

American Express: rue du Mont-Blanc 7 (tel. 73 17 60; fax 732 72 11). Mail held. All banking services; good exchange rates. **ATM** service with AmEx card. Hotel (20SFr) and train (10SFr) reservations. Open in summer Mon.-Fri. 8:30am-6pm, Sat. 9am-noon; off-season Mon.-Fri. 8:30am-5:30pm, Sat. 9am-noon.

Flights: Cointrin Airport (tel. 717 71 11) is naturally one of Swissair's hubs. There are daily direct flights to New York, Paris, London, Amsterdam, and Rome.

Trains: Gare Cornavin, pl. Cornavin, is the primary station and departure point for all major Swiss and foreign cities. To: Lausanne (40min., 19.40SFr), Bern (1¾hr.,

48SFr), Zurich (3hr., 74SFr), Basel (2¾hr., 67SFr), Montreux (1hr., 27SFr), Interlaken (2¾hr., 60SFr), Paris (3½hr., 66-81SFr for ages under 26, 82-97SFr for those over age 26), and Rome (10hr., 84SFr under 26, 109SFr over 26). The busy reservation and information office is open Mon.-Fri. 8:45am-7:40pm, Sat. 8:30am-5:40pm.

Public Transportation: Transport Publics Genevois, next to the tourist office in Gare Cornavin (tel. 308 34 34; open daily 6:15am-8pm), provides a free but confusing map of the local bus routes called *Le Réseau.* 2.20SFr buys an hour of unlimited travel on any bus; 3 stops or less costs 1.50SFr; 6 1hr. trips for 12SFr, or 12 1hr. trips for 22SFr. Your best bet is a full day pass for 5SFr. Buses are free with Swisspass, but not with Eurail. Buy multi-fare and day tickets at train station, others at automatic vendors at every stop. Buses run daily 5:30am-midnight.

Ferries: Hugely popular **CGN ferries** (tel. 732 39 16) depart from the quai du Mont-Blanc at the foot of rue des Alpes for Lausanne (3hr., 29SFr one way) and Montreux (4½hr., 34SFr one way). Round-trip tickets include the option of returning by train.

Bike Rental: At Gare Cornavin's baggage check (tel. 715 22 20). 22-29SFr per day. Open Mon.-Fri. 6:50am-6:45pm, Sat.-Sun. 7am-12:30pm and 1:30-5:45pm.

Hitchhiking: Those headed to Germany or northern Switzerland take bus 4/44 to "Jardin Botanique." For France, hitchers take bus 4/44 to "Palettes" and then line D to "St. Julien." In summer, **Telstop** lists rides in front of the CAR info-bus.

Gay and Lesbian Organization: Dialogai, Case Postale 27, av. Wendt 57 (tel. 340 00 00; fax 340 03 98). Bus 3, 9, or 10 to "Servette-Ecole." Publishes *Dialogai,* a guide to Switzerland's gay scene. Mostly men; women are welcome. Open Wed. 8-10pm.

Travelers with Disabilities: CCIPH (Centre de Coordination et d'Information pour Personnes Handicapées), rte de Chée 54 (tel. 736 38 10). The tourist office also provides a free guide entitled *Guide à l'Usage des Personnes Handicapées.*

Laundromat: Salon Lavoir St-Gervais, rue Vallin 9, off pl. St-Gervais. Wash 4SFr, dry 1SFr per 12min. Open Mon.-Sat. 7:30am-9pm, Sun. 10am-9pm.

Crisis Line: Lifeline (tel. (059) 504 23 704), a 24hr. hotline for problems ranging from drug addiction to extreme depression.

Medical Services: Hôpital Cantonal, rue Micheli-du-Crest 24 (tel. 372 81 20). Door 3 for outpatient care. Walk-in clinics dot the city; call 320 25 11.

Emergencies: Fire: tel. 118. **Ambulance:** tel. 144.

Police: rue Pecolat 5 (tel. 117), next to the post office.

Post Office: Poste Centrale, rue du Mont-Blanc 18, a block from the Gare Cornavin. Open Mon.-Fri. 7:30am-6pm, Sat. 8-11am. Address *Poste Restante* to: CH-1211 Genève 1 Mont-Blanc. **Postal Code:** CH-1211.

Telephones: PTT, Gare Cornavin. Has phone-now-pay-later system that takes Visa, MasterCard, AmEx, and Diners. Open daily 8am-10pm. **Telephone Code:** 022.

ACCOMMODATIONS AND CAMPING

You can usually find dorm beds and hostel rooms in Geneva, but hotels fill quickly, so reserve in advance. If the places listed below are booked, try one of the 25 others listed in *Info Jeunes,* which you can pick up at the tourist office.

Auberge de Jeunesse (HI), rue Rothschild 28-30 (tel. 732 62 60; fax 738 39 87). Walk left from the station down rue de Lausanne and then turn right onto rue Rothschild, or ride Bus 1 ("Wilson.") Bureaucratic feel, but also a restaurant, kitchen, and TV room. Reception open in summer daily 6:30-10am and 4pm-midnight; off-season 6:30-10am and 5pm-midnight. Curfew midnight. 23SFr, nonmembers 28SFr. Doubles 70-80SFr. Triples 85-120SFr. Showers, sheets, and breakfast included.

Centre St. Boniface, av. du Mail 14 (tel. 321 88 44; fax 320 47 94). Take bus 1 or 4/44 to "Cirque," and continue down av. du Mail. Spartan but quiet rooms just minutes from the *vieille ville.* Kitchen. Reception open Mon-Fri. 9:30-11:30am, 4:30-6:30pm, and 7:30-8:30pm, Sat. 10am-noon. Dorms 16SFr. Sheets 8SFR. From mid-July to late Sept. there are singles (34-39SFr) and a few doubles (57-62SFr).

Hôme St-Pierre, cours St-Pierre 4 (tel. 310 37 07), opposite the west end of the cathedral in the heart of the *vieille ville.* From the train station, cross the Rhône at Pont du Mont-Blanc, then head up the Rampe de la Treille and take the third right. You can also take bus 5 to "pl. Neuve." A well-decorated, homey hostel for women only (ages 17-30). Reception open Mon.-Sat. 8:30am-1pm and 4-8pm, Sun. 9am-

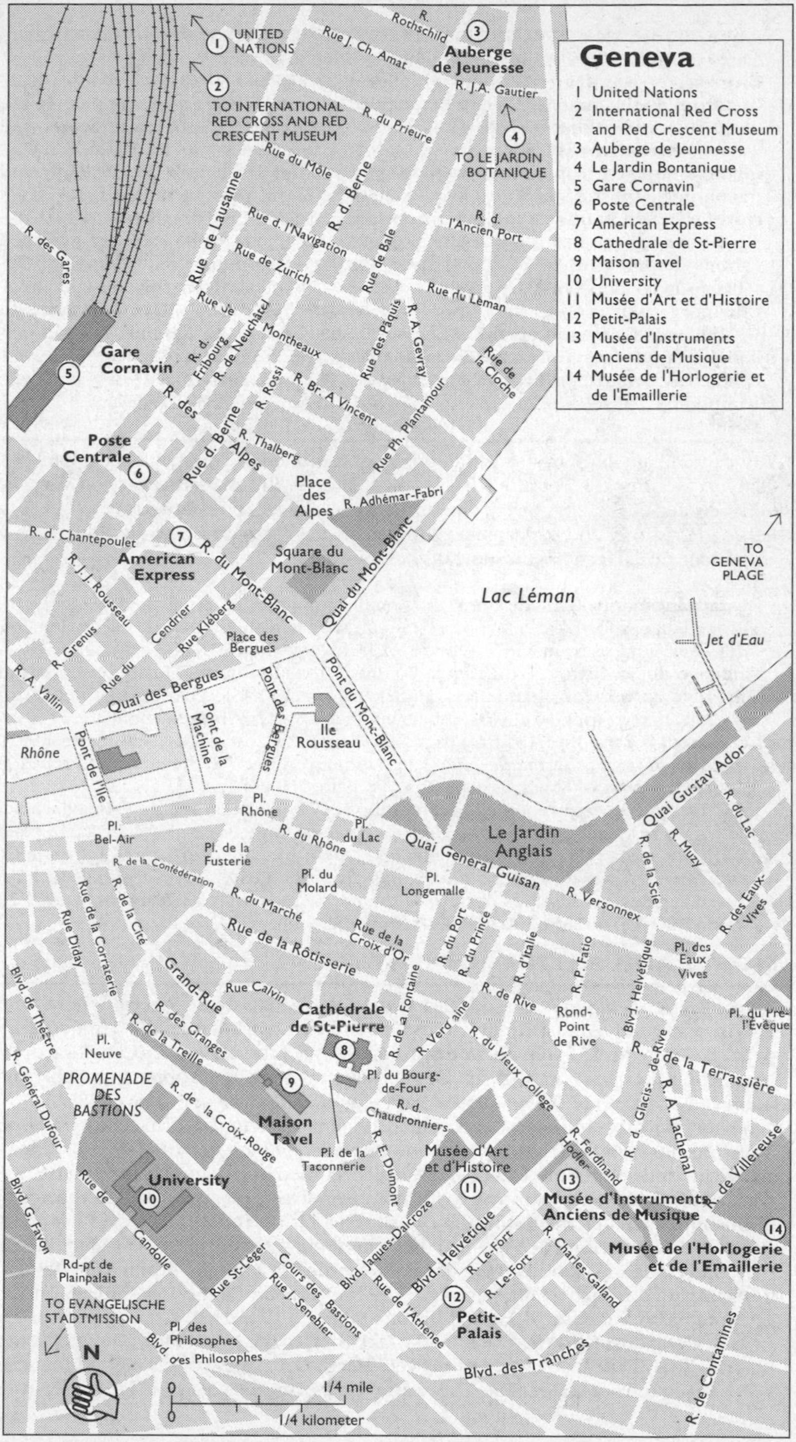
Geneva
1 United Nations
2 International Red Cross and Red Crescent Museum
3 Auberge de Jeunesse
4 Le Jardin Bontanique
5 Gare Cornavin
6 Poste Centrale
7 American Express
8 Cathedrale de St-Pierre
9 Maison Tavel
10 University
11 Musée d'Art et d'Histoire
12 Petit-Palais
13 Musée d'Instruments Anciens de Musique
14 Musée de l'Horlogerie et de l'Emaillerie
UNITED NATIONS
TO INTERNATIONAL RED CROSS AND RED CRESCENT MUSEUM
Auberge de Jeunesse
TO LE JARDIN BOTANIQUE
Gare Cornavin
Poste Centrale
American Express
Place des Alpes
Square du Mont-Blanc
Place des Bergues
Lac Léman
TO GENEVA PLAGE
Jet d'Eau
Rhône
Ile Rousseau
Le Jardin Anglais
Cathédrale de St-Pierre
Maison Tavel
PROMENADE DES BASTIONS
University
Musée d'Art et d'Histoire
Musée d'Instruments Anciens de Musique
Musée de l'Horlogerie et de l'Emaillerie
Petit-Palais
TO EVANGELISCHE STADTMISSION
Rd-pt de Plainpalais
Pl. des Philosophes
N
1/4 mile
1/4 kilometer

1pm. Big breakfast (Mon.-Sat.) 7.50SFr. No lockout or curfew. Dorms 22SFr. Singles 35SFr. Doubles 50SFr. Showers and lockers included. Reserve ahead.

Cité Universitaire, av. Miremont 46 (tel. 839 22 11; fax 839 22 23). From pl. de 22 Cantons on the right as you exit the station, ride bus 3 ("Crêts-de-Champel") to the last stop. Institutional college with TV rooms, restaurant, disco, tennis courts, and even **Internet access.** Reception open Mon.-Fri. 8am-noon and 2-10pm, Sat.-Sun. 8am-noon and 6-10pm. Curfew 11:30pm. Lockout 10am-6pm. Dorms (July and Sept. only) 15SFr. Singles 36-43SFr. Doubles 52-58SFr. Shower included.

Hotel Pension Saint-Victor, rue François-le-Fort 1 (tel. 346 17 18; fax 346 10 46). Take bus 1, 3, or 5 to "pl. Claparède." Outstanding hotel with clean, distinguished rooms in the old town. Reception open Mon.-Fri. 7:30-8pm, Sat.-Sun. 8am-8pm. Singles from 65SFr. Doubles from 90SFr. Breakfast included. Reservations imperative.

Camping: Sylvabelle, chemin de Conches 10 (tel. 347 06 03); take bus 8 to "Conches." Reception open Easter to Oct. daily 7-10am and 7-10pm. 6SFr per person, 4SFr per tent. To reach **Pointe-à-la-Bise** (tel. 752 12 96), ride bus 9 to "Rive," then bus E (north) to "Bise." 6SFr per person, 9SFr per tent. Open April to mid-Oct.

FOOD

You can find anything from sushi to *paella* in Geneva, but you may need a banker's salary to foot the bill. For a quick bite to eat shop at the **supermarkets** on virtually every corner of the city, or try one of the many university **cafeterias** listed in *Info Jeunes*. *Patisseries* and pasta/pizza parlors permeate **Place du Bourg-de-Four,** below Cathédrale de St-Pierre, as do some of the best cafés.

Restaurant Manora, rue de Cornavin 4, 3min. from the station in the Placette Dept. Store. Huge, affordable self-serve restaurant with a fresh, high-quality selection. Salads 4SFr. Entrees from 11SFr. Open Mon.-Sat. 7am-9:30pm, Sun. 9am-9pm.

Auberge de Saviese, rue du Pâquis 20. Bus 1 to "Monthoux." Rustic interior and massive barrels for chandeliers. *Plats du jour* 13-14SFr. Excellent *fondue au cognac* 19SFr. Open Mon.-Fri. 8:30am-midnight, Sat. 2:30pm-midnight.

Le Rozzel, Grand-Rue 18. Breton-style *crêperie* with outdoor seating amid the antique shops of the *vieille ville.* Large dinner crepes 7-16SFr. Dessert crepes 5-14SFr. Open Mon.-Thurs. 7:30am-9pm, Fri.-Sun. 7:30am-1am.

La Crise, rue de Chantepoulet 13. From the station, right on rue de Cornavin, then left. Tiny restaurant with big portions. Huge meal (large slice of quiche and a plate full of veggies) 7SFr. Hearty soup 3.50SFr. Open Mon.-Fri. 6am-8pm, Sat. 6am-3pm.

Les 5 Saveurs, rue du Prieuré 22. Seconds from the hostel. *Very* health-conscious. Fresh veggies and luscious desserts at the noon-time buffet 12Sfr for 400g. *Plat du soir* 15SFr. Open Mon.-Fri. noon-2pm and 6:30-9pm.

SIGHTS AND ENTERTAINMENT

A visit to the *vieille ville* should start at the **Cathédrale de St-Pierre,** where John Calvin preached against indulgences and the extravagance of the 16th-century papacy. Climb the 157-step **north tower** for a view of the old town. (Cathedral open June-Sept. daily 9am-7pm; Oct. and March-May 9am-noon and 2-6pm; Nov.-Feb. 9am-noon and 2-5pm. Free. Tower closes 30min. before the cathedral. Tower 3SFr.)

A short walk from the west end of the cathedral leads to the 14th-century **Maison Tavel,** rue du Puits-St-Pierre 6, which now stores everything from a 1799 guillotine to a vast zinc-and-copper model of the city in 1850 (open Tues.-Sun. 10am-5pm; free). A walk along **Grand-Rue** takes you to the commemorative plaque at #40, birthplace of philosopher Jean-Jacques Rousseau. Rest for a bit on the 394ft. **world's longest bench,** below the Hôtel de Ville, and then check out the stony gazes of Calvin, Cromwell, and company along **Le Mur des Réformatuers,** facing the Promenade des Bastions. Bearded monks shuffle about inside the **Russian Orthodox Church** on rue Toepffer, near the Musée d'Art et d'Histoire (1SFr).

Stroll along quai Gustave-Ardor, by the lakefront, to the 140m high plume of water from the **Jet-d'Eau;** at any given time (well, March-Oct.), the world's highest fountain keeps seven tons of water aloft. The nearby **Jardin Anglais** pays homage to Geneva's watch industry with the much-touted **floral clock.** Two beaches front the lake: *Genevois* frequent the laid-back **Pâquis Plage** at quai du Mont-Blanc (1SFr), while upscale **Genève Plage** (6SFr) offers a waterslide, volleyball, and an Olympic-size pool.

A veritable sub-city of organizational headquarters awaits on the *rive droite,* a 15-minute walk from the train station or a short hop on bus 8. The rather dull guided tour of the **United Nations** (info tel. 907 45 60), at the end of rue Montbrillant, pales before the constant traffic of international diplomats, brightly clothed in native garb. (Open July-Aug. daily 9am-6pm; April-June and Sept.-Oct. 10am-noon and 2-4pm; Nov.-March Mon.-Fri. 10am-noon and 2-4pm. 8.50SFr, students 6.50SFr.) Even better is the excellent **International Red Cross and Red Crescent Museum,** av. de la Paix 17 (bus 8, F, V, or Z to "Appia"), which reflects on the organization's work with powerful displays and videos (open Wed.-Mon. 10am-5pm; 10SFr, students 5SFr).

Pick up *Genève Agenda* and *What's On in Geneva* at the tourist office to plan your fun. Summer nightlife offerings center on lakeside quais, cafés in **pl. du Bourg-de-Four,** and in the village of **Carouge** (tram 12 to "pl. du Marché"). Befriend a native to find this week's **squat bar,** a moving party that attracts a trendy and artsy crowd. Or, join a hip college crowd at **Casting Café,** rue de la Servette 6, a two-minute walk behind the station. (Open Mon.-Fri. 11am-2am, Sat.-Sun. 2pm-2am; DJs play house music Sat.-Sun. 4:30-8am.) **La Clémence,** pl. du Bourg-de-Four 20, attracts students with breakfast and beer (beer 4-8SFr; open Mon.-Fri. 7am-1am, Sat.-Sun. 7am-2am), while **Au Chat Noir,** rue Vautier 13 in Carouge, features jazz, rock, and blues (open Mon.-Thurs. 6pm-4am, Fri. 6pm-5am, Sat. 9pm-5am, Sun. 9pm-4am).

In July and August, **Cinélac** shows movies on a screen over the lake near Genève Plage. *The* party in Geneva is **L'Escalade,** commemorating the dramatic repulse of the invading Savoyard troops from the city walls. The revelry lasts a full weekend in mid-December. Summer festivals include the biggest celebration of **American Independence Day** outside the U.S., and the **Fêtes de Genève,** August 7-10, an international music and art celebration. **La Bâtie Festival,** an experimental-rock festival held in late August and early September, draws music lovers for a two-week orgy of cabarets, theater, and concerts (many events free; otherwise 10-32SFr, students half-price).

Lausanne

In its past, Lausanne was the haunt of literary luminaries such as Dickens, Thackery, and T.S. Eliot (who wrote *The Waste Land* here). Hardly a waste land, Lausanne is now the locus of a well-oiled tourist machine whose hum is tactfully muted by the soft lull of Lac Léman's waves and breezes from the Alps. As it did with literati, Lausanne lures visitors with sunny decadence, cosmopolitan airs, and an endless succession of free performances and festivals during the summer.

The **International Olympic Committee's** magnificent **Musée Olympique,** quai d'Ouchy 1 (tel. (021) 621 65 11), unites sport, art, and culture with paintings and statues, video highlights of past Olympics, and sleek presentations on the philosophy and history of the games. (Open May-Sept. Mon.-Wed. and Fri.-Sun. 10am-7pm, Thurs. 10am-8pm; Oct.-April Tues.-Wed. and Fri.-Sun. 10am-6pm, Thurs. 10am-8pm. 14SFr, students and seniors 9SFr.) Connected by a short uphill path, the **Musée de l'Elysée,** av. de l'Elysée (tel. (021) 617 48 21; email dgirardin@ping.ch) features stunning photography and film exhibits. (Bus 2 to "Croix-d'Ouchy." Open Tues.-Wed. and Fri.-Sun. 10am-6pm, Thurs. 10am-9pm. 5SFr, students 2.50SFr.) The more macabre **Collection de l'Art Brut** (tel. (021) 647 54 35; bus 2 or 3 to "Jomini") features chilling works by the criminally insane, institutionalized, and other non-traditional artists (open Tues.-Sun. 11am-1pm and 2-6pm; 6SFr, students and seniors 4SFr). To return to the sacred, walk up the covered medieval steps (or bus 16) to the Gothic **Cathédrale,** consecrated by Pope Gregory X in 1275 but stripped of much of its ornamentation during the Reformation. Fortunately, the rose window in the south transept was spared. (Open July to mid-Sept. daily 7am-7pm; mid-Sept. to June 7am-5pm. Free guided tours July-Sept., call (021) 323 84 34. Tower open 8:30-11:30am and 1:30-5:30pm. 2SFr.) The **quai de Belgique** and **la Place de la Navigation** are lakeside promenades flanked by flowers, gardens, and fountains; the best beach area is in the **Bellerive Complex.** (Bus 2 to "Bellerive." Open mid-May to Aug. daily 9:30am-dusk. 4.50SFr, students and seniors 3SFr; 0.50SFr discount after 5pm.)

Practical Information, Accommodations, and Food Although there is a branch in the train station, the main **tourist office,** av. de Rhodanie 2 (tel. (021) 613 73 21, for general info 617 73 73; fax 616 86 47; email information@lausanne-tourisme.ch; http://www.lausanne.tourisme.ch), is located across from the lake. Take the Métro (2.20SFr) or bus 2 to "Ouchy." The staff is superb, the map and information guides free, and the wait short; the office also makes hotel reservations for 4-6SFr. (Open April-Sept. Mon.-Fri. 8am-7pm, Sat. 9am-6pm, Sun. 9am-1pm and 2-6pm; Oct.-March Mon.-Fri. 8am-6pm, Sat. 9am-1pm and 2-6pm.) They offer museum passports (26SFr for a 3-day pass; students and seniors 20SFr) which give visitors free entry to all museums, public transportation, and one film at the **Swiss Film Archive,** allée E. Ansemel 3 (tel. (021) 331 01 00). Frequent **trains** serve Geneva (40min., 19.40SFr), Basel (2½hr., 57SFr), Montreux (20min., 8.40SFr), Zurich (2½hr., 62SFr), and other cities; visit the station on pl. de la Gare (open Mon.-Fri. 8am-7pm, Sat. 8am-5pm, Sun. 11am-7pm) or call (021) 157 22 22 for more info. A vast, barracks-like complex, **Jeunotel,** Chemin du Bois-de-Vaux 36 (tel. (021) 626 02 22; fax 626 02 26), is Lausanne's only official youth hostel. Take bus 2 ("Bourdonette") to "Bois-de-Vaux," then cross the street and follow the signs. (Reception open 24hr. Dorms 26SFr; singles 65SFr, with shower 75SFr; doubles 37SFr, with shower 46SFR; triples or quads 26SFr. Breakfast 3SFr. V, MC.) **Hotel "Le Chalet,"** av. d'Ouchy 49 (tel. (021) 616 52 06), has a limited number of rooms in a gardened 19th-century chalet. Take the Métro or bus 2 to "Jordils." (Arrive before 11pm. Singles 62SFr; doubles 87SFr; smaller rooms 48SFr. Breakfast 8SFr.) To get to the lakeside **Camping de Vidy,** take bus 2 to "Bois-de-Vaux," then cross the street, go down the Chemin du Bois-de-Vaux past Jeunotel and underneath the overpass. The reception office is straight ahead across the road. A restaurant, supermarket, and playground are close by. (Reception open daily 8am-8pm. 6.50SFr, students 6SFr; tents 7-11SFr; 1- to 2-person bungalows 54SFr; 3- to 4-person bungalows 86SFr; city tax 1.20SFr per person and 2.50SFr per car. Wheelchair access.)

Many Lausanne restaurants are just spectator sports for the budget traveler. Visit produce **markets** Wednesday and Saturday on rue de Bourg behind the Eglise St.-François (open 7am-1pm), Sunday at Ouchy (open April to mid-Oct. 9am-8pm), and Friday mornings at rue du Petit-Chêne off pl. St-François. At the end of August, find a flower and honey market at Derrière-Bourg in the *vieille ville* (open 8am-11pm). **Manora,** pl. St-François 17, is a popular self-service restaurant with fantastic salad, fruit, and dessert bars. (*Menus du jour* 7-14SFr. Open Mon.-Sat. 7am-10:30pm, Sun. 9am-10:30pm; hot food served 11am-10pm.) The **Crêperie "La Chandeleur,"** rue Mercerie 9, offers countless dinner and dessert crepes (4-18SFr; open Tues.-Thurs. 11am-10pm, Fri.-Sat. 11am-11:30pm). **Au Couscous,** rue Enning 2, at the top of rue de Bourg, serves fashionable, vegetarian-friendly Maghreb and Tunisian cuisine (15-22SFr; open Sun.-Thurs. 6pm-12:30am, Fri.-Sat. 6pm-midnight). Wander along the bar-lined **pl. St-François** for drinks and entertainment. **Dolce Vita,** rue de César Roux 30, features frequent live shows of rap, indie, world, and blistering acid jazz. (Beer 4-5SFr. Open Sun. and Wed. 10pm-2am, Fri.-Sat. 10pm-4am, in summer also Thurs. 10pm-3am.) The *vieille ville* springs to life the first two weeks of July with theater and dance events, most free, during the **Festival de la Cité.**

Montreux

Montreux is postcard Switzerland at its swanky, but genteel, best. The crystal-blue water of Lac Léman and the snow-capped Alps are a photographer's dream, and can be seen with breathtaking perfection from **St-Vincent,** the parish church, on rue de Temple. Montreux's 13th-century **Château de Chillon** features all the comforts of home—prison cells, a torture chamber, a weapons room—and inspired narratives by

Rousseau and Hugo as well as Lord Byron's *The Prisoner of Chillon.* (Open April-June and Sept. daily 9am-5:45pm; July-Aug. 9am-6:15pm; Oct. 10am-4:45pm; Nov.-Feb. 10am-noon and 1:30-4pm; March 10am-noon and 1:30-4:45pm. 6.50SFr, students 5.50SFr.) The biggest attraction, however, is the fabulous **Montreux Jazz Festival,** (tickets 49-129SFr; standing room 29-69SFr), which lasts for 15 days after the first Friday in July and is one of the biggest parties in Europe. From mid-March the jazz hotline is (021) 983 82 82. The tourist office has info and tickets; write months in advance for tickets at rue du Théâtre 5. (Booking desk tel. (021) 623 45 67; http://www.grolier.fr/festival/montreux. Open Mon.-Fri. 9am-noon and 1:30-6pm; 24hr. during the festival.) Tickets are also available from Société de Banque Suisse ticket counters or the Swiss National Tourist offices at 608 Fifth Ave., New York, NY 10020 (tel. (212) 757-5944) or at Swiss Court, London W1V 8EE (tel. (0171) 734 19 21). During the festival, **Jazz Off** offers 500 free hours of concerts.

Montreux's **tourist office,** pl. du Débarcadère (tel. (021) 962 84 84; fax 963 78 95; email tourism@montreux.ch; http://www.montreux.ch), sits on the lake. Descend the stairs opposite the train station and head left on Grand-Rue. The office is set back on the right hand side (open June-Aug. daily 9am-7pm; Sept.-May 9am-noon and 1:30-6pm). A branch office is at Gare de Montreux. **Trains** roll frequently into the station on av. des Alpes from Geneva (1hr., 27SFr), Bern (1½hr., 37SFr), and Lausanne (20min., 8.40SFr). Direct trains also go to Martigny, Aigle, Sion, and Brig and through the mountains of Gstaad. Walk along the lake for 20 minutes to the **Auberge de Jeunesse Montreux (HI),** passage de l'Auberge 8 (tel. (021) 963 49 34; fax 963 27 29), or take bus 1 ("Villeneuve") to "Territet" and follow the signs downhill. Despite the rumbling trains above, visitors pack the hostel for its view of the lake, fantastic showers, and airy comforters, so make reservations. (Reception open April-Sept. daily 7:30-10am and 5-11pm; Oct.-March 7:30-9:30am and 5-11pm. Checkout 9:30am. Lockout 10am-5pm. Curfew midnight; groups and families can request a key. 27SFr first night, then 24.50SFr; doubles 72SFr, then 67SFr; additional 5SFr for nonmembers. Breakfast included. Wheelchair access. V, MC.) A family business since 1870, the **Hôtel Pension Wilhelm,** rue du Marché 13-15 (tel. (021) 963 14 31; fax 963 32 85), sports sunny rooms with sinks. From the station, walk left three minutes up av. des Alpes and turn left onto rue du Marché, up the hill and past the police station (reception open all day and at night by prior notice; 37SFr, with shower 60SFr). Nearby **Villeneuve** has lakeside camping at **Les Horizons Bleus** (tel. (021) 960 15 47). Take bus 1 to Villeneuve, then walk along the lake to the left (reception open daily 8am-10pm; 7SFr per person, tax 1SFr; showers free).

Lakeside dining is sadly unaffordable. **Caveau des Vignerons,** rue Industrielle 30bis, serves fondue (20SFr), *raclette* (5.50SFr), and local wines (35-40SFr a bottle). (Open Mon.-Fri. 7am-midnight, Sat. 3pm-midnight. Closed last weekend in July and first 2 weeks in Aug.) The **Marché de Montreux,** pl. du Marché, a covered, outdoor market of culinary staples and specialties along both quai de la Rouvenaz and quai Jaccoud, may be more affordable (open Fri. 7am-3pm).

From late August to early October, the **Montreux-Vevey Classical Music Festival** (tickets 20-140SFr) reigns, featuring philharmonics from Moscow to Memphis. Write to the Office of the Classical Music Festival, rue du Théâtre 5, 1st Floor, Case Postale 162, CH-1820 Montreux 2 (tel.(021) 963 54 50; fax 963 25 06). Try your luck at the **Casino de Montreux,** rue du Théâtre 9 (tel. (021) 962 83 83), which features a cabaret, piano bar, restaurant, gambling tables, and slot machines (must be 20 or over; open nightly 5pm-3am). One of the jazz festival venues, **Duke's,** Grand-Rue 97, approximates the festive spirit year-round. (Beer 6-7.50SFr. Open Sun.-Thurs. until 1am, Fri.-Sat. until 3am, during Jazz Festival until 6am. Happy hour 6-8pm.)

■ Near Montreux: Gstaad

Lying at the juncture of four Alpine valleys, Gstaad is in the heart of ski country. But as small Alpine villages go, Gstaad is an anomaly. While its neighbor, Saanen, has a goat for a mascot, Gstaad's emblems are its glitzy five-star hotels and designer boutiques. The main reason to come to Gstaad is for its superlative sports scene, including hard-core **mountain-bike** and **hiking** trails (the tourist office publishes a helpful map and guide) and, most notably, **skiing.** With 250km of runs and 69 lifts, the town generally has something open from mid-December through April. The **Top Card ski pass** (tel. (033) 748 82 82; fax 748 82 60; email ski.gstaad@gstaad.ch) is 50SFr for one day on all sectors. More limited passes are slightly cheaper.

Gstaad's very friendly, well-organized **tourist office** (tel. (033) 748 81 81, for direct reservations 748 81 84; fax 748 81 31; email tvsl@gstaad.ch; http://www.gstaad.ch) is just past the railway bridge on the main road to the right of the station and publishes a list of budget accommodations. (Open July-Aug. Mon.-Sat. 9am-6pm; Sept.-June Mon.-Fri. 8:30am-noon and 2-6pm, Sat. 9am-noon.) The **Jugendherberge** (tel. (033) 744 13 43), 2 mi. away in Saanen, is a godsend. From Gstaad, take the train (every hr., 2.40SFr) or post bus (every hr., 2.40SFr). (Reception open 7:30am-9am and 5pm-10pm. Dorms 25.30SFr; doubles 37.50SFr. Breakfast, sheets, and showers included. Closed Nov. and May.) **Camping Bellerive** (tel. (033) 744 63 30) rests between Gstaad and Saanen (6.40-7.50SFr, 5.30SFr per tent). Budget diners should take advantage of the **Co-op,** left on the main street from the train station. (Restaurant open Mon.-Fri. 7:30am-6:30pm, Sat. 7:30am-4:30pm. Supermarket open Mon.-Fri. 8am-12:15pm and 1:30-6:30pm, Sat. 8am-4pm.)

ITALIAN SWITZERLAND (TICINO)

The Italian-speaking canton of Ticino (Tessin, in German and French) is renowned for its refreshing mix of Swiss efficiency and Italian *dolce vita.* Language is not the only thing that sets the region apart from the rest of Switzerland. The white and charred-wood chalets of the Graubünden and Berner Oberland fade away, replaced by jasmine-laced villas the bright colors of Italian *gelato.* Lush, almost Mediterranean vegetation, emerald lakes, and shaded castles render Ticino's hilly countryside as romantic as its famed resorts, Lugano and Locarno.

Lugano

Lugano, Switzerland's third-largest banking center, hides from German Switzerland in the crevassed bay between San Salvatore and Monte Brè. Traditionally a magnet for older retirees, this sun-drenched oasis increasingly draws younger crowds who fill Lugano's garden's with relaxed laughter. The leafy frescoes of the 16th-century **Cathedral San Lorenzo,** just below the train station, gleam through centuries of dust. **Basilica Sacro Cuore,** on corso Elevezia, and the **Chiesa Santa Maria degli Angioli,** on P. B. Luini, both feature striking frescoes as well. A variety of museums offers rainy day amusement. The statues from Samoa, Papua-New Guinea, and Africa in the **Museo delle Culture Extraeuropee,** 324 via Cortivo, on the footpath to Gandria in the Villa Helenum, provide a break from the usual paintings and cuckoo clocks (open March-Oct. Tues.-Sun. 10am-5pm; 5SFr, 3SFr). Lugano's waterfront parks are ideal places to spend a few hours. Summer **festivals** celebrate jazz and blues in early July and late August. Hiking the region is supplemented by adrenaline-intensive activities ranging from skiing (full-day 89SFr) to paragliding (150SFr) to "canyoning" down waterfalls (89SFr) to rock-climbing (89SFr), all arranged by **ASBEST Adventure Company,** via Basilea 28, CH-6900 Lugano (tel. (091) 966 11 14; fax 966 12 13).

The **tourist office,** 5 riva Albertolli (tel. (091) 921 46 64; fax 922 76 53), offers maps and books rooms for 4SFr. Take bus 5 to "Centro," walk toward the lake, and turn on riva Albertolli. (Open April-Oct. Mon.-Fri. 9am-6:30pm, Sat. 9am-12:30pm and 1:30-5pm, Sun. 10am-2pm; Nov.-March Mon.-Sat. 9am-12:30pm and 1:30-5pm.) **Trains** (tel. (091) 157 22 22) go to Basel (4½hr., 77SFr), Bern (5hr., 74SFr), Zurich (3hr., 59SFr), Locarno (1hr., 16SFr), and Milan (1½hr., 14SFr). **Ostello della Gioventù (HI),** Lugano-Savosa (*not* downtown Lugano), 13 via Cantonale (tel. (091) 966 27 28; 928

23 63), is like staying in a villa resort, but with bunk beds. Take bus 5 to "Crocifisso" (6th stop), then backtrack a few steps and turn left up via Cantonale. (Reception open daily 7am-noon and 3-10pm. Curfew 10pm. Dorms 17SFr; singles 32-42SFr; doubles 40-60SFr. Open mid-March to Oct.) **Hotel Pestalozzi,** 9 P. Indipendenza (tel. (091) 921 46 46), is an upscale version of a budget hotel (reception open 24hr.; singles 54-92SFr, doubles 96-148SFr). There are five **campsites** nearby, all in **Agno.** Take the Ferrovia-Lugano-Ponte-Tresa (FLP) train across the street from the station (all 7.50SFr per person, 4-15SFr per tent; open April-Oct.).

Lugano's many outdoor restaurants and cafés pay homage to the canton's Italian heritage. **La Tinèra,** 2 via dei Gorini, is a low-lit, romantic, underground restaurant with authentic Ticinese ambience (daily specials 10-15SFr; open Mon.-Sat. 11am-2:30pm and 6-10pm). **Pestalozzi,** 9 P. Indipendenza, offers vegetarian dishes starting at 10.50SFr (open Mon.-Sat. 11am-2:30pm and 6-10pm), while **Ristorante Cantinone,** in P. Cioccaro, does pasta and pizza for 10.50-17SFr (open 9pm-midnight). Shop at **Migros,** 15 via Pretoria, in the center of town, or around the corner from the hostel. The arcades of the *città vecchia* (old city) come alive at night. The outdoor cafés of the P. della Riforma are especially lively. The **Pave Pub,** riva Albertolli 1, pours out an English pub atmosphere (beer 4-5SFr; open daily 11am-1am). **B-52,** 4 via al Forte, mixes and mingles a young crowd (open Tues.-Sun. 10pm-3am), while the Latin-American **Mango Club,** 8 P. Dante, gets nice and spicy (opens daily from 11pm).

Locarno

On the shores of Lago Maggiore, Locarno basks in warm near-Mediterranean breezes and bright Italian sun, with luxuriant palm trees replacing the ruggedness of the Alps. Above the city towers the striking church, **Madonna del Sasso** (Madonna of the Rock). The lady of the house, the Madonna, is in the museum next door, as are masterpieces by Ciseri and Raphael. (Grounds open March-Oct. daily 7am-10pm; Nov.-Feb. 7am-9pm. Museum open April-Oct. Mon.-Fri. 2-5pm, Sun. 10am-noon and 2-5pm. Museum 2.50SFr, students 1.50SFr.)

To reach the **tourist office,** Largo Zorzi, on P. Grande (tel. (091) 751 03 33), walk diagonally to the right from the train station, cross via della Stazione, follow this street through the pedestrian walkway, and then cross the street on your left. The office is in the same building as the casino. (Open March-Oct. Mon.-Fri. 8am-7pm, Sat.-Sun. 9am-5pm; Nov.-Feb. Mon.-Fri. 8am-noon and 2-6pm.) **Pensione Città Vecchia,** 13 via Toretta (tel./fax (091) 751 45 54), has great prices and location (reception open daily 8am-9pm; 22SFr; singles 33SFr; open March-Oct.). **Reginetta,** 8 via della Motta (tel./fax (091) 752 35 53), has newly renovated spacious rooms. Walk along the arcades to the end of P. Grande, and make a right (reception open daily 8am-9pm; 39SFr; open March-Oct.). **Ostello Giaciglio,** 7 via Rusca (tel. (091) 751 30 64), has a sauna (20SFr) and tanning salon (10SFr), as well as dorms for 30SFr. To get to the hostel from the end of P. Grande, turn right on via della Motta, and take the left fork in the road.

Turkey (Türkiye)

US$1 = 165,370TL (Turkish Lira)	**100,000TL = US$0.60**
CDN$1 = 118,672TL	**100,000TL = CDN$0.84**
UK£1 = 263,831TL	**100,000TL = UK£0.38**
IR£1 = 238,464TL	**100,000TL = IR£0.42**
AUS$1 = 122,903TL	**100,000TL = AUS$0.81**
NZ$1 = 105,903TL	**100,000TL = NZ$0.94**
SAR1 = 35,003TL	**100,000TL = SAR2.86**
Country Code: 90	**International Dialing Prefix: 00**

All prices are quoted in U.S. dollars because inflation in Turkey is running high.

Turkey has served as both a battleground and a canvas for Eastern and Western cultures and traditions. The iron-forging Hittites controlled Asia Minor in the second millennium BC, developed systems of government and law, and spoke an early Indo-European language. Metropolises emerged after the 2nd century BC, when the coastline became the commercial and political core of the Roman province of Asia Minor. Following the creation of the Eastern Roman Empire in Byzantium (renamed "Constantinople"), Asia Minor became the center of Greek Orthodox Christian culture, and oversaw an empire stretching from the Balkans through Greece to the Levant and Egypt. The Seljuk Turks held sway from the 11th to the 14th centuries.

The Ottomans ruled their vast empire of Turkey (and parts of the Eastern Mediterranean) from the early 15th century to the end of World War I. The reign of Süleyman the Magnificent, from 1520 to 1566, marked the apex of the empire, after which corruption began to take its toll. Modern Turkey's existence is due to early 20th-century leader Mustafa Kemal (Atatürk), who expelled foreign armies. Equating modernization with Westernization, Atatürk abolished the Ottoman Caliphate, romanized the alphabet, outlawed Muslim tribunals, and installed a replica of democratic government; for a time he even ordered *muezzin* (prayer callers) to sing in modern Turkish, even though, according to Muhammad, the Quran is immutable, and untranslatable.

Atatürk's autocratic reforms, however, could go only so far. Beyond Istanbul and a few other large cities, traditional Islamic customs and attitudes prevailed. In the late 1970s, democracy began to falter as street warfare erupted in Istanbul. Elections in 1983 ushered in the centrist party of Turgut Özal, who died in 1993; in that year Tansu Çiller was elected Turkey's first female Prime Minister. In spring of 1994, Çiller turned the problem of Kurdish terrorism over to the military and they began razing villages suspected of harboring rebel activity. Thousands of Kurdish villagers subsequently began fleeing to the cities. While Turkey was a crucial ally of the U.S. and Israel during the Cold War, but its current position is more vague, and in early 1995, Turkey was conditionally accepted into the European Customs Union, but some of the conditions have still not been met. Meanwhile, Turkey has sought economic opportunity in the East with Muslim former Soviet republics. In June 1996 Tansu Çiller formed a coalition government with Necmettin Erbakan, the Fundamentalist Islam leader of the Welfare Party. Under pressure from Turkey's military, which sees itself as the guardian of secularism, Erbakan resigned as prime minister in June 1997. A new coalition of Mesut Yılmaz and Çiller brings together the political forces of Turkey's Left and Right, but faces strong challenges. At press time, the next elections were scheduled to be held in September or October 1997.

For a true Turkish delight, consult *Let's Go: Greece & Turkey 1998.*

GETTING THERE

Bus travel is one of the cheapest methods of getting to Turkey. **Eurolines,** 4 Cardiff Rd., Luton LU1 1PP (tel. (01582) 40 45 11), operates buses to Turkey. Although **trains** link Turkey to major cities (such as Athens and Vienna) in other European

countries, they are not the most convenient way to travel: **Eurail** is *not* valid in Turkey, and the Turkish rail system is very antiquated and inefficient. Always ask for a top bunk and wrap your luggage straps around your limbs when you sleep.

Reservations are recommended for many **ferries,** which run on irregular schedules. Check in at least two hours in advance. Bring toilet paper, motion sickness medication, and food. From Çeşme, an Ertürk ferry offers service to Chios, Greece (May-June 3-4 per week; July-April 1 per week). Prices are US$25 one way, same-day return US$30, open round-trip US$35. Rhodes is linked by ferry to Marmaris (one way 10,000dr, round-trip 12,000dr), Limassol, Cyprus (2 per week, 17hr., 18,500-22,000dr), and Haifa, Israel (2 per week, 36hr., 28,500-33,000dr). Limassol and Haifa services give student and youth discounts of 20% year-round. **Hydrofoils (Flying Dolphins)** run more frequently than ferries, at twice the speed, but cost twice as much. If you have **flown** to Greece on a European charter flight, you cannot travel to Turkey.

GETTING AROUND

> Road travel in Turkey is dangerous by European and U.S. standards, with rates of deaths per vehicle kilometer 22 times as high as in the United States. Professional bus drivers are known to drive excessively fast and recklessly. *Let's Go* recommends using other forms of transportation, such as trains or ferries.

Frequent and cheap **buses** run between all sizeable cities. Many lines provide a 10% discount to ISIC-carrying students who ask. More expensive companies usually offer larger seats, air-conditioning, a toilet, and tea for about 50% more. Reputable companies include Varan Tours, Ulusoy, Kamıl Koç, Pamukkale, and Çanakkale Seyahat. The trade-off for inexpensive **trains** (10% student discount) is the long rides. **Shared taxis,** known as *dolmuş,* usually vans, fill gaps left by the bus system and follow fixed routes. They are almost as cheap as buses and leave whenever they fill up (*dolmuş* means "stuffed"). You can get on and off *dolmuş* whenever you like. Those who **hitchhike** generally pay half what the trip would cost by bus. The hitching signal is a waving hand, but *Let's Go* urges you to consider the safety risks. **Turkish Airlines** has direct flights once or twice weekly from Istanbul to Trabzon, Van, Diyarbakır, Erzurum, Izmir, and Ankara. Domestic flights average US$80 one-way, but passengers 12 to 24 years old may receive a discount. **Ferries** do not serve the west coast, but a **Turkish Maritime Lines** cruise ship sails from Istanbul to Izmir (1 per week, 21hr.).

ESSENTIALS

Turkish government **tourist offices** and tourist police exist in most major cities and resort areas. Some English, German, or French is usually spoken. They help find accommodations and often provide the usual slew of services without charge. In places without an official office, travel agents often serve the same function.

If you're coming from Greece, spend your drachmae before arriving; the few banks that offer **currency exchange** do so at a heinous rate. Persistent haggling in shops, over accommodations, and over some transportation fares can save you money. Examine what you buy at bazaars carefully; exporting antiques is a jailable offense, even if you play ignorant. If you're caught doing drugs in Turkey, you're screwed. Horror stories of lengthy prison sentences and dealer-informers are true; embassies are utterly helpless in all cases. Turkish law also provides for "guilt by association"—those in the company of a person caught are subject to prosecution.

Everything closes on the national **holidays:** January 1, January 29-February 1, April 7-10, April 23, May 1, August 30, and October 29. During Ramadan (*Ramazan* in Turkish; Dec. 30, 1997 to Jan. 28, 1998 and Dec. 19, 1998 to Jan. 17, 1999), pious Muslims abstain from eating, drinking, smoking, or sex between dawn and sunset. Businesses may have shorter hours, few restaurants are open at that time, and public eating is inappropriate. Hotel rooms are more available during this period. Large celebrations mark Ramadan's conclusion; bus and train tickets or hotel rooms are scarce. During *Kurban Bayramı* (the Festival of Sacrifice; April 7-10, 1998), similar disruption occurs. On the first day of the celebration, families of an appropriate standing slaughter a sheep. Museums and archaeological sites in Turkey are open Tuesday through Sunday 9am to 5pm. At all state-run museums, students with **ISIC** receive 50% off. Entrance to many museums is free with a **GO25** (FIYTO) youth card.

Communication Turkey's **post offices (PTTs)** are typically open from 8:30am to 12:30 and 1:30 to 5:30pm; offices in resort towns and central post offices in larger towns keep longer hours. Address *Poste Restante (Postrestant)* to the *Merkez Postanesi* (Central Post Office). Turkey has a surprisingly good phone system; beware, however, of obsolete listings, as the system was revised in 1994: all area codes have three digits and all phone numbers have seven. Make international calls at post offices, or buy a phone card *(telekart)*. Calling North America is expensive. Make **collect calls** from a post office or any phone. Callers to the U.S. can dial 00 800 122 77 for an AT&T Direct operator. For **MCI WorldPhone,** dial 00 800 111 77; for **Sprint Access,** dial 00 800 144 77. To call **Canada Direct,** dial 00 800 16 67 77; **BT Direct,** 00 800 44 11 77; **Ireland Direct,** 00 800 353 11 77; **Australia Direct,** 00 800 61 11 77. Pay phones usually terminate calling card calls after three minutes.

It's rarely a problem finding English-speakers in well touristed areas. Off the beaten track, sign language and a pocket dictionary usually suffice. Remember that in Turkey a raise of the chin, sometimes accompanied by a clicking noise made with the tongue, means "no"; waving a hand up and down at you, palm toward the ground, means "come," not "good-bye." The habit of snapping the fingers of one hand and then slapping the top of the other fist is considered obscene

Yes/No	*Evet/Hayır*	EH-vet/HIGH-yuhr
Hello	*Merhaba*	MEHR-hah-bah
Please	*Lütfen*	LEWT-fen
Thank you	*Teşekkürler*	teh-shehk-keur-LEHR
Pardon me	*Affedersiniz*	ahf-feh-DEHR-see-neez
Do you speak English?	*İngilizçe biliyor musunuz?*	EEN-ghee-leez-jeh bee-lee-YOHR-moo-soo-nooz
I don't speak Turkish.	*Türkçe bilmiyorum.*	TEWRK-cheh BEEHL-mee-yohr-oom

Where is...?	*...nerede?*	NEHR-eh-deh
Help!	*Hol van!*	hawl von

Health, Safety, and Climate Toiletries are cheap and readily available in Turkey, although tampons may be harder to find in the east and in small towns. Always carry toilet paper; expect to encounter quite a number of pit toilets. There are rumors that some of eastern Turkey's feisty mosquitoes carry malaria; to be on the safe side, start a course of anti-malaria pills before you go. Ask your doctor about typhoid and tetanus shots, as well as immune globulin to help fight Hepatitis A. In Turkey, you should never drink unbottled water that you have not purified yourself—the risk of contracting diarrhea or other diseases is high. Don't brush your teeth or even rinse your toothbrush with tap water. Avoid salads as uncooked vegetables contain untreated water. Peel all fruits and vegetables yourself, and avoid watermelon (which often has water injected into it) and ice cubes. Avoid ground beef, any sort of uncooked meat including raw shellfish, unpasteurized milk, and sauces containing raw eggs. In the event that you get diarrhea or food poisoning, see **On-the-Road Ailments,** p. 28. Dial 122 for **emergency medical service.**

Due to political sporadic fighting with Kurds and tensions with Armenia, the areas surrounding **Diyarbakır** and the **border with Armenia** are **not safe** to travel through. **Women** traveling in Turkey may have a less pleasant experience than men. When not in heavily touristed areas, women should dress conservatively. Always wear a bra and avoid short shorts and tank tops; in the east, wear long skirts and sleeves, even a head scarf. If you feel threatened, visible and audible anger—particularly in public—can be a deterrent. Holler "eem-DAHT" (help) if the situation gets out of hand. The **emergency police number** is 155. Invest in secure accommodations, especially ones with the word *"aile"* (family-style) in their names. Your best bet is to not travel alone.

Climate in Turkey varies substantially. The Mediterranean and Aegean coasts are known for being extremely hot and dry during July and August; in central and eastern Anatolia, winter cold and summer heat are severe. Coastal regions are in general most pleasant and least crowded in the spring and autumn. The Black Sea Coast, moderate almost all year, contains areas where rain falls 200 days per year.

Accommodations, Camping, and Food A night's budget accommodation averages US$5-8. Make sure your hotel has water before paying; when traveling in winter, check for heating. Don't expect toilet paper or towels in low-budget hotels. Most Turkish towns have a *hamam,* or bathhouse, where you can get a steam bath for US$3. *Hamamlar* schedule different times for men and women. It is not wise for women traveling alone to visit the *hamam.* **Camping** is popular in Turkey, and cheap campgrounds abound (around US$2 per person), although many official ones still aren't registered with the Ministry of Culture and Tourism. Official government campsites are open from April or May to October.

In many restaurants *(lokanta),* guests are shown into the back kitchen and encouraged to order by pointing. The availability of shepherd's salad, lentil soup, rice pilaf, or yogurt; their availability is understood. Usually, you can't bargain in restaurants, except when ordering fish. Tourists who prefer water to soft drinks at meals should buy bottled spring water cheaply at a corner grocery store and bring it along. *Kebap* (kabob), the most famous of Turkish dishes, means any food broiled or roasted in small pieces. Usually involving lamb or chicken, *kebap* cooking ranges from skewer *(şiş)* or spit *(döner)* broiling, to oven roasting. After *kebap*, the most popular food served is the medallion-sized, grilled hamburger patty (*köfte*). *Et* is the generic word for meat: lamb is *kuzu,* veal *dana eti.* Chicken, usually known as *tavuk,* becomes *piliç* when roasted. Over 8333km of coastline inspire Turks to cook *kılıç* (swordfish), *kalkan* (turbot), *hamsi* (anchovies), *kalamar* (squid), *karides* (shrimp), and *midye* (mussels). **Vegetarians** often choose to subsist on Turkey's wide variety of *meze* (appetizers). *İmambayıldı,* a cold concoction of split eggplant, tomatoes, onions, and olive oil, literally means "the priest fainted" (from its delicious taste). One cannot talk about Turkish food without mentioning *dolma*—yes, stuffed, like the taxis. *Dol-*

TURKEY

mas can be served hot or cold, and with or without meat. Turkish **tea** *(çay)* is served hot, with sugar. Specify a level of sweetness for your *kahve* (coffee): *sade* (unsweetened), *orta* (medium-sweet), or *şekerli* (sweet). Ice-cold *rakı,* an aniseed liquor tasting like licorice, is Turkey's **national drink.** Customarily mixed in equal parts with water, which clouds it, *rakı* has acquired the name "lion's milk." There's an endless array of **sweet things**—*baklava,* a flaky pastry jammed with nuts and soaked in honey; *kadayıf,* a shredded-wheat dough filled with nuts and sugar; and *helva,* a crumbly sesame and honey loaf. Of course, there's always the delicious Turkish Delight *(lokum)*and Turkish marzipan *(acıbadem kurabiyesi).*

Istanbul

The only city in the world that straddles two continents, Istanbul has always been a meeting place of diverse cultures and peoples. Constantine consolidated Roman power here in the 4th century, and the following centuries brought Christian and Greek influences under the Byzantine Empire. Eventually, internal crises and unruly Crusaders weakened the western stronghold, and in 1453 Mehmet II conquered the city and established the reign of the Ottoman Empire. The magnificent legacies of these three great empires coexist today with a new set of cultures and customs. Sophisticated Euro-chic tourists cross paths with conservative, veiled Muslims on their way to prayer, and thousands of solemn mosques and ancient ruins share street space with boisterous markets and teahouses throughout the city.

ORIENTATION AND PRACTICAL INFORMATION

Waterways divide Istanbul into three sections. The **Bosphorus Strait** (Boğaziçi) splits the European (west) and Asian (east) sections. The Turks call the western, European side "Arupa" and the eastern, Asian side "Asya." The area south of the **Golden Horn** is known as **Haliç,** where most of the sites of interest are located. Most directions in Istanbul are further specified by city precinct or district. Budget travelers converge in **Sultanahmet** and **Laleli** (Askaray), the area around the Aya Sophia mosque, south of and up the hill from Sirkeci. The main boulevard—leading west from Sultanahmet towards the university, the Grand Bazaar, and Aksaray—changes names from **Divan Yolu** to **Ordu Caddesi** as it nears Aksaray. Shoppers crowd the district between the **Grand Bazaar,** east of the university, and the less touristy **Egyptian Bazaar,** southeast of Eminönü. The **Kumkapı** district is south of the university and Yeniçeriler Caddesi. Stay near landmarks and use the tourist office's free map and you won't get lost.

As always, be aware of common tourist pitfalls. Don't exchange money with people on the street—they're most likely passing off counterfeits. Make sure that taxi drivers restart their meters when you get in. Most areas of Istanbul are relatively safe even at night, but districts to avoid after sunset include the **Galata tower, Beyazıt,** and the back streets of **Beyoğlu,** the area north of İstiklâl Cad. Women are often targets of harassment on the streets, and getting around alone can be unpleasant.

Tourist Office: Free country and city maps in various offices. **Sultanahmet,** 3 Divan Yolu (tel./fax 518 18 02), at the north end of the Hippodrome, across from the Sultan Pub (open daily 9am-5pm). **Taksim,** in the Hilton Hotel Arcade (tel. 233 05 92; open Mon.-Sat. 9am-5pm) and near the French Consulate (tel. 245 68 76; same hours). Also in the **Karaköy Maritime Station** (tel. 249 57 76; open daily 8:30am-5pm), the **Sirkeci Train Station** (tel. 511 58 88; open daily 8:30am-5:30pm), and the **Atatürk Airport** (tel. 663 07 93; open 24hr.).

Budget Travel Offices: Gençtur, Prof. K. Ismail Gürkan Cad. Cağaloğlu, Hamamı, Sok. Kardeşler Iştlan, 4th fl. (tel. 520 52 74, -5; fax 519 08 64), in central Sultanahmet. Sells ISICs and GO25 cards. *Poste Restante.* Open Mon.-Fri. 9:30am-noon and 1-5pm, Sat. 9:30am-1pm. **Seventur Travel Shop,** 2-C Alemdar Cad. (tel. 512 41 83; fax 512 36 41). Follow the Sirkeci tram tracks past Aya Sophia. Sells ISIC and youth ID, offers shuttle to airport, and sells reliable plane and bus tickets. *Poste Restante.* Open Mon.-Sat. 9am-1pm, Sat. 9am-6pm. **Indigo Tourism and Travel Agency,** 24

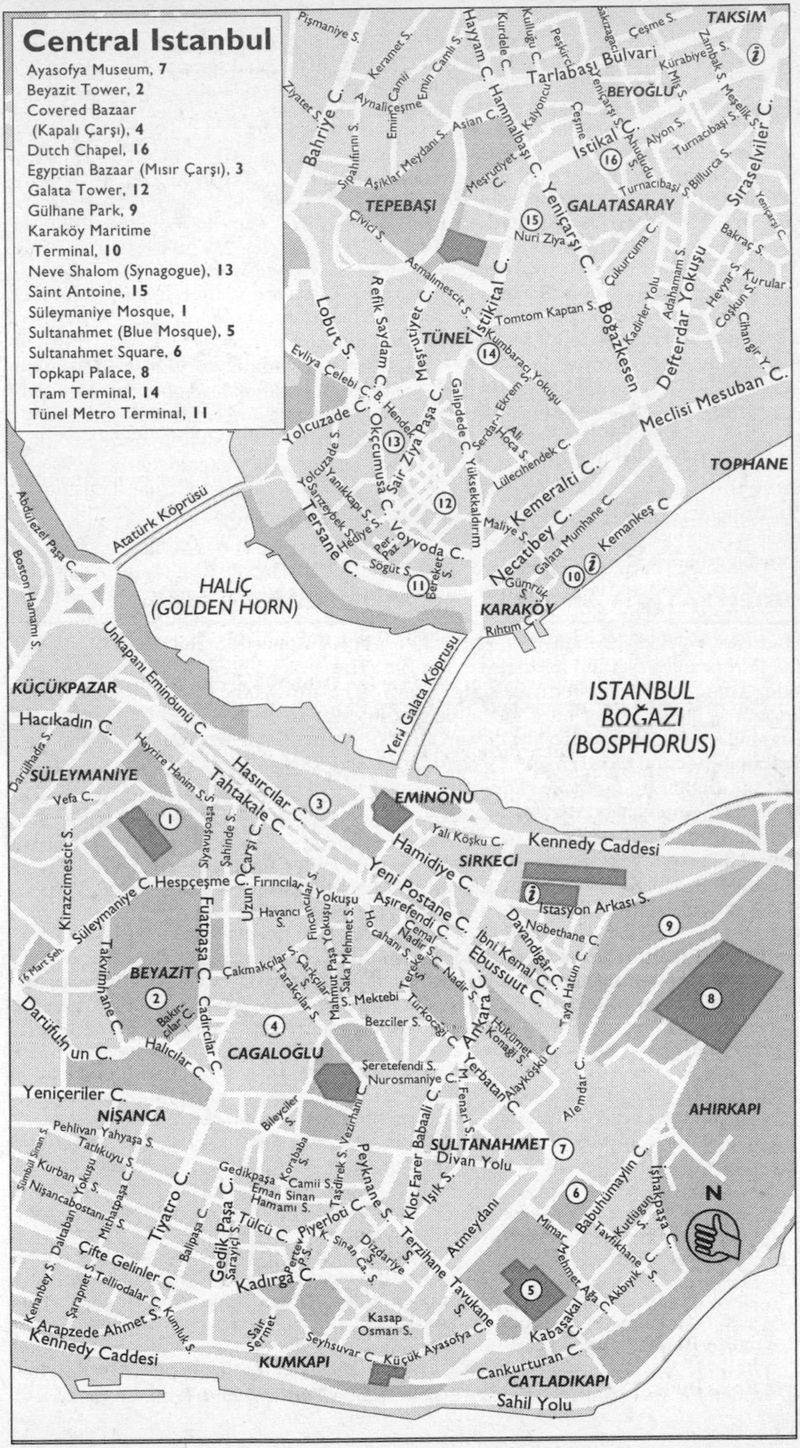
Central Istanbul
Ayasofya Museum, 7
Beyazit Tower, 2
Covered Bazaar (Kapalı Çarşı), 4
Dutch Chapel, 16
Egyptian Bazaar (Mısır Çarşı), 3
Galata Tower, 12
Gülhane Park, 9
Karaköy Maritime Terminal, 10
Neve Shalom (Synagogue), 13
Saint Antoine, 15
Süleymaniye Mosque, 1
Sultanahmet (Blue Mosque), 5
Sultanahmet Square, 6
Topkapı Palace, 8
Tram Terminal, 14
Tünel Metro Terminal, 11
TAKSİM
BEYOĞLU
Tarlabaşı Bulvari
İstiklal C.
TEPEBAŞI
GALATASARAY
TÜNEL
TOPHANE
KARAKÖY
HALİÇ (GOLDEN HORN)
ISTANBUL BOĞAZI (BOSPHORUS)
Atatürk Köprüsü
Yeni Galata Köprusu
Meclisi Mesuban Y. C.
Kemeraltı C.
Necatibey C.
Unkapanı Eminönü C.
KÜÇÜKPAZAR
Hacıkadın C.
SÜLEYMANİYE
EMİNÖNÜ
SİRKECİ
Kennedy Caddesi
Hasırcılar C.
Tahtakale C.
Hamidiye C.
Yeni Postane C.
BEYAZIT
CAGALOĞLU
SULTANAHMET
Divan Yolu
AHIRKAPI
NİŞANCA
KUMKAPI
CATLADIKAPI
Cankurturan C.
Sahil Yolu
N

TURKEY

Akbıyık Cad. (tel. 517 72 66; fax 518 53 33), is located in the heart of the cluster of hotels in Sultanahmet. Sells ISIC, GO25, bus, plane, and ferry tickets. *Poste Restante*. Open in summer daily 8:30am-7:30pm; off-season Mon.-Sat. 9:30am-6pm.

Consulates: All are open Mon.-Fri. **Australia,** 58 Tepecik Yolu, Etiler (tel. 257 70 50, -1). **Canada,** 107/3 Büyükdere Cad., Gayrettepe (tel. 272 51 74; fax 272 34 27). **Ireland** (honorary), 26-a Cumhuriyet Cad., Mobil Altı, Elmadağ (tel. 246 60 25). **New Zealand** nationals should get in touch with the embassy in Ankara, at 24/1 Kız Kulesi Sok. (tel. (312) 445 05 56). **South Africa,** 106 Büyükdere Cad., Esentepe (tel. 275 47 93; fax 288 25 04). **U.K.,** 34 Meşrutiyet Cad., Beyoğlu/Tepebaşı (tel. 293 75 45). **U.S.,** 104-108 Meşrutiyet Cad., Tepebaşı (tel. 251 36 02).

Currency Exchange: Banks' exchange counters are open Mon.-Fri. 8:30am-noon and 1:30-5pm. Most don't charge commission. **ATMs** are scattered across the city. **Garanti Bankası** branches are open on Sat. and during noon breaks.

American Express: Türk Express, 91 Cumhuriyet Cad., 2nd fl. (tel. 230 15 15), up the hill from Taksim Sq., handles lost checks and cards. Open Mon.-Fri. 9am-6pm. The office in the **Hilton Hotel lobby,** Cumhuriyet Cad. (tel. 241 02 48), deals with lost cards only when Türk Express is closed. Open daily 8:30am-8pm. Wire money through **Koç Bank,** 233 Cumhuriyet Cad. (tel. 232 26 00). Open Mon.-Fri. 8:45am-12:30pm and 1:30-4:30pm.

Flights: Atatürk Airport, 30km from the city, has a domestic and an international terminal connected by bus (6am-10pm, every 20min.). Take a *Havaş* bus from either terminal to the city (5:50am-10:50pm, 30min., US$2.50). The bus stops at Aksaray, where you can catch the tram to Sultanahmet, and at Şişhane.

Trains: Haydarpaşa Station (tel. (216) 336 04 75 or 336 20 63), on the Asian side. Ferries (US$0.50) run daily 6am-midnight from the station to Karaköy pier 7, on the European side. This station serves destinations in Turkey. Europe-bound trains leave from **Sirkeci Station** (tel. 527 00 50, -1), in Eminönü. To: Sofia (US$31), Athens (US$62.50), and Munich (US$212).

Buses: Intercity buses leave from the **Esenler Otobüs Terminalı** *(otogar)*. To get there from Sultanahmet, take the tram 6 stops to **Yusufpaşa,** then walk to the **Aksaray Metro station** on the Adnan Menderes Blvd. Take the metro to *otogar* (15min., US$0.35), where dozens of bus companies have offices. **Varan Tours** (tel. 658 02 77; fax 658 02 80) operates throughout Western Europe; **Ulusoy** (tel. 658 30 00; fax 658 30 10) serves Greece as well as domestic destinations; **Kamıl Koç** (tel. 658 20 00; fax 658 20 08), **Pamukkale** (tel./fax 658 22 22), and **Çanakkale Seyahat** (tel. 658 36 40, -1) are also recommended. Unlicensed companies have been known to offer discounts to western countries and then abandon passengers in Eastern Europe—be very cautious. Frequent buses leave for Ankara (6hr., US$12-15), Izmir (9hr., US$14-17), and Bodrum (13hr., US$21.25). European destinations include Athens (16hr., US$24-27) and Vienna (1 per week, 36hr., US$95).

Public Transportation: AKBİL, or the Akıllı Bilet, are new electronic tickets for metros, trams, seabuses, public buses, and double-decker buses. Deposit an initial US$3.50, then add credit to your AKBİL from any of the IETT bus booths with the sign "AKBİL satılır." AKBİL ticket prices are usually 30-50% cheaper than cash fares.

Ferries: Turkish Maritime Lines, the blue-awninged "*Denizcilik İşletmeleri*" building, is near Pier 7 at Karaköy, just west of Haydarpaşa ferry terminal. Combination ticket to Izmir ($10-25): sails to Bandırma, then takes the train (3 per week). For **local ferries** head to the Sirkeci area, around the Galata Bridge. Pier 1 serves Üsküdar (6:30am-11pm), Pier 2 serves Kadıköy (7:30am-9pm, US$0.50), and Pier 3 sends cruises along the Bosphorus (round-trip US$4) and to the Princes Islands. Pier 4 serves Kadıköy (8am-7:25pm, US$0.60); Pier 5 Adalar; Pier 6 Bağlat (past the Galata Bridge). Pier 7, in Kadıköy across the Galata Bridge, serves the Haydarpaşa railway station (6am-midnight, US$0.50). Timetables are posted at each terminal.

Taxis: Make sure the meter is on and don't pay more than it says. One light on the meter indicates the day rate; two lights the night rate (50% higher; midnight-8am). Steer away from taxis at the airport or from drivers who approach you in Sultanahmet. If you don't speak Turkish, have your destination written down.

English Bookstores: Aypa Bookstore, 19 Mimar Mehmet Ağa Cad., Sultanahmet (tel. 517 44 92), behind the Blue Mosque. Open daily 6:30am-8pm. **International Press Büffe,** 91 İstiklâl Cad., has international magazines and newspapers.

Laundromat: Star Laundry, 18 Akbıyık Cad. (tel. 638 23 02), below Star Pension. Wash and dry US$1.25 per kg, minimum 2kg. Open daily 8am-10pm.

Hospitals: American Hospital, Admiral Bristol Hastanesi, 20 Güzelbahçe Sok., Nişantaşı (tel. 231 40 50). The **German Hospital,** 119 Sıraselviler Cad., Taksim (tel. 293 21 50), is more convenient to Sultanahmet.

Emergencies: Tourist Police (tel. 527 45 03 or 528 53 69; fax 512 76 76), in Sultanahmet at the beginning of Yerebatan Cad., behind the obelisk in the park across from the tourist office. Open 24hr. In **emergencies** call 155.

Post Office (PTT): Main branch at 25 Büyük Postane Sok. Better for those in Sultanahmet is the booth opposite the Aya Sophia entrance. Open daily 8:30am-7pm.

Telephone Code: 212 (European side) or 216 (Asian side).

ACCOMMODATIONS AND CAMPING

Istanbul's budget rooms (and all *Let's Go* recommendations) concentrate in the comparatively safe, central **Sultanahmet** district. Hotels around **Sirkeci** railway station are US$5-10. **Aksaray** offers hotels in every price range. Hotels in **Laleli,** the city's center of prostitution, should be avoided. Rates rise about 20% in July and August.

Yücelt Hostel (HI), 6/1 Caferiye Cad. (tel. 513 61 50, -1; fax 512 76 28). From the Sultanahmet tram stop, follow the tracks downhill toward Sirkeci; Aya Sophia is the red-tinted mosque on your right, and the hostel is in the alley to the left as you face the mosque's gate. Free storage and showers. Dorms US$4-9. Doubles US$8-11 per person. 10% *Let's Go* discount. Laundry US$1.25 per kg. Reserve 2 weeks ahead.

Orient Youth Hostel, 13 Akbıyık Cad. (tel. 517 94 93; fax 518 38 94), near Topkapı Palace. A/C, cable TV. Bring own toilet paper and towel. Luggage room, safe, and a travel agency. Dorms US$4.50. Doubles US$5.50 per person. Quads US$5.

Sultan Turist Otel, 3 Terbıyık Sok. (tel. 516 92 60; fax 517 16 26). Around the corner from the Orient Hostel. Immaculate and professional. Roof restaurant/bar. Safe-deposit and laundry services. In-house travel office, and international phone services. Dorms US$6.90. Singles US$16.50. Doubles US$20. Triples US$25.

Hotel Anadolu, Yerebatan Cad. 3 Salkım Söğüt Sok. (tel. 512 10 35; fax 527 76 95). From the Sultanahmet tram, walk 50m down to Sirkeci along the tram tracks; take a left at the major intersection (Yerebatan Cad.), then the first right. Rudimentary, well-kept rooms. US$12 per person. Roof beds US$7.

Alp Guesthouse, Akbıyık Cad. 4 Adliye Sok. (tel. 517 95 70 or 518 57 28). Spacious, spotless rooms and Mediterranean-style ambience. Drinks served until 11pm. Airport transportation service, safe, and luggage room. All rooms with bath and shower. Singles US$35. Doubles US$45-50. Breakfast US$5.

Bahaus Guesthouse, Akbıyık Cad. Bayram Fırını Sok. #11 (tel./fax 517 66 97). Comfortable. View of the Bosphorus. Singles US$15. Doubles US$25-30. Triples US$35-40. Basement US$5. 10% *Let's Go* discount.

Hotel Pamphylia, Yerebatan Cad. 47 (tel. 526 89 35 or 513 95 48; fax 513 95 49). Immaculate rooms, some with balcony and TV. Terrace with a great view. Safe deposit. Singles US$25. Doubles US$35. Triples US$50. Rates US$5 less off season.

Hanedan Hotel, Akbıyık Cad., 3 Adliye Sok. (tel. 516 48 69; fax 517 45 24). Pleasant view from terrace. Beautiful cafeteria. Currency exchange. 24hr. airport transport. 24hr. hot water. Doubles US$20-$26. Breakfast included.

Hotel Side Pension, 20 Utangaç Sok. (tel./fax 517 65 90). Basic little pension. 3rd floor walls are lined with beautiful Ottoman-style tiles. Large, well-kept rooms. Singles US$6-15. Doubles US$20-30. Breakfast included.

Camping: Londra Camping (tel. 560 42 00), 1km from the airport. No bus stop; take a taxi. The site has a cafeteria, bar, and showers. US$2.50 per person, US$1.90 per tent. Two-person bungalows US$12.50.

FOOD

If you like eating, you'll love Istanbul. The **Kumkapı** district, south of the Grand Bazaar, is justly famous for its seafood, and **Beyoğlu** boasts a wide variety of establishments around İstiklâl Cad. To get there from Sultanahmet, follow the tram lines to Sirkeci, take a left, and follow the water, crossing the Galata Bridge and taking a left onto the first major thoroughfare; the Tünel, which will take you to İstiklâl Cad., will be on the right. **Cengelköy** is known for its fish restaurants. **Ortaköy** has fine restaurants with Bosphorus views. Two **open-air markets** are centrally located: one next to Çiçek Pasajı, in Beyoğlu, and a fruit market next to the *Mısır Çarşısı* (Egyptian Spice Bazaar). The **Egyptian Spice Bazaar** sells a mouth-watering collection of oriental sweets. Stop at a *büfe* (snack shop) for *tost* and a soft drink, both for less than US$1.

Türkistan Aşevi, 36 Tavukhane Sok. A feast for the eyes and taste buds. 7-course lunch US$14. 8-course dinner US$17. No alcohol served.

Dârüzziyâfe, 6 Şifahane Cad., in the Süleymaniye Mosque. Main courses US$4.50-6. Mellow atmosphere. *Sülemaniye Çorbası* is a must (meat and veggie soup, US$1.75). Live Ottoman music Sat. nights. No alcohol. Open noon-11pm.

Pudding Shop, 6 Divan Yolu, was a major pitstop on the Hippie Trail to the Far and Middle East in 1970s. Self-serve restaurant. Meat dishes US$2-2.50. Veggie dishes US$1.50. Super dessert stop. The cappuccino rocks at only US$0.65.

Cennet, 90 Divan Yolu, on the right as you walk along Divan Yolu from Sultanahmet towards Aksaray, 3min. from the Sultanahmet tram. A full meal is US$3-6. Specializes in Anatolian pancakes *(gözeme)*. Open daily 10am-midnight.

Pandeli Restaurant, 1 Egyptian Spice Bazaar. Main courses US$5-7. Starters US$4.75. Tasty *yaprak dolması* (stuffed vine leaves). *Hünkâr beğendi* (mashed eggplant with kebap) US$5.75. Open Mon.-Sat. noon-3pm.

House of Medusa Restaurant, Yerebatan Cad. 19 Muhteremefendi Sok., on a cross street off Divan Yolu. Excellent Turkish cuisine in the 1st fl. garden (open in summer), the 3rd fl. divan area, and a 4th floor bar. Delicious *piliç* (chicken stuffed with vegetables) US$3.75. Veggie specialties US$2.75-4.25. Tasty pudding US$1.75. All are best capped with the delicious Turkish coffee. Open daily 8am-midnight.

Şampiyon, Balık Pazarı. Famous all around Turkey; believed to prepare the best *kokoreç* in the country. Lamb innards are grilled, then cooked with spices and tomatoes. Try the smallest portion *(çeyrek ekmek kokoreç)* US$1.50.

Cumhuriyet Meyhanesi, at the far end of the fruit market. Turkey's top poets, artists, and journalists gather here in the evenings. Serves delectable items such as eggplant salad for US$2.25. Open daily 10am-1am, possibly later.

SIGHTS

Istanbul's incomparable array of attractions could keep an ardent sightseer busy for weeks; try to allow at least a few days to hit the highlights listed here. A FIYTO card grants free entry to many museums. An ISIC is generally good for half price.

Built in 537 by Emperor Justinian, the **Aya Sophia** (Haghia Sophia) has served both as a cathedral and a mosque but now functions as a museum featuring wall mosaics. (Museum open Tues.-Sun. 9:30am-4:30pm. Gallery with mosaics open Tues.-Sun. 9:30-11:30am and 1-4pm. US$3.30, students US$1.30.) Sultan Ahmet I built the **Blue Mosque** *(Sultanahmet Camii)*, opposite Aya Sophia, in an attempt to one-up Justinian. The mosque's silhouette is unforgettable, and the interior, with its blue Iznik tiles, is stunning. You may visit the mosque outside of the five daily prayer times; modest dress is required. Across the street to the right from the Aya Sophia is the **Yerebatan Cistern,** a vast underground cavern whose shallow water reflects the 336 columns that support the structure (open daily 9am-5pm; US$1.65). To the northwest is the **Hippodrome,** where Byzantine emperors presided over chariot races and put down uprisings. Across from the Hippodrome, the 16th-century **İbrahim Paşa Palace** houses a museum of Turkish and Islamic art (open Tues.-Sun. 10am-5pm).

From the mid-15th century until the mid-19th century, the **Topkapı Sarayı** (Topkapı Palace) was the nerve center of the Ottoman Empire. This magnificent maze of buildings was originally the site of the Ottoman government and the home of the Sultan. Don't miss the **Second Court** and its huge East Asian porcelain collection, or the **Treasury,** with an inestimable wealth of diamonds, emeralds, gold, and jade. Nearby, the **Pavilion of Holy Relics** contains remnants of the prophet Muhammad: his footprint, a lock of hair, a tooth, his original seal, and a letter written by his hand. You can also take a tour of the **Harem** (every 30min.; US$2.50) and view beautiful blue-green

Umm...

We've all heard stories about foreign hosts who inadvertently make sexual innuendoes, inviting their English-speaking guests to take advantage of the washerwoman or cordially asking them not to have children at the bar. Likewise, an American who is a little shaky on her Turkish may miss the significance of the guffaws that her repeated *ums* elicit. On the lips of a Turk, this oft-repeated American stammer has a more *private* significance. The fluent and modest American, knowing better, will only discuss her *am* with her gynecologist.

tiles in the ominous-sounding **Circumcision Chamber** (palace grounds open daily 9:30am-5pm; US$3.30, students US$1.30).

A museum complex is located through a gate marked "Archaeological Museum" downhill from the Topkapı Palace. The **Tiled Pavilion** *(Çinili Köşk),* once a petite pleasure retreat attached to the Topkapı Palace, now houses the **Tile Museum.** Replete with yellows, blues, and greens, the building's own tiles constitute one of Turkey's best examples of the Tabrizi Persian style (open May-Sept. Tues.-Thurs. and Sat.-Sun. 9am-4pm; US$1.35). The **Museum of the Ancient Orient** has a buffet of Hittite, Babylonian, Sumerian, Assyrian, and Egyptian artifacts including tablets of the Hammurabi Code and a peace treaty by Egyptian Pharoah Ramses II (open daily May-Sept. 9am-4pm; US$1.35). The **Archaeological Museum** has an excellent collection of Greek, Hellenistic, and Roman marbles and bronzes, including a famous sarcophagus with carvings of Alexander the Great (open May-Sept. daily 9am-4pm; US$1.35).

To get to the vast, ornate, and chaotic **Grand Bazaar** *(Kapalı Çarşı)* from Sultanahmet, follow the tram tracks toward Askaray until you see the mosque on your right. Enter the mosque's side gate, and walk, with the park to your left, to the bazaar entrance. You will get lost, but you'll enjoy it. Beware, though, that hawkers prey on tourists and that prices skyrocket in the summer (open Mon.-Sat. 9am-7pm). At the opposite entrance of the bazaar is the **Sahaflar Çarşısı** (used book market) which sells a wide selection of books along with Quranic inscriptions, artwork, and university texts. The market opens onto a bustling square. Opposite stands the huge gate of **Istanbul University,** where peaceful respites are interrupted only by the frequent appearance of riot police, often on Fridays after prayer. The campus contains **Beyazıt Camii,** the oldest mosque in Istanbul. Just north of the university is the **Süleymaniye** mosque complex. Together with the **Şehzade Mehmet** (a few blocks southwest) and the **Selimiye** (in the city of Edirne), the Süleymaniye (completed 1557) is one of the three masterpieces of Sinan, who almost single-handedly codified Ottoman Classical architecture. The complex includes a mosque, seven religious schools, a charitable soup kitchen, and the tomb of Süleyman the Magnificent.

In the northwest corner of the city, the impeccably preserved **Kariye Camii,** with its superb 14th-century frescoes is a mandatory stop for Byzantine art connoisseurs. The museum is a long way up Fevzipaşa Cad. near the Edirne Gate and is accessible by *dolmuş*, bus 58 from Eminönü, or any bus in the direction Edirnekapı (open Wed.-Mon. 9:30am-4:30pm).

Across the Galata Bridge, the 62m high **Galata Tower,** built by Justinian in 528 and rebuilt for spying purposes in 1348 by the Genoese, offers spectacular views of the Golden Horn. Along the Bosphorus, **Dolmabahçe Palace** was the home of sultans from 1856 until the demise of the Ottoman Empire after World War I, and soldiers still guard the collection of imperial treasures (open Tues.-Sun. 9:30am-4pm; US$5). To reach the palace from Eminönü, take the ferry (US$0.50) or bus 58 to Beşiktaş. The number of visitors per day is limited, so go early. For a closer look at the waters around Istanbul, take a **Bosphorus cruise;** boats leave from Pier 3, beside the Galata Bridge in Eminönü (US$3.35). When the ferry reaches the Asian side, treat yourself to street vendors' fish *kebap* and mussels. Double-decker bus 210 runs every hour from behind the tourist office to points along the European side (2 bus tickets each way).

Ferries from Eminönü or Kabataş travel to four of the beautiful, undeveloped islands in the **Princes Isles.** Look for the "Sirkeci Adalar" signs (round-trip US$2.50).

Büyükada, the largest and most picturesque of the islands, offers great swimming at a rocky **beach.** In Heybeliada, you can take a horse-carriage starting from İsa Çelebi Sok. **St. George's Monastery** is the highest point on the island. Ask about **hiking trails,** as some areas of the dense forest are forbidden. The **Ideal Aile Pansion,** 14 Kadıyoran Cad. (tel. (216) 382 68 57), is a haunted-house style masterpiece, with large rooms and communal bathrooms (US$10 per person).

Eyüp, a popular Muslim pilgrimage site, houses the 15th-century tomb of Job, the companion of Muhammad who died during an Arab siege of the city in the 7th century. The Golden Horn ferries ride the waves to Eyüp twice per hour from pier 6 in Eminönü, above the Galata Bridge (35min., US$0.45), or catch bus 55. Today Eyüp is mostly a religious site, with Quran shops, the Eyüp Mosque, and lovely, spacious cemeteries. Dress modestly, and avoid traveling in packs, making excessive hand gestures, or drinking alcohol in the open.

ENTERTAINMENT

Nightlife rages from midnight to dawn in the Taksim district. Do not club-hop here in a haphazard manner: some clubs are reputable, but some are run by hustlers who have ties to the nearby red-light district. Stick to places which have been specifically recommended by *Let's Go* or trustworthy locals. Keep in mind as well that several of the clubs mentioned here will not let you in if you are shabbily dressed. Nightclubs are located on İstiklâl Cad., Sıraselviler Cad. (the other main street which runs from Taksim Sq. to the Bosphorus), and on the little side streets which run off them.

Kemançı, Sıraselviler Cad., on an alley off İstiklâl Cad. Wild and loud rock bar that frequently hosts live bands. US$5 cover on weekends includes a drink.

Bilsak, Sıraselviler Cad., Soğana Sk. 7. The place for a more mellow and artsy scene.

Carnival Pub, in the fruit market beside the Flower Passage. Hosts heavy metal and punk bands nightly. Beers US$2.

Leman Kültür, İmam Adman alley off İstiklâl Cad. Dimly lit bar with billiards.

Hayal Kahvesi, Büyükparmakkapı Sok., an alley off İstiklâl Cad. Popular haven for artists. Live music starts at 11pm. House special Hayal cocktail US$4.25.

North Shield, Çalıkuşu Sok. in Levent. Authentic British pub with an incredible variety of European beers. Foreigners tend to hang here.

2019, Atatürk 100, Tıl Oto Sanayi Sitesi. Hard rock with car wreck decor. Gays, Istanbul's jet-set, and assorted funky types frequent this bar.

VAT 69, İmam Adnan Sok. Popular with gay men. Open until early morning.

The much-publicized **Cağaloğlu Hamamı** (tel. 522 24 24), in Sultanahmet on Yerebatan Cad., is a fancy **Turkish Bath** *(hamam).* Avoid it if you are at all claustrophobic (open daily 8am-10pm; US$10-20). Istanbul's other famous *hamam,* the historical **Çemberlitaş Bath,** 8 Vezirhan Cad. (tel. 522 79 74; fax 511 25 35), is the 1584 product of master architect Mimar Sinan (open daily 6am-midnight; US$10). Turkish massages are often severe by European and American standards.

Edirne

An easy *dolmuş* ride from the Greek and Bulgarian borders (though 227km from Istanbul), **Edirne** nourished the genius of quintessentially Ottoman architect Sinan. His masterpiece, the **Selimiye Camii** (Selim's Mosque), presides over the city with 71m minarets and 999 windows. The vast interior, ornately decorated from dome to floor, is even more impressive. Edirne's other major sight is the **Beyazıt Complex,** a spiritual and physical welfare facility a couple of kilometers from town. The centerpiece is the **Beyazıt Camii,** a beautiful, single-domed mosque surrounded by multi-domed buildings which were designed to be schools, storehouses, and asylums. To make the long but scenic trek, walk along Talat Paşa Cad. to the river (don't cross it), then turn right and walk along the dirt path. After about 10 minutes you will see a bridge below on your left; cross it, and walk another five minutes until you see the mosque. When you get back into town, you may want to relax in one of Edirne's excellent **Turkish baths.** Sinan's 16th-century **Sokollu Hamamı,** beside the Üç Şerefeli Camii, combines superior service with inspiring architecture (open daily 8am-10pm for men; 10am-5pm for women; US$2.25, with massage US$5).

Buses arrive from Istanbul (3hr., US$6), Ankara (10hr., US$20), and Bursa (US$9.50); when you arrive at the *otogar,* walk across the street and take a *dolmuş* into Edirne. The **tourist office,** 17 Talat Paşa Cad. (tel. (284) 213 92 08), about 200m west of the Eski Camii, gives out free maps (open June-Aug. daily 9am-6pm; Sept.-May Mon.-Sat. 8:30am-5pm). The wonderful **Hotel Kervansaray** (tel. (284) 225 21 95; fax 225 04 62), along Hürriyet Meydanı, built in the 16th century as a resting place for camel caravans, now has small but comfortable rooms with bath, TV, and phone. The call to prayer which resonates down the corridors at 4:30am will undoubtedly fill you with the joy of experiencing this unique Turkish tradition (singles US$18, doubles US$32, triples US$42; breakfast included). **Efe Hotel,** 13 Maarif Cad. (tel. (284) 213 61 66 or 213 64 66), has spotless rooms with modern bathrooms (singles US$16, doubles US$22; breakfast included). A few doors down is **Hotel Aksaray** (tel. (284) 212 60 35), with cheaper but much more basic rooms (singles US$27, doubles US$38). Do not leave Edirne without taking *çay* (small US$0.20, large US$0.35) at **Sera** teahouse, in the park between Selimiye Camii and Eski Camii.

Bursa

Along with Konya, Bursa is one of Turkey's two holy cities of pilgrimage. Although the city is now an industrial center and wealthy resort area, the well preserved Ottoman monuments scattered throughout town and the thermal baths in the **Çekirge** (Grasshopper) district remain excellent attractions. Despite their names, **Yeşil Camii** (Green Mosque) and **Yeşil Türbe** (Green Mausoleum), in the eastern part of town, feature rich turquoise and cobalt blue Iznik tiles (open in summer daily 8:30am-5:30pm; off-season 8am-5pm; US$0.25 donation). Nearby, the **Turkish and Islamic Art Museum,** including the **Ethnographic Museum,** houses 16th-century ivory boxes, costumes and musical instruments of the dervishes, exquisite bath tools, and other exhibits (open daily 8:30am-12:30pm and 1:30-5pm; US$1, students US$0.50, free with ISIC). Built in the Turkish style common before the conquest of Constantinople, the **Ulu Camii** (Great Mosque) was commissioned by Beyazıt to commemorate his victory in Nikopolis in 1396. It's said that Beyazıt vowed to build 20 mosques if he won the war, but later skimped by just building Ulu Camii's 20 domes. To get to the **Eski Kaplıca** (Old Springs) bathing complex, built by Justinian in the 6th century, take the Çekirge *dolmuş* and get off at the Kervansaray Hotel. After a long day of travel, ask for the "rubbing" and have your skin treated with a special cloth. (Open daily 7:30am-11pm. Entrance to baths US$7.50. Rubbing and massage US$3 each.)

Mt. Uludağ (Mt. Olympus), home of Turkey's leading ski resort, gives the city its nickname, "Green Bursa." To reach the **Uludağ cable car** station, take a *dolmuş* marked "Teleferik" (US$0.30) from behind Adliye and Heykel. The cable car runs to the mid-station (8am-10pm every 40min., round-trip US$5.75), and from the mid-station to Sarıalan from where you take a minibus to the resort area (bus 10 min, US$1). Plan for a cooler climate, changing weather, and high-priced hotels.

Practical Information, Accommodations, and Food Bursa is accessible by **ferry** from Istanbul (US$2.50); the ferries land in Yalova, where you can hop on a *dolmuş* or bus. **Buses** arrive from Istanbul's Esenler Bus Station (4hr., US$7) and connect to Ankara, Izmir, and other cities. To reach the center of town from the bus station, take a *dolmuş* marked "Heykel" and get off at Ulu Camii. The **tourist office** (tel. (224) 221 23 59) is near the *heykel* (a huge statue of Atatürk) and down the stairs by the big fountain. (Open June-Sept. Mon.-Sat. 8:30am-noon and 1-5:30pm; Oct.-May Mon.-Fri. 8:30am-noon and 1-5pm.)

The charming **Özen Şükran Otel,** 39 İnönü Cad. (tel. (224) 221 54 53), is a small hotel with old furniture (singles US$8, doubles US$12, triples US$15). **Otel Deniz,** 19

Tahtakale Cad. (tel. (224) 222 92 38), is more expensive, but also more comfortable (singles US$8, doubles US$13.50). Bursa is home to *İskender kebap,* a yogurt, tomato, and lamb dish which you can sample at many restaurants between the Atatürk statue and the *Yeşil Camii.* **Kebapçı İskender,** 7 Ünlü Cad., at the corner of Atatürk Blv. and İnönü Cad., claims to have invented the *İskender kebap* (US$3.15).

AEGEAN COAST

With a rich collection of classical ruins and a sinuous coastline that conceals sublime beaches, the once tranquil Aegean Coast is becoming an increasingly popular destination. No legal barriers prevent tourists from traveling from the Greek islands to Turkey, though some travelers have reported complications and high port taxes.

Gallipoli to Troy

Gallipoli (Gelibolu) Each year thousands of New Zealanders and Aussies make pilgrimages to the battlefield of **Gallipoli,** where many of their brethren died in the World War I battle which launched its hero, Atatürk, on an ascent to the status of Turkey's founding father. To tour the battle sights and memorials try **Ana-Tur,** Cumhuriyet Meydani Özay İşhani Kat. 2, No. 30 (tel. (286) 271 58 42 or 217 07 71), or **Troyanzac Travel Agency** (tel. (286) 217 58 47; fax 217 58 49), both based in Çanakkale. Bring a bathing suit, as many tours stop for a dip at **Brighton Beach.** To explore on your own take a *dolmuş* from **Eceabat,** available by frequent ferries from Çanakkale (US$0.50), to the **Kabatepe Museum** (open daily 8:30am-noon and 1-5:30pm; US$0.75). From the museum it is 4km to **Anzac Cove,** and 7km uphill to the Australian **Lone Pine Memorial.** From here, walk to the highest point on the peninsula, **Chunuk Bair**—the ground taken by Atatürk. Today, the **New Zealand Memorial** shares space with Atatürk's statued image. To see the memorials on the southern tip of the peninsula where tours often don't cover, take the ferry from Çanakkale to Kilitbakik and then a minibus to the **Çanakkale Memorial** at **Melles Point.** Be sure to check the minibus service before returning to Kilitbakik.

Gallipoli Town is a quiet place to relax on the sandy beach 1.5km down the road, before touring the battlefields only kilometers away. Gallipoli is connected by Radar Tur **buses** (tel. (286) 566 64 24) to Istanbul (8 per day, US$7) and Izmir (1 per day, US$9). The bus station is in the **Liman Meydani** square where hotels, restaurants, and taxis cluster. The **Yilmaz Hotel**'s English-speaking staff approximates tourist office service. Across from the hotel, the street Atatürk Cad. leads to other hotels.

Çanakkale Blessed with inexpensive accommodations and bus connections to major cities and sights, **Çanakkale** is an easy base from which to explore Gallipoli and Troy. As many Australian and New Zealander troops lost their lives in nearby Gallipoli during World War I, Aussies and Kiwis are particularly welcome. A handful of pubs cater to those nationals. **Buses** arrive often from Bursa (5½hr., US$8), Istanbul (5hr., US$11), Izmir (5hr., US$9), and other cities. From the bus station, take a left out the main doors, then the next right onto Demircio|lu Cad. (following the "feribot" sign), and continue to the docks. The **tourist office,** 67 İskele Meydanı (tel./fax (286) 217 11 87), is on your left (open Mon.-Fri. 8:30am-7:30pm). Large rooms and hot showers await at **Yellow Rose Pension,** 5 Yeni Sok. (tel./fax (286) 217 33 43), around a corner from the clock tower (singles US$5, doubles US$10, triples US$15).

Troy (Truva) lies 32km south of Çanakkale. The site slept under a blanket of mythology until Heinrich Schliemann, millionaire-*cum*-archaeologist, uncovered the ancient city to prove that Homeric stories were not merely fiction. The remaining Bronze Age fortifications are remarkably well-preserved. Nine distinct strata have been identified and are explained in the **Excavation House.** (Site and house open in summer daily

8am-7:30pm; off-season 8am-5pm. US$1.50, students US$0.75.) Take a *dolmuş* (US$1) from the station in Çanakkale, and ask it to wait while you explore. **Anzac House** (tel. 217 01 56) leads tours leaving at 9am (US$8). Make sure to bring water.

Pergamon to Çeşme

Pergamon The ancient hilltop city of Pergamon was a dazzling center of cultural activity with one of the richest libraries in the ancient world. Today, ruins spread over 30,000 acres, but many attractions cluster around two principal sites. The **Acropolis** looms majestically above the town. (Open June-Oct. daily 8:30am-7pm; Nov.-May 8:30am-5:30pm. US$1.75, students US$0.70.) The **Asclepion** (medical center) lies in the valley below. An impressive portion of the Asclepion remains, including a marble colonnade, theater, and healing rooms. (Both sites open June-Oct. daily 8:30am-7pm; Nov.-May 8:30am-5:30pm. US$1.75, students US$0.70.) The ruins of a huge gymnasium, a Roman circus, several temples, and the lavishly frescoed **House of Attalus** are also scattered about. The most notable attraction is the mammoth **amphitheater,** capable of seating 10,000 spectators. On your way to the **Royal Palaces,** write down a secret desire and tie it to the "wishing tree" on your left. Pergamon gazes across the river at the pleasant, modern town of **Bergama,** where buses travel to and from Bursa (5hr., US$7), Izmir (1½hr.,US$2), and Istanbul (9hr., US$14). Call (232) 31 10 82 35 46 for more info. Bergama's **tourist office** (tel. (232) 632 18 62) is a 1km walk to the right from the main bus station (open April-Sept. daily 8:30am-7pm; Oct.-March Mon.-Sat. 8:30am-5:30pm). **Pension Athena** (tel. (232) 633 34 20), on the road beyond İstiklal Meydanı in a restored Ottoman house, boasts "Not the best, but we're trying to get there." Strike one up for honest advertising. (US$5.25, with shower US$7; 10% *Let's Go* discount; laundry US$5).

Izmir From the rubble of the 1922 Turkish War of Independence, **Izmir,** formerly the ancient **Smyrna,** has risen to become Turkey's third-largest city. Industrial fumes now linger over parts of the city, but along Anafartalar Cad., *çay salonu* (teahouses), the cries of children and vendors, and a full-fledged **bazaar** (open Mon.-Sat. 8:30am-7pm) provide energy and excitement amid the concrete buildings. Izmir's **archaeological museum,** near Konak Sq., displays statues of Poseidon and Demeter among other antiquities (open Tues.-Sun. 8:30am-5:30pm; US$2, students US$1). In late June and early July, an **international festival** brings folk and classical music to Izmir, Çeşme, and Ephesus (call (232) 441 60 60 for info). An astounding number of budget hotels and cheap restaurants, along with several bus company offices and the Alsancak **train station,** are located at the center of the Basmane district. **Buses** run to Istanbul (9hr., US$22), Bursa (5hr., US$7), and many other cities. The **tourist office,** 1/1D Gazi Osman Paşa Blv. (tel. (232) 484 21 48 or 489 92 78; fax 489 92 78), near the tall Hilton Hotel, offers maps and info. (Open May-Oct. Mon.-Fri. 8:30am-7pm, Sat.-Sun. 8:30am-5:30pm; Nov.-April Mon.-Sat. 8:30am-5:30pm.) **Bilen Palas Otel,** 1369 Sok. No. 68 (tel. (232) 483 92 46), has communal showers and the traditional Turkish "pit" toilet (singles US$7, doubles US$12.40, triples US$17.25, quads US$27.60). Most rooms at **Otel Divan,** 1369 Sok No. 61 (tel. (232) 483 36 75; fax 483 22 43), have TV, toilet, and shower (prices same as Bilen Palas).

Çeşme One hour west of Izmir is the popular seaside resort of Çeşme. **Buses** leave every half hour from the Üçkuyular bus lot in Izmir (US$2). **Ertürk Tourism** (tel. (232) 712 67 68) sends ferries from Çeşme to Chios in Greece (July-Sept. daily; May-June 3-5 per week; round-trip US$35). The **tourist office** (tel. (232) 712 66 53) is down the main road toward the water. (Open in summer Mon.-Fri. 8:30am-7pm, Sat.-Sun. 8:30am-5pm; off-season daily 8:30am-5:30pm.) **Tarhan Pension,** Musalla Mah. 9 Çarşı Sok. (tel. (232) 712 65 99), has hot-water showers and comfy rooms (singles US$7, doubles US$14, triples US$24; breakfast US$1.75), while the family-style **Tani Pension,** Musalla Mah., 15 Çarşı Sok. (tel. (232) 712 62 38), has clean rooms with marble floors (singles US$7, doubles US$14, triples US$21).

Kuşadasi

Kuşadası's population quintuples during the summer as countless pubs, clothiers, and restaurants greet the new round of tourists. Although expensive, The **Grand Bazaar** and **Barbados Mayrettin** can assuage the shopper's browsing urges. The area's **beaches,** accessible by *dolmuş,* are clean but overcrowded. When you tire of the crowds, nearby Ephesus and Selçuk feature beautiful scenery and superb relics of the Romand and early Christian eras.

You must pay a US$10 port tax upon entering, generally best paid in U.S. dollars to avoid commissions and weak exchange rates. **Ferries** run to Samos, Greece (one way US$30, same-day round-trip US$35). Contact **Ekol Travel** (tel. (256) 614 92 55), and flash *Let's Go* for a discount. The main **bus station** is about 2km east of the port area, but many *dolmuş* provide transportation to the city center. Buses run to Istanbul (11hr., US$18), Bodrum (2½hr., US$6.66), and Ankara (10hr.,US$16.66). The **tourist office,** No. 13 on İskele Meydanı (tel. (256) 614 11 03), offers maps, bus schedules, and accommodations listings. (Open June-Sept. daily 8am-6pm; Oct.-May 8am-noon and 1:30-5:30pm). To get to the office from the bus station, it's best to take a taxi.

Use discretion when dealing with the hustlers offering "bargain accommodations" who meet buses and ferries. You'll find many cheap pensions along **Aslanlar Caddesi. Hülya Pension,** 39 İleri Sok. (tel. (256) 614 20 75), offers clean, bright rooms (doubles US$8-10, triples US$12-15). **Hotel Rose,** 7 Aslanlar Cad. (tel. (256) 612 25 88; fax 614 11 13), boasts a bar and lounge, 24-hour hot water, **Internet access,** laundry service (US$2 per kg), free luggage storage, and transport to Ephesus. (Dorms US$4, private rooms with bath US$10. 15% *Let's Go* discount. Breakfast US$2.50.) Down the street from Hotel Rose, **Park Pension** (tel. (256) 614 39 17 or 612 69 12) offers comfort in colorful rooms (singles US$6.70; breakfast included; reserve ahead). Bring your sleeping bag and tent to **Yat Camping** (tel. (256) 614 13 33), 2km north of town on Atatürk Bulvarı (US$2.50 per person, US$1.50-2 per tent; caravans US$2.50). There are many cheap restaurants along **Kahramanlar Caddesi** and its alley tributaries. Parallel to Kahramanlar Cad., **Barlar Sok** houses nightclubs (open until 4am).

Near Kuşadasi

For an archaeological fix, search no farther than **Ephesus** (Efes), where ruins from the Roman and early Christian era are extensive and well preserved. If you see Ephesus on your own, you'll approach the ruins from the road between Kuşadası and Selçuk; your first glimpse of the site will be the outskirts of the ancient city. The most important of these remains is the **Vedius Gymnasium,** to the left as you proceed down the road to the main entrance. Farther along lies an enormous **stadium** (the seats were removed to build the Byzantine city walls). Once you pass through the main entrance, marvel at the **Arcadian Street,** a magnificent, colonnaded marble avenue. Uphill, the imposing ruins of the **Temple of Hadrian** dominate the left side of the road. Farther up the hill are the ruins of the exquisite **Fountain of Trajan.** To get to Ephesus from the Kuşadası bus station, take a *dolmuş* to Selçuk, and tell the driver you want to get off at Ephesus. From the Selçuk train station, take any *dolmuş* towards Kuşadası. Guided tours of the ruins are expensive (about US$25 per day); instead, get a good guidebook at the entrance (US$5) and tour the site on your own (site open daily 8am-6pm; US$4.75, with ISIC US$2.40).

The authentic "Turkishness" of the small and beautiful **Selçuk** has made it both preferable to Kuşadasi and aggressively touristed. It is easy to escape the town's commercial fervor by escaping to the breathtaking landscape surrounding town. The colossal and comparatively unadvertised **Basilica of Saint John** was constructed in the 6th century under the Byzantine emperor Justinian (open daily 8am-6pm; US$1.33, students US$0.66). The **Temple of Artemis,** one of the seven wonders of the ancient world, used to be the largest temple on the planet; now a lone reconstructed column twists toward the heavens. Selçuk's **Ephesus Museum** holds most of the archaeological finds unearthed in the region since World War II (open daily 8:30am-6pm; US$2, students US$1).

The **tourist office,** Atatürk Mah. Agora Çarşısı, 35-6 Mirza Karşısı (tel. (232) 892 63 28), provides free maps. (Open in summer Mon.-Fri. 8am-7pm, Sat.-Sun. 9am-5pm; off-season Mon.-Fri. 9am-5pm.) Facing away from the office, walk four blocks left on Atatürk Cad.; nearby, the **train** and **bus stations** send *dolmuş* to Kuşadası and buses to Izmir (US$1.50). **Pansiyon Karahan** (Smiley's Place), 9 I. Okul Sok. (tel. (232) 892 25 75), the second right after the bus station heading north, has clean rooms with showers and secure locks (US$6.66 per person; breakfast US$2.50; reserve ahead). Behind the Ephesus Museum, the friendly **Australian New Zealand Pension,** 7 Prof. Miltner Sok. (tel. (232) 892 60 50), has a lively garden (US$8 per person, dorm beds US$4; 15% *Let's Go* discount). The **Ekselans Café and Bar,** Okul Sok. No. 18, has beer (US$1), cognac (US$0.66), and backgammon (open daily 11am-midnight).

Pamukkale and Aphrodisias

Whether as ancient Hierapolis or modern **Pamukkale,** this village has been drawing the weary its thermal springs for over 23 centuries. The Turkish name—literally "cotton castle"—refers to the snow-white regional cliffs, shaped over millennia by the accumulation of calcium deposited by mineral springs. Don't leave Pamukkale without a dip in the **sacred fountain** at the Pamukkale Motel, 75m past the archaeological museum. Warm, fizzy waters bubble at the spring's source (open for pool use daily 8am-8pm; US$3.33 per 2hr.). Most of the direct **buses** that run to Pamukkale leave from Selçuk and Kuşadası (5-6 per day, 4½hr., US$4.50). From Pamukkale, there are buses to Bodrum (5hr., US$6.25), Selçuk and Kuşadası (4½hr., US$7.50), and Izmir (4hr., US$6.25). Three **tourist offices** serve the town; one is toward the main road on the way to the site (open in summer daily 8am-7pm, off-season 8am-5pm). **Koray Hotel,** (tel. 272 2300; fax 272 2095) in the middle of Pamukkale Village, toward the right of the bus stop, has rooms which face a beautiful garden and a thermal water pool. All rooms come with bathroom and shower (singles US$5-7; breakfast US$2).

In ancient times, **Aphrodisias** (Geyre) gained fame for its exquisite sculptures, and evolved into a metropolis after Pergamon became Roman. Particularly worth seeing is the Greek **stadium,** with its seating capacity of 30,000, and the elegant **Temple of Aphrodite.** (Museum and site open daily in summer 8:30am-7pm; off-season 8:30am-5pm. US$2 per site, students US$1.) The easiest way to see the ruins is as a daytrip from Pamukkale; **buses** leave at 10am and return at 5pm (2hr., round-trip US$6.70).

Bodrum

Bodrum, Herodotus's home town, seems to be in a world of its own. Here travelers come to a nexus of divine beaches, forests, and quaint little islands known for their exquisite swimming coves. Turn left onto Saray Sok. from Neyzen Tevfik Cad. to reach the scanty remains of the **Mausoleum of Halicarnassus,** yet another of the seven wonders of the ancient world (open Tues.-Sun. 8:30am-5:30pm; US$1.40, students US$0.70). Guarding the harbor, the **Kale,** built on an acropolis, now houses Bodrum's **Museum of Underwater Archaeology,** a unique assortment of shipwreck flotsam from sites along the surrounding coastline. (*Kale* open Tues.-Sun. 8:30am-5pm. US$1.33, students US$0.66. Museum open Tues.-Fri. 8:30am-5pm. US$1.33, students US$0.66.) Nightlife rages all week long. Despite the high cover, your destination should be the large open-air **Halicarnassus Disco,** at the end of Cumhuriyet Cad., 1500m from the center of town. Different shows every night include live music and a laser show (cover US$14; open until the early morning). Another hotspot is the **Red Lion Bar,** on Cumhuriyet Cad., one of the most popular bars (no cover).

The **tourist office,** 12 Eylül Meydanı (tel. (252) 316 10 91), at the foot of the castle, has room listings, bus info, and free brochures with maps (open April-Oct. daily 8:30am-7:30pm; Nov.-March Mon.-Fri. 8am-noon and 1-5pm). Pensions are plentiful, but reservations are wise. Solo travelers may need to find a roommate in the high season. The **Yenilmez Pansiyon** (tel. 316 2520), along Neyzen Tevfik Cad., the road along the water to the right as you face the harbor, has spotless rooms and 24hr. hot water. Turn right at the alley after Lowry's Irish Pub (but before Sini Restaurant), and walk up the winding path (doubles US$20). **Polyanna Pension,** No. 5 Ortanca Sok. (tel. 316 1528), a side street just before the Halicarnassis Disco end of Cumhuriyet Cad., offers clean rooms with toilets and showers (doubles with breakfast US$16.70). Bodrum is famous for its seafood, especially octopus and squid. Trendy **Café Mavsoleion,** on the harborfront on Neyzen Tevfik Cad., serves dishes at reasonable prices.

Near Bodrum: The Bodrum Peninsula

Bodrum's popularity among Turks stems largely from its location at the head of the enchanting **Bodrum Peninsula.** After day of swimming and sunning along the peninsula's many beaches, you can partake of Bodrum's rousing nightlife. A few of the beaches on the southern coast of the peninsula are accessible only by tour boats, which leave from the front of Bodrum's castle (daily 9-11am, returning 5-6pm). Itineraries for the tours vary widely (check the tour schedule at the dock); some popular destinations include **Kara Island,** the village of **Akyarlar,** and the beaches at **Baradakçı, Çapa Tatil, Kargı Bay, Bağla,** and **Karaincir.** Boat tours cost around US$12 per person for the day, US$18 with lunch. In summer, boats also leave daily from the castle to tranquil **Orak Island** (same prices). These are some of the best swimming spots on the peninsula, but there are few budget accommodations nearby. Daytrips are your best bet. **Gölköy** and **Türkbükü,** once idyllic villages, are now hives for Turkish tourists. Words cannot do justice to **Gümüşlük,** a tiny seaside paradise at the west tip of the Bodrum Peninsula, whose sparkling vistas, cool sea breezes, and relaxed atmosphere make it a escape from the frenetic hedonism of Bodrum.

MEDITERRANEAN COAST

Reaching from the edges of Greece to the Syrian border, Turkey's Mediterranean coast is alternately chic, garish, and remote. Pine forests, hidden coves, and beaches line the stretch between Fethiye and Antalya. Accommodations along the west segment are cheap, and excellent seafood abounds. Farther east, swatches of sand and concrete dotted with castles and ruins mark the shore dubbed the "Turquoise Coast."

Marmaris and the Datça Peninsula

Urban **Marmaris** is easily accessible to Rhodes and serves as a good base for exploring in the southern Aegean and Mediterranean coasts. Its small **castle** built by Süleyman the Magnificent in 1522 is a worth a visit. **Ferries** travel to Rhodes. (Fri. leaves Marmaris at 9:15am and leaves Rhodes at 2:30pm. 1½hr. US$14 plus. Same day return US$27.33. Open ticket US$36. US$5 per port entered.) Contact **Yeşil Marmairis** for more info (tel. (252) 412 10 33 or 412 22 90; fax 412 07 78). Frequent **buses** run to Izmir (5hr., US$8), Bodrum (3hr., US$5), and many other cities. From the station, cross the bridge over a channel of water and follow the coast to the **tourist office,** 2 İskele Meydanı, near the harborfront Roman statue. (Tel. (252) 412 10 35. Fax 412 72 77. Open in summer daily 8:30am-7:30pm; off-season Mon.-Fri. 8:30am-5pm).

The **Interyouth Hostel,** Tepe Mah. #45 42nd Sok. (tel. (252) 412 36 87; fax 412 78 23), is one of the most professionally run hostels on the coast. There is a less appealing copycat hostel at the outskirts of town; to get to the real Interyouth Hostel from the Atatürk statue, walk straight up Ulusal Egemenlik Bd., look for signs, and take a right (dorms US$4.25, doubles US$6; 10% discount with ISIC, IYH, and GO25 cards). To reach **Maltepe Pansiyon** (tel. (252) 412 16 29), make a right (as you face the water) from the centrum, and then turn right at the disco and cabaret and follow this road across the footbridge (singles US$10, doubles US$16.66). Head to the **bazaar,** where several affordable restaurants await. Get no frills Turkish food (meals US$1-2) at **Özyiğut Restaurant,** Tepe Mah. 53 Çarşı İçi No. 21. To meet other tourists, head to the row of pubs behind the tourist office or to the **Greenhouse** or the **B-52 Bar.**

From Marmaris hop on a bus to the resplendent **Datça Peninsula** (1½hr., US$3.33). Boats depart from Bodrum daily at 9am and 5pm (2hr., round-trip US$13.33). **Antalyalı Pension** (tel. (252) 712 38 12) is centrally located and easy to find (on Yalı Cad., a main road on the peninsula). From the bus station, pass the PTT and take the left fork (doubles US$16.70, triples US$20). **Ilıca Camping** (tel. (252) 712 34 00), on the beach beyond the harbor (right at the taxi station), has a restaurant and two-person bungalows (camping US$3.40 per person; bungalows US$6.70 per person).

The ancient city of **Caunos,** where archaeologists are turning up new structures as fast as they can dig, is located by the river leading out of nearby Lake Küyceğiz. The ruins are accessible only by boat from the nearby town of **Dalyan.** If you decide to camp at the nearby Lake Köyceğiz, your stay will undoubtedly coincide with the annual convention of the Voracious Mosquitoes Union. Dalyan's **Kristal Pansiyon** (tel. 284 22 63 or 284 31 53), off Maraş Sok., provides palatial rooms and all-important screened windows (singles US$10, doubles US$16.66; breakfast included).

CENTRAL TURKEY

The high, dry mountain ranges of Central Anatolia form Turkey's bread basket. While the Aegean and Mediterranean coasts have suffered the affects of rampant tourism, the beautiful mountains of this region boast some of the most authentic and hospitable towns and villages in all of Turkey.

Ankara

Travelers have often scorned this sprawling, polluted, windy capital, and so miss its pockets of traditional Turkish life and windows to the soul of modern Turkey. Catch the city on a sunny summer day, and you may find it more lively and engaging than its poor reputation would suggest. The **Ethnographic Museum,** about 1km south of Ulus off Atatürk Blv., contains a beautiful collection of clothing, calligraphy, ironwork, and woodwork, including some carvings from mosques (open Tues.-Sun. 8:30am-12:30pm and 1:30-5:30pm; US$2.80). The fantastic **Anadolu Medeniyetleri Müzesi** (Museum of Anatolian Civilizations), northeast of the Ethnographic Museum, lies at the feet of the citadel that dominates the old town. Walk to the top of Hisarpark Cad., turn right at the Citadel steps, and follow the Citadel boundaries. The museum's unique setting—a restored 15th-century Ottoman *han* (inn) and *bedesten* (covered bazaar)—complements the collection of astoundingly old artifacts inside (open Tues.-Sun. 8:30am-5:30pm; US$2.10, students $1.05). Also in town, the pure white **Kocatepe Mosque** is one of the world's largest and most beautiful. Inside the mosque a gold sphere, surrounded by smaller spheres, hangs from the ceiling. Don't leave town without visiting **Anıt Kabir,** Atatürk's mausoleum. The structure, nearly a kilometer long, houses Atatürk's sarcophagus and many personal effects. To reach the site from the tourist office, walk left (northwest) up Gazi Mustafa Kemal Blv. until you reach the square. As you approach the square, the next major street to your left, Anıt Cad., exiting the traffic circle, leads to the sprawling grounds and mausoleum.

Practical Information, Accommodations, and Food The **train** station *(gar)* is 1½km southwest of Ulus Sq. Fast blue trains *(Mavi Tren)* travel to Istanbul and Izmir (each US$8.50); normal trains to these two cities cost US$7-8. The **bus** terminal *(Otogar)*, in Söğütözü 5km west of Kızılay, is connected to all points in the city by local buses, *dolmuş,* and taxis. Buses depart frequently for Konya (3½hr., US$5.60), Istanbul (7½hr., US$10.50), and Izmir (8½hr., US$12). The **tourist office** is at 121 Gazi Mustafa Kemal Blv. (tel. (312) 488 70 07 or 231 55 72). From the train station's main platform, descend to the shop-lined tunnel to Tandoğan (marked Tandoğan Kapalı Çarşı); at the end of the tunnel turn left onto Gazi Mustafa Kemal Blv. The staff gives out free maps (open Mon.-Fri. 8:30am-6:30pm, Sat.-Sun. 9am-5pm;

reduced hours off season). There is a **branch office** at the airport (open 24hr.). The embassies in Ankara include: **Australia,** 83 Nenehatun Cad., Gaziomanpaşa (tel. (312) 446 11 80); **Bulgaria,** 124 Atatürk Blv. (tel. (312) 426 74 55); **Canada,** 75 Nenehatun Cad. (tel. (312) 436 12 75); **Greece,** 9-11 Zia Ül-Rahman Cad., Gaziomanpaşa (tel. (312) 436 88 60); **New Zealand,** 13/4 İran Cad., Kavaklıdere (tel. (312) 467 90 56); **South Africa,** 27 Filistin Sok. (tel. (312) 446 40 56); **U.K.,** 46A Şehit Ersun Cad. (tel. (312) 468 62 30); and **U.S.,** 110 Atatürk Blv. (tel. (312) 468 61 10).

Of the two main accommodations centers, Ulus is cheaper, but Kızılay is safer and cleaner. Going south along Atatürk Blv., take the fourth left after the McDonald's and the third right onto Selanik Cad. to reach peaceful **Otel Ertan,** 70 Selanik Cad. (tel. (312) 418 40 84), which is convenient to Kızılay nightlife (singles US$12.30, doubles US$17.60). **Hotel Ergen,** 48 Karamfil Sok (tel. (312) 417 59 06), is recommended by the tourist office and has small, clean rooms (singles US$25). **M.E.B. Özel Çağdaş Erkek Öğrenci Yurt,** 15 Neyzen Tevfik Sok., Maltepe (tel. 232 2954, -5), has dormitories located between G.M.K. Blv. and Gençlik Cad. that are used for a co-ed hostel from June 1-Sept. 1. Coming out of the Maltepe Ankaray stop onto G.M.K. Blv., make a right (away from the tourist office) uphill onto Neyzen Tevfik Sok (US$12).

Kızılay has many mid-range restaurants and cafés; Gençlike Park has cheaper eateries, and the Citadel and Kavaklıdere more upscale establishments. In Kızılay, **Cafe M,** on Selanik Cad., draws students and young travelers. Right on the square in the Citadel, **Kale Washington** serves tasty dishes on a canopied terrace (main courses about US$5.25). The **Gıma supermarket** is on Anafartalar Cad. in Ulus. At night, students crowd tree-lined **Yüksel Sok.,** one block south of Kızılay on the left. To the right is the café-laden **Selanik Sok.,** which runs parallel to Atatürk Blv. Pub life centers on two streets: **İnkilâp Sok.** and the livelier **Bayındır Sok.,** two and three blocks to the left of Kızılay Sq. as you look south. Beer flows freely at the crowded **Büyük Ekspress,** 11 Bayındır Sok.

Carpet Buying in Turkey

Carpet and *kilim* buying in Turkey is a task for the expert bargainer. Merchandise is always overpriced, sometimes by as much as 50%, but the high quality can make it worth your while. "Shop around" is an understatement—you should seek out advice from several carpet/*kilim* vendors who speak English (as most do). The name of the game is bargaining, so don't be afraid to stick by your bid if you know it's fair. Always get several independent opinions on the value of a carpet before you buy. Be sure to flip the carpet over to feel for knots (if you cannot feel any, it is probably machine made). Also, pull out a strand from the carpet and burn it; if it smells like wool, you know it is real. Be careful not to leave the store without a copy of insurance and shipping contracts, as well as a certificate of guarantee.

Ukraine (Україна)

US$1	**= 1.87hv (Ukrainian hryvny)**	**1hv =**	**US$0.54**
CDN$1	**= 1.34hv**	**1hv =**	**CDN$0.74**
UK£1	**= 3.00hv**	**1hv =**	**UK£0.33**
IR£1	**= 2.75hv**	**1hv =**	**IR£0.36**
AUS$1	**= 1.36hv**	**1hv =**	**AUS$0.73**
NZ$1	**= 1.18hv**	**1hv =**	**NZ$0.85**
SAR1	**= 0.40hv**	**1hv =**	**SAR2.52**

Country Code: 380 **International Dialing Prefix: 810**

Compared to many of its more westernized neighbors, Ukraine is anarchic and dour. Foreign tourism is practically non-existent in this huge and diverse land; one need not seek to depart from any beaten paths because—aside from an ugly and expensive Intourist trail—there is none. This does not necessarily mean a lack of comfort, but rather that when traveling in Ukraine, you will see people, not just touristy roads and souvenir shops. Museums cost nothing and are empty; medieval castles are still huge, dark, and unsupervised; and cobbled roads remain unpaved. The ascent of the new rich, however, has pushed some prices well above the normal standard of living, creating a split between the ritzy world of plenty which Ukrainians expect foreigners to be a part of (and to pay for) and the impoverished world inhabited by the majority of

Ukrainians themselves. There are treasures here, but you'll have to find them on your own, because Ukraine, with enough problems of its own, isn't inclined to play host.

For more detailed coverage of Ukraine, refer to *Let's Go: Eastern Europe 1998.*

GETTING THERE

Foreign travelers arriving in Ukraine must have not only a **visa,** but also an **invitation** from a citizen or official organization or a tourist voucher from a travel agency. Regular visa processing at an embassy (invitation in hand) takes up to nine days and costs US$50 (double-entry US$80); three-day rush, available to citizens of Australia, Canada, Great Britain, Ireland, New Zealand, and South Africa but *not* the United States costs US$80 (double entry US$120). For more info, contact an **embassy** (see **Government Information Offices,** p. 1). Some private organizations, such as **Russia House** (U.S. tel. (202) 986-6010; fax 667-4244), arrange visas and invitations. **Host Families Association,** 5-25 Tavricheskaya, 193015 St. Petersburg, Russia (tel./fax 812 275 1992; email hofa@usa.net), provides invitations for HOFA guests.

If you arrive at the **Kiev airport** without a visa, you can buy a **tourist voucher,** which will then permit you to buy a visa. This allows you to go through customs, where you must declare all valuables and foreign currency to facilitate leaving the country. Carry a copy of your invitation and letters of introduction at all times. Upon arrival in Ukraine you should check into a hotel or register with the hall of nightmares that is the **Office of Visas and Registration** (OVIR), in Kiev at bulv. Tarasa Shevchenka, 34 (Тараса Шевченка), or in police stations in smaller cities, within your first three days in the country (US$10). Visas may also be extended here. Your visa not only lets you in; it also allows you to leave. *Do not lose it.*

Air Ukraine International (in the U.S., tel. (312) 337-0004) flies from European capitals, Chicago, New York, and Washington. Swiss Air, Air France, ČSA, Lufthansa, LOT, Malév, and SAS also fly to Kiev. **Trains** run to Ukraine from all neighboring states. When coming from the west, prepare for a two-hour stop at the border. **Ferries** cross the Black Sea from Odessa and Yalta to Istanbul.

GETTING AROUND

Trains are dirt cheap, reasonably comfortable, and go everywhere. Getting tickets, however, can drive you batty. Try to buy tickets two or three days in advance.You may be told there are no more seats when in fact only the first two classes are full; ask about the other classes as well. Conductors are often willing to seat those without tickets (charging the ticket price and pocketing the money themselves), and scalpers sell what are usually valid tickets. **Buses** are more expensive, but the best for short distances. Buy tickets at the regular ticket windows (the night before in large cities).

Taxis overcharge everyone; agree on a price before getting in. State taxis (with checkered signs) are supplemented by unregulated "private transport," which is at your own risk. Both can be hailed by holding the hand at a downward salute.

ESSENTIALS

The breakup of the Soviet Union technically brought about the demise of the state travel agency, **Intourist,** which was responsible for foreigners traveling to Ukraine. Nonetheless, they still have an office in every city, sometimes under another name. It's not a bad idea to register with your embassy once you arrive in Ukraine. Besides making the process of recovering lost passports much quicker, the embassy staff may be able to offer important information on travel in Ukraine.

On September 2, 1996, Ukraine replaced **karbovanets** (Krb; a.k.a. kupon) with a new currency, **hryvnia** (hv; гривна), which eradicates five zeroes—each hryvnia (pl hryvny) is worth 100,000 karbovantsi. The new coins are **kopeks** (100kp=1hv). Beware individuals who might try to hand over karbovantsi as change; US$10 worth of change might quickly become US¢0.01. Hotels usually request hryvny, only occasionally asking for dollars. International train tickets are usually sold partly in hryvny, partly in dollars. **Exchange** of US$ and DM is fairly simple and can be done at Обмін

Валют (*Obmin Valyut*) kiosks. Exchange of other currencies is difficult; **traveler's checks** are not accepted but can be changed to dollars at small commissions in almost every city in Ukraine. **X-Change Points,** in major cities, have Western Union and give Visa cash advances. *Don't* use the private money exchangers.

Communication **Telephones** are struggling out of the Dark Ages. Order international calls at the post office for the cheapest rates. In Kiev, **Utel** (Ukraine telephone) produces electronic **phonecards.** Utel's new technology lets you make collect calls from some phones; dial 27 10 36 and ask for an "ITNT" (AT&T) operator. **AT&T Direct** (tel. (8) 100 11—wait for another tone after the 8) and **MCI Direct** (tel. (8) 100 13) are available from Utel and private phones. Otherwise you must make international calls at the post office—cheaper, but a hassle. **Local calls** are free from any gray pay phone in most cities. In Lviv, buy tokens at the post office or at kiosks. **Mail** is cheap but slow (at least two to three weeks from Kiev to any foreign destination). In case of **fire,** dial 01; to reach the **police,** call 02; and for an **ambulance,** dial 03.

Ease your trip with a few Ukrainian or Russian phrases (see **Russia: Essentials,** p. 740). Ukrainian or sometimes Polish is preferred in the West, but Russian is still more common in Crimea and most of Eastern Ukraine, even Kiev. The Ukrainian alphabet resembles Russian with only a few character and pronunciation differences. Ukrainian adds "і" (*ee* sound) and "ї" (*yee* sound)—"и" is closest to "s*i*t." The "ґ" (hard g) has been reintroduced since independence but is not widely used, and the "г," pronounced "g" in Russian, comes out like an "h."

Yes/No	Так/Ні	tak/nee
Hello	Добрий день	DOH-bree dehn
Please	Прошу	PRO-shoo
Thank you	Дякую	DYA-kou-yoo
Excuse me	Вибачте	VIH-bach-te
Do you speak English?	Ви говорите по-англиськи?	vih ho-VOR-ih-te poh-anh-lih-skih
I don't understand	Я не розумію	ya ne roh-zoo-MEE-yu
Where?	Де?	deh
How much?	Скільки?	SKEEL-kih
I'd like...	Я хочу...	ya KHO-choo
Help!	Поможіт	poh-moh-ZHEET

Accommodations, Camping, and Food **Hotels** fall into two categories, "hotels" and "tourist bases" called "турбаза" (TOOR-bah-zah). The latter usually form part of a complex aimed at motoring tourists but are otherwise nearly indistinguishable from hotels. Hotel prices in Kiev are astronomical, but singles run anywhere from 5hv to 90hv per night in the rest of the country. Check your bill carefully. Your passport may be kept for the duration of your stay. Conditions are usually adequate, although you'll need your own toilet paper (buy it at kiosks or markets), and hot water is a rare gift. Do not leave valuables in your room unattended. Most cities have a **campground** on the edge of town. These old Soviet complexes can be quite posh, with saunas and restaurants. Space in a bungalow with electricity runs 10-20hv per night; tent space costs 5-15hv. Free camping is illegal. **Private rooms** are available through overseas agencies and bargaining at the train station (2-5hv per person).

There are few choices between new, expensive restaurants and the cheap, sometimes risky bars and *stolovayas.* A decent *stolovaya* (столовая) or cafeteria (кафе) offers a choice of two main dishes, soups, and a fruit drink (all for 1-2hv). Most foreigners leave tips of 10%; locals do not tip. Public markets fill large warehouses and are usually jam-packed (open daily 7am-5pm). State food stores are classified by content: Гастроном mostly sells packaged goods, Молоко dairy products, Овочі-Фрукти fruits and veggies, Мясо meat, Хліб bread, Ковбаси sausage, and Риба fish.

Kiev Київ

"Most often of all I soothe my aged imagination with pictures of gold-domed, garden-cloaked and poplar-crowned Kiev," wrote Taras Shevchenko from exile. The poet's praise was once justified, when Kiev ruled the first Slavic empire and artfully sculpted houses lined the city streets. Today, economic crisis rages throughout Ukraine, and the capital city struggles to rebuild a country as its own houses crumble and citizens beg in the streets. Meanwhile, a gaudy rich caste glories in its opulent *couture* and German cars. Kiev will need years to return to the magnificence of which Shevchenko wrote, although tourists will find the sights worth a prolonged stop.

ORIENTATION AND PRACTICAL INFORMATION

Almost all attractions and services lie on the right bank of the Dnipro River, in western Kiev. The train station is at M: Vokzalna (Вокзальна). Two metro stops away, **Khreshchatik** (Хрещатик), a busy boulevard, satisfies most tourist needs except housing. The parallel **Volodimirska vul.** (Володимирська вул.) brims with history.

Tourist Office: Intercity Travel, vul. Hospitalna, 4, 3rd fl., room 304 (Госпітальна; tel. 294 31 11; fax 220 54 46), inside Hotel Rus (Готел Рус). *Kiev Pocket* guides are available in the lobby downstairs (10hv). Open Mon.-Fri. 9am-8pm, Sat. 10am-4pm. **Hotel Kievska's lobby** (Київська), behind Hotel Rus at vul. Hospitalna, 12, also has info. Both hotels are at M: Respublikansky stadion (Республіканський стадіон).

Embassies: Australia, vul. Kominternu, 18 (Комінтерну; tel. 225 75 86). **Belarus,** vul. Sichnevoho Povstaniya, 6 (Січневого Повстанія; tel. 290 02 01). **Canada,** vul. Yaroslaviv Val, 31 (Ярославів Вал; tel. 224 53 60). **Russia,** pr. Kutuzova, 8 (Кутузова; tel. 294 79 36). **South Africa,** Chervonoarmiska vul., 9/2 (Червоноармийська; tel. 227 71 72). **U.K.,** Sichnevoho Povstaniya, 6 (tel. 290 73 17). Open Mon.-Fri. 9am-noon. **U.S.,** vul. Y. Kotsyubinskoho, 10 (Ю. Коцюбинського; tel. 244 73 49, emergency 216 38 05). Open Mon.-Fri. 2-6pm.

Currency Exchange: Look for *Obmin-Valyut* (Обмін-Валют) windows on every street and in every café-bar. They usually take only US$ and DM and don't deal in traveler's checks or credit card advances. For those services, try a bank.

Flights: Kiev-Borispil Airport receives international flights. A **city bus** (2.5hv) runs to M: Livoberezhna (Лівобережна), across the river from central Kiev (every 2hr.).

Trains: Kiev-Passazhirski (Київ-Пассажирський), Vokzalna pl. (Вокзальна пл.). M: Vokzalna or tram 2. Buy international **tickets** at Intourist window 10, 2nd fl. Open daily 8am-1pm, 2-7pm, and 8pm-7am. To: Odessa (19hr., 16hv), Lviv (12hr., 16hv), Prague (34hr., 149hv), Warsaw (15hr., 66hv), and Moscow (15-17hr.,43-61hv).

Buses: Tsentralni Avtovokzal (Централний Автовокзал), Moskovska pl., 3 (Московська), serves long-distance destinations. **Pivdenna** (Південна), pr. Akademika Hlushkova, 3 (Академика Глушкова), connects to Odessa; **Podil** (Поділ), vul. Nizhny Val, 15a (Нижній Вал), serves Crimea.

Public Transportation: Kiev's **Metro** has 3 intersecting lines. Buy tokens at the "Каса" *(Kasa)* for 0.30hv or a monthly pass from a numbered kiosk for 10hv (good on all public transport). Tickets for **trams, trolleys,** and **buses** are sold at kiosks (0.30hv) and must be punched on board.

Medical Assistance: Emergency Care Center, vul. Mechnikova, 1 (Мечникова; tel. 22 42 02 or 227 92 30), also has a dental clinic (tel. 227 42 40).

Emergencies: Fire: tel. 01. **Police:** tel. 02. **Ambulance:** tel. 03.

Post Office: vul. Khreshchatik, 22 (Хрещатик), next to Maidan Nezalezhnosti (Майдан Незалежності). *Poste Restante* at counters 26-27. Info at counter 10; no English. Open Mon.-Sat. 8am-8pm, Sun. 9am-7pm. **Postal Code:** 252 001.

Telephones: Mizhmisky Perehovorny Punkt (Мижміський Переговорний Пункт), at the post office, or **Telefon-Telefaks** (Телефон-Телефакс) around the corner (entry on Khreshchatik). Both offices open 24hr. Buy **Utel phonecards** (10, 20, and 40hv) from the post office and upscale hotels to make international calls at the post office, hotels, airport, train station, fancy restaurants, and the Dim Ukrainski (Дім Український) across from Hotel Dnipro. **Telephone Code:** 044.

ACCOMMODATIONS AND FOOD

Kiev's hotel prices, aimed at foreign businesspeople, seem rude at best, but cheap lodgings await on the distant horizons. **Diane Sadovnikov**—a former missionary living and working here—and her husband Yuri find accommodations in a private apartment (45-75hv), with a family, or in a hotel/dorm. They also arrange invitations (US$30; tel./fax 516 05 48; call between 9am-5pm one month in advance). In a pinch, contact **Eric,** the owner of Club Sofia (tel. 229 88 16). Ask at the tourist office for directions to the **Grazhdanski Aviatski Institut Student Hotel,** vul. Nizhinska, 29E. (Ніжінська. Tel. 484 90 59. Singles 13.20-17.80hv; doubles 22-33hv. No English spoken.) **Hotel Universitetsky** (Університетський), vul. Lomonosova, 81 (Ломоносова), offers rooms a half hour from the center: call 266 74 44 before 5pm and ask for the director (30-33hv per person). Alternatively, camp at **Motel-Camping "Prolisok,"** pr. Peremohy, 179 (tel. 444 12 93; dim comfy motel doubles 107hv; tent space 8.80hv per person). From M: Svyatoshin (Святошин), take trolley 7 west to "Автостанція Дачна" *(Avtostantsiya Dachna)* and walk 2km down the highway.

Many restaurants in Kiev cater to the newly rich; with few exceptions meals cost 12hv and up even at a cheaper restaurant. Supermarkets such as **7/24,** vul. Baseina 1/2 (Басеина; open 24hr.) are convenient but more expensive than markets and smaller shops. Enjoy cutlets with french fries and veggies for 4.50hv at **Stary Agat** (Старий Агат), vul. Sahaydochnoho, 6 (Сагайдочного; M: Поштова площа; open daily 10am-midnight), or Lebanese dishes at **Montannya Snack** (Монтання Снак), vul. Volodimirska, 68. (Володимирська. M: Площа Льва Толстого. Open Mon.-Fri. noon-11pm, Sat.-Sun. noon-midnight.) For good hardy Ukrainian food, try **Stalovaya** (Столовая), Kudryavsky Uzviz 7 (Кудрявський Узвіз), in the same building as the U.S. Commercial Service (potato soup and bread 0.38hv; open daily noon-3pm). For lighter fare, **Kavyarnya Svitoch** (Кав'ярня Світоч), vul. Velika Zhitomirska, 8a (Велика Житомирська), has great coffee and chocolates (open daily 9am-9pm). **Bessarabsky Rynok** (Бессарабський Ринок), vul. Khreshchatik and bulv. Shevchenka (Шевченка), is a large **market** (open Mon. 7am-5pm, Tues.-Sun. 7am-7pm).

SIGHTS AND ENTERTAINMENT

Downtown Kiev lies on **vul. Khreshchatik** (Хрещатик), a broad commercial avenue built largely after World War II. At the center of town, **Maidan Nezalezhnosti** (Independence Plaza, formerly October Revolution Square), enclosing large fountains, is filled with book vendors, musicians, and angel-headed hipsters. At the center of **Khreshchaty Park,** the **Arch of Brotherhood,** resembling a huge silver croquet wicket, celebrates the Russian-Ukrainian union. Locals refer to it as the "Yoke." Also in the park is the monument to the **brave football players.** As the story goes, Nazi troops forced the Dynamo soccer team to play the German army's Luftwaffe team. The Kiev team proudly won the match 3-0 and were promptly executed. At bulv. Tarasa Shevchenka, the **V.I. Lenin monument** is one of Kiev's rare undesecrated Communist monuments. Dedicated to the poet, bulv. Tarasa Shevchenko sweeps past many-domed **Volodimirsky Cathedral,** built to commemorate 900 years of Christianity in Kiev. At #12, **Taras Shevchenko Museum** is a large and beautiful literary museum. Exhibits are labeled in Ukrainian and Russian, but an English tour costs 20hv or 10hv for students (open Tues.-Sun. 10am-5pm; closed last Fri. of the month).

At the end of vul. Volodimirska (Володимирська), an ancient, winding road leads to the oldest section of Kiev—**Andrivsky uzviz** (Андріївський узвіз), lined with cafés, souvenir vendors, and galleries. **St. Andrew's Cathedral** looms proudly over the street; learn all about it at the **Andrivsky Uzviz Museum** (open Wed.-Sun. 11am-7pm; 1hv). From the end of the street near Volodimirska, a scenic **funicular** goes to upper Kiev (0.30hv; open daily 6:30am-11pm), where the golden onion domes, decorated facades, and 11th-century Byzantine icons of the **St. Sophia Monastery Complex** recall its past as cultural center of Kievan Rus and the site of the first library in Rus. Back toward Tarasa Shevchenka, the **Zoloty vorota** (Золотои Ворота; Golden Gates) have marked the entrance to Kiev since 1037. A museum sits inside the gates (open daily May-Oct. 10am-5pm; 2hv, students 1hv).

Kiev's oldest and holiest religious site is the mysterious **Kievo-Pecherska Lavra** (Києво-Печерська Лавра; Kiev-Pechery Monastery; M: Arsenalna), once the center of Orthodox Christianity. Its monks were subsequently mummified and entombed in the **caves.** Buy a candle as you enter if you want to see anything. Women should cover their heads and shoulders; men should wear pants. When in the caves, you're supposed to look only at the monks whose palms are facing up (open Wed.-Mon. 9-11:30am and 1-4pm). The 18th-century **Velyka lavrska dzvinytsya** (Велика лаврська дзвіниця; Great Cave Bell Tower; open daily 9:30am-8pm; 2hv, students 1hv) and the 12th-century **Troitska Nadzramna Tserkva** (Троїцька надзрамна церква; Holy Trinity Church) on the grounds are particularly worth visiting. (Complex open daily 9:30am-7pm; in winter until 6pm. Ticket for all churches and exhibitions (but no museums) 7hv, students 3hv. English guides 2-3hv.)

Perhaps it is the foreboding presence of the many cathedrals, or the fact that by midnight many people are too drunk to walk, but the capital simply doesn't live up to its big-city billing when it comes to nightlife. Fortunately, **Club Sofia,** vul. Sofiivska, 7 (Софіївська; tel. 229 88 16), off Maydan Nezalezhnosti, is an exception to this rule. Unofficially "Eric's Bar," this smoky cellar will already be jam-packed with young artists, intellectuals, foreigners, and Ukrainians of all sorts early in the evening.

Lviv Львів

Lviv's cobblestone alleys lead past towering spires, hulking homes, and several centuries of artistic and architectural achievement. These monuments see few of the tourists so familiar to other Austro-Hungarian cities like Kraków and Prague, but the vendors, storekeepers, and café owners on the streets below are ready and waiting.

Lviv's historical center is best seen on foot; start on prosp. Svobody (Свободи), next to the ornate Neoclassical **Teatr Opera ta Baletu** (Театр Опери та Балету), which opens onto a pedestrian mall. The **Mickiewicz statue,** honoring the Polish poet and patriot, is the site of concerts and political discussions. Turn left at the movie theater and head to the stone-gray facade of the **Church of St. Andrew,** which boasts a frescoed interior and a massive gilt altar. A sharp left here leads to **pl. Rynok** (Ринок), the historic market square. On pl. Katedralna (Катедральна) rises the Polish **Roman Catholic Cathedral** (open Mon.-Sat. 6am-noon and 6-8pm, Sun. 6am-3pm and 5:30-8pm). Follow vul. Ruska (Руська) east to the massive **Assumption Church,** next to the 60m **Kornyakt's belltower,** and the Baroque cupola of the **Muzey Istorii Religii** (Музей Исторії Релігії; Museum of Religious History). This former Dominican monastery displays masterfully carved wooden figures (open Fri.-Wed. 10am-6pm). The **Arsenal Museum,** Arsenalna vul., 3 (Арсенальна), at vul. Pidvalna, has an impressive collection of weapons (open Thurs.-Tues. 10am-5:45pm; 1hv, students 0.50hv).

To catch a performance at the **Opera** or the **Symphony,** vul. Chaikovskovo, visit the ticket windows (театральни каси; *teatralny kasy*) at pr. Svobody, 37 (open Mon.-Sat. 11am-2pm and 4-7pm). At night, shabbily dressed artsy types do shots while arguing with the sophisticated black-clad wine-sippers at **Club-Café Lyalka** (Клуб-Кафе Лялька), vul. Halytska, 1 (Галицька; cover 2hv; open Mon.-Thurs. 11am-11pm, Fri.-Sun. 11am-1 or 2am). Another oh-so-mellow crowd hangs out at **Klub-Kafé za Kulisami** (Клуб-Кафе 'за Кулісами'), vul. Tchaikovskoho, 7 (Чайковського). There's decent background music and liquor, but without coffee and a cigarette you'll feel out of place (open daily noon-midnight).

UKRAINE

Practical Information, Accommodations, and Food The **travel bureau** in the Hotel George is the best place to schedule flights and buy train tickets (open daily 9am-noon and 2-6pm). The **train station,** at the end of Vokzalna vul. (Вокзальна вул.), serves Kiev (11-16hr., 17-25hv), Moscow (29hr., 67hv), and Warsaw (13hr., 48hv). Buy **bus** tickets to Poland (Kraków 7-9hr., 20hv) at the station on the edge of town at vul. Stryska (вул. Стрийська). The **Hotel George** (Готель Жорж), pl. Mitskievycha 1 (Міцкевича; tel. (0322) 72 59 52), is a restored turn-of-the-century luxury hotel; take tram 1 from the train station to "Дорошенка." (Singles US$17, with bath US$56; doubles US$23, with bath US$59. Pay in US$ only. Breakfast included.) **Hotel Karpaty** (Карпати), vul. Kleparivska, 3 (Клепарівська; tel. (0322) 33 34 27), has clean rooms; take tram 4 from vul. 700-richcha Lvova (700-річчя Львова; singles 48hv, doubles 60hv; bring toilet paper).

Lviv is full of quick eateries serving Ukrainian fast food (beef and potatoes, borscht, etc.), especially around pl. Rynok. The most convenient **market** is behind the flower stands across from St. Andrew's Church. The sparkling new **Acropolis** (Акрополіс), Sh. Rystaveli, 2 (Ш. Руставелі), off vul. Zelena (Зелена), is a favorite among vegetarians and carnivores alike (entrees 2.50-6hv; open daily 10am-10pm). Lviv's coolest citizens sip coffee in a 16th-century Italian courtyard at **Italysky Dvorik** (Італійський Дворик), pl. Rynok, 6 (open daily 10am-7:30pm).

Yalta Ялта

The Most Popular Resort in Crimea has much to offer, but after the sun and Black Sea, everything else is garnish. Strolling along the promenade is a favorite pastime after a hard day of sun-bathing. Get off the trolleybus at **Sovetskaya pl.** (Советская) and walk 100m down **Moskovskaya ul.** (Московская) to reach the sea. Many **hiking trails** begin in Yalta; consult the *Polyana Skazok* (Поляна Сказок) campground for advice on reaching the **Uchan-Su waterfall** and other natural wonders. In the luxuriant **Primorsky Park Gagarina** at the southwest end of nab. Lenina (Ленина), you can see the **exotic fish aquarium** (open daily 10am-8pm; 2hv).

Playwright **Anton Chekhov** called Yalta home for the last five years of his life, and his house and garden at ul. Kirova, 112 (Кирова) are now a museum. Bus 8 takes you there every 40 minutes from the *Kinoteatr Spartak* (Кинотеатр Спартак) stop on Pushkinskaya ul. (Пушкинская; open Tues.-Sun. 10am-5pm; 2hv). Shuttle 5 from the *Kinoteatr Spartak* in Yalta stops every 40-50 minutes in the town of **Livadia** (Лівадія) across from the **Veliky Palats** (Великий Палац; Great Palace), Nicholas II's ornate summer palace. In 1945, Churchill, Roosevelt, and Stalin met here during the "Yalta" Conference to finalize post-war spheres of influence (palace-museum open Thurs.-Tues. 10am-5pm; 5hv). The most extravagant *dacha* in Greater Yalta—**Palats Vorontsova** (open Tues.-Sun. 9am-5pm; 4hv)—resides in the nearby city of **Alupka** (Алупка), where you can also take a magnificent **cable car** (Fri.-Wed. 10am-4pm; 8hv). Water shuttles leave hourly for Alupka from Yalta (1hr., 3hv).

Practical Information, Accommodations, and Food To get to Yalta, take a **train** to Simferopol from Kiev (16hr., 22hv), Odessa (14hr., 13hv), or Moscow (26hr., 45hv), and then get on one of the frequent **trolleybuses** to Yalta (4.20hv). Tickets for buses to nearby points can be purchased on board or at the **bus station,** Moskovskaya ul., 57; across the street is the **trolley station.** In the city, trolley 1 is most useful (.20hv on board). The prices at Yalta's hotels have recently increased dramatically. The best deal is to book ahead or get a room from one of the *babushki* (old women) at the bus station. The prices at **Gostinitsa Krym** (Гостиница Крым), Moskovskaya ul., 1/2 (tel. (0654) 32 60 01), with its small, clean rooms and hall shower and bath, can't be beaten for a downtown hotel (singles 19hv, doubles 28hv; 5hv registration fee). **Massandra** (Массандра), ul. Drazhinskovo, 48 (Дражинского; tel. (0654) 35 25 91), is at the edge of the old quarter (doubles with sink 27hv; with shower, telephone, and fridge 54hv). For a beautiful campground with showers and kitchen, trek to **Motel-Camping Polyana Skazok** (Поляна Сказок), ul. Kirova, 167 (Кирова; tel. (0654) 39 52 19). Take bus 26, 27, or 11 from the station's upper platform to "Polyana Skazok" and walk 20 minutes uphill (tents 5hv per person; bungalows for two 18hv; motel doubles 65hv). For traditional Russian food, try **Café Siren** (Кафе Сирень), ul. Roosevelta, 6 (Рузевельта), with its freshly made Russian borscht, ***kasha, kakdet,*** and ***kompot*** (full meal 3-4hv; open daily 8am-8pm), or the **Café Krym** (Крым), Moskovskaya ul., 1/2 (full meal 3hv; open daily 7am-8pm).

Odessa (Odesa) Одесса

Odessa (Ukrainian: Odesa) owes its physical existence to Russians under French influence, but its spiritual debt is to Jews, Turks, and the Black Sea. The pedestrian **Deribasovskaya ul.** (Дерибасовская ул.), the port city's commercial center, is home to performers, artists, and a thriving café culture. Turn left on Rishelevskaya (Ришельевская) to find the **Opera and Ballet Theater** (Театр оперы и балета), an imposing edifice that towers over the surrounding gardens. Tickets for nightly shows run 1-5hv at the box office next door (open daily 8am-8pm). At ul. Lanzheronovskaya, 4 (Ланжероновская; old Lastochkina), the **Arkheologichesky muzey** (Археологический музей) houses artifacts found in the Black Sea region (open Tues.-Sun. 11am-6:30pm; 2hv). Take a right here onto shady **ul. Primorskaya** (ул. Приморская), the most popular spot for strolling and people-watching. Down Primorskaya, a statue of the **Duc de Richelieu,** the city founder, gazes toward the **Potemkinskaya lestnitsa** (Потемкинская лестница; Potemkin Stairs). Director Sergei Eisenstein used these stairs in his epic 1925 film *Battleship Potemkin* and the name has stuck. Facing the sea, turn left to reach a **monument** commemorating the actual mutiny of the *Potemkin.* At Primorskaya's end, the **Palace of Vorontsov** offers a superb sunset view. The rock used to build Odessa was mined under the city, forming the world's longest series of **catacombs.** During the Nazi occupation, the **resistance** was based here, and the city has set up an excellent **museum** re-creating their camp. The tourist office can arrange for a car and an English-speaking guide (US$12 per person).

Most of Odessa's sandy shore is accessible by public transportation. Tram 5 stops at **Lanzheron** (Ланжерон), the beach closest to central Odessa, and at **Arkadiya** (Аркадия), the most popular for its wide stretches of sand.

Practical Information, Accommodations, and Food You can leave Odessa by **train** for Kiev (12hr., 17hv), Lviv (15hr., 15hv), Moscow (26hr., 45hv), and Rīga (47hr., 60hv). The station lies on pl. Privokzalnaya (Привокзальная), at the south end of ul. Pushkinskaya (Пушкинская). Tram 2, 3, or 12 takes you along ul. Preobrazhenskaya (Преображенская; old Советской Армии) to the west end of ul. Deribasovskaya; from there, take a right onto ul. Pushkinskaya. The **bus** station, ul. Dzerzhinskovo 58 (Дзержинского), along the tram 5 and 15 lines, also serves Kiev (12hr., 17hv). The **Intourist office,** ul. Pushkinskaya, 17 (tel. (0482) 25 24 58), in Hotel Krasnaya's lobby, sells train, plane, and bus tickets. Ride trolley 1 or 4 from the train station (open daily 9am-5pm). Register at the **Office of Visas and International Registration (ОВИР),** Krasny Pereulok, 5 (Красный Переулок; tel. (0482) 25 89 74; US$10), and keep the registration card to avoid a heavy "fine" at the border.

Accommodations are few and far between in Odessa. Private **apartments** are by far the cheapest option (US$3 per person and up), but they tend to be far from the center. Take tram 3 or 12 from the train station to reach several hotels in the downtown area. Grand old **Spartak** (Спартак), ul. Deribasovskaya, 25 (tel. (0482) 26 89 24), rents large, sparsely furnished rooms (singles 40-42hv, doubles 42-80hv). Or, camp at **Camping Delphin** (Кемпинг "Дельфин"), dor. Kotovskovo, 307 (дор. Котовського; tel. (0482) 55 50 52). From the train station, take trolley 4 or 10 to the terminus (a small loop in the road) and transfer to tram "любой" (#7); get off 20min. later at "Лузанівка" (*Luzanivka*) and continue 500m. A cheap restaurant, sauna, bar, and beach make up for the distance (bungalows 40hv; cottages 46hv; tents 14hv; all prices per person).

Odessa is blessed with a few good restaurants, an amazing market (Привоз; *privoz*) on ul. Privoznaya (Привозьная), and hip cafés. Good options line ul. Preobrazhenskaya south of ul. Deribasovskaya. Point to what you want at the friendly Ukrainian **Kartoplyanki** (Картоплянки), ul. Ekaterininskaya, 3 (Екатерининская; entrees US$1-2; open daily 9am-9pm). The hyper-cool sip foreign liquor at **Café na Grecheskoy** (Кафе на Греческой), ul. Grecheskaya, 11 (Греческая). Regular folk just enjoy the juicy cutlets. The party town of the former USSR never sleeps—ul. Deribasovskaya hops all night with music ranging from Euro-techno to Slavic folk.

Yugoslavia (Југославиа)

US$1	**= 4.85DIN (Yugoslavian dinar)**	**1DIN =**	**US$0.21**
CDN$1	**= 3.51DIN**	**1DIN =**	**CDN$0.29**
UK£1	**= 7.72DIN**	**1DIN =**	**UK£0.13**
IR£1	**= 7.11DIN**	**1DIN =**	**IR£0.14**
AUS$1	**= 3.53DIN**	**1DIN =**	**AUS$0.28**
NZ$1	**= 3.08DIN**	**1DIN =**	**NZ$0.33**
SAR1	**= 1.03DIN**	**1DIN =**	**SAR0.97**

Country Code: 381 **International Dialing Prefix: 99**

Yugoslavia has been born again, three times: in 1929, 1946, and most recently in 1992, after four of six constituent republics broke off as independent states. Serbia and Montenegro are the only two remaining countries in this Serb-dominated republic, along with the semi-autonomous provinces Vojvodina and Kosovo. The towns that hide in Yugoslavia's hills are now accustomed to hardship, and Belgrade has gone gray trying to recover from years of an international economic embargo. When Serbian President Slobodon Milosević, dictator of Serbia for 10 years, annulled local elections held in November 1996, months of protests followed. In July 1997, up against his two-term constitutional limit as the President of Serbia, Milosević ran for the President of Yugoslavia, with the intention of transferring power to this ceremonial post. Montenegro was disgruntled by Milosević's move and has made noises of secession. As Yugoslavia struggles to retain its political legitimacy, it is clear that Serbia is the power holding the federation together.

For more information on Yugoslavia, see *Let's Go: Eastern Europe 1998*.

ESSENTIALS

Visas (US$20 for Americans, US$22 for other citizens) are required of nationals from Australia, Canada, Ireland, New Zealand, South Africa, the U.K., and the U.S. Visa processing usually takes seven working days. Citizens of Ireland and Great Britain require letters of invitation to support their visa. Do not expect to receive a visa on the border. Entrants are required to declare the amount of cash they are bringing into the country and take no more out of the country than the amount on the entry receipt.

The border between Serbia and Croatia is officially closed (as of summer 1997), but Yugoslavia is accessible through Hungary, Romania, Bulgaria, Greece, Macedonia, and (allegedly) Albania. Belgrade is the main entry point, and is accessible by plane, train, bus, and car. **Yugoslavia Airlines** (YAT) flies into Belgrade, as well as European carriers including Lufthansa, British Airways, SwissAir, Air France, and LOT airlines. **Trains** are designated *brzi* (fast) or *putnički* (slow); reservations are generally required for couchettes and international trains, which come from Budapest, Thessaloniki, Skopje, Sofia, and Istanbul. **Buses** are more far reaching and less expensive.

With the exception of the tourist center in Belgrade, most **tourist offices** are geared toward organizing tours for locals going abroad and offer little info to international travelers. Most brochures are long out of date. State-run **hotels** dominate the accommodations scene in Serbia and Montenegro; you will be required to leave your passport at the desk when you register, but you will regain it when you leave. Hotels are virtually empty yet inexplicably expensive, and **private rooms** are few and far between. **Camping** is an option along the Danube and the Adriatic coast.

Yugoslav dinars come in denominations of 1, 5, 10, and 20; they are subdivided into the para (100 para = 1 dinar). While all transactions are legally supposed to take place in local currency, many establishments take Deutschmarks. Banks, hotels, and exchange booths (especially in Belgrade) offer exchange services; remember to get rid of excess dinars before you leave. Bring enough cash to cover your trip; restocking is difficult and can only be done in Belgrade. You can cash **AmEx** checks at several banks in Belgrade, but remuneration is in dollars, and sometimes banks run out of dollars. **Credit cards** are merely decorations for your wallet.

Poste Restante services are available in Belgrade only. **Post offices** are identified by the yellow PTT (ПТТ) signs. Telephones are coin- or card- operated; telephone coins, available at the post offices, are cheaper and more convenient. The only place to make an **international call** is at the main post office in Belgrade. You cannot make **collect calls** from Yugoslavia; dial 0801 to make an **AT&T** credit card call. Emergency numbers are 91 for **fire** and 94 for **police.**

Belgrade Београд

Ruled by the Byzantines, the Bulgarians, and then the Austro-Hungarians, Belgrade asserted itself briefly in the 15th century as the capital of Serbia before falling to the Turks. Ottoman control lasted until 1867, yet by the turn of the 19th century, Belgrade had a modern European look. Today a busy metropolis struggling to overcome a worsening economic situation and large population of war refugees, Belgrade welcomes foreigners warmly. Serbia's tumultuous history is documented in the **Narodni Muzej** (National Museum), Trg Republike. (Take bus 31 or 75. Open Tues.-Wed. and Fri-Sat. 10am-5pm, Thurs. noon-8pm, Sun. 10am-2pm.) Across the way is the **Narodno Pozorište** (National Theater), Trg Republike 2, which was decorated by Viennese artists and features nightly entertainment (closed July-Aug.; get tickets at the Bilet Servis on Trg Republike 5). Past the fountains across the square begins **Knez Mihaila,** a commercial street lined with shops, restaurants, and galleries. Out of the square, down Sima Markovica at #8, lies **Knoak Knjeginje Ljubice** (Night-quarters of Princess Ljubice), with 19th-century Balkan decorations and temporary exhibits of Yugoslavian art (open Tues.-Fri. 10am-5pm, Sat.-Sun. 9am-4pm; 5dn). Nearby, at 7.

Jula 5, the **Muzej Srpske Pravoslavne Crkve** (Museum of Serbian Orthodox Church), is a small place on the 2nd floor of a building which also houses the episcopal administration. On display are 16th-century prayer books and icons, as well as the first printed book in Belgrade (open Tues.-Sat. 8am-2pm, Sun. 11am-3pm; 1dn). The most notable landmark in Belgrade are the well-preserved remains of the huge fortress **Kalemedan,** which consists of the Upper and Lower cities. The first is a popular park, while the second, a gang hangout, should be avoided at night.

Other worthwhile places to visit lie across the Sava River in Novi Beograd and Zamun. The **Muzej Savremene Umetnosti** (Museum of Contemporary Art), Ušće Save bb, is a must (buses 15 or 84; open Wed.-Mon. 10am-6pm; free). The old town of **Zemun,** northwest along the Danube, was built in the Austro-Hungarian style. The 18th-century Orthodox **Sveti Nikola** sits at the base of Sindelićeva and harbors exquisite religious artwork (open daily 9am-1pm and 5-7pm).

The TIC **tourist office** (tel. (011) 63 56 22), in the pedestrian underground passage at the north end of Terazije, is an excellent source of information and books accommodations (open Mon.-Fri. 9am-8pm, Sat. 9am-4pm). The **Australian** embassy is at Čika Ljubina (tel. (011) 62 46 55); **Canadian,** Kneza Miloša 75 (tel. (011) 64 46 66); **U.K.,** Generala Ždanova 46 (tel. (011) 64 50 55); **U.S.,** Kneza Miloša 50 (tel. (011) 64 56 55). **New Zealanders** should contact their embassy in Bonn (Bundeskanzlerpl. 2-10; tel. (0228) 22 80 70). The **Aerodrum Beograd** airport (tel. (011) 60 15 55, tourist info ext. 2980, general info ext. 2580) is 25km west of Belgrade. **Trains** run from the Glavna železnička stanica (tel. (011) 63 62 99) to Sofia (3 per day, 10hr., 130dn) and elsewhere. **Buses** departing from the "Beograd" bus station (tel. (011) 63 62 99) are faster, cheaper, and offer more destinations. Exchange money at **Beobanka,** Kneza Mihailova 22 (tel. (011) 62 30 32; open Mon.-Fri. 8am-7pm, Sat. 9am-3pm), or look for signs with the word *"device"* (currency). The tourist office can help you find rooms, or try **Taš,** Beogradska 71 (tel. (011) 324 35 07), 2km from the bus station by tram 2 or 7 (doubles only; 148dn per bed). **Beograd,** Balkanska 52 (tel. (011) 64 51 78 or 64 53 61; fax 64 37 46), is nicer and pricier (singles 160-180dn). **Camp Košutujak,** Kneza Višeslava 17 (tel. (011) 54 21 66; fax 55 95 38), is accessible by buses 23 and 53 from the bus station (tents DM10 per person). The gastronomical center is the area called **Skadarlija,** where classy locals dine. Common folk can get the cheaper version at the bottom end of the street. **Pivnica Aleksandar,** Cetinjska 15, serves a mixed crowd under huge straw umbrellas (chicken wings 33dn per kg). **Grmeč,** Makedonska 32, features excellent Yugoslavian cuisine.

Peć (Peja)

Located in the semi-autonomous province of Kosovo, Peć (PEHCH), or Peja (PEY-uh), as the Albanian locals will correct you, fills its Oriental-style bazaar with citizens in traditional dress, while the mountains of Rugovska Klisura prop up the sky in the background. The oldest mosque is **Quarši Djamija,** in the old-town quarter on Zhemajl Školozi, near the intersection of Nemanjina and Krala Petrar (open after the 1pm and 7pm prayers). About 2km along the river stands the **Patrijaršija Monastery,** the center of Serbian spiritual and cultural life in medieval times. To get there, take Boro Vukmirovig from behind Radio Metohija (downtown), going west out of town. One of Serbia's most beautiful monasteries is near Peć: **Visoki Dečani Monastery,** intended as a mausoleum for the nation's kings. Below the 1000 stunning renditions of Biblical scenes, Dečani is still thriving; the 22 monks inhabiting it continue the traditional monastic activities of translating and publishing books and Web pages (http://www.prishtina.com/Religion/Decani/decani.htm).

To reach Peć, **buses** run through Priština, a transportation hub for the rest of Yugoslavia. **Kosmet Tours** at Nemanjina 102 and **Punik Tourist,** farther down toward the town center, are primarily travel agencies for locals but may be able to answer questions about the town. **Motel Jusaj,** Rr. Buriqa 48 (tel./fax (39) 211 49), is your best bet for accommodations (DM15). Across the street sits the new, private **Hotel Dypon** (tel. (39) 315 93; DM40-50). **Restoran Stari Most** stradles the Bistrica River and offers standard local fare (open Mon.-Sat. 7am-10pm).

Rail Planner

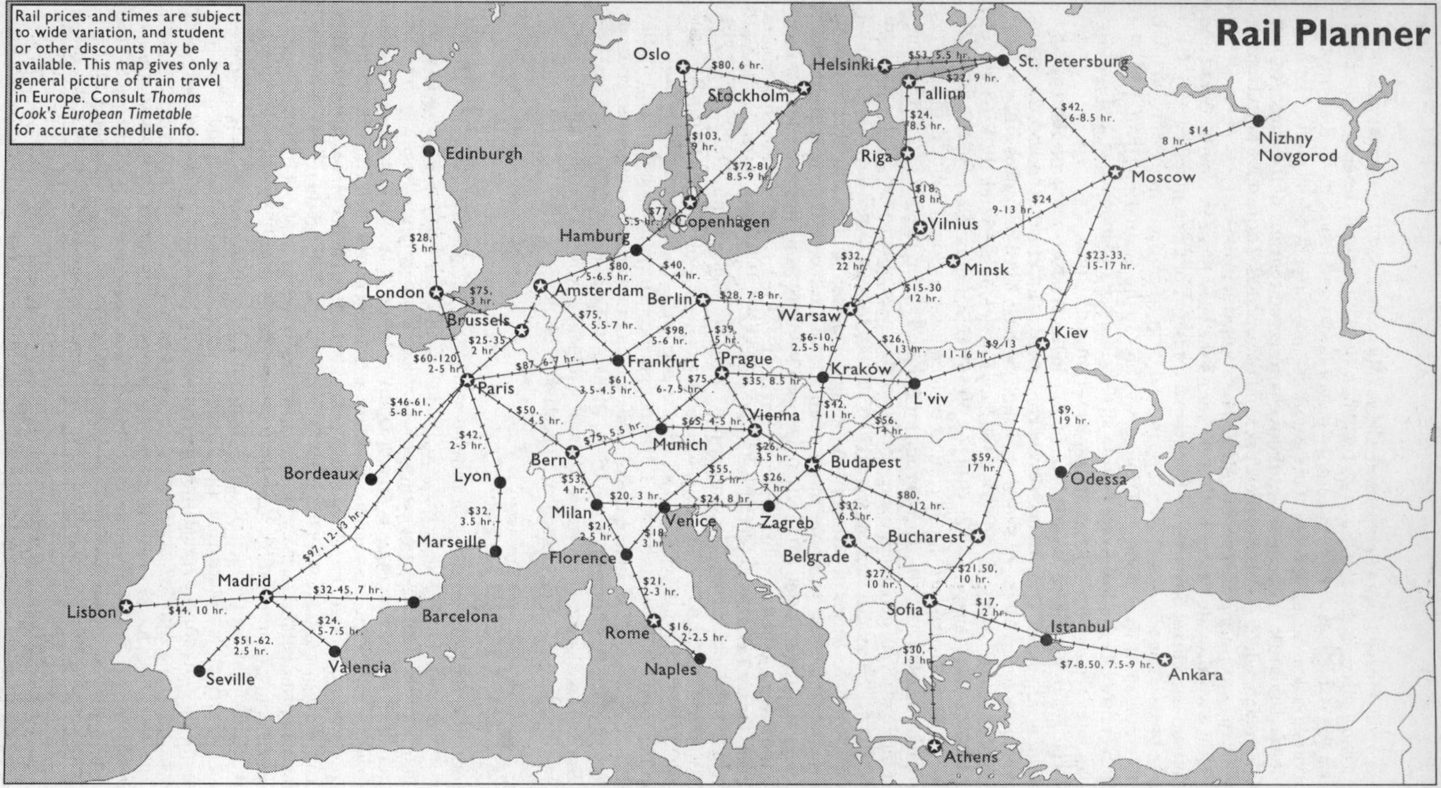

Rail prices and times are subject to wide variation, and student or other discounts may be available. This map gives only a general picture of train travel in Europe. Consult *Thomas Cook's European Timetable* for accurate schedule info.

Index

Key

The following abbreviations denote the country chapter in which the reference is contained.

AND: Andorra
AUS: Austria
BLR: Belarus
BEL: Belgium
BRI: Britain
BOS: Bosnia
BUL: Bulgaria
CRO: Croatia
CYP: Cyprus
CZE: Czech Rep.
DEN: Denmark
ESS: Essentials
EST: Estonia
FIN: Finland
FRA: France
GER: Germany
HUN: Hungary
ICE: Iceland
IRE: Ireland
ITA: Italy
LAT: Latvia
LIE: Liechtenstein
LIT: Lithuania
LUX: Luxembourg
MAL: Malta
NETH: Netherlands
NOR: Norway
POL: Poland
POR: Portugal
ROM: Romania
RUS: Russia
SLK: Slovakia
SLN: Slovenia
SPA: Spain
SWE: Sweden
SWI: Switzerland
TUR: Turkey
UKR: Ukraine
YUG: Yugoslavia

Symbols

A

B

C

INDEX

INDEX

INDEX

INDEX

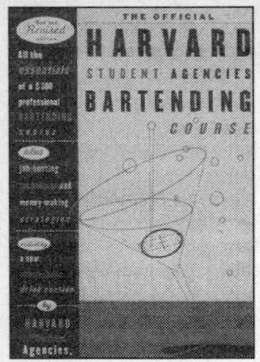

★Let's Go 1998 Reader Questionnaire★

Please fill this out and return it to **Let's Go, St. Martin's Press,** 175 Fifth Ave., New York, NY 10010-7848. All respondents will receive a free subscription to ***The Yellowjacket,* the Let's Go Newsletter**.

Name: ______________________________

Address: ______________________________

City: ______________ **State:** ______ **Zip/Postal Code:** ________

Email: ______________ **Which book(s) did you use?** __________

How old are you? under 19 19-24 25-34 35-44 45-54 55 or over

Are you (circle one) in high school in college in graduate school employed retired between jobs

Have you used Let's Go before? yes no **Would you use it again?** yes no

How did you first hear about Let's Go? friend store clerk television bookstore display advertisement/promotion review other

Why did you choose Let's Go (circle up to two)? reputation budget focus price writing style annual updating other: __________

Which other guides have you used, if any? Frommer's $-a-day Fodor's Rough Guides Lonely Planet Berkeley Rick Steves other: ______________

Is Let's Go the best guidebook? yes no

If not, which do you prefer? ______________

Please rank each of the following parts of Let's Go 1 to 5 (1=needs improvement, 5=perfect). packaging/cover practical information accommodations food cultural introduction sights practical introduction ("Essentials") directions entertainment gay/lesbian information maps other: ______________

How would you like to see the books improved? (continue on separate page, if necessary) ______________________________

____

How long was your trip? one week two weeks three weeks one month two months or more

Which countries did you visit? ______________________________

What was your average daily budget, not including flights? __________

Have you traveled extensively before? yes no

Do you buy a separate map when you visit a foreign city? yes no

Have you seen the Let's Go Map Guides? yes no

Have you used a Let's Go Map Guide? yes no

If you have, would you recommend them to others? yes no

Did you use the Internet to plan your trip? yes no

Would you use a Let's Go: recreational (e.g. skiing) guide gay/lesbian guide adventure/trekking guide phrasebook general travel information guide

Which of the following destinations do you hope to visit in the next three to five years (circle one)? South Africa China South America Russia Caribbean Scandinavia other: ______________

Where did you buy your guidebook? Internet chain bookstore independent bookstore college bookstore travel store other: ______________

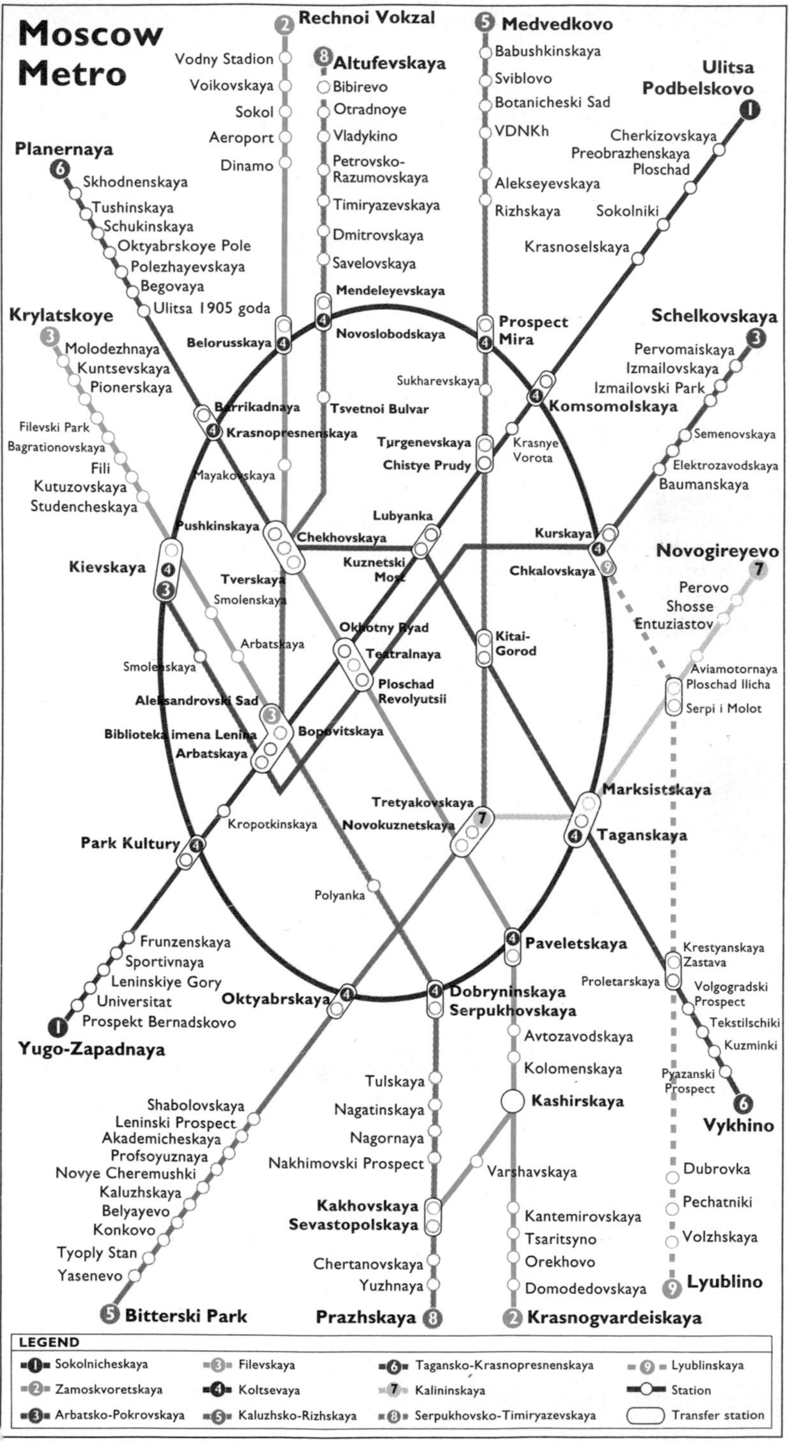
Moscow Metro
2 Rechnoi Vokzal
Vodny Stadion
Voikovskaya
Sokol
Aeroport
Dinamo
8 Altufevskaya
Bibirevo
Otradnoye
Vladykino
Petrovsko-Razumovskaya
Timiryazevskaya
Dmitrovskaya
Savelovskaya
Mendeleyevskaya
Novoslobodskaya
5 Medvedkovo
Babushkinskaya
Sviblovo
Botanicheski Sad
VDNKh
Alekseyevskaya
Rizhskaya
Prospect Mira
Sukharevskaya
Tsvetnoi Bulvar
Turgenevskaya
Chistye Prudy
Ulitsa Podbelskovo
1
Cherkizovskaya
Preobrazhenskaya Ploschad
Sokolniki
Krasnoselskaya
Komsomolskaya
Krasnye Vorota
Schelkovskaya
3
Pervomaiskaya
Izmailovskaya
Izmailovski Park
Semenovskaya
Elektrozavodskaya
Baumanskaya
Kurskaya
Chkalovskaya
Novogireyevo
7
Perovo
Shosse Entuziastov
Aviamotornaya
Ploschad Ilicha
Serpi i Molot
Planernaya
6
Skhodnenskaya
Tushinskaya
Schukinskaya
Oktyabrskoye Pole
Polezhayevskaya
Begovaya
Ulitsa 1905 goda
Belorusskaya
Krylatskoye
Molodezhnaya
Kuntsevskaya
Pionerskaya
Filevski Park
Bagrationovskaya
Fili
Kutuzovskaya
Studencheskaya
Barrikadnaya
Krasnopresnenskaya
Mayakovskaya
Pushkinskaya
Chekhovskaya
Tverskaya
Lubyanka
Kuznetski Most
Kievskaya
Smolenskaya
Arbatskaya
Smolenskaya
Okhotny Ryad
Teatralnaya
Ploschad Revolyutsii
Kitai-Gorod
Aleksandrovski Sad
Biblioteka imena Lenina
Arbatskaya
Borovitskaya
Marksistskaya
Taganskaya
Tretyakovskaya
Novokuznetskaya
Kropotkinskaya
Park Kultury
Polyanka
Paveletskaya
Frunzenskaya
Sportivnaya
Leninskiye Gory
Universitat
Prospekt Bernadskovo
Yugo-Zapadnaya
Oktyabrskaya
Dobryninskaya
Serpukhovskaya
Proletarskaya
Krestyanskaya Zastava
Volgogradski Prospect
Tekstilschiki
Kuzminki
Pyazanski Prospect
Vykhino
Avtozavodskaya
Kolomenskaya
Kashirskaya
Tulskaya
Nagatinskaya
Nagornaya
Nakhimovski Prospect
Shabolovskaya
Leninski Prospect
Akademicheskaya
Profsoyuznaya
Novye Cheremushki
Kaluzhskaya
Belyayevo
Konkovo
Tyoply Stan
Yasenevo
Bitterski Park
Varshavskaya
Kakhovskaya
Sevastopolskaya
Chertanovskaya
Yuzhnaya
Prazhskaya
Kantemirovskaya
Tsaritsyno
Orekhovo
Domodedovskaya
Krasnogvardeiskaya
Dubrovka
Pechatniki
Volzhskaya
Lyublino
LEGEND
1 Sokolnicheskaya
2 Zamoskvoretskaya
3 Arbatsko-Pokrovskaya
3 Filevskaya
4 Koltsevaya
5 Kaluzhsko-Rizhskaya
6 Tagansko-Krasnopresnenskaya
7 Kalininskaya
8 Serpukhovsko-Timiryazevskaya
9 Lyublinskaya
Station
Transfer station

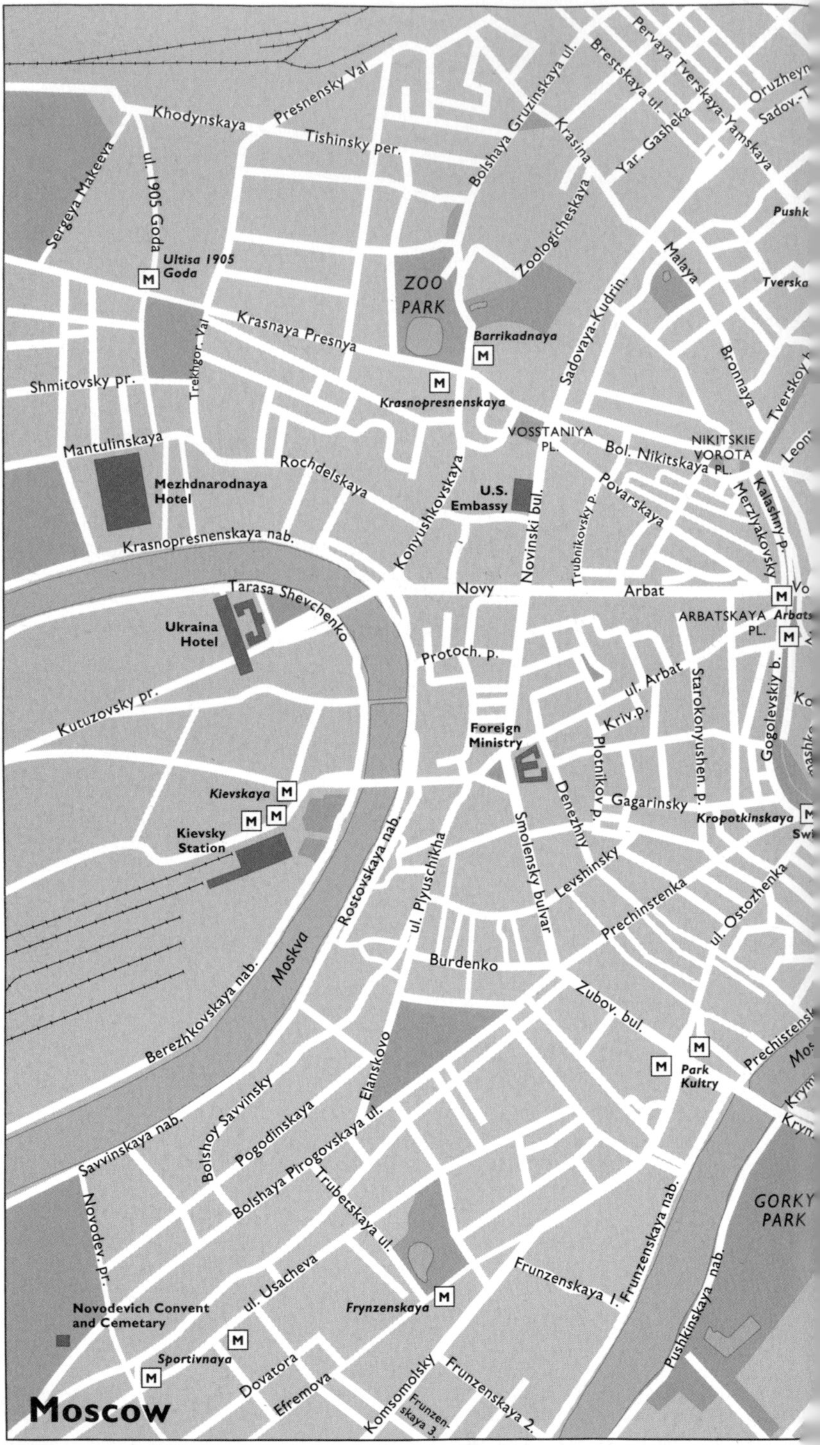
Presnensky Val
Khodynskaya
Tishinsky per.
Sergeya Makeeva
ul. 1905 Goda
Ultisa 1905 Goda
Bolshaya Gruzinskaya ul.
Brestskaya ul.
Pervaya Tverskaya-Yamskaya
Krasina
Yar. Gasheka
Zoologicheskaya
Malaya
ZOO PARK
Krasnaya Presnya
Trekhgor. Val
Barrikadnaya
Krasnopresnenskaya
Sadovaya-Kudrin.
Bronnaya
Shmitovsky pr.
Mantulinskaya
VOSSTANIYA PL.
Bol. Nikitskaya
NIKITSKIE VOROTA PL.
Rochdelskaya
Mezhdnarodnaya Hotel
U.S. Embassy
Konyushkovskaya
Novinski bul.
Trubnikovsky p.
Povarskaya
Merzlyakovsky
Kalashny p.
Krasnopresnenskaya nab.
Tarasa Shevchenko
Novy
Arbat
ARBATSKAYA PL.
Ukraina Hotel
Protoch. p.
ul. Arbat
Starokonyushen. p.
Gogolevskiy b.
Kutuzovsky pr.
Kriv.p.
Foreign Ministry
Plotnikov p.
Kievskaya
Gagarinsky
Kropotkinskaya
Kievsky Station
Denezhny
Smolensky bulvar
Rostovskaya nab.
ul. Plyuschikha
Levshinsky
Prechinstenka
ul. Ostozhenka
Moskva
Burdenko
Berezhkovskaya nab.
Zubov. bul.
Park Kultry
Elanskovo
Bolshoy Savvinsky
Pogodinskaya
Savvinskaya nab.
Bolshaya Pirogovskaya ul.
Trubetskaya ul.
GORKY PARK
Frunzenskaya nab.
Novodev. pr.
ul. Usacheva
Frunzenskaya 1.
Pushkinskaya nab.
Frynzenskaya
Novodevich Convent and Cemetary
Sportivnaya
Dovatora
Efremova
Komsomolsky
Frunzenskaya 2.
Frunzen-skaya 3.
Moscow

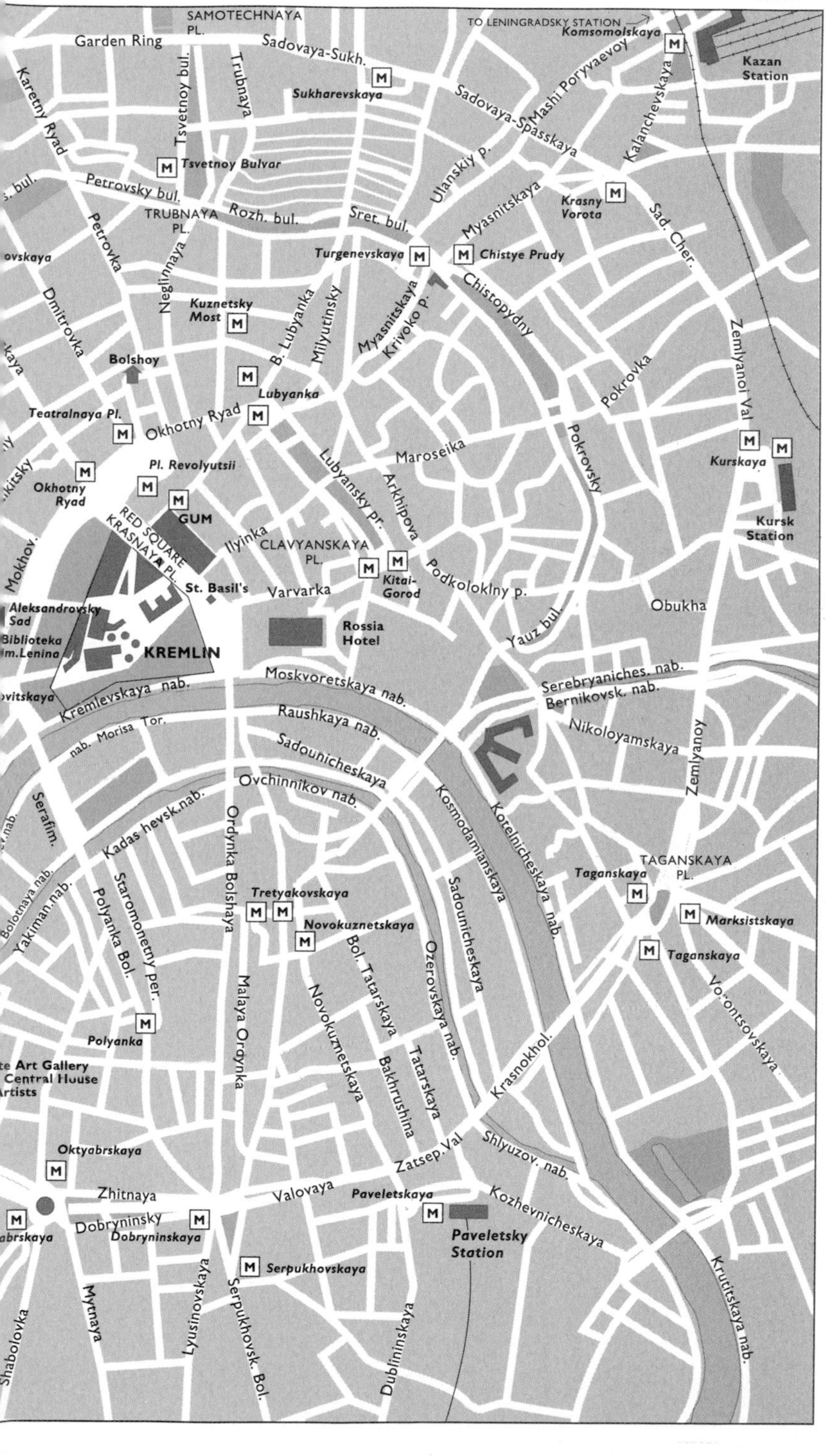
SAMOTECHNAYA PL.
TO LENINGRADSKY STATION
Komsomolskaya
Kazan Station
Garden Ring
Sadovaya-Sukh.
Karetny Ryad
Tsvetnoy bul.
Trubnaya
Sukharevskaya
Sadovaya-Spasskaya
Mashi Poryvaevoy
Kalanchevskaya
Tsvetnoy Bulvar
Petrovsky bul.
TRUBNAYA PL.
Rozh. bul.
Sret. bul.
Ulanskiy p.
Myasnitskaya
Krasny Vorota
Sad. Cher.
Petrovka
Neglinnaya
Turgenevskaya
Chistye Prudy
Chistopydny
Dmitrovka
Kuznetsky Most
B. Lubyanka
Milyutinsky
Myasnitskaya
Krivoko p.
Zemlyanoi Val
Bolshoy
Lubyanka
Pokrovka
Teatralnaya Pl.
Okhotny Ryad
Pokrovsky
Maroseika
Kurskaya
Pl. Revolyutsii
Lubyansky pr.
Arkhipova
Okhotny Ryad
GUM
Kursk Station
RED SQUARE
KRASNAYA PL.
Ilyinka
CLAVYANSKAYA PL.
Mokhov.
Kitai-Gorod
Podkoloklny p.
St. Basil's
Varvarka
Obukha
Aleksandrovsky Sad
Rossia Hotel
Biblioteka im.Lenina
KREMLIN
Yauz bul.
Moskvoretskaya nab.
Serebryaniches. nab.
Bernikovsk. nab.
Kremlevskaya nab.
Raushkaya nab.
Nikoloyamskaya
nab. Morisa Tor.
Sadounicheskaya
Zemlyanoy
Ovchinnikov nab.
Serafim.
Kadas hevsk.nab.
Ordynka Bolshaya
Kosmodamianskaya
Kotelnicheskaya nab.
TAGANSKAYA PL.
Taganskaya
Sadounicheskaya
Tretyakovskaya
Marksistskaya
Bolotnaya nab.
Yakiman.nab.
Polyanka Bol.
Staromonetny per.
Novokuznetskaya
Bol. Tatarskaya
Ozerovskaya nab.
Taganskaya
Novokuznetskaya
Vo-ontsovskaya
Polyanka
Malaya Ordynka
Bakhrushina
Tatarskaya
Krasnokhol.
Central House
Artists
Oktyabrskaya
Zatsep.Val
Shlyuzov. nab.
Zhitnaya
Valovaya
Paveletskaya
Kozhevnicheskaya
Dobryninsky
Dobryninskaya
Paveletsky Station
Serpukhovskaya
Krutitskaya nab.
Shabolovka
Mytnaya
Lysinovskaya
Serpukhovsk. Bol.
Dublininskaya

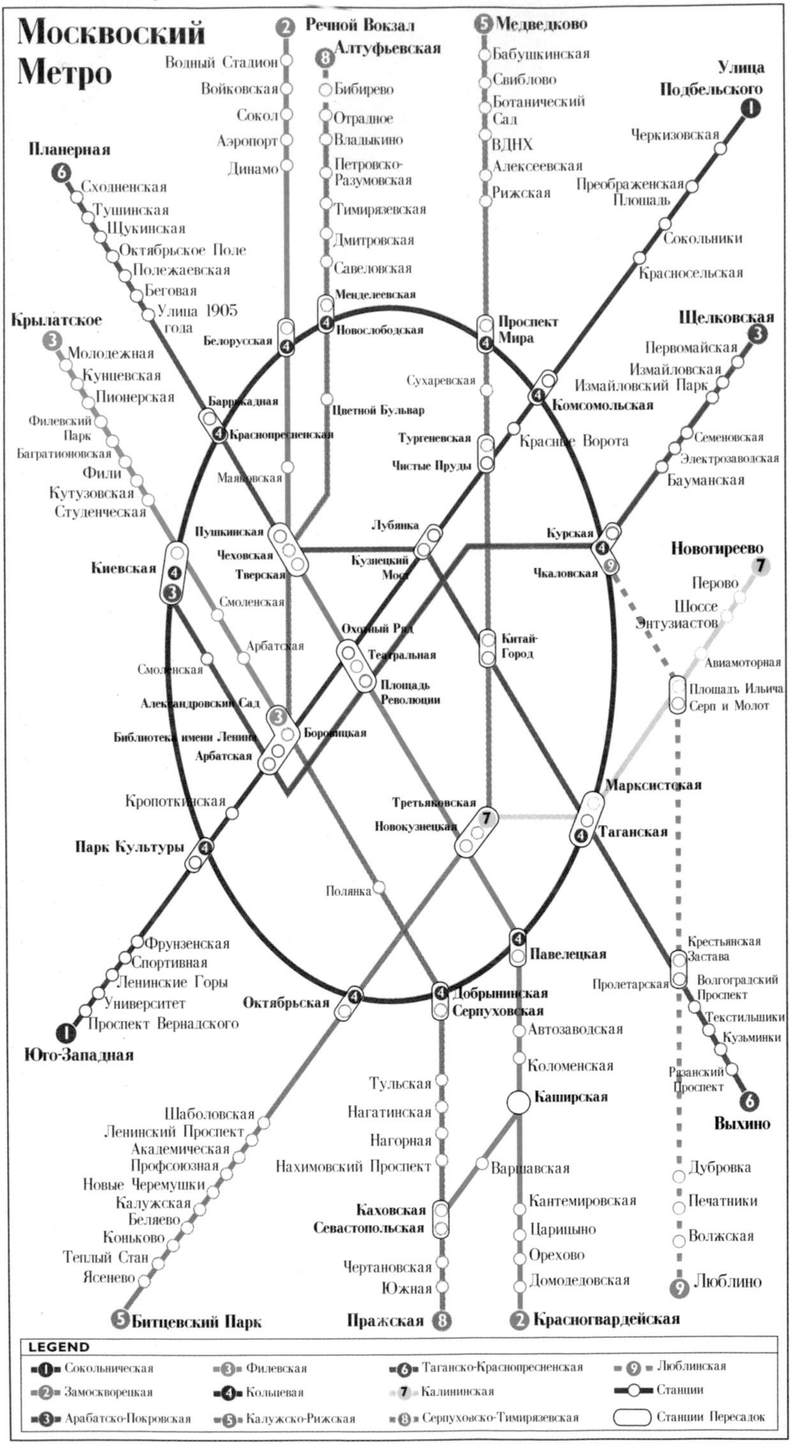
Москвоский Метро
Речной Вокзал
Водный Стадион
Войковская
Сокол
Аэропорт
Динамо
Алтуфьевская
Бибирево
Отрадное
Владыкино
Петровско-Разумовская
Тимирязевская
Дмитровская
Савеловская
Менделеевская
Новослободская
Медведково
Бабушкинская
Свиблово
Ботанический Сад
ВДНХ
Алексеевская
Рижская
Проспект Мира
Сухаревская
Тургеневская
Чистые Пруды
Улица Подбельского
Черкизовская
Преображенская Площадь
Сокольники
Красносельская
Комсомольская
Красные Ворота
Щелковская
Первомайская
Измайловская
Измайловский Парк
Семеновская
Электрозаводская
Бауманская
Курская
Чкаловская
Новогиреево
Перово
Шоссе Энтузиастов
Авиамоторная
Площадь Ильича
Серп и Молот
Планерная
Сходненская
Тушинская
Щукинская
Октябрьское Поле
Полежаевская
Беговая
Улица 1905 года
Белорусская
Баррикадная
Краснопресненская
Цветной Бульвар
Маяковская
Крылатское
Молодежная
Кунцевская
Пионерская
Филевский Парк
Багратионовская
Фили
Кутузовская
Студенческая
Киевская
Пушкинская
Чеховская
Тверская
Лубянка
Кузнецкий Мост
Смоленская
Арбатская
Охотный Ряд
Театральная
Площадь Революции
Китай-Город
Смоленская
Александровский Сад
Библиотека имени Ленина
Боровицкая
Арбатская
Кропоткинская
Парк Культуры
Третьяковская
Новокузнецкая
Марксистская
Таганская
Полянка
Павелецкая
Крестьянская Застава
Пролетарская
Волгоградский Проспект
Текстильщики
Кузьминки
Рязанский Проспект
Выхино
Фрунзенская
Спортивная
Ленинские Горы
Университет
Проспект Вернадского
Юго-Западная
Октябрьская
Добрынинская
Серпуховская
Автозаводская
Коломенская
Каширская
Тульская
Нагатинская
Нагорная
Нахимовский Проспект
Варшавская
Каховская
Севастопольская
Кантемировская
Царицыно
Орехово
Домодедовская
Чертановская
Южная
Пражская
Красногвардейская
Шаболовская
Ленинский Проспект
Академическая
Профсоюзная
Новые Черемушки
Калужская
Беляево
Коньково
Теплый Стан
Ясенево
Битцевский Парк
Дубровка
Печатники
Волжская
Люблино
LEGEND
Сокольническая
Замоскворецкая
Арабатско-Покровская
Филевская
Кольцевая
Калужско-Рижская
Таганско-Краснопресненская
Калининская
Серпуховско-Тимирязевская
Люблинская
Станции
Станции Пересадок

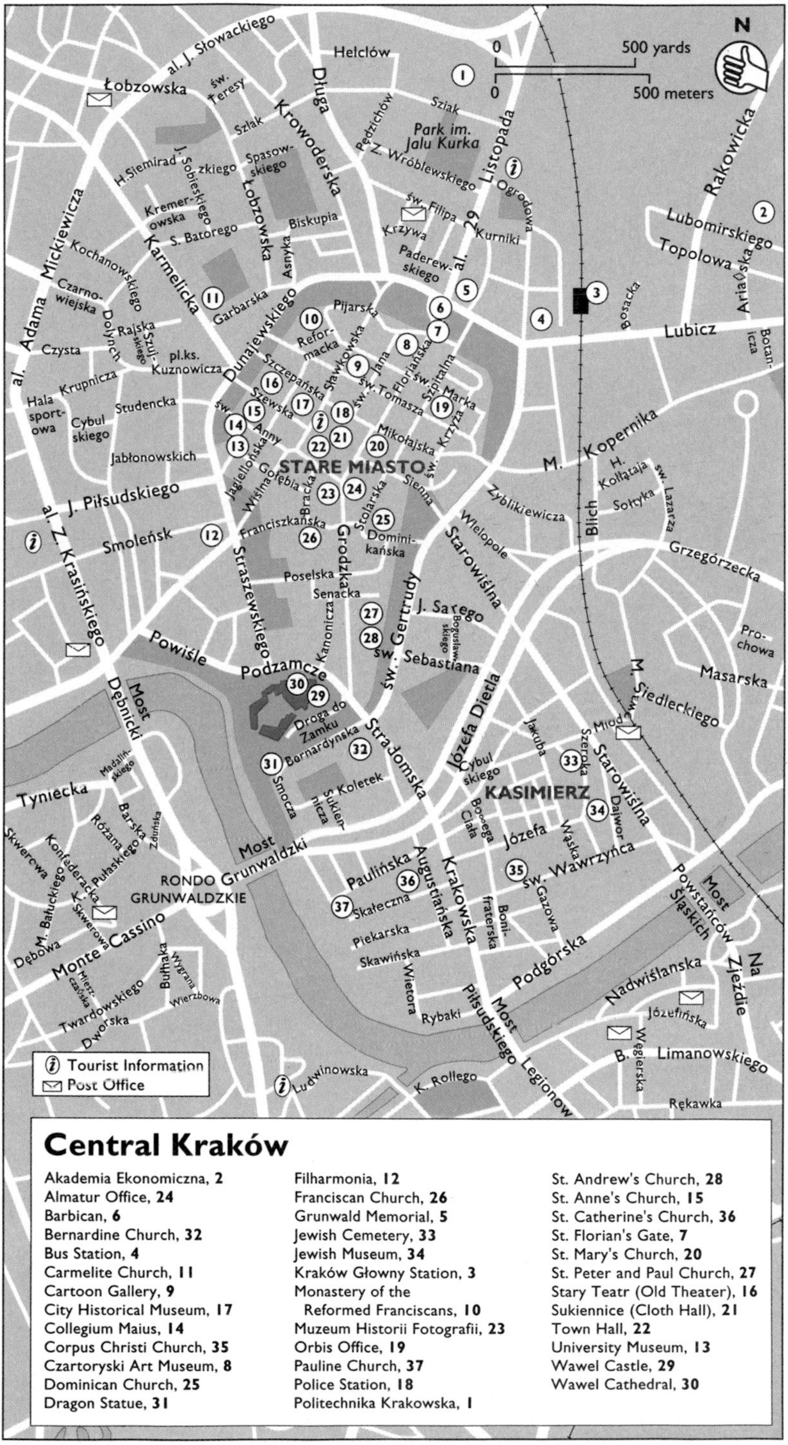

Central Kraków

Akademia Ekonomiczna, **2**
Almatur Office, **24**
Barbican, **6**
Bernardine Church, **32**
Bus Station, **4**
Carmelite Church, **11**
Cartoon Gallery, **9**
City Historical Museum, **17**
Collegium Maius, **14**
Corpus Christi Church, **35**
Czartoryski Art Museum, **8**
Dominican Church, **25**
Dragon Statue, **31**
Filharmonia, **12**
Franciscan Church, **26**
Grunwald Memorial, **5**
Jewish Cemetery, **33**
Jewish Museum, **34**
Kraków Głowny Station, **3**
Monastery of the Reformed Franciscans, **10**
Muzeum Historii Fotografii, **23**
Orbis Office, **19**
Pauline Church, **37**
Police Station, **18**
Politechnika Krakowska, **1**
St. Andrew's Church, **28**
St. Anne's Church, **15**
St. Catherine's Church, **36**
St. Florian's Gate, **7**
St. Mary's Church, **20**
St. Peter and Paul Church, **27**
Stary Teatr (Old Theater), **16**
Sukiennice (Cloth Hall), **21**
Town Hall, **22**
University Museum, **13**
Wawel Castle, **29**
Wawel Cathedral, **30**

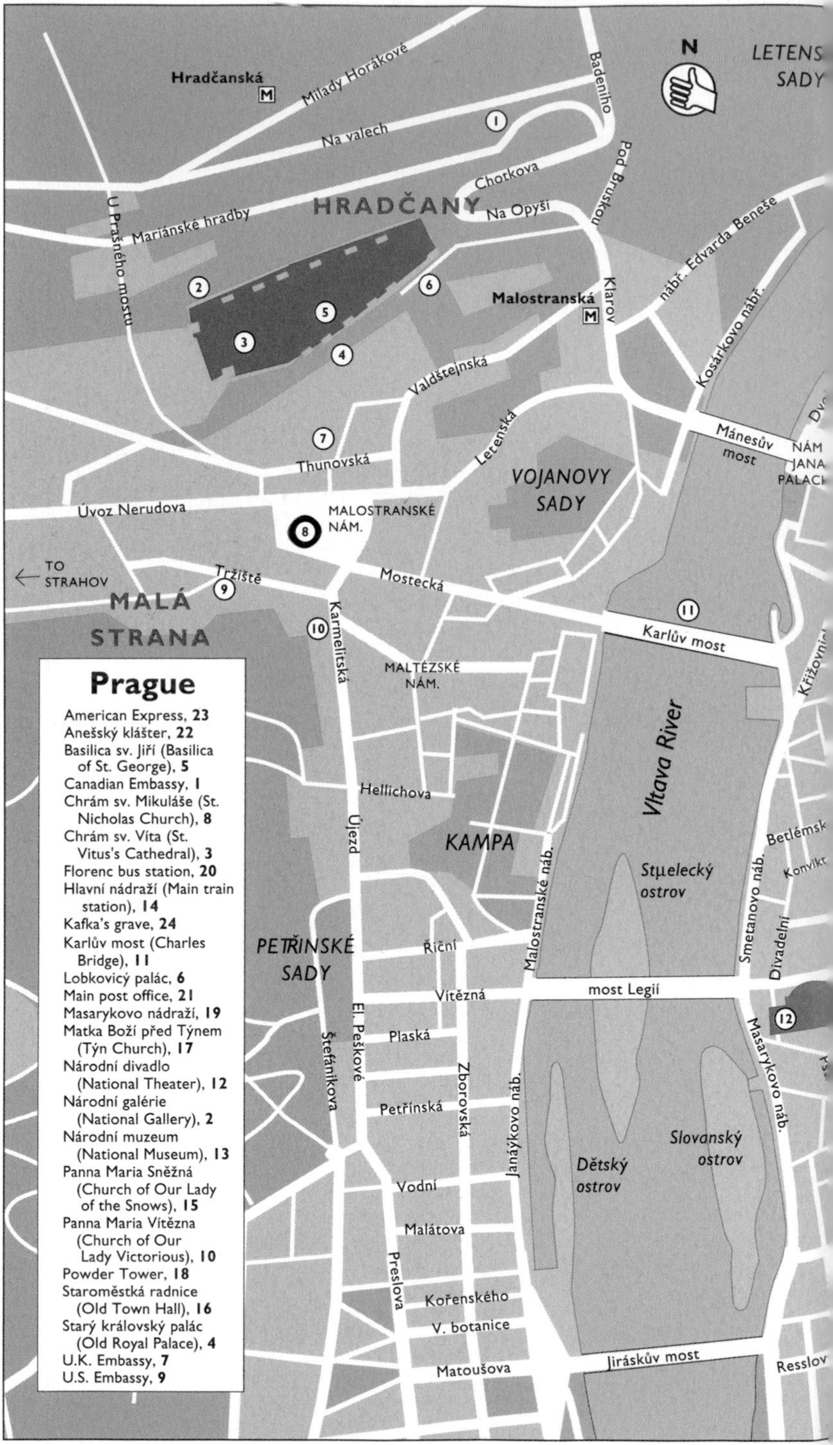
Prague
American Express, 23
Anešský klášter, 22
Basilica sv. Jiří (Basilica of St. George), 5
Canadian Embassy, 1
Chrám sv. Mikuláše (St. Nicholas Church), 8
Chrám sv. Víta (St. Vitus's Cathedral), 3
Florenc bus station, 20
Hlavní nádraží (Main train station), 14
Kafka's grave, 24
Karlův most (Charles Bridge), 11
Lobkovicý palác, 6
Main post office, 21
Masarykovo nádraží, 19
Matka Boží před Týnem (Týn Church), 17
Národní divadlo (National Theater), 12
Národní galérie (National Gallery), 2
Národní muzeum (National Museum), 13
Panna Maria Sněžná (Church of Our Lady of the Snows), 15
Panna Maria Vítězna (Church of Our Lady Victorious), 10
Powder Tower, 18
Staroměstká radnice (Old Town Hall), 16
Starý královský palác (Old Royal Palace), 4
U.K. Embassy, 7
U.S. Embassy, 9
N
Hradčanská
HRADČANY
Malostranská
MALOSTRANSKÉ NÁM.
VOJANOVY SADY
TO STRAHOV
MALÁ STRANA
MALTÉZSKÉ NÁM.
KAMPA
PETŘINSKÉ SADY
Vltava River
Stμelecký ostrov
Dětský ostrov
Slovanský ostrov
Milady Horákové
Na valech
Badeniho
Pod Bruskou
Chotkova
Na Opyši
Mariánské hradby
U Prašného mostu
nábř. Edvarda Beneše
Klarov
Kosárkovo nábř.
Valdštejnská
Letenská
Mánesův most
Thunovská
Úvoz Nerudova
Tržiště
Mostecká
Karmelitská
Karlův most
Hellichova
Újezd
Malostranské nab.
Smetanovo nab.
Divadelni
Betlémsk
Konvikt
Křížovni
Říční
Vítězná
most Legií
Masarykovo náb.
Plaská
El. Peškové
Štefánikova
Zborovská
Janáčkovo náb.
Petřínská
Vodní
Malátova
Preslova
Kořenského
V. botanice
Matoušova
Jiráskův most
Resslov

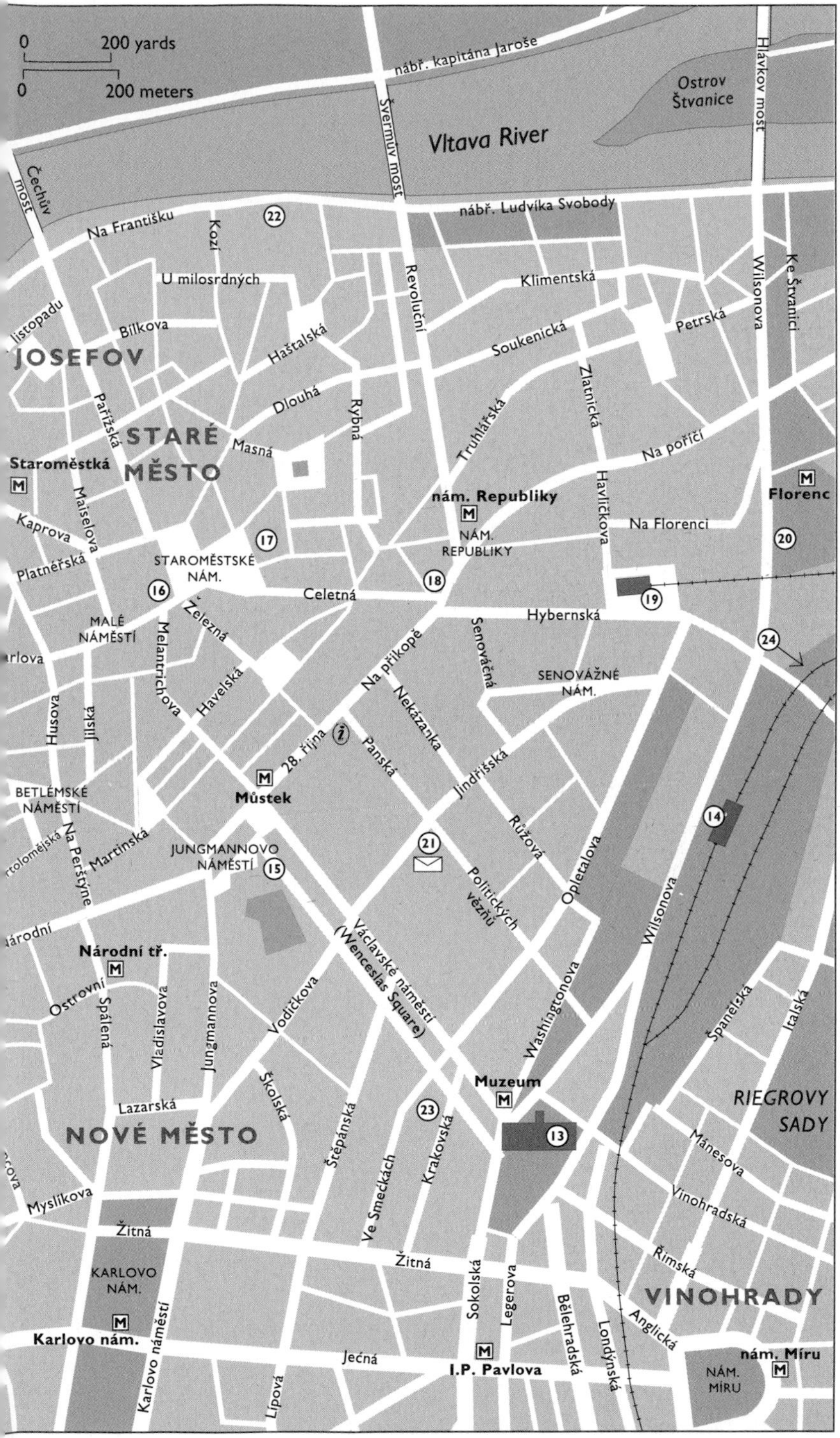

0 200 yards
0 200 meters
nábř. kapitána Jaroše
Ostrov Štvanice
Hlávkov most
Vltava River
Švermův most
Čechův most
nábř. Ludvíka Svobody
Na Františku
Kozí
22
U milosrdných
Revoluční
Klimentská
Wilsonova
Ke Štvanici
listopadu
Bílkova
Haštalská
Soukenická
Petrská
JOSEFOV
Dlouhá
Rybná
Truhlářská
Zlatnická
Pařížská
STARÉ MĚSTO
Masná
Na poříčí
Staroměstská
M
Maiselova
Havlíčkova
nám. Republiky
M
Florenc
M
Kaprova
17
NÁM. REPUBLIKY
Na Florenci
20
Platnéřská
STAROMĚSTSKÉ NÁM.
18
16
Celetná
19
MALÉ NÁMĚSTÍ
Železná
Hybernská
Senovážná
Melantrichova
24
rlova
Havelská
Na příkopě
SENOVÁŽNÉ NÁM.
Husova
Jilská
Nekázanka
28. října
Panská
Jindřišská
M
Můstek
BETLÉMSKÉ NÁMĚSTÍ
14
Růžová
Na Perštýne
Martinská
JUNGMANNOVO NÁMĚSTÍ
15
21
Politických vězňů
Opletalova
Wilsonova
árodní
Václavské náměstí (Wenceslas Square)
Národní tř.
M
Washingtonova
Vodičkova
Ostrovní
Spálená
Vladislavova
Jungmannova
Španělská
Italská
Školská
Muzeum
M
RIEGROVY SADY
Lazarská
23
NOVÉ MĚSTO
13
Štěpánská
Krakovská
Mánesova
Myslíkova
Ve Smečkách
Vinohradská
Žitná
Žitná
Římská
KARLOVO NÁM.
Sokolská
Legerova
Bělehradská
VINOHRADY
M
Karlovo nám.
Karlovo náměstí
Anglická
Londýnská
Ječná
M
I.P. Pavlova
nám. Míru
M
NÁM. MÍRU
Lípová

Central Budapest

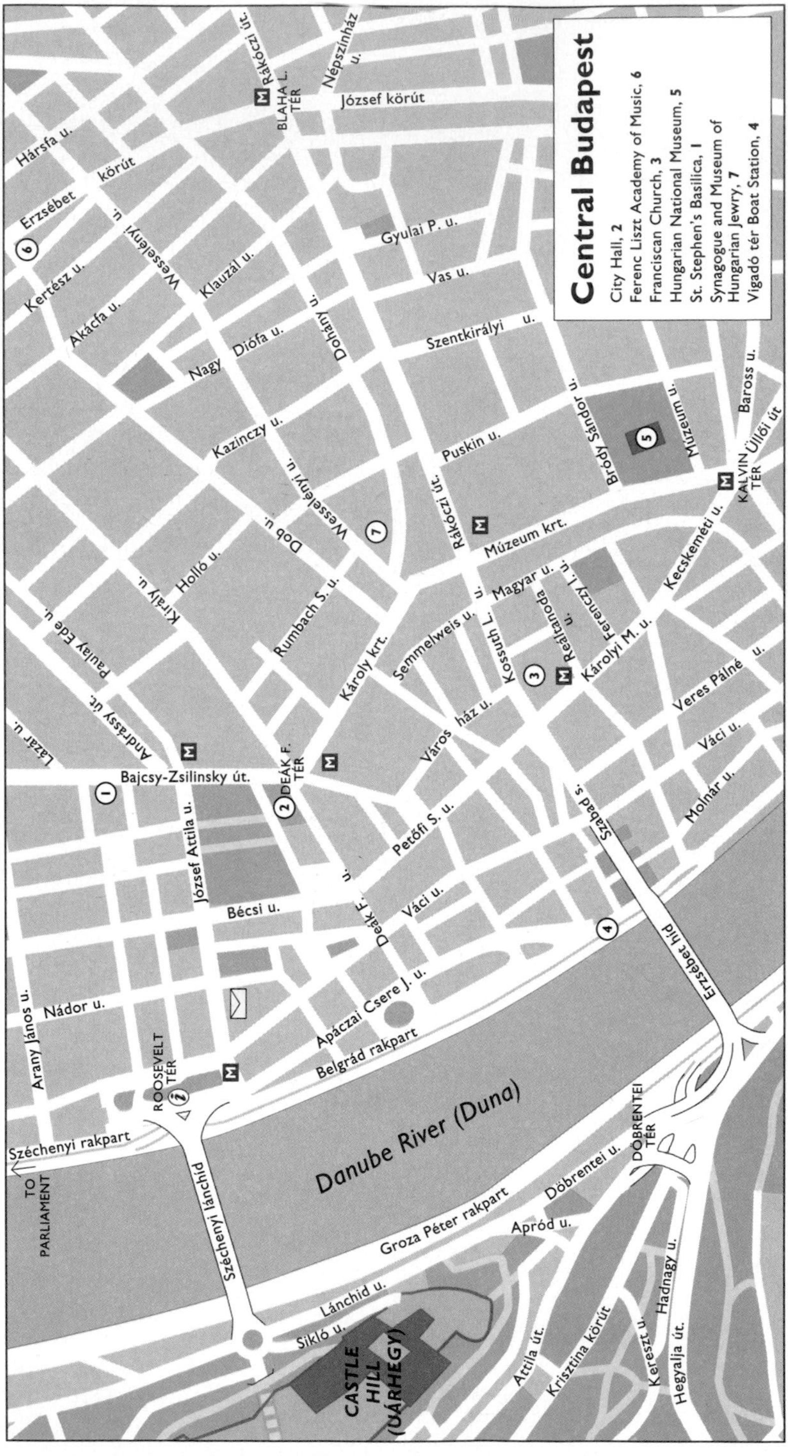

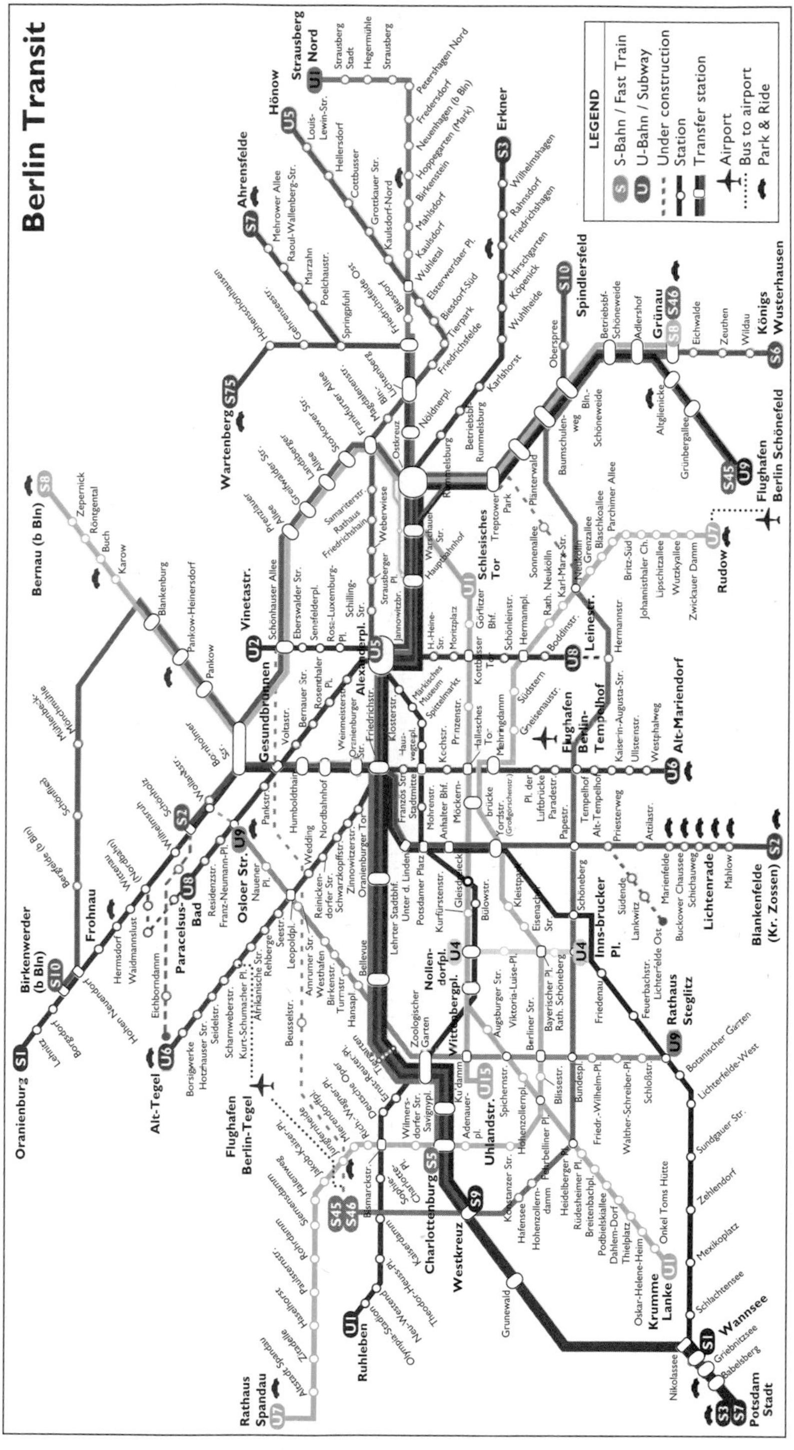
Berlin Transit
LEGEND
S-Bahn / Fast Train
U-Bahn / Subway
Under construction
Station
Transfer station
Airport
Bus to airport
Park & Ride
Oranienburg
Lehnitz
Borgsdorf
Birkenwerder (b Bln)
Hohen Neuendorf
Frohnau
Hermsdorf
Waidmannslust
Wittenau (Nordbahn)
Wilhelmsruh
Schönholz
Wollankstr.
Bornholmer Str.
Gesundbrunnen
Bergfelde (b Bln)
Schönfließ
Mühlenbeck-Mönchmühle
Blankenburg
Pankow-Heinersdorf
Pankow
Bernau (b Bln)
Zepernick
Röntgental
Buch
Karow
Wartenberg
Hohenschönhausen
Gehrenseestr.
Ahrensfelde
Mehrower Allee
Raoul-Wallenberg-Str.
Marzahn
Poelchaustr.
Springpfuhl
Hönow
Louis-Lewin-Str.
Hellersdorf
Cottbusser
Grottkauer Str.
Kaulsdorf-Nord
Strausberg Nord
Strausberg Stadt
Hegermühle
Strausberg
Petershagen Nord
Fredersdorf
Neuenhagen (b Bln)
Hoppegarten (Mark)
Birkenstein
Mahlsdorf
Kaulsdorf
Wuhletal
Elsterwerdaer Pl.
Biesdorf-Süd
Tierpark
Friedrichsfelde
Biesdorf
Friedrichsfelde Ost
Lichtenberg
Magdalenenstr.
Frankfurter Allee
Storkower Str.
Landsberger Allee
Greifswalder Str.
Prenzlauer Allee
Schönhauser Allee
Vinetastr.
Erkner
Wilhelmshagen
Rahnsdorf
Friedrichshagen
Hirschgarten
Köpenick
Wuhlheide
Karlshorst
Nöldnerpl.
Ostkreuz
Betriebsbf Rummelsburg
Rummelsburg
Spindlersfeld
Oberspree
Baumschulenweg
Betriebsbf. Schöneweide
Adlershof
Grünau
Eichwalde
Zeuthen
Wildau
Königs Wusterhausen
Altglienicke
Grünbergallee
Flughafen Berlin Schönefeld
Plänterwald
Treptower Park
Warschauer Str.
Schlesisches Tor
Görlitzer Bhf.
Kottbusser Tor
Moritzplatz
Heinrich-Heine-Str.
Jannowitzbr.
Alexanderpl.
Weberwiese
Strausberger Pl.
Samariterstr.
Rathaus Friedrichshain
Frankfurter Tor
Schilling-Str.
Rosa-Luxemburg-Pl.
Senefelderpl.
Eberswalder Str.
Rosenthaler Pl.
Bernauer Str.
Voltastr.
Weinmeisterstr.
Oranienburger Str.
Friedrichstr.
Hackescher Markt
Klosterstr.
Märkisches Museum
Spittelmarkt
Hausvogteipl.
Stadtmitte
Französische Str.
Kochstr.
Prinzenstr.
Hallesches Tor
Mehringdamm
Gneisenaustr.
Südstern
Hermannpl.
Schönleinstr.
Boddinstr.
Leinestr.
Hermannstr.
Rathaus Neukölln
Karl-Marx-Str.
Neukölln
Sonnenallee
Grenzallee
Blaschkoallee
Parchimer Allee
Britz-Süd
Johannisthaler Ch.
Lipschitzallee
Wutzkyallee
Zwickauer Damm
Rudow
Flughafen Berlin-Tempelhof
Platz der Luftbrücke
Paradestr.
Tempelhof
Kaiserin-Augusta-Str.
Ullsteinstr.
Westphalweg
Alt-Mariendorf
Alt-Tempelhof
Priesterweg
Attilastr.
Marienfelde
Buckower Chaussee
Schichauweg
Lichtenrade
Mahlow
Blankenfelde (Kr. Zossen)
Südende
Lankwitz
Lichterfelde Ost
Yorckstr.
Möckernbrücke
Gleisdreieck
Anhalter Bhf.
Potsdamer Platz
Mohrenstr.
Unter d. Linden
Lehrter Stadtbhf.
Humboldthain
Nordbahnhof
Wedding
Pankstr.
Osloer Str.
Nauener Pl.
Leopoldpl.
Amrumer Str.
Westhafen
Birkenstr.
Turmstr.
Hansapl.
Bellevue
Zoologischer Garten
Tiergarten
Beusselstr.
Seestr.
Rehberge
Afrikanische Str.
Kurt-Schumacher-Pl.
Scharnweberstr.
Seidelstr.
Holzhauser Str.
Borsigwerke
Alt-Tegel
Eichborndamm
Paracelsus-Bad
Residenzstr.
Franz-Neumann-Pl.
Reinickendorfer Str.
Schwartzkopffstr.
Zinnowitzer Str.
Oranienburger Tor
Flughafen Berlin-Tegel
Ernst-Reuter-Pl.
Deutsche Oper
Richard-Wagner-Pl.
Mierendorffpl.
Jungfernheide
Jakob-Kaiser-Pl.
Halemweg
Siemensdamm
Rohrdamm
Paulsternstr.
Haselhorst
Zitadelle
Altstadt Spandau
Rathaus Spandau
Bismarckstr.
Sophie-Charlotte-Pl.
Kaiserdamm
Theodor-Heuss-Pl.
Neu-Westend
Olympia-Stadion
Ruhleben
Charlottenburg
Wilmersdorfer Str.
Savignypl.
Kurfürstendamm
Uhlandstr.
Adenauerpl.
Wittenbergpl.
Nollendorfpl.
Kurfürstenstr.
Bülowstr.
Kleistpark
Eisenacher Str.
Viktoria-Luise-Pl.
Bayerischer Pl.
Rathaus Schöneberg
Innsbrucker Pl.
Schöneberg
Augsburger Str.
Spichernstr.
Hohenzollernpl.
Berliner Str.
Blissestr.
Bundespl.
Friedrich-Wilhelm-Pl.
Walther-Schreiber-Pl.
Schloßstr.
Rathaus Steglitz
Friedenau
Feuerbachstr.
Botanischer Garten
Lichterfelde-West
Sundgauer Str.
Zehlendorf
Mexikoplatz
Schlachtensee
Wannsee
Nikolassee
Griebnitzsee
Babelsberg
Potsdam Stadt
Grunewald
Westkreuz
Halensee
Hohenzollerndamm
Heidelberger Pl.
Fehrbelliner Pl.
Konstanzer Str.
Rüdesheimer Pl.
Breitenbachpl.
Podbielskiallee
Dahlem-Dorf
Thielplatz
Oskar-Helene-Heim
Onkel Toms Hütte
Krumme Lanke

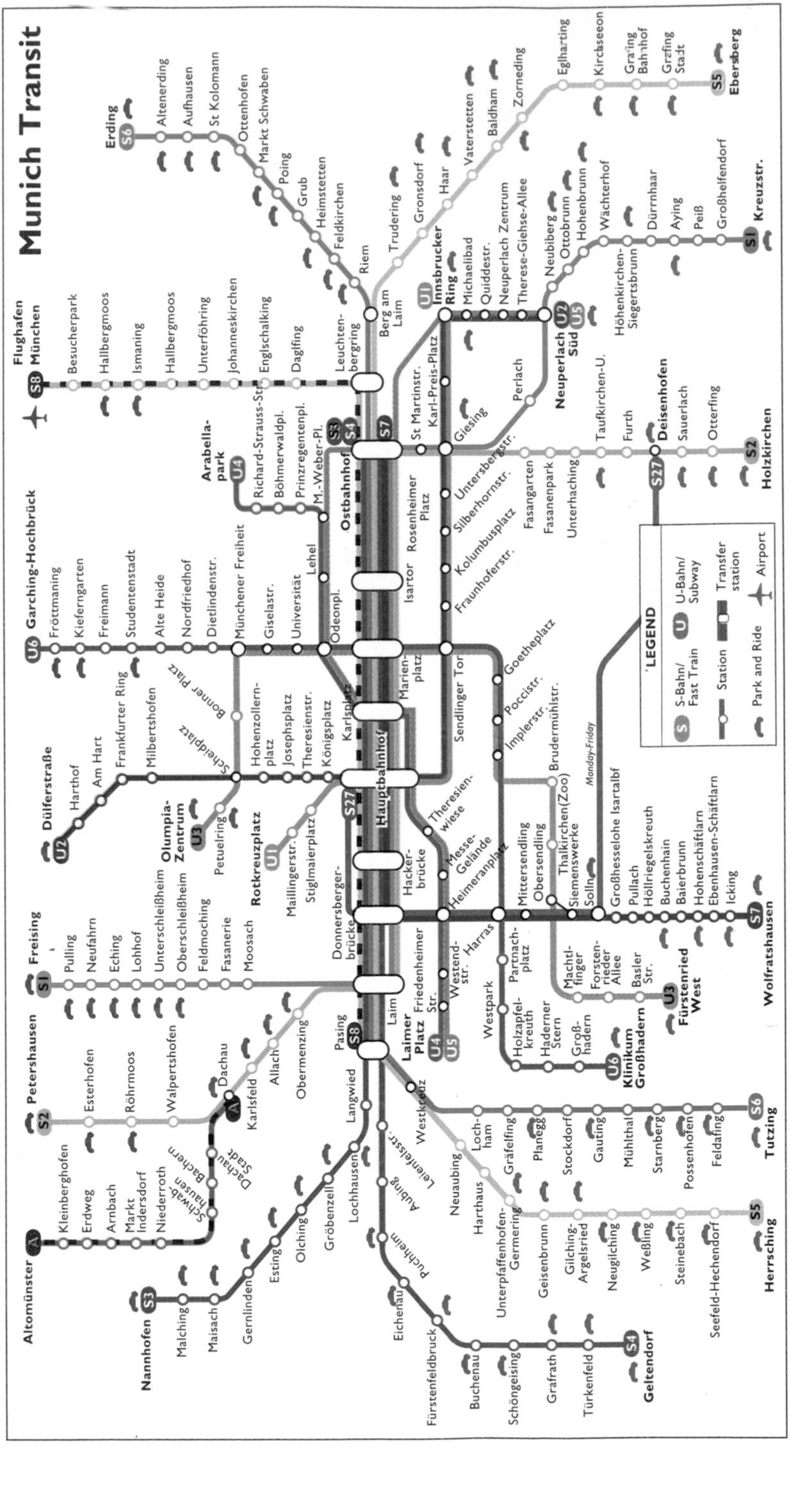

Munich Transit
Flughafen München
S8
Besucherpark
Hallbergmoos
Ismaning
Unterföhring
Johanneskirchen
Englschalking
Daglfing
Leuchtenbergring
Erding
S6
Altenerding
Aufhausen
St Kolomann
Ottenhofen
Markt Schwaben
Poing
Grub
Heimstetten
Feldkirchen
Riem
Berg am Laim
Trudering
Gronsdorf
Haar
Vaterstetten
Baldham
Zorneding
Eglharting
Kirchseeon
Grafing Bahnhof
Grafing Stadt
S5
Ebersberg
U1
Innsbrucker Ring
Michaelibad
Quiddestr.
Neuperlach Zentrum
Therese-Giehse-Allee
Neuperlach Süd
U2
U5
Neubiberg
Ottobrunn
Hohenbrunn
Wächterhof
Höhenkirchen-Siegertsbrunn
Dürrnhaar
Aying
Peiß
Großhelfendorf
S1
Kreuzstr.
Garching-Hochbrück
U6
Fröttmaning
Kieferngarten
Freimann
Studentenstadt
Alte Heide
Nordfriedhof
Dietlindenstr.
Münchener Freiheit
Giselastr.
Universität
Odeonpl.
Arabellapark
U4
Richard-Strauss-Str.
Böhmerwaldpl.
Prinzregentenpl.
M.-Weber-Pl.
Lehel
S3
S4
S7
Ostbahnhof
St Martinstr.
Karl-Preis-Platz
Giesing
Perlach
Untersbergstr.
Silberhornstr.
Kolumbusplatz
Fraunhoferstr.
Fasangarten
Fasanenpark
Unterhaching
Taufkirchen-U.
Furth
Deisenhofen
S27
Sauerlach
Otterfing
S2
Holzkirchen
Rosenheimer Platz
Isartor
Marienplatz
Sendlinger Tor
Goetheplatz
Poccistr.
Implerstr.
Brudermühlstr.
Thalkirchen (Zoo)
Obersendling
Siemenswerke
Mittersendling
Solln
Monday-Friday
Großhesselohe Isartalbf
Pullach
Höllriegelskreuth
Buchenhain
Baierbrunn
Hohenschäftlarn
Ebenhausen-Schäftlarn
Icking
S7
Wolfratshausen
LEGEND
S-Bahn/ Fast Train
U-Bahn/ Subway
Station
Transfer station
Park and Ride
Airport
Dülferstraße
U2
Harthof
Am Hart
Frankfurter Ring
Milbertshofen
Bonner Platz
Scheidplatz
Hohenzollernplatz
Josephsplatz
Theresienstr.
Königsplatz
Karlsplatz
Hauptbahnhof
Olympia-Zentrum
U3
Petuelring
Rotkreuzplatz
U1
Maillingerstr.
Stiglmaierplatz
Theresienwiese
Hackerbrücke
Messe-Gelände
Heimeranplatz
Harras
Partnachplatz
Westpark
Holzapfelkreuth
Haderner Stern
Großhadern
U6
Klinikum Großhadern
Machtlfinger
Forstenrieder Allee
Basler Str.
U3
Fürstenried West
Freising
S1
Pulling
Neufahrn
Eching
Lohhof
Unterschleißheim
Oberschleißheim
Feldmoching
Fasanerie
Moosach
Donnersbergerbrücke
Laim
Friedenheimer Str.
Westend-str.
Laimer Platz
U4
U5
Petershausen
S2
Esterhofen
Röhrmoos
Walpertshofen
Dachau
A
Karlsfeld
Allach
Obermenzing
Pasing
S8
Langwied
Westkreuz
Leienfelsstr.
Aubing
Puchheim
Eichenau
Fürstenfeldbruck
Buchenau
Schöngeising
Grafrath
Türkenfeld
S4
Geltendorf
Altomünster
Kleinberghofen
Erdweg
Arnbach
Markt Indersdorf
Niederroth
Schwabhausen
Bachern
Dachau Stadt
Nannhofen
S3
Malching
Maisach
Gernlinden
Esting
Olching
Gröbenzell
Lochhausen
Neuaubing
Harthaus
Lochham
Gräfelfing
Planegg
Stockdorf
Gauting
Mühlthal
Starnberg
Possenhofen
Feldafing
S6
Tutzing
Unterpfaffenhofen-Germering
Geisenbrunn
Gilching-Argelsried
Neugilching
Weßling
Steinebach
Seefeld-Hechendorf
S5
Herrsching

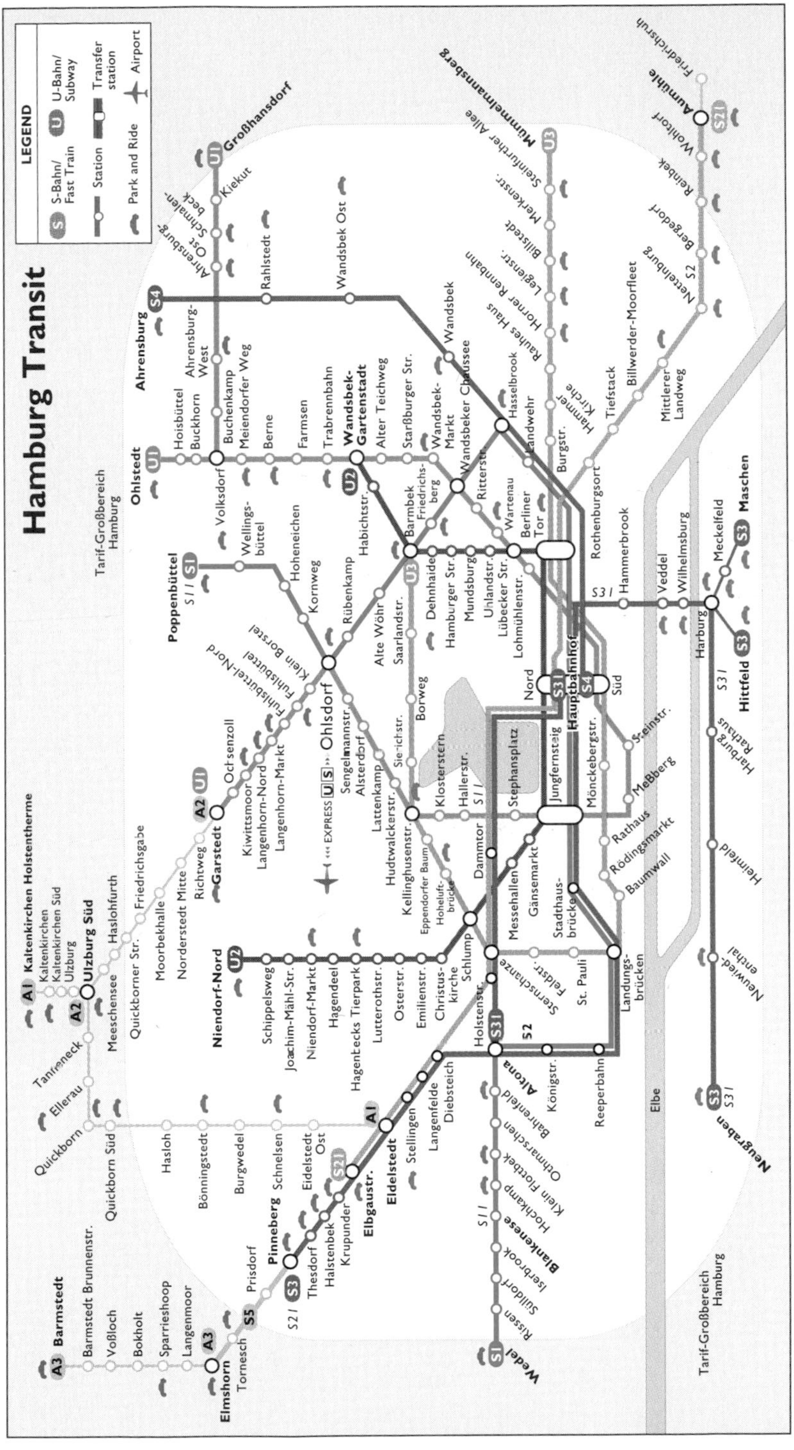
Hamburg Transit
LEGEND
S-Bahn/ Fast Train
U-Bahn/ Subway
Station
Transfer station
Park and Ride
Airport
Tarif-Großbereich Hamburg
Kaltenkirchen Holstentherme
Kaltenkirchen
Kaltenkirchen Süd
Ulzburg
Ulzburg Süd
Haslohfurth
Tanneneck
Meeschensee
Ellerau
Quickborn
Quickborn Süd
Hasloh
Bönningstedt
Burgwedel
Schnelsen
Eidelstedt Ost
Barmstedt
Barmstedt Brunnenstr.
Voßloch
Bokholt
Sparrieshoop
Langenmoor
Elmshorn
Tornesch
Prisdorf
Pinneberg
Thesdorf
Halstenbek
Krupunder
Elbgaustr.
Eidelstedt
Stellingen
Langenfelde
Diebsteich
Altona
Holstenstr.
Sternschanze
Christus-kirche
Schlump
Friedrichsgabe
Moorbekhalle
Quickborner Str.
Norderstedt Mitte
Richtweg
Garstedt
Ochsenzoll
Kiwittsmoor
Langenhorn-Nord
Langenhorn-Markt
Fuhlsbüttel-Nord
Fuhlsbüttel
Klein Borstel
Ohlsdorf
Poppenbüttel
Wellingsbüttel
Hoheneichen
Kornweg
Ohlstedt
Hoisbüttel
Buckhorn
Volksdorf
Ahrensburg
Ahrensburg-West
Buchenkamp
Meiendorfer Weg
Berne
Farmsen
Trabrennbahn
Wandsbek-Gartenstadt
Großhansdorf
Kiekut
Schmalenbeck
Ahrensburg-Ost
Rahlstedt
Wandsbek Ost
Wandsbek
Niendorf-Nord
Schippelsweg
Joachim-Mähl-Str.
Niendorf-Markt
Hagendeel
Hagenbecks Tierpark
Lutterothstr.
Osterstr.
Emilienstr.
Sengelmannstr.
Alsterdorf
Lattenkamp
Hudtwalckerstr.
Kellinghusenstr.
Eppendorfer Baum
Hoheluft-brücke
Siemersplatz
Borgweg
Saarlandstr.
Alte Wöhr
Rübenkamp
Habichtstr.
Barmbek
Alter Teichweg
Straßburger Str.
Wandsbek-Markt
Wandsbeker Chaussee
Friedrichs-berg
Ritterstr.
Wartenau
Hasselbrook
Landwehr
Dehnhaide
Hamburger Str.
Mundsburg
Uhlandstr.
Lübecker Str.
Lohmühlenstr.
Berliner Tor
Klosterstern
Hallerstr.
Dammtor
Stephansplatz
Jungfernstieg
Hauptbahnhof
Nord
Süd
Mönckebergstr.
Steinstr.
Meßberg
Rathaus
Rödingsmarkt
Baumwall
Messehallen
Gänsemarkt
Stadthaus-brücke
Landungs-brücken
St. Pauli
Feldstr.
Königstr.
Reeperbahn
Bahrenfeld
Othmarschen
Klein Flottbek
Hochkamp
Blankenese
Iserbrook
Sülldorf
Rissen
Wedel
Elbe
Burgstr.
Hammer Kirche
Rauhes Haus
Horner Rennbahn
Legienstr.
Billstedt
Merkenstr.
Steinfurther Allee
Mümmelmannsberg
Rothenburgsort
Tiefstack
Billwerder-Moorfleet
Mittlerer Landweg
Nettelnburg
Bergedorf
Reinbek
Wohltorf
Aumühle
Friedrichsruh
Hammerbrook
Veddel
Wilhelmsburg
Harburg
Meckelfeld
Maschen
Hittfeld
Harburg Rathaus
Heimfeld
Neuwiedenthal
Neugraben
EXPRESS
S1
S11
S2
S21
S3
S31
S4
S5
U1
U2
U3
A1
A2
A3

Frankfurt Transit

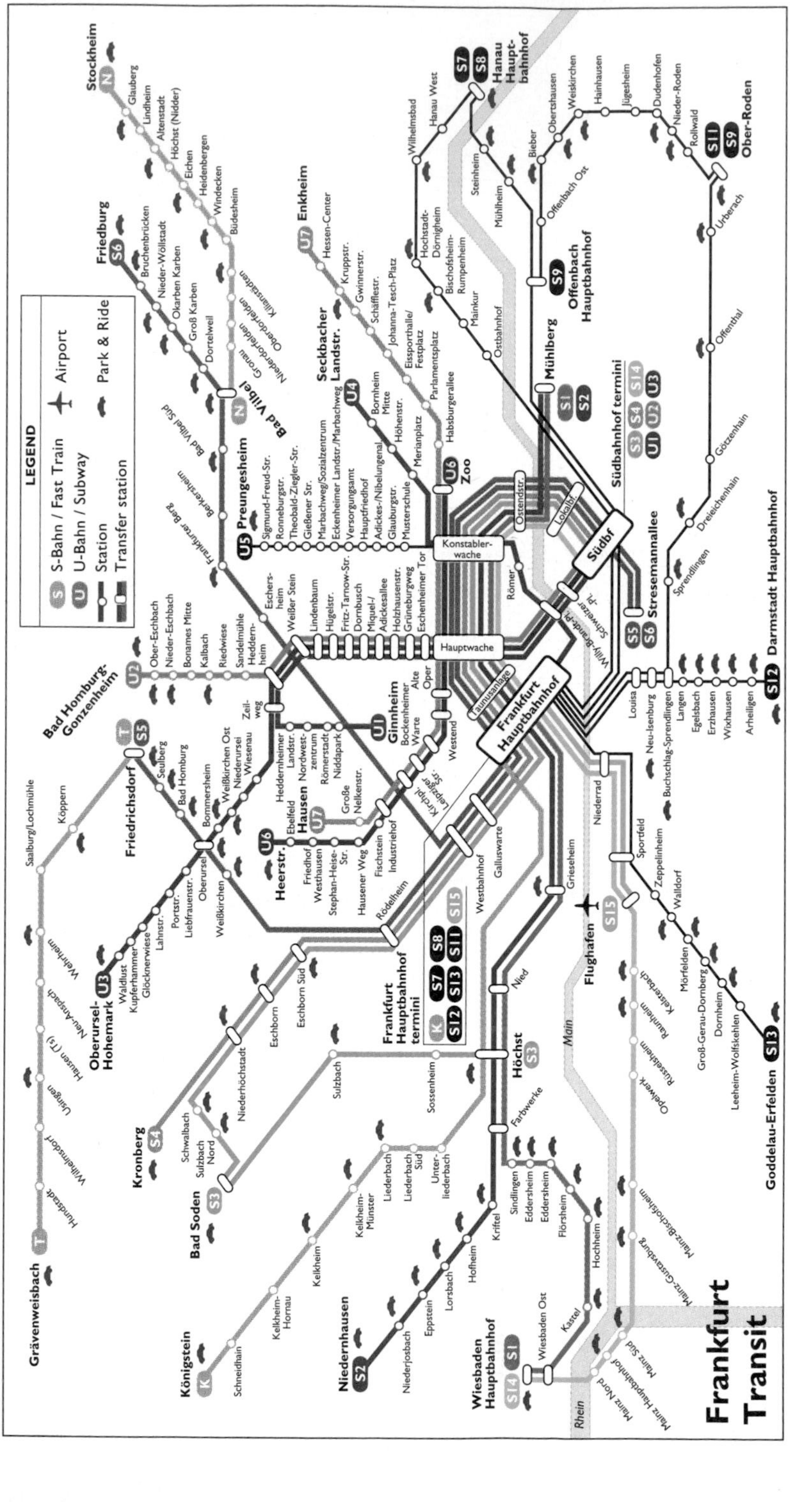

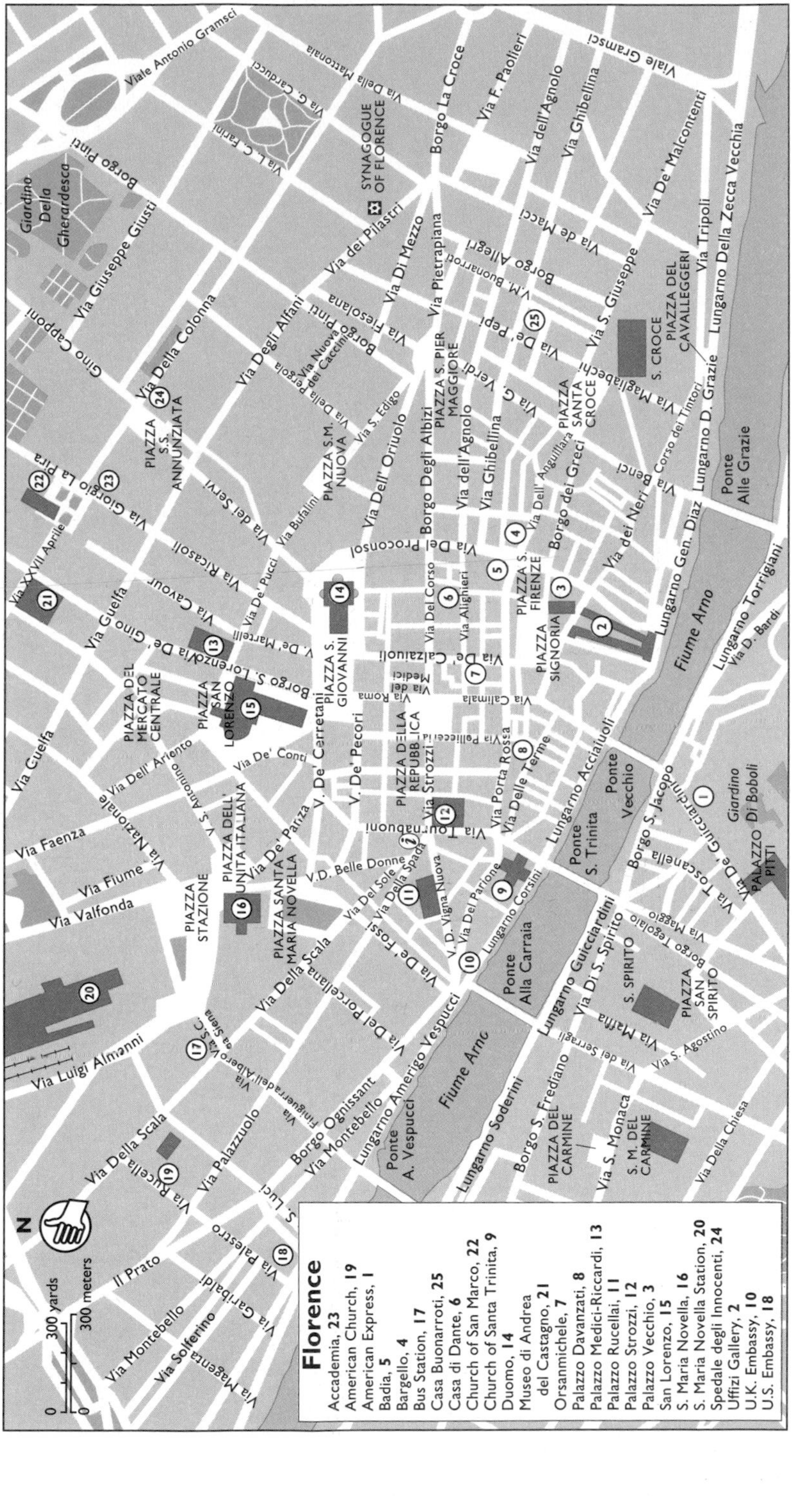
Florence
Accademia, 23
American Church, 19
American Express, 1
Badia, 5
Bargello, 4
Bus Station, 17
Casa Buonarroti, 25
Casa di Dante, 6
Church of San Marco, 22
Church of Santa Trinita, 9
Duomo, 14
Museo di Andrea del Castagno, 21
Orsanmichele, 7
Palazzo Davanzati, 8
Palazzo Medici-Riccardi, 13
Palazzo Rucellai, 11
Palazzo Strozzi, 12
Palazzo Vecchio, 3
San Lorenzo, 15
S. Maria Novella, 16
S. Maria Novella Station, 20
Spedale degli Innocenti, 24
Uffizi Gallery, 2
U.K. Embassy, 10
U.S. Embassy, 18
N
0
300 yards
300 meters

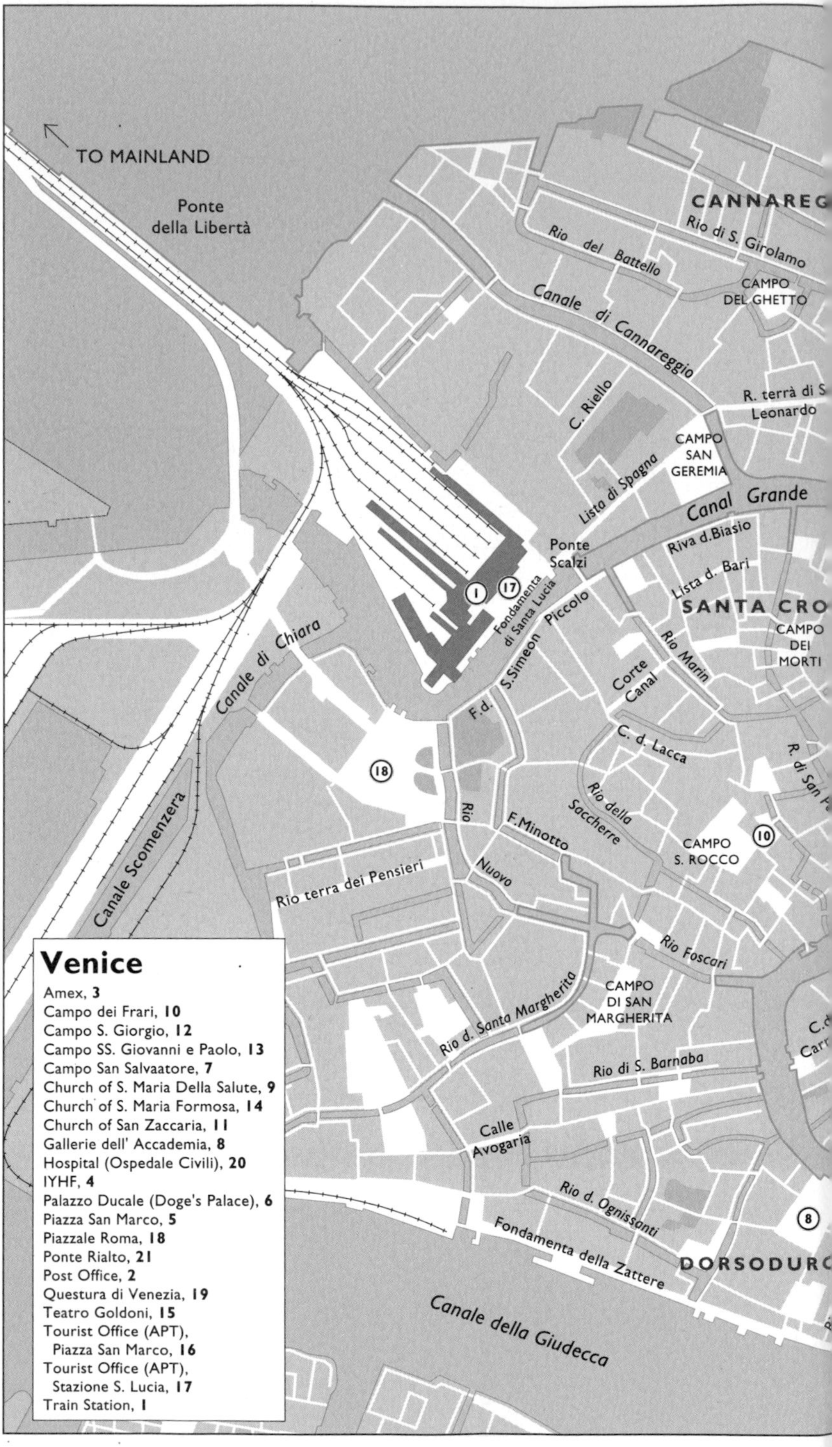
TO MAINLAND
Ponte della Libertà
Rio di S. Girolamo
Rio del Battello
CAMPO DEL GHETTO
Canale di Cannareggio
C. Riello
Leonardo
CAMPO SAN GEREMIA
Lista di Spagna
Canal Grande
Ponte Scalzi
Riva d.Biasio
Lista d. Bari
Fondamenta di Santa Lucia
F.d. S.Simeon Piccolo
CAMPO DEI MORTI
Rio Marin
Corte Canal
Canale di Chiara
C. d. Lacca
Rio della Saccherre
Rio F.Minotto
Rio Nuovo
CAMPO S. ROCCO
Canale Scomenzera
Rio terra dei Pensieri
Rio Foscari
CAMPO DI SAN MARGHERITA
Rio d. Santa Margherita
Rio di S. Barnaba
Calle Avogaria
Rio d. Ognissanti
Fondamenta della Zattere
Canale della Giudecca
Venice
Amex, 3
Campo dei Frari, 10
Campo S. Giorgio, 12
Campo SS. Giovanni e Paolo, 13
Campo San Salvaatore, 7
Church of S. Maria Della Salute, 9
Church of S. Maria Formosa, 14
Church of San Zaccaria, 11
Gallerie dell' Accademia, 8
Hospital (Ospedale Civili), 20
IYHF, 4
Palazzo Ducale (Doge's Palace), 6
Piazza San Marco, 5
Piazzale Roma, 18
Ponte Rialto, 21
Post Office, 2
Questura di Venezia, 19
Teatro Goldoni, 15
Tourist Office (APT), Piazza San Marco, 16
Tourist Office (APT), Stazione S. Lucia, 17
Train Station, 1

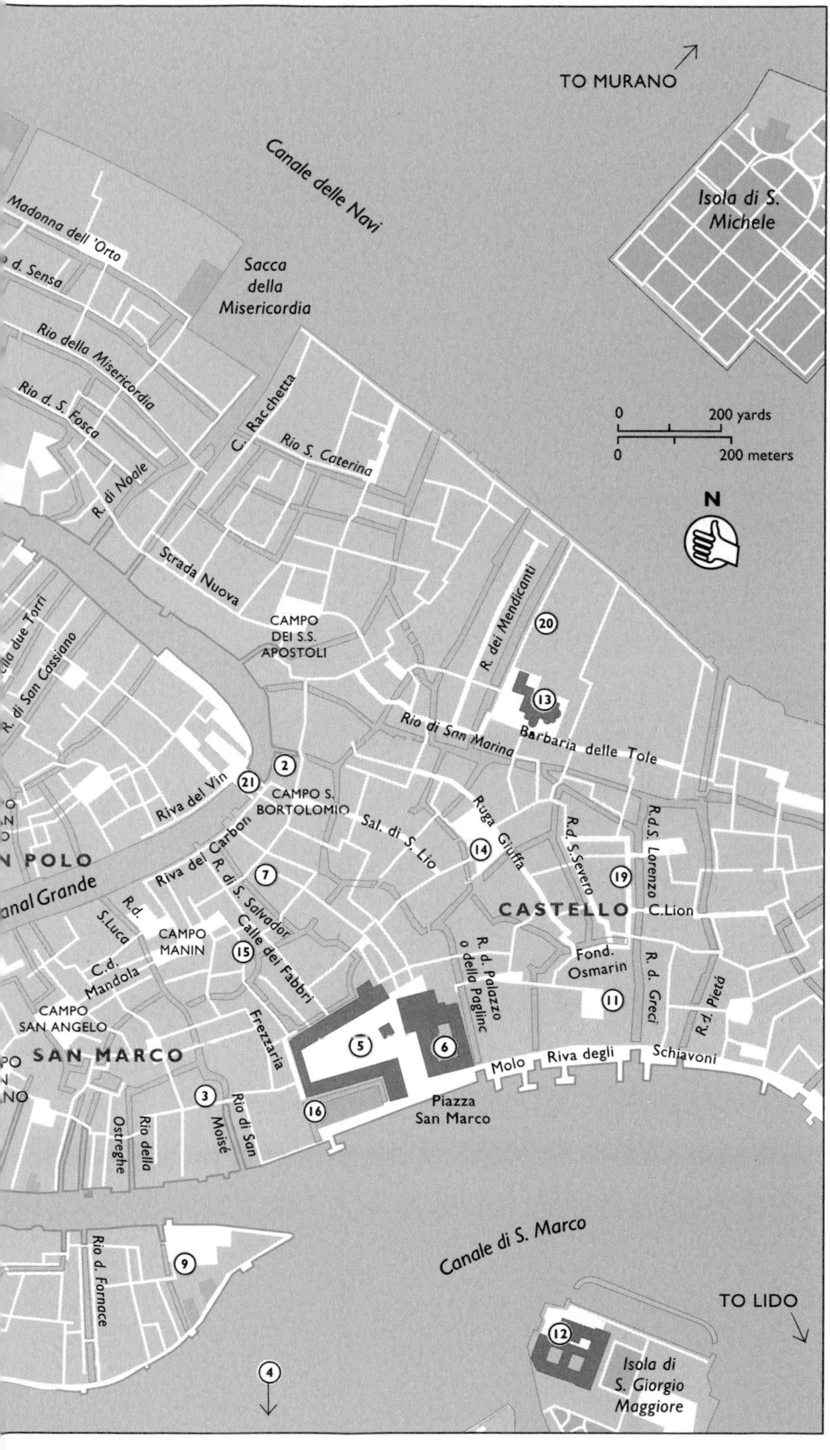
TO MURANO
Canale delle Navi
Isola di S. Michele
Madonna dell 'Orto
d. Sensa
Sacca della Misericordia
Rio della Misericordia
Rio d. S. Fosca
C. Racchetta
Rio S. Caterina
0 200 yards
0 200 meters
N
R. di Noale
Strada Nuova
R. dei Mendicanti
CAMPO DEI S.S. APOSTOLI
due Torri
R. di San Cassiano
Rio di San Marina
Barbaria delle Tole
Riva del Vin
CAMPO S. BORTOLOMIO
Sal. di S. Lio
Ruga Giuffa
R.d. S.Severo
R.d.S. Lorenzo
POLO
Riva del Carbon
R. di S. Salvador
anal Grande
R.d. S.Luca
CAMPO MANIN
Calle dei Fabbri
CASTELLO
C.Lion
C.d. Mandola
R. d. Palazzo o della Paglinc
Fond. Osmarin
R. d. Greci
R.d. Pietà
CAMPO SAN ANGELO
Frezzaria
SAN MARCO
Molo
Riva degli Schiavoni
Piazza San Marco
Rio di San Moisé
Rio della Ostreghe
Canale di S. Marco
Rio d. Fornace
TO LIDO
Isola di S. Giorgio Maggiore
2
3
4
5
6
7
9
11
12
13
14
15
16
19
20
21

Milan

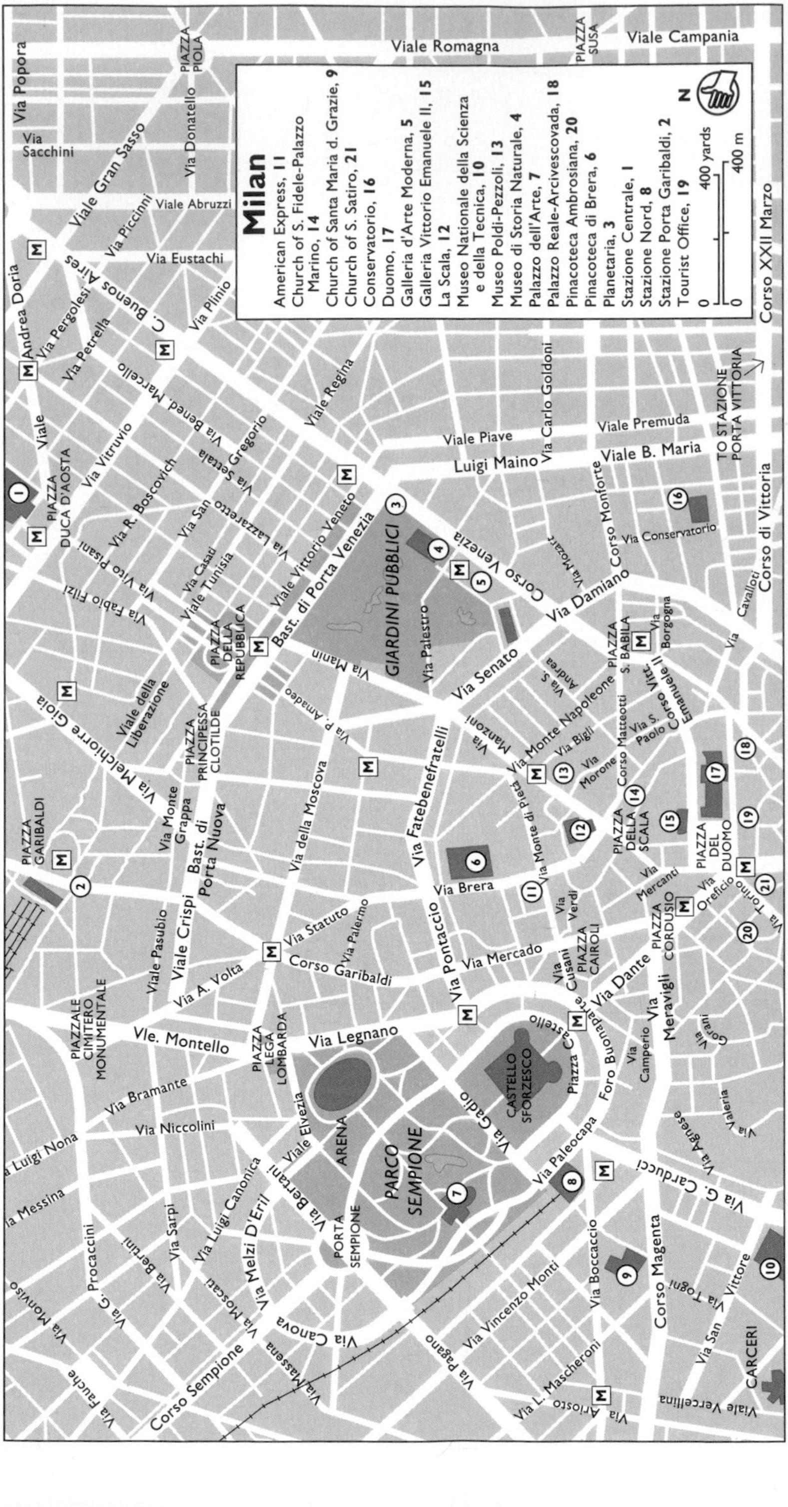
Milan
American Express, 11
Church of S. Fidele-Palazzo Marino, 14
Church of Santa Maria d. Grazie, 9
Church of S. Satiro, 21
Conservatorio, 16
Duomo, 17
Galleria d'Arte Moderna, 5
Galleria Vittorio Emanuele II, 15
La Scala, 12
Museo Nationale della Scienza e della Tecnica, 10
Museo Poldi-Pezzoli, 13
Museo di Storia Naturale, 4
Palazzo dell'Arte, 7
Palazzo Reale-Arcivescovada, 18
Pinacoteca Ambrosiana, 20
Pinacoteca di Brera, 6
Planetaria, 3
Stazione Centrale, 1
Stazione Nord, 8
Stazione Porta Garibaldi, 2
Tourist Office, 19
0
400 yards
0
400 m
N
Viale Romagna
Viale Campania
PIAZZA SUSA
PIAZZA PIOLA
Via Popora
Via Sacchini
Viale Gran Sasso
Via Donatello
Viale Abruzzi
Via Piccinni
Via Eustachi
C. Buenos Aires
Via Plinio
Via Andrea Doria
Via Pergolesi
Via Petrella
Via Bened. Marcello
Via Settala
Via San Gregorio
Viale Regina
Viale Piave
Viale Premuda
Viale B. Maria
Luigi Maino
Via Carlo Goldoni
TO STAZIONE PORTA VITTORIA
Corso XXII Marzo
Corso di Vittoria
PIAZZA DUCA D'AOSTA
Via Vitruvio
Via R. Boscovich
Via Lazzaretto
Via San
Viale Vittorio Veneto
GIARDINI PUBBLICI
Corso Venezia
Via Conservatorio
Corso Monforte
Via Mozart
Via Damiano
Via Cavallotti
Via Vito Pisani
Via Fabio Filzi
Via Casati
Viale Tunisia
PIAZZA DELLA REPUBBLICA
Bast. di Porta Venezia
Via Manin
Via Palestro
Via Senato
PIAZZA S. BABILA
Via Borgogna
Via S. Andrea
Via Manzoni
Via Monte Napoleone
Via Bigli
Via Morone
Corso Matteotti
Via S. Paolo
Corso Vitt. Emanuele II
Viale della Liberazione
PIAZZA PRINCIPESSA CLOTILDE
Via P. Amadeo
Via Melchiorre Gioia
Via Monte Grappa
Bast. di Porta Nuova
Via della Moscova
Via Fatebenefratelli
Via Monte di Pietà
PIAZZA DELLA SCALA
PIAZZA DEL DUOMO
Via Mercanti
Via Orefici
Via Torino
PIAZZA GARIBALDI
Viale Pasubio
Viale Crispi
Via Statuto
Via Palermo
Via Brera
Via Verdi
PIAZZA CAIROLI
PIAZZA CORDUSIO
Corso Garibaldi
Via Mercado
Via Pontaccio
Via Cusani
Via Dante
Via Meravigli
Via A. Volta
PIAZZALE CIMITERO MONUMENTALE
Vle. Montello
PIAZZA LEGA LOMBARDA
Via Legnano
Piazza Castello
CASTELLO SFORZESCO
Foro Buonaparte
Via Camperio
Via Gorani
Via Bramante
Via Niccolini
Viale Elvezia
ARENA
PARCO SEMPIONE
Via Gadio
Via Paleocapa
Via Valeria
Via Agnese
Via G. Carducci
Via Luigi Nona
Via Messina
Via Sarpi
Via Luigi Canonica
Via Bertani
Via Melzi D'Eril
PORTA SEMPIONE
Via Procaccini
Via Bertini
Via Moscati
Via Canova
Via Monviso
Via G.
Via Fauche
Corso Sempione
Via Massena
Via Pagano
Via Vincenzo Monti
Via Boccaccio
Corso Magenta
Via Togni
Via San Vittore
CARCERI
Via L. Mascheroni
Via Ariosto
Viale Vercellina

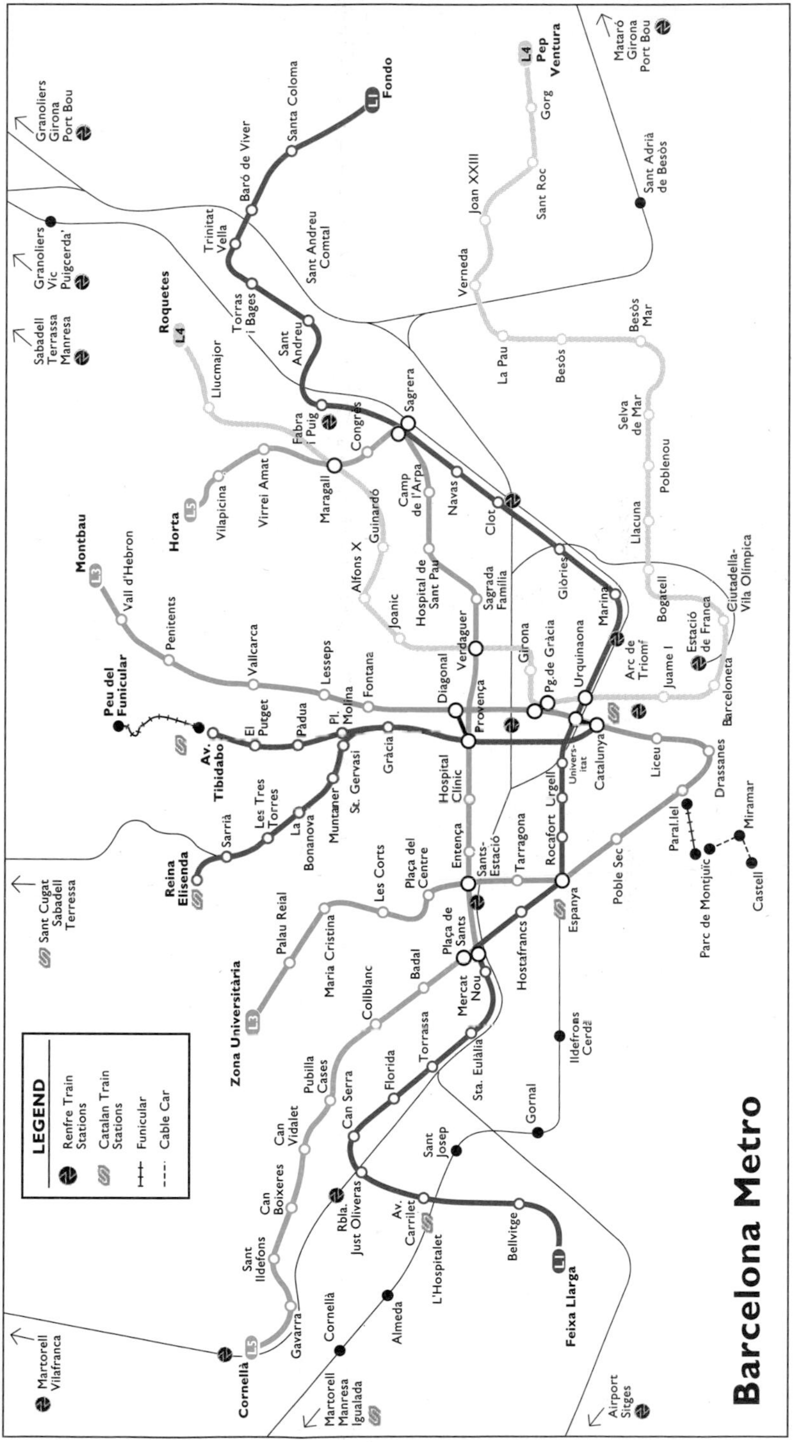
Barcelona Metro
LEGEND
Renfe Train Stations
Catalan Train Stations
Funicular
Cable Car
L1
Fondo
Feixa Llarga
L3
Montbau
Zona Universitària
L4
Pep Ventura
Roquetes
L5
Horta
Cornellà
Santa Coloma
Baró de Viver
Trinitat Vella
Torras i Bages
Sant Andreu
Fabra i Puig
Sagrera
Navas
Clot
Glòries
Marina
Arc de Triomf
Urquinaona
Catalunya
Universitat
Urgell
Rocafort
Espanya
Hostafrancs
Plaça de Sants
Mercat Nou
Sta. Eulàlia
Torrassa
Florida
Can Serra
Rbla. Just Oliveras
Av. Carrilet
Bellvitge
Vall d'Hebron
Penitents
Vallcarca
Lesseps
Fontana
Diagonal
Liceu
Drassanes
Paral.lel
Poble Sec
Tarragona
Sants-Estació
Plaça del Centre
Les Corts
Maria Cristina
Palau Reial
Gorg
Sant Roc
Joan XXIII
Verneda
La Pau
Besòs
Besòs Mar
Selva de Mar
Poblenou
Llacuna
Bogatell
Ciutadella-Vila Olímpica
Barceloneta
Juame I
Estació de França
Girona
Verdaguer
Joanic
Alfons X
Guinardó
Maragall
Llucmajor
Vilapicina
Virrei Amat
Congrés
Camp de l'Arpa
Hospital de Sant Pau
Sagrada Família
Provença
Pg. de Gràcia
Hospital Clínic
Entença
Badal
Collblanc
Pubilla Cases
Can Vidalet
Can Boixeres
Sant Ildefons
Gavarra
Peu del Funicular
Av. Tibidabo
El Putget
Pàdua
Pl. Molina
Gràcia
Sant Gervasi
Muntaner
La Bonanova
Les Tres Torres
Sarrià
Reina Elisenda
Parc de Montjuïc
Miramar
Castell
Sant Andreu Comtal
Sant Adrià de Besòs
Ildefons Cerdà
Gornal
Sant Josep
L'Hospitalet
Almeda
Cornellà
Granoliers Girona Port Bou
Granoliers Vic Puigcerdà'
Sabadell Terrassa Manresa
Sant Cugat Sabadell Terressa
Martorell Vilafranca
Martorell Manresa Igualada
Airport Sitges
Mataró Girona Port Bou

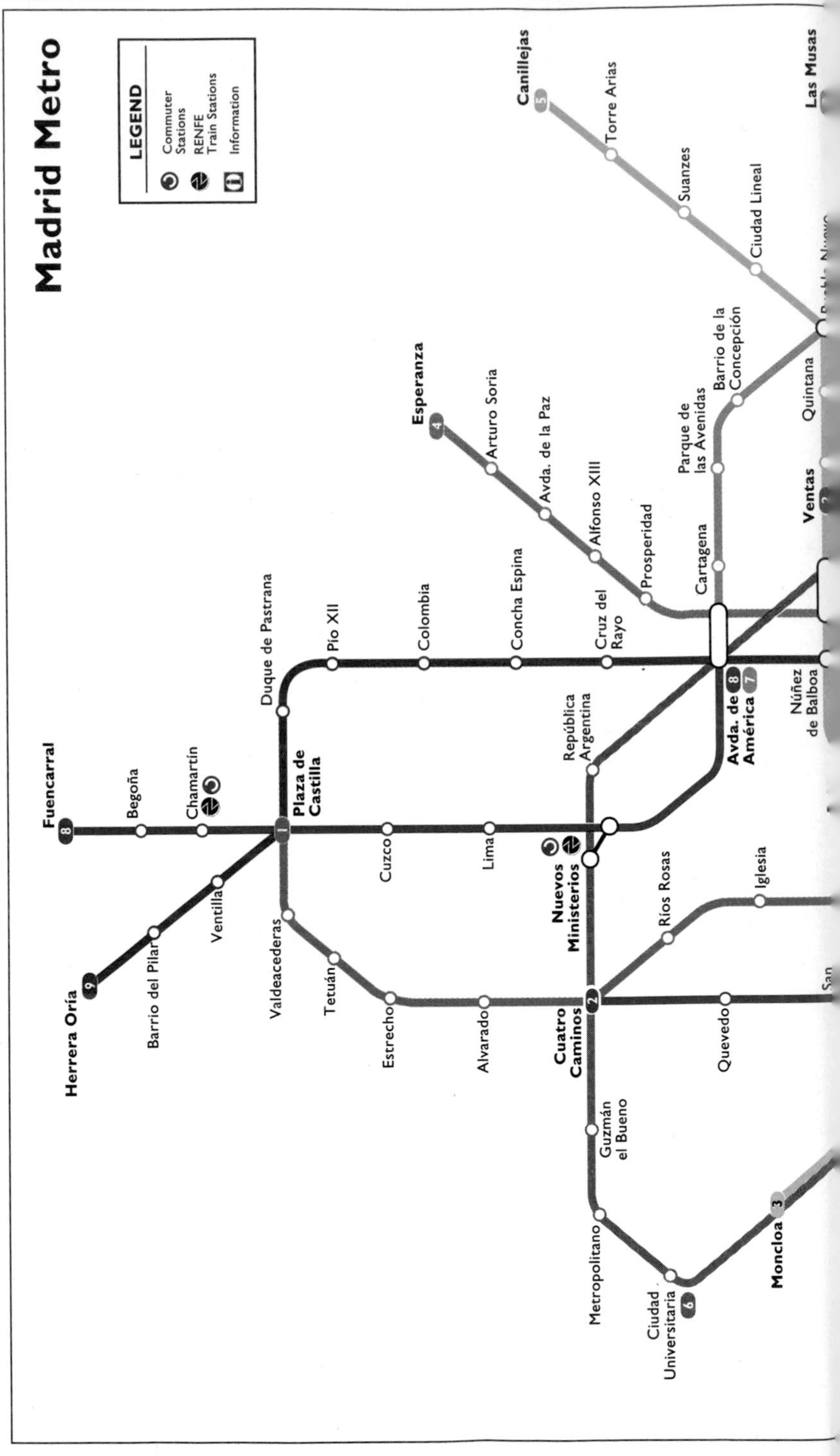
Madrid Metro
LEGEND
Commuter Stations
RENFE Train Stations
Information
Canillejas
Torre Arias
Suanzes
Ciudad Lineal
Las Musas
Esperanza
Arturo Soria
Avda. de la Paz
Alfonso XIII
Prosperidad
Cartagena
Parque de las Avenidas
Barrio de la Concepción
Quintana
Ventas
Duque de Pastrana
Pío XII
Colombia
Concha Espina
Cruz del Rayo
República Argentina
Avda. de América
Núñez de Balboa
Fuencarral
Begoña
Chamartín
Plaza de Castilla
Cuzco
Lima
Nuevos Ministerios
Herrera Oría
Barrio del Pilar
Ventilla
Valdeacederas
Tetuán
Estrecho
Alvarado
Cuatro Caminos
Ríos Rosas
Iglesia
Quevedo
Guzmán el Bueno
Metropolitano
Ciudad Universitaria
Moncloa

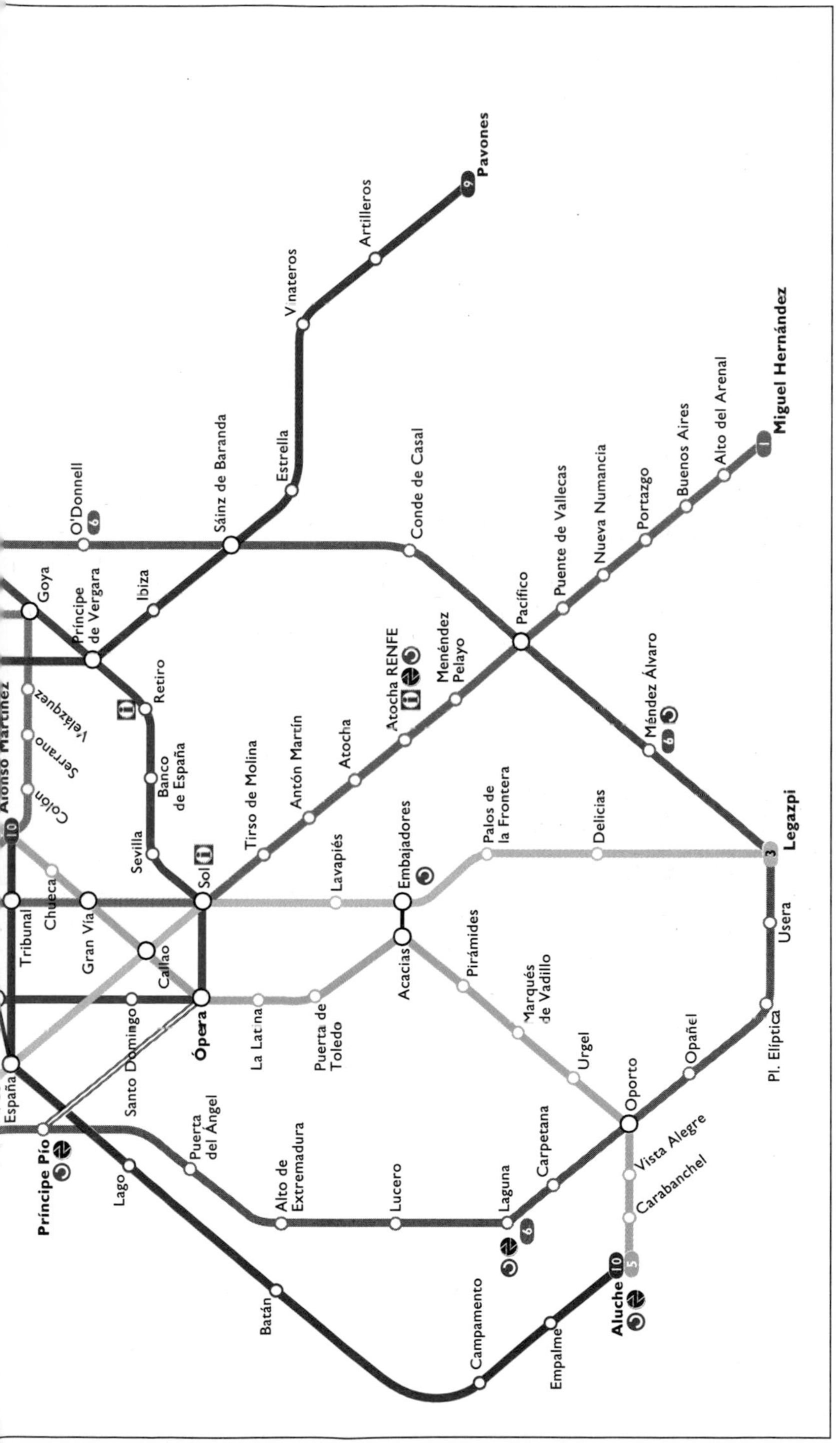
Pavones
9
Artilleros
Vinateros
Estrella
Sáinz de Baranda
O'Donnell
6
Conde de Casal
Miguel Hernández
1
Alto del Arenal
Buenos Aires
Portazgo
Nueva Numancia
Puente de Vallecas
Pacífico
Goya
Príncipe de Vergara
Ibiza
Retiro
Banco de España
Sevilla
Atocha RENFE
Menéndez Pelayo
Méndez Álvaro
6
Atocha
Antón Martín
Tirso de Molina
Alonso Martínez
10
Colón
Serrano
Velázquez
Sol
Lavapiés
Embajadores
Palos de la Frontera
Delicias
Legazpi
3
Tribunal
Chueca
Gran Vía
Callao
Acacias
Pirámides
Marqués de Vadillo
Usera
Santo Domingo
Ópera
La Latina
Puerta de Toledo
Urgel
Oporto
Opañel
Pl. Elíptica
España
Príncipe Pío
Puerta del Ángel
Lago
Alto de Extremadura
Lucero
Laguna
6
Carpetana
Vista Alegre
Carabanchel
5
10
Aluche
Batán
Campamento
Empalme

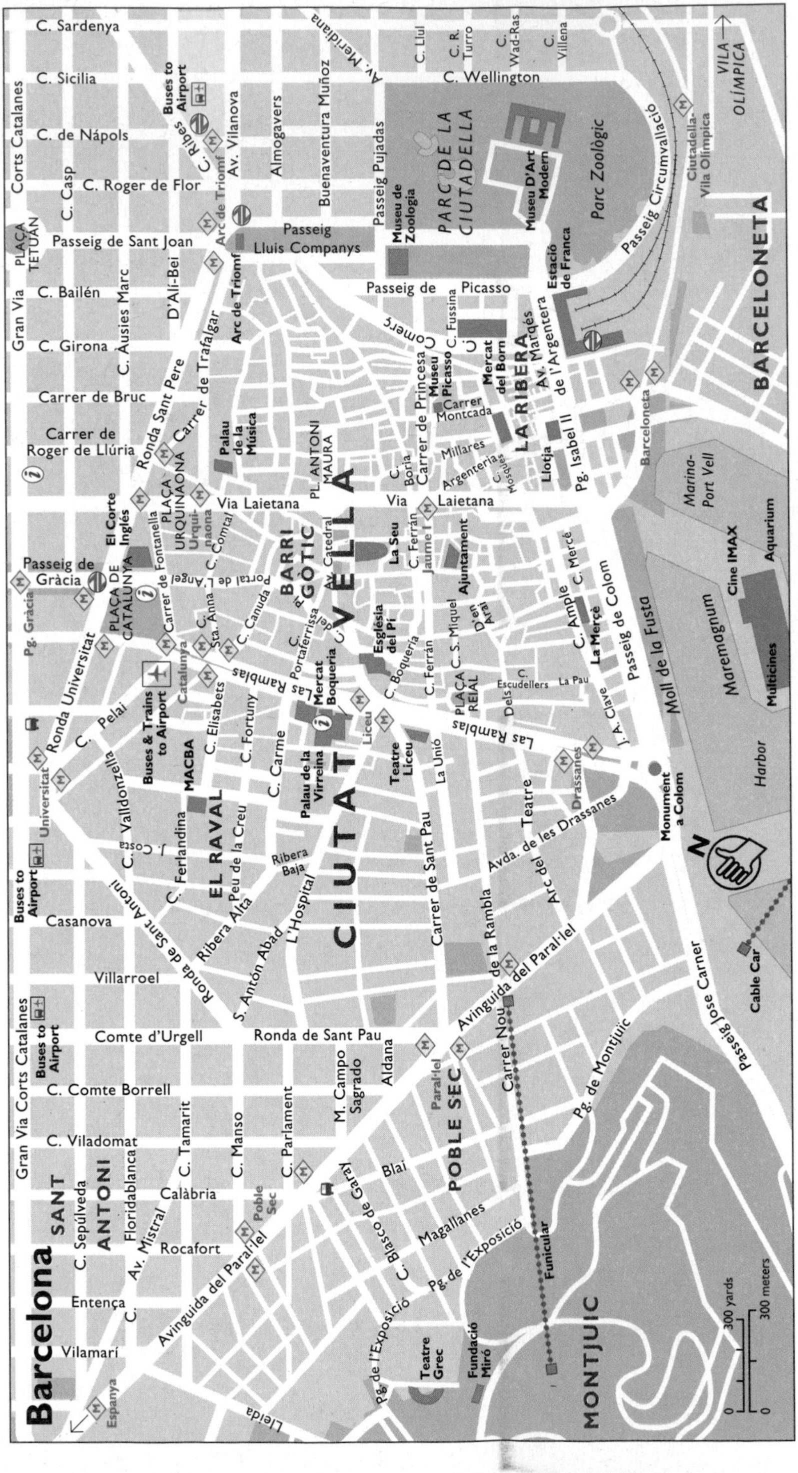
Barcelona
C. Sardenya
C. Sicilia
C. de Nàpols
Corts Catalanes
C. Casp
C. Roger de Flor
PLAÇA TETUAN
Passeig de Sant Joan
Gran Via
C. Bailén
C. Àusies Marc
D'Alí-Bei
C. Girona
Carrer de Bruc
Carrer de Roger de Llúria
Ronda Sant Pere
Carrer de Trafalgar
Arc de Triomf
Buses to Airport
C. Ribes
Av. Vilanova
Almogavers
Buenaventura Muñoz
Av. Meridiana
Passeig Pujadas
Passeig Lluis Companys
Museu de Zoologia
PARC DE LA CIUTADELLA
C. Wellington
C. Llul
C. R. Turro
C. Wad-Ras
C. Villena
VILA OLÍMPICA
Museu D'Art Modern
Parc Zoològic
Passeig Circumvallació
Ciutadella-Vila Olímpica
Estació de França
Passeig de Picasso
Comerç
C. Fussina
Mercat del Born
Museu Picasso
Carrer de Princesa
Carrer Montcada
LA RIBERA
Av. Marquès de l'Argentera
BARCELONETA
Barceloneta
Millares
Argenteria
C. Mosques
Llotja
Pg. Isabel II
C. Boria
Palau de la Música
PL. ANTONI MAURA
Via Laietana
PLAÇA URQUINAONA
Urquinaona
El Corte Inglés
C. Comtal
C. de Fontanella
Passeig de Gràcia
Pg. Gràcia
PLAÇA DE CATALUNYA
Portal de L'Angel
Catalunya
C. Sta. Anna
C. Canuda
BARRI GÒTIC
Av. Catedral
La Seu
C. Ferrán
Jaume I
Ajuntament
CIUTAT VELLA
Església del Pi
C. del Pi
C. Portaferrissa
Mercat Boqueria
Las Ramblas
C. Boquería
C. S. Miquel
D'en Arai
PLAÇA REIAL
C. Escudellers
Dels
La Pau
C. Ample
C. Mercè
La Mercè
Passeig de Colom
Moll de la Fusta
Marina-Port Vell
Aquarium
Cine IMAX
Maremagnum
Multicines
Harbor
J. A. Clave
Monument a Colom
Drassanes
Avda. de les Drassanes
Arc del Teatre
Ronda Universitat
C. Pelai
Buses & Trains to Airport
MACBA
C. Elisabets
C. Fortuny
C. Carme
Palau de la Virreina
Liceu
Teatre Liceu
La Unió
Universitat
C. Valldonzella
C. Ferlandina
J. Costa
EL RAVAL
Peu de la Creu
Ribera Baja
Ribera Alta
L'Hospital
Carrer de Sant Pau
de la Rambla
Ronda de Sant Antoni
Casanova
Villarroel
S. Antón Abad
Comte d'Urgell
Ronda de Sant Pau
Gran Via Corts Catalanes
C. Comte Borrell
M. Campo Sagrado
Aldana
Paral·lel
POBLE SEC
Avinguida del Paral·lel
Carrer Nou
Pg. de Montjuïc
Passeig Jose Carner
Cable Car
C. Viladomat
C. Tamarit
C. Manso
C. Parlament
Blai
C. Blasco de Garay
Magallanes
Pg. de l'Exposició
Poble Sec
Calàbria
SANT ANTONI
C. Sepúlveda
Floridablanca
Av. Mistral
Rocafort
Entença
C.
Vilamarí
Espanya
Teatre Grec
Fundació Miró
Funicular
MONTJUIC
Lleida
0
300 yards
300 meters
N

RESIDENTIAL
REWARDS
UNITED AIRLINES
MILEAGE PLUS®
3 BEDROOMS.
2 1/2 BATHS.
25,000 MILES.
Now a Countrywide home loan
can make earning miles easy.